EMERGENCY TELEPHONE NU

DOCTOR	
HOSPITAL	
POLICE	
FIRE	
LOCATION OF FIRST AID KIT	
RESCUE SQUAD	
POISON CONTROL CENTER	
NEIGHBOR	
NEIGHBOR	
AMBULANCE	

SEE PAGES 147–151 FOR FIRST AID

Add below other telephone numbers you may need quickly, for example, the schools your children attend, the places where members of your family work, homes and offices of relatives upon whom you can always count, your local taxi company, auto service station, and clergyman.

Webster's New World Dictionary
with
Student Handbook

YOUNG PEOPLE'S EDITION

THE SOUTHWESTERN COMPANY
Nashville, Tennessee

Illustration credits. Sources for the illustrations appear below. When two or more illustrations appear on a page, they are credited in the order in which they appear on the page, left to right and top to bottom.

ACKNOWLEDGMENTS: Copyrighted Materials: Pages 5, 7, 8 © Suzanne Opton, 21 © 1978 Fred Ward/Black Star, 124 © Allen Green/Photo Researchers, 126 © J. Allan Cash/Rapho/Photo Researchers, 127 © 1976 Sam Dasher/Photo Researchers, 314 © Rand McNally & Co., 329, 332 © Georg Gerster/Rapho/Photo Researchers, 334 © 1972 Carl Frank/Photo Researchers, 338 © Christa Armstrong/Photo Researchers, 341 © Georg Gerster/Rapho/Photo Researchers, 346 © 1975 Georg Gerster/Rapho/Photo Researchers, 348 © George Holton/Photo Researchers, 350 Gullers AB/Rapho/Photo Researchers, 353 © 1976 S. Duroy/Rapho/Photo Researchers, 357 © 1975 Serraillier/Rapho/Photo Researchers, 357 © 1973 Lily Solmssen/Photo Researchers, 358, 361, 369 (bottom) © Georg Gerster/Rapho/Photo Researchers
    Page 1 Chris Reeberg/DPI, 12 E. P. Dutton & Co., Inc., 16 Culver Pictures, 17 Little, Brown & Co., 18 Bradley Smith/Photo Researchers, 20 Bantam-Skylark, 59 Culver Pictures, 61 (both) Culver Pictures, 90 The American Red Cross, 93 New York Public Library Collection, 96 The National Foundation March of Dimes, Culver Pictures, 97 Culver Pictures, 99 UPI, 101 (both) New York Public Library Collection, 105 Painting by John Trumbull from Library of Congress Collection, 112 M.E. Warren/Photo Researchers, 113 SYGMA, 115 Elizabeth Hibbs/Monkmeyer, 117 From the book Equal Justice Under Law, courtesy of the Foundation of the Federal Bar Assn., 125 Grant Heilman, 128 Bethlehem Steel Corp., 129 Grant Heilman, 131 Erika/Peter Arnold Photo Archives, 140, 141, 142, 143 Illustrations by Diane L. Nelson, AMI, 157 Peter Arnold Photo Archives, 160 Culver Pictures, UPI, 161 Wide World Photos, 164 Ken Regan/Camera 5, 168 Wide World, UPI, 169 UPI, Yale University, 176 Wide World, 183 (both) Keystone, 184 Keystone, Marlow/SYGMA, 189 Curt Gunther/Camera 5, 192 J. P. Laffont/SYGMA, 193 Ken Regan/Camera 5, 195, 199 Martha Swope/Taurus Photos, 204 New York Public Library Collection, 207 Pictorial Parade, 253 Culver Pictures, 255 Wide World, 258 Swedish Information Service, The Bettmann Archive, Yale University, Swedish Information Service, 259 French Embassy Press, German Information Service, Culver Pictures, Keystone, 261 Pictorial Parade, University of California, Columbia University, UPI, 276 Brookhaven National Laboratory, 282 Culver Pictures, Austrian Information Service, UPI, 285 Dan O'Neill/Editorial Photocolor Archives, 286 (both) Laima Turnley/Editorial Photocolor Archives, 287 NASA, 290 U.S. Department of the Interior, 295 M. Williams/National Park Service, 300 U.S. Department of Commerce, Weather Bureau, 301 (all) National Oceanic and Atmospheric Administration, 311 Hale Observatories, Mt. Wilson and Palomar Observatories, 323 NASA, 324 (both) NASA, 325 NASA, 327 United Nations, 331 Carl Frank/Photo Researchers, 336 Carl Frank/Photo Researchers, 342 Jerry Frank, 343 Van Bucher/Photo Researchers, 345 Jerry Frank, 351 Carl Frank/Photo Researchers, 355 Klaus D. Francke/Peter Arnold Photo Archives, Photo Researchers, 364 Grant Heilman, 367 Photo Researchers, 368 Lord/Monkmeyer, 369 (top) Photo Researchers.

Contents

STUDENT HANDBOOK

HOW TO STUDY 1–8

IMPORTANCE OF PLANNING 2
Plan Your Homework 3 • Plan Your Recreation 3 • One
Successful Student's Study Schedule 4

THE STRATEGY OF STUDY 5
Reading for Study Purposes 6 • A Good Way to Learn
Vocabulary 6 • Preparing for Tests 7 • Study as a Lifetime
Activity 8

A GUIDE TO READING 9–20

THE PLEASURE OF READING 10
Folk Tales and Fairy Tales 10 • Myths and Legends 12
Fantastic Stories 12 • Science Fiction 13 • Ghosts and
Ghouls 13 • Adventure 14 • Animal Stories 14 • Mysteries 15
Realistic Stories 15 • Historical Novels 16 • History 17
Biography 18 • Poetry 18 • Nature, Science, and Ecology 19
Funny Stories 20 • Hobbies and Special Interests 20

USING THE LANGUAGE 21–58

HOW TO IMPROVE YOUR READING 22
Three Hints for Improving Your Study Reading 22 • How to
Increase Your Reading Speed 23

HOW TO IMPROVE YOUR WRITING 24
Begin with an Outline 24 • Preparing Your Final Copy 25

DIAGRAMING SENTENCES   26

SPECIAL USES OF LANGUAGE   27

CONJUGATING THE ENGLISH VERB   28

GLOSSARY OF GRAMMATICAL TERMS   30

USEFUL RULES OF PUNCTUATION   31
Period 31 • Exclamation Point 31 • Question Mark 32
Comma 32 • Colon 33 • Semicolon 33 • Apostrophe 33
Quotation Marks 33 • Dash 34 • Hyphen 34 • Parentheses 34
Brackets 34

RULES OF CAPITALIZATION   35

SEVEN HELPFUL SPELLING RULES   36
Four Valuable Spelling Hints 38 • One Hundred Words Frequently
Misspelled 38

SYNONYMS AND ANTONYMS   39

THE UNITED STATES 59–130

UNITED STATES HISTORY   60

IMPORTANT EVENTS IN AMERICAN HISTORY   62

FACTS ABOUT THE PRESIDENTS   72

INFLUENTIAL MEN AND WOMEN   90

WORDS THAT SHAPED U.S. HISTORY   98

DECLARATION OF INDEPENDENCE   103
Text of the Declaration of Independence 104 • The Signers of the
Declaration 106 • The Thirteen Original Colonies (with map) 107

THE CONSTITUTION   108

BILL OF RIGHTS   109

THE FEDERAL GOVERNMENT   111
The Legislative Branch 112 • The Executive Branch 114 • The
Judicial Branch 116 • The Federal Bureaucracy 117

GLOSSARY OF GOVERNMENT TERMS   119

THE STATES   122
Essential Information, Listed by State 122 • Map of Territorial
Acquisitions 123 • Population Density of the U.S.   130 • State
Populations Compared 130

HEALTH AND HOME 131–156

HEALTHY AND VIGOROUS LIVING   132

Table of Basic Four Food Groups 132 • Dieting 133 • Table of Recommended Nutritional Requirements 133 • Vitamins: Their Importance and Sources 134 • Caring for Your Skin and Hair 135 Caring for Your Teeth 135 • The Importance of Exercise 135 Preventing Health Problems 137 • Immunization Schedule 137 Tips for Adolescents 137 • The Uses and Effects of Some Drugs 138

The Skeletal and Muscular Systems 140 • Organs of the Body 141 The Nervous System 142 • The Circulatory System 143 • Some Infectious Diseases 144

SAFETY   145

Tips for Home Safety 145 • How to Put out Fires 146

FIRST AID   147

Shock 148 • Mouth-to-Mouth Resuscitation 149

FIRST-AID FACTS YOU SHOULD KNOW   150

THE HOME   152

Smart Food-Buying Habits 152 • Buying Meat 152 • Buying Poultry 153 • Buying Fish and Shellfish 153 • Vegetables and Fruits 154 • Stain Removal Chart 154 • Household Cleaning Tips 155 • Care and Cleaning of Furniture 155 • Consumer Protection 155 • Common Deceptions 156

SPORTS 157–194

BASEBALL: THE NATIONAL PASTIME   158

Professional Baseball Today 159 • Some Major League Records 160 • Amateur Baseball Today 161 • How to Play Baseball 162 • Some Little-Known Dimensions of Baseball 163

GLOSSARY OF BASEBALL TERMS   164

FOOTBALL: BRUISING CONTACT SPORT   166

Professional Football 166 • Key Dates in the Development of Modern Football 167 • Amateur Football 168 • How to Play Football 169 • Some Little-Known Football Dimensions 172

GLOSSARY OF FOOTBALL TERMS   174

BASKETBALL: THE ACTION SPORT   175

Professional Basketball 175 • Amateur Basketball 176 • How to Play Basketball 177 • Basketball for Women 179

GLOSSARY OF BASKETBALL TERMS   180

TENNIS: FASTEST GROWING SPORT 181

Lawn Tennis 181 • Women's Tennis 182 • International
Competition Today 183 • How to Play Tennis 183

GLOSSARY OF TENNIS TERMS 186

SOCCER: THE FAVORITE WORLD-WIDE 187

How to Play Soccer 187 • Equipment 189 • Professional
Soccer 190 • Amateur Soccer 190

GLOSSARY OF SOCCER TERMS 190

THE OLYMPIC GAMES 191

Olympic Sports 191 • The Decathlon: World's Toughest
Event 192 • Olympic Records 193

MUSIC 195–208

THE STUDY OF MUSIC 196

BANDS 196

THE SYMPHONY ORCHESTRA 196

LISTENING TO MUSIC ON YOUR OWN 198

GLOSSARY OF MUSIC 200

FAMOUS COMPOSERS 203

MATHEMATICS 209–252

PLACE VALUE 210

WHOLE-NUMBER OPERATIONS 211

Addition of Whole Numbers 211 • Table of Roman Numerals 213
Subtraction of Whole Numbers 216 • Multiplication of Whole
Numbers 218 • Division of Whole Numbers 223

OPERATIONS WITH FRACTIONS 227

Factoring 227 • Reducing Fractions 230 • Finding the Least
Common Multiple (LCM) 231 • Finding the Least Common
Denominator (LCD) 232 • Renaming Fractions as Fractions with a
Given Denominator 233 • Renaming Whole Numbers as
Fractions 233 • Renaming Whole Numbers as Fractions with a
Given Denominator 234 • Renaming Mixed Numbers as
Fractions 234

Addition of Fractions 235 • Addition of Mixed Numbers 237
Subtraction of Fractions 238 • Subtraction of Mixed Numbers 238

Multiplication of Fractions 240 • Multiplication of Mixed
Numbers 240 • Division of Fractions 241 • Division of Mixed
Numbers 241

EXPONENTS 242

DECIMALS 244
Operations on Decimals 244 • Writing Fractions as Decimals 247
Writing Decimals as Fractions 248

HAND-HELD CALCULATORS 249

LIST OF MATHEMATICAL SYMBOLS 251

GLOSSARY OF TERMS USED IN MATHEMATICS 252

SCIENCE 253–286

CHEMISTRY AND PHYSICS 254
What Is Science? 254 • Subjects Covered by Chemistry and
Physics 254 • Table of Metric Weights and Measures 262
Table of Equivalent Measures 262 • Conversion Table 264
Facts About Some Important Elements 266 • Man-Made Textile
Fibers 272 • Atomic Particles 273

IMPORTANT EVENTS IN CHEMISTRY AND PHYSICS 256

GLOSSARY OF CHEMISTRY AND PHYSICS 274

LIFE SCIENCE 276
Subjects Covered by Life Science 276 • The Ecosystem: The Web
of Life 277 • The Plant Kingdom 278 • The Animal
Kingdom 279 • Prehistoric Man 280 • Major Human Fossil
Discoveries 280

IMPORTANT EVENTS IN LIFE SCIENCE 281

GLOSSARY OF LIFE SCIENCE 283

CAREERS IN SCIENCE 285

EARTH AND SPACE SCIENCE 287–326

OUR PLANET EARTH 288
The Structure of the Earth 288 • How the Continents Are
Formed 288 • Above and Below the Surface of the Earth 289
Diagram of the Formation of Continents 291 • Volcanoes and
Earthquakes 290 • Schematic of an Active Volcano 292
Glaciation 293 • Geologic Time Table 294 • North American

Glacial Stages 295 • Schematic of a Glacier 296 • Map of Glacial
Stages 297 • The Ice Ages 297

Earth's Weather and Atmosphere 298 • The Layers of the
Atmosphere 298 • Composition of Earth's Atmosphere 298
Wind 299 • Special Wind Storms 299 • Weather and
Climate 300 • Air Masses 300 • Types of Clouds 301 • Modern
Weather Instruments 302

GLOSSARY OF TERMS USED IN EARTH SCIENCE 303

BEYOND THE EARTH 304
Facts About the Planets 304 • Diagram of the Solar System 305
Lunar and Solar Eclipses 307 • Total Lunar Eclipses
1978–1990 307 • Total Solar Eclipses 1978–1990 307 • Schematic
of Eclipses 308 • Phases of the Moon 309 • The Seasons 310
Galaxies 311 • Stars 311 • Luminosity 312 • Classification of
Stars 312 • Death of Stars 313 • Star Chart 314
Cosmology 315 • Important Events in Astronomy 316

SPACE EXPLORATION 318
Manned Space Flight 318 • Table of Manned Space Flights 320
Salyut Space Laboratory 323 • Skylab 324 • Space Shuttle
Orbiter 325 • Viking Mars Lander 325 • Other Space Probes 326

GLOSSARY OF ASTRONOMY AND SPACE SCIENCE 326

THE WORLD 327–370

COUNTRIES OF THE WORLD 328

WORLD GEOGRAPHY 363
Earth's Measurements 363 • The Continents 364 • Table of
Statistics: The Continents 366 • Ten Largest Islands 366 • Ten
Largest Countries 366 • World Population 367 • Ten Largest
Countries by Population 367 • Fifteen Largest Cities 367
Oceans of the World 368 • Ten Largest Seas 368 • Ten Largest
Lakes 368 • Ten Longest Rivers 368 • Ten Highest
Waterfalls 368 • Ten Highest Mountains 369 • Recently Active
Volcanoes 369 • Great Deserts of the World 369

MAPS OF THE WORLD 370

Student Handbook

Editorial development of the Student Handbook was directed by
The Hudson Group, Inc., Pleasantville, New York.

EUGENE EHRLICH / *Editor-in-Chief*   GORTON CARRUTH / *Sponsoring Editor*

Bruce Wetterau / *Managing Editor*

David H. Scott / *Senior Editor*   Natalie Goldstein / *Picture Editor*

Associate Editors:
   Lilian Brady, Renee Cohen, Nancy Hayes, Emma G. Peirce, Katherine G. Scott

Editorial Assistants:
   Hayden Carruth, Edward Fields, Susan Horton

CONTRIBUTING EDITORS

Everett J. Arthur	Norma S. Ehrlich	Harold P. Menninger
Patrick Beausoleil	Gladys Hager	David Morrill
David M. Brownstone	Murray Halwer	John A. Peirce
Gerard G. Chamberland	Gene R. Hawes	Edgar M. Reilly, Jr.
Phillip Cole	Waldeck Mainville	Richard H. Sturgeon
		Ann Waterhouse

The Student Handbook was designed by Edward Aho Design Associates, Inc.,
Pleasantville, New York.

Edward Aho / *Director*

Laurel Casazza, Pam Forde
Designers / Art Directors

Assistants: Gregory Brownstone, Deborah Hughes

ILLUSTRATION

James Barkley	Peter Loewer
Ken Marcus Daly	Diane L. Nelson
Nick Forde	Publisher's Graphics
Graphic Presentation, Inc.	Jan Pyk
Robert Handville	Michael Vivo

Composition for the Student Handbook was by Monotype Composition Company, Inc.,
Baltimore, Maryland.

HOW TO STUDY

Every serious student wants to learn as much as possible about how the world functions. Another important educational goal is to gain an understanding of the great ideas that have shaped human lives. A third goal is to develop the skills needed to meet life's demands.

The single most important skill you can learn in school is *how to learn*. If you expect to do well in the career you one day will choose, know from the start that your learning will not end when school days are over. To be ready for all the opportunities that lie ahead, you will always have to learn more. For this reason, your *Student Handbook* begins with valuable tips on how to study. In addition, many other parts of this volume and of the Concise Edition give you information that will help you. Make the most of your opportunity. Become the best learner you can possibly be.

Importance of Planning

Who doesn't want to do well in school? We all know that the better we do in school, the more we enjoy every day of the year. With homework done on time, with all our lessons learned, we can look forward to the next day's classes.

With work left undone, with information only half understood, we worry about whether our teachers will call on us the next day and show up the fact that we are not prepared.

Will there be a surprise quiz? Will a teacher insist that we give up sports activities or club activities so we can make up work we have neglected?

Do you ever ask yourself, "How is it that some students are always well prepared? Are they just naturally smarter than I am—or do they have a secret way of studying, a way I can use if someone will tell me what it is."

The truth is there is no secret way to study successfully. It is also true that the smartest students do not always get the best marks, learn the most in school, or have the greatest success once the years of schooling are over.

What makes the difference between doing your best in school and doing less than your best is careful planning and keeping to your plan so you achieve your goals.

- *You can use all your natural ability.*
- *You can use your time well.*
- *You can make the most of your opportunities.*

Talk with anyone who is successful in life: your local bank president, the supermarket manager, the school principal, a prominent attorney, or any leader in your community. Find out how they plan each day's activities. You can be sure that such people do not merely let things happen to them. They keep a diary in which they schedule everything they have to do. Busy men and women do not trust themselves to keep their appointments in their heads. They don't guess what they have to do next. They cannot accomplish all the work they do unless they plan carefully.

While you are in school, preparing for your life work, you can benefit from careful planning. Students are among the busiest people in the world. Every week is filled with classes, after-school recreation, home chores or jobs, and many hours of study. By planning your study hours as carefully as any other busy person does, you will make the most of your time, your opportunities, and your many assets—your talents, your intelligence, your future.

8:00	STAFF MEETING
8:30	INTERVIEW JOB APPLICANT
9:00	ANSWER MAIL
9:30	REVIEW NEXT YEAR'S BUDGET
10:00	
10:30	
11:00	
11:30	REVIEW NOTES FOR LUNCHEON MEETING WITH FINANCE COMMITTEE
12:00	LUNCH IN EXECUTIVE DININGROOM
12:30	
1:00	
1:30	OUTLINE AND FIRST DRAFT OF QUARTERLY REPORT
2:00	
2:30	
3:00	BOARD MEETING
3:30	
4:00	
4:30	REVIEW SALES FORECASTS

A page from a busy person's diary. In order to make good use of time, an executive plans each hour of every business day as precisely as possible.

PLAN YOUR HOMEWORK

Few of us always find homework interesting. Yes, there will be some assignments you look forward to—a science project, a special book report, a part in a class play, or any one of the many assignments that fit your special interests. But there will be other assignments you would gladly skip—if the world would only let you.

Yet you must do every assignment, and you must do it on time. A wise man has said that *work expands to fill the time available for it.* This means that if you do not set aside a particular period in which to do a particular assignment, it will take up all your time.

The best way to get a job done, then, whether you like the work or not, is to set aside a particular time slot in your day or evening that you will devote to that work.

And you will get it done. You will find, for example, that if you budget one hour for a certain assignment and the following hour for another assignment, you will get both jobs done on time. If you don't budget your time this way, but merely sit down to work one afternoon or evening, the first assignment will take all the time you have available. You may never get to the second one.

Let's say you have a math assignment and an English assignment to do in the same evening. You want to do the math first because math is harder for you and you want to be as alert as possible for the work. By setting a time of one hour for the math, you will find that you can complete it or nearly complete it in that time. You then can take a break for a few minutes to clear your head. During the break you might take a quick walk or do some other physical exercise. When you sit down to work again, you are refreshed and can plunge into the English assignment, again budgeting one hour or whatever time you think the homework should take. Thus, in the two hours or so you have budgeted, you complete all your work for that evening.

In this manner *you control your assignments instead of letting your assignments control you.* You get much more work done in a given time, and you have time left for your hobbies or for reading for pleasure.

Learning the habit of controlling your time by careful scheduling is one of the best things you can do for yourself during the years of schooling.

PLAN YOUR RECREATION

Happy, productive school years are the result of worthwhile use of your time—recreation time as well as study time. Use your spare time for vigorous physical exercise and your hobbies, and you will find that your school work will benefit.

	MONDAY	TUESDAY	WEDNESDAY	THURSDAY	FRIDAY	SATURDAY
9	English Class Theme Due	English Class	English Class	English Class	English Class	Review For Math Test
10	Math Test	Math Class	Math Class	Math Class	Free Period Review History	
11	History Class	History Class	Free Period Library Research	History Class	History Test	Final Draft of English Theme
12	LUNCH	LUNCH	Lunch, Band Practice	LUNCH	LUNCH	
1	French Conversation	French Translation		French Grammar	French Grammar	TIME OFF
2	Phys. Ed.	Swimming Team Practice	Phys. Ed.	Phys. Ed.	Swimming Team Practice	
3				Nature Club		
4	Reading	Reading	Reading	Supermarket Job	Supermarket Job	
5						
6	DINNER					
7	French Homework	Math Homework	French Homework	First Draft English Theme	French Homework	
8	English Homework	English Homework	Math Homework		English Homework	
9	Math Homework	Practice Music	History Homework	History Test Review		Have Fun!

ONE SUCCESSFUL STUDENT'S STUDY SCHEDULE

Organizing your own study schedule will take some time, but it will pay off in better grades. Expect to change your schedule a few times each term until you find out how much time you need for each subject. Schedule study time for the day before the class and include recreation time in your schedule.

The Romans had the slogan *Mens sana in corpore sano*: a sound mind in a sound body. This was and is the goal of education, and you must not neglect your physical and emotional health as you pursue your studies. To achieve this goal, you must be sure to take part in physical exercise and games as well as other things you like to do on your own.

This does not mean that you must let your studies play second fiddle to the games you love. A boy who puts high school football ahead of high school studies may be unhappy when he leaves high school with varsity letters but little else. Your future demands more preparation than football practice. Thus, while you should not neglect to develop your sports ability, remember the importance of acquiring a good education. Many famous athletes—Supreme Court Justice Byron "Whizzer" White, for example—show us that studies can be combined with excellence in sports.

Take part in the games and clubs your school offers, but leave ample time for your studies. In your weekly schedule, budget your time for recreation in the same way you budget your study hours.

The Strategy of Study

Many students do not realize that effective study begins with understanding just what teachers expect of their students. Good students soon learn to do their work in the way their teachers want it done.

Teachers emphasize various types of learning when they assign homework. One teacher may expect a great deal of memorization. Another may place special emphasis on learning *principles* rather than on learning *details*. Another may want students to develop the ability to *think for themselves* instead of relying on what others do and say. Yet another may want students to learn *just what the teacher thinks* and be able to give it back exactly the way the teacher said it.

These different ways of teaching all have their places in education, and you must learn to meet these various demands. As

Teachers are always willing to give you extra time if you need it. Be sure to ask for time when you have a problem, but be sure to make appointments with teachers well in advance.

early as possible in each semester, then, try to size up your teachers and find out what they expect of you. As you study, prepare yourself for the next day's classes in just the manner that will meet your various teachers' expectations. If you are expected to memorize facts and details, memorize them. If you are expected to learn principles rather than details, concentrate on principles. If you are expected to learn to think for yourself, concentrate on that. If your teacher expects you to remember just what the teacher has said in class, do just that.

Meeting your teachers' expectations is a valuable strategy in successful study.

READING FOR STUDY PURPOSES

When you read an assignment, you must understand that such reading is quite dif-

ferent from the kind of reading you do when you are reading a story for pleasure or when you are reading a newspaper.

Reading for study purposes means learning what you read and being able to tell somebody what you have learned. Such reading demands that you stop from time to time to test your understanding of what you have read.

The best way to do this is to *skim* the assigned reading first, noting what the assignment covers. A few minutes spent finding out what the assignment covers will prepare your mind for what you are about to read. Skimming in this manner can be thought of as *finding out what questions the material asks and answers*. Once you have found this out, you are ready to begin doing your careful reading.

When reading, keep in mind that *you are looking for the answers to the questions you located* when you skimmed. In a sense

---

A GOOD WAY TO LEARN VOCABULARY

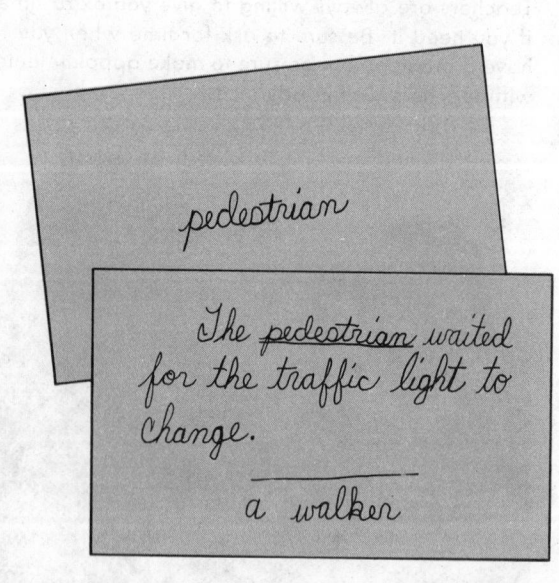

Ordinary index cards can become valuable tools in learning new words. On one side of each card, write a word you want to learn.

On the back of the card, write the sentence in which you found the word *plus* the dictionary definition of the word.

Keep your word cards with you as you go about your daily school program. In your spare time during the day, take out your pack of cards and drill yourself. Looking at the face of a card, see whether you can remember the meaning of the word and the sentence in which you found it. When you know a word, place a check mark on the face of the card and put it back in your pack. When a card has three check marks, you know that word. Put that card away in your desk. About once a month, go through all the cards you have put away to make sure you still remember the words on them.

you are setting up a quiz for yourself on what the assignment covers. As you find the full answer to the first question, stop reading, put the book aside, and *answer the question from memory*. The best way to answer the question is in writing. If you work this way, you will be preparing for the test you will take at the end of a unit of study or for the test your teacher will give you at the end of the term.

When you have finished the entire assignment this way, put your book aside and try to *ask and answer every question raised in your reading*. If you cannot answer all the questions, go back to the answers you have written in order to refresh your memory. Once you are able to summarize an entire assignment in this way, you have learned what you are supposed to have learned. You are ready for the next day's class and you have made an important advance toward preparing for a written test.

PREPARING FOR TESTS

If you study in the manner just described, you will be getting ready for tests from the first day in each of your courses. All that will remain to be done is finish the final review all of us need to do our best on important tests. If you neglect your day-by-day studying, preparing for a test becomes a race against time that is thoroughly unpleasant. Cramming may get you through a test, but you can be sure you will not remember much of what you crammed once the test is over. Study takes time, and trying to learn in one night what should have been learned in a month or more is an uphill battle that makes school an unhappy experience.

When you do your final review, make sure you know what kind of test your teacher is planning to give. Short-answer tests usually concentrate on details. Essay

School gives you a great deal of pleasure as well as the foundation for a successful life—if you study effectively. Good work habits in the classroom mean effective use of time. Pay careful attention to teachers' advice and directions so that you do your work on time and in the manner expected of you.

Don't neglect your hobbies and other interests. Collecting stamps, butterflies, rocks, or coins may become the start of serious study leading to a fine career that will give you satisfaction.

tests usually test learning of broad principles. Thus, while you are studying for a test, keep in mind that you are trying to meet the teacher's expectations.

Does the teacher expect knowledge of facts and dates? Formulas and definitions? Plot summaries of stories or poems? Knowledge of themes and characters? Whatever a teacher has stressed during class sessions is what that teacher will concentrate on in examinations.

Remember that your teachers do not give examinations in order to torture you. They want you to succeed. The happiest teacher is one who can pass all students with high grades.

As you do your final reviewing for a quiz or examination, do not just pore over your textbooks, trying to stuff information into your head. Instead, *ask yourself the questions your teacher probably will ask you.* You can make up a final examination as well as a teacher can if you have studied carefully all term and paid attention in class. When you have decided what the most likely questions are, *answer those questions in writing.* Practice of this kind is the best preparation for a test.

STUDY AS A LIFETIME ACTIVITY

Study does not end when high school or college days are over. So much is being discovered and improved in the modern world each day that we must struggle to keep up with new information and new ideas. In addition, people live longer lives in the advanced countries of the world. This means that we spend more and more years learning new things. Farmers must understand modern machinery in order to make a living. Engineers must study constantly to keep up with ever-growing technology. The members of every profession must study new developments in their fields.

If you do not yet realize it, learn now that you have entered into a program of study that will not end until you are no longer alive. This study will enrich your life as well as enable you always to earn your living. When something interests you, follow it up. Don't put it off by saying, "Someday I'm going to find out more about that." "When I have the time, I think I'll go into that more deeply." The time is right now, and the library is the place to begin.

The more you read, the more you will know of the exciting ideas, skills, and knowledge that are yours for the asking. Work at this process of discovery to build a satisfying life now and in the future.

A GUIDE TO READING

Hours spent with good books are hours of pleasure—if you select books that match your interests. Each year tens of thousands of books are published. Some of them are practical books, giving information you may need to pursue a hobby or interest. Some are books of entertainment, designed to lighten your hours. Others may be called biographies or histories but, by their examples of great lives and great events, they really become books of inspiration. Though such books carry you into the past, they help you see yourself now and in the future.

In addition to these, there are works of fiction and collections of poetry. Their creators are limited only by their imaginations, and as a reader you are completely free to go along with the novelist or poet as the work unfolds. Give yourself the great gift of reading by using the following pages to find books you will treasure.

The Pleasure of Reading

The books listed on the following pages are to be read for pleasure. You will find them interesting, entertaining, and exciting. The books are grouped under many categories to help you find titles that interest you, but your search through these lists should not be confined to any single category. Every one of them contains books you will want to read.

For instance, many of the books of poetry are humorous and two of them are about events in American history. So, even if you have not yet found how interesting poetry can be, be sure to sample the Poetry list. Fairy Tales, Myths, Ghost Stories, and Science Fiction are also Fantastic Stories. As far as we know, the stories on these lists could not really have happened. The books on the Realistic Stories list are mostly about young people who have had experiences and problems that may resemble your own or those of people you know.

If you don't yet care much for reading, but like to make things with your own hands, try one of the books on the Hobbies list. Or make a windmill—one of the books on the Nature, Science, and Ecology list tells you how. Or you might try one of the Funny Books and become a comedian. Whatever your interests, you will surely find books here to give you many hours of pleasure.

To help you find a book that suits you, most of the lists are divided into three parts, with the easiest books appearing first, then the more advanced, and finally the most advanced. Choose your subject, find a good title, get the book, and settle down to enjoy good reading.

FOLK TALES AND FAIRY TALES

Africa

Animals Mourn for Da Leopard by Peter G. Dorliae.
Anansi the Spider by Gerald McDermott.
The Time-Ago Tales of Jahdu by Virginia Hamilton.
Black Fairy Tales by Terry Berger.
Tales Told Near a Crocodile by Humphrey Harman.

Asia and the Pacific

The Emperor and the Kite by Jane Yolen. Chinese legend.
Fairy Tales of the Orient by Pearl Buck.
The Journey of Akbar by Aline Glasgow. Indian folklore.
Kap and the Wicked Monkey by Betty Jean Lifton. Based on a Japanese folk story.
The Talkative Beasts: Myths, Fables and Poems of India by Gwendolyn Reed.
Serendipity Tales by Elizabeth Jamison Hodges. Tales from Persia, India, and Ceylon.
Backbone of the King: The Story of Paka'a and His Son Ku by Marcia Brown. Hawaiian legend.

"The Old Hunting Dog," from *Aesop's Fables*.

From a collection of *Grimm's Fairy Tales*.

British Isles

The Hound of Ulster by Rosemary Sutcliff.

The High Deeds of Finn MacCool by Rosemary Sutcliff.

Favorite Fairy Tales Told in England by Virginia Haviland.

Favorite Fairy Tales Told in Scotland by Virginia Haviland.

Duffy and the Devil, a Cornish Tale by Harve Zemach.

The Girl Who Sat by the Ashes by Padraic Colum.

The Caribbean and Latin America

The Piece of Fire and Other Haitian Tales by Harold Courlander.

The Tiger and the Rabbit and Other Tales by Pura Belpré.

Latin American Tales by Genevieve Barlow.

Tales from Silver Lands by Charles Finger.

Europe

The Complete Fairy Tales of George Macdonald by George Macdonald.

Aesop's Fables.

Grimm's Fairy Tales.

Hans Christian Andersen.

The White Cat and Other Old French Fairy Tales by Rachel Field.

Zlateh the Goat and Other Stories by Isaac Bashevis Singer.

Awake and Dreaming by Harve Zemach.

Middle East

Once the Hodja by Alice Green Kelsey.

Arabian Nights by Andrew Lang.

Persian Folk and Fairy Tales by Anne Sinclair Mehdevi.

United States and Canada

Bowleg Bill: Seagoing Cowpuncher by Harold W. Felton. Other books by the same author: *Pecos Bill and the Mustang, True Tall Tales of Stormalong,* and *Mike Fink, Best of the Keelboatmen.*

The Talking Cat and Other Stories of French Canada by Natalie Savage Carlson. Other books by the same author: *Alphonse, That Bearded One;* and *Sashes Red and Sashes Blue.*

John Henry: An American Legend by Ezra Jack Keats.

Eagle Mask: A West Coast Indian Tale by James Houston. Other books by the same author: *The White Archer: An Eskimo Legend* and *Akarak: An Eskimo Journey.*

Cover of a modern version of *Beowulf*.

The Legend of Sleepy Hollow by Washington Irving.
Uncle Remus: His Songs and His Sayings by Joel Chandler Harris.
Down from the Lonely Mountain by Jane Louise Curry.
Yankee Doodle's Cousins by Anne Malcolmsen.

MYTHS AND LEGENDS

Greek Gods and Heroes and **The Siege and Fall of Troy** by Robert Graves. Myths retold by a famous poet.
Beowulf retold by Rosemary Sutcliff. The oldest English epic.
The Children's Homer: The Adventures of Odysseus and the Tales of Troy by Padraic Colum. By the same author: *The Golden Fleece and the Heroes Who Lived Before Ulysses.*
Adventures of Rama retold by Joseph Gaer. A Hindu myth-epic.
Tales of Charlemagne by Jennifer Westwood. Six great sagas of medieval Europe.
Story of King Arthur and His Knights by Howard Pyle. By the same author: *The Merry Adventures of Robin Hood.*
Stories of the Gods and Heroes by Sally Benson.
How the People Sang the Mountains Up by Maria Leach.
The Golden Treasury of Myths and Legends by Anne Terry White.
Thunder of the Gods by Dorothy Hosford. Norse myths.

The Children of Odin: The Book of Northern Myths by Padraic Colum.

FANTASTIC STORIES

The Borrowers by Mary Norton. A story about tiny people who live in walls and borrow everything they need. This is just one of many books about these people by the same author.
The Town Cats by Lloyd Alexander. Eight stories about cats that try to set the world aright. By the same author: *The Book of Three, The Castle of Llyr,* and *The Black Cauldron.* Adventure and intrigue in the imaginary kingdom of Prydain, from which Taran, the Assistant Pig-keeper goes forth to overcome the evil Horned King.
The 21 Balloons by William Pène du Bois. Comedy, science, and adventure in this story of a balloon trip.
Half Magic by Edward Eager. Jane, along with her two sisters and brother, uses a half-magic coin to travel to King Arthur's Court and other exciting places. By the same author: *The Time Garden* and *Magic by the Lake,* and others.
Pippi Longstocking by Astrid Lindgren. Nine-year-old Pippi lives alone with a monkey and a horse and creates fun and excitement wherever she goes.
The Children of Green Knowe by Lucy M. Boston. Tolly is sent to live with his grandmother, who helps him see and play with children who lived long ago. This is just one of many books in the Green Knowe series.
Mary Poppins by P. L. Travers. Adventures of the gravity-defying nursemaid and the children she looks after. There are other good Mary Poppins books.
A Furl of Fairy Wind by Mollie Hunter. Four modern fairy tales.

The Jungle Book by Rudyard Kipling. The adventure of Mowgli, a human baby raised by wolves. Kipling was also the author of the *Just So Stories,* humorous tall tales about animals. Millions have loved these books.
Charlie and the Chocolate Factory by Roald Dahl. The story of Willie Wonka's amazing factory told by a master story-teller.
The Court of the Stone Children by Eleanor Cameron. A young visitor to a San Francisco museum becomes involved with a girl of the time of Napoleon whose home and its furnishings now

From *The Wind in the Willows*
by Kenneth Grahame.

are part of a museum. Mysterious story well told.

Charlotte's Web by E. B. White. A spider saves a pig by spinning messages in her web. A classic story that is read and enjoyed by people of all ages. By the same author: *Stuart Little* and *The Trumpet of the Swan*.

The Phantom Tollbooth by Norton Juster. Miles is given a tollbooth and goes to a fantastic world you will enjoy.

The Lion, the Witch, and the Wardrobe by C. S. Lewis. Four children sent to the country to escape the bombing of London during World War II meet exciting adventures in the land of Narnia, which lies just beyond the wardrobe in a vacant room. The story is continued in *The Magician's Nephew, The Last Battle,* and others.

The Hobbitt by J. R. R. Tolkien. The very popular story of how Bilbo Baggins helped the dwarves recover stolen wealth from Smaug the dragon.

Alice's Adventures in Wonderland and **Through the Looking Glass** by Lewis Carroll. These classic stories have been read again and again for over one hundred years.

The Wind in the Willows by Kenneth Grahame. Mole, Water Rat, Badger, and Toad live in the woods and give joy to millions of readers.

SCIENCE FICTION

Miss Pickerell Goes to Mars by Ellen MacGregor. Miss Pickerell gives a stranger a lift and suddenly finds herself on the way to Mars. Some other books about Miss Pickerell are: *Miss Pickerell Goes Undersea* and *Miss Pickerell Goes to the Arctic*.

Danny Dunn and the Weather Machine by Jay Williams. Even readers who have trouble getting into a book will like this amusing story of two boys on a flight into space. Other good ones by this author are *Danny Dunn and the Anti-Gravity Paint, Danny Dunn and the Homework Machine,* and *Danny Dunn on a Desert Island*.

Down to Earth by Patricia Wrightson. Martin the Martian is befriended by some children in Australia until he can return to his home planet.

The Pool of Fire by John Christopher. In the twenty-first century, Earth is conquered by the Tripods. A small group of men survive and try to recapture their planet.

A Wrinkle in Time by Madeleine L'Engle. Three children are spirited to a world in outer space by three supernatural beings. If you enjoy this one, try *The Arm of the Starfish* by the same author.

Another World by Gardner Dozois. A collection of eleven exciting stories.

Shakespeare's Planet by Clifford Simak. Horton and his comedian robot companion land on a mysterious planet, where they meet weird inhabitants.

Time for the Stars by Robert Heinlein. Twins Tom and Pat take part in an experiment in which one is sent into space while the other remains on Earth. Other good stories by this author are *Tunnel in the Sky, Citizen of the Galaxy,* and *Have Space Suit—Will Travel*.

Operation Time Search by André Norton. Ray finds himself back in the time of Atlantis and gets involved in a conflict. By the same author: *The Zero Stone, Moon of Three Rings, Steel Magic,* and others.

20,000 Leagues Under the Sea by Jules Verne. This exciting story of Captain Nemo and his submarine can serve as your introduction to the many exciting books by this author. *Around the World in 80 Days* is another favorite.

GHOSTS AND GHOULS

Ghosts I Have Been by Richard Peck. A girl impersonates a ghost and finds she herself has second sight.

The Wednesday Witch by Ruth Chew. A witch rides a flying vacuum cleaner instead of a broom and meets adventure. Mysterious and funny.

Poltergeists: Hauntings and the Haunted by David C. Knight. Twelve factual reports of what are called noisy ghosts. The stories come from the seventeenth century as well as modern times.

The Phantom Cyclist and Other Ghost Stories by Ruth Ainsworth. Make sure you keep a light on in every room while you read these chillers.

Meet the Werewolf by Georgess McHargue. Everything you ever wanted to know about werewolves.

Dreamland Lake by Richard Peck. Two boys in the seventh grade find a body lying in the woods.

The House with a Clock in Its Walls by John Bellairs. A boy discovers that his uncle is a real wizard and then dabbles in magic himself. A ghost story filled with suspense.

The Eyes of the Amaryllis by Natalie Babbitt. A story about a shipwreck that can be called either a ghost story or a love story. Read it and make up your own mind.

Encounters with the Invisible World by Marilynne K. Roach. Ten tales of ghosts, witches, and the devil—based on old New England legends.

The Shadow Cage and Other Tales of the Supernatural by Philippa Pearce. One of the interesting characters in this book is a dog that vanquishes invisible rats.

Escape If You Can—13 Tales of the Preternatural by Eva-Lis Wuorio. Mysterious stories of many different places—Lebanon, London, Finland, Canada.

A Host of Ghosts by Christine Bernard. These retold stories concern doppelgängers, remembered lives, telepathy, and other mysterious subjects.

ADVENTURE

The Bushbabies by William Stevenson. Jackie, her interesting pet, and an old African hunter travel over miles of wild country in Kenya.

Boy Alone by Reginald Ottley. A story about a boy and a dog in Australia. Also by this author: *The Roan Colt* and *Rain Comes to Yambroorah*.

Call It Courage by Armstrong Perry. The son of a Polynesian chieftain has harrowing adventures while trying to conquer his fears.

The Devil's Triangle by Elwood D. Baumann. Strange occurrences and disappearances that have been recorded since the time of Columbus until the present, all in the waters known as the Bermuda Triangle.

Treasure Island by Robert Louis Stevenson. This is everyone's favorite pirate story.

North to Freedom by Anne Holm. Twelve-year-old David escapes from a concentration camp and makes his way across Europe.

Tiktá-'Liktak by James Houston. An Eskimo boy survives a winter alone on an ice floe.

Julie of the Wolves by Jean C. George. Lost and without food or compass on the North Slope of Alaska, thirteen-year-old Julie is accepted by a pack of Arctic wolves who help her survive.

(There are many more exciting stories of adventure listed under **Animal Stories** and **Historical Novels**.)

ANIMAL STORIES

Fish Head by Jean Fritz. Excellent story of a seagoing cat.

The Midnight Fox by Betsy C. Byars. A boy tries to save a black fox from being shot. By the same author: *Rama the Gypsy Cat*.

Stormy, Misty's Foal by Marguerite Henry. A good horse story.

Rabbit Hill and **The Tough Winter** by Robert Lawson. Two good adventure stories about a community of animals large and small who live on Rabbit Hill.

Stranger at Green Knowe by Lucy M. Boston. A friendship between a Chinese boy and a gorilla who meet in a London zoo. In the same series: *The River at Green Knowe*.

The Black Stallion by Walter Farley. Exciting story of a boy, a wild horse, a shipwreck, and a horse race. Other books by this writer: *Son of Black Stallion, The Black Stallion and Satan,* and *The Island Stallion*.

Cranes in My Corral by Dayton O. Hyde. An Oregon rancher raises four sandhill cranes.

Flight of the White Wolf by Mel Ellis. A boy and a white wolf flee to the northern woods.

Runaway Stallion by Walt Morey. Thrilling story of a runaway race horse and the boy who befriends him in the old West.

Sam Savitt's True Horse Stories by Sam Savitt. Sixteen exciting and moving true stories for horse lovers.

The Incredible Journey, A Tale of Three Animals by Sheila Burnford. A Siamese cat, an English bull terrier, and a Labrador retriever travel hundreds of miles to get home.

From *Call of the Wild* by Jack London.

Dr. Watson and the famous Sherlock Holmes.

The Yearling by Marjorie Kinnan Rawlings. The story of a boy and his pet fawn that is loved by people of all ages.

Old Yeller by Fred Gipson. A stray dog attaches himself to a Texas family in 1860 and defends them against all dangers.

Rascal by Sterling North. Popular story of a boy and his pet raccoon.

The Red Pony by John Steinbeck. A classic story by one of America's most popular writers.

Call of the Wild by Jack London. Buck goes from a comfortable home in California to become a great sled dog in Alaska and finally returns to the wild as the leader of a wolf pack. Millions of readers have enjoyed this one.

MYSTERIES

Encyclopedia Brown by Donald J. Sobel. This is just the first of a series about a remarkable boy detective.

How to Write Codes and Send Secret Messages by John Peterson. Directions for writing and deciphering space codes, hidden word codes, and alphabet codes.

Who Really Killed Cock Robin? An Ecological Mystery by Jean Craighead. A mystery that deals with the cycles of nature and problems of modern living.

The Case of the Stolen Code Book by Barbara Rinkoff. Let's see whether you can solve this one.

The Gift by Peter Dickinson. Thriller about a boy who can read other people's minds.

The Mystery of the Great Swamp by Marjorie A. Zapf. Wait until you fall into this one.

Mystery and More Mystery, Thrillers and More Thrillers, Spies and More Spies by Robert Arthur.

Tuck Everlasting by Natalie Babbitt. A kidnapping, murder, a jailbreak.

The Clairvoyant Countess by Dorothy Gilman. A psychic countess, a murder, and humorous misadventure.

The Strange Case of Dr. Jekyll and Mr. Hyde by Robert Louis Stevenson. A doctor turns into a monster.

The Purloined Letter and the Murders in the Rue Morgue by Edgar Allan Poe. The inventor of the modern mystery story is at his best here.

The Adventures of Sherlock Holmes by Sir Arthur Conan Doyle. Match wits with the greatest detective of them all.

REALISTIC STORIES

The Eighteenth Emergency by Betsy Byars. Benjie wins out over the bully who threatens to beat him up.

Franklin Stein by Ellen Raskin. A lonely boy creates a pet from such things as a mop, a coffee pot, and a Venetian blind. And he wins a prize in the pet show.

The Adventures of Tom Sawyer by Mark Twain.

The Good Master by Kate Seredy. A headstrong city girl's adventures on her uncle's ranch in Hungary before World War II.

Harriet the Spy by Louise Fitzhugh. Harriet keeps a secret notebook that falls into the wrong hands. *The Long Secret* by the same author.

Sounder by William H. Armstrong. A black sharecropper is driven to steal in order to support his family and his dog Sounder. A boy loves them both.

And Now Miguel by Joseph Krumgold. The struggle of a twelve-year-old boy to become an expert shepherd like all the other men in his family.

Little Women by Louisa May Alcott. Three or four generations of your family may have read and enjoyed this story. It's your turn now.

The Adventures of Tom Sawyer by Mark Twain. An American classic of life in a small Missouri town.

The Loner by Ester Weir. An orphan boy is taken in by a sheep woman who tries to teach him to become a shepherd. He struggles to succeed, finding that it is not easy.

Freaky Friday by Mary Rogers. What happens when a thirteen-year-old girl finds she is her own mother and has to deal with a mother's daily problems?

The Summer of the Swans by Betsy Byars. A shy eighth-grade girl tries to protect her younger brother, who is retarded.

Mine for Keeps by Jean Little. A girl who has cerebral palsy is helped by her pet dog to find friends and security.

It's Not the End of the World by Judy Blume. The problems of three children when they realize their parents are going to be divorced.

But I'm Ready to Go by Louise Albert. Judy, a fifteen-year-old with an invisible handicap, takes stock of her plusses and sets out to put her life together.

His Enemy, His Friend by John R. Tunis. On a soccer field, Jean-Paul confronts the man who presided over his father's execution twenty years earlier. By the same author: *Silence over Dunkerque, Schoolboy Johnson,* and *All-American.*

David in Silence by Veronica Robinson. A deaf boy tries to share the activities of boys who can hear.

Grandma Didn't Wave Back by Rose Blue. Debbie watches her grandmother slip into senility.

HISTORICAL NOVELS

Ben and Me by Robert Lawson. The life of Benjamin Franklin, the American patriot, told humorously by his mouse. By the same author: *Mr. Revere and I.*

The Courage of Sarah Noble by Alice Dalgliesh. A story based on the true adventures of an eight-year-old girl who takes care of her father while he builds a house for his family in the wilderness. By the same author: *The Columbus Story.*

Winter Danger, Buffalo Knife, Tomahawks and Trouble, The Far Frontier by William O. Steele. Four exciting novels of boys growing up on the frontier.

The Matchlock Gun by Walter D. Edmonds. A boy and his mother fight off Indians. A suspense story you won't put down.

Viking Adventure by Clyde Bulla. A Viking boy on an exciting voyage to Vinland.

By the Great Horn Spoon by Sid Fleischman. Account of a trip to the California gold fields by way of Cape Horn. A funny book.

The Witch of Blackbird Pond by Elizabeth G. Speare. A young teen-ager finds herself accused of witchcraft in Puritan New England. *The Bronze Bow* is another good one by the same author.

Across Five Aprils by Irene Hunt. An Illinois farm boy growing up during the Civil War finds himself the head of the family.

Johnnie Tremain by Esther Forbes. An apprentice to a silversmith becomes a courier for the Whigs at the beginning of the American Revolution.

Cover of *Ben and Me* by Robert Lawson.

Little House in the Big Woods by Laura Ingalls Wilder. A pioneer family lives in Wisconsin in the 1870s. There are many other books in this popular series.

Caddie Woodlawn by Carol Ryrie Brink. The exciting adventures of a tomboy on the frontier during the 1860s.

Calico Bush by Rachel Field. The adventures of an indentured servant-girl in Indian country in 1743. By the same author: *Hitty, Her First Hundred Years.*

Island of the Blue Dolphins by Scott O'Dell. The true story of a courageous Indian girl who survived alone for eighteen years on an island off California. *Sing Down the Moon,* by the same author, is the story of a Navajo girl whose people are conquered by the white man.

The Spanish Letters by Mollie Hunter. Scottish nobles plot to take King James prisoner and help Spain invade England in 1589. Secret codes, hidden tunnels, roof-top chases, plus more.

Beyond the Frontier by Franklin Folsom. Exciting story based on the real-life experience of a boy captured by Seneca Indians during the Revolutionary War.

So Ends This Day by James Forman. A young man on an exciting three-year voyage aboard a whaling ship before the Civil War.

The Ghost in the Noonday Sun by Sid Fleischman. A twelve-year-old boy is shanghaied aboard a pirate ship.

HISTORY

The Aztec Indians of Mexico by Sonia Bleeker.

The Lion in the Gateway by Mary Renault. Ancient Greece, especially how the Greeks defeated the Persians. Excitingly told.

America Is Born, America Grows Up, and **America Moves Forward** by Gerald Johnson. A three-volume history of the United States.

The Norman Conquest by Walter C. Hodges. History plus how people lived about one thousand years ago.

The California Gold Rush by Mary McNeer. An exciting account of one of our most colorful periods.

The Pony Express by Samuel Hopkins Adams. Excitement and suspense.

George Washington's World, Abraham Lincoln's World, The World of Captain John Smith, Augustus Caesar's World, The World of Columbus and Sons by Genevieve Foster. Five books telling what the world was like during five heroes' lives. A view of history not often found in school books.

The First Book of Ancient Egypt and **The First Book of Ancient Mesopotamia and Persia** by Charles C. Robinson.

The Story of D-Day: June 6, 1944 by Bruce Bliven, Jr. The Allied landing in France during World War II.

The American Revolution by Bruce Bliven, Jr. Exciting account of the War of Independence.

30 Seconds over Tokyo by Bob Considine and Ted Lawson. Jimmy Doolittle's famous and daring raid during World War II. Told as a first-hand account.

The Dark Ages, The Egyptians, The Near East, Greeks: A Great Adventure, Roman Empire, and **Races and People** by Isaac Asimov. A masterful story-teller opens up worlds for us.

The Rise and Fall of Adolf Hitler and **The Sinking of the Bismarck** by William L. Shirer. The award-winning journalist gives us two dramatic histories of World War II.

The Endless Steppe by Esther Hautzig. A personal story of five years of a childhood spent in Siberia in a camp for political refugees.

Snow Treasure by Marie McSwigan. Norwegian children smuggle gold out of their country under the noses of their Nazi guards.

Watergate: America in Crisis by Jules Archer.

The Story of Mankind by Willem Van Loon. A classic work covering man's history from the beginning through World War II.

BIOGRAPHY

Abraham Lincoln, Benjamin Franklin, Leif the Lucky, Pocahontas, Buffalo Bill, Columbus by Ingri and Edgar Parin d'Aulaire. Six books on interesting and important people. All with pictures.

They Showed the Way by Charlemae Rollins. The lives of important figures in black history, some well known and others less famous.

Malcolm X by Arnold Adoff. An interesting account of this black leader.

The Remarkable Ride of the Abernathy Boys by Robert B. Jackson. The Abernathy boys, ages six and ten, rode horseback by themselves from Oklahoma to New York City.

Amos Fortune, Free Man by Elizabeth Yates. Story of an African prince who became a slave but finally regained his freedom.

George Washington, Leader of the People and **Abraham Lincoln, Friend of the People** by Clara Ingram Judson.

Armed with Courage by May McNeer and Lynd Ward. Stories about seven great humanitarians.

Invincible Louisa by Cornelia Meigs. Life of Louisa May Alcott, author of *Little Women*.

America's Ethan Allen by Stewart Holbrook. Exciting story of the daring leader of the Green Mountain Boys.

Andrew Jackson by Margaret L. Coit. Story of a colorful and courageous president.

Six Feet Six: The Heroic Story of Sam Houston by Marquis and Bessie James.

Blue Jacket by Allan W. Eckert. The story of a seventeen-year-old white boy who was captured by the Shawnees in 1771 and became a famous war chief.

Profiles in Courage by John F. Kennedy. Biographies of Americans in public life who made courageous decisions.

Weaver of Dreams: The Girlhood of Charlotte Bronte by Elfrida Vipont. Story of the author of *Jane Eyre* and of her strange family.

Anne Frank: The Diary of a Young Girl by Anne Frank. The sad, courageous life of a Dutch teenager forced to hide from the Nazis during World War II.

Langston Hughes by Milton Meltzer. Life of the great black poet.

The Story of My Life by Helen Keller. The amazing autobiography of a blind and deaf mute woman who became an inspiration to the world.

Helen Keller, author of *The Story of My Life*.

Lee of Virginia by Douglas Southall Freeman. Another book about Lee.

Dancing Star: The Story of Anna Pavlova by Gladys Malvern. Story of the Russian ballerina.

Harriet Tubman: Conductor on the Underground Railroad by Ann Petry. Born a slave, Harriet Tubman escaped and led three hundred other slaves to freedom.

Pioneer in Blood Plasma: Dr. Charles Drew by Robert Lickello. A black physician who was a great medical scientist.

Shakespeare of London by Marchette Chute. Story of the greatest writer in the English language and the world he lived in.

POETRY

Poetry is much like music in that the rhythms and sounds are important. That's why it is best to read poetry aloud. You might want to tap your feet to it or even dance. The more often you read it, the better it will sound. It's also good to share poetry with other people—a friend, a brother or sister, your parents. Poetry often means different things to different people, especially if they are of different ages and experiences. If you read poetry aloud with a younger sister or brother and with your grandmother, you can share your impressions. If you are one of those people who think poetry is not for them, try some of the humorous poetry first. When you first experience the magic of poetry, you will find that you will want to go on and try more.

Piper, Pipe that Song Again and **Piping Down the Valleys Wide** compiled by Nancy Larrick.

You Come Too by Robert Frost. The famous poet's own selections for young people. A recording of these poems is available.

All Day Long: Fifty Rhymes of the Never Was and Always Is by David McCord. Amusing and very modern verses. By the same poet: *Take Sky* and *Far and Few*. Also on records.

The Birds and the Beasts Were There; A Book of Nature Poems; Oh, How Silly!; Poems of Magic and Spells compiled by William Cole. All kinds of poems, some humorous. Good reading for the entire family.

———————————

Arrow Book of Poetry selected by Ann McGovern.

The Gold Journey compiled by Louise Bogan and William Jay Smith. Poems old and new on many different subjects.

First Voices edited by Geoffrey Summerfield. Four collections of new and old poetry, some of it by children.

Cricket Songs, Japanese Haiku translated by Harry Behn. *Haiku* is a special kind of poetry written with only seventeen-syllables in three lines. It is always about a single small aspect of nature.

    O cricket, from your cheery cry
    No one could ever guess
    How quickly you must die.

Many American children enjoy writing their own *haiku*.

Don't Tell the Scarecrow and Other Japanese Poems by Issa, Yayu, and others. Another interesting collection of *haiku*.

Concrete Is Not Always Hard edited by A. Barbara Pilon. A new kind of poetry you can see as well as hear.

Peacock Pie by Walter De la Mare. These imaginative and beautiful poems are great favorites. Also: *Bells and Grass*, by the same poet.

———————————

Wind Song, Early Moon by Carl Sandburg. Two collections of poetry by one of America's best poets. Full of humor, imagination, and fun with words and sound. Some of the poems are on a record called *Carl Sandburg's Poems for Children*.

There Is No Rhyme for Silver, It Doesn't Always Have to Rhyme, Catch a Little Rhyme by Eve Merriam. Playful, modern free verse. By the same author: *Independent Voices,* a collection of true glimpses into American history that is especially good for reading aloud.

Don't You Turn Back and **The Dream Keeper** by Langston Hughes. Many poems by the great black poet. *The Dream Keeper* is available as a recording.

Prayers from the Ark, poems by Carmen Bernos de Gasztold, translated by Rumer Godden. Prayers of twenty-six animals in Noah's Ark. Amusing and moving. This collection is available as a recording.

I Heard a Scream in the Street edited by Nancy Larrick. A collection of city poems by city kids.

Pop/Rock Songs of the Earth edited by Jerry L. Walker. Twenty-five songs sung by popular singers and all dealing with the environment. Illustrated.

NATURE, SCIENCE, AND ECOLOGY

Great Whales by Patricia Lauber. Recent discoveries and a true story.

Growing Up Green by Alice Skelsey and Gloria Huckaby. Discovering nature, and projects for you and your parents.

Terrariums by John Hoke. Do it yourself.

The Hidden Country: Nature on Your Doorstep by John Richards.

Science Magic with Chemistry and Biology by Ted Johnson.

Asimov's Guide to Science by Isaac Asimov.

Find the Constellations by H. A. Rey.

———————————

The Only Earth We Have by Lawrence Pringle.

Metric Science Can Be Fun by Munro Leaf.

Science Magic with Physics by Kay Richards.

The I Hate Mathematics! Book by Marilyn Burns. Games to help you understand mathematics.

All About Dinosaurs by Roy Chapman Andrews. By the same author: *All About Strange Beasts of the Past.*

———————————

The Sea Around Us by Rachel L. Carson. The magic and mystery of the ocean and how the ocean affects all of us.

Sunshine Makes the Seasons by Franklin M. Branley.

Our Six-Legged Friends and Allies by Hilda Simon. Ecology in your backyard.

Cover of a collection of modern fables.

Indian Harvest by William C. Grimm. How to find wild plants the Indians used for food.

Catch the Wind by Landt Sennis. History of windmills as a source of energy. How to build windmills and generators.

FUNNY STORIES

Laughing by Charles Keller. A collection of American humor—short stories and jokes.

How to Care for Your Monster by Norman Bridweil. You will need this book to take proper care of your monsters, mummies, and vampires.

Dragon, Dragon and Other Tales by John Gardner. Fairy tales turned into humorous modern fables.

Laughing Together by Barbara K. Walker. Young people's jokes from all over the world.

The Whim Wham Book by Duncan Emrich. Riddles, jokes, and superstitions. By the same author: *Nonsense Book* and *Hodgepodge Book*.

You Can't Eat Peanuts in Church and Other Little-Known Laws by Barbara Seuling. Unusual and amusing laws from all over the United States.

Felton and Fowler's Best, Worst and Most Unusual by Bruce Felton and Mark Fowler. Hundreds of funny, shocking, and fascinating facts.

How to Eat Fried Worms by Thomas Rockwell. Billy makes a bet that he can eat fifteen worms, one a day.

The Day the Circus Came to Lone Tree by Glen Rounds. What happened when cowboys thought the lady lion-tamer was about to be devoured.

HOBBIES AND SPECIAL INTERESTS

Paint All Kinds of Pictures by Arnold Spilka.

Give a Magic Show! by Burton and Rita Marks.

Taking Pictures by Nina Leen.

Puppet Fun by Nellie McCaslin.

Exciting Things to Do with Nature Materials by Judy Allen.

Dollhouse Magic by P. K. Roche. How to make dollhouse furnishings inexpensively.

Clay, Wood and Wire: A How-to-Do-It Book of Sculpture by Harvey Weiss.

Collage and Construction by Harvey Weiss.

Modeling in Clay, Plaster and Papier-Mâché by Richard Stade.

Snips and Snails and Walnut Whales by Phyllis Fiarotta. Things to make from natural materials. By the same author: *Sticks and Stones and Ice Cream Cones*. More things to make.

Paper Cutting by Eric Hawkesworth. Things to make from paper plus how to create your own stories and give performances.

Bake Bread by Hannah Solomon.

Christmas Cookbook by Susan Purdy.

How to Star in Basketball by Herman L. Masin.

Football for Young Champions by Robert J. Antonacci and Jene Barr.

The Kids' Kitchen Takeover by Sara Bonnett Stein. All kinds of fun in the kitchen—not just cooking.

The Colonial Cookbook by Lucille Recht Penner.

CB Bible by Porter Bibb.

Great Pets! An Extraordinary Guide to Usual and Unusual Family Pets by Sara Stein.

The Kids' Money-Making Book by Jim and Jean Young.

Pinch of Sunshine, ½ Cup of Rain: Natural Food Recipes for Young People by Ruth Cavin.

American Folksongs for Children by Ruth C. Seeger.

The Art of Cartooning by Syd Hoff.

Act Now! Plays and Ways to Make Them by Nellie McCaslin.

Grand Slam by Jim Bunning, Whitey Ford, Mickey Mantle, and Willie Mays. Tips on playing baseball.

Sportsmath: How It Works by Lee Arthur. How to work out all kinds of sports statistics.

The New Junior Illustrated Encyclopedia of Sports by Herbert Kamm.

Basic Hockey Strategy by Richard B. Lyttle.

Women in Sports: Figure Skating by Elizabeth Van Steenwyk.

USING THE LANGUAGE

It is customary at great events of state and at important moments in our lives to ask for words of wisdom and beauty from those gifted in language. When John F. Kennedy was inaugurated thirty-fifth President of the United States, America's uncrowned poet laureate Robert Frost was invited to read from his work to mark the occasion. With all the leaders of the nation in attendance, the poet stood in the cold wind and recited. Yet it was other words spoken that day — John Kennedy's words—we remember best: ''Ask not what America will do for you, but what together we can do for the freedom of man.''

In trying to improve your own grasp of language, you will find certain information helpful. The following pages present useful suggestions for reading and writing. Follow them so that one day you will be able to hold the attention of others through excellent use of language.

How to Improve Your Reading

One of the most important skills you can learn is effective reading. Effective reading means reading as rapidly as you can with good understanding. There is no point in racing through a chapter of a book without getting from that chapter what the author put in it and what you set out to get from it.

This means that you must be able to adjust your reading speed to the type of material you are reading—*easy books should be read quickly, difficult books slowly*—and you must be sure that you understand just what the material says. This also means that you must be able to read in different ways, depending on the reason for your reading.

If you are reading for pleasure, read as quickly or as slowly as you wish to get the greatest pleasure from your reading. A good story often is enjoyed most when it is read quickly. The story comes to life before your eyes, and the action unfolds almost as fast as it might in real life. On the other hand, a particular story may say so much to you that you want to linger over certain sentences, getting every last bit of meaning from them. Poetry usually should be read slowly to understand everything the poet has said. In fact, most poetry is best read aloud, which means reading much more slowly than you can read silently.

If you are reading for study purposes, it is best to adopt a reading speed somewhere between the speed at which you read easy stories and the speed at which you read difficult poems. But many times while you are reading for study purposes, you will want to stop to ask yourself whether you understand and remember what you are reading. For this reason, reading for study purposes actually takes longer than any other kind of reading. Such reading becomes a quiz in which you act as teacher as well as student. You read for a while and stop. Then you ask yourself: "What did the author say?" "If I were asked a question on this material, what would my answer be?" When you finish the entire reading assignment, it is best to stop once more and try to recall and summarize everything important that you have covered.

THREE HINTS FOR IMPROVING YOUR STUDY READING

1. *Sit in a straight chair.* Reading in bed or in a comfortable armchair invites sleep—not careful attention. Sitting upright in a straight chair helps you keep alert. You will get through your reading assignments faster and better.
2. *Work with the author of the book you are studying.* Go after the author's ideas and

information; don't sit back and let the words pass before your eyes like clouds in a summer sky. Study reading is an active process. The author has laid out certain information for you. Look for it. Remember that you are trying to learn a lesson. When you work hard with an author's ideas and facts, your study time becomes productive.

3. *Set goals for each study session.* By looking through an assignment to see what it covers, you will find that the material falls into a certain number of parts. Each part answers certain questions, and learning these answers establishes your goals. What is the first question to be answered? Once you know what the question is, you are ready to begin reading. As you read, look for the answer to that question. Once you have read it, stop reading and ask yourself the question. Then recite the answer. When you can recite the answer from memory, you are ready to go on to the next part of the reading. Each of your goals will be met one at a time. When you have finished an entire assignment, you should be ready to recite from memory the main information in that assignment.

HOW TO INCREASE YOUR READING SPEED

The single best way to increase your reading speed is to read many exciting books—one after another. Such books grip your interest, making you want to read on as quickly as possible to find out what happens next. No one who has read a great deal in childhood—without any urging from parents or teachers—grows up to be a slow reader.

In the television age, we all have the temptation to satisfy our need for adventure stories of one type or another by turning on the television set. Too often we sit back to let stories come to us with practically no effort on our part. There is nothing wrong with watching television; it enables us to see far-off places, to share in exciting experiences, to appreciate visual beauty. Unfortunately, television usually asks little of our brains. We become mere spectators instead of active participants. Everything is done for us, and we do not grow as individuals.

Reading demands active participation. The reader must go after the story and pursue the information. And as we seek out what a book provides, we become stronger and stronger readers.

If you have not yet developed the habit of reading, you may find that you do not read as quickly as others do. As long as your eyesight is good and your vocabulary rich enough for the books you want to read or must read, you can soon become a fast and accurate reader simply by *becoming a reader.* All you have to do, then, to increase your reading speed is to begin reading regularly. Each time you read, try to read a little

faster than is comfortable for you. Don't try to double your reading speed overnight. The advertisements that promise such miracles cannot be trusted. Just read a little faster than is comfortable for you, and be sure to read every day. You can easily find the time for reading. Every time you reach for the switch on the television set, ask yourself whether you have done your reading for the day. If you have not, then stay away from that switch until you have finished reading.

By using the **Guide to Reading** in this volume, you will be able to find books that are at least as interesting as any television program. If you read through all those books, you will find that you have become a rapid and careful reader. By the time you are ready for college or whatever other training you undertake after high school, you can be sure you will not be held back by poor reading habits. Furthermore, good reading habits will help you in your career as well as in enjoyment of leisure time.

How to Improve Your Writing

BEGIN WITH AN OUTLINE

An outline organizes reports, essays, and compositions. By providing a framework for whatever you are going to write, it helps you understand the relationships between the parts of your writing. It also helps your reader follow your thoughts.

An *informal outline* is simply a listing of the main ideas or topics you are going to cover. In writing such an outline, you should leave spaces between the items for facts, examples, and other supporting information. As these ideas occur to you, you fill them in where they are appropriate.

A *formal outline* follows a prescribed pattern, as shown in the **Form for a Formal Outline**. Remember that an outline must serve your needs while you are writing. Thus, it can be revised whenever you find it necessary. You must not slavishly follow an outline that turns out to be less than ideal.

The following suggestions are helpful in constructing an outline:

1. Use Roman numerals for main topics.
2. Use capital letters for subtopics.
3. Use Arabic numerals for subdivisions of subtopics.
4. Use small letters for the next lower division of information.
5. Use Arabic numerals enclosed in parentheses for the next lower order of information.
6. Indent an additional amount of space when you move to a lower order of information. Use the same indentation for information of the same rank.
7. Express topics and subtopics as nouns, noun phrases, or questions.
8. Introduce a subtopic only when the topic will have at least two subdivisions.

USING THE LANGUAGE

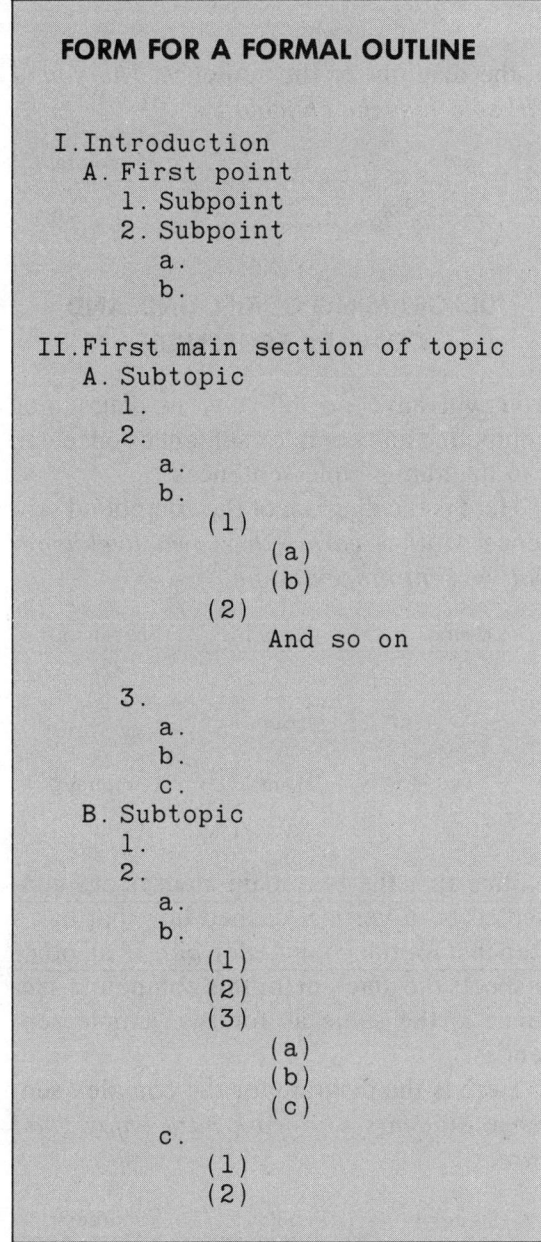

FORM FOR A FORMAL OUTLINE

I. Introduction
  A. First point
    1. Subpoint
    2. Subpoint
      a.
      b.

II. First main section of topic
  A. Subtopic
    1.
    2.
      a.
      b.
        (1)
          (a)
          (b)
        (2)
          And so on

    3.
      a.
      b.
      c.
  B. Subtopic
    1.
    2.
      a.
      b.
        (1)
        (2)
        (3)
          (a)
          (b)
          (c)
      c.
        (1)
        (2)

PREPARING YOUR FINAL COPY

Most of the papers you are writing now are class assignments—book reports, themes, and other kinds of compositions. After you have done your research, organized your ideas, and written the paper, you have one more step to go—preparing the final copy

to hand in. Here are some suggestions.

1. *Proofread your final draft carefully.* Check spelling, capitalization, and punctuation. Look up words you're not sure of. Read your whole paper through to be sure it makes sense and says what you really want to say.

2. *Now make your final copy.* Your teacher may tell you what kind of paper to use and whether to use pencil or pen. In most cases, use standard size paper (8½″ × 11″). If you are writing longhand, use black or blue pen on lined theme paper. If you have a typewriter, use white bond paper.

3. *Leave comfortable margins at the top, bottom, and sides of the paper.*

4. *Remember to indent each new paragraph.* If you are typing your composition, be sure to double space.

5. *Write on only one side of the paper.* Number each page and make sure your pages are in order before you turn in the paper.

6. *Don't forget to put your name, the date, and any other information your teacher asks for on the first page.* You've worked hard on this composition—make sure you identify it as yours!

Diagraming sentences

Many people find diagrams helpful in understanding English sentences. The following discussion shows you how to diagram various types of sentences.

SIMPLE SENTENCE DIAGRAM

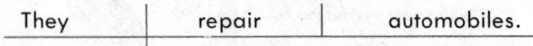

The base line represents the entire clause. The vertical line cutting through the base line divides the subject and the predicate. The vertical line rising from the base line represents the object of the verb.

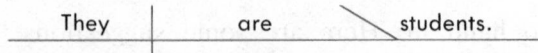

A line slanting back toward the verb divides the verb and its complement.

DIAGRAMING MODIFIERS

Any modifiers in a sentence are placed below the base line. They are attached by slanting lines to the words they modify. Here is the diagram of the sentence *The bright sun hurt our tired eyes.*

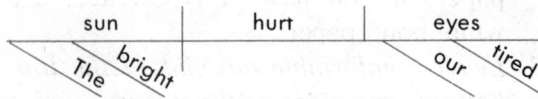

Modifiers of modifiers are attached to the words they modify. Here is the diagram of the sentence *Many bright yellow flowers very quickly cheered the old man.*

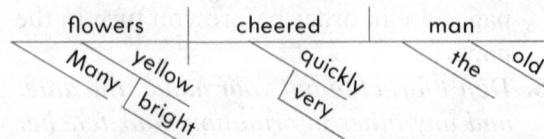

Indirect objects are treated as modifiers of the verb and placed below the line. Here

is the diagram of the sentence *The young girl sold him the chocolates.*

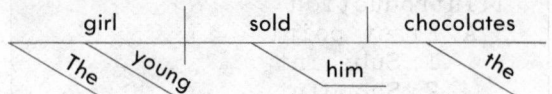

DIAGRAMING COMPOUND AND COMPLEX SENTENCES

You will have no difficulty in diagraming compound and complex sentences once you can diagram simple sentences.

Here is the diagram of the compound sentence *Mother earned her own livelihood, but we sent money home.*

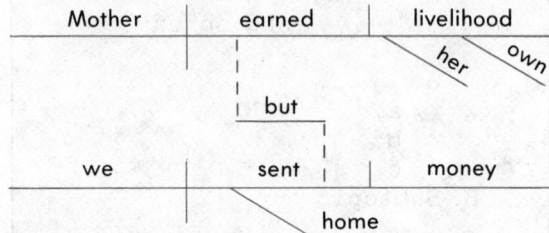

Notice that the two main clauses are connected by a vertical dashed line that has a step in it for the conjunction *but.* In all other respects the diagram for this compound sentence is the same as for two simple sentences.

Here is the diagram for the complex sentence *Students who work hard enjoy good careers.*

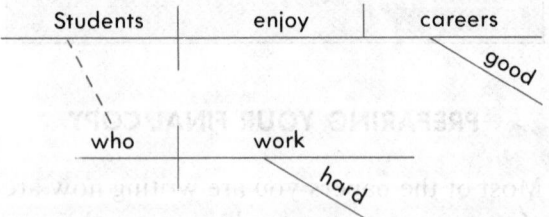

Notice that the dashed line connecting the dependent clause to the main clause is slanted back toward the word the dependent clause modifies.

USING THE LANGUAGE

Special uses of language

To improve the way you speak and write, learn these techniques used by poets and prose writers.

Alliteration. Deliberate repetition of sounds. "The *f*air breeze blew, the white *f*oam *f*lew,/The *f*urrow *f*ollowed *f*ree. . . ."

Hyperbole. Obvious and deliberate exaggeration, used to emphasize but not deceive. *I was scared to death by the way she looked at me. I would walk a million miles for one of her smiles.*

Irony. Conveying meaning emphatically by using words that say the opposite of what we mean. Mark Twain: *"The reports of my death are greatly exaggerated." He loved trees the way any convicted horse thief does.*

Metaphor. A figure of speech in which a word or phrase is applied to an object, idea, or person to which it is not literally related. *The clouds were small puffs of cotton. He was an elephant of a man.*

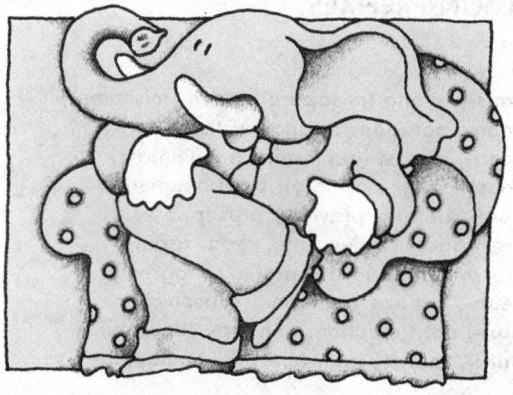

Onomatopoeia. Use of words that suggest by their sounds the object or idea being named. *sizzle, twitter, buzz, hiss, coo, roar.*

Personification. A figure of speech in which human qualities are given to animals, objects, or ideas. *The leaves shivered in anticipation of winter. His ideas sang themselves to sleep as he waited for the teacher to call on him. You could hear the tulips say, "We'll be back next year. Don't fear."*

His life was so gentle,
* and the elements*
So mix'd in him,
* that Nature might stand up*
And say to all the
* world, This was a man!*
                    —William Shakespeare.

Rhetorical question. A question that is not intended to be answered, but is used to emphasize a point or draw attention to it. Shakespeare's Shylock: *"If you tickle us, do we not laugh? If you poison us, do we not die? And if you wrong us, shall we not revenge?"*

Simile. A metaphor employing *like* or *as*. *His complexion was as fresh as a three-day-old pizza. Eddie stood by the dance floor like a supertanker waiting to discharge five hundred tons of crude oil. "Once let slavery get planted in a locality by ever so weak or doubtful a title, and in ever so small numbers, and it is like the Canadian thistle or Bermuda grass—you cannot root it out."*—Abraham Lincoln.

Conjugating the English verb

ACTIVE VOICE	SINGULAR	PLURAL
Present Tense	I find you find he, she, it finds	we find you find they find
Past Tense	I found you found he, she, it found	we found you found they found
Future Tense	I shall find you will find he, she, it will find	we shall find you will find they will find
Perfect Tense	I have found you have found he, she, it has found	we have found you have found they have found
Past Perfect Tense	I had found you had found he, she, it had found	we had found you had found they had found
Future Perfect Tense	I shall have found you will have found he, she, it will have found	we shall have found you will have found they will have found

MEANINGS OF COMMON PREFIXES

a-, not (aharmonic, amoral)
ante-, before (antecedent, anteroom)
anti-, against (antibiotic, antidote)
bi-, two (bicycle, bicameral)
co-, together (coeducation, coexist)
dis-, not (disability, disagreeable)
e-, ex-, out, away (emigrate, exhale)
in-, im-, into (income, immigrate)
in-, im-, ir-, not (insane, inimical, impossible, impractical, irregular)

mis-, wrong (misapprehension, misnomer)
non-, not (nonstop, nonpartisan)
pen-, almost (peninsula, penultimate)
post-, after postnatal, postponement)
pre-, before (preview, presuppose)
re-, again (redecorate, redo, rerun)
retro-, backward (retrofit, retrogress)
sub-, under (submarine, subsonic)
un-, not (unbutton, unhappy, unusual)
uni-, mono-, one, (unicorn, monoplane)

USING THE LANGUAGE

Conjugating the English verb

PASSIVE VOICE	SINGULAR	PLURAL
Present Tense	I am found you are found he, she, it is found	we are found you are found they are found
Past Tense	I was found you were found he, she, it was found	we were found you were found they were found
Future Tense	I shall be found you will be found he, she, it will be found	we shall be found you will be found they will be found
Perfect Tense	I have been found you have been found he, she, it has been found	we have been found you have been found they have been found
Past Perfect Tense	I had been found you had been found he, she, it had been found	we had been found you had been found they had been found
Future Perfect Tense	I shall have been found you will have been found he, she, it will have been found	we shall have been found you will have been found they will have been found

MEANINGS OF COMMON SUFFIXES

-ed, forms past tense of regular verbs (acted, happened, looked, whistled)

-en, forms a verb from a noun or adjective (darken, lengthen, shorten)

-ful, forms words that show a particular quality (joyful, playful) or a particular amount (roomful, spoonful)

-ing, forms present participle or gerund, a verb form that functions as a noun (eating, singing, winging)

-less, forms an adjective with the meaning of *without* (careless, hatless, homeless)

-ly, forms adjectives or adverbs with the meaning of *in a certain way* (badly, quickly, motherly, friendly)

-ment, forms a noun that shows a result or state of being (improvement, merriment, shipment)

-ness, forms a noun showing quality or condition (sadness, likeness)

-ous, forms an adjective showing a certain quality (joyous, mountainous, suspicious)

-tion, forms a noun showing action or process (action, resignation)

GLOSSARY OF GRAMMATICAL TERMS

active voice. Verb form in which the subject performs the action of the verb: She *chose*. See **passive voice.**

adjective. Word that modifies a noun or pronoun, telling what kind, how many, which (a *black* hat, *four* questions, *this* one). A predicate adjective, or adjective complement, follows a linking verb: She is *ill*. I feel *happy*.

adverb. Word that modifies anything except a noun or pronoun, telling how, when, where, in what manner, to what extent: She swims *well*. I worked *today*. We swam *farther*. She has *evenly* spaced teeth.

article. The words *a, an,* and *the.*

auxiliary. Verb form (usually some form of *be, do,* or *have*) combined with another verb to show tense or voice: He *is* going home. She *is* satisfied. They *were* hit.

clause. Group of related words with a subject and verb: *they are eating their dinner.*

complement. Word or phrase that completes the meaning of a linking verb. There are two types of complements: predicate adjectives (She is *sad*) and predicate nouns (Anne is a *physician*).

complex sentence. Sentence consisting of a main clause and dependent clause: *The dog barked* (main clause) *while the man slept* (dependent clause).

compound sentence. Sentence with two main clauses: *The dog barked* and *the man slept.* The two main clauses are usually joined by *and, or, but,* or *or.* They sometimes are separated by semicolons: *The dog barked; the man slept.*

conjunction. Word that connects words or clauses or phrases: *and, or, however, thus,* etc.

dependent clause. Clause that cannot stand alone as a sentence: *while you sat; when you left.*

direct object. Word telling who or what a verb acts on: The cat ate the *meat*. Linda hid her *face*.

indirect object. Word naming the receiver of the action of verbs of giving or telling: Bert passed *him* the ball. Ask *Jane* that question.

intransitive verb. Verb that does not have a direct object or complement. Examples: *sleep, look, sit.*

linking verb. Verb that links a subject and complement: I *feel* fine. He *is* a student.

modifier. Word, phrase, or clause describing or limiting the meaning of a word or group of words. Modifiers function as adjectives or adverbs.

nominative case. Also called subjective case. Form of a pronoun indicating it functions as subject or complement: *I, he, she, we, they* love baseball. It is *I, he, she, we, they.* See **objective case.**

noun. Word that names a person, place, thing, or idea: *woman, town, couch, honesty.* A proper noun names someone or something specific: *Prince Hal, Nashville.*

objective case. Also called accusative case. Form of a pronoun indicating it functions as object. Indirect object: I gave *him, me, her, us, them* a treat. Direct object: *Whom* did you accuse? I gave *her* a treat.

participle. Form of verb that combines with an auxiliary to form tense or voice: I am *going* home tomorrow. He has been *dispossessed.*

passive voice. Verb form in which the subject receives the action of the verb: She *was chosen.* The police *have been informed.*

phrase. Group of related words not containing both a subject and verb: *the big red barn; thousands of miles.* Phrases can function as subjects, objects, complements, and modifiers.

predicate. The full verb, including its objects and modifiers: They *have been looking for a new car.*

predicate adjective. Adjective after a linking verb that completes the statement of the verb: They were *friendly.* Are you *happy*?

predicate noun. Noun after a linking verb that functions to rename the subject of the verb: Elizabeth II now is *Queen.* She is an interesting *woman.*

preposition. Word or words that relate a noun or pronoun to other words in a sentence: *to, in, toward, among, in, between,* etc.

pronoun. A word that stands for a noun. Examples: I, you, he, she, it, we, they, me, him, us, them, theirs.

subject. Performer of the action of active verb: *John* went to the circus. Receiver of the action of passive verb: The *store* was closed.

tense. Characteristic of verb that shows the time of the action or condition expressed: I *see*; I *saw*; I *will see*; I *will have seen*, etc.

transitive verb. Verb that takes a direct object: I *hit* the ball. They *felt* the cloth.

verb. Word or words in a sentence that express action or state of being: I *run*. I *wonder. Have* you *known* her long?

Useful Rules of Punctuation

PERIOD

Use a period after a declarative sentence or imperative sentence:

> I like to swim in salt water lakes.
>
> Please finish your lunch.

Use a period after an abbreviation:

> Col. Mr. Mrs. Ms. lb. oz.

When a sentence ends in an abbreviation, only one period is needed.

EXCLAMATION POINT

Use an exclamation mark after an interjection:

> Fire! Help!
>
> Hello!

Use an exclamation point after an exclamatory sentence:

> Drop that gun!
>
> **Run for your life!**

QUESTION MARK

Use a question mark after an interrogative sentence:

> Are you sure you want to attend?

When an interrogative sentence ends in an abbreviation, a question mark is needed after the period:

> Did the recipe actually call for 6 oz.?

COMMA

Use a comma to separate main clauses in a compound sentence, taking care to place the comma before the conjunction:

> He went to the movies, and I stayed home.
>
> They bought new dresses, but I did not.

Use a comma after an adverbial clause at the beginning of a sentence:

> If that is the correct answer, I surely failed the test.
>
> When you come to the end of the road, stop and wait for us.

Use a pair of commas to set off phrases and clauses that can be omitted without loss of meaning:

> John Steinbeck, who won the Nobel Prize for Literature, long has been a best-selling American author.
>
> My high school, for many years the largest in our region, has always had outstanding athletic programs.

Use commas to set off nouns of direct address:

> Will you help her, John, with the cooking?

Use commas to set off appositives that can be omitted without loss of meaning:

> President Carter, the commander-in-chief, reviewed the regiment.

Use commas to set off items in addresses and dates:

> We were told to mail the package to 2245 West Sports Street, Fulton, Texas.
>
> He was born in Watertown, South Dakota, on June 13, 1961.

Use commas to set off independent phrases and clauses:

> That man, for better or for worse, is our candidate and must be supported.
>
> Miss Stewart, I believe, will be chosen as principal next year.

Use a comma to set off the tag line for a quotation:

> The butcher said, "You cannot have good beef if you are not willing to pay the price."
>
> "Will you try," asked the small boy, "to help me find my dog?"

Do not use a comma before quotation marks that enclose a title:

> John Greenleaf Whittier wrote "Snowbound."

Use a comma to set off mild exclamations at the beginning of a sentence:

> No, I could not find the dog.
>
> Oh, what a beautiful day!

Use commas to separate words or groups of words in a series of three or more expressions:

> She ordered ham, eggs, toast, and milk.
>
> We swam in the lake, fished in the river, and hunted in the woods.

Use commas to separate adjectives not connected by conjunctions:

> The steep, winding, narrow path came to an end.

When you are not certain about whether to use a comma between such adjectives, ask yourself whether an *and* would be appropriate between them. If the answer is yes, a comma is needed. If the answer is no, a comma is wrong:

> The lovely young girl spoke forcefully.

Use a comma after the salutation in a friendly letter:

> Dear Bill,   Dear Sally,

Use a comma after the complimentary close in a friendly letter or business letter:

> Sincerely,   Sincerely yours,
> Yours truly,

Use a comma to separate transitional words in a sentence:

> I plan to attend the meeting. However, I may be an hour late.

COLON

Use a colon after the salutation in a business letter:

> Gentlemen: Dear Mrs. Gwinn:

Use a colon between hours, minutes, and seconds to show time:

> The class begins at 8:15:00 not 8:25:45.

Use a colon to introduce a list, statement, question, or formal quotation:

> She asked me to invite the following people: Mary Wodehouse, Harry Schepps, and Sue Koch.

> I intend to stress three factors: study habits, extracurricular activities, and graduation requirements.

SEMICOLON

Use a semicolon to separate main clauses of a compound sentence when a conjunction is omitted:

> We planned to extend the vacation for two weeks; the factory refurbishment was not complete.

Use a semicolon between clauses of a compound sentence when the clauses are connected by such conjunctive adverbs as *therefore, however, nevertheless, thus,* and *moreover:*

> The school seemed extraordinarily quiet during that time; moreover, the entire community seemed so subdued that we could not help but worry about what might be happening.

Notice that a comma is needed after the conjunction.

Use semicolons to separate long clauses that are joined by conjunctions, or clauses that already have commas within them:

> Jane got to her own party late, I was told; and when she got to the front door, she was greeted by angry guests.

APOSTROPHE

Use an apostrophe to indicate a contraction:

> He isn't going to attend.

> They haven't done their share.

Use an apostrophe to form the possessive of nouns naming people or units of time:

> John's friends will be there.

> An hour's delay is more than we can forgive.

Use an apostrophe to form the plurals of letters, signs, symbols, and words considered merely as words:

> There are two c's and two m's in *accommodate.*

> He used thirty *and's* in a single paragraph.

QUOTATION MARKS

Use quotation marks to set off the exact words of a speaker:

> Father said, "Would you please remove that dog."

Notice that the quoted sentence is not a question even though it appears to be a question. For this reason, a period is used instead of a question mark.

Use quotation marks to set off the titles of

articles, short poems, stories, and chapters of a book:

> I enjoyed Longfellow's "The Wreck of the Hesperus."

Notice that titles of full-length books, magazines, newspapers, and plays appear as italics in print and are underlined in typing and handwriting.

Use quotation marks to set off a word used as a word rather than as its meaning:

> We used "work" as a noun rather than as a verb.

Notice that words used as words appear in italics in print.

> We used *work* as a noun.

Use single quotation marks for quotations within quotations:

> "I can recite Shakespeare's 'All the world's a stage,'" she said.

DASH

Use a dash to indicate a break or change in direction of thought:

> The bird flew—where did it fly?
>
> "I can't remember—" the child's voice broke.

Use a dash to show where words or letters have been omitted:

> He turned quickly so as not to confront his questioner and K— stared sternly from the bench.

Use a dash instead of parentheses if parenthetical material is closely related to the thought of the sentence:

> Mary told me—not you—that the family was extremely poor.

Use a dash before a summary statement at the end of a sentence:

> He worked, he saved, he went without —he did all this to provide the money for your education.

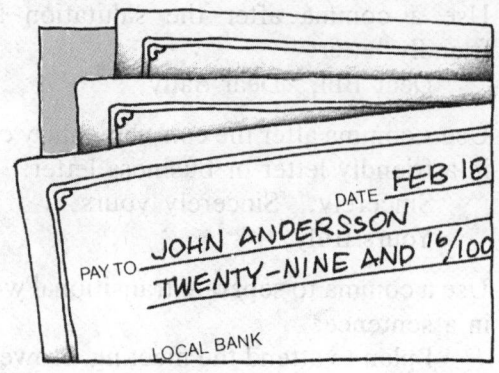

HYPHEN

Use a hyphen to divide a word at the end of a line. The general rule is to divide between syllables, and you would do well to check your dictionary when dividing a word. Use a hyphen for compound numbers from twenty-one to ninety-nine:

> sixty-eight   one hundred sixty-eight
> three hundred and eighty-four

Use a hyphen when combining two or more words to make a single modifier:

> Self-supporting individuals form the bulk of our population.

Check uncommon words in the dictionary.

PARENTHESES

Use parentheses to set off material separate from the main idea of a sentence:

> When the picnic finally is held (and I am sure it will be), will you go with me?

See the dash rule for setting material off within a sentence.

BRACKETS

Use brackets when you insert material of your own in a quotation:

> "It [Evangeline] was a long narrative poem that told a story based on actual events."

Rules of Capitalization

Capitalize the first word of every sentence:
> It was a great day.

Capitalize the first word of every line of poetry unless the poet has not used a capital letter in writing the poem:
> "Here once the embattled farmer stood,
> And fired the shot heard round the world."

Capitalize the first word of a direct quotation unless you work the quotation into one of your own sentences:
> Father said, "There will be no dinner for you tonight."
>
> Who can doubt the greatness of a nation "conceived in liberty"?

Capitalize all proper nouns and proper adjectives (adjectives derived from proper nouns):
> Joan of Arc was a French military leader.
>
> He was overly fond of British clothes and Chinese food.

Capitalize all important events in history and important places:
> French and Indian Wars
> White House   World Trade Center

Capitalize school subjects only when they come from proper nouns or when they are official names of courses:
> English   German   Biology II
> literature   history   mathematics

Capitalize directions when they represent regions of a country:
> He moved to the Southwest.
>
> He tracked the escaped prisoner south to the edge of town.

Capitalize the following words in a title: first word, last word, important words, words containing five letters or more; articles, prepositions, and conjunctions are not important words:
> *For Whom the Bell Tolls*
> "The Man Who Corrupted Hadleyburg"
> "The Birth of Venus"

Capitalize the names of places, mountains, rivers, cities, states, and streets:
> Tennessee   Great Smoky Mountains
> Cumberland River   Fifth Avenue
> Pacific Ocean

Capitalize nouns and personal pronouns referring to God:
> I know He is the Lord.

Capitalize the titles of sacred words:
Koran   Bible   Old Testament

Capitalize the words *I* and *O*.

Capitalize titles used with names or when the titles refer to specific people:
We listened attentively to Colonel Moriarty.

The President of the United States will now speak to us on the radio.

Capitalize common nouns when they are part of a particular name:
Is Johnson High School going to be closed during the holidays?

We will register at the Holiday Inn.

You will be president of the Acme Tire Works some day.

I spent many hours in Central Park, most of them in the Aquatic Bird House.

Seven Helpful Spelling Rules

1. Use *i* before *e* except after *c*. When the sound is *e*, write *ie* except after *c:*

ie	ei
believe	ceiling
brief	conceit
chief	deceive
piece	receipt
yield	perceive

When the sound is other than *e*, usually write *ei:*

eight	reign	their
heir	rein	veil
neigh	skein	vein
neighbor	sleigh	weigh

Exceptions: counterfeit, either, forfeit, leisure, neither, seize, weird

2. In words ending in *y*, when the *y* comes before a consonant, change the *y* to *i* before adding any suffix, except *-ing:*
beauty + ful = beautiful
carry + ed = carried
carry + er = carrier
carry + ing = carrying

defy + ance = defiance
happy + ness = happiness
mercy + ful = merciful
modify + er = modifier
modify + ing = modifying
Exceptions: shy + ness = shyness
dry + ness = dryness

In words ending in *y* when *y* comes after a vowel (a, e, i, o, u), do not change the *y* before adding a suffix:
annoy + ed = annoyed
annoy + ing = annoying
delay + ed = delayed
delay + ing = delaying
employ + ed = employed
employ + er = employer
employ + ing = employing
Exceptions: day + ly = daily
pay + d = paid
say + d = said

3. Follow a word ending in *c* with a *k* before adding an ending that begins with *e* or *i:*
mimic   mimicked   mimicking
picnic   picnicked   picknicking

4. Double the final consonant of a word before adding a suffix that begins with a vowel if the consonant ends a word of one syllable, or if the consonant follows a single vowel:

admit	admitting	pat	patted
fit	fitting	slap	slapping
knit	knitted	spin	spinning

Exception: If the final consonant comes after two vowels, the single consonant is left before adding a suffix that begins with a vowel:

boot booted booting
kneel kneeled kneeling
sail sailed sailing

Exception: If the final consonant comes after another consonant, the final consonant is left before adding a suffix that begins with a vowel:

stalk stalked stalker stalking
stock stocked stocker stocking
talk talked talker talking

5. Double the final consonant of a word containing two or more syllables when adding a suffix beginning with a vowel unless the consonant follows two vowels, the consonant follows another consonant, or the accent does not fall on the final syllable:

doubled final consonant

compel compelled compelling
expel expelled expelling
occur occurrence occurring
permit permitted permitting
refer referred referring
regret regrettable regretted

final consonant not doubled

benefit benefited benefiting
cancel canceled canceling
contain container containing
debit debited debiting
model modeled modeling
offer offered offering

refer referee reference
Exception: cancellation

6. Drop the silent *e* when adding a suffix beginning with a vowel to words ending in silent *e:*

argue arguable arguing
bone bony
change changing
come coming
debate debatable debating
make making
move movable moving
sale salable
size sizable

Keep the silent *e* at the end of the word if the suffix being added begins with a consonant:

care careful
complete completeness
engage engagement
grace graceful
sure sureness surely
true trueness
vague vaguely
waste wasteful

Exceptions: acknowledge
 acknowledgment
 argue argument
 due duly
 judge judgment
 true truly

7. Keep the final *e* before adding a suffix beginning with *a* or *o* to a word ending in *ce* or *ge:*

advantage + ous = advantageous
courage + ous = courageous
imagine + able = imaginable
machine + able = machinable
notice + able = noticeable
peace + able = peaceable
service + able = serviceable
trace + able = traceable

Exception: practice + able = practicable

FOUR VALUABLE SPELLING HINTS

1. Possessive pronouns are never written with an apostrophe, because their possessive case form shows ownership: *its, hers, ours.*
2. Adverbs often are formed by adding *-ly* to adjectives, but some end in *ally: accidentally, finally, occasionally, practically.*
3. Only one English word ends in *full,* the adjective *full.* All other adjectives having the sound of *full* end in *ful: cheerful, cupful, graceful, handful, hopeful.*
4. Only three English verbs end in *ceed: exceed, proceed,* and *succeed.* All other verbs with that sound end in *cede: accede, cede, concede, intercede, precede, recede,* and *secede.* The word *supersede* is spelled with an *s,* not a *c.*

ONE HUNDRED WORDS FREQUENTLY MISSPELLED

accommodate	environment	performance	repetition
achievement	exaggerate	personal	rhythm
acquire	existence	personnel	sense
affect	existent	possession	separate
all right	experience	possible	separation
apparent	explanation	practical	shining
argument	fascinate	precede	similar
belief	height	prejudice	studying
believe	interest	prepare	succeed
beneficial	its (it's)	prevalent	succession
benefited	led	principal	surprise
category	lose	principle	technique
coming	losing	privilege	than
comparative	marriage	probably	their
conscious	medieval	procedure	then
controversy	necessary	proceed	there
controversial	occasion	profession	they're
definitely	occurred	professor	thorough
definition	occurrence	prominent	to (too, two)
describe	occurring	pursue	transferred
description	opinion	quiet	unnecessary
device	opportunity	quite	villain
disastrous	paid	receive	woman
effect	paralyze	recommend	write
embarrass	particular	referring	writing

Synonyms and Antonyms

Synonyms are words having the same or nearly the same meaning in one or more senses. Thus, after the entry word *beautiful* in the following list, these words are shown as synonyms: fine, handsome, pretty, bewitching, attractive, comely. The synonyms share one characteristic: they all, in one or more senses, have the meaning or nearly the meaning of *beautiful*. Antonyms (opposite meanings) follow in parentheses.

A

abandon, leave, forsake, desert, renounce, surrender, relinquish, quit, forgo, waive. (Keep, hold, maintain, cherish.)

abandoned, deserted, forsaken, wicked, reprobate, dissolute, profligate, flagitious, corrupt, depraved, vicious. (Virtuous.)

abandonment, leaving, desertion, dereliction, renunciation, defection.

abasement, degradation, fall, degeneracy, humiliation, abjection, debasement, servility. (Honor.)

abash, embarrass, humiliate, mortify, bewilder, disconcert, discompose, confound, confuse, shame. (Encourage, cheer, embolden.)

abate, decrease, ebb, dwindle, subside, moderate, reduce, lessen. (Increase, revive, enlarge, aggravate, enhance.)

abbreviate, shorten, abridge, curtail, contract, condense, reduce. (Extend.)

abdicate, give up, resign, renounce, abandon, forsake, relinquish, quit, forgo.

abet, sanction, support, uphold, help, encourage, instigate, incite, stimulate, aid, assist. (Deter, dissuade, hinder, impede.)

abettor, assistant, accessory, accomplice, promoter, instigator, particeps criminis, coadjutor, associate, companion, cooperator. (Opponent.)

abhor, despise, dislike, hate, detest, abominate, loathe, nauseate. (Love, admire, esteem, approve.)

abide, endure, tolerate, bear, continue, wait. (Avoid, resist, abandon, shun.)

ability, capability, talent, faculty, capacity, qualification, aptitude, aptness, expertness, skill, efficiency, accomplishment, attainment. (Incompetency.)

abject, groveling, low, mean, base, ignoble, worthless, despicable, servile, vile, contemptible. (Noble.)

abjure, recant, forswear, disclaim, recall, revoke, retract, renounce. (Maintain.)

able, strong, powerful, muscular, stalwart, vigorous, athletic, robust, brawny, skillful, adroit, competent, efficient, capable, clever, self-qualified, telling, fitted. (Weak.)

abode, residence, habitation, dwelling, domicile, home quarters, lodging.

abolish, quash, destroy, revoke, abrogate, annul, cancel, annihilate, extinguish, vitiate, invalidate, nullify, end, remove, repeal. (Establish, continue, support, sustain, enforce.)

abominable, hateful, detestable, odious, vile, execrable. (Lovable.)

abortive, fruitless, ineffectual, idle, inoperative, vain, futile. (Effectual.)

about, concerning, regarding, relative to, with regard to, as to, respecting, referring to, around, nearly, approximately.

abscond, run off, steal away, decamp, bolt, depart, disappear.

absent, inattentive, abstracted, not present, away, dreamy. (Present.)

absolute, entire, complete, unconditional, unqualified, unrestricted, despotic, arbitrary, tyrannous, imperative, authoritative, imperious, autocratic, positive, unequivocal. (Limited, conditional, accountable.)

absorb, engross, swallow up, engulf, imbibe, consume, merge. (Eject, exude, emit, disgorge.)

absurd, silly, foolish, preposterous, ridiculous, irrational, unreasonable, nonsensical, inconsistent, ludicrous, (Wise, solemn, logical, sensible.)

abuse, *v.,* asperse, revile, vilify, reproach, calumniate, defame, slander, scandalize, malign, traduce, disparage, depreciate, ill-use, defile, desecrate. (Praise, protect, eulogize, laud, extol.)

abuse, *n.,* scurrility, ribaldry, contumely, obloquy, opprobrium, foul invective, vituperation, illusage. (Praise, protection.)

accede, assent, consent, acquiesce, comply, agree, coincide, concur, approve. (Protest.)

accelerate, hasten, hurry, expedite, forward, quicken, dispatch. (Retard.)

accept, receive, take, admit. (Refuse.)

acceptable, agreeable, pleasing, gratifying, pleasurable, welcome. (Displeasing.)

accident, casualty, incident, contingency, mishap, adventure, chance.

accommodate, serve, oblige, adapt, adjust, fit, suit. (Disoblige, impede.)

accomplice, confederate, accessory, abettor, coadjutor, assistant, ally, associate, particeps criminis. (Adversary.)

accomplish, do, effect, finish, execute, achieve, complete, perfect, consummate. (Fail.)

accomplishment, attainment, qualification, acquirement. (Defect.)

account, narrative, description, narration, relation, detail, recital, reckoning, bill, charge.

accountable, punishable, answerable, amenable, responsible, liable.

accumulate, bring together, amass, collect, gather. (Scatter, dissipate.)

accumulation, collection, store, mass, congeries, concentration. agglomeration.

accurate, correct, exact, precise, nice, truthful. (Erroneous, careless.)

achieve, do, accomplish, effect, fulfill, execute, gain, win.

achievement, feat, exploit, accomplishment, attainment, performance, acquirement, gain. (Failure.)

acknowledge, admit, confess, own, avow, grant, recognize, allow, concede. (Deny.)

acquaint, inform, enlighten, apprise, make aware, make known, notify, communicate. (Deceive.)

acquaintance, familiarity, intimacy, cognizance, fellowship, companionship, friendship, knowledge. (Unfamiliarity.)

acquiesce, agree, accede, assent, comply, consent, give way, coincide, concur. (Protest.)

acquit, pardon, forgive, discharge, set free, clear, absolve. (Condemn, convict.)

acrimony, harshness, severity, unkindness, asperity, bitterness, malignity, virulence. (Gentleness, amiability, kindness, mildness, courtesy, sweetness.)

act, do, operate, make, perform, play, enact.

action, deed, achievement, feat, exploit, accomplishment, battle, engagement, agency, instrumentality.

active, lively, sprightly, alert, agile, nimble, brisk, quick, supple, prompt, vigilant, bustling, energetic, busy, laborious, industrious. (Lazy, idle, inactive, slow, sluggish, indolent, passive.)

actual, real, positive, genuine, certain. (Fictitious.)

acute, shrewd, intelligent, penetrating, piercing, keen. (Dull.)

adapt, accommodate, suit, fit, conform.

addicted, devoted, wedded, attached, accustomed, habituated, given up to, boring, beside, close, nigh. (Distant, dedicated, averse, unaccustomed.)

addition, increase, accession, augmentation, reinforcement. (Subtraction, separation.)

address, *n.,* speech, discourse, appeal, oration, tact, skill, ability, dexterity, deportment, demeanor.

address, *v.,* greet, accost, salute, hail. (Shun, pass, avoid, ignore.)

adequate, fit, equal, capable, able, suited, qualified, competent. (Inferior, unfit, unequal, inadequate, incompetent.)

adjacent, near to, adjoining, contiguous, coterminous, bordering, neighboring, abutting. (Distant, remote.)

adjourn, defer, prorogue, postpone.

adjunct, appendage, appurtenance, appendency, dependency.

adjust, set right, fit, accommodate, adapt, arrange, settle, regulate, organize. (Confuse.)

admirable, striking, surprising, wonderful, astonishing. (Detestable.)

admire, esteem, love, extol, respect, venerate, honor, adore, approve, enjoy, applaud. (Abhor, detest, scorn, execrate, dislike, despise, abominate.)

admit, allow, permit, suffer, tolerate. (Deny.)

advantageous, beneficial. (Hurtful.)

adverse, opposed, unfavorable, inimical, antagonistic, contrary, hostile. (Helpful, favorable, aiding, assisting, cooperative.)

affront, insult, offend, irritate, exasperate, vex, provoke, annoy, displease, aggravate. (Gratify, please, conciliate.)

afraid, apprehensive, scared, fearful, timid, alarmed, cautious, anxious. (Audacious, brave, confident, bold, gallant, heroic, intrepid, valiant, daring, courageous.)

agree, accord, acquiesce, concur, harmonize, assent, coincide. (Contradict, differ, oppose, disagree, dissent.)

agreeable, pleasant, pleasing, charming. (Disagreeable.)

alacrity, briskness, swiftness, promptness, speed, celerity, alertness, activity. (Apathy, laziness, sluggishness, slowness, indolence, aversion, repugnance.)

alarm, fright, panic, terror, fear, dread, dismay, affront. (Confidence, assurance, calmness, security.)

alert, nimble, active, prompt, brisk, lively. (Dull, inactive, slow, sluggish.)

allay, pacify, quiet, soothe, still, compose, calm, alleviate, mollify, appease. (Excite, rouse, stir, provoke, agitate, arouse.)

altercation, dispute, discord, contention, argument, row, quarrel, scrap, disturbance, brawl. (Harmony, unanimity, agreement, union.)

alternating, intermittent. (Continual.)

amazement, surprise, awe, wonder, bewilderment, confusion, astonishment. (Indifference, steadiness, coolness, stoicism, calmness, composure.)

ambassador, envoy, plenipotentiary, minister.

amend, improve, correct, better, mend, rectify, repair. (Impair, harm, spoil, injure.)

anger, ire, wrath, indignation, resentment, animosity, displeasure, rage. (Good nature, amiability.)

appropriate, assume, ascribe, arrogate, usurp.

argue, debate, dispute, reason upon.

arise, flow, emanate, spring, proceed, rise, issue.

artful, disingenuous, sly, tricky, insincere. (Candid.)

artifice, trick, stratagem, finesse.

association, combination, company, partnership, society. (Isolation, solitude, separation.)

attack, assail, assault, encounter. (Defend.)

attain, gain, master, accomplish, achieve, win, reach, get, acquire. (Forfeit, abandon, lose.)

audacity, boldness, effrontery, hardihood, temerity. (Meekness.)

austere, rigid, rigorous, severe, stern. (Dissolute.)

avaricious, niggardly, miserly, parsimonious. (Generous.)

aversion, antipathy, dislike, hatred, repugnance. (Affection.)

awe, dread, fear, reverence. (Familiarity.)

awkward, clumsy, uncouth, ungainly. (Graceful, adroit.)

B

babble, chatter, prattle, prate, murmur, cackle.

bad, wicked, evil. (Good.)

baffle, confound, defeat, disconcert. (Aid, abet.)

barbarous, cruel, merciless, pitiless, atrocious, brutal, inhuman, savage, uncivilized. (Humane, polite, civilized, cultured, refined, urbane.)

beat, defeat, overpower, overthrow, rout.

beautiful, fine, handsome, pretty, bewitching, attractive, comely. (Homely, ugly, hideous, horrid, unattractive.)

becoming, decent, fit, seemly, suitable, befitting, graceful. (Unbecoming, unsuitable, unfitting, misplaced.)

beg, beseech, crave, entreat, implore, solicit, supplicate. (Give.)

behavior, carriage, conduct, deportment, bearing, manner, demeanor.

belief, credit, faith, trust. (Doubt.)

beneficent, bountiful, generous, liberal, munificent. (Covetous, miserly.)

benefit, favor, advantage, kindness, civility. (Injury.)

benevolence, beneficence, benignity, humanity, kindness, tenderness, generosity, liberality, unselfishness. (Malevolence, selfishness, unkindness.)

blame, censure, condemn, reprove, reproach, upbraid. (Praise.)

bleak, cheerless, bare, dismal, blank, desolate, waste, unsheltered, dreary. (Cheery, balmy, sunny, warm, mild.)

blemish, defect, disfigurement, imperfection, flaw, speck, spot, stain. (Ornament.)

blind, sightless, heedless. (Farsighted.)

blot, cancel, efface, expunge, erase, obliterate.

bold, brave, daring, fearless, intrepid, undaunted. (Timid.)

brave, daring, bold, courageous, adventurous, heroic, intrepid, fearless, valiant, dauntless. (Afraid, timid, cowardly, fearful.)

bravery, courage, valor. (Cowardice.)

break, crack, split, smash, bruise, crush, pound, squeeze.

breeze, blast, gale, gust, hurricane, storm, tempest.

bright, brilliant, luminous, resplendent, clear, radiant, shining. (Dull.)

C

calamity, disaster, misfortune, mischance, mishap. (Good fortune.)

calm, cool, mild, quiet, peaceful, still, tranquil, collected, composed, placid, serene. (Stormy, disturbed, agitated, excited, ruffled, violent, unsettled.)

cancel, nullify, abolish, annul, rescind, quash, revoke, repeal. (Maintain, establish, sustain, uphold, approve.)

candid, sincere, honest, truthful, frank, fair, impartial, unbiased. (Cunning, adroit, crafty, sly, shrewd, tricky, wily, subtle, deceitful, artful.)

caress, fondle, pet, kiss, embrace. (Spurn, buffet.)

carnage, butchery, massacre, slaughter.

catch, grasp, grip, capture, clutch, clasp, seize, snatch, secure, take. (Miss, lose, restore, release.)

cause, motive, reason. (Effect, consequence.)

cavity, hollow, indentation, hole, opening, bore, perforation, fissure. (Lump, hill, mound, knoll, elevation.)

cease, finish, quit, stop, terminate, discontinue, leave off, end. (Continue, begin, inaugurate, start.)

censure, animadvert, criticize. (Praise.)

certain, secure, sure. (Doubtful.)

cessation, intermission, rest, stop. (Continuance.)

chance, fate, fortune. (Design.)

change, barter, exchange, substitute.

changeable, fickle, inconstant, mutable, variable. (Unchangeable.)

character, reputation, repute, standing.

charm, captivate, enchant, enrapture, fascinate.

cheap, inexpensive, inferior, common. (Dear.)

cheerful, gay, merry, sprightly. (Mournful.)

chief, chieftain, head, leader. (Subordinate, attendant, follower.)

circumstance, fact, incident.

class, degree, order, rank.

clear, bright, lucid, vivid. (Opaque, ambiguous, dim, obscure, vague.)

clever, adroit, dexterous, expert, skillful. (Stupid, awkward, bungling.)

combination, cabal, conspiracy, plot.

command, injunction, order, precept.

commodity, goods, merchandise, ware.

common, mean, ordinary, vulgar. (Uncommon, extraordinary.)

compassion, sympathy, pity, clemency. (Cruelty, severity.)

compel, force, oblige, necessitate, make, coerce. (Coax, lead.)

compendium, compend, abridgment. (Enlargement.)

compensation, amends, recompense, remuneration, requital, reward.

complain, lament, murmur, regret, repine. (Rejoice.)

comply, accede, conform, submit, yield. (Refuse.)

comprehend, comprise, include, embrace, grasp, understand, perceive. (Exclude, mistake.)

comprise, comprehend, contain, embrace, include.

conceal, hide, secrete. (Uncover.)

conceive, comprehend, understand.

conclusion, inference, deduction.

condemn, censure, blame, disapprove, reprove. (Justify, exonerate, acquit, approve.)

conduct, direct, guide, lead, govern, regulate, manage.

confirm, corroborate, approve, attest. (Contradict.)

conflict, combat, contest, contention, struggle. (Peace, quiet.)

conquer, master, beat, overcome, subdue, surmount, vanquish. (Defeat, lose, capitulate.)

consequence, effect, event, issue, result. (Cause.)

consider, reflect, ponder, weigh.

consistent, constant, compatible. (Inconsistent.)

console, comfort, solace. (Harrow, worry.)

constancy, firmness, stability, steadiness. (Fickleness.)

contaminate, corrupt, defile, pollute, taint.

contemplate, meditate, muse.

contemptible, despicable, paltry, pitiful, vile, mean. (Noble.)

contend, contest, dispute, strive, struggle, combat.

continual, constant, continuous, perpetual, incessant. (Intermittent.)

continuance, continuation, duration. (Cessation.)

continue, persist, persevere, pursue, prosecute. (Cease.)

contradict, deny, gainsay, oppose. (Confirm.)

contrast, compare, discriminate, differentiate.

convey, transfer, shift, move, change, carry, transport, transmit, give. (Keep, hold, possess, retain.)

covetousness, avarice, cupidity. (Beneficence.)

cowardice, fear, timidity, pusillanimity. (Courage.)

crime, sin, vice, misdemeanor. (Virtue.)

criminal, convict, culprit, felon, malefactor.

crooked, bent, curved, oblique. (Straight.)

cruel, barbarous, brutal, inhuman, savage. (Kind.)

cultivation, culture, refinement.

cursory, desultory, hasty, slight. (Thorough.)

custom, fashion, manner, practice.

D

danger, hazard, peril. (Safety.)

dark, somber, gloomy, dismal, opaque, obscure, dim. (Light, bright, clear, radiant.)

deadly, fatal, destructive, mortal.

deceit, cheat, imposition, trick, delusion, guile, beguilement, treachery, sham. (Truthfulness.)

deceive, delude, impose upon, overreach, gull, dupe, cheat.

decide, determine, settle, adjudicate, terminate, resolve.

decipher, read, spell, interpret, solve.

decision, determination, conclusion, resolution, firmness (Vacillation.)

declamation, oratory, elocution, harangue, effusion, debate.

declaration, avowal, manifestation, statement, profession.

decrease, diminish, lessen, wane, decline, retrench, curtail, reduce. (Growth.)

dedicate, devote, consecrate, offer, set, apportion.

deed, act, action, commission, achievement, instrument, document.

deem, judge, estimate, consider, think, suppose, conceive.

deep, profound, subterranean, submerged, designing, abstruse, learned. (Shallow.)

deface, mar, spoil, injure, disfigure. (Beautify.)

default, lapse, forfeit, omission, absence, want, failure.

defect, imperfection, flaw, fault, blemish. (Beauty, improvement.)

defend, guard, protect, justify.

defense, excuse, plea, vindication, bulwark, rampart.

defer, delay, postpone, put off, prorogue, adjourn. (Force, expedite.)

deficient, short, wanting, inadequate, scanty, incomplete. (Complete.)

defile, *v.*, pollute, corrupt, sully, befoul, contaminate, spoil. (Beautify, clean, purify.)

define, fix, settle, determine, limit.

defray, meet, liquidate, pay, discharge.

delicacy, nicety, daintiness, refinement, tact, softness, modesty. (Boorishness, indelicacy.)

delicate, tender, fragile, dainty, refined. (Coarse.)

delicious, sweet, palatable, luscious, savory. (Nauseous, bitter, unpalatable.)

delight, enjoyment, pleasure, happiness, transport, ecstasy, gladness, rapture, bliss. (Annoyance.)

deliver, liberate, free, rescue, pronounce, give, hand over. (Retain.)

demonstrate, prove, show, exhibit, illustrate.

depart, leave, quit, decamp, retire, withdraw, vanish (Remain.)

derision, scorn, contempt, contumely, disrespect.

derivation, origin, source, beginning, cause, etymology, root.

describe, delineate, portray, explain, illustrate, define, picture.

desecrate, profane, secularize, misuse, abuse, pollute. (Keep holy.)

deserve, merit, earn, justify, win.

design, *n.*, delineation, sketch, drawing, cunning, artfulness, contrivance.

desirable, expedient, advisable, valuable, acceptable, proper, judicious, beneficial, profitable, good.

desire, *n.*, longing, affection, craving, coveting, wish.

desist, cease, stop, discontinue, drop, abstain, forbear. (Continue, persevere.)

desolate, bereaved, forlorn, forsaken, deserted, wild, waste, bare, bleak, lonely. (Pleasant, happy.)

desperate, wild, daring, audacious, determined, reckless.

despised, degraded, worthless. (Admired.)

destiny, fate, decree, doom, end.

destructive, detrimental, hurtful, noxious, injurious, deleterious, baleful, baneful, subversive. (Creative.)

deter, warn, stop, dissuade, terrify, scare. (Encourage.)

detriment, loss, harm, injury, deterioration. (Benefit.)

develop, unfold, amplify, expand, enlarge.

device, artifice, expedient, contrivance.

devoid, void, wanting, destitute, unendowed, unprovided. (Full, complete.)

devoted, attached, fond, absorbed, dedicated.

dictate, prompt, suggest, enjoin, order, command.

dictatorial, imperative, imperious, domineering, arbitrary, tyrannical, overbearing. (Submissive.)

die, perish, decease, expire, depart, decline, languish, wane, sink, fade, decay.

diet, foods, victuals, nourishment, nutriment, sustenance, fare.

difference, variation, contrast, disparity, separation, disagreement, discord, dissent, estrangement, variety.

different, various, manifold, diverse, unlike, separate, distinct. (Similar.)

difficult, severe, arduous, laborious, trying, hard, intricate, involved, perplexing, obscure, unmanageable. (Easy.)

dilatory, tardy, procrastinating, behindhand, lagging, dawdling. (Prompt.)

diligence, care, assiduity, attention, heed, industry. (Negligence.)

diminish, lessen, reduce, contract, curtail, retrench. (Increase.)

disability, unfitness, incapacity.

discern, behold, descry, observe, recognize, see, discriminate, separate, perceive.

discipline, order, strictness, training, coercion, punishment, organization. (Confusion, demoralization.)

discover, disclose, detect, make known, find, invent, contrive, expose, reveal.

discreditable, shameful, disgraceful, scandalous, disreputable. (Creditable.)

discreet, cautious, prudent, wary, judicious. (Indiscreet.)

discrepancy, disagreement, difference, variance. (Agreement.)

discrimination, acuteness, discernment, judgment, caution.

disease, illness, unhealthiness, complaint, malady, disorder, ailment, sickness.

disgrace, *n.*, disrepute, reproach, dishonor, shame, odium. (Honor.)

disgrace, *v.* debase, degrade, defame, discredit. (Exalt.)

disgust, dislike, distaste, loathing, abomination, abhorrence. (Admiration.)

dishonest, unjust, fraudulent, unfair, deceitful, cheating, deceptive, wrongful. (Honest.)

dismiss, send off, discharge, discard, banish. (Retain.)

dispel, scatter, drive away, disperse, dissipate. (Collect.)

display, show, spread out, exhibit, expose. (Hide.)

dispose, arrange, place, order, give, bestow.

dispute, *v.*, argue, contest, contend, question, impugn. (Assent.)

dispute, *n.*, argument, debate, controversy, quarrel, disagreement. (Harmony.)

dissent, disagree, differ, vary. (Assent.)

distinct, clear, plain, obvious, different, separate. (Obscure, indistinct.)

distinguish, perceive, discern, mark out, divide, discriminate.

distinguished, famous, glorious, far-famed, noted, illustrious, eminent, celebrated. (Obscure, unknown, ordinary.)

distract, perplex, bewilder. (Calm, concentrate.)

distribute, allot, share, dispense, apportion, deal. (Collect.)

disturb, derange, discompose, agitate, rouse, interrupt, confuse, trouble, annoy, vex, worry. (Pacify, quiet.)

disuse, discontinuance, abolition, desuetude. (Use.)

do, effect, make, perform, accomplish, finish, transact, achieve, complete, realize, perpetrate, execute.

docile, tractable, teachable, compliant, tame. (Stubborn, determined, inflexible, firm, resolute.)

doctrine, tenet, article of belief, creed, dogma, teaching.

doleful, dolorous, woebegone, rueful, dismal, piteous. (Joyous.)

doom, *n.*, sentence, verdict, judgment, fate, lot, destiny.

doubt, *n.*, uncertainty, suspense, hesitation, scruple, ambiguity. (Certainty.)

draw, pull, haul, drag, attract, inhale, sketch, describe.

dread, *n.*, fear, horror, terror, alarm, dismay, awe. (Boldness, assurance.)

dreadful, fearful, frightful, shocking, awful, horrible, horrid, terrific.

dress, *n.*, clothing, attire, apparel, garments, costume, garb, livery, raiment.

drown, inundate, swamp, submerge, overwhelm, engulf.

dry, *a.*, arid, parched, lifeless, dull, tedious, uninteresting, meager. (Moist, interesting, succulent.)

due, owing to, attributable to, just, fair, proper, debt, right.

dull, stupid, gloomy, sad, dismal, commonplace. (Bright.)

dunce, simpleton, fool, ninny, idiot. (Sage.)

duplicate, facsimile, replica, likeness, imitation, copy, counterpart, reproduction. (Model, original, pattern, prototype.)

durable, lasting, permanent, abiding, continuing. (Ephemeral, perishable.)

dwell, stay, stop, abide, sojourn, linger, tarry.

dwindle, pine, waste, diminish, decrease, fall off. (Grow.)

E

eager, fervent, desirous, hot, ardent, impassioned, forward, impatient. (Diffident, apathetic, indifferent, unconcerned.)

earn, acquire, obtain, win, gain, achieve.

earnest, *a.*, ardent, serious, grave, solemn, warm. (Trifling.)

earnest, *n.*, pledge, pawn.

ease, *n.*, comfort, rest. (Worry.)

ease, *v.*, calm, alleviate, allay, mitigate, appease, assuage, pacify, disburden, rid. (Annoy, worry.)

easy, light, comfortable, unconstrained. (Difficult, hard.)

eccentric, irregular, anomalous, singular, odd, abnormal, wayward, particular, strange. (Regular, ordinary.)

economical, sparing, saving, provident, thrifty, frugal, careful, niggardly. (Wasteful.)

efface, blot out, expunge, obliterate, wipe out, cancel, erase.

effect, *n.*, consequence, result, issue, event, execution, operation.

effect, *v.*, accomplish, fulfill, realize, achieve, execute, operate, complete.

effective, efficient, operative, serviceable. (Vain, ineffectual.)

efficacy, efficiency, energy, agency, instrumentality.

efficient, effectual, effective, competent, capable, able, fitted.

eliminate, drive out, expel, thrust out, eject, cast out, oust, dislodge, banish, proscribe.

eloquence, oratory, rhetoric, declamation.

elucidate, make plain, explain, clear up, illustrate.

elude, evade, escape, avoid, shun.

embarrass, perplex, entangle, distress, trouble. (Assist.)

embellish, adorn, decorate, bedeck, beautify, deck. (Disfigure.)

embolden, inspirit, animate, encourage, cheer, urge, impel, stimulate. (Discourage.)

eminent, distinguished, signal, conspicuous, noted, prominent, elevated, renowned, famous, glorious, illustrious. (Obscure, unknown.)

emit, give out, throw out, exhale, discharge, vent.

emotion, perturbation, agitation, trepidation, tremor, mental conflict.

employ, occupy, busy, take up with, engross.

employment, business, avocation, engagement, office, function, trade, profession, occupation, calling, vocation.

enclose, surround, shut in, fence in, cover, wrap.

encourage, countenance, sanction, support, foster, cherish, inspirit, embolden, animate, cheer, incite, urge, impel, stimulate. (Deter.)

end, *n.*, aim, object, purpose, result, conclusion, upshot, close, expiration, termination, extremity, sequel.

endeavor, attempt, try, essay, strive, aim.

endorse, ratify, confirm, superscribe.

endurance, continuation, duration, fortitude, patience, resignation.

endure, *v.*, last, continue, support, bear, sustain, suffer, brook, submit to, undergo, tolerate. (Perish, succumb, yield.)

enemy, foe, antagonist, adversary, opponent. (Friend.)

energetic, industrious, effectual, efficacious, powerful, binding, stringent, forcible, nervous. (Lazy.)

engage, employ, busy, occupy, attract, invite, allure, entertain, engross, take up, enlist.

enjoyment, pleasure, gratification. (Grief, sorrow, sadness.)

enlarge, increase, extend, augment, broaden, swell. (Diminish.)

enlighten, illumine, illuminate, instruct, inform. (Befog, becloud.)

enliven, cheer, vivify, stir up, animate, inspire, exhilarate. (Sadden, quiet.)

enmity, animosity, hostility, ill will, maliciousness. (Friendship.)

enormous, gigantic, colossal, huge, vast, immense, prodigious. (Insignificant.)

enough, sufficient, plenty, abundance. (Want.)

enraged, infuriated, raging, wrathful. (Pacified.)

enrapture, enchant, fascinate, charm, captivate, bewitch. (Repel.)

enroll, enlist, list, register, record.

enterprise, undertaking, endeavor, venture, energy.

entertain, beguile, amuse, cheer, divert, interest, please. (Annoy, disturb, tire, bore, weary, distract.)

enthusiasm, fervor, warmth, intensity, earnest, devotion, zeal, ardor. (Ennui, timidity, wariness, lukewarmness.)

entrance, ingress, access, door, approach, inlet, entry, gate, opening, portal. (Ejection, refusal, expulsion, exit, egress, withdrawal.)

equal, equable, even, like, alike, uniform. (Unequal.)

eradicate, root out, extirpate, exterminate.

erroneous, incorrect, inaccurate, inexact. (Exact.)

error, blunder, mistake. (Truth.)

especially, chiefly, particularly, principally. (Generally.)

essay, dissertation, tract.

establish, build up, confirm. (Overthrow.)

esteem, regard, respect. (Contempt.)

estimate, appraise, appreciate, esteem, compute, rate.

USING THE LANGUAGE

eternal, imperishable, perpetual, undying, timeless, unceasing, endless, everlasting. (Finite.)

evade, equivocate, prevaricate.

even, level, plain, smooth. (Uneven.)

event, accident, adventure, incident, occurrence.

evil, ill, harm, mischief, misfortune. (Good.)

exact, nice, particular, punctual. (Inexact.)

exalt, ennoble, dignify, raise. (Humble.)

examination, investigation, inquiry, research, search, scrutiny.

exceed, excel, outdo, surpass, transcend. (Fall short.)

exceptional, uncommon, rare, extraordinary. (Common.)

excess, profusion, surplus, superfluity, waste, lavishness, luxuriance, dissipation, extravagance. (Poverty, want, need, lack, scantiness, frugality, economy, dearth, destitution.)

excite, awaken, provoke, rouse, stir up. (Lull.)

excursion, jaunt, ramble, tour, trip.

execute, fulfill, perform.

exempt, free, cleared. (Subject.)

exercise, practice.

exhaustive, thorough, complete. (Cursory.)

exigency, emergency.

experiment, proof, trial, test.

explain, expound, interpret, illustrate, elucidate.

express, declare, signify, utter, tell.

exterminate, expel, banish, destroy, remove, annihilate, eradicate. (Beget, develop, breed, increase, replenish, populate, propagate, augment.)

extravagant, lavish, profuse, prodigal. (Parsimonious.)

F

fable, apologue, novel, romance, tale.

face, visage, countenance.

facetious, pleasant, jocular, jocose. (Serious.)

factor, agent.

fail, to fall short, be deficient. (Accomplish.)

faint, weak, irresolute, faltering, feeble, languid. (Forcible, fresh, hearty, resolute.)

fair, clear. (Stormy.)

fair, equitable, honest, reasonable. (Unfair.)

faith, creed. (Unbelief, infidelity.)

faithful, staunch, devoted, trusty, true, loyal, constant. (Faithless, false, untrue.)

faithless, perfidious, treacherous. (Faithful.)

fall, drop, droop, sink, tumble. (Rise.)

fame, renown, reputation, distinction, eminence.

famous, celebrated, renowned, illustrious. (Obscure.)

fanciful, capricious, fantastical, whimsical.

fancy, imagination.

fast, rapid, quick, fleet, expeditious. (Slow.)

fatigue, weariness, lassitude. (Vigor.)

fear, timidity, timorousness, fright, apprehension, trepidation. (Bravery.)

feeling, sensation, sense.

feeling, sensibility, susceptibility. (Insensibility.)

ferocious, fierce, savage, wild, barbarous. (Mild.)

fertile, fruitful, prolific, plenteous, productive. (Sterile.)

feud, bitterness, contest, affray, animosity, brawl, dispute, fray, enmity, riot, quarrel, strife, row, controversy, dissension.

fickle, fluctuating, changeable, inconstant, restless, irresolute, uncertain, unreliable, versatile, wavering, vacillating. (Constant, firm, fixed, determined, resolute, stable, sure, steady, uniform, decided, unchanging.)

firm, constant, solid, steadfast, fixed, stable. (Weak.)

first, foremost, chief, earliest. (Last.)

fit, accommodate, adapt, adjust, suit.

fix, determine, establish, settle, limit, decide.

flame, blaze, flare, flash, glare.

flat, level, even.

flexible, pliant, pliable, ductile, supple. (Inflexible.)

flourish, prosper, thrive. (Decay.)

fluctuating, wavering, hesitating, oscillating, vacillating, change. (Firm, steadfast, decided.)

fluent, flowing, glib, voluble, unembarrassed, ready. (Hesitating.)

folks, persons, people, individuals.

follow, succeed, ensue, imitate, copy, pursue.

follower, partisan, disciple, adherent, retainer, pursuer, successor.

folly, silliness, foolishness, imbecility, weakness. (Wisdom.)

fond, enamored, attached, affectionate. (Distant.)

fondness, affection, attachment, kindness, love. (Aversion.)

foolhardy, venturesome, incautious, hasty, adventurous, rash. (Cautious.)

foolish, simple, silly, irrational, brainless, imbecile, crazy, absurd, preposterous, ridiculous, nonsensical. (Discreet, wise.)

forecast, forethought, foresight, premeditation, prognostication.

forego, quit, relinquish, let go, waive.

foregoing, antecedent, anterior, preceding, previous, prior, former.

forerunner, herald, harbinger, precursor, omen.

foresight, forethought, forecast, premeditation.

forge, coin, invent, frame, feign, fabricate, counterfeit.

forgive, pardon, remit, absolve, acquit, excuse, except.

forlorn, forsaken, abandoned, deserted, desolate, lone, lonesome.

form, *n.,* ceremony, solemnity, observance, rite, figure, shape, conformation, fashion, appearance, representation, resemblance.

form, *v.,* make, create, produce, constitute, arrange, fashion, mold.

formal, ceremonious, precise, exact, stiff, methodical, affected. (Informal, natural.)

former, antecedent, anterior,

previous, prior, preceding, foregoing.

forsaken, abandoned, forlorn, deserted, desolate, lone, lonesome.

fortunate, lucky, happy, auspicious, prosperous, successful. (Unfortunate.)

fortune, chance, fate, luck, doom, destiny, property, possession, riches.

foster, cherish, nurse, tend, harbor, nurture. (Neglect.)

foul, impure, nasty, filthy, dirty, unclean, defiled. (Pure, clean.)

fragile, brittle, frail, delicate, feeble. (Strong.)

fragments, pieces, scraps, leavings, chips, remains, remnants.

frailty, weakness, failing, foible, imperfection, fault, blemish. (Strength.)

frame, *v.,* construct, invent, coin, fabricate, forge, mold, feign, make, compose.

franchise, right, exemption, immunity, privilege, freedom, suffrage.

frank, artless, candid, sincere, free, easy, familiar, open, ingenuous, plain. (Tricky, insincere.)

frantic, distracted, mad, furious, raving, frenzied. (Quiet, subdued.)

fraud, deceit, deception, duplicity, guile, cheat, imposition. (Honesty.)

freak, fancy, humor, vagary, whim, caprice, crotchet. (Purpose, resolution.)

free, *a.,* liberal, generous, bountiful, bounteous, munificent, frank, artless, candid, familiar, open, independent, unconfined, unreserved, unrestricted, exempt, clear, loose, easy, careless. (Slavish, stingy, artful, costly.)

free, *v.,* release, set free, deliver, rescue, liberate, enfranchise, affranchise, emancipate, exempt. (Enslave, bind.)

freedom, liberty, independence, unrestraint, familiarity, license, franchise, exemption, privilege. (Slavery.)

frequent, often, common, usual, general. (Rare.)

fret, gall, chafe, agitate, irritate, vex.

friendly, cordial, fond, companionable, affable, amicable, genial, kind, hearty, neighborly, sociable, social. (Antagonistic, belligerent, cold, alienated, frigid, hostile, distant, unfriendly, unkind, indifferent.)

frightful, fearful, dreadful, dire, direful, terrific, awful, horrible, horrid.

frivolous, trifling, trivial, petty. (Serious, earnest.)

frugal, provident, economical, saving. (Wasteful, extravagant.)

frugality, parsimony, prudence, economy, miserliness, scrimping, saving, thrift, sparing. (Luxury, riches, waste, wealth, opulence, liberality, bounty, abundance, affluence, extravagance.)

fruitful, fertile, prolific, productive, abundant, plentiful, plenteous. (Barren, sterile.)

fruitless, vain, useless, idle, abortive, bootless, unavailing, without avail.

furious, violent, boisterous, vehement, dashing, sweeping, rolling, impetuous, frantic, distracted, stormy, angry, raging, fierce. (Calm.)

futile, trifling, trivial, frivolous, useless, (Effective.)

G

gain, *n.,* profit, emolument, advantage, benefit, winnings, earnings. (Loss.)

gain, *v.,* get, acquire, obtain, attain, procure, earn, win, achieve, reap, realize, reach. (Lose.)

gallant, brave, bold, courageous, gay, fine, showy, intrepid, heroic, fearless.

galling, chafing, irritating, vexing. (Soothing.)

game, play, pastime, diversion, sport, amusement.

gang, band, horde, company, troop, crew.

gap, breach, chasm, hollow, cavity, cleft, crevice, rift, chink.

garnish, embellish, adorn, beautify, deck, decorate.

gather, pick, cull, assemble, muster, infer, collect. (Scatter.)

gaudy, showy, flashy, tawdry, gay, glittering, bespangled. (Somber.)

gaunt, emaciated, scraggy, skinny, meager, lank, attenuated, spare, lean, thin. (Well-fed.)

gay, cheerful, merry, lively, jolly, sprightly, blithe. (Solemn.)

generate, form, make, beget, produce.

generation, formation, race, breed, stock, kind, age, era.

generous, beneficent, noble, honorable, bountiful, liberal, free, magnanimous. (Niggardly, greedy, miserly, stingy, parsimonious.)

genial, cordial, hearty, festive, joyous, (Distant, cold.)

genius, intellect, invention, talent, nature, character, adept. (Stupidity, dullness.)

genteel, refined, polished, fashionable, polite, well-bred. (Boorish.)

gentle, placid, bland, mild, meek, tame, docile. (Rough, uncouth.)

get, obtain, earn, gain, attain, procure, achieve, acquire.

ghastly, pallid, wan, hideous, grim, shocking.

ghost, specter, sprite, apparition, shade, phantom.

gift, donation, benefaction, grant, alms, bequest, present, gratuity, boon, faculty, talent.

gigantic, colossal, huge, enormous, vast, prodigious, immense. (Diminutive.)

give, cede, deliver, grant, bestow, confer, yield, impart.

glad, pleased, cheerful, joyful, gladsome, gratified, cheering. (Sad.)

gleam, glimmer, glance, glitter, shine, flash.

glee, gaiety, merriment, mirth, joviality, joy, hilarity. (Sorrow.)

gloom, cloud, darkness, dimness, blackness, dullness, sadness. (Light, brightness, joy.)

gloomy, lowering, lurid, dim, dusky, sad, glum. (Bright, clear.)

glorify, magnify, celebrate, adore, exalt.

glorious, famous, renowned,

distinguished, noble, exalted. (Infamous.)

glory, honor, fame, renown, splendor, grandeur. (Infamy.)

glut, gorge, stuff, cram, cloy, satiate, block up.

go, depart, proceed, move, budge, stir.

godly, righteous, devout, holy, pious, religious.

good, *n.,* benefit, weal, advantage, profit, boon. (Evil.)

good, *a.,* virtuous, righteous, upright, just, true. (Wicked, bad.)

gorge, glut, fill, cram, stuff, satiate.

gorgeous, superb, grand, magnificent, splendid. (Plain, simple.)

govern, control, rule, direct, manage, command.

government, rule, state, control, sway.

graceful, becoming, comely, elegant, beautiful. (Awkward.)

grand, majestic, stately, dignified, lofty, elevated, exalted, splendid, gorgeous, superb, magnificent, sublime, pompous. (Shabby.)

grant, *v.,* bestow, impart, give, yield, cede, allow, confer, invest.

grant, *n.,* gift, boon, donation.

graphic, forcible, telling, picturesque, vivid, pictorial.

grasp, catch, seize, grip, clasp, grapple.

grateful, agreeable, pleasing, welcome, thankful. (Harsh.)

gratification, enjoyment, pleasure, delight, reward. (Disappointment.)

grave, *a.,* serious, sedate, solemn, sober, pressing, heavy. (Giddy.)

grave, *n.,* tomb., sepulcher, vault.

great, big, huge, large, majestic, vast, grand, noble, august. (Small.)

greediness, avidity, eagerness, voracity. (Generosity.)

grief, affliction, sorrow, trial, woe, tribulation, sadness, melancholy. (Joy.)

grieve, mourn, lament, sorrow, pain, hurt, wound, bewail. (Rejoice.)

grievous, painful, afflicting, heavy, baleful, unhappy.

grind, crush, oppress, grate, harass, afflict.

grisly, terrible, hideous, grim, ghastly, dreadful. (Pleasing.)

gross, coarse, outrageous, unseemly, shameful, indelicate. (Delicate.)

group, assembly, cluster, collection, clump, order, class.

grovel, crawl, cringe, fawn, sneak.

grow, increase, vegetate, expand, advance. (Decay, diminish.)

growl, grumble, snarl, murmur, complain.

grudge, malice, rancor, spite, pique, hatred, aversion.

gruff, rough, rugged, blunt, rude, harsh, surly, bearish (Pleasant.)

guile, deceit, fraud. (Candor.)

guiltless, harmless, innocent.

guilty, culpable, sinful, criminal.

H

habit, custom, practice, fashion, routine, system.

hail, accost, address, greet, salute, welcome.

happiness, beatitude, blessedness, bliss, felicity, contentment, joy, merriment, rapture, pleasure, enjoyment. (Unhappiness.)

harbor, haven, port.

hard, firm, solid, arduous, difficult. (Soft, easy.)

harm, injury, hurt, wrong, affliction. (Benefit.)

harmless, safe, innocuous, innocent. (Hurtful.)

harsh, rough, rigorous, severe, gruff, morose. (Gentle.)

harvest, crop, fruit, growth, result, return, yield, proceeds, product, increase.

hasten, accelerate, dispatch, expedite, speed. (Delay.)

hasty, hurried, ill-advised. (Deliberate.)

hateful, odious, detestable. (Lovable.)

hatred, enmity, ill will, rancor, animosity, hostility, revenge, spite, hate. (Friendship.)

hazard, peril, chance, risk, venture.

healthy, hale, vigorous, well, salubrious, salutary, wholesome, (Unhealthy, diseased, fragile, ill, sick.)

heap, accumulate, amass, pile.

hearty, cordial, sincere, warm. (Insincere.)

heavy, burdensome, ponderous, weighty. (Light.)

heed, care, attention.

heighten, enhance, exalt, elevate, raise.

help, abet, encourage, aid, assist, relieve, succor. (Hinder, oppose, thwart, discourage.)

heretic, pervert, renegade, traitor, sectary, sectarian, schismatic, dissenter, nonconformist.

hesitate, falter, stammer, stutter.

hide, cover, disguise, cloak, conceal, bury, veil, suppress, screen, entomb, secrete. (Betray, confess, admit, avow, exhibit, divulge, expose, show, reveal, publish, advertise, tell, uncover.)

hinder, retard, hamper, delay, deter, check, balk, impede, obstruct, prevent. (Help.)

hint, allude, refer, suggest, intimate, insinuate.

hold, detail, keep, retain.

holiness, sanctity, piety, sacredness.

holy, devout, pious, religious.

home, habitation, dwelling, fireside, hearth, house, residence, domicile, abode.

homely, plain, ugly, coarse. (Beautiful.)

honesty, integrity, probity, uprightness. (Dishonesty.)

honor, respect, reverence, esteem. (Dishonor.)

hope, confidence, expectation, trust.

hopeless, desperate.

hot, ardent, burning, fiery. (Cold.)

however, nevertheless, notwithstanding, yet.

humane, kind, merciful, human, tender, gentle, gracious, sympathetic, forgiving, charitable, benevolent, benignant, pitying.

humble, *a.,* modest, submissive, plain, unostentatious, simple. (Haughty.)

humble, *v.,* degrade, humiliate, mortify, abase. (Exalt.)

humor, mood, temper.

hunt, pursuit, search, seek, chase.

hurtful, noxious, pernicious. (Beneficial.)

hypocrite, cheat, deceiver, dissembler, impostor.

I

idea, thought, imagination.

ideal, imaginary, fancied. (Actual.)

idle, indolent, lazy. (Industrious.)

ignominious, shameful, scandalous, infamous. (Honorable.)

ignominy, shame, disgrace, obloquy, infamy, reproach.

ignorant, unlearned, illiterate, uninformed, uneducated. (Knowing.)

illegal, unlawful, illicit, contraband, illegitimate. (Legal.)

illimitable, boundless, immeasurable, unlimited, infinite.

illiterate, unlettered, unlearned, untaught, uninstructed. (Learned, educated.)

illusion, fallacy, deception, phantasm.

illusory, imaginary, chimerical, visionary. (Real.)

illustrate, explain, elucidate, clear.

illustrious, celebrated, noble, eminent, famous, renowned. (Obscure.)

image, likeness, picture, representation, effigy.

imaginary, ideal, fanciful, illusory. (Real.)

imagine, conceive, fancy, apprehend, think, presume.

imbecility, silliness, senility, dotage.

imitate, copy, ape, mimic, mock, counterfeit.

immaculate, unspotted, spotless, unsullied. (Soiled.)

immediate, pressing, instant, next, proximate.

immediately, instantly, forthwith, directly, presently.

immense, vast, enormous, huge, prodigious, monstrous.

immunity, privilege, prerogative, exemption.

impair, injure, diminish, decrease.

impart, reveal, divulge, disclose, discover, bestow, afford.

impartial, just, equitable, unbiased. (Partial.)

impeach, accuse, charge, arraign, censure.

impede, hinder, retard, obstruct, prevent. (Help.)

impediment, obstruction, hindrance, obstacle, barrier, bar, clog, encumbrance. (Aid, assistance, benefit, help.)

impel, animate, induce, incite, instigate, embolden. (Retard.)

impending, imminent, threatening.

imperative, commanding, despotic, authoritative.

imperfection, fault, blemish, defect, vice.

imperil, endanger, hazard, jeopardize.

impertinent, intrusive, meddling, officious, rude, saucy, impudent, insolent.

impetuous, violent, boisterous, furious, vehement. (Calm.)

implicate, involve, entangle, embarrass, compromise.

imply, involve, comprise, infold, import, denote, signify.

importance, signification, significance, avail, consequence, weight, gravity, moment.

imposing, impressive, striking, majestic, august, noble, grand. (Insignificant.)

impressive, stirring, forcible, exciting, affecting, moving.

imprison, incarcerate, shut up, immure, confine. (Liberate.)

imprisonment, captivity, durance.

improve, amend, better, mend, reform, rectify, ameliorate, apply, use, employ. (Deteriorate.)

impudence, forwardness, boldness, effrontery, assurance, impertinence, confidence, insolence, rudeness.

impudent, saucy, brazen, bold, impertinent, forward, rude, insolent, immodest, shameless.

impulse, incentive, incitement, motive, instigation.

impulsive, rash, hasty, forcible, violent. (Deliberate.)

incentive, motive, inducement, impulse.

incite, instigate, excite, provoke, stimulate, encourage, urge, impel.

inclination, leaning, slope, disposition, tendency, bent, bias, affection, attachment, wish, liking, desire. (Aversion.)

incline, *v.,* slope, lean, slant, tend, bend, turn, bias, dispose.

include, comprehend, comprise, contain, embrace, take in.

incompetent, incapable, unable, inadequate, insufficient. (Competent.)

incongruous, contrary, discrepant, conflicting, absurd, inconsistent, mismated, incoherent, irreconcilable, incompatible. (Consistent, harmonious, suitable, accordant, compatible.)

increase, *v.,* extend, enlarge, augment, dilate, expand, amplify, raise, enhance, aggravate, magnify, grow. (Diminish.)

increase, *n.,* augmentation, accession, addition, enlargement, extension. (Decrease.)

indefinite, vague, uncertain, unsettled, loose, lax. (Definite.)

indicate, point out, show, mark.

indifference, apathy, carelessness, listlessness, insensibility. (Application, assiduity.)

indigence, want, neediness, penury, poverty, destitution, privation. (Affluence.)

indignation, anger, wrath, ire, resentment.

indignity, insult, affront, outrage, obloquy, opprobrium, reproach, ignominy. (Honor.)

indiscriminate, promiscuous, indistinct, chance, confused (Select, chosen.)

indispensable, essential, necessary, requisite, expedient. (Unnecessary, supernumerary.)

indisputable, undeniable, undoubted, incontestable, indubitable, unquestionable, sure, infallible.

indulge, foster, cherish, fondle. (Deny.)

ineffectual, vain, useless, unavailing, fruitless, abortive, inoperative. (Effective.)

inequality, disparity, disproportion, dissimilarity, unevenness. (Equality.)

inevitable, unavoidable, not to be avoided, certain.

infamous, scandalous, shameful, ignominious, opprobrious, disgraceful. (Honorable.)

inference, deduction, corollary, conclusion, consequence.

infinite, eternal, absolute, boundless, countless, limitless, unbounded, numberless, unlimited, unfathomable. (Brief, bounded, restricted, small, moderate, limited, little, measurable.)

infirm, weak, feeble, enfeebled. (Robust.)

inflame, anger, irritate, enrage, chafe, incense, nettle, aggravate, embitter, exasperate. (Allay, soothe.)

infringe, invade, intrude, contravene, break, transgress, violate.

ingenuous, artless, candid, generous, open, frank, plain, sincere. (Crafty.)

inherent, ingrained, inbred, inborn, native, natural, intrinsic. (Casual, accidental, incidental, superfluous, subsidiary, supplemental.)

inhuman, cruel, brutal, savage, barbarous, ruthless, merciless, ferocious. (Humane.)

iniquity, injustice, wrong, grievance.

injure, damage, hurt, deteriorate, wrong, aggrieve, harm, spoil, mar, sully. (Benefit.)

injurious, hurtful, baneful, pernicious, deleterious, noxious, prejudicial, wrongful, damaging. (Beneficial.)

injustice, wrong, iniquity, grievance, unfairness. (Right.)

innocent, guiltless, sinless, harmless, inoffensive, innocuous, exemplary, stainless, virtuous. (Guilty.)

inquiry, investigation, examination, research, scrutiny, disquisition, question, query, interrogation.

inquisitive, prying, peeping, curious, peering, searching

insane, mad, deranged, delirious, demented. (Sane.)

insanity, madness, mental aberration, lunacy, delirium, craziness, derangement, hallucination. (Sanity.)

insinuate, hint, intimate, suggest, infuse, introduce, ingratiate.

insipid, dull, flat, mawkish, tasteless, vapid, inanimate, lifeless. (Bright, sparkling.)

insolent, rude, saucy, pert, impertinent, abusive, scurrilous, opprobrious, insulting, offensive.

inspire, animate, exhilarate, enliven, cheer, breathe, inhale.

instigate, stir up, persuade, animate, incite, urge, stimulate, encourage.

instill, implant, inculcate, infuse, insinuate.

instruct, inform, teach, educate, enlighten, initiate.

instrumental, conducive, assistant, helping, ministerial.

insufficiency, inadequacy, incompetency, incapability, deficiency, lack.

insult, affront, outrage, indignity, blasphemy. (Honor.)

insulting, insolent, rude, saucy, impertinent, abusive.

integrity, uprightness, honesty, probity, entirety, entireness, completeness, rectitude, purity. (Dishonesty.)

intellect, understanding, sense, brains, mind, intelligence, ability, talent, genius. (Body.)

intellectual, mental, ideal, metaphysical. (Brutal.)

intelligible, clear, obvious, plain, distinct. (Abstruse.)

intemperate, immoderate, excessive, drunken, nimious, inordinate. (Temperate.)

intense, ardent, earnest, glowing, fervid, burning, vehement.

intent, design, purpose, intention, drift, view, aim, purport, meaning.

interfere, meddle, intermeddle, interpose.

interminable, endless, interminate, infinite, unlimited, illimitable, boundless, limitless. (Brief, concise.)

interpose, intercede, arbitrate, mediate, interfere, meddle.

interpret, explain, expound, elucidate, unfold, decipher.

intimate, hint, suggest, insinuate, express, signify, impart, tell.

intimidate, dishearten, alarm, frighten, scare, appall, daunt, cow, browbeat. (Encourage.)

intolerable, insufferable, unbearable, insupportable, unendurable.

intrepid, bold, brave, daring, fearless, dauntless, undaunted, courageous, valorous, valiant, heroic, gallant, chivalrous, doughty. (Cowardly, fainthearted.)

intrigue, plot, cabal, conspiracy, combination, artifice, ruse, amour.

invasion, incursion, irruption, inroad, aggression, raid, fray.

invent, devise, contrive, frame, find out, discover, design.

investigation, examination, search, inquiry, research, scrutiny.

invigorate, brace, harden, nerve, strengthen, fortify. (Enervate.)

invincible, unconquerable, impregnable, insurmountable.

invisible, unseen, imperceptible, impalpable, unperceivable.

invite, ask, call, bid, request, allure, attract, solicit.

invoke, invocate, call upon, appeal, refer, implore, beseech.

involve, implicate, entangle, compromise, envelop.

irksome, wearisome, tiresome, tedious, annoying. (Pleasant.)

irony, sarcasm, satire, ridicule, raillery.

irrational, foolish, silly, imbecile, brutish, absurd, ridiculous. (Rational.)

irregular, eccentric, anomalous, inordinate, intemperate. (Regular.)

irreligious, profane, godless, impious, sacrilegious, desecrating.

irritable, excitable, irascible, susceptible, sensitive. (Calm.)

irritate, aggravate, worry, embitter, madden, exasperate.

issue, *v.,* emerge, rise, proceed, flow, spring, emanate.

issue, *n.,* end, upshot, effect, result, offspring, progeny.

J

jade, harass, weary, tire, worry.

jangle, wrangle, conflict, disagree.

jarring, conflicting, discordant, inconsonant, inconsistent.

jaunt, ramble, excursion, trip.

jealousy, suspicion, envy.

jeopardy, hazard, peril, danger.

jest, joke, sport, divert, make game of.

journey, travel, tour, passage, excursion, voyage, trip.

joy, gladness, mirth, delight. (Grief.)

joyful, glad, rejoicing, exultant. (Mournful.)

judge, justice, referee, arbitrator, arbiter.

judgment, discernment, discrimination, understanding.

justice, equity, right. Justice is right as established by law; equity according to the circumstances of each particular case. (Injustice.)

justness, accuracy, correctness.

K

keep, preserve, save. (Abandon.)

kill, execute, massacre, assassinate, murder, slay.

kindred, affinity, consanguinity, relationship.

knowledge, intelligence, wisdom, comprehension, erudition, learning, science. (Ignorance, illiteracy, unfamiliarity.)

L

labor, toil, work, effort, drudgery. (Idleness.)

lack, need, deficiency, scarcity, insufficiency. (Plenty.)

lament, mourn, grieve, weep. (Rejoice.)

language, dialect, idiom, speech, tongue, vocabulary.

large, ample, big, capacious, abundant, coarse, colossal, commodious, enormous, vast, huge, gigantic, great, massive, spacious. (Little, petty, paltry, scanty, small, tiny, trivial, brief, diminutive, insignificant.)

lascivious, loose, unchaste, lustful, lewd, lecherous. (Chaste.)

last, final, latest, ultimate. (First.)

laudable, commendable, praiseworthy. (Blamable.)

laughable, comical, droll, ludicrous. (Serious.)

learned, erudite, scholarly. (Ignorant.)

leave, *v.,* quit, relinquish.

leave, *n.,* liberty, permission, license. (Prohibition.)

life, existence, animation, spirit, vivacity. (Death.)

lifeless, dead, inanimate.

lift, erect, elevate, exalt, raise. (Lower.)

light, clear, bright. (Dark.)

lightness, flightiness, giddiness, levity, volatility. (Seriousness.)

likeness, resemblance, similarity. (Unlikeness.)

linger, lag, loiter, tarry, saunter. (Hasten.)

little, diminutive, small. (Great.)

livelihood, living, maintenance, subsistence, support.

lively, jocund, sprightly, vivacious, merry, sportive. (Slow, languid, sluggish.)

long, extended, extensive. (Short.)

look, appear. seem.

look, gaze, discern, behold, glance, see, stare, view, watch, scan, inspect.

lose, miss, forfeit. (Gain.)

loss, detriment, damage, deprivation. (Gain.)

loud, clamorous, high-sounding, noisy. (Low, quiet.)

love, fondness, attachment, devotion, affection. (Hatred.)

low, abject, mean. (Noble.)

lunacy, derangement, insanity, mania, madness. (Sanity.)

luster, brightness, brilliancy, splendor.

luxuriant, exuberant. (Sparse.)

M

mad, crazy, insane, delirious, rabid, violent, frantic. (Sane, rational, quiet.)

madness, insanity, fury, rage, frenzy.

make, form, create, produce, build, construct. (Destroy.)

malediction, anathema, curse, imprecation, execration.

malevolent, malicious, virulent, malignant. (Benevolent.)

malice, spite, rancor, ill feeling, ill will, grudge, animosity. (Benignity.)

malicious. See malevolent.

manacle, *v.,* shackle, fetter, chain. (Free.)

manage, contrive, concert, direct.

management, direction, superintendence, care, economy.

mangle, tear, lacerate, mutilate, cripple, maim.

mania, madness, insanity, lunacy.

manly, masculine, vigorous, courageous, brave, heroic. (Effeminate.)

manner, habit, custom, way, air, look, appearance.

manners, morals, habits, behavior, carriage.

mar, spoil, ruin, disfigure. (Improve.)

march, tramp, tread, walk, step, space.

margin, edge, rim, border, brink, verge.

martial, military, warlike, soldierlike.

marvel, wonderful, miracle, prodigy.

marvelous, wondrous, wonderful, amazing, miraculous.

masculine, manly, mannish, virile, male, manful, manlike.

massive, bulky, heavy, weighty, ponderous, solid, substantial. (Flimsy.)

mastery, dominion, rule, sway, ascendancy, supremacy.

matchless, unrivaled, unequaled unparalleled, peerless, incomparable, inimitable, surpassing. (Common, ordinary.)

mean, *a.,* stingy, niggardly, low, abject, vile, ignoble, degraded, contemptible, vulgar, despicable. (Generous.)

USING THE LANGUAGE

mean, v., design, purpose, intent, contemplate, signify, denote, indicate.

meaning, signification, import, acceptation, sense, purport.

meek, unassuming, mild, gentle, soft, demure, humble. (Proud, arrogant, bold, haughty, impudent, presumptuous.)

melancholy, low-spirited, dispirited, dreamy, sad. (Jolly, buoyant.)

mellow, ripe, mature, soft. Immature.)

melodious, tuneful, musical, silver, dulcet, sweet. (Discordant.)

memorable, signal, distinguished, marked.

memorial, monument, memento, commemoration.

memory, reminiscence, remembrance, recollection.

mend, repair, amend, correct, better, ameliorate, improve, rectify.

mention, tell, name, communicate, impart, divulge, reveal, disclose, inform, acquaint.

merciful, compassionate, lenient, clement, tender, gracious, kind. (Cruel.)

merciless, hard-hearted, cruel, unmerciful, pitiless, remorseless, unrelenting. (Kind.)

mercy, favor, grace, kindness, leniency, pardon, tenderness, pity, compassion, benevolence, clemency, benignity, blessing. (Revenge, cruelty, harshness, severity, sternness, punishment, implacability, hardness.)

merriment, mirth, joviality, jollity, hilarity. (Sorrow.)

merry, cheerful, mirthful, joyous, gay, lively, sprightly, hilarious, jovial, blithe, blithesome, sportive, jolly. (Sad.)

mien, air, look, manner, aspect, appearance.

migratory, roving, strolling, wandering, vagrant. (Settled, sedate, permanent.)

mimic, imitate, ape, mock.

mind, intellect, brain, instinct, reason, sense, soul, thought, understanding, intelligence.

mindful, observant, attentive, heedful, thoughtful. (Heedless.)

miscellaneous, promiscuous, indiscriminate, mixed.

mischief, injury, harm, damage, evil, hurt, ill. (Benefit.)

miscreant, caitiff, villain, ruffian.

miserable, unhappy, wretched, distressed, afflicted. (Happy.)

miserly, stingy, niggardly, avaricious, gripping.

misery, wretchedness, woe, destitution, penury, privation, beggary. (Happiness.)

mix, blend, combine, amalgamate, associate, fuse, join, unite, mingle, compound. (Divide, sift, part, segregate, sort, unravel, disjoin, classify, assort, analyze.)

moderate, temperate, abstemious, sober, abstinent. (Immoderate.)

modest, chaste, virtuous, bashful, reserved. (Immodest.)

moist, wet, damp, dank, humid. (Dry.)

monotonous, unvaried, dull, undiversified, tiresome. (Varied.)

monstrous, shocking. dreadful, horrible, huge, immense.

monument, memorial, record, remembrance, cenotaph.

mood, humor, disposition, vein, temper.

morbid, sick, ailing, sickly, diseased, corrupted. (Normal, sound.)

morose, gloomy, sullen, surly, fretful, crabbed, crusty, sour, sulky. (Joyous, pleasant, friendly, amiable.)

mortal, deadly, fatal, human.

mount, arise, rise, ascend, soar, tower, climb, scale.

mournful, sad, sorrowful, lugubrious, grievous, doleful, heavy. (Happy.)

move, actuate, impel, induce, prompt, instigate, persuade, stir, agitate, propel, push.

muse, v., mediate, contemplate, reflect, think, cogitate, ponder.

music, harmony, melody, symphony.

musical, tuneful, melodious, harmonious, dulcet, sweet.

musty, stale, sour, fetid. (Fresh, sweet.)

mute, dumb, silent, speechless.

mutilate, maim, cripple, disable, disfigure.

mutinous, insurgent, seditious, tumultuous, turbulent, riotous. (Obedient, orderly.)

mutual, reciprocal, interchanged, correlative. (Sole, solitary.)

mysterious, dark, obscure, hidden, secret, dim, mystic, enigmatical, unaccountable, inexplicable, abstruse. (Open, clear.)

mystify, confuse, perplex, puzzle. (Clear, explain.)

N

naked, nude, bare, uncovered, rude, unclothed, rough, simple. (Covered, clad.)

narrate, tell, relate, detail, recount, describe, enumerate, rehearse, recite.

nasty, filthy, foul, dirty, unclean, indecent, impure, gross, vile.

nation, people, community, realm, state.

native, indigenous, inborn, vernacular.

neat, natty, nice, orderly, clean, dapper, tidy, trim, prim, spruce. (Dirty, rough, disorderly, unkempt, soiled, untidy, negligent.)

necessary, needful, expedient, essential, requisite, indispensable. (Useless.)

necessitate, compel, force, oblige.

necessity, need, occasion, exigency, emergency, urgency, requisite.

need, n., necessity, distress, poverty, indigence, want, penury.

need, v., require, want, lack.

neglect, v., disregard, slight, omit, overlook.

neglect, n., omission, failure, default, negligence, remissness, carelessness, slight.

neighborhood, environs, vicinity, adjacency, nearness, proximity.

nice, exact, accurate, good, particular, precise, fine, delicate. (Careless, coarse, unpleasant.)

nimble, spry, active, brisk,

lively, alert, quick, agile, prompt. (Awkward, slow, clumsy.)

nobility, aristocracy, greatness, grandeur, peerage.

noble, exalted, elevated, illustrious, great, grand, lofty. (Low.)

notable, plain, evident, remarkable, signal, striking, rare. (Obscure.)

note, *n.,* token, symbol, mark, sign, indication, remark, comment.

noted, distinguished, remarkable, renowned, eminent. (Obscure.)

notice, *n.,* advice, notification, intelligence, information.

notice, *v.,* mark, note, observe, attend to, regard, heed.

notify, *v.,* publish, acquaint, apprise, inform, declare.

notion, conception, idea, belief, opinion, sentiment.

notorious, conspicuous, open, obvious, ill-famed. (Unknown.)

nourish, nurture, cherish, foster, supply. (Starve, famish.)

nourishment, food, diet, sustenance, nutrition.

novel, modern, new, fresh, recent, unused, strange, rare. (Old.)

noxious, hurtful, deadly, poisonous, deleterious, baneful. (Beneficial.)

nullify, annual, vacate, invalidate, repeal, quash, cancel. (Affirm.)

nutrition, food, diet, nutriment, nourishment.

O

obedient, complaint, submissive, dutiful, respectful. (Obstinate.)

obese, corpulent, fat, adipose, fleshy. (Attenuated.)

obey, *v.,* conform, comply, submit. (Rebel, disobey.)

object, *n.,* aim, end, purpose, design, mark, butt.

object, *v.,* oppose, except to, contravene, impeach, deprecate. (Assent.)

obnoxious, offensive. (Agreeable.)

obscure, dense, deep, pro-found, undistinguished, unknown. (Distinguished.)

obsolete, old, rare, obsolescent, ancient, disused, antiquated, archaic.

obstinate, contumacious, headstrong, stubborn, obdurate. (Yielding.)

obstruct, block, hinder, clog, bar, arrest, retard, stay, barricade, impede, oppose, interrupt. (Aid, clear, promote, facilitate, free, advance, accelerate.)

occasion, opportunity.

offense, affront, misdeed, misdemeanor, transgression, trespass.

offensive, insolent, abusive, obnoxious. (Inoffensive.)

old, aged, superannuated, ancient, antique, antiquated, obsolete, old-fashioned, senile, elderly, venerable. (Young, new.)

opaque, dark. (Bright, transparent.)

open, candid, unreserved, clear, fair. (Hidden, dark.)

opinion, notion, view, judgment, belief, sentiment.

opinionated, conceited, egotistical. (Modest.)

oppose, resist, withstand, thwart. (Give way.)

option, choice.

order, method, rule, system, regularity. (Disorder.)

origin, cause, occasion, source, beginning. (End.)

outlive, survive.

outward, external, outside, exterior. (Inner.)

over, above. (Under.)

overbalance, outweigh, preponderate.

overbear, bear down, overwhelm, overpower, subdue.

overbearing, haughty, proud, arrogant. (Gentle.)

overflow, inundation, deluge.

overrule, supersede, suppress.

overturn, invert, overthrow, reverse, subvert. (Establish, fortify.)

overwhelm, crush, defeat, vanquish.

P

pain, suffering, qualm, pang, agony, anguish, torment, ache, torture. (Pleasure, delight, rapture.)

pallid, pale, wan. (Florid.)

part, division, portion, share, fraction. (Whole.)

perceive, note, observe, discern, distinguish, comprehend, understand.

perception, conception, notion, idea.

perfect, ideal, sinless, spotless, stainless, holy, complete, immaculate, unblemished, consummate, correct, faultless. (Bad, defaced, corrupt, blemished, spoiled, worthless, perverted, inferior, marred, defective, faulty, deficient, imperfect.)

peril, danger, pitfall, snare. (Safety.)

permanent, fixed, constant, lasting, perpetual, stable, steadfast, unchanging, imperishable, durable, enduring, changeless.

permission, constant, liberty, leave, permit, license, allowance, authority. (Denial, objection, refusal, prevention.)

permit, allow, tolerate. (Forbid.)

perplexity, confusion, doubt, distraction, amazement, astonishment, bewilderment.

persuade, coax, convince, urge, allure, entice, prevail upon.

pertness, sauciness, smartness, boldness, briskness, flippancy, impudence, liveliness. (Modesty, diffidence, shyness, demureness, bashfulness.)

physical, corporeal, bodily, material. (Mental.)

picture, engraving, print, representation, illustration, image.

piteous, doleful, woeful, rueful. (Joyful.)

pitiful, mournful, pathetic, pitiable, woeful, sorrowful, abject, lamentable, mean, miserable, wretched. (Glorious, great, grand, mighty, lofty, noble, superb, exalted, commanding, august, superior.)

pitiless. See merciless.

pity, mercy, condolence, compassion, sympathy. (Cruelty, brutality, harshness, severity, sternness, barbarity.)

plain, open, manifest, evident. (Secret.)

play, game, sport, amusement. (Work.)

plead, beseech, ask, beg, entreat, implore, urge, solicit, argue, advocate.

plentiful, abundant, ample, copious, plenteous, rich, teeming, luxuriant, full, bountiful, affluent. (Scarce, deficient, impoverished, scant.)

poise, balance.

polite, cultured, courtly, elegant, genteel, civil, urbane, gracious, obliging, courteous, accomplished. (Awkward, coarse, boorish, raw, rude, uncivil, insulting, uncouth, impolite, impudent.)

positive, absolute, peremptory, decided, certain. (Negative).

possessor, owner, proprietor.

possible, practical, practicable. (Impossible.)

poverty, penury, indigence, need, want. (Wealth.)

power, authority, force, strength, dominion.

powerful, mighty, potent (Weak.)

praise, acclaim, approbation, commendation, eulogy, plaudit, commend, extol, laud. (Blame.)

prayer, entreaty, petition, request, suit.

precarious, perilous, risky, uncertain, hazardous, dubious, doubtful. (Firm, assured, infallible, sure, undeniable.)

pretense, *n.*, pretext, subterfuge.

prevailing, predominant, prevalent, general. (Isolated, sporadic.)

prevent, obviate, preclude.

previous, antecedent, introductory, preparatory, preliminary. (Subsequent.)

pride, haughtiness, vainglory, arrogance, vanity, conceit. (Humility.)

principally, chiefly, mainly, essentially.

principle, ground, reason, motive, impulse, maxim, rule, rectitude, integrity.

privilege, immunity, advantage, favor, prerogative, exemption, right, claim.

profession, business, trade, occupation, vocation, office, employment, engagement, avowal.

proffer, volunteer, offer, propose, tender.

profligate, abandoned, dissolute, depraved, vicious, degenerate, corrupt, demoralized. (Virtuous.)

profound, deep, fathomless, penetrating, solemn, abstruse, recondite. (Shallow.)

profuse, extravagant, prodigal, lavish, improvident, excessive, copious, plentiful. (Succinct.)

prohibit, forbid, hinder, prevent, debar, disallow, interdict. (Permit, license, sanction, allow, tolerate, authorize.)

prominent, eminent, marked, important, conspicuous, leading. (Obscure.)

promiscuous, mixed, unarranged, indiscriminate, mingled. (Select.)

prop, *v.*, maintain, sustain, support, stay.

proper, legitimate, right, just, fair, equitable, honest, suitable, fit, decent, meet, becoming, befitting, adapted, pertinent, appropriate. (Wrong.)

prosper, flourish, succeed, grow rich, thrive, advance. (Fail.)

prosperity, well-being, weal, welfare, happiness, good luck. (Poverty.)

proxy, agent, representative, substitute, delegate, deputy.

prudence, carefulness, judgment, discretion, wisdom. (Indiscretion.)

punctual, exact, precise, nice, particular, prompt, timely. (Dilatory.)

putrefy, rot, decompose, corrupt, decay.

puzzle, *v.*, perplex, confound, embarrass, bewilder, confuse, pose, mystify. (Enlighten.)

Q

quack, imposter, pretender, charlatan, empiric, mountebank. (Savant.)

quaint, artful, curious, far-fetched, fanciful, odd, singular.

qualified, competent, fitted, adapted. (Incompetent.)

quality, attribute, rank, distinction.

queer, odd, peculiar, singular, quaint, unique, strange, unusual, ridiculous, preposterous, bizarre, curious, eccentric, ludicrous, fantastic, funny. (Common, natural, usual, normal, ordinary, regular.)

question, query, inquiry, interrogatory.

quibble, cavil, evade, equivocate, prevaricate, shuffle.

quick, lively, brisk, expeditious, impetuous, adroit, fleet, rapid, swift, sweeping, dashing, clever, sharp, ready, prompt, alert, nimble, agile, active. (Slow.)

quote, note, repeat, cite, adduce.

R

rabid, mad, furious, raging, frantic. (Rational.)

race, course, match, pursuit, career, family, clan, house, ancestry, lineage, pedigree.

rack, agonize, wring, torture, excruciate, distress, harass. (Soothe.)

racy, spicy, pungent, smart, spirited, lively, vivacious. (Dull, insipid.)

radiance, splendor, brightness, brilliance, brilliancy, luster, glare. (Dullness.)

rancor, malignity, hatred, hostility, antipathy, animosity, enmity, ill will, spite. (Forgiveness.)

rank, order, degree, dignity, nobility, consideration.

ransack, rummage, pillage, overhaul, explore, plunder.

rapt, ecstatic, transported, ravished, entranced, charmed. (Distracted.)

rapture, ecstasy, transport, delight, bliss. (Dejection.)

rare, curious, unique, unusual, strange, peculiar, odd, extraordinary, scarce, singular, uncommon.

rascal, scoundrel, rogue, knave, vagabond, scamp.

rash, hasty, precipitate, foolhardy, adventurous, heedless, reckless, careless. (Deliberate.)

rate, value, compute, appraise, estimate, chide, abuse.

ratify, confirm, establish, substantiate, sanction. (Protest, oppose.)

rational, reasonable, sagacious, judicious, wise, sensible, sound. (Unreasonable.)

ravage, overrun, overspread, desolate, despoil, destroy.

ravish, enrapture, enchant, charm, delight, abuse.

raze, demolish, destroy, overthrow, ruin, dismantle. (Build up.)

reach, touch, stretch, attain, gain, arrive at.

ready, prepared, ripe, apt, prompt, adroit, handy. (Slow, dilatory.)

real, authentic, actual, literal, practical, positive, certain, genuine, true. (Unreal.)

realize, accomplish, achieve, effect, gain, get, acquire, comprehend.

reap, gain, get, acquire, obtain.

reason, *n.,* motive, design, end, proof, cause, ground, purpose.

reason, *v.,* deduce, draw from, trace, infer, conclude.

reasonable, rational, wise, honest, fair, right, just. (Unreasonable.)

rebellion, insurrection, revolt.

rebellious, mutinous, seditious, refractory, disobedient, ungovernable, insubordinate, contumacious. (Docile, obedient, yielding, tractable, subservient, compliant, gentle.)

recant, recall, abjure, retract, revoke.

recede, retire, retreat, withdraw, ebb.

recreation, sport, pastime, amusement, play, game, fun.

redeem, ransom, recover, rescue, deliver, save, free.

redress, remedy, repair, remission, abatement, relief.

reduce, abate, lessen, decrease, lower, shorten, conquer.

refined, polite, courtly, polished, cultured, genteel, purified. (Boorish.)

reflect, consider, cogitate, think, ponder, muse, censure.

reform, amend, correct, better, restore, improve. (Corrupt.)

refute, disprove, falsify, negative. (Affirm.)

regard, *v.,* mind, heed, notice, behold, view, consider, respect.

regret, *n.,* grief, sorrow, lamentation, repentance, remorse.

regular, orderly, uniform, customary, ordinary, stated. (Irregular.)

regulate, methodize, arrange, adjust, organize, govern, rule. (Disorder.)

reimburse, refund, repay, satisfy, indemnify.

relevant, fit, proper, suitable, appropriate, pertinent, apt. (Irrelevant.)

reliance, trust, hope, dependence, confidence. (Suspicion.)

relief, succor, aid, help, redress, alleviation.

relinquish, give up, forsake, resign, surrender, quit, leave, forego. (Retain.)

remedy, help, relief, redress, cure, specific, reparation.

remorseless, pitiless, relentless, merciless, cruel, ruthless, barbarous. (Merciful, humane.)

remote, distant, far, secluded, indirect. (Near.)

renounce, disown, recant, refute, reject, retract, revoke, repudiate, recall, discard, deny, abandon, disclaim, disavow. (Assert, avow, advocate, acknowledge, cherish, claim, uphold, defend, vindicate, proclaim, retain.)

report, record, rumor, story, tale, statement, narrative, account, description, recital.

reproduce, propagate, imitate, represent, copy.

repudiate, disown, discard, disavow, renounce, disclaim. (Acknowledge.)

repugnant, antagonistic, distasteful. (Agreeable.)

repulsive, forbidding, odious, ugly, disagreeable, revolting. (Attractive.)

respite, reprieve, interval, stop.

reverence, *n.,* honor, respect, awe, veneration, deference,

homage, worship. (Execration.

revise, review, reconsider.

revive, refresh, renew, renovate, animate, resuscitate, vivify, cheer, comfort.

rich, wealthy, affluent, opulent, copious, ample, abundant, exuberant, plentiful, fertile, fruitful, superb, gorgeous. (Poor.)

rival, *n.,* antagonist, opponent, competitor.

road, way, highway, route, course, path, pathway, anchorage.

roam, ramble, rove, stray, wander, stroll.

robber, footpad, bandit, brigand, burglar, pirate, thief, raider, plunderer, pillager, marauder, forager, buccaneer.

robust, strong, lusty, vigorous, sinewy, stout, sturdy, stalwart, ablebodied. (Puny.)

rout, *v.,* discomfit, beat, defeat, overthrow, scatter.

route, road, course, march, way, path, journey, direction.

rude, rugged, rough, uncouth, unpolished, harsh, gruff, impertinent, impudent, saucy, flippant, insolent, churlish. (Polished, polite.)

ruthless, cruel, savage, barbarous, inhuman, merciless, remorseless, relentless, unrelenting. (Considerate.)

S

sacred, holy, hallowed, divine, consecrated, dedicated, devoted. (Profane.)

safe, secure, harmless, trustworthy, reliable. (Perilous, dangerous.)

sanction, confirm, countenance, encourage, support, ratify, authorize. (Disapprove.)

sane, sober, lucid, sound, rational. (Crazy.)

saucy, impertinent, rude, impudent, insolent, flippant, forward. (Modest.)

scandalize, shock, disgust, offend, calumniate, vilify, revile, malign, traduce, defame, slander.

scanty, bare, pinched, insufficient, slender, meager. (Ample.)

scatter, strew, spread, disseminate, disperse, dissipate, dispel. (Collect.)

secret, clandestine, concealed, hidden, sly, underhand, latent, private. (Open.)

send, fling, hurl, emit, drive, dispatch, cast, delegate, throw, launch, project. (Get, bring, carry, convey, hand, keep, receive, retain, hold.)

sense, discernment, appreciation, perception, view, opinion, feeling, sensibility, susceptibility, thought, signification, judgment, import, significance, meaning, purport, wisdom.

sensible, wise, intelligent, reasonable, sober, sound, conscious, aware. (Foolish.)

settle, arrange, adjust, regulate, conclude, determine.

several, sundry, divers, many, various.

severe, austere, inexorable, strict, harsh, stern, stringent, unmitigated, rough, unyielding. (Lenient, affable, easy, indulgent.)

shake, tremble, shudder, shiver, quiver, quake.

shallow, superficial, flimsy, slight. (Deep, thorough.)

shame, disgrace, dishonor. (Honor.)

shameful, degrading, scandalous, disgraceful, outrageous. (Honorable.)

shameless, immodest, impudent, indecent, indelicate, brazen.

shape, form, fashion, mold, model.

share, portion, lot, division, quantity, quota, contingent.

sharp, acute, keen. (Dull.)

shine, glare, glitter, radiate, sparkle.

short, brief, concise, succinct, summary. (Long.)

sick, diseased, sickly, unhealthy, morbid. (Healthy.)

sickness, illness, indisposition, disease, disorder. (Health.)

significant, *a.*, expressive, material, important. (Insignificant.)

signification, import, sense, meaning.

silence, speechlessness, dumbness. (Noise.)

silent, dumb, mute, speechless. (Talkative.)

simple, single, uncompounded, plain, artless. (Complex, compound.)

sincere, candid, hearty, honest, pure, genuine, real. (Insincere.)

situation, condition, plight, predicament, state, position.

size, bulk, greatness, magnitude, dimension.

skeptic, deist, agnostic, atheist, doubter, infidel, freethinker, unbeliever. (Believer, Christian.)

slander, defame, detract, revile, vilify, traduce, libel, malign, disparage, asperse, decry, calumniate. (Defend, extol, laud, praise, eulogize.)

slavery, servitude, enthrallment, thralldom. (Freedom.)

sleep, doze, drowse, nap, slumber.

sleepy, somnolent. (Wakeful.)

slow, dilatory, tardy, lingering, sluggish. (Fast.)

smell, fragrance, odor, scent, perfume.

smooth, even, level, mild. (Rough.)

soak, drench, imbue, steep.

social, sociable, friendly, communicative. (Unsocial.)

soft, gentle, meek, mild. (Hard.)

solicit, importune, urge.

solitary, sole, only, single.

sorry, grieved, poor, paltry, insignificant. (Glad, respectable.)

soul, mind, spirit. (Soul is opposed to body, mind to matter.)

sound, *a.*, healthy, sane. (Unsound.)

sound, *n.*, tone, noise.

space, room.

sparse, scanty, thin. (Luxuriant.)

speak, converse, talk, say, tell, confer, articulate, express, utter.

special, particular, specific. (General.)

spend, expend, exhaust, consume, dissipate, waste, squander. (Save.)

sporadic, isolated, rare. (General, prevalent.)

spread, disperse, diffuse, expand, disseminate, scatter.

spring, fountain, source.

staff, prop, support, stay.

stagger, reel, totter.

stain, soil, discolor, spot, sully, tarnish, color, blot.

state, commonwealth, realm.

sterile, barren, unfruitful. (Fertile.)

stifle, choke, suffocate, smother.

stormy, rough, boisterous, tempestuous. (Calm.)

straight, direct, right. (Crooked.)

strait, *a.*, narrow, confined.

stranger, alien, foreigner. (Friend.)

strengthen, fortify, invigorate, encourage. (Weaken.)

strong, robust, sturdy, powerful. (Weak.)

stupid, dull, foolish, obtuse, witless. (Clever.)

stupor, swoon, torpor, unconsciousness, syncope, lethargy, coma, fainting, apathy, asphyxia.

subject, exposed to, liable. (Exempt.)

subject, inferior, subordinate. (Superior to, above.)

subsequent, succeeding, following. (Previous.)

substantial, solid, durable. (Unsubstantial.)

suit, accord, agree. (Disagree.)

superficial, flimsy, shallow, untrustworthy. (Thorough.)

superfluous, unnecessary, excessive. (Necessary.)

surrender, cede, give, yield, sacrifice, relinquish, abandon, capitulate, alienate.

surround, encircle, encompass, environ.

sustain, maintain, support.

symmetry, proportion.

sympathy, commiseration, compassion, condolence.

synonymous, alike, corresponding, equivalent, like, same, identical, similar, synonymic.

system, rule, manner, method, plan, order.

systematic, orderly, regular, methodical. (Chaotic.)

T

taciturn, silent, reticent, mute, reserved, close, dumb, speechless, uncommunicative. (Talkative, unreserved, loquacious, garrulous, free, communicative.)

take, accept, receive. (Give.)

talkative, garrulous, communicative, loquacious. (Silent.)

taste, flavor, relish, savor. (Tastelessness.)

tax, custom, duty, impost, excise, toll.

tax, assessment, rate.

tease, taunt, tantalize, torment, vex.

temerity, rashness, presumption, recklessness, audacity, hastiness, foolhardiness, heedlessness, precipitation. (Care, caution, timidity, wariness, hesitation, cowardice, circumspection.)

temporary, *a.,* fleeting, transient, transitory. (Permanent.)

tenacious, pertinacious, retentive.

tendency, aim, drift, scope.

tenet, position, view, conviction, belief.

term, boundary, limit, period, time.

territory, dominion.

thankful, grateful, obliged. (Thankless.)

thankless, ungracious, profitless, ungrateful, unthankful.

thaw, melt, dissolve, liquefy. (Freeze.)

theatrical, dramatic, showy, ceremonious, meretricious.

theft, robbery, depredation, spoliation.

theme, subject, topic, text, essay.

theory, speculation, scheme, plea, hypothesis, conjecture.

therefore, accordingly, consequently, hence.

thick, dense, close, compact, solid, coagulated, muddy, turbid, misty, foggy, vaporous. (Thin.)

thin, slim, slender, slight, flimsy, attenuated, lean, scraggy.

think, cogitate, consider, reflect, ponder, contemplate, meditate, muse, conceive, fancy, imagine, apprehend, hold, esteem, reckon, consider, regard, deem, believe, opine.

thorough, accurate, correct, trustworthy, reliable, complete. (Superficial.)

thought, idea, conception, imagination, fancy, conceit, notion, supposition, care, provision, consideration, opinion, view, sentiment, reflection, deliberation.

thoughtful, considerate, careful, reflective, cautious, heedful, contemplative, provident, pensive, dreamy. (Thoughtless.)

thoughtless, inconsiderate, rash, improvident, precipitate, heedless.

tie, *v.,* bind, restrain, restrict, oblige, secure, unite, join. (Loose.)

tie, *n.,* band, ligament, ligature.

time, duration, season, period, era, age, date, span, spell.

tolerate, allow, admit, receive, suffer, permit, let, endure, abide. (Oppose.)

top, summit, apex, head, crown, surface. (Bottom, base.)

torrid, burning, hot, parching, scorching, sultry.

tortuous, twisted, winding, crooked, indirect.

torture, torment, anguish, agony.

touching, tender, affecting, moving, pathetic.

tractable, docile, manageable, amenable.

trade, traffic, commerce, dealing, occupation, employment, office.

traditional, oral, uncertain, transmitted.

traffic, trade, exchange, commerce, intercourse.

trammel, *n.,* fetter, shatter, clog, bond, chain, impediment, hindrance.

tranquil, still, unruffled, peaceful, quiet, hushed. (Noisy, boisterous.)

transaction, negotiation, occurrence, proceeding, affair.

trash, nonsense, twaddle, trifles.

travel, trip, ramble, peregrination, excursion, journey, tour, voyage.

treacherous, traitorous, treasonable, disloyal, faithless, falsehearted, perfidious, sly, false. (Trustworthy, faithful.)

trite, stale, old, ordinary, commonplace, hackneyed. (Novel.)

triumph, achievement, ovation, victory, conquest, jubilation. (Failure, defeat.)

trivial, trifling, petty, small, frivolous, unimportant, insignificant. (Important.)

true, genuine, actual, sincere, truehearted, unaffected, honest, upright, veritable, real, veracious, authentic, exact, accurate, correct.

tumultuous, turbulent, riotous, disorderly, disturbed, confused, unruly. (Orderly.)

tune, tone, air, melody, strain.

turbid, foul, thick, muddy, impure, unsettled.

type, emblem, symbol, figure, sign, letter, sort, kind.

tyro, novice, beginner, learner.

U

ugly, unsightly, plain, homely, illfavored, hideous. (Beautiful.)

umbrage, offense, dissatisfaction, displeasure, resentment.

umpire, referee, arbitrator, judge, arbiter.

unanimity, accord, agreement, unity, concord. (Discord.)

unanimous, agreeing, likeminded.

unbridled, wanton, licentious, dissolute, loose, lax.

uncertain, doubtful, dubious, questionable, fitful, equivocal, ambiguous, indistinct, variable, fluctuating.

uncivil, discourteous, disrespectful, disobliging, rude. (Civil.)

unclean, dirty, filthy, sullied. (Clean.)

uncommon, rare, strange, scarce, singular, choice. (Common, ordinary.)

unconcerned, careless, indifferent, apathetic. (Anxious.)

uncouth, strange, odd, clumsy, ungainly. (Graceful.)

uncover, reveal, strip, expose, lay bare, divest. (Hide.)

under, below, underneath, beneath, subordinate, lower, inferior. (Above.)

understanding, knowledge, intellect, intelligence, faculty, comprehension, mind, reason, brains.

undertake, engage in, embark on, agree, promise.

undo, annul, frustrate, unfasten, destroy.

uneasy, restless, disturbed, unquiet, stiff, awkward. (Quiet.)

unequal, uneven, not alike, irregular, insufficient. (Even.)

unequaled, matchless, unique, novel, new, unheard of.

unfair, wrongful, dishonest, unjust. (Fair.)

unfit, *a.,* improper, unsuitable, inconsistent, untimely, incompetent. (Fit.)

unfit, *v.,* disable, disqualify, incapacitate. (Fit.)

unfortunate, calamitous, ill-fated, unlucky, wretched, unhappy, miserable. (Fortunate.)

ungainly, clumsy, awkward, lumbering, uncouth. (Pretty.)

unhappy, miserable, wretched, distressed, afflicted, painful, disastrous, drear, dismal. (Happy.)

uniform, regular, symmetrical, even, equal, alike, unvaried. (Irregular.)

uninterrupted, continuous, perpetual, unceasing, incessant, endless. (Intermittent.)

union, junction, combination, alliance, confederacy, league, coalition, agreement, concert. (Disunion, separation.)

unique, unequal, uncommon, rare, choice, matchless. (Common, ordinary.)

unite, join, conjoin, combine, concert, add, attach, incorporate, embody, clench, merge. (Separate, disrupt, sunder.)

universal, general, all, entire, total, catholic. (Sectional.)

unlimited, absolute, boundless, undefined, infinite. (Limited.)

unreasonable, foolish, silly, absurd.

unrivaled, unequaled, unique, unexampled, incomparable, matchless. (Mediocre.)

unroll, unfold, open, discover.

unruly, ungovernable, unmanageable, refractory. (Tractable, docile)

unusual, rare, unwonted, singular, uncommon, remarkable, strange, extraordinary. (Common.)

uphold, maintain, defend, sustain, support, vindicate. (Desert, abandon.)

upright, vertical, perpendicular, just, erect, equitable, fair, pure, honorable. (Prone, horizontal.)

uprightness, honesty, integrity, fairness, goodness, probity, honor, virtue. (Dishonesty.)

urge, incite, impel, push, drive, instigate, stimulate, press, solicit, induce.

urgent, pressing, important, imperative, immediate, serious, wanted. (Unimportant.)

usage, custom, fashion, practice, prescription.

use, *n.,* usage, practice, habit, custom, avail, advantage, utility, benefit, application. (Disuse, desuetude.)

use, *v.,* employ, exercise, occupy, accustom, practice, inure. (Abuse.)

useful, advantageous, serviceable, available, helpful, beneficial, good. (Useless.)

useless, unserviceable, fruitless, idle, profitless. (Useful.)

usual, ordinary, common, accustomed, habitual, wonted, customary, general, prevalent, regular. (Unusual, exceptional, rare, singular, strange.)

usurp, arrogate, seize, appropriate, assume.

utmost, farthest, remotest, uttermost, greatest.

utter, *a.,* extreme, excessive, sheer, mere, pure.

utter, *v.,* speak, articulate, express, pronounce, issue.

utterly, totally, completely, wholly, quite, altogether, entirely.

V

vacant, empty, unfilled, unoccupied, thoughtless, unthinking, void, vacuous. (Occupied, crowded, full, jammed, packed.)

vagrant, *n.,* wanderer, beggar, tramp, vagabond, rogue.

vague, unsettled, undetermined, uncertain, pointless, indefinite. (Definite.)

vain, useless, fruitless, empty, worthless, inflated, proud, conceited, unreal, unavailing, frivolous. (Effectual, humble, real.)

valiant, brave, bold, valorous, courageous, gallant. (Cowardly.)

valid, weighty, strong, powerful, efficient, sound, binding. (Invalid.)

valor, courage, gallantry, boldness, bravery, heroism. (Cowardice.)

value, *v.,* appraise, assess, reckon, appreciate, estimate, prize, treasure, esteem. (Despise, condemn.)

vanish, disappear, fade, melt, dissolve.

vanity, emptiness, conceit, self-conceit, affectedness.

vapid, dull, flat, insipid, stale, tame. (Sparkling.)

vapor, fume, smoke, mist, fog, steam.

variable, changeable, unsteady, shifting, inconstant wavering, fickle, fitful, restless. (Constant.)

variety, difference, diversity, change, diversification, mixture, medley, miscellany. (Sameness, monotony.)

vast, spacious, boundless, mighty, immense, enormous, colossal, gigantic, huge, prodigious. (Confined.)

vaunt, boast, brag, puff, hawk, advertise, flourish, parade.

venerable, grave, sage, wise, old, reverend.

venial, pardonable, excusable, justifiable. (Grave, serious.)

venom, poison, virus, spite, malice, malignity.

venture, *n.,* speculation, chance, peril, stake.

venture, *v.,* dare, adventure, risk, hazard, jeopardize.

veracity, truth, truthfulness, credibility, accuracy, candor, verity, honesty. (Falsehood, deception, fabrication, lie, untruth.)

verbal, oral, spoken, literal, parole, unwritten.

verdict, judgment, finding, decision, answer.

vexation, chagrin, mortification. (Pleasure.)

vibrate, oscillate, swing, sway, wave, undulate, thrill.

vice, vileness, corruption, depravity, pollution, immorality, wickedness, guilt, iniquity, crime. (Virtue.)

vicious, corrupt, depraved, debased, bad, contrary, unruly, demoralized, profligate, faulty. (Virtuous, gentle.)

victim, sacrifice, food, prey, sufferer, dupe, gull.

victuals, viands, bread, meat, repast, provisions, fare, food.

view, prospect, survey.

violent, boisterous, furious, impetuous, vehement. (Gentle.)

virtue, honesty, morality, honor, truth, worth, uprightness, virtuousness, probity, purity, integrity, chastity, goodness, duty, rectitude, faithfulness. (Vice, viciousness, evil, wrong, wickedness.)

virtuous, upright, honest, moral. (Profligate.)

vision, apparition, ghost, phantom, specter.

voluptuary, epicure, sensualist.

vote, suffrage, voice.

vouch, affirm, asseverate, aver, assure.

W

wait, await, expect, look for, wait for.

wakeful, vigilant, watchful. (Sleepy.)

wander, range, ramble, roam, rove, stroll, stray, deviate.

want, lack, need. (Abundance.)

wary, circumspect, cautious. (Foolhardy.)

wash, clean, rinse, wet, moisten, tint, stain.

waste, v., squander, dissipate, lavish, destroy, decay, dwindle, wither.

wasteful, extravagant, profligate. (Economical.)

wave, breaker, billow, surge.

way, method, plan, system, means, manner, mode, form, fashion, course, process, road, route, track, path, habit, practice.

wealth, money, pelf, plenty, opulence, means, riches, prosperity, lucre, luxury, assets, abundance, affluence, property. (Need, destitution, lack, beggary, misery, poverty, privation, want, scarcity, mendicancy, pauperism, impecuniosity.)

wearisome, tedious, tiresome. (Interesting, entertaining.)

weary, harass, jade, tire, fatigue. (Refresh.)

win, get, obtain, gain, procure, effect, realize, accomplish, achieve. (Lose.)

winning, attractive, charming, fascinating, bewitching, enchanting, dazzling, brilliant. (Repulsive.)

wisdom, prudence, foresight, sagacity, far-sightedness, judiciousness, sense. (Foolishness, absurdity, idiocy, silliness, stupidity, nonsense.)

wit, humor, satire, fun, raillery.

wonder, v., admire, amaze, astonish, surprise.

wonder, n., marvel, miracle, prodigy.

word, n., expression, term.

work, labor, task, toil, occupation, business, employment, exertion. (Play.)

worthless, valueless. (Valuable.)

writer, author, penman.

wrong, injustice, injury. (Right.)

Y

yawn, gape, open wide.

yearn, hanker after, long for, desire, crave.

yell, bellow, cry out, scream.

yellow, golden, saffronlike.

yelp, bark, sharp cry, howl.

yet, besides, nevertheless, however, ultimately, notwithstanding, still, at last, so far, thus far.

yield, bear, give, afford, impart, communicate, confer, bestow, abdicate, resign, cede, surrender, relinquish, relax, quit,

forego, give up, let go, waive, comply, accede, assent, acquiesce, succumb, submit. (Withdraw, withhold, retain, deny, refuse, vindicate, assert, claim, disallow, resist, dissent, protest, struggle, strive.)

yielding, conceding, producing, surrendering, supple, pliant, submissive, accommodating, unresisting. (Firm, defiant, hard, unyielding, resisting, unfruitful.)

yoke, v., couple, link, connect, conjoin, enslave, subjugate. (Dissever, divorce, disconnect, liberate, release, manumit, enfranchise.)

yore, long ago, long since. (Recently, today, now.)

youth, boy, lad, minority, adolescence, juvenility. (Old, ancient, antiquated, elderly, senile, patriarchal, primeval, time-honored, olden.)

youthful, young, juvenile, boyish, girlish, puerile, immature, adolescent. (Aged, senile, mature, decrepit, decayed, venerable, antiquated, superannuated.)

Z

zeal, energy, fervor, ardor, earnestness, enthusiasm, eagerness. (Indifference, apathy, torpor, coldness, carelessness, sluggishness.)

zealot, partisan, bigot, fanatic, devotee, visionary, enthusiast. (Traitor, deserter, renegade.)

zealous, warm, ardent, fervent, enthusiastic, anxious, eager, earnest, steadfast, bold, (Indifferent, dispassioned, apathetic, passionless, phlegmatic, platonic.)

zenith, height, highest point, pinnacle, summit, culmination, maximum. (Depth, lowest point, minimum.)

zephyr, mild breeze, west wind, gentle wind. (Gale, furious wind.)

zero, nothing, naught, cipher. (Something.)

zest, flavor, appetizer, gusto, pleasure, enjoyment, relish, sharpener, enhancement. (Distaste, disgust, disrelish, detriment.)

USING THE LANGUAGE

THE UNITED STATES

The third century of a great experiment in democratic government has begun in the United States of America. We recall with pride such events as the Boston Tea Party, but our history is more than the story of protest and battle. It began with the efforts of freedom-loving people eager to meet the challenges of a new land. Our history is renewed in generation after generation by the continuing desire of courageous men and women who want to keep alive our free government.

As you prepare to play a part in our country's destiny, you will want to learn as much as possible about the United States. In the following pages you will read of American history, our leaders, and our famous documents. You will find in that record the strengths and the struggles of our past. The Concise Edition of the *Student Handbook* provides additional information about our history and government.

United States History

American history does not begin with Columbus or the Vikings or the Pilgrims who landed at Plymouth Rock. It begins with a few Indian tribes that crossed the Bering Straits from Asia to North America—about 20,000 years ago, during the Ice Age. Over the next few thousand years, many more tribes migrated, gradually spreading over most of the continent.

Scientists who have studied these ancient North American Indians have decided that there were about 400 different tribal groups, with different customs, cultures, and languages. Some, such as the Plains Indians, were nomads, who traveled about, hunting and fishing, and gathering food that grew wild. The Pueblos, on the other hand, settled down in large cliff villages and began to plant crops. Eastern Indians were hunters and fishermen who settled in villages near lakes and rivers.

No one can be sure how many Indians lived in North America before the Europeans came, but there were probably about 23 million.

Most people now believe that the first Europeans to land in North America were the Norsemen. Sailing from their settlements in Greenland, they landed somewhere on the coast about 990. A few years later, according to the Norse sagas, Leif Ericson explored the land to the south, naming it Vinland. Other Norse expeditions also came.

The great age of New World exploration began with Christopher Columbus's voyages to the Caribbean in 1492, 1493, and 1502. He never reached the mainland but discovered the islands of Cuba, Jamaica, Hispaniola (the Dominican Republic and Haiti), and Puerto Rico—all of which he believed were near India. Soon, however, explorers realized that they had found a new continent, not a new way to the Orient. In the early 1500s other Spanish and Portuguese sailors and *conquistadores* explored and conquered Mexico and Central and South America. Ponce de Leon landed in Florida in 1513, and Hernando de Soto discovered the Mississippi River in 1539. In 1565 the Spanish founded St. Augustine, Florida, the first permanent European town in America.

English and French explorers were concentrating on lands to the north. In 1497, only five years after Columbus, John Cabot landed in North America. Other expeditions explored the coast, and in 1535 Jacques Cartier sailed up the St. Lawrence River. Many of these explorers sailed far

Pilgrims on their way to church. Plymouth Colony was established by the Pilgrims at Plymouth, Massachusetts, in 1620. Half the colonists died during the harsh first winter, including their leader, Governor John Carver. In 1691 Plymouth Colony became part of Massachusetts Bay Colony.

to the north, looking for a northwest passage to Asia. Others looked for pleasant lands where they could found colonies.

Plains Indians on a buffalo hunt. The Spaniards introduced horses into North America toward the end of the sixteenth century and greatly influenced the Indian way of life. Even today, descendants of this horse survive as mustangs on the plains of the Western states.

In 1585 Sir Walter Raleigh tried to start an English colony on Roanoke Island, Virginia (which he had named after Queen Elizabeth). No one knows exactly what happened to the Roanoke colonists. When a ship returned to the colony from England in 1590, they were found to have disappeared.

The time chart that follows begins with the decade 1600–1609, the time of the first lasting European settlements. The chart is divided into four sections, listing events in different areas.

The "political" section gives such events as elections and treaties. The "military" section includes wars and other armed actions. The "science and arts" listings include important inventions, famous books, and other events in cultural history. Finally, the "people and society" section lists important events that have affected the way people live in the United States.

Important events in American history

	POLITICS	MILITARY
1600–1609	Treaties with Spain allow French and English right to New World colonies, 1604 onward.	Iroquois Indian tribes form league, the "Five Nations," about 1600, and dominate New York and New England.
1610–1619	First colonial legislature meets, Virginia, 1619; **New England settlers sign Mayflower Compact, 1620.**	
1620–1629	Virginia becomes Royal Colony, 1624, after charter is revoked.	British capture Quebec, 1629, during continuing conflicts with French.
1630–1639	Church-dominated civil government set up in Massachusetts Bay, 1630–35; Connecticut adopts *Fundamental Orders*, 1639 (first written constitution).	New England settlers war with Pequot Indians, 1637.
1640–1649	**Civil War in England deposes king,** sets up Parliamentary rule, 1642–51; New England Confederation (of colonies) formed, 1643.	Iroquois league destroys Huron nation, 1649, wars against other tribes and their French allies.
1650–1659	Oliver Cromwell and the Protectorate rule England, 1653–59.	English capture Acadia (Nova Scotia) from the French, 1654.
1660–1669	**Monarchy restored in England, 1660;** Navigation Acts, 1660 and 1663, put restrictions on colonial trade.	**English conquer Dutch colonies of New Netherlands, 1661–64;** New Amsterdam renamed New York, 1664; English ally with Iroquois Five Nations, 1664.
1670–1679	New Hampshire made separate royal colony, 1679.	King Philip's War (New England settlers vs. Indians), 1675–76; Bacon leads rebellion against royal governor of Virginia, 1675–76.

THE UNITED STATES

SCIENCE & ARTS

Jamestown settlers begin farming, corn planting, 1609; Captain John Smith writes *A True Relation of . . . Virginia*, 1608.

Gov. Bradford writes history of Plymouth colony, 1630–47; New England laws require towns to establish schools, after 1636; Harvard College founded, 1636.

Bay Psalm Book, 1640, is first book printed in colonies; education made compulsory in New England colonies, 1640s; first ironworks, 1643.

Traveling portrait painters are first colonial artists, 1650s; *Tenth Muse*, poems by Anne Bradstreet, 1650.

John Eliot makes Indian translation of Bible, 1663; first colonial astronomers begin work, 1665.

PEOPLE & SOCIETY

Jamestown colony founded, 1607; Champlain founds Quebec, 1608; Spanish build Santa Fe, 1609; Hudson explores east coast, 1609.

First blacks arrive in America, as indentured servants, 1619.

Mayflower Pilgrims land near Cape Cod, 1620; Dutch immigrants buy Manhattan Island, 1626; English Puritans establish Massachusetts Bay Colony, 1628–30.

Maryland founded as Catholic colony, 1634; Roger Williams leaves Massachusetts to found Rhode Island, 1636; Swedes settle Delaware, 1638; **"Great Migration" from England, 1630–42.**

Rhode Island constitution, 1647, gives religious freedom, separates church and state authority; Toleration Act passed in Maryland, 1649.

Dutch settle in Delaware, 1655; Quakers persecuted in New England colonies, 1656–61.

French explore Great Lakes region, found Sault Ste. Marie, 1668.

Virginia passes slave laws, 1670; first successful settlement in Carolinas is Charles Town, 1670; Marquette and Joliet explore Mississippi Valley, 1673.

THE UNITED STATES

	POLITICS	MILITARY
1680–1689	King James II makes Andros governor of combined New York, New Jersey, New England colonies, 1686; Revolution in England, 1688; **Parliament passes Declaration of Rights, 1689.**	Protestants and Catholics clash in Maryland, 1685–88; King William's War, between English, French, and Indian allies, reflects French-English wars in Europe, 1689–97. 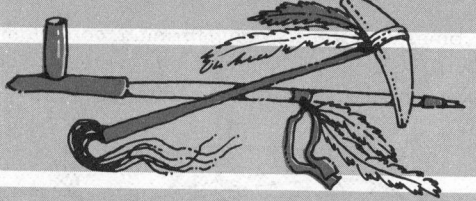
1690–1699	Maryland becomes royal province, 1691.	
1700–1709	Charter of Privileges, 1701, gives Pennsylvania colony a liberal form of government.	Queen Anne's War begins in New England, 1702, as one phase of wars in Europe.
1710–1719	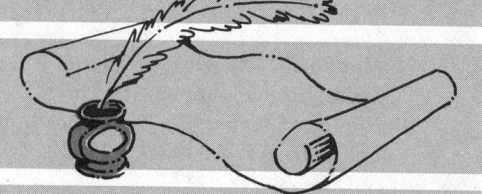	Tuscarora Indian War in the Carolinas, 1711–13; Treaty of Utrecht, 1713, ends Queen Anne's War, gives England lands in Canada.
1720–1729	North and South Carolina become royal colonies, 1729.	
1730–1739	Hat Act, 1732, and Molasses Act, 1733, restrict colonial industry and trade; **trial of John Peter Zenger establishes freedom of the press, 1735.**	English colonists in Georgia attack Spanish settlements in Florida as part of War of Jenkins' Ear, 1739.
1740–1749	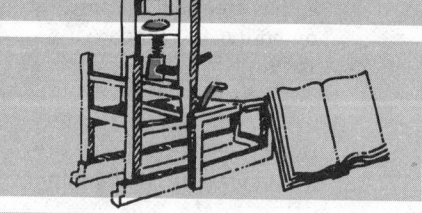	King George's War, 1740–48, between English and French, reflects continuing wars in Europe.
1750–1759	Albany Congress tries to form union of northern colonies, 1754.	**French and Indian War begins, 1754;** French build Ft. Duquesne (Pittsburgh), 1754; Acadians exiled from Nova Scotia, 1755; English under General Wolfe win Battle of Quebec, 1759.
1760–1769	George III becomes king of England, 1760; **Parliament passes Stamp Act, 1765;** colonists protest and Act is repealed, 1766; Townshend Acts impose new taxes, 1767.	Treaty of Paris, 1763, ends war and destroys French power in North America; Pontiac leads Great Lakes Indians against British, 1763–66.

64

SCIENCE & ARTS	PEOPLE & SOCIETY
	**LaSalle claims Mississippi Valley for France, names it Louisiana, 1682;** Penn establishes Pennsylvania, makes treaty with Indians, 1682.
New England Primer published, 1690; William and Mary College founded in Virginia, 1693.	**Witchcraft trials in Massachusetts, 1692–93;** French establish settlements along Gulf Coast and Mississippi River, 1699.
Cotton Mather writes *Ecclesiastical History of New England,* 1702; Yale College founded, 1701.	French build fort at Detroit, 1701, and trading posts along Mississippi; Ben Franklin born, 1706.
"Mother Goose" rhymes published, 1715.	George I of the German House of Hanover succeeds Anne of England, 1714. French found New Orleans, 1718.
Colonial naturalists begin studies, 1720s; John Bartram sets up first American botanical garden, 1728.	French settle in Illinois country, 1720–26.
New instruments for navigation and surveying developed, 1730–35; long rifle improved, 1730s; Ben Franklin publishes *Poor Richard's Almanack,* 1732–57.	George Washington born, 1732; colony of Georgia founded, 1733; "Great Awakening" religious movement begins, 1734.
First American magazine, 1741; Ben Franklin invents Franklin stove, 1742, experiments with electricity, 1747; first American theatrical company formed, 1749–50.	**Alaska discovered by Bering and claimed by Russia, 1741;** Jefferson born, 1743; settlers from Pennsylvania and Virginia move into Ohio Valley, 1744.
First Conestoga wagons built, about 1750; Ben Franklin invents lightning rod, 1752. 	James Madison born, 1751; first general hospital in colonies, 1752; Ben Franklin runs first post-office service, 1753–55; Alexander Hamilton born, 1755.
David Rittenhouse builds first instruments for astronomy in colonies, 1769; first American medical school opens, 1765.	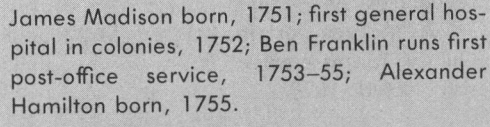 **Proclamation of 1763 prohibits settlement west of Appalachians;** Mason-Dixon Line, 1767, settles Maryland boundary dispute; Spanish priests found missions in California, 1769–82.

	POLITICS	MILITARY
1770–1779	Boston Tea Party protests tea tax, 1773; "Intolerable Acts" passed, 1774; Continental Congresses meet, 1774–75; **Declaration of Independence issued, July 4, 1776.**	Boston Massacre, 1770; **colonists and British troops fight at Lexington and Concord, April 1775;** Congress names George Washington commander, May 1775; army winters at Valley Forge, 1777.
1780–1789	Articles of Confederation adopted as first constitution, 1781; convention meets to write new Constitution, 1787; **electors choose Washington as first President under Constitution, 1789.**	**Cornwallis surrenders to Washington at Yorktown, 1781;** Treaty of Paris, 1783, ends American Revolution. 
1790–1799	**Bill of Rights is added to Constitution, 1791.** Whiskey Rebellion protests federal taxes, 1794; John Adams elected President, 1796; Alien and Sedition Acts passed, 1798.	Undeclared war with France, 1798–1800; Napoleon becomes the all-powerful First Consul of France, 1799.
1800–1809	Jefferson elected President after tie vote with Burr, 1801; Louisiana Purchase, 1803; Madison elected, 1808. Supreme Court establishes its right to decide constitutionality of laws, in Marbury vs. Madison, 1803.	Naval war with Barbary Coast pirates, 1801–16; Napoleonic wars in Europe halt shipping trade, 1803–09.
1810–1819	"War Hawks" from the West dominate Congress, 1811; President Madison blamed for War of 1812; Monroe's election, 1816, begins "Era of Good Feeling."	**War with Britain, 1812–14,** over land in Canada and shipping; Battle of Lake Erie, 1813; Harrison defeats Indians at Tippecanoe, 1811, and in Canada, 1813; Battle of New Orleans, 1815.
1820–1829	**Missouri Compromise on slavery, 1820;** U.S. recognizes new Latin American republics, 1822; **"Monroe Doctrine" stated, 1823;** John Quincy Adams elected, 1824; Andrew Jackson elected, 1828.	
1830–1839	Webster-Hayne debates in Congress on states' rights, 1830; Texas Republic formed, 1836; Van Buren elected, 1836.	Indians attempt to win back land in Blackhawk War, 1832; Seminole Wars in Florida, 1835; **Mexicans besiege Alamo, 1836;** Anglo-American clashes on Canadian border, 1838–39.

66

SCIENCE & ARTS	PEOPLE & SOCIETY
Thomas Paine's *Common Sense*, 1776, and *Crisis* papers, 1776–83; poetry by Philip Freneau, 1770s. 	Daniel Boone leads settlers to Kentucky through Cumberland Gap, 1775; Congress approves design for U.S. flag, June 14, 1777.
Webster's *Blue-Backed Speller*, 1783; Franklin invents bifocals, 1783; *The Federalist Papers* published, 1787–88, in favor of new Constitution.	Loyalists emigrate to Canada and England, after 1783; Northwest Ordinance, 1787, sets pattern for settlement and statehood in West and Midwest.
Paine's *Rights of Man*, 1792, and *Age of Reason*, 1794–95; Gilbert Stuart paints portraits, 1792; Eli Whitney invents cotton gin, 1793; Bowditch's *American Practical Navigator* published, 1799.	**First national census gives population of U.S. as 4 million, 1790;** Columbia River (Oregon) discovered, 1792; yellow fever epidemic in Philadelphia, 1793.
Smallpox vaccine introduced in U.S., 1800; Fulton builds steamboat *Clermont*, 1807; Washington Irving's *Knickerbocker History of New York*, 1809.	Slave trade outlawed by Congress, 1808; **Lewis and Clark expedition explores West, 1803–06;** Abraham Lincoln born, 1809.
Star-Spangled Banner written, 1814; first steamship crosses Atlantic, 1819.	West Florida (entire Gulf Coast) annexed, 1810; third national census shows population of more than 7 million, 1810; Colonization Society, 1817, plans to return blacks to Africa.
Erie Canal completed, 1825; James Fenimore Cooper's *Last of the Mohicans* published, 1826; Audubon paints *Birds of America*, 1827.	Emma Willard founds first women's college, 1821; first public high school begun, Boston, 1821; Irish and German immigrants arrive after 1826.
"Tom Thumb," first U.S. steam locomotive, 1830; first clipper ship built, 1833; Emerson leading figure of New England Transcendentalists, 1830s; "penny daily" papers start in New York, 1833–35.	Nat Turner leads slave rebellion, 1831; financial panic of 1837 causes depression, 1839; underground railroad (system of safe hiding places) helps escaping slaves, 1830–60.

THE UNITED STATES

	POLITICS	MILITARY
1840–1849	W. H. Harrison elected, 1840, in vicious political campaign; dies, 1841; Tyler succeeds him; Democrats ask annexation of Texas and Oregon; Polk elected, 1844; Gen. Taylor elected, 1848.	U.S. troops sent to Mexican border, 1845; Texas annexed as state, 1845; **war with Mexico, 1846–48;** U.S. troops occupy California, 1846–47.
1850–1859	Congress debates slavery question, passes "Compromise of 1850"; Fillmore becomes President after Taylor's death, 1850; Buchanan elected in 1856; Lincoln-Douglas debates, 1858.	Abolitionist John Brown raids Harpers Ferry, Virginia, and is captured by U.S. troops, 1859.
1860–1869	**Lincoln elected, 1860; Southern states secede, 1860–61, and organize Confederate States of America;** Jefferson Davis becomes president of Confederacy, 1861. **Lincoln assassinated, 1865;** Andrew Johnson becomes President; Civil Rights Act, 1866; **Johnson acquitted in impeachment trial, 1868;** U.S. Grant elected President, 1868.	**Confederacy fires on Ft. Sumter, and Civil War begins, 1861;** some major battles are Bull Run, 1861; Gettysburg, 1863; Atlanta, 1864; **General Robert E. Lee surrenders, 1865;** Army and militia conquer Cheyenne and Arapaho in Colorado, 1865; first Sioux War, 1865–68.
1870–1879	Disputed 1876 election makes Hayes President, 1877; Congress passes laws against Ku Klux Klan, 1870–71; New York's Tweed Ring broken up, 1871.	Apaches massacred in Arizona, 1871; Custer and his cavalry wiped out at Little Bighorn, 1876; army pursues and captures Nez Percé Indians, 1877.
1880–1889	Garfield elected, 1880, succeeded by Arthur after assassination, 1881; Pendleton Civil Service Act, 1883; Cleveland elected, 1884; Benjamin Harrison elected, 1888.	U.S. signs Geneva Convention, 1882, international agreement for care of war wounded.
1890–1899	Sherman Anti-Trust Act, 1890; Cleveland elected, 1892; U.S. involved in Cuban rebellion, 1896; William Jennings Bryan makes "Cross of Gold" speech, but loses election to McKinley, 1896.	Troops put down Indian "Ghost Dance" movement, 1890; battleship "Maine" blown up in Havana, **war with Spain begins, 1898;** U.S. gains Puerto Rico and Philippines, 1899.

THE UNITED STATES

SCIENCE & ARTS

Edgar Allan Poe's tales published, 1840; Morse demonstrates telegraph and Morse Code, 1844; Goodyear patents vulcanized rubber, 1844; sewing machine invented, 1846.

Melville's *Moby-Dick* and Hawthorne's *House of Seven Gables* published, 1851; Harriet Beecher Stowe's *Uncle Tom's Cabin* is a best seller, 1852; Thoreau's *Walden*, 1854; Whitman's *Leaves of Grass*, 1855.

Pony Express mail service begins, 1860; Mathew B. Brady begins photographic coverage of Civil War, 1862; first Bessemer steel plant, 1864; Pullman builds first comfortable sleeping car, 1864; first book by Horatio Alger, 1867; Louisa May Alcott's *Little Women*, 1868; **transcontinental railroad completed, with two lines meeting in Utah, 1869.**

P. T. Barnum's "Greatest Show on Earth" opens, 1871; first U.S. nursing school, 1873; **Bell demonstrates telephone, 1876;** Mark Twain's *Tom Sawyer*, 1876.

Edison patents incandescent light, 1880; A. A. Michelson measures speed of light, 1880; Clara Barton starts U.S. Red Cross, 1881; Eastman perfects hand camera, 1888.

U.S. Weather Bureau organized, 1890; first gasoline and electric-powered autos, 1892.

PEOPLE & SOCIETY

Many people migrate to the West, 1842–47; **gold found in California, 1848;** first women's rights convention, 1848; mass immigrations follow European revolutions of 1848.

Chinese laborers immigrate to work on Western railroads, 1854; Supreme Court "Dred Scott decision" upholds slavery in territories, 1857; Gold Rush in Rockies, 1858–59.

Emancipation Proclamation abolishes slavery in the South, 1863; **13th Amendment prohibits slavery, 1865;** Alaska bought from Russia, 1867; first professional baseball team, Cincinnati, 1869; Knights of Labor organized, 1869.

Chicago Fire, 1871; financial panic of 1873 causes depression; many immigrants from Europe, Ireland, 1873; baseball's National League founded, 1876; Woolworth opens first "5 & 10" 1879.

Peak immigration from Germany, China, 1882; immigrants begin to come from Russia, southern Europe, 1885; American Federation of Labor formed, 1886; Oklahoma land rush, 1889.

Basketball invented, 1891; financial panic, 1893, causes depression and major strikes, 1894; "Coxey's Army" of unemployed marches to Washington, 1894; Alaska Gold Rush, 1896–97.

THE UNITED STATES

	POLITICS	MILITARY
1900–1909	Hawaii annexed, 1900; **McKinley reelected, 1900, but assassinated, 1901; Theodore Roosevelt succeeds him**; U.S. leases Panama Canal Zone, 1908; Taft elected, 1908.	International force takes part in China's Boxer Rebellion, 1900; U.S. Navy makes world cruise, 1907.
1910–1919	LaFollette founds Progressive Republican party, 1911; era of municipal reform, 1912; **Wilson elected, 1912, presents "14 Points" for peace, 1918**; U.S. rejects League of Nations, 1919.	Troops sent to Mexican border, 1911; **World War I begins in Europe, 1914**; German U-boat sinks "Lusitania," 1915; U.S. enters war, 1917; **Armistice signed, November 11, 1918.**
1920–1929	Harding elected, 1920; "Teapot Dome" oilfield scandal, 1922; Coolidge becomes president on Harding's death, 1923; PanAmerican conference, 1928; Hoover elected, 1928.	World War I peace treaties signed, 1921; French and Belgian troops occupy Ruhr to enforce reparations, 1923; Germany agrees to demilitarize Rhineland and secure French and Belgian frontiers, 1925; Kellogg-Briand Peace Pact signed, 1928.
1930–1939	**Franklin D. Roosevelt elected, 1932; initiates "New Deal" economic and social policies to fight Depression**; reelected 1936.	U.S. passes Neutrality Acts, 1935–37; individual Americans fight in Spanish Civil War, 1936–1939; **German aggression, 1938–39, involves much of Europe in war.**
1940–1949	Roosevelt reelected, 1940, 1944 (for 4th term); Atlantic Charter, 1941; Yalta Conference, 1945; Truman becomes President on FDR's death, April 1945; United Nations charter written, 1945; **first United Nations General Assembly meets**, 1946; Marshall Plan for postwar aid, 1946; Truman defeats Dewey in election, 1948.	German troops overrun Europe, 1940–41; Battle of Britain, 1940; Japan attacks Pearl Harbor, Hawaii, December 7, 1941; U.S. declares war on Japan, Germany, Italy, 1941; **Allies invade Europe on D-day, June 6, 1944**; Germany surrenders, May 1945; **atomic bombs dropped on Japan, August 1945**, and Japan surrenders; peace treaties signed, 1946. USSR blockades Berlin, 1948.
1950–1959	**Senator Joseph McCarthy makes widespread accusations of communism in government, 1950–53**; Eisenhower wins election over Adlai Stevenson, 1952; Army-McCarthy hearings in Senate, 1954.	**War begins in Korea, 1950**; U.S. gives aid to new government in Saigon, Vietnam, 1950; Truman ousts General Douglas McArthur in dispute over Korean War policy, 1951; U.S. aids French war in Indo-china, leading to Vietnam partition, 1954; Soviet troops crush Hungarian uprising, 1956; Fidel Castro takes over in Cuba, 1959.

THE UNITED STATES

SCIENCE & ARTS

Wright Brothers make first flight, 1903; **Model T Ford invented, 1908;** first daily newspaper comic strip, 1907; Admiral Peary reaches North Pole, 1909.

Armory Show of modern art, 1913; Hollywood becomes center of movie industry, 1913–15; **Panama Canal completed, 1914;** Goddard patents rocket, 1914; first air mail service, 1918.

First national radio broadcast, 1920; Gershwin writes "Rhapsody in Blue," 1924; *The Jazz Singer* is first full-length sound movie, 1927; **Lindbergh makes solo flight across Atlantic, 1927;** first "Mickey Mouse" cartoon, 1928; Admiral Byrd flies over North and South Poles, 1926 and 1929.

Planet Pluto first seen, 1930; Sinclair Lewis is first U.S. writer to win Nobel Prize, 1930; Empire State Building built, 1931; Boulder Dam, 1936; *Gone With the Wind* published, 1936.

Electron microscope developed, 1940; first controlled nuclear chain reaction, 1942; **post-war boom in television, 1946 on;** Bikini A-bomb tests, 1946; **transistor invented, 1947;** Einstein develops unified field theory, 1945; first show by abstract painter Jackson Pollock, 1943.

First hydrogen bomb test, 1952; Cinemascope process developed, 1953; Hemingway wins Nobel Prize, 1954; Salk polio vaccine used, 1954; **USSR launches *Sputnik*, 1957;** first atomic submarine, *Nautilus*, crosses under ice of North Pole, 1958; St. Lawrence Seaway opens, 1959.

PEOPLE & SOCIETY

San Francisco earthquake and fire, 1906; financial panic of 1907 causes unemployment and inflation.

Boy Scouts of America founded, 1910; "Titanic" sinks, 1912; worldwide flu epidemic kills 20 million, 1918–19.

Prohibition begins, 1920; **women win right to vote, 1920;** limits set on immigration, 1921; **stocks decline sharply, stock market crashes, 1929.**

Banks close, 1930–31; **Depression unemployment and inflation reach peak, July 1931;** migrants move from Southwest "dust bowl," 1935; first Social Security Act, 1935.

OPA (Office of Price Administration) sets up price controls, rationing of food, tires, metals, 1941; West Coast Japanese moved to relocation camps, 1942; Displaced Persons Act, 1948, allows immigration of European war refugees.

Cabinet Department of Health, Education and Welfare established, 1953; **Supreme Court outlaws school segregation, 1954;** blacks boycott Montgomery, Alabama, buses in first major civil rights action, 1955; federal troops enforce desegregation in Little Rock, Arkansas, 1957; Alaska and Hawaii become states, 1959.

THE UNITED STATES

	POLITICS	MILITARY
1960–1969	Kennedy-Nixon TV debates, 1960; John F. Kennedy wins election, 1960, calls for "New Frontier" program; **Kennedy assassinated Nov. 22, 1963,** and Lyndon Johnson becomes President; Johnson announces "War on Poverty," 1964; withdraws from Presidential race, 1968; **Robert Kennedy assassinated, 1968;** Richard Nixon elected over Hubert H. Humphrey, 1968.	Berlin Wall built, 1961; U.S. supports Cuban "Bay of Pigs" invasion, 1961; **Cuban missile crisis, 1962;** economic and military aid sent to South Vietnam, 1962; U.S. troops sent to Laos, 1964; **Tonkin Gulf resolution, 1964, supports more U.S. military action in Vietnam;** Senators begin to criticize war in Vietnam, 1966; widespread antiwar protests begin, 1967–68.
1970–1978	Supreme Court allows newspaper publication of "Pentagon Papers," 1971; **Nixon visits China and USSR, 1972;** Communist China admitted to UN, 1972; Nixon defeats Senator George McGovern in 1972 election; Watergate scandal engulfs Nixon. House begins impeachment proceedings, 1974; **Nixon resigns, 1974;** Gerald Ford becomes first President under terms of the 25th Amendment. Jimmy Carter defeats Gerald Ford in 1976 election. President Carter emphasizes "Human Rights" as fundamental part of foreign policy.	U.S. invasion of Cambodia, 1970, arouses antiwar protests; Congress debates withholding funds for war in Vietnam, 1971–72. Strategic Arms Limitation Talks (SALT talks) between U.S. and Soviet Union begun, 1972. **United States troops leave Vietnam, which falls to North Vietnamese troops, 1974.** Israel and Arab nations fight fourth war in 30 years over continuation of Israel, 1973.

Facts about the Presidents

George Washington (1732–1799)
1ST PRESIDENT, 1789–97

Born: February 22, 1732, Westmoreland County, Virginia.

Died: December 14, 1799, Mount Vernon, Virginia.

Education: Schooled at home and then trained in surveying.

Occupation: Soldier, surveyor, planter. Led troops under General Braddock in French and Indian Wars; named head of Continental armies in 1775, led the major battles of the Revolution and accepted British surrender at Yorktown, 1781. Retired from army, 1783.

Religion: Episcopalian.

Family life: Married Martha Dandridge

SCIENCE & ARTS

U.S. auto industry makes first compact cars, 1960; Telstar is first communications satellite, 1961; **U.S. makes its first manned space flight, 1961;** *Silent Spring* published, 1962; "pop" art exhibited, 1962; first heart transplant operation, 1967; **U.S. Apollo 11 lands first men on the moon, 1969.**

Environmental Protection Agency set up, 1970, as federal coordinator of antipollution efforts. OPEC (Organization of Petroleum Exporting Countries) oil embargo, 1973, focuses attention on energy consumption. President Carter calls for new energy policy of conservation and use of alternative energy sources.

PEOPLE & SOCIETY

Anti-Castro Cubans emigrate to U.S., 1960 on; Civil Rights Act, 1960; Peace Corps established, 1961; civil rights march on Washington, 1963; Selma, Alabama, civil rights march, 1965; Martin Luther King receives Nobel Peace Prize, 1965; Medicare bill passed, 1965; **Martin Luther King assassinated, 1968.**

Kent State students killed during Vietnam War demonstration, 1970; **wage-price freeze ordered in attempt to stop inflation, 1971;** 26th Amendment lowers voting age to eighteen, 1971. Equal Rights Amendment is debated and approaches ratification in 1977. Women's rights becomes strong political and social movement.

Custis (1731–1802), a widow with two children, in 1759.

Political career: As a prominent planter, became member of Virginia House of Burgesses, 1758, and gradually became active in colonial politics. Delegate to Continental Congresses, 1774–75, and elected commander. After war, became involved in organization of new federal government; presided over Constitutional Convention; unanimously elected first president, 1789. Attempted to balance politics of new country; refused third term in office, 1796, and retired to Mount Vernon.

● *Highlights of his presidency:* Established the Bank of the United States and a postal system, created West Point, put down the Whiskey Rebellion. His farewell address warned about permanent alliances with other countries.

Appearance: Tall (6 feet 2 inches) and powerfully built, sandy hair, blue eyes.

John Adams (1735–1826)
2ND PRESIDENT, 1797–1801

Born: October 30, 1735, Braintree (Quincy), Massachusetts.
Died: July 4, 1826, Quincy, Massachusetts.
Education: Graduated from Harvard College (Cambridge, Massachusetts).
Occupation: Lawyer, diplomat, public official.
Religion: Unitarian.
Family life: Married Abigail Smith (1744–1818) in 1764; they had three sons and two daughters. Abigail Adams, an exceptional and brilliant woman, left an interesting record of the times in her letters.

Political career: An early leader of the Revolution, Adams attended the Continental Congresses and was on the committee to write the Declaration of Independence. A leading diplomat, 1778–88, he helped Washington's career and was vice-president, 1789–97. Elected in 1796 as a Federalist; was badly defeated for reelection, 1800, and retired.

● *Highlights of his presidency:* Prospective treaty with the French marred by XYZ affair; French officials demanded bribes. Alien and Sedition laws passed with Adams neutral. Because of his lack of support in Congress, Adams did not accomplish much in his four years in office.

Appearance: Short and stout, with strong, stern features.

Thomas Jefferson (1743–1826)
3RD PRESIDENT, 1801–09

Born: April 13, 1743, Goochland (Albemarle) County, Virginia.
Died: July 4, 1826, Charlottesville, Virginia.
Education: College of William and Mary (Williamsburg, Virginia).
Occupation: Lawyer, writer, public official; talented in music, languages, science, architecture; interested in education and political philosophy. Founded and organized University of Virginia; designed its buildings as well as his own home, Monticello.
Religion: No formal affiliation.
Family life: Married Martha Wayles Skelton (1748–1782), a widow, in 1772. They had six children; only two daughters survived infancy.
Political career: Became early leader in Revolution; in Virginia House of Burgesses, 1769–74; attended Continental Congress. Author of the Declaration of Independence, 1776. After war, was governor of Virginia and diplomat for new United States govern-

ment; Washington's secretary of state, 1790–93. Political leader of Democratic-Republicans and vice-president under Adams. As president, made Louisiana Purchase from France.

● *Highlights of his presidency:* Authorized the Louisiana Purchase, attacked the Barbary Pirates with naval forces. Forced the Embargo Act through Congress as a measure against British and French, who were at war. Jefferson did much to rid the presidency of its royal trappings and to reduce the power of the federal government.

Appearance: Tall and slender (6 feet 2 inches) with reddish-blond hair.

James Madison (1751–1836)
4TH PRESIDENT, 1809–17

Born: March 16, 1751, Port Conway, Virginia.
Died: June 28, 1836, Montpelier, Virginia.
Education: Graduated from College of New Jersey (now Princeton).
Occupation: Lawyer, public official.
Religion: Episcopalian.
Family life: Married a popular and attractive widow, Dolly Paine Todd (1768–1849), in 1794. Dolly Madison courageously rescued paintings and papers from the White House during the British invasion, 1814.
Political career: Entered Virginia politics in 1774; very influential at the Constitutional Convention, 1787; wrote part of Federalist papers explaining the new government. Served in Congress, 1789–97, and was Jefferson's secretary of state before becoming Democratic-Republican candidate, 1808.

● *Highlights of his presidency:* Called for war against Britain in 1812.

Appearance: The smallest President— 5 feet 4 inches tall, about 100 pounds— blond and blue-eyed.

Washington *John Adams* *Th Jefferson* *James Madison* *James Monroe*

James Monroe (1758–1831)
5TH PRESIDENT, 1817–25

Born: April 28, 1758, Westmoreland County, Virginia.

Died: July 4, 1831, New York, New York.

Education: Attended College of William and Mary (Williamsburg, Virginia), studied law with Jefferson.

Occupation: Lawyer, diplomat, public official; fought in the American Revolution, 1775–78.

Religion: Episcopalian.

Family life: Married Elizabeth Kortwright (1768–1830) in 1786; they had two daughters and one son.

Political career: Elected to Virginia legislature during Revolution; a member of Congress, 1783–86; served in United States Senate, 1790–94. Held several diplomatic posts and was Madison's secretary of state, 1811–17. Served two terms as president (Democratic-Republican), a peaceful period known as the "Era of Good Feeling."

● *Highlights of his presidency:* Missouri Compromise admitted that state as a "slave" state. Acquired Florida from Spain. Announced the Monroe Doctrine as fundamental foreign policy position.

Appearance: Tall (6 feet), rugged, and athletic.

John Quincy Adams (1767–1848)
6TH PRESIDENT, 1825–29

Born: July 11, 1767, Braintree (Quincy), Massachusetts.

Died: February 23, 1848, Washington, D.C.

Education: Attended school in Europe, graduated from Harvard College.

Occupation: Lawyer, diplomat, public official.

Religion: Unitarian.

Family life: Married Louisa Catherine Johnson (1775–1852), daughter of the United States consul in London, 1797. They had three sons and one daughter.

Political career: Held diplomatic posts under his father, President John Adams, and later was minister to several European countries, 1794–1801. Served in United States Senate from Massachusetts, 1803–08. Negotiated treaty ending War of 1812; served as Monroe's secretary of state, 1817–25. Disputed election of 1824 was decided by House of Representatives; after his term, Adams returned to Congress, 1831–48.

- *Highlights of his presidency:* Advocated passage of "Tariff of Abominations" whose high rates favored New England manufacturers and hurt Southern farmers.

Appearance: Short and stocky, balding, stern-featured.

Andrew Jackson (1767–1845)
7TH PRESIDENT, 1829–37

Born: March 15, 1767, Waxhaw, South Carolina.

Died: June 8, 1845, at The Hermitage, near Nashville, Tennessee.

Education: Studied law, but never attended college.

Occupation: Primarily a soldier, also a lawyer, planter, merchant. Fought in the Revolution (at age thirteen), later led expeditions against the Creek Indians, defeated the British at New Orleans (1815), and fought in Seminole Wars; then became military governor of Florida.

Religion: Presbyterian.

Family life: Married Rachel Donelson Robards (1767–1828) in 1791; remarried after her divorce was granted.

Political career: Served in Congress as representative and senator from Tennessee (1796–98); again in the Senate, 1823–25. A military hero, ran unsuccessfully for president, 1824; won in 1828; renominated by Democratic-Republicans, 1832, in first party convention.

- *Highlights of his presidency:* Used "spoils system" in appointments (friendship rather than merit). Opposed Bank of United States. Opposed secession of South Carolina.

Appearance: Tall and rawboned, blue eyes, bushy gray hair.

Martin Van Buren (1782–1862)
8TH PRESIDENT, 1837–41

Born: December 5, 1782, Kinderhook, New York.

Died: July 24, 1862, Kinderhook, New York.

Education: Studied law but never attended college.

Occupation: Lawyer, public official.

Religion: Dutch Reformed.

Family life: Married Hannah Hoes (1783–1819) in 1807; they had four sons. One of his daughters-in-law was White House hostess.

Political career: A rival of DeWitt Clinton for leadership of the New York Republicans; held state offices before becoming United States senator, 1821–28, then succeeded Clinton as governor. A trusted advisor and secretary of state to Andrew Jackson; became his vice-president, 1833–37. Succeeded Jackson as president; nominated again in 1840 but defeated. Nominated in 1848 by the dissident Free-Soil Party; retired after his defeat.

- *Highlights of his presidency:* Opposed annexation of Texas. Fought unpopular war with Seminole Indians in Florida.

Appearance: Small (5 feet 6 inches) and erect, with graying reddish hair.

William Henry Harrison (1773–1841)
9TH PRESIDENT, March–April 1841

Born: February 9, 1773, Charles City County, Virginia.

Died: April 4, 1841, Washington, D.C., while in office.

Education: Attended Hampden-Sydney College (Virginia).

Occupation: Soldier. Left school to fight Indians in 1791; became a hero in Indian wars and in War of 1812. Nicknamed "Old Tippecanoe" for one of his victories.

Religion: Episcopalian.

Family life: Eloped with Anna Symmes (1775–1864) in 1795; they had six sons and four daughters. Their grandson, Benjamin Harrison, was also president.

Political career: Delegate to United States Congress from Northwest Territory,

John Quincy Adams *Andrew Jackson* *M Van Buren* *W H Harrison* *John Tyler*

then territorial governor and superintendent of Indian affairs, 1801–13. Served in Congress as representative, then senator from Ohio. Defeated as Whig candidate for president, 1836; won in 1840 with slogan "Tippecanoe and Tyler Too."

● *Highlights of his presidency:* Slogan "Tippecanoe and Tyler Too" was campaign's most notable success. Died one month after inauguration.

Appearance: Tall and thin.

John Tyler (1790–1862)
10TH PRESIDENT, 1841–45

Born: March 29, 1790, Charles City County, Virginia.

Died: January 18, 1862, Richmond, Virginia.

Education: College of William and Mary (Williamsburg, Virginia).

Occupation: Lawyer, public official; college chancellor.

Religion: Episcopalian.

Family life: Married Letitia Christian (1790–1842) in 1813; they had five daughters and three sons. After her death, married Julia Gardiner (1820–1889) in a White House ceremony; they had five sons and two daughters.

Political career: Son of the governor of Virginia, entered politics in state legislature, 1811; was United States representative and then senator from Virginia; also state governor, 1823–25. Broke with Democrats to join Whigs, who nominated him for vice-president; became president on Harrison's death, but lost power in conflict with Whig leader Henry Clay. Retired from politics until 1861, when he attempted to bring about North-South compromise.

● *Highlights of his presidency:* Reorganized Navy. Ended Seminole War. Signed treaty with China.

Appearance: Tall, thin, and fair.

James Knox Polk (1795–1849)
11TH PRESIDENT, 1845–49

Born: November 2, 1795, Mecklenburg County, North Carolina.

Died: June 15, 1849, Nashville, Tennessee.

Education: Graduated from University of North Carolina (Chapel Hill).

Occupation: Lawyer, politician.

Religion: Presbyterian.

Family life: Married Sarah Childress (1803–1891) in 1824.

Political career: Highly successful in

THE UNITED STATES

local politics; helped by Andrew Jackson, became United States representative from Tennessee, 1825–39; Speaker of the House, 1835–39; governor of Tennessee, 1839–41; returned to Washington; nominated in 1844 as a "dark horse" candidate. Never in good health, died three months after leaving office.

● *Highlights of his presidency:* Went to war with Mexico over territorial acquisitions. Gained California and New Mexico.

Appearance: Small, sharp-featured, with white hair worn long.

Zachary Taylor (1784–1850)
12TH PRESIDENT, 1849–50

Born: November 24, 1784, Orange County, Virginia.

Died: July 9, 1850, Washington, D.C. (while in office).

Education: Taylor had almost no schooling before joining the army.

Occupation: Soldier. The son of an army colonel, Taylor served in the War of 1812; was recommissioned in 1816 and served against the Indians in the West for more than twenty years, then in Florida's Seminole Wars. Became a national hero ("Old Rough and Ready") in Mexican War, 1846–47.

Religion: Episcopalian.

Family life: Married Margaret Mackall Smith (1788–1852) in 1810; they had five daughters and one son.

Political career: Nominated for the presidency by the Whigs in 1848 because of popularity as war hero. Died suddenly after becoming ill at a July 4th celebration.

● *Highlights of his presidency:* Became antislavery in bitter divisions over whether slavery would be permitted in newly acquired territory. Died after only sixteen months in office.

Appearance: Stocky (5 feet 8 inches tall) and short-legged, with a square, ruddy face.

Millard Fillmore (1800–1874)
13TH PRESIDENT, 1850–53

Born: January 7, 1800, Cayuga County, New York.

Died: March 8, 1874, Buffalo, New York.

Education: Attended country schools, taught himself law.

Occupation: Lawyer, politician.

Religion: Unitarian.

Family life: Married Abigail Powers (1798–1853) in 1826; they had a son and a daughter. After her death, married Caroline McIntosh (1814–1881) in 1858.

Political career: Served in New York state assembly; then in Congress, 1833–35 and 1837–43; ran as a Whig for governor of New York, 1844. Elected vice-president in 1848; became president on Taylor's death, but not renominated. Defeated for presidency as "Know-Nothing" candidate, 1856.

● *Highlights of his presidency:* Tried to steer a middle course between the pro-slavery forces to preserve the Union.

Appearance: Medium height, fair, and blue-eyed.

Franklin Pierce (1804–1869)
14TH PRESIDENT, 1853–57

Born: November 23, 1804, Hillsboro, New Hampshire.

Died: October 8, 1869, Concord, New Hampshire.

Education: Graduated from Bowdoin College (Brunswick, Maine).

Occupation: Lawyer, politician; served in Mexican War, 1847–48.

Religion: Episcopalian.

Family life: Married Jane Means Appleton (1806–1863) in 1834; they had three sons, all of whom died while still children.

Political career: Son of governor of New Hampshire, served in state legislature, then went to Congress as representative (1833–37) and senator (1837–42). Nominated by

the Democrats in 1852 as surprise "dark horse" candidate; unqualified and inept, was not renominated in 1856.

● *Highlights of his presidency:* Expansionist, but not able to gain territory he wanted—Alaska, Hawaii, Cuba. Succeeded in Gadsden Purchase. Used federal troops to restore order after Kansas-Nebraska Act became law.

Appearance: Stiffly erect in posture (5 feet 10 inches tall) gray-eyed.

James Buchanan (1791–1868)
15TH PRESIDENT, 1857–61

Born: April 23, 1791, Cove Gap, near Mercersburg, Pennsylvania.

Died: June 1, 1868, Lancaster, Pennslyvania.

Education: Graduated from Dickinson College (Carlisle, Pennsylvania).

Occupation: Lawyer, diplomat, public official; served briefly in War of 1812.

Religion: Presbyterian.

Family life: A lifelong bachelor.

Political career: Served in Pennsylvania legislature, then became a Jacksonian Democrat. Representative in Congress from Pennsylvania, 1821–31; senator, 1834–45. Was minister to Russia and to Great Britain;

served as Polk's secretary of state. Hoped for Democratic presidential nomination in 1844, 1848, 1852; elected in 1856.

● *Highlights of his presidency:* Failed to move decisively on secession of South Carolina, taking narrow view of presidential power.

Appearance: Tall (6 feet), muscular.

Abraham Lincoln (1809–1865)
16TH PRESIDENT, 1861–65

Born: February 12, 1809, Hodgenville, Hardin County, Kentucky.

Died: April 15, 1865, Washington, D.C. (fatally shot by John Wilkes Booth).

Education: Self-taught; studied law on his own.

Occupation: Lawyer, public official. As a young man was a farmer, store clerk, pilot for river flatboats.

Religion: No formal affiliation.

Family life: Married Mary Todd (1818–1882) in 1842; they had four sons. She was hot-tempered and highly emotional.

Political career: Elected to Illinois state legislature as a Whig, 1834, while still studying law; known as excellent debater, named floor leader; United States representative from Illinois, 1847–49. Joined antislavery

Republicans, ran for Senate and debated Stephen Douglas, 1858. Became known nationally and nominated for president, 1860; reelected 1864 because of Union successes in Civil War, but assassinated early in 1865.

● *Highlights of his presidency:* Opposed secession, prosecuted war to save Union. Issued Emancipation Proclamation. Was assassinated five days after Lee surrendered.

Appearance: Very tall (6 feet 4 inches) and rawboned, with black hair and beard.

Andrew Johnson (1808–1875)
17TH PRESIDENT, 1865–69

Born: December 29, 1808, Raleigh, North Carolina.

Died: July 31, 1875, Carter's Station, Tennessee.

Education: Never attended school; his future wife taught him to read and write when he was seventeen years old.

Occupation: Tailor, politician.

Religion: No formal affiliation.

Family life: Married Eliza McCardle (1810–1876) in 1827; they had three sons and two daughters.

Political career: As leader of local workingmen's party, entered Tennessee politics; served in United States House of Representatives (1843–53), then as governor of Tennessee; United States senator (1857–62). Nominated as vice-president, 1864, and succeeded after Lincoln's assassination, 1865. The first president to face an impeachment trial, Johnson later was reelected to the Senate, 1875.

● *Highlights of his presidency:* Tried to move toward peace. Thirteenth and Fourteenth Amendments passed. Opposed by radicals in Congress who ultimately tried to impeach him.

Appearance: Stocky (5 feet 10 inches), with brown hair worn long.

Ulysses Simpson Grant (1822–1885)
18TH PRESIDENT, 1869–77

Born: April 27, 1822, Point Pleasant, Ohio (named Hiram Ulysses Grant).

Died: July 23, 1885, Mount McGregor, New York.

Education: Graduated from United States Military Academy (West Point, New York).

Occupation: Soldier. Served in Mexican War after graduating from West Point; resigned from army, 1854, but unsuccessful in farming, business. Returned to army, 1861, and was leading Union general in Civil War.

Religion: Methodist.

Family life: Married Julia Dent (1826–1902) in 1848; they had three sons and one daughter.

Political career: As a hero of the Civil War, was nominated by the Republicans in 1868. After serving two terms, was defeated for renomination in 1880.

● *Highlights of his presidency:* Chose not to press terms of Fourteenth Amendment. Second administration marred by scandal— his appointees charged with accepting bribes.

Appearance: Short and stocky, with bushy, dark brown beard.

Rutherford Birchard Hayes (1822–1893)
19TH PRESIDENT, 1877–81

Born: October 4, 1822, Delaware, Ohio.

Died: January 17, 1893, Fremont, Ohio.

Education: Kenyon College (Gambier, Ohio); Harvard Law School.

Occupation: Lawyer, politician. Served as officer during Civil War.

Religion: No formal affiliation.

Family life: Married Lucy Webb (1831–1889) in 1852; she was the first president's wife with a college degree. They had seven sons and a daughter; celebrated their silver wedding anniversary in the White House.

Political career: Elected to United States

Abraham Lincoln   *Andrew Johnson*   *U. S. Grant*   *R.B. Hayes*   *James A Garfield*   *Chester A Arthur*

House of Representatives at end of army career; governor of Ohio, 1868–72 and 1876–77. Nominated by Republicans, 1876, to run for president against Samuel J. Tilden; the election, the most disputed in history, was decided by a special bipartisan commission in March 1877. Resigned after one term and worked for various social reforms.

● *Highlights of his presidency:* Elected by an election commission despite receiving a minority of popular votes. Removed federal troops from South. Urged civil service reform.

Appearance: About 5 feet 9 inches tall, brown hair and sandy red beard.

James Abram Garfield   (1831–1881)
20TH PRESIDENT, March–September 1881

Born: November 19, 1831, Orange, Ohio.

Died: September 19, 1881, in Elberon, New Jersey after being shot July 2 by a man who had been refused a political job.

Education: Graduated from Williams College (Williamstown, Massachusetts).

Occupation: College professor; taught ancient languages and literature at Hiram College and was college president, 1857–61. Served in Civil War as officer of Ohio volunteers.

Religion: Disciples of Christ.

Family life: Married Lucretia Rudolph (1832–1918) in 1858; they had five sons and two daughters.

Political career: Served as United States representative from Ohio, 1863–80; House minority leader, 1876; named to serve in Senate in 1880. Nominated as a "dark horse" by Republican convention, 1880; assassinated, 1881.

● *Highlights of his presidency:* Fought corruption in Post Office system. Promoted better Latin-American relations. Assassinated during first year in office.

Appearance: Tall (6 feet), strongly built, light brown beard.

Chester Alan Arthur   (1830–1886)
21ST PRESIDENT, 1881–85

Born: October 5, 1830, Fairfield, Vermont.

Died: November 18, 1886, New York, New York.

Education: Graduated from Union College (Schenectady, New York).

Occupation: Lawyer. Served with New York militia in Civil War, held political posts in army.

Religion: Episcopalian.

Family life: Married Ellen Herndon

(1837–1880) in 1859; they had two sons and a daughter.

Political career: Active in New York Republican party; named collector of customs of port of New York, 1871, but removed during civil service reform. Nominated for vice-president in 1880 to please pro-Grant wing of Republican party; became president on Garfield's death. Supported civil service reform and lost support of party leaders; not renominated, 1884.

● *Highlights of his presidency:* Recommended Civil Service Reform Act of 1883. Vetoed a Chinese Exclusion Bill (overridden). Organized the Alaska territory.

Appearance: Tall (6 feet 2 inches), handsome, with mustache and side whiskers.

Grover Cleveland   (1837–1908)
22ND PRESIDENT, 1885–89
24TH PRESIDENT, 1893–97

Born: March 18, 1837, Caldwell, New Jersey (full name Stephen Grover Cleveland).

Died: June 24, 1908, Princeton, New Jersey.

Education: Began as clerk in a law firm and became a lawyer; never attended college.

Occupation: Lawyer, public official.

Religion: Presbyterian.

Family life: Elected while still a bachelor, Cleveland married Frances Folsom (1864–1947) in 1886 in a White House wedding. They had three daughters (two born in the White House) and two sons.

Political career: Active in local Democratic politics in New York; served as sheriff and district attorney; elected reform mayor of Buffalo, 1881, governor of New York, 1883–85. Elected president, 1884, but defeated for second term; reelected in 1892, but gradually lost influence within party, left politics.

● *Highlights of his presidency:* For tariff reform. Supported the new Civil Service Commission. Induced Congress to repeal the Tenure Office Act. Regained presidency after Harrison. Had to deal with panic of 1893—bank failures, bankruptcies, and unemployment. Broke Pullman strike (to move the mail).

Appearance: Cleveland was a large man —5 feet 11 inches tall—weighing over 250 pounds.

Benjamin Harrison   (1833–1901)
23RD PRESIDENT, 1889–93

Born: August 20, 1833, North Bend, Ohio.

Died: March 13, 1901, Indianapolis, Indiana.

Education: Graduated from Miami University (Oxford, Ohio).

Occupation: Lawyer, politician. Fought in Civil War as head of infantry regiment.

Religion: Presbyterian.

Family life: Married Caroline Scott (1831–1892) in 1853; they had a son and a daughter. After her death, married her widowed niece, Mary Scott Dimmick (1859–1948); they had a daughter.

Political career: A prosperous corporation lawyer, prominent in local politics, ran for governor, 1876; became senator from Indiana, 1881–87. Nominated by Republicans in 1888; defeated in 1892 election.

● *Highlights of his presidency:* United States claimed Samoa. Aided in passage of Sherman Antitrust Act.

Appearance: Short and stocky (5 feet 6 inches), blue-eyed, with full beard.

William McKinley   (1843–1901)
25TH PRESIDENT, 1897–1901

Born: January 29, 1843, Niles, Ohio.

Died: September 14, 1901, Buffalo, New York, a week after being shot by an anarchist.

Education: Attended Allegheny College (Meadville, Pennsylvania).

Occupation: Lawyer, politician. Enlisted in Union army, served 1861–65.

Religion: Methodist.

Family life: Married Ida Saxton (1847–1907) in 1871; they had two daughters who died in infancy. Mrs. McKinley was an invalid.

Political career: Became active in Ohio Republican politics after the Civil War; served in United States House of Representatives, 1877–83 and 1885–91; defeated for Congress but elected governor of Ohio, 1892–96. Defeated William Jennings Bryan in presidential elections of 1896 and 1900; tried to prevent Spanish-American War. Shot early in second term.

● *Highlights of his presidency:* Presided during Spanish-American War. Philippines, Guam, and Puerto Rico ceded to United States. Assassinated early in second term.

Appearance: Medium height, with a high, broad forehead.

Theodore Roosevelt (1858–1919)
26TH PRESIDENT, 1901–09

Born: October 27, 1858, New York, New York.

Died: January 6, 1919, Oyster Bay, New York.

Education: Graduated from Harvard, attended Columbia Law School.

Occupation: Rancher, lawyer, public official, big-game hunter. Became a national hero leading "Rough Riders" in Spanish-American War. Led expeditions to Africa, South America.

Religion: Dutch Reformed.

Family life: Married Alice Hathaway Lee (1861–1884) in 1880; they had a daughter. In 1886 married Edith Kermit Carow (1861–1948); they had four sons and a daughter.

Political career: Entered New York state assembly as independent Republican, 1881; retired to ranch after deaths of wife and mother in 1884. Was United States Civil Service Commissioner, 1889–95, and held other posts as a reform official. Elected governor of New York and then nominated for vice-president, 1900; became President after McKinley's assassination, reelected in 1904. Given Nobel Peace Prize, 1905, for work in ending Russo-Japanese War. Tried unsuccessfully for renomination in 1912; formed own Progressive Party.

● *Highlights of his presidency:* For regulation of business trusts. Advocate of "big stick" in diplomacy. Encouraged building

THE UNITED STATES

83

of Panama Canal. Won Nobel Prize for mediating end to Russo-Japanese War.

Appearance: Medium height (5 feet 10 inches), bushy eyebrows and mustache, wide mouth, prominent teeth.

William Howard Taft (1857–1930)
27TH PRESIDENT, 1909–13

Born: September 15, 1857, Cincinnati, Ohio.

Died: March 8, 1930, Washington, D.C.

Education: Graduated from Yale University and Cincinnati Law School.

Occupation: Lawyer, jurist, public official. After his term, became law professor at Yale, 1913–21, and then United States Chief Justice, 1921–30.

Religion: Unitarian.

Family life: Married Helen ("Nellie") Herron (1861–1943) in 1886; they had two sons (one of them Senator Robert A. Taft) and a daughter.

Political career: Entered local Republican politics; appointed a judge, 1887; United States solicitor general, 1890. Governor of the Philippines, 1901; then, as secretary of war, was advisor to President Theodore Roosevelt. Later led conservative Republicans opposing Roosevelt, but lost 1912 election.

● *Highlights of his presidency:* Sixteenth Amendment added. Alaska gained full territorial government. Department of Labor established.

Appearance: A very large man, about 6 feet 2 inches tall, weighing over 300 pounds.

Woodrow Wilson (1856–1924)
28TH PRESIDENT, 1913–21

Born: December 28, 1856, Staunton, Virginia (named Thomas Woodrow Wilson).

Died: February 3, 1924, Washington, D.C.

Education: Attended Princeton University, University of Virginia Law School; Ph.D. from Johns Hopkins.

Occupation: Educator, lawyer, public official. A college professor, 1885–1902; president of Princeton University, 1902–10, before entering politics.

Religion: Presbyterian.

Family life: Married Ellen Axson (1860–1914) in 1885; they had three daughters. After her death he married a widow, Edith Galt (1872–1961), who took many duties during his illness.

Political career: Nominated for New Jersey governor, 1910; then by the Democrats for president, 1912. Reelected in 1916 on slogan "He kept us out of war." Urged United States membership in League of Nations; his health failed, 1919. Awarded Nobel Peace Prize, 1920.

● *Highlights of his presidency:* Federal Reserve System created. Clayton Antitrust Act passed. Strained relations with Mexico. In second term confronted World War I. Advocate of League of Nations. Lost bitter fight with Senate over peace treaty.

Appearance: Tall, lean, with narrow, face; scholarly appearance.

Warren Gamaliel Harding (1865–1923)
29TH PRESIDENT, 1921–23

Born: November 2, 1865, Corsica (Blooming Grove), Ohio.

Died: August 2, 1923, San Francisco, California.

Education: Graduated from Ohio Central College (Iberia, Ohio).

Occupation: Newspaper editor, politician. Bought Marion (Ohio) *Star* in 1884; its success made him influential in local politics.

Religion: Baptist.

Family life: Married Florence Kling DeWolfe (1860–1924) in 1891; she ran the business side of the newspaper.

Political career: Became prominent in

THE UNITED STATES

Ohio Republican politics, served in state senate, 1899–1903 and as lieutenant governor; served in United States Senate, 1915–21, and was nominated as "dark horse" candidate in 1920. Administration corrupt, with many rumored scandals; he died suddenly while on a national tour.

● *Highlights of his presidency:* Convened Washington Disarmament Conference, resulting in treaty. Picked strong Cabinet members such as Herbert Hoover and Charles Evans Hughes. Teapot Dome scandal involving others in administration marred his presidency. Died in office.

Appearance: Tall (6 feet), regarded as handsome, with silver-gray hair.

Calvin Coolidge (1872–1933)
30TH PRESIDENT, 1923–29

Born: July 4, 1872, Plymouth, Vermont.
Died: January 5, 1933, Northampton, Massachusetts.
Education: Graduated from Amherst College (Amherst, Massachusetts).
Occupation: Lawyer, politician.
Religion: Congregationalist.
Family life: Married Grace Anna Goodhue (1879–1957), a teacher, in 1905; they had two sons.

Political career: Entered politics in Massachusetts and rose steadily; state senator, 1912–15; lieutenant governor and governor, 1916–20. Became known for firm, quiet settlement of Boston police strike and given Republican vice-presidential nomination, 1920. Succeeded after Harding's death and reelected, 1924. Known for brief speeches; said simply, "I do not choose to run . . ." in 1928.

● *Highlights of his presidency:* Probusiness . . . "The business of America is business." Opposed to joining League of Nations, but for Kellogg-Briand Pact outlawing war. Relations with Mexico improved.

Appearance: Medium height (5 feet 10 inches), slim, with expressionless features.

Herbert Clark Hoover (1874–1964)
31ST PRESIDENT, 1929–33

Born: August 10, 1874, West Branch, Iowa.
Died: October 20, 1964, New York, New York.
Education: Graduated from Stanford University (Palo Alto, California).
Occupation: Mining engineer, philanthropist, public official. Successful engineering career made him a millionaire,

1895–1914. Headed numerous war relief organizations during and after World War I.

Religion: Quaker.

Family life: Married Lou Henry (1874–1944) in 1899. They had two sons.

Political career: Became internationally known for war relief administration; secretary of commerce for Harding and Coolidge, 1921–28. Republican nominee for president, 1928, defeated in 1932 because of economic crash and Depression. Headed postwar European relief and "Hoover commissions" on government reform, 1947–49, 1953–55.

● *Highlights of his presidency:* Seven months after inaugural stock market crashed, bringing on Great Depression. Used troops to disband veterans marching in Washington for bonuses. Urged withdrawal of American troops from Nicaragua and Haiti.

Appearance: 5 feet 11 inches, solidly built, square-faced, ruddy complexion, graying blond hair.

Franklin Delano Roosevelt (1882–1945)
32ND PRESIDENT, 1933–45

Born: January 30, 1882, Hyde Park, New York.

Died: April 12, 1945, Warm Springs, Georgia (while in office).

Education: Graduated from Harvard; attended Columbia Law School.

Occupation: Lawyer, public official.

Religion: Episcopalian.

Family life: Married Eleanor Roosevelt (1884–1962), a cousin, in 1905; her uncle, Theodore Roosevelt, gave her away. They had five sons and one daughter; a son died in infancy. In her own right, Eleanor Roosevelt was outstanding for her work in human rights and politics.

Political career: Entered politics in New York State, named assistant Navy secretary, 1913–20; Democratic vice-presidential candidate, 1920. Remained active despite polio attack, 1921; elected New York governor, 1929–33, and easily won 1932 presidential election. Because of Depression and World War II, reelected three times, but died in office.

● *Highlights of his presidency:* Reaction to Depression was action. First one hundred days marked by major legislation—New Deal. Fought the Supreme Court, which declared several acts unconstitutional. Committed United States to Allied cause in World War II, working closely with Churchill. Strong advocate of United Nations.

Appearance: Tall and solidly built, with high forehead; after crippling polio attack, wore leg braces, later used wheelchair. Wore pince-nez glasses.

Harry S. Truman (1884–1972)
33RD PRESIDENT, 1945–53

Born: May 8, 1884, Lamar, Missouri.

Died: December 26, 1972, Independence, Missouri.

Education: Went to work after high school; attended law school, 1923–25.

Occupation: Judge, businessman, politician. Worked on farm, 1906–17, then joined army; fought in World War I until 1919, discharged as major; ran haberdashery business, 1919–21.

Religion: Baptist.

Family life: Married Bess Wallace (1885–   ) in 1919; they had one daughter, Margaret.

Political career: Appointed to local Democratic offices and judgeships in 1920s; elected to United States Senate from Missouri, 1934–45; became known as head of Senate committee investigating defense projects. Nominated for vice-president, 1944, and became President on death of Roosevelt; reelected, 1948, in upset election; retired in 1953.

- *Highlights of his presidency:* Extension of New Deal (Fair Deal). Frustrated by "do-nothing" Republican Congress. European recovery promoted by Marshall Plan. Created North Atlantic Treaty Organization (NATO). Presided over beginning of Cold War.

Appearance: Medium height, with graying hair, round face, bright eyes behind glasses.

Dwight David Eisenhower (1890–1969)
34TH PRESIDENT, 1953–61

Born: October 14, 1890, Denison, Texas.
Died: March 28, 1969, Washington, D.C.
Education: Graduated from United States Military Academy (West Point, New York).
Occupation: Army officer. A career soldier, Eisenhower served in various parts of the world; became Third Army chief of staff, 1941, as brigadier general; named commander of European Theater, World War II, in 1942; and supreme Allied commander, 1944; led D-Day invasion, 1944; chief of staff, 1945–48; retired from active duty, but named NATO commander, 1950.
Religion: Presbyterian.
Family life: Married Mamie Geneva

Doud (1896–   ) in 1916; they had two sons, one of whom died in childhood. Eisenhower's grandson later married the daughter of President Richard Nixon.

Political career: A war hero, was nominated for the presidency in 1952; reelected in 1956.

- *Highlights of his presidency:* Ended Korean War. Promoted highway building program. Refused to oppose Senator Joseph McCarthy. Sent federal troops to Arkansas to enforce school desegregation. Broke diplomatic relations with Cuba.

Appearance: About 5 feet 11 inches tall, athletic build; bald.

John Fitzgerald Kennedy (1917–1963)
35TH PRESIDENT, 1960–63

Born: May 29, 1917, Brookline, Massachusetts.
Died: November 22, 1963, Dallas, Texas, shot by an assassin.
Education: Graduated from Harvard.
Occupation: Writer, politician; his *Profiles in Courage* (1954) won a Pulitzer Prize. Became a hero in World War II as PT-boat commander.
Religion: Roman Catholic.
Family life: Married Jacqueline Lee

Bouvier (1929–   ) in 1953; their children were Caroline and John, Jr.

Political career: The son of a powerful political family, entered Massachusetts politics after World War II. Congressman from Massachusetts, 1946–51; elected United States senator in 1952. Contender for Democratic vice-presidential nomination, 1956; nominated for president, 1960; the youngest man and first Roman Catholic to be elected. Fatally shot while riding in a motorcade in Dallas, Texas.

● *Highlights of his presidency:* Dealt with steel crisis when companies raised prices after unions held the line. Approved Bay of Pigs invasion in Cuba, which failed. Succeeded in getting Russians to withdraw missiles from Cuba. Assassinated in office.

Appearance: Tall and athletic looking, widely regarded as handsome.

Lyndon Baines Johnson (1908–1973)
36TH PRESIDENT, 1963–69

Born: August 27, 1908, near Stonewall, Texas.
Died: January 22, 1973, Johnson City, Texas.
Education: Graduated from Southwest Texas State Teachers College.
Occupation: Rancher, teacher, politician.
Religion: Church of Christ.
Family life: Married Claudia Alta (Lady Bird) Taylor (1912–   ) in 1934; they had two daughters, Luci and Lynda.
Political career: Began as aide to Texas congressman; elected congressman in 1937, served until elected senator in 1948. Became Senate Democratic leader, 1953, and majority leader, 1955; skillful in passing legislation. Contender for presidential nomination, 1960, but named to be vice-president; became president, 1963, after Kennedy's assassination. Began program of "Great Society," reelected 1964; in

1968, because of Vietnam controversy, announced he would not run again.
● *Highlights of his presidency:* Guided 1964 Civil Rights Act through Congress. Initiated "Great Society" programs aimed at medical care for aged, aid to education, improved housing. Intervened militarily in Dominican Republic. Dominant foreign policy issue was the Vietnam War.

Appearance: Tall and rangy, added weight as president; strong features.

Richard Milhous Nixon (1913–   )
37TH PRESIDENT, 1969–74

Born: January 9, 1913, Yorba Linda, California.
Education: Graduated from Whittier College (California) and Duke University Law School (Durham, North Carolina).
Occupation: Lawyer, public official.
Religion: Quaker background.
Family life: Married Thelma (Patricia) Ryan (1913–   ) in 1940; they have two daughters, Julie and Patricia.
Political career: Entered politics after World War II naval service; congressman from California, 1946–51; elected United States senator in 1950; vice-president under Eisenhower, 1953–61. Nominated by Republicans for president in 1960, but defeated by Kennedy after television debates. Defeated for governor of California in 1962 and announced retirement from politics; nominated for presidency in 1968 and again in 1972.
● *Highlights of his presidency:* Preoccupied with trying to end war in Indochina in first term. Promoted more normal relations with Russia and China through detente. Second term marred by Watergate scandal, which put him under increasing pressure to resign or face impeachment trial. Resigned from office, August 9, 1974.

Appearance: Medium height; dark hair, gray at temples; turned-up nose.

Richard M Nixon   *Gerald Ford*   *Jimmy Carter*

Gerald R. Ford (1913–   )
38TH PRESIDENT, 1974–77

Born: July 14, 1913, Omaha, Nebraska.

Education: Graduated from University of Michigan and Yale University Law School.

Occupation: Lawyer, public official.

Religion: Episcopalian.

Family life: Married Elizabeth Bloomer Warren (1918–   ), whose first marriage ended in divorce, in 1948. They have three sons and one daughter.

Political career: Practiced law briefly in Grand Rapids, Michigan, before entering the 1948 Republican Party primary. He upset the incumbent congressman and was elected that fall. He continued to be elected and spent twenty-five years in the House of Representatives, eight as Republican Leader. After Vice-President Spiro Agnew resigned in October, 1973, Ford was nominated by President Nixon to replace him. The Senate approved by 92–3 on November 27 and the House by 387–35 on December 6, and Ford became vice-president that day. He became president August 9, 1974, when President Nixon resigned.

● *Highlights of his presidency:* Pardoned Richard Nixon. Provided continuity from Nixon foreign policy by deciding on Henry Kissinger as secretary of state.

Appearance: Tall, broad-shouldered, trim. Large head, balding gray-blond hair.

Jimmy (James Earl) Carter (1924–   )
39TH PRESIDENT

Born: October 1, 1924, Plains, Georgia.

Education: Attended Georgia Institute of Technology and graduated from the United States Naval Academy at Annapolis.

Occupation: Farmer, warehouse operator, public official.

Religion: Baptist.

Family life: Married Rosalynn Smith (1927–   ) in 1946. They have three sons and a daughter.

Political career: Resigned his commission in the Navy to take over family business when his father died in 1953. Elected to the Georgia State Senate, ran unsuccessfully for governor in 1966, but won in 1970. Limited by Georgia law to one term, he devoted full time from 1974–1976 to his quest for the presidency.

● *Highlights of his presidency:* Has advocated policy on energy to conserve oil while developing alternative sources. Advocate of human rights as part of foreign policy.

Appearance: Medium height, graying hair, jowly but otherwise trim. Famous for his smile.

Influential Men and Women

Anthony, Susan Brownell

Born: February 15, 1820, in Adams, Massachusetts.

Died: March 13, 1906, in Rochester, New York.

Susan B. Anthony grew up in a Quaker family and was educated at her father's school. She was a schoolteacher herself from 1846 to 1849, when she gave up teaching to become a social reformer. She later became a leader of the women's suffrage movement. Her first efforts at social reform were directed at temperance (abstaining from drinking alcoholic beverages). She was among the organizers of the Woman's State Temperance Society of New York. She also took part in the abolitionist movement, but her major effort was directed at gaining voting rights for women. She tried to attach a provision to the Fourteenth Amendment to give women the right to vote. In 1869 she became president of the National Woman Suffrage Association. She died before passage of the Nineteenth Amendment, which established women's voting rights.

Barton, Clara

Born: December 25, 1821, in Oxford, Massachusetts.

Died: April 12, 1912, at Glen Echo, Maryland.

Clara Barton taught school in New Jersey, but gave it up in 1854 to go to Washington, D.C., where at the beginning of the Civil War she organized supply and nursing services for sick and wounded Union Army troops. As an unpaid worker she did her

Red Cross nurses in Cuba caring for wounded Spanish-American War soldiers. Clara Barton founded the American Red Cross.

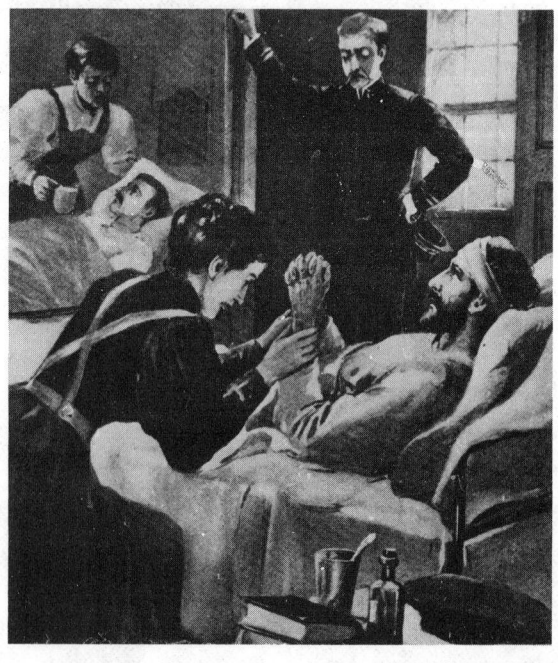

work behind the lines and on the battlefields. With the Army of the James, she acted as superintendent of nurses. After the war she was in charge of a government effort to locate missing soldiers. During the Franco-Prussian War she was active in relief activities for the International Red Cross at Geneva. When she returned to the United States, she conducted a campaign to establish an American Red Cross. As a result of her efforts, a National Society of the Red Cross was organized in 1881, with Miss Barton as its president. She served until 1904, active in relieving suffering caused by wars and disasters, such as the Spanish-American War, the Boer War, and the Galveston flood of 1900. She was responsible for getting the "American Amendment" included at the Geneva International Conference in 1884. This amendment specified that in extreme peacetime emergencies the Red Cross should carry out humanitarian work as it had been doing during wars.

Bell, Alexander Graham

Born: March 3, 1847, in Edinburgh, Scotland.

Died: August 2, 1922, on Cape Breton Island in Nova Scotia.

Alexander Graham Bell was the inventor of the telephone, which grew out of his work as an educator of the deaf. He was educated in the secondary schools of Edinburgh and became an assistant to his father, who invented the Visible Speech System in 1867. The family moved to Canada in 1870, and young Bell began giving instructions in his father's system to teachers of the deaf throughout New England. From 1873 through 1877 he was a professor of vocal physiology and the mechanics of speech at Boston University. His interest in the deaf and in acoustics led to a series of experiments, out of which came the first practical demonstration, at Boston in 1876, of the magneto-electric telephone. The Bell Telephone Company was organized in 1877, and development of the telephone proceeded rapidly after that. Bell became an American citizen in 1882 and continued his work with the deaf along with further experimentation in the transmission of sound.

Carnegie, Andrew

Born: November 25, 1835, in Dunfermline, Scotland.

Died: August 11, 1919, at Lenox, Massachusetts.

Andrew Carnegie came to the United States with his parents in 1848 and went to work in a textile mill in Allegheny, Pennsylvania. He became a messenger in the Pittsburgh telegraph office in 1849, personal telegrapher to the superintendent of the Pennsylvania railroad in 1853, and head of the eastern military telegraph lines during the Civil War. After the war, he organized businesses in the iron and steel industry. After 1873 he concentrated on the steel industry and for the next thirty years accumulated holdings that by 1900 made him the dominant figure in the steel industry. In 1901 he sold his interests to what became the United States Steel Corporation. He established the Carnegie trusts, foundations for the advancement of teaching and for peace. His enormous wealth was used to endow numerous libraries all over the world. This strong commitment to libraries and learning is almost as important a legacy as his contributions to the steel industry.

Carver, George Washington

Born: In 1860, near Diamond Grove, Missouri.

Died: January 5, 1943, at Tuskegee, Alabama.

George Washington Carver was born of slave parents and worked his way through high school in Kansas and through Iowa

State College, where he was awarded a Bachelor of Science degree in 1894 and a Master of Science degree in 1896. He stayed at Iowa State as head of the college greenhouse while pursuing his degrees, but moved to Tuskegee Institute afterwards as the director of agricultural research, remaining there the rest of his life. He worked on the diversified use of common agricultural products. This had an important influence on the diversification of southern agriculture from a single-crop basis. From the peanut and sweet potato he developed more than a hundred different products, including peanut butter, plastics, lubricants, dyes, medicines, and ink.

Edison, Thomas Alva

Born: February 11, 1847, in Milan, Ohio.
Died: October 18, 1931, at West Orange, New Jersey.
Thomas Edison was taught at home by his mother because he was considered a slow learner in school. As a boy he sold candy, newspapers, and other articles on trains. He became interested in the telegraph, becoming a telegraph operator himself in 1863. In 1868 he joined the Western Union Telegraph Company in Boston. The next year he patented his first invention—an electrographic vote recorder. That same year he moved to New York and formed a partnership called Pope, Edison and Company, which was dissolved in 1870. In 1876 he started the Edison research laboratories at Menlo Park, New Jersey. He later moved it to larger quarters in Orange, New Jersey, where it became known as the Edison General Electric Company, later to be absorbed into what is now General Electric. In 1877 he invented the phonograph, later the incandescent lamp (light bulbs). Edison was granted more than 1000 patents. Most of them were the result of the collective effort of people working in his laboratories.

Among his patents are those for the storage battery, dictaphone, mimeograph, telegraph signal box, ore separator, electric safety lantern, and electric locomotive.

Ford, Henry

Born: July 30, 1863, near Dearborn, Michigan.
Died: April 7, 1947, at Dearborn.
Henry Ford quit school at the age of fifteen and went to work as a machine shop apprentice in Detroit. He later became a traveling repairman for a farm machinery company. For several years after that, he was the operator of his own sawmill. In 1887 he became chief engineer for the Edison Illuminating Company in Detroit. He built his first automobile in 1896, organized the Ford Motor Company in 1903, and produced the first Model T automobile in 1909. This was done by using standardized features and assembly line production, which made Ford the symbol of modern technology. In 1914 he instituted the eight-hour day and the minimum five-dollar daily wage. He worked for world peace and, with his son, Edsel, established the Ford Foundation, which has carried on a diversified philanthropic program, mainly in education.

Franklin, Benjamin

Born: January 17, 1706, in Boston, Massachusetts.
Died: April 17, 1790, in Philadelphia, Pennsylvania.
Benjamin Franklin was a statesman, diplomat, editor, and scientist. He went to work in his father's tallow shop after very little schooling; later he worked in his brother's printing shop. In 1723 he moved to Philadelphia and worked as a printer. In 1729 he bought a newspaper called the *Pennsyl-*

Benjamin Franklin was a writer, publisher, scientist inventor, and statesman. He represented his country at the French court during the American Revolution.

vania Gazette, which published an annual edition of a publication called *Poor Richard's Almanack* from 1732 until 1757. He gained international fame by inventing the Franklin stove in 1742, and by identifying the relation of lightning to electricity in 1752. He was a member of the Second Continental Congress, and the first postmaster general of the United States. He helped draft the Declaration of Independence, and was a member of the Constitutional Convention. At the Constitutional Convention, he was instrumental in working out the compromise that led to the representation of the states in the House of Representatives according to state population.

Gompers, Samuel

Born: January 27, 1850, in London, England.

Died: December 13, 1924, in San Antonio, Texas.

Samuel Gompers was an apprentice cigarmaker in London, England. He came to the United States in 1863, joined the Cigarmaker's Union, and became its president in 1877. Samuel Gompers was one of the principal organizers of the Federation of Organized Trades and Labor Unions in 1881. This was reorganized in 1886 as the American Federation of Labor. Gompers was its president from then until his death, with the exception of one year, 1895. He became labor's most influential spokesman, stressing practical goals such as wages, hours, and safety. He opposed radicals in the movement, active identification with a particular political party, and the formation of a separate labor party.

King, Martin Luther, Jr.

Born: January 15, 1929, in Atlanta, Georgia.

Died: April 4, 1968, in Memphis, Tennessee, killed by an assassin.

Martin Luther King was graduated from Morehouse College in 1948, received the Bachelor of Divinity degree from Crozer Theological Seminary in 1951 and the Doctor of Philosophy degree from Boston University in 1955. As pastor of a Baptist church in Montgomery, Alabama, he organized a Black bus boycott. He was an advocate of nonviolent demonstration. His "Letter from a Birmingham Jail" inspired the growing civil rights movement. Martin Luther King was the founder of the Southern Christian Leadership Conference, out of which have come other leaders such as Jesse Jackson and Andrew Young. He led the 1963 march on Washington of over 200,000 followers. It was there that he delivered the eloquent and memorable "I Have a Dream" address. King was awarded the Nobel Peace Prize in 1964. He opposed the Vietnam War in 1967 and was turning his attention to a nationwide campaign to help the poor at the time of his death.

Marshall, John

Born: September 24, 1755, in Germantown, Virginia.

Died: July 6, 1835, in Philadelphia, Pennsylvania.

John Marshall served in the American Revolution as an officer, briefly attended law school at the College of William and Mary and was admitted to the bar in 1783. He served as a Federalist Party Congressman for one term and then became secretary of state under John Adams. He became chief justice of the Supreme Court in 1801 and served for thirty-four years in that office. During those years the Court became an important shaper of American politics and gained significant prestige. Among his most important opinions were: *Marbury* v. *Madison* in 1803, in which the right of judicial review (not established in the Constitution) was asserted; *McCulloch* v. *Maryland* in 1819, with its doctrine of implied constitutional powers; and *Gibbons* v. *Ogden* in 1824, with its broad interpretation of the Commerce clause of the Constitution.

Morse, Samuel Finley Breese

Born: April 27, 1791, in Charlestown, Massachusetts.

Died: April 2, 1872, in New York City.

After graduating from Yale in 1810, Samuel F. B. Morse went to England to study art. Returning four years later, he opened a studio in Boston. He was not able to attract enough customers so he moved to Charleston, South Carolina. There he was more successful, but he left and settled in New York City in 1823. In 1825 he was commissioned to do two portraits of Lafayette,

which he painted in Washington, D.C. He was the chief founder of the National Academy of Design and served as its first president from 1826 to 1842. About 1837 he abandoned painting and devoted himself to experimenting with the transmission of signals by electricity. Out of this came his invention of a series of dots and dashes known as the Morse code. His most significant contribution was his system of electromagnetic relays, which made possible the transmission of messages over great distances.

Nader, Ralph

Born: February 27, 1934, in Winstead, Connecticut.

The name Ralph Nader has become almost synonymous with "consumer advocate." He was graduated from Princeton in 1955 and from Harvard Law School in 1958. He gained national attention with the publication of his book *Unsafe at Any Speed* in 1965. This book was a broad attack on the automobile industry, which he charged with placing style, comfort, and horsepower above safety. He has investigated health and safety conditions in the coal industry, the meat industry, gas pipelines, and old-age homes. Almost single-handedly Nader has been the driving force behind consumer protection in the 1960s and 1970s.

Ochs, Adolph Simon

Born: March 12, 1858, in Cincinnati, Ohio.

Died: April 8, 1935, at Chattanooga, Tennessee.

Adolph Ochs received most of his schooling from his parents. He served an apprenticeship on the *Knoxville Chronicle* and, in 1878, bought a controlling interest in the *Chattanooga Times*. In 1896 he became the publisher of the *New York Times,* which was then on the verge of bankruptcy. He changed its policy from that of sensational journalism to responsible reporting; the *New York Times* became the most respected newspaper in the United States. It is known as the "newspaper of record" because of its responsible coverage of events. The *Times* has become an indispensable medium of information for governments as well as for the general reading public.

Oppenheimer, J. Robert

Born: April 22, 1904, in New York City.
Died: February 18, 1967, at Princeton, New Jersey.
Robert Oppenheimer was graduated from Harvard in 1925 and took his Ph.D. degree at Gottingen, Germany, in 1927. In 1929 he joined the physics faculty at both the University of California, Berkeley, and the California Institute of Technology. Because of his grasp of a broad range of physics, he was appointed director of the Los Alamos Science Laboratory in 1942. There, he supervised the work of some 4000 scientists, which resulted in production of the atomic bomb in 1945. He was the main author of the Baruch Plan, which proposed international control of the use of atomic energy. He later headed the Institute for Advanced Study at Princeton.

Rockefeller, John Davison

Born: July 8, 1839, in Richford, New York.
Died: May 23, 1937, at Ormond Beach, Florida.
John D. Rockefeller was educated in Cleveland, Ohio, where he later worked as a clerk and bookkeeper. After the 1859 discovery of oil at Titusville, Pennsylvania, Rockefeller, along with Samuel Andrews

John D. Rockefeller, 1884. Rockefeller established the first great American oil fortune. He was successful in railroads, banks, finance, and other enterprises. The Rockefellers became, and have remained, one of the truly influential American families, whose members are active in government, banking, and real estate.

(inventor of a cheap process for refining oil) and his brother, William Rockefeller, established the firm of William Rockefeller and Company and the Standard Oil Works of Cleveland. This led to the organization of the Standard Oil Company in 1867, which became the first great industrial combination. In the next several years it was able to eliminate almost all competition and became known as the Standard Oil trust. The company, throughout its history, has had to defend itself against charges of monopolistic practices. Rockefeller amassed a fortune estimated at $1 billion by the time he retired. He spent his later years in various philanthropic efforts, including the endowment of the University of Chicago, the Rockefeller Institute of Medical Research, and the Rockefeller Foundation.

Salk, Jonas

Born: October 28, 1914, in New York City.

Jonas Salk was graduated from City College in New York in 1934 and was awarded the M.D. degree in 1939 by the New York University College of Medicine. He carried on virus research under Thomas Francis, Jr. at the N.Y.U. College of Medicine. When Francis moved to the University of Michigan's School of Public Health, Salk joined him to carry on research on influenza vaccine. In 1947 Salk switched to the University of Pittsburgh School of Medicine as director of the Virus Research Laboratory. With funds provided by the National Foundation for Infantile Paralysis, Salk experimented with various strains of virus on monkey tissue, killing the viruses in the vaccine with formaldehyde. The vaccine was pronounced safe for humans in 1955 and was found to be 80 to 90 percent effective. Through his pioneering efforts, the disease poliomyelitis has been almost totally eradicated. Dr. Salk remains active in medical research.

Washington, Booker T.

Born: April 5, 1856, at Hale's Ford, Virginia.

Died: November 14, 1915, at Tuskegee, Alabama.

Booker T. Washington worked his way through Hampton Institute as a janitor and was graduated in 1875. He later taught there, before being asked to organize Tuskegee Institute, a college for Black students who wanted to become teachers or get training for industry. He felt that education and training of Blacks would better serve the cause of their advancement than political activism. He served as principal of the institute until his death.

Dr. Jonas Salk, developer of a vaccine against polio in 1955. Dr. Albert Sabin developed another polio vaccine in 1961. These vaccines have greatly reduced incidence of the disease.

Booker T. Washington. Born a slave, Washington became the founder and head of Tuskegee Institute in Tuskegee, Alabama. He told his life story in *Up from Slavery.*

THE UNITED STATES

Whitney, Eli

Born: December 8, 1765, in Westboro, Massachusetts.

Died: January 8, 1825, in New Haven, Connecticut.

Eli Whitney's father operated a metalworking shop, and young Whitney learned about mechanical crafts as he was growing up. He was graduated from Yale in 1789 and went south to study law. While he was there, he designed the cotton gin, a machine that overcame the tedious job of cleaning green seed cotton by hand. His large model, on which he received a patent in 1794, revolutionized the agriculture of the South. Whitney returned to New Haven and entered the firearms business. He was awarded a government contract for 10,000 muskets in 1798 and devised a system of interchangeable parts to manufacture them. The idea of interchangeable parts became the key to modern mass production.

Wiener, Norbert

Born: November 26, 1894, in Columbia, Missouri.

Died: March 18, 1964, in Stockholm, Sweden.

Norbert Wiener was the son of a Harvard professor. A child prodigy, he was graduated from Tufts University at the age of fourteen and earned the Ph.D. degree at Harvard at the age of nineteen. He studied in Europe before returning to college teaching at Harvard and Maine and then, from 1919 until 1960, at the Massachusetts Institute of Technology. He was both a mathematician and a philosopher. His early interest in the flow of information along a wave was continued in his work for the government in World War II. He helped develop radar, coding, and gun-aiming devices, but his major contribution was in computers. He coined the term *cybernetics* to define the new science of automation.

The flying machines built by Orville and Wilbur Wright marked the beginning of the aviation era. Here, Wilbur mans the crude wooden levers that controlled the machine in flight.

Wright, Wilbur and Orville

Born: April 16, 1867, in Millville, Indiana; August 19, 1871, in Dayton Ohio.

Died: May 30, 1912, at Dayton, Ohio; January 30, 1948, in Dayton, Ohio.

Neither of the Wright brothers had much formal education. In 1892 they opened a shop in Dayton and began manufacturing bicycles. They became fascinated with aviation about 1898 and read articles and books on kites, gliders, and aeronautics. They went to Kitty Hawk, North Carolina, to experiment with gliders. That led to development of their own wind tunnel and testing of hundreds of wing and airplane surfaces. In October of 1902 they began construction of a powered aircraft. It weighed 750 pounds and carried a 170-pound, 12-horsepower gasoline motor. This was completed at Kitty Hawk, where on December 17, 1903, Orville Wright made the first piloted flight of a powered airplane. They returned to Dayton to improve the machine, and the results enabled them to stay aloft much longer. Their improved model was patented in May of 1906.

Zenger, John Peter

Born: In 1697, in Germany.
Died: July 28, 1746, in New York City.
Peter Zenger arrived in New York City in 1710 and served as an apprentice printer. In 1726 he started an independent printing business, and in 1733 he became the editor and publisher of the *New York Weekly Journal.* The *Journal* opposed the provincial administration in a series of articles. In 1734 Zenger, as the publisher, was arrested and imprisoned for ten months before he was brought to trial in 1735 for seditious libel. His lawyer, Andrew Hamilton of Philadelphia, succeeded in gaining Zenger's acquittal. The case is a landmark in the history of freedom of the press in the United States.

Words That Shaped U.S. History

The world will little note, nor long remember what we say here, but it can never forget what they did here. It is for us the living, rather, to be dedicated here to the unfinished work which they who fought here have thus far so nobly advanced. It is rather for us to be here dedicated to the great task remaining before us—that from these honored dead we take increased devotion to that cause for which they here gave the last full measure of devotion—that we here highly resolve that these dead shall not have died in vain—that this nation, under God, shall have a new birth of freedom—and that government of the people, by the people, for the people, shall not perish from the earth.

Abraham Lincoln
(from *The Gettysburg Address,* 1863)

In the long history of the world, only a few generations have been granted the role of defending freedom in its hour of maximum danger. I do not shrink from this responsibility—I welcome it. I do not believe that any of us would exchange places with any other people or any other generation. The energy, the faith, the devotion which we bring to this endeavor will light our country and all who serve it—and the glow from that fire can truly light the world.

And so, my fellow Americans: Ask not what your country can do for you—ask what you can do for your country.

My fellow citizens of the world: Ask not what America will do for you, but what together we can do for the freedom of man. . . .

John F. Kennedy
(from Inaugural Address, 1961)

THE UNITED STATES

Sir, we have done everything that could be done to avert the storm which is now coming on. We have petitioned; we have remonstrated; we have supplicated; we have prostrated ourselves before the tyrannical hands of the ministry and parliament. Our petitions have been slighted; our remonstrances have produced additional violence and insult; our supplications have been disregarded; and we have been spurned, with contempt, from the foot of the throne. In vain, after these things, may we indulge the fond hope of peace and reconciliation. There is no longer any room for hope. If we wish to be free . . . we must fight! I repeat it sir, we must fight! . . . Why stand we here idle? What is it that gentlemen wish? What would they have? Is life so dear or peace so sweet as to be purchased at the price of chains and slavery? Forbid it, Almighty God! I know not what course others may take—but as for me, give me liberty, or give me death!

Patrick Henry
(from "Give Me Liberty . . ." 1775)

. . . I still have a dream. It is a dream deeply rooted in the American dream. I have a dream that one day this nation will rise up, live out the true meaning of its creed: "We hold these truths to be self-evident, that all men are created equal."

. . . I have a dream that my four little children will one day live in a nation where they will not be judged by the color of their skin but by the context of their character.

. . . I have a dream today . . . I have a dream that one day every valley shall be exalted, every hill and mountain shall be made low. The rough places will be made plain, and the crooked places will be made straight. And the glory of the Lord shall be revealed, and all flesh shall see it together. This is our hope. This is the faith that I go back to the South with.

Martin Luther King, Jr. (1929–1968). The noted Black leader was awarded the Nobel Peace Prize in 1964 but fell victim to an assassin in Memphis, Tennessee, in 1968.

With this faith we will be able to hew out of the mountain of despair a stone of hope. . . . With this faith we will be able to work together, to pray together, to struggle together, to go to jail together, to stand up for freedom together, knowing that we will be free one day.

Martin Luther King
(from "I Have a Dream," 1963)

By the rude bridge that arched the flood,
Their flag to April's breeze unfurled,
Here once the embattled farmers stood,
And fired the shot heard round the world.

Ralph Waldo Emerson
("Concord Hymn," 1st stanza)
Sung at the completion of the Concord
Monument, April 19, 1863.

You may fire when ready, Gridley.

George Dewey
(At battle of Manila Bay, May 1, 1898)

THE UNITED STATES

O Columbia, the gem of the ocean,
  The home of the brave and the free,
The shrine of each patriot's devotion,
  A world offers homage to thee.
Thy mandates make heroes assemble
  When Liberty's form stands in view;
Thy banners make tyranny tremble
  When borne by the red, white and blue.
When borne by the red, white and blue,
When borne by the red, white and blue,
Thy banners make tyranny tremble
When borne by the red, white and blue.

Author Unknown
("Columbia, the Gem of the Ocean," 1st stanza)
First sung in Philadelphia about 1843.

Give me your tired, your poor,
Your huddled masses yearning to breathe
  free,
The wretched refuse of your teeming shore.
Send these, the homeless, tempest-tossed
  to me,
I lift my lamp beside the golden door!

Emma Lazarus
(from "The New Colossus")

Mine eyes have seen the glory of the
  coming of the Lord:
He is trampling out the vintage where
  the grapes of wrath are stored;
He hath loosed the fateful lightning
  of his terrible swift sword:
His truth is marching on.

Julia Ward Howe
(from the "Battle Hymn of the Republic")

So it's home again, and home again,
  America for me!
My heart is turning home again, and
  there I long to be
In the land of youth and freedom beyond
  the ocean bars,
Where the air is full of sunlight
  and the flag is full of stars.

Henry Van Dyke
("America for Me," 2nd stanza)

When a man assumes a public trust, he should consider himself as public property.

Thomas Jefferson

The God who gave us life, gave us liberty at the same time.

Thomas Jefferson

Equal and exact justice to all men, of whatever state or persuasion, religious or political; peace, commerce, and honest friendship with all nations, — entangling alliances with none; the support of State governments in all their rights, as the most competent administrations for our domestic concerns, and the surest bulwarks against anti-republican tendencies; the preservation of the general government in its whole constitutional vigour, as the sheet anchor of our peace at home and safety abroad; . . . freedom of religion; freedom of the press; freedom of person under the protection of the habeas corpus; and trial by juries impartially selected—these principles form the bright constellation which has gone before us, and guided our steps through an age of revolution and reformation.

Thomas Jefferson

I hold the maxim no less applicable to public than to private affairs, that honesty is always the best policy.

George Washington
(Farewell Address)

The battle, sir, is not to the strong alone; it is to the vigilant, the active, the brave.

Patrick Henry

I am not a Virginian, but an American.

Patrick Henry

These are the times that try men's souls.

Thomas Paine

Patrick Henry (1736–1799). A prominent figure in Virginia political life during the eighteenth century, Henry was a champion of the Revolutionary cause and supported adoption of the Bill of Rights.

Daniel Webster (1782–1852). This great American statesman rose to prominence during service in the U.S. Senate, where he participated in debates on states rights and nullification.

Tarquin and Caesar each had his Brutus, Charles the First his Cromwell, and George the Third ["Treason!" cried the Speaker] *may profit by their example*. If *this* be treason, make the most of it.

Patrick Henry
(Speech on the Stamp Act, May 29, 1765)

National honor is national property of the highest value.

James Monroe
(First Inaugural Address)

The American continents . . . are henceforth not to be considered as subjects for future colonization by any European powers.

James Monroe
(Annual Message to Congress, December 1823, the Monroe Doctrine)

America has furnished to the world the character of Washington. And if our American institutions had done nothing else, that alone would have entitled them to the respect of mankind.

Daniel Webster

Liberty and Union, now and forever, one and inseparable.

Daniel Webster

Our country! In her intercourse with foreign nations may she always be in the right; but our country, right or wrong.

Stephen Decatur

Liberty exists in proportion to wholesome restraint.

Daniel Webster

We admit of no government by divine right . . . the only legitimate right to govern is an express grant of power from the governed.

William Henry Harrison
(Inaugural Address)

Government is a trust, and the officers of the government are trustees; and both the trust and the trustees are created for the benefit of the people.

Henry Clay

The office of government is not to confer happiness, but to give men opportunity to work out happiness for themselves.

William Ellery Channing

The very essence of a free government consists in considering offices as public trusts, bestowed for the good of the country, and not for the benefit of an individual or a party.

J. C. Calhoun

We have met the enemy, and they are ours.

Oliver Hazard Perry
(September 10, 1813)

I only regret that I have but one life to lose for my country.

Nathan Hale
(Before his execution, 1775)

War is cruel and you cannot refine it . . . . War is hell.

William Tecumseh Sherman
(A composite of two statements made by him in Atlanta in 1864 and in 1879.)

Ideals are like stars; you will not succeed in touching them with your hands. But like the seafaring man on the desert of waters, you choose them as your guides, and following them you will reach your destiny.

Carl Schurz

Millions for defense, but not one cent for tribute.

Charles Cotesworth Pinckney
(When Ambassador to France, 1796)

Men are not superior by reason of the accidents of race or color. They are superior who have the best heart—the best brain.

Robert Ingersoll

Do not pray for easy lives. Pray to be stronger men! Do not pray for tasks equal to your powers. Pray for powers equal to your tasks.

Philip Brooks

There is a homely adage which runs, ''Speak softly and carry a big stick; you will go far.'' If the American nation will speak softly and yet build and keep at a pitch of the highest training a thoroughly efficient navy, the Monroe Doctrine will go far.

Theodore Roosevelt
(Speech, September 2, 1901)

Absolute freedom of the press to discuss public questions is a foundation stone of American liberty.

Herbert Clark Hoover

The only thing we have to fear is fear itself.

Franklin D. Roosevelt
(First Inaugural Address)

In the field of world policy I would dedicate this nation to the policy of the good neighbor.

Franklin D. Roosevelt
(First Inaugural Address)

Labor to keep alive in your breast that little spark of celestial fire—conscience.

George Washington

Declaration of Independence

IN CONGRESS, JULY 4, 1776

The unanimous declaration of the thirteen united States of America.

When in the Course of human events, it becomes necessary for one people to dissolve the political bands which have connected them with another, and to assume among the powers of the earth, the separate and equal station to which the Laws of Nature and of Nature's God entitle them, a decent respect to the opinions of mankind requires that they should declare the causes which impel them to the separation.

We hold these truths to be self-evident, that all men are created equal, that they are endowed by their Creator with certain unalienable Rights, that among these are Life, Liberty and the pursuit of Happiness.—That to secure these rights, Governments are instituted among Men, deriving their just powers from the consent of the governed,—That whenever any Form of Government becomes destructive of these ends it is the Right of the People to alter or to abolish it, and to institute new Government, laying its foundation on such principles and organizing its powers in such form, as to them shall seem most likely to effect their Safety and Happiness.

There were many years of discontent and protest in the American Colonies before the colonists actually declared their independence from Britain in 1776. The battles of Lexington and Concord were fought more than a year earlier. Several tries at peace were made, though in New York and New England colonists and British soldiers were already fighting.

Finally the Continental Congress observed that American public opinion had swung to the side of complete independence. In June 1776, they named a committee to write a declaration. Its members were Thomas Jefferson, Benjamin Franklin, John Adams, Roger Sherman, and Robert R. Livingston. Jefferson actually wrote the Declaration of Independence, although the others made suggestions. On July 4, 1776, the Congress accepted the Declaration.

The first signer was John Hancock, who, the story goes, wrote his name very large "so the king could read it without his spectacles."

The writers of the Declaration hoped for the approval of other countries, and so they carefully stated their complaints against King George and his government. (Later, when the Constitution and Bill of Rights were written, they protected citizens against these same problems.) In fact, the Declaration inspired many other moves toward freedom, including the French Revolution a few years later and the revolutions in South America in the 1820s.

Text of Declaration of Independence

When in the Course of human events, it becomes necessary for one people to dissolve the political bands which have connected them with another, and to assume among the powers of the earth, the separate and equal station to which the Laws of Nature and of Nature's God entitle them, a decent respect to the opinions of mankind requires that they should declare the causes which impel them to the separation.

We hold these truths to be self-evident, that all men are created equal, that they are endowed by their Creator with certain unalienable Rights, that among these are Life, Liberty and the pursuit of Happiness. —That to secure these rights, Governments are instituted among Men, deriving their just powers from the consent of the governed,—That whenever any Form of Government becomes destructive of these ends it is the Right of the People to alter or to abolish it, and to institute new Government, laying its foundation on such principles and organizing its powers in such form, as to them shall seem most likely to effect their Safety and Happiness.

Prudence, indeed, will dictate that Governments long established should not be changed for light and transient causes; and accordingly all experience hath shewn, that mankind are more disposed to suffer, while evils are sufferable, than to right themselves by abolishing the forms to which they are accustomed. But when a long train of abuses and usurpations, pursuing invariably the same Object evinces a design to reduce them under absolute Despotism, it is their right, it is their duty, to throw off such Government, and to provide new Guards for their future security. Such has been the patient sufferance of these Colonies; and such is now the necessity which constrains them to alter their former Systems of Government. The history of the present King of Great Britain is a history of repeated injuries and usurpations, all having in direct object the establishment of an absolute Tyranny over these States. To prove this, let Facts be submitted to a candid world.

He has refused his Assent to Laws, the most wholesome and necessary for the public good. He has forbidden his Governors to pass Laws of immediate and pressing importance, unless suspended in their operation till his Assent should be obtained; and when so suspended, he has utterly neglected to attend to them. He has refused to pass other Laws for the accommodation of large districts of people, unless those people would relinquish the right of Representation in the Legislature, a right inestimable to them and formidable to tyrants only. He has called together legislative bodies at places unusual, uncomfortable, and distant from the depository of their public Records, for the sole purpose of fatiguing them into compliance with his measures. He has dissolved Representative Houses repeatedly, for opposing with manly firmness his invasions on the rights of the people. He has refused for a long time, after such dissolutions, to cause others to be elected; whereby the Legislative powers, incapable of Annihilation, have returned to the People at large for their exercise; the State remaining in the mean time exposed to all the dangers of invasion from without, and convulsions within.

He has endeavoured to prevent the population of these States; for that purpose obstructing the Laws for Naturalization of Foreigners; refusing to pass others to encourage their migrations hither, and raising the conditions of new Appropriations of Lands. He has obstructed the Administration of Justice, by refusing his Assent to Laws for establishing Judiciary powers. He has made Judges dependent on his Will alone, for the tenure of their offices, and the amount and payment of their salaries. He has erected a multitude of New Offices, and sent hither swarms of Officers to harass our people, and eat out their substance. He has kept among us, in times of peace, Standing Armies without the Consent of our legislatures. He has affected to render the Military independent of and superior to the Civil power.

He has combined with others to subject us to a jurisdiction foreign to our constitution, and unacknowledged by our laws; giving his Assent to their Acts of pretended Legislation: For Quartering large bodies of armed troops among us: For protecting them, by a mock Trial, from punishment for any Murders which they should commit on the Inhabitants of these States: For cutting off our Trade with all parts of the world: For imposing Taxes on us without our Consent: For depriving us in many cases of the benefits of Trial by Jury: For transporting us beyond Seas to be tried for pretended offences: For abolishing the free System of English Laws in a neighbouring Province, establishing therein an Arbitrary government, and enlarging its Boundaries so as to render it at once an example and fit instrument for introducing the same absolute rule into these Colonies: For taking away our Charters, abolishing our most valuable Laws, and altering fundamentally the Forms of our Governments: For suspending our own Legislatures, and declaring themselves invested with power to legislate for us in all cases whatsoever.

He has abdicated Government here, by declaring us out of his Protection and waging War against us. He has plundered our seas, ravaged our Coasts, burnt our towns, and destroyed the Lives of our people. He is at this time transporting large Armies of foreign Mercenaries to compleat the works of death, desolation and tyranny, already begun with circumstances of Cruelty & perfidy scarcely paralleled in the most barbarous ages, and totally unworthy the Head of a civilized nation. He has constrained our fellow Citizens taken Captive on the high Seas to bear Arms against their Country, to become the executioners of their friends and Brethren, or to fall themselves by their Hands. He has excited domestic insurrections amongst us, and has endeavoured to bring on the inhabitants of our frontiers, the merciless Indian Savages, whose known rule of warfare is an undistinguished destruction of all ages, sexes and conditions.

In every stage of these Oppressions We have Petitioned for Redress in the most humble terms: Our repeated Petitions have been answered only by repeated injury. A Prince, whose character is thus marked by every act which may define a Tyrant, is unfit to be the ruler of a free people. Nor have We been wanting in attentions to our British brethren. We have warned them from time to time of attempts by their legislature to extend an unwarrantable jurisdiction over us. We have reminded them of the circumstances of our emigration and settlement here. We have appealed to their native justice and magnanimity, and we have conjured them by the ties of our common kindred to disavow these usurpations, which would inevitably interrupt our connections and correspondence. They too have been deaf to the voice of justice and of consanguinity. We must, therefore, acquiesce in the necessity, which denounces our Separation, and hold them, as we hold the rest of mankind, Enemies in War, in Peace Friends.

We, therefore, the Representatives of the UNITED STATES OF AMERICA, in General Congress, Assembled, appealing to the Supreme Judge of the world for the rectitude of our intentions, do, in the Name, and by Authority of the good People of these Colonies, solemnly publish and declare, That these United Colonies are, and of Right ought to be FREE AND INDEPENDENT STATES; that they are Absolved from all Allegiance to the British Crown, and that all political connection between them and the State of Great Britain, is and ought to be totally dissolved; and that as Free and Independent States, they have full Power to levy War, conclude Peace, contract Alliances, establish Commerce, and to do all other Acts and Things which Independent States may of right do. And for the support of this Declaration, with a firm reliance on the protection of divine Providence, we mutually pledge to each other our Lives, our Fortunes and our sacred Honor.

Declaration of Independence is presented to Continental Congress, June 28, 1776. Jefferson and Franklin are seen in this painting by colonial artist John Trumbull.

THE UNITED STATES

THE SIGNERS OF THE DECLARATION OF INDEPENDENCE

John Adams, Massachusetts, lawyer, age 40 (1735–1826).

Samuel Adams, Massachusetts, politician, age 53 (1722–1803).

Josiah Bartlett, New Hampshire, physician, age 46 (1729–1795).

Carter Braxton, Virginia, planter, age 39 (1736–1797).

Charles Carroll of Carrollton, Maryland, planter, age 38 (1737–1832).

Samuel Chase, Maryland, lawyer, age 35 (1741–1811).

Abraham Clark, New Jersey, farmer, lawyer, age 40 (1726–1794).

George Clymer, Pennsylvania, merchant, age 37 (1739–1813).

William Ellery, Rhode Island, lawyer, age 48 (1727–1820).

William Floyd, New York, farmer, age 41 (1734–1821).

Benjamin Franklin, Pennsylvania, writer, scientist, statesman, age 70 (1706–1790).

Elbridge Gerry, Massachusetts, shipping merchant, age 31 (1744–1814).

Button Gwinnett, Georgia, planter, about 41 (c. 1735–1777).

Lyman Hall, Georgia, physician, age 52 (1724–1790).

John Hancock, Massachusetts, shipping merchant, age 39 (1737–1793).

Benjamin Harrison, Virginia, planter, about 50 (c. 1726–1791).

John Hart, New Jersey, farmer, about 65 (c. 1711–1779).

Joseph Hewes, North Carolina, businessman, age 46 (1730–1779).

Thomas Heyward, South Carolina, planter, lawyer, age 29 (1746–1809).

William Hooper, North Carolina, lawyer, age 34 (1742–1790).

Stephen Hopkins, Rhode Island, farmer, public official, publisher, age 69 (1707–1785).

Francis Hopkinson, New Jersey, lawyer, musician, writer, age 38 (1737–1791).

Samuel Huntington, Connecticut, lawyer, age 45 (1731–1796).

Thomas Jefferson, Virginia, lawyer, planter, writer, age 33 (1743–1826).

Richard Henry Lee, Virginia, planter, lawyer, age 44 (1732–1794).

Francis Lightfoot Lee, Virginia, planter, age 41 (1734–1797).

Francis Lewis, New York, businessman, age 63 (1713–1802).

Philip Livingston, New York, merchant, age 60 (1716–1778).

Thomas Lynch, South Carolina, planter, age 26 (1749–1779).

Thomas McKean, Delaware, lawyer, age 42 (1734–1817).

Arthur Middleton, South Carolina, planter, age 34 (1742–1787).

Lewis Morris, New York, landowner, age 50 (1726–1798).

Robert Morris, Pennsylvania, merchant, financier, age 42 (1734–1806).

John Morton, Pennsylvania, surveyor, farmer, about 52 (c. 1724–1777).

Thomas Nelson, Virginia, planter, merchant, age 41 (1738–1789).

William Paca, Maryland, lawyer, age 37 (1740–1799).

Robert Treat Paine, Massachusetts, lawyer, age 45 (1731–1814).

John Penn, North Carolina, lawyer, age 36 (1740–1788).

George Read, Delaware, lawyer, age 42 (1733–1798).

Caesar Rodney, Delaware, landowner, legislator, age 48 (1728–1784).

George Ross, Delaware, lawyer, age 46 (1730–1779).

Benjamin Rush, Pennsylvania, physician, age 30 (1745–1813).

Edward Rutledge, South Carolina, lawyer, age 26 (1749–1800).

Roger Sherman, Connecticut, merchant, judge, age 55 (1721–1793).

James Smith, Pennsylvania, lawyer, age about 57 (c. 1719–1806).

Richard Stockton, New Jersey, lawyer, age 46 (1730–1781).

Thomas Stone, Maryland, lawyer, planter, age 33 (1743–1787).

George Taylor, Pennsylvania, ironmaster, age 60 (1716–1781).

Matthew Thornton, New Hampshire, physician, age 62 (c. 1714–1803).

George Walton, Georgia, lawyer, age 35 (1741–1804).

William Whipple, New Hampshire, merchant, age 46 (1730–1785).

William Williams, Connecticut, businessman, official, age 45 (1731–1811).

James Wilson, Pennsylvania, lawyer, political writer, age 33 (1742–1798).

John Witherspoon, New Jersey, clergyman, educator, age 53 (1723–1794).

Oliver Wolcott, Connecticut, lawyer, judge, age 49 (1726–1797).

George Wythe, Virginia, lawyer, age 50 (1726–1806).

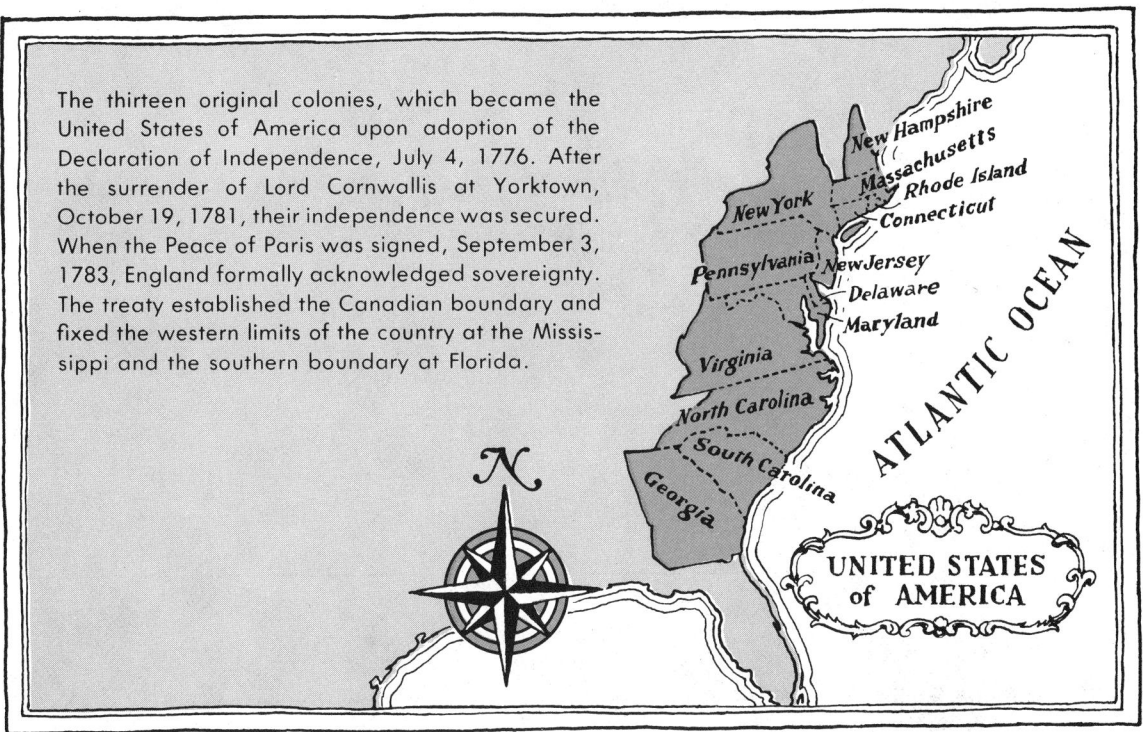

The thirteen original colonies, which became the United States of America upon adoption of the Declaration of Independence, July 4, 1776. After the surrender of Lord Cornwallis at Yorktown, October 19, 1781, their independence was secured. When the Peace of Paris was signed, September 3, 1783, England formally acknowledged sovereignty. The treaty established the Canadian boundary and fixed the western limits of the country at the Mississippi and the southern boundary at Florida.

THE THIRTEEN ORIGINAL COLONIES

Colony	First permanent settlement	First European settlers	Ratified Constitution
Virginia	Jamestown, 1607	English	June 25, 1788
Massachusetts	Plymouth, 1620	English	February 6, 1788
New Hampshire	Little Harbour (Rye), 1623	English	June 21, 1788
New York	Fort Orange (Albany), 1624	Dutch	July 26, 1788
Maryland	St. Mary's, 1634	English	April 28, 1788
Connecticut	Hartford, 1635	English	January 9, 1788
Rhode Island	Providence, 1636	English	May 29, 1790
Delaware	Christina (Wilmington), 1638	Swedish	December 7, 1787
Pennsylvania	Tinicum Island, 1643	Swedish, Finnish	December 12, 1787
North Carolina	Albemarle Sound, 1653	English	November 21, 1789
New Jersey	Elizabeth, 1664	English	December 18, 1787
South Carolina	Albemarle Point, 1670	English	May 23, 1788
Georgia	Savannah, 1733	English	January 2, 1788

The Constitution

In 1787 the newly written Constitution of the United States was an unusual document. Not only was it the first written national constitution since ancient times, but it was also the first to create what is called the federal system. Under this system sovereign power comes from the people. Some governmental powers are given to the national government, others to the states.

This was a different system from the one under which the new nation had been governed since the end of the American Revolution in 1781. The Articles of Confederation left nearly all the power in the hands of the states—they could cooperate with the central government or ignore it if they chose. There were no executive branch, no national court system, nor power in Congress to impose taxes. Many people opposed the new form of government, but eventually its strongest supporters, known as the Federalists, won out by agreeing to a series of compromises, and by 1789 all the states had ratified (approved) the Constitution.

Since the loss of personal and civil rights had been the original reason for rebellion against the British, the anti-Federalists insisted that the first order of business under the new Congress should be to add to the Constitution a guarantee of these rights. Accordingly, the Bill of Rights became the first ten amendments of the Constitution on December 15, 1791.

The Constitution was divided into seven sections, called articles. The first four formed the basis of the government: Article

I established the Congress, the legislative (lawmaking) branch; Article II described the executive branch (the presidency), and Article III dealt with the judicial branch (the court system). Article IV discussed the relationships between states and the rules for territories. Article V provided for changing the Constitution by amending it. Article VI established the supremacy of federal laws, and Article VII provided the means by which the Constitution was to be adopted.

In establishing a new system of government, the Constitution gave the country a political framework that has endured for nearly 200 years. Moreover, by distributing certain powers among the executive, legislative, and judicial branches of government, a system of "checks and balances" was established which has prevented any one branch from monopolizing power.

Another constitutional principle—Federalism—calls for political authority to be distributed between the national government and the states.

The amending process is the method set forth by the Constitution itself for changing the Constitution. The process of amendment was deliberately designed to be time-consuming; large majorities are required for the approval of an amendment. As a result, only twenty-six amendments have been adopted (including the first ten, which almost have to be considered part of the original document).

A twenty-seventh amendment, the Equal Rights Amendment, has been proposed by the Congress and, so far, has been approved by thirty-five of the states; approval (or ratification) by thirty-eight of the states is needed for adoption.

Interpretation of the Constitution by the Supreme Court has brought about its most profound changes. Practically every part of the Constitution has been tested before the Supreme Court at some time. In this process the Court has shaped and reshaped the document.

Legislation has also altered the Constitution—the sizes of the House of Representatives and the Supreme Court have been legislated. The Cabinet, Boards, and services—such as Social Security—were all created by Congressional action.

Custom, though less precise in bringing about change, has contributed to it, nonetheless. Political parties, nominating conventions, and the committee system in Congress are all practices which were not foreseen by the framers of the Constitution.

This flexibility has enabled the Constitution to adapt to changing times and conditions—incredible geographic expansion, the transformation of the country from a predominantly rural one to a modern industrial giant—while remaining closely attuned to the needs of the people.

BILL OF RIGHTS

The first ten amendments, called the *Bill of Rights,* were added to the Constitution in 1791. They are still the basic source of such important individual rights as freedom of speech and religion and freedom of the press.

Many of the later amendments were needed to change provisions of the original Constitution, such as the procedure for electing a president and vice-president. Through several other amendments, the right to vote has been extended to all men and women over eighteen years old.

AMENDMENT 1

*Freedom of Religion, Speech,
Press, Assembly, and Petition*

Congress shall make no law respecting an establishment of religion, or prohibiting the free exercise thereof; or abridging the free-

The Second Amendment to the U.S. Constitution protects the right to bear arms; the Fourth Amendment requires a search warrant before private property may be searched or seized.

dom of speech, or of the press, or the right of the people peaceably to assemble, and to petition the government for a redress of grievances.

AMENDMENT 2

Right to Bear Arms

A well-regulated militia, being necessary to the security of a free state, the right of the people to keep and bear arms, shall not be infringed.

AMENDMENT 3

Quartering Soldiers

No soldier shall, in time of peace be quartered in any house, without the consent of the owner, nor in time of war, but in a manner to be prescribed by law.

AMENDMENT 4

Searches and Seizures

The right of the people to be secure in their persons, houses, papers, and effects, against unreasonable searches and seizures, shall not be violated, and no warrants shall issue, but upon probable cause, supported by oath or affirmation, and particularly describing the place to be searched, and the persons or things to be seized.

AMENDMENT 5

Rights

No person shall be held to answer for a capital, or otherwise infamous crime, unless on a presentment or indictment of a grand jury, except in cases arising in the land or naval forces, or in the militia, when in actual service in time of war or public danger; nor shall any person be subject for the same offense to be twice put in jeopardy of life or limb; nor shall be compelled in any criminal case to be a witness against himself, nor be deprived of life, liberty, or property, without due process of law; nor shall private property be taken for public use, without just compensation.

AMENDMENT 6

Jury in Criminal Cases

In all criminal prosecutions, the accused shall enjoy the right to a speedy and public trial, by an impartial jury of the state and district wherein the crime shall have been committed, which district shall have been previously ascertained by law, and to be informed of the nature and cause of the accusation; to be confronted with the witnesses against him; to have compulsory process for obtaining witnesses in his favor, and to have the assistance of counsel for his defense.

AMENDMENT 7

Jury in Civil Cases

In suits at common law, where the value in controversy shall exceed twenty dollars, the right of trial by jury shall be preserved, and no fact tried by a jury shall be otherwise reexamined in any court of the United States, than according to the rules of the common law.

AMENDMENT 8

Excessive Penalties

Excessive bail shall not be required, nor excessive fines imposed, nor cruel and unusual punishments inflicted.

AMENDMENT 9

Other Rights

The enumeration in the Constitution, of certain rights, shall not be construed to deny or disparage others retained by the people.

AMENDMENT 10

State Powers

The powers not delegated to the United States by the Constitution, nor prohibited by it to the states, are reserved to the states respectively, or to the people.

The Federal Government

The organization of the federal government in three main branches is described in the first three articles of the Constitution: the legislative (lawmaking) branch in Article I, the executive branch in Article II, and the judicial (court) branch in Article III. (See Concise Edition for complete text). Although the Constitution describes the guidelines and relationships among the three major branches of the government, it does not provide the details of their administration. Within the framework of the Constitution, the Cabinet, departments, political parties, and congressional committees have been organized and developed.

Each branch acts as a check on the others. For example, every law passed by the legislative branch must go to the President for approval before it can become a "law of the land." The President can reject, or *veto*, the law proposed by the legislature. However, even if it has been vetoed, Congress can pass it with a two-thirds majority vote in both houses.

The third branch of government, the judiciary, includes the Supreme Court, the federal district courts, and the courts of appeal. With its ability to declare laws unconstitutional, the Supreme Court can put a check on the legislative and executive branches. The Supreme Court, in turn, is balanced by the other two branches. For example, the President nominates judges, and the Senate must approve his nominees. By setting up this system of checks and balances within the federal government, the authors of the Constitution sought to prevent domination by any one of the branches.

THE LEGISLATIVE BRANCH

The legislative branch of the federal government is called the Congress. The Congress is a *bicameral* system; that is, it is divided into two parts. These are the Senate and the House of Representatives. The nominal leader of the Senate is the Vice-President of the United States. However, he is simply the presiding officer when the Senate convenes. He votes only in the event of a tie. The real leader is the Senate Majority Leader, chosen by the majority party members. The leader of the House of Representatives is called the Speaker of the House and is also chosen from the majority party.

Congressional Powers

Congress has the authority to judge the elections and qualifications of its own members and to decide the rules for running its own meetings, but its most important power is to make and pass laws.

In economic matters Congress has the power to establish and collect federal taxes and duties, and import and excise taxes; to pay federal debts; to borrow money on United States credit; to regulate trade with foreign nations and among the states; to coin money and provide substitutes (such as paper money) as well as make provisions for controlling their value, and to make uniform laws of bankruptcy.

Congress also has the power to provide

The United States Capitol in Washington, D.C. The statue on top of the dome represents Freedom. When Congress is in session, a light shines on the dome.

for the common defense and welfare. It can declare war and provide funds for the armed forces to carry on war.

Congress also fixes standards for weights and measures, establishes uniform rules of naturalization, and defines and punishes crimes on the high seas and offenses against international law. It also governs all districts that are used by the federal government for civil and military purposes, including the District of Columbia.

The Senate has three powers that the House of Representatives does not have. First, it has the right to approve or reject presidential appointments. Second, with the President, it can make treaties with foreign powers. Third, it has the sole power to judge government officials impeached by the House of Representatives.

The House of Representatives has two powers that the Senate does not have. It originates all bills for raising revenue (tariffs

112

THE UNITED STATES

Members of the Senate Select Committee on Presidential Campaign Activities, chaired by Senator Sam Ervin, North Carolina. The hearings of this committee were important in the events leading to resignation of President Richard M. Nixon in 1974. Vice-President Gerald Ford then succeeded to the presidency.

and taxes), although the Senate can amend them. It also has the power of impeaching government officials for misconduct.

Qualifications for Senators

Each state, regardless of its area or population, has two senators, who are elected for six-year terms. In order to provide continuity, the terms are staggered so that only one-third of the Senate members are elected (or reelected) at one time. Unlike representatives, each senator represents an entire state. Since 1913 senators have been elected by the direct vote of the people. Before then they were elected by the state legislatures.

To be eligible for election to the Senate, a person must be thirty years of age, a citizen of the United States for at least nine years, and a resident of the state from which he or she is chosen.

Qualifications for Representatives

The population of a state determines its number of congressional representatives. The apportionment (number) of representatives to each state is determined every ten years, after each federal census. The total population of the country is divided by the number of United States representatives (fixed at 435 since 1912) to determine the number of people entitled to one representative (called the unit of representation). After the 1970 census, the unit of representation was 468,971 citizens to every representative. The number of representatives to which a state is entitled is determined by dividing its population by the unit of representation. Each state, however, is entitled to one representative no matter how small its population.

Each representative serves for two years. To be eligible for election, a candidate must be at least twenty-five years of age, a citizen of the United States for at least seven years, and a resident of the state from which he or she is chosen. By custom, each representative is selected from a congressional district, unless a representative is congressman-at-large and represents an entire state. In 1977 the salaries of senators and representatives were increased to $57,500. The Speaker of the House received $80,000 and both the Majority and Minority Leaders of the Senate, $65,000.

THE EXECUTIVE BRANCH

The Constitution gives the executive power of the government to the President of the United States. The President serves a four-year term and may not serve more than two consecutive terms. The Vice-President, who is elected with the President for a four-year term, has no executive authority.

Qualifications for President and Vice-President

The qualifications for President and Vice-President are the same. They must be natural-born citizens of the United States, have lived within the United States for fourteen years (ambassadors and civil servants abroad are considered to be on United States territory), and be at least thirty-five years of age.

In 1977 the President's salary was $200,000 a year with an expense allowance of $50,000. He also received a nontaxable expense allowance of up to $100,000 for travel and official entertainment. The Vice-President received $80,000 in salary and $10,000 for expenses (all taxable).

Presidential Elections

Every four years, on the first Tuesday after the first Monday in November, an election for President and Vice-President is held. When a person votes for President and Vice-President, the vote is actually cast for electors who represent a particular political party's choice for these offices. Each state has as many electors as it has representatives in Congress. All the electors from a state are pledged to vote for the candidate who receives the majority of the votes in that state. The entire number of electors (538, including 3 from Washington, D.C.) chosen from all the states form the electoral college.

The electors meet in their respective state capitals on the first Wednesday after the second Monday in December to vote for the two candidates to whom they are pledged. The votes are totaled and sent to Congress. Congress then announces the result of the election.

In order to win, a candidate must receive a majority of the electoral votes cast. If no one has the required number of electoral votes, the procedure to be followed is as given in the Twelfth Amendment to the Constitution: the House of Representatives selects the President, and the Senate selects the Vice-President from among the candidates running.

Since 1937 the President and Vice-President have taken office on January 20 under the provisions of the Twentieth Amendment. Before the Twentieth Amendment was adopted, they took office on March 4.

Presidential Powers

The President has the power to appoint justices to the Supreme Court and other federal courts, ambassadors, ministers, consuls to foreign countries, United States district attorneys and marshals, the three highest classes of postmaster, and the members of the Cabinet. All these appointments must have the consent of a majority

North Portico of the White House. Located at 1600 Pennsylvania Avenue, Washington, D.C., the White House provides living quarters for the President and family and offices for some of his staff. Other staffers have offices in the Executive Office Building on the White House grounds. Theodore Roosevelt officially adopted the name "White House" in 1902.

vote of the Senate. Minor appointments are made by department heads, but the responsibility for them rests with the President. Any appointments the President makes during a recess of the Senate are valid without the Senate's consent until the end of the next session of Congress.

The President also has the power to make treaties with foreign nations. Treaties, however, must have the consent of two-thirds of the senators present at any session.

The President is commander in chief of the armed forces of the United States and of the state militia when it is called into military service. Presidents Johnson and Nixon used this power to carry on wars in Korea and Vietnam without a formal declaration by Congress.

Annually, in January, the President makes a report to the Congress on the state of the nation, with recommendations for needed legislation. This is known as the "State of the Union" message. The President also has the power to veto bills passed by Congress or to return bills to Congress for further consideration. However, Congress may pass a bill without the President's signature with a two-thirds vote. If a bill is not signed by the President and is returned to Congress within ten days, it automatically becomes a law. However, if Congress adjourns before ten days have passed and the bill has not been signed, the bill is automatically vetoed (this is called a pocket veto).

The President has the power to call special sessions of Congress and can adjourn them if they cannot agree on a time of adjournment (this has never happened).

The President also has the power to grant reprieves (a reprieve is the postponement of punishment—usually the execution of a condemned person) in cases involving federal law. He may grant pardons for offenses against the United States, except in cases of impeachment. President Ford's pardon of Richard Nixon occurred after articles of impeachment had been voted in the House Judiciary Committee but before the full House had voted to send the case to the Senate for judgment.

The President receives ambassadors and ministers of foreign countries. An ambassador represents the person who governs his country and is entitled to meet with the President in person at all convenient times.

The Cabinet

The Cabinet, made up of the President's personally selected advisers, has been organized to meet the administrative needs of the executive branch. It is not specifically mentioned in the Constitution, but has become accepted through custom. Each Cabinet member is the principal officer of a department in the executive branch.

The Cabinet members are the secretaries of the treasury; state; defense; interior; agriculture; commerce; labor; transportation; health, education, and welfare; and housing and urban development. A new post, secretary of energy, has been created by President Carter. The Cabinet also includes the attorney general. The President may invite the Vice-President to attend meetings of the Cabinet. Cabinet members serve at the pleasure of the President, usually during his full term. In 1977 each Cabinet member received a salary of $67,500.

THE JUDICIAL BRANCH

The third branch of the federal government established by the Constitution is the judiciary. It is made up of the Supreme Court,

circuit courts of appeals, and district courts. The federal courts judge both civil and criminal cases, but have no connection with the courts established by the states. The Constitution established the Supreme Court as the highest judicial power in the nation.

The Supreme Court is composed of one chief justice and eight associate justices, all appointed by the president for life terms. In 1977 the salary for chief justice was $80,000 and for each associate justice, $77,500. Their salaries cannot be reduced during their terms of office. The Supreme Court is usually in session from October to May.

Supreme Court Powers

The Supreme Court has two kinds of authority—original jurisdiction and appellate jurisdiction. Original jurisdiction is the power to try cases that have not been tried before in other courts. Appellate jurisdiction is the power to give final decisions on cases that have been tried in other courts. These cases are often appealed to the Supreme Court, which may choose to hear them. More often, the Supreme Court may choose not to hear them. In this case the decision of the next lower court becomes the final decision.

The powers of original jurisdiction include all cases affecting ambassadors, other public ministers, and consuls; all cases of admiralty and maritime law; all controversies in which the United States is one of the parties; all controversies between two or more states; all controversies between one state and citizens of another state or between citizens of different states; and all controversies between a state or its citizens and a foreign state or its citizens.

The power of appellate jurisdiction is the source of the Supreme Court's power to declare an act of Congress or a state law unconstitutional. It is only by implication and

The Supreme Court Building, Washington, D.C. Above the main entrance is a group of nine sculpted figures, the center being the Goddess of Liberty. In this marble building, the nine Justices of the Supreme Court hear cases publicly and carry on their deliberations. Visitors may attend the public sessions.

custom that the Supreme Court enjoys this authority. The Constitution does not mention it but gives the Supreme Court "appellate jurisdiction . . . with such exceptions and under such regulations as the Congress shall make."

Lower Courts

The Constitution does not name the lower federal courts specifically but provides for their creation. In 1977 there were twelve circuit courts of appeals and United States district courts.

District courts serve an entire state or part of a state or territory. They hear cases involving federal offenses and certain classes of controversies between states. District courts also try cases involving violations of federal laws connected with the revenue and postal departments, smuggling, counterfeiting, and bankruptcy.

The circuit courts of appeals hear appeals from decisions in the district courts. This function helps relieve the Supreme Court, since the circuit court's decision is usually considered final. Only cases involving important constitutional questions are passed on to the Supreme Court for review of lower court decisions.

THE FEDERAL BUREAUCRACY

The federal bureaucracy carries out most of the work of governing. The huge growth of the national government, beginning with the Depression and continuing with World War II, has produced an administrative system of enormous size and complexity.

The structure of this bureaucracy can be broken down into the *Executive Office of the President,* the *Cabinet Departments,*

Executive Agencies, and *Regulatory Commissions.* The Executive Office of the president was established in 1939 to advise and assist the President in managing the bureaucracy. It has grown steadily in size and influence, and its three most important agencies are the *White House Staff,* the *National Security Council,* and the *Office of Management and Budget.* The size of the White House Staff has grown from about 250 members under President Kennedy to twice that number under President Carter. Its members have substantial power and are not subject to Senate approval. For example, in the Nixon administration Messrs. Haldeman, Ehrlichman, and Kissinger (before he was named secretary of state) became extremely influential with respect to government policy.

The National Security Council was established in 1947 to help the President coordinate American military and foreign policies. The Council has representatives from the State and Defense Departments as well as the Central Intelligence Agency (CIA).

The Office of Management and Budget (OMB) was created in 1970 and supersedes the Bureau of the Budget. Departments of the executive branch submit their estimates of anticipated needs to the OMB, where priorities are established and the total budget is put together.

The Cabinet departments are the principal agencies of the federal government. Originally, there were only three—the Departments of State, War, and Treasury. Today there are twelve, including the newest, the Department of Energy. Each one is headed by a secretary who is appointed by the President and approved by the Senate. A secretary has no fixed term and serves as long as the President wishes. Together, these department heads make up the Cabinet. Some Presidents have consulted the Cabinet on a regular basis, while others have sought advice from individual members.

The Executive Agencies are part of the presidency but not part of the departments. Examples are the Veteran's Administration (VA), the National Aeronautics and Space Agency (NASA), and the Central Intelligence Agency (CIA). There are two government corporations which should be noted here: the Tennessee Valley Authority (TVA) and the United States Postal Service.

The regulatory commissions have the responsibility of overseeing certain parts of the economy. Some examples are the Interstate Commerce Commission (ICC), which regulates railroads, buses, and trucking; the Federal Communications Commission (FCC), which supervises the radio and television industry; and the Environmental Protection Agency (EPA), which monitors industry to minimize pollution. These commissions are relatively independent. Their members are appointed by the President; they serve longer terms than he does (so both parties are represented); and the President has no veto over their decisions.

The federal bureaucracy is often the target of criticism because of its size and what is thought to be its incompetence, red-tape, and impersonal nature. Presidential candidates pledge that they will streamline the bureaucracy; once elected, they find this difficult to do.

The Civil Service Reform Act of 1883 created a Civil Service Commission, which selects government employees on the basis of merit as demonstrated by the examinations they take. This ended the "spoils system," which had seen new presidents fill government jobs with their loyal followers after each election. Now 85 percent of the federal bureaucracy is made up of civil servants who gained their place on merit. A substantial number of these people stay on in the federal bureaucracy throughout their careers, while presidents come and go.

GLOSSARY OF GOVERNMENT TERMS

absentee voting. The privilege of casting a ballot without appearing in person.

ambassador. A foreign diplomat of the highest rank. He represents the head of his nation to the head of the nation to which he is sent. He has personal access to the head of the government to which he is sent.

amendment. A change made in a law, a constitution, or a legislative bill.

amnesty. A pardon and forgiveness granted by a government.

antitrust. A term denoting any policy or legislation designed to protect trade or commerce from conspiracies to limit competition.

apportionment. The number of representatives each state is allowed to have in the United States House of Representatives. It also applies to state legislatures. As total population changes, reapportionment takes place to provide fair representation.

appropriation. Setting aside a particular amount of money for a particular purpose.

arbitration. Settling disputes between two parties, by referring the matter to a third party called the arbitrator. The arbitrator hears and receives evidence, then makes a decision which is binding by prior agreement of the parties.

balance of payments. The difference between a nation's imports and exports over a given period. Consists of goods, services, gold, capital.

balance of trade. The difference in value between the trade exports and imports of a country over a given period.

ballot. A means of secret voting. The Australians originated paper balloting in which the voter marks his ballot and puts it into a locked box. Now, voting machines record and count votes automatically in many parts of the United States.

bill. A draft or form of a proposed act or statute, submitted to a legislature for enactment into law.

bureaucracy. Government by bureaus; also a term used to describe a narrow, rigid form of government which is so bound up in administrative rules that it is unresponsive to public opinion.

checks and balances. Precautions against one division of government having too much power. For example, the power of the Supreme Court to declare federal or state laws unconstitutional is a check on Congress.

civil rights. Claims to civil liberties given legal standing by laws upheld in courts. The acquisition of civil rights by groups or individuals involves custom, legislative and judicial recognition, and legal enforcement. It also involves the interaction of social, political, and economic considerations. The basis for civil rights in the United States is the Bill of Rights.

civil service. The duties of all government employees not in the army, navy, legislative or judicial branches of the government; or the whole body of civil servants chosen by examination, not elected or appointed.

cloture (closure) rules. Regulations limiting debate in the legislature. If a specified number of legislators vote to end discussion on a measure, further debate is barred and a vote is taken.

communism. A theory of government and social order in which property and the instruments of production belong to the people, and the profits arising from all labor are devoted to the general good.

cost-of-living index. A price index that measures changes in the cost of living over a period of time. The most frequently used is the "consumer price index" issued by the United States Department of Labor.

deficit. A shortage of money, when expenditures are greater than income, or when liabilities are greater than assets.

democracy. Rule by the people. It may refer to a form of government or a way of life.

department. A division of the executive branch of government. The United States Constitution mentions departments, which have since been created by statute. The President's Cabinet officers are the heads of their departments.

depression. A time when there is little activity in business, high unemployment, low production, and little consumer buying.

diplomatic service. The governmental organization that handles foreign affairs and international relations. The personnel of this organization in the United States are appointed by the President or chosen on the basis of examination.

due process of law. The legal steps that must be taken whenever a person is charged with breaking the law. Every citizen is guaranteed *due process* by the United States Constitution.

economic growth. An increase in the amount of goods or services produced in a nation or area, coupled with an increase in personal income.

election. The method by which qualified voters choose government officials. A run-off election is held in case of a tie vote or insufficient votes to qualify for election.

eminent domain. The power of government to take and pay for any property for the public use or good.

executive. The branch of government that enforces laws.

federal government. A union of two or more political units, such as states or provinces, under a single government of limited powers.

filibuster. A word used to describe the tactics, usually long speeches, used to delay the course of legislative business.

fiscal year. Any period of twelve consecutive months chosen as the basis for annual financial reporting, planning, or budgeting.

free enterprise system. An economic system and an important part of the American way of life. Under this system, almost all means of production are privately owned, and each person is free to make his own economic decisions.

gross national product (GNP). The total amount of goods and services of a country.

home rule. The right of cities to frame their own charters in order to check the legislative interests and the influence of rural areas.

impeachment. An accusation of wrongdoing brought against a government official by an authorized legislative body. The House of Representatives, by majority vote, can impeach an officer of the United States government. The Senate, by a two-thirds vote of the senators present, tries the case under the direction of the chief justice of the Supreme Court. Andrew Johnson, the only United States President to be impeached (1868), was acquitted.

income tax. A tax levied by a government on individual and corporate incomes.

inflation. A steady upward movement in the level of prices.

initiative. One form of direct legislation by the voters of a state. The people of some states and cities are granted the right to originate laws by securing a petition signed by a certain number of voters or a certain percentage of the total number of voters. The proposed measure is voted on and becomes law if approved by a majority voting.

internal revenue. The federal government's income from domestic taxes. Among the main sources are corporation taxes, income taxes, estate and gift taxes, and retailers' excise and stamp taxes.

law. A set of rules which public governments make and enforce.

legislation. Lawmaking, usually in the sense of making statutes or ordinances through a body called a legislature, assembly, or council— usually a group representing the people. In a wider sense there is legislation by the courts as they interpret the law made by the legislature.

legislature. The lawmaking body of a state or nation, consisting of one or two branches, usually called the Senate and House of Representatives.

logrolling. The exchanging of votes by legislators. "You vote for my bill (in which you have no special interest) and I'll vote for yours."

martial law. In United States procedure, the control of the civil population through the use of military force. This occurs when the civil authorities have shown themselves unable to meet an emergency situation. It may be declared by the President of the United States, or by the governor of a state, and in rare cases by a ranking military officer.

mayor. The chief executive officer of a city, except in those cities with charters calling for a manager or commission government. In the United States mayors are now elected by popular vote, a method used for about a century.

minimum wage. The lowest wage payable to employees by law or contract. The Fair Labor Standards Act establishes the legal minimum wage to be paid workers engaged in interstate commerce.

monarchy. A form of government in which one person who inherits, or is elected to, a throne holds executive power for life.

monopoly. In economics a market situation in which there is only one seller of a commodity or service.

net income. The income remaining after all possible deductions, offsets, or allowances are made from a gross income.

panic. A sudden widespread financial fright marked by a wild effort to convert all securities into cash and to withdraw all deposits from banks. A panic results from a business or commercial crisis and arises from the fear that banks will fail and the securities will become worthless.

party government. A system of government based on selection of public officials from the candidates nominated by political parties. In a democratic nation there are two or more parties, and each has its own platform, a program it hopes to enact.

petition. A formal written request by citizens made to some governmental authority. The right of petition, however, does not necessitate government consideration. For instance, the Constitution guarantees the right of petition, but the House of Representatives may table any petition without referring it to a committee.

platform. A declaration of a political party's principles, the basis on which the candidates stand; a formal statement appealing for votes. Party platforms are adopted at national conventions or drafted by party councils.

plebiscite. A vote of the people on any question.

plurality. The largest number of votes cast in an election. A majority is more than half the votes cast. If there are two candidates, the one receiving the majority of votes also receives the plurality.

plural voting. The right to cast more than one vote in an election. For instance, in Britain a person can vote in more than one parliamentary borough if he owns property in more than one borough.

primary election. The selection by a political party of candidates for public office to run for election on the party ticket. A direct primary is held at an officially designated time before an election. In open primaries a voter is given separate ballots for each of the parties. He chooses one and uses it to cast his vote. The others are destroyed.

public debt. The financial obligations of a government, national, state or local, to the public.

quorum. The minimum number of members of a body who, when assembled, are legally competent to transact business. This is usually a majority unless there is a provision to the contrary.

referendum. Submitting an act passed by the legislature to the people, who must approve it before it becomes effective. The usual procedure is to draw up a petition and have it signed by the required number of voters. It is then submitted to the designated official to be placed on the ballot at the next election.

rider. An additional piece of legislation attached to another, usually larger, one. Riders are often added to legislation for the purpose of holding up the legislation to which the rider is attached or insuring the passage of the rider as part of the whole.

socialism. An economic system and also a way of life. Socialists believe that a country's principal means of production should be owned or controlled by the government.

sovereignty. The supreme power of a country over its own affairs.

standard of living. The minimum of goods required by an individual or class to maintain a certain status.

statute. A law passed by a legislature such as Congress.

table a bill. The motion to "lay on the table" is not debatable and is usually used to take a bill out of action.

taxation. The usual method of obtaining funds for public use by assessing persons who are subject to the jurisdiction of the government. Federal taxes range from import taxes and duties to a variety of internal excise taxes. State and local taxes have generally been on land and personal property.

totalitarianism. A form of government in which the state claims control of all the activities of the people.

treaties. Executive proposals on foreign policy which, to take effect, must be approved by a two-thirds vote of the senators present.

veto. The power to invalidate a law, especially such a power lodged in a single official. For example, the President of the United States can veto a law, but can be overruled by a two-thirds vote in each House. In the United Nations, certain members of the Security Council can veto proposals of that body.

welfare state. A term sometimes applied to a country in which the government assumes important responsibility for the social welfare of the people.

whip. A member of a political party in the legislature appointed to enforce discipline among the members of the party. Whips act to persuade party members to vote with their party in order to secure passage or defeat of a bill.

woman suffrage. The right of women to vote on equal terms with men. The Nineteenth Amendment to the Constitution gave women this right.

The States

(Population data are 1976 official estimates except where otherwise stated.)

Alabama

Area: 51,609 square miles (including 758 square miles of water)
Population: 3,665,000
Capital: Montgomery
State bird: Yellowhammer
State tree: Southern pine
State flower: Camellia
State motto: Audemus iura nostra defendere (We dare defend our rights)
Governor's term: 4 years
U.S. Representatives: 7
State legislature: senate 35; house 106

Alaska

Area: 586,412 square miles (including 19,980 square miles of water)
Population: 382,000
Capital: Juneau
State bird: Willow ptarmigan
State tree: Sitka spruce
State flower: Forget-me-not
Governor's term: 4 years
U.S. Representatives: 1
State legislature: senate 20; house 40

Arizona

Area: 113,909 square miles (including 346 square miles of water)

Population: 2,270,000
Capital: Phoenix
State bird: Cactus wren
State tree: Paloverde
State flower: Saguaro
State motto: Ditat Deus (God enriches)
Governor's term: 4 years
U.S. Representatives: 4
State legislature: senate 30; house 60

Arkansas

Area: 53,104 square miles (including 929 square miles of water)
Population: 2,109,000
Capital: Little Rock
State bird: Mockingbird
State tree: Pine
State flower: Apple blossom
State motto: Regnat populus (The people rule)
Governor's term: 2 years
U.S. Representatives: 4
State legislature: senate 35; house 100

California

Area: 158,693 square miles (including 2,156 square miles of water)
Population: 21,520,000
Capital: Sacramento
State bird: California valley quail
State tree: California redwood
State flower: Golden poppy
State motto: Eureka (I have found it)

Governor's term: 4 years
U.S. Representatives: 43
State legislature: senate 40; assembly 80

Colorado

Area: 104,247 square miles (including 453 square miles of water)
Population: 2,583,000
Capital: Denver
State bird: Lark bunting
State tree: Blue spruce
State flower: Rocky Mountain columbine
State motto: Nil sine Numine (Nothing without Providence)
Governor's term: 4 years
U.S. Representatives: 5
State legislature: senate 35; house 65

Connecticut

Area: 5,009 square miles (including 139 square miles of water)
Population: 3,117,000
Capital: Hartford
State bird: Robin
State tree: White oak
State flower: Mountain laurel
State motto: Qui transtulit sustinet (He who transplanted will sustain)
Governor's term: 4 years
U.S. Representatives: 6
State legislature: senate 36; house 177

Delaware

Area: 2,057 square miles (including 75 square miles of water)
Population: 582,000
Capital: Dover
State bird: Blue hen chicken
State tree: American holly
State flower: Peach blossom
State motto: Liberty and independence
Governor's term: 4 years
U.S. Representatives: 1
State legislature: senate 19; house 39

District of Columbia

Area: 67 square miles
Population: 756,510 (1970 census); Metropolitan Area, 2,861,123

Florida

Area: 58,560 square miles (including 4,424 square miles of water)
Population: 8,421,000
Capital: Tallahassee
State bird: Mockingbird
State tree: Sabal palm
State flower: Orange blossom
State motto: In God we trust
Governor's term: 4 years
U.S. Representatives: 15
State legislature: senate 48; house 119

Georgia

Area: 58,876 square miles (including 679 square miles of water)
Population: 4,970,000
Capital: Atlanta
State bird: Brown thrasher
State tree: Live oak
State flower: Cherokee rose
State motto: Wisdom, justice, and moderation
Governor's term: 4 years
U.S. Representatives: 10
State legislature: senate 56; house 195

Hawaii

Area: 6,450 square miles (including 25 square miles of water)
Population: 887,000
Capital: Honolulu
State bird: Nene (Hawaiian goose)
State tree: Kukui (Candlenut)
State flower: Hibiscus

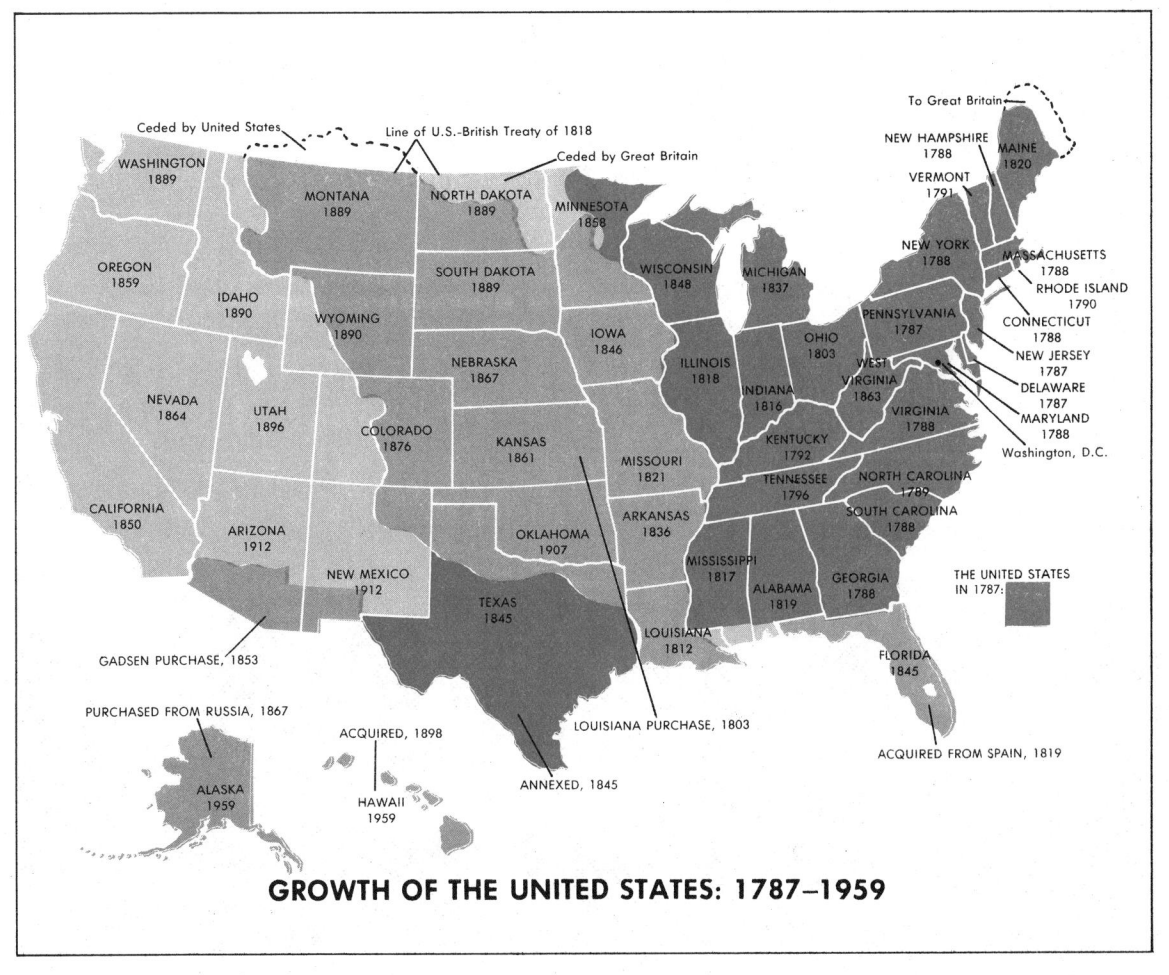

GROWTH OF THE UNITED STATES: 1787–1959

State motto: Ua mau ke ea o ka aina i ka pono (The life of the land is perpetuated in righteousness)
Governor's term: 4 years
U.S. Representatives: 2
State legislature: senate 25; house 51

Idaho

Area: 83,557 square miles (including 880 square miles of water)
Population: 831,000
Capital: Boise
State bird: Mountain bluebird
State tree: White pine
State flower: Syringa
State motto: Esto perpetua (May she endure forever)
Governor's term: 4 years
U.S. Representatives: 2
State legislature: senate 35; house 70

Illinois

Area: 56,400 square miles (including 523 square miles of water)
Population: 11,229,000
Capital: Springfield
State bird: Cardinal
State tree: Native oak
State flower: Native violet
State motto: State sovereignty—national union

Governor's term: 4 years
U.S. Representatives: 24
State legislature: senate 58; house 117

Indiana

Area: 36,291 square miles including 102 square miles of water)
Population: 5,302,000
Capital: Indianapolis
State bird: Cardinal
State tree: Tulip tree
State flower: Peony
State motto: The crossroads of America
Governor's term: 4 years
U.S. Representatives: 11
State legislature: senate 50; house 100

Iowa

Area: 56,290 square miles (including 247 square miles of water)
Population: 2,870,000
Capital: Des Moines
State bird: Eastern goldfinch
State tree: Oak
State flower: Wild rose
State motto: Our liberties we prize and our rights we will maintain
Governor's term: 2 years
U.S. Representatives: 6
State legislature: senate 50; house 100

Kansas

Area: 82,264 square miles (including 208 square miles of water)
Population: 2,310,000
Capital: Topeka
State bird: Western meadowlark
State tree: Cottonwood
State flower: Wild sunflower
State motto: Ad astra per aspera (To the stars through difficulties)
Governor's term: 2 years
U.S. Representatives: 5
State legislature: senate 40; house 125

Kentucky

Area: 40,395 square miles (including 544 square miles of water)
Population: 3,428,000
Capital: Frankfort
State bird: Cardinal
State tree: Tulip poplar
State flower: Goldenrod
State motto: United we stand, divided we fall
Governor's term: 4 years
U.S. Representatives: 7
State legislature: senate 38; house 100

Louisiana

Area: 48,523 square miles (in-

Farmer plows a wheat field in Kansas. The state ranks first as a wheat-producer and plays a leading role in feeding the nations of the world.

THE UNITED STATES

cluding 3,368 square miles of water)
Population: 3,841,000
Capital: Baton Rouge
State bird: Brown pelican
State tree: Bald cypress
State motto: Union, justice, and confidence
Governor's term: 4 years
U.S. Representatives: 8
State legislature: senate 39; house 105

Maine

Area: 33,215 square miles (including 2,282 square miles of water)
Population: 1,070,000
Capital: Augusta
State bird: Chickadee
State tree: White pine
State flower: White pine cone and tassel
State motto: Dirigo (I direct, or I guide)
Governor's term: 4 years
U.S. Representatives: 2
State legislature: senate 32; house 151

Maryland

Area: 10,577 square miles (including 686 square miles of water)
Population: 4,144,000

Capital: Annapolis
State bird: Baltimore oriole
State tree: White oak
State flower: Black-eyed Susan
State motto: Fatti maschii, parole femine (Manly deeds, womanly words)
Governor's term: 4 years
U.S. Representatives: 8
State legislature: senate 43; house 42

Massachusetts

Area: 8,257 square miles (including 424 square miles of water)
Population: 5,809,000
Capital: Boston
State bird: Chickadee
State tree: American elm
State flower: Mayflower
State motto: Ense petit placidam sub libertate quietem (By the sword we seek peace, but peace only under liberty)
Governor's term: 4 years
U.S. Representatives: 12
State legislature: senate 40; house 240

Michigan

Area: 58,216 square miles (including 1,398 square miles of water)
Population: 9,104,000

Capital: Lansing
State bird: Robin
State tree: White pine
State flower: Apple blossom
State motto: Si quaeris peninsulam amoenam circumspice (If you seek a pleasant peninsula, look about you)
Governor's term: 4 years
U.S. Representatives: 19
State legislature: senate 38; house 110

Minnesota

Area: 84,068 square miles (including 4,779 square miles of water)
Population: 3,965,000
Capital: St. Paul
State bird: Common loon
State tree: Norway pine
State flower: Pink and white lady's slipper
State motto: L'etoile du nord (The star of the north)
Governor's term: 4 years
U.S. Representatives: 8
State legislature: senate 67; house 135

Mississippi

Area: 47,716 square miles (including 358 square miles of water)
Population: 2,354,000
Capital: Jackson

Pulp logs at a paper mill in Rumford, Maine. Forests, covering four-fifths of the land area of Maine, supply the state's wood-processing industry.

Desert valley lying between ranges of the Sierra Nevada west of the border of Nevada and California. The visitor to the West is treated to many such vistas.

State bird: Mockingbird
State tree: Magnolia
State flower: Magnolia
State motto: Virtute et armis (By valor and arms)
Governor's term: 4 years
U.S. Representatives: 5
State legislature: senate 52; house 122

Missouri

Area: 69,686 square miles (including 640 square miles of water)
Population: 4,778,000
Capital: Jefferson City
State bird: Bluebird
State tree: Flowering dogwood
State flower: Hawthorn
State motto: Salus populi suprema lex esto (Let the welfare of the people be the supreme law)
Governor's term: 4 years
U.S. Representatives: 10
State legislature: senate 34; house 163

Montana

Area: 147,138 square miles (including 1,535 square miles of water)
Population: 753,000
Capital: Helena
State bird: Western meadowlark

State tree: Ponderosa pine
State flower: Bitterroot
State motto: Oro y plata (Gold and silver)
Governor's term: 4 years
U.S. Representatives: 2
State legislature: senate 55; house 104

Nebraska

Area: 77,227 square miles (including 705 square miles of water)
Population: 1,553,000
Capital: Lincoln
State bird: Western meadowlark
State tree: American elm
State flower: Goldenrod
State motto: Equality before the law
Governor's term: 4 years
U.S. Representatives: 3
State legislature: unicameral body of 49 members all designated senators

Nevada

Area: 110,540 square miles (including 65 square miles of water)
Population: 610,000
Capital: Carson City
State bird: Mountain bluebird
State tree: Single-leaf piñon
State flower: Sagebrush

State motto: All for our country
Governor's term: 4 years
U.S. Representatives: 1
State legislature: senate 20; assembly 40

New Hampshire

Area: 9,304 square miles (including 271 square miles of water)
Population: 822,000
Capital: Concord
State bird: Purple finch
State tree: White birch
State flower: Purple lilac
State motto: Live free or die
Governor's term: 2 years
U.S. Representatives: 2
State legislature: senate 24; house 400

New Jersey

Area: 7,836 square miles (including 304 square miles of water)
Population: 7,336,000
Capital: Trenton
State bird: Eastern goldfinch
State tree: Red oak
State flower: Purple violet
State motto: Liberty and prosperity
Governor's term: 4 years
U.S. Representatives: 15
State legislature: senate 20; assembly 40

Lower Manhattan skyline, New York City, showing the twin towers of the World Trade Center among other skyscrapers in the nation's cultural and business center.

New Mexico

Area: 121,666 square miles (including 221 square miles of water)
Population: 1,168,000
Capital: Sante Fe
State bird: Roadrunner, or chaparral
State tree: Piñon, or nut pine
State flower: Yucca
State motto: Crescit eundo (It grows as it goes)
Governor's term: 2 years
U.S. Representatives: 2
State legislature: senate 42; house 70

New York

Area: 49,576 square miles (including 1,707 square miles of water)
Population: 18,084,000
Capital: Albany
State bird: Bluebird (unofficial)
State tree: Sugar maple
State flower: Rose
State motto: Excelsior (Ever upward)
Governor's term: 4 years
U.S. Representatives: 39
State legislature: senate 57; house 150

North Carolina

Area: 52,586 square miles (including 3,706 square miles of water)
Population: 5,469,000
Capital: Raleigh
State bird: Cardinal
State tree: Pine
State flower: Flowering dogwood
State motto: Esse quam videri (To be rather than to seem)
Governor's term: 4 years
U.S. Representatives: 11
State legislature: senate 50; house 120

North Dakota

Area: 70,665 square miles (including 1,385 square miles of water)
Population: 643,000
Capital: Bismarck
State bird: Western meadowlark
State tree: American elm
State flower: Wild prairie rose
State motto: Liberty and union, now and forever, one and inseparable
Governor's term: 4 years
U.S. Representatives: 1
State legislature: senate 49; house 98

Ohio

Area: 41,222 square miles (including 204 square miles of water)
Population: 10,690,000
Capital: Columbus
State bird: Cardinal
State tree: Buckeye
State flower: Scarlet carnation
State motto: With God, all things are possible
Governor's term: 4 years
U.S. Representatives: 23
State legislature: senate 33; house 99

Oklahoma

Area: 69,919 square miles (including 935 square miles of water)
Population: 2,766,000
Capital: Oklahoma City
State bird: Scissor-tailed flycatcher
State tree: Redbud
State flower: Mistletoe
State motto: Labor omnia vincit (Labor conquers all things)
Governor's term: 4 years
U.S. Representatives: 6
State legislature: senate 48; house 99

Oregon

Area: 96,981 square miles (including 772 square miles of water)
Population: 2,329,000
Capital: Salem
State bird: Western meadowlark
State tree: Douglas fir

Molten iron being poured at the Bethlehem Steel Corporation, Bethlehem, Pa. One fourth of the nation's supply of steel is produced in Pennsylvania.

State flower: Oregon grape
State motto: The union
Governor's term: 4 years
U.S. Representatives: 4
State legislature: senate 30; house 60

Pennsylvania

Area: 45,333 square miles (including 308 square miles of water)
Population: 11,862,000
Capital: Harrisburg
State bird: Ruffed grouse
State tree: Hemlock
State flower: Mountain laurel
State motto: Virtue, liberty, and independence
Governor's term: 4 years
U.S. Representatives: 25
State legislature: senate 50; house 203

Rhode Island

Area: 1,214 square miles (including 165 square miles of water)
Population: 927,000
Capital: Providence
State bird: Rhode Island red
State tree: Red maple
State flower: Violet
State motto: Hope
Governor's term: 2 years
U.S. Representatives: 2

State legislature: senate 50; house 100

South Carolina

Area: 31,055 square miles (including 775 square miles of water)
Population: 2,848,000
Capital: Columbia
State bird: Carolina wren
State tree: Palmetto
State flower: Carolina jessamine
State motto: Animis opibusque parati (Prepared in mind and resources); Dum spiro spero (While I breathe I hope)
Governor's term: 4 years
U.S. Representatives: 6
State legislature: senate 46; house 124

South Dakota

Area: 77,047 square miles (including 1,091 square miles of water)
Population: 686,000
Capital: Pierre
State bird: Ring-necked pheasant
State tree: Black Hills spruce
State flower: American pasque-flower
State motto: Under God the people rule
Governor's term: 4 years

U.S. Representatives: 2
State legislature: senate 35; house 75

Tennessee

Area: 42,244 square miles (including 879 square miles of water)
Population: 4,214,000
Capital: Nashville
State bird: Mockingbird
State tree: Tulip poplar
State flower: Iris
State motto: Agriculture and commerce
Governor's term: 4 years
U.S. Representatives: 8
State legislature: senate 33; assembly 99

Texas

Area: 267,339 square miles (including 4,369 square miles of water)
Population: 12,487,000
Capital: Austin
State bird: Mockingbird
State tree: Pecan
State flower: Bluebonnet
State motto: Friendship
Governor's term: 2 years
U.S. Representatives: 24
State legislature: senate 31; house 150

THE UNITED STATES

Herd of Holstein cows on a Wisconsin farm. Wisconsin ranks first in the nation in production of milk products. In 1975 there were over a million cows in Wisconsin.

Utah

Area: 84,916 square miles (including 2,535 square miles of water)
Population: 1,228,000
Capital: Salt Lake City
State bird: Sea gull
State tree: Blue spruce
State flower: Sego lily
State motto: Industry
Governor's term: 4 years
U.S. Representatives: 2
State legislature: senate 28; house 69

Vermont

Area: 9,609 square miles (including 335 square miles of water)
Population: 476,000
Capital: Montpelier
State bird: Hermit thrush
State tree: Sugar maple
State flower: Red clover
State motto: Freedom and unity
Governor's term: 2 years
U.S. Representatives: 1
State legislature: senate 30; house 8

Virginia

Area: 40,817 square miles (including 976 square miles of water)
Population: 5,032,000
Capital: Richmond
State bird: Cardinal
State flower: Flowering dogwood
State motto: Sic semper tyrannis (Thus always with tyrants)
Governor's term: 4 years
U.S. Representatives: 10
State legislature: senate 40; house 100

Washington

Area: 68,192 square miles (including 1,529 square miles of water)
Population: 3,612,000
Capital: Olympia
State bird: Willow goldfinch
State tree: Western hemlock
State flower: Coast rhododendron
State motto: Al-ki (By and by)
Governor's term: 4 years
U.S. Representatives: 7
State legislature: senate 49; house 99

West Virginia

Area: 24,181 square miles (including 97 square miles of water)
Population: 1,821,000
Capital: Charleston
State bird: Cardinal
State tree: Sugar maple
State flower: Rhododendron
State motto: Montani semper liberi (Mountaineers are always free)
Governor's term: 4 years
U.S. Representatives: 4
State legislature: senate 34; house 100

Wisconsin

Area: 56,154 square miles (including 1,690 square miles of water)
Population: 4,609,000
Capital: Madison
State bird: Robin
State tree: Sugar maple
State flower: Violet
State motto: Forward
Governor's term: 4 years
U.S. Representatives: 9
State legislature: senate 33; house 100

Wyoming

Area: 97,914 square miles (including 633 square miles of water)
Population: 390,000
Capital: Cheyenne
State bird: Meadowlark
State tree: Cottonwood
State flower: Indian paintbrush
State motto: Equal rights
Governor's term: 4 years
U.S. Representatives: 1
State legislature: senate 30; house 61

U.S. POPULATION DENSITY, 1790-1980
(in people per square mile of U.S. territory)
PEOPLE PER SQUARE MILE
60
50
40
30
20
10
0
1790
1800
1810
1820
1830
1840
1850
1860
1870
1880
1890
1900
1910
1920
1930
1940
1950
1960
1970
1980
CENSUS YEAR

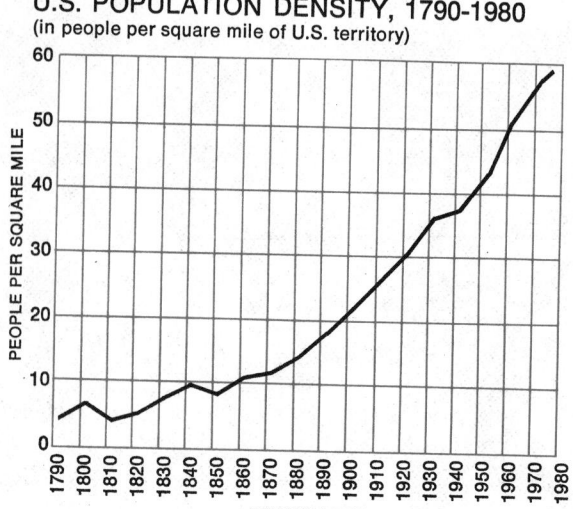

The population density of the United States has risen markedly but is still far less than that of many countries. New York, an old and well-established state, and California, a rapidly developing one, are shown below as having the largest populations of all the states.

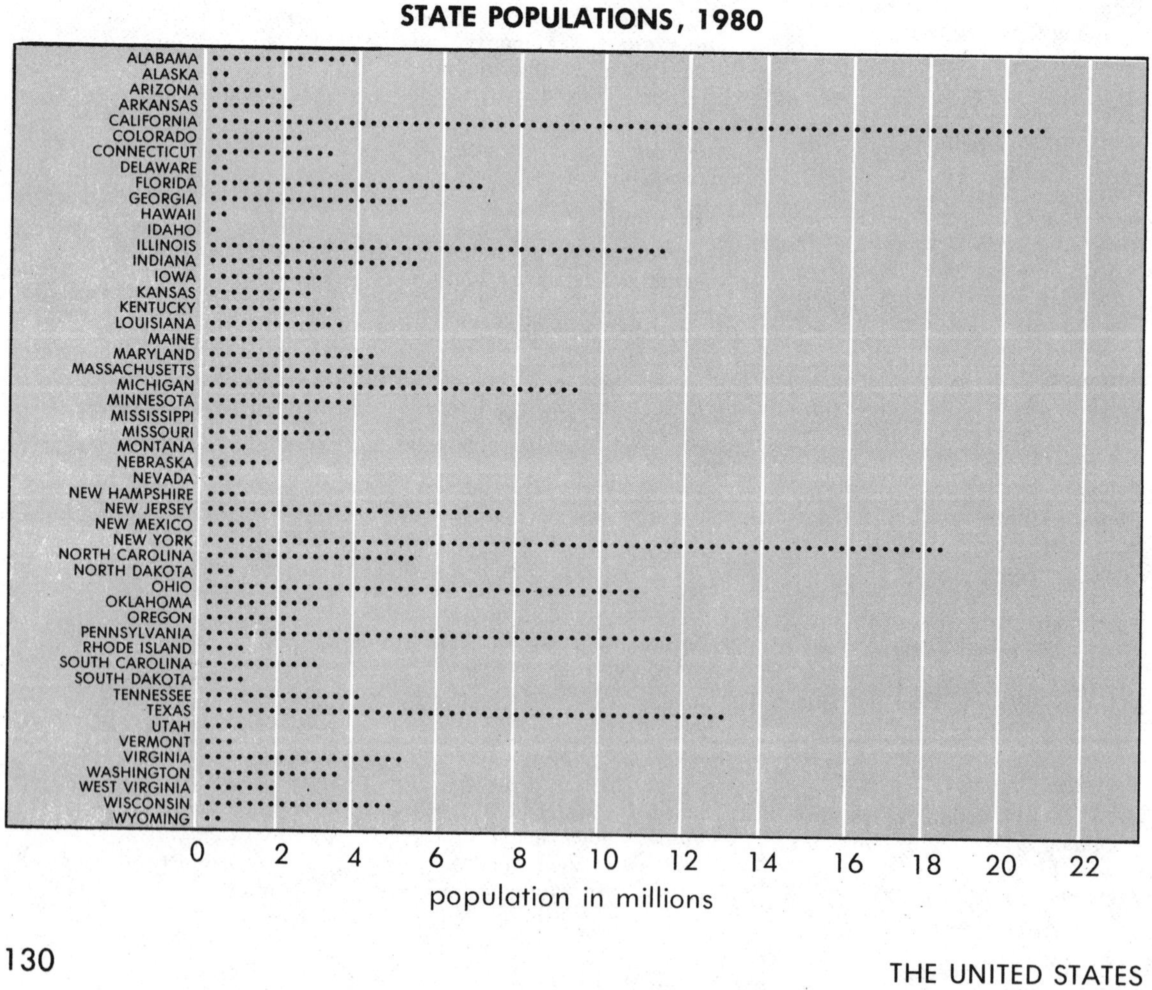

STATE POPULATIONS, 1980
ALABAMA
ALASKA
ARIZONA
ARKANSAS
CALIFORNIA
COLORADO
CONNECTICUT
DELAWARE
FLORIDA
GEORGIA
HAWAII
IDAHO
ILLINOIS
INDIANA
IOWA
KANSAS
KENTUCKY
LOUISIANA
MAINE
MARYLAND
MASSACHUSETTS
MICHIGAN
MINNESOTA
MISSISSIPPI
MISSOURI
MONTANA
NEBRASKA
NEVADA
NEW HAMPSHIRE
NEW JERSEY
NEW MEXICO
NEW YORK
NORTH CAROLINA
NORTH DAKOTA
OHIO
OKLAHOMA
OREGON
PENNSYLVANIA
RHODE ISLAND
SOUTH CAROLINA
SOUTH DAKOTA
TENNESSEE
TEXAS
UTAH
VERMONT
VIRGINIA
WASHINGTON
WEST VIRGINIA
WISCONSIN
WYOMING
0
2
4
6
8
10
12
14
16
18
20
22
population in millions

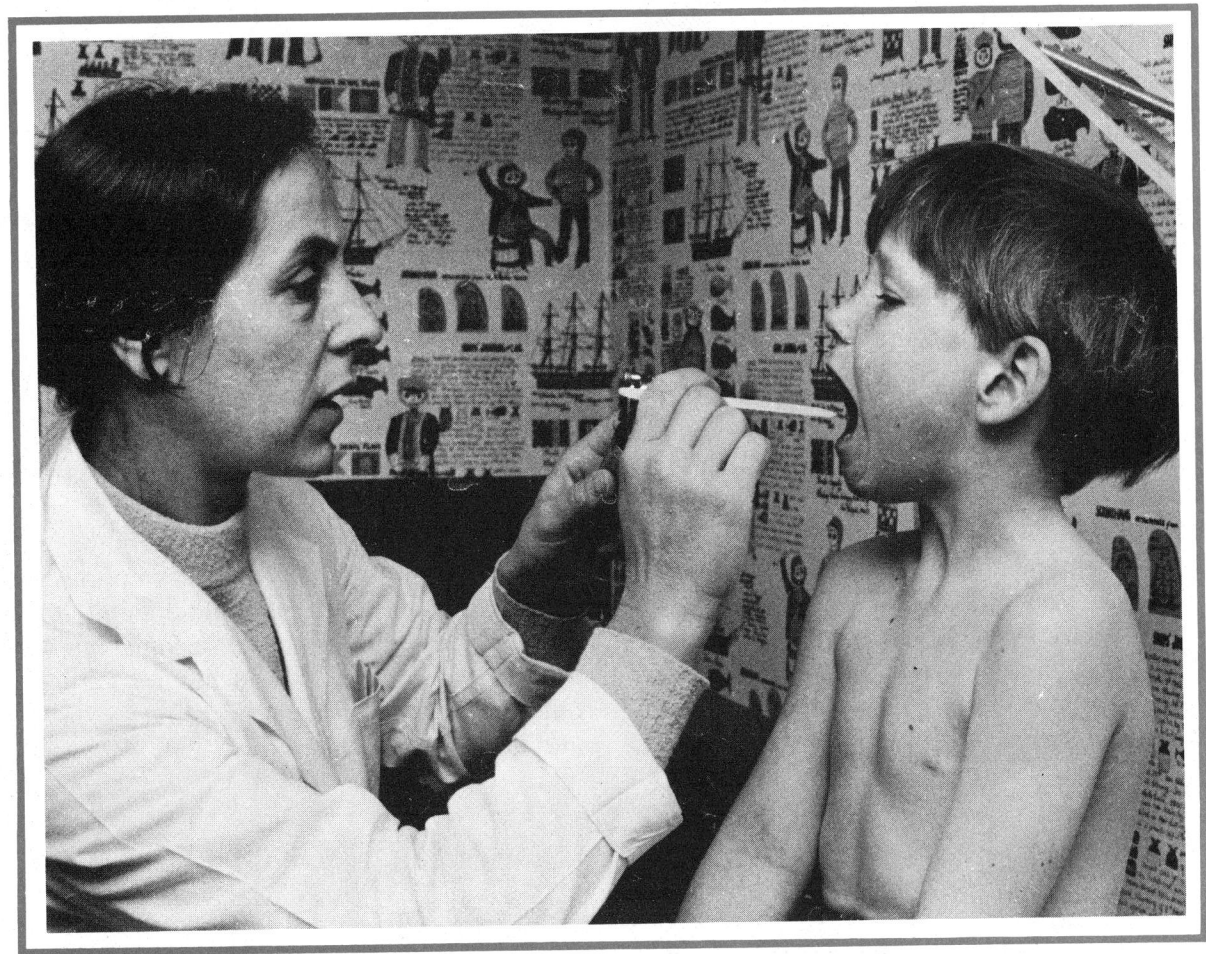

HEALTH AND HOME

We owe it to ourselves and those we love to keep ourselves in good health. By following sensible rules of diet, personal care, and exercise, we do much toward achieving happy lives. In addition to caring for ourselves, we must provide safe environments at home, school, and work. Good safety practices, knowledge of first aid, and sound ways of managing our affairs are equally important.

For these reasons, the pages that follow provide information you will want to consult often, not just in an emergency. You would do well to read these pages now to learn recommended procedures and to know where to look for quick help when you need it. The Concise Edition of the *Student Handbook* also has information on the vocational arts, planning your future, and managing your money that will help you achieve the goals of this section.

Healthy and Vigorous Living

Good health is something that takes effort. If you pay no attention to the food you eat, the care you take of your body, or the kind of exercise you get, your neglect will show —in how you *look* (your complexion, your weight, your hair, and your body's overall appearance) and in how you *feel* (full of pleasure and vigor or too tired to bother).

Proper diet is the single most important factor in good health, but difficult to achieve. Many of us have become interested in organic foods and natural foods, but just as many live on french fries, colas, and quick-service hamburgers.

THE BASIC FOUR FOOD GROUPS

GROUP I. Enriched or Whole Grain Bread, Flour, Cereals

Every day, choose four servings from the following grain foods:

All enriched breads	Brown rice or
Whole wheat bread	converted rice
Dark rye bread	Corn meal, whole
Rolled oat cereal	grain or enriched
Whole wheat cereal	Macaroni, noodles,
Other cereals, whole	spaghetti, enriched
grain or enriched	

GROUP II. Meats, Eggs, Dried Beans

Each day select two or more servings of meat or other protein-rich foods. Serve at least one of these every day:

Beef	Veal	Poultry
Lamb	Variety meats	Fish
Mutton	Game	Luncheon meats

Other protein-rich food to include:

Eggs	Cheese	Soy beans
Lentils	Peanut butter	Soya flour and
Nuts	Dried beans	grits
Peanuts	or peas	

GROUP III. Milk, Ice Cream, Cheese

Daily milk needs:

Adults	2 or more cups
Children	3 to 4 cups
Teen agers	1 quart or more
Pregnant women	1 quart or more
Nursing mothers	$1\frac{1}{2}$ quarts or more

GROUP IV. Vegetables and Fruits

Serve at least four from this group:

Broccoli	Carrots
Cabbage (raw)	Squash
Salad greens	Spinach
Citrus fruits	Sweet potatoes
Peppers	Other greens
Strawberries	Other vegetables
Tomatoes	and fruits

Americans, young and old, tend to have poor eating habits. We eat rich foods and ignore the simpler, better ones like fruits and vegetables. We also use many convenience foods, which are filled with chemicals and questionable artificial additives.

Eating properly does take thought, but it is a habit that pays off in better health. Professional suggestions are available for our guidance. Foods are arranged in basic *groups* according to their sources and the vitamins or food essentials they provide. The most common grouping is the basic four.

Each day your body needs certain amounts of food from each group in order to give you a balanced amount of the food essentials—proteins, fats, carbohydrates—as well as vitamins and minerals.

Get in the habit of eating three meals a day. A sound meal provides you with the energy needed to keep going until the next meal. This is why breakfast is so important. It should include eggs or other foods that supply protein. If you snack, choose healthful foods, such as fresh fruit, cheese, peanut butter or meat sandwiches, raw vegetables, and milk or fruit juice. These are better for you than potato chips, candy, soda, and other snacks, all of which fail to provide useful nutrients.

DIETING

Your nutritional requirements depend on your body type and on the amount of energy you use every day. Don't gauge what you must eat by the amount a friend may eat. Your growth pattern and needs are your own. If you want, or need, to lose a great deal of weight, check with your doctor and follow the diet pattern he or she recommends. Be sure you really are overweight

RECOMMENDED DAILY NUTRITIONAL REQUIREMENTS

| | Age | Wt. (lbs.) | Ht. (in.) | Calories | Protein (gms) | Calcium (mgs) | Iron (mgs) | Vitamins | | | | | |
								A (I.U.)	B₁ (mgs)	B₂ (mgs)	Niacin (mgs)	C (mgs)	D (I.U.)
Men	18–35	154	69	2,900	70	800	10	5,000	1.2	1.7	19	70	
	35–55	154	69	2,600	70	800	10	5,000	1.0	1.6	17	70	
	55–75	154	69	2,200	70	800	10	5,000	0.9	1.3	15	70	
Women	18–35	128	64	2,100	58	800	15	5,000	0.8	1.3	14	70	
	35–55	128	64	1,900	58	800	15	5,000	0.8	1.2	13	70	
	55–75	128	64	1,600	58	800	10	5,000	0.8	1.2	13	70	
Children	1–3	29	34	1,300	32	800	8	2,000	0.5	0.8	9	40	400
	3–6	40	42	1,600	40	800	10	2,500	0.6	1.0	11	50	400
	6–9	53	49	2,100	52	800	12	3,500	0.8	1.3	14	60	400
Boys	9–12	72	55	2,400	60	1,100	15	4,500	1.0	1.4	16	70	400
	12–15	98	61	3,000	75	1,400	15	5,000	1.2	1.8	20	80	400
	15–18	134	68	3,400	85	1,400	15	5,000	1.4	2.0	22	80	400
Girls	9–12	72	55	2,200	55	1,100	15	4,500	0.9	1.3	15	80	400
	12–15	103	62	2,500	62	1,300	15	5,000	1.0	1.5	17	80	400
	15–18	117	64	2,300	58	1,300	15	5,000	0.9	1.3	15	70	400

Vitamins: Their importance and sources

The essential vitamins and the quantities we need to maintain good health are officially established by the National Research Council of the Food and Nutrition Board of the National Academy of Sciences.

vitamin A. Important for growth in children, good vision, healthy skin and hair; essential to the epithelial tissues of the body.

Source: butter, eggs, cream, whole milk, fortified margarine, cheddar cheese; kidneys, liver, Chinook salmon; deep green leafy vegetables (spinach, broccoli, brussels sprouts); yellow vegetables (carrots, squash); fish liver oils; tomatoes, apricots, cantaloupe.

vitamin B (thiamine). Essential to the circulatory and nervous systems; prevents beriberi.

Source: milk, eggs; whole grain or enriched cereals and breads; liver, poultry, fish, pork; yeast; peanuts and peanut butter; oysters.

vitamin B2 (riboflavin). Essential for the building and maintenance of body tissues, including the epithelial tissues; also helpful in controlling the eyes' sensitivity to light.

Source: milk, eggs; bread (whole wheat or enriched); kidney, liver; dried yeast; deep green leafy vegetables (spinach, kale, broccoli, mustard greens).

vitamin B6 (pyridoxine). Important for healthy teeth and gums; essential to the nervous system, the blood vessels, and the red blood cells.

Source: milk, eggs; whole grain cereals; meat, especially liver; deep green leafy vegetables (see vitamin A and vitamin B2), corn; peanuts, soybeans, beans; molasses.

vitamin B12 (cobalamin). Important for the nervous system and for growth in children; prevents certain forms of anemia.

Source: milk, eggs; kidney, liver, saltwater fish and shellfish, lamb, poultry, veal.

niacin (niacinamide). Essential to the conversion of food into energy; aids the nervous system; prevents pellagra.

Source: eggs; whole grain cereals, enriched and whole grain bread; liver, kidney, meat, fish, poultry; peanuts.

vitamin C (ascorbic acid). Essential to the strength of body cells and blood vessels, and important for healthy teeth, gums, and bones; fights infections; prevents scurvy.

Source: citrus fruits (oranges, lemons, grapefruits), strawberries, green peppers, tomatoes, pineapples, bananas, avocados, artichokes, deep green leafy vegetables, cabbage, cauliflower.

vitamin D. Essential to the growth and maintenance of strong teeth and bones, necessary in the process of utilizing calcium and phosphorus; prevents rickets.

Source: fortified milk, egg yolks, fortified margarine; fish liver oils, salmon, tuna, herring, sardines, liver.

folic acid. Essential for the protection of the gastrointestinal tract.

Source: deep green leafy vegetables; chicken liver, meats; food yeast.

pantothenic acid. Essential to the nervous system and the adrenal gland and to the manufacture of antibodies.

Source: in all plant and animal tissue, particularly in foods such as kidney, liver, peanuts, fresh vegetables, egg yolks.

biotin. Essential to the health of the skin and mucous membranes; necessary for the maintenance of red blood cells and the circulatory system.

Source: manufactured by microorganisms in the intestines; also can be found in eggs, deep green leafy vegetables, liver, kidneys, string beans.

vitamin E (tocopherol). Important for protection of fat within the body tissues and control of the rate of its breakdown; essential to the red blood cells.

Source: milk, butter, eggs; whole grain or enriched cereals; meats; vegetable oils, deep green leafy vegetables.

vitamin K. Essential to the process of blood clotting.

Source: manufactured by microorganisms in the intestines; can also be found in deep green leafy vegetables, tomatoes, soybeans, liver.

and are not just wishing to be thinner than you should be. Even when you are dieting, eat well-balanced meals. Cut down on fattening foods, but do not skip entire meals or throw your system out of balance by eating just one thing. Even if you want to lose only a few pounds, do it slowly and carefully, not with a crash diet. Above all, don't try to lose weight with diet pills or liquid proteins.

Basic foods for dieters include two servings a day of meat, fish, eggs, or protein-rich beans (such as navy beans); four servings of green and yellow vegetables and citrus fruits; and four servings of milk, cheese, or cottage cheese. You lose weight not by skipping basic foods, but by cutting down on rich and fatty foods. A list of daily nutritional requirements is provided to help you plan better eating habits. Use the list daily whenever you diet.

CARING FOR YOUR SKIN AND HAIR

Projecting a good personal appearance is not really as difficult as most of us imagine. Frequent baths or showers will help keep your skin healthy. If you are very active physically, you may need to bathe more than once a day. Be sure to use a soap that is not too strong for your skin. Foods high in protein and vitamin A help to produce a clear complexion.

Your hair reflects the condition of your overall health. Brushing is probably the most important thing you can do to keep it shiny and manageable. Brushing brings the blood closer to your scalp, removes dirt and dead cells, and distributes natural body oils throughout the hair and scalp. Wash your hair at least once a week.

CARING FOR YOUR TEETH

In order to have clean, healthy teeth, you must give them special care. The enamel that acts as a protective covering cannot replace itself. When it wears away, the tooth decays.

Germs can also be responsible for irritated gums. Brushing and flossing regularly are the keys to keeping healthy teeth and gums. Brush your teeth after every meal. If you can't, brush them after breakfast and before going to bed.

THE IMPORTANCE OF EXERCISE

Fresh air and sunlight are as important for humans as they are for other living things, and outdoor activity is doubly beneficial. Walking, jogging, hiking, and skating combine exercise with recreation and can be enjoyed alone or in the company of others.

Normal activity burns up energy and provides some exercise, but it is wise to take advantage of the physical exercise and training provided by team sports and gym classes.

Calisthenics are exercises performed without equipment. They are intended to stretch, rather than build, your muscles and to keep your body in tone. In the "windmill": stand erect, hands extended at shoulder height; bend and touch toes with opposite hands, alternating sides. Repeat.

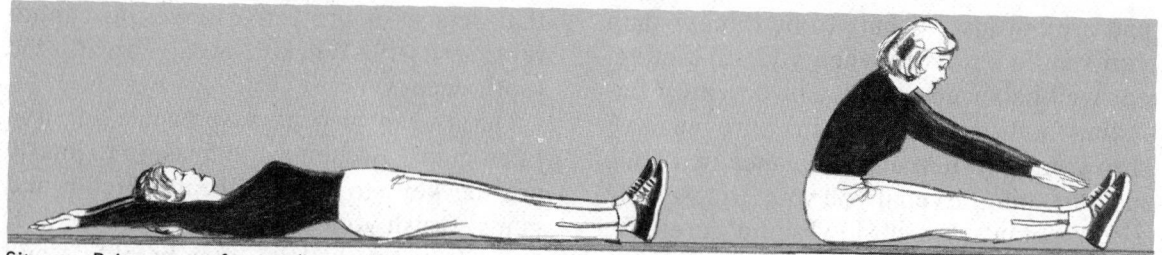

Sit-ups: Bring arms forward over head; roll to a sitting position; touch ankles. Repeat.

Push-ups. Men: hands and toes. Women: hands and lower legs. Keep body straight; lower to 2 inches of floor; push up. Repeat.

The "twister": Stand erect with hands on hips and feet apart. Bend forward from waist, then twist to right. Bend back from waist, then twist to left. Repeat.

Running in place: Stand straight with hands clenched, elbows bent. While running, pump arms vigorously. Athletes often perform this exercise to loosen up.

136

How to Exercise

If your daily schedule does not involve physical activity, you probably need a regular exercise program. Exercising does not have to be a dull routine of touching your toes every morning. The best exercise, in fact, is probably the kind you get outdoors —swimming, tennis, other sports, and brisk walking. But calisthenics—an organized series of exercises for specific muscles and specific kinds of toning up—are also important in physical fitness. The calisthenics suggested here are good for limbering up, for warm-up exercises, and for regular exercising.

PREVENTING HEALTH PROBLEMS

Checkups are important. Begin now to develop the habit of taking care of yourself before you get sick.

1. See your doctor for a checkup at least once a year.

2. Have a dental check twice a year.

3. Have your eyes examined once a year. Study and read with the proper lighting and posture to avoid eye strain.

Get shots as your doctor recommends them. If you are planning to travel, go to camp, or work in a summer camp, you may need shots beforehand, or you may need booster shots for earlier immunizations.

Be very careful in your use of drugs: drugs can harm your body. Avoid diet pills, sleeping pills, and stay-awake aids unless your doctor prescribes or suggests them. Know and think about the consequences of using drugs, such as alcohol, tobacco, marijuana, "speed," or other drugs. Do not get involved with them. Don't use harmful drugs just because somebody else does. A

IMMUNIZATION SCHEDULE

The following is a suggested schedule for immunization during a baby's first year. It is based on recommendations of the American Medical Association and the American Academy of Pediatrics.

Diphtheria, Whooping Cough, Tetanus

Age for First Dose	6 weeks to 2 months.
Number of Doses	3 shots, one month apart.
Boosters	At 1 year and again at 4 years; repeated as recommended by physician.

Polio

Age for First Dose	6 weeks to 3 months.
Number of Doses	3 oral doses, four to six weeks apart.
Boosters	Every year, as recommended by physician.

Smallpox

Age for First Dose	15 to 18 months.
Number of Doses	1 vaccination.
Boosters	Every 3 to 5 years, and if exposed.

Measles

Age for First Dose	12 months.
Number of Doses	"live" type: 1 shot; "killed" type: 3 shots, one month apart.
Boosters	As recommended by physician.

table is provided to show you the effects of certain drugs on your body.

TIPS FOR ADOLESCENTS

Skin Problems. A good diet and general good health will do a lot to make your skin healthy and glowing. Skin problems are troublesome for adolescents, and serious cases of acne or other teenage skin problems need a doctor's care. Young women with skin problems should be especially careful about the use of makeup—choosing cosmetics carefully and using them sparingly or not at all. Nonallergenic lipsticks are obtainable.

The uses and effects of some drugs

Narcotics	Medical Uses	Physical Addiction	Harmful Effects
Heroin	None legal	High	Extreme dependence; loss of coordination; stupor; intellectual dysfunctioning; constipation; appetite loss; death by overdose
Morphine	Relief from pain; in severe cases, coughing, diarrhea, and anxiety	High	
Methadone	Treating heroin and morphine addicts	High	
Stimulants			
Amphetamines (Methedrine, Benzedrine, Dexedrine)	Treating narcolepsy, hyper-kinesis, and in rare instances, obesity and fatigue	Addictive in large doses	Possible brain damage; dependence; delusions; hallucinations; toxic psychosis; appetite loss; insomnia; exhaustion; nervousness
Cocaine	Local anesthetic	None	Dependence; depression; appetite loss; irritability; insomnia; exhaustion; nervousness
Caffeine	None	Slight	Slight dependence; insomnia; restlessness; nervousness
Nicotine (tobacco)	None	None	Emphysema; lung cancer; cardio-vascular disease; dependence; chronic cough
Depressants			
Barbiturates (Seconal, Nembutal, Amytal)	Sedative, treatment of high blood pressure, epilepsy, hyperthyroidism	High	Dependence; toxic psychosis; depression; drowsiness; loss of coordination; stupor; overdose may be fatal
Tranquilizers	Treatment of psychosis, anxiety, tension, neurosis	None	Slight dependence; drowsiness; dryness of mouth; overdose may be fatal
Alcohol	Rarely used as a sedative	May be addictive	Cirrhosis; brain damage; dependence; psychosis; loss of coordination; stupor; intellectual dysfunction
Hallucinogens			
LSD	Controlled experiments only	None	Hallucination; panic; may cause psychosis
Mescaline	None	None	Hallucination; panic; may cause psychosis
Marijuana	Controlled experiments only	None	Slight dependence; reduced coordination

138

Regular Exercise. This is important at all times, including the menstrual period, unless your doctor advises against exercise at that time. Moderate exercise is often helpful for cramps or queasy stomachs. Though menstrual periods will probably be irregular during adolescence, watch for unusual pain or bleeding and report it to your doctor or to the school nurse.

Rest and Relaxation. Rest and relaxation are also important. The amount of sleep you need will vary with your age and rate of growth or use of energy. Between the ages of twelve and fourteen, most adolescents need about nine hours of sleep each night. If you need a great deal of sleep or feel lethargic, check with your doctor. You may not be eating properly, or your body may just need more rest. Try to rest at intervals throughout the day, especially after meals. If you are involved in physical activity, take a break and do something involving mental activity or just relax. If you are studying and become fatigued, take a physical-activity break. Balance your work and recreation. All study or all play limits your experience. You need outside interests and activities that will expand your world and help to keep you from becoming too one-sided. A hobby or a volunteer job will give you something to do and may help develop an interesting career possibility. You will also find that the proper amount of rest and relaxation will add hours of productive time to your day, because you will work better after a break.

Know Yourself. You should learn to recognize your individual pattern of growth and development. When you notice changes in your body or its functions, report them to your doctor and find out if treatment is needed. They may not be natural adolescent fluctuations.

HARD FACTS ABOUT SUGAR

In January, 1977, the Senate Select Committee on Nutrition and Human Needs urged Americans to reduce their sugar consumption by 40 percent.

- Sugar (like starch) is a carbohydrate.

- **In 1900:** The average American consumed 77 pounds of sugar a year, of which 65 percent was sucrose.

- **Today:** The average American consumes 125 pounds of sugar a year, of which 95 percent is sucrose.

• Twenty percent of the daily caloric intake of the average American is sugar. Refined sugar has no nutrient content; it is "empty calories." Unrefined sugars do not provide enough trace nutrients to make a difference in food value.

• Food that has sugar as one of the main ingredients rarely contains enough other ingredients to make the food more than "empty calories." Seventy percent of the sugar in the American diet is hidden in processed foods. Check labels and notice how often sugar occurs in cereals, soups, peanut butter, ketchup, salad dressings, sauces, soft drinks, dessert mixes, etc.

• Sugar does not *cause* diabetes, heart disease, obesity. *But* the treatment of these diseases includes a reduced caloric intake—a weight loss. Sugar is a problem food to sufferers of these conditions.

• Sugar promotes tooth decay. Dentists recommend rinsing the mouth after eating or drinking anything sweet to remove sugar left on teeth. Dentists suggest avoiding sweets between meals.

• Americans thoughtlessly make their main carbohydrate source the processed, sugar-sweetened foods, so their diet lacks bulk and essential ingredients.

• Get sweets from natural sources. Keep down the empty calories. Three pounds of apples contain about the same number of calories as one candy bar.

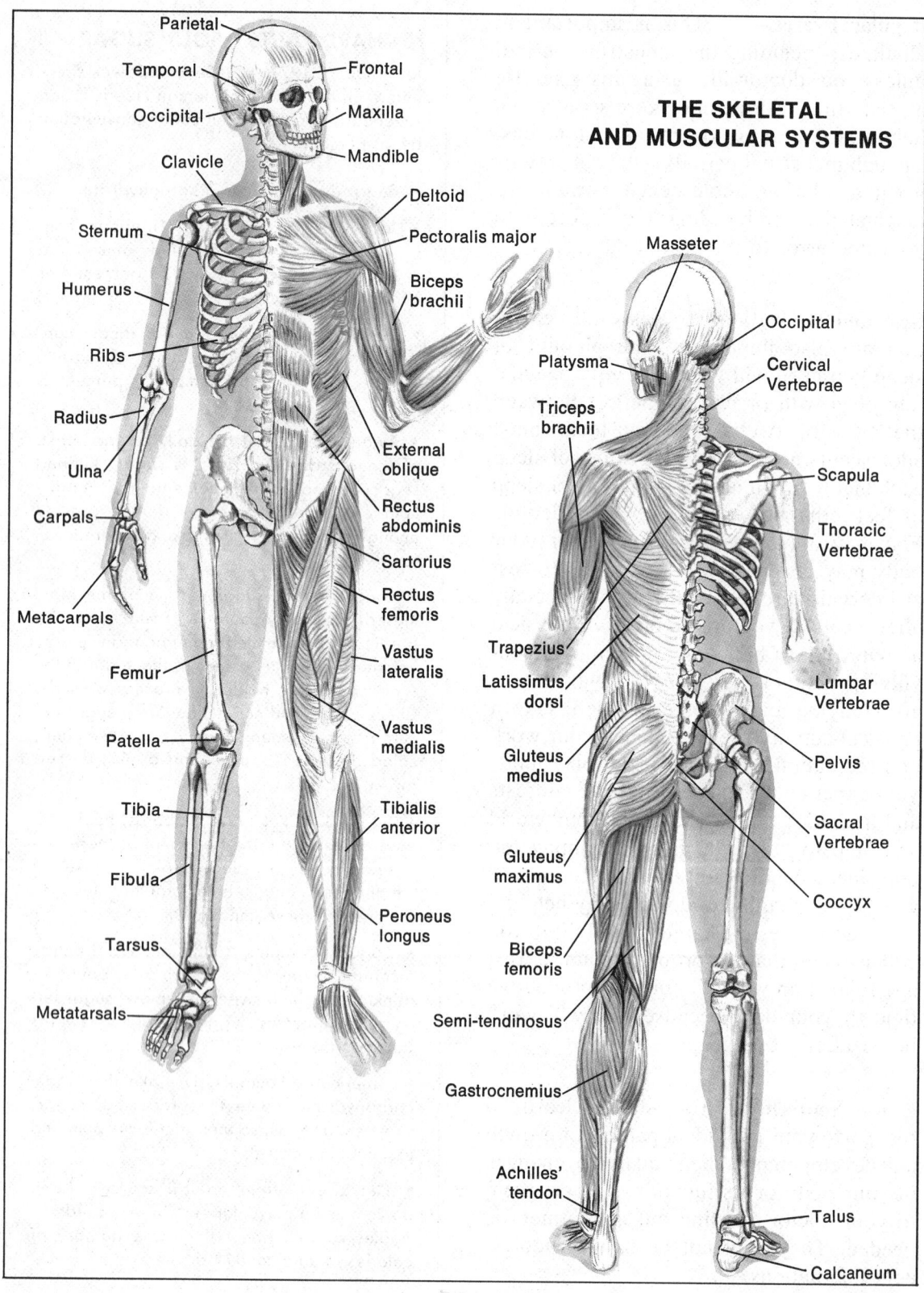

THE SKELETAL
AND MUSCULAR SYSTEMS

Parietal
Temporal
Occipital
Frontal
Maxilla
Mandible
Clavicle
Sternum
Humerus
Ribs
Radius
Ulna
Carpals
Metacarpals
Femur
Patella
Tibia
Fibula
Tarsus
Metatarsals

Deltoid
Pectoralis major
Biceps brachii
External oblique
Rectus abdominis
Sartorius
Rectus femoris
Vastus lateralis
Vastus medialis
Tibialis anterior
Peroneus longus

Masseter
Platysma
Triceps brachii
Trapezius
Latissimus dorsi
Gluteus medius
Gluteus maximus
Biceps femoris
Semi-tendinosus
Gastrocnemius
Achilles' tendon

Occipital
Cervical Vertebrae
Scapula
Thoracic Vertebrae
Lumbar Vertebrae
Pelvis
Sacral Vertebrae
Coccyx
Talus
Calcaneum

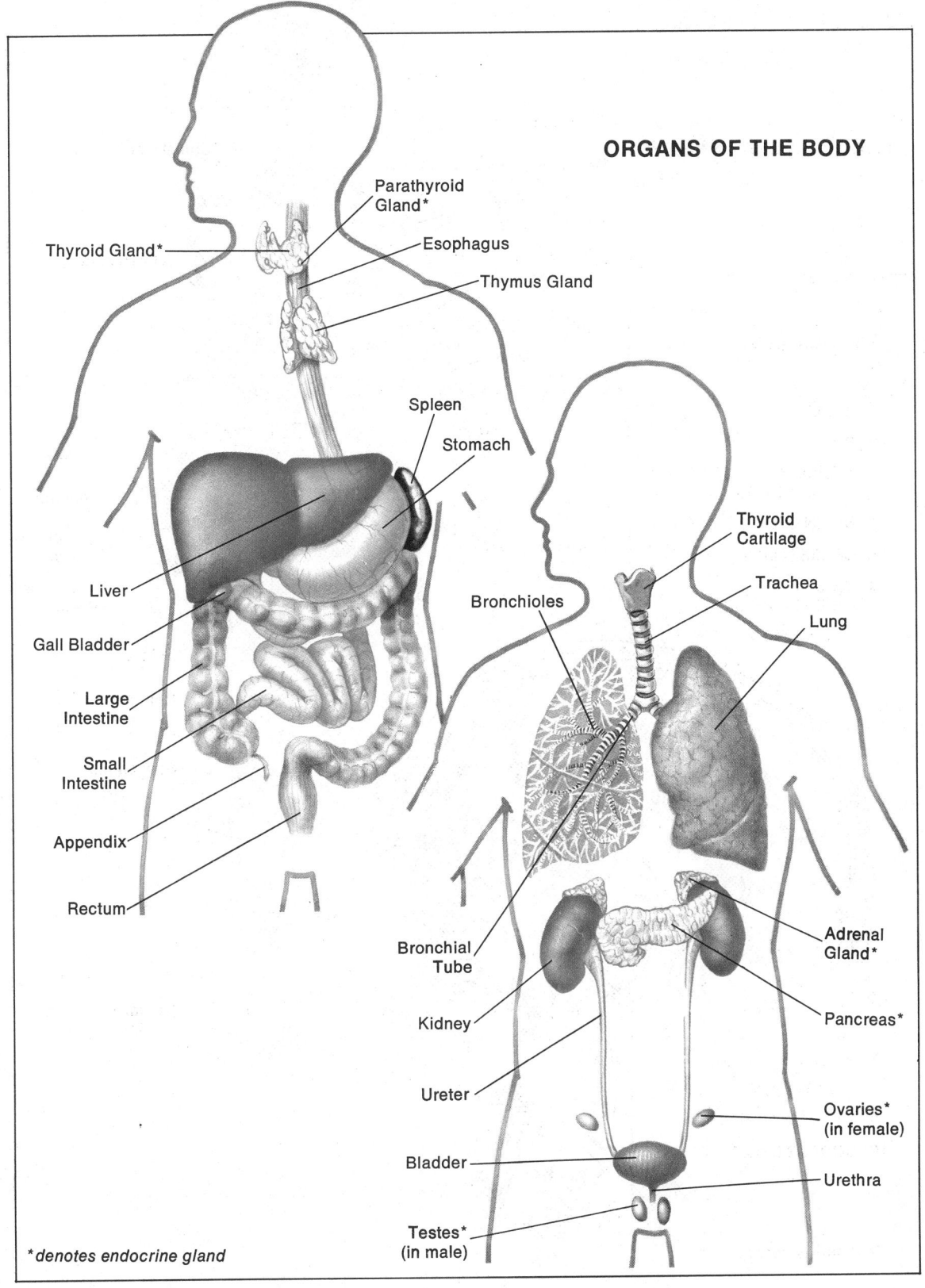

ORGANS OF THE BODY

Parathyroid Gland*

Thyroid Gland*

Esophagus

Thymus Gland

Spleen

Stomach

Thyroid Cartilage

Trachea

Liver

Bronchioles

Lung

Gall Bladder

Large Intestine

Small Intestine

Appendix

Rectum

Bronchial Tube

Adrenal Gland*

Kidney

Pancreas*

Ureter

Ovaries* (in female)

Bladder

Urethra

Testes* (in male)

*denotes endocrine gland

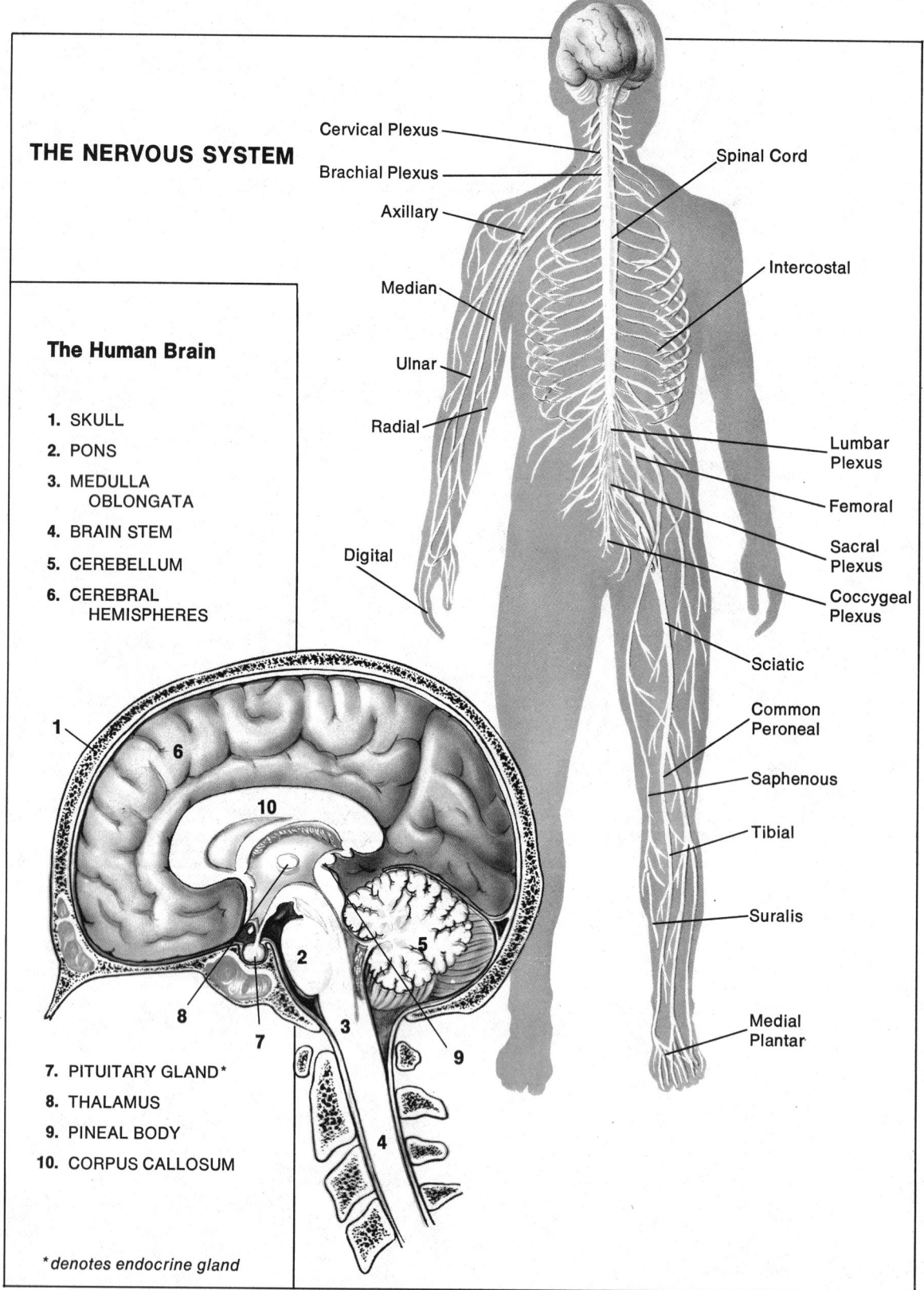

THE NERVOUS SYSTEM

Cervical Plexus

Brachial Plexus

Axillary

Median

Ulnar

Radial

Digital

Spinal Cord

Intercostal

Lumbar Plexus

Femoral

Sacral Plexus

Coccygeal Plexus

Sciatic

Common Peroneal

Saphenous

Tibial

Suralis

Medial Plantar

The Human Brain

1. SKULL
2. PONS
3. MEDULLA OBLONGATA
4. BRAIN STEM
5. CEREBELLUM
6. CEREBRAL HEMISPHERES

7. PITUITARY GLAND*
8. THALAMUS
9. PINEAL BODY
10. CORPUS CALLOSUM

*denotes endocrine gland

142   HEALTH AND HOME

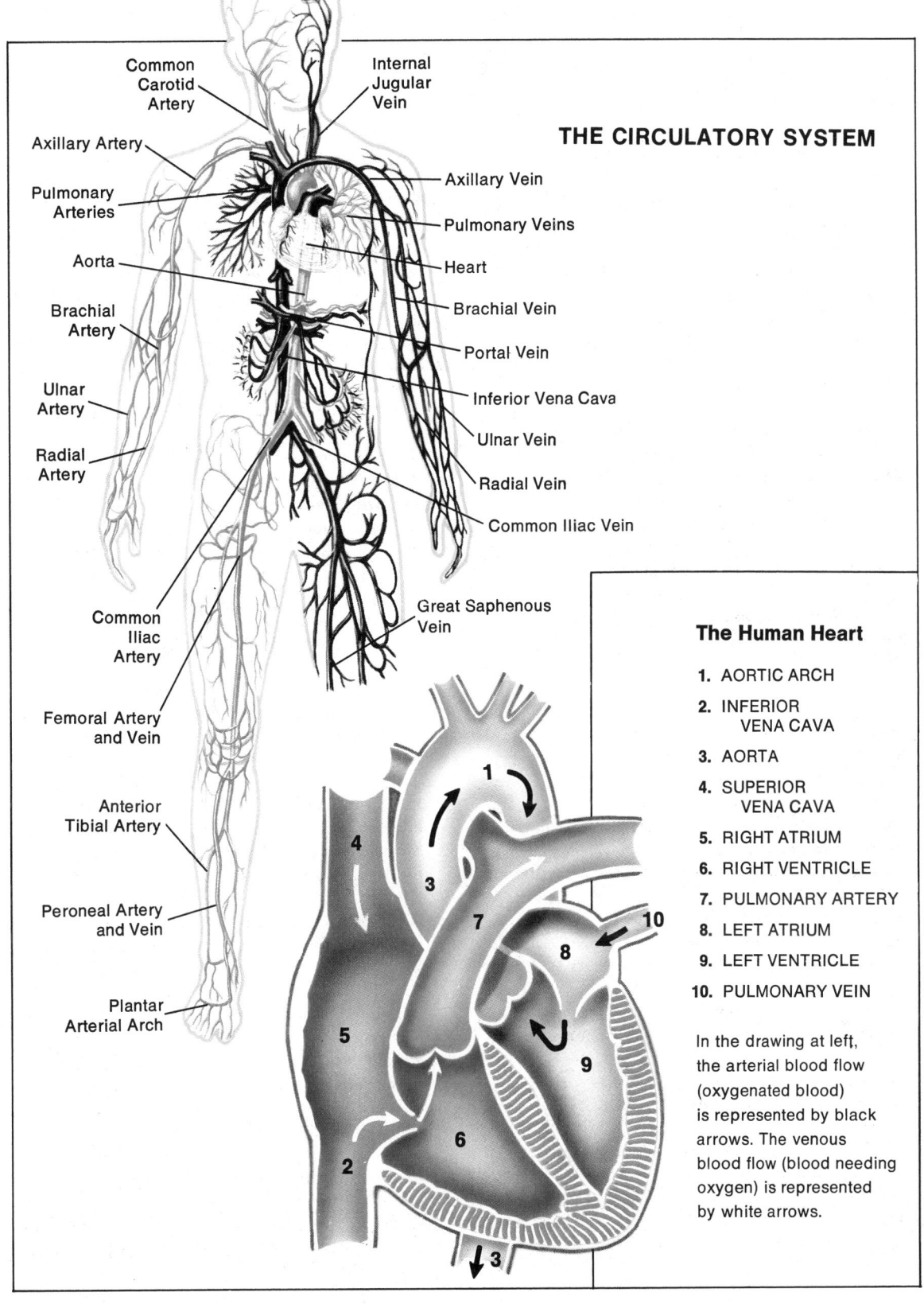

THE CIRCULATORY SYSTEM

Common Carotid Artery

Internal Jugular Vein

Axillary Artery

Pulmonary Arteries

Aorta

Brachial Artery

Ulnar Artery

Radial Artery

Common Iliac Artery

Femoral Artery and Vein

Anterior Tibial Artery

Peroneal Artery and Vein

Plantar Arterial Arch

Axillary Vein

Pulmonary Veins

Heart

Brachial Vein

Portal Vein

Inferior Vena Cava

Ulnar Vein

Radial Vein

Common Iliac Vein

Great Saphenous Vein

The Human Heart

1. AORTIC ARCH
2. INFERIOR VENA CAVA
3. AORTA
4. SUPERIOR VENA CAVA
5. RIGHT ATRIUM
6. RIGHT VENTRICLE
7. PULMONARY ARTERY
8. LEFT ATRIUM
9. LEFT VENTRICLE
10. PULMONARY VEIN

In the drawing at left, the arterial blood flow (oxygenated blood) is represented by black arrows. The venous blood flow (blood needing oxygen) is represented by white arrows.

Some infectious diseases

chicken pox. A childhood viral disease characterized by rash, fever, headache, and loss of appetite. Transmitted by inhalation of infected airborne droplets. Usually lasts three to five days.

common cold. A disease caused by the transfer of viruses from one person to another, often by sneezing or coughing. Usually lasts two to three days. Characterized by sneezing, coughing, sore throat, and fever.

diphtheria. A bacterial disease that primarily affects children. Transmitted by airborne droplets from the throat of an infected person. Accompanied by breathing difficulty caused by a membrane that forms across the throat. Most infants are inoculated against diphtheria.

German measles (rubella or three-day measles). A viral disease characterized by skin rash and swollen lymph glands. Transmitted by contact with an infected person and usually lasts two to four days. Ordinarily affects children; if it affects a pregnant woman, can be extremely dangerous to the fetus. Controlled by inoculation.

hepatitis, infectious. A viral disease of the liver, transmitted by close contact with carriers or contaminated food or water. Usually lasts four to six weeks. Causes fever, skin rash, weakness, loss of appetite, chills, nausea, jaundice.

hepatitis, serum. A viral disease of the liver. Transmitted by contact with infected blood and contaminated hypodermic needles. Usually lasts four to six weeks, with symptoms similar to those of infectious hepatitis.

influenza. A viral disease that often occurs in epidemics. Transmitted by airborne droplets and causes chills, fever, muscle and eye pain, and sneezing. Can lead to pneumonia. Vaccines may provide temporary immunity.

measles (rubeola). A viral disease that usually infects children. Symptoms include red and watery eyes, fever, nasal discharge, congestion, and rash. Usually lasts four to ten days. There is a vaccine against it.

mumps. A viral disease transmitted by direct contact with infected persons. Usually affects children and lasts four to five days. Attacks the salivary glands, causing pain, swelling, and fever. Complications may involve other glands.

pneumonia. A respiratory disease that may be caused by viruses, bacteria, or fungi that attack the lungs when resistance is low, often because of a cold or other minor aliment. Characterized by fever, coughing, chest aches, chills.

poliomyelitis (infantile paralysis). A viral disease transmitted by carriers or contaminated food. Usually lasts seven to ten days, but if the nerve cells controlling muscles are attacked, permanent partial paralysis may result. May produce fever, sore throat, or headaches. Polio vaccines have nearly eliminated polio.

rabies. A viral disease transmitted by the saliva of infected animals. Usually lasts six to ten days. Fever, headaches, breathing spasms, convulsions, and fits are characteristic of the disease. Unless vaccine injections are begun at once, death almost certainly results.

rheumatic fever. A disease that usually affects children. Develops after a bacterial respiratory infection. Aches that move from joint to joint, nosebleeds, abdominal pains, and skin eruptions are common symptoms. Rheumatic fever may damage the heart.

scarlet fever. A bacterial disease, related to "strep" throat, usually affecting children. Transmitted by infected carriers or contaminated food. Fever, vomiting, headache, sore throat, and rash are common symptoms. Usually lasts two to five days.

tetanus (lockjaw). A bacterial disease caused by the contamination of wounds. Symptoms include muscle spasms and difficulty in breathing and may last from a few days to several years. Immediate treatment is necessary to prevent death. Can be controlled by inoculation.

tuberculosis. A bacterial disease transmitted by infected carriers or contaminated milk. In its early stage, tuberculosis is characterized by fever, fatigue, and loss of weight. Later, chest pains, bloody sputum, and sweating develop. Vaccine is available.

typhoid fever. A bacterial disease carried in contaminated food or water. Usually lasts five to six weeks. Symptoms include headaches, fever, chills, nausea, coughing, constipation, and nosebleeds. Can be controlled with inoculation.

whooping cough. Children are the usual victims of this bacterial disease. Characterized by an explosive cough, convulsions, and possible lung complications. Inoculation is available.

Safety

TIPS FOR HOME SAFETY

Accidents in the home are the second leading cause of accidental death. A thoughtful review of the entire home environment—house, yard, and garage—will reveal objects and areas with potential for wounds, burns, falls, poisoning, and electric shock. Children and adults should learn the proper use and handling of appliances, utensils, and tools, and the importance of their safe storage.

The following are a few general safety *precautions* that will help your family:

1. Keep stairs free from litter and toys.
2. Be sure stair pads are securely fastened down.
3. Dispose of broken glass and tin cans in covered containers.
4. Cover electrical outlets when not in use.
5. Never leave a tub of hot water unattended.
6. Never leave a young child unattended, particularly in the bathtub.
7. Never use electrical appliances while taking a bath.
8. Keep medicines and cleaning supplies out of reach of younger children.
9. Never use charcoal in a fireplace inside your house.
10. Check paints for lead content. (Children will chew anything.)
11. Be sure rugs are nonskid.
12. Keep sharp objects out of reach of children.
13. Check fabric labels to see if they are flame retardant.

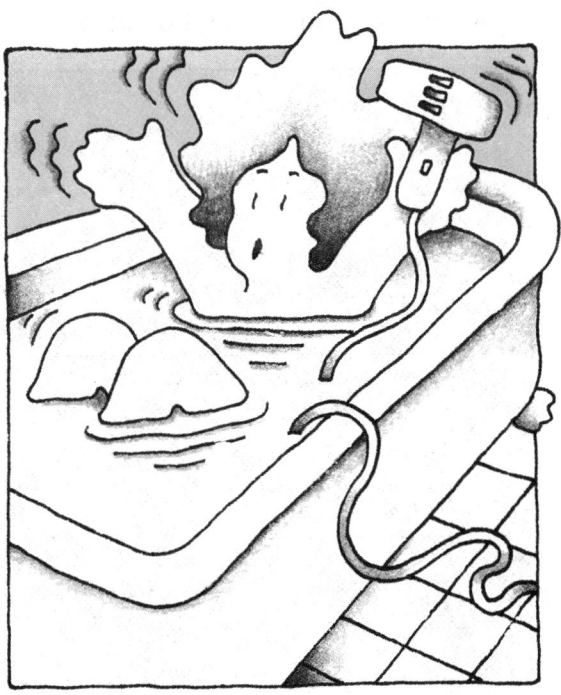

Precautions Against Fire

1. See that all wiring is properly installed and maintained.
2. Check insulation of electric appliances. Never use an electric appliance not in good repair.
3. Always keep a screen in front of the fireplace.
4. Never smoke in bed. Get up if you must smoke.
5. Never allow oily rags to accumulate.
6. In case of fire at night, feel the door. If it seems hot, don't open it. Seek another way of escape.
7. Never leave irons, toasters, etc. turned on when you leave the room.

Precautions Against Electrical Shock and Fire

1. Provide sufficient outlets and circuits to serve all lamps and appliances with safety.
2. Locate switches so they help light the way. For example, at entrances to rooms and at the head and foot of stairs.
3. Do not overload wiring.
4. Do not place too many small appliances on one circuit.
5. Never touch electrical equipment when any part of the body is in contact with a wet surface.
6. Follow manufacturer's recommendations in using Christmas lighting and use it only where specifically stated.
7. If service line is overhead, check it for signs of wear caused by moving tree limbs or other kinds of friction.
8. Replace frayed and damaged cords and blown fuses. Major repairs and installations should be made by a licensed electrician.

Precautions Against Theft

1. When you are away on vacation don't tell the world. Tell the milkman and the newsboy to stop deliveries.
2. Leave a light burning in the living room when you are out for the evening.
3. When you plan to be away for some time, arrange to have the lawn cut or the paths shovelled.

HOW TO PUT OUT FIRES

1. Fire from grease	Smother flames with soda. Cover pan with lid. For grease fire in the oven, close oven door and turn off oven. NEVER USE WATER.
2. Fire from electricity	Unplug or shut off electricity. If plug is pulled out, it is safe to use water.
3. Fire from coal or wood	Cover with water.
4. Fire from kerosene or gasoline	If it is a small fire, smother with soda, sand, or dirt. For a larger one, get away and call fire department.

IF YOUR CLOTHING CATCHES FIRE, DO NOT RUN. STAND STILL. SMOTHER THE FLAMES BY WRAPPING A BLANKET OR RUG AROUND YOU.

4. Don't advertise your absence or leave timetables of your activities by leaving notes in the mailbox, etc.
5. Never leave the key under the doormat. Leave it with a neighbor if you must leave it for a member of the family.
6. If your home is burglarized, give the police a complete list of what was stolen, but don't tell the newspapers what the burglars missed. That information may invite a second burglary.

Precautions Against Kitchen Accidents

1. Never mix cleaning aids. Dangerous fumes can be released.
2. Close doors and drawers immediately after use.
3. Wipe up spills immediately.
4. Never leave cooking spoons in pans. Use wooden spoons when working at the range.
5. Use flat-bottomed and well-balanced pots and pans with handles turned away from edge of range or table.
6. Remove lids directed away from body to avoid steam burns.
7. Pick up broken glass with a damp paper towel.
8. Carry pans with pot holders, not dish-towels.
9. Use sturdy stepladders or stepstools for reaching high places.
10. Keep knives sharp; cut with knife edge directed away from body.
11. Wash knives separately from other utensils and store them separately.
12. Follow directions for using pressure cookers and saucepans.

First Aid

SOME FIRST AID SUPPLIES

Get a tin box for your first aid kit. Paint it a bright red. A box you can store on a convenient shelf is better than a drawer or a cabinet, because you can carry it to the scene of an accident. Prepare another kit for your car.

Make certain that you store your first aid kits where they belong and that everyone in your family knows where the kits are. Instruct your family in the correct use of all the supplies. Replace supplies as they are used.

For burns:
  Plastic food wrap.
  Do not use waxed paper.
  Plastic covered bandage, individually wrapped.
  Vaseline
  Vitamin A & D ointment

For bites:
  Calamine lotion
  Vaseline

For cuts:
  Plastic covered bandage, as for burns
  Rolls of bandage. Ask your druggist for two or three of the most common sizes.
  Roll of adhesive tape
  Band-Aids of various sizes

For nose bleeds:
  Roll of sterile cotton
  Cotton balls

To induce vomiting:
  Ipecac syrup

SHOCK

Shock is a state of prostration in which all bodily functions are affected: blood circulation, breathing, etc.

Shock may be mild or severe. It may occur soon after injury or hours later. For this reason, all seriously hurt people should be treated for shock whether or not symptoms are present. Untreated shock may prove fatal. *Only cardiac arrest, stoppage of breathing, heavy bleeding, and poisoning are treated before shock.*

The symptoms of shock are general weakness; pale, cold, clammy skin; bluish lips and nails; feeble, fast, irregular breathing; weak pulse; lightheadedness; dilation of eye pupils. The victim may become semiconscious or totally unconscious; restless, anxious, or unresponsive.

TREATMENT

Send for help at once.

Keep victim lying down.

Cover victim with coat or blanket to maintain body temperature, but do not overheat.

Stop any bleeding by hand pressure on a pad over wound.

Do not give fluids.

Be calm, reassuring, and attentive.

CAUSES

Shock can result from a severe burn, cut, or fall, as in:

a fall from a bicycle causing cuts, abrasions, and lacerations

an injury from a knife or razor

a fall downstairs with small wounds, but bruising and fright evident

To relieve choking, place arm around body with thumb-side of fist against stomach. Grasp fist with other hand and pull sharply upwards. Repeat. Apply mouth-to-mouth resuscitation.

For poisoning, read poison label and follow directions. Telephone a doctor or take patient to emergency room of nearest hospital. Bring poison to doctor.

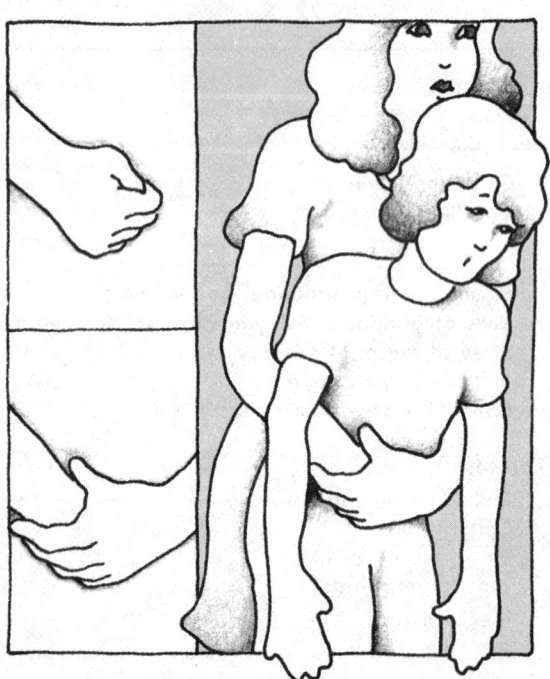

Mouth-to-mouth resuscitation

Mouth-to-mouth resuscitation is a vital first aid technique.
It is used in the event of electric shock, drowning, or asphyxiation.

1. Tilt the victim's head back with victim on his back, neck fully extended.

2. Lift the victim's jaw into jutting-out position by inserting thumb between teeth, grasping lower jaw and lifting it forcefully upward.

3. If air passage is not yet cleared, clear at once with fingers or with several sharp blows between shoulder blades.

4. With lower jaw lifted, open your mouth wide and cover victim's mouth by placing your mouth over his with airtight contact, also closing victim's nose by pinching it between thumb and finger.

5. Blow air into victim's lungs until you see the chest rise; remove your mouth and let him exhale. If chest does not rise, check steps above. Repeat step approximately 12 times a minute until victim revives. (20 times a minute for children.)

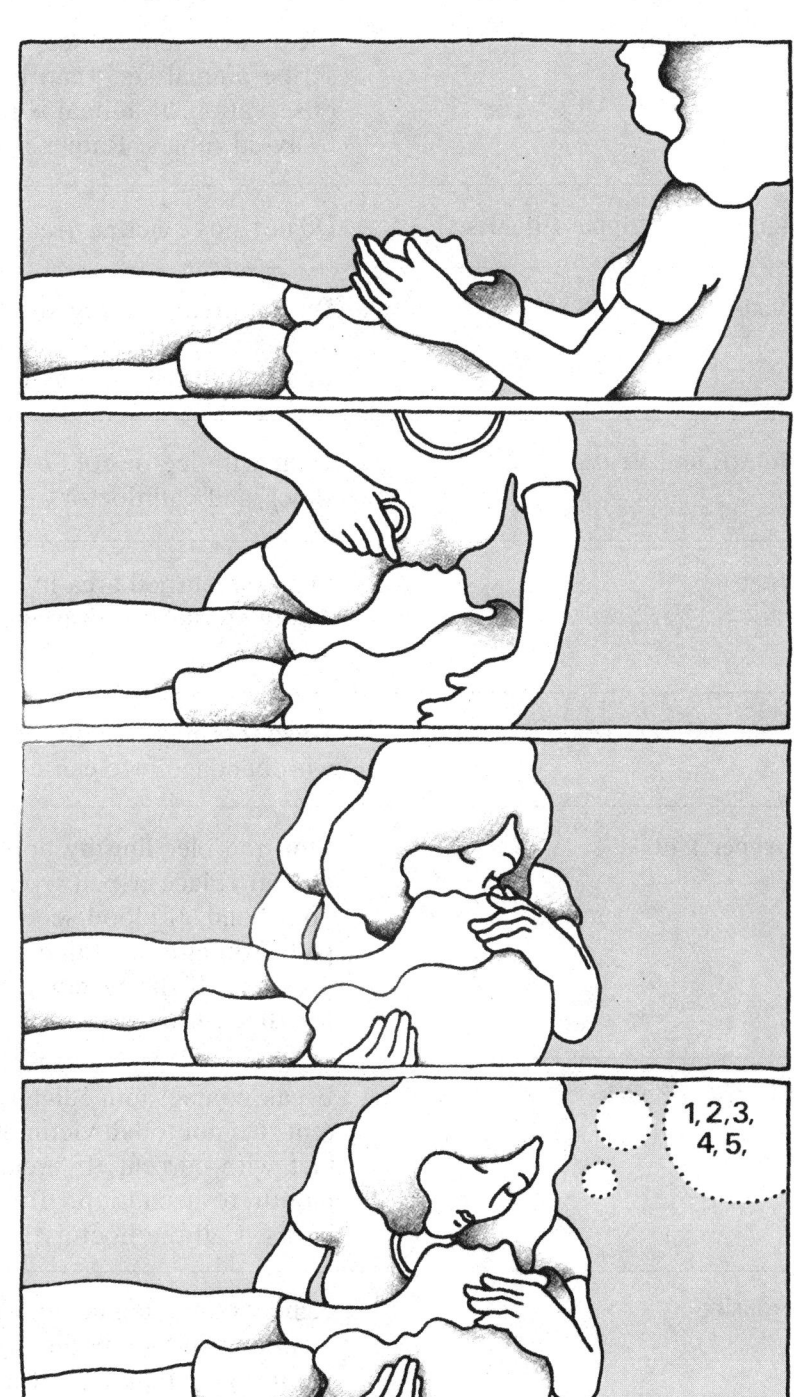

HEALTH AND HOME

First-aid facts you should know

Animal Bites	Clean wound with soap and water. Call doctor. Describe animal so it can be picked up and kept under observation. If animal is rabid, victim must be treated to avoid rabies. Rabies is fatal to animals and man.
Back, Neck, Spine Injuries	Do not move victim. Treat for shock and call the doctor.
Blisters	Do not break—apply sterile bandage. If blister breaks or has broken, clean as wound with soap and warm water. Blot dry. Cover with sterile bandage.
Bumps and Bruises	Treat with ice or cold compresses. If severe, treat for shock and call doctor.
Burns	Immerse burned area in cold water for 2 to 5 minutes. Apply sterile wet dressing. If burns are severe, call a doctor.
Cuts and Scrapes	Wash thoroughly with soap and water. Blot dry. Cover with bandage or clean cloth.
Deeper Cuts	Stop the bleeding by applying direct pressure on the wound. Place a pad over the wound and press with your hand. If blood seeps through, do not remove the pad. Add more padding over the first pad and continue pressure. If the bleeding persists, call a doctor. Treat for shock if the wound is severe.
Electrical Shock	Break contact immediately by turning off electric current. Do not touch victim while he or she is still in contact with current. If breathing stops, start mouth-to-mouth resuscitation. Treat for shock and attend to burns. Call the doctor.
Fainting	Keep victim lying down. Tilt head backward to chin-up position. This keeps airway open. Cover with blankets. Do not give liquids, but moisten lips.

Fire	If clothing catches on fire, smother flames with blanket, rug, coat, or towel. Roll victim over to put all flames out. Treat for shock and call doctor.
Foreign Bodies in Nose and Ears	Encourage the victim to blow his nose. If the object is not removed by blowing, do not probe. A doctor must remove the object.
Foreign Body in Eye	If object is on surface, flush with clear water. An object sometimes can be removed with a moist piece of soft, clean cloth. If the object is embedded, have a doctor remove it.
Fractures	Keep victim quiet and treat for shock. Call doctor.
Insect Bites and Stings	Use cold compress to relieve pain. If victim is allergic to stings, call doctor immediately. Multiple stings can cause severe reaction. Some people are allergic to spider bites and have a serious reaction.
Nosebleeds	Sit victim upright if possible. Pinch nostrils together firmly and keep victim quiet. Prolonged bleeding requires medical attention.
Poisons	Obtain medical help immediately. Keep container. Observe directions on container as to antidotes to be given.
Shock	Keep victim lying down. Cover with coat or blanket but do not overheat victim. Do not give fluids. Call a doctor at once.
Sprains and Strains	Use cold compresses on injured area. Elevate injured part. Call doctor if swelling or pain becomes severe.
Swallowed Objects	If object is smooth, it should go through digestive tract easily. Watch for its expulsion in bowel movements. If object is caught in windpipe of a child, turn child upside down and slap on back. If this does not work, get medical help immediately.
Vomiting	Place victim on side or in semi-sitting position. Keep victim quiet. Apply cool wet cloth to forehead and face.

The Home

Running a home today requires a body of knowledge unknown a few generations ago. A lot is expected of the modern homemaker, who is now a dietitian, bookkeeper, repairman, interior decorator, and informed citizen as well as nurturer of the young.

The information presented here is designed to save precious time, provide data not readily available elsewhere, and assist in running the home in a thoroughly professional manner.

SMART FOOD BUYING HABITS

Make out a shopping list, but be flexible should you spot an unadvertised special. Buy in quantity, but only what you can reasonably store and use. Buy in season, but not at the beginning of the season. Prices drop as supplies increase.

When buying meat and vegetables, remember that the price per serving counts, not the price per pound.

Buying Meat

Meat is the single most expensive item on a shopping list, so it is wise to understand the labeling and grading of meat.

Federal Inspection Mark and Label. The federal government inspects all meat which is marketed across state lines. Meat so inspected and passed carries a stamp saying it has passed the United States Department of Agriculture (USDA) inspection. This tells consumers that the meat came from a healthy animal, that it was processed under sanitary conditions, and that it is honestly labeled.

Grade Stamp or Packer's Brand. The USDA grade stamp is a purple shield-shape. Some meat packers use brands instead of grades to represent the quality levels of their products. Beef, lamb, mutton, veal, and calf are federally graded and are in most markets. Pork is not usually graded. Beef is the meat most often found with a USDA grade stamp. Beef grades are:

- *U.S. Prime. Excellent quality and flavor. Most prime meat goes to restaurants. It has the most marbling (flecks of fat within the lean), which makes it tender and juicy.*

- *U.S. Choice. This grade is the most popular and is commonly found in retail markets. It has slightly less marbling, but is still good quality.*

- *U.S. Good. Relatively tender beef with a high ratio of lean to fat. Lacks some juiciness and flavor.*

- *U.S. Standard and Commercial. Little is sold in retail markets. Most such meat is acceptable only in dishes requiring long simmering, since it lacks sufficient marbling.*

- *U.S. Utility, Cutter, and Canner. Used mostly in processed meat products.*

Buying Poultry

Most poultry is marketed ready to cook and is sold either chilled or frozen. Cut-up poultry spoils faster than whole birds, and turkey spoils faster than chicken. Watch out for brownish spots on frozen poultry, which indicate freezer burn.

Chickens. Chickens marked "broiler," "fryer," or "frying," generally weigh up to $3\frac{1}{2}$ pounds. They are good for either broiling or frying. The largest birds of this class are also roasted. Roasting chickens and capons are young birds that have grown to larger size, with full flavor and tender thick meat. Stewing chickens or hens are older, good only for stewed chicken, casseroles, or salads.

Turkeys. Turkeys marked "fryer" or "roaster" weigh 4 to 5 pounds and are suitable for frying or broiling as well as roasting. Other turkeys labeled "young hen," "young tom," or "young turkey" weigh from 6 to 24 pounds and are roasted. If the word "young" or "yearling" is not used on the label, the bird may be assumed to be suitable for stewing. Boneless turkey roasts and boneless turkey rolls are popular convenience items.

Ducks and Geese. These are marked "young." Ducks are usually sold frozen and marketed as duckling. Geese generally weigh 6 to 12 pounds.

Buying Fish and Shellfish

Look for freshness in the fish. If it is frozen, be sure it is frozen solid, has little odor or discoloration. Wrapping should be moisture-proof. Keep fish frozen until ready to use. To insure freshness of fresh fish, look for the following:

- *Eyes: bright, clear, full and bulging.*

- *Gills: reddish-pink, free from slime or odor.*

- *Scales: adhering tightly to skin.*

- *Flesh: firm and elastic.*

- *Odor: fresh, free of strong smell, especially around gills and belly.*

If there is a doubt about the freshness of a fish, place it in cold water. If it is fresh, it will float.

Fish is marketed in the following forms:

- *Whole: in its natural state, about 45 percent is edible.*

- *Drawn: only the entrails removed, about half of the drawn fish is edible.*

- *Dressed: with scales and entrails removed, one pound usually can serve two.*

- *Steaks: in slices cut crosswise and ready to cook, one pound serves two.*

- *Fillets: the entire side section cut away from the backbone.*

All fresh whole shellfish, except shrimp, should be alive when purchased. Shrimp is also available frozen.

Buying Vegetables and Fruits

To maintain quality in fresh vegetables and fruits, store them in the refrigerator in the crisper or in plastic bags. Bananas are not refrigerated. Potatoes and onions are stored in a cool, dry place.

Canned fruits and vegetables lose quality if stored much longer than a year but they remain safe to eat indefinitely if the seal is not broken.

When buying frozen vegetables, select firm packages. Frozen food is safe to eat as long as the package remains frozen, but a storage temperature of 0°F or lower is necessary to maintain high quality.

STAIN REMOVAL CHART

animal stains. Sponge out immediately with warm water and an absorbent cloth. Old stains are sometimes removed by sponging with a solution of one part soapless lather and five parts water, plus three tablespoonfuls of white vinegar to each quart water. Repeat if necessary.

blood, sugar, or catsup. Soak immediately in cold water for thirty minutes or longer. Work detergent into stain and rinse. If stain persists, put a few drops of ammonia on stain and repeat detergent treatment. Bleach if necessary.

candle wax. Place stain between clean white blotters or several layers of facial tissues and press with warm iron. To remove remaining stain, sponge with a cleaning fluid.

chewing gum. Harden lump with ice, then scrape off with knife blade. Follow with cleaning fluid if necessary.

chocolate or cocoa. Soak in cold water for thirty minutes, followed by a warm or hot detergent wash, depending on fabric. If brown stain remains, treat with peroxide. If greasy spot remains, use cleaning fluid.

coffee or tea. Rub synthetic shampoo on spot, then wash regularly.

grass or foliage. Sponge with equal parts of alcohol and water. Then launder. If yellow stain remains, use liquid bleach.

grease, oil, and tar. Rub spot with lard, then sponge with cleaning fluid over a pad. Follow quickly with regular wash.

ink. Some inks are impossible to remove. Others wash out in regular wash, especially if fresh. For all inks, first rub with synthetic shampoo and let stand fifteen minutes before rinsing. Repeat if necessary. For ballpoint ink, sponge repeatedly with acetone or amyl acetate. Use amyl acetate on acetate and acrylic. Use acetone on all other fabrics.

iron rust. Dip in hot oxalic acid solution (1 tablespoon to 1 cup water). Rinse immediately. Follow with regular wash.

lipstick and rouge. Apply undiluted liquid detergent to stain, or dampen and rub in soap or detergent until thick suds form. Work in until outline of stain is gone, then rinse.

mildew. Remove mildew spots. Brush off any surface growth outdoors to prevent scattering the mildew spores. Sun and air fabric thoroughly. Wash articles at once with soap and water. On upholstered articles or mattresses, sponge lightly with thick suds of soap or synthetic detergent, and wipe with a clean, damp cloth. If stain remains on washable items, bleach with lemon juice and salt, sodium perborate bleach, or a dilute solution of sodium hydrochlorite or other household chlorine bleach.

milk and cream. Soak in cool or lukewarm water, then wash.

perspiration. Soak whites for a short time in diluted bleaching solution or in sodium hydrosulfite solution (1 teaspoon to 1 cup water). Hold colored fabrics over open bottle of household ammonia, then sponge with vinegar solution.

scorch. Wash according to fabric. Bleach in sun.

soft drinks. Sponge immediately with cool water. Soak in cool water before washing.

HOUSEHOLD CLEANING TIPS

1. Treat all stains promptly.
2. Use stain removers that suit both stain and fabric. Test remover first on unexposed part of garment.
3. If stain is unknown, avoid hot water.
4. Use most gentle treatment first. Use light, rapid strokes from center of stain to outside edge in a random pattern to avoid forming a ring. Work over a blotter or other absorbent pad, never over folds of the garment. Rinse thoroughly before washing.
5. Take difficult stains to the dry cleaner.

Care and Cleaning of Furniture

Many furniture finishes are available, and they vary in their resistance to stains, scratches, and wear. Any labels or tags on new pieces should be carefully saved for future reference.

A few rules to prevent damage to furniture:

1. Don't put hot dishes on a table without a protective pad.
2. Don't put damp items, or objects that are apt to collect condensation, such as a vase of flowers, on a wood surface without a protective pad.
3. Maintain a good, protective wax finish at all times.
4. Never slide any item such as a flower pot or knick-knack across a table top.
5. Don't place furniture close to a radiator, fireplace, or window.
6. Use polish on a dusting cloth to keep dust from being ground into the wood.
7. Change dusting cloths when they become soiled or damp.
8. Polish only a small section at a time and rub with the grain of the wood.

For *plastic surfaces,* clean with a liquid wax or multi-surface cleaner-polisher. Both protect against scratching from dust and grit, and keep spills from sticking.

When an area is badly worn, or spotted by fruit juices, ink, or rust, use an auto cleaner-wax to restore the finish. Use long, gentle even strokes.

Vinyl upholstery can be cleaned with a liquid wax or multi-surface cleaner-polish. They do not contain abrasives.

Painted furniture can be protected with any wax. A paste wax will give darker finishes a high luster. A liquid wax will add gloss to lighter finishes.

Self-adhesive vinyl coverings used by do-it-yourselfers to re-cover cabinets, walls, tabletops, etc., need frequent cleaning. The dirt and finger marks they collect can be removed and the surface protected with either a multi-surface cleaner-polish, or a liquid wax.

Marble can stain as badly as wood and should be waxed. Remove oily food stains before waxing. Place a white blotter, soaked in non-flammable dry cleaning fluid, over the spot and allow it to dry. If the spot remains, add one or two drops of ammonia to hydrogen peroxide and apply. You may have to repeat the process several times.

CONSUMER PROTECTION

More and more cities and states are establishing consumer protection agencies. The Federal Trade Commission is concerned with protecting the public against abuse in the market place. They have compiled the following list of the more common deceptions practiced on the American public.

If you will learn your rights as a consumer, you will find that you are fully capable of protecting those rights. Businesses you deal with tend to be honest in their practices, but it is always proper for you to be alert when dealing with businesses that are new to you. Your alertness will pay off.

COMMON DECEPTIONS

Bait and Switch. This occurs when an item is advertised, usually at a low price, but is down-graded by the seller or appears to be shabby or inferior. The seller attempts to deter the purchaser from buying it while at the same time pushing the sale of a higher profit item.

Contest Winner (see also *free goods*). In this deceptive practice, an individual is told that he has won a contest (whether he has entered or not) but finds that there are conditions to be met before he receives his prize. In addition he may be solicited to purchase additional goods after he has received his prize.

Debt Collection Deception. This includes the use of any forms, letters, questionnaires, or other printed or written material that does not clearly and conspicuously disclose that they are being used to collect a debt or to obtain information about a debtor; or the false representation that the writer is affiliated with a branch of government, or is a credit bureau.

Deceptive Guarantees. These include any guarantee which does not make clear what product, or part of the product is guaranteed, what characteristics are covered or excluded, and the time it covers.

Fair Packaging and Labeling. The failure to include a label on the product which specifies its identity; the name and place of business of the manufacturer, packer, or distributor; the net quantity of the contents; and the net amount in a serving when the number of servings is represented.

False Testimonials, Endorsements or Certification. Falsely stating or implying that a product is endorsed or approved by anyone when this is not so is a violation. Other violations include implying an entire product has been endorsed when only a portion of it has; misuse of a union label; false claims that products or services have won awards while implying that the awards were based on comparisons with competing products; false contests followed by fake awards.

Foreign Origin. Failing to disclose the country of origin when marketing an imported product is prohibited. Usually this information must be marked on the package as well as on the product. The words "import" or "imported" are not enough.

Free Goods Not Free. Estimates for repair work or the sale of goods or services advertised or solicited as being "free" when there are charges or conditions which were not revealed.

Lotteries. The use of lottery devices to sell merchandise is a violation if a purchase is required. Elements of a classic lottery are (1) consideration, (2) chance, and (3) prize. However, any method designed to appeal to gambling instincts may be a violation, even though not technically a lottery.

Product Effectiveness, Nature and Quality. The misrepresentation of products concerning (1) what they can do, (2) how they are made, and (3) their durability is a violation.

Substitution of Merchandise. The substitution of a variety, make, model, or quality of goods in place of goods actually believed to be purchased is a violation.

Truth in Lending. On open-end credit accounts, such as revolving charge accounts, all relevant terms, including the finance charge and annual percentage rate, must be revealed. On installment credit sales and on installment loans, the failure to disclose all relevant terms, including the finance charge and annual percentage rate at the time of the purchase is prohibited. In advertising of certain credit terms, the failure to disclose all relevant terms including the annual percentage rate is prohibited.

Used for New. The advertising or sale of goods as "new" when in fact they are reconditioned, repossessed or used is a violation.

SPORTS

The growth of spectator sports throughout the world has been so rapid that we sometimes appear to be spending all our waking hours watching sports events on television. Each week of the year many of us are tuned to the TV set to see the greatest, the most, the unforgettable. While Americans will never give up their weekend football or the excitement of an October World's Series game, we must not forget that the benefit of sports comes from playing rather than watching.

So while many interesting records of professional sports appear in the following pages, you will also find rules and other useful facts about how to play the most popular games. If your favorite is baseball, football, basketball, tennis, or soccer, this section will be of special interest to you. The section closes with records of the Olympic games.

Baseball: The National Pastime

The legend that Abner Doubleday invented the game of baseball in Cooperstown, New York, in 1839 has been shown to have no support in fact. On the contrary, sports historians have proved that the game, regarded as the "great American pastime," was popular in England at least a hundred years earlier. For a time it was even known under the same name "baseball." Some believe that its origins go back to a barnyard game played by milkmaids and farmhands in England in the fourteenth century. They used a soft ball that was tossed underhand and hit with a closed fist; milk stools were used as bases.

By the early nineteenth century this English game, by then played with a bat, was generally known as "rounders." Among its rules (according to a game book published in 1829) was one that called for using four "stones" or "posts" for bases. Another rule declared a batter "out" when he missed three balls thrown to him, when he hit a fly ball that was caught before it hit the ground, or when he hit one foul ball. In "rounders," a base runner was "out" if he was hit with a thrown ball while running to a "stone" or "post." The ball used was so soft it could not be hit far and did not hurt when it struck a base runner.

The American form of this game came into existence in 1845. In that year Alexander J. Cartwright wrote his set of rules for the game. This established how the game would be played by the Knickerbocker Base Ball Club of New York, of which Mr. Cartwright was a member-player, in its games with other private gentlemen's clubs in the New York metropolitan area. Cartwright decided that 90 feet was the right distance between bases. (Before this the distance had varied widely, to suit a club's members or its playing field.) Cartwright also scrapped the old method of putting a player "out" by hitting him with the ball, in favor of requiring him to be touched with it. These two rules together required a hard ball that could be thrown a long distance accurately. Cartwright's rules were soon adopted by clubs in the Boston and Philadelphia areas. Although many of his rules had to be changed later—for example, to permit pitching overhand—baseball American style advanced steadily along the course Cartwright put it on.

Baseball was highly popular as a sport among soldiers on both sides during the Civil War. It was spread throughout the country when the fighting men returned home at the war's end. The first fully professional player was Alfred J. Reach of Philadelphia (1864). The first all-profes-

A close play—the base runner times his slide into the base to avoid being tagged out. The fielder protects his base but keeps clear of the runner's spikes. The umpire positions himself to have a clear view of the play. A play is never too close to call. A tie is ruled in favor of the runner.

sional team was the Cincinnati Red Stockings (1869); they toured the country, winning 56 of 57 games. The other game was a tie. In 1876 The National League of Professional Base Ball Clubs was formed, the same National League (but with different cities represented) that exists today. In 1900 the American League was formed. The first World Series between the pennant winners of the two leagues was played in 1903.

PROFESSIONAL BASEBALL TODAY

Today professional baseball is organized in "major" and "minor" leagues. There are two major leagues, the National League and the American League. Each has an eastern and a western division, with six clubs in each division. The minor leagues are supported by the major league clubs and are the source of many major league play-

ers. The top minor leagues—those with players of near major-league ability—are classified AAA. Down the ladder of player-skills are leagues classified AA and A. At the bottom are the Rookie Leagues. In the 1970s the number of minor leagues in all classes has averaged about eighteen.

Nearly all the clubs in the minor leagues are owned outright by major league clubs. These minor league clubs are called farm teams, and the owners are referred to as the "parent" clubs. Other minor league clubs are merely affiliated with a major league club, which temporarily assigns to them its younger or less skillful players in the hope that with proper training they may eventually be able to play in the big leagues. All contracts between clubs and players in the major and minor leagues are under the jurisdiction of the Commissioner of Baseball. The Commissioner's office was created by the club owners in 1920. This was at the time of the Black Sox scandal, which grew

SOME MAJOR LEAGUE RECORDS

Highest Batting Average: Lifetime, .367, Ty Cobb (Detroit Tigers and Philadelphia Athletics). Season, .424, Rogers Hornsby (St. Louis Cardinals) in 1924.

Most Hits: Lifetime, 4,191, Ty Cobb. Season, 257, George Sisler (St. Louis Browns) in 1920.

Most Runs: Lifetime, 2,244, Ty Cobb. Season, 177, Babe Ruth (New York Yankees) in 1921.

Most Home Runs: Lifetime, Hank Aaron, 755 (Milwaukee Braves, Atlanta Braves, and Milwaukee Brewers). Season, 154-game schedule, 60, Babe Ruth (New York Yankees) in 1927; 162-game schedule, 61, Roger Maris (New York Yankees) in 1961.

Most Runs Batted In: Lifetime, 2,297, Hank Aaron. Season, 190, Hack Wilson (Chicago Cubs) in 1930.

Most Bases on Balls: Lifetime, 2,056, Babe Ruth. Season, 170, Babe Ruth (New York Yankees) in 1923.

Most Stolen Bases: Lifetime, 900, Lou Brock (Chicago Cubs and St. Louis Cardinals, as of April 1, 1978). Season, 118, Lou Brock, in 1974.

Most Games Won by a Pitcher: Lifetime, 511, Cy Young (Cleveland Spiders, St. Louis Cardinals, Boston Red Sox, Cleveland Indians and Boston Braves). Season, 41, Jack Chesbro (New York Highlanders) in 1904.

Most Shutouts by a Pitcher: Lifetime, 113, Walter Johnson (Washington Senators). Season, 16, Grover Cleveland Alexander (Philadelphia Phillies) in 1916.

Most Strikeouts by a Pitcher: Lifetime, 3,508, Walter Johnson. Season, 383, Nolan Ryan (California Angels) in 1973.

Longest Winning Streak by a Pitcher: 24, Carl Hubbell (New York Giants) across two seasons, 1936 and 1937. In one season, 19, Rube Marquard (New York Giants) in 1912.

Longest Consecutive Games Hitting Streak: 56, Joe DiMaggio (New York Yankees) in 1941.

Most Consecutive Games Played: 2,130, Lou Gehrig (New York Yankees) in 1925–1939.

George Herman "Babe" Ruth, possibly the greatest baseball player of all time, puts one into the right-field bleachers. Known as "The Sultan of Swat," Ruth had 714 lifetime home runs.

Ty Cobb, the short-tempered Detroit Tigers outfielder, adds to his grand total of 4,191 hits. Cobb led the league in hitting 12 times, and his lifetime average of .367 is still a record.

out of the "throwing" of games by several Chicago White Sox players, bribed by gamblers during the 1919 World Series.

The major league playing season is from early April to early October. Each team now plays 162 games (for many years it was 154). Of these, 90 are with the other five teams in their own division of their league (18 with each) and 72 with the six teams in the other division (12 with each). Half of a team's games with each rival are played "at home," the other half "away." At the end of the season the two divisional champions in each league meet in play-offs. The first team to win 3 games is the league champion, the pennant winner. The two pennant winners then meet in the annual World Series to determine the world championship. The winner is the first team to win 4 games. It is already conceivable that, in the future, championship teams of Japan and Latin America, where baseball is extremely popular, will have to be included in play-offs leading up to the World Series.

AMATEUR BASEBALL TODAY

Baseball is the most widely played amateur sport in the United States.

The best-known amateur league is the Little League, an international organization founded in Williamsport, Pennsylvania, in 1939. Today the Little League is comprised of more than 9,000 locally sponsored leagues (over 55,000 teams) in which any child between the ages of 8 and 12 may play. (Girls have been included since 1974.) Over 2 million boys and girls now participate. After a season of scheduled six-inning games and regional play-offs, a Little League World Series is played annually in Williamsport in August. Smaller fields are used than in the adult game, the bases being 60 feet apart.

For teenagers there are the Pony, Babe

Lou Brock, St. Louis Cardinals outfielder, steals second on his way to breaking Ty Cobb's record of 892 lifetime stolen bases. In 1974 Brock stole a record 118 bases.

Ruth, and Connie Mack Leagues. For those over the age of 18 there is American Legion Junior Baseball. The majority of high schools in the United States also have teams.

Baseball is regaining its popularity on college campuses, especially in the South and Southwest, where the climate provides a long playing season. There are several intercollegiate leagues, most of which participate in the National Collegiate Athletic Association's annual tournament for the college championship. Many college players today move quickly into the major leagues.

In addition to all these, there are amateur leagues and teams sponsored by city park districts, chambers of commerce, industrial corporations, police athletic leagues, fraternal organizations, and others.

A large percentage of organized amateur baseball for adults is devoted to *softball* rather than to regular baseball. In softball, pitching must be underhand, whether the "fast-pitch" or "slow-pitch" variety is played. The ball has a 12-inch circumference (sometimes larger in slow-pitch softball) and is not as lively as a standard baseball. The bases are 60 feet apart. The

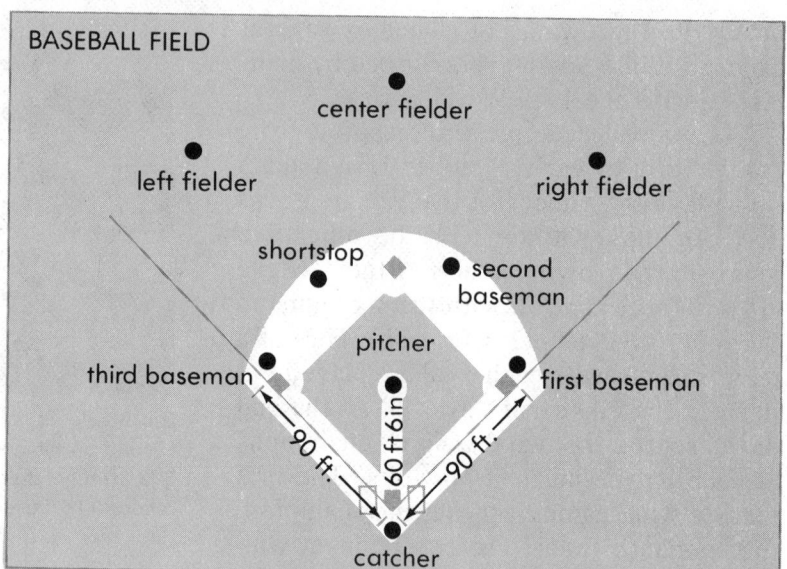

BASEBALL FIELD

center fielder

left fielder

right fielder

shortstop

second baseman

pitcher

third baseman

first baseman

90 ft.

60 ft 6 in

90 ft.

catcher

Standard positions of the defensive team. For some batters, especially those known to pull the ball, the defense shifts markedly. There is no restriction on where fielders stand.

pitcher stands 46 feet from home plate, and a baserunner must remain on the base until the ball leaves the pitcher's hand. It has been estimated that 20 million persons in over 40 countries now play softball in an organized way.

HOW TO PLAY BASEBALL

The game is played on a baseball field between two teams of nine players each—ten, if the teams adopt the American League's use of a "designated hitter" to bat for the pitcher. Each game consists of nine innings of play (or any number the teams have agreed to play). An inning consists of each team taking its turn at bat and in the field. The team playing on its own ("home") playing field bats last in each inning. After nine innings, the team with the most runs wins. In case of a tie, play continues until the end of a complete inning in which the tie is broken.

The team at bat tries to get its players on base, around the bases, and back to home plate without their being put out and before three batters have been called out. Each player who crosses home plate in this way scores a run for his team.

While one team is batting, the other is in the field, trying to put the batters or runners out. When the team at bat makes three outs, it takes its turn in the field.

The Pitch. Play begins when the pitcher delivers the ball to the batter, who is standing in the batter's box at home plate, ready to swing at the ball. There is a batter's box (marked in white) on either side of home plate. The batter may take his position in either box. If he uses the box on the third base side of home plate, he is known as a right-handed batter. If he chooses the box toward first base, he is a left-handed batter. The pitched ball may be either *inside* or *outside* the strike zone. The strike zone is the area above the plate which begins just above the level of the batter's knees and extends upwards to just below the batter's shoulders. If the pitch cuts through this strike zone, the batter must either swing at it or pay a penalty for letting it pass by. If he lets the ball go by, swings and misses, or hits it into foul territory, a "strike" is called by the umpire standing behind the catcher. A foul ball hit after a second strike is not counted against the batter, unless it is a foul tip caught by the catcher before it hits the ground. Three strikes make an out (a strike-out), and the next batter in the lineup moves into the batter's box.

If the pitched ball is thrown *outside* the strike zone and the batter does not swing at it, the umpire declares it a "ball." After four balls the batter "walks" to first base. A batter may also walk to first base if hit with a pitched ball or if the catcher interferes with his swing in any way.

The Hit.　When the batter hits the ball, he becomes a runner. If the ball he hits is caught on the fly in fair or foul territory, the runner is out. If the hit ball is not caught on the fly, it will fall into either foul territory or fair territory. If it falls into foul territory, the runner simply returns to the batter's box and a strike is called against him. If it falls into fair territory, the runner must run to first base before the fielders get the ball there. If, before the runner reaches first base, a fielder holding the ball tags him with it or touches first base, the runner is out.

Once a batter has reached first base safely for a single, he may continue running in an effort to reach second for a double, third for a triple, and home plate for a home run, so long as he is not tagged out along the way by a fielder holding the ball in his hand or glove.

The Runner.　A runner who has stopped at one of the bases is "safe" as long as he is touching the base. He may advance whenever he thinks he can reach the next base without being put out. This is generally when a later batter makes a hit or when another runner forces him to advance. But he may also, for example, try to advance on a fair grounder or a wild pitch, or to "steal" a base while the pitcher is delivering a pitch.

There can be only one runner on a base at a time. Thus, a runner on first base must

SOME LITTLE-KNOWN DIMENSIONS OF BASEBALL

The Baseball: Circumference, at least 9 and not more than 9¼ inches
　Weight, at least 5 and not more than 5¼ ounces

The Bat: Length, not more than 42 inches, and rounded its entire length
　Diameter, not more than 2¾ inches at its fattest part
　Weight, there is no regulation.
　　Most professional batters choose bats weighing between 32 and 36 ounces.

The Pitcher's Rubber: Length, 2 feet
　Width, 6 inches
　　Actually the "rubber" is a 6 × 6 inch beam, 2 feet long, sunk into the pitcher's mound exactly 60 feet 6 inches from the rear point of home plate.

The Pitcher's Mound: Height, not to exceed 15 inches above the level of home plate

Home Plate: Width, 1 foot
　Length, 17 inches

The Batter's Box: Width, 4 feet
　Length, 6 feet
　Distance from inner line to home plate, 6 inches
　The batter may stand, and step forward or backward, anywhere within the box when swinging at the ball.

The Bases: Length and width, 15 inches
　Height (thickness), 3 to 4 inches

run to second if the batter hits a fair grounder and heads for first. If the fielders can get the ball to second base before the runner arrives there, he is forced out. In a force-out situation, the runner need not be tagged with the ball. Similarly, if there are runners on first and second, they must advance to second and third if the batter hits a fair grounder. In this case, force-outs can occur at second and third. If there are runners on first, second, and third, force-outs

Hank Aaron watching one go by. Aaron did what was for years thought impossible when he broke Babe Ruth's longstanding home run record. When Aaron retired, his home run output totaled 755.

can occur at second, third, or home on a fair grounder.

If a hit ball is caught on the fly, the runners must return to their bases and "tag up" before trying to take another base. If they are off their base when a fly is caught, or leave before it is actually caught, they may be put out by the return of the ball to the base they left, provided the ball reaches that base ahead of the runner.

A runner may not skip a base, but must run the bases in order. He may not pass a runner ahead of him. He may not run outside the base paths or interfere with a fielder attempting to play a batted ball. A player who breaks any of these rules is declared out automatically by the umpire best positioned to judge the play in question.

A game may be called (stopped) by the umpire for bad weather or other important reasons, such as lack of daylight in a park without lights. If, in a called game, five innings have been played (or four and one-half innings, if the home team is ahead) the game is considered completed. In such a case the score is "official," including the hits, runs, errors, etc., of the individual players. If less than an "official" game has been completed, the game must be replayed from the start, and individual records for that game are not considered official.

When baseball is played just for fun, many of these rules are relaxed. For example, balls and strikes are commonly not called. The only strikes recorded in such games are foul balls or swings-and-misses. Similarly, runners are sometimes not allowed to steal bases.

GLOSSARY OF BASEBALL TERMS

assist. A play in which one fielder helps another put out a batter or base runner.

balk. An illegal motion by the pitcher with men on base; the penalty advances the runner or runners one base.

ball. A pitch outside the strike zone.

batting average. The percentage of times a batter makes a hit, computed by dividing hits by times at bat.

bunt. A ball tapped gently by the batter, usually by holding the bat loosely, with hands well up on the bat handle.

designated hitter. A batter who hits for the pitcher through the game, but does not play in the field. He may bat anywhere in the batting order his team decides.

diamond. The infield; sometimes, by extension, the playing field. The diamond formed by the baselines (as seen from home plate) is actually a square, standing on one corner, each side 90 feet long.

double. A hit on which a batter advances two bases.

doubleheader. Two games played on one day, for

a single price of admission. A twi-night double-header is two games, started in daylight, finished under lights.

double play. A play in which a batter and a runner, or two runners, are put out in one play.

earned run. A run that results from the batting team's play rather than a fielder's misplay or a pitcher's wildness.

earned-run average (ERA). The percentage of earned runs charged against a pitcher, computed by dividing earned runs by innings pitched, including fractions.

fielder's choice. A play in which the fielder chooses (or attempts) to put out a runner instead of the batter of a fair ground ball. The batter is charged with a time at bat and is not credited with a hit.

fly ball. A ball hit into the air, fair or foul.

force-out. A putout of a baserunner made by tagging a base (usually with the fielder's foot) to which the runner is forced to advance by another runner behind him.

foul ball. A fly ball landing or caught outside the foul lines. A ground ball that passes over first or third base, or inside them, and then rolls into foul territory in the outfield is a fair ball.

foul territory. That portion of the playing field outside the foul lines.

foul tip. A pitched ball that glances off the batter's bat and continues its flight in the direction of the catcher.

hit. A single, double, triple, or home run.

home run. A hit on which the batter circles the bases successfully to home plate without the help of a fielding error.

infield fly rule. A rule under which an umpire calls a batter automatically out if he hits a fly ball which in the umpire's judgment an infielder can catch without difficulty, at a time when there is no more than one out and when there are runners on first and second, or on all three bases; the baserunners are permitted to advance, but at their own risk.

inning. That portion of a game during which both teams bat until three outs have been made.

line drive. A hard-hit fly ball that travels in almost a horizontal line. Also called a "liner."

line up. A written list of players in their order of batting.

out. This occurs when a batter is retired when at bat, at a base, or between bases.

passed ball. A pitched ball that goes by the catcher and allows a baserunner to advance one or more bases. If the catcher is at fault, it is a passed ball; if the pitcher is at fault, it is a "wild pitch."

pinch hitter. A substitute batter. To pinch-hit is to substitute for another player at bat.

run. The official unit of score, made by the safe circuit of all the bases and a final touching of home plate.

runs batted in (RBI). A run driven in by a batter.

runner. A player who has hit a fair ball or who is on base.

pop fly. A fly ball hit so high that an infielder or outfielder has enough time to get under it. Also called a "pop-up."

relief pitcher. A pitcher who replaces a team's starting pitcher.

sacrifice. A play in which the batter intentionally hits the ball in such a way as to advance a runner rather than try to get on base himself.

squeeze play. A play in which a runner is brought home from third base on a bunt. In the *suicide squeeze*, the runner starts for home with the pitcher's motion to the plate; in the *safety squeeze*, the runner waits near third base until he sees that the batter has actually bunted.

stolen base. A base taken by a runner without the aid of a fair hit by a teammate or of a misplay by the fielding team.

strike. A penalty against the batter if: (1) he lets a pitched ball that passes through the strike zone go by; (2) he swings and misses; or (3) he hits a foul ball that is not caught (not counted on a third strike).

strike zone. The area over home plate, above the knees and below the shoulders of a batter.

tag up. Return to the base occupied, during the catch of a fly ball, before attempting to advance to the next base after the catch.

triple. A hit on which the batter reaches third base without an error by the team in the field.

triple play. A play in which a batter and two runners or three runners are put out in one continuous play.

umpire. An official who calls the plays in a game. These number four in the major leagues; the minimum in other games is usually two.

walk. A base on balls, or "free pass" to first base. This occurs when the pitches pitches four "balls" before the batter is out. A batter also receives a "free pass" when a pitcher hits the batter with a pitched ball.

Football: Bruising Contact Sport

American football is a game that was developed in the United States from soccer, with later borrowings from the British game of rugby. It reached the form we know today only about 1912, after much trial and error and many innovative rule changes urged by players, coaches, collegiate associations, and even a President, Theodore Roosevelt.

To most of the rest of the world, the word "football" refers to the game that Americans call soccer. Soccer is a kicking game and uses a round ball. Touching the ball with the hands, let alone running with it, is illegal in soccer. These rules were used for the earliest American football, which was much like soccer, in the years following the Civil War. The objective of the American version of soccer was to kick a ball across the other team's goal line. This feat was made more difficult by the use of as many as thirty players to a side, and fields 140 yards or more in length. The first recorded American football game between colleges, played November 6, 1869 (Rutgers 6, Princeton 4), was a game much like soccer.

Rugby made its contribution to our autumn sport in 1874, when Harvard played a three-game football series with McGill University of Toronto, Canada. In two of these games Canadian rugby rules were followed. These rules permitted picking up the oval ball used in rugby and running with it. A team could score points by carrying or kicking the ball over the goal line, and tackling was permitted. Fifteen players comprised a team. The Harvard players liked this new form of the game. They introduced it to the rest of the football-playing eastern universities, and American football was on its way.

PROFESSIONAL FOOTBALL

The first professional football game on record was played on August 31, 1895, between teams from Latrobe and Jeannette, two small towns in Pennsylvania. Latrobe won, 12 to 0.

Until the 1920s, professional football was a small-town game, played mostly as a Sunday afternoon pastime. It was especially popular among workers in the industrial areas of Pennsylvania, western New York State, and northern Ohio. Several towns, such as Latrobe, supported teams, but most were sponsored by factories, mills, mines, and railroads. The rivalries were intense.

From this small-town beginning, professional football gradually grew into one of

KEY DATES IN THE DEVELOPMENT OF MODERN FOOTBALL

1876 The first college football organization was formed. Its members were Harvard, Yale, Princeton, Rutgers, and Columbia.

1880–1885 A "first down" rule was adopted: 5 yards in three plays. This eliminated the "scrum" of rugby and allowed one team to retain possession as long as it was advancing downfield, making first downs. It also brought about planned plays and signal calling. The number of players was reduced to eleven. The field was shortened to 110 yards. The goal area to score points by kicking was first sharply reduced in size, and then posts were erected to kick between; finally, a crossbar was raised to be kicked over. Touchdowns were set at 4 points, the conversion 2, a safety 2.

1889 Walter Camp, Yale coach, with sportswriter Casper Whitney, started his yearly selection of the eleven best players of the nation, called the All-American team, a selection he continued until his death in 1924.

1905–1906 President Theodore Roosevelt, reacting to a wave of serious injuries caused by the bruising, massed-blocking, and rushing of college football, ordered the violence ended. Rules were changed to open up the game. Specifically, a *forward* pass from one back to another back or an end was permitted. This opened up offenses and prevented massed defenses. The forward pass was much used by the smaller colleges, especially in 1906–1912. The widely publicized game in which small Notre Dame beat Army 35–13 in 1913, with a combined running and passing attack, further advanced the cause of more open football.

1912 The field was reduced to 100 yards, plus 10-yard end zones where a pass could legally be caught. The first-down rule was changed to 10 yards in four downs. A touchdown was raised to 6 points, a conversion lowered to 1 point.

1936 The ball was reduced in thickness and made more pointed. This made it possible to throw longer and more accurate passes, and to hold the ball in the palm of the hand while running. Also, the passer no longer needed to throw at least five yards behind the line of scrimmage; he was able to run up to the line of scrimmage before throwing.

1945 The free-substitution rule was adopted. In the 1950s this rule was temporarily modified in various ways but was finally again accepted. It led to two-platoon football and the use of kicking and other specialists.

1958 The 2-point option on a conversion after a touchdown, by run or pass, was adopted in intercollegiate football.

the most popular spectator sports in the United States. As the game became organized and stabilized under the National Football League after 1921, more former college stars were attracted to the professional ranks, and more spectators wanted to see them play.

Probably the most important single factor in the growth of professional football was television. Before television, only the people who lived in cities that had league teams knew much about professional football. But television brought the game into the home of nearly every American. And television income made it possible for teams to pay players on a much higher level than ever dreamed of by the pioneering professionals of the 1920s.

Paul "Bear" Bryant is one of the most successful coaches in the history of collegiate football. His University of Alabama eleven has won nine conference and four Sugar Bowl championships.

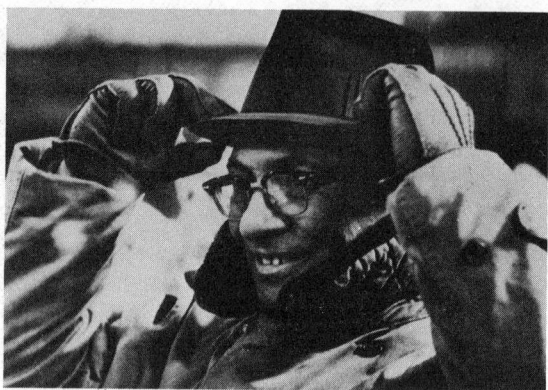

Vince Lombardi, committed to excellence and total dedication, led his Green Bay Packers to five NFL championships and two Super Bowl victories in eight years as head coach.

National Football League. The leading professional teams in the United States belong to the National Football League (NFL). This is the direct descendant of the league organized in 1921 by the operators of various small-town and industrial teams, and since then it has guided the development of professional football in the United States.

Teams within conferences play each other according to a schedule arranged by the NFL. Toward the end of the playing season, in early January, the conference champions are determined in play-off games. The two conference champions then meet in the Super Bowl, which is played in a warm-weather city in mid-January. The Super Bowl winner is the world champion of the year.

AMATEUR FOOTBALL

The most popular of all college and high school sports, in terms of number of spectators, is football. Students and alumni everywhere look forward to the crisp autumn Saturday afternoons of the football season when they can see their varsity teams play. Such extras as marching bands,

cheerleaders, and mascots rouse school spirit and add to the color of the game.

Nearly all medium-sized and large high schools field football teams, which today need squads of at least thirty-five fully uniformed players to play the game successfully in league competition. High schools of approximately the same size, and within easy bus travel of each other, tend to form leagues, each team in the league playing every other team once. The larger high schools often play a freshman-team schedule also. Younger boys get their first experience of football in school peewee leagues (under various names) that play their games at times that do not compete with the big team's games.

Intercollegiate play is governed and administered by various football leagues operating within the framework of the National Collegiate Athletic Association (NCAA). On the East Coast there are (among others less well known) the Ivy League and the Atlantic Conference; in the South, the Southeastern and Southern Conferences; in the Midwest, the Big Ten and Big Eight; and in the West, the Pacific Eight and the Southwest Conference. Some large schools, such as Notre Dame, Penn

Knute Rockne diagrams a play for the Notre Dame football team. In his 13 years as head coach, the Fighting Irish played five undefeated seasons and six in which they lost only once.

Walter Camp revolutionized the game of football. Known as "The Father of American Football," he was responsible for initiating intercollegiate play as well as many important rule changes.

State, Army (United States Military Academy), and Navy (United States Naval Academy) do not belong to a conference.

At the end of the football season, conference champions and leading independents are paired off in the various bowl games. The most famous of these games is the Rose Bowl in Pasadena, California, in which the Big Ten champion meets the champion of the Pacific Eight, before a crowd of more than 100,000 onlookers. The Rose Bowl game has been played on New Year's Day since 1916, and is preceded by the famous Rose Bowl parade.

Other famous New Year's Day bowl games, to which league champions and other strong teams are invited, are the Orange Bowl in Miami (since 1933), the Sugar Bowl in New Orleans (since 1935), and the Cotton Bowl in Dallas (since 1937).

HOW TO PLAY FOOTBALL

Because football is a rough contact sport, players wear various kinds of protective equipment. All players must wear shoulder pads and football pants with special knee and thigh padding; some may also put on girdle pads, rib guards, and arm and hand pads. To protect the head, all players must wear a helmet with an attached face mask, and a mouth guard. To maintain a firm grip on the turf, the players wear special shoes fitted with blunt spikes.

Brightly colored jerseys are also worn, each team using its own school or team colors, with large numbers on front and back for easy identification of each player. Quarterbacks wear numbers 1 to 19; halfbacks and fullbacks, 20 to 49; centers and linebackers, 50 to 59; guards, 60 to 69; tackles, 70 to 79; ends and wide receivers, 80 to 99.

The Basic Game. The game is played on a regulation field between two teams of eleven players. Each team tries to get the ball and move it across the other team's goal line for a score (a "touchdown") or kick it through the opponent's goal posts by means of a "placekick." (The rules given here are for collegiate play.)

The game begins with a kickoff. The referee tosses a coin to decide which team kicks off, the visiting team's captain calling heads or tails. The captain of the team that wins the toss has the choice of (1) kicking off or receiving; or (2) choosing the goal his team will defend. At the start of the second half, the other captain makes a similar first choice.

During play, the two teams face each other on the field, their goal lines behind them. Once the kickoff has been completed, the offensive team has possession of the ball. Through a series of planned attacks or plays, it tries to carry, pass, or kick the ball down the field. Meanwhile, the other team (the defense) tries to stop the advance, either by tackling the ball carrier, intercepting a pass, recovering a fumble, or catching and running back a kick.

Each play lasts from the time the ball is centered until it is downed. The ball is centered by a lineman, called the center, who snaps the ball from the scrimmage line, through his legs, usually to the quarterback, who puts it into play in a variety of ways. The ball is "down" when its forward movement has been stopped—generally when the ball carrier is tackled or forced out of bounds, when a pass is incomplete, or when a ball is fumbled and recovered by one side or the other. The point at which the ball is downed establishes the line of scrimmage for the next play.

Back now to the first play after the kickoff. The offensive team has four plays, or "downs," in which to move the ball toward their opponent's goal. If in these four downs, the offensive team gains 10 yards, as measured by the "chain gang" on the sideline, it is entitled to another four downs. This is called "making a first down." If it fails to advance 10 yards, it loses possession of the ball. It also loses possession of the ball when a pass is intercepted, when a fumble is recovered by the defense, or when it gives up possession with a punt. (A punt is the usual action for an offensive team, unless it is deep in the

This is only one of the many formations used for offensive and defensive plays. Many teams use a five-man defensive line, with three linebackers, two defensive halfbacks, and one safety. At the goal line, the defense often moves into a 7-2-2 formation to stop a plunge.

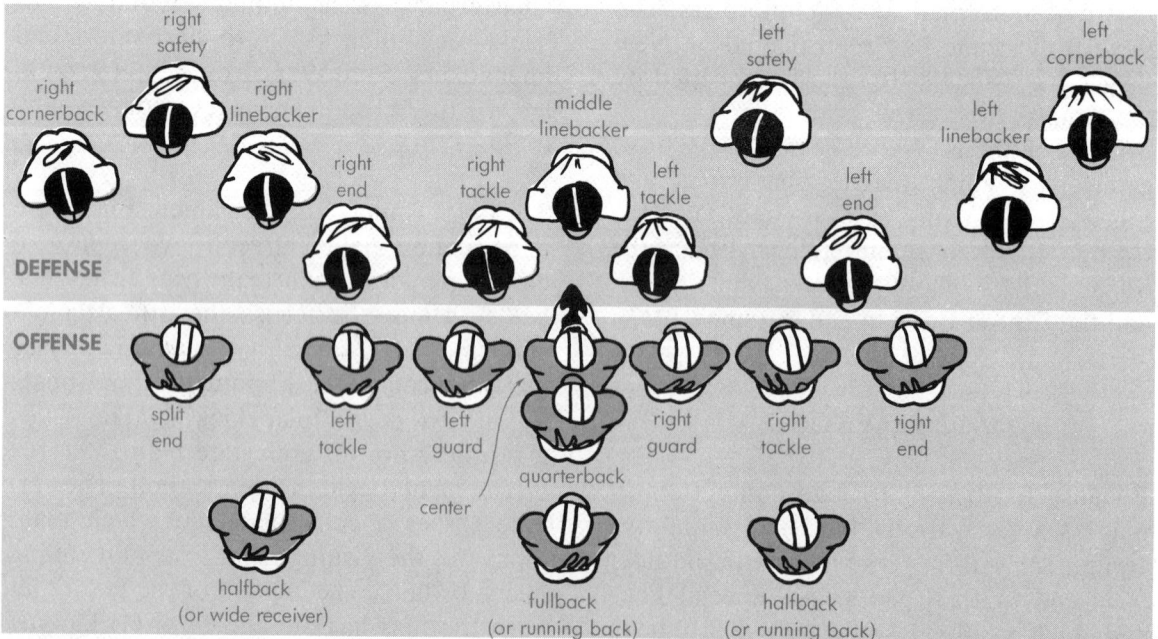

defensive team's territory, when it fears it will not be able to make a first down on its final, fourth-down try.)

The ball is moved back and forth on the playing field during alternative series of downs and first downs until one team or the other scores by moving the ball over the other team's goal line, that is, by scoring a "touchdown," or kicks a field goal through the goal posts. After the time-out following a touchdown or field goal, the scoring team kicks off as at the opening of the game.

The Kickoff.   The ball is placed on a tee at the 40-yard line of the kicking team. The players stand in the kickoff formation (see diagram), the kicking team lining up across the field a few yards behind the ball, ready to run downfield to tackle the opponent who catches the ball. As soon as the referee gives the signal to start play, the kicker runs forward, followed by his team-

mates, and kicks the ball. If the ball stays within the playing field, any player on the receiving team may catch the ball and run it back until he is tackled or forced out of bounds. At that point the ball is dead, the head linesman marks the position of the ball on the sideline, and the 10-yard chain is set in position. If the kick goes out of bounds, the kicking team is penalized 5 yards and must kick again from its 35-yard line.

Scrimmage.   Before each scrimmage the offensive team usually goes into a huddle, during which the quarterback tells his team-mates which play will be used. He chooses a play that has been planned and practiced before the game, so that each player knows his job in carrying out the plan of attack.

After a huddle, the offensive team takes its positions in a formation suited to the play chosen. The defense also assumes a

Typical kick-off formation in collegiate football. Five members of the receiving team (in foreground) must remain between their 45-yard line and the midfield stripe until the ball has been kicked. This rule prevents formation of a wedge of blockers ahead of the ball-carrier.

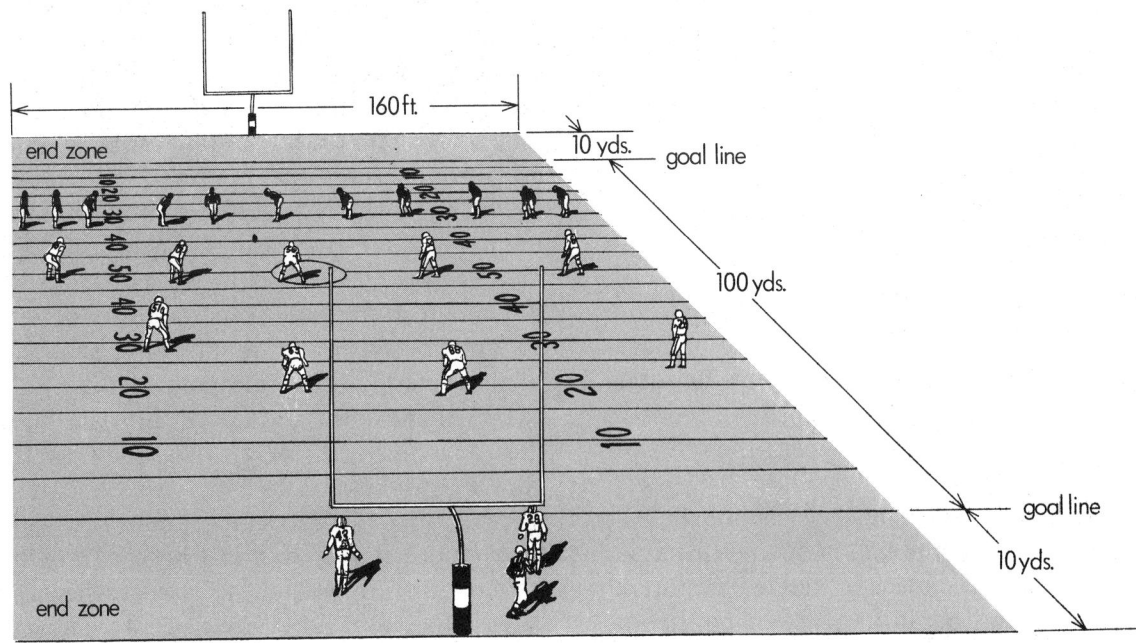

SOME LITTLE-KNOWN FOOTBALL DIMENSIONS

The Field: 120 yards long, including two 10-yard end zones. 53⅓ yards (160 feet) wide

The Football: Approximately 11 inches long, made of cowhide with a rubber lining
7 inches (minimum) in diameter at the center
12½ to 13½ pounds per inch of air pressure
14 to 15 ounces in weight
Oval-shaped and pointed at ends

The Goal Posts: College and school football: posts centered on the end-lines; posts 23 feet 4 inches apart; crossbar 10 feet high
Professional football: posts centered on the goal lines; posts 18 feet 6 inches apart; crossbar 10 feet high

The In-Bounds Markers: (Also Called Hash Marks) College and school football: 53⅓ feet from the sidelines
Professional football: 60 feet from the sidelines

formation based on the kind of play it expects from the offense. The teams face each other, half-kneeling, half-crouching, at the line of scrimmage. The ball is in the neutral zone between them and directly in front of the center.

The center bends over the ball, his legs straddling it. At a predetermined moment he snaps it back, usually handing it quickly to the quarterback, and the play begins.

The backs and ends handle the ball—carrying it, passing it, receiving it, or kicking it. At the same time, the linemen block the defense, make a path through the defensive line for the ball carrier, or hold the line until the receivers are running their patterns downfield and the quarterback has thrown the ball.

Meanwhile, the defense is reacting to the offensive play, trying to tackle the ball carrier, to block a kick, or to block or intercept a pass. When the defense succeeds in downing the ball (or when the offense scores) the play is ended.

The line of scrimmage is established at the point where the ball is downed, that is, where the ball carrier is tackled or forced out of bounds or, in the case of an incomplete pass, at the previous line of scrimmage. If the ball carrier is forced out of bounds or tackled outside the inbounds lines, the ball is moved to the point on the inbounds line where it intersects the new line of scrimmage.

Punts. If after three downs, the offense is short of the yardage needed for a first down, the quarterback may call for a punt. In this play the offense turns the ball over to the opposition, but in doing so kicks it as far as possible from its own goal line. The ball is snapped to the punter standing 10 to 15 yards behind the center. The punter holds the ball in front of him, about shoulder high. He steps forward, releases the ball and, before it hits the ground, kicks it downfield. If the punt is in bounds, a defensive player may catch it and run it back, as in the kickoff, or he may signal for a fair catch. If the punt goes over the goal line, the receiving team may run it back or accept a "touchback," which sets the ball in play on its 20-yard line. If it goes out of bounds, it is put into play on the inbounds line opposite the point where it went out.

Scoring. To score, the offense must move the ball across its opponent's goal line. The offense may carry or pass the ball over the line to make a touchdown, worth 6 points and the chance to make an additional point (or 2 points) after touchdown.

To make the extra point or points, the offense lines up for scrimmage on the defense's 3-yard line. They may try either to kick the ball between the goal posts and over the crossbar for 1 point, or to run or pass the ball over the goal line for 2 points.

Any time a team is within kicking distance of the other team's goal, it may try for a field goal, worth 3 points. A field goal must be kicked over the crossbar and between the goal posts. If the field goal is missed, the ball is played as in a punt.

A safety is a scoring play in which the defense may make 2 points by tackling an offensive ball carrier behind his own goal line. The distinction between a safety and a touchback is made clear in the Glossary.

Playing Time. In collegiate or professional football, there is officially one hour of play. However, since the clock is stopped for the halftime rest period, for time-outs, and sometimes between plays, a game may last two to three hours.

The hour is divided into thirty-minute halves, with a fifteen-minute rest period between them. At the start of each half, the ball is put into play with a kickoff. Each half is divided into fifteen-minute quarters. At the end of the first and third quarters, during a one-minute intermission, the teams switch goals, and the ball is then played from the corresponding position at the other end of the field.

Fouls and Penalties. When a player on either team breaks a rule, an official drops a colored flag and calls a foul. The offending team is charged with a penalty unless the opponents choose to decline the penalty and let the play stand. For example, a team that has scored a touchdown will naturally

A play begins when the center either hands or tosses the ball to another player, usually the quarterback. The teams are at the line of scrimmage. The quarterback (10) looks over the defense as he calls signals to his teammates. He wants to be sure he is calling the right play.

decline a penalty called on the defense during the touchdown play; it wants the touchdown, not the penalty.

If the offended team chooses to let the play stand, the down is counted and play continues from the line of scrimmage established in the play.

If the offended team chooses to accept the penalty, the scrimmage line is moved from the enforcement spot (usually the previous line of scrimmage or the spot of the foul) 5 or 15 yards toward the offending team's goal, depending on the kind of foul called. However, the ball may not be moved more than half the distance between the enforcement spot and the goal line, except for pass interference. Penalties for more serious violations may include the loss of a down or of the possession of the ball; players who commit serious personal fouls may be suspended from the game.

Five of the most common fouls and their penalties (in collegiate play) are listed below:

Delay of the game: using more than 25 seconds to put the ball into play (5 yards).

Offside: moving across the scrimmage line before the ball is centered (5 yards).

Backfield in motion: forward movement of an offensive back before the ball is centered (5 yards).

Clipping: blocking a defensive player from behind (15 yards).

Holding: illegal use of hands or arms by an offensive player while blocking (15 yards).

GLOSSARY OF FOOTBALL TERMS

back. An offensive player who is at least 1 yard behind the line of scrimmage when the ball is snapped.

block. To stop, nudge aside, or knock down an opponent by using the body but not the hands or arms.

chain gang. The head linesman's assistants at the end of the line of scrimmage, who at his direction keep the record of downs and of the position of the ball after downs. They operate a chain exactly 10 yards long.

conversion attempt. The opportunity to make a point or 2 points, given to a team that has scored a touchdown.

eligible receiver. The other three backs and the two ends comprise the receivers eligible to receive a forward pass.

enforcement spot. The place from which the penalty for a foul is stepped off by the referee.

fair catch. A catch of a kicked ball by a member of the receiving team after he gives a hand-waving signal that indicates his intentions; if the ball is caught, the receiver may not be tackled, nor may he run with the ball.

field goal. A kick through the goal posts and over the crossbar (worth 3 points).

forward pass. A pass toward the opponent's goal line from behind the line of scrimmage. It may only be made to an eligible receiver.

free ball. A live ball (one not blown dead by a whistle), not in a player's possession.

fumble. The unintentional loss of the ball while it is being carried.

huddle. The meeting of players before the snap, in which the next plays or formations are chosen. Normally, both offensive and defensive teams huddle before each play.

incomplete pass. A pass that is not caught before it hits the ground.

intercepted pass. A pass caught by a member of the opposing team.

interference. The prevention of a pass receiver from catching a pass by illegal means.

kickoff. A kick that puts the ball in play at the beginning of the first and second halves, and after touchdowns, field goals, and safeties.

lateral pass. A pass toward either side of the field or away from the opponent's goal line. A ball

SPORTS

may be so passed anywhere on the field, to any player.

line of scrimmage. The line across the field at which a play begins.

lineman. A player on the scrimmage line when the ball is snapped.

live ball. See *free ball*.

officials. Referee, umpire, head linesman, field judge, back judge, and line judge; each official has special duties.

penalty. Action taken against a team for having committed a foul.

place kick. A kick of a ball that is placed on a tee or held point-to-the-ground by another player.

punt. A kick toward the opposing team's goal line during scrimmage.

referee. The chief official of the game.

safety. A play in which an *offensive* ball carrier is tackled behind his own goal line (worth 2 points for the defense). If a *defensive* ball carrier (punt receiver, pass interceptor, or recoverer of an opponent's fumble into the end zone) is tackled behind his own goal line, it is a *touchback*, and the ball is put into play at the 20-yard line.

scrimmage. The interaction of two teams during a down (play).

scrimmage line. See *line of scrimmage*.

snap. A pass from the center to a back or kicker at the beginning of a scrimmage.

tackle. To bring the ball carrier down; also the name of two linesmen.

touchback. Called when a team takes possession of a ball behind its own goal line following a kickoff, punt, intercepted pass, or recovery of an opponent's fumble into the end zone; also called when a kickoff goes over the goal line and out of the end zone. In either case the ball is put into play at the 20-yard line, with the receiving team in possession.

touchdown. A play in which the offense carries the ball or completes a pass over the opponent's goal line (worth 6 points).

Basketball: The Action Sport

The game of basketball was invented by a Canadian clergyman, Dr. James A. Naismith, then an instructor at the Young Men's Christian Association (YMCA) training school in Springfield, Massachusetts. At the 1891 summer session for instructors, the major complaint was that students disliked the formal calisthenics used in winter physical education classes. The head of the physical education department assigned Naismith the task of inventing a game that was enjoyable, provided good exercise, and could be played indoors during the long winter months. The result was basketball, the only major modern sport that did not evolve from an older game.

By 1900 basketball was being played in Canada and in Europe, having been introduced there by foreign students and YMCA instructors. After the turn of the century, it spread to Latin America and to the Orient —the Philippines, China, and Japan—and it became an official Olympic event in 1936. Today basketball is second only to soccer as an international sport.

PROFESSIONAL BASKETBALL

Soon after basketball was introduced at the YMCA gyms in the late 1890s, it became so popular that many Y's banned the game in order to keep their facilities free for other activities. When the north branch of the Philadelphia YMCA outlawed basketball in

NBA EASTERN CONFERENCE

Atlantic Division
Boston Celtics
Buffalo Braves
New Jersey Nets
New York Knickerbockers
Philadelphia 76ers

Central Division
Atlanta Hawks
Houston Rockets
New Orleans Jazz
Cleveland Cavaliers
San Antonio Spurs
Washington Bullets

NBA WESTERN CONFERENCE

Midwest Division
Chicago Bulls
Denver Nuggets
Detroit Pistons
Indiana Pacers
Kansas City Kings
Milwaukee Bucks

Pacific Division
Los Angeles Lakers
Phoenix Suns
Portland Trail Blazers
Golden State Warriors
Seattle SuperSonics

1897, the members formed independent teams. They played before spectators who paid for admission, and thus they became the first "semiprofessionals."

Many professional leagues have since been formed, but the game was not officially organized until 1947, when the National Basketball Association (NBA) was formed. This was the first professional league that attracted top college stars; it dominates professional basketball today.

The American Basketball Association (ABA) was founded in 1967 but proved unsuccessful. In 1976, the remaining ABA teams were allowed to join the NBA. This brought the number of teams in the National Basketball Association to twenty-two.

AMATEUR BASKETBALL

Basketball is a major sport in schools, colleges, and universities throughout the United States. In addition, thousands play it for fun and exercise. Many are members of teams sponsored by churches, business firms, industrial plants, or clubs. Most of these teams belong to an amateur league or conference. The best known amateur league for nonschool teams is the Amateur Athletic Union (AAU), which each year sponsors a championship tournament.

The best known college conference is the National Collegiate Athletic Association (NCAA), which governs most college play. It has two major divisions—university and college. At the end of the playing season, conference winners and independent teams are selected to compete for the NCAA basketball championship.

Among the many high school athletic associations, there are active state leagues and conferences, which are organized differently within each state. At the end of the season, most states hold tournaments to choose state championship teams.

In 1950, "Biddy" basketball was organized for boys under 12 and girls under 13. Players use smaller balls, and the baskets are 8 feet above the floor. Each year an international tournament is held to determine the world champions. "Biddy" basketball success has led to the formation of many leagues for younger players, increasing even more the popularity of this sport.

HOW TO PLAY BASKETBALL

The object of the game is for a team to get possession of the ball, move it toward the offensive basket, and shoot it through for a field goal. The visiting team chooses its offensive basket for the first half; the teams switch baskets for the second half.

Each team has five players on the court—the center, two forwards, and two guards. All players are allowed to shoot baskets and move the ball on the court.

Generally the center, usually the tallest member of the team, starts the game with a jump against the opposing center. During offensive play, the center usually stays near the offensive basket. If a field goal is not successful, he usually is the chief rebounder, the man who, because of his height, can most easily grab the ball and keep possession of it for his team.

The two forwards, on the offense, also operate near their offensive basket. The guards are usually responsible for moving the ball to an area where any offensive player can most easily shoot for a basket.

Starting Play. The ball is put into play at the start of a game by the centers with a "jump." They stand in the center restraining circle marked on the court, facing each other and their own offensive baskets. The other players are outside the circle, the forwards in front of their center and the guards behind him.

The referee tosses the ball up between the centers. As the ball reaches its highest point, each center tries to tap it toward his teammates. As soon as a player gets the ball, his team becomes the offense.

Moving the Ball. The offensive team tries to advance the ball toward its offensive basket. To do this, players may pass the ball back and forth, or bounce it off the floor between them. They may also dribble the ball, that is, bounce it along the floor with one hand.

Meanwhile, the defense tries to prevent the offense from getting into a position from which the offense can shoot a basket and score. The two major kinds of defense are *man-to-man*, in which each player guards a specified opponent; and *zone*, in which a player guards those opponents who come into a particular area of the court. In either case, the defense discourages shots and tries to keep the offense off balance and confused. More important, the defense tries to intercept the ball as it is passed or as it rebounds off the backboard after an attempted shot. The defense also tries to steal the ball by knocking it from a player's hands, usually as he dribbles it down the court. When the defensive team gets the

Many a game has been won at the free throw line. Practice and cool nerves are needed.

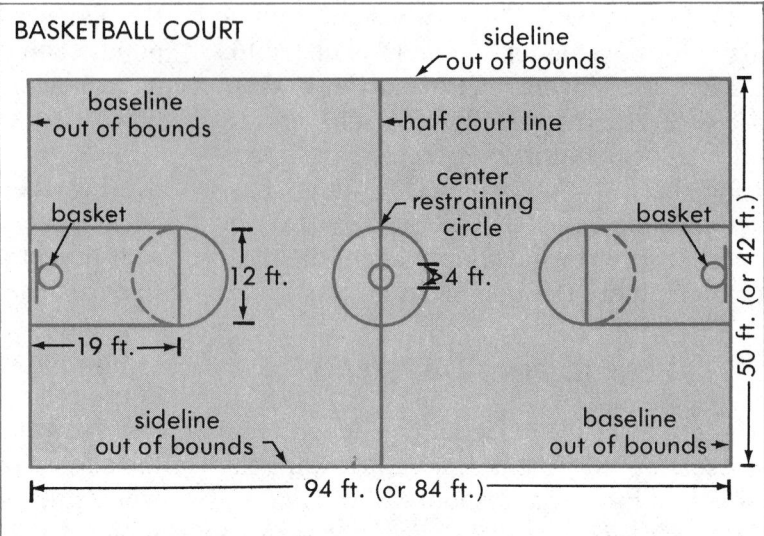

BASKETBALL COURT

sideline out of bounds

baseline out of bounds

half court line

center restraining circle

basket

basket

12 ft.

24 ft.

19 ft.

50 ft. (or 42 ft.)

sideline out of bounds

baseline out of bounds

94 ft. (or 84 ft.)

Dimensions of the court for regulation basketball. The rim of the basket is exactly 10 feet above the floor. Only ten players are permitted on the court during play.

ball, it tries to move it down the court into a position from which it—as the offensive team—can shoot before the team that lost the ball can recover to set up its defense. This is called the "fast-break."

The ball is automatically turned over to the defense if an offensive player "double dribbles" or "travels" with the ball. Once a player stops dribbling and holds the ball with both hands, he must either pass it to another player or shoot for a basket; he cannot dribble it again. Also, a player may not travel with the ball, that is, he may not hold it and walk or run. In either case, the ball is "dead," and the official turns it over to a member of the other team, who stands outside the boundary line of the court near the spot of infraction and makes a "throw-in"—he tosses it to a teammate inbounds within five seconds—and play begins again.

A ball may also be turned over to the defense if it goes out-of-bounds. In this case, too, the ball is dead and an official must decide who touched it last. He gives the ball to a player on the opposite team, who makes a throw-in from the spot where it went out. If an official cannot decide who touched it last, he calls for a jump ball in the nearest restraining circle. He may also

call for a jump ball if two opposing players both have a firm hold on the ball at the same time.

Shooting the Basket. Players may shoot for a basket from anywhere on the court, but it is best to move the ball as close as possible to the goal before shooting. A team scores a field goal, worth 2 points, when it shoots the ball through the basket. After each basket, the ball is put into play by a member of the opposite team, who throws in from behind the baseline.

Fouls and Free Throws. The only way other than the field goal that a team may score is with a "free throw," which is awarded to a player when an opponent has committed a foul against him. He takes his free throw (unhindered by opponents) from the free throw line 15 feet from the backboard; if he succeeds, his team scores one point. Two free throws are awarded the player if the foul was made while he was shooting for a field goal and he missed the shot. (If he has made the shot, he is given only one free throw.)

While the free throw is being attempted, the other players stand outside the free throw lane (marked on the court) on either side of the basket. After the attempt (or second attempt if two throws were awarded) the ball is live, and it may be grabbed on the rebound by any player for his team.

There are two different kinds of fouls—personal and technical. Personal fouls are those resulting from contact with an opponent. Any player who collides with or aggressively pushes, trips, shoves, or charges into his opponents is charged with a personal foul. A player who commits five personal fouls (six in a professional game) is taken out of the game.

For a personal foul that is unintentional, the offended player gets one free throw. If such a foul is committed after four fouls in a quarter of a game played in quarters, or after six fouls in a half of a game played in halves, the offended player has two chances to make a point (or three chances to make two points).

If a foul is intentional, the offended player gets two free throws. If the officials judge the personal foul to be "flagrant," the offending player may be thrown out of the game.

Technical fouls do not ordinarily involve player contact. They are usually the result of a team's breaking the rules—taking more than five time-outs, delaying the game, having too many men on the court, unsportsmanlike conduct, and so forth.

If these violations are minor and unintentional, one free throw is awarded to the offended team. For intentional, serious violations, two free throws are awarded.

Periods of Play. The game is divided into periods of actual play, but the clock is stopped for time-outs and when the ball is dead. Teams younger than high school age play four quarters, or periods, of 6 minutes each, with intermissions of 1 minute after the first and third quarters and 10 minutes

At the opening whistle, each team seeks the advantage of possession of the ball. From then on, the action moves up and down the court.

after the first half. High school teams play four quarters of 8 minutes with the same intermissions. College teams play two halves of 20 minutes each with a 15-minute rest period. Professional teams play four 12-minute quarters.

If the game is tied at the end of the last period, overtime periods are played—3 minutes in high school games and 5 minutes for college or professional games.

BASKETBALL FOR WOMEN

The rules for women were formally established in 1899. They limited the dribble to three floor contacts and assessed a foul for holding the ball longer than 3 seconds. Each team had six players—three forwards and three guards. With the exception of one roving guard and one roving forward, the players were not allowed to cross over the center area of the court. The forwards of one team played against the guards of the other at one end of the court and vice-versa. Only the forwards could shoot for a basket. When the guards intercepted or recovered the ball, it was moved to the center line and given to the forwards, who moved it toward the goal and attempted to score.

These rules made the game slow and less exciting than men's basketball. As basketball for women gained in popularity and their skills improved, the style of the game and the rules were changed. Today there is little distinction between a men's or women's game. There are large crowds at some women's games, and women's basketball has recently been recognized as an essential part of the Olympic Games.

GLOSSARY OF BASKETBALL TERMS

bonus free throw. The bonus free throw is awarded to a team when their opponents commit a certain number of personal fouls: the number is different for college and high school play.

bounce pass. A pass that is bounced between two players.

defensive press. Defense in which players guard opponents closely at all times.

double dribble. To dribble once, then hold the ball, and dribble again. This is a violation of the rules, which results in a turnover of the ball to the other team.

double foul. When two opponents commit personal fouls against each other, no free throws are awarded.

dribble. To move the ball by bouncing it on the floor with one hand.

field goal. A "basket," made by shooting the ball through the team's own basket, worth 2 points.

foul. An infraction of the rules involving personal contact or team conduct; the penalty is one or more free throws.

free throw. A chance to score one or more points given to a player when a foul is committed against him (or in some cases, against his team).

guard. To try to prevent an offensive player from scoring; also the name of two players on a team.

held ball. A ball held tightly by two players of opposing teams. An official declares the ball dead and it is put into play with a jump ball in the nearest restraining circle.

in-bounding. Throwing the ball from out-of-bounds to a teammate who is in-bounds.

jump ball. A ball that the referee tosses up between two players who are standing in a restraining circle; each tries to tap it toward a teammate.

officials. The referee is the chief official of the game; one or two umpires assist him on the court. There are also scorers and timers on the sidelines.

personal foul. A foul that involves contact with another player while the ball is live or after it is given to a player for a throw-in.

technical foul. A non-contact foul usually involving team conduct.

ten-second free throw rule. A rule forcing a player to shoot a free throw within 10 seconds after he is awarded the ball; failure to do so results in a turnover.

ten-second rule. A rule requiring a team to move the ball from its back court into its front court within 10 seconds after gaining possession; failure to do so results in a turnover.

three-second rule. A rule making it illegal for a player to remain in the free throw lane under the offensive basket for more than 3 seconds when his team has possession of the ball.

turnover. Loss of possession of the ball, usually due to a violation of the rules or to an intercepted pass.

traveling. Taking two steps or more while holding the ball. This is a violation of the rules, which results in a turnover.

Tennis: Fastest Growing Sport

Tennis, the world's most popular sport involving one player against another, is a truly international game. In its present form tennis goes back hardly more than a century, but it has an ancestry traceable probably to the twelfth century and certainly the thirteenth century in France.

LAWN TENNIS

A rule book for the game of lawn tennis was prepared by a Major Walter Wingfield in England in 1873. The game was played on an outdoor lawn court of an hour-glass shape, with a net 5 feet across its waist. Credit for establishing the rules of tennis is generally given to the Marylebone Cricket Club, which stabilized a game that was spreading like wildfire under various rules wherever level lawns were found. In the United States popularity of the game spread quickly to suburbs of New York; to Newport, Rhode Island; Boston; Philadelphia; and New Orleans.

By 1877 the English had decided finally on a rectangular court 26 yards long. The server was allowed one fault, so that he or she had two chances to put the ball in play. The All-England Croquet Club emerged as the powerful group in tennis. In 1877 it expanded its name to include Lawn Tennis,

and it initiated the first championship tournament at its grounds in Wimbledon, a suburb of London. Modern tennis was on its way.

The height of the net was fixed in 1880 at 3 feet at the center of the court and 3 feet 6 inches at the posts outside the alley lines. Little has been done to the rules since then, except to increase the weight of the ball from $1\frac{1}{4}$–$1\frac{1}{2}$ ounces to 2–$2\frac{1}{16}$ ounces. The first official United States championship for men was held in 1881 at Newport; for women, in 1887.

Although the rules had been relatively stable during the first three decades of championship tennis, the tennis racket left behind its early flat-topped and lopsided shape in favor of the oval shape used today.

A landmark in tennis was the arrival on the scene of Maurice McLoughlin, known as the "California Comet." McLoughlin brought a slashing style of play to the game. The slow-moving, backcourt, fencing-for-an-opening style employed by most of the previous masters of the game gave way to McLoughlin's all-out attack, which meant net play, volleys, half-volleys, and smashes. The result was that ever-larger numbers of players and spectators enjoyed championship play.

Interest in international competition had

its start in 1900, when Dwight F. Davis, himself a United States championship doubles player, donated the Davis Cup. For nearly two decades, virtually the only contenders were Great Britain, Australia, and the United States. After William T. ("Big Bill") Tilden and William ("Little Bill") Johnston brought the Davis Cup back from Australia in 1919, Tilden dominated the world tennis scene for seven years and thrilled spectators for twelve. His fluid strokes, cannonball serve, mastery of spin and pace, and ability to raise his game to the need of the moment made him supreme.

From Tilden's era to the present, the stream of gifted tennis players has been uninterrupted. To mention United States men players only, and only the greatest, there have been Ellsworth Vines, Don Budge (he won all four major national championships in 1938), Jack Kramer, Pancho Gonzales, Tony Trabert, and Jimmy Connors. Each year produces an ever-larger crop of young players ready to step into the limelight.

WOMEN'S TENNIS

From the time of the first United States women's tennis champion, Ellen Hansell (1887), to Billy Jean King and Christine Evert is a long journey in styles of play and court dress. In the nineteenth century, the well-dressed female players wore a long white dress with leg-of-mutton sleeves, a sailor hat, and ornamented tennis shoes. May Sutton, of California, astounded Wimbledon in 1905 and 1907 with a masculine-style forehand drive. Helen Hotchkiss (later Mrs. George Wightman, who donated the Wightman Cup) won the United States women's championship consistently in the second decade of this century with an all-court game. Her incisive volleying stepped up the tempo of the women's game.

Suzanne Lenglen, of France, probably advanced tennis even more in the popularity polls by her speed of foot and her daring costume, which liberated women tennis players from the constricting dress prescribed by traditional standards of the times.

After Lenglen, players of first rank came tumbling forward: Helen Wills Moody, Helen Jacobs, Sarah Palfrey, Alice Marble, Pauline Betz, Maureen ("Little Mo") Connolly, Althea Gibson, Billy Jean King, Christine Evert, and many others broke into prominence.

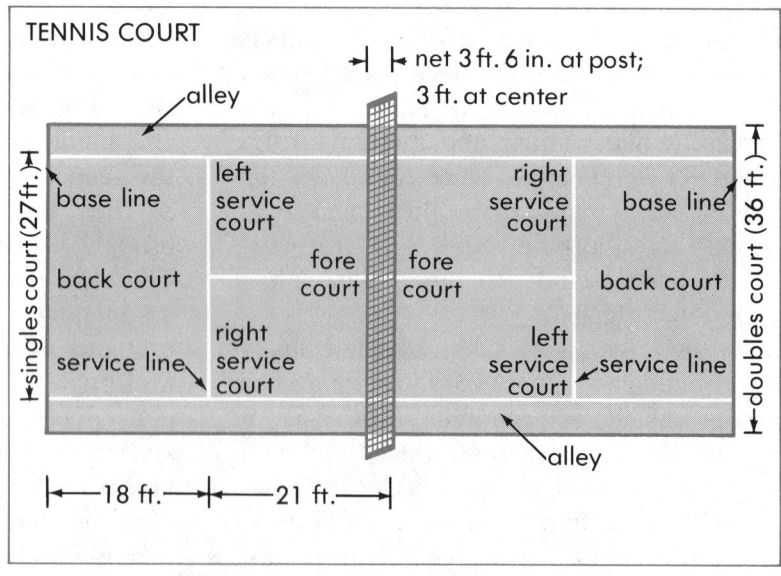

Dimensions of a regulation tennis court. The court surface may vary but the court must always be the same size. The alleys are used only for doubles games.

Billie Jean King lunges for a forehand in a memorable 1975 victory over Chris Evert. King is among a handful of tennis players who have won three consecutive Wimbledon championships.

Chris Evert follows through on a backhand on her way to winning her second Wimbledon championship in 1976. Evert began to dominate international women's competition after 1975.

INTERNATIONAL COMPETITION TODAY

Davis Cup competition has expanded so widely that four zone or regional elimination trials are necessary: European A and B, Eastern (Asia), and American (North and South). For women the annual Wightman Cup matches between the United States and Great Britain are played as spiritedly as ever. Another trophy for women's international team play, the Federation Cup, was donated in 1962 by the International Lawn Tennis Association (ILTA) on its 50th anniversary.

Once a sport for the well-to-do, tennis is now available to nearly everybody. More free public and school courts are built each year, and the growth in the number of low-cost commercial tennis clubs has been phenomenal, offering covered and open-air courts in many parts of the United States for daytime or night play. Whereas grass courts were once considered ideal for the game, their number has decreased steadily. They are expensive to maintain and are unable to withstand constant play. Clay courts have been standard in the South and on the West Coast from the turn of the century, and there now are several types of asphalt and concrete surfaces in use, as well as a bewildering number of synthetic court surfaces. The manufacture of tennis rackets has also experienced many innovations, such as the availability of nylon as a substitute for gut in stringing the racket, and of laminated wood, lightweight metal, or plastic for solid wood frames.

HOW TO PLAY TENNIS

Lawn tennis is played either by two persons (singles) or four persons (doubles) on a rectangular court with a racket and a ball.

Rod Laver stretches for a backhand at Wimbledon. A powerful, aggressive player despite his slight build, Laver won two grand slams during his successful career in the 1960s and 1970s.

Jimmy Connors, once known as "The Bad Boy of Tennis," braces for one of his powerful two-handed backhands at Wimbledon in 1977. Connors is known for his aggressive, forcing game.

Tennis rackets are about 27 inches long and 9 inches wide at the face.

Singles

In a singles match, two players are on the court, one on each side of the net. Before the first game, a coin is tossed or a racket spun to decide who will be the server. The winner of the toss may instead choose the side of the net he or she will take in the first game. The opponent then makes whichever of these choices is left. The players are ready to take their positions on the court.

The ball is put into play with the serve. For the first point in each game, the server stands behind the right-hand half of the baseline (see diagram). The position of the server is anywhere between the alley line and the point on the baseline that would be intersected by an extension of the center line dividing the service courts. The inter-section point usually is marked in white-wash in tournament play. When the opposing player is ready, the server throws the ball into the air and, at arm's length upward, hits the ball with the racket. For the serve to be valid, or "good," the ball must land in the service court (including the service lines) on the opposite side of the net, and diagonally across from the side on which the server is standing. Failure to make a valid serve is a "fault." If the server fails twice to deliver a serve into the proper service court, the server has committed a double fault, and the opponent has scored a point.

If the receiver then returns a valid serve within the boundaries of the server's court, the ball is in play. The players then hit the ball back and forth until one player hits it into the net, knocks it out of bounds, misses it, or lets it bounce more than once. The opponent then scores a point.

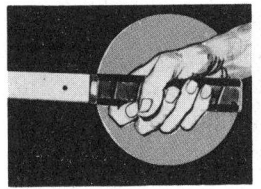

FOREHAND

OVERHEAD
SERVICE

BACKHAND

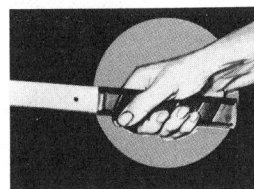

The server continues to serve until a game is won or lost. The serve is always delivered from behind the base line, alternating from the right and left-hand sides of the server's base line. When a game is won, the service is passed on to the other player. The players change sides after the odd-numbered games of each set, that is, after the first, third, fifth, etc.

Scoring. If the server makes a double fault (fails to make a valid serve twice), the receiver scores a point. After the game is under way, either player can score a point if the opposing player fails to make a return within the other's court. All serves that land on the service line, and all returns thereafter that land on the outer lines of the court being used, are good. The winner of a game is the player who first scores four points. The first point in a game is 15, the second 30, the third 40, and the fourth "game." However, if the scores reach "deuce" (40 to 40), a player must score two successive points from deuce to win the game. The first point after deuce is called "advantage" or simply "ad." If the other side wins the next point to even the score, the game goes back to deuce, and so

on until one player scores two consecutive points from deuce.

The player who first wins six games wins a set. Traditionally, as in game score, if the set is "deuce" (five games to five), a player must win two consecutive games from deuce to win. Since 1970, however, most tied sets in tournaments have been decided in a "sudden death" play-off by means of a 9-point tie-breaker system. In this, Player A serves the first two points, Player B the third and fourth points, A the fifth and sixth, and B the seventh, eighth, and ninth. The first player to win five points wins the set.

In men's national and regional championships, a player must win three out of five sets. In matches of lesser importance, and in all women's play, a match is won by the first player to win two sets.

Doubles

In a doubles match, there are four players on a slightly larger court, two on each side of the net. (See diagram for court size.) Given the larger court, the rules for doubles are the same as those for singles, except in the order of service. After the toss, the team that has won the service decides which will serve first; the other team decides which player will receive first (play the right-hand service court) and which the left. When the first game is completed, the service is passed to the opponents, one of whom will serve first for them. After the second game, the partner of the initial server becomes the server. After the third game, the other opponent becomes the server. Once the order has been decided in the second game, it is kept throughout the set.

GLOSSARY OF TENNIS TERMS

ace. A valid serve that the receiver does not touch at all with his or her racket.

advantage. The point scored after deuce. When the server scores the point, it is called "advantage in"; when the receiver scores, it is called "advantage out."

backhand. One of the basic strokes by which a right-handed player hits a ball played to his or her left side, and a left-handed player one played to his or her right side.

deuce. A tie score (40 to 40); also any return thereafter to an equal point-score.

double fault. Two serves that are not valid that are delivered in succession. See **fault.**

fault. A serve that is not valid, not "in," including a footfault.

footfault. A server's failure to keep both feet on the ground or behind the baseline between the center mark and the side boundary during a serve; it counts as a fault.

forehand. One of the basic strokes by which a right-handed player hits the ball played to his right side; and a left-handed player, one played to his left side.

game. The score when one side has won four points, or two consecutive points after deuce is reached.

ground stroke. A ball hit after it has bounced once. Ground strokes are the forehand and the backhand, but they may be played in different manners.

half-volley. A ball played directly after it has hit the ground, sometimes called a pick-up.

let or **let ball.** A served ball that lands in the proper service court, but only after touching the net in getting there. It is not counted as a fault, and the serve is replayed. After the serve, any ball that touches the net in passing over it is played as if nothing had happened, provided the ball lands within the playing area.

lob. A high, arched ball, usually played to allow a player time to regain good court position, but sometimes employed as an attacking tactic.

love. The score of zero, said either of points in a game or of games in a set.

officials. In tournament play, the referee is the chief official, and is in charge of the tournament; the umpire is in charge of the match; and the linesmen determine and indicate whether a ball is hit within the boundaries of the court.

rally. To hit the ball back and forth over the net until one player fails to return it properly. Also, to practice, to limber up.

serve. To put the ball in play by hitting it into the opponent's proper service court.

set. The score when one player wins six games. In the case of a set that becomes "deuced" at 5-all, the ways of breaking the tie will have been established by the referee or by the players themselves (in informal play).

smash. A hard overhand stroke used to return a lob or finish off a point.

volley. A stroke, usually made in the forecourt, in which an opponent's return is played on the fly, that is, before it hits the ground. "To volley" means to stroke in this manner.

Soccer: The Favorite World-Wide

Soccer is the most popular team sport in the world today. It is played in 143 countries and is considered the national sport of many European and South American countries. Crowds watching championship matches are often twice as large as those attending the baseball World Series or the football Superbowl in the United States. No other sport can claim a true world championship such as the soccer World Cup that has been awarded every four years since 1930.

Various football games are said to have been played for centuries, but it was not until the late 1800s that clear distinctions were made among them. The modern version of soccer developed in 1863 in England when the supporters of the kicking, heading, and no-hands variety of football formed The Football Association. The name "soccer" came from a corruption of "association" or its abbreviation "assoc." At the same time rugby emerged, with rules including both kicking and carrying the ball. American football later developed into what is essentially a carrying and passing game.

Soccer has several good features: it is easy to understand; it can be played by both sexes; its costs are low; and serious injury is relatively rare.

HOW TO PLAY SOCCER

Outdoor soccer is played by two teams of 10 field players and one goal-keeper each. The objective is to kick, pass, or head a ball into the opponent's goal.

The rules for soccer as it is played around the world were drawn up by the Federation of International Football Association (FIFA) and are known as the "Laws of the Game." They apply to such regulations as those concerning the field of play, method of scoring, fouls, misconduct, duration of the game, and officials. These rules have brought conformity to international competition. Only in the United States have they been modified to satisfy professional, collegiate, and high-school governing bodies.

The field is rectangular and may vary from 100 to 130 yards long and 50 to 100 yards wide. (In intercollegiate competition in the United States, the length may be from 110 to 120 yards and the width from 65 to 75 yards.) The field is divided into two halves by a center line, in the middle of which is the center spot. It is here that the kick-off starts the game and re-starts it after a goal is scored.

The goals are placed in the center of the goal line at each end of the field and consist of two posts 24 feet apart, joined by a crossbar 8 feet above the ground. From the crossbar a net is suspended to catch the ball and verify the goal. In front of each goal are two rectangular areas. The smaller one, the goal area, is 60 feet wide and extends 18 feet in front of the goal; the larger one, the penalty area, is 132 feet wide by 54 feet deep. This is the area where the goalkeeper may use his hands and where penalty kicks are made from the penalty spot 12 yards from the center of the goal. Only the goalkeeper may attempt to block a penalty kick.

The team consists of the goalkeeper, two full-backs, a center half-back, two wing half-backs, and five forwards behind the center line.

The officials of the game are the referee, who acts as timekeeper and enforces the rules; and two linesmen, who notify the referee of out-of-bounds, offsides, and fouls committed.

The action of the game is very fast. The ball often passes from one team to the other within seconds, and the roles of the players change from attacker to defender accordingly. The game is played for 90 minutes, usually in two 45-minute halves. (United States college games are played in four 22-minute quarters.) The most popular formations (or line-ups) used today are 4-2-4 and 4-3-3. In each case the back line of defense has four players. The midfield varies between two and three, and the forward line between four and three. The speed of the game limits the use of set plays and depends on improvisation by the individual players. Under international rules, no more than two substitutions are allowed. (This rule varies in the United States.)

Players may not hold, push, or trip an

Soccer is growing in popularity, but Americans are not as familiar with this sport as with many others. The dimensions of the soccer field shown are regulation. Where space is not available, teams practice on small fields.

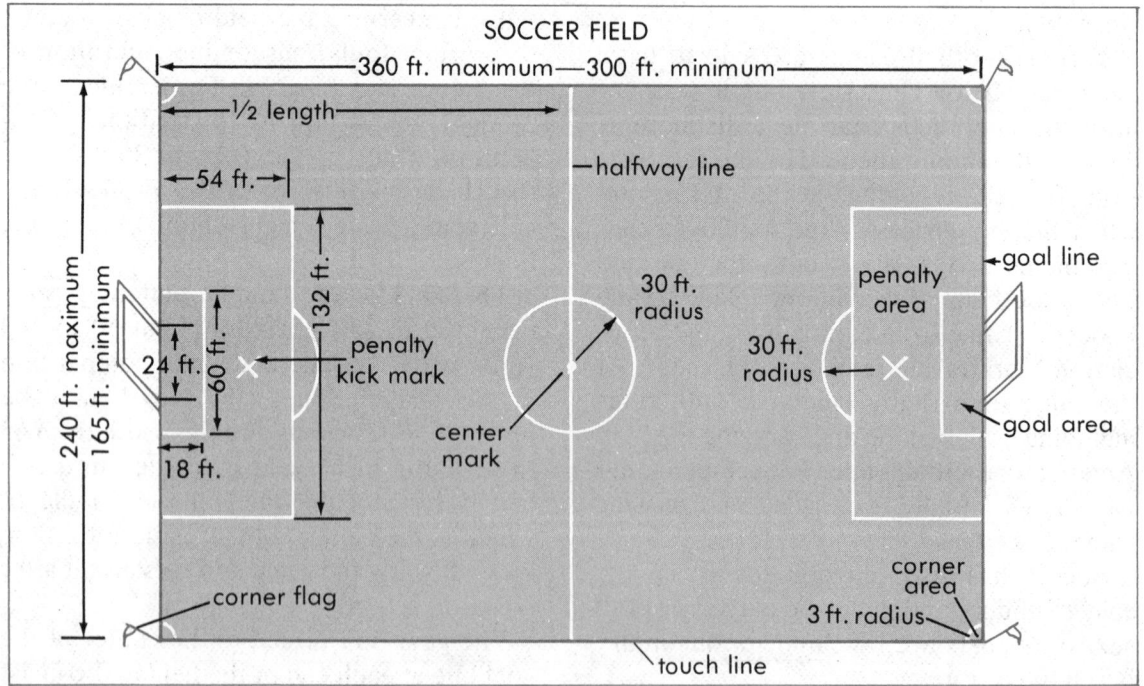

SOCCER FIELD

SPORTS

opponent or use their hands on the ball. If a foul is committed, the referee may send a player off the field for the rest of the game or award a free kick to a player on the opposing team. A ball is out of play if it goes outside the touch line (side line) and is put back in play by a member of the team not responsible for sending it out. The ball is thrown inbounds by a two-handed, over-the-head delivery. When the ball crosses the goal line, the referee determines whether the offense or defense was responsible and gives the ball to the opposite side to put into play. The offense does this by a corner kick from the side on which the ball went out; the defense, by a kick from the goal area.

The winner of the match is the team that scores the greater number cf goals (one point each). If the game is tied at the end of regulation time, the game ends as a tie. One exception to this rule is in tournament competition in the United States, where overtime periods are used to break a tie.

The quality of play depends on physical fitness, technique, and tactical skills. Fitness training for young players must include soccer-related drills with the ball. A player must have endurance to cope with the continuous play, quickness of movement and agility to control the ball, and strength for any action or movement on the field. Players must also have good technique—the ability to control the ball by trapping, passing, dribbling, heading, and shooting. They must be able to execute that technique under pressure from opponents while attempting to attack and score a goal, or defend and prevent a goal. A player has a responsibility to the team for his or her own tactics and for team tactics.

EQUIPMENT

A soccer ball is round, usually a rubber bladder with a leather casing, having a

LEADING PLAYERS IN NASL 1977

Gordon Banks	Goalkeeper
	Ft. Lauderdale
Ken Cooper	Goalkeeper
	Dallas
Steve David	Forward
	Los Angeles
Pélé	Forward
	Cosmos
George Best	Midfield
	Los Angeles
Alan West	Midfield
	Minnesota
Mike England	Defender
	Seattle
Franz Beckenbauer	Defender
	Cosmos
Giorgio Chinaglia	Forward
	Cosmos
Kyle Rote, Jr.	Forward*
	Dallas

* Rote was the first native-born American to star in the professional ranks, which in its first 10 years has been dominated by players from other parts of the world.

circumference of 27–28 inches and weighing 14–16 ounces. A smaller and lighter ball is used in youth games.

Players are equipped with shorts, shirts or jerseys with 8-inch numbers on the back, calf-length socks, and football boots (with studs or cleats up to ½ inch). Shin guards, worn under socks, are optional.

PROFESSIONAL SOCCER

The American Soccer League has been playing competitively since 1934, but at first without the enthusiastic support that baseball and football have enjoyed. In 1967, however, the North American Soccer League (NASL) was formed with a franchise in Atlanta. Ten years later, the league had prospered and grown to 24 teams representing cities in the United States and Canada. Average attendance in 1967 was less than 2000 per game but increased to 14,640 per game for the 251 scheduled NASL games in 1977.

AMATEUR SOCCER

Reports from high school and college soccer associations demonstrate clearly that soccer is the fastest growing sport. Over 4200 schools now sponsor high-school soccer, compared to 2300 in 1971. More surprising is the growth of women's soccer from 28 teams in 1970 to over 600 in 1976. Collegiate soccer has grown from 153 teams in 1957 to 429 in 1976. In addition, figures from the American Youth Soccer Association and the United States Youth Soccer Association demonstrate that a national trend toward soccer at the under-18 level is rapidly taking hold.

GLOSSARY OF SOCCER TERMS

Caution. A warning by the referee to a player who persistently fouls, who argues with the referee, or who is guilty of bad sportsmanship.

Charge. Use of the shoulder to attempt to knock an opponent off balance. A legal tactic.

Dangerous play. Any action by a player that the referee considers to be dangerous or likely to cause injury.

Dribbling. Using the feet to move the ball through or around an opponent. Usually consists of a series of short taps.

Half volley. A ball kicked just as it is rebounding off the ground.

Heading. Propelling the ball by butting it with the head, usually with the forehead.

Holding. Obstructing an opponent's progress or movement by using one's hands.

Marking. Shadowing or closely guarding an opponent.

Offside. A player who is nearer to the opponent's goal line than the ball when the ball is played to him is offside unless (1) there are two opponents nearer to the goal line; (2) he is in his own half of the field; (3) the ball last touches an opponent; (4) he receives the ball directly from a corner kick, goal kick, throw-in, or a drop ball.

Penalty kick. Any direct free kick awarded to the offensive team in the penalty area. The kick is taken from the penalty spot, and only the kicker and the goalkeeper may remain in the penalty area while the kick is being made.

Screening. Keeping a player's body between an opponent and the ball.

Striker. The player positioned in the center of the offensive line, formerly known as the center forward.

Sweeper. A defender who plays behind the defensive line to counter any breakthrough by the offense.

Tackling. Using the feet to try to take the ball away from an opponent.

Trapping. Gaining control of the ball with some part of the body other than the hands and arms.

Volley. A ball kicked while it is in the air.

The Olympic Games

The first Olympic Games known positively to have been held were those of 776 B.C., twenty-three years before Rome was founded. (Games held prior to that time take us out of history into legend.) From 776 B.C. the Greeks computed their time on a four-year basis. Each such period was called an Olympiad. An event was reckoned as happening in the first, second, third or fourth year in a given Olympiad. At the end of each Olympiad, another celebration was held on the Plain of Olympia, in northwest Greece, on the Peloponnesus.

The glory days of the Olympic Games faded after 400 B.C. The decline was gradual at first, but the pace increased after Rome defeated Greece in 197 B.C. and controlled the Games. By 393 A.D. the Emperor Theodosius I, a Christian, terminated the games on the ground that they were pagan and totally corrupted. After a 1200-year history the Olympic Games disappeared from the scene. They remained almost forgotten for about 1500 years. Their revival at Athens in 1896 reawakened international interest in a modern Olympic Games, modeled on the ideals of their ancient counterpart.

Not every modern holding of the Games has been free of troubles. In 1908, the London Games were tarnished by disputes over the actions of officials. In 1912, Jim Thorpe of the United States, perhaps the greatest all-round athlete of all time, who had won the gold medal in the pentathlon and decathlon at Stockholm, was determined afterwards to have been a professional athlete (in baseball) and hence

---

OLYMPIC SPORTS

SUMMER GAMES

Archery	Fencing	Rowing	Weightlifting
Basketball	Field Hockey	Shooting	Wrestling,
Boxing	Gymnastics	Soccer	Freestyle
Canoeing	Handball	Swimming	Wrestling,
Cycling	Judo	Track and Field	Greco-Roman
Diving	Modern	Volleyball	Yachting
Equestrian	Pentathlon	Water Polo	

WINTER GAMES

Biathlon	Skiing,
Bobsled	Alpine
Figure	Skiing,
Skating	Nordic
Ice Hockey	Speed
Luge	Skating

Bruce Jenner concludes his record-breaking 1976 performance in the decathlon.

Event	Jenner's Performance
100 meter dash	0:10.94
long jump	23'8¼"
shot put	50'4¼"
high jump	6'8"
400 meter run	47.51
110 meter high hurdles	14.84
discus throw	164'2"
pole vault	15'9"
javelin throw	224'9½"
1,500 meter run	4:12.61

Elsewhere in this section a list of sports contested today is printed. To be placed on the schedule, a sport must be demonstrated to be widely enjoyed in forty or more nations spread across three or more continents. The sport must then be approved for inclusion in the Games by the International Olympic Committee (IOC). The IOC elects its own members, and only countries that have held Games are entitled to two representatives on it.

Each country has a national Olympic committee that determines who will represent their nation and raises funds to defray expenses. These national committees certify that their nation's Olympic contenders meet the Olympic standards for eligibility. Generally speaking, each nation may qualify three athletes in each individual event and one team in each team event. In the most popular sports of the Games, in terms of entrants—track and field, and swimming—a nation is entitled to enter only one athlete per event unless it can demonstrate that its entrants meet a minimum standard for the event set by the IOC.

THE DECATHLON: WORLD'S TOUGHEST EVENT

The most difficult and exhausting event in the Olympic games is the decathlon, a Greek word meaning "ten contests." Each contestant must compete in all ten and is given points for performance in each. The entrant with the largest total is the winner. Five events are held on one day, the others on the next day. The winner of the decathlon is the best track and field athlete of the games and is regarded as the world's greatest athlete until the next Olympics.

At the 1976 games held in Montreal the decathlon was won by Bruce Jenner of the United States, with a record-breaking total of 8,618 points.

ineligible for the Games, according to Olympic rules. His Olympic titles were taken from him. In 1936, Hitler poisoned the Berlin holding of the Games by his efforts to make it a showpiece for Nazi ideology and military trappings. In 1972, at Munich, a group of armed terrorists invaded the training camp before the Games and gunned down athletes representing Israel.

The torch-lighting ceremony marks the beginning of another Olympic Games. The Olympic tradition is thousands of years old, but the first modern Games were held in Athens in 1896.

OLYMPIC RECORDS

MEN'S SWIMMING

100 Meter Freestyle	
Jim Montgomery, U.S., 1976	0:49.99
200 Meter Freestyle	
Bruce Furniss, U.S., 1976	1:50.29*
400 Meter Freestyle	
Brian Goodell, U.S., 1976	3:51.93*
1,500 Meter Freestyle	
Brian Goodell, U.S., 1976	15:02.40*
100 Meter Backstroke	
John Naber, U.S., 1976	0:55.49*
200 Meter Backstroke	
John Naber, U.S., 1976	1:59.19*
100 Meter Breaststroke	
John Hencken, U.S., 1976	1:03.11
200 Meter Breaststroke	
David Wilkie, Great Britain, 1976	2:15.11*
100 Meter Butterfly	
Mark Spitz, U.S., 1972	0:54.3
200 Meter Butterfly	
Michael Bruner, U.S., 1976	1:59.23*
400 Meter Individual Medley	
Rod Strachan, U.S., 1976	4:23.68*
800 Meter Freestyle Relay	
United States, 1976	7:23.22*
400 Meter Medley Relay	
United States, 1976	3:42.22*

* indicates world record also

Springboard Diving
Phil Boggs, U.S., 1976   619.52 points
Platform Diving
Klaus DiBiasi, Italy, 1976   600.51 points

WOMEN'S SWIMMING

100 Meter Freestyle	
Kornelia Ender, E. Germany, 1976	0:55.65*
200 Meter Freestyle	
Kornelia Ender, E. Germany, 1976	1:59.26*
400 Meter Freestyle	
Petra Thumer, E. Germany, 1976	4:09.89
800 Meter Freestyle	
Petra Thumer, E. Germany, 1976	8:37.14
100 Meter Backstroke	
Ulrike Richter, E. Germany, 1976	1:01.83
200 Meter Backstroke	
Ulrike Richter, E. Germany, 1976	2:13.43
100 Meter Breaststroke	
Hannelore Anke, E. Germany, 1976	1:11.16
200 Meter Breaststroke	
Marina Koshevaya, U.S.S.R., 1976	2:33.35*
100 Meter Butterfly	
Kornelia Ender, E. Germany, 1976	1:00.13
200 Meter Butterfly	
Andrea Pollack, E. Germany, 1976	2:11.41

400 Meter Individual Medley
    Ulrike Tauber, E. Germany, 1976   4:42.77*
400 Meter Freestyle Relay
    United States, 1976   3:44.82*
400 Meter Medley Relay
    E. Germany, 1976   4:07.95*
Springboard Diving
    Jennifer Chandler, U.S., 1976   506.19 points
Platform Diving
    Yelena Vaitsekhovskaya,
      U.S.S.R., 1976   406.49 points

MEN'S TRACK AND FIELD

100 Meter Dash
    James Hines, U.S., 1968   0:0.9
200 Meter Dash
    Tommie Smith, U.S., 1968   0:19.8
400 Meter Dash
    Lee Evans, U.S., 1968   0:43.8
800 Meter Run
    Alberto Juantorena, Cuba, 1976   1:43.50*
1,500 Meter Run
    Kipchoge Keino, Kenya, 1968   3:34.9
5,000 Meter Run
    Lasse Viren, Finland, 1976   13:24.76
10,000 Meter Run
    Lasse Viren, Finland, 1972   27:38.4
Marathon
    Waldemar Cierpinski,
      E. Germany, 1976   2 hrs. 9:55
110 Meter Hurdles
    Rod Milburn, U.S., 1972   0:13.2
400 Meter Hurdles
    Edwin Moses, U.S., 1976   0:47.64
3,000 Meter Steeplechase
    Anders Garderud, Sweden, 1976   8:08.20*
400 Meter Relay
    United States, 1968, 1972   0:38.2
1,600 Meter Relay
    United States, 1968   2:56.1
20,000 Meter Walk
    Daniel Bautista, Mexico, 1976   1 hr. 24:40.6
Long Jump
    Robert Beamon, U.S., 1968   29'2¼"

* indicates world record also

Triple Jump
    Viktor Saneyev, U.S.S.R., 1968   57'¾"
High Jump
    Jacek Wszola, Poland, 1976   7'4½"
Pole Vault
    Wolfgang Nordwig, E. Germany, 1972   18'½"
    Tadeusz Slusarski, Poland, 1976   18'½"
Shot Put
    Udo Beyer, E. Germany, 1976   69'6.7"
Discus Throw
    Mac Wilkins, U.S., 1976   221'5.4"
Javelin Throw
    Miklos Nemeth, Hungary, 1976   310'4½"*
Hammer Throw
    Yuri Sedykh, U.S.S.R., 1976   254'4"
Decathlon
    Bruce Jenner, U.S., 1976   8,618 points

WOMEN'S TRACK AND FIELD

100 Meter Dash
    Wilma Rudolph, U.S., 1960   0:11.0
    Wyomia Tyus, U.S., 1968   0:11.0
200 Meter Dash
    Baerbel Eckert, E. Germany, 1976   0:22.37
400 Meter Dash
    Irena Szewinska, Poland, 1976   0:49.29*
800 Meter Run
    Tatyana Kazankina, U.S.S.R., 1976   1:54.94
1,500 Meter Run
    Tatyana Kazankina, U.S.S.R., 1976   4:05.48
100 Meter Hurdles
    Annelie Erhardt, E. Germany, 1972   0:12.6
400 Meter Relay
    East Germany, 1976   0:42.55
1,600 Meter Relay
    East Germany, 1976   3:19.23*
Long Jump
    Viorica Viscopoleanu, Rumania, 1968   22'4½"
High Jump
    Rosemarie Ackermann, E. Germany, 1976   6'4"
Discus Throw
    Evelin Schlaak, E. Germany, 1976   226'4½"
Shot Put (8 lb. 13 oz.)
    Ivanka Khristova, Bulgaria, 1976   69'5"
Javelin Throw
    Ruth Fuchs, E. Germany, 1976   216'4"
Pentathlon
    Mary Peters, Great Britain, 1972   4,801 points

MUSIC

The study of music has long been a tradition in our schools and colleges. Students are encouraged to join glee clubs, bands, and orchestras. Church and social groups also encourage active participation. The rest of us, who may have less talent or no desire to find out whether or not we have talent, still enjoy listening to music — popular, classical, or both. Everywhere we have the opportunity to listen to rock groups, country western groups, blue grass groups, chamber music trios and quartets, and symphony orchestras.

Whether you only listen or whether you take a more active role, you will find your enjoyment of music heightened by reading the following pages. They give you the opportunity to learn more about bands and orchestras, musical compositions, musical terms, and lives of famous classical composers.

The Study of Music

Music has become a significant part of everyday life in twentieth-century America. We are surrounded by music—from the background music of a film or television program to the constant musical programs on AM and FM radio. Music is an accompaniment to athletic events and forms a central part of religious services. There are increasing numbers of bands and orchestras on every level. An understanding of musical terms and basic musical concepts is relevant to our daily lives and adds to our enjoyment of music.

The word "music" was borrowed from Greek mythology: the Muses were nine sister goddesses who were in charge of song, poetry, art, and science. Music is the organization of tone within a span of time. Tone is produced when a vibrator (vocal chords, reed, string) is set in motion by some energy (breath, bow). The tone is then enlarged by a resonator (chest, clarinet, trumpet, etc.). Tone has four characteristics that always affect it: pitch, intensity, duration, and quality. Tones are arranged in succession to create melodies. Melodies are then combined to produce longer compositions with organization and structure. Melodies can be supported by chordal accompaniment (harmony) to produce a richer sound.

The lists of musical terms and famous composers supplied here will be helpful if you desire to enlarge your knowledge of music.

BANDS

Concert bands and marching bands are undoubtedly the most numerous and popular musical groups in the country. Bands are organized at elementary, junior high, and senior high, as well as college levels. Many communities also sponsor bands for adult instrumentalists. The Navy, Army, Marine Corps, and Air Force maintain many bands of superior quality.

There is great variety in the seating arrangement of a concert band, depending on the number of instruments in each section as well as the type of sound desired by the conductor, but the louder instruments (brasses and percussion) generally are placed to the rear of the group.

THE SYMPHONY ORCHESTRA

The players in a modern symphony orchestra sit in an arrangement much like the one shown. Some conductors arrange their players slightly differently, and some compositions call for a different arrangement.

196

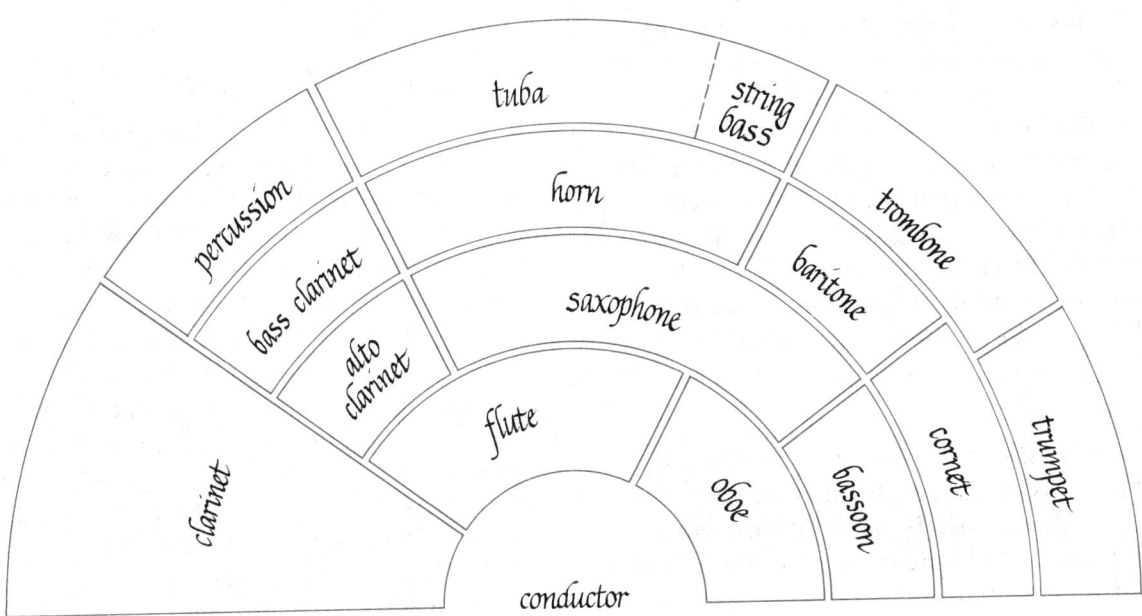

CONCERT BAND. The seating arrangement and the types of instruments included are appropriate for the music most often played by bands. At a band concert, we expect to hear the brasses play a leading role. Thus, at a band concert, we often hear the works of composers such as John Philip Sousa.

SYMPHONY ORCHESTRA. The prominence given to the strings in a full orchestra shows the importance of this section in most symphonic works. The violins frequently serve as the voice of the symphony orchestra. As the number and mix of instruments change, the sound also changes.

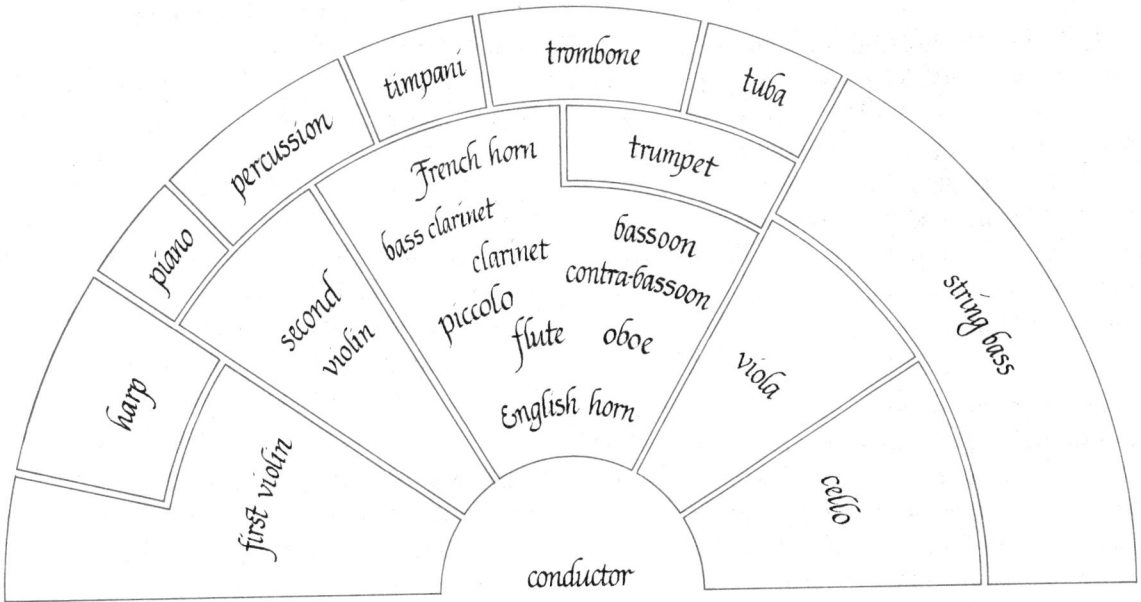

For instance, if the orchestra were playing a concerto for piano and orchestra, a grand piano would be placed somewhere near the conductor's podium. On the other hand, if the orchestra were playing eighteenth-century music written for a small orchestra, there might be only half as many instrumentalists on stage and no percussion instruments at all. Some modern composers have used many more instruments than are named here.

There are four basic kinds of instruments in the symphony. The **strings,** named because their tone is produced by vibrating strings, include the violins (usually divided into two sections), the slightly larger violas, the cellos, and the string basses. The harp, the guitar, and the piano are also string instruments.

The **brasses** are made of metal, and their tone is produced by blowing into a cup-shaped mouthpiece. Brasses in the orchestra include the trumpet, trombone, tuba, and French horn. Other brass instruments are used in band music.

Both the brasses and the woodwinds are wind instruments. The **woodwinds'** sound is produced by blowing into a reed or a long mouthpiece. Orchestra woodwinds include the flute and piccolo, the oboe, clarinet, English horn, and bassoon. The recorder and the saxophone are also wind instruments, as are the bagpipes, the accordion, and the harmonica.

The **percussion** section includes instruments that are shaken or struck. Some, like the kettledrum and xylophone, have a definite pitch, while others simply make a distinctive sound, such as the bass drum, triangle, cymbals, and castanets.

LISTENING TO MUSIC ON YOUR OWN

Here is a list of works to help you become acquainted with the styles and periods of music. All the works listed here have been recorded. You may be able to borrow phonograph records from your school or local library or from your friends.

Many record companies have put out their own "history of music" series of records; these can be very helpful, especially in finding medieval and Renaissance music to listen to. In addition, there are groups that specialize in singing and playing such music on ancient instruments.

This list gives representative works of the last 250 years, from the baroque period to the present.

Orchestral Works
Bach: *Brandenburg Concertos*
Handel: *Water Music*
Haydn: *Surprise Symphony*
Mozart: *Eine Kleine Nachtmusik*
Beethoven: *Sixth ("Pastoral") Symphony*
Schubert: *Great C-Major Symphony*
Brahms: *First Symphony*
Dvorak: *"New World" Symphony*
Schoenberg: *Transfigured Night*
Bartok: *Concerto for Orchestra*
Vaughan Williams: *Fantasia on "Greensleeves"*
Mozart: *Piano Concerto No. 17*
Beethoven: *"Emperor" Piano Concerto*
Tchaikovsky: *Piano Concerto No. 1*
Rachmaninoff: *Piano Concerto No. 2*
Bach: *Concerto for Two Violins*
Tchaikovsky: *Violin Concerto*
Vivaldi: *Guitar Concerto in D*

Solo and Chamber Works
Bach: *Well-Tempered Clavier*
Bach: *Toccata and Fugue in D Minor for Organ*

Beethoven: *"Kreutzer" Sonata*
Schubert: *"Trout" Quintet*
Brahms: *Hungarian Dances*
Liszt: *Hungarian Rhapsodies*
Chopin: Polonaises, waltzes, mazurkas, études (for piano)
String quartets by Mozart, Beethoven, Brahms

Program Music
Mendelssohn: *Italian Symphony*
Tchaikovsky: *1812 Overture*
Moussorgsky: *Pictures at an Exhibition*
Saint-Saens: *Carnival of the Animals*
Debussy: *Afternoon of a Faun*
R. Strauss: *Thus Spake Zarathustra*
Dukas: *The Sorcerer's Apprentice*
De Falla: *Nights in the Gardens of Spain*
Respighi: *The Fountains of Rome*
Gershwin: *An American in Paris*
Prokofiev: *Peter and the Wolf*
Copland: *Appalachian Spring*
Vaughan Williams: *Antarctic Symphony*

Choral Works
Purcell: *Come Ye Sons of Art*
Handel: *Messiah*
Bach: *Coffee Cantata*
Haydn: *The Creation*
Beethoven: *9th ("Choral") Symphony*

Mahler: *Das Lied von der Erde*
Schoenberg: *Gurrelieder*
Orff: *Carmina Burana*

Opera
Mozart: *The Marriage of Figaro*
Rossini: *The Barber of Seville*
Bizet: *Carmen*
Verdi: *Rigoletto*
J. Strauss: *Die Fledermaus*
Wagner: *Die Meistersinger*
Gilbert and Sullivan: *H.M.S. Pinafore*
Gershwin: *Porgy and Bess*

Comparing Styles
In comparing styles and periods of music, it often helps to hear how different composers have treated similar themes or subjects. Here are some groups for you to compare.

Beethoven's *Moonlight Sonata* and Debussy's *Clair de lune*
Tchaikovsky's *Romeo and Juliet*, Prokofiev's *Romeo and Juliet*, and Bernstein's *West Side Story*
Vivaldi's *The Four Seasons*, Haydn's, *The Seasons*, and Stravinsky's *The Rite of Spring*
Mozart's *Jupiter Symphony* and Prokofiev's *Classical Symphony*

New York Philharmonic Society orchestra in rehearsal for one of its concerts at Lincoln Center, New York. This famous orchestra also goes on concert tour outside New York each year.

GLOSSARY OF MUSIC

You can find the meanings of many of the music words you want to know by looking in your dictionary. Some of the words that are in the dictionary are also included in this glossary. In addition, the glossary contains musical signs and symbols, as well as many other words and terms that you will meet in music courses or while learning to sing or play an instrument.

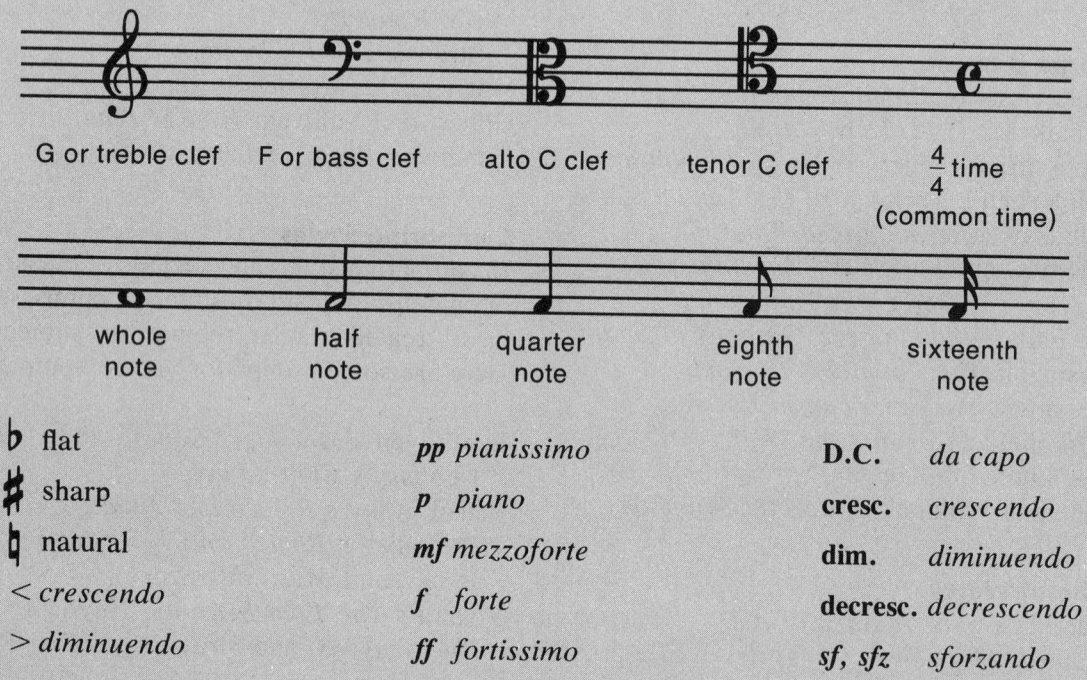

G or treble clef	F or bass clef	alto C clef	tenor C clef	$\frac{4}{4}$ time (common time)

whole note	half note	quarter note	eighth note	sixteenth note

♭ flat

♯ sharp

♮ natural

< *crescendo*

> *diminuendo*

pp pianissimo

p piano

mf mezzoforte

f forte

ff fortissimo

D.C. *da capo*

cresc. *crescendo*

dim. *diminuendo*

decresc. *decrescendo*

sf, sfz sforzando

a capella (Italian, "in the chapel style"). Choral music sung without accompaniment is sung a capella.

accelerando. Gradual increase in the speed of the beats.

adagio (Italian, "slow"). Indicates that a piece of music should be played at a slow tempo.

allegro (Italian, "happy"). Fast, lively.

andante (Italian, "to go"). Moderately slow.

arpeggio (Italian, "like a harp"). A method of playing a chord in which the notes are played quickly one after the other, lowest to highest, instead of all together.

augmented chord. A triad in which the fifth is raised one-half tone.

baroque. Musical period following the Renaissance, extending roughly from 1600 to 1750.

bass. Lowest male voice, or the largest string instrument, same as the double bass.

cadenza (Italian, "cadence"). A difficult and showy passage near the end of a solo, allowing the performer to show his skill.

cantata. A musical setting of a religious text for soloists and chorus with piano or orchestra accompaniment. It is shorter than an oratorio and is not meant to be acted.

capriccio (Italian, "whim"). A lively piece of music written according to the composer's fancy, rather than according to some particular form.

chamber music. Instrumental music written to be played in a room, rather than in a church or concert hall. Each part is taken by one instrument.

chord. Three or more notes that are sounded at the same time. A chord usually supports a melody.

clavichord. A piano-like instrument popular until the 1800s, when it was largely replaced by the piano.

clef. A sign at the beginning of a musical staff, used to show the pitch on that staff.

coda (Italian, "tail"). A final passage or section ending a work or movement.

concerto. A composition in three or four movements for solo instrument (piano, violin, etc.) and full orchestra.

concerto grosso. A baroque instrumental form for two to four soloists and string orchestra.

counterpoint. Music in which two or more separate melodic lines (voices) are played at the same time, rather than one melodic line with harmony.

da capo or D.C. (Italian, "from the beginning"). Indicates that the piece should be repeated from the beginning. D.C. al fine means "from the beginning to the end."

diminished chord. A triad in which both the third and the fifth are lowered one-half step from the major.

dissonance. Intervals or chords that produce a disagreeable sound and tend to produce tension.

dominant. Another name for the fifth, or fifth tone, of an ascending diatonic scale. The dominant chord in the key of C is a G chord.

expression marks. Marks in a musical score that tell how the music should be played, rather than what notes to play.

forte or f (Italian, "strong"). Loud.

fortissimo or ff (Italian, "very strong"). Very loud.

fugue. A composition in polyphonic texture for either voices or instruments and written according to prescribed procedures.

gavotte. A dance of French origin in a moderate quadruple meter.

gigue. A dance of English origin (jig) in a rapid triple meter. It is usually included in a baroque dance suite.

Gregorian chant. A form of singing used since before the Middle Ages in the Roman Catholic Church. Its text is usually from the Bible; its melody is sung in unison without harmony, accompaniment, or set tempo.

harmony. The sounding of two or more different tones at the same time, as opposed to melody, in which tones are sounded one after another.

interval. The distance between two tones. A harmonic interval is the distance between two tones played at the same time; a melodic interval is the distance between two tones played one after another.

key note. The first note of a scale, the note that determines the key.

key signature. The sharps or flats written at the beginning of a musical staff to show what key the music is in. For example, no sharps or flats means the key of C; one flat means F, five sharps means B.

largo. Very slow and stately.

lento. Slowly.

libretto. A book containing the words of an opera or oratorio.

lieder (German, "songs"). German poems set to music for solo voice and piano accompaniment.

madrigal. A kind of song, often about love, popular in Elizabethan England. Madrigals were usually written to be sung by small groups in several parts.

Mass. A musical setting of the principal service of the Roman Catholic Church.

mazurka. A Polish dance in a moderate triple meter, with the accent on the third beat.

meter. The organization of beats or pulses into meaningful groups within each measure.

minuet. A dance of French origin in a triple meter that was included in the baroque dance suite and later in the symphony.

moderato. Moderately (refers to tempo).

modulation. Changing from one key to another during a composition.

monophonic. A musical texture consisting of one melodic line without any accompaniment.

octave. The interval that contains eight steps of the diatonic scale.

oratorio. An oratorio has the same structure as opera but is usually on a religious subject and is not meant to be acted.

percussion. The family of instruments that produces sounds by being struck: drums, gongs, etc.

pianoforte (Italian, "soft-loud"). The original name for the piano. The piano is a string instrument, not a percussion instrument.

pitch. The highness or lowness of a tone that is measured in frequencies per second. The desired pitch is indicated by its position on the staff.

polyphonic music. Music in which there is more than one part, with each part carrying its own melody.

presto (Italian, "very fast"). A dynamic mark meaning very fast.

program music. A general term for music that tells

a story or describes something, rather than existing for the sake of its pleasing sound.

quartet. A group of four musicians, or music to be performed by them. A string quartet consists of two violins, a viola, and a cello; a barbershop quartet consists of two tenors, a baritone, and a bass, singing in close harmony.

Renaissance. A period in musical history, from about 1400 to about 1600. Renaissance composers such as Byrd, Lassus, Palestrina, and Gabrieli developed polyphonic music to a high degree in Masses, motets, madrigals, instrumental variations, and dances.

requiem. A setting of the Catholic Mass for the dead.

rest. Signs that correspond to the note values but indicate a similar period of silence.

Rococo. A period in musical history, from about 1710 to about 1775. Rococo music was generally more elegant and frivolous than baroque music. Telemann and Couperin were the best-known composers of this period.

Romantic. A period in musical history, extending from about 1820 well into the twentieth century. In romanticism, emotions became more important than form. Composers in this style include Beethoven in his later works, Chopin, Mendelssohn, Brahms, Wagner, and Richard Strauss.

rondo. A musical form in which the first section is repeated like a refrain after other sections. The rondo form is often used as the last movement of a sonata, a symphony, or, especially, a concerto.

round. A type of polyphonic song in which each successive voice begins the first line as the previous voice is beginning the second, and so on; two examples: "Frere Jacques" and "Three Blind Mice."

scale. An arrangement of tones between one note and its octave, in ascending or descending order. A diatonic scale (either major or minor) contains eight tones including the octave; a chromatic scale contains thirteen tones including the octave, that is, all the tones between the note and its octave.

scherzo (Italian, "joke"). A musical form in a lively 3/4 or 3/8 tempo, often used as the third movement of a sonata, symphony, or string quartet.

sforzando (Italian, "forcing"). Indicates that a note or chord should be accented strongly (abbr. *sf*, *sfz*). Also called forzando (*fz*).

sonata. The commonest form of instrumental composition in serious music. Usually contains four movements: a fast movement, a slow movement, a dance movement in 3/4 or 3/8 time, and a fast concluding movement. Music in this form for piano or other solo instrument, with or without piano accompaniment, is also called a sonata. If it is for three or four instruments, it is a trio or a quartet. If it is for a whole orchestra, it is a symphony.

symphonic band. A band that performs in concert rather than merely playing at football games. Many famous modern composers have written music for symphonic band.

symphony. An extended composition of four movements for full orchestra. The symphonic form has been greatly used by composers from the classical period to the present.

syncopation. The displacement of the normal accent. Strong accents that occur on weak beats or unexpected places.

tempo. Rate of speeds of the beats of a composition. The tempo is indicated by terms such as andante, adagio, allegro, allegretto, presto, etc.

time signature. Two numbers placed after the key signature at the beginning of a piece of music, showing the rhythm of the piece. For example, 3/4 time shows that there are three beats to a measure, and that a quarter note gets one beat.

toccata (Italian, "touched"). A type of composition for organ or harpsichord, popular in the baroque period, usually difficult enough to show off the skills of the instrument, the composer, and the performer.

tremolo. A rapid back and forth motion of the bow on a string.

triad. A chord with three notes: the key note, the third, and the fifth.

trill. A rapid alternation between a note and the note above.

twelve-tone music. A system of composing music developed by Schoenberg about 1920. It takes its name from the twelve tones of the chromatic scale (not including the octave). Twelve-tone music is composed according to traditional ideas of melody and harmony, and it is usually atonal, that is, not written in any one key.

vibrato (Italian, "vibrated"). In stringed instruments and in singing, a slight wavering of the tone without changing the pitch.

whole-tone scale. A seven-note scale made up of only whole-tone steps, used by Debussy and other impressionists.

Famous Composers

Bach, Johann Sebastian (1685–1750), German. Bach was the greatest composer of the baroque period, and many people call him the greatest composer of all time. He served as organist and music director to the courts of Weimer and Cöthen and to the town of Leipzig. During his lifetime, Bach was known as the foremost organist in Europe, but today he is famed chiefly for the music he wrote.

Bach's work includes music for organ and other keyboard instruments; chamber music for solo instruments and ensembles; and vocal music, mainly religious. Some of his best-known works are the Brandenburg Concertos, the Well-Tempered Clavier, the St. Matthew and St. John Passions, and the Mass in B-Minor.

Bartok, Bela (1881–1945), Hungarian. Bartok was born in a district of Hungary that is now part of Romania. He attended the Royal Academy of Music in Budapest and quickly established himself as a brilliant pianist. He developed an avid interest in the folk music of his area and, with his friend Kodaly, collected thousands of songs from Slovakia, Romania, and Bulgaria. The folk element greatly influenced his compositional style. He taught piano at the Royal Academy and composed in his spare time.

His compositions were somewhat advanced for public consumption. He came to the United States in 1940 on the advice of his friends, who feared for his safety. He taught folklore research at Columbia. Stricken with leukemia, he died in New York City. In addition to operas, ballets, and string quartets, he wrote the Concerto for Orchestra and three piano concertos.

Beethoven, Ludwig van (1770–1827), German. Beethoven's early music was written in the classical style of the eighteenth century, but from about the age of thirty he developed a new style, more emotional and less formal. His most famous works are his nine symphonies, of which the best known are the third, or Eroica; the fifth; the sixth, or Pastoral; and the ninth, or Choral. Other familiar works are the Emperor piano concerto, the Moonlight Sonata, and the opera Fidelio. Beethoven became entirely deaf in his later years. He wrote some of his greatest works while deaf, even though he could never hear them performed.

Berlioz, Hector (1803–1869), French. Berlioz is probably the most innovative composer of the French romantic movement. At eighteen he entered the Paris Medical School but soon left to study music. He

MUSIC

Ludwig van Beethoven, whose works are played often by symphony orchestras everywhere. The opening notes of his famous Fifth Symphony have come to symbolize triumph over despair.

wrote for large orchestras and choral groups. He made great demands on the instrumentalists. He furthered the cause of program music. As his compositions were not in great demand, he made a living by writing reviews and articles for newspapers. His first great work was the imaginative Symphonie Fantastique.

Brahms, Johannes (1833–1897), German. As a young man, Brahms wrote and studied by day and played piano in the taverns and bars of Hamburg by night. He embarked on a European concert tour at the age of twenty and became the protégé of various well-known musicians. Eventually settling in Vienna, he gave up playing and conducting to spend his time on composing. Brahms combined classical form and romantic style in his music. His works include four symphonies, each one a masterpiece; the Hungarian dances; the Academic Fes-

tival Overture; Variations on a Theme by Haydn; chamber works, concertos, and choral works (German Requiem); and many songs, of which the most famous is his "Lullaby."

Chopin, Frederic Francois (1810–1849), Polish. Although Chopin left Poland at the age of twenty and settled in Paris, his interest in Polish folk music was reflected in his compositions for the rest of his life. Tuberculosis forced him to give up a concert career, and he became one of the most popular teachers and influential composers of the romantic period. Chopin composed almost exclusively for the piano; he was largely responsible for making it a virtuoso instrument. His works include polonaises, mazurkas, nocturnes, etudes, preludes, and waltzes.

Debussy, Claude Achille (1862–1918), French. Debussy originated the Impressionist school in music with his Prelude to the Afternoon of a Faun, an orchestral piece largely inspired by the painting and poetry of the time. Debussy ignored the rules of form and harmony that had always been considered necessary in serious composition; instead, he tried to give a musical impression of his subject. Other pieces in this style are his La Mer (The Sea); Clair de Lune (Moonlight), an ever-popular piano piece; and his opera Pelléas et Mélisande.

Dvorak, Antonin (1841–1904), Czechoslovakian. Dvorak was born in Bohemia in a little town near Prague. He studied voice, violin, organ, and viola and eventually developed an interest in nationalistic music. In 1892 he was invited to become the director of the National Conservatory of Music in New York. It was natural that he developed an interest in Black and Indian music. He urged young American composers to incorporate their native music in their compositions. His most famous composition, the Symphony in E Minor (From the New World), was written in 1893 while he was still in the United States.

Foster, Stephen Collins (1826–1864), American. Foster occupies a special place in American music. His more than 200 songs express a heartfelt feeling for the people and country. Some of his most famous songs were written for minstrel shows. They include "Oh! Susanna," "Camptown Races," "My Old Kentucky Home," "Old Black Joe," and "Jeannie with the Light Brown Hair."

Gershwin, George (1898–1937), American. Gershwin studied formal composition, but started his career writing popular songs, of which the first was "Swanee." Paul Whiteman, a jazz dance bandleader, commissioned him to write Rhapsody in Blue, his most popular work. Gershwin also wrote musical comedies, with lyrics by his brother Ira (Lady Be Good, Of Thee I Sing). His other orchestral works include the Concerto in F for piano and An American in Paris. Gershwin was an innovator in the composition of truly American music. He used elements from jazz and blues in the American opera Porgy and Bess.

Grieg, Edward (1843–1907), Norwegian. Grieg is considered the musical spokesman for Norway. Although he studied music in Germany, he developed a great interest in the folk music of his country. He has written what is probably the most popular and most often played piano concerto, Concerto in A Minor.

Handel, George Frederick (1685–1789), German. Handel overcame his father's insistence that he study law and became a church organist and composer. After a long trip to Italy, where his works were highly praised, he became chief court musician to the elector of Hanover (Germany). When the elector was named King of England as George I, Handel settled in London. There he produced operas and, when operas went out of fashion, oratorios; among them was his most famous work, The Messiah. His other works include cantatas, music for organ and harpsichord, and instrumental music, including the well-known Water Music. Handel was the last of the great baroque composers, and his death marked the end of the baroque period in music.

Haydn, Franz Joseph (1732–1809), Austrian. Haydn had very little formal training in music, but his natural talent so impressed Hungarian Prince Esterhazy that he made Haydn chief musician to his court. Haydn stayed at this post for many years; there he worked out the forms followed by Mozart, Beethoven, and others in writing classical symphonies and string quartets. He was the first composer of the classical period.

Haydn wrote an enormous amount of music: chamber works, concertos, operas, songs, twelve masses, over 100 symphonies, and a well-known hymn tune that has been both the Austrian and the German national anthem.

Liszt, Franz (1811–1886), Hungarian. Liszt is generally considered the greatest pianist of the last century. For his own use, he wrote a large number of piano pieces that were considered some of the most difficult of his time. At the height of his concert career, he gave up playing to become a teacher and conductor.

Mahler, Gustav (1860–1911), Austrian. Mahler made his name as a conductor of opera, but wrote only one opera that was produced. He wrote ten symphonies, the last of which was unfinished when he died. He also wrote several song cycles, of which the best-known is Das Lied von der Erde (Song of the Earth). His Eighth Symphony for orchestra and chorus is called Symphony of a Thousand because of the number of performers required to play it. He is considered the last of the German romantics.

Mendelssohn, Felix (full name **Jakob Ludwig Felix Mendelssohn-Bartholdy**) (1809–1847), German. At the age of seventeen, Mendelssohn wrote his well-known overture for Shakespeare's Midsummer Night's Dream. At twenty he conducted a performance of Bach's St. Matthew Passion, starting a revival of interest in Bach that has continued to the present.

Mendelssohn's compositions, and his performances in the music capitals of the world, influenced the romantic school. His other works include the Italian and Scotch symphonies, the oratorio Elijah, a violin concerto, and the piano pieces Songs Without Words.

Mozart, Wolfgang Amadeus (1756–1791), Austrian. Mozart learned to play the harpsichord at the age of three and began composing two years later. His father, his sister, and he toured Europe as concert musicians until he was sixteen. When his operas had made him famous, he settled in Vienna.

Mozart was the foremost composer of the classical period and had great influence on nineteenth-century composers. His works include many keyboard pieces, concertos for most orchestral instruments of his time, and symphonies. His operas, which are still among the most popular of all time, include

The Marriage of Figaro, The Magic Flute, and Don Giovanni, often called the greatest opera ever written.

Prokofiev, Sergei Sergeevich (1891–1953), Russian. Prokofiev's first symphony, the Classical, written in the style of Mozart, made him known in Europe. After touring Europe and the United States, he settled in Russia. For a children's concert, he wrote his famous Peter and the Wolf, which was designed to introduce children to the instruments of the orchestra. Prokofiev also wrote the operas The Love of Three Oranges and The Fiery Angel as well as musical scores for the films Lieutenant Kije and Alexander Nevsky.

Ravel, Maurice (1875–1937), French. Ravel was born in France, near the Spanish border, of a Swiss father and a Basque mother. His early association with Spanish music resulted in many compositions with the flavor of that country. Ravel studied at the Paris Conservatory for several years. He developed as a brilliant pianist and composer of dazzling piano and orchestral works. Ravel's compositional practice was to write his pieces for piano and then arrange them for orchestra. His best known piano piece is the Pavane for a Dead Princess. One of the most popular orchestral compositions is his Bolero.

Rimsky-Korsakov, Nikolai (1844–1908), Russian. Rimsky-Korsakov is the best known of the Russian nationalistic composers. He was born into an aristocratic family and was trained for a career in the Navy. He began to compose in his spare time and eventually was appointed Inspector of Naval Bands. He left the Navy to teach composition at the St. Petersburg Conservatory of Music. He wrote several operas on Russian subjects. His best known work is the symphonic suite, Scheherazade, which is based on The Thousand and One Nights.

Schoenberg, Arnold (1874–1951), Austrian. Schoenberg was an almost entirely self-taught musician. When his music became known, he was able to become a teacher and to spend more time composing. He gradually abandoned the traditional idea of writing a piece in a particular key; from this atonal music he developed twelve-tone music, a system that rejects classical melody and harmony.

Driven out of Europe by the Nazis, Schoenberg became a United States citizen. His works include Transfigured Night, the symphonic poem Pelléas and Mélisande, and the melodrama Pierrot Lunaire.

Schubert, Franz (1797–1828), Austrian. Schubert's life is a classical example of the starving artist whose work is not appreciated until after his death. He made very little money from his composing and, except for a short period as a teacher, never held a steady job. He wrote a great number of art songs for voice and piano, setting to music the greatest German poetry of his day. Such songs have since been known as lieder (German for "songs"). His lieder include "The Wanderer," "Death and the Maiden," "Who Is Sylvia?" and "Ave Maria."

Schubert also produced a number of operatic, choral, and chamber works, as well as orchestral pieces. They include the Unfinished and Great C-Major symphonies, the Trout quintet, and the Rosamunde overture.

Strauss, Richard (1864–1949), German. Strauss first made his reputation as an operatic and orchestral conductor. He had no interest in politics, but the Nazis consid-

Igor Stravinsky, shown conducting his famous Petrouchka ballet. The music of this Russian master lends itself to brilliant choreography in the modern vein. His symphonic works are played everywhere.

ered him one of their official composers, and his reputation abroad suffered accordingly. His best-known compositions are operas and tone poems. The operas include Salome, Elektra, and Der Rosenkavalier; among his richly emotional tone poems, perhaps the best known are Don Juan, Till Eulenspiegel's Merry Pranks, Don Quixote, and Thus Spake Zarathustra.

Stravinsky, Igor (1882–1971), Russian. Stravinsky's first two ballets, Firebird and Petrouchka, were well received, but he first caught the world's attention in 1913 with The Rite of Spring, a ballet whose music was so startling and unusual that the first-night audience rioted over it.

During his middle years, Stravinsky composed in the neoclassical style; during his later years, he wrote twelve-tone music. When World War II broke out, he became a

United States citizen. His later works include the ballet Orpheus, the opera The Rake's Progress, symphonies, concertos, and chamber music.

Tchaikovsky, Peter Ilich (1840–1893), Russian. Tchaikovsky began a career as a law clerk but continued to study music; after graduating from the St. Petersburg Conservatory, he taught harmony in Moscow. He also made a reputation as a composer, and after several years the wealthy Madame von Meck became his patroness and gave him an income. He never met her, but her generosity enabled him to give up teaching to compose.

Tchaikovsky was a member of the romantic school. His melodic music has always been very popular. Best known are his ballets Swan Lake and The Nutcracker. He also wrote six symphonies, including the sixth or Pathétique; the operas Queen of Spades and Eugene Onegin; and such popular orchestral works as Romeo and Juliet, the 1812 Overture, and concertos for piano and for violin.

Verdi, Giuseppe (1813–1901), Italian. Verdi came from a poor family, and his musical education was insufficient to get him into the Milan Conservatory; but he became music master in his village and began to write operas. His operas were produced at La Scala in Milan, but when the second one, King for a Day, was booed off the stage, he was ready to give up. He was persuaded to write a third, Nabucco, which was a great success. From then on, Verdi produced one masterpiece after another for the next fifty years.

His operas, mostly romantic melodramas, include Rigoletto, Il Trovatore, La Traviata, Don Carlo, Aida, Otello, and A Masked Ball. Many consider his last opera, Falstaff, to be his best. Also well known are his sacred choral works, the Stabat Mater and the Requiem.

Vivaldi, Antonio (1678–1741), Italian. Vivaldi was ordained as a priest but could never say Mass because of his asthma. Instead he became a teacher and concert violinist in Venice. He wrote over 400 concertos and a number of concerti grossi, of which the best known is The Four Seasons. He also wrote forty-six operas, but it was his instrumental music that influenced later composers by its clear, lyric quality.

Wagner, Richard (1813–1883), German. After a stormy and sometimes scandalous early career, Wagner was given a theater for his operas by the city of Bayreuth in Germany. There he was at last able to produce his greatest work, The Ring of the Nibelung, a cycle of four long operas (Das Rheingold, Die Walküre, Siegfried, and Götterdämmerung). His family continued to produce his works at Bayreuth after he died, and the yearly Bayreuth Festival became world famous.

Wagner revolutionized the opera form. His operas were no longer arias strung together by recitative but an endless melody. He introduced the leitmotif, a melody used to identify a recurring theme or character. His other works include Lohengrin, Tannhäuser, Tristan and Isolde, The Flying Dutchman, Die Meistersinger von Nürnberg, and Parsifal.

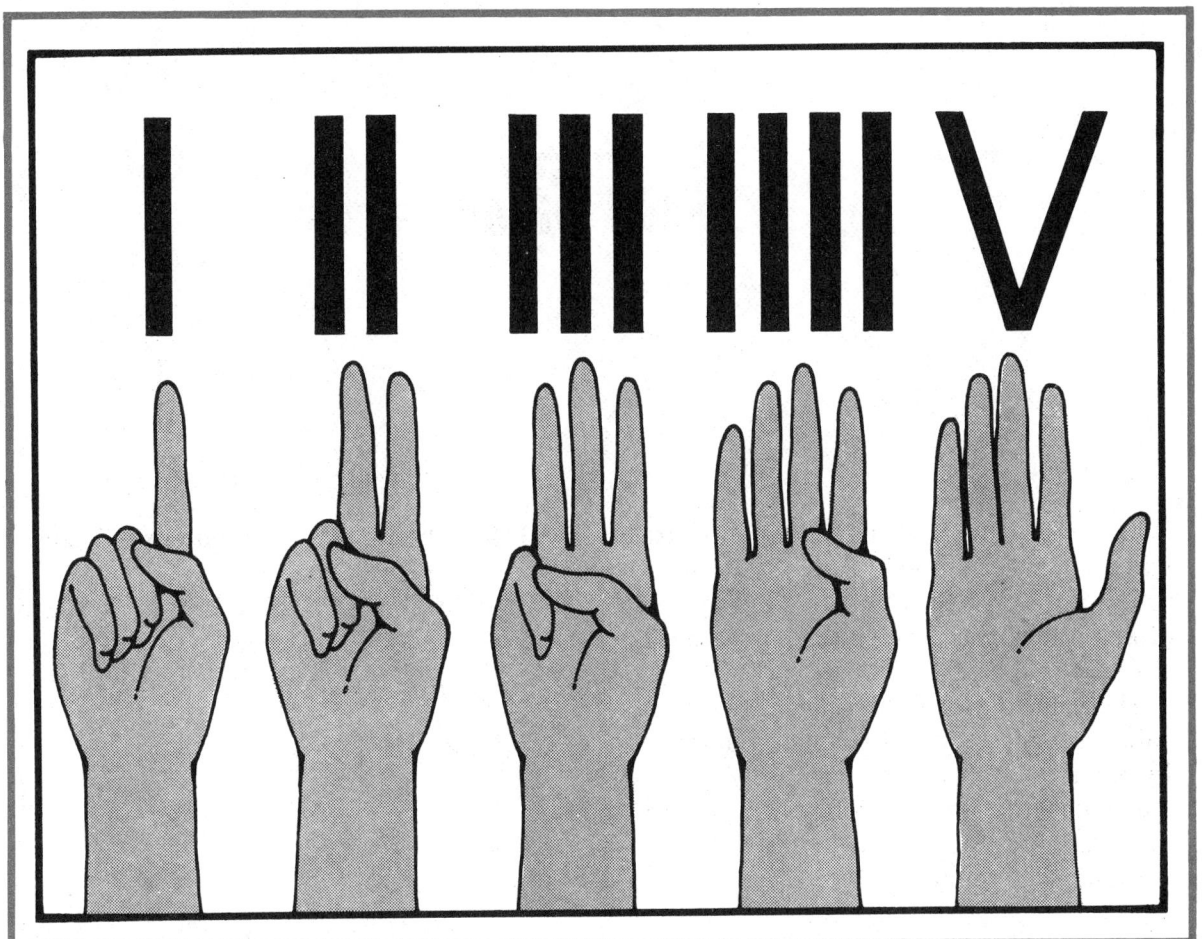

MATHEMATICS

Knowledge of arithmetic and more advanced branches of mathematics is essential for all of us. Since earliest times man has dealt with problems involving counting, and we have evidence that early man performed remarkable calculations to learn when to plant his fields and how to keep records of business transactions. Today, when too many of us are apt to leave important calculations to machines, people are losing the ability to do their own computations.

Surely it is better for you to become fully competent in arithmetic. Above all, if you intend to pursue a professional career, you will want to know a great deal about mathematics. For this reason, the following pages review basic arithmetic, and the Concise Edition of the *Student Handbook* takes you much deeper into mathematics. Here is your chance to become proficient in basic and advanced mathematics.

Place Value

When you count or when you do arithmetic you use ten digits (numerals): 0, 1, 2, 3, 4, 5, 6, 7, 8, and 9. Thus, we say that our system of numbering is a decimal system—a base-ten system.

The value of a digit or numeral (its place value) depends upon its place in a number. In order to add, subtract, multiply, or divide numbers correctly, you must pay careful attention to place value.

Look at the number 37:

$$37 = 3 \text{ tens} + 7 \text{ ones}$$
$$= 30 + 7$$

The place (or position) of the 7 tells you that its value is 7 ones—or 7. The position of the 3 tells you that its value is 3 tens—or 30. We say that the 7 is in the ones place or ones column, and that the 3 is in the tens place or tens column.

Here are some other examples:

$$26 = 2 \text{ tens} + 6 \text{ ones}$$
$$= 20 + 6$$

$$234 = 2 \text{ hundreds} + 3 \text{ tens} + 4 \text{ ones}$$
$$= 200 + 30 + 4$$

$$506 = 5 \text{ hundreds} + 0 \text{ tens} + 6 \text{ ones}$$
$$= 500 + 0 + 6$$

$$4,932 = 4 \text{ thousands} + 9 \text{ hundreds} + 3 \text{ tens} + 2 \text{ ones}$$
$$= 4,000 + 900 + 30 + 2$$

If you write 26 as

$$20 + 6,$$

or if you write 506 as

$$500 + 0 + 6,$$

then you are writing these numbers in *expanded form* or *expanded notation*.

To make place value clear, a place value chart is often used. This place value chart shows the number 74,316.

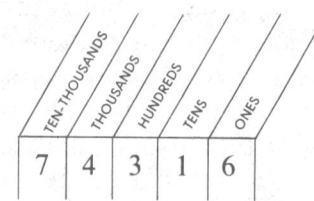

Using the chart, you can easily read the value of each numeral. Thus, the value of the 7 is 7 ten-thousands (70,000); the value of the 4 is 4 thousands (4,000); and so on.

Whole–Number Operations

ADDITION OF WHOLE NUMBERS

PROBLEM 1.

$$\begin{array}{r} 5 \\ +3 \\ \hline \end{array}$$

You can solve this problem by using the table of basic addition facts shown here. Read down to row 5 (see the arrow on the side of the table) and across to column 3 (see the arrow at the top of the table). Row 5 and column 3 meet at the number 8, which is the answer.

$$5 + 3 = 8$$

+	0	1	2	3	4	5	6	7	8	9
0	0	1	2	3	4	5	6	7	8	9
1	1	2	3	4	5	6	7	8	9	10
2	2	3	4	5	6	7	8	9	10	11
3	3	4	5	6	7	8	9	10	11	12
4	4	5	6	7	8	9	10	11	12	13
5	5	6	7	8	9	10	11	12	13	14
6	6	7	8	9	10	11	12	13	14	15
7	7	8	9	10	11	12	13	14	15	16
8	8	9	10	11	12	13	14	15	16	17
9	9	10	11	12	13	14	15	16	17	18

TABLE OF ADDITION FACTS

NOTE TO PARENTS

The four basic algorithms (procedures) you learned in elementary school (to add, subtract, multiply, and divide) are still the preferred algorithms today. Ultimately, each child should know how to compute with these algorithms. They are the quickest and most practical paper-and-pencil algorithms which are known.

We teach these algorithms in a two-stage process. We first concentrate on understanding why the algorithms work, then we concentrate on using these algorithms skillfully. When teaching for understanding, we sometimes use longer and more elaborate algorithms. Some of these algorithms are illustrated in this section with a ◆ symbol.

◆ If you can't remember the basic addition facts or can't find a table, you can easily solve the problem by using a number line.

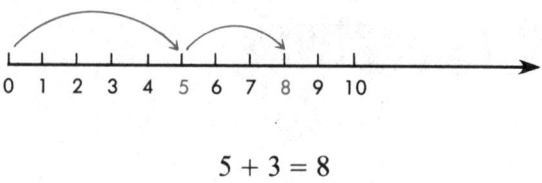

$$5 + 3 = 8$$

PROBLEM 2.

$$\begin{array}{r} 4 \\ 3 \\ +6 \\ \hline \end{array}$$

You can use a table of addition facts to solve this problem if you break it up into two steps.

Step 1

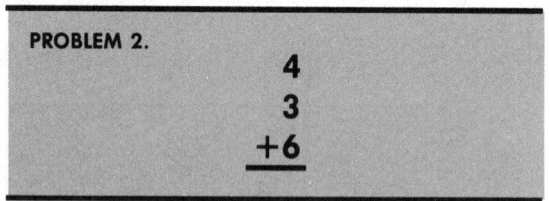

$$\left.\begin{array}{r} 4 \\ 3 \end{array}\right\} 7 \qquad \text{Add one pair}$$
$$+6 \qquad\qquad \text{of numbers.}$$

Step 2

$$\begin{array}{r} 7 \\ +6 \\ \hline 13 \end{array} \qquad \begin{array}{l}\text{Add this sum}\\\text{to the third number.}\end{array}$$

◆ If you can't remember the basic addition facts or if you can't find a table, you can still solve this problem by using a number line.

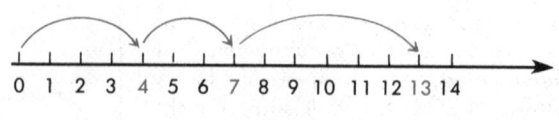

$$4 + 3 + 6 = 13$$

212

PROBLEM 3.

$$\begin{array}{r} 23 \\ + 4 \\ \hline \end{array}$$

Using a place value chart is a good way of solving problems like this.

TENS	ONES
2	3
+	4

Step 1

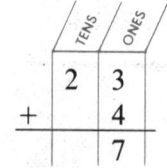

Add the numbers in the ones column: $3 + 4 = 7$. Write the 7 at the bottom of the ones column.

Step 2

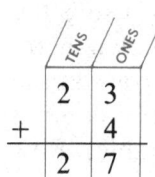

Add the numbers in the tens column: 2 tens + 0 tens = 2 tens. Write the 2 at the bottom of the tens column. Your answer is 27.

If you have trouble adding the numbers in the ones column or the tens column, you can use a table or a number line, as shown in **PROBLEM 1**.

PROBLEM 4.

$$\begin{array}{r} 27 \\ + 9 \\ \hline \end{array}$$

Using a place value chart is a good way of solving problems like this.

TENS	ONES
2	7
+	9

ROMAN NUMERALS

Roman numerals—the symbols used in ancient Rome—are the most familiar of ancient counting systems. You still see them on buildings, clock faces, and many other places. One thing that makes Roman numerals difficult to read is that the position of the letter symbols matters. If a smaller number (like I, or 1) is placed before a larger one (like V, or 5) it is subtracted. If it comes after the larger number, it is added. So IV = 4, but VI = 6.

Here are the Roman numerals from 1 to 10, along with some of the symbols for larger numbers.

I = 1	VI = 6	XX = 20	C = 100
II = 2	VII = 7	XL = 40	D = 500
III = 3	VIII = 8	L = 50	M = 1,000
IV = 4	IX = 9	LXXV = 75	
V = 5	X = 10		

And here is how a modern date looks in Roman numerals: **MCMLXXVIII** 1978

Step 1

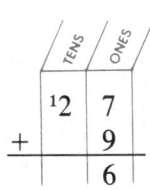

Add the numbers in the ones column: 7 + 9 = 16. Rename 16 as 1 ten and 6 ones. Write the 6 at the bottom of the ones column and the 1 at the top of the tens column.

Step 2

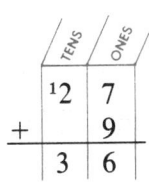

Add the numbers in the tens column: 2 tens + 1 ten = 3 tens. Write the 3 at the bottom of the tens column. Your answer is 36.

If you have trouble adding the numbers in the ones column or the tens column, you can use a table or a number line, as shown in **PROBLEM 1**.

PROBLEM 5.
$$\begin{array}{r} 13 \\ +44 \\ \end{array}$$

Step 1

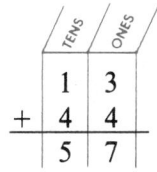

Add the numbers in the ones column: 3 + 4 = 7. Write the 7 at the bottom of the ones column.

Step 2

Add the numbers in the tens column: 1 ten + 4 tens = 5 tens. Write the 5 at the bottom of the tens column.

If you have trouble adding the numbers in either column, use an addition table or a number line, as shown in **PROBLEM 1**.

MATHEMATICS

PROBLEM 6.

$$37$$
$$+26$$

Step 1

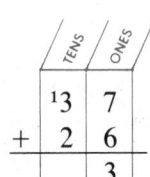

Add the numbers in the ones column: $7 + 6 = 13$.
Rename 13 as 1 ten and 3 ones. Write the 3 at the bottom of the ones column and write the 1 at the top of the tens column.

Step 2

Add the numbers in the tens column: 1 ten $+ 3$ tens $+ 2$ tens $= 6$ tens. Write the 6 at the bottom of the tens column.

If you have any trouble adding the numbers in either column, use an addition table or a number line, as shown in **PROBLEM 1**.

PROBLEM 7.

$$57$$
$$+88$$

Step 1

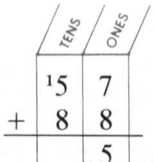

Add the numbers in the ones column: $7 + 8 = 15$.
Rename 15 as 1 ten and 5 ones. Write the 5 at the bottom of the ones column and write the 1 at the top of the tens column.

Step 2

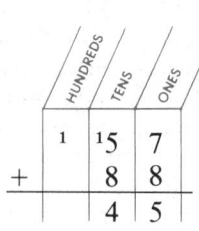

Add the numbers in the tens column: 1 ten $+ 5$ tens $+ 8$ tens $= 14$ tens. Rename 14 tens (or 140) as 1 hundred and 4 tens. Write the 4 at the bottom of the tens column and write the 1 at the top of the hundreds column.

Step 3

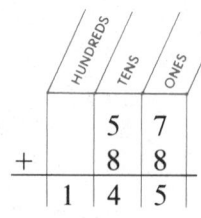

Add the numbers in the hundreds column: 1 hundred $+ 0$ hundreds $= 1$ hundred.
Write the 1 at the bottom of the hundreds column.

If you have trouble adding the numbers in any of the columns, use an addition table or a number line, as shown in **PROBLEM 1**.

PROBLEM 8.

$$24$$
$$32$$
$$+46$$

Problems like these can be solved in two different ways. The most common way is to use a place value chart, as in **PROBLEM 7**.

Step 1

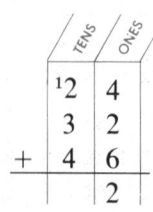

Add the numbers in the ones column: $4 + 2 + 6 = 12$.
Rename 12 as 1 ten and 2 ones. Write the 2 at the bottom of the ones column and the 1 at the top of the tens column.

MATHEMATICS

Step 2

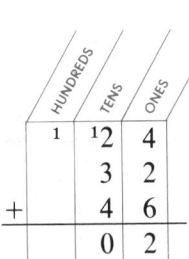

Add the numbers
in the tens column:
1 ten + 2 tens + 3 tens
+ 4 tens = 10 tens.
Rename 10 tens as
1 hundred and 0 tens.
Write the 0 at the
bottom of the tens
column and the 1
at the top of the
hundreds column.

Step 3

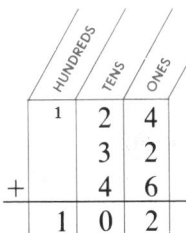

Add the numbers
in the hundreds column:
1 hundred + 0 hundreds
= 1 hundred.
Write the 1 at the
bottom of the
hundreds column.

If you have any trouble adding the numbers
in the ones column or the tens column, you
can use a table of addition facts or a number
line, as shown in **PROBLEM 1**.

◆ If adding all three numbers at once is
too difficult, you can break the problem
into parts.

Step 1

Take the top two numbers, write them
in a place value chart, and add them as
shown in **PROBLEM 6**.

```
 2 4 ⎫        2 4
 3 2 ⎬      + 3 2
+ 4 6         5 6
```

Step 2

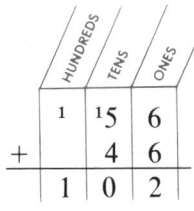

Add the sum from **Step 1**
to the third number
in the problem.
Again, follow
the steps in **PROBLEM 6**.

| PROBLEM 9. | 731 |
| | +569 |

Step 1

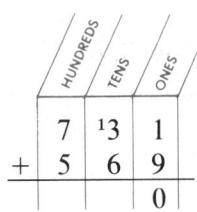

Add the numbers
in the ones column:
1 + 9 = 10.
Rename 10 as 1 ten
and 0 ones.
Write the 0 at the
bottom of the ones
column and the 1
at the top
of the tens column.

Step 2

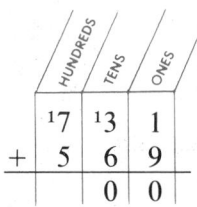

Add the numbers
in the tens column:
1 ten + 3 tens
+ 6 tens = 10 tens.
Rename 10 tens as
1 hundred and 0 tens.
Write the 0
at the bottom
of the tens column
and the 1 at the top
of the hundreds column.

Step 3

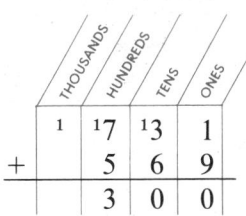

Add the numbers
in the hundreds
column: 1 hundred
+ 7 hundreds +
5 hundreds = 13
hundreds. Rename
13 hundreds as 1
thousand and 3 hun-
dreds.
Write the 3 at the
bottom of the
hundreds column
and the 1 at the
top of the thousands
column.

Step 4

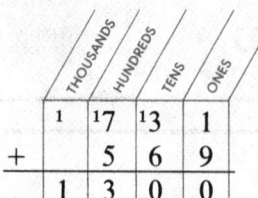

Add the numbers in the thousands column.
Write the 1 at the bottom of the thousands column.

SUBTRACTION OF WHOLE NUMBERS

PROBLEM 10.

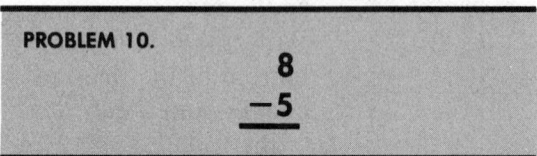

You can solve this problem by consulting the table of basic subtraction facts shown below.

–	0	1	2	3	4	5	6	7	8	9
0	0									
1	1	0								
2	2	1	0							
3	3	2	1	0						
4	4	3	2	1	0					
5	5	4	3	2	1	0				
6	6	5	4	3	2	1	0			
7	7	6	5	4	3	2	1	0		
8	8	7	6	5	4	3	2	1	0	
9	9	8	7	6	5	4	3	2	1	0

TABLE OF SUBTRACTION FACTS

Read down the left side of the table to row **8** and across to column **5**. Row **8** and column **5** meet at the number **3**, the answer.

$$8 - 5 = 3$$

◆ This problem may also be solved by using a number line.

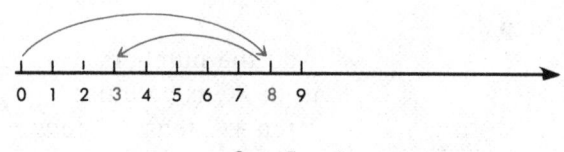

$$8 - 5 = 3$$

PROBLEM 11.

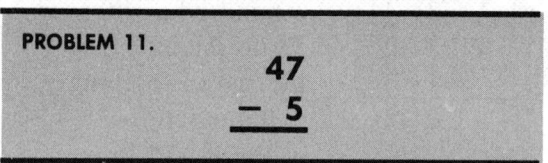

Using a place value chart is a good way of solving problems like this.

Step 1

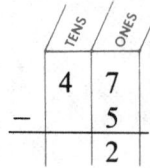

Subtract in the ones column:
$7 - 5 = 2$.
Write the 2 at the bottom of the ones column.

Step 2

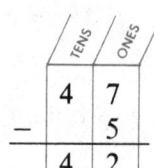

Subtract in the tens column:
4 tens – 0 tens = 4 tens.
Write the 4 at the bottom of the tens column.

If you have trouble subtracting in either column, use a subtraction table or a number line, as shown in **PROBLEM 10.**

PROBLEM 12.

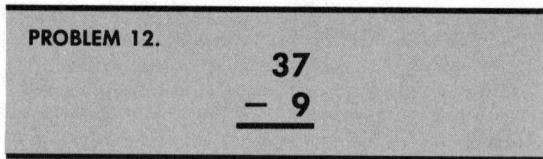

Step 1

Before subtracting in the ones column, you have to do some renaming, since 9 cannot be subtracted from 7.

MATHEMATICS

Rename the 3 tens as 2 tens and 10 ones. This gives you 17 ones in the ones column:

$$37 = 3 \text{ tens} + 7 \text{ ones}$$
$$= 2 \text{ tens} + 17 \text{ ones}$$

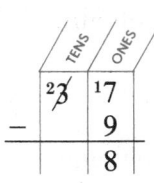 Now you can subtract in the ones column: $17 - 9 = 8$. Write the 8 at the bottom of the ones column.

Step 2

 Subtract in the tens column: $2 \text{ tens} - 0 = 2 \text{ tens}$. Write the 2 at the bottom of the tens column.

If you have trouble subtracting numbers in either column after you rename, use a subtraction table or a number line, as shown in **PROBLEM 10.**

PROBLEM 13.
$$68$$
$$-52$$

Step 1

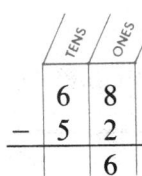 Subtract in the ones column: $8 - 2 = 6$. Write the 6 at the bottom of the ones column.

Step 2

Subtract in the tens column: $6 \text{ tens} - 5 \text{ tens} = 1 \text{ ten}$. Write the 1 at the bottom of the tens column.

If you have trouble subtracting in either column, use a subtraction table or a number line, as shown in **PROBLEM 10.**

PROBLEM 14.
$$70$$
$$-45$$

Step 1

Before subtracting in the ones column, you have to do some renaming, since 5 cannot be subtracted from 0. Rename 7 tens as 6 tens and 10 ones. This gives you 10 ones in the ones column.

$$70 = 7 \text{ tens} + 0 \text{ ones}$$
$$= 6 \text{ tens} + 10 \text{ ones}$$

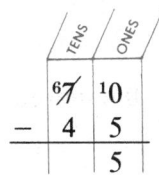 Now you can subtract in the ones column: $10 - 5 = 5$. Write the 5 at the bottom of the ones column.

Step 2

Subtract in the tens column: $6 \text{ tens} - 4 \text{ tens} = 2 \text{ tens}$. Write the 2 at the bottom of the tens column.

If you have any trouble subtracting in either column after you rename, use a subtraction table or a number line, as shown in **PROBLEM 10.**

PROBLEM 15.
$$682$$
$$- 47$$

Step 1

Before subtracting in the ones column, you have to rename, since 7 cannot be subtracted from 2. Rename the 8 tens as 7 tens and 10 ones. This gives you 12 ones in the ones column.

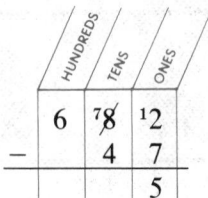

Now you can subtract:
12 − 7 = 5.

Step 2

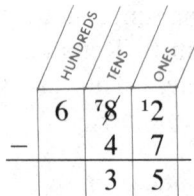

Subtract
in the tens column:
7 tens − 4 tens = 3 tens.
Write the 3
at the bottom
of the tens column.

Step 3

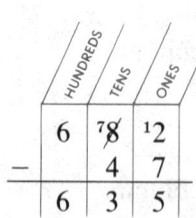

Subtract
in the hundreds
column:
6 hundreds − 0 hundreds
= 6 hundreds.
Write the 6
at the bottom
of the hundreds column.

PROBLEM 16.

$$503 - 46$$

Step 1

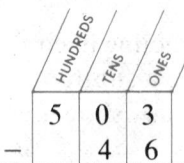

Before subtracting
in the ones column,
you have to rename,
since 6 cannot be
subtracted from 3.

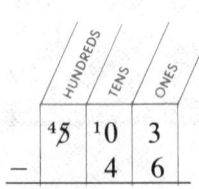

Since there are no
tens to rename,
you have to go to
the hundreds column.
Rename the 5 hundreds
as 4 hundreds
and 0 tens as 10 tens.

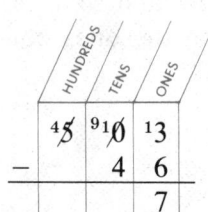

Now you have 10 tens,
which can be renamed
as 9 tens and 10 ones.
Now you can subtract:
13 − 6 = 7.
Write the 7
at the bottom
of the ones column.

Step 2

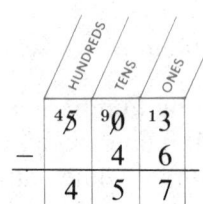

Subtract
in the tens column:
9 tens − 4 tens = 5 tens.
Write the 5
at the bottom
of the tens column.

Step 3

Subtract
in the hundreds column:
4 hundreds − 0 hundreds
= 4 hundreds.
Write the 4
at the bottom
of the hundreds column.

If you have trouble subtracting the numbers in any column after you rename, use a subtraction table or a number line, as shown in **PROBLEM 10**.

MULTIPLICATION OF WHOLE NUMBERS

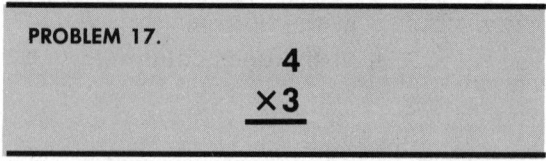

PROBLEM 17.

$$4 \times 3$$

You can solve this problem by using the table of multiplication facts on the next page.

×	0	1	2	3	4	5	6	7	8	9
0	0	0	0	0	0	0	0	0	0	0
1	0	1	2	3	4	5	6	7	8	9
2	0	2	4	6	8	10	12	14	16	18
3	0	3	6	9	12	15	18	21	24	27
4	0	4	8	12	16	20	24	28	32	36
5	0	5	10	15	20	25	30	35	40	45
6	0	6	12	18	24	30	36	42	48	54
7	0	7	14	21	28	35	42	49	56	63
8	0	8	16	24	32	40	48	56	64	72
9	0	9	18	27	36	45	54	63	72	81

TABLE OF MULTIPLICATION FACTS

Read down to row **4** and across to column **3**. Row **4** and column **3** meet at the number **12**, which is the answer:

$$4 \times 3 = 12$$

◆ You can also find the answer by adding 3 fours or by counting the elements in 3 sets of four.

```
  4        ○ ○ ○
  4        ○ ○ ○
 +4        ○ ○ ○
 ──        ○ ○ ○
 12
```

12 elements

Or you can use a number line.

0 1 2 3 4 5 6 7 8 9 10 11 12 13 14

$$4 + 4 + 4 = 12$$

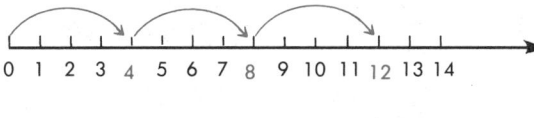

PROBLEM 18.

26
× 3

The number 26 does not appear in the table of basic multiplication facts. But 2 and 6 do. We can attack this problem by multiplying ones and tens separately. We can do this because 26 = 2 tens and 6 ones.

Step 1

	TENS	ONES
	2	6
×		3
	1	8

Multiply ones by ones: $6 \times 3 = 18$. Write the partial product.

Step 2

	TENS	ONES
	2	6
×		3
	1	8
	6	0

Multiply tens by ones: 2 tens × 3 ones = 6 tens = 60. Write the partial product.

Note that 2 tens × 3 ones is 6 tens—not 6 ones.

Step 3

	TENS	ONES
	2	6
×		3
	1	8
	6	0
	7	8

Add the partial products: $18 + 60 = 78$.

You will find the following form a bit faster.

Step 1

	TENS	ONES
	¹2	6
×		3
		8

Multiply ones by ones: $6 \times 3 = 18$ = 1 ten and 8 ones. Write the 8 at the bottom of the ones column, and write the 1 in the tens column.

Step 2

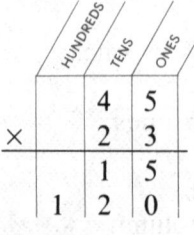

Multiply tens by ones:
$20 \times 3 = 60$.
Now add the 10
indicated by
the small 1
in the tens column:
$60 + 10 = 70 = 7$ tens.
Write the 7
in the tens column.

PROBLEM 19.

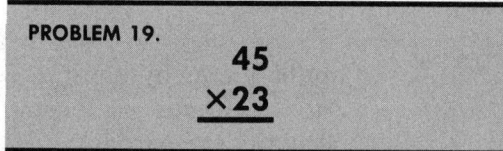

$$\begin{array}{r} 45 \\ \times 23 \\ \hline \end{array}$$

Neither 45 nor 23 appears in the table of basic multiplication facts. But 4, 7, 2, and 3 do. We can attack this problem by multiplying ones and tens separately. We can do this because $45 = 4$ tens and 5 ones, and $23 = 2$ tens and 3 ones.

Step 1

Multiply ones by ones:
$5 \times 3 = 15$.
Write the partial
product.

Step 2

Multiply tens by ones:
4 tens $\times$ 3 ones
$= 12$ tens $= 120$.
Write the partial
product.

Note that 4 tens $\times$ 3 ones is 12 tens, not 12 ones.

Step 3

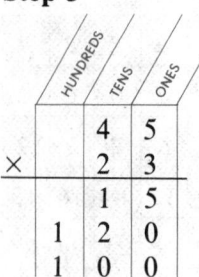

Multiply ones by tens:
5 ones by 2 tens
$= 10$ tens.
Write the partial
product.

Note again that 5 ones $\times$ 2 tens is 10 tens, not 10 ones.

Step 4

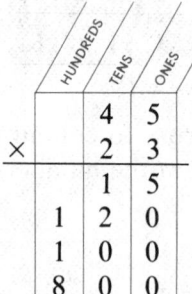

Multiply tens by tens:
4 tens $\times$ 2 tens
is 8 hundreds.

Note that tens $\times$ tens is hundreds—not tens.

Step 5

Add the
partial products.

You will find that the following form is faster.

Step 1

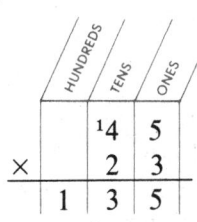

	TENS	ONES
	1 4	5
×	2	3
		5

Multiply ones by ones:
5 × 3 = 15
= 1 ten and 5 ones.
Write the 5
at the bottom
of the ones column
and the 1
in the tens column.

Step 2

	HUNDREDS	TENS	ONES
		1 4	5
×		2	3
	1	3	5

Multiply tens by ones:
4 tens × 3 ones = 12 tens
= 120.
Now add to this
the 10 indicated
by the small 1
in the tens column:
120 + 10 = 130
= 1 hundred and 3 tens.
Write the 1
in the hundreds column
and the 3
in the tens column.

Step 3

	HUNDREDS	TENS	ONES
	1	~~1~~4	5
×		2	3
	1	3	5
		0	

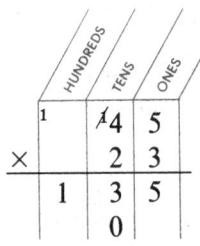

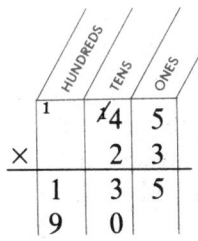

Multiply ones by tens:
5 ones × 2 tens = 10 tens
= 1 hundred.
Write a 0
in the tens column
and a 1
at the top of
the hundreds column.

Step 4

	HUNDREDS	TENS	ONES
	1	~~1~~4	5
×		2	3
	1	3	5
	9	0	

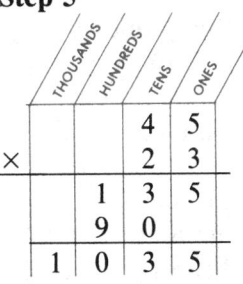

Multiply tens by tens:
4 tens × 2 tens
= 8 hundreds.
Add to this
the hundred indicated
by the small 1:
8 hundreds + 1 hundred
= 9 hundred. Write the 9
in the hundreds column.

Step 5

	THOUSANDS	HUNDREDS	TENS	ONES
			4	5
×			2	3
		1	3	5
		9	0	
	1	0	3	5

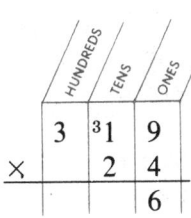

Add the partial products.

PROBLEM 20.

$$\begin{array}{r} 319 \\ \times\ 24 \\ \hline \end{array}$$

Step 1

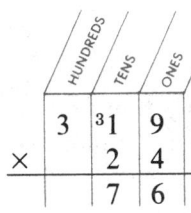

	HUNDREDS	TENS	ONES
	3	3 1	9
×		2	4
			6

Multiply ones by ones:
9 × 4 = 36
= 3 tens and 6 ones.
Write the 6
at the bottom
of the ones column
and the 3
in the tens column.

Step 2

	HUNDREDS	TENS	ONES
	3	3 1	9
×		2	4
		7	6

Multiply tens by ones:
1 ten × 4 ones = 4 tens.
Add to this the 3 tens
indicated by the small 3
in the tens column:
4 tens + 3 tens = 7 tens.
Write the 7
in the tens column.

Step 3

	THOUSANDS	HUNDREDS	TENS	ONES
		3	3 1	9
×			2	4
	1	2	7	6

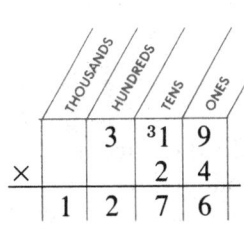

Multiply hundreds
by ones:
3 hundreds × 4 ones
= 12 hundreds
= 1 thousand and
2 hundred.
Write the 2
in the hundreds
column and the 1
in the thousands
column.

Step 4

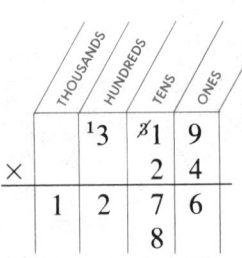

Multiply ones by tens: 9 ones × 2 tens = 18 tens = 1 hundred and 8 tens. Write the 8 in the tens column and the 1 at the top of the tens column.

Step 5

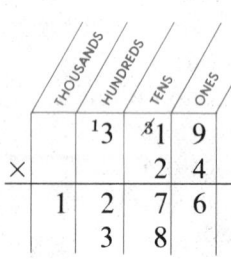

Multiply tens by tens: 1 ten × 2 tens = 2 hundreds. Add to this the hundred indicated by the small 1: 2 hundred + 1 hundred = 3 hundred. Write the 3 in the hundreds column.

Step 6

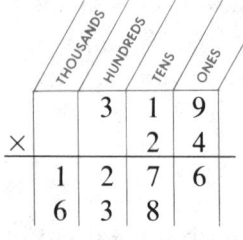

Multiply hundreds by tens: 3 hundreds × 2 tens = 6 thousands. Write the 6 in the thousands column.

Step 7

THOUSANDS	HUNDREDS	TENS	ONES
	3	1	9
×		2	4
1	2	7	6
6	3	8	
7	6	5	6

Add the partial products.

This problem, and those with even larger factors, can be solved using the method shown in **PROBLEMS 18–20**. It involves multiplying ones, tens, and hundreds separately.

```
      3 1 9
    × 5 2 4
  ─────────
        3 6    ones × ones
        4 0    tens × ones
    1 2 0 0    hundreds × ones
      1 8 0    ones × tens
      2 0 0    tens × tens
    6 0 0 0    hundreds × tens
    4 5 0 0    ones × hundreds
    5 0 0 0    tens × hundreds
  1 5 0 0 0 0  hundreds × hundreds
  ───────────
  1 6 7 1 5 6  add partial products
```

The following method is faster.

Step 1

```
      3 1 9    Multiply ones, tens,
    × 5 2 4    and hundreds by ones.
  ─────────
    1 2 7 6
```

Step 2

```
      3 1 9    Multiply ones, tens,
    × 5 2 4    and hundreds by tens.
  ─────────
    1 2 7 6
    6 3 8
```

Step 3

```
        3 1 9    Multiply ones, tens,
      × 5 2 4    and hundreds
    ─────────    by hundreds.
      1 2 7 6
      6 3 8
  1 5 9 5
```

MATHEMATICS

Step 4

```
        3   1   9
    ×   5   2   4
      1   2   7   6     Add the partial
        6   3   8       products.
  1   5   9   5
  1   6   7   1   5   6
```

DIVISION OF WHOLE NUMBERS

PROBLEM 22.   2⟌8

This problem is asking, "How many twos are there in eight?" There are several ways of answering this question. The usual way is based on simple subtraction: we find out how many twos there are in eight by taking twos away until we can't take any more.

```
      8
    − 2        (1 two subtracted)
      6
    − 2        (1 two subtracted)
      4
    − 2        (1 two subtracted)
      2
    − 2        (1 two subtracted)
      0        (4 twos subtracted in all)
```

We see from this that there are exactly 4 twos in 8.

We might, however, save time by subtracting several twos at once:

```
      8
    − 6        (3 twos subtracted)
      2
    − 2        (1 two subtracted)
      0        (4 twos subtracted in all)
```

We might even get the right answer in one try and subtract them all at once:

```
      8
    − 8        (4 twos subtracted)
      0
```

This is the idea behind the division algorithm:

```
        4
    2⟌ 8
      −8
        0
```

The number at the top simply shows that 4 twos were subtracted—all at once—below.

PROBLEM 23.   2⟌9

This problem is asking, "How many twos are there in nine?" We can use the subtraction method shown in **PROBLEM 25** to solve this problem. That is, we can find out how many twos there are in nine by taking twos away until we can't take any more.

```
      9
    − 2        (1 two subtracted)
      7
    − 2        (1 two subtracted)
      5
    − 2        (1 two subtracted)
      3
    − 2        (1 two subtracted)
      1        (4 twos subtracted in all)
```

We can't take away any more twos, but we still have 1 left over from the 9. This is a remainder.

As we saw in **PROBLEM 22**, the idea behind the division algorithm is subtraction.

$$
\begin{array}{r}
9 \\
-\ 8 \\
\hline
1
\end{array}
\quad \text{(4 twos subtracted)} \quad
\begin{array}{r}
4 \\
2\,\overline{)\,9} \\
-8 \\
\hline
1
\end{array}
$$

The number at the top simply shows that 4 twos were subtracted, all at once.

PROBLEM 24.

$$2\,\overline{)\,16}$$

This problem is asking, "How many twos are there in sixteen?" We can use the same subtraction method as in **PROBLEMS 22** and **23** to solve this problem—we can take away twos until we can't take any more.

$$
\begin{array}{r}
16 \\
-\ 2 \\
\hline
14 \\
-\ 2 \\
\hline
12 \\
-\ 2 \\
\hline
10 \\
-\ 2 \\
\hline
8 \\
-\ 2 \\
\hline
6 \\
-\ 2 \\
\hline
4 \\
-\ 2 \\
\hline
2 \\
-\ 2 \\
\hline
0
\end{array}
$$

(1 two subtracted)
(1 two subtracted)
(1 two subtracted)
(1 two subtracted)
(1 two subtracted)
(1 two subtracted)
(1 two subtracted)
(1 two subtracted)
(8 twos subtracted in all)

As we saw in **PROBLEMS 22** and **23**, subtraction is the basis for the division algorithm.

$$
\begin{array}{r}
16 \\
-16 \\
\hline
0
\end{array}
\quad \text{(8 twos subtracted)} \quad
\begin{array}{r}
8 \\
2\,\overline{)\,16} \\
-16 \\
\hline
0
\end{array}
$$

The number at the top of the algorithm indicates that 8 twos were subtracted.

PROBLEM 25.

$$2\,\overline{)\,80}$$

This problem is asking, "How many twos are there in 80?" We could use the subtraction method and take away twos, one at a time, until we couldn't take away any more. It would be much faster, however, to take away twos *ten* at a time.

$$
\begin{array}{r}
80 \\
-20 \\
\hline
60 \\
-20 \\
\hline
40 \\
-20 \\
\hline
20 \\
-20 \\
\hline
0
\end{array}
$$

(10 twos subtracted)
(10 twos subtracted)
(10 twos subtracted)
(10 twos subtracted)
(40 twos subtracted in all)

Subtracting ten-at-a-time is the basis for the division algorithm.

$$
\begin{array}{r}
80 \\
-80 \\
\hline
0
\end{array}
\quad \text{(40 twos subtracted)} \quad
\begin{array}{r}
40 \\
2\,\overline{)\,80} \\
-80 \\
\hline
0
\end{array}
$$

You can solve this problem in the algorithm form quite easily if you think of 80 as 8 tens.

$$
\begin{array}{r}
4 \text{ tens} \ = \ 40 \\
2\,\overline{)\,8 \text{ tens}} \\
-8 \text{ tens} \\
\hline
0
\end{array}
$$

MATHEMATICS

The standard division algorithm is:

$$2 \overline{)\, 80} \quad \begin{array}{r} 40 \\ \hline -8 \\ \hline 0 \\ -0 \\ \hline 0 \end{array}$$

In effect, if you can solve the problem $8 \div 2$, you can solve any of the following problems:

$$2 \overline{)\, 800} \;=\; 2 \overline{)\, 8 \text{ hundreds}} \quad \begin{array}{l} 4 \text{ hundreds} = 400 \\ \hline -8 \text{ hundreds} \\ \hline 0 \end{array}$$

$$2 \overline{)\, 8000} \;=\; 2 \overline{)\, 8 \text{ thousands}} \quad \begin{array}{l} 4 \text{ thousands} = 4000 \\ \hline -8 \text{ thousands} \\ \hline 0 \end{array}$$

And so on. This fact makes it possible to attack division problems digit-by-digit.

PROBLEM 26.

$$2 \overline{)\, 88}$$

As you saw in **PROBLEM 25**, you only need to know how to divide 8 by 2 in order to divide 88 by 2. This is so because 88 is 8 tens + 8 ones. Therefore the problem can be rewritten as follows:

$$2 \overline{)\, 8 \text{ tens} + 8 \text{ ones}}$$

Step 1

$$2 \overline{)\, 8 \text{ tens} + 8 \text{ ones}} \quad \begin{array}{l} 4 \text{ tens} \\ \hline -8 \text{ tens} \\ \hline 0 \end{array}$$ Divide the tens.

If you are not sure how to divide 8 by 2, go back to **PROBLEM 22**. If you are not sure

how to divide 8 tens by 2, go back to **PROBLEM 25**.

Step 2

$$2 \overline{)\, 8 \text{ tens} + 8 \text{ ones}} \quad \begin{array}{l} 4 \text{ tens} + 4 \text{ ones} \;= 44 \\ \hline -8 \text{ tens} - 8 \text{ ones} \\ \hline \quad 0 \qquad 0 \end{array}$$ Divide the ones.

The problem can be solved more quickly by taking out the words "tens" and "ones":

Step 1

$$2 \overline{)\, 8\ 8} \quad \begin{array}{r} 4 \\ \hline -8 \\ \hline 0 \end{array}$$

Step 2

$$2 \overline{)\, 8 \quad 8} \quad \begin{array}{r} 4 \quad 4 \\ \hline -8 \; -8 \\ \hline 0 \quad 0 \end{array}$$

And finally, we are ready for the standard form:

$$2 \overline{)\, 88} \quad \begin{array}{r} 4 \\ \hline -8 \\ \hline 8 \end{array}$$

Note that there is really nothing new in this. The 8 merely shows that we are subtracting 8 tens from the 88. The 8 is a remainder—we have not yet taken away as many twos as we can.

$$2 \overline{)\, 88} \quad \begin{array}{r} 44 \\ \hline -8 \\ \hline 8 \\ -8 \\ \hline 0 \end{array}$$

PROBLEM 27.

$$3\overline{)78}$$

As you saw in **PROBLEM 26,** this sort of problem can be attacked by dividing each digit separately.

Step 1

$$
\begin{array}{r}
2 \\
3\overline{)78} \\
-60 \\
\hline
18
\end{array}
$$
    Divide the tens.

If you aren't sure how to divide 7 by 3, go back to **PROBLEM 22.** If you aren't sure why 60 was subtracted, go back to **PROBLEM 26.**

Step 2

$$
\begin{array}{r}
26 \\
3\overline{)78} \\
-60 \\
\hline
18 \\
-18 \\
\hline
0
\end{array}
$$
    Divide the remainder.

And finally, we are ready for the standard form:

$$
\begin{array}{r}
26 \\
3\overline{)78} \\
-6 \\
\hline
18 \\
-18 \\
\hline
0
\end{array}
$$

PROBLEM 28.

$$3\overline{)528}$$

Step 1

$$
\begin{array}{r}
1 \\
3\overline{)528} \\
-3 \\
\hline
2
\end{array}
$$
    Divide the first digit.

Here, using the standard algorithm, we write only a 3 to note that we have subtracted 3 hundreds. We write the remainder as 2, although the remainder at this point is actually 228.

Step 2

$$
\begin{array}{r}
1 \\
3\overline{)528} \\
-3 \\
\hline
22
\end{array}
$$
    Bring down the second digit.

Step 3

$$
\begin{array}{r}
17 \\
3\overline{)528} \\
-3 \\
\hline
22 \\
-21 \\
\hline
1
\end{array}
$$
    Divide the 22 by 3.

Step 4

$$
\begin{array}{r}
17 \\
3\overline{)528} \\
-3 \\
\hline
22 \\
-21 \\
\hline
18
\end{array}
$$
    Bring down the third digit.

Step 5

$$
\begin{array}{r}
176 \\
3\overline{)528} \\
-3 \\
\hline
22 \\
-21 \\
\hline
18 \\
-18 \\
\hline
0
\end{array}
$$
    Divide the 18 by 3.

In this problem the divisor, 6, is greater than the first digit of the dividend. Thus we can't divide the first digit. We could indicate this with a zero.

$$6\overline{)\begin{matrix}0\\528\end{matrix}}\\-0\\\overline{5}$$

We would then go on to bring down the second digit and divide.

$$6\overline{)\begin{matrix}0\\528\end{matrix}}\qquad 6\overline{)\begin{matrix}08\\528\end{matrix}}\\-0\qquad\qquad-0\\\overline{52}\qquad\qquad\overline{52}\\\qquad\qquad\qquad-48\\\qquad\qquad\qquad\overline{4}$$

This step is usually not done. When the divisor is greater than the first digit, we simply divide the first *two* digits.

Step 1

$$6\overline{)\begin{matrix}8\\528\end{matrix}}\\-48\\\overline{4}$$ Divide the first two digits by 6.

Step 2

$$6\overline{)\begin{matrix}8\\528\end{matrix}}\\-48\\\overline{48}$$ Bring down the third digit.

Step 3

$$6\overline{)\begin{matrix}88\\528\end{matrix}}\\-48\\\overline{48}\\-48\\\overline{0}$$ Now divide the 48 by 6.

Operations with Fractions

FACTORING

Factoring is a skill you will need in working with fractions. It is a simple operation. To factor a number, you find its factors: the whole numbers that can be multiplied together to give the number. This can be done with a "factor tree."

Nine and 1 are both factors of 9. But knowing this is not very useful, since every number has itself and 1 as factors. What other whole numbers might be factors of 9: 5? 7? 2? 3? Let's start with the smallest number after 1 and see.

Step 1

Divide 9 by 2.

$$9 \div 2 = ?$$

Nine is not divisible evenly by 2. Therefore 2 is not one of its factors. Let's try the next whole number.

Step 2

Divide 9 by 3.

$$9 \div 3 = 3$$

Since 9 is divisible by 3, 3 is one of its factors.

Now we have factored 9 completely.

$$9 = 3 \times 3$$

Step 1

Divide 8 by 2.

$$8 \div 2 = 4$$

We have found two factors of 8:

$$8 = 2 \times 4$$

But what about 4? The number 4 can also be factored.

Step 2

Divide 4 by 2.

$$4 \div 2 = 2$$

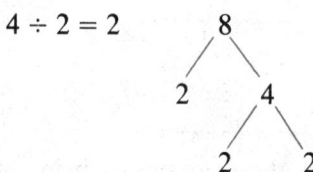

Now we have factored 8 completely.

$$8 = 2 \times 2 \times 2$$

Step 1

Divide 30 by 2.

$$30 \div 2 = 15$$

Is this a complete factorization? We must also test 15 for its factors.

Step 2

Divide 15 by 2.

$$15 \div 2 = ?$$

Fifteen is not divisible by 2.

Step 3

Divide 15 by 3.

$15 \div 3 = 5$

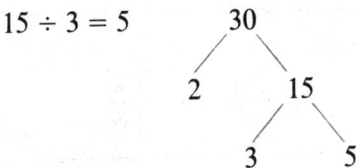

Since 5 is not divisible by 2 or 3, we have factored 30 completely.

$$30 = 2 \times 3 \times 5$$

PROBLEM 33.

Factor: 735

Step 1

Divide 735 by 2.

$$735 \div 2 = ?$$

Two is not a factor of 735.

Step 2

Divide 735 by 3.

$$735 \div 3 = 245$$

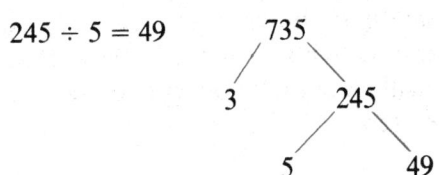

Now we must go on to factor 245.

Step 3

Divide 245 by 2.

$$245 \div 2 = ?$$

Two is not a factor of 245.

Step 4

Divide 245 by 3.

$$245 \div 3 = ?$$

Three is not a factor of 245.

Step 5

Divide 245 by 5. (There is no point in testing 4; if 245 were divisible by 4, it would have been divisible by 2.)

$$245 \div 5 = 49$$

Now we must go on to factor 49.

Step 6

Divide 49 by 2.

$$49 \div 2 = ?$$

Two is not a factor of 49.

Step 7

Divide 49 by 3.

$$49 \div 3 = ?$$

Three is not a factor of 49.

Step 8

Divide 49 by 5.

$$49 \div 5 = ?$$

Five is not a factor of 49.

Step 9

Divide 49 by 7. (There is no point in testing 6; if 49 were divisible by 6 it would have been divisible by 2 and 3.)

$$49 \div 7 = 7$$

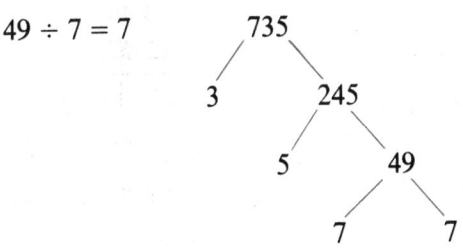

Seven is not divisible by 2, 3, or 5. Therefore we have factored 735 completely.

$$735 = 3 \times 5 \times 7 \times 7$$

The method shown above can be used to factor any whole number. With practice, you will find that you can omit some of these steps.

REDUCING FRACTIONS

PROBLEM 34.

Reduce: $\dfrac{4}{6}$

Being able to reduce fractions will simplify much of your later work.

Step 1

Factor the numerator and the denominator.

$$\frac{4}{6} = \frac{2 \times 2}{2 \times 3}$$

If you aren't sure how to factor 4 and 6, go back to **PROBLEM 30**.

Step 2

Cross out common factors.

$$\frac{4}{6} = \frac{\cancel{2} \times 2}{\cancel{2} \times 3}$$

Step 3

Rewrite.

$$\frac{4}{6} = \frac{2}{3}$$

PROBLEM 35.

Reduce: $\dfrac{12}{16}$

Step 1

Factor the numerator and the denominator.

$$\frac{12}{16} = \frac{2 \times 2 \times 3}{2 \times 2 \times 2 \times 2}$$

Step 2

Cross out common factors.

$$\frac{12}{16} = \frac{\cancel{2} \times \cancel{2} \times 3}{\cancel{2} \times \cancel{2} \times 2 \times 2}$$

Step 3

Rewrite.

$$\frac{12}{16} = \frac{3}{2 \times 2} = \frac{3}{4}$$

PROBLEM 36.

Reduce: $\dfrac{105}{110}$

Step 1

Factor the numerator and the denominator.

$$\frac{105}{110} = \frac{3 \times 7 \times 5}{2 \times 5 \times 11}$$

Step 2

Cross out common factors.

$$\frac{105}{110} = \frac{3 \times 7 \times \cancel{5}}{2 \times \cancel{5} \times 11}$$

Step 3

Rewrite.

$$\frac{105}{110} = \frac{3 \times 7}{2 \times 11} = \frac{21}{22}$$

PROBLEM 37.

Reduce: $\frac{4}{4}$

A fraction like $\frac{4}{4}$ is usually reduced, because it is another name for 1.

$$\frac{4}{4} = 1$$

PROBLEM 38.

Reduce: $\frac{12}{3}$

Whenever the numerator is larger than the denominator, the fraction can be reduced to a whole number or to a whole number and a fraction.

Step 1

Rename the numerator as a sum of addends equal to the denominator.

$$\frac{12}{3} = \frac{3 + 3 + 3 + 3}{3}$$

Step 2

Rename as separate fractions.

$$\frac{3 + 3 + 3 + 3}{3} = \frac{3}{3} + \frac{3}{3} + \frac{3}{3} + \frac{3}{3}$$

Step 3

Reduce.

$$\frac{3}{3} + \frac{3}{3} + \frac{3}{3} + \frac{3}{3} = 1 + 1 + 1 + 1 = 4$$

Therefore, $\frac{12}{3} = 4$. This can be done quicker by dividing the numerator by the denominator:

$$\frac{12}{3} = 12 \div 3 = 4$$

PROBLEM 39.

Reduce: $\frac{127}{8}$

Step 1

$$\begin{array}{r} 15 \\ 8\overline{)127} \\ -8 \\ \hline 47 \\ -40 \\ \hline 7 \end{array}$$

Divide the numerator by the denominator.

This takes care of 120 of the 127 eighths, since 8×15 is 120. The remainder is 7 eighths.

Step 2

Write the whole number and the fractional remainder.

$$\frac{127}{8} = 15\frac{7}{8}$$

FINDING THE LEAST COMMON MULTIPLE (LCM)

PROBLEM 40.

Find the LCM of 2 and 3.

Being able to find the LCM of two numbers is a skill you will need in finding lowest common denominators.

The multiples of a number are what you get by multiplying that number by whole numbers. For example, multiples of 2 are 2, 4, 6, 8, 10, 12, and so on. Multiples of 3 are 3, 6, 9, 12, 15, 18, and so on.

Multiples of 2:
    2 4 6 8 10 12 . . .

Multiples of 3:
    3 6 9 12 15 18 . . .

If you look at these lists you will see certain numbers that appear in both. These are the *common* multiples. If you were to continue the lists, you would find many more common multiples for 2 and 3: 18, 24, 30, 36, and so on. But the smallest, or least, of these common multiples is 6. Therefore the LCM of 2 and 3 is 6.

PROBLEM 41.
Find the LCM of 4 and 6.

Step 1

List the multiples of both numbers.
    Multiples of 4:
        4   8   12   16   20
    Multiples of 6:
        6   12   18   24   30

Step 2

Find the LCM.
    Multiples of 4:
        4   8   12   16   20
    Multiples of 6:
        6   12   18   24   30

The LCM of 4 and 6 is 12.

This method can be used to find the LCM of any two numbers.

FINDING THE LEAST COMMON DENOMINATOR (LCD)

PROBLEM 42.
Find the LCD for $\frac{8}{8}$ and $\frac{2}{3}$.

The least common denominator of any two fractions is the least common multiple of the two denominators.

Step 1

Find the least common multiple of the denominators, 8 and 3.
    Multiples of 8:
        8   16   24   32
    Multiples of 3:
        3   6   9   12   15   18   21   24

The least common multiple of 8 and 3 is 24. If you are not sure how to find the least common multiple of two numbers, go back to **PROBLEM 40**.

The least common denominator for $\frac{5}{8}$ and $\frac{2}{3}$ is 24.

PROBLEM 43.
Find the LCD for $\frac{1}{6}$ and $\frac{3}{4}$.

Step 1

Find the least common multiple of the denominators.
    Multiples of 6:
        6   12   18
    Multiples of 4:
        4   8   12

The least common multiple of 6 and 4 is 12. Therefore, the least common denominator for $\frac{1}{6}$ and $\frac{3}{4}$ is 12.

RENAMING FRACTIONS AS FRACTIONS WITH A GIVEN DENOMINATOR

> **PROBLEM 44.**
>
> $$\frac{2}{3} = \frac{?}{6}$$

To add or subtract fractions, you often have to rename one or both as a fraction with a different denominator. You do this by multiplying the fraction by some fraction equal to 1. Because 1 is the identity element for multiplication, multiplying a number by 1 does not change its value.

$$\frac{2}{2} \times \frac{2}{3} = \frac{2 \times 2}{2 \times 3} = \frac{4}{6}$$

Multiplying $\frac{2}{3}$ by $\frac{2}{2}$ changes its denominator to 6; but it does not change its value, because $\frac{2}{2}$ is simply a name for 1. If you are not sure how to multiply fractions, go to **PROBLEM 67**.

> **PROBLEM 45.**
>
> $$\frac{3}{5} = \frac{?}{20}$$

The following fractions are equal to 1:

$$\frac{2}{2}, \frac{3}{3}, \frac{4}{4}, \frac{5}{5}, \frac{6}{6}, \frac{7}{7}, \cdots$$

One of them can be used to change $\frac{3}{5}$ to a fraction with a denominator of 20.

$$\frac{\Box}{\Box} \times \frac{3}{5} = \frac{?}{20}$$

We see it must be $\frac{4}{4}$, since $4 \times 5 = 20$. We could also reach this by division:

$$20 \div 5 = 4$$

Therefore $\frac{4}{4}$ is the fraction we must use to change $\frac{3}{5}$ to a fraction with a denominator of 20.

$$\frac{4}{4} \times \frac{3}{5} = \frac{4 \times 3}{4 \times 5} = \frac{12}{20}$$

> **PROBLEM 46.**
>
> $$\frac{4}{9} = \frac{?}{45}$$

Step 1

Divide 45 by 9.

$$45 \div 9 = 5$$

Step 2

Write a fraction equal to 1 that has the denominator 5.

$$1 = \frac{5}{5}$$

Step 3

Multiply $\frac{4}{9}$ by $\frac{5}{5}$.

$$\frac{5}{5} \times \frac{4}{9} = \frac{5 \times 4}{5 \times 9} = \frac{20}{45}$$

RENAMING WHOLE NUMBERS AS FRACTIONS

> **PROBLEM 47.**
>
> ### Rename 4 as a fraction.

Any whole number can be renamed as a fraction by writing it as a numerator over the denominator 1. Therefore,

$$4 = \frac{4}{1}$$

PROBLEM 48.

Rename 257 as a fraction.

Write 257 as a numerator over the denominator 1.

$$257 = \frac{257}{1}$$

RENAMING WHOLE NUMBERS AS FRACTIONS WITH A GIVEN DENOMINATOR

PROBLEM 49.

$$4 = \frac{?}{3}$$

Step 1

Rename 4 as a fraction with the denominator 1.

$$4 = \frac{4}{1}$$

If you are not sure how to do this, go back to **PROBLEM 47**. Now that 4 is in fractional form, it can be renamed in the same way as the fractions in **PROBLEMS 44–46**.

Step 2

Rename $\frac{4}{1}$ as thirds.

$$\frac{3}{3} \times \frac{4}{1} = \frac{12}{3}$$

If you are not sure how to do this, go back to **PROBLEM 44**.

PROBLEM 50.

$$257 = \frac{?}{4}$$

Step 1

Rename 257 as a fraction with the denominator 1.

$$257 = \frac{257}{1}$$

Step 2

Rename $\frac{257}{1}$ as fourths.

$$\frac{4}{4} \times \frac{257}{1} = \frac{1028}{4}$$

RENAMING MIXED NUMBERS AS FRACTIONS

PROBLEM 51.

$$2\frac{1}{3} = \frac{?}{3}$$

Step 1

Rename 2 as a fraction with the denominator 3.

$$\frac{3}{3} \times \frac{2}{1} = \frac{6}{3}$$

If you are not sure how to do this, go back to **PROBLEM 49**.

Step 2

Add $\frac{6}{3}$ to $\frac{1}{3}$.

$$\frac{6}{3} + \frac{1}{3} = \frac{6+1}{3} = \frac{7}{3}$$

If you are not sure how to add these fractions, go to **PROBLEM 53**.

go to **PROBLEM 53**

PROBLEM 52.
$$4\frac{2}{7} = \frac{?}{7}$$

Step 1

Rename 4 as a fraction with the denominator 7.

$$\frac{7}{7} \times \frac{4}{1} = \frac{28}{7}$$

Step 2

Add $\frac{28}{7}$ to $\frac{2}{7}$.

$$\frac{28}{7} + \frac{2}{7} = \frac{28 + 2}{7} = \frac{30}{7}$$

A shortcut in renaming mixed numbers: Multiply the whole number by the denominator of the fraction and add the result to the numerator of the fraction: $(4 \times 7) + 2 = 30$. This gives you the numerator of the target fraction.

ADDITION OF FRACTIONS

PROBLEM 53.
$$\frac{1}{5} = \frac{3}{5}$$

Adding fractions that have a common denominator is very simple.

Step 1

Rewrite the numerator addends over the common denominator.

$$\frac{1}{5} + \frac{3}{5} = \frac{1 + 3}{5}$$

Step 2

Add the numerators.

$$\frac{1 + 3}{5} = \frac{4}{5}$$

GEOMETRIC FIGURES

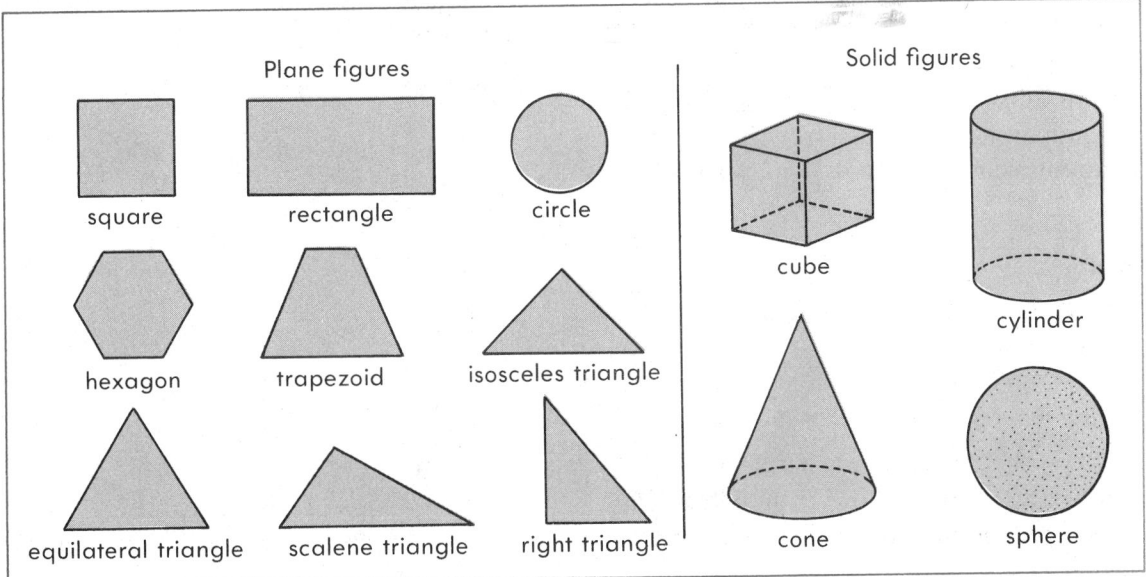

Plane figures

square   rectangle   circle

hexagon   trapezoid   isosceles triangle

equilateral triangle   scalene triangle   right triangle

Solid figures

cube   cylinder

cone   sphere

$$\frac{3}{8} + \frac{2}{8}$$

Step 1

Rewrite the numerator addends over the common denominator.

$$\frac{3}{8} + \frac{2}{8} = \frac{3+2}{8}$$

Step 2

Add the numerators.

$$\frac{3+2}{8} = \frac{5}{8}$$

PROBLEM 55.

$$\frac{1}{3} + \frac{1}{2}$$

Before adding two fractions with different denominators, you must rewrite them as fractions with a common denominator.

Step 1

Find the least common denominator for $\frac{1}{3}$ and $\frac{1}{2}$.

The least common denominator for $\frac{1}{3}$ and $\frac{1}{2}$ is 6.

If you are not sure how to find the least common denominator, go back to **PROBLEM 42.**

Step 2

Rename $\frac{1}{3}$ and $\frac{1}{2}$ as sixths.

$$\frac{2}{2} \times \frac{1}{3} = \frac{2}{6} \quad \text{and} \quad \frac{3}{3} \times \frac{1}{2} = \frac{3}{6}$$

If you are not sure how to rename fractions, go back to **PROBLEM 44.**

Step 3

Add $\frac{2}{6}$ and $\frac{3}{6}$.

$$\frac{2}{6} + \frac{3}{6} = \frac{2+3}{6} = \frac{5}{6}$$

If you are not sure how to add fractions, go back to **PROBLEM 53.**

PROBLEM 56.

$$\frac{2}{5} + \frac{3}{7}$$

Step 1

Find the least common denominator for $\frac{2}{5}$ and $\frac{3}{7}$.

The least common denominator for $\frac{2}{5}$ and $\frac{3}{7}$ is 35.

Step 2

Rename $\frac{2}{5}$ and $\frac{3}{7}$ as thirty-fifths.

$$\frac{7}{7} \times \frac{2}{5} = \frac{14}{35} \quad \text{and} \quad \frac{5}{5} \times \frac{3}{7} = \frac{15}{35}$$

Step 3

Add $\frac{14}{35}$ and $\frac{15}{35}$.

$$\frac{14}{35} + \frac{15}{35} = \frac{14+15}{35} = \frac{29}{35}$$

Any two fractions with unlike denominators can be added in this way.

PROBLEM 57.

$$2 + \frac{1}{9}$$

Adding a whole number and a fraction is very easy.

$$2 + \frac{1}{9} = 2\tfrac{1}{9}$$

ADDITION OF MIXED NUMBERS

PROBLEM 58.

$$2\frac{1}{9} + \frac{4}{9}$$

Adding a mixed number and a fraction is easy once you have renamed the mixed number as a fraction.

Step 1

Rename $2\frac{1}{9}$ as a fraction.

$$2\tfrac{1}{9} + \frac{4}{9} = \frac{19}{9} + \frac{4}{9}$$

If you are not sure how to do this, go back to **PROBLEM 51**.

Step 2

Add.

$$\frac{19}{9} + \frac{4}{9} = \frac{23}{9}$$

Step 3

Reduce.

$$\frac{23}{9} = 2\tfrac{5}{9}$$

If you are not sure how to reduce this fraction, go back to **PROBLEM 39**.

PROBLEM 59.

$$2\frac{1}{9} + 16\frac{4}{9}$$

Step 1

Rename both addends as fractions.

$$2\tfrac{1}{9} + 16\tfrac{4}{9} = \frac{19}{9} + \frac{148}{9}$$

Step 2

Add.

$$\frac{19}{9} + \frac{148}{9} = \frac{19 + 148}{9} = \frac{167}{9}$$

Step 3

Reduce.

$$\frac{167}{9} = 18\tfrac{5}{9}$$

PROBLEM 60.

$$3\frac{1}{8} + 6\frac{2}{5}$$

Adding two mixed numbers with fractions having different denominators combines the steps shown in **PROBLEMS 55–59**.

Step 1

Rename both addends as fractions.

$$3\tfrac{1}{8} + 6\tfrac{2}{5} = \frac{25}{8} + \frac{32}{5}$$

Step 2

Rewrite as fractions with a common denominator.

$$\frac{25}{8} + \frac{32}{5} = \frac{125}{40} + \frac{256}{40}$$

If you are not sure how to do this, go back to **PROBLEMS 42 and 44.**

Step 3

Add.

$$\frac{125}{40} + \frac{256}{40} = \frac{125 + 256}{40} = \frac{381}{40}$$

Step 4

Reduce.

$$\frac{381}{40} = 9\frac{21}{40}$$

SUBTRACTION OF FRACTIONS

PROBLEM 61.
$$\frac{3}{5} - \frac{1}{5}$$

Subtracting fractions that have a common denominator is very simple.

Step 1

Rewrite the numerators over the common denominator.

$$\frac{3}{5} - \frac{1}{5} = \frac{3-1}{5}$$

Step 2

Subtract.

$$\frac{3-1}{5} = \frac{2}{5}$$

PROBLEM 62.
$$\frac{1}{2} - \frac{1}{3}$$

Before subtracting two fractions with different denominators, you must rewrite them as fractions with a common denominator.

Step 1

Find the least common denominator for $\frac{1}{2}$ and $\frac{1}{3}$.
The least common denominator for $\frac{1}{2}$ and $\frac{1}{3}$ is 6.
If you are not sure how to do this, go back to **PROBLEM 43.**

Step 2

Rename $\frac{1}{2}$ and $\frac{1}{3}$ as sixths.

$$\frac{3}{3} \times \frac{1}{2} = \frac{3}{6} \quad \text{and} \quad \frac{2}{2} \times \frac{1}{3} = \frac{2}{6}$$

If you are not sure how to do this, go back to **PROBLEM 44.**

Step 3

Subtract.

$$\frac{3}{6} - \frac{2}{6} = \frac{3-2}{6} = \frac{1}{6}$$

If you are not sure how to do this, go back to **PROBLEM 61.**

SUBTRACTION OF MIXED NUMBERS

PROBLEM 63.
$$2\frac{4}{9} - \frac{2}{9}$$

To subtract a fraction from a mixed number, you can rename the mixed number as a fraction.

Step 1

Rename $2\frac{4}{9}$ as a fraction.

$$2\frac{4}{9} - \frac{2}{9} = \frac{22}{9} - \frac{2}{9}$$

If you are not sure how to rename mixed numerals, go back to **PROBLEM 51**.

Step 2

Subtract.

$$\frac{22}{9} - \frac{2}{9} = \frac{22 - 2}{9} = \frac{20}{9}$$

Step 3

Reduce.

$$\frac{20}{9} = 2\frac{2}{9}$$

If you are not sure how to do this, go back to **PROBLEM 39**.

PROBLEM 64. $\dfrac{30}{7} - 3\dfrac{3}{7}$

Step 1

Rewrite $3\frac{3}{7}$ as a fraction.

$$\frac{30}{7} - 3\frac{3}{7} = \frac{30}{7} - \frac{24}{7}$$

Step 2

Subtract.

$$\frac{30}{7} - \frac{24}{7} = \frac{30 - 24}{7} = \frac{6}{7}$$

PROBLEM 65. $3\dfrac{7}{8} - 2\dfrac{4}{8}$

Step 1

Rename both mixed numbers as fractions.

$$3\frac{7}{8} - 2\frac{4}{8} = \frac{31}{8} - \frac{20}{8}$$

Step 2

Subtract.

$$\frac{31}{8} - \frac{20}{8} = \frac{31 - 20}{8} = \frac{11}{8}$$

Step 3

Reduce.

$$\frac{11}{8} = 1\frac{3}{8}$$

PROBLEM 66. $2\dfrac{5}{8} - 1\dfrac{1}{3}$

Step 1

Rename both mixed numbers as fractions.

$$2\frac{5}{8} - 1\frac{1}{3} = \frac{21}{8} - \frac{4}{3}$$

Step 2

Rewrite as fractions with a common denominator.

$$\frac{21}{8} - \frac{4}{3} = \frac{63}{24} - \frac{32}{24}$$

If you are not sure how to do this, go back to **PROBLEMS 42** and **44**.

Step 3

Subtract.

$$\frac{63}{24} - \frac{32}{24} = \frac{63 - 32}{24} = \frac{31}{24}$$

Step 4

Reduce.

$$\frac{31}{24} = 1\frac{7}{24}$$

MULTIPLICATION OF FRACTIONS

PROBLEM 67.

$$\frac{1}{2} \times \frac{1}{3}$$

Multiplication of fractions is a very simple process: you simply multiply numerators and denominators.

$$\frac{1}{2} \times \frac{1}{3} = \frac{1 \times 1}{2 \times 3} = \frac{1}{6}$$

PROBLEM 68.

$$\frac{2}{9} \times \frac{6}{7}$$

Step 1

Multiply numerators and denominators.

$$\frac{2}{9} \times \frac{6}{7} = \frac{2 \times 6}{9 \times 7} = \frac{12}{63}$$

Step 2

Reduce.

$$\frac{12}{63} = \frac{4}{21}$$

If you are not sure how to reduce this fraction, go back to **PROBLEM 34**.

PROBLEM 69.

$$6 \times \frac{3}{8}$$

To multiply a whole number by a fraction, you can rewrite the whole number as a fraction.

$$6 = \frac{6}{1}$$

If you are not sure how to do this, go back to **PROBLEM 47**.

You can then go on to multiply and reduce.

$$\frac{6}{1} \times \frac{3}{8} = \frac{18}{8} = 2\frac{2}{8} = 2\frac{1}{4}$$

MULTIPLICATION OF MIXED NUMBERS

PROBLEM 70.

$$2\frac{3}{7} \times 9$$

Step 1

Rename both factors as fractions.

$$2\frac{3}{7} \times 9 = \frac{17}{7} \times \frac{9}{1}$$

If you are not sure how to do this renaming, go back to **PROBLEMS 47** and **51**.

Step 2

Multiply.

$$\frac{17}{7} \times \frac{9}{1} = \frac{17 \times 9}{7} = \frac{153}{7}$$

MATHEMATICS

Step 3

Reduce.

$$\frac{153}{7} = 21\frac{6}{7}$$

PROBLEM 71.
$$5\frac{2}{13} \times 2\frac{3}{9}$$

Step 1

Rename both factors as fractions.

$$5\frac{2}{13} \times 2\frac{3}{9} = \frac{67}{13} \times \frac{21}{9}$$

Step 2

Multiply.

$$\frac{67}{13} \times \frac{21}{9} = \frac{67 \times 21}{13 \times 9} = \frac{1407}{117}$$

Step 3

Reduce.

$$\frac{1407}{117} = 12\frac{3}{117}$$

DIVISION OF FRACTIONS

PROBLEM 72.
$$\frac{1}{2} \div \frac{2}{3}$$

It is useful to know that dividing by a fraction gives the same result as multiplying by its *reciprocal*. The reciprocal of $\frac{2}{3}$ is $\frac{3}{2}$. Therefore,

$$\frac{1}{2} \div \frac{2}{3} = \frac{1}{2} \times \frac{3}{2}$$

Dividing fractional numbers then becomes a simple problem of multiplication.

$$\frac{1}{2} \times \frac{3}{2} = \frac{1 \times 3}{2 \times 2} = \frac{3}{4}$$

PROBLEM 73.
$$\frac{2}{3} \div \frac{4}{7}$$

Step 1

Rewrite as a multiplication problem.

$$\frac{2}{3} \div \frac{4}{7} = \frac{2}{3} \times \frac{7}{4}$$

Step 2

Multiply.

$$\frac{2}{3} \times \frac{7}{4} = \frac{14}{12}$$

Step 3

Reduce.

$$\frac{14}{12} = 1\frac{2}{12} = 1\frac{1}{6}$$

If you are not sure how to reduce these fractions, go back to **PROBLEMS 39** and **34**.

DIVISION OF MIXED NUMBERS

PROBLEM 74.
$$2\frac{5}{8} \div 3$$

Step 1

Rename $2\frac{5}{8}$ and 3 as fractions.

$$2\frac{5}{8} \div 3 = \frac{21}{8} \div \frac{3}{1}$$

If you are not sure how to rename 3 as a fraction, go back to **PROBLEM 47**.

Step 2

Rewrite as a multiplication problem.

$$\frac{21}{8} \div \frac{3}{1} = \frac{21}{8} \times \frac{1}{3}$$

Step 3

Multiply.

$$\frac{21}{8} \times \frac{1}{3} = \frac{21 \times 1}{8 \times 3} = \frac{21}{24}$$

Step 4

Reduce.

$$\frac{21}{24} = \frac{7}{8}$$

PROBLEM 75.

$$1\frac{5}{6} \div 4\frac{2}{7}$$

Step 1

Rename $1\frac{5}{6}$ and $4\frac{2}{7}$ as fractions.

$$1\frac{5}{6} \div 4\frac{2}{7} = \frac{11}{6} \div \frac{30}{7}$$

Step 2

Rewrite as a multiplication problem.

$$\frac{11}{6} \div \frac{30}{7} = \frac{11}{6} \times \frac{7}{30}$$

Step 3

Multiply.

$$\frac{11}{6} \times \frac{7}{30} = \frac{11 \times 7}{6 \times 30} = \frac{77}{180}$$

Exponents

An easy way to show when a number has been multiplied by itself two or more times is to use exponents. Look at the following examples:

$$6 \times 6 = 6^2$$
$$5 \times 5 \times 5 = 5^3$$
$$9 \times 9 \times 9 \times 9 = 9^4$$

The 2, 3, and 4 are being used as exponents. They tell us how many times the numbers 6, 5, and 9, called bases, are being multiplied together. The numbers 6^2, 5^3, and 9^4 are called powers of the bases. The number 6 is raised to the second power (squared),

five is raised to the third power (cubed), and nine is raised to the fourth power.

PROBLEM 76.

Find the value of 4^3

Step 1

Rewrite 4^3 as a multiplication problem.

$$4^3 = 4 \times 4 \times 4$$

MATHEMATICS

Step 2

Multiply

$$4 \times 4 \times 4 = 64$$

PROBLEM 77.

Simplify: $2^4 \times 2^5$

Step 1

Rewrite 2^4 and 2^5 as multiplication problems.

$$2^4 = 2 \times 2 \times 2 \times 2$$
$$2^5 = 2 \times 2 \times 2 \times 2 \times 2$$

Step 2

Multiply.

$$2^4 \times 2^5 =$$
$$(2 \times 2 \times 2 \times 2) \times (2 \times 2 \times 2 \times 2 \times 2)$$

Step 3

Count how many twos are being multiplied together. There are 4 twos, then 5 twos being multiplied together.

$$2^{4+5} = 2^9$$

This could be written as

$$2^4 \times 2^5 = 2^{4+5} = 2^9$$

PROBLEM 78.

Simplify: $3^7 \div 3^4$

Step 1

Rewrite 3^7 and 3^4 as multiplication problems.

$$3^7 = 3 \times 3 \times 3 \times 3 \times 3 \times 3 \times 3$$
$$3^4 = 3 \times 3 \times 3 \times 3$$

Step 2

Divide

$$\frac{3^7}{3^4} = \frac{\cancel{3} \times \cancel{3} \times \cancel{3} \times \cancel{3} \times 3 \times 3 \times 3}{\cancel{3} \times \cancel{3} \times \cancel{3} \times \cancel{3}}$$

Step 3

Count how many threes are left. There are 3 threes.

$$3 \times 3 \times 3 = 3^{7-4} = 3^3$$

This could be written as

$$3^7 \div 3^4 = 3^{7-4} = 3^3$$

PROBLEM 79.

Simplify: $(5^3)^2$

Step 1

Rewrite 5^3 as a multiplication problem.

$$5^3 = 5 \times 5 \times 5$$

Step 2

Rewrite as $(5 \times 5 \times 5)^2$.

$$(5 \times 5 \times 5) \times (5 \times 5 \times 5)$$

Step 3

Count how many fives are being multiplied together.
There are six fives.

$$(5 \times 5 \times 5) \times (5 \times 5 \times 5) = 5^{3 \times 2} = 5^6$$

This could be written

$$(5^3)^2 = 5^{3 \times 2} = 5^6$$

When 1 is used as an exponent, such as 7^1, it means one seven.

$$7^1 = 7$$

Zero may be used as an exponent as long as its base is not zero. A nonzero number may be raised to the zero power. The value is always one.

$$5^0 = 1 \qquad 3^0 = 1$$

Zero raised to the zero power (0^0) has no value.

PROBLEM 80.

Simplify: $6^2 \div 6^2$

Follow the steps for solving PROBLEM 78.

$$6^2 \div 6^2 = 6^{2-2} = 6^0 = 1$$

Decimals

You can use the idea of place value (see page 210) to show fractions. This is done by placing a decimal point after the ones place in a number. All digits after the decimal point show numbers of fractional parts. Let us look at the number 563.241, using a place-value chart.

In expanded notation, this number could be written as

5 hundreds + 6 tens + 3 ones + 2 tenths + 4 hundredths + 1 thousandth

or

$$500 + 60 + 3 + \frac{2}{10} + \frac{4}{100} + \frac{1}{1000}$$

Here are some fractions written as decimals and in expanded notation.

$$7.54 = 7 + \frac{5}{10} + \frac{4}{100}$$

$$0.078 = 0 + 0 + \frac{7}{100} + \frac{8}{1000}$$

$$42.6 = 40 + 2 + \frac{6}{10}$$

OPERATIONS ON DECIMALS

Addition, subtraction, multiplication, and division with decimals follow the same rules as the whole number operations, except that the decimal point must be kept straight.

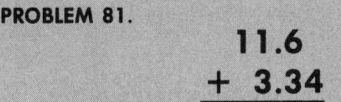

$$11.6$$
$$+\ 3.34$$

Using a place value chart is a good way of solving problems like this.

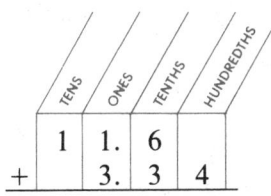

Step 1

Add the numbers in the four columns, as before.

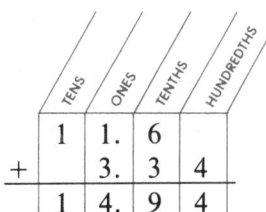

Write the answer at the bottom.

$$6.14$$
$$-2.05$$

Step 1

Subtract the numbers in the three columns, as before.

$$
\begin{array}{r}
6.\ 1\ 4 \\
-\ 2.\ 0\ 5 \\
\hline
4.\ 0\ 9
\end{array}
$$

Write the answer at the bottom.

$$20.$$
$$-\ 0.37$$

Step 1

Enter two zeros to the right of the decimal in the first number. This does not change the value of the number since

$$20. = 20.00$$

Step 2

Subtract the numbers in the four columns, as before.

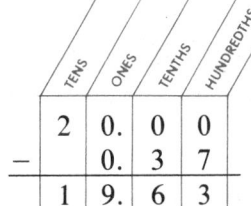

Write the answer at the bottom.

You may have noticed that we entered a zero in the ones column in the number 0.37 (and in the number 0.078 shown earlier). This is done to emphasize the location of the decimal.

$$12.96$$
$$\times\ \ 1.8$$

The number 12.96 is close to 13 and the number 1.8 is close to 2 so the product of these two numbers should be close to $13 \times 2 = 26$. This method of estimating can be used to check on the final location of the decimal point.

Step 1

1296	Multiply the numbers
× 18	as you would have
10368	done earlier,
1296	by temporarily
23328	forgetting the
	decimal points.

Step 2

12.96	(two places)	Count the number
1.8	(one place)	of places which
		are used
		on the right
		of the decimal.

Step 3

12.96	(two places)	Add the number
1.8	+(one place)	of places.

Step 4

23.328   Enter a decimal point
in the product so that
number of places on the
right of the decimal
is the same as that
found in **Step 3** above.

23.328 has three places to the right of the decimal.

Notice that 23.328 is near the approximate product of 26 which we found earlier.

PROBLEM 85.

$$6.1\overline{)43.31}$$

The number 6.1 is close to 6 and the number 43.31 is close to 42. The quotient of these two numbers should be close to $42 \div 6 = 7$.

Step 1

71	
61) 4331	Divide the numbers
427	as you would have
61	done earlier,
61	by temporarily
0	forgetting the
	decimal points.

Step 2

43.31	(two places)	Count the number
6.1	(one place)	of places which
		are used on the right
		of the decimal
		in each number.

Step 3

Subtract the number of places in the divisor from the number of places in the dividend.

43.31	(two places)	(dividend)
6.1	−(one place)	(divisor)
	(one place)	

Step 4

Enter a decimal point in the quotient so that it has the same number of places to the right of the decimal point as found in **Step 3** above. This gives us the quotient 7.1.

7.1 has one place to the right of the decimal.

Notice that 7.1 is near the approximate quotient of 7, which we found earlier.

MATHEMATICS

WRITING FRACTIONS AS DECIMALS

All fractions can be rewritten as decimals. There are, however, two kinds of decimals which result.

If the denominator of the fraction, when written in reduced form, can divide exactly into 10 or a power of 10 (i.e., 100, 1000, 10,000, . . .), then the decimal will end. A decimal ends if you can count the places which are used to the right of the decimal.

If the denominator of the fraction, when written in reduced form, cannot divide exactly into 10 or a power of 10, then the decimal will continue without end and the numbers to the right of the decimal will repeat.

The next two problems show an example of each kind of fraction.

PROBLEM 86.

Write $\dfrac{21}{56}$ as a decimal

Step 1

$\dfrac{21}{56} = \dfrac{3}{8}$ Reduce the fraction.

Step 2

Divide the denominator, 8, into 10 or one of its powers.

Since 8 divides exactly into 1000, the decimal will end.

Step 3

$$\begin{array}{r} 375 \\ 8\,\overline{)\,3.000} \\ \underline{2\,4} \\ 60 \\ \underline{56} \\ 40 \\ \underline{40} \end{array}$$

Divide the denominator into the numerator. Add zeros to the right of the decimal point in the dividend, as needed.

Step 4

Position the decimal point.

There are three places in the dividend, and no places in the divisor. Therefore, there will be three places in the quotient.

$$\frac{21}{56} = 0.375$$

PROBLEM 87.

Write $\dfrac{10}{12}$ as a decimal

Step 1

$\dfrac{10}{12} = \dfrac{5}{6}$ Reduce the fraction.

Step 2

Divide the denominator into 10 or one of its powers.

Since 6 will not divide exactly into 10, 100, 1000, . . . , the decimal will not end.

Step 3

$$6 \overline{)5.00} \atop \begin{array}{r} 833\ldots \\ \hline \end{array}$$

$$\begin{array}{r} 833\ldots \\ 6\overline{)5.00} \\ \underline{4\,8} \\ 20 \\ \underline{18} \\ 20 \\ \underline{18} \\ 2 \end{array}$$

Divide the denominator into the numerator.

Add zeros to the right of the decimal point in the dividend, until the decimal begins to repeat.

Step 4

Position the decimal point.

We can use approximation to check on the final location of the decimal point. $6 \div 5$ is close to $6 \div 6$, which is 1. Our answer should be close to 1, which it is.

$$\frac{10}{12} = 0.833\ldots$$

WRITING DECIMALS AS FRACTIONS

Not all decimals can be rewritten as fractions. All decimals, however, can be approximated by fractions.

Decimals which end and decimals which continue without end but repeat can be written exactly as fractions.

PROBLEM 88.
Write 2.56 as a fraction.

Step 1

Expand the decimal (write in expanded notation).

$2.56 = 2$ ones $+ 5$ tenths $+ 6$ hundredths

$2.56 = 2 + \dfrac{5}{10} + \dfrac{6}{100}$

Step 2

Add the numbers.

$$2 + \frac{5}{10} + \frac{6}{100} = \frac{200}{100} + \frac{50}{100} + \frac{6}{100} = \frac{256}{100}$$

Step 3

$$\frac{256}{100} = \frac{64}{25}$$

Reduce the fraction.

PROBLEM 89.
Write 1.376376 . . . as a fraction.

Step 1

Count the number of places in the part of the decimal which repeats.

Since 376 repeats, there are 3 places.

Step 2

Multiply the decimal by ten raised to that power.

3 places means 10^3 or $10 \times 10 \times 10$.

$1.376376\ldots \times 10 \times 10 \times 10$
$$= 1376.376\ldots$$

Step 3

$$\begin{array}{r} 1376.376\ldots \\ -\quad 1.376376\ldots \\ \hline 1375. \end{array}$$

Subtract the smaller decimal from the larger.

Step 4

Divide the result by the power of 10 used in **Step 2** (10^3) minus one.

$$(10 \times 10 \times 10) - 1 = 999$$
$$1375 \div 999 = \frac{1375}{999}$$

Hand-held calculators

Hand-held calculators are so inexpensive that most families and many schools now have them. These calculators make problems with addition, subtraction, multiplication, and division very easy. They are also used to solve problems involving decimals and percents.

Although no two calculators look exactly alike, all have common characteristics (keys) and the arithmetic is performed in the same way on all of them. Problems involving decimals are solved in the same way as problems involving whole numbers. The only difference is that the decimal point key must be depressed when needed.

Simple addition, subtraction, multiplica-

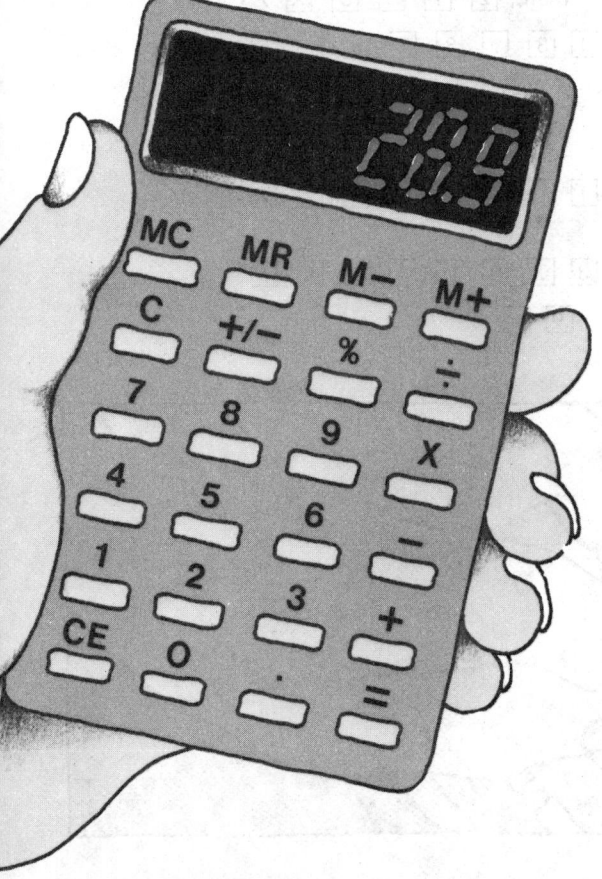

tion, and division problems are solved by depressing the correct keys for the numbers operations, or symbols. A more complicated problem must be broken down into a series of simpler problems.

The c key on the calculator is used to clear the calculator of all previous entries. On some calculators it is also used to turn the calculator on.

The ce key on the calculator is used to clear only the last key depressed. This key is used if a mistake has been made.

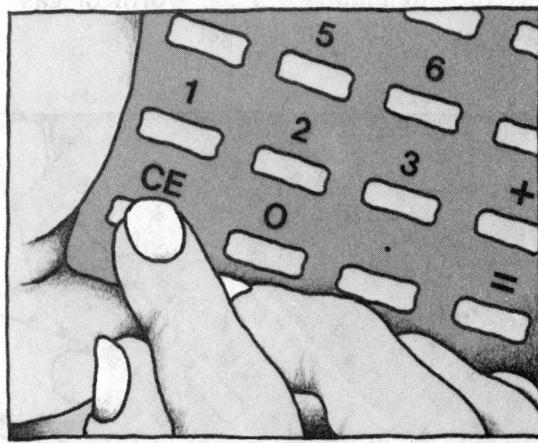

The chart on the next page illustrates some of the kinds of problems which can be done on hand-held calculators.

To solve the following problems on a hand-held calculator:

Depress in order the following keys. The symbol △, which is shown in some examples, indicates a partial answer.

$7 + 6 + 5$ [7] [+] [6] [+] [5] [=]

$18 - 4$ [1] [8] [−] [4] [=]

3×7 [3] [×] [7] [=]

$1.86 \div 3$ [1] [.] [8] [6] [÷] [3] [=]

5% of 18   [.] [0] [5] [×] [1] [8] [=]

9^5 [9] [×] [9] [×] [9] [×] [9] [×] [9] [=]

$(3 + 7) \div (10 - 2)$ [1] [0] [−] [2] [=] △ [c]
then, [3] [+] [7] [÷] △ [=]

$(21 - 6) \times (3 + 5)$ [3] [+] [5] [=] △ [c]
then, [2] [1] [−] [6] [×] △ [=]

$13.876 - 5.934$ [1] [3] [.] [8] [7] [6] [−] [5]
[.] [9] [3] [4] [=]

If 454 grams of peanuts costs $1.39, how much does each gram cost?

[1] [.] [3] [9] [÷] [4] [5] [4] [=]

A liter of gasoline costs 15.9 cents. You ask the attendant for $3.00 worth of gas. How many liters do you get?

[3] [.] [0] [0] [÷] [.] [1] [5]
[9] [=]

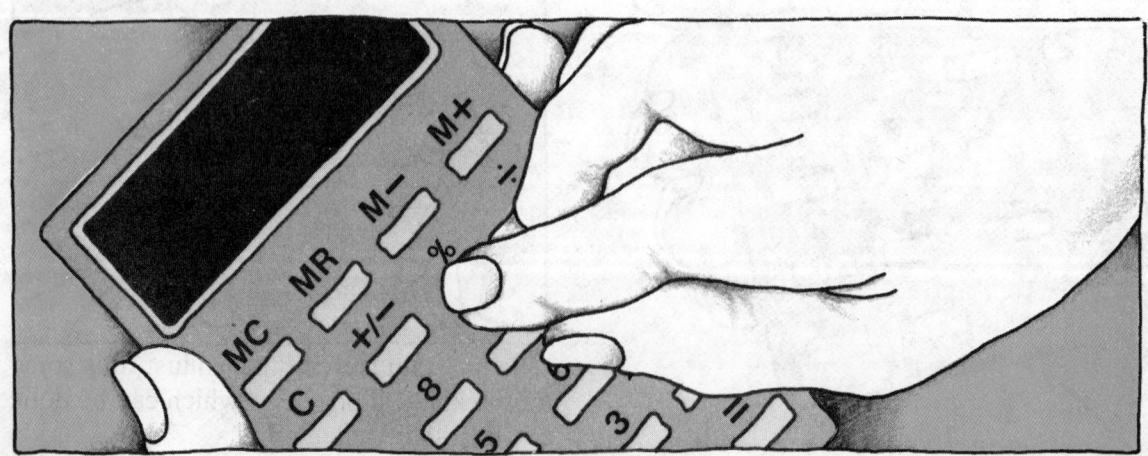

LIST OF SYMBOLS

a^n	**a** to the **n**th power		$\leq$	is less than or equal to
$\lvert a \rvert$	absolute value of **a**		$\overleftrightarrow{AB}$	line **AB**
$+$	addition		m(AB)	measure (length) of segment **AB**
$-a$	additive inverse of **a**		m $\angle a$	measure (number of degrees) of angle **a**
$\angle a$	angle **a**			
$\angle ABC$	angle **ABC**		$\times$ or $\cdot$	multiplication
$\doteq$ or $\approx$	approximately equal		-3	a negative number
A-B-C	**B** is between **A** and **C**		$\sim$ $\sqrt[n]{\ }$	not, or it is false that the **n**th root of a number
$\wedge$	conjunction (and)			
$\ldots$	continues unendingly		n(A)	number of elements (members) of set **A**
$\cdot$	decimal point			
$\vee$	disjunction (or)		$\parallel$	parallel
$\div$	division		$\%$	per cent
$\in$	is an element (member) of		$\perp$	perpendicular
$\notin$	is not an element (member) of		$+3$	a positive number
$\varnothing$	empty set		n'	**n** prime
$=$	equals		$\subset$	proper subset of
$\neq$	does not equal		$\overrightarrow{AB}$	ray **AB** (vector **AB**)
$\leftrightarrows$	equivalent to (in one-to-one correspondence with)		a^{-1}	reciprocal of **a** $\left(\text{i.e.,}\ \dfrac{1}{a}\right)$
$\rightarrow$	if, . . . then . . . , or implies		$\llcorner$	right angle
$>$	is greater than		$\overline{AB}$	segment **AB**
$\geq$	is greater than or equal to		$\{\ \}$	set
i	$\sqrt{-1}$ ($i^2 = -1$) imaginary number		$\subseteq$	subset of
			n_3	subscript (**n** sub **3**)
$\cap$	intersection		$-$	subtraction
$<$	is less than		$\cup$	union

GLOSSARY OF TERMS USED IN MATHEMATICS

addend. The numbers that are added together in addition. In the equation $3 + 2 = 5$, the numbers 3 and 2 are addends.

angle. A figure formed by two lines or rays diverging from a common point, called the vertex.

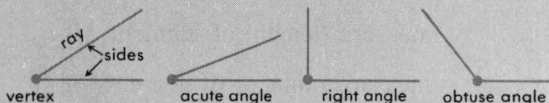

vertex   acute angle   right angle   obtuse angle

area. A two-dimensional measure of the surface inside a plan (flat) geometric figure. The area of this figure is 12 square units.

circumference. The total length of the distance around a circle.

denominator. In a fraction, the quantity below the fraction bar. The denominator in the fraction $\frac{2}{3}$ is 3.

dividend. In division, the quantity that is to be divided. In the division problem, $36 \div 9 = 4$, the dividend is 36.

divisor. The quantity by which the dividend is divided. In the division problem, $36 \div 9 = 4$, the divisor is 9.

element. Any member of a set. The set $\{11, 12, 13\}$ has three elements: 11, 12, and 13.

numerator. In a fraction, the quantity above the fraction bar. In the fraction $\frac{3}{4}$, 3 is the numerator.

quotient. The result of a division problem. In the division problem $36 \div 9 = 4$, the quotient is 4.

product. The result of a multiplication problem.

$4 \times 5 = 20$ In this multiplication problem, the product is 20.

factors. In multiplication, the numbers that are multiplied together.

$7 \times 8 = 56$ In this multiplication problem, 7 and 8 are factors.

sum. The answer to an addition problem.

$$\begin{array}{r} 2 \\ +\ 3 \\ \hline 5 \end{array}$$

In this addition problem, the sum is 5.

set. A collection or group, made up of elements. The elements of a set may be numbers, objects, or any other thing that can be collected. A set is usually shown as $\{1, 2, 3, 4\}$, where the elements of the set are placed inside brackets.

SCIENCE

Men and women of science devote themselves to acquiring basic information that may eventually help us conquer disease, increase food supplies, and unravel the secrets of weather, energy, and other vital forces that shape our lives.

Like America's Thomas Edison, we should all strive toward a better understanding of how and why nature behaves as it does. As we move to the end of the present century, science will play an ever-greater role in our daily activities, making it increasingly important for us to learn as much about it as we can. In the following pages you will find valuable information on chemistry, physics, and life science. To help you even more, the section after this one deals with earth and space science, and the Concise Edition of the *Student Handbook* supplies more advanced information on biology, chemistry, and physics.

Chemistry and Physics

WHAT IS SCIENCE?

For many thousands of years, human beings scarcely changed the way they lived. Then, only about four hundred years ago, a great change occurred in the way people lived and in the way they thought about the world and themselves.

The reason for this sudden change was that science began to develop. The development was slow at first, but then became quite rapid. As science and applied science —technology—have developed faster and faster, they have become the main shaping forces in today's world. They have given us enormous power, which can be very beneficial or very dangerous, depending on our wisdom in using it. They have also brought us an understanding of the world around us and of the nature of life. This understanding was impossible for even the wisest of people in prescientific days. The necessary facts were not then available.

People began to ask questions about nature and were not satisfied with the explanations given in ancient books or by people thought of as wise.

The early scientists demanded proof. They tested theories, whenever they could, by performing experiments. They made the results public, so other scientists could think about the results and repeat the experiments if they wished. All this is part of the scientific attitude, which demands facts, reasoning, and experimentation whenever possible. This, in essence, is the *scientific method*. By using this method, scientists have transformed our world.

SUBJECTS COVERED BY CHEMISTRY AND PHYSICS

Chemistry studies the substances that are found in nature and the ways in which new substances are formed. A change in a substance is a *chemical change* only if new substances are formed. Cutting a sheet of paper into shreds is not a chemical change because the shreds are still paper. Burning paper is a chemical change, because new substances are formed, such as carbon dioxide and water. The simplest possible chemical substance is called an *element*. At present, 105 elements are known.

Inorganic chemistry deals with the chemical changes of all the elements except carbon, which is considered separately.

Organic chemistry deals with compounds of the element carbon. Carbon is unique because it forms more *compounds* (chemical substances) than all the other elements combined. Living organisms depend on organic chemistry for their life processes.

Biochemistry deals with the chemical changes that take place in living things, such as the digestion of food.

Analytical chemistry tries to find out what compounds are present in unknown samples and how much of each compound is present.

Physical chemistry studies chemical changes from a more basic point of view. It asks questions like: Why does one chemical reaction take place much faster than another? Why does one chemical reaction produce a great deal of heat, while another produces little or none?

Physics deals with energy and the way it changes from one form to another. It also studies the basic nature of the physical world. It is easy to understand why physics was once called "natural philosophy." Physics is subdivided into six branches:

1. *Mechanics* is concerned with the laws that govern the motion of bodies, and with the forces that act on bodies.

2. *Heat* is concerned with the energy that is due to the random motion of molecules, and with the ways in which this energy can be put to use.

3. *Sound* is concerned with the nature of wave motion to which our ears are sensitive.

4. *Electricity and magnetism* are concerned with the laws that govern the attraction or repulsion of substances having electric charges. The laws of electricity in motion, and the laws of magnetic attraction and repulsion, which are closely connected with the electricity in motion, are also included in the study of these subjects.

5. *Electromagnetic radiation* is concerned with wave motion that includes light, ultraviolet, X rays, infrared, microwaves, and radio.

6. *"Modern"* physics is concerned with such topics as the theory of relativity, radioactivity, nuclear energy, quantum theory, and the nature of the atom. Modern physics is growing rapidly.

Albert Einstein (1879–1955) is considered one of the greatest scientists of all time. His brilliant insights and formulations served as the basis for much modern research in physics. Born in Germany, he fled to the United States to escape persecution by the Nazis. Although an ardent pacifist, Einstein helped the United States in the conquest of the Axis powers.

IMPORTANT EVENTS IN CHEMISTRY AND PHYSICS

Date	Scientist	Accomplishment
c. 500 B.C.	Leucippus (exact dates unknown), Greek philosopher.	Believed that every natural event had a natural cause. Helped develop the atomic theory of matter.
c. 400 B.C.	Democritus (c. 460–c. 370 B.C.), Greek philosopher.	A student of Leucippus. Developed the atomic theory of matter with Leucippus.
c. 300 B.C.	Archimedes (c. 287–c. 212 B.C.), Greek mathematician and physicist.	Discovered the laws of floating bodies, establishing the science of hydrostatics.
1556	Georg Bauer; in Latin, Georgius Agricola (1494–1555), German mineralogist.	Published De re metallica which established the science of mineralogy.
1582–92	Galileo Galilei (1564–1642), Italian mathematician, physicist, and astronomer.	One of the first to make a scientific study of the motion of bodies.
1600	William Gilbert (1540–1603), English physicist.	Published De magnete, magneticisque corporibus, which established the basis for future work on gravitational theory.
1643	Evangelista Torricelli (1608–1647), Italian physicist and mathematician.	Proved that air has weight; invented the barometer.
1661–62	Robert Boyle (1627–1691), English scientist.	Discovered the laws governing the relationship between pressure and volume of gases. Formulated the difference between a chemical element and a chemical compound.
1676	Olaus Römer (1644–1710), Danish astronomer.	Measured the velocity of light for the first time.
1677	Christian Huygens (1629–1695), Dutch mathematician, astronomer, physicist.	Developed the wave theory of light.
1687	Isaac Newton (1642–1727), English physicist and mathematician.	Published his Principia setting forth the three laws of motion and the law of universal gravitation.
1724	Gabriel Daniel Fahrenheit (1686–1736), German physicist.	Published his Philosophical Transactions, which outlined his work in thermometry.
1729	Stephen Gray (1667–1736), English physicist.	Showed that some substances are conductors of electricity and others are insulators.

IMPORTANT EVENTS IN CHEMISTRY AND PHYSICS (continued)

Date	Scientist	Accomplishment
1733	Charles François de Cisternay du Fay (1698–1739), French physicist.	Formulated the basic laws of electrical charges and showed the difference between positive and negative charges.
1774	Joseph Priestley (1733–1804), English chemist.	Discovered oxygen as a chemical element.
1785	Charles Augustin de Coulomb (1736–1806), French physicist.	Formulated the basic law of electrostatics by measuring the forces between electric charges.
1787	Jacques Alexandre César Charles (1746–1823), French physicist.	Discovered the relation between temperature and volume for a gas at a constant pressure.
1789	Antoine Laurent Lavoisier (1743–1794), French scientist.	Studied the chemical changes involved in combustion.
1799	Joseph Louis Proust (1754–1826), French chemist.	Formulated the law of definite proportions between the elements and compounds.
1800	Count Alessandro Volta (1745–1827), Italian physicist.	Discovered how to produce an electric current and made the first primary wet cell.
1803	John Dalton (1766–1844), English chemist and physicist.	Rediscovered the atomic nature of matter.
1809	Joseph Louis Gay-Lussac (1778–1850), French chemist and physicist.	Discovered the laws governing the volumes of gases in chemical combinations.
1811	Amedeo Avogadro (1776–1856), Italian physicist.	Discovered the law that equal volumes of gases at the same temperature and pressure contain equal numbers of molecules.
1820	Hans Christian Oersted (1777–1851), Danish chemist and physicist.	Discovered electromagnetism.
1822	André Marie Ampère (1775–1836), French mathematician and physicist.	One of the first to understand the phenomenon of electrical current.
1826	Baron Jöns Jacob Berzelius (1779–1848), Swedish chemist.	Developed the table of atomic weights.
1827	Georg Simon Ohm (1787–1854), German physicist.	Showed how electrical resistance, current, and voltage are related.
1828	Friedrich Wöhler (1800–1882), German chemist.	The first to synthesize an organic compound from inorganic matter.

Date	Scientist	Accomplishment
1831	Michael Faraday (1791–1867), English chemist and physicist.	Discovered principle of electric motor and generator
1840s	Julius R. von Mayer (1814–1878), German physicist.	A formulator of the first law of thermodynamics (the conservation of energy).
1840s	James Prescott Joule (1818–1889), English physicist.	A formulator of the first law of thermodynamics (the conservation of energy).
1840s	Hermann L. F. von Helmholtz (1821–1894), German scientist.	A formulator of the first law of thermodynamics (the conservation of energy).
1850	Rudolf J. E. Clausius (1822–1888), German physicist.	Formulated the second law of thermodynamics (the law of entropy).
1850s	Gustav R. Kirchhoff (1824–1887), German physicist.	One of the men who established the science of spectroscopy.
1850s	Robert W. Bunsen (1811–1899), German chemist.	One of the men who established the science of spectroscopy.
1861	Friedrich A. Kekulé (1829–1896), German chemist.	Established the science of organic chemistry as the study of carbon compounds.
1864	James C. Maxwell (1831–1879), English physicist.	Formulated the theory of electromagnetic radiation.
1869	Dmitri I. Mendeleev (1834–1907), Russian chemist.	Developed the periodic table of the elements.
1876–78	Josiah Willard Gibbs (1839–1903), U.S. physicist.	Adapted the laws of thermodynamics to chemistry.

Jöns Jakob Berzelius   James Clerk Maxwell   Josiah Willard Gibbs   Savante Arrhenius

Date	Scientist	Accomplishment
1884	Svante A. Arrhenius (1859–1927), Swedish chemist.	Developed the concept of ionization.
1887	Henri Louis Le Chatelier (1850–1936), French chemist.	Formulated laws governing chemical equilibrium.
1887	Heinrich R. Hertz (1857–1894), German physicist.	Discovered principle of radio transmission and reception.
1895	Wilhelm K. Roentgen (1845–1923), German physicist.	Discovered the X ray.
1896	Antoine H. Becquerel (1852–1908), French physicist.	Discovered radioactivity.
1897	Sir Joseph J. Thomson (1856–1940), English physicist.	Discovered the electron.
1898–99	Sir James Dewar (1842–1923), Scottish physicist.	The first to liquefy and solidify hydrogen.
1900	Max Planck (1858–1947), German physicist.	Formulated the quantum theory.
1901	Jacobus Hendricus Van't Hoff (1852–1911), Dutch physicist.	Explained optical rotation of organic compounds. Applied thermodynamics to solutions.
1903	Ernest Rutherford (1871–1937), English chemist.	Explained the nature of radioactive disintegration.
1903	Marie Curie (1867–1934) and Pierre Curie (1859–1906), French physicists.	Did research on radioactive phenomena, which led to their discovery of polonium and radium.

Antoine Becquerel

Max Planck

Ernest Rutherford

Enrico Fermi

SCIENCE

Date	Scientist	Accomplishment
1905–16	Albert Einstein (1879–1955), U.S. physicist.	Developed the general and special theories of relativity.
1911	Charles T. R. Wilson (1869–1959), British physicist.	Built the first cloud chamber for viewing nuclear particles.
1910–22	Francis William Aston (1877–1945), English chemist and physicist.	Developed the mass spectroscope to study the structure of molecules; with it he discovered chemical isotopes.
1912–15	Sir William H. Bragg (1862–1942), English physicist.	Developed the X-ray spectrometer to study the structure of crystals.
1913	Henry G. J. Moseley (1887–1915), English physicist.	Established that the atomic number of an element is equal to the charge of the nucleus.
1913	Niels H. D. Bohr (1885–1962), Danish physicist.	Formulated the concept of the planetary atom.
1923	Arthur Holly Compton (1892–1962), U.S. physicist.	Discovered the change in the wavelengths of X rays when scattered by matter (the Compton effect).
1924	Louis V. de Broglie (1892–), French physicist.	Discovered the wave nature of the electron.
1925	Werner Heisenberg (1901–), German physicist.	Formulated the uncertainty principle in atomic physics.
1926	Erwin Schrodinger (1887–1961), German physicist.	Developed wave theory of quantum mechanics.
1931	Wolfgang Pauli (1900–1958), German physicist.	Developed the exclusion principle in quantum mechanics, which led him to postulate the existence of the neutrino.
1932	Carl D. Anderson (1905–), U.S. physicist, and James Chadwick (1891–1974), English physicist.	Discovered the positron.
1932	Ernest Thomas Sinton Walton (1903–), Irish physicist, and Sir J. D. Cockcroft (1897–1967), English physicist.	Built the first high-energy particle accelerator.

IMPORTANT EVENTS IN CHEMISTRY AND PHYSICS (continued)

Date	Scientist	Accomplishment
1934	Enrico Fermi (1901–1954), U.S. physicist.	Bombarded uranium with neutrons and produced new elements.
1947	Willard F. Libby (1908–), U.S. chemist.	Developed carbon-14 dating of organic matter.
1948	John Bardeen (1908–), American physicist.	Invented transistor with Shockley and Brattain.
1954	Linus Carl Pauling (1901–), U.S. chemist.	Studied nature of the chemical bond, investigated structure of proteins.
1955	Emilio G. Segre (1905–), U.S. physicist, and Owen Chamberlain (1920–), U.S. physicist.	Produced and detected the antiproton.
1964	C. H. Townes (1915–), American physicist.	Worked out the principles of the maser and laser.
1964	R. B. Woodward (1917–), American chemist.	Achieved total synthesis of chlorophyll.
1969	Murray Gell-Mann (1929–), American physicist.	Developed theory of subatomic particles.
1971	Dennis Gabor (1900–), Hungarian inventor.	Invented holographic photography.
1977	Rosalind Yalow (1922–), American chemist.	Devised radio-immune assay procedure.

Willard F. Libby

Linus G. Pauling

Charles H. Townes

Rosalind Yalow

METRIC WEIGHTS AND MEASURES

Lengths

1 centimeter (cm.) = 10 millimeters (mm.)
1 decimeter (dm.) = 10 centimeters
1 meter (m.) = 10 decimeters
1 dekameter (dkm.) = 10 meters
1 hectometer (hm.) = 10 dekameters
1 kilometer (km.) = 10 hectometers = 1,000 meters

Areas

1 square centimeter = 100 square millimeters
1 square meter = 10,000 square centimeters
1 square kilometer = 1,000,000 square meters

Volumes

1 centiliter (cl.) = 10 milliliters (ml.)
1 deciliter (dl.) = 10 centiliters
1 liter (l.) = 10 deciliters = 1,000 milliliters
   = 0.001 cubic meter
1 dekaliter (dkl.) = 10 liters
1 hectoliter (hl.) = 10 dekaliters
1 kiloliter (kl.) = 10 hectoliters = 1,000 liters
1 cubic centimeter = 1,000 cubic millimeters
1 cubic meter = 1,000,000 cubic centimeters

Weights

1 centigram (cg.) = 10 milligrams (mg.)
1 decigram (dg.) = 10 centigrams
1 gram (g.) = 10 decigrams
1 dekagram (dkg.) = 10 grams
1 hectogram (hg.) = 10 dekagrams
1 kilogram (kg.) = 10 hectograms = 1,000 grams
1 metric ton (t.) = 1,000 kilograms

EQUIVALENTS

1 acre = 43,560 square feet = 4,840 square yards
1 angstrom = 0.1 millimicron = 0.0001 micron = 0.0000001 millimeter = 0.000000004 inch = 10^{-10} meter
1 assay ton = 29.167 grams
1 bushel (U.S.) = 2,150.42 cubic inches = 35.239 liters = 4 pecks = 32 quarts
1 carat = 200 milligrams = 3.086 grains
1 centimeter = 0.3937 inch
1 cord = 128 cubic feet
1 cubic centimeter = 0.061 cubic inch
1 cubic decimeter = 61.024 cubic inches
1 cubic foot = 7.481 gallons = 1,728 cubic inches
1 cubic inch = 0.554 fluid ounce = 4.433 fluid drams = 16.387 cubic centimeters
1 cubic meter = 1.308 cubic yards
1 cubic yard = 0.765 cubic meter = 27 cubic feet
1 cup, measuring = 8 fluid ounces = ½ liquid pint
1 decimeter = 3.937 inches
1 dekaliter = 2.642 gallons = 1.135 pecks
1 dekameter = 32.808 feet
1 dram, fluid or liquid (U.S.) = ⅛ fluid ounce = 0.226 cubic inch = 3.697 milliliters
1 fathom = 6 feet = 1.8288 meters
1 foot = 0.3048 meter = 12 inches
1 furlong = 660 feet = ⅛ statute mile = 201.169 meters

1 gallon (U.S.) = 231 cubic inches = 3.785 liters = 0.833 British gallon = 128 U.S. fluid ounces
        = 4 liquid quarts

1 grain = 64.79891 milligrams

1 gram = 15.432 grains = 0.035 ounce, avoirdupois

1 hand = 4 inches

1 inch = 2.54 centimeters

1 kilogram = 2.205 pounds

1 kilometer = 0.621 mile

1 league (land) = 3 statute miles = 4.828 kilometers

1 liter = 1.057 liquid quarts = 0.908 dry quart = 61.024 cubic inches

1 meter = 39.37 inches = 1.094 yards

1 microgram = 0.000001 gram

1 micron = 0.001 millimeter = 0.00003937 inch

1 mile, statute = 5,280 feet = 1.609 kilometers

1 mile, nautical = 1.852 kilometers = 1.151 statute miles = 6,076.1155 feet

1 milligram = 0.015 grain

1 milliliter = 0.271 fluid dram = 0.061 cubic inch

1 millimeter = 0.03937 inch

1 millimicron = 0.001 micron = 0.00000003937 inch

1 ounce, avoirdupois = 437.5 grains = 0.911 troy ounce = 28.350 grams

1 ounce, troy or apothecaries = 480 grains = 1.097 avoirdupois ounces = 31.103 grams

1 peck = 8.810 liters = ¼ bushel (U.S.) = 8 quarts = 16 pints

1 pint, dry = 33.600 cubic inches = 0.551 liter

1 pint, liquid = 28.875 cubic inches = 0.473 liter = 2 cups = 16 ounces

1 point = 0.01 carat = 2 milligrams

1 point (typography) = 0.013837 inch = $1/72$ inch = 0.351 millimeter

1 pound, avoirdupois = 7,000 grains = 16 ounces = 1.215 troy or apothecaries
        pounds = 453.59237 grams

1 pound, troy or apothecaries = 5,760 grains = 0.823 avoirdupois pound
        = 373.242 grams

1 quart, dry (U.S.) = 67.201 cubic inches = 1.101 liters

1 quart, liquid (U.S.) = 57.75 cubic inches = 0.946 liter = 2 pints = 32 ounces

1 rod = 16½ feet = 5½ yards = 5.0292 meters

1 square centimeter = 0.155 square inch

1 square decimeter = 15.5 square inches

1 square foot = 929 square centimeters = 144 square inches

1 square inch = 6.45 square centimeters

1 square kilometer = 0.386 square mile = 247.105 acres

1 square meter = 1.196 square yards = 10.764 square feet

1 square mile = 640 acres

1 square millimeter = 0.00155 square inch

1 square rod = 25.293 square meters = 272.25 square feet = 30.25 square yards

1 square yard = 0.836 square meter = 9 square feet = 1,296 square inches

1 tablespoon = 3 teaspoons = 4 fluid drams = ½ fluid ounce

1 teaspoon = ⅓ tablespoon = 1⅓ fluid drams

1 ton, gross or long = 2,240 pounds = 1.12 net tons = 1.016 metric tons

1 ton, metric = 2,204.623 pounds = 0.984 gross ton = 1.102 net tons

1 ton, net or short = 2,000 pounds = 0.907 metric ton = 0.893 gross ton

1 yard = 0.9144 meter = 3 feet = 36 inches

CONVERSION TABLE

to convert	into	multiply by
acres	square feet	43,560.0
acres	square miles	0.001562
ampere-hours	coulombs	3,600.0
angstroms	microns	0.0001
BTUs	kilocalories	0.252
centimeters	feet	0.03281
centimeters	inches	0.3937
cubic centimeters	cubic inches	0.06102
cubic centimeters	pints (liq.)	0.002113
cubic feet	cubic meters	0.02832
cubits	inches	18.0
days	seconds	86,400.0
degrees (angle)	radians	0.01745
em, pica	inches	0.167
ergs	kilowatt-hours	2.778×10^{-14}
fathoms	feet	6.0
feet	centimeters	30.48
feet	meters	0.3048
feet	miles (nautical)	1.645×10^{-4}
feet	miles (statute)	1.894×10^{-4}
feet/min.	centimeters/sec.	0.5080
feet/sec.	knots	0.5921
feet/sec.	statute miles/hr.	0.6818
furlongs/hr.	statute miles/hr.	0.125
furlongs	feet	660.0
gallons (liq.)	liters	3.785
gallons of water	pounds of water	8.3453
grams	ounces (avoirdupois)	0.03527
grams	ounces (troy)	0.03215
grams	pounds	0.002205
hand	centimeters	10.16
hours	days	0.04167
hours	weeks	0.005952
inches	centimeters	2.540

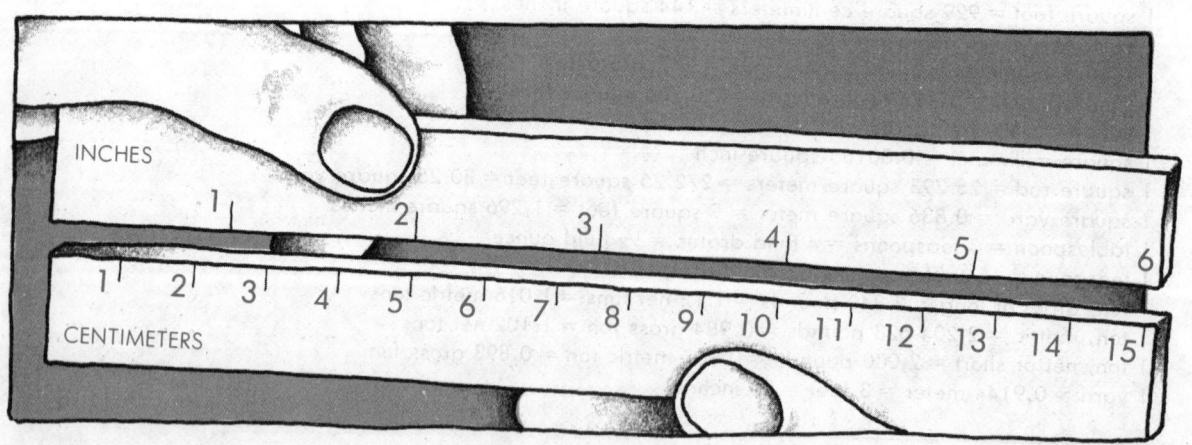

CONVERSION TABLE (continued)

to convert	into	multiply by
inches	miles (statute)	1.578×10^{-5}
joules	ergs	1×10^{7}
kilograms	pounds	2.205
kilometers	feet	3,280.8
kilometers	miles (statute)	0.6214
knots	feet/hr.	6,080.0
knots	nautical miles/hr.	1.0
knots	statute miles/hr.	1.151
league	miles (statute)	3.0
light year	miles (statute)	5.9×10^{12}
liters	cubic centimeters	1,000.0
liters	cubic inches	61.025
liters	gallons (liq.)	0.2642
liters	pints (liq.)	2.113
meters	feet	3.281
meters	miles (nautical)	5.396×10^{-4}
meters	miles (statute)	6.214×10^{-4}
microns	meters	0.000001
miles (nautical)	feet	6,076.115
miles (statute)	feet	5,280.0
miles (nautical)	kilometers	1.852
miles (statute)	kilometers	1.609
miles (nautical)	miles (statute)	1.1508
miles (statute)	miles (nautical)	0.8684
miles (statute)/hr.	feet/min.	88.0
millimeters	inches	0.03937
ounces (avoirdupois)	grams	28.3495
ounces (avoirdupois)	pounds (avoirdupois)	0.0625
ounces (troy)	ounces (avoirdupois)	1.09714
pints (liq.)	cubic centimeters	473.2
pints (liq.)	cubic inches	28.875
pints (liq.)	gallons (liq.)	0.125
pints (liq.)	quarts (liq.)	0.5
pounds (avoirdupois)	kilograms	0.4536

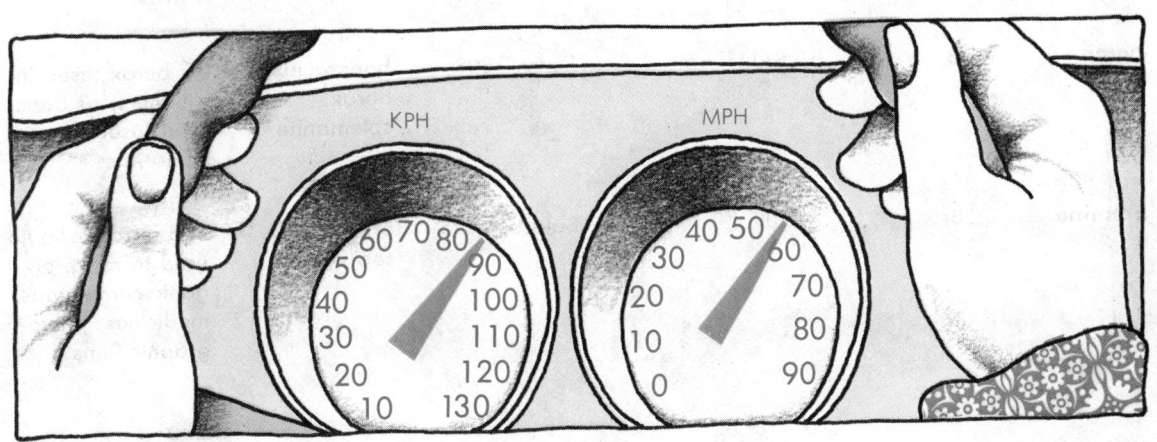

FACTS ABOUT SOME IMPORTANT ELEMENTS

All matter is made up of 105 known elements which combine with one another to form immense numbers of chemical compounds. In the table below, important properties of the commonest elements and the industrially most important elements are listed. The *atomic weight* is the mass of the atom compared with carbon 12, an isotope of carbon that has been assigned the value 12. The *atomic number* is the number of protons in the nucleus of the atom. Atomic number is the most important factor in determining the chemical properties of the element.

Element	Symbol	Atomic Weight	Atomic Number	Discovery	Occurrence	Properties, uses
aluminum	Al	26.9815	13	Oersted, 1825	cryolite, bauxite, clays	White metal, used in construction where light weight is important. As oxide, used as abrasive.
antimony	Sb	121.75	51	ancient times	native or in stibnite	Brittle metal used in bearings.
arsenic	As	74.92	33	ancient times	native or as sulfide, arsenate	Gray, brittle semi-metal, used in pesticides, lead shot, war gases.
bismuth	Bi	208.98	83	ancient times	native or as sulfide	Brittle metal used in electric fuses, fire sprinkler systems, safety valves.
boron	B	10.811	5	Davy, 1808	boric acid, borax, colemanite	As borax, used in cleaners; as boric acid, used in antiseptics.
bromine	Br	79.909	35	Balard, 1826	brine wells, sea water	Red corrosive liquid used to make organic compounds, medicines, photographic films.

FACTS ABOUT SOME IMPORTANT ELEMENTS (continued)

Element	Symbol	Atomic Weight	Atomic Number	Discovery	Occurrence	Properties, uses
cadmium	Cd	112.40	48	Stromeyer, 1817	zinc ores	Blue-white metal used in electroplating, bearings, batteries, atomic reactors
calcium	Ca	40.08	20	Davy, 1808	limestone, gypsum	Silvery, active metal. Compounds used in mortar, plaster, cement, agriculture.
carbon	C	12.011	6	ancient times	Carbon dioxide in air, carbonates, petroleum, coal. Free as diamond, graphite	Black or transparent nonmetal. As diamond, used in jewelry, abrasives; as graphite, in lubricants. Forms innumerable compounds. Basis of all life.
chlorine	Cl	35.453	17	Scheele, 1774	sea water, salt deposits	Green corrosive gas. Used in bleach, germicides, drugs, manufacture of organic chemicals.
chromium	Cr	51.996	24	Vauquelin, 1797	chromite ore	Hard white metal used in electroplating, stainless steel. Compounds used in tanning, paints.
cobalt	Co	58.933	27	Brandt, 1735	sulfide or arsenide ores	Brittle metal used in stainless steel, electroplating. As oxide, gives blue color to glass, enamel.

Element	Symbol	Atomic Weight	Atomic Number	Discovery	Occurrence	Properties, uses
copper	Cu	63.54	29	ancient times	native, or as oxide, sulfide, carbonate	Reddish metal used as electrical conductor, to make brass, bronze, other alloys. Compounds used in water purification.
fluorine	F	18.9984	9	Moissan, 1886	fluorspar, cryolite	Yellow gas, very corrosive. Used to make refrigerants, plastics. As hydrofluoric acid, etches glass.
gold	Au	196.97	79	ancient times	native, or telluride ores	Yellow metal, used in coins, jewelry, dentistry.
helium	He	4.003	2	Ramsay, 1895	well gas, air	Inert gas, used in balloons.
hydrogen	H	1.008	1	Cavendish, 1766	water, petroleum	Gas used for heat, to make ammonia, many chemical processes.
iodine	I	126.90	53	Courtois, 1811	sea water, brines, saltpeter	Black solid, used as germicide, for organic chemicals, photography.
iron	Fe	55.85	26	ancient times	hematite, magnetite, many other ores	White, hard metal. Chief component of steel. Compounds used in medicine, blueprints.
lead	Pb	207.21	82	ancient times	galena, silver ores	White metal used in plumbing, solder, type metal, batteries. Compounds used as pigments.

FACTS ABOUT SOME IMPORTANT ELEMENTS (continued)

Element	Symbol	Atomic Weight	Atomic Number	Discovery	Occurrence	Properties, uses
lithium	Li	6.940	3	Arfvedson, 1817	lepidolite, spodumene	Light, very active metal. Salts used in medicine, fireworks.
magnesium	Mg	24.32	12	H. Davy, 1808	magnesite, dolomite	Light, white metal, used to make light alloys for airplanes. Salts used in medicine.
manganese	Mn	54.938	25	Gahn, 1774	pyrolusite, braunite, hausmannite, other ores	Gray-white, brittle metal. Used in stainless steel, other alloys.
mercury	Hg	200.59	80	ancient times	native, or as cinnabar	Liquid, silvery metal, used in thermometers, barometers, other instruments. Alloys called amalgams, used in dentistry. Salts used in pigments.
molybdenum	Mo	95.94	42	Scheele, 1778	molybdenite, wulfenite	Hard, white metal, used in tool steels, boiler plate, radio tubes.
neon	Ne	20.183	10	Ramsay, 1898	air	Inert gas used in electric signs.
nickel	Ni	58.71	28	Cronstedt, 1751	pyrrhotite, nickel glance	Hard, white metal, used in stainless steel, coins, many alloys, electroplating, as catalyst.
nitrogen	N	14.007	7	Rutherford, 1772	main ingredient of air	Colorless gas, used to make ammonia, nitric acid, many organic compounds.

Element	Symbol	Atomic Weight	Atomic Number	Discovery	Occurrence	Properties, uses
oxygen	O	15.999	8	Priestley, 1774	air, water	colorless gas, essential for life, used in oxyacetylene flames, aid to respiration.
palladium	Pd	106.4	46	Wollaston, 1803	platinum ores	White, hard metal used in jewelry, instruments, catalyst in chemical processes.
phosphorus	P	30.98	15	Brand, 1669	apatite, bones, teeth	Yellow, waxy form; red, crystalline form. Compounds used in fertilizer, detergents.
platinum	Pt	195.09	78	Scaliger, 1557	native, or as arsenide	Silvery metal used in jewelry, instruments, laboratory ware, catalysts.
potassium	K	39.096	19	Davy, 1807	sea water, salt mines	Soft, silvery, very active metal. Salts used in fertilizers, medicine.
radium	Ra	226.05	88	Curie, 1898	pitchblende, uranium ores	Radioactive metal, used in medicine, to make luminous watch dials.
selenium	Se	78.96	34	Berzelius, 1817	flue dust of industrial processes	Red, amorphous or gray, semimetallic, used in photocells, ceramics.
silicon	Si	28.086	14	Berzelius, 1823	very abundant in earth's crust	Brown nonmetal. Compounds used in glass, cement, ceramics, photoelectric cells.

Element	Symbol	Atomic Weight	Atomic Number	Discovery	Occurrence	Properties, uses
silver	Ag	107.870	47	ancient times	native or as sulfide, chloride	White metal, used in jewelry, coins, photography, tableware, medicine, electroplating.
sodium	Na	22.9898	11	Davy, 1807	sea water, salt mines	Silvery, very active metal. Salts used in seasoning, fertilizers, detergents.
sulfur	S	32.064	16	ancient times	native, or as sulfides, sulfates	Yellow solid, used to vulcanize rubber, make sulfuric acid; sulfur dioxide used as fumigant, bleach.
thorium	Th	232.038	90	Berzelius, 1828	thorite, monazite	Dense gray metal used in atomic reactors
tin	Sn	118.70	50	ancient times	cassiterite	White metal, used to plate steel, make pewter, solder, bronze, type metal. Salts used in textiles.
titanium	Ti	47.90	22	Gregor, 1791	as oxide, titanates	Lustrous white metal, used in alloys. Oxide used as paint pigment.
tungsten	W	183.85	74	d'Elhuyar, 1783	wolframite, scheelite	Brittle metal, used in light filaments, steel alloys.
uranium	U	238.029	92	Klaproth, 1789	pitchblende	White, dense metal, radioactive, used in glass and china, source of atomic energy.

FACTS ABOUT SOME IMPORTANT ELEMENTS (continued)

Element	Symbol	Atomic Weight	Atomic Number	Discovery	Occurrence	Properties, uses
vanadium	V	50.9414	23	Sefström, 1830	vanadinite, patronite	Gray metal, used to make steel alloys. Oxide used as catalyst.
zinc	Zn	65.37	30	ancient times	blende, smith-sonite, cala-mine	Blue-white metal, used in brass, many other alloys, metal plating. Compounds used in paints, antiseptics.
zirconium	Zr	91.22	40	Klaproth, 1789	zircon, silicate ores	Gray metal used in alloys, to deoxidize and desulfurize steel. Oxide used in paints, abrasives.

MAN-MADE TEXTILE FIBERS

Name	Type	Uses
rayon	regenerated cellulose	clothing, tire cord, industrial belts, hoses
cellulose acetate	modified cellulose	garments
nylon	polyamide synthetic	wash and wear fabrics, carpets, stretch fabrics, tire cord, rope, human artery replacement
acrylics	polyacrylonitrile synthetic	blankets, carpets, dresses, "fake" fur
polyesters	polymerized esters	carpets, industrial fabrics, apparel
polypropylene	synthetic from propylene	carpets, upholstery
spun glass	inorganic	curtains, home furnishings, reinforced plastics

ATOMIC PARTICLES

Name	Description	Charge
alpha particle	The nucleus of a helium atom, which is produced by the radioactive decay of certain atoms.	+
beta particle	An electron emitted during the radioactive decay of certain atoms.	−
electron	An electrically charged particle; electrons make up the non-nuclear part of an atom.	−
gamma ray	High energy radiation emitted by radioactive decay.	0
mesons	About a dozen subatomic particles with a mass between that of the electron and that of the proton. Mesons are very unstable, with a lifetime of about 0.000001 second.	−, +, 0
neutrino	A particle emitted from the nucleus of a radioactive atom when an electron is emitted or captured by the atom. The neutrino has no measurable mass.	0
neutron	An electrically neutral particle found in the nucleus of most atoms.	0
photon	The smallest indivisible quantity of light energy.	0
positron	Positive beta particles emitted during the radioactive decay of certain elements.	+
proton	An electrically charged particle found in the nucleus of an atom.	+
quarks	Theoretically, three types of high-energy particles believed to form the basis of all matter. Quarks have not yet been produced or found.	−

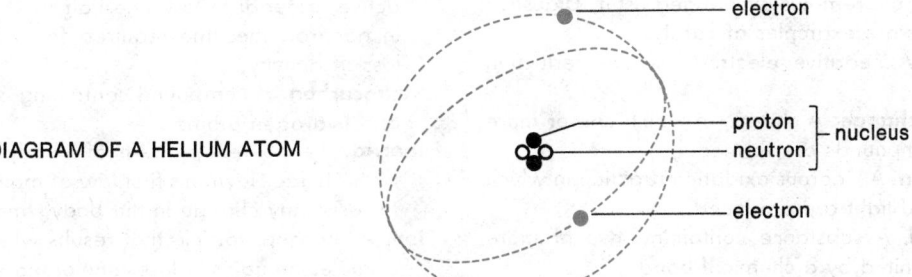

DIAGRAM OF A HELIUM ATOM

GLOSSARY OF CHEMISTRY AND PHYSICS

absolute zero. The temperature at which molecules cease moving and perfect gases exert no pressure. This temperature has been shown to be unattainable but would be equal to $-273.15°$ C. or $-459.67°$ F.

acceleration. The rate of change of velocity (speeding up or slowing down) with time. *Angular acceleration* is the speeding up or slowing down of a rotating body. *Acceleration of gravity* is a change in velocity caused by gravitational attraction; on Earth, it is equal to 32.2 feet per second per second.

acid. A substance that gives a hydrogen ion to a base.

alloy. A substance consisting of two or more metals that are intimately combined, usually by dissolving one in the other.

ampere. A unit of electrical current. A milliampere is equal to 0.001 ampere, and a microampere is equal to 0.000001 ampere.

anode. A positive electrode where oxidation occurs.

atom. The smallest part of a chemical element that can exist alone or in combination.

atomic number. The number of protons in the nucleus of an atom.

atomic weight. The weight of an atom compared with the weight of an atom of carbon 12.

base. A substance which accepts a hydrogen ion from an acid.

buffer. A substance that helps to keep the acidity or basicity of a solution from changing.

calorie. A unit quantity of heat energy. A gram calorie is the quantity of heat that must be supplied to 1 gram of water to raise its temperature by $1°$ C.

catalyst. A substance that speeds up a chemical reaction but remains unchanged itself. Digestive enzymes are examples of catalysts.

cathode. A negative electrode where reduction occurs.

chemical change. A change in which one or more new compounds are formed.

combustion. A vigorous oxidation reaction in which heat and light are produced.

compound. A substance containing two or more atoms united by a chemical bond.

cosmic rays. Radiation originating in interstellar space and reaching Earth's surface. The rays consist primarily of protons, but may also consist of electrons, mesons, and positrons.

density. The mass per unit volume of a material. Density is usually expressed in terms of pounds per cubic foot or grams per cubic centimeter.

diffusion. The scattering of light in all directions during transmission or reflection. During transmission, it is caused by the light waves striking minute particles. During reflection, diffusion is caused by irregularities in the reflecting surface.

electrolysis. Chemical decomposition of a substance by passing an electric current through the substance in a dissolved or molten state.

electron volt (EV). A small unit of energy defined as the kinetic energy possessed by an electron that has been subjected to a potential difference of one volt. The energy of nuclear particles in particle accelerators is usually expressed in millions of electron volts (MeV) or billions of electron volts (GeV).

element. A substance composed of one kind of atom.

energy. The ability to do work. There are many forms of energy such as heat, light, chemical, radiant, mechanical, and nuclear energy. There are two kinds of mechanical energy: a body possesses *kinetic energy* by virtue of its motion, and it possesses *potential energy* by virtue of its position in relation to any specific reference point.

force. Any action that will impart an acceleration to any mass that is free to move.

gamma rays. Very high energy X rays. Gamma rays are emitted by radioactive substances.

gravity. Attraction of a body for other bodies due to their masses.

half-life. The period of time it takes for a radioactive material to lose one-half its strength. Or, in general, the time required for a 50 percent loss of activity.

hydrocarbon. A compound containing only carbon and hydrogen atoms.

inertia. The inherent property of a body (as defined by Sir Isaac Newton's first law of motion) to tend to resist any change in the body's motion.

ion. A charged particle that results when an atom or molecule gains or loses one or more electrons. A positive ion is an atom or molecule that has lost an electron; a negative ion is an atom or molecule that has gained an electron.

isomers. Molecules that have different configurations but have the same number and kinds of atoms.

isotopes. Elements of the same atomic number but having different numbers of neutrons in the nucleus.

kinetic energy. Energy due to motion.

mass. An inherent property of matter that is a measure of the amount of matter present in a body. Masses are generally measured by comparing the force of gravitation acting upon them; this is called their *weight*. Thus, the weight of a body is proportional to its mass.

matter. Anything that has mass and occupies space.

molecular weight. The sum of the atomic weights of the atoms in a molecule.

momentum. The property of a body in motion that determines the amount of time it will take to bring the body to rest when a constant force is applied to it. Momentum is the product of the body's mass multiplied by its velocity.

nuclear fission. Splitting the nucleus of an atom into two parts by bombarding it with neutrons. When the atom splits, it emits neutrons and large quantities of energy in the form of light and heat.

nuclear fusion. Joining the nuclei of two or more atoms to form the single nucleus of another heavier element.

nucleon. A proton or a neutron.

ohm. A unit of electrical resistance.

oxidation. The combination of a substance with oxygen, or the loss of electrons in a chemical reaction.

pH. The negative logarithm of the hydrogen ion concentration of a solution. It is a measure of acidity or basicity.

physical change. A change in a substance that does not change its molecular composition.

radiation. Transmission of energy by electromagnetic waves.

radical. A group of atoms that always functions as a unit in a chemical reaction.

radioactivity. Disintegration of the nuclei of the atoms of certain elements accompanied by the emission of rays and elementary particles.

resistance. The opposition offered to the flow of an electrical current by a substance through which it is passing.

salt. The product, other than water, of the reaction between an acid and a base.

solution. A homogeneous mixture of a gas, liquid, or solid, called the *solute*, with a liquid, called the *solvent*. The solute is usually dispersed as individual molecules or ions.

specific gravity. The ratio of the weight of any substance to that of an equal volume of fresh water. A specific gravity of less than 1.0 indicates a density less than that of water; a specific gravity greater than 1.0, a density greater than that of water.

ultrasonic. A sound wave having a frequency above 20,000 cycles per second.

ultraviolet. Wavelengths of light shorter than visible light but longer than X rays.

valence. A number that represents the combining power of an atom or radical.

velocity. The rate of displacement, or rate of change of position, per unit time. Velocity includes direction, but *speed* does not. Thus an airplane that has a velocity of 600 miles per hour east will have a speed of 600 miles per hour. The distinction between velocity and speed is not always made, especially in nontechnical usage.

volt. The unit of electrical potential difference.

watt. A unit of electric power. Electric power (measured in watts) is the product of the current (measured in amperes) and the potential difference (measured in volts).

work. The product of a force acting through a distance. Thus, work is done when a 5-pound weight is raised 10 feet above the ground, the amount of work being 50 (5×10) foot-pounds.

Life Science

SUBJECTS COVERED BY LIFE SCIENCE

Taxonomy attempts to find relations and possible common origins of different forms of life by classifying them into orderly groups.

Biogeography is a study in which the world is divided into zones on the basis of climate and location, and the kinds of plants and animals found in each zone are studied.

Ecology is the study of the way creatures react with one another and with their environment. The environment causes changes in the plant and animal populations, but the reverse is also true. The introduction of a new plant or animal can cause large changes in the environment.

Genetics is the study of how one generation of organisms passes its characteristics on to the next generation. The sciences of plant and animal breeding have done much to increase our food supplies, and these sciences are branches of genetics. We now know that the basis of heredity is the *gene,* which consists of molecules of DNA.

Anatomy is the study of the structure of organisms; *embryology* is the study of how organisms develop.

Histology is the study of organs, and *cytology* is the study of the interior of cells.

Biochemistry and biophysics are applications of the physical sciences to life processes.

Subjects like *botany* (the study of plants) and *zoology* (the study of animals) are not considered as fundamental as the above.

Brookhaven National Laboratory, N.Y. Biologists examine the first hybrid plant ever grown from genetic cells of different species. New strains are important in research.

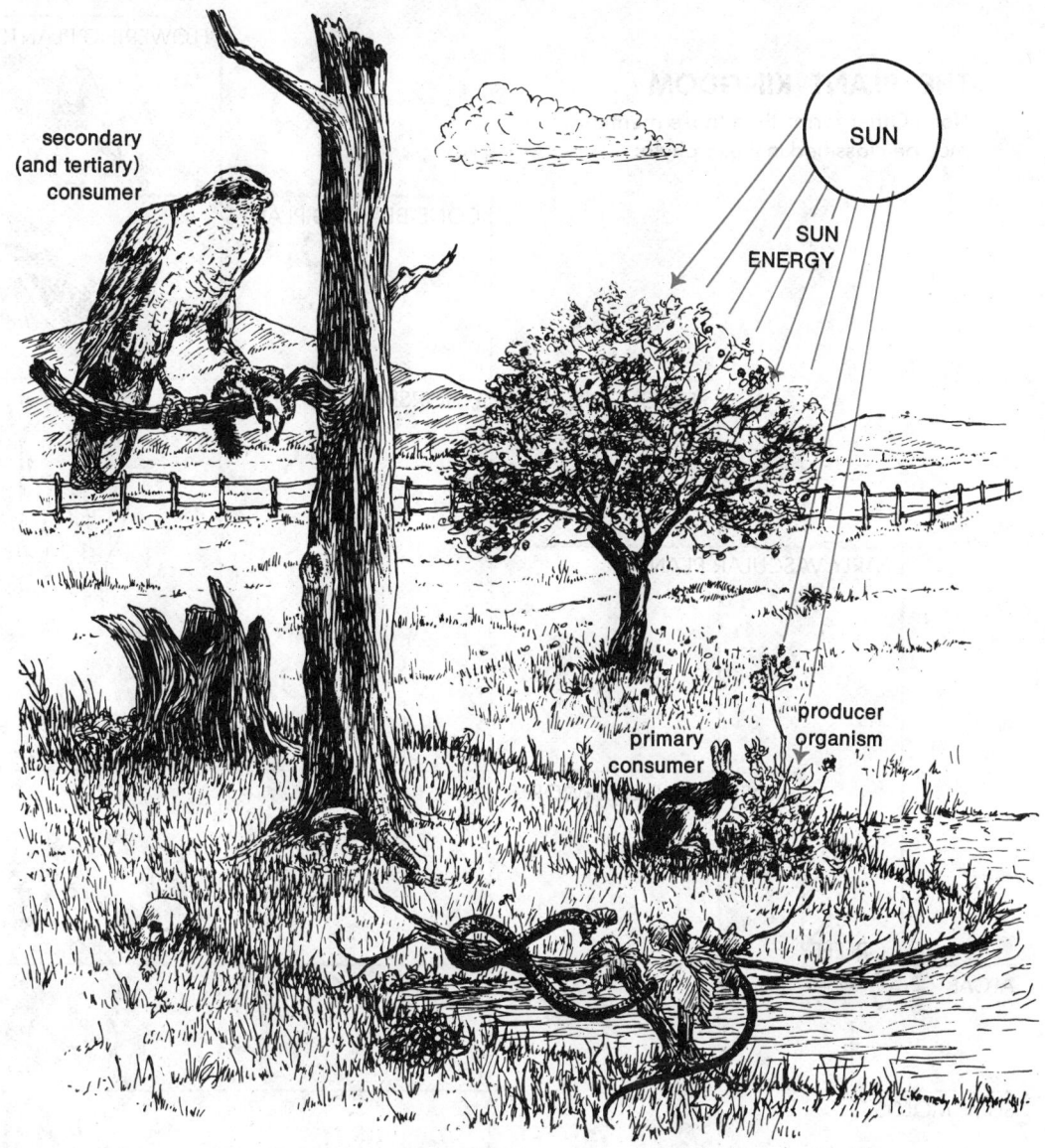

secondary
(and tertiary)
consumer

SUN

SUN
ENERGY

producer
organism

primary
consumer

THE ECOSYSTEM: THE WEB OF LIFE

Survival of all living things depends on a carefully balanced system called an
ecosystem. All life needs energy, and the original source of energy in an ecosystem
is the sun. Green plants, called producer organisms, use the sun's energy to
make their food. Animals, which get their energy by eating plants or other animals,
are called consumers. There are different kinds of consumers. A rabbit, which
eats plant material, is called a primary consumer. An eagle is called a secondary
consumer when it gets its energy from eating animals that eat plants. A snake is
called a secondary consumer because it eats animals that eat plants. When an
eagle eats a snake, the eagle is called a tertiary consumer. There are other
organisms in an ecosystem, such as bacteria that decompose dead animals and
plant material. Such organisms, called reducer organisms, return minerals and
organic material to the air and soil. They are not shown here.

SCIENCE

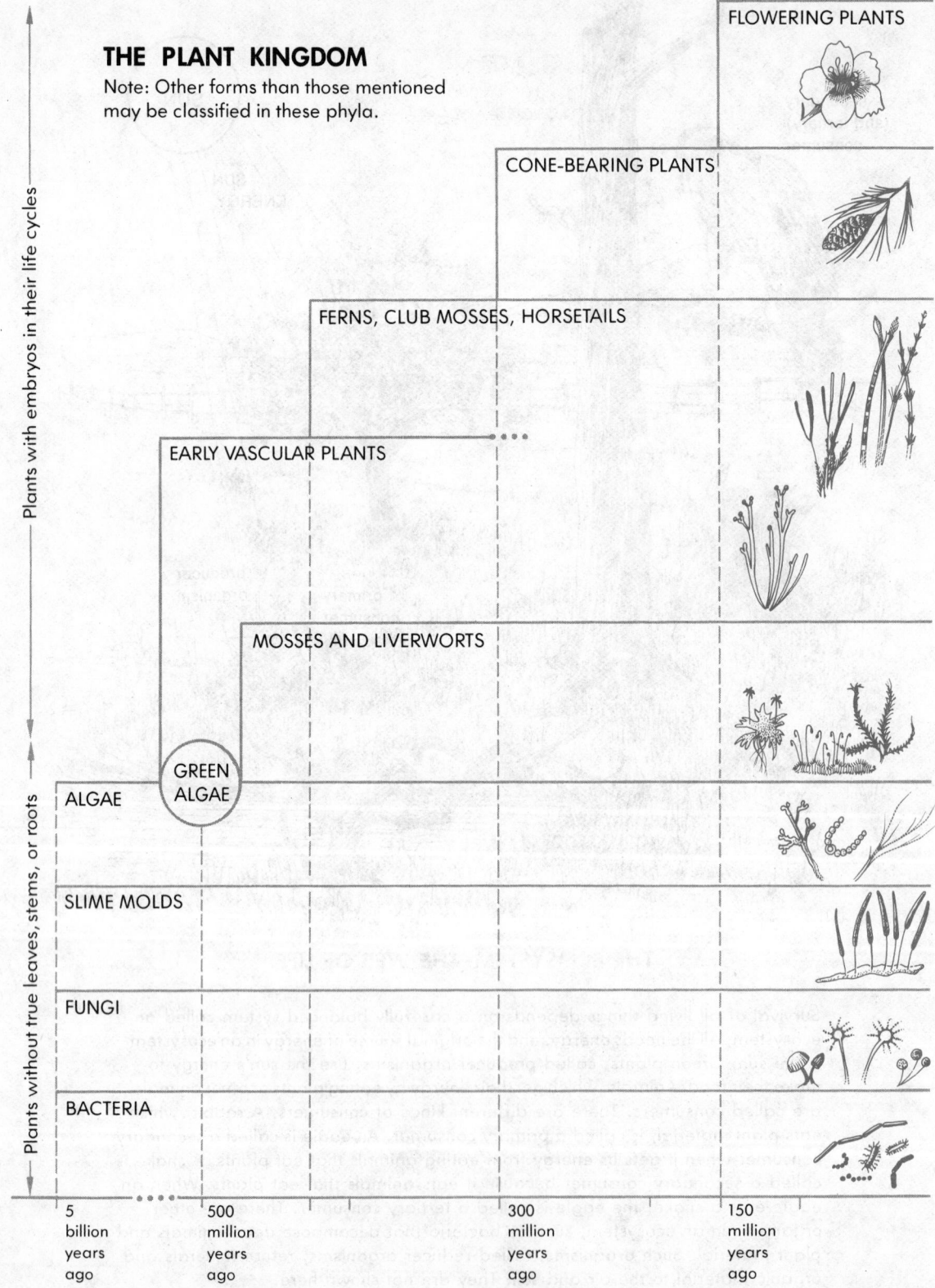

THE PLANT KINGDOM

Note: Other forms than those mentioned may be classified in these phyla.

FLOWERING PLANTS

CONE-BEARING PLANTS

FERNS, CLUB MOSSES, HORSETAILS

EARLY VASCULAR PLANTS

MOSSES AND LIVERWORTS

GREEN ALGAE

ALGAE

SLIME MOLDS

FUNGI

BACTERIA

Plants with embryos in their life cycles

Plants without true leaves, stems, or roots

5 billion years ago

500 million years ago

300 million years ago

150 million years ago

278

SCIENCE

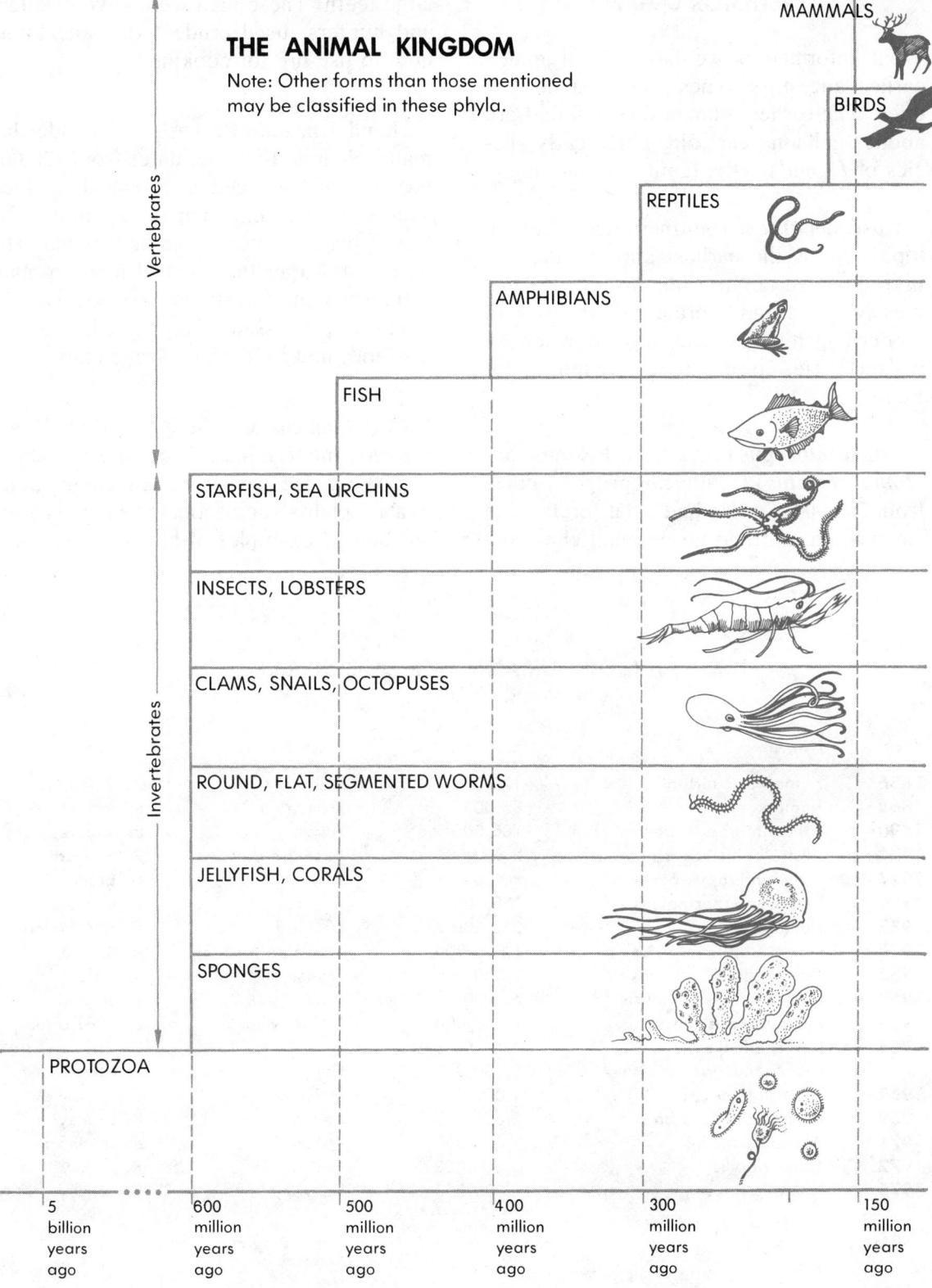

THE ANIMAL KINGDOM

Note: Other forms than those mentioned may be classified in these phyla.

MAMMALS

BIRDS

REPTILES

AMPHIBIANS

FISH

STARFISH, SEA URCHINS

INSECTS, LOBSTERS

CLAMS, SNAILS, OCTOPUSES

ROUND, FLAT, SEGMENTED WORMS

JELLYFISH, CORALS

SPONGES

PROTOZOA

Vertebrates

Invertebrates

| 5 billion years ago | 600 million years ago | 500 million years ago | 400 million years ago | 300 million years ago | 150 million years ago |

PREHISTORIC MAN

What information we have about man's earliest ancestors comes from fossil discoveries. The earliest human fossils found are about 5 million years old. Some early species of *Homidae*, the family of man, are:

Australopithecus (Southern ape). Australopithecus is the earliest known man and first appeared about 5 million B.C. He had massive jaws and a brain half the size of modern man's, and he stooped when he walked. He used stone weapons for hunting.

Pithecanthropus (Java man, Peking man, *Homo erectus*). Pithecanthropus dates from 700,000 B.C. He had a flat forehead, a small brain, a broad nose, small chin, and large teeth. These men were cave dwellers and hunters, used crude tools, and knew how to use fire for cooking.

Homo neanderthalensis (Neanderthal man). Neanderthal man dates from 120,000 B.C. He had a receding forehead, a thick skull, a short chin, and thick limbs. The top of his head was more or less flat. His brain was larger than that of modern man, and he was short in stature. *Homo neanderthalensis* possessed a language, hunted for his food, and used crude stone axes.

Homo sapiens (Cro-Magnon man). *Homo sapiens,* modern man, first appeared about 35,000 B.C. He used stone implements, cultivated plants, domesticated animals, and left behind examples of his art in caves.

MAJOR HUMAN FOSSIL DISCOVERIES

Year	Name	Est. date B.C.	Location	Discoverer
1856	Homo neanderthalensis	120,000	Germany	J. C. Fuhlrott
1868	Homo sapiens	35,000	France	E. Lartet
1890	Pithecanthropus erectus	700,000	Java	E. Dubois
1924	Australopithecus africanus	2,000,000	Bechuanaland	R. A. Dart
1927	Pithecanthropus pekinensis	400,000	China	D. Black
1929	Homo neanderthalensis	120,000	Israel	D. Garrod
1935	Homo erectus	250,000	England	A. T. Marston
1938	Paranthropus robustus	1,000,000	Transvaal	R. Broom
1953	Telanthropus capensis	1,000,000	Transvaal	R. Broom
1957	Homo neanderthalensis	45,000	Iraq	R. Solecki
1959	Zinjanthropus bosei	1,750,000	Tanganyika	L. S. B. Leakey
1965	Homo erectus paleohungaricus	450,000 and 2,500,000	Hungary	L. Vertes
1969	Australopithecus	4,000,000	Ethiopia	F. C. Howell
1969	Australopithecus bosei	2,600,000	Kenya	R. Leakey
1971	Australopithecus	5,000,000	Kenya	A. Lewis
1972	Homo habilis	2,500,000	Kenya	R. Leakey
1975	Homo erectus	1,500,000	Kenya	R. Leakey

IMPORTANT EVENTS IN LIFE SCIENCE

Date	Scientist	Accomplishment
c. 300 B.C.	Theophrastus (c. 372–c. 287 B.C.), Greek botanist.	Considered to be the father of the science of botany.
c. 350 B.C.	Aristotle (384–322 B.C.), Greek physician and naturalist.	Began a scientific study of all known animals. He is called the "father of zoology."
1543	Andreas Vesalius (1514–1564), Flemish anatomist.	Published De Humani Corporis Fabrica, which is the first illustrated work on human anatomy.
1551–87	Konrad von Gesner (1516–1565), Swiss naturalist.	Published Historia Animalium, which is considered the basis of modern zoology.
c. 1560	Leonhard Fuchs (1501–1566), German botanist.	Published the first glossary of botanical terminology.
1665	Robert Hooke (1635–1703), English microbiologist.	Discovered that cork was made of microscopic cells.
1673	Anthony van Leeuwenhoek (1632–1723), Dutch physicist.	Invented the microscope.
c. 1750	Carolus Linnaeus (1707–1778), Swedish botanist.	Founded the systematic study of botany. Developed the generic system of animal and plant classification.
1838–39	Mattias Schleiden (1804–1881) and Theodor Schwann (1810–1882), German microbiologists.	Proposed the theory that all plants and animals are made of cells.
1859	Charles Darwin (1809–1882), English naturalist.	Published On the Origin of Species by Means of Natural Selection, which proposed his theory of evolution.
1862	Louis Pasteur (1822–1895), French chemist and bacteriologist.	Proved that all life comes from pre-existing life. Disproved the theory of spontaneous generation.
1866	Gregor Johann Mendel (1822–1884), Austrian monk and botanist.	The father of genetics. Showed how traits are transmitted from parent to offspring.
1870–90	Robert Koch (1843–1910), German physician.	Demonstrated that certain diseases are caused by specific bacteria.
1878	Wilhelm Kuhne (1837–1900), German physiologist.	Studied the nature of enzyme action.
1887	Edouard van Beneden (1846–1910), Belgian biologist.	Discovered the process of cell division called meiosis.

Date	Scientist	Accomplishment
1926	Hermann J. Muller (1890–1967), U.S. biologist.	Discovered that X rays could cause genetic mutations in offspring.
1929	Alexander Fleming (1881–1955), Scottish physician.	Discovered the antibacterial action of penicillin.
1944–46	M. H. F. Wilkins (1916–), Irish biophysicist.	Studied the structure of DNA with X rays for the first time.
1949	Willard F. Libby (1908–), U.S. biochemist.	Developed the carbon-14 method of dating plant and animal remains.
1950	P. S. Hench (1896–), and E. C. Kendall (1886–1972), U.S. biochemists.	Discovered cortisone.
1952	J. Lederberg (1925–), American geneticist.	Showed that genetic material can be transferred from one type of microorganism to another.
1953	P. B. Medawar (1915–), British biologist.	Showed that mice can be treated in such a way that they will not reject transplanted tissue from another mouse.
1953	James W. Watson (1928–), U.S. biochemist, and F. H. C. Crick (1916–), English molecular biologist.	Discovered the molecular structure of DNA.
1955	Severo Ochoa (1905–), U.S. biochemist.	Synthesized RNA for the first time.

Charles Darwin

Louis Pasteur

Gregor Mendel

Rachel L. Carson

Date	Scientist	Accomplishment
1958	G. W. Beadle (1903–), with E. J. Tatum and J. Lederberg.	Showed that chemical processes in cells are regulated by genes.
1962	Rachel L. Carson (1907–1964), U.S. biologist.	Published *Silent Spring*, exposing the dangers of pesticide control to animal life.
1967	Arthur Kornberg (1918–), U.S. biochemist.	Synthesized DNA for the first time.
1968	M. W. Nirenbert (1927–), American biochemist.	With R. W. Holley and H. S. Khorana deciphered the genetic code of DNA.
1975	H. M. Temin (1934–), American biologist.	With R. Dulbecco and D. Baltimore showed that tumor viruses can interact with the genetic material of cells, a discovery of possible importance in cancer research.

GLOSSARY OF LIFE SCIENCE

acquired characteristic. A physical trait of an organism that is brought about by its environment.

adaptations. Features of structure and function that make an organism better suited for living and reproducing in a particular environment.

amino acids. Chemical compounds that contain amino and acid groups. All proteins are made from about 23 amino acids.

anabolism. Those phases of metabolism which make more complex substances from simpler ones.

anatomy. The study of the structure of organisms.

angiosperms. Plants that form true flowers as their structures of reproduction. The seeds of angiosperms are enclosed in structures of the parent plant. These structures are usually called *fruits*.

asexual reproduction. Reproduction from one parent organism without the union of germ cells.

ATP. Adenosine triphosphate, a compound which produces metabolic energy by releasing a phosphate.

autotrophic organisms. Organisms that require only inorganic material for food. These organisms are mainly plants and some bacteria.

balance of nature. The natural condition in which plant and animal communities continue unchanged in either numbers or composition.

biogeography. The study of the plants and animals found in various climatic and geographic zones.

biome. The largest ecological unit. A biome includes all of the plants and animals of a particular region of the earth. The arctic tundra is an example of a biome.

catabolism. The phases of metabolism that make simpler substances from more complex ones.

cell. The smallest unit of living matter, composed of a nucleus, cytoplasm, and a membrane.

cell membrane. The thin outer layer of animal and plant cells.

chlorophyll. A green pigment in plants that transforms sunlight into usable energy for the process of photosynthesis.

chloroplast. An intracellular structure in higher plants that contains chlorophyll.

chromosomes. Threadlike structures in a cell nucleus that contain the hereditary material used in reproduction. Chromosomes are made up of genes.

conjugation. A form of sexual reproduction in which two cells join and transfer genetic material. Conjugation is usually associated with single-celled organisms.

cytology. The study of the protoplasmic structure of cells.

cytoplasm. Semifluid material surrounding the nucleus of a cell and enclosed by the cell membrane.

DNA (deoxyribonucleic acid). Nucleic acid found in cell chromosomes, which duplicates itself and transfers genetic information during reproduction.

ecology. The study of organisms in relation to each other and their environment.

ecosystem. A living community that contains an energy source, abiotic chemicals, and organisms that function as producers, consumers, and reducers.

embryo. The developing plant or animal before birth or germination. In humans, "embryo" usually refers to the developing individual during the first three months of pregnancy.

environment. The total surroundings of a living thing.

evolution. Genetic change in a species that, over a period of time, better adapts it to its environment.

fertilization. The union of a sperm (male sex cell) and an egg (female sex cell) to produce a new individual.

fetus. A developing animal before birth. In humans, "fetus" usually refers to the developing individual after the first three months of pregnancy.

gametes. Mature germ cells having half the number of chromosomes found in body cells.

genes. The hereditary material that makes up chromosomes.

genetics. The study of how one generation of organisms passes its characteristics on to the next generation.

genus. A group of related species.

germ cell. A sex cell (sperm or ovum) as differentiated from the other cells of the body.

gymnosperm. A seed plant that has exposed ovules. Gymnosperms are often referred to as conifers or evergreens.

habitat. The natural home of an animal or plant.

heredity. The traits that are genetically passed from parent to offspring; biological inheritance.

hermaphrodite. An animal or plant possessing both male and female reproductive organs.

heterotrophic. Organisms that require organic compounds for food.

histology. The study of organs.

hybrid. A cross between different species.

meiosis. A special kind of cell division in organisms that have sexual reproduction; it reduces the chromosome number in the mature germ cells by half.

metabolism. The set of interrelated chemical processes characteristic of life.

metamorphosis. Radical changes in the development of some animals as they mature. It is usually associated with insects and amphibians.

mitosis. Cell division in which the two daughter cells have the same genetic material as the parent cell.

morphology. The study of the form and structure of living things.

mutation. An inheritable change in a chromosome or gene.

nucleus. An inner body in a cell that contains the cell's hereditary material (chromosomes, genes, and DNA) and controls the activity of the cytoplasm.

ontogeny. The developmental history of an individual organism.

parasite. An organism which takes its food from another living organism.

photosynthesis. The process by which green plants manufacture food (glucose) from carbon dioxide, water, and light.

phylogeny. The evolutionary history of a group of organisms.

physiology. Study of the processes which occur in living organisms.

protoplasm. All the material in a living cell.

reduction division. See *meiosis*.

RNA (ribonucleic acid). Chemical compounds that aid in the duplication of DNA.

sexual reproduction. Reproduction that requires the combination of genetic material from the germ cells of two individuals.

species. A particular kind of plant or animal which maintains its distinctness over many generations.

spontaneous generation. The belief that living things can emerge from nonliving material.

spore. A single-celled reproductive body produced by all major kinds of plants.

symbiosis. A relationship in which two dissimilar organisms live together and benefit each other.

taxonomy. Classification of plants and animals according to evolutionary relationships.

transpiration. The process by which plants lose water through evaporation.

zygote. An egg cell at the moment of fertilization.

Careers in Science

Science enables us to understand nature and is also of great practical importance. The United States is a high-technology society, meaning that much of its industry is based on recent scientific discoveries. Continuing research is also necessary to cope with many problems, such as the energy shortages that appear to lie ahead. Job opportunities look good in many fields requiring some degree of scientific training, ranging from high school or vocational school science courses to advanced college degrees.

For the following occupations, high school or vocational school courses in science are important:

Machinist, instrument maker,
    tool-and-die maker
Photoengraver
Boilermaker
Stationary engineer
Welder
Electrician
Elevator constructor
Plumber, pipefitter
Jeweler, watch repairman
Television and radio serviceman
Photographer
Electric light, power line worker
Radio and TV broadcast technician
Sheet-metal worker
Airplane mechanic
Telephone line installation worker
Automobile mechanic
Air conditioning worker

Electronics repair shop. Employing complex meters and test equipment, a highly skilled technician repairs an electronic component. Research laboratories employ skilled repairmen to maintain equipment.

Chemistry laboratory. Students use laboratory equipment to perform experiments and record the results in laboratory notebooks as part of their training.

Physician examines x-ray. Training beyond high school and college can lead to interesting and rewarding careers in hospitals and research laboratories.

The following occupations require college training in life science and some chemistry and physics:

Conservation: Forestry, soil conservation
Life scientist: Biochemistry, soil science
Optometrist
Dentist, dental hygienist
Doctor of medicine
Veterinarian
Occupational and physical therapist
Dietician
Pharmacist
Psychologist
Home economist

The following occupations require training in applied science beyond the high school level:

Draftsman, science and engineering technician, surveyor
Business machine repairman, computer serviceman
Medical technician: X-ray, operating room, etc.
Dispensing optician

The following occupations require college training in chemistry or physics or both:

Science teacher
Engineer: Aerospace, agricultural, biomedical, ceramic, chemical, civil, electrical, industrial, mining, petroleum
Environmental scientist: Geology, meteorology, oceanography
Physical scientist: Astronomy, chemistry, physics
Geographer
Architect
Technical writer

EARTH AND SPACE SCIENCE

What Jules Verne presented a few generations ago as fiction in his novel *From the Earth to the Moon*, astronauts and cosmonauts have now established as fact. Man not only has voyaged to the moon but has mapped it, explored it, prospected it. In the following pages you will find information about the planets and outer space, but you will first find much about our own planet.

Even as we venture into space we know we cannot ignore our immediate environment. Only through continuing studies of Earth's natural features and processes can we hope to provide our growing population with food, clothing, and shelter. As you read these pages, do not forget that the preceding section offers additional information on science and that the Concise Edition of the *Student Handbook* provides more advanced information on biology, physics, and chemistry.

Our Planet Earth

Earth is 93 million miles from the sun. It travels around the sun once every 365 days, 6 hours, 9 minutes, and 9.54 seconds. Two other planets are closer than Earth to the sun, and six are farther away. Earth also spins on its axis every 23 hours, 56 minutes, and 4.09 seconds. The surface of Earth is about 70 percent water. The deepest part of the ocean is Challenger Deep, in the Pacific Ocean southwest of Guam. At this point, it is 36,198 feet deep. The highest point of land is Mount Everest in Asia, which is 29,028 feet above sea level.

THE STRUCTURE OF EARTH

Earth is not a perfect sphere, since its diameter is 7927 miles through the equator and 7900 miles through the poles. If we could drill through Earth, we would find it is made up of four fairly definite layers. The top layer, called the *crust,* averages about 20 miles thick. Below this is the *mantle,* about 1800 miles thick; then the *outer core,* about 1375 miles thick; and then the *inner core,* with a radius of about 800 miles. The line between the crust and the mantle is called the *Mohorovicic discontinuity* or the "Moho."

Earth's crust is mostly silicate rock. The mantle is thought to be another silicate, called olivene. Below this comes the outer core, which is believed to be molten iron containing some nickel. Finally, there is the inner core, which is also iron and nickel but which is solid because of the immense pressure inside Earth.

Below the surface, Earth is hot and becomes hotter the closer one gets to the center. The main source of the heat is now believed to be radioactivity from uranium, thorium, and an isotope of potassium. The upper part of the mantle has a temperature of about 1600°F rising to 4000°F at the bottom. The outer core ranges from 4000° to 9000°F, and the inner core is about 9000°F.

HOW THE CONTINENTS ARE FORMED

Most scientists believe that about 200 million years ago all the land on Earth was joined together, forming a single large land mass. By using computers, scientists have been able to show how today's continents may have fitted together like the pieces of a puzzle. This single large continent is sometimes called Pangaea. About 180 million years ago, Pangaea began to break apart to form three separate continents. The large block to the north (very much later to become Europe, Asia, North America, and Greenland) is called Laurasia. Laurasia broke away from the other two land masses, which together are called Gondwanaland.

The northern block of Gondwanaland was to become South America and Africa; the southern block was to become Antarctica and Australia with New Zealand. A small piece of land broke away between the northern and southern parts of Gondwanaland and began moving northward. It was to become India.

These land masses continued to drift. About 65 million years ago, the continents began to look as they do today. South America and Africa had drifted apart, and soon North America and Greenland would break away from Laurasia. India was about to collide with Eurasia, forming the Himalaya Mountains. The southern block of

Our tallest structures and deepest mines are tiny compared to the heights and depths man has explored. In 1968 Apollo 8 flew 234,672 miles high.

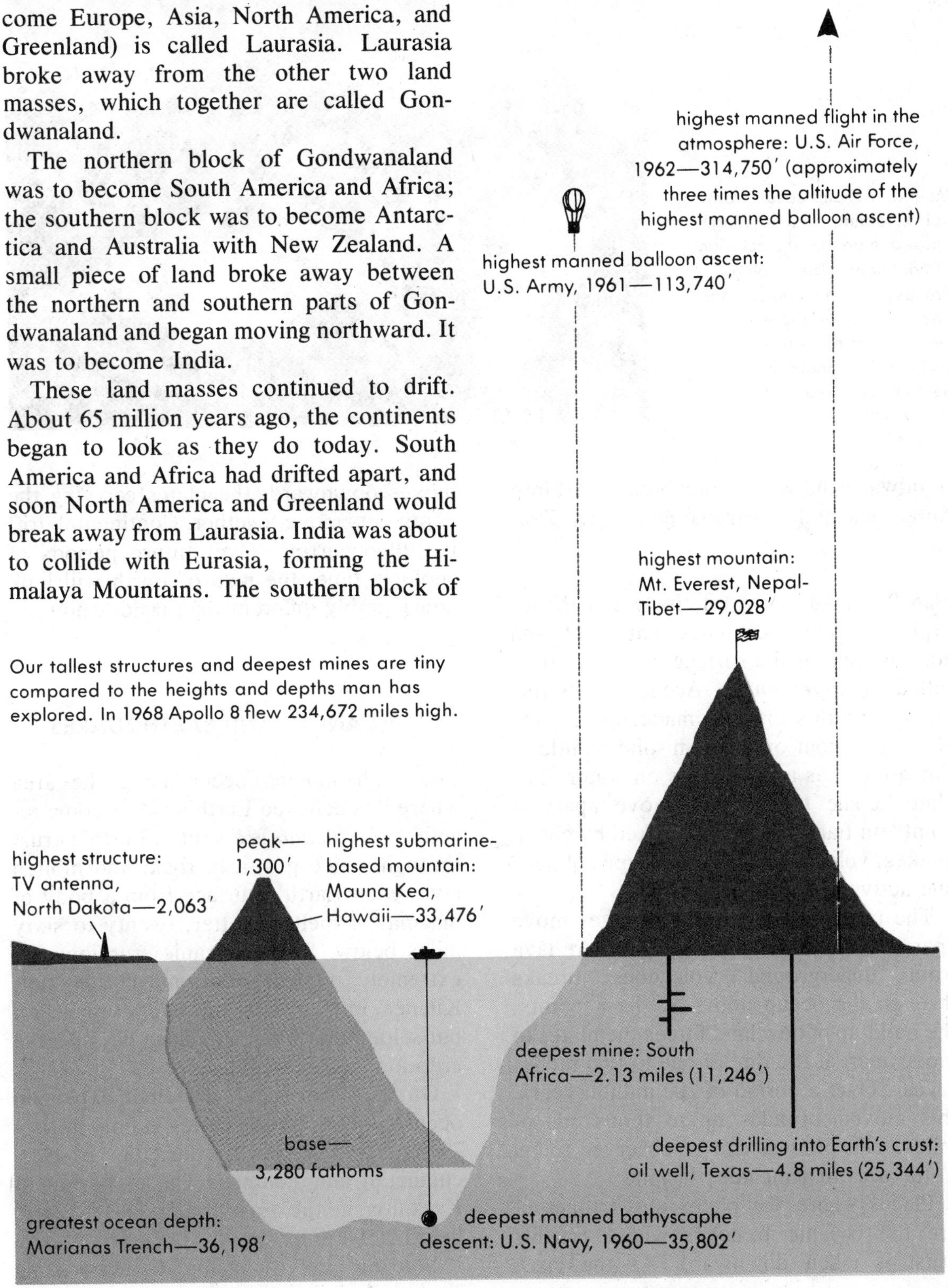

highest manned flight in the atmosphere: U.S. Air Force, 1962—314,750' (approximately three times the altitude of the highest manned balloon ascent)

highest manned balloon ascent: U.S. Army, 1961—113,740'

highest mountain: Mt. Everest, Nepal-Tibet—29,028'

highest structure: TV antenna, North Dakota—2,063'

peak— 1,300'

highest submarine-based mountain: Mauna Kea, Hawaii—33,476'

deepest mine: South Africa—2.13 miles (11,246')

base— 3,280 fathoms

deepest drilling into Earth's crust: oil well, Texas—4.8 miles (25,344')

greatest ocean depth: Marianas Trench—36,198'

deepest manned bathyscaphe descent: U.S. Navy, 1960—35,802'

Mountain chains result from uplift, folding, and faulting caused in part by the collision of continents. The geologic process known as *volcanism* also causes variations in the elevation of the earth's surface. Volcanoes are the best-known manifestation of volcanism.

Gondwanaland would soon break apart into Antarctica and Australia plus New Zealand.

Plate Tectonics. A relatively new theory explaining how these large masses of land float around on the surface of the Earth is called *plate tectonics.* According to this theory, Earth's crust is made up of large plates that float on the semisolid mantle of Earth much as a boat floats on water. The plates come together or move apart at points on Earth's surface marked by earthquakes, volcanoes, and other types of seismic activity.

The major areas where the plates move apart are the mid-ocean ridges, where lava from underground volcanoes breaks through the ocean floor. At these points, the build-up of new land forces the plates to move apart at the rate of one to two inches a year. Over a period of 200 million years, this movement adds up to thousands of miles. This process can be observed today in the area that includes Iceland.

Places where the plates move together are the oceanic trenches where Earth's crust is taken downward. As the crust

moves downward, the plates carrying the continents move together. Continental drift is still occurring. Over future periods of geologic time, the map of Earth will look considerably different than it does now.

VOLCANOES AND EARTHQUAKES

These phenomena occur along the area where it is believed Earth's plates come together. A *volcano* is a vent in Earth's crust through which gas, ash, rock, and molten lava reach Earth's surface from a body of magma, or melted matter, twenty to sixty miles below. Some volcanic eruptions are extremely violent, but most are not. Kilauea, in Hawaii, erupts every few years, but seldom does much damage because the eruptions are not explosive.

On the other hand, a violent explosion occurred in Mount Vesuvius in Italy in A.D. 79, completely burying the cities of Herculaneum and Pompeii. The explosion of Krakatoa in the East Indies in 1883 was heard 2,500 miles away.

Volcanic activity is found in the same

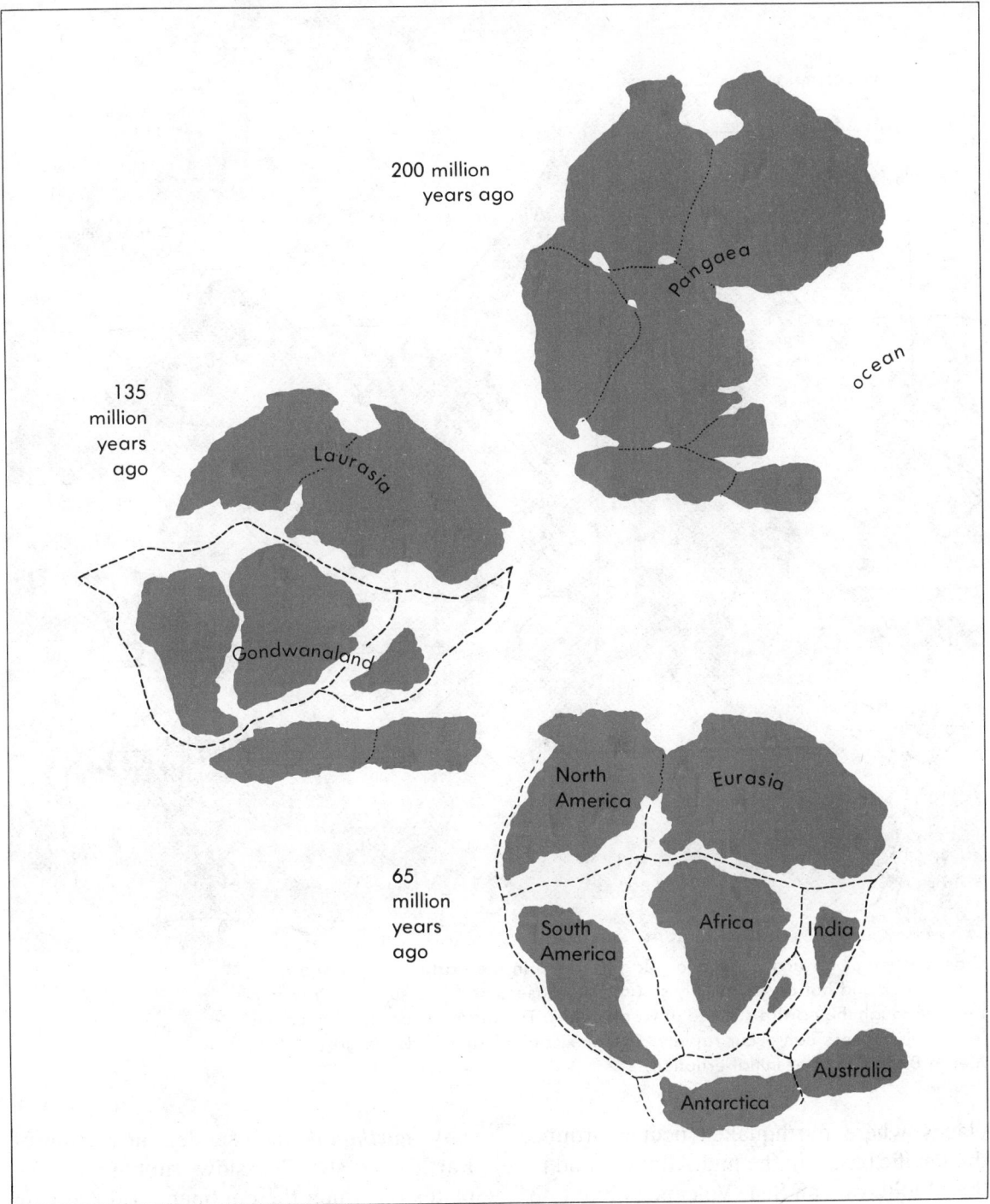

200 million
years ago

Pangaea

ocean

135
million
years
ago

Laurasia

Gondwanaland

North
America

Eurasia

65
million
years
ago

South
America

Africa

India

Antarctica

Australia

About 200 million years ago all land was one large continent, Pangaea, from which our familiar continents were eventually formed. These land masses still float on the earth's surface, producing areas of tension, where there are frequent earthquakes and volcanoes. You can see that the surface of our planet is still in process of change, even though that change is almost imperceptible in a human lifetime.

EARTH AND SPACE SCIENCE

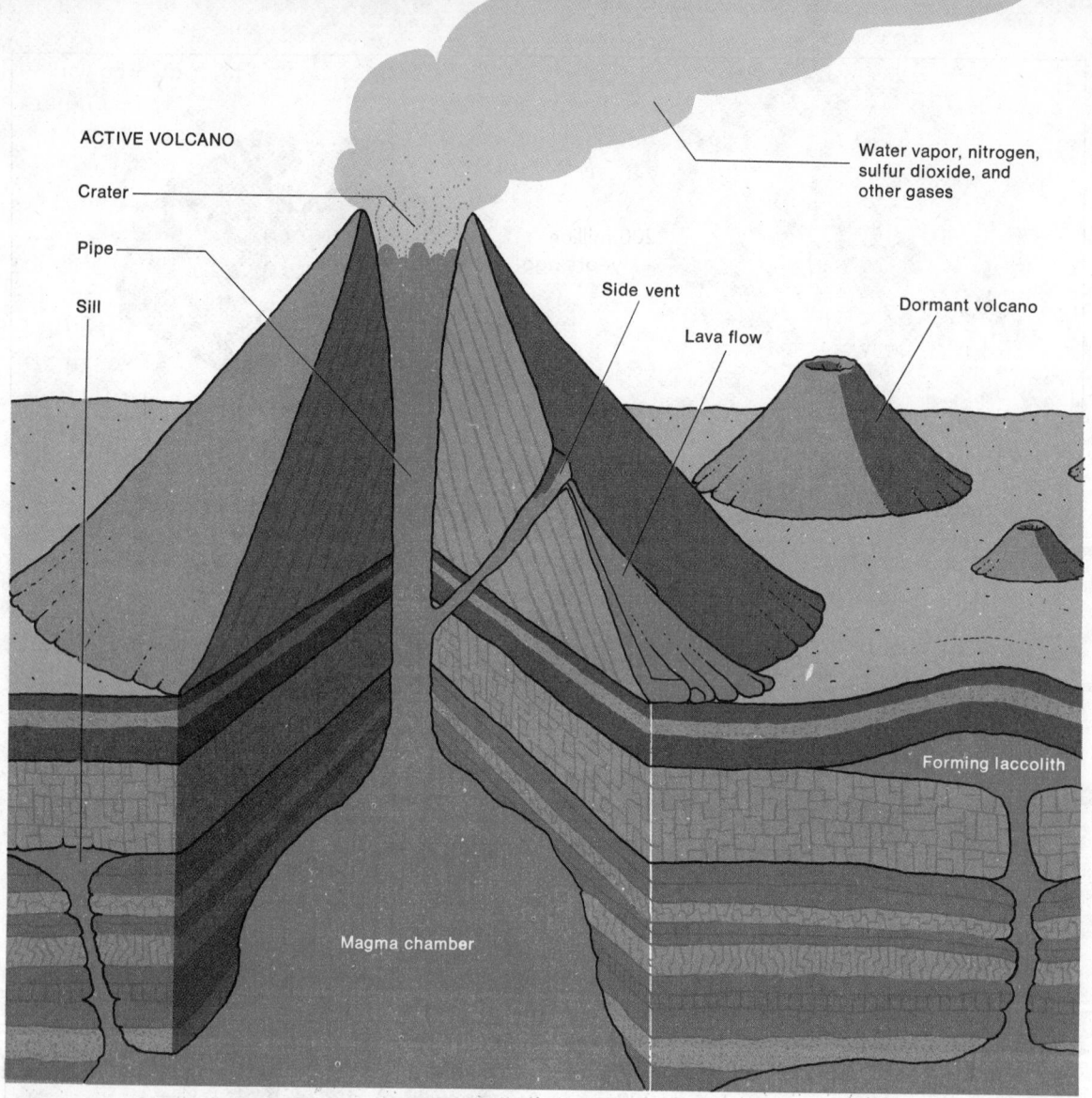

ACTIVE VOLCANO

Crater

Pipe

Sill

Water vapor, nitrogen, sulfur dioxide, and other gases

Side vent

Lava flow

Dormant volcano

Forming laccolith

Magma chamber

Cross-section of an active volcano. Magma deep in the earth is composed of molten rock and hot gases, mostly steam. The gases exert pressure until magma bursts through the earth's surface at weak points. The magma cools and becomes lava. This process can occur rapidly. The Mexican volcano, Parícutin grew 1,500 feet in 8 months after initial eruption.

places where earthquakes occur: around the Pacific basin, in the mid-Atlantic, and in the Mediterranean Sea. Volcanoes build up new land areas. The Hawaiian Islands were built by volcanoes, a process which is still going on. In 1963, the island of Surtsey, near Iceland, was formed by an underwater volcano.

An *earthquake* is a sudden movement of Earth's crust. The slow rubbing of the plates on which the continents ride sets up forces that are suddenly relieved by slippage, which we feel as an earthquake. Or, the earthquake may be caused by volcanic activity. The *focus,* or source, of the earthquake is the spot under Earth's surface where the slippage occurs. The *epicenter* is the spot on the surface directly above the focus. It is estimated that there are about a million earthquakes a year, most of them very small. About 80 percent occur along the edges of the Pacific Ocean.

An earthquake produces waves that can be picked up by an instrument called a *seismograph,* which tells us where the earthquake occurred and how severe it was. There are several types of waves: P waves are longitudinal, or push-pull, waves. The material, which may be solid or liquid, moves back and forth in the direction of the wave. S waves are transverse, or shake, waves. The material moves up and down across the direction of the wave. Since S waves travel more slowly than P waves, we can tell how far away the earthquake occurred by computing the difference in the time it takes for the two waves to arrive at the seismograph. Using seismographs at three or more different locations enables us to calculate where the earthquake occurred. This type of information tells us that Earth's core must be liquid. At certain locations, S waves never arrive at all. Since S waves cannot travel through a liquid, we know a liquid must have been in its path. There are also long surface, or L, waves. These travel on the surface and do the most damage. The strength of an earthquake is indicated on a scale called the *Richter Scale,* which is based on the height, or amplitude, of the peaks that the tremors produce on the seismograph recording. There is no fixed upper or lower limit to the Richter Scale. A magnitude of 2.5 on this scale is just enough to be felt nearby; a 6.0 causes moderate destruction; a very large earthquake may register 8.6 or as high as 8.9. Even larger earthquakes are possible.

GLACIATION

In Antarctica and Greenland, and on the upper slopes of high mountains elsewhere, there are *glaciers*—accumulations of snow and ice that move slowly over the ground. Some 10,000 to 20,000 years ago, during the Ice Age, the northern parts of North

Prominent features of the earth's surface are created by the coming together (*at the left*) and the separating (*at the right*) of crustal plates. Deep trenches and high mountains are formed at coastlines, and ridges are created in mid-ocean. Knowledge of the topography of the ocean floor is becoming increasingly necessary as we move into an era of ocean mining.

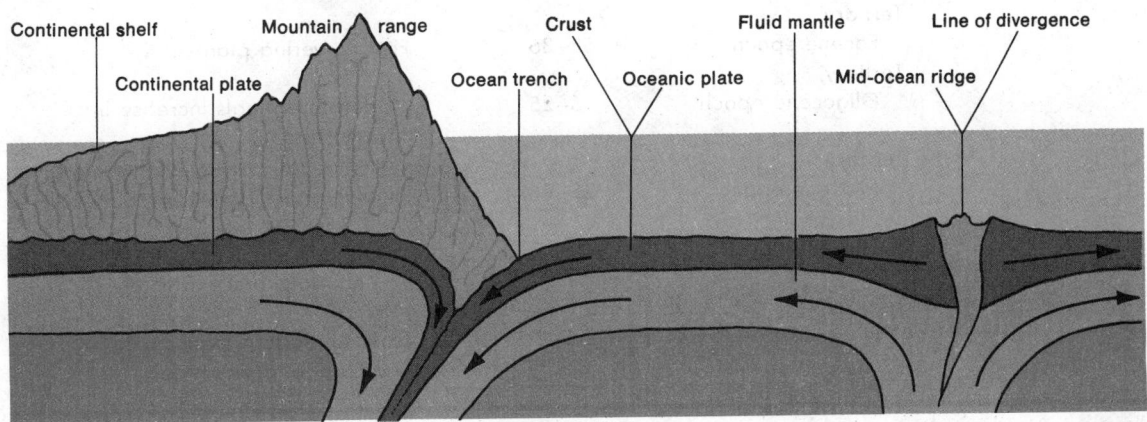

Continental shelf   Mountain range   Crust   Fluid mantle   Line of divergence

Continental plate   Ocean trench   Oceanic plate   Mid-ocean ridge

GEOLOGIC TIME TABLE

Life on earth originated about 2,000 million years ago. The oldest fossil remains are from about 550 million years ago, and man first appeared about 5 million years ago.

Era	Period	Millions of Years Ago	Forms of Life
Pre-Cambrian	Archaean	2,000+	No fossil remains of life
	Lower Pre-Cambrian	2,000–1,200	No fossil remains of life
	Middle Pre-Cambrian	1,200–900	No fossil remains of life
	Upper Pre-Cambrian	900–700	No fossil remains of life
	Late Pre-Cambrian	700–600	Small primitive plants and animals
Paleozoic	Cambrian	600–500	First invertebrate sea life
	Ordovician	500–425	First fishes and crustaceans
	Silurian	425–405	First land plants
	Devonian	405–345	First amphibians
	Mississippian	345–310	Ferns and fern-like trees
	Pennsylvanian	310–280	First reptiles
	Permian	280–230	Reptiles develop and increase in numbers
Mesozoic	Triassic	230–181	First dinosaurs appear
	Jurassic	181–135	Age of dinosaurs begins; first small mammals; primitive birds
	Cretaceous	135–65	Age of dinosaurs ends; modern vegetation appears
Cenozoic	Tertiary, Paleocene epoch	65–58	First placental mammals; first primates
	Tertiary, Eocene epoch	58–36	First flowering plants
	Tertiary, Oligocene epoch	36–25	Modern mammals increase in numbers
	Tertiary, Miocene epoch	25–7	Whales and apes appear
	Tertiary, Pliocene epoch	7–2.5	Mammoths and other large mammals; first evidence of man
	Tertiary, Pleistocene epoch	2.5–0	Early to modern man; present animal and plant life

EARTH AND SPACE SCIENCE

NORTH AMERICAN GLACIAL STAGES

Exact dating for the glacial and interglacial periods is not now possible, but some geologists have established general time periods by means of radiocarbon dating of wood found in deposits left by the glaciers. These periods are shown here.

Glacial	Interglacial	Years Ago
Nebraskan		perhaps 900,000
	Aftonian	
Kansan		perhaps 700,000
	Yarmouth	
Illinois		perhaps 300,000
	Sangamon	
Wisconsin		
Farmdale		25–29,000
Iowan		21–23,000
Tazewell		15–19,000
Cary		13–14,000
Mankato		12,000
Valders		11,000

Tyndall Glacier flows from Mount St. Elias, an 18,000-foot peak on the boundary of Alaska and Canada. Glacier ice, moving only inches a day, consists of highly compressed snow.

America, Europe, Asia, and much of southern South America were covered with ice, just as Greenland and Antarctica are today. It is thought that these glaciers moved at a rate of 100 to 200 feet per year and covered the greatest area 16,000 to 18,000 years ago, when they began to recede. These massive "continents" of ice were 5 to 10 thousand feet thick. Many other glacial ages have occurred over the past three and a half million years of the Pleistocene epoch.

It is believed that a lowering of the world atmospheric temperature brings on a glacial age. The last ice age probably resulted from a drop of 6°C in world temperatures. The causes of such temperature changes are not known.

Glaciers are generally divided into two types: mountain, or alpine, glaciers; and continental glaciers, or ice sheets. Alpine glaciers have been compared to rivers of ice, but they are more like bulldozers that slowly plow down a valley, straightening it out and deepening it. When an alpine glacier eventually disappears, it leaves a U-shaped valley with steep sides and a cirque, or amphitheaterlike depression, in the mountainside at its head. The cirque often contains a lake. Alpine glaciers produced the rugged landscapes of the Alps and Himalayas.

Continental glaciers, on the other hand, tend to smooth out the surface over which they move. At the margin of the ice, a continental glacier pushes up a mass of irregular, unsorted rock debris called an end *moraine.* On the side of the moraine away from the ice is a relatively level area, called an *outwash plain,* composed of fine material washed away from the end moraine by meltwater from the glacier. There are irregular kettle holes in both the moraine and the outwash plain, caused by the melting of buried blocks of ice. Behind the end moraine is the *till plain,* or *ground moraine,* a wide, gently undulating area of unsorted debris called *till,* which was carried in and under the ice and was dropped when the glacier receded. Continental glaciers also form *eskers,* or winding ridges of sorted till, and *drumlins,* or long, narrow hills of unsorted till. When it melts back, the ice also deposits *erratics,* or single boulders composed of rock foreign to the area. There may be many lakes in end moraines, but few in ground moraines or outwash plains.

Alpine glaciation. An alpine glacier carves a U-shaped valley and leaves cinques at its head, which may become lakes. Shallower valleys overhang main valleys, sometimes resulting in waterfalls. The mountains become more rugged as a result of the glacial action and erosion. We might expect that glaciation and erosion would eventually level the surface of our planet but they will not, because they are offset by volcanism and other processes.

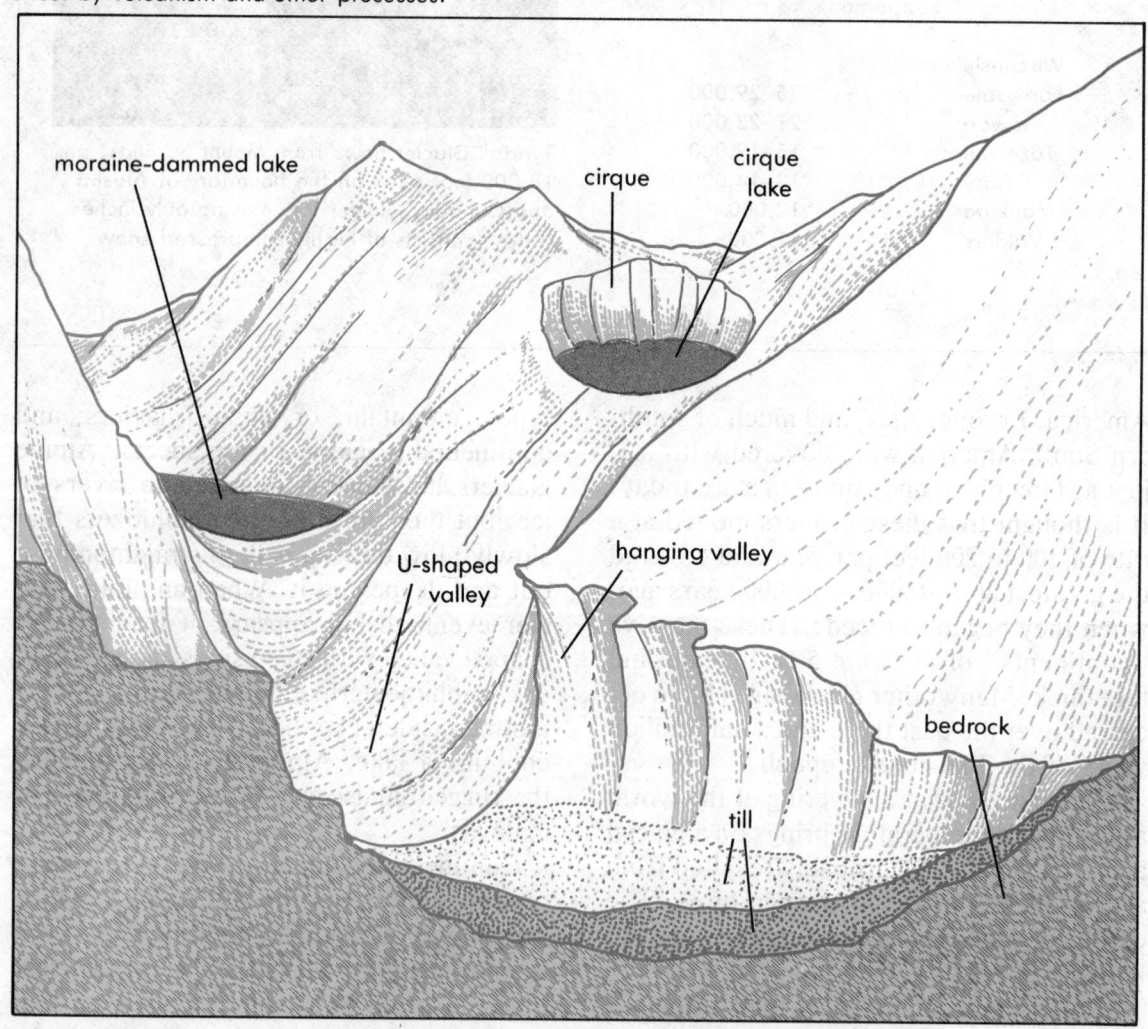

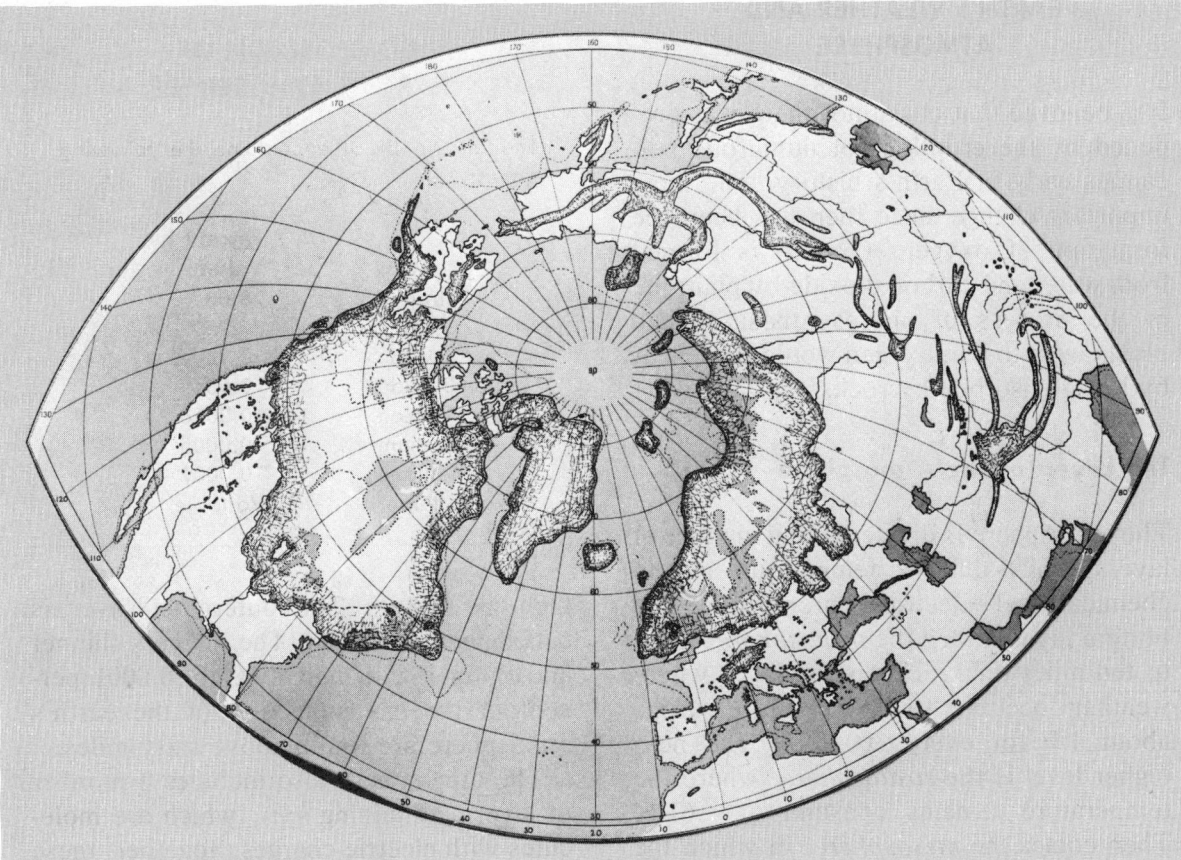

Extent of Glaciation in the Northern Hemisphere

THE ICE AGES

There is evidence that glaciers occurred in Pre-Cambrian times, as early as 600 million years ago. The glaciers that have left the clearest marks began in the Pleistocene. There were four major Ice Ages, with warmer periods between them. The map shows the greatest extent of the last glaciation throughout the Northern Hemisphere. In North America the ice sheet covered nearly all of Canada and extended well down into the United States. Its southern edge made a line roughly from New York City through Pennsylvania to the Ohio River, then up the Missouri River to central Montana. In the Far West, the glaciers in what is now the United States were mostly alpine glaciers, not the huge continental ice sheet that blanketed the eastern half of the continent. Some of the remains of glaciation that can be seen today include great scratch marks on rocks; the many lakes that dot Midwestern states like Minnesota, Michigan, and Wisconsin; long ridges called moraines; and flat prairie land where glacial drift has been spread over the bedrock.

The Ice Age began about two and one-half million years ago, about the time of early man. Some scientists speculate that our present age may be only another period between glaciations.

EARTH'S WEATHER AND ATMOSPHERE

It is believed that our atmosphere was produced by the eruptions of numerous volcanoes early in Earth's history. The most important change since then has been the formation of oxygen. Oxygen is formed from water and carbon dioxide by plant life in the process of photosynthesis. If all plants were to die, oxygen would disappear by being absorbed by rocks.

The Layers of the Atmosphere

The atmosphere is divided into a number of layers, which differ in temperature and in chemical and electrical properties. The bottom layer, called the *troposphere*, is six to ten miles thick. This is the layer where weather occurs. Its temperature drops about 1°F for every 300 feet. The next higher level is the *stratosphere*, where the temperature remains constant at −67°F. Then comes the *mesosphere*, in which the temperature first gradually rises and then gradually falls to −90°F at a height of about sixty miles. This is followed by the *thermosphere*, where the temperature rises as

	COMPOSITION OF EARTH'S ATMOSPHERE	

The air we breathe contains the following gases:

Gas	Percent by Volume
Nitrogen	78.08
Oxygen	20.95
Argon	0.93
Carbon Dioxide	0.03
Neon	0.0018
Helium	0.0005
Methane	0.0002
Water Vapor	Variable

high as 1800°F. The outermost layer is called the *exosphere*. The air gets thinner and thinner with height. Only 0.0001 percent of the gas molecules of the earth's atmosphere are found above sixty miles.

The atmosphere also includes a number of layers containing *ions*, which are molecules with electric charges. Together, these layers make up the *ionosphere*, part of which is in the mesosphere and part in the thermosphere. These charged particles reflect long radio waves, making radio trans-

Scientists divide the atmosphere into five zones, or layers, according to temperature and other factors. The ionosphere (not shown) is a special zone of electrically charged particles extending about 50 to 300 miles from the earth. In it appear the northern lights.

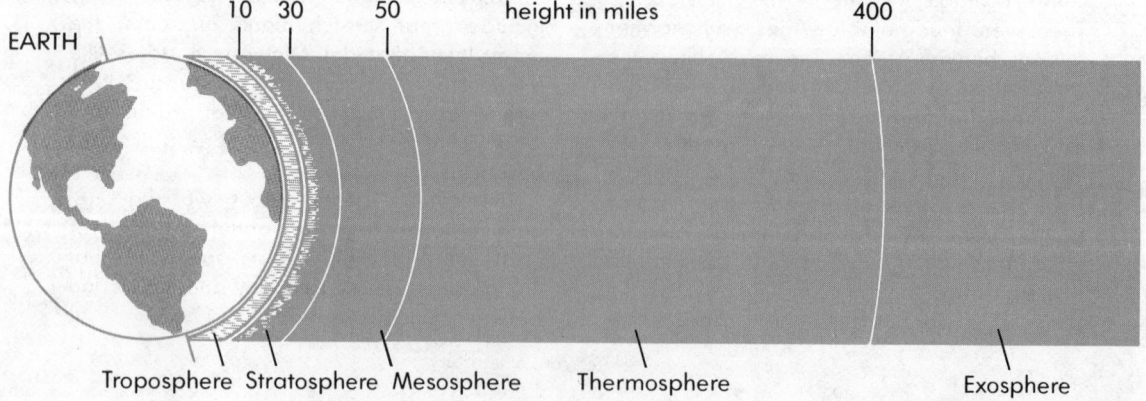

EARTH   10   30   50   height in miles   400

Troposphere   Stratosphere   Mesosphere   Thermosphere   Exosphere

mission beyond the horizon possible. Short waves, which strike the ionosphere more nearly perpendicularly, will pass through. The ionosphere is also responsible for the colorful display of the *aurora borealis,* or northern lights.

Wind

Wind, or air in motion, is produced by temperature differences on different parts of the earth. These temperature differences produce pressure differences, and the air flows from high pressure areas to low pressure areas. The direction of the wind is influenced by Earth's rotation (called the *Coriolis force*) and by friction with Earth's surface. Earth has several fairly steady wind systems, such as the *prevailing westerlies* in the temperate zones and the *trade winds* in the tropics. The *jet stream* is a special, high-altitude wind generally found 30,000 to 35,000 feet above the ground. It flows from west to east in both hemispheres, and its speed averages 175 miles per hour.

Wind Measurement. In some regions, the direction from which the wind blows can be associated with a particular kind of weather. For example, in many sections of the United States, a south wind signals the approach of warmer weather, and a north wind indicates the opposite. A wind from the west will most often bring fair weather; an easterly wind will most often bring rain or snow. A change in wind direction can serve as a useful indicator of a change in the weather.

An instrument that shows wind direction is called a *weather vane*. The most common weather vane is an arrow with a large tail. This arrow rotates freely on a fixed base and points into the wind in the direction from which the wind blows.

An instrument used to measure wind speed is called an *anemometer*. The cup anemometer is made up of three or four hollow, hemispherical cups attached to horizontal arms extending from a vertical axis. The force of the wind on the cups causes the apparatus to turn on the axis; the higher the wind speed, the faster the cups turn. The spinning apparatus is linked mechanically to a pointer that moves over a scale and indicates wind speed in knots or miles per hour.

Some instruments are designed to measure wind direction and wind speed simultaneously. One of these instruments looks like a weather vane, but has a hollow tube in the head of the arrow. The wind speed is measured in terms of the pressure of the air blowing into the tube. Another instrument that measures wind speed and direction simultaneously is the *aerovane,* which looks like a miniature airplane without wings. A tail fin keeps the instrument facing into the wind, and the wind speed is established by a spinning propeller.

Special Wind Storms

Hurricanes. One of the most destructive of all storms is the *hurricane.* A hurricane is a seasonal storm (most prevalent in August and September) that originates over the tropical regions of the Atlantic Ocean. Sometimes more than 300 miles in diameter, hurricanes move at speeds of ten to twenty miles per hour and have winds of over seventy-five miles per hour. (A hurricane generates more energy in one hour than all the electric power generated in the United States in one year.) At the center, or eye, of a hurricane is an area about five miles wide where the winds are usually calm and the sky above is sometimes clear. Hurricanes usually last from five to ten days. They lose force rapidly when they

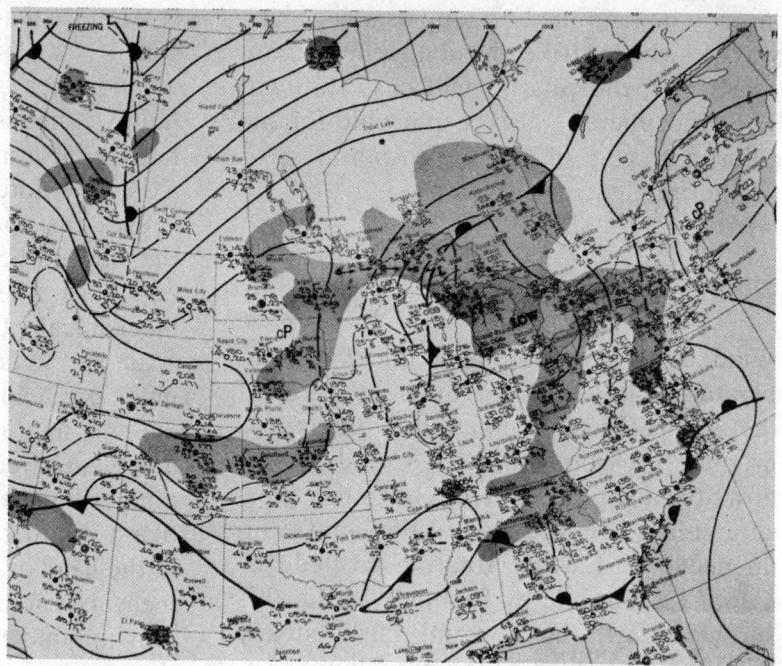

Daily weather maps are published in many newspapers to show the movement and development of weather patterns. Farmers follow weather information carefully, as do pilots, sailors, and thousands of amateur meteorologists.

move over land. On the average, two hurricanes strike in the United States each year.

A *typhoon* is the Pacific version of a hurricane. Typhoons occur mainly during February and March.

Tornadoes. Although limited in size and duration, *tornadoes* are the most violent and deadly of all storms. Ranging from 100 to 500 feet wide, they move at speeds of from twenty-five to forty miles per hour for distances up to fifty miles. A tornado has a dark funnel shape descending from a low cloud. A tornado that occurs over water is a *waterspout*. Most tornadoes occur in Australia and in the southern and western parts of the United States.

Tornadoes present a double hazard: high-speed winds and low pressure. Their wind speeds have been estimated to be as high as 500 miles per hour. The air pressure at the center of a tornado is very low, perhaps two-thirds that of the surroundings. Thus, closed houses over which a tornado passes

may actually explode from the normal air pressure within.

Weather and Climate

Climate is the average weather in a certain area. Many factors influence climate, such as distance from the equator, closeness to large bodies of water, altitude, nearness of mountains, and other factors. The climate is often cool and wet on the side of a mountain range toward the wind, and warm and dry on the other side. One reason the Pacific Coast is warm is because the Rocky Mountains block cold winter air from the east. Oceans tend to stabilize the climate of nearby land, because they are warmer than the land in winter and cooler in summer.

Air Masses

Air masses are large portions of air that are relatively uniform in temperature, pressure, and moisture. They are named according to the place where they originate. The most

TYPES OF CLOUDS

Cumulus. Puffy, cottony cloud typical of fair summer days. Under certain conditions, cumulus grows tall and becomes cumulonimbus.

Cirrus. Thin, feathery, white cloud formed of ice crystals, at very high altitudes (about 30,000 ft.). Cirrus carries very strong winds.

Nimbostratus. A true rain cloud, low in the sky. The base of a nimbostratus cloud looks dark and wet, with dark streaks running to the ground.

Cumulonimbus. A tall billowy cloud (thunderhead) that signals a coming storm. Formed by vertical winds, the cloud may tower 5 miles.

Altocumulus. Large tufts of patchy white or gray-shadowed cloud at middle altitudes in the sky (6,500–20,000 ft.).

Stratocumulus. Low clouds (under 6,500 ft.) in layers of rolls and patches that blend together. Stratocumulus may bring showers.

EARTH AND SPACE SCIENCE

important ones are *polar* and *tropical,* sometimes called P and T on a weather map. They are also called *arctic* (A) and *equatorial* (E). An air mass that begins on land is called *continental* (C); one that starts over water is called *maritime* (M). In general, MT (maritime tropical) air is warm and humid, CT (continental tropical) is warm and dry, MP (maritime polar) is cold and moist, and CP (continental polar) is cold and dry.

Fronts. Major weather changes occur at the boundaries separating air masses, called *fronts.* When cold air is advancing at the boundary, the boundary line is called a *cold front.* Cold fronts are usually accompanied by heavy showers and followed by lower temperatures. When warm air is advancing at the boundary, the boundary line is called a *warm front.* Gentle rains usually precede a warm front, followed by higher temperatures. A boundary line that is not moving is called a *stationary front.*

Frontal boundaries are shown as lines on a weather map, but they really extend upward from the ground. Since cold air is heavier than warm air, the cold air forms a wedge underneath the warm air. When cold and warm fronts meet, one of the air masses is lifted from the ground, thus forming what is known as an *occluded front.*

Modern Weather Instruments

Satellites. Since 1960, many Tiros weather satellites have been launched by the National Aeronautics and Space Administration. The cloud pictures taken by cameras in these satellites are used by weather bureaus to supplement other reports. Satellites are of great value to forecasters, because they provide information about vast areas of Earth where few weather observations are made. Satellite photographs also provide early storm warnings. Tiros satellites have demonstrated their effectiveness by identifying and tracking storms. When significant weather developments, such as hurricane and typhoon formations, are detected by the satellites, the weather bureaus issue special bulletins to nations that may be affected.

Radar. The National Weather Service maintains many long-range and medium-range radar installations at strategic points in the United States. This equipment is used to track severe storms.

Automatic Stations. In addition to manned installations, the National Weather Service also maintains automatic stations to provide weather information from remote, inaccessible locations. These automatic stations observe cloud height, visual range at airports for pilots, air pressure, and other weather conditions. They transmit these observations over teletype circuits. For extremely remote locations, an atomic-powered weather station was developed through the efforts of the Atomic Energy Commission (now the Nuclear Regulatory Commission) and the National Weather Service. One such station, installed in the Canadian Arctic during the summer of 1961, has been operating satisfactorily ever since.

Computers. To aid the weatherman in assembling and analyzing the wealth of weather data received, high-speed electronic computers have been installed at the National Meteorological Center, the National Weather Satellite Center, the National Weather Records Center at Asheville, North Carolina, and at various other research and forecast centers.

GLOSSARY OF TERMS USED IN EARTH SCIENCE

aerovane. An instrument that measures wind speed and direction at the same time.

air mass. A large portion of air with relatively uniform properties, especially temperature, pressure, and moisture.

anemometer. An instrument for measuring wind speed.

aurora borealis. A glow sometimes seen in the Northern Hemisphere, which is caused by ionized particles in the atmosphere, also called northern lights.

climate. The average weather conditions prevailing in a given area.

continental air mass. One originating over land.

Coriolis force. A force due to Earth's rotation that deflects winds to the right in the Northern Hemisphere and to the left in the Southern Hemisphere.

crust. The outermost part of Earth.

drumlin. Long, narrow hills of unsorted till left by a continental glacier.

earthquake. A movement of the Earth's surface due to faults in rocks, volcanic forces, and motion of the crustal plates.

epicenter. The point on the surface of Earth directly above the origin of an earthquake.

esker. Winding ridges of sorted till formed by a continental glacier.

exosphere. The outermost part of Earth's atmosphere.

front. The boundary between two air masses of different densities.

glaciation. Action that causes formation of glaciers.

hurricane. A severe storm with winds of greater than 75 miles per hour.

ionosphere. A region of Earth's atmosphere containing ionized particles that reflect radio waves of long wave lengths.

jet stream. A narrow band of very fast-moving westward wind in the upper troposphere.

mantle. The first layer beneath Earth's crust.

maritime air mass. One that forms over water.

Mohorovicic discontinuity ("Moho"). The boundary between Earth's crust and mantle.

moraine. A ridge of soil and rock deposited by a glacier.

occluded front. A weather front formed by a cold air mass entering under and uplifting a warm air mass.

plate tectonics. A theory that the continents float on plates, or sections of Earth's crust that rest on the mantle.

polar air mass. One originating in cold polar regions.

Richter Scale. A method of measuring earthquake intensity, based on seismograph tracings.

seismograph. An instrument that detects earthquake waves.

stratosphere. The second lowest layer of Earth's atmosphere.

thermosphere. The fourth layer of Earth's atmosphere.

tornado. A short-lived, violent cyclonic storm with winds up to 500 miles per hour.

trade wind. An almost constant wind that blows toward the equator from the northeast in the Northern Hemisphere and from the southeast in the Southern Hemisphere.

tropical air mass. One originating in the tropics.

troposphere. The lowest layer of Earth's atmosphere.

typhoon. A severe tropical storm in the Pacific region.

volcano. A vent in Earth's crust from which molten rock and gases issue.

waterspout. A tornado occurring over water.

wind vane. An instrument for determining wind direction. Also called a weather vane.

Beyond the Earth

THE SOLAR SYSTEM

Earth is one of nine planets that revolve around a star we call the sun. There are also thirty-one moons that revolve around the various planets. In addition there are asteroids, meteors, comets, dust, and gas. The whole, taken together, makes up the *solar system*. Mercury, Venus, Earth, and Mars are called the *inner planets*. They are small in size, have thin atmospheres, high densities, and only three moons among them. The rest are called the *outer planets* and are large (except Pluto), have heavy atmospheres, low densities, and a total of twenty-eight moons.

In addition to the planets in our solar system, a belt of asteroids lies between the orbits of Mars and Jupiter. Over 1,600 have been found, and scientists believe that more than 44,000 asteroids exist. They range in size from less than a mile to 470 miles in diameter.

Scientists are not certain of the origin of the asteroid belt. Some believe the asteroids are the remains of a planet that once existed between Mars and Jupiter. Other scientists believe that the large mass of Jupiter prevented the formation of another planet, so many small "planets" formed instead.

The diagram on the facing page shows the relative sizes of the planets.

FACTS ABOUT THE PLANETS

Mercury

Distance from Sun: 36,000,000 miles
Length of year: 87.96 days
Diameter: 3,000 miles
Length of day: 58.65 Earth days
Mass relative to Earth: 0.054
Surface temperature: 660°F (dayside)
Atmosphere: carbon dioxide
Weight of 150-lb. person: 55 lbs.
Number of moons: none

Venus

Distance from Sun: 67,000,000 miles
Length of year: 224.70 days
Diameter: 7,600 miles
Length of day: about 243 Earth days
Mass relative to Earth: 0.815
Surface temperature: 800°F
Atmosphere: carbon dioxide, water, and perhaps nitrogen
Weight of 150-lb. person: 130 lbs.
Number of moons: none

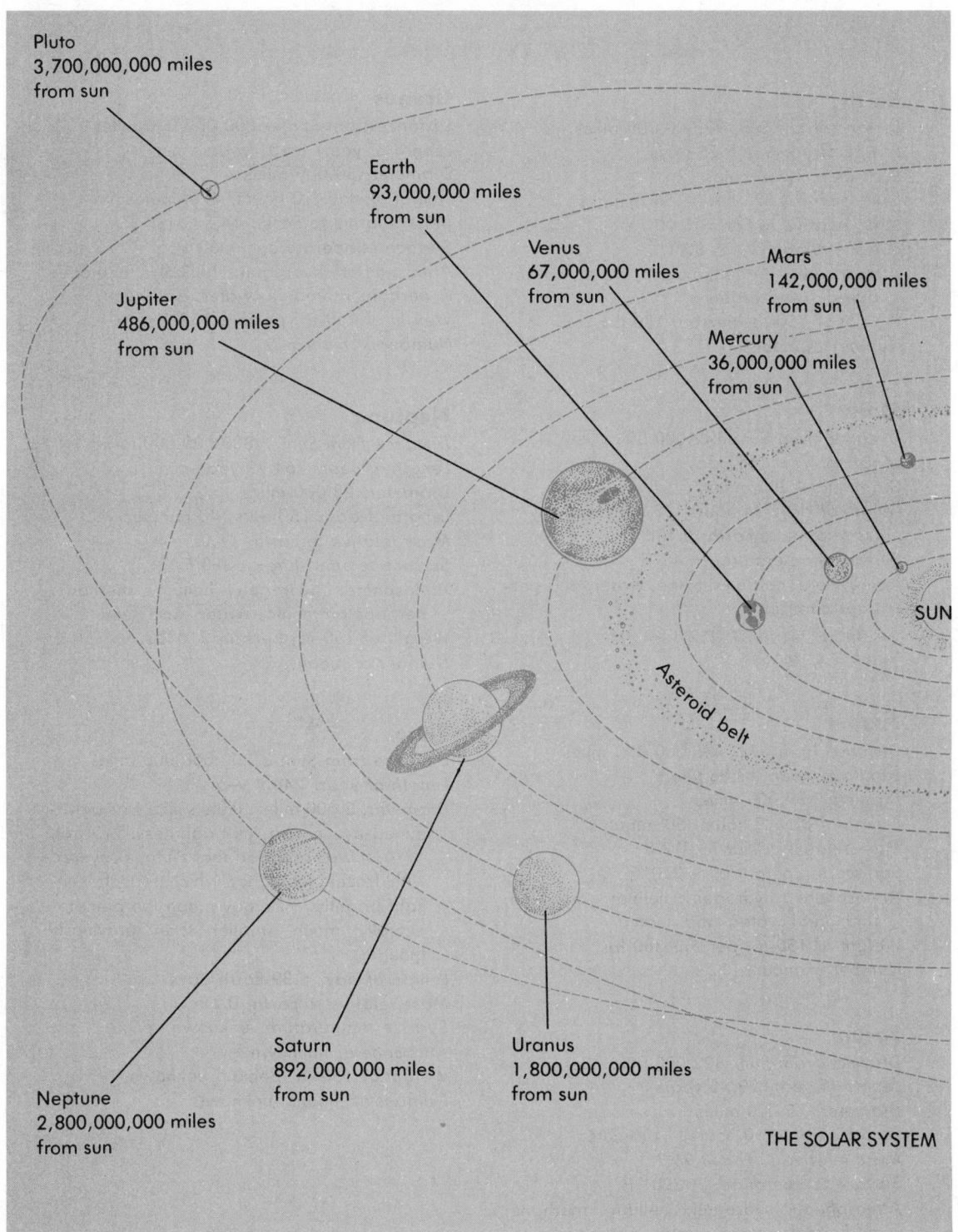

Pluto
3,700,000,000 miles
from sun

Earth
93,000,000 miles
from sun

Venus
67,000,000 miles
from sun

Mars
142,000,000 miles
from sun

Jupiter
486,000,000 miles
from sun

Mercury
36,000,000 miles
from sun

SUN

Asteroid belt

Saturn
892,000,000 miles
from sun

Uranus
1,800,000,000 miles
from sun

Neptune
2,800,000,000 miles
from sun

THE SOLAR SYSTEM

The solar system is composed of a sun, nine planets, and 31 moons as well as
dust, gas, meteoroids, asteroids, and comets. The planets are drawn to scale here
(there is doubt about the size of Pluto), but their distances from the sun are not.

Earth

Distance from Sun: 93,000,000 miles
Length of year: 365.25 days
Diameter: 7,900 miles
Length of day: 23 hours, 56 minutes
Mass relative to Earth: 1.00
Surface temperature: 60°F
Atmosphere: nitrogen, oxygen, water, carbon dioxide, and argon
Weight of 150-lb. person: 150 lbs.
Number of moons: 1

Mars

Distance from Sun: 142,000,000 miles
Length of year: 687 days
Diameter: 4,200 miles
Length of day: 24 hours, 37 minutes
Mass relative to Earth: 0.108
Surface temperature: −45°F
Atmosphere: carbon dioxide, water, and perhaps nitrogen
Weight of 150-lb. person: 55 lbs.
Number of moons: 2

Jupiter

Distance from Sun: 486,000,000 miles
Length of year: 11.86 years
Diameter: 89,000 miles
Length of day: 9 hours, 50 minutes
Mass relative to Earth: 317.8
Surface temperature: −240°F
Atmosphere: hydrogen, helium, methane; ammonia, water, and neon
Weight of 150-lb. person: 380 lbs.
Number of moons: 12

Saturn

Distance from Sun: 892,000,000 miles
Length of year: 29.45 years
Diameter: 75,000 miles
Length of day: 10 hours, 14 minutes
Mass relative to Earth: 95.2
Surface temperature: −290° F
Atmosphere: hydrogen, helium, methane; perhaps ammonia, water, and neon
Weight of 150-lb person: 160 lbs.
Number of moons: 10

Uranus

Distance from Sun: 1,800,000,000 miles
Length of year: 84.01 years
Diameter: 30,000 miles
Length of day: 10 hours, 49 minutes
Mass relative to Earth: 14.5
Surface temperature: −360°F
Atmosphere: hydrogen, helium, methane; perhaps ammonia, water, and neon
Weight of 150-lb. person: 155 lbs.
Number of moons: 5

Neptune

Distance from Sun: 2,800,000,000 miles
Length of year: 164.79 years
Diameter: 28,000 miles
Length of day: 15 hours, 48 minutes
Mass relative to Earth: 17.2
Surface temperature: −380°F
Atmosphere: hydrogen, helium, methane; perhaps ammonia, water, and neon
Weight of 150-lb. person: 210 lbs.
Number of moons: 2

Pluto

Distance from Sun: 3,700,000,000 miles
Length of year: 248.4 years
Diameter: 3,600 miles. Pluto's size was determined by, in part, its brightness. In April, 1976, it was reported that Pluto is covered with frozen methane, which reflects sunlight brightly. This may mean the planet is actually much smaller than previously thought.
Length of day: 6.39 Earth days
Mass relative to Earth: 0.18
Surface temperature: unknown
Atmosphere: unknown
Weight of 150-lb. person: unknown
Number of moons: unknown

LUNAR AND
SOLAR ECLIPSES

A celestial body casts a shadow into space when it is lighted from one side. The light usually comes from a sun. If another celestial body passes into this shadow, it is eclipsed. For example, when Earth passes between the sun and the moon, a lunar *eclipse* occurs. When the moon passes between the sun and Earth, a solar eclipse occurs. The shadow that is cast by Earth or the moon is really of two different darknesses. The inner shadow, which is very dark, is called the *umbra*. Outside the umbra is a shadow of semidarkness called the *penumbra*.

A lunar eclipse can only occur during a full moon, when sun, Earth, and moon are in a straight line. Most of the time, the moon's orbit takes it out of Earth's shadow. When Earth's umbra covers the moon's surface, a total eclipse of the moon can be seen from an entire hemisphere on Earth.

A solar eclipse occurs when sun, moon, and Earth are in a straight line. Because of the sun's size compared with the moon's, the umbra cast by the moon is small, covering an area about 167 miles wide. The penumbra covers an area about 2,000 miles wide. People in the area where the umbra falls see a total solar eclipse. Those in the area of the penumbra see a partial solar eclipse. Solar eclipses happen less often than lunar eclipses and are over more quickly.

Eclipses are great astronomical spectacles that are eagerly anticipated by laymen and scientists in the civilized world. Primitive peoples regard these celestial events with fear and awe, since they cannot understand how such phenomena occur. The explanations they are apt to offer are based usually on displeasure of the gods.

TOTAL LUNAR ECLIPSES 1978–1990

Date	Duration (minutes)
1978—March 24	218
1978—September 16	214
1979—September 6	206
1982—January 9	214
1982—July 6	224
1982—December 30	210
1985—May 4	212
1985—October 28	204
1986—April 24	210
1986—October 17	212
1989—February 20	212
1989—August 17	220
1990—February 9	204

TOTAL SOLAR ECLIPSES 1978–1990

Date	Duration (minutes)
*1979—February 26	3
1980—February 16	4
1981—July 31	2
1983—June 11	5
1984—November 22	2
1985—November 12	—
1986—October 3	—
1987—March 29	0.4
1988—March 18	4
1990—July 22	3

*to be seen on North American continent

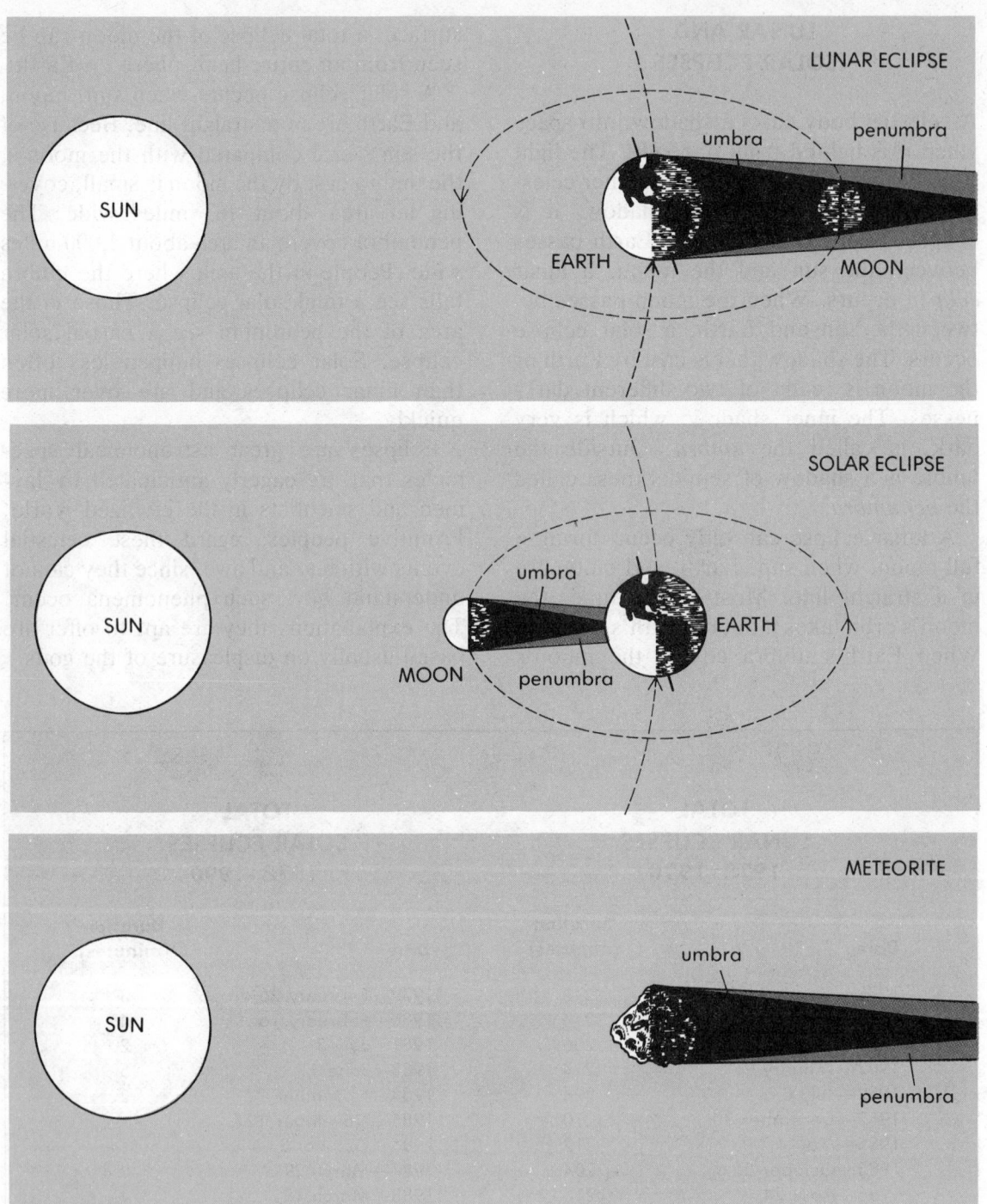

The earth's umbra (top) covers the moon in a total lunar eclipse. In a partial lunar eclipse, only a portion of the moon is in the umbra. In a solar eclipse (middle), the moon's umbra falls on the earth's surface. A partial solar eclipse is seen where the penumbra falls. Any celestial body (bottom) can cast a shadow in space.

EARTH AND SPACE SCIENCE

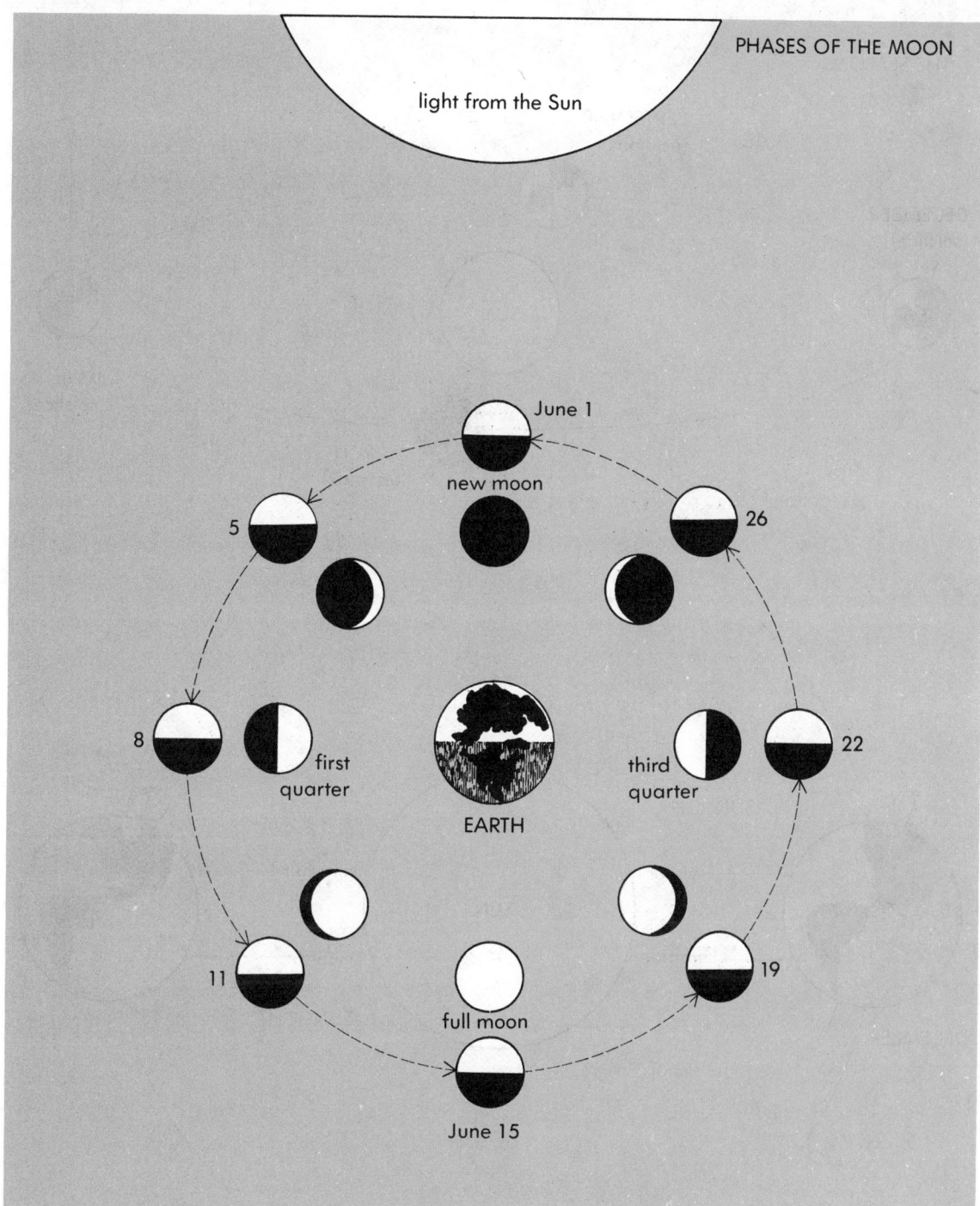

light from the Sun

June 1

new moon

5

26

8

first quarter

EARTH

third quarter

22

11

19

full moon

June 15

The phases of the moon relate to the amount of sunlight reflected by the moon to earth, determining how much of the moon we see. Actually, the moon always receives the same amount of sunlight. During the 29½ days the moon takes to circle the earth, it waxes to a full and then wanes to a new moon.

EARTH AND SPACE SCIENCE

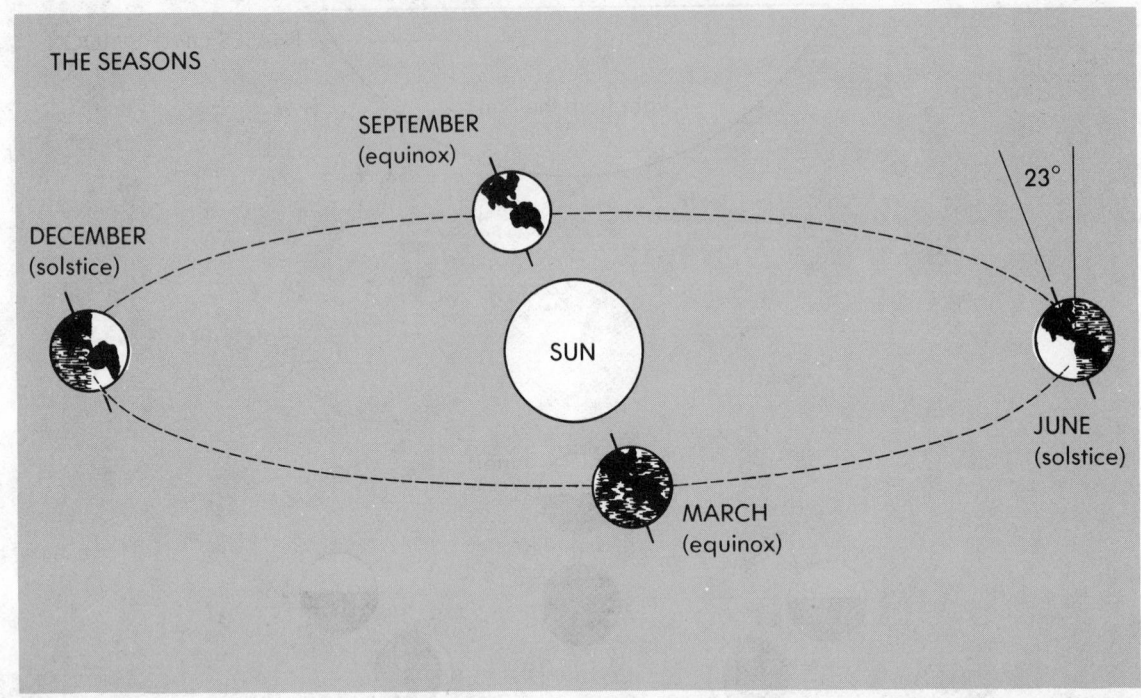

THE SEASONS

SEPTEMBER
(equinox)

DECEMBER
(solstice)

23°

SUN

JUNE
(solstice)

MARCH
(equinox)

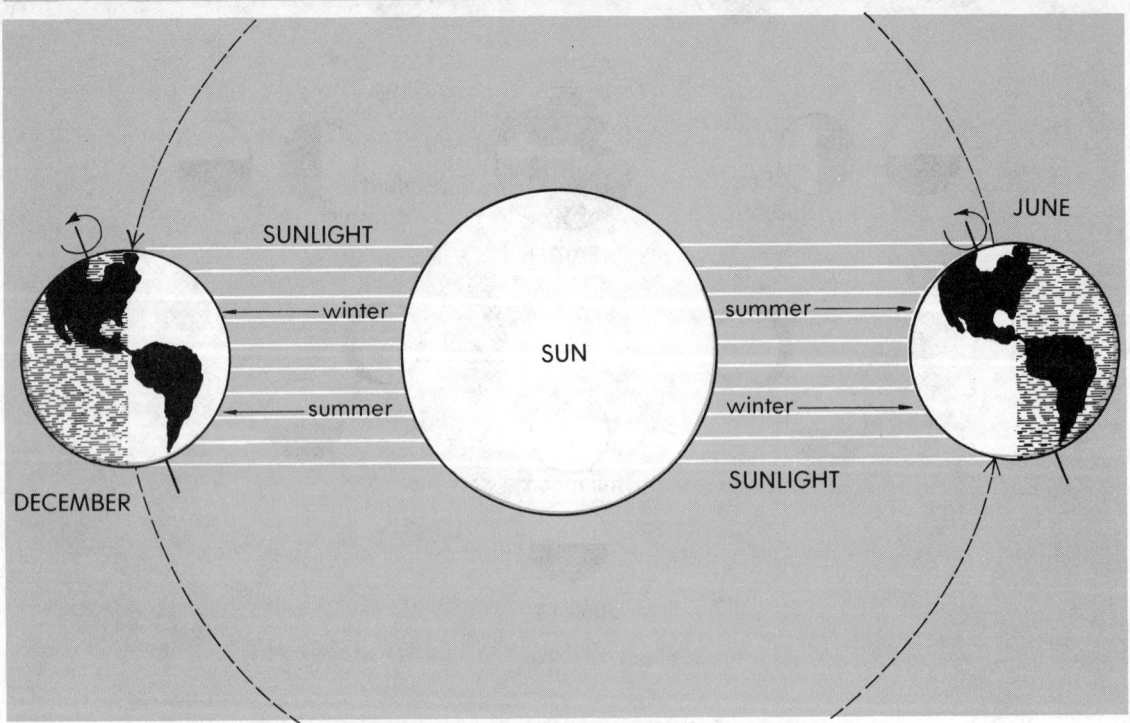

SUNLIGHT

winter

SUN

summer

summer

winter

JUNE

DECEMBER

SUNLIGHT

Seasonal changes (top) occur because areas of the earth receive different amounts
of sunlight through the year. When the North Pole tilts towards the sun, the
northern hemisphere is in summer and the southern hemisphere is in winter. When
it tilts away, the opposite is true. In summer, the sun's rays (bottom) hit the earth
more directly than in winter.

EARTH AND SPACE SCIENCE

GALAXIES

Our solar system is a small part of a *galaxy,* which is a very large collection of stars, gas, dust, and other objects traveling through space as a unit. Our galaxy is called the *Milky Way,* because if we look at the sky at night, we see millions of stars whose light combines to give a milky haze. The Milky Way is relatively thin and flat, something like a wristwatch, but it also has spiral arms, something like a pinwheel. Our sun is located in one of these arms, far from the center of the galaxy.

Distances in astronomy are so great that the unit most often used is the *light-year,* which is the distance that light travels in a year, or about six trillion miles. Another unit is the *parsec,* which is 3.26 light-years. The Milky Way has a diameter of about 100,000 light-years and is believed to be about 5,000 light-years thick. It contains about 100 billion stars, as well as huge amounts of dust and gas. The entire galaxy rotates very slowly, taking about 200 million years to complete one revolution.

The universe contains many billions of galaxies like our own—some larger, and some smaller. Each galaxy contains billions of stars. The galaxy closest to us is called Andromeda and is similar to the Milky Way, having spiral arms and about 100 billion stars. It is the only galaxy visible to the naked eye, but it is very faint, in spite of its great size, because it is two million light-years away. Many galaxies occur in groups called *clusters,* containing as many as 10,000 galaxies, all held together by gravitational force. Not all galaxies are spirals, like ours. About 20 percent are elliptical, and a small number are irregular in shape.

STARS

Many billions of years ago, the galaxies were vast clouds of hydrogen gas with a small percentage of helium. The laws of physics predict that such a cloud will break up into many smaller clouds under the influence of gravity, and that gravity will

Famous Whirlpool Nebula, or Galaxy, in Canes Venatici, photographed through the Hale telescope. Note the connecting arm of stars between the parent galaxy and its satellite.

Horsehead Nebula in Orion is one of the most spectacular objects in the sky, as seen in this photo made at Mt. Palomar Observatory, California, long a distinguished astronomical center.

also cause the smaller clouds to contract. As the hydrogen atoms in such a cloud fall faster and faster toward the center, the cloud becomes hot and starts to glow. Finally it becomes so hot at the core that a nuclear reaction begins, in which four hydrogen atoms are fused to form helium. This reaction produces huge amounts of energy, serving as the source of the energy of the stars, including our sun. The energy that is produced exerts an outward pressure, and at this point the gas cloud stops contracting. This is how stars are born. New stars still are being born from the gas in our galaxy.

Luminosity

One of the most important facts about a star is its brightness, or *luminosity,* which is the rate at which the star radiates energy. Astronomers generally use the term *magnitude* to express the brightness of a star. There are two kinds of magnitude. *Apparent magnitude* is the brightness as it appears to us, without making corrections for the distance of the star from us. *Absolute magnitude* is brightness after allowing for the fact that stars are at different distances from us. By agreement, the bright stars Aldeberan and Altair are given a magnitude of one and are first-magnitude stars. A first-magnitude star is 2.5 times as bright as a second-magnitude star and $2.5 \times 2.5 = 6.25$ times as bright as a third-magnitude star, and so on. The human eye can see stars down to the sixth magnitude, which is about 100 times fainter than a first-magnitude star. Since magnitude is a logarithmic scale, a star brighter than our standard has a negative magnitude. Apparent magnitudes range from -26.5 for the sun to $+24$, which can be detected only by the largest telescopes.

To calculate absolute magnitude, we must correct for the different distances of the stars. One star may look much fainter than another although it is actually putting out much more energy. It appears fainter because it is farther away. The apparent brightness of a star is inversely proportional to the square of its distance. That is, the farther away a star is, the less its apparent brightness. By agreement, the absolute magnitude is the value we would measure if the star or other celestial object were at a distance of ten parsecs (32.6 light-years) from us. This is easily calculated from the inverse square law if the distance is known. On this scale, the stars show a magnitude range of -10 to $+19$. Our sun is somewhere in the middle with $+5$. In size and energy output, ours is an average star.

The simplest way to find the distance of a star from Earth is to observe its position from two different points in Earth's orbit around the sun. From the shift in the position, the distance can be calculated. This method is useful only up to a distance of 100 light-years. There are many indirect methods for measuring more distant stars. The closest star is Alpha Centauri, about 4.5 light-years away.

Classification of Stars

Our eyes tell us that stars vary in color, some being a brilliant blue-white, others yellow, and still others red. The color depends on the surface temperature of the star, which can be measured fairly accurately by means of a spectroscope. Astronomers have classified stars into groups based on temperature. These groups are:

O	50,000°C	G	5,500°C
B	20,000°C	K	4,500°C
A	10,000°C	M	3,000°C
F	7,500°C		

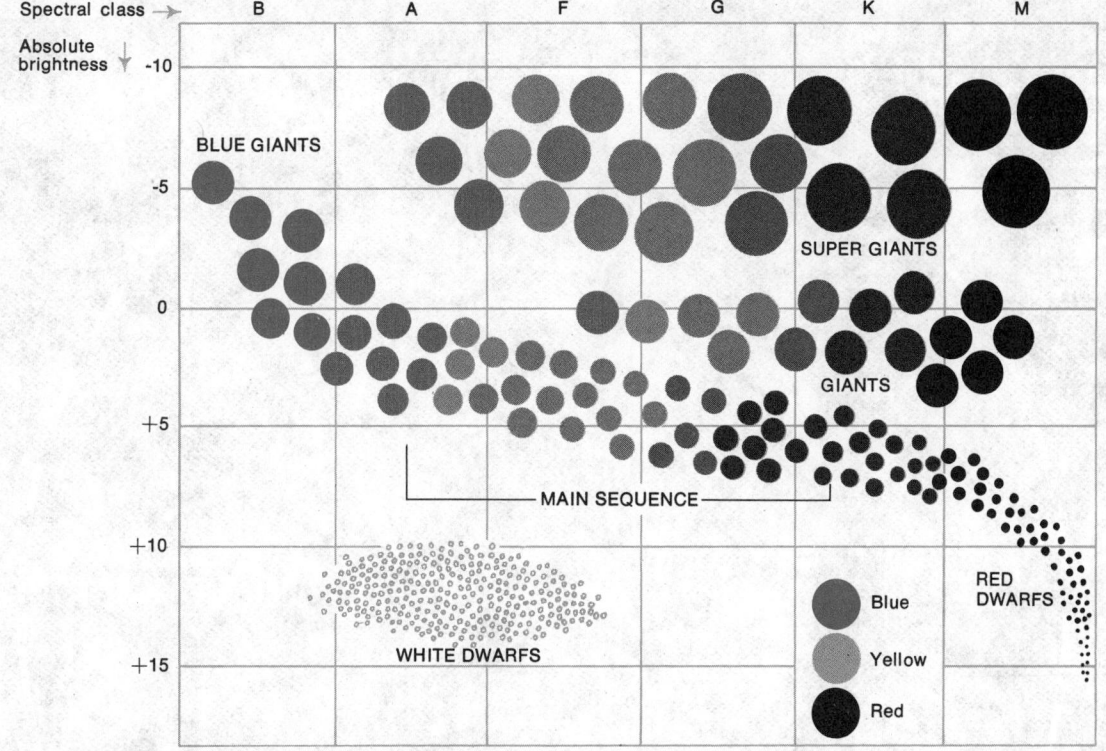

Spectral class →

Absolute brightness ↓

| | B | A | F | G | K | M |

BLUE GIANTS

SUPER GIANTS

GIANTS

MAIN SEQUENCE

RED DWARFS

Blue

Yellow

Red

WHITE DWARFS

Star field diagram plots the spectral class of a star (based on temperature) against its absolute brightness. The main sequence ranges from blue giants through yellow stars to red dwarfs. Outside the normal range are yellow and red giants and white dwarf stars.

Each major class is further subdivided. Our sun is class G2, temperature 6000°C.

The astronomers Herzsprung and Russell made a plot of the absolute magnitude (brightness) of many stars against their spectral class (surface temperature) and produced a diagram, called the H-R diagram. Most stars fall into a regular order called the *main sequence.* A star's position in the main sequence depends on its mass, or the amount of hydrogen gas in the star. The very massive stars have a high temperature and appear blue, whereas the smaller stars have a lower temperature and appear yellow, like our sun, or red. There are stars (giants and white dwarfs) which do not fall in the main sequence. It has been found that these represent dying stars, which are running out of hydrogen fuel.

The Death of Stars

When a star begins to run out of hydrogen at its core, the first thing that happens is that the star expands and its surface cools. It becomes a *red giant.* For most stars, the next stage is loss of the energy that kept the star from shrinking. It contracts and becomes a *white dwarf,* which eventually radiates away all its heat and becomes cold and black. This is going to be the fate of our sun. If a star is very large to begin with, however, its collapse will produce such high temperatures that the star will explode, forming a spectacular *supernova.* These are easily visible to the naked eye during daylight. The most recent supernova in our galaxy was seen in 1604. The core of a supernova can become a *pulsar,* or *neutron*

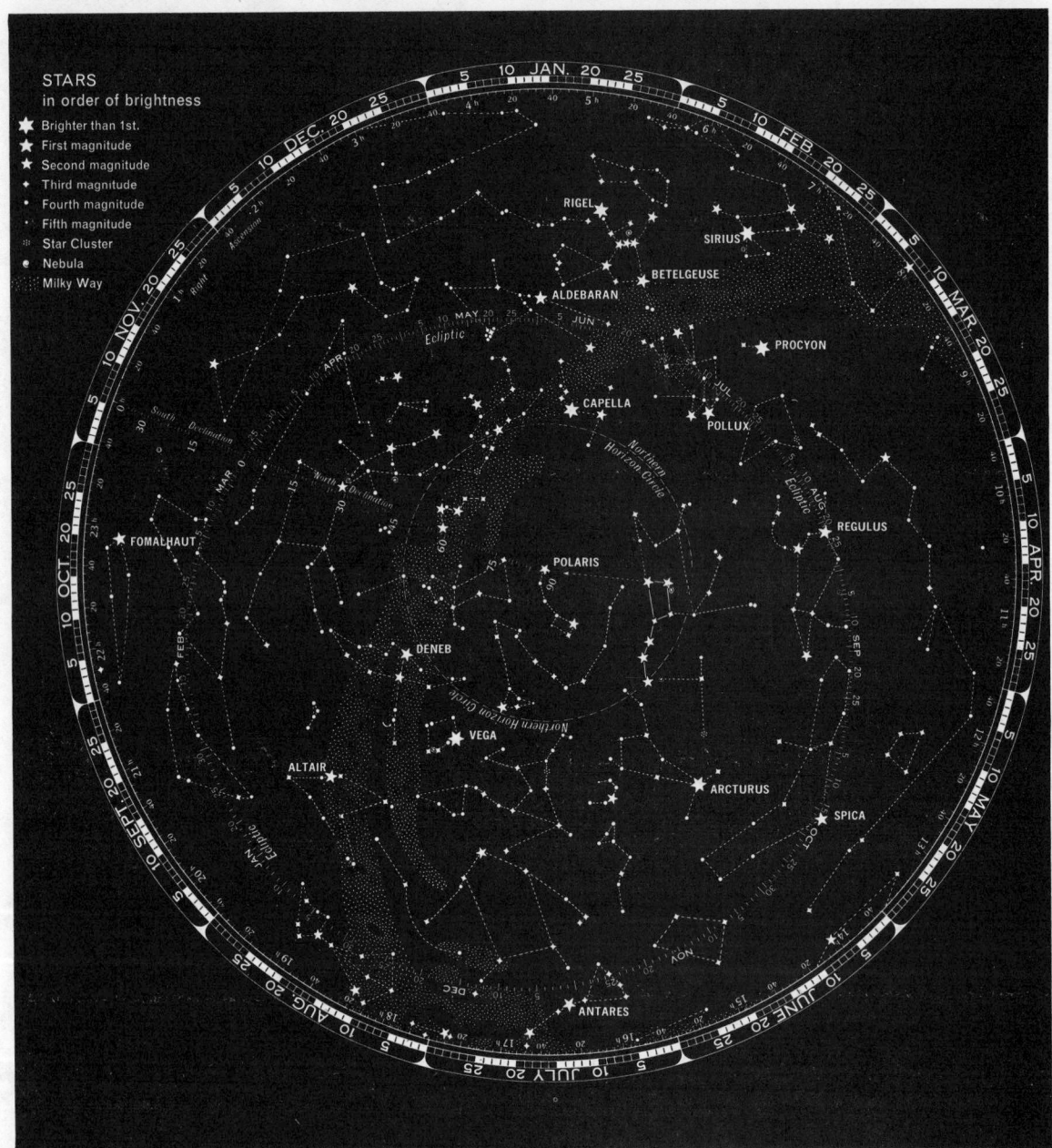

Star chart of the northern sky can be used by anyone in North America. Face north
and rotate the book until the current date is at the top. Stars in the upper two-thirds
of the chart are those visible at about 9 P.M. The star nearly at the center of
the chart is Polaris, the North Star. Stars within the northern horizon circle
correspond to the stars that rotate counter-clockwise around the North Star and
are always visible above the horizon for anyone living at 40° north latitude.
Stars to the right of center are visible in the eastern sky; those to the left of center
are visible in the western sky. Stars close to the upper edge of the chart are close
to the southern horizon. Amateur star-watchers are found everywhere, using even
modest telescopes to enjoy the great celestial hobby.

EARTH AND SPACE SCIENCE

star. This is an extremely dense object spinning at a rapid rate and putting out energy we detect as regular pulses. Or, the star can end up as a *black hole,* an object whose gravity is so great that even radiation such as light cannot escape from it. The star remnant must be at least twice the mass of the sun in order to form a black hole. As yet, there is no definite evidence that black holes exist.

The greater the mass of a star, the faster it burns out. The total life of the sun should be about ten billion years, but a star ten times the sun's mass will last only fifty million years or less.

COSMOLOGY

Cosmology is the study of the way the universe as a whole is organized, how it began, and what will eventually happen to it. One of the most important events in the history of astronomy was the discovery by the American astronomer Hubble, around 1920, that the universe is expanding. He observed that light from distant galaxies is shifted in its wavelengths toward the red end of the spectrum, and the farther away the galaxy, the greater the shift. The explanation accepted by nearly all is that the galaxies are receding from one another, and the farther they are from us, the faster they are traveling away.

The *red shift* is caused by the well-known *Doppler effect,* which causes light from a receding object to seem to have longer wavelengths. This led the Belgian astronomer Lemaitre and the Russian-American physicist Gamov to formulate the *Big-Bang* theory. This states that about fifteen billion years ago, all the matter and energy in the universe were concentrated in a huge fireball, which exploded and became clouds of hydrogen. The clouds, in turn, formed galaxies of stars. The expansion that began with the original explosion will continue forever, and eventually all energy will be lost by radiation and the entire universe will be dead.

Another theory, called the *oscillating universe,* accepts the initial explosion but states that the force of gravity will eventually cause the galaxies to slow down, stop, then come together again, reforming the original fireball, which will then expand again, and so on, a process which has already occurred an infinite number of times and will continue to occur forever.

A third theory, due to the work of the English astronomers Gold, Bondi, and Hoyle, rejects the Big-Bang theory entirely. They assume that the universe has always had the same average appearance as today and will continue in the same state forever. This is called the *Steady State* theory. To make up for the galaxies that move away beyond our reach, they assume that hydrogen atoms are being created continuously out of nothing and that these in time form new galaxies.

There is strong evidence that the Steady State theory is incorrect. Studies have shown that the rate of expansion of the universe is slowing down. This cannot be explained by the Steady State theory. Also, the Big-Bang theory predicts that the earth should be receiving microwave radiation of certain wavelengths as remains of the original fireball. This radiation was found in 1965 by Penzias and Wilson of Bell Laboratories.

It is not possible to decide at present between the expanding universe idea and the oscillating universe theory. For all matter to return to the original fireball requires that the total matter in the universe be more than a certain amount. Otherwise, the force of gravity is too small to stop the expansion. So far, there seems to be too little matter by a factor of about 30. However, it is entirely possible that additional matter will one day be discovered.

IMPORTANT EVENTS IN ASTRONOMY

Date	Scientist	Accomplishment
c. 270 B.C.	Aristarchus of Samos (fl.280–264 B.C.), Greek astronomer.	Was the first to maintain that the earth moves around the sun.
c. 150 B.C.	Hipparchus (fl.c.160–c.126 B.C.), Greek astronomer.	Measured the size of the moon and how far it is from the earth.
c. 100 A.D.	Ptolemy, in Latin, Claudius Ptolemaeus (fl.100s A.D.), Greek astronomer.	Published the *Almagest*, which developed his view of the universe with the earth at its center.
1472	Regiomontanus, pseudonym of Johann Müller (1436–1476), German astronomer.	Studied the comet that became known as Halley's Comet.
1543	Nicolaus Copernicus (1473–1543), Polish astronomer.	Published *De revolutionibus orbium coelestium*, which explained his ideas of a sun-centered universe.
1580	Tycho Brahe (1546–1601), Danish astronomer.	Completed his observatory from which he studied planetary motion.
1609–19	Johannes Kepler (1571–1630), German astronomer.	Formulated the laws of the motions of the planets.
1610	Galileo Galilei (1564–1642), Italian astronomer.	Published *Sidereus nuncius*, which supported the Copernican theory of the universe.
1682	Edmund Halley (1656–1742), British astronomer.	Calculated the correct orbit of the great comet of 1682, now known as Halley's Comet. He was the first to prove that comets orbited the sun.
1772	Johann Elert Bode (1747–1826), German astronomer.	Stated "Bode's law," which is a formula for determining the relative distances of the planets from the sun.
1781	Sir William Herschel (1738–1822), British astronomer.	Discovered the planet Uranus.
1796	Pierre Simon LaPlace (1749–1827), French astronomer.	Put forth the nebular hypothesis for the origin of the solar system.
1842	Christian Johann Doppler (1803–1853), Austrian astronomer.	His theory, called the Doppler effect, made it possible to calculate how fast stars move away from or toward the earth.

EARTH AND SPACE SCIENCE

Date	Scientist	Accomplishment
1846	Urbain Jean Joseph Leverrier (1811–1877), French astronomer.	Predicted the existence of Neptune by studying the motions of Uranus.
1846	Johann Gottfried Galle (1812–1910), German astronomer.	Using Leverrier's information, he was the first to see Neptune.
1912	Henrietta Swan Leavitt (1868–1921), U.S. astronomer.	Discovered the relationship between the periods and luminosities of variable stars, which aided in determining the distances to galaxies.
1914	Percival Lowell (1855–1916), U.S. astronomer.	Made the calculations that led to the discovery of Pluto.
1927	Abbé George Le Maitre (1894–1966), Belgian astronomer.	Proposed "Big Bang" theory of the universe.
1930	Clyde William Tombaugh (1906–), U.S. astronomer.	Was the first to see Pluto using Percival Lowell's calculations.
1931–32	Karl G. Jansky (1905–1950), U.S. astronomer.	Discovered radio waves from outer space. Radio astronomy was founded with this discovery.
1938	Hans Bethe (1906–), American physicist.	Showed that the source of energy in stars is a nuclear reaction in which hydrogen is converted into helium.
1958	James Alfred Van Allen (1912–), U.S. astronomer.	Discovered the Van Allen Radiation Belt surrounding the earth.
1960	Allen R. Sandage (1926–), U.S. astronomer.	With Thomas Matthews, was the first to identify radio emissions from quasars.
1963	Maarten Schmidt (1929–), Dutch astronomer.	Used red light shift to show that quasars are probably traveling away from us at extreme speeds.
1965	Arno A. Penzias (1933–), with Robert W. Wilson, American physicists.	Discovered the primordial background radiation of the universe which strongly supports the "Big Bang" theory of the universe.
1967	Anthony Hewish (1924–), British astronomer.	Discovered pulsars, stars which emit energy in regular pulses.

Space Exploration

On October 4, 1957, a new era in science and technology opened with the launching of Sputnik I by the Soviet Union. This four-ton missile went into Earth orbit and remained aloft for three months until it burned up in the lower atmosphere. The United States launched its first orbiting satellite on January 31, 1958. The technology advanced rapidly, and on July 16, 1969, Neil A. Armstrong and Edwin A. Aldrin, Jr., were launched in the Apollo spacecraft on a successful mission to the moon.

Manned Space Flight

The first manned flight took place on April 12, 1961, when Yuri Gagarin (killed seven years later in a jet accident) went into orbit in the Soviet Vostok 1 spacecraft. Gagarin made one revolution of Earth, and his total flight time was one hour, forty-eight minutes.

On May 5, 1961, the United States sent up its first astronaut, Alan B. Shepard, Jr. In a Mercury capsule boosted by a Redstone launch vehicle, Shepard made a suborbital, fifteen minute flight that took him to an altitude of 117 miles.

Vostok, U.S.S.R. Vostok was a cylindrical spacecraft, nine feet in diameter, about seventeen feet long, and weighing slightly more than five tons. It was an elementary one-man spacecraft, designed to prove man's survivability in space. The spacecraft was lowered to Earth by parachute after reentry. The cosmonaut ejected at a low altitude and parachuted separately. The Vostok program consisted of six flights between 1961 and 1963, including the first manned flight, the first missions of more than twenty-four hours in space (Vostok 2), and the first spacecraft piloted by a woman (Vostok 6).

Mercury, U.S. Like Vostok, Mercury was an elementary spacecraft, designed only for the initial steps of manned space flight. Mercury was a bell-shaped capsule, nine feet, seven inches long and six feet, two inches wide at its widest point. Its weight was about 3,000 pounds, varying slightly with each mission. The program consisted of six flights between 1961 and 1963, two of them suborbital and the rest orbital. The Redstone launch vehicle was used for the suborbital flights, and the more powerful Atlas rocket boosted the orbital missions. The program included the first

United States orbital flight (Mercury-Atlas 6) and the first flight of more than twenty-four hours by a United States spacecraft (Mercury-Atlas 9).

Voskhod, U.S.S.R. The second-generation Soviet manned spacecraft, Voskhod, made only two flights (1964–65), but it represented a considerable advance over its predecessor. Voskhod was the first spacecraft capable of carrying more than one person. Voskhod, at 11,700 pounds, was only slightly heavier than Vostok, but it was much larger—twenty-five feet long and thirteen feet in diameter. Voskhod was designed to stay a long time in space (up to two weeks), and an air-lock system permitted the cosmonauts to leave the spacecraft for extra-vehicular activity. An improved parachute landing system and shock absorbing system allowed the cosmonauts to return to Earth with the spacecraft rather than ejecting. Voskhod's first flight on October 12, 1964, marked the first multi-man space mission. A crew of three made the twenty-four-hour flight. The second flight on March 18 and 19, 1965, was notable because the co-pilot Alexei Leonov became the first space walker. He spent ten minutes outside the spacecraft in a special multi-layered extravehicular suit.

Gemini, U.S. The United States' second-generation manned spacecraft, Gemini, offered a great many improvements over Mercury. Among the most important, it was a two-man craft and it was maneuverable. All previous manned spacecraft had been unable to change course or altitude. Gemini was similar in shape to Mercury but a great deal larger—eleven feet long, seven and a half feet in diameter at its base, weighing about 7,000 pounds. Gemini was a two-part spacecraft, including a reentry module containing the crew and an adapter section containing some of the fuel and equipment. The latter section was jettisoned before reentry. Like Mercury, Gemini was a water-lander. After a parachute descent, it was capable of staying afloat on the ocean by means of a flotation system built into the base.

The first Gemini was launched March 23, 1965, and the program continued through ten manned flights; the last was launched November 11, 1966. The program included a number of highlights: the first orbital maneuvering by a manned spacecraft (Gemini 3); the first United States multi-man flight (Gemini 3); the first United States space walk (Gemini 4); a flight of exceptionally long duration—330 hours and 30 minutes—for that time (Gemini 7); the first rendezvous between two spacecraft (Gemini 6 and 7); the first docking in space (Gemini 8).

Soyuz, U.S.S.R. In 1967, the Soviet Union introduced its third-generation manned spacecraft, Soyuz. The first flight, on April 23 of that year, ended tragically when the parachute descent system became fouled, killing Vladimir Komarov, the first man killed on a space mission. Soyuz is a three-module spacecraft, more than thirty-four feet long, nine and three-quarters feet wide at its maximum diameter, weighing about 13,000 pounds (weights vary because Soyuz may be flown as a one-, two-, or three-man spacecraft). It was the first Soviet manned spacecraft capable of maneuvering, rendezvousing, and docking. Soyuz is an earthlander. In addition to the usual parachute descent system, it has a number of solid propellant braking rockets for softening the landing shock. It is a very long duration spacecraft, believed capable of thirty days or more in space. Among the highlights of the Soyuz program are the

MANNED SPACE FLIGHT

Mission/Crew	Country	Launch Date	Duration (days)	Mission/Crew	Country	Launch Date	Duration (days)

VOSTOK 1
  Yuri A. Gagarin[1]
	U.S.S.R.	April 12, 1961	0.075	GEMINI 7
				  Frank Borman
				  James A. Lovell, Jr.
					U.S.	December 4, 1965	13.8

MERCURY-REDSTONE 3
  Alan B. Shepard, Jr.
	U.S.	May 5, 1961	0.01	GEMINI 6
				  Walter M. Schirra, Jr.
				  Thomas P. Stafford
					U.S.	December 15, 1965	1.1

MERCURY-REDSTONE 4
  Virgil I. Grissom[2]
	U.S.	July 21, 1961	0.01	GEMINI 8
				  Neil A. Armstrong
				  David R. Scott
					U.S.	March 16, 1966	0.45

VOSTOK 2
  Gherman S. Titov
	U.S.S.R.	August 6, 1961	1.05	GEMINI 9A
				  Thomas P. Stafford
				  Eugene A. Cernan
					U.S.	June 3, 1966	3.0

MERCURY-ATLAS 6
  John H. Glenn, Jr.
	U.S.	February 20, 1962	0.2	GEMINI 10
				  John W. Young
				  Michael Collins
					U.S.	July 18, 1966	2.9

MERCURY-ATLAS 7
  M. Scott Carpenter
	U.S.	May 24, 1962	0.2	GEMINI 11
				  Charles Conrad, Jr.
				  Richard F. Gordon, Jr.
					U.S.	September 12, 1966	3.0

VOSTOK 3
  Andrian G. Nikolayev
	U.S.S.R.	August 11, 1962	3.9	GEMINI 12
				  James A. Lovell, Jr.
				  Edwin E. Aldrin, Jr.
					U.S.	November 11, 1966	4.0

VOSTOK 4
  Pavel R. Popovich
	U.S.S.R.	August 12, 1962	3.0	SOYUZ 1
				  Vladimir M. Komarov
					U.S.S.R.	April 23, 1967	1.1

MERCURY-ATLAS 8
  Walter M. Schirra, Jr.
	U.S.	October 3, 1962	0.38	APOLLO 7
				  Walter M. Schirra, Jr.
				  Donn F. Eisele
				  R. Walter Cunningham
					U.S.	October 11, 1968	10.9

MERCURY-ATLAS 9
  L. Gordon Cooper, Jr.
	U.S.	May 15, 1963	1.4	SOYUZ 3
				  Georgi T. Beregovoi
					U.S.S.R.	October 26, 1968	4.0

VOSTOK 5
  Valery F. Bykovsky
	U.S.S.R.	June 14, 1963	5.0	APOLLO 8
				  Frank Borman
				  James A. Lovell, Jr.
				  William A. Anders
					U.S.	December 21, 1968	6.1

VOSTOK 6
  Valentina V. Tereshkova
	U.S.S.R.	June 16, 1963	3.0	SOYUZ 4
				  Vladimir A. Shatalov
					U.S.S.R.	January 15, 1969	3.0

VOSKHOD 1
  Vladimir M. Komarov[3]
  Konstantin Feoktistov
  Boris G. Yegorov
	U.S.S.R.	October 12, 1964	1.0	SOYUZ 5
				  Boris V. Volynov
				  Alexei S. Yeliseyev
				  Yevgeny V. Khrunov
					U.S.S.R.	January 15, 1969	3.0

VOSKHOD 2
  Alexei A. Leonov
  Pavel I. Belyayev
	U.S.S.R.	March 18, 1965	1.1	APOLLO 9
				  James A. McDivitt
				  David R. Scott
				  Russell L. Schweikart
					U.S.	March 3, 1969	10.0

GEMINI 3
  Virgil I. Grissom[2]
  John W. Young
	U.S.	March 23, 1965	0.21				

GEMINI 4
  James A. McDivitt
  Edward H. White, 2nd[2]
	U.S.	June 3, 1965	4.1				

GEMINI 5
  L. Gordon Cooper, Jr.
  Charles Conrad, Jr.
	U.S.	August 21, 1965	8.0				

1. Since deceased; killed in jet training accident, March 27, 1968.
2. Since deceased; killed in Apollo pad fire, January 27, 1967.
3. Since deceased; killed on descent on Soyuz 1, April 24, 1967, when parachute system fouled.

Mission/Crew	Country	Launch Date	Duration (days)
APOLLO 10 Thomas P. Stafford Eugene A. Cernan John W. Young	U.S.	May 18, 1969	8.1
APOLLO 11 Neil A. Armstrong Edwin E. Aldrin, Jr. Michael Collins	U.S.	July 16, 1969	8.2
SOYUZ 6 Georgi Shonin Valery M. Kubasov	U.S.S.R.	October 11, 1969	5.0
SOYUZ 7 Anatoly V. Filipchenko Viktor V. Gorbatko Vladislav N. Volkov[4]	U.S.S.R.	October 12, 1969	5.0
SOYUZ 8 Vladimir A. Shatalov Alexei S. Yeliseyev	U.S.S.R.	October 13, 1969	5.0
APOLLO 12 Charles Conrad, Jr. Alan L. Bean Richard F. Gordon, Jr.	U.S.	November 14, 1969	10.5
APOLLO 13 James A. Lovell, Jr. Fred W. Haise, Jr. John L. Swigert, Jr.	U.S.	April 11, 1970	6.0
SOYUZ 9 Andrian G. Nikolayev Vitaly Sevastianov	U.S.S.R.	June 2, 1970	17.8
APOLLO 14 Alan B. Shepard, Jr. Edgar D. Mitchell Stuart A. Roosa	U.S.	January 31, 1971	9.1
SOYUZ 10 Vladimir A. Shatalov Alexei S. Yeliseyev Nikolai Rukavishnikov	U.S.S.R.	April 22, 1971	1.9
SOYUZ 11 Georgi Dobrovolsky[5] Vladislav N. Volkov[5] Viktor Patsayev[5]	U.S.S.R.	June 6, 1971	23.8
APOLLO 15 David R. Scott Alfred M. Worden James B. Irwin	U.S.	July 26, 1971	11.1
APOLLO 16 Charles M. Duke, Jr. Thomas K. Mattingly John K. Young	U.S.	April 16, 1972	12.4
APOLLO 17 Eugene A. Cernan Ronald E. Evans Harrison H. Schmitt	U.S.	December 7, 1972	12.6
SKYLAB SL-2 Charles Conrad, Jr. Joseph P. Kerwin Paul J. Wertz	U.S.	May 25, 1973	28
SKYLAB SL-3 Alan L. Bean, Jr. Jack R. Lousma Owen K. Garriott	U.S.	July 28, 1973	60
SOYUZ 12 V. G. Lazarev O. G. Markarov	U.S.S.R.	September 27, 1973	3
SKYLAB SL-4 Gerald Carr Edward Gibson William Pogue	U.S.	November 16, 1973	84
SOYUZ 14 P. Popovich Y. Artyushkin	U.S.S.R.	July 3, 1974	15
SOYUZ 16 A. V. Filipchenko N. N. Dukavishnikov	U.S.S.R.	December 2, 1974	7
SOYUZ 17 A. Gubarey G. Grechko	U.S.S.R.	February 9, 1975	22
SOYUZ 18 P. I. Klimuk V. I. Sevastyanov	U.S.S.R.	May 24, 1975	64
SOYUZ 22 V. Bykovsky V. Askenov	U.S.S.R.	September 15, 1976	9
SOYUZ 24 V. V. Gorbatko Y. Glazkov	U.S.S.R.	February 7, 1977	19

4. Since deceased; killed on descent of Soyuz 11, June 30, 1971.
5. Killed during descent of Soyuz 11.

first Soviet rendezvous and docking (the manned Soyuz 3 docked with an unmanned Soyuz 2); the first transfer of men from one spacecraft in orbit to another (Soyuz 4 and 5); the first triple launch and rendezvous of manned spacecraft (Soyuz 6, 7, and 8); the longest duration in space, set first by Soyuz 9 and topped by Soyuz 11 before the latter mission ended in tragedy.

Soyuz 11 was part of a three-spacecraft experiment in space-station development. The first segment, a prototype space laboratory called Salyut 1, was sent into orbit unmanned on April 19, 1971. Soyuz 10, launched April 22 and carrying a three-man crew, docked with Salyut and the cosmonauts transferred to the laboratory, where they conducted experiments for almost two days. They returned to Earth in the Soyuz 10. On June 7, Soyuz 11 docked with Salyut, and its three astronauts worked in the laboratory for twenty-three days. After undocking and starting the reentry phase, the cosmonauts died during the descent.

Apollo, U.S.   The third-generation of the United States manned spacecraft, Apollo, is the world's most advanced spacecraft, as demonstrated in repeated lunar landings. Apollo includes a command module; the reentry capsule, which also serves as crew quarters and command post; the lunar module, in which two of the three astronauts descend to the lunar surface; and the service module, a jettisonable segment which contains much of the fuel, expendables, and other equipment. Fully assembled, Apollo is about sixty feet long and weighs about 100,000 pounds—weights vary with each mission. A main propulsion engine (located in the service module and producing 20,500 pounds of thrust), together with sixteen small thrusters mounted around the cylindrical wall of the spacecraft, give Apollo extraordinary maneuver-

ability. The lunar module has separate descent and ascent engines for its trip to the lunar surface. Like all United States manned spacecraft, Apollo is a water-lander that descends to the ocean landing site by means of a three-parachute system. The first manned Apollo mission (Apollo 7), an eleven-day Earth-orbital flight, was flown October 11–21, 1968. The highlight of the program was the first manned lunar landing on July 20, 1969. Apollo 11 astronauts Armstrong and Aldrin were the first men to set foot on the moon. They performed a solar wind experiment; set up a seismometer to measure vibrations on the moon's surface; assembled a laser reflector to bounce back laser beams sent from Earth, enabling scientists to measure the distance between the moon and Earth to within inches; and collected forty-eight pounds of surface material.

On November 19, 1969, the Apollo 12 lunar module landed on the moon. On one of their two trips outside the lunar module, the astronauts walked to the lunar probe Surveyor 3, which had landed on the moon in April 1967. Some parts of Surveyor 3 were brought back to Earth so the effects of the moon's environment on them could be studied. The astronauts set up a seismometer, conducted experiments, and collected more lunar samples. After the astronauts had boarded the command module for return to Earth, the lunar module was crashed into the moon's surface so the vibrations it set up could be studied.

Apollo 13 was launched nine months after Apollo 11, but the mission had to be aborted because of a leak in an oxygen tank. The craft was already 205,000 miles from Earth. By using the engines of the lunar module, the astronauts were able to make a safe and dramatic return to Earth.

Apollo 14 was next sent to the moon. Shortly after its launch, it was feared that the mission would have to be aborted be-

Apollo 16 astronaut bounces over the lunar surface. In the background are the lunar module and the Lunar Rover. The entire world watched as men planted a plastic flag, suggesting territorial rights to the moon, rights that time and technological developments will confirm or refute. Of greater importance is full scientific understanding of the universe. Space flights can play a great role in gaining this understanding.

cause of a water leak. However, the problem was corrected and the flight continued on schedule. The astronauts on Apollo 14 carried out numerous experiments and spent more time exploring the moon's surface than had any previous expedition.

Apollo 15 made a perfect lift-off on July 26, 1971, and on July 30 landed on the moon. For the first time, the moon was explored with a lunar Rover, which carried the astronauts for several miles over the lunar surface.

Apollo 16 was successfully launched on April 16, 1972. Just eight months later, on December 7, Apollo 17 marked the last manned lunar space flight.

Salyut Space Laboratory

This USSR program is similar to the U.S. Skylab program. The first Salyut orbiting laboratory, weighing about twenty tons, was launched April 19, 1971. The first crew, consisting of G. T. Dobrovolsky, V. N. Volkov, and V. I. Patsayev, was sent up to man it on June 7, 1971, and spent twenty-four days doing experiments. The mission ended in tragedy, however, when the crew was killed during the return to earth. Since then there have been several other Salyut missions. In Salyut 4 A. Gubarey and G. Grechko spent twenty-eight days aboard a space laboratory beginning February 9, 1975. Salyut 5 was orbited June 22, 1976, and B. Volynov and V. Zholobov were sent up to man it on July 6, 1976. They spent forty-eight days in space doing experiments. Y. Romanenko and G. Grechko were sent up to man the orbiting Salyut 6 December 10, 1977, and during this mission completed a space walk of one hour and twenty-eight minutes.

Space Shuttle Orbiter taken aloft for first solo test flight, Oct. 12, 1977. This great piggyback duo has performed well so far and soon will be called on to start the United States space shuttle service for scientists, astronauts, and their equipment.

Skylab

The United States followed the Apollo program with Skylab, which uses modified Apollo hardware to create a prototype manned space station. Skylab is a large orbital laboratory weighing close to eighty-five tons. Its major elements are a large workshop, including laboratory and living quarters; a manned astronomical observatory; and a docking port for docking manned spacecraft.

Skylab was launched on May 14, 1973, as a single unmanned unit. A Saturn 5 rocket placed the space station 271 miles above the Earth. During the launch a metal covering protecting part of the space laboratory tore away, and two of the largest solar panels failed to open.

On May 25, 1973, the Skylab 1 astronauts—Charles Conrad Jr., Joseph P. Kerwin, and Paul J. Wertz—were launched to the space station for a twenty-eight-day stay in space. Their first assignment was to rig a sun shield to protect the laboratory and to fix the disabled solar panels. After successfully completing these tasks, they set about performing solar and Earth

Viking Orbiter and Lander being assembled on launch pad at Kennedy Space Center in 1975. Launched by a Titan III/Centaur rocket, it landed successfully on Mars.

324

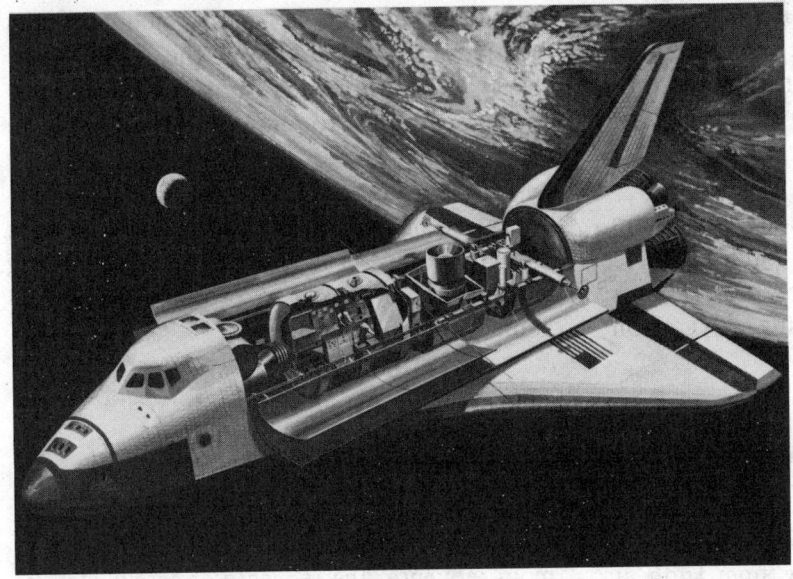

Artist's conception of a Space Lab, shown carried by the NASA Space Shuttle. In this flying laboratory, space scientists are able to perform many types of experiments while actually living in space. In time this capability will increase.

resources experiments. On June 22, 1973, the astronauts made a successful return landing in the Pacific.

On July 28, 1973, the Skylab 2 astronauts —Alan L. Bean, Jack R. Lousma, and Owen K. Garriott—set out to link up with the station. After being in space for fifty-nine days, they returned on September 25, 1973. The astronauts brought back 77,600 pictures of the sun's corona, 14,000 pictures of Earth, and 18 miles of magnetic tape data.

Space Shuttle Orbiter

This United States space vehicle is designed to be reusable, which should greatly reduce the cost of space flight. Its rocket engines will be dropped in the ocean after use so they can be recovered. The Space Shuttle Orbiter will carry a crew of seven, with supplies for thirty days, and will be used to ferry men and equipment to orbiting space stations and to rescue stranded spacemen. The Space Shuttle Orbiter will return to Earth with a glide landing and be ready for reuse in two weeks. A total of five are to be built. The first model was unveiled on September 17, 1976, and preliminary testing is well advanced.

Viking Mars Lander

This United States unmanned space vehicle is designed to land on Mars, photograph the terrain, measure wind velocities, and analyze the atmosphere. The Viking Mars Lander will even scoop up samples of Martian soil, analyze it, and try to detect evidence of life. This is designed to be done by adding some of the soil to a nutrient medium containing radioactive carbon. If organisms are in the soil, they should grow and produce radioactive carbon dioxide, which the instrument package is designed to detect. Viking 1 was launched August 20, 1975, and landed on Mars July 20, 1976. Viking 2 was launched September 9, 1975, and landed September 3, 1976. Both sent back very sharp pictures of Martian terrain and showed that the polar caps are ice, not frozen carbon dioxide, as some believed. They also showed dried river beds, evidence that Mars once had abundant water.

However, the tests for living organisms have been judged negative, although the possibility has not been entirely ruled out.

Other Space Probes

The Soviet Union has landed its Venera series probes on Venus. The landings have shown that Venus is extremely hot. This is caused by the large amount of carbon dioxide in its atmosphere, which prevents the planet from radiating the sun's heat. The United States has sent probes to Mercury and Jupiter to photograph and analyze those planets.

The international interest in space exploration has produced impressive amounts of knowledge for scientists. Continuing efforts are expected to produce additional benefits to mankind.

GLOSSARY OF ASTRONOMY AND SPACE SCIENCE

absolute magnitude. The apparent magnitude a star would have at a distance from Earth of ten parsecs.

apparent magnitude. A measure of the brightness of a star or other body as observed from Earth, with no correction for distance.

asteroid. A small planet, ranging in size from less than a mile to a few hundred miles in diameter.

Big-Bang theory. The theory that the universe was once concentrated into a fireball, which expanded in a violent manner.

black hole. A hypothetical body, resulting from the collapse of a star. Its gravity is so great that even light cannot escape it.

comet. A small body with a luminous tail, which revolves around the sun.

cosmology. The science that deals with the organization and probable future of the universe.

crescent moon. A phase of the moon when it appears to be less than half full.

Doppler effect. An apparent change in the wavelength of a wave motion due to the motion of the body producing the wave.

eclipse. The cut-off of light from a celestial body by the passage of another celestial body.

equinox. The time of year when the sun crosses the equator, and day and night are equal.

full moon. The phase of the moon in which its entire face is visible from Earth.

galaxy. A large collection of stars traveling through space as a unit.

gibbous moon. A phase when the moon is more than half full but not yet full.

light-year. The distance light travels in a year, about six trillion miles.

luminosity. The brightness of a celestial object.

main sequence. The sequence of normal stars on the H-R diagram relating brightness to surface temperature.

meteor. An object from the solar system that burns up in Earth's atmosphere.

neutron star. A star composed entirely of neutrons; one of the end states in the evolution of stars.

new moon. The phase of the moon in which its face is invisible.

oscillating universe. The theory that the universe expands and contracts repeatedly.

parsec. A measure of distance equal to 3.26 light-years, or the distance at which the radius of Earth's orbit subtends an angle of one degree of arc.

penumbra. The portion of a shadow in which only part of the light source is blocked.

pulsar. A star that emits regular, rapid radio pulses; thought to be a neutron star.

red giant. A large, cool star of high luminosity; an initial stage of a dying star.

solar system. The sun and the bodies that revolve around it.

solstice. The time of year when the sun reaches its farthest distance north or south from the equator.

steady-state theory. A theory of cosmology that postulates that the average composition of the universe is unchanging in space and time.

supernova. An explosion of a star releasing great amounts of energy and matter.

umbra. The central, very dark part of a shadow.

white dwarf. A very small, luminous star; one of the last phases in the life of a star.

THE WORLD

By late 1977 the flags of 149 member states flew at the headquarters of the United Nations in New York City. In 1945, when the UN was founded to maintain world peace, only 51 nations were members. The past decade has seen national boundaries change dramatically, particularly in Africa, where former colonies have achieved independence. Too few of us know the names of these new nations or other vital facts about them. Yet, as responsible citizens, we must keep informed about other countries and peoples as well as about ourselves.

The following pages tell us about new and old nations and contain up-to-date maps of all parts of the globe. Refer to these pages when you need geographic information. To find additional information about geography as well as about other social sciences, consult the Concise Edition of the *Student Handbook*.

Countries of the World

Afghanistan

Official name: Republic of Afghanistan
Area: 250,775 square miles
Location: South-central Asia, just north of Pakistan, landlocked
Natural features: The Hindu Kush mountain range runs through the center of the country. Mountains and desert country are interspersed with small, fertile valleys, irrigated by mountain streams.
Population: 19,500,000 (1977 est.)
Capital: Kabul
Other principal cities: Kandahar, Baghlan, Herat
Languages: Pushtu, Dari
Religion: Moslem
Leading industries: Agriculture, textile weaving, flour milling

Albania

Official name: People's Socialist Republic of Albania
Area: 11,100 square miles
Location: Southeast Europe, on the west coast of the Balkan peninsula
Natural features: More than two-thirds of Albania consists of hills and mountains, often covered with scrub forest. Only the coastal plain is level and rolling.
Population: 2,500,000 (1977 est.)
Capital: Tirana
Other principal cities: Durrës, Vlorë, Shkodër
Languages: Albanian (based on Tosk), Gheg
Religions: Moslem, Orthodox Christian, Roman Catholic. All religious institutions were closed by the government in 1967.
Leading industries: Agriculture; oil production and refining; manufacturing of chemicals, fertilizers, construction materials, and textiles

Algeria

Official name: Democratic and Popular Republic of Algeria
Area: 919,591 square miles
Location: North Africa, on the Mediterranean Sea between Morocco and Tunisia
Natural features: Most of Algeria is covered by the Sahara Desert. In the north, where most of the people live, there are a narrow coastal plain and two east-west mountain ranges—the Tell Atlas and the Saharan Atlas—separated by a plateau.
Population: 17,800,000 (1977 est.)
Capital: Algiers
Other principal cities: Oran, Constantine, Annaba
Languages: Arabic, French
Religion: Moslem
Leading industries: Agriculture, livestock raising, fishing, mining, food and leather processing

Andorra

Official name: Principality of Andorra
Area: 190 square miles
Location: Europe. One of the smallest states in Europe, Andorra is located in the eastern Pyrenees, between France and Spain.
Natural features: Drained by the Valira River, Andorra has a rugged landscape, dominated by mountains and cut by deep gorges.
Population: 27,200 (1977 est.)
Capital: Andorra la Vella
Other principal cities: Sant Juliá, Encamp
Language: Catalan
Religion: Roman Catholic
Leading industries: Tourism, agriculture and livestock raising, timber production

Angola

Official name: People's Republic of Angola
Area: 481,351 square miles
Location: West-central Africa. Bordered by Atlantic Ocean on the west, South-West Africa on the south, and Zaïre and Zambia on the north and east.
Natural features: A narrow coastal strip rises sharply toward an interior plateau (3000–5000 feet); a highland area of 6000 to 7000 feet lies in west-central region.
Population: 6,800,000 (1977 est.)
Capital: Luanda
Other principal cities: Huambo, Lobito, Benguela
Languages: Portuguese, African languages, chiefly of Bantu origin
Religions: Majority, tribal religions; 40 percent Christian
Leading industries: Agriculture, fishing, oil refining, paper and metal products, timber

Argentina

Official name: Argentine Republic
Area: 1,068,296
Location: Southern South America, next to Chile. The second largest Latin American country, Argentina dominates the southern half of the continent.
Natural features: Argentina has four major land regions: rich, fertile pampas in the heartland of the country, fanning out from the east-central section; subtropical lowlands in the north; the Andes mountain range in the west; and the Patagonian steppe and rainy Tierra del Fuego in the south.
Population: 26,100,000 (1977 est.)
Capital: Buenos Aires
Other principal cities: Córdoba, Rosario, Lanús
Language: Spanish
Religion: Roman Catholic
Leading industries: Agriculture and livestock raising; petroleum production; mining; iron and steel production; manufacturing of automobiles, machinery, chemicals, and cement

Australia

Official name: Commonwealth of Australia
Area: 2,967,909 square miles
Location: Southern hemisphere. Australia is a large island continent that lies southeast of Asia, between the Indian and Pacific oceans.
Natural features: Most of the continent is a low plateau, with a flat, arid center. Some mountain chains lie close to the coast, and on the southeastern corner is a huge fertile plain of about 500,000 square miles.
Population: 13,987,600 (1977 est.)
Capital: Canberra
Other principal cities: Sydney, Melbourne, Brisbane, Adelaide, Perth, Hobart
Language: English
Religions: Anglican, Roman Catholic

Souf, Algeria. Situated in the drifting sands of the Sahara, Souf is a group of oases famous for the golden Deglet Mir dates. There would be no life in the area, much of which is below sea level, without water from these oases.

Leading industries: Agriculture and livestock raising (particularly sheep; Australia produces almost one-third of the world's wool); manufacturing of steel, automobiles, ships, textiles, chemicals, and electrical equipment; petroleum refining; mining

Austria

Official name: Republic of Austria
Area: 32,375 square miles
Location: Central Europe. A landlocked nation, Austria is located just south of West Germany and Czechoslovakia.
Natural features: The country is 70 percent mountainous, dominated in the western and southern sections by the Austrian Alps. The eastern provinces are drained by the Danube River.
Population: 7,600,000 (1977 est.)
Capital: Vienna
Other principal cities: Graz, Linz, Salzburg, Innsbruck
Language: German
Religion: Roman Catholic
Leading industries: Iron and steel production; food processing; manufacturing of machinery, chemicals, textiles, ceramics, and metal goods; stone and glass

Bahamas

Official name: Commonwealth of the Bahamas
Area: 5,382 square miles
Location: An archipelago located in northern portion of the West Indies in the Atlantic Ocean
Natural features: Includes 700 islands and 2000 rocks and cays; less than 30 of the islands are inhabited. Islands are low and flat with excellent beaches.
Population: 210,000 (1977 est.)
Capital: Nassau
Other principal city: Freeport
Language: English
Religions: Primarily Baptist, Anglican, and Roman Catholic
Leading industry: Tourism is the main source of income.

Bahrain

Official name: State of Bahrain
Area: 240 square miles
Location: Southwest Asia. Bahrain is a tiny island nation in the Gulf of Bahrain, an inlet of the Persian Gulf.
Natural features: Bahrain is an archipelago. The islands are generally low and level, composed of sand and bare rock.
Population: 300,000 (1977 est.)
Capital: Manama
Other principal city: Muharraq
Language: Predominantly Arabic
Religion: Moslem

Leading industries: Petroleum refining and production of crude oil

Bangladesh

Official name: People's Republic of Bangladesh
Area: 55,126 square miles
Location: South Asia, in the eastern part of the Indian subcontinent, on the Bay of Bengal. Bangladesh is bordered on the west, north, and east by India; on the southeast by Burma; and by the Bay of Bengal on the south.
Natural features: Bangladesh is a subtropical alluvial plain, drained by the Ganges and the Jamuna rivers.
Population: 77,000,000 (1977 est.)
Capital: Dacca
Other principal cities: Chittagong, Khulna
Language: Bengali
Religions: Moslem, Buddhist, Hindu, (some Christian)
Leading industry: Agriculture (principal crop, jute)

Barbados

Official name: Barbados
Area: 166 square miles
Location: West Indies. The most easterly of the islands in the Caribbean, Barbados lies just east of the Windward Islands and about 270 miles northeast of South America.
Natural features: Barbados, a coral island, is flat except for a small area of highlands in the northeast.
Population: 250,000 (1977 est.)
Capital and principal city: Bridgetown
Language: English
Religion: Anglican
Leading industries: Agriculture (principal crop, sugarcane), sugar refining, fishing, tourism

Belgium

Official name: Kingdom of Belgium
Area: 11,781 square miles
Location: Northwest Europe, on the North Sea next to the Netherlands
Natural features: Most of Belgium is relatively flat, except for the hilly, wooded Ardennes region in the southeast.
Population: 9,820,000 (1977 est.)
Capital: Brussels
Other principal cities: Antwerp, Liège, Ghent
Languages: French, Flemish, German
Religion: Roman Catholic
Leading industries: Mining (coal); diamond cutting; shipbuilding; manufacturing of steel, textiles, chemicals, glass

Benin (Dahomey)

Official name: People's Republic of Benin
Area: 43,483 square miles

Location: West Africa, just west of Nigeria

Natural features: On the south is a narrow, sandy coastline; to the north and farther inland is a flat region (the main oil-palm producing area); still farther north are the Atakora Mountains and grasslands.

Population: 3,250,000 (1977 est.)

Capital: Porto Novo

Other principal cities: Cotonou, Natatingou, Abomey

Languages: French, African dialects

Religions: Animist, Moslem, Roman Catholic

Leading industries: Agriculture (particularly oil palm), processing of palm oil products, fishing

Bhutan

Official name: Kingdom of Bhutan

Area: 18,147 square miles

Location: Central Asia, on the Indian subcontinent in the eastern Himalayas

Natural features: In the north are the peaks of the Himalayas that tower up to 25,000 feet; in the densely populated central region are fertile valleys; and in the south is the low Duar Plain covered with semitropical forest.

Population: 1,200,000 (1977 est.)

Capital and largest city: Thimphu

Languages: Dzongka, Nepali

Religion: Buddhist

Leading industry: Agriculture

Bolivia

Official name: Republic of Bolivia

Area: 424,163 square miles

Location: Central South America, next to Brazil; a landlocked country

Natural features: Between the two ranges of the Andes Mountains is a bleak, densely populated plateau, the Altiplano; in the intermediary region (yungas) are the eastern mountain slopes and valleys, and to the north and southeast are the sparsely populated Amazon-Chaco lowlands.

Population: 4,800,000 (1977 est.)

Capital: La Paz (administrative); Sucre (legal and judicial)

Other principal cities: Cochabamba, Santa Cruz

Languages: Spanish, Indian dialects

Religion: Roman Catholic

Leading industries: Mining (particularly tin); agriculture; food processing; manufacturing of textiles, leather goods, cement, ceramics

Botswana

Official name: Botswana

Area: 224,764 square miles

Location: Southern Africa. A landlocked country just north of South Africa.

Natural features: Western and central Botswana is covered mostly by the Kalahari Desert; the north-west is drained by the Okavango River, forming a great inland delta known as the Okavango Swamps; in the east the land is well-watered and fertile.

Population: 700,000 (1977 est.)

Capital: Gaborone

Other principal cities: Francistown, Selebi-Pikwe

Languages: English; Setswana, the main African language; Khoisan (spoken by the Bushmen)

Religions: Tribal religions, Christian

Leading industries: Animal husbandry (particularly cattle), agriculture, meat processing, mining

Brazil

Official name: Federative Republic of Brazil

Area: 3,286,470 square miles

Location: South America. The largest nation in South America and the fifth largest in the world, Brazil dominates the northern half of the continent.

Natural features: The country is divided into four major regions: the tropical basin of the Amazon in the north; the semiarid scrub land of the northeast; the agricultural-mineral heartland of the south-central plains; and the fertile coastal belt extending from Natal to Porto Alegre.

Population: 107,000,000 (1977 est.)

Capital: Brasília

Principal cities: São Paulo, Rio de Janeiro, Belo Horizonte, Recife, Salvador

Language: Portuguese

Indians dancing at Copacabana on Lake Titicaca in Bolivia. Half of all Bolivians are Indians. The men wear wool hats with ear flaps, the women high hats and many petticoats.

Religion: Roman Catholic
Leading industries: Agriculture (principal crop, coffee); mining of iron, manganese, bauxite, gold, and diamonds; food processing; manufacturing of chemicals, textiles, and metallurgical products

Bulgaria

Official name: People's Republic of Bulgaria
Area: 42,823 square miles
Location: Southeast Europe on the Balkan peninsula, bordered on the east by the Black Sea, on the north by Rumania, on the south by Turkey and Greece, and on the west by Yugoslavia.
Natural features: Bulgaria is divided roughly into three parallel east-west zones: the Danube basin tableland in the north, the Stara Planina Mountains in the central region, and the Thracian Plain and Rhodope Mountains in the south and southwest.
Population: 8,800,000 (1977 est.)
Capital: Sofia
Other principal cities: Plovdiv, Varna, Ruse, Burgas
Language: Bulgarian
Religion: Bulgarian Orthodox
Leading industries: Agriculture, food processing, iron and steel production, mining

Burma

Official name: Socialist Republic of the Union of Burma
Area: 261,789 square miles
Location: Southeast Asia, on the Andaman Sea
Natural features: Mountain ranges form a horseshoe on the north, east, and west of diamond-shaped Burma. The Irrawaddy River drains the center and fertile southern regions. The coasts are rocky and steep, and many islands dot the shore.
Population: 31,500,000 (1977 est.)
Capital: Rangoon
Other principal cities: Mandalay, Moulmein
Language: Burmese
Religion: Buddhist
Leading industries: Agriculture (mainly rice), forestry, fishing, petroleum production

Burundi

Official name: Republic of Burundi
Area: 10,747 square miles
Location: East-central Africa on Lake Tanganyika
Natural features: Grassy uplands and high plateaus
Population: 4,000,000 (1977 est.)
Capital and principal city: Bujumbura
Languages: Kirundi, French
Religions: Roman Catholic, Animist
Leading industries: Agriculture, food processing

Cambodia

Official name: Democratic Kampuchea
Area: 69,898 square miles
Location: Southeast Asia. Cambodia is bordered by

Between the ninth and twelfth centuries A.D., the Khmers dominated most of what is now Southeast Asia. Angkor Wat is the best preserved temple in the Khmer ruins, Cambodia.

Laos and Thailand on the north, by Vietnam on the southeast, by Thailand on the west, and by the Gulf of Thailand on the southwest.
Natural features: Cambodia is composed of an alluvial plain situated in a mountain-rimmed basin; it is drained by the Mekong River.
Population: 7,735,279 (1976 est.)
Capital: Phnom Penh
Other principal cities: Battambang, Kompong Cham
Languages: Cambodian (Khmer), French
Religion: Theravada Buddhist
Leading industry: Agriculture (particularly rice)

Cameroon

Official name: United Republic of Cameroon
Area: 183,568 square miles
Location: West-central Africa on the Gulf of Guinea
Natural features: Cameroon has four distinct regions: low, rolling savanna in the north; mountainous forests in the west; a central plateau; and a low, coastal plain with rain forests in the south.
Population: 6,700,000 (1977 est.)
Capital: Yaoundé
Other principal cities: Douala, N'Kongsamba
Languages: French, English, African languages
Religions: Christian, Moslem, Animist
Leading industries: Agriculture, manufacture of aluminum and chemicals, mining (particularly bauxite)

Canada

Official name: Canada
Area: 3,851,809 square miles
Location: North America, occupying all the continent north of the United States, except Alaska and the French islands of St. Pierre and Miquelon. Canada is the second largest country in the world.
Natural features: In the north is the Arctic archipelago; in the east and central region is the Canadian Shield, a rugged area of pre-Cambrian rock; to the west, stretching to the mountains, is a vast prairie; mountain ranges, including the Canadian Rockies, cover the far west.
Population: 23,306,000 (1977 est.)
Capital: Ottawa
Other principal cities: Montreal, Toronto, Winnipeg, Vancouver, Calgary
Languages: English, French; both official
Religions: Roman Catholic, Protestant
Leading industries: Pulp and paper production, iron and steel production, petroleum refining, forestry, fishing, trapping

Cape Verde

Official name: Republic of Cape Verde
Area: 1,557 square miles
Location: In Atlantic Ocean, 390 miles west of Dakar, Senegal, off the coast of Africa (ten islands and five islets)
Natural features: Three of the islands are flat; the other seven are mountainous, volcanic in origin.
Population: 310,000 (1977 est.)
Capital: Praia
Other principal cities: Mindelo, Espargos
Language: Officially Portuguese, most speaking a dialect
Religions: Roman Catholic, Animist
Leading industries: Main economic functions are shipping and aircraft refueling. Fishing important.

Central African Empire

Official name: Central African Empire
Area: 236,293 square miles
Location: A landlocked nation in Africa, in almost the exact center of the continent
Natural features: Central African Republic is a huge plateau, well drained by two river systems, the Shari and the Ubangi and their tributaries.
Population: 1,900,000 (1977 est.)
Capital: Bangui
Other principal cities: Berberati, Bambari
Languages: French, Sangho
Religions: Animist, Christian (mainly Protestant)
Leading industries: Agriculture, livestock raising; mining of diamonds, uranium, and gold

Ceylon

See Sri Lanka

Chad

Official name: Republic of Chad
Area: 495,752 square miles
Location: A landlocked country in north-central Africa
Natural features: Chad is a shallow basin, rimmed by mountains on the north and east. Part of the Sahara extends into the north part of the country; there are savanna in the central region and in the south, where there are many wild animals. Lake Chad is on the western border.
Population: 4,200,000 (1977 est.)
Capital: N'Djamena
Other principal cities: Moundou, Sarh
Languages: French, Arabic, tribal languages
Religions: Moslem, Animist
Leading industries: Agriculture (particularly cotton), livestock raising, fishing on Lake Chad

Chile

Official name: Republic of Chile
Area: 292,256 square miles
Location: Southwest coast of South America
Natural features: Chile stretches 2,650 miles along the Pacific Ocean, and is only 250 miles wide at its widest point. The north is desert, the central region agricultural, and the south forest land; the eastern frontier is dominated by the Andes.
Population: 10,700,000 (1977 est.)
Capital: Santiago
Other principal cities: Valparaíso, Concepción, Viña del Mar
Language: Spanish
Religion: Roman Catholic
Leading industries: Mining (particularly copper and iron ore); steel production; manufacturing of paper, paper products, and chemicals

China

Official name: People's Republic of China
Area: 3,691,000 square miles
Location: East Asia; China is the third largest nation in the world.
Natural features: Two-thirds of China is mountainous or semidesert; the eastern part consists of fertile plains and deltas.
Population: 835,000,000 (1977 est.)
Capital: Peking
Other principal cities: Shanghai, Tientsin, Lüta, Canton, Wuhan, Harbin, Mukden, Chungking, Nanking
Language: Chinese, spoken with many phonetical differences, but written in a uniform script
Religions: Confucian, Buddhist, Taoist. However, during the Cultural Revolution most places of worship were closed.
Leading industries: Agriculture (particularly rice and wheat), mining, petroleum production, manufacture of textiles

China (Taiwan)

Official name: Republic of China

Area: 13,971 square miles

Location: On the island of Taiwan, also called Formosa, ninety miles off the southeast coast of the Chinese mainland. It includes all the islands in the Taiwan group, sixty-four in the Penghu group (the Pescadores), and the islands of Quemoy and Matsu.

Natural features: A chain of mountains runs from the northeast to the southwest, covering two-thirds of the island. A flat, coastal plain, which supports most of the population, lies on the western third.

Population: 16,583,050 (1977 est.)

Capital: Taipei

Other principal cities: Kaohsiung, Tainan, Taichung

Languages: Mandarin Chinese, Amoy and Hakka dialects, Japanese, and English

Religion: Blend of Buddhist and Taoist

Leading industries: Agriculture, food processing, manufacturing of textiles, chemicals, electrical appliances; agriculture accounts for 14 percent of GNP; industry, 44 percent.

Colombia

Official name: Republic of Colombia

Area: 439,735 square miles

Location: Northwest South America

Tobacco fields in Colombia where agriculture, especially coffee, is the main industry. The Andes and thick tropical jungles limit arable land—only about 5% of Colombia is cultivated.

Natural features: Colombia is sharply divided by the Andes into a coastal flatland, a high plateau region, and an eastern plains area. Because of the natural mountain barriers, climate, people, and ways of life differ radically from area to area.

Population: 25,200,000 (1977 est.)

Capital: Bogotá

Other principal cities: Medellin, Cali, Barranquilla

Language: Spanish

Religion: Roman Catholic

Leading industries: Agriculture (particularly coffee), cattle raising, petroleum production, food processing, textile weaving, chemicals

Comoro Islands

Official name: Republic of the Comoros

Area: 719 square miles

Location: Islands in Mozambique Channel of Indian Ocean, 300 miles northwest of Madagascar. Three main islands: Anjouan, Mohéli, and Grand Comoro.

Natural features: Of volcanic origin; Karthala (8,399 feet) on Grand Comoro is still active.

Population: 280,000 (1977 est.)

Capital and main city: Moroni

Languages: Arabic, French, Swahili

Religions: Moslem; some Christian

Leading industries: Agriculture, fishing, and stock raising

Congo (Brazzaville)

Official name: People's Republic of the Congo

Area: 132,046 square miles

Location: West-central Africa; its southwest corner touches the Atlantic Ocean.

Natural features: The country consists of a low, coastal plain, highlands in the center, and a plateau to the north. About half the land is covered with dense equatorial forest; about a quarter is marshland.

Population: 1,400,000 (1977 est.)

Capital: Brazzaville

Other principal city: Pointe Noire

Languages: French, Lingala, Kikongo

Religions: About evenly divided between Animist and Roman Catholic

Leading industries: Agriculture, forestry, fishing

Congo (Kinshasa)

See Zaïre

Costa Rica

Official name: Republic of Costa Rica

Area: 19,652 square miles

Location: Central America

Natural features: A volcanic mountain system crosses the country lengthwise, and on each side of it is a coastal plain. About two-thirds of the country is covered by forests.

Population: 2,100,000 (1977 est.)
Capital: San José
Other principal cities: Alajuela, Heredia, Limón
Languages: Spanish, English with a Jamaican dialect
Religion: Roman Catholic
Leading industries: Agriculture, forestry, fishing, food processing, mining, manufacturing of textiles, fertilizer, and furniture

Cuba

Official name: Republic of Cuba
Area: 42,827 square miles
Location: An island nation, Cuba lies at the entrance of the Gulf of Mexico, about ninety miles south of Florida.
Natural features: Most of Cuba consists of flat or gently rolling, fertile terrain; some is mountainous.
Population: 9,500,000 (1977 est.)
Capital: Havana
Other principal cities: Santiago de Cuba, Camagüey, Guantánamo, Holguín
Language: Spanish
Religion: Roman Catholic
Leading industries: Agriculture (particularly sugar and tobacco), sugar refining, mining, manufacturing of cigars and cigarettes, rum, and textiles; 41 percent of the GNP is derived from industry.

Cyprus

Official name: Republic of Cyprus
Area: 3,572 square miles
Location: An island nation of the eastern Mediterranean, lying forty-four miles south of Turkey and sixty miles west of Syria
Natural features: A fertile central plain, the Mesaoria, lies between two mountain ranges that dominate the land—the Troodos Mountains in the southwest and the Kyrenia range along the northern coast.
Population: 670,000 (1977 est.)
Capital: Nicosia
Other principal cities: Limassol, Famagusta
Languages: Greek, Turkish, English
Religions: Predominantly Greek Orthodox; Moslem
Leading industries: Agriculture, mining (particularly copper and asbestos), wine making

Czechoslovakia

Official name: Czechoslovak Socialist Republic
Area: 49,373 square miles
Location: Central Europe, below Poland
Natural features: In the west is Bohemia, a plateau surrounded by mountains; in the central region is Moravia, a hilly region; and in the east is Slovakia, an area that has both mountains and lowlands.
Population: 15,000,000 (1977 est.)

Capital: Prague
Other principal cities: Brno, Bratislava, Ostrava
Languages: Czech, Slovak
Religion: Roman Catholic. However, all churches are under government control.
Leading industries: Iron and steel production; brewing; manufacture of glass, leather products, textiles; agriculture (Czechoslovakia is one of Europe's most industrialized nations.)

Denmark

Official name: Kingdom of Denmark
Area: 16,629 square miles
Location: Northwest Europe. Denmark is composed of several islands between the Baltic and North seas, as well as a peninsula that extends into the North Sea.
Natural features: Nearly all of Denmark is flat and rolling.
Population: 5,100,000 (1977 est.)
Capital: Copenhagen
Other principal cities: Aarhus, Odense, Aalborg
Language: Danish
Religion: Lutheran
Leading industries: Agriculture, dairying, food processing, manufacture of machinery and chemicals

Djibouti

Official name: Republic of Djibouti
Area: 8,880 square miles
Location: Northeastern Africa. Bordered on the north, west, and southwest by Ethiopia, on southeast by Somalia, at southern entrance of Red Sea.
Natural features: Arid rocky coastal plain with interior plateau, no rivers
Population: 190,000 (1977 est.)
Capital: Djibouti
Languages: Chiefly Hamitic languages of Somali and Afar (French and Arabic also used)
Religions: Predominantly Sunni Moslem with Christian minorities
Leading industries: Foodstuffs (bottling), liquid gas, herding, and shipbuilding

Dominican Republic

Official name: Dominican Republic
Area: 18,816 square miles
Location: West Indies, occupying the eastern two-thirds of the island of Hispaniola
Natural features: The country is crossed by four mountain ranges, the principal one being the Cordillera Central. In the upper central part is the Cibao valley, the nation's "food basket."
Population: 5,000,000 (1977 est.)
Capital: Santo Domingo
Other principal city: Santiago

Language: Spanish
Religion: Roman Catholic
Leading industries: Agriculture, livestock raising, sugar refining, processing of other food products

Ecuador

Official name: Republic of Ecuador
Area: 109,483 square miles
Location: Northwest South America, on the Pacific Ocean; the country lies on the equator. Its territory includes the Galápagos Islands, which are about 600 miles west of the mainland.
Natural features: About a quarter of the country consists of a coastal plain; another quarter is the Sierra (highlands) between two chains of the Andes; and the other half is a jungle, the Oriente.
Population: 6,900,000 (1977 est.)
Capital: Quitó
Other principal city: Guayaquil
Languages: Spanish, Quechua
Religion: Roman Catholic
Leading industries: Agriculture, forestry, fishing, manufacture of textiles

Egypt

Official name: Arab Republic of Egypt
Area: 386,659 square miles

Plaza Independencia, Quito, Ecuador.
A picturesque city, Quito existed before Columbus saw America. Quito lies near
the equator, but high in the Andes,
and enjoys a cool climate.

Location: Northeast Africa, on the Mediterranean and Red seas
Natural features: About 95 percent of the country is desert; the only fertile land is in the Nile River Valley and delta.
Population: 38,600,000 (1977 est.)
Capital: Cairo
Other principal cities: Alexandria, Giza, Suez
Language: Arabic
Religions: Predominantly Sunni Moslem; Coptic Christian
Leading industries: Agriculture (the Aswan Dam provides water for irrigation); food processing, petroleum products, manufacture of textiles and chemicals

El Salvador

Official name: Republic of El Salvador
Area: 8,260 square miles
Location: Central America, on the Pacific Ocean
Natural features: Mountain ranges divide the country into a narrow Pacific coastal belt on the south; a populated, subtropical central region of valleys and plateaus; and a mountainous northern region.
Population: 4,200,000 (1977 est.)
Capital: San Salvador
Other principal cities: Santa Ana, San Miguel
Language: Spanish
Religion: Roman Catholic
Leading industries: Agriculture, cattle raising, food processing

England

See United Kingdom

Equatorial Guinea

Official name: Republic of Equatorial Guinea
Area: 10,831 square miles
Location: West Africa, at the equator. Equatorial Guinea consists of two provinces—Rio Muni on the Atlantic coast of the continent, and Macías Nguema Biyogo, consisting of two main islands and several smaller ones.
Natural features: On the main island of Macías Nguema Biyogo, there are two large volcanic mountain formations separated by a valley. Rio Muni consists of a coastal plain that gives way to valleys, low hills, and finally spurs of the Crystal Mountains.
Population: 325,000 (1977 est.)
Capital: Malabo
Other principal city: Bata
Languages: Spanish, Bantu languages
Religions: Majority Roman Catholic; Protestant, Animist
Leading industries: Agriculture, forestry, fishing

Ethiopia

Official name: Ethiopia
Area: 471,776 square miles
Location: Eastern Africa, on the Red Sea
Natural features: The center of the country consists of a high, mountainous plateau, split diagonally by the Rift Valley. The terrain slopes to the lowlands to the west and to a plain in the southeast.
Population: 28,500,000 (1977 est.)
Capital: Addis Ababa
Other principal city: Asmara
Languages: Amharic, English, Arabic
Religions: Equal proportions of the population Coptic Christian and Moslem; Animist
Leading industries: Agriculture, livestock raising

Fiji

Official name: Fiji
Area: 7,055 square miles
Location: Southwest Pacific, Fiji consists of about 320 islands in the Koro Sea, about 1,100 miles north of New Zealand; the largest of the islands is Viti Levu.
Natural features: The larger islands are volcanic in origin, mountainous, partly covered with dense tropical forests, and surrounded by coral reefs.
Population: 590,000 (1977 est.)
Capital: Suva
Other principal city: Lautoka
Language: English
Religions: Christian (mainly Methodist); Indian population, Hindu
Leading industries: Agriculture (particularly sugar and coconuts), mining, sugar refining, coconut oil production

Finland

Official name: Republic of Finland
Area: 130,128 square miles
Location: Northern Europe; part of Finland lies above the Arctic Circle. The Åland Islands between the Baltic Sea and the Gulf of Bothnia also belong to Finland.
Natural features: Much of Finland, with its 60,000 lakes, is low and swampy. Beyond the coastal belt is a wooded plateau; in the north are mountains.
Population: 4,750,000 (1977 est.)
Capital: Helsinki
Other principal cities: Turku, Tampere
Languages: Finnish, Lappish, Swedish
Religion: Evangelical Lutheran
Leading industries: Mining, forestry, shipbuilding, manufacture of wood and paper products

France

Official name: French Republic
Area: 210,038 square miles
Location: Western Europe; includes the island of Corsica. France is the largest country in Western Europe.
Natural features: Two-thirds of France (the northern, central, and western portions) consist of flat or gently rolling terrain; about one-third, particularly around the land borders, is mountainous.
Population: 53,100,000 (1977 est.)
Capital: Paris
Other principal cities: Marseilles, Lyons, Toulouse, Nice
Language: French
Religion: Roman Catholic
Leading industries: Agriculture (particularly wheat and grapes); wine making (France is the leading producer of wines); mining; fishing; iron and steel production; manufacture of machinery, chemicals, motor vehicles, textiles and clothing

Gabon

Official name: Gabonese Republic
Area: 103,346 square miles
Location: West-central Africa, on the Gulf of Guinea just south of the equator
Natural features: Much of the country is covered with a dense equatorial rain forest. Inland there are plateaus and mountains through which rivers have carved valleys and channels.
Population: 560,000 (1977 est.)
Capital: Libreville
Other principal cities: Port-Gentil, Lambaréné
Languages: French, Fang, Bantu languages
Religions: Nearly evenly divided between Christian (mainly Roman Catholic) and Animist
Leading industries: Agriculture, mining (particularly manganese and iron ore), forestry, processing of timber and minerals; world's largest exporter of manganese.

Gambia

Official name: Republic of The Gambia
Area: 4,127 square miles
Location: West Africa, on the Atlantic Ocean; it is nearly surrounded by Senegal.
Natural features: Gambia is only a few miles wide, but stretches inland from the coast about 200 miles on either side of the Gambia River; most of the land is covered with mangrove swamps.
Population: 540,000 (1977 est.)
Capital and largest city: Banjul
Languages: English, Malinke, Wolof
Religions: Predominantly Moslem; Christian, Animist
Leading industry: Agriculture (particularly peanut growing)

Germany, East

Official name: German Democratic Republic
Area: 41,768 square miles
Location: North-central Europe, on the Baltic Sea; the eastern portion of a divided nation

Hull of a new ship in Hamburg, West Germany, one of the biggest centers of ship-building in Europe. Heavily damaged by bombs and fire during World War II, Hamburg has been largely rebuilt. Shipbuilding is one of many industries that have made Germany a major economic power in the West.

Natural features: Northern East Germany, the Baltic coast, has lakes and low hills; in the center are mountains as well as a sandy arid section and a fertile plain; the south is a heavily forested region of mountains and lowlands.

Population: 16,700,000 (1977 est.)

Capital: East Berlin

Other principal cities: Leipzig, Dresden, Karl-Marx-Stadt, Halle, Magdeburg

Language: German

Religions: Predominantly Protestant; Roman Catholic. (However, under the Communist regime all churches are closely regulated by the state.)

Leading industries: Agriculture; iron and steel production; manufacture of chemicals, fertilizers, machinery, synthetic rubber and fibers, drugs, plastics, and vehicles

Germany, West

Official name: Federal Republic of Germany

Area: 95,985 square miles

Location: North-central Europe, on the North Sea; the western portion of a divided nation

Natural features: Germany is flat in the north and hilly in the central and western portions; there are low mountains in the Black Forest, and the Alps rise to nearly 10,000 feet along the southern border. The Rhine and its tributaries, including the Moselle, flow through central Germany.

Population: 62,000,000 (1977 est.)

Capital: Bonn

Other principal cities: Hamburg, Munich, Cologne, Essen, Düsseldorf, Frankfurt-am-Main, Dortmund, Stuttgart; West Berlin (pop. 1,984,837) is not legally part of, but is closely allied with West Germany.

Language: German

Religions: Largely Protestant (mainly Lutheran); and Roman Catholic

Leading industries: Iron and steel production, mining (particularly coal), shipbuilding, manufacture of chemicals, machinery, vehicles; the leading industrial nation of Europe.

Ghana

Official name: Republic of Ghana

Area: 92,099 square miles

Location: West Africa, on the Gulf of Guinea

Natural features: Ghana is a low, sometimes hilly country, well drained by the Volta River and its tributaries. Away from the coast there are grassland plains, savanna, and a belt of tropical rain forest.

Population: 10,200,000 (1977 est.)

Capital: Accra

Other principal cities: Kumasi, Sekondi-Takoradi

Languages: English, about fifty tribal languages

Religions: Largely Christian; Moslem, Animist

Leading industries: Agriculture (world's leading producer of cocoa), mining (gold and diamonds), livestock raising, fishing, food processing

Great Britain

See United Kingdom

Greece

Official name: Republic of Greece (Hellenic Republic)
Area: 50,944 square miles
Location: Southeast Europe, occupying the southern part of the Balkan peninsula and islands in the Ionian and Aegean seas
Natural features: Most of Greece is mountainous, with dry and rocky land.
Population: 9,100,000 (1977 est.)
Capital: Athens
Other principal cities: Piraeus, Salonika
Language: Modern Greek
Religion: Greek Orthodox
Leading industries: Agriculture (including wheat, tobacco, olives, and grapes, despite the fact that very little land is suitable for cultivation); sheep and goat raising; food processing; manufacture of textiles, aluminum, and chemicals

Grenada

Official name: State of Grenada
Area: 133 square miles
Location: The southernmost of the Windward Islands in the West Indies; includes the southern Grenadines, the largest of which is Carriacou
Natural features: Volcanic origin, chiefly mountainous
Population: 100,000 (1977 est.)
Capital: St. George's
Other principal cities: Gouyave, Grenville, Victoria
Languages: English with rare use of Franco-African patois
Religions: Roman Catholic, Protestant
Leading industries: Agriculture (sugar, coconuts, nutmeg, cocoa, and bananas), increasing tourism, offshore exploration for gas and oil in progress, forestry, fishing

Guatemala

Official name: Republic of Guatemala
Area: 42,042 square miles
Location: Central America, just south of Mexico
Natural features: Guatemala is largely mountainous, except for the Caribbean lowlands in the southeast, the lowland forest of Petén in the north, and the narrow coastal plain that borders the Pacific coast. The highest peak in the Central American Cordillera, Mt. Tajumulco, is located there.
Population: 6,000,000 (1977 est.)
Capital: Guatemala
Other principal cities: Quezaltenango, Tiquisate, Escuintla

Languages: Spanish, Maya-Quiché Indian dialects
Religion: Roman Catholic
Leading industries: Agriculture (coffee, cotton, bananas), mining, forestry, manufacture of paper products and tobacco

Guinea

Official name: Republic of Guinea
Area: 94,925 square miles
Location: West Africa, on the Atlantic Ocean between Sierra Leone and Guinea-Bissau
Natural features: Guinea consists of a low coastal plain, a pastoral middle area, a forest region along the Liberian border, and a dry area in the north. The east is drained by the Niger River.
Population: 4,700,000 (1977 est.)
Capital and principal city: Conakry
Languages: French, Peul, Mandé
Religions: Predominantly Moslem; Animist
Leading industries: Agriculture (particularly bananas), forestry, fishing, mining (mostly bauxite), alumina production

Guinea-Bissau

Official name: Republic of Guinea-Bissau
Area: 13,948 square miles
Location: On the west coast of Africa; the Atlantic Ocean on the west, Senegal on the north, and Guinea on the east and south
Natural features: Low lying coastal plain with savanna, swamp, and rainforest (eighteen offshore islands including Bijagós Archipelago).
Population: 575,000 (1977 est.)
Capital: Bissau
Other principal city: Bafata
Languages: Portuguese and Crioulo
Religions: Predominantly Animist; Moslem, Christian
Leading industries: Agriculture (cashew nuts, rice, palm kernels), timber

Guyana

Official name: Cooperative Republic of Guyana
Area: 83,000 square miles
Location: South America, on the northeast coast
Natural features: Guyana is divided into a low coastal region, a forested interior, and a region of mountains and savanna in the south and west.
Population: 800,000 (1977 est.)
Capital: Georgetown (a new capital site at Konawaruk designated in 1976)
Other principal cities: New Amsterdam, Linden
Language: English
Religions: Majority Christian (mainly Anglican); Hindu, Moslem
Leading industries: Agriculture (particularly sugar), mining (mainly bauxite, diamonds, and gold), sugar refining, aluminum smelting, forestry, manufacture of wood and pulp products

Haiti

Official name: Republic of Haiti
Area: 10,683 square miles
Location: West Indies. Haiti occupies the western third of the island of Hispaniola in the Caribbean Sea.
Natural features: About two-thirds of the country is mountainous; the rest consists of plains and valleys.
Population: 4,900,000 (1977 est.)
Capital and principal city: Port-au-Prince
Languages: French, Creole
Religions: Mostly Roman Catholic; Voodoo
Leading industries: Agriculture (although most of the country is unsuitable for cultivation), mining (particularly bauxite and copper), tourism, processing of coffee, sugar, sisal, and edible oils

Honduras

Official name: Republic of Honduras
Area: 43,277 square miles
Location: Central America, on the Gulf of Honduras in the Caribbean Sea
Natural features: Honduras is mostly mountainous, dominated by the Central American Andes. A fertile plain stretches inland from the "Mosquito Coast" along the Caribbean; another plain along the Pacific coast.
Population: 2,900,000 (1977 est.)
Capital: Tegucigalpa
Other principal cities: San Pedro Sula, La Ceiba
Languages: Spanish, English (in the north and on the Bay Islands)
Religion: Roman Catholic
Leading industries: Agriculture (particularly bananas), forestry, mining (especially silver), food processing

Hungary

Official name: Hungarian People's Republic
Area: 35,919 square miles
Location: East-central Europe. A landlocked country, Hungary lies just above Yugoslavia.
Natural features: Most of Hungary is a low, flat plain, with the exception of some low mountains in the northeast and north-central portions and around Lake Balaton. It is drained by the Danube River.
Population: 10,620,000 (1977 est.)
Capital: Budapest
Other principal cities: Miskolc, Debrecen, Pécs, Szeged
Language: Hungarian (or Magyar)
Religions: Mostly Roman Catholic; Protestant. (However, under the Communists, all churches are closely regulated by the state.)
Leading industries: Mining (particularly bauxite); iron and steel production; manufacture of chemicals, construction machinery, and railroad equipment; agriculture

Iceland

Official name: Republic of Iceland
Area: 39,768 square miles
Location: North Atlantic. Iceland is an island nation that lies about 645 miles west of Norway.
Natural features: Three-fourths of Iceland consists of glaciers, lakes, mountainous lava desert, and other wasteland; the rest, particularly along the southwest coast where most of the people live, is cultivated or used for grazing.
Population: 222,000 (1977 est.)
Capital: Reykjavik
Other principal cities: Kópavogur, Akureyri, Hafnarfjödür
Language: Icelandic
Religion: Evangelical Lutheran
Leading industries: Fishing and fish processing, agriculture, sheep grazing, manufacture of motors, fertilizer, chemicals, textiles, and clothing

India

Official name: Republic of India
Area: 1,269,339 square miles
Location: South-central Asia. India occupies the major portion of the Indian subcontinent.
Natural features: India consists of three major topographical areas: the Himalayas along the northern border; the northern Gangetic Plain, a fertile and heavily populated region drained by the Ganges River; the peninsula in the south (Deccan Plateau), which is hilly (an average of 1,000 to 3,000 feet).
Population: 600,000,000 (1977 est.). India is one of the most densely populated nations in the world.
Capital: New Delhi
Principal cities: Bombay, Delhi, Calcutta, Madras, Ahmedabad, Hyderabad, Bangalore, Kanpur, Poona
Languages: Hindi, English. In addition, there are fourteen other constitutionally recognized languages and more than 1,652 dialects spoken.
Religions: Predominantly Hindu; Moslem, Christian
Leading industries: Agriculture (particularly grains), iron and steel production, mining (largely coal), manufacture of textiles, chemicals, cement, and industrial machinery and equipment. (India has great economic problems because there is not enough farming or industry to support its population.)

Indonesia

Official name: Republic of Indonesia
Area: 788,430 square miles
Location: Southeast Asia, in the Malay archipelago. Indonesia consists of six large islands (the Greater Sunda: Java, Sumatra, Borneo, Bali, and Celebes) and more than 3,000 small islands that form an arc between Asia and Australia. Portuguese Timor was annexed by Indonesia on May 3, 1976.

Natural features: The larger islands have mountain ranges that rise from extensive coastal lowland plains. Many of the smaller islands are dotted with volcanoes, some active.
Population: 130,000,000 (1977 est.). Indonesia is the fifth most populous nation in the world.
Capital: Djakarta
Other principal cities: Bandung, Surabaja, Medan
Languages: Bahasa Indonesia, English
Religions: Predominantly Moslem; Christian, Buddhist/Hindu on the island of Bali
Leading industries: Agriculture (particularly rubber), mining (largely tin), forestry, petroleum production, food processing

Iran

Official name: Iran; formerly known as Persia
Area: 636,293 square miles
Location: Southwest Asia, on the Caspian Sea in the north and the Persian Gulf in the south
Natural features: Iran lies on a large plateau, mostly barren desert and high mountains. There are some fertile lowlands along the country's seacoasts.
Population: 34,000,000 (1977 est.)
Capital: Tehran
Other principal cities: Isfahan, Meshed, Tabriz
Languages: Persian (Farsi), Kurdish, Turkic, Arabic
Religion: Moslem
Leading industries: Petroleum production (Iran con-

tains 10 percent of the world's known resources), agriculture, livestock raising (including camels), fishing, food processing

Iraq

Official name: Republic of Iraq
Area: 172,476 square miles
Location: Southwest Asia, just west of Iran
Natural features: Iraq has a rugged highland region in the northeast, a vast desert in the west and southwest, and a fertile lowland region in between, drained by the Tigris and Euphrates rivers.
Population: 11,600,000 (1977 est.)
Capital: Bagdad
Other principal cities: Mosul, Basra
Languages: Arabic, Kurdish (the Kurds make up about 20 percent of the population)
Religion: Moslem
Leading industries: Petroleum production, agriculture (in the Tigris-Euphrates Valley), sheep herding

Ireland

Official name: Ireland
Area: 27,136 square miles
Location: Western Europe, on the second largest of the British Isles. It occupies all the island except for the six counties in the north (Ulster) that belong to the United Kingdom.

The Golden Mosque, Bagdad, Iraq, is a symbol of former magnificence now obscured by modern construction. An important city since the 8th century, Bagdad reached its zenith during the times of the *Thousand and One Nights,* when it was known for its many gardens.

Natural features: Shaped like a basin, Ireland is hilly along the coasts and has low-lying central plains, drained by the Shannon River.

Population: 3,200,000 (1977 est.)

Capital: Dublin

Other principal cities: Cork, Limerick, Waterford, Galway

Languages: English, Gaelic (Irish)

Religion: Roman Catholic

Leading industries: Agriculture, food processing, manufacture of textiles (particularly linen) and clothing

Israel

Official name: State of Israel

Area: 7,847 square miles

Location: Southwest Asia (the Middle East), on the Mediterranean Sea; bordered on the north by Lebanon, on the east by Syria and Jordan, on the south by Egypt and on the west by the Mediterranean

Natural features: Northern Israel is hilly; the center is a coastal plain; while the Negev Desert, in the south, covers about 50 percent of the country.

Population: 3,700,000 (1977 est.)

Capital: Jerusalem. Tel Aviv is the diplomatic capital.

Other principal city: Haifa

Languages: Hebrew, Arabic, English

Religions: Judaism predominant; Moslem, Greek Catholic and Orthodox

Leading industries: Agriculture (accomplished with intense irrigation); oil refining; mining; quarrying; manufacture of machinery, chemicals, textiles, and petroleum products

Italy

Official name: Italian Republic

Area: 116,303 square miles

Location: Southern Europe. Italy is on a boot-shaped peninsula that extends into the Mediterranean Sea; the Adriatic Sea, an arm of the Mediterranean, is on the east coast.

Natural features: Italy is rugged and mountainous, except for the Po River valley in the north and the heel of the boot in the south, which are plains areas.

Population: 56,323,000 (1977 est.)

Capital: Rome

Other principal cities: Milan, Naples, Turin, Genoa

Language: Italian

Religion: Roman Catholic

Leading industries: Manufacture of automobiles, textiles, machinery, metal products, and chemicals; oil refining; agriculture (in the Po Valley and less successfully in the south); food processing; mining (particularly mercury); quarrying; tourism

Ivory Coast

Official name: Republic of Ivory Coast

Area: 127,520 square miles

Location: West Africa, on the Gulf of Guinea; between Ghana on the east and Guinea and Liberia on the west

Natural features: A rain forest stretches inland from the coast and covers about 40 percent of the country; the rest is a wooded and grassy savanna, with some mountains in the northwest.

Population: 7,000,000 (1977 est.)

An open-air market, Ivory Coast. Produce for local consumption is brought to such markets, which also serve as centers of social life. A major exporter of coffee, Ivory Coast is primarily an agricultural country.

342

Capital: Abidjan
Other principal cities: Bouaké, Gagnoa
Languages: French, Dioula
Religions: Largely Animist; Moslem, Roman Catholic
Leading industries: Agriculture, forestry, sawmilling, fishing, food processing

Jamaica

Official name: Jamaica
Area: 4,244 square miles
Location: West Indies. An island nation, Jamaica lies about ninety miles south of Cuba.
Natural features: Most of the island is mountainous. There are lowlands in the west and a narrow plain along the southern coast.
Population: 2,100,000 (1977 est.)
Capital: Kingston
Other principal cities: Montego Bay, Spanish Town
Languages: English; Jamaican Creole, a local patois of archaic English and African words
Religions: Predominantly Protestant; Roman Catholic
Leading industries: Agriculture, mining (Jamaica is the world's largest producer of bauxite), sugar refining, rum and beer production, forestry, fishing, tourism

Japan

Official name: Japan
Area: 145,730 square miles
Location: Northwest Pacific. Japan is a 2,360 mile-long archipelago off the east coast of Asia, consisting of four main islands (Hokkaido, Honshu, Shikoku, and Kyushu) and more than 3,000 smaller islands.
Natural features: Most of Japan is covered with either hills or mountains, some of which are active volcanoes; only 15 percent of the land is suitable for cultivation.
Population: 110,000,000 (1977 est.)
Capital: Tokyo (the most populous city in the world)
Other principal cities: Osaka, Yokohama, Nagoya, Kyoto, Kobe, Kitakyushu, Sapporo
Language: Japanese
Religions: Buddhist, Shinto. (Many subscribe to both religions.)
Leading industries: Manufacture of textiles, metals and metal products, machinery (particularly precision machinery), automobiles, cameras; agriculture (although declining since World War II), fishing, forestry. Japan is one of the most highly industrialized nations on earth.

Jordan

Official name: Hashemite Kingdom of Jordan
Area: 37,737 square miles
Location: Southwest Asia (the Middle East), just east of Israel

Assembly plant, Japan. With its disciplined labor force and advanced technology Japan is now the third richest industrialized nation.

Natural features: Most of Jordan is barren desert. The Great Rift Valley runs along the western border; the northern part is drained by the Jordan River. West of the Jordan is the very fertile Judaean Hill region, which was seized by Israel in 1967.
Population: 2,800,000 (1977 est.)
Capital: Amman
Other principal cities: Irbid, Nablus, Zarqa. (A sector of Jerusalem once belonged to Jordan, but has been occupied by Israel since 1967.)
Language: Arabic
Religions: Mostly Sunni Moslem; Christian
Leading industries: Agriculture (although less than 10 percent of Jordan's land is suitable for cultivation), mining (phosphate, potash, and marble), oil refining, tanning; manufacture of cement, tobacco products, and soap

Kampuchea, Democratic

See Cambodia

Kenya

Official name: Republic of Kenya
Area: 224,960 square miles
Location: East Africa, on the Indian Ocean at the equator
Natural features: The Great Rift Valley runs through western and central Kenya, between rugged plains and mountains; eastern Kenya is dry bush land and a humid coastal region, while the north is scrub and

desert. Kenya has many lakes, including a portion of Lake Victoria.

Population: 13,900,000 (1977 est.)
Capital: Nairobi
Other principal city: Mombasa
Languages: English, Swahili, Kikuyu, Luo
Religions: Majority Christian; large Animist population; Moslem, Hindu
Leading industries: Agriculture (largely on European-owned plantations), food processing, oil refining, mining (soda ash), forestry, fishing, tourism

Korea, North

Official name: Democratic People's Republic of Korea
Area: 46,540 square miles
Location: Northeast Asia. North Korea is part of a divided nation on the Korean Peninsula.
Natural features: North Korea is very mountainous; less than one-fifth of the land is suitable for cultivation.
Population: 16,700,000 (1977 est.)
Capital: Pyongyang
Other principal cities: Chongjin, Hamhung, Sinuiju, Wonsan
Language: Korean
Religions: Buddhist, Confucian, Shaman, Ch'ondokyo (a combination of Buddhism and Christianity). However, religious practice is discouraged by the Communist Party.
Leading industries: Iron and steel production; mining (coal); manufacture of chemicals, cement, and machinery; agriculture, fishing, forestry

Korea, South

Official name: Republic of Korea
Area: 38,175 square miles
Location: Northeast Asia. South Korea is one half of a divided nation on the Korean Peninsula.
Natural features: Like North Korea, South Korea is mountainous, with some limited land suitable for cultivation in the south.
Population: 35,900,000 (1977 est.)
Capital: Seoul
Other principal cities: Pusan, Taegu, Inchon, Kwangju
Language: Korean
Religions: Buddhist, Confucian, Shaman, Ch'ondokyo (a mixture of Buddhism and Christianity), Christian (largely Protestant)
Leading industries: Agriculture, food processing; manufacture of textiles, chemicals, and machinery

Kuwait

Official name: State of Kuwait
Area: 6,532 square miles
Location: Southwest Asia. Kuwait is in the northeast corner of the Arabian peninsula on the Persian Gulf.

Natural features: Kuwait is virtually all desert, with a few oases.
Population: 1,100,000 (1977 est.)
Capital: Kuwait
Other principal cities: Salimiya, Hawalli
Languages: Arabic, English
Religion: Moslem
Leading industry: Petroleum production

Laos

Official name: Lao People's Democratic Republic
Area: 91,428 square miles
Location: Southeast Asia, just west of Vietnam
Natural features: Northern Laos, drained by the Mekong River and its tributaries, consists of jungle-covered mountains and plateaus. In the south are the foothills of the Annam Mountains, sloping westward to the Mekong River valley.
Population: 3,500,000 (1977 est.)
Capital: Vientiane
Other principal cities: Savannakhet, Pakse, Luang Prabang
Languages: Lao, French
Religions: Predominantly Theravada Buddhist
Leading industry: Agriculture (rice, corn, coffee); industry little developed

Lebanon

Official name: Republic of Lebanon
Area: 4,015 square miles
Location: Southwest Asia (the Middle East), on the Mediterranean Sea just north of Israel
Natural features: Next to a narrow coastal plain are the high Lebanese Mountains. Farther east are the fertile Beqaa Valley and the Anti-Lebanon Mountains.
Population: 3,300,000 (1977 est.)
Capital: Beirut
Other principal city: Tripoli
Languages: Arabic, French, English
Religions: Majority Moslem; Christian
Leading industries: Commerce, agriculture, food processing, forestry (cedars), oil refining, manufacture of textiles and cement, tourism

Lesotho

Official name: Kingdom of Lesotho
Area: 11,720 square miles
Location: South Africa. Lesotho is an enclave within the Republic of South Africa.
Natural features: About one-fourth of the western region is lowland; the rest is mountainous.
Population: 1,100,000 (1977 est.)
Capital and principal city: Maseru
Languages: Sesotho, English
Religions: Largely Christian; Animist

Class in nutrition, Liberia. Founded by Americans in 1822, Liberia was a haven for freed Blacks whose descendants now constitute only a small fraction of today's population.

Leading industries: Agriculture, mining (one of the world's largest diamonds—600 carats—was found in Lesotho).

Liberia

Official name: Republic of Liberia
Area: 43,000 square miles
Location: West Africa, on the Atlantic Ocean, west of Ivory Coast
Natural features: Liberia is mostly flat land covered by tropical woodlands. There are some hills in the northwest and a belt of mountains along the Guinea border.
Population: 1,800,000 (1977 est.)
Capital and principal city: Monrovia
Languages: English, about thirty African dialects
Religions: Predominantly Animist; Christian, Moslem
Leading industries: Mining (particularly iron ore and diamonds), agriculture, rubber tree plantations, forestry, fishing

Libya

Official name: Socialist People's Libyan Arab Jamahiriya
Area: 679,358 square miles
Location: North Africa, on the Mediterranean Sea, just west of Egypt

Natural features: Most of Libya consists of barren, rocky plains and sand dunes, with scattered oases. In the northwest and northeast, there are highlands, and in the south are mountains of the central Sahara.
Population: 2,550,000 (1977 est.)
Capital: Tripoli
Other principal cities: Benghazi, Zawia, Misurata
Language: Arabic (official); English, Italian
Religion: Sunni Moslem
Leading industries: Petroleum production (Libya is one of the world's largest producers of oil), agriculture (date palms on desert oases and other crops along the coast), livestock grazing (by nomads), fishing

Liechtenstein

Official name: Principality of Liechtenstein
Area: 61 square miles
Location: Western Europe, in the Rhine River valley between Austria and Switzerland
Natural features: The land is fairly flat in the river valley and mountainous elsewhere.
Population: 25,000 (1977 est.)
Capital and principal city: Vaduz
Language: German; Alemannic dialect
Religion: Roman Catholic
Leading industries: Manufacture of precision instruments, agriculture, dairying, tourism, postage stamp sales. Many international corporations headquarter in Liechtenstein because taxes are low.

Luxembourg

Official name: Grand Duchy of Luxembourg
Area: 999 square miles
Location: Western Europe. A landlocked country, Luxembourg is situated between Western Germany and France.
Natural features: The rugged uplands of the Ardennes plateau form the northern part of Luxembourg, while the south consists of rolling terrain and broad valleys.
Population: 360,000 (1977 est.)
Capital: Luxembourg
Other principal city: Esch/Alzette
Languages: French, German, Luxembourgeois (Letzeburgesch). Many Luxembourgers are bilingual or trilingual.
Religion: Roman Catholic
Leading industries: Iron and steel production, agriculture, dairying, brewing and distilling; manufacture of chemicals, fertilizer, tires, tobacco, and metal products

Madagascar

Official name: Democratic Republic of Madagascar
Area: 226,657 square miles

Location: Indian Ocean. Madagascar occupies the fourth largest island in the world, situated about 250 miles off the east coast of Africa, from which it is separated by the Mozambique Channel.
Natural features: The terrain is dominated by an eroded central plateau that rises to as high as 9,450 feet. In the east it slopes steeply to a narrow, swampy coast and in the west, more gradually to lowlands.
Population: 8,000,000 (1977 est.)
Capital: Antananarivo
Other principal cities: Tamatave, Majunga, Fianarantsoa
Languages: Malagasy, French, Hova, several other dialects. There are 18 different ethnic groups on the island.
Religions: Majority Animist; Christian, Moslem
Leading industries: Agriculture, mining (particularly graphite)

Malawi

Official name: Republic of Malawi
Area: 45,747 square miles
Location: East Africa. Malawi is a landlocked country next to Mozambique.
Natural features: The Great Rift Valley runs the length of Malawi (from north to south) and contains the 360-mile-long Lake Nyasa (Malawi). There are high plateaus on each side of the lake and mountains to the north and south of it.
Population: 5,300,000 (1977 est.)
Capital: Lilongwe
Other principal cities: Blantyre, Zomba
Languages: English, Bantu languages
Religions: Largely Christian; Moslem, Animist
Leading industries: Agriculture (particularly tea and tobacco), production of tung oil (used in paints).

Malaysia

Official name: Malaysia
Area: 128,308 square miles
Location: Southeast Asia. Malaysia includes Malaya on the southern end of the Malay Peninsula (East Malaysia), and Sarawak and Sabah on the island of Borneo (West Malaysia), about 400 miles away across the Red China Sea.
Natural features: In East Malaysia, a mountain range flanked by coastal plains runs north and south. Similarly in West Malaysia, coastal plains rise to mountain interiors. About 70 percent of the total land area is covered with dense tropical jungle.
Population: 12,600,000 (1977 est.)
Capital: Kuala Lumpur
Other principal cities: Ipoh, Pinang (Penang, Georgetown)
Languages: Malay, English, variety of native Chinese and Indian dialects
Religions: Moslem (most Malays); Hindu (most In-

dians); Confucian, Buddhist (most Chinese); Animist. Islam is the state religion.
Leading industries: Rubber production, agriculture, mining (particularly tin and iron ore), tin smelting, forestry, fishing

Maldive Islands (Maldives)

Official name: Republic of Maldives
Area: 115 square miles
Location: Indian Ocean. The Maldive Islands are an archipelago of 2,000 coral islands about 400 miles southwest of Sri Lanka (Ceylon).
Natural features: The Maldives rest on a submarine ridge, probably of volcanic origin, and are grouped into 19 atolls (coral rings), each encircling a lagoon.
Population: 139,000 (1977 est.)
Capital and principal city: Malé
Language: Divehi (dialect of Sinhalese), Arabic
Religion: Moslem (Sunni)
Leading industries: Fishing (largely tuna and bonito from which they make "Maldive fish"—dried bonito), copra, coconut oil production, weaving

Mali

Official name: Republic of Mali
Area: 464,873 square miles
Location: West Africa. Mali is a landlocked country that lies between Mauritania and Niger.
Natural features: Mali is largely flat and dry, with

In Mopti, Mali, Arab traders haggle over salt slabs. Though poverty-stricken today, Mali was once the seat of a great 14th century empire whose chief export was gold.

occasional striking sandstone mountains and plateaus. From north to south there are the desolate Sahara, some agricultural and pasture land, and finally savanna scrub land, drained by the Niger River.

Population: 6,100,000 (1977 est.)
Capital: Bamako
Other principal cities: Mopti, Ségou, Kayes
Languages: French, native languages
Religions: Predominantly Moslem; Animist
Leading industries: Agriculture, livestock raising, fishing (on the Niger River)

Malta

Official name: Republic of Malta
Area: 122 square miles
Location: Mediterranean Sea. Malta is composed of two main islands, Malta and Gozo, and the smaller island of Comino; they are about fifty-eight miles south of Sicily.
Natural features: The terrain is rather flat, consisting of limestone rock covered with a thin layer of soil.
Population: 326,000 (1977 est.)
Capital and principal city: Valletta
Languages: Maltese, English, Italian
Religion: Roman Catholic
Leading industries: Fishing; food processing; manufacture of textiles and clothing, rubber products, chemicals; shipbuilding

Mauritania

Official name: Islamic Republic of Mauritania
Area: 452,702 square miles
Location: West Africa, on the Atlantic Ocean between Spanish Sahara and Senegal
Natural features: The northern two-thirds of Mauritania is covered with desert (the Sahara), but in the south and southwest near the Senegal River, there is some land suitable for cultivation.
Population: 1,400,000 (1977 est.)
Capital and principal city: Nouakchott
Languages: Arabic (Hassaniyah), French, Wolof, Tukolor
Religion: Moslem
Leading industries: Agriculture, livestock raising (including camels), mining (particularly iron ore), fishing

Mauritius

Official name: Mauritius
Area: 790 square miles
Location: Indian Ocean. Mauritius is a tropical island nation about 500 miles east of Madagascar, just above the Tropic of Capricorn. It includes several other smaller islands.
Natural features: Mauritius is composed of a central plateau surrounded by mountains, probably the rim of an ancient volcano; the island is entirely surrounded by coral reefs.
Population: 900,000 (1977 est.). Mauritius is one of the most densely populated nations in the world.
Capital: Port Louis
Other principal cities: Beau-Bassin and Rose Hill, Curepipe
Languages: English, Creole, Chinese, Hindi, Urdu, French
Religions: Majority Hindu; Moslem, Christian
Leading industries: Growing of sugarcane, sugar refining, fishing.

Mexico

Official name: United Mexican States
Area: 761,600 square miles
Location: North America, just below the western United States
Natural features: Mexico consists of a large, temperate central plateau flanked on the east and west with mountain ranges of the Sierra Madre. There are tropical lowlands along the coasts.
Population: 60,000,000 (1977 est.)
Capital: Mexico City
Other principal cities: Guadalajara, Monterrey, Ciudad Juárez, Puebla, León
Languages: Spanish, Indian dialects
Religion: Roman Catholic
Leading industries: Agriculture, livestock raising, mining (Mexico is the world's largest producer of silver), forestry, fishing; manufacture of automobiles, industrial machinery, steel, and chemicals

Monaco

Official name: Principality of Monaco
Area: (0.578 square miles) 374 acres
Location: Western Europe, on the Mediterranean Sea. Monaco is an enclave in southeastern France.
Natural features: Monaco is situated on steep cliffs surrounding a harbor. It has three sections, Monte Carlo, La Condamine, and Monaco-Ville, which is located on a high promontory extending into the Mediterranean.
Population: 25,000 (1977 est.)
Capital and principal city: Monaco-Ville
Languages: French, Monégasque (mixture of French and Italian), English, and Italian
Religion: Roman Catholic
Leading industries: Tourism, gambling. Many foreign companies headquarter in Monaco because of low taxation.

Mongolia

Official name: Mongolian People's Republic
Area: 606,163 square miles
Location: Central Asia. Mongolia is a landlocked nation between China and the Soviet Union.

Natural features: Mongolia is composed of a huge steppe plateau fringed by mountains in the north, northwest, and east. In the southeast is the Gobi Desert.
Population: 1,500,000 (1977 est.)
Capital and principal city: Ulan Bator
Languages: Khalkha Mongolian, Turkic
Religion: Lamaistic Buddhism. However, religious practice is limited by the Communist Party.
Leading industries: Animal husbandry, processing of livestock products, mining (particularly coal)

Morocco

Official name: Kingdom of Morocco
Area: 241,224 square miles
Location: Northwest Africa, on the Mediterranean and Atlantic coasts, west of Algeria
Natural features: In the center of Morocco are the dry, rocky Atlas Mountains, which slope to narrow, fertile coastal plains in the north and west. In the south is the Sahara Desert.
Population: 18,000,000 (1977 est.)
Capital: Rabat
Other principal cities: Casablanca, Marrakech, Fez, Meknès
Languages: Arabic, Berber, French
Religion: Sunni Moslem
Leading industries: Agriculture (Morocco supplies most of the fruits and vegetables for Western Europe), food processing, mining, commerce

Mozambique

Official name: People's Republic of Mozambique
Area: 308,641 square miles
Location: East coast of Africa. The Mozambique Channel is on the east, Swaziland on the south, South Africa on the south and west, Rhodesia on the west, Zambia and Malawi on the northwest, and Tanzania on the north.
Natural features: Lowlands along 1700 miles of coast rise to plateau (9000 feet) with high mountains to north.
Population: 9,300,000 (1977 est.)
Capital: Naputo
Other principal cities: Beira, Nampula
Languages: African languages, Portuguese
Religions: Traditional African; some Moslem and Christian
Leading industries: Agriculture, tourism, mining (copper, coal, semi-precious stones)

Nauru

Official name: Republic of Nauru
Area: 7.7 square miles
Location: Central Pacific. The island of Nauru lies just south of the equator, about 1,300 miles northeast of Australia.
Natural features: The interior of Nauru consists of a

barren plateau, with a narrow strip of fertile land around the coast. The island is surrounded by coral reefs.
Population: 7,100 (1977 est.)
Capital: Yaren (district)
Other principal cities: Virtually all the people live in settlements along the coast.
Languages: Nauruan, English
Religion: Christian (mainly Protestant)
Leading industry: Phosphate mining. This lucrative industry gives the islanders one of the highest per capita incomes in the world.

Nepal

Official name: Kingdom of Nepal
Area: 54,663 square miles
Location: South Asia, in the Himalaya Mountains
Natural features: Nepal is largely mountainous; along the northern border are the High Himalaya, with Mount Everest and seven other of the world's highest mountains. In the center are high ranges and fertile valleys and in the south, the Terai, a region of swamps and plains.
Population: 13,000,000 (1977 est.)
Capital: Kathmandu
Other principal cities: Lalitpur, Biratnagar
Languages: Nepali, Tibeto-Burman languages, Munda, various Indo-Aryan dialects, English

Sherpas from Mt. Makalu, Nepal, wearing kurri knives. These mountain people are famous for guiding expeditions to the highest peaks of the Himalaya, among them Mt. Everest.

Religions: In the south Hindu; Mahayana Buddhist in the north. Hinduism is the official religion.

Leading industries: Agriculture (livestock herding, grains), forestry

The Netherlands

Official name: Kingdom of the Netherlands

Area: 15,892 square miles

Location: Western Europe, on the North Sea between Belgium and Germany

Natural features: The Netherlands is largely flat and low (much of it is below sea level and protected by dikes), except for a few hills in the southeast.

Population: 13,825,000 (1977 est.)

Capital: Amsterdam (seat of government at the Hague)

Other principal cities: Rotterdam, The Hague, Utrecht, Eindhoven

Languages: Dutch, Frisian (in the northern province of Friesland)

Religions: Largely Roman Catholic; Protestant

Leading industries: Commerce, shipbuilding, agriculture, food processing; manufacture of machinery and metal products, textiles, and chemicals

New Zealand

Official name: New Zealand

Area: 103,736 square miles

Location: South Pacific. New Zealand, located about 1,200 miles southeast of Australia, has two principal islands—North Island and South Island (separated by Cook Strait)—as well as Stewart Island, off the southern tip of South Island, and the Chatham islands about 400 miles east of South Island.

Natural features: North Island, the most populous, has rolling hills and low mountains in the north, volcanic peaks in the center, and fertile coastal plains in the south. South Island is mountainous.

Population: 3,148,000 (1977 est.)

Capital: Wellington

Other principal cities: Auckland, Christchurch, Dunedin, Manukau, Hamilton

Languages: English, Maori

Religions: Majority Protestant; Roman Catholic

Leading industries: Sheep raising, dairying, food processing, oil refining; manufacture of textiles, cement, fertilizers; mining

Nicaragua

Official name: Republic of Nicaragua

Area: 50,193 square miles

Location: Central America. The largest of the Central American republics, Nicaragua lies between Honduras and Costa Rica.

Natural features: Nicaragua is largely mountainous (Central American Cordilleras) and sparsely populated in the interior. On the Caribbean coast there is a wide plain, the "Mosquito Coast," and on the Pacific, a narrow coastal plain.

Population: 2,300,000 (1977 est.)

Capital: Managua

Other principal cities: León, Granada, Chinandega, Masaya

Languages: Spanish, English

Religion: Roman Catholic

Leading industries: Agriculture (cotton, coffee), mining (especially gold, silver, and copper), forestry, fishing, sugar refining, food processing, commerce

Niger

Official name: Republic of Niger

Area: 489,189 square miles

Location: West-central Africa. A landlocked country, Niger is surrounded by Algeria, Libya, Chad, Nigeria, Benin, Upper Volta, and Mali.

Natural features: Niger is virtually one big plain; the north is part of the Sahara, the south, arable savanna.

Population: 4,750,000 (1977 est.)

Capital: Niamey

Other principal cities: Zinder, Maradi, Tahoua

Languages: French, African languages

Religion: Moslem

Leading industries: Agriculture (peanuts, grains), livestock raising, mining

Nigeria

Official name: Federal Republic of Nigeria

Area: 379,628 square miles

Location: West Africa, on the Gulf of Guinea between Benin and Cameroon

Natural features: The coastal land is a belt of mangrove swamps, interspersed with Niger River delta branches and numerous other rivers and creeks; inland, a belt of tropical rain forest rises gradually to a high plateau (about 6,000 feet).

Population: 75,000,000 (1977 est.)

Capital: Lagos

Other principal cities: Ibadan, Ogbomosho, Mushin, Oshogbo

Languages: English, African languages (particularly Hausa, Yoruba, Ibo, Fulani)

Religions: Animist, Moslem (in the north), Christian (in the south and west)

Leading industries: Agriculture (world's leading exporter of peanuts and African oil palm products), petroleum production, mining, fishing, forestry, food processing

Norway

Official name: Kingdom of Norway

Area: 125,053 square miles

Location: Northern Europe. Norway stretches along the western portion of the Scandinavian peninsula; nearly half its length is north of the Arctic Circle.

Natural features: The coast of Norway is deeply indented with fjords. Farther inland, the land rises

Norwegian vessels carry their hardy fishermen throughout the cold waters of the Atlantic in search of herring and other fish that are staples of the Scandinavian diet.

to high, rugged plateaus and mountains, with well-watered fertile valleys. The country also has numerous glaciers, including Jostedalsbreen, Europe's largest ice field.

Population: 4,035,000 (1977 est.)
Capital: Oslo
Other principal cities: Trondheim, Bergen, Stavanger, Kristiansand
Languages: Norwegian, Lappish and Finnish (in the north)
Religion: Evangelical Lutheran
Leading industries: Merchant shipping, fishing (particularly whaling), forestry, agriculture, animal husbandry; manufacture of pulp and paper products, metal and metal products, machinery

Oman

Official name: Sultanate of Oman
Area: 120,000 square miles
Location: Northeast Africa on the southeast corner of the Arabian peninsula on the Arabian Sea
Natural features: Oman has a relatively fertile coastal plain from which a range of mountains rises sharply; the interior is a low, barren plateau.
Population: 800,000 (1977 est.)
Capital: Muscat
Other principal cities: Matrah, Salala, Nizwa
Language: Arabic
Religion: Moslem

Leading industries: Petroleum production, agriculture (particularly dates), date drying, fishing

Pakistan

Official name: Islamic Republic of Pakistan
Area: 310,403 square miles
Location: South Asia, on the Indian subcontinent. Pakistan lies northeast of India on the Arabian Sea.
Natural features: In the north and northwest are towering mountain ranges (including the Himalayas); along their foothills is a barren plain, and toward the east, the Indus plain drained by the Indus River.
Population: 70,000,000 (1977 est.)
Capital: Islamabad
Other principal cities: Karachi, Lahore, Lyallpur, Hyderabad, Multan, Rawalpindi
Languages: Urdu, Bengali, English, Punjabi
Religions: Predominantly Moslem; Hindu
Leading industries: Agriculture (particularly wheat and jute), food processing; manufacture of textiles, chemicals, cement, and paper

Panama

Official name: Republic of Panama
Area: 29,208 square miles
Location: Latin America. Panama occupies the southern end of the Isthmus of Panama and forms the land connection between the North and South American continents.
Natural features: Panama is largely mountainous, with lowlands along both coastlines. Eastern Panama is covered with tropical rain forests. The Panama Canal links the Pacific and Atlantic oceans.
Population: 1,772,000 (1977 est.)
Capital: Panama
Other principal cities: Colón, San Miguelito
Languages: Spanish, English
Religion: Roman Catholic
Leading industries: Providing goods and services for the Canal Zone, agriculture (bananas, rice), food processing

Papua New Guinea

Official name: Papua New Guinea
Area: 183,540 square miles
Location: Southwest Pacific about one hundred miles northeast of Australia. Eastern half of island of New Guinea, bordered on west by Indonesia
Natural features: High mountain ridge separating New Guinea, broad upland valley plains, vast swamps along much of coast
Population: 2,900,000 (1977 est.)
Capital: Port Moresby
Other principal cities: Rabaul, Lae
Languages: Melanesion Pidgin and Hiri (Police) Motu, English, about 750 localized languages
Religion: Largely Christian (Protestant, Roman Catholic); traditional forms

Leading industries: Agriculture, fishing, mining (copper, gold, silver), search for oil and gas started

Paraguay

Official name: Republic of Paraguay
Area: 157,047 square miles
Location: South America, southwest of Brazil
Natural features: Paraguay is topographically divided by the Paraguay River. The eastern part consists of fertile, rolling terrain, wooded hills, and tropical forest. In the west is the Chaco, a low plain covered with marshes and dense scrub forests.
Population: 2,805,000 (1977 est.)
Capital and principal city: Asunción
Languages: Spanish, Guarani (virtually all the people are bilingual)
Religion: Roman Catholic
Leading industries: Agriculture, cattle raising, forestry, food processing, commerce

Peru

Official name: Republic of Peru
Area: 496,222 square miles
Location: South America. Peru lies on the west coast, just above Chile.
Natural features: Peru consists of a narrow, coastal desert, a high sierra (Andean Cordilleras), and the eastern lowlands, made up of uncharted tropical jungles.
Population: 16,242,000 (1977 est.)
Capital: Lima

Other principal cities: Callao, Arequipa, Chimbote, Chiclayo
Languages: Spanish, Quechua, Aymara
Religion: Roman Catholic
Leading industries: Agriculture, forestry, fishing, mining, smelting, food processing, and refining

Philippines

Official name: Republic of the Philippines
Area: 115,707 square miles
Location: Southeast Asia. The Philippines include about 7,000 islands that stretch about 1,000 miles along the southeast rim of Asia.
Natural features: Most of the total land area lies on eleven main islands characterized by wide coastal plains and mountainous interiors, with wide valleys, volcanoes, hot and mineral springs.
Population: 44,010,000 (1977 est.)
Capital: Manila
Other principal cities: Cebu, Davao, Iloilo, Bacolod
Languages: Filipino (Tagalog), more than 70 other Philippine languages and dialects, English, Spanish
Religions: Predominantly Roman Catholic; Protestant; Moslem
Leading industries: Agriculture (rice, copra), fishing, forestry, mining, manufacture of textiles

Poland

Official name: Polish People's Republic
Area: 120,725 square miles

Indian watching sheep near Sacahuaman, an Incan fortress of 200-ton stone blocks fitted without mortar. Peru has a considerable livestock industry, with an estimated 14,000,000 sheep as well large numbers of cattle and swine. The animals graze over sites once inhabited by the ancient Incans.

Location: Eastern Europe, on the Baltic Sea, next to the Soviet Union
Natural features: Poland consists mainly of lowlands, except for the Sudeten Range and the Carpathian Mountains along the southern border.
Population: 34,530,000 (1977 est.)
Capital: Warsaw
Other principal cities: Lodz, Krakow, Wroclaw, Poznan, Gdansk
Language: Polish
Religion: Roman Catholic
Leading industries: Mining (particularly coal), manufacture of machinery and chemicals, iron and steel production, shipbuilding (Poland is the ninth largest producer of ships), agriculture, food processing

Portugal

Official name: Portuguese Republic
Area: 35,549 square miles
Location: Western Europe. Portugal occupies the western portion of the Iberian peninsula; the island groups of Madeira and the Azores are considered part of the country.
Natural features: Northern Portugal is mountainous; the south, below the Tagus River, consists of rolling plains.
Population: 9,800,000 (1977 est.)
Capital: Lisbon
Other principal city: Oporto
Language: Portuguese
Religion: Roman Catholic
Leading industries: Agriculture, wine making (particularly port and Madeira), food processing, forestry (Portugal is one of the world's leading suppliers of cork), fishing

Qatar

Official name: State of Qatar
Area: 4,247 square miles
Location: Southwest Asia, on a peninsula that stretches into the Persian Gulf
Natural features: Qatar consists of a flat limestone plain thinly covered by sand; it is low, hot, and dry.
Population: 170,000 (1977 est.)
Capital: Doha
Other principal cities: Umm Said, Dukhan
Language: Arabic
Religion: Sunni Moslem (Wahobi Sect)
Leading industries: Petroleum production (the only source of national income), herding of goats and camels, fishing, pearl diving

Rhodesia

Official name: Rhodesia
Area: 150,803 square miles
Location: South-central Africa. A landlocked nation, Rhodesia lies between Mozambique on the Indian Ocean and Botswana, north of South Africa.

Natural features: Most of Rhodesia is a high, rolling plateau, covered with grassland and scattered shrubs or trees.
Population: 6,600,000 (1977 est.)
Capital: Salisbury
Other principal cities: Bulawayo, Gwelo, Umtali
Languages: English, Bantu languages
Religions: The predominant religion is a combination of Animism and Christianity; Moslem; Christian (largely Anglican)
Leading industries: Mining (Wankie colliery is the largest coal mine in the world); manufacture of metals and metal products, textiles and clothing, tobacco products, and chemicals; agriculture; food processing

Rumania

Official name: Socialist Republic of Rumania
Area: 91,699 square miles
Location: Southeastern Europe. Rumania is a Balkan state on the Black Sea between the Soviet Union and Bulgaria.
Natural features: Two arc-shaped mountain systems, the Carpathians and the Transylvanian Alps, dominate Rumania's landscape; they separate a plains region in the east and south from the Transylvanian plateau in the northwest.
Population: 21,425,000 (1977 est.)
Capital: Bucharest
Other principal cities: Constanta, Ploiesti, Iasi, Timisoara
Language: Rumanian
Religions: Predominantly Rumanian Orthodox; Greek Uniate, Roman Catholic
Leading industries: Iron and steel production, petroleum production, agriculture, forestry, food processing; manufacture of machinery, chemicals, and textiles

Russia

See Soviet Union

Rwanda

Official name: Republic of Rwanda
Area: 10,160 square miles
Location: East-central Africa, partly in the Great Rift Valley, just north of Burundi and east of Zaïre; a land-locked country
Natural features: Rwanda, called "Land of a Thousand Hills," consists largely of grassy hills that roll southeastward from a chain of volcanoes in the northwest. Kagera National Park in the northeast covers a tenth of the country and preserves the native flora and fauna; Lake Kivu on the western border is considered one of Africa's most beautiful.
Population: 4,300,000 (1977 est.)
Capital and principal city: Kigali
Languages: Kinyarwanda, French, Kiswahili

Oil refinery on Ras Tannura, Saudi Arabia. Most of the country's oil production facilities are found along the Persian Gulf. Pipe lines connect the refinery to inland oil fields, storage tanks, and oil tankers.

Religions: Predominantly Christian (mainly Roman Catholic); Animist, Moslem
Leading industries: Mining (mostly cassiterite), agriculture (bananas and coffee), cattle raising

San Marino

Official name: Most Serene Republic of San Marino
Area: 23.4 square miles
Location: Europe. San Marino is an exclave in Italy, in the Apennines southwest of Rimini.
Natural features: San Marino lies almost entirely on one mountain, the three-peaked Mt. Titano, which rises more than 2,700 feet.
Population: 21,000 (1977 est.)
Capital and principal city: San Marino
Language: Italian
Religion: Roman Catholic
Leading industries: Agriculture (grapes and wheat), dairying, wine making, quarrying, tourism, sales of postage stamps

São Tomé and Príncipe

Official name: Democratic Republic of São Tomé and Príncipe
Area: 372 square miles
Location: Two islands in the Gulf of Guinea, about 125 miles off the west coast of Africa
Natural features: Hilly, wooded interiors, flat coastal plains

Population: 85,000 (1977 est.)
Capital: São Tomé
Other principal city: Santo António
Language: Portuguese; a local Creole
Religion: Roman Catholic
Leading industries: Agriculture, industries: copra, palm oil, and fish processing

Saudi Arabia

Official name: Kingdom of Saudi Arabia
Area: 829,995 square miles
Location: Southwest Asia (Middle East), on the Arabian peninsula.
Natural features: Most of Saudi Arabia, particularly in the uninhabited interior, is a barren desert plateau. In the west along the Red Sea are a narrow coastal plain and the Hejaz Mountains; in the east along the Persian Gulf are more rolling coastal plains.
Population: 7,900,000 (1977 est.)
Capital: Riyadh is the royal capital; Jidda is the administrative capital. Taif is summer capital.
Other Principal city: Mecca
Language: Arabic
Religion: Sunni Moslem
Leading industries: Petroleum production (Saudi Arabia is believed to have 10 percent of the world's oil reserves), oil refining, agriculture, herding (sheep, goats, camels), pearl diving, fishing, tourism (mostly by Moslem pilgrims)

Senegal

Official name: Republic of Senegal
Area: 76,124 square miles
Location: West Africa. Senegal is on the Atlantic Ocean between Mauritania and Guinea-Bissau.
Natural features: A transitional zone between the Sahara and the equatorial jungle, Senegal is semi-desert in the northwest, with savanna in the center and south.
Population: 5,300,000 (1977 est.)
Capital: Dakar
Other principal city: Thiès
Languages: French, African languages (Wolof, Fulani)
Religions: Predominantly Moslem; Christian, Animist
Leading industries: Commerce, agriculture (principal crop, peanuts), manufacture of peanut oil, phosphate mining, food processing, fishing

Seychelles

Official name: Republic of Seychelles
Area: 107 square miles
Location: Indian Ocean, about 1000 miles east of Kenya, just south of the Equator
Natural features: An archipelago of about 90 islands. Divided between a Granitic Group and a Coralline Group (about equally). The main island, Mahé, is mountainous and contains about 85 percent of population.
Population: 60,000 (1977 est.)
Capital and largest city: Victoria
Languages: Creole (predominant), English, and French
Religions: Predominantly Roman Catholic; Anglican
Leading industries: Tourism, processing of coconut and vanilla, agriculture, fishing

Sierra Leone

Official name: Republic of Sierra Leone
Area: 27,925 square miles
Location: West Africa, on the Atlantic Ocean, between Guinea and Liberia
Natural features: The coast of Sierra Leone is a plain of swamps and mangrove; this gives way to wooded hills and a plateau in the interior, and there are mountains near the eastern border.
Population: 3,200,000 (1977 est.)
Capital and principal city: Freetown
Languages: English, Creole (Krio), Mende, Temne
Religions: Predominantly Animist; Moslem, Christian
Leading industries: Agriculture (including palm kernels, cacao, kola nuts, and ginger), mining (Sierra Leone is one of the world's largest suppliers of diamonds; iron ore is also mined).

Singapore

Official name: Republic of Singapore
Area: 226 square miles
Location: Southeast Asia. An island nation, Singapore is just south of the Malay Peninsula, separated from it by the Johore Strait. A causeway connects the island with Malaysia.
Natural features: Except for a central plateau, Singapore is low (originally swamp and jungle); the city occupies land reclaimed from the sea.
Population: 2,300,000 (1977 est.)
Capital and principal city: City of Singapore
Languages: Malay, English, Chinese, Tamil, Hindi
Religions: The Chinese are Buddhist, Taoist, or Confucian; the Malays and Pakistanis are Moslem; the Indians are Hindu, and the Europeans and Eurasians are almost all Christian.
Leading industries: Commerce and trade (the commercial and financial center of Southeast Asia, with the world's fourth largest port), tourism, shipbuilding; food, rubber, and lumber processing; agriculture, fishing

Somalia

Official name: Somali Democratic Republic
Area: 246,200 square miles
Location: East Africa, on the Indian Ocean, just south of the Gulf of Aden
Natural features: Northern Somalia is mountainous; central and southern Somalia is largely desert or semiarid land, except for a large fertile area in the south, crossed by the Juba and Shebelli rivers.
Population: 3,400,000 (1977 est.)
Capital and principal city: Mogadishu
Languages: Somali (national language with no generally accepted written form); Arabic, Italian, English (official written languages)
Religion: Sunni Moslem
Leading industries: Livestock raising (cattle, camels, sheep, goats), agriculture (particularly bananas and spices), fishing, sales of wild animal skins (particularly Somali leopard skins)

South Africa

Official name: Republic of South Africa
Area: 472,359 square miles
Location: Southern tip of the African continent, between the South Atlantic Ocean and the Indian Ocean. Walvis Bay on the Atlantic coast of South-West Africa is part of South Africa.
Natural features: South Africa consists of a large interior plateau with a narrow belt of lowlands along the coasts.
Population: 26,100,000 (1977 est.)
Capital: Cape Town
Other principal cities: Johannesburg, Pretoria, Durban
Languages: English, Afrikaans, Bantu languages. The Indian population speaks Tamil, Hindi, Gujarati and Telugu.

The 16th century Cathedral of St. Basil, Red Square, Moscow. Legend has it that Ivan the Terrible blinded its Italian architect so he could not build anything else so beautiful.

Casa Milá, Barcelona, Spain, designed by the famous architect Gaudi (1852–1926), Barcelona has many notable buildings and wide boulevards.

Religions: Majority Christian (Chiefly Protestant), various Bantu religions, Aniniest
Leading industries: Mining (world leader in production of gold, diamonds, and antimony), iron and steel production; manufacture of machinery, textiles, automobiles, chemicals, and fertilizers; agriculture

Soviet Union

Official name: Union of Soviet Socialist Republics
Area: 8,649,490 square miles
Location: Northern Eurasia. The largest nation in the world, the Soviet Union extends from the Baltic Sea to the Pacific Ocean, with the Arctic Ocean to the north.
Natural features: In the west, from the Pripet Marshes (near Poland) to the Ural Mountains, there is a broad plain with occasional hills, crossed by numerous rivers, including the Volga and Dnieper. The Caucasus Mountains lie between the Black and Caspian seas. East of the lower Urals are the Siberian lowlands and deserts of Central Asia, beyond which are the Siberian highlands and mountain ranges of the Soviet Far East. There are also high mountains to the south of the central desert.
Population: 255,300,000 (1977 est.)
Capital: Moscow
Other principal cities: Leningrad, Kiev, Tashkent, Baku, Kharkov, Gorki, Novosibirsk, Kuibyshev, Sverdlovsk, Minsk
Languages: Russian (spoken by about 60 percent of the population as a first language and as a second language by nearly all the rest). About 260 other languages and dialects are also spoken.
Religions: Predominantly atheist; of those professing a religion, most are Russian Orthodox; also, Moslem (in central Asia), Christian, and Jewish. The government discourages all religious practice.
Leading industries: Iron and steel production; manufacture of heavy machinery, electrical equipment, chemicals, cement, textiles and clothing; food processing, mining, agriculture (grains). There are more than 2,000,000 square miles of arable land in the Soviet Union.

Spain

Official name: Spanish State
Area: 194,881 square miles
Location: Southwest Europe. Spain occupies most of the Iberian peninsula, and includes the Balearic Islands in the Mediterranean, the Canary Islands in the Atlantic, and Ceuta and Melilla in Africa.
Natural features: Most of Spain consists of a high tableland (the Meseta) divided by east-west mountain ranges. Along the coasts is a narrow coastal plain, which widens in the Andalusian lowlands in

the south. The Pyrenees run along the French-Spanish border.

Population: 36,100,000 (1977 est.)

Capital: Madrid

Other principal cities: Barcelona, Valencia, Seville, Saragossa

Languages: Spanish; regional dialects of Catalan, Galician, and Basque

Religion: Roman Catholic

Leading industries: Agriculture (grains, vegetables, olives, grapes, oranges), wine making, cork production, mining; manufacture of textiles, paper, automobiles, and cement

Sri Lanka

Official name: Republic of Sri Lanka (formerly Ceylon)

Area: 25,332 square miles

Location: Island in Indian Ocean, off the southeastern tip of India

Natural features: A low plain covers the northern half of the island of Sri Lanka and the coast of the southern half; the south-central region is hilly and mountainous.

Population: 14,100,000 (1977 est.)

Capital: Colombo

Other principal cities: Dehiwala-Mount Lavinia, Jaffna, Moratuwa, Kandy, Kotte

Languages: Sinhala, Tamil, English

Religions: Predominantly Buddhist; Hindu, Christian (mainly Roman Catholic), and Moslem

Leading industries: Agriculture (tea, rice), rubber growing, forestry, fishing, mining (graphite and precious gems); processing of tea, rubber, and coconuts; manufacture of tobacco products, chemicals, tires, paper

Sudan

Official name: Democratic Republic of the Sudan

Area: 967,494 square miles

Location: Northeast Africa, on the Red Sea between Egypt and Ethiopia. Sudan is the largest country in Africa.

Natural features: There are three distinct regions in Sudan: the bleak Libyan and Sahara deserts in the north; grassy, fertile plains in the center; and swamp and tropical rain forests in the south. The Nile River flows through the center of the country.

Population: 18,300,000 (1977 est.)

Capital: Khartoum

Other principal cities: Omdurman, Port Sudan

Languages: Arabic, many African languages (in the south)

Religions: In the north, predominantly Moslem; mostly Animist in the south; some small Christian communities

Leading industries: Agriculture (principal crops, cotton and gum arabic, of which Sudan produces 80 percent of the world's supply), livestock raising, manufacture of food and vegetable oils

Surinam

Official name: Republic of Surinam

Area: 60,239 square miles

Location: Northeast coast of South America; bordered on the north by the Atlantic Ocean, on the east by French Guiana, and on the south by Brazil

Natural features: There are three principal zones: a coastal belt which is flat (with dikes for agriculture), a central area with forests and swamp, and a southern hilly zone comprising 75 percent of the area.

Population: 430,000 (1977 est.)

Capital and principal city: Paramaribo

Languages: Dutch and English

Religions: Evenly divided among Hindu, Moslem, Protestant, and Roman Catholic

Leading industries: Mining (bauxite) and agriculture (rice, coffee, sugar, citrus fruits)

Swaziland

Official name: Kingdom of Swaziland

Area: 6,705 square miles

Location: Southern Africa. Swaziland is almost entirely surrounded by South Africa.

Natural features: Swaziland consists of three distinct regions of about equal size: the high veldt in the west is mountainous; the middle veldt, a plateau; and the low veldt in the east, a low plain.

Population: 500,000 (1977 est.)

Capital: Mbabane

Other principal city: Manzini

Languages: English, siSwati

Religions: About evenly divided between Animist and Christian

Leading industries: Agriculture, cattle raising, mining (particularly asbestos and iron ore), food processing, forestry

Sweden

Official name: Kingdom of Sweden

Area: 173,655 square miles

Location: Northern Europe. Sweden occupies the eastern part of the Scandinavian peninsula.

Natural features: Northern Sweden is mountainous; in the south there is gently rolling terrain. There are numerous lakes, and about half the country is wooded.

Population: 8,236,179 (1977 est.)

Capital: Stockholm

Other principal cities: Göteborg, Malmö, Uppsala, Norrköping

Languages: Swedish; Lappish and Finnish (by a small minority in the north)

Religion: Lutheran

Leading industries: Forestry, mining (particularly iron ore), agriculture (grains, potatoes), dairying, fishing, shipbuilding; manufacture of metal products, paper, vehicles, scientific instruments, porcelain and glass

Switzerland

Official name: Swiss Confederation
Area: 15,943 square miles
Location: Central Europe, surrounded by Germany, Austria, Italy, and France
Natural features: Switzerland is largely mountainous; it is crossed by two mountain ranges, the Alps and the Jura, between which is a plateau. The headwaters of the Rhine and the Rhone are in the Swiss Alps, as is Mont Blanc (15,771 feet), the highest peak in western Europe.
Population: 6,550,000 (1977 est.)
Capital: Bern
Other principal cities: Zürich, Basel, Geneva, Lausanne
Languages: German, French, Italian, Romansch (a form of Latin) in the southeast; many Swiss are bi- or trilingual.
Religions: Majority Protestant; Roman Catholic; small Jewish community
Leading industries: Commerce; manufacture of machinery, chemicals, and watches; agriculture, dairying. Switzerland has abundant hydroelectric power.

Syria

Official name: Syrian Arab Republic
Area: 71,498 square miles
Location: Southwest Asia (Middle East), on the Mediterranean Sea, south of Turkey.
Natural features: A narrow fertile plain along the coast rises into rugged mountains. East of the mountains are the central plains, and the Syrian desert in the southeast. In the north is the fertile Euphrates River valley.
Population: 7,800,000 (1977 est.)
Capital: Damascus
Other principal cities: Aleppo, Homs
Language: Arabic
Religions: Predominantly Sunni Moslem; also Christian and other Moslem
Leading industries: Agriculture, goat and sheep herding, food processing, commerce, oil refining; manufacture of textiles, leather products, cement, glass, and soap

Tanzania

Official name: United Republic of Tanzania (formerly the states of Tanganyika and Zanzibar)
Area: 363,708 square miles
Location: East Africa, on the Indian Ocean, between Kenya and Mozambique. It includes the island of Zanzibar, twenty miles east.

Paper factory, Lessebo, Sweden. About half of Sweden is covered with forests, and their cutting is strictly controlled. Reforestation is required on private as well as public lands.

Zuos in the Engadine Valley, Switzerland. The Inn River flows through this beautiful valley of eastern Switzerland, which boasts such famous resorts as St. Moritz.

Drying sisal fibers, Tanzania. One of Tanzania's chief exports, sisal is used to make the binding twine used in harvesting machines. This new East African country's principal exports are agricultural goods and diamonds.

Natural features: Tanganyika, on the mainland, consists of a low-lying coastal area, a high central plateau, and scattered mountainous areas, including Mount Kilimanjaro (19,340 feet). Lake Victoria and the Serengeti Plain are in the north. Zanzibar is a low coral island.

Population: 16,000,000 (1977 est.)

Capital: Dar es Salaam

Other principal city: Zanzibar

Languages: English, Swahili; about 120 other dialects, mostly Bantu

Religions: Largest group, Moslem; also, Christian, Animist

Leading industries: Agriculture (sisal for rope; cotton, coffee, nuts, cloves [world's largest producer]), fishing, food processing, diamond mining

Thailand

Official name: Kingdom of Thailand (called Siam until 1939)

Area: 198,455 square miles

Location: Southeast Asia, just west of Laos, on the Malay Peninsula.

Natural features: There are north-south mountain ranges in the north and east of Thailand, extending into the Malay Peninsula. In the center is a plain, watered by canals, east of which is the barren Khorat plateau.

Population: 43,200,000 (1977 est.)

Capital: Bangkok

Other principal cities: Thonburi, Chiengmai

Language: Thai

Religion: Buddhist

Leading industries: Agriculture (principal crop, rice), forestry (Thai forests produce teak), fishing, mining (one of the world's greatest producers of tin), smelting, saw milling, manufacture of textiles (silk), cement, and glass

Togo

Official name: Republic of Togo

Area: 21,622 square miles

Location: West Africa, on the Gulf of Guinea, between Ghana and Nigeria

Natural features: Togo is divided from the northeast to the southwest by the Chaine du Togo hills, on either side of which are large plains.

Population: 2,300,000 (1977 est.)

Capital and principal city: Lomé

Languages: French; forty-four other dialects including Ewe, Twi, and Hausa

Religions: Predominantly Animist; also Christian, Moslem

Leading industries: Agriculture (main crops, coffee, cacao, copra), coconut oil production, mining (phosphate), food processing, manufacture of cement and textiles

Tonga

Official name: Kingdom of Tonga
Area: 270 square miles
Location: Southwest Pacific Ocean. Tonga, an archipelago of 150 islands (45 inhabited), is about 400 miles east of Fiji.
Natural features: The islands are mostly low-lying coral, though some are volcanic; the majority, including Tongatapu, on which the capital is located, have no natural sources of fresh water.
Population: 92,000 (1977 est.)
Capital and principal city: Nuku'alofa
Languages: Tongan, English
Religion: Christian (mostly Methodist)
Leading industries: Agriculture (particularly coconuts and bananas), fishing

Trinidad and Tobago

Official name: Republic of Trinidad and Tobago
Area: 1,980 square miles
Location: West Indies. The most southern of the Lesser Antilles, the islands lie about seven miles northeast of the Venezuelan coast; they are separated by a nineteen-mile channel.
Natural features: Three low mountain ranges, interspersed with well-watered lowlands, cross Trinidad from east to west. Tropical forests cover about half the island. Tobago is mountainous and rugged with some flat land at the southwestern tip.
Population: 1,175,000 (1977 est.)
Capital: Port-of-Spain
Other principal city: San Fernando
Languages: English; Hindi and other Indian languages are spoken by the East Indian population.
Religions: Predominantly Christian; Hindu, Moslem
Leading industries: Petroleum and natural asphalt production, agriculture (principal crop, sugarcane), oil and sugar refining, food processing, manufacture of cotton textiles, tourism

Tunisia

Official name: Republic of Tunisia
Area: 63,170 square miles
Location: North Africa, on the Mediterranean Sea, between Algeria and Libya
Natural features: Tunisia consists of a wooded, fertile region in the north, into which the Tell Atlas Mountains extend; a central coastal plain; and a desert, part of the Sahara, in the south.
Population: 5,850,000 (1977 est.)
Capital: Tunis
Other principal cities: Sfax, Bizerte, Sousse
Languages: Arabic, French
Religion: Moslem
Leading industries: Agriculture (Tunisia is one of the world's largest producers of olive oil), livestock raising (by the nomads), mining (principally phosphate and iron ore), food processing

Turkey

Official name: Republic of Turkey
Area: 300,946 square miles
Location: Asia Minor and southeast Europe, between the Mediterranean and Black seas. About 97 percent of Turkey is in Asia.
Natural features: The center of Asiatic Turkey is the semiarid Anatolian plateau, surrounded by hills and mountains, and fertile coastal strips. European Turkey consists of rolling arable land.
Population: 40,500,000 (1977 est.)
Capital: Ankara
Other principal cities: Istanbul, Izmir, Adana, Bursa
Languages: Turkish; Kurdish and Arabic (by minorities)
Religion: Sunni Moslem
Leading industries: Agriculture, livestock raising (especially on the Anatolian plain), forestry, mining (one of the world's largest producers of chrome), iron and steel production, food processing; manufacture of textiles, fertilizers, paper, and chrome products

Uganda

Official name: Republic of Uganda
Area: 91,076 square miles
Location: East Africa. Uganda is a landlocked nation between Kenya on the east and Zaïre on the west.
Natural features: Most of Uganda is a plateau, with numerous lakes—Victoria, George, Albert, Edward—making up about 18 percent of the total area. There are thick forests in the south and savanna in the north.
Population: 12,000,000 (1977 est.)
Capital: Kampala
Other principal cities: Jinja, Mbale, Entebbe
Languages: Swahili, English; Ganda (Luganda), and many other local languages
Religions: About half Christian; Moslem, traditional religions
Leading industries: Agriculture, cattle raising, fishing, mining (particularly copper), food and mineral processing, manufacture of textiles and tobacco products

Union of Soviet Socialist Republics (USSR)

See Soviet Union

United Arab Emirates

Official name: United Arab Emirates (formerly known as the Trucial States, Trucial Oman, or Trucial Shiekdoms)
Area: 32,278 square miles
Location: Southwest Asia (Middle East). The seven emirates (from west to east: Abu Dhabi, Dubai, Sharjah, Ajman, Umm al-Qaiwain, Ras al-Khaimah, Fujairah) are on the Persian Gulf, be-

tween Qatar and Oman; inland they border on Saudi Arabia.

Natural features: Most of the region is low and flat, except for some hills and mountains on the eastern end. The climate is hot and dry, sometimes reaching 140 degrees.

Population: 260,000 (1977 est.)
Capital: Abu Dhabi
Other principal city: Dubai
Language: Arabic
Religion: Sunni Moslem
Leading industries: Petroleum production, herding, growing of dates, fishing

United Kingdom

Official name: United Kingdom of Great Britain and Northern Ireland
Area: 94,399 square miles
Location: Northwest Europe. England, Scotland, and Wales are on the island of Great Britain, which is separated from continental Europe by the North Sea, the Strait of Dover, and the English Channel. On the west, the Irish Sea and the North Channel separate Great Britain from the island of Ireland, six northern counties of which make up Northern Ireland (Ulster).
Natural features: England is hilly in the north, west, and southwest, with undulating downs, fens, and low plains in the east and southeast; central England (Midlands) has low, rolling plains. The Cheviot Hills separate England from Scotland and make up the Southern Uplands of Scotland. In Scotland are also the Central Lowlands and the Northern Highlands, rising to 4,406 feet (Ben Nevis), the highest point in the British Isles. Wales is largely mountainous; Northern Ireland contains many plateaus and hills.
Population: 56,100,000 (1977 est.)
Capital: London
Other principal cities: In England, Birmingham, Liverpool, Manchester, Sheffield, Leeds; in Scotland, Glasgow and Edinburgh; in Wales, Swansea and Cardiff; in Northern Ireland, Belfast
Languages: English, Gaelic (in parts of Scotland and Northern Ireland), Welsh (in Wales)
Religions: Church of England (Anglican), Church of Scotland (Presbyterian)
Leading industries: Iron and steel production; mining (particularly coal); manufacture of motor vehicles, aircraft, textiles, chemicals; food processing; and in Wales, Northern Ireland, and Scotland, agriculture, grazing of sheep, dairying, and fishing

United States

Official name: United States of America
Area: 3,615,123 square miles
Location: North America, between Canada on the north and Mexico on the southwest, and stretching from the Atlantic to the Pacific oceans. It includes

Alaska, a large land mass on the western end of Canada; and the Hawaiian Islands, about 2,000 miles off the United States west coast.
Natural features: The United States from east to west consists of an Atlantic coastal plain; the Appalachian Mountains; a vast region of interior plains drained by the Mississippi River and its tributaries; the rugged, steep Rocky Mountains, and the lower mountains and rolling valleys of the Pacific border. About one-third of the country is covered with forests. Alaska has four main physical divisions: the Pacific mountain system, the Central plateau, the Arctic mountain system, and the Arctic slope. Hawaii is an archipelago of 122 mountainous islands of volcanic origin.
Population: 215,000,000 (1977 est.)
Capital: Washington, D.C.
Other principal cities: New York City, Chicago, Los Angeles, Philadelphia, Detroit, Houston, Baltimore, Dallas, Cleveland
Languages: English; Spanish by sizable minorities in New York City, Florida, and near the Mexican border.
Religions: The largest group is Protestant. Also Roman Catholic, Jewish.
Leading industries: Iron and steel production; metal processing; manufacture of heavy machinery, transportation equipment, textiles, chemicals, petroleum products, furniture, clothing, household appliances; agriculture (one of the world's leading producers of grains, tobacco, and cotton), cattle raising, dairying, forestry, fishing. The United States is the richest of the world's major nations.

Upper Volta

Official name: Republic of Upper Volta
Area: 105,869 square miles
Location: West Africa. Upper Volta is a landlocked nation that lies just south of Mali.
Natural features: Upper Volta consists of a large plateau, with numerous valleys formed by three main rivers, the Black, White, and Red Voltas.
Population: 6,400,000 (1977 est.)
Capital: Ouagadougou
Other principal cities: Bobo-Dioulasso, Koudougou
Languages: French, Mossi, other African languages
Religions: Majority, Animist; Moslem, Christian
Leading industries: Agriculture, livestock raising

Uruguay

Official name: Oriental Republic of Uruguay
Area: 68,536 square miles
Location: South America, on the southeast coast, just south of Brazil
Natural features: Uruguay has low hills and grassy plains, watered by numerous streams.
Population: 2,800,000 (1977 est.)
Capital: Montevideo

Other principal cities: Las Piedras, Salto
Language: Spanish
Religion: Roman Catholic
Leading industries: Livestock raising (cattle and sheep), agriculture; manufacture of textiles, construction materials, and chemicals; wine making; meat packing

Vatican City

Official name: State of the Vatican City
Area: 108.7 acres (or 0.17 square miles). The Vatican is the world's smallest sovereign state.
Location and features: Southern Europe. Vatican City lies near the west bank of the Tiber River in Rome, Italy, bordered on the west and south by the Leonine Wall. It includes St. Peter's Basilica, St. Peter's Square, the Vatican palaces, Belvedere Park, and the Vatican Gardens, and is the administrative center for the Roman Catholic Church. It also exercises extraterritorial sovereignty over a dozen buildings and some territory in and near Rome.
Population: 724 (1975 est.)
Languages: Italian, Latin (the official language of the Holy See)
Leading industries: Tourism, sale of Vatican stamps and publications. (Economically, it depends on the Roman Catholic Church.)

Venezuela

Official name: Republic of Venezuela
Area: 352,143 square miles
Location: South America, on the northern (Caribbean) coast, between Colombia and Guyana
Natural features: Venezuela has four major geographic regions: the Andes Mountains in the northwest; the coastal zone along Lake Maracaibo and the Caribbean; the llanos (plains) that stretch from the Andes to the Orinoco River; and the Guayana Highlands, high plateaus and rolling plains beyond the Orinoco.
Population: 12,700,000 (1977 est.)
Capital: Caracas
Other principal cities: Maracaibo, Valencia, Barquisimeto
Language: Spanish
Religion: Roman Catholic
Leading industries: Petroleum production and refining; mining (mainly iron ore); manufacture of textiles and clothing, building materials, chemicals; commerce; agriculture; food processing; pearl fishing (especially on Margarita Island)

Vietnam

Official name: Socialist Republic of Vietnam
Area: 128,405 square miles
Location: Southeast Asia, eastern part of Indochina bordered by China on the north, the South China Sea on the east, and Laos and Cambodia on the west

Natural features: Jungle-covered hills in the north rise in the southeast to the Annamese Cordilleras and outlying plateaus; east of the mountains are fertile coastal lowlands.
Population: 47,300,000 (1977 est.)
Capital: Hanoi
Other principal cities: Ho Chi Minh City (formerly Saigon), Da Nang, and Hue
Languages: Vietnamese, Chinese, and French
Religions: Buddhist and Animist
Leading industries: Basically agriculture (rice, sugar, tea), mining (coal, iron ore, apatite, phosphates)

Western Samoa

Official name: Western Samoa
Area: 1,133 square miles
Location: South Pacific. Western Samoa is composed of the main islands of Savai'i and Upolu and several others, which lie midway between Honolulu and Sydney, Australia.
Natural features: The islands are rugged and mountainous, mainly of volcanic origin; most have coral reefs surrounding them.
Population: 151,500 (1977 est.)
Capital and principal city: Apia
Languages: Samoan, English
Religion: Christian (predominantly Congregationalist, Methodist, and Roman Catholic)

Caracas, capital of Venezuela. Founded in 1567, Caracas is nevertheless a modern city, made prosperous by the country's oil production. It is an educational and cultural center.

Leading industries: Agriculture (principally taro, coconuts, cocoa, bananas, and pineapples); fishing; food processing; manufacture of handicrafts, clothing, soap, and furniture

Yemen

Official name: Yemen Arab Republic
Area: 77,220 square miles
Location: Northeast Asia, just off the southwest corner of Arabia, bordered on the west by the Red Sea
Natural features: Yemen is largely mountainous and receives abundant rainfall. There is semidesert land on the coastal strip along the Red Sea.
Population: 5,600,000 (1977 est.)
Capital: San'a
Other principal cities: Hodeida, Ta'izz
Language: Arabic
Religion: Moslem
Leading industry: Agriculture (principal crops, gat [a mildly narcotic shrub], cotton, and coffee), mining (salt)

Yemen, Southern

Official name: People's Democratic Republic of Yemen (often called Aden)
Area: 111,101 square miles
Location: Northeast Asia, off the southeastern corner of Arabia, bordered on the south by the Gulf of Aden. Some of the country's land borders are undefined.
Natural features: Along the coast of Southern Yemen is a sandy plain that gives way to mountainous interior terrain. The deserts of the Empty Quarter of Arabia extend into the north of the country.
Population: 1,800,000 (1977 est.)
Capital: Aden
Other principal cities: Mukalla, Seiyun
Languages: Arabic, English
Religion: Moslem
Leading industries: Agriculture, fishing

Yugoslavia

Official name: Socialist Federal Republic of Yugoslavia
Area: 98,766 square miles
Location: Southeast Europe, on the Adriatic Sea, between Italy and Albania. It includes six republics: Slovenia, Croatia, Serbia, Bosnia-Herzegovina, Macedonia, and Montenegro.
Natural features: About two-thirds of Yugoslavia is mountainous, while the other third in the north and east consists of lowland hills and plains, drained by the Danube River.
Population: 21,672,000 (1977 est.)
Capital: Belgrade

Other principal cities: Zagreb, Skopje, Sarajevo, Ljubljana
Languages: Serbo-Croatian, Slovenian, Macedonian
Religions: Largest proportion Orthodox Christian; Roman Catholic, Moslem
Leading industries: Agriculture (mainly cereal grains), mining, petroleum production, tourism, food processing; manufacture of metals, wood products, chemicals, textiles

Zaïre (Congo Kinshasa)

Official name: Republic of Zaïre (formerly known as Congo Kinshasa)
Area: 918,962 square miles
Location: South-central Africa. Zaïre occupies a large area of the interior; a narrow strip of land running between Congo (Brazzaville) and Angola joins it to the Atlantic Ocean.
Natural features: The vast central basin-shaped plateau slopes to the west and is covered by tropical rain forests; it is rimmed by highlands and mountains, with huge lakes on the eastern border. In the northwest are dense grasslands, drained by the Zaïre (Congo) River.
Population: 26,000,000 (1977 est.)
Capital: Kinshasa
Other principal cities: Kananga, Lubumbashi
Languages: French; about 700 African languages and dialects
Religions: Evenly divided between Christian (mainly Roman Catholic), and traditional religions (mainly Animist)
Leading industries: Agriculture, food processing, mining (particularly industrial diamonds, also copper and cobalt), forestry, light manufacturing

Zambia

Official name: Republic of Zambia
Area: 290,586 square miles
Location: Central Africa. Zambia is a landlocked nation located just south of Zaïre.
Natural features: Most of Zambia is a high plateau, with mountains and highlands in the north and east. The Zambezi River flows through the country, forming Victoria Falls. There are many lakes.
Population: 5,200,000 (1977 est.)
Capital: Lusaka
Other principal cities: Kitwe, Ndola
Languages: English, Afrikaans, about forty different Bantu languages
Religions: African population, mostly traditional religions; Christian
Leading industries: Quarrying and mining (particularly copper), agriculture, food processing, manufacture of textiles and construction materials

World Geography

If you were fortunate enough to travel throughout the world, you would discover an almost endless variety in the world's geographic features. You would see the beauty and majesty of the world's highest mountains, the Himalayas in Nepal, and the highest peak, Mt. Everest, which rises to 29,028 feet. On the western edge of Asia, on the border of Israel and Jordan, you would find the lowest point on the earth, the Dead Sea, which is almost 1,300 feet below sea level. In Africa you would see the largest desert, the Sahara, and the longest river, the Nile. In North America, you would find five of the largest freshwater lakes, including Superior, Huron, and Michigan.

On this marvelous journey, you would see all the places you learn about in your geography classes as well as thousands of others. But in your travels you would also learn firsthand of the immense size of the world, its oceans, continents, mountains, rivers, and deserts.

The tables in this section and the maps in the World Atlas section present the most important geographic features in a way that will help you understand the full scope of the world, its natural wonders and its man-made cities.

EARTH'S MEASUREMENTS

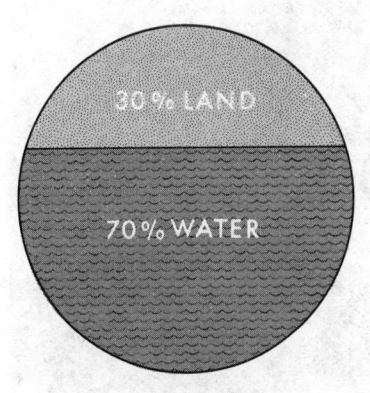

Equatorial diameter	7,908 miles
Polar diameter	7,882 miles
Circumference around equator	24,894 miles
Circumference around poles	24,811 miles
Estimated mass	5,883,000,000,000,000,000,000 tons
Estimated volume	260,052,000,000 cubic miles
Total surface area	197,272,000 square miles
Total ocean area	140,000,000 square miles
Total land area	57,272,000 square miles
Average land elevation	2,700 feet
Average ocean depth	12,500 feet
Greatest ocean depth	35,000 feet

THE CONTINENTS

About 29 percent of the earth's surface is divided into seven continents that include almost 99 percent of all the land. Earth is about 4½ billion years old, but many scientists believe the continents took their present shape about 150 million years ago. Before then, scientists believe, the continents were joined together in one or two large land masses. As time went by, these land masses began to break apart. After millions of years these smaller land masses took the shapes and positions they have today. This movement of land masses is called *continental drift* and is still going on at a rate of one to six feet a century.

Asia

Asia, largest of the continents, is home of half the world's population. It is divided from Europe by the Ural Mountains.

The far northern part of Asia is cold, flat, and sparsely populated. The central part of the continent is mountainous and dry. The southern part is hot, wet, and tropical. Long months of heavy monsoon rains make the land in the south rich and moist for rice growing.

China, Japan, India, Korea, and the eastern part of the Soviet Union are among the most important countries of Asia. Petroleum, iron, coal, rubber, copra, and tin are some of the products mined or cultivated.

Africa

Africa, the second largest continent, is made up of many different peoples and ways of life. In central Africa, where life in small villages is much as it was hundreds of years ago, the climate is hot and damp. Much of the land is covered by thick rain forests and large grassy plains. Northwest

Africa is dry, sandy desert. In the northeast, along the Nile, rich fertile land is used for agriculture. West Africa, highly influenced by Europe, is modern and industrialized, while southern Africa is famous for its diamond mines.

North America

North America is made up of only three countries, Canada, the United States, and Mexico. The far northern part of the continent is very cold and sparsely populated. Much of the south is hot and dry, and the southernmost part of Mexico is tropical. Mountain ranges are found in the west.

North America is rich in natural resources. Although the United States and Canada are both industrial nations, they contain enormous stretches of farmland. Mexico's economy relies heavily on agriculture, but it also has vast supplies of silver, zinc, sulfur, and petroleum.

South America

South America ranges from a cool, dry climate to a tropical one. The western coast is dominated by the lofty Andes Mountains. Much of the jungle in the central highlands is unexplored. In the southern lowlands, sweeping grasslands, called *pampas,* are used for cattle grazing.

Many minerals are found in South America. Agricultural products include nuts, sugar, and coffee.

Antarctica

Antarctica is the least-known continent. It is covered by snow and ice that average about 8,000 feet in thickness. Temperatures in the coastal areas average about zero. In the central area, around the South Pole, the average temperature is about $-80°F.$, $-62°C.$ Much of Antarctica has not been explored.

Antarctica is largely mountainous, and only the most primitive forms of plans live there. As yet, few mineral deposits have been found.

Europe

Europe is highly industrialized. About 20 percent of the world's population lives there, in several kinds of climate and topography. Scandinavia, in the north, is cold and snowy. In the south, the countries around the Mediterranean Sea are hot. In some parts of the Netherlands, the land lies below sea level, while central Europe has mountains as high as 18,000 feet.

About 40 percent of the land area of Europe is used for agriculture. Urban areas are crowded and modern. Manufacturing is very important to Europe's economy.

Australia

Australia is an island continent. Because it lies so far south, the climate ranges from warm to tropical. Most Australians live in modern coastal cities, but the interior is largely occupied by native peoples, called aborigines. Australia is located far from any other land, so many plants and animals found there are not found elsewhere. The kangaroo, the platypus, and the koala bear are native to the continent.

Eastern Australia is composed of mountains, forest, farms, and grazing lands. The west, partly desert and partly grasslands, supports a large cattle industry. Sheep and cattle raising are important in Australia's economy. Coal, iron ore, lead, gold, and zinc are found in great quantities.

THE CONTINENTS

Name	Area (sq. mi.)	% World land	Highest point (ft.)	Lowest point below sea level (ft.)
Asia	17,129,000	29.7	Mt. Everest (29,028), Nepal/Tibet	Dead Sea (1,296), Israel/Jordan
Africa	11,707	20.0	Mt. Kibo (19,340), Tanzania	Lake Assal (510), Djibouti
North America	9,362,000	16.3	Mt. McKinley (20,320), Alaska	Death Valley (282), southwestern U.S.
South America	6,886,000	12.0	Mt. Aconcagua (22,834), Argentina	Salinas Grandes (131), Argentina
Antarctica	5,500,000	9.6	Vinson Massif (16,860)	Lowest point is at sea level
Europe	4,057,000	6.5	Mt. Elbruz (18,510), USSR	Caspian Sea (92), USSR
Australia	2,942,000	5.1	Mt. Kosciusko (7,310), New South Wales	Lake Eyre (52), southern Australia

TEN LARGEST ISLANDS

	Island	Ocean	Size (sq. mi.)	Population
1.	Greenland	N. Atlantic	840,000	50,000
2.	New Guinea	Pacific	315,000	4,000,000+
3.	Borneo	Pacific	287,000	6,000,000
4.	Madagascar	Indian	227,000	6,500,000
5.	Baffin Island	N. Atlantic	265,949	3,300
6.	Sumatra	Indian	183,000	20,000,000
7.	Great Britain	N. Atlantic	89,000	54,000,000
8.	Honshu	Pacific	89,000	77,000,000+
9.	Ellesmere Island	Arctic	82,000	uninhabited
10.	Victoria Island	Arctic	82,000	500

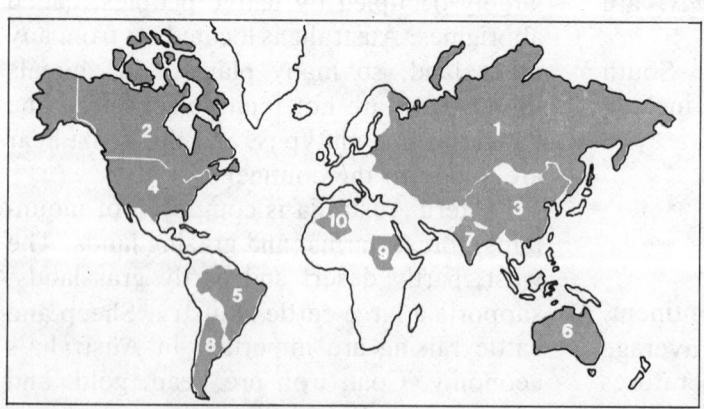

TEN LARGEST COUNTRIES

	Country	Area (sq. mi.)
1.	U.S.S.R.	8,650,000
2.	Canada	3,850,000
3.	China	3,690,000
4.	U.S.A.	3,610,000
5.	Brazil	3,290,000
6.	Australia	2,970,000
7.	India	1,180,000
8.	Argentina	1,070,000
9.	Sudan	967,000
10.	Algeria	919,000

WORLD POPULATION

There are almost four billion people in the world, according to latest estimates. Here are the populations of the continents. The figures for Asia and Europe leave out the population of the USSR, which lies on both continents. Oceania includes Australia, New Zealand, and the many other islands in that area of the Pacific.

Asia	2,056,000,000
Europe	462,000,000
Africa	344,000,000
North America	321,000,000
USSR	255,000,000
South America	190,000,000
Oceania	19,400,000
Antarctica	0

THE TEN LARGEST COUNTRIES BY POPULATION

There are 149 member nations in the United Nations. China, with approximately 835 million people, is the largest. The smallest, Pitcairn Island, has approximately 125 people. Here, in order of size, are the population figures for the twelve largest.

1.	China	835,000,000
2.	India	600,000,000
3.	U.S.S.R.	255,000,000
4.	United States	215,000,000
5.	Indonesia	130,000,000
6.	Japan	110,000,000
7.	Brazil	107,000,000
8.	Bangladesh	77,000,000
9.	Nigeria	75,000,000
10.	Pakistan	70,000,000

THE FIFTEEN LARGEST CITIES

1.	Shanghai	10,820,000
2.	Tokyo	8,642,000
3.	New York	7,800,000
4.	Mexico City	7,690,000
5.	Moscow	7,580,000
6.	Peking	7,570,000
7.	London	7,028,000
8.	Bombay	5,970,000
9.	Sao Paulo	5,816,000
10.	Tehran	4,400,000
11.	Rio de Janeiro	4,252,000
12.	Chicago	3,173,000
13.	Calcutta	3,149,000
14.	Buenos Aires	2,976,000
15.	Paris	2,600,000

THE WORLD

OCEANS OF THE WORLD

Ocean	Area (sq. mi.)	Avg. depth (ft.)	Max. depth (ft.)
Pacific	64,186,300	14,048	36,198
Atlantic	33,420,000	12,880	28,374
Indian	28,350,500	13,002	25,344
Arctic	5,105,700	5,010	17,880

TEN LARGEST SEAS

Sea	Area (sq. mi.)	Avg. depth (ft.)	Max. depth (ft.)
1. Caribbean	970,000	8,685	24,720
2. Mediterranean	969,100	4,926	16,896
3. South China	895,400	5,400	15,000
4. Bering	875,000	4,893	15,800
5. Gulf of Mexico	600,000	4,874	12,300
6. Okhotsk	590,000	2,749	11,069
7. East China	482,300	617	9,500
8. Hudson Bay	317,500	420	2,846
9. Japan	391,100	5,468	12,275
10. Andaman	308,000	2,854	12,392

TEN LARGEST LAKES

Lake	Location	Area (sq. mi.)	Length (mi.)
1. Caspian Sea	USSR/Iran	143,243	746
2. Superior	U.S./Canada	31,700	383
3. Victoria	E. Cent. Africa	26,724	250
4. Aral	USSR	25,676	266
5. Huron	U.S./Canada	23,010	247
6. Michigan	U.S.	22,300	321
7. Tanganyika	E. Cent. Africa	12,650	321
8. Great Bear	Canada	12,096	190
9. Baykal	USSR	11,780	395
10. Nyasa	S.E. Africa	11,555	360

TEN LONGEST RIVERS

River	Length (mi.)	Location
1. Nile	4,145	N.E. Africa
2. Amazon	3,915	S. America
3. Mississippi-Missouri	3,710	United States
4. Ob-Irtysh	3,362	USSR
5. Yangtze	3,400	China
6. Huang	2,900	China
7. Congo	2,718	Africa
8. Amur	2,700	USSR
9. Lena	2,734	USSR
10. Mackenzie	2,635	Canada

TEN HIGHEST WATERFALLS

Name	Country	Height (ft.)
1. Angel	Venezuela	3,212
2. Tugela	South Africa	3,110
3. Cuquenan	Venezuela	2,000
4. Sutherland	New Zealand	1,904
5. Takkakaw	Canada	1,650
6. Ribbon	United States	1,612
7. Upper Yosemite	United States	1,430
8. Gavarnie	France	1,385
9. Krimml	Austria	1,247
10. Silverstrand	United States	1,170

TEN HIGHEST MOUNTAINS

	Mountain	Range	Location	Height (ft.)
1.	Everest	Himalayas	Nepal/Tibet	29,028
2.	Godwin-Austen	Karakoram	India/Kashmir	28,250
3.	Kanchenjunga	Himalayas	Nepal/Sikkim	28,208
4.	Makalu	Himalayas	Nepal/Tibet	27,824
5.	Dhaulagiri	Himalayas	Nepal	26,810
6.	Nanga Parbat	Himalayas	Kashmir	26,660
7.	Annapurna	Himalayas	Nepal	26,504
8.	Gasherbrum	Karakoram	Kashmir	26,470
9.	Gosainthan	Himalayas	Tibet	26,291
10.	Nanda Devi	Himalayas	India	25,645

RECENTLY ACTIVE VOLCANOES

Name	Location	Height (ft.)	Last eruption
Etna	Sicily	10,902	1971
Fuego	Guatemala	12,582	1967
Hekla	Iceland	4,892	1970
Izalco	El Salvador	6,184	1967
Kilauea	Hawaii	4,077	1974
Merapi	Java	9,548	1969
Nyamiagira	Congo	10,028	1976
Nyiragongo	Congo	11,385	1977
Pacaya	Guatemala	8,346	1970
Stromboli	Lipari Is. (near Sicily)	3,038	1971

GREAT DESERTS OF THE WORLD

	Desert	Location	Size (sq. mi.)
1.	Sahara	N. Africa	3,500,000
2.	Great Australian	Australia	1,300,000
3.	Gobi	Central Asia	500,000
4.	Kara Kum	Central Asia	115,000
5.	Thar	N.W. India	150,000
6.	Takla Makan	W. China	180,000
7.	Kalahari	S. Africa	225,000
8.	Nubian	N.E. Africa	150,000
9.	Arabian	Egypt	70,000
10.	Atacama	Chile	140,000

Maps of the World

Map Symbols   5

World (physical features)   6–7

World (political divisions)   8–9

Northern Lands and Seas   10

North America   11

Canada   12–13

United States of America   14–15

Gulf and Caribbean Lands   16–17

South America   18

Southern Lands and Seas (Antarctica)   19

Europe and Western Asia   20–21

Soviet Union   22–23

Asia   24–25

Australia and New Zealand   26–27

Africa   28

Index

Page		Lat. °′	Long. °′
20	Aberdeen, Scot.	57·10 N	2·05 W
14	Aberdeen, S.D.	45·28 N	98·29 W
28	Abidjan, Ivory Coast	5·26 N	4·06 W
28	Accra, Ghana	5·40 N	0·15 W
24	Aden, P.D.R. of Yem.	12·48 N	45·00 E
28	Addis Ababa, Eth.	9·00 N	38·44 E
24	Afghanistan, Asia	33·00 N	63·00 E
28	Africa		
24	Agra, India	27·18 N	78·00 E
15	Akron, Ohio	41·05 N	81·30 W
15	Alabama (State), U.S.	32·50 N	87·30 W
25	Al Aqabah, Jor. (Palestine In.)	29·45 N	35·55 E
14	Alaska (State), U.S.	65·00 N	158·00 W
20	Albania, Eur.	41·45 N	20·00 E
15	Albany, Ga.	31·35 N	84·10 W
15	Albany, N.Y.	42·40 N	73·50 W
14	Albany, Ore.	44·38 N	123·06 W
13	Albany (R.), N.A.	51·45 N	83·30 W
12	Alberta (Prov.), Can.	54·33 N	117.10 W
14	Albuquerque, N.Mex.	35·05 N	106·40 W
21	Aleppo, Syria	36·10 N	37·18 E
28	Alexandria, Eg.	31·12 N	29·58 E
15	Alexandria, Va.	38·50 N	77·05 W
28	Algeria, Afr.	34·58 N	4·00 E
28	Algiers (Alger), Alg.	36·51 N	2·56 E
24	Allahabad, India	25·32 N	81·53 E
21	Al Masul, Iraq	36·00 N	42·53 E
20	Alps (Mts.), Eur.	46·18 N	8·42 E
15	Altoona, Pa.	40·25 N	78·25 W
18	Amazon (R.), Braz.	2·03 S	53·18 W
25	Amman, Jordan (Palestine In.)	31·57 N	35·57 E
20	Amsterdam, Neth.	52·21 N	4·52 E
23	Amur R., China-Sov. Un.	49·38 N	137·25 E
25	Amyun, Leb. (Palestine In.)	34·18 N	35·48 E
14	Anaconda, Mont.	46·07 N	112·55 W
14	Anchorage, Alsk.	61·12 N	149·48 W
15	Anderson, S.C.	34·30 N	82·40 W
20	Andorra, Eur.	42·32 N	1·18 E
23	Angarsk, Sov. Un.	52·48 N	104·15 E
28	Angola, Afr.	14·15 S	16·00 E
17	Anguilla, N.A.	18·15 N	62·54 W
24	Ankara, Tur.	39·55 N	32·50 E
15	Annapolis, Md.	39·00 N	76·25 W
15	Ann Arbor, Mich.	42·15 N	83·45 W
28	Antananarivo, Mad.	18·51 S	47·40 E
19	Antarctica		
17	Antigua I., N.A.	17·07 N	61·32 E
18	Antofagasta, Chile	23·32 S	70·21 W
18	Araguaia (R.), Braz.	8·37 S	49·43 W
21	Aral Sea, Sov. Un.	45·17 N	60·02 E
22	Ararat (Mtn.), Tur.	39·50 N	44·20 E
10	Arctic Ocean		
18	Arequipa, Peru	16·27 S	71·30 W
18	Argentina, S.A.	35·30 S	67·00 W
14	Arizona (State), U.S.	34·00 N	113·00 W
15	Arkansas (State), U.S.	34·50 N	93·40 W
14	Arkansas R., U.S.	37·50 N	103·15 W
21	Arkhangelsk, Sov. Un.	64·30 N	40·25 E
24	Asia		
28	Asmara, Eth.	15·17 N	38·56 E
18	Asunción, Par.	25·25 S	57·30 W
28	Aswân, Eg.	25·05 N	32·57 E
28	Asyut, Eg.	27·10 N	31·10 E
20	Athens, Grc.	38·00 N	23·38 E
15	Atlanta, Ga.	33·45 N	84·23 W
15	Atlantic City, N.J.	39·20 N	74·30 W
6	Atlantic Ocean		
15	Auburn, Maine	44·04 N	70·24 W
27	Auckland, N.Z. (In.)	37·43 S	174·53 E
15	Augusta, Ga.	33·26 N	82·00 W
15	Augusta, Maine	44·19 N	69·42 W
14	Austin, Tex.	30·15 N	97·42 W
26	Australia		
20	Austria, Eur.	47·15 N	11·53 E
25	Az Zarqa, Jordan (Palestine In.)	32·03 N	36·07 E
11	Baffin I., Can.	67·20 N	71·00 W
24	Baghdad, Iraq	33·14 N	44·22 E
17	Bahamas, N.A.	26·15 N	76·00 W
27	Bairnsdale, Austl.	37·50 S	147·39 E
14	Baker, Ore.	44·46 N	117.42 W
14	Bakersfield, Calif.	35·23 N	119·00 W
20	Baleares, Islas, Sp.	39·25 N	1·28 E
22	Balkhash, L., Sov. Un.	45·58 N	72·15 E
20	Baltic Sea, Eur.	55·20 N	16·50 E
15	Baltimore, Md.	39·20 N	76·38 W
28	Bamako, Mali	12·45 N	7·50 W
24	Bangalore, India	13·03 N	77·39 E
24	Bangkok, Thai.	13·50 N	100·29 E
24	Bangladesh, Asia	24·00 N	90·00 E
15	Bangor, Maine	44·47 N	68·47 W
28	Bangui, Cen. Afr. Emp.	4·28 N	18·35 E
28	Banjul, Gam.	13·23 N	16·45 W
17	Barbados, N.A.	13·30 N	59·48 W
17	Barbuda I., Antigua	17·40 N	61·37 W
27	Barcaldine, Austl.	28·30 S	145·43 E
20	Barcelona, Sp.	41·25 N	2·08 E
18	Barranquilla, Col.	10·57 N	75·00 W
13	Barrie, Can.	44·25 N	79·45 W
28	Bata, Equat. Gui.	1·53 N	9·48 E
15	Baton Rouge, La.	30·28 N	91·10 W
23	Baykal, L., Sov. Un.	53·00 N	109·28 E
28	Beira, Moz.	19·46 S	34·58 E
24	Beirut, Leb.	33·53 N	35·30 E
18	Belém, Braz.	1·18 S	48·27 W
20	Belfast, N. Ire.	54·36 N	5·45 W
20	Belgium, Eur.	51·00 N	2·52 E
20	Belgrade, Yugo.	44·48 N	20·32 E
11	Belize, N.A.	17·00 N	88·40 W
16	Belmopan, Belize	17·15 N	88·47 W
15	Beloit, Wis.	42·31 N	89·04 W
28	Bengasi, Libya	32·08 N	20·06 E
28	Benin, Afr.	8·48 N	2·00 E
20	Bergen, Nor.	60·24 N	5·20 E
11	Bering Sea, Asia-N.A.	58·00 N	175·00 W
14	Berkeley, Calif.	37·52 N	122·17 W
20	Berlin, East, G.D.R.	52·30 N	13·25 E
20	Berlin, West, F.R. of Ger.	52·30 N	13·20 E
17	Bermuda I., N.A.	32·20 N	65·45 W
20	Bern, Switz.	46·55 N	7·25 E
24	Bhutan, Asia	28·00 N	90·00 E
20	Bialystok, Pol.	53·08 N	23·12 E
20	Bilbao, Sp.	43·12 N	2·48 W
14	Billings, Mont.	45·47 N	108·29 W
15	Biloxi, Miss.	30·24 N	88·50 W
15	Birmingham, Ala.	33·31 N	86·49 W
20	Birmingham, Eng.	52·29 N	1·53 W
14	Bismarck, N.D.	46·48 N	100·46 W
28	Bissau, Gui.-B.	11·52 N	15·47 W
21	Black Sea, Asia-Eur.	43·01 N	32·16 E
23	Blagoveshchensk, Sov. Un.	55·03 N	56·00 E
18	Bogotá, Col.	4·38 N	74·06 W
14	Boise, Idaho	43·38 N	116·12 W
18	Bolivia, S.A.	17·00 S	64·00 W
20	Bologna, It.	44·30 N	11·18 E
28	Boma, Zaire	5·45 S	13·05 E
24	Bombay, India	18·58 N	72·50 E
20	Bonn, F.R. of Ger.	50·44 N	7·06 E
20	Bordeaux, Fr.	44·50 N	0·37 W
7	Borneo I., Asia	0·25 N	112·39 E
15	Boston, Mass.	42·15 N	71·07 W
28	Botswana, Afr.	22·10 S	23·13 E
14	Boulder, Colo.	40·02 N	105·19 W
20	Braila, Rom.	45·15 N	27·58 E
18	Branco (R.), Braz.	2·21 N	60·38 W
18	Brasília, Braz.	15·49 S	47·39 W
20	Bratislava, Czech.	48·09 N	17·07 E
18	Brazil, S.A.	9·00 S	53·00 W
28	Brazzaville, Con.	4·10 S	15·18 E
20	Bremen, F.R. of Ger.	53·05 N	8·50 E
15	Bridgeport, Conn.	41·12 N	73·12 W
17	Bridgetown, Barb.	13·08 N	59·37 W
27	Brisbane, Austl.	27·30 S	153·10 E
12	British Columbia (Prov.), Can.	56·00 N	124·53 W
25	Brunei, Asia	4·52 N	113·38 W
20	Brussels, Bel.	50·51 N	4·21 E
20	Bucharest, Rom.	44·23 N	26·10 E
20	Budapest, Hung.	47·30 N	19·05 E
18	Buenos Aires, Arg.	34·20 S	58·30 W
15	Buffalo, N.Y.	42·54 N	78·51 W
28	Bujumbura, Burundi	3·19 S	29·28 E
28	Bulawayo, Rh.	20·12 S	28·43 E
20	Bulgaria, Eur.	42·12 N	24·13 E
24	Burma, Asia	21·00 N	95·15 E
21	Bursa, Tur.	40·10 N	28·10 E
28	Burundi, Afr.	3·00 S	29·30 E
15	Butte, Mont.	46·00 N	112·31 W
20	Cagliari, It.	39·16 N	9·08 E
28	Cairo, Eg.	30·03 N	31·17 E
18	Calcutta, India	22·32 N	88·22 E
12	Calgary, Can.	51·03 N	114·05 W
14	California (State), U.S.	38·10 N	121·20 W
16	California, Gulf of, Mex.	30·30 N	113·45 W
18	Callao, Peru	12·80 S	77·07 W
25	Cambodia, Asia	14·00 N	105·45 E
15	Camden, N.J.	39·56 N	75·06 W
28	Cameroon, Afr.	5·48 N	11·00 E
12	Camrose, Can.	53·08 N	112·50 W
11	Canada, N.A.	50·00 N	100·00 W
26	Canberra, Austl.	35·21 S	149·10 E
28	Cape Town, S. Afr.	33·48 S	18·28 E
18	Caracas, Ven.	10·30 N	66·58 W
17	Caribbean Sea, N.A.-S.A.	14·30 N	75·30 W
14	Carson City, Nev.	39·10 N	119·45 W
13	Cartwright, Can.	53·36 N	57·00 W
28	Casablanca, Mor.	33·32 N	7·41 W
22	Caspian Sea, Asia	39·30 N	52·00 E
18	Cayenne, Fr. Gu.	4·56 N	52·18 W
15	Cedar Rapids, Iowa	42·00 N	91·43 W
16	Celaya, Mex.	20·33 N	100·49 W
7	Celebes (Is.), Indon.	2·15 S	120·30 E
28	Central African Empire, Afr.	7·50 N	21·00 E
28	Chad, Afr.	17·48 N	19·00 E
28	Chad, L., Afr.	14·00 N	14·28 E
15	Champaign, Ill.	40·10 N	88·15 W
15	Charleston, S.C.	32·47 N	79·56 W
15	Charleston, W. Va.	38·20 N	81·35 W
15	Charlotte, N.C.	35·15 N	80·50 W
17	Charlotte Amalie (St. Thomas), Vir. Is. (U.S.A.) (St. Thomas In.)	18·21 N	64·54 W
15	Chattanooga, Tenn.	35·01 N	85·15 W
21	Chelyabinsk, Sov. Un.	55·10 N	61·25 E
23	Cheremkhovo, Sov. Un.	52·58 N	103·18 E
14	Cheyenne, Wyo.	41·10 N	104·49 W
15	Chicago, Ill.	41·49 N	87·37 W
23	Chichihaerh, China	47·18 N	124·00 E
16	Chihuahua, Mex.	28·37 N	106·06 W
18	Chile, S.A.	53·24 N	72·53 W
24	China, Asia	36·45 N	93·00 E
23	Chita, Sov. Un.	52·09 N	113·39 E
15	Cincinnati, Ohio	39·08 N	84·30 W
17	Ciudad Bolívar, Ven.	8·07 N	63·41 W
16	Ciudad Juárez, Mex.	31·44 N	106·28 W
15	Clarksburg, W. Va.	39·15 N	80·20 W
15	Cleveland, Ohio	41·30 N	81·42 W
20	Coimbra, Port.	40·14 N	8·23 W
20	Cologne (Köln), F.R. of Ger.	50·56 N	6·57 E
18	Colombia, S.A.	3·30 N	72·30 W
24	Colombo, Sri Lanka	6·58 N	79·52 E
16	Colón, Pan. (In.)	9·22 N	79·54 W
14	Colorado (State), U.S.	39·30 N	106·55 W
14	Colorado (R.), Mex.-U.S.	36·25 N	112·00 W
14	Colorado Springs, Colo.	38·49 N	104·48 W
15	Columbia, S.C.	34·00 N	81·00 W
14	Columbia (R.), Can.-U.S.	46·20 N	123·00 W
15	Columbus, Ohio	40·00 N	83·00 W
28	Comoros, Afr.	12·30 S	42·45 E
28	Conakry, Gui.	9·29 N	13·45 W
18	Concepción, Chile	36·51 S	72·59 W
15	Concord, N.H.	43·10 N	71·30 W
28	Congo, Afr.	3·00 S	13·48 E
28	Congo R., Afr.	2·00 S	17·01 E
15	Connecticut (State), U.S.	41·40 N	73·10 W
20	Constantine, Alg.	36·28 N	6·38 E
20	Copenhagen, Den.	55·43 N	12·27 E
18	Copiapó, Chile	27·16 S	70·28 W
18	Coquimbo, Chile	29·58 S	71·31 W
18	Córdoba, Arg.	30·20 S	64·03 W
20	Cork, Ire.	51·54 N	8·25 W
18	Corrientes, Arg.	27·25 S	58·39 W
20	Corsica (I.), Eur.	42·10 N	8·55 E
11	Costa Rica, N.A.	10·30 N	84·30 W
15	Covington, Ky.	39·05 N	84·31 W
20	Crete (I.), Eur.	35·15 N	24·30 E
11	Cuba, N.A.	22·00 N	79·00 W
24	Cyprus, Asia	34·56 N	31·28 E
20	Czechoslovakia, Eur.	49·28 N	16·00 E
24	Dacca, Bngl.	23·45 N	90·29 E
28	Dakar, Senegal	14·39 N	17·28 W
14	Dallas, Tex.	32·45 N	96·48 W
25	Damascus, Syria (Palestine In.)	33·31 N	36·18 E
20	Danube R., Eur.	43·51 N	17·30 E
28	Dar es Salaam, Tan.	6·58 S	39·13 E
27	Darling (R.), Austl.	31·50 S	143·20 E
15	Davenport, Iowa	41·34 N	90·38 W
15	Dayton, Ohio	39·45 N	85·15 W
20	Debrecen, Hung.	47·32 N	21·40 E
15	Delaware (State), U.S.	38·40 N	75·30 W
24	Delhi, India	28·54 N	77·13 E
24	Demavend (Mt.), Iran	36·05 N	52·05 E
20	Denmark, Eur.	56·14 N	8·30 E
14	Denver, Colo.	39·44 N	104·59 W
15	Des Moines, Iowa	41·35 N	93·37 W
15	Detroit, Mich.	42·22 N	83·10 W
28	Diégo-Suarez, Mad.	12·18 S	49·16 E
21	Diyarbakir, Tur.	38·00 N	40·10 E
25	Djakarta, Indon.	6·17 S	106·45 E
28	Djibouti, Djibouti	11·34 N	43·00 E
28	Djibouti, Afr.	11·35 N	45·08 E
22	Dnepr (Dnieper) (R.), Sov. Un.	46·47 N	32·57 E
10	Dominican Republic, N.A.	18·59 N	70·40 W
21	Donetsk, Sov. Un.	48·00 N	37·35 E

Dov–Lyo

Page		Lat.	Long.
15	Dover, Del.	39·10 N	75·30 W
20	Drogobych, Sov. Un.	49·21 N	23·31 E
20	Dublin, Ire.	53·20 N	6·15 W
15	Dubuque, Iowa	42·30 N	90·43 W
14	Duluth, Minn.	46·50 N	92·07 W
27	Dunedin, N.Z.	45·48 S	170·32 E
28	Durban, S. Afr.	29·48 S	31·00 E
15	Durham, N.C.	36·00 N	78·55 W
25	East China Sea, Asia	30·28 N	125·52 E
18	Ecuador, S.A.	0·00 N	78·30 W
20	Edinburgh, Scot.	55·57 N	3·10 W
12	Edmonton, Can.	53·30 N	113·45 W
28	Egypt, Afr.	26·58 N	27·01 E
28	El Aaiún, W. Sah.	26·45 N	13·15 W
20	Elbe R., Ger.	53·47 N	12·30 E
21	Elbrus, Mt., Sov. Un.	43·20 N	42·25 E
28	El Obeid, Sud.	13·15 N	30·15 E
14	El Paso, Tex.	31·47 N	106·27 W
11	El Salvador, N.A.	14·00 N	89·30 W
28	Equatorial Guinea, Afr.	2·20 N	7·37 E
15	Erie, L., Can.-U.S.	42·15 N	81·25 W
21	Esfahan, Iran	32·38 N	51·30 E
21	Eskisehir, Tur.	39·40 N	30·20 E
20	Essen, F.R. of Ger.	51·26 N	6·59 E
28	Ethiopia, Afr.	7·53 N	37·55 E
14	Eugene, Ore.	44·02 N	123·06 W
14	Euphrates, R., Asia	34·52 N	42·53 E
24	Europe		
15	Evansville, Ind.	38·00 N	87·30 W
14	Everett, Wash.	47·59 N	122·11 W
24	Everest, Mt., China-Nep.	32·58 N	86·57 E
26	Eyre, Austl.	32·15 S	126·20 E
14	Fairbanks, Alsk.	64·50 N	147·48 W
18	Falkland Is., S.A.	50·45 S	61·00 W
14	Fargo, N.D.	46·53 N	96·48 W
6	Fiji, Oceania	18·50 S	175·00 E
20	Finland, Eur.	62·45 N	26·13 E
20	Florence, It.	43·47 N	11·15 E
14	Flores (I.), Indon.	8·14 S	121·08 E
15	Florida (State), U.S.	30·30 N	84·40 W
17	Fort-de-France, Mart.	14·37 N	61·06 W
15	Fort Smith, Ark.	35·23 N	94·24 W
12	Fort Smith, Can.	60·09 N	112·08 W
20	France, Eur.	46·39 N	0·47 E
15	Frankfort, Ky.	38·10 N	84·55 W
15	Frankfurt, F.R. of Ger.	50·07 N	8·40 E
22	Franz Josef Land (Is.), Sov. Un.	81·32 N	40·00 E
15	Frederick, Md.	39·25 N	77·25 W
28	Freetown, S.L.	8·29 N	13·16 W
18	French Guiana, S.A.	4·20 N	53·00 W
28	Gabès, Tun.	33·51 N	10·04 E
28	Gabon, Afr.	0·30 N	10·45 E
28	Gaborone, Bots.	24·28 S	25·59 E
15	Gainesville, Fla.	28·43 N	82·25 W
20	Galdhøpiggen (Mtn.), Nor.	61·39 N	8·12 E
28	Gambia, Afr.	13·38 N	19·38 W
13	Gander, Can.	48·59 N	54·32 W
24	Ganges (R.), India	24·32 N	80·00 E
15	Gary, Ind.	41·35 N	87·21 W
20	Gävle, Swe.	60·40 N	17·07 E
20	Gdansk (Danzig), Pol.	54·20 N	18·40 E
27	Geelong, Austl.	38·06 S	144·13 E
20	Geneva, Switz.	46·14 N	6·04 E
20	Genoa, It.	44·23 N	9·52 E
18	Georgetown, Guy.	7·45 N	58·04 W
15	Georgia (State), U.S.	32·40 N	83·50 W
13	Geraldton, Can.	49·43 N	87·00 W
20	German Democratic Republic, Eur.	52·00 N	12·30 E
20	Germany, Federal Republic of, Eur.	51·00 N	9·00 E
28	Ghana, Afr.	8·00 N	2·00 W
20	Glasgow, Scot.	55·20 N	5·03 W
20	Gorkiy, Sov. Un.	56·15 N	44·20 E
20	Göteborg, Swe.	57·39 N	11·56 E
14	Grand Forks, N.D.	47·55 N	97·05 W
14	Grand Island, Nebr.	40·56 N	98·20 W
15	Grand Rapids, Mich.	43·00 N	85·45 W
21	Graz, Aus.	47·05 N	15·26 E
27	Great Barrier Rf., Austl.	16·43 S	146·34 E
13	Great Falls, Can.	48·58 N	55·37 W
14	Great Falls, Mont.	47·30 N	111·15 W
14	Great Salt L., Utah	41·19 N	112·48 W
20	Greece, Eur.	39·00 N	21·30 E
15	Greeley, Colo.	40·25 N	104·41 W
15	Green Bay, Wis.	44·30 N	88·04 W
11	Greenland, N.A.	74·00 N	40·00 W
15	Greensboro, N.C.	36·04 N	79·45 W
15	Greenville, S.C.	34·50 N	82·25 W
17	Guadalajara, Mex.	20·41 N	103·21 W
16	Guanajuato, Mex.	21·01 N	101·16 W
17	Guantánamo, Cuba	20·10 N	75·10 W
11	Guatemala, Guat.	14·37 N	90·32 W
11	Guatemala, N.A.	15·45 N	91·45 W
18	Guayaquil, Ec.	2·16 S	79·53 W
28	Guinea, Afr.	10·48 N	12·28 W
28	Guinea-Bissau, Afr.	12·00 N	16·00 W
18	Guyana, S.A.	7·00 N	59·40 W
23	Hailun, China	47·18 N	126·50 E
11	Haiti, N.A.	19·00 N	72·15 W
21	Hamadan, Iran	34·45 N	48·07 E
15	Hammond, Ind.	41·37 N	87·31 W
21	Hanoi, Viet.	21·04 N	105·50 E
28	Harar, Eth.	9·43 N	42·10 E
28	Hargeisa, Som.	9·20 N	43·57 E
15	Harrisburg, Pa.	40·15 N	76·50 W
14	Havana, Cuba	23·08 N	82·23 W
14	Hawaii (State), U.S.	20·00 N	157·40 W
15	Helena, Ark.	34·33 N	90·35 W
14	Helena, Mont.	46·35 N	112·01 W
20	Helsinki, Fin.	60·10 N	24·53 E
24	Himalaya Mts., Asia	29·30 N	85·02 E
27	Hispaniola (I.), N.A.	17·30 N	73·15 W
27	Hobart, Austl.	43·00 S	147·30 E
25	Ho Chi Minh City (Saigon), Viet.	10·46 N	106·34 E
25	Hokkaido (I.), Jap.	43·30 N	142·45 E
21	Homs, Syr.	34·42 N	36·52 E
11	Honduras, N.A.	14·30 N	88·00 W
25	Hong Kong, Asia	22·15 N	114·40 E
14	Honolulu, Hawaii (Hawaii In.)	21·18 N	157·50 W
14	Hood, Mt., Ore.	45·20 N	121·43 W
15	Hot Springs, Ark.	34·29 N	93·02 W
14	Houston, Tex.	29·46 N	95·21 W
25	Hsian (Sian), China	34·20 N	109·00 E
28	Huambo, Ang.	12·45 S	15·45 E
18	Huascarán, Mt., Peru	9·05 S	77·50 W
13	Hudson B., Can.	60·15 N	85·30 W
20	Hungary, Eur.	46·44 N	17·55 E
15	Huntington, W. Va.	38·25 N	82·25 W
15	Huron, L., Can.-U.S.	45·15 N	82·40 W
20	Iasi, Rom.	47·10 N	27·40 E
28	Ibadan, Nig.	7·26 N	3·48 E
20	Iceland, Eur.	65·12 N	19·45 W
14	Idaho (State), U.S.	44·00 N	115·10 W
14	Idaho Falls, Idaho	43·30 N	112·01 W
15	Illinois (State), U.S.	40·25 N	90·40 W
15	India, Asia	23·00 N	77·30 E
15	Indiana (State), U.S.	39·50 N	86·45 W
15	Indianapolis, Ind.	39·46 N	86·08 W
7	Indian Ocean		
28	Indonesia, Asia	4·38 S	118·45 E
24	Indus (R.), Pak.	26·43 N	67·41 E
12	Innisfail, Can.	52·01 N	113·57 W
15	Iowa (State), U.S.	42·05 N	94·20 W
18	Iquitos, Peru	3·39 S	73·18 W
21	Iran (Persia), Asia	31·15 N	53·30 E
24	Iraq, Asia	32·00 N	42·30 E
20	Ireland (Eire), Eur.	53·33 N	13·00 W
23	Irkutsk, Sov. Un.	52·16 N	104·00 E
24	Islamabad, Pak.	33·55 N	73·05 E
25	Israel, Asia (Palestine In.)	31·00 N	35·00 E
21	Istanbul, Tur.	41·02 N	29·00 E
20	Italy, Eur.	43·58 N	11·14 E
28	Ivory Coast, Afr.	7·43 N	6·30 W
21	Izmir, Tur.	38·25 N	27·05 E
15	Jackson, Miss.	32·17 N	90·10 W
15	Jacksonville, Fla.	30·20 N	81·40 W
11	Jamaica (I.), N.A.	18·21 N	77·31 W
25	Japan, Asia	36·30 N	133·30 E
25	Japan, Sea of, Asia	40·08 N	132·55 E
25	Jarash, Jordan (Palestine In.)	32·17 N	35·53 E
7	Java (I.), Indon.	8·35 S	111·11 E
15	Jefferson City, Mo.	38·34 N	92·10 W
25	Jerusalem, Isr.-Jordan (Palestine In.)	31·46 N	35·14 E
28	Johannesburg, S. Afr.	26·08 S	27·54 E
24	Jordan, Asia	30·15 N	38·00 E
28	Jos, Nig.	9·53 N	8·56 E
14	Juneau, Alsk.	58·25 N	134·30 W
16	Juticalpa, Hond.	14·35 N	86·17 W
24	Kabul, Afg.	34·39 N	69·14 E
14	Kailua, Hawaii (Hawaii In.)	19·49 N	155·59 W
28	Kalahari Des., Bots.	23·00 S	22·03 E
28	Kampala, Ug.	0·14 N	32·34 E
28	Kano, Nig.	12·03 N	8·32 E
14	Kansas (State), U.S.	38·30 N	99·40 W
15	Kansas City, Mo.	39·05 N	94·35 W
24	Karachi, Pak.	24·59 N	68·56 E
24	Karikal, India	10·58 N	79·49 E
24	Kathmandu, Nep.	27·49 N	85·21 E
15	Kenosha, Wis.	42·34 N	87·50 W
15	Kentucky (State), U.S.	37·30 N	87·35 W
28	Kenya, Afr.	1·00 N	36·53 E
28	Kenya, Mt., Ken.	0·15 S	37·16 E
21	Kerman, Iran	30·23 N	57·08 E
28	Khartoum, Sud.	15·34 N	32·36 E
21	Kiev, Sov. Un.	50·27 N	30·30 E
28	Kigali, Rw.	1·59 S	30·05 E
28	Kilimanjaro (Mtn.), Tan.	3·09 S	37·19 E
28	Kimberley, S. Afr.	28·40 S	24·50 E
11	Kingston, Jam.	18·00 N	76·45 W
17	Kingstown, St. Vincent	13·10 N	61·14 W
28	Kinshasa (Léopoldville), Zaire	4·28 S	15·16 E
21	Kirkuk, Iraq	35·28 N	44·22 E
20	Kirovsk, Sov. Un.	59·52 N	30·59 E
28	Kisangani (Stanleyville), Zaire	0·32 N	25·14 E
28	Kisumu, Ken.	0·05 S	34·49 E
15	Knoxville, Tenn.	35·58 N	83·55 W
25	Kobe, Jap.	34·30 N	135·10 E
23	Komsomolsk-na-Amure, Sov. Un.	50·46 N	137·14 E
25	Korea, North, Asia	38·45 N	130·00 E
25	Korea, South, Asia	38·45 N	130·00 E
20	Krakow, Pol.	50·05 N	20·00 E
22	Krasnoufimsk, Sov. Un.	56·38 N	57·46 E
21	Krivoy Rog, Sov. Un.	47·54 N	33·22 E
25	Kuala Lumpur, Mala. (Singapore In.)	3·08 N	101·42 E
21	Kurgan, Sov. Un.	55·28 N	65·14 E
24	Kuwait, Asia	29·00 N	48·45 E
24	Kuwait, Kuw.	29·04 N	47·59 E
21	Kuybyshev, Sov. Un.	53·10 N	50·05 E
13	Labrador (Reg.), Can.	53·05 N	63·30 W
12	Lacombe, Can.	52·29 N	113·41 W
15	Lafayette, La.	30·15 N	92·02 W
28	Lagos, Nig.	6·31 N	3·15 E
24	Lahore, Pak.	32·00 N	80·00 E
15	Lansing, Mich.	42·45 N	84·35 W
24	Laos, Asia	19·30 N	102·45 E
18	La Paz, Bol.	16·31 S	68·03 W
14	Laramie, Wyo.	41·20 N	105·40 W
14	Las Cruces, N. Mex.	32·20 N	106·50 W
14	Las Vegas, Nev.	36·12 N	115·10 W
27	Launceston, Austl.	41·35 S	147·22 E
15	Laurel, Miss.	31·42 N	89·07 W
15	Leavenworth, Kans.	39·19 N	94·54 W
24	Lebanon, Asia	34·00 N	35·00 E
20	Leeds, Eng.	53·48 N	1·33 W
20	Le Havre, Fr.	49·31 N	0·07 E
20	Leningrad, Sov. Un.	59·57 N	30·20 E
22	Leninogorsk, Sov. Un.	50·29 N	83·25 E
28	Lesotho, Afr.	29·45 S	28·07 E
15	Lewiston, Maine	44·05 N	70·14 W
15	Lexington, Ky.	38·05 N	84·30 W
28	Liberia, Afr.	6·30 N	9·55 W
28	Libreville, Gabon	0·29 N	9·26 E
28	Libya, Afr.	27·38 N	15·00 E
20	Liechtenstein, Eur.	47·14 N	9·15 E
20	Lille, Fr.	50·38 N	3·01 E
28	Lilongwe, Malawi	13·59 S	33·44 E
18	Lima, Peru	12·06 S	76·55 W
14	Lincoln, Nebr.	40·49 N	96·43 W
20	Lisbon, Port.	38·42 N	9·05 W
15	Little Rock, Ark.	34·42 N	92·16 W
20	Liverpool, Eng.	53·25 N	5·10 W
28	Livingstone, Zambia	17·51 S	25·48 E
28	Lobito, Ang.	12·15 S	13·35 E
20	Lodz, Pol.	51·46 N	19·13 E
14	Logan, Utah	41·46 N	111·51 W
20	Loire (R.), Fr.	47·19 N	3·11 W
28	Lomé, Togo.	6·13 N	1·14 E
20	London, Eng.	51·30 N	0·07 W
14	Los Angeles, Calif.	34·00 N	118·15 W
15	Louisiana (State), U.S.	30·50 N	92·50 W
15	Louisville, Ky.	38·15 N	85·45 W
15	Lowell, Mass.	42·38 N	71·18 W
27	Lower Hutt, N.Z. (In.)	41·08 S	175·00 E
28	Luanda, Ang.	8·50 S	13·15 E
28	Lubumbasi (Elisabethville), Zaire	11·41 S	27·32 E
28	Lusaka, Zambia	15·19 S	28·15 E
20	Luxembourg, Lux.	49·38 N	6·30 E
20	Luxembourg, Eur.	49·30 N	6·22 E
20	Luzon (I.), Phil.	17·10 N	119·45 E
20	Lyon, Fr.	45·44 N	4·52 E

Page		Lat. ° ′	Long. ° ′
12	Mackenzie (R.), Can...	63·28 N	124·23 W
11	McKinley, Mt., Alsk...	63·00 N	151·02 W
15	Macon, Ga...	32·49 N	83·39 W
28	Madagascar, Afr...	18·05 S	43·12 E
18	Madeira, R., Braz...	6·48 S	62·43 W
15	Madison, Wis...	43·05 N	89·23 W
20	Madrid, Sp...	40·26 N	3·42 W
28	Mafeking, S. Afr...	25·46 S	24·45 E
28	Mai-Ndombe (L.), Zaire...	2·16 S	19·00 E
16	Maine (State), U.S...	45·25 N	69·50 W
20	Mainz, F.R. of Ger...	49·59 N	8·16 E
28	Malabo, Equat. Gui...	3·43 N	8·42 E
28	Malawi, Afr...	11·15 S	33·45 E
28	Malawi, Lake, Afr...	11·32 S	35·15 E
15	Malaysia, Asia...	4·10 N	101·22 E
24	Maldives, Asia...	4·30 N	71·30 E
28	Mali, Afr...	15·45 N	0·15 W
20	Malta, Eur...	35·52 N	14·26 E
11	Managua, Nic...	12·10 N	86·16 W
20	Manchester, Eng...	53·28 N	2·14 W
15	Manchester, N.H...	43·00 N	71·30 W
23	Manchuria (Reg.), China...	48·00 N	124·58 E
24	Mandalay, Bur...	22·00 N	96·08 E
14	Mandan, N.D...	46·49 N	100·54 W
25	Manila, Phil...	14·37 N	121·00 E
12	Manitoba (Prov.), Can...	55·12 N	97·29 W
17	Manzanillo, Cuba...	20·20 N	77·05 W
28	Maputo, Moz...	26·14 S	33·30 E
18	Maracaibo, Ven...	10·38 N	71·45 W
15	Marion, Ind...	40·35 N	85·45 W
28	Marrakech, Mor...	31·38 N	8·00 W
28	Marree, Austl...	29·38 S	137·55 E
17	Martinique I., N.A...	14·30 N	60·37 W
15	Maryland (State), U.S...	39·10 N	76·25 W
28	Marzuq, Libya...	26·00 N	14·09 E
15	Massachusetts (State), U.S...	42·20 N	72·30 W
28	Masuru, Leso...	29·09 S	27·11 E
28	Mauritania, Afr...	19·38 N	13·30 W
7	Mauritius, Afr...	20·18 S	57·36 E
28	Mbandaka, Zaire...	0·01 N	18·17 E
28	Mecca, Sau. Ar...	21·27 N	39·45 E
18	Medellín, Col...	6·15 N	75·34 W
7	Mediterranean Sea, Afr.-Asia-Eur...	36·22 N	13·25 E
27	Melbourne, Austl...	37·52 S	145·08 E
21	Melitopol, Sov. Un...	46·49 N	35·19 E
15	Memphis, Tenn...	35·07 N	90·03 W
15	Mendoza, Arg...	32·48 S	68·45 W
15	Meridian, Miss...	32·21 N	88·41 W
21	Mersin, Tur...	37·00 N	34·40 E
11	Mexico, N.A...	23·45 N	104·00 W
16	Mexico, Gulf of, N.A...	25·15 N	93·45 W
16	Mexico City, Mex...	19·28 N	99·09 W
14	Miami, Ariz...	33·20 N	110·55 W
15	Miami, Fla...	25·45 N	80·11 W
15	Michigan (State), U.S...	45·55 N	87·00 W
15	Michigan, L., U.S...	43·20 N	87·10 W
20	Milan, It...	45·29 N	9·12 E
15	Milwaukee, Wis...	43·03 N	87·55 W
14	Minatitlán, Mex...	17·59 N	94·33 W
25	Mindanao (I.), Phil...	7·30 N	125·10 E
15	Minneapolis, Minn...	44·58 N	93·15 W
12	Minnedosa, Can...	50·16 N	99·50 W
15	Minnesota (State), U.S...	46·10 N	90·20 W
14	Minot, N.D...	48·13 N	101·16 W
20	Miskolc, Hung...	48·07 N	20·50 E
15	Mississippi (State), U.S...	32·30 N	89·45 W
15	Mississippi (R.), U.S...	31·50 N	91·30 W
15	Missouri (State), U.S...	38·00 N	93·40 W
15	Missouri (R.), U.S...	40·40 N	96·00 W
15	Mitchell, Mt., N.C...	35·47 N	82·15 W
15	Mobile, Ala...	30·42 N	88·03 W
28	Moçambique, Moz...	15·07 S	40·48 E
28	Mogadiscio, Som...	2·08 N	45·22 E
28	Mombasa, Ken...	4·01 S	39·43 E
20	Monaco, Eur...	43·43 N	7·47 E
24	Mongolia, Asia...	46·00 N	100·00 E
15	Monroe, La...	32·30 N	92·06 W
15	Monrovia, Lib...	6·21 N	10·59 W
14	Montana (State), U.S...	47·10 N	111·50 W
18	Montevideo, Ur...	34·50 S	56·10 W
15	Montgomery, Ala...	32·23 N	86·17 W
15	Montpelier, Vt...	44·20 N	72·35 W
13	Montreal, Can...	45·30 N	73·35 W
26	Moonta, Austl...	34·05 S	137·42 E
28	Morocco, Afr...	32·00 N	7·00 W
21	Moscow, Sov. Un...	55·45 N	37·37 E
28	Mozambique, Afr...	20·15 S	33·53 E
15	Muncie, Ind...	40·10 N	85·30 W
27	Mungana, Austl...	17·15 S	144·18 E
20	Munich, F.R. of Ger...	48·08 N	11·35 E
24	Murmansk, Sov. Un...	69·00 N	33·20 E
24	Muscat, Om...	23·23 N	58·30 E
15	Muskogee, Okla...	35·44 N	95·21 W
17	Nadir, Vir. Is. (U.S.A.) (St. Thomas In.)...	18·19 N	64·53 W
28	Nairobi, Ken...	1·18 S	36·47 E
28	Namibia, Afr...	19·30 S	16·13 E
14	Nampa, Idaho...	43·35 N	116·35 W
20	Naples, It...	40·37 N	14·12 E
15	Nashua, N.H...	42·47 N	71·23 W
15	Nashville, Tenn...	36·10 N	86·48 W
17	Nassau, Ba...	25·05 N	77·20 W
18	Natal, Braz...	6·00 S	35·13 W
28	Ndjamena, Chad...	12·15 N	15·04 E
12	Nebraska (State), U.S...	41·45 N	101·30 W
12	Nelson, Can...	49·27 N	117·24 W
23	Nenchiang, China...	49·02 N	125·15 E
24	Nepal, Asia...	28·45 N	83·00 E
20	Netherlands, Eur...	53·01 N	3·57 E
15	Nevada (State), U.S...	39·30 N	117·00 W
15	Newark, Del...	39·40 N	75·45 W
15	Newark, N.J...	40·44 N	74·10 W
15	New Bedford, Mass...	41·35 N	70·55 W
13	New Brunswick (Prov.), Can...	47·14 N	66·30 W
27	New Caledonia (I.), Oceania...	21·28 S	164·15 E
24	New Delhi, India...	28·43 N	77·18 E
13	Newfoundland (Prov.), Can...(In.)	48·15 N	56·53 W
7	New Guinea (I.), Pap. N. Gui...	5·45 S	140·00 E
15	New Hampshire (State), U.S...	43·55 N	71·40 W
15	New Haven, Conn...	41·20 N	72·55 W
27	New Hebrides (Is.), Oceania...	16·02 S	169·15 E
15	New Jersey (State), U.S...	40·30 N	74·50 W
14	New Mexico (State), U.S...	34·30 N	107·10 W
15	New Orleans, La...	30·00 N	90·05 W
15	New York (State), U.S...	42·45 N	78·05 W
15	New York, N.Y...	40·40 N	73·58 W
27	New Zealand, Oceania...	39·14 S	169·30 E
28	Niamey, Niger...	13·33 N	2·08 E
28	Nicaragua, N.A...	12·45 N	86·15 W
24	Nicosia, Cyprus...	35·10 N	33·22 E
28	Niger, Afr...	18·02 N	8·30 E
28	Niger (R.), Afr...	12·30 N	2·30 E
28	Nigeria, Afr...	8·57 N	6·30 E
28	Nile (R.), Afr...	29·30 N	32·00 E
14	Nome, Alsk. (Alaska In.)...	64·30 N	165·20 W
14	Norfolk, Nebr...	42·10 N	97·25 W
15	Norfolk, Va...	36·55 N	76·15 W
11	North America		
15	North Carolina (State), U.S...	35·40 N	81·30 W
14	North Dakota (State), U.S...	47·20 N	101·55 W
20	North Sea, Eur...	56·09 N	3·16 E
20	Norway, Eur...	63·48 N	11·17 E
12	Northwest Territories (Prov.), Can...	64·42 N	119·09 W
28	Nouakchott, Mauritania...	18·15 N	15·56 W
13	Nova Scotia (Prov.), Can...	44·28 N	65·00 W
22	Novaya Zemlya (I.), Sov. Un...	72·00 N	54·46 E
21	Novosibirsk, Sov. Un...	55·00 N	82·58 E
14	Oakland, Calif...	37·48 N	122·16 W
14	Ogden, Utah...	41·14 N	111·58 W
15	Ohio (State), U.S...	40·30 N	83·15 W
15	Ohio R., U.S...	37·25 N	88·05 W
23	Okayama, Japan...	34·39 N	133·54 E
23	Okhotsk, Sea of, Asia...	54·45 N	146·00 E
14	Oklahoma (State), U.S...	36·00 N	98·20 W
14	Oklahoma City, Okla...	35·27 N	97·32 W
15	Olympia, Wash...	47·02 N	122·52 W
15	Omaha, Nebr...	41·18 N	95·57 W
24	Oman, Asia...	18·50 N	56·45 E
21	Omsk, Sov. Un...	55·12 N	73·19 E
13	Ontario (Prov.), Can...	50·47 N	88·50 W
13	Ontario, L., Can.-U.S...	43·35 N	79·05 W
28	Oran, Alg...	35·46 N	0·45 W
14	Oregon (State), U.S...	43·40 N	121·50 W
16	Orizaba, Mex...	18·52 N	97·05 W
15	Orlando, Fla...	28·32 N	81·22 W
23	Osaka, Jap...	34·40 N	135·27 E
13	Oshawa, Can...	43·50 N	78·50 W
15	Oshkosh, Wis...	44·01 N	88·35 W
20	Oslo, Nor...	59·56 N	10·41 E
13	Ottawa, Can...	45·25 N	75·43 W
28	Ouagadougou, Upper Volta...	12·20 N	1·43 W
15	Owensboro, Ky...	37·45 N	87·05 W
6	Pacific O.		
24	Pakistan, Asia...	28·00 N	67·30 E
25	Palawan (Is.), Phil...	9·50 N	117·38 E
20	Palermo, It...	38·08 N	13·24 E
25	Palestine, Asia (Palestine In.)...	31·33 N	35·00 E
11	Panama, N.A...	8·35 N	81·08 W
11	Panama, Gulf of, Pan...	7·45 N	79·20 W
25	Panay (Is.), Phil...	11·15 N	121·38 E
27	Papua New Guinea, Oceania...	7·00 S	142·15 E
18	Paraguay, S.A...	24·00 S	57·00 W
18	Paraguay (R.), S.A...	21·12 S	57·31 W
18	Paramaribo, Sur...	5·50 N	55·15 W
18	Paraná (R.), Arg...	32·15 S	60·55 W
20	Paris, Fr...	48·51 N	2·20 E
15	Parkersburg, W. Va...	39·15 N	81·35 W
12	Peace (R.), Can...	57·29 N	117·32 W
21	Pechora (R.), Sov. Un...	66·00 N	52·30 E
25	Peking, China...	39·55 N	116·23 E
14	Pendleton, Ore...	45·41 N	118·47 W
15	Pennsylvania (State), U.S...	41·00 N	78·10 W
15	Pensacola, Fla...	30·25 N	87·13 W
15	Peoria, Ill...	40·45 N	89·35 W
21	Perm, Sov. Un...	58·00 N	56·15 E
26	Perth, Austl...	31·50 S	116·10 E
18	Peru, S.A...	10·00 S	75·00 W
15	Petersburg, Va...	37·12 N	77·30 W
21	Petropavlovsk, Sov. Un...	54·44 N	69·07 E
23	Petrovsk-Zabaykalskiy, Sov. Un...	51·13 N	109·08 E
15	Philadelphia, Pa...	40·00 N	75·13 W
25	Philippines, Asia...	14·25 N	125·00 E
25	Phnom Penh, Camb...	11·39 N	104·53 E
14	Phoenix, Ariz...	33·30 N	112·00 W
14	Pierre, S.D...	44·22 N	100·20 W
14	Pikes Pk., Colo...	38·49 N	105·03 W
15	Pittsburgh, Pa...	40·26 N	80·01 W
14	Platte (R.), U.S...	40·50 N	100·40 W
20	Plovdiv, Bul...	42·09 N	24·43 E
28	Pocatello, Idaho...	42·54 N	112·30 W
28	Pointe Noire, Con...	4·48 S	11·50 E
20	Poland, Eur...	52·37 N	17·01 E
17	Ponce, P.R. (Puerto Rico In.)...	18·01 N	66·43 W
11	Port-au-Prince, Hai...	18·35 N	72·20 W
15	Portland, Maine...	43·40 N	70·16 W
14	Portland, Ore...	45·31 N	123·41 W
20	Pôrto, Port...	41·10 N	8·38 W
17	Port of Spain, Trin...	10·44 N	61·24 W
15	Portsmouth, N.H...	43·05 N	70·50 W
15	Portsmouth, Va...	36·50 N	76·19 W
24	Port Said, Eg...	31·15 N	32·19 E
28	Port Sudan, Sud...	19·30 N	37·10 E
20	Portugal, Eur...	38·15 N	8·08 W
20	Prague, Czech...	50·05 N	14·30 E
14	Prescott, Ariz...	34·30 N	112·30 W
28	Pretoria, S. Afr...	25·43 S	28·16 E
13	Prince Edward Island (Prov.), Can...	46·45 N	63·10 W
12	Prince of Wales (Is.), Alsk...	55·48 N	133·46 W
15	Providence, R.I...	41·50 N	71·23 W
14	Provo, Utah...	40·15 N	111·40 W
14	Pueblo, Colo...	38·15 N	104·36 W
17	Puerto Rico, N.A. (Puerto Rico In.)...	18·16 N	66·50 W
18	Purús (R.), S.A...	6·45 S	64·34 W
25	Pyongyang, Kor., N...	39·03 N	125·48 E
20	Pyrenees (Mts.), Fr.-Sp...	43·00 N	0·05 E
24	Qatar, Asia...	25·00 N	52·45 E
13	Quebec, Can...	46·49 N	71·14 W
13	Quebec (Prov.). Can...	51·07 N	70·25 W
25	Quezon City, Phil...	14·40 N	121·02 E
18	Quito, Ec...	0·17 S	78·32 W
28	Rabat, Mor...	33·59 N	6·47 W
14	Rainier, Mt., Wash...	46·52 N	121·46 W
15	Raleigh, N.C...	35·45 N	78·39 W
24	Rangoon, Bur...	16·46 N	96·09 E
14	Rapid City, S.D...	44·06 N	103·14 W

Rec–Zam

Page		Lat. °'	Long. °'
18	Recife (Pernambuco), Braz.	8·09 S	34·59 W
14	Red (R.), Can.-U.S.	48·10 N	97·00 W
28	Red Sea, Afr.-Asia	23·15 N	37·00 E
12	Regina, Can.	50·31 N	104·30 W
15	Reims, Fr.	49·16 N	4·00 E
14	Reno, Nev.	39·32 N	119·49 W
20	Reykjavik, Ice.	64·09 N	21·39 W
20	Rhine R., Eur.	50·34 N	7·21 E
15	Rhode Island (State), U.S.	41·35 N	71·40 W
28	Rhodesia, Afr.	17·50 S	29·30 E
20	Rhône (R.), Fr.	45·14 N	4·53 E
15	Richmond, Va.	37·35 N	77·30 W
15	Rio de Janeiro, Braz.	22·50 S	43·20 W
18	Rio Grande, Braz.	31·04 S	52·14 W
14	Rio Grande (R.), Mex.-U.S.	37·44 N	106·51 W
24	Riyadh, Sau. Ar.	24·31 N	46·47 E
15	Roanoke, Va.	37·16 N	79·55 W
15	Rochester, N.Y.	43·15 N	77·35 W
15	Rockford, Ill.	42·16 N	89·07 W
14	Rock Springs, Wyo.	41·35 N	109·13 W
20	Romania, Eur.	46·18 N	22·53 E
20	Rome, It.	41·52 N	12·37 E
18	Rosario, Arg.	32·58 S	60·42 W
20	Rotterdam, Neth.	51·55 N	4·28 E
28	Rwanda, Afr.	2·10 S	29·37 E
25	Ryukyu Is., Jap.	25·00 N	126·00 E
14	Sacramento, Calif.	38·35 N	121·30 W
13	St. John, Can.	45·19 N	66·04 W
15	St. Joseph, Mo.	39·44 N	94·49 W
13	St. Lawrence R., Can.-U.S.A.	48·24 N	69·03 W
15	St. Louis, Mo.	38·39 N	90·15 W
17	St. Lucia Is., N.A.	13·54 N	60·40 W
12	St. Paul, Can.	53·58 N	111·30 W
15	St. Paul, Minn.	44·57 N	93·05 W
15	St. Petersburg, Fla.	27·47 N	82·38 W
17	St. Thomas (Is.), Vir. Is. (U.S.A.) (St. Thomas In.)	18·22 N	64·57 W
17	St. Vincent (Is.) N.A.	13·14 N	60·50 W
23	Sakhalin (Is.), Sov. Un.	51·52 N	144·15 E
14	Salem, Ore.	44·55 N	123·03 W
14	Salina, Kans.	38·50 N	97·37 W
28	Salisbury, Rh.	17·49 S	30·52 E
20	Salonika (Thessaloniki), Grc.	40·38 N	22·59 E
14	Salt Lake City, Utah	40·45 N	111·52 W
18	Salto, Ur.	31·18 S	57·45 W
25	Samar (Is.), Phil.	11·30 N	126·07 E
24	Sana, Yemen	15·45 N	44·00 E
14	San Antonio, Tex.	29·25 N	98·30 W
14	San Bernardino, Calif.	34·07 N	117·19 W
14	San Diego, Calif.	32·43 N	117·10 W
14	San Francisco, Calif.	37·45 N	122·26 W
14	San Jose, Calif.	37·20 N	121·54 W
17	San José, C.R.	9·57 N	84·05 W
17	San Juan, P.R. (Puerto Rico In.)	18·30 N	66·10 W
20	San Marino, Eur.	43·52 N	12·38 E
17	San Miguel, Sal.	13·28 N	88·11 W
11	San Salvador, Sal.	13·45 N	89·11 W
16	Santa Ana, Sal.	14·02 N	89·35 W
17	Santa Clara, Cuba	22·25 N	80·00 W
14	Santa Fe, N. Mex.	35·10 N	106·00 W
14	Santiago, Chile	33·26 S	70·40 W
10	Santo Domingo, Dom. Rep.	18·30 N	69·55 W
18	São Francisco (R.), Braz.	8·56 S	40·20 W
18	São Paulo, Braz.	23·34 S	46·38 W
18	Sarajevo, Yugo.	43·15 N	18·26 E
21	Saratov, Sov. Un.	51·50 N	45·00 E
20	Sardinia (Is.), Eur.	40·08 N	9·05 E
12	Saskatchewan (Prov.), Can.	54·46 N	107·40 W
12	Saskatchewan (R.), Can.	53·30 N	103·41 W
12	Saskatoon, Can.	52·11 N	106·42 W
24	Saudi Arabia, Asia	22·40 N	46·00 E
15	Sault Ste. Marie, Mich.	46·29 N	84·21 W
15	Savannah, Ga.	32·04 N	81·07 W
15	Scranton, Pa.	41·45 N	75·45 W
14	Seattle, Wash.	47·36 N	122·20 W
28	Sénégal, Afr.	14·53 N	14·58 W
28	Sénégal R., Mauritania-Sénégal	16·45 N	14·37 W
25	Seoul, Kor., S.	37·35 N	127·03 E
25	Seranggung, Indon (In.)	0·49 N	104·11 E
25	Seville, Sp.	37·29 N	5·58 W
25	Shanghai, China	31·14 N	121·27 E
15	Sheboygan, Wis.	43·45 N	87·44 W
15	Sherbrooke, Can.	45·25 N	72·00 W
14	Sheridan, Wyo.	44·48 N	106·56 W
14	Sherman, Tex.	33·39 N	96·37 W
25	Shikoku (Is.), Jap.	33·43 N	133·33 E
15	Shreveport, La.	32·30 N	93·46 W
28	Sicily (Is.), It.	37·38 N	13·30 E
28	Sierra Leone, Afr.	8·48 N	12·30 E
25	Singapore, Singapore (Singapore In.)	1·18 N	103·52 E
25	Singapore, Asia.	1·22 N	103·45 E
15	Sioux City, Iowa	42·30 N	96·25 W
14	Sioux Falls, S.D.	43·33 N	96·43 W
20	Skopje, Yugo.	42·02 N	21·26 E
21	Smolensk, Sov. Un.	54·46 N	32·03 E
14	Snake (R.), Idaho	43·33 N	116·18 W
21	Sochi, Sov. Un.	43·35 N	39·50 E
20	Sofia, Bul.	42·43 N	23·20 E
7	Solomon Is., Oceania	7·00 S	148·00 E
28	Somalia, Afr.	3·28 N	44·47 E
25	Sour (Tyre), Leb. (Palestine In.)	33·16 N	35·11 E
28	South Africa, Afr.	31·50 S	28·05 E
18	South America		
15	South Carolina (State), U.S.	34·15 N	81·10 W
14	South Dakota (State), U.S.	44·20 N	101·55 W
24	Soviet Union, Asia-Eur.	60·30 N	64·00 E
20	Spain, Eur.	40·15 N	4·30 W
17	Spanish Town, Jam.	18·00 N	76·55 W
14	Spokane, Wash.	47·39 N	117·25 W
15	Springfield, Ill.	39·46 N	89·37 W
15	Springfield, Mass.	42·05 N	72·35 W
15	Springfield, Mo.	37·13 N	93·17 W
24	Sri Lanka, Asia	8·45 N	82·30 E
20	Stockholm, Swe.	59·23 N	18·00 E
20	Stuttgart, F.R. of Ger.	48·48 N	9·15 E
18	Sucre, Bol.	19·06 S	65·16 W
28	Sudan, Afr.	14·00 N	28·00 E
28	Suez, Eg.	29·58 N	32·34 E
7	Sumatra (Is.), Indon.	2·06 N	99·40 E
15	Superior, L., Can.-U.S.	47·38 N	89·20 W
18	Surinam, S.A.	3·45 N	56·30 W
21	Sverdlovsk, Sov. Un.	57·50 N	60·37 E
28	Swaziland, Afr.	26·30 S	31·30 E
20	Sweden, Eur.	60·10 N	14·10 E
20	Switzerland, Eur.	46·30 N	7·43 E
21	Syktyvkar, Sov. Un.	61·35 N	50·40 E
15	Syracuse, N.Y.	43·05 N	76·10 W
24	Syria, Asia	35·00 N	37·15 E
12	Taber, Can.	49·47 N	112·20 W
14	Tacoma, Wash.	47·14 N	122·27 W
23	Taegu, Kor., S.	35·49 N	128·41 E
25	Taipei, Taiwan	25·02 N	121·38 E
25	Taiwan (Is.), Asia	23·30 N	122·20 E
23	Talien (Dairen), China	38·54 N	121·35 E
15	Tallahassee, Fla.	30·25 N	84·17 W
15	Tampa, Fla.	27·57 N	82·25 W
16	Tampico, Mex.	22·14 N	97·51 W
28	Tanganyika, L., Afr.	6·00 S	30·15 E
28	Tanger, Mor.	35·52 N	5·55 W
28	Tanzania, Afr.	6·48 S	33·58 E
27	Tasmania (Is.), Austl.	41·28 S	142·30 E
17	Tegucigalpa, Hond.	14·08 N	87·15 W
24	Tehran, Iran	35·45 N	51·30 E
15	Tennessee (State), U.S.	35·50 N	88·00 W
15	Tennessee (R.), U.S.	35·10 N	88·20 W
15	Terre Haute, Ind.	39·25 N	87·25 W
14	Texas (State), U.S.	31·00 N	101·00 W
24	Thailand, Asia	16·30 N	101·00 E
20	The Hague, Neth.	52·05 N	4·16 E
13	Thunder Bay, Can.	48·28 N	89·12 W
25	Tientsin, China	39·08 N	117·14 E
18	Tierra del Fuego (Reg.), Arg.-Chile	53·50 S	68·45 W
24	Tigris, R., Asia	34·30 N	44·00 E
26	Timor (Is.), Indon.	10·08 S	125·00 E
20	Tiranë, Alb.	41·18 N	19·50 E
18	Titicaca, L., S.A.	16·12 S	70·33 W
28	Togo, Afr.	8·00 N	0·52 E
25	Tokyo, Jap.	35·41 N	139·44 E
28	Tombouctou (Timbuktu), Mali.	16·52 N	2·53 W
39	Topeka, Kans.	39·02 N	95·41 W
20	Toubkal Pk., Mor.	31·15 N	7·46 W
20	Tours, Fr.	47·23 N	0·39 E
20	Trenton, N.J.	40·13 N	74·46 W
17	Trinidad and Tobago, N.A.	11·00 N	61·00 W
28	Tripoli, Libya	31·00 N	12·26 E
28	Tucson, Ariz.	32·15 N	111·00 W
28	Tuléar, Mad.	20·16 S	43·44 E
28	Tulsa, Okla.	36·08 N	95·58 W
28	Tunis, Tun.	36·59 N	10·06 E
28	Tunisia, Afr.	35·00 N	10·11 E
21	Turkestan, Sov. Un.	42·40 N	65·00 E
24	Turkey, Asia-Eur.	38·45 N	32·00 E
20	Turku, Fin.	60·28 N	22·12 E
15	Tuscaloosa, Ala.	33·10 N	87·35 W
14	Twin Falls, Idaho	42·33 N	114·29 W
18	Ucayali (R.), Peru	8·58 S	74·13 W
21	Ufa, Sov. Un.	54·45 N	55·57 E
28	Uganda, Afr.	2·00 N	32·28 E
24	Ulan Bator, Mong.	47·56 N	107·00 E
24	United Arab Emirates, Asia	23·30 N	53·00 E
20	United Kingdom, Eur.	54·00 N	2·00 W
11	United States, N.A.	38·00 N	110·00 W
21	Upper Volta, Afr.	11·46 N	3·18 W
21	Ural (R.), Sov. Un.	49·50 N	51·30 E
21	Uralsk, Sov. Un.	51·15 N	51·10 E
18	Uruguay, S.A.	32·45 S	56·00 W
14	Utah (State), U.S.	39·25 N	112·40 W
15	Utica, N.Y.	43·05 N	75·10 W
20	Vaduz, Liech.	47·10 N	9·32 E
18	Valdivia, Chile	39·47 S	73·13 W
20	Valencia, Sp.	39·26 N	0·23 W
18	Valencia, Ven.	10·11 N	68·00 W
20	Valladolid, Sp.	41·41 N	4·41 W
20	Valletta, Malta	35·50 N	14·29 E
11	Vancouver Is., Can.	49·47 N	128·23 W
18	Venezuela, S.A.	8·00 N	65·00 W
16	Veracruz, Mex.	19·13 N	96·07 W
15	Vermont (State), U.S.	43·50 N	72·50 W
25	Victoria, Hong Kong.	22·10 N	114·18 E
28	Victoria (L.), Afr.	2·00 S	32·16 E
11	Victoria Is., Can.	70·13 N	107·45 W
20	Vienna, Aus.	48·13 N	16·22 E
24	Vientiane, Laos.	18·07 N	102·33 E
25	Vietnam, Asia	16·00 N	108·00 E
19	Vinson Massif (Mtn.), Ant.	77·40 S	87·00 W
15	Virginia (State), U.S.	37·00 N	80·45 W
18	Vitória, Braz.	20·09 S	40·17 W
21	Vladivostok, Sov. Un.	43·06 N	131·47 E
22	Volga (R.), Sov. Un.	47·30 N	46·20 E
14	Waipahu, Hawaii (Hawaii In.)	21·20 N	158·02 W
20	Warsaw, Pol.	52·15 N	21·05 E
11	Washington, D.C., U.S.	38·50 N	77·00 W
14	Washington (State), U.S.	47·30 N	121·10 W
27	Wellington, N.Z. (In.)	41·15 S	174·45 E
28	Western Sahara, Afr.	23·05 N	15·33 W
15	West Virginia (State), U.S.	39·00 N	80·50 W
14	Whitney, Mt., Calif.	36·34 N	118·18 W
15	Wichita, Kans.	37·42 N	97·21 W
15	Wilmington, Del.	39·45 N	75·33 W
15	Wilmington, N.C.	34·12 N	77·56 W
28	Windhoek, Namibia	21·05 S	17·10 E
15	Windsor, Can.	42·19 N	83·00 W
14	Winnemucca, Nev.	40·59 N	117·43 W
12	Winnipeg, Can.	49·55 N	97·09 W
12	Winnipeg, L., Can.	53·29 N	98·41 W
12	Winnipegosis, Can.	51·40 N	100·01 W
15	Winona, Minn.	44·03 N	91·40 W
15	Winston-Salem, N.C.	36·05 N	80·15 W
15	Wisconsin (State), U.S.	44·30 N	91·00 W
27	Wollongong, Austl.	34·26 S	151·05 E
13	Woodstock, Can.	46·09 N	67·36 W
15	Worcester, Mass.	42·16 N	71·49 W
23	Wrangel, Sov. Un.	71·25 N	173·38 E
14	Wyoming (State), U.S.	42·50 N	108·30 W
18	Xingú (R.), Braz.	6·20 S	52·34 W
23	Yakutsk, Sov. Un.	62·13 N	129·49 E
25	Yangtze (R.), China	30·00 N	117·25 E
28	Yaoundé, Cam.	3·58 N	11·45 E
7	Yellow Sea, Asia	35·20 N	122·15 E
24	Yemen, Asia	15·45 N	44·30 E
24	Yemen, People's Democratic Republic of, Asia	14·45 N	46·45 E
25	Yokohama, Jap.	35·37 N	139·40 E
20	Yugoslavia, Eur.	44·48 N	17·29 E
12	Yukon R., Can.-U.S.	65·10 N	163·10 W
23	Yuzhno-Sakhalinsk, Sov. Un.	47·11 N	143·04 E
20	Zagreb, Yugo.	45·50 N	15·58 E
28	Zaire, Afr.	1·00 S	22·15 E
28	Zambezi (R.), Afr.	16·33 S	29·22 E
28	Zambia, Afr.	14·23 S	24·15 E

MAP SYMBOLS

CULTURAL FEATURES

Political Boundaries

— — — — (over water) International (Demarcated, Undemarcated, and Administrative)

—■—■—■— Disputed de facto

—·—·—·— Disputed de jure

▬ ▬ ▬ ▬ Indefinite or Undefined

——— (over water) Secondary, State, Provincial, etc.

⬚ Parks, Indian Reservations

⬚ City Limits   ▪ Built-up Areas

Cities, Towns and Villages

PARIS 1,000,000 and over (Metropolitan Area Population)

◉ Ufa 500,000 to 1,000,000 (Metropolitan Area Population)

⊙ Gyor 50,000 to 500,000

○ Agadir 25,000 to 50,000

○ Moreno 0 to 25,000

TOKYO National Capitals

Boise Secondary Capitals

Note: On maps at 1:20,000,000 and smaller, and on maps at 1:1,000,000, the type size indicates the relative importance of cities, not the specific population classification shown above.

Transportation

Railroads

———— Railroads (On 1:1,000,000 scale maps)

- - - - - - Railroad Ferries

Roads

Major
———— On 1:1,000,000 scale maps
Other

Major
———— On 1:4,000,000 scale maps
Other

———— On other scale maps

········· Caravan Routes

✈ Airports

Other Cultural Features

⌒ Dams

·-·-·-·-· Pipelines

▲ Pyramids

∴ Ruins

LAND FEATURES

△ Peaks, Spot Heights

✕ Passes

Sand

Contours

WATER FEATURES

Lakes and Reservoirs

Fresh Water

Fresh Water: Intermittent

Salt Water

Salt Water: Intermittent

Other Water Features

Salt Basins, Flats

Swamps

Ice Caps and Glaciers

Rivers

Intermittent Rivers

Aqueducts and Canals

Ship Channels

Falls

Rapids

♪ Springs

△ Water Depths

Fishing Banks

Sand Bars

Reefs

The two illustrations below represent the same imaginary area.
The upper illustration demonstrates how the Atlas maps symbolize land and water features.
The lower illustration shows how these same features on the earth's surface would appear if viewed obliquely from an airplane.

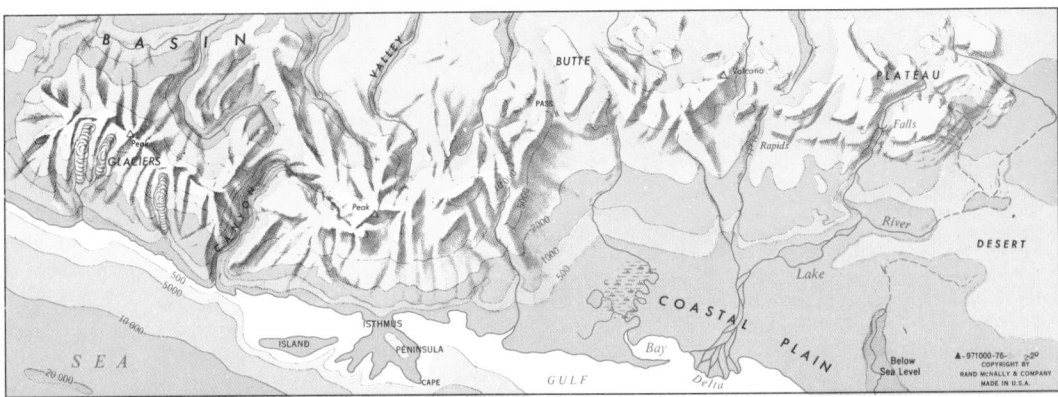

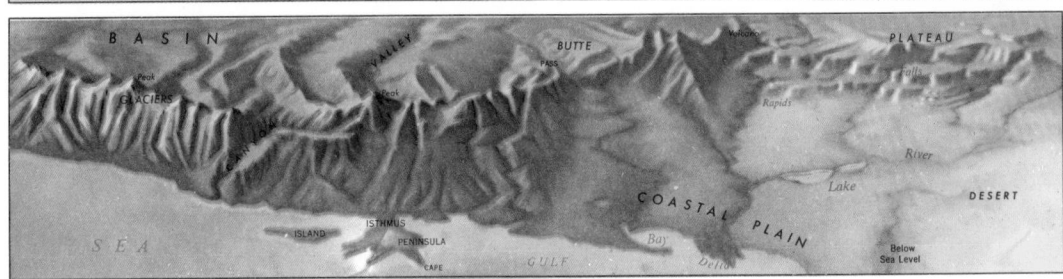

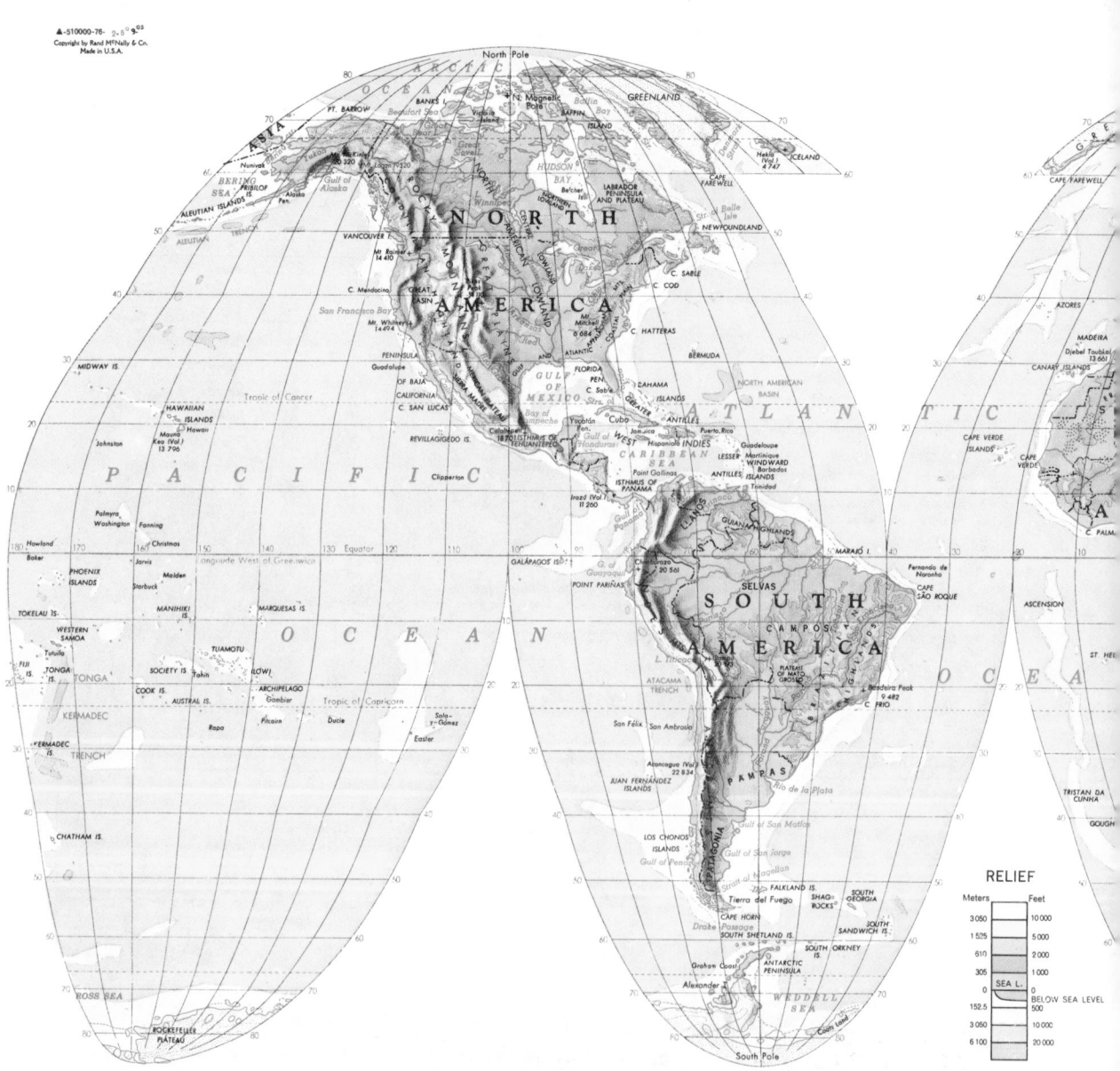

RELIEF

WORLD • Physical

GOODE'S HOMOLOSINE EQUAL AREA PROJECTION

Up to latitude 40° distances on all
parallels and midmeridians are true;
beyond 40° they are approximate

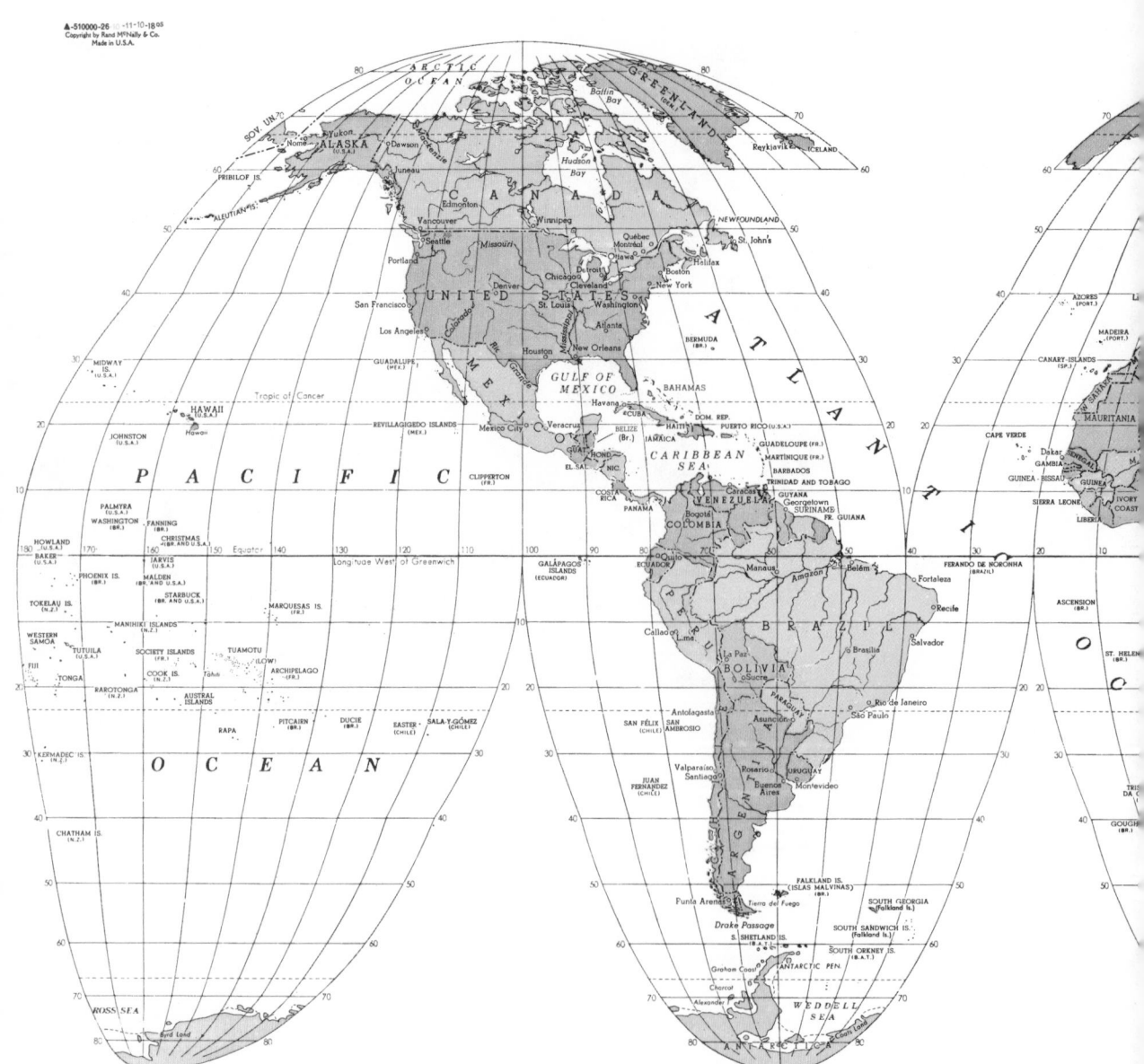

ARCTIC OCEAN

GREENLAND

Baffin Bay

SOV. UN.
Nome Yukon
Dawson
ALASKA
Juneau
PRIBILOF IS.
ALEUTIAN IS.

C A N A D A

NEWFOUNDLAND
Reykjavik ICELAND

Edmonton
Vancouver
Seattle
Winnipeg
Missouri
Portland
St. John's
Québec
Montreal
Ottawa
Halifax
Denver
Chicago Detroit
Cleveland
San Francisco
UNITED STATES
St. Louis
Boston
New York
Washington
Los Angeles
Atlanta
Colorado
BERMUDA
(BR.)

MIDWAY
IS.
(U.S.A.)
Houston
New Orleans
GUADALUPE
(MEX.)
Tropic of Cancer

HAWAII
(U.S.A.)
Hawaii
GULF OF MEXICO
BAHAMAS
Havana
CUBA
DOM. REP.
PUERTO RICO (U.S.A.)

JOHNSTON
(U.S.A.)
REVILLAGIGEDO ISLANDS
(MEX.)
Mexico City
Veracruz
HAITI
JAMAICA
GUADELOUPE (FR.)
MARTINIQUE (FR.)
BARBADOS

PALMYRA
(U.S.A.)
WASHINGTON
(BR.)
FANNING
(BR.)
CLIPPERTON
(FR.)
BELIZE
(Br.)
GUAT.
HOND.
EL SAL.
NIC.
CARIBBEAN
SEA
TRINIDAD AND TOBAGO

P A C I F I C

CHRISTMAS
(BR. AND U.S.A.)
Equator
COSTA
RICA
PANAMA
Caracas
VENEZUELA
GUYANA
Georgetown
SURINAME
FR. GUIANA

HOWLAND
(U.S.A.)
BAKER
(U.S.A.)
JARVIS
(U.S.A.)
GALÁPAGOS
ISLANDS
(ECUADOR)
Bogotá
COLOMBIA
ECUADOR
Longitude West of Greenwich

PHOENIX IS.
(BR.)
MALDEN
(BR. AND U.S.A.)
STARBUCK
(BR. AND U.S.A.)
MARQUESAS IS.
(FR.)
Manaus
Amazon
Belém
FERANDO DE NORONHA
(BRAZIL)
Fortaleza
Recife

TOKELAU IS.
(N.Z.)
MANIHIKI ISLANDS
(N.Z.)
Callao
Lima
B R A Z I L

WESTERN
SAMOA
TUTUILA
(U.S.A.)
SOCIETY ISLANDS
(FR.)
TUAMOTU
Tahiti
Brasília
Salvador

FIJI
TONGA
RAROTONGA
(N.Z.)
COOK IS.
(N.Z.)
AUSTRAL
ISLANDS
ARCHIPELAGO
(FR.)
La Paz
BOLIVIA
Sucre
Rio de Janeiro
São Paulo

PITCAIRN
(BR.)
DUCIE
(BR.)
EASTER
(CHILE)
SALA-Y-GÓMEZ
(CHILE)
PARAGUAY
Asunción

RAPA
SAN FÉLIX
(CHILE)
SAN
AMBROSIO
Antofagasta

KERMADEC IS.
(N.Z.)
JUAN
FERNÁNDEZ
(CHILE)
Valparaíso
Santiago
Rosario
URUGUAY
Montevideo
Buenos
Aires

O C E A N

CHATHAM IS.
(N.Z.)

FALKLAND IS.
(ISLAS MALVINAS)
(BR.)
SOUTH GEORGIA
(Falkland Is.)

Punta Arenas
Tierra del Fuego
SOUTH SANDWICH IS.
(Falkland Is.)

Drake Passage
S. SHETLAND IS.
SOUTH ORKNEY IS.
(B.A.T.)

ROSS SEA
Byrd Land
Graham Coast
Charcot
ANTARCTIC PEN.
W E D D E L L
S E A

Alexander
Coast Land
A N T A R C T I C A

ATLANTIC

AZORES
(PORT.)
MADEIRA
(PORT.)
CANARY ISLANDS
(SP.)
MAURITANIA

CAPE VERDE
Dakar
SENEGAL
GAMBIA
GUINEA-BISSAU
GUINEA
SIERRA LEONE
IVORY COAST
LIBERIA

OCEAN
ASCENSION
(BR.)
ST. HELENA
(BR.)

TRIS-
TAN DA C
GOUGH

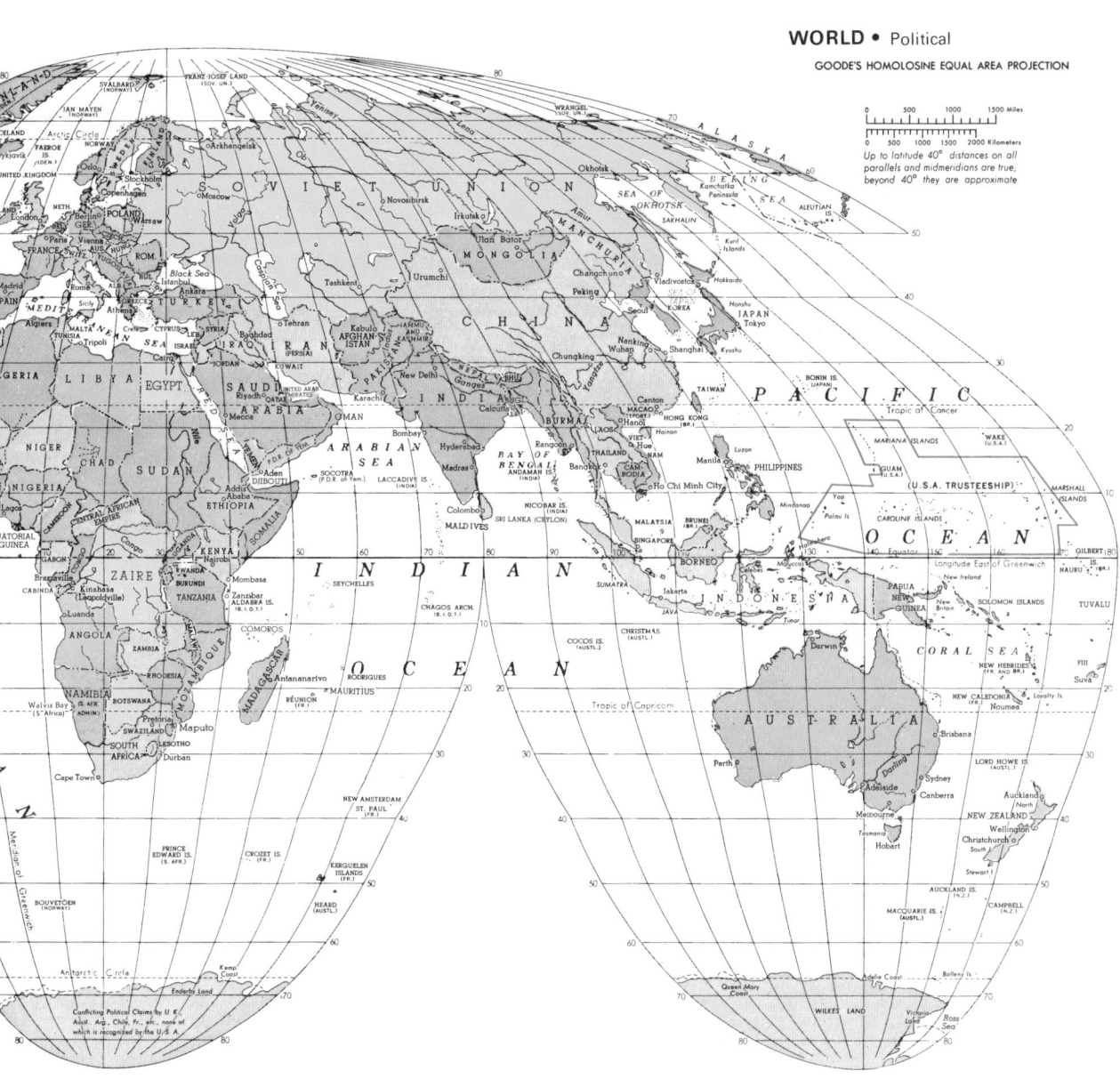

WORLD • Political

GOODE'S HOMOLOSINE EQUAL AREA PROJECTION

Up to latitude 40° distances on all
parallels and midmeridians are true;
beyond 40° they are approximate

NORTHERN LANDS AND SEAS

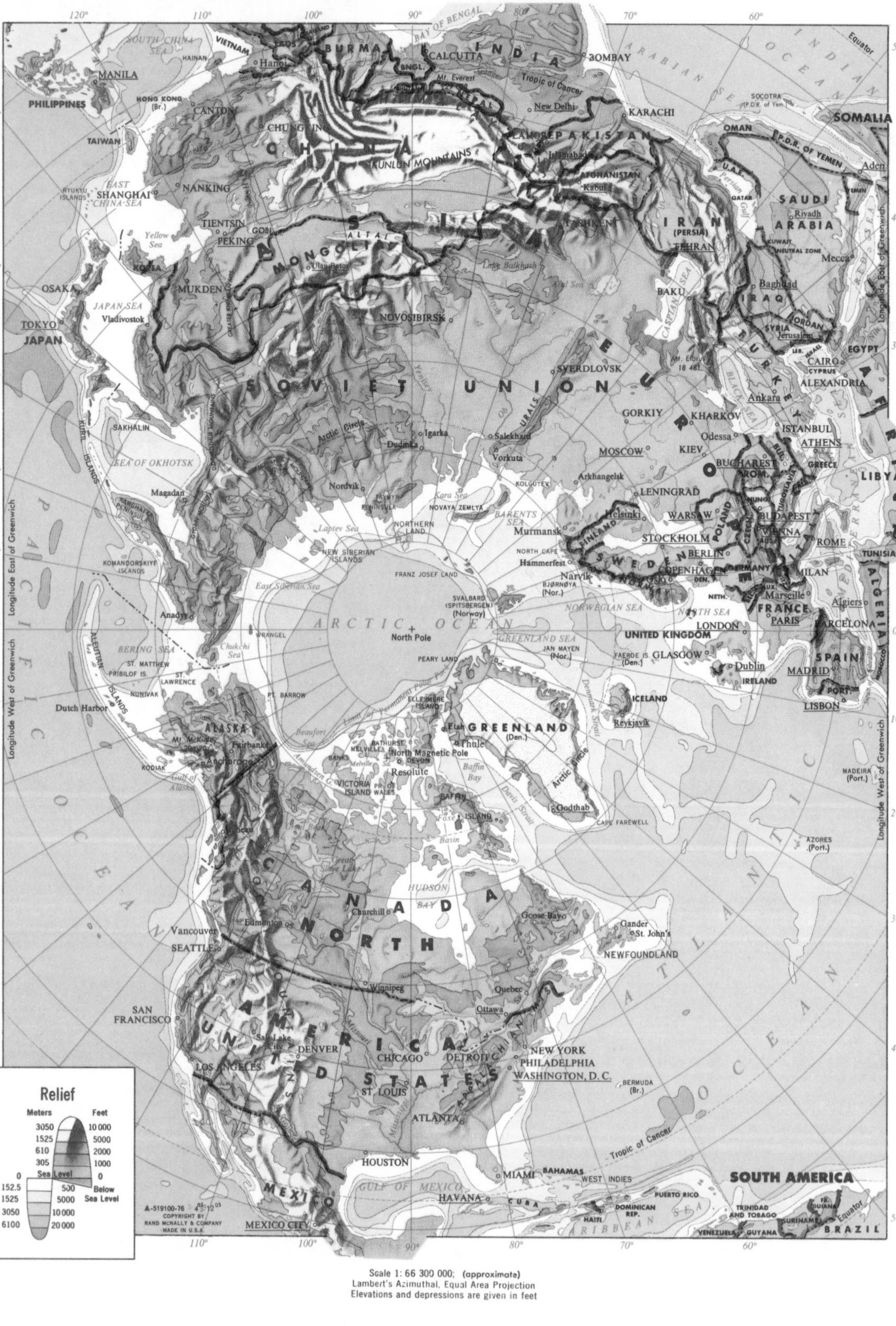

Relief

Meters		Feet
3050		10 000
1525		5000
610		2000
305		1000
0	Sea Level	0
		Below
152.5	500	Sea Level
1525	5000	
3050	10 000	
6100	20 000	

A-519100-76
COPYRIGHT BY
RAND McNALLY & COMPANY
MADE IN U.S.A.

Scale 1: 66 300 000; (approximate)
Lambert's Azimuthal, Equal Area Projection
Elevations and depressions are given in feet

NORTH AMERICA

Relief

Meters		Feet
3050		10 000
1525		5000
610		2000
305		1000
0	Sea Level	0
		500 Below
152.5		Sea Level
1525		5000
3050		10 000
6100		20 000

▲-520000-76-
COPYRIGHT BY
RAND McNALLY & COMPANY
MADE IN U.S.A.

Lambert's Azimuthal, Equal Area Projection
Elevations and depressions are given in feet

0   200   400   600   800   1000 Miles
0   400   800   1200   1600 Kilometers

Conic Projection

Elevations and depressions are given in feet

CANADA

All islands within bays and straits
lie within Northwest Territories.

60° Longitude West of Greenwich 55°

Same scale as
main map

QUEBEC

Gulf of
St. Lawrence

NEWFOUNDLAND

ATLANTIC OCEAN

Relief

Meters		Feet
3050		10 000
1525		5000
610		2000
305		1000
152.5		500
Sea Level		0
152.5		500
1525		5000
3050		10000

▲-820200-76-
COPYRIGHT BY
RAND McNALLY & COMPANY
MADE IN U.S.A.

0 25 50 75 100   200   300   400   500 Miles
0   100   200   400   600   800 Kilometers

Polyconic Projection
Elevations and depressions are given in feet

UNITED STATES OF AMERICA

Polyconic Projection
Elevations and depressions are given in feet

CENTRAL

CALIFORNIA ARIZONA
SAN DIEGO
Tijuana Mexicali
Ensenada

NEW MEXICO
Phoenix Santa Fe
Albuquerque

KANSAS MISSOURI
Springfield Evansville
ILL. KEN.
Cairo Bowling Gre
Hopkinsville

Amarillo Oklahoma City
OKLAHOMA
Tulsa Muskogee
Fort Smith
ARKANSAS
Little Rock

TENNESSEE
Nashville Chattanoo
Memphis

BAJA
CALIFORNIA
NORTE
GUADALUPE
(Mex.)
CEDROS

Tucson
Nogales
Bisbee
Douglas
Ciudad Juárez
El Paso
Deming
Las Cruces

SONORA
Puerto Peñasco
ANGEL DE LA GUARDA
TIBURON

CHIHUAHUA
Chihuahua

T E X A S
Pecos
San Angelo
Del Rio
Piedras Negras
Eagle Pass
Nueces

Wichita Falls
Lubbock
Childress
Lawton
Fort Worth
DALLAS
Waco
Austin Beaumont
San Antonio
Corpus Christi

Hot Springs
Pine Bluff
Texarkana
Corsicana
Shreveport
Vicksburg
Natchez
LOUISIANA
Baton Rouge
New Orleans
CAPE SAN BLA

Birmingham
ALABAMA
Montgome
Jackson
Greenvill
Mobile
Pensacola

BAJA
CALIFORNIA
SUR
STA. MARGARITA
STA. GENOVEVA 7100
C. SAN LÁZARO
C. SAN LUCAS

Guaymas
Hermosillo
Ciudad Obregón
Navojoa

COAHUILA
Salado
Sabinas
Monclova
Saltillo
Laredo
Nuevo Laredo
Brownsville
Matamoros

Culiacán
Topolobampo
Los Mochis

DURANGO
Gómez Palacio
Lerdo
Torreón
Jiménez
Francisco I. Madero
Concepción del Oro
NUEVO LEON
Monterrey

Mazatlán
Escuinapa
(de Hidalgo)
Durango

ZACATECAS
Zacatecas
Matehuala

GULF OF MEX

Tropic of Cancer

NAYARIT
Islas Tres Marías
Tepic
San Blas
Tuxpan

AGUASCALIENTES
Aguascalientes
SAN LUIS
POTOSI
San Luis Potosí
Salinas
Ciudad del Maíz
Ciudad Victoria
Ciudad Mante
Tampico

CAPE CORRIENTES
Guadalajara
León
JALISCO
GUANAJUATO
Guanajuato
Querétaro
HIDALGO
Pachuca
Tuxpan
Nautla

REVILLAGIGEDO
ISLANDS
(Mex.)

Ciudad Guzmán
Colima
Manzanillo
Celaya
MICHOACÁN
Morelia
Toluca
MEXICO CITY
Puebla
Jalapa Enríquez
Veracruz
Orizaba
Bay of
Campeche

Progreso
Sisal
Mérida
YUCATÁN
Valladolid
Cozumel
C. CATOCHE
Temax

Campeche
CAMPECHE
PENINSULA
QUINTANA ROO
Ciudad Chetumal
(Payo Obispo)

Acapulco
GUERRERO
Chilpancingo
OAXACA
Oaxaca
Tehuantepec
Gulf of
Tehuantepec

San Andrés Tuxtla
Coatzacoalcos
(Puerto México)
Minatitlán
TABASCO
Villahermosa
Ciudad del
Carmen

BELIZE
Belize
TURNEFFE
BELIZE
(Br.)

CHIAPAS
Tuxtla Gutiérrez
Comitán
Quezaltenango
Mazatenango
GUATEMALA
Guatemala
Cobán
Pto. Cortés
La Ceiba
Tela
HONDURAS
Tegucigalpa

SALVADOR
Santa Ana
San Salvador
San Miguel
Gulf of
Fonseca
León
Managua
NICARA

PACIFIC OCEAN

COCO
(Costa Rica)

San Juan del Sur
Granada

Canal Zone Inset:

Caribbean Sea
Limón Bay
Colón
Cristóbal
Margarita
GATUN LOCKS
Gatún
2200
Isaoca Mt. 1847
Sabaldo Mt.
Nuevo San Juan
PANAMA
Gatún Lake
Salud Mt. 1182
East Mt. 608
West Mt. 537
CANAL ZONE
(U.S.A.)
North Gamboa
Balboa Mt. 1149
Chilibre
Madden Lake
GAILLARD CUT
Gold Hill 662
Paraíso
Pedro Miguel
PEDRO MIGUEL LOCKS
MIRAFLORES LOCKS
Cocolí
Diablo Hts.
Balboa Heights
Gamboa Mt. 1205
Panamá
PANAMA
La Chorrera
Bay of Panama
TABOGA
TABOGUILLA

0 10 Miles
0 4 8 12 16 Kilometers

80° 79°30'

©RMcN

A -530000-76 5-62°
COPYRIGHT BY
RAND McNALLY & COMPANY
MADE IN U.S.A.

GULF AND CARIBBEAN LANDS

PUERTO RICO

ATLANTIC OCEAN

Aguadilla • Arecibo • San Juan
POINT HIGUERO • Utuado • CABEZAS DE • ST. THOMAS • TORTOLA
Mayagüez • Caguas • SAN JUAN (U.S.A.) • Charlotte • Amalie • ST. JOHN (U.S.A.)
(U.S.A.) • Coamo • Cayey • CULEBRA • Vieques
CABO ROJO • Ponce • Salinas • Guayama • VIEQUES
Humacao

CARIBBEAN SEA

Christiansted
SAINT CROIX (U.S.A.)

0 10 20 30 40 Miles
0 10 20 30 40 50 60 Kilometers

ST. THOMAS

LITTLE HANS LOLLIK • OUTER BRASS
INNER BRASS • HANS LOLLIK
STORMY PT • PICARA PT • THATCH CAY • GRASS CAY
ST. THOMAS (U.S.A.) • Charlotte Amalie
Crown Mt. (St. Thomas) Nadir
1558 • St. Thomas Harbor

0 1 2 3 4 6 Miles
0 2 4 6 Kilometers

Relief

Meters	Feet
3050	10 000
1525	5000
610	2000
305	1000
152.5	500
Sea Level	0
152.5	500
1525	5000
3050	10 000
6100	20 000

0 50 100 200 300 400 500 Miles
0 100 200 400 600 800 Kilometers

Longitude West of Greenwich

SOUTH AMERICA

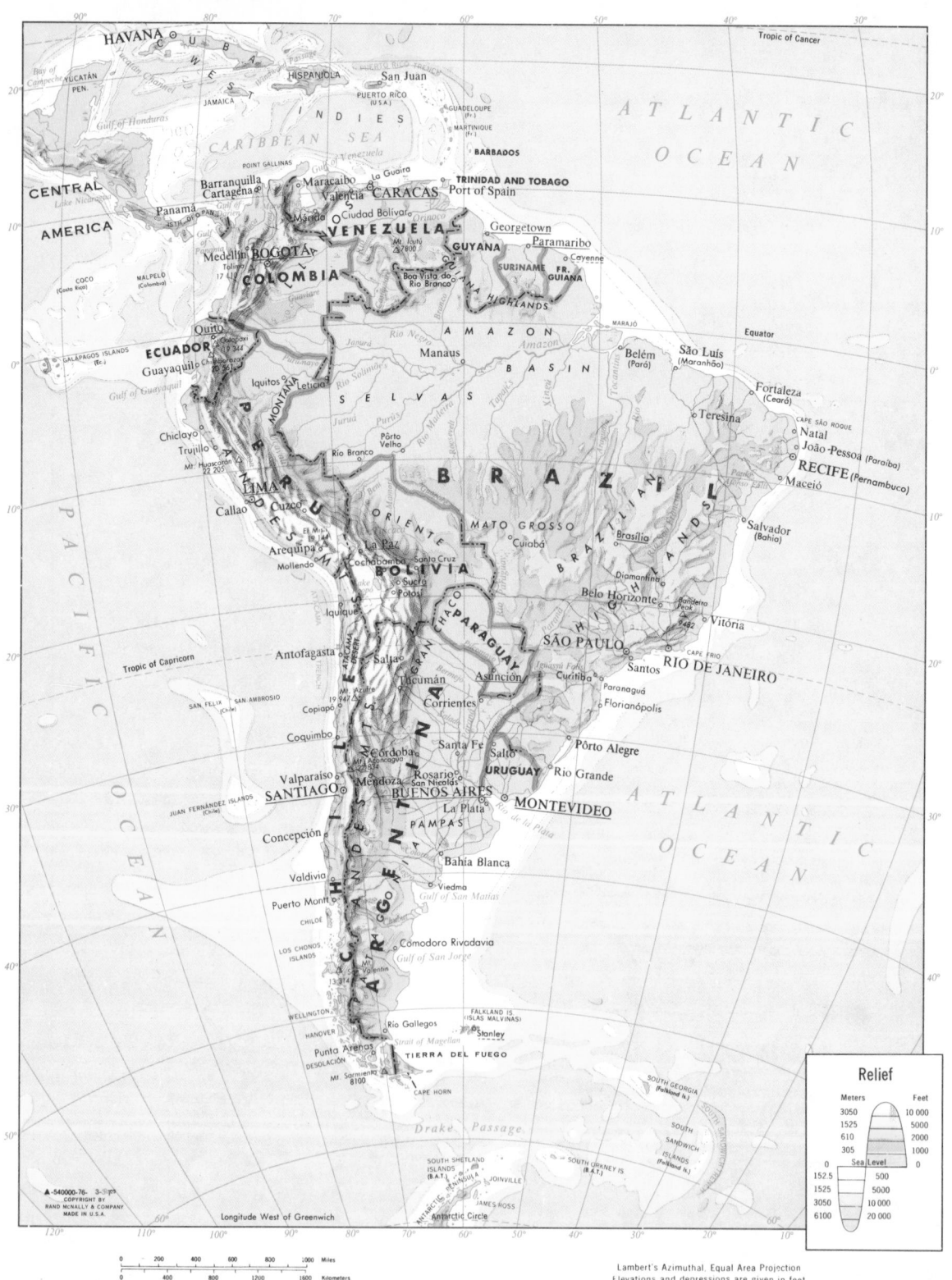

HAVANA

Bay of Campeche
YUCATÁN PEN.

CUBA

Yucatan Channel

JAMAICA

Gulf of Honduras

CENTRAL

Lake Nicaragua

AMERICA

COCO (Costa Rica)

MALPELO (Colombia)

Panamá
ISTH. OF PAN.

GALÁPAGOS ISLANDS (Ec.)

QUITO

ECUADOR

Guayaquil

Gulf of Guayaquil

Chiclayo

Trujillo

Mt. Huascarán 22,205

LIMA

Callao

ANDES

Arequipa

Mollendo

Iquique

PACIFIC

Antofagasta

SAN FELIX (Chile)

SAN AMBROSIO (Chile)

Copiapó

Coquimbo

OCEAN

JUAN FERNÁNDEZ ISLANDS (Chile)

Valparaíso

SANTIAGO

Concepción

Valdivia

Puerto Montt

CHILOE

LOS CHONOS ISLANDS

WELLINGTON

HANOVER

DESOLACIÓN

Punta Arenas

HISPANIOLA

San Juan

PUERTO RICO TRENCH

PUERTO RICO (U.S.A.)

GUADELOUPE (Fr.)

MARTINIQUE (Fr.)

BARBADOS

INDIES

CARIBBEAN SEA

POINT GALLINAS

Gulf of Venezuela

TRINIDAD AND TOBAGO
Port of Spain

Barranquilla

Cartagena

Maracaibo

La Guaira

Valencia

CARACAS

Mérida

Medellín

BOGOTÁ

Tolima 17,110

COLOMBIA

Ciudad Bolívar

Orinoco

VENEZUELA

Mt. Roraima 9,800

Georgetown

GUYANA

Paramaribo

SURINAME

Cayenne

FR. GUIANA

Boa Vista do Rio Branco

GUIANA HIGHLANDS

Guaviare

Río Negro

AMAZON

Equator

MARAJÓ

Manaus

Amazon

BASIN

Belém (Pará)

São Luís (Maranhão)

Iça

Japurá

Iquitos

Leticia

Río Solimões

MONTAÑA

SELVAS

Juruá

Purús

Río Madeira

Tapajós

Xingu

Fortaleza (Ceará)

Teresina

CAPE SÃO ROQUE

Natal

João Pessoa (Paraíba)

RECIFE (Pernambuco)

Maceió

Río Branco

Pôrto Velho

B R A Z I L

PERU

Cuzco

ORIENTE

MATO GROSSO

Cuiabá

São Francisco

Salvador (Bahia)

La Paz

Cochabamba

Santa Cruz

BOLIVIA

Sucre

Potosí

EL MISTI 19,101

BRAZILIAN

Brasília

Diamantina

Belo Horizonte

Bandeira Peak 9492

Vitória

CHACO

GRAN CHACO

PARAGUAY

Asunción

São Paulo

Santos

RIO DE JANEIRO

CAPE FRIO

Salta

Tucumán

Mt. Azufre 19,947

ARGENTINA

Corrientes

Iguaçu Falls

Curitiba

Paranaguá

Florianópolis

PAMPAS

Copiapó

Córdoba

Aconcagua 23,834

Mendoza

Santa Fe

Rosario

San Nicolás

Salto

Pôrto Alegre

URUGUAY

Río Grande

BUENOS AIRES

La Plata

MONTEVIDEO

Río de la Plata

Bahía Blanca

Viedma

Gulf of San Matías

Comodoro Rivadavia

Gulf of San Jorge

Mt. Valentín 13,314

ANDES

Río Gallegos

FALKLAND IS. (ISLAS MALVINAS)

Stanley

Strait of Magellan

Mt. Sarmiento 8100

TIERRA DEL FUEGO

CAPE HORN

Drake Passage

ATLANTIC

OCEAN

ATLANTIC

OCEAN

Tropic of Cancer

Tropic of Capricorn

Equator

Tropic of Capricorn

SOUTH GEORGIA (Falkland Is.)

SOUTH SANDWICH ISLANDS (Falkland Is.)

SOUTH SHETLAND ISLANDS (B.A.T.)

SOUTH ORKNEY IS. (B.A.T.)

JOINVILLE

ANTARCTIC PENINSULA

JAMES ROSS

Antarctic Circle

Longitude West of Greenwich

▲ 540000-76- 3-S-pt
COPYRIGHT BY
RAND MCNALLY & COMPANY
MADE IN U.S.A.

Relief		
Meters		Feet
3050		10 000
1525		5000
610		2000
305		1000
Sea Level		0
152.5		500
1525		5000
3050		10 000
6100		20 000

0 200 400 600 800 1000 Miles

0 400 800 1200 1600 Kilometers

Lambert's Azimuthal, Equal Area Projection
Elevations and depressions are given in feet

SOUTHERN LANDS AND SEAS

Relief

Meters		Feet
3050		10 000
1525		5000
610		2000
305		1000
Sea Level		0
152.5	500	Below Sea Level
1525	5000	
3050	10 000	
6100	20 000	

▲ -594000-76- 4 12 05
COPYRIGHT BY
RAND M9NALLY & COMPANY
MADE IN U.S.A.

Tropic of Capricorn

PERU
La Paz
BOLIVIA
Sucre
SOUTH
BRAZIL
AMERICA
PARAGUAY
Asunción
Brasília
SANTIAGO
CHILE
Rosario
ARGENTINA
URUGUAY
BUENOS AIRES
MONTEVIDEO
SÃO PAULO
Santos
RIO DE JANEIRO

SALA-Y-GÓMEZ
(Chile)
SAN FÉLIX
(Chile)
SAN AMBROSIO
(Chile)
EASTER I.
(Chile)
JUAN FERNÁNDEZ
ISLANDS
(Chile)
TUAMOTU
(LOW) ARCHIPELAGO
(Fr.)
LOS CHONOS
ISLANDS

Punta Arenas
Strait of Magellan
CAPE HORN
Drake Passage
FALKLAND IS.
(ISLAS MALVINAS)
(Br.)

SOUTH SHETLAND
ISLANDS (B.A.T.)
ADELAIDE
SOUTH
ORKNEY IS.
(B.A.T.)
SOUTH GEORGIA
(Falkland Is.)

BELLINGSHAUSEN
SEA
ALEXANDER
Antarctic Circle
THURSTON I.
AMUNDSEN
SEA
Mt. Rex
3 625
WEDDELL
SEA
SOUTH
SANDWICH IS.
(Falkland Is.)
TRISTAN DA
CUNHA
(Br.)
GOUGH
(Br.)

Mt. Siple
10 171
Mt. Ulmer
8 451
Mt. Hope
ELLSWORTH
MTS.
RONNE
ICE SHELF
BERKNER
ISLAND
FILCHNER ICE SHELF
COATS
LAND

Mt. Sidley
13 712
ROCKEFELLER
PLATEAU
WHITMORE
MTS.
PENSACOLA
MTS.
THIEL
MTS.

ROOSEVELT
QUEEN
MAUD
MTS.
South Pole
10 000
QUEEN MAUD LAND
BOUVETØYA
(BOUVET)
(Nor.)

ROSS
SEA
ROSS
ICE SHELF
SCOTT
Mt. Erebus
McMurdo
Mt. Sabine
12 280
VICTORIA
LAND
Mt. Markham
14 272
Mt. Albert Markham
10 522
Mt. McClintock 11 457
ANTARCTICA
MÜHLIG-
HOFMANN
MTS.

C. OF GOOD HOPE
Cape Town

NEW
ZEALAND
CHATHAM IS.
(N.Z.)
BOUNTY IS.
(N.Z.)
CAMPBELL
(N.Z.)
AUCKLAND IS.
(N.Z.)
BALLENY IS.
South
Magnetic Pole
WILKES   LAND
AMERICAN
HIGHLAND
ENDERBY
LAND
Antarctic Circle
BELGICA MTS.
QUEEN FABIOLA
MTS.
NAPIER MTS.

AFRICA
SOUTH
AFRICA
PRINCE
EDWARD IS.
(S. Africa)
LESOTHO
Durban
SWAZILAND

MACQUARIE
(Austl.)
DIBBLE ICEBERG
TONGUE
SHACKLETON ICE
SHELF
WEST ICE SHELF
AMERY
ICE SHELF
LAMBERT
GLACIER

MOZAMBIQUE

TASMAN
SEA
Hobart
TASMANIA
MELBOURNE
Adelaide
HEARD
(Austl.)
McDONALD
(Austl.)
CROZET IS.
(Fr.)
KERGUELEN IS.
(Fr.)
C. STE. MARIE
MADAGASCAR
COMOROS
Antananarivo

AUSTRALIA
GREAT
SANDY
DESERT
GREAT VICTORIA
DESERT
C. LEEUWIN
Perth
NORTH WEST
CAPE
NEW AMSTERDAM
(Fr.)
ST. PAUL
(Fr.)
Tropic of Capricorn
RÉUNION
(Fr.)
MASCARENE IS.
MAURITIUS
AMIRANTE IS.
(Sey.)
Meuzambique Channel

TIMOR
SEA
Timor
FLORES
INDONESIA
INDIAN   OCEAN
SEYCHELLES

PACIFIC   OCEAN

ATLANTIC   OCEAN

ANTARCTICA IN PROFILE
SECTION ALONG LINE AB

15000		South Pole		15000
10000	Horlick Mts.		Frœmnes Mts.	10000
5000				5000
Feet (A)	Byrd Basin	Polar Basin	Sea Level	(B) Feet
5000				5000

Scale 1: 66 300 000; (approximate)
Lambert's Azimuthal, Equal Area Projection
Elevations and depressions are given in feet

Relief

Meters		Feet
3050		10 000
1525		5000
610		2000
305		1000
152.5		500
0	Sea Level	0
152.5		500
1525		5000
3050		10 000

Below Sea Level

Conic Projection

Elevations and depressions are given in feet

Longitude West of Greenwich   0°   Longitude East of Greenwich

EUROPE AND WESTERN ASIA

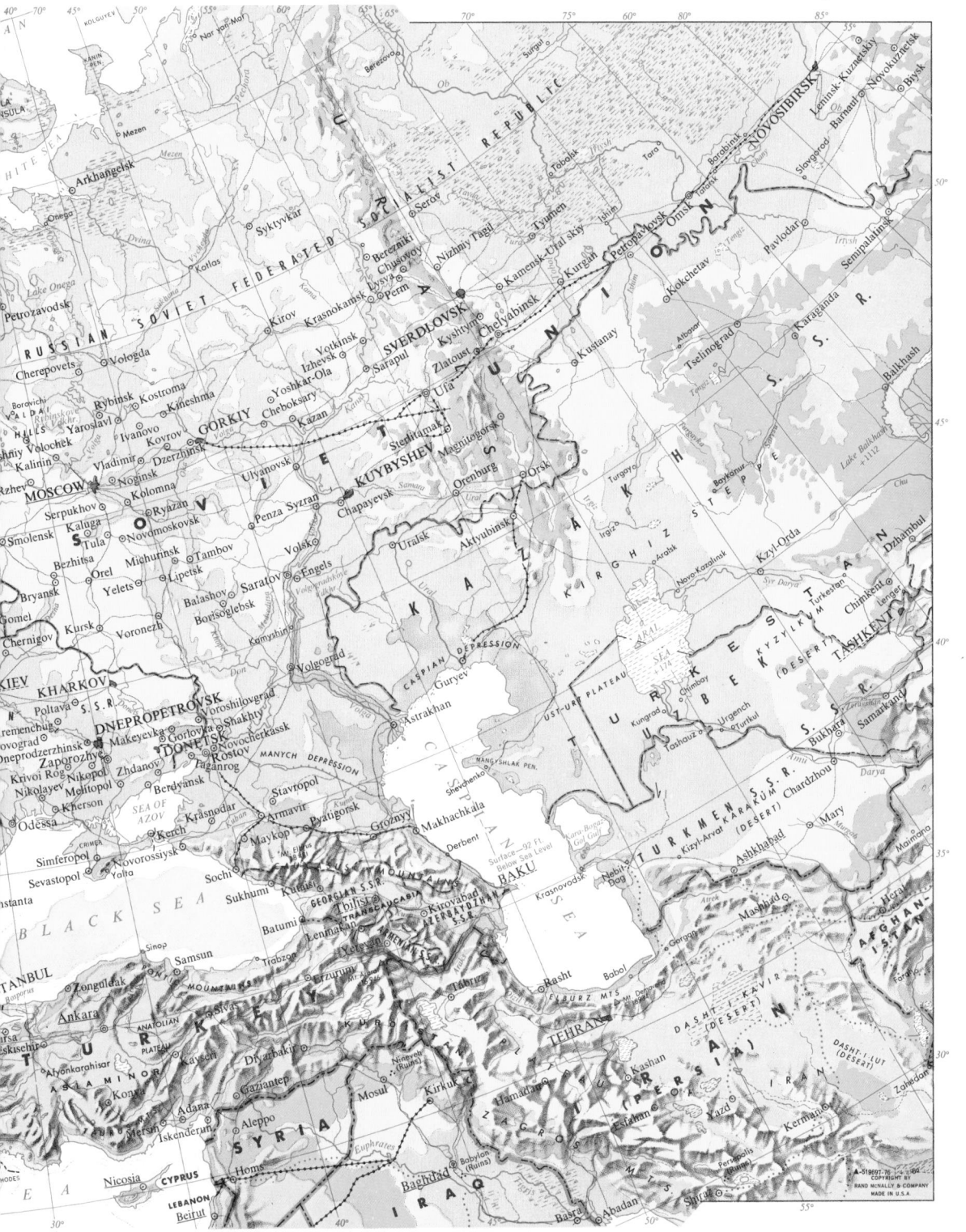

SOVIET UNION

Relief

Meters		Feet
3050		10 000
1525		5000
610		2000
305		1000
152.5		500
	Sea Level	
152.5		500
1525		Below Sea Level
3050		5000
		10 000

Longitude East of Greenwich

Relief

Meters		Feet
3050		10 000
1525		5000
610		2000
305		1000
0	Sea Level	0
		Below
		Sea Level
152.5		500
1525		5000
3050		10 000
6100		20 000

▲-519695-76 II 8-5912 ℗
COPYRIGHT BY
RAND MCNALLY & COMPANY
MADE IN U.S.A.

Lambert's Azimuthal, Equal Area Projection
Elevations and depressions are given in feet

Relief

Meters		Feet
3050		10 000
1525		5000
610		2000
305		1000
152.5		500
0	Sea Level	0
152.5		500	Below Sea Level
1525		5000
3050		10 000
6100		20 000

A-590200-76
COPYRIGHT BY
RAND McNALLY & COMPANY
MADE IN U.S.A.

Longitude 115° East of Greenwich

Lambert's Azimuthal, Equal Area Projection
Elevations and depressions are given in feet

AUSTRALIA AND NEW ZEALAND

Same scale as main map

AFRICA

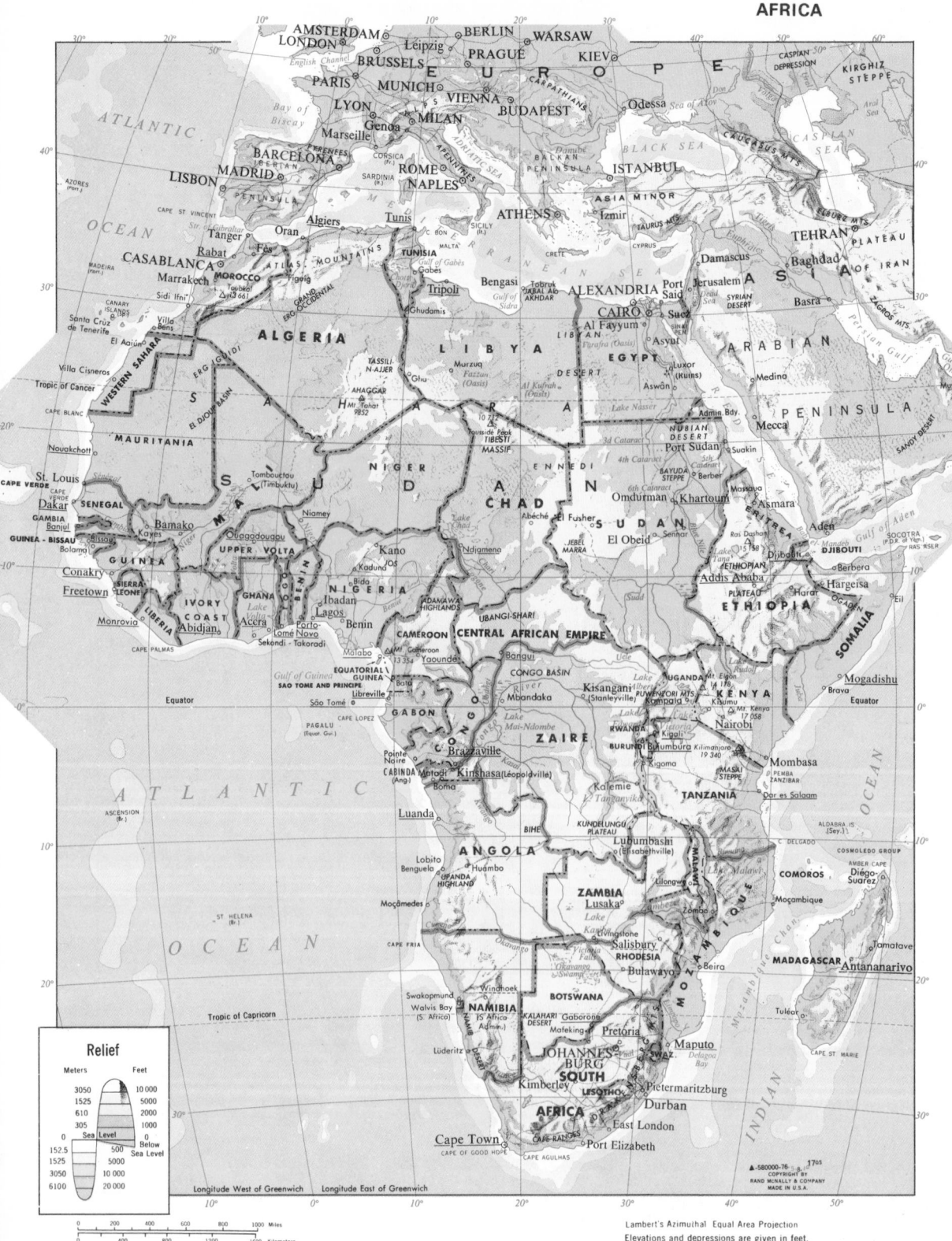

Lambert's Azimuthal Equal Area Projection
Elevations and depressions are given in feet.

Relief		
Meters		Feet
3050		10 000
1525		5000
610		2000
305		1000
0 Sea Level		0 Below Sea Level
152.5		500
1525		5000
3050		10 000
6100		20 000

WEBSTER'S
New World
DICTIONARY

YOUNG PEOPLE'S EDITION

DAVID B. GURALNIK

Editor in Chief

Contents

Editorial Staff and Advisory Council iv

Foreword v

GUIDE TO USING THE DICTIONARY *Guide 1*

What You Can Find in Your Dictionary .... *Guide 1*

The Problem of Spelling .... *Guide 6*

Consonant and Vowel Sounds .... *Guide 7*

Steps To Remember .... *Guide 8*

What Does the Word Mean? .... *Guide 8*

How To Pronounce the Words .... *Guide 10*

The Pronunciation Key .... *Guide 12*

Guides for Writing, Speaking, and Reading .... *Guide 13*

A DICTIONARY OF AMERICAN ENGLISH 1–808

EDITORIAL STAFF

ADVISORY COUNCIL

iv

FOREWORD

This dictionary was prepared especially for young people in Grades 4 through 8. The editors studied lists showing the words that students are most likely to see or hear. They checked textbooks and reading materials to find the words now being used in science, social studies, English, and other subjects. Teachers and educators throughout the country were consulted to secure their views on contents and arrangement. The editors drew on their own records of words in general use, records built up through years spent in editing dictionaries for high-school and college students and for adults. In addition, they asked a number of educators and teachers to serve as an Advisory Council. This Council examined the work of the editors and offered valuable suggestions. The result of this program is a dictionary specifically prepared for young students, tailored to their needs, their skills, and their perspectives.

All entries in this dictionary are presented in one alphabetical listing. In addition to words of general vocabulary, these entries include proper names, abbreviations, suffixes and prefixes, and compounds of two or more words. The main entry is followed by its pronunciation, a part-of-speech label, numbered definitions, and abundant phrase and sentence illustrations of the various meanings in context. Meanings which apply to the use of the word as a noun, for example, are listed separately from those which apply to the use of the word as a verb, adjective, etc.

One of the features of this dictionary is the inclusion in the entry of many common idioms incorporating the entry word, plus words formed from that word: irregular principal parts of verbs, comparative and superlative forms of adjectives and adverbs, and plurals of nouns, as well as derivatives formed by the addition of suffixes. Each of these "formed words" shows syllabification and accent and is identified according to use.

One feature that teachers and students will welcome is the simplified pronunciation key that eliminates the confusion caused by using too many diacritical marks. The complete key will be found on p. *Guide 11*. An abbreviated form of this key will be found on every right-hand page of the dictionary proper. The pronunciations shown are those of General American, as they are sounded in the context of phrases and sentences. The symbols used are broad enough in application to allow speakers of other varieties of American English to apply them to their own pronunciation patterns. Only the commonest variant pronunciations are given.

A special feature of this dictionary is the help it provides in word study and in writing and speaking. Note, for example, the full and well-illustrated treatment of prefixes and suffixes. The meanings, the examples, and the editorial notes guide students in using words that best express the meaning intended and that suit the occasion.

The many pictures are planned not only to brighten the columns of print, but also to add information about the words that they illustrate. An average size is given for every animal pictured. Diagrams and cross sections help the student to visualize complicated concepts. Of particular interest are the drawings for words like *scowl, incongruous, cringe,* and *askew,* illustrating actions and abstract or relative terms in a way that vividly reinforces the definition.

The many helps which students can find in this dictionary are pointed out and explained in the introductory materials that follow, prepared for classroom study.

David B. Guralnik

v

GUIDE TO USING THE DICTIONARY

WHAT YOU CAN FIND IN YOUR DICTIONARY

Are you puzzled every so often by the meaning of a word new to you? Or by a word you already know that is being used with a meaning that seems to be different? Do you ever have trouble spelling or pronouncing a word? Or when you are writing, do you sometimes reach the end of a line and wonder how to divide a word into syllables?

The book that can help you deal with all these problems, and more, is the dictionary. The dictionary you are now holding was prepared especially for you. It gives the meanings of the words you hear most often over the radio and television, and the words you see most often in newspapers, magazines, and books. It shows you how they are used. It can help you with your spelling and your grammar too.

You may sometimes hear or read an especially hard word or a technical word that is not explained in this dictionary. Then you will need to look in a larger, more advanced dictionary, where such words may be found.

Think of your dictionary as a guidebook, telling you how words are used by educated people. It is not a rule book, telling you how words *should* be used. This explains why you may find in it two ways of spelling one word, as *theater* and *theatre*. Both spellings can be found in good magazines and books and are, therefore, considered "correct." You may also find two pronunciations, as for *news*, since some educated people pronounce it one way (nōōz) and some pronounce it another way (nyōōz).

When there is any reason why you should hesitate to use a word, or a certain meaning of a word, you will find a special note in your dictionary. The special note follows the word or meaning. (See "Notes for Special Uses," beginning on p. *Guide 14*.)

You need a guidebook because our language is always changing. New words are added, like *aerospace, defoliate,* and *hertz*. Some older words are now seldom used. Have you heard anyone refer to his "steed" lately? Or use the word *troth* instead of *truth*? Then there are familiar words used in combinations to give new meanings: *tape recorder, paperback, iron curtain, spaceship, drive-in, audio-visual, chalkboard, hang-up*.

To find any word in the dictionary, you need to know how the words in it are arranged.

Entry Words

Suppose that your class is studying South America, and in one book you read that over two thousand years ago the Indians of Peru raised cotton, beans, and gourds. What are gourds? Were they used for food? If not, why did these ancient people raise them? Your dictionary answers your questions. Here is what you find:

gourd (gôrd *or* goord), *n.* **1.** a vine with large fruit containing many seeds. Gourds belong to the same family as the squash and pumpkin. **2.** the fruit of this vine, not fit for eating but often dried and used for cups, bowls, etc.

gourds

Notice that the word **gourd** is listed first, in dark bold type that quickly catches your eye. Every word you find listed this way in the dictionary is called an "entry word" or a "main entry." All the information about it—including the word itself—is called an "entry."

Following the entry word comes the pronunciation. In this case, two common pronunciations are shown. Either one can be used. (See the section on pronunciation beginning on p. *Guide 10*.)

Two meanings come next, each numbered separately. By reading these meanings you learn how gourds are related to other common plants, and why their fruit was useful to the Indians of long ago.

The picture will help you to recognize different kinds of gourds.

The entry words are arranged in the same order as the letters in the alphabet. They may be single words or compound words, names of people or of places, abbreviations, prefixes, suffixes, etc. All of them are listed in alphabetical order, from A to Z. When all the words in a group begin with the same letter, you must look for the first letter that is different. It may be the second letter:

> abacus
> Andes
> art
> atomic bomb
> azure

or the third letter:

> backhand
> badminton
> barn dance
> bath

or the fourth letter:

> disdain
> dismal
> distance

In some words, you may have to go down to the last letter. Notice that the two-word entries, *atomic bomb* and *barn dance*, are arranged in the same order as single-word entries.

Order of All Entries

The following list shows you how the different kinds of entries are arranged. In the case of proper names such as Robert E. Lee, the last name is given first. No matter what kind of entry you are looking for, you will find it listed in alphabetical order.

-able	*a suffix*
alphabet	*a noun*
A.M.	*an abbreviation*
barbarous	*an adjective*
evening star	*a two-word compound*
Lee, Robert E.	*a proper name (person)*
Mount Vernon	*a proper name (place)*
S	*a chemical symbol*
un-	*a prefix*
will-o'-the-wisp	*a noun formed with hyphens*
willy-nilly	*an adverb formed with hyphens*
zoom	*a verb or noun*

Guide Words

There are two words printed in dark bold type at the top of each page in your dictionary. They are called "guide words." When you are looking for an entry, these guide words are helpful. Suppose you want to look up the word **daffodil**. As you search through the D's, you will come to page 180, with these guide words:

> **daddy-longlegs**   **damp**

This means that the first entry on that page is **daddy-longlegs** and the last entry is **damp.** All the other entries on this page come in alphabetical order after **daddy-longlegs** and before **damp. Daffodil** belongs here because **daf-** comes after **dad-** and before **dam-.** Which of the following words will appear on that page?

> dachshund
> **Dallas**
> damage
> dark

Words Formed From Entry Words

Sometimes the word you want to find is not listed as a main entry, in the same way that the words **gourd** and **daffodil** are. In that case, you need to do a little detective work. For example, to find the plural form **cherries,** you will have to look up the entry word **cherry.** To find the participle **smiling,** you will have to look up the entry word **smile.** To find the adverb **loudly,** you will have to look up the entry word **loud.** Such words formed from entry words are usually listed after the definitions for the entry word, as in these examples:

ad·mire (əd mīr′), v. to regard with wonder, delight, and pleased approval [The painting was *admired* by everyone.] —**ad·mired′,** *p.t. & p.p.;* **ad·mir′ing,** *pr.p.* —**ad·mir′er,** *n.* —**ad·mir′ing·ly,** *adv.*

fool·ish (fool′ish), *adj.* without good sense; silly. —**fool′ish·ly,** *adv.* —**fool′ish·ness,** *n.*

grub·by (grub′ē), *adj.* dirty or untidy. —**grub′-bi·er,** *compar.;* **grub′bi·est,** *superl.*

As a rule, you will find the following kinds of words at the end of an entry, in dark bold type of a smaller size, after the meanings:

1. Plurals of nouns
2. Comparative and superlative forms of adjectives and adverbs
3. Principal parts of verbs
4. Words formed by adding a suffix to the entry word

Plurals

Most nouns form the plural in a regular way, by adding *-s* or *-es* to the singular. For instance, the plural of *boy* is *boys* and the plural of *glass* is *glasses.* Plurals formed in this regular way need not be shown in a dictionary, unless they have a special use or meaning. In the entries for words like **bird, moon,** and **stadium,** the plural is not given, because it is formed by merely adding *-s.*

But many nouns form plurals in a way that is not regular, and for these words, the plural form (abbreviated *pl.*) is shown. For example:

sky . . . . —**skies,** *pl.*
beau . . . . —**beaus** or **beaux** (bōz), *pl.*
child . . . . —**chil′dren,** *pl.*
ver·min . . . . —*n. sing. & pl.* (This label means that the plural form is exactly the same as the singular.)

These plurals are listed at the end of the entry. In a few instances, the plural is also listed as a main entry followed by the pronunciation:

chil·dren (chil′drən), *n.* plural of **child.**
geese (gēs), *n.* plural of **goose.**

Principal Parts of Verbs

The principal parts of most verbs, such as *look,* are formed in a regular way. You add *-ed* to form the past tense (abbreviated *p.t.*). You add *-ed* to form the past participle (abbreviated *p.p.*). You add *-ing* to form the present participle (abbreviated *pr.p.*).

> look looked (*p.t.*) looked (*p.p.*)
> looking (*pr.p.*)
> walk walked (*p.t.*) walked (*p.p.*)
> walking (*pr.p.*)

Your dictionary lists **look** and **walk** as main entries. It does not show the other forms because they are regular.

Quite a few verbs, however, are not regular. One or more principal parts may be quite different from the main entry. Or a letter may be dropped from the main form or added to it before the endings are added. The principal parts for such verbs are listed at the end of the entry:

buy..........—**bought,** *p.t. & p.p.;* **buy′ing,** *pr.p.*
go...........—**went,** *p.t.;* **gone,** *p.p.;* **go′ing,** *pr.p.*
ed·u·cate...—**ed′u·cat·ed,** *p.t. & p.p.;* **ed′-u·cat·ing,** *pr.p.*
re·fer.......—**re·ferred′,** *p.t. & p.p.;* **re·fer′-ring,** *pr.p.*
build.......—**built** *or older* **build′ed,** *p.t. & p.p.;* **build′ing,** *pr.p.*

When a principal part is not the same for every meaning, that fact is also noted in the entry:

fly....**7.** to hit a fly in baseball ... —**flew,** *p.t.;* **flown,** *p.p.* (**flied** *is p.t. & p.p. for meaning 7*); **fly′ing,** *pr.p.*

A sports announcer would say, "Jones flied out to left field."

You will find these irregular principal parts at the end of the entry in dark bold type, marked to show syllables and accents. The pronunciation is shown only when it is unusual. When a principal part is quite different from the main entry, it may also be listed as a main entry, as in these instances:

bought (bôt), past tense and past participle of **buy.**
built (bilt), a past tense and past participle of **build.**
flied (flīd), a past tense and past participle of **fly,** in its meaning in baseball.
went (went), past tense of **go.**

Comparative and Superlative Forms of Adjectives and Adverbs

Many adjectives have a comparative form (abbreviated *compar.*) and a superlative form (abbreviated *superl.*). The adjective *small,* for example, has the comparative form *smaller* to describe something that is "more small." It also has the superlative form *smallest* to describe something that is "most small." When these forms are made in a regular way, by simply adding *-er* or *-est,* they need not be shown in a dictionary. A few adverbs (such as *soon*) have comparative and superlative forms, and the same rule is followed for them.

Comparative and superlative forms that are made in a way that is not regular are shown in the dictionary, at the end of the entry. Such forms are also shown if the spelling is changed when *-er* and *-est* are added. For example:

large...—**larg′er,** *compar.;* **larg′est,** *superl.*
big.....—**big′ger,** *compar.;* **big′gest,** *superl.*
ros·y...—**ros′i·er,** *compar.;* **ros′i·est,** *superl.*
lit·tle..—**lit′tler** or **less** or **less′er,** *compar. of adj.;* **lit′tlest** or **least,** *superl. of adj.* —**less,** *compar. of adv.;* **least,** *superl. of adv.*

In some instances, as with **less** and **least,** these forms are also listed as main entries.

Words Formed by Adding Suffixes

Many words are formed by adding an ending to another word. For example, *clearly* is formed from *clear; goodness* is formed from *good.* Endings like *-ly* and *-ness* are called suffixes and are usually added to a root or base. The root word for *clearly* is *clear.* Suffixes let you use the root word to form a related word that is a different part of speech.

In this dictionary, every common suffix is listed as a main entry. In the following examples, notice how adding the suffix to the root word lets you form a related word:

sad	+ -ness	= sadness
sleeve	+ -less	= sleeveless
cheer	+ -ful	= cheerful
local	+ -ize	= localize
compar(e)	+ -ative	= comparative
pit(y)	+ -ful	= pitiful

Notice in the last two examples above that the *e* in *compare* is dropped before the suffix *-ative* is added, and that the *y* in *pity* is changed to *i* before the suffix *-ful* is added.

More than one suffix can be added to a word. In the following examples, notice how *two* related words can be formed by adding a suffix and then adding another suffix to the new word. First, a suffix is added to a root word, as *-y* is added to *greed*. Then, another suffix, *-ness* is added to a word, *greedy*, that already has a suffix, after changing the *-y* to *-i*.

greed greed*y* greed*iness*
wonder wonder*ful* wonderful*ly*

Some of the words formed by adding suffixes are listed as main entries, as, for example, **hopeful**. Others, whose meanings can be easily understood, are shown at the end of an entry, as **hopefully** and **hopefulness**. Notice in the following examples that each word formed with a suffix is followed by a part-of-speech label that tells you how the word is to be used.

hope·ful (hōp′fəl), *adj.* **1.** feeling or showing hope. **2.** causing or giving hope [a *hopeful* sign]. — **hope′ful·ly**, *adv.* —**hope′ful·ness**, *n.*

in·ves·ti·gate (in ves′tə gāt), *v.* to search into so as to learn the facts; examine in detail [to *investigate* an accident]. —**in·ves′ti·gat·ed**, *p.t.* & *p.p.*; **in·ves′ti·gat·ing**, *pr.p.* —**in·ves′ti·ga′tion**, *n.* —**in·ves′ti·ga·tor**, *n.*

To find the meaning of a word formed by adding a suffix, look for the root word first. Suppose you don't know the meaning of *astonishment*. When you look for this word in the dictionary, you find it listed in the entry for **astonish**:

as·ton·ish (ə stän′ish), *v.* to surprise greatly; fill with wonder; amaze. —**as·ton′ish·ing**, *adj.* —**as·ton′ish·ing·ly**, *adv.* —**as·ton′ish·ment**, *n.*

Your next step is to find the meaning of the suffix **-ment**:

-ment (mənt), a suffix meaning: **1.** the act or result of [*Improvement* is the act or result of improving.] **2.** a means or thing for [An *adornment* is a thing for adorning.] **3.** the condition or fact of being [*Disappointment* is the condition or fact of being disappointed.]

From these two entries, you learn the meaning of *astonishment*: "the condition or fact of being greatly surprised."

Words Formed by Adding Prefixes

Prefixes are also used to form words. A prefix is a syllable or a group of syllables joined to the beginning of a word to form a related word. Some common prefixes are **bi-, in-, pre-, un-.**

In this dictionary, every common prefix is listed as a main entry. In the following examples, notice how adding the prefix to the root word lets you form a related word:

weekly	+ bi-	= biweekly
school	+ pre-	= preschool
important	+ un-	= unimportant

Some of the words formed by adding prefixes are listed as main entries. You can often find the meaning of other words formed with prefixes by adding the meaning of the prefix to the meaning of the word itself. In this way, you can understand the meaning of *nonactive* or of *antiwar*, even though they are not entries in the dictionary.

Words whose meaning is not easily understood even if you know the meaning of the root word and prefix are usually given as main entries in the dictionary. For example, **antifreeze,** formed from **anti-** and **freeze,** is a main entry.

A great many words are formed in English by using the prefix **un-,** meaning "not." A special list of these words, with their spelling, accents, and syllable divisions, appears on the page with the entry word **un-** and on a number of the following pages. "Un-" words with special meanings are given in the main alphabetical listing.

One of the best ways to improve your reading is to learn the prefixes and suffixes. Then you can tell at a glance which part is the root or base word. Often you know the meaning of the root word and can quickly arrive at the meaning of the whole word.

THE PROBLEM OF SPELLING

Finding an entry is a problem when you do not know how to spell the word you are looking up. The English language gives us many problems in spelling. The main reason that we have these problems is that we have always been slow to change the spelling of a word when we change the way we pronounce it. For instance, the word *knee* was at an earlier time pronounced with the sound of (k) at the beginning. We no longer use the (k) in pronouncing the word, but we still spell it *knee*. Some attempts have been made to simplify our spelling, as by spelling *through* as *thru*, to make it fit the way we pronounce it. But most of the problems remain.

Another reason for these spelling problems is that many letters have more than one sound. Say the sound of the letter *a* in the words *ate, cat,* and *father*. And notice that the letter *o* in *both* is not sounded like the *o* in *hot* or the *o* in *form*. The *o* in *people* or in *leopard* does not spell a sound at all. Our language is full of surprises like these. You must be prepared for them as you read and as you write.

Also, the same sound can have a number of different spellings. Say the sound of the letter *a* in the word *ape*. Now see the way the same sound is spelled in the words *aid, break, eight, say, they,* and *vein.* Or think of how you would go about finding out how to spell the word *choir* if you had only heard it spoken. You might have thought that it was spelled *kwire.* If you looked in the K section of the dictionary, you would not find such a word. Perhaps you thought of *quire,* because you know that *qu* in *quire* has the sound (kw). And you did find an entry for *quire,* but as you read the meaning, you realized that "a set of 24 or 25 sheets of paper" has nothing to do with "a group of people trained to sing together, especially as part of a church service."

By using the chart that follows you can discover how *choir* is spelled. In the group of "consonant sounds" you will find in the column of "sounds" the sound "k as in *keep*". In the column of "letters" you will find "ch". And in the column of "examples" you will find "chrome." And so on. Soon you will have discovered that *choir* is one of the surprises in English spelling. The (k) sound is spelled as *ch,* and the (wī) sound is spelled as *oi.*

Very few students know all the letters, and combinations of letters, which stand for the different sounds of the English language. The chart that follows can help you whenever you are not sure of a spelling.

CONSONANT SOUNDS

SOUNDS	LETTERS	EXAMPLES
b as in *bat*	b, bb	rub, rubber
ch as in *chin*	ch, tch, te, ti, tu	chair, catch, righteous, question, nature
d as in *do*	d, dd, ed	nod, riddle, called
f as in *fine*	f, ff, gh, ph, lf	fix, differ, laugh, phrase, calf
g as in *go*	g, gg, gh, gu	give, egg, ghost, guard
h as in *high*	h, wh	her, who
j as in *jump*	j, g, gg, d, di, dg, dj	jig, magic, exaggerate, graduate, soldier, judgment, adjust
k as in *keep*	k, lk, c, cc, ch, ck, cqu, cu, qu	kite, walk, can, account, chrome, lack, lacquer, biscuit, liquor
l as in *let*	l, ll, sl	leave, call, isle
m as in *me*	m, mm, mb, mn, lm	drum, drummer, limb, hymn, calm
n as in *no*	n, nn, gn, kn, pn	near, dinner, gnome, kneel, pneumonia
ng as in *wing*	ng, n, ngue	long, think, tongue
p as in *pat*	p, pp	copy, dipper
r as in *run*	r, rr, rh, wr	river, berry, rhyme, wrong
s as in *sew*	s, ss, sc, c, ps, sch	sit, miss, scene, cent, psychology, schism
sh as in *ship*	sh, s, ss, sch, sci, si, ssi, ce, ch, ci, ti	share, sure, issue, schwa, conscience, mansion, mission, ocean, machine, facial, nation
t as in *top*	t, th, tt, ght, ed	tear, Thomas, better, bought, walked
v as in *very*	v, lv, f	dove, salve, of
w as in *we*	w, o, u	wail, choir, quaint
y as in *you*	y, i, j	yellow, union, hallelujah
z as in *zebra*	z, zz, s, ss, x	zone, buzzer, busy, scissors, xylophone
zh as in *pleasure*	z, g, s, si, zi	azure, garage, leisure, confusion, glazier

VOWEL SOUNDS

SOUNDS	LETTERS	EXAMPLES
a as in *cat*	a, ai	lad, plaid
a as in *cake*	a, ai, au, ay, ea, ei, ey, et	lane, rain, gauge, ray, break, veil, obey, sachet
a as in *care*	a, ai, ay, e, ea, ei	dare, fair, prayer, there, wear, their
ah as in *father*	a, ea, o	far, hearth, stop
aw as in *saw*	aw, au, a, o, oa, ou	law, caught, wall, order, broad, fought
e as in *bed*	e, ea, eo, ie, a, ae, ai, ay, u	berry, heavy, leopard, friend, any, aerate, said, says, bury
e as in *we*	e, ee, ea, ei, eo, ey, i, ie, ae, oe	equal, free, lean, receive, people, key, machine, field, alumnae, phoebe
i as in *it*	i, ie, ee, o, u, ui, y	give, sieve, been, women, busy, build, hymn
i as in *kite*	i, ie, ei, ey, ai, uy, y	ice, tie, height, eye, aisle, buy, fly
o as in *go*	o, oa, oe, ou, ow, au, eau, ew	pole, boat, toe, soul, grow, mauve, beau, sew
oo as in *tool*	oo, o, oe, u, ue, ui, eu, ew, ough	moose, move, shoe, rule, blue, fruit, maneuver, threw, through
oo as in *book*	oo, o, ou, u	wood, wolf, would, pull
ow as in *now*	ow, ou, ough	crowd, out, bough
oy as in *boy*	oy, oi	toy, toil
uh as in *cuff*	u, o, oo, oe, ou	summer, son, flood, does, double
ur as in *hurt*	er, ear, ar, ir, or, our, ur, yr	germ, heard, forward, bird, worry, courage, turn, myrtle
u as in *fuse*	u, ue, ui, eau, eu, ew, iew, yu, you	use, cue, suit, beauty, feud, few, view, yule, youth
ə as in the first syllable of *asleep:* see p. Guide 11	a, e, i, o, u, and many combinations of these letters	ago, agent, sanity, confess, focus, etc.

STEPS TO REMEMBER

When you are looking for a word in the dictionary, you will save time and effort if you follow these steps:

1. Begin with the first letter of the word. Turn to the part of the dictionary containing that letter.

2. Use the guide words to find the page on which the word is listed.

3. Look first at the main entries. Use alphabetical order to find the word quickly.

4. If you find the word, but the meanings do not seem right, look at the next main entry. Sometimes two or more main entries are spelled the same way but have different meanings.

5. If you do not find the word listed as a main entry, look at the word again. Is there a word from which this word could have been formed? Look up the root word and check the words printed in dark bold type at the end of that entry.

6. Make sure you are thinking of the correct spelling. Look at the chart of English spellings on p. *Guide 7*.

WHAT DOES THE WORD MEAN?

Every main entry in the dictionary is followed by one or more meanings. For example:

out·put . . . . **1.** the amount made or done [the daily *output* of one factory worker]. **2.** the information delivered by a computer. **3.** the electric current or power delivered by an electric circuit or by an electric machine, as a generator.

Suppose that you have never seen the word *output*. You are reading an article that speaks of the *output* of a dynamo. When you look up the word *output* in the dictionary, which of the three meanings will help you understand the article?

Context: A Clue to the Right Meaning

You must find the meaning which fits into the place where you want to use it. This place—a sentence or a group of words—is called the "context" of the word. Any words coming just before and just after a particular word form the context of that word. Find the meanings of the word in the dictionary. Try out each of the meanings in the context. You will soon find the one that fits. Always check all the meanings of a word before you decide that you have chosen the right one for use in the place where you need it.

Sometimes you find that none of the meanings in an entry are right for the context of the word. Perhaps you are looking at the wrong entry. There may be another entry or entries—following this one—spelled and pronounced exactly the same but with different meanings, as in the case of *brake*.

brake (brāk), *n.* a thing used to slow down or stop a car, machine, etc. It is often a block or band that is pressed against a wheel or other moving part. —*v.* to slow down or stop with a brake. —**braked,** *p.t. & p.p.;* **brak′ing,** *pr.p.*
brake (brāk), *n.* a thick growth of bushes, tall grasses, etc.; thicket.
brake (brāk), *n.* a large, coarse fern; bracken.

Order of Meanings

Your dictionary usually gives the most common meaning first. The next meaning or two may be closely related to the first one. Other meanings, less common, may be listed next. After these, come the meanings used only in special subjects or fields, such as science, business, poetry, or sports. Next you may find a meaning that was once common but is now rare. Last of all, usually, come the meanings of the word that are heard only in everyday talk, and any meanings that are considered slang. Each meaning is given a number, to set it off from the rest, with a new series of numbers for each part of speech. Here is the dictionary entry for a word with many different meanings:

cov·er (kuv′ər), *v.* **1.** to place one thing over another; spread over [*Cover* the bird cage at night. *Cover* the wall with white paint. Water *covered* the fields.] **2.** to hide; keep from being seen [He tried to *cover* up his mistake.] **3.** to protect, as from harm or loss. **4.** to provide for; take care of [Is this case *covered* by the rules?] **5.** to have to do with; be about; include [His talk *covered* his travels in Europe.] **6.** to go; travel [The camel *covered* 65 miles that day.] **7.** to keep a gun aimed at [*Cover* him while I call the police.] **8.** to get the news or pictures of: *used by newspapermen* [He *covers* the police court.] **9.** to guard or defend: *used in sports* [*Cover* first base.] —*n.* **1.** anything that covers, as a lid, a blanket, the binding of a book, etc. **2.** anything that hides or protects [under *cover* of darkness]. —**take cover,** to seek shelter.

You will sometimes find a meaning that used to be common, but is now rare. A good example is meaning 2 for **closet**: "a small private room where one can be alone." This is followed by the note, "*no longer much used in this meaning.*"

Part–of–Speech Labels

Many words may be used in more than one way. Notice the way the word *change* is used in each of these sentences:

I must *change* my shirt.
Do you have *change* for a dollar?

In the first sentence, *change* is used as a verb, an action word. In the second sentence, it is used as a noun, a naming word. In your dictionary, the meanings for each part of speech are grouped together. The noun meanings are grouped together after *n.* (the abbreviation for noun). The verb meanings are grouped together after *v.* (the abbreviation for verb). Each group is numbered separately. Look back at the entry for **cover.** For the verb, there are nine separate meanings. For the noun, there are two.

The noun group and the verb group are separated by a long dash. Here is the list of part-of-speech labels used in your dictionary:

n.	noun
v.	verb
pron.	pronoun
adj.	adjective
adv.	adverb
prep.	preposition
conj.	conjunction
interj.	interjection

Common Idioms

You may not realize it, but you use idioms all the time.

Bob was down *in the dumps* because he didn't make the team. He had *set his heart on* it. Carl was *in the same boat.* Their only hope was that the coach might have a *change of heart* and give them one more chance to *try out.*

An idiom is "a phrase or expression that has a meaning different from what the words suggest in their usual meaning." When you read the above paragraph, you knew, of course, that Bob was not really in a place where rubbish is dumped, nor was Carl in a real boat. If you did not know the meaning of the idioms, you would have trouble understanding the paragraph.

In this dictionary, you will find a great many idioms. They are listed after the meanings of the entry word.

close (klōz), *v.* **1.** to make no longer open; shut [*Close* the door.] **2.** to fill up or stop up [to *close* a hole]. **3.** to bring or come to a finish; end [to *close* a speech]. **4.** to bring or come together [to *close* ranks]. —*n.* an end; finish. —**close down,** to shut or stop entirely. —**close in,** to draw near from different directions, cutting off escape. —**close out,** to sell goods at a low price so as to get completely rid of stock. —**close up, 1.** to draw nearer together. **2.** to shut or stop up entirely. —**closed,** *p.t. & p.p.;* **clos′- ing,** *pr.p.*

Here is an interesting fact: the idiom **how come?** is listed in the entry for **come,** not for **how.** When you are looking for an idiom, look under what seems to be the most important word. That is not always the first word in the idiom.

The four idioms listed below are fairly common. See how quickly you can find them.

> **keep house**
> **bring up**
> **go Dutch**
> **frame of mind**

Examples

Your dictionary uses many examples to show you exactly how a word is used. For instance, as in these entries:

saw . . . —*v.* **1.** to cut or form with a saw [to *saw* wood]. **2.** to move the arms through, as if sawing [He *sawed* the air as he argued.] **3.** to be sawed [This plank *saws* easily.] . . .

change (chānj), *v.* **1.** to make or become different in some way; alter [Time *changes* all things. The quiet town has *changed* into a busy city.] **2.** to put or take one thing in place of another; substitute [He has *changed* jobs twice this year.] **3.** to give or take one thing in return for another; exchange [The two boys *changed* seats. Can you *change* this dollar bill for four quarters?] **4.** to get off one train, bus, or plane and get on another [The passengers *change* at Chicago.] —*n.* **1.** the act of changing in some way [There will be a *change* in the weather tomorrow.] **2.** something put in place of something else [a fresh *change* of clothing]. **3.** the money returned when one has paid more than the amount owed [If you give the clerk a dollar for a toy that costs 70 cents, your *change* will be 30 cents.] **4.** a number of coins or bills whose total value equals a single larger coin or bill [I have *change* for your $10 bill.] **5.** small coins [The *change* jingled in his pocket.] —**changed,** *p.t. & p.p.;* **chang'ing,** *pr.p.*

The examples may be phrases or sentences. Every example is put into brackets [ ]. Notice that the word itself is printed in *italic* or *slanting* type.

HOW TO PRONOUNCE THE WORDS

If someone asked you what language you speak, you would probably answer, "English." A better answer would be "American English," for the way you speak differs somewhat from the way English people speak. You can understand them, of course, but they sound different.

People in the Midwest, in New England, and in the South all speak the English language. Yet they pronounce many words differently. These differences are not important. The dialect or speech of the educated people of one region of the country is no "better" or "more correct" than that of another region. The speech used by most people in the greater part of the United States has been called General American English but is now called the Midland dialect. This dictionary shows you how words are pronounced by educated people who speak this most common dialect. You may live in a region where certain words are pronounced differently. For instance, people who live in New England tend usually to "drop the *r*" in such words as *father*. If so, you will naturally use the same pronunciation as your parents, teachers, and most of the people in your community.

The Pronunciation Symbols

After each entry in your dictionary, you will see the same word written with special symbols and enclosed in parentheses. This tells you how the word sounds.

> **band·age** (ban'dij)
> **dem·on·stra·tion** (dem'ən strā'shən)

Say the word aloud as you look at the sound symbols. All but two of the symbols used in this dictionary are formed from letters of the alphabet. Some have special marks above them called "diacritical marks."

Here are some names you might use when referring to these marks:

long mark a, e, i, o   (ā, ē, ī, ō)
   (or macron a, e, i, o)
two-dot a   (ä)
circumflex o   (ô)
tilde u   (ũ)

Here are the names of the symbols which are not letters:

schwa   (ə)
apostrophe   (')

A list of all the symbols used in the pronunciations is called "The Pronunciation Key." Each symbol is followed by key words that show the sound of the symbol.

THE PRONUNCIATION KEY

Symbol	Key Words	Symbol	Key Words
a	fat, lap	b	bed, dub
ā	āpe, dāte	d	did, had
ä	cär, fäther	f	fall, off
e	ten, berry	g	get, dog
ē	ēven, mēet	h	he, ahead
i	hit, mirror	j	joy, jump
ī	bīte, hīre	k	kill, bake
ō	gō, tōne	l	let, ball
ô	hôrn, lông	m	met, trim
ōō	tōōl, trōōp	n	not, ton
yōō	u in cute	p	put, tap
oo	book, moor	r	red, dear
yoo	u in unite	s	sell, pass
oi	oil, point	t	top, hat
ou	out, pound	v	vat, have
u	up, cut	w	will, always
ũ	fũr, tũrn	y	yet, yard
		z	zebra, haze
ə	a in ago	ch	chin, arch
	e in agent	ng	ring, singer
	e in father	sh	she, dash
	i in sanity	th	thin, truth
	o in confess	*th*	*th*en, fa*th*er
	u in focus	zh	s in pleasure
		'	as in able (ā'b'l)

This Key also appears on the inside of the front and back covers of this dictionary.

Key Words

There is a short list of key words below the entries on each right-hand page in your dictionary. This gives you a quick way to check the sound of a certain symbol. Each key word gives you the sound of one symbol. The key word "āpe", for example, gives you the sound of the symbol (ā). The key word "hôrn" gives you the sound of the symbol (ô). The key words are arranged in the same order as the symbols in the Pronunciation Key. When you come to a new word like **Barcelona** (bär′sə lō′nə), you can quickly find the sound of ä, ə, and ō in the key words. Sometimes you may need to refer to the complete Key.

Special Symbols

The Schwa

Say in a natural way "He is about ten years old." Notice that you did not pronounce the third word (ā bout′) or (ä bout′). You used a soft "uh" sound. The symbol for this sound is called the schwa, and it looks like this (ə). When a vowel occurs in an unstressed syllable, it does not have its usual sound. The schwa stands for the neutral vowel sound in words like these:

ef·fect (ə fekt′)
fu·gi·tive (fyōō′jə tiv)
col·lect (kə lekt′)
ap·peal (ə pēl′)
cam·pus (kam′pəs)
anx·ious (angk′shəs)
fa·ther (fä′*th*ər)

The ng Symbol

The (ng) symbol stands for the sound at the end of *sing* and *wing*. In this dictionary, it is also used to show the sound of *n* when followed by *g*, as in *finger* (fing′gər) and the sound of *n* when followed by *k*, as in *drink* (dringk).

The Apostrophe

Another symbol is the apostrophe ('), which you will find only before the sounds of *l*, *m*, or *n* in an unstressed syllable. Take the word *apple*, for example. Most people go directly from the sound of *p* to the sound of *l* with almost no vowel sound in between: (ap′′l). Some people do put a vowel sound in: (ap′əl). In this dictionary, you will find only the first of these two possible pronunciations, as also in *rhythm* (rith′m) and in *cotton* (kät′′n).

Vowel Sounds Followed by r

When you speak a word, you do not say each sound separately. You blend the sounds together. When *r* follows a vowel, the sound of the vowel changes a little. (Say *cost* and *cord*.) This change is so slight, however, that we use the same symbol (ô) for the vowel sound in each word. For example:

mitt, mirror } i
bet, berry } e
calm, car } ä

Remember that the same sound may be spelled in a number of ways:

ir as in *mirror* is also heard in: here (hir), near (nir), cheer (chir)

er as in *berry* is also heard in: air (er), fair (fer), care (ker)

ũ as in *her* is also heard in: fur (fũr), fir (fũr), learn (lũrn), worm (wũrm), squirm (skwũrm)

Accents

In pronouncing most words of more than one syllable, you put a heavier accent, or stress, on one of the syllables than on the others. Say aloud the words *picture* and *above*. Did you notice how you accented the first syllable in the first word and the second syllable in the second word? In this dictionary, a dark accent mark (′) is placed after the syllable that is stressed: (pik′chər), (ə buv′).

In many words of more than two syllables, one will get a heavy stress, and another will get a lighter stress. Say the word *dictionary*. Notice that the first syllable gets the main emphasis, but the third syllable is also accented, although the stress is lighter. This lighter stress is shown by a light accent mark, as in **dic·tion·ar·y** (dik′shən er′ē).

Many words of three syllables, especially verbs such as *aggravate* and *supervise*, have the main accent, or stress, on the first syllable and a much lighter accent on the last syllable. It is not necessary in most cases to show this lighter accent for such words: (ag′rə vāt), (sōō′pər vīz).

Some words have two equally heavy stresses. This happens most often with compound words written with a hyphen. In such cases, a heavy accent mark is shown after each stressed syllable, as in **good-sized** (good′sīzd′).

When There Is More Than One Pronunciation

Many words are pronounced in different ways even by people who speak the same variety of English. For the word *either*, some people say (ē′thər) and others say (ī′thər). For *duty*, some say (dōō′tē) while others say (dyōō′tē). When two or more pronunciations are given for the same word, any one of them may be used. The fact that one is given first does not mean that it is "better" than another. It simply means that the first one seems to be used more often than the other or others.

Sometimes a word will be pronounced one way when it is used as one part of speech, and some other way when it is used as another part of speech. Read these sentences aloud:

That object is a bottle opener.
I object to your leaving now.

In the first sentence, *object* is a noun. In the second sentence, *object* is a verb. Look for the word **object** in your dictionary. You will find the pronunciation (äb′jikt) and the meanings for *object* used as a noun. In the second part of the entry, you will find the pronunciation (əb jekt′) and the meanings for *object* used as a verb.

In checking pronunciations, always read the entire entry. There may be special ways to pronounce the word when it is used as different parts of speech or when it has a special meaning.

pa·tent (pat′'nt), . . . —*adj.* **1.** protected by a patent. **2.** (pā′t'nt) easy to see or recognize; plain; evident [a *patent* lie].

GUIDES FOR WRITING, SPEAKING, AND READING

As you can see, your dictionary is very helpful as a guidebook. It guides you in:

Spelling words
Pronouncing words
Finding the meaning you need
for a word
Choosing the right word to
express your meaning
Forming words with prefixes
and suffixes

There are other ways in which your dictionary can help you in your writing, speaking, and reading.

Dividing Words Into Syllables

When you are writing sentences, you sometimes find that you cannot fit a whole word at the end of a line. You must decide where to divide the word. Where would you divide the word *elephant?*

We went to the zoo to see the elephant.

or:

We went to the zoo to see the elephant.

There is no easy rule for dividing words into syllables, but your dictionary can help you. Each entry word of more than one syllable is shown this way:

ab·bre·vi·a·tion
mean·ing·less

The small center dots separate the word into syllables. You may divide a word at any place where a dot appears. Try not to divide short words. A syllable of one or two letters on a line by itself might be hard to read.

No center dots are shown for compound entries like **double boiler,** because the syllable division has already been given in the entries for **dou·ble** and **boil·er.**

Notes for Special Uses

In this dictionary, you will find many notes about the ways in which words are used or about meanings that are special to a particular kind of work. You will find two notes of this sort in the entry for **cover,** printed on page *Guide 9: used by newspapermen,* and *used in sports.* The following sections tell about other kinds of notes.

Everyday Talk

Many of the words and expressions you hear and use at home and with friends you would not expect to hear in a serious lecture or see in most of your schoolbooks, because they would sound out of place. Take the words *lovely* and *mighty,* for example. When you say, "It was a lovely party," or "I'm mighty hungry," you are using these words in a special way—as you do in everyday talk.

love·ly (luv′lē), *adj.* **1.** very pleasing in looks or character; beautiful [a *lovely* girl]. **2.** very enjoyable: *used only in everyday talk* [We had a *lovely* time.]. . . .

might·y (mīt′ē), *adj.* **1.** very strong; powerful [a *mighty* blow]. **2.** great; very large [a *mighty* forest]. —*adv.* very; extremely: *used only in everyday talk* [*mighty* tired] . . . .

Notice that in both entries a colon (:) comes before the note. The other uses and meanings are proper in all kinds of speaking and writing.

Slang words and phrases are usually out of place in any serious speech or writing. Many slang words become popular but are in use for only a short time. Since you will need to understand or want to use today's slang at certain times, a few slang words and meanings that have been in use for a longer time are included in this dictionary. They are followed by a special note:

gim·mick (gim′ik), *n.* a clever gadget, trick, or idea: *a slang word.*

chow (chou), *n.* **1.** a dog that was first bred in China, with a thick, brown or black coat and a black tongue. **2.** food: *slang in this meaning.*

Words Used Only in Some Regions

Just as there are differences in pronunciations between one region and another, there are differences in the words that are used in speaking of the same thing. As you travel around this country, you will hear *lug* and *tote*, as well as *carry*. You will hear *skillet* and *spider*, as well as *frying pan*. Do you know what a *critter* is? Or a *poke* of candy? Often such words are entered in this dictionary with a special note:

crit·ter or **crit·tur** (krit′ər), *n.* a creature: *used in some regions.*

poke (pōk) *n.* a sack; bag: *now used only in some regions.*

These words are perfectly "correct" in the parts of the country where they are commonly used. The notes in the dictionary simply remind you that such dialect words may not be understood by people in other regions.

If you travel to other countries where English is spoken, you will also hear and read words not commonly used in the United States. In England, for example, you hear *lift* for *elevator* and *lorry* for *truck*. Some of the words that are used mainly in Great Britain are also used in Canada. The following entries will show you some of these special notes.

mi·ka·do or **Mi·ka·do** (mi kä′dō), *n.* a title for the emperor of Japan, used by foreigners but not the Japanese. —**mi·ka′dos**, *pl.*

cheque (chek), *n.* a bank check: *this spelling is mainly British.*

gaol (jāl), *n.* a jail: *a British spelling.* —**gaol′er**, *n.*

draughts (drafts), *n.pl.* the game of checkers: *the British name.*

ken (ken), *n.* knowledge or understanding [Nuclear physics is beyond his *ken.*] —*v.* to know: *used mainly in Scotland.* —**kenned**, *p.t. & p.p.*; **ken′ning**, *pr.p.*

trek (trek), *v.* **1.** to travel slowly or with difficulty. **2.** to travel by ox wagon: *an old meaning in South Africa.* —*n.* a long, slow journey. —**trekked**, *p.t. & p.p.*; **trek′king**, *pr.p.*

Words No Longer in General Use

Your language is constantly changing as new words are created and some of the old words go out of use. You can see this change by comparing the language of today with the language of the Bible, as in the King James Version (1611), or of poems and stories written long ago. Many of the older words that you may need to know are listed in this dictionary, followed by a special note.

mayst (māst), an older form of **may,** used with *thou,* as in the Bible.

meet (mēt), *adj.* fitting or proper: *no longer much used.*

or·i·son (ôr′i z′n), *n.* a prayer: *now seldom used except in poetry.*

thou (*th*ou), *pron.* an older form of **you,** used as the subject of a verb: *now used only in poetry, prayers, etc.*

Notes of Special Interest

Sometimes the plural of a word has its own special meaning. In the entry for **bearing,** the fourth meaning of the word is followed by a note showing the plural and an example of the word in use in this meaning. In **arms,** the plural is listed as a main entry, followed by three meanings and three idioms.

bear·ing (ber′ing), *n.* . . . . **4.** direction or position in relation to something else: *usually used in the plural,* **bearings** [The ship lost her *bearings* in the fog.] . . . .

arms (ärmz), *n.pl.* **1.** weapons; tools used for fighting. **2.** fighting; warfare. **3.** pictures of animals, designs, etc. put on a shield or flag as the sign of a noble family, a country, etc.: see **coat of arms.** —**bear arms,** to serve as a soldier, sailor, etc. —**take up arms,** to go to war or join a rebellion. —**up in arms,** angry and ready to fight.

Sometimes a word has a different meaning when the first letter is written or printed as a capital. The capitalized form is then shown in the entry, in dark bold type, along with its own special meaning.

west (west), *n.* **1.** the direction toward the point where the sun sets. **2.** a place or region in or toward this direction. In the United States, **the West** usually means the part west of the Mississippi River. **3. West,** the Western Hemisphere. . . .

Sometimes a word or phrase appears within the entry for a related word, set off in dark bold type, as **bay leaf** below.

bay (bā), *n.* an evergreen tree with tough, shiny leaves; laurel tree. The sweet-smelling leaf (**bay leaf**) is dried and used for flavor in cooking.

cof·fee (kôf′ē), *n.* **1.** a dark-brown drink made by brewing the roasted and ground seeds of a tropical plant in boiling water. **2.** these seeds (also called **coffee beans**) or the plant on which they grow.

Rather than repeat information given elsewhere in the dictionary, the editors will occasionally suggest that you turn to another entry, sometimes for the meaning of a word, sometimes for additional facts. The directions "see," "see also," or "same as" mean that you should "turn to" the other entry for the meaning that will help you. For example:

Scotch (skäch), *adj.* Scottish. —*n.* the English spoken in Scotland. See **Scottish.**

shall (shal), *a helping verb used with other verbs in speaking of the future* [I *shall* leave tomorrow. *Shall* we eat?] See the note following **will.** See also **should.**

en·quire (in kwīr′), *v.* same as **inquire.** —**en·quired′,** *p.t. & p.p.;* **en·quir′ing,** *pr.p.*

The History of Words

English words were not all invented on one certain day when people decided to "speak English." The words we use have developed over a period of thousands of years. Most of them come from languages that existed long before the time

that English began to be thought of as a separate language. Our words have come from many sources. A large number of our words were borrowed from Latin and Greek and from earlier forms of French and German. *Circus* was once a Latin word. *Theater* comes from French, where it is a word borrowed from ancient Greek. Some sources of English are more surprising. *Algebra,* for example, comes from an Arabic word. A dictionary planned for the use of college students shows the history of each entry in a special note, called an "etymology." Such etymologies often will show how a word has changed in meaning or how it has developed a new meaning.

For a number of entries in this dictionary, the editors have included interesting or helpful notes based on the etymology of the word. And often the definition itself, as for **T-bar** or **T square,** will tell you how the word got its name. The history of a word may help you to understand its use today. For example:

century plant, a desert plant that is a kind of agave. It gets its name from the mistaken belief that it blooms only once a century.

tre·men·dous (tri men′dəs), *adj.* **1.** very large or great; enormous: the earlier meaning was "so great or dreadful as to make one tremble." **2.** wonderful, very fine, etc.: *used only in everyday talk.* —**tre·men′dous·ly,** *adv.*

On the following two pages you will find a column of words from the C section of the dictionary and a column from the I section. Along the side of each column are words and phrases that you have learned in reading this *Guide to Using the Dictionary.* These words and phrases, with lines running from them, point to the many different kinds of information you can find in your dictionary. Studying these two pages will help you review most of what you have learned in reading the *Guide.*

GUIDE WORD ──────────── co·operative

PRONUNCIATION ──── **co·op·er·a·tive** (kō äp′ər ā′tiv *or* kō äp′rə tiv), *adj.* **1.** willing to co-operate; helpful. **2.** that is or belongs to a group whose members produce goods together or sell them and share the profits [The farmers of this area started a *co-operative* store.] —*n.* such a group, store, etc. Also written VARIANT SPELLING ──── **cooperative.**

co·or·di·nate (kō ôr′də nit), *adj.* of equal importance. —*v.* (kō ôr′də nāt), to bring together in the proper relation; make work together well [By *co-ordinating* our efforts, we moved the piano.] Also written **coordinate.** —**co·or′·di·nat·ed,** *p.t. & p.p.;* **co·or′di·nat·ing,** *pr.p.*

HYPHENATED WORD ──── **co·or·di·na·tion** (kō ôr′də nā′shən), *n.* a being co-ordinated, or working together smoothly [*Co-ordination* of both hands is important in playing the piano.] Also written **coordination.**

coot (kōōt), *n.* a water bird with webbed feet, that swims and dives like a duck.

coot (16 in. long)

A SLANG WORD ──── **cop** (käp), *n.* a policeman: *a slang word.*

cope (kōp), *v.* to be able to manage in a struggle; take care of successfully [She was able to *cope* with the unruly children.] PRINCIPAL PARTS of a verb ──── —**coped,** *p.t. & p.p.;* **cop′ing,** *pr.p.*

A PROPER NAME (place) ──── **Co·pen·ha·gen** (kō′pən hā′gən), *n.* a seaport and the capital of Denmark.

A PROPER NAME (person) ──── **Co·per·ni·cus, Nic·o·la·us** (nik′ə lā′əs kō·pūr′ni kəs), 1473–1543; Polish astronomer, who taught that the planets move around the sun.

co·pi·lot (kō′pī lət), *n.* the assistant pilot of an aircraft.

cop·ing (kōp′ing), *n.* the sloping top layer of a stone or brick wall.

coping saw, a saw with a narrow blade for cutting curves in wood.

co·pi·ous (kō′pi əs), *adj.* more than enough; plentiful [*copious* praise]. —**co′·pi·ous·ly,** *adv.*

ILLUSTRATION showing use ────

coping saw

cop·per (käp′ər), *n.* **1.** a reddish-brown metal that is a chemical element. Copper is easily beaten or stretched into various shapes, and it is a good conductor of heat and electricity. **2.** something made of copper or of a copper alloy, as a penny. **3.** reddish brown.

cop·per·head (käp′ər hed), *n.* a poisonous snake of North America, that has a copper-colored head.

cop·pice (käp′is), *n.* CROSS REFERENCE ──── same as **copse.**

cop·ra (käp′rə), *n.* dried coconut meat.

copse (käps), *n.* a number of small trees and shrubs growing thickly; thicket.

ILLUSTRATION showing size ────

copperhead (2 ft. long)

SPELLING AND————
SYLLABIFICATION

im·pugn (im pyōōn′), *v.* to doubt or question [Do you *impugn* my sincerity?]

im·pulse (im′puls), *n.* **1.** a sudden feeling that makes one want to do something [She had an *impulse* to scream.] **2.** the force that starts some action; push or thrust [The *impulse* of the propeller drives the ship through the water.]

im·pul·sion (im pul′shən), *n.* an impulse.

im·pul·sive (im pul′siv), *adj.* **1.** acting or likely to act suddenly and without thinking [The *impulsive* child dashed into the street.] **2.** done or made on a sudden impulse [an *impulsive* state-

WORD FORMED BY————
ADDING A SUFFIX

ment]. **—im·pul′sive·ly, adv.**

im·pu·ni·ty (im pyōō′nə tē), *n.* freedom from the danger of being punished or harmed [You can't ignore the rules of health with *impunity*.]

EXAMPLES OF THE WORD IN USE————
in various meanings

im·pure (im pyoor′), *adj.* **1.** not clean; dirty [Smoke made the air *impure*.] **2.** mixed with things that do not belong [*impure* gold]. **3.** not decent or proper [*impure* thoughts].

im·pur·i·ty (im pyoor′ə tē), *n.* **1.** the condition of being impure. **2.** something mixed in that makes another thing impure [Strain the oil to

PLURAL OF NOUN————

remove *impurities*.] **—im·pu′ri·ties, pl.**

im·pute (im pyōōt′), *v.* to consider to be guilty of; blame; charge [to *impute* a crime to someone].

PRINCIPAL PARTS of a verb————
WORD FORMED FROM AN ENTRY WORD————

—im·put′ed, p.t. & p.p.; im·put′ing, pr.p.

—im·pu·ta·tion (im′pyoo tā′shən), *n.*

in (in), *prep.* **1.** contained by, covered by, or surrounded by [to live *in* town; to dress *in* furs; caught *in* a storm]. **2.** during or after [to do *in* a second; to leave *in* an hour]. **3.** not beyond [still *in* sight]. **4.** having or showing [*in* trouble; *in* tears]. **5.** having to do with; with regard to [*in* business; *in* my opinion; the best *in* the

EXAMPLES OF THE WORD IN USE————
as various parts of speech

school]. **6.** by means of; using [written *in* ink]. **7.** because of [to shout *in* anger]. **8.** into [Go *in* the house.] **—adv. 1.** inside or toward the inside [He walked *in* slowly.] **2.** within a certain place [Keep the cat *in*.] **—adj. 1.** that has power or control [the *in* group]. **2.** that is inside or leads inside [Use the *in* door.] **—n. 1.** *usually*

NOTE FOR USE OF THE PLURAL————
NOTE FOR SPECIAL USE OF A MEANING————

ins, *pl.* those who are in power or in office. **2.** a way to get special favor: *used only in everyday talk* [Do you have an *in* with him?] **—in for,** certain to have [He's *in for* a big surprise.] **—ins**

COMMON IDIOMS————

and outs, all the parts or details. **—in that,** for this reason; because. **—in with,** being friends or partners with.

PREFIXES————

in-, a prefix meaning "in," "into," "within," "on," or "toward": it is usually seen in words coming from Latin, such as *induct* and *infer*.

in-, a prefix meaning "not" [*Incorrect* means not correct.]

ABBREVIATION————

in., abbreviation for **inch** or **inches.**

WORDS FORMED BY————

in·a·bil·i·ty (in′ə bil′ə tē), *n.* the condition of being unable; lack of ability or power.

ADDING A PREFIX

in·ac·ces·si·ble (in′ak ses′ə b'l), *adj.* impossible or hard to reach or get to [Their cottage is *inaccessible* except by boat.] **—in′ac·ces′-si·bil′i·ty, n.**

KEY WORDS FOR PRONUNCIATION

fat, ape, cär, ten, ēven, hit, bīte, gō, hôrn, tōōl, book up, fûr;
get, joy, yet, chin, she, thin, *th*en; zh = s in pleasure; ′ as in able (ā′b'l);
ə = a in ago, e in agent, i in sanity, o in confess, u in focus.

A

A, a (ā), *n.* the first letter of the English alphabet. —**A's, a's** (āz), *pl.*

A (ā), *n.* **1.** the highest grade, meaning "excellent" or "best." **2.** the symbol for the chemical element *argon.*

a (ə *or* ā), *adj.* **1.** one; one sort of [Mother baked *a* cake.] **2.** each; any one [A dog that bites should be tied up.] *A* is also called an *indefinite article.* See also **the. 3.** in or for each [It costs ten cents *a* box.] See also **an.**

Aar·on (er′ən), *n.* in the Bible, the older brother of Moses. He was first high priest of the ancient Jews.

A.B., Bachelor of Arts: also **B.A.**

a·back (ə bak′), *adv.* backward; back: *now seldom used.* —**taken aback,** surprised and confused [She was *taken aback* by my angry answer.]

ab·a·cus (ab′ə kəs), *n.* a frame with groups of beads sliding back and forth on wires. The abacus is used in a system of doing arithmetic quickly without writing. —**ab′a·cus·es** or **ab·a·ci** (ab′ə sī), *pl.*

a·baft (ə baft′), *adv.* at or toward the stern or rear of a ship. —*prep.* behind; back of: *a sailor's word.*

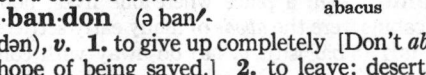

abacus

a·ban·don (ə ban′dən), *v.* **1.** to give up completely [Don't *abandon* hope of being saved.] **2.** to leave; desert [The crew *abandoned* the burning ship.] —*n.* uncontrolled freedom of actions or emotions [She danced with wild *abandon.*] —**a·ban′don·ment,** *n.*

a·ban·doned (ə ban′dənd), *adj.* **1.** forsaken; deserted [an *abandoned* shack]. **2.** shamefully wicked [He led an *abandoned* life.]

a·base (ə bās′), *v.* to make lower in position or more humble [The king's subjects *abased* themselves before him.] —**a·based′,** *p.t. & p.p.;* **a·bas′ing,** *pr.p.* —**a·base′ment,** *n.*

a·bash (ə bash′), *v.* to embarrass or make ill at ease; make self-conscious [She was *abashed* by his kindness after she had insulted him.]

a·bate (ə bāt′), *v.* to make or become less or weaker; diminish; decrease [The hurricane winds *abated.*] —**a·bat′ed,** *p.t. & p.p.;* **a·bat′ing,** *pr.p.* —**a·bate′ment,** *n.*

ab·bé (ab′ā), *n.* a title of respect used in France for a priest or other clergyman.

ab·bess (ab′is), *n.* a woman who is head of an abbey of nuns.

ab·bey (ab′ē), *n.* **1.** a monastery headed by an abbot or a nunnery headed by an abbess. **2.** a building, especially a church, belonging to an abbey.

ab·bot (ab′ət), *n.* a man who is head of an abbey of monks.

ab·bre·vi·ate (ə brē′vi āt), *v.* to make shorter by cutting out part [*Abbreviate* your speech. *Abbreviate* "street" to "st."] —**ab·bre′vi·at·ed,** *p.t. & p.p.;* **ab·bre′vi·at·ing,** *pr.p.*

ab·bre·vi·a·tion (ə brē′vi ā′shən), *n.* **1.** a making or becoming shorter. **2.** a shortened form of a word or phrase, as *N.Y.* for *New York, U.S.A.* for *United States of America, in.* for *inch.*

ABC (ā′bē′sē′), *n.* **1.** the alphabet: *usually in plural,* **ABC's. 2.** the simplest facts of a subject, or the first, basic steps of some activity [His father taught him the *ABC's* of baseball.]

ab·di·cate (ab′də kāt), *v.* to give up some high position or power; especially, to resign as king. —**ab′di·cat·ed,** *p.t. & p.p.;* **ab′di·cat·ing,** *pr.p.* —**ab′di·ca′tion,** *n.*

---

fat,　āpe,　cär,　ten,　ēven,　hit,　bīte,　gō,　hôrn,　tōol,　book,　up,　fûr;
get,　joy,　yet,　chin,　she,　thin,　*then;*　zh = s in pleasure;　′ as in able (ā′b'l);
ə = a in ago,　e in agent,　i in sanity,　o in confess,　u in focus.

ab·do·men (ab′də mən *or* ab dō′mən), *n.* **1.** the part of the body between the chest and pelvis; belly. It contains the stomach, intestines, liver, etc. **2.** the part of an insect's body furthest back.

abdomen

ab·dom·i·nal (ab däm′ə n'l), *adj.* of, in, or for the abdomen [*Abdominal* pains may be caused by eating too much.]

ab·duct (ab dukt′), *v.* to carry a person away unlawfully and by force; kidnap [Bold Lochinvar *abducted* his sweetheart just before she was to marry another.] —**ab·duc′tion,** *n.* —**ab·duc′tor,** *n.*

a·bed (ə bed′), *adv.* in bed; on a bed: *now seldom used.*

A·bel (ā′b'l), *n.* in the Bible, the second son of Adam and Eve, killed by his brother, Cain.

Ab·er·deen (ab ər dēn′), *n.* a city in eastern Scotland, on the North Sea.

ab·er·ra·tion (ab′ər ā′shən), *n.* **1.** a turning away from what is right, true, etc. [Stealing is an *aberration* in conduct.] **2.** an abnormal or unusual act or condition [*Aberrations* of the mind are sometimes called insanity.] **3.** the failure of light rays from one point to meet at a single focus. A faulty lens or mirror causes aberration and results in a blurred image.

aberration

a·bet (ə bet′), *v.* to urge on, approve, or help, especially in something wrong [He was guilty of aiding and *abetting* the young thief.] —**a·bet′ted,** *p.t. & p.p.;* **a·bet′ting,** *pr.p.*

a·bey·ance (ə bā′əns), *n.* a stopping for a while, as during some activity [Hold the game in *abeyance* until we check the rules.]

ab·hor (ab hôr′), *v.* to feel great fear, disgust, or hatred for [He *abhors* fighting.]—**ab·horred′,** *p.t. & p.p.;* **ab·hor′ring,** *pr.p.*

ab·hor·rence (ab hôr′əns), *n.* **1.** a hating [I can't hide my *abhorrence* for her.] **2.** something feared, hated, or considered disgusting [His behavior is an *abhorrence* to all of us.]

ab·hor·rent (ab hôr′ənt), *adj.* causing fear, disgust, hatred, etc. [His cruelty is *abhorrent*.]

a·bide (ə bīd′), *v.* **1.** to remain; go on being; stay; dwell: *now seldom used except in poetry, the Bible, etc.* [*Abide* with me. They will all *abide* in peace.] **2.** to await [We shall *abide* your return.] **3.** to put up with; bear; stand [Some people cannot *abide* loud noises.] —**abide by, 1.** to remain true to a promise, etc. [You must *abide by* our agreement.] **2.** to give in to and carry out [I shall *abide by* the decision.] —**a·bode′** or **a·bid′ed,** *p.t. & p.p.;* **a·bid′ing,** *pr.p.*

a·bid·ing (ə bīd′ing), *adj.* lasting without change [*abiding* faith in the goodness of man.]

a·bil·i·ty (ə bil′ə tē), *n.* **1.** a being able; power to do something [Does he have the *ability* to pay?] **2.** a natural skill or talent [Mozart showed a special *ability* for music at a very early age.] —**a·bil′i·ties,** *pl.*

ab·ject (ab jekt′ *or* ab′jekt), *adj.* **1.** causing unhappiness; wretched [*abject* misery]. **2.** low in spirit and self-respect; mean; deserving to be scorned [an *abject* coward]. —**ab·ject′ly,** *adv.*

ab·jure (ab joor′), *v.* to swear publicly that one will give up certain rights, opinions, etc. [Galileo was forced to *abjure* his ideas about astronomy.] —**ab·jured′,** *p.t. & p.p.;* **ab·jur′ing,** *pr.p.* —**ab·ju·ra·tion** (ab′joo rā′shən), *n.*

a·blaze (ə blāz′), *adj.* **1.** burning with flames [The barn was *ablaze*.] **2.** shining brightly; brilliant [The courtyard was *ablaze* in the noonday sun.] **3.** very excited or eager [He was *ablaze* with anger.]

a·ble (ā′b'l), *adj.* **1.** having the means or power to do something [He is *able* to take care of himself.] **2.** having the necessary skill or talent [an *able* mechanic]. —**a′bler,** *compar.;* **a′blest,** *superl.*

-a·ble (ə b'l), a suffix meaning: **1.** that can be [A *drinkable* liquid is one that can be drunk.] **2.** tending to [*Perishable* goods tend to perish.]

a·ble-bod·ied (ā′b'l bäd′id), *adj.* healthy and strong.

able-bodied seaman, a trained, skillful sailor: *now often* **able seaman.**

ab·lu·tion (ab loō′shən), *n.* a washing of the body, especially as part of a religious ceremony.

a·bly (ā′blē), *adv.* in an able manner; skillfully,

ab·ne·ga·tion (ab′ni gā′shən), *n.* a giving up of rights, claims, wishes, etc. [A hermit lives a life of *abnegation*.]

ab·nor·mal (ab nôr′məl), *adj.* not normal; not regular or average; not usual or typical [Snow in July is *abnormal* here.] —**ab·nor′mal·ly,** *adv.*

ab·nor·mal·i·ty (ab′nôr mal′ə tē), *n.* **1.** the condition of being abnormal. **2.** an abnormal thing or part [A sixth finger on the hand is an *abnormality*.] —**ab′nor·mal′i·ties,** *pl.*

a·board (ə bôrd′), *adv.* on, in, or into a ship, airplane, etc. —*prep.* on; in [They are *aboard* the airplane.]

a·bode (ə bōd′), a past tense and past participle of **abide.** —*n.* a place where one lives; home [Log cabins were the *abode* of many early settlers.]

a·bol·ish (ə bäl′ish), *v.* to do away with completely; get rid of [Congress may *abolish* a law.]

ab·o·li·tion (ab′ə lish′ən), *n.* an abolishing or being abolished [the *abolition* of slavery.]

ab·o·li·tion·ist or **Ab·o·li·tion·ist** (ab′ə lish′ən ist), *n.* a person who wanted to abolish or put an end to Negro slavery in the United States.

A-bomb (ā′bäm′), *n.* an atomic bomb.

a·bom·i·na·ble (ə bäm′ə nə b'l), *adj.* **1.** nasty and disgusting; hateful [an *abominable* crime.]

2. very unpleasant; disagreeable [He finds this music *abominable*.] **—a·bom′i·na·bly,** *adv.*

a·bom·i·na·tion (ə bäm′ə nā′shən), *n.* **1.** hatred and disgust for a thing or person. **2.** anything hateful and disgusting ["Lying lips are an *abomination* to the Lord."]

ab·o·rig·i·nal (ab′ə rij′ə n′l), *adj.* of, like, or being aborigines.

ab·o·rig·i·nes (ab′ə rij′ə nēz′), *n.pl.* the first persons who ever lived in a certain area or place; natives [The Indians were the *aborigines* of the United States.] **—ab′o·rig′i·ne′,** *sing.*

a·bort (ə bôrt′), *v.* **1.** to stop an action or operation that is already in progress [The flight of the missile was *aborted* when it began to veer off course.] **2.** to have a miscarriage.

a·bor·tion (ə bôr′shən), *n.* the birth of an offspring before it is developed enough.

a·bor·tive (ə bôr′tiv), *adj.* **1.** born before it is developed enough to live. **2.** failing to succeed; fruitless [an *abortive* plan.]

a·bound (ə bound′), *v.* **1.** to exist in large numbers or amounts [Tropical plants *abound* in the jungle.] **2.** to have plenty; be filled [These woods *abound* with birds.]

a·bout (ə bout′), *adv.* **1.** on every side; all around [Look *about*.] **2.** here and there; in all directions [Birds fly *about*.] **3.** near [It is somewhere *about*.] **4.** in or to the opposite direction; around [Turn yourself *about*.] **5.** nearly; more or less [*about* forty years old]. **6.** almost: *used only in everyday talk* [I'm just *about* ready.] **—adj.** **1.** active; awake or recovered [He is up and *about* again.] **2.** existing in the area [There is much illness *about*.] **—prep.** **1.** around; on all sides of [The waves rose *about* the boat.] **2.** here and there in; everywhere in [Stop running *about* the house.] **3.** near to [He was born *about* 1920.] **4.** with [He has his brains *about* him.] **5.** taking care of [Go *about* your business.] **6.** almost ready [I am *about* to cry.] **7.** having to do with; in regard to [This book is *about* ships.]

a·bout-face (ə bout′fās′), *n.* **1.** a turning or facing in the opposite direction. **2.** a change to the opposite opinion or attitude. **—v.** (ə bout′-fās′), to turn or face in the opposite direction.

a·bove (ə buv′), *adv.* **1.** in or at a higher place; up [See the birds flying *above*.] **2.** before or earlier in a book or paragraph [This is my goal, as I have stated *above*.] **—prep.** **1.** higher than; over [We flew *above* the clouds.] **2.** beyond; past [the road *above* the town]. **3.** better than [*above* the average]. **4.** more than [It cost *above* five dollars.] **—adj.** placed, found, or mentioned above or earlier [The *above* facts are correct.] **—above all,** most of all; mainly.

a·bove·board (ə buv′bôrd′), *adv. & adj.* hiding nothing; open and honest; straightforward.

ab·ra·ca·dab·ra (ab′rə kə dab′rə), *n.* **1.** a word supposed to have magic powers, used in casting spells. **2.** foolish or meaningless talk.

A·bra·ham (ā′brə ham), *n.* in the Bible, the first patriarch and ancestor of the Jews.

ab·ra·sion (ə brā′zhən), *n.* **1.** a scraping off of skin. **2.** a wearing away by rubbing or scraping [the *abrasion* of rock by wind and water]. **3.** a place where the surface has been scraped off.

ab·ra·sive (ə brā′siv), *adj.* causing abrasion; scraping or rubbing. **—n.** something that grinds, scrapes, polishes, etc., as a rubbing powder.

a·breast (ə brest′), *adv. & adj.* side by side, as in moving forward. **—abreast of** or **abreast with,** in line with; not behind.

a·bridge (ə brij′), *v.* **1.** to make shorter, smaller, or fewer; especially, to shorten a talk, book, etc. by using fewer words. **2.** to take away [Congress shall make no law *abridging* the freedom of speech.] **—a·bridged′,** *p.t. & p.p.;* **a·bridg′-ing,** *pr.p.*

a·bridg·ment or **a·bridge·ment** (ə brij′-mənt), *n.* **1.** the act of abridging. **2.** a shortened form or version [an *abridgment* of a novel].

a·broad (ə brôd′), *adv.* **1.** generally known or rumored [A report is *abroad* that the king is ill.] **2.** out-of-doors [Couples strolled *abroad* in the park.] **3.** outside one's own country [He will go *abroad* to Europe this winter.] **—from abroad,** from a foreign land or lands.

ab·ro·gate (ab′rə gāt), *v.* to put an end to; repeal; cancel [to *abrogate* a law]. **—ab′ro·gat·ed,** *p.t. & p.p.;* **ab′ro·gat·ing,** *pr.p.*

a·brupt (ə brupt′), *adj.* **1.** coming or happening suddenly, without warning [He made an *abrupt* stop.] **2.** speaking or spoken bluntly or gruffly [He answered with an *abrupt* "no!"] **3.** very steep [an *abrupt* cliff]. **—a·brupt′ly,** *adv.*

ab·scess (ab′ses), *n.* an inflamed place in the body in which pus gathers, causing a swelling.

ab·scessed (ab′sest), *adj.* having an abscess.

ab·scond (ab skänd′), *v.* to run away and hide, especially in order to escape the law.

ab·sence (ab′s'ns), *n.* **1.** the fact of being absent [During the *absence* of the president, the vice-president will preside.] **2.** the fact of being without; lack [In the *absence* of proof, a man cannot be held guilty.]

ab·sent (ab′s'nt), *adj.* **1.** not present; away [He was *absent* from school for a week.] **2.** not existing; lacking [If calcium is *absent* from your diet, your bones will become soft.] **3.** not paying attention or not listening [an *absent* manner]. **—v.** (ab sent′), to take or keep oneself away [He *absents* himself from classes.]

ab·sen·tee (ab s'n tē′), *n.* a person who is absent, as from home, school, work, etc.

ab·sent·ly (ab′s'nt lē), *adv.* in an absent manner; not paying attention.

ab·sent-mind·ed (ab′s'nt mīn′did), *adj.* **1.** thinking or dreaming of something else and not paying attention. **2.** having a poor memory.

ab·so·lute (ab′sə lōōt), *adj.* **1.** perfect; complete; whole [I demand *absolute* silence.] **2.** not

fat, āpe, cär, ten, ēven, hit, bīte, gō, hôrn, tōōl, book, up, fûr;
get, joy, yet, chin, she, thin, *then;* zh = s in pleasure; ′ as in able (ā′b'l).
ə = a in ago, e in agent, i in sanity, o in confess, u in focus.

mixed; pure [*absolute* alcohol]. **3.** not limited; without any restrictions [Dictators are *absolute* rulers.] **4.** positive; definite [It's an *absolute* certainty that he will pass.] **5.** actual; real [an *absolute* truth]. **—ab'so·lute'ly,** *adv.*

absolute zero, the supposed temperature at which a substance would have no movement of its molecules and no heat. On the Fahrenheit scale, absolute zero is about 460° below zero.

ab·so·lu·tion (ab'sə lōō'shən), *n.* a freeing from guilt or from punishment for sin [The priest gave her *absolution* after she had confessed and repented her sin.]

ab·solve (ab solv'), *v.* **1.** to free a person from guilt or blame or from punishment for sin [I was *absolved* of the crime. The priest *absolved* the sinner.] **2.** to free from a promise or duty. **—ab·solved',** *p.t. & p.p.;* **ab·solv'ing,** *pr.p.*

ab·sorb (əb sôrb' *or* ab zôrb'), *v.* **1.** to suck up [A sponge *absorbs* water.] **2.** to take in and make part of itself [The city *absorbed* that small town.] **3.** to take up the full attention of [He was so *absorbed* in his work that he forgot to eat.] **4.** to take in and not reflect or throw back [The black wall *absorbs* light. The rubber mat *absorbed* the shock of his fall.]

ab·sorb·ent (əb sôrb'ənt *or* ab zôrb'ənt), *adj.* able to absorb moisture, light, etc. [an *absorbent* cloth].

ab·sorb·ing (əb sôrb'ing *or* ab zôrb'ing), *adj.* very interesting ["The Three Musketeers" is an *absorbing* tale of adventure.]

ab·sorp·tion (əb sôrp'shən *or* ab zôrp'shən), *n.* **1.** an absorbing or being absorbed [The walls are insulated to prevent the *absorption* of heat.] **2.** great interest or full attention [His *absorption* in the book made him late.]

ab·stain (ab stān'), *v.* to do without willingly; hold oneself back [He *abstains* from meat on Friday.]

ab·ste·mi·ous (ab stē'mi əs), *adj.* eating, drinking, etc. sparingly; moderate [Monks lead an *abstemious* life.]

ab·sten·tion (ab sten'shən), *n.* an abstaining; a holding back [An *abstention* in voting is a refusal to vote either "yes" or "no."]

ab·sti·nence (ab'stə nəns), *n.* doing without some or all food, drink, or other pleasures willingly [*Abstinence* alone sometimes means *abstinence* from alcoholic liquor.]

ab·stract (ab'strakt *or* ab strakt'), *adj.* **1.** thought of apart from any particular instance [an *abstract* idea of justice]. **2.** expressing a quality thought of apart from any real thing having this quality ["Beauty" is an *abstract* word.] **3.** hard to understand [His explanation is too *abstract*.] **4.** having a design or form that is not actually like any real object or being [an *abstract* painting]. **—n.** (ab'strakt), a brief report of an article, record, etc.

abstract picture

—v. (ab strakt'), to make a brief report of; summarize [He *abstracted* the main facts of the story.]

ab·stract·ed (ab strak'tid), *adj.* lost in thought; absent-minded.

ab·strac·tion (ab strak'shən), *n.* **1.** an abstract idea, quality, word, etc. **2.** an abstract picture or piece of sculpture. **3.** the condition of being lost in thought; absent-mindedness.

ab·struse (ab strōōs'), *adj.* hard to understand [Dictionary definitions should not be *abstruse*.]

ab·surd (əb surd' *or* ab zurd'), *adj.* so clearly untrue or unreasonable as to be laughable or ridiculous [It is *absurd* to eat peas with a knife.] **—ab·surd'ly,** *adv.*

ab·surd·i·ty (əb sur'də tē *or* ab zur'də tē), *n.* the condition of being absurd; foolishness; nonsense. **—ab·surd'i·ties,** *pl.*

a·bun·dance (ə bun'dəns), *n.* a great supply; an amount more than enough [Where there is an *abundance* of goods, prices go down.]

a·bun·dant (ə bun'dənt), *adj.* **1.** very plentiful; more than enough [We have an *abundant* supply of meat for the winter.] **2.** rich; well-supplied [a lake *abundant* in fish.]

a·buse (ə byōōz'), *v.* **1.** to use in a wrong or improper way [Don't *abuse* the privilege of recess.] **2.** to hurt by treating badly; mistreat [He thought the lion tamer *abused* the caged beasts.] **3.** to scold or speak harshly about or to. **—n.** (ə byōōs'), **1.** wrong, bad, or unjust use or practice [We object to any *abuse* of voting rights.] **2.** unkind, cruel, or unfair treatment. **3.** insulting or harshly scolding language. **—a·bused',** *p.t. & p.p.;* **a·bus'ing,** *pr.p.*

a·bu·sive (ə byōō'siv), *adj.* **1.** abusing; mistreating. **2.** harshly scolding; insulting.

a·but (ə but'), *v.* to touch at one end; border [Our north pasture *abuts* on their farm.] **—a·but'-ted,** *p.t. & p.p.;* **a·but'ting,** *pr.p.*

a·but·ment (ə but'mənt), *n.* something that abuts or borders upon something else; especially, a part on the ground that supports an arch or the end of a bridge.

a·bys·mal (ə biz'm'l), *adj.* of or like an abyss; too deep to measure. **—a·bys'mal·ly,** *adv.*

a·byss (ə bis'), *n.* **1.** a great, deep crack or gap in the earth; chasm. **2.** anything too deep to measure [an *abyss* of shame.]

Ab·ys·sin·i·a (ab'ə sin'i ə), *n.* former name of Ethiopia. **—Ab·ys·sin'i·an,** *adj. & n.*

A.C., a.c., alternating current (of electricity).

a·ca·cia (ə kā'shə), *n.* **1.** a tree or shrub of warm regions with feathery leaves and clusters of yellow or white flowers. **2.** the locust tree.

ac·a·dem·ic (ak'ə-dem'ik), *adj.* **1.** having to do with schools, colleges, or teaching [the *academic* life of a college professor]. **2.** having to do with general rather than

acacia

technical education [Literature, languages, and social studies are included in an *academic* course.] **3.** not practical; merely theoretical [an *academic* discussion about life on Mars]. Also **ac·a·dem'·i·cal.** —**ac'·a·dem'·i·cal·ly,** *adv.*

a·cad·e·my (ə kad'ə mē), *n.* **1.** a place of higher learning. **2.** a private high school. **3.** any school for special training, as in music, art, or military science. **4.** a society of scholars, writers, artists etc. working in the interests of the arts or sciences. —**a·cad'e·mies,** *pl.*

ac·cede (ak sēd'), *v.* **1.** to enter upon a high position [Elizabeth II *acceded* to the British throne in 1952.] **2.** to give one's consent; agree [We *acceded* to his request.] —**ac·ced'ed,** *p.t. & p.p.;* **ac·ced'ing,** *pr.p.*

ac·cel·er·ate (ak sel'ər āt), *v.* **1.** to increase the speed of [to *accelerate* an engine]. **2.** to hasten or bring about sooner [New industries *accelerated* the growth of the city.] **3.** to go faster. —**ac·cel'er·at·ed,** *p.t. & p.p.;* **ac·cel'·er·at·ing,** *pr.p.*

ac·cel·er·a·tion (ak sel'ər ā'shən), *n.* **1.** an accelerating, or increase in speed. **2.** the rate at which speed is increased.

ac·cel·er·a·tor (ak sel'ər ā'tər), *n.* a thing that accelerates an action; especially, the foot throttle of an automobile, for making it go faster by feeding the engine more gasoline.

ac·cent (ak'sent), *n.* **1.** extra force, or stress, given to some syllables or words in speaking [The *accent* in "establish" is on the second syllable.] **2.** a mark used to show such stress, either as strong (ˊ) or weak (ˋ) [Note the strong and weak *accents* in "ac·cel'er·a'tor."] **3.** the special way of pronouncing used by people from a certain region or country [She speaks English with an Irish *accent*.] **4.** extra force given to certain beats in music to make rhythm. —*v.* (*also* ak sent'), **1.** to pronounce with special stress [*Accent* the second syllable of "Detroit."] **2.** to mark with an accent. **3.** to emphasize.

ac·cen·tu·ate (ak sen'choo āt), *v.* **1.** to pronounce or mark with an accent, or stress. **2.** to emphasize [The low windows *accentuated* the height of the room.] —**ac·cen'tu·at·ed,** *p.t. & p.p.;* **ac·cen'tu·at·ing,** *pr.p.* —**ac·cen'tu·a'tion,** *n.*

ac·cept (ak sept'), *v.* **1.** to take what is offered or given [The dealer *accepted* $50 for the used stove.] **2.** to receive with favor; approve [We *accepted* his apology. Hoop skirts were once *accepted* as the fashion.] **3.** to agree to; consent to [He will not *accept* defeat.] **4.** to answer "yes" to [We *accept* your invitation.]

ac·cept·a·ble (ak sep'tə b'l), *adj.* worth accepting; satisfactory; proper [an *acceptable* answer]. —**ac·cept'a·bly,** *adv.*

ac·cept·ance (ak sep'təns), *n.* **1.** an accepting or being accepted. **2.** approval or belief [This theory has the *acceptance* of most scientists.]

ac·cess (ak'ses), *n.* **1.** a way of approach [The *access* to the farm is by this road.] **2.** a being able or allowed to approach, enter, or use [May I have *access* to the information?]

ac·ces·si·ble (ak ses'ə b'l), *adj.* **1.** that can be approached or entered [The atomic power plant is *accessible* only to employees.] **2.** that can be got; obtainable [Fresh fruit is now *accessible* all winter long.] —**ac·ces'si·bil'i·ty,** *n.*

ac·ces·sion (ak sesh'ən), *n.* **1.** a coming to the throne, power, etc. [the *accession* of Queen Victoria in 1837.] **2.** increase by something added [The United States expanded west by the *accession* of a vast region in 1803.] **3.** something added [The museum's new *accession* is a Picasso painting.]

ac·ces·so·ry (ak ses'ə rē), *adj.* extra; going with or helping the more important thing [The electric stove has outlets for *accessory* appliances.] —*n.* **1.** something extra; something added, as for convenience, comfort, or decoration [A radio and heater are *accessories* on an automobile. A purse, gloves, and belt are *accessories* to an outfit.] **2.** a person who helps another to break the law, although he is absent at the time of the crime [He became an *accessory* by helping the murderer escape.] —**ac·ces'so·ries,** *pl.*

ac·ci·dent (ak'sə dənt), *n.* **1.** a happening that is not expected or planned [Our meeting was a happy *accident*.] **2.** an unfortunate happening or instance of bad luck that causes damage or injury [He's had three *accidents* since he's been driving a car.] **3.** fortune; chance [I won by *accident*.]

ac·ci·den·tal (ak'sə den't'l), *adj.* happening by chance [Goodyear's discovery of how to vulcanize rubber was *accidental*.] —**ac'ci·den'tal·ly,** *adv.*

ac·claim (ə klām'), *v.* **1.** to greet with loud applause or strong approval [The audience *acclaimed* the soprano for her brilliant solo.] **2.** to announce or recognize by clapping hands, cheering, or some other show of approval [They *acclaimed* him president.] —*n.* loud praise, approval, or welcome.

ac·cla·ma·tion (ak'lə mā'shən), *n.* **1.** loud applause or strong approval [The hero was received with wild *acclamation*.] **2.** a vote made by voice that need not be counted because all or most of those voting clearly approve [The chairman was elected by *acclamation*.]

ac·cli·mate (ə klī'mit *or* ak'li māt), *v.* to get used to a new climate or different surroundings [George is still not *acclimated* to the new neighborhood.] —**ac·cli'mat·ed,** *p.t. & p.p.;* **ac·cli'·mat·ing,** *pr.p.*

ac·cli·ma·tize (ə klī'mə tīz), *v.* to acclimate. —**ac·cli'ma·tized,** *p.t. & p.p.;* **ac·cli'ma·tiz·ing,** *pr.p.*

ac·co·lade (ak ə lād' *or* ak'ə lād), *n.* something done or given as a sign of great respect [The loud applause of the orchestra was the highest *accolade* the pianist ever received.]

ac·com·mo·date (ə käm'ə dāt), *v.* **1.** to make

fat, āpe, cär, ten, ēven, hit, bīte, gō, hôrn, tōōl, book, up, fûr; get, joy, yet, chin, she, thin, *th*en; zh = s in pleasure; ' as in able (ā'b'l); ə = a in ago, e in agent, i in sanity, o in confess, u in focus.

fit; adjust [He *accommodated* his walk to the slow steps of his friend.] **2.** to do a favor for [I can *accommodate* you with a loan.] **3.** to find room for; lodge [This motel will *accommodate* fifty people.] **4.** to become adjusted in focusing [My eyes have trouble *accommodating* to faraway objects.] —**ac·com′·mo·dat·ed,** *p.t. & p.p.;* **ac·com′·mo·dat·ing,** *pr.p.*

ac·com·mo·dat·ing (ə käm′ə dāt ing), *adj.* willing to please; ready to help; obliging [The *accommodating* waiter let us sit by the window.]

ac·com·mo·da·tion (ə käm′ə dā′shən), *n.* **1.** a change so as to fit new conditions; adjustment [the *accommodation* of old ideas to a new plan]. **2.** a help or convenience [Our store has a public telephone as an *accommodation* to the customers.] **3. accommodations,** *pl.* room or room and board [We need hotel *accommodations* for six.]

ac·com·pa·ni·ment (ə kum′pə ni mənt), *n.* something that goes along with another thing; especially, music played along with a solo part, etc. [the piano *accompaniment* to a song.]

ac·com·pa·nist (ə kum′pə nist), *n.* a person who plays a musical accompaniment.

ac·com·pa·ny (ə kum′pə nē), *v.* **1.** to go along with; be together with [He *accompanied* her to the movies. The bleating of the sheep was *accompanied* by the barking of the dog.] **2.** to play a musical accompaniment for or to. —**ac·com′·pa·nied,** *p.t. & p.p.;* **ac·com′·pa·ny·ing,** *pr.p.*

ac·com·plice (ə käm′plis), *n.* a person who helps another break the law [The driver of the car was an *accomplice* in the robbery.]

ac·com·plish (ə käm′plish), *v.* to do; carry out [The task was *accomplished* in record time.]

ac·com·plished (ə käm′plisht), *adj.* **1.** done; completed [an *accomplished* program]. **2.** trained; skilled [an *accomplished* pianist].

ac·com·plish·ment (ə käm′plish mənt), *n.* **1.** an accomplishing; completion. **2.** a task that has been successfully completed; achievement [Crossing the desert was a great *accomplishment*.] **3.** a social art or skill [Not the least of Mary's *accomplishments* is her talent for cooking.]

ac·cord (ə kôrd′), *v.* **1.** to give, grant, or award [He was *accorded* many honors.] **2.** to be in agreement or harmony [The story he tells does not *accord* with the facts.] —*n.* agreement; harmony [Everyone was in *accord* on the new plan for lower taxes.] —**of one's own accord,** willingly, without being asked.

ac·cord·ance (ə kôr′d'ns), *n.* agreement; harmony [He built it in *accordance* with the plans.] —**ac·cord′·ant,** *adj.*

ac·cord·ing (ə kôr′ding), *adj.* agreeing; in harmony. —**according to, 1.** in agreement with [The bus left *according to* schedule.] **2.** in the order of [They were seated *according to* age.] **3.** as stated or reported by [*According to* the newspaper, the fire caused great damage.]

ac·cord·ing·ly (ə kôr′ding lē), *adv.* **1.** in a way that is fitting or proper [He was a hero and was treated *accordingly*.] **2.** therefore [The lawyer felt the claim was just. *Accordingly*, he filed suit for damages.]

ac·cor·di·on (ə kôr′di ən), *n.* a musical instrument with keys, metal reeds, and a bellows. It is played by pulling out and pressing together the bellows to force air through the reeds, which are opened by fingering the keys.

accordion

ac·cost (ə kôst′), *v.* to approach and speak to; greet first, before being greeted [A stranger *accosted* him in the station and asked directions.]

ac·count (ə kount′), *v.* **1.** to consider or judge to be [The new process was *accounted* of little value in cutting costs.] **2.** to give a reckoning of money handled [He had to *account* to his father for every penny he spent.] **3.** to give a satisfactory reason; explain [How do you *account* for the sudden drop in prices?] **4.** to do away with [He *accounted* for five of the enemy.] —*n.* **1.** a statement of money received, paid, or owed; record of business dealings. **2.** worth; importance [a thing of small *account*]. **3.** an explanation [No satisfactory *account* of their failure has been given.] **4.** a report; story [This is the *account* of their travels.] —**call to account,** to demand an explanation of. —**on account,** as partial payment [He received the radio by paying five dollars *on account*.] —**on account of,** because of. —**on no account,** not under any circumstances. —**take into account** or **take account of,** to take into consideration. —**turn to account,** to get use or profit from.

ac·count·a·ble (ə koun′tə b'l), *adj.* **1.** obliged to account for one's acts; responsible [A baby is not *accountable* for its conduct.] **2.** that can be accounted for [His absence is *accountable*.] —**ac·count′·a·bly,** *adv.*

ac·count·ant (ə koun′t'nt), *n.* a person whose work is keeping or examining accounts, or business records.

ac·count·ing (ə koun′ting), *n.* **1.** the system or work of keeping accounts, or business records. **2.** a settling or balancing of accounts.

ac·cou·ter (ə kōō′tər), *v.* to dress or outfit [The princes were *accoutered* in silken robes.]

ac·cou·ter·ments or **ac·cou·tre·ments** (ə kōō′tər mənts), *n.pl.* **1.** clothes; dress. **2.** a soldier's equipment except clothes and weapons.

ac·cou·tre (ə kōō′tər), *v.* to accouter. —**ac·cou′·tred,** *p.t. & p.p.;* **ac·cou′·tring,** *pr.p.*

ac·cred·it (ə kred′it), *v.* **1.** to give someone the official power to act; authorize [She was *accredited* as a delegate to the convention.] **2.** to believe in [Smith's report of the expedition is the only one now *accredited*.] **3.** to approve of as coming up to the necessary standards [an *accredited* college].

ac·cre·tion (ə krē′shən), *n.* a coming or joining together of separate particles or parts [Some rocks are formed by *accretion*.]

ac·crue (ə krōō′), *v.* **1.** to come as a natural result or as an advantage [Power *accrues* to the wealthy.] **2.** to come as a regular addition or growth [Interest *accrues* to your savings account from July 1.] —**ac·crued′**, *p.t. & p.p.;* **ac·cru′ing,** *pr.p.* —**ac·cru·al** (ə krōō′əl), *n.*

ac·cu·mu·late (ə kyōōm′yoo lāt), *v.* to pile up; collect; gather [Broken furniture *accumulated* in the attic. He has *accumulated* a large library.] —**ac·cu′mu·lat·ed,** *p.t. & p.p.;* **ac·cu′mu·lat·ing,** *pr.p.*

ac·cu·mu·la·tion (ə kyōōm′yoo lā′shən), *n.* **1.** the act of accumulating or collecting. **2.** a collection of things [an *accumulation* of books].

ac·cu·ra·cy (ak′yoo rə sē), *n.* a being accurate or without mistakes; precision.

ac·cu·rate (ak′yoo rit), *adj.* careful and exact; correct; without mistakes or errors [an *accurate* report; an *accurate* worker; an *accurate* thermometer]. —**ac′cu·rate·ly,** *adv.*

ac·curs·ed (ə kûr′sid *or* ə kûrst′), *adj.* **1.** under a curse; sure to end badly. **2.** very bad, unpleasant, or annoying [an *accursed* chore].

ac·cu·sa·tion (ak′yoo zā′shən), *n.* a claim or charge that a person is guilty of doing wrong or of breaking the law [He denied the *accusation* that he had lied.]

ac·cu·sa·tive (ə kyōō′zə tiv), *adj.* showing the direct object of a verb or the object of a preposition. In Latin and some other languages, nouns, pronouns, and adjectives have certain endings to show that they are in the accusative case. In English the objective case is sometimes called the accusative case. —*n.* the accusative case.

ac·cuse (ə kyōōz′), *v.* **1.** to charge someone with doing wrong or breaking the law [I am *accusing* him of taking my book.] **2.** to find fault with; blame [You can't *accuse* her of carelessness.] —**ac·cused′**, *p.t. & p.p.;* **ac·cus′ing,** *pr.p.* —**ac·cus′er,** *n.*

ac·cus·tom (ə kus′təm), *v.* to make familiar by habit or use [He *accustomed* himself to his new house.]

ac·cus·tomed (ə kus′təmd), *adj.* customary; usual [He greeted us with his *accustomed* charm.] —**accustomed to,** used to; in the habit of [He is *accustomed to* obeying orders.]

ace (ās), *n.* **1.** a playing card or a face of dice marked with one spot. **2.** an expert in something [A U.S. Air Force pilot who has destroyed five enemy planes is called an *ace.*] **3.** a point, as in tennis, won by a single stroke. —*adj.* expert; first-rate: *used only in everyday talk* [an *ace* salesman].

ace

ac·e·tate (as′ə tāt), *n.* a salt of acetic acid [Cellulose *acetate*, formed from acetic acid and cellulose, is used in making rayon.]

a·ce·tic acid (ə sē′tik), a sour, colorless liquid that has a sharp smell. It is found in vinegar.

a·cet·y·lene (ə set′ə lēn), *n.* a colorless, poisonous gas that burns brightly with a hot flame. It is used in blowtorches for welding.

ache (āk), *v.* **1.** to have or give a dull, steady pain [My head *aches.*] **2.** to want very much; long: *used only in everyday talk* [I'm *aching* to go with you.] —*n.* a dull, steady pain. —**ached,** *p.t. & p.p.;* **ach′ing,** *pr.p.*

a·chieve (ə chēv′), *v.* **1.** to do; succeed in doing; accomplish [The legislature *achieved* very little in its last session.] **2.** to get or reach by trying hard; gain [We *achieved* a great victory.] —**a·chieved′**, *p.t. & p.p.;* **a·chiev′ing,** *pr.p.*

a·chieve·ment (ə chēv′mənt), *n.* **1.** an achieving. **2.** a thing achieved or done, especially by skill, work, courage, etc. [The climb to the top of Mt. Everest was a remarkable *achievement.*]

A·chil·les (ə kil′ēz), *n.* a hero of Greek legend, a leader of the Greeks in the Trojan War. He was killed by an arrow that struck his heel, the only part of his body that could be injured.

ac·id (as′id), *n.* a chemical compound that contains hydrogen and forms a salt when combined with a base. Acids dissolve in water, taste sour, and make blue litmus turn red. —*adj.* **1.** of or like an acid. **2.** sour; sharp and biting to the taste [A lime is an *acid* fruit.] —**ac′id·ly,** *adv.*

a·cid·i·ty (ə sid′ə tē), *n.* the quality or condition of being acid; sourness.

ac·knowl·edge (ak n, näl′ij), *v.* **1.** to admit to be true [I *acknowledge* that you are right.] **2.** to recognize the authority of [They *acknowledged* him as their king.] **3.** to recognize and answer or express one's thanks for [He *acknowledged* my greeting with a nod. Have you written to your aunt to *acknowledge* the gift?] —**ac·knowl′edged,** *p.t. & p.p.;* **ac·knowl′edg·ing,** *pr.p.*

ac·knowl·edg·ment *or* **ac·knowl·edge·ment** (ak näl′ij mənt), *n.* **1.** an acknowledging. **2.** something given or done in acknowledging.

ac·me (ak′mē), *n.* the highest point; peak [Playing Hamlet was the *acme* of his career.]

ac·ne (ak′nē), *n.* a common skin disease of young people in which pimples keep appearing on the face, back, and chest.

ac·o·lyte (ak′ə līt), *n.* someone who assists a priest at Mass, as an altar boy.

ac·o·nite (ak′ə nīt), *n.* **1.** a poisonous plant with flowers shaped like hoods. **2.** a medicine made from the roots of one kind of aconite.

a·corn (ā′kôrn), *n.* the nut, or fruit, of the oak tree.

a·cous·tic (ə kōōs′tik), *adj.* having to do with hearing or with sound [The *acoustic* tile on the walls muffled the noise in the room.]

acorns

a·cous·tics (ə kōōs′tiks), *n.pl.* **1.** the qualities of a theater,

fat, āpe, cär, ten, ēven, hit, bīte, gō, hôrn, tōol, book, up, fûr;
get, joy, yet, chin, she, thin, *th*en; zh = s in pleasure; ′ as in able (ā′b'l);
ə = a in ago, e in agent, i in sanity, o in confess, u in focus.

room, etc. that are responsible for how clearly sounds can be heard in it. **2.** the science of sound: *used with a singular verb.*

ac·quaint (ə kwānt′), *v.* **1.** to give knowledge of; inform [He *acquainted* himself with all the facts.] **2.** to cause to know personally; make familiar with [Are you *acquainted* with Sarah?]

ac·quaint·ance (ə kwān′t'ns), *n.* **1.** knowledge of a thing or person gained from personal experience [a thorough *acquaintance* with modern music]. **2.** a person one knows only slightly. **—make someone's acquaintance,** to become acquainted with someone.

ac·qui·esce (ak′wi es′), *v.* to accept without arguing; agree or give in quietly [Our nation will never *acquiesce* to the enemy's demands.] **—ac′qui·esced′,** *p.t. & p.p.;* **ac′qui·esc′ing,** *pr.p.*

ac·qui·es·cence (ak′wi es′'ns), *n.* an acquiescing; acceptance or agreement without arguing. **—ac′qui·es′cent,** *adj.*

ac·quire (ə kwīr′), *v.* to get as one's own; become the owner of [The museum *acquired* an Egyptian mummy for its collection.] **—acquired′,** *p.t. & p.p.;* **ac·quir′ing,** *pr.p.*

ac·quire·ment (ə kwīr′mənt), *n.* **1.** the act of acquiring. **2.** something acquired; especially, a skill or ability gained by learning.

ac·qui·si·tion (ak′wə zish′ən), *n.* **1.** the act of acquiring. **2.** something acquired [Our library's new *acquisitions* include an encyclopedia.]

ac·quis·i·tive (ə kwiz′ə tiv), *adj.* eager to acquire; greedy [a miser's *acquisitive* nature].

ac·quit (ə kwit′), *v.* **1.** to declare to be not guilty [The court *acquitted* the prisoner.] **2.** to conduct oneself; behave [Although shunned, she *acquitted* herself with great dignity.] **—ac·quit′·ted,** *p.t. & p.p.;* **ac·quit′ting,** *pr.p.*

ac·quit·tal (ə kwit′'l), *n.* the freeing of an accused person by a verdict of "not guilty."

a·cre (ā′kər), *n.* **1.** a measure of land, 43,560 square feet. **2. acres,** *pl.* lands or fields [golden *acres* of grain].

a·cre·age (ā′kər ij), *n.* **1.** the number of acres in a piece of land. **2.** land as made up of acres.

ac·rid (ak′rid), *adj.* **1.** sharp, bitter, or irritating to the taste or smell [the *acrid* smell of ammonia]. **2.** bitter or sarcastic in speech [*acrid* comments].

ac·ri·mo·ni·ous (ak′rə mō′ni əs), *adj.* bitter or sharp in temper, manner, or speech.

ac·ri·mo·ny (ak′rə mō′nē), *n.* bitterness or sharpness of temper, manner, or speech.

ac·ro·bat (ak′rə bat), *n.* a performer who does tricks in tumbling or on the trapeze, tightrope, etc.

ac·ro·bat·ic (ak′rə bat′ik), *adj.* **1.** of an acrobat. **2.** like an acrobat or his tricks [an *acrobatic* dancer].

ac·ro·bat·ics (ak′rə bat′iks), *n.pl.* **1.** an acrobat's tricks. **2.** any difficult tricks [mental *acrobatics*].

acrobats

A·crop·o·lis (ə kräp′ə lis), *n.* a fortified hill in ancient Athens, on which the Parthenon was built.

a·cross (ə krôs′ *or* ə kräs′), *adv.* from one side to the other [The new bridge makes it easy to get *across.*] **—prep. 1.** from one side to the other of [He swam *across* the river.] **2.** on the other side of; over [He lives *across* the street.] **3.** into contact with [I came *across* an old friend yesterday.]

act (akt), *n.* **1.** a thing done; deed [an *act* of bravery]. **2.** an action; a doing of something [caught in the *act* of telling a lie]. **3.** a law; decree [an *act* of Congress]. **4.** one of the main divisions of a play, opera, etc. [The first *act* of "Hamlet" has five scenes.] **5.** any of the separate performances on a variety program [Her dancing *act* came next.] **—v. 1.** to perform on the stage; play the part of [She *acted* Juliet.] **2.** to behave like [He always *acts* the fool.] **3.** to behave; conduct oneself [Please *act* like a gentleman.] **4.** to do something; function; work [Because of the emergency, we must *act* immediately.] **5.** to have an effect [Acids *act* on metal.] **—act for, 1.** to do the work of. **2.** to act in behalf of. **—act up,** to behave playfully or to misbehave: *used only in everyday talk.*

act·ing (ak′ting), *adj.* taking over another's duties for a while [While the mayor was ill, the law director was *acting* mayor.]

ac·tion (ak′shən), *n.* **1.** the doing of something [An emergency calls for quick *action.*] **2.** an act or thing done. **3. actions,** *pl.* behavior [the *actions* of a coward]. **4.** the effect produced by something [the *action* of a drug]. **5.** the way of moving, working, etc. [the *action* of a washing machine]. **6.** a lawsuit. **7.** combat in war; battle [He was wounded in *action.*] **—in action,** active; in motion. **—take action, 1.** to become active. **2.** to start a lawsuit.

ac·ti·vate (ak′tə vāt), *v.* to make active; put into action. **—ac′ti·vat·ed,** *p.t. & p.p.;* **ac′ti·vat·ing,** *pr.p.* **—ac′ti·va′tion,** *n.*

ac·tive (ak′tiv), *adj.* **1.** acting; working; in operation [That company is no longer *active.*] **2.** full of action; lively; busy; quick [an *active* mind; an *active* boy]. **3.** having the verb in the form (called *voice*) that shows its subject as doing the action: opposite of *passive* [In the sentence "He threw the ball," the verb "threw" is in the *active* voice.] **—ac′tive·ly,** *adv.*

ac·tiv·i·ty (ak tiv′ə tē), *n.* **1.** the condition of being active; action; motion [slow business *activity*]. **2.** normal power of mind or body; liveliness; alertness [His mental *activity* did not lessen in old age.] **3.** a recreation or pastime that keeps one busy [She took part in many *activities* after school.] **—ac·tiv′i·ties,** *pl.*

ac·tor (ak′tər), *n.* a person who acts in plays, movies, etc.

ac·tress (ak′tris), *n.* a woman or girl actor.

ac·tu·al (ak′chōō əl), *adj.* as it really is; in fact; real; true [The *actual* cost was lower than the estimate. The king's brother was the *actual* ruler.]

ac·tu·al·i·ty (ak′chōō al′ə tē), *n.* actual fact or condition; reality [In *actuality*, Columbus never set foot upon the American continent.]

ac·tu·al·ly (ak′chōō əl ē *or* ak′choo lē), *adv.* really; in fact [The man *actually* cried.]

ac·tu·ate (ak′choo āt), *v.* **1.** to put into action [The starter of the car is *actuated* by turning the key.] **2.** to cause to take action [What motives *actuated* him?] —**ac′tu·at·ed**, *p.t. & p.p.;* **ac′tu·at·ing**, *pr.p.*

a·cu·men (ə kyoo′mən), *n.* keenness and quickness in understanding and dealing with a situation; shrewdness [political *acumen*].

a·cute (ə kyoot′), *adj.* **1.** having a sharp point [a leaf with an *acute* tip]. **2.** very keen and sensitive; sharp and quick [*acute* eyesight or hearing]. **3.** intense and sharp [*acute* pain; *acute* jealousy]. **4.** severe and serious for a short time; not chronic [an *acute* disease]. **5.** very severe; critical [There was an *acute* shortage of trained workers.] **6.** less than 90 degrees: said of angles. —**a·cute′ly**, *adv.* —**a·cute′ness**, *n.*

acute accent, a mark (′) over some letters, as in French words [*divorcée*].

ad (ad), *n.* an advertisement: *used only in everyday talk.*

A.D., of the Christian era; from the year in which Jesus Christ was believed to have been born [Nero, emperor of Rome, was born in 37 *A.D.*] *A.D.* is the abbreviation of *Anno Domini*, Latin for "in the year of the Lord."

ad·age (ad′ij), *n.* an old saying that has been accepted as a truth ["Where there's smoke, there's fire" is an *adage*.]

Ad·am (ad′əm), *n.* in the Bible, the first man.

ad·a·mant (ad′ə mənt), *adj.* not giving in easily; firm; not yielding [The king remained *adamant* to her pleas for mercy.]

Ad·ams, John (ad′əms), 1735–1826; second president of the United States, from 1797 to 1801.

Adams, John Quin·cy (kwin′sē), 1767–1848; sixth president of the United States, from 1825 to 1829. He was the son of John Adams.

Adam's apple, a bulge in the throat, seen especially in men. It is formed by the cartilage of the voice cords.

a·dapt (ə dapt′), *v.* **1.** to change so as to make fit or usable [This radio can be *adapted* for use with direct current.] **2.** to change oneself to fit new conditions [It was hard for the colonists to *adapt* themselves to the new land.]

Adam's apple

a·dapt·a·ble (ə dap′tə b'l), *adj.* **1.** that can be adapted or made to fit. **2.** able to adapt easily.

ad·ap·ta·tion (ad′ap tā′shən), *n.* **1.** an adapting or changing so as to fit. **2.** a thing adapted from something else, as a play from a novel.

add (ad), *v.* **1.** to join or put something to another thing so that there will be more or so as to mix into one thing [We *added* some books to our library. *Add* two cups of sugar to the batter.] **2.** to say further [Jack agreed to come but *added* that he would be late.] **3.** to join numbers so as to get a total [*Add* 3 and 5.] **4.** to cause an increase of [Music *adds* to my pleasure at meals.] —**add up to,** to reach a total of.

ad·der (ad′ər), *n.* **1.** a small, poisonous snake of Europe. **2.** a harmless snake of North America.

ad·dict (ad′ikt), *n.* a person who has a habit so strong that he cannot easily give it up [a drug *addict*]. —*v.* (ə dikt′), to give oneself up to some strong habit [Many people are *addicted* to watching television.] —**ad·dic′tion**, *n.*

adding machine, a machine that prints numbers and then adds them up when one presses certain keys. Some adding machines can also subtract, divide, and multiply.

ad·di·tion (ə dish′ən), *n.* **1.** an adding of numbers to get a sum or total. **2.** a joining of one thing to another thing [The lemonade was improved by the *addition* of sugar.] **3.** a thing or part added [The gymnasium is a new *addition* to our school.] —**in addition to,** besides.

ad·di·tion·al (ə dish′ən 'l), *adj.* more; extra; added [We must order an *additional* supply of notebooks this year.] —**ad·di′tion·al·ly**, *adv.*

ad·di·tive (ad′ə tiv), *n.* a substance added to another in small amounts for a special reason, as a preservative added to food.

ad·dle (ad′'l), *v.* **1.** to make or become confused [His mind is *addled*.] **2.** to make or become rotten: said of an egg. —**ad′dled**, *p.t. & p.p.;* **ad′dling**, *pr.p.*

ad·dress (ə dres′), *v.* **1.** to speak to or write to; direct one's words to [She *addressed* her remarks to the editor. The principal will *address* our first assembly.] **2.** to write on a letter or package the name, street number, city, etc. of the one to whom it is being sent. **3.** to get oneself working [We must *address* ourselves to the problem.] —*n.* **1.** a written or spoken speech. **2.** (ə dres′ *or* ad′rəs), the place to which mail, etc. can be sent to one; place where one lives or works.

ad·duce (ə doos′), *v.* to give as a reason or proof [To show that the earth is not flat he *adduced* the fact that ships disappear below the horizon.] —**ad·duced′**, *p.t. & p.p.;* **ad·duc′ing**, *pr.p.*

ad·e·noids (ad′'n oidz), *n.pl.* growths of tissue in the upper part of the throat, behind the nose. Adenoids sometimes swell up and make it hard to breathe and speak.

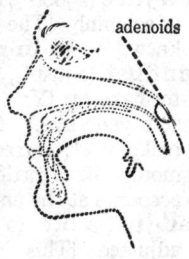

adenoids

a·dept (ə dept′), *adj.* highly skilled; expert [*adept* at tennis].

ad·e·qua·cy (ad′ə kwə sē), *n.* a being enough or good enough for what is needed.

ad·e·quate (ad′ə kwit), *adj.*

enough or good enough for what is needed; ~~sufficient; suitable~~ [an *adequate* supply of food; *adequate* skills]. —**ad′e·quate·ly,** *adv.*

ad·here (ad hir′), *v.* **1.** to stick and not come loose; stay attached [This stamp won't *adhere* to the envelope.] **2.** to stay firm in supporting or approving [to *adhere* to a plan or a decision]. —**ad·hered′,** *p.t. & p.p.;* **ad·her′ing,** *pr.p.*

ad·her·ence (ad hir′əns), *n.* a supporting or approving of a person, idea, etc.

ad·her·ent (ad hir′ənt), *n.* a supporter of a person, idea, etc. —*adj.* sticking fast; attached.

ad·he·sion (ad hē′zhən), *n.* a sticking to something or being stuck together.

ad·he·sive (ad hē′siv), *adj.* **1.** sticking and not coming loose; clinging. **2.** having a sticky surface [*Adhesive* tape is used to hold bandages in place.] —*n.* a sticky substance [Glue is an *adhesive.*]

a·dieu (ə dyōō′ *or* ə dōō′), *interj. & n.* good-by.

a·di·os (ä di ōs′), *interj.* good-by: *a Spanish word.*

ad·i·pose (ad′ə pōs), *adj.* having to do with animal fat; fat; fatty [*adipose* tissue].

Ad·i·ron·dacks (ad′ə rän′daks), *n.pl.* a mountain range in northeastern New York State: also called **Adirondack Mountains.**

adj., abbreviation for **adjective.**

ad·ja·cent (ə jā′s'nt), *adj.* near or next [The playground is *adjacent* to the school.] —**ad·ja′-cent·ly,** *adv.*

ad·jec·tive (aj′ik tiv), *n.* a word used with a noun or pronoun to tell which, what kind of, how many, or whose [In the sentence "Every pupil was good," the words "every" and "good" are *adjectives.*] —**ad·jec·ti·val** (aj′ik tī′v'l), *adj.*

ad·join (ə join′), *v.* **1.** to be next to [The bell tower *adjoins* the church.] **2.** to be next to each other; be side by side. —**ad·join′ing,** *adj.*

ad·journ (ə jūrn′), *v.* **1.** to close a session or meeting for the day or for a time [Congress has *adjourned* for two weeks.] **2.** to change the place of meeting: *used only in everyday talk* [Let's *adjourn* to the porch.] —**ad·journ′ment,** *n.*

ad·judge (ə juj′), *v.* to decide, declare, or award [The boy was *adjudged* innocent. A sum of $5,000 was *adjudged* to the accident victim.] —**ad·judged′,** *p.t. & p.p.;* **ad·judg′ing,** *pr.p.*

ad·junct (aj′ungkt), *n.* a less important thing added to something more important [He planted an orchard as an *adjunct* to his farm.]

ad·jure (ə joor′), *v.* to command or ask earnestly or solemnly [The judge *adjured* him to tell all he knew.] —**ad·ju·ra·tion** (aj′oo rā′shən), *n.*

ad·just (ə just′), *v.* **1.** to change or move so as to make fit [You can *adjust* the driver's seat to suit your size.] **2.** to arrange the parts of to make work correctly; regulate, as a watch or motor. **3.** to settle or put in order [We *adjust* our accounts at the end of the month.]

ad·just·a·ble (ə jus′tə b'l), *adj.* that can be adjusted [This ironing board is *adjustable* to several heights.]

ad·just·er or **ad·jus·tor** (ə jus′tər), *n.* a person or thing that adjusts something [The *adjuster* came to settle the insurance claims.]

ad·just·ment (ə just′mənt), *n.* **1.** a changing or settling of things to bring them into proper order or relation [The immigrant made a quick *adjustment* to his new life.] **2.** a way or device by which parts are adjusted [An *adjustment* on our television set can make the picture brighter.]

ad·ju·tant (aj′ə tənt), *n.* **1.** an assistant; especially, an army officer who serves as a secretary to the commanding officer. **2.** a large stork of India and Africa: also called **adjutant stork.**

ad·lib (ad′lib′), *v.* to make up and insert words, gestures, etc. not in the script as one is performing: *used only in everyday talk* [A good actor learns to *ad-lib* when he forgets his lines.] —**ad′-libbed′,** *p.t. & p.p.;* **ad′-lib′bing,** *pr.p.*

ad·min·is·ter (əd min′ə stər), *v.* **1.** to manage or direct [The principal *administers* the school.] **2.** to give out, as punishment or justice [My father *administered* the spanking.] **3.** to give or apply medicine, treatment, etc. [She is trained to *administer* first aid in emergencies.] **4.** to direct the taking of an oath [The Chief Justice *administers* the oath of office of a president-elect.] **5.** to give help [She *administered* to the sick.] Also **ad·min·is·trate** (əd min′ə strāt).

ad·min·is·tra·tion (əd min′ə strā′shən), *n.* **1.** an administering; management; direction. **2.** *often* **Administration,** the officials of a government or institution and their policies or principles [The *Administration* was criticized for its foreign policy.] **3.** their term of office [Barkley was vice-president during Truman's *administration.*] —**ad·min′is·tra′tive,** *adj.*

ad·min·is·tra·tor (əd min′ə strā′tər), *n.* **1.** a person who administers or directs something; executive. **2.** a person appointed by a law court to manage the distribution of a dead person's property.

ad·mi·ra·ble (ad′mə rə b'l), *adj.* deserving to be admired or praised; excellent [William Tell showed *admirable* courage.] —**ad′mi·ra·bly,** *adv.*

ad·mi·ral (ad′mə rəl), *n.* **1.** the commanding officer of a navy or of a fleet of ships. **2.** a naval officer of the highest rank.

ad·mi·ral·ty (ad′mə rəl tē), *n.* **1.** the department of government that is in charge of navy affairs. **2.** the system of law governing the sea, shipping, etc. —**ad′mi·ral·ties,** *pl.*

ad·mi·ra·tion (ad′mə rā′shən), *n.* **1.** a feeling of delight and pleased approval at anything fine, skillful, beautiful, etc. [The guests stood in *admiration* of the garden.] **2.** a thing or person bringing about such feelings [Her golden hair was the *admiration* of all the girls.]

admiral

ad·mire (əd mīr′), *v.* to regard with wonder, delight, and pleased approval [The painting was *admired* by everyone.] —**ad·mired′,** *p.t. & p.p.;* **ad·mir′ing,** *pr.p.* —**ad·mir′er,** *n.* —**ad·mir′ing·ly,** *adv.*

ad·mis·si·ble (əd mis′ə b'l), *adj.* that can be

admitted, accepted, or allowed [The witness's opinions were not *admissible* evidence.]

ad·mis·sion (əd mish′ən), *n.* **1.** an admitting or being admitted. **2.** the right of entering [The reporters were denied *admission* to the house.] **3.** the price paid for entering [*Admission* to the zoo is fifty cents.] **4.** an admitting of the truth of something; confession [His silence was an *admission* of guilt.]

ad·mit (əd mit′), *v.* **1.** to permit or give the right to enter [One ticket *admits* two persons.] **2.** to have room for [The hall *admits* 500 people.] **3.** to grant the truth of; confess [Lucy will never *admit* that she was mistaken.] —**ad·mit′ted,** *p.t. & p.p.;* **ad·mit′ting,** *pr.p.*

ad·mit·tance (əd mit′′ns), *n.* the right to enter [Can I get *admittance* to the army camp?]

ad·mit·ted·ly (əd mit′id lē), *adv.* by one's own admission or confession [I am *admittedly* afraid.]

ad·mix·ture (ad miks′chər), *n.* **1.** a mixture. **2.** a thing added in mixing.

ad·mon·ish (əd män′ish), *v.* **1.** to warn a person that he must correct some fault [The judge *admonished* him to drive more slowly.] **2.** to criticize in a mild way [Mother *admonished* Bill for coming home late.]

ad·mo·ni·tion (ad′mə nish′ən), *n.* **1.** an admonishing; a warning to improve some fault. **2.** mild criticism.

a·do (ə dōō′), *n.* fuss; trouble [Much *ado* was made about his going away for a week.]

a·do·be (ə dō′bē), *n.* **1.** brick made of clay dried in the sun instead of baked by fire. **2.** the clay of which such brick is made. **3.** a building made of adobe.

adobe

ad·o·les·cence (ad′ə les′′ns), *n.* the time of life between childhood and adulthood; youth.

ad·o·les·cent (ad′ə les′′nt), *adj.* **1.** growing up; developing from a child to an adult. **2.** of or like an adolescent; youthful; not yet grown up. —*n.* a boy or girl between childhood and adulthood; person in his teens.

a·dopt (ə däpt′), *v.* **1.** to choose and take into one's family by a legal procedure [They *adopted* their son Jim when he was one year old.] **2.** to take and use as one's own [Most inventors *adopt* and develop the earlier ideas of others.] **3.** to choose or follow [We must *adopt* a new plan of action.] —**a·dop′tion,** *n.*

a·dor·a·ble (ə dôr′ə b'l), *adj.* **1.** worthy of being adored: *not now in common use.* **2.** delightful; charming: *used only in everyday talk* [What an *adorable* cottage!]

ad·o·ra·tion (ad′ə rā′shən), *n.* **1.** the act of worshiping. **2.** great love and respect.

a·dore (ə dôr′), *v.* **1.** to worship as divine ["O come let us *adore* Him."] **2.** to love greatly or honor highly [He *adored* his wife.] **3.** to like very much: *used only in everyday talk* [She *adored* the hat.] —**a·dored′,** *p.t. & p.p.;* **a·dor′ing,** *pr.p.*

a·dorn (ə dôrn′), *v.* to add beauty or splendor to; decorate [A gold vase *adorned* the table.]

a·dorn·ment (ə dôrn′mənt), *n.* **1.** the act of adorning. **2.** something that adorns; decoration; ornament [Paintings, tapestries, and other *adornments* covered the walls.]

A·dri·at·ic (ā′dri at′ik *or* ad′ri at′ik), *n.* a sea between Italy and Yugoslavia. It is an arm of the Mediterranean.

a·drift (ə drift′), *adv. & adj.* **1.** drifting; floating freely without being steered [The boat was *adrift* in the ocean.] **2.** without any particular aim or purpose [Having no work, he felt *adrift* in life.]

a·droit (ə droit′), *adj.* skillful and clever [his *adroit* handling of an awkward situation]. —**a·droit′ly,** *adv.* —**a·droit′ness,** *n.*

ad·u·la·tion (aj′ə lā′shən), *n.* greater flattery or praise than is proper or deserved [The singer was greeted by the *adulation* of his fans.]

a·dult (ə dult′ *or* ad′ult), *adj.* **1.** grown up; having reached full size and strength [an *adult* person or plant]. **2.** of or for grown men or women [an *adult* novel or play]. —*n.* **1.** a man or woman who is fully grown up; mature person. **2.** an animal or plant that is fully developed. —**a·dult′hood,** *n.*

a·dul·ter·ate (ə dul′tər āt), *v.* to make impure or inferior by adding a harmful or unnecessary substance [The milk was *adulterated* with water.] —**a·dul′ter·at·ed,** *p.t. & p.p.;* **a·dul′ter·at·ing,** *pr.p.* —**a·dul′ter·a′tion,** *n.*

a·dul·ter·ous (ə dul′tər əs), *adj.* guilty of adultery.

a·dul·ter·y (ə dul′tər ē), *n.* the act of being sexually unfaithful to one's husband or wife. —**a·dul′ter·ies,** *pl.*

adv., abbreviation for **adverb.**

ad·vance (əd vans′), *v.* **1.** to go or bring forward; move ahead [He *advanced* his foot a bit.] **2.** to suggest; offer [A new plan has been *advanced*.] **3.** to help to grow or develop; promote [This law *advances* the building of new homes.] **4.** to cause to happen earlier [The date of the test was *advanced* from May 10 to May 5.] **5.** to make or become higher; increase [The cost of food continues to *advance*.] **6.** to lend [We can *advance* him $2,000.] **7.** to rise in rank, importance, etc. [She *advanced* from assistant principal to principal of the school.] —*n.* **1.** a moving forward or ahead; progress [the new *advances* in science]. **2.** a rise in value or cost [His wages did not keep up with the *advance* in prices.] **3.** a payment made before it is due, as of wages [He asked for an *advance* of next week's allowance.] **4.** an attempt to gain favor or become friendly [Our new neighbors have made several *advances* toward us.] —*adj.* **1.** in front [an *advance guard*]. **2.** ahead of time [*advance information*]. —**in advance, 1.** in front [He kept *in advance* as we walked.] **2.** before due; ahead of time [They paid the rent *in advance*.] —**ad·vanced',** *p.t. & p.p.;* **ad·vanc'ing,** *pr.p.*

ad·vanced (əd vanst'), *adj.* **1.** in advance; in front. **2.** far on in life; old [He became a painter at an *advanced* age.] **3.** ahead of the times; not as yet accepted [*advanced* ideas].

ad·vance·ment (əd vans'mənt), *n.* **1.** an advancing. **2.** promotion; progress; improvement [We work for the *advancement* of mankind.]

ad·van·tage (əd van'tij), *n.* **1.** a more favorable position; better chance [His speed gave him an *advantage* over me.] **2.** a thing, condition, or event that can help one; benefit [A friendly manner is an *advantage* in business.] —**take advantage of,** to make use of for one's own benefit [*Take advantage of* your opportunities.] —**to advantage,** to a good effect [I can use that money *to advantage*.]

ad·van·ta·geous (ad'vən tā'jəs), *adj.* giving advantage; favorable; helpful [The fort stood in an *advantageous* position above the road.]

Ad·vent (ad'vent), *n.* **1.** the period including the four Sundays just before Christmas. **2.** Christ's birth. **3. advent,** a coming or arrival [the *advent* of spring].

ad·ven·ture (əd ven'chər), *n.* **1.** an exciting and dangerous undertaking [The story tells of his *adventures* on the moon.] **2.** an unusual, stirring experience [Going to a circus is an *adventure* for a child.]

ad·ven·tur·er (əd ven'chər ər), *n.* **1.** a person who has or looks for adventures. **2.** a person who tries to become rich in a dishonest or tricky way.

ad·ven·ture·some (əd ven'chər səm), *adj.* adventurous.

ad·ven·tur·ous (əd ven'chər əs), *adj.* **1.** liking adventure; willing to take chances; daring [an *adventurous* explorer]. **2.** full of danger; risky [an *adventurous* hunting trip].

ad·verb (ad'vərb), *n.* a word used with a verb, adjective, or another adverb to tell when, where, how, what kind, or how much. *Quickly* tells how in "run *quickly*." *Always* tells when in "*always* sad." *Bright* tells what kind in "*bright* red dress." *Very* tells how much in "run *very* quickly." —**ad·ver·bi·al** (əd vūr'bi əl), *adj.*

ad·ver·sar·y (ad'vər ser'ē), *n.* an enemy or opponent. —**ad'ver·sar'ies,** *pl.*

ad·verse (əd vūrs'), *adj.* **1.** opposed; coming against someone or something [*adverse* currents in the river; *adverse* criticism]. **2.** not helpful; harmful [The hot sun had an *adverse* effect on the crops.] —**ad·verse'ly,** *adv.*

ad·ver·si·ty (əd vūr'sə tē), *n.* misfortune; bad luck; poverty and trouble. —**ad·ver'si·ties,** *pl.*

ad·ver·tise (ad'vər tīz), *v.* **1.** to tell people about or praise publicly some product so as to make them want to buy it [They will *advertise* the new cars in magazines and on television.] **2.** to announce or ask for publicly, as in a newspaper [to *advertise* a house for rent; to *advertise*

for a servant]. —**ad'ver·tised,** *p.t. & p.p.;* **ad'ver·tis·ing,** *pr.p.* —**ad'ver·tis·er,** *n.*

ad·ver·tise·ment (ad'vər tīz'mənt *or* əd vūr'tiz mənt), *n.* a public announcement, as in a newspaper, advertising something.

ad·ver·tis·ing (ad'vər tīz'ing), *n.* **1.** an advertisement or advertisements. **2.** the work of preparing and issuing advertisements [*Advertising* is now a major industry in this country.]

ad·vice (əd vīs'), *n.* opinion given as to what to do or how to do something [We followed his *advice* in selecting a new home.]

ad·vis·a·ble (əd vīz'ə b'l), *adj.* being good advice; wise; sensible [It is *advisable* to wear rubbers when it rains.] —**ad·vis'a·bil'i·ty,** *n.*

ad·vise (əd vīz'), *v.* **1.** to give advice or an opinion to [The doctor *advised* me to have an operation.] **2.** to offer something as advice; recommend [I should *advise* a long ocean trip.] **3.** to notify; inform [The letter *advised* us that the meeting was to be on Tuesday.] —**ad·vised',** *p.t. & p.p.;* **ad·vis'ing,** *pr.p.*

ad·vise·ment (əd vīz'mənt), *n.* careful consideration [He will take our suggestion under *advisement* before he decides what to do.]

ad·vis·er *or* **ad·vi·sor** (əd vīz'ər), *n.* a person who advises or gives his opinion.

ad·vi·so·ry (əd vī'zə rē), *adj.* advising; able to advise; giving advice [*advisory* experts].

ad·vo·ca·cy (ad'və kə sē), *n.* an advocating; a speaking or writing in support of something.

ad·vo·cate (ad'və kāt), *v.* to speak or write in support of; be in favor of [The senator *advocated* a new housing bill.] —*n.* (ad'və kit *or* ad'və-kāt), **1.** a person who speaks or writes in favor of something. **2.** a person who argues another's case; especially, a lawyer. —**ad'vo·cat·ed,** *p.t. & p.p.;* **ad'vo·cat·ing,** *pr.p.*

adz *or* **adze** (adz), *n.* a tool that is a little like an ax, but has a curved blade. It is used for trimming and smoothing wood.

Ae·ge·an (ē jē'ən), *n.* a sea between Greece and Turkey. It is an arm of the Mediterranean.

ae·gis (ē'jis), *n.* sponsorship or support [He spoke under the *aegis* of the university.]

adz

Ae·ne·as (i nē'əs), *n.* a famous Trojan warrior of Greek and Roman legend. The Roman poet Virgil tells of his adventures after the Trojan War in a long poem called the **Ae·ne·id** (i nē'id).

ae·on (ē'ən *or* ē'än), *n.* same as **eon.**

aer·ate (er'āt), *v.* **1.** to place out in the open air. **2.** to force air or a gas into [If you *aerate* water with carbon dioxide, you have soda water.] —**aer'at·ed,** *p.t. & p.p.;* **aer'at·ing,** *pr.p.*

aer·i·al (er'i əl), *adj.* **1.** of or in the air. **2.** like air; light as air. **3.** of or for aircraft or flying [*aerial* maps]. —*n.* an antenna for radio or television.

aer·i·al·ist (er'i əl ist), *n.* an acrobat who does stunts on a trapeze, high wire, etc.

aer·ie or **aer·y** (er′ē), *n.* the nest of an eagle or other bird of prey, built in a high place.

aer·o·nau·tics (er′ə-nô′tiks), *n.pl.* the science of making and flying aircraft; aviation. —**aer′o·nau′tic** or **aer′o·nau′ti·cal**, *adj.*

aer·o·plane (er′əplān), *n.* an airplane.

aer·o·space (er′ōspās), *n.* the earth's atmosphere and the space outside it.

Ae·sop (ē′səp *or* ē′säp), *n.* Greek writer of fables who lived in the 6th century B.C.

aerie

aes·thet·ic (es thet′ik), *adj.* 1. of beauty or the study of beauty. 2. keenly aware of what is beautiful; artistic. —**aes·thet′i·cal·ly**, *adv.*

a·far (ə fär′), *adv.* at or to a distance: *now seldom used except in poetry.* —**from afar,** from a distance [We heard the barking *from afar.*]

af·fa·ble (af′ə b'l), *adj.* easy to talk to; friendly; pleasant and polite. —**af′fa·bil′i·ty,** *n.* —**af′fa·bly,** *adv.*

af·fair (ə fer′), *n.* 1. a happening or event; occurrence [The meeting will be a long, tiresome *affair.*] 2. **affairs,** *pl.* matters of business [His *affairs* will be taken care of by his secretary while he is away.]

af·fect (ə fekt′), *v.* 1. to bring about a change in; have an effect on [Bright light *affects* the eyes.] 2. to make feel sad or sympathetic [The little boy's accident has *affected* us deeply.]

af·fect (ə fekt′), *v.* 1. to like to have, use, wear, etc. [She *affects* plaid coats.] 2. to pretend to be, have, feel, like, etc. [Although he disliked sports, he *affected* an interest in baseball.]

af·fec·ta·tion (af′ek tā′shən), *n.* unnatural behavior that is meant to impress others [Ed's use of long words is just an *affectation.*]

af·fect·ed (ə fek′tid), *adj.* 1. injured or diseased [She rubbed powder on the *affected* part of the skin.] 2. feeling sad or sympathetic [The president's death left them deeply *affected.*]

af·fect·ed (ə fek′tid), *adj.* unnatural; artificial in a way meant to impress people [*affected* politeness].

af·fect·ing (ə fek′ting), *adj.* making one feel sadness, sympathy, or pity [The book "Oliver Twist" is an *affecting* story of an orphan.]

af·fec·tion (ə fek′shən), *n.* 1. a fond or tender feeling; warm liking [The *affection* one feels for a pet is not the same as love.] 2. a disease [an *affection* of the liver].

af·fec·tion·ate (ə fek′shən it), *adj.* gentle and loving. —**af·fec′tion·ate·ly,** *adv.*

af·fi·da·vit (af′ə dā′vit), *n.* a statement written by a person who swears that it is the truth [He signed an *affidavit* saying that he returned the borrowed money.]

af·fil·i·ate (ə fil′i āt), *v.* to take in or be taken in as a member or another part; join [Three new stores have become *affiliated* with the chain of supermarkets.] —*n.* (ə fil′i it), an affiliated person or organization [The women's college is an *affiliate* of the University.] —**af·fil′i·at·ed,** *p.t. & p.p.;* **af·fil′i·at·ing,** *pr.p.* —**af·fil′i·a′tion,** *n.*

af·fin·i·ty (ə fin′ə tē), *n.* 1. close relationship or kinship [Folk ballads show the close *affinity* of music with poetry.] 2. the special attraction that one person has for another. 3. a person who especially attracts another. —**af·fin′i·ties,** *pl.*

af·firm (ə fūrm′), *v.* to say something and be willing to stand by its truth; assert positively [I cannot *affirm* that Smith is guilty of any crime.] —**af·fir·ma·tion** (af′ər mā′shən), *n.*

af·firm·a·tive (ə fūr′mə tiv), *adj.* saying that it is true; answering "yes" [an *affirmative* reply]. —*n.* 1. a word, phrase, or action showing that one approves or agrees [She nodded her head in the *affirmative.*] 2. the side that favors or agrees with the point being debated [There were more votes in the negative than in the *affirmative.*]

af·fix (ə fiks′), *v.* 1. to fasten; attach; stick [*Affix* a label to the jar.] 2. to add at the end [You must *affix* your signature to the contract.] —*n.* (af′iks), a prefix or suffix. —**af·fixed** or **af·fixt** (ə fikst′), *p.t. & p.p.;* **af·fix′ing,** *pr.p.*

af·flict (ə flikt′), *v.* to cause pain or suffering to; trouble [She is *afflicted* with a skin rash.]

af·flic·tion (ə flik′shən), *n.* pain; trouble; suffering or the cause of suffering.

af·flu·ence (af′lōō əns), *n.* great plenty; abundance, as of riches; wealth. —**af′flu·ent,** *adj.*

af·ford (ə fôrd′), *v.* 1. to have money enough to spare for: *usually used with* can *or* be able [Can we *afford* a vacation in Canada this year?] 2. to be able to do something without taking great risks [I can *afford* to speak frankly.] 3. to give; furnish [Music *affords* her pleasure.]

af·fray (ə frā′), *n.* a noisy fight or quarrel.

af·fright (ə frīt′), *v.* to frighten; terrify: *now seldom used.*

af·front (ə frunt′), *v.* to insult right to one's face and on purpose [He *affronted* us by yawning in a bored way.] —*n.* speech or conduct that is meant to be rude or offensive; insult [Criticism of her cooking is an *affront* to a hostess.]

Af·ghan (af′gan), *n.* 1. a person born or living in Afghanistan. 2. **afghan,** a crocheted or knitted soft wool blanket or shawl.

Af·ghan·i·stan (af gan′ə stan), *n.* a country in southwestern Asia, between Iran and India.

a·field (ə fēld′), *adv.* 1. in, on, or to the field. 2. away from home; astray.

a·fire (ə fīr′), *adv. & adj.* on fire; burning.

a·flame (ə flām′), *adv. & adj.* 1. in flames; burning. 2. glowing [fields *aflame* with sunlight].

AFL-CIO, American Federation of Labor and Congress of Industrial Organizations. It is the largest organization of labor unions in the United States.

a·float (ə flōt′), *adj.* **1.** floating on the surface [We set some paper boats *afloat* on the river.] **2.** on board ship; at sea [As a sailor, he spent most of his life *afloat.*] **3.** flooded [The ship sprang a leak and soon the deck was *afloat.*] **4.** current; circulating [Rumors were *afloat.*]

a·foot (ə foot′), *adv. & adj.* **1.** on foot; walking [They set out *afoot* for the beach.] **2.** in operation; in progress; astir [There is trouble *afoot.*]

a·fore (ə fôr′), *adv., prep., conj.* before: *now seldom used except in compound words and in sailors' talk.*

a·fore·men·tioned (ə fôr′men′shənd), *adj.* mentioned before or earlier [The *aforementioned* people all passed the test.]

a·fore·said (ə fôr′sed′), *adj.* aforementioned.

a·fore·time (ə fôr′tīm′), *adv.* in times now past; formerly [He had visited us *aforetime.*]

a·foul (ə foul′), *adv. & adj.* in a mess or a tangle. —**run afoul of,** to get into trouble with [He ran *afoul* of the law.]

a·fraid (ə frād′), *adj.* feeling fear; frightened [*afraid* of the dark]. *Afraid* is often used in everyday talk to show regret [I'm *afraid* I can't go.]

a·fresh (ə fresh′), *adv.* again; anew [He tore up the letter and started writing *afresh.*]

Af·ri·ca (af′ri kə), *n.* the second largest continent. It is south of Europe, between the Atlantic and Indian oceans.

Af·ri·can (af′ri kən), *adj.* of Africa, its people, cultures, etc. —*n.* **1.** a person born or living in Africa. **2.** a member of an African race; Negro.

aft (aft), *adj. & adv.* at, near, or toward the stern of a ship.

af·ter (af′tər), *adv.* **1.** behind; coming next [You go on ahead, and we'll follow *after.*] **2.** later; following in time [They met in May and were married three months *after.*] —*prep.* **1.** behind [The soldiers marched one *after* the other.] **2.** in search of [What are you *after*?] **3.** later than [He worked *after* quitting time.] **4.** as a result of; because of [*After* what has happened, he won't go.] **5.** in spite of [*After* all the bad luck he has had, he is still cheerful.] **6.** next to in rank or importance [A captain comes *after* a major.] **7.** in the manner of [a novel *after* the style of Dickens]. **8.** for; in honor of [He is named *after* Lincoln.] **9.** about; concerning [She asked *after* you.] —*conj.* following the time when [They left the party *after* we did.] —*adj.* next; later [in an *after* period of his career.]

af·ter·ef·fect (af′tər ə fekt′), *n.* an effect coming later, or as a result of a main effect [This drug has no harmful *aftereffects.*]

af·ter·glow (af′tər glō), *n.* the glow that is left after a light has gone, as after a sunset.

af·ter·math (af′tər math), *n.* a result or effect, especially a bad one [Her headaches are an *aftermath* of the accident.]

af·ter·noon (af tər nōōn′), *n.* the time of day from noon to evening.

af·ter·thought (af′tər thôt), *n.* a thought coming later, especially too late to be helpful [The day following the test, he had many *afterthoughts* about his answers.]

af·ter·ward (af′tər wərd) or **af·ter·wards** (af′tər wərdz), *adv.* later; at a later time [We had dinner and went for a drive *afterward.*]

Ag, the symbol for the chemical element *silver.*

a·gain (ə gen′ *or* ə gān′), *adv.* **1.** once more; one more time [If you don't understand the sentence, read it *again.*] **2.** back; as before [He is home *again.*] **3.** on the other hand [She wants to sing and, then *again,* she's afraid to.] —**again and again,** often; many times.

a·gainst (ə genst′ *or* ə gānst′), *prep.* **1.** acting in an opposite way to; opposed to [the fight *against* disease]. **2.** toward so as to strike [Throw the ball *against* the wall.] **3.** opposite to the direction of [He drove *against* the traffic.] **4.** so as to be prepared for [We provided *against* a poor crop.]

a·gape (ə gāp′), *adv. & adj.* gaping; with the mouth wide open, as in surprise or wonder [We stared at the strange sight *agape.*]

ag·ate (ag′it), *n.* **1.** a hard stone with striped or clouded coloring, used in jewelry. **2.** a small glass ball that looks like this, used in marbles.

a·ga·ve (ə gā′vē), *n.* an American desert plant, especially the century plant, with thick, fleshy leaves. Fiber for making rope is obtained from some kinds of agave.

agave

age (āj), *n.* **1.** the time that a person or thing has existed from birth or beginning [He left school at the *age* of fourteen.] **2.** a stage of life [She is at the awkward *age.*] **3.** the latter part of a lifetime; old age [*Age* had turned his hair gray.] **4.** a generation [Future *ages* will read his books.] **5.** a period of time in history [the Middle *Ages,* the Stone *Age*]. **6.** a long time: *used only in everyday talk, usually in the plural,* **ages** [It has been *ages* since I've seen him.] —*v.* to grow old or make old [He is *aging* rapidly. Hard work has *aged* him.] —**of age,** having reached the time of life when one is considered an adult with full legal rights [A man comes *of age* at twenty-one.] —**aged,** *p.t. & p.p.;* **ag′ing** or **age′ing,** *pr.p.*

-age (ij), a suffix meaning: **1.** the act of [*Marriage* is the act of marrying.] **2.** amount or number of [*Acreage* is the number of acres.] **3.** cost of [*Postage* is the cost of posting a letter.] **4.** group of [*Peerage* is a group of peers.] **5.** home of [A *hermitage* is the home of a hermit.]

a·ged (ā′jid), *adj.* **1.** grown old [his *aged* aunt]. **2.** (ājd), of the age of [a girl *aged* ten years].

a·gen·cy (ā′jən sē), *n.* **1.** that by which something is done; means [Electricity is the *agency* by which our homes are lighted.] **2.** the business of a person, company, etc. that acts for someone else [an insurance *agency*]. —**a′gen·cies,** *pl.*

a·gen·da (ə jen′də), *n.pl.* a list of things to be done or talked about, as at a meeting: *now often* used with a singular verb [The *agenda* for the session was prepared last week.]

a·gent (ā′jənt), *n.* **1.** a person or thing that brings about a certain result [Education is a powerful *agent* in helping people to understand one another.] **2.** a person or company that acts for another [Most actors have *agents* to handle their business matters.]

ag·gran·dize (ag′rən dīz *or* ə gran′dīz), *v.* to make more powerful, richer, etc. [Some public officials used their office to *aggrandize* themselves.] —**ag′gran·dized,** *p.t. & p.p.;* **ag′gran·diz·ing,** *pr.p.* —**ag·gran·dize·ment** (ə gran′dizmənt), *n.*

ag·gra·vate (ag′rə vāt), *v.* **1.** to make worse; make more troublesome [He *aggravated* his sprained ankle by walking.] **2.** to make impatient; annoy; bother; irritate: *used only in everyday talk* [You'll *aggravate* Dad if you're late for dinner again.] —**ag′gra·vat·ed,** *p.t. & p.p.;* **ag′gra·vat·ing,** *pr.p.* —**ag′gra·va′tion,** *n.*

ag·gre·gate (ag′ri git), *adj.* gathered into a whole; considered as a group; total [the *aggregate* number of schools in this area]. —*n.* the complete number; total; collection [The *aggregate* of books in the library amounts to over 1,000.]

ag·gre·ga·tion (ag′ri gā′shən), *n.* a group or collection of distinct things thought of as a whole.

ag·gres·sion (ə gresh′ən), *n.* the starting of a fight or war by one person or nation with another; any warlike act by one country against another without just cause.

ag·gres·sive (ə gres′iv), *adj.* **1.** ready to start fights or quarrels [an *aggressive* bully]. **2.** bold and active; full of energy and ideas [an *aggressive* leader]. —**ag·gres′sive·ly,** *adv.* —**ag·gres′sive·ness,** *n.*

ag·gres·sor (ə gres′ər), *n.* a person or country that starts a fight or war.

ag·grieve (ə grēv′), *v.* to make feel injured or insulted; offend [The colonists were much *aggrieved* by the stamp tax.] —**ag·grieved′,** *p.t. & p.p.;* **ag·griev′ing,** *pr.p.*

a·ghast (ə gast′), *adj.* feeling great horror or dismay; horrified [*aghast* at the sight of blood].

ag·ile (aj′əl), *adj.* moving with quickness and ease; active; nimble [an *agile* jumper]. —**ag′ile·ly,** *adv.*

a·gil·i·ty (ə jil′ə tē), *n.* the ability to move with quickness and ease [Tennis requires *agility*.]

ag·i·tate (aj′ə tāt), *v.* **1.** to stir or shake up; move violently. **2.** to excite or disturb the feelings of [The news of the disaster *agitated* him.] **3.** to stir up interest and support through speeches and writing so as to cause change [He *agitated* for better working conditions.] —**ag′i·tat·ed,** *p.t. & p.p.;* **ag′i·tat·ing,** *pr.p.*

ag·i·ta·tion (aj′ə tā′shən), *n.* **1.** the act of stirring or shaking violently. **2.** a disturbing or exciting of the feelings. **3.** discussion in order to stir up people and produce changes.

ag·i·ta·tor (aj′ə tā′tər), *n.* a person or thing that agitates.

a·glow (ə glō′), *adv. & adj.* in a glow; flushed with color, as from excitement [Her face was *aglow* with joy.]

ag·nos·tic (ag näs′tik), *n.* a person who believes that it is impossible to know whether or not there is a God.

a·go (ə gō′), *adj.* gone by; past [They were married five years *ago.*] —*adv.* in the past [long *ago*].

a·gog (ə gäg′), *adv. & adj.* full of excitement or interest [The children are all *agog* over the puppy.]

ag·o·nize (ag′ə nīz), *v.* to suffer or make suffer pain so great that the body or mind can hardly bear it. —**ag′o·nized,** *p.t. & p.p.;* **ag′o·niz·ing,** *pr.p.*

ag·o·ny (ag′ə nē), *n.* **1.** pain so great that the body or mind can hardly bear it. **2.** a last great struggle of the body or mind, as in dying. —**ag′o·nies,** *pl.*

a·grar·i·an (ə grer′i ən), *adj.* **1.** having to do with land as it is owned for farming [The large estates were divided among the peasants to solve the *agrarian* problem.] **2.** of farming or farmers; agricultural. —*n.* a person in favor of a more even division of land among those who work it. —**a·grar′i·an·ism,** *n.*

a·gree (ə grē′), *v.* **1.** to say "yes"; consent [John *agreed* to go if we paid him.] **2.** to grant; admit [The waiter *agreed* that the steak was overdone.] **3.** to be alike or similar; be in accord [Our tastes in art *agree.* I *agree* with my father in matters of politics.] **4.** to be healthful, proper, etc.: *followed by* with [This climate *agrees* with him.] **5.** in grammar, to have the same number, person, case, or gender [The verb *agrees* with its subject in number and person.] —**a·greed′,** *p.t. & p.p.;* **a·gree′ing,** *pr.p.*

a·gree·a·ble (ə grē′ə b'l), *adj.* **1.** pleasing; pleasant [an *agreeable* odor]. **2.** willing or ready to say "yes" [She was *agreeable* to our plan.] —**a·gree′a·bly,** *adv.*

a·gree·ment (ə grē′mənt), *n.* **1.** an agreeing; a being in harmony [The news report was not in *agreement* with the facts.] **2.** a fixing of terms between two or more people, countries, etc., as in a treaty [The U.S. has trade *agreements* with many nations.]

ag·ri·cul·tur·al (ag′ri kul′chər əl), *adj.* of agriculture; having to do with farming.

ag·ri·cul·ture (ag′ri kul′chər), *n.* the science and art of growing crops and raising livestock; farming.

ag·ri·cul·tur·ist (ag′ri kul′chər ist) *or* **ag·ri·cul·tur·al·ist** (ag′ri kul′chər əl ist), *n.* **1.** an expert in agriculture. **2.** a farmer.

a·ground (ə ground′), *adv. & adj.* on or onto the shore, the bottom, a reef, etc. [The ship ran *aground* in the shallow bay.]

---

fat, āpe, cär, ten, ēven, hit, bīte, gō, hôrn, tōōl, book, up, fŭr; get, joy, yet, chin, she, thin, *th*en; zh = s in pleasure; ′ as in able (ā′b'l); ə = a in ago, e in agent, i in sanity, o in confess, u in focus.

a·gue (ā′gyōō), *n.* **1.** a disease, especially malaria, in which the patient has both fever and chills, one after the other. **2.** a chill; fit of shivering.

ah (ä), *interj.* a sound made in various ways to show pain, delight, regret, disgust, surprise, etc.

a·ha (ä hä′), *interj.* a sound made to show satisfaction, pleasure, triumph, etc.

a·head (ə hed′), *adv. & adj.* in or to the front; forward [The lighthouse was directly *ahead* of the ship. He moved *ahead* halfway through the race.] —**ahead of,** in advance of; before [He arrived *ahead of* the other guests.] —**get ahead of,** to do better than; outdo.

a·hem (ə hem′), *interj.* a cough or slight noise in the throat made to get someone's attention, to show doubt, etc.

a·hoy (ə hoi′), *interj.* a call used by sailors in hailing a person or ship [Ship *ahoy!*]

aid (ād), *v.* to give help to; assist [The medicine *aided* him in his recovery.] —*n.* **1.** help; assistance [The compass is an *aid* to navigation.] **2.** a helper; assistant [Sue is a nurse's *aid*.]

aide (ād), *n.* an officer in the army, navy, etc. who is an assistant to an officer of higher rank.

aide-de-camp or **aid-de-camp** (ād′də kamp′), *n.* an aide to a general or marshal. —**aides′-de-camp′** or **aids′-de-camp′,** *pl.*

ai·grette (ā′gret *or* ā gret′), *n.* **1.** a heron with long, white plumes: usually **egret. 2.** a plume of these feathers, once worn for ornament by women.

ail (āl), *v.* **1.** to cause pain to; trouble; distress [The doctor doesn't know what *ails* me.] **2.** to be ill; feel sick [Grandfather is *ailing* today.]

ai·le·ron (ā′lə rän), *n.* a hinged flap on the back edge of the wing of an airplane. It is moved up or down in keeping the plane steady or in making a turn in the air.

ail·ment (āl′mənt), *n.* an illness; sickness.

aim (ām), *v.* **1.** to point a gun, missile, etc. or direct a blow or remark [He *aimed* the dart at the target's center. She *aimed* the insult at her brother.] **2.** to have as one's goal or purpose; try [We *aimed* at complete victory. We *aim* to please.] —*n.* **1.** the aiming of a weapon at a target [My *aim* is blocked by that tree.] **2.** intention, object, or purpose [His chief *aim* in life is to help others.] —**take aim,** to point at a target; direct a bullet, blow, remark, etc.

aim·less (ām′lis), *adj.* without aim or purpose [a vagabond's *aimless* life]. —**aim′less·ly,** *adv.*

ain't (ānt), a shortened everyday form of *am not, is not, are not, has not,* or *have not. Ain't* is not now usually regarded as standard English, although it is sometimes defended as a useful contraction of *am not* in asking a question [I'm going too, *ain't* I?]

air (er), *n.* **1.** the mixture of gases that is all around the earth. Air cannot be seen, but it can spread to fill a space and it can move in currents. It consists mainly of nitrogen, oxygen, hydrogen, and carbon dioxide. **2.** space above the earth; sky [The lark flew into the *air*.] **3.** the general feeling one gets from someone or something [An *air* of luxury fills the room. The stranger had an *air* of mystery.] **4.** a melody or tune; song.

—*adj.* having to do with airplanes, air forces, etc. [a country with *air* power]. —*v.* **1.** to let air into or through in order to dry, cool, or freshen [We must *air* the rooms before we move in.] **2.** to make widely known [I wish Jane wouldn't *air* her troubles.] —**give oneself airs** or **put on airs,** to act as though one were better or more important than other people. —**on the air,** broadcasting or being broadcast over radio. —**up in the air,** not settled; not decided. —**walk on air,** to feel very happy or lively.

air base, an airport for military airplanes.

air-con·di·tion (er′kən dish′ən), *v.* to provide with air conditioning. —**air′-con·di′tioned,** *adj.*

air conditioning, any system in buildings, cars, etc. for cleaning the air and changing the amount of moisture and heat in it. Air conditioning is usually used to make an enclosed place cooler and drier.

air·craft (er′kraft), *n. sing. & pl.* any machine or machines for flying [Airplanes, dirigibles, balloons, and helicopters are all *aircraft*.]

aircraft carrier, a warship that carries small airplanes and is used as their base. It has a large, flat deck for taking off and landing.

air·drome (er′drōm), *n.* **1.** an airport. **2.** an airfield. **3.** a hangar. *Mainly a British word.*

Aire·dale (er′dāl), *n.* a large terrier having a hard, wiry, tan coat with black markings.

aircraft carrier

air·field (er′fēld), *n.* a field where aircraft can take off and land.

air force, armed forces made up of the airplanes, men, and equipment needed for air warfare.

air·i·ly (er′ə lē), *adv.* in an airy or gay, light manner; jauntily [He spoke *airily* of the dangers he had faced.]

Airedale (24 in. high at shoulder)

air·ing (er′ing), *n.* **1.** the condition of being left open to the air for drying, freshening, etc. [These blankets need an *airing*.] **2.** a making known to the public [The newspapers gave the scandal an *airing*.] **3.** a walk or ride outdoors.

air·less (er′lis), *adj.* without air; especially, without fresh air [a musty, *airless* attic].

air line, 1. a system or company for moving freight and passengers by aircraft. **2.** a route for travel by air.

air liner, a large passenger airplane.

air mail, 1. mail carried by aircraft. **2.** the system of carrying mail by aircraft. —**air-mail** (er′māl′), *adj.*

air·man (er'mən), *n.* **1.** a pilot or crew member of an airplane. **2.** an enlisted person in the U.S. Air Force. —**air'men,** *pl.*

air·plane (er'plān), *n.* an aircraft that is kept up by the force of air upon its wings and is driven forward by a screw propeller or by jet propulsion.

air pocket, a condition of the air that causes an airplane to make sudden, short drops.

air·port (er'pôrt), *n.* a place where aircraft can land to get fuel, be repaired, take on passengers and freight, etc.

air raid, an attack by aircraft, usually bombers.

air rifle, a rifle in which the force of air under pressure is used to shoot BB's, etc.

air·ship (er'ship), *n.* any aircraft that is filled with a gas lighter than air and is moved through the air by propellers; dirigible.

air·sick (er'sik), *adj.* feeling sick or vomiting from traveling in an aircraft.

air·strip (er'strip), *n.* an airfield prepared quickly, as for use in warfare.

air·tight (er'tīt'), *adj.* **1.** closed so tightly that air cannot get in or out [an *airtight* can of coffee]. **2.** that cannot be criticized or proved to be false [an *airtight* alibi].

air·y (er'ē), *adj.* **1.** open to the air; breezy [an *airy* room]. **2.** flimsy as air; not solid or practical [*airy* schemes]. **3.** light as air; delicate [*airy* music]. **4.** lighthearted; gay [*airy* merriment]. **5.** of or in the air [the *airy* heights of the Alps]. —**air'i·er,** *compar.;* **air'i·est,** *superl.* —**air'i·ly,** *adv.*

aisle (īl), *n.* **1.** an open way for passing between or along rows of seats, as in a theater. **2.** a part of a church along the inside wall, set off by a row of columns or pillars.

aisle of a theater

a·jar (ə jär'), *adv.* & *adj.* slightly open [The door stood *ajar*.]

A·jax (ā'jaks), *n.* either of two warriors in Greek myths who were heroes of the Trojan War.

a·kim·bo (ə kim'bō), *adv.* & *adj.* with the hands on the hips and the elbows bent outward.

a·kin (ə kin'), *adj.* **1.** of the same family or kin; related. **2.** somewhat alike; similar [The lemon and the lime are *akin* in taste.]

Ak·ron (ak'rən), *n.* a city in northeastern Ohio.

-al (əl), a suffix meaning: **1.** of, like, or suitable for [*Musical* sounds are sounds of or like music.] **2.** the act

girl with arms akimbo

or process of [*Denial* is the act of denying.]

Al, symbol for the chemical element *aluminum.*

Al·a·bam·a (al'ə bam'ə), *n.* a State in the southeastern part of the United States: abbreviated **Ala.**

al·a·bas·ter (al'ə bas'tər), *n.* a smooth, white stone that is carved into statues, vases, etc. —*adj.* smooth and white like alabaster.

à la carte (ä'lə kärt'), with a separate price for each dish on the menu instead of a single price for a whole meal [Dinners served *à la carte* are usually more expensive.]

a·lack (ə lak'), *interj.* an exclamation used in olden times to show regret, surprise, etc.

a·lac·ri·ty (ə lak'rə tē), *n.* quick, lively action; eager quickness [She ran to the door with *alacrity*.]

A·lad·din (ə lad''n), *n.* a boy in *The Arabian Nights* who found a magic lamp and a magic ring. Whenever he rubbed these, a genie would appear to do whatever he asked.

Al·a·mo (al'ə mō), *n.* a mission, later a fort, at San Antonio, Texas. Mexican troops captured it from the Texans in 1836.

a la mode or **à la mode** (ä'lə mōd'), *adj.* **1.** made or served in a certain style; especially, served with ice cream [pie *a la mode*]. **2.** in the fashion; stylish.

a·larm (ə lärm'), *n.* **1.** a signal that is a warning of danger [He blew his bugle to sound the *alarm*.] **2.** a bell, siren, etc. that gives such a warning [a fire *alarm*]. **3.** sudden fear caused by possible danger [The village was filled with *alarm* when the river started to flood.] —*v.* to make suddenly afraid or anxious [He was *alarmed* to find the house empty.]

alarm clock, a clock that can be set to ring or buzz at any particular time, as to awaken a person from sleep.

a·larm·ing (ə lär'ming), *adj.* that can make one suddenly afraid or anxious; frightening [There has been an *alarming* increase in traffic deaths.] —**a·larm'ing·ly,** *adv.*

a·larm·ist (ə lär'mist), *n.* **1.** a person who sounds unnecessary alarms. **2.** a person who is easily frightened and usually expects the worst to happen.

a·lar·um (ə ler'əm), *n.* an older spelling of **alarm,** now used only in poetry.

a·las (ə las'), *interj.* an exclamation showing sorrow, pity, regret, or fear.

A·las·ka (ə las'kə), *n.* a State of the United States in northwestern North America, separated from Asia by the Bering Strait: abbreviated **Alas.** —**A·las'kan,** *adj.* & *n.*

Alaska Highway, a highway extending from British Columbia, Canada, to central Alaska.

alb (alb), *n.* a long, white linen robe, worn by a priest at Mass.

Al·ba·ni·a (al bā'ni ə), *n.* a country in southern Europe. —**Al·ba'ni·an,** *adj.* & *n.*

---

fat, āpe, cär, ten, ēven, hit, bīte, gō, hôrn, tōōl, book, up, fûr; get, joy, yet, chin, she, thin, *th*en; zh = s in pleasure; 'as in able (ā'b'l); ə = a in ago, e in agent, i in sanity, o in confess, u in focus.

Al·ban·y (ôl′bə nē), *n.* the capital of New York State, on the Hudson River.

al·ba·tross (al′bə trôs), *n.* a large sea bird with long, narrow wings, webbed feet, and a large, hooked beak.

al·be·it (ôl bē′it), *conj.* although; even though; nevertheless: *now seldom used* [He was an un-learned man, *albeit* no fool.]

Al·ber·ta (al bŭr′tə), *n.* a province of south-western Canada.

al·bi·no (al bī′nō), *n.* **1.** a person or animal whose skin, hair, and eyes lack normal coloring. Albinos have a pale skin, whitish hair, and pink eyes. **2.** a plant lacking normal coloring. —**al·bi′nos,** *pl.*

albatross
(wing spread is 10 ft.)

Al·bi·on (al′bi ən), *n.* England: *a name used in poetry.*

al·bum (al′bəm), *n.* **1.** a book with blank pages for collecting pic-tures, clippings, stamps, etc. **2.** a booklike holder for phonograph records, or a set of such records. **3.** a single, long-playing record containing a collection of musical pieces.

picture album

al·bu·men (al byoo′mən), *n.* **1.** the white of an egg. **2.** albumin.

al·bu·min (al byoo′min), *n.* a protein found in egg white, milk, muscle, blood, and in many plant tissues and fluids.

Al·bu·quer·que (al′bə kŭr′kē), *n.* a city in central New Mexico.

Al·can Highway (al′kan), Alaska Highway.

al·che·mist (al′kə mist), *n.* a person who worked in alchemy.

al·che·my (al′kə mē), *n.* **1.** an early form of chemistry, often mixed with magic, studied in the Middle Ages. The chief aims of alchemy were to change iron or lead into gold and to find a drink that would keep people young forever. **2.** a magical power to bring about change.

al·co·hol (al′kə hôl), *n.* **1.** a colorless, strong-smelling liquid that evaporates easily and burns with a hot flame. Alcohol is made from fer-mented grain, potatoes, etc. and is used in indus-try and as an antiseptic in medicine. It is the substance in whisky, beer, wine, etc. that makes people drunk. **2.** any liquor that has alcohol in it [The doctor warned against the use of *alcohol.*]

al·co·hol·ic (al′kə hôl′ik), *adj.* of or contain-ing alcohol. —*n.* a person suffering from alco-holism.

al·co·hol·ism (al′kə hôl′iz′m), *n.* the diseased condition of mind and body caused by drinking too much alcoholic liquor.

Al·cott, Louisa May (ôl′kət), 1832–1888; American writer of novels.

al·cove (al′kōv), *n.* a small part of a room that is set back from the main part [The *alcove* off the kitchen serves as a breakfast nook.]

al·der (ôl′dər), *n.* a small tree like the birch. It has woody cones and grows in wet soils.

al·der·man (ôl′dər-mən), *n.* in some cities, a member of the city council; coun-cilman. —**al′der-men,** *pl.* —**al·der-man·ic** (ôl′dər man′ik), *adj.*

alcove

ale (āl), *n.* a drink very much like beer, made from malt and hops.

a·lert (ə lŭrt′), *adj.* **1.** watchful and ready [an *alert* guard]. **2.** quick in thought or action; active; nimble [Grandmother is very *alert* for a woman of eighty-five.] —*n.* **1.** a warning signal, as of an expected air raid. **2.** the time from such a warning until the danger is over. —*v.* to warn to be ready [The soldiers were *alerted* before the attack.] —**on the alert,** watchful and ready. —**a·lert′ly,** *adv.* —**a·lert′ness,** *n.*

A·leu·tian Islands (ə loo′shən), a part of Alaska consisting of a chain of islands off the southwest coast.

Al·ex·an·der the Great (al′ig zan′dər), 356–323 B.C.; king of Macedonia who conquered Persia, Syria, Egypt, etc.

Al·ex·an·dri·a (al′ig zan′dri ə), *n.* a city in Egypt, on the Mediterranean.

al·fal·fa (al fal′fə), *n.* a plant with purple, cloverlike flowers and long, deep roots. It is grown as food for cattle, horses, etc.

Al·fred the Great (al′-frid), 849–899 A.D.; an early king of England who fur-thered English culture.

al·gae (al′jē), *n.pl.* a group of simple plants, often grow-ing in colonies in water or on damp surfaces. Algae have no true root, stem, or leaf. Most seaweeds are algae.

al·ge·bra (al′jə brə), *n.* a form of mathematics that uses letters as well as num-bers in formulas, equations, etc. to solve prob-lems. Example: if $2x^2 + 3x + 15 = 29$, then $x = 2$.

alfalfa
(plant and roots)

al·ge·bra·ic (al′jə brā′ik), *adj.* of, like, or used in algebra. —**al·ge·bra/i·cal·ly,** *adv.*

Al·ger·i·a (al jir′i ə), *n.* a country in northern Africa, formerly under French control. —**Al·ger/i·an,** *adj. & n.*

Al·giers (al jirs′), *n.* the capital of Algeria.

Al·gon·qui·an (al gäng′kwi ən) or **Al·gon·quin** (al gäng′kwin), *adj.* of or having to do with a large group of North American Indian tribes. —*n.* **1.** the family of languages spoken by these tribes. **2.** a member of any of these tribes.

a·li·as (ā/li əs), *n.* a name that is not one's real name, used by a person to hide who he really is. —*adv.* having the alias of [John Bell *alias* Paul Jones].

A·li Ba·ba (al/i bab/ə *or* ä/li bä/bə), in *The Arabian Nights,* a poor woodcutter who found the treasure of forty thieves in a cave. He made the door of the cave open by saying "Open sesame!"

al·i·bi (al/ə bī), *n.* **1.** the plea of a person accused of a crime that he was not at the scene of the crime when it took place. **2.** any excuse: *used only in everyday talk* [What is your *alibi* for being late?] —*v.* to give an excuse: *used only in everyday talk.* —**al/i·bis,** *pl.*

al·ien (āl/yən), *adj.* belonging to another country or people; foreign; strange [*alien* customs]. —*n.* **1.** a foreigner. **2.** a person living in a country of which he is not a citizen. —**alien to,** strange to; not natural to [Cruel words were *alien to* his lips.]

al·ien·ate (āl/yən āt), *v.* to make lose the friendship or love once felt; make unfriendly [His bad temper *alienated* us.] —**al/ien·at·ed,** *p.t. & p.p.;* **al/ien·at·ing,** *pr.p.* —**al/ien·a/tion,** *n.*

al·ien·ist (āl/yən ist), *n.* a doctor who treats patients who are mentally ill: a name used in law courts for a psychiatrist.

a·light (ə līt/), *v.* **1.** to get down or off; dismount [She *alighted* from her horse.] **2.** to come down after flight; settle [The bird *alighted* on the ground.] **3.** to come by chance; happen on or upon. —**a·light/ed,** or **a·lit/,** *p.t. & p.p.;* **a·light/ing,** *pr.p.*

a·light (ə līt/), *adj.* lighted up; glowing [a face *alight* with joy].

a·lign (ə līn/), *v.* **1.** to put or come into a straight line [*Align* the chairs along the wall.] **2.** to get into agreement, close co-operation, etc. [Senator Blake has *aligned* himself with the conservatives.]

a·lign·ment (ə līn/mənt), *n.* **1.** arrangement in a straight line [The front wheels are out of *alignment.*] **2.** a getting into agreement or co-operation [a new *alignment* of western European nations].

a·like (ə līk/), *adj.* like one another; similar [His mother and sister look *alike.*] —*adv.* in the same way; similarly [Their father treated them *alike.* They dress *alike.*]

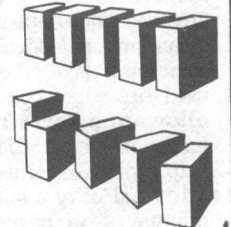

upper blocks in alignment; lower blocks out of alignment

al·i·men·ta·ry (al/ə men/tə rē), *adj.* having to do with food or digestion [The *alimentary* canal is the passage from the mouth through the stomach and intestines.]

al·i·mo·ny (al/ə mō/nē), *n.* money that a court orders a man to pay regularly to support a woman from whom he has been divorced.

a·line (ə līn/), *v.* to align. —**a·lined/,** *p.t. & p.p.;* **a·lin/ing,** *pr.p.* —**a·line/ment,** *n.*

a·live (ə līv/), *adj.* **1.** having life; living. **2.** going on; in action; not ended or destroyed [to keep old memories *alive*]. **3.** lively; alert. —**alive to,** fully aware of [Are you *alive to* the risks you are taking?] —**alive with,** full of living or moving things [a hive *alive with* bees].

al·ka·li (al/kə lī), *n.* any chemical substance, such as soda or potash, that neutralizes acids and forms salts with them. Alkalis dissolved in water have a soapy feel and taste. —**al/ka·lis** or **al/ka·lies,** *pl.*

al·ka·line (al/kə līn *or* al/kə lin), *adj.* of, like, or containing an alkali [Lime is an *alkaline* substance used to neutralize acid soil.] —**al·ka·lin·i·ty** (al/kə lin/ə tē), *n.*

al·ka·loid (al/kə loid), *n.* any of a group of bitter compounds, such as caffeine, morphine, and quinine, which are found mostly in plants. Alkaloids have many uses in medicine.

all (ôl), *adj.* **1.** the whole part or amount of [in *all* England; *all* the gold]. **2.** every one of [*All* men must eat. *All* the men went.] **3.** as much as possible [My apology was made in *all* sincerity.] **4.** any; any whatever [true beyond *all* question]. **5.** alone; only [Life is not *all* pleasure.] —*pron.* **1.** everyone: *used with a plural verb* [*All* of us are here.] **2.** everything; the whole matter [*All* is over between them.] **3.** every part or bit [*All* of the candy is gone.] —*n.* **1.** everything one has [He gave his *all* to the cause.] **2.** the whole amount [That is *all* you're going to get.] —*adv.* **1.** completely; entirely [*all* worn out; *all* through the night]. **2.** each; apiece [The score is thirty *all.*] —**above all,** before all other things. —**after all,** in spite of everything. —**all but, 1.** all except. **2.** almost. —**all in,** very tired: *used only in everyday talk.* —**all in all, 1.** keeping everything in mind. **2.** as a whole. —**all over, 1.** ended. **2.** everywhere. —**at all, 1.** in the least; to the smallest amount. **2.** in any way. **3.** under any conditions; in spite of. —**in all,** altogether.

Al·lah (al/ə *or* ä/lə), *n.* the name for God used in the Moslem religion.

all-A·mer·i·can (ôl/ə mer/ə kən), *adj.* **1.** made up entirely of Americans [an *all-American* group of scientists]. **2.** having to do with a make-believe football team made up of college players chosen as the best of the year in the United States.

all-a·round (ôl/ə round/), *adj.* able to do many things or be used for many purposes [A tractor is a piece of *all-around* farm machinery.]

al·lay (ə lā/), *v.* **1.** to put to rest; quiet; calm [His confident manner helped to *allay* their fears.] **2.** to make lighter or less; relieve, as pain or grief. —**al·layed/,** *p.t. & p.p.;* **al·lay/ing,** *pr.p.*

al·le·ga·tion (al'ə gā'shən), *n.* **1.** the act of alleging. **2.** a positive statement, often one without proof [a false *allegation* of bribery].

al·lege (ə lej'), *v.* **1.** to declare, usually without proof [He *alleged* that he had seen a flying saucer.] **2.** to give as an excuse or reason [In his defense he *alleged* insanity at the time of the crime.] —**al·leged'**, *p.t. & p.p.*; **al·leg'ing**, *pr.p.*

Al·le·ghe·ny Mountains (al'ə gā'nē), a mountain range in central Pennsylvania, Maryland, West Virginia, and Virginia: also called **the Al'le·ghe'nies.**

al·le·giance (ə lē'jəns), *n.* **1.** a being loyal to one's country or ruler [We pledge *allegiance* to the flag as a symbol of our country.] **2.** loyalty or devotion, as to friends or a cause.

al·le·go·ry (al'ə gôr'ē), *n.* a story used for teaching or explaining something. In allegories people, animals, things, and happenings have some meaning besides the one that is readily seen [Aesop's fables are short *allegories*.] —**al'le·go'ries**, *pl.* —**al'le·gor'i·cal**, *adj.*

al·le·gro (ə lā'grō *or* ə leg'rō), *adj. & adv.* fast; lively: an Italian word used in music to tell how fast a piece should be played.

al·le·lu·ia (al'ə loo'yə), *interj. & n.* same as **hallelujah.**

al·ler·gic (ə lur'jik), *adj.* **1.** of or caused by an allergy. **2.** having an allergy.

al·ler·gy (al'ər jē), *n.* a condition in which one becomes sick by breathing in, touching, eating, etc. some particular substance that is not harmful to most people [Hay fever is often caused by an *allergy* to certain pollens.] —**al'ler·gies**, *pl.*

al·le·vi·ate (ə lē'vi āt), *v.* to make easier to bear; lighten or relieve [Drugs are sometimes used to *alleviate* pain.] —**al·le'vi·at·ed**, *p.t. & p.p.*; **al·le'vi·at·ing**, *pr.p.* —**al·le'vi·a'tion**, *n.*

al·ley (al'ē), *n.* **1.** a narrow street or walk between or behind buildings. **2.** a long, narrow lane of polished wood, along which the balls are rolled in bowling. **3.** a place that has several such lanes for bowling. —**al'leys**, *pl.*

al·ley (al'ē), *n.* a large marble used as the shooter in playing marbles. —**al'leys**, *pl.*

bowling alley

al·li·ance (ə lī'əns), *n.* **1.** a joining or coming together for some purpose; uniting of families by marriage, of nations by treaty, etc. **2.** the agreement made for such a uniting. **3.** the nations or persons united in such a way.

al·lied (ə līd' *or* al'īd), *adj.* **1.** united by treaty, agreement, etc. [*allied* nations]. **2.** closely related [Anatomy and biology are *allied* sciences.]

al·lies (al'īz *or* ə līz'), *n.* plural of **ally.** The nations who joined to fight against Germany in World Wars I and II were called **the Allies.**

al·li·ga·tor (al'ə gā'tər), *n.* a large lizard like the crocodile, found in warm rivers and marshes of the United States and China. A scaly leather is made from its hide.

alligator pear, the avocado.

al·lit·er·a·tion (ə lit'ər·ā'shən), *n.* a repeating of the same sound at the beginning of two or more words, as in a line of poetry [There is an *alliteration* of *s* in "Sing a song of sixpence."]

alligator (8 to 12 ft. long)

al·lo·cate (al'ə kāt), *v.* **1.** to set aside for a special purpose [Congress has *allocated* funds for building large dams.] **2.** to divide in shares or according to a plan; allot [He *allocated* his time between work and play.] —**al'lo·cat·ed**, *p.t. & p.p.*; **al'lo·cat·ing**, *pr.p.* —**al'lo·ca'tion**, *n.*

al·lot (ə lät'), *v.* **1.** to divide or give out in shares or by lot [The land was *allotted* equally to the settlers.] **2.** to give to a person as his share [Each speaker is *allotted* five minutes.] —**al·lot'ted**, *p.t. & p.p.*; **al·lot'ting**, *pr.p.*

al·lot·ment (ə lät'mənt), *n.* **1.** an allotting, or giving out in shares. **2.** a thing allotted; share.

all-out (ôl'out'), *adj.* complete or wholehearted: *used only in everyday talk* [an *all-out* effort].

al·low (ə lou'), *v.* **1.** to let be done; permit; let [*Allow* us to pay. No smoking *allowed*.] **2.** to let have [She *allowed* herself no candy.] **3.** to let enter or stay [Dogs are not *allowed* on buses.] **4.** to admit to be true or right [His claim for $50 was *allowed*.] **5.** to give or keep an extra amount so as to have enough [*Allow* an inch for shrinkage.] —**allow for,** to keep in mind [In comparing Jack's skill with Jerry's, you must *allow for* the difference in their ages.]

al·low·a·ble (ə lou'ə b'l), *adj.* that can be allowed; permissible.

al·low·ance (ə lou'əns), *n.* **1.** an amount of money, food, etc. given regularly to a child or to anyone who depends on others for support. **2.** an amount added or taken off to make up for something [We give an *allowance* of $2 on your used tire when you buy a new one.] —**make allowance for. 1.** to leave room, time, etc. for; allow for. **2.** to keep in mind things that will help explain or excuse something.

al·loy (al'oi *or* ə loi'), *n.* **1.** a metal that is a mixture of two or more metals, or of a metal and something else [Bronze is an *alloy* of copper and tin.] **2.** a common metal, as copper, mixed with a precious metal, as gold, often to give hardness. —*v.* (ə loi'), **1.** to mix metals into an alloy. **2.** to make less worthy by adding something not so good [His kindness is *alloyed* by his desire to be praised.]

all right, 1. satisfactory; adequate; good or well [Your work is *all right*.] **2.** yes; very well [*All right*, I'll do it.] **3.** certainly [She'll go *all right*, but she wants to be coaxed.]

all·round (ôl′round′), *adj.* all-around.

all·spice (ôl′spīs), *n.* **1.** the berry of a West Indian tree related to the myrtle. **2.** a spice made from this berry. Its flavor is like that of several spices mixed together.

all-star (ôl′stär′), *adj.* made up of outstanding or star performers [an *all-star* team].

al·lude (ə lōōd′), *v.* to mention without going into any detail; refer in a general way [He *alluded* to secrets which he could not reveal.] —**al·lud′ed,** *p.t.* & *p.p.;* **al·lud′ing,** *pr.p.*

al·lure (ə loor′), *v.* to tempt with something desirable; attract; entice. —*n.* charm; fascination [the *allure* of faraway places]. —**al·lured′,** *p.t.* & *p.p.;* **al·lur′ing,** *pr.p.*

al·lure·ment (ə loor′mənt), *n.* **1.** an alluring, or tempting. **2.** fascination; charm. **3.** something that allures.

al·lur·ing (ə loor′ing), *adj.* tempting strongly; highly attractive [an *alluring* offer].

al·lu·sion (ə lōō′zhən), *n.* a brief mention without going into details [The poem contains several *allusions* to Greek mythology.]

al·lu·vi·al (ə lōō′vi əl), *adj.* made up of the sand or clay washed down by flowing water [*alluvial* deposits at the mouth of the river].

al·ly (ə lī′), *v.* **1.** to join together by agreement; unite for a special purpose [Nations often *ally* themselves by treaty.] **2.** to relate by close likenesses [The onion is *allied* to the lily.] —*n.* (al′ī), a country or person joined with another for a special purpose [England was our *ally* during World War II.] —**al·lied′,** *p.t.* & *p.p.;* **al·ly′ing,** *pr.p.* —**al′lies,** *pl.*

al·ma ma·ter or **Al·ma Ma·ter** (al′mə mä′tər *or* äl′mə mä′tər), **1.** the college or school that one attended. **2.** its official song.

al·ma·nac (ôl′mə nak), *n.* a yearly calendar with notes about coming events and information about the weather, tides, planting, etc.

al·might·y (ôl mī′tē), *adj.* having power with no limit; all-powerful. —**the Almighty,** God.

al·mond (ä′mənd *or* am′ənd), *n.* **1.** an oval nut that is the seed of a fruit which looks like a small peach. **2.** the small tree that this fruit grows on.

al·most (ôl′mōst), *adv.* not completely but very nearly [She tripped and *almost* fell. Dan is *almost* twelve.]

alms (ämz), *n.* money, food, etc. given to help poor people: used with either a singular *or* plural verb.

almond (shell and kernel)

alms·house (ämz′hous), *n.* a home for people too poor to take care of themselves.

al·oe (al′ō), *n.* **1.** a plant of South Africa with long, fleshy leaves and a tall spike of flowers. **2.** aloes, *pl.* a bitter drug made from the juice of aloe leaves and used as a laxative: used with a singular verb.

a·loft (ə lôft′), *adv.* **1.** high up; far above the ground [The boy swung *aloft* into the upper

branches of the tree.] **2.** high above the deck of a ship; near the top of the mast.

a·lo·ha (ə lō′ə *or* ä lō′hä), *n.* & *interj.* love: a Hawaiian word used for "hello" or "good-by."

a·lone (ə lōn′), *adj.* & *adv.* **1.** away or from anything or anyone else [The hut stood *alone* on the prairie.] **2.** without any other person [She likes to walk *alone*.] **3.** without anything else; only [The carton *alone* weighs five pounds.] —**let alone, 1.** not to bother or interfere with. **2.** not to speak of [I haven't a dime, *let alone* a dollar.] —**let well enough alone,** to be satisfied with things as they are.

a·long (ə lông′), *prep.* on or beside the length of [Put these planks *along* the wall.] —*adv.* **1.** forward or onward [The policeman told us to move *along*.] **2.** together [Come *along* with us.] **3.** with one [Take your camera *along*.] —**all along,** from the very beginning [She knew our secret *all along*.] —**along with, 1.** together with. **2.** in addition to. —**get along, 1.** to go forward. **2.** to manage [How can you *get along* on $50 a week?] **3.** to succeed. **4.** to agree.

a·long·side (ə lông′sīd′), *prep.* at the side of; side by side with [You will find the car *alongside* the building.] —**alongside of,** at the side of; beside.

a·loof (ə lōōf′), *adj.* & *adv.* keeping oneself apart or at a distance; showing no interest or sympathy [He stood *aloof* from the others. She has few friends because of her *aloof* manner.]

a·loud (ə loud′), *adv.* **1.** in a voice that can be heard; loudly [You may whisper in the library, but do not talk *aloud*.] **2.** with the voice [Read the letter *aloud* to the class.]

al·pac·a (al pak′ə), *n.* **1.** a sheeplike animal of South America, related to the llama. **2.** its long, silky wool. **3.** a cloth woven from this wool. **4.** a shiny cloth made of wool mixed with cotton, etc., and used for linings, suits, etc.

al·pha (al′fə), *n.* **1.** the first letter of the Greek alphabet. **2.** the beginning of anything: used especially in the phrase **alpha and omega,** meaning "the beginning and the end."

alpaca (5 ft. high at head)

al·pha·bet (al′fə bet), *n.* **1.** the letters of a language, given in the regular order [The English *alphabet* goes from A to Z.] **2.** any system of symbols used in writing [the Braille *alphabet*].

al·pha·bet·i·cal (al′fə bet′i k'l), *adj.* **1.** of the alphabet. **2.** arranged in the regular order of the alphabet [The entries in this dictionary are in *alphabetical* order.] Also **al·pha·bet′ic.** —**al′pha·bet′i·cal·ly,** *adv.*

al·pha·bet·ize (al′fə bə tīz′), *v.* to arrange in alphabetical order. —**al′pha·bet·ized′,** *p.t.* & *p.p.;* **al′pha·bet·iz′ing,** *pr.p.*

---

fat,   āpe,   cär,   ten,   ēven,   hit,   bīte,   gō,   hôrn,   tōol,   book,   up,   fur;
get,   joy,   yet,   chin,   she,   thin,   *then;*   zh = s in pleasure;   ′ as in able (ā′b'l);
ə = a in ago,   e in agent,   i in sanity,   o in confess,   u in focus.

Al·pine (al′pīn), *adj.* **1.** of the Alps or the people who live there. **2. alpine,** of or like high mountains.

Alps (alps), *n.pl.* a mountain system in Europe, with ranges in France, Switzerland, Germany, Italy, Austria, and Yugoslavia.

al·read·y (ôl red′ē), *adv.* by or before this time; even now [When we arrived, dinner had *already* begun. I am *already* ten minutes late.]

Al·sace-Lor·raine (al′sās lô rān′), *n.* a region in northeastern France. It was seized by Germany in 1871 and returned to France in 1919. During World War II it was again under German rule.

al·so (ôl′sō), *adv.* in addition; too; besides [He wrote the play and *also* acted in it.]

Alta., abbreviation for **Alberta.**

al·tar (ôl′tər), *n.* **1.** a high place on which sacrifices or offerings are made to a god. **2.** a table, stand, etc. used for certain religious rituals as in a church [The bride and groom knelt before the *altar*.]

al·ter (ôl′tər), *v.* to change; make or become different in part [The weather *alters* with the seasons. The tailor *altered* the shoulders on the jacket.] —**al′ter·a·ble,** *adj.*

al·ter·a·tion (ôl′tər ā′shən), *n.* an altering; change.

al·ter·ca·tion (ôl′tər kā′shən), *n.* a quarrel; angry argument.

al·ter·nate (ôl′tər nit), *adj.* **1.** coming by turns; first one and then the other [The skirt has *alternate* stripes of blue and yellow.] **2.** every other [We take piano lessons on *alternate* Tuesdays.] —*n.* a person chosen to take the place of another if needed [Since Dick Burke cannot accept the appointment to West Point, his *alternate*, Art Peters, will receive it.] —*v.* (ôl′tər nāt), **1.** to do, use, act, happen, etc. by turns [Good times *alternate* with bad.] **2.** to take turns [The boys and girls *alternate* in using the swimming pool.] —**al′ter·nat·ed,** *p.t.* & *p.p.;* **al′ter·nat·ing,** *pr.p.* —**al′ter·nate·ly,** *adv.* —**al′ter·na′tion,** *n.*

alternating current, an electric current whose direction is reversed at a regular frequency, usually 60 cycles per second.

al·ter·na·tive (ôl tūr′nə tiv), *adj.* allowing a choice between two, or sometimes more than two, things [There are *alternative* routes you can take to town.] —*n.* **1.** a choice between two or more things. **2.** any one of the things that can be chosen. —**al·ter′na·tive·ly,** *adv.*

al·though (ôl thō′), *conj.* in spite of the fact that; even if; though: sometimes spelled **altho** [*Although* the sun is shining, it may rain later.]

al·tim·e·ter (al tim′ə tər *or* al′tə mē′tər), *n.* an instrument for measuring altitude, especially one that shows how high an airplane is flying.

al·ti·tude (al′tə tood *or* al′tə tyood), *n.* **1.** height; especially, the height of a thing above the earth's surface or above sea level. **2.** a high place.

al·to (al′tō), *n.* **1.** the lowest kind of singing voice of women, girls, or young boys. **2.** a singer with such a voice, or an instrument with a range like this. —*adj.* of or for an alto. —**al′tos,** *pl.*

al·to·geth·er (ôl′tə geth′ər), *adv.* **1.** to the full extent; wholly; completely [You're not *altogether* wrong.] **2.** when everything is considered; on the whole [*Altogether*, the best thing would be for us to stay here.]

al·tru·ism (al′troo iz′m), *n.* a putting the good of others ahead of one's own interests; unselfish action. —**al′tru·ist,** *n.*

al·tru·is·tic (al′troo is′tik), *adj.* putting the good of others ahead of one's own interests; unselfish. —**al′tru·is′ti·cal·ly,** *adv.*

al·um (al′əm), *n.* a mineral salt used in making baking powders, dyes, and paper. It is also used to stop bleeding from small cuts.

a·lu·mi·num (ə loo′mi nəm), *n.* a silvery, lightweight metal that is a chemical element. It does not rust and is used to make many things. —*adj.* of or containing aluminum.

a·lum·na (ə lum′nə), *n.* a girl or woman alumnus. —**a·lum·nae** (ə lum′nē), *pl.*

a·lum·nus (ə lum′nəs), *n.* a person who has gone to or is a graduate of a particular school or college [He is an *alumnus* of Harvard.] —**a·lum·ni** (ə lum′nī), *pl.*

al·ways (ôl′wiz *or* ôl′wāz), *adv.* **1.** at all times; at every time [We *always* have potatoes at dinner.] **2.** all the time; continually; forever [He swore to love her *always*.]

am (am), the form of the verb *be* that is used to show the present time with *I* [I *am* happy. *Am* I late?]

AM or **A.M.,** amplitude modulation: a method of radio broadcasting in which the strength of the radio wave changes according to the sound being broadcast: see also **FM.**

A.M., a.m., in the time from midnight to noon: *A.M.* is the abbreviation of *ante meridiem,* Latin for "before noon" [Be here at 8:30 *A.M.*]

a·mal·gam (ə mal′gəm), *n.* **1.** an alloy of mercury with another metal or other metals [Silver *amalgam* is used to fill teeth.] **2.** any mixture or blend.

a·mal·gam·ate (ə mal′gə māt), *v.* to join together into one; mix; combine [Five small businesses were *amalgamated* to form the corporation.] —**a·mal′ga·mat·ed,** *p.t.* & *p.p.;* **a·mal′ga·mat·ing,** *pr.p.* —**a·mal′ga·ma′tion,** *n.*

am·a·ryl·lis (am′ə ril′is), *n.* a plant that grows from a bulb, bearing several lilylike flowers on a single stem.

a·mass (ə mas′), *v.* to pile up; collect or gather together [to *amass* much money].

am·a·teur (am′ə choor *or* am′ə toor), *n.* **1.** a person who does something because he enjoys it rather than for money; one who is not a professional. **2.** a person who does something without much skill. —*adj.* **1.** of or done by amateurs [an *amateur* performance]. **2.** being an amateur [an *amateur* athlete].

am·a·teur·ish (am′ə choor′ish *or* am′ə toor′ish), *adj.* like an amateur; unskillful; not expert.

am·a·to·ry (am′ə tôr′ē), *adj.* having to do with or showing love [Romeo's *amatory* speech].

a·maze (ə māz´), *v.* to cause to feel great surprise or sudden wonder; astonish [They were *amazed* at the great height of the waterfall.] —**a·mazed´**, *p.t. & p.p.;* **a·maz´ing**, *pr.p.*

a·maze·ment (ə māz´mənt), *n.* great surprise or wonder; astonishment.

a·maz·ing (ə māz´ing), *adj.* causing amazement; astonishing. —**a·maz´ing·ly**, *adv.*

Am·a·zon (am´ə zän), *n.* **1.** in Greek myths, any member of a race of women warriors that fought against the Greeks. **2. amazon,** a woman who is large and strong like a man. **3.** a river in South America, about 4,000 miles long, flowing across Brazil into the Atlantic.

am·bas·sa·dor (am bas´ə dər), *n.* **1.** an official of highest rank sent to represent his government in a foreign country. **2.** any person sent as a representative or messenger.

am·ber (am´bər), *n.* **1.** a brownish-yellow substance found in the ground and used in jewelry, etc. It is the hardened resin of pine trees that grew millions of years ago. **2.** the color of amber. —*adj.* **1.** made of amber. **2.** having the color of amber.

am·ber·gris (am´bər grēs *or* am´bər gris), *n.* a grayish, waxy substance that comes from the intestines of certain whales. It has a strong, sweet smell and is used in making perfumes.

am·bi·dex·trous (am´bə dek´strəs), *adj.* able to use the right or left hand with equal ease, as in writing or throwing.

am·bi·gu·i·ty (am´bi gyōō´ə tē), *n.* **1.** the condition of being ambiguous; a being unclear or indefinite. **2.** an ambiguous remark or expression. —**am´bi·gu´i·ties,** *pl.*

am·big·u·ous (am big´yōō əs), *adj.* **1.** having two or more possible meanings ["Henry is a funny boy" is an *ambiguous* remark. It can mean that Henry is comical or that he is strange.] **2.** not clear; indefinite [Don't be so *ambiguous* in your answers.] —**am·big´u·ous·ly,** *adv.*

am·bi·tion (am bish´ən), *n.* **1.** strong desire to be successful or to gain fame, power, or wealth. **2.** the thing that one desires so strongly [His *ambition* is to be an engineer.]

am·bi·tious (am bish´əs), *adj.* **1.** full of ambition [The senator is *ambitious* and wants to be president.] **2.** showing ambition or great hopes [an *ambitious* plan]. —**am·bi´tious·ly,** *adv.*

am·ble (am´b'l), *v.* **1.** to move at a smooth, easy pace by raising first both legs on one side, then both legs on the other: said of horses, camels, etc. **2.** to walk in a slow, relaxed manner. —*n.* **1.** a horse's ambling gait. **2.** a slow, relaxed walking pace. —**am´bled,** *p.t. & p.p.;* **am´bling,** *pr.p.*

am·bro·sia (am brō´zhə), *n.* **1.** the food of the ancient Greek and Roman gods. **2.** anything that tastes or smells very delicious. —**am·bro´sial,** *adj.*

am·bu·lance (am´byoo ləns), *n.* an automo-

bile or wagon built for carrying sick or injured people.

am·bus·cade (am bəs kād´), *n. & v.* ambush. —**am·bus·cad´ed,** *p.t. & p.p.;* **am·bus·cad´-ing,** *pr.p.*

am·bush (am´boosh), *n.* **1.** a group, as of soldiers, waiting in hiding to make a surprise attack on someone. **2.** the place where they are hiding. —*v.* **1.** to hide for a surprise attack [*Ambush* your troops in the woods.] **2.** to attack from hiding [He was *ambushed* and captured as he approached the bridge.]

a·me·ba (ə mē´bə), *n.* same as **amoeba.** —**a·me´bas** or **a·me·bae** (ə mē´bē), *pl.*

a·mel·io·rate (ə mēl´yə rāt), *v.* to make or become better; improve [The workers sought to *ameliorate* their working conditions.] —**a·mel´-io·rat·ed,** *p.t. & p.p.;* **a·mel´io·rat·ing,** *pr.p.* —**a·mel´io·ra´tion,** *n.*

a·men (ā´men´ *or* ä´men´), *interj.* a Hebrew word meaning "may it be so!" or "so it is": *used after a prayer or to express approval.*

a·me·na·ble (ə mē´nə b'l *or* ə men´ə b'l), *adj.* able to be controlled or influenced; responsive [Bob is *amenable* to kindness, but not to force.] —**a·me´na·bil´i·ty,** *n.* —**a·me´na·bly,** *adv.*

a·mend (ə mend´), *v.* **1.** to make better; improve; correct [Harold was told to *amend* his manners.] **2.** to change or revise [Some selfish groups try to get laws *amended* to favor them.]

a·mend·ment (ə mend´mənt), *n.* **1.** a change for the better; improvement; correction. **2.** a change in or an addition to a bill, law, constitution, etc. [The first ten *amendments* to the Constitution are called the Bill of Rights.]

a·mends (ə mendz´), *n. sing. & pl.* something given or done by a person to make up for an injury, insult, or loss that he has caused; compensation [He tried to make *amends* for his rudeness by apologizing.]

a·men·i·ty (ə men´ə tē), *n.* **1.** pleasant quality; attractiveness [The *amenity* of the Mexican climate attracted us.] **2. amenities,** *pl.* polite acts; pleasant manners [The *amenities* require her to thank him.] —**a·men´i·ties,** *pl.*

A·mer·i·ca (ə mer´ə kə), *n.* **1.** either North America or South America. **2.** North America, South America, and Central America, all together. **3.** the United States.

A·mer·i·can (ə mer´ə kən), *adj.* **1.** of or in America [the *American* Indians]. **2.** of or in the United States [*American* foreign policy]. —*n.* **1.** a person born or living in America. **2.** a citizen of the United States.

A·mer·i·can·ism (ə mer´ə kən iz'm), *n.* **1.** a custom, belief, or habit of the people of the United States. **2.** a word or phrase of American English, especially one that was first used in the United States ["Juke box" and "squaw" are *Americanisms*.] **3.** loyalty to the United States, or to its customs, beliefs, etc.

---

fat, āpe, cär, ten, ēven, hit, bīte, gō, hôrn, tōōl, book, up, fũr;
get, joy, yet, chin, she, thin, *th*en; zh = s in pleasure; ´ as in able (ā´b'l);
ə = a in ago, e in agent, i in sanity, o in confess, u in focus.

A·mer·i·can·ize (ə mer′ə kən īz′), *v.* to make or become American, as in customs, habits, speech, or beliefs. —**A·mer′i·can·ized′**, *p.t. & p.p.*; **A·mer′i·can·iz′ing**, *pr.p.* —**A·mer′i·can·i·za′tion**, *n.*

American Revolution, the revolution from 1763 to 1783 by which the American colonies won their independence from England. It became the Revolutionary War in 1775.

am·e·thyst (am′ə thist), *n.* a purple stone, especially a kind of quartz, that is used as a jewel. —*adj.* purple or violet.

a·mi·a·ble (ā′mi ə b′l), *adj.* pleasant and friendly; good-natured [an *amiable* companion; an *amiable* remark]. —**a′mi·a·bly**, *adv.*

am·i·ca·ble (am′i kə b′l), *adj.* friendly; peaceable; not quarrelsome [an *amicable* discussion]. —**am′i·ca·bly**, *adv.*

a·mid (ə mid′), *prep.* among; in the middle of [Weeds grew *amid* the flowers.]

a·mid·ships (ə mid′ships), *adv.* in or toward the middle of the ship [The larger vessel struck us *amidships*.]

a·midst (ə midst′), *prep.* amid; among.

a·mi·go (ə mē′gō), *n.* friend: *a Spanish word.* —**a·mi′gos**, *pl.*

a·miss (ə mis′), *adv. & adj.* in a wrong way; out of order; faulty or faultily; wrong [If nothing goes *amiss*, he will return on Monday.]

am·i·ty (am′ə tē), *n.* friendly, peaceful relations, as between nations or groups; friendship.

am·mo·ni·a (ə mōn′yə), *n.* **1.** a colorless gas that is made up of nitrogen and hydrogen and has a very sharp smell. It is used in making fertilizers, etc. **2.** a liquid made by dissolving this gas in water: also called **ammonia water.**

am·mu·ni·tion (am′yoo nish′ən), *n.* **1.** anything that is hurled by a weapon or is exploded as a weapon, such as bullets, shells, bombs, rockets, etc. **2.** anything that can be used in attack or defense [The encyclopedia provided him with *ammunition* for his argument.]

am·ne·si·a (am nē′zhə), *n.* the condition of suddenly forgetting all or some of the past, as because of brain injury or shock.

am·nes·ty (am′nəs tē), *n.* a general pardon, especially for political offenses against a government [The king granted *amnesty* to the imprisoned rebels.] —**am′nes·ties**, *pl.*

a·moe·ba (ə mē′bə), *n.* a tiny animal made up of just one cell, found usually in foul, standing water. It can be seen only through a microscope and it moves by changing its shape. —**a·moe′bas** or **a·moe·bae** (ə mē′bē), *pl.*

amoeba

a·mong (ə mung′), *prep.* **1.** in the company of; together with [You are *among* friends.] **2.** from place to place in [He passed *among* the crowd.] **3.** in the group or class of [She is the fairest *among* women.] **4.** with a share for each of [The estate was divided *among* the relatives.] **5.** with one another [Don't quarrel *among* yourselves.]

a·mongst (ə mungst′), *prep.* among.

am·o·rous (am′ə rəs), *adj.* **1.** full of or showing love; loving [*amorous* words; an *amorous* suitor]. **2.** in love. —**am′o·rous·ly**, *adv.*

a·mor·phous (ə môr′fəs), *adj.* **1.** not having a definite form or shape [The amoeba is a tiny, *amorphous* animal.] **2.** of no definite type or kind [an old mansion of a rambling, *amorphous* style]. **3.** solid but not made up of crystals [a lump of *amorphous* charcoal].

A·mos (ā′məs), *n.* **1.** a Hebrew prophet in the Bible. **2.** a book of the Old Testament.

a·mount (ə mount′), *v.* **1.** to add up; total [The bill *amounts* to $4.50.] **2.** to be equal in meaning or effect [His failure to answer our request *amounts* to a refusal.] —*n.* **1.** the sum; total [The *amount* of the expenses was $13.50.] **2.** a quantity [a small *amount* of rain].

a·mour (ə moor′), *n.* a love affair, especially a secret one.

am·pere (am′pir), *n.* a unit for measuring the strength of an electric current. It is the amount of current sent by one volt through a resistance of one ohm. Abbreviated **amp.**

am·phib·i·an (am fib′i ən), *adj.* **1.** belonging to a class of cold-blooded animals with a backbone, that live both on land and in water. **2.** amphibious. —*n.* **1.** any amphibian animal, as the frog, which has lungs but begins life

amphibian (truck)

in water as a tadpole with gills. **2.** any animal that lives both on land and in water, as the seal or beaver. **3.** an airplane that can take off from or come down on either land or water. **4.** a tank, truck, etc. that can travel on either land or water.

am·phib·i·ous (am fib′i əs), *adj.* **1.** that can live both on land and in water [an *amphibious* plant]. **2.** that can operate or travel on both land and water [an *amphibious* truck].

am·phi·the·a·ter or **am·phi·the·a·tre** (am′fə thē′ə tər), *n.* **1.** a round or oval building having rising rows of seats around an open space in which sports events, plays, etc. are held. **2.** a level place surrounded by hills.

am·ple (am′p′l), *adj.* **1.** having plenty of space; roomy; large [A family of ten can eat together in the *ample* kitchen.] **2.** more than enough; abundant [From his *ample* funds he gave to many in need.] **3.** enough; adequate [Our coal supply is just *ample* for the winter.]

am·pli·fi·ca·tion (am′plə fi kā′shən), *n.* **1.** an amplifying, or making larger or stronger; increase. **2.** additional matter or details [Your report needs some *amplification*.]

am·pli·fi·er (am′plə fī′ər), *n.* **1.** a person or thing that amplifies. **2.** a vacuum tube or other device, as in a radio or phonograph, for making electric or radio waves stronger before they are changed into sounds.

am·pli·fy (am′plə fī), *v.* **1.** to make larger, stronger, louder, etc. **2.** to make fuller or more complete [He bored us by *amplifying* every small point in the story.] —**am′pli·fied,** *p.t. & p.p.;* **am′pli·fy·ing,** *pr.p.*

am·pli·tude (am′plə tōōd *or* am′plə tyōōd), *n.* **1.** great size or extent; largeness. **2.** an amount that is more than enough; abundance.

am·ply (am′plē), *adv.* in an ample manner; fully [You will be *amply* rewarded.]

am·pu·tate (am′pyoo tāt), *v.* to cut off, as by surgery [The doctor *amputated* his leg below the knee.] —**am′pu·tat·ed,** *p.t. & p.p.;* **am′pu·tat·ing,** *pr.p.* —**am′pu·ta′tion,** *n.*

Am·ster·dam (am′stər dam), *n.* a seaport and one of the two capitals of the Netherlands.

a·muck (ə muk′), *adv.* in a mad rage to kill. —**run amuck,** to rush about in a mad rage.

am·u·let (am′yoo lit), *n.* something worn on the body because it is supposed to have magic to protect against harm or evil; a charm.

a·muse (ə myōōz′), *v.* **1.** to keep busy or interested with something pleasant or enjoyable; entertain [We *amused* ourselves with games.] **2.** to make laugh or smile by being comical or humorous [His jokes *amused* me.] —**a·mused′,** *p.t. & p.p.;* **a·mus′ing,** *pr.p.*

a·muse·ment (ə myōōz′mənt), *n.* **1.** the condition of being amused. **2.** something that amuses or entertains; entertainment [The merry-go-round is my favorite *amusement* in the park.]

a·mus·ing (ə myōōz′ing), *adj.* causing laughter or smiles. —**a·mus′ing·ly,** *adv.*

an (ən *or* an), *adj.* **1.** one; one sort of [He drives *an* automobile to work.] **2.** each; any one [*An* ant is a kind of insect.] *An* is also called an *indefinite article*. See also **the.** **3.** in or for each [He earns one dollar *an* hour.] *An* is used before all words beginning with a vowel sound [*an* orange, *an* honor, *an* usher]. *A* is used before a consonant sound [*a* pear, *a* home, *a* uniform (yōō′nə fôrm)].

-an (ən), a suffix meaning: **1.** of or having to do with [A *diocesan* bishop is the bishop of a diocese.] **2.** born in or living in [A *European* is a person born or living in Europe.]

a·nach·ro·nism (ə nak′rə niz′m), *n.* **1.** the connecting of a person, thing, or happening with another that came later in history [Shakespeare was guilty of an *anachronism* when he had a clock striking in "Julius Caesar."] **2.** anything that is or seems to be out of its proper time in history [A belief in magic today is an *anachronism*.]

an·a·con·da (an′ə kän′də), *n.* a very long, heavy snake of South America. Anacondas kill their prey by crushing it in their coils.

a·nae·mi·a (ə nē′mi ə) *n.* same as **anemia.**

an·aes·the·sia (an′əs thē′zhə), *n.* same as **anesthesia.** —**an′aes·thet′ic,** *adj. & n.*

an·al·ge·sic (an′al jē′sik), *adj.* stopping or easing pain. —*n.* a drug that eases pain.

a·nal·o·gous (ə nal′ə gəs), *adj.* alike or the same in some ways [An electronic calculating machine is *analogous* to the human brain.]

a·nal·o·gy (ə nal′ə jē), *n.* likeness in some ways

between things that are otherwise unlike; resemblance in part [He explained how a jet airplane flies by showing an *analogy* with air escaping fast from a toy balloon.] —**a·nal′o·gies,** *pl.*

a·nal·y·sis (ə nal′ə sis), *n.* a separating or breaking up of something into its parts so as to examine them and see how they fit together [Chemical *analysis* of the rock proved that it contained uranium. This book has a fine *analysis* of the Civil War.] —**a·nal′y·ses** (ə nal′ə sēz), *pl.*

an·a·lyst (an′ə list), *n.* a person who analyzes.

an·a·lyt·i·cal (an′ə lit′i k′l) *or* **an·a·lyt·ic** (an′ə lit′ik), *adj.* **1.** having to do with analysis [an *analytical* process]. **2.** skilled in analyzing [an *analytical* person]. —**an′a·lyt′i·cal·ly,** *adv.*

an·a·lyze (an′ə līz), *v.* to separate or break up any thing or idea into its parts so as to examine them and see how they fit together [to *analyze* a chemical; to *analyze* the causes of war]. —**an′a·lyzed,** *p.t. & p.p.;* **an′a·lyz·ing,** *pr.p.*

an·ar·chism (an′ər kiz′m), *n.* the belief that all forms of government act unjustly against the liberty of the individual and should therefore be done away with.

an·arch·ist (an′ər kist), *n.* **1.** a person who believes in anarchism. **2.** a person who mocks at or ignores rules, duties, orderly behavior, etc.

an·arch·y (an′ər kē), *n.* **1.** the complete absence of government and law. **2.** a condition of disorder or confusion. —**an·ar·chic** (an är′kik), *adj.*

a·nath·e·ma (ə nath′ə mə), *n.* **1.** a terrible curse against a person or thing, often one putting a person out of a church. **2.** a person or thing that is accursed or hated.

a·nath·e·ma·tize (ə nath′ə mə tīz′), *v.* to utter an anathema against; curse. —**a·nath′e·ma·tized,** *p.t. & p.p.;* **a·nath′e·ma·tiz′ing,** *pr.p.*

an·a·tom·i·cal (an′ə täm′i k′l), *adj.* of or having to do with anatomy.

a·nat·o·mist (ə nat′ə mist), *n.* a person who is skilled in anatomy.

a·nat·o·my (ə nat′ə mē), *n.* **1.** a cutting apart of an animal or plant in order to study its parts. **2.** the study of the form or structure of animals or plants. Anatomy deals with the different tissues, parts, and organs of a body. **3.** the structure of the body [The *anatomy* of a frog is in many ways like that of a person.]

-ance (əns), a suffix meaning: **1.** the act of [*Assistance* is the act of assisting.] **2.** the state of being [*Vigilance* is the state of being vigilant.] **3.** a thing that [A *conveyance* is a thing that conveys.]

an·ces·tor (an′ses tər), *n.* **1.** a person who comes before one in a family line, especially a great-grandparent or someone earlier; forefather [His *ancestors* lived in Italy.] **2.** an early kind of animal from which later kinds have developed [The *ancestor* of the elephant was the mammoth.] —**an·ces·tress** (an′ses tris), *n. fem.*

an·ces·tral (an ses′trəl), *adj.* of or inherited

---

fat, āpe, cär, ten, ēven, hit, bīte, gō, hôrn, tōōl, book, up, fŭr; get, joy, yet, chin, she, thin, *th*en; zh = s in pleasure; ′ as in able (ā′b′l); ə = a in ago, e in agent, i in sanity, o in confess, u in focus.

from an ancestor or ancestors [*ancestral* jewels].

an·ces·try (an′ses trē), *n.* one's ancestors as a group; family descent [a man of noble *ancestry*].

an·chor (ang′kər), *n.* **1.** a heavy object let down into the water by a chain to keep a ship from drifting. It is usually a metal piece with hooks which grip the ground at the bottom of the water. **2.** anything that keeps something else steady or firm [In time of trouble, faith was his only *anchor*.] —*v.* **1.** to keep from drifting or coming loose by using an anchor. **2.** to attach or fix firmly [The shelves are *anchored* to the wall.] —**weigh anchor, 1.** to pull up the anchor. **2.** to go away; leave.

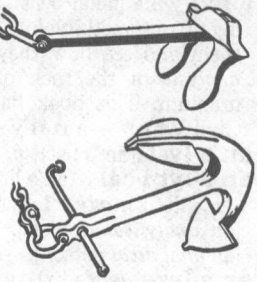

anchors

an·chor·age (ang′kər ij), *n.* **1.** the act of anchoring. **2.** a place to anchor ships. **3.** a strong support that keeps something steady.

an·cho·rite (ang′kə rīt), *n.* **1.** a person who lives away from other people in order to think deeply about religious matters. **2.** any hermit.

anchor man, the last runner on a relay team.

an·cho·vy (an′chə vē *or* an chō′vē), *n.* a very small fish of the herring family. Anchovies are usually salted and canned in oil, or made into a salty paste. —**an′cho·vies,** *pl.*

an·cient (ān′shənt), *adj.* **1.** of times long past; belonging to the early history of man, before about 500 A.D. **2.** having lasted a long time; very old [their *ancient* quarrel]. —**the an·cients,** the people who lived in ancient times.

an·cient·ly (ān′shənt lē), *adv.* in ancient times [The world was *anciently* believed to be flat.]

-an·cy (ən sē), same as **-ance.**

and (and *or* ənd *or* ən), *conj.* **1.** also; in addition; as well as [Come to the party *and* bring your friend.] **2.** plus; added to [6 *and* 2 makes 8.] **3.** as a result [Help me *and* I'll be grateful.] **4.** to: *used only in everyday talk* [Try *and* come.]

An·da·lu·sia (an′də lōō′zhə), *n.* a region of southern Spain. —**An′da·lu′sian,** *adj. & n.*

an·dan·te (an dan′tē *or* än dän′tā), *adj. & adv.* rather slow: an Italian word used in music to tell how fast a piece should be played.

An·der·sen, Hans Christian (an′dər s'n), 1805–1875; Danish writer of fairy stories.

An·des (an′dēz), *n.pl.* a mountain system along the length of western South America.

and·i·ron (and′ī′ərn), *n.* either one of a pair of metal supports on which to rest logs in a fireplace.

an·ec·dote (an′ik dōt), *n.* a short, interesting or amusing story of some happening or about some person [He told an *anecdote* about the first time he tried to ski.] —**an′ec·do′tal,** *adj.*

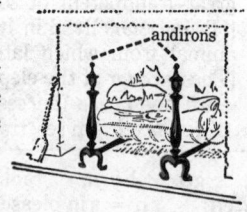

andirons

a·ne·mi·a (ə nē′mi ə), *n.* a condition in which a person's blood does not have enough red corpuscles or hemoglobin so that it does not carry a normal amount of oxygen.

a·ne·mic (ə nē′mik), *adj.* of or having anemia.

an·e·mom·e·ter (an′ə mäm′ə tər), *n.* a device for measuring the speed of the wind.

a·nem·o·ne (ə nem′ə nē), *n.* **1.** a plant with white, purple, or red flowers, that are shaped like small cups. **2.** a sea anemone, a water animal that looks like a flower.

an·es·the·sia (an′əs thē′zhə), *n.* a condition in which one has no feeling of pain, heat, touch, etc. in all or part of the body.

an·es·thet·ic (an′əs thet′ik), *adj.* of or producing anesthesia [an *anesthetic* drug]. —*n.* a drug, gas, etc.

sea anemones

used to produce anesthesia, as before surgery [A *local anesthetic* causes numbness in just a part of the body. A *general anesthetic* can make one completely unconscious.]

an·es·the·tist (ə nes′thə tist), *n.* a person trained to give anesthetics.

an·es·the·tize (ə nes′thə tīz), *v.* to cause anesthesia in as by giving anesthetics. —**an·es′the·tized,** *p.t. & p.p.;* **an·es′the·tiz·ing,** *pr.p.*

a·new (ə nōō′ *or* ə nyōō′), *adv.* **1.** once more; again [The truce ended and the war began *anew.*] **2.** in a new way; differently [They tore down the slums and began to build *anew.*]

an·gel (ān′jəl), *n.* **1.** a being that is supposed to live in heaven and have more power and goodness than human beings. Angels are often mentioned in the Bible as messengers of God. They are usually pictured as wearing white robes and having wings and a halo. **2.** a person thought of as being as beautiful or as good as an angel. **3.** a helping or guiding spirit [your good *angel*].

angel

angel cake or **angel food cake,** a light, spongy, white cake made without shortening or egg yolks, but with many egg whites.

an·gel·ic (an jel′ik) or **an·gel·i·cal** (an jel′i·k'l), *adj.* **1.** of the angels; heavenly. **2.** as beautiful, good, or innocent as an angel.

An·ge·lus or **an·ge·lus** (an′jə ləs), *n.* **1.** a prayer said at morning, noon, and evening in the Roman Catholic Church. **2.** the bell rung to tell the time for this prayer.

an·ger (ang′gər), *n.* a feeling of being very annoyed and wanting to fight back at a person or thing that hurts one or is against one; wrath; rage. —*v.* to make angry [Her rude reply *angered* her brother.]

an·gle (ang'g'l), *n.* **1.** the shape made by two straight lines meeting in a point, or by two surfaces meeting along a line. **2.** the space between such lines or surfaces. It is measured in degrees. **3.** the way one looks at something; point of view [Consider the problem from all *angles.*] —*v.* **1.** to move or bend at an angle. **2.** to tell or write a story or report in a way that tries to make others have certain feelings about it: *used only in everyday talk.* —**an'gled,** *p.t. & p.p.;* **an'gling,** *pr.p.*

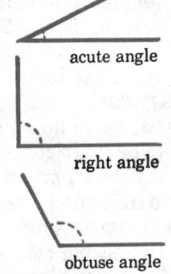

acute angle

right angle

obtuse angle

an·gle (ang'g'l), *v.* **1.** to fish with a hook and line. **2.** to use tricks or schemes to get something [to *angle* for a compliment by flattering another]. —**an'gled,** *p.t. & p.p.;* **an'gling,** *pr.p.*

an·gler (ang'glər), *n.* **1.** a fisherman who uses a hook and line. **2.** a salt-water fish that eats smaller fish which it attracts with its long rays.

an·gle·worm (ang'g'l wurm'), *n.* an earthworm, used for bait in fishing.

An·gli·can (ang'gli kən), *adj.* of the Church of England. —*n.* a member of the Church of England. —**An'gli·can·ism,** *n.*

An·gli·cize (ang'glə sīz), *v.* to make English in form, pronunciation, customs, manners, etc. [*Patio* is a Spanish word that has been *Anglicized.*] —**An'gli·cized,** *p.t. & p.p.;* **An'gli·ciz·ing,** *pr.p.*

an·gling (ang'gling), *n.* the act of fishing with a hook and line.

An·glo- (ang'glō), a word root combined with a word or another root, meaning "English" or "England" [An *Anglo*-American treaty is one between England and America.]

An·glo-Sax·on (ang'glō sak's'n), *n.* **1.** a member of the German peoples who invaded England and were living there at the time of the Norman Conquest. **2.** their language, from which modern English developed: also called *Old English.* **3.** an Englishman or a person whose ancestors were English. —*adj.* **1.** of the Anglo-Saxons, their language, etc. **2.** having English ancestors.

An·go·ra (ang gôr'ə), *n.* **1.** a kind of cat with long, silky fur. **2.** a kind of goat with long, silky hair. This hair, called **Angora wool,** is used in making mohair. **3.** the fine, silky hair of a domestic rabbit, called **Angora rabbit.** It is used in making a soft yarn which is woven into sweaters, mittens, etc.

an·gri·ly (ang'grə lē), *adv.* in an angry manner.

an·gry (ang'grē), *adj.* **1.** feeling or showing anger; enraged [*angry* words; an *angry* crowd]. **2.** wild and stormy [an *angry* sea]. **3.** inflamed and sore [an *angry* wound]. —**an'gri·er,** *compar.;* **an'gri·est,** *superl.*

an·guish (ang'gwish), *n.* great suffering, as

from worry, grief, or pain; agony [She was in *anguish* until her child was found.] —**an'guished,** *adj.*

an·gu·lar (ang'gyoo lər), *adj.* **1.** having angles or sharp corners. **2.** measured by an angle [the *angular* motion of a pendulum]. **3.** with bones that jut out; gaunt [an *angular* face].

an·gu·lar·i·ty (ang'gyoo lar'ə tē), *n.* **1.** the condition of being angular or having angles. **2.** a sharp corner; angle. —**an'gu·lar'i·ties,** *pl.*

an·i·line (an'l in *or* an'l ēn), *n.* a poisonous, oily liquid that is made from benzene and is used in making dyes. —*adj.* made from aniline [*aniline* dyes].

an·i·mal (an'ə m'l), *n.* **1.** any living being that can move about by itself but does not make its own food as plants do [Insects, snakes, fish, birds, cattle, and people are all *animals.*] **2.** any such being other than man; especially, any four-footed animal; beast. **3.** a person who is like a beast or brute. —*adj.* **1.** of or from an animal [*animal* fats]. **2.** like an animal or beast; coarse, gross, wild, etc. [He lives an *animal* existence.]

an·i·mate (an'ə māt), *v.* **1.** to give life to. **2.** to make cheerful or lively [A smile *animated* her face.] **3.** to cause to act; inspire [She is *animated* only by a desire to help others.] —*adj.* (an'ə mit), living; having life [*animate* beings]. —**an'i·mat·ed,** *p.t. & p.p.;* **an'i·mat·ing,** *pr.p.*

an·i·mat·ed (an'ə māt'id), *adj.* **1.** alive or seeming to be alive [An *animated* cartoon is a kind of motion picture in which drawn figures seem to move as if alive.] **2.** vigorous; lively; gay [an *animated* conversation]. —**an'i·mat·ed·ly,** *adv.*

an·i·ma·tion (an'ə mā'shən), *n.* **1.** life. **2.** liveliness; enthusiasm; spirit [They spoke with *animation* of their trip to Mexico.]

an·i·mos·i·ty (an'ə mäs'ə tē), *n.* a feeling of strong dislike or hatred; ill will [He aroused her *animosity* by making fun of her.] —**an'i·mos'i·ties,** *pl.*

an·ise (an'is), *n.* **1.** a plant of the carrot family, whose seeds have a strong, pleasant smell. **2.** this seed, used for flavoring and in medicine.

An·ka·ra (äng'kə rə), *n.* the capital of Turkey.

an·kle (ang'k'l), *n.* the part that joins the foot to the leg.

an·klet (ang'klit), *n.* **1.** a band worn around the ankle, usually as an ornament. **2.** a short sock worn by girls or women.

an·nals (an''lz), *n.pl.* **1.** a record of events year by year, put down in the order in which they happened. **2.** a history [Joan of Arc holds a unique place in the *annals* of France.]

anklets

An·nap·o·lis (ə nap''l is),

n. the capital of Maryland, on Chesapeake Bay. The United States Naval Academy is there.

an·neal (ə nēl′), *v.* to make glass or metal less brittle by heating it and then cooling it slowly.

an·nex (ə neks′), *v.* to add on or attach a smaller thing to a larger one [Texas was *annexed* to the Union in 1845.] —*n.* (an′eks), something added on; especially, an extra part built on or near a building to give more space. —**an′nex·a′tion,** *n.*

an·ni·hi·late (ə nī′ə lāt), *v.* to destroy completely; put out of existence; demolish [An atomic war could *annihilate* whole nations.] —**an·ni′hi·lat·ed,** *p.t. & p.p.;* **an·ni′hi·lat·ing,** *prp.* —**an·ni′hi·la′tion,** *n.*

an·ni·ver·sa·ry (an′ə vûr′sər ē), *n.* **1.** the date on which something happened in an earlier year [June 4 will be the tenth *anniversary* of their wedding.] **2.** the celebration of such a date. —*adj.* of or connected with an anniversary [an *anniversary* party]. —**an′ni·ver′sa·ries,** *pl.*

an·no·tate (an′ō tāt′), *v.* to add notes that explain something or give one's opinions [Scholars *annotate* the plays of Shakespeare.] —**an′no·tat·ed,** *p.t. & p.p.;* **an′no·tat′ing,** *prp.*

an·no·ta·tion (an′ō tā′shən), *n.* **1.** an annotating. **2.** a note or notes added to a book to explain something or offer opinions.

an·nounce (ə nouns′), *v.* **1.** to tell the public about; proclaim [to *announce* the opening of a new store]. **2.** to say; tell [He *announced* that he wasn't going with us.] **3.** to say that someone has arrived [The butler *announced* each guest as he entered.] **4.** to make known or clear [Footsteps *announced* his return.] —**an·nounced′,** *p.t. & p.p.;* **an·nounc′ing,** *prp.*

an·nounce·ment (ə nouns′mənt), *n.* **1.** an announcing of something that has happened or will happen. **2.** something announced, often in the form of a written or printed notice [Wedding *announcements* are usually engraved.]

an·nounc·er (ə noun′sər), *n.* **1.** a person who announces. **2.** a person who introduces radio or television programs, reads the news, etc.

an·noy (ə noi′), *v.* to irritate, bother, or make slightly angry [Their loud talk *annoyed* the librarian.] —**an·noy′ing,** *adj.*

an·noy·ance (ə noi′əns), *n.* **1.** an annoying or being annoyed [He showed his *annoyance* by frowning.] **2.** a thing or person that annoys [A barking dog is an *annoyance* to neighbors.]

an·nu·al (an′yōō əl), *adj.* **1.** that comes or happens once a year; yearly [an *annual* summer vacation]. **2.** for a year's time, work, etc. [an *annual* wage]. **3.** living or lasting for only one year or season [The marigold is an *annual* plant.] —*n.* **1.** a book or magazine published once a year. **2.** a plant that lives only one year or season.

an·nu·al·ly (an′yōō ə lē), *adv.* each year; every year.

an·nu·i·ty (ə nōō′ə tē *or* ə nyōō′ə tē), *n.* **1.** a kind of insurance from which a person gets regular payments of money after he reaches a certain age. **2.** a yearly payment of money [The widow receives an *annuity* of $5,000 from the trust fund.] —**an·nu′i·ties,** *pl.*

an·nul (ə nul′), *v.* to do away with; put an end to; make no longer binding under the law; cancel [The marriage was *annulled* after a week.] —**an·nulled′,** *p.t. & p.p.;* **an·nul′ling,** *prp.* —**an·nul′ment,** *n.*

an·num (an′əm), *n.* a year: a Latin word used in the phrase *per annum* meaning "yearly."

An·nun·ci·a·tion (ə nun′si ā′shən), *n.* **1.** in the Bible, the angel Gabriel's announcement to Mary that she was to give birth to Jesus. **2.** a church festival on March 25 in memory of this.

an·ode (an′ōd), *n.* the pole or piece by which positive electricity enters an electric battery, electron tube, etc.; positive electrode.

a·noint (ə noint′), *v.* **1.** to rub oil or ointment on. **2.** to put oil on in a ceremony of making holy or placing in a high office [David was *anointed* king of Israel by Samuel.]

a·nom·a·lous (ə näm′ə ləs), *adj.* not following the general rule or the usual pattern; abnormal [Horthy of Hungary held the *anomalous* title of admiral in a state that had no navy.]

a·nom·a·ly (ə näm′ə lē), *n.* anything anomalous [The duckbill, which lays eggs, is an *anomaly* among mammals.]

a·non (ə nän′), *adv.* **1.** in a short time; soon. **2.** at another time [I leave now, but I shall see you *anon.*] *This word is now seldom used.*

anon., abbreviation for **anonymous.**

an·o·nym·i·ty (an′ə nim′ə tē), *n.* the condition of being anonymous.

a·non·y·mous (ə nän′ə məs), *adj.* **1.** whose name is not known [an *anonymous* writer]. **2.** given, written, etc. by a person whose name is kept secret [an *anonymous* letter; an *anonymous* gift]. —**a·non′y·mous·ly,** *adv.*

an·oth·er (ə nuth′ər), *adj.* **1.** one more [May I have *another* cup of tea?] **2.** a different; not the same [She exchanged the dress for *another* one.] **3.** one of the same sort as [As a boy, he dreamed he would be *another* John Paul Jones.] —*pron.* **1.** one more [I've had a cooky, but I'd like *another.*] **2.** a different one [If one store doesn't have it, try *another.*]

ans., abbreviation for **answer.**

an·swer (an′sər), *n.* **1.** something said, written, or done in return to a question, argument, letter, action, etc.; reply; response [The only *answers* required for the test were "true" or "false." His *answer* to the insult was to turn his back.] **2.** a solution to a problem, as in arithmetic. —*v.* **1.** to give an answer; reply or react, as to a question or action. **2.** to serve or be usable for [A small tack will *answer* my purpose.] **3.** to be responsible [You must *answer* for the children's conduct.] —**answer to a description,** to be just as described.

an·swer·a·ble (an′sər ə b'l), *adj.* **1.** responsible; obliged to give an accounting or explanation

[He is old enough to be *answerable* for his actions.] **2.** that can be answered or shown to be wrong [an *answerable* argument].

ant (ant), *n.* a small insect, usually without wings, that lives in or on the ground, in wood, etc. Ants live together in large, well-organized groups.

ant (⅛ in. long)

-ant (ənt), a suffix meaning: **1.** that has, shows, or does [A *defiant* person is one who shows defiance.] **2.** a person or thing that [An *occupant* is a person who occupies.]

ant·ac·id (ant as′id), *adj.* that neutralizes or weakens acids. —*n.* an antacid substance [Baking soda is an *antacid.*]

an·tag·o·nism (an tag′ə niz′m), *n.* the condition of being opposed to or feeling unfriendly toward another.

an·tag·o·nist (an tag′ə nist), *n.* a person who opposes, fights, or competes with another; opponent; rival.

an·tag·o·nis·tic (an tag′ə nis′tik), *adj.* showing antagonism; opposing; hostile; unfriendly. —**an·tag·o·nis′ti·cal·ly,** *adv.*

an·tag·o·nize (an tag′ə nīz), *v.* to make someone dislike oneself; make an enemy of [She *antagonized* us by her rudeness.] —**an·tag′o·nized,** *p.t. & p.p.;* **an·tag′o·niz·ing,** *pr.p.*

ant·arc·tic (ant ärk′tik), *adj.* of or near the South Pole or the region around it. —*n.* the region around the South Pole.

Ant·arc·ti·ca (ant ärk′ti kə), *n.* a large area of land, mainly covered with ice, about the South Pole: also called the **Antarctic Continent.**

Antarctic Ocean, the ocean around Antarctica.

ante-, a prefix meaning "before" [To *antedate* is to come before in time.]

ant·eat·er (ant′ēt′ər), *n.* an animal with a long snout and a long, sticky tongue. It feeds mainly on ants.

an·te·ced·ent (an′tə sēd′′nt), *adj.* coming or happening before; previous [The witness told of an event *antecedent* to the robbery.] —*n.* **1.** a thing or happening coming before something else [One's *antecedents* can mean "one's past history."] **2.** the word or group of words to which a pronoun refers [In "the girl who sang," "girl" is the *antecedent* of "who."]

anteater (4 ft. long)

an·te·cham·ber (an′ti chām′bər), *n.* an anteroom.

an·te·date (an′ti dāt), *v.* **1.** to come or happen before [The American Revolution *antedated* the French Revolution.] **2.** to give an earlier date to

[You *antedate* a check written on May 3 if you put May 1 on it.]

an·te·di·lu·vi·an (an′ti di loo′vi ən), *adj.* **1.** of the time before the Flood. **2.** very old or old-fashioned [*antediluvian* ideas]. —*n.* a person or thing that is antediluvian.

an·te·lope (an′t'l ōp), *n.* a swift, graceful animal that is a little like a deer. Antelopes have horns and are related to oxen and goats.

antelope
(2½ ft. high at shoulder)

an·ten·na (an ten′ə), *n.* **1.** either of a pair of slender feelers on the head of an insect, crab, lobster, etc. **2.** a wire or set of wires used in radio and television to send and receive electric waves; aerial. —**an·ten·nae** (an ten′ē) or **an·ten′nas,** *pl. for meaning 1;* **an·ten′nas,** *pl. for meaning 2.*

an·te·ri·or (an tir′i ər), *adj.* **1.** at or toward the front; forward. **2.** coming before; earlier.

an·te·room (an′ti room), *n.* a room leading to a larger or more important room; waiting room.

an·them (an′thəm), *n.* **1.** the official song of a country [Our national *anthem* is "The Star-Spangled Banner."] **2.** a religious song or hymn, usually with words from the Bible.

television antenna

an·ther (an′thər), *n.* the part of a flower's stamen that holds the pollen. Anthers are the small heads on the slender stems that grow at the center of a flower.

ant hill, a heap of dirt carried by ants from their underground nest and piled around its entrance.

an·thol·o·gy (an thäl′ə jē), *n.* a collection of poems, stories, or other writings. —**an·thol′o·gies,** *pl.*

anthers

An·tho·ny, Su·san B. (soo′z'n an′thə nē), 1820–1906; American teacher who helped women gain the right to vote in the U.S.

an·thra·cite (an′thrə sīt), *n.* hard coal, which burns with much heat and little smoke.

an·thrax (an′thraks), *n.* a disease of cattle, sheep, etc. that is caused by bacteria and can be passed on to human beings.

an·thro·poid (an′thrə poid), *adj.* like a human being in form; manlike [The gorilla, chimpanzee, and orangutan are *anthropoid* apes.] —*n.* any anthropoid ape.

---

an·thro·pol·o·gist (an'thrə päl'ə jist), *n.* an expert in anthropology.

an·thro·pol·o·gy (an'thrə päl'ə jē), *n.* the science that studies mankind, especially its origin, development, divisions, and customs. —**an'thro·po·log'i·cal,** *adj.*

anti-, a prefix meaning: **1.** against, opposed to [*Antislavery* means opposed to slavery.] **2.** that acts against [An *antitoxin* is a substance that acts against the toxin of a disease.]

an·ti·bi·ot·ic (an'ti bī ät'ik), *n.* a chemical substance produced by bacteria, fungi, etc. It can kill, or stop the growth of, germs. Antibiotics, such as penicillin, are used in treating diseases.

an·tic (an'tik), *adj.* odd and funny; grotesque; ludicrous. —*n.* an antic act; playful or silly trick; prank [The children laughed at the *antics* of Punch and Judy.]

An·ti·christ (an'ti krīst), *n.* in the Bible, the great opponent of Christ: see I John 2:18.

an·tic·i·pate (an tis'ə pāt), *v.* **1.** to look forward to; expect [He *anticipated* great pleasure from his visit to the ranch.] **2.** to be aware of or take care of ahead of time [Our host *anticipated* our every wish.] **3.** be ahead of in doing or achieving [Some think that the vikings *anticipated* Columbus in discovering America.] —**an·tic'i·pat·ed,** *p.t.* & *p.p.*; **an·tic'i·pat·ing,** *pr.p.* —**an·tic'i·pa'tion,** *n.*

an·ti·cli·max (an'ti klī'maks), *n.* a dropping from the important or serious to the unimportant or silly [Last week he wrecked his car, broke his leg, and then, as an *anticlimax,* caught cold.]

an·ti·dote (an'ti dōt), *n.* **1.** a substance that is taken to weaken the effect of a poison. **2.** anything that works against an evil or unwanted condition [The gay party was a good *antidote* to the sadness we felt.]

An·tie·tam (an tē'təm), *n.* a creek in western Maryland. A battle of the Civil War was fought near there in 1862.

an·ti·freeze (an'ti frēz), *n.* a substance with a low freezing point, such as alcohol, put in the water of automobile radiators to prevent freezing.

an·ti·his·ta·mine (an'ti his'tə mēn), *n.* a medicine used to relieve asthma, hay fever, and, sometimes, the common cold.

an·ti·knock (an'ti näk'), *n.* a substance added to gasoline to do away with noise caused by too fast combustion in an engine.

An·til·les (an til'ēz), *n.pl.* a group of islands in the West Indies. The **Greater Antilles** include Cuba, Jamaica, Hispaniola, and Puerto Rico. The **Lesser Antilles** include many small islands to the east and south.

an·ti·mo·ny (an'tə mō'nē), *n.* a silvery-white, brittle metal that is a chemical element. It is used in alloys and in certain medicines and pigments.

an·tip·a·thy (an tip'ə thē), *n.* **1.** great dislike; strong feeling against [Tom has an *antipathy* toward dogs.] **2.** the thing for which one feels such dislike. —**an·tip'a·thies,** *pl.*

an·tip·o·des (an tip'ə dēz), *n.pl.* a region on the other side of the earth: *used with a plural or singular verb* [The British call New Zealand and Australia the *antipodes.*]

an·ti·quar·i·an (an'ti kwer'i ən), *adj.* having to do with antiques or antiquaries. —*n.* an antiquary.

an·ti·quar·y (an'ti kwer'ē), *n.* a person who collects or studies relics and ancient works of art. —**an'ti·quar·ies,** *pl.*

an·ti·quat·ed (an'ti kwāt'id), *adj.* no longer used; old-fashioned; out-of-date [*antiquated* styles; *antiquated* ideas].

an·tique (an tēk'), *adj.* very old; of former times; made or used a long time ago. —*n.* a piece of furniture or silverware, a tool, etc. made many years ago [He sells *antiques* of colonial America.]

an·tiq·ui·ty (an tik'wə tē), *n.* **1.** the early period of history, especially before the Middle Ages; ancient times [Aristotle was a writer of *antiquity.*] **2.** great age; oldness [The pyramids are of great *antiquity.*] **3.** the people, works of art, customs, etc. of ancient times: *usually used in plural* [a student of Roman *antiquities*]. —**an·tiq'ui·ties,** *pl.*

an·ti·Sem·i·tism (an'ti sem'ə tiz'm), *n.* **1.** prejudice against Jews. **2.** unfair or cruel treatment of Jews. —**an·ti·Se·mit·ic** (an'ti sə mit'ik), *adj.*

an·ti·sep·tic (an'ti sep'tik), *adj.* preventing infection by killing germs. —*n.* any substance that does this, as alcohol or iodine.

an·ti·slav·er·y (an'ti slāv'ər ē), *adj.* against slavery.

an·ti·so·cial (an'ti sō'shəl), *adj.* **1.** not liking to be with other people [She was so *antisocial* that she never had visitors.] **2.** harmful to society in general [All crimes are *antisocial* acts.]

an·tith·e·sis (an tith'ə sis), *n.* **1.** the exact opposite [Joy is the *antithesis* of sorrow.] **2.** an opposing of things or ideas, as in the sentence "You are going; I am staying." —**an·tith·e·ses** (an tith'ə sēz), *pl.*

an·ti·tox·in (an'ti täk'sin), *n.* a substance formed in the body which acts against a disease, such as tetanus. An antitoxin formed in the blood of a diseased animal is sometimes injected into human beings to prevent their getting the disease.

an·ti·trust (an'ti trust'), *adj.* opposed to, or having control over, trusts, or large businesses that are monopolies.

ant·ler (ant'lər), *n.* **1.** the horn of any animal of the deer family. **2.** a branch of such a horn. Antlers are grown and shed once every year. —**ant·lered** (ant'lərd), *adj.*

an·to·nym (an'tə nim), *n.* a word that is opposite in meaning to another word ["Sad" is an *antonym* of "happy."]

antlers

Ant·werp (ant'wərp), *n.* a seaport in northern Belgium.

a·nus (ā'nəs), *n.* the opening in the body through which waste matter leaves the intestines.

an·vil (an′vil), *n.* an iron or steel block on which heated metal objects, such as horseshoes, are hammered into shape.

anvil

anx·i·e·ty (ang zī′ə tē), *n.* **1.** a feeling uneasy or worried about what may happen; concern [Her *anxiety* is caused by John's delay in coming home.] **2.** an eager but often uneasy desire [He fumbled the ball in his *anxiety* to do well.] —**anx·i′e·ties,** *pl.*

anx·ious (angk′shəs), *adj.* **1.** having anxiety; uneasy in mind; worried [She was *anxious* all during the airplane flight.] **2.** full of anxiety or worry [an *anxious* hour]. **3.** eagerly wishing [*anxious* to do his best.] —**anx′ious·ly,** *adv.*

an·y (en′ē), *adj.* **1.** one, no matter which one, of more than two [*Any* pupil in the class may answer.] **2.** some, no matter how much, how many, or what kind [Do you have *any* apples?] **3.** even one; the least number of [I haven't *any* dimes.] **4.** every [*Any* person knows this.] —*pron.* any one or ones; any amount or number [I lost my pencils; do you have *any*?] —*adv.* to any degree; at all [Is he *any* better today?]

an·y·bod·y (en′ē bud′ē *or* en′ē bäd′ē), *pron.* any person; anyone [Is *anybody* home?]

an·y·how (en′ē hou), *adv.* **1.** no matter in what way [I like eggs *anyhow* they may be prepared.] **2.** no matter what else may be true; in any case [I don't like the color, and *anyhow* it's not my size.] **3.** in a careless way [Don't do it just *anyhow*, do it right.]

an·y·one (en′ē wun), *pron.* any person; anybody [Does *anyone* know where he lives?]

any one, 1. any single [*Any one* boy should be able to carry it by himself.] **2.** any single person or thing [Take one; *any one* you want.]

an·y·thing (en′ē thing), *pron.* any thing; any event, fact, etc. [Did *anything* important happen while I was gone?] —*n.* a thing, no matter of what kind [When she shops she buys *anything* and everything.] —*adv.* in any way; at all [Her hat isn't *anything* like yours.] —**anything but,** not at all [I'm *anything but* lonely.]

an·y·way (en′ē wā), *adv.* anyhow.

an·y·where (en′ē hwer), *adv.* **1.** in or at any place [She always has a good time *anywhere* she is.] **2.** to any place [He isn't going *anywhere*.]

A-OK (ā′ō kā′), *adj.* in excellent condition, working order, etc.: *used only in everyday talk.*

a·or·ta (ā ôr′tə), *n.* the main artery of the body. It carries blood from the heart to all parts except the lungs. —**a·or′tas** *or* **a·or·tae** (ā ôr′tē), *pl.*

a·pace (ə pās′), *adv.* at a fast rate; swiftly [The plans went forward *apace*.]

A·pach·e (ə pach′ē), *n.* a member of a tribe of nomadic Indians of northern Mexico and the southwestern United States. —**A·pach′es** *or* **A·pach′e,** *pl.*

a·part (ə pärt′), *adv.* **1.** separately or away from one another [The eruptions of the geyser come about one hour *apart*. He tried to get the fighting boys *apart*.] **2.** reserved for a particular use or function [Each year I set one week *apart* to go to the seashore.] **3.** in or to pieces [The ship was blown *apart* by the bomb. He took the motor *apart*.] —*adj.* separated; not together [During the war, we were *apart* for three years.] —**apart from,** except for; other than [*Apart from* newspapers he reads very little.]

a·part·ment (ə pärt′mənt), *n.* a group of connected rooms, or a single large room, to live in. It is usually a single suite in a building (called an **apartment house**) of several suites.

ap·a·thet·ic (ap′ə thet′ik), *adj.* **1.** having no strong feeling; not feeling or showing love, hate, fear, etc. [Her pitiful plea touched her father who usually seemed *apathetic*.] **2.** not interested; indifferent [It was hard to arouse the *apathetic* public to danger.] —**ap′a·thet′i·cal·ly,** *adv.*

ap·a·thy (ap′ə thē), *n.* **1.** a lack of strong feeling, as love, fear, etc. **2.** a lack of interest or concern [Public *apathy* resulted in a light vote.]

ape (āp), *n.* **1.** a large monkey that has no tail and can walk in an almost upright position [The gorilla and chimpanzee are *apes*.] **2.** any monkey. **3.** a person who imitates or mimics another. —*v.* to imitate or mimic. —**aped,** *p.t. & p.p.;* **ap′ing,** *pr.p.*

Ap·en·nines (ap′ə nīnz), *n.pl.* a mountain range in central Italy.

ap·er·ture (ap′ər chər), *n.* an opening or hole [Light enters a camera through the *aperture* when the shutter is opened.]

a·pex (ā′peks), *n.* the highest point of anything; peak [the *apex* of a pyramid; the *apex* of his career]. —**a′pex·es** *or* **ap·i·ces** (ap′i-sēz), *pl.*

a·phid (ā′fid *or* af′id), *n.* an insect that lives on plants by sucking their juice.

aph·o·rism (af′ə riz′m), *n.* a short, clear statement telling a general truth ["A book you haven't read is a new book" is an *aphorism*.]

a·piece (ə pēs′), *adv.* for each one; each [Candy bars are ten cents *apiece*.]

A.P.O. *or* **APO,** Army Post Office.

A·poc·a·lypse (ə päk′ə lips), *n.* the last book of the New Testament; book of Revelation.

A·poc·ry·pha (ə päk′rə fə), *n.pl.* certain books that are included in the Roman Catholic version of the Bible but are not accepted in the Protestant versions or in Jewish Scriptures.

a·poc·ry·phal (ə päk′rə f'l), *adj.* **1.** coming from a source that is doubtful or unknown, and therefore probably false [The story of George Washington and the cherry tree is *apocryphal*.]

2. Apocryphal, of or like the Apocrypha.

A·pol·lo (ə päl′ō), *n.* **1.** the Greek and Roman god of music, poetry, and medicine. In later times he was also regarded as the god of the sun. **2.** any handsome young man.

a·pol·o·get·ic (ə päl′ə jet′ik), *adj.* making an apology or showing that one is sorry for doing something wrong, etc. **—a·pol′o·get′i·cal·ly,** *adv.*

a·pol·o·gist (ə päl′ə jist), *n.* a person who defends a certain idea, religion, etc.

a·pol·o·gize (ə päl′ə jīz), *v.* to make an apology; say that one is sorry for doing something wrong or being at fault [John *apologized* to Mary for interrupting her.] **—a·pol′o·gized,** *p.t. & p.p.;* **a·pol′o·giz·ing,** *pr.p.*

a·pol·o·gy (ə päl′ə jē), *n.* **1.** a statement that one is sorry for doing something wrong or being at fault; the act of begging a person's pardon [Miss Smith wrote an *apology* to the person she had insulted.] **2.** a statement that defends some idea, religion, etc. **—a·pol′o·gies,** *pl.*

ap·o·plec·tic (ap′ə plek′tik), *adj.* **1.** of or like apoplexy [an *apoplectic* fit]. **2.** likely to have apoplexy [He was *apoplectic* with rage.]

ap·o·plex·y (ap′ə plek′sē), *n.* a condition in which one is suddenly unable to move, think, or feel, as a result of the breaking or blocking of a blood vessel in the brain.

a·pos·ta·sy (ə päs′tə sē), *n.* a turning away from the religion, faith, principles, etc. that one used to believe in.

a·pos·tate (ə päs′tāt), *n.* a person who has turned away from the religion, faith, principles, etc. that he used to believe in.

a·pos·tle (ə päs′'l), *n.* **1.** *usually* **Apostle,** any of the twelve followers of Jesus chosen by him to spread his teachings. **2.** any early Christian missionary or leader. **3.** any leader of a new movement to bring about a reform [Susan B. Anthony was an *apostle* of women's suffrage.]

ap·os·tol·ic (ap′əs täl′ik), *adj.* **1.** having to do with the Apostles or their teachings, or times. **2.** of or from the Pope [an *apostolic* letter].

a·pos·tro·phe (ə päs′trə fē), *n.* the mark (′) used: **1.** in a shortened word or phrase to show that a letter or letters have been omitted [*ne′er* for *never; I′ll* for *I will*]. **2.** to show the possessive case [*Mary's* dress; the *girls'* club]. **3.** to form certain plurals [There are two *6's* in my address.]

a·poth·e·car·y (ə päth′ə ker′ē), *n.* a person who makes and sells drugs and medicines; druggist; pharmacist. **—a·poth′e·car′ies,** *pl.*

Ap·pa·la·chi·an Mountains (ap′ə lā′chi ən *or* ap′ə lach′ən), a mountain system in eastern North America, reaching from Canada to Alabama: also called **the Appalachians.**

ap·pall *or* **ap·pal** (ə pôl′), *v.* to cause to feel horror; shock; dismay [The sight of the wreck *appalled* him.] **—ap·pal′ling,** *adj.*

ap·pa·ra·tus (ap′ə rā′təs *or* ap′ə rat′əs), *n.* the tools, instruments, or equipment needed to do a certain job, experiment, etc. [Beakers and Bunsen burners are the *apparatus* of the chemist.] **—ap′-pa·ra′tus** *or* **ap′pa·ra′tus·es,** *pl.*

ap·par·el (ə par′əl), *n.* clothing; garments; dress

[They sell only women's *apparel*.] **—v.** to dress; clothe [The king was *appareled* in his robes of state.] **—ap·par′eled** *or* **ap·par′elled,** *p.t. & p.p.;* **ap·par′el·ing** *or* **ap·par′el·ling,** *pr.p.*

ap·par·ent (ə par′ənt *or* ə per′ənt), *adj.* **1.** easily seen or understood; obvious; clear [His poorly written letter makes it *apparent* that he will not get the job.] **2.** that appears to be, but is perhaps not really so; seeming [His *apparent* genius is only a good memory.] **—ap·par′ent·ly,** *adv.*

ap·pa·ri·tion (ap′ə rish′ən), *n.* a strange figure appearing suddenly and thought to be a ghost.

ap·peal (ə pēl′), *v.* **1.** to ask earnestly for help, an opinion, etc. [He *appealed* to me for a loan.] **2.** to be interesting or attractive [a book that *appeals* to both boys and girls]. **3.** to ask that a decision in a law case be reviewed by a higher court. **—n. 1.** an earnest request for help, sympathy, etc. **2.** a quality that makes someone or something interesting or attractive [Her great *appeal* lay in her kindness.] **3.** a request to have a decision in a law case reviewed by a higher court; also, the right to make such a request.

ap·pear (ə pir′), *v.* **1.** to come into sight or into being [A ship *appeared* on the horizon. Freckles *appear* on his face every summer.] **2.** to come before the public [He has *appeared* on television. The magazine *appears* monthly.] **3.** to be present; present oneself [I must *appear* in court on Friday.] **4.** to seem; look [He *appears* to be in good health.]

ap·pear·ance (ə pir′əns), *n.* **1.** the act of appearing. **2.** the way a person or thing looks [From his *appearance*, we knew he was angry.] **3.** a false or wrong impression [Anne gives the *appearance* of being busy, but she gets little done.]

ap·pease (ə pēz′), *v.* to satisfy or make calm by giving what is wanted [Water *appeases* thirst. Primitive people tried to *appease* their gods by making sacrifices.] **—ap·peased′,** *p.t. & p.p.;* **ap·peas′ing,** *pr.p.* **—ap·pease′ment,** *n.*

ap·pel·late (ə pel′it), *adj.* that is appealed to [An *appellate* court can hear appeals and change the decisions of lower courts.]

ap·pel·la·tion (ap′ə lā′shən), *n.* **1.** a name or title that describes someone or something [King Richard's *appellation* is "the Lion-Hearted."] **2.** the act of calling by a name.

ap·pend (ə pend′), *v.* to add or attach as an extra part [*Append* a list of the books you used at the end of your report.]

ap·pend·age (ə pen′dij), *n.* a thing that is attached or grows out as a natural, but less important part [A branch of a tree and the tail of a dog are both *appendages*.]

ap·pen·dec·to·my (ap′ən dek′tə mē), *n.* an operation by which a surgeon removes a person's appendix. **—ap′pen·dec′to·mies,** *pl.*

ap·pen·di·ci·tis (ə pen′də sī′tis), *n.* a diseased condition of a person's appendix in which it becomes swollen and inflamed.

ap·pen·dix (ə pen′diks), *n.* **1.** an extra section added at the end of a book [The *appendix* to a book often contains notes of explanation.] **2.** a small closed tube growing out of the large intestine. It serves no known purpose. **—ap·pen′-dix·es** or **ap·pen·di·ces** (ə pen′də sēz), *pl.*

ap·per·tain (ap ər tān′), *v.* to belong naturally or be a part; have to do with [Scientists are solving problems that *appertain* to space travel.]

ap·pe·tite (ap′ə tīt), *n.* **1.** a desire or wish for food [Exercise gave him a strong *appetite*.] **2.** any strong desire [an *appetite* for good books].

ap·pe·tiz·er (ap′ə tīz′er), *n.* a small bit of a tasty food or a drink for giving one a bigger appetite at the beginning of a meal [Olives, tomato juice, etc. are used as *appetizers*.]

ap·pe·tiz·ing (ap′ə tīz′ing), *adj.* that gives one a bigger appetite; tasty.

ap·plaud (ə plôd′), *v.* to show that one enjoys or approves of something, especially by clapping one's hands or cheering.

ap·plause (ə plôz′), *n.* the act of showing that one enjoys or approves of something, especially by clapping the hands or cheering.

ap·ple (ap′′l), *n.* **1.** a round, firm fruit with juicy flesh, a green, yellow, or red skin, and small seeds. **2.** the tree this fruit grows on. **—apple of one's eye,** a person or a thing that is especially dear to one.

apple butter, a kind of jam made from apples cooked with spices.

ap·ple·sauce (ap′′l sôs), *n.* a food made by cooking pieces of apple in sweetened water until they become a soft, pulpy mass.

ap·pli·ance (ə plī′əns), *n.* a machine or device for doing a certain task, especially one that is worked mechanically or by electricity, etc. [Stoves, irons, etc. are household *appliances*.]

ap·pli·ca·ble (ap′li kə b′l), *adj.* that can be applied or used; suitable [Your suggestions are not *applicable* to the problems we face.] **—ap′-pli·ca·bil′i·ty,** *n.*

ap·pli·cant (ap′li kənt), *n.* a person who applies or asks for something [There are five *applicants* for this job.]

ap·pli·ca·tion (ap′li kā′shən), *n.* **1.** the act of applying or putting something on [the *application* of paint to a wall]. **2.** the act of putting something to use [This job calls for the *application* of many skills.] **3.** a thing that is applied, especially a remedy or medicine [*Applications* of mustard paste are sometimes used in treating chest colds.] **4.** a way of applying or of being used [The word "run" has various *applications*.] **5.** an asking for something; request [an *application* for membership in a club]. **6.** a form on which questions must be answered when applying for something, as for a job. **7.** continued effort of the mind or body; the act of paying close attention [He became an honor student by *application* to his studies.]

ap·plied (ə plīd′), *adj.* used in actual practice; practical [An *applied* science uses what is already known to make something; it does not seek to work out new theories.]

ap·pli·qué (ap li kā′), *n.* a decoration made of one material, sewed or pasted to another material.

ap·ply (ə plī′), *v.* **1.** to put or spread on [*Apply* glue to the surface.] **2.** to put into use [*Apply* your knowledge to this problem.] **3.** to work hard

appliqué

and steadily [He *applied* himself to his studies.] **4.** to ask in a formal way [Why don't you *apply* for permission to leave early?] **5.** to have to do with or be suitable to [This rule *applies* to you.] **—ap·plied′,** *p.t. & p.p.;* **ap·ply′ing,** *pr.p.*

ap·point (ə point′), *v.* **1.** to fix or set; decide upon [Let's *appoint* a time for our meeting.] **2.** to name or choose for an office or position [Federal judges are *appointed* by the President.]

ap·point·ee (ə poin′tē′), *n.* a person who has been appointed to some position.

ap·poin·tive (ə poin′tiv), *adj.* to which one is appointed rather than elected, as some jobs.

ap·point·ment (ə point′mənt), *n.* **1.** the act of appointing or a being appointed [The *appointment* of Jones as chairman came as no surprise.] **2.** a position held by an appointed person [He worked hard for the party, hoping to receive an *appointment*.] **3.** an arrangement to meet someone or be somewhere at a certain time [She did not keep her *appointment* with me for lunch today.] **4. appointments,** *pl.* furniture [a hotel with fine *appointments* in every room].

Ap·po·mat·tox (ap′ə mat′əks), *n.* a town in Virginia, where Lee surrendered to Grant in 1865, ending the Civil War.

ap·por·tion (ə pôr′shən), *v.* to divide and give out in shares [The money that was collected will be *apportioned* to the various charities.] **—ap·por′tion·ment,** *n.*

ap·po·si·tion (ap′ə zish′ən), *n.* the relationship between one word or phrase and another that follows and explains it [In the sentence "The Nile, a river in Africa, is longer than the Mississippi," the phrase "a river in Africa" is in *apposition* with "Nile."]

ap·prais·al (ə prāz′′l), *n.* **1.** the act of appraising something. **2.** the value decided on in appraising.

ap·praise (ə prāz′), *v.* **1.** to set a price for; decide how much something is worth [The agent *appraised* the house at $25,000.] **2.** to judge the quality or value of [It is the literary critic's work to *appraise* books.] **—ap·praised′,** *p.t. & p.p.;* **ap·prais′ing,** *pr.p.* **—ap·prais′er,** *n.*

ap·pre·ci·a·ble (ə prē′shi ə b′l *or* ə prē′shə b′l), *adj.* enough to be seen or noticed; noticeable [There is an *appreciable* difference in their sizes.] **—ap·pre′ci·a·bly,** *adv.*

ap·pre·ci·ate (ə prē′shi āt), *v.* **1.** to think well of; understand and enjoy [He has learned to

fat,   āpe,   cär,   ten,   ēven,   hit,   bīte,   gō,   hôrn,   tool,   book,   up,   fur;
get,   joy,   yet,   chin,   she,   thin,   *then;*   zh = s in pleasure;   ′ as in able (ā′b′l);
ə = a in ago,   e in agent,   i in sanity,   o in confess,   u in focus.

appreciate good music.] **2.** to recognize and be grateful for [We *appreciate* all you have done for our family.] **3.** to be fully aware of [I can *appreciate* your problem in making a decision.] **4.** to make or become more valuable [The new shopping center will *appreciate* the homes in the area.] —**ap·pre′ci·at·ed,** *p.t. & p.p.;* **ap·pre′-ci·at·ing,** *prp.* —**ap·pre′ci·a′tion,** *n.*

ap·pre·ci·a·tive (ə prē′shi ā′tiv *or* ə prē′shi ə-tiv), *adj.* feeling or showing that one appreciates something [The *appreciative* audience cheered.]

ap·pre·hend (ap′ri hend′), *v.* **1.** to capture or arrest [The police have not yet *apprehended* the burglar.] **2.** to catch the meaning of; understand [He quickly *apprehended* the problem and solved it.] **3.** to expect anxiously or with fear; dread [I *apprehended* disaster in the snowstorm ahead.]

ap·pre·hen·sion (ap′ri hen′shən), *n.* **1.** a capturing or arresting [the *apprehension* of a criminal]. **2.** understanding [He has no *apprehension* of my meaning.] **3.** an anxious feeling that something bad will happen; dread [He opened the telegram with *apprehension*.]

ap·pre·hen·sive (ap′ri hen′siv), *adj.* feeling anxious or fearful about what may happen; uneasy [Talk about war made us *apprehensive*.]

ap·pren·tice (ə pren′tis), *n.* **1.** a person who is learning a trade by helping a worker skilled in that trade. In earlier times, an apprentice was legally bound to work for his master a certain number of years to pay for his training. **2.** any beginner or learner. —*v.* to place or receive as an apprentice [Benjamin Franklin was *apprenticed* to a printer at an early age.] —**ap·pren′ticed,** *p.t. & p.p.;* **ap·pren′tic·ing,** *prp.*

ap·pren·tice·ship (ə pren′tis ship), *n.* the condition or period of being an apprentice.

ap·prise *or* **ap·prize** (ə prīz′), *v.* to give information to; inform; notify [The spy *apprised* General Washington of the enemy's failure to fortify Trenton.] —**ap·prised′** *or* **ap·prized′,** *p.t. & p.p.;* **ap·pris′ing** *or* **ap·priz′ing,** *prp.*

ap·proach (ə prōch′), *v.* **1.** to come closer or draw nearer [He saw three riders *approaching*. Vacation time *approaches*.] **2.** to be like or similar to [The painter used a green paint that *approached* what we wanted.] **3.** to go to someone with a plan or request [Have you *approached* your father about letting you have a bicycle?] —*n.* **1.** a coming closer or drawing nearer [The first robin marks the *approach* of spring.] **2.** a path or road that leads to some place [The *approaches* to the city are clogged with traffic.]

ap·pro·ba·tion (ap′rə bā′shən), *n.* approval; a telling or showing that one is satisfied with something [Our plans have Mother's *approbation*.]

ap·pro·pri·ate (ə prō′pri āt), *v.* **1.** to set aside for a special use [Congress has *appropriated* money for building roads.] **2.** to take for one's own use [Jane *appropriated* her sister's pearl necklace.] —*adj.* (ə prō′pri it), suitable or right for the purpose [The chorus sang songs *appropriate* to Christmas.] —**ap·pro′pri·at·ed,** *p.t. & p.p.;* **ap·pro′pri·at·ing,** *prp.* —**ap·pro′-pri·ate·ly,** *adv.*

ap·pro·pri·a·tion (ə prō′pri ā′shən), *n.* **1.** the act of appropriating. **2.** a sum of money set aside for a special use.

ap·prov·al (ə prōv′'l), *n.* **1.** the thought or feeling that someone or something is good or worthwhile [The audience showed its *approval* by applauding.] **2.** consent given because of such feeling [He sent that letter without my *approval*.] —**on approval,** for the customer to examine and decide whether to buy or return.

ap·prove (ə prōv′), *v.* **1.** to think or declare to be good, worthwhile, etc.; feel favorable toward: *often used with* of [She doesn't *approve* of most television shows.] **2.** to give one's consent to [Have these plans been *approved* by the mayor?] —**ap·proved′,** *p.t. & p.p.;* **ap·prov′ing,** *prp.*

ap·prox·i·mate (ə präk′sə mit), *adj.* very similar or close to; more or less correct or exact [The painting is an *approximate* copy of one by Raphael. The *approximate* area of the United States is 3,000,000 square miles.] —*v.* (ə präk′sə-māt), to be or make almost the same as or very much like [These artificial flavors do not even *approximate* real fruit flavors.] —**ap·prox′i-mat·ed,** *p.t. & p.p.;* **ap·prox′i·mat·ing,** *prp.*

ap·prox·i·mate·ly (ə präk′sə mit lē), *adv.* not exactly but nearly; almost [It cost *approximately* $337,000,000 to build the Panama Canal.]

ap·prox·i·ma·tion (ə präk′sə mā′shən), *n.* **1.** an approximating, or coming close. **2.** an estimate or guess that is approximately correct or exact; rough idea [The contractor gave us an *approximation* of the cost of building the house.]

ap·pur·te·nance (ə pûr′t'n əns), *n.* an extra, less important part that goes with the main thing [He sold the house and all *appurtenances*, as the barn, garage, and sheds.]

a·pri·cot (ā′pri kät *or* ap′ri kät), *n.* **1.** a pale orange fruit that is a little like a peach. **2.** the tree it grows on. **3.** a pale orange color.

A·pril (ā′prəl), *n.* the fourth month of the year. It has 30 days. Abbreviated **Apr.**

April Fools' Day, April 1. On this day it is a custom to play harmless tricks on people.

a·pron (ā′prən), *n.* **1.** a garment of cloth, leather, plastic, etc. worn over the front part of the body, to cover and protect one's clothes. **2.** the paved area in front of a garage, etc. **3.** the part of a stage in front of the curtain.

ap·ro·pos (ap rə pō′), *adj.* fitting the occasion; suitable; apt [an *apropos* suggestion]. —**apropos of,** in connection with; regarding [*Apropos of* your vacation, what will you do?]

apse

apse (aps), *n.* a part of a church that is set back, usually at the east end of the nave. It is generally in the shape of a half circle with a domed roof.

apt (apt), *adj.* **1.** likely or almost certain; inclined [It is *apt* to rain today.] **2.** suited to the thing for which it is used; appropriate; fitting [an *apt* remark]. **3.** quick to learn or understand [John is an *apt* student.] —**apt′ly**, *adv.*

ap·ti·tude (ap′tə tōōd *or* ap′tə tyōōd), *n.* **1.** an ability that one has naturally; talent [Napoleon had an *aptitude* for military planning.] **2.** quickness to learn or understand [a scholar of great *aptitude*].

aq·ua·lung (ak′wə lung), *n.* a kind of scuba: **Aqualung** is a trademark.

aq·ua·ma·rine (ak′wə mə rēn′), *n.* **1.** a clear, pale blue-green mineral, used in jewelry. **2.** a pale blue-green color. —*adj.* blue-green.

aq·ua·naut (ak′wə nôt), *n.* a person trained to work in a watertight underwater chamber.

aq·ua·plane (ak′wə plān), *n.* a board that is towed by a motorboat while a person stands on it for a ride over the water. —*v.* to ride on such a board as a sport. —**aq′·ua·planed**, *p.t. & p.p.;* **aq′ua·plan·ing**, *pr.p.*

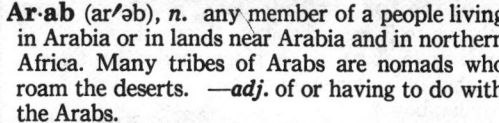
aquaplane

a·quar·i·um (ə-kwer′i əm), *n.* **1.** a glass tank or bowl in which live fishes, water animals, and water plants are kept. **2.** a building where collections of such animals and plants are shown to the public. —**a·quar′-i·ums** or **a·quar-i·a** (ə kwer′i ə), *pl.*

aquarium

a·quat·ic (ə kwat′-ik), *adj.* **1.** growing or living in or upon water [Seaweeds are *aquatic* plants.] **2.** done in or upon the water [Sailing is an *aquatic* sport.]

aq·ue·duct (ak′wi dukt), *n.* **1.** a large pipe or channel for bringing water from one place to another. Aqueducts are usually sloped a little so that the water will flow down. **2.** a high structure like a bridge, for carrying such a pipe across a river bed, etc.

aqueduct

a·que·ous (ā′kwi əs *or* ak′wi əs), *adj.* containing water or like water; watery [an *aqueous* solution].

aq·ui·line (ak′wə lin *or* ak′wə līn), *adj.* **1.** of or like an eagle. **2.** curved or hooked like an eagle's beak [an *aquiline* nose].

Ar·ab (ar′əb), *n.* any member of a people living in Arabia or in lands near Arabia and in northern Africa. Many tribes of Arabs are nomads who roam the deserts. —*adj.* of or having to do with the Arabs.

ar·a·besque (ar ə besk′), *n.* **1.** a complicated design of flowers, leaves, lines, circles, etc. twisted together. **2.** a position in ballet dancing (*see the picture at the right*). —*adj.* of or done in arabesque [an *arabesque* pattern in a rug].

arabesque

A·ra·bi·a (ə rā′bi ə), *n.* a large peninsula in southwestern Asia. It is mostly a desert region.

A·ra·bi·an (ə rā′bi ən), *adj.* of Arabia or the Arabs. —*n.* a person born or living in Arabia.

Arabian Nights, The, a collection of very old stories from Arabia, India, Persia, etc. The stories of Ali Baba, Sinbad the Sailor, and Aladdin are in this collection.

Arabian Sea, a part of the Indian Ocean between India and Arabia.

Ar·a·bic (ar′ə bik), *adj.* of Arabia, the Arabs, or their language. —*n.* the language of the Arabs. It is related to Hebrew and Aramaic.

Arabic numerals, the figures 1, 2, 3, 4, 5, 6, 7, 8, 9, and the 0 (zero).

ar·a·ble (ar′ə b'l), *adj.* in a fit condition for plowing [The flooded land is no longer *arable*].

Ar·a·by (ar′ə bē), *n.* Arabia: *now seldom used except in poetry.*

a·rach·nid (ə rak′nid), *n.* any of a large group of animals related to the insects. They have eight legs and a body that is usually divided into two sections [Spiders and scorpions are *arachnids*.]

Ar·a·gon (ar′ə gän), *n.* a region in northeastern Spain that was once a kingdom.

Ar·a·ma·ic (ar′ə mā′ik), *n.* a Semitic language spoken in Biblical times.

ar·bi·ter (är′bi tər), *n.* **1.** a person who has the power to judge or decide [The *arbiter* in a baseball game is the umpire.] **2.** an arbitrator.

ar·bi·trar·y (är′bə trer′ē), *adj.* based only on one's own will or judgment; ignoring rules or others' opinions [an *arbitrary* decision; an *arbitrary* person]. —**ar′bi·trar′i·ly**, *adv.*

ar·bi·trate (är′bə trāt), *v.* **1.** to settle a dispute by choosing someone to hear both sides and make a decision [Labor and management have decided to *arbitrate* their dispute over wages.] **2.** to give a decision as an arbitrator [The United Nations will *arbitrate* in the border dispute.] —**ar′bi·trat·ed**, *p.t. & p.p.;* **ar′bi·trat·ing**, *pr.p.* —**ar′bi·tra′tion**, *n.*

ar·bi·tra·tor (är′bə trā′tər), *n.* **1.** a person chosen to judge a dispute. **2.** an arbiter.

ar·bor (är′bər), *n.* a place shaded by trees or bushes or by vines on a trellis; bower.

ar·bo·re·al (är bôr′i əl), *adj.* **1.** of or like trees. **2.** living in trees [Squirrels are *arboreal* animals.]

arbor

ar·bor·vi·tae or **ar·bor vi·tae** (är′bər vī′tē), *n.* a small evergreen tree with flattened sprays of leaves that look like scales.

ar·bu·tus (är byoo′təs), *n.* an evergreen plant that trails along the ground and bears clusters of white or pink flowers in the spring.

arc (ärk), *n.* **1.** a part of the line that forms a circle or any curve. **2.** the streak of bright light made by an electric current passing between two electrodes.

arc

ar·cade (är kād′), *n.* **1.** a covered passageway, as through a building, often with an arched roof; especially, such a passage with small shops on both sides. **2.** a row of arches supported by columns.

arcade

arch (ärch), *n.* **1.** a curved part of a structure that holds up the weight of material over an open space. Arches are used in doors, windows, bridges, etc. **2.** anything shaped like an arch [the *arch* of the foot]. —*v.* **1.** to curve into an arch [The cat *arched* its back.] **2.** to form an arch over [The bridge *arches* over the valley.]

arch (ärch), *adj.* **1.** main; chief [the *arch* villain]. **2.** playful or full of mischief; pert [an *arch* smile].

arch-, a prefix meaning "main," "chief" [An *archangel* is a chief angel, or angel of the highest rank.]

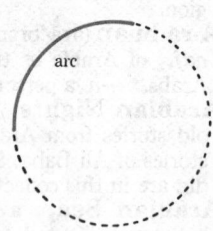

arch

ar·chae·ol·o·gy (är′ki äl′ə jē), *n.* the study of ancient times and ancient peoples. Such study is carried on mainly by digging up the remains of ancient cities, buildings, tombs, etc. —**ar·chae·o·log·i·cal** (är′ki ə läj′i k′l), *adj.* —**ar′chae·ol′o·gist,** *n.*

ar·cha·ic (är kā′ik), *adj.* **1.** belonging to an earlier time; ancient or old-fashioned [The yard was enclosed by an *archaic* iron fence.] **2.** that is now seldom used except in poetry, the Bible, etc.

["Thou art" is an *archaic* form of "you are."]

arch·an·gel (ärk′ān′jəl), *n.* a chief angel.

arch·bish·op (ärch′bish′əp), *n.* a bishop of the highest rank.

arch·duke (ärch′dook′ *or* ärch′dyook′), *n.* a son of the emperor in the old Austrian Empire. —**arch·duch·ess** (ärch′duch′is), *n.fem.*

ar·che·ol·o·gy (är′ki äl′ə jē), *n.* same as **archaeology.**

arch·er (ärch′ər), *n.* a person who shoots with bow and arrow.

arch·er·y (ärch′ər ē), *n.* **1.** the skill or sport of shooting with bow and arrow. **2.** archers as a group.

ar·che·type (är′kə tīp), *n.* the first one, that serves as a model for others [The Constitution of the U.S. has served as the *archetype* for many constitutions.]

archer

Ar·chi·me·des (är′ki mē′dēz), *n.* 287?–212 B.C.; Greek mathematician and inventor.

ar·chi·pel·a·go (är′kə pel′ə gō), *n.* a group or chain of many islands in a sea. —**ar′chi·pel′a·goes** or **ar′chi·pel′a·gos,** *pl.*

ar·chi·tect (är′kə tekt), *n.* a person who works out the plans for buildings, bridges, etc. and sees that these plans are carried out by the builders.

ar·chi·tec·ture (är′ki tek′chər), *n.* **1.** the science or work of planning and putting up buildings. **2.** a style or special way of building [Modern *architecture* makes much use of straight lines and simple forms.] —**ar′chi·tec′tur·al,** *adj.* —**ar′chi·tec′tur·al·ly,** *adv.*

archipelago

ar·chives (är′kīvz), *n.pl.* **1.** a place where old public records and papers of historical interest are kept. **2.** such records and papers.

arch·ly (ärch′lē), *adv.* in a playful or mischievous way; pertly.

arch·way (ärch′wā), *n.* a passage or entrance under an arch.

arc·tic (ärk′tik *or* är′tik), *adj.* of or near the North Pole or the region around it. —*n.* the region around the North Pole.

Arctic Ocean, the ocean around the North Pole.

ar·dent (är′d′nt), *adj.* full of eagerness; very enthusiastic; passionate. —**ar′dent·ly,** *adv.*

ar·dor (är′dər), *n.* very warm feeling; passion; eagerness; enthusiasm [Patrick Henry spoke with *ardor* in the fight for liberty.] The usual British spelling is **ardour.**

ar·du·ous (är′joo əs), *adj.* **1.** hard to do; difficult [*arduous* work]. **2.** using much energy; strenuous [*arduous* efforts]. —**ar′du·ous·ly,** *adv.*

are (är), the form of the verb *be* used to show the

present time with *you*, *we*, and *they*, and with plural nouns [*Are* we late? You *are*.]

ar·e·a (er′i ə), *n.* **1.** the amount or size of a surface, measured in square units [If a floor is 10 feet wide and 20 feet long, its *area* is 200 square feet.] **2.** a part of the earth's surface; region [Bananas grow in tropical *areas*.] **3.** a space used for a special purpose [a picnic *area*].

a·re·na (ə rē′nə), *n.* **1.** the open field in the middle of a Roman amphitheater, where gladiators fought. **2.** any place where there is struggle or conflict [an *arena* for boxing matches; the *arena* of politics].

aren't (ärnt), are not [They *aren't* going.] *Aren't* is sometimes used in place of *am not* in questions [I'm going too, *aren't* I?]

Ar·es (er′ēz), *n.* the Greek god of war. The Romans called this god *Mars*.

ar·gent (är′jənt), *adj.* of silver; silvery: *now used mainly in poetry.*

Ar·gen·ti·na (är′jən tē′nə), *n.* a country in southern South America.

Ar·gen·tine (är′jən tēn), *adj.* of Argentina or its people. —*n.* a person born or living in Argentina.

ar·gon (är′gän), *n.* a chemical element that is a gas without color or smell. It is found in the air in very small amounts, and is used in electric light bulbs, radio tubes, etc.

Ar·go·naut (är′gə nôt), *n.* any of the men in a Greek legend who sailed with Jason to search for the Golden Fleece.

ar·go·sy (är′gə sē), *n.* **1.** a large ship, especially one carrying cargo. **2.** a fleet of such ships. *Now used only in poetry.* —**ar′go·sies,** *pl.*

ar·gue (är′gyōō), *v.* **1.** to give reasons for or against something [to *argue* against a bill in Congress]. **2.** to have a disagreement; quarrel [Ruth and her father are always *arguing* about politics.] **3.** to seem to prove; show; indicate [His fine manners *argue* a good upbringing.] **4.** to make do something by giving reasons [They *argued* me into staying a week.] —**ar′gued,** *p.t. & p.p.;* **ar′gu·ing,** *pr.p.*

ar·gu·ment (är′gyōō mənt), *n.* **1.** the act of arguing; discussion in which people disagree; dispute. **2.** a reason given for or against something [The senator gave good *arguments* for lowering taxes.] **3.** a short statement of what a book, article, etc. is about.

ar·gu·men·ta·tive (är′gyōō men′tə tiv), *adj.* always ready to argue; quarrelsome.

Ar·gus (är′gəs), *n.* **1.** a giant in Greek myths, with a hundred eyes. **2.** a careful watchman.

a·ri·a (ä′ri ə *or* er′i ə), *n.* a song in an opera or oratorio, that is sung by one person accompanied by musical instruments.

ar·id (ar′id), *adj.* **1.** not having enough water for things to grow; dry and barren [A desert is an *arid* region.] **2.** not interesting; dull. —**a·rid·i·ty** (ə rid′ə tē), *n.* —**ar′id·ly,** *adv.*

Ar·i·el (er′i əl), *n.* an airy spirit in Shakespeare's play "The Tempest."

a·right (ə rīt′), *adv.* correctly; rightly [Did I hear you *aright*?]

a·rise (ə rīz′), *v.* **1.** to get up, as from sleeping or sitting; rise. **2.** to move upward; ascend [Clouds of dust *arose* from the dry plains.] **3.** to begin to be; originate [Many new businesses have *arisen* in the town.] **4.** to come as a result [Prejudice *arises* from ignorance.] —**a·rose′,** *p.t.;* **a·ris·en** (ə riz′'n), *p.p.;* **a·ris·ing** (ə rīz′-ing), *pr.p.*

ar·is·toc·ra·cy (ar′ə stäk′rə sē), *n.* **1.** an upper or ruling class of society whose wealth and high social position are inherited; nobility. **2.** government by such an upper class. **3.** those considered the best in some way [an *aristocracy* of scientists in the Atomic Age.] —**ar′is·toc′ra·cies,** *pl.*

a·ris·to·crat (ə ris′tə krat), *n.* **1.** a member of the aristocracy; nobleman or noblewoman. **2.** a person whose tastes, manners, beliefs, etc. are those of the upper class.

ar·is·to·crat·ic (ə ris′tə krat′ik), *adj.* **1.** belonging to the aristocracy. **2.** like an aristocrat; proud, noble, etc. (*in a good sense*) or haughty, snobbish, etc. (*in a bad sense*). —**ar·is′to·crat′i·cal·ly,** *adv.*

Ar·is·tot·le (ar′is tät′'l), *n.* 384–322 B.C.; Greek philosopher.

a·rith·me·tic (ə rith′mə tik), *n.* the science or art of using numbers, especially in adding, subtracting, multiplying, and dividing. —**ar·ith·met·i·cal** (ar′ith met′i k'l), *adj.*

Ar·i·zo·na (ar′ə zō′nə), *n.* a State in the southwestern part of the United States: abbreviated **Ariz.**

ark (ärk), *n.* **1.** in the Bible, the ship in which Noah, his family, and two of every kind of animal lived during the great flood. **2.** the chest holding the two stone tablets on which the Ten Commandments were inscribed. It was kept in the holiest part of the ancient Jewish Temple. Its full name was the **ark of the covenant.**

Ar·kan·sas (är′kən sô), *n.* a State in the south central part of the United States: abbreviated **Ark.**

arm (ärm), *n.* **1.** the part of the body between the shoulder and the hand; an upper limb. **2.** anything thought of as being like an arm, as the raised side of a chair, the sleeve of a coat, an inlet of the sea, or a branch of government. —**arm in arm,** with arms joined, as two people walking together. —**with open arms,** in a warm and friendly way.

arm (ärm), *n.* any weapon: see **arms.** —*v.* **1.** to furnish with a weapon or weapons. **2.** to furnish with some kind of protection [*armed* against the cold with a heavy coat].

ar·ma·da (är mä′də), *n.* **1.** a fleet of warships [The Spanish *Armada* sent against England in 1588 was defeated.] **2.** a fleet of warplanes.

---

fat, āpe, cär, ten, ēven, hit, bīte, gō, hôrn, tool, book, up, fur; get, joy, yet, chin, she, thin, then; zh = s in pleasure; ' as in able (ā′b'l); ə = a in ago, e in agent, i in sanity, o in confess, u in focus.

ar·ma·dil·lo (är'mə dil'ō), *n.* a burrowing animal with an armor of bony plates around its back and head. It is found in Texas, Central America, and South America. Some armadillos can roll up into a ball when in danger. —**ar'ma·dil'los,** *pl.*

armadillo (2½ ft. long)

ar·ma·ment (är'mə mənt), *n.* **1.** *often* **armaments,** *pl.* all the guns, bombs, ships, planes, etc. for waging war. **2.** all the weapons of a warship, warplane, tank, etc.

ar·ma·ture (är'mə chər), *n.* **1.** that part of an electric generator in which the current is brought into being; also, that part of a motor in which the movement is produced. In both cases, it is an iron core wound around with wire, and it is usually a rotating part. **2.** a soft iron bar placed across the poles of a magnet. **3.** the part moved by a magnet in an electric relay or bell. **4.** armor or protective covering.

arm·chair (ärm'cher), *n.* a chair with supports at the sides for the arms or elbows.

armed forces (ärmd), all the military, naval, and air forces of a country.

armchair

Ar·me·ni·a (är mē'ni ə), *n.* a former country in southwestern Asia, now divided between the Soviet Union, Turkey, and Iran. —**Ar·me'ni·an,** *adj. & n.*

arm·ful (ärm'fool), *n.* as much as the arms or one arm can hold. —**arm'fuls,** *pl.*

arm·hole (ärm'hōl), *n.* an opening for the arm at the shoulder of a shirt, coat, etc.

ar·mi·stice (är'mə stis), *n.* an agreement to stop fighting, as before getting together to draw up a peace treaty; truce [The *armistice* of Nov. 11, 1918, ended fighting in World War I.]

Armistice Day, see **Veterans Day.**

ar·mor (är'mər), *n.* **1.** covering worn to protect the body against weapons [The knight's suit of *armor* was made of metal plate.] **2.** any protective covering, as the shell of a turtle or the metal plates on a warship. The usual British spelling is **armour.**

ar·mored (är'mərd), *adj.* **1.** covered with armor [an *armored* car]. **2.** furnished with tanks and other armored vehicles [the *armored* divisions of an army].

ar·mor·er (är'mər ər), *n.* a soldier or sailor whose job is to take care of the small guns of his company, warship, etc.

ar·mo·ri·al (är môr'i əl), *adj.* having to do with coats of arms; heraldic.

armor

ar·mor·y (är'mər ē), *n.* **1.** a place where weapons are stored; arsenal. **2.** a building where a National Guard unit drills. **3.** a factory where pistols, rifles, etc. are made. —**ar'mor·ies,** *pl.*

arm·pit (ärm'pit), *n.* the hollow place under the arm where it joins the shoulder.

arms (ärmz), *n.pl.* **1.** weapons; tools used for fighting. **2.** fighting; warfare. **3.** pictures of animals, designs, etc. put on a shield or flag as the sign of a noble family, a country, etc.: see **coat of arms.** —**bear arms,** to serve as a soldier, sailor, etc. —**take up arms,** to go to war or join a rebellion. —**up in arms,** angry and ready to fight.

ar·my (är'mē), *n.* **1.** a large group of soldiers trained for war, especially on land; also, all the soldiers of a country. **2.** a large group of persons organized to work for some cause [the Salvation *Army*]. **3.** any large number of persons, animals, etc. [an *army* of campers]. —**ar'mies,** *pl.*

ar·ni·ca (är'ni kə), *n.* **1.** a medicine made from a thistle plant, for rubbing on sprains or bruises. **2.** this plant, which has bright yellow flowers on long stalks.

Ar·nold, Benedict (är'nəld), 1741–1801; American general in the Revolution who became a traitor.

a·ro·ma (ə rō'mə), *n.* a pleasant smell, as of a plant or of something cooking.

ar·o·mat·ic (ar'ə mat'ik), *adj.* having a pleasant, often spicy, smell; fragrant [*aromatic* herbs].

a·rose (ə rōz'), the past tense of **arise.**

a·round (ə round'), *adv.* **1.** in a circle [The wheel turned *around*.] **2.** in circumference [A baseball measures about nine inches *around*.] **3.** on all sides [The valley is hemmed *around* by mountains.] **4.** in the opposite direction [We turned *around* and went back home.] **5.** in various places; here and there [The women went into the store to look *around*.] **6.** near by: *used only in everyday talk* [Stay *around* in case we need you.] —*prep.* **1.** in a circle that surrounds [Pine trees grew *around* the lake.] **2.** on all sides of [the suburbs *around* the city]. **3.** here and there in; about [Toys were scattered *around* the room.] **4.** close to; about: *used only in everyday talk* [It cost *around* four dollars.] See also **round.**

a·rouse (ə rouz'), *v.* **1.** to awaken, as from sleep. **2.** to work up; bring into being; excite [The trembling animal *aroused* our pity.] —**a·roused',** *p.t. & p.p.;* **a·rous'ing,** *pr.p.*

ar·que·bus (är'kwi bəs), *n.* a firearm of the 15th century that was held up by a hooked stick while being fired.

ar·raign (ə rān'), *v.* to bring before a law court to answer a charge with either "guilty" or "not guilty." —**ar·raign'ment,** *n.*

ar·range (ə rānj'), *v.* **1.** to put in a certain order. **2.** to make plans; prepare [I *arranged* to meet him at his office.] **3.** to change so as to fit; adapt; adjust [This violin solo has been *arranged* for the guitar.] —**ar·ranged',** *p.t. & p.p.;* **ar·rang'ing,** *pr.p.*

ar·range·ment (ə rānj'mənt), *n.* **1.** an arranging or putting in order. **2.** the way in which something is arranged [a new *arrangement* of furniture in the room]. **3.** a preparation; plan: *usually used in plural,* **arrangements** [*Arrangements* have been made for the party.]

ar·rant (ar′ənt), *adj.* that is very plainly such; absolute; complete [an *arrant* fool].

ar·ray (ə rā′), *v.* **1.** to put in the proper order [The troops were *arrayed* for battle.] **2.** to dress in fine clothes [*arrayed* in an elegant silk gown]. —*n.* **1.** arrangement in the proper order [soldiers in battle *array*]. **2.** a large display [an *array* of fine china]. **3.** fine clothes; finery.

ar·rears (ə rirz′), *n.pl.* a debt or duty not yet taken care of; unfinished business [*arrears* of unanswered letters]. —**in arrears,** behind in paying a debt, or in one's work.

ar·rest (ə rest′), *v.* **1.** to stop from growing or spreading [A coat of paint will *arrest* the rust.] **2.** to catch and hold [The canary's song *arrested* her attention.] **3.** to seize or take to jail on a charge of breaking the law [The policeman *arrested* him for careless driving.] —*n.* the act of arresting by the police. —**under arrest,** held as a prisoner on a charge of breaking the law.

ar·rest·ing (ə res′ting), *adj.* causing interest or attention; striking [an *arresting* performance].

ar·riv·al (ə rīv′'l), *n.* **1.** the act of arriving [to welcome the *arrival* of spring]. **2.** a person or thing that has arrived [He is a recent *arrival* to the U.S. from France.]

ar·rive (ə rīv′), *v.* **1.** to come to a place after a journey [When does the bus from Chicago *arrive* here?] **2.** to come [The time has *arrived* to say good-by.] **3.** to get success or fame [The pianist had *arrived* by the age of 25.] —**arrive at, 1.** to reach by traveling. **2.** to reach by work, thinking, etc. [Have you *arrived* at a decision?] —**ar·rived′,** *p.t. & p.p.;* **ar·riv′ing,** *pr.p.*

ar·ro·gance (ar′ə gəns), *n.* a feeling of too great pride or confidence that makes one act as though he were better than others; haughtiness.

ar·ro·gant (ar′ə gənt), *adj.* having or showing arrogance. —**ar′ro·gant·ly,** *adv.*

ar·row (ar′ō), *n.* **1.** a slender rod that is shot from a bow. Arrows usually have a point at the front end and feathers at the back end. **2.** anything that looks or is used like an arrow; especially, a sign (→) used to point out a direction or place.

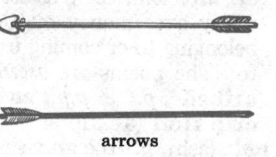

arrows

ar·row·head (ar′ō hed′), *n.* the pointed tip of an arrow.

ar·row·root (ar′ō rōōt′), *n.* a starch from the roots of a tropical plant, used as food.

ar·se·nal (är′s'n əl), *n.* a place where guns and ammunition are made or stored.

ar·se·nic (är′s'n ik), *n.* a silvery-white metal, a chemical element sometimes found in the form of a powder. It is very poisonous and is used in powders and sprays for killing insects, rats, and mice.

ar·son (är′s'n), *n.* the crime of setting fire to a building or other property on purpose.

art (ärt), *n.* **1.** the making or doing of things that have form and beauty [Drawing, painting, sculpture, architecture, music, literature, drama, and the dance are *arts*.] See also **fine arts. 2.** paintings, drawings, statues, or other things made by artists. **3.** any of certain fields of study, as literature, languages, history, philosophy, music, etc.: *usually used in pl.,* **arts.** In this meaning the *arts* are considered as separate from the *sciences.* **4.** the ability to make or do things; skill [the *art* of cooking]. **5.** any craft or profession [the cobbler's *art*]. **6.** a sly or cunning trick; wile [She used all her *arts* to gain his love.]

art (ärt), the older form of **are,** used with *thou,* as in the Bible.

Ar·te·mis (är′tə mis), *n.* the Greek goddess of the moon and hunting. The Romans called this goddess *Diana.*

ar·te·ri·al (är tir′i əl), *adj.* **1.** of or like an artery or arteries. **2.** having to do with the blood in the arteries [*Arterial* blood is a brighter red than the blood in the veins because it has taken up oxygen from the lungs.]

ar·ter·y (är′tər ē), *n.* **1.** any of the tubes that carry blood from the heart to all parts of the body: see also **vein. 2.** a main road or channel [a railroad *artery*]. —**ar′ter·ies,** *pl.*

ar·te·sian well (är tē′zhən), a deep well in which the water gushes up because of the pressure under the ground.

art·ful (ärt′fəl), *adj.* **1.** skillful or clever [*artful* reasoning]. **2.** sly or cunning; crafty [an *artful* swindle]. —**art′ful·ly,** *adv.*

ar·thri·tis (är thrī′tis), *n.* a disease in which the joints of the body swell up and become sore. —**ar·thrit·ic** (är thrit′ik), *adj.*

Ar·thur (är′thər), *n.* the hero of many old legends, a king of Britain who led the knights of the Round Table. Such a king is supposed to have lived in the 6th century A.D.

Ar·thur, Ches·ter A. (ches′tər är′thər), 1830–1886; 21st president of the United States, from 1881 to 1885.

ar·ti·choke (är′tə chōk), *n.* **1.** a plant that looks like a large thistle. **2.** its flower head, which is cooked and eaten as a vegetable.

ar·ti·cle (är′ti k'l), *n.* **1.** a thing of a certain kind; separate thing [an *article* of clothing]. **2.** a section that deals with a separate point in a constitution, treaty, contract, etc. **3.** a complete piece of writing on a single subject, as in a newspaper or

artichoke

magazine. **4.** any of the words *a, an,* or *the.*

ar·tic·u·late (är tik′yoo lit), *adj.* **1.** spoken in such a way that all the sounds and words are clear and distinct [an *articulate* reply]. **2.** able to speak in this way; also, able to tell one's thoughts clearly so they are understood [an *articulate* spokesman for a cause]. **3.** having joints [The legs are *articulate* limbs.] —*v.* (är tik′yoo lāt), **1.** to say in a clear, distinct way. **2.** to put or come together by means of a joint [The arm *articulates* with the body at the shoulder.] —**ar·tic′u·lat·ed,** *p.t. & p.p.;* **ar·tic′u·lat·ing,** *pr.p.*

ar·tic·u·la·tion (är tik′yoo lā′shən), *n.* **1.** way of talking or pronouncing. **2.** the way parts are joined together. **3.** a joint, as between bones.

ar·ti·fact (är′tə fakt), *n.* a thing made by human work or skill.

ar·ti·fice (är′tə fis), *n.* a clever method or sly trick [using every *artifice* to avoid capture].

ar·tif·i·cer (är tif′ə sər), *n.* a skillful maker of things; expert workman.

ar·ti·fi·cial (är′tə fish′əl), *adj.* **1.** made by man, not by nature; not natural [Man-made satellites are called *artificial* moons.] **2.** put on just for an effect; not sincere; false [an *artificial* smile]. —**ar·ti·fi·ci·al·i·ty** (är′tə fish′i al′ə tē), *n.* —**ar′ti·fi′cial·ly,** *adv.*

artificial respiration, the act of trying to start or keep a person breathing by forcing air into and out of his lungs, as in cases of drowning, shock, etc.

ar·til·ler·y (är til′ər ē), *n.* large guns, too heavy to carry; mounted guns. —**the artillery,** the branch of an army that uses such guns.

ar·ti·san (är′tə z′n), *n.* a worker who is skilled in some trade; craftsman.

art·ist (är′tist), *n.* **1.** a person who works in any of the fine arts, especially in painting, drawing, sculpture, etc. **2.** a person who does something with skill [His cook is an *artist* with pastries.]

ar·tis·tic (är tis′tik), *adj.* **1.** of art or artists. **2.** done skillfully and with a good sense of color, form, design, etc. [an *artistic* job of redecorating]. **3.** having a feeling for what is beautiful. —**ar·tis′ti·cal·ly,** *adv.*

art·ist·ry (är′tis trē), *n.* artistic work or skill.

art·less (ärt′lis), *adj.* **1.** without art or skill; clumsy. **2.** without artificial tricks; simple; natural [an *artless* way of speaking].

-ar·y (er′ē *or* ər ē), a suffix meaning: **1.** having to do with [*Customary* means having to do with customs.] **2.** a person or thing connected with [A *missionary* is a person connected with missions.]

as (az), *adv.* **1.** to the same amount or degree; equally [Are you *as* tall as your father?] **2.** for instance; thus [Some plants, *as* corn and potatoes, are native to America.] —*conj.* **1.** to the same amount or degree that [It flew straight *as* an arrow. I'm *as* hungry *as* you are.] **2.** in the way that [Do *as* I tell you.] **3.** at the same time that; while [She wept *as* she spoke.] **4.** because; since [*As* I am tired, I'll stay home.] **5.** that the result was [She was so brave *as* to put us all to

shame.] **6.** though [Full *as* he was, he kept on eating.] —*pron.* a fact that [She's tired, *as* anyone can see.] —*prep.* in the role or character of [He poses *as* a friend.] —**as for** or **as to,** in regard to; concerning [*As for* me, I'll have milk.] —**as if** or **as though,** as it (or one) would if [He looked *as if* he wanted to fight.] —**as is,** just as it is: *a slang phrase.* —**the same as,** like; resembling [Your hat is *the same as* mine.]

As, symbol for the chemical element *arsenic.*

as·a·fet·i·da or **as·a·foet·i·da** (as′ə fet′i də), *n.* a gummy substance that is gotten from certain plants and has a bad smell. It is used in medicine.

as·bes·tos (as bes′təs *or* az bes′təs), *n.* a grayish mineral found in long fibers which can be made into a kind of cloth or paper. Asbestos will not burn and so it is used in fireproof curtains, roofing, insulation, etc.

as·cend (ə send′), *v.* to go up; move upward; rise; climb [The procession *ascended* the hill.]

as·cend·an·cy or **as·cend·en·cy** (ə sen′dən sē), *n.* a position in which one has control or power; supremacy; domination [For centuries ancient Rome held *ascendancy* over Europe.]

as·cend·ant or **as·cend·ent** (ə sen′dənt), *adj.* **1.** rising; ascending. **2.** in control; dominant. —**in the ascendant,** becoming more powerful or important.

as·cen·sion (ə sen′shən), *n.* a rising; ascent. —**the Ascension,** in the Bible, the ascent of Jesus into heaven after rising from the dead.

as·cent (ə sent′), *n.* **1.** an ascending or rising; climbing [an *ascent* in a balloon; a rapid *ascent* to leadership]. **2.** a way leading up; slope.

as·cer·tain (as ər tān′), *v.* to find out in such a way as to be sure [He *ascertained* the metals in the ore by using chemical tests.] —**as·cer·tain′a·ble,** *adj.* —**as·cer·tain′ment,** *n.*

as·cet·ic (ə set′ik), *n.* a person who chooses to live without the usual pleasures and comforts of man; especially, one who lives this way for religious reasons. —*adj.* of or like ascetics or their way of life. —**as·cet′i·cism,** *n.*

as·cribe (ə skrīb′), *v.* **1.** to think to be the result of: *used with* to [He *ascribed* his poor work to worry over money matters.] **2.** to think of as belonging to or coming from; attribute. *used with* to [The poems are *ascribed* to Homer.] —**as·cribed′,** *p.t. & p.p.;* **as·crib′ing,** *pr.p.* —**as·crip·tion** (ə skrip′shən), *n.*

ash (ash), *n.* the grayish powder left after something has been burned. See also **ashes.**

ash (ash), *n.* a shade tree whose tough wood has a straight, close grain.

a·shamed (ə shāmd′), *adj.* **1.** feeling shame because something bad, wrong, or foolish was done [The boy was *ashamed* of his tears.] **2.** not willing because of a fear that one will feel shame [He was *ashamed* to be seen in his old suit.]

ash·en (ash′'n), *adj.* **1.** of ashes. **2.** like ashes, especially in color; pale [an *ashen* face].

ash·en (ash′'n), *adj.* of the ash tree or its wood.

ash·es (ash′iz), *n.pl.* **1.** the particles, grayish powder, etc. remaining after something has been burned. **2.** the body of a dead person; especially, the part of the body that is left after cremation.

a·shore (ə shôr′), *adv. & adj.* to or on the shore [He jumped overboard and swam *ashore*].

ash tray, a kind of dish into which smokers drop their tobacco ashes, etc.

Ash Wednesday, the Wednesday that is the first day of Lent. In some churches on this day ashes are put on the forehead.

ash·y (ash′ē), *adj.* **1.** full of or covered with ashes. **2.** having the gray color of ashes; pale.

A·sia (ā′zhə), *n.* the largest continent, about 17,000,000 square miles in area. It has the Pacific Ocean on the east and is separated from northern Europe by the Ural Mountains.

Asia Minor, a peninsula in western Asia, between the Black Sea and the Mediterranean Sea. It includes most of Turkey.

A·si·at·ic (ā′zhi at′ik) or **A·sian** (ā′zhən), *adj.* having to do with Asia or its people. —*n.* a person born or living in Asia.

a·side (ə sīd′), *adv.* **1.** on or to one side [She pulled the curtains *aside*.] **2.** away; for use later [Put a piece of cake *aside* for me.] **3.** out of the way; out of thought [All joking *aside*, I mean what I said.] —*n.* words spoken so that they will not be heard by certain people [An actor's *aside* to the audience is not supposed to be heard by the other actors.] —**aside from,** except for [*Aside from* tennis, I don't enjoy sports.]

as·i·nine (as′ə nīn), *adj.* stupid, silly, or foolish.

ask (ask), *v.* **1.** to use words in trying to find out; seek the answer to [We *asked* how much it cost. Why do you *ask* so many questions?] **2.** to put a question to; seek information from [*Ask* her where she's going.] **3.** to tell what is wanted; make a request [We *asked* the bank for a loan. John *asked* to be excused from school.] **4.** to demand or expect as a price [They are *asking* one dollar a pound for coffee.] **5.** to invite [We weren't *asked* to the party.]

a·skance (ə skans′), *adv.* **1.** sidewise; with a glance to the side. **2.** with doubt or suspicion [They looked *askance* at the plan for moving.]

a·skew (ə skyōō′), *adv. & adj.* on or to one side; not straight [He wore his hat *askew*.]

a·slant (ə slant′), *adv. & adj.* on a slant; in a slanting direction. —*prep.* on a slant across.

a·sleep (ə slēp′), *adj.* **1.** sleeping; in a state of sleep. **2.** numb except for a prickly feeling [I have been sitting on my foot so long that it is *asleep*.] —*adv.* into a sleeping condition [to fall *asleep*].

asp (asp), *n.* a small, poisonous snake of Africa and Europe.

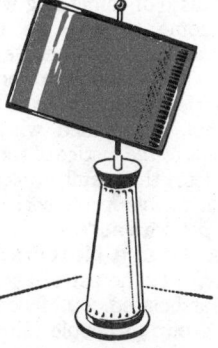
a lamp shade askew

as·par·a·gus (ə spar′ə gəs), *n.* a plant with small leaves that look like scales. Its young shoots are cooked and eaten as a vegetable.

as·pect (as′pekt), *n.* **1.** look or appearance [In the shadows his face had a frightening *aspect*.] **2.** a way that one may look at or think about something [Have you considered all the *aspects* of the problem?] **3.** the side facing in a particular direction [the eastern *aspect* of the house].

asparagus

as·pen (as′pən), *n.* a kind of poplar tree whose leaves flutter in the lightest breeze.

as·per·i·ty (as per′ə tē), *n.* **1.** roughness or harshness, as of weather. **2.** sharpness of temper. —**as·per′i·ties,** *pl.*

as·per·sion (ə spûr′zhən), *n.* a false or unfair remark that can hurt one; slander [The candidate cast *aspersions* on his opponent's character.]

as·phalt (as′fôlt), *n.* **1.** a dark, sticky substance like tar, that is found in the ground. **2.** a mixture of this with sand or gravel, used to cover roads, roofs, floors, etc.

as·phyx·i·ate (as fik′si āt), *v.* to make unconscious by cutting down the supply of oxygen in the blood [When a person suffocates, as in drowning, he has been *asphyxiated*.] —**as·phyx′i·at·ed,** *p.t. & p.p.;* **as·phyx′i·at·ing,** *pr.p.* —**as·phyx′i·a·tion,** *n.*

as·pic (as′pik), *n.* a jelly of meat juice, tomato juice, etc., molded and eaten as a relish.

as·pir·ant (ə spīr′ənt *or* as′pə rənt), *n.* a person who is trying to get honors or a high position [an *aspirant* to the presidency].

as·pi·rate (as′pə rāt), *v.* to pronounce with the sound of *h* [The "h" in "home" is *aspirated;* the "h" in "honor" is not.] —*n.* the sound of *h* in *home.* —*adj.* pronounced with this sound. —**as′pi·rat·ed,** *p.t. & p.p.;* **as′pi·rat·ing,** *pr.p.*

as·pi·ra·tion (as′pə rā′shən), *n.* **1.** a strong wish, hope, or ambition [his *aspirations* to become a doctor]. **2.** the act of breathing; breath. **3.** an aspirating.

as·pire (ə spīr′), *v.* to be ambitious to get or do something; seek [Napoleon *aspired* to create a French empire. Most writers *aspire* after fame.] —**as·pired′,** *p.t. & p.p.;* **as·pir′ing,** *pr.p.*

as·pi·rin (as′pər in), *n.* a medicine used for headaches and other pains or to bring down fever. It is a white powder that is now usually pressed into tablets.

ass (as), *n.* **1.** a donkey. **2.** a stupid or silly person; fool.

as·sa·fet·i·da or **as·sa·foet·i·da** (as′ə fet′i də), *n.* same as **asafetida.**

---

fat, āpe, cär, ten, ēven, hit, bīte, gō, hôrn, tōōl, book, up, fûr;
get, joy, yet, chin, she, thin, *th*en; zh = s in pleasure; ′ as in able (ā′b'l);
ə = a in ago, e in agent, i in sanity, o in confess, u in focus.

as·sail (ə sāl′), *v.* **1.** to attack by hitting, punching, etc. **2.** to attack with questions, arguments, or doubts. —**as·sail′a·ble**, *adj.*

as·sail·ant (ə sāl′ənt), *n.* a person who assails; attacker.

as·sas·sin (ə sas′in), *n.* a murderer, especially one hired or chosen to kill a government leader.

as·sas·si·nate (ə sas′ə nāt), *v.* to murder; especially, to murder a government leader. —**as·sas′si·nat·ed**, *p.t.* & *p.p.*; **as·sas′si·nat·ing**, *pr.p.* —**as·sas′si·na′tion**, *n.*

as·sault (ə sôlt′), *n.* **1.** a sudden attack with great force [The soldiers made an *assault* on the fortress.] **2.** a direct threat to harm someone. The carrying out of such a threat is called *assault and battery.* —*v.* to make a violent attack upon.

as·say (ə sā′), *v.* **1.** to test an ore or alloy to find out how much of a certain metal is in it. **2.** to try; attempt: *now seldom used.* —*n.* the testing of an ore or alloy. —**as·say′er**, *n.*

as·sem·blage (ə sem′blij), *n.* **1.** a group of persons or things gathered together; gathering or collection [an *assemblage* of musicians]. **2.** a fitting together of parts, as of a machine.

as·sem·ble (ə sem′b'l), *v.* **1.** to gather together into a group; collect [The members of the family *assembled* for a reunion.] **2.** to put together the parts of [His hobby is *assembling* model trains.] —**as·sem′bled**, *p.t.* & *p.p.*; **as·sem′bling**, *pr.p.*

as·sem·bly (ə sem′blē), *n.* **1.** a gathering together of people [The Bill of Rights includes the right of peaceful *assembly.*] **2.** a group of persons gathered together; meeting. **3. Assembly,** the lower branch of the legislature in some States. **4.** a fitting together of parts, as in making automobiles. **5.** the parts so fitted together [the tail *assembly* of an airplane]. **6.** a signal on a bugle or drum for soldiers to come together in formation. —**as·sem′blies**, *pl.*

as·sent (ə sent′), *v.* to say "yes"; give one's consent; agree [to *assent* to a proposal]. —*n.* consent or agreement [We would not give our *assent* to the plan.]

as·sert (ə sŭrt′), *v.* **1.** to say in a clear, sure way; declare [His doctors *assert* that his health is good.] **2.** to insist on or defend, as one's rights or a claim. —**assert oneself, 1.** to insist on one's rights. **2.** to be too bold in dealing with others.

as·ser·tion (ə sŭr′shən), *n.* **1.** the act of asserting something. **2.** a strong or positive statement [Do you believe his *assertion* that he is innocent?]

as·ser·tive (ə sŭr′tiv), *adj.* **1.** sure; positive. **2.** too sure of oneself; too bold in dealing with others. —**as·ser′tive·ly**, *adv.*

as·sess (ə ses′), *v.* **1.** to set a value on property in order to figure the tax on it [A county official *assessed* the house at $10,000.] **2.** to set the amount, as of a fine or tax. **3.** to put a tax, fine, or dues on [The club *assessed* each member twenty dollars.]

as·sess·ment (ə ses′mənt), *n.* **1.** an assessing. **2.** the amount that is assessed.

as·ses·sor (ə ses′ər), *n.* a person whose work is to set a value on property in order to figure the tax on it.

as·set (as′et), *n.* **1.** anything owned that has value [The *assets* of the company include its land, buildings, machinery, stock, cash, and money owed to it.] **2.** a fine or valuable thing to have [Charm is her chief *asset.*]

as·sev·er·ate (ə sev′ə rāt), *v.* to say in a serious, positive way. —**as·sev′er·a′tion**, *n.*

as·si·du·i·ty (as′ə dyōō′ə tē), *n.* hard and steady effort; diligence.

as·sid·u·ous (ə sij′ōō əs), *adj.* working or done with hard, steady effort; diligent [an *assiduous* student]. —**as·sid′u·ous·ly**, *adv.*

as·sign (ə sīn′), *v.* **1.** to set apart for a special purpose; designate [Let's *assign* a day for the meeting.] **2.** to place at some task or work; appoint [I was *assigned* to guard the bicycles.] **3.** to give out as a task; allot [The teacher *assigned* a new lesson.] **4.** to give or hand over to another [The author has *assigned* all rights in his book to his wife.]

as·sign·ment (ə sīn′mənt), *n.* **1.** the act of assigning. **2.** something assigned, as a lesson.

as·sim·i·late (ə sim′'l āt), *v.* **1.** to take something in and make it part of oneself; absorb [The body *assimilates* food. Did you *assimilate* what you just read? America has *assimilated* people of many nations.] **2.** to make or become like or alike [The immigrant *assimilated* his ways to those of the new land.] —**as·sim′i·lat·ed**, *p.t.* & *p.p.*; **as·sim′i·lat·ing**, *pr.p.* —**as·sim′i·la′tion**, *n.*

as·sist (ə sist′), *v.* to help; aid [He *assisted* me in preparing the program.] —*n.* an act of helping.

as·sist·ance (ə sis′təns), *n.* help; aid.

as·sist·ant (ə sis′tənt), *n.* a person who assists or helps another; helper; aid [an *assistant* to the president]. —*adj.* assisting or helping the person under whom one works [an *assistant* principal].

as·siz·es (ə sīz′əz), *n.pl.* court sessions held at regular times in each county of England.

assn., abbreviation for **association.**

as·so·ci·ate (ə sō′shi āt), *v.* **1.** to connect in one's mind; think of together [We *associate* the taste of something with its smell.] **2.** to bring or come together as friends or partners [Don't *associate* with people who gossip.] —*n.* (ə sō′shi it), a person with whom one is joined in some way; friend, partner, or fellow worker. —*adj.* (ə sō′shi it), **1.** joined with others in some way [an *associate* justice of the Supreme Court]. **2.** having less than full rank; of a lower position [an *associate* professor]. —**as·so′ci·at·ed**, *p.t.* & *p.p.*; **as·so′ci·at·ing**, *pr.p.*

as·so·ci·a·tion (ə sō′si ā′shən *or* ə sō′shi ā′shən), *n.* **1.** the act of associating or the fact of being associated. **2.** fellowship or partnership. **3.** a group of people joined in some way or for some purpose; society. **4.** a connection in the mind of one idea or feeling with another [the *association* of the color blue with coolness].

as·sort·ed (ə sôr′tid), *adj.* **1.** of different sorts; of various kinds; miscellaneous [a box of *assorted* candies]. **2.** sorted into groups according to

kind [These buttons are *assorted* as to size.]
3. matched [a poorly *assorted* pair].

as·sort·ment (ə sôrt′mənt), *n.* **1.** the act of sorting or arranging into groups; classification. **2.** a collection of various sorts or things; variety [an *assortment* of books].

asst., abbreviation for **assistant.**

as·suage (ə swāj′), *v.* to make easier or calmer; lessen; lighten [Her kind words *assuaged* my grief. Nothing will *assuage* his anger.] —**as·suaged′,** *p.t. & p.p.;* **as·suag′ing,** *pr.p.*

as·sume (ə sōōm′ *or* ə syōōm′), *v.* **1.** to take on a certain look, form, or role [In a Greek myth, Zeus *assumes* the form of a bull.] **2.** to take upon oneself; take over [to *assume* an obligation; to *assume* control]. **3.** to suppose something to be a fact; take for granted [Let's *assume* that he will be on time.] **4.** to pretend to have; put on [Although afraid, he *assumed* an air of bravery.] —**as·sumed′,** *p.t. & p.p.;* **as·sum′ing,** *pr.p.*

as·sump·tion (ə sump′shən), *n.* **1.** the act of assuming [an *assumption* of power]. **2.** anything taken for granted [Our *assumption* that she was guilty proved correct.] **3. Assumption,** in Roman Catholic belief, the taking up of the Virgin Mary, whole in body, into heaven; also, the church festival on August 15 celebrating this.

as·sur·ance (ə shoor′əns), *n.* **1.** a being sure about something; confidence [I have no *assurance* that we will win.] **2.** something said or done to make one feel confident [The flood victims received *assurances* of government aid.] **3.** self-confidence; belief in one's own abilities [The young lawyer lacked *assurance*.] **4.** insurance: *the word used in England.*

as·sure (ə shoor′), *v.* **1.** to make a person sure of something; convince [What can we do to *assure* him of our friendship?] **2.** to tell or promise positively [I *assure* you I'll be there.] **3.** to make a doubtful thing certain; guarantee [His gift of money *assured* the success of our campaign.] —**as·sured′,** *p.t. & p.p.;* **as·sur′ing,** *pr.p.*

as·sured (ə shoord′), *adj.* **1.** made sure; guaranteed [an *assured* income]. **2.** confident; sure of oneself [an *assured* manner]. —**as·sur′ed·ly,** *adv.*

As·syr·i·a (ə sir′i ə), *n.* an ancient empire in western Asia. It reached its height in the seventh century B.C. —**As·syr′i·an,** *adj. & n.*

as·ter (as′tər), *n.* a plant with purple, pink, or white flowers. The simple types look like daisies, but some asters are large and have many petals.

as·ter·isk (as′tər isk), *n.* a sign in the shape of a star (*) used in printing and writing. It is used to call attention to a footnote or other explanation or to show that something has been left out.

a·stern (ə stûrn′), *adj. & adv.* **1.** behind a ship. **2.** at or toward the back part of a ship. **3.** backward.

as·ter·oid (as′tər oid), *n.* any of the many small planets found between Mars and Jupiter.

They move in their own orbits around the sun.

asth·ma (az′mə), *n.* a disease in which there are attacks of wheezing, coughing, and hard breathing. It is usually caused by an allergy.

a·stig·ma·tism (ə stig′mə tiz′m), *n.* a fault in the lens of the eye, which keeps the light rays from coming to a focus. Astigmatism makes things look blurred or irregular.

a·stir (ə stûr′), *adv. & adj.* moving about; in motion; active [The town is *astir* with visitors.]

as·ton·ish (ə stän′ish), *v.* to surprise greatly; fill with wonder; amaze. —**as·ton′ish·ing,** *adj.* —**as·ton′ish·ing·ly,** *adv.* —**as·ton′ish·ment.**

as·tound (ə stound′), *v.* to surprise so greatly as to make confused or speechless. —**as·tound′ing,** *adj.* —**as·tound′ing·ly,** *adv.*

a·stray (ə strā′), *adv. & adj.* away from the right path or way [The cows went *astray* and trampled the flower garden.]

a·stride (ə strīd′), *adv. & adj.* with one leg on each side [She sits *astride* when riding horseback.] —*prep.* with one leg on each side of [He sat *astride* the bench.]

as·trin·gent (ə strin′jənt), *n.* a medicine or lotion that tightens up body tissues. Astringents are used to stop bleeding in small cuts or to give the skin a fresh, tingling feeling. —*adj.* that has the effect of an astringent.

as·trol·o·gy (ə sträl′ə jē), *n.* a false science based on a belief that the stars, planets, and moon affect people's lives and that one can tell the future by studying the stars. —**as·trol′o·ger,** *n.* —**as·tro·log·i·cal** (as′trə läj′i k′l), *adj.*

as·tro·naut (as′trō nôt), *n.* a person trained to make rocket flights in outer space.

as·tro·nau·tics (as′trō nô′tiks), *n.pl.* the science that studies the problems of traveling in outer space: *used with a singular verb.*

as·tron·o·mer (ə strän′ə mər), *n.* an expert in astronomy.

as·tro·nom·i·cal (as′trə näm′i k′l), *adj.* **1.** of astronomy. **2.** extremely great [The distances and quantities of astronomy are measured in *astronomical* figures.]

as·tron·o·my (ə strän′ə mē), *n.* the science that studies the motion, size, and make-up of the stars, planets, comets, etc.

as·tute (ə stōōt′ *or* ə styōōt′), *adj.* having or showing a clever or shrewd mind; keen. —**as·tute′ly,** *adv.* —**as·tute′ness,** *n.*

a·sun·der (ə sun′dər), *adv.* into pieces or bits; apart [The boat struck the rock and fell *asunder*.]

a·sy·lum (ə sī′ləm), *n.* **1.** a place where one is safe and secure; refuge. **2.** a place for housing large groups of helpless people, such as orphans or those who are very old or mentally ill [Today, mental hospitals, foster homes, etc. are taking the place of the old-fashioned *asylums*.]

at (at), *prep.* **1.** on; in; near; by [Are they *at* home?] **2.** to or toward [Look *at* her. Aim *at*

---

fat, āpe, cär, ten, ēven, hit, bīte, gō, hôrn, tōōl, book, up, fûr;
get, joy, yet, chin, she, thin, *then;* zh = s in pleasure; ′ as in able (ā′b′l);
ə = a in ago, e in agent, i in sanity, o in confess, u in focus.

the target.] **3.** attending [Tom was *at* the party.] **4.** busy with [men *at* work]. **5.** in a condition of [England and France were *at* war.] **6.** in the manner of [The boy ran *at* a trot.] **7.** because of [terrified *at* the sight]. **8.** in the amount, rate, or price of [*at* five cents each]. **9.** on or close to the time or age of [Byron died *at* thirty-six.]

ate (āt), past tense of **eat.**

-ate (āt; *for meaning 3,* it), a suffix meaning: **1.** to make, become, or form [To *invalidate* is to make invalid. To *ulcerate* is to form an ulcer.] **2.** to treat with [To *vaccinate* is to treat with vaccine.] **3.** of or like [*Collegiate* activities are activities of college students.]

a·the·ist (ā′thē ist), *n.* a person who believes that there is no God. —**a′the·ism,** *n.* —**a′-the·is′tic,** *adj.*

A·the·na (ə thē′nə) or **A·the·ne** (ə thē′nē), *n.* the Greek goddess of wisdom and skills. The Romans called this goddess *Minerva.*

A·the·ni·an (ə thē′ni ən), *adj.* of Athens or its people. —*n.* a person born or living in Athens; especially, a citizen of ancient Athens.

Ath·ens (ath′inz), *n.* the capital of Greece, in the southeastern part. In ancient times this city was the center of Greek culture.

a·thirst (ə thũrst′), *adj.* **1.** thirsty: *now seldom used except in poetry.* **2.** eager; longing [*athirst* for knowledge].

ath·lete (ath′lēt), *n.* a person who is skilled at games or sports in which one needs strength, skill, and speed.

athlete's foot, a skin disease of the feet in which little blisters form and there is itching. It is caused by a tiny fungus.

ath·let·ic (ath let′ik), *adj.* **1.** of or for athletes or athletics. **2.** like an athlete; physically strong and active. —**ath·let′i·cal·ly,** *adv.*

ath·let·ics (ath let′iks), *n.pl.* games and sports in which one needs strength, skill, and speed: *sometimes used with a singular verb.*

a·thwart (ə thwôrt′), *prep.* **1.** across; from one side to the other of. **2.** against [to come *athwart* opposition]. **3.** across the course of [A school of sharks passed *athwart* the ship.]

a·tin·gle (ə ting′g'l), *adj.* tingling, as with excitement.

-a·tion (ā′shən), a suffix meaning: **1.** the act of [*Alteration* is the act of altering.] **2.** the condition of being [*Gratification* is the condition of being gratified.] **3.** the result of [A *complication* is the result of complicating.]

-a·tive (ā′tiv *or* ə tiv), a suffix meaning "of," "serving to," or "tending to" [An *informative* talk is one that serves to inform. A *talkative* person is one who tends to talk too much.]

At·lan·ta (at lan′tə), *n.* the capital of Georgia, in the northern part.

At·lan·tic (at lan′tik), *n.* the ocean lying between the American continents to the west and Europe and Africa to the east. —*adj.* of, in, on, or near this ocean.

At·lan·tis (at lan′tis), *n.* an island or continent mentioned in legends. It was supposed to have sunk into the Atlantic.

At·las (at′ləs), *n.* **1.** a giant in Greek myths who held up the heavens on his shoulders. **2. at-las,** a book of maps. —**at′las·es,** *pl.*

at·mos·phere (at′məs fir), *n.* **1.** all the air around the earth. **2.** the gases around any planet or star. **3.** the air in any particular place. **4.** the general feeling or spirit of a place or thing [the cheerful *atmosphere* of a gaily painted room].

at·mos·pher·ic (at′məs fer′ik), *adj.* **1.** of or in the atmosphere [Lightning is an *atmospheric* disturbance.] **2.** caused or produced by the atmosphere [*Atmospheric* pressure at sea level is equal to 14.69 pounds per square inch.]

at·oll (at′ôl *or* at′äl), *n.* a coral island that is shaped like a ring around a lagoon.

atoll

at·om (at′əm), *n.* **1.** any of the tiny particles of which the chemical elements are made. Atoms, which combine to form molecules, are themselves made up of various smaller particles. An atom of helium, for example, consists of a nucleus with two electrons revolving around it. **2.** a tiny particle of anything; jot [He hasn't an *atom* of sense.]

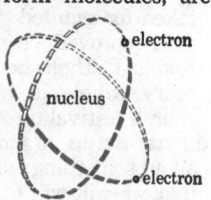
atom of helium

a·tom·ic (ə täm′ik), *adj.* **1.** having to do with an atom or atoms. **2.** very small; tiny; minute. —**a·tom′i·cal·ly,** *adv.*

atomic bomb or **atom bomb,** a very destructive kind of bomb in which the nuclei of atoms of plutonium or uranium are split, releasing energy in an explosion with enormous force and heat. See also **hydrogen bomb.**

atomic energy, the energy released when the nuclei of atoms are split or fused.

atomic number, a number showing the position of a chemical element in a table (called the **periodic table**) in which all the elements are arranged according to their characteristics. The atomic number is the number of protons in the nucleus of an atom [The *atomic number* of hydrogen is 1; that of gold is 79.]

atomic weight, a number showing the relative weight of an atom of an element, using oxygen (with a number of 16) as the basis of comparison [The *atomic weight* of hydrogen is 1.008; that of gold is 197.2.]

at·om·iz·er (at′əm īz′ər), *n.* a device used to shoot out a fine spray, as of medicine or perfume.

a·tone (ə tōn′), *v.* to make up for doing something wrong or harmful; make amends [He tried to *atone* for his sins by giving his wealth to charity.] —**a·toned′,** *p.t. & p.p.;* **a·ton′ing,** *pr.p.*

a·tone·ment (ə tōn′mənt), *n.* **1.** the act of atoning. **2.** something done to make up for doing something wrong or harmful; amends.

a·top (ə täp′), *adj. & adv.* on or at the top [The lightning rod stood *atop* of the chimney.] —*prep.* on the top of [a feather *atop* his hat].

a·tro·cious (ə trō′shəs), *adj.* **1.** very cruel or

evil; brutal ["Uncle Tom's Cabin" tells of Simon Legree's *atrocious* treatment of slaves.] **2.** very bad or unpleasant: *used only in everyday talk* [an *atrocious* climate]. —**a·tro′cious·ly,** *adv.*

a·troc·i·ty (ə träs′ə tē), *n.* **1.** great cruelty or wickedness; brutality. **2.** a cruel or wicked act [the *atrocities* of the Nazi concentration camps]. **3.** a very bad or unpleasant thing: *used only in everyday talk.* —**a·troc′i·ties,** *pl.*

at·ro·phy (at′rə fē), *n.* a wasting away or shrinking up [Paralysis of the arm resulted in the *atrophy* of its muscles.] —*v.* to waste away or fail to grow [Muscles can *atrophy* from lack of use and so can the mind.] —**at′ro·phied,** *p.t. & p.p.;* **at′ro·phy·ing,** *pr.p.*

at·tach (ə tach′), *v.* **1.** to fasten or join together, as by sticking or tying [*Attach* a stamp to the letter.] **2.** to bring close together by feelings of love or affection [Most people become *attached* to their pets.] **3.** to add or affix [Will you *attach* your signature to this petition?] **4.** to think of as belonging to; ascribe [I *attach* great importance to this bit of news.] **5.** to assign to some position [The lieutenant is temporarily *attached* to our regiment.] **6.** to seize property from a person by order of a court of law [We had to *attach* Smith's salary to collect what he owed us.] —**attach to,** to come with; belong to [Certain duties *attach to* this position.]

at·ta·ché (at ə shā′), *n.* a member of the staff of an ambassador or minister to a foreign country.

at·tach·ment (ə tach′mənt), *n.* **1.** the act of attaching something. **2.** anything used for attaching; fastening. **3.** strong liking or love; great affection. **4.** anything added or attached [Her sewing machine has an *attachment* for making buttonholes.]

at·tack (ə tak′), *v.* **1.** to start a fight with; strike out at; make an assault [The prisoner *attacked* the guard. Our regiment will *attack* at dawn.] **2.** to speak or write against; oppose [The senator *attacked* the proposed law with strong words.] **3.** to begin working on with vigor [to *attack* a problem.] **4.** to begin acting upon harmfully [The disease *attacked* him suddenly.] —*n.* **1.** the act of attacking [the enemy's *attack;* an *attack* on someone's character]. **2.** a beginning or case of a disease [an *attack* of flu].

at·tain (ə tān′), *v.* **1.** to get by working hard; gain; achieve [to *attain* success]. **2.** to reach or come to [He *attained* the age of ninety.] —**at·tain′a·ble,** *adj.*

at·tain·der (ə tān′dər), *n.* a taking away of the property and civil rights of a person who has been sentenced to death [The U.S. Constitution forbids the passing of a *bill of attainder,* that would set such additional punishment.]

at·tain·ment (ə tān′mənt), *n.* **1.** the act of attaining [the *attainment* of one's ambitions]. **2.** something that has been attained, especially a skill or knowledge; accomplishment [a doctor famous for his great *attainments* in surgery].

at·taint (ə tānt′), *v.* **1.** to disgrace or dishonor. **2.** to punish by attainder.

at·tar (at′ər), *n.* a perfume made from the petals of flowers, especially of roses.

at·tempt (ə tempt′), *v.* to try, or to try to do or get [to *attempt* to swim the English Channel; to *attempt* a hard task]. —*n.* **1.** a try [He succeeded in his first *attempt.*] **2.** an attack [An *attempt* was made on his life.] —**attempt the life of,** to try to kill.

at·tend (ə tend′), *v.* **1.** to be present at [We *attend* school five days a week.] **2.** to take care of; wait upon [Susan *attended* the bride as she dressed for the wedding.] **3.** to go with or follow [Success *attended* his efforts.] —**attend to, 1.** to pay attention to. **2.** to take care of [I'll *attend to* the matter soon.]

at·tend·ance (ə ten′dəns), *n.* **1.** the act of attending. **2.** the number of persons present [The *attendance* at the ball game was 48,321.]

at·tend·ant (ə ten′dənt), *adj.* **1.** attending or taking care [an *attendant* nurse]. **2.** that goes along; joined with; accompanying [Every job has its *attendant* problems.] —*n.* a person who attends, or serves; servant, keeper, etc. [an *attendant* at the zoo; the queen and her *attendants*].

at·ten·tion (ə ten′shən), *n.* **1.** the act of keeping one's mind closely on something or the ability to do this; heed; notice [Your *attention* was very poor during the lecture.] **2.** notice or observation [Her loud laugh caught my *attention.*] **3.** a kind or thoughtful act or behavior; courtesy [The soldiers were grateful for the letters, packages, and other *attentions* from home.] **4.** a position of standing straight and still, as in waiting for a command [The soldier stood at *attention.*]

at·ten·tive (ə ten′tiv), *adj.* **1.** that pays attention, or listens closely [A performer likes an *attentive* audience.] **2.** kind, thoughtful, courteous, etc. [an *attentive* husband]. —**at·ten′tive·ly,** *adv.* —**at·ten′tive·ness,** *n.*

at·ten·u·ate (ə ten′yōō āt′), *v.* **1.** to make thin or slender [a vase *attenuated* at its mouth]. **2.** to weaken; take away the force of [The power of King John was *attenuated* by the Magna Charta.] —**at·ten′u·at·ed,** *p.t. & p.p.;* **at·ten′u·at·ing,** *pr.p.* —**at·ten′u·a′tion,** *n.*

at·test (ə test′), *v.* **1.** to declare that something is true or genuine [The purity of the diamond was *attested* by the jeweler.] **2.** to be a witness; testify [I can *attest* to the time of his arrival.]

at·tic (at′ik), *n.* the room or space just below the roof of a house; garret.

At·ti·ca (at′i kə), *n.* a state of ancient Greece. Its capital was Athens.

At·ti·la (at′l ə), *n.* king of the Huns in the fifth century. He died in 453 A.D.

at·tire (ə tīr′), *v.* to dress, especially in very fine clothes; dress up; array [a bride *attired* in white]. —*n.* clothes, especially very fine clothes.

fat, āpe, cär, ten, ēven, hit, bīte, gō, hôrn, tool, book, up, fur;
get, joy, yet, chin, she, thin, *th*en; zh = s in pleasure; ′ as in able (ā′b'l);
ə = a in ago, e in agent, i in sanity, o in confess, u in focus.

—at·tired′, *p.t.* & *p.p.;* **at·tir′ing,** *pr.p.*

at·ti·tude (at′ə tōōd *or* at′ə tyōod), *n.* **1.** the position or posture of the body in doing a particular thing [We knelt in an *attitude* of prayer.] **2.** a way of acting or behaving that shows what one is thinking or feeling [a friendly *attitude*].

at·tor·ney (ə tūr′nē), *n.* **1.** a person who has been given the right to act for another, as in business dealings. This right is called a **power of attorney. 2.** a lawyer. **—at·tor′neys,** *pl.*

attorney general, the chief law officer of a country or State [The U.S. *Attorney General* is the head of the Justice Department.] **—attorneys general** or **attorney generals,** *pl.*

at·tract (ə trakt′), *v.* **1.** to make come closer; pull toward oneself [A magnet *attracts* iron and steel.] **2.** to be admired or noticed by [Her beauty *attracted* people.]

at·trac·tion (ə trak′shən), *n.* **1.** the act or power of attracting [Money has a great *attraction* for him.] **2.** anything that attracts.

at·trac·tive (ə trak′tiv), *adj.* **1.** that has the power to attract; attracting. **2.** pleasing, charming, pretty, etc. [an *attractive* dress].

at·trib·ut·a·ble (ə trib′yoo tə b′l), *adj.* that can be attributed [His errors are *attributable* to carelessness.]

at·trib·ute (ə trib′yoot), *v.* to think of something as belonging to or coming from a particular person or thing [a poem *attributed* to Homer]. **—n.** (at′rə byōot), **1.** a feature or quality that is thought of as a natural part of some person or thing [Freedom of speech is an *attribute* of democracy.] **2.** an object used as a symbol [Cupid's *attribute* is the bow and arrow.] **—at·trib′ut·ed,** *p.t.* & *p.p.;* **at·trib′ut·ing,** *pr.p.* **—at′tri·bu′tion,** *n.*

at·tri·tion (ə trish′ən), *n.* a wearing down or weakening little by little [The long siege turned into a war of *attrition.*]

at·tune (ə tōōn′ *or* ə tyōon′), *v.* to bring into harmony or agreement [Their minds have become *attuned* to scientific reasoning.] **—at·tuned′,** *p.t.* & *p.p.;* **at·tun′ing,** *pr.p.*

atty., abbreviation for **attorney.**

Au, the symbol for the chemical element *gold.*

au·burn (ô′bərn), *adj.* & *n.* reddish brown.

auc·tion (ôk′shən), *n.* a public sale at which each thing is sold to the person offering to pay the highest price. **—v.** to sell at an auction.

auc·tion·eer (ôk shən ēr′), *n.* a person whose work is selling things at auctions.

au·da·cious (ô dā′shəs), *adj.* **1.** daring or bold; fearless. **2.** too bold; lacking respect; impudent.

au·dac·i·ty (ô das′ə tē), *n.* **1.** bold courage; daring. **2.** too much boldness; impudence.

au·di·ble (ô′də b′l), *adj.* that can be heard; loud enough to be heard [an *audible* whisper]. **—au′di·bil′i·ty,** *n.* **—au′di·bly,** *adv.*

au·di·ence (ô′di əns), *n.* **1.** a group of persons gathered together to hear and see a speaker, a play, a musical program, etc. **2.** all those persons who are listening to a radio program or watching a television program. **3.** an interview with a person of high rank [an *audience* with the Pope].

au·di·o (ô′di ō), *adj.* having to do with the part that is heard on a telecast: see also **video.**

au·di·o-vis·u·al (ô′di ō vizh′ōō əl), *adj.* involving both hearing and sight [Motion pictures and recordings are *audio-visual* aids used in teaching.]

au·dit (ô′dit), *n.* an examination of the accounts or records of a business to see that they are right. **—v.** to make such an examination.

au·di·tion (ô dish′ən), *n.* a short performance by an actor or musician who is being tested for a particular job. **—v. 1.** to judge someone in an audition. **2.** to perform in an audition.

au·di·tor (ô′də tər), *n.* **1.** a listener or hearer. **2.** a person whose work is auditing accounts.

au·di·to·ri·um (ô′də tôr′i əm), *n.* a building or room where an audience can gather.

au·di·to·ry (ô′də tôr′ē), *adj.* having to do with the sense of hearing [the *auditory* nerve].

Au·du·bon, John J. (ô′də bän), 1785–1851; U.S. nature artist, famous for his study of birds.

Aug., abbreviation for **August.**

au·ger (ô′gər), *n.* a tool for boring holes, as in wood or in the earth.

aught (ôt), *n.* **1.** anything whatever; any little part [Do you have *aught* to show for your work?] **2.** a zero; naught.

aug·ment (ôg ment′), *v.* to make or become greater or larger [The teacher *augmented* his income by selling insurance.]

aug·men·ta·tion (ôg′mən tā′shən), *n.* **1.** the act of augmenting. **2.** an addition; increase.

au·gur (ô′gər), *n.* **1.** a priest in ancient Rome who claimed to foretell the future by explaining certain omens and signs. **2.** any fortuneteller. **—v.** to be a sign of something that will happen [Cloudy skies *augur* rain.] **—augur ill** (or **augur well**), to be a sign that something bad (or something good) will happen.

au·gu·ry (ô′gyər ē), *n.* **1.** the practice of trying to foretell the future from omens or signs. **2.** an omen or sign. **—au′gu·ries,** *pl.*

Au·gust (ô′gəst), *n.* the eighth month of the year. It has 31 days. Abbreviated **Aug.**

au·gust (ô gust′), *adj.* causing one to feel awe and respect [an *august* assembly of scholars].

Au·gus·ta (ô gus′tə), *n.* the capital of Maine.

Au·gus·tus (ô gus′təs), *n.* 63 B.C.–14 A.D.; first emperor of Rome, from 27 B.C. to 14 A.D.

auk (ôk), *n.* a diving bird of the northern seas, with webbed feet and short wings. The **great auk,** which is now extinct, could not fly.

aunt (ant *or* änt), *n.* **1.** a sister of one's mother or father. **2.** the wife of one's uncle.

au·ra (ô′rə), *n.* a general feeling that seems to come out from and surround a particular person or thing [There was an *aura* of gentleness about the old doctor.]

auk (1 ft. high)

au re·voir (ô'rə vwär'), until we meet again: *a French phrase used for "good-by."*

au·ri·cle (ô'ri k'l), *n.* **1.** the outer part of the ear. **2.** either of the two top sections of the heart. The blood flows into these from the veins. *See the picture for* **heart.**

au·ro·ra bo·re·a·lis (ô rôr'ə bôr'i al'is *or* bôr'i-ā'lis), very bright bands of light that are sometimes seen at night in the sky of the Northern Hemisphere; northern lights.

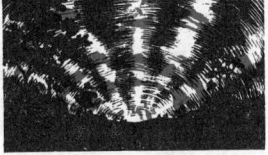

aurora borealis

aus·pic·es (ôs'pis-iz), *n.pl.* approval and help [a plan under government *auspices*].

aus·pi·cious (ôs pish'əs), *adj.* seeming to show that success will follow; favorable [He scored 100 on his first test, an *auspicious* beginning for the new school year.] —**aus·pi'cious·ly**, *adv.*

aus·tere (ô stir'), *adj.* **1.** very strict or stern in one's morals or behavior; harsh. **2.** very simple and plain; without decoration or luxury [Pioneers usually lead an *austere* life.] —**aus·tere'ly**, *adv.* —**aus·ter·i·ty** (ô ster'ə tē).

Aus·tin (ôs'tin), *n.* the capital of Texas.

Aus·tral·ia (ô strāl'yə), *n.* **1.** an island continent in the Southern Hemisphere, southeast of Asia. **2.** a British Commonwealth made up of this continent and Tasmania. —**Aus·tral'ian**, *adj. & n.*

Aus·tri·a (ôs'tri ə), *n.* a country in central Europe. —**Aus'tri·an**, *adj. & n.*

au·then·tic (ô then'tik), *adj.* **1.** that can be trusted; reliable; true [an *authentic* news report]. **2.** that is genuine; real [an *authentic* antique]. —**au·then'ti·cal·ly**, *adv.*

au·then·ti·cate (ô then'ti kāt), *v.* to prove that something is genuine or real; show the truth of. —**au·then'ti·cat·ed**, *p.t. & p.p.;* **au·then'ti·cat·ing**, *pr.p.*

au·then·tic·i·ty (ô'thən tis'ə tē), *n.* the condition of being authentic; genuineness.

au·thor (ô'thər), *n.* **1.** a person who writes something, as a book, story, or play [Mark Twain was the *author* of "Tom Sawyer."] **2.** a person who makes or begins something; creator [Darwin was the *author* of the theory of evolution.] —*v.* to be the author of.

au·thor·i·ta·tive (ə thôr'ə tā'tiv), *adj.* **1.** having or showing authority; official [He gave orders in an *authoritative* manner.] **2.** that can be trusted because it comes from an expert or authority [an *authoritative* opinion]. —**au·thor'i·ta'tive·ly**, *adv.*

au·thor·i·ty (ə thôr'ə tē), *n.* **1.** the right to give orders, make decisions, or take action [He learned to respect the *authority* of his teachers.] **2.** a person who has the right to govern or the power to enforce laws [The *authorities* are searching for the missing child.] **3.** a person,

book, etc. that can be trusted to give correct information or advice [Years of study made Dr. Hall an *authority* on tropical diseases.] —**au·thor'i·ties**, *pl.*

au·thor·i·za·tion (ô'thər i zā'shən), *n.* **1.** the act of authorizing something. **2.** the right or permission given by someone with authority.

au·thor·ize (ô'thə rīz), *v.* **1.** to give permission for something [The city *authorized* the building of a housing project.] **2.** to give someone the right or power to do something [The President has *authorized* him to sign the treaty.] —**au'thor·ized**, *p.t. & p.p.;* **au'thor·iz·ing**, *pr.p.*

au·thor·ship (ô'thər ship), *n.* the origin of a book, idea, etc. [This is a story of unknown *authorship*.]

au·to (ô'tō), *n.* an automobile. —**au'tos**, *pl.*

auto-, a prefix meaning: **1.** of or for oneself. **2.** by oneself or itself. *See the words that follow below.*

au·to·bi·og·ra·phy (ô'tə bī äg'rə fē), *n.* the story of one's own life written by oneself. —**au'to·bi·og'ra·phies**, *pl.* —**au·to·bi·o·graph·ic** (ô'tə bī'ə graf'ik) *or* **au'to·bi'o·graph'i·cal**, *adj.*

au·toc·ra·cy (ô täk'rə sē), *n.* government in which one person has all the power; dictatorship. —**au·toc'ra·cies**, *pl.*

au·to·crat (ô'tə krat), *n.* **1.** a ruler who has complete power; dictator. **2.** a person who forces others to do as he wishes.

au·to·crat·ic (ô'tə krat'ik), *adj.* of or like an autocrat; having complete power over others; dictatorial. —**au'to·crat'i·cal·ly**, *adv.*

au·to·graph (ô'tə graf), *n.* something written in a person's own handwriting, especially his name [Some people collect *autographs* of famous persons.] —*v.* to write one's name on [Please *autograph* my program.]

au·to·mat·ic (ô'tə mat'ik), *adj.* **1.** done without thinking about it, as though by a machine; unconscious [The blinking of the eyes is usually *automatic*.] **2.** moving or working by itself [A thermostat is an *automatic* device that turns heat on and off.] —*n.* a pistol or rifle that keeps firing shots rapidly until the trigger is released. —**au'to·mat'i·cal·ly**, *adv.*

au·to·ma·tion (ô'tə mā'shən), *n.* a system of manufacturing in which many or all of the operations are done automatically and are controlled by machines instead of by people.

au·tom·a·ton (ô täm'ə tän), *n.* **1.** a machine that can move or act of itself. **2.** a person who acts in an automatic way, like a machine.

au·to·mo·bile (ô'tə mə bēl' *or* ô'tə mō'bēl), *n.* a car moved by an engine that is part of it, and used for traveling on streets or roads; motorcar.

au·to·mo·tive (ô'tə mō'tiv), *adj.* **1.** moving by means of its own power; self-moving [an *automotive* vehicle]. **2.** having to do with automobiles [the *automotive* industry].

au·ton·o·mous (ô tän'ə məs), *adj.* governing

itself; having self-government; independent [an *autonomous* nation]. **—au·ton′o·mous·ly,** *adv.*

au·ton·o·my (ô tän′ə mē), *n.* self-government; independence [a town with local *autonomy*].

au·top·sy (ô′täp sē), *n.* an examination of a dead body to find the cause of death or the damage done by a disease. **—au′top·sies,** *pl.*

au·tumn (ô′təm), *n.* the season of the year that comes between summer and winter; fall. **—***adj.* of or like autumn. **—au·tum·nal** (ô tum′n'l), *adj.*

aux·il·ia·ry (ôg zil′yə rē), *adj.* that helps or aids; acting as an extra help [*Auxiliary* firemen were called out.] **—***n.* an auxiliary person, group, or thing [This club has a women's *auxiliary*]. **—aux·il′ia·ries,** *pl.*

auxiliary verb, a verb that is used to form tenses, moods, or voices of other verbs. *Have, be, may, can, must, do, shall, will* are used as auxiliary verbs. In the sentence "He will be late," *will* is an auxiliary verb.

av., abbreviation for *avoirdupois.*

a·vail (ə vāl′), *v.* to be of use, help, or advantage to [His pleas to his uncle for help *availed* him nought.] **—***n.* use or help; advantage [He tried, but to no *avail*.] **—avail oneself of,** to take advantage of, as an opportunity.

a·vail·a·ble (ə vāl′ə b'l), *adj.* that can be got, used, or reached [The dress is *available* in three colors.] **—a·vail′a·bil′i·ty,** *n.*

av·a·lanche (av′ə lanch), *n.* **1.** a large mass of snow, ice, rocks, etc. sliding swiftly down a mountain. **2.** anything that comes down on one suddenly and in large numbers [an *avalanche* of mail; an *avalanche* of blows].

av·a·rice (av′ə ris), *n.* too great a desire to have wealth; greed for riches.

av·a·ri·cious (av′ə rish′əs), *adj.* too eager to have wealth; greedy for riches; miserly. **—av′a·ri′cious·ly,** *adv.*

a·vast (ə vast′), *interj.* stop! halt! *A sailor's word.*

a·vaunt (ə vônt′), *interj.* begone! go away! *Now seldom used.*

Ave. or **Av.,** abbreviations for **Avenue.**

A·ve Ma·ri·a (ä′vi mə rē′ə), **1.** "Hail, Mary": the first words of a Latin prayer to the Virgin Mary used in the Roman Catholic Church. **2.** this prayer.

a·venge (ə venj′), *v.* to get revenge for; pay back a wrong or injury [to *avenge* an insult; to *avenge* a murder]. **—a·venged′,** *p.t. & p.p.;* **a·veng′ing,** *pr.p.* **—a·veng′er,** *n.*

a·ve·nue (av′ə nyōō *or* av′ə nōō), *n.* **1.** a street, especially a wide one. **2.** a road, path, or drive with trees along both sides. **3.** a way to something [Books are *avenues* to knowledge.]

a·ver (ə vur′), *v.* to state as the truth; declare positively [He *averred* his innocence all the way to the gallows.] **—a·verred′,** *p.t. & p.p.;* **a·ver′ring,** *pr.p.*

av·er·age (av′ər ij *or* av′rij), *n.* **1.** the number gotten by dividing the sum of two or more quantities by the number of quantities added [The *average* of 7, 9, and 17 is 11 (7 + 9 + 17 =

33 ÷ 3 = 11).] **2.** the usual kind or amount; that which is found most often [His intelligence is above the *average*.] **—***adj.* **1.** being the average [The *average* score on this test was 82.] **2.** of the usual kind; normal; ordinary [the *average* man]. **—***v.* **1.** to figure the average of [Will you *average* these prices for me?] **2.** to be, do, have, etc. on an average [He *averages* eight hours of sleep a day.] **—on the average,** as an average amount, rate, etc. [He earns $80 a week *on the average*.] **—av′er·aged,** *p.t. & p.p.;* **av′er·ag·ing,** *pr.p.*

a·verse (ə vurs′), *adj.* not willing; opposed [She is *averse* to lending money.]

a·ver·sion (ə vur′zhən), *n.* **1.** a strong dislike [He has an *aversion* to parties.] **2.** a thing so disliked [Spinach is her chief *aversion*.]

a·vert (ə vurt′), *v.* **1.** to turn away [to *avert* one's eyes]. **2.** to keep from happening; prevent [He apologized to *avert* trouble.]

a·vi·ar·y (ā′vi er′ē), *n.* a large cage or building for keeping many birds. **—a′vi·ar′ies,** *pl.*

a·vi·a·tion (ā′vi ā′shən), *n.* the science, skill, or work of flying airplanes.

a·vi·a·tor (ā′vi ā′tər), *n.* a person who flies airplanes; pilot; airman.

a·vi·a·trix (ā′vi ā′triks), *n.* a woman aviator.

av·id (av′id), *adj.* very eager or greedy [an *avid* reader of books; *avid* for power]. **—av′id·ly,** *adv.*

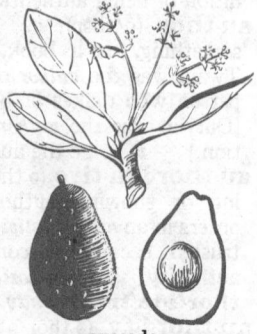
aviary

a·vid·i·ty (ə vid′ə tē), *n.* great eagerness or greed.

av·o·ca·do (av′ə kä′dō), *n.* **1.** a tropical fruit that is shaped like a pear and has a thick, green or purplish skin and a single large seed. Its yellow, buttery flesh is used in salads. **2.** the tree that it grows on. **—av′o·ca′dos,** *pl.*

av·o·ca·tion (av′ə kā′shən), *n.* something one does besides his regular work, often just for pleasure; hobby [The doctor's *avocation* was making furniture.]

avocado

a·void (ə void′), *v.* to keep away from; get out of the way of; shun [to *avoid* crowds; to *avoid* trouble]. **—a·void′a·ble,** *adj.* **—a·void′ance,** *n.*

av·oir·du·pois (av′ər də poiz′), *n.* the system of weights used in England and America, in which 16 ounces equal 1 pound: also called **avoirdupois weight.** See also **troy** (**weight**).

a·vouch (ə vouch′), *v.* **1.** to declare to be true or right [Her innocence was *avouched* by three witnesses.] **2.** to assure or guarantee.

a·vow (ə vou′), *v.* to say or admit openly or frankly [He *avowed* that he had been mistaken.] —**a·vow′al,** *n.*

a·vowed (ə voud′), *adj.* openly declared or frankly admitted; confessed [Robin Hood was an *avowed* opponent of injustice.] —**a·vow·ed·ly** (ə vou′id lē), *adv.*

a·wait (ə wāt′), *v.* **1.** to wait for; be looking for [We are *awaiting* your arrival.] **2.** to be waiting for; be ready for [A pleasant vacation in Europe *awaits* you.]

a·wake (ə wāk′), *v.* **1.** to bring or come out of sleep; wake. **2.** to make or become active; stir up [to *awake* old memories]. —*adj.* **1.** not asleep. **2.** active; alert. —**a·woke′** or **a·waked′,** *p.t.;* **a·waked′** or **a·woke′,** *p.p.;* **a·wak′ing,** *pr.p.*

a·wak·en (ə wāk′ən), *v.* to awake; rouse.

a·wak·en·ing (ə wāk′ən ing), *n.* a waking up; rousing.

a·ward (ə wôrd′), *v.* **1.** to give by the decision of a judge [The court *awarded* her $2,000 in damages.] **2.** to give as the result of judging in a contest [His essay was *awarded* first prize.] —*n.* **1.** a decision, as by a judge. **2.** something awarded; prize.

a·ware (ə wer′), *adj.* knowing or understanding; conscious; informed [Are you *aware* of the problem facing us?]

a·way (ə wā′), *adv.* **1.** to another place [Tom Sawyer ran *away* from home.] **2.** far [*away* behind]. **3.** off; aside [The janitor cleared the snow *away*.] **4.** from one's keeping [Don't give *away* the secret.] **5.** out of hearing or out of sight [The sound faded *away*.] **6.** at once [Fire *away*!] **7.** without stopping [He worked *away* all night.] —*adj.* **1.** not here; absent; gone [She is *away* on vacation.] **2.** at a distance [ten miles *away*]. —*interj.* go away! begone! —**away with,** take away [*Away with* the knave!] —**do away with,** to get rid of; put an end to.

awe (ô), *n.* deep respect mixed with fear and wonder [They looked up at the starry sky and were filled with *awe*.] —*v.* to make have a feeling of awe [The crowds were *awed* by the daring leap of the diver.] —**stand** (or **be**) **in awe of,** to respect and fear. —**awed,** *p.t.* & *p.p.;* **aw′ing,** *pr.p.*

awe·some (ô′səm), *adj.* **1.** causing one to feel awe [The explosion of an atomic bomb is an *awesome* sight.] **2.** showing or feeling awe [an *awesome* look on his face].

awe-strick·en (ô′strik″n), *adj.* awe-struck.

awe-struck (ô′struk′), *adj.* filled with awe.

aw·ful (ô′fool), *adj.* **1.** making one feel awe or dread; causing fear [an *awful* scene of destruction]. **2.** very bad, ugly, great, etc.: used only in everyday talk [an *awful* joke].

aw·ful·ly (ô′fool ē *or* ô′flē), *adv.* **1.** in an awful or dreadful way. **2.** very; extremely: *used only in everyday talk* [an *awfully* pretty dress].

a·while (ə hwīl′), *adv.* for a while; for a short time [Sit down and rest *awhile*.]

awk·ward (ôk′wərd), *adj.* **1.** not having grace or skill; clumsy; bungling [an *awkward* dancer; an *awkward* workman]. **2.** hard to use or manage; not convenient [The long handle makes this an *awkward* tool.] **3.** uncomfortable; cramped [He was sitting in an *awkward* position.] **4.** embarrassing [His *awkward* remark was followed by an even more *awkward* pause.] —**awk′ward·ly,** *adv.* —**awk′ward·ness,** *n.*

awl (ôl), *n.* a small, pointed tool for making holes in wood or leather.

awn·ing (ôn′ing), *n.* a shade made of canvas, metal, or wood fixed to a frame over a window, door, etc. to keep off the sun and rain.

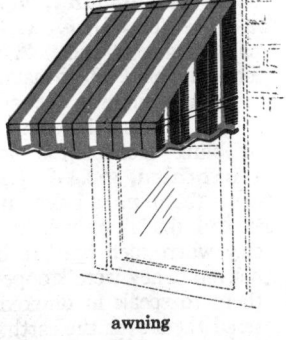
awl

a·woke (ə wōk′), the usual past tense and sometimes a past participle of **awake.**

a·wry (ə rī′), *adv.* & *adj.* **1.** twisted to one side; askew [He pulled the covers *awry* in his sleep.] **2.** wrong; amiss [Our plans went *awry*.]

ax or **axe** (aks), *n.* a tool for chopping or splitting wood. —**ax′es,** *pl.*

ax·i·al (ak′si əl), *adj.* of, like, or around an axis [an *axial* rod; *axial* rotation].

ax·i·om (ak′si əm), *n.* a statement that needs no proof because its truth can be plainly seen [It is an *axiom* that no one lives forever.]

awning

ax·i·o·mat·ic (ak′si ə mat′-ik), *adj.* **1.** of or like an axiom; plainly true. **2.** full of axioms. —**ax′i·o·mat′-i·cal·ly,** *adv.*

ax·is (ak′sis), *n.* **1.** a real or imaginary straight line about which something turns: *see picture on the next page.* [The *axis* of the earth passes through the North and South poles.] **2.** a central line around which the parts of a thing are arranged in a balanced way. —**the Axis,** Germany, Italy, and Japan as allies in World War II. —**ax·es** (ak′sēz), *pl.*

ax

ax·le (ak/s'l), *n.* **1.** a rod on which a wheel turns, or one connected to a wheel so that they turn together. **2.** *also* **ax·le·tree** (ak/s'l trē), the bar joining two opposite wheels, as of an automobile.

aye or **ay** (ā), *adv.* always; ever: *now seldom used except in poetry.*

aye or **ay** (ī), *adv.* yes. —*n.* a vote of "yes."

a·zal·ea (ə zāl/yə), *n.* a shrub having narrow, pointed leaves, and flowers of various colors.

axis

A·zores (ə zôrz/ *or* ā/zôrz), *n.pl.* a group of Portuguese islands west of Portugal.

Az·tec (az/tek), *n.* **1.** a member of a people who lived in Mexico and had a highly developed civilization before they were conquered by Spain in 1519. **2.** their language. —*adj.* of the Aztecs.

az·ure (azh/ər), *n.* the blue color of a clear sky; sky blue. —*adj.* of this color.

Aztec

B

B, b (bē), *n.* the second letter of the English alphabet. —**B's, b's** (bēz), *pl.*

B, the symbol for the chemical element *boron.*

Ba, the symbol for the chemical element *barium.*

B.A., Bachelor of Arts: also **A.B.**

baa (bä), *n.* the sound made by a sheep, lamb, or goat. —*v.* to make this sound; bleat. —**baaed,** *p.t. & p.p.;* **baa/ing,** *pr.p.*

bab·ble (bab/'l), *v.* **1.** to make sounds like a baby trying to talk. **2.** to talk or say fast or foolishly; blab. **3.** to make a low, bubbling sound, as a brook running over stones. —*n.* **1.** jumbled speech sounds. **2.** foolish or silly talk. **3.** a low bubbling sound [the *babble* of the stream]. —**bab/bled,** *p.t. & p.p.;* **bab/bling,** *pr.p.*

babe (bāb), *n.* a baby; infant.

Ba·bel (bā/b'l *or* bab/'l), *n.* **1.** in the Bible, a city where men tried to build a tower to reach heaven. They were stopped by God, who caused them to speak in different languages and scattered them over the earth. **2.** *also* **babel,** noisy confusion, as of many people talking at once.

ba·boon (ba bōōn/), *n.* a fierce ape of Africa and Arabia, with a large head shaped like a dog's.

ba·bush·ka (bə-boosh/kə), *n.* a scarf worn on the head by a woman or girl. It is tied under the chin.

ba·by (bā/bē), *n.* **1.** a very young child; infant. **2.** a person who seems helpless, cries easily, etc., like a baby. **3.** the youngest or smallest in a group. —*adj.* **1.** of or for a baby [*baby* food]. **2.** very young or small [a *baby* fox]. **3.** like a baby; childish [*baby* talk]. —*v.* to treat like a baby; pamper. —**ba/bies,** *pl.* —**ba/bied,** *p.t. & p.p.;* **ba/by·ing,** *pr.p.*

ba·by·hood (bā/bē hood), *n.* the time or stage when one is a baby.

ba·by·ish (bā/bē ish), *adj.* like a baby; helpless, timid, etc.

baboon (body is 2 ft. long)

Bab·y·lon (bab/i lən), *n.* the ancient capital of Babylonia, known for its wealth and wickedness.

Bab·y·lo·ni·a (bab/'l ō/ni ə), *n.* an ancient, powerful empire of southwestern Asia, north of Arabia. —**Bab/y·lo/ni·an,** *adj. & n.*

ba·by-sit (bā/bē sit/), *v.* to be a baby sitter. —**ba/by-sat/,** *p.t. & p.p.;* **ba/by-sit/ting,** *pr.p.*

baby sitter, a person hired to take care of a child or children, as when the parents are away for the evening.

Bac·chus (bak/əs), *n.* an ancient Greek and Roman god of wine and merrymaking.

Bach, Jo·hann Se·bas·tian (yō/hän si bäs/-tyən bäk/), 1685–1750; German composer of music.

bach·e·lor (bach/ə lər *or* bach/lər), *n.* **1.** a man who has not married. **2.** a person who has received the first degree from a college or university for completing a four-year course [He is a *Bachelor* of Science in chemistry.]

bach·e·lor's-but·ton (bach/ə lərz but/'n), *n.* a plant with flowers shaped a little like buttons and usually blue.

ba·cil·lus (bə sil/əs), *n.* any of the bacteria that are shaped like a rod. Some bacilli cause diseases, such as tuberculosis. —**ba·cil/li** (bə sil/ī), *pl.*

back (bak), *n.* **1.** the part of the body that is opposite to the chest and belly. In most animals other than man, it is the part opposite the underside. **2.** the backbone [He broke his *back* falling down the stairs.] **3.** the part of a chair or seat that supports one's back. **4.** the part of something behind or opposite the front [the *back* of the cupboard; the *back* of his leg]. **5.** the side of something that is less often used or seen; reverse [the *back* of the hand; the *back* of a rug]. **6.** a football player whose position is behind the line. —*adj.* **1.** at the rear or back; behind [the *back* wheel of a bicycle]. **2.** of or for a time in the past [a *back* copy of a newspaper; *back* pay]. **3.** in the opposite direction; reversed [the *back* stroke of a piston]. —*adv.* **1.** at or to the back; backward [Please move *back* in the bus.] **2.** to the place that it came from [I threw the ball to him and he threw it *back*.] **3.** to an earlier condition or time [We nursed him *back* to health.] **4.** in return [Give *back* the money you borrowed.] —*v.* **1.** to move backward or to the rear [The truck *backed* up to the platform.] **2.** to help or support [The plan can't fail if we all *back* it.] **3.** to put something on the back of [The rug is *backed* with rubber.] —**back and forth,** backward and forward or from side to side. —**back down,** to give up an action that one has started. —**back out** or **go back on,** to refuse to do something one has promised to do: *used only in everyday talk.* —**behind one's back,** without one's knowing or allowing it. —**in back of,** at or to the rear of; behind.

back·bite (bak′bīt), *v.* to say unkind or untrue things about a person who is absent. —**back′-bit,** *p.t.;* **back′·bit·ten** or **back′·bit,** *p.p.;* **back′·bit·ing,** *pr.p.*

back·bone (bak′bōn), *n.* **1.** the long row of connected bones in the back of man and many other animals; spine. **2.** the main support of anything [The cavalry formed the *backbone* of the attack.] **3.** will power, courage, determination, etc. [It takes *backbone* to be a pioneer.]

back·er (bak′ər), *n.* a person who gives help or support; supporter; sponsor.

back·field (bak′fēld), *n.* in football, the players whose usual position is behind the line; especially, the quarterback, halfbacks, and fullback.

back·fire (bak′fīr), *n.* an explosion of gas that takes place at the wrong time in the cylinder of an engine, as of an automobile; also, one that occurs in the wrong place, as in the exhaust pipe, making a loud noise. —*v.* **1.** to have a backfire [The truck *backfired* twice.] **2.** to have a bad or unexpected result [His plan *backfired*.] —**back′-fired,** *p.t. & p.p.;* **back′·fir·ing,** *pr.p.*

back·gam·mon (bak′gam′ən), *n.* a game played on a special board by two people. Each player has fifteen pieces, which he moves after throwing dice to get a number.

back·ground (bak′-ground), *n.* **1.** the part of a scene or picture that is or seems to be toward the back. **2.** a surface against which

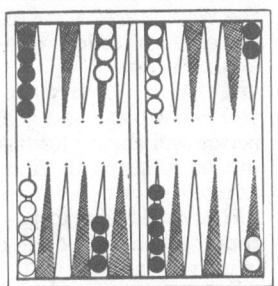
backgammon board

something is shown or seen [The flag has white stars on a blue *background*.] **3.** a less important position where one is not likely to be noticed [The mayor's wife tried to stay in the *background*.] **4.** a person's training and experience [She has a good *background* for office work.] **5.** the events that came before; causes [This book tells about the *background* of the Civil War.]

back·hand (bak′hand), *n.* a kind of stroke as in tennis, in which the back of the hand swings out toward the ball, etc. The arm is brought forward from across the body. —*adj.* made or done with such a stroke [a *backhand* swing]. —*adv.* with a backhand swing.

backhand stroke

back·hand·ed (bak′han′-did), *adj.* **1.** backhand. **2.** finding fault while seeming to praise; not sincere ["You don't look nearly so fat in that dress" is a *backhanded* compliment.]

back·ing (bak′ing), *n.* **1.** anything placed in back for support or strength [The photograph has a *backing* of cardboard.] **2.** support or aid [He has the *backing* of the President.]

back·log (bak′lôg), *n.* a piling up, as of work to be done or orders to be filled.

back·slide (bak′slīd), *v.* to go back to wrong ways of believing or acting; often, to lose religious faith. —**back′slid,** *p.t.;* **back′slid** or **back′-slid·den,** *p.p.;* **back′slid·ing,** *pr.p.*

back·stage (bak′stāj′), *adv. & adj.* in or to the part of a theater where the actors get ready to go on stage, where the sets are kept, etc.

back·stroke (bak′strōk), *n.* **1.** a backhand stroke. **2.** a stroke made by a swimmer lying on his back and moving head first. —**back′stroked,** *p.t. & p.p.;* **back′-strok·ing,** *pr.p.*

backstroke

back talk, impolite answers that show a lack of respect: *used only in everyday talk.*

back·track (bak′trak), *v.* to go back by the same way that one has come.

back·ward (bak′wərd), *adv.* **1.** toward the back; behind [to look *backward*]. **2.** with the back toward the front [If a person rides *backward* he can see where he has been.] **3.** in a way opposite to the usual way [Noel is Leon spelled *backward*.] **4.** from a better to a worse condition. —*adj.* **1.** turned toward the back or in an opposite way [a *backward* glance]. **2.** not eager; bashful; shy. **3.** making progress slowly; retarded [*backward* children; *backward* nations].

back·wards (bak′wərdz), *adv.* backward.

back·wa·ter (bak′wô′tər), *n.* **1.** water moved backward or held back, as by the tide or by a dam. **2.** a place or condition where there is no progress or growth.

back·woods (bak′woodz′), *n.pl.* wild land covered with forests, far from towns.

back·woods·man (bak′woodz′mən), *n.* a man who lives in the backwoods. —**back′woods′-men,** *pl.*

fat, āpe, cär, ten, ēven, hit, bīte, gō, hôrn, tool, book, up, fűr;
get, joy, yet, chin, she, thin, *then;* zh = s in pleasure; ' as in able (ā′b'l).
ə = a in ago, e in agent, i in sanity, o in confess, u in focus.

ba·con (bā′kən), *n.* salted and smoked meat from the sides or back of a hog.

bac·te·ri·a (bak tir′i ə), *n.pl.* living things that have only one cell and are so small that they can be seen only with a microscope. Some bacteria cause diseases and others make milk turn sour, cause cheese to ripen, or help make plant food from nitrogen in the air. —**bac·te·ri·um** (bak tir′i əm), *sing.* —**bac·te′ri·al,** *adj.*

bac·te·ri·ol·o·gy (bak tir′i äl′ə jē), *n.* the science or study of bacteria.

bad (bad), *adj.* **1.** not good; not what it should be; poor; unfit [*bad* lighting; *bad* workmanship]. **2.** not pleasant; not what one would like [*bad* news]. **3.** rotten; spoiled [a *bad* apple]. **4.** in error; wrong; faulty [*bad* spelling]. **5.** wicked; evil [a *bad* man]. **6.** causing injury; harmful [Reading in poor light is *bad* for the eyes.] **7.** serious; severe [a *bad* mistake; a *bad* storm]. **8.** sorry; unhappy [George felt *bad* about losing the money.] —*adv.* badly: *used only in everyday talk* [He wants to go so *bad.*] —*n.* **1.** a bad thing or condition [to go from *bad* to worse]. **2.** those who are wicked [In fairy tales the *bad* are always punished.] —**not bad,** fairly good: *used only in everyday talk.* —**worse,** *compar.;* **worst,** *superl.* —**bad′ness,** *n.*

bad blood, a feeling of being enemies.

bade (bad), a past tense of **bid.**

badge (baj), *n.* **1.** a pin, emblem, or ribbon worn to show that one belongs to a certain group or has done something special [a policeman's *badge;* a boy scout's *badge*]. **2.** any sign or symbol [His battle wound is a red *badge* of courage.]

badg·er (baj′ər), *n.* **1.** an animal with a broad back, thick fur, and short legs. It lives in holes which it digs in the ground. **2.** the fur of this animal. —*v.* to annoy; pester [a speaker *badgered* by interruptions].

badger (2 ft. long)

bad·lands (bad′landz), *n.pl.* any land without trees or grass, where the wind and rain have worked the soil and soft rocks into strange shapes.

bad·ly (bad′lē), *adv.* **1.** in a bad way; harmfully, unpleasantly, incorrectly, wickedly, etc. **2.** very much; greatly: *used only in everyday talk.*

bad·min·ton (bad′min tən), *n.* a game like tennis, in which a cork with feathers in one end is batted back and forth across a high net by players using light rackets.

bad-tem·pered (bad′tem′pərd), *adj.* having a bad temper; getting angry easily; irritable.

baf·fle (baf′'l), *v.* **1.** to confuse so as to keep from understanding or solving; puzzle [The crime

badminton

has *baffled* the police for months.] **2.** to interfere with; hold back; hinder [to *baffle* sound]. —*n.* a wall or screen that holds back or turns to one side a flow, as of a fluid, heat, or sound waves. —**baf′fled,** *p.t. & p.p.;* **baf′fling,** *pr.p.*

bag (bag), *n.* **1.** paper, cloth, or other soft material made up so as to have a closed bottom and sides, used for holding or carrying things [Unlike a box, a *bag* can take the shape of what it is holding.] **2.** a suitcase, woman's purse, etc. **3.** anything shaped or bulging like a bag [*bags* under the eyes]. **4.** game that a hunter catches or kills. **5.** in baseball, a base. —*v.* **1.** to put into a bag. **2.** to bulge like a full bag [His trousers *bag* at the knees.] **3.** to catch or kill in hunting [The hunter *bagged* two ducks.] —**bagged,** *p.t. & p.p.;* **bag′ging,** *pr.p.*

Bag·dad or **Bagh·dad** (bag′dad), *n.* the capital of Iraq, on the Tigris River.

bag·gage (bag′ij), *n.* **1.** the trunks, suitcases, etc. that a person takes on a trip; luggage. **2.** the equipment and supplies of an army.

bag·gy (bag′ē), *adj.* hanging loosely and bulging in places [*baggy* trousers]. —**bag′gi·er,** *compar.;* **bag′gi·est,** *superl.* —**bag′gi·ness,** *n.*

bag·pipe (bag′pīp) *n. often* **bagpipes,** *pl.* a musical instrument with a leather bag into which the player blows air. The air is then forced with the arm through several pipes to make shrill tones. Bagpipes are now played mainly in Scotland.

bah (bä *or* ba), *interj.* a sound made to show a feeling of disgust or scorn.

Ba·ha·ma Islands (bə hä′mə *or* bə hä′mə), a group of British islands in the West Indies, north of Cuba. Also called **the Ba·ha′mas.**

bagpipe

bail (bāl), *n.* money left with a law court as a guarantee that an arrested person will appear for trial. If he fails to appear, the court keeps the money. —*v.* to have an arrested person set free by giving bail [His friends *bailed* him out.] —**jump bail,** to fail to appear for trial after bail has been paid: *used only in everyday talk.*

bail (bāl), *v.* to take water out of a boat, as by dipping with a bucket. —**bail out,** to make a parachute jump from an aircraft.

bail (bāl), *n.* a curved handle, as on a bucket.

bail·iff (bāl′if), *n.* **1.** a sheriff's assistant. **2.** an officer who has charge of prisoners and jurors in a court. **3.** a steward or manager of an estate.

bairn (bern), *n.* a child: *a Scottish word.*

bait (bāt), *n.* **1.** food put on a hook or trap to attract and catch fish or animals. **2.** anything used to tempt or attract a person. —*v.* **1.** to put bait on a hook or trap. **2.** to set attacking dogs against [People used to *bait* chained bears for amusement.] **3.** to torment or tease by saying annoying or cruel things [The boys *baited* Paul by calling him "Fatty."]

baize (bāz), *n.* thick woolen cloth, usually dyed green, used to cover a billiard table.

bake (bāk), *v.* **1.** to cook in an oven, with little or no water or other liquid [She *baked* a cake. The potatoes *baked* for an hour.] **2.** to make or become dry and hard by heat [to *bake* bricks in a kiln]. —**baked,** *p.t. & p.p.;* **bak′ing,** *pr.p.*

bak·er (bāk′ər), *n.* a person whose work or business is baking bread, cakes, and pastry.

baker's dozen, thirteen. At one time bakers added an extra roll to each dozen they sold.

bak·er·y (bāk′ər ē), *n.* a place where bread, cakes, etc. are baked or sold. —**bak′er·ies,** *pl.*

bak·ing powder (bāk′ing), a white powder containing baking soda and an acid substance, used in cakes, biscuits, etc. to make them rise.

baking soda, a white powder that neutralizes acids and is also used in or like baking powder.

Ba·laam (bā′ləm), *n.* in the Bible, a prophet who was scolded by his donkey after he had beaten it for balking.

bal·ance (bal′əns), *n.* **1.** equality in amount, weight, value, or importance, as between two things or the parts of a single thing [the *balance* of two boys on a seesaw; the *balance* of light and dark in a painting]. **2.** the ability to keep one's body steady without falling [He lost his *balance* when he looked down from the ladder.] **3.** one's normal, steady state of mind. **4.** an equal condition between the amount of money that one owes and the amount that is owed to one. **5.** the amount of money one has in a bank account. **6.** the amount still owed after part of a bill has been paid. **7.** the part left over; remainder: *used only in everyday talk* [I carried some of the groceries, and the store delivered the *balance*.] **8.** a device for weighing, having two shallow pans hanging from the ends of a bar supported in the middle. **9.** a wheel that controls the speed of moving parts, as in a clock: also called **balance wheel.** —*v.* **1.** to compare two things to see which is heavier, better, or more important. **2.** to keep oneself or something else from falling, by holding steady [The seal *balanced* the ball on his nose. The dancer *balanced* on her toes.] **3.** to make two things or parts equal in weight, value, or importance [If you and I sit in the front and father in the back, we can *balance* the boat.] **4.** to make up for by acting in an opposite way; counteract [His kind acts *balanced* his rough manner.] **5.** to find the difference, if any, between the amount of money that one has or that is owed to one and the amount one owes or has spent; also, to make these

balance for weighing

amounts equal [to *balance* a checking account].
  —**in the balance,** not yet settled or decided.
  —**bal′anced,** *p.t. & p.p.;* **bal′anc·ing,** *pr.p.*

Bal·bo·a (bal bō′ə), *n.* 1475–1517; Spanish explorer who discovered the Pacific Ocean.

bal·co·ny (bal′kə nē), *n.* **1.** a platform with a low wall or railing, that juts out from the side of a building. **2.** an upper floor of rows of seats in a theater, etc. It often juts out over the main floor. —**bal′co·nies,** *pl.*

balcony

bald (bôld), *adj.* **1.** having no hair on all or part of the scalp [Many men become *bald,* but few women do.] **2.** not covered by natural growth [a *bald,* rocky hill]. **3.** plain and frank [the *bald* facts]. —**bald′ly,** *adv.* —**bald′ness,** *n.*

bald eagle, a large, strong eagle of North America, which has a white-feathered head and neck when it is full-grown. It is the eagle shown on the coat of arms of the United States. *See the picture for* **eagle.**

bal·der·dash (bôl′dər dash), *n.* talk or writing that is nonsense.

bal·dric (bôl′drik), *n.* a belt worn over one shoulder and across the chest to hold a sword, bugle, etc.

bale (bāl), *n.* a large bundle of tightly packed cotton, hay, straw, etc., wrapped up for shipping. —*v.* to make into bales [to *bale* hay]. —**baled,** *p.t. & p.p.;* **bal′ing,** *pr.p.*

bale

bale·ful (bāl′fəl), *adj.* harmful or evil; sinister [a *baleful* glance]. —**bale′ful·ly,** *adv.* —**bale′ful·ness,** *n.*

balk (bôk), *v.* **1.** to stop and stubbornly refuse to move or act. **2.** to bring to a stop; block [The project was *balked* by a lack of funds.] —*n.* **1.** something that blocks or hinders. **2.** in baseball, the action by a pitcher of starting a pitch but not finishing it. This allows any base runners to move up one base.

Bal·kan (bôl′kən), *adj.* of the Balkans or their people.

Bal·kans (bôl′kənz), *n.pl.* the countries on a peninsula (**Balkan Peninsula**) in southeastern Europe; Yugoslavia, Romania, Bulgaria, Albania, Greece, and part of Turkey. Also called **Balkan States.**

balk·y (bôk′ē), *adj.* in the habit of balking [a *balky* mule]. —**balk′i·er,** *compar.;* **balk′i·est,** *superl.*

---

fat,   āpe,   cär,   ten,   ēven,   hit,   bīte,   gō,   hôrn,   tool,   book,   up,   fŭr;
get,   joy,   yet,   chin,   she,   thin,   then;   zh = s in pleasure;   ′ as in able (ā′b'l);
    ə = a in ago,   e in agent,   i in sanity,   o in confess,   u in focus.

ball (bôl), *n.* **1.** any round object; sphere [a meat *ball; ball* of yarn]. **2.** a solid or hollow object, round or egg-shaped, used in playing various games [a golf *ball;* a foot*ball*]. **3.** a game played with a ball, especially baseball [Let's play *ball.*] **4.** the throw, pitch, or flight of a ball [to throw a fast *ball;* to hit a long *ball*]. **5.** in baseball, a pitch that is not a strike and is not swung at by the batter. **6.** a round shot for a rifle or cannon. —*v.* to form into a ball.

ball (bôl), *n.* a large, formal dancing party.

bal·lad (bal′əd), *n.* **1.** a song or poem that tells a story in short verses. **2.** a popular love song.

bal·last (bal′əst), *n.* **1.** heavy material, such as metal or sand, carried in a ship, balloon, etc. to keep it steady. **2.** crushed rock or gravel used to make a firm bed for railroad tracks. —*v.* to make steady by adding ballast.

ball bearing, 1. a part of a machine in which the moving parts revolve or slide on rolling metal balls so that there is very little friction. **2.** any of these metal balls. —**ball′-bear′ing,** *adj.*

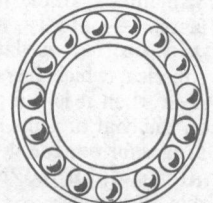
ball bearing

bal·le·ri·na (bal′ə rē′nə), *n.* a woman ballet dancer.

bal·let (bal′ā *or* ba lā′), *n.* **1.** a dance performed on a stage, usually by a group of dancers in costume. It often tells a story by means of its graceful, fixed movements. **2.** a group of such dancers.

bal·lis·tics (bə lis′tiks), *n.pl.* the science that has to do with the shooting of bullets, rockets, etc.: *used with a singular verb.* —**bal·lis′tic,** *adj.*

bal·loon (bə lōōn′), *n.* **1.** a large bag that floats high above the ground when filled with a gas lighter than air. Balloons are now often used to carry instruments for studying the upper air. **2.** a small rubber bag blown up with air or gas and used as a toy. —*v.* to swell like a balloon.

bal·lot (bal′ət), *n.* **1.** a piece of paper on which a person marks his choice in voting. **2.** the act or a way of voting. —*v.* to vote by ballot.

ball point pen, a kind of fountain pen whose writing point is a tiny ball that rolls the ink onto the writing surface.

ball·room (bôl′rōōm), *n.* a large room or hall for dancing.

balm (bäm), *n.* **1.** a sweet-smelling oil that is gotten from certain trees and is used as an ointment. **2.** any salve or lotion used for healing or for relieving pain. **3.** anything that soothes [Sleep was a *balm* to his troubles.]

balm·y (bäm′ē), *adj.* like balm; soothing, mild, or pleasant [a *balmy* day]. —**balm′i·er,** *compar.;* **balm′i·est,** *superl.* —**balm′i·ness,** *n.*

ba·lo·ney (bə lō′nē), *n.* **1.** bologna. **2.** nonsense; foolishness: *slang in this meaning.*

bal·sa (bôl′sə), *n.* **1.** a tree growing in tropical America that has a very lightweight wood used for airplane models, rafts, etc. **2.** the wood.

bal·sam (bôl′səm), *n.* **1.** the same as **balm** (*in meaning 1*). **2.** any tree or plant from which balm is gotten; especially, a kind of fir tree.

3. a garden plant whose pods burst open when ripe and scatter their seeds.

Bal·tic (bôl′tik), *n.* a sea in northern Europe bounded on the west by Sweden and leading into the North Sea: in full, **Baltic Sea.** —*adj.* of or on the Baltic Sea [Lithuania, Latvia, and Estonia are sometimes called the *Baltic* States.]

Bal·ti·more (bôl′tə môr), *n.* a seaport in northern Maryland, on Chesapeake Bay.

Baltimore oriole, a black and orange songbird of North America. *See the picture for* **oriole.**

bal·us·ter (bal′əs tər), *n.* any of the small posts that support the upper rail of a railing.

bal·us·trade (bal ə strād′), *n.* a railing held up by balusters, as on a staircase.

bam·boo (bam bōō′), *n.* a tropical plant with woody stems that are hollow and jointed. It is a kind of grass that grows as tall as trees, and its stems are used in making canes, furniture, fishing poles, etc.

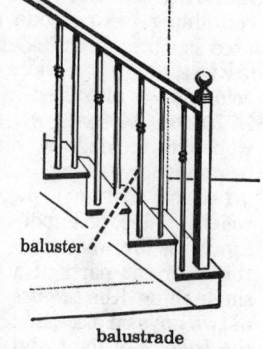
baluster
balustrade

bam·boo·zle (bam-bōō′z'l), *v.* **1.** to trick or cheat. **2.** to confuse or puzzle [The riddle has us *bamboozled.*] *This word is used only in everyday talk.* —**bam·boo′-zled,** *p.t. & p.p.;* **bam-boo′zling,** *pr.p.*

ban (ban), *v.* to have a rule against doing, saying, using, etc.; forbid [Some cities have tried to *ban* certain books.] —*n.* **1.** an official order forbidding something [The city placed a *ban* on the burning of rubbish.] **2.** a curse. —**banned,** *p.t. & p.p.;* **ban′ning,** *pr.p.*

ba·nal (bā′n'l), *adj.* said or told so often that it has become dull or stale; trite [His speech was full of *banal* jokes.]

ba·nan·a (bə nan′ə), *n.* **1.** a large tropical plant with long, broad leaves and a large bunch of fruit growing on a single stalk. **2.** its narrow, slightly curved fruit. It has a sweet, creamy flesh covered by a yellow or reddish skin.

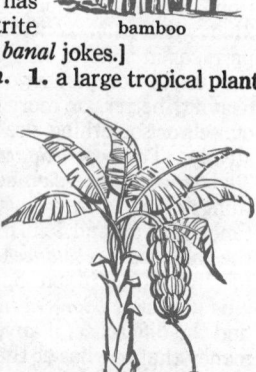
bamboo
banana plant

band (band), *n.* **1.** a cord or wire, or a strip of some material, used to encircle something or to bind something together [The iron *bands* around the barrel broke. A wedding ring is sometimes called a *band*.] **2.** a stripe of some different color or material [a *band* of chrome along the side of the car]. **3.** a range of frequencies for radio broadcasting [a short-wave *band*]. **4.** a group of people joined together to do something [a *band* of explorers]. **5.** a group of musicians playing together, especially on wind instruments [a dance *band;* a marching *band*]. —*v.* **1.** to put a band on or mark with a band [The pigeons were *banded* on the leg.] **2.** to join together or unite [The neighbors *banded* together to build the barn.]

band·age (ban'dij), *n.* a strip of cloth, gauze, etc. used to cover a sore or wound or to bind up an injured part of the body. —*v.* to bind or cover with a bandage. —**band'aged,** *p.t. & p.p.;* **band'ag·ing,** *pr p.*

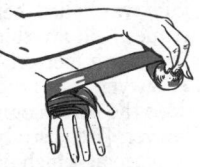
bandage

ban·dan·na or **ban·dan·a** (ban dan'ə), *n.* a large, colored handkerchief, usually with a pattern printed on it. Bandannas are often worn around the neck or head.

band·box (band'bäks), *n.* a light, cardboard box for holding hats, collars, etc.

ban·deau (ban dō'), *n.* a narrow ribbon worn around the head to hold the hair in place. —**bandeaux** (ban dōz'), *pl.*

ban·dit (ban'dit), *n.* a robber, especially one who robs travelers on the road.

band·mas·ter (band'mas'tər), *n.* the leader of a band of musicians.

band saw, a saw whose blade is a long, narrow loop of metal that runs over pulleys. It is usually worked by electricity.

band·stand (band'stand), *n.* **1.** a platform from which a band of musicians can give a concert out-of-doors. It usually has a roof, but is open on all sides. **2.** any platform for a band of musicians, as in a ballroom.

bandstand

band · wag · on (band'wag''n), *n.* a gaily decorated wagon for a band of musicians to ride in, as in a parade. —**on the bandwagon,** on the winning or popular side, as in an election: *used only in everyday talk.*

ban·dy (ban'dē), *v.* to toss or pass back and forth; give and get back [to *bandy* gossip]. —**bandy words,** to have an argument. —**ban'-died,** *p.t. & p.p.;* **ban'dy·ing,** *pr.p.*

ban·dy (ban'dē), *adj.* bending outward at the knees; bowed [*bandy* legs].

ban·dy-leg·ged (ban'dē leg'id *or* ban'dē legd'), *adj.* having bandy legs; bowlegged.

bane (bān), *n.* something that causes worry, ruin, or death. —**bane'ful,** *adj.*

bang (bang), *v.* **1.** to hit hard and noisily [He *banged* his fist on the door. The shutters *banged* against the house.] **2.** to shut noisily [Don't *bang* the door.] **3.** to make a loud noise [The drums were *banging.* He heard a gun *bang* twice.] —*n.* **1.** a hard blow or loud knock [a *bang* on the door]. **2.** a sudden loud noise [The dynamite went off with a *bang.*] —*adv.* hard, noisily, and suddenly [The car ran *bang* into the wall.] —**bang up,** to hurt or damage.

bang (bang), *v.* to cut hair short and straight across. —*n.* banged hair worn across the forehead: *usually used in the plural,* **bangs.**

Bang·kok (bang'käk), *n.* the capital of Thailand.

ban·gle (bang'g'l), *n.* a bracelet or anklet worn as an ornament.

ban·ian (ban'yən), *n.* same as **banyan.**

ban·ish (ban'ish), *v.* **1.** to force a person to leave his country as a punishment; exile. **2.** to put away; get rid of [She tried to *banish* all thoughts of the tragedy.] —**ban'ish·ment,** *n.*

ban·is·ter (ban'is tər), *n.* a row of small posts (*balusters*) holding up a railing, as along a staircase: *often used in the plural,* **banisters.**

ban·jo (ban'jō), *n.* a stringed musical instrument with a long neck and a round body covered with tightly stretched skins. It has, usually, four or five strings that are plucked with the fingers or a pick. —**ban'jos** or **ban'joes,** *pl.* —**ban'jo·ist,** *n.*

banjo

bank (bangk), *n.* **1.** a place of business for keeping, exchanging, and lending money. Banks make a profit by charging interest for the money they lend. **2.** a place for keeping a supply of something for use later on [a blood *bank*]. —*v.* to put or keep money in a bank. —**bank on,** to depend on: *used only in everyday talk.*

bank (bangk), *n.* **1.** a large or long mound or pile [a *bank* of earth; a *bank* of clouds]. **2.** the land along the sides of a river or stream. **3.** a shallow place in a sea or lake [The ship ran aground on the sand *bank.*] —*v.* **1.** to pile up so as to form a bank [The snow was *banked* along the driveway.] **2.** to slope a road where it goes

fat,   āpe,   cär,   ten,   ēven,   hit,   bīte,   gō,   hôrn,   tool,   book,   up,   fũr;
get,   joy,   yet,   chin,   she,   thin,   *th*en;   **zh** = s in pleasure;   ' as in able (ā'b'l);
ə = a in ago,   e in agent,   i in sanity,   o in confess,   u in focus.

around a curve. **3.** to tilt an airplane while making a turn so that the wing on the inside of the turn is lower. **4.** to cover a fire with ashes or more fuel so that it will burn slower.

bank (bangk), *n.* **1.** a row or tier of oars, as in an ancient galley. **2.** a row or tier of objects [a *bank* of lights; a *bank* of keys on an organ].

bank·er (bangk′ər), *n.* a person who owns or manages a bank.

bank·ing (bangk′ing), *n.* the work of a banker; the business of managing a bank.

bank·rupt (bangk′rupt), *adj.* **1.** not able to pay one's debts and freed by law from the need for doing so [Any property a *bankrupt* person may still have is usually divided among those to whom he owes money.] **2.** left without any value or worth [a *bankrupt* policy]. —*n.* a person who is bankrupt. —*v.* to make bankrupt.

bank·rupt·cy (bangk′rupt sē), *n.* state or case of being bankrupt. —**bank′rupt·cies,** *pl.*

ban·ner (ban′ər), *n.* **1.** a piece of cloth with an emblem or words on it [The *banner* behind the President's desk bears the seal of the U.S.] **2.** a flag [the Star-Spangled *Banner*]. **3.** a headline across a newspaper page. —*adj.* top; leading [Our company had a *banner* year in sales.]

banns (banz), *n.pl.* a public announcement in church that two persons are soon to be married.

ban·quet (bang′kwit), *n.* a formal dinner or feast for many people. Banquets, at which speeches are made, are often held to celebrate something or to raise money. —*v.* **1.** to have a banquet for. **2.** to dine well; feast.

ban·shee or **ban·shie** (ban′shē), *n.* in Irish and Scottish folk tales, a female spirit who is supposed to wail or shriek as a sign that someone in a family is about to die.

ban·tam or **Ban·tam** (ban′təm), *n.* a breed of chicken of small size. The male is often a fighter.

ban·ter (ban′tər), *n.* playful teasing or joking. —*v.* to joke or tease in a playful way.

ban·yan (ban′yən), *n.* a fig tree of the East Indies whose branches take root in the ground, forming many new trunks.

bap·tism (bap′tiz′m), *n.* **1.** the religious ceremony of taking a person into a Christian church by dipping him in water or sprinkling water on

banyan

him. **2.** a first experience, especially one that is hard or severe [new troops receiving their *baptism* of fire]. —**bap·tis′mal,** *adj.*

Bap·tist (bap′tist), *n.* **1.** a member of a Christian church which believes that baptism should be given only to an adult and only by dipping the entire body in water. **2.** a person who baptizes [John the *Baptist*].

bap·tis·ter·y or **bap·tis·try** (bap′tis trē), *n.* a place used for baptism, usually in a church. —**bap′tis·ter·ies** or **bap′tis·tries,** *pl.*

bap·tize (bap tīz′ or bap′tīz), *v.* **1.** to take a

person into a Christian church by baptism. **2.** to give a name to at baptism; christen. —**bap·tized′,** *p.t. & p.p.;* **bap·tiz′ing,** *pr.p.*

bar (bär), *n.* **1.** a long, fairly narrow piece of wood, metal, etc. Bars are often used to block the way, to fasten something, or as a lever [The prison has *bars* on the windows. He pried open the box with a steel *bar*.] **2.** a solid piece of something, having an even shape [*bar* of soap; chocolate *bar*]. **3.** anything that prevents or stands in the way [The sand *bar* blocked the river channel. Foreign birth is a *bar* to becoming president.] **4.** a stripe or band of color or light [*Bars* of sunlight came through the clouds.] **5.** a law court [She was called before the *bar* to answer for her crimes.] **6.** anything that acts like a law court in judging a person [the *bar* of public opinion]. **7.** lawyers as a group [Which candidate for judge does the *bar* recommend?] **8.** the profession of a lawyer [He is studying for the *bar*.] **9.** a counter or place at which drinks, and sometimes food, are served. **10.** any of the lines that run from top to bottom of a musical staff, dividing it into equal groups of beats, called measures; also, any of these measures [The band played the opening *bars* of "America."] —*v.* **1.** to fasten with a bar [The door is *barred* and bolted.] **2.** to block; shut off; obstruct [A fallen tree *bars* the path.] **3.** to stand in the way; prevent; forbid [State law *bars* convicts from voting.] **4.** to keep out; refuse to let in [The dog was *barred* from the house.] **5.** to mark with stripes or bands. —*prep.* except; leaving out: *now used only in the phrase* **bar none,** *meaning* "with no exception." —**barred,** *p.t. & p.p.;* **bar′ring,** *pr.p.*

barb (bärb), *n.* a sharp point sticking out in an opposite direction from the main point of a fishhook, arrow, etc. —*v.* to put a barb or barbs on.

Bar·ba·dos (bär bā′dōz), *n.* a country on an island in the West Indies.

bar·bar·i·an (bär ber′i ən), *n.* **1.** a person living in a savage or primitive state. **2.** a cruel or crude person; brute. —*adj.* **1.** not civilized; savage; primitive. **2.** cruel; brutal.

bar·bar·ic (bär ber′ik), *adj.* of or like barbarians; not civilized; wild; crude.

fishhook with barbs

bar·bar·ism (bär′bə riz′m), *n.* **1.** an action or behavior that is brutal or savage. **2.** a word or phrase that is not considered in good use ["Youse" is a *barbarism* for "you."]

bar·bar·i·ty (bär ber′ə tē), *n.* **1.** brutal or savage act or behavior; cruelty. **2.** a crude or coarse style or taste. —**bar·bar′i·ties,** *pl.*

bar·ba·rous (bär′bə rəs), *adj.* **1.** not civilized; primitive. **2.** cruel, savage, or brutal. **3.** crude or coarse [a *barbarous* style or taste]. **4.** using words or phrases that are not considered in good use. —**bar′ba·rous·ly,** *adv.*

Bar·ba·ry (bär′bə rē), *n.* the Moslem areas of North Africa west of Egypt.

bar·be·cue (bär′bə kyōō), *n.* **1.** a pig, ox, etc. roasted whole on a spit over an open fire. **2.** any meat roasted over an open fire. **3.** a picnic or party at which such meat is cooked and eaten. **4.** a stove or pit for cooking out-of-doors. —*v.* **1.** to roast on a spit over an open fire. **2.** to broil or roast meat or fish in a highly seasoned sauce (called **barbecue sauce**). —**bar′be·cued,** *p.t. & p.p.*; **bar′be·cu·ing,** *pr.p.*

barbed (bärbd), *adj.* **1.** having a barb or barbs. **2.** sharp and painful [*barbed* remarks].

barbed wire, wire with sharp points all along it. It is used for fences or barriers.

bar·ber (bär′bər), *n.* a person whose work is cutting hair, shaving beards. etc.

bar·ber·ry (bär′ber′ē), *n.* **1.** a shrub with small thorns and small, red berries. **2.** this berry. —**bar′ber′ries,** *pl.*

bar·ber·shop (bär′bər-shäp), *n.* a barber's place of business.

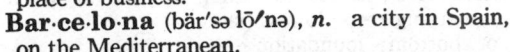
barbed wire

Bar·ce·lo·na (bär′sə lō′nə), *n.* a city in Spain, on the Mediterranean.

bard (bärd), *n.* **1.** a person who composed and sang poems in ancient times. **2.** a poet.

bare (ber), *adj.* **1.** not covered or clothed; naked; stripped [*bare* legs; a *bare* spot in the lawn]. **2.** not furnished; empty [a *bare* room]. **3.** simple; plain [the *bare* facts]. **4.** no more than; mere [a *bare* ten inches away]. —*v.* to make bare; uncover; expose. —**lay bare,** to make clear; expose; reveal. —**bar′er,** *compar.*; **bar′est,** *superl.* —**bared,** *p.t. & p.p.*; **bar′ing,** *pr.p.*

bare (ber), a former past tense of **bear.**

bare·back (ber′bak), *adv. & adj.* on a horse with no saddle [to ride *bareback*].

bare·faced (ber′fāst), *adj.* feeling or showing no shame; impudent; bold [a *barefaced* lie].

bare·foot (ber′foot), *adj. & adv.* with bare feet; without shoes and stockings.

bare·foot·ed (ber′foot′id), *adj.* barefoot.

bare·head·ed (ber′hed′id), *adj. & adv.* wearing no hat or other covering on the head.

bare·ly (ber′lē), *adv.* **1.** only just; no more than; scarcely [It is *barely* a year old.] **2.** in a bare way; poorly [a *barely* furnished office].

bar·gain (bär′g'n), *n.* **1.** an agreement to give or do something in return for something else [Let's make a *bargain* to help each other with our chores.] **2.** something offered or gotten for less than the usual cost [This dress was a *bargain* at only $5.00.] —*v.* to talk over a sale or trade, trying to get the best possible terms [He *bargained* with the salesman for an hour before buying the car.] —**bargain for,** to expect; be ready for [more trouble than he had *bargained for*]. —**into the bargain,** in addition; as well.

barge (bärj), *n.* **1.** a large boat with a flat bot-

tom, for carrying goods on rivers or canals. **2.** any large or clumsy looking boat of this kind. —*v.* to enter in a clumsy or rude way: *used only in everyday talk* [He *barged* in without knocking.] —**barged,** *p.t. & p.p.*; **barg′ing,** *pr.p.*

bar·i·tone (bar′ə tōn), *n.* **1.** a man's voice that is lower than a tenor but higher than a bass. **2.** a singer with such a voice, or an instrument with a range like this. —*adj.* of or for a baritone.

bar·i·um (ber′i əm), *n.* a chemical element that is a silver-white metal. Its salts are used in medicine and in making paints.

bark (bärk), *n.* the outside covering of the trunk and branches of a tree. —*v.* **1.** to peel the bark from. **2.** to scrape some skin off [He *barked* his shins on the low table.]

bark (bärk), *v.* **1.** to make the short, sharp cry of a dog. **2.** to make a sound like this [The rifles *barked.*] **3.** to speak or shout sharply [to *bark* orders]. —*n.* the sound made in barking.

bark (bärk), *n.* **1.** a kind of ship with three masts. **2.** any sailing ship: *used mainly in poetry.*

bark·er (bär′kər), *n.* a person in front of a theater, carnival tent, etc. who tries to get people to go inside by talking in a loud and lively way.

bar·ley (bär′lē), *n.* **1.** a cereal grass whose seed, or grain, is used in making malt, soups, etc. **2.** this grain.

bar·ley·corn (bär′lē kôrn′), *n.* **1.** barley grass or its grain. **2.** whisky: also **John Barleycorn.**

barn (bärn), *n.* a farm building for sheltering cows, farm machines, etc. and for storing crops.

bar·na·cle (bär′nə k'l), *n.* a small sea animal with a shell, which fastens itself to rocks, the bottoms of ships, etc.

barn dance, a party, sometimes held in a barn, where people do square dances.

barn·storm (bärn′-stôrm), *v.* to go about the country from one small town

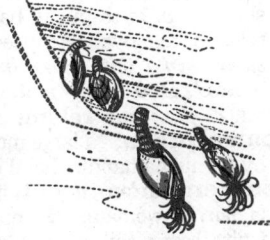
barnacles

to another acting in plays, giving concerts, etc.

barn·yard (bärn′yärd), *n.* the yard or ground near a barn, often with a fence around it.

ba·rom·e·ter (bə räm′ə tər), *n.* **1.** an instrument that measures the pressure of the air around us. It is used in forecasting changes in the weather and to find the height above sea level. **2.** anything that shows changes in conditions [The stock market is a *barometer* of business.] —**bar·o·met·ric** (bar′ə met′rik), *adj.*

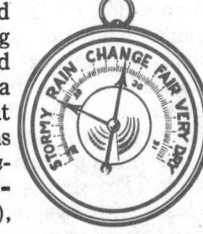
barometer

bar·on (bar′ən), *n.* **1.** a

British nobleman of the lowest rank in the House of Lords. **2.** a nobleman in a few other countries.

bar·on·ess (bar/ə nis), *n.* **1.** a baron's wife or widow. **2.** a woman with a baron's rank.

bar·on·et (bar/ə nit), *n.* a man with a British rank below a baron but above a knight.

ba·ro·ni·al (bə rō/ni əl), *adj.* of or fit for a baron [a *baronial* mansion].

ba·roque (bə rōk/), *adj.* having many ornaments and fancy designs [*baroque* architecture].

barque (bärk), *n.* same as **bark** (a ship).

bar·racks (bar/əks), *n.pl.* a building or group of buildings where soldiers live: *used with either a singular or plural verb* [This *barracks* is old. These *barracks* are old.]

bar·ra·cu·da (bar/ə kōō/də), *n.* a large, fierce fish found in warm seas. —**bar·ra·cu/da** or **bar·ra·cu/das,** *pl.*

bar·rage (bə räzh/), *n.* **1.** the continued shooting of many cannons or machine guns against a part of the enemy's line. It protects one's own troops when moving forward or retreating. **2.** any heavy attack [a *barrage* of insults].

bar·rel (bar/əl), *n.* **1.** a large, round container that has bulging sides and a flat top and bottom. It is usually made of wooden slats bound together by metal hoops. **2.** the amount a barrel will hold: the standard barrel in the United States holds 31½ gallons. **3.** the straight tube of a gun through which the bullet or shell is shot. —*v.* **1.** to put in barrels. **2.** to move fast; speed: *slang in this meaning.* —**bar/reled** or **bar/relled,** *p.t. & p.p.;* **bar/rel·ing** or **bar/rel·ling,** *pr.p.*

barrel

barrel organ, a large music box usually played by turning a handle; hand organ.

bar·ren (bar/ən), *adj.* **1.** unable to have children [a *barren* woman]. **2.** not producing crops or fruit [*barren* soil; a *barren* tree]. **3.** not bringing useful results; not worthwhile [a *barren* plan]. **4.** not having any; empty [*barren* of charm]. —*n.* an area of barren land. —**bar/ren·ness,** *n.*

bar·rette (bə ret/), *n.* a clasp for holding a girl's or woman's hair in place.

bar·ri·cade (bar/ə kād or bar ə kād/), *n.* **1.** a pile of things built up quickly to block a road or entrance, especially in order to hold off an attack. **2.** anything that blocks the way; barrier. —*v.* **1.** to put up barricades in; block [The streets were *barricaded* with logs and barbed wire.] **2.** to keep out or shut in with a barricade [She *barricaded* herself in her room.] —**bar/ri·cad·ed,** *p.t. & p.p.;* **bar/ri·cad·ing,** *pr.p.*

barrette

bar·ri·er (bar/i ər), *n.* **1.** a fence, wall, or other thing that blocks the way or keeps one from going on. **2.** anything that keeps people apart or

prevents progress [The caste system of India created many *barriers.*]

bar·ring (bär/ing), *prep.* unless there should be; excepting [*Barring* rain, we leave tonight.]

bar·ris·ter (bar/is tər), *n.* in England, a lawyer who pleads cases in court.

bar·room (bär/rōōm), *n.* a room with a bar or counter at which alcoholic drinks are sold.

bar·row (bar/ō), *n.* **1.** a shallow, open box with handles at each end, used for carrying small loads. **2.** a wheelbarrow. **3.** a small cart with two wheels, pushed by hand.

bar·row (bar/ō), *n.* a heap of earth or rocks used in olden times to mark a grave.

Bart., abbreviation for **Baronet.**

bar·tend·er (bär/ten/dər), *n.* a man who serves alcoholic drinks at a bar.

bar·ter (bär/tər), *v.* to pay for goods with other goods instead of with money; trade [He *bartered* his overcoat for food.] —*n.* the act of bartering.

bas·al (bā/s'l), *adj.* basic (*in meaning 1*).

ba·salt (bə sôlt/ or bas/ôlt), *n.* a hard, dark rock found in lava that has cooled and hardened.

base (bās), *n.* **1.** the thing or part on which something rests; lowest part or bottom; foundation [A cement slab forms the *base* of the statue.] **2.** the main part, on which the rest depends; basis [A man's *base* pay is the rate he is paid per hour or per week, not counting overtime, bonuses, etc.] **3.** any of the four goals which a baseball player must safely reach one after the other before scoring a run. **4.** any goal or safety point in certain other games. **5.** a center or headquarters; especially, the place from which troops, planes, ships, or explorers set out or from which they get their orders and supplies. **6.** a chemical substance that acts on an acid to form a salt [Sodium hydroxide, a *base,* acts with hydrochloric acid to form sodium chloride, or common table salt.] —*v.* to put or rest on a base or on something that acts as a support [love *based* on respect]. —**based,** *p.t. & p.p.;* **bas/ing,** *pr.p.*

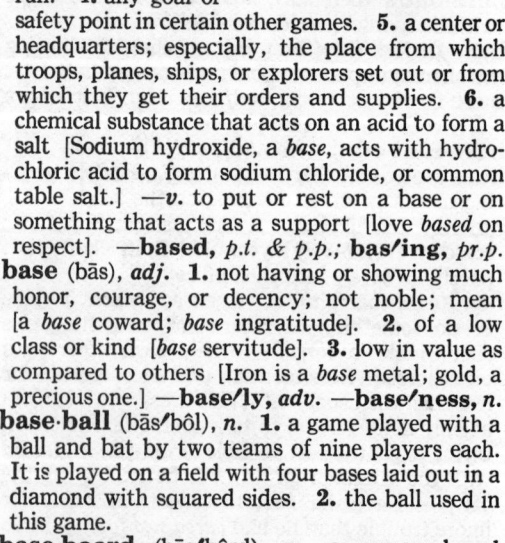

base

base (bās), *adj.* **1.** not having or showing much honor, courage, or decency; not noble; mean [a *base* coward; *base* ingratitude]. **2.** of a low class or kind [*base* servitude]. **3.** low in value as compared to others [Iron is a *base* metal; gold, a precious one.] —**base/ly,** *adv.* —**base/ness,** *n.*

base·ball (bās/bôl), *n.* **1.** a game played with a ball and bat by two teams of nine players each. It is played on a field with four bases laid out in a diamond with squared sides. **2.** the ball used in this game.

base·board (bās/bôrd), *n.* a narrow board covering the edge of a wall next to the floor.

base·less (bās/lis), *adj.* not based on fact or truth; without good reason [*baseless* beliefs].

base·ment (bās/mənt), *n.* the cellar or lowest rooms of a building, below the main floor and at least partly below the surface of the ground.

bash (bash), *v.* to hit or damage with a heavy blow; smash: *used only in everyday talk.*

bash·ful (bash′fəl), *adj.* timid and shy when among people. —**bash′ful·ly,** *adv.* —**bash′-ful·ness,** *n.*

bas·ic (bās′ik), *adj.* **1.** at the base; being the base or basis; fundamental; main [the *basic* rules of a science]. **2.** of or containing a chemical base; alkaline. —**bas·i·cal·ly** (bās′ik lē), *adv.*

bas·il (baz′l), *n.* a plant with a pleasant smell, used as a seasoning in cooking.

ba·sil·i·ca (bə sil′i kə), *n.* an ancient building consisting of a long room with a part shaped like a half circle at the far end. It had a row of columns along each side.

bas·i·lisk (bas′ə lisk), *n.* a monster like a lizard, told about in myths. Its breath and glance were supposed to kill people.

ba·sin (bā′s'n), *n.* **1.** a wide, shallow bowl for holding a liquid. **2.** a washbowl or sink. **3.** a bay or sheltered part of a sea or lake [a yacht *basin*]. **4.** all the land drained by a river and its branches.

ba·sis (bā′sis), *n.* the thing or part on which something rests or depends; support [There is no *basis* for the rumor.] —**ba·ses** (bā′sēz), *pl.*

bask (bask), *v.* **1.** to warm oneself pleasantly, as in the sunlight. **2.** to enjoy any kind of warm or pleasant feeling [He *basked* in her favor.]

bas·ket (bas′kit), *n.* **1.** a container made by weaving together cane, rushes, wood strips, etc. It often has a handle or handles [a bushel *basket;* a clothes *basket*]. **2.** the amount a basket holds [Apples are $2.00 a *basket*.] **3.** anything that looks like a basket or is used as one [a wastepaper *basket* made of metal]. **4.** the open net through which the ball is tossed in basketball; also, a goal scored by tossing the ball through this net.

bas·ket·ball (bas′kit bôl′), *n.* **1.** a game played between two teams of five players each, usually indoors. Points are scored by tossing a ball through a raised net, like an open basket, at either end of the playing court. **2.** the large ball used in this game. It is covered with leather and filled with air.

bas-re·lief (bä′ri lēf′), *n.* sculpture in which figures are carved in a flat surface so that they stand out a little from the background [Lincoln's head on the penny is a kind of *bas-relief*.]

bass (bās), *n.* **1.** the lowest kind of man's singing voice. **2.** a singer with such a voice, or an instrument with the lowest range of tones. **3.** the lowest part of harmony in a piece of music. —*adj.* **1.** of or for a bass. **2.** having low, deep sounds or tones [a *bass* drum].

bass (bas), *n.* a fish found in both fresh and salt water and used for food. —**bass** or **bass′es,** *pl.*

bass clef (bās), a sign on a musical staff showing that the notes on the staff are below middle C. *See the picture for* **clef.**

bas·set (bas′it), *n.* or **basset hound,** a hunting dog with a long body, short legs, and long ears.

bas·si·net (bas ə net′), *n.* a large basket used as a baby's bed, often with a hood at one end.

bas·soon (ba sōōn′), *n.* a wood-wind musical instrument with deep, low tones. Its long, curved mouthpiece has two reeds.

bass viol (bās), a stringed musical instrument that looks like a huge violin and has deep, low tones.

bass·wood (bas′wood), *n.* a kind of linden tree, or its soft, but strong wood.

bassoon

bast (bast), *n.* a strong fiber gotten from plants and used in making ropes and mats.

bas·tard (bas′tərd), *n.* a child born to a woman who is not married to the child's father. *This word is now considered impolite or unkind.*

baste (bāst), *v.* to sew with long, loose stitches so as to hold the parts in place until the final sewing is done. After a hem is properly sewed, these stitches are pulled out. —**bast′ed,** *p.t. & p.p.;* **bast′ing,** *pr.p.*

baste (bāst), *v.* to keep meat juicy during roasting by pouring juices or melted fats over it. —**bast′ed,** *p.t. & p.p.;* **bast′ing,** *pr.p.*

bass viol

Bas·tille (bas tēl′), *n.* **1.** a famous prison in Paris that was destroyed by mobs on July 14, 1789. This action was the beginning of the French Revolution. **2. bastille,** any prison.

bas·tion (bas′chən), *n.* **1.** a part of a fort that juts out to give the defenders a better place to shoot from. **2.** any strong defense.

bat (bat), *n.* **1.** a wooden club used in hitting the ball in baseball. **2.** any strong, sturdy stick. **3.** a turn at batting in baseball [He got three hits in four times at *bat*.] **4.** a hard blow or hit: *used only in everyday talk.* —*v.* **1.** to hit with a bat or something like a bat. **2.** to take a turn at batting in baseball. —**not bat an eye,** to show no surprise: *used only in everyday talk.* —**bat′-ted,** *p.t. & p.p.;* **bat′ting,** *pr.p.*

basket

bat (bat), *n.* a furry animal that looks like a mouse but has wings of stretched skin. Bats usually fly at night. **—blind as a bat,** completely blind. Bats do not see well.

bat (3½ in. long)

batch (bach), *n.* **1.** the amount of something made at one time [a *batch* of cookies; wool yarn from different *batches*]. **2.** an amount of something to be used or worked on at one time [a *batch* of dishes to wash].

bat·ed (bāt′id), *adj.* held in: *now mainly in the phrase* **with bated breath,** in a frightened or excited way, as if holding one's breath.

bath (bath), *n.* **1.** a washing or dipping of something in a liquid; especially, a washing of the body with water [Give the dog a *bath.*] **2.** water or other liquid for bathing, or for dipping or soaking anything [The *bath* is too hot. The hot metal was dipped in an oil *bath.*] **3.** a bathtub. **4.** a bathroom. **5.** a bathhouse (*in meaning 2*). **—baths** (ba*thz*), *pl.*

bathe (bāth), *v.* **1.** to take a bath or give a bath to; wash. **2.** to put into or cover with a liquid; wet or soak [to *bathe* a wound in alcohol]. **3.** to go swimming [to *bathe* in the sea]. **4.** to cover or fill with a liquid or something spoken of as if it were a liquid [Sweat *bathed* his brow. The trees were *bathed* in moonlight.] **—bathed,** *p.t. & p.p.;* **bath′ing,** *pr.p.* **—bath′er,** *n.*

bath·house (bath′hous), *n.* **1.** a building where people change clothes for swimming. **2.** a public building where people can take baths.

bathing cap, a tight rubber cap to keep the hair dry while bathing or swimming.

bathing suit, a garment worn for swimming.

bath·robe (bath′rōb), *n.* a long, loose garment worn to and from the bath or while relaxing.

bath·room (bath′rōōm), *n.* a room with a bathtub, toilet, washstand, etc.

bath·tub (bath′tub), *n.* a large tub in which a person takes a bath. Nowadays it is usually fastened to water pipes in a bathroom.

ba·tiste (ba tēst′), *n.* a light, thin, linen or cotton cloth, used for shirts, dresses, etc.

ba·ton (ba tän′), *n.* **1.** a slender stick used by a conductor in directing an orchestra. **2.** a short staff that is the sign of authority of an officer or official [a marshal's *baton*]. **3.** a metal rod twirled in a showy way, as by a drum major.

Ba·ton Rouge (bat′n rōōzh′), the capital of Louisiana, on the Mississippi River.

baton

bat·tal·ion (bə tal′yən), *n.* **1.** a large group of soldiers, especially a unit forming part of a regiment and made up of several companies. **2.** any large group working at the same thing [A *battalion* of newspaper reporters followed the President on his trip.]

bat·ten (bat′n), *n.* a thin strip of wood; especially, any of the strips used to nail down canvas over a ship's hatches, as in a storm. **—v.** to fasten with battens [The sailors *battened* down the hatches.]

bat·ter (bat′ər), *v.* **1.** to beat with blow after blow; pound noisily [The waves *battered* the rocks on the shore.] **2.** to break to pieces by pounding [The firemen *battered* down the door.] **3.** to damage or wear out by rough use [The furniture was *battered.*] **—n.** a thin, flowing mixture of flour, milk, eggs, etc. beaten together for making such things as cakes, waffles, and cookies.

bat·ter (bat′ər), *n.* the player whose turn it is to bat in baseball.

bat·ter·ing-ram (bat′ər ing ram′), *n.* a heavy wooden beam, used for battering down gates, doors, and walls. As used in ancient warfare, it sometimes had an iron ram's head at one end.

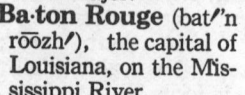

battering-ram

bat·ter·y (bat′ər ē), *n.* **1.** a set of things connected or used together [A *battery* of microphones surrounded the Mayor.] **2.** an electric cell or a group of connected cells that furnishes an electric current [*Batteries* are used in automobiles and flashlights.] **3.** a beating: see **assault. 4.** a number of heavy guns, or cannons, used together in warfare; also, the group of soldiers manning these. **5.** in baseball, the pitcher and catcher as a unit. **—bat′ter·ies,** *pl.*

bat·ting (bat′ing), *n.* **1.** the act of a person who bats in baseball. **2.** a sheet or wad of cotton or wool fiber used in bandages, quilts, etc.

bat·tle (bat′l), *n.* **1.** a particular fight between armed forces during a war [The naval *battle* lasted two days.] **2.** armed fighting generally; warfare [He limps from a wound received in *battle.*] **3.** any fight or struggle; conflict [a *battle* of ideas]. **—v.** to fight or struggle [The little ship *battled* against the storm.] **—give battle** or **do battle,** to take part in a battle; fight. **—bat′tled,** *p.t. & p.p.;* **bat′tling,** *pr.p.* **—bat′tler,** *n.*

bat·tle-ax or **bat·tle-axe** (bat′l aks), *n.* a heavy ax used in the past as a weapon of war.

battle cry, a cry or slogan used to encourage those in a battle or struggle.

bat·tle·dore (bat′l dôr), *n.* the racket used to hit the shuttlecock in a game (called **battledore and shuttlecock**) like badminton.

bat·tle·field (bat′l fēld), *n.* the place where a battle is fought or was fought.

bat·tle·ground (bat′l ground), *n.* a battlefield.

bat·tle·ment (bat′'l mənt), *n.* **1.** a low wall on a tower, with open spaces to shoot through. **2.** decoration like this on any building.

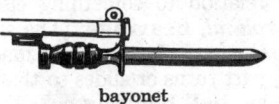
battlement

bat·tle·ship (bat′'l-ship), *n.* a large warship with big guns and very heavy armor.

bau·ble (bô′b'l), *n.* a bright, showy thing that has little value.

baux·ite (bôk′sīt *or* bō′zīt), *n.* the claylike ore from which aluminum is gotten.

Ba·var·i·a (bə ver′i ə), *n.* a state in southern Germany. —**Ba·var′i·an,** *adj. & n.*

bawd·y (bô′dē), *adj.* not decent or proper; vulgar; obscene. —**bawd′i·er,** *compar.;* **bawd′i·est,** *superl.*

bawl (bôl), *v.* **1.** to call out in a loud, rough voice; bellow ["Forward march!" *bawled* the sergeant.] **2.** to weep and wail loudly, as a child does: *used only in everyday talk.* —**bawl out,** to scold angrily: *a slang phrase.*

bay (bā), *n.* a part of a sea or lake that cuts into a coastline to form a hollow curve.

bay (bā), *n.* **1.** a part of a room or building that is partly set off from the rest of the building, as by pillars or screens [Tools and lumber are kept in different *bays* in the warehouse.] **2.** a part of a room built out from the wall line, forming an alcove inside: see also **bay window.**

bay (bā), *v.* to bark or howl with long, deep sounds [The hound *bayed* at the moon.] —*n.* **1.** the sound of baying. **2.** the condition of a hunted animal that has been cornered and is forced to turn and fight [The deer was brought to *bay* at the end of the canyon.] **3.** the condition of being held off by a cornered animal [The deer kept the hunters at *bay* with his antlers.]

bay (bā), *n.* an evergreen tree with tough, shiny leaves; laurel tree. The sweet-smelling leaf (**bay leaf**) is dried and used for flavor in cooking.

bay (bā), *n.* **1.** a reddish-brown color. **2.** a horse, etc. of this color. —*adj.* having this color.

bay·ber·ry (bā′ber′ē), *n.* **1.** a shrub that bears gray berries with a waxy coating that is used in making some candles. **2.** any of these berries. —**bay′ber′ries,** *pl.*

bay·o·net (bā′ə nit), *n.* a blade like a dagger that can be put on the front end of a rifle. —*v.* to stab or kill with a bayonet. —**bay′o·net·ed,** *p.t. & p.p.;* **bay′o·net·ing,** *pr.p.*

bayonet

bay·ou (bī′oo), *n.* in the southern United States, a slow-moving, marshy body of water, often one that joins a river or lake with a gulf.

bay window, a window or set of windows in a bay that is built out from the wall of a building.

ba·zaar or **ba·zar** (bə zär′), *n.* **1.** a sale of many kinds of articles, usually to raise money for a club, church, or charity. **2.** in Oriental countries, a market or a street where there are many shops.

bay window

ba·zoo·ka (bə zoo′kə), *n.* a rocket gun that can be carried, first used in World War II.

BB (bē′bē′), *n.* a tiny metal ball to be shot from an air rifle (**BB gun**). —**BB's,** *pl.*

bbl., abbreviation for **barrel.** —**bbls.** or **bbl.,** *pl.*

B.C., before Christ; before the year in which Jesus Christ was believed to have been born [Julius Caesar died in 44 *B.C.*]

B.C., abbreviation for **British Columbia.**

be (bē), *v. Be* is used to join a subject with a word or words that tell something about it. It is also used to tell that something exists or takes place, and as a helping verb with other verb forms. In the present tense *be* has these forms: I *am;* he, she, or it *is;* we, you, or they *are.* **1.** *Be* may join a subject with a noun, adjective, or pronoun [Ed and Lois *are* students. Mary *is* pretty. Who *is* he?] **2.** *Be* may mean "to live," "to happen or take place," or "to stay or continue" [Lincoln *is* no more. The wedding will *be* next Saturday. I will *be* here until Monday.] **3.** *Be* may be used as a helping verb with a past participle, a present participle, or an infinitive [Bill *is* gone. Jane *is* going. Fred *is* to go later.] —**was** or **were,** *p.t.;* **been,** *p.p.;* **being,** *pr.p.*

be-, a prefix meaning: **1.** around [To *beset* is to set around, or surround.] **2.** completely [To *besmear* is to smear completely.] **3.** away [To *betake* oneself is to take oneself away.] **4.** about [To *bemoan* someone is to moan about someone.] **5.** to make [To *becalm* is to make calm.] **6.** to furnish or cover with [To *begrime* is to cover with grime.]

Be, symbol for the chemical element *beryllium.*

beach (bēch), *n.* a smooth, sloping stretch of sand and pebbles at the edge of a sea or lake. —*v.* to run onto a beach [to *beach* a boat].

beach·head (bēch′hed), *n.* an area controlled by troops that have invaded an enemy shore.

bea·con (bē′k'n), *n.* **1.** a light for warning or guiding [They started a bonfire on the hill as a *beacon* for the approaching ship.] **2.** a tower which sends out beams of light or radio waves to guide ships or airplanes in stormy or foggy weather.

bead (bēd), *n.* **1.** a small, usually round piece of glass, metal, etc. with a small hole in it so that it can be put on a string [Her only

fat,   āpe,   cär,   ten,   ēven,   hit,   bīte,   gō,   hôrn,   tool,   book,   up,   fŭr;
get,   joy,   yet,   chin,   she,   thin,   *then;*   zh = s in pleasure;   ′ as in able (ā′b'l);
ə = a in ago,   e in agent,   i in sanity,   o in confess,   u in focus.

jewelry was a string of *beads*.] **2.** a drop or bubble [There were *beads* of sweat on his forehead.] —*v.* to decorate or cover with beads [a *beaded* handbag]. —**draw a bead on,** to take careful aim at. —**tell one's beads,** to say prayers with a rosary.

bead·ing (bēd′ing), *n.* **1.** a trimming or design made of beads. **2.** a narrow molding with a pattern of small balls like beads. **3.** any narrow trimming with such a pattern.

bea·dle (bē′d'l), *n.* in earlier times, a church officer whose duty was to keep order in church.

bead·y (bēd′ē), *adj.* small, round, and sparkling [the *beady* eyes of a snake].

bea·gle (bē′g'l), *n.* a small hunting dog with a smooth coat, short legs, and drooping ears.

beak (bēk), *n.* **1.** a bird's bill, especially the sharp, hooked bill of the eagle, hawk, owl, etc. **2.** a part or thing that is like a beak.

beak·er (bēk′ər), *n.* **1.** a large cup or goblet. **2.** a wide glass with a lip for pouring, used by chemists and druggists.

beam (bēm), *n.* **1.** a long, thick piece of timber or metal. Beams are used in buildings and ships as horizontal supports for roofs, floors, and decks. **2.** the distance from one side of a ship to the other at its widest place. **3.** the crossbar of a balance, with a scale hanging from each end. **4.** a ray of light. **5.** a bright, joyful look or smile. **6.** a stream of radio or radar signals sent out to guide airplanes or ships in their course. —*v.* **1.** to shine brightly [A light *beamed* from the window.] **2.** to show one's pleasure with a bright look or smile. **3.** to aim a radio signal, radio program, etc. [to *beam* the program to France.] —**on the beam, 1.** following the guiding beam, as an airplane. **2.** doing things exactly right: *slang in this meaning.*

beaker

bean (bēn), *n.* **1.** the smooth, hard seed taken from the pods of certain plants for use as food. Kidney beans and lima beans are seeds of this kind. **2.** a pod with such seeds [String *beans* are cooked and eaten as a green vegetable, pod and all.] **3.** any plant that bears beans. **4.** any seed or fruit that looks like a bean or a bean pod [coffee *bean*].

bean·bag (bēn′bag), *n.* a small cloth bag filled with dried beans and used in certain games.

bean plant and seeds in pod

bean·stalk (bēn′stôk), *n.* the main stem of a bean plant.

bear (ber), *v.* **1.** to take from one place to another; carry [The guests arrived *bearing* gifts.] **2.** to have or show [She *bears* a resemblance to you. The letter *bore* his signature.] **3.** to hold up [Will the walls *bear* the weight of the roof?]

4. to give birth to [She has *borne* three children.] **5.** to bring into being; produce [Our pear tree *bore* no fruit.] **6.** to hold or behave oneself in a certain way [He *bears* himself with pride.] **7.** to be able to stand something painful or annoying; put up with; endure [I can't *bear* this heat.] **8.** to take care of; pay for [to *bear* all expenses]. **9.** to keep hold of [She *bears* a grudge for a long time.] **10.** to carry or move along [The current *bore* the boat toward the falls. The ship *bore* west.] **11.** to call for; need [His suspicious actions *bear* watching.] —**bear down, 1.** to press or push down. **2.** to try hard. —**bear on,** to have to do with; apply to [This evidence does not *bear on* the crime.] —**bear out,** to show to be true; prove. —**bear up,** to hold up, as under a strain; keep one's spirits up. —**bear with,** to put up with; endure. —**bore,** *p.t.;* **borne,** *p.p.* (see also **born**); **bear′ing,** *pr.p.* —**bear′-a·ble,** *adj.* —**bear′er,** *n.*

bear (ber), *n.* **1.** a large, heavy animal with shaggy fur and a very short tail. Common kinds of bear are the brown bear, grizzly bear, and polar bear. **2.** a person who is clumsy, rude, and rough. —**bear·ish,** *adj.*

brown bear (3 ft. high at shoulder)

beard (bird), *n.* **1.** the hair growing on the lower part of a man's face; whiskers. **2.** any growth like a beard, as the hair on a goat's chin or the stiff fibers on a spike of wheat. —*v.* to come face to face with and defy. —**beard′ed,** *adj.*

bear·er (ber′ər), *n.* **1.** a person or thing that bears or carries something [a *bearer* of good news]. **2.** the person who presents a check, note, or money order for payment.

beards

bear·ing (ber′ing), *n.* **1.** the way one stands or walks; carriage [the upright *bearing* of a soldier]. **2.** the way one behaves; manner [a kindly *bearing*]. **3.** the fact of having something to do with; connection [The price of feed has a direct *bearing* on the cost of beef.] **4.** direction or position in relation to something else: *usually used in the plural,* **bearings** [The ship lost her *bearings* in the fog.] **5.** a part of a machine on which another part turns or slides so that there is little friction: see **ball bearing.**

beast (bēst), *n.* **1.** any large, four-footed animal [A horse is a *beast* of burden (used for carrying things). A lion is a *beast* of prey (that kills other animals for food).] **2.** a cruel or stupid person.

beast·ly (bēst′lē), *adj.* **1.** like a beast; cruel, stupid, etc. **2.** unpleasant: *used only in everyday talk* [*beastly* weather]. —**beast′li·er,** *compar.;* **beast′li·est,** *superl.* —**beast′li·ness,** *n.*

beat (bēt), *v.* **1.** to hit or strike again and again; pound [Stop *beating* that drum. Rain was *beating* on the roof.] **2.** to punish by hitting or whipping [He doesn't approve of *beating* children.] **3.** to mix by stirring strongly with a fork, spoon, or beater [*Beat* the whites of two eggs.] **4.** to move up and down; flap [The robin *beat* his wings against the window.] **5.** to make flat by pounding, tramping, etc. [We *beat* a path through the tall grass.] **6.** to force or push [He *beat* his way through the crowd.] **7.** to move or sound in an even, regular way; throb [He could feel his heart *beat*.] **8.** to make a sound when struck [We heard war drums *beating*.] **9.** to mark time in music, as by tapping. **10.** to win over; defeat [Our football team *beat* Central High twice.] **11.** to confuse or puzzle: *used only in everyday talk* [It *beats* me how she gets so much done.] —*n.* **1.** a beating or throbbing, as of the heart. **2.** a blow, stroke, etc. made again and again [the *beat* of the hail on the window]. **3.** a route that one follows in his work [a policeman's *beat*]. **4.** the unit of rhythm or accent in music [Waltz time has three *beats* in each measure.] —**beat a retreat,** to pull back; retreat. —**beat back** or **beat off,** to drive or force back. —**beat,** *p.t.;* **beat'en,** *p.p.;* **beat'ing,** *pr.p.*

beat·en (bēt'n), past participle of **beat**. —*adj.* **1.** that has been hit with many blows [He cringed like a *beaten* dog.] **2.** made flat by being much walked on [a *beaten* path through the fields]. **3.** shaped or made thin by hammering [*beaten* gold]. **4.** that has lost; defeated.

beat·er (bēt'ər), *n.* a thing that is used for beating [an egg *beater*].

be·a·tif·ic (bē'ə tif'ik), *adj.* full of bliss or joy.

be·at·i·fy (bi at'ə fī), *v.* **1.** to make blessed or full of bliss. **2.** in the Roman Catholic Church, to say that a certain dead person is among the blessed in heaven. —**be·at'i·fied,** *p.t. & p.p.;* **be·at'i·fy·ing,** *pr.p.* —**be·at·i·fi·ca·tion** (bi·at'ə fi kā'shən), *n.*

be·at·i·tude (bi at'ə tōōd *or* bi at'ə tyōōd), *n.* complete happiness; bliss. —**the Beatitudes,** the part of the Sermon on the Mount, in the Book of Matthew, which begins "Blessed are the poor in spirit."

beau (bō), *n.* **1.** a man who is courting a woman; sweetheart. **2.** a man who pays much attention to fashion in clothes and manners: *now seldom used.* —**beaus** or **beaux** (bōz), *pl.*

beau·te·ous (byōō'ti əs), *adj.* beautiful.

beau·ti·ful (byōō'tə fəl), *adj.* very pleasant to look at or hear; giving delight to the mind [a *beautiful* face]. —**beau'ti·ful·ly,** *adv.*

beau·ti·fy (byōō'tə fī), *v.* to make beautiful or more beautiful. —**beau'ti·fied,** *p.t. & p.p.;* **beau'ti·fy·ing,** *pr.p.* —**beau·ti·fi·ca·tion** (byōō'tə fi kā'shən), *n.*

beau·ty (byōō'tē), *n.* **1.** that quality in a person or thing which makes it pleasant for one to look at, hear, or think about [the *beauty* of a sunset]. **2.** a beautiful person or thing; especially, a beautiful woman. —**beau'ties,** *pl.*

beauty shop or **beauty salon** or **beauty parlor,** a place where women can go to get their hair dressed, their nails manicured, etc.

bea·ver (bē'vər), *n.* **1.** an animal that has soft, brown fur and a flat, broad tail, and can live on land and in water. It cuts down trees with its teeth and builds dams across rivers. **2.** the fur of a beaver.

beaver (2½ ft. long)

bea·ver (bē'vər), *n.* a part of a helmet used in the Middle Ages, that could be moved down to protect the mouth and chin.

be·calmed (bi kämd'), *adj.* not able to move because there is no wind [The sailboat was *becalmed* in the still lagoon.]

be·came (bi kām'), past tense of **become.**

be·cause (bi kôz'), *conj.* for the reason that; since [I'm late *because* I overslept.] —**because of,** on account of; as a result of [He was absent from school *because of* illness.]

beck (bek), *n.* a movement of the hand or head that tells someone to come closer. —**at the beck and call of,** obeying every order of.

beck·on (bek'n), *v.* to call closer by a motion of the head or hand.

be·come (bi kum'), *v.* **1.** to come to be [He *became* ill last week. Her baby brother had *become* a young man.] **2.** to be right or suitable for; make attractive [That hat *becomes* you.] —**become of,** to happen to [What *became* of John after he left home?] —**be·came',** *p.t.;* **be·come',** *p.p.;* **be·com'ing,** *pr.p.*

be·com·ing (bi kum'ing), *adj.* right or suitable; attractive [a *becoming* gown].

bed (bed), *n.* **1.** a piece of furniture for sleeping or resting on. **2.** any place or thing used for sleeping or resting [A park bench was his *bed*.] **3.** sleep [Farmers go to *bed* early.] **4.** a piece of ground where plants are grown [a flower *bed*]. **5.** the ground at the bottom of a river, lake, etc. **6.** any flat base or foundation [They placed the printing press on a *bed* of concrete.] **7.** a layer of something in the ground [a *bed* of coal]. —*v.* to go or put to sleep; prepare a place for sleeping [We'll *bed* down here in the woods.] —**bed and board,** a place to sleep and meals. —**bed'ded,** *p.t. & p.p.;* **bed'ding,** *pr.p.*

bed·bug (bed'bug), *n.* a small, flat, biting insect that is sometimes found in beds, etc.

bed·cham·ber (bed'chām'bər), *n.* a bedroom.

bed·clothes (bed'klōz *or* bed'klō*th*z), *n.pl.* sheets, pillows, blankets, etc.

bed·ding (bed/ing), *n.* **1.** mattresses and bed-clothes. **2.** straw, etc. for animals to sleep on.

be·deck (bi dek/), *v.* to decorate or adorn.

be·dew (bi dōō/ *or* bi dyōō/), *v.* to make wet, as with dew [cheeks *bedewed* with tears].

bed·fel·low (bed/fel/ō), *n.* a person who shares one's bed.

be·diz·en (bi dī/z'n), *v.* to dress or decorate in a cheap, showy way.

bed·lam (bed/ləm), *n.* a place or condition of noise and confusion, as in the old-fashioned insane asylum [The children were screaming, the radio was blaring, the house was a *bedlam*.]

Bed·ou·in (bed/ōō in), *n.* an Arab who belongs to any of the tribes that wander in the deserts of Arabia, Syria, or North Africa.

be·drag·gled (bi drag/'ld), *adj.* wet and dirty, as with mud; untidy; messy.

bed·rid·den (bed/rid/'n), *adj.* having to stay in bed for a long time because of sickness.

bed·roll (bed/rōl), *n.* a roll of bedding carried by campers for sleeping outdoors.

bed·room (bed/rōōm), *n.* a room to sleep in.

bed·side (bed/sīd), *n.* the space beside a bed [The nurse was at his *bedside* constantly.]

bed·spread (bed/spred), *n.* a cover spread over a bed when it is not being slept in.

bed·spring (bed/spring), *n.* a framework of springs in a bedstead on which a mattress lies.

bed·stead (bed/sted), *n.* the frame of a bed, holding the bedspring and mattress.

bed·time (bed/tīm), *n.* the time when one usually goes to bed.

bee (bē), *n.* **1.** a hairy insect that has four wings and feeds on the nec-tar of flowers. Some bees live together in colonies or hives and make honey and wax. **2.** a meeting of people for working at some-thing together [a quilting *bee*].

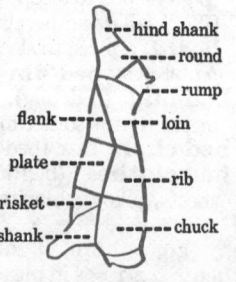

bee (¾ in. long)

beech (bēch), *n.* **1.** a tree with smooth bark, dark-green leaves, and nuts that may be eaten. **2.** the hard wood of this tree. —**beech/-en,** *adj.*

beech·nut (bēch/nut), *n.* the small, three-cornered nut of the beech tree.

beef (bēf), *n.* **1.** meat from a steer, cow, or bull. **2.** a full-grown steer, cow, or bull, raised for its meat. —**beeves** or **beefs,** *pl.*

beef·steak (bēf/stāk), *n.* a thick slice of beef to be broiled or fried.

beef·y (bēf/ē), *adj.* fleshy and solid; having much muscle [a *beefy* football player]. —**beef/i·er,** *compar.;* **beef/i·est,** *superl.*

hind shank
round
rump
flank — loin
plate
rib
brisket
shank — chuck

beef cuts

bee·hive (bē/hīv), *n.* **1.** a box or other shelter for a colony of bees, in which they make and store honey. **2.** any place where there is much ac-tivity.

bee·line (bē/līn), *n.* a straight line from one place to another; direct route.

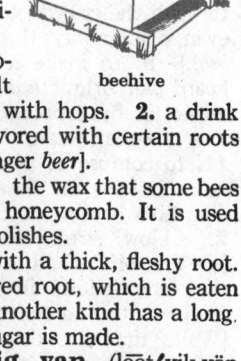

beehive

been (bin), past parti-ciple of **be.**

beer (bir), *n.* **1.** an alco-holic drink made of malt and water, and flavored with hops. **2.** a drink that is not alcoholic, flavored with certain roots and plants [root *beer;* ginger *beer*].

bees·wax (bēz/waks), *n.* the wax that some bees make for building their honeycomb. It is used in making candles and polishes.

beet (bēt), *n.* a plant with a thick, fleshy root. One kind has a round, red root, which is eaten as a cooked vegetable. Another kind has a long white root from which sugar is made.

Bee·tho·ven, Lud·wig van (lōōt/vik vän bā/tō vən), 1770–1827; German composer.

bee·tle (bē/t'l), *n.* an insect that has two pairs of wings. The hard front wings cover the thin hind wings when these are folded.

bee·tling (bēt/ling), *adj.* sticking out; overhanging [*beetling* eyebrows].

beetle (½ in. long)

beeves (bēvz), *n.* a plural of **beef.**

be·fall (bi fôl/), *v.* to hap-pen to [Many adventures *befell* Robin Hood.] —**be·fell** (bi fel/), *p.t.;* **be·fall·en** (bi fôl/ən), *p.p.;* **be·fall/ing,** *pr.p.*

be·fit (bi fit/), *v.* to be right or proper for. —**be·fit/ted,** *p.t. & p.p.;* **be·fit/ting,** *pr.p.*

be·fog (bi fôg/ *or* bi fäg/), *v.* **1.** to cover with fog; make foggy. **2.** to confuse; muddle [His mind is *befogged* by lack of sleep.] —**be·fogged/,** *p.t. & p.p.;* **be·fog/ging,** *pr.p.*

be·fore (bi fôr/), *prep.* **1.** ahead of [The long valley stretched *before* him.] **2.** in front of ["a dainty dish to set *before* a king"]. **3.** earlier than; previous to [Will you finish *before* noon?] **4.** rather than; instead of [I'd choose death *before* dishonor.] —*adv.* **1.** in the past; earlier [I've heard that song *before*.] **2.** at an earlier time; sooner [The doctor can see you at ten o'clock, but not *before*.] **3.** ahead; in front [They marched off, the banners going *before*.] —*conj.* **1.** earlier than the time that [Wash your hands *before* you eat.] **2.** rather than [I'd go hungry *before* I'd eat snails.]

be·fore·hand (bi fôr/hand/), *adv. & adj.* ahead of time [Let's arrange the seating *beforehand*.]

be·friend (bi frend/), *v.* to act as a friend to.

be·fud·dle (bi fud/'l), *v.* to confuse; make dull or stupid [The wine *befuddled* him.] —**be·fud/-dled,** *p.t. & p.p.;* **be·fud/dling,** *pr.p.*

beg (beg), *v.* **1.** to ask for as charity or as a gift [The tramp *begged* for food at the farmhouse door.] **2.** to ask as a favor; ask seriously or humbly [She *begged* me not to tell the secret.] **3.** to ask for in a polite way [I *beg* your pardon.] —**beg off,** to ask to be excused from doing something. —**go begging,** to be unwanted. —**begged,** *p.t. & p.p.;* **beg′ging,** *pr.p.*

be·gan (bi gan′), past tense of **begin.**

be·get (bi get′), *v.* **1.** to be the father of [God told Jacob he would *beget* many children.] **2.** to cause to be; produce [Poverty *begets* crime.] —**be·got′,** *p.t.;* **be·gat** (bi gat′), old *p.t.;* **be·got′ten** or **be·got′,** *p.p.;* **be·get′ting,** *pr.p.*

beg·gar (beg′ər), *n.* **1.** a person who begs, especially one who lives by begging. **2.** a person who is very poor. —*v.* **1.** to make a beggar of; make poor. **2.** to make seem poor or useless [Her beauty *beggars* description.]

beg·gar·ly (beg′ər lē), *adj.* like or fit for a beggar; poor or worthless.

be·gin (bi gin′), *v.* to start being, doing, acting, etc.; get under way [Work *begins* at 8:00 A.M. His cold *began* with a sore throat.] —**be·gan′,** *p.t.;* **be·gun′,** *p.p.;* **be·gin′ning,** *pr.p.*

be·gin·ner (bi gin′ər), *n.* a person who is just beginning to learn something; novice.

be·gin·ning (bi gin′ing), *n.* a start or starting; first part or first action [A handshake may be the *beginning* of a friendship.]

be·gone (bi gôn′), *interj.* go away! get out!

be·go·nia (bi gōn′yə), *n.* a plant with showy red, white, or pink flowers and large leaves.

be·got (bi gät′), the past tense and a past participle of **beget.**

be·got·ten (bi gät′'n), a past participle of **beget.**

be·grime (bi grīm′), *v.* to cover with grime or dirt; make dirty; soil. —**be·grimed′,** *p.t. & p.p.;* **be·grim′ing,** *pr.p.*

begonia

be·grudge (bi gruj′), *v.* **1.** to envy someone because of something he has [They *begrudged* him his good fortune.] **2.** to give without wanting to; complain while giving [He *begrudges* her every cent of her allowance.] —**be·grudged′,** *p.t. & p.p.;* **be·grudg′ing,** *pr.p.*

be·guile (bi gīl′), *v.* **1.** to cheat or trick into doing or believing something wrong [Delilah *beguiled* Samson into telling her the secret of his strength.] **2.** to pass time pleasantly [They *beguiled* the long evening with singing.] **3.** to please greatly; charm [Her beauty *beguiled* us.] —**be·guiled′,** *p.t. & p.p.;* **be·guil′ing,** *pr.p.*

be·gun (bi gun′), past participle of **begin.**

be·half (bi haf′), *n.* support or interest [Many of his friends spoke in his *behalf*.] —**on behalf of, 1.** in the interest of. **2.** speaking or acting for; representing.

be·have (bi hāv′), *v.* **1.** to act in a certain way; to conduct oneself [The boys *behaved* badly at the picnic.] **2.** to act in a proper way; do the right things [Try to *behave* yourself in public.] —**be·haved′,** *p.t. & p.p.;* **be·hav′ing,** *pr.p.*

be·hav·ior (bi hāv′yər), *n.* the way a person or thing behaves, or acts; conduct or action [Her *behavior* at the dance was rude. Marie Curie studied the *behavior* of radium.]

be·head (bi hed′), *v.* to cut off the head of.

be·held (bi held′), past tense and past participle of **behold.**

be·hest (bi hest′), *n.* an order or command [I have come at the *behest* of the king.]

be·hind (bi hīnd′), *adv.* **1.** in or to the rear or back [The children trailed *behind*.] **2.** in an earlier time or condition [He tried to leave his past *behind*.] **3.** late or slow in action or progress [He fell *behind* in his studies.] —*prep.* **1.** in the rear of; in back of [He sits *behind* me.] **2.** later or slower than [He is two grades *behind* me in school. The train was *behind* schedule.] **3.** supporting; in favor of [Everyone is *behind* the campaign for a new school.] —*adj.* that is to the rear or in back of [Everyone pass his paper to the student *behind*.] —*n.* the lower back part of the body; rump: *used only in everyday talk.*

be·hind·hand (bi hīnd′hand′), *adv. & adj.* late or slow in action or progress; behind time.

be·hold (bi hōld′), *v.* to look at; see [He never *beheld* a sadder sight.] —*interj.* look! see! —**be·held′,** *p.t. & p.p.;* **be·hold′ing,** *pr.p.*

be·hold·en (bi hōl′d'n), *adj.* obliged to feel grateful; owing thanks [I am *beholden* to you for your advice.]

be·hoove (bi hōōv′), *v.* to be necessary or right for; be the duty of [It *behooves* you to think for yourself.] —**be·hooved′,** *p.t. & p.p.;* **be·hoov′ing,** *pr.p.*

beige (bāzh), *n. & adj.* the color of sand; grayish yellow.

be·ing (bē′ing), present participle of **be.** —*n.* **1.** existence; life [The Boy Scouts came into *being* in 1908.] **2.** a living creature [a human *being*]. —**for the time being,** for now.

be·la·bor (bi lā′bər), *v.* **1.** to beat hard; whip. **2.** to attack with words; scold or criticize.

be·lat·ed (bi lāt′id), *adj.* too late; not on time [I sent him a *belated* greeting after his birthday had passed.] —**be·lat′ed·ly,** *adv.*

be·lay (bi lā′), *v.* to make a rope hold tight by winding it around a pin (called **belaying pin**). —*interj.* stop! [*Belay* there!] *A sailor's word.* —**be·layed′,** *p.t. & p.p.;* **be·lay′ing,** *pr.p.*

belch (belch), *v.* **1.** to let gas from the stomach out through the mouth, usually with a noise. **2.** to throw out with force [The volcano *belched* flame.] —*n.* a belching.

bel·dam or **bel·dame** (bel′dəm), *n.* an old

woman, especially an ugly, unpleasant one; hag.

be·lea·guer (bi lē′gər), *v.* to besiege; surround as with an attacking army.

Bel·fast (bel′fast), *n.* a seaport and the capital of Northern Ireland.

bel·fry (bel′frē), *n.* a tower, or the part of a tower in which a bell or bells are hung. —**bel′fries,** *pl.*

belfry

Bel·gian (bel′jən), *adj.* of Belgium or its people. —*n.* a person born or living in Belgium.

Bel·gium (bel′jəm), *n.* a country in western Europe, on the North Sea.

Bel·grade (bel′grād), *n.* the capital of Yugoslavia.

be·lie (bi lī′), *v.* 1. to give a false idea of; hide [His smile *belies* his anger.] 2. to show to be false [Her cruelty *belied* her kind words.] —**be·lied′,** *p.t. & p.p.;* **be·ly′-ing,** *pr.p.*

be·lief (bə lēf′), *n.* 1. a believing or feeling that certain things are true or real; faith [He could not destroy my *belief* in the honesty of most people.] 2. trust or confidence [I have *belief* in his ability.] 3. anything believed or accepted as true; opinion [What are your religious *beliefs?*]

be·lieve (bə lēv′), *v.* 1. to take to be true or real [Can we *believe* his story?] 2. to have religious faith [to *believe* in a life after death]. 3. to have trust or confidence in [I know you will win; I *believe* in you.] 4. to suppose; guess. —**be·lieved′,** *p.t. & p.p.;* **be·liev′ing,** *pr.p.* —**be·liev′a·ble,** *adj.* —**be·liev′er,** *n.*

be·like (bi līk′), *adv.* likely: *now seldom used.*

be·lit·tle (bi lit′'l), *v.* to make seem little or unimportant ["Anyone could score 100 on that test," she said in *belittling* tones.] —**be·lit′-tled,** *p.t. & p.p.;* **be·lit′tling,** *pr.p.*

bell (bel), *n.* 1. a hollow, metal object that rings when it is struck. The common bell is shaped like an upside-down cup, with a clapper hanging inside. 2. the sound made by a bell. 3. anything shaped like a common bell [a *bell* of a trumpet]. 4. a stroke of a bell rung every half hour on shipboard to mark the periods of a watch [Eight *bells* mark the end of each four-hour watch.] —*v.* 1. to put a bell on [to *bell* a cow]. 2. to flare out like a bell.

bell

Bell, Alexander Gra·ham (grā′əm bel), 1847-1922; American inventor of the telephone.

bel·la·don·na (bel′ə dän′ə), *n.* 1. a poisonous plant with reddish flowers and black berries. 2. a drug made from this plant.

bell·boy (bel′boi), *n.* a boy or man whose work in a hotel is to carry luggage and do errands.

belle (bel), *n.* a pretty woman or girl; often, the one who is the prettiest or most popular [the *belle* of the ball].

bel·li·cose (bel′ə kōs), *adj.* eager to fight or quarrel; warlike.

bel·lig·er·ent (bə lij′ər ənt), *adj.* 1. at war; engaged in a war. 2. showing a readiness to fight or quarrel [a *belligerent* gesture or tone]. —*n.* a person or nation that is fighting or at war. —**bel·lig′er·ence** or **bel·lig′er·en·cy,** *n.* —**bel·lig′er·ent·ly,** *adv.*

bel·low (bel′ō), *v.* 1. to roar loudly as a bull does. 2. to shout out, as in anger or pain. —*n.* the sound of bellowing; roar.

bel·lows (bel′ōz), *n. sing. & pl.* 1. a device that blows out air when its sides are squeezed together. It is used especially to make fires burn strongly. 2. anything like a bellows, as the folding part of some cameras.

bellows

bel·ly (bel′ē), *n.* 1. the lower front part of the human body between the chest and thighs; abdomen. 2. the underside of an animal's body. 3. the stomach. 4. the part deep inside [the *belly* of a ship]. 5. a bulging part [the *belly* of a sail]. —*v.* to swell out; bulge [The sails *bellied* out in the wind.] —**bel′lies,** *pl.* —**bel′lied,** *p.t. & p.p.;* **bel′ly·ing,** *pr.p.*

bel·ly·but·ton (bel′ē but′'n), *n.* the navel: *used only in everyday talk.*

be·long (bi lông′), *v.* to have its proper place [This chair *belongs* in the corner.] —**belong to,** 1. to be part of; go with [The gray buttons *belong to* my dress.] 2. to be owned by [The magic lamp *belonged to* Aladdin.] 3. to be a member of [He *belongs to* the Boy Scouts.]

be·long·ings (bi lông′ingz), *n.pl.* those things that belong to a person; possessions.

be·lov·ed (bi luv′id *or* bi luvd′), *adj.* much loved [my *beloved* son]. —*n.* a beloved person.

be·low (bi lō′), *adv. & adj.* in or to a lower place; beneath [I'll take the upper bunk and you can sleep *below*.] —*prep.* lower than in place, position, price, rank, etc. [the people living *below* us; a price *below* $5.00].

belt (belt), *n.* 1. a strip of leather, cloth, etc. worn around the waist to hold up clothing or as an ornament. 2. a solid strip or band of something [The Cotton *Belt* is the region in the South where cotton is grown.] 3. a strap looped around two or more wheels. When one wheel turns, it moves the strap, which turns the other wheel or wheels. —*v.* 1. to put a belt on. 2. to strike hard, as with a belt: *used only in everyday talk.*

belt *(meaning 3)*

be·moan (bi mōn′), *v.* to moan or cry about; lament [to *bemoan* one's fate].

bench (bench), *n.* 1. a long, hard seat for several persons, with or without a back. 2. a strong table on which work with tools is done [a carpenter's *bench*]. **3.** the place where judges sit in a courtroom. **4.** *sometimes* **Bench,** the work or position of a judge; also, judges as a group [a member of the *Bench*]. —*v.* to keep from playing in a game [The coach *benched* his star player for fighting.]

bend (bend), *v.* **1.** to pull or press something hard or stiff into a curve or angle [*Bend* the branch down so we can reach the cherries.] **2.** to be curved in this way [The tree *bent* under the weight of the snow.] **3.** to turn in a certain direction [He *bent* his steps from the path.] **4.** to give in or make give in [He *bends* to her wishes.] **5.** to stoop [*Bend* over and touch your toes.] —*n.* **1.** a bending. **2.** a bent or curving part. —**bent,** *p.t.* & *p.p.;* **bend′ing,** *pr.p.*

bend·ed (bend′id), *adj.* that is bent [on *bended* knee].

be·neath (bi nēth′), *adv.* & *adj.* in a lower place; below or just below; underneath [Look *beneath* the table. The cups are on the shelf *beneath.*] —*prep.* **1.** lower than; below or just below; under [*beneath* sunny skies; the ground *beneath* his feet; a rank *beneath* that of colonel]. **2.** not worthy of [*beneath* one's dignity].

Ben·e·dict, Saint (ben′ə dikt), an Italian monk who lived in the 6th century.

Ben·e·dic·tine (ben′ə dik′tin), *adj.* having to do with the religious order founded by Saint Benedict. —*n.* a Benedictine monk or nun.

ben·e·dic·tion (ben′ə dik′shən), *n.* **1.** an asking for God's blessing, as by a minister at the end of a church service. **2.** a blessing.

ben·e·fac·tion (ben′ə fak′shən), *n.* the act of doing good or giving help to those in need [His *benefactions* included a gift of $500 to the hospital.]

ben·e·fac·tor (ben′ə fak′tər), *n.* a person who has given money or other help to someone in need. —**ben′e·fac′tress,** *n.fem.*

be·nef·i·cence (bə nef′ə s′ns), *n.* **1.** the fact or quality of being kind or doing good; charity. **2.** something given or done to help others; kind act or gift. —**be·nef′i·cent,** *adj.*

ben·e·fi·cial (ben′ə fish′əl), *adj.* being of help or use; helpful; favorable [*beneficial* advice].

ben·e·fi·ci·ar·y (ben′ə fish′ər ē *or* ben′ə fish′i-er′ē), *n.* **1.** a person who gets benefit. **2.** a person who gets money or property from a will or insurance policy. —**ben′e·fi′ci·ar·ies,** *pl.*

ben·e·fit (ben′ə fit), *n.* **1.** help or advantage; also, anything that helps [Speak louder for the *benefit* of those in the rear.] **2.** *often* **benefits,** *pl.* money paid by an insurance company, the government, etc., as during old age or sickness, or for death. **3.** any public event put on to raise money for a certain person, group, or cause [Tonight's show is a *benefit* for crippled children.] —*v.* **1.** to do good for; aid; help [The new tax law *benefits* large businesses.] **2.** to get good from; be helped by; profit [The children *benefited* from the fresh air and exercise in camp.] —**ben′-**

e·fit·ed, *p.t.* & *p.p.;* **ben′e·fit·ing,** *pr.p.*

be·nev·o·lence (bə nev′ə ləns), *n.* a wanting to do good; kindliness; generosity [Mr. Jones showed his *benevolence* by giving a college scholarship to his office boy.]

be·nev·o·lent (bə nev′ə lənt), *adj.* doing or wanting to do good; kind; generous.

Ben·gal (beng gôl′), *n.* a former province of British India divided into **East Bengal** (in Pakistan) and **West Bengal** (in India).

be·night·ed (bi nīt′id), *adj.* being in darkness or ignorance; backward; ignorant [a poor, *be-nighted* people, held back by superstition].

be·nign (bi nīn′), *adj.* **1.** good-natured or kindly [a *benign* smile]. **2.** doing good; helpful; favorable [The sickly child was taken west in search of a more *benign* climate.] **3.** doing little or no harm; not likely to cause death [a *benign* tumor]. —**be·nign′ly,** *adv.*

be·nig·nant (bi nig′nənt), *adj.* benign (*in meanings 1 and 2*).

ben·i·son (ben′ə z′n), *n.* a blessing.

Ben·ja·min (ben′jə mən), *n.* **1.** in the Bible, the youngest son of Jacob. **2.** the tribe of Israel descended from him.

bent (bent), past tense and past participle of **bend.** —*adj.* **1.** made curved or crooked; not straight [He used a *bent* pin for a fishhook.] **2.** wanting very much; determined [Hitler was *bent* on conquering Europe.] —*n.* a natural liking or skill [a *bent* for working with numbers].

be·numb (bi num′), *v.* to make numb; cause to have no feeling [She was *benumbed* by grief.]

ben·zene (ben′zēn), *n.* a clear liquid gotten from coal tar. It is a compound of carbon and hydrogen, used in making varnishes and dyes.

ben·zine (ben′zēn), *n.* a clear liquid that burns easily, gotten from petroleum. It is used in dry cleaning and as a motor fuel.

ben·zo·ate (ben′zō it), *n.* a chemical compound used to keep food from spoiling.

ben·zol (ben′zôl), *n.* same as **benzene.**

be·queath (bi kwēth′ *or* bi kwēth′), *v.* **1.** to leave one's money, etc. to another when one dies [He *bequeathed* his entire fortune to his nephew.] **2.** to leave behind; pass on [The artist *bequeathed* his talent to his son.]

be·quest (bi kwest′), *n.* a bequeathing or something bequeathed [Henry received a *bequest* of $5,000 from his aunt.]

be·rate (bi rāt′), *v.* to scold in a harsh way. —**be·rat′ed,** *p.t.* & *p.p.;* **be·rat′ing,** *pr.p.*

be·reave (bi rēv′), *v.* to take away something or someone dear to one; leave sad and lonely [He was *bereaved* by his wife's death.] —**be·reaved′** or **be·reft′,** *p.t.* & *p.p.;* **be·reav′ing,** *pr.p.* —**be·reave′ment,** *n.*

be·reft (bi reft′), a past tense and past participle of **bereave.** —*adj.* left sad, lonely, or empty by having had something taken away [*Bereft* of all power, Napoleon was exiled to St. Helena.]

---

fat, ape, cär, ten, ēven, hit, bīte, gō, hôrn, tool, book, up, fur;
get, joy, yet, chin, she, thin, *then;* zh = s in pleasure; ' as in able (ā′b'l).
ə = a in ago, e in agent, i in sanity, o in confess, u in focus.

be·ret (bə rā′), *n.* a flat, round cap of a soft material, such as felt or wool.

berg (bŭrg), *n.* an iceberg.

ber·i·ber·i (ber′ē ber′ē), *n.* a disease in which the body grows weak and crippled. It is caused by a lack of vitamin B_1 in the diet.

beret

Ber·ing Sea (ber′ing *or* bir′ing), the northern part of the Pacific Ocean.

Bering Strait, the narrow waterway between Siberia and Alaska, in the Bering Sea.

Ber·lin (bər lin′), *n.* a city in eastern Germany that was the capital of the former German Empire. After World War II it was divided into an eastern district (the capital of East Germany) and a western district.

Ber·mu·da (bər myōō′də), *n.* a group of British Islands in the Atlantic, east of South Carolina.

Bermuda shorts, short trousers that reach down almost to the knees: also called **walking shorts.**

Bern or **Berne** (bŭrn *or* bern), *n.* the capital of Switzerland.

ber·ry (ber′ē), *n.* any small, juicy fruit with seeds and a soft pulp, as a strawberry, black-berry, or blueberry. In scientific use, many fleshy fruits having a skin are classed as berries, for example, the tomato, banana, and grape. **—go berrying,** to look for and pick berries. **—ber′ries,** *pl.*

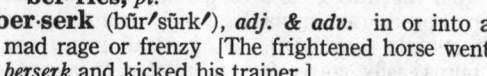
Bermuda shorts

ber·serk (bŭr′sŭrk′), *adj. & adv.* in or into a mad rage or frenzy [The frightened horse went *berserk* and kicked his trainer.]

berth (bŭrth), *n.* **1.** a bed or bunk along a wall, on a ship, train, etc. **2.** a place where a ship anchors or ties up to a dock. **3.** a position or job [He applied for a *berth* as an engineer.] **—give a wide berth to,** to stay a safe distance away from.

berth

ber·yl (ber′il), *n.* a very hard, bright mineral, often bluish-green, as the emerald.

be·ryl·li·um (bə ril′i əm), *n.* a chemical element that is a grayish, lightweight metal. It is used in making strong alloys.

be·seech (bi sēch′), *v.* to ask in a pleading way; implore. **—be·sought′** or **be·seeched′,** *p.t. & p.p.;* **be·seech′ing,** *pr.p.*

be·seem (bi sēm′), *v.* to be fitting or proper for; suit; befit [It ill *beseems* him to be so selfish when he is so rich.]

be·set (bi set′), *v.* to attack from all sides; surround [He was *beset* with worries.] **—be·set′,** *p.t. & p.p.;* **be·set′ting,** *pr.p.*

be·side (bi sīd′), *prep.* **1.** by or at the side of; close to [The garage is *beside* the house.] **2.** compared with [My share seems small *beside* yours.] **3.** in addition to; besides. **—beside oneself,** wild or upset because of anger or worry. **—beside the point,** having nothing to do with what is being talked about.

be·sides (bi sīdz′), *adv.* in addition; as well; furthermore [We'll have games and dancing and food *besides*.] **—prep.** in addition to; as well as [Will anyone be there *besides* you?]

be·siege (bi sēj′), *v.* **1.** to surround a place with soldiers and keep it under attack so as to force a surrender. **2.** to crowd around or make many demands on [He was *besieged* with reporters and requests for more information.] **—be·sieged′,** *p.t. & p.p.;* **be·sieg′ing,** *pr.p.*

be·smear (bi smir′), *v.* to smear over; smudge.

be·smirch (bi smŭrch′), *v.* to make dirty; soil [a name *besmirched* by scandal].

be·som (bē′zəm), *n.* a broom made of a bunch of twigs tied to a handle.

be·sot·ted (bi sät′id), *adj.* dull or dazed, as from drinking liquor.

be·sought (bi sôt′), a past tense and past participle of **beseech.**

be·span·gle (bi spang′g'l), *v.* to decorate with spangles. **—be·span′gled,** *p.t. & p.p.;* **be·span′gling,** *pr.p.*

be·spat·ter (bi spat′ər), *v.* to spatter over, as with spots of mud.

be·speak (bi spēk′), *v.* **1.** to make plain or clear; be a sign of; show [His large mansion *bespeaks* his wealth.] **2.** to order ahead of time; reserve [Are these seats *bespoken*?] **—be·spoke** (bi spōk′), *p.t.;* **be·spok·en** (bi spōk′'n) or **be·spoke′,** *p.p.;* **be·speak′ing,** *pr.p.*

Bes·se·mer process (bes′ə mər), a method of making steel by forcing air through melted iron.

best (best), *adj.* **1.** above all others, as in worth or ability; most excellent, most fit, most desirable, etc. [Peter is the *best* player on the team. What is the *best* time to plant tulips?] **2.** being the most; almost all [Driving to work takes the *best* part of an hour.] *Best* is the superlative of **good.** **—adv. 1.** in a way that is best or most excellent, fit, etc. [Which choir sang *best*?] **2.** more than any other; most [Of all your dresses I like the pink one *best*.] *Best* is the superlative of **well. —n. 1.** a person or thing that is most excellent, most fit, etc. [That doctor is among the *best* in his profession. When he buys shoes, he buys the *best*.] **2.** the most that a person can do; utmost [He did his *best* to win.] **—v.** to win out over; defeat [We *bested* them at tennis.] **—all for the best,** turning out to be good or fortunate after all. **—at best,** as the most that can be expected; at most. **—get the best of,** to defeat. **—had best,** ought to; should. **—make the best of,** to do as well as one can with.

bes·tial (bes′chəl), *adj.* like a beast; brutal or cruel. **—bes·ti·al·i·ty** (bes′chi al′ə tē), *n.*

be·stir (bi stŭr′), *v.* to stir up; make busy [She *bestirred* herself and made lunch.] **—be·stirred′,** *p.t. & p.p.;* **be·stir′ring,** *pr.p.*

best man, the man who stands with the bridegroom at a wedding and hands him the ring.

be·stow (bi stō′), *v.* to give as a gift or as charity [Andrew Carnegie *bestowed* millions of dollars on libraries.] **—be·stow′al,** *n.*

be·strew (bi strōō′), *v.* to scatter or be scattered over [a lawn *bestrewed* with leaves]. **—be·strewed′,** *p.t.;* **be·strewed′** or **be·strewn** (bi strōōn′) *p.p.;* **be·strew′ing,** *pr.p.*

be·stride (bi strīd′), *v.* to sit on something, or stand over something, with one leg on each side [to *bestride* a horse or a ditch]. **—be·strode** (bi strōd′), *p.t.;* **be·strid·den** (bi strid′'n), *p.p.;* **be·strid′ing,** *pr.p.*

bet (bet), *n.* **1.** an agreement between two persons that the one who is proved wrong about something must pay or do something [Let's make a *bet* about who will finish first.] **2.** the thing to be paid or done [The *bet* will be one candy bar.] **—v. 1.** to risk something in a bet [I'll *bet* one candy bar that I finish first.] **2.** to make a bet or be willing to make a bet [I *bet* he'll be late.] **—bet** or **bet′ted,** *p.t.* & *p.p.;* **bet′ting,** *pr.p.*

be·ta (bā′tə), *n.* the second letter of the Greek alphabet.

be·take (bi tāk′), *v.* to take oneself; go [The knight *betook* himself to his castle.] **—be·took′,** *p.t.;* **be·tak′en,** *p.p.;* **be·tak′ing,** *pr.p.*

be·think (bi thingk′), *v.* to think of or remind [I suddenly *bethought* myself of what I had come for.] **—be·thought** (bi thôt′), *p.t.* & *p.p.;* **be·think′ing,** *pr.p.*

Beth·le·hem (beth′li əm *or* beth′li hem′), *n.* an ancient town in Judea (now in western Jordan) where Jesus was born.

be·tide (bi tīd′), *v.* to happen to: *now used mainly in the phrase* **woe betide (someone),** meaning "may bad luck happen to (someone)."

be·times (bi tīmz′), *adv.* early [He awoke *betimes* to journey forth before daylight.]

be·to·ken (bi tō′kən), *v.* to be a sign of; show [This ring *betokens* our friendship.]

be·took (bi took′), past tense of **betake.**

be·tray (bi trā′), *v.* **1.** to help the enemy of one's country, side, or friends; be a traitor to [Benedict Arnold planned to *betray* the Colonies in 1780.] **2.** to fail to keep a promise, secret, agreement, etc.; be unfaithful [He *betrayed* his parents' trust by wasting money at college.] **3.** to make plain to see; show signs of; reveal [His shaky voice *betrayed* his fear.] **—be·tray′al,** *n.*

be·troth (bi trôth′ *or* bi trōth′), *v.* to promise in marriage [to *betroth* a daughter].

be·troth·al (bi trôth′əl *or* bi trō′thəl), *n.* a betrothing; engagement to be married.

be·trothed (bi trôtht′ *or* bi trōthd′), *n.* the person to whom one is engaged to be married.

bet·ter (bet′ər), *adj.* **1.** above another, as in worth or ability; more excellent, more fit, more desirable, etc. [Peter is a *better* player than Mike. I have a *better* idea.] **2.** being more than half

[It takes the *better* part of a day to get there.] **3.** not so sick; more healthy than before. *Better* is the comparative of **good. —adv. 1.** in a way that is better or more excellent, fit, etc. [They will sing *better* with more practice.] **2.** more [I like your pink dress *better* than the green.] *Better* is the comparative of **well. —n. 1.** a person or thing that is more excellent, more fit, etc. [This ball is the *better* of the two.] **2.** a person with more authority [Obey your *betters*.] **—v.** to make or become better; improve; surpass [He has *bettered* the record for the mile run by two seconds.] **—better off,** in a better or improved condition. **—for the better,** to a better or improved condition [His work has changed *for the better*.] **—get the better of,** to defeat. **—had better,** ought to; should. **—think better of,** to change one's mind about.

bet·ter or **bet·tor** (bet′ər), *n.* one who bets.

bet·ter·ment (bet′ər mənt), *n.* a making or being made better; improvement.

be·tween (bi twēn′), *prep.* **1.** in the space, time, or degree that separates [a lake *between* the U.S. and Canada; office hours *between* one and five o'clock; a color *between* blue and green]. **2.** having to do with; involving [the war *between* the North and the South]. **3.** that connects [a road *between* Cleveland and Chicago; a bond *between* friends]. **4.** with a part for or from each of. Although *between* and *among* are sometimes used in place of each other, *between* is usually used of only two and *among* of more than two [*Between* them they landed the fish. The men had fifty dollars *between* them.] **5.** one or the other of [You must choose *between* love and duty.] **6.** because of both [*Between* work and study, he had no time for play.] **—between you and me,** as a secret that you and I share. **—in between, 1.** in a middle position. **2.** in the midst of.

be·twixt (bi twikst′), *prep.* between: *now seldom used except in the phrase* **betwixt and between,** meaning "not completely one nor the other."

bev·el (bev′'l), *n.* **1.** a sloping edge between two parallel surfaces. **2.** a tool used for measuring and marking angles. **—v.** to cut or grind so as to give a slope to [*Bevel* the edges of the mirror.] **—adj.** sloped; beveled [a *bevel* edge]. **—bev′eled** or **bev′elled,** *p.t.* & *p.p.;* **bev′el·ing** or **bev′el·ling,** *pr.p.*

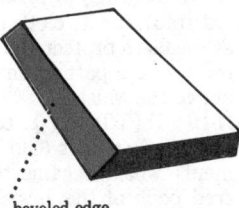

beveled edge

bev·er·age (bev′ər ij), *n.* any kind of drink, as milk, coffee, or lemonade.

bev·y (bev′ē), *n.* **1.** a group, as of women. **2.** a flock, especially of quail. **—bev′ies,** *pl.*

be·wail (bi wāl′), *v.* to weep over; complain about [to *bewail* one's bad luck].

be·ware (bi wer′), *v.* to be careful; be on one's

---

fat,   āpe,   cär,   ten,   ēven,   hit,   bīte,   gō,   hôrn,   tōōl,   book,   up,   fûr;
get,   joy,   yet,   chin,   she,   thin,   *th*en;   zh = s in pleasure;   ′ as in able (ā′b'l);
ə = a in ago,   e in agent,   i in sanity,   o in confess,   u in focus.

guard against [*Beware* of ice on the sidewalks.]

be·wil·der (bi wil/dər), *v.* to make confused; puzzle very much [The city's winding streets *bewildered* us.] —**be·wil/der·ment**, *n.*

be·witch (bi wich/), *v.* **1.** to use magic on; put a spell on [Circe *bewitched* Ulysses' companions and turned them into pigs.] **2.** to charm and delight very much; fascinate [The youth was *bewitched* by her beauty.] —**be·witch/ing**, *adj.*

be·yond (bi yänd/), *prep.* **1.** on the far side of; farther away than [The town is just *beyond* the hill.] **2.** later than [I stayed up *beyond* midnight.] **3.** outside the reach or power of [He is *beyond* help.] **4.** more or better than [He says nothing *beyond* what we already know.] —*adv.* farther away [The field is behind the house; the forest lies *beyond*.] —**the beyond** or **the great beyond,** whatever follows death.

Bhu·tan (bo͞o tän/), *n.* a country in the Himalayas, northeast of India.

bi-, a prefix meaning: **1.** having two [A *bicuspid* tooth has two points on its crown.] **2.** happening every two [A *biennial* election takes place every two years.] **3.** happening twice during every [*biannual* meetings held twice a year].

Bi, symbol for the chemical element *bismuth.*

bi·an·nu·al (bī an/yo͞o əl), *adj.* coming twice a year. —**bi·an/nu·al·ly**, *adv.*

bi·as (bī/əs), *n.* **1.** a slanting line cut or sewn across the weave of cloth. **2.** a leaning in favor of or against something or someone; partiality or prejudice. —*v.* to give a bias in thinking to; prejudice; influence [The jury had been *biased* by newspaper stories.] —**on the bias,** diagonally across the weave [cloth cut *on the bias*]. —**bi/ased** or **bi/assed**, *p.t. & p.p.;* **bi/as·ing** or **bi/as·sing**, *pr.p.*

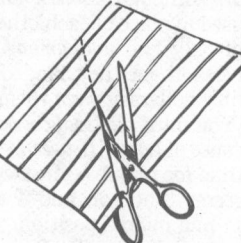

cutting on the bias

bib (bib), *n.* **1.** cloth tied around a child's neck at meals to protect the clothing. **2.** the part of an apron above the waist.

Bi·ble (bī/b'l), *n.* **1.** the collection of writings (Old Testament) which became the sacred book of the Jewish religion, or these writings along with the New Testament, which became the sacred book of the Christian religion. **2.** the sacred book of any religion [The Koran is the Moslem *Bible.*] —**Bib·li·cal** or **bib·li·cal** (bib/li k'l), *adj.*

bib

bib·li·og·ra·phy (bib/li äg/rə fē), *n.* a list of writings about a certain subject or by a certain author. —**bib/li·og/ra·phies**, *pl.* —**bib·li·o·graph·i·cal** (bib/li ə graf/i k'l), *adj.*

bi·cam·er·al (bī kam/ər əl), *adj.* having two groups in the lawmaking body [The *bicameral*

U.S. Congress is made up of the Senate and House of Representatives.]

bi·car·bon·ate of soda (bī kär/bə nit), baking soda.

bi·ceps (bī/seps), *n.* the large muscle in the front of the upper arm.

bick·er (bik/ər), *v.* to have a small quarrel over an unimportant matter; squabble.

biceps

bi·cus·pid (bī kus/pid), *n.* a tooth with two points on its top surface [An adult has eight *biscuspids.*] *See the picture.*

bi·cy·cle (bī/si k'l), *n.* a machine to ride on that has two wheels, one behind the other. It is moved by foot pedals and steered by bars. —*v.* to ride a bicycle. —**bi/cy·cled**, *p.t. & p.p.,* **bi/cy·cling**, *pr.p.* —**bi/cy·clist** (bī/si klist), *n.*

bicuspid

bid (bid), *v.* **1.** to command or ask [Do as you are *bidden.*] **2.** to tell [He *bade* his friend farewell.] **3.** to offer as the price for something [She *bid* ten dollars for the chair at the auction.] —*n.* **1.** a bidding of an amount; the amount bid [The builder whose *bid* for the work is the lowest will win the contract.] **2.** an attempt or try [a *bid* for fame]. —**bid fair,** to seem likely to [This winter *bids fair* to be a cold one.] —**bade** or **bid**, *p.t.;* **bid·den** (bid/'n) or **bid**, *p.p.* (for meaning 3, only *bid* is used as the *p.t. & p.p.*); **bid/ding**, *pr.p.*

bicycle

bid·der (bid/ər), *n.* a person who bids, as at an auction.

bide (bīd), *v.* **1.** to stay or wait. **2.** to dwell; live. *This word is now seldom used except in the phrase* **bide one's time,** meaning "to wait patiently for a chance." —**bid/ed** or **bode** (bōd), *p.t.;* **bid/ed**, *p.p.;* **bid/ing**, *pr.p.*

bi·en·ni·al (bī en/i əl), *adj.* **1.** happening once every two years [a *biennial* meeting]. **2.** lasting for two years [a *biennial* plant]. —*n.* a plant that lives for two years, as the pansy. It usually produces its flowers in the second year.

bier (bir), *n.* a stand on which a coffin or dead body is placed before or during a funeral.

bi·fo·cals (bī/fō k'lz), *n.pl.* eyeglasses in which each lens has two parts, one for seeing close things, as in reading, and the other for seeing things far away.

bifocals

big (big), *adj.* **1.** of

great size; large [a *big* cake; a *big* city]. **2.** loud [a *big* voice]. **3.** important; outstanding [a *big* day in his life]. **4.** showy and boastful; exaggerated [a lot of *big* talk]. **5.** noble; generous [a *big* heart]. —*adv.* in a showy or boastful way [to talk *big*]; also, in a broad way; showing imagination [Think *big!*]: *used only in everyday talk.* —**big'ger,** *compar.;* **big'gest,** *superl.* —**big'ness,** *n.*

big·a·my (big'ə mē), *n.* the crime of marrying someone while one is still married to another person. —**big'a·mist,** *n.* —**big'a·mous,** *adj.*

big·horn (big'hôrn), *n.* a wild sheep with long, curved horns, found in the Rocky Mountains.

bight (bīt), *n.* **1.** a loop in a rope. **2.** a curve in a coast line. **3.** a bay.

big·ot (big'ət), *n.* a person who stubbornly and without thinking holds to certain opinions and will not listen to other views; prejudiced and narrow-minded person. —**big'-ot·ed,** *adj.*

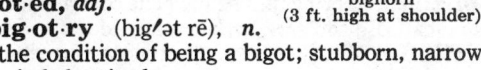

bighorn
(3 ft. high at shoulder)

big·ot·ry (big'ət rē), *n.* the condition of being a bigot; stubborn, narrow-minded attitude.

big top, a circus tent; also, the circus itself: *used only in everyday talk.*

bike (bīk), *n. & v.* bicycle: *used only in everyday talk.* —**biked,** *p.t. & p.p.;* **bik'ing,** *pr.p.*

bi·lat·er·al (bī lat'ər əl), *adj.* **1.** of, on, or having two sides. **2.** by or for two sides or parties [a *bilateral* treaty].

bile (bīl), *n.* **1.** the bitter, yellow or greenish fluid that is made by the liver and stored in the gall bladder. It helps in digestion. **2.** bad temper; anger.

bilge (bilj), *n.* **1.** the rounded, lower part of a ship's hold. **2.** the stale, dirty water that gathers there: also called **bilge water. 3.** nonsense: *slang in this meaning.*

bil·ious (bil'yəs), *adj.* **1.** having something wrong with the bile or liver. **2.** bad-tempered; cross. —**bil'ious·ness,** *n.*

bilk (bilk), *v.* to cheat or swindle.

bill (bil), *n.* **1.** a listing of money owed for certain goods or services [a grocery *bill*]. **2.** a list of things offered, as a menu or a theater program [a *bill* of fare]. **3.** an advertising poster or a handbill. **4.** a piece of paper money [a dollar *bill*]. **5.** a proposed law that is to be voted on by a group of lawmakers [a housing *bill* now before Congress]. —*v.* to send a bill to, showing money owed [This store *bills* us on the first day of the month.]

bill (bil), *n.* **1.** the horny jaws of a bird, usually coming out to a point; beak. **2.** a part like this, as a turtle's mouth. —*v.* to show affection: *used*

mostly in the phrase **bill and coo,** meaning "to act in a loving way."

bill·board (bil'bôrd), *n.* a large board outdoors, on which advertisements are posted.

bil·let (bil'it), *v.* to give soldiers lodging in private homes by military order [The troops were *billeted* in farms along the border.] —*n.* lodging gotten by military order.

bill·fold (bil'fōld), *n.* a thin, flat case for carrying paper money in the pocket; wallet.

bil·liards (bil'yərdz), *n.* a game played with hard balls on a special table covered with green felt and having cushioned edges. The balls are struck with a long stick called a cue.

bil·lion (bil'yən), *n. & adj.* **1.** in the United States and France, a thousand millions (1,000,000,000). **2.** in Great Britain and Germany, a million millions (1,000,000,000,000).

man playing billiards

Bill of Rights, the first ten amendments to the Constitution of the United States, which protect such rights as freedom of speech and religion.

bill of sale, a paper showing that something has been sold by one person to another.

bil·low (bil'ō), *n.* **1.** a large ocean wave. **2.** anything that sweeps along and swells like a wave [Great *billows* of smoke poured from the chimney.] —*v.* to swell out in billows [The sails *billowed* in the wind.] —**bil'low·y,** *adj.*

bil·ly (bil'ē), *n.* a short, heavy stick carried by some policemen. —**bil'lies,** *pl.*

billy goat, a male goat: *used only in everyday talk.*

bi·month·ly (bī munth'lē), *adj. & adv.* **1.** once every two months [A *bimonthly* magazine comes out six times a year.] **2.** twice a month: *in this meaning,* semimonthly *is the preferred word.*

bin (bin), *n.* an enclosed space for storing things, such as flour, coal, or tools.

bind (bīnd), *v.* **1.** to tie together, as with rope; tie tightly [*Bind* these logs together to make a raft.] **2.** to stick or fasten by sticking; hold [The swallow uses mud to *bind* its nest.] **3.** to bring or keep together by a feeling of love or duty [Sharing a favorite story *binds* the family together.] **4.** to hold or keep; tie down [What *binds* you to your job?] **5.** to force to do something because of a promise, law, or contract [The witness is *bound* by oath to tell the truth] **6.** to put a bandage on [The nurse will *bind* your wounds.] **7.** to fasten printed sheets together and put them between covers, thus making a book. **8.** to decorate or make stronger with a band of tape or thread [*Bind* the edges of the rug to keep them from raveling.] **9.** to constipate. —**bound,** *p.t. & p.p.;* **bind'ing,** *pr.p.*

bind·er (bīn′dər), *n.* **1.** a person who works in a bindery. **2.** a material that binds things together [Tar is used as a *binder* for gravel in paving.] **3.** a folder for holding sheets of paper together. **4.** the part of a reaper that ties the grain into bundles; also, a machine that both cuts and binds grain.

bind·er·y (bīn′dər ē), *n.* a place where books are bound. **—bind′er·ies,** *pl.*

bind·ing (bīn′ding), *adj.* that holds one to a promise or agreement [a *binding* contract]. **—n.** **1.** the covers and backing of a book. **2.** the work done in a bindery. **3.** a tape used in sewing to make seams and edges stronger.

bin·na·cle (bin′ə k'l), *n.* a box that holds a ship's compass, located near the steering wheel.

bin·oc·u·lars (bi näk′yə lərz), *n.pl.* a pair of small telescopes fastened together for use with both eyes [Field glasses and opera glasses are two kinds of *binoculars*.]

binoculars

bi·o·chem·is·try (bī′ō kem′is trē), *n.* the science that studies the chemistry of plant and animal life.

bi·o·de·grad·a·ble (bī′ō di grā′də b'l), *adj.* that is easily decomposed, especially by the action of bacteria [a *biodegradable* detergent].

bi·og·ra·pher (bī äg′rə fər), *n.* a person who writes a biography or biographies.

bi·og·ra·phy (bī äg′rə fē), *n.* the story of a person's life written by another person. **—bi·og′ra·phies,** *pl.* **—bi·o·graph·i·cal** (bī′ə graf′i k'l), *adj.*

bi·o·log·i·cal (bī′ə läj′i k'l), *adj.* having to do with biology. **—bi′o·log′i·cal·ly,** *adv.*

bi·ol·o·gy (bī äl′ə jē), *n.* the science of plants and animals; the study of living things and the way they live and grow. **—bi·ol′o·gist,** *n.*

bi·par·ti·san (bī pär′tə z'n), *adj.* made up of or by two political parties [a *bipartisan* plan].

bi·ped (bī′ped), *n.* any animal with only two legs [Men and birds are *bipeds*.]

bi·plane (bī′plān), *n.* the earlier type of airplane with two main wings, one above the other.

birch (bûrch), *n.* **1.** a tree that has a thin, smooth bark that is easily peeled in papery strips from the trunk. **2.** its hard wood, used in making furniture. **3.** a birch rod or a bunch of birch twigs, used for whipping. **—v.** to whip with a birch.

birch (bark and leaves)

bird (bûrd), *n.* **1.** a warm-blooded animal that has a backbone, two feet, and wings, and is covered with feathers. Birds lay eggs and can usually fly. **2.** the feather-tipped cork used in the game of badminton; shut-

tlecock. **3.** a person; especially, an odd sort of person: *slang in this meaning.* **—birds of a feather,** people with the same tastes or interests.

bird·bath (bûrd′bath), *n.* a basin of water set on a stand outdoors, for birds to bathe in.

bird dog, a dog trained to hunt birds.

bird·ie (bûr′dē), *n.* **1.** a small bird: *a child's word.* **2.** in the game of golf, a score of one stroke less than par for any hole.

bird·lime (bûrd′līm), *n.* a sticky substance spread on twigs to catch birds.

bird of paradise, a brightly colored bird of New Guinea, with long, lacy tail feathers.

bird of prey, a bird that kills other animals for food, as the eagle or hawk.

bird's-eye (bûrdz′ī′), *adj.* seen from high above [We get a *bird's-eye* view from the tower.]

Bir·ming·ham (bûr′ming ham), *n.* **1.** a city in north central Alabama. **2.** (bûr′ming əm), a city in central England.

birth (bûrth), *n.* **1.** the act of being born [the anniversary of Lincoln's *birth*]. **2.** origin or background [Alexander Hamilton was West Indian by *birth*.] **3.** the beginning of something new [1942 marks the *birth* of the Atomic Age.] **—give birth to,** to bring into being [The cow *gave birth to* a calf. Edison *gave birth to* many ideas.]

birth·day (bûrth′dā), *n.* **1.** the day on which a person is born or something is begun. **2.** the anniversary of this day.

birth·mark (bûrth′märk), *n.* a mark or spot found on the skin at birth.

birth·place (bûrth′plās), *n.* the place where a person was born or a thing had its beginning.

birth rate, the average number of births during a year for each thousand of the total number of people in any country, area, or group.

birth·right (bûrth′rīt), *n.* the rights that a person has because he was born in a certain family or place or because he was the first-born son [Freedom of speech is part of our American *birthright*. Esau sold his *birthright* to his younger brother, Jacob.]

Bis·cay, Bay of (bis′kā), a bay formed by the Atlantic Ocean north of Spain and west of France.

bis·cuit (bis′kit), *n.* **1.** a small bread roll made of dough quickly raised with baking powder. **2.** a cracker or cooky: *mainly a British meaning.*

bi·sect (bī sekt′), *v.* **1.** to cut into two parts [Budapest is *bisected* by the Danube River.] **2.** to divide into two equal parts [A circle is *bisected* by its diameter.]

bish·op (bish′əp), *n.* **1.** a minister or priest of high rank, who is the head of a church district or diocese.

bisected angle

2. a chess piece that can move diagonally across any number of empty squares.

bish·op·ric (bish′əp rik), *n.* **1.** the church district of a bishop; diocese. **2.** the position or rank of a bishop.

Bis·marck (biz′märk), *n.* the capital of North Dakota.

Bismarck, Otto von, 1815–1898; German chancellor who helped found the German Empire.

bis·muth (biz′məth), *n.* a chemical element that is a brittle, grayish-white metal. Bismuth is used in alloys of low melting point, and its salts are used in medicine.

bi·son (bī′s'n *or* bī′z'n), *n.* a wild animal of the ox family, with a shaggy mane, short, curved horns, and a humped back. The American bison is often called a *buffalo.* —**bi′son,** *pl.*

bison (10 ft. long)

bit (bit), *n.* **1.** a metal bar that is the part of a bridle that fits in a horse's mouth. It is used for controlling the horse. **2.** the cutting part of a drilling or boring tool. See the picture of **brace and bit. 3.** the part of a key that turns the lock.

bit (bit), *n.* **1.** a small piece or amount [a *bit* of candy; torn to *bits*]. **2.** a short time; moment: *used only in everyday talk* [Wait a *bit* longer.] —*adj.* very small [a *bit* part in a movie]. —**a bit of,** rather; something of [He's *a bit of* a bully.] —**bit by bit,** little by little; gradually. —**two bits,** twenty-five cents (*four bits* is fifty cents, etc.): *used only in everyday talk.*

bitch (bich), *n.* a female dog, wolf, etc.

bite (bīt), *v.* **1.** to seize, snap at, or cut with the teeth or with parts like jaws [The dog *bit* the mailman's leg. The trap *bit* into his foot. Don't *bite* off such large pieces.] **2.** to sting, as a mosquito or bee. **3.** to hurt in a sharp, stinging way [The cold wind *bites* my face.] **4.** to press hard into; grip [The wheels of the car *bit* into the snow.] **5.** to be tricked into swallowing bait [The fish won't *bite.*] —*n.* **1.** the act of biting [The *bite* of a dog can be dangerous.] **2.** a wound or sting from biting [arms covered with mosquito *bites*]. **3.** a stinging or painful feeling [the *bite* of an October wind]. **4.** a mouthful [Don't take such big *bites.*] **5.** a small meal; snack: *used only in everyday talk.* **6.** the way the upper and lower teeth come together [She wears braces to correct her *bite.*] —**bite the dust,** to be killed, as in fighting. —**bit** (bit), *p.t.;* **bit′ten** or **bit,** *p.p.;* **bit′ing,** *pr.p.*

bit·ing (bīt′ing), *adj.* sharp, stinging, or cutting [a *biting* wind; a *biting* criticism].

bit·ten (bit′'n), a past participle of **bite.**

bit·ter (bit′ər), *adj.* **1.** having a strong, often unpleasant taste [The seed in a peach pit is *bitter.*] **2.** full of sorrow, pain, or discomfort [They suffered *bitter* hardships during the war.] **3.** sharp or stinging [a *bitter* wind]. **4.** with strong feelings of hatred or dislike [*bitter* enemies]. —*adv.* in a bitter or unpleasant way [The night was *bitter* cold.] —**bit′ter·ly,** *adv.* —**bit′ter·ness,** *n.*

bit·tern (bit′ərn), *n.* a bird that looks like a small heron and lives in marshes. It has a loud, deep, hollow cry.

bit·ter·sweet (bit′ər swēt′), *n.* **1.** a poisonous vine with purple flowers and red berries that taste bitter and sweet. **2.** a woody vine with bright orange seedcases that split open to show red seeds. —*adj.* both bitter and sweet; also, both sad and happy.

bittern (2 ft. long)

bi·tu·men (bi tōō′mən *or* bi-tyōō′mən), *n.* a mineral that burns easily and is found in nature as asphalt. It can also be made from petroleum or coal.

bi·tu·mi·nous coal (bi tōō′mə nəs *or* bi-tyōō′mə nəs), soft coal, which burns easily and with more smoke than hard coal (anthracite).

bi·valve (bī′valv), *n.* a water animal whose soft, boneless body is enclosed in a shell of two parts hinged together, as a clam or oyster.

biv·ou·ac (biv′ōō ak′ *or* biv′wak), *n.* a camp   bittersweet (*meaning 2*) of soldiers outdoors with little or no shelter, set up for a short time. —*v.* to camp outdoors. —**biv′-ou·acked′,** *p.t. & p.p.;* **biv′ou·ack′ing,** *pr.p.*

bi·week·ly (bī wēk′lē), *adj. & adv.* once every two weeks.

bi·zarre (bi zär′), *adj.* very odd or unusual; queer; fantastic; grotesque.

blab (blab), *v.* **1.** to tell a secret; tattle. **2.** to gossip. —**blabbed,** *p.t. & p.p.;* **blab′bing,** *pr.p.*

black (blak), *adj.* **1.** opposite of white; of the color of coal or pitch. Although we speak of black as a color, it is really the absence of all color. A surface is black only when it absorbs all the light rays that make color and reflects none back. **2.** without any light [a *black* and moonless night]. **3.** having dark-colored skin and hair; Negro. **4.** evil; wicked [*black* deeds]. **5.** full of sorrow or suffering; sad; unhappy; gloomy [*black* thoughts; a *black* day]. **6.** angry or sullen [*black* looks]. —*n.* **1.** black color, black paint, black dye, etc. **2.** black clothes, especially when worn in mourning. **3.** a person with a dark-colored skin; Negro: *black* is now the word that many people prefer. —*v.* **1.** to make black; blacken. **2.** to polish with blacking. —**black out, 1.** to put out or hide all lights that might be seen by an enemy at night. **2.** to become unconscious. —**black′ness,** *n.*

black-and-blue (blak′ən blōō′), *adj.* discolored or turned dark, as by a bruise or bruises.

black·ball (blak′bôl), *v.* to vote against letting a certain person join a club, etc.

black·ber·ry (blak′ber′ē), *n.* **1.** the small, dark purple or black fruit of a prickly bush or vine. **2.** this bush or vine. —**black′ber′ries,** *pl.*

black·bird (blak′bŭrd), *n.* any of various birds such as the cowbird and red-winged blackbird. All male blackbirds have black feathers.

black·board (blak′bôrd), *n.* a large piece of slate or other smooth, dark material on which to write or draw with chalk.

black·en (blak′′n), *v.* **1.** to make or become black; darken [Rain clouds *blacken* the sky.] **2.** to hurt by telling bad things about one.

black eye, a bruise on the flesh around the eye, as from a hard blow.

black-eyed Su·san (blak′- id sōō′z′n), a plant having yellow flowers like daisies, with a dark-brown center.

black·guard (blag′ərd *or* blag′ärd), *n.* a wicked person; scoundrel; villain.

black·head (blak′hed), *n.* a pimple with a black tip, caused by a bit of fatty matter clogging a pore.

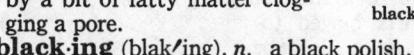

black eye

black·ing (blak′ing), *n.* a black polish.

black·jack (blak′jak), *n.* **1.** a short, thick club that is covered with leather and has a flexible handle. It is used as a hitting weapon. **2.** a card game in which each player tries to get cards that add up to 21 points. —*v.* to hit with a blackjack.

black·list (blak′list′), *v.* to put a person's name on a black list.

black list, a list of people that one does not like or that are to be punished in some way.

black·mail (blak′māl), *n.* **1.** the crime of threatening to tell something harmful about someone unless he pays some money. **2.** money gotten in this way. —*v.* to get or try to get such money from someone.

black·out (blak′out), *n.* **1.** a putting out or hiding of all lights that might be seen by an enemy at night. **2.** a becoming unconscious.

Black Sea, a sea south of the Soviet Union and north of Turkey.

black sheep, a person who is considered to be not so respectable or successful as the other members of his family or group.

black·smith (blak′smith), *n.* a man who makes or fixes iron things by heating them in a forge and then hammering them on an anvil. A blacksmith often makes and fits horseshoes.

black·snake (blak′snāk), *n.* a harmless, dark-colored snake found in North America.

black·thorn (blak′thôrn), *n.* **1.** a shrub that grows in Europe and has thorns and white flowers. Its purple fruit looks like a plum and is called a *sloe.* **2.** a cane or stick made from its stem.

black·top (blak′täp), *n.* an asphalt mixture for paving roads. —*v.* to cover with blacktop. *For principal parts see* **top.**

black widow, a black spider with red marks on its belly. The female is poisonous and eats its mate.

blad·der (blad′ər), *n.* **1.** a part like a bag inside the body that holds a fluid; especially, the organ that collects the urine coming from the kidneys. **2.** something like this bag [a football *bladder*].

blade (blād), *n.* **1.** a broad, flat part of something [the *blade* of an oar; the shoulder *blade*]. **2.** the sharp, cutting part of a knife, saw, sword, etc. **3.** a sword or a swordsman. **4.** a gay young man. **5.** the leaf of grass or of a cereal. **6.** the broad, flat part of any leaf.

blame (blām), *v.* **1.** to say or think that someone or something is the cause of what is wrong or bad [Don't *blame* others for your own mistakes.] **2.** to find fault with; disapprove of; criticize [I can't *blame* you for being angry.] —*n.* **1.** the fact of being responsible for what is wrong or bad [I will take the *blame* for the broken window.] **2.** the act of blaming or finding fault [a letter full of *blame*]. —**be to blame,** to be the one who ought to be blamed. —**blamed,** *p.t. & p.p.;* **blam′ing,** *pr.p.*

blame·less (blām′lis), *adj.* not deserving to be blamed; having done no wrong; innocent.

blame·worth·y (blām′wŭr′thē), *adj.* deserving to be blamed; having done wrong.

blanch (blanch), *v.* **1.** to turn pale; lose color in the face [to *blanch* with fear]. **2.** to make lighter in color; whiten [Gardeners *blanch* celery by covering the stalks with soil.] **3.** to remove the skin of almonds, etc. with boiling water.

bland (bland), *adj.* **1.** pleasant and polite [His *bland* manner won many friends.] **2.** smooth and mild; not sharp [Custard is a *bland* food]. —**bland′ly,** *adv.* —**bland′ness,** *n.*

blan·dish·ment (blan′dish mənt), *n.* coaxing or flattery to get what one wants [Delilah's *blandishments* lured Samson to his death.]

blank (blangk), *adj.* **1.** not marked or written on [a *blank* sheet of paper]. **2.** showing no expression or interest [His face remained *blank*.] **3.** empty of any thought [It is hard to keep your mind *blank*.] —*n.* **1.** a paper with empty spaces to be written in [an application *blank*]. **2.** an empty space on such a paper [Fill in all the *blanks*.] **3.** a cartridge that has no bullet, fired only to make a noise: the full name is **blank car·tridge.** —**blank′ly,** *adv.* —**blank′ness,** *n.*

blan·ket (blang′kit), *n.* **1.** a large, soft piece of cloth used as a covering for warmth, especially in bed. **2.** any covering that is spread out [a *blanket* of snow]. —*adj.* taking care of a number of things; general [The captain issued *blanket* instructions to cover all emergencies.] —*v.* to cover with a blanket [Leaves *blanketed* the lawn.]

blare (bler), *v.* to sound out with loud, harsh tones [Car horns *blared*.] —*n.* such a loud, harsh sound. —**blared,** *p.t. & p.p.;* **blar′ing,** *pr.p.*

blar·ney (blär′nē), *n.* smooth talk used in flattering or coaxing [People who kiss a famous stone in Blarney Castle in Ireland are supposed to become skilled at using *blarney*.]

bla·sé (blä zā′), *adj.* bored with the pleasures of life; never surprised or pleased.

blas·pheme (blas fēm′), *v.* to show lack of

respect for God or for anything considered sacred; curse or swear. **—blas·phemed′,** *p.t. & p.p.;* **blas·phem′ing,** *pr.p.*

blas·phe·my (blas′fi mē), *n.* words or action showing a lack of respect for God or for anything considered sacred. **—blas′phe·mies,** *pl.* **—blas′phe·mous,** *adj.*

blast (blast), *n.* **1.** a strong rush of air or gust of wind. **2.** the sound of a rush of air, as through a trumpet or factory whistle. **3.** an explosion, as of dynamite; also, the amount of dynamite, etc. used. **—v. 1.** to blow up with dynamite, etc. [to *blast* rock]. **2.** to blight or destroy [The sudden frost *blasted* our lemon tree.] **—at full blast,** at full speed or in full operation.

blast furnace, a tall furnace for smelting ore, in which a blast of air is used to produce the very high heat needed.

bla·tant (blā′t'nt), *adj.* very loud and noisy, in a vulgar way. **—bla′tan·cy,** *n.* **—bla′tant·ly,** *adv.*

blaze (blāz), *n.* **1.** a bright flame or fire. **2.** any bright light [the *blaze* of searchlights]. **3.** a sudden or showy outburst; flash [a *blaze* of glory]. **4.** a bright display [The garden was a *blaze* of color.] **—v. 1.** to burn brightly. **2.** to shine brightly [At night the carnival *blazed* with lights.] **3.** to burst out with strong feeling [to *blaze* with anger]. **—blazed,** *p.t. & p.p.;* **blaz′ing,** *pr.p.*

blaze (blāz), *n.* **1.** a white spot on the face of a horse, etc. **2.** a mark made on a tree by cutting off a piece of bark [We marked the trail by cutting *blazes* as we went along.] **—v.** to mark a tree or trail with blazes. **—blazed,** *p.t. & p.p.;* **blaz′ing,** *pr.p.*

blaz·er (blāz′ər), *n.* a lightweight sports jacket, often brightly colored.

bla·zon (blā′z'n), *v.* **1.** to decorate or paint a coat of arms. **2.** to make known all over [a deed that *blazoned* his name far and wide]. **—n.** a coat of arms.

blaze

bldg., abbreviation for **building.**

bleach (blēch), *v.* to make or become white or pale by means of chemicals or by the action of sunshine. **—n.** any chemical used in bleaching.

bleach·ers (blēch′ərz), *n.pl.* a section of seats, usually bare benches without a roof, for watching outdoor sports.

bleak (blēk), *adj.* **1.** open to wind and cold; not sheltered; bare [the *bleak* plains]. **2.** cold and cutting; harsh [a

bleachers

bleak wind]. **3.** not cheerful; gloomy [a *bleak* future]. **—bleak′ly,** *adv.* **—bleak′ness,** *n.*

blear (blir), *v.* to make dim or blurred.

blear·y (blir′ē), *adj.* made dim or blurred [His eyes were *bleary* from lack of sleep.] **—blear′i·er,** *compar.;* **blear′i·est,** *superl.*

bleat (blēt), *v.* **1.** to make the sound of a sheep, goat, or calf. **2.** to talk or say in a weak, trembling voice. **—n.** the sound made in bleating.

bled (bled), past tense and past participle of **bleed.**

bleed (blēd), *v.* **1.** to lose blood [The wound stopped *bleeding*.] **2.** to feel pain, grief, or sympathy [Her heart *bleeds* for the poor.] **3.** to draw blood from [In earlier times, doctors often *bled* people to try to make them well.] **4.** to get money from, as by blackmail: *used only in everyday talk.* **—bled,** *p.t. & p.p.;* **bleed′ing,** *pr.p.*

blem·ish (blem′ish), *n.* a mark that spoils or damages; flaw; defect [skin *blemishes;* a *blemish* in his character]. **—v.** to put a blemish on.

blench (blench), *v.* to shrink back, as in fear.

blend (blend), *v.* **1.** to mix different kinds together in order to get a certain flavor, color, etc. [to *blend* tea or paint]. **2.** to come together or mix so that the parts are no longer distinct [The sky *blended* with the sea at the horizon.] **3.** to go well together; be in harmony [Her blue sweater *blends* with her gray skirt.] **—n.** a mixture of different kinds [a *blend* of coffee].

bless (bles), *v.* **1.** to make or call holy. **2.** to ask God's favor for [The minister *blessed* the congregation.] **3.** to bring happiness or good fortune to [God *bless* you!] **4.** to praise or glorify [to *bless* the Lord]. *Bless* is often used in exclamations of mild surprise [*Bless* me if it isn't Jane!] **—blessed** (blest) or, less often, **blest,** *p.t. & p.p.;* **bless′ing,** *pr.p.*

bless·ed (bles′id *or* blest), *adj.* **1.** holy; sacred. **2.** full of bliss; fortunate [*blessed* in having two fine children]. **—bless′ed·ness,** *n.*

bless·ing (bles′ing), *n.* **1.** a prayer asking God's favor for something. **2.** good wishes or approval [The parents gave the engaged couple their *blessing*.] **3.** anything that brings joy or comfort [Rain now would be a *blessing*.]

blest (blest) a past tense and past participle of **bless.**

blew (blōō), past tense of **blow.**

blight (blīt), *n.* **1.** any disease that hurts or kills plants. **2.** anything that hurts or destroys [Slums are a *blight* on a city.] **—v.** to damage or destroy; ruin [Our hopes were *blighted*.]

blimp (blimp), *n.* a small, egg-shaped airship: *used only in everyday talk.*

blind (blīnd), *adj.* **1.** not able to see; having no sight. **2.** not able to notice, understand, or judge [The father was *blind* to his son's faults.] **3.** hidden from sight [a *blind* stitch]. **4.** having no opening [a *blind* wall]. **5.** closed at one end [a *blind* alley]. **6.** done by instruments only [*blind* flying in a fog]. —v. 1. to make blind; make unable to see. 2. to make unable to understand or judge well [His eagerness *blinded* him to the danger.] —n. 1. a window shade of stiffened cloth, metal slats, etc. 2. a person or thing used to mislead. —**blind′ly,** adv. —**blind′ness,** n.

blind·ers (blīn′dərz), n.pl. two leather flaps that keep a horse from see-ing to the sides.

blind·fold (blīnd′fōld), v. to cover someone's eyes, as by tying a cloth around the head. —adj. with the eyes covered; not seeing. —n. a cloth used to cover the eyes.

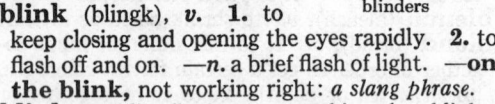

blinders

blind·man's buff (blīnd′-manz buf′), a game in which a blindfolded player has to catch another player and then tell who it is.

blink (blingk), v. 1. to keep closing and opening the eyes rapidly. 2. to flash off and on. —n. a brief flash of light. —**on the blink,** not working right: *a slang phrase.*

blink·er (bling′kər), n. something that blinks; especially, a flashing signal that warns.

bliss (blis), n. great joy or happiness.

bliss·ful (blis′fəl), adj. full of great joy or happiness [a *blissful* marriage].

blis·ter (blis′tər), n. 1. a small swollen place on the skin, filled with watery matter and caused by a burn or by rubbing. 2. any part that swells like a blister [*blisters* in a coat of paint]. —v. 1. to make blisters on [The sun *blistered* my nose.] 2. to form blisters [Old paint may *blister.*]

blithe (blīth), adj. gay; carefree [Shelley called the skylark a "*blithe* spirit."] —**blithe′ly,** adv.

blithe·some (blīth′səm), adj. blithe; gay.

bliz·zard (bliz′ərd), n. a heavy snowstorm with a very strong wind.

bloat (blōt), v. to puff up as when swollen with water or air. —**bloat′ed,** adj.

blob (bläb), n. a small lump of something soft and moist [a *blob* of jelly].

bloc (bläk), n. a group of people or nations working together for a particular purpose.

block (bläk), n. 1. a thick piece of wood, stone, etc., with some flat sur-faces [a butcher's *block;* a set of toy *blocks*]. 2. the platform used at an auction. 3. a mold on which things are shaped [a hat *block*]. 4. anything that stops movement or progress [A *block* behind the back wheels will keep the car from moving. Laziness is a *block* to suc-cess.] 5. a number of things thought of as a single unit [We have re-served a *block* of seats for the concert.] 6. the

butcher's block

square formed by four streets [The city hall takes up the whole *block.*] 7. the distance from one street to the next along a street that crosses them. 8. a pulley in a frame. —v. 1. to stop movement or progress [The fallen tree *blocked* the path.] 2. to shape [*Block* the sweater after you wash it.] —**block in** or **block out,** to sketch in a rough, quick way; plan an outline. —**block up,** to fill up so that nothing can pass through.

block·ade (blä kād′), n. a shutting off of a place by enemy troops or warships to keep people or supplies from moving in or out. —v. to put under a blockade. —**run the blockade,** to break through a blockade. —**block·ad′ed,** p.t. & p.p.; **block·ad′ing,** pr.p.

block and tackle, pulley blocks and ropes, used for lifting large, heavy ob-jects.

block·head (bläk′hed), n. a stupid person.

block·house (bläk′hous), n. a strong wooden fort with openings in the walls to shoot from and a second story that sticks out.

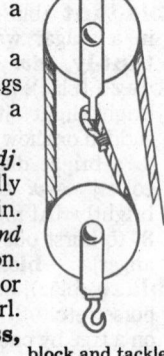

block and tackle

blond or **blonde** (bländ), adj. 1. having light-colored, especially yellow, hair and a very light skin. 2. light-colored [*blond* hair; *blond* furniture]. —n. a blond person. *Blond* is usually used of a man or boy and *blonde* of a woman or girl. —**blond′ness** or **blonde′ness,** n.

blood (blud), n. 1. the red liquid that is pumped through the arteries and veins by the heart. The blood carries oxygen and cell-building ma-terial to the body tissues and carries carbon dioxide and waste matter away from them. 2. ancestors or family line; descent: this meaning is based on the false idea that the blood of related persons has something special that shows this relationship [They are of the same *blood.*] —**bad blood,** anger; hatred. —**in cold blood,** on purpose, but without anger or other strong feeling [to kill *in cold blood*].

blood·cur·dling (blud′kŭr′dling), adj. very frightening [a *bloodcurdling* scream].

blood·ed (blud′id), adj. of fine stock or breed [a *blooded* horse].

blood·hound (blud′hound), n. a large dog with a wrinkled face and long, drooping ears. Bloodhounds have a keen sense of smell and are often used in tracking escaped pris-oners.

blood·less (blud′lis), adj. 1. without blood or without enough blood; pale [*bloodless* cheeks]. 2. without life; dead. 3. without killing [a *bloodless* revolution].

bloodhound (2 ft. high)

blood poisoning, a diseased condition of the blood caused by germs or toxins.

blood pressure, the pressure of the blood against the walls of the arteries and other blood vessels. It varies according to age, health, etc.

blood·shed (blud′shed), *n.* the shedding of blood; killing [War brings much *bloodshed*.]

blood·shot (blud′shät), *adj.* red because the small blood vessels are swollen or broken [*bloodshot* eyes].

blood·suck·er (blud′suk′ər), *n.* **1.** a leech or other animal that sucks blood. **2.** a person who uses his power to get all he can from others.

blood·thirst·y (blud′thŭrs′tē), *adj.* eager to hurt or kill; murderous.

blood vessel, any of the many tubes in the body through which the blood flows; any artery, vein, or capillary.

blood·y (blud′ē), *adj.* **1.** full of or covered with blood [a *bloody* nose]. **2.** with much killing or wounding [a *bloody* battle]. **3.** bloodthirsty. —*v.* to cover or smear with blood. —**blood′i·er,** *compar.*; **blood′i·est,** *superl.* —**blood′ied,** *p.t. & p.p.*; **blood′y·ing,** *pr.p.*

bloom (bloom), *n.* **1.** a flower or blossom. **2.** the time or condition of bearing blossoms [The lilies are in *bloom* again.] **3.** a time or condition of beauty, freshness, or growth [She was in the *bloom* of girlhood.] **4.** the healthy glow of youth [the *bloom* on her cheeks]. **5.** the powdery coating on certain fruits, as the plum or grape. —*v.* **1.** to bear blossoms [Tulips *bloom* in the spring.] **2.** to be healthy and fresh; be at one's best [The children *bloomed* at camp this summer.]

bloom·ers (bloom′ərz), *n.pl.* **1.** short baggy pants fitting snugly at the waist and thighs, worn by girls for sports. **2.** an undergarment somewhat like this.

blos·som (bläs′əm), *n.* **1.** a flower, especially of a plant that bears fruit [apple *blossoms*]. **2.** a condition or time of flowering [The cherry trees are in *blossom*.] —*v.* **1.** to bear blossoms; bloom. **2.** to unfold or develop [The ugly duckling *blossomed* into a beautiful swan.]

blot (blät), *n.* **1.** a spot or stain, especially of ink. **2.** anything that spoils or mars [That shack is a *blot* on the landscape.] —*v.* **1.** to make blots on; spot; stain [The ink ran and *blotted* the writing.] **2.** to erase, hide, or get rid of [These memories were soon *blotted* from her mind.] **3.** to dry by soaking up the wet liquid [You can *blot* ink with a piece of soft paper.] —**blot′ted,** *p.t. & p.p.*; **blot′ting,** *pr.p.*

blotch (bläch), *n.* **1.** any spot or patch that spoils the even color or smoothness of the skin. **2.** any large spot or stain. —*v.* to mark with blotches. —**blotch′y,** *adj.*

blot·ter (blät′ər), *n.* **1.** a piece of thick, soft paper used to blot ink dry. **2.** a book for writing down things as they happen [A police *blotter* is a record of arrests and charges.]

blouse (blous), *n.* **1.** a loose outer garment like a shirt, worn by women and children. **2.** the jacket of a military uniform.

blouse

blow (blō), *v.* **1.** to move with some force, as air [There is a wind *blowing*.] **2.** to force air out, as from the mouth [*Blow* on your hands to warm them.] **3.** to force air into or through in order to clear [to *blow* one's nose]. **4.** to breathe hard and fast; pant. **5.** to make sound by blowing or being blown [The noon whistle is *blowing*. *Blow* your trumpet.] **6.** to be carried by the wind [My hat suddenly *blew* off.] **7.** to drive by blowing [The fan *blew* the paper out the window.] **8.** to form or cause to swell by forcing in air or gas [to *blow* bubbles]. —*n.* **1.** the act of blowing. **2.** a strong wind; gale. —**blow out, 1.** to put out a fire or flame by blowing. **2.** to burst suddenly, as a tire. **3.** to melt, as a fuse, from too much electric current. —**blow over, 1.** to move away, as rain clouds. **2.** to pass over; be forgotten. —**blow up, 1.** to fill with air or gas, as a balloon. **2.** to burst or explode. **3.** to lose one's temper: *used only in everyday talk.* —**blew,** *p.t.*; **blown,** *p.p.*; **blow′ing,** *pr.p.*

blow (blō), *n.* **1.** a hard hit, as with the fist. **2.** a sudden attack [One swift *blow* can win the battle.] **3.** a sudden misfortune; shock [His death was a great *blow* to all of us.] —**come to blows,** to begin fighting.

blow·er (blō′ər), *n.* **1.** a person who blows [a glass *blower*]. **2.** a fan, etc. for blowing air, as from a furnace.

blow·gun (blō′gun), *n.* a long tube through which darts are blown by mouth.

blown (blōn), past participle of **blow.** —*adj.* out of breath [*blown* from running].

blow·out (blō′out), *n.* the bursting of a tire.

blow·pipe (blō′pīp), *n.* a tube for blowing air or gas into a flame to make it hotter.

blow·torch (blō′tôrch), *n.* a small torch that shoots out a hot flame. It is used to melt metal, burn off old paint, etc.

blowtorch

blub·ber (blub′ər), *n.* the fat of whales and other sea animals, from which an oil is gotten. —*v.* to weep loudly.

bludg·eon (bluj′ən), *n.* a short club with a thick, heavy end. —*v.* **1.** to hit with a bludgeon. **2.** to threaten or bully.

blue (bloo), *adj.* **1.** having the color of the clear sky or the deep sea. **2.** feeling sad or gloomy; in low spirits. —*n.* **1.** the color of the clear sky or the deep sea. **2.** any blue paint or dye. **3.** anything colored blue, as the sky or the sea. —*v.* to use bluing on laundry. **—out of the blue,** suddenly and without being expected; as if from the sky. **—the blues, 1.** a sad, gloomy feeling: *used only in everyday talk.* **2.** a type of Negro folk song, having a slow jazz rhythm and sad words. **—blu′er,** *compar.;* **blu′est,** *superl.* **—blued,** *p.t. & p.p.;* **blu′ing** or **blue′ing,** *pr.p.*

blue·bell (blōō′bel), *n.* any of several plants that have blue flowers shaped like bells.

blue·ber·ry (blōō′ber′ē), *n.* **1.** a small, round, dark blue berry that is eaten. **2.** the shrub on which it grows. **—blue′ber′ries,** *pl.*

blue·bird (blōō′bûrd), *n.* a small songbird of North America that has a blue back and wings.

blue·bon·net (blōō′bän′it), *n.* a small wild flower of the pea family, having blue blossoms.

blue·bot·tle (blōō′bät′'l), *n.* a large, hairy fly with a shiny blue body.

blue·fish ((blōō′fish), *n.* a silvery-blue sea fish that is used for food.

blue·grass (blōō′gras), *n.* a grass with bluish-green stems.

blue·jack·et (blōō′jak′it), *n.* a sailor in the navy.

blue·jay (blōō′jā), *n.* a bird with a blue back and a crest of feathers on its head. It has a loud, rough call. Also written **blue jay.**

blue laws, strict, harsh laws like those passed by the Puritans; especially, laws that forbid dancing, shows, sports, etc. on Sunday.

blue·print (blōō′print), *n.* a photographic copy, as of the plans for a building. It has white lines and letters on a blue background.

bluejay (11 in. long)

blue ribbon, first prize in a competition.

blu·et (blōō′it), *n.* a small plant that grows in low tufts and has blue flowers.

bluff (bluf), *v.* to fool or try to fool by acting very sure of oneself. —*n.* **1.** an act of bluffing [His threat is just a *bluff.*] **2.** a person who bluffs.

bluff (bluf), *n.* a high, steep bank or cliff. **—adj. 1.** having a broad, flat front that slopes steeply [*bluff* river banks]. **2.** rough and frank; blunt.

blu·ing or **blue·ing** (blōō′ing), *n.* a blue dye put into the rinse water when doing laundry. It keeps white fabrics from turning yellow.

blu·ish (blōō′ish), *adj.* somewhat blue.

blun·der (blun′dər), *n.* a foolish or stupid mistake. —*v.* **1.** to make such a mistake. **2.** to move clumsily or carelessly; stumble.

blun·der·buss (blun′dər bus), *n.* a short gun with a wide muzzle, used about 300 years ago.

blunderbuss

blunt (blunt), *adj.* **1.** having a dull edge or point; not sharp [a *blunt* ax]. **2.** speaking plainly and honestly, without trying to be polite [His *blunt* reply was "I don't like you."] —*v.* to

make dull [The knife was *blunted* from long use.] **—blunt′ly,** *adv.* **—blunt′ness,** *n.*

blur (blûr), *v.* **1.** to make less clear or sharp; confuse [The face in the picture is *blurred*. The medicine *blurred* his sight.] **2.** to smear or smudge [His leaking pen *blurred* the paper.] —*n.* **1.** a being blurred or unclear; dim or confused condition. **2.** a stain or blot. **—blurred,** *p.t. & p.p.;* **blur′ring,** *pr.p.*

blurt (blûrt), *v.* to say suddenly without stopping to think [to *blurt* out a secret].

blush (blush), *v.* to become red in the face, as from shyness or shame [Helen *blushed* at the compliment.] —*n.* **1.** a reddening of the face, as from shyness or shame. **2.** a rosy color [the *blush* of dawn]. **—at first blush,** without stopping to think further.

blus·ter (blus′tər), *v.* **1.** to blow in a stormy way [*blustering* winds]. **2.** to speak in a noisy, boastful, or bullying way. —*n.* **1.** stormy noise. **2.** noisy or boastful talk. **—blus′ter·y,** *adj.*

blvd., abbreviation for **boulevard.**

bo·a (bō′ə), *n.* **1.** a very large tropical snake that winds about its prey and crushes it to death. The python is a kind of boa. **2.** a long, fluffy scarf of feathers, etc., worn by women.

boa con·stric·tor (kən strik′tər), a kind of boa that reaches a length of 10 to 15 feet.

boar (bôr), *n.* **1.** a male pig. **2.** a wild pig of Europe, Africa, and Asia.

board (bôrd), *n.* **1.** a long, broad, flat piece of sawed wood, used in building. **2.** a flat piece of wood or other hard material made for a special use [a checker *board;* a bulletin *board;* an ironing *board*]. **3.** a table at which meals are eaten. **4.** food served at a table; especially, meals given regularly for pay. **5.** a group of people who manage or control a business, school, department, etc. [*board* of education]. **6.** the side of a ship [to jump over*board*]. —*v.* **1.** to cover up with boards [The windows of the old house were *boarded* up.] **2.** to give or get meals, or room and meals, regularly for pay. **3.** to get on a ship, airplane, bus, etc. **—on board,** on a ship, etc.

ironing board

board·er (bôr′dər), *n.* a person who lives, or eats his meals. in another's home for pay.

board·ing·house (bôrd′ing hous′), *n.* a house where meals, or room and meals, can be had for pay: also **boarding house.**

boarding school, a school where the pupils live during the school year.

board·walk (bôrd′wôk), *n.* a walk made of thick boards, especially along a beach.

boast (bōst), *v.* **1.** to talk about with too much pride and pleasure; praise too highly; brag [We tired of hearing him *boast* of his bravery.] **2.** to be proud of having [Our city *boasts* a fine new zoo.] —*n.* **1.** a boasting or bragging. **2.** something that one can boast of [It was his *boast* that he had never been late to school.] —**boast′er,** *n.*

boast·ful (bōst′fəl), *adj.* boasting; always ready to brag.

boat (bōt), *n.* **1.** a small vessel for traveling on water, such as a rowboat, sailboat, lifeboat, or motorboat. In popular use, but not by sailors, a ship of any size is sometimes called a boat. **2.** a dish shaped a little like a boat [gravy *boat*]. —*v.* to row or sail in a boat [We *boated* down the river for a mile. —**in the same boat,** facing the same kind of problem.

boat·swain (bō′s'n *or* bōt′swān), *n.* a petty officer on a ship who directs the work of the crew.

bob (bäb), *v.* **1.** to move with short, jerky motions [His head *bobbed* up and down as the car bounced over the ruts.] **2.** to cut off short [to *bob* a dog's tail]. —*n.* **1.** a short, jerky movement [He greeted us with a *bob* of his head.] **2.** a style of short haircut for women or girls. **3.** a hanging weight at the end of a plumb line. **4.** a cork on a fishing line. —**bobbed,** *p.t. & p.p.;* **bob′bing,** *pr.p.*

bob·bin (bäb′in), *n.* a kind of spool around which thread, yarn, etc. is wound. Bobbins are used in weaving, on sewing machines, etc.

bob·by (bäb′ē), *n.* a policeman: *a British slang word.* —**bob′bies,** *pl.*

bobby pin, a small metal hairpin with the sides pressing close together.

bobby socks, girls' socks that reach just above the ankle: *used only in everyday talk.*

bob·cat (bäb′kat), *n.* a wildcat.

bob·o·link (bäb′'l ingk′), *n.* a North American songbird of the blackbird family. Its name comes from its call.

bob·sled (bäb′sled), *n.* a long sled ridden in races down a slide by a team of two or four men. It has a steering wheel and a brake.

bobby pin

bobsled

bob·tail (bäb′tāl), *n.* **1.** a tail that has been cut short. **2.** an animal with its tail cut short. —*adj.* having its tail cut short [a *bobtail* cat].

bob·white (bäb-hwīt′), *n.* a small North American quail with brown and white markings on a gray body. Its name comes from its call.

bode (bōd), *v.* to be a sign or omen of [That black cloud *bodes* rain.] —**bode ill,** to be a bad sign. —**bode well,** to be a good sign. —**bod′ed,** *p.t. & p.p.;* **bod′ing,** *pr.p.*

bod·ice (bäd′is), *n.* **1.** the tightly fitting upper part of a woman's dress. **2.** a kind of vest worn by women and girls, usually laced down the front.

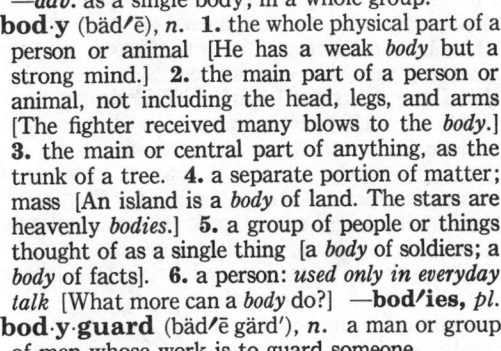
bodice

bod·ied (bäd′ēd), *adj.* having a certain kind of body [able-*bodied;* full-*bodied* flavor].

bod·i·less (bäd′i lis), *adj.* not having a body [a *bodiless* spirit].

bod·i·ly (bäd′'l ē), *adj.* of, in, by, or to the body [*bodily* labor; *bodily* harm]. —*adv.* as a single body; in a whole group.

bod·y (bäd′ē), *n.* **1.** the whole physical part of a person or animal [He has a weak *body* but a strong mind.] **2.** the main part of a person or animal, not including the head, legs, and arms [The fighter received many blows to the *body*.] **3.** the main or central part of anything, as the trunk of a tree. **4.** a separate portion of matter; mass [An island is a *body* of land. The stars are heavenly *bodies*.] **5.** a group of people or things thought of as a single thing [a *body* of soldiers; a *body* of facts]. **6.** a person: *used only in everyday talk* [What more can a *body* do?] —**bod′ies,** *pl.*

bod·y·guard (bäd′ē gärd′), *n.* a man or group of men whose work is to guard someone.

Boer (bôr), *n.* a South African whose ancestors were Dutch colonists. —*adj.* of the Boers.

bog (bäg *or* bôg), *n.* wet, spongy ground; a small marsh or swamp. —*v.* to sink or become stuck, as in a bog. —**bogged,** *p.t. & p.p.;* **bog′ging,** *pr.p.* —**bog′gy,** *adj.*

bo·gey (bō′gē), *n.* a bogy. —**bo′geys,** *pl.*

bo·gus (bō′gəs), *adj.* not genuine; false; counterfeit [a *bogus* dollar bill].

bo·gy (bō′gē), *n.* **1.** an imaginary evil spirit; goblin. **2.** a person or thing that causes unnecessary fear. —**bo′gies,** *pl.*

Bo·he·mi·a (bō hē′mi ə), *n.* a region in western Czechoslovakia, once a kingdom.

Bo·he·mi·an (bō hē′mi ən), *n.* **1.** a person born or living in Bohemia. **2.** the language of Bohemia; Czech. **3.** an artist, writer, musician, etc. who feels free to live according to his own rules and morals, which are different from those of most people. —*adj.* **1.** of Bohemia, its people, or their language. **2.** of or like a Bohemian (*in meaning 3*); unconventional.

boil (boil), *v.* **1.** to bubble up and become steam or vapor by being heated [Water *boils* at 212° F.] **2.** to heat a liquid until it bubbles up in this way. **3.** to cook in a boiling liquid [to *boil* potatoes]. **4.** to be stirred up, as with anger; rage. —*n.* the condition of boiling [Bring the soup to a *boil*.] —**boil down, 1.** to make less by boiling. **2.** to make shorter by using fewer words; abridge.

boil (boil), *n.* a painful, red swelling on the skin.

Boils are filled with pus and caused by infection.

boil·er (boil′ər), *n.* **1.** a pot or tub in which things are boiled. **2.** a large tank in which water is heated until it becomes steam, which is then used for heating or power. **3.** a tank for heating and storing hot water.

Boi·se (boi′sē), *n.* the capital of Idaho.

bois·ter·ous (bois′tər əs), *adj.* **1.** rough and stormy. **2.** noisy and lively [a *boisterous* party].

bold (bōld), *adj.* **1.** ready to take risks or face danger; daring; fearless [a *bold* explorer]. **2.** too free in manner; not polite or respectful; impudent. **3.** so sharp or clear as to stand out [*bold* handwriting]. **—bold′ly,** *adv.* **—bold′ness,** *n.*

bole (bōl), *n.* the trunk of a tree.

bo·le·ro (bō ler′ō), *n.* **1.** a Spanish dance with a lively rhythm. **2.** the music for this dance. **3.** a short, open vest, often with sleeves, worn by men and women. **—bo·ler′os,** *pl.*

Bol·í·var, Si·món (sē mōn′ bō lē′vär *or* sī′mən bäl′ə vər), 1783–1830; Venezuelan general who helped free South America from Spain.

Bo·liv·i·a (bə liv′i ə), *n.* a country in western South America. **—Bo·liv′i·an,** *adj. & n.*

boll (bōl), *n.* the seed pod of certain plants, especially of cotton, which contains the fiber.

boll weevil, a small, gray beetle whose larvae are hatched in cotton bolls and do much damage to the cotton.

Bo·lo·gna (bə lō′nyä), *n.* a city in northern Italy.

bo·lo·gna (bə lō′nə *or* bə- lō′nē), *n.* a large sausage made of various meats.

Bol·she·vik or **bol·she·vik** (bäl′shə vik *or* bōl′shə vik), *n.* **1.** a member of the political party that came into power in Russia after the revolution of 1917. It became the Communist Party of the Soviet Union. **2.** a radical in politics.

boll weevils on cotton boll

Bol·she·vism or **bol·she·vism** (bäl′shə viz′m *or* bōl′shə viz′m), *n.* the beliefs and practices of the Bolsheviks. **—Bol′she·vist** or **bol′she·vist,** *adj. & n.*

bol·ster (bōl′stər), *n.* a long, narrow pillow or cushion. **—v.** to prop up, as if with a bolster; support [His jokes *bolstered* up my spirits.]

bolt (bōlt), *n.* **1.** a heavy metal pin that is threaded like a screw. It is used with a nut to hold parts together. **2.** a metal bar that slides into a part across a door for keeping it shut. **3.** the part of a lock that is moved by the key. **4.** a large roll of cloth. **5.** a flash of lightning. **6.** a short arrow shot from a crossbow. **7.** the act of one who bolts [He made a sudden *bolt* from the room.] **—v. 1.** to fasten with a bolt.

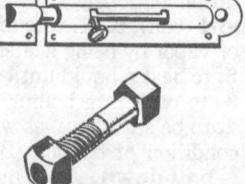
upper: bolt for door
lower: bolt and nut

2. to run out or run away suddenly [He *bolted* from the room.] **3.** to swallow quickly; gulp down [to *bolt* one's lunch]. **4.** to stop being a member or supporter of [to *bolt* a political party]. **—a bolt from the blue,** sudden surprise or shock. **—bolt upright,** very straight up.

bolt (bōlt), *v.* to sift through a sieve.

bomb (bäm), *n.* a hollow case filled with an explosive, a harmful gas, etc. Bombs are blown up by a fuse or by being dropped or thrown against something with force. **—v.** to attack or destroy with bombs.

bom·bard (bäm bärd′), *v.* **1.** to attack with artillery; shell. **2.** to keep on directing questions, requests, etc. at. **—bom·bard′ment,** *n.*

bom·bard·ier (bäm bər dir′), *n.* the member of a bomber crew who releases the bombs.

bom·bast (bäm′bast), *n.* talk or writing that sounds grand and important but has little meaning. **—bom·bas′tic,** *adj.*

Bom·bay (bäm bā′), *n.* a city in western India.

bomb·er (bäm′ər), *n.* an airplane made for dropping bombs in warfare.

bomb·shell (bäm′shel), *n.* **1.** a bomb. **2.** a sudden or shocking surprise.

bo·na fi·de (bō′nə fī′dē *or* bō′nə fīd′), in good faith; genuine [a *bona fide* contract].

bo·nan·za (bə nan′zə), *n.* **1.** a very rich deposit of ore. **2.** anything that gives wealth or great profit: *used only in everyday talk.*

Bonaparte, see **Napoleon Bonaparte.**

bon·bon (bän′bän), *n.* a small piece of candy.

bond (bänd), *n.* **1.** anything that binds or ties [Handcuffs or shackles are called *bonds.*] **2.** a force that unites; tie [the *bonds* of friendship]. **3.** a written agreement by which a person must pay a sum of money if certain things are done or if certain other things fail to be done. **4.** a certificate sold by a government or business as a way of raising money. It promises that the buyer will get back by a certain date the money he paid, along with interest [The city will issue *bonds* to build a new swimming pool.] **5.** the way bricks, stones, etc. are lapped upon one another in building a wall. **—v.** to furnish a bond or bonds for.

bond·age (bän′dij), *n.* slavery.

bond·ed (bän′did), *adj.* **1.** insured or protected by bonds. **2.** stored in a warehouse (called a **bonded warehouse**) under government care, until taxes are paid [*bonded* imports].

bond·man (bänd′mən), *n.* a slave or serf. **—bond′men,** *pl.*

bonds·man (bändz′mən), *n.* **1.** a person who becomes responsible for another by furnishing a bond (*in meaning 3*). **2.** a slave or serf. **—bonds′men,** *pl.*

bond·wom·an (bänd′woom′ən), *n.* a woman slave or serf. **—bond′wom′en,** *pl.*

bone (bōn), *n.* **1.** any of the hard pieces that are joined together to form the skeleton of a person or animal [There are about 200 *bones* in a person's body.] **2.** the material of which these are formed. **3.** a substance like bone or a thing made of bone [Ivory is often called *bone.*] **—v.** to take the bones out of [to *bone* fish]. **—make**

no bones about, to admit freely. **—boned,** *p.t. & p.p.;* **bon′ing,** *pr.p.*

bon·er (bōn′ər), *n.* a silly or stupid mistake: *a slang word.*

bon·fire (bän′fīr), *n.* a fire built outdoors.

bon·go (bäng′gō), *n.* either of a pair of small drums, played with the hands. **—bon′gos,** *pl.*

bo·ni·to (bə nē′tō), *n.* an ocean fish of the mackerel family. It is one of the kinds of tuna whose flesh is canned.

Bonn (bän), *n.* the capital of West Germany.

bon·net (bän′it), *n.* **1.** a hat for women and children that is held in place by a ribbon tied under the chin. **2.** a soft cap worn by men and boys in Scotland.

bonnet

bon·ny or **bon·nie** (bän′ē), *adj.* handsome or pretty in a healthy, cheerful way: *now used mainly in Scotland and parts of England.* **—bon′ni·er,** *compar.;* **bon′ni·est,** *super l.*

bo·nus (bō′nəs), *n.* anything given in addition to what is due or expected; gift of something extra **—bo·nus·es** (bō′nəs iz), *pl.*

bon voy·age (bōn′ vwä yäzh′), a pleasant journey: *a French phrase of farewell to a traveler.*

bon·y (bōn′ē), *adj.* **1.** of or like bone [The skull is a *bony* structure.] **2.** full of bones [a *bony* piece of fish]. **3.** having bones that stick out; thin; lean [Lincoln's *bony* face]. **—bon′i·er,** *compar.;* **bon′i·est,** *super l.*

boo (bōō), *interj. & n.* a long, drawn-out sound made in showing dislike or scorn; also, a short sound like this made in order to startle a person. **—v.** to shout "boo" at in showing dislike. **—booed,** *p.t. & p.p.;* **boo′ing,** *pr.p.*

boo·by (bōō′bē), *n.* **1.** a stupid or foolish person. **2.** a large, heavy sea bird: in full, **booby gannet. —boo′bies,** *pl.*

booby prize, a silly prize given in fun to the person with the lowest score in a game, etc.

booby trap, 1. a hidden bomb that is fixed to some harmless-looking object so that it will explode when someone touches or lifts the object. **2.** any hidden trick or trap.

boo·hoo (bōō′hōō′), *n.* noisy weeping.

book (book), *n.* **1.** printed sheets of paper fastened together at one side, between hard or stiff covers; volume [Our library has 50,000 *books*.] **2.** a long piece of writing such as a novel, a history, a long poem, etc. [His *book* will be published in two volumes.] **3.** a main part of a long piece of writing ["Genesis" is the first *book* of the Bible.] **4.** a number of blank pages bound together between covers [an account *book*; a note*book*]. **5.** a number of small things bound together in a cover [a *book* of matches; a *book* of tickets]. **—v. 1.** to write down the name of in a book or record; list [The police *book* arrested people who are brought into the station.] **2.** to

enter a name on a list, as in reserving something [to *book* passage on a ship]. **—an open book,** something plain to see or understand. **—by the book,** according to the rules. **—keep books,** to keep accounts or business records. **—know like a book,** to know very well. **—the Book** or **the Good Book,** the Bible.

book·case (book′kās), *n.* a set of shelves or a cabinet for holding books.

book end, a fancy weight or bracket put at the end of a row of books to keep them standing up.

book·ish (book′ish), *adj.* **1.** spending much time reading or studying. **2.** more like books than like real life; too formal; dry [a *bookish* style of writing].

book ends

book·keep·er (book′kēp′ər), *n.* a person whose work is to keep accounts for a business.

book·keep·ing (book′kēp′ing), *n.* the work of keeping business accounts.

book·let (book′lit), *n.* a little book, often with paper covers.

book·mark (book′märk), *n.* anything slipped between the pages of a book to mark a place.

book·mo·bile (book′mə bēl), *n.* a traveling library in a truck that goes to places which do not have a regular library.

book·shelf (book′shelf), *n.* a shelf on which books may be kept. **—book′shelves,** *pl.*

book·worm (book′wûrm), *n.* **1.** an insect larva that bores holes in books. **2.** anyone who reads or studies a great deal.

boom (bōōm), *v.* to make a deep, hollow sound like a bass drum. **—n.** such a sound.

boom (bōōm), *n.* **1.** a pole that comes out from a mast to keep the bottom of a sail stretched out. **2.** a beam that comes out from a derrick for lifting and guiding a load. **3.** a heavy chain or other barrier put in a harbor or river to keep ships out or to keep floating logs in.

boom (bōōm), *v.* **1.** to grow suddenly or swiftly; thrive [Industry *boomed* after the war.] **2.** to try to make well-known or popular [Returning soldiers *boomed* the general for president.] **—n.** a sudden, rapid growth; especially, a time of business prosperity.

boom·er·ang (bōōm′ər ang), *n.* **1.** a flat, curved stick that can be thrown so it will come back to the thrower. It is used as a weapon by natives of Australia. **2.** something said or done to harm a person that turns out to hurt the one who started it. **—v.** to act as a boomerang.

boon (bōōn), *n.* **1.** a welcome gift; blessing [The early spring was a *boon* to the farmers.] **2.** favor; request: *now seldom used in this meaning* ["Grant me a *boon*, oh King!"]

boon companion, a close friend who often joins one in seeking fun and pleasure.

Boone, Daniel (bōōn), 1734–1820; American frontiersman.

boor (boor), *n.* a person who has bad manners and is very rude to others. —**boor′ish,** *adj.*

boost (bōōst), *v.* **1.** to raise by pushing from below; push up [Tom *boosted* the child into the tree.] **2.** to make higher or greater [A transformer *boosts* the voltage in an electric line.] **3.** to urge others to support [Let's form a club to *boost* the football team.] —*n.* a pushing up; a raise or help [Lower prices resulted in a *boost* in sales.] *This word is used mainly in everyday talk.* —**boost′er,** *n.*

boot (bōōt), *n.* **1.** a covering of leather, rubber, etc. for the foot and part of the leg. **2.** a patch put over a break on the inside of an automobile tire. **3.** a kick with the foot. The slang phrase *to get the boot* means "to be fired from a job." —*v.* **1.** to put boots on. **2.** to kick [to *boot* a football].

boot (bōōt), *v.* to benefit or profit: *now seldom used* [It *boots* us little to object.] —**to boot,** in addition; besides [We ate up the cake and a pie *to boot.*]

boot·black (bōōt′blak), *n.* a person whose work is shining boots and shoes.

boot·ee (bōō′tē), *n.* a baby's soft shoe, knitted or made of cloth.

booth (bōōth), *n.* a small space all or partly closed off so as to form a stall or shed [a *booth* at a market; a voting *booth;* a telephone *booth;* a restaurant *booth*].

bootee

boot·leg (bōōt′leg), *v.* to sell alcoholic liquor when it is against the law, as during Prohibition. —**boot′legged,** *p.t. & p.p.;* **boot′leg·ging,** *pr.p.* —**boot′leg·ger,** *n.*

boot·less (bōōt′lis), *adj.* doing no good; useless [a *bootless* effort].

boo·ty (bōō′tē), *n.* **1.** goods taken from the enemy in war. **2.** any goods taken by force or stolen; plunder [The robbers divided their *booty.*] **3.** any gifts, prizes, etc.: *a humorous usage.*

bo·rax (bôr′aks), *n.* a white salt used in making glass, enamel, and soaps.

Bor·deaux (bôr dō′), *n.* **1.** a city in southwestern France. **2.** a white or red wine originally from France.

bor·der (bôr′dər), *n.* **1.** the line that divides one country or state from another; frontier. **2.** an edge or a narrow strip along an edge; margin [a red tablecloth with a blue *border;* a *border* of flowers along the driveway]. —*v.* **1.** to put a border on [The dress is *bordered* with lace.] **2.** to lie along the edge of [Lilies *border* the path.] —**border on** or **border upon,** to be next to; be close to [Canada *borders on* the United States. His grief *borders on* madness.]

bor·der·land (bôr′dər land), *n.* **1.** the land near a border between countries. **2.** an uncertain condition that is not quite one thing nor the other [the *borderland* between waking and sleeping].

bor·der·line (bôr′dər līn), *n.* a border or boundary between countries or states. —*adj.* **1.** on a border [a *borderline* town]. **2.** not quite one thing nor another; uncertain; doubtful [a *borderline* type of mental illness].

bore (bôr), *v.* **1.** to make a deep, round hole by drilling or digging [A tunnel was *bored* through the mountain.] **2.** to make tired by being dull or uninteresting [The speaker *bored* the audience with his old jokes.] —*n.* **1.** the hollow part inside a tube or pipe [This gun has a narrow *bore.*] **2.** a tool for boring. **3.** a hole made by boring. **4.** a dull or uninteresting person or thing. —**bored,** *p.t. & p.p.;* **bor′ing,** *pr.p.*

bore (bôr), past tense of **bear.**

Bo·re·as (bôr′i əs), *n.* the north wind.

bore·dom (bôr′dəm), *n.* the condition of being bored by something dull or uninteresting.

bor·er (bôr′ər), *n.* **1.** a tool for boring. **2.** an insect or worm that bores holes in fruit, etc.

bo·ric acid (bôr′ik), a white powder dissolved in water for use as a weak antiseptic.

born (bôrn), a past participle of **bear,** meaning "given birth to" [The twins were *born* an hour apart.] —*adj.* **1.** brought into life or being [a newly *born* idea]. **2.** by birth or nature [She is a *born* musician.]

borne (bôrn), the usual past participle of **bear** [She has *borne* a child. He has *borne* much pain.]

Bor·ne·o (bôr′ni ō), *n.* a large island in the East Indies, southwest of the Philippines.

bo·ron (bôr′än), *n.* a chemical element that is found only in certain compounds, such as borax. It is used in making glass, metal alloys, etc.

bor·ough (bur′ō), *n.* **1.** a town or village that has a charter to govern itself. **2.** one of the five main divisions of New York City.

bor·row (bär′ō *or* bôr′ō), *v.* **1.** to get to use something for a while by agreeing to return it later [You can *borrow* that book from the library.] **2.** to take another's word, idea, etc. and use it as one's own [The Romans *borrowed* many of their myths from the Greeks.] —**borrow trouble,** to worry before one has to.

bosh (bäsh), *n. & interj.* nonsense: *used only in everyday talk.*

bos·om (booz′əm), *n.* **1.** a person's breast [Rest your head on my *bosom.*] **2.** the breast thought of as the place where feelings begin [Deep within his *bosom,* he knew he was wrong.] **3.** the inside; central part [in the *bosom* of her family]. **4.** the part of a garment that covers the breast. —*adj.* very close and dear [a *bosom* friend].

boss (bôs), *n.* **1.** a person who is in charge of workers, as an employer, a manager, or a foreman. **2.** a person who controls a political group [the Republican Party *boss* in Fayette County]. —*v.* to act as boss or give orders to. *This word is used mainly in everyday talk.*

boss (bôs), *n.* a small knob or stud sticking out as a decoration. —*v.* to decorate with bosses.

boss·y (bôs′ē), *adj.* acting like a boss; fond of giving orders: *used only in everyday talk.*

Bos·ton (bôs′t'n), *n.* a seaport that is the capital of Massachusetts.

bo·sun (bō′s'n), *n.* a boatswain.

bo·tan·i·cal (bə tan′i k'l), *adj.* having to do

with botany [Plants are raised for study and exhibit in a *botanical* garden.] Also **bo·tan′ic.**

bot·a·ny (bät′ə nē), *n.* the science that studies plants and how they grow. —**bot′a·nist,** *n.*

botch (bätch), *v.* to fix or patch in a clumsy way; to spoil by poor or careless work; bungle [He failed to match the color and so *botched* the paint job.] —*n.* a poor or careless piece of work.

both (bōth), *adj. & pron.* the two, or the two of them [*Both* birds are small, and *both* sing well.] —*conj. & adv.* equally; as well; not only: *used in phrases with* and [I am *both* tired and hungry.]

both·er (bä*th*′ər), *v.* **1.** to annoy; cause worry or trouble to; pester [Does the noise *bother* you?] **2.** to take the time or trouble [Don't *bother* to answer this letter.] —*n.* something that annoys or causes worry or trouble [Flies are a *bother.*]

both·er·some (bä*th*′ər səm), *adj.* annoying.

Bot·swa·na (bät swä′nə), *n.* a country in southern Africa, north of South Africa.

bot·tle (bät′'l), *n.* **1.** a container, especially for liquids, usually made of glass. Bottles generally have a narrow neck and no handles. **2.** the amount that a bottle holds [He drank a *bottle* of milk.] —*v.* to put into a bottle. —**bottle up,** to hold back; restrain [to *bottle up* the enemy]. —**bot′tled,** *p.t. & p.p.;* **bot′tling,** *pr.p.*

bot·tle·neck (bät′'l nek), *n.* anything that slows up movement or progress [This narrow street is a *bottleneck* during rush hours.]

bot·tom (bät′əm), *n.* **1.** the lowest part [Sign your name at the *bottom* of this paper.] **2.** the part on which a thing rests; underside; base [Any side on which a crate rests becomes its *bottom.*] **3.** the part of a chair, etc. on which one sits [There's a new cane *bottom.*] **4.** the ground under a body of water [The ship sank to the *bottom.*] **5.** *often* **bottoms,** *pl.* low land along a river. **6.** the true facts or the main reason; basis or cause [Get to the *bottom* of the problem.] —*adj.* of or at the bottom; lowest [the *bottom* shelf].

bot·tom·less (bät′əm lis), *adj.* so deep that it seems to have no bottom [a *bottomless* lake].

bou·doir (bōō′dwär), *n.* a woman's bedroom or dressing room.

bouf·fant (bōō fänt′), *adj.* puffed out; full [a *bouffant* skirt].

bough (bou), *n.* a large branch of a tree.

bought (bôt), past tense and past participle of **buy.**

bouil·lon (bool′yän), *n.* a clear soup.

boul·der (bōl′dər), *n.* a large rock made round and smooth by weather and water.

boul·e·vard (bool′ə värd), *n.* a wide street, often lined with trees: abbreviated **blvd.**

bouffant skirt

bounce (bouns), *v.* **1.** to hit against a surface so as to spring back; bound or rebound [to *bounce* a ball against a wall; to *bounce* up and down on a sofa]. **2.** to move suddenly; jump; leap [He *bounced* out of bed when the alarm clock rang.] —*n.* **1.** a springing or bounding; leap. **2.** the ability to bound or rebound [This ball has lost its *bounce.*] —**bounced,** *p.t. & p.p.;* **bounc′ing,** *pr.p.* —**bounc′er,** *n.*

bounc·ing (boun′sing), *adj.* big, healthy, strong, etc. [It's a *bouncing* baby boy.]

bound (bound), *v.* **1.** to move with a leap or leaps [The dog came *bounding* down the path.] **2.** to spring back from a surface; rebound; bounce. —*n.* **1.** a jump; leap [He reached the door with one *bound.*] **2.** a bounce.

bound (bound), past tense and past participle of **bind.** —*adj.* **1.** sure; certain [He's *bound* to lose.] **2.** having a binding or cover [a *bound* book]. **3.** determined: *used only in everyday talk* [a team *bound* on winning]. —**bound up in,** very busy with [a man *bound up in* his work].

bound (bound), *adj.* ready to go or going; headed [We are *bound* for home.] This word is sometimes used as a suffix, as in *northbound.*

bound (bound), *n.* a boundary line or limit. —*v.* to form a boundary of [The river *bounds* the town on the south.] —**out of bounds, 1.** outside the playing limits, as of a football field. **2.** not to be entered or used; forbidden.

bound·a·ry (boun′də rē *or* boun′drē), *n.* a line or thing that marks the outside edge or limit [The Ohio River forms the southern *boundary* of Indiana.] —**bound′a·ries,** *pl.*

bound·en (boun′dən), *adj.* that one is bound by; that one must do [a *bounden* duty].

bound·less (bound′lis), *adj.* having no bounds or limits [the *boundless* skies].

boun·te·ous (boun′ti əs), *adj.* **1.** giving much gladly; generous [a *bounteous* patron]. **2.** more than enough; plentiful [a *bounteous* harvest].

boun·ti·ful (boun′ti fəl), *adj.* bounteous.

boun·ty (boun′tē), *n.* **1.** a giving of much gladly; generosity [We are grateful for your *bounty.*] **2.** something given freely; generous gift. **3.** a reward given by a government, as for killing harmful animals. —**boun′ties,** *pl.*

bou·quet (bō kā′ *or* bōō kā′), *n.* **1.** a bunch of flowers. **2.** (bōō kā′), fragrant smell.

Bour·bon (boor′bən *or* bŭr′bən), *n.* **1.** a former ruling family in France and Spain. **2. bourbon,** a whisky made chiefly from corn.

bour·geois (boor zhwä′), *n.* a person of the middle class, or bourgeoisie. —*adj.* of or like the middle class or its way of life: *now usually used to mean* respectable, ordinary,

bouquet

fat,   āpe,   cär,   ten,   ēven,   hit,   bīte,   gō,   hôrn,   tōōl,   book,   up,   fŭr;
get,   joy,   yet,   chin,   she,   thin,   *th*en;   zh = s in pleasure;   ′ as in able (ā′b′l);
ə = a in ago,   e in agent,   i in sanity,   o in confess,   u in focus.

smugly comfortable, etc. —**bour·geois′**, pl.

bour·geoi·sie (boor′zhwä zē′), n. sing. & pl. the social class between the working class and the very wealthy; middle class.

bourn or **bourne** (bôrn or boorn), n. a brook.

bourn or **bourne** (bôrn or boorn), n. **1.** a boundary. **2.** a goal; aim. Now seldom used.

bout (bout), n. **1.** a contest; fight [a boxing bout]. **2.** a spell; term [a bout of the flu].

bo·vine (bō′vīn), adj. **1.** of an ox or cow. **2.** like an ox or cow; slow, dull, without feeling, etc.

bow (bou), v. **1.** to bend the head or body in respect, worship, greeting, etc. **2.** to give up or yield [I shall bow to your wishes.] **3.** to bend or weigh down [His back was bowed down by the load.] —n. a bending of the head or body, as in respect, etc. —**take a bow,** to come back on stage in answer to applause.

bow (bō), n. **1.** a weapon for shooting arrows, made of a curved strip of wood with a cord tied to both ends. See the picture for **archer. 2.** a slender stick with horsehairs tied along its length. It is drawn across the strings of a violin, cello, etc. to play it. **3.** anything curved or bent [a rainbow]. **4.** a knot tied with loops in it [Shoelaces are tied with a bow.] —v. **1.** to bend or curve [The wall bowed outward.] **2.** to play a violin, etc. with a bow.

bow (bou), n. the front part of a ship, boat, etc.

bow·els (bou′əlz), n.pl. **1.** the intestines, especially of a human being. **2.** the part deep inside [the bowels of the earth].

bow·er (bou′ər), n. a place shaded by trees or bushes or by vines on a trellis; arbor.

bow·ie knife (bō′ē or boo′ē), a long knife with a single edge, used by hunters.

bowl (bōl), n. **1.** a deep, rounded dish. **2.** as much as a bowl will hold [He ate two bowls of soup.] **3.** a thing or part shaped like a bowl [Tobacco is put in the bowl of a pipe.]

bowie knife

bowl (bōl), n. **1.** the heavy ball used in the game of bowls. **2.** a rolling of the ball in bowling. —v. **1.** to play at bowling or take a turn at bowling. **2.** to move swiftly and smoothly [The car bowled along the highway.] —**bowl over, 1.** to knock over. **2.** to surprise very much; shock: used only in everyday talk. —**bowl′er,** n.

bow·leg·ged (bō′leg′id or bō′legd), adj. having legs that are bowed outward.

bowl·ing (bō′ling), n. **1.** a game in which each player rolls a heavy ball along a wooden lane (**bowling alley**), trying to knock down ten wooden pins at the far end. **2.** the game of bowls.

bowls (bōlz), n. an old game played on a smooth lawn (**bowling green**) with a heavy wooden ball.

bowlegged man

Each player tries to roll his ball as close as possible to another ball at the far end.

bow·man (bō′mən), n. a man armed with bow and arrows; archer. —**bow′men,** pl.

bow·sprit (bou′sprit or bō′sprit), n. a large pole sticking out forward from the bow of a sailing ship. Ropes from the front mast and sails are tied to it.

bow·string (bō′string), n. the string of an archer's bow.

bow tie (bō), a necktie tied in a small bow.

box (bäks), n. **1.** cardboard, wood, or other stiff material made up in a form to hold or carry things in. It usually has four sides, a bottom, and a lid on top. **2.** as much as a box will hold [I ate two boxes of popcorn.] **3.** anything that is more or less like a box, as an enclosed place with seats for a jury, a booth, the marked-off place where the batter must stand in baseball, etc. —v. to put into a box [Box the oranges for shipping.] —**box in** or **box up,** to shut in or keep in.

bow tie

box (bäks), n. a blow or slap with the hand or fist, especially on the ear. —v. **1.** to hit with such a blow or slap. **2.** to fight with the fists: see **boxing.**

box (bäks), n. an evergreen shrub or small tree with leathery leaves: also called **box′wood.**

box·car (bäks′kär), n. a railroad car for carrying freight, with a roof and closed sides.

box·er (bäk′sər), n. **1.** a man who boxes. **2.** a large dog with a stocky body and small ears.

boxcar

box·ing (bäk′sing), n. the skill or sport of fighting with the fists, especially in padded leather mittens (**boxing gloves**).

box office, a place where tickets are sold, as in a theater.

boy (boi), n. **1.** a male child before he becomes a man. **2.** any man; fellow: used only in everyday talk [The boys at the office formed a bowling team.]

boxing

3. a man servant, porter, etc.: now considered an impolite use. —interj. an exclamation used to show pleasure, surprise, etc.

boy·cott (boi′kät), v. to join together in refusing to buy, sell, or use something or to have any dealings with someone [The whole town boycotted the dairy because of unclean conditions there.] —n. the act of boycotting a business, etc.

boy·hood (boi′hood), *n.* the time of being a boy [He delivered papers in his *boyhood*.]

boy·ish (boi′ish), *adj.* of, like, or fit for a boy [a *boyish* prank]. —**boy′ish·ly,** *adv.*

boy scout, a member of the **Boy Scouts,** a club for boys that trains them in outdoor skills and in citizenship.

Br, the symbol for the chemical element *bromine.*

Br., abbreviation for **Britain** or **British.**

bra (brä), *n.* a brassiere: *only in everyday talk.*

brace (brās), *v.* **1.** to make stronger by propping up [We can *brace* the shelf by nailing a wedge under it.] **2.** to make ready for a jolt, shock, etc. [I *braced* myself for the crash.] **3.** to give energy to; stimulate [The cool, fresh air will *brace* you.] —*n.* **1.** a pair or couple [a *brace* of pistols]. **2.** a thing for supporting a weak part or for keeping parts in place [A timber propping up floor boards, a stiff frame for supporting a weak leg, etc., and a metal band on the teeth to help them grow straight are all called *braces*.] **3. braces,** *pl.* suspenders: *used in Great Britain.* **4.** either of the signs { }, used to group together words, lines, or staves of music. **5.** a tool for holding and turning a bit, or drill. —**brace up,** to become strong or brave again after defeat, disappointment, etc. —**braced,** *p.t. & p.p.;* **brac′ing,** *pr.p.*

brace for the leg

brace·let (brās′lit), *n.* a band or chain worn as an ornament about the wrist or arm.

brac·ing (brās′ing), *adj.* filling with energy; refreshing [the *bracing* air at the seashore].

brack·en (brak′ən), *n.* a large, coarse fern.

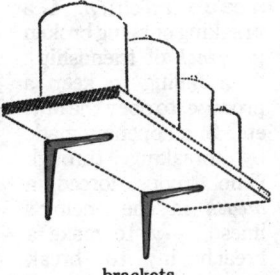
brace and bit

brack·et (brak′it), *n.* **1.** a support fastened to a wall for holding up a shelf, balcony, etc. **2.** a shelf or fixture sticking out from a wall. **3.** either of the signs [ ], used to enclose words, figures, etc. that are put in to explain something or make a comment [In this dictionary examples showing how words are used are in *brackets*.] **4.** a grouping into classes according to a system [the $5,000 to $10,000 income *bracket*]. —*v.* **1.** to fasten or support with

brackets

brackets. **2.** to put a word or words between brackets. **3.** to group or think of together [Grant and Lee are *bracketed* in history.]

brack·ish (brak′ish), *adj.* **1.** a little salty, as the water of some marshes near the sea. **2.** having an unpleasant taste.

bract (brakt), *n.* a leaf that grows at the base of a flower or on the flower stem. Bracts usually look like small scales.

brad (brad), *n.* a thin nail with a small head.

brae (brā), *n.* a hillside: *a Scottish word.*

brag (brag), *v.* to boast. —*n.* the act of boasting. —**bragged,** *p.t. & p.p.;* **brag′ging,** *pr.p.*

brag·gart (brag′ərt), *n.* a person who is always boasting about himself.

Brah·ma (brä′mə), *n.* in the Hindu religion, the god who created the universe.

Brah·man or **Brah·min** (brä′mən), *n.* a member of the highest caste of Hindus. It is the social class of priests and scholars.

Brahms, Jo·han·nes (yō hä′nəs brämz′), 1833–1897; German composer of music.

braid (brād), *v.* to weave together three or more strands of hair, straw, ribbon, etc. —*n.* **1.** a rope of braided hair. **2.** a band of braided cloth, ribbon, etc. used for trimming or decoration.

Braille or **braille** (brāl), *n.* a system of printing and writing for blind people. The letters, numbers, etc. are formed by patterns of raised dots which are felt with the fingers.

Braille

brain (brān), *n.* **1.** the gray and white tissue inside the skull of a person or of any animal with a backbone. It is the main part of the nervous system, by which one thinks and feels. **2. brains,** *pl.* intelligence; understanding [Use your *brains*.] —*v.* to hit hard on the head. —**beat one's brains,** to try hard to remember, understand, etc.

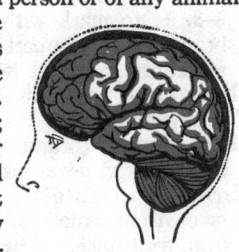
brain

brain·less (brān′lis), *adj.* foolish; stupid.

brain storm, a sudden, brilliant idea: *used only in everyday talk.*

brain·y (brān′ē), *adj.* having a good mind; intelligent: *used only in everyday talk.* —**brain′i·er,** *compar.;* **brain′i·est,** *superl.*

braise (brāz), *v.* to brown in fat and then cook over a low fire in a covered pan with a little liquid [to *braise* meat]. —**braised,** *p.t. & p.p.;* **brais′ing,** *pr.p.*

brake (brāk), *n.* a thing used to slow down or stop a car, machine, etc. It is often a block or band that is pressed against a wheel or other moving part. —*v.* to slow down or stop with a brake. —**braked,** *p.t. & p.p.;* **brak'ing,** *pr.p.*

brake (brāk), *n.* a thick growth of bushes, tall grasses, etc.; thicket.

brake (brāk), *n.* a large, coarse fern; bracken.

brake·man (brāk'mən), *n.* a man who works brakes on a train; now, usually, an assistant to the conductor. —**brake'men,** *pl.*

bram·ble (bram'b'l), *n.* any prickly shrub, as the raspberry or blackberry.

bran (bran), *n.* the husks of ground wheat, rye, etc. that are left after sifting the flour.

branch (branch), *n.* 1. any part of a tree growing from the trunk or from a main limb. 2. anything coming out like a branch from the main part [the *branch* of a river or of a railroad]. 3. a division or part [Chemistry is a *branch* of science.] 4. a part that is away from the main unit [Our public library has *branches* in the suburbs.] —*v.* to divide into branches [The road *branches* two miles east of the town.] —**branch off,** to go off in another direction. —**branch out,** to make one's interests or activities greater or broader.

brand (brand), *n.* 1. a piece of burning wood. 2. a mark burnt on the skin with a hot iron [*Brands* are put on cattle to show who owns them.] 3. the iron so used: also called **branding iron.** 4. a mark of shame [He bore the *brand* of traitor.] 5. a mark or name put on the goods of a particular company; trademark. 6. a particular kind or make [a new *brand* of cigarettes]. —*v.* 1. to mark with a brand. 2. to set apart as something shameful [to *brand* him a liar].

several brands and branding iron

bran·dish (bran'dish), *v.* to shake or wave in a threatening way [to *brandish* a sword].

brand-new (brand'nōō' *or* brand'nyōō'), *adj.* entirely new; never used before.

bran·dy (bran'dē), *n.* 1. an alcoholic liquor made from wine. 2. an alcoholic liquor made from fruit juice. —**bran'dies,** *pl.*

brant (brant), *n.* a small, dark wild goose.

brash (brash), *adj.* 1. acting too quickly; rash. 2. bold in a rude way; impudent.

Bra·sil·i·a (brə sil'i ə), *n.* the capital of Brazil.

brass (bras), *n.* 1. a yellow metal that is an alloy of copper and zinc. 2. **brasses,** *pl.* brass-wind musical instruments. 3. rude boldness; impudence: *used only in everyday talk.*

bras·siere *or* **bras·sière** (brə zir'), *n.* an undergarment worn by women to support the breasts.

brass winds, musical instruments made of coiled metal tubes and having a cup-shaped mouthpiece [The trumpet and tuba are *brass winds.*] —**brass'-wind',** *adj.*

brass·y (bras'ē), *adj.* 1. of or like brass. 2. bold in a rude way; impudent. 3. loud and blaring

[a *brassy* voice]. —**brass'i·er,** *compar.;* **brass'- i·est,** *superl.* —**brass'i·ness,** *n.*

brat (brat), *n.* a child who doesn't behave or is hard to manage: *sometimes used jokingly.*

bra·va·do (brə vä'dō), *n.* a pretending to be brave or bold when one is really afraid.

brave (brāv), *adj.* 1. willing to face danger, pain, or trouble; not afraid; full of courage. 2. fine, grand, or splendid [a *brave* new world]. —*n.* an American Indian warrior. —*v.* to face without fear; defy [to *brave* a storm]. —**braved,** *p.t. & p.p.;* **brav'ing,** *pr.p.* —**brave'ly,** *adv.*

brav·er·y (brāv'ər ē), *n.* 1. a being brave; courage. 2. a fine display or showy clothes [dressed in their holiday *bravery*]. —**brav'er·ies,** *pl.*

bra·vo (brä'vō), *interj. & n.* a word shouted to mean "very good! well done! excellent!" [The audience shouted "*Bravo!*" when Caruso finished his solo.] —**bra'vos** or **bra'voes,** *pl.*

brawl (brôl), *n.* a rough, noisy quarrel or fight. —*v.* to quarrel or fight noisily. —**brawl'er,** *n.*

brawn (brôn), *n.* big, strong muscles, or muscular strength [The bully was all *brawn* and no brain.] —**brawn'i·er,** *compar.;* **brawn'i·est,** *superl.* —**brawn'y,** *adj.*

bray (brā), *n.* 1. the loud, harsh cry that a donkey makes. 2. a sound like this. —*v.* to make a cry or noise of this kind.

bra·zen (brā'z'n), *adj.* 1. of or like brass. 2. bold and impudent; showing no shame [a *brazen* lie or a *brazen* liar]. —**brazen it out,** to act in a bold way as if one need not be ashamed [Although caught cheating, she tried to *brazen it out.*] —**bra'zen·ly,** *adv.*

bra·zier (brā'zhər), *n.* a heavy pan for holding burning coals or charcoal.

Bra·zil (brə zil'), *n.* a country in eastern and central South America. —**Bra·zil·ian** (brə zil'- yən), *adj. & n.*

Brazil nut, a three-sided nut that is the seed of a tree growing in South America. It has a dark shell and a white, oily kernel, and grows in a hard shell that holds a number of such nuts.

Brazil nuts

breach (brēch), *n.* 1. a breaking or being broken [a *breach* of friendship]. 2. a failing to keep a promise, to obey the law, etc. 3. an opening made by breaking through [The troops forced a *breach* in the enemy's lines.] —*v.* to make a breach in; to break through.

bread (bred), *n.* 1. a common food baked from a dough made with flour or meal and water, and often milk, yeast, etc. 2. any baked goods like bread but made with a batter [quick *breads*; corn*bread*]. 3. food or the means of living ["Give us this day our daily *bread.*"] —*v.* to cover with bread crumbs or meal before cooking [*breaded* pork chops]. —**break bread,** to eat, especially to eat with someone else. —**know which side one's bread is buttered on,** to know what is best for oneself.

bread·fruit (bred/frōōt), *n.* the large, round fruit of a tree growing on South Pacific islands. It has a starchy pulp which becomes like bread when it is cooked.

breadth (bredth), *n.* **1.** the distance from side to side of a thing; width. **2.** amount or extent; largeness [*breadth* of understanding].

break (brāk), *v.* **1.** to come or make come apart by force; split or crack sharply into pieces [*Break* an egg into the bowl. The rusty hinge *broke.*] **2.** to get out of working order; make or become useless [You can *break* your watch by winding it too tightly.] **3.** to cut open the surface of [to *break* ground for a new building]. **4.** to tame by using force [The cowboys *broke* the wild ponies.] **5.** to do better than; outdo [to *break* a record]. **6.** to upset the order of [The soldiers *broke* ranks and ran.] **7.** to fail to carry out or follow [to *break* an agreement; to *break* the law]. **8.** to end, stop, or interrupt [The net *broke* his fall. The fuse melted and *broke* the electric circuit.] **9.** to make poor or bankrupt [Another such loss will *break* me.] **10.** to change suddenly or become choked [The old man's voice *broke* as he sobbed out his story.] **11.** to begin or come suddenly [Dawn was *breaking.*] **12.** to become known or make known [The news story *broke* today. Who will *break* the sad news to her?] **13.** to curve suddenly near the plate: said of a pitched baseball. —*n.* **1.** a breaking open or apart. **2.** a broken place [The X ray showed a small *break* in the bone.] **3.** a beginning [We left at the *break* of day.] **4.** an interruption [Recess is a relaxing *break* in our school day.] **5.** an escape, as from jail. **6.** a chance: *slang in this meaning* [Give me a *break.* That was a lucky *break.*] —**break away,** to leave suddenly. —**break down, 1.** to lose control of oneself; begin to cry. **2.** to go out of working order. **3.** to separate into parts for study. —**break in, 1.** to enter by force. **2.** to interrupt. **3.** to train a beginner. —**break into, 1.** to enter by force. **2.** to begin suddenly to speak or perform. **3.** to interrupt. —**break off, 1.** to stop suddenly. **2.** to stop being friendly. —**break out, 1.** to develop a rash on the skin. **2.** to begin suddenly. **3.** to escape. —**break up, 1.** to take apart or fall apart; wreck. **2.** to stop; put an end to. **3.** to make feel upset; disturb. —**break with, 1.** to stop being friendly with. **2.** to stop following [The Indian *broke with* the customs of his people.] —**broke,** *p.t.;* **brok/en,** *p.p.;* **break/ing,** *pr.p.*

break·a·ble (brāk/ə b'l), *adj.* that can be broken or that is likely to break.

break·age (brāk/ij), *n.* **1.** a breaking or being broken. **2.** loss or damage by breaking [*Breakage* on the shipment amounted to $100.]

break·down (brāk/doun), *n.* **1.** a getting out of working order, or a falling apart. **2.** a becoming sick in body or mind. **3.** a separating into parts; analysis [a *breakdown* of costs].

break·er (brāk/ər), *n.* a person or thing that breaks, as a wave that breaks on the shore.

break·fast (brek/fəst), *n.* the first meal of the day. —*v.* to eat breakfast.

break·neck (brāk/nek), *adj.* likely to cause an accident; unsafe [He drove at *breakneck* speed.]

break·wa·ter (brāk/wô/tər), *n.* a wall built to break the force of waves, as near a harbor.

bream (brēm), *n.* any of several fresh-water or salt-water fishes, related to the carp. —**bream** or **breams,** *pl.*

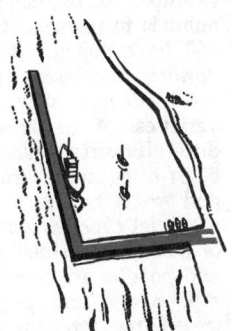
breakwater

breast (brest), *n.* **1.** the upper, front part of the body, between the neck and the belly. **2.** either of the two glands on this part of a woman's body, from which babies get milk. **3.** the breast thought of as the center of feelings [Anger raged through his *breast.*] —*v.* to face or meet bravely. —**make a clean breast of,** to confess everything.

breast·bone (brest/bōn), *n.* the thin, flat bone to which most of the ribs are joined in the front of the chest; sternum.

breast·plate (brest/plāt), *n.* a piece of armor for protecting the breast.

breast·work (brest/wŭrk), *n.* a low wall put up quickly as a defense in battle.

breath (breth), *n.* **1.** air taken into the lungs and then let out. **2.** easy or natural breathing [Wait till I get my *breath* back.] **3.** life or spirit [While there is *breath* in me, I will resist.] **4.** a slight breeze [There wasn't a *breath* of air.] —**below one's breath** or **under one's breath,** in a whisper. —**catch one's breath, 1.** to gasp or pant. **2.** to pause or rest. —**in the same breath,** at almost the same moment. —**save one's breath,** to keep quiet.

breathe (brēth), *v.* **1.** to take air into the lungs and then let it out. **2.** to live [While I *breathe,* you are safe.] **3.** to speak quietly; whisper [Don't *breathe* a word of it to anyone.] **4.** to stop for breath; rest [to *breathe* a horse after a long run]. —**breathed,** *p.t. & p.p.;* **breath/ing,** *pr.p.*

breath·er (brēth/ər), *n.* a pause for rest: *used only in everyday talk.*

breath·less (breth/lis), *adj.* **1.** breathing hard; panting [He was *breathless* after the long run.] **2.** not breathing for a moment because of excitement, fear, etc. **3.** without breath.

breath·tak·ing (breth/tāk/ing), *adj.* very exciting; thrilling [a *breath-taking* sight].

bred (brĕd), past tense and past participle of **breed.**

breech (brēch), *n.* a lower, back part; especially, the part of a gun behind the barrel.

breech·es (brich′iz), *n.pl.* 1. short trousers reaching just below the knees. 2. any trousers: *used only in everyday talk.*

breed (brēd), *v.* 1. to give birth to young; hatch; reproduce [Mosquitoes *breed* in swamps.] 2. to keep and raise animals in pairs, so that they will have young. 3. to raise flowers, vegetables, etc. and try to develop new or better varieties. 4. to cause or produce [Poverty *breeds* crime.] 5. to bring up, or train [born and *bred* to be a farmer]. —*n.* a special type of some animal or plant; race; stock [Spaniels and poodles are *breeds* of dogs.] —**bred,** *p.t. & p.p.;* **breed′ing,** *pr.p.* —**breed′er,** *n.*

breeches

breed·ing (brēd′ing), *n.* 1. the producing or raising of young; especially, the raising of plants and animals for developing new or better types. 2. upbringing or training as shown in one's behavior [His manners show good *breeding.*]

breeze (brēz), *n.* a light and gentle wind. —*v.* to move briskly or gaily: *slang in this meaning.* —**breezed,** *p.t. & p.p.;* **breez′ing,** *pr.p.*

breez·y (brēz′ē), *adj.* 1. with breezes blowing; slightly windy [a *breezy* day]. 2. light and gay [*breezy* talk]. —**breez′i·er,** *compar.;* **breez′i·est,** *superl.* —**breez′i·ly,** *adv.*

breth·ren (breth′rin), *n.pl.* brothers: *now used mainly of fellow members of a church.*

Bret·on (bret′'n), *adj.* of Brittany, its people, or their language. —*n.* 1. a person born or living in Brittany. 2. the Celtic language of Brittany.

brevi·ar·y (brē′vi er′ē), *n.* a book containing the daily prayers, hymns, etc. to be said by a Roman Catholic priest. —**bre′vi·ar′ies,** *pl.*

brev·i·ty (brev′ə tē), *n.* a being brief; shortness [the *brevity* of a speech]. —**brev′i·ties,** *pl.*

brew (broo), *v.* 1. to make by steeping, boiling, and fermenting malt and hops [to *brew* beer]. 2. to make by steeping in boiled water [to *brew* tea]. 3. to plan or scheme [The boys are *brewing* mischief.] 4. to begin to form [A storm is *brewing.*] —*n.* a drink that has been brewed.

brew·er (broo′ər), *n.* a person whose work or business is brewing beer and ale.

brew·er·y (broo′ər ē), *n.* a place where beer and ale are brewed. —**brew′er·ies,** *pl.*

bri·ar (brī′ər), *n.* same as **brier.**

bribe (brīb), *n.* anything given or promised to a person to get him to do something that he should not do or does not want to do [A gift offered to a congressman to influence his vote is called a *bribe.*] —*v.* to offer or give a bribe to. —**bribed,** *p.t. & p.p.;* **brib′ing,** *pr.p.*

brib·er·y (brīb′ər ē), *n.* the giving or taking of bribes. —**brib′er·ies,** *pl.*

bric-a-brac (brik′ə brak′), *n.* small objects placed about a room for decoration, as little china figures, small vases, etc.

brick (brik), *n.* 1. a block of baked clay, used in building. 2. bricks as a material [The house is built of *brick.*] 3. anything shaped like a brick [a *brick* of ice cream]. —*adj.* built of brick [a *brick* wall]. —*v.* to cover or fill in with brick.

brick·bat (brik′bat), *n.* 1. a broken bit of brick thrown as a weapon. 2. a strong criticism.

brick·lay·er (brik′lā′ər), *n.* a person whose work is building with bricks. —**brick′lay′ing,** *n.*

brick·work (brik′wûrk), *n.* a thing or part built of bricks.

brid·al (brīd′'l), *adj.* of a bride or wedding [a *bridal* gown; a *bridal* feast].

bride (brīd), *n.* a woman on her wedding day or just after the wedding.

bride·groom (brīd′groom), *n.* a man on his wedding day or just after the wedding.

brides·maid (brīdz′mād), *n.* one of the young women who attend the bride at a wedding.

bridge (brij), *n.* 1. something built over a river, railroad, etc. to serve as a road or path across. 2. the upper, bony part of the nose. 3. the part of a pair of eyeglasses that fits over the nose. 4. the thin curved piece over which the strings of a violin, cello, etc. are stretched. 5. the high platform on a ship from which the officer in charge controls it. 6. a small frame for false teeth, that is fastened to a real tooth or teeth: also **bridge′work.** —*v.* to make or be a bridge over [to *bridge* a river]. —**bridged,** *p.t. & p.p.;* **bridg′ing,** *pr.p.*

bridge of false teeth

bridge (brij), *n.* a card game for two pairs of players.

bridge·head (brij′hed), *n.* a strong position taken by an attacking army on the enemy's side of a bridge, river, etc.

bri·dle (brī′d'l), *n.* the part of a horse's harness for the head. It has a bit for the mouth to which the reins are fastened. —*v.* 1. to put a bridle on. 2. to hold back or control as with a bridle [You must *bridle* your anger.] 3. to pull one's head back quickly with the chin drawn in, as in showing anger at an insult. —**bri′dled,** *p.t. & p.p.;* **bri′dling,** *pr.p.*

bridle

bridle path, a path for horseback riding.

brief (brēf), *adj.* 1. not lasting very long; short in time [a *brief* visit]. 2. using just a few words; not wordy; concise [a *brief* news report]. —*n.* a statement giving the main points of a law case, for use in court. —*v.* to give the main points or necessary facts to [to *brief* pilots before a flight]. —**hold a brief for,** to argue in favor of. —**in brief,** in a few words. —**brief′ly,** *adv.*

brief case, a flat case or bag, usually of leather,

used for carrying papers, books, and the like.

bri·er (brī′ər), *n.* any prickly or thorny bush, as the wild rose.

bri·er (brī′ər), *n.* **1.** a low shrub of Europe whose root is used in making tobacco pipes. **2.** this root.

brig (brig), *n.* **1.** a ship with two masts and square sails. **2.** the prison on a warship.

bri·gade (bri gād′), *n.* **1.** a former unit of the U.S. Army made up of two or more regiments. **2.** any group of people who work together as a unit [a fire *brigade*].

brig·a·dier general (brig ə dir′), a military officer who ranks just above a colonel.

brig·and (brig′ənd), *n.* a bandit, especially one of a roaming band.

brig·an·tine (brig′ən tēn), *n.* a kind of brig that has square sails on the foremast only.

bright (brīt), *adj.* **1.** shining; giving light; full of light [a *bright* star; a *bright* day]. **2.** very strong or brilliant in color or sound [a *bright* red; the *bright* tones of a cornet]. **3.** lively; cheerful [a *bright* smile]. **4.** having a quick mind; clever [a *bright* child]. **5.** full of hope; cheerful [a *bright* future]. —*adv.* in a bright manner [stars shining *bright*]. —**bright′ly,** *adv.* —**bright′ness,** *n.*

bright·en (brīt′'n), *v.* **1.** to make or become bright or brighter [The new lamps *brighten* up the room.] **2.** to make or become happy or happier; cheer [Her smile has *brightened* my day.]

bril·liance (bril′yəns) or **bril·lian·cy** (bril′-yən sē), *n.* the fact of being brilliant; great brightness, splendor, intelligence, etc.

bril·liant (bril′yənt), *adj.* **1.** very bright; glittering or sparkling [the *brilliant* sun on the water]. **2.** very splendid or distinguished [a *brilliant* gathering of authors]. **3.** very clever or intelligent [a *brilliant* discovery]. —*n.* a diamond or other gem cut in such a way that it will sparkle. —**bril′liant·ly,** *adv.*

brim (brim), *n.* **1.** the top rim of a cup, bowl, etc. [filled to the *brim*]. **2.** a rim or edge that sticks out [the *brim* of a hat]. —*v.* to fill or be full to the brim [eyes *brimming* with tears]. —**brimmed,** *p.t. & p.p.;* **brim′ming,** *pr.p.*

brim·ful (brim′fool′), *adj.* full to the brim.

brim·stone (brim′stōn), *n.* sulfur.

brin·dle (brin′d'l), *adj.* brindled. —*n.* **1.** a brindled color. **2.** a brindled animal.

brin·dled (brin′d'ld), *adj.* having a gray or tan coat streaked or spotted with a darker color [a *brindled* cow].

brindled cow

brine (brīn), *n.* **1.** water full of salt [*Brine* is used for pickling meat, etc.] **2.** the ocean.

bring (bring), *v.* **1.** to carry or lead here or to the place where the speaker will be [Take this book back and *bring* me another. *Bring* your friend to my party next week.] **2.** to cause to happen or come [War *brings* death and famine.] **3.** to persuade or influence [I can't *bring* myself to tell her.] **4.** to sell for [Eggs *bring* a high price today.] —**bring about,** to cause; make happen. —**bring around** or **bring round,** **1.** to persuade by arguing, urging, etc. **2.** to bring back to consciousness: *used only in everyday talk.* —**bring forth,** **1.** to give birth to. **2.** to make known. —**bring forward,** to introduce or show. —**bring off,** to make happen; carry out. —**bring on,** to cause to begin or happen. —**bring out,** **1.** to make known or make clear. **2.** to publish a book or bring a play, person, etc. before the public. —**bring over,** **1.** to convince. **2.** to bring on a visit. —**bring to,** **1.** to bring back to consciousness. **2.** to stop, as a ship. —**bring up, 1.** to take care of during childhood; raise; rear. **2.** to mention or suggest in a discussion. **3.** to cough up or vomit. **4.** to cause to stop suddenly. —**brought,** *p.t. & p.p.;* **bring′ing,** *pr.p.*

brink (brink), *n.* **1.** the edge of a cliff or other steep place. **2.** the point just short of [on the *brink* of a discovery; at the *brink* of war].

brin·y (brīn′ē), *adj.* of or like brine; very salty. —**brin′i·er,** *compar.;* **brin′i·est,** *superl.*

brisk (brisk), *adj.* **1.** quick and full of energy [We started to walk at a *brisk* pace.] **2.** cool, dry, and bracing [a *brisk* October morning]. —**brisk′ly,** *adv.* —**brisk′ness,** *n.*

bris·ket (bris′kit), *n.* meat cut from the breast of a beef.

bris·tle (bris′'l), *n.* **1.** any short, stiff, prickly hair, especially of a hog. **2.** such a hair, or an artificial hair like it, used for brushes. —*v.* **1.** to stand up stiffly, like bristles [The hair on the cat's back *bristled* as the dog came near.] **2.** to become tense with anger; be ready to fight back [He *bristled* at the insult.] **3.** to be thickly covered with [The tournament field *bristled* with lances and banners.] —**bris′tled,** *p.t. & p.p.;* **bris′-tling,** *pr.p.* —**bris·tly** (bris′lē), *adj.*

Bris·tol (bris′t'l), *n.* a seaport in southwestern England.

Brit·ain (brit′'n), *n.* same as **Great Britain.**

Bri·tan·ni·a (bri tan′i ə), *n.* Great Britain.

Brit·ish (brit′ish), *adj.* **1.** of Great Britain or its people. **2.** of the British Commonwealth of Nations. —**the British,** the people born or living in Great Britain.

British Columbia, a province of Canada, in the southwestern part.

British Commonwealth of Nations, a group of countries, including Great Britain (and its colonies), Australia, Canada, India, etc., joined together under the British monarch. Called, in earlier times, **British Empire.**

Brit·ish·er (brit′ish ər), *n.* a person living in

Great Britain, especially an Englishman.

British Honduras, a British colony in Central America, on the Caribbean.

British Isles, a group of islands northwest of France, including Great Britain, Ireland, and several smaller islands.

British West Indies, the British colonies in the West Indies, including, formerly, Jamaica.

Brit·on (brit′n), *n.* **1.** a person born or living in Great Britain. **2.** one of the native Celtic people living in southern Britain before it was invaded by the Anglo-Saxons.

Brit·ta·ny (brit′n ē), *n.* a region in France, on a peninsula in the northwestern part.

brit·tle (brit′l), *adj.* easily broken because it is hard and not flexible [As a person grows older, his bones become more *brittle.*]

broach (brōch), *v.* **1.** to start talking about [I'll *broach* the subject to him at dinner.] **2.** to make a hole in so as to let out liquid; tap [to *broach* a cask of wine].

broad (brôd), *adj.* **1.** large from side to side; wide [a *broad* room]. **2.** clear and open [*broad* daylight]. **3.** easy to understand; not subtle; obvious [a *broad* hint; *broad* humor]. **4.** wide in range; not limited [a *broad* variety; a *broad* education]. **5.** broad-minded; liberal or tolerant. **6.** main or general [the *broad* outlines of a subject]. —**broad′ly,** *adv.*

broad·cast (brôd′kast), *v.* **1.** to send over the air by means of radio [to *broadcast* a program]. **2.** to scatter or spread widely. —*n.* **1.** a broadcasting. **2.** a radio program [Did you hear the six o'clock news *broadcast?*] —*adv.* scattered about; far and wide [Seed may be sown either *broadcast* or in rows.] —**broad′cast** *or,* also for meaning 1, **broad′cast·ed,** *p.t. & p.p.;* **broad′cast·ing,** *pr.p.*

broad·cloth (brôd′klôth), *n.* **1.** a fine, smooth cotton or silk cloth, used for shirts, pajamas, etc. **2.** a fine, smooth woolen cloth.

broad·en (brôd′n), *v.* to make or become broad or broader; widen.

broad jump, an athletic contest to see who can jump the farthest: see also **high jump.**

broad·loom (brôd′lōōm), *adj.* woven on a wide loom [*broadloom* rugs and carpets].

broad-mind·ed (brôd′mīn′did), *adj.* keeping one's mind open to others' beliefs, to different ways of life, etc.; not having prejudice; tolerant. —**broad′-mind′ed·ness,** *n.*

broad·side (brôd′sīd), *n.* **1.** the entire side of a ship above the water line. **2.** the firing at one time of all the guns on one side of a ship. **3.** a sheet of paper printed on one side, as with advertising. **4.** a strong or insulting attack in words. —*adv.* **1.** directly in the side [The train rammed the car *broadside.*] **2.** without choosing targets [She criticized the class *broadside.*]

broad·sword (brôd′sôrd), *n.* a sword with a broad blade, for slashing rather than thrusting.

Broad·way (brôd′wā), *n.* a street in New York City known as the center of the theater section.

bro·cade (brō kād′), *n.* a rich cloth with a raised design woven into it.

broc·co·li (bräk′ə lē), *n.* a vegetable whose green stalks and loose heads of tiny green flower buds are cooked for eating.

broccoli

bro·gan (brō′gən), *n.* a brogue (shoe).

brogue (brōg), *n.* a heavy oxford shoe.

brogue (brōg), *n.* the way the people of a particular region pronounce words; especially, the way English is spoken by the Irish.

broil (broil), *v.* **1.** to cook or be cooked close to a flame or other high heat [to *broil* steaks over charcoal]. **2.** to make or be very hot [a *broiling* summer day].

broil·er (broil′ər), *n.* **1.** a pan or grill for broiling. **2.** the part of a stove used for broiling. **3.** a young chicken for broiling.

broke (brōk) past tense of **break.** —*adj.* having no money; bankrupt: *a slang use.*

bro·ken (brō′kən), past participle of **break.** —*adj.* **1.** split or cracked into pieces [a *broken* dish; a *broken* leg]. **2.** not in working condition [a *broken* watch]. **3.** not kept or carried out [a *broken* promise]. **4.** interrupted; not even [*broken* sleep]. **5.** not following the usual rules of grammar or word order [He speaks *broken* English.] **6.** sick, weakened, or beaten [a *broken* spirit].

bro·ken-down (brō′kən doun′), *adj.* **1.** sick or worn out, as by old age or disease. **2.** out of order; useless [a *broken-down* automobile].

bro·ken·heart·ed (brō′kən här′tid), *adj.* full of sorrow or despair; very unhappy.

bro·ker (brō′kər), *n.* a person who buys and sells stocks, real estate, etc. for others.

bro·ker·age (brō′kər ij), *n.* **1.** the business of a broker. **2.** the fee paid to a broker.

bro·mide (brō′mīd), *n.* **1.** a salt containing bromine. Some bromides are used as a drug to calm the nerves. **2.** a popular saying used so often that it has become stale and dull. Example: "Every cloud has its silver lining."

bro·mine (brō′mēn), *n.* a reddish-brown liquid that gives off a strong vapor. It is one of the chemical elements.

bron·chi (bräng′kī), *n.pl.* the two main branches of the windpipe. —**bron·chus** (bräng′kəs), *sing.*

bron·chi·al (bräng′ki əl), *adj.* having to do with the bronchi or with the smaller tubes leading from the bronchi into the lungs [A *bronchial* cold makes one cough.]

bron·chi·tis (bräng kī′tis), *n.* an illness in which the lining of the bronchial tubes is inflamed and there is painful coughing.

bron·co *or* **bron·cho** (bräng′kō), *n.* a small horse of the western United States, that is only partly tamed. —**bron′cos** *or* **bron′chos,** *pl.*

bron·to·sau·rus (brän′tə sô′rəs), *n.* a huge dinosaur whose fossil bones are found in the western United States.

bronze (bränz), *n.* **1.** a metal that is an alloy

of copper and tin. **2.** a statue or other work of art made of bronze ["The Thinker" is a famous *bronze*.] **3.** a reddish-brown color like that of bronze. —*adj.* of or like bronze. —*v.* to make or become bronze in color.

brooch (brōch *or* brōoch), *n.* a large pin with a clasp, worn mainly as an ornament at the bosom or neck of a woman's dress.

brood (brōod), *n.* **1.** a group of birds hatched at one time and cared for together. **2.** all the children in a family. —*v.* **1.** to sit on and hatch eggs. **2.** to keep thinking in a worried or troubled way [She *brooded* over the loss of her money.]

brooch

brood·er (brōod/ər), *n.* **1.** a person or animal that broods. **2.** a heated shelter for raising young chicks, ducklings, etc.

brook (brook), *n.* a small stream.

brook (brook), *v.* to put up with; stand for; bear; endure [I will *brook* no interference.]

brook·let (brook/lit), *n.* a little brook.

Brook·lyn (brook/lin), *n.* a former city in New York, now a borough of New York City.

broom (brōom), *n.* **1.** a brush with a long handle, used for sweeping. **2.** a shrub with small leaves, slender branches, and usually yellow flowers.

broom·stick (brōom/stik), *n.* the handle of a broom.

bros., abbreviation for **brothers.**

broth (brôth), *n.* water in which meat or a vegetable has been boiled; a thin, clear soup.

broth·er (bruth/ər), *n.* **1.** a boy or man as he is related to the other children of his parents. **2.** a person who is close to one in some way; especially, a fellow member of the same race, religion, profession, club, etc. —**broth/ers,** *pl.* —**breth/ren** *is an older pl.*

broth·er·hood (bruth/ər hood), *n.* **1.** the tie between brothers or between people who feel they all belong in one big family [the *brotherhood* of man]. **2.** a group of men joined together in some interest, work, belief, etc.

broth·er·in·law (bruth/ər in lô/), *n.* **1.** the brother of one's husband or wife. **2.** the husband of one's sister. —**broth/ers·in·law/,** *pl.*

broth·er·ly (bruth/ər lē), *adj.* **1.** of or like a brother. **2.** friendly, loyal, kindly, etc. [*brotherly* advice]. —**broth/er·li·ness,** *n.*

brougham (brōom), *n.* a closed carriage with the driver's seat outside.

brought (brôt), past tense and past participle of **bring.**

brow (brou), *n.* **1.** the eyebrow. **2.** the forehead. **3.** the top edge of a steep hill or cliff.

brow·beat (brou/bēt), *v.* to frighten a person into doing something by using rough talk or fierce looks; bully. —**brow/beat,** *p.t.;* **brow/beat·en,** *p.p.;* **brow/beat·ing,** *pr.p.*

brown (broun), *n.* the color of chocolate or

coffee, a mixture of red, black, and yellow. —*adj.* having this color. —*v.* to make or become brown [The turkey is *browning* in the oven.]

Brown, John (broun), 1800–1859; an American who fought slavery before the Civil War.

brown·ie (broun/ē), *n.* **1.** a small elf in folk tales who does good deeds for people at night. **2.** a small, flat bar of chocolate cake with nuts in it. **3. Brownies,** *pl.* the youngest branch of the Girl Scouts for girls who are seven and eight years old.

Brown·ing, Robert (broun/-ing), 1812–1889; English poet.

brown·ish (broun/ish), *adj.* somewhat brown.

brown rice, rice that has not been polished.

brownie

brown sugar, sugar that has not been refined or is only partly refined. It is brown in color.

browse (brouz), *v.* **1.** to nibble at leaves, twigs, shoots, etc. [deer *browsing* in the forest]. **2.** to look through a book or books, stopping to read a bit here and there. —**browsed,** *p.t. & p.p.;* **brows/ing,** *pr.p.*

bru·in (brōo/in), *n.* a bear: *a name used in children's tales.*

bruise (brōoz), *v.* **1.** to hurt a part of the body, as by a blow, without breaking the skin [His *bruised* knee turned black-and-blue.] **2.** to hurt the outside of [Several of the peaches were *bruised.*] **3.** to cause pain or injury to [Her feelings were *bruised* by his remarks.] —*n.* an injury to the outer part or flesh that doesn't break the skin but discolors it. —**bruised,** *p.t. & p.p.;* **bruis/ing,** *pr.p.*

bruit (brōot), *v.* to make widely known, as by rumor [His fame has been *bruited* about.]

brunch (brunch), *n.* breakfast and lunch eaten as one meal late in the morning.

bru·nette *or* **bru·net** (brōo net/), *adj.* having black or dark-brown hair, dark eyes, and a dark skin. —*n.* a brunette person. *Brunette* is usually used of a woman or girl and *brunet* of a man or boy.

brunt (brunt), *n.* the heaviest or hardest part [to bear the *brunt* of the blame, etc.].

brush (brush), *n.* **1.** a bunch of bristles, hairs, or wires fastened into a hard back or handle and used for cleaning, polishing, grooming, painting, etc. **2.** the act of rubbing with a brush. **3.** a light, grazing stroke [a *brush* of the hand]. **4.** a bushy tail; especially, the tail of a fox. **5.** low, shrubby growth; brushwood [The wounded bird hid in the *brush.*] **6.** land overgrown with brush where few people live. **7.** a short, sharp fight or quarrel [The gang had several *brushes* with the police.] —*v.* **1.** to use a brush on; clean; polish, paint, smooth etc. with a brush [*Brush* your shoes. *Brush* the paint on evenly.] **2.** to

fat, āpe, cär, ten, ēven, hit, bīte, gō, hôrn, tōol, book, up, fûr;
get, joy, yet, chin, she, thin, *then;* zh = s in pleasure; ' as in able (ā/b'l);
ə = a in ago, e in agent, i in sanity, o in confess, u in focus.

touch or graze in passing [The tire is scuffed where it *brushed* against the curb.] **3.** to remove by a stroke, as of the hand [*Brush* the flies away from that cake.] **—brush off,** to get rid of; dismiss. **—brush up,** to study something again so as to refresh one's memory about it.

brush·wood (brush′wood), *n.* **1.** tree branches that have been chopped or broken off. **2.** a thick growth of small trees and shrubs; underbrush.

brusque (brusk), *adj.* rough and abrupt in manner or speech [His answer to our request was a *brusque* "No!"] **—brusque′ly,** *adv.*

Brus·sels (brus′'lz), *n.* the capital of Belgium, in the central part.

Brussels sprouts, 1. a vegetable whose stem bears green buds that look like tiny cabbage heads and are cooked for eating. **2.** these buds.

Brussels sprouts

bru·tal (broo′t'l), *adj.* like a brute; cruel and without feeling; savage, rough, violent, etc. **—bru′tal·ly,** *adv.*

bru·tal·i·ty (broo tal′ə-tē), *n.* **1.** the fact of being brutal; cruelty. **2.** a brutal or savage act. **—bru·tal′i·ties,** *pl.*

brute (broot), *n.* **1.** a beast. **2.** a person who is very stupid or cruel, coarse, and rude. —*adj.* of or like a beast; without reasoning; brutal, savage, stupid, etc. [War is the use of *brute* force to get one's way.] **—brut′ish,** *adj.*

Bru·tus (broo′təs), *n.* 85?–42 B.C.; a Roman statesman who helped kill Julius Caesar.

B.S., abbreviation for **Bachelor of Science.**

bu., abbreviation for **bushel** or **bushels.**

bub·ble (bub′'l), *n.* **1.** a very thin film of liquid forming a ball around air or gas [soap *bubbles*]. **2.** a tiny ball of air or gas in a liquid [The *bubbles* in the soda water tickled her nose.] **3.** any plan, idea, etc. that bursts or falls apart as easily as a bubble. —*v.* **1.** to make bubbles; rise in bubbles; foam [Boiling water *bubbles*.] **2.** to make a boiling or gurgling sound [a *bubbling* brook]. **—bubble over,** to be unable to hold back one's excitement. **—bub′bled,** *p.t. & p.p.;* **bub′-bling,** *pr.p.*

bu·bon·ic plague (byoo bän′ik), a deadly disease that spreads rapidly and is carried by rats. In olden times it killed large groups of people.

buc·ca·neer (buk ə nir′), *n.* a pirate.

Bu·chan·an, James (byoo kan′ən), 1791–1868; fifteenth president of the United States, from 1857 to 1861.

Bu·cha·rest (boo kə rest′), *n.* the capital of Romania.

buck (buk), *n.* **1.** the male of certain animals, especially of the deer, goat, or rabbit. **2.** a dollar: *slang in this meaning.* —*v.* **1.** to jump upward quickly, with the head down and the back curved, as a horse does when it tries to throw its rider. **2.** to plunge forward with the head down, as a goat [In football, the fullback often *bucks* the

opponents' line.] **3.** to resist in a stubborn way: *used only in everyday talk.* **—buck up,** to cheer up; brace up: *used only in everyday talk.* **—pass the buck,** to try to make someone else take the blame or responsibility.

buck·board (buk′bôrd), *n.* a light, open carriage with a single seat placed on a platform that joins the two axles.

buck·et (buk′it), *n.* **1.** a round container with a flat bottom and a curved handle, used to hold or carry water, coal, etc.; pail. **2.** a thing like a bucket, as the scoop or dipper on a steam shovel. **3.** a bucketful.

bucket (*meaning 2*)

buck·et·ful (buk′it fool), *n.* as much as a bucket can hold. **—buck′et·fuls,** *pl.*

buck·eye (buk′ī), *n.* **1.** a tree very much like the horse chestnut. **2.** its large, brown, glossy seed, contained in a bur.

buck·le (buk′'l), *n.* **1.** a clasp on one end of a strap or belt for fastening the other end in place. **2.** an ornament like a clasp, as on shoes. —*v.* to fasten with a buckle. **—buckle down,** to set to work with real effort. **—buck′led,** *p.t. & p.p.;* **buck′ling,** *pr.p.*

buck·le (buk′'l), *v.* to bend, warp, or crumple [The bridge began to *buckle* under the weight of the truck.] —*n.* a part that is buckled. **—buck′-led,** *p.t. & p.p.;* **buck′ling,** *pr.p.*

buck·ler (buk′lər), *n.* a small, round shield worn on the arm.

buck·ram (buk′rəm), *n.* a coarse, stiff cloth used in binding books or as lining in clothes.

buck·saw (buk′sô), *n.* a saw set in a frame and held with both hands in cutting wood.

buck·shot (buk′shät), *n.* large lead shot for shooting deer and other large animals.

buck·skin (buk′skin), *n.* **1.** a soft, strong, tan leather made from the skins of deer or sheep. **2.** **buckskins,** *pl.* clothes or shoes of buckskin.

bucksaw

buck·toothed (buk′tootht), *adj.* having large front upper teeth that stick out.

buck·wheat (buk′hwēt), *n.* **1.** a plant grown for its dark-brown, three-cornered seeds. **2.** this seed, which is used as fodder and is ground into a dark flour. **3.** this flour, used in pancakes.

bu·col·ic (byoo käl′ik), *adj.* **1.** of shepherds; pastoral [the *bucolic* poems of Virgil]. **2.** of country life or farms; rural [It was surprising to find such a *bucolic* scene so near the city.]

bud (bud), *n.* **1.** a small swelling on a plant, from which a shoot, a flower, or leaves will grow. **2.** an early stage of growth or blossoming [Our lilacs are in *bud*.] —*v.* **1.** to begin to show buds. **2.** to begin to grow or blossom [When he was only three years old, Mozart was recognized as a *budding* genius.] —**nip in the bud,** to stop something when it is just beginning to develop. —**bud′ded,** *p.t. & p.p.;* **bud′ding,** *pr.p.*

Bu·da·pest (boo′də pest), *n.* the capital of Hungary, on the Danube.

Bud·dha (bood′ə), *n.* 563?–483? B.C.; a religious leader of India, who founded Buddhism.

Bud·dhism (bood′iz′m), *n.* a religion of Asia, founded by Buddha. It teaches that by right living and right thinking the soul is freed from pain, sorrow, and desire. —**Bud′dhist,** *adj. & n.*

statue of Buddha

bud·dy (bud′ē), *n.* a close friend; comrade: *used only in everyday talk.* —**bud′dies,** *pl.*

budge (buj), *v.* to move even a little [Both of us together could not *budge* the rock.] —**budged,** *p.t. & p.p.;* **budg′ing,** *pr.p.*

budg·et (buj′it), *n.* a careful plan for spending the money that is received in a certain period. —*v.* **1.** to plan the spending of money; make a budget. **2.** to fit something into a plan [I *budget* my time as well as my money.]

Bue·nos Ai·res (bwā′nəs ī′rās *or* er′ēz), the capital of Argentina, a seaport.

buff (buf), *n.* **1.** a heavy, soft, dark-yellow leather made from the skin of a buffalo or ox. **2.** a stick or wheel covered with leather, used for cleaning and shining. **3.** a dark-yellow color. —*adj.* dark-yellow. —*v.* to clean or shine, as with a buff.

Buf·fa·lo (buf′l ō), *n.* a city in New York.

buf·fa·lo (buf′l ō), *n.* a wild ox, sometimes tamed as a work animal, as the water buffalo of India. The American bison is also commonly called a *buffalo.* —**buf′fa·loes** or **buf′fa·los** or **buf′-fa·lo,** *pl.*

buffalo (5 ft. high)

Buffalo Bill, the nickname of **William F. Cody.**

buff·er (buf′ər), *n.* **1.** a person who buffs. **2.** a wheel or stick for buffing. **3.** anything that cushions the shock of a blow or bump. **4.** any person, country, etc. that comes between two others that are likely to fight.

buf·fet (buf′it), *n.* **1.** a slap or punch. **2.** any blow or shock [Hamlet felt the *buffets* of misfortune.] —*v.* to hit, punch, slap, etc. [The strong winds *buffeted* the old elm.]

buf·fet (bə fā′ *or* boo fā′), *n.* **1.** a piece of furniture with drawers and cupboards in which silverware, table linens, etc. are stored. **2.** platters of food on a buffet or table from which people serve themselves.

buf·foon (bu foon′), *n.* a person who is always clowning and trying to be funny; clown.

buf·foon·er·y (bu foon′ər ē), *n.* the jokes and tricks of a buffoon; clowning.

bug (bug), *n.* **1.** a crawling insect with sucking mouth parts. In common talk, any insect is often called a *bug.* **2.** a germ that causes disease: *used only in everyday talk.*

bug·a·boo (bug′ə boo), *n.* a bugbear. —**bug′-a·boos,** *pl.*

bug·bear (bug′ber), *n.* **1.** a frightening person or thing made up in stories to scare children into being good. **2.** a thing that one keeps being afraid of for no good reason.

bug·gy (bug′ē), *n.* **1.** a light carriage with one double seat, pulled by one horse. **2.** a baby's carriage. —**bug′gies,** *pl.*

bu·gle (byoo′g′l), *n.* a type of small trumpet, usually without keys or valves. Bugles are used mainly for sounding calls and signals, as in the army. —**bu·gler** (byoo′glər), *n.*

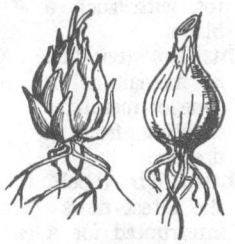

bugle

build (bild), *v.* **1.** to make by putting together materials or parts; construct [to *build* a house]. **2.** to bring into being; create, develop, etc. [to *build* a business; a theory *built* on facts]. —*n.* the way a thing is built or shaped; form or figure [a stocky *build*]. —**built** *or older* **build′ed,** *p.t. & p.p.;* **build′ing,** *pr.p.*

build·er (bil′dər), *n.* one that builds; especially, a person whose business is putting up houses and other buildings.

build·ing (bil′ding), *n.* **1.** anything that is built with walls and a roof; a structure, as a house, factory, school, etc. **2.** the act or work of one who builds.

built (bilt), *a past tense and past participle of* **build.**

built-in (bilt′in′), *adj.* made as part of the building; not movable [*built-in* cabinets].

bulb (bulb), *n.* **1.** the round, fleshy, underground growth of the onion, lily, etc., made up of layers of scales. It is the bud from which the stem and roots grow. **2.** an underground stem that looks like a bulb [A crocus *bulb* is not a true *bulb*.] **3.** anything shaped like a bulb [an electric light *bulb*].

bulbs

bulb·ous (bul′bəs), *adj.* **1.** growing from bulbs. **2.** shaped like a bulb [a *bulbous* nose].

Bul·gar·i·a (bul ger′i ə), *n.* a country in southeastern Europe, on the Black Sea. —**Bul·gar′i-an,** *adj. & n.*

bulge (bulj), *n.* a part that swells out [The marbles made a *bulge* in his pocket.] —*v.* to swell outward [The postman's bag *bulged* with mail.] —**bulged,** *p.t. & p.p.;* **bulg′ing,** *pr.p.*

bulk (bulk), *n.* **1.** a greatness of size or mass [The light carton was hard to carry because of its *bulk*.] **2.** the largest or main part [He lost the *bulk* of his fortune.] —*v.* to seem large or important. —**in bulk,** not put up in packages [to sell rice *in bulk*].

bulk·head (bulk′hed), *n.* any of the strong walls that divide a ship or airplane into sections. They keep water or fire from spreading in case of an accident.

bulk·y (bul′kē), *adj.* having great bulk; especially, so big as to be clumsy to handle [a *bulky* box]. —**bulk′i·er,** *compar.;* **bulk′i·est,** *superl.*

bull (bool), *n.* **1.** the male of any animal of the ox family. **2.** the male of some other large animals, as the elephant, moose, or whale. —*adj.* male [a *bull* moose].

bull (bool), *n.* an official letter or order from the Pope.

bull (bool), *n.* a silly but funny mistake in something said or written.

bull·dog (bool′dôg), *n.* a short-haired, stocky dog with a square jaw and a stubborn grip. —*v.* to throw a steer by seizing its horns and twisting its head around. —**bull′dogged,** *p.t. & p.p.;* **bull′dog·ging,** *pr.p.*

bull·doze (bool′dōz), *v.* to frighten by using force or threats; bully: *used only in everyday talk.* —**bull′-dozed,** *p.t. & p.p.;* **bull′-dozing,** *pr.p.*

bulldog (1½ ft. high)

bull·doz·er (bool′dōz′ər), *n.* **1.** a person who bulldozes. **2.** a large blade like a shovel on the front of a tractor, for pushing earth or rubble; also, a tractor with such a blade.

bul·let (bool′it), *n.* a small ball or cone of metal for shooting from a firearm.

bulldozer

bul·le·tin (bool′ə t'n), *n.* **1.** a short report of the latest news [The television program was interrupted for a *bulletin* on the plane crash.] **2.** a magazine or paper published regularly for the members of some group.

bulletin board, a board or wall space on which bulletins or notices are put up.

bull·fight (bool′fīt), *n.* a public show in which a bull is first stirred up to anger and is then killed by a matador with a sword. —**bull′fight·er,** *n.* —**bull′fight·ing,** *n.*

bull·finch (bool′finch), *n.* a small songbird of Europe and Asia, with a short, rounded beak.

bull·frog (bool′frôg *or* bool′fräg), *n.* a large frog that has a deep, loud croak.

bul·lion (bool′yən), *n.* bars of gold or silver before they have been made into coins.

bull·ock (bool′ək), *n.* an ox or steer.

bull's-eye (boolz′ī′), *n.* **1.** the round center of a target. **2.** a shot that hits this mark.

bul·ly (bool′ē), *n.* a person who likes to hurt or frighten those who are smaller or weaker. —*v.* to hurt or frighten as a bully does; browbeat; bull-doze. —*adj. & interj.* very good; fine: *used only in everyday talk.* —**bul′lies,** *pl.* —**bul′lied,** *p.t. & p.p.;* **bul′ly·ing,** *pr.p.*

bul·rush (bool′rush), *n.* a tall plant that grows in shallow water and marshy places.

bul·wark (bool′wərk), *n.* **1.** a wall of earth, stone, etc. for defending against an enemy. **2.** a person or thing that is a defense or protection [The Bill of Rights is a *bulwark* of our civil liberties.] **3.** **bulwarks,** *pl.* the part of a ship's side above the deck.

bum (bum), *n.* a person who does no work but spends his time loafing; a useless person; vagrant. —*v.* **1.** to loaf; idle away time. **2.** to beg for [to *bum* a ride]. —*adj.* bad; not good. *The word* bum *is slang in all its meanings.* —**bummed,** *p.t. & p.p.;* **bum′ming,** *pr.p.*

bum·ble·bee (bum′b'l bē′), *n.* a large, hairy, yellow-and-black bee that buzzes loudly.

bump (bump), *v.* **1.** to knock against something; hit with a jolt [The bus *bumped* the car ahead of it. Don't *bump* into the wall.] **2.** to move with jerks or jumps; jolt [The old car *bumped* down the road.] —*n.* **1.** a knock or blow; light jolt. **2.** a part that bulges out, causing an uneven surface. **3.** a swelling caused by a blow.

bump·er (bump′ər), *n.* **1.** a bar across the front or back of a car, etc. to give some protection if the car bumps into something. **2.** a cup or glass filled to the brim. —*adj.* very large or full [a *bumper* crop].

bump·kin (bump′kin), *n.* a person from the country who does not have city manners.

bump·y (bump′ē), *adj.* full of bumps; rough [a *bumpy* road]. —**bump′i·er,** *compar.;* **bump′-i·est,** *superl.* —**bu·mp′i·ly,** *adv.*

bun (bun), *n.* **1.** a small bread roll, often sweetened. **2.** hair worn in a twisted knot on the back of a woman's head.

bunch (bunch), *n.* **1.** a group of things of the same kind growing or placed together [a *bunch* of bananas; a *bunch* of keys]. **2.** a group of people: *used only in everyday talk* [A whole *bunch* of us are going.] —*v.* to gather into a bunch [Passengers *bunched* up at the front of the bus.]

bun·dle (bun′d'l), *n.* **1.** a group of things tied or wrapped up together [a *bundle* of dirty clothes]. **2.** any package or parcel. —*v.* **1.** to wrap or tie together into a bundle [*Bundle* your old newspapers together.] **2.** to send or go quickly [The children were *bundled* off to bed.] —**bundle up,** to put on plenty of warm clothing. —**bun′dled,** *p.t. & p.p.;* **bun′dling,** *pr.p.*

bung (bung), *n.* **1.** a cork or other stopper for the hole in a barrel or cask. **2.** such a hole, through which liquid can be drawn out: also called **bunghole.** —*v.* to close with a bung; stop up.

bun·ga·low (bung′gə lō), *n.* a small house with one story and an attic.

bun·gle (bung′g'l), *v.* to spoil by clumsy work; botch [He became nervous and *bungled* his part in the play.] —*n.* **1.** the act of bungling. **2.** a bungled piece of work. —**bun′gled,** *p.t. & p.p.;* **bun′gling,** *pr.p.* —**bun′gler,** *n.*

bun·ion (bun′yən), *n.* a red, painful swelling at the base of the big toe, with a thickening of the skin.

bunk (bungk), *n.* **1.** a bed that sticks out from the wall like a shelf. **2.** any narrow bed. —*v.* **1.** to sleep in a bunk. **2.** to use a makeshift sleeping place [Gene and I *bunked* in the barn.]

bunk (bungk), *n.* talk that is silly or misleading; nonsense; humbug: *a slang word.*

bunk·er (bung′kər), *n.* **1.** a large bin, as for storing fuel on a ship. **2.** a hollow or a mound of earth making an obstacle on a golf course.

Bun·ker Hill (bung′kər), a hill in Boston, Massachusetts. In 1775 a battle of the American Revolution took place nearby.

bun·ny (bun′ē), *n.* a rabbit: *pet name used by children.* —**bun′nies,** *pl.*

bunt (bunt), *v.* to bat a pitched baseball lightly so that it does not go out of the infield. —*n.* **1.** the act of bunting. **2.** a bunted ball.

bunt·ing (bun′ting), *n.* **1.** a thin cloth used in making flags. **2.** flags or pieces of cloth in the colors and patterns of the flag, used as decorations. **3.** a closed, warm blanket for wrapping a baby, with a hood for the head.

bunt·ing (bun′ting), *n.* a small bird that looks something like the sparrow.

bunting

Bunyan, Paul, see **Paul Bunyan.**

buoy (boo′ē *or* boi), *n.* **1.** an object floating in water and held in place by an anchor, to warn of danger or to mark a channel. It often has a light or bell. **2.** a life preserver: also called **life buoy.** —*v.* **1.** to keep afloat. **2.** to lift up or keep up in spirits; encourage [The team was *buoyed* up by hopes of victory.]

buoys

buoy·an·cy (boi′ən sē *or* boo′yən sē), *n.* **1.** the power to float or rise in liquid or air [Balsa wood is used in rafts because of its great *buoyancy.*] **2.** the power to keep something afloat [Blimps cannot fly high where the air is thin and has little *buoyancy.*] **3.** a cheerful spirit not easily kept down.

buoy·ant (boi′ənt *or* boo′yənt), *adj.* **1.** able to float or rise in liquid or air. **2.** able to keep things afloat [The Great Salt Lake in Utah is more *buoyant* than the ocean.] **3.** cheerful and lively [*buoyant* spirits]. —**buoy′ant·ly,** *adv.*

bur or **burr** (bŭr), *n.* **1.** a seedcase that is rough and prickly on the outside. **2.** a plant with burs. **3.** a thing that sticks like a bur. See also **burr.**

bur., abbreviation for **bureau.**

Bur·bank, Luther (bŭr′bangk), 1849–1926; U.S. scientist who bred many new kinds of fruits, flowers, and vegetables.

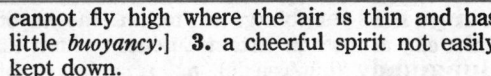

burs

bur·den (bŭr′d'n), *n.* **1.** anything that is carried; load [a light *burden*]. **2.** anything one has to bear or put up with; heavy load [a *burden* of responsibility]. —*v.* to put a burden on; load; weigh down [I won't *burden* you with my problems.] —**burden of proof,** the obligation to prove something.

bur·den (bŭr′d'n), *n.* **1.** the chorus of a song. **2.** the main or central idea; theme.

bur·den·some (bŭr′d'n səm), *adj.* hard to bear; troublesome [a *burdensome* duty].

bur·dock (bŭr′däk), *n.* a plant with burs, large leaves, and a strong smell.

bu·reau (byoo′rō), *n.* **1.** a chest of drawers for holding clothes. It usually has a mirror. **2.** an office, as for a certain part of a business [an information *bureau*]. **3.** a department of the government [The *Bureau* of Internal Revenue is in charge of collecting Federal taxes.] —**bu′reaus** or **bu·reaux** (byoo′rōz), *pl.*

bu·reauc·ra·cy (byoo räk′rə sē), *n.* **1.** government by appointed officials who follow all rules without question and without exceptions. **2.** such officials, as a group, or the way they govern. —**bu·reauc′ra·cies,** *pl.*

bu·reau·crat (byoo′rə krat), *n.* **1.** an official in a bureaucracy. **2.** any official who follows rules and routines blindly without thinking. —**bu′reau·crat′ic,** *adj.*

burg (bŭrg), *n.* a city, town, or village: *used only in everyday talk.*

bur·gess (bŭr′jis), *n.* **1.** a citizen of a borough. **2.** a member of the lower house of the legislature of Maryland or Virginia before the Revolution.

burgh (bŭrg *or* bŭr′ō), *n.* a chartered town in Scotland.

burgh·er (bŭr′gər), *n.* a citizen of a burgh or town.

bur·glar (bŭr′glər), *n.* a person who breaks into a building, especially in order to steal.

bur·gla·ry (bŭr′glə rē), *n.* the act of breaking into a building, especially at night in order to steal. —**bur′gla·ries,** *pl.*

fat, āpe, cär, ten, ēven, hit, bīte, gō, hôrn, tōōl, book, up, fŭr; get, joy, yet, chin, she, thin, *th*en; zh = s in pleasure; ' as in able (ā′b'l); ə = a in ago, e in agent, i in sanity, o in confess, u in focus.

bur·go·mas·ter (bŭr′gə mas′tər), *n.* the mayor of a city or town in certain European countries.

Bur·gun·dy (bŭr′gən dē), *n.* **1.** a district of eastern France that was once a kingdom. **2.** a red or white wine, originally from France.

bur·i·al (ber′i əl), *n.* the act of burying a dead body in a grave, tomb, or the sea.

bur·lap (bŭr′lap), *n.* a coarse cloth made of jute or hemp. It is used for making bags, etc.

bur·lesque (bər lesk′), *n.* **1.** a funny or sarcastic imitation of something serious [This musical comedy is a *burlesque* of a tragic Italian opera.] **2.** a stage show consisting of songs, dances, and comic skits, usually of a vulgar kind. —*adj.* imitating in a funny or sarcastic way [The play is a *burlesque* romance.] —*v.* to imitate in a funny or sarcastic way. —**bur·lesqued′**, *p.t.* & *p.p.*; **bur·les′quing**, *pr.p.*

bur·ly (bŭr′lē), *adj.* big and strong; husky. —**bur′li·er**, *compar.*; **bur′li·est**, *superl.*

Bur·ma (bŭr′mə), *n.* a country in southeastern Asia, on the Indian Ocean. —**Bur·mese** (bər mēz′), *adj.* & *n.*

burn (bŭrn), *v.* **1.** to be on fire; blaze [The candle *burned* for a long time.] **2.** to set on fire in order to give heat or light [They *burn* coal in their furnace.] **3.** to destroy or be destroyed by fire [We *burn* our rubbish at the dump.] **4.** to injure or be injured by fire or heat, or by something that has the same effect, as acid or friction; scorch, singe, scald, etc. **5.** to make by fire, acid, etc. [He *burned* a hole in his coat.] **6.** to make feel hot [Pepper *burned* his throat.] **7.** to feel hot [My head is *burning* with fever.] **8.** to excite or be excited, as with anger, curiosity, or desire. —*n.* an injury or damage caused by fire, heat, wind, acid, etc. —**burned** or **burnt**, *p.t.* & *p.p.*; **burn′ing**, *pr.p.*

burn (bŭrn), *n.* a brook: *a Scottish word.*

burn·er (bŭr′nər), *n.* **1.** the part of a stove, furnace, etc. from which the flame comes. **2.** a stove, furnace, etc. [an oil *burner*]. **3.** a person whose work is to burn something.

bur·nish (bŭr′nish), *v.* to make or become shiny by rubbing; polish [*burnished* gold]. —*n.* a gloss or polish.

bur·noose (bər nōōs′ *or* bŭr′nōōs), *n.* a long cloak with a hood, worn by Arabs and Moors.

Burns, Robert (bŭrnz), 1759–1796; Scottish poet.

burnt (bŭrnt), a past tense and past participle of **burn.** —*adj.* that has been burned.

burp (bŭrp), *n.* & *v.* belch: *a slang word.*

burr (bŭr), *n.* **1.** a rough edge left on metal, etc. after it has been cut or drilled. **2.** a dentist's drill. **3.** a strong rolling of the sound of the letter *r* [a Scottish *burr*]. **4.** a whirring or buzzing sound. See also **bur.**

burnoose

bur·ro (bŭr′ō), *n.* a donkey, especially one used as a pack animal in the southwestern U.S. —**bur′ros**, *pl.*

bur·row (bŭr′ō), *n.* a hole or tunnel dug in the ground by an animal [Woodchucks live in *burrows*.] —*v.* **1.** to dig a burrow. **2.** to live or hide as in a burrow. **3.** to search or work hard, as if by digging.

burst (bŭrst), *v.* **1.** to break open suddenly with force, especially because of pressure from the inside; fly into pieces; explode [A balloon will *burst* if you blow too much air into it.] **2.** to go, come, start, or appear suddenly and with force [He *burst* into the room. She *burst* into tears.] **3.** to be as full or as crowded as possible [a room *bursting* with people; people *bursting* with joy]. —*n.* **1.** a sudden outbreak; explosion [He was greeted with a *burst* of cheers.] **2.** a sudden, forceful effort or action; spurt [a *burst* of speed]. —**burst**, *p.t.* & *p.p.*; **burst′ing**, *pr.p.*

Bu·run·di (boo roon′dē), *n.* a country in east central Africa, east of Congo.

bur·y (ber′ē), *v.* **1.** to put a dead body into the earth, a tomb, or the sea [The Egyptians *buried* the Pharaohs in pyramids.] **2.** to cover up so as to hide [She *buried* her face in the pillow.] **3.** to put away and forget [Let's *bury* our feud.] **4.** to put oneself deeply into [He *buried* himself in his work.] —**bur′ied**, *p.t.* & *p.p.*; **bur′y·ing**, *pr.p.*

bus (bus), *n.* a large motor coach for carrying many passengers, usually along a regular route. —**bus′es** or **bus′ses**, *pl.*

bush (boosh), *n.* **1.** a woody plant, smaller than a tree and having many stems branching out low instead of one main stem or trunk; shrub. **2.** wild land that has not been cleared and settled [The hunting party was lost in the *bush*.] —*v.* to spread or grow out like a bush. —**beat around the bush,** to talk around a subject without getting to the point.

bush·el (boosh′əl), *n.* **1.** a measure of volume for grain, fruit, vegetables, etc. It is equal to 4 pecks, or 32 quarts. **2.** a basket or other container that holds a bushel.

bush·ing (boosh′ing), *n.* a metal lining used to keep moving parts of a machine from wearing down. It can be replaced when it is worn out.

bush·mas·ter (boosh′mas′tər), *n.* a large, poisonous snake of South America.

bush·y (boosh′ē), *adj.* **1.** thick and spreading out like a bush [*bushy* eyebrows]. **2.** overgrown with bushes [*bushy* land]. —**bush′i·er**, *compar.*; **bush′i·est**, *superl.*

bus·i·ly (biz′'l ē), *adv.* in a busy way.

busi·ness (biz′nis), *n.* **1.** what one does for a living; one's work or occupation [Shakespeare's *business* was writing plays.] **2.** what one has a right or a duty to do [You had no *business* telling her I was here.] **3.** a matter or affair [Let's settle the whole *business* of what I'm to do.] **4.** the buying and selling of goods and services; commerce; trade. **5.** a place where things are made or sold; store or factory [He owns three *businesses*.] —*adj.* of or for business [a *business* office; *business* hours]. —**mean business,** to be in earnest: *used only in everyday talk.*

busi·ness·like (biz′nis līk′), *adj.* working with care and good system; efficient.

busi·ness·man (biz′nis man′), *n.* a man who is the owner or manager of a business. —**busi′-ness·men′**, *pl.* —**busi′ness·wom′an**, *n.fem.*

bus·kin (bus′kin), *n.* a kind of boot worn long ago. The laced buskin worn by tragic actors in ancient Athens is a symbol of Greek tragedy.

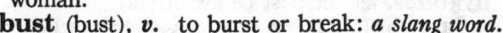

buskins

buss (bus), *n. & v.* kiss: *now seldom used.*

bus·ses (bus′iz), *n.* a plural of **bus.**

bust (bust), *n.* **1.** a piece of sculpture showing the head and upper chest of a person. **2.** the bosom of a woman.

bust (bust), *v.* to burst or break: *a slang word.*

bus·tle (bus′'l), *v.* to hurry busily or with much fuss and bother. —*n.* a bustling; busy and noisy activity [the *bustle* of traffic during the rush hour]. —**bus′tled**, *p.t. & p.p.;* **bus′-tling**, *pr.p.*

bust

bus·tle (bus′'l), *n.* a padding or frame worn at the back by women to puff out the skirt.

bus·y (biz′ē), *adj.* **1.** doing something; active; at work; not idle [The students are *busy* at their desks.] **2.** full of activity; with much action or motion [a *busy* morning; a *busy* store]. **3.** being used [Short buzzes on the phone tell that the line is *busy.*] —*v.* to make or keep busy [The women *busied* themselves in the kitchen.] —**bus′i·er,** *compar.;* **bus′i·est,** *superl.* —**bus′ied,** *p.t. & p.p.;* **bus′y·ing,** *pr.p.*

bus·y·bod·y (biz′ē bäd′ē), *n.* a person who mixes into other people's business; meddler. —**bus′y·bod′ies,** *pl.*

bustle

but (but), *prep.* except; other than [Nobody came *but* me.] —*conj.* **1.** yet; however [The story is long, *but* it is never dull.] **2.** on the contrary [I am old, *but* you are young.] **3.** except that; unless [It never rains *but* it pours.] **4.** that [I don't question *but* you're correct.] —*adv.* **1.** only [if I had *but* known]. **2.** no more than; merely [He is *but* a child.] —**all but,** almost. —**but for,** if it were not for. —**cannot but,** have no choice except to.

butch·er (booch′ər), *n.* **1.** a person whose work is killing animals for use as food. **2.** a person who cuts up meat for sale. **3.** a cruel person who causes many deaths or much suffering. —*v.* **1.** to kill animals for use as food. **2.** to kill in a cruel, senseless way; slaughter [The army *butchered* the helpless civilians.] **3.** to mess up; spoil by poor work; botch.

butch·er·y (booch′ər ē), *n.* cruel slaughter.

but·ler (but′lər), *n.* a man servant, usually one in charge of the other servants.

butt (but), *n.* **1.** the thick end of anything [a rifle *butt*]. **2.** the end left after something is used; stub [a cigar *butt*]. **3.** a person who is made fun of or teased [The fat boy was the *butt* of their unkind jokes.]

butt (but), *v.* to strike or push with the head; ram [Goats *butt.*] —*n.* a butting; push with the head. —**butt in** or **butt into,** to mix into someone else's business: *a slang phrase.*

butt (but), *n.* a large cask for wine or beer.

butte (byōōt), *n.* a steep hill standing alone in a plain; often, a small mesa: see **mesa.**

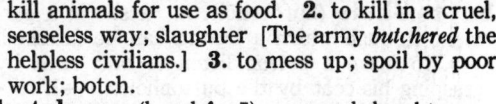

butte

but·ter (but′ər), *n.* **1.** the yellow fat gotten by churning cream. It is used as a spread on bread and in cooking. **2.** a thing that looks like butter or is used like butter [peanut *butter*]. —*v.* to spread with butter [*Butter* the toast.]

but·ter·cup (but′ər kup), *n.* a plant with yellow, cup-shaped flowers, growing in fields.

but·ter·fat (but′ər fat), *n.* the fatty part of milk, from which butter is made.

but·ter·fly (but′ər flī), *n.* an insect with a slender body and four broad wings, usually brightly colored. —**but′ter·flies,** *pl.*

but·ter·milk (but′ər milk), *n.* the sour liquid left after churning butter from milk.

but·ter·nut (but′ər nut) *n.* **1.** the oily nut of the white walnut tree. **2.** this walnut tree.

buttercup

but·ter·scotch (but′ər skäch), *n.* a hard, sticky candy made from brown sugar and butter.

but·tocks (but′əks), *n.pl.* the fleshy parts where the legs join the back of the body; rump.

but·ton (but′'n), *n.* **1.** a small disk or knob sewed to a garment. It is pushed through a slit to fasten parts together or is just a decoration. **2.** a small knob that is pushed or turned to work a bell, light, machine, etc. —*v.* to fasten or close with a button or buttons [*Button* up your overcoat.]

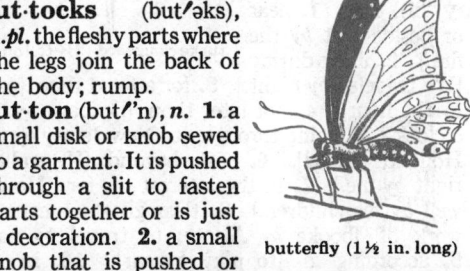

butterfly (1½ in. long)

but·ton·hole (but'′n hōl), *n.* a slit in a garment through which a button can be fastened. —*v.* to make a person listen to one, as if by grasping his coat by the buttonholes. —**but'·ton·holed,** *p.t. & p.p.;* **but'ton·hol·ing,** *pr.p.*

but·ton·wood (but'′n wood), *n.* **1.** the American sycamore tree. **2.** its wood.

but·tress (but'ris), *n.* **1.** a support built against a wall to make it strong. **2.** any support or prop. —*v.* to prop up or support [to *buttress* a wall; to *buttress* an argument].

bux·om (buk'səm), *adj.* plump, healthy, and good-natured [Only women are called *buxom.*]

buy (bī), *v.* to get by paying money or something else; purchase [The Dutch *bought* Manhattan Island for about $24.] —*n.* the value of a thing compared with its price [Turnips are your best *buy* in January vegetables.] —**buy off,** to bribe. —**buy out,** to buy all the stock or business rights of. —**buy up,** to buy all of something that can be gotten. —**bought,** *p.t. & p.p.;* **buy'ing,** *pr.p.* —**buy'er,** *n.*

buttress

buzz (buz), *v.* **1.** to make a humming sound like a long, steady *z* [Bees *buzz* in flight.] **2.** to talk in low, excited tones [The town *buzzed* with the news.] **3.** to fly an airplane low over [A pilot was fined for *buzzing* the tower.] **4.** to signal with a buzzer. —*n.* **1.** a humming sound like a long, steady *z.* **2.** a confused sound, as of many excited voices. —**buzz about** or **buzz around,** to scurry around. —**give someone a buzz,** to telephone someone: *slang.*

buz·zard (buz'ərd), *n.* **1.** a kind of hawk that is slow and heavy in flight. **2.** a vulture with a naked, reddish head: also **turkey buzzard.**

buz·zer (buz'ər), *n.* an electrical device that makes a buzzing sound used as a signal.

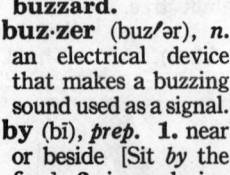
turkey buzzard (2½ ft. long)

by (bī), *prep.* **1.** near or beside [Sit *by* the fire.] **2.** in or during [We traveled *by* night.] **3.** for a fixed time [paid *by* the hour]. **4.** not later than [Be back *by* ten o'clock.] **5.** going through [to New Jersey *by* the Holland Tunnel]. **6.** past; beyond [He walked right *by* me.] **7.** in the interest of; for [He did well *by* his children.] **8.** through the means or work of [books *by* Alcott; to travel *by* car]. **9.** according to [to play *by* ear]. **10.** in [It grows dark *by* degrees.] **11.** with permission of [*by* your leave]. **12.** in the amount of [cheaper *by* the dozen; cloth *by* the yard]. —*adv.* **1.** near; close at hand [Stand *by!*] **2.** away; aside [Put some money *by* for a rainy day.] **3.** past [We watched the parade go *by.*] —**by and by,** after a while. —**by and large,** on the whole; considering everything. —**by the by** or **by the bye,** by the way.

by-, a prefix meaning: **1.** close by; near [A *bystander* stands near the scene of action.] **2.** on the side; of lesser importance [A *by-product* is of lesser importance than the main product.]

by-and-by (bī'′n bī'), *n.* a future time.

Bye·lo·rus·sia (bye'lə rush'ə), *n.* a republic in the western part of the Soviet Union.

by·gone (bī'gôn), *adj.* past; gone by. —*n.* anything that is gone or past. —**let bygones be bygones,** let the past be forgotten.

by·law (bī'lô), *n.* a rule passed by a club, a board of directors, etc. for use in its own meetings.

by·line (bī'līn'), *n.* a line at the head of a newspaper article telling who wrote it.

by·pass (bī'pas'), *n.* a road, pipe, etc. that leaves the main route in order to get around an obstacle [Route 2A is a *by-pass* around the town.] —*v.* to go around instead of through.

by-pass

by·path or **by-path** (bī'path'), *n.* side path; path away from the main roads.

by·play (bī'plā), *n.* action going on aside from the main action, as in a scene of a play.

by·prod·uct (bī'präd'əkt), *n.* anything made from the things left over in making a main product [Glue is a *by-product* of meat packing.]

by·road (bī'rōd), *n.* a side road; bypath.

By·ron, George Gor·don (gôr'd'n bī'rən), 1788–1824; English poet: called **Lord Byron.**

by·stand·er (bī'stan'dər), *n.* a person who stands near but does not take part in what is happening; onlooker.

by·way (bī'wā), *n.* a side path; bypath.

by·word (bī'wûrd), *n.* **1.** a common saying; proverb ["Waste not, want not" is a *byword* with him.] **2.** a person or thing considered typical of something bad [His cruelty has made him a *byword.*]

By·zan·tine (biz'′n tēn *or* biz'′n tīn), *adj.* having to do with the eastern part of the later Roman Empire (395–1435 A.D.). Byzantine architecture had domes over square areas, round arches, and mosaic art work.

By·zan·ti·um (bi zan'shi əm *or* bi zan'ti əm), *n.* an ancient city where Istanbul now stands. It was the capital of the Byzantine Empire.

C

C, c (sē), *n.* the third letter of the English alphabet. —**C's, c's** (sēz), *pl.*

C, *n.* **1.** the Roman numeral for 100. **2.** the symbol for the chemical element *carbon.*

C., c., abbreviation for **cent** or **cents, centi-grade, centimeter, century, chapter, copyright, cubic.**

Ca, symbol for the chemical element *calcium.*

cab (kab), *n.* **1.** a carriage or an automobile (**taxicab**) that can be hired along with its driver. **2.** the place in a locomotive, truck, crane, etc. where the driver or engineer sits.

ca·bal (kə bal′), *n.* **1.** a small group of persons who are joined in a secret scheme or plot. **2.** the scheme or plot of such a group.

ca·ba·na (kə bä′nyä *or* kə ban′ə), *n.* **1.** a cabin or hut. **2.** a small shelter where one can change his clothes to go swimming.

cab·a·ret (kab ə rā′), *n.* a restaurant with dancing and singing as entertainment.

cab·bage (kab′ij), *n.* a vegetable with thick leaves folded tightly over each other to form a hard, round head.

cab·in (kab′in), *n.* **1.** a small house built in a simple, rough way, usually of wood [Lincoln was born in a log *cabin.*] **2.** a room on a ship, especially one with berths for sleeping. **3.** the space in an aircraft where the passengers ride.

cab·i·net (kab′ə nit), *n.* **1.** a case or cupboard with drawers or shelves for holding or storing things [a china *cabinet;* a medicine *cabinet*]. **2.** *often* **Cabinet,** a group of officials appointed by the head of a nation to advise him. The President's cabinet is made up of the heads of the departments of our government.

china cabinet

cab·i·net·mak·er (kab′ə nit māk′ər), *n.* a workman who makes fine furniture or woodwork.

ca·ble (kā′b'l), *n.* **1.** a thick, heavy rope, often made of strands of wire [The bridge is supported by *cables.*] **2.** a bundle of insulated wires through which electric current can be sent [Telephone and telegraph *cables* are often laid under the ground or on the ocean floor.] **3.** a cablegram. —*v.* to send a cablegram to. —**ca′bled,** *p.t. & p.p.;* **ca′bling,** *pr.p.*

ca·ble·gram (kā′b'l gram), *n.* a message sent across an ocean by telegraph cable.

ca·boose (kə bōos′), *n.* a car for the trainmen on a freight train. It is usually the last car.

Cab·ot, John (kab′ət), 1450–1498; Italian explorer who discovered North America in 1497 while he sailed in the service of England.

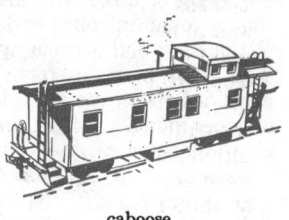
caboose

ca·ca·o (kə kā′ō *or* kə kä′ō), *n.* **1.** a small tropical tree from whose seeds cocoa and chocolate are made. **2.** these seeds. —**ca·ca′os,** *pl.*

cache (kash), *n.* **1.** a place for hiding or storing something, as food or supplies. **2.** anything so hidden. —*v.* to hide or store in a cache. —**cached,** *p.t. & p.p.;* **cach′ing,** *pr.p.*

cack·le (kak′'l), *v.* **1.** to make the shrill, broken sounds of a hen. **2.** to laugh or talk in a shrill way. —*n.* the act or sound of cackling. —**cack′led,** *p.t. & p.p.;* **cack′ling,** *pr.p.*

cac·tus (kak′təs), *n.* a plant with fleshy stems that bear spines or scales instead of leaves, often having showy flowers. Cactuses grow in hot, dry places. —**cac′tus·es** or **cac·ti** (kak′tī), *pl.*

cactus

cad (kad), *n.* a man who treats others in a way that is not right or honorable.

ca·dav·er·ous (kə dav′ər əs), *adj.* looking as pale, thin, and bony as one might in death.

cad·die *or* **cad·dy** (kad′ē), *n.* a person whose work is carrying golfers' clubs on the golf course. —*v.* to do the work of a caddie. —**cad′dies,** *pl.* —**cad′died,** *p.t. & p.p.;* **cad′dy·ing,** *pr.p.*

ca·dence (kā′d'ns), *n.* **1.** flow or rhythm with a regular beat [the *cadence* of waves breaking on the shore; to march in a fast *cadence*]. **2.** the rise or fall of the voice in speaking; also, the tone of the voice [a quiet *cadence*]. **3.** the final chords or other ending of a section of music.

ca·det (kə det′), *n.* **1.** a student in training to become an officer in the army, navy, or air force. **2.** a student at any military school.

cad·mi·um (kad′mi əm), *n.* a blue-white metal that is a chemical element. It is used in alloys and pigments.

Cae·sar (sē′zər), *n.* **1.** 100?–44 B.C.; Roman general and dictator who built up the Roman

Empire: also called **Julius Caesar. 2.** the title of some of the Roman emperors who followed Caesar. **3.** an emperor or dictator.

ca·fé (ka fā′), *n.* a restaurant or barroom.

caf·e·te·ri·a (kaf′ə tir′i ə), *n.* a restaurant in which people go to a counter to get their food before they sit down to eat.

caf·feine or **caf·fein** (kaf′ēn), *n.* a substance that is found in coffee and tea. It is a stimulant to the heart and nervous system.

cage (kāj), *n.* **1.** a box or closed-off space with wires or bars on the sides, in which to keep birds or other animals. **2.** a thing that looks like this, as an elevator car. —*v.* to shut up in a cage. —**caged**, *p.t. & p.p.;* **cag′ing**, *pr.p.*

cage·y (kāj′ē), *adj.* sly, tricky, or cunning: *used only in everyday talk.* —**cag′i·er**, *compar.;* **cag′i·est**, *superl.*

Cain (kān), *n.* in the Bible, the oldest son of Adam and Eve. He killed his brother Abel. —**raise Cain,** to make much noise, trouble, etc.: *a slang phrase.*

cairn (kern), *n.* a heap of stones in the form of a cone, built long ago as a tomb or landmark.

Cai·ro (kī′rō), *n.* the capital of the United Arab Republic, in Egypt on the Nile River.

cais·son (kā′sən), *n.* **1.** a trailer cart for carrying artillery ammunition. **2.** a watertight box inside of which men do building under water.

cai·tiff (kā′tif), *n.* a wicked or cowardly person; villain. —*adj.* wicked or cowardly.

ca·jole (kə jōl′), *v.* to coax with flattery or false promises; wheedle. —**ca·joled′**, *p.t. & p.p.;* **ca·jol′ing**, *pr.p.* —**ca·jol′er·y**, *n.*

cake (kāk), *n.* **1.** a mixture of flour, eggs, milk, sugar, etc., baked in a loaf and often covered with icing. **2.** a small, flat mass of batter or of some hashed food, that is fried or baked [a griddle *cake;* a fish *cake*]. **3.** any solid mass with a definite shape [a *cake* of soap]. —*v.* to form into a hard mass [The paint was old and had *caked* in the can.] —**caked**, *p.t. & p.p.;* **cak′ing**, *pr.p.*

Cal., an abbreviation for **California.**

cal·a·bash (kal′ə bash), *n.* **1.** a tropical American tree with a fruit that looks like a gourd. **2.** this fruit. **3.** a bowl, tobacco pipe, etc. made from the dried shell of this fruit.

cal·a·mine (kal′ə mīn), *n.* a zinc compound that is used in skin lotions.

ca·lam·i·tous (kə lam′ə təs), *adj.* bringing calamity or disaster [a *calamitous* winter].

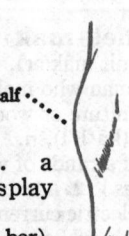

man smoking
a calabash

ca·lam·i·ty (kə lam′ə tē), *n.* **1.** deep trouble or misery [the *calamity* of war]. **2.** a happening that brings great loss and sorrow; disaster. —**ca·lam′i·ties**, *pl.*

cal·ci·fy (kal′sə fī), *v.* to turn hard and stony from deposits of lime or calcium salts. —**cal′ci·fied**, *p.t. & p.p.;* **cal′ci·fy·ing**, *pr.p.*

cal·ci·mine (kal′sə mīn), *n.* a white or colored, watery liquid used as a thin paint for plastered ceilings or walls. —*v.* to cover with calcimine.

—**cal′ci·mined**, *p.t. & p.p.;* **cal′ci·min·ing**, *pr.p.*

cal·cine (kal′sīn), *v.* to heat or burn something until it dries out and turns into powder or ashes. —**cal′cined**, *p.t. & p.p.;* **cal′cin·ing**, *pr.p.*

cal·ci·um (kal′si əm), *n.* a chemical element that is a soft, silver-white metal. It is found combined with other elements in the bones of animals and in limestone, marble, chalk, etc.

cal·cu·late (kal′kyoo lāt′), *v.* **1.** to find out by using arithmetic; compute [*Calculate* the amount of cloth you will need for the skirt.] **2.** to find out by reasoning; estimate [He tried to *calculate* the effect of his decision.] **3.** to plan or intend [His joke was *calculated* to shock us.] —**cal′cu·lat′ed**, *p.t. & p.p.;* **cal′cu·lat′ing**, *pr.p.*

cal·cu·lat·ing (kal′kyoo lā′ting), *adj.* full of sly schemes; shrewd or cunning.

cal·cu·la·tion (kal′kyoo lā′shən), *n.* **1.** the act of calculating. **2.** the answer found by calculating. **3.** careful thought or planning.

cal·cu·la·tor (kal′kyoo lā′tər), *n.* **1.** a person who calculates. **2.** a machine that adds, subtracts, etc. rapidly. **3.** an electronic machine that can work out complicated problems in mathematics.

cal·cu·lus (kal′kyoo ləs), *n.* a branch of mathematics that can be used to solve hard problems in science and statistics.

Cal·cut·ta (kal kut′ə), *n.* a seaport in northeastern India.

cal·dron (kôl′drən), *n.* a large pot or kettle.

cal·en·dar (kal′ən dər), *n.* **1.** a system for arranging time into days, weeks, months, and years [Most countries now use the Gregorian *calendar.*] **2.** a table or chart showing such an arrangement, usually for a single year [Do you have an old 1950 *calendar?*] **3.** a list or schedule [A court *calendar* lists the cases to be heard.]

cal·en·der (kal′ən dər), *n.* a machine with rollers for giving paper or cloth a smooth or glossy surface. —*v.* to press in such a machine.

calf (kaf), *n.* **1.** a young cow or bull. **2.** a young elephant, whale, hippopotamus, seal, etc. **3.** calfskin. —**calves,** *pl.*

calf (kaf), *n.* the fleshy back part of the leg between the knee and the ankle. —**calves,** *pl.*

calf·skin (kaf′skin), *n.* **1.** the skin of a calf. **2.** a soft, flexible leather made from this.

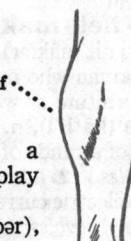

calf

Cal·i·ban (kal′ə ban), *n.* a savage slave in Shakespeare's play *The Tempest.*

cal·i·ber or **cal·i·bre** (kal′ə bər), *n.* **1.** the size of a bullet or gun shell as measured by its diameter [A bullet of .45 *caliber* is 45/100 inch in diameter.] **2.** the diameter of the inside of a gun barrel or other tube [A gun of .45 *caliber* fires a .45 *caliber* bullet.] **3.** ability or quality [a statesman of high *caliber*].

cal·i·brate (kal′ə brāt), *v.* **1.** to find out the caliber of. **2.** to check or correct the markings for the degrees on a measuring instrument, as a thermometer. **—cal′i·brat·ed,** *p.t. & p.p.;* **cal′i·brat·ing,** *pr.p.* **—cal′i·bra′tion,** *n.*

cal·i·co (kal′ə kō), *n.* a cheap cotton cloth, usually printed with a colored pattern. **—adj.** **1.** made of calico. **2.** spotted like calico [a *calico* cat]. **—cal′i·coes** or **cal′i·cos,** *pl.*

Cal·i·for·nia (kal′ə fôr′nyə), *n.* a State in the southwestern part of the United States, on the Pacific Coast: abbreviated **Calif.** or **Cal.** **—Cal′i·for′nian,** *adj. & n.*

cal·i·pers (kal′ə pərz), *n.pl.* an instrument made up of a pair of hinged legs, for measuring the thickness or diameter of a thing.

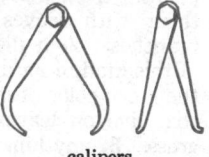
calipers

ca·liph or **ca·lif** (kā′lif), *n.* supreme ruler: the title taken by some of the heads of Moslem states in past times.

cal·is·then·ics (kal′əs then′iks), *n.pl.* exercises or drills that are done to develop a strong, trim body.

boys doing calisthenics

calk (kôk), *v.* to fill up cracks or seams with putty, tar, etc. [Boats are *calked* to make them watertight. Windows are *calked* to keep the warm air inside.] Also spelled **caulk.**

call (kôl), *v.* **1.** to say in a loud voice; cry out; shout [The sergeant *called* the roll. *Call* for help.] **2.** to order to come; summon [Mother is *calling* me home.] **3.** to visit for a short time [The minister *called*, but he didn't stay long.] **4.** to telephone. **5.** to give a name to [George is *called* Bud by his friends.] **6.** to give a signal to, as in order to awaken [Ask the hotel clerk to *call* you at 7 o'clock.] **7.** to think of as being [I *call* such gossip shameful.] **8.** to stop [The umpire *called* the game because of rain.] **—n. 1.** the act of calling; shout or cry [a *call* for help.] **2.** an order to come; summons or invitation [He answered the *call* to arms.] **3.** strong attraction [Do you feel the *call* of the sea?] **4.** need or necessity [There's no *call* for you to laugh at us.] **5.** a signal or message [Did you get your telephone *call* from New York?] **6.** the special cry or sound of a particular animal or bird. **7.** a short visit [The doctor is out making *calls.*] **—call for, 1.** to make a strong request for; demand. **2.** to come and get; stop for. **—call forth,** to bring into action or being [*Call forth* your courage.] **—call off, 1.** to order away [*Call off* the dog.] **2.** to read out loud from a list [*Call off* the roll.] **3.** to decide not to have an event that was supposed to take place: *only in everyday talk.* **—call on, 1.** to visit for a short time. **2.** to ask a person to speak. **—call out,** to speak in a loud voice; shout. **—call up, 1.** to recall. **2.** to order to come, especially for

duty in the armed forces. **3.** to telephone. **—on call,** ready when called for. **—call′er,** *n.*

cal·la (kal′ə), *n.* a plant with a large, white leaf that looks like a flower surrounding a long, yellow spike that is the true flower: also **calla lily.**

call·ing (kôl′ing), *n.* **1.** the action of one that calls. **2.** one's trade, occupation, or profession.

cal·li·o·pe (kə lī′ə pē *or* kal′i ōp), *n.* a musical instrument with a series of steam whistles. It is played like an organ.

calliope

cal·lis·then·ics (kal′əs then′iks), *n.pl.* calisthenics.

cal·lous (kal′əs), *adj.* **1.** having a callus or calluses; thick-skinned [the *callous* hands of a blacksmith]. **2.** not having any feeling for the suffering of others; unfeeling [a *callous* remark]. **—v.** to make or become callous.

cal·low (kal′ō), *adj.* young and without experience; immature [a *callow* lad].

cal·lus (kal′əs), *n.* a hard, thickened place on the skin. **—cal′lus·es,** *pl.*

calm (käm), *adj.* not disturbed, excited, or stirred up; quiet; still [a *calm* sea; a *calm* mind; a *calm* answer]. **—n.** a lack of wind or motion; stillness; quiet [The ship lies motionless in the *calm.*] **—v.** to make or become calm. **—calm′ly,** *adv.* **—calm′ness,** *n.*

cal·o·mel (kal′ə m'l), *n.* a white, tasteless powder that is a compound of mercury. It is used as a medicine to make the bowels move.

ca·lor·ic (kə lôr′ik), *adj.* **1.** of heat. **2.** of calories [Nuts have a high *caloric* content.]

cal·o·rie (kal′ə rē), *n.* the unit for measuring heat. It is also the unit for measuring the energy that food supplies to the body [One large egg supplies about 100 *calories.*]

cal·u·met (kal′yoo met), *n.* a pipe smoked by American Indians as a sign of peace.

cal·um·ny (kal′əm nē), *n.* a false and mean statement that is made to hurt someone's reputation; slander. **—cal′um·nies,** *pl.*

calumet

Cal·va·ry (kal′və rē), *n.* in the Bible, the place near Jerusalem where Jesus was put to death.

calves (kavz), *n.* plural of **calf.**

Cal·vin, John (kal′vin), 1509–1564; French Protestant leader.

Cal·vin·ism (kal′vin iz'm), *n.* the religious system of John Calvin, which teaches that God has

fat, āpe, cär, ten, ēven, hit, bīte, gō, hôrn, tōol, book, up, fûr;
get, joy, yet, chin, she, thin, *th*en; zh = s in pleasure; ′ as in able (ā′b'l);
ə = a in ago, e in agent, i in sanity, o in confess, u in focus.

decided the fate of each man. —**Cal′vin·ist,** *adj.* & *n.*

ca·lyp·so (kə lip′sō), *adj.* describing a kind of West Indian song that is made up as it is being sung. Calypso songs have a strong rhythm and are often about current events.

ca·lyx (kā′liks), *n.* the outer ring of leaves, or sepals, growing at the base of a flower. It forms the outer cover of the unopened bud. —**ca′lyx·es** or **cal·y·ces** (kal′ə sēz), *pl.*

calyx

cam (kam), *n.* a wheel with an irregular shape or with a part sticking out, which gives an irregular motion to another wheel or to a shaft moving along its edge. Cams are used to change circular motion to a back-and-forth motion.

ca·ma·ra·de·rie (kä′mə rä′dər ē), *n.* the warm friendship that comrades feel for one another.

cam·ber (kam′bər), *n.* a slight arch, as in the surface of an airplane wing. —*v.* to arch slightly.

cam·bi·um (kam′bi əm), *n.* the layer of soft tissue under the bark of trees and other woody plants. New bark and wood grow from it.

Cam·bo·di·a (kam bō′di ə), *n.* a country in a large peninsula south of central China.

cam·bric (kām′brik), *n.* a thin, closely woven cloth of linen or cotton.

Cam·bridge (kām′brij), *n.* **1.** a city in England, home of Cambridge University. **2.** a city in Massachusetts, home of Harvard University.

came (kām), past tense of **come.**

cam·el (kam′′l), *n.* a large, cud-chewing animal with a humped back, that is the common beast of burden in Asian and North African deserts. When food and drink are scarce, it can keep going for a few days on the fat and water stored in its body tissue. The **Arabian camel** has one hump; the **Bac·tri·an** (bak′tri ən) camel has two.

Arabian camel
(about 7 ft. high)

ca·mel·li·a (kə mēl′yə), *n.* a plant with shiny evergreen leaves and large white or red flowers.

Cam·e·lot (kam′ə lät), *n.* in British legend, the city where King Arthur held court.

cam·e·o (kam′i ō), *n.* a gem with a figure carved in it. Its two layers are usually of different colors, so that when the top is carved, the bottom serves as a background. —**cam′e·os,** *pl.*

cameo

cam·er·a (kam′ər ə), *n.* **1.** a closed box for taking pictures. The light that enters when a lens or hole at one end is opened forms an image on the film or plate at the other end. **2.** that part of a television transmitter which picks up the picture to be sent.

Cam·e·roun (kam ə rōōn′), *n.* a country in western Africa, on the Atlantic Ocean.

cam·o·mile (kam′ə mīl), *n.* a plant whose flowers, which look like daisies, are dried and brewed into a kind of tea for use as a medicine.

cam·ou·flage (kam′ə fläzh), *n.* **1.** the act of hiding soldiers, guns, etc. from the enemy by making them look like part of the landscape, as by painting them or covering them with leaves and branches. **2.** a disguise of this kind in nature, as the green color of insects that live on leaves and grass. **3.** anything used to disguise or mislead. —*v.* to disguise in order to hide. —**cam′ou·flaged,** *p.t.* & *p.p.;* **cam′ou·flag·ing,** *pr.p.*

soldier protected
by camouflage

camp (kamp), *n.* **1.** a group of tents, huts, or other rough shelters to live in for a time. **2.** a place with barracks or tents where soldiers, sailors, etc. live while they are being trained or when they are not in combat. **3.** a place in the country where people, especially children, can have an outdoor vacation. —*v.* **1.** to set up a camp [Let's *camp* by the river tonight.] **2.** to live in a camp for a time. —**break camp,** to take down a camp and go away.

cam·paign (kam pān′), *n.* **1.** a series of battles or other military actions having a special goal [Napoleon's Russian *campaign* ended with the defeat of his armies.] **2.** a series of planned actions for getting something done [a *campaign* to get someone elected]. —*v.* to take part in a campaign. —**cam·paign′er,** *n.*

cam·pa·ni·le (kam′pə nē′lē), *n.* a tower with bells in it, often standing alone.

camp·er (kamp′ər), *n.* **1.** a person who spends his vacation at a camp. **2.** a motor vehicle or trailer having the special things needed for camping.

camp·fire (kamp′fīr), *n.* an outdoor fire, as at a camp.

Camp Fire Girls, a club for girls that seeks to help them become healthy women of good character.

cam·phor (kam′fər), *n.* a substance with a strong smell, that comes from the wood of an Oriental tree. It is used to protect clothes from moths and in skin ointments.

campanile

cam·pus (kam′pəs), *n.* the grounds of a college or school.

can (kan), *a helping verb used with other verbs and meaning:* **1.** to know how to [He *can* add and subtract.] **2.** to be able to [The baby *can* walk.]

3. to have the right to [He *can* vote when he is twenty-one.] **4.** to have permission to; may [*Can* I go out to play?] **—could,** *p.t.*

can (kan), *n.* **1.** a metal container of various kinds [a milk *can;* a *can* of shoe polish]. **2.** a metal container in which foods are sealed so as to keep in good condition for some time. **3.** as much as a can holds; canful. **—v.** to put into airtight cans or jars so as to keep in good condition for later use. **—canned,** *p.t. & p.p.;* **can′ning,** *pr.p.* **—can′ner,** *n.*

Can., abbreviation for **Canada.**

Ca·naan (kā′nən), *n.* in the Bible, the land promised by God to Abraham and his descendants. Canaan is an old name for Palestine.

Ca·naan·ite (kā′nən īt), *n.* a person who lived in Canaan before the Israelites settled there.

Can·a·da (kan′ə də), *n.* a country north of the United States. It is a member of the British Commonwealth of Nations.

Canada goose, a large wild goose of North America. It is gray, with a black head and neck. *See the picture for* **goose.**

Ca·na·di·an (kə nā′di ən), *adj.* of Canada or its people. **—n.** a person born or living in Canada.

ca·nal (kə nal′), *n.* **1.** a ditch filled with water to allow ships to cross a stretch of land. Canals are also used to carry water for irrigating crops. **2.** a tube in the body [the alimentary *canal*].

Canal Zone, the strip of land ten miles wide in Central America that surrounds the Panama Canal. It is governed by the United States.

ca·na·pé (kan′ə pē), *n.* a cracker or bit of toast spread with cheese, spiced meat, or fish, etc. and served as an appetizer.

ca·nard (kə närd′), *n.* a false rumor that is meant to hurt someone's reputation.

ca·nar·y (kə ner′ē), *n.* **1.** a small, yellow songbird, kept as a pet in a cage. **2.** a light yellow: also **canary yellow. —ca·nar′ies,** *pl.*

Canary Islands, a group of islands off the northwest coast of Africa, belonging to Spain.

ca·nas·ta (kə nas′tə), *n.* a card game played with two decks of cards.

Can·ber·ra (kan′bər ə), *n.* the capital of Australia, in the southeastern part.

can·cel (kan′s'l), *v.* **1.** to cross out with lines or mark in some other way [Postage stamps and checks are *canceled* to show that they have already been used.]

canceled stamp

2. to do away with; wipe out; say that it will no longer be [to *cancel* an order or an appointment]. **3.** to balance something so that it has no effect [His vote of "no" *canceled* my vote of "yes."] **—can′celed** or **can′celled,** *p.t. & p.p.;* **can′cel·ing** or **can′cel·ling,** *pr.p.*

can·cel·la·tion (kan′s'l ā′shən), *n.* **1.** the act of canceling. **2.** something canceled. **3.** a mark that cancels, as on a postage stamp.

can·cer (kan′sər), *n.* **1.** a disease in which certain cells grow wild and spread throughout the body. **2.** a growth made up of such cells. See also **Tropic of Cancer. —can′cer·ous,** *adj.*

can·de·la·bra (kan′d'l ä′brə *or* kan′d'l ā′brə), *n.* a candelabrum. **—can′de·la′bras,** *pl.*

can·de·la·brum (kan′d'l ä′brəm *or* kan′d'l ā′brəm), *n.* a large candlestick with branches for several candles. **—can′de·la′bra** or **can′de·la′brums,** *pl.*

candelabrum

can·did (kan′did), *adj.* saying what one honestly thinks; frank, honest, and fair [a *candid* opinion]. **—can′did·ly,** *adv.*

can·di·da·cy (kan′də də sē), *n.* the fact of being a candidate [Jones announced his *candidacy* for the Senate.] **—can′di·da·cies,** *pl.*

can·di·date (kan′də dāt), *n.* a person who offers himself or is suggested by others for an office or award [a *candidate* for mayor; a *candidate* for the Nobel prize].

can·died (kan′dēd), *adj.* **1.** cooked in or glazed with sugar [*candied* apples]. **2.** partly or wholly turned to sugar [*candied* sirup].

can·dle (kan′d'l), *n.* a stick or piece of tallow or wax with a wick through it, which gives light when burned. **—v.** to examine eggs for freshness by holding in front of a light. **—not hold a candle to,** not be nearly so good as. **—can′dled,** *p.t. & p.p.;* **can′dling,** *pr.p.*

can·dle·light (kan′d'l līt), *n.* the light given by candles [We dined by *candlelight.*]

candle power, a measure of how strong a light is, based on the light given off by a candle of a standard size.

can·dle·stick (kan′d'l stik), *n.* a holder with a small cup in which a candle can be fixed.

can·dor (kan′dər), *n.* a being open, honest, and fair in saying what one thinks; frankness.

can·dy (kan′dē), *n.* a sweet food, usually in small pieces, made mainly from sugar or sirup, with flavor, coloring, fruits, nuts, etc. added. **—v. 1.** to preserve by cooking with sugar [to *candy* orange peel]. **2.** to form into crystals of sugar [The sirup has *candied.*] **—can′dies,** *pl.* **—can′died,** *p.t. & p.p.;* **can′dy·ing,** *pr.p.*

candlestick

cane (kān), *n.* **1.** the hollow, jointed stem of some plants, as bamboo or rattan. **2.** a plant with such a stem. **3.** a stick carried when walking. **4.** sugar cane. **5.** thin strips of rattan used in weaving baskets, chair seats, etc.

—v. 1. to beat with a cane or stick. 2. to make or fix with cane [to cane a chair seat]. —caned, p.t. & p.p.; can′ing, pr.p.

ca·nine (kā′nīn), adj. of or like a dog or the family of animals that includes dogs [Wolves and foxes are canine animals.] —n. a dog.

canine tooth, any of the four pointed teeth next to a person's incisors; eyetooth.

can·is·ter (kan′is tər), n. a box or can with a lid, for keeping coffee, tea, etc.

can·ker (kang′kər), n. 1. an open sore in the mouth. 2. any bad influence that gradually destroys something [Idleness was a canker eating away at his ambition.] —can′ker·ous, adj.

can·na (kan′ə), n. a tall tropical plant with large leaves and brightly colored flowers.

canned (kand), adj. put into airtight cans or jars so as to keep in good condition [canned milk or fruits].

can·ner·y (kan′ər ē), n. a factory where foods are canned. —can′ner·ies, pl.

can·ni·bal (kan′ə b′l), n. 1. a person who eats human flesh. 2. any animal that eats its own kind. —can′ni·bal·ism, n. —can′ni·bal·is′tic, adj.

can·non (kan′ən), n. a large gun mounted on some base; piece of artillery. —can′nons or can′non, pl.

can·non·ade (kan ən ād′), n. a constant firing of cannon.

cannon ball, a type of heavy metal ball that used to be fired from cannons.

can·not (kan′ät or ka nät′), can not.

can·ny (kan′ē), adj. shrewd and careful in one's actions or dealings; clever and cautious [a canny bargainer]. —can′ni·er, compar.; can′ni·est, superl. —can′ni·ly, adv.

ca·noe (kə nōō′), n. a narrow, light boat with its sides meeting in a sharp edge at each end. It is moved by one or more pad-dles [The wood-land Indians used birch bark to cover the frames of their canoes.] —v. to ride in a canoe.

canoe

—ca·noed′, p.t. & p.p.; ca·noe′ing, pr.p.

can·on (kan′ən), n. 1. a law or all the laws of a church [the Roman Catholic canon]. 2. a rule or principle of greatest importance [Free speech is a canon of democracy.] 3. a standard to judge something by [His remarks violated all canons of good taste.] 4. an official list, as of saints or of those books of the Bible which are accepted by a particular church. 5. a clergyman who is on the staff of a cathedral. —ca·non·i·cal (kə nän′i-k′l), adj.

ca·ñon (kan′yən), n. a canyon.

can·on·ize (kan′ən īz), v. to say that a certain dead person is among the saints in heaven [St. Francis was canonized by the Roman Catholic Church in 1228.] —can′on·ized, p.t. & p.p.; can′on·iz·ing, pr.p. —can′on·i·za′tion, n.

can·o·py (kan′ə pē), n. 1. a cloth or other cover-ing fastened as a roof above a throne, bed, etc., or held on poles over a person or sacred thing. 2. any covering or top shel-ter [We walked beneath the canopy of flowering trees.] —v. to put or form a canopy over. —can′o-pies, pl. —can′o·pied, p.t. & p.p.; can′o·py·ing, pr.p.

canst (kanst), the older form of can used with thou, as in the Bible.

cant (kant), n. 1. the special words and phrases used by a particular group or class of people; jargon [Thieves have a cant of their own.] 2. talk in which the speaker pretends to be good, religious, etc. although he is not.

cant (kant), n. a tilt or slant. —v. to tilt, slant, or tip.

can't (kant), can not.

can·ta·loupe or can·ta·loup (kan′tə lōp), n. a muskmelon, especially a kind that has a hard, rough skin and sweet, juicy orange-colored flesh.

can·tan·ker·ous (kan tang′kər əs), adj. hav-ing a bad temper; ready to quarrel.

can·ta·ta (kən tä′tə), n. a piece of music sung by soloists and a chorus. A cantata tells a story, like an opera, but is not acted.

can·teen (kan tēn′), n. 1. a store where food, drink, and personal sup-plies are sold, especially one in or near an army camp. 2. a small con-tainer for carrying drink-ing water, as on a hike.

can·ter (kan′tər), n. an easy gallop [The horse went at a canter.] —v. to ride or go at an easy gallop.

Can·ter·bur·y (kan′tər ber′ē), n. a city in southeastern England. It has a large cathedral.

can·ti·cle (kan′ti k′l), n. a song or hymn with words from the Bible.

canteen

can·ti·le·ver (kan′t′l ev′ər or kan′t′l ē′vər), n. a beam or support that is fastened to a wall or pier at only one end.

cantilever bridge, a bridge formed by cantilevers that jut out toward each other from piers and meet to form a span.

cantilevers

can·to (kan′tō), n. any of the main sections of a long poem. —can′tos, pl.

Can·ton (kan tän′), n. a large seaport city in southeastern China.

can·ton (kan′tən or kan tän′), n. any of the

political divisions or districts of Switzerland.

can·ton·ment (kan tän′mənt), *n.* any place where troops are stationed for a time.

can·tor (kan′tər), *n.* a singer of the solos that are part of the service in a Jewish synagogue.

can·vas (kan′vəs), *n.* **1.** a strong, heavy cloth of hemp, cotton, or flax, used for tents, sails, oil paintings, etc. **2.** an oil painting on canvas. —*adj.* made of canvas. —**under canvas, 1.** in tents. **2.** with sails unfurled.

can·vas·back (kan′vəs bak), *n.* a wild duck of North America, with a grayish back.

can·vass (kan′vəs), *v.* **1.** to go among people asking for votes, opinions, donations, etc. or trying to sell something. **2.** to examine or discuss in detail [The club will *canvass* ways of raising money at today's meeting.] —*n.* the act of canvassing. —**can′vass·er,** *n.*

can·yon (kan′yən), *n.* a long, narrow valley with high cliffs on each side. It usually has a river running through it.

caou·tchouc (koō′chook *or* kou chook′), *n.* crude natural rubber as it comes from the plant.

cap (kap), *n.* **1.** a covering for the head, that fits closely and has only a visor or no brim at all. Some caps show the rank or work of the wearer [a cardinal's *cap;* a nurse's *cap;* a fool's *cap*]. **2.** anything like a cap, as a cover, lid, or top [a bottle *cap;* the *cap* of a mushroom; mountain *caps*]. **3.** a dot of gunpowder set in paper for firing in a toy gun. —*v.* **1.** to put a cap on [*Cap* that bottle.] **2.** to cover the top of [Snow *capped* the hills.] **3.** to do as well as or better than [The other runners could not *cap* John's winning time.] —**capped,** *p.t. & p.p.;* **cap′ping,** *pr.p.*

upper: bottle cap
lower: boy's cap

cap., abbreviation for **capital.**

ca·pa·bil·i·ty (kā′pə bil′ə tē), *n.* the power to do something; ability. —**ca′pa·bil′i·ties,** *pl.*

ca·pa·ble (kā′pə b'l), *adj.* able to do things well; fit or skilled [a *capable* teacher]. —**capable of, 1.** able or ready to [He's quite *capable* of telling a lie.] **2.** having what is necessary for [This table is *capable of* seating ten persons.] —**ca′pa·bly,** *adv.*

ca·pa·cious (kə pā′shəs), *adj.* able to hold much; spacious; roomy [a *capacious* trunk].

ca·pac·i·ty (kə pas′ə tē), *n.* **1.** the amount of space that can be filled; room for holding [a jar with a *capacity* of 2 quarts; a stadium with a seating *capacity* of 80,000]. **2.** the ability to be, learn, become, etc.; skill or fitness [He has the *capacity* to be a doctor.] **3.** position or character [He's acting in the *capacity* of an adviser.] —**ca·pac′i·ties,** *pl.*

ca·par·i·son (kə par′ə s'n), *n.* **1.** a decorated covering and harness for a horse. **2.** the dress and ornaments of a person. —*v.* to dress with rich clothes.

cape (kāp), *n.* a garment without sleeves that is fastened at the neck and hangs over the back and shoulders.

cape (kāp), *n.* a piece of land that sticks out into a lake or sea.

ca·per (kā′pər), *v.* to skip about in a playful way. —*n.* **1.** a playful skip or leap. **2.** a playful or silly trick; prank. —**to cut a caper, 1.** to caper. **2.** to play tricks.

ca·pers (kā′pərz), *n.pl.* the green flower buds of a Mediterranean bush. They are pickled and used as a flavoring.

cape

Cape Town *or* **Cape·town** (kāp′toun′), *n.* a seaport city in South Africa. The legislature meets there.

cap·il·lar·y (kap′′l er′ē), *n.* **1.** a tube that is very narrow inside [The ordinary thermometer is a *capillary*.] **2.** any of the tiny blood vessels joining the arteries and the veins. —*adj.* of or like a capillary. —**cap′il·lar′ies,** *pl.*

cap·i·tal (kap′ə t'l), *adj.* **1.** that can be punished by death [Murder is a *capital* crime.] **2.** most important; chief [Honesty is a *capital* virtue.] **3.** where the government is located [a *capital* city]. **4.** very fine; excellent [a *capital* performance]. See also **capital letter.** —*n.* **1.** a capital letter. **2.** a city or town where the government of a state or nation is located. **3.** money or property, especially when used in business to make more money. **4.** the top part of a column. —**make capital of,** to make the most of; get advantage from.

capital of a column

cap·i·tal·ism (kap′ə t'l iz'm), *n.* a system in which the land, factories, etc. used in making goods are owned and operated by individuals for profit.

cap·i·tal·ist (kap′ə t'l ist), *n.* a person who owns much capital; especially, one whose wealth is used in business for making more money.

cap·i·tal·is·tic (kap′ə t'l is′tik), *adj.* of or like capitalists, or favoring capitalism.

cap·i·tal·i·za·tion (kap′ə t'l i zā′shən), *n.* **1.** the act of capitalizing. **2.** the stocks and bonds that stand for the total capital, or funds, of a business.

cap·i·tal·ize (kap′ə t'l īz′), *v.* **1.** to begin with a capital letter or write in capital letters. **2.** to change into capital, or wealth, that can be used in a business. **3.** to use for one's own advantage [He *capitalized* on my errors.] —**cap′i·tal·ized′,** *p.t. & p.p.;* **cap′i·tal·iz′ing,** *pr.p.*

capital letter, the form of a letter that is

fat, āpe, cär, ten, ēven, hit, bīte, gō, hôrn, tool, book, up, fŭr;
get, joy, yet, chin, she, thin, *th*en; zh = s in pleasure; ′ as in able (ā′b'l);
ə = a in ago, e in agent, i in sanity, o in confess, u in focus.

used to begin a sentence or a name [THIS IS PRINTED IN CAPITAL LETTERS.]

capital punishment, the killing of someone by law as punishment for a crime.

Cap·i·tol (kap′ə t'l), *n.* **1.** the building in which the United States Congress meets, at Washington, D.C. **2.** *often* **capitol,** the building in which a State legislature meets.

ca·pit·u·late (kə pich′ə lāt), *v.* to surrender or give up on certain conditions. —**ca·pit′u·lat·ed,** *p.t. & p.p.;* **ca·pit′u·lat·ing,** *pr.p.* —**ca·pit′u·la′tion,** *n.*

ca·pon (kā′pän), *n.* a rooster with its sex glands removed, fattened for eating.

ca·price (kə prēs′), *n.* a sudden change in the way one thinks or acts that seems to be without reason.

ca·pri·cious (kə prish′əs), *adj.* likely to change suddenly and for no reason plain to see; flighty [a *capricious* child; a *capricious* breeze].

Capricorn, see **Tropic of Capricorn.**

cap·size (kap sīz′), *v.* to overturn or upset [The lifeboat *capsized* in the stormy sea.] —**cap·sized′,** *p.t. & p.p.;* **cap·siz′ing,** *pr.p.*

cap·stan (kap′stən), *n.* an upright drum, as on ships, around which cables are wound so as to haul them in. Capstans are turned by a bar or bars at the top or, now usually, by machinery.

cap·sule (kap′s'l *or* kap′syool), *n.* **1.** a small container holding a dose of medicine. A capsule is made of gelatin and dissolves quickly after being swallowed. **2.** a case containing the seeds of some plants. **3.** an enclosed section, as for men in a spacecraft.

capstan

Capt., abbreviation for **Captain.**

cap·tain (kap′t'n), *n.* **1.** a chief or leader of some group or activity [a police *captain;* a *captain* of industry; the *captain* of a football team]. **2.** an army or air force officer who ranks just above a first lieutenant. **3.** a navy officer who ranks just above a commander. **4.** the master of a ship. —*v.* to be captain of [Joe *captains* the chess team.] —**cap′tain·cy,** *n.*

upper: seed
capsule
lower: med-
icine capsule

cap·tion (kap′shən), *n.* a title or heading, as of an article or picture in a newspaper.

cap·tious (kap′shəs), *adj.* **1.** eager to point out others' mistakes; carping. **2.** made only in order to argue or find fault [*captious* objections].

cap·ti·vate (kap′tə vāt), *v.* to be highly interesting or pleasing to; fascinate. —**cap′ti·vat·ed,** *p.t. & p.p.;* **cap′ti·vat·ing,** *pr.p.*

cap·tive (kap′tiv), *n.* a person caught and held prisoner, as in war. —*adj.* held as a prisoner.

cap·tiv·i·ty (kap tiv′ə tē), *n.* the condition of being held as a prisoner [the largest lion in *captivity*].

cap·tor (kap′tər), *n.* a person who takes another as a prisoner.

cap·ture (kap′chər), *v.* to catch and hold by force or skill [to *capture* enemy troops; to *capture* the attention]. —*n.* **1.** a capturing or being captured; seizure [*Capture* of the spy is certain.] **2.** something that has been captured. —**cap′tured,** *p.t. & p.p.;* **cap′tur·ing,** *pr.p.*

car (kär), *n.* **1.** anything that moves on wheels, for carrying people or things; especially, an automobile. **2.** a railroad car or streetcar. **3.** the part of an elevator where people ride; cage.

car·a·bao (kä′rə bä′ō), *n.* a water buffalo of the Philippine Islands. —**ca′ra ba′os,** *pl.*

Ca·ra·cas (kə rä′kəs), *n.* the capital of Venezuela, in the northern part.

car·a·cul (kar′ə kəl), *n.* the fleece of certain Asian lambs, having loose, flat curls. It is used as a fur.

ca·rafe (kə raf′), *n.* a glass bottle for holding water, hot coffee, etc.

car·a·mel (kar′ə m'l *or* kär′m'l), *n.* **1.** burnt sugar used to color or flavor food. **2.** a chewy candy made from sugar, milk, etc.

car·at (kar′ət), *n.* **1.** the unit used for weighing gems. It is equal to 1/5 of a gram. **2.** one 24th part of pure gold [14 *carat* gold is 14 parts pure gold and 10 parts other metal.] Also spelled **karat.**

carafe

car·a·van (kar′ə van), *n.* **1.** a group of merchants, nomads, etc. traveling together for safety, as through a desert. **2.** a large covered wagon or car for carrying people, animals, etc.; van [a circus *caravan*].

car·a·way (kar′ə wā), *n.* **1.** a plant with spicy, strong-smelling seeds. **2.** these seeds, used to flavor bread, cakes, cheese, etc.

car·bine (kär′bīn *or* kär′bēn), *n.* a small, light kind of rifle.

car·bo·hy·drate (kär′bə hī′drāt), *n.* any of a group of substances made up of carbon, hydrogen, and oxygen, including the sugars and starches. Carbohydrates are an important part of our diet.

car·bol·ic acid (kär bäl′ik), a poisonous acid gotten from coal tar and used in weak form as a disinfectant to kill germs.

car·bon (kär′bən), *n.* **1.** a chemical element that is not a metal, found in all plant and animal matter. Coal and charcoal are forms of impure carbon, while diamonds and graphite are pure forms. **2.** a sheet of carbon paper. **3.** a copy made with this: *the full name is* **carbon copy.**

car·bon·ate (kär′bən āt), *n.* a salt of carbonic acid. —*v.* to put carbon dioxide in so as to make bubble [Soda pop is a *carbonated* drink.] —**car′bon·at·ed,** *p.t. & p.p.;* **car′bon·at·ing,** *pr.p.*

carbon dioxide, a gas of carbon and oxygen that has no color and no smell and is heavier than air. It is breathed out of the lungs and is taken in by plants, which use it to make their food.

car·bon·ic acid (kär bän′ik), a weak acid formed of carbon dioxide dissolved in water.

car·bon·if·er·ous (kär′bə nif′ər əs), *adj.* containing carbon or coal [*carboniferous* layers in the earth].

car·bon·ize (kär′bə nīz), *v.* **1.** to change into carbon, as by burning. **2.** to coat with carbon. —**car′bon·ized,** *p.t. & p.p.;* **car′bon·iz·ing,** *pr.p.*

carbon monoxide, a very poisonous gas that has no color and no smell. It is found in the fumes given off by automobile engines.

carbon paper, very thin paper coated on one side with a carbon substance. It is put between sheets of paper, and typing or writing on the upper sheet makes a copy on the lower ones.

car·bun·cle (kär′bung k'l), *n.* **1.** a painful red swelling beneath the skin, filled with pus and caused by infection. It is larger than a boil. **2.** a dark-red gem; especially, a garnet.

car·bu·re·tor (kär′bə rē′tər), *n.* the part of an engine in an automobile, etc. that mixes air with gasoline spray to make the mixture that explodes in the cylinders.

car·cass (kär′kəs), *n.* **1.** the dead body of an animal. **2.** a human body: *used in a joking or mocking way.* **3.** the framework or shell of a building, ship, tire, etc.

card (kärd), *n.* **1.** a flat piece of cardboard or stiff paper, often with something printed on it [A calling *card* carries a person's name, address, etc. Greeting *cards* are sent on holidays, birthdays, etc. A show *card* is used for advertising something.] See also **playing card, post card. 2.** a comical person: *used only in everyday talk.* —**put** or **lay one's cards on the table,** to be frank; tell everything.

card (kärd), *n.* a tool like a metal comb or wire brush used to comb or separate fibers of wool, cotton, etc., before spinning. —*v.* to use such a tool on.

carding wool

card·board (kärd′bôrd), *n.* a thick, stiff kind of paper used for making cards, light boxes, book covers, etc.

car·di·ac (kär′di ak′), *adj.* of the heart.

car·di·gan (kär′di gən), *n.* a knitted jacket or a sweater that has long sleeves and that buttons down the front.

car·di·nal (kär′d'n əl), *adj.* **1.** of main importance; chief [The *cardinal* points of the compass are north, south, east, and west.] **2.** bright-red. —*n.* **1.** one of the Roman Catholic officials whom the Pope elects to his council. When the Pope dies, the cardinals elect a new pope. **2.** an American songbird that is bright red and has a black face.

cardigan

cardinal number, any number used in counting or in showing how many [Three, sixty, and 169 are *cardinal numbers.*] See also **ordinal number.**

cards (kärdz), *n.pl.* a game, such as bridge or rummy, played with playing cards.

care (ker), *n.* **1.** the condition of being troubled by fear or worry [His mind was filled with *care* for his son's safety.] **2.** a watching over or tending; protection [Mother's *care* helped me get well.] **3.** serious attention or interest; regard [He does his homework with *care.*] **4.** something to worry about [A sick pet is such a *care!*] —*v.* **1.** to feel an interest, worry, regret, etc. [Do you *care* if I go? I don't *care* if I did lose.] **2.** to wish or desire [Do you *care* to come along?] —**care for, 1.** to watch over; take charge of [Will you *care for* my canary while I am gone?] **2.** to love or like [She doesn't *care for* dancing.] **3.** to wish for; want [Do you *care for* any gravy?] —**care of** or **in care of,** in the charge of; at the address of: abbreviated **c/o** or **c.o.** [Send the letter (*in*) *care of* my parents.] —**have a care** or **take care,** be careful; watch out. —**take care of, 1.** to watch over; protect [*Take care of* my little girl.] **2.** to look after; do what needs to be done about [I *took care of* that matter quickly.] —**cared,** *p.t. & p.p.;* **car′ing,** *pr.p.*

ca·reen (kə rēn′), *v.* **1.** to lean or tip to one side, as a sailing ship under a strong wind. **2.** to lurch from side to side while moving fast [The car *careened* down the bumpy hill.]

careening car

ca·reer (kə rir′), *n.* **1.** a running rapidly; speed [The sailboat sped through the waves in full *career.*] **2.** the way one earns his living; profession or occupation [Have you thought of teaching as a *career?*] **3.** one's progress through life or in one's work [He had a long and successful *career* in politics.] —*v.* to rush wildly; speed along.

care·free (ker′frē), *adj.* without care or worry; happy.

care·ful (ker′fəl), *adj.* **1.** taking care so as not to have mistakes, accidents, or the like; cautious [Be *careful* in crossing streets.] **2.** done or made with care [*careful* work]. —**care′ful·ly,** *adv.* —**care′ful·ness,** *n.*

care·less (ker′lis), *adj.* **1.** not paying enough attention; not thinking before one acts or speaks [*Careless* drivers cause many accidents.] **2.** done or made without care; full of mistakes [*careless* writing]. **3.** without worry; carefree; happy [*careless* vacation days]. —**care′less·ly,** *adv.* —**care′less·ness,** *n.*

ca·ress (kə res′), *v.* to touch or stroke in a loving or gentle way [He *caressed* his dog fondly. The breeze *caressed* the trees.] —*n.* a loving or gentle touch, kiss, or embrace.

---

fat, āpe, cär, ten, ēven, hit, bīte, gō, hôrn, tōōl, book, up, fűr;
get, joy, yet, chin, she, thin, *th*en; zh = s in pleasure; ′ as in able (ā′b'l);
ə = a in ago, e in agent, i in sanity, o in confess, u in focus.

car·et (kar′it *or* ker′it), *n.* the mark ∧, used to show where something is to be added in a written or printed line.

care·tak·er (ker′tāk′ər), *n.* a person whose work is to take care of some thing or place; custodian [the *caretaker* of an estate].

care·worn (ker′wôrn), *adj.* worn out by sadness and worry [a *careworn* face].

car·go (kär′gō), *n.* the load of goods carried by a ship or airplane. —**car′goes** or **car′gos,** *pl.*

Car·ib·be·an Sea (kar′ə bē′ən *or* kə rib′i ən), a sea bounded by the West Indies, Central America, and South America.

car·i·bou (kar′ə bōō), *n.* any of several kinds of North American reindeer.

car·i·ca·ture (kar′i kə chər), *n.* **1.** a picture or imitation of a person or thing in which certain features or parts are exaggerated in a joking or mocking way. **2.** the skill or work of making such pictures, etc. —*v.* to make or be a caricature of. —**car′i·ca·tured,** *p.t.* & *p.p.;* **car′i·ca·tur·ing,** *pr.p.* —**car′i·ca·tur·ist,** *n.*

caricature

car·ies (ker′ēz), *n.* decay of teeth or bones [Tooth cavities are caused by *caries.*]

car·il·lon (kar′ə län), *n.* a set of bells on which melodies can be played, now usually from a keyboard.

car·load (kär′lōd), *n.* a load that will fill a car [two *carloads* of coal].

car·mine (kär′min *or* kär′mīn), *n.* a red or purplish-red color. —*adj.* red or purplish-red.

car·nage (kär′nij), *n.* a bloody killing of many people, especially in battle; slaughter.

car·nal (kär′nəl). *adj.* of the flesh or body, not of the spirit; worldly [*carnal* desires].

car·na·tion (kär nā′shən), *n.* **1.** a plant of the pink family with white, pink, or red flowers having ragged petals and a strong smell like cloves. **2.** its flower.

car·ni·val (kär′nə v′l), *n.* **1.** an entertainment with side shows, amusement rides, refreshments, etc. **2.** feasting and merrymaking with many people joining in parades, dances, and masquerades; especially, such a festival in the week before Lent.

carnation

car·niv·o·rous (kär niv′ə rəs), *adj.* feeding on flesh [Lions are *carnivorous* animals.]

car·ol (kar′əl), *n.* a song of joy or praise, especially a Christmas song. —*v.* to sing in joy or praise. —**car′oled** or **car′olled,** *p.t.* & *p.p.;* **car′ol·ing** or **car′ol·ling,** *pr.p.*

Car·o·li·na (kar′ə lī′nə), *n.* North Carolina or South Carolina.

ca·rouse (kə rouz′), *v.* to join with others in drinking and having a noisy, merry time. —*n.* a carousing. —**ca·roused′,** *p.t.* & *p.p.;* **ca·rous′ing,** *pr.p.* —**ca·rous′al,** *n.*

carp (kärp), *n.* a fresh-water fish with soft fins and large scales, that is used for food. —**carp** or **carps,** *pl.*

carp (kärp), *v.* to find fault in a petty or nagging way; keep complaining.

Car·pa·thi·an Mountains (kär pā′thi ən), mountain ranges reaching into parts of Czechoslovakia, Poland, the Ukraine, and Romania.

car·pel (kär′p′l), *n.* the part of a flower in which the seeds grow. The pistil is formed of one or more carpels See also **pistil.**

carpel

car·pen·ter (kär′pən tər), *n.* a workman who builds and repairs wooden things, especially the wooden parts of buildings, ships, etc.

car·pen·try (kär′pən trē), *n.* the work or trade of a carpenter.

car·pet (kär′pit), *n.* **1.** a thick, heavy fabric used to cover floors. **2.** anything that covers like a carpet [a *carpet* of snow]. — *v.* to cover with a carpet. —**on the carpet,** getting a strong scolding or criticism.

car·pet·bag (kär′pit bag′), *n.* an old-fashioned kind of traveling bag, made of carpeting.

car·pet·bag·ger (kär′pit bag′ər), *n.* a Northerner who went into the South just after the Civil War to profit from the confusion there.

car·pet·ing (kär′pit ing), *n.* carpets or the fabrics used for carpets.

car·port (kär′pôrt), *n.* a shelter for an automobile, built against the side of a building.

car·riage (kar′ij), *n.* **1.** a vehicle with wheels, usually one drawn by horses, for carrying people. **2.** a frame on wheels for carrying something heavy [a gun *carriage*]. **3.** a moving part of a machine for carrying something along [The *carriage* of a typewriter holds the paper.] **4.** the way one stands or walks; posture; bearing. **5.** a carrying of goods in trains, ships, trucks, etc.; transportation. **6.** (kar′i ij), the cost of carrying goods.

baby carriage

car·ried (kar′ēd), past tense and past participle of **carry.**

car·ri·er (kar′i ər), *n.* **1.** a person or thing that carries [a mail *carrier;* an aircraft *carrier*]. **2.** a company that is in the business of transporting goods or passengers. Railroad, bus, and truck companies are called **common carriers.**

car·ri·on (kar′i ən), *n.* the flesh of a dead body that is rotting.

Car·roll, Lew·is (lōō′is kar′əl), 1832–1898; the pen name of Charles L. Dodgson, the English author of *Alice in Wonderland.*

car·rot (kar′ət), *n.* a plant with a long, thick, orange-red root that is eaten as a vegetable.

car·rou·sel (kar′oo sel′), *n.* a merry-go-round.

car·ry (kar′ē), *v.* **1.** to take from one place to another; transport, convey, or conduct [Please help me *carry* these books home. The large pipe *carries* water. Air *carries* sounds.] **2.** to cause to go; lead [A love of travel *carried* him around the world.] **3.** to bring over a figure from one column to the next in adding a row of figures. **4.** to win [John easily *carried* the argument.] **5.** to hold or support; bear [These beams *carry* the weight of the roof.] **6.** to have in it; contain [The letter *carried* a threat.] **7.** to sit, stand, or walk in a certain way [The captain *carried* himself stiffly.] **8.** to have for sale [Does this store *carry* toys?] **9.** to be able to reach over a distance [His voice *carries* well.] **10.** to sing or play the notes of correctly [I just can't *carry* a tune.] —**carry away,** to stir the feelings so deeply that one cannot think clearly. —**carry off, 1.** to kill [The disease *carried off* thousands.] **2.** to win a prize. —**carry on, 1.** to do or manage, as a business. **2.** to go on as before. **3.** to behave in a wild or silly way: *used only in everyday talk.* —**carry out,** to get done; accomplish; bring to a finish [to *carry out* a threat]. —**car′ried,** *p.t. & p.p.;* **car′ry·ing,** *pr.p.*

car·sick (kär′sik′), *adj.* sick from riding in a car, so that one feels like vomiting.

Car·son City (kär′s'n), the capital of Nevada.

cart (kärt), *n.* a small wagon, often with only two wheels, moved by hand or drawn by an animal [a pony *cart;* a grocery *cart*]. —*v.* to carry in a cart, truck, or the like. —**put the cart before the horse,** to do things backward or in the wrong order. —**cart′er,** *n.*

pony cart

cart·age (kär′tij), *n.* **1.** the carrying or delivering of goods. **2.** the charge for this.

carte blanche (kärt′ blänsh′), full freedom or the right to do as one thinks best.

car·tel (kär tel′), *n.* a group of companies joined together to have complete control over the production and prices of certain products; trust or monopoly.

Car·thage (kär′thij), *n.* an ancient city and state in northern Africa, near where Tunis now is. It was destroyed by the Romans in 146 B.C. —**Car·tha·gin·i·an** (kär′thə jin′i ən), *adj. & n.*

car·ti·lage (kär′t'l ij), *n.* a tough, flexible tissue that is connected with the bones and forms parts of the skeleton; gristle [The tough part of the outer ear is *cartilage.*] —**car·ti·lag·i·nous** (kär′tə laj′ə nəs), *adj.*

car·ton (kär′t'n), *n.* a box or other container made of cardboard.

car·toon (kär tōōn′), *n.* **1.** a drawing, as in a newspaper or magazine, that shows how the editor or artist feels about some person or thing in the news. It is often a caricature that criticizes or praises. **2.** any comic drawing, or a comic strip. **3.** an animated cartoon. —*v.* to draw cartoons. —**car·toon′ist,** *n.*

car·tridge (kär′trij), *n.* **1.** the metal or cardboard case that holds the gunpowder and the bullet or shot for use in a firearm. **2.** any container more or less like this, as for camera film or for the needle of a phonograph.

cart wheel, a handspring done sidewise.

carve (kärv), *v.* **1.** to make by cutting or as if by cutting [to *carve* a statue in marble; to *carve* a ca-reer]. **2.** to cut into slices or pieces [Will you *carve* the turkey?] —**carved,** *p.t. & p.p.;* **carv′ing,** *pr.p.* —**carv′er,** *n.*

cart wheel

Car·ver, George Wash-ington (kär′vər), 1864–1943; U.S. scientist who developed many products from peanuts and other plants.

carv·ing (kär′ving), *n.* **1.** the work or art of one who carves. **2.** a carved figure or design.

cas·cade (kas kād′), *n.* **1.** a small, steep water-fall. **2.** something like this, as sparks falling in a shower. —*v.* to fall in a cascade. —**cas·cad′ed,** *p.t. & p.p.;* **cas·cad′ing,** *pr.p.*

cas·car·a (kas ker′ə), *n.* a medicine made from the bark of a California tree, used to help the bowels move.

case (kās), *n.* **1.** a single example or happening [a *case* of carelessness; four *cases* of measles]. **2.** a set of facts or conditions connected with a certain thing [the *case* of the missing jewels]. **3.** a matter to be decided by a court of law; lawsuit [Two attorneys will handle his *case*.] **4.** a person being treated or helped, as by a doctor or social worker. **5.** in grammar, the form of a noun, pronoun, or adjective that shows its relation to the other words around it [In the sentence "He hit me," the subject *he* is in the nominative *case* and the object *me* is in the objective *case*.] —**in any case,** no matter what else may be true; anyhow. —**in case,** if; should it be that. —**in case of,** if there should happen to be. —**in no case,** not under any conditions; never.

case (kās), *n.* **1.** a container for holding and pro-tecting something [a watch *case;* a brief *case;* a seed *case;* a violin *case*]. **2.** as much as a case will hold [A *case* of root beer is 24 bottles.] **3.** a frame, as for a window. —*v.* to put or hold in a case. —**cased,** *p.t. & p.p.;* **cas′ing,** *pr.p.*

ca·se·in (kā′sēn *or* kā′si in), *n.* the main pro-tein of milk that is left when the water, butterfat, and sugar are removed. It is used in making plas-tics, glues, coatings, etc.

case·ment (kās′mənt), *n.* a window frame that opens on hinges along the side, like a door.

cash (kash), *n.* **1.** money on hand in coins or bills; ready money. **2.** money or a check paid at the time of buying something [I always pay *cash* and never buy on credit.] —*v.* to give or get cash for [to *cash* a check]. —*adj.* of or for cash [a *cash* sale]. —**cash in on,** to get profit from.

casement

cash·ew (kash′o͞o), *n.* **1.** a soft, curved nut that is the seed of a tropical evergreen tree. **2.** this tree.

cash·ier (ka shir′), *n.* a person in a store, restaurant, bank, etc. who handles the money.

cash·ier (ka shir′), *v.* to remove from a position of trust as a punishment; especially, to discharge a military officer with dishonor.

cash·mere (kash′mir), *n.* **1.** a very fine, soft wool, especially that from goats of Kashmir and Tibet. **2.** a soft cloth made of this wool. **3.** a shawl made of cashmere.

cash register, a machine used in business, that is an adding machine with a drawer for holding money. The drawer is opened by punching keys to show the amount of money received for each sale. *See the picture for* **register.**

cas·ing (kās′ing), *n.* **1.** a covering that protects, as the outer part of an automobile tire or the skin of a sausage. **2.** the framework around a window or door.

ca·si·no (kə sē′nō), *n.* **1.** a room or building for shows, dancing, gambling, etc. **2.** same as **cassino.** —**ca·si′nos,** *pl.*

cask (kask), *n.* **1.** a barrel for holding liquids. **2.** as much as a cask will hold.

cas·ket (kas′kit), *n.* **1.** a small box for holding valuable things, as jewelry. **2.** a coffin.

Cas·pi·an Sea (kas′pi ən), an inland sea between the Caucasus and Asia.

casque (kask), *n.* a helmet.

Cas·san·dra (kə san′drə), *n.* a Trojan princess in Greek legend who kept foretelling that Troy would be destroyed but was never believed.

cas·sa·va (kə sä′və), *n.* a tropical plant whose starchy roots are used in making tapioca.

cas·se·role (kas′ə rōl), *n.* **1.** a covered baking dish in which food can be cooked and then served. **2.** the food baked and served in such a dish.

cas·sette (ka set′), *n.* **1.** a case with a roll of film in it, for loading a camera quickly and easily. **2.** a similar case with recording tape in it, for use in a tape recorder.

cas·sia (kash′ə), *n.* **1.** a tropical tree whose bark is used like cinnamon. **2.** the bark. **3.** a tropical plant whose pods and leaves are used in medicines that make the bowels move.

cas·si·no (kə sē′nō), *n.* a card game in which the players win cards by matching them with others in their hand.

cas·sock (kas′ək), *n.* a long, usually black robe worn by some clergymen.

cast (kast), *v.* **1.** to throw out or down; toss; fling; hurl [to *cast* stones into the water; to *cast* a line in fishing]. **2.** to let fall; turn or direct [to *cast* one's eyes or attention on a thing; to *cast* light on a mystery]. **3.** to throw off; shed [The snake *casts* its skin.] **4.** to shape melted metal, plastic, etc. by pouring or pressing into a mold and letting it harden; also, to make by this method [John is *casting* book ends in the metal shop today.] **5.** to choose actors for a play [The director had difficulty *casting* "The Tempest." Morris was *cast* in the leading role.] —*n.* **1.** the act of casting or throwing; a throw. **2.** a way of casting or how far something is thrown. **3.** something formed in a mold [a bronze *cast* of a statue]. **4.** a stiff plaster form for keeping a broken arm or leg in place while it is healing. **5.** the set of actors in a play. **6.** a condition in which the eye is turned a little out of focus; squint. **7.** a form or appearance [His face had the *cast* of a typical Navaho Indian.] **8.** a slight coloring; tinge [The water is blue with a greenish *cast*.] —**cast about, 1.** to look; search. **2.** to make plans. —**cast aside** or **cast away,** to throw away or get rid of; discard. —**cast off, 1.** to get rid of; discard. **2.** to free a ship from a dock, as by untying the lines. —**cast one's ballot** or **cast one's vote,** to vote. —**cast,** *p.t. & p.p.;* **cast′ing,** *pr.p.*

cassock

cas·ta·nets (kas tə nets′), *n.pl.* a pair of small, hollowed pieces of hard wood or ivory that are held in the hand and clicked together to beat time to music. Castanets are used especially in Spanish dances.

cast·a·way (kast′ə wā), *n.* a shipwrecked person. *adj.* **1.** thrown away; discarded. **2.** shipwrecked.

caste (kast), *n.* **1.** any of the social classes into which Hindus are born. At one time Hindus of one caste could not mix with those of another. **2.** any system in which people are separated into classes because of their rank, wealth, etc.; also, any such class. —**lose caste,** to lose the respect that upper-class people usually get.

castanets

cast·er (kas′tər), *n.* **1.** a person or thing that casts. **2.** a small container for vinegar, salt, mustard, etc. at the table. **3.** a small wheel on a swivel that is attached to each leg of a

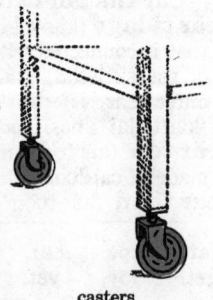

casters

piece of furniture so that it can be moved easily. Also spelled **castor** in meanings 2 and 3.

cas·ti·gate (kas′tə gāt), *v.* to punish harshly, now usually by scolding or criticizing sharply. —**cas′ti·gat·ed,** *p.t. & p.p.;* **cas′ti·gat·ing,** *pr.p.* —**cas′ti·ga′tion,** *n.* —**cas′ti·ga′tor,** *n.*

Cas·tile (kas tēl′), *n.* a region in central and northern Spain that was once a kingdom.

Cas·tile soap (kas′tēl *or* kas tēl′), a fine, hard soap made from olive oil.

Cas·til·ian (kas til′yən), *adj.* having to do with Castile, its people, etc. [The *Castilian* form of Spanish is the standard literary language of Spain.] —*n.* 1. a person born or living in Castile. 2. Castilian Spanish.

cast·ing (kas′ting), *n.* a thing, especially of metal, cast in a mold.

cast iron, hard, brittle iron shaped by casting.

cast-i·ron (kast′ī′ərn), *adj.* 1. made of cast iron. 2. hard, strong, and able to take rough treatment, like cast iron [a *cast-iron* stomach].

cas·tle (kas′'l), *n.* 1. a large building or group of buildings that was the home of a king or noble in the Middle Ages. Castles had thick walls, moats, etc. to protect them against attack. 2. any very large and solid house. 3. a piece used in playing chess, that is shaped like a castle tower.

castle in the air, something that one imagines and wants but is not likely to get; daydream.

cast·off (kast′ôf). *adj.* thrown away; discarded; abandoned. —*n.* a person or thing cast off.

cas·tor (kas′tər) *n.* caster (*in meanings 2 & 3*).

castor oil, a thick oil gotten from the bean of a tropical plant. It is used as a medicine to make the bowels move.

cas·trate (kas′trāt), *v.* to remove the male sex glands of; geld [A capon is a *castrated* rooster.] —**cas′trat·ed,** *p.t. & p.p.;* **cas′trat·ing,** *pr.p.*

cas·u·al (kazh′ōō əl), *adj.* 1. happening by chance; not planned [a *casual* visit]. 2. not having any particular purpose [a *casual* glance; a *casual* remark]. 3. not regular; occasional [*casual* labor]. 4. for wear at times when dressy clothes are not needed [*casual* sports clothes]. —**cas′u·al·ly,** *adv.* —**cas′u·al·ness,** *n.*

cas·u·al·ty (kazh′ōō əl tē *or* kazh′ool tē), *n.* 1. an accident, especially one that causes death. 2. anyone hurt or killed in an accident. 3. a soldier, sailor, etc. lost to service, as because of being wounded, captured, etc. —**cas′u·al·ties,** *pl.*

cas·u·ist·ry (kazh′ōō is trē), *n.* the deciding of questions of right or wrong in conduct; now, often, the use of clever but false reasoning to prove that one is right. —**cas′u·ist,** *n.*

cat (kat), *n.* 1. a small animal with soft fur, often kept as a pet or for killing mice. 2. any larger animal related to this, as the lion, tiger, or

leopard. 3. a woman who says mean things about others. 4. a cat-o′-nine-tails. —**let the cat out of the bag,** to let a secret be found out.

cat·a·clysm (kat′ə kliz′m), *n.* any sudden anr, violent change, as a great flood, earthquake, wad or revolution. —**cat′a·clys′mic,** *adj.*

cat·a·comb (kat′ə kōm), *n.* any of a group of connected halls and rooms underground for burying dead people. The Catacombs of Rome were used by the early Christians as a place to hide.

cat·a·log (kat′'l ôg), *n. & v.* catalogue.

cat·a·logue (kat′'l ôg), *n.* 1. a card file in alphabetical order giving a complete list of things in a collection, as of all the books in a library. 2. a book or paper listing all the things for sale or on display. 3. any complete list. —*v.* to make a list of or put into a list. —**cat′a·logued,** *p.t. & p.p.;* **cat′a·logu·ing,** *pr.p.* —**cat′a·logu·er,** *n.*

Cat·a·lo·ni·a (kat′ə lō′ni ə), *n.* a region in northeastern Spain. —**Cat′a·lo′ni·an,** *adj. & n.*

ca·tal·pa (kə tal′pə), *n.* a tree with large, heart-shaped leaves and long, slender pods.

cat·a·lyst (kat′'l ist), *n.* a substance that causes a chemical change when added to something but is not changed itself. —**cat·a·lyt·ic** (kat′'l it′ik), *adj.*

cat·a·mount (kat′əmount), *n.* a wild cat, as a cougar or lynx.

cat·a·pult (kat′ə pult), *n.* 1. a large weapon that worked like a slingshot, used in olden times to throw spears, arrows, rocks, etc. against the enemy. 2. a modern machine for launching an airplane from the deck of a ship. —*v.* 1. to throw from or as if from a catapult; hurl. 2. to move suddenly and quickly, as if thrown from a catapult [Lindbergh *catapulted* into fame by crossing the Atlantic.]

catalpa leaves and pods

ancient catapult

cat·a·ract (kat′ə rakt), *n.* 1. a large waterfall. 2. any strong flood or rush of water. 3. an eye disease in which the lens becomes clouded, causing gradual loss of sight.

ca·tarrh (kə tär′), *n.* an old-fashioned name for a condition in which there is a thick flow of mucus from the nose and throat, as in a cold.

ca·tas·tro·phe (kə tas′trə fē), *n.* a thing that happens suddenly and causes great loss, suffering,

---

fat, āpe, cär, ten, ēven, hit, bīte, gō, hôrn, tool, book, up, fūr; get, joy, yet, chin, she, thin, then; zh = s in pleasure; ′ as in able (ā′b'l); ə = a in ago, e in agent, i in sanity, o in confess, u in focus.

or damage; terrible disaster. —cat·a·stroph·ic (kat'ə sträf'ik), *adj.*

cat·bird (kat'bŭrd), *n.* a gray American songbird whose call is like the mewing of a cat.

cat·boat (kat'bōt), *n.* a sailboat with a single sail on a mast set forward in the bow.

cat·call (kat'kôl), *n.* a hooting or whistling sound made as a rude way of showing that one does not like a certain speaker, actor, etc.

catch (kach), *v.* **1.** to take hold of, as after a chase; capture [to *catch* a thief]. **2.** to get by a hook, trap, or the like [to *catch* fish; to *catch* mice]. **3.** to stop by grasping with the hands or arms [to *catch* a ball]. **4.** to become held or entangled; snag [My sleeve *caught* on the doorknob.] **5.** to get to in time [to *catch* a bus]. **6.** to get from someone or something; be seized by [to *catch* the flu]. **7.** to get by seeing, hearing, or thinking [to *catch* sight of a thing; to *catch* what a person says or means]. **8.** to come upon or see by surprise; discover [She *caught* him reading a comic book in the study hall.] **9.** to strike suddenly [The blow *caught* him by surprise. Her hat *caught* my fancy.] **10.** to take hold and spread [The dry grass *caught* fire from a spark.] **11.** to act as a catcher in baseball [You pitch; I'll *catch*.] —*n.* **1.** the act of catching a ball, etc. [The outfielder made a running *catch*.] **2.** anything that is caught [a *catch* of 14 fish]. **3.** a thing that catches or fastens [Fix the *catch* on that cupboard door.] **4.** a musical round. **5.** a break in the voice, as when speaking with deep feeling. **6.** a hidden or tricky part: *used only in everyday talk* [There's a *catch* in his offer.] —**catch it,** to get a scolding or other punishment: *used only in everyday talk.* —**catch on, 1.** to become popular. **2.** to understand. *This phrase is used only in everyday talk.* —**catch up, 1.** to come up even, as by hurrying or by extra work. **2.** to take up suddenly; snatch. —**caught,** *p.t. & p.p.*; **catch'ing,** *pr.p.*

catch·er (kach'ər), *n.* **1.** one who catches. **2.** in baseball, the player behind home plate, who catches pitched balls that are not hit away.

catch·ing (kach'ing), *adj.* **1.** easily passed on to another; contagious [Measles are *catching*. His joy is *catching*.] **2.** pleasing; attractive.

catch·up (kach'əp *or* kech'əp), *n.* ketchup.

catch·y (kach'ē), *adj.* **1.** pleasing and easy to remember [a *catchy* tune]. **2.** tricky or difficult [That question's *catchy*.] —**catch'i·er,** *compar.*; **catch'i·est,** *superl.*

cat·e·chism (kat'ə kiz'm), *n.* **1.** a set of questions and answers used in teaching religion. **2.** any long set of questions asked of someone, as in testing him.

cat·e·chize or **cat·e·chise** (kat'ə kīz), *v.* **1.** to teach by means of question and answer. **2.** to question closely, as in testing. —**cat'e·chized** or **cat'e·chised,** *p.t. & p.p.*; **cat'e·chiz·ing** or **cat'e·chis·ing,** *pr.p.* —**cat'e·chist,** *n.*

cat·e·gor·i·cal (kat'ə gôr'i k'l), *adj.* without any conditions; without an "if" or "maybe"; absolute [a *categorical* refusal]. —**cat'e·gor'i·cal·ly,** *adv.*

cat·e·go·ry (kat'ə gôr'ē), *n.* a division of a main subject or group; class [Biology is divided into two *categories*, zoology and botany.] —**cat'e·go'ries,** *pl.*

ca·ter (kā'tər), *v.* **1.** to provide food and service [His business is *catering* for large parties.] **2.** to try to please by doing or giving what is wanted [This store *caters* to young people.] —**ca'ter·er,** *n.*

cat·er·pil·lar (kat'ər pil'ər), *n.* the wormlike larva of the moth or butterfly, that hatches from the egg. It later becomes the pupa.

Caterpillar Tractor, a kind of tractor used for heavy work on rough or muddy ground. It has an endless metal belt on each side, that moves over toothed wheels. *A trademark.*

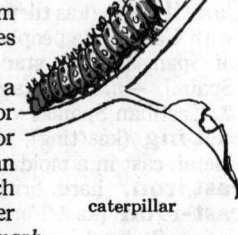

caterpillar

cat·er·waul (kat'ər wôl), *n.* the howling or screeching sound sometimes made by a cat; shriek. —*v.* to make such a sound.

cat·fish (kat'fish), *n.* a fish without scales, and with feelers about the mouth that are a little like a cat's whiskers.

cat·gut (kat'gut), *n.* a tough cord made from the dried intestines of sheep, etc. It is used to sew up wounds in surgery and to string musical instruments, tennis rackets, etc.

ca·thar·tic (kə thär'tik), *n.* a strong medicine to make the bowels move, as castor oil.

Ca·thay (ka thā'), *n.* an old name for China.

ca·the·dral (kə thē'drəl), *n.* **1.** the main church of a bishop's district, containing his throne. **2.** any large, important church.

cath·ode (kath'ōd), *n.* the pole or piece that is negatively charged in an electric battery, electron tube, etc.; negative electrode.

cath·o·lic (kath'ə lik), *adj.* **1.** including many or all kinds; broad; liberal [He has *catholic* tastes in art.] **2. Catholic,** having to do with the Christian church whose head is the Pope; Roman Catholic. —*n.* **Catholic,** a member of the Roman Catholic Church. —**Ca·thol·i·cism** (kə thäl'ə siz'm), *n.*

cath·o·lic·i·ty (kath'ə lis'ə tē), *n.* the fact of including many or all kinds; broadness.

cat·kin (kat'kin), *n.* the blossom of certain trees, as the willow, consisting of a cluster of small flowers along a drooping spike.

cat nap, a short, light sleep.

cat·nip (kat'nip), *n.* a plant of the mint family, with downy leaves. Cats like its smell.

cat·o'·nine·tails (kat'ə nīn'tālz), *n. sing. & pl.* a whip made of nine knotted cords fixed to a handle. It was once used for punishment.

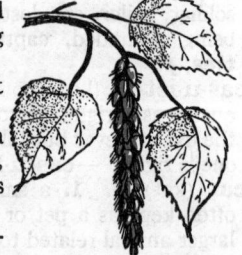

catkin of the aspen

cat's cradle, a game played by looping a string over the fingers to make various designs.

Cats·kill Mountains (kats′kil), a group of mountains in southern New York: also called **the Catskills.** It is famous as a vacation area.

cat's cradle

cat's-paw (kats′pô′), *n.* a person led by another into doing something for him that is bad or dangerous.

cat·sup (kech′əp *or* kat′səp), *n.* ketchup.

cat·tail (kat′tāl), *n.* a tall plant that grows in marshes. It has long, flat leaves and long, brown, fuzzy spikes.

cat·tle (kat′'l), *n.* animals of the cow family that are raised on farms and ranches, as cows, bulls, steers, and oxen. In earlier times this word was used to mean all kinds of livestock.

cat·tle·man (kat′'l mən), *n.* a man who raises cattle for the market. —**cat′tle·men,** *pl.*

cat·ty (kat′ē), *adj.* 1. of or like a cat. 2. saying mean things about others. —**cat′ti·er,** *compar.*; **cat′ti·est,** *superl.*

cat·walk (kat′wôk), *n.* a narrow path or platform, as along the edge of a bridge.

Cau·ca·sian (kô kā′zhən), *adj.* 1. having to do with or belonging to the division of mankind that is loosely called the "white race." Most Europeans are Caucasian. 2. of the Caucasus. —*n.* a member of the Caucasian group of mankind.

Cau·ca·sus (kô′kə səs), *n.* a mountain range, or the region around it, in the southernmost part of Soviet Russia, between the Black Sea and the Caspian Sea.

cau·cus (kô′kəs), *n.* a special meeting of the leaders or of a committee of a political party to pick candidates or make plans for bringing up at the main meeting. —*v.* to hold a caucus.

cau·dal (kô′d'l), *adj.* 1. that is a tail or is like a tail [the *caudal* fin of a fish]. 2. at or near the tail.

caught (kôt), past tense and past participle of **catch.**

caul·dron (kôl′drən), *n.* same as **caldron.**

cau·li·flow·er (kô′lə flou′ər), *n.* a kind of cabbage with a head of white, fleshy flower clusters growing tightly together. It is eaten as a vegetable.

caulk (kôk), *v.* to fill up cracks or seams with putty, tar, etc. Also spelled **calk.**

cause (kôz), *n.* 1. a person or thing that brings about some action or result [A spark from the wire was the *cause* of the fire.] 2. a reason for some action, feeling, etc. [John has given me no *cause* to admire him.] 3. an activity or interest that a number of people work for and support; movement [They have formed a group to work in the *cause* of peace.] —*v.* to be the cause of; make happen; bring about [The icy streets *caused* several accidents.] —**caused,** *p.t. & p.p.*; **caus′ing,** *pr.p.* —**cause′less,** *adj.*

cause·way (kôz′wā), *n.* 1. a raised road or path, as across a marsh. 2. a highway.

caus·tic (kôs′tik), *adj.* 1. that can burn or eat away living tissue by chemical action [Lye is a *caustic* substance.] 2. very sarcastic; sharp or biting [*caustic* comments]. —*n.* a caustic substance. —**caus′ti·cal·ly,** *adv.*

cau·ter·ize (kô′tər īz), *v.* to burn with a hot iron or needle, or with a caustic substance [Warts can be removed by *cauterizing* them.] —**cau′ter·ized,** *p.t. & p.p.*; **cau′ter·iz·ing,** *pr.p.*

cau·tion (kô′shən), *n.* 1. a being careful to keep away from danger, risks, or mistakes; wariness [Use *caution* in crossing streets.] 2. a warning [a word of *caution*]. —*v.* to warn; tell of danger [The sign *cautioned* us to slow down.]

cau·tious (kô′shəs), *adj.* careful to keep away from danger, risks, or mistakes; wary [a *cautious* chess player]. —**cau′tious·ly,** *adv.*

cav·al·cade (kav′'l kād), *n.* 1. a parade of people on horseback, in carriages, etc. 2. any procession or series [a *cavalcade* of events].

cav·a·lier (kav ə lir′), *n.* 1. a horseman; especially, a knight. 2. a gentleman who is very polite and attentive to women. —*adj.* 1. free and easy; gay [*cavalier* wit]. 2. proud in a scornful way; arrogant [*cavalier* contempt].

cav·al·ry (kav′'l rē), *n.* soldiers who serve on horseback or, now usually, in armored cars.

cav·al·ry·man (kav′'l rē mən), *n.* a member of the cavalry. —**cav′al·ry·men,** *pl.*

cave (kāv), *n.* a hollow place inside the earth, often an opening in a hillside. —**cave in,** to fall in or sink in; collapse. —**caved,** *p.t. & p.p.*; **cav′ing,** *pr.p.*

cave man, a human being of the time when man lived in caves, many thousands of years ago.

cav·ern (kav′ərn), *n.* a cave, especially a large cave.

cav·ern·ous (kav′ər nəs), *adj.* 1. like a cavern; hollow or deep [*cavernous* cheeks]. 2. full of caverns [*cavernous* hills].

cave man

cav·i·ar or **cav·i·are** (kav′i är), *n.* the salted eggs of sturgeon or of certain other fish, eaten as an appetizer.

cav·il (kav′'l), *v.* to object when there is little reason to do so; criticize unimportant things. —*n.* an unnecessary objection about something unimportant. —**cav′iled** or **cav′illed,** *p.t. & p.p.*; **cav′il·ing** or **cav′il·ling,** *pr.p.*

cav·i·ty (kav′ə tē), *n.* **1.** a hole or hollow place [the mouth *cavity*]. **2.** a hollow place caused by decay, as in a tooth. —**cav′i·ties,** *pl.*

ca·vort (kə vôrt′), *v.* to leap about; prance or caper; also, to frolic.

caw (kô), *n.* the loud, harsh cry of a crow or raven. —*v.* to make this sound.

cay·enne (kī en′ *or* kā en′), *n.* a very hot red pepper made from the dried seeds or fruit of a pepper plant (*in meaning 1*).

cay·use (kī yōōs′), *n.* an Indian pony.

cc. or **c.c.,** abbreviation for **cubic centimeter** or **cubic centimeters.**

Cd, symbol for the chemical element *cadmium.*

cease (sēs), *v.* to bring or come to an end; stop. —**ceased,** *p.t. & p.p.;* **ceas′ing,** *pr.p.*

cease·less (sēs′lis), *adj.* going on and on; continuous. —**cease′less·ly,** *adv.*

ce·dar (sē′dər), *n.* **1.** an evergreen tree having clusters of needlelike leaves, small cones, and sweet-smelling, reddish wood. **2.** this wood, which is used to make chests and closets for storing clothes.

cede (sēd), *v.* to give up one's rights in; surrender [Spain *ceded* Puerto Rico to the United States in 1898.] —**ced′ed,** *p.t. & p.p.;* **ced′ing,** *pr.p.*

cedar leaves and cones

ceil·ing (sēl′ing), *n.* **1.** the inside top part of a room, opposite the floor. **2.** a limit set on how high something may go [a *ceiling* on prices]. **3.** a covering of clouds that limits the view for airplanes.

cel·an·dine (sel′ən dīn), *n.* a plant of the poppy family, with small yellow flowers.

cel·e·brate (sel′ə brāt), *v.* **1.** to honor a victory, the memory of something, etc. in some special way [to *celebrate* a birthday with a party; to *celebrate* the Fourth of July with fireworks]. **2.** to honor or praise among people [Aesop's fables have been *celebrated* for centuries.] **3.** to go through the proper ceremony in an act of worship [to *celebrate* Mass]. —**cel′e·brat·ed,** *p.t. & p.p.;* **cel′e·brat·ing,** *pr.p.* —**cel′e·bra′tion,** *n.*

cel·e·brat·ed (sel′ə brāt′id), *adj.* famous; well-known [a *celebrated* pianist].

ce·leb·ri·ty (sə leb′rə tē), *n.* **1.** a famous person [The singer Caruso became a *celebrity.*] **2.** a being well-known and honored; fame; renown [He seeks no *celebrity.*] —**ce·leb′ri·ties,** *pl.*

ce·ler·i·ty (sə ler′ə tē), *n.* an acting or moving quickly; swiftness; speed.

cel·er·y (sel′ər ē), *n.* a plant whose crisp, long stalks are eaten as a vegetable.

ce·les·tial (sə les′chəl), *adj.* **1.** of the heavens or sky [The stars are *celestial* bodies.] **2.** of the finest or highest kind; perfect [*celestial* bliss].

cel·i·ba·cy (sel′ə bə sē), *n.* the condition of being unmarried, or remaining single.

cel·i·bate (sel′ə bīt), *n.* a person who is not married, especially a priest, monk, etc. who has vowed not to marry. —*adj.* unmarried.

cell (sel), *n.* **1.** a small, plainly furnished room, as in a prison or a monastery. **2.** any one of a number of small, hollow, connected spaces, as in a honeycomb. **3.** the basic unit of living matter, or tissue, usually very small [All plants and animals are made up of one or more *cells.*] **4.** a container holding metal or carbon pieces in a liquid or paste, for making electricity by chemical action [A battery is made up of one or more *cells.*]

living cell (enlarged many times)

cel·lar (sel′ər), *n.* a room or rooms underground, usually beneath a building, for storing things.

cel·list or **'cel·list** (chel′ist), *n.* a person who plays the cello.

cel·lo or **'cel·lo** (chel′ō), *n.* a musical instrument like a violin but larger and having a deeper tone: its full name is **violoncello.** —**cel′los** or **'cel′los,** *pl.*

cel·lo·phane (sel′əfān), *n.* a material made from cellulose in the form of thin, clear, waterproof sheets. It is used as a wrapping for food and other things.

cel·lu·lar (sel′yoo lər), *adj.* of, like, or containing cells [*cellular* tissue].

cello

cel·lu·loid (sel′yoo loid), *n.* a substance made from cellulose and used for combs, etc. It can catch on fire easily. **Celluloid** is a trademark.

cel·lu·lose (sel′yoo lōs), *n.* the main substance in the woody part of plants and trees. It is used in making paper, rayon, and explosives.

Celt (selt *or* kelt), *n.* a member of a people speaking a Celtic language.

Celt·ic (sel′tik *or* kel′tik), *n.* a family of languages that includes those spoken by the Britons and Gauls in ancient times and modern Welsh, Irish, and Scottish. —*adj.* of the Celts or their languages.

ce·ment (sə ment′), *n.* **1.** a powder made of lime and clay, mixed with water, and often sand, to make a thick mixture which hardens like stone when it dries. It is used for floors and walks and for holding stones or bricks together. **2.** a substance like this used for filling cavities in teeth. **3.** any soft substance that fastens things together when it hardens, as paste or glue. —*v.* **1.** to fasten together or cover with cement [to *cement* the pieces of a broken cup; to *cement* a driveway]. **2.** to make stronger [to *cement* a friendship].

cem·e·ter·y (sem′ə ter′ē), *n.* a place for burying the dead; graveyard. —**cem′e·ter′ies,** *pl.*

cen·ser (sen′sər), *n.* a container in which incense is burned, as in some church services.

cen·sor (sen′sər), *n.* **1.** an official who has the power to examine books, news stories, mail, movies, etc., and to remove or change anything the government does not wish people to see or hear. **2.** anyone who tells others what they should not do, say, see, etc. **3.** an official in ancient Rome who took the census and watched over the conduct of the people. —*v.* to examine books, letters, movies, etc. and to remove or hold back anything thought not right for people to see or hear. —**cen'sor·ship,** *n.*

cen·so·ri·ous (sen sôr'i əs), *adj.* always finding fault; criticizing. —**cen·sor'i·ous·ly,** *adv.*

cen·sure (sen'shər), *n.* a blaming or finding fault; disapproval. —*v.* to blame or find fault with; criticize harshly. —**cen'sured,** *p.t. & p.p.;* **cen'sur·ing,** *pr.p.*

cen·sus (sen'səs), *n.* an official counting of all the people in a country or area to find out how many there are and of what sex, ages, occupations, etc. [The United States *census* has been taken every ten years since 1790.]

cent (sent), *n.* a 100th part of a dollar, or a coin worth one cent; penny.

cen·taur (sen'tôr), *n.* a creature in Greek myths that was part man and part horse.

cen·te·nar·y (sen'tə ner'ē *or* sen·ten'ə rē), *n.* **1.** a period of 100 years; century. **2.** a centennial. —**cen'-te·nar·ies,** *pl.*

cen·ten·ni·al (sen ten'-i əl), *adj.* **1.** of or lasting for 100 years. **2.** happening once in 100 years. **3.** of a 100th anniversary. —*n.* a 100th anniversary or its celebration [Our nation celebrated its *centennial* in 1876.]

centaur

cen·ter (sen'tər), *n.* **1.** a point inside a circle or sphere that is the same distance from all points on the circumference or surface. **2.** the middle point or part; place at the middle [A vase of flowers stood at the *center* of the table.] **3.** a person or thing at the middle point [The *center* in basketball stands in the middle of the floor at the beginning of play.] **4.** a main point or place, where there is much activity or attraction [a shopping *center;* a *center* of interest]. —*v.* **1.** to place in or at the center [Try to *center* the design on the page.] **2.** to collect in one place; concentrate [We *centered* all our attention on the baby.]

center of gravity, that point in a thing around which its weight is evenly balanced.

cen·ti·grade (sen'tə grād), *adj.* **1.** having a basic scale of 100 degrees [The *centigrade* thermometer marks the freezing point of water as 0° and the boiling point as 100°.] **2.** as measured by the centigrade thermometer [10° *centigrade*].

cen·ti·gram *or* **cen·ti·gramme** (sen'tə-gram), *n.* a unit of weight, equal to 1/100 gram.

cen·time (sän'tēm), *n.* the 100th part of the French franc.

cen·ti·me·ter *or* **cen·ti·me·tre** (sen'tə mē'tər), *n.* a unit of measure, equal to 1/100 meter.

cen·ti·pede (sen'tə pēd), *n.* a small animal like a worm with many pairs of legs along its body. The two front legs are poison fangs.

cen·tral (sen'trəl), *adj.* **1.** in or at the center; forming the center [the *central* part of Ohio]. **2.** at about the same distance from different points [We chose a *central* meeting place.] **3.** most important; main; principal [the *central* plot in a novel]. —**cen'-tral·ly,** *adv.*

centipede (1 in. long)

Central African Republic, a country in central Africa, south of Chad.

Central America, the narrow part of America between Mexico and South America. It includes Guatemala, Nicaragua, Panama, etc.

cen·tral·ize (sen'trə līz), *v.* **1.** to make or become central; bring or come to a center. **2.** to bring under one control [All government powers were *centralized* under a dictator.] —**cen'-tral·ized,** *p.t. & p.p.;* **cen'tral·iz·ing,** *pr.p.* —**cen'tral·i·za'tion,** *n.*

Central Standard Time, see **Standard Time.**

cen·tre (sen'tər), *n. & v.* center: *a British spelling.* —**cen'tred,** *p.t. & p.p.;* **cen'tring,** *pr.p.*

cen·trif·u·gal force (sen trif'yoo g'l), the force that pulls a thing outward when it is spinning rapidly around a center [If you swing a ball on a string around your head, the *centrifugal force* of the ball's weight will keep the string taut and the ball swinging. The *centripetal force* of your hand holding the string will keep the ball from flying away.]

cen·trip·e·tal force (sen trip'ə t'l), the force that pulls a thing inward when it is spinning rapidly around a center: see **centrifugal force.**

cen·tu·ri·on (sen toor'i ən *or* sen tyoor'i ən), *n.* the commander of a group of about 100 soldiers in ancient Rome.

cen·tu·ry (sen'chə rē), *n.* **1.** any of the 100-year periods counted forward or backward from the beginning of the Christian Era [From 500 to 401 B.C. was the fifth *century* B.C.; from 1901 to 2000 is the twentieth *century* A.D.] **2.** any period of 100 years [He was born more than a *century* ago.] —**cen'tu·ries,** *pl.*

century plant, a desert plant that is a kind of agave. It gets its name from the mistaken belief that it blooms only once a century.

ce·ram·ics (sə ram'iks), *n.pl.* **1.** the art or work of making objects of baked clay, as pottery, porcelain, etc.: *used with a singular verb.* **2.** objects made of baked clay. —**ce·ram'ic,** *adj.*

Cer·ber·us (sûr′bər əs), *n.* a three-headed dog in Greek and Roman myths, that guarded the entrance to Hades.

ce·re·al (sir′i əl), *n.* **1.** any grass that bears seeds used for food [Rice, wheat, and oats are common *cereals*.] **2.** the seeds of such a grass; grain. **3.** food made from grain, especially breakfast food, as oatmeal or corn flakes. —*adj.* of or having to do with grain or the grasses bearing it.

cer·e·bel·lum (ser′ə bel′əm), *n.* the part of the brain behind and below the cerebrum.

cer·e·bral (ser′ə brəl *or* sə rē′brəl), *adj.* having to do with the brain or with the cerebrum.

cerebral palsy, a condition caused by injury to the brain, usually during birth, in which there is some difficulty in moving or speaking.

cer·e·brum (ser′ə brəm *or* sə rē′brəm), *n.* the upper, main part of the brain.

cer·e·ment (ser′ə mənt), *n.* the shroud or garment in which a dead person is buried.

cer·e·mo·ni·al (ser′ə mō′ni əl), *adj.* of or for a ceremony [The Indians put on their *ceremonial* robes for the war dance.] —*n.* **1.** a system of rules for ceremonies, especially in religion [a *ceremonial* for baptism]. **2.** a ceremony.

cer·e·mo·ni·ous (ser′ə mō′ni əs), *adj.* **1.** full of ceremony. **2.** very polite and formal [a *ceremonious* bow]. —**cer′e·mo′ni·ous·ly,** *adv.*

cer·e·mo·ny (ser′ə mō′nē), *n.* **1.** an act or set of acts done in a special way, with all the correct details for the occasion [a wedding *ceremony* in church; the *ceremony* of inaugurating the President]. **2.** very polite behavior that follows strict rules; formality [She served the tea with great *ceremony*.] —**stand on ceremony,** to pay strict attention to the rules of polite, formal behavior. —**cer′e·mo′nies,** *pl.*

Ce·res (sir′ēz), *n.* the Roman goddess of plants and farming. The Greeks called her *Demeter*.

ce·rise (sə rēz′), *n. & adj.* bright red.

cer·tain (sûr′t'n), *adj.* **1.** without any doubt or question; sure; positive [Are you *certain* of your facts?] **2.** bound to happen; not failing or missing [Such clouds bring *certain* rain. His aim was *certain*.] **3.** not named or described, though perhaps known [It happened in a *certain* town in Algeria.] **4.** some, but not much [to a *certain* extent]. —**for certain,** surely; without doubt.

cer·tain·ly (sûr′t'n lē), *adv.* without any doubt; surely [I shall *certainly* be there.]

cer·tain·ty (sûr′t'n tē), *n.* **1.** the condition of being certain; sureness [The weather cannot be predicted with *certainty*.] **2.** anything that is certain; positive fact [I know for a *certainty* that they are related.] —**cer′tain·ties,** *pl.*

cer·tif·i·cate (sər tif′ə kit), *n.* a written or printed statement that can be used as proof of something because it is official [a birth *certificate*].

cer·ti·fy (sûr′tə fī), *v.* **1.** to say in an official way that something is true or correct; verify [The doctor's letter *certified* that Harry's absence was due to illness.] **2.** to guarantee; vouch for [A *certified* check is one that the bank guarantees to be good.] **3.** to give a certificate to [A *certified* public accountant has a certificate of approval from the State.] —**cer′ti·fied,** *p.t. & p.p.* **cer′ti·fy·ing,** *pr.p.* —**cer′ti·fi·ca′tion,** *n.*

ce·ru·le·an (se rōō′li ən), *adj.* sky-blue.

ce·si·um (sē′zi əm), *n.* a soft, blue-gray metal that is a chemical element. It is used in electric eyes.

ces·sa·tion (se sā′shən), *n.* a ceasing or stopping, either forever or for some time [There will be a *cessation* of work during the holidays.]

ces·sion (sesh′ən), *n.* a ceding or giving up of rights or land [The *cession* of Guam to the U.S. by Spain took place in 1898.]

cess·pool (ses′pōōl), *n.* a deep hole in the ground for collecting the waste matter from the sinks and toilets of a house.

Cey·lon (si län′), *n.* a country in the British Commonwealth, on an island south of India.

cf., compare: *cf.* is the abbreviation of *confer*, the Latin word for "compare."

ch., abbreviation for **chapter.** —**chs.,** *pl.*

Chad (chad), *n.* a country in central Africa, south of Libya.

chafe (chāf), *v.* **1.** to rub so as to make warm [to *chafe* one's hands]. **2.** to make or become sore by rubbing [The stiff collar *chafed* his neck.] **3.** to make or become angry or annoyed [The delay *chafed* her. He *chafed* at his loss.] —**chafe at the bit,** to be impatient, as from having to wait. —**chafed,** *p.t. & p.p.* **chaf′ing,** *pr.p.*

chaff (chaf), *n.* **1.** the husks of wheat or other grain, separated from the seed by threshing. **2.** any worthless thing or part [His opinions are mere *chaff*.] **3.** friendly teasing or joking; banter. —*v.* to tease or make fun of in a friendly way.

chaf·finch (chaf′inch), *n.* a small songbird of Europe. It is often kept in a cage as a pet.

chaf·ing dish (chāf′ing), a pan placed in a frame over a small heating device. It is used to cook food at the table or to keep food hot.

cha·grin (shə grin′), *n.* a feeling of embarrassment and annoyance because one has failed or has been disappointed. —*v.* to embarrass and annoy [Our hostess was *chagrined* when the guest of honor failed to appear.] —**cha·grined′,** *p.t. & p.p.* **cha·grin′ing,** *pr.p.*

chafing dish

chain (chān), *n.* **1.** a number of links or loops joined together in a line that can be bent [a *chain* of steel; a *chain* of daisies]. **2. chains,** *pl.* anything that binds or holds someone prisoner; especially, bonds or shackles. **3.** a series of things joined together [a *chain* of mountains; a *chain* of events]. **4.** an instrument like a chain used for measuring length [A surveyor's *chain* is 66 feet long.] —*v.* **1.** to fasten or bind with chains. **2.** to hold down; bind [Dad is *chained* to his job.]

chain mail, armor that is made of metal links joined together, so that it will bend.

chain reaction, a series of actions, changes, or events, each of which in turn starts another. Atomic energy is produced by a chain reaction in which some particles of atoms are set free to strike other atoms in a mass, setting free more particles that strike still other atoms, and so on. When this happens very quickly, it causes an explosion.

chain store, any of a group of stores owned and run by the same company.

chair (cher), *n.* **1.** a piece of furniture that has a back and is a seat for one person. **2.** an important or official position [Professor Lane holds the *chair* of Latin at the college.] **3.** a chairman.

chair·man (cher′mən), *n.* a person who is in charge of a meeting or is the head of a committee or board. —**chair′men,** *pl.* —**chair′man-ship,** *n.*

chaise (shāz), *n.* a light carriage, especially one with two wheels and a folding top.

chaise longue (shāz′ lông′), a chair built like a couch, having a seat long enough to hold the out-stretched legs. —**chaise longues,** *pl.*

chaise longue

Chal·de·a (kal dē′ə), *n.* an ancient land in a region that is now the southern part of Iraq.

cha·let (sha lā′), *n.* **1.** a kind of Swiss house (*see the picture*). **2.** any house like this.

chal·ice (chal′is), *n.* a drinking cup; especially, the wine cup used in the Communion service.

Swiss chalet

chalk (chôk), *n.* **1.** a whitish lime-stone that is soft and easily crushed into a powder. It is made up mainly of small sea shells. **2.** a piece of chalk or of a material like it, for writing on blackboards. —*v.* to mark with chalk. —**chalk up, 1.** to score, as points in a game. **2.** to charge or credit [*Chalk* it *up* to experience.] —**chalk′y,** *adj.*

chalk·board (chôk′bôrd), *n.* a blackboard, especially one of a light-colored material.

chal·lenge (chal′ənj), *v.* **1.** to question the right or rightness of; refuse to believe unless proof is given [to *challenge* a claim; to *challenge* something said or the person who says it]. **2.** to call to take part in a fight or contest; dare [He *challenged* me to a game of checkers.] **3.** to refuse to let pass unless a certain sign is given [The sentry waited for the password after *challenging* the soldier.] —*n.* **1.** the act of challenging. **2.** the thing that is said, done, or called for in challenging. —**chal′lenged,** *p.t. & p.p.;* **chal′leng·ing,** *pr.p.* —**chal′leng·er,** *n.*

chal·lis or **chal·lie** (shal′ē), *n.* a soft, light cloth, usually printed with a pattern.

cham·ber (chām′bər), *n.* **1.** a room, often a bedroom. **2. chambers,** *pl.* a group of connected rooms or offices [a judge's *chambers*]. **3.** a large hall or meeting room. **4.** a number of people working together as a group for some purpose [A *chamber* of deputies is a legislature. A *chamber* of commerce promotes business activities.] **5.** an enclosed space in the body of a plant or animal [a *chamber* of the heart]. **6.** the part of a gun that holds the cartridge or shell.

cham·ber·lain (chām′bər lin), *n.* **1.** a man in charge of the household of a ruler or lord. **2.** a high official in certain royal courts.

cham·ber·maid (chām′bər mād), *n.* a woman whose work is taking care of bedrooms, as in hotels.

chamber music, music that is meant to be played by small groups [Sonatas, trios, and quartets are forms of *chamber music.*]

cham·bray (sham′brā), *n.* a smooth cotton cloth made by weaving white threads across colored ones.

cha·me·le·on (kə mē′li ən), *n.* **1.** a small lizard that can change the color of its skin. **2.** a person who keeps changing his opinions.

cham·ois (sham′ē), *n.* **1.** a small antelope like a goat, found in the mountains of Europe and southwestern Asia. **2.** a soft leather made from its skin or from the skin of sheep, deer, or goats [Pieces of *chamois* are used as polishing cloths.] —**cham′ois,** *pl.*

chamois (2½ ft. high)

champ (champ), *v.* **1.** to chew hard and noisily. **2.** to bite down on hard and restlessly [The horse *champed* at the bit.]

champ (champ), *n.* a champion: *a slang word.*

cham·pagne (sham pān′), *n.* pale yellow wine that bubbles like soda water.

cham·paign (sham pān′), *n.* flat, open country.

cham·pi·on (cham′pi ən), *n.* **1.** a person or thing that wins first place or is judged to be best, as in a contest or sport [a spelling *champion;* a tennis *champion*]. **2.** a person who fights for another or for a cause; defender [a *champion* of the poor]. —*adj.* winning over all others; being the best of its kind [a *champion* bull]. —*v.* to fight for or defend [Carrie Chapman Catt *championed* women's right to vote.]

cham·pi·on·ship (cham′pi ən ship′), *n.* **1.** the position or title of a champion; first place. **2.** the act of championing, or defending.

chance (chans), *n.* **1.** the way things turn out;

fat,   āpe,   cär,   ten,   ēven,   hit,   bīte,   gō,   hôrn,   tool,   book,   up,   fur;
get,   joy,   yet,   chin,   she,   thin,   *th*en;   zh = s in pleasure;   ′ as in able (ā′b'l);
ə = a in ago,   e in agent,   i in sanity,   o in confess,   u in focus.

happening of events by accident [They left it to *chance* when they would meet again.] **2.** a possibility or probability [There is little *chance* that he will play.] **3.** a time to take advantage of; opportunity [This is your *chance* to succeed.] **4.** a risk; gamble [to take a *chance* on winning]. —*adj.* happening by chance; accidental [a *chance* meeting of friends]. —*v.* **1.** to happen by chance [I *chanced* to be passing by.] **2.** to leave to chance; risk [This plan may fail, but let's *chance* it.] —**by chance,** accidentally. —**chance on** or **chance upon,** to find or meet by chance. —**chanced,** *p.t. & p.p.;* **chanc'ing,** *pr.p.*

chan·cel (chan's'l), *n.* the part of a church around the altar, used by the clergy and choir.

chan·cel·lor (chan'sə lər), *n.* any of certain high officials, as a minister of state in some countries, the chief judge in some law courts, or the head of some universities.

chan·de·lier (shan də lir'), *n.* a lighting fixture hanging from the ceiling with branches for several lights.

chandelier

chan·dler (chan'dlər), *n.* a person who sells supplies and groceries [A ship *chandler* sells provisions for ships.]

change (chānj), *v.* **1.** to make or become different in some way; alter [Time *changes* all things. The quiet town has *changed* into a busy city.] **2.** to put or take one thing in place of another; substitute [He has *changed* jobs twice this year.] **3.** to give or take one thing in return for another; exchange [The two boys *changed* seats. Can you *change* this dollar bill for four quarters?] **4.** to get off one train, bus, or plane and get on another [The passengers *change* at Chicago.] —*n.* **1.** the act of changing in some way [There will be a *change* in the weather tomorrow.] **2.** something put in place of something else [a fresh *change* of clothing]. **3.** the money returned when one has paid more than the amount owed [If you give the clerk a dollar for a toy that costs 70 cents, your *change* will be 30 cents.] **4.** a number of coins or bills whose total value equals a single larger coin or bill [I have *change* for your $10 bill.] **5.** small coins [The *change* jingled in his pocket.] —**changed,** *p.t. & p.p.;* **chang'ing,** *pr.p.*

change·a·ble (chān'jə b'l), *adj.* changing often or likely to change [*changeable* weather].

change·less (chānj'lis), *adj.* not changing; constant [a *changeless* love].

change·ling (chānj'ling), *n.* a child secretly put in the place of another; especially, in folk tales, one exchanged in this way by fairies. •

chan·nel (chan''l), *n.* **1.** the bed of a river or stream. **2.** the deeper part of a river, harbor, etc. **3.** a body of water joining two larger bodies of water [The English *Channel* links the Atlantic Ocean to the North Sea.] **4.** any tube or groove through which a liquid flows. **5.** any means by which something moves or passes [We get news

through newspapers and other *channels*.] **6.** the band of frequencies on which a single radio station or television station sends out its programs. —*v.* **1.** to make a channel in. **2.** to send through a channel. —**chan'neled** or **chan'nelled,** *p.t. & p.p.;* **chan'nel·ing** or **chan'nel·ling,** *pr.p.*

Channel Islands, some British islands in the English Channel, including Jersey and Guernsey.

chant (chant), *n.* **1.** a song, especially one in which strings of words or syllables are sung in the same tone [*Chants* are used in some church services.] **2.** a singsong way of speaking [the *chant* of an auctioneer]. —*v.* to sing or say in a chant [to *chant* a prayer].

chan·tey or **chan·ty** (shan'tē *or* chan'tē), *n.* a song that sailors sing in rhythm with their motions while working. —**chan'teys** or **chan'ties,** *pl.*

chan·ti·cleer (chan'ti klir'), *n.* a rooster.

Cha·nu·kah (hä'noo kä), *n.* same as **Hanukkah.**

cha·os (kā'äs), *n.* the greatest confusion and disorder.

cha·ot·ic (kā ät'ik), *adj.* in the greatest confusion and disorder. —**cha·ot'i·cal·ly,** *adv.*

chap (chap), *n.* a man or boy; fellow: *used only in everyday talk.*

chap (chap), *v.* to crack open; make or become rough [The wind will *chap* your skin.] —**chapped,** *p.t. & p.p.;* **chap'ping,** *pr.p.*

chap., abbreviation for **chapter.**

chap·el (chap''l), *n.* **1.** a place of Christian worship smaller than a church. **2.** a small room in a church, having its own altar. **3.** any room or building for holding religious services, as in a hospital, college, or army camp.

chap·er·on or **chap·er·one** (shap'ə rōn), *n.* an older person who goes along with young, unmarried people to a party, dance, etc. to see that they behave properly. —*v.* to be a chaperon to. —**chap'er·oned,** *p.t. & p.p.;* **chap'er·on·ing,** *pr.p.*

chap·lain (chap'lin), *n.* a minister, priest, or rabbi serving in the army, navy, etc. or in a hospital, prison, etc.

chap·let (chap'lit), *n.* **1.** a wreath for the head. **2.** a string of beads, especially a short rosary.

chaps (chaps), *n.pl.* leather coverings worn over trousers by cowboys to protect their legs.

chap·ter (chap'tər), *n.* **1.** any of the main parts into which a book is divided. **2.** a thing like a chapter; part; episode [a *chapter* of one's life]. **3.** a branch of a club or society that has a number of branches.

char (chär), *v.* **1.** to change to charcoal by burning. **2.** to burn slightly; scorch. —**charred,** *p.t. & p.p.;* **char'ring,** *pr.p.*

chaps

char·ac·ter (kar'ik tər), *n.* **1.** the total of things that a person does, feels, and thinks by which he is judged as being good or bad, strong or weak, etc. [That insulting remark showed his true *character*.] **2.** these things when thought of as being especially good or strong [Men of *character* are needed in high positions.] **3.** the total of things that makes one person or thing different from others; special quality; nature [The surrounding fields and woods gave the school a rural *character*.] **4.** any letter, figure, or symbol used in writing and printing. **5.** a person in a story or play. **6.** an odd or unusual person: *used only in everyday talk.*

char·ac·ter·is·tic (kar′ik tər is′tik), *adj.* that helps make up the special character of some person or thing; typical; like no other [the *characteristic* tail feathers of the peacock]. —*n.* something that makes a person or thing different from others; special part or quality [The pointed arch is a *characteristic* of Gothic style.] —**char′-ac·ter·is′ti·cal·ly,** *adv.*

char·ac·ter·ize (kar′ik tər īz′), *v.* **1.** to describe or show as having certain characteristics [Tennyson *characterized* King Arthur as wise and brave.] **2.** to be characteristic or typical of [Great energy *characterized* Henry Ford.] —**char′-ac·ter·ized′,** *p.t.* & *p.p.*; **char′ac·ter·iz′ing,** *pr.p.* —**char′ac·ter·i·za′tion,** *n.*

cha·rade (shə rād′), *n.* a game in which players try to guess the word or phrase that another player is acting out without speaking, often syllable by syllable.

char·coal (chär′kōl), *n.* a black form of carbon made by heating wood to a high degree in a closed container without air. It is used as a fuel, filter, crayon, etc.

charge (chärj), *v.* **1.** to load or fill [to *charge* a gun with ammunition; to *charge* a battery with electricity]. **2.** to give a task, duty, etc. to; make responsible for [I *charge* you with delivering this message.] **3.** to give instructions to [A judge *charges* a jury.] **4.** to accuse of doing wrong; blame [Charles I of England was *charged* with treason.] **5.** to set as a price; ask for payment [Barbers once *charged* a quarter for a haircut. We do not *charge* for gift wrappings.] **6.** to write down as something owed, to be paid for later [If you have no cash, this store will *charge* your purchase.] **7.** to rush at with force; attack [Our troops *charged* the enemy.] —*n.* **1.** the thing or amount used to load or fill a gun, battery, etc. **2.** a person or thing that one must take care of; responsibility [The children were the nurse's *charges*.] **3.** instruction or order [The judge gave his *charge* to the jury.] **4.** a claim that one has done wrong; accusation [He denied the *charge* that he had cheated.] **5.** price or cost [Is there any *charge* for delivering?] **6.** same as **charge account**; also, a single entry in a charge account. **7.** an attack, as by soldiers. **8.** the signal for such an attack [The bugler sounded the *charge*.] —**charge off, 1.** to put down as a loss. **2.** to

think of as due to a certain cause [*Charge off* his mistake to a lack of experience.] —**in charge,** having the responsibility or control. —**charged,** *p.t.* & *p.p.*; **charg′ing,** *pr.p.* —**charge′a·ble,** *adj.*

charge account, a plan by which a customer may buy things from a store or business and pay for them at a later time.

charg·er (chär′jər), *n.* **1.** a war horse. **2.** a machine that charges batteries.

charg·er (chär′jər), *n.* a large, flat dish.

char·i·ly (cher′ə lē), *adv.* in a chary way; with care, caution, shyness, etc.

char·i·ot (char′i ət), *n.* an open car with two wheels, drawn by horses. It was used in ancient times in battles, races, etc.

Greek chariot

char·i·ot·eer (char′-i ə tir′), *n.* the driver of a chariot.

cha·ris·ma (kə-riz′mə), *n.* a special quality of leadership that inspires loyalty and deep respect.

char·i·ta·ble (char′ə tə b′l), *adj.* **1.** kind and generous in giving money or other help to people in need; benevolent. **2.** for the poor, the sick, and others needing help [a *charitable* institution]. **3.** kind and forgiving in judging other people. —**char′i·ta·bly,** *adv.*

char·i·ty (char′ə tē), *n.* **1.** a giving of money or help to people in need. **2.** an institution, fund, etc. for giving such help. **3.** kindness in judging other people. **4.** love for one's fellow men: *now mainly in religious use,* as in the phrase "faith, hope, and charity." —**char′i·ties,** *pl.*

char·la·tan (shär′lə t′n), *n.* a person who tricks others into thinking he is an expert or highly skilled in something; quack; fake.

Char·le·magne (shär′lə mān), *n.* 742-814; king of the Franks and first emperor of the Holy Roman Empire.

Charles I (chärlz), 1600-1649; king of England from 1625 to 1649. He was beheaded for treason.

Charles·ton (chärlz′tən), *n.* **1.** the capital of West Virginia. **2.** a seaport in South Carolina.

char·ley horse (chär′lē), a cramp in muscles of the leg or arm: *used only in everyday talk.*

charm (chärm), *n.* **1.** an act, thing, word, or phrase that is supposed to have magic power to do good or evil. **2.** any small object worn as a decoration on a bracelet, necklace, etc. **3.** the quality or a feature in someone or something that attracts or delights people [His greatest *charm* is his smile.] —*v.* **1.** to act on as if by magic. **2.** to attract or delight; enchant. —**charmed life,** a life that

charms on a bracelet

seems to be protected from harm, as if by magic. **—charm′er,** *n.*

charm·ing (chärm′ing), *adj.* very pleasing; attractive; delightful. **—charm′ing·ly,** *adv.*

Cha·ron (ker′ən), *n.* the boatman in Greek myths who carried the souls of the dead across the river Styx to Hades.

chart (chärt), *n.* **1.** a map of an ocean or sea for use by sailors. It shows coast lines, depths, currents, etc. **2.** a group of facts about something set up in the form of a diagram, graph, table, etc. **—v. 1.** to make a map of. **2.** to show on a chart [to *chart* the weather].

char·ter (chär′tər), *n.* **1.** an official paper in which certain rights are given by a government to a person or business [a royal *charter* to settle a colony; a city *charter* to operate a bus line]. **2.** an official paper setting forth aims and principles of a group [the *Charter* of the United Nations]. **3.** written permission from a society to organize a local chapter [a *charter* for a troop of boy scouts]. **—v. 1.** to give a charter to. **2.** to hire or lease for the special use of a group [to *charter* a bus].

char·treuse (shär trooz′), *n. & adj.* pale, yellowish green.

char·wom·an (chär′woom′ən), *n.* a woman whose work is cleaning and scrubbing offices, etc. **—char′wom′en,** *pl.*

char·y (cher′ē), *adj.* **1.** not taking chances; careful; cautious [Be a little more *chary* of offending them.] **2.** not giving freely; sparing [He was *chary* of his favors to friends.] **—char′i·er,** *compar.;* **char′i·est,** *superl.*

Cha·ryb·dis (kə rib′dis), *n.* a whirlpool off the coast of Sicily, opposite the rock Scylla. A person is said to be "between Scylla and Charybdis" when he must choose between two dangers.

chase (chās), *v.* **1.** to go after or keep following in order to catch or harm. **2.** to drive away [He waved his hand to *chase* the flies away.] **—n. 1.** the act of chasing; pursuit. **2.** the act of hunting animals. **3.** anything that is hunted. **—give chase,** to chase or pursue. **—chased,** *p.t. & p.p.;* **chas′ing,** *pr.p.* **—chas′er,** *n.*

chasm (kaz′m), *n.* **1.** a deep crack in the earth; narrow gorge. **2.** any break or gap.

chas·sis (chas′ē *or* shas′-ē), *n.* **1.** the framework of an automobile, including all parts except the engine and body. **2.** the framework and all the working parts of a radio or television set, not including the cabinet. **—chas·sis** (chas′ēz *or* shas′ēz), *pl.*

chasm

chaste (chāst), *adj.* **1.** behaving in a moral way, especially about sex; pure. **2.** pure and simple in style; not fancy.

chas·ten (chās′'n), *v.* **1.** to punish in order to make better [to *chasten* a disobedient child]. **2.** to hold down the high spirits or wildness of.

chas·tise (chas tīz′), *v.* to punish, especially by beating. **—chas·tised′,** *p.t. & p.p.;* **chas-**

tis′ing, *pr.p.* **—chas·tise·ment** (chas′tiz-mənt *or* chas tīz′mənt), *n.*

chas·ti·ty (chas′tə tē), *n.* the quality of being chaste, moral, or pure; virtue.

chat (chat), *v.* to talk in an easy, relaxed way. **—n.** easy, relaxed talk or conversation. **—chat′-ted,** *p.t. & p.p.;* **chat′ting,** *pr.p.*

châ·teau (sha tō′), *n.* a castle or large country house, especially in France. **—châ·teaux** (sha-tōz′), *pl.*

Chat·ta·noo·ga (chat′ə nōō′gə), *n.* a city in southeastern Tennessee.

chat·tel (chat′'l), *n.* a piece of property that can be moved [Land and buildings are not *chattels;* furniture, automobiles, livestock, etc. are *chattels.*]

chat·ter (chat′ər), *v.* **1.** to make short, quick sounds that seem almost like talk [Birds and apes *chatter.*] **2.** to talk fast and in a foolish way, without stopping. **3.** to make fast clicking sounds with the teeth, when the lower jaw trembles because of fear or cold. **—n. 1.** the noise of chattering. **2.** fast, foolish talk. **—chat′ter·er,** *n.*

chat·ty (chat′ē), *adj.* **1.** always ready to chat [I get all the gossip from my *chatty* neighbor.] **2.** full of easy, friendly talk [a *chatty* letter]. **—chat′ti·er,** *compar.;* **chat′ti·est,** *superl.*

Chau·cer, Geof·frey (jef′rē chô′sər), 1340?–1400; English poet who wrote *The Canterbury Tales.*

chauf·feur (shō′fər *or* shō fūr′), *n.* a person whose work is to drive an automobile for another person. **—v.** to act as a chauffeur to.

cheap (chēp), *adj.* **1.** low in price [Vegetables are *cheaper* in summer than in winter.] **2.** charging low prices [a chain of *cheap* cafeterias]. **3.** worth more than it costs [That suit would be *cheap* at twice the price.] **4.** gotten with not much work or trouble; easily got [a *cheap* victory]. **5.** of low value or of poor quality [That radio is made of *cheap* parts that will wear out.] **6.** not worth having respect for [Don't make yourself *cheap* by getting rowdy.] **—adv.** at a low cost [I bought these shoes *cheap* at a sale.] **—cheap′-ly,** *adv.* **—cheap′ness,** *n.*

cheap·en (chēp′ən), *v.* to make or become cheap or cheaper.

cheap skate, a person who hates to give or spend money; stingy person: *a slang phrase.*

cheat (chēt), *v.* **1.** to act in a way that is not fair or honest in order to get what one wants [to *cheat* a person out of money; to *cheat* in a test]. **2.** to escape by tricks or by good luck [to *cheat* death]. **—n. 1.** a person who cheats: also **cheat′er. 2.** an act of cheating; a trick, fraud, or swindle.

check (chek), *n.* **1.** a sudden stop [We must put a *check* to so much tardiness.] **2.** a condition of being kept under control [He held his temper in *check.*] **3.** a person or thing that holds back or controls [High tariffs act as a *check* on trade.] **4.** a test to find out if something is as it should be [Add the column of numbers backwards as a *check* on your answer.] **5.** the mark √, used to show that something is right, or to call attention to something. **6.** a ticket or other token that shows one's right to claim an article left in a checkroom, etc. [a hat *check;* baggage *check*]. **7.** a piece of paper telling how much one owes, as for a meal at a restaurant. **8.** a written order to a bank to pay a certain amount of money from one's account to a certain person. **9.** a pattern of small squares like a checkerboard; also, any of the squares in such a pattern. **10.** in chess, the condition of a king that is in danger and must be put into a safe position. —*v.* **1.** to stop suddenly. **2.** to hold back or control. **3.** to prove to be right or find what is wanted by examining, comparing, etc. [These figures *check* with mine. *Check* the records for this information.] **4.** to mark with a check (*see meaning 5 of the noun*). **5.** to mark with a pattern of squares [a *checked* suit]. **6.** to put in a checkroom for a time. **7.** in chess, to place an opponent's king in check (*see meaning 10 of the noun*). —*interj.* I agree. I shall do it. Right!: *used only in everyday talk.* —**check in,** to write one's name on a list as a guest at a hotel, convention, etc. —**check out,** to settle one's bill and leave a hotel. —**in check,** under control. —**check′er, n.**

check·book (chek′book), *n.* a book that contains forms for writing checks (*meaning 8*).

check·er (chek′ər), *n.* **1.** a small square, as on a checkerboard. **2.** a pattern of such squares. **3.** one of the flat, round pieces used in playing certain games: see **checkers.** —*v.* to mark off in squares, or in patches of different colors.

check·er·board (chek′ər bôrd), *n.* a board divided into 64 squares of two colors. It is used in the games of checkers and chess (*see the picture for* **chess**).

check·ered (chek′ərd), *adj.* **1.** having a pattern of squares. **2.** broken up into many parts; full of changes, ups and downs, etc. [Captain Kidd had a *checkered* career.]

checkered tablecloth

check·ers (chek′-ərz), *n.pl.* a game played on a checker-board by two players, each of whom tries to capture all 12 pieces of the other player: *used with a singular verb.*

check·mate (chek′māt), *n.* **1.** the winning move in chess that ends the game by putting the opponent's king in a position where it cannot be saved; also, such a position. **2.** hopeless danger or complete defeat. —*v.* to place in checkmate; defeat completely. —**check′mat·ed,** *p.t. & p.p.;* **check′mat·ing,** *pr.p.*

check·rein (chek′rān), *n.* a short rein for pulling the bridle to keep a horse's head up.

check·room (chek′rōōm), *n.* a room where hats, coats, baggage, etc. may be left in safekeeping for a time.

check·up (chek′up), *n.* an examination of something to find out its condition, see if it is true or real, etc. [a *checkup* by one's doctor].

cheek (chēk), *n.* **1.** the side of the face between the nose and the ear and below the eye. **2.** the kind of boldness that shows no respect; impudence: *used only in everyday talk* [She had the *cheek* to push into line ahead of us.]

cheep (chēp), *n.* the short, peeping sound of a young bird; chirp. —*v.* to make such a sound.

cheer (chir), *n.* **1.** a glad, excited shout of welcome, joy, or approval [The crowd gave their hero three *cheers*.] **2.** good or glad feelings; joy, hope, comfort, etc. [That song brings *cheer* to my heart.] —*v.* **1.** to give cheer to. **2.** to urge on or applaud with cheers. —**be of good cheer,** to be glad or hopeful. —**cheer up,** to make or become glad or hopeful.

cheer·ful (chir′fəl), *adj.* **1.** full of cheer; glad; joyful [a *cheerful* smile]. **2.** filling with cheer; bright and gay [a *cheerful* room]. **3.** willing; glad to help [a *cheerful* worker]. —**cheer′ful·ly,** *adv.* —**cheer′ful·ness, n.**

cheer·less (chir′lis), *adj.* not cheerful; sad; dreary. —**cheer′less·ly, adv.**

cheer·y (chir′ē), *adj.* cheerful; lively and happy [They gave us a *cheery* welcome.] —**cheer′i·er,** *compar.;* **cheer′i·est,** *superl.* —**cheer′i·ly, adv.** —**cheer′i·ness, n.**

cheese (chēz), *n.* a solid food made by pressing together the curds of soured milk.

cheese·cloth (chēz′klôth), *n.* a thin, cotton cloth with a very loose weave.

chee·tah (chē′tə), *n.* an animal found in Africa and southern Asia that is like the leopard but smaller. It can be trained to hunt.

cheetah (7 ft. long, including tail)

chef (shef), *n.* **1.** a head cook. **2.** any cook.

chem·i·cal (kem′i-k′l), *adj.* **1.** of or in chemistry [a *chemical* process]. **2.** made by or used in chemistry [*chemical* compounds]. —*n.* any substance used in chemistry or gotten by a chemical process [Various *chemicals* are used in making plastics.] —**chem′i·cal·ly, adv.**

che·mise (shə mēz′), *n.* a kind of loose undergarment like a slip, that women used to wear.

chem·ist (kem′ist), *n.* **1.** an expert in chemistry. **2.** a druggist: *a British meaning.*

chem·is·try (kem′is trē), *n.* the science in which substances are examined to find out what they are made of, how they act under various conditions, and how they are combined or separated to form other substances.

cheque (chek), *n.* a bank check: *this spelling is mainly British.*

---

fat, āpe, cär, ten, ēven, hit, bīte, gō, hôrn, tōōl, book, up, fûr; get, joy, yet, chin, she, thin, *th*en; zh = s in pleasure; ′ as in able (ā′b'l); ə = a in ago, e in agent, i in sanity, o in confess, u in focus.

cher·ish (cher′ish), *v.* **1.** to treat with love or care; hold dear; take good care of [to *cherish* one's family; to *cherish* one's rights]. **2.** to keep firmly in the mind; cling to the idea or feeling of [to *cherish* fame, a hope, etc.].

Cher·o·kee (cher′ə kē), *n.* a member of an Indian tribe most of whom were moved in times past from the southeastern United States to the Southwest. —**Cher′o·kee** or **Cher′o·kees,** *pl.*

cher·ry (cher′ē), *n.* **1.** a small, round fruit with sweet flesh covering one seed. Cherries are bright red, dark red, or yellow. **2.** the tree that this fruit grows on in clusters. **3.** the wood of this tree. **4.** bright red. —**cher′ries,** *pl.*

cher·ub (cher′əb), *n.* **1.** a kind of angel mentioned in the Bible. A cherub is now usually shown in pictures as a chubby child with little wings. **2.** any healthy-looking child with a pretty face. —**cher′ubs** *or also, for meaning 1,* **cher·u·bim** (cher′ə bim), *pl.*

che·ru·bic (chə rōō′bik), *adj.* of or like a cherub; plump and sweet-looking [a baby's *cherubic* face].

Ches·a·peake Bay (ches′ə pēk), a bay of the Atlantic Ocean that reaches into Maryland and Virginia.

Chesh·ire cat (chesh′ir), a grinning cat in *Alice in Wonderland* that fades away leaving only its grin.

chess (ches), *n.* a game played on a checkerboard by two players. Each in turn moves one of his 16 pieces (called **chess′-men**) with which he tries to capture the other's pieces. See **check-mate.**

chess

chest (chest), *n.* **1.** a heavy box with a lid [a toy *chest;* a tool *chest*]. **2.** a piece of furniture with drawers; bureau: also called **chest of drawers.** **3.** the part of the body inside the ribs; also, the outside front part of this [a cold in the *chest;* a tattoo on the *chest*].

chest·nut (ches′nut), *n.* **1.** a dark-brown nut with a smooth, thin shell and a prickly husk. It is usually eaten cooked or roasted. **2.** the tree of the beech family that this nut grows on. **3.** the wood of this tree. **4.** dark reddish brown. **5.** an old, stale joke, story, etc.: *used only in everyday talk.*

chestnuts

chev·a·lier (shev ə lir′), *n.* **1.** in olden times, a knight or cavalier. **2.** now, a person who has been honored by being made a member of the French Legion of Honor.

chev·i·ot (shev′i ət), *n.* a rough woolen cloth that is woven with raised diagonal lines.

chev·ron (shev′rən), *n.* a badge of rank shaped like an upside-down V, worn on the sleeve of a military or police uniform.

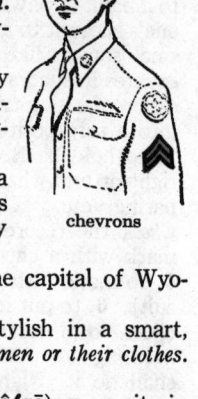
chevrons

chew (chōō), *v.* to bite and grind up with the teeth. —*n.* something chewed or for chewing. —**chew′y,** *adj.*

chewing gum, a gummy substance, such as chicle, flavored and sweetened for chewing.

che·wink (chi wingk′), *n.* a North American bird that nests on the ground and has a cry that sounds like its name.

Chey·enne (shī en′), *n.* the capital of Wyoming.

chic (shēk *or* shik), *adj.* stylish in a smart, pleasing way: *used only of women or their clothes.* —*n.* a chic look.

Chi·ca·go (shə kä′gō *or* shə kô′gō), *n.* a city in northeastern Illinois, on Lake Michigan.

chi·can·er·y (shi kān′ər ē), *n.* the use of clever but tricky talk or acts in order to fool or confuse. —**chi·can′er·ies,** *pl.*

chick (chik), *n.* **1.** a young chicken. **2.** a young bird.

chick·a·dee (chik′ə dē), *n.* a small, gray bird with a black cap and throat.

chick·en (chik′ən), *n.* **1.** the common fowl raised for use as food, especially the young of this fowl; hen or rooster. **2.** the flesh of a chicken.

chick·en-heart·ed (chik′ən här′tid), *adj.* afraid to take a chance; timid or cowardly.

chickadee (5 in. long)

chicken pox, a children's disease in which there is a mild fever and small, watery blisters form on the skin.

chick·weed (chik′wēd), *n.* a common weed with small, oval leaves and tiny, white flowers.

chic·le (chik′'l), *n.* a gummy substance made from the sap of a tropical American tree. It is used in chewing gum.

chic·o·ry (chik′ə rē), *n.* **1.** a plant with blue flowers and leaves that look like those of the dandelion. **2.** the root of this plant, which is sometimes roasted, ground, and mixed with coffee. —**chic′o·ries,** *pl.*

chide (chīd), *v.* to scold because of some fault; rebuke [She *chided* John for being rude.] —**chid′ed** or **chid** (chid), *p.t. & p.p.;* **chid′-ing,** *pr.p.*

chief (chēf), *n.* the leader or head of some group [an Indian *chief;* the *chief* of a hospital staff]. —*adj.* **1.** having the highest position; being at the head [the *chief* executive]. **2.** main; most important [Bill's *chief* interest is baseball.] —**in chief,** in the highest position [commander *in chief*].

chief justice, the judge who is in charge of a court made up of several judges [The *Chief Justice* of the U.S. is the judge in charge of the Supreme Court.]

chief·ly (chēf′lē), *adv.* most of all; especially; mainly [A watermelon is *chiefly* water.]

chief·tain (chēf′tən), *n.* **1.** a chief of a tribe or clan. **2.** any leader of a group.

chif·fon (shi fän′), *n.* a thin, soft cloth of silk, nylon, etc., used in women's clothes.

chig·ger (chig′ər), *n.* the tiny, red larva of certain mites. It bores under the skin and causes itching.

Chi·hua·hua (chi wä′wä), *n.* a very small, lively dog with large, pointed ears. It originally came from Mexico.

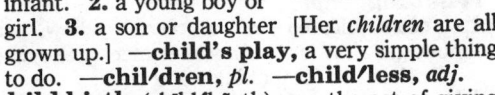
Chihuahua (8 in. high)

chil·blain (chil′blān), *n.* a red swelling on the feet or hands that itches and burns. It is caused by being out too long in freezing cold.

child (chīld), *n.* **1.** a baby; infant. **2.** a young boy or girl. **3.** a son or daughter [Her *children* are all grown up.] —**child's play,** a very simple thing to do. —**chil′dren,** *pl.* —**child′less,** *adj.*

child·birth (chīld′bûrth), *n.* the act of giving birth to a child.

child·hood (chīld′hood), *n.* the time or condition of being a child.

child·ish (chīl′dish), *adj.* **1.** of or fit for a child [*childish* games]. **2.** more like a child's than a grownup's; foolish, simple, etc. [The angry woman gave a *childish* answer.] —**child′-ish·ly,** *adv.* —**child′ish·ness,** *n.*

child·like (chīld′līk), *adj.* like a child, as in innocence, honesty, trust, etc. [He was *childlike* in his frankness.]

chil·dren (chil′drən), *n.* plural of **child.**

Chil·e (chil′ē), *n.* a country on the southwestern coast of South America. —**Chil′e·an,** *adj. & n.*

chil·e con car·ne (chil′ē kän kär′nē), a Mexican food made of beans, meat, red peppers, and spices. Also spelled **chili con carne.**

chil·i (chil′ē), *n.* **1.** the dried pod of red pepper, used as a very hot seasoning. **2.** same as **chile con carne.** Also spelled **chil′e** or **chil′li.** —**chil′ies,** *pl.*

chili sauce, tomato sauce spiced with chilies.

chill (chil), *n.* **1.** a feeling of coldness that makes one shiver. **2.** a coolness that is uncomfortable [There's a *chill* in the air.] —*adj.* chilly. —*v.* **1.** to make or become cool or cold [Melons taste better if they are *chilled*.] **2.** to cause a chill in [The wind *chilled* her.]

chil·ly (chil′ē), *adj.* **1.** so cool as to be uncomfortable; rather cold [a *chilly* room]. **2.** not friendly [a *chilly* reception]. —**chil′li·er,** *compar.*; **chil′li·est,** *superl.* —**chil′li·ness,** *n.*

chime (chīm), *n.* **1.** a bell that is part of a set of bells on which tunes can be played. **2.** a single bell struck by a small hammer, as in a clock or doorbell. **3. chimes,** *pl.* the music or sounds made by such bells. —*v.* to ring, as a chime or chimes. —**chime in, 1.** to join in. **2.** to agree. —**chimed,** *p.t. & p.p.*; —**chim′ing,** *pr.p.*

Chi·me·ra (kə mir′ə *or* kī mir′ə), *n.* **1.** a monster in Greek myths that breathed fire and was part lion, part goat, and part serpent. **2. chimera,** any imaginary monster or any foolish or wild idea. Also spelled **Chimaera** or **chi-maera.** —**chi·mer′i·cal,** *adj.*

chim·ney (chim′nē), *n.* **1.** a pipe or shaft going up through a roof to carry off smoke and fumes from a furnace, fireplace, or stove. Chimneys are usually enclosed with brick or stone. **2.** a glass tube around the flame of a lamp. —**chim′neys,** *pl.*

chim·pan·zee (chim′pan zē′ *or* chim pan′zē), *n.* an ape of Africa that is smaller than a gorilla and is one of the most intelligent of all the lower animals.

chimpanzee (4½ ft. tall)

chin (chin), *n.* the part of the face below the lower lip; front part of the lower jaw. —*v.* to pull oneself up, while hanging by the hands from a bar, until the chin is even with the bar. —**chinned,** *p.t. & p.p.*; **chin′ning,** *pr.p.*

Chi·na (chī′nə), *n.* a country in eastern Asia.

chi·na (chī′nə), *n.* **1.** a fine kind of porcelain that was first made in China. **2.** dishes or ornaments made of this. **3.** any dishes made of earthenware. Also **chi·na·ware** (chī′nə wer).

boy chinning himself

Chi·na·man (chī′nə mən), *n.* a Chinese. *This is not a polite name for a Chinese.*

China Sea, a part of the Pacific Ocean east of China.

chinch bug (chinch), a small black bug with white wings that damages grain plants.

chin·chil·la (chin chil′ə), *n.* **1.** a small, ratlike animal found in the Andes Mountains in South America. **2.** its soft, gray fur, which is very expensive. **3.** a heavy woolen cloth with a rough surface, used for making overcoats.

chinchilla (15 in. long)

---

fat,　āpe,　cär,　ten,　ēven,　hit,　bīte,　gō,　hôrn,　tōōl,　book,　up,　fûr;
get,　joy,　yet,　chin,　she,　thin,　*th*en;　zh = s in pleasure;　′ as in able (ā′b'l);
ə = a in ago,　e in agent,　i in sanity,　o in confess,　u in focus.

Chi·nese (chī nēz′), *n.* **1.** a member of a people whose native country is China. **2.** the language of China. —*adj.* of China, its people, language, or culture. —**Chi·nese′**, *pl.*

chink (chingk), *n.* a narrow opening; crack. —*v.* **1.** to form chinks in. **2.** to fill the chinks in.

chink (chingk), *n.* a sharp, clinking sound, as of coins striking together. —*v.* to make this sound or cause to make this sound.

chi·nook (chi nŏŏk′), *n.* a warm, moist wind blowing from the southwest over the sea onto the coast of Oregon and Washington.

chintz (chints), *n.* a cotton cloth printed in colors with flower designs or other patterns. It usually has a hard, glossy surface.

chip (chip), *v.* **1.** to break or cut a small piece or thin slice from. **2.** to break off into small pieces [This glass *chips* easily.] **3.** to shape by cutting or chopping with an ax, chisel, etc. [*Chip* a hole in the ice.] —*n.* **1.** a small, thin piece broken or cut off [A potato *chip* is a thin slice of potato fried crisp.] **2.** a place where a small piece has been chipped off [a *chip* on the edge of a plate]. **3.** a small, round disk used in gambling games in place of money. —**chip in,** to share in giving money or help: *used only in everyday talk.* —**chip off the old block,** a person who is much like his father. —**chipped,** *p.t. & p.p.;* **chip′ping,** *pr.p.*

chip·munk (chip′mungk), *n.* a small squirrel of North America with striped markings on its back. It lives in holes in the ground.

chip·per (chip′ər), *adj.* feeling healthy and cheerful: *used only in everyday talk.*

chi·rop·o·dist (ki rāp′ə dist), *n.* a person whose work is taking care of feet, as by removing corns, strengthening arches, etc.

chipmunk (9 in. long)

chi·ro·prac·tor (kī′rə prak′tər), *n.* a person who practices a system of treating diseases by pressing and moving the spine and joints of the body with the hands.

chirp (chûrp), *v.* to make a short, sharp sound, as some birds or insects do. —*n.* this sound.

chir·rup (chir′əp), *v.* to keep on chirping, as a cricket does. —*n.* the sound of chirruping.

chis·el (chiz′'l), *n.* a tool having a strong blade with a sharp edge for cutting or shaping wood, stone, or metal. —*v.* **1.** to cut or shape with a chisel. **2.** to get something by cheating: *used only in everyday talk.* —**chis′-eled** or **chis′elled,** *p.t. & p.p.;* **chis′el·ing** or **chis′-el·ling,** *pr.p.* —**chis′el·er** or **chis′el·ler,** *n.*

chisel

chit·chat (chit′chat), *n.* light

talk about common, everyday things; small talk.

chiv·al·rous (shiv′'l rəs), *adj.* **1.** helping the weak and protecting women as the knights of old were supposed to do; gallant, brave, etc. **2.** having to do with chivalry. —**chiv′al·rous·ly,** *adv.*

chiv·al·ry (shiv′'l rē), *n.* **1.** the way of life followed by the knights of the Middle Ages. **2.** the noble qualities a knight was supposed to have, such as courage, honor, and a readiness to help the weak and protect women.

chive (chīv), *n.* a plant of the onion family, with slender hollow leaves that are chopped up and used for flavoring.

chlo·ral (klôr′əl), *n.* a chemical prepared from chlorine and alcohol. A drug made with chloral is used to cause sleep.

chlo·ride (klôr′īd), *n.* a chemical compound of chlorine and another element or elements [Sodium *chloride*, formed of sodium and chlorine, is common table salt.]

chlo·ri·nate (klôr′ə nāt), *v.* to add chlorine to in order to make pure [to *chlorinate* a swimming pool]. —**chlo′ri·nat·ed,** *p.t. & p.p.;* **chlo′-ri·nat·ing,** *pr.p.*

chlo·rine (klôr′ēn), *n.* a greenish-yellow, poisonous gas that is a chemical element. It is used in bleaches and for making water pure.

chlo·ro·form (klôr′ə fôrm), *n.* a sweetish, colorless liquid that changes into a vapor easily. It is used by doctors to make a person unconscious, as before an operation. —*v.* **1.** to make unconscious by giving chloroform. **2.** to kill with chloroform [He *chloroforms* the insects before putting them in his collection.]

chlo·ro·phyll or **chlo·ro·phyl** (klôr′ə fil), *n.* the green coloring matter in plants. Sunlight causes it to change carbon dioxide and water into the carbohydrates that are the food of the plant.

chock (chäk), *n.* a block or wedge placed under a wheel, barrel, etc. to keep it from rolling. —*v.* to wedge firmly with a chock.

chock-full (chäk′fool′), *adj.* as full as possible [He added coal until the bin was *chock-full*.]

choc·o·late (chôk′lit *or* chäk′ə lit), *n.* **1.** a paste, powder, sirup, or bar made from cacao seeds that have been ground and roasted. **2.** a drink made of chocolate, sugar, and milk or water. **3.** a candy made of chocolate or covered with chocolate. **4.** reddish brown. —*adj.* made of or flavored with chocolate.

choice (chois), *n.* **1.** a choosing or picking from others; selection [You may have two books of your own *choice*.] **2.** the right or chance to choose [You will be assigned to a seat; you have no *choice* in the matter.] **3.** a person or thing chosen [He is my *choice* for captain.] **4.** a group of things from which to choose [We have a *choice* of three movies; which one shall we see?] —*adj.* especially good; of the best kind [*choice* fruits].

choir (kwīr), *n.* **1.** a group of people trained to sing together, especially as part of a church service. **2.** the part of a church where the choir sings.

choke (chōk), *v.* **1.** to keep from breathing by blocking the windpipe or squeezing the throat; strangle; suffocate. **2.** to have a hard time breathing [The smoke in the room made me *choke*.] **3.** to block up a passage; clog [Garbage *choked* the drain in the sink.] **4.** to hold back the growth or action of; smother [Weeds are *choking* the grass in the lawn.] **5.** to cut off some air from a carburetor so as to make a richer gasoline mixture, as in cold weather. —*n.* **1.** the act or sound of choking. **2.** a valve that chokes a carburetor. —**choke back,** to hold back, as sobs or tears. —**choke down,** to swallow hard. —**choke off,** to bring to an end; stop the growth of. —**choke up, 1.** to block up; clog. **2.** to be unable to speak, act, etc., as because of fear or nervousness: *used only in everyday talk.* —**choked,** *p.t. & p.p.;* **chok'-ing,** *pr.p.*

chok·er (chōk'er), *n.* **1.** a thing that chokes. **2.** a necklace that fits closely around the neck.

chol·er (käl'er), *n.* great anger: *an old-fashioned word.*

chol·er·a (käl'er ə), *n.* a deadly disease that spreads quickly, as a plague, especially in places where sanitation is poor.

chol·er·ic (käl'er ik), *adj.* easily made angry; having a quick temper.

choose (chooz), *v.* **1.** to pick out one or more from a number or group [*Choose* a topic from this list.] **2.** to make up one's mind; decide or prefer [He did not *choose* to run for mayor.] —**chose,** *p.t.;* **cho'sen,** *p.p.;* **choos'ing,** *pr.p.*

choos·y (chooz'ē), *adj.* very careful or fussy in choosing: *used only in everyday talk.*

chop (chäp), *v.* **1.** to cut by strokes with an ax or the like [to *chop* down a tree]. **2.** to make a quick, cutting stroke [The batter *chopped* at the ball.] **3.** to cut into small bits [*Chop* some nuts for the filling.] —*n.* **1.** a quick, cutting stroke or blow. **2.** a slice of lamb, pork, or veal cut with a piece of bone from the rib, loin, or shoulder.

rib chop

—**chopped,** *p.t. & p.p.;* **chop'ping,** *pr.p.* —**chop'per,** *n.*

chop (chäp), *n.* a jaw: see also **chops.**

chop (chäp), *v.* to shift suddenly, as the wind. —**chopped,** *p.t. & p.p.;* **chop'ping,** *pr.p.*

Cho·pin, Frédéric (shō'pan), 1810–1849; Polish pianist and composer who lived in France.

chop·py (chäp'ē), *adj.* **1.** having rough, broken waves [A strong wind made the lake *choppy*.] **2.** with short, quick movements; jerky [He runs fast in spite of his *choppy* stride.] —**chop'pi·er,** *compar.;* **chop'pi·est,** *superl.*

chops (chäps), *n.pl.* **1.** the jaws. **2.** the flesh about the mouth.

chop·sticks (chäp'stiks), *n.pl.* a pair of small thin sticks used mainly by the Chinese, to lift food to the mouth.

chop su·ey (chäp'soo'ē), a mixture of meat, bean sprouts, mushrooms, etc. cooked in a sauce and served with rice. Chop suey was first made by Chinese in America.

chopsticks

cho·ral (kôr'əl), *adj.* **1.** of or for a choir or chorus. **2.** sung or recited by a chorus.

cho·rale or **cho·ral** (kô ral'), *n.* a simple hymn tune, often sung in unison.

chord (kôrd), *n.* a combination of three or more musical tones that make harmony when sounded together.

chord (kôrd), *n.* **1.** a straight line joining any two points on an arc or circle. **2.** a string of a harp or lyre: *used in poetry.* **3.** a feeling or emotion thought of as being played on like the string of a harp [to strike a sympathetic *chord*].

chord

chore (chôr), *n.* **1.** a common, everyday task, as on a farm or in the home [His *chores* included mowing the lawn.] **2.** any hard or boring task [Scrubbing pans is a *chore* for her.]

chor·e·og·ra·phy (kô'ri äg'rə fē), *n.* the planning of dance steps and movements of a ballet. —**chor'e·og'ra·pher,** *n.*

chor·is·ter (kôr'is tər), *n.* a singer in a choir, especially a boy singer.

chor·tle (chôr't'l), *v.* to chuckle in a loud, gleeful way. —**chor'tled,** *p.t. & p.p.;* **chor'-tling,** *pr.p.*

chor·us (kôr'əs), *n.* **1.** a group of people trained to speak or sing together [Greek plays usually had a *chorus* which explained what the actors were doing.] **2.** music to be sung by a chorus ["The Anvil *Chorus*" is a famous song from an Italian opera.] **3.** singers and dancers who work as a group, not soloists, as in a musical play. **4.** a number of voices speaking at once [The teacher was answered by a *chorus* of eager replies.] **5.** the part of a song that is repeated after each verse; refrain [The *chorus* of "The Bluetail Fly" begins "Jimmy crack corn . . . ."] —*v.* to speak or sing together or at the same time [The Senators *chorused* their approval.] —**in chorus,** all at once; together.

chose (chōz), past tense of **choose.**

cho·sen (chō'z'n), past participle of **choose.** —*adj.* picked out by choice; selected [A *chosen* few soldiers formed the king's guard.]

fat,   āpe,   cär,   ten,   ēven,   hit,   bīte,   gō,   hôrn,   tool,   book,   up,   fūr;
get,   joy,   yet,   chin,   she,   thin,   *then;*   zh = s in pleasure;   ' as in able (ā'b'l);
ə = a in ago,   e in agent,   i in sanity,   o in confess,   u in focus.

chow (chou), *n.* **1.** a dog that was first bred in China, with a thick, brown or black coat and a black tongue. **2.** food: *slang in this meaning.*

chow (20 in. high)

chow·der (chou′dər), *n.* a thick soup made of fish or clams cooked with onions, potatoes, milk or tomatoes, etc.

chow mein (chou′ mān′), a mixture of meat, onions, celery, bean sprouts, etc. cooked in a sauce and served with fried noodles. Chow mein was first made by Chinese in America.

Christ (krīst), *n.* Jesus of Nazareth, regarded by Christians as the Messiah: the title *Christ* is from the Greek word for "messiah."

chris·ten (kris′n), *v.* **1.** to baptize or give a name to at baptism [The baby was *christened* Thomas.] **2.** to give a name to [We *christened* the boat Speedwell II.] —**chris′ten·ing,** *n.*

Chris·ten·dom (kris′n dəm), *n.* **1.** all the Christian people. **2.** those parts of the world where Christianity is the most common religion.

Chris·tian (kris′chən), *n.* a person who believes in Jesus as the Messiah and in the religion based on the teachings of Jesus. —*adj.* **1.** of Jesus or his teachings. **2.** belonging to the religion based on these teachings. **3.** having the qualities that Christians are supposed to have, as kindness, charity, and humbleness.

Chris·ti·an·i·ty (kris′chi an′ə tē), *n.* **1.** the Christian religion. **2.** all the Christian people.

Chris·tian·ize (kris′chən īz), *v.* to make Christian. —**Chris′tian·ized,** *p.t. & p.p.;* **Chris′tian·iz·ing,** *pr.p.*

Christian name, the name given in baptism, to go with the family name; first name.

Christian Science, a religion and system of healing founded by Mary Baker Eddy in 1866. It teaches that sin, disease, and death are errors of the mind which proper thinking will correct.

Christ·like (krīst′līk), *adj.* like Jesus Christ, especially in qualities or spirit.

Christ·mas (kris′məs), *n.* a holiday on December 25 celebrating the birth of Jesus Christ.

Christmas tree, an evergreen tree decorated with ornaments and lights at Christmas time.

chro·mat·ic (krō mat′ik), *adj.* **1.** of color or having color or colors. **2.** in music, with a half tone between each note [There are thirteen half tones in an octave of the *chromatic* scale.]

chrome (krōm), *n.* chromium, especially when it is used to plate steel or other metal.

chro·mi·um (krō′mi əm), *n.* a very hard metal that is a chemical element. Chromium does not rust easily and is used in steel alloys and as a plating for metals. Chromium compounds are used in many paints and dyes.

chro·mo·some (krō′mə sōm), *n.* any of certain tiny particles in the nucleus of cells. Chromosomes contain the genes that carry the inherited characteristics of an animal or plant.

chron·ic (krän′ik), *adj.* **1.** going on for a long time or coming back again and again [a *chronic* disease]. **2.** having been one for a long time; constant or habitual [a *chronic* complainer; a *chronic* invalid]. —**chron′i·cal·ly,** *adv.*

chron·i·cle (krän′i k'l), *n.* a history or story; especially, a record of happenings in the order in which they happened. —*v.* to tell or write the history of; record. —**chron′i·cled,** *p.t. & p.p.;* **chron′i·cling,** *pr.p.* —**chron′i·cler,** *n.*

Chron·i·cles (krän′i k'lz), *n.* either of two books of the Old Testament.

chron·o·log·i·cal (krän′ə läj′i k'l), *adj.* **1.** arranged in the order in which things happened [a *chronological* chart of English history]. **2.** of chronology. —**chron′o·log′i·cal·ly,** *adv.*

chro·nol·o·gy (krə näl′ə jē), *n.* **1.** the science of measuring time and of finding the correct dates for happenings. **2.** arrangement of happenings in the order in which they happened. —**chro·nol′o·gies,** *pl.*

chro·nom·e·ter (krə näm′ə tər), *n.* a very accurate clock or watch, as for scientific use.

chrys·a·lis (kris′'l is), *n.* **1.** the form of a butterfly when it is in a cocoon, between the time when it is a larva and the time when it is a winged adult. **2.** the cocoon.

chrys·an·the·mum (kris an′thə məm), *n.* **1.** a plant with round flowers that bloom in late summer and fall. It is grown in a wide variety of sizes and colors. **2.** any of these flowers.

chrys·o·lite (kris′ə līt), *n.* a green or yellow stone sometimes used as a gem.

chrysalis as seen from front and side

chub·by (chub′ē), *adj.* round and plump [a *chubby* little boy]. —**chub′bi·er,** *compar.;* **chub′bi·est,** *superl.* —**chub′bi·ness,** *n.*

chuck (chuk), *v.* **1.** to tap or pat under the chin in a gentle, playful way. **2.** to throw with a quick, short toss. **3.** to get rid of: *used only in everyday talk.* —*n.* **1.** a gentle tap under the chin. **2.** a toss.

chuck (chuk), *n.* a cut of beef from the shoulder, between the neck and the ribs.

chuck·le (chuk′'l), *v.* to laugh softly in a low tone. —*n.* a soft laugh. —**chuck′led,** *p.t. & p.p.;* **chuck′ling,** *pr.p.*

chuck wagon, a wagon equipped as a kitchen for feeding cowboys or other outdoor workers.

chug (chug), *n.* a short, exploding sound, such as that made by steam escaping from a steam engine. —*v.* to move while making such sounds. —**chugged,** *p.t. & p.p.;* **chug′ging,** *pr.p.*

chum (chum), *n.* a close friend. —*v.* to go about together as close friends do. *This word is used only in everyday talk.* —**chummed,** *p.t. & p.p.;* **chum′ming,** *pr.p.*

chum·my (chum′ē), *adj.* very friendly; like a chum: *used only in everyday talk.* —**chum′mi·er,** *compar.;* **chum′mi·est,** *superl.*

chump (chump), *n.* a stupid or silly person; fool: *used only in everyday talk.*

Chung·king (choong′king′), *n.* a city in central China, on the Yangtze River.

chunk (chungk), *n.* a short, thick piece [a *chunk* of meat]. —**chunk′y,** *adj.*

church (chûrch), *n.* **1.** a building for holding religious services, especially one for Christian worship. **2.** religious services [*Church* will be held earlier than usual next Sunday.] **3.** all Christians as a group, or a particular sect or denomination [the Methodist *Church*].

Church·ill, Sir **Win·ston** (win′stən chûrch′-il), 1874–1965; British statesman; prime minister from 1940 to 1945 and from 1951 to 1955.

church·man (chûrch′mən), *n.* **1.** a clergyman. **2.** a member of a church. —**church′men,** *pl.*

Church of England, the Episcopal Church of England, that has the sovereign as its head.

church·yard (chûrch′yärd), *n.* the yard around a church, often used as a burial ground.

churl (chûrl), *n.* **1.** a person of the lowest class in England long ago; peasant or rustic. **2.** a person who is rough and impolite; boor. —**churl′ish,** *adj.* —**churl′ish·ness,** *n.*

churn (chûrn), *n.* a container in which milk or cream is stirred hard or shaken to make butter. —*v.* **1.** to stir or shake milk or cream in a churn so as to make butter. **2.** to stir or move about with much force [The motorboats *churned* up the water of the lake.]

churn

chute (shoot), *n.* **1.** a part of a river where the water moves swiftly; also, a waterfall. **2.** a tube or slide in which things are dropped or slid down to a lower place [We have a laundry *chute* going from the bedroom to the basement.]

chute or **'chute** (shoot), *n.* a parachute: *only in everyday talk.*

ci·ca·da (si kā′də), *n.* an insect that is like a large fly with transparent wings. The male makes a loud, shrill sound.

Cic·er·o (sis′ə rō), *n.* 106–43 B.C.; Roman statesman who was a famous orator.

-cide (sīd), a suffix meaning "killer" or "killing" [*Suicide* is the act of killing oneself.]

ci·der (sī′dər), *n.* juice pressed from apples, used as a drink or made into vinegar.

ci·gar (si gär′), *n.* tobacco leaves formed into a tight roll for smoking.

cig·a·rette or **cig·a·ret** (sig ə ret′ *or* sig′ə ret), *n.* a small roll of finely cut tobacco wrapped in thin paper for smoking.

cicada
(3 in. long)

cil·i·a (sil′i ə), *n.pl.* **1.** the eyelashes. **2.** fine hairlike parts growing out from some plant and animal cells. Certain one-celled animals move by waving their cilia. —**cil·i·um** (sil′i əm), *sing.*

cinch (sinch), *n.* **1.** a band put around the belly of a horse or other animal to keep a saddle or pack in place. **2.** something that is easy to do or is sure to happen: *slang in this meaning* [It's a *cinch* our team will win.] —*v.* **1.** to tighten a cinch, as on a horse. **2.** to make sure of: *slang in this meaning* [The salesman *cinched* the deal.]

cin·cho·na (sin kō′nə), *n.* **1.** a tree that grows in the tropics and has a bitter bark from which quinine is gotten. **2.** this bark.

Cin·cin·nat·i (sin′sə nat′ē), *n.* a city in southwestern Ohio, on the Ohio River.

cinc·ture (singk′chər), *n.* a belt or girdle.

cin·der (sin′dər), *n.* **1.** a tiny bit of partly burned coal, wood, or the like [The wind blew a *cinder* in his eye.] **2. cinders,** *pl.* the ashes from coal or wood.

Cin·der·el·la (sin′dər el′ə), *n.* a girl in a fairy tale who is a drudge in the house of her stepmother until her fairy godmother helps her to meet a prince, who marries her.

cin·e·ma (sin′ə mə), *n.* **1.** a movie or the movies; motion picture. **2.** a movie theater. *Now mainly a British word.*

cin·na·mon (sin′ə mən), *n.* **1.** the light brown spice made from the inner bark of a tree that grows in the East Indies. **2.** this bark or the tree it comes from. **3.** a light reddish brown.

ci·pher (sī′fər), *n.* **1.** a zero; the symbol 0. **2.** a person or thing that has no importance. **3.** secret writing that can be understood only by those who have the key to it; code. **4.** the key to such a code. —*v.* to work problems in arithmetic; figure: *now seldom used.*

cir·ca (sûr′kə), *prep.* about: *used with figures or dates* [Euclid lived *circa* 300 B.C.]

Cir·ce (sûr′sē), *n.* a witch in Homer's *Odyssey* who turned men into pigs.

cir·cle (sûr′k'l), *n.* **1.** a closed curved line forming a perfectly round, flat figure. Every point on this line is the same distance from a point inside called the center. **2.** the figure formed by such a line. **3.** anything round like a circle or ring [a *circle* of children playing "drop the handkerchief"]. **4.** any series that ends the way it began or is repeated over and over; cycle [We wash the dishes, dirty them, wash them again, and so on—it's a tiresome *circle!*] **5.** a group of people joined together by the same interests [the Ladies' Sewing *Circle;* a *circle* of friends]. —*v.* **1.** to form a circle around; surround [The children *circled* the Maypole.] **2.** to move around, as in a circle [The planets

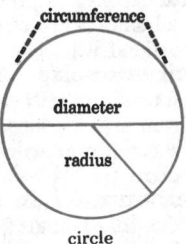

circle

circle the sun.] —**cir′cled,** *p.t. & p.p.;* **cir′-cling,** *pr.p.*

cir·clet (sûr′klit), *n.* **1.** a small circle. **2.** a round band worn as an ornament on the finger, arm, neck, or head; ring, bracelet, etc.

cir·cuit (sûr′kit), *n.* **1.** a going around something; course or journey in a circle [The moon's *circuit* of the earth takes about 28 days.] **2.** the regular journey through a district of a person in his work; also, the district itself [the mailman's *circuit;* a judge's *circuit*]. **3.** the line or distance around some area. **4.** a group of theaters owned or managed by the same person or company. **5.** the complete path of an electric current; also, any hookup, wiring, etc. that is connected into this path.

cir·cu·i·tous (sər kyōō′i təs), *adj.* roundabout; not direct [a *circuitous* explanation].

cir·cu·lar (sûr′kyōō lər), *adj.* **1.** having the shape of a circle; round [a *circular* saw]. **2.** of a circle [*circular* measurement]. **3.** moving in a circle [a *circular* railway]. —*n.* a letter or advertisement that is prepared in many copies for sending to many people.

cir·cu·late (sûr′kyōō lāt), *v.* **1.** to move in a regular course and return to the same point [Blood *circulates* through the body from the heart.] **2.** to move or send about from person to person or place to place [That rumor has been *circulating* through the town.] —**cir′cu·lat·ed,** *p.t. & p.p.;* **cir′cu·lat·ing,** *pr.p.*

cir·cu·la·tion (sûr′kyōō lā′shən), *n.* **1.** a moving around from place to place [An electric fan kept the air in *circulation*.] **2.** the movement of the blood through the veins and arteries. **3.** the passing of something from person to person or place to place [Gold money has been taken out of *circulation* in the U.S.] **4.** the average number of copies of a magazine or newspaper sent out in a certain period [Our school paper has a weekly *circulation* of 630.]

cir·cu·la·to·ry (sûr′kyōō lə tôr′ē), *adj.* having to do with circulation, as of the blood.

circum-, a prefix meaning "around, about, on all sides" [To *circumnavigate* the earth is to sail around it.]

cir·cum·cise (sûr′kəm sīz), *v.* to cut off the foreskin of, either as a religious ceremony or for sanitary reasons. —**cir′cum·cised,** *p.t. & p.p.;* **cir′cum·cis·ing,** *pr.p.* —**cir·cum·ci·sion** (sûr′kəm sizh′ən), *n.*

cir·cum·fer·ence (sər kum′fər əns), *n.* **1.** the line that bounds a circle or other rounded surface. See the picture for **circle. 2.** the distance measured by this line [The *circumference* of our swimming pool is 70 feet.]

cir·cum·flex (sûr′kəm fleks), *n.* the mark ^, used over a vowel to show pronunciation, as in some French words.

cir·cum·lo·cu·tion (sûr′kəm lō kyōō′shən), *n.* a roundabout or long way of saying something ["To become the recipient of" is a *circumlocution* for "to get."]

cir·cum·nav·i·gate (sûr′kəm nav′ə gāt), *v.* to sail around [to *circumnavigate* the earth]. —**cir′-**

cum·nav′i·gat·ed, *p.t. & p.p.;* **cir′cum·nav′-i·gat·ing,** *pr.p.* —**cir′cum·nav′i·ga′tion,** *n.*

cir·cum·scribe (sûr kəm scrīb′), *v.* **1.** to draw a line around or encircle; especially, to draw a figure around another figure so as to touch it at certain points; also, to be drawn in this way. **2.** to hold in closely; confine or restrict [His interests were very *circumscribed* until he went away to college.] —**cir·cum·scribed′,** *p.t. & p.p.;* **cir·cum·scrib′ing,** *pr.p.*

cir·cum·spect (sûr′kəm spekt), *adj.* careful to consider everything before acting, deciding, etc.; cautious and prudent. —**cir′cum·spect·ly,** *adv.* —**cir′cum·spec′tion,** *n.*

cir·cum·stance (sûr′kəm stans), *n.* **1.** a fact or event connected in some way with a situation [What were the *circumstances* that led up to his arrest?] **2.** formal acts and much splendor; ceremony [the pomp and *circumstance* of a coronation]. **3. circumstances,** *pl.* the condition in which one lives, especially with regard to money [in comfortable *circumstances*]. —**under no circumstances,** never; under no conditions. —**under the circumstances,** if one considers the special facts of the case.

cir·cum·stan·tial (sûr′kəm stan′shəl), *adj.* **1.** based on certain circumstances or facts [His fingerprints on the gun were *circumstantial* evidence that he might be guilty.] **2.** complete in every detail [a *circumstantial* account of one's day].

cir·cum·vent (sûr kəm vent′), *v.* to get the better of a person or prevent a plan by using tricks or cleverness.

cir·cus (sûr′kəs), *n.* **1.** a traveling show held in tents or in a hall, with clowns, trained animals, acrobats, etc. **2.** a very funny or entertaining person or thing: *used only in everyday talk.* **3.** a stadium or arena in ancient Rome, where games, races, or the like were held.

cir·rus (sir′əs), *n.* a kind of cloud that looks like thin strips of woolly curls. —**cir·ri** (sir′ī), *pl.*

cirrus

cis·tern (sis′tərn), *n.* a tank for storing water, especially rain water.

cit·a·del (sit′ə d'l *or* sit′ə del), *n.* a fort on a high place, for defending a town.

ci·ta·tion (sī tā′shən), *n.* **1.** an order to appear in a law court [A traffic ticket for speeding is a *citation*.] **2.** a mentioning or quoting of something written in a book, article, etc.; also, the piece of writing mentioned. **3.** an official mention that praises [He received a *citation* from the President for bravery in war.]

cite (sīt), *v.* **1.** to order to appear in a law court [He was *cited* for bad brakes.] **2.** to mention or quote [She *cited* four books to prove her point.] **3.** to mention for praise [The brave Army nurse was *cited* in official reports.] —**cit′ed,** *p.t. & p.p.;* **cit′ing,** *pr.p.*

cit·i·zen (sit′ə z'n), *n.* **1.** a person who is a member of a country or state either because he was born there or because he has been made a member by law. Citizens have certain duties to their country and are entitled to certain rights. **2.** a member of some group, as of a school [Good *citizens* help keep their classrooms neat.]

cit·i·zen·ry (sit'ə z'n rē), *n.* all citizens as a group.

cit·i·zen·ship (sit'ə z'n ship'), *n.* the condition of being a citizen; also, the rights and duties of a citizen [*Citizenship* includes the right to vote and the duty to serve on a jury.]

cit·ric (sit'rik), *adj.* having to do with, or coming from, citrus fruit [*Citric* acid is a weak acid found in oranges, lemons, etc.]

cit·ron (sit'rən), *n.* **1.** a fruit that is like a large lemon with a thick skin. **2.** the thorny tree that it grows on. **3.** the candied peel of this fruit, used in cakes, puddings, etc.

cit·rus (sit'rəs), *n.* **1.** any fruit of the family that includes oranges, lemons, limes, and grapefruit. **2.** a tree on which such a fruit grows. —*adj.* of these trees or fruits. *The adj. is sometimes spelled* **citrous.**

cit·y (sit'ē), *n.* a large, important town, especially, in the United States, one having a population over a certain number and organized under a charter from the State in which it is located. —**cit'ies,** *pl.*

city hall, a building in which the offices of a city government are located.

city manager, a person appointed by a city council to manage the affairs of the city.

civ·et (siv'it), *n.* **1.** an animal of Africa and Asia that looks like a small hyena: also called **civet cat. 2.** a substance with a strong smell, that comes from the glands of this animal. It is used in making some perfumes.

civ·ic (siv'ik), *adj.* **1.** of a city [plans for *civic* development]. **2.** of citizens or citizenship [Voting is a *civic* duty.]

civ·ics (siv'iks), *n.pl.* the study of how one's government works and of one's duties and rights as a citizen: *used with a singular verb.*

civ·il (siv'l), *adj.* **1.** of a citizen or citizens [*civil* rights]. **2.** of or within a country or its government [*civil* service; *civil* war]. **3.** polite; courteous [Stop shouting and give me a *civil* answer.] **4.** not connected with military or religious affairs [*civil* marriage]. —**civ'il·ly,** *adv.*

civil engineering, the planning and building of highways, bridges, harbors, and the like. —**civil engineer.**

ci·vil·ian (sə vil'yən), *n.* a person who is not a member of the armed forces. —*adj.* of or for civilians; not military.

ci·vil·i·ty (sə vil'ə tē), *n.* politeness or a polite act; courtesy. —**ci·vil'i·ties,** *pl.*

civ·i·li·za·tion (siv''l i zā'shən), *n.* **1.** the stage in the progress of man when he is no longer a savage and when arts, sciences, government,

etc. are developed [*Civilization* came to Asia before it appeared in Europe.] **2.** the countries and peoples that are civilized [The explorer returned to *civilization* after a year in the jungle.] **3.** the way of life of a people, nation, or period [the *civilization* of the Middle Ages].

civ·i·lize (siv'l īz), *v.* to bring out of a savage and ignorant condition and educate in the arts, sciences, government, etc. —**civ'i·lized,** *p.t. & p.p.;* **civ'i·liz·ing,** *pr.p.*

civil liberties, the freedom, guaranteed by law, to think, speak, and act as one likes so long as one does not harm others.

civil rights, the rights of all citizens, regardless of race, religion, sex, etc., to enjoy life, liberty, property, and the equal protection of the law. The 13th, 14th, 15th, and 19th Amendments to the Constitution guarantee these rights in the United States.

civil service, all those people who work for the government except in the armed forces or in certain other posts; especially, a system under which government jobs are gotten by those who score highest on examinations open to everyone.

civil war, war between sections or groups of the same nation. —**the Civil War,** the war from 1861 to 1865 between the North and the South in the United States.

Cl, symbol for the chemical element *chlorine.*

clack (klak), *v.* **1.** to make a sudden, sharp sound or cause to make this sound [Spanish dancers *clack* their heels on the floor.] **2.** to chatter. —*n.* a sudden, sharp sound [The door closed with a *clack.*]

clad (klad), a past tense and past participle of **clothe.** —*adj.* clothed; dressed [a poorly *clad* boy].

claim (klām), *v.* **1.** to demand or ask for something that belongs to one or is due to one [He *claimed* the package at the post office.] **2.** to call for; need; deserve [This problem *claims* our attention.] **3.** to state as a fact or as one's belief; assert [He *claimed* that he had been cheated.] —*n.* **1.** a demand for something that belongs to one or is due to one [He presented a *claim* for damages done to his car.] **2.** a right or title to something [a *claim* to a throne]. **3.** something claimed, as a piece of land staked out by a settler. **4.** a statement of something as a fact [False *claims* are sometimes made about used cars.] —**lay claim to,** to say that one has a right or title to.

claim·ant (klām'ənt), *n.* a person who makes a claim.

clair·voy·ance (kler voi'əns), *n.* the supposed ability to see things that are not in sight [He seemed to know who was in the other room, as though by *clairvoyance.*]

clair·voy·ant (kler voi'ənt), *adj.* **1.** of clairvoyance. **2.** seeming to have clairvoyance. —*n.* a person who seems to have clairvoyance.

clam (klam), *n.* an animal like an oyster, with a soft body enclosed in two hard shells hinged together. Clams live in sand along the seashore or in fresh water. Some kinds are used as food. —*v.* to dig for clams. —**clammed,** *p.t.* & *p.p.*; **clam′ming,** *pr.p.*

clam (3 in. wide)

clam·bake (klam′bāk), *n.* a picnic at which clams steamed or baked with chicken, corn, etc. are served.

clam·ber (klam′bər), *v.* to climb with effort, especially by using the hands as well as the feet [He *clambered* up the side of the cliff.]

clam·my (klam′ē), *adj.* moist and cold [His hands became *clammy* when he was frightened.] —**clam′mi·er,** *compar.*; **clam′mi·est,** *superl.*

clam·or (klam′ər), *n.* a loud, continued noise or uproar, as of a crowd demanding something or complaining. —*v.* to cry out or demand noisily. —**clam′or·ous,** *adj.*

clamp (klamp), *n.* a device for holding things together; especially, a device with two parts that are brought together by a screw for gripping something. —*v.* to fasten with a clamp. —**clamp down,** to become more strict. *This phrase is used only in everyday talk.*

clamp holding
two boards

clan (klan), *n.* **1.** a group of families who claim to be descended from a common ancestor. **2.** a group of people who have the same interests; clique; set.

clan·des·tine (klan des′tin), *adj.* kept secret because of guilty feelings [a *clandestine* meeting]. —**clan·des′tine·ly,** *adv.*

clang (klang), *n.* a loud, ringing sound, as of a large bell. —*v.* to make such a sound.

clan·gor (klang′gər), *n.* **1.** a clang. **2.** a continued clanging [the *clangor* of church bells].

clank (klangk), *n.* a sound like a clang but not so ringing [The hammer hit the anvil with a *clank*.] —*v.* to make such a sound.

clan·nish (klan′ish), *adj.* **1.** of a clan. **2.** sticking closely to one's own group and staying away from other people [We objected to the club because its members were so *clannish*.]

clans·man (klanz′mən), *n.* a member of a clan. —**clans′men,** *pl.*

clap (klap), *v.* **1.** to make the sudden, loud sound of two flat surfaces being struck together. **2.** to strike the palms of the hands together, as in applauding. **3.** to strike with the palm of the hand ["Good work!" he said, *clapping* me on the shoulder.] **4.** to put or bring swiftly [He was *clapped* into jail.] —*n.* **1.** the sudden, loud sound of clapping [a *clap* of thunder]. **2.** a sharp blow; slap. —**clapped,** *p.t.* & *p.p.*; **clap′ping,** *pr.p.*

clap·board (klab′ərd *or* klap′bôrd), *n.* a thin board with one edge thicker than the other, used for siding on the outside of a wooden house.

clap·per (klap′ər), *n.* one that claps; especially, the tongue of a bell.

clar·et (klar′ət), *n.* **1.** a dry red wine. **2.** purplish red.

clar·i·fy (klar′ə fī), *v.* **1.** to make or become clear and pure [Strain the liquid to *clarify* it.] **2.** to make or become easier to understand [He *clarified* the problem by drawing a diagram.] —**clar′i·fied,** *p.t.* & *p.p.*; **clar′i·fy·ing,** *pr.p.* —**clar′i·fi·ca′tion,** *n.*

clar·i·net (klar ə net′), *n.* a wood-wind musical instrument whose mouthpiece has one reed and whose lower end is shaped like a bell.

clar·i·on (klar′i ən), *adj.* clear, sharp, and shrill [the *clarion* sounds of a trumpet].

clar·i·ty (klar′ə tē), *n.* clearness.

clarinet

clash (klash), *n.* **1.** a loud, harsh noise, as of metal striking against metal with great force. **2.** a sharp disagreement; conflict [a *clash* of ideas]. —*v.* **1.** to strike with a clash [He *clashed* the cymbals together.] **2.** to go against each other; come into conflict; disagree sharply [They *clashed* in debate. Her orange scarf *clashed* with her red blouse.]

clasp (klasp), *n.* **1.** a fastening, as a hook or catch, for holding two things or parts together [The *clasp* on my pocketbook is loose.] **2.** a holding in the arms; embrace. **3.** a holding with the hand; grip. —*v.* **1.** to fasten with a clasp. **2.** to hold tightly in the arms [The little girl fell asleep *clasping* her doll.] **3.** to grip with the hand [I *clasped* his hand in greeting.]

class (klas), *n.* **1.** a number of people or things thought of as a group because they are alike in certain ways [Whales belong to the *class* of mammals. He is a member of the working *class*.] **2.** a group of students meeting together to be taught; also, a meeting of this kind [My English *class* is held at nine o'clock.] **3.** a group of students graduating together [the *class* of 1966]. **4.** a division according to grade or quality [to travel first *class*]. **5.** very fine style or appearance; excellence: *slang in this meaning* [a golfer with a lot of *class*]. —*v.* to put in a class; classify [My teacher *classes* me with his best students.]

clas·sic (klas′ik), *adj.* **1.** of the highest quality or rank; that is a model of its kind [a *classic* example of modern architecture]. **2.** of the art, literature, and culture of the ancient Greeks and Romans. **3.** having a formal style that is simple and restrained [the *classic* balance of a Haydn symphony]. **4.** famous because it is typical and has become a tradition [Turkey is the *classic* dish for Thanksgiving dinner.] —*n.* **1.** a book, painting, symphony, etc. of the highest excellence. **2.** a person who creates such works. **3.** a famous event that is held regularly [The World Series is baseball's "fall *classic*."] —**the classics,** the literature of the ancient Greeks and Romans.

clas·si·cal (klas/i k'l), *adj.* **1.** classic (*in meanings* 1, 2, 3). **2.** describing a kind of music that is not simple in form and that requires much study and training to write and perform [Symphonies, concertos, sonatas, chamber music, etc. are called *classical* music.]

clas·si·fi·ca·tion (klas/ə fi kā/shən), *n.* arrangement into classes or groups according to some system.

clas·si·fy (klas/ə fī), *v.* to arrange by putting into classes or groups according to some system [Plants and animals are *classified* into various orders, families, species, etc.] —**clas/si·fied,** *p.t. & p.p.;* **clas/si·fy·ing,** *pr.p.*

class·mate (klas/māt), *n.* a member of the same class at a school or college.

class·room (klas/rōōm), *n.* a room in a school or college where classes meet to be taught.

clat·ter (klat/ər), *n.* **1.** a series of sharp, clashing sounds [the *clatter* of children running through the halls]. **2.** a noisy chatter; hubbub. —*v.* to make a clatter or move with a clatter.

clause (klôz), *n.* **1.** a group of words that includes a subject and verb, but that forms only part of a sentence. In the sentence "She will visit us if she can," *She will visit us* is a clause that could be a complete sentence, and *if she can* is a clause that depends on the first clause. **2.** any of the separate points or articles in a law, contract, treaty, etc.

clav·i·cle (klav/ə k'l), *n.* the narrow bone joining the breastbone to the shoulder blade; collarbone.

claw (klô), *n.* **1.** a sharp, curved nail on the foot of an animal or bird. **2.** a foot with such nails [The eagle holds its victims in its *claws.*] **3.** the grasping part on each front leg of a lobster, crab, or scorpion. **4.** anything like a claw, as the curved part on a type of hammer (called **claw hammer**) used for pulling nails: see picture of **hammers.** —*v.* to scratch, pull, or tear with claws or as if with claws.

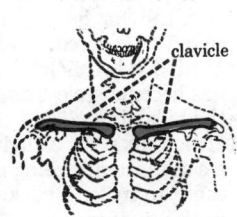
clavicle

clay (klā), *n.* **1.** a stiff, sticky earth that becomes hard when it is baked. It is used in making bricks, pottery, tile, and china. **2.** the human body: *used with this meaning in the Bible.*

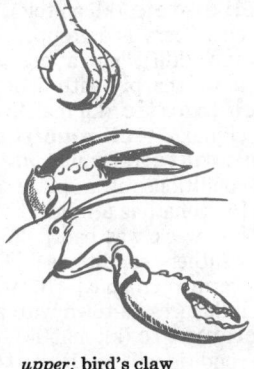
upper: bird's claw
lower: lobster's claws

clay·ey (klā/ē), *adj.* **1.** of, like, or full of clay. **2.** smeared with clay. —**clay/i·er,** *compar.;* **clay/i·est,** *superl.*

clean (klēn), *adj.* **1.** without dirt or impure matter [*clean* dishes; *clean* oil]. **2.** without evil or wrongdoing [He has led a *clean* life.] **3.** neat and tidy [a *clean* housekeeper]. **4.** done in a skillful, exact way [a *clean* dive into the pool]. **5.** having no flaws or weak spots [a *clean* record]. **6.** complete or thorough [a *clean* shave; a *clean* sweep]. —*adv.* **1.** so as to be clean. **2.** completely; entirely [He has gone *clean* out of his mind.] —*v.* to make clean. —**clean out, 1.** to make empty. **2.** to use up the money of: *only in everyday talk.* —**clean up, 1.** to make clean or neat. **2.** to finish some work: *only in everyday talk.* —**clean/ness,** *n.*

clean-cut (klēn/kut/), *adj.* **1.** having a clear, sharp outline; distinct. **2.** having a healthy, trim, neat look [a *clean-cut* young fellow].

clean·er (klēn/ər), *n.* **1.** a person whose work is cleaning. **2.** a tool or substance used for cleaning.

clean·ly (klen/lē), *adj.* always keeping clean or kept clean. —**clean/li·ness,** *n.*

clean·ly (klēn/lē), *adv.* in a clean manner.

cleanse (klenz), *v.* to make clean or pure [to feel *cleansed* of sin]. —**cleansed,** *p.t. & p.p.;* **cleans/ing,** *pr.p.*

cleans·er (klenz/ər), *n.* a substance, as scouring powder, used for cleansing.

clear (klir), *adj.* **1.** bright or sunny; without clouds or mist [a *clear* day]. **2.** that can be seen through; transparent [*clear* glass]. **3.** having no spots, scars, or flaws [a *clear* skin]. **4.** sharp and distinct; not dim or blurred [a *clear* outline; a *clear* tone]. **5.** able to see or think well [*clear* vision; a *clear* mind]. **6.** easy to understand; not confusing [a *clear* explanation]. **7.** plain; obvious [a *clear* case of carelessness]. **8.** complete or certain [a *clear* majority of votes; a *clear* title to property]. **9.** not guilty; innocent [a *clear* conscience]. **10.** left over after expenses or charges [a *clear* profit of $10,000]. **11.** without anything in the way; not blocked; open [a *clear* view; a *clear* passage]. —*adv.* **1.** in a clear manner; clearly [The bells rang out *clear.*] **2.** all the way: *used only in everyday talk* [We walked *clear* through the town.] —*v.* **1.** to make or become clear [The sky *cleared* after the storm. This salve will *clear* your skin.] **2.** to empty or remove [*Clear* the trash from the basement. They *cleared* the ship of cargo.] **3.** to free from guilt or blame [to *clear* a suspect of a crime]. **4.** to pass over, under, or by with space to spare [The horse leaped and *cleared* the fence by two feet. The tug barely *cleared* the bridge.] **5.** to make as a profit [He *cleared* $5 on that sale.] —**clear away** or **clear off,** to take away so as to leave a cleared space. —**clear out, 1.** to empty. **2.** to go away: *used only in everyday talk.* —**clear up, 1.** to make or become clear. **2.** to explain. **—in the clear, 1.** in the open; not shut in, blocked, or hidden by anything. **2.** not suspected of being guilty: *used only in everyday talk.* **—clear′ly,** *adv.* **—clear′ness,** *n.*

clear·ance (klir′əns), *n.* **1.** the act of clearing. **2.** the clear space between a moving thing and that which it passes through, under, etc.

clearance

clear-cut (klir′kut′), *adj.* **1.** having a clear, sharp outline. **2.** distinct; definite; not doubtful [a *clear-cut* victory].

clear·ing (klir′ing), *n.* a piece of land from which the trees have been cleared.

cleat (klēt), *n.* **1.** a piece of metal or wood fastened to something for support or strength or to keep one from slipping. Cleats are used under shelves, on the soles of shoes, etc. **2.** a wooden or metal piece on which ropes are fastened on a ship.

cleats

cleav·age (klēv′ij), *n.* a splitting in two; division [a *cleavage* in rock; the *cleavage* between North and South over slavery].

cleave (klēv), *v.* to divide by a sharp blow; split [The tree was *cleft* by lightning.] **—cleft** or **cleaved** or **clove,** *p.t.;* **cleft** or **cleaved** or **clo′ven,** *p.p.;* **cleav′ing,** *pr.p.*

cleave (klēv), *v.* to cling closely; stick [barnacles *cleaving* to a rock; to *cleave* to a belief]. **—cleaved,** *p.t. & p.p.;* **cleav′ing,** *pr.p.*

cleav·er (klēv′ər), *n.* a heavy cutting tool with a broad blade, used by butchers.

clef (klef), *n.* a sign at the beginning of a musical staff that shows the pitch of the notes on the staff [The notes in the treble or G *clef* are mainly above middle C. The notes in the bass or F *clef* are mainly below middle C.]

cleaver

cleft (kleft), a past tense and past participle of **cleave.** **—adj.** split open; divided [a *cleft* palate]. **—n.** an opening or hollow made by or as if by splitting [a passage through a *cleft* in the rocks; a *cleft* in the chin].

upper: treble clef
lower: bass clef

clem·a·tis (klem′ə tis), *n.* a climbing plant, or vine, with brightly colored flowers.

clem·en·cy (klem′ən sē), *n.* **1.** kindness in judging or punishing someone; mercy [The judge showed *clemency* because the prisoner was ill.] **2.** mildness, as of the weather.

Clem·ens, Samuel Lang·horne (lang′hôrn

klem′ənz), the real name of **Mark Twain.**

clem·ent (klem′ənt), *adj.* **1.** showing mercy. **2.** pleasant or mild: *used of the weather.*

clench (klench), *v.* **1.** to close or press tightly together [to *clench* the fist; to *clench* the teeth]. **2.** to grip firmly. **—n.** a firm grip.

Cle·o·pa·tra (klē′ə pat′rə *or* klē′ə pā′trə), 69–30 B.C.; queen of Egypt who was loved by Julius Caesar and Mark Anthony.

cler·gy (klûr′jē), *n.* all ministers, priests, rabbis, etc. as a group. **—cler′gies,** *pl.*

cler·gy·man (klûr′jē mən), *n.* a minister, priest, rabbi, etc. **—cler′gy·men,** *pl.*

cler·ic (kler′ik), *n.* a clergyman.

cler·i·cal (kler′i k'l), *adj.* **1.** having to do with a clergyman or the clergy. **2.** having to do with office clerks or their work.

clerk (klûrk; *the British pronounce it* klärk), *n.* **1.** an office worker who keeps records, types letters, etc. [Some *clerks,* as a *clerk* of courts or a city *clerk,* have special duties.] **2.** a person who sells in a store; salesman or saleswoman.

Cleve·land (klēv′lənd), *n.* a city in northeastern Ohio, on Lake Erie.

Cleve·land, Gro·ver (grō′vər klēv′lənd), 1837–1908; 22nd president of the United States (1885–1889); 24th president (1893–1897).

clev·er (klev′ər), *adj.* **1.** quick in thinking or learning; smart; intelligent. **2.** skillful [Watchmakers are *clever* with their hands.] **3.** showing skill or fine thinking [a *clever* move in chess]. **—clev′er·ly,** *adv.* **—clev′er·ness,** *n.*

clew (kloo), *n.* **1.** a ball of thread or yarn. **2.** same as **clue. 3.** a metal loop in the corner of a sail for holding ropes by which the sail is raised or lowered.

cli·ché (klē shā′), *n.* an expression or idea that has become stale from too much use ["As old as the hills" is a *cliché.*]

click (klik), *n.* a slight, sharp sound like that of a snap fastener being closed. **—v. 1.** to make or cause to make a click. **2.** to be a success: *slang in this meaning.*

cli·ent (klī′ənt), *n.* **1.** a person or company for whom a lawyer, etc. is acting. **2.** a customer.

cli·en·tele (klī ən tel′), *n.* all of one's clients or customers as a group.

cliff (klif), *n.* a high, steep rock that comes down sharply with little or no slope.

cli·mac·tic (klī mak′tik), *adj.* of or forming a climax. **—cli·mac′ti·cal·ly,** *adv.*

cli·mate (klī′mit), *n.* **1.** the average weather conditions of a place over a period of years [Arizona has a mild, dry *climate,* but its weather last week was bad.] **2.** a region with particular weather conditions [They went south to a warmer *climate.*] **3.** the usual conditions and influences [a town with an intellectual *climate*].

cli·mat·ic (klī mat′ik), *adj.* of climate [*climatic* conditions]. **—cli·mat′i·cal·ly,** *adv.*

cli·max (klī′maks), *n.* the final and strongest idea or event in a series; highest point of interest or excitement [The *climax* of the movie came when the hero saved the heroine.]

climb (klīm), *v.* **1.** to go up or, sometimes,

down by using the feet and often the hands [to *climb* the stairs; to *climb* up or down a tree]. **2.** to rise to a higher position [He *climbed* to power in ten years. The airplane *climbed* to 20,000 feet.] **3.** to grow upward on some support [The ivy *climbed* the wall.] —*n.* the act of climbing; rise; ascent [a tiring *climb*]. —**climb′er,** *n.*

clime (klīm), *n.* a country, region, or climate: *used mainly in poetry.*

clinch (klinch), *v.* **1.** to fasten a nail that has been driven through something by bending down the end that sticks out. **2.** to settle definitely; fix [The extra $100 *clinched* the deal.] **3.** to hold on tight in boxing so as to keep one's opponent from punching. —*n.* the act of clinching. —**clinch′er,** *n.*

cling (kling), *v.* to bold on tightly; stick; adhere [The child *clung* to his father's hand. The vine *clings* to the wall.] —**clung,** *p.t. & p.p.;* **cling′-ing,** *pr.p.*

clin·ic (klin′ik), *n.* **1.** a place where patients are examined or treated by a group of doctors who are specialists. **2.** a place in a hospital or medical school where poor people can come for free treatment or advice. **3.** a place where special problems are studied or treated [a child guidance *clinic*]. **4.** the teaching of medicine by examining and treating patients while students watch. —**clin′i·cal,** *adj.*

clink (klingk), *n.* a short, tinkling sound, as of coins struck together. —*v.* to make such a sound or cause to make such a sound.

clink·er (klingk′ər), *n.* a stony mass formed in a coal fire from the impure parts of coal.

clip (klip), *v.* **1.** to cut short or cut off as with shears or scissors [to *clip* wool from a sheep; to *clip* pictures from a magazine]. **2.** to cut the hair or wool of [We had our dog *clipped*.] **3.** to hit with a quick, sharp punch: *used only in everyday talk.* **4.** to move with speed: *used only in everyday talk* [The car *clipped* right along.] —*n.* **1.** the act of clipping. **2.** a quick, sharp punch: *used only in everyday talk.* **3.** a high rate of speed: *used only in everyday talk* [to move at a *clip*]. —**clipped,** *p.t. & p.p.;* **clip′ping,** *pr.p.*

clip (klip), *n.* anything that is used to hold or fasten two or more things together [a paper *clip*]. —*v.* to fasten with a clip. —**clipped,** *p.t. & p.p.;* **clip′ping,** *pr.p.*

clip·per (klip′ər), *n.* **1.** a person who clips. **2.** *often* **clippers,** *pl.* a tool for clipping or shearing [a *clipper* for trimming hedges; a barber's *clippers*]. **3.** a sailing ship with a sharp bow and narrow beam, built for speed. Many clippers were built in the middle 19th century.

clip·ping (klip′ing), *n.* **1.** a piece cut off or out of something [a *clipping* from a plant].

nail clippers

2. an item cut out of a newspaper or magazine.

clique (klēk *or* klik), *n.* a small group of people who are friendly only with one another and have little to do with outsiders.

cloak (klōk), *n.* **1.** a loose outer garment, usually without sleeves. **2.** something that covers or hides [The fog dropped a *cloak* over the city.] —*v.* **1.** to cover as with a cloak. **2.** to conceal; hide [She *cloaked* her disappointment with gay talk.]

cloak·room (klōk′rōōm), *n.* a room where coats, hats, etc. may be left for a time.

clob·ber (kläb′ər), *v.* to hit many times; maul: *a slang word.*

clock (kläk), *n.* a device for measuring and showing the time, usually by means of pointers moving around a dial. Clocks, unlike watches, are not meant to be worn or carried about. —*v.* to measure the time of a race or runner.

cloak

clock (kläk), *n.* a long, narrow design on the side of a stocking, going up from the ankle.

clock·wise (kläk′wīz), *adv. & adj.* in the direction in which the hands of a clock move [When you turn the knob *clockwise*, the radio goes on.]

clock·work (kläk′würk), *n.* the springs, gears, and wheels of a clock, or of anything that works like a clock. —**like clockwork,** very regularly and exactly.

clod (kläd), *n.* **1.** a lump of earth or clay. **2.** a dull, stupid person.

clog (kläg), *n.* **1.** anything that blocks up or gets in the way. **2.** a heavy shoe, usually with a wooden sole. —*v.* **1.** to slow up or stop movement. **2.** to block up or become blocked up [Dirt *clogged* the drainpipe.] —**clogged,** *p.t. & p.p.;* **clog′ging,** *pr.p.*

clois·ter (klois′tər), *n.* **1.** a place where monks or nuns live; monastery or convent. **2.** any peaceful place where one can get away from people. **3.** a covered walk along an inside wall, as of a convent, that borders on a courtyard. —*v.* to shut away as in a cloister. —**clois′tered,** *adj.*

close (klōs), *adj.* **1.** with not much space between; near. **2.** having parts near together; compact; dense [a *close* weave]. **3.** as near to the surface as possible [a *close* shave]. **4.** very near in relationship; very dear [a *close* friend]. **5.** very nearly like the original [a *close* copy]. **6.** thorough or careful [Pay *close* attention.] **7.** nearly equal or even [a *close* contest]. **8.** shutting in with not much free space; confining [*close* quarters]. **9.** carefully guarded [a *close* secret]. **10.** not frank or open; secretive [He is very *close* about his business affairs.] **11.** stingy [She is *close* with her money.] **12.** stuffy and full of stale air [a *close* room]. —*adv.* so as to be close or near; closely [Follow *close* behind.] —*n.* an enclosed place. —**clos′er,** *compar.;* **clos′est,** *superl.* —**close′ly,** *adv.* —**close′ness,** *n.*

close (klōz), *v.* **1.** to make no longer open; shut [*Close* the door.] **2.** to fill up or stop up [to *close* a hole]. **3.** to bring or come to a finish; end [to *close* a speech]. **4.** to bring or come together [to *close* ranks]. —*n.* an end; finish. —**close down,** to shut or stop entirely. —**close in,** to draw near from different directions, cutting off escape. —**close out,** to sell goods at a low price so as to get completely rid of stock. —**close up, 1.** to draw nearer together. **2.** to shut or stop up entirely. —**closed,** *p.t. & p.p.;* **clos′-ing,** *pr.p.*

close call (klōs), a narrow escape from danger: *used only in everyday talk.*

close·fist·ed (klōs′fis′tid), *adj.* stingy.

close-mouthed (klōs′mou*th*d′), *adj.* not talking much; telling little.

clos·et (kläz′it), *n.* **1.** a small room or cupboard for clothes, linens, supplies, etc. **2.** a small private room where one can be alone: *no longer much used in this meaning.* —*v.* to shut up in a room for a private talk [The chairman was *closeted* with his close advisers.]

close-up (klōs′up′), *n.* a picture taken with the camera very close to the subject.

clo·sure (klō′zhər), *n.* a closing or being closed; especially, the ending of debate in a legislature by having the issue put to a vote.

clot (klät), *n.* a lump formed when matter in a liquid thickens [a blood *clot*]. —*v.* to form a clot or clots. —**clot′ted,** *p.t. & p.p.;* **clot′ting,** *pr.p.*

cloth (klôth), *n.* **1.** a material made, especially by weaving, from threads of cotton, wool, silk, nylon, etc. **2.** a piece of such material for a particular use [a table*cloth;* a wash*cloth*]. —**the cloth,** the clergy. —**cloths** (klô*th*z *in the meaning* "pieces of cloth"; klôths *in the meaning* "kinds of cloth"), *pl.*

clothe (klō*th*), *v.* **1.** to put clothes on; dress. **2.** to provide with clothes [It costs much to *clothe* a large family.] **3.** to cover or surround [a field *clothed* in snow; a hero *clothed* in glory]. —**clothed** or **clad,** *p.t. & p.p.;* **cloth′ing,** *pr.p.*

clothes (klōz *or* klō*th*z), *n.pl.* **1.** cloth or other material made up in different shapes and styles to wear on the body; dresses, suits, hats, under-wear, etc.; garments. **2.** bedclothes.

clothes·line (klōz′līn), *n.* a rope or wire on which clothes are hung for drying or airing.

clothes·pin (klōz′pin), *n.* a small clip of wood or plastic for holding clothes on a line.

cloth·ier (klō*th*′yər), *n.* a person who makes or sells clothes.

cloth·ing (klō*th*′ing), *n.* clothes.

clo·ture (klō′chər), *n.* same as **closure** (when used of the ending of debate).

cloud (kloud), *n.* **1.** a mass of fine drops of water or tiny crystals of ice floating in the air above the earth. **2.** a mass of smoke, dust, or

steam. **3.** a great number of things moving in a solid mass [a *cloud* of locusts]. **4.** any dark marking or mass, as in marble or in a liquid. **5.** anything that threatens or spreads gloom [under a *cloud* of suspicion]. —*v.* **1.** to cover or make dark as with clouds [The sun is *clouded* over. His reputation is *clouded* with gossip.] **2.** to make or become gloomy or troubled [Her face *clouded* with worry.] **3.** to make or become muddy or foggy [The water *clouded*.] —**in the clouds, 1.** high up in the sky. **2.** not practical; fanciful. **3.** having a daydream.

cloud·burst (kloud′bûrst), *n.* a sudden, very heavy rain.

cloud·less (kloud′lis), *adj.* free from clouds; clear; bright [a *cloudless* sky].

cloud·y (kloud′ē), *adj.* **1.** covered with clouds; overcast. **2.** marked with spots or streaks, as marble. **3.** not clear; muddy, foggy, vague, dim, etc. [*cloudy* water; *cloudy* ideas]. —**cloud′i·er,** *compar.;* **cloud′i·est,** *superl.*

clout (klout), *n.* a sharp blow or knock. *v.* to strike or knock sharply. *This word is used only in everyday talk.*

clove (klōv), *n.* the dried flower bud of a tropical evergreen tree, used as a spice.

clove (klōv), *n.* a section of a bulb, as of garlic.

clove (klōv), a past tense of **cleave** (split).

clo·ven (klō′vən), a past participle of **cleave** (split). —*adj.* divided; split [*cloven* hoof].

clo·ver (klō′vər), *n.* a low-growing plant with leaves in three parts and small, sweet-smelling flowers. *Red clover* is grown for fodder. *White clover* is often found in lawns. —**in clover,** living a pleasant, easy life.

clo·ver·leaf (klō′vər lēf), *n.* a place where highways meet, with one going under the other and with curving ramps, so that traffic can move easily and smoothly. —**clo′-ver·leafs,** *pl.*

clown (kloun), *n.* **1.** a person who en-tertains, as in a cir-cus, by doing comical tricks and silly stunts; jester; buffoon. **2.** a rude or clumsy per-son; boor. —*v.* **1.** to perform as a clown.

cloverleaf

2. to play practical jokes and act silly. —**clown′-ish,** *adj.*

cloy (kloi), *v.* to make weary or displeased with too much of something [Our appetites were *cloyed* with rich food.]

club (klub), *n.* **1.** a heavy wooden stick, used as a weapon. **2.** any stick made for some special purpose [a golf *club*]. **3.** the mark ♣, used on a black suit of playing cards; also, a card of this suit. **4.** a group of people who meet together for pleasure or for some special purpose [a bridge *club;* athletic *club*]. **5.** the building or place where they meet. —*v.* **1.** to hit as with a club. **2.** to join together for some purpose. —**clubbed,** *p.t. & p.p.;* **club′bing,** *pr.p.*

cluck (kluk), *v.* to make a low, sharp, clicking sound, like that made by a hen calling her chickens. —*n.* this sound or a sound like it.

clue (klōō), *n.* a fact or thing that helps to solve a puzzle or mystery [Deep footprints were a *clue* to the fat man's guilt.]

clump (klump), *n.* **1.** a group of things close together; cluster [a *clump* of trees]. **2.** a mass or lump [a *clump* of dirt]. **3.** the sound of heavy footsteps. —*v.* to walk heavily.

clum·sy (klum′zē), *adj.* **1.** not having good control; awkward [The *clumsy* boy dropped his fork.] **2.** badly made or done; crude [a *clumsy* shelter made of old boards]. —**clum′si·er,** *compar.;* **clum′si·est,** *superl.* —**clum′si·ly,** *adv.* —**clum′si·ness,** *n.*

clung (klung), past tense and past participle of **cling.**

clus·ter (klus′tər), *n.* a number of things growing together or seen together [a *cluster* of grapes; a *cluster* of stars]. —*v.* to grow or gather together [Pigeons *clustered* around her.]

clutch (kluch), *v.* **1.** to grasp; hold tightly. **2.** to reach or grab for; snatch [Drowning men are said to *clutch* at straws.] —*n.* **1.** the grasp of a hand or claw; a clutching [The robber made a *clutch* at her pearls.] **2. clutches,** *pl.* power or control [The heroine was in the villain's *clutches*.] **3.** a device in an automobile, etc. that puts moving parts into gear or takes them out of gear.

clut·ter (klut′ər), *n.* a number of things scattered in confusion; disorder [We poked through the *clutter* in Grandma's attic.] —*v.* to make untidy and confused [Don't *clutter* up your mind with comics.]

cm., abbreviation for **centimeter.**

Co, symbol for the chemical element *cobalt.*

co-, a prefix meaning: **1.** together with [A *co*-worker is a person who works together with another.] **2.** equally: to the same extent [A *co*-owner is a person who owns something equally with another.]

Co. or **co.,** abbreviation for **company** or **county.**

c/o or **c.o.,** an abbreviation meaning "in care of" or "at the address of" [Send me the box *c/o* my mother.]

coach (kōch), *n.* **1.** a large, closed carriage drawn by horses, with the driver's seat outside. **2.** a railroad car with seats for passengers. **3.** a bus. **4.** a person who teaches and trains students, athletes, singers, etc. [a football *coach*]. —*v.* to teach, train, or tutor [Will you *coach* me for the test in French?]

coach

coach·man (kōch′mən), *n.* the driver of a coach. —**coach′men,** *pl.*

co·ag·u·late (kō ag′yoo lāt), *v.* to turn into a soft, thick mass, as blood does in a wound; clot. —**co·ag′u·lat·ed,** *p.t. & p.p.;* **co·ag′u·lat·ing,** *pr.p.* —**co·ag′u·la′tion,** *n.*

coal (kōl), *n.* **1.** a black, solid substance that is dug up from the ground for use as a fuel. Coal is mostly carbon, formed from decaying plant growth pressed together for millions of years. **2.** a piece of glowing or charred coal, wood, etc.; ember —*v.* **1.** to supply with coal. **2.** to take in a supply of coal.

co·a·lesce (kō ə les′), *v.* to grow or come together into one mass or body; unite [Several political groups *coalesced* in 1854 to form the Republican Party.] —**co·a·lesced′,** *p.t. & p.p.;* **co·a·lesc′ing,** *pr.p.* —**co·a·les′cence,** *n.*

co·a·li·tion (kō′ə lish′ən), *n.* a joining together of persons or groups for some purpose, as of political parties or nations in wartime.

coal oil, 1. kerosene. **2.** petroleum.

coal tar, a black, thick liquid formed from the vapors given off when soft coal is burned [Dyes, medicines, and explosives have been developed from *coal tar*.]

coarse (kôrs), *adj.* **1.** made up of rather large particles; not fine [*coarse* sand]. **2.** rough or harsh to the touch [*coarse* cloth]. **3.** not refined or polite; vulgar; crude [a *coarse* joke]. **4.** of a poor or cheap kind [*coarse* shoes]. —**coarse′ly,** *adv.* —**coarse′ness,** *n.*

coars·en (kôr′s'n), *v.* to make or become coarse [Outdoor life *coarsened* his skin.]

coast (kōst), *n.* **1.** land along the sea; seashore. **2.** a slide or ride downhill, as on a sled. —*v.* **1.** to sail along a coast, especially from port to port. **2.** to ride or slide downhill, as on a sled. **3.** to keep on moving after the driving power is cut off [We ran out of gas, but the car *coasted* to the gas station.]

coast·al (kōs′t'l), *adj.* of, near, or along a coast [a *coastal* city].

coast·er (kōs′tər), *n.* **1.** a person or thing that coasts. **2.** a ship that sails from port to port along a coast. **3.** a sled or wagon for coasting. **4.** a small tray placed under a glass or bottle to protect a table top, etc.

coaster under a glass

coast guard, 1. a group of people whose work for the government is to defend coasts, stop smuggling, help ships in trouble, etc. **2. Coast Guard,** such a group in the United States. It is a branch of the Treasury Department except in wartime, when it is under the Navy Department. **3.** a member of a coast guard.

coast line, the outline or shape of a coast.

coat (kōt), *n.* **1.** an outer garment with sleeves, that opens down the front [an over*coat;* the *coat* of a suit]. **2.** the natural covering of an animal, as of skin or fur [Our dog has a curly black *coat*.] **3.** any outer covering or layer

[Our house has three *coats* of paint.] —*v.* to cover with a coat or layer of something [The street is *coated* with ice.]

coat·ing (kōt'ing), *n.* **1.** a layer of something covering a surface [a *coating* of enamel]. **2.** cloth for making coats.

coat of arms, a group of designs and figures arranged as on a shield, to serve as the special mark of some person, family, or institution.

coat of mail, a suit of armor that was made of metal rings linked together or of small metal plates overlapping one another.

coat of arms

coax (kōks), *v.* to keep on asking for something in a pleasant and gentle way [He *coaxed* his parents to let him go swimming.]

co·ax·i·al cable (kō ak'si əl), a specially insulated cable for sending telephone, telegraph, or television signals.

cob (käb), *n.* **1.** the part of an ear of corn on which the kernels grow; corncob. **2.** a male swan. **3.** a short, stout horse.

co·balt (kō'bôlt), *n.* a hard, shiny-gray metal that is a chemical element. It is used in alloys and in making blue pigments.

cob·ble (käb''l), *v.* to mend, especially shoes. —**cob'bled,** *p.t. & p.p.;* **cob'bling,** *pr.p.*

cob·bler (käb'lər), *n.* a person whose work is mending shoes.

cob·bler (käb'lər), *n.* a fruit pie with no bottom crust and a top crust of biscuit dough.

cob·ble·stone (käb''l stōn), *n.* a rounded stone. At one time cobblestones were much used for paving streets.

co·bra (kō'brə), *n.* a very poisonous snake of Asia and Africa. When it is excited, the skin around its neck swells into a hood.

cob·web (käb'web), *n.* a web spun by a spider. Since a cobweb is often found in a quiet, undisturbed place, it is used in figures of speech about unused or inactive things [to blow the *cobwebs* from one's brain].

cobblestones

co·caine or **co·cain** (kō-kān'), *n.* a drug that deadens the nerves, much used in dentistry and medicine at one time to lessen pain.

coc·cus (käk'əs), *n.* any of a group of round or oval bacteria [Scarlet fever is caused by the bacteria called strepto*coc·cus*.] —**coc·ci** (käk'sī), *pl.*

cobra (6 ft. long)

cock (käk), *n.* **1.** a male bird; especially, a rooster. **2.** a faucet or valve for controlling the flow of a liquid or gas. **3.** the hammer of a gun;

also, its position when set for firing. —*v.* **1.** to tip to one side; tilt [He *cocked* his hat over his ear.] **2.** to turn up or toward something [The dog *cocked* his ear.] **3.** to set the hammer of a gun in firing position.

cock (käk), *n.* a small pile, as of hay, shaped like a cone.

cock·ade (käk ād'), *n.* a knot of ribbon or other decoration, worn on a hat as a badge.

cock-a-doo·dle-doo (käk'ə dōō'd'l dōō'), *n.* an imitation of the sound made by a rooster.

cock·a·too (käk'ə tōō), *n.* a large parrot of Australia, etc., that is brightly colored and has a high crest. —**cock'a·toos,** *pl.*

cock·a·trice (käk'ə tris), *n.* a serpent in legends that was supposedly able to kill by a look.

cock·er·el (käk'ər əl), *n.* a young rooster.

cock·er spaniel (käk'ər), a small dog with long, drooping ears, long, silky hair, and short legs.

cockatoos
(about 16 in. long)

cock·eyed (käk'īd), *adj.* **1.** cross-eyed. **2.** crooked or lopsided; off at an angle: *slang in this meaning.* **3.** silly or ridiculous: *slang in this meaning.*

cock·horse (käk'hôrs'), *n.* a hobbyhorse.

cock·le (käk''l), *n.* **1.** a shellfish that is used for food and has two hinged shells with ridges. **2.** one of these shells: also called **cock'le·shell.** **3.** a small, shallow boat: also called **cock'le·boat.** **4.** a wrinkle or pucker. —**cockles of one's heart,** one's deepest feelings.

cock·le (käk''l), *n.* a kind of weed that grows in grain fields.

cock·ney (käk'nē), *n.* **1.** a person who comes from the East End of London, England, and speaks the kind of English that is heard in that district. **2.** this kind of English [In *cockney,* the "h" sound is often dropped, so that "his" is spoken as "is."] —*adj.* of or like cockneys or their speech. —**cock'neys,** *pl.*

cock·pit (käk'pit), *n.* in a small airplane, the space where the pilot and passengers sit.

cock·roach (käk'rōch), *n.* an insect that is sometimes found as a pest in kitchens. It has a flat, brown or black body and long feelers.

cocks·comb (käks'kōm), *n.* **1.** the red, fleshy growth on the head of a rooster. **2.** a plant with flowers that look like this.

cock·sure (käk'shoor'), *adj.* absolutely sure; especially, sure of oneself in a stubborn way.

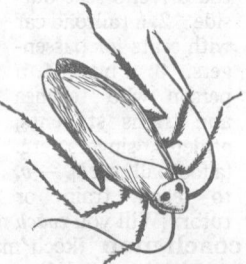

cockroach (1½ in. long)

cock·tail (käk'tāl), *n.* **1.** a mixed alcoholic drink made in any of various ways. **2.** an appetizer served at the beginning of a meal, such as tomato juice, or sea food in a sharp sauce.

cock·y (käk′ē), *adj.* sure of oneself in a rude and bold way; conceited: *used only in everyday talk.* —**cock′i·er**, *compar.*; **cock′i·est**, *superl.* —**cock′i·ly**, *adv.* —**cock′i·ness**, *n.*

co·co (kō′kō), *n.* **1.** the coconut palm. **2.** a coconut.

co·coa (kō′kō), *n.* **1.** a powder made from roasted cacao seeds, used in making chocolate. **2.** a drink made from this powder by adding sugar and hot water or milk.

co·co·nut or **co·coa·nut** (kō′kə nut), *n.* the large, round fruit of a tall, tropical palm tree (called the **coconut palm** or **coco palm**). Coconuts have a thick, hard, brown shell that has an inside layer of sweet white matter used as a food. The hollow center is filled with a sweet, milky liquid.

coconut palm, husk, and nut

co·coon (kə kōōn′), *n.* the silky case that caterpillars spin to shelter themselves while they are changing into butterflies or moths.

cocoon of a moth

cod (käd), *n.* an important large food fish of the North Atlantic. —**cod** or **cods**, *pl.*

C.O.D. or **c.o.d.**, collect on delivery [When goods are sent *C.O.D.*, the receiver must pay for them when they are delivered.]

Cod, Cape (käd), a peninsula in southeastern Massachusetts.

cod·dle (käd′'l), *v.* **1.** to cook slowly in water that is very hot but not boiling. **2.** to treat tenderly, as a baby or a sick person; pamper. —**cod′dled**, *p.t. & p.p.*; **cod′dling**, *pr.p.*

code (kōd), *n.* **1.** a set of laws, as of a nation, city, or organization, arranged in an orderly way. **2.** any set of rules of conduct [a moral *code*]. **3.** a set of signals used in sending messages, as by telegraph or flags [the Morse *code*]. **4.** a system of secret writing in which words, letters, figures, etc. are given certain meanings [Wartime messages are often sent in *code*.] —*v.* to put a message into a code. —**cod′ed**, *p.t. & p.p.*; **cod′ing**, *pr.p.*

co·deine (kō′dēn), *n.* a drug gotten from opium, used in medicine to lessen pain.

cod·fish (käd′fish), *n.* same as **cod**.

codg·er (käj′ər), *n.* a fellow; especially, a queer, old fellow: *used only in everyday talk.*

cod·i·fy (käd′ə fī *or* kō′də fī), *v.* to arrange in

an orderly way [Justinian *codified* Roman law in the 6th century.] —**cod′i·fied**, *p.t. & p.p.*; **cod′i·fy·ing**, *pr.p.* —**cod′i·fi·ca′tion**, *n.*

cod·ling moth (käd′ling), a small moth whose larva ruins various fruits [The worm you find in an apple is the larva of the *codling moth*.]

cod-liv·er oil (käd′liv′ər), oil that is gotten from the livers of cod and certain other fish. It is rich in vitamins A and D.

Co·dy, William F. (kō′dē), 1846–1917; U.S. scout, hunter, and showman. He was called **Buffalo Bill.**

co·ed or **co-ed** (kō′ed′), *n.* a girl student at a coeducational college: *used only in everyday talk.*

co·ed·u·ca·tion·al (kō′ej oo kā′shən 'l), *adj.* that is or has to do with a school or college in which both boys and girls or men and women attend classes together.

co·erce (kō ûrs′), *v.* to force into doing something; compel [He was *coerced* by threats into helping them.] —**co·erced′**, *p.t. & p.p.*; **co·erc′ing**, *pr.p.* —**co·er·cion** (kō ûr′shən), *n.*

co·ex·ist (kō′ig zist′), *v.* to go on living or existing together at the same time. —**co·ex·ist′ence**, *n.*

cof·fee (kôf′ē), *n.* **1.** a dark-brown drink made by brewing the roasted and ground seeds of a tropical plant in boiling water. **2.** these seeds (also called **coffee beans**) or the plant on which they grow.

coffee table, a small, low table on which refreshments can be served, as in a living room.

cof·fer (kôf′ər), *n.* **1.** a box or chest in which money or valuables are kept; money box. **2. coffers**, *pl.* a treasury; funds [The king emptied his *coffers* to pay his son's ransom.]

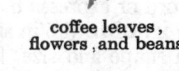

coffee leaves, flowers, and beans

cof·fin (kôf′in), *n.* the case or box in which a dead body is buried.

cog (käg), *n.* **1.** any one of a row of teeth on the rim of a wheel, which fit between the teeth on another wheel: see also **gear**. **2.** a person thought of as just one small part in the working of a business, etc.: *used only in everyday talk.*

co·gent (kō′jənt), *adj.* strong and to the point; convincing [a *cogent* reason or argument]. —**co′gen·cy**, *n.* —**co′gent·ly**, *adv.*

cog·i·tate (käj′ə tāt), *v.* to think hard; consider with care. —**cog′i·tat·ed**, *p.t. & p.p.*; **cog′i·tat·ing**, *pr.p.* —**cog′i·ta′tion**, *n.*

co·gnac (kōn′yak), *n.* a French brandy.

cog·nate (käg′nāt), *adj.* related by coming from the same source [English and Swedish are *cognate* languages.]

cog·ni·zance (käg′ni zəns), *n.* the fact of being

aware; attention. —**take cognizance of,** pay attention to; notice. —**cog′ni·zant,** *adj.*

co·here (kō hir′), *v.* **1.** to stick together, as parts of a mass. **2.** to be connected in a proper way [The ideas in your report do not *cohere.*] —**co·hered′,** *p.t. & p.p.;* **co·her′ing,** *pr.p.*

co·her·ent (kō hir′ənt), *adj.* **1.** sticking together [a *coherent* blob of jelly]. **2.** having all parts connected in a proper way; clear [Grandfather's rambling stories were not very *coherent.*] —**co·her′ence,** *n.* —**co·her′ent·ly,** *adv.*

co·he·sion (kō hē′zhən), *n.* a sticking together; also, the power to stick together. —**co·he·sive** (kō hē′siv), *adj.*

co·hort (kō′hôrt), *n.* **1.** a group of from 300 to 600 soldiers in ancient Rome. There were ten cohorts in a legion. **2.** any group moving or working together [Brigham Young led a *cohort* of Mormons to Utah.] **3.** a fellow worker; associate [The mayor came with his *cohorts.*]

coif (koif), *n.* a cap that is shaped like a hood and fits the head closely.

coif·fure (kwä fyoor′), *n.* the style in which a woman's hair is worn.

coil (koil), *v.* to wind around and around in circles or in a spiral [The sailors *coiled* the ropes on the deck of the ship. The vine *coiled* around the tree.] —*n.* **1.** anything wound in circles or in a spiral [a *coil* of wire]. **2.** each turn of something wound in this way [This spring has weak *coils.*]

coin (koin), *n.* **1.** a piece of metal money having a certain value. **2.** metal money in general [The United States Mint produces *coin.*] —*v.* **1.** to make metal into coins. **2.** to make up or invent [The word "gas" was *coined* by a Belgian chemist in the 17th century.]

coin·age (koin′ij), *n.* **1.** the act of coining [the *coinage* of money; the *coinage* of new words]. **2.** coins; metal money [The United States no longer issues gold *coinage.*] **3.** a newly invented word or expression.

co·in·cide (kō′in sīd′), *v.* **1.** to be exactly alike in shape and size [If one circle fits exactly over another, they *coincide.*] **2.** to happen at the same time [Since our birthdays *coincide,* let's celebrate together.] **3.** to agree; be the same [Our interests do not *coincide.*] —**co′in·cid′ed,** *p.t. & p.p.;* **co′in·cid′ing,** *pr.p.*

co·in·ci·dence (kō in′sə dəns), *n.* **1.** a happening of events that seem to be connected but are not actually; accidental occurrence [It is just a *coincidence* that both my roommate and I are named Jones.] **2.** the fact of coinciding [the *coincidence* of two triangles.]

co·in·ci·dent (kō in′sə dənt), *adj.* **1.** happening at the same time; coinciding [Winter in the United States is *coincident* with summer in Australia.] **2.** exactly alike in shape and size.

co·in·ci·den·tal (kō in′sə den′t'l), *adj.* being a coincidence; happening by accident and not actually having a connection [Our meeting in Paris was purely *coincidental.*]

coke (kōk), *n.* coal from which most of the gases have been removed by heating. It burns with great heat and little smoke.

Col., an abbreviation for **Colonel** and **Colorado.**

col·an·der (kul′ən dər *or* käl′ən dər), *n.* a pan with holes in the bottom for draining off liquids, as in washing vegetables.

colander

cold (kōld), *adj.* **1.** of a temperature much lower than that of the human body; very chilly; frigid [a *cold* day; a *cold* climate]. **2.** without the proper heat or warmth [Your bath will get *cold.*] **3.** feeling chilled [If you are *cold,* put on your coat.] **4.** without any feeling; unkind, unfriendly, or gloomy [a *cold* welcome; a *cold* stare]. **5.** that suggests coldness [Green and blue are *cold* colors.] —*n.* **1.** a lack of heat or warmth [the intense *cold* of the arctic regions]. **2.** a common illness in which there is sneezing and coughing and a discharge from the nose. —**catch cold,** to become ill with a cold. —**throw cold water on,** to discourage. —**cold′ly,** *adv.* —**cold′ness,** *n.*

cold-blood·ed (kōld′blud′id), *adj.* **1.** having blood that becomes colder or warmer as the air or water around the animal changes [Fishes and snakes are *cold-blooded* animals.] **2.** not having normal human feelings of kindness and pity; cruel [a *cold-blooded* murderer].

cold cream, an oily preparation used to make the skin clean and smooth.

cold-heart·ed (kōld′här′tid), *adj.* not feeling sympathy or kindness; unkind.

cold sore, little blisters that form about the mouth when one is ill with a cold or fever.

cold war, strong disagreement between nations in their diplomatic and economic relations, without actual warfare.

cole·slaw or **cole slaw** (kōl′slô), *n.* a salad made of shredded raw cabbage, often mixed with salad dressing and seasoning.

col·ic (käl′ik), *n.* sharp pain in the bowels.

Col·i·se·um (käl′ə sē′əm), *n.* **1.** same as **Colosseum. 2. coliseum,** a large building or stadium for sports events, shows, etc.

col·lab·o·rate (kə lab′ə rāt), *v.* **1.** to work together in preparing something [Charles and Mary Lamb *collaborated* in writing "Tales from Shakespeare."] **2.** to help or work with an enemy that has invaded one's country. —**col·lab′o·rat·ed,** *p.t. & p.p.;* **col·lab′o·rat·ing,** *pr.p.* —**col·lab′o·ra′tion,** *n.* —**col·lab′o·ra·tor,** *n.*

col·lapse (kə laps′), *v.* **1.** to fall down or fall to pieces, as when the sides fail to hold [The bridge *collapsed* when the flood waters weakened its piers.] **2.** to break down or lose strength suddenly; fail [Our hope has *collapsed.* The wounded soldier *collapsed* from loss of blood.] **3.** to fold together neatly in a small space [A convertible automobile has a top that *collapses.*] —*n.* the act of collapsing; a falling in, breakdown, failure, etc. [the *collapse* of a burning building; a nervous *collapse*]. —**col·lapsed′,** *p.t. & p.p.;* **col·laps′ing,** *pr.p.* —**col·laps′i·ble,** *adj.*

col·lar (käl′ər), *n.* **1.** the part of a garment that fits around the neck. It is sometimes a separate piece or a folded-over band. **2.** a band of leather or metal for a dog's neck. **3.** the part of a horse's harness that fits around its neck. **4.** a metal ring or band that is used to connect pipes or rods or to keep some part of a machine steady. —*v.* **1.** to put a collar on. **2.** to grab by the collar; seize [The thief was *collared* as he left the store.]

horse's collar

col·lar·bone (käl′ər bōn), *n.* the clavicle.

col·lat·er·al (kə lat′ər əl), *adj.* **1.** that goes along with the main thing, but in a less important way; additional or secondary [*collateral* evidence]. **2.** having the same ancestors but in a different branch of the family [Your cousins are your *collateral* relatives.] —*n.* stocks, bonds, or other property that is given to a lender of money to hold as a pledge that the loan will be repaid.

col·league (käl′ēg), *n.* a fellow worker in the same office or in the same profession.

col·lect (kə lekt′), *v.* **1.** to gather in one place; assemble [*Collect* the rubbish and burn it. Water *collects* around the drain in the sink.] **2.** to gather things for a hobby [Paul began *collecting* stamps when he was ten.] **3.** to call for and get money owed [The building manager *collects* the rent.] —*adj. & adv.* with payment to be made by the person receiving [Telephone her *collect*.]

col·lect·ed (kə lek′tid), *adj.* **1.** gathered together in one book or set [the *collected* works of Shakespeare]. **2.** in control of oneself; calm [He remained *collected* during the quarrel.]

col·lec·tion (kə lek′shən), *n.* **1.** the act of collecting [Rubbish *collection* is on Friday.] **2.** things collected [a *collection* of coins]. **3.** something gathered into a mass or pile [a *collection* of dust]. **4.** money collected [a *collection* for a church].

col·lec·tive (kə lek′tiv), *adj.* **1.** of or as a group; by or of all in the group [The team made a *collective* effort to win.] **2.** having to do with a project in which a number of people work together as a group [a *collective* farm]. **3.** that is singular in form but is the name for a group of individual persons or things [Army, orchestra, and crowd are *collective* nouns.] —**col·lec′-tive·ly,** *adv.*

col·lec·tor (kə lek′tər), *n.* a person or thing that collects [George is a *collector* of rare coins. She works as a bill *collector*.]

col·leen (käl′ēn), *n.* a girl: *an Irish word.*

col·lege (käl′ij), *n.* **1.** a school of higher education that offers studies beyond the high school and gives degrees to graduating students. A college is often a part of a university, which may have a number of special colleges, as of law or medicine. **2.** a school that offers training in some special work [a business *college*]. **3.** a group of persons having certain powers and duties [the electoral *college*].

col·le·gi·an (kə lē′jən), *n.* a college student.

col·le·gi·ate (kə lē′jit), *adj.* of or like a college or college students [*collegiate* life].

col·lide (kə līd′), *v.* **1.** to come together with force; bump into [The car *collided* with a train.] **2.** to be opposed; disagree; clash [Our ideas *collide* on this matter.] —**col·lid′ed,** *p.t. & p.p.;* **col·lid′ing,** *pr.p.*

col·lie (käl′ē), *n.* a large dog with long hair and a narrow head, often used to herd sheep.

col·lier (käl′yər), *n.* **1.** a coal miner. **2.** a ship for carrying coal.

col·lier·y (käl′yər ē), *n.* a coal mine and its buildings, equipment, etc.

collie (2 ft. high at shoulder)

col·li·sion (kə lizh′ən), *n.* **1.** the act of colliding, or coming together with force; crash [an automobile *collision*]. **2.** a clash of interests, ideas, etc.

col·loid (käl′oid), *n.* a thick substance formed when very fine particles that cannot be dissolved stay scattered throughout a liquid without sinking. —**col·loi·dal** (kə loi′d'l), *adj.*

col·lo·qui·al (kə lō′kwi əl), *adj.* being or containing the words and phrases that are used only in everyday talk and in writing that is like everyday talk ["My buddy flunked the exam" is a *colloquial* way of saying "My close friend failed the examination."] —**col·lo′qui·al·ly,** *adv.*

col·lo·qui·al·ism (kə lō′kwi əl iz'm), *n.* a colloquial word or phrase.

col·lo·quy (käl′ə kwē), *n.* a talk or conversation; especially, a formal discussion [a *colloquy* between diplomats]. —**col′lo·quies,** *pl.*

col·lu·sion (kə lōō′zhən), *n.* a secret agreement for a wrong or unlawful purpose [The cashier had worked in *collusion* with the thieves.]

Colo., an abbreviation for **Colorado.**

Co·logne (kə lōn′), *n.* a city in western Germany, on the Rhine.

co·logne (kə lōn′), *n.* a sweet-smelling liquid like perfume, but not so strong.

Co·lom·bi·a (kə lum′bi ə), *n.* a country in northwestern South America.

co·lon (kō′lən), *n.* a punctuation mark (:) used before a long quotation, example, series, etc. It is also used after the greeting of a formal letter [Dear Sir:].

co·lon (kō′lən), *n.* the main part of the large intestine, above the rectum.

---

fat, āpe, cär, ten, ēven, hit, bīte, gō, hôrn, tōōl, book, up, fur;
get, joy, yet, chin, she, thin, then; zh = s in pleasure; ′ as in able (ā′b'l);
ə = a in ago, e in agent, i in sanity, o in confess, u in focus.

col·o·nel (kur'n'l), *n.* an army or air force officer ranking just above a lieutenant colonel.

co·lo·ni·al (kə lō'ni əl), *adj.* **1.** of or living in a colony or colonies. **2.** of or in the thirteen British colonies in North America that became the United States. —*n.* a person who lives in a colony.

col·o·nist (käl'ə nist), *n.* **1.** one of the first settlers of a colony. **2.** a person who lives in a colony.

col·o·nize (käl'ə nīz), *v.* **1.** to start a colony or colonies in [Spain was the first nation to *colonize* the New World.] **2.** to settle in a colony. —**col'·o·nized,** *p.t. & p.p.;* **col'o·niz·ing,** *pr.p.* —**col'o·ni·za'tion,** *n.*

col·on·nade (käl ə nād'), *n.* a row of columns, as along the side of a building.

col·o·ny (käl'ə nē), *n.* **1.** a group of people who settle in a distant, undeveloped land but remain under the rule of the country from which they came. **2.** the place where they settle [the Pilgrim *colony* at Plymouth]. **3.** a land that is ruled by a country some distance away [Java was a Dutch *colony* for many years.] **4.** a group of people who live together in a city and have the same interests or background [an artists' *colony;* the Chinese *colony* in San Francisco]. **5.** a group of animals or plants living or growing together [a *colony* of ants]. —**col'·o·nies,** *pl.*

colonnade

col·or (kul'ər), *n.* **1.** the effect that light rays of different wave lengths have on the eyes [The *colors* of a rainbow lie in bands shading from red (formed by the longest rays), through orange, yellow, green, blue, and violet (formed by the shortest rays).] **2.** anything used to produce color; dye; pigment; paint. Black, white, and gray are often called colors, but see **black, white, gray. 3. colors,** *pl.* a flag or banner. **4.** look, appearance, or sound [Her writings have the *color* of truth.] —*v.* **1.** to give color to or change the color of [Billy *colored* the drawings with crayons. The fever *colored* her cheeks.] **2.** to take on a color or to change color. **3.** to change or affect in some way [His opinions *color* his reports.] —**call to the colors,** to draft into the armed forces. —**show one's colors,** to show one's true self or one's real feelings. —**with flying colors,** with great success.

Col·o·rad·o (käl'ə rad'ō *or* käl'ə rä'dō), *n.* **1.** a State in the southwestern part of the United States: abbreviated **Colo.** or **Col. 2.** a river flowing southwestward from Colorado.

col·or·a·tion (kul'ər ā'shən), *n.* the way in which a thing is colored; coloring.

col·or-blind (kul'ər blīnd'), *adj.* unable to see the differences between certain colors or, sometimes, between any colors.

col·ored (kul'ərd), *adj.* **1.** having color [*colored* paper; a green-*colored* tie]. **2.** of a race other than the white, especially of the Negro race.

col·or·ful (kul'ər fəl), *adj.* **1.** full of color; bright [*colorful* wallpaper]. **2.** full of variety or interest; vivid; picturesque [The circus is a *colorful* setting for a novel.]

col·or·ing (kul'ər ing), *n.* **1.** the act or art or adding colors. **2.** anything used to color; dye; pigment; paint. **3.** the way in which a thing is colored [the bright *coloring* of tropical birds].

col·or·less (kul'ər lis), *adj.* **1.** without color [*colorless* glass]. **2.** not having variety or interest; dull [a *colorless* piece of music].

co·los·sal (kə läs'l), *adj.* very large or very great; enormous. —**co·los'sal·ly,** *adv.*

Col·os·se·um (käl'ə sē'əm), *n.* a stadium in Rome which was built in the first century A.D. A large part of it is still standing.

co·los·sus (kə läs'əs), *n.* a very large or important person or thing. The **Colossus of Rhodes** was a huge statue of Apollo built at Rhodes by the Greeks in the third century B.C. —**co·los·si** (kə läs'ī) or **co·los'sus·es,** *pl.*

col·our (kul'ər), *n. & v.* color: *British spelling.*

colt (kōlt), *n.* a young male horse, donkey, etc.

Co·lum·bi·a (kə lum'bi ə), *n.* **1.** the United States: *a name used in poetry.* **2.** the capital of South Carolina. **3.** a river rising in British Columbia and flowing between Washington and Oregon to the Pacific.

col·um·bine (käl'əm bīn), *n.* a plant having showy flowers with spurs on them.

Co·lum·bus (kə lum'bəs), *n.* the capital of Ohio.

Co·lum·bus, Chris·topher (kə lum'bəs), 1446?-1506; Italian explorer who discovered America in 1492, while sailing in the service of Spain.

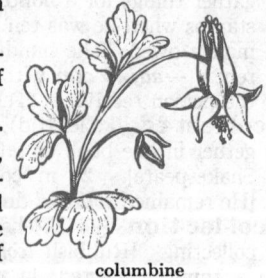
columbine

col·umn (käl'əm), *n.* **1.** a long, generally round, upright support; pillar. Columns usually stand in groups to hold up a roof or other part of a building, but they are sometimes used just for decoration. **2.** any long, upright thing like a column [a *column* of water; the spinal *column*]. **3.** any of the long sections of print lying side by side on a page and separated by a line or blank space [Each page of this book has two *columns*.] **4.** a series of articles that appear regularly in a newspaper or magazine and are written by one writer or on a special subject [a chess *column*]. **5.** a group of soldiers, ships, etc. placed in a row, one behind another

col·um·nist (käl'əm nist), *n.* a person who writes a column in a newspaper or magazine [a sports *columnist*].

com-, a prefix meaning "with" or "together" [To *compress* a mass is to press it together.]

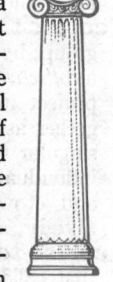
column

co·ma (kō′mə), *n.* a condition like a deep, long sleep, often caused by injury or disease.

Co·man·che (kō man′chē), *n.* **1.** a member of a tribe of American Indians who lived in the Western plains. **2.** their language.

comb (kōm), *n.* **1.** a thin strip of hard rubber, plastic, metal, etc. with teeth. It is passed through the hair to smooth or arrange it, or is put in the hair to hold it in place. **2.** a tool like this, used for cleaning and straightening wool or flax. **3.** the red, fleshy growth on the head of a rooster, etc. **4.** a honeycomb. —*v.* **1.** to smooth, arrange, or clean with a comb. **2.** to search carefully through [We've *combed* the house for that book.]

comb.

com·bat (käm′bat; *also, for the v.,* kəm bat′), *v.* to fight or struggle; oppose [Sir Galahad rode out to *combat* the dragon.] —*n.* **1.** battle [He was wounded in *combat*.] **2.** a struggle or conflict. —**com′bat·ed** or **com′bat·ted,** *p.t. & p.p.;* **com′bat·ing** or **com′bat·ting,** *pr.p.*

com·bat·ant (käm′bə tənt *or* kəm bat′ənt), *adj.* fighting or ready to fight. —*n.* a person who is fighting; fighter.

com·ba·tive (kəm bat′iv *or* käm′bə tiv), *adj.* fond of fighting; ready or eager to fight.

comb·er (kōm′ər), *n.* **1.** a person or machine that combs wool or flax. **2.** a large wave that breaks on a beach.

com·bi·na·tion (käm′bə nā′shən), *n.* **1.** a combining or being combined [He succeeded by a *combination* of hard work and luck.] **2.** a thing made by combining other things [This green paint is a *combination* of blue and yellow.] **3.** a number of people united together for some purpose. **4.** the series of numbers or letters that must be turned to in the right order to open a kind of lock called a **combination lock** [Most safes have a *combination lock*.]

com·bine (kəm bīn′), *v.* to come or bring together; join; unite [to *combine* work with pleasure; to *combine* chemical elements]. —*n.* **1.** (käm′bīn), a machine that gathers grain and threshes it at the same time. **2.** (käm′bīn *or* kəm bīn′), a group of people or businesses joined together, as for controlling trade: *used only in everyday talk.* —**com·bined′,** *p.t. & p.p.;* **com·bin′ing,** *pr.p.*

combine

com·bus·ti·ble (kəm bus′tə b'l), *adj.* **1.** that catches fire and burns easily [Be careful of *combustible* cleaning fluids.] **2.** easily excited [He has a *combustible* temper.]

com·bus·tion (kəm bus′chən), *n.* the act or process of burning [An internal-*combustion* engine is one in which the fuel is burned within the engine itself.]

come (kum), *v.* **1.** to move from "there" to "here" [*Come* to me. Will you *come* to our party?] **2.** to arrive or appear [Help will *come* soon.] **3.** to be in a certain order [After 9 *comes* 10.] **4.** to be descended [He *comes* from a large family.] **5.** to be caused; result [Poor grades may *come* from lack of study.] **6.** to get to be; become [My shoe *came* loose.] **7.** to be made or sold [This dress *comes* in four colors.] **8.** to add up; amount [Your grocery bill *comes* to $10.78.] *Come* is often used as an exclamation to show that one is angry, impatient, suspicious, etc. [*Come, come!* You can't play ball in here!] —**come about,** to happen; occur. —**come across** or **come upon,** to meet or find by accident. —**come at,** to approach angrily, as if to attack. —**come back,** to return. —**come between,** to separate or make unfriendly [Don't let a little quarrel *come between* us.] —**come by,** to get; gain [This rare stamp is hard to *come by*.] —**come into, 1.** to join. **2.** to get or inherit [He *came into* a fortune.] —**come off, 1.** to become separated or unfastened. **2.** to happen [The whole affair *came off* badly.] —**come out, 1.** to be shown or told [Your secret will *come out*.] **2.** to be offered for sale [This book *came out* last month.] **3.** to end up. —**come over,** to happen to [What's *come over* you?] —**come to,** to become conscious again. —**come up,** to be mentioned, as in a discussion. —**come up to,** to equal. —**how come?** how is it that? why?: *used only in everyday talk.* —**came,** *p.t.;* **come,** *p.p.;* **com′ing,** *pr.p.*

co·me·di·an (kə mē′di ən), *n.* an actor who plays comic parts, or one who tells jokes and does funny things to make people laugh.

co·me·di·enne (kə mē′di en′), *n.* a woman comedian.

com·e·dy (käm′ə dē), *n.* **1.** a play or movie that is more or less humorous and has a happy ending. **2.** a comical happening in real life [The mix-up with the twins was quite a *comedy*.]

come·ly (kum′lē), *adj.* pleasant to look at; pretty [a *comely* woman]. —**come′li·er,** *compar.;* **come′li·est,** *superl.* —**come′li·ness,** *n.*

com·er (kum′ər), *n.* one who comes [The contest is open to all *comers*.]

com·et (käm′it), *n.* a heavenly body that has a bright center and, usually, a fiery tail, and that moves in a regular course around the sun.

com·fit (kum′fit), *n.* a candy.

com·fort (kum′fərt), *v.* to make feel less sad

or sorrowful; ease the pain of; soothe [How can we *comfort* the boy who lost his dog?] —*n.* **1.** the condition of having one's pain or sorrow made easier [Your kind words have given me *comfort*.] **2.** someone or something that brings such comfort or cheer [The blind man's radio was a great *comfort* to him.] **3.** the condition of not having hardships, worry, pain, etc. [to live in *comfort*].

com·fort·a·ble (kum′fər tə b'l; *now often* kumf′tər b'l), *adj.* **1.** giving comfort or ease; not giving pain [a *comfortable* pair of shoes]. **2.** feeling comfort; not uneasy [Are you *comfortable* in that chair?] —**com′fort·a·bly,** *adv.*

com·fort·er (kum′fər tər), *n.* **1.** one who brings comfort. **2.** a quilted bed covering.

com·ic (käm′ik), *adj.* **1.** having to do with comedy. **2.** funny or amusing; making one laugh. —*n.* **1.** a comedian. **2. comics,** *pl.* same as **comic strip**; also, a section of comic strips, as in a newspaper.

com·i·cal (käm′i k'l), *adj.* funny or amusing [The clown was a *comical* fellow.]

comic book, a paper booklet of comic strips.

comic strip, a series of cartoons or drawings that tells a comical or exciting story.

com·ing (kum′ing), *adj.* that will come; approaching; on the way [Let's go this *coming* Friday.] —*n.* arrival; approach [Cold mornings warn of the *coming* of winter.]

com·ma (käm′ə), *n.* a punctuation mark (,) used to show a pause that is shorter than the pause at the end of a sentence [The *comma* is often used between clauses or after the opening phrase of a sentence. Words, numbers, or phrases in a series are separated by *commas*.]

com·mand (kə mand′), *v.* **1.** to give an order to; direct [I *command* you to halt!] **2.** to be in control of [Captain Stone *commands* Company B.] **3.** to deserve to have [His wisdom *commands* our respect.] —*n.* **1.** an order or direction [Obey my *command*!] **2.** the power or ability to control or command; control [Who is in *command* here? He had no *command* of his temper.] **3.** a military force, a district, etc. under someone's control [The general took charge of his new *command*.]

com·man·dant (käm ən dant′ *or* käm ən dänt′), *n.* an officer in charge of a command; commander.

com·man·deer (käm ən dir′), *v.* to take by force or by authority, especially for military use [The army *commandeered* the school for use as a hospital.]

com·man·der (kə man′dər), *n.* **1.** a person who commands, especially one in charge of a military force. **2.** an officer in the navy who ranks just under a captain.

commander in chief, the top commander of the armed forces of a nation [In the U.S., the President is the *Commander in Chief*.] —**commanders in chief,** *pl.*

com·mand·ing (kə man′ding), *adj.* **1.** in command or control [a *commanding* officer]. **2.** that has or seems to have authority [a *commanding* voice].

com·mand·ment (kə mand′mənt), *n.* a law or order; especially, in the Bible, any of the ten laws (**Ten Commandments**) that God gave to Moses.

com·man·do (kə man′dō), *n.* any member of a small group of specially trained soldiers who make surprise raids behind enemy lines. —**com·man′dos** or **com·man′does,** *pl.*

com·mem·o·rate (kə mem′ər āt), *v.* to honor or keep alive the memory of [The Washington Monument *commemorates* our first President.] —**com·mem′o·rat·ed,** *p.t.* & *p.p.;* **com·mem′o·rat·ing,** *pr.p.*

com·mem·o·ra·tion (kə mem′ər ā′shən), *n.* **1.** a commemorating. **2.** a celebration or ceremony in memory of someone or something. —**in commemoration of,** in honor of the memory of.

com·mence (kə mens′), *v.* to begin or start. —**com·menced′,** *p.t.* & *p.p.;* **com·menc′ing,** *pr.p.*

com·mence·ment (kə mens′mənt), *n.* **1.** a beginning or start. **2.** the graduation ceremony of a school or college, when graduates receive their degrees or diplomas.

com·mend (kə mend′), *v.* **1.** to mention with approval; praise [The general *commended* the troops for their bravery.] **2.** to put in someone's care or keeping; commit. —**com·men·da·tion** (käm′ən dā′shən), *n.*

com·mend·a·ble (kə men′də b'l), *adj.* deserving to be praised [a *commendable* plan].

com·men·su·rate (kə men′shoor it), *adj.* **1.** equal in measure or size. **2.** in the right proportion; of equal value [His punishment is not *commensurate* with his crime.]

com·ment (käm′ent), *n.* **1.** a remark or note that explains or gives an opinion about [The teacher's *comments* on the essay helped us to understand it.] **2.** talk or gossip [His absence caused much *comment*.] —*v.* to make comments or remarks [The doctor would not *comment* on his patient's illness.]

com·men·tar·y (käm′ən ter′ē), *n.* **1.** a series of comments or notes on a book, etc. [The scholar prepared a *commentary* on Milton's poems.] **2.** a comment. —**com′men·tar′ies,** *pl.*

com·men·ta·tor (käm′ən tā′tər), *n.* **1.** a person who writes a commentary on a book, etc. **2.** a person whose work is reporting the news and giving his opinions about it, as on the radio.

com·merce (käm′ərs), *n.* the buying and selling of goods, especially when done on a large scale between cities, states, or countries; trade.

com·mer·cial (kə mur′shəl), *adj.* **1.** having to do with commerce or trade [*commercial* relations between countries]. **2.** in, for, or concerned with the making of profit [The book was an artistic success but a *commercial* failure.] —*n.* a paid advertisement on radio or television. —**com·mer′cial·ly,** *adv.*

com·mer·cial·ize (kə mur′shəl īz), *v.* to make into a business matter, especially so as to make profit [Radio and television in the U.S. are largely *commercialized*.] —**com·mer′cial·ized,** *p.t. & p.p.;* **com·mer′cial·iz·ing,** *pr.p.* —**com·mer′cial·ism,** *n.*

com·min·gle (kə ming′g'l), *v.* to mingle or mix together; blend. —**com·min′gled,** *p.t. & p.p.;* **com·min′gling,** *pr.p.*

com·mis·er·ate (kə miz′ər āt), *v.* to feel or show sorrow or pity for another's troubles; sympathize [His friends *commiserated* with him on his loss.] —**com·mis′er·at·ed,** *p.t. & p.p.;* **com·mis′er·at·ing,** *pr.p.* —**com·mis′er·a′tion,** *n.*

com·mis·sar (käm′ə sär), *n.* at one time, the head of any of the government departments in the Soviet Union: now called *minister.*

com·mis·sar·i·at (käm′ə ser′i ət), *n.* the branch of an army that furnishes food and other supplies.

com·mis·sar·y (käm′ə ser′ē), *n.* a store, as in a military camp or lumber camp, where food and other small supplies may be bought. —**com′·mis·sar′ies,** *pl.*

com·mis·sion (kə mish′ən), *n.* **1.** the right to perform certain duties or to have certain powers; also, a paper giving this right [Officers in the U.S. armed forces hold their rank by a *commission* from the President.] **2.** a thing that a person is given the power to do for another. **3.** a group of people chosen to do a certain thing [A *commission* was appointed to study the traffic problem.] **4.** the act of committing, or doing [the *commission* of a crime]. **5.** a part of the money taken in on sales that is paid to the person making the sale [He received 10% of the price as his *commission*.] —*v.* **1.** to give a commission to [Generals, colonels, majors, captains, and lieutenants are called *commissioned* officers.] **2.** to give the right to do something; authorize. **3.** to put a ship into service. —**in commission, 1.** in use. **2.** in fit condition for use. —**out of commission, 1.** not in use. **2.** not in fit condition for use.

com·mis·sion·er (kə mish′ən ər), *n.* **1.** a member of a commission. **2.** the head of a government department [a water *commissioner*].

com·mit (kə mit′), *v.* **1.** to give in charge; place as a trust [to *commit* a patient to a mental hospital]. **2.** to do or perform something bad or wrong [to *commit* a crime; to *commit* suicide]. **3.** to do or say something that will involve or pledge one [If you join that book club, you *commit* yourself to buying six books.] —**commit to memory,** to memorize. —**com·mit′ted,** *p.t. & p.p.;* **com·mit′ting,** *pr.p.*

com·mit·ment (kə mit′mənt), *n.* **1.** a committing or being committed. **2.** a promise; pledge.

com·mit·tee (kə mit′ē), *n.* a group of people chosen to study some matter or to do a certain thing [a *committee* to set up rules].

com·mode (kə mōd′), *n.* **1.** a chest of drawers. **2.** a washstand. **3.** a toilet.

com·mo·di·ous (kə mō′di əs), *adj.* having plenty of room; roomy; not crowded.

com·mod·i·ty (kə mäd′ə tē), *n.* anything that is bought and sold; article of trade or commerce. —**com·mod′i·ties,** *pl.*

com·mo·dore (käm′ə dôr), *n.* **1.** at one time, an officer in the navy who ranked just above a captain. **2.** a title given to the president of a yacht club, etc.

com·mon (käm′ən), *adj.* **1.** belonging equally to each or all [England, Canada, and the U.S. share a *common* language.] **2.** belonging to all the people; public [a *common* park]. **3.** of, from, by, or to all [the *common* good]. **4.** often seen or heard; widespread; usual [Squirrels are *common* in these woods. That's a *common* saying.] **5.** of the usual kind; ordinary; not outstanding [the *common* man]. **6.** having no rank [Privates are *common* soldiers.] **7.** coarse or crude; vulgar [He has such *common* manners.] —*n.* often **commons,** *pl.* land that is owned or used by all the people of a town or village; public land. —**in common,** owned, used, or shared equally by all. —**com′mon·ness,** *n.*

com·mon·er (käm′ən ər), *n.* any person who is not a nobleman.

com·mon·ly (käm′ən lē), *adv.* as a general rule; usually; ordinarily.

common noun, any noun that is not the name of a particular person or thing and is not begun with a capital letter [Some *common nouns* are "man," "cat," "road," and "sea."] See also **proper noun.**

com·mon·place (käm′ən plās), *adj.* not new or interesting; ordinary. —*n.* a common or ordinary thing, idea, remark, etc.

com·mons (käm′ənz), *n.pl.* all the people who are not nobles; common people [The House of *Commons* is the group of elected representatives in the British parliament.]

common sense, ordinary good sense; intelligence that comes from experience [It is *common sense* to dress warmly in cold weather.]

com·mon·weal (käm′ən wēl), *n.* the public good; the general welfare.

com·mon·wealth (käm′ən welth), *n.* **1.** the people of a nation or state. **2.** a nation or state in which the people run the government; democracy or republic. **3.** sometimes, any State of the United States.

com·mo·tion (kə mō′shən), *n.* a noisy rushing about; confusion [There was a great *commotion* as the ship began to sink.]

com·mu·nal (käm′yoo n'l *or* kə myōō′n'l), *adj.* of or belonging to the community; public [This park is *communal* property.]

com·mune (kə myōōn′), *v.* to meet or deal with in close understanding [It was thought that witches *communed* with the Devil.] —**com·muned′,** *p.t. & p.p.;* **com·mun′ing,** *pr.p.*

com·mune (käm′yōōn), *n.* the smallest district

that has a local government in France, Belgium, and some other countries in Europe.

com·mu·ni·ca·ble (kə myōō′ni kə b′l), *adj.* that can be passed along from person to person [*communicable* ideas; a *communicable* disease].

com·mu·ni·cant (kə myōō′ni kənt), *n.* **1.** a person who receives or who may receive Holy Communion [a *communicant* of the Catholic Church]. **2.** a person who passes along information.

com·mu·ni·cate (kə myōō′nə kāt), *v.* **1.** to pass along; transmit [Copper wire can *communicate* electricity.] **2.** to make known; give or exchange information [to *communicate* by telephone; to *communicate* an idea by the use of signals]. **3.** to be connected [The living room *communicates* with the dining room.] —**com·mu′ni·cat·ed,** *p.t. & p.p.;* **com·mu′ni·cat·ing,** *pr.p.*

com·mu·ni·ca·tion (kə myōō′nə kā′shən), *n.* **1.** the act of communicating [the *communication* of disease; the *communication* of news]. **2.** a way or means of communicating [The hurricane broke down all *communication* between both cities.] **3.** information, message, letter, etc. [He received the news in a *communication* from his lawyer.]

com·mu·ni·ca·tive (kə myōō′nə kā′tiv *or* kə myōō′ni kə tiv), *adj.* willing to talk or tell something; talkative.

com·mun·ion (kə myōōn′yən), *n.* **1.** a sharing; holding of things in common [They have no *communion* of interests.] **2.** a close relationship with deep understanding; fellowship [In his walks in the woods, the boy felt a *communion* with nature.] **3. Communion,** a sharing in, or celebrating of, Holy Communion.

com·mu·ni·qué (kə myōō′nə kā′), *n.* an official message or bulletin, as of military plans.

com·mu·nism (käm′yoo niz′m), *n.* **1.** a system in which the means of producing goods are owned by the community, and all of the people share in the work and the goods produced. **2. Communism,** a political movement for setting up such a system.

com·mu·nist (käm′yoo nist), *n.* **1.** a person who favors or supports communism. **2. Communist,** a member of a political party that seeks to set up communism.

com·mu·ni·ty (kə myōō′nə tē), *n.* **1.** all the people who live in a particular district, city, etc. [The new swimming pool is for the use of the entire *community*.] **2.** a group of people living together and having similar interests and work [a college *community*]. **3.** a sharing in common [a *community* of interests]. —**com·mu′ni·ties,** *pl.*

com·mu·ta·tion (käm′yoo tā′shən), *n.* **1.** a substituting of one kind of payment for another [a *commutation* of money for services owed]. **2.** the travel of a commuter. **3.** the changing of a punishment to one that is less harsh [a *commutation* of a death sentence to one of life in prison].

com·mute (kə myōōt′), *v.* **1.** to travel as a commuter. **2.** to change a punishment, duty, etc. to one that is less harsh [to *commute* a prisoner's sentence from five to three years]. —**com·mut′ed,** *p.t. & p.p.;* **com·mut′ing,** *pr.p.*

com·mut·er (kə myōōt′ər), *n.* a person who travels daily by train, etc. between his home in a suburb and his place of work in the city.

com·pact (kəm pakt′ *or* käm′pakt), *adj.* **1.** closely and firmly packed together [His clothes were tied in a neat, *compact* bundle.] **2.** having parts fitted together so as not to waste space [a *compact* kitchen]. **3.** having no unnecessary words; brief [a *compact* report]. —*n.* (käm′pakt), **1.** a small case containing a mirror, face powder, etc. **2.** an agreement [a *compact* among all nations to promote peace].

woman's compact

com·pan·ion (kəm pan′yən), *n.* **1.** a person who goes along with another; especially, one who often shares or supports the other's activities; comrade; associate. **2.** either one of a pair of matched things [Where's the *companion* to this glove?]

com·pan·ion·a·ble (kəm pan′yən ə b′l), *adj.* easy to be friends with; friendly; sociable.

com·pan·ion·ship (kəm pan′yən ship), *n.* the state of being companions; fellowship.

com·pan·ion·way (kəm pan′yən wā′), *n.* the stairway leading from the deck of a ship to the space below.

com·pa·ny (kum′pə nē), *n.* **1.** a group of people; especially, a group joined together in some work or activity [a *company* of actors; a business *company*]. **2.** a group of soldiers that is usually under the command of a captain. **3.** the state of being companions; companionship [We enjoy each other's *company*.] **4.** friends or companions [A man is judged by the *company* he keeps.] **5.** a guest or guests: *used only in everyday talk* [We shall have *company* for dinner tomorrow.] —**keep company, 1.** to go together, as a couple that plans to marry. **2.** to be a companion to [I'll stay at home to *keep* you *company*.] —**com′pa·nies,** *pl.*

com·pa·ra·ble (käm′pər ə b′l), *adj.* **1.** that can be compared; of more or less the same kind [Rugby is a game *comparable* with football.] **2.** worthy to be compared [No one is *comparable* to her in charm.] —**com′pa·ra·bly,** *adv.*

com·par·a·tive (kəm par′ə tiv), *adj.* **1.** that compares [*Comparative* anatomy studies and compares the differences in the structure of man and the lower animals.] **2.** judged by comparison with others; relative [Our campaign to raise money was a *comparative* success.] **3.** being the form of adjectives and adverbs that shows a greater but not the greatest degree in meaning ["Better" is the *comparative* degree of "good" and "well."] —*n.* the comparative degree ["Softer" and "more thoughtful" are the *comparatives* of "soft" and "thoughtful."] —**com·par′a·tive·ly,** *adv.*

com·pare (kəm per′), *v.* **1.** to describe as being the same; liken [He *compared* the sound of thunder to the roll of drums.] **2.** to examine certain things in order to find out how they are alike or different [Let's *compare* our report cards.] **3.** to equal or come close to by comparison [Few dogs can *compare* with the Great Dane in size.] **4.** to form the positive, comparative, and superlative degrees of an adjective or adverb. —**beyond compare,** without equal. —**compared′,** *p.t. & p.p.;* **com·par′ing,** *pr.p.*

com·par·i·son (kəm par′ə s'n), *n.* **1.** a comparing or being compared. **2.** enough likeness or similarity to make comparing worthwhile [There is just no *comparison* between fresh and canned fruit.] **3.** the change in an adjective or adverb to show the positive, comparative, and superlative degrees [The degrees of *comparison* of "long" are "long," "longer," "longest."] —**in comparison with,** compared with.

com·part·ment (kəm pärt′mənt), *n.* any of the parts into which an enclosed space is divided.

com·pass (kum′pəs), *n.* **1.** an instrument for showing direction, especially one with a moving needle that always points to magnetic north. **2.** often **compasses,** *pl.* an instrument with two hinged legs, used for drawing circles or measuring distances. **3.** boundary; circumference [He spent his life within the *compass* of his home.] **4.** the full range or extent; reach [within the *compass* of one's experience; the *compass* of a singer's voice]. —*v.* **1.** to go or move round; make or form a circle around; surround. **2.** to accomplish or gain. **3.** to grasp with the mind; understand.

magnetic compass

drawing compass

com·pas·sion (kəm pash′ən), *n.* a feeling of being sorry for others and wanting to help them; deep sympathy; pity.

com·pas·sion·ate (kəm pash′ən it), *adj.* feeling or showing compassion; full of sympathy. —**com·pas′sion·ate·ly,** *adv.*

com·pat·i·ble (kəm pat′ə b'l), *adj.* able to live or be together; getting along well together; in agreement [A dog and cat can be *compatible.* Violence is not *compatible* with reason.] —**com·pat′i·bil′i·ty,** *n.* —**com·pat′i·bly,** *adv.*

com·pa·tri·ot (kəm pā′tri ət), *n.* a person who comes from the same country as another.

com·peer (kəm pir′), *n.* **1.** a person of the same rank; equal; peer. **2.** a companion.

com·pel (kəm pel′), *v.* to force; make do something [The Governor *compelled* William Tell to shoot the apple off his son's head.] —**com·pelled′,** *p.t. & p.p.;* **com·pel′ling,** *pr.p.*

com·pen·sate (käm′pən sāt), *v.* to make up for; take the place of; pay or repay [He worked late to *compensate* for time off.] —**com′pen·sat·ed,** *p.t. & p.p.;* **com′pen·sat·ing,** *pr.p.*

com·pen·sa·tion (käm′pən sā′shən), *n.* **1.** the act of compensating. **2.** something given or done to make up for something else [He will receive a pension as *compensation* for his injury.]

com·pete (kəm pēt′), *v.* to take part in a contest; be a rival for something [Two hundred students *competed* for the scholarship.] —**com·pet′ed,** *p.t. & p.p.;* **com·pet′ing,** *pr.p.*

com·pe·tence (käm′pə təns) or **com·pe·ten·cy** (käm′pə tən sē), *n.* enough skill or intelligence to do something; ability.

com·pe·tent (käm′pə tənt), *adj.* having enough ability to do what is needed; capable [a *competent* typist]. —**com′pe·tent·ly,** *adv.*

com·pe·ti·tion (käm′pə tish′ən), *n.* the act of competing; contest or rivalry.

com·pet·i·tive (kəm pet′ə tiv), *adj.* having to do with competition or based on competition [*competitive* sports]. —**com·pet′i·tive·ly,** *adv.*

com·pet·i·tor (kəm pet′ə tər), *n.* a person who competes; rival [business *competitors*].

com·pi·la·tion (käm′pə lā′shən), *n.* something that is compiled [A dictionary is a *compilation* of facts about words.]

com·pile (kəm pīl′), *v.* to bring together in an orderly way, as facts, writings, statistics, etc. [He *compiled* a book of rules for games.] —**compiled′,** *p.t. & p.p.;* **com·pil′ing,** *pr.p.* —**com·pil′er,** *n.*

com·pla·cent (kəm plā′s'nt), *adj.* satisfied with the way one is or with what one has done [A *complacent* team will often lose the game.] —**com·pla′cen·cy** or **com·pla′cence,** *n.*

com·plain (kəm plān′), *v.* **1.** to find fault with something or show pain or displeasure [Mother is always *complaining* about our lack of neatness.] **2.** to make a report about something bad [We *complained* to the police about the noise.]

com·plain·ant (kəm plān′ənt), *n.* a person who brings charges in a law case.

com·plaint (kəm plānt′), *n.* **1.** the act of complaining or finding fault. **2.** something to complain about [My main *complaint* is his carelessness.] **3.** an illness [They all had a cold or some other common *complaint*.]

com·plai·sant (kəm plā′z'nt), *adj.* willing to please; obliging. —**com·plai′sance,** *n.*

com·ple·ment (käm′plə mənt), *n.* **1.** something that completes a whole or makes perfect [A lace tablecloth would be the perfect *complement* for my china.] **2.** the full number needed [This ship has a *complement* of 300 men.] **3.** the word or words that complete a predicate [In "We made him our captain," "our captain" is a *complement*.] —*v.* (käm′plə ment), to make complete or perfect by supplying what is needed [A bright scarf would *complement* your black dress.]

com·ple·men·ta·ry (käm′plə men′tər ē), *adj.* supplying what is missing in one another; completing [Any two colors, as blue and yellow, that

fat,   āpe,   cär,   ten,   ēven,   hit,   bīte,   gō,   hôrn,   tool,   book,   up,   fur;
get,   joy,   yet,   chin,   she,   thin,   *then;*   zh = s in pleasure;   ′ as in able (ā′b'l);
ə = a in ago,   e in agent,   i in sanity,   o in confess,   u in focus.

combine to form white light are called *com-plementary* colors.]

com·plete (kəm plēt′), *adj.* **1.** having no parts missing; full; whole [a *complete* deck of cards]. **2.** finished; ended [No one's education is ever really *complete*.] **3.** thorough; perfect [She has *complete* confidence in her doctor.] —*v.* to make complete; finish or make whole, full, perfect, etc. [When will the new road be *completed?*] —**com·plet′ed,** *p.t.* & *p.p.;* **com·plet′ing,** *pr.p.* —**com·plete′ly,** *adv.*

com·ple·tion (kəm plē′shən), *n.* a making or being completed, full, perfect, etc.; finishing.

com·plex (kəm pleks′ *or* käm′pleks), *adj.* made up of different parts connected in a way that is hard to understand; not simple; intricate [An electronic calculator is a *complex* machine. Juvenile delinquency is a *complex* problem.] —*n.* (käm′pleks), **1.** a complex whole [Inside the radio there was a *complex* of wires.] **2.** a mixed-up feeling about something that makes one show fear, dislike, etc. [an inferiority *complex;* a *complex* about traveling in airplanes].

com·plex·ion (kəm plek′shən), *n.* **1.** the color and appearance of the skin, especially of the face. **2.** the general look or nature [The *complexion* of our lives is changed by war.]

com·plex·i·ty (kəm plek′sə tē), *n.* **1.** the quality of being complex. **2.** a complex thing. —**com·plex′i·ties,** *pl.*

complex sentence, a sentence made up of a main clause and one or more dependent clauses.

com·pli·ance (kəm plī′əns), *n.* **1.** a complying, or giving in to a request or demand. **2.** a being too ready to give in to others. —**in compliance with,** in agreement with or obedience to. —**com·pli′ant,** *adj.*

com·pli·cate (käm′plə kāt), *v.* to make difficult, mixed-up, or involved [Heavy debts have *complicated* his life.] —**com′pli·cat·ed,** *p.t.* & *p.p.;* **com′pli·cat·ing,** *pr.p.*

com·pli·cat·ed (käm′plə kāt′id), *adj.* complex; not simple [a *complicated* jigsaw puzzle].

com·pli·ca·tion (käm′plə kā′shən), *n.* **1.** a complicated or mixed-up condition; confusion or intricacy. **2.** a happening that makes something more complicated or involved [the *complications* of a plot; a disease with *complications*].

com·plic·i·ty (kəm plis′ə tē), *n.* the fact of being involved with another in doing something wrong or unlawful [*complicity* in a crime].

com·pli·ment (käm′plə mənt), *n.* **1.** something said when one wants to praise, approve, or admire. **2.** a polite or respectful act [The audience paid him the *compliment* of listening quietly.] **3. compliments,** *pl.* polite greetings; respects [Please give your mother my *compliments*.] —*v.* (käm′plə ment), to pay a compliment to; congratulate [We *complimented* the actors on their performance.]

com·pli·men·ta·ry (käm′plə men′tər ē), *adj.* **1.** paying a compliment; giving praise or admiring [*complimentary* remarks]. **2.** given free [a *complimentary* ticket to a play].

com·ply (kəm plī′), *v.* to do what is asked or demanded; yield; submit to [He wouldn't *comply* with the rules of the game.] —**com·plied′,** *p.t.* & *p.p.;* **com·ply′ing,** *pr.p.*

com·po·nent (kəm pō′nənt), *n.* any of the main parts of a whole; constituent; ingredient [the *components* of a phonograph]. —*adj.* helping to form a whole [*component* parts].

com·port (kəm pôrt′), *v.* **1.** to behave in a certain way [He *comported* himself properly.] **2.** to agree or fit [His comic remarks did not *comport* with the seriousness of the matter.]

com·pose (kəm pōz′), *v.* **1.** to make by combining [Mortar is *composed* of lime, sand, and water.] **2.** to put together in proper order [The figures in this painting are well *composed*.] **3.** to create or write [to *compose* a song or poem]. **4.** to adjust or settle [to *compose* a quarrel]. **5.** to put into a calm condition; quiet [Try to *compose* yourself before you speak.] **6.** to put together pieces of type for printing. —**com·posed′,** *p.t.* & *p.p.;* **com·pos′ing,** *pr.p.*

com·posed (kəm pōzd′), *adj.* calm; peaceful.

com·pos·er (kəm pōz′ər), *n.* a person who composes, especially one who composes music.

com·pos·ite (kəm päz′it), *adj.* made up of distinct parts; compound [The head of a *composite* flower, as the aster, is made up of many small flowers.] —*n.* a thing made up of distinct parts [The picture is a *composite* of two photographs.]

com·po·si·tion (käm′pə zish′ən), *n.* **1.** the act, work, or style of composing something. **2.** something composed, as a piece of writing or a musical work. **3.** the parts or materials of a thing and the way they are put together [We shall study the *composition* of this gas.] **4.** a mixture [a *composition* of various metals].

com·post (käm′pōst), *n.* a mixture of rotten vegetable matter, manure, etc. for fertilizer.

com·po·sure (kəm pō′zhər), *n.* calmness of mind; self-control; serenity.

com·pound (käm′pound), *n.* **1.** anything made up of two or more parts or materials; mixture. **2.** a chemical substance formed by combining two or more elements [Water (H_2O) is a *compound*.] —*adj.* made up of two or more parts ["Handbag" is a *compound* word.] —*v.* (kämpound′), to combine or make by combining; mix [to *compound* a medical prescription].

compound sentence, a sentence made up of two or more main clauses. Example: The sun is shining and the birds are singing.

com·pre·hend (käm′pri hend′), *v.* **1.** to understand [I cannot *comprehend* this book.] **2.** to include; take in.

com·pre·hen·si·ble (käm′pri hen′sə b'l), *adj.* that can be understood; understandable.

com·pre·hen·sion (käm′pri hen′shən), *n.* the act of understanding or the power to understand [a good *comprehension* of science].

com·pre·hen·sive (käm′pri hen′siv), *adj.* **1.** including much; covering many details [a *comprehensive* survey]. **2.** understanding fully [a *comprehensive* mind]. —**com′pre·hen′sive·ly,** *adv.*

com·press (kəm pres′), *v.* to press or squeeze closely together; press into a smaller space [The air in a tire is *compressed*.] —*n.* (käm′pres), a pad of hot or cold cloth, often wet, pressed on a part of the body to make it less sore, to stop bleeding, etc. —**com·pres′-sion** (-presh′ən), *n.* —**com·pres′sor**, *n.*

a compress

com·prise (kəm prīz′), *v.* to consist of; be made up of; contain [His library *comprises* 2,000 books.] —**com·prised′**, *p.t. & p.p.*; **com·pris′ing**, *pr.p.*

com·pro·mise (käm′prə mīz), *n.* a settling of an argument or dispute in which each side gives up part of what it wants. —*v.* **1.** to settle by a compromise [The boys *compromised* by taking turns on the bicycle.] **2.** to put in danger of being criticized or disgraced [Do not *compromise* your reputation by cheating.] —**com′pro-mised**, *p.t. & p.p.*; **com′pro·mis·ing**, *pr.p.*

comp·trol·ler (kən trōl′ər), *n.* same as **con-troller** (*meaning 1*).

com·pul·sion (kəm pul′shən), *n.* a forcing or being forced to do something [Only *compulsion* can make him agree.] —**com·pul′sive**, *adj.*

com·pul·so·ry (kəm pul′sər ē), *adj.* that must be done; required [*compulsory* training].

com·punc·tion (kəm pungk′shən), *n.* a feel-ing sorry or guilty about doing something [He had no *compunctions* about being late.]

com·pute (kəm pyoot′), *v.* to figure something by arithmetic; calculate [to *compute* the tax]. —**com·put′ed**, *p.t. & p.p.*; **com·put′ing**, *pr.p.* —**com·pu·ta·tion** (käm′pyoo tā′shən), *n.*

com·put·er (kəm pyoo′tər), *n.* **1.** a person who computes. **2.** an electronic machine used as a calculator or to store and select data.

com·put·er·ize (kəm pyoo′tər īz), *v.* to equip with or operate by electronic computers [a bank's *computerized* accounting system]. —**com·put′-er·ized**, *p.t. & p.p.*; **com·put′er·iz·ing**, *pr.p*

com·rade (käm′rad), *n.* a close friend; com-panion or fellow worker. —**com′rade·ship**, *n.*

con (kän), *adv.* against ["Pro and *con*" means "for and against" something.] —*n.* a reason or vote against [the pros and *cons* of the plan].

con (kän), *v.* to study or learn carefully. —**conned**, *p.t. & p.p.*; **con′ning**, *pr.p.*

con-, the form of the prefix **com-** that is used before certain consonants.

con·cave (kän′kāv *or* kän kāv′), *adj.* hollow and rounded like the inside of a bowl. —**con·cave′ly**, *adv.* —**con·cav·i·ty** (kän kav′ə tē), *n.*

con·ceal (kən sēl′), *v.* to hide or keep secret; put or keep out of sight [She *concealed* her amusement. The robber *con-cealed* his gun.]

concave lenses

con·ceal·ment (kən sēl′mənt), *n.* **1.** the act of concealing. **2.** a hiding place.

con·cede (kən sēd′), *v.* **1.** to admit to be true; say that it is so [He will not *concede* that he has failed.] **2.** to let have; grant [We *concede* you the victory.] —**con·ced′ed**, *p.t. & p.p.*; **con-ced′ing**, *pr.p.*

con·ceit (kən sēt′), *n.* too high an opinion of oneself; vanity [A pretty woman's *conceit* can make her unattractive.] —**con·ceit′ed**, *adj.*

con·ceiv·a·ble (kən sēv′ə b′l), *adj.* that can be imagined or thought of [He had no *conceivable* reason for lying.] —**con·ceiv′a·bly**, *adv.*

con·ceive (kən sēv′), *v.* **1.** to form or develop in the mind; think of; imagine [I have *conceived* a plan for making a fortune.] **2.** to understand [It is difficult to *conceive* how this motor works.] **3.** to become pregnant. —**con·ceived′**, *p.t. & p.p.*; **con·ceiv′ing**, *pr.p.*

con·cen·trate (kän′s'n trāt), *v.* **1.** to gather all one's thoughts or efforts [I must *concentrate* on this problem.] **2.** to bring or come closely together in one place [The troops are *concen-trated* at the border.] **3.** to make or become stronger or thicker [You can *concentrate* the jam by boiling off some of the water.] —*n.* a substance that has been concentrated [Evaporated milk is a *concentrate*.] —**con′cen·trat·ed**, *p.t. & p.p.*; **con′cen·trat·ing**, *pr.p.*

con·cen·tra·tion (kän′s'n trā′shən), *n.* **1.** a concentrating or being concentrated. **2.** careful, close attention [Chess is a game that requires *concentration*.] **3.** strength or thickness [the *concentration* of an acid].

concentration camp, a prison camp for holding people who are thought to be dangerous to the ruling group. These camps were much used in Nazi Germany.

con·cen·tric (kən sen′trik), *adj.* having the same center [*concentric* cir-cles].

con·cept (kän′sept), *n.* an idea; especially, a general idea of what a thing or class of things is [Jefferson's *con-cept* of democracy differed from Hamilton's.]

concentric circles

con·cep·tion (kən sep′-shən), *n.* **1.** the act of con-ceiving or forming an idea [You will get credit for the *conception* of this plan.] **2.** a general idea; concept [A baby has almost no *conception* of time.] **3.** the start of pregnancy.

con·cern (kən surn′), *v.* **1.** to have a relation to; be important to; interest [This matter *con-cerns* all of us.] **2.** to make anxious or unhappy; trouble [Don't let the loss of a game *concern* you.] —*n.* **1.** something that concerns or is important to one [The way I dress is no one's *concern* but my own.] **2.** worry or anxiety [The doctor showed no *concern* as he spoke.] **3.** a business or company

fat,   āpe,   cär,   ten,   ēven,   hit,   bīte,   gō,   hôrn,   tool,   book,   up,   fur;
get,   joy,   yet,   chin,   she,   thin,   *then*;   zh = s in pleasure;   ′ as in able (ā′b'l);
ə = a in ago,   e in agent,   i in sanity,   o in confess,   u in focus.

[a manufacturing *concern*]. —**as concerns,** in regard to; about.

con·cerned (kən sûrnd′), *adj.* **1.** interested. **2.** worried or anxious.

con·cern·ing (kən sûrn′ing), *prep.* having to do with; relating to; about.

con·cert (kän′sərt), *n.* a musical program, especially one in which a number of musicians perform together. —**in concert,** with all in agreement, or acting together as one ["Yes!" they shouted *in concert.*]

con·cert·ed (kən sûr′tid), *adj.* planned or agreed upon by all; combined [to make a *concerted* effort].

con·cer·ti·na (kän′sər tē′nə), *n.* a musical instrument like a small accordion.

con·cer·to (kən cher′tō), *n.* a piece of music for a solo instrument or instruments with an orchestra. It usually has three movements. —**con·cer′tos** or **con·cer·ti** (kən cher′tē), *pl.*

concertina

con·ces·sion (kən sesh′ən), *n.* **1.** a conceding, or giving in. **2.** a thing conceded [We shall need to make *concessions* in order to get the contract.] **3.** a right or lease given by a government, company, etc. [Who has the refreshment *concession* at the ball park?]

conch (kängk), *n.* **1.** a shellfish with a large spiral shell. **2.** this shell.

con·cil·i·ate (kən sil′i āt), *v.* to win over by friendly acts; make friendly [Traders *conciliated* the Indians with gifts of beads.] —**con·cil′i·at·ed,** *p.t. & p.p.;* **con·cil′i·at·ing,** *pr.p.* —**con·cil′i·a′tion,** *n.*

conch

con·cil·i·a·to·ry (kən sil′i ə tôr′ē), *adj.* that serves to win over or make friendly [a *conciliatory* act].

con·cise (kən sīs′), *adj.* telling much in few words; short and clear [a *concise* statement]. —**con·cise′ly,** *adv.* —**con·cise′ness,** *n.*

con·clave (kän′klāv), *n.* a private meeting, as the one held by cardinals to elect a pope.

con·clude (kən klōōd′), *v.* **1.** to come or bring to an end [The play *concludes* with the death of Hamlet.] **2.** to settle or arrange [to *conclude* an agreement]. **3.** to decide; make up one's mind [I *concluded* that he was right.] —**con·clud′ed,** *p.t. & p.p.;* **con·clud′ing,** *pr.p.*

con·clu·sion (kən klōō′zhən), *n.* **1.** the end; last part [We left at the *conclusion* of the show.] **2.** an opinion reached by thinking; judgment [My *conclusion* is that you are both right.] **3.** the act of settling or arranging something [the *conclusion* of an agreement]. —**in conclusion,** finally; as a last statement.

con·clu·sive (kən klōō′siv), *adj.* that settles a question; convincing [His fingerprint would be *conclusive* evidence.] —**con·clu′sive·ly,** *adv.*

con·coct (kən käkt′), *v.* to make up, prepare,

or invent [to *concoct* a new recipe; to *concoct* an excuse].

con·coc·tion (kən käk′shən), *n.* **1.** the act of concocting. **2.** something concocted.

con·com·i·tant (kən käm′ə tənt), *adj.* going along with; accompanying [*concomitant* events]. —*n.* something that goes along; accompaniment [Coughing is often a *concomitant* to smoking.]

Con·cord (käng′kərd), *n.* **1.** the capital of New Hampshire. **2.** a town in Massachusetts, where an early battle of the American Revolution was fought on April 19, 1775.

con·cord (käng′kôrd), *n.* harmony; peaceful agreement [*concord* between nations].

con·cord·ance (kən kôr′d'ns), *n.* **1.** concord; agreement [I must act in *concordance* with the rules.] **2.** a kind of index that lists the words used by an author or in a book, and tells where they appear [a Bible *concordance*].

con·course (kän′kôrs), *n.* **1.** a running or flowing together [a *concourse* of rivers]. **2.** a crowd of people. **3.** a large, open place where crowds gather, as in a railroad station. **4.** a broad boulevard.

con·crete (kän′krēt *or* kän krēt′), *n.* a hard substance made of cement, sand, gravel, and water. It is used for making roads, bridges, buildings, etc. —*adj.* **1.** real or exact; not imaginary or vague [to offer *concrete* help; to give a *concrete* example]. **2.** made of concrete.

con·cu·bine (käng′kyoo bīn′), *n.* a woman who lives with a man but is not actually his wife. Among some peoples, a man could have several wives and concubines.

con·cur (kən kûr′), *v.* **1.** to agree in an opinion or decision [Dr. Smith *concurred* in Dr. Black's diagnosis.] **2.** to act or happen together [Several events *concurred* to cause this result.] —**con·curred′,** *p.t. & p.p.;* **con·cur′ring,** *pr.p.*

con·cur·rence (kən kûr′əns), *n.* **1.** agreement [I am in complete *concurrence* with you.] **2.** an acting or happening together.

con·cur·rent (kən kûr′ənt), *adj.* **1.** acting or happening together [*concurrent* causes]. **2.** in agreement.

con·cus·sion (kən kush′ən), *n.* **1.** a shaking with great force; shock [An earthquake can cause *concussion* miles away.] **2.** an injury to the brain or spine from a hard blow, fall, etc.

con·demn (kən dem′), *v.* **1.** to say that a person or thing is wrong or bad [Our teachers *condemn* comic books about crime.] **2.** to declare to be guilty; convict [A jury tried and *condemned* him.] **3.** to give as punishment; sentence [The judge *condemned* him to life imprisonment.] **4.** to take property by law for public use [The land was *condemned* for use as an army base.] **5.** to declare to be unfit for use [The old school was *condemned* for lack of fire escapes.] —**con·dem·na·tion** (kän′dem nā′shən), *n.*

con·den·sa·tion (kän′den sā′shən), *n.* **1.** a condensing or being condensed. **2.** something that is condensed.

con·dense (kən dens′), *v.* **1.** to make or become thicker, denser, or more closely packed together

[Milk is *condensed* by evaporation. Steam *condenses* to water when it strikes a cold surface.] **2.** to put into fewer words [The author *condensed* his book into a magazine article.] **—con·densed′,** *p.t. & p.p.;* **con·dens′ing,** *pr.p.*

con·dens·er (kən den′sər), *n.* **1.** a person or thing that condenses. **2.** a part in an electric hookup for storing an electric charge.

con·de·scend (kän′di send′), *v.* **1.** to act too proud or haughty while doing a favor; be patronizing [The actor *condescended* to sign just a few autographs.] **2.** to be politely willing to do something thought to be beneath one's dignity [The judge *condescended* to join in the game.] **—con·de·scen·sion** (kän′di sen′shən), *n.*

con·di·ment (kän′də mənt), *n.* a seasoning for food, as salt, pepper, mustard, etc.

con·di·tion (kən dish′ən), *n.* **1.** the particular way a person or thing is [What is the *condition* of the patient? Weather *conditions* won't allow us to go.] **2.** the right or healthy way to be [The whole team is in *condition.*] **3.** position in life; rank [a man of low *condition*]. **4.** anything which must be or must happen before something else can take place [Some consider wealth a *condition* of happiness.] **—v. 1.** to bring into fit condition [Spring training helps to *condition* baseball players.] **2.** to form a habit in; accustom [Our dog is *conditioned* to bark at strangers.] **3.** to be a condition of; determine [the things that *condition* our happiness].

con·di·tion·al (kən dish′ən 'l), *adj.* **1.** depending on a condition [Your trip is *conditional* on your good behavior.] **2.** telling of a condition ["If Jane arrives on time" is a *conditional* clause.] **—con·di′tion·al·ly,** *adv.*

con·dole (kən dōl′), *v.* to show sympathy with someone in sorrow [Her friends came to *condole* with her in mourning.] **—con·doled′,** *p.t. & p.p.;* **con·dol′ing,** *pr.p.*

con·do·lence (kən dō′ləns), *n.* a showing of sympathy with someone in sorrow.

con·done (kən dōn′), *v.* to forgive or overlook a wrong done [Many mothers *condone* the mistakes of their own children.] **—con·doned′,** *p.t. & p.p.;* **con·don′ing,** *pr.p.*

con·dor (kän′dər), *n.* a large vulture with a bare head and neck, found in the Andes Mountains and in California.

condor (9 ft. wingspread)

con·duce (kən dōōs′ *or* kən dyōōs′), *v.* to help to bring about; contribute [Eating the right foods *conduces* to good health.] **—con·duced′,** *p.t. & p.p.;* **con·duc′ing,** *pr.p.*

con·du·cive (kən dōō′siv *or* kən dyōō′siv), *adj.* helping to bring about; contributing [Soft music is often *conducive* to sleep.]

con·duct (kän′dukt), *n.* **1.** the way one acts or behaves; behavior [The teacher praised her students for their good *conduct* in class.] **2.** way of handling or managing; management [We all approve of his *conduct* of the business.] **—v.** (kən dukt′), **1.** to lead or guide [The waiter *conducted* us to our table.] **2.** to manage; direct; be the leader of [to *conduct* a meeting; to *conduct* an orchestra]. **3.** to behave [He *conducted* himself like a gentleman.] **4.** to be a means for carrying; transmit [Copper *conducts* electricity.]

con·duc·tion (kən duk′shən), *n.* the passing along or letting through, as of liquid in a pipe or electricity in a wire.

con·duc·tiv·i·ty (kän′duk tiv′ə tē), *n.* the ability to conduct heat, electricity, or sound.

con·duc·tor (kən duk′tər), *n.* **1.** a person who conducts; director [the *conductor* of an orchestra]. **2.** the person in charge who collects fares on a train, streetcar, etc. **3.** something that conducts electricity, heat, or sound [Air is a good *conductor* of heat.]

con·duit (kän′dit *or* kän′dōō it), *n.* **1.** a pipe or passage through which fluids pass [Gutters, water pipes, gas pipes, and sewers are all called *conduits.*] **2.** a tube for protecting electric wires and cables.

cone (kōn), *n.* **1.** a solid object that narrows evenly from a flat circle at one end to a point at the other. **2.** anything shaped like this, as a shell of pastry for holding ice cream. **3.** the fruit of some evergreen trees, containing seeds.

co·ney (kō′nē), *n.* same as **cony.** **—co′neys,** *pl.*

con·fec·tion (kən fek′shən), *n.* any kind of candy or other sweet thing like candy.

con·fec·tion·er (kən fek′shən ər), *n.* a person who makes or sells candies and other sweets.

ice-cream
cone

con·fec·tion·er·y (kən fek′shən·er′ē), *n.* **1.** candies and other sweets. **2.** a shop where candies, etc. are sold. **—con·fec′tion·er′ies,** *pl.*

con·fed·er·a·cy (kən fed′ər ə sē), *n.* a union of people, groups, or states for a certain purpose; league. **—the Confederacy,** the eleven Southern States that seceded from the United States in 1860 and 1861: also called **Confederate States of America. —con·fed′er·a·cies,** *pl.*

evergreen cones

con·fed·er·ate (kən fed′ər it), *adj.* **1.** joined in a confederacy. **2. Confederate,** of the Confederacy. **—n. 1.** a person who joins with others especially to do something not lawful; ally or accomplice. **2. Confederate,** a supporter of the Confederacy. **—v.** (kən fed′ər āt),

con·fed·er·a·tion (kən fed′ər ā′shən), *n.* **1.** the act of confederating. **2.** a union of nations; league; alliance.

con·fer (kən fūr′), *v.* **1.** to give or grant [Many honors were *conferred* upon the scientist.] **2.** to meet for a discussion; have a talk [The president *conferred* with his advisers.] —**con·ferred′**, *p.t. & p.p.;* **con·fer′ring**, *pr.p.*

con·fer·ence (kän′fər əns), *n.* **1.** a meeting of people to discuss something [A *conference* on education was held in Washington.] **2.** an association, as of college athletic teams.

con·fess (kən fes′), *v.* **1.** to tell what one has done that is bad; admit a fault or crime [John *confessed* that he had started the fight.] **2.** to tell what one really thinks; acknowledge [I *confess* that operas bore me.] **3.** to tell one's sins to a priest. **4.** to listen to a person tell his sins, as a priest does.

con·fes·sion (kən fesh′ən), *n.* **1.** a confessing; telling of one's faults, sins, etc. **2.** something confessed.

con·fes·sion·al (kən fesh′ən 'l), *n.* the place in a church where a priest hears confessions.

con·fes·sor (kən fes′ər), *n.* **1.** a person who confesses. **2.** a priest who hears confessions.

con·fet·ti (kən fet′ē), *n.pl.* bits of colored paper thrown about at carnivals, parades, etc.: *used with a singular verb* [The *confetti* is in that box.]

con·fi·dant (kän fə dant′), *n.* a close, trusted friend to whom one tells secrets.

con·fide (kən fīd′), *v.* **1.** to tell or talk about as a secret [She *confided* her troubles to me.] **2.** to trust in someone who can keep one's secrets [He *confided* in his sister.]

girl throwing confetti

3. to give into the keeping of a trusted person [She *confided* the care of her fortune to her lawyer.] —**con·fid′ed**, *p.t. & p.p.;* **con·fid′ing**, *pr.p.*

con·fi·dence (kän′fə dəns), *n.* **1.** strong belief or trust in someone or something; reliance [I have *confidence* in his abilities.] **2.** a belief in oneself; self-confidence [He began to play with *confidence*.] **3.** trust in another to keep one's secrets [I told it to him in *confidence*.] **4.** a secret [Don't burden her with your *confidences*.]

con·fi·dent (kän′fə dənt), *adj.* full of confidence; sure; certain; assured [*confident* of victory; a *confident* manner]. —**con′fi·dent·ly**, *adv.*

con·fi·den·tial (kän′fə den′shəl), *adj.* **1.** told in confidence; secret [a *confidential* report]. **2.** trusted with private matters [a *confidential* agent]. —**con′fi·den′tial·ly**, *adv.*

con·fig·u·ra·tion (kən fig′yoo rā′shən), *n.* the shape, form, or outline of a thing.

con·fine (kən fīn′), *v.* **1.** to keep within limits; restrict [Please *confine* your talk to five minutes.] **2.** to keep shut up [to *confine* in prison; *confined* to the house by illness]. —*n.* (kän′fīn), a boundary or limit: *usually used in the plural*, **confines** [the *confines* of a town]. —**con·fined′**, *p.t. & p.p.;* **con·fin′ing**, *pr.p.* —**con·fine′ment**, *n.*

con·firm (kən fūrm′), *v.* **1.** to make sure or firm by agreeing or approving [The Senate *confirmed* the treaty.] **2.** to prove to be true; verify [to *confirm* a rumor]. **3.** to make a person a full member in a church.

con·fir·ma·tion (kän′fər mā′shən), *n.* **1.** the act of confirming, or making sure. **2.** something that confirms or proves. **3.** a ceremony in which a person is made a full member in a church.

con·firmed (kən fūrmd′), *adj.* **1.** set in one's ways or habits [a *confirmed* bachelor]. **2.** proved to be true [a *confirmed* theory].

con·fis·cate (kän′fis kāt), *v.* to seize with authority [to *confiscate* land in order to build a highway]. —**con′fis·cat·ed**, *p.t. & p.p.;* **con′fis·cat·ing**, *pr.p.* —**con′fis·ca′tion**, *n.*

con·fla·gra·tion (kän′flə grā′shən), *n.* a big fire that does great damage.

con·flict (kän′flikt), *n.* **1.** a fight or battle. **2.** a clash or sharp disagreement, as of interests or ideas. —*v.* (kən flikt′), to be or act against; be opposed to [His ideas *conflict* with mine.]

con·flu·ence (kän′floo əns), *n.* **1.** a flowing together, as of two streams. **2.** a coming together, as of people. —**con′flu·ent**, *adj.*

confluence of rivers

con·form (kən fôrm′), *v.* **1.** to make the same or similar [He *conformed* his thinking to ours.] **2.** to be or act in the required way; be in agreement with [to *conform* to rules]. —**con·form′a·ble**, *adj.* —**con·form′ist**, *adj. & n.*

con·for·ma·tion (kän′fôr mā′shən), *n.* the way in which a thing is formed or shaped; arrangement of parts; structure [The *conformation* of the land was changed by an earthquake.]

con·form·i·ty (kən fôr′mə tē), *n.* **1.** a being in agreement; likeness or similarity. **2.** a following of rules, orders, customs, or accepted ideas [Extreme *conformity* often prevents original thought.] —**con·form′i·ties**, *pl.*

con·found (kän found′), *v.* to mix up or confuse; bewilder [The old man was so *confounded* by the traffic, he was afraid to move.] **Confound it!** is a phrase of mild swearing which shows that one is annoyed or angry.

con·front (kən frunt′), *v.* **1.** to meet face to face, especially in a bold way; stand up against [to *confront* an enemy]. **2.** to bring face to face [He confessed when *confronted* with the evidence.]

con·fron·ta·tion (kän′frən tā′shən), *n.* a face-to-face meeting, as of two persons who hold opposite views on some matter.

Con·fu·cius (kən fyoo′shəs), *n.* 551?–479 B.C.; Chinese philosopher and teacher.

con·fuse (kən fyooz′), *v.* **1.** to mix up, especially in the mind; put into disorder; bewilder [You will *confuse* her with so many questions.] **2.** to fail to see or remember the difference between; mistake [You are *confusing* wisdom and knowledge.] —**con·fused′**, *p.t.* & *p.p.*; **con·fus′ing,** *pr.p.* —**con·fus·ed·ly** (kən fyōōz′id lē), *adv.*

con·fu·sion (kən fyōō′zhən), *n.* **1.** a being confused; disorder or bewilderment [There was *confusion* in the room when fire broke out.] **2.** a confusing or failing to see the difference [His *confusion* of colors comes from color blindness.]

con·fute (kən fyōōt′), *v.* to prove to be false or wrong [to *confute* an opponent in a debate; to *confute* an argument point by point]. —**con·fut′ed,** *p.t.* & *p.p.*; **con·fut′ing,** *pr.p.* —**con·fu·ta·tion** (kän′fyoo tā′shən), *n.*

con·geal (kən jēl′), *v.* to make or become solid or thick, as by cooling or freezing; thicken [Melted fat *congeals* as it cools.]

con·gen·ial (kən jēn′yəl), *adj.* **1.** able to get along well together; having the same interests [*congenial* friends]. **2.** fitting one's needs or mood; agreeable [*congenial* surroundings].

con·gen·i·tal (kən jen′ə t'l), *adj.* present from the time of birth [a *congenital* disease].

con·gest (kən jest′), *v.* **1.** to fill up with too much blood [A cold causes the nose to become *congested*.] **2.** to make too full; make crowded [The market is always *congested* on Saturday.] —**con·ges′tion,** *n.*

con·glom·er·ate (kən gläm′ər āt), *v.* to form or collect into a round mass. —*adj.* (kən gläm′ər it), made up of separate parts or materials formed into one mass [A *conglomerate* rock is made up of pebbles and stones cemented together in hard clay and sand.] —*n.* (kən gläm′ər it), a conglomerate mass. —**con·glom′er·at·ed,** *p.t.* & *p.p.*; **con·glom′er·at·ing,** *pr.p.* —**con·glom′er·a′tion,** *n.*

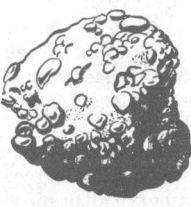

conglomerate rock

Con·go (käng′gō), *n.* **1.** a river in central Africa, flowing into the Atlantic. **2.** a country in central Africa, once called **Belgian Congo. 3.** a country west of this, at one time a colony of France.

con·grat·u·late (kən grach′ə lāt), *v.* to tell a person that one is happy for his success or good luck [I *congratulate* you on your marriage.] —**con·grat′u·lat·ed,** *p.t.* & *p.p.*; **con·grat′u·lat·ing,** *pr.p.*

con·grat·u·la·tion (kən grach′ə lā′shən), *n.* the act of congratulating; words that tell of one's happiness at another's success or good luck: *usually used in the plural,* **congratulations** [Let's send *congratulations* to the winner.]

con·gre·gate (käng′grə gāt), *v.* to come together; assemble [We *congregated* around the piano.] —**con′gre·gat·ed,** *p.t.* & *p.p.*; **con′gre·gat·ing,** *pr.p.*

con·gre·ga·tion (käng′grə gā′shən), *n.* **1.** a gathering, especially of a group of people. **2.** a group meeting for a religious service.

con·gre·ga·tion·al (käng′grə gā′shən 'l), *adj.* **1.** of or like a congregation. **2. Congregational,** of a Protestant faith in which each member congregation governs itself. —**Con′gre·ga′tion·al·ist,** *n.* & *adj.*

con·gress (käng′grəs), *n.* **1.** a coming together; meeting; convention. **2. Congress,** the group of elected officials in the United States government that makes the laws. It consists of the Senate and the House of Representatives.

con·gres·sion·al (kən gresh′ən 'l), *adj.* having to do with a congress or with Congress.

con·gress·man (käng′grəs mən), *n.* a member of Congress, especially of the House of Representatives. —**con′gress·men,** *pl.*

con·gress·wom·an (käng′grəs woom′ən), *n.* a woman member of Congress, especially of the House of Representatives. —**con′gress·wom′-en,** *pl.*

con·gru·ent (käng′grōō ənt), *adj.* in agreement or harmony; corresponding.

con·gru·ous (käng′grōō əs), *adj.* **1.** same as **congruent. 2.** fitting in a proper way; suitable.

con·i·cal (kän′i k'l), *adj.* **1.** of a cone. **2.** shaped like a cone. —**con′i·cal·ly,** *adv.*

co·ni·fer (kō′nə fər *or* kän′ə fər), *n.* a tree or shrub that bears cones, as the pine, spruce, etc. —**co·nif·er·ous** (kō nif′ər əs), *adj.*

conj., abbreviation for **conjunction.**

con·jec·ture (kən jek′chər), *n.* a guess or guessing; opinion formed without sure facts [What we know of Shakespeare's life is based mainly on *conjecture*.] —*v.* to make a conjecture. —**con·jec′tured,** *p.t.* & *p.p.*; **con·jec′tur·ing,** *pr.p.* —**con·jec′tur·al,** *adj.*

con·join (kən join′), *v.* to join together; unite. —**con·joint′,** *adj.* —**con·joint′ly,** *adv.*

con·ju·gal (kän′joo gəl), *adj.* of marriage.

con·ju·gate (kän′joo gāt), *v.* to list the different forms of a verb in person, number, and tense [*Conjugate* "to be," beginning "I am, you are, he is."] —**con′ju·gat·ed,** *p.t.* & *p.p.*; **con′ju·gat·ing,** *pr.p.* —**con′ju·ga′tion,** *n.*

con·junc·tion (kən jungk′shən), *n.* **1.** a joining together; combination [High winds, in *conjunction* with rain, made travel difficult.] **2.** a word used to join other words, phrases, or clauses [*And, but, or, if,* etc. are *conjunctions*.]

con·jure (kun′jər *or* kän′jər), *v.* **1.** to practice magic or witchcraft, as in supposedly making evil spirits come to do one's bidding. **2.** (kən joor′), to beg or plead with in a very serious way [For your mother's sake, I *conjure* you not to leave home.] —**conjure up,** to make appear, as if by magic [The music *conjured up* memories.] —**con′jured,** *p.t.* & *p.p.*; **con′jur·ing,** *pr.p.*

con·jur·er *or* **con·jur·or** (kun′jər ər *or* kän′jər ər), *n.* a magician.

con·nect (kə nekt/), *v.* **1.** to join together; unite [Many bridges *connect* North and South London.] **2.** to relate in some way; think of together [Do you *connect* Bill's silence with Ann's arrival?] **3.** to meet so that passengers can change to another train, plane, etc. [Does this train *connect* with the bus for Marysville?]

Con·nect·i·cut (kə net/i kət), *n.* a New England State of the United States: abbreviated **Conn.**

con·nec·tion (kə nek/shən), *n.* **1.** a connecting or being connected. **2.** a part or thing that connects. **3.** a being related in some way; relationship [What is the *connection* between lightning and thunder?] **4.** a person with whom one is associated in some way [He has some important *connections*.] **5.** the meeting of buses, trains, etc. so that people can change from one to another [If you miss your *connection* in Chicago, you will need to wait six hours.] —**in connection with, 1.** together with. **2.** referring to.

con·nec·tive (kə nek/tiv), *adj.* that connects; connecting. —*n.* a word that connects others, as a conjunction or a preposition.

conn·ing tower (kän/ing), a low tower on a submarine, used as a place for observation.

con·niv·ance (kə nīv/əns), *n.* a conniving.

con·nive (kə nīv/), *v.* **1.** to pretend not to see something wrong or evil, so that one seems to be giving his consent. **2.** to help someone secretly in wrongdoing; conspire. —**con·nived/**, *p.t. & p.p.*; **con·niv/ing,** *pr.p.*

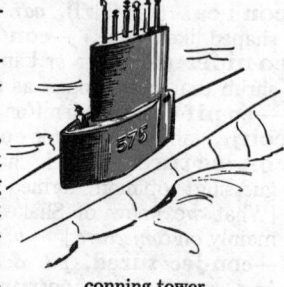
conning tower

con·nois·seur (kän ə sur/), *n.* a person who has much knowledge and good taste in some fine art [a *connoisseur* of music].

con·no·ta·tion (kän/ə tā/shən), *n.* something connoted; idea associated with a word or phrase in addition to its actual meaning.

con·note (kə nōt/), *v.* to suggest some idea or feeling in addition to the actual meaning [The word "mother" means "female parent," but it usually *connotes* love, care, and tenderness.] —**con·not/ed,** *p.t. & p.p.*; **con·not/ing,** *pr.p.*

con·quer (käng/kər), *v.* **1.** to get or gain by using force, as by winning a war [The Spaniards *conquered* Mexico.] **2.** to overcome by trying hard; defeat [He *conquered* his bad habits.] —**con·quer·or** (käng/kər ər), *n.*

con·quest (käng/kwest), *n.* **1.** the act of conquering. **2.** something conquered, as a country.

con·quis·ta·dor (kän kwis/tə dôr), *n.* any of the early Spanish conquerors of Mexico, Peru, etc.

con·science (kän/shəns), *n.* a sense of right and wrong; feeling that keeps one from doing bad things [His *conscience* bothered him after he told the lie.] —**on one's conscience,** making one feel guilty.

con·sci·en·tious (kän/shi en/shəs), *adj.* **1.** always trying to do the right thing [a *conscientious* worker]. **2.** made or done with care in a way one knows is right [*conscientious* work]. —**con/sci·en/tious·ly,** *adv.*

conscientious objector, a person who will not take part in war because his conscience tells him it is wrong.

con·scious (kän/shəs), *adj.* **1.** aware of one's own feelings or of things around one [*conscious* of a slight noise; *conscious* of having a fever]. **2.** able to feel and think; in the normal waking state [She became *conscious* a few minutes after she had fainted.] **3.** done or doing with awareness or on purpose [*conscious* humor]. —**con/scious·ly,** *adv.*

con·scious·ness (kän/shəs nis), *n.* **1.** a being conscious; awareness. **2.** all the thoughts and feelings a person has when awake [The memory of the event was gone from his *consciousness*.]

con·script (kən skript/), *v.* to force to serve in the armed forces; draft. —*n.* (kän/skript), a person forced to serve in the armed forces; draftee. —**con·scrip/tion,** *n.*

con·se·crate (kän/sə krāt), *v.* **1.** to set apart as holy; make sacred for religious use [The priest *consecrated* the water.] **2.** to give up to a purpose; devote [He *consecrated* his life to helping the poor.] —**con/se·crat·ed,** *p.t. & p.p.*; **con/se·crat·ing,** *pr.p.* —**con/se·cra/tion,** *n.*

con·sec·u·tive (kən sek/yoo tiv), *adj.* coming in regular order without a break [It snowed three *consecutive* days.] —**con·sec/u·tive·ly,** *adv.*

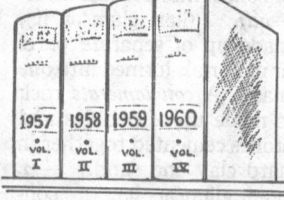
consecutive volumes

con·sen·sus (kən sen/səs), *n.* agreement of all or most in some opinion [It was the *consensus* of the parents that a new school should be built.]

con·sent (kən sent/), *v.* to agree or give approval [He *consented* to serve as president.] —*n.* agreement or approval [May I have your *consent* to leave early?]

con·se·quence (kän/si kwens), *n.* **1.** a result or outcome [What were the *consequences* of your decision?] **2.** importance [a matter of great *consequence*]. —**take the consequences,** to accept the results of one's actions.

con·se·quent (kän/si kwent), *adj.* coming as a result; resulting [his trial and *consequent* imprisonment]. —*n.* something coming as a result.

con·se·quen·tial (kän/si kwen/shəl), *adj.* **1.** same as **consequent. 2.** acting important.

con·se·quent·ly (kän/si kwent lē), *adv.* as a result; therefore [The frost spoiled the crops and *consequently* prices rose.]

con·ser·va·tion (kän/sər vā/shən), *n.* a conserving, or protecting from loss, waste, or harm [The *conservation* of forests, rivers, etc. is important to our economy.]

con·serv·a·tism (kən sur/və tiz'm), *n.* a feeling

or working against change and reform, especially in political and social matters.

con·serv·a·tive (kən sür′və tiv), *adj.* **1.** wanting to keep things as they are and being against change and reform [One of the political parties of Great Britain is the *Conservative* Party.] **2.** cautious or safe; not risky [a *conservative* taste in music; a *conservative* estimate of costs]. —*n.* a conservative person.

con·ser·va·to·ry (kən sür′və tôr′ē), *n.* **1.** a small, private greenhouse. **2.** a school of music, art, etc. —**con·ser′va·to′ries,** *pl.*

con·serve (kən sürv′), *v.* to keep from being hurt, lost, or wasted [to *conserve* one's strength]. —*n.* (kän′sərv), a kind of jam made of two or more fruits. —**con·served′,** *p.t. & p.p.;* **con·serv′ing,** *pr.p.*

con·sid·er (kən sid′ər), *v.* **1.** to think about in order to make up one's mind [Please *consider* my suggestion.] **2.** to keep in mind; take into account [His health is fine, if you *consider* his age.] **3.** to be thoughtful about [to *consider* the feelings of others]. **4.** to think to be; believe [I *consider* him a fine scholar.]

con·sid·er·a·ble (kən sid′ər ə b'l), *adj.* **1.** worth considering; important [a *considerable* man]. **2.** much or large [*considerable* success].

con·sid·er·a·bly (kən sid′ər ə blē), *adv.* much; a great deal [I feel *considerably* better.]

con·sid·er·ate (kən sid′ər it), *adj.* thoughtful of other people's feelings; kind [It was *considerate* of you to invite her too.] —**con·sid′er·ate·ly,** *adv.*

con·sid·er·a·tion (kən sid′ə rā′shən), *n.* **1.** the act of considering; careful thought [After long *consideration,* Lincoln decided to run for president.] **2.** a reason for doing something [His sense of duty was his chief *consideration* in accepting the offer.] **3.** something paid for a favor or service [He repairs clocks for a *consideration.*] **4.** a being thoughtful about other people's feelings; kindness. —**in consideration of, 1.** because of. **2.** in return for. —**take into consideration,** to keep in mind; take into account. —**under consideration,** being thought over.

con·sid·ered (kən sid′ərd), *adj.* decided after careful thought [a *considered* judgment].

con·sid·er·ing (kən sid′ər ing), *prep.* keeping in mind; taking into account [He's done well, *considering* all that's happened.]

con·sign (kən sīn′), *v.* **1.** to give over; entrust [I *consign* my books to your care.] **2.** to send or address [This shipment is *consigned* to our New York office.]

con·sign·ment (kən sīn′mənt), *n.* **1.** the act of consigning. **2.** something consigned [We have shipped you a *consignment* of hats.]

con·sist (kən sist′), *v.* **1.** to be made up of; contain [Bronze *consists* of copper and tin.] **2.** to be contained in as a cause or quality [Wisdom does not *consist* only in knowing facts.]

con·sist·ence (kən sis′təns), *n.* consistency.

con·sist·en·cy (kən sis′tən sē), *n.* **1.** thickness or firmness [Flour is added to gravy to increase its *consistency.*] **2.** a being consistent; action that is always the same or suitable [He is unpredictable because he lacks *consistency.*]

con·sis·tent (kən sis′tənt), *adj.* **1.** acting or thinking always in the same way [Parents should be *consistent* in their discipline.] **2.** in agreement or harmony; suitable [His words are not *consistent* with his acts.] —**con·sis′tent·ly,** *adv.*

con·sis·to·ry (kən sis′tə rē), *n.* a church council or court. —**con·sis′to·ries,** *pl.*

con·so·la·tion (kän′sə lā′shən), *n.* **1.** the act of consoling. **2.** something that consoles, or makes one less sad or troubled; comfort.

con·sole (kən sōl′), *v.* to make less sad or troubled; comfort [A toy *consoled* the lost child.] —**con·soled′,** *p.t. & p.p.;* **con·sol′ing,** *pr.p.*

con·sole (kän′sōl), *n.* **1.** the part of an organ at which the player sits, containing the keyboard, pedals, etc. **2.** a radio, phonograph, or television cabinet that stands on the floor.

console of an organ

con·sol·i·date (kən säl′ə dāt), *v.* **1.** to join together into one; unite; merge [The corporation was formed by *consolidating* many companies.] **2.** to make or become strong or firm [The troops *consolidated* their position by bringing up heavy guns.] —**con·sol′i·dat·ed,** *p.t. & p.p.;* **con·sol′i·dat·ing,** *pr.p.* —**con·sol′i·da′tion,** *n.*

con·som·mé (kän sə mā′), *n.* a clear meat soup that is served hot or cold.

con·so·nance (kän′sə nəns), *n.* agreement or harmony.

con·so·nant (kän′sə nənt), *adj.* in agreement or harmony [His actions were *consonant* with his principles.] —*n.* **1.** a speech sound made by stopping or partly stopping the breath with the tongue, teeth, or lips. **2.** any of the letters used to show these sounds [Most letters except *a, e, i, o,* and *u* are usually *consonants; w* and *y* are sometimes *consonants.*]

con·sort (kän′sôrt), *n.* a wife or husband, especially of a ruling king or queen. —*v.* (kən sôrt′), to spend much time; associate [She *consorts* with snobs.]

con·spic·u·ous (kən spik′yōō əs), *adj.* **1.** easy to see; plainly seen [a *conspicuous* sign]. **2.** getting attention by being unusual; remarkable [He received a medal for *conspicuous* bravery.] —**con·spic′u·ous·ly,** *adv.*

con·spir·a·cy (kən spir′ə sē), *n.* **1.** a secret plan by two or more people to do something bad or unlawful; plot [a *conspiracy* to kill the king]. **2.** a working or joining together [A *conspiracy* of

---

fat,   āpe,   cär,   ten,   ēven,   hit,   bīte,   gō,   hôrn,   tool,   book,   up,   fūr;
get,   joy,   yet,   chin,   she,   thin,   *then;*   zh = s in pleasure;   ′ as in able (ā′b'l);
ə = a in ago,   e in agent,   i in sanity,   o in confess,   u in focus.

events kept me from the party.] —**con·spir′a·cies,** *pl.*

con·spir·a·tor (kən spir′ə tər), *n.* a person who takes part in a conspiracy; plotter.

con·spire (kən spīr′), *v.* **1.** to plan together secretly, as to commit a crime. **2.** to join or act together toward some result [Rain and cold *conspired* to spoil our vacation.] —**con·spired′,** *p.t. & p.p.;* **con·spir′ing,** *pr.p.*

con·sta·ble (kän′stə b'l *or* kun′stə b'l), *n.* a policeman.

con·stab·u·lar·y (kən stab′yoo ler′ē), *n.* a police force.

con·stan·cy (kän′stən sē), *n.* a staying the same; faithfulness or firmness.

con·stant (kän′stənt), *adj.* **1.** not changing; staying the same; fixed [To be a pilot is Al's *constant* goal.] **2.** loyal; faithful [a *constant* friend]. **3.** going on all the time; never stopping [I'm tired of his *constant* complaints.] —*n.* something that never changes [Pi (π) is a *constant* used in figuring measurements of all circles.] —**con′stant·ly,** *adv.*

Con·stan·ti·no·ple (kän′stan tə nō′p'l), *n.* the old name for Istanbul, a city in Turkey.

con·stel·la·tion (kän′stə lā′shən), *n.* a group of stars, usually named after something that it is supposed to suggest [Orion is a *constellation* seen in the winter sky.]

con·ster·na·tion (kän′stər nā′shən), *n.* great fear that makes one feel helpless; dismay [The earthquake filled us with *consternation*.]

con·sti·pate (kän′stə pāt), *v.* to cause constipation in. —**con′sti·pat·ed,** *p.t. & p.p.;* **con′sti·pat·ing,** *pr.p.*

the constellation Orion

con·sti·pa·tion (kän′stə pā′shən), *n.* a condition in which waste matter from the bowels does not empty easily or often enough.

con·stit·u·en·cy (kən stich′oo ən sē), *n.* **1.** all the voters of a particular district. **2.** the district itself. —**con·stit′u·en·cies,** *pl.*

con·stit·u·ent (kən stich′oo ənt), *adj.* **1.** needed to form a whole; used in making a thing [a *constituent* part]. **2.** having the right to vote or elect. **3.** having the power to make or change a constitution [a *constituent* assembly]. —*n.* **1.** one of the parts that make up a thing [Oxygen is one of the *constituents* of air.] **2.** any of the voters represented by a particular official.

con·sti·tute (kän′stə toōt *or* kän′stə tyoōt), *v.* **1.** to make up; form; compose [Twelve people *constitute* a jury.] **2.** to set up; establish [A committee was *constituted* to study the problem.] **3.** to give a certain right or duty to; appoint [We *constitute* you our spokesman.] —**con′sti·tut·ed,** *p.t. & p.p.;* **con′sti·tut·ing,** *pr.p.*

con·sti·tu·tion (kän′stə toō′shən *or* kän′stə tyoō′shən), *n.* **1.** the act of constituting. **2.** the way in which a person or thing is formed; make-up; structure [His strong *constitution* helped him

to recover from his illness.] **3.** the system of basic laws or rules of a government, society, etc. [The *Constitution* of the United States is the supreme law of the land.]

con·sti·tu·tion·al (kän′stə toō′shən 'l *or* kän′stə tyoō′shən 'l), *adj.* **1.** of or in the make-up of a person or thing; basic [a *constitutional* weakness]. **2.** of or in agreement with a nation's constitution [Freedom of speech is one of our *constitutional* rights.] —*n.* a short walk taken as exercise: *used only in everyday talk.* —**con′sti·tu·tion·al·ly,** *adv.*

con·sti·tu·tion·al·i·ty (kän′stə toō′shən al′ə tē *or* kän′stə tyoō′shən al′ə tē), *n.* the fact of being in agreement with a nation's constitution [to test the *constitutionality* of an act].

con·strain (kən strān′), *v.* to hold in or keep back by force or strain; force; compel [*constrained* to agree; a *constrained* laugh].

con·straint (kən strānt′), *n.* **1.** a constraining or being constrained; force. **2.** the holding in of one's feelings [She spoke of her sorrow with *constraint*.]

con·strict (kən strikt′), *v.* to make smaller or narrower by pressing together; squeeze; contract [The tight collar *constricted* his neck.] —**con·stric′tion,** *n.* —**con·stric′tive,** *adj.* —**con·stric′tor,** *n.*

con·struct (kən strukt′), *v.* to make or build with a plan [to *construct* a house or a theory].

con·struc·tion (kən struk′shən), *n.* **1.** the act of constructing or building. **2.** the way something is built or put together [a house of brick *construction*]. **3.** something built; structure [The Great Wall of China is a remarkable *construction*.] **4.** an explanation or meaning [Don't put the wrong *construction* on what I said.] **5.** the arrangement of words in a sentence ["Of what is it made?" is a more formal *construction* than "What's it made of?"]

con·struc·tive (kən struk′tiv), *adj.* able or helping to construct or build up; making suggestions [*Constructive* criticism helps us to correct our mistakes.]

con·strue (kən stroō′), *v.* **1.** to explain the meaning of; interpret [We *construed* her silence to mean that she agreed.] **2.** to find out or show how the parts of a sentence are related. —**con·strued′,** *p.t. & p.p.;* **con·stru′ing,** *pr.p.*

con·sul (kän′s'l), *n.* **1.** an official who lives in a certain foreign city to look after his country's interests and to help its citizens there. **2.** either of the two chief officials of the ancient Roman republic. —**con′su·lar,** *adj.*

con·su·late (kän′s'l it), *n.* **1.** the position and duties of a consul. **2.** the building where a consul works and often lives.

con·sult (kən sult′), *v.* **1.** to talk things over in order to decide [Let's *consult* about our vacation plans.] **2.** to go to for information or advice [If your coughing continues, *consult* a doctor.] **3.** to keep in mind; consider [*Consult* your own wishes in the matter.]

con·sult·ant (kən sul′t'nt), *n.* an expert who is called on for special advice or services.

con·sul·ta·tion (kän's'l tā'shən), *n.* **1.** the act of consulting. **2.** a meeting to talk over some problem.

con·sume (kən soom' *or* kən syoom'), *v.* **1.** to destroy, as by fire. **2.** to use up; spend or waste [The meeting *consumed* most of the day.] **3.** to drink up or eat up [He *consumed* two rolls.] —**consumed with,** filled with [to be *consumed with* envy]. —**con·sumed',** *p.t. & p.p.;* **con·sum'ing,** *pr.p.*

con·sum·er (kən soom'ər *or* kən syoom'ər), *n.* a person or thing that consumes; especially, a person who buys goods for his own needs and not to sell to others or to use in making other goods for sale.

con·sum·mate (kän'sə māt), *v.* to make complete; finish; fulfill [to *consummate* a project]. —*adj.* (kən sum'it), complete; absolute [*consummate* happiness]. —**con'sum·mat·ed,** *p.t. & p.p.;* **con'sum·mat·ing,** *pr.p.* —**con'sum·ma'tion,** *n.*

con·sump·tion (kən sump'shən), *n.* **1.** a consuming or using up. **2.** the amount used up [What is the annual *consumption* of paper in the U.S.?] **3.** tuberculosis of the lungs.

con·sump·tive (kən sump'tiv), *adj.* having tuberculosis of the lungs. —*n.* a person who has this disease.

con·tact (kän'takt), *n.* **1.** a touching or meeting [The light is turned on by the *contact* of the switch with the wire.] **2.** the condition of associating [You will come into *contact* with many people.] **3.** connection [The pilot tried to make *contact* with the airport.] —*v.* to get in touch with; communicate with: *used only in everyday talk.*

con·ta·gion (kən tā'jən), *n.* **1.** the spreading of disease from one person to another by contact. **2.** any disease spread in this way. **3.** the spreading of a feeling or idea from person to person [a *contagion* of gaiety at a carnival].

con·ta·gious (kən tā'jəs), *adj.* **1.** spread by contact [a *contagious* disease]. **2.** quickly spreading from person to person [*contagious* laughter]. —**con·ta'gious·ly,** *adv.*

con·tain (kən tān'), *v.* **1.** to have in it; hold; enclose or include [This bottle *contains* cream. Your list *contains* 25 names.] **2.** to be able to hold; be equal to [This jug *contains* a gallon. A gallon *contains* four quarts.] **3.** to hold back; control or restrain [Try to *contain* your tears.]

con·tain·er (kən tān'ər), *n.* a thing for holding something; box, can, bottle, pot, etc.

con·tam·i·nate (kən tam'ə nāt), *v.* to make dirty or impure by touching or mixing with; pollute; corrupt [Automobile fumes are *contaminating* the air.] —**con·tam'i·nat·ed,** *p.t. & p.p.;* **con·tam'i·nat·ing,** *pr.p.* —**con·tam'i·na'tion,** *n.*

con·temn (kən tem'), *v.* to scorn or despise.

con·tem·plate (kän'təm plāt), *v.* **1.** to look at or think about carefully or seriously; study;

consider [He *contemplated* the problem for a long time.] **2.** to have as a plan; expect; intend [I *contemplate* going to Mexico next summer.] —**con'tem·plat·ed,** *p.t. & p.p.;* **con'tem·plat·ing,** *pr.p.* —**con'tem·pla'tion,** *n.*

con·tem·pla·tive (kän'təm plā'tiv *or* kən tem'plə tiv), *adj.* thoughtful; contemplating.

con·tem·po·ra·ne·ous (kən tem'pə rā'ni əs), *adj.* existing or happening in the same period of time [*contemporaneous* events].

con·tem·po·rar·y (kən tem'pə rer'ē), *adj.* existing or happening in the same period of time. —*n.* a person living in the same period as another [Dickens and Longfellow were *contemporaries*.] —**con·tem'po·rar'ies,** *pl.*

con·tempt (kən tempt'), *n.* **1.** the feeling one has toward someone or something he considers low, worthless, or evil; scorn [to feel *contempt* for a cheat]. **2.** the condition of being despised or scorned [to be held in *contempt*]. **3.** the act of showing a lack of respect for a court or legislature, as by refusing to obey a lawful order [to be fined for *contempt* of court].

con·tempt·i·ble (kən temp'tə b'l), *adj.* that should be treated with contempt; deserving scorn [a *contemptible* liar].

con·temp·tu·ous (kən temp'choo əs), *adj.* full of contempt; scornful [a *contemptuous* smile].

con·tend (kən tend'), *v.* **1.** to fight or struggle [to *contend* with greed and envy]. **2.** to strive in a contest; compete [Jones will *contend* for the prize]. **3.** to argue; hold to be a fact [We *contend* that he is guilty.] —**con·tend'er,** *n.*

con·tent (kən tent'), *adj.* happy with what one has or is; not wanting anything else; satisfied [Are you *content* with the food here?] —*v.* to satisfy; make content [I must *content* myself with reading about travel.] —*n.* a being satisfied or contented [a sigh of *content*].

con·tent (kän'tent), *n.* **1.** the amount held or contained [The *content* of a barrel is 31½ gallons. Cast iron has a high carbon *content*.] **2.** **contents,** *pl.* all that is contained; everything inside [the *contents* of a trunk]. **3.** *often* **contents,** *pl.* the things dealt with in a piece of writing, etc. [a table of *contents* in a book].

con·tent·ed (kən ten'tid), *adj.* satisfied.

con·ten·tion (kən ten'shən), *n.* **1.** the act of contending; argument, struggle, or strife [*contention* about a point of law]. **2.** something that one argues for as right or true [It was his *contention* that we should all pay.]

con·ten·tious (kən ten'shəs), *adj.* always ready to argue; quarrelsome.

con·tent·ment (kən tent'mənt), *n.* a being contented; feeling of quiet satisfaction.

con·test (kən test'), *v.* **1.** to try to prove that something is not true, right, or lawful; dispute [to *contest* a will]. **2.** to fight for; struggle to win or keep [to *contest* a prize]. —*n.* (kän'test), **1.** a fight, struggle, or argument. **2.** a race, game,

---

fat, āpe, cär, ten, ēven, hit, bīte, gō, hôrn, tool, book, up, fûr; get, joy, yet, chin, she, thin, *th*en; zh = s in pleasure; ' as in able (ā'b'l); ə = a in ago, e in agent, i in sanity, o in confess, u in focus.

etc. in which there is a struggle to be the winner.

con·test·ant (kən tes′tənt), *n.* a person who takes part in a contest.

con·text (kän′tekst), *n.* the words just before or after a certain word or sentence that help make clear what it means [A remark taken out of *context* may be misunderstood.]

con·tig·u·ous (kən tig′yōō əs), *adj.* 1. touching along all or most of one side [The United States is *contiguous* with Canada.] 2. lying near; neighboring [*contiguous* houses]. —**con·ti·gu·i·ty** (kän′ti gyōō′ə tē), *n.*

con·ti·nence (kän′tə nəns), *n.* control of oneself and one's appetites; not eating, drinking, etc. too much. —**con′ti·nent,** *adj.*

con·ti·nent (kän′tə nənt), *n.* any of the main large land areas of the earth. The continents are Africa, Asia, Australia, Europe, North America, South America, and, often, Antarctica. —**the Continent,** all of Europe except the British Isles.

con·ti·nen·tal (kän′tə nen′t'l), *adj.* 1. of or like a continent. 2. **Continental,** of or like the Continent of Europe [a *Continental* tour]. 3. **Continental,** of the American colonies at the time of the American Revolution [the *Continental* Congress]. —*n.* **Continental,** 1. a person living on the Continent of Europe. 2. a soldier of the American Revolutionary army.

con·tin·gen·cy (kən tin′jən sē), *n.* 1. the chance that something might happen; possibility [We cannot plan our lives on the *contingency* of future events.] 2. a possible happening; chance; accident [On camping trips, you must be ready for any *contingency.*] —**con·tin′gen·cies,** *pl.*

con·tin·gent (kən tin′jənt), *adj.* 1. that may or may not happen; possible [*contingent* events]. 2. depending on something uncertain; conditional [His promotion is *contingent* on his passing the final test.] —*n.* 1. a chance happening; accident. 2. a group forming part of a larger one; especially, one's share of workers, delegates, etc. [the Chicago *contingent* at the convention].

con·tin·u·al (kən tin′yōō əl), *adj.* 1. happening over and over again; repeated often [his *continual* jokes]. 2. continuous; going on without stopping [the *continual* roar of the waterfall]. —**con·tin′u·al·ly,** *adv.*

con·tin·u·ance (kən tin′yōō əns), *n.* 1. a continuing; keeping up or going on [The treaty provides for a *continuance* of trade.] 2. the putting off of something to a later time [His lawyer asked for a *continuance* of the trial.]

con·tin·u·a·tion (kən tin′yōō ā′shən), *n.* 1. a keeping up or going on without stopping. 2. a taking up or beginning again after stopping. 3. a part or thing added on, as a sequel to a story or an extension of a highway.

con·tin·ue (kən tin′yōō), *v.* 1. to keep on being or doing [The war *continued* for four years. In spite of the noise, I *continued* reading.] 2. to stay in the same place or position [The chairman will *continue* in office for another year.] 3. to go on or start again after a stop; resume [After a sip of water, the speaker *continued.*] 4. to go on or

extend; stretch [This road *continues* to the main highway.] 5. to put off to a later time [The trial will be *continued* until Monday.] —**con·tin′-ued,** *p.t. & p.p.;* **con·tin′u·ing,** *pr.p.*

con·ti·nu·i·ty (kän′tə nōō′ə tē), *n.* 1. the condition of being continuous. 2. something that is continuous or connected, not broken up. 3. the remarks made by an announcer, etc. that tie together the parts of a radio or television program. —**con′ti·nu′i·ties,** *pl.*

con·tin·u·ous (kən tin′yōō əs), *adj.* going on without a stop or break; connected [a *continuous* line of trees]. —**con·tin′u·ous·ly,** *adv.*

con·tort (kən tôrt′), *v.* to twist or force out of its usual form [a face *contorted* with pain].

con·tor·tion (kən tôr′shən), *n.* a contorting or being contorted, as of the face or body.

con·tour (kän′toor), *n.* the outline of something, or a line drawn to represent this.

contour farming, farming in which sections are plowed along the natural lines of ridges, slopes, etc., to keep the land from eroding.

contour farming

con·tra·band (kän′tra band), *n.* goods that may not be legally imported or exported, and that are smuggled into a country.

con·tract (kän′trakt), *n.* 1. an agreement, especially a written agreement that one can be held to by law [a *contract* to build a house]. 2. a form of bridge, the card game. —*v.* (kən trakt′; *for meaning 1, often* kän′trakt), 1. to make a contract to do, buy, or sell something. 2. to get; come to have [to *contract* a disease]. 3. to make or become smaller; draw together; shrink [Cold *contracts* metals. His brows were *contracted* in a frown.]

con·trac·tion (kən trak′shən), *n.* 1. a contracting or being contracted. 2. a shortened form of a word or phrase, as *I'm* for *I am.*

con·trac·tor (kän′trak tər), *n.* a person or company that contracts to do or supply something; especially, one whose business is contracting work in any of the building trades.

con·tra·dict (kän trə dikt′), *v.* 1. to say the opposite of; deny the things said by someone [The witness *contradicted* the story told by the suspect. Stop *contradicting* me.] 2. to be opposite to or different from; go against [The facts *contradict* your theory.]

con·tra·dic·tion (kän′trə dik′shən), *n.* 1. a contradicting or being contradicted. 2. a remark or act that contradicts another.

con·tra·dic·to·ry (kän′trə dik′tər ē), *adj.* contradicting; saying the opposite; contrary [*contradictory* statements].

con·tral·to (kən tral′tō), *n.* 1. a woman's singing voice with the lowest tones; alto. 2. a woman singer with such a voice. —*adj.* of or for a contralto. —**con·tral′tos,** *pl.*

con·trap·tion (kən trap′shən), *n.* any strange-looking device or machine that one does not fully understand; gadget: *used only in everyday talk.*

con·tra·ri·wise (kän′trer i wīz′), *adv.* **1.** in an opposite or stubbornly different way. **2.** as opposed to what has been said; on the contrary.

con·tra·ry (kän′trer ē), *adj.* **1.** opposite; completely different [to hold *contrary* opinions; to move in a *contrary* direction]. **2.** opposed; being or acting against [*contrary* to the rules]. **3.** (*often* kən trer′i), opposing in a stubborn way; perverse [A *contrary* child says "No!" to every request.] —*n.* the opposite [Just the *contrary* of what you say is true.] —**on the contrary,** the opposite is true.

con·trast (kən trast′), *v.* **1.** to compare in such a way as to show the differences [to *contrast* two systems]. **2.** to show differences when compared [Their methods *contrast* sharply with ours.] —*n.* (kän′trast), **1.** a difference between things being compared [the *contrast* between air and rail travel]. **2.** something showing such a difference [The tall, lean man is quite a *contrast* to his short, stout wife.]

con·trib·ute (kən trib′yoot), *v.* **1.** to give together with others [He *contributes* to his church.] **2.** to write an article, poem, etc. as for a magazine or newspaper. —**contribute to,** to have a part in bringing about [His jokes *contributed to* our fun.] —**con·trib′ut·ed,** *p.t. & p.p.;* **con·trib′ut·ing,** *pr.p.*

con·tri·bu·tion (kän′trə byoo′shən), *n.* **1.** the act of contributing. **2.** something contributed, as money to a charity or a poem to a magazine.

con·trib·u·tor (kən trib′yoo tər), *n.* a person or thing that contributes.

con·trib·u·to·ry (kən trib′yoo tôr′ē), *adj.* having a part in bringing something about; contributing [*contributory* factors to a victory].

con·trite (kən trīt′ *or* kän′trīt), *adj.* **1.** feeling very sorry for having done something bad. **2.** showing such feeling [a *contrite* apology]. —**con·tri·tion** (kən trish′ən), *n.*

con·triv·ance (kən trīv′əns), *n.* **1.** the act or a way of contriving. **2.** something contrived, as an invention, a device, a plan, etc.

con·trive (kən trīv′), *v.* **1.** to think up; scheme; plan [We must *contrive* a way to help her.] **2.** to invent or design [He *contrived* a new kind of car.] **3.** to bring about or manage in some way [I'll *contrive* to meet you there.] —**con·trived′,** *p.t. & p.p.;* **con·triv′ing,** *pr.p.*

con·trol (kən trōl′), *v.* **1.** to have the power of ruling, guiding, or managing [The secretary of state *controls* the foreign affairs of the nation.] **2.** to hold back; curb [*Control* your temper!] —*n.* **1.** power to direct or manage [She has no *control* over her children.] **2.** a holding back; restraint [The truck went out of *control* on the hill.] **3.** a part or thing that controls a machine [the *controls* of an airplane]. —**con·trolled′,** *p.t. & p.p.;* **con·trol′ling,** *pr.p.* —**con·trol′la·ble,** *adj.*

con·trol·ler (kən trōl′ər), *n.* **1.** a person in charge of spending, as for a company or government: also spelled **comptroller.** **2.** a person or thing that controls.

con·tro·ver·sial (kän′trə vur′shəl), *adj.* that is or can be much argued about; debatable [a *controversial* book]. —**con′tro·ver′sial·ly,** *adv.*

con·tro·ver·sy (kän′trə vur′sē), *n.* argument or debate. —**con′tro·ver′sies,** *pl.*

con·tro·vert (kän′trə vərt), *v.* **1.** to argue against; deny. **2.** to argue about; debate.

con·tu·ma·cious (kän′too mā′shəs *or* kän′tyoo-mā′shəs), *adj.* disobeying or rebelling in a stubborn way. —**con·tu·ma·cy** (kän′too mə sē *or* kän′tyoo mə sē), *n.*

con·tu·me·ly (kän′too mə lē *or* kän′tyoo mə lē), *n.* **1.** insulting acts or words; scorn. **2.** a scornful insult. —**con′tu·me·lies,** *pl.*

con·tu·sion (kən tōo′zhən), *n.* a bruise; injury in which the skin is not broken.

co·nun·drum (kə nun′drəm), *n.* a riddle whose answer is a pun. Example: "What is the difference between a jeweler and a jailer?" "One sells watches and the other watches cells."

con·va·lesce (kän və les′), *v.* to get back health and strength after an illness. —**con·va·lesced′,** *p.t. & p.p.;* **con·va·lesc′ing,** *pr.p.*

con·va·les·cence (kän′və les′′ns), *n.* the act or time of convalescing.

con·va·les·cent (kän′və les′′nt), *adj.* getting back health and strength after illness. —*n.* a convalescent person.

con·vec·tion (kən vek′shən), *n.* a carrying or passing along, as of heat in air, gas, or liquid currents [In a house heated by *convection*, hot air or water moves through pipes from the furnace to the rooms.]

con·vene (kən vēn′), *v.* to come or call together for a meeting; assemble [Congress regularly *convenes* in January. In a crisis, the President can *convene* Congress for a special session.] —**con·vened′,** *p.t. & p.p.;* **con·ven′ing,** *pr.p.*

con·ven·ience (kən vēn′yəns), *n.* **1.** a being convenient or making things easier [He lives near his store for the sake of *convenience*.] **2.** personal comfort or advantage [This telephone is for the *convenience* of customers.] **3.** anything that adds to one's comfort or saves work [vacuum cleaners, refrigerators, and other modern *conveniences*]. —**at one's convenience,** at a time or in a way that suits one.

con·ven·ient (kən vēn′yənt), *adj.* adding to one's comfort; making things easier; causing little trouble or work [a *convenient* place for a meeting]. —**con·ven′ient·ly,** *adv.*

con·vent (kän′vent), *n.* a group of nuns living together under strict religious vows, or the place where they live.

con·ven·tion (kən ven′shən), *n.* **1.** a meeting of members or delegates from various places, held every year or every few years [the State *conven-*

tion of a political party; a national *convention* of English teachers]. **2.** an agreement between persons or nations. **3.** a custom or way of doing something that most people follow [It is a *convention* to say "How do you do?" on being introduced to someone.]

con·ven·tion·al (kən ven′shən 'l), *adj.* **1.** that is a convention or custom; usual or customary ["Yours truly" is a *conventional* closing to a letter.] **2.** behaving in the way that most people do or in ways that most people approve of [a *conventional* person]. **3.** according to fixed rules and customs; not original; formal [a *conventional* painting of fruit arranged on a table]. —**con·ven′tion·al·ly,** *adv.*

con·ven·tion·al·i·ty (kən ven′shən al′ə tē), *n.* **1.** the quality of being conventional. **2.** a conventional form, rule, or way of doing things. —**con·ven′tion·al′i·ties,** *pl.*

con·verge (kən vûrj′), *v.* to bring, come, or seem to come together at a point; move toward the same place [Railroad tracks *converge* as they move off into the distance. The crowds *converged* on the stadium.] —**con·verged′,** *p.t. & p.p.;* **con·verg′ing,** *pr.p.*

fences converging

con·ver·gence (kən vûr′jəns), *n.* a converging or the point at which things converge. —**con·ver′gent,** *adj.*

con·ver·sant (kən vûr′s'nt *or* kän′vər s'nt), *adj.* knowing about through study or experience; familiar or acquainted [People can now become *conversant* with great music through records.]

con·ver·sa·tion (kän′vər sā′shən), *n.* a talk or a talking together.

con·ver·sa·tion·al (kän′vər sā′shən 'l), *adj.* **1.** of, for, or like conversation [His writing has a *conversational* style.] **2.** fond of conversation; liking to talk with others.

con·verse (kən vûrs′), *v.* to talk; have a conversation. —*n.* (kän′vərs), talk; conversation. —**con·versed′,** *p.t. & p.p.;* **con·vers′ing,** *pr.p.*

con·verse (kän′vərs), *adj.* turned about; opposite or contrary. —*n.* the opposite ["Wet" is the *converse* of "dry."] —**con·verse′ly,** *adv.*

con·ver·sion (kən vûr′zhən), *n.* **1.** a converting or being converted; change [An atomic explosion is based on the *conversion* of matter into energy.] **2.** a change from one belief or religion to another.

con·vert (kən vûrt′), *v.* **1.** to change from one form or use to another; transform [The mill *converts* grain into flour.] **2.** to change from one belief or religion to another [Missionaries tried to *convert* them to Christianity.] **3.** to exchange for something of equal value [She *converted* her cash into jewels.] **4.** to score an extra point or points after a touchdown in football. —*n.* (kän′vərt), a person who has changed from one religion or belief to another. —**con·vert′er,** *n.*

con·vert·i·ble (kən vûr′tə b'l), *adj.* that can be converted [Matter is *convertible* into energy.] —*n.* an automobile with a top that can be folded back.

con·vex (kän′veks *or* kän veks′), *adj.* curving outward like the outside of a ball [a *convex* lens]. —**con·vex′i·ty,** *n.* —**con·vex′ly,** *adv.*

convex lenses

con·vey (kən vā′), *v.* **1.** to take from one place to another; carry or transport [The cattle were *conveyed* in trucks to market.] **2.** to be the means through which something moves or flows; transmit [The chimney *conveys* the smoke to the outside.] **3.** to make known; give [Did you *convey* my message to him?] **4.** to hand over, as land, from one owner to another.

con·vey·ance (kən vā′əns), *n.* **1.** the act of conveying. **2.** anything used for conveying, as an automobile or truck.

con·vey·er *or* **con·vey·or** (kən vā′ər), *n.* a person or thing that conveys; especially, a moving endless chain or belt (called, in full, **conveyer belt**).

con·vict (kən vikt′), *v.* to judge and find guilty, as in a court trial [The jury *convicted* him of robbery.] —*n.* (kän′vikt), a person found guilty of a crime, especially one who is serving a sentence in prison.

con·vic·tion (kən vik′shən), *n.* **1.** a convicting or being convicted of a crime. **2.** a fixed idea or strong belief [No one could shake her *conviction* that he was innocent.]

con·vince (kən vins′), *v.* to make feel sure; persuade [I'm *convinced* you're right.] —**con·vinced′,** *p.t. & p.p.;* **con·vinc′ing,** *pr.p.*

con·vinc·ing (kən vin′sing), *adj.* causing one to feel sure or to agree [*convincing* reasons].

con·viv·i·al (kən viv′i əl), *adj.* enjoying a good time, as at parties; loving fun; sociable.

con·vo·ca·tion (kän′və kā′shən), *n.* a meeting called for some purpose; assembly.

con·voke (kən vōk′), *v.* to call together for a meeting. —**con·voked′,** *p.t. & p.p.;* **con·vok′ing,** *pr.p.*

con·vo·lu·tion (kän′və loo′shən), *n.* **1.** a twisting or coiling together. **2.** a twist, coil, or fold [The surface of the brain has *convolutions*.]

con·voy (kän′voi′), *v.* to go along with as an escort or in order to protect [Two destroyers *convoyed* the oil tanker.] —*n.* (kän′voi), **1.** a convoying or being convoyed. **2.** a group of ships, vehicles, etc. traveling together, as in order to protect one another.

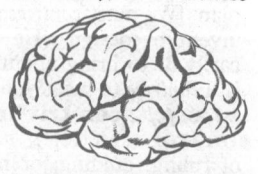
convolutions of the brain

con·vulse (kən vuls′), *v.* **1.** to shake or disturb violently and suddenly [The building was *convulsed* by an explosion.] **2.** to cause to shake or twitch [*convulsed* with laughter; *convulsed* with pain]. —**con·vulsed′,** *p.t. & p.p.;* **con·vuls′ing,** *pr.p.*

con·vul·sion (kən vul′shən), *n.* **1.** a sudden, sharp tightening or twitching of the muscles, as in certain diseases. **2.** any strong disturbance, as an earthquake or a riot.

con·vul·sive (kən vul′siv), *adj.* convulsing or like a convulsion [*convulsive* laughter].

co·ny (kō′nē), *n.* **1.** a rabbit. **2.** rabbit fur. —**co′nies,** *pl.*

coo (kōō), *n.* the soft, murmuring sound made by doves and pigeons. —*v.* **1.** to make this sound. **2.** to speak or say in a soft, loving way.

cook (kook), *v.* **1.** to prepare food by heating; boil, roast, bake, etc. **2.** to be cooked [The roast should *cook* longer.] —*n.* a person who prepares food for eating. —**cook up,** to think up, as a scheme: *used only in everyday talk.*

cook·er (kook′ər), *n.* something in which food is cooked, as a stove or pot [pressure *cooker*].

cook·er·y (kook′ər ē), *n.* the art of cooking.

cook·y or **cook·ie** (kook′ē), *n.* a small, flat, sweet cake. —**cook′ies,** *pl.*

cool (kōōl), *adj.* **1.** a little cold; not warm but not very cold [The days grow *cool* in October.] **2.** not too hot; comfortable [*cool* clothes; a *cool* place to sleep]. **3.** calm; not excited [Keep *cool* in an emergency.] **4.** not friendly or interested; showing dislike [a *cool* manner]. **5.** all of; no less than: *used only in everyday talk* [He won a *cool* thousand dollars.] **6.** that does not suggest warmth [Gray, green, and blue are *cool* colors.] —*n.* a place, time, etc. that is cool [the *cool* of the night]. —*v.* **1.** to become cool [The soup is *cooling*.] **2.** to make cool [He blew on the soup to *cool* it.] —**cool′ly,** *adv.* —**cool′ness,** *n.*

cool·er (kōōl′ər), *n.* a box or room in which things are cooled or kept cool [a meat *cooler*].

Coo·lidge, Calvin (kōō′lij), 1872–1933; 30th president of the United States (1923–1929).

coo·lie (kōō′lē), *n.* an unskilled worker, especially formerly, in India, China, Burma, etc.

coon (kōōn), *n.* a raccoon.

coop (kōōp), *n.* a cage or pen for fowl or small animals. —*v.* to shut up in a coop or small space [He felt *cooped* up in the cabin.]

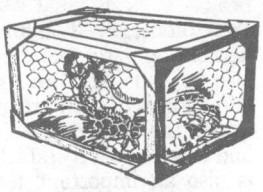

chicken coop

co-op or **co·öp** (kō′äp), *n.* a co-operative store, group, etc.: *used only in everyday talk.*

coop·er (kōōp′ər), *n.* a person who makes or repairs barrels and casks.

Coop·er, James Fen·i·more (fen′ə môr kōō′pər), 1789–1851; American writer of novels.

co-op·er·ate (kō äp′ər āt), *v.* to work together to get something done [If we all *co-operate*, we can finish the job in a week.] Also written **cooperate.** —**co-op′er·at·ed,** *p.t. & p.p.;* **co-op′er·at·ing,** *pr.p.* —**co-op′er·a′tion** or **co-op′er·a′tion,** *n.*

co-op·er·a·tive (kō äp′ər ā′tiv *or* kō äp′rə tiv), *adj.* **1.** willing to co-operate; helpful. **2.** that is or belongs to a group whose members produce goods together or sell them and share the profits [The farmers of this area started a *co-operative* store.] —*n.* such a group, store, etc. Also written **cooperative.**

co-or·di·nate (kō ôr′də nit), *adj.* of equal importance. —*v.* (kō ôr′də nāt), to bring together in the proper relation; make work together well [By *co-ordinating* our efforts, we moved the piano.] Also written **coordinate.** —**co-or′di·nat·ed,** *p.t. & p.p.;* **co-or′di·nat·ing,** *pr.p.*

co-or·di·na·tion (kō ôr′də nā′shən), *n.* a being co-ordinated, or working together smoothly [*Co-ordination* of both hands is important in playing the piano.] Also written **coordination.**

coot (kōōt), *n.* a water bird with webbed feet, that swims and dives like a duck.

cop (käp), *n.* a policeman: *a slang word.*

cope (kōp), *v.* to be able to manage in a struggle; take care of successfully [She was able to *cope* with the unruly children.] —**coped,** *p.t. & p.p.;* **cop′ing,** *pr.p.*

coot (16 in. long)

Co·pen·ha·gen (kō′pən hā′gən), *n.* a seaport and the capital of Denmark.

Co·per·ni·cus, Nic·o·la·us (nik′ə lā′əs kō·pūr′ni kəs), 1473–1543; Polish astronomer, who taught that the planets move around the sun.

co·pi·lot (kō′pī lət), *n.* the assistant pilot of an aircraft.

cop·ing (kōp′ing), *n.* the sloping top layer of a stone or brick wall.

coping saw, a saw with a narrow blade for cutting curves in wood.

coping saw

co·pi·ous (kō′pi əs), *adj.* more than enough; plentiful [*copious* praise]. —**co′pi·ous·ly,** *adv.*

cop·per (käp′ər), *n.* **1.** a reddish-brown metal that is a chemical element. Copper is easily beaten or stretched into various shapes, and it is a good conductor of heat and electricity. **2.** something made of copper or of a copper alloy, as a penny. **3.** reddish brown.

cop·per·head (käp′ər hed), *n.* a poisonous snake of North America, that has a copper-colored head.

cop·pice (käp′is), *n.* same as **copse.**

cop·ra (käp′rə), *n.* dried coconut meat.

copse (käps), *n.* a number of small trees and shrubs growing thickly; thicket.

copperhead (2 ft. long)

cop·y (käp′ē), *n.* **1.** a thing made just like another; imitation or likeness [a *copy* of a statue; a *copy* of a letter]. **2.** any one of a number of books, magazines, pictures, etc. printed from the same plates [Our library has five *copies* of this book.] **3.** something to be used as a model or pattern [His handwriting makes a good *copy* for us to practice.] **4.** a piece of writing that is to be set in type for printing [Reporters must write clear *copy*.] —*v.* **1.** to make a copy or copies of [*Copy* the questions on the blackboard.] **2.** to act or be the same as; imitate. —**cop′ies,** *pl.* —**cop′ied,** *p.t. & p.p.;* **cop′y·ing,** *pr.p.*

cop·y·cat (käp′ē kat′), *n.* a person who copies or imitates others: *a child's word.*

cop·y·right (käp′ē rīt′), *n.* the only legal right to publish, produce, or sell a particular piece of writing, art, or music. In the U.S., a copyright lasts for 28 years, but may be renewed once for another 28 years. —*v.* to protect by copyright [Books are not *copyrighted* until they are published.]

co·quette (kō ket′), *n.* a vain girl or woman who tries to get men to notice and admire her; flirt. —**co·quet′tish,** *adj.*

cor·a·cle (kôr′ə k'l), *n.* a short, wide boat made of a wooden frame covered with an animal skin or other waterproof material.

cor·al (kôr′əl), *n.* **1.** a hard, stony substance made up of the skeletons of many tiny sea animals. Reefs of coral are found in tropical seas. **2.** a piece of coral, especially a red kind used in jewelry. **3.** a yellowish red. —*adj.* **1.** made of coral. **2.** yellowish-red in color.

coral

cord (kôrd), *n.* **1.** a thick string or thin rope. **2.** any part of the body that is like a cord [the spinal *cord;* vocal *cords*]. **3.** a wire or wires covered with rubber or other insulation and used to carry electricity from an outlet to a lamp, machine, etc. **4.** a rib on certain kinds of cloth, as on corduroy; also, such a cloth. **5.** a measure of cut firewood. A cord is a pile 8 feet long, 4 feet wide, and 4 feet high. —*v.* **1.** to fasten or provide with a cord or cords. **2.** to pile up firewood in cords.

cord·age (kôr′dij), *n.* cords and ropes, especially the ropes in a ship's rigging.

cor·dial (kôr′jəl), *adj.* deeply felt; hearty; sincere [a *cordial* welcome]. —*n.* a sirupy alcoholic drink. —**cor′dial·ly,** *adv.*

cor·dial·i·ty (kôr′ji al′ə tē *or* kôr jal′ə tē), *n.* cordial quality; warm, friendly feeling.

cor·don (kôr′d'n), *n.* a line or circle, as of policemen, soldiers, or ships, placed around an area to guard it.

cor·do·van (kôr′də vən), *n.* a soft, colored leather, usually of sheepskin or horsehide.

cor·du·roy (kôr′də roi), *n.* **1.** a heavy cotton cloth having a surface like velvet with raised ribs, or ridges. **2. corduroys,** *pl.* trousers made of this cloth. —*adj.* **1.** of or like corduroy. **2.** made of logs laid crosswise [a *corduroy* road].

cord·wood (kôrd′wood), *n.* firewood sold in cords.

core (kôr), *n.* **1.** the hard center of some fruits, as the apple or pear, containing the seeds. **2.** the central or innermost part of anything. **3.** the most important part [the *core* of a problem]. —*v.* to cut out the core of a fruit. —**cored,** *p.t. & p.p.;* **cor′ing,** *pr.p.*

Cor·inth (kôr′inth), *n.* an ancient city in Greece.

Co·rin·thi·an (kə rin′thi ən), *adj.* **1.** of Corinth. **2.** of a highly decorated style of ancient Greek architecture.

Co·rin·thi·ans (kə rin′thi ənz), *n.* either of two books of the New Testament, letters from Paul to the Christians of Corinth.

cork (kôrk), *n.* **1.** the thick outer bark of a certain tree of the oak family that grows in the Mediterranean area. Cork is very light and tough and is used for various purposes. **2.** a piece of cork, especially one used as a stopper for a bottle or cask. **3.** a stopper made of any material, as of glass or rubber. —*v.* to stop or shut up, as with a cork [to *cork* a bottle].

cork·screw (kôrk′skroo), *n.* a tool for pulling corks out of bottles.

corm (kôrm), *n.* an underground stem of certain plants, that looks like a bulb [The crocus grows from a *corm.*]

corkscrew

cor·mo·rant (kôr′mə rənt), *n.* a large sea bird with webbed toes and a long, hooked beak.

corn (kôrn), *n.* **1.** a kind of grain that grows in kernels on large ears; maize: also called **Indian corn.** Some kinds of corn are ground into meal. Others are cooked and eaten as a vegetable. Corn is also an important feed for livestock. **2.** any kind of grain [In England, *corn* usually means "wheat."] —*v.* to keep meat from spoiling by packing it in salt or soaking it in strong salt water.

cormorant
(3 ft. long)

corn (kôrn), *n.* a hard, thick, painful growth of skin on a toe, usually caused by rubbing or tightness of a shoe.

corn bread, bread made of corn meal.

corn·cob (kôrn′käb), *n.* the hard, woody part of an ear of corn, on which the kernels grow.

cor·ne·a (kôr′ni ə), *n.* the clear outer layer of the eyeball, covering the iris and pupil.

corned (kôrnd), *adj.* kept from spoiling by the use of salt or strong salt water [*corned* beef].

cor·ner (kôr′nər), *n.* **1.** the place where two lines or surfaces come together to form an angle. **2.** the space between such lines or surfaces [a lamp in the *corner* of a room]. **3.** the place where two streets meet. **4.** a place or region; quarter [the *corners* of the earth]. **5.** the act of buying up all or most of a certain stock or article of trade so as to raise its price [to have a *corner* in cotton]. —*v.* **1.** to put into a corner. **2.** to force into a corner, or into a difficult position from which it is hard to escape. **3.** to get a corner in some stock or article of trade. —*adj.* at, on, or in a corner. —**cut corners, 1.** to take a shorter route by going across corners. **2.** to cut down on expenses, time, labor, etc.

cor·ner·stone (kôr′nər stōn), *n.* **1.** a stone at the corner of a building; especially, such a stone laid at a ceremony that marks the beginning of building. **2.** the most important part; foundation [The Bill of Rights is often called the *cornerstone* of our liberties.]

cor·net (kôr net′), *n.* a musical instrument like a trumpet, but with a mellower tone.

corn·flow·er (kôrn′-flou′ər), *n.* same as **bachelor's-button.**

cor·nice (kôr′nis), *n.* a molding that sticks out along the top of an outside or inside wall.

cornet

Cor·nish (kôr′nish), *adj.* of Cornwall or its people. —*n.* the ancient Celtic language once spoken in Cornwall.

corn sirup, a sweet sirup made from cornstarch.

corn·starch (kôrn′stärch), *n.* a fine, starchy flour made from corn and used in cooking.

cor·nu·co·pi·a (kôr′nə kō′pi ə *or* kôr′nyoo kō′-pi ə), *n.* **1.** a goat's horn filled to overflowing with fruits, flowers, and grains. It is also called **the horn of plenty** and is used as a symbol of plenty in art, sculpture, etc. **2.** any container shaped like this.

cornucopia

Corn·wall (kôrn′wôl), *n.* a county in the southwestern tip of England.

Corn·wal·lis, Charles (kôrn wôl′is), 1738–1805; commander of the British forces during the American Revolution.

corn·y (kôr′nē), *adj.* old-fashioned, stale, or sentimental in a foolish way: *a slang word.*

co·rol·la (kə räl′ə), *n.* the petals of a flower.

cor·ol·lar·y (kôr′ə ler′ē), *n.* something that can be taken for granted once another thing has been proved or has become a fact [If two angles of a triangle are equal, it follows as a *corol-*

lary that two of its sides are equal.] —**cor′-ol·lar′ies,** *pl.*

co·ro·na (kə rō′nə), *n.* the ring of light seen around the sun during a total eclipse.

cor·o·nar·y throm·bo·sis (kôr′ə ner′ē thräm-bō′sis), the blocking by a blood clot of any branch of the two arteries (**coronary arteries**) that feed blood to the heart tissues.

cor·o·na·tion (kôr′ə nā′shən), *n.* the crowning of a king or queen.

cor·o·ner (kôr′ə nər), *n.* an official whose duty is to find out the cause of any death that does not seem to be due to natural causes.

cor·o·net (kôr′ə net), *n.* **1.** a small crown worn by princes and nobles of high rank. **2.** a band of jewels, flowers, etc. worn around the head.

Corp., abbreviation for **Corporal** or **Corporation.**

cor·po·ral (kôr′pər əl), *n.* a noncommissioned officer in the armed forces below a sergeant.

cor·po·ral (kôr′pər əl), *adj.* of the body; bodily [A whipping is *corporal* punishment.]

cor·po·rate (kôr′pər it), *adj.* **1.** united by law into one body, as a business; forming a corporation. **2.** of a corporation [*corporate* debts].

cor·po·ra·tion (kôr′pə rā′shən), *n.* a group of people who get a charter that gives the group some of the legal powers and rights that a single person has [Cities and colleges, as well as businesses, can be organized as *corporations.*]

cor·po·re·al (kôr pôr′i əl), *adj.* **1.** of, for, or like the body; bodily [*corporeal* appetites]. **2.** real or material [*corporeal* property].

corps (kôr), *n.* **1.** a section or a special branch of the armed forces [the Signal *Corps;* the Marine *Corps*]. **2.** a group of people working together under a leader [a diplomatic *corps*]. —**corps** (kôrz), *pl.*

corpse (kôrps), *n.* the dead body of a person.

cor·pu·lent (kôr′pyoo lənt), *adj.* fat and fleshy; stout in build. —**cor′pu·lence, n.**

cor·pus·cle (kôr′pəs 'l), *n.* any of the red cells or white cells that float in the blood [Red *corpuscles* carry oxygen to the body tissues. Certain white *corpuscles* kill harmful germs.]

cor·ral (kə ral′), *n.* **1.** a place fenced in for holding horses, cattle, sheep, etc. **2.** wagons drawn round in a circle for defending a camp —*v.* **1.** to round up or shut up, as in a corral. **2.** to form wagons into a corral. —**cor·ralled′,** *p.t. & p.p.;* **cor·ral′ling,** *pr.p.*

corral

cor·rect (kə rekt′), *v.* **1.** to make right; get rid of mistakes in [*Correct* your spelling before you turn in your papers.]

fat, āpe, cär, ten, ēven, hit, bīte, gō, hôrn, tōol, book, up, fûr;
get, joy, yet, chin, she, thin, *th*en; zh = s in pleasure; ' as in able (ā′b'l)
ə = a in ago, e in agent, i in sanity, o in confess, u in focus.

2. to point out the mistakes of; sometimes, to punish or scold for such mistakes [to *correct* a child's behavior]. —*adj.* **1.** without a mistake; right; true [a *correct* answer]. **2.** agreeing with what is considered proper [*correct* behavior]. —**cor·rect′ly,** *adv.* —**cor·rect′ness,** *n.*

cor·rec·tion (kə rek′shən), *n.* **1.** a correcting or being corrected. **2.** a change that corrects a mistake [Write your *corrections* in the margin.] **3.** punishment or scolding to correct faults.

cor·rec·tive (kə rek′tiv), *adj.* that corrects or is meant to correct [a *corrective* device].

cor·re·late (kôr′ə lāt), *v.* to bring things into proper relation with one another; connect related things [to *correlate* the results of several experiments]. —**cor′re·lat·ed,** *p.t. & p.p.;* **cor′re·lat·ing,** *pr.p.*

cor·re·la·tion (kôr′ə lā′shən), *n.* the relation or connection between things [the high *correlation* between ignorance and prejudice].

cor·rel·a·tive (kə rel′ə tiv), *adj.* having a relation with one another; especially, describing either of a pair of words that show such a relation [In "Neither John nor I will go," "neither" and "nor" are *correlative* conjunctions.]

cor·re·spond (kôr ə spänd′), *v.* **1.** to be in agreement with; match [His opinions *correspond* with mine.] **2.** to be the same as or equal to [A general in the army *corresponds* to an admiral in the navy.] **3.** to write letters to and receive letters from someone.

cor·re·spond·ence (kôr′ə spän′dəns), *n.* **1.** the fact of corresponding; agreement or sameness. **2.** the writing and receiving of letters [to engage in *correspondence*]. **3.** the letters written or received [the *correspondence* on the Acme contract].

cor·re·spond·ent (kôr′ə spän′dənt), *n.* **1.** a person with whom one exchanges letters. **2.** a person hired by a newspaper or magazine to send news regularly from a distant city or country.

cor·ri·dor (kôr′ə dər), *n.* a long hall or passageway, especially one into which rooms open.

cor·rob·o·rate (kə räb′ə rāt), *v.* to make more sure; add proof to; confirm [Two witnesses *corroborated* his story.] —**cor·rob′o·rat·ed,** *p.t. & p.p.;* **cor·rob′o·rat·ing,** *pr.p.* —**cor·rob′o·ra′tion,** *n.*

cor·rode (kə rōd′), *v.* to eat into or wear away slowly, as by the action of acid or rust. —**cor·rod′ed,** *p.t. & p.p.;* **cor·rod′ing,** *pr.p.* —**cor·ro·sion** (kə rō′zhən), *n.*

cor·ro·sive (kə rō′siv), *adj.* corroding or causing corrosion [a *corrosive* acid]. —*n.* something that corrodes things.

cor·ru·gate (kôr′ə gāt), *v.* to form ridges and furrows in so as to give a wavy surface [*corrugated* paper]. —**cor′ru·gat·ed,** *p.t. & p.p.;* **cor′ru·gat·ing,** *pr.p.* —**cor′ru·ga′tion,** *n.*

corrugated surface

cor·rupt (kə rupt′), *adj.* changed from good to bad; having become rotten, dishonest, impure, or the like [*corrupt* officials; *corrupt* business practices; a *corrupt* version of a writing]. —*v.* to make

or become corrupt; debase. —**cor·rupt′ly,** *adv.*

cor·rupt·i·ble (kə rup′tə b'l), *adj.* that can be corrupted.

cor·rup·tion (kə rup′shən), *n.* **1.** a change from good to bad. **2.** evil or wicked ways. **3.** bribery or other dishonest dealings [*corruption* in government]. **4.** decay or rottenness.

cor·sage (kôr säzh′), *n.* a small bunch of flowers for a woman to wear, usually at the waist or shoulder.

cor·sair (kôr′ser), *n.* **1.** a pirate. **2.** a pirate ship.

corse·let (kôrs′lit), *n.* a kind of armor once worn on the upper part of the body.

cor·set (kôr′sit), *n.* an undergarment that fits tightly around the waist and hips. It is worn, mainly by women, to support or shape the body.

Cor·si·ca (kôr′si kə), *n.* a French island in the Mediterranean Sea, southeast of France.

cor·tege or **cor·tège** (kôr tāzh′), *n.* **1.** a solemn parade or procession, as at a funeral. **2.** a number of followers or attendants; retinue.

Cor·tés or **Cor·tez, Her·nan·do** (hər nan′dō kôr tez′), 1485–1547; Spanish soldier who conquered Mexico.

cor·tex (kôr′teks), *n.* **1.** the layer of gray matter covering most of the brain. **2.** the bark of trees. —**cor·ti·ces** (kôr′ti sēz), *pl.* —**cor·ti·cal** (kôr′ti k'l), *adj.*

cos·met·ic (käz met′ik), *n.* any substance used to make the skin or hair beautiful [Hair lotion and lipstick are *cosmetics*.] —*adj.* for improving the looks; beautifying.

cos·mic (käz′mik), *adj.* **1.** having to do with the whole universe. **2.** huge; enormous; vast.

cosmic rays, strong atomic rays that keep striking the earth from outer space.

cos·mo·pol·i·tan (käz′mə päl′ə t'n), *adj.* **1.** having to do with the world as a whole. **2.** interested in and liking the people and cultures of all countries; feeling at home anywhere. —*n.* a cosmopolitan person.

cos·mos (käz′məs), *n.* **1.** the universe as a system with order. **2.** any whole system with order. **3.** a tall plant with slender leaves and white or colored flowers. It blooms in the fall.

Cos·sack (käs′ak), *n.* a member of a people of southern Russia, famous as horsemen.

cost (kôst), *v.* **1.** to be priced at; be sold for [It *costs* a dime.] **2.** to cause the giving up of; be gotten for [This small kindness will *cost* you little effort.] —*n.* **1.** amount of money, time, work, etc. asked or paid for something; price [the high *cost* of meat]. **2.** loss or sacrifice [staying up late at the *cost* of one's health]. **3. costs,** *pl.* expenses of a law trial, usually paid by the loser. —**at all costs** or **at any cost,** by any means needed. —**cost,** *p.t. & p.p.;* **cost′ing,** *pr.p.*

cosmos

Cos·ta Ri·ca (käs′tə rē′kə), a country in Central America. —**Cos′ta Ri′can.**

cos·ter·mon·ger (käs′tər mung′gər), *n.* a person who sells fruits, vegetables, etc. from a cart or street stand: *used mainly in England.*

cost·ly (kôst′lē), *adj.* costing much; expensive or valuable [a *costly* error; *costly* clothes]. —**cost′·li·er,** *compar.;* **cost′li·est,** *superl.* —**cost′li·ness,** *n.*

cost of living, the average cost of the necessities of life, as food, clothing, and shelter.

cos·tume (käs′tōōm *or* käs′tyōōm), *n.* **1.** the way or style of dressing of a certain place or time or for a certain purpose [a Japanese *costume;* an eighteenth-century *costume;* a riding *costume*]. **2.** clothing worn by an actor in a play or by a person at a masquerade [a pirate *costume*]. —*v.* to dress in a costume. —**cos′tumed,** *p.t. & p.p.;* **cos′tum·ing,** *pr.p.*

cos·tum·er (käs′tōōm ər *or* käs′tyōōm ər), *n.* a person who makes, sells, or rents costumes.

co·sy (kō′zē), *adj. & n.* cozy. —**co′si·er,** *compar.;* **co′si·est,** *superl.* —**co′sies,** *pl.*

cot (kät), *n.* a narrow bed, especially a folding bed with a wooden or metal frame.

cot (kät), *n.* **1.** a cottage: *used mainly in poetry.* **2.** a cote. **3.** a covering for a hurt finger.

cote (kōt), *n.* a small shelter for birds or farm animals [a dove *cote*].

folding cot

co·te·rie (kō′tər ē), *n.* a close circle of friends or fellow workers; clique.

cot·tage (kät′ij), *n.* a small house [a peasant's *cottage;* a summer *cottage* at the beach].

cottage cheese, a soft, white cheese made from the curds of sour milk.

cot·ter or **cot·tar** (kät′ər), *n.* a Scottish farmer who rents his land and cottage from a large landholder.

cotter pin, a split pin used to hold parts together. Its ends are spread apart after it is fitted into a slot or hole.

cot·ton (kät′'n), *n.* **1.** the soft, white fibers that grow around the seeds of a shrub called the **cotton plant. 2.** this plant. **3.** thread or cloth made of these fibers. —*adj.* of cotton [a *cotton* field; a *cotton* shirt].

cotton gin, a machine for pulling cotton fibers away from the seeds.

cot·ton·mouth (kät′'n mouth), *n.* the water moccasin, a poisonous snake of the southern U.S.

cot·ton·seed (kät′'n sēd), *n.* the seed of the cotton plant, from which an oil (**cottonseed oil**) is gotten for use in shortening, soap, etc.

cot·ton·tail (kät′'n tāl), *n.* the common American rabbit with a short, white, fluffy tail.

cot·ton·wood (kät′'n wood), *n.* **1.** a kind of poplar tree that has seeds covered with cottonlike

hairs. **2.** the wood of this tree or of any poplar.

cot·y·le·don (kät′'l ē′d'n), *n.* the first leaf, or either of the pair of first leaves, growing out of a seed.

couch (kouch), *n.* **1.** a piece of furniture for sitting or lying on; sofa. **2.** any resting place [A pile of hay was his *couch.*] —*v.* **1.** to lie or put on a couch. **2.** to bring down to a position for attacking [to *couch* a spear]. **3.** to put into words [His speech was *couched* in flowery language.]

cou·gar (kōō′gər), *n.* a large animal of the cat family, with a slender, tan body and a long tail: also called **puma, mountain lion.**

cougar (6 ft. long)

cough (kôf), *v.* **1.** to force air from the lungs with a sudden, loud noise, as to clear the throat. **2.** to get out of the throat by coughing [to *cough* up phlegm]. —*n.* **1.** the act or sound of coughing. **2.** a condition of coughing often [He has a bad *cough.*]

could (kood), past tense of **can** [At one time you *could* buy a hamburger for five cents.] *Could* is also used as a helping verb with about the same meaning as *can,* but showing less force or sureness [You *could* be right. I *could* do it tomorrow.]

couldn't (kood′'nt), could not.

couldst (koodst), the older form of **could,** used with *thou,* as in the Bible.

cou·lee (kōō′lē), *n.* **1.** a stream of lava. **2.** a deep ravine, usually dry in the summer.

coun·cil (koun′s'l), *n.* **1.** a group of people meeting together to plan or decide something or to give advice. **2.** a group of people elected to make the laws for a city or town.

coun·cil·man (koun′s'l mən), *n.* a member of a council, as of a city. —**coun′cil·men,** *pl.*

coun·ci·lor or **coun·cil·lor** (koun′s'l ər), *n.* a member of a council.

coun·sel (koun′s'l), *n.* **1.** a talking together in order to exchange ideas or opinions; discussion [Let us take *counsel* with each other.] **2.** advice or opinion [What is your *counsel* in this matter?] **3.** the lawyer or lawyers who are handling a case. —*v.* **1.** to give advice to; advise. **2.** to recommend. —**coun′seled** or **coun′selled,** *p.t. & p.p.;* **coun′sel·ing** or **coun′sel·ling,** *pr.p.*

coun·se·lor or **coun·sel·lor** (koun′s'l ər), *n.* **1.** a person who advises; adviser. **2.** a lawyer. **3.** a person in charge of children at a camp.

count (kount), *v.* **1.** to name numbers in a regular order [Can you *count* to ten in French?] **2.** to add up so as to get a total [*Count* the money in your pocket.] **3.** to take or be taken into account [There will be ten at dinner, *counting* the host and hostess. This practice game won't *count*.] **4.** to consider to be [I *count* myself lucky.] **5.** to be important; have value [Every bit of help *counts*.] —*n.* **1.** a counting or adding up. **2.** the total number counted. **3.** any of the crimes that a person is charged with [He was found guilty on two *counts*.] —**count off,** to separate into equal groups by counting [*Count off* by groups of four.] —**count on,** to depend on.

count (kount), *n.* a nobleman in some European countries.

coun·te·nance (koun′tə nəns), *n.* **1.** the look on a person's face that shows his nature or feelings [a noble *countenance*]. **2.** the face [A smile spread over his *countenance*.] **3.** approval or support [to give *countenance* to a plan]. —*v.* to approve or support [I will not *countenance* such rudeness.] —**coun′te·nanced,** *p.t. & p.p.;* **coun′te·nanc·ing,** *pr.p.*

count·er (koun′tər), *n.* **1.** a person or thing that counts. **2.** a small disk for keeping count, as in games. **3.** a long table in a store or restaurant for serving customers, showing goods, etc.

count·er (koun′tər), *adv.* in the opposite direction or way; contrary [I failed because I went *counter* to your advice.] —*adj.* being or acting in the opposite direction or way; contrary; opposed [a *counter* blow]. —*v.* to act or do counter to; oppose; give another in return [to *counter* one plan with another; to *counter* a punch in boxing].

counter-, a prefix meaning "opposite," "against," or "in return" [To *counteract* something is to act against it. A *counterattack* is an attack in return for another attack.]

coun·ter·act (koun tər akt′), *v.* to act against; stop or undo the effect of [The rains will help *counteract* the dry spell.]

coun·ter·at·tack (koun′tər ə tak′), *n.* an attack made in return for another attack. —*v.* to make a counterattack.

coun·ter·bal·ance (koun′tər bal′əns), *n.* a weight, power, force, etc. that balances or acts against another. —*v.* (koun′tər bal′əns), to be a counterbalance to. —**coun′ter·bal′anced,** *p.t. & p.p.;* **coun′ter·bal′anc·ing,** *pr.p.*

coun·ter·claim (koun′tər klām), *n.* an opposing claim in answer to a claim against one.

coun·ter·clock·wise (koun′tər kläk′wīz), *adj. & adv.* in a direction opposite to that in which the hands of a clock move. *See the picture.*

counterclockwise direction shown by arrows

coun·ter·feit (koun′tər fit), *adj.* made in imitation of the real thing so as to fool or cheat people [*counterfeit* money]. —*n.* a thing that is counterfeit. —*v.* **1.** to make an imitation of in order to cheat [to *counterfeit* money]. **2.** to pretend; feign [to *counterfeit* sorrow]. —**coun′ter·feit·er,** *n.*

coun·ter·mand (kount ər mand′), *v.* to take back a command by giving an opposite one.

coun·ter·pane (koun′tər pān), *n.* a bedspread.

coun·ter·part (koun′tər pärt), *n.* **1.** a person or thing that is very much like another [He is his father's *counterpart*.] **2.** a thing that goes with another thing to form a set [This cup is the *counterpart* to that saucer.]

coun·ter·point (koun′tər point), *n.* the art or way of putting two or more melodies together so that they fit together in harmony ["Swanee River" and "Humoresque" can be sung in *counterpoint*.]

coun·ter·poise (koun′tər poiz), *n.* **1.** a weight, power, or force that balances another. **2.** the condition of being in balance. —*v.* to be a counterpoise to. —**coun′ter·poised,** *p.t. & p.p.;* **coun′ter·pois·ing,** *pr.p.*

coun·ter·rev·o·lu·tion (koun′tər rev′ə lōō′-shən), *n.* a movement to overthrow a government set up by a revolution.

coun·ter·sign (koun′tər sīn), *n.* a secret signal or password that must be given to a guard or sentry. —*v.* to sign a paper already signed by someone else, in order to confirm it.

coun·ter·sink (koun′tər singk), *v.* **1.** to widen the top part of a hole for a bolt or screw so that the head will not stick out from the surface. **2.** to fit a bolt or screw into such a hole. —**coun·ter·sunk** (koun′tər sungk), *p.t. & p.p.;* **coun′ter·sink·ing,** *pr.p.*

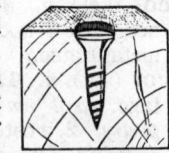

countersunk screw

count·ess (koun′tis), *n.* the wife or widow of a count or earl.

count·ing·house (koun′ting hous′), *n.* an office in which a business firm keeps its accounts.

count·less (kount′lis), *adj.* too many to be counted; innumerable [the *countless* stars].

coun·tri·fied (kun′tri fīd), *adj.* looking or acting like plain people from the country.

coun·try (kun′trē), *n.* **1.** an area of land; region [wooded *country*]. **2.** the whole land of a nation [The *country* of Japan is made up of islands.] **3.** the people of a nation [The speech was broadcast to the whole *country*.] **4.** the nation to which one belongs ["My *country*, 'tis of thee"]. **5.** land with farms and small towns; land outside of cities [Let's drive out to the *country*.] —*adj.* of, in, from, or like the country; rural ["To home" is *country* talk for "at home."] —**coun′tries,** *pl.*

coun·try·man (kun′trē mən), *n.* **1.** a man of one's own country. **2.** a man who lives in the country, as on a farm. —**coun′try·men,** *pl.*

coun·try·side (kun′trē sīd), *n.* the country (*meaning 5*) or people who live in the country.

coun·ty (koun′tē), *n.* **1.** in the United States, any of the sections into which a State is divided. Each county has its own officials. **2.** any of the districts into which Great Britain is divided. **3.** the people of a county. —**coun′ties,** *pl.*

coup (kōō), *n.* a sudden, bold, and clever move that brings about some striking change, as in a government. —**coups** (kōōz), *pl.*

coupe (kōōp *or, sometimes,* kōō pā′), *n.* an automobile with two doors and a closed body that is smaller than that of a sedan.

cou·pé (kōō pā′), *n.* **1.** a closed carriage that seats two riders and has a raised seat outside for the driver. **2.** a coupe.

cou·ple (kup′'l), *n.* **1.** two things of the same kind that go together; pair [A *couple* of book ends held the books in place.] **2.** a man and woman who are married or engaged or who are partners as in a dance or game. **3.** a few; several: *used only in everyday talk.* —*v.* to join together; unite; connect; pair [Hard work *coupled* with good luck made him a rich man.] —**cou′pled,** *p.t. & p.p.;* **cou′pling,** *pr.p.*

cou·plet (kup′lit), *n.* two lines of poetry that go together and are usually rhymed. Example:

O, what may man within him hide,
Though angel on the outward side!

cou·pling (kup′ling), *n.* **1.** the act of joining together. **2.** a device for joining parts or things together [a *coupling* for cars in a railroad train; a *coupling* for pipes].

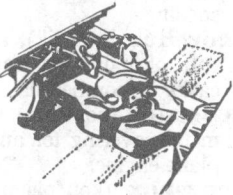

railroad-car coupling

cou·pon (kōō′pän *or* kyōō′pän), *n.* **1.** a ticket or part of a ticket that gives the holder certain rights [The *coupon* on this bar of soap is worth 10c toward the purchase of another bar.] **2.** a part of a bond which is cut off at certain times and turned in for payment of interest.

cour·age (kur′ij), *n.* a being able to control one's fear and so to face danger, pain, or trouble willingly; bravery.

cou·ra·geous (kə rā′jəs), *adj.* having or showing courage; brave. —**cou·ra′geous·ly,** *adv.*

cou·ri·er (koor′i ər *or* kur′i ər), *n.* a messenger sent in a hurry with an important message.

course (kôrs), *n.* **1.** a going on from one point to the next; progress in space or time [the *course* of history; the *course* of a journey; in the *course* of a week]. **2.** a way or path along which something moves; channel, track, etc. [a golf *course;* race*course*]. **3.** the direction taken [His *course* was directly south.] **4.** a way of acting or proceeding [The law must take its *course.*] **5.** a number of like things in regular order; series [a *course* of exercises to build the muscles]. **6.** a part of a meal served at one time [The main *course* was roast beef.] **7.** a complete series of studies [He took a business *course* in high school.] **8.** any of these studies [an algebra *course*]. **9.** a single row of bricks or stones in a wall. —*v.* to run; race through or after [blood *coursing* through the veins; hounds *coursing* rabbits]. —**a matter of course,** a regular or natural thing. —**in the course of,** during. —**of course, 1.** as one expects; naturally. **2.** without doubt; certainly. —**coursed,** *p.t. & p.p.;* **cours′ing,** *pr.p.*

cours·er (kôr′sər), *n.* a swift, graceful horse: *used mainly in poetry.*

court (kôrt), *n.* **1.** an open space with buildings or walls around it; courtyard. **2.** a short street, often closed at one end. **3.** a space marked out for playing some game [a basketball *court;* a handball *court*]. **4.** the palace of a king or other ruler. **5.** the family, advisers, and attendants who gather at a ruler's court. **6.** a formal meeting held by a ruler. **7.** courtship. **8.** a person or persons who examine and decide cases of law; judge or judges. **9.** a place where law trials are held. **10.** a meeting of all the persons who are to seek justice in a case of law, including the judge or judges, the lawyers, and the jury [The *court* will convene at nine tomorrow morning.] —*v.* **1.** to pay attention to or try to please in order to get something [Politicians usually *court* the voters before an election.] **2.** to try to get the love of in order to marry; woo [He's been *courting* her for five years.] **3.** to try to get or seem to be trying to get [to *court* praise; to *court* danger].

cour·te·ous (kur′ti əs), *adj.* polite and kind; thoughtful of others. —**cour′te·ous·ly,** *adv.*

cour·te·sy (kur′tə sē), *n.* **1.** courteous or polite behavior; good manners [Thank you for your *courtesy* in writing to me.] **2.** a polite act or remark. —**cour′te·sies,** *pl.*

court·house (kôrt′hous), *n.* **1.** a building in which law courts are held. **2.** a building that contains the offices of a county government.

cour·ti·er (kôr′ti ər), *n.* **1.** any of the attendants or other persons who gather in a ruler's court. **2.** a person who flatters or tries too hard to please in order to get something.

court·ly (kôrt′lē), *adj.* polite and dignified in a way thought proper for a ruler's court [a *courtly* knight]. —**court′li·ness,** *n.*

court-mar·tial (kôrt′mär′shəl), *n.* **1.** a court of military or naval officers for the trial of persons accused of breaking military law. **2.** a trial by such a court. —*v.* to try by a court-martial. —**courts′-mar′tial** *or, for meaning 2,* **court′-mar′tials,** *pl.* —**court′-mar′tialed,** *p.t. & p.p.;* **court′-mar′tial·ing,** *pr.p.*

court·room (kôrt′rōōm), *n.* a room in which a law court is held.

court·ship (kôrt′ship), *n.* the courting of a woman in order to marry her.

court·yard (kôrt′yärd), *n.* an open space with buildings or walls around it.

cous·in (kuz′'n), *n.* **1.** the son or daughter of one's uncle or aunt: also called **first cous·in.** You are a *second cousin* to the children of your parents' first cousins, and you are a *first cousin once removed* to the children of your first cousins. **2.** a distant relation.

courtyard

cove (kōv), *n.* a small, sheltered bay.

cov·e·nant (kuv′ə nənt), *n.* a serious agreement between persons, groups, or nations. —*v.* to make such an agreement.

Cov·en·try (kuv′ən trē), *n.* a city in central England. —**send to Coventry,** to refuse to have anything to do with.

cov·er (kuv′ər), *v.* **1.** to place one thing over another; spread over [*Cover* the bird cage at night. *Cover* the wall with white paint. Water *covered* the fields.] **2.** to hide; keep from being seen [He tried to *cover* up his mistake.] **3.** to protect, as from harm or loss. **4.** to provide for; take care of [Is this case *covered* by the rules?] **5.** to have to do with; be about; include [His talk *covered* his travels in Europe.] **6.** to go; travel [The camel *covered* 65 miles that day.] **7.** to keep a gun aimed at [*Cover* him while I call the police.] **8.** to get the news or pictures of: *used by newspapermen* [He *covers* the police court.] **9.** to guard or defend: *used in sports* [*Cover* first base.] —*n.* **1.** anything that covers, as a lid, a blanket, the binding of a book, etc. **2.** anything that hides or protects [under *cover* of darkness]. —**take cover,** to seek shelter.

cov·er·age (kuv′ər ij), *n.* the amount or extent covered by something.

cov·er·alls (kuv′ər ôlz), *n.pl.* a one-piece work garment with sleeves and legs, worn by mechanics, etc.

covered wagon, a large wagon with an arched cover of canvas, used in pioneer days.

cov·er·ing (kuv′ər ing), *n.* anything that covers.

cov·er·let (kuv′ər lit), *n.* a bedspread.

coveralls

cov·ert (kuv′ərt), *adj.* done in a hidden or secret way [a *covert* look at his neighbor's work]. —*n.* a sheltered place; especially, underbrush where animals can hide. —**cov′ert·ly,** *adv.*

cov·et (kuv′ət), *v.* to want greedily something belonging to another ["Thou shalt not *covet* thy neighbor's house . . ."]

cov·et·ous (kuv′ə təs), *adj.* wanting greedily what belongs to another. —**cov′et·ous·ly,** *adv.*

cov·ey (kuv′ē), *n.* **1.** a small flock of birds, especially partridges or quail. **2.** a small group of people. —**cov′eys,** *pl.*

cow (kou), *n.* **1.** the full-grown female of any animal of the ox family; especially, the common farm animal kept for its milk. **2.** the female elephant, seal, whale, etc.

cow (kou), *v.* to make afraid or meek.

cow·ard (kou′ərd), *n.* a person who is unable to control his fear and so shrinks from danger or trouble.

cow·ard·ice (kou′ər dis), *n.* the way a coward acts or feels; lack of courage.

cow·ard·ly (kou′ərd lē), *adj.* of or like a coward. —*adv.* in the manner of a coward.

cow·bird (kou′bŭrd), *n.* a small blackbird that often lays its eggs in other birds' nests.

cow·boy (kou′boi), *n.* **1.** a ranch worker who

herds or tends cattle: also **cow′hand. 2.** in stories, movies, etc., any Western character who rides a horse and carries a gun.

cow·er (kou′ər), *v.* to bend over or tremble, as from fear or cold; crouch or cringe.

cow·herd (kou′hŭrd), *n.* a person whose work is herding cattle at pasture.

cow·hide (kou′hīd), *n.* **1.** the hide of a cow. **2.** leather made from it. **3.** a whip made from this leather, often a braided whip.

cowl (koul), *n.* **1.** a monk's hood, usually fastened to the back of a cloak. **2.** the part of an automobile body between the hood and the windshield. **3.** a cowling.

monk's cowl

cow·lick (kou′lik), *n.* a tuft of hair that cannot easily be combed flat.

cowl·ing (koul′ing), *n.* a metal covering for an airplane engine.

cow·pox (kou′päks), *n.* a disease of cows. People are vaccinated with a mild virus of cowpox to keep them from getting smallpox.

cow·punch·er (kou′pun′chər), *n.* a cowboy: *used only in everyday talk.*

cow·slip (kou′slip), *n.* a wild flower with yellow blossoms.

cox·comb (käks′kōm), *n.* a vain, conceited man who keeps showing off his clothes and looks.

cox·swain (käk′s'n *or* käk′swān), *n.* the man who steers a boat, especially a racing shell.

coy (koi), *adj.* shy or bashful, or pretending to be so, often in a flirting way. —**coy′ly,** *adv.*

coy·ote (kī′ōt *or* kī ō′tē), *n.* a small wolf of the prairies of western North America.

coz·en (kuz′'n), *v.* to cheat or fool. —**coz′en·age,** *n.*

co·zy (kō′zē), *adj.* warm and comfortable; snug [It was *cozy* sitting around the campfire.] —*n.* a padded cover for a teapot, to keep the tea hot. —**co′zi·er,** *compar.;* **co′zi·est,** *superl.* —**co′zies,** *pl.* —**co′zi·ly,** *adv.*

coyote (4 ft. long)

C.P.A. or **c.p.a.,** abbreviation for **Certified Public Accountant.**

Cpl., an abbreviation for **Corporal.**

Cr, symbol for the chemical element *chromium.*

crab (krab), *n.* a broad, flat shellfish with four pairs of legs and a pair of claws. Some kinds are used as food.

crab (krab), *n.* **1.** a crab apple. **2.** a person who is always cross and complaining. —*v.* to complain or find fault: *used only in everyday talk* [The soldiers

crab (shell about 4 in. wide)

crabbed about the food.] —**crabbed,** *p.t. &
p.p.;* **crab′bing,** *pr.p.*

crab apple, 1. a small, very sour apple, used
for making jellies and preserves. **2.** the tree it
grows on.

crab·bed (krab′id), *adj.* **1.** crabby. **2.** hard
to read or make out [*crabbed* handwriting].

crab·by (krab′ē), *adj.* cross and complaining;
hard to please. —**crab′bi·er,** *compar.;* **crab′-
bi·est,** *superl.* —**crab′bi·ly,** *adv.*

crab grass, a coarse grass that spreads quickly
and can spoil the looks of a lawn.

crack (krak), *v.* **1.** to make or cause to make a
sudden, sharp noise, as of something breaking
[Thunder rolled and lightning *cracked.*] **2.** to
break or split, with or without the parts falling
apart [The snowball *cracked* the window. *Crack*
the coconut open.] **3.** to become harsh or change
pitch suddenly [Her voice *cracked* when she sang
the highest note.] **4.** to hit with a sudden, sharp
blow: *used only in everyday talk* [I *cracked* my
knee against the desk.] **5.** to break down; lose
control of oneself: *slang in this meaning* [He
cracked under the strain.] **6.** to break into: *slang
in this meaning* [The burglar *cracked* the safe.]
7. to say in a joking or mocking way: *slang in
this meaning.* —*n.* **1.** a sudden, sharp noise, as of
something breaking [the *crack* of a whip]. **2.** a
break, usually with the parts still holding together [a *crack* in a cup]. **3.** a narrow opening;
crevice [The cat slipped through a *crack* in the
fence.] **4.** a loud, hard blow: *used only in everyday
talk* [a *crack* on the head]. **5.** a try: *slang in this
meaning* [Let me have a *crack* at that problem.]
6. a joking or mocking remark: *slang in this
meaning.* —*adj.* excellent; first-rate: *used only
in everyday talk* [a *crack* athlete]. —**crack
down on,** to become strict or stricter with:
used only in everyday talk. —**cracked up to be,**
thought or said to be: *used only in everyday talk.*

cracked (krakt), *adj.* **1.** having cracks in it.
2. sounding harsh [a *cracked* voice]. **3.** crazy;
insane: *used only in everyday talk.*

crack·er (krak′ər), *n.* **1.** a thin, crisp biscuit
made of dough that has not been raised; wafer.
2. a firecracker.

crack·le (krak′'l), *v.* to make sharp, snapping
sounds [The dry wood *crackled* as it
burned.] —*n.* **1.** a number of such
sounds. **2.** fine, irregular cracks on
the surface of some kinds of pottery,
china, etc. —**crack′led,** *p.t. &
p.p.;* **crack′ling,** *pr.p.*

crack·ling (krak′ling), *n.* **1.** a series of sharp, snapping sounds. **2.**
the crisp rind of roast pork.

crack-up (krak′up′), *n.* **1.** a crash.
2. a breakdown of body or mind.

-cra·cy (krə sē), a suffix meaning
"government" [*Democracy* is government by the people.]

crackle on
a vase

cra·dle (krā′d'l), *n.* **1.** a baby's small bed,
usually on rockers. **2.** the
place where something
began [Boston is often
called the *cradle* of the
American Revolution.] **3.**
anything that looks like a
cradle or that is used for
holding, rocking, etc. [the
cradle for holding a tele-
phone receiver; a miner's *cradle* for washing gold
out of sand]. **4.** a frame on a scythe for laying
the cut grain evenly. —*v.* to rock or hold as in a
cradle. —**cra′dled,** *p.t. & p.p.;* **cra′dling,** *pr.p.*

baby's cradle

craft (kraft), *n.* **1.** special skill or ability. **2.**
work that takes special skill, especially with the
hands [the *craft* of weaving]. **3.** the members of a
skilled trade. **4.** skill in fooling or tricking others;
slyness. **5.** a boat, ship, or aircraft: **craft** is the
pl. for this meaning

crafts·man (krafts′mən), *n.* a skilled workman; one in a skilled trade. —**crafts′men,** *pl.*

craft·y (kraf′tē), *adj.* skillful in fooling or tricking others; sly; cunning. —**craft′i·er,** *compar.;*
craft′i·est, *superl.* —**craft′i·ly,** *adv.*

crag (krag), *n.* a steep, rugged rock that rises
above or juts out from others.

crag·gy (krag′ē), *adj.* having many crags;
steep and rugged. —**crag′gi·er,** *compar.;*
crag′gi·est, *superl.* —**crag′gi·ness,** *n.*

cram (kram), *v.* **1.** to pack full or too full
[The cupboard was *crammed* with dishes.] **2.** to
stuff or force [He *crammed* the papers into a
drawer.] **3.** to study many facts in a hurry, as for
a test: *used only in everyday talk.* —**crammed,**
p.t. & p.p.; **cram′ming,** *pr.p.*

cramp (kramp), *n.* **1.** a sharp, painful tightening of a muscle, as from a chill or strain. **2.**
cramps, *pl.* sharp pains in the belly. **3.** a metal
bar with both ends bent, used for holding together blocks of stone or timbers. —*v.* **1.** to
cause a cramp in. **2.** to keep from moving or
acting freely; confine; hamper.

cran·ber·ry (kran′ber′ē), *n.* **1.** a hard, sour,
red berry used in sauces and jellies. **2.** the marsh
shrub it grows on. —**cran′ber′ries,** *pl.*

crane (krān), *n.* **1.** a large wading bird with
very long legs and neck, and a long, straight bill:
see picture on next page. **2.** a machine for lifting
heavy weights by means
of a long, movable arm.
—*v.* to stretch the neck,
as in trying to see over
something. —**craned,**
p.t. & p.p.; **cran′ing,**
pr.p.

cra·ni·um (krā′ni əm), *n.*
the skull, especially the
part containing the brain.
—**cra·ni·a** (krā′ni ə), *pl.*
—**cra′ni·al,** *adj.*

crane for lifting

fat, āpe, cär, ten, ēven, hĭt, bīte, gō, hôrn, tool, book, up, fûr;
get, joy, yet, chin, she, thin, *th*en; zh = s in pleasure; ′ as in able (ā′b'l);
ə = a in ago, e in agent, i in sanity, o in confess, u in focus.

crank (krangk), *n.* **1.** a handle or arm that is bent at right angles and connected to a shaft of a machine in order to turn it. **2.** a person who has odd, stubborn notions about something: *used only in everyday talk.* **3.** a cross, complaining person: *used only in everyday talk.* —*v.* to start or work by turning a crank.

crane (4 ft. tall)

crank·case (krangk'-kās), *n.* the metal case enclosing a crankshaft, as in an automobile.

crank·shaft (krangk'shaft), *n.* a shaft that turns a crank or is turned by a crank, as in an automobile engine.

crank·y (krang'kē), *adj.* cross or complaining. —**crank'i·er,** *compar.;* **crank'i·est,** *superl.*

cran·ny (kran'ē), *n.* a small, narrow opening; chink or crack, as in a wall. —**cran'nies,** *pl.*

crape (krāp), *n.* a thin, crinkled cloth [Black *crape* is a sign of mourning.] See also **crepe.**

crash (krash), *v.* **1.** to fall, hit, or break with force and with a loud, smashing noise. **2.** to fall to the earth so as to be damaged or smashed [The airplane *crashed.*] **3.** to get into a party, theater, etc. without an invitation or ticket: *used only in everyday talk.* —*n.* **1.** a loud, smashing noise. **2.** the crashing of a car, airplane, etc. **3.** a sudden failure or ruin, as of a business; also, a general business depression.

crash (krash), *n.* a coarse linen cloth.

crass (kras), *adj.* very stupid and coarse [a *crass* insult]. —**crass'ly,** *adv.* —**crass'ness,** *n.*

crate (krāt), *n.* a box made of wooden slats, for packing things. —*v.* to pack in a crate. —**crat'-ed,** *p.t. & p.p.;* **crat'ing,** *pr.p.*

cra·ter (krā'tər), *n.* **1.** a hollow, shaped like a bowl, as at the mouth of a volcano or on the surface of the moon. **2.** any hollow like this, as one made by a bomb explosion.

craters of the moon

cra·vat (krə vat'), *n.* a necktie.

crave (krāv), *v.* **1.** to long for very much; want badly [to *crave* food]. **2.** to beg for [to *crave* pardon]. —**craved,** *p.t. & p.p.;* **crav'ing,** *pr.p.*

cra·ven (krā'vən), *adj.* cowardly. —*n.* a coward. —**cra'ven·ly,** *adv.*

crav·ing (krāv'ing), *n.* a strong longing or appetite [He has a *craving* for sweets.]

craw (krô), *n.* **1.** the crop of a bird. **2.** the stomach of any animal.

craw·fish (krô'fish), *n.* a crayfish.

crawl (krôl), *v.* **1.** to move slowly by dragging the body along the ground as a worm does. **2.** to go on hands and knees; creep. **3.** to move slowly [The truck *crawled* up the steep hill.] **4.** to be full of crawling things [The rotten log was *crawling* with worms.] **5.** to feel as if insects were crawling on the skin [It makes my flesh *crawl* to hear ghost stories.] —*n.* **1.** a crawling; slow, creeping movement. **2.** a swimming stroke in which the head is kept low in the water and the legs are kicked.

cray·fish (krā'fish), *n.* **1.** a small, fresh-water shellfish that looks like a small lobster. **2.** a sea shellfish that is like the lobster, but does not have large claws.

cray·on (krā'ən *or* krā'än), *n.* a small stick of chalk, charcoal, or a colored kind of wax, used for drawing or writing. —*v.* to draw with crayons.

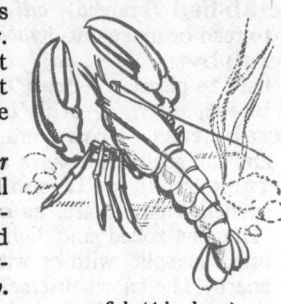

crayfish (4 in. long)

craze (krāz), *v.* **1.** to make sick in the mind, or insane [*crazed* by grief]. **2.** to make fine cracks or crackle in: *see the picture for* **crackle.** —*n.* something that is the fashion for a short while; fad. —**crazed,** *p.t. & p.p.;* **craz'ing,** *pr.p.*

cra·zy (krā'zē), *adj.* **1.** having a sick mind; insane. **2.** very foolish or mad [a *crazy* idea]. **3.** very eager or enthusiastic: *used only in everyday talk* [She's *crazy* about the movies.] —**cra'zi·er,** *compar.;* **cra'zi·est,** *superl.* —**cra'zi·ly,** *adv.* —**cra'zi·ness,** *n.*

crazy quilt, a quilt made of pieces of cloth of various colors, sizes, and shapes.

creak (krēk), *v.* to make a harsh, squeaking sound, as rusted hinges or old floor boards. —*n.* such a sound. —**creak'y,** *adj.*

cream (krēm), *n.* **1.** the oily, yellowish part of milk that rises to the top and contains the butterfat. **2.** any food that is made of cream or is like cream [ice *cream*]. **3.** a smooth, oily substance used to clean and soften the skin. **4.** the best part [the *cream* of the crop]. **5.** yellowish white. —*v.* **1.** to beat, as butter and sugar, until creamy. **2.** to form a creamy foam on top.

cream cheese, a soft, white cheese made of cream or of milk and cream.

cream·er·y (krēm'ər ē), *n.* **1.** a place where milk and dairy products are prepared. **2.** a store where these are sold. —**cream'er·ies,** *pl.*

cream·y (krēm'ē), *adj.* of, like, or full of cream; smooth and rich. —**cream'i·er,** *compar.;* **cream'i·est,** *superl.*

crease (krēs), *n.* **1.** a line or ridge made by folding or pressing [the *crease* in trousers]. **2.** a fold or wrinkle [*creases* in an old man's face]. —*v.* to make a crease or creases in. —**creased,** *p.t. & p.p.;* **creas'ing,** *pr.p.*

cre·ate (krē āt'), *v.* to bring into being; cause to be; make; form; put together [Rembrandt *created* many fine works of art. The President *created* three new generals.] —**cre·at'ed,** *p.t. & p.p.;* **cre·at'ing,** *pr.p.*

cre·a·tion (krē ā'shən), *n.* **1.** the act of creating. **2.** the whole world and everything in it; universe. **3.** anything created or brought into being.

cre·a·tive (krē ā'tiv), *adj.* creating or able to create; inventive; having imagination and ability.

cre·a·tor (krē ā′tər), *n.* a person that creates. —**the Creator,** God.

crea·ture (krē′chər), *n.* a living being; any person or animal.

cre·dence (krē′d′ns), *n.* belief or trust in what someone says [to give *credence* to gossip].

cre·den·tials (kri den′shəlz), *n.pl.* a letter or paper carried by a person to show who he is, or to prove his right to do something.

cred·i·ble (kred′ə b′l), *adj.* that can be believed; believable [a *credible* idea]. —**cred·i·bil·i·ty** (kred′ə bil′ə tē), *n.* —**cred′i·bly,** *adv.*

cred·it (kred′it), *n.* **1.** belief; trust [I place full *credit* in what the boy says.] **2.** praise or approval [I give her *credit* for trying.] **3.** official recognition in a record [You will receive *credit* for two days' work.] **4.** a person or thing that brings praise [He is a *credit* to the team.] **5.** trust that a person will be able and willing to pay later [They do not give *credit* in this store.] **6.** amount of money in someone's account [This deposit gives him a *credit* of $50.00.] —*v.* **1.** to believe; accept as true [He wouldn't *credit* my excuse.] **2.** to add to a person's account [*Credit* him with $3.50.] —**credit someone with,** to believe that someone has or give recognition to someone for [to *credit someone with* honesty]. —**do credit to,** bring honor to. —**on credit,** by agreeing to pay later [to buy a car *on credit*]. —**to one's credit,** bringing honor to one.

cred·it·a·ble (kred′it ə b′l), *adj.* deserving credit or praise. —**cred′it·a·bly,** *adv.*

cred·i·tor (kred′i tər), *n.* a person to whom one owes something.

cre·du·li·ty (krə dōō′lə tē *or* krə dyōō′lə tē), *n.* a willingness to believe, even without proof.

cred·u·lous (krej′oo ləs), *adj.* willing to believe things, even without proof; easily fooled.

creed (krēd), *n.* **1.** a statement of the main beliefs of a religion. **2.** any belief or set of beliefs that guide a person.

creek (krēk *or* krik), *n.* **1.** a small river or stream. **2.** a narrow inlet or bay.

creel (krēl), *n.* a basket for holding fish, often worn by fishermen.

creep (krēp), *v.* **1.** to move along with the body close to the ground, as a baby on hands and knees. **2.** to move in a slow or sneaking way [The cars *crept* along in the heavy traffic. The thieves *crept* into the store at night.] **3.** to come on gradually and almost without being noticed [Old age *crept* up on him.] **4.** to grow along the ground or a wall, as ivy. —*n.* the act of creeping. —**make**

creel

one's flesh creep, to make one feel fear or disgust, as if insects were creeping on one's skin: *also, in everyday talk,* **give one the creeps.** —**crept,** *p.t. & p.p.;* **creep′ing,** *pr.p.*

creep·er (krēp′ər), *n.* **1.** a person or thing that creeps. **2.** any plant that grows along the ground or a wall.

creep·y (krēp′ē), *adj.* having or causing a feeling of fear or disgust, as if insects were creeping on one's skin [a *creepy* tale of murder]. —**creep′i·er,** *compar.;* **creep′i·est,** *superl.*

cre·mate (krē′māt), *v.* to burn a dead body to ashes. —**cre′mat·ed,** *p.t. & p.p.;* **cre′mat·ing,** *pr.p.* —**cre·ma′tion,** *n.*

Cre·ole (krē′ōl), *n.* **1.** a person descended from the original French settlers of Louisiana. **2.** French as spoken by such people. **3.** a person with French or Spanish ancestors, born in Latin America or the West Indies. —*adj.* of or having to do with Creoles [*Creole* cooking].

cre·o·sote (krē′ə sōt), *n.* an oily liquid with a sharp smell, made from wood tar or coal tar and used on wood to keep it from rotting.

crepe *or* **crêpe** (krāp), *n.* **1.** a thin cloth with a crinkled surface. Such black cloth worn as a sign of mourning is usually spelled **crape. 2.** thin paper crinkled like crepe: also **crepe paper.**

crept (krept), past tense and past participle of **creep.**

cre·scen·do (krə shen′dō), *adj. & adv.* gradually becoming louder or stronger: *a direction in music shown by the sign* <. —*n.* a gradual increase in loudness. —**cre·scen′dos,** *pl.*

cres·cent (kres′'nt), *n.* **1.** the shape of the moon in its first or last quarter. **2.** anything shaped like this, as a curved bun or roll. —*adj.* shaped like a crescent.

cress (kres), *n.* a small plant whose sharp-tasting leaves are used in salads.

crest (krest), *n.* **1.** a tuft of feathers or fur, on the head of certain birds and animals. **2.** a plume of feathers or other decoration worn on a helmet. **3.** a design, as of a crown or an eagle's head, placed at the top of a coat of arms, or used as a family mark on silverware, stationery, etc. **4.** the top of anything [the *crest* of a wave; a mountain *crest*].

crescent

crest·ed (kres′tid), *adj.* having a crest.

crest

crest·fall·en (krest′fôl′'n), *adj.* having lost one's spirit or courage; made sad or humble [The players trooped into the locker room, *crestfallen* at losing the game.]

Crete (krēt), *n.* a Greek island in the eastern Mediterranean. —**Cre′tan,** *adj. & n.*

cre·tonne (kri tän′ *or* krē′tän), *n.* a heavy

cotton or linen cloth with patterns printed in colors, used for curtains, chair covers, etc.

cre·vasse (krə vas′), *n.* a deep crack or crevice, especially in a glacier.

crev·ice (krev′is), *n.* a narrow opening caused by a crack or split, as in rock.

crew (krōō), *n.* **1.** all the men working on a ship, aircraft, etc. [A ship's *crew* is usually thought of apart from its officers.] **2.** any group of people working together [a railroad *crew*]. **3.** a group or gang; mob. **4.** a rowing team.

crew (krōō), a past tense of **crow**.

crew cut, a style of man's haircut in which the hair is cut very close to the head.

crib (krib), *n.* **1.** a small bed with high sides, for a baby. **2.** a rack or box for feeding animals. **3.** a bin for storing grain, salt, etc. **4.** a framework of slats and bars for support, as in a mine shaft. **5.** notes, a translation, etc. used in a dishonest way to do schoolwork: *used only in everyday talk.*

baby's crib

—*v.* to use a crib to do schoolwork; also, to pass off another's ideas as one's own: *used only in everyday talk.* —**cribbed,** *p.t. & p.p.;* **crib′bing,** *pr.p.*

crib·bage (krib′ij), *n.* a card game in which score is kept by moving pegs on a small board.

crick (krik), *n.* a painful cramp, as in the neck.

crick·et (krik′it), *n.* a leaping insect related to the grasshopper. Male crickets make a chirping noise by rubbing the wings together.

crick·et (krik′it), *n.* **1.** an outdoor game played with a ball, bats, and wickets, by two teams of eleven men each. Cricket is played mainly in England. **2.** fair play; sportsmanship: *used only in everyday talk.*

cricket (1 in. long)

cried (krīd), past tense and past participle of **cry.**

cri·er (krī′ər), *n.* **1.** a person who cries or shouts. **2.** a person whose work was shouting out public announcements, news, etc. through the streets.

cries (krīz), **1.** the form of the verb **cry** used in the present with *he, she,* or *it.* **2.** the plural of the noun **cry.**

crime (krīm), *n.* **1.** the doing of something that is against the law; serious wrongdoing that breaks the law. **2.** an evil or foolish act; sin [It would be a *crime* to waste this food.]

Cri·me·a (krī mē′ə), *n.* a peninsula in Soviet Russia, jutting into the Black Sea. —**Cri·me′an,** *adj.*

crim·i·nal (krim′ə n'l), *adj.* **1.** being a crime; that is a crime [a *criminal* act]. **2.** having to do with crime [*criminal* law]. —*n.* a person guilty of a crime. —**crim′i·nal·ly,** *adv.*

crimp (krimp), *v.* **1.** to press into narrow, even folds; pleat [The lace ruffles on her dress were *crimped.*] **2.** to make hair wavy or curly. —*n.* **1.** the act of crimping. **2.** a fold or wave [The rain put a *crimp* in her hair.]

crim·son (krim′z'n), *adj. & n.* deep red [Blood is *crimson.*] —*v.* to make or become crimson.

cringe (krinj), *v.* to draw back, bend over, or tremble with fear [The dog *cringed* and put its tail between its legs.] —**cringed,** *p.t. & p.p.;* **cring′ing,** *pr.p.*

crin·kle (kriŋ′k'l), *v.* **1.** to make or become full of wrinkles or creases [Old paper money is usually *crinkled* from use.] **2.** to make a sound like that of paper being crushed. —**crin′kled,** *p.t. & p.p.;* **crin′kling,** *pr.p.* —**crin′kly,** *adj.*

crin·o·line (krin′'l in), *n.* **1.** a coarse, stiff cloth used as a lining or in petticoats for puffing out skirts. **2.** a hoop skirt.

child cringing

crip·ple (krip′'l), *n.* a person or animal that is lame or injured so as to be unable to move in a normal way. —*v.* **1.** to make a cripple of; lame [*crippled* by polio]. **2.** to hurt or weaken [The snowstorm *crippled* railroad service.] —**crip′pled,** *p.t. & p.p.;* **crip′pling,** *pr.p.*

cri·sis (krī′sis), *n.* **1.** the turning point in a disease that shows whether the patient will get well or die. **2.** any turning point, as in history. **3.** a time of great danger or trouble.

crisp (krisp), *adj.* **1.** hard or firm, but easily broken or snapped [*crisp* bacon; *crisp* lettuce]. **2.** sharp, clear, lively, etc.; not dull or slow [a *crisp* way of speaking]. **3.** fresh and bracing [*crisp* air]. **4.** tightly curled and wiry [*crisp* hair]. —*v.* to make or become crisp. —**crisp′ly,** *adv.* —**crisp′ness,** *n.*

crisp·y (kris′pē), *adj.* same as **crisp** (*meaning* 1). —**crisp′i·er,** *compar.;* **crisp′i·est,** *superl.*

criss·cross (kris′krôs), *adj.* crossing or marked by crossing lines [a *crisscross* pattern]. —*v.* to move crosswise or mark with crossing lines [Railroad tracks *crisscross* the valley.]

cri·ter·i·on (krī tir′i ən), *n.* a rule or test by which something can be judged; measure of value [A student's grades are not always the best *criterion* of his ability.] —**cri·ter·i·a** (krī tir′i ə) or **cri·ter′i·ons,** *pl.*

crit·ic (krit′ik), *n.* **1.** a person who forms judgments of people or things; especially, one whose work is to write such judgments of books, music, plays, etc., as for a newspaper or magazine. **2.** a person who is quick to find fault.

crit·i·cal (krit′i k'l), *adj.* **1.** tending to find fault or to disapprove [You're too *critical* of others.] **2.** based on sound, careful judgment [a *critical* opinion]. **3.** having to do with critics or criticism. **4.** dangerous or risky; causing worry [a *critical* situation which could lead to war]. **5.** of or forming a crisis [the *critical* stage of a disease]. —**crit′i·cal·ly,** *adv.*

crit·i·cism (krit′ə siz'm), *n.* **1.** the forming of judgments, especially about books, music, etc. **2.** a piece of writing by a critic; review. **3.** the act of finding fault; disapproval.

crit·i·cize (krit′ə sīz), *v.* **1.** to judge as a critic. **2.** to find fault with; disapprove of [His wife *criticizes* everything he does.] —**crit′i·cized,** *p.t. & p.p.;* **crit′i·ciz·ing,** *prp.*

cri·tique (kri tēk′), *n.* **1.** a piece of writing that gives a careful judgment of a book, play, etc. **2.** the art of a critic; criticism.

crit·ter or **crit·tur** (krit′ər), *n.* a creature: *used in some regions.*

croak (krōk), *v.* **1.** to make a deep, hoarse sound in the throat [Frogs and ravens *croak*.] **2.** to say in a deep, hoarse voice [The tired runner *croaked* a warning.] —*n.* a croaking sound.

Cro·a·tia (krō ā′shə), *n.* a state in northwestern Yugoslavia. —**Cro·a′tian,** *adj. & n.*

cro·chet (krō shā′), *n.* a kind of knitting done with one hooked needle. —*v.* to knit with such a needle. —**cro·cheted** (krō shād′), *p.t. & p.p.;* **cro·chet·ing** (krō shā′ing), *prp.*

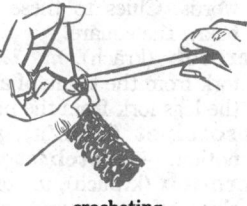
crocheting

crock (kräk), *n.* a pot or jar made of baked clay.

crock·er·y (kräk′ər ē), *n.* pots, jars, and dishes made of baked clay; earthenware.

croc·o·dile (kräk′ə dīl), *n.* a large lizard like the alligator, that lives in and near tropical rivers. It has a thick, tough skin, a long tail, large jaws, and pointed teeth.

crocodile (15 ft. long)

cro·cus (krō′kəs), *n.* a small plant that grows from a corm and has a yellow, purple, or white flower. It is one of the first plants to bloom in the spring. —**cro′cus·es,** *pl.*

Croe·sus (krē′səs), *n.* **1.** a very rich king in Asia Minor in the 6th century B.C. **2.** any very rich man.

crocuses

Cro-Ma·gnon (krō mag′nän), *adj.* of a race of tall men who lived in Europe in the Stone Age.

Crom·well, Oliver (kräm′wel), 1599–1658; English general and statesman.

crone (krōn), *n.* a wrinkled old woman; hag.

cro·ny (krō′nē), *n.* a close friend or companion. —**cro′nies,** *pl.*

crook (krook), *n.* **1.** a thing or part that is bent or curved [the *crook* of one's arm; a *crook* in the road]. **2.** a shepherd's staff with a hook at the end to collar sheep. **3.** a person who steals or cheats: *used only in everyday talk.* —*v.* to bend or curve [to *crook* one's arm].

crook·ed (krook′id), *adj.* **1.** not straight; bent, curved, or twisted [a *crooked* road]. **2.** not honest; cheating.

croon (kroon), *v.* to sing or hum in a low, gentle tone [to *croon* lullabies].

crop (kräp), *n.* **1.** any farm product grown in the soil, as wheat, cotton, fruit, etc.; also, the amount of such a product grown at one time. **2.** a group of things or persons [a new *crop* of students; a *crop* of complaints]. **3.** a pouch in a bird's gullet where food is softened for digestion. **4.** the handle of a whip, or a short whip with a loop at the end. **5.** hair cut very short [a close *crop*]. —*v.* **1.** to cut or bite off the tops or ends of [The goat *cropped* the grass.] **2.** to cut short; trim [to *crop* hair]. —**crop out** or **crop up,** to come up in a way that is not expected. —**cropped,** *p.t. & p.p.;* **crop′ping,** *prp.*

crop·per (kräp′ər), *n.* a person or thing that crops. —**come a cropper, 1.** to fall headlong. **2.** to fail or be ruined. *The phrase is used only in everyday talk.*

cro·quet (krō kā′), *n.* an outdoor game in which the players use mallets to drive a wooden ball through hoops in the ground.

croquet

cro·quette (krō ket′), *n.* a little ball of chopped meat, fish, etc. fried in deep fat.

cro·sier (krō′zhər), *n.* the staff of a bishop or abbot, that is a symbol of his office.

cross (krôs), *n.* **1.** an upright post with a bar across it near the top, on which the ancient Romans put criminals to death. **2.** the figure of a cross used as a symbol of the crucifixion of Jesus and of the Christian religion. **3.** any trouble that one has to bear [A sick husband has been her *cross*.] **4.** any design or mark made by crossing lines. **5.** a mixing of different breeds of animals or plants. **6.** the result of such mixing [A bull terrier is a *cross* between a bulldog and a terrier.] —*v.* **1.** to make

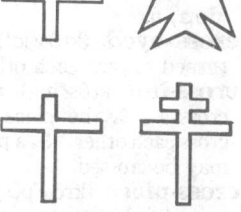
types of cross

the sign of the cross over, as a religious act [to *cross* oneself]. **2.** to place across or crosswise [*Cross* your fingers.] **3.** to draw a line or lines across [*Cross* your "t's."] **4.** to go from one side to the other of; go or extend across [He *crossed* the ocean. The bridge *crosses* the river.] **5.** to pass each other while moving in opposite directions [Our letters *crossed* in the mail.] **6.** to go against; oppose; hinder [No one likes to be *crossed*.] **7.** to mix different breeds of animals or plants. —*adj.* **1.** lying or passing across; crossing [a *cross* street]. **2.** cranky or irritable; having a bad temper. —**cross off** or **cross out,** to do away with or cancel as by drawing lines across. —**cross one's mind,** to come to one's mind; occur to one. —**cross one's path,** to meet one. —**cross′ly,** *adv.*

cross·bar (krôs′bär), *n.* a bar or line placed crosswise, as a bar between goal posts.

cross·bones (krôs′bōnz), *n.* the figure of two bones placed across each other, under a skull, used as a sign of death or deadly danger.

cross·bow (krôs′bō), *n.* a weapon of the Middle Ages, consisting of a bow set across a wooden stock. The stock had a groove that held the arrow and a trigger that released the bow-string.

crossbow

cross·breed (krôs′brēd), *v.* to mix different breeds of animals or plants. —*n.* an animal or plant produced by crossbreeding. —**cross·bred** (krôs′bred), *p.t. & p.p.;* **cross′breed·ing,** *pr.p.*

cross-coun·try (krôs′kun′trē), *adj.* across open country or fields instead of on roads [a *cross-country* race].

cross·cut (krôs′kut), *adj.* used for cutting across [A *crosscut* saw cuts wood across the grain.] —*n.* a cut or way across. —*v.* to cut across. —**cross′cut,** *p.t. & p.p.;* **cross′cut·ting,** *pr.p.*

cross-ex·am·ine (krôs′ig zam′in), *v.* to question again, as a witness already questioned by the other side during a trial, in order to check the earlier answers or to get more information. —**cross′-ex·am′ined,** *p.t. & p.p.;* **cross′-ex·am′in·ing,** *pr.p.* —**cross′-ex·am·i·na′tion,** *n.*

cross-eyed (krôs′īd′), *adj.* having the eyes turned toward each other.

cross·ing (krôs′ing), *n.* **1.** the act of one that crosses. **2.** the place where lines, streets, etc. cross each other. **3.** a place where a street or river may be crossed.

cross·piece (krôs′pēs), *n.* a piece, as of wood or metal, lying across something else.

cross-pur·pose (krôs′pūr′pəs), *n.* an opposing purpose. —**at cross-purposes,** having a mistaken idea as to each other's purposes.

cross-ques·tion (krôs′kwes′chən), *v.* to cross-examine.

cross reference, a notice to look in another part of a book, list, etc. for more information.

cross·road (krôs′rōd), *n.* **1.** a road that crosses

another road. **2.** a road that connects two or more main roads. **3.** *usually* **crossroads,** *pl.* the place where roads cross each other.

cross section, 1. the act of cutting something straight across. **2.** a piece cut off in this way. **3.** a sample that has enough of each kind in it to show what the whole is like [The newspaper polled a *cross section* of the city's voters.]

cross·walk (krôs′wôk), *n.* a lane marked off for people to use in walking across a street.

cross·way (krôs′wā), *n.* a crossroad.

cross·ways (krôs′wāz), *adv.* crosswise.

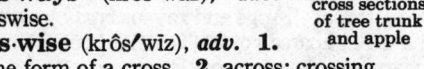
cross sections
of tree trunk
and apple

cross·wise (krôs′wīz), *adv.* **1.** in the form of a cross. **2.** across; crossing.

cross·word puzzle (krôs′wûrd), a puzzle that consists of a square made up of blank spaces, which are to be filled with letters that form certain words. Clues to these words are usually given below the square.

crotch (kräch), *n.* **1.** a place where branches fork from the trunk of a tree. **2.** the place where the legs fork from the human body.

crotch·et (kräch′it), *n.* a queer or stubborn notion. —**crotch′et·y,** *adj.*

crouch (krouch), *v.* to stoop with the legs bent close to the ground, as an animal about to leap. —*n.* the act or position of crouching.

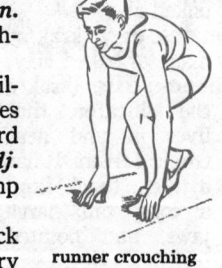

croup (krōōp), *n.* a children's disease that causes hoarse coughing and hard breathing. —**croup′y,** *adj.*

croup (krōōp), *n.* the rump of a horse.

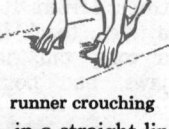
runner crouching

crow (krō), *n.* a large black bird known for its harsh cry or caw. —**as the crow flies,** in a straight line between two places.

crow (krō), *v.* **1.** to make the shrill cry of a rooster. **2.** to make loud sounds like this, as in happiness, delight, or boasting. —*n.* the shrill cry of a rooster. —**crowed** *or, for meaning 1,* **crew,** *p.t. & p.p.;* **crow′ing,** *pr.p.*

crow (1½ ft. long)

crow·bar (krō′bär), *n.* a long metal bar with one end like a chisel, for prying or lifting things.

crowd (kroud), *n.* **1.** a large group of people together [*crowds* of Christmas shoppers]. **2.** the common people; the masses. **3.** a group of people having something in common; set: *used only in everyday talk* [His brother's *crowd* is too old for him.] —*v.* **1.** to push or squeeze [Can we all *crowd* into one car?] **2.** to come together in a large group [People *crowded* to see the show.] **3.** to pack or fill too full.

crown (kroun), *n.* **1.** a headdress of gold, jewels, etc., worn by a king or queen. **2.** the power of being the ruler [The nobles fought for the *crown*.] **3.** the king or queen [arrested by order of the *crown*]. **4.** a wreath worn on the head as a sign of honor or victory. **5.** first place in a contest; championship [The boxer won the heavyweight *crown*.] **6.** anything like a crown; especially, the top part [a *crown* of golden hair; the *crown* of a hill; the *crown* of a hat]. **7.** the top part of the head. **8.** the part of a tooth that sticks out from the gum. **9.** a British silver coin equal to five shillings. —*v.* **1.** to make a king or queen by putting a crown on [Elizabeth I was *crowned* in 1558.] **2.** to honor or reward [The victor was *crowned* with glory.] **3.** to be at the top of [Woods *crowned* the hill.] **4.** to cover the crown of a tooth with gold, etc. to protect it. **5.** to end or complete [Success *crowned* his efforts.] **6.** to hit over the head: *used only in everyday talk.*

king's crown

crow's-nest (krōz'nest'), *n.* a small box or platform near the top of a ship's mast, where the lookout stands.

cru·cial (krōō'shəl), *adj.* of the most importance; that decides something [The final examination is the *crucial* test.] —**cru'cial·ly,** *adv.*

cru·ci·ble (krōō'sə b'l), *n.* a pot or vat in which ores and metals are melted.

crow's-nest

cru·ci·fix (krōō'sə fiks), *n.* a figure of a cross with Jesus on it. It is a Christian symbol.

cru·ci·fix·ion (krōō'sə fik'shən), *n.* **1.** a crucifying. **2.** the Crucifixion, the crucifying of Jesus, or a picture or painting of this.

cru·ci·fy (krōō'sə fī), *v.* **1.** to put to death by nailing or tying to a cross. **2.** to treat in a cruel way; torture or abuse. —**cru'ci·fied,** *p.t. & p.p.;* **cru'ci·fy·ing,** *pr.p.*

crude (krōōd), *adj.* **1.** looking or acting rough or clumsy [a *crude* drawing; a *crude* backwoodsman]. **2.** in its natural or raw condition, before it has been prepared for use [*crude* oil]. —**crude'ly,** *adv.* —**crude'ness,** *n.*

cru·el (krōō'əl), *adj.* **1.** liking to make others suffer; having no mercy or pity [The *cruel* Pharaoh made slaves of the Israelites.] **2.** causing pain and suffering [*cruel* insults; a *cruel* winter]. —**cru'el·ly,** *adv.*

cru·el·ty (krōō'əl tē), *n.* **1.** a being cruel. **2.** a cruel act. —**cru'el·ties,** *pl.*

cru·et (krōō'it), *n.* a small glass bottle for serving oil, vinegar, etc. at the table.

cruise (krōōz), *v.* **1.** to sail or drive about from place to place, as for pleasure or in searching for something. **2.** to move smoothly at a speed that is not strained [The airplane *cruised* at 300 miles per hour.] —*n.* a ship voyage from place to place for pleasure. —**cruised,** *p.t. & p.p.;* **cruis'ing,** *pr.p.*

cruets

cruis·er (krōōz'ər), *n.* **1.** a fast warship, smaller than a battleship. **2.** anything that cruises, as a police car, motorboat, etc.

crul·ler (krul'ər), *n.* a kind of twisted doughnut made with a rich dough.

crumb (krum), *n.* **1.** a tiny piece broken off, as of bread or cake. **2.** any bit or scrap [*crumbs* of knowledge]. —*v.* to break into crumbs, as bread.

crum·ble (krum'b'l), *v.* to break into crumbs or small pieces [He *crumbled* the crackers into his soup. The old plaster walls began to *crumble*.] —**crum'bled,** *p.t. & p.p.;* **crum'bling,** *pr.p.*

crum·bly (krum'blē), *adj.* likely to crumble; easily crumbled [*crumbly* rocks; *crumbly* cake].

crum·ple (krum'p'l), *v.* **1.** to crush together into creases; wrinkle [He *crumpled* the paper in his hand. This fabric won't *crumple*.] **2.** to fall to pieces; break down: *used only in everyday talk.* —**crum'pled,** *p.t. & p.p.;* **crum'pling,** *pr.p.*

crunch (krunch), *v.* **1.** to chew with a noisy, crackling sound [to *crunch* carrots]. **2.** to grind or move over with a noisy, crushing sound [The wheels *crunched* the pebbles in the drive.] —*n.* the act or sound of crunching.

crunch·y (krun'chē), *adj.* making a crunching sound [*crunchy* celery]. —**crunch'i·er,** *compar.;* **crunch'i·est,** *superl.*

crup·per (krup'ər), *n.* **1.** a leather strap fastened to a harness and passed under a horse's tail. **2.** the rump of a horse.

cru·sade (krōō sād'), *n.* **1.** *sometimes* **Crusade,** any of the wars which Christians from the West fought in the 11th, 12th, and 13th centuries to capture the Holy Land from the Moslems. **2.** any fight for a cause thought to be good or against something thought to be bad [a *crusade* for better housing; a *crusade* against cancer]. —*v.* to take part in a crusade. —**cru·sad'ed,** *p.t. & p.p.;* **cru·sad'ing,** *pr.p.* —**cru·sad'er,** *n.*

cruse (krōōz *or* krōōs), *n.* a small jar for water, oil, etc. *This word is now seldom used.*

crush (krush), *v.* **1.** to press or squeeze with force so as to break, hurt, or put out of shape [He *crushed* the walnut in his hand. His hat was *crushed* when he sat on it.] **2.** to grind or pound into bits [This machine *crushes* rocks.] **3.** to bring to an end by force; subdue; suppress [The government *crushed* the revolt.] **4.** to become crumpled or wrinkled [Her cotton dress *crushes* easily.] —*n.* **1.** a crushing or squeezing; strong pressure. **2.** many people or things crowded together [He was caught in the *crush* of people leaving the stadium.] **3.** a strong attraction toward someone: *used only in everyday talk* [John has a *crush* on Mary.]

Cru·soe, Rob·in·son (räb'in s'n kroo'sō), the hero of Daniel Defoe's novel, *Robinson Crusoe,* who is shipwrecked on a desert island.

crust (krust), *n.* **1.** the hard, crisp, outer part of bread; also, a piece of this. **2.** any dry, hard piece of bread. **3.** the shell or cover of a pie, made of flour and shortening. **4.** any hard covering or top layer, as of snow or soil. —*v.* to cover or become covered with a crust [The roofs were *crusted* with ice and snow.]

crus·ta·cean (krus tā'shən), *n.* an animal with a hard outer shell, that usually lives in water [Shrimps, crabs, and lobsters are *crustaceans*.]

crust·y (krus'tē), *adj.* **1.** having a crust or like a crust [*crusty* snow]. **2.** having a bad temper; rude and impolite. —**crust'i·er,** *compar.*; **crust'i·est,** *superl.* —**crust'i·ly,** *adv.*

crutch (kruch), *n.* **1.** a support used under the arm by a lame person to help in walking. **2.** any kind of support or help.

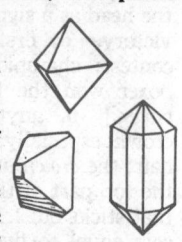

crux (kruks), *n.* the most important or deciding point [The *crux* of the matter is that we can't afford a new car.]

cry (krī), *v.* **1.** to make a loud sound with the voice; call out or shout [She *cried* out in fright when she saw the face at the window.] **2.** to show sorrow, pain, etc. by sobbing or shedding tears. **3.** to say loudly; shout; exclaim ["Help! Help!" she cried.] —*n.* **1.** a loud sound made by the voice; shout or call [I heard his *cry* for help.] **2.** a call or slogan that is supposed to rouse people [a battle *cry*]. **3.** a fit of sobbing and weeping [She had a good *cry* and fell asleep.] **4.** the sound an animal makes [the *cry* of a lost sheep]. —**a far cry, 1.** a long way [It was *a far cry* from the farm to the town.] **2.** a thing much different [The new school was *a far cry* from the old one.] —**cry for, 1.** to plead for. **2.** to need greatly. —**cry one's eyes out,** to weep much and bitterly. —**cried,** *p.t. & p.p.*; **cry'ing,** *pr.p.* —**cries,** *pl.*

crutches

cry·ba·by (krī'bā'bē), *n.* **1.** a child who cries often without much reason. **2.** a person who complains when he fails to win or get his own way.

cry·ing (krī'ing), *adj.* that must be taken care of [a *crying* need].

cry·o·gen·ics (krī'ə jen'iks), *n.* the science that deals with the production of very low temperatures and the effects they have on things.

crypt (kript), *n.* an underground room, espe-cially one under a church, for burying the dead.

cryp·tic (krip'tik), *adj.* having a hidden or difficult meaning; secret; mysterious [a *cryptic* answer]. —**cryp'ti·cal·ly,** *adv.*

cryp·to·gram (krip'tə gram), *n.* something written in a code or secret writing.

crys·tal (kris't'l), *n.* **1.** a clear, transparent quartz that looks like glass. **2.** a very clear, sparkling glass. **3.** something made of such glass, as a goblet or bowl. **4.** the glass or plastic cover over the face of a watch. **5.** any of the regularly shaped pieces into which many substances are formed when they become solids. A crystal has a number of flat surfaces in an orderly arrangement [Salt, sugar, and snow are made up of *crystals*.] —*adj.* **1.** made of crystal. **2.** clear as crystal [the *crystal* waters of a stream].

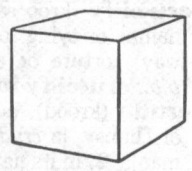

types of crystal

crystal ball, a large glass ball in which fortune-tellers pretend to see the future.

crys·tal·line (kris't'l in), *adj.* **1.** made of crystal. **2.** clear as crystal. **3.** formed of crystals or like a crystal.

crys·tal·lize (kris't'l īz), *v.* **1.** to form crystals [Boil the maple sirup until it will *crystallize*.] **2.** to take on or give a definite form [Their customs were *crystallized* into law.] —**crys'tal·lized,** *p.t. & p.p.*; **crys'tal·liz·ing,** *pr.p.* —**crys·tal·li·za·tion** (kris't'l ə zā'shən), *n.*

Cs, symbol for the chemical element *cesium.*

C.S.T., abbreviation for **Central Standard Time.**

ct., abbreviation for **cent.** —**cts.,** *pl.*

Cu, symbol for the chemical element *copper.*

cu., abbreviation for **cubic.**

cub (kub), *n.* the young of certain animals, such as the bear, lion, and whale.

Cu·ba (kyōō'bə), *n.* a country on an island in the West Indies. —**Cu'ban,** *adj. & n.*

cub·by·hole (kub'ē hōl'), *n.* a small, snug room, closet, or compartment.

cube (kyōōb), *n.* **1.** a solid with six square sides, all the same size. **2.** the result gotten by multiplying a number by itself and then multiplying the product by the same number [The *cube* of 3 is 27 (3 × 3 × 3 = 27).] —*v.* **1.** to get the cube of a number [5 *cubed* is 125.] **2.** to cut into cubes [She *cubed* the fruit for a salad.] —**cubed,** *p.t. & p.p.*; **cub'ing,** *pr.p.*

cube

cu·bic (kyōō'bik), *adj.* **1.** having the shape of a cube. **2.** having measure in three directions [A *cubic* foot is the volume of a cube that is one foot long, one foot wide, and one foot high.]

cu·bi·cle (kyōō'bi k'l), *n.* a small, separate room or compartment, as for study or sleep.

cu·bit (kyōō'bit), *n.* a measure of length used in olden times, about 18 to 22 inches.

cuck·oo (koo'koo *or* kook'oo), *n.* **1.** a dull-brown bird with a long, slender body. The

European cuckoo lays its eggs in the nests of other birds. **2.** the cry of a cuckoo, which sounds a little like its name. *—adj.* crazy or silly: *slang in this meaning.*

cu·cum·ber (kyōō′kum bər), *n.* **1.** a long vegetable with green skin and firm, white flesh. It is used in salads and made into pickles. **2.** the vine that it grows on. **—cool as a cucumber,** calm; not excited.

cucumber

cud (kud), *n.* a mouthful of swallowed food that cattle, sheep, goats, etc. bring back up from the first stomach to chew again slowly a second time.

cud·dle (kud′'l), *v.* **1.** to hold lovingly and gently in one's arms [to *cuddle* a baby]. **2.** to lie close and snug; nestle [to *cuddle* up in a chair]. **—cud′dled,** *p.t. & p.p.;* **cud′dling,** *pr.p.*

cudg·el (kuj′əl), *n.* a short, thick stick or club. *—v.* to beat with such a club. **—cudgel one's brains,** to think hard. **—cudg′eled** or **cudg′elled,** *p.t. & p.p.;* **cudg′el·ing** or **cudg′el·ling,** *pr.p.*

cue (kyōō), *n.* **1.** the last few words in an actor's speech that are a signal to another actor to enter or to speak. **2.** a few notes of music that are a signal to another musician or to a singer to begin. **3.** any signal, hint, or suggestion [If you are not sure of which fork to use, take a *cue* from your hostess.] *—v.* to give a cue to. **—cued,** *p.t. & p.p.;* **cu′ing,** *pr.p.*

cue (kyōō), *n.* **1.** a long stick used in pool and billiards to strike the ball. **2.** a queue.

cuff (kuf), *v.* to hit with the open hand; slap. *—n.* a slap.

cuff (kuf), *n.* **1.** a band at the wrist of a sleeve, either fastened to the sleeve or separate. **2.** a fold turned up at the bottom of a trouser leg. **3.** a handcuff.

cuff links, a pair of linked buttons for keeping some kinds of shirt cuff closed.

cui·rass (kwi ras′), *n.* a piece of armor that covers the breast and the back.

cui·ras·sier (kwi rə sir′), *n.* a cavalry soldier in olden times who wore a cuirass.

cui·sine (kwi zēn′), *n.* **1.** style of cooking [a Swedish *cuisine*]. **2.** the food prepared, as at a restaurant.

cu·li·nar·y (kyōō′lə ner′ē), *adj.* having to do with cooking or cookery.

cull (kul), *v.* **1.** to pick out; select and gather. **2.** to look over in order to choose those wanted [to *cull* a cornfield for ripe ears]. *—n.* a thing taken out as not being good enough.

cul·mi·nate (kul′mə nāt), *v.* to reach its highest point [His career *culminated* in his being elected president.] **—cul′mi·nat·ed,** *p.t. & p.p.;* **cul′mi·nat·ing,** *pr.p.* **—cul′mi·na′tion,** *n.*

cul·pa·ble (kul′pə b'l), *adj.* deserving blame; guilty. **—cul′pa·bly,** *adv.* **—cul·pa·bil·i·ty** (kul′pə bil′ə tē), *n.*

cul·prit (kul′prit), *n.* **1.** a person who is guilty of a crime or wrongdoing. **2.** a person accused of a crime in court.

cult (kult), *n.* **1.** a way of worshiping; system of religious rites [a *cult* of snake worshipers]. **2.** a fashion or belief that a number of people are enthusiastic about [the *cult* of sun bathing].

cul·ti·vate (kul′tə vāt), *v.* **1.** to prepare and use land for growing crops; till. **2.** to grow plants or crops. **3.** to break up the soil around plants in order to kill weeds and help the plants grow. **4.** to help to grow by care, training, or study [*Cultivate* your mind.] **5.** to try to become friendly with, as in order to get or learn something [to *cultivate* a person]. **—cul′ti·vat·ed,** *p.t. & p.p.;* **cul′ti·vat·ing,** *pr.p.*

cul·ti·va·tion (kul′tə vā′shən), *n.* **1.** the cultivating of land or plants. **2.** the improving of something through care, training, or study. **3.** the result of improving one's mind, tastes, and manners; culture; refinement.

cul·ti·va·tor (kul′tə vā′tər), *n.* **1.** a person who cultivates. **2.** a tool or machine for loosening the earth and killing weeds around plants.

cul·ture (kul′chər), *n.* **1.** the cultivating of soil. **2.** the raising or improving of some plant, animal, etc. [bee *culture*]. **3.** a growth of bacteria specially made, as for medical research. **4.** improvement by study or training, especially of the mind, manners, and taste; refinement. **5.** the ideas, skills, arts, tools, and way of life of a certain people in a certain time; civilization [the *culture* of the Aztecs]. **—cul′tur·al,** *adj.* **—cul′tur·al·ly,** *adv.*

cul·tured (kul′chərd), *adj.* **1.** produced by cultivation. **2.** having culture or refinement.

cul·vert (kul′vərt), *n.* a drain or waterway passing under a road.

cum·ber (kum′bər), *v.* same as **encumber.**

cum·ber·some (kum′bər səm), *adj.* hard to handle or deal with, as because of size, weight, or many parts; clumsy; unwieldy.

culvert

cum·brous (kum′brəs), *adj.* cumbersome.

cu·mu·la·tive (kyōōm′yə lā′tiv), *adj.* growing stronger, larger, etc. by being added to [The evidence against him has been *cumulative.*]

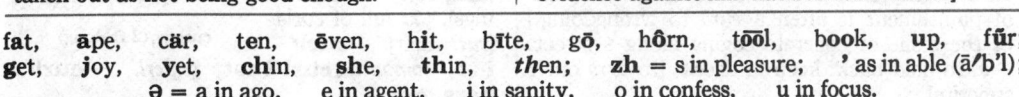

cu·mu·lus (kyoom/yə ləs), *n.* a kind of cloud in which round masses are piled up on each other.

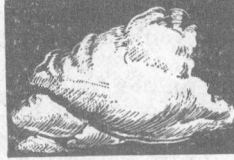
cumulus

cu·ne·i·form (kyoo nē/ə fôrm), *adj.* shaped like a wedge; especially, describing the characters used in the writings of ancient Assyria, Persia, etc.

cun·ning (kun/ing), *adj.* **1.** clever or skillful. **2.** skillful in cheating or tricking; crafty; sly. **3.** pretty in a sweet or delicate way [a *cunning* child]. —*n.* skill, especially in cheating or tricking. —**cun/ning·ly,** *adv.*

god   sun   man
cuneiform characters

cup (kup), *n.* **1.** a small container for drinking from, usually in the shape of a bowl and having a handle. **2.** as much as a cup will hold; cupful [He drank two *cups* of tea.] **3.** anything shaped like a cup, as a silver bowl given as a prize. **4.** one's share [a full *cup* of happiness]. **5.** the hole on a golf green into which the ball is hit. —*v.* to shape like a cup [*Cup* your hands.] —**cupped,** *p.t. & p.p.;* **cup/ping,** *pr.p.*

cup·bear·er (kup/ber/ər), *n.* a person who served cups of wine at banquets in olden times.

cup·board (kub/ərd), *n.* a closet or cabinet with shelves for holding dishes, food, etc.

cup·cake (kup/kāk), *n.* a small cake, sometimes baked in a paper cup.

cup·ful (kup/fool), *n.* as much as a cup will hold, usually half a pint. —**cup/fuls,** *pl.*

Cu·pid (kyoo/pid), *n.* the Roman god of love. He is usually pictured as a small boy with wings who carries a bow and arrow.

cu·pid·i·ty (kyoo pid/ə tē), *n.* strong desire or greed, especially for money.

cu·po·la (kyoo/pə lə), *n.* **1.** a rounded roof or ceiling. **2.** a small dome on a roof.

cur (kŭr), *n.* **1.** a dog of mixed breed; mongrel. **2.** a mean, cowardly person.

cur·a·ble (kyoor/ə b'l), *adj.* that can be cured.

cu·rate (kyoor/it), *n.* a clergyman who helps a vicar or rector in his duties.

cur·a·tive (kyoor/ə tiv), *adj.* curing or helping to cure. —*n.* a cure or remedy.

cu·ra·tor (kyoo rā/tər), *n.* a person in charge of a museum, library, etc.

cupola

curb (kŭrb), *n.* **1.** a chain or strap fastened to a horse's bit and passed under his lower jaw. It holds back the horse when the reins are pulled. **2.** anything that checks or holds back [Fear of punishment is often a *curb* to wrongdoing.] **3.** the stone or concrete edging along a street. —*v.* to hold back; keep in check [to *curb* one's appetite].

curd (kŭrd), *n.* the thick, clotted part of soured milk, used for making cheese.

cur·dle (kŭr/d'l), *v.* to form into curd or clots. —**curdle one's blood,** to frighten very much. —**cur/dled,** *p.t. & p.p.;* **cur/dling,** *pr.p.*

cure (kyoor), *n.* **1.** anything that makes a sick person well; remedy [Penicillin is a *cure* for pneumonia.] **2.** a healing or being healed. **3.** a way of making well or healing [There is no *cure* for my sadness.] —*v.* **1.** to make well; heal [to *cure* a sick person or a disease]. **2.** to stop or get rid of something bad [Low grades *cured* me of neglecting my homework.] **3.** to keep meat, fish, etc. from spoiling, as by salting or smoking. —**cured,** *p.t. & p.p.;* **cur/ing,** *pr.p.*

cu·ré (kyoo rā/), *n.* a parish priest: *a French word.*

cure-all (kyoor/ôl/), *n.* something supposed to cure all illness or all bad conditions.

cur·few (kŭr/fyoo), *n.* **1.** in the Middle Ages, the ringing of a bell in the evening to warn all people to cover their fires and go to bed. **2.** a time in the evening beyond which certain persons or all people must not be on the streets [Our town has a nine o'clock *curfew* for children.]

Cu·rie, Marie (kyoo rē/), 1867–1934; Polish scientist in France who, with her husband Pierre, discovered radium.

cu·ri·o (kyoor/i ō), *n.* any unusual or rare article [Whalers brought carved jade and other *curios* from the Far East.] —**cu/ri·os,** *pl.*

cu·ri·os·i·ty (kyoor/i äs/ə tē), *n.* **1.** a strong feeling of wanting to know or learn [A baby's *curiosity* is his best teacher.] **2.** such a feeling about something that is not one's business [*Curiosity* killed the cat.] **3.** a strange or unusual thing [A fire engine pulled by horses is now a *curiosity.*] —**cu/ri·os/i·ties,** *pl.*

cu·ri·ous (kyoor/i əs), *adj.* **1.** full of curiosity; wanting very much to know; inquisitive. **2.** strange or unusual [*curious* spellings on an old map]. —**cu/ri·ous·ly,** *adv.*

curl (kŭrl), *v.* **1.** to twist into ringlets or coils [to *curl* hair]. **2.** to move in circles or rings [The fog *curled* around our feet.] **3.** to curve or bend around; roll up [The dampness *curled* the pages of the book. I *curled* up on the sofa.] —*n.* **1.** a little coil of hair. **2.** anything curled or curved [a *curl* of smoke from the chimney.]

cur·lew (kŭr/loo), *n.* a bird with long legs and a long, curved bill, that lives on the shore.

curl·i·cue (kŭr/li kyoo), *n.* a fancy curve or twist, as in a design or in handwriting.

curl·y (kŭr/lē), *adj.* **1.** curled or curling [long, *curly* wood shavings]. **2.** full of curls [*curly* hair]. —**curl/i·er,** *compar.;* **curl/i·est,** *superl.* —**curl/i·ness,** *n.*

curlew (2 ft. long)

cur·rant (kŭr′ənt), *n.* **1.** a small, sweet, black raisin, used in cooking. **2.** a small, sour berry, either white, black, or red, used in jams and jellies; also, the bush it grows on.

cur·ren·cy (kŭr′ən sē), *n.* **1.** money in common use; legal coins and bills [Gold coins were once part of American *currency*.] **2.** a going around from person to person. **3.** general use; popularity [Slang words usually lose *currency* quickly.] —**cur′ren·cies,** *pl.*

cur·rent (kŭr′ənt), *adj.* **1.** of the present time; now going on; most recent [the *current* decade; *current* events]. **2.** going around from person to person [*current* gossip]. **3.** commonly accepted [Belief in witchcraft was *current* in early colonial days.] —*n.* **1.** a flow of water or air in a definite direction; stream. **2.** the flow of electricity in a wire or other conductor. **3.** the general movement or drift, as of opinion. —**cur′rent·ly,** *adv.*

cur·ric·u·lum (kə rik′yoo ləm), *n.* the course or plan of study in a school [Is French in the *curriculum* at your school?] —**cur·ric′u·lums** or **cur·ric·u·la** (kə rik′yoo lə), *pl.*

cur·ry (kŭr′ē), *v.* to smooth and clean an animal's coat with a comb (**cur′ry·comb**) having strong metal teeth. —**curry favor,** to try to win favor from someone by flattery. —**cur′ried,** *p.t. & p.p.;* **cur′ry·ing,** *pr.p.*

cur·ry (kŭr′ē), *n.* **1.** a spicy powder or sauce made with many herbs and seasonings. **2.** food flavored with this. —**cur′ries,** *pl.*

curse (kŭrs), *n.* **1.** a calling on God or the gods to bring evil on some person or thing. **2.** a word or words used in swearing at someone. **3.** a cause of evil or trouble; misfortune [Is atomic power a blessing or a *curse*?] —*v.* **1.** to call on God or the gods to harm or punish; damn. **2.** to swear at; use bad or profane language. **3.** to bring evil or trouble on; afflict [*cursed* with illness]. —**cursed,** *p.t. & p.p.;* **curs′ing,** *pr.p.*

curs·ed (kŭr′sid *or* kŭrst), *adj.* **1.** under a curse. **2.** deserving to be cursed; evil; bad.

cur·sive (kŭr′siv), *adj.* written with the strokes of the letters joined in each word.

cur·so·ry (kŭr′sər ē), *adj.* done in a hurry and without attention to details; superficial [He gave the book a *cursory* reading.] —**cur′so·ri·ly,** *adv.*

curt (kŭrt), *adj.* so short or abrupt as to seem rude; brusque [a *curt* dismissal; a *curt* reply]. —**curt′ly,** *adv.*

cur·tail (kər tāl′), *v.* to cut short; reduce [to *curtail* expenses]. —**cur·tail′ment,** *n.*

cur·tain (kŭr′t'n), *n.* **1.** a piece of cloth or the like hung at a window, in front of a stage, etc. to decorate or to cover, hide, or shut off. **2.** anything that hides, covers, or shuts off [The ship could not be seen through the *curtain* of fog.] —*v.* to furnish or hide as with a curtain [Her life was *curtained* in secrecy.]

curt·sy or **curt·sey** (kŭrt′sē), *n.* a bow that women and girls make by bending the knees and lowering the body a little. —*v.* to make a curtsy as a greeting or a mark of respect. —**curt′sies** or **curt′seys,** *pl.* —**curt′sied** or **curt′seyed,** *p.t. & p.p.;* **curt′sy·ing** or **curt′sey·ing,** *pr.p.*

woman curtsying

cur·va·ture (kŭr′və chər), *n.* a curving or a curve [*curvature* of the spine].

curve (kŭrv), *n.* **1.** a line that has no straight part; bend with no angles [A circle is a continuous *curve*. Their house is on a *curve* in the road.] **2.** a baseball pitched with a spin so that it curves to one side before crossing the plate. —*v.* **1.** to turn or bend so as to form a curve [The trail *curves* to the left.] **2.** to move in a curved path [The next pitch *curved* in to the batter.] —**curved,** *p.t. & p.p.;* **curv′ing,** *pr.p.*

cush·ion (koosh′ən), *n.* **1.** a pillow or soft pad for sitting on or leaning against [the *cushions* of a sofa]. **2.** something soft or springy like a cushion, as the rim of a billiard table, where the balls hit. —*v.* **1.** to furnish with a cushion [a *cushioned* seat]. **2.** to protect from shock by means of a cushion [Grass *cushioned* his fall.]

cusp (kusp), *n.* **1.** a point formed where two curves meet [the *cusps* of a crescent moon]. **2.** any of the high points on the chewing part of a tooth.

cus·pid (kus′pid), *n.* a tooth with one cusp; canine tooth.

cus·pi·dor (kus′pə dôr), *n.* same as **spittoon.**

cuss (kus), *n. & v.* curse: *only in everyday talk.*

cuss·ed (kus′id), *adj.* **1.** cursed. **2.** stubborn. *Used only in everyday talk.*

cus·tard (kus′tərd), *n.* a soft food made of eggs, milk, and sugar, either boiled or baked.

cus·to·di·an (kus tō′di ən), *n.* **1.** a person who is the keeper or guardian of something [the *custodian* of a private library]. **2.** a person whose work is to take care of a building; janitor.

cus·to·dy (kus′tə dē), *n.* a guarding or keeping safe; care [The tax records are in the *custody* of the county auditor.] —**in custody,** in the keeping of the police; in jail or prison. —**take into custody,** to arrest.

cus·tom (kus′təm), *n.* **1.** a usual thing to do; habit [It is his *custom* to have tea after dinner.] **2.** something that has been done for a long time and so has become the common or regular thing to do [It is the *custom* to have a turkey dinner at Thanksgiving.] **3.** **customs,** *pl.* taxes collected by a government on goods brought in from other countries; also, the government agency that collects these taxes. **4.** the support given to a

fat,   āpe,   cär,   ten,   ēven,   hit,   bīte,   gō,   hôrn,   tōōl,   book,   up,   fŭr;
get,   joy,   yet,   chin,   she,   thin,   *th*en;   zh = s in pleasure;   ' as in able (ā′b'l)
ə = a in ago,   e in agent,   i in sanity,   o in confess,   u in focus.

business by buying regularly from it [That baker has had the *custom* of our family for many years.] —*adj.* **1.** made to order; made for a certain customer [*custom* shoes]. **2.** making things to order [a *custom* tailor].

cus·tom·ar·y (kus′tə mer′ē), *adj.* in keeping with custom; usual [It is *customary* to tip a waitress.] —**cus′tom·ar′i·ly,** *adv.*

cus·tom·er (kus′təm ər), *n.* **1.** a person who buys, especially one who buys regularly [He has been a *customer* of this shop for ten years.] **2.** any person with whom one has dealings: *used only in everyday talk* [a rough *customer*].

cus·tom·house (kus′təm hous), *n.* a building or office where customs are paid.

cus·tom-made (kus′təm mād′), *adj.* made especially for a certain customer; made to order.

cut (kut), *v.* **1.** to make an opening in with a knife or other sharp tool; pierce; gash [He *cut* his chin while shaving.] **2.** to divide into parts with such a tool; sever [Will you *cut* the cake?] **3.** to make by cutting [He *cut* a path through the underbrush.] **4.** to make shorter by trimming [to *cut* one's hair]. **5.** to make less; reduce; decrease [Prices were *cut*.] **6.** to hurt as if with sharp strokes [*cut* by the cold wind]. **7.** to be cut [This wood *cuts* easily.] **8.** to go through or across, usually to make a shorter way [The path *cuts* across the meadow. The tunnel *cuts* through the mountain.] **9.** to have a new tooth grow through the gum. **10.** to hit a ball so that it spins or glances off. **11.** to pretend not to see or know a person; snub: *used only in everyday talk.* —*n.* **1.** a cutting or being cut. **2.** a stroke or blow that is sharp or cutting. **3.** an opening made by a knife or other sharp tool. **4.** a piece cut off [a *cut* of beef]. **5.** a making less; reduction [a *cut* in pay]. **6.** the shortest way across: usually **short cut. 7.** the style in which a thing is cut; fashion [the *cut* of his suit]. **8.** something said or done that hurts one's feelings. **9.** a block or plate engraved for printing; also, a picture, etc. made from this. **10.** a share, as of profits: *slang in this meaning.* —**cut and dried,** dull or boring. —**cut back,** to make shorter as by cutting off the end. —**cut down, 1.** to cause to fall by cutting. **2.** to make less; reduce. —**cut in, 1.** to move in suddenly [A car *cut in* ahead of ours.] **2.** to break in on; interrupt. —**cut off, 1.** to separate from other parts by cutting; sever. **2.** to stop suddenly; shut off. —**cut out, 1.** to remove by cutting. **2.** to remove; leave out; omit. **3.** to make by cutting. **4.** to stop; discontinue: *used only in everyday talk.* —**cut out for,** suited for. —**cut short,** to stop suddenly before the end. —**cut up, 1.** to cut into pieces. **2.** to joke; clown: *slang in this meaning.* —**cut,** *p.t. & p.p.*; **cut′ting,** *pr.p.*

cute (kyōōt), *adj.* **1.** clever or shrewd [a *cute* trick]. **2.** pretty or pleasing in a dainty way. *Used only in everyday talk.* —**cut′er,** *compar.*; **cut′est,** *superl.* —**cute′ly,** *adv.*

cut·i·cle (kyōō′ti k'l), *n.* **1.** the outer layer of the skin. **2.** hardened skin, as at the base and sides of a fingernail.

cut·lass or **cut·las** (kut′ləs), *n.* a short, curved sword, with a sharp edge on one side.

cut·ler (kut′lər), *n.* a person who makes, sells, or repairs knives or other cutting tools.

cut·ler·y (kut′lər ē), *n.* **1.** cutting tools such as knives and scissors. **2.** knives, forks, and spoons, for use in eating.

cut·let (kut′lit), *n.* **1.** a small slice of meat from the ribs or leg, for frying or broiling. **2.** a small, flat cake of chopped meat or fish.

cutlass

cut·off (kut′ôf), *n.* **1.** a road that is a short cut. **2.** a valve or other part that shuts off a flow of steam, water, etc.

cut-rate (kut′rāt′), *adj.* selling or on sale at a lower price [*cut-rate* drugs].

cut·ter (kut′ər), *n.* **1.** a person or thing that cuts, as a person who cuts cloth into the sections that are sewed together to form a garment. **2.** a small, swift boat or ship, as an armed ship used by the coast guard for patrolling.

cut·throat (kut′thrōt), *n.* a murderer. —*adj.* without mercy; ruthless.

cut·ting (kut′ing), *n.* **1.** the act of one that cuts. **2.** a piece cut off, as a shoot cut from a plant for starting a new plant. —*adj.* **1.** that cuts; sharp [a *cutting* edge]. **2.** chilling or piercing [a *cutting* wind]. **3.** rude; harsh [a *cutting* remark].

cut·tle·fish (kut′'l fish), *n.* a sea animal with ten arms and a hard inside shell that is called a **cut′tle·bone** and is used as a bird food. Some cuttlefishes squirt out a black fluid when in danger.

cut·worm (kut′wûrm), *n.* a caterpillar that feeds on young plants, as cabbage or corn, which it cuts near the ground.

cuttlefish (about 8 in. long)

cwt., abbreviation for **hundredweight.**

-cy (sē), a suffix meaning: **1.** quality or condition of being [*Hesitancy* is the quality of being hesitant.] **2.** position or rank of [*Captaincy* is the rank of captain.]

cy·a·nide (sī′ə nīd), *n.* any of certain highly poisonous compounds.

cy·cle (sī′k'l), *n.* **1.** a complete set of events that keep coming back in the same order; also, the time it takes for one complete set to take place [the *cycle* of the four seasons; the business *cycle* of prosperity and depression]. **2.** a very long period of time; an age. **3.** a bicycle, tricycle, or motorcycle. **4.** a complete set of stories, songs, or poems about a certain hero or event. —*v.* to ride a bicycle, tricycle, or motorcycle. —**cy′-cled,** *p.t. & p.p.*; **cy′cling,** *pr.p.*

cy·clic (sī′klik *or* sik′lik), *adj.* of or like a cycle; happening in cycles.

cy·clist (sī′klist), *n.* a person who rides a bicycle, tricycle, or motorcycle.

cy·clone (sī′klōn), *n.* a storm with very strong winds moving around a center of low pressure.

cy·clon·ic (sī klän′ik), *adj.* of or like a cyclone.

cy·clo·pe·di·a or **cy·clo·pae·di·a** (sī′klə pē′di ə), *n.* same as **encyclopedia**.

Cy·clops (sī′kläps), *n.* any of a race of giants in Greek myths, who had only one eye, in the forehead. —**Cy·clo·pes** (sī klō′pēz), *pl.*

cy·clo·tron (sī′klə trän), *n.* a large apparatus for giving such high speed to atomic particles that they will break into other atoms and cause changes in the nuclei.

cyg·net (sig′nit), *n.* a young swan.

cyl·in·der (sil′in dər), *n.* **1.** a round figure with two flat ends that are parallel circles: *see the picture.* **2.** anything shaped like this, as the part of a revolver that holds the cartridges, or the chamber in which a piston of an engine moves up and down.

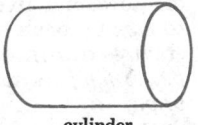
cylinder

cy·lin·dri·cal (si lin′dri k'l), *adj.* having the shape of a cylinder.

cym·bal (sim′b'l), *n.* a round brass plate, used in orchestras and bands, that makes a sharp, ringing sound when it is hit. Cymbals can be used in pairs that are struck together.

cymbals

cyn·ic (sin′ik), *n.* a person who is cynical.

cyn·i·cal (sin′i k'l), *adj.* **1.** doubting that people are ever sincere, honest, or good. **2.** gloomy and bitter about life; sarcastic, sneering, or the like. —**cyn′i·cal·ly**, *adv.*

cyn·i·cism (sin′ə siz'm), *n.* **1.** the feelings or beliefs of a cynical person. **2.** a cynical idea or remark.

cy·no·sure (sī′nə shoor *or* sin′ə shoor), *n.* a person or thing that is a center of attention [As he dropped his fork, he felt he was the *cynosure* of all eyes.]

cy·press (sī′prəs), *n.* **1.** an evergreen tree with cones and dark leaves. **2.** the hard wood of this tree.

Cy·prus (sī′prəs), *n.* a country on an island in the Mediterranean, south of Turkey. —**Cyp·ri·an** (sip′ri ən) or **Cyp·ri·ot** (sip′ri ət), *adj. & n.*

Cy·rus (sī′rəs), *n.* 600?–529 B.C.; king of Persia and founder of the Persian empire.

cyst (sist), *n.* a small bag or pouch growing in some part of the body, especially one filled with fluid or hard matter.

czar (zär), *n.* the title of any of the former emperors of Russia.

cza·ri·na (zä rē′nə), *n.* the wife of a czar.

Czech (chek), *n.* **1.** a person born or living in Czechoslovakia, especially a Slav of the western part. **2.** the Slavic language of the Czechs. —*adj.* of Czechoslovakia or its people.

Czech·o·slo·vak (chek′ə slō′vak *or* chek′ə slō′väk), *adj.* of Czechoslovakia or its people. —*n.* **1.** a person born or living in Czechoslovakia. **2.** any of the Slavic dialects spoken in Czechoslovakia.

Czech·o·slo·va·ki·a (chek′ə slō vä′ki ə), *n.* a country in central Europe. —**Czech′o·slo·va′ki·an**, *adj. & n.*

D

D, d (dē), *n.* the fourth letter of the English alphabet. —**D's, d's** (dēz), *pl.*

D, *n.* the Roman numeral for 500.

d., abbreviation used in England for **penny** or **pence.** It actually stands for the Latin word *denarius,* a small coin of ancient Rome.

D.A., abbreviation for **District Attorney.**

dab (dab), *v.* to stroke lightly and quickly; pat with soft, gentle strokes [to *dab* one's face with lotion; to *dab* paint on a surface]. —*n.* **1.** a light, quick stroke; tap; pat. **2.** a small bit of something soft or moist [a *dab* of butter]. —**dabbed,** *p.t. & p.p.;* **dab′bing,** *pr.p.*

dab·ble (dab′'l), *v.* **1.** to dip the hands lightly in and out of water, as in play. **2.** to do something lightly or playfully, not in a serious or thorough way [He *dabbles* in music.] —**dab′bled,** *p.t. & p.p.;* **dab′bling,** *pr.p.* —**dab′bler,** *n.*

dace (dās), *n.* a small fish of the carp family, found in fresh water. —**dace** or **dac′es,** *pl.*

dachs·hund (däks′hoont *or* daks′hund), *n.* a small dog with a long body and very short legs.

Da·cron (dā′krän), *n.* a man-made fiber or a fabric made from this that is washable and does not wrinkle easily: *a trademark.*

dachshund (8 in. high at shoulder)

dac·tyl·ic (dak til′ik), *adj.* describing poetry made up of measures of three syllables each, with the accent on the first syllable ["Take′ her up/ ten′der ly" is a *dactylic* line.]

dad (dad), *n.* father: *used in familiar talk.*

dad·dy (dad′ē), *n.* father: *mainly a child's word.* —**dad′dies,** *pl.*

---

fat, āpe, cär, ten, ēven, hit, bīte, gō, hôrn, tool, book, up, fûr;
get, joy, yet, chin, she, thin, *th*en; zh = s in pleasure; ′ as in able (ā′b'l);
ə = a in ago, e in agent, i in sanity, o in confess, u in focus.

dad·dy-long·legs (dad′ē lông′legz), *n.* an animal that is like a spider but with much longer and thinner legs.—**dad′dy-long′-legs,** *pl.*

daf·fo·dil (daf′ə dil), *n.* a plant that grows from a bulb and has long, narrow leaves and yellow flowers.

daddy-longlegs

daft (daft), *adj.* silly, foolish, crazy, etc.

dag·ger (dag′ər), *n.* **1.** a weapon with a short, pointed blade, used for stabbing. **2.** the mark †, used in printing to call attention to a footnote or the like.

da·guerre·o·type (də ger′ə-tīp), *n.* an old kind of photograph made on a chemically treated metal or glass plate.

dahl·ia (dal′yə), *n.* a tall plant having large, showy flowers in various bright colors.

Da·ho·mey (dä hō′mā), *n.* a country in western Africa, on the Atlantic Ocean.

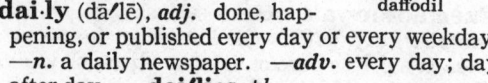
daffodil

dai·ly (dā′lē), *adj.* done, happening, or published every day or every weekday. —*n.* a daily newspaper. —*adv.* every day; day after day. —**dai′lies,** *pl.*

dain·ty (dān′tē), *adj.* **1.** pretty or lovely in a delicate way [a *dainty* lace handkerchief]. **2.** showing a delicate or fussy taste [a *dainty* appetite]. **3.** delicious and choice [a *dainty* dish]. —*n.* a choice food; delicacy. —**dain′ties,** *pl.* —**dain′ti·ly,** *adv.* —**dain′ti·ness,** *n.*

dair·y (der′ē), *n.* **1.** a building where milk and cream are kept and butter and cheese are made. **2.** a farm on which milk, butter, cheese, etc. are produced. **3.** a store that sells milk, butter, cheese, etc. —**dair′ies,** *pl.*

dair·y·maid (der′ē mād), *n.* a girl or woman who works in a dairy.

dair·y·man (der′ē mən), *n.* **1.** a man who works for a dairy. **2.** a man who owns or manages a dairy. —**dair′y·men,** *pl.*

da·is (dā′is), *n.* a platform at one end of a room [The throne stood on a *dais*.] —**da′is·es,** *pl.*

dai·sy (dā′zē), *n.* **1.** a common plant with flowers that have white or pink rays in the shape of petals around a yellow center. **2.** such a flower. —**dai′sies,** *pl.*

Da·ko·ta (də kō′tə), *n.* the U.S. territory from which North Dakota and South Dakota were formed.

dale (dāl), *n.* a valley.

Dal·las (dal′əs), *n.* a city in northeastern Texas.

daisy

dal·li·ance (dal′i əns), *n.* the act of dallying; flirting, toying, trifling, or the like.

dal·ly (dal′ē), *v.* **1.** to deal with in a light and playful way; toy; flirt; trifle [to *dally* with an idea]. **2.** to waste time; loiter. —**dal′lied,** *p.t. & p.p.;* **dal′ly·ing,** *pr.p.*

Dal·ma·tia (dal mā′shə), *n.* a region of southwestern Yugoslavia.

Dal·ma·tian (dal mā′shən), *n.* a large dog with short hair and a black-and-white coat.

dam (dam), *n.* a wall built to hold back flowing water, or the water held back in this way. —*v.* to hold back as by a dam; keep back the flow of [to *dam* a river; to *dam* up one's energy]. —**dammed,** *p.t. & p.p.;* **dam′ming,** *pr.p.*

dam (dam), *n.* the female parent of a horse, cow, sheep, etc.

dam

dam·age (dam′ij), *n.* **1.** the hurting or breaking of a thing so as to make it of less value [The storm caused some *damage* to the barn.] **2. damages,** *pl.* money asked or paid to make up for harm or damage done [The victim of the accident sued for $10,000 in *damages*.] —*v.* to do damage to [The frost *damaged* the crops.] —**dam′aged,** *p.t. & p.p.;* **dam′ag·ing,** *pr.p.*

Da·mas·cus (də mas′kəs), *n.* the capital of Syria. It is one of the oldest cities in the world.

dam·ask (dam′əsk), *n.* **1.** a rich cloth, as of silk or linen, decorated with woven designs and used for tablecloths, furniture covering, draperies, etc. **2.** a deep pink or rose color. **3.** steel having a pattern of wavy lines, once used for making swords. —*adj.* **1.** of or like damask. **2.** deep-pink or rose.

dame (dām), *n.* **1.** a lady: *an old word, not much used now.* **2.** a title of honor held by some British women. **3.** any woman: *slang in this meaning.*

damn (dam), *v.* **1.** to say strongly that something is very bad [All critics *damned* the play.] **2.** to doom to everlasting punishment [His own sins have *damned* him.] **3.** to swear at by saying "damn"; curse. —*n.* the saying of "damn" as a curse, or to show anger, etc. —**damned** (damd), *p.t. & p.p.;* **damn·ing** (dam′ing), *pr.p.* —**dam·na·tion** (dam nā′shən), *n.*

dam·na·ble (dam′nə b'l), *adj.* deserving to be damned; very bad, hateful, outrageous, etc. [a *damnable* villain]. —**dam′na·bly,** *adv.*

Dam·o·cles (dam′ə klēz), *n.* a man in Greek legend who was given a lesson in the dangers of a ruler's life when the king seated him at a feast under a sword hanging by a single hair.

Da·mon and Pyth·i·as (dā′mən ən pith′i əs), two men in a Roman legend who were such close friends that one risked his life for the other.

damp (damp), *adj.* slightly wet; moist or foggy [*damp* clothes; *damp* weather]. —*n.* **1.** a slight wetness; moisture [The *damp* in the cave was chilling.] **2.** a harmful gas sometimes found in coal mines. —*v.* **1.** to make damp; dampen. **2.** to check or partly smother [to *damp* a fire]. —**damp′ly,** *adv.* —**damp′ness,** *n.*

damp·en (dam′pən), *v.* **1.** to make or become slightly wet or moist [*Dampen* the shirts before ironing them.] **2.** to make low or dull; deaden; check [His cold reply *dampened* our enthusiasm.]

damp·er (dam′pər), *n.* **1.** a plate in a flue, as of a furnace or stove, that can be turned to control the draft. **2.** anything that dulls or deadens [Her sadness cast a *damper* on our fun.]

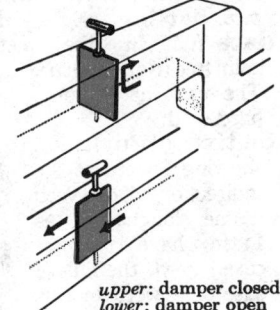
upper: damper closed
lower: damper open

dam·sel (dam′z'l), *n.* a girl or maiden: *now seldom used.*

dam·son (dam′z'n), *n.* **1.** a small, purple plum. **2.** the tree it grows on.

dance (dans), *v.* **1.** to move the body and feet in some kind of rhythm, usually to music [to *dance* a waltz or a minuet]. **2.** to jump up and down lightly or excitedly [waves *dancing* in the moonlight; children *dancing* with joy]. —*n.* **1.** the act of dancing, or one round of dancing [May I have the next *dance* with you?] **2.** the special steps of a particular kind of dancing [My favorite *dance* is the polka.] **3.** a party for dancing. **4.** a piece of music for dancing. —**danced,** *p.t.* & *p.p.;* **danc′ing,** *pr.p.*

danc·er (dan′sər), *n.* a person who dances.

dan·de·li·on (dan′di li′ən), *n.* a common weed with yellow flowers on long, hollow stems and jagged leaves that can be eaten.

dan·dle (dan′d'l), *v.* to dance a child up and down playfully, as on the knee. —**dan′dled,** *p.t.* &*p.p.;***dan′dling,** *pr.p.*

dandelion

dan·druff (dan′druf), *n.* small, white flakes of dead skin formed on the scalp.

dan·dy (dan′dē), *n.* **1.** a man who is very fussy about his clothes and looks. **2.** a thing that is very good: *a slang meaning.* —*adj.* very good; fine: *a slang meaning.* —**dan′dies,** *pl.*

Dane (dān), *n.* a person born or living in Denmark.

dan·ger (dān′jər), *n.* **1.** a condition in which there could be harm, trouble, loss,

mother dandling a child

etc.; risk; peril [to live in constant *danger*]. **2.** a thing that may cause harm [Explorers in the jungle face many *dangers*.]

dan·ger·ous (dān′jər əs), *adj.* full of danger; likely to cause harm; unsafe [This shaky old bridge is *dangerous*.] —**dan′ger·ous·ly,** *adv.*

dan·gle (dang′g'l), *v.* **1.** to hang loosely so as to swing back and forth [A long tail *dangled* from the kite.] **2.** to hold so that it dangles [The girl *dangled* her doll by one arm.] —**dan′gled,** *p.t.* & *p.p.;* **dan′gling,** *pr.p.*

Dan·iel (dan′yəl), *n.* a Hebrew prophet in the Bible who was saved from a den of lions by his faith in God.

Dan·ish (dān′ish), *adj.* of Denmark or the Danes. —*n.* the language of the Danes.

dank (dangk), *adj.* unpleasantly damp; moist and chilly [a *dank* dungeon]. —**dank′ness,** *n.*

Dan·te (dän′tā *or* dan′tē), *n.* 1265–1321; Italian poet, who wrote *The Divine Comedy.*

Dan·ube (dan′yo͞ob), *n.* a river in southern Europe, flowing eastward into the Black Sea.

dap·per (dap′ər), *adj.* **1.** neat, trim, and dressed with care. **2.** small and brisk [The *dapper* jockey mounted his horse.]

dap·ple (dap′'l), *adj.* marked with spots; mottled [a *dapple* horse]. —*v.* to mark with spots or patches [Clumps of daisies *dappled* the meadow.] —**dap′pled,** *p.t.* & *p.p.;* **dap′pling,** *pr.p.*

Dar·da·nelles (där də nelz′), *n.* the strait joining the Aegean Sea and the Sea of Marmara.

dare (der), *v.* **1.** to be brave or bold enough to do a certain thing [I wouldn't *dare* to oppose him.] **2.** to face bravely or boldly; defy [The hunter *dared* the dangers of the jungle.] **3.** to call on someone to do a certain thing to show that he is not afraid; challenge [He *dared* me to swim across the lake.] —*n.* a challenge to prove that one is not afraid [I accepted his *dare* to swim across the lake.] —**dare say,** to think it very likely. —**dared,** *p.t.* & *p.p.;* **dar′ing,** *pr.p.*

dare·dev·il (der′dev′'l), *n.* a bold, reckless person. —*adj.* bold and reckless.

dar·ing (der′ing), *adj.* bold enough to take risks; fearless. —*n.* bold courage.

Da·ri·us I (də rī′əs), 558?–486 B.C.; king of Persia from 521 to 486 B.C.

dark (därk), *adj.* **1.** having little or no light [a *dark* room; a *dark* night]. **2.** closer to black than to white; deep in shade; not light [*dark* green]. **3.** hidden; full of mystery [a *dark* secret]. **4.** gloomy or hopeless [Things looked *dark* for him.] **5.** with little or no learning; ignorant [The Middle Ages are sometimes called the *Dark* Ages.] —*n.* **1.** a being dark; darkness, as of night [Are you afraid of the *dark*?] **2.** a dark color or shade [the contrast of lights and *darks* in a picture]. —**in the dark,** not knowing or informed; ignorant [I'm *in the dark* about your plans.] —**dark′ly,** *adv.* —**dark′ness,** *n.*

dark·en (där′kən), *v.* to make or become dark.

dark horse, one who wins or may win a contest without being expected to: *used only in everyday talk.*

dar·ling (där′ling), *n.* a person whom one loves very much [People in love often call each other "*Darling.*"] —*adj.* very dear; beloved [She is my *darling* child.]

darn (därn), *v.* to mend a hole or tear in cloth by sewing stitches back and forth over it. —*n.* a place that has been darned.

dart (därt), *n.* **1.** a short arrow with a sharp point that is thrown as a weapon, or at a target in games. **2.** a sudden, quick move [The boy made a *dart* into the street.] —*v.* **1.** to send out suddenly and fast [The beacon *darted* its beam into the sky.] **2.** to move suddenly and fast [birds *darting* through the trees].

game of darts

Dar·win, Charles Robert (där′win), 1809–1882; English scientist and writer who is known for his theory of evolution.

dash (dash), *v.* **1.** to throw so as to break; smash [He *dashed* the bottle to the floor.] **2.** to hit roughly [The high wind *dashed* the boat on the rocks.] **3.** to splash [We *dashed* some water in his face.] **4.** to put an end to; destroy [Her hopes are *dashed.*] **5.** to do or write something quickly [I'll *dash* off a note to Agnes.] **6.** to move quickly; rush [The thief *dashed* down the alley.] —*n.* **1.** a heavy blow; smash [the *dash* of waves on the beach]. **2.** a little bit; pinch [Put a *dash* of salt in the salad.] **3.** a short, fast run or race [a 100-yard *dash*]. **4.** energy or liveliness [Leslie always adds *dash* to a party.] **5.** the mark (—), used in printing or writing to show a break in a sentence, or to show that something has been left out. This mark also stands for the long click used in forming letters in the Morse code.

dash·board (dash′bôrd), *n.* the panel in an automobile, etc. that has the controls and gauges on it.

dash·ing (dash′ing), *adj.* **1.** full of dash or energy; lively [a *dashing* young man]. **2.** colorful or showy [a *dashing* costume].

das·tard (das′tərd), *n.* a mean, sneaky coward. —**das′tard·ly,** *adj.*

da·ta (dā′tə *or* dat′ə), *n.pl.* facts or figures from which something can be learned: *used with either a singular or plural verb* [This *data* is listed in tables. These *data* are listed in tables.] —**da′tum,** *sing.*

date (dāt), *n.* **1.** the time at which a thing happens [The *date* of Lincoln's birth was February 12, 1809.] **2.** the day of the month [What's the *date* today?] **3.** the words or figures on a coin, letter, etc. that tell when it was made. **4.** an agreement to meet at a certain time, as between a couple going out together; also, the person with whom one goes out: *used only in everyday talk.*

—*v.* **1.** to mark with a date [The letter is *dated* May 15.] **2.** to find out or give the date or age of [A tree can be *dated* by counting the rings in its trunk.] **3.** to be dated; belong to a particular time [a painting that *dates* from the artist's earliest work]. **4.** to have a date with: *used only in everyday talk* [Sarah is *dating* Joe tonight.] —**out of date,** no longer in use; old-fashioned. —**up to date,** keeping up with the latest ideas, facts, styles, etc.; modern. —**dat′ed,** *p.t. & p.p.;* **dat′ing,** *pr.p.* —**date′less,** *adj.*

date (dāt), *n.* the sweet, fleshy fruit of a tall palm tree (**date palm**). The fruit has a long, hard seed.

da·tive (dā′tiv), *adj.* showing a word as the indirect object of a verb [Some languages, as Latin, have a *dative* case.] —*n.* the dative case or a word in this case.

da·tum (dā′təm *or* dat′əm), *n.* singular of **data.**

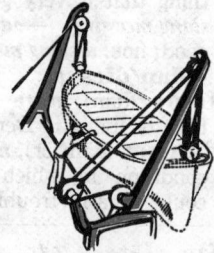
date palm

daub (dôb), *v.* **1.** to cover or smear with sticky, soft stuff [She *daubed* salve on his burned finger.] **2.** to paint in a sloppy way. —*n.* **1.** something daubed on [*daubs* of plaster]. **2.** a poorly painted picture. —**daub′er,** *n.*

daugh·ter (dô′tər), *n.* **1.** a girl or woman as she is related to a parent or to both parents. **2.** a girl or woman thought of as being related to someone or something [a *daughter* of France].

daugh·ter-in-law (dô′tər ′n lô′), *n.* the wife of one's son. —**daugh′ters-in-law′,** *pl.*

daunt (dônt), *v.* to make afraid or discouraged [She was never *daunted* by misfortune.]

daunt·less (dônt′lis), *adj.* that cannot be frightened or discouraged; fearless [The *dauntless* rebels fought on.] —**daunt′less·ly,** *adv.*

dau·phin (dô′fin), *n.* in earlier times, the title of the oldest son of the king of France.

dav·en·port (dav′ən pôrt), *n.* a large sofa.

Da·vid (dā′vid), *n.* the second king of Israel, whose story is told in the Bible.

da Vinci, see **Vinci.**

Da·vis, Jefferson (dā′vis), 1808–1889; president of the Confederacy from 1861 to 1865.

dav·it (dav′it), *n.* either of a pair of posts on a ship, which support a small boat and are used in lowering it into the water.

Da·vy Jones (dā′vē jōnz), the spirit of the sea: *a joking name used by sailors.* **Davy Jones's locker** is the bottom of the sea thought of as the grave of those drowned or buried at sea.

davits

daw (dô), *n.* same as **jackdaw.**

daw·dle (dô'd'l), *v.* to waste time by being slow; idle; loiter. —**daw'dled,** *p.t. & p.p.;* **daw'dling,** *pr.p.*

dawn (dôn), *v.* **1.** to begin to grow light as the sun rises [Day is *dawning.*] **2.** to come into being; begin to develop [With the discovery of electricity, a new age *dawned.*] **3.** to begin to be understood or felt [The meaning suddenly *dawned* on me.] —*n.* **1.** the beginning of day; daybreak. **2.** the beginning of anything [the *dawn* of the Space Age].

day (dā), *n.* **1.** the time of light between sunrise and sunset. **2.** a period of 24 hours, measured from midnight to midnight. This is nearly equal to the time that it takes the earth to revolve once on its axis. **3.** a period or time [the best writer of his *day*]. **4.** time of power, glory, or success [He has had his *day*.] **5.** the time one works each day [an eight-hour *day*]. **6. days,** *pl.* life [He spent his *days* in study.] —**call it a day,** to stop working for the day: *used only in everyday talk.* —**win the day,** to win the day's battle or contest.

day·break (dā'brāk), *n.* the time in the morning when light begins to show; dawn.

day·dream (dā'drēm), *n.* pleasant, dreamy thinking or wishing. —*v.* to have daydreams.

day·light (dā'līt), *n.* **1.** the light of day; sunlight. **2.** dawn; daybreak. **3.** daytime.

day·light-sav·ing time (dā'līt sāv'ing), time that is one hour later than standard time, generally used in the summer [9 p.m. *daylight-saving time* is 8 p.m. standard time.]

day·time (dā'tīm), *n.* the time of daylight, between dawn and sunset.

Day·ton (dā't'n), *n.* a city in southwestern Ohio.

daze (dāz), *v.* to stun or bewilder, as by a shock or blow [He was *dazed* by the news of her marriage.] —*n.* a dazed condition; bewilderment. —**dazed,** *p.t. & p.p.;* **daz'ing,** *pr.p.*

daz·zle (daz''l), *v.* **1.** to make nearly blinded, as with great brightness [I was *dazzled* by the headlights of approaching cars.] **2.** to be so brilliant or splendid as to overcome the mind or cause admiration [the *dazzling* skill of the pianist]. —*n.* a dazzling, or a thing that dazzles. —**daz'zled,** *p.t. & p.p.;* **daz'zling,** *pr.p.*

D.C., abbreviation for **District of Columbia.**

D.C. or **d.c.,** abbreviation for **direct current.**

D.D., abbreviation for **Doctor of Divinity** (a college degree held by some ministers).

D.D.S., abbreviation for **Doctor of Dental Surgery** (a college degree held by dentists).

DDT, a chemical compound for killing insects.

de-, a prefix meaning: **1.** away from; off [A train is *derailed* when it goes off the tracks.] **2.** down [To *descend* is to come down.] **3.** entirely; completely [A *despoiled* city is one that is completely plundered.] **4.** do in reverse; undo [To *defrost* food is to unfreeze it.]

dea·con (dē'k'n), *n.* **1.** a clergyman who ranks just below a priest. **2.** a church officer who helps the minister, especially in matters not having to do with worship.

dead (ded), *adj.* **1.** no longer living; without life [Throw out these *dead* flowers.] **2.** no longer in use [Sanskrit is a *dead* language.] **3.** without feeling, motion, or power [His arm hung *dead* at his side.] **4.** without warmth, brightness, sharpness, etc.; dull [a *dead* color]. **5.** not active; not working [a *dead* telephone]. **6.** sure or exact [a *dead* shot; *dead* center]. **7.** complete [a *dead* loss]. —*adv.* **1.** completely; entirely [I am *dead* tired from running.] **2.** directly; straight [Steer *dead* ahead.] —*n.* the time of most cold, most darkness, etc. [the *dead* of winter; the *dead* of night]. —**the dead,** those who have died.

dead·en (ded''n), *v.* **1.** to take away feeling; make numb [The dentist *deadens* the nerve before he drills.] **2.** to dull or weaken [Heavy curtains will *deaden* street noises.]

dead end, a street, alley, etc. closed at one end. —**dead'-end',** *adj.*

dead letter, a letter that is not claimed or delivered, as because of a wrong address.

dead·line (ded'līn), *n.* the latest time by which something must be done or finished.

dead·lock (ded'läk), *n.* a halt in a struggle because both sides are equally strong and neither will give in [The Vice President's vote breaks the *deadlock* of a tie in Senate voting.] —*v.* to bring or come to a deadlock.

dead·ly (ded'lē), *adj.* **1.** causing death; that can kill [The cobra is a *deadly* snake.] **2.** full of hate or violence [*deadly* combat; *deadly* enemies]. **3.** as in death [a *deadly* paleness]. **4.** very boring or dull: *used only in everyday talk.* —*adv.* **1.** as if dead [She turned *deadly* white.] **2.** very; extremely [He is *deadly* serious.] —**dead'li·er,** *compar.;* **dead'li·est,** *superl.*

dead reckoning, a way of figuring the position of a ship by means of the compass and ship's log, rather than by the sun or stars.

Dead Sea, a salt lake between Israel and Jordan.

deaf (def), *adj.* **1.** not able to hear or not able to hear well. **2.** not willing to hear; not paying attention [He was *deaf* to warnings of danger.] —**deaf'ness,** *n.*

deaf·en (def''n), *v.* **1.** to make deaf. **2.** to make such noise that it becomes hard to hear.

deaf-mute (def'myōōt'), *n.* a person who has been deaf from birth and cannot talk because he has never heard the sounds of words. Most deaf-mutes can now be taught to talk.

deal (dēl), *v.* **1.** to have to do with; handle, take care of, give attention to, etc. [Science *deals* with facts.] **2.** to act or behave [I don't think he *dealt* fairly with me.] **3.** to buy and sell; make a business of [My uncle *deals* in rare books.] **4.** to buy from or sell to; trade [Do you *deal* with our grocer?] **5.** to give; deliver [He *dealt* the knight a stout blow on the head.] **6.** to pass out to a number of persons; especially, to hand playing cards, one at a time, to players. —*n.* **1.** an agreement, as in business; sale, contract, or bargain [They made a *deal* to rent the building. The senator made a *deal* to get extra votes.] **2.** any arrangement or plan [The New *Deal* was the government's plan to end a depression.] **3.** the act of dealing playing cards, or the cards dealt. **4.** an amount; quantity. —**a good deal** or **a great deal,** very much [I have *a good deal* of time. Walk *a good deal* faster.] —**dealt,** *p.t. & p.p.;* **deal'ing,** *pr.p.*

deal·er (dēl'ər), *n.* **1.** a person in business; one who buys and sells [a hardware *dealer*]. **2.** the one who passes out the cards in a card game.

deal·ing (dēl'ing), *n.* usually **dealings,** *pl.* way of acting toward others; relations [In his *dealings* with friends, he was fair; in business *dealings,* he was dishonest.]

dealt (delt), past tense and past participle of **deal.**

dean (dēn), *n.* **1.** an official in a school or college who is in charge of the students or teachers. **2.** a clergyman in charge of a cathedral. **3.** the member of a group who has been in it the longest [the *dean* of American poets].

dear (dir), *adj.* **1.** much loved; beloved [a *dear* friend]. **2.** much valued; highly thought of: used in letters to show politeness [*Dear* Sir]. **3.** costing much; high in price; expensive [Meat is too *dear* for us to buy much.] —*adv.* at a high cost [You'll pay *dear* for saying that.] —*n.* a person whom one loves; darling [Her father said, "Let's go home, *dear.*"] —*interj.* a word said to show surprise, pity, etc. [Oh *dear!* What shall I do?] —**dear'ly,** *adv.* —**dear'ness,** *n.*

dearth (dûrth), *n.* a too small supply; scarcity [a *dearth* of good books].

dear·y or **dear·ie** (dir'ē), *n.* dear; darling: used only in everyday talk. —**dear'ies,** *pl.*

death (deth), *n.* **1.** the act or fact of dying; ending of life. **2.** any end that is like dying [the *death* of our hopes]. **3.** the condition of being dead [as still as *death*]. **4.** the cause of death [The atomic bomb was *death* to thousands.] —**put to death,** to kill; execute. —**to death,** very much [She worries me *to death*.]

death·bed (deth'bed), *n.* the bed on which a person dies, or the last hours of one's life.

death·less (deth'lis), *adj.* that can never die; immortal [the poet's *deathless* words].

death·like (deth'līk), *adj.* like death or as in death [a *deathlike* calm].

death·ly (deth'lē), *adj.* **1.** causing death; deadly [a *deathly* poison]. **2.** like death or as in death [a *deathly* stillness]. —*adv.* in a deathlike way [She is *deathly* ill.]

death rate, the number of deaths among a certain number of people over a certain period of time; usually, the average number of deaths for every thousand people during a year.

death's-head (deths'hed'), *n.* a human skull as a symbol of death.

Death Valley, a dry, hot region in eastern California. It is 276 feet below sea level.

de·ba·cle (dā bä'k'l or di bak''l), *n.* a sudden great disaster or upset [Napoleon's invasion of Russia was a *debacle* that ended in his defeat.]

de·bar (di bär'), *v.* to keep from some right or privilege [He was *debarred* from voting.] —**de·barred',** *p.t. & p.p.;* **de·bar'ring,** *pr.p.*

de·base (di bās'), *v.* to make lower in value or character [to *debase* oneself by lying; to *debase* money by raising the price of gold or silver]. —**de·based',** *p.t. & p.p.;* **de·bas'ing,** *pr.p.* —**de·base'ment,** *n.*

de·bat·a·ble (di bāt'ə b'l), *adj.* that can be debated; that has strong points on both sides [a *debatable* question].

de·bate (di bāt'), *v.* **1.** to give reasons for or against; argue about something, especially in a formal contest between two opposite sides [The Senate *debated* the question of foreign treaties.] **2.** to consider reasons for and against [He *debated* the problem in his own mind.] —*n.* the act of debating something; discussion or formal argument. —**de·bat'ed,** *p.t. & p.p.;* **de·bat'ing,** *pr.p.* —**de·bat'er,** *n.*

de·bauch (di bôch'), *v.* to lead into bad or evil ways; lead astray; corrupt.

de·bauch·er·y (di bôch'ər ē), *n.* the satisfying of one's desires and appetites in a bad or wild way; dissipation. —**de·bauch'er·ies,** *pl.*

de·bil·i·tate (di bil'ə tāt), *v.* to weaken [Too much bed rest after surgery can be *debilitating* to the body.] —**de·bil'i·tat·ed,** *p.t. & p.p.;* **de·bil'i·tat·ing,** *pr.p.*

de·bil·i·ty (di bil'ə tē), *n.* weakness.

deb·it (deb'it), *n.* an entry in an account book of money owed. —*v.* to charge with a debt.

deb·o·nair or **deb·o·naire** (deb ə ner'), *adj.* cheerful and pleasant in a carefree way.

de·brief (dē brēf'), *v.* to question someone who has ended a mission, so as to get information.

de·bris or **dé·bris** (də brē' or dā'brē), *n.* broken, scattered remains; rubbish [the *debris* from an explosion; the *debris* on picnic grounds].

debt (det), *n.* **1.** something that one owes to another [a *debt* of five dollars; a *debt* of gratitude]. **2.** the condition of owing [I am greatly in *debt* to him.]

debt·or (det'ər), *n.* one who owes a debt.

de·bunk (di bungk'), *v.* to show how false something really is: used only in everyday talk.

de·but or **dé·but** (di byōō' or dā'byōō), *n.* **1.** a first appearance before the public, as of an actor. **2.** the entering of a girl into high society, usually by means of a formal party.

deb·u·tante or **dé·bu·tante** (deb'yoo tänt'), *n.* a girl making her debut into high society.

Dec., abbreviation for **December.**

deca- or **dec-,** a prefix meaning "ten" [A *decagon* is a plane figure with ten sides.]

dec·ade (dek'ād), *n.* a period of ten years.

de·ca·dence (di kā'd'ns or dek'ə dəns), *n.* a becoming bad, immoral, or impure [A love of cruel sports showed the *decadence* of Nero's court.] —**de·ca'dent,** *adj.*

dec·a·gon (dek′ə gän), *n.* a plane figure with ten sides and ten angles.

de·cal (di kal′), *n.* a picture or design that is transferred from a specially prepared paper onto glass, wood, etc.: a shortened form of **de·cal·co·ma·ni·a** (di kal′kə mā′ni ə).

Dec·a·logue or **Dec·a·log** (dek′ə lôg), *n.* the Ten Commandments.

de·camp (di kamp′), *v.* **1.** to pack up and leave a camp. **2.** to leave suddenly and secretly [The treasurer *decamped* with the tax money.]

de·cant (di kant′), *v.* to pour off carefully, as into another bottle, without stirring up the sediment [to *decant* wine].

de·cant·er (di kan′tər), *n.* a decorative glass bottle for serving wine or liquor.

de·cap·i·tate (di kap′ə tāt), *v.* to cut off the head of; behead. —**de·cap′i·tat·ed,** *p.t.* & *p.p.;* **de·cap′i·tat·ing,** *pr.p.* —**de·cap′i·ta′tion,** *n.*

de·cath·lon (di kath′län), *n.* an athletic contest that tests skills in ten events, including running, jumping, and throwing.

de·cay (di kā′), *v.* **1.** to become rotten by the action of bacteria [The fallen apples *decayed* on the ground.] **2.** to fall into ruin; become no longer sound, powerful, rich, beautiful, etc. [Spain's power *decayed* after her fleet was destroyed.] —*n.* a rotting or falling into ruin.

decanter

de·cease (di sēs′), *n.* death [He will inherit the estate upon the *decease* of his uncle.]

de·ceased (di sēst′), *adj.* dead. —**the deceased,** the dead person or dead persons.

de·ceit (di sēt′), *n.* **1.** a deceiving or lying. **2.** a lie or a dishonest act or acts.

de·ceit·ful (di sēt′fəl), *adj.* full of deceit; lying or misleading; not to be trusted. —**de·ceit′ful·ly,** *adv.* —**de·ceit′ful·ness,** *n.*

de·ceive (di sēv′), *v.* to make someone believe what is not true; fool or trick; mislead [The queen *deceived* Snow White by pretending to be her friend.] —**de·ceived′,** *p.t.* & *p.p.;* **de·ceiv′ing,** *pr.p.* —**de·ceiv′er,** *n.*

De·cem·ber (di sem′bər), *n.* the last month of the year. It has 31 days. Abbreviated **Dec.**

de·cen·cy (dē′s′n sē), *n.* **1.** the quality of being decent; proper behavior, modesty, courtesy, etc. [You might have the *decency* to thank her.] **2.** **decencies,** *pl.* things needed to lead a decent life. —**de′cen·cies,** *pl.*

de·cent (dē′s′nt), *adj.* **1.** proper and fitting; not to be ashamed of; respectable [*decent* manners; *decent* language]. **2.** fairly good; satisfactory [a *decent* wage]. **3.** kind; generous; fair [It was *decent* of him to lend you his car.] —**de′cent·ly,** *adv.*

de·cen·tral·ize (dē sen′trəl īz), *v.* to turn over power from a main center, as a national government, to local groups or branches. —**de·cen′tral·ized,** *p.t.* & *p.p.;* **de·cen′tral·iz·ing,** *pr.p.* —**de·cen′tral·i·za′tion,** *n.*

de·cep·tion (di sep′shən), *n.* **1.** a deceiving or fooling. **2.** something that fools, as a fraud.

de·cep·tive (di sep′tiv), *adj.* deceiving; not what it seems to be. —**de·cep′tive·ly,** *adv.*

de·cide (di sīd′), *v.* **1.** to choose after some thought; make up one's mind [She can't *decide* which dress to wear.] **2.** to end a contest or argument by giving one side the victory; settle [A jury will *decide* this case.] —**de·cid′ed,** *p.t.* & *p.p.;* **de·cid′ing,** *pr.p.*

de·cid·ed (di sīd′id), *adj.* **1.** clear and sharp; definite [There was a *decided* change in the weather.] **2.** sure or firm; without doubt [He has very *decided* ideas on the subject.] —**de·cid′ed·ly,** *adv.*

de·cid·u·ous (di sij′ōō əs), *adj.* **1.** falling off at a certain time of the year, as the leaves of some trees. **2.** shedding its leaves every year; not evergreen [Elms are *deciduous* trees.]

dec·i·mal (des′ə m'l), *adj.* of or based upon the number ten; counted by tens [The metric system of measure is a *decimal* system.] —*n.* a fraction with a denominator of 10, or of 100 or 1,000, etc. It is shown by a point (**decimal point**) before the numerator, as .5 (5/10) or .63 (63/100).

dec·i·mate (des′ə māt), *v.* to destroy or kill one tenth of or, now, any large part of [The city was *decimated* by the bombing attacks.] —**dec′i·mat·ed,** *p.t.* & *p.p.;* **dec′i·mat·ing,** *pr.p.* —**dec′i·ma′tion,** *n.*

de·ci·pher (di sī′fər), *v.* **1.** to translate from secret writing or code into ordinary language. **2.** to make out the meaning, as of scrawled or blurred writing.

de·ci·sion (di sizh′ən), *n.* **1.** the act of deciding or settling something, or the opinion or choice decided on [The *decision* of the judges will be final.] **2.** firmness of mind; determination [a man of *decision*].

de·ci·sive (di sī′siv), *adj.* **1.** that settles or could settle a question or argument [a *decisive* battle in a war]. **2.** showing firmness or determination [a *decisive* tone of voice].

deck (dek), *n.* **1.** any of the floors of a ship, reaching from side to side. The main deck is usually a roof over the ship's hold. **2.** a pack of playing cards. —*v.* to dress or adorn with fine clothes or decorations [She *decked* herself in expensive furs.] —**clear the decks,** to get ready for action.

de·claim (di klām′), *v.* to speak loudly and with strong feeling, as some orators do in trying to sway an audience.

dec·la·ma·tion (dek′lə mā′shən), *n.* **1.** the act or skill of declaiming. **2.** a speech, poem, etc. that is or can be declaimed.

de·clam·a·to·ry (di klam′ə tôr′ē), *adj.* **1.** of or fit for declaiming [a *declamatory* poem]. **2.** speaking loudly and with great feeling.

dec·la·ra·tion (dek′lə rā′shən), *n.* **1.** a declaring or being declared [The *declaration* of a holiday is always good news.] **2.** a public statement; proclamation [The *Declaration* of Independence was the formal statement by the thirteen American colonies in 1776 declaring them to be independent of Great Britain.]

de·clar·a·tive (di klar′ə tiv), *adj.* making a statement, not asking a question ["I shall go away" is a *declarative* sentence.]

de·clare (di kler′), *v.* **1.** to make known; say or announce openly [Let us *declare* a war on disease. "I'm leaving for good!" he *declared*.] **2.** to tell what taxable goods one is bringing into a country [At the customs office, we *declared* the camera we bought in Canada.] **—I declare!** I am surprised, startled, etc. **—de·clared′,** *p.t. & p.p.;* **de·clar′ing,** *pr.p.*

de·clen·sion (di klen′shən), *n.* **1.** a class of nouns, pronouns, and adjectives that have the same endings or other changes to show case, or how they are used in a sentence. **2.** the changing of the forms of such words. English has such declension only for pronouns, as *he, him, his.*

de·cline (di klīn′), *v.* **1.** to bend or slope downward [The lawn *declines* to the sidewalk.] **2.** to become less, as in health, power, or value; decay [A person's strength usually *declines* in old age.] **3.** to refuse something, especially in a polite way [I am sorry I must *decline* your invitation.] **4.** to give the different case forms of a noun, pronoun, or adjective in order. **—n. 1.** a becoming less, smaller, or weaker; decay [a *decline* in employment]. **2.** the last part [the *decline* of day]. **3.** a downward slope [We slid down the *decline.*] **—de·clined′,** *p.t. & p.p.;* **de·clin′ing,** *pr.p.*

de·cliv·i·ty (di kliv′ə tē), *n.* a downward slope of the ground. **—de·cliv′i·ties,** *pl.*

de·code (dē kōd′), *v.* to figure out the meaning of something written in code. **—de·cod′ed,** *p.t. & p.p.;* **de·cod′ing,** *pr.p.*

de·com·pose (dē kəm pōz′), *v.* **1.** to rot or decay. **2.** to break up into its separate basic parts [Electrolysis will *decompose* water into hydrogen and oxygen.] **—de·com·posed′,** *p.t. & p.p.;* **de·com·pos′ing,** *pr.p.* **—de·com·po·si·tion** (dē′käm pə zish′ən), *n.*

de·con·gest·ant (dē′kən jes′tənt), *n.* a medicine used to relieve congestion in a nose caused by a cold, hay fever, etc.

dec·o·rate (dek′ə rāt), *v.* **1.** to add something to so as to make prettier or more pleasing; ornament; adorn [to *decorate* a blouse with embroidery]. **2.** to plan and arrange the colors and furnishings of a room or house. **3.** to give a medal, ribbon, or other sign of honor to [The general *decorated* the soldier for bravery.] **—dec′or·at·ed,** *p.t. & p.p.;* **dec′or·at·ing,** *pr.p.*

dec·o·ra·tion (dek′ə rā′shən), *n.* **1.** the act of decorating. **2.** anything used for decorating; ornament [Christmas tree *decorations*]. **3.** a medal, ribbon, etc. given as a sign of honor.

Decoration Day, same as **Memorial Day.**

dec·o·ra·tive (dek′ə rə tiv *or* dek′ə rā′tiv), *adj.* that serves to decorate; ornamental.

dec·o·ra·tor (dek′ə rā′tər), *n.* a person who decorates; especially, one whose work is decorating and furnishing rooms.

dec·o·rous (dek′ə rəs), *adj.* having or showing dignity and good taste; behaving properly.

de·co·rum (di kôr′əm), *n.* that which is suitable or fitting; proper and dignified behavior, speech, etc. [Loud laughter in the library shows a lack of *decorum.*]

de·coy (di koi′ *or* dē′koi), *n.* **1.** an artificial bird or animal used to attract wild birds or animals to a place where they can be shot or trapped; also, a live bird or animal used in the same way. **2.** a thing or person used to lure someone into a trap. **—v.** (di koi′), to lure into a trap or danger.

decoy for ducks

de·crease (di krēs′), *v.* to make or become gradually less or smaller [Father has been *decreasing* my allowance for several weeks. The pain is *decreasing.*] **—n.** (dē′krēs), **1.** a decreasing or growing less [a *decrease* in profits]. **2.** the amount of decreasing [The sales *decrease* last month was $300.] **—on the decrease,** decreasing. **—de·creased′,** *p.t. & p.p.;* **de·creas′ing,** *pr.p.*

de·cree (di krē′), *n.* an official order or decision, as of a government or court. **—v.** to order or decide by decree [The governor *decreed* an increase in taxes.] **—de·creed′,** *p.t. & p.p.;* **de·cree′ing,** *pr.p.*

de·crep·it (di krep′it), *adj.* broken down or worn out by old age or long use.

de·crep·i·tude (di krep′ə tōod *or* di krep′ə tyōod), *n.* the condition of being decrepit.

de·cre·scen·do (dē′krə shen′dō), *adj. & adv.* gradually becoming softer: *a direction in music usually shown by the sign >.* **—n.** a decrease in loudness. **—de′cre·scen′dos,** *pl.*

de·cry (di krī′), *v.* to speak out against strongly and openly; condemn [to *decry* dishonesty in government]. **—de·cried′,** *p.t. & p.p.;* **de·cry′ing,** *pr.p.*

ded·i·cate (ded′ə kāt), *v.* **1.** to set aside for a special purpose [The church was *dedicated* to the worship of God. The doctor has *dedicated* his life to cancer research.] **2.** to say at the beginning of a book, etc. that it was written in honor of, or out of affection for, a certain person [The author *dedicated* the novel to his wife.] **—ded′i·cat·ed,** *p.t. & p.p.;* **ded′i·cat·ing,** *pr.p.* **—ded′i·ca′tion,** *n.*

ded·i·ca·to·ry (ded′ə kə tôr′ē), *adj.* of or as a dedication [a *dedicatory* speech].

de·duce (di dōōs′ *or* di dyōōs′), *v.* to figure out by reasoning from known facts or general principles; infer [The existence of the planet Neptune was *deduced* before its actual discovery.] —**de-duced′**, *p.t. & p.p.;* **de·duc′ing**, *pr.p.*

de·duct (di dukt′), *v.* to take away; subtract [to *deduct* $10 from a price for paying cash].

de·duc·tion (di duk′shən), *n.* **1.** the act of deducting; subtraction. **2.** the amount deducted. **3.** reasoning from known facts or general principles to a logical conclusion [Detectives in stories solve crimes by *deduction.*] **4.** a conclusion reached in this way. —**de·duc′tive,** *adj.*

deed (dēd), *n.* **1.** a thing done; act; action ["*Deeds* speak louder than words."] **2.** a paper drawn up according to law that hands over a property to someone. —*v.* to hand over a property by such a paper.

deem (dēm), *v.* to think, believe, or judge [He *deems* it necessary that we go along.]

deep (dēp), *adj.* **1.** reaching far down, far in, or far back [a *deep* lake; a *deep* wound; a *deep* closet]. **2.** reaching a certain distance down, in, or back [This drawer is only ten inches *deep.*] **3.** having a low tone or low tones [a *deep* groan; a *deep* bass voice]. **4.** hard to understand [a *deep* subject]. **5.** great, heavy, or serious [*deep* disgrace; a *deep* sleep]. **6.** strongly felt [*deep* love]. **7.** dark and rich [*deep* colors]. **8.** very much taken up; greatly involved [*deep* in thought; *deep* in debt]. —*n.* **1.** a deep place. **2.** the middle or darkest part [the *deep* of the night]. —*adv.* far down, far in, or far back [to dig *deep*]. —**the deep,** the sea or ocean: *used mainly in poetry.* —**deep′ly,** *adv.* —**deep′ness,** *n.*

deep·en (dēp′'n), *v.* to make or become deeper.

deep-root·ed (dēp′rōot′id), *adj.* **1.** having deep roots. **2.** firmly fixed; hard to remove [*deep-rooted* prejudice].

deep-seat·ed (dēp′sēt′id), *adj.* firmly fixed; hard to remove; deep-rooted.

deer (dir), *n.* a swift-running, hoofed animal that chews its cud. The male usually has antlers that are shed every year. —**deer,** *pl.*

deer·skin (dir′skin), *n.* **1.** the hide of a deer. **2.** leather made from this hide.

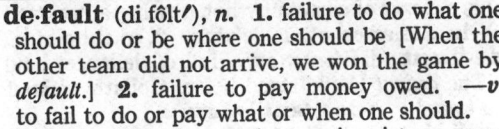
deer

de·face (di fās′), *v.* to spoil the looks of; mar [to *deface* a picture by writing on it]. —**de-faced′,** *p.t. & p.p.;* **de-fac′ing,** *pr.p.*

def·a·ma·tion (def′ə mā′shən), *n.* a defaming or being defamed; slander or libel.

de·fam·a·to·ry (di fam′ə tôr′ē), *adj.* defaming; hurting a person's reputation.

de·fame (di fām′), *v.* to say false and harmful things so as to hurt the reputation of; slander or libel. —**de·famed′,** *p.t. & p.p.;* **de·fam′ing,** *pr.p.* —**de·fam′er,** *n.*

de·fault (di fôlt′), *n.* **1.** failure to do what one should do or be where one should be [When the other team did not arrive, we won the game by *default.*] **2.** failure to pay money owed. —*v.* to fail to do or pay what or when one should.

de·feat (di fēt′), *v.* **1.** to win victory over; overcome; beat [to *defeat* a foe]. **2.** to bring to nothing; make fail; balk [His hopes were *defeated* by a stroke of bad luck.] —*n.* **1.** a being defeated; failure to win [Germany's *defeat* in World War II]. **2.** a defeating; victory over [the Allies' *defeat* of Germany].

de·feat·ist (di fēt′ist), *n.* a person who gives up a fight before it is lost. —*adj.* of or like a defeatist. —**de·feat′ism,** *n.*

de·fect (dē′fekt *or* di fekt′), *n.* a fault or flaw; imperfect part; weakness [a *defect* in a diamond; a *defect* in one's vision]. —*v.* (di fekt′), to desert one's cause or group; forsake. —**de·fec′tion,** *n.*

de·fec·tive (di fek′tiv), *adj.* having a defect or defects; imperfect; faulty.

de·fence (di fens′), *n.* British spelling of **defense.**

de·fend (di fend′), *v.* **1.** to keep safe from harm or danger; guard; protect [Soldiers swear to *defend* their country.] **2.** to uphold something that is under attack; especially, to be the lawyer for a person accused or sued in a law court. **3.** to make an excuse for; justify [Can you *defend* your rudeness?] —**de·fend′er,** *n.*

de·fend·ant (di fen′dənt), *n.* the person in a law court who is being accused or sued.

de·fense (di fens′), *n.* **1.** a defending against attack [to fight in *defense* of liberty]. **2.** something that defends; means of protecting [The army built *defenses* along the coast.] **3.** arguments given to support or uphold something under attack. **4.** a defendant and his lawyers.

de·fense·less (di fens′lis), *adj.* having no defense; not able to protect oneself.

de·fen·si·ble (di fen′sə b'l), *adj.* that can be defended or shown to be right.

de·fen·sive (di fen′siv), *adj.* protecting from attack; defending [*defensive* barricades]. —*n.* a defensive position or act [The weaker team was soon on the *defensive.*] —**de·fen′sive·ly,** *adv.*

de·fer (di fur′), *v.* to put off until a later time; postpone [The judge *deferred* the trial until the following week.] —**de·ferred′,** *p.t. & p.p.;* **de·fer′ring,** *pr.p.* —**de·fer′ment,** *n.*

de·fer (di fur′), *v.* to give in to the wishes or opinion of another, as in showing respect [He *deferred* to his father's decision.] —**de·ferred′,** *p.t. & p.p.;* **de·fer′ring,** *pr.p.*

def·er·ence (def′ər əns), *n.* polite respect for the wishes or opinion of another. —**in deference to,** out of respect for.

def·er·en·tial (def′ər en′shəl), *adj.* showing deference; very respectful.

de·fi·ance (di fī′əns), *n.* the act of defying or opposing a powerful person or thing [He showed

fat, āpe, cär, ten, ēven, hĭt, bīte, gō, hôrn, tool, book, up, fur;
get, joy, yet, chin, she, thin, *then;* zh = s in pleasure; ′ as in able (ā′b'l).
ə = a in ago, e in agent, i in sanity, o in confess, u in focus.

his *defiance* of custom by not wearing a necktie.]
—**in defiance of, 1.** defying. **2.** in spite of.

de·fi·ant (di fī′ənt), *adj.* full of defiance; bold [The *defiant* David stood before Goliath without a sword.] —**de·fi′ant·ly,** *adv.*

de·fi·cien·cy (di fish′ən sē), *n.* an amount short of what is needed; shortage [A vitamin *deficiency* causes poor health.] —**de·fi′cien·cies,** *pl.*

de·fi·cient (di fish′ənt), *adj.* not having enough; lacking [A mentally *deficient* person lacks normal intelligence.]

def·i·cit (def′ə sit), *n.* a shortage in the amount of money needed [After taxes were collected, the town still had a *deficit* of $50,000.]

de·file (di fīl′), *v.* to make dirty or impure [The well was *defiled* by flood waters.] —**de·filed′,** *p.t. & p.p.;* **de·fil′ing,** *pr.p.* —**de·file′ment,** *n.*

de·file (di fīl′), *v.* to march in single file. —*n.* a steep valley or narrow pass, through which soldiers must go in single file.

de·fine (di fīn′), *v.* **1.** to tell the meaning or meanings of; explain [This paragraph *defines* the word "define."] **2.** to describe in detail; make clear [Can you *define* your duties as a secretary?] **3.** to mark clearly the outline or limits of [to *define* a boundary]. —**de·fined′,** *p.t. & p.p.;* **de·fin′ing,** *pr.p.*

defile

def·i·nite (def′ə nit), *adj.* **1.** having exact limits [a *definite* boundary]. **2.** clear and exact in meaning [*definite* orders]. **3.** certain; positive [It's *definite* that he'll go.] —**def′i·nite·ly,** *adv.*

definite article, the word "the."

def·i·ni·tion (def′ə nish′ən), *n.* **1.** a defining or being defined. **2.** a statement that tells what a thing is or what a word means. **3.** the clearness or sharpness of an outline.

de·fin·i·tive (di fin′ə tiv), *adj.* that is positive and final; that decides [a *definitive* answer].

de·flate (di flāt′), *v.* **1.** to make smaller or flatter by letting out air or gas [to *deflate* a tire]. **2.** to make smaller or less important [He felt *deflated* when they ignored his arrival.] —**de·flat′ed,** *p.t. & p.p.;* **de·flat′ing,** *pr.p.*

de·fla·tion (di flā′shən), *n.* **1.** a deflating or being deflated. **2.** a lessening of the amount of money in circulation, making it more valuable.

de·flect (di flekt′), *v.* to turn or make go to one side [to *deflect* a ball with one's leg]. —**de·flec′tion,** *n.*

De·foe, Daniel (di fō′), 1659?–1731; English writer who wrote *Robinson Crusoe.*

de·fo·li·ate (dē fō′li āt), *v.* to remove the leaves from plants, especially trees. —**de·fo′li·at·ed,** *p.t. & p.p.;* **de·fo′li·at·ing,** *pr.p.*

de·for·est (dē fôr′ist), *v.* to remove the trees or forests from a piece of land.

de·form (di fôrm′), *v.* to spoil the form or look of; disfigure [a tree *deformed* by disease].

de·form·i·ty (di fôr′mə tē), *n.* **1.** the condition of being deformed. **2.** a part that is deformed. —**de·form′i·ties,** *pl.*

de·fraud (di frôd′), *v.* to take away money, rights, etc. from by cheating or tricking.

de·fray (di frā′), *v.* to pay or supply the money for [to *defray* expenses]. —**de·fray′al,** *n.*

de·frost (dē frôst′), *v.* to get rid of frost or ice from [to *defrost* a refrigerator].

de·fros·ter (dē frôs′tər), *n.* any device used to melt ice and frost, as from a windshield.

deft (deft), *adj.* quick but sure; skillful [the *deft* strokes of an artist's brush]. —**deft′ly,** *adv.*

de·funct (di fungkt′), *adj.* no longer living or existing; dead; extinct [a *defunct* law].

de·fy (di fī′), *v.* **1.** to stand up against or oppose boldly and openly [to *defy* authority]. **2.** to have difficulties that cannot be overcome; resist completely [This problem *defies* solution.] **3.** to dare or challenge [I *defy* you to prove me wrong.] —**de·fied′,** *p.t. & p.p.;* **de·fy′ing,** *pr.p.*

de·gen·er·a·cy (di jen′ər ə sē), *n.* the fact of being or becoming degenerate.

de·gen·er·ate (di jen′ər it), *adj.* having sunk into a lower, worse, or less developed condition [the *degenerate* life of the Roman emperors; a *degenerate* form of plant life]. —*n.* a degenerate person, especially one who does not know right from wrong and does evil things. —*v.* (di jen′ər āt), to become degenerate; sink into something low or bad. —**de·gen′er·at·ed,** *p.t. & p.p.;* **de·gen′er·at·ing,** *pr.p.* —**de·gen′er·a′tion,** *n.*

de·grade (di grād′), *v.* **1.** to bring down to a lower rank, as in punishing; demote. **2.** to make lower or worse; make lose self-respect; disgrace [He would not *degrade* himself by cheating on the test.] —**de·grad′ed,** *p.t. & p.p.;* **de·grad′ing,** *pr.p.* —**deg·ra·da·tion** (deg′rə dā′shən), *n.*

de·gree (di grē′), *n.* **1.** a step in a series; stage in the progress of something [He advanced by *degrees* from clerk to president.] **2.** a unit used in measuring temperature. *The symbol for degree is* ° [The boiling point of water is 212° Fahrenheit.] **3.** a unit used in measuring angles and arcs of circles [There are 360 *degrees* in the circumference of a circle.] **4.** rank or position in life or in some group [a lady of high *degree*]. **5.** a rank given by a college to a student who has satisfactorily completed a course of study, or to an outstanding person as an honor [a B.A. *degree*]. **6.** amount or extent [A burn of the third *degree* is one that does the greatest amount of damage to the skin and flesh.] **7.** any of the three forms that an adjective or adverb takes when it is compared [The positive *degree* is "dark," the comparative *degree* is "darker," and the superlative *degree* is "darkest."]

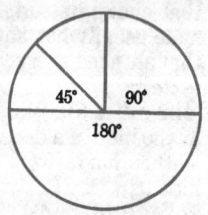

degrees in a circle

de·hu·mid·i·fi·er (dē′hyōō mid′ə fī ər), *n.* a device that removes moisture from the air.

de·hy·drate (dē hī′drāt), *v.* **1.** to remove water from; dry [Powdered milk is milk that has been *dehydrated*.] **2.** to lose water; become dry. —**de·hy′drat·ed**, *p.t. & p.p.*; **de·hy′drat·ing**, *pr.p.* —**de′hy·dra′tion**, *n.*

de·i·fy (dē′ə fī), *v.* to make a god of; worship as a god [The Romans *deified* their emperors.] —**de′i·fied**, *p.t. & p.p.*; **de′i·fy·ing**, *pr.p.* —**de·i·fi·ca·tion** (dē′ə fi kā′shən), *n.*

deign (dān), *v.* to think of as not being beneath one's dignity; condescend; lower oneself [Would you *deign* to have dinner with us?]

de·ist (dē′ist), *n.* a person who believes that there is a God because there is order in nature, but who does not believe in any formal religion. —**de′ism**, *n.*

de·i·ty (dē′ə tē), *n.* **1.** a god or goddess [the *deities* of ancient Greece]. **2.** the condition of being a god [a tribe that believed in the *deity* of animals]. —**the Deity**, God. —**de′i·ties**, *pl.*

de·ject·ed (di jek′tid), *adj.* low in spirit; sad; discouraged. —**de·ject′ed·ly**, *adv.*

de·jec·tion (di jek′shən), *n.* lowness of spirits; sadness; discouragement.

Del·a·ware (del′ə wer), *n.* **1.** a State on the Eastern coast of the United States. **2.** a river flowing between Pennsylvania and New Jersey into the Atlantic. Abbreviated **Del.**

de·lay (di lā′), *v.* **1.** to put off to a later time; postpone [The bride's illness will *delay* the wedding.] **2.** to make late; hold back; keep from going on [I was *delayed* by the storm.] —*n.* a delaying or being delayed [Engine trouble caused a *delay* in the plane's take-off.]

de·lec·ta·ble (di lek′tə b'l), *adj.* very pleasing; delightful [*delectable* to the taste].

de·lec·ta·tion (dē′lek tā′shən), *n.* delight; enjoyment; great pleasure [a fashion show for the *delectation* of the ladies].

del·e·gate (del′ə gāt *or* del′ə git), *n.* a person sent to speak and act for his group or branch; representative [Our union will send a *delegate* to the national convention.] —*v.* (del′ə gāt), **1.** to send or appoint as a delegate. **2.** to give over a right or duty to another; entrust [The people *delegate* the power to make laws to a legislature.] —**del′e·gat·ed**, *p.t. & p.p.*; **del′e·gat·ing**, *pr.p.*

del·e·ga·tion (del′ə gā′shən), *n.* **1.** a delegating or being delegated [the *delegation* of a power]. **2.** a group of delegates [The Iowa *delegation* voted as a unit.]

de·lete (di lēt′), *v.* to take out or cross out something printed or written [His name had been *deleted* from the original list.] —**de·let′ed**, *p.t. & p.p.*; **de·let′ing**, *pr.p.*

del·e·te·ri·ous (del′ə tir′i əs), *adj.* harmful to health or well-being; injurious.

Del·hi (del′ē), *n.* a city in northern India. See **New Delhi.**

de·lib·er·ate (di lib′ər it), *adj.* **1.** carefully thought out and made or done on purpose [a *deliberate* refusal]. **2.** careful in making up one's

mind; not hasty [He was very *deliberate* in choosing a partner.] **3.** slow; unhurried [Take *deliberate* aim.] —*v.* (di lib′ər āt), to think or discuss carefully in order to make up one's mind [The jury *deliberated* for six hours before reaching a verdict.] —**de·lib′er·at·ed**, *p.t. & p.p.*; **de·lib′er·at·ing**, *pr.p.* —**de·lib′er·ate·ly**, *adv.*

de·lib·er·a·tion (di lib′ər ā′shən), *n.* **1.** a careful thinking through [Choose now, as there is no time for *deliberation*.] **2.** *often* **deliberations,** *pl.* a talking about or debating of some problem before deciding [the *deliberations* of statesmen before drawing up a treaty].

del·i·ca·cy (del′i kə sē), *n.* **1.** the condition of being delicate; fineness in skill or work; fragile beauty, sensitiveness, weakness, etc. [the *delicacy* of spun glass or of a rose petal; *delicacy* in dealing with risky matters; *delicacy* in health]. **2.** a choice food or dainty [smoked oysters and other *delicacies*]. —**del′i·ca·cies**, *pl.*

del·i·cate (del′i kit), *adj.* **1.** pleasing in its lightness, mildness, or softness [a *delicate* flavor, odor, color, etc.] **2.** beautifully fine in quality or form [*delicate* linen; *delicate* workmanship]. **3.** slight and not easily felt or seen [a *delicate* difference]. **4.** easily hurt or spoiled; not strong; frail or fragile [*delicate* glassware; *delicate* health]. **5.** needing careful handling [a *delicate* problem]. **6.** having a quick and sensitive reaction to small differences or details [a *delicate* ear for music; a *delicate* gauge].

del·i·ca·tes·sen (del′i kə tes′'n), *n.* **1.** a store that sells prepared foods, such as cooked meats, cheeses, salads, relishes, etc. **2.** the foods sold in such a store.

de·li·cious (di lish′əs), *adj.* very pleasing, especially to the taste; delightful.

de·light (di līt′), *v.* **1.** to give great pleasure to [This feast would *delight* a king.] **2.** to be greatly pleased; rejoice [We *delighted* in our good fortune.] —*n.* **1.** great joy or pleasure [a child's *delight* with a new toy]. **2.** something giving great joy or pleasure [His daughter was his constant *delight*.]

de·light·ful (di līt′fəl), *adj.* giving delight or pleasure; very pleasing [a *delightful* party]. —**de·light′ful·ly**, *adv.*

de·lin·e·ate (di lin′i āt′), *v.* **1.** to draw or sketch; portray. **2.** to describe or picture in words [The hero of the story is *delineated* as a man of courage.] —**de·lin′e·at·ed**, *p.t. & p.p.*; **de·lin′e·at·ing**, *pr.p.* —**de·lin′e·a′tion**, *n.*

de·lin·quen·cy (di ling′kwən sē), *n.* **1.** failure to do what is needed; neglect of duty. **2.** the doing of bad or unlawful things [juvenile *delinquency*]. —**de·lin′quen·cies**, *pl.*

de·lin·quent (di ling′kwənt), *adj.* **1.** failing to do what is needed [*delinquent* in paying a bill]. **2.** overdue [His taxes are now *delinquent*.] —*n.* a person, especially a child or youth (**juvenile delinquent**), who is guilty of doing such unlawful things as stealing, street fighting, or the like.

de·lir·i·ous (di lir′i əs), *adj.* **1.** in a delirium; raving [*delirious* from a high fever]. **2.** wildly excited [*delirious* with joy].

de·lir·i·um (di lir′i əm), *n.* **1.** a condition of the mind, as during a fever or insanity, in which one is very restless and excited, has queer thoughts, and keeps talking wildly. **2.** any very great excitement.

de·liv·er (di liv′ər), *v.* **1.** to bring or carry and hand over; transfer [*Deliver* the groceries to my house. I *delivered* your message by phone.] **2.** to take around and pass out in a number of places; distribute [Milkmen *deliver* milk.] **3.** to speak or read aloud [to *deliver* a speech.] **4.** to strike [to *deliver* a blow]. **5.** to set free or rescue [Lincoln *delivered* the slaves.] **6.** to help a mother give birth to a baby [The doctor *delivered* the twins.] —**deliver oneself of,** to say aloud; express.

de·liv·er·ance (di liv′ər əns), *n.* a freeing or being freed; rescue.

de·liv·er·y (di liv′ər ē), *n.* **1.** the act of delivering; a transferring or distributing [daily *deliveries* to customers; the *delivery* of a prisoner into custody]. **2.** the way in which a person speaks [the fast *delivery* of a radio announcer]. **3.** the act of giving birth to a child. **4.** the act of throwing, striking, etc. or the way this is done [the pitcher's *delivery* of the ball]. —**de·liv′er·ies,** *pl.*

dell (del), *n.* a small valley or sheltered low place, usually with trees in it.

del·ta (del′tə), *n.* **1.** the fourth letter of the Greek alphabet, shaped like a triangle. **2.** the triangle-shaped piece of land formed when sand and soil are deposited at the mouth of a large river.

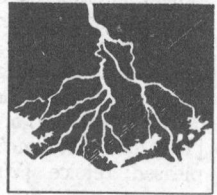
delta of a river

de·lude (di lōōd′), *v.* to fool, as by false promises; mislead; trick. —**de·lud′ed,** *p.t. & p.p.;* **de·lud′ing,** *pr.p.*

del·uge (del′yōōj), *n.* **1.** a great flood. **2.** a heavy rain; downpour. **3.** a rush or flood of anything [A *deluge* of questions followed his talk.] —*v.* to flood or overflow. —**the Deluge,** the great flood told about in the story of Noah. —**del′uged,** *p.t. & p.p.;* **del′ug·ing,** *pr.p.*

de·lu·sion (di lōō′zhən), *n.* **1.** a deluding or misleading. **2.** a false or mistaken belief, especially when it is a sign of mental illness.

de·lu·sive (di lōō′siv), *adj.* misleading; false [a *delusive* hope of finding wealth].

de luxe (di looks′ *or* di luks′), of extra fine quality; luxurious [a *de luxe* model of a car].

delve (delv), *v.* to search for facts [to *delve* into books; *delve* into the past]. —**delved,** *p.t. & p.p.;* **delv′ing,** *pr.p.*

Dem., abbreviation for **Democrat** or **Democratic.**

dem·a·gogue or **dem·a·gog** (dem′ə gôg), *n.* a person who stirs up the feelings and prejudices of people to win them over quickly and use them to get power.

dem·a·gog·y (dem′ə gō jē), *n.* the ways of a demagogue.

de·mand (di mand′), *v.* **1.** to ask for as a right, or as if one had the right; ask with authority [They *demanded* to see the mayor.] **2.** to call for; need [This work *demands* great care.] —*n.* **1.** a demanding or the thing demanded. **2.** a claim or need [This job makes great *demands* on my time.] **3.** the desire for a certain product by buyers who are ready to buy at the stated price [When the *demand* is greater than the supply, prices go up.] —**in demand,** wanted.

de·mar·ca·tion (dē′mär kā′shən), *n.* **1.** the setting and marking of limits or boundaries. **2.** a limit or boundary.

de·mean (di mēn′), *v.* to behave [He *demeaned* himself like a gentleman.]

de·mean (di mēn′), *v.* to make low or cheap [You *demean* yourself by telling a lie.]

de·mean·or (di mēn′ər), *n.* behavior or conduct; manner [a quiet, humble *demeanor*].

de·ment·ed (di men′tid), *adj.* sick in the mind.

de·mer·it (dē mer′it), *n.* **1.** a fault or failing. **2.** a mark put down against a person, as for poor work or conduct.

de·mesne (di mān′ *or* di mēn′), *n.* **1.** a lord's mansion and the land around it. **2.** a region or domain.

De·me·ter (di mē′tər), *n.* the Greek goddess of plants and farming. The Romans called her *Ceres.*

dem·i·god (dem′i gäd), *n.* in Greek and Roman myths, a being who was part god and part human.

dem·i·john (dem′i jän), *n.* a large bottle or jug with a wicker covering.

de·mil·i·ta·rize (dē mil′ə tə rīz), *v.* to take away the army and the power to wage war [to *demilitarize* a captured country]. —**de·mil′i·ta·rized,** *p.t. & p.p.;* **de·mil′i·ta·riz·ing,** *pr.p.* —**de·mil′i·ta·ri·za′tion,** *n.*

demijohn

de·mise (di mīz′), *n.* death.

de·mo·bi·lize (dē mō′b′l īz), *v.* to release soldiers, sailors, etc. from military service, as at the end of a war. —**de·mo′bi·lized,** *p.t. & p.p.;* **de·mo′bi·liz·ing,** *pr.p.* —**de′mo·bi·li·za′tion,** *n.*

de·moc·ra·cy (də mäk′rə sē), *n.* **1.** government in which the people hold the ruling power, usually giving it over to representatives whom they elect to make the laws and run the government. **2.** a country, state, etc. with such government. **3.** equal rights, opportunity, and treatment for all [We have real *democracy* in our school.] —**de·moc′ra·cies,** *pl.*

dem·o·crat (dem′ə krat), *n.* **1.** a person who believes in and supports democracy; believer in rule by the people, equal rights for all, etc. **2. Democrat,** a member of the Democratic Party.

dem·o·crat·ic (dem′ə krat′ik), *adj.* **1.** of, belonging to, or supporting democracy [a *democratic* nation]. **2.** treating people of all classes in the same way [a *democratic* employer]. **3. Democratic,** of or belonging to the Democratic Party. —**dem'o·crat'i·cal·ly,** *adv.*

Democratic Party, one of the two major political parties in the United States.

de·moc·ra·tize (də mäk'rə tīz), *v.* to make or become democratic. —**de·moc'ra·tized,** *p.t. & p.p.;* **de·moc'ra·tiz·ing,** *pr.p.*

de·mol·ish (di mäl'ish), *v.* to tear down; smash; destroy or ruin [The tornado *demolished* the barn. Our hopes were *demolished* by his refusal.]

dem·o·li·tion (dem'ə lish'ən *or* dē'mə lish'ən), *n.* a demolishing or wrecking; destruction.

de·mon (dē'mən), *n.* **1.** a devil; evil spirit. **2.** a very evil or cruel person or thing [the *demon* of jealousy].

de·mo·ni·ac (di mō'ni ak), *adj.* **1.** of or like a demon; devilish. **2.** filled with or showing wild fury; frenzied; frantic.

de·mo·ni·a·cal (dē'mə nī'ə k'l), *adj.* demoniac.

de·mon·stra·ble (di män'strə b'l), *adj.* that can be demonstrated or proved. —**de·mon'stra·bly,** *adv.*

dem·on·strate (dem'ən strāt), *v.* **1.** to show or prove by facts, actions, feelings, etc. [He *demonstrated* his desire for an education by working at night.] **2.** to explain by the use of examples or experiments [We can *demonstrate* the laws of heredity by breeding fruit flies.] **3.** to show how something works or is used [The salesman *demonstrated* the carpet sweeper.] **4.** to show one's feelings by taking part in a public meeting, parade, etc. [Thousands joined in the march to *demonstrate* for peace.] —**dem'on·strat·ed,** *p.t. & p.p.;* **dem'on·strat·ing,** *pr.p.*

dem·on·stra·tion (dem'ən strā'shən), *n.* **1.** the act or means of demonstrating something; a showing, proving, or explaining [a *demonstration* of grief; a *demonstration* of an automobile]. **2.** a meeting or parade of many people to show publicly how they feel about something.

de·mon·stra·tive (di män'strə tiv), *adj.* **1.** showing one's feelings in a very open way [a *demonstrative* child]. **2.** that points out ["That" and "these" are *demonstrative* pronouns.]

dem·on·stra·tor (dem'ən strā'tər), *n.* a person or thing that demonstrates; especially, a person who takes part in a public demonstration.

de·mor·al·ize (di môr'ə līz), *v.* **1.** to spoil the morals of; make bad [Are children *demoralized* by comic books showing violence?] **2.** to weaken the spirit or discipline of [The soldiers were *demoralized* by a lack of supplies.] —**de·mor'al·ized,** *p.t. & p.p.;* **de·mor'al·iz·ing,** *pr.p.* —**de·mor'al·i·za'tion,** *n.*

De·mos·the·nes (di mäs'thə nēz), *n.* 385?–322 B.C.; a famous Greek orator.

de·mote (di mōt'), *v.* to put in a lower grade or rank [The soldier was *demoted* from sergeant to private.] —**de·mot'ed,** *p.t. & p.p.;* **de·mot'ing,** *pr.p.* —**de·mo'tion,** *n.*

de·mur (di mur'), *v.* to be unwilling to do something; hold back [I want to help, but I *demur* at doing all the work.] —**de·murred',** *p.t. & p.p.;* **de·mur'ring,** *pr.p.*

de·mure (di myoor'), *adj.* modest and shy or pretending to be modest and shy. —**de·mure'ly,** *adv.* —**de·mure'ness,** *n.*

den (den), *n.* **1.** a cave or other place where a wild animal makes its home; lair. **2.** a secret place where criminals meet. **3.** a small, cozy room where one can be alone to read, work, etc.

fox's den

de·na·ture (dē nā'chər), *v.* to change the nature of; especially, to make alcohol unfit for drinking without spoiling it for other uses. —**de·na'tured,** *p.t. & p.p.;* **de·na'tur·ing,** *pr.p.*

de·ni·al (di nī'əl), *n.* **1.** a saying "no" to a request; refusal. **2.** a saying that something is not true or right [a *denial* of the policeman's charges]. **3.** a taking away or holding back [a *denial* of privileges]. **4.** a refusing to recognize as one's own [a *denial* of one's family].

den·im (den'im), *n.* a coarse cotton cloth that will take hard wear and is used for work clothes or play clothes.

den·i·zen (den'i z'n), *n.* a person, animal, or plant that lives in a certain place [*denizens* of the city; winged *denizens* of the air].

Den·mark (den'märk), *n.* a country in northern Europe, between the North and Baltic seas.

de·nom·i·nate (di näm'ə nāt), *v.* to give a name to; call. —**de·nom'i·nat·ed,** *p.t. & p.p.;* **de·nom'i·nat·ing,** *pr.p.*

de·nom·i·na·tion (di näm'ə nā'shən), *n.* **1.** the name of a thing or of a class of things [The cent, nickel, and dime are the smaller *denominations* of U.S. coins.] **2.** a religious group or sect [Lutherans and Baptists are two Protestant *denominations*.] —**de·nom'i·na'tion·al,** *adj.*

de·nom·i·na·tor (di näm'ə nā'tər), *n.* the number or quantity below the line in a fraction. It shows the number of equal parts into which the whole has been divided [In the fraction 2/5, 5 is the *denominator*. John ate 2/5 of a pie, or 2 of the 5 equal parts.]

de·no·ta·tion (dē'nō tā'shən), *n.* **1.** a denoting; indication. **2.** the exact meaning of a word, without the added ideas that it may have taken on: see also **connotation.**

de·note (di nōt'), *v.* **1.** to be a sign of; show [Dark, low clouds *denote* rain.] **2.** to mean; be the name of [The words "metaphor" and "simile" *denote* two different figures of speech.] —**de·not'ed,** *p.t. & p.p.;* **de·not'ing,** *pr.p.*

de·nounce (di nouns'), *v.* **1.** to speak out

against in a strong way; say that something is bad. **2.** to give information against someone to the police; inform against. **3.** to announce that one will no longer honor a certain treaty. —**de-nounced′**, *p.t. & p.p.*; **de-nounc′ing**, *pr.p.*

dense (dens), *adj.* **1.** having its parts close together; crowded; thick [a *dense* woods]. **2.** slow in understanding; stupid. —**dense′ly**, *adv.* —**dense′ness**, *n.*

den-si-ty (den′sə tē), *n.* **1.** a being dense, thick, or crowded. **2.** the quantity or mass of something for each unit of area or volume [the *density* of population per square mile; the *density* of a gas]. —**den′si-ties**, *pl.*

dent (dent), *n.* a hollow made in a hard surface by a blow or by pressure. —*v.* **1.** to make a dent in. **2.** to become dented.

den-tal (den′t'l), *adj.* having to do with the teeth or with a dentist's work.

dents in a pan

den-ti-frice (den′tə fris), *n.* any paste, powder, or liquid used to clean the teeth.

den-tine (den′tēn) or **den-tin** (den′tin), *n.* the hard, bony material forming the main part of a tooth, under the enamel.

den-tist (den′tist), *n.* a doctor whose work is preventing and taking care of diseased or crooked teeth, or replacing them with artificial teeth.

den-tist-ry (den′tis trē), *n.* the work or profession of a dentist.

den-ture (den′chər), *n.* a fitting for the mouth, with artificial teeth, often a full set.

de-nude (di nōōd′ *or* di nyōōd′), *v.* to make bare or naked; strip [land *denuded* of trees]. —**de-nud′ed**, *p.t. & p.p.*; **de-nud′ing**, *pr.p.*

de-nun-ci-a-tion (di nun′si ā′shən), *n.* the act of denouncing; a condemning, informing, etc.

Den-ver (den′vər), *n.* the capital of Colorado.

de-ny (di nī′), *v.* **1.** to say that something is not true or right; contradict [He *denied* that he had ever been in Chicago.] **2.** to refuse to grant or give [to *deny* permission]. **3.** to refuse to recognize as one's own; disown [to *deny* one's religion]. **4.** to refuse the use of [to *deny* a golf course to all except members]. —**deny oneself**, to do without things that one wants. —**de-nied′**, *p.t. & p.p.*; **de-ny′ing**, *pr.p.*

de-o-dor-ant (dē ō′dər ənt), *adj.* that stops or gets rid of bad smells. —*n.* a deodorant cream, salve, etc.

de-o-dor-ize (dē ō′dər īz), *v.* to stop or get rid of the smell of. —**de-o′dor-ized**, *p.t. & p.p.*; **de-o′dor-iz-ing**, *pr.p.*

de-part (di pärt′), *v.* **1.** to go away; set out; leave [The train will *depart* on time.] **2.** to turn aside; change [to *depart* from custom]. **3.** to die.

de-part-ed (di pär′tid), *adj.* gone away; dead [the *departed* years; our *departed* ancestors]. —**the departed**, the dead person or persons.

de-part-ment (di pärt′mənt), *n.* a separate part or branch, as of a government or business [the police *department*; the shipping *department*; the *department* of history in a college]. —**de-part-men-tal** (dē′pärt men′t'l), *adj.*

department store, a large store with separate departments for selling many kinds of goods.

de-par-ture (di pär′chər), *n.* **1.** a departing; going away; leaving. **2.** a turning aside, or changing to something new [Office work is a new *departure* for him.] **3.** death.

de-pend (di pend′), *v.* **1.** to be controlled or decided by [The attendance at the game *depends* on the weather.] **2.** to put one's trust in; be sure of [You can't *depend* on the weather.] **3.** to rely for help or support [Carl *depends* on his brother for money.] **4.** to hang down.

de-pend-a-ble (di pen′də b'l), *adj.* that can be depended on; reliable [a *dependable* friend]. —**de-pend′a-bil′i-ty**, *n.*

de-pend-ence (di pen′dəns), *n.* **1.** a being controlled or decided by something else. **2.** a depending on another for help or support. **3.** trust; reliance [I place *dependence* in his word.]

de-pend-en-cy (di pen′dən sē), *n.* **1.** dependence. **2.** a land or country that is controlled by another country. —**de-pend′en-cies**, *pl.*

de-pen-dent (di pen′dənt), *adj.* **1.** controlled or decided by something else [The size of her allowance is *dependent* on her father's wages.] **2.** relying on another for help or support [A baby is completely *dependent* on his parents.] —*n.* a person who depends on someone else for his support.

dependent clause, same as **subordinate clause**.

de-pict (di pikt′), *v.* **1.** to be a picture of; portray [This painting *depicts* a London street.] **2.** to picture in words; describe [His novel *depicts* life in a small town.] —**de-pic′tion**, *n.*

de-plete (di plēt′), *v.* to empty or use up; exhaust [Our water supply will be *depleted* unless it rains soon. His energy was *depleted*.] —**de-plet′ed**, *p.t. & p.p.*; **de-plet′ing**, *pr.p.* —**de-ple′tion**, *n.*

de-plor-a-ble (di plôr′ə b'l), *adj.* that can or should be deplored; regrettable; wretched [*deplorable* slums]. —**de-plor′a-bly**, *adv.*

de-plore (di plôr′), *v.* to be sorry about; feel or show deep regret about [The editorial *deplored* the lack of playgrounds in the city.] —**de-plored′**, *p.t. & p.p.*; **de-plor′ing**, *pr.p.*

de-pop-u-late (dē päp′yoo lāt), *v.* to lessen the number of people in [A plague *depopulated* Europe in the 14th century.] —**de-pop′u-lat-ed**, *p.t. & p.p.*; **de-pop′u-lat-ing**, *pr.p.* —**de-pop′u-la′tion**, *n.*

de-port (di pôrt′), *v.* **1.** to force to leave a country by official order; banish [He was *deported* for having entered the country illegally.] **2.** to behave in a certain way [Billy *deported* himself like a little gentleman.]

de-por-ta-tion (dē′pôr tā′shən), *n.* a deporting or being deported from a country.

de-port-ment (di pôrt′mənt), *n.* the way a person behaves himself; behavior.

de-pose (di pōz′), *v.* **1.** to remove from a position of power, especially from a throne. **2.** to state under oath; testify. —**de-posed′**, *p.t. & p.p.*; **de-pos′ing**, *pr.p.*

de·pos·it (di päz′it), *v.* **1.** to place for safe-keeping, as money in a bank. **2.** to give as part payment or as a pledge [They *deposited* $500 on a new car.] **3.** to lay down [He *deposited* his books on the chair. The river *deposits* tons of mud at its mouth.] —*n.* **1.** something placed for safekeeping, as money in a bank. **2.** the state of being so placed [I have $200 on *deposit*.] **3.** money given as a pledge or part payment. **4.** something left lying by forces in nature [a mud *deposit* at a river's mouth; a coal *deposit*].

dep·o·si·tion (dep′ə zish′ən), *n.* **1.** the act of removing someone from a position of power [the *deposition* of a king]. **2.** something stated under oath, especially written testimony [The witness in the hospital made a *deposition*.]

de·pos·i·tor (di päz′i tər), *n.* a person who deposits, especially money in a bank.

de·pos·i·to·ry (di päz′ə tôr′ē), *n.* a place where things are put for safekeeping; storehouse. —**de·pos′i·to′ries,** *pl.*

de·pot (dē′pō), *n.* **1.** a storehouse or warehouse. **2.** a railroad station. **3.** (dep′ō), a place for storing military supplies.

de·prave (di prāv′), *v.* to make bad, wicked, or corrupt [Life in prison had *depraved* him.] —**de·praved′,** *p.t. & p.p.;* **de·prav′ing,** *pr.p.*

de·prav·i·ty (di prav′ə tē), *n.* a depraved condition or act; wickedness. —**de·prav′i·ties,** *pl.*

dep·re·cate (dep′rə kāt), *v.* to feel and show disapproval of [The speaker *deprecated* our lack of interest.] —**dep′re·cat·ed,** *p.t. & p.p.;* **dep′re·cat·ing,** *pr.p.* —**dep′re·ca′tion,** *n.*

dep·re·ca·to·ry (dep′rə kə tôr′ē), *adj.* that deprecates or shows disapproval [a *deprecatory* remark].

de·pre·ci·ate (di prē′shi āt), *v.* **1.** to make or become less in value [An automobile *depreciates* with age.] **2.** to make seem unimportant; belittle [I don't like to hear you *depreciate* yourself.] —**de·pre′ci·at·ed,** *p.t. & p.p.;* **de·pre′ci·at·ing,** *pr.p.* —**de·pre′ci·a′tion,** *n.*

dep·re·da·tion (dep′ri dā′shən), *n.* a robbing, plundering, or destroying, as by enemy troops.

de·press (di pres′), *v.* **1.** to make sad or gloomy; discourage. **2.** to press down; lower [*Depress* the gas pedal slowly.] **3.** to make less active; weaken [High tariffs have *depressed* world trade.]

de·pres·sion (di presh′ən), *n.* **1.** sadness; gloominess [to suffer from a fit of *depression*.] **2.** a pressing down, or lowering. **3.** a hollow or low place [Water collected in the *depressions* in the ground.] **4.** a period during which there is less business and many people lose their jobs.

de·prive (di prīv′), *v.* **1.** to take away from by force; dispossess [The Indians were *deprived* of their lands.] **2.** to keep from having or enjoying [I hope this won't *deprive* me of your company.] —**de·prived′,** *p.t. & p.p.;* **de·priv′ing,** *pr.p.* —**dep·ri·va·tion** (dep′rə vā′shən), *n.*

dept., abbreviation for **department.**

depth (depth), *n.* **1.** the fact of being deep, or how deep a thing is; deepness [the *depth* of the ocean; a closet five feet in *depth;* the *depth* of a color; the great *depth* of his love]. **2.** *often* **depths,** the inner or middle part; also, the deep or deepest part [in the *depth* of night; from the *depths* of one's heart]. —**out of one's depth** or **beyond one's depth,** beyond what one can do or understand.

dep·u·ta·tion (dep′yoo tā′shən), *n.* **1.** the act of deputing. **2.** a group of people sent to act for others; delegation [Our neighborhood sent a *deputation* to the mayor to ask for street repairs.]

de·pute (di pyoot′), *v.* to choose a person to take one's place or to do one's work [Early painters often *deputed* helpers to finish their paintings.] —**de·put′ed,** *p.t. & p.p.;* **de·put′ing,** *pr.p.*

dep·u·tize (dep′yoo tīz), *v.* to make a person one's deputy. —**dep′u·tized,** *p.t. & p.p.;* **dep′u·tiz·ing,** *pr.p.*

dep·u·ty (dep′yoo tē), *n.* a person chosen to take the place of another or to do his work [a sheriff's *deputy*]. —**dep′u·ties,** *pl.*

de·rail (dē rāl′), *v.* to cause to go off its rails [to *derail* a train]. —**de·rail′ment,** *n.*

de·range (di rānj′), *v.* **1.** to make a person lose his mind; make insane. **2.** to upset the order or working of; mix up [Our routine was *deranged* by their visit.] —**de·ranged′,** *p.t. & p.p.;* **de·rang′ing,** *pr.p.* —**de·range′ment,** *n.*

Der·by (dur′bē), *n.* **1.** any of certain famous races, especially horse races [the Kentucky *Derby*]. **2. derby,** a stiff felt hat with a round crown. —**Der′bies** or **der′bies,** *pl.*

derby

der·e·lict (der′ə likt), *adj.* **1.** that has been deserted and given up as lost [a *derelict* ship at sea]. **2.** not doing what one should do; neglectful [to be *derelict* in one's duty]. —*n.* **1.** a ship deserted at sea. **2.** a poor, homeless person who has no one to care for him.

der·e·lic·tion (der′ə lik′shən), *n.* **1.** an abandoning or being abandoned. **2.** a failing to do one's duty.

de·ride (di rīd′), *v.* to make fun of; laugh at in a scornful way; ridicule. —**de·rid′ed,** *p.t. & p.p.;* **de·rid′ing,** *pr.p.*

de·ri·sion (di rizh′ən), *n.* a deriding; jeering or ridicule.

de·ri·sive (di rī′siv), *adj.* deriding, or making fun; ridiculing. —**de·ri′sive·ly,** *adv.*

der·i·va·tion (der′ə vā′shən), *n.* **1.** a deriving or developing from some source. **2.** the source or origin of anything [an American of Greek *derivation*]. **3.** the way in which a word has

fat, āpe, cär, ten, ēven, hit, bīte, gō, hôrn, tōōl, book, up, fur;
get, joy, yet, chin, she, thin, *th*en; zh = s in pleasure; ′ as in able (ā′b'l);
ə = a in ago, e in agent, i in sanity, o in confess, u in focus.

developed from some source [Some dictionaries give the *derivations* as well as the meanings of words.]

de·riv·a·tive (də riv′ə tiv), *adj.* derived from something else. —*n.* something derived from something else [Certain medicines are *derivatives* of coal tar.]

de·rive (də rīv′), *v.* **1.** to get or receive from a source [We *derive* gasoline from petroleum. Many English words are *derived* from Latin. He *derived* enjoyment from the music.] **2.** to come from a certain source [Our laws *derive* from those of England.] —**de·rived′**, *p.t. & p.p.;* **de·riv′- ing,** *pr.p.*

der·ma (dur′mə) or **der·mis** (dur′mis), *n.* the layer of skin just below the outer skin.

de·rog·a·to·ry (di räg′ə tôr′ē), *adj.* meant to make someone or something seem lower or of less value; belittling [*derogatory* remarks].

der·rick (der′ik), *n.* **1.** a large machine for lifting and moving heavy things. It has a long beam that is supported and moved by ropes and pulleys. **2.** a tall framework, as over an oil well, that holds machinery for drilling or pumping, etc.

der·vish (dur′vish), *n.* a member of any of various Moslem religious groups which live a life of poverty.

des·cant (des kant′), *v.* to hold a long talk on some subject.

derrick over an oil well

de·scend (di send′), *v.* **1.** to move down to a lower place [to *descend* from a hilltop; to *descend* a staircase]. **2.** to become lower or smaller [Prices have *descended* during the past month.] **3.** to come from a certain source [He is *descended* from pioneers.] **4.** to be passed on to an heir [This house will *descend* to my son.] **5.** to lower oneself in dignity [He has *descended* to begging for money.] **6.** to make a sudden attack [The troops *descended* upon the enemy camp.]

de·scend·ant (di sen′dənt), *n.* a person who is descended from a certain ancestor.

de·scent (di sent′), *n.* **1.** a descending, or moving down to a lower place. **2.** a way or slope downward [a steep *descent* down the mountain]. **3.** a sudden attack. **4.** a becoming lower; decline [a sharp *descent* in the price of corn]. **5.** a family from which one descends; ancestry [He is of French *descent*.]

de·scribe (di skrīb′), *v.* **1.** to tell or write about in some detail [to *describe* a trip one has taken]. **2.** to trace or form the outline of [His hand *described* a circle in the air.] —**de·scribed′,** *p.t. & p.p.;* **de·scrib′ing,** *pr.p.* —**de·scrib′a- ble,** *adj.*

de·scrip·tion (di skrip′shən), *n.* **1.** the act of describing something or words that describe [Give us a *description* of your lost dog.] **2.** sort or kind [books of every *description*].

de·scrip·tive (di skrip′tiv), *adj.* describing; that describes [*descriptive* writing].

de·scry (di skrī′), *v.* to catch sight of something far away or hard to see [We suddenly *descried* land straight ahead.] —**de·scried′,** *p.t. & p.p.;* **de·scry′ing,** *pr.p.*

des·e·crate (des′i krāt), *v.* to use something sacred in a wrong or bad way; treat as not sacred [to *desecrate* a Bible by marking it up]. —**des′- e·crat·ed,** *p.t. & p.p.;* **des′e·crat·ing,** *pr.p.* —**des′e·cra′tion,** *n.*

de·seg·re·gate (dē seg′rə gāt), *v.* to stop the practice of keeping people of different races separate, as in public schools. —**de·seg′re- gat·ed,** *p.t. & p.p.;* **de·seg′re·gat·ing,** *pr.p.* —**de·seg′re·ga′tion,** *n.*

de·sert (di zurt′), *v.* **1.** to go away from someone or something that one ought not to leave; abandon [to *desert* one's wife]. **2.** to leave a military post without permission and with no idea of coming back. —**de·sert′er,** *n.* —**de· ser′tion,** *n.*

des·ert (dez′ərt), *n.* a dry, sandy region with little or no plant life. —*adj.* of or like a desert; especially, wild and not lived in [a *desert* island].

de·sert (di zurt′), *n.* what a person deserves, either as reward or punishment: *usually used in the plural,* **deserts** [The villains in fairy tales usually get their just *deserts*.]

de·serve (di zurv′), *v.* to have a right to; be one who ought to get [This matter *deserves* thought. Bill *deserves* a scolding.] —**de·served′,** *p.t. & p.p.;* **de·serv′ing,** *pr.p.* —**de·serv′ed·ly,** *adv.*

de·serv·ing (di zur′ving), *adj.* that ought to get help or a reward [a *deserving* student].

des·ic·cate (des′i kāt), *v.* to dry out; remove the water from [Prunes are *desiccated* plums.] —**des′ic·cat·ed,** *p.t. & p.p.;* **des′ic·cat·ing,** *pr.p.*

de·sign (di zīn′), *v.* **1.** to think up and draw plans for [to *design* a new model of a car]. **2.** to arrange the parts, colors, etc. of [Who *designed* this lovely book?] **3.** to set apart for a certain use; intend [This table was not *designed* to be sat on.] —*n.* **1.** a drawing or plan to be followed in making something [the *designs* for an airplane]. **2.** the arrangement of parts, colors, etc.; pattern or decoration [the *design* in a table- cloth]. **3.** a plan or purpose [It was his *design* to study law.] **4.** **designs,** *pl.* a secret plan, usually a dishonest or selfish one [He had *designs* on her money.] —**by design,** on purpose.

des·ig·nate (dez′ig nāt), *v.* **1.** to point out; show [Capital cities are *designated* on this map by circled dots.] **2.** to choose or appoint [We have *designated* Smith to be chairman.] **3.** to give a name to; call [The top grade of beef is *desig- nated* as "prime."] —**des′ig·nat·ed,** *p.t. & p.p.;* **des′ig·nat·ing,** *pr.p.* —**des′ig·na′tion,** *n.*

de·sign·er (di zīn′ər), *n.* a person who designs or makes original plans [a dress *designer*].

de·sign·ing (di zīn′ing), *adj.* **1.** that designs or makes plans or patterns. **2.** plotting or scheming. —*n.* the art or work of making designs.

de·sir·a·ble (di zīr′ə b'l), *adj.* worth wanting or having; pleasing, excellent, beautiful, or the like. —**de·sir′a·bil′i·ty,** *n.* —**de·sir′a·bly,** *adv.*

de·sire (di zīr′), *v.* **1.** to wish or long for; want strongly [to *desire* success]. **2.** to ask for; request [The principal *desires* to see you in his office.] —*n.* **1.** a strong wish. **2.** the thing wished for. —**de·sired′**, *p.t. & p.p.;* **de·sir′ing**, *pr.p.*

de·sir·ous (di zīr′əs), *adj.* desiring; wanting [to be *desirous* of learning].

de·sist (di zist′), *v.* to stop doing something; cease [*Desist* from fighting.]

desk (desk), *n.* a piece of furniture with a smooth top at which one can write, draw, or read. It often has drawers for storing things.

Des Moines (də moin′), the capital of Iowa.

des·o·late (des′ə lit), *adj.* **1.** left alone; lonely; forlorn [a *desolate* tree on a rocky crag]. **2.** not lived in; deserted [a *desolate* wilderness]. **3.** ruined or destroyed [the *desolate* farms in a drought area]. **4.** very unhappy; miserable [Her death left him *desolate*.] —*v.* (des′ə lāt), **1.** to make unfit for life; ruin; destroy [The tornado *desolated* many towns.] **2.** to leave alone; forsake; abandon. **3.** to make unhappy or miserable. —**des′o·lat·ed**, *p.t. & p.p.;* **des′o·lat·ing**, *pr.p.* —**des′o·la′tion**, *n.*

De So·to, Hernando (di sō′tō), 1500?–1542; Spanish explorer who discovered the Mississippi.

de·spair (di sper′), *n.* **1.** a giving up or loss of hope [He was in *despair* of ever winning back his fortune.] **2.** a person or thing that causes one to lose hope [Harry is the *despair* of his teachers.] —*v.* to lose or give up hope [The prisoner *despaired* of ever being free again.]

des·patch (di spach′), *v. & n.* same as **dispatch.**

des·per·a·do (des′pə rä′dō *or* des′pə rä′dō), *n.* a dangerous, reckless criminal; bold outlaw. —**des′per·a′does** *or* **des′per·a′dos**, *pl.*

des·per·ate (des′pər it), *adj.* **1.** reckless because one has lost hope [a *desperate* criminal; a *desperate* leap from a burning building]. **2.** making one lose hope; very dangerous or serious [a *desperate* illness]. —**des′per·ate·ly**, *adv.*

des·per·a·tion (des′pər ā′shən), *n.* **1.** the condition of being desperate. **2.** recklessness that comes from despair [In *desperation* the deer leaped across the chasm.]

des·pi·ca·ble (des′pik ə b′l), *adj.* that deserves to be despised; contemptible [a *despicable* bully]. —**des′pi·ca·bly**, *adv.*

de·spise (di spīz′), *v.* to dislike strongly and feel scorn for [He *despises* cheaters.] —**despised′**, *p.t. & p.p.;* **de·spis′ing**, *pr.p.*

de·spite (di spīt′), *prep.* in spite of; regardless of [We started out *despite* the storm.] —*n.* a wanting to harm others; malice; spite.

de·spoil (di spoil′), *v.* to rob or plunder [The museum was *despoiled* of its treasures.]

de·spond·ent (di spän′dənt), *adj.* having lost one's hope or courage; discouraged [He was *despondent* over the loss of his job.] —**despond′en·cy** *or* **de·spond′ence**, *n.*

des·pot (des′pət), *n.* a person who treats those under his control in any way he cares to; especially, a cruel and unjust ruler; tyrant. —**des·pot·ic** (des pät′ik), *adj.* —**des′pot·ism**, *n.*

des·sert (di zurt′), *n.* something sweet served at the end of a meal, as fruit, pie, or cake.

des·ti·na·tion (des′tə nā′shən), *n.* the place that a person or thing is going to [We shall visit Belgium, but our *destination* is Paris.]

des·tine (des′tin), *v.* to head toward some goal or end, as if by fate [The play seemed *destined* to be a success.] —**destined for, 1.** intended for [My old clothes are *destined for* the rummage sale.] **2.** bound for [We were *destined for* home.] —**des′tined**, *p.t. & p.p.;* **des′tin·ing**, *pr.p.*

des·tin·y (des′tə nē), *n.* **1.** that which is bound to happen; one's fate [Was it his *destiny* to become President?] **2.** that which seems to make things happen the way they do; fate [*Destiny* brought him here.] —**des′tin·ies**, *pl.*

des·ti·tute (des′tə tōōt *or* des′tə tyōōt), *adj.* **1.** having no money or means by which to live; very poor. **2.** not having; being without; lacking [The desert is *destitute* of trees.]

des·ti·tu·tion (des′tə tōō′shən *or* des′tə tyōō′shən), *n.* the condition of being destitute or very poor; complete poverty.

de·stroy (di stroi′), *v.* to put an end to by breaking up, tearing down, ruining, or spoiling [The flood *destroyed* 300 homes.]

de·stroy·er (di stroi′ər), *n.* **1.** a person or thing that destroys. **2.** a small, fast warship.

de·struc·tion (di struk′shən), *n.* a destroying or being destroyed; ruin [The forest fire caused much *destruction*.]

de·struc·tive (di struk′tiv), *adj.* destroying or likely to destroy [a *destructive* child].

des·ue·tude (des′wi tōōd *or* des′wi tyōōd), *n.* the condition of not being used any more; disuse [That custom has fallen into *desuetude*.]

des·ul·to·ry (des′′l tôr′ē), *adj.* passing from one thing to another in an aimless way [Their talk at lunch was *desultory*.]

de·tach (di tach′), *v.* **1.** to unfasten and take away; disconnect [Five cars were *detached* from the train.] **2.** to choose and send on a special task [Soldiers were *detached* to guard the President's train.] —**de·tach′a·ble**, *adj.*

de·tached (di tacht′), *adj.* **1.** separate; not connected [a *detached* garage]. **2.** not taking sides or having feelings one way or the other; aloof [a *detached* observer].

de·tach·ment (di tach′mənt), *n.* **1.** a detaching; separation. **2.** troops or ships chosen and sent on a special task [a *detachment* of guards]. **3.** a being detached or aloof [Try to look at your troubles with *detachment*.]

de·tail (di tāl′ *or* dē′tāl), *n.* **1.** any of the small parts that go to make up something; item [He left out the minor *details* of the plan. You must use care on the *details* of your painting.] **2.** a dealing with things item by item [Don't go into *detail* about your trip.] **3.** a small group of soldiers or sailors chosen for a special task; also, the special task [A *detail* was sent to blow up the bridge.] —*v.* (di tāl′), **1.** to give all the details of [The salesman had to *detail* all expenses in his report.] **2.** to send a soldier, etc. on a detail. —**in detail,** item by item; leaving out no detail.

de·tain (di tān′), *v.* to keep from going on; hold back [A long freight train *detained* us.]

de·tect (di tekt′), *v.* to discover something hidden or not easily noticed [to *detect* a slight flaw]. —**de·tec′tion,** *n.*

de·tec·tive (di tek′tiv), *n.* a person, usually on a police force, whose work is trying to solve crimes, getting secret information, etc. —*adj.* of detectives and their work.

de·tec·tor (di tek′tər), *n.* **1.** a person or thing that detects. **2.** a crystal or vacuum tube in a radio, for picking up the signal wave.

de·ten·tion (di ten′shən), *n.* a detaining or being detained; forced delay or confinement [his long *detention* in the county jail].

de·ter (di tŭr′), *v.* to keep a person from doing something through fear, doubt, etc.; discourage [Does capital punishment *deter* crime?] —**de·terred′,** *p.t. & p.p.;* **de·ter′ring,** *pr.p.*

de·ter·gent (di tŭr′jənt), *adj.* that cleans [a *detergent* wax that cleans and polishes]. —*n.* a substance used for cleaning, especially one that looks like soap but is made from certain chemicals, not from fats and lye.

de·te·ri·o·rate (di tir′i ə rāt′), *v.* to make or become worse; turn bad [His health has *deteriorated* during the past year.] —**de·te′ri·o·rat′ed,** *p.t. & p.p.;* **de·te′ri·o·rat′ing,** *pr.p.* —**de·te′ri·o·ra′tion,** *n.*

de·ter·mi·nant (di tŭr′mə nənt), *adj.* that determines or decides. —*n.* a thing that determines; deciding factor.

de·ter·mi·na·tion (di tŭr′mə nā′shən), *n.* **1.** a deciding or finding out for sure. **2.** firmness of purpose; fixed aim [Lincoln's *determination* to save the Union never weakened.]

de·ter·mine (di tŭr′min), *v.* **1.** to settle or decide on [I haven't *determined* whether to go to college.] **2.** to set one's mind on something; resolve [He was *determined* to succeed.] **3.** to find out exactly [First *determine* the area of the floor.] **4.** to be the thing that decides; have an important effect on [A boy's hobbies often *determine* his choice of a career.] —**de·ter′mined,** *p.t. & p.p.;* **de·ter′min·ing,** *pr.p.*

de·ter·mined (di tŭr′mind), *adj.* **1.** having one's mind set; decided; resolved [*Determined* to pass, the pupil studied hard.] **2.** firm and unwavering [a *determined* knock on the door].

de·ter·rent (di tŭr′ənt *or* di ter′ənt), *adj.* that deters. —*n.* a thing that deters.

de·test (di test′), *v.* to dislike with strong feeling; hate; abhor. —**de·test′a·ble,** *adj.* —**de·tes·ta·tion** (dē′tes tā′shən), *n.*

de·throne (dē thrōn′), *v.* to remove from a throne or from any high position. —**de·throned′,** *p.t. & p.p.;* **de·thron′ing,** *pr.p.*

det·o·nate (det′ə nāt), *v.* to explode with much noise [to *detonate* a bomb]. —**det′o·nat·ed,** *p.t. & p.p.;* **det′o·nat·ing,** *pr.p.* —**det·o·na·tion** (det′ə nā′shən), *n.*

det·o·na·tor (det′ə nā′tər), *n.* a fuse or the like for setting off an explosive.

de·tour (dē′toor), *n.* **1.** a turning aside from the direct or regular route. **2.** a route used when the regular route is closed to traffic. —*v.* to go or send by a detour.

de·tract (di trakt′), *v.* to take away something, especially something worthwhile or attractive [Weeds *detract* from the beauty of a lawn.] —**de·trac′tion,** *n.* —**de·trac′tor,** *n.*

det·ri·ment (det′rə mənt), *n.* damage or harm, or something that causes this [He watches television all evening to the *detriment* of his studies.] —**det′ri·men′tal,** *adj.*

De·troit (di troit′), *n.* a city in southeastern Michigan.

deuce (doos *or* dyoos), *n.* **1.** a playing card with two spots. **2.** a tie score of 40 points each or 5 games each in tennis. **3.** the devil or bad luck: *used as a mild curse to show that one is annoyed, surprised, etc.*

Deu·ter·on·o·my (doo′tər än′ə mē *or* dyoo′tər än′ə mē), *n.* the fifth book of the Old Testament.

dev·as·tate (dev′əs tāt), *v.* to ruin or destroy completely; make waste [An atomic war could *devastate* the world.] —**dev′as·tat·ed,** *p.t. & p.p.;* **dev′as·tat·ing,** *pr.p.* —**dev′as·ta′tion,** *n.*

deuce of hearts

de·vel·op (di vel′əp), *v.* **1.** to make or become larger, fuller, better, etc.; grow or expand [The seedling *developed* into a tree. Reading *develops* one's knowledge.] **2.** to bring or come into being and work out gradually; evolve [Dr. Salk *developed* a vaccine for polio. A fungous growth *developed* on the plants.] **3.** to treat an exposed photographic film or plate with chemicals, so as to show the picture. **4.** to become known [It *developed* that Sally had won several contests.]

de·vel·op·ment (di vel′əp mənt), *n.* **1.** the act of developing; a causing to grow, expand, improve, etc. **2.** a thing that has developed [a real estate *development*]. **3.** a happening; event [an unexpected *development* in a case].

de·vi·ate (dē′vi āt), *v.* to turn aside from the usual or expected way, goal, rule, standard, etc. [to *deviate* from the truth]. —**de′vi·at·ed,** *p.t. & p.p.;* **de′vi·at·ing,** *pr.p.* —**de′vi·a′tion,** *n.*

de·vice (di vīs′), *n.* **1.** something made or invented for some special use; tool, machine, etc. [A windmill is a *device* for putting wind power to work.] **2.** a plan that has been worked out to bring about a certain result; scheme [The errand was a *device* to get John out of the house.] **3.** a design or emblem, as on a shield or badge. —**leave someone to his own devices,** to let someone do as he wishes.

dev·il (dev′l), *n.* **1.** any of the evil spirits of hell in religious belief and in folk tales; especially, **the Devil,** the chief evil spirit, who is also called Satan. He is usually shown as a man with horns, a forked tail, etc. **2.** an evil or cruel person or spirit. **3.** a person who is very lively, playful, daring, etc. **4.** a very unhappy or unlucky person. **5.** a printer's helper. —*v.* to annoy or tease. —**dev′iled** or **dev′-illed,** *p.t. & p.p.;* **dev′il·ing** or **dev′il·ling,** *pr.p.* —**dev′il·ish,** *adj.*

the Devil

dev·iled or **dev·illed** (dev′ld), *adj.* chopped up fine and highly seasoned [*deviled* ham].

dev·il·fish (dev′l fish), *n.* **1.** the largest kind of ray, a fish with a broad, flat body and a long tail. **2.** an octopus.

dev·il-may-care (dev′l mā ker′), *adj.* reckless or careless; happy-go-lucky.

dev·il·ment (dev′l mənt), *n.* mischief.

dev·il's-food cake (dev′lz food′), a rich chocolate cake.

dev·il·try (dev′l trē), *n.* mischief; wild fun. —**dev′il·tries,** *pl.*

de·vi·ous (dē′vi əs), *adj.* **1.** not in a straight path; roundabout; winding [We approached by a *devious* trail that followed a creek.] **2.** that strays from what is right or usual; not frank [*devious* behavior]. —**de′vi·ous·ly,** *adv.*

de·vise (di vīz′), *v.* **1.** to work out; think up; plan or invent something [to *devise* a training program]. **2.** to give or leave in a will. —**de·vised′,** *p.t. & p.p.;* **de·vis·ing,** *pr.p.*

de·void (di void′), *adj.* without any; empty [a man *devoid* of pity; a room *devoid* of color].

de·volve (di välv′), *v.* to be passed on [In my absence, these duties will *devolve* on you.] —**de·volved′,** *p.t. & p.p.;* **de·volv′ing,** *pr.p.*

de·vote (di vōt′), *v.* to give up to some purpose, activity, or person [He has *devoted* his life to painting.] —**de·vot′ed,** *p.t. & p.p.;* **de·vot′-ing,** *pr.p.*

de·vot·ed (di vōt′id), *adj.* very loving or loyal [a *devoted* father; a *devoted* supporter].

dev·o·tee (dev ə tē′), *n.* a person who is strongly devoted to something or someone [a *devotee* of the theater; a *devotee* of Bach].

de·vo·tion (di vō′shən), *n.* **1.** a devoting or being devoted [his *devotion* to his wife; her *devotion* to the cause]. **2.** *often* **devotions,** *pl.* prayers. —**de·vo′tion·al,** *adj.*

de·vour (di vour′), *v.* **1.** to eat up in a hungry or greedy way. **2.** to ruin or destroy [The little town was *devoured* by the landslide.] **3.** to take in greedily with the eyes or ears [My nephew *devours* fairy tales.] **4.** to swallow up; absorb [He was *devoured* by curiosity.]

de·vout (di vout′), *adj.* **1.** very religious; pious. **2.** serious and with deep feeling; sincere [a *devout* wish for success]. —**de·vout′ly,** *adv.*

dew (doo *or* dyoo), *n.* **1.** water from the air that forms in little drops on cool surfaces at night. **2.** anything like dew, as droplets of sweat. —**dew′y,** *adj.*

dew·drop (doo′dräp *or* dyoo′dräp), *n.* a drop of dew.

dew·lap (doo′lap *or* dyoo′lap), *n.* a fold of skin hanging under the throat of cattle, etc.

dex·ter·i·ty (dek ster′ə tē), *n.* skill and quickness in the use of one's hands, body, or mind [The barber shows *dexterity* with the scissors. He has the *dexterity* of a diplomat.]

dex·ter·ous (dek′strəs *or* dek′-stər əs), *adj.* skillful and quick in the use of the hands, body, or mind; deft or clever [a *dex-terous* surgeon]. —**dex′ter-ous·ly,** *adv.*

dewlap

dex·trose (dek′strōs), *n.* a sugar found in plants and animals; glucose.

dex·trous (dek′strəs), *adj.* dexterous.

di-, a prefix meaning "two" or "double" [Carbon *dioxide* has two atoms of oxygen per molecule.]

di·a-, a prefix meaning "through" or "across" [A *diagonal* line slants across a figure.]

di·a·be·tes (dī′ə bē′tis *or* dī′ə bē′tēz), *n.* a sickness in which the body produces little or no insulin to break down and use the sugar eaten. It can be controlled by taking prepared insulin regularly. Also called **sugar diabetes.**

di·a·bet·ic (dī′ə bet′ik *or* dī′ə bē′tik), *adj.* of or having diabetes. —*n.* a person who has diabetes.

di·a·bol·ic (dī′ə bäl′ik) or **di·a·bol·i·cal** (dī′ə-bäl′i k′l), *adj.* of or like a devil; very wicked or cruel; fiendish; devilish [*diabolical* torture]. —**di′a·bol′i·cal·ly,** *adv.*

di·a·crit·ic (dī′ə krit′ik), *n.* a diacritical mark.

di·a·crit·i·cal mark (dī′ə krit′i k′l), a mark added to a letter to show how to pronounce it. Examples: ä, ā. ô.

di·a·dem (dī′ə dem), *n.* **1.** a crown. **2.** any band worn on the head as an ornament.

di·ag·nose (dī əg nōs′), *v.* to make a diagnosis of. —**di·ag·nosed′,** *p.t. & p.p.;* **di·ag·nos′-ing,** *pr.p.*

di·ag·no·sis (dī′əg nō′sis), *n.* **1.** the act or practice of examining a patient and studying his symptoms to find out what disease he has. **2.** a careful examination of all the facts in a situation to find out how it has been brought about [a *diagnosis* of the last election]. **3.** the decision or opinion that results from such examinations. **—di·ag·no·ses** (dī/əg nō/sēz), *pl.*

di·ag·o·nal (dī ag/ə n'l), *adj.* **1.** slanting from one corner to the opposite corner, as of a square. **2.** going in a slanting direction [a tie with *diagonal* stripes]. **—n.** a diagonal line, plane, course, or part. **—di·ag/-o·nal·ly,** *adv.*

diagonal line

di·a·gram (dī/ə gram), *n.* a drawing, plan, or chart that helps explain a thing by showing all its parts, how it is put together, how it works, etc. [a *diagram* showing how to assemble a radio set; a *diagram* of all the rooms in a museum]. **—v.** to show or explain by means of a diagram; make a diagram of. **—di/a·gramed** or **di/a·grammed,** *p.t. & p.p.;* **di/a·gram·ing** or **di/a·gram·ming,** *pr.p.* **—di/-a·gram·mat/ic,** *adj.*

di·al (dī/əl), *n.* **1.** the face of a watch, clock, or sundial. **2.** the face of certain other instruments, as a compass, gauge, meter, or radio, having marks on which a moving pointer can show amount, direction, place, etc. **3.** a disk on a telephone that can be turned for making connections automatically. **—v. 1.** to tune in a radio or television station. **2.** to call on a telephone by using a dial. **—di/aled** or **di/alled,** *p.t. & p.p.;* **di/al·ing** or **di/al·ling,** *pr.p.*

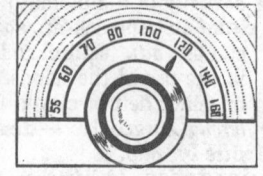

upper: dial of a radio
lower: dial of a clock

di·a·lect (dī/ə lekt), *n.* the form of a language that is used only in a certain place or among a certain group [Southern *dialect* or Irish *dialect* of English]. **—di·a·lec/tal,** *adj.*

di·a·logue or **di·a·log** (dī/ə lôg), *n.* **1.** a talking together, especially an open exchange of ideas, as in an effort to understand each other's views. **2.** the parts of a play, novel, etc. that are conversation.

di·am·e·ter (dī am/ə tər), *n.* **1.** a straight line passing through the center of a circle or sphere, from one side to the other. *See the picture for* **circle. 2.** the length of such a line [The *diameter* of the moon is about 2,160 miles.]

di·a·met·ri·cal (dī/ə met/ri k'l) or **di·a·met·ric** (dī/ə met/rik), *adj.* **1.** of or along a diameter. **2.** directly opposite. **—di/a·met/ri·cal·ly,** *adv.*

di·a·mond (dī/mənd *or* dī/ə mənd), *n.* **1.** a very precious stone, usually colorless, formed of nearly pure carbon. It is the hardest known mineral and is used as a gem, in the cutting edge of tools, as the tip of a phonograph needle, etc. **2.** a

diamonds

figure shaped like this: ◇. **3.** a playing card of a suit marked with this figure in red. **4.** the infield of a baseball field or the whole playing field.

Di·an·a (dī an/ə), *n.* the Roman goddess of the moon and of hunting. The Greeks called this goddess *Artemis.*

di·a·pa·son (dī/ə pā/z'n), *n.* **1.** the whole range of a voice or musical instrument. **2.** either of two organ stops that cover the whole range and cause each note played to sound in two or more octaves.

di·a·per (dī/ə pər *or* dī/pər), *n.* a cloth pinned around a baby as a kind of underpants.

di·a·phragm (dī/ə fram), *n.* **1.** the wall of muscles and tendons between the cavity of the chest and the cavity of the abdomen. **2.** a vibrating disk that makes or receives sound waves, as in a telephone receiver or mouthpiece, a loudspeaker, etc. **3.** a disk with a center hole to control the amount of light that goes through a camera lens.

di·ar·rhe·a or **di·ar·rhoe·a** (dī/ə rē/ə), *n.* a condition in which bowel movements come too often and are too loose.

di·a·ry (dī/ə rē), *n.* **1.** a record written day by day of some of the things done, seen, or thought by the writer. **2.** a book for keeping such a record. **—di/a·ries,** *pl.*

di·a·tribe (dī/ə trīb), *n.* a speech or writing that attacks some person or thing in a very harsh way.

dice (dīs), *n.pl.* small cubes marked on each side with a different number of dots (from one to six). Dice are used, usually in pairs, in various games of chance. **—v.** to cut into small cubes [to *dice* beets]. **—die** or **dice,** *sing.* **—diced** (dīst), *p.t. & p.p.;* **dic/ing,** *pr.p.*

dick·ens (dik/'nz), *n. & interj.* a mild word used instead of *devil* [What the *dickens*!]

Dick·ens, Charles (dik/'nz), 1812–1870; English novelist.

dick·er (dik/ər), *v.* to make or try to make a trade by bargaining.

dick·ey or **dick·y** (dik/ē), *n.* a kind of bib or shirt front, often with a collar, worn under a suit or on a dress. **—dick/eys** or **dick/ies,** *pl.*

dic·ta·phone (dik/tə fōn), *n.* a machine that makes a record of words spoken into it so that they can be played back. It is used in offices for dictating letters, etc. to be typed. The name **Dictaphone** is a trademark.

dic·tate (dik/tāt), *v.* **1.** to speak or read something aloud for someone else to write down [to *dictate* a letter to a secretary]. **2.** to say or tell with authority; command or order [Let your conscience *dictate* what you do.] **—n.** an order or command given with authority [It was a *dictate* of the court that he leave town.] **—dic/tat·ed,** *p.t. & p.p.;* **dic/tat·ing,** *pr.p.*

dic·ta·tion (dik tā/shən), *n.* **1.** the dictating of words for another to write down [rapid *dictation*]. **2.** the words dictated [a notebook filled with *dictation*]. **3.** the giving of orders or commands with authority [to rebel against *dictation* by one's elders].

dic·ta·tor (dik′tā tər), *n.* **1.** a ruler who has complete power over his country. **2.** any person with much power, whose word is obeyed [She set herself up as *dictator* of manners.] **3.** a person who dictates words for another to write down. —**dic′ta·tor·ship,** *n.*

dic·ta·to·ri·al (dik′tə tôr′i əl), *adj.* of or like a dictator; overbearing; tyrannical [a *dictatorial* foreman].

dic·tion (dik′shən), *n.* **1.** the way in which something is put into words; choice and arrangement of words [The *diction* of everyday talk is different from that of a formal essay.] **2.** a way of speaking or pronouncing words; enunciation [An actor must have good, clear *diction.*]

dic·tion·ar·y (dik′shən er′ē), *n.* **1.** a book in which some or most of the words of a language, or of some special field, are listed in alphabetical order with their meanings, pronunciations, etc. [a school *dictionary;* a medical *dictionary*]. **2.** a book like this in which words of one language are explained in words of another language [a Spanish-English *dictionary*]. —**dic′tion·ar′ies,** *pl.*

dic·tum (dik′təm), *n.* a saying; especially, an opinion given with authority [the *dictums* of a critic]. —**dic′tums** or **dic·ta** (dik′tə), *pl.*

did (did), past tense of **do.**

di·dac·tic (dī dak′tik), *adj.* **1.** used for teaching, or meant to teach a lesson [Many of Aesop's fables are *didactic.*] **2.** too willing to teach others [She is a *didactic* person, always correcting another's speech.] —**di·dac′ti·cal·ly,** *adv.*

did·n't (did′′nt), did not.

didst (didst), a form of **did** used with *thou,* as in the Bible.

die (dī), *v.* **1.** to stop living; become dead. **2.** to stop going, moving, acting, etc. [The motor sputtered and *died.*] **3.** to lose force; become weak, faint, etc. [The sound of music *died* away.] **4.** to want greatly: *used only in everyday talk* [She's *dying* to know my secret.] —**die off,** to die one by one until all are gone. —**died,** *p.t.* & *p.p.;* **dy′ing,** *pr.p.*

die (dī), *n.* **1.** either of a pair of dice: see **dice.** **2.** a tool or device used to give a certain form to some object [*Dies* are used to punch holes in metal, cut threads on screws, stamp the design on coins, etc.] —**the die is cast,** the decision has been made and there is no turning back from it. —**dice** (dīs), *pl. for meaning 1;* **dies** (dīz), *pl. for meaning 2.*

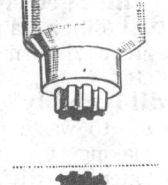

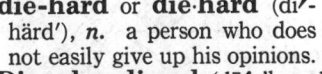
stamping die

die-hard or **die·hard** (dī′härd′), *n.* a person who does not easily give up his opinions.

Die·sel or **die·sel** (dē′z′l or dē′s′l), *n.* a kind of internal-combustion engine that burns crude oil by using heat produced by compressing air. Also called **Diesel engine** or **Diesel motor.**

di·et (dī′ət), *n.* **1.** what a person or animal usually eats or drinks; usual food [Rice is a basic food in the *diet* of many Asian countries.] **2.** a special choice as to kinds and amounts of food eaten, as for one's health or to gain or lose weight [a sugar-free *diet;* a reducing *diet*]. —*v.* to eat certain kinds and amounts of food, especially in order to lose weight.

di·et (dī′ət), *n.* a formal meeting for discussion; especially, the law-making assembly of certain countries [the Japanese *Diet*].

di·e·tar·y (dī′ə ter′i), *adj.* having to do with a food diet [the *dietary* laws of the Moslems].

di·e·tet·ic (dī′ə tet′ik), *adj.* of or for a food diet.

di·e·tet·ics (dī′ə tet′iks), *n.pl.* the study of the kinds and amounts of food needed for good health: *used with a singular verb.*

di·e·ti·tian or **di·e·ti·cian** (dī′ə tish′ən), *n.* a person whose work is planning diets that will give people the kinds and amounts of food that they need.

dif·fer (dif′ər), *v.* **1.** to be not the same; be unlike [Our tastes in music *differ.*] **2.** to have unlike or opposite opinions or ideas; disagree [We *differed* about the meaning of the poem.]

dif·fer·ence (dif′ər əns *or* dif′rəns), *n.* **1.** a being unlike one another or a way in which people or things are unlike [the *difference* between black and white; a *difference* in size]. **2.** a differing in opinions; disagreement or argument [They are friends in spite of their *differences* over politics.] **3.** the amount by which one quantity is greater or less than another [The *difference* between 11 and 7 is 4.] —**make a difference,** to have some effect or importance; to matter.

dif·fer·ent (dif′ər ənt *or* dif′rənt), *adj.* **1.** not alike; unlike [John's hobbies are quite *different* from his brother's.] **2.** not the same; separate; distinct [There are three *different* colleges in the city.] **3.** not like most others; unusual [Their house is really *different.*] —**dif′fer·ent·ly,** *adv.*

dif·fer·en·tial (dif′ər en′shəl), *adj.* that differ according to conditions [*differential* rates]. —*n.* **1.** a difference in rates, charges, or the like. **2.** an arrangement of gears, as in the rear axle of an automobile, which lets the outside wheel turn faster around curves than the inside wheel: *the full name is* **differential gear.**

dif·fer·en·ti·ate (dif′ər en′shi āt), *v.* **1.** to tell or see the difference [Only an expert could *differentiate* between the original painting and the copy.] **2.** to be or make different [What *differentiates* the polar bear from other bears?] —**dif′fer·en′ti·at·ed,** *p.t.* & *p.p.;* **dif′fer·en′ti·at·ing,** *pr.p.* —**dif′fer·en′ti·a′tion,** *n.*

dif·fi·cult (dif′i kult), *adj.* **1.** hard to do, make, or understand; that takes much trouble, thought, or skill [This algebra problem is *difficult.*] **2.** hard to please; not easy to get along with [Scrooge was a *difficult* employer.]

fat, āpe, cär, ten, ēven, hit, bīte, gō, hôrn, tool, book, up, fûr;
get, joy, yet, chin, she, thin, *th*en; zh = s in pleasure; ′ as in able (ā′b′l);
ə = a in ago, e in agent, i in sanity, o in confess, u in focus.

dif·fi·cul·ty (dif′i kul′tē), *n*. **1.** how difficult, or hard to deal with, a thing is [These problems are arranged in order of their *difficulty*.] **2.** something that is difficult [Columbus overcame many *difficulties* to cross the Atlantic.] **3.** trouble or the cause of trouble [Did you have *difficulty* in doing your homework?] —**dif′fi·cul′ties,** *pl*.

dif·fi·dent (dif′i dənt), *adj*. not sure of oneself; bashful or shy. —**dif′fi·dence,** *n*. —**dif′fi·dent·ly,** *adv*.

dif·frac·tion (di frak′shən), *n*. the breaking up of a ray of light into dark or light bands or into the colors of the spectrum.

dif·fuse (di fyo͞os′), *adj*. **1.** spread out; not centered in one place [This lamp gives *diffuse* light.] **2.** using more words than are needed; wordy [a *diffuse* style]. —*v*. (di fyo͞oz′), **1.** to spread out in every direction; scatter widely [to *diffuse* light, heat, information, etc.]. **2.** to mix together, as gases or liquids; intermingle. —**dif·fused′,** *p.t. & p.p.;* **dif·fus′ing,** *pr.p.* —**dif·fuse′ly,** *adv*. —**dif·fu·sion** (di fyo͞o′zhən), *n*.

dig (dig), *v*. **1.** to turn up or remove ground with a spade, the hands, claws, etc. [The pirates *dug* for buried treasure.] **2.** to make by digging [to *dig* a well]. **3.** to make a way by digging [The miners are *digging* through a wall of clay.] **4.** to get out by digging [to *dig* potatoes]. **5.** to find out, as by careful study [to *dig* out the truth]. **6.** to nudge or poke [to *dig* someone in the ribs]. **7.** to work or study hard: *used only in everyday talk*. —*n*. **1.** a nudge or poke. **2.** an insulting or sneering remark: *used only in everyday talk*. —**dug,** *or in older use* **digged,** *p.t. & p.p.;* **dig′ging,** *pr.p.*

di·gest (di jest′ *or* dī jest′), *v*. **1.** to change food in the stomach and intestines into a form that can be used by the body [Small babies cannot *digest* solid food.] **2.** to be digested [Some foods do not *digest* easily.] **3.** to think over so as to understand fully [Read and *digest* that article.] —*n*. (dī′jest), a short account or report of a longer story, article, etc.; summary [a *digest* of recent law cases].

di·gest·i·ble (di jes′tə b′l *or* dī jes′tə b′l), *adj*. that can be digested.

di·ges·tion (di jes′chən *or* dī jes′chən), *n*. **1.** the act or process of digesting food. **2.** the ability to digest food. —**di·ges′tive,** *adj*.

dig·ger (dig′ər), *n*. a person or thing that digs.

dig·it (dij′it), *n*. **1.** any number from 0 through 9. **2.** a finger or toe.

dig·i·ta·lis (dij′i tal′is), *n*. a medicine made from the dried leaves of one kind of foxglove: see **foxglove**. It is used in heart disease to speed up the action of the heart.

dig·ni·fied (dig′nə fīd), *adj*. having dignity; noble, proper, self-respecting, etc.

dig·ni·fy (dig′nə fī), *v*. to give dignity or honor to; make seem worthy or noble [to *dignify* a politician by calling him a statesman]. —**dig′ni·fied,** *p.t. & p.p.;* **dig′ni·fy·ing,** *pr.p.*

dig·ni·tar·y (dig′nə ter′ē), *n*. a person holding a high position, as in a government or church. —**dig′ni·tar′ies,** *pl*.

dig·ni·ty (dig′nə tē), *n*. **1.** the quality of being worthy or noble; real worth [He respects the *dignity* of all men.] **2.** a noble or stately appearance or manner [the *dignity* with which swans move in water]. **3.** high rank or position that deserves respect [We must uphold the *dignity* of our courts.] **4.** proper pride and self-respect [It would be beneath my *dignity* to notice his insults.] —**dig′ni·ties,** *pl*.

di·gress (də gres′ *or* dī gres′), *v*. to wander from the subject that one has been talking or writing about. —**di·gres′sion,** *n*.

dike (dīk), *n*. a wall or dam built to keep a sea or river from flooding over land. —*v*. to protect with a dike. —**diked,** *p.t. & p.p.;* **dik′ing,** *pr.p.*

dike

di·lap·i·dat·ed (di lap′ə dāt′id), *adj*. falling to pieces; broken down; shabby and neglected [a *dilapidated* barn].

di·lap·i·da·tion (di lap′ə dā′shən), *n*. a dilapidated or run-down condition; ruin.

di·late (dī lāt′ *or* di lāt′), *v*. to make or become wider or larger; expand; swell [The pupils of the eyes become *dilated* in the dark.] —**di·lat′ed,** *p.t. & p.p.;* **di·lat′ing,** *pr.p.* —**di·la′tion,** *n*.

dil·a·to·ry (dil′ə tôr′ē), *adj*. slow or late in doing things; delaying [I am *dilatory* in answering my mail.]

di·lem·ma (di lem′ə), *n*. a situation in which one must choose between things that are equally unpleasant or dangerous; difficult choice.

dil·et·tan·te (dil′ə tan′tē *or* dil ə tänt′), *n*. a person who loves the fine arts; now especially, one who is interested in art, literature, etc., but not in a deep or serious way. —**dil′et·tan′tes** or **dil·et·tan·ti** (dil′ə tan′tē), *pl*.

dil·i·gence (dil′ə jəns), *n*. careful and steady work or effort; industry.

dil·i·gent (dil′ə jənt), *adj*. doing one's work in a careful, steady way; working hard; industrious. —**dil′i·gent·ly,** *adv*.

dill (dil), *n*. a plant whose spicy seeds and stems are used to flavor pickles, etc.

dil·ly·dal·ly (dil′ē dal′ē), *v*. to waste time by not making up one's mind; loiter. —**dil′ly·dal′lied,** *p.t. & p.p.;* **dil′ly·dal′ly·ing,** *pr.p.*

di·lute (di lo͞ot′ *or* dī lyo͞ot′), *v*. **1.** to thin out or weaken by adding water or other liquid [to *dilute* condensed milk]. **2.** to weaken by mixing with something else [The force of his writing is *diluted* by his use of too many words.] —*adj*. diluted [*dilute* acid]. —**di·lut′ed,** *p.t. & p.p.;* **di·lut′ing,** *pr.p.* —**di·lu′tion,** *n*.

dill

dim (dim), *adj.* **1.** not bright or clear; somewhat dark; shadowy; gloomy [the *dim* twilight; a *dim* view of the future]. **2.** not clear to the hearing or mind; faint; indistinct [a *dim* sound in the distance; a *dim* recollection]. **3.** not seeing or understanding clearly [*dim* vision; a mind *dim* with age]. —*v.* to make or grow dim [Approaching cars should *dim* their lights.] —**dim′mer,** *compar.*; **dim′mest,** *superl.* —**dimmed,** *p.t.* & *p.p.*; **dim′ming,** *pr.p.* —**dim′ly,** *adv.* —**dim′ness,** *n.*

dime (dīm), *n.* a silver coin of the United States and of Canada, worth ten cents; one-tenth of a dollar.

di·men·sion (də men′shən), *n.* **1.** a measurement of something in length, width, or height [The *dimensions* of the box are 40 inches in length, 30 inches in height, and 24 inches in width.] **2.** size or importance [a project of vast *dimensions*].

di·min·ish (də min′ish), *v.* to make or become smaller in size or less in force, importance, etc. [An early winter quickly *diminishes* the squirrel's store of nuts. The danger of frost begins to *diminish* after the first of April.]

di·min·u·en·do (də min′yŏŏ en′dō), *adj.* & *adv.* gradually becoming less loud: a direction in music usually shown by the sign >. —*n.* a gradual decrease in loudness. —**di·min′u·en′dos,** *pl.*

dim·i·nu·tion (dim′ə nyŏŏ′shən *or* dim′ə nŏŏ′-shən), *n.* a lessening in size, amount, etc.

di·min·u·tive (də min′yoo tiv), *adj.* **1.** very small; tiny. **2.** showing that something is smaller [The word "booklet" is formed by adding the *diminutive* suffix "-let" to "book."] —*n.* a word formed by adding a diminutive suffix.

dim·i·ty (dim′ə tē), *n.* a thin cotton cloth used for dresses and curtains. —**dim′i·ties,** *pl.*

dim·ple (dim′p'l), *n.* **1.** a small hollow spot, as on the chin or cheek. **2.** any slight hollow, as in the surface of water. —*v.* to form dimples [Her cheeks *dimple* when she smiles.] —**dim′pled,** *p.t.* & *p.p.*; **dim′pling,** *pr.p.*

din (din), *n.* a loud, steady noise; confused uproar [the *din* of a boiler factory]. —*v.* **1.** to make a din. **2.** to keep repeating; say again and again [He *dinned* the warning into my ears.] —**dinned,** *p.t.* & *p.p.*; **din′-ning,** *pr.p.*

dimples

dine (dīn), *v.* **1.** to eat dinner. **2.** to give a dinner to [to *dine* a visitor]. —**dined,** *p.t.* & *p.p.*; **din′ing,** *pr.p.*

din·er (dīn′ər), *n.* **1.** a person eating dinner. **2.** a railroad car in which meals are served to passengers. **3.** a restaurant built to look like such a car.

din·ette (dī net′), *n.* a small room or an alcove, used as a dining room.

ding (ding), *n.* the sound of a bell. —*v.* to make this sound.

ding-dong (ding′dông′), *n.* the sound of a bell struck again and again.

din·ghy (ding′gē), *n.* a small boat, usually a rowboat. —**din′ghies,** *pl.*

din·gy (din′jē), *adj.* having a dull, dirty look; not bright or clean [a *dingy* room]. —**din′gi·er,** *compar.*; **din′gi·est,** *superl.* —**din′gi·ness,** *n.*

dining room, a room where meals are eaten.

din·ner (din′ər), *n.* **1.** the main meal of the day, whether eaten in the evening or about noon. **2.** a banquet in honor of some person or event.

di·no·saur (dī′nə sôr), *n.* any of a group of reptiles that lived millions of years ago. Dinosaurs had four legs and a long, tapering tail, and some were almost 100 feet long.

dint (dint), *n.* strength or power; force [By *dint* of great effort he got what he wanted.]

dinosaur (75 ft. long)

di·oc·e·san (dī äs′ə s'n), *adj.* of a diocese. —*n.* the bishop of a diocese.

di·o·cese (dī′ə sis *or* dī′ə sēs), *n.* the church district under the control of a bishop.

Di·og·e·nes (dī äj′ə nēz), *n.* 412?-323 B.C.; Greek philosopher: according to legend, he searched with a lantern for an honest man.

Di·o·ny·sus (dī′ə nī′səs), *n.* an earlier Greek name for the god Bacchus.

di·ox·ide (dī äk′sīd), *n.* an oxide containing two atoms of oxygen in each molecule.

dip (dip), *v.* **1.** to put into a liquid and quickly pull out again [to *dip* a brush into paint]. **2.** to go down into a liquid and quickly come out again [The oars of the galley *dipped* in rhythm.] **3.** to lower and quickly raise or rise again [The airplane *dipped* its right wing. The treetops *dipped* in the wind.] **4.** to slope downward, as a road. **5.** to take out by scooping up with a dipper, the hand, etc. [to *dip* water from a bucket]. **6.** to make a candle by putting a wick into melted tallow or wax again and again. **7.** to look into or study for a little while [to *dip* into a book]. —*n.* **1.** a dipping or being dipped; a plunge into water, a quick drop, a downward slope, etc. **2.** something dipped or scooped out [a *dip* of ice cream]. **3.** a liquid into which things are dipped, as in cleaning or dyeing. —**dipped** *or* **dipt,** *p.t.* & *p.p.*; **dip′ping,** *pr.p.*

diph·the·ri·a (dif thir′i ə *or* dip thir′i ə), *n.* a disease of the throat that is spread by a germ, causes fever and soreness, and makes breathing difficult.

diph·thong (dif′thông *or* dip′thông), *n.* a sound made by pronouncing two vowels one right after the other without stopping [The "ou" in "mouse" is a *diphthong* formed by the vowel sounds ä and ōō.]

di·plo·ma (di plō'mə), *n.* a paper given to a student by a school or college to show that he has been graduated.

di·plo·ma·cy (di plō'mə sē), *n.* **1.** the carrying on of relations between nations, as in building up trade, making treaties, etc. **2.** skill in dealing with people so as to get their help and keep them friendly; tact. —**di·plo'ma·cies,** *pl.*

dip·lo·mat (dip'lə mat), *n.* **1.** a person who acts for his country in dealing with other nations. **2.** a person who has tact in dealing with others.

dip·lo·mat·ic (dip'lə mat'ik), *adj.* **1.** having to do with diplomacy. **2.** tactful [a *diplomatic* salesman]. —**dip'lo·mat'i·cal·ly,** *adv.*

dip·per (dip'ər), *n.* **1.** a person or thing that dips. **2.** a cup with a long handle, used for scooping up liquids; ladle. **3.** either of two groups of stars in the shape of a dipper. One is called the **Big Dipper,** the other the **Little Dipper.**

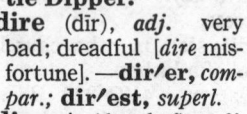

upper: water dipper
lower: the Big Dipper

dire (dīr), *adj.* very bad; dreadful [*dire* misfortune]. —**dir'er,** *compar.;* **dir'est,** *superl.*

di·rect (də rekt'), *adj.* **1.** by the shortest way, without turning or stopping; straight [a *direct* route home]. **2.** honest and to the point; frank [a *direct* question]. **3.** with no one or nothing between; immediate [The wire was in *direct* contact with the ground.] **4.** traced from father to child to grandchild, etc. [a *direct* descendant]. **5.** exact; complete [the *direct* opposite]. **6.** in the exact words used by the speaker [a *direct* quotation]. —*v.* **1.** to be in charge of; manage; control; supervise [to *direct* the building of a bridge; to *direct* a glee club; to *direct* a play]. **2.** to command or order [You are *directed* to appear in court.] **3.** to tell someone the way to a place [Will you please *direct* me to the city hall?] **4.** to aim or steer; point [His remarks were *directed* at me.] —*adv.* directly [Go *direct* to your house.] —**di·rect'ness,** *n.*

direct current, an electric current that flows in one direction only.

di·rec·tion (də rek'shən), *n.* **1.** a directing or managing; control [The choir is under the *direction* of Mr. Jones.] **2.** an order or command. **3.** *usually* **directions,** *pl.* instructions on how to get to some place or how to do something [*directions* for driving to New York; *directions* for building a model boat]. **4.** the point toward which something faces or the line along which something moves or lies ["North," "up," "forward," and "left" are *directions*.] **5.** line along which a thing develops [to plan in the *direction* of a longer school year]. —**di·rec'tion·al,** *adj.*

di·rec·tive (də rek'tiv), *n.* an order or instruction coming from a central office.

di·rect·ly (də rekt'lē), *adv.* **1.** in a direct line or way; straight [Come *directly* home after school. The town lies *directly* to the north.] **2.** with nothing coming between; immediately [He is *directly* responsible to me.] **3.** exactly; completely [*directly* opposite].

direct object, the word in a sentence that tells who or what receives the action of the verb [In "John wrote a story," "story" is the *direct object*.] See also **indirect object.**

di·rec·tor (də rek'tər), *n.* **1.** a person who directs or manages the work of others [the *director* of a play, a band, a government bureau]. **2.** a member of a group chosen to direct the affairs of a business. —**di·rec'tor·ship,** *n.*

di·rec·to·ry (də rek'tə rē), *n.* a book or list of names, addresses, etc. [a telephone *directory;* an office *directory*]. —**di·rec'to·ries,** *pl.*

dire·ful (dīr'fəl), *adj.* same as **dire.**

dirge (dūrj), *n.* a slow, sad piece of music showing grief for the dead, as at a funeral.

dir·i·gi·ble (dir'i jə b'l), *n.* a large, long airship that can be steered.

dirk (dūrk), *n.* a short dagger.

dirt (dūrt), *n.* **1.** mud, dust, soot, or other matter that makes things unclean; filth. **2.** earth or soil. **3.** indecent talk, writing, or action.

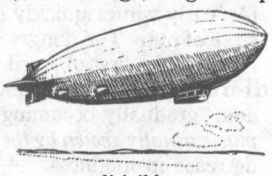

dirigible

dirt·y (dūr'tē), *adj.* **1.** having dirt on or in it; not clean; soiled. **2.** foul or indecent; not nice; mean [a *dirty* trick]. **3.** muddy or clouded in color [a *dirty* yellow]. **4.** rough or stormy [*dirty* weather]. —*v.* to make or become dirty; soil. —**dirt'i·er,** *compar.;* **dirt'i·est,** *superl.* —**dirt'ied,** *p.t. & p.p.;* **dirt'y·ing,** *pr.p.* —**dirt'i·ness,** *n.*

dis-, a prefix meaning: **1.** away, away from, or out of [*Displace* means to move away from its place.] **2.** the opposite of [*Dishonest* means the opposite of honest.] **3.** to fail, stop, or refuse to [*Disagree* means to fail to agree.]

dis·a·bil·i·ty (dis'ə bil'ə tē), *n.* **1.** the condition of not being able or fit to do something. **2.** something that disables, as an illness or injury. —**dis'a·bil'i·ties,** *pl.*

dis·a·ble (dis ā'b'l), *v.* to make unable to move or act in a normal way; cripple [She is *disabled* by arthritis.] —**dis·a'bled,** *p.t. & p.p.;* **dis·a'bling,** *pr.p.*

dis·a·buse (dis ə byōōz'), *v.* to free from false ideas; put right [She *disabused* her pupils of their belief in fairies.] —**dis·a·bused',** *p.t. & p.p.;* **dis·a·bus'ing,** *pr.p.*

dis·ad·van·tage (dis'əd van'tij), *n.* **1.** anything that stands in the way of success; handicap; drawback [Weak arches are a *disadvantage* on long hikes.] **2.** loss or harm [This decision will work to your *disadvantage*.] —**dis·ad·van·ta·geous** (dis ad'vən tā'jəs), *adj.*

dis·ad·van·taged (dis'əd van'tijd), *adj.* kept from having decent living conditions, an education, etc., because of being poor.

dis·af·fect·ed (dis'ə fek'tid), *adj.* no longer friendly or loyal; discontented [The *disaffected* sailors talked of mutiny.] —**dis'af·fec'tion,** *n.*

dis·a·gree (dis ə grē'), *v.* **1.** to differ in opinion; often, to quarrel or argue [to *disagree* on politics]. **2.** to be different; differ [His story of the accident *disagreed* with hers.] **3.** to be harmful or unpleasant to [Corn *disagrees* with me.] —**dis·a·greed',** *p.t. & p.p.;* **dis·a·gree'ing,** *pr.p.*

dis·a·gree·a·ble (dis'ə grē'ə b'l), *adj.* **1.** not pleasing to one; unpleasant; offensive [a *disagreeable* odor]. **2.** hard to get along with; bad-tempered; cross. —**dis'a·gree'a·bly,** *adv.*

dis·a·gree·ment (dis'ə grē'mənt), *n.* **1.** a quarrel or argument. **2.** a difference of opinion. **3.** a being unlike; difference.

dis·ap·pear (dis ə pir'), *v.* to stop being seen or to stop existing; vanish [The car *disappeared* around a curve. Dinosaurs *disappeared* millions of years ago.] —**dis'ap·pear'ance,** *n.*

dis·ap·point (dis ə point'), *v.* to fail to give or do what is wanted, expected, or promised; leave unsatisfied [We were *disappointed* in the weather. Although all promised to come, two of the boys *disappointed* us.]

dis·ap·point·ment (dis'ə point'mənt), *n.* **1.** a disappointing or being disappointed [one's *disappointment* over not winning]. **2.** a person or thing that disappoints [The team has been a *disappointment* to us.]

dis·ap·pro·ba·tion (dis'ap rə bā'shən), *n.* disapproval.

dis·ap·prov·al (dis'ə proov''l), *n.* a refusing to approve; opinion or feeling against something [The crowd showed its *disapproval* by booing.]

dis·ap·prove (dis ə proov'), *v.* to refuse to approve; have an opinion or feeling against; think to be wrong [The Puritans *disapproved* of dancing.] —**dis·ap·proved',** *p.t. & p.p.;* **dis·ap·prov'ing,** *pr.p.* —**dis·ap·prov'ing·ly,** *adv.*

dis·arm (dis ärm'), *v.* **1.** to take away weapons from [The policeman *disarmed* the robbers.] **2.** to make smaller or get rid of a nation's armed forces or its weapons of war [When all nations *disarm,* there will be peace.] **3.** to make harmless or friendly [the *disarming* manner of a child].

dis·ar·ma·ment (dis är'mə mənt), *n.* **1.** a disarming. **2.** a making smaller or getting rid of a nation's armed forces or weapons of war.

dis·ar·range (dis ə rānj'), *v.* to upset the order or arrangement of; make less neat [Do not *disarrange* the papers on my desk.] —**dis·ar·ranged',** *p.t. & p.p.;* **dis·ar·rang'ing,** *pr.p.* —**dis·ar·range'ment,** *n.*

dis·ar·ray (dis ə rā'), *n.* an untidy condition; disorder or confusion.

dis·as·sem·ble (dis'ə sem'b'l), *v.* to take apart [to *disassemble* a motor]. —**dis'as·sem'bled,** *p.t. & p.p.;* **dis'as·sem'bling,** *pr.p.*

dis·as·ter (di zas'tər), *n.* a happening that causes much damage or suffering, as a flood or earthquake; catastrophe. —**dis·as'trous,** *adj.*

dis·a·vow (dis ə vou'), *v.* to say that one knows nothing about or does not approve of; disclaim [He can never *disavow* the letter he wrote.]

dis·band (dis band'), *v.* to break up as a group or organization [The principal *disbanded* all fraternities at our school.]

dis·bar (dis bär'), *v.* to take away from a lawyer the right to practice law. —**dis·barred',** *p.t. & p.p.;* **dis·bar'ring,** *pr.p.* —**dis·bar'ment,** *n.*

dis·be·lief (dis bi lēf'), *n.* a not believing; lack of belief [He stared at me in *disbelief.*]

dis·be·lieve (dis bi lēv'), *v.* to have no belief in; refuse to believe. —**dis·be·lieved',** *p.t. & p.p.;* **dis·be·liev'ing,** *pr.p.*

dis·bur·den (dis bûr'd'n), *v.* to get rid of a burden, as of something weighing on one's mind.

dis·burse (dis bûrs'), *v.* to pay out, especially from public funds. —**dis·bursed',** *p.t. & p.p.;* **dis·burs'ing,** *pr.p.* —**dis·burse'ment,** *n.*

disc (disk), *n.* same as **disk.**

dis·card (dis kärd'), *v.* **1.** to throw away or get rid of something that is no longer wanted. **2.** in playing cards, to remove an unwanted card from one's hand. —*n.* (dis'kärd), **1.** a discarding or being discarded. **2.** something that is discarded.

dis·cern (di zûrn' *or* di sûrn'), *v.* to see or make out clearly; recognize [Can you *discern* a sail on the horizon? I cannot *discern* what reason he might have had.] —**dis·cern'i·ble,** *adj.* —**dis·cern'ment,** *n.*

dis·cern·ing (di zûrn'ing *or* di sûrn'ing), *adj.* having good judgment or understanding.

dis·charge (dis chärj'), *v.* **1.** to release from something that controls or holds in [to *discharge* a soldier from the army, a patient from a hospital, or a prisoner from jail]. **2.** to dismiss from a job; fire. **3.** to remove a burden or load; unload [The boat *discharged* its cargo.] **4.** to give forth or let out [The steam is *discharged* through this pipe.] **5.** to pay a debt or perform a duty [I have *discharged* all my obligations.] **6.** to shoot or fire, as a gun. **7.** to use up the electricity in [to *discharge* a battery]. —*n.* (*also* dis'chärj), **1.** a discharging or being discharged. **2.** a certificate that discharges [He has an honorable *discharge* from the army.] **3.** something discharged [His shirt was stained by the *discharge* from the wound.] —**dis·charged',** *p.t. & p.p.;* **dis·charg'ing,** *pr.p.*

dis·ci·ple (di sī'p'l), *n.* **1.** a person who follows another as his teacher or leader. **2.** any of the early followers of Jesus.

dis·ci·pli·nar·i·an (dis'ə pli ner'i ən), *n.* a person who enforces strict discipline.

dis·ci·pli·nar·y (dis'ə pli ner'ē), *adj.* of or for discipline [to take *disciplinary* action].

dis·ci·pline (dis'ə plin), *n.* **1.** training that teaches one to obey rules and control his behavior [the strict *discipline* of army life]. **2.** the result of such training; self-control; orderliness [The

---

fat, āpe, cär, ten, ēven, hit, bīte, gō, hôrn, tool, book, up, fûr; get, joy, yet, chin, she, thin, *th*en; zh = s in pleasure; ' as in able (ā'b'l); ə = a in ago, e in agent, i in sanity, o in confess, u in focus.

pupils showed perfect *discipline*.] **3.** punishment [cruel prison *discipline*]. —*v.* **1.** to train in discipline [Regular chores help to *discipline* children.] **2.** to punish. —**dis'ci·plined,** *p.t.* & *p.p.*; **dis'ci·plin·ing,** *pr.p.*

dis·claim (dis klām'), *v.* to deny that one has any claim to or connection with; refuse to admit or accept; deny [to *disclaim* one's rights to property; to *disclaim* knowledge of a crime].

dis·close (dis klōz'), *v.* **1.** to bring into view; uncover [He opened his hand and *disclosed* a silver dollar.] **2.** to make known; reveal [to *disclose* a secret]. —**dis·closed',** *p.t.* & *p.p.*; **dis·clos'ing,** *pr.p.*

dis·clo·sure (dis klō'zhər), *n.* **1.** a disclosing. **2.** a thing disclosed [The reporter made startling *disclosures* about prison conditions.]

dis·col·or (dis kul'ər), *v.* to change in color by fading, streaking, or staining [The strong soap *discolored* his socks.] —**dis·col'or·a'tion,** *n.*

dis·com·fit (dis kum'fit), *v.* to make confused, as by spoiling plans; upset or embarrass. —**dis·com·fi·ture** (dis kum'fi chər), *n.*

dis·com·fort (dis kum'fərt), *n.* **1.** lack of comfort; being uneasy in body or mind. **2.** anything that causes this.

dis·com·pose (dis kəm pōz'), *v.* to make nervous and ill at ease; fluster; upset [Unexpected guests always *discompose* Mother.] —**dis·com·posed',** *p.t.* & *p.p.*; **dis·com·pos'ing,** *pr.p.* —**dis·com·po·sure** (dis'kəm pō'zhər), *n.*

dis·con·cert (dis kən surt'), *v.* to bring confusion or disorder to, as by surprising; upset [to be *disconcerted* by a sudden change in plans].

dis·con·nect (dis kə nekt'), *v.* to undo the connection of; separate; unfasten [*Disconnect* the radio by pulling the plug from the socket.] —**dis·con·nec'tion,** *n.*

dis·con·so·late (dis kän'sə lit), *adj.* so sad or unhappy that nothing will comfort [Billy was *disconsolate* over the loss of his bicycle.]

dis·con·tent (dis kən tent'), *n.* a feeling of not being satisfied and of wanting something different; dissatisfaction.

dis·con·tent·ed (dis'kən ten'tid), *adj.* wanting things different than they are; not satisfied.

dis·con·tin·ue (dis'kən tin'yōō), *v.* to stop doing, using, etc.; give up [to *discontinue* a subscription to a magazine]. —**dis'con·tin'ued,** *p.t.* & *p.p.*; **dis'con·tin'u·ing,** *pr.p.*

dis·con·tin·u·ous (dis'kən tin'yōō əs), *adj.* not continuous; full of interruptions or gaps.

dis·cord (dis'kôrd), *n.* **1.** a failing to get along well together; lack of agreement; conflict [*Discord* among nations may lead to war.] **2.** a harsh, unpleasant sound. **3.** a sounding together of musical notes that do not harmonize.

dis·cord·ance (dis kôr'd'ns), *n.* discord.

dis·cord·ant (dis kôr'd'nt), *adj.* **1.** not agreeing or going well together; conflicting [His speech was full of *discordant* notes.] **2.** sounding harsh or unpleasant. **3.** not in harmony [*discordant* music]. —**dis·cord'ant·ly,** *adv.*

dis·count (dis'kount), *n.* an amount taken off a price, bill, or debt [a 5% *discount* on cash

sales]. —*v.* **1.** to give a certain amount as a discount from a price, bill, etc. **2.** to allow for exaggeration; believe only in part.

dis·coun·te·nance (dis koun'tə nəns), *v.* **1.** to make ashamed or embarrassed [He was *discountenanced* by their laughter.] **2.** to disapprove of; discourage. —**dis·coun'te·nanced,** *p.t.* & *p.p.*; **dis·coun'te·nanc·ing,** *pr.p.*

dis·cour·age (dis kur'ij), *v.* **1.** to prevent by disapproving or interfering [We *discouraged* him from risking his money. The storm *discouraged* any further boating.] **2.** to cause to lose hope or confidence [The singer was *discouraged* by the lack of applause.] —**dis·cour'aged,** *p.t.* & *p.p.*; **dis·cour'ag·ing,** *pr.p.* —**dis·cour'age·ment,** *n.*

dis·course (dis'kôrs), *n.* **1.** talk or conversation. **2.** a formal speech or writing on a serious subject. —*v.* (dis kôrs'), to give a long or formal talk [The professor *discoursed* on early church music.] —**dis·coursed',** *p.t.* & *p.p.*; **dis·cours'ing,** *pr.p.*

dis·cour·te·ous (dis kur'ti əs), *adj.* not polite; rude. —**dis·cour'te·ous·ly,** *adv.*

dis·cour·te·sy (dis kur'tə sē), *n.* rude or impolite behavior or a rude act or remark. —**dis·cour'te·sies,** *pl.*

dis·cov·er (dis kuv'ər), *v.* **1.** to be the first to find, see, or learn about [Newton *discovered* the laws of gravity.] **2.** to come upon; learn or find out about [I *discovered* many facts I never knew in the almanac.]

dis·cov·er·y (dis kuv'ər ē), *n.* **1.** a discovering or being discovered. **2.** a thing discovered. —**dis·cov'er·ies,** *pl.*

dis·cred·it (dis kred'it), *v.* **1.** to give or be a reason for not believing or trusting [His earlier lies *discredit* anything he may say.] **2.** to make seem not reliable or honest; hurt the reputation of [The judge has been *discredited* by the newspapers.] —*n.* **1.** doubt or lack of belief [These facts throw *discredit* on his story.] **2.** disgrace or dishonor [He ran away, much to his *discredit*.]

dis·cred·it·a·ble (dis kred'it ə b'l), *adj.* that discredits or brings disgrace or dishonor.

dis·creet (dis krēt'), *adj.* careful about what one says or does; prudent. —**dis·creet'ly,** *adv.*

dis·crep·an·cy (dis krep'ən sē), *n.* a difference or disagreement [There are several *discrepancies* in their reports.] —**dis·crep'an·cies,** *pl.*

dis·cre·tion (dis kresh'ən), *n.* **1.** carefulness in what one says or does; prudence [A person should use *discretion* in dealing with strangers.] **2.** judgment or opinion [Use your own *discretion* in choosing a topic.]

dis·cre·tion·ar·y (dis kresh'ə ner'ē), *adj.* left to one's own free judgment or choice [*discretionary* powers].

dis·crim·i·nate (dis krim'ə nāt), *v.* **1.** to see the difference between; distinguish [He is color-blind and cannot *discriminate* between red and green.] **2.** to show prejudice by treating in a less favorable way [Some businesses *discriminate* against women in hiring.] —**dis·crim'i·nat·ed,** *p.t.* & *p.p.*; **dis·crim'i·nat·ing,** *pr.p.*

dis·crim·i·na·tion (dis krim′ə nā′shən), *n.* **1.** a discriminating or distinguishing [*discrimination* between right and wrong]. **2.** the practice of treating persons or things in different ways because of prejudice [*discrimination* against minority groups]. **3.** good taste or judgment [to show *discrimination* in buying clothes].

dis·cur·sive (dis kŭr′siv), *adj.* going from one topic to another in a rambling way [a *discursive* speech].

dis·cus (dis′kəs), *n.* a heavy disk of metal and wood that is thrown in an athletic contest as a test of strength and skill.

dis·cuss (dis kus′), *v.* to talk or write about, with various opinions and ideas being given [Congress is *discussing* a new tax law.] **—dis·cus·sion** (dis kush′-ən), *n.*

man throwing a discus

dis·dain (dis dān′), *v.* to look down on with scorn; act as though something were beneath one's dignity [She *disdained* their insulting remarks.] **—*n.* scorn for a person or thing one considers beneath one. **—dis·dain′ful,** *adj.*

dis·ease (di zēz′), *n.* a condition of not being healthy; sickness; illness [Measles is a common children's *disease.* Some funguses cause *disease* in animals and plants.] **—dis·eased′,** *adj.*

dis·em·bark (dis im bärk′), *v.* to put or go ashore from a ship; land. **—dis·em·bar·ka·tion** (dis′em bär kā′shən), *n.*

dis·em·bod·ied (dis′im bäd′id), *adj.* separated from the body [*disembodied* spirits].

dis·en·chant (dis in chant′), *v.* to free from a false idea; make see the truth about something [Anyone who thinks it never rains in Mexico City will be *disenchanted* by a visit there.] **—dis·en·chant′ment,** *n.*

dis·en·cum·ber (dis′in kum′bər), *v.* to free from something that burdens or troubles.

dis·en·gage (dis in gāj′), *v.* to free from something that holds, binds, or connects; unfasten; detach [to *disengage* oneself from a pledge; to *disengage* troops from battle; to *disengage* gears]. **—dis·en·gaged′,** *p.t. & p.p.;* **dis·en·gag′ing,** *pr.p.* **—dis·en·gage′ment,** *n.*

dis·en·tan·gle (dis′in tang′g'l), *v.* to free from tangles or confusion; straighten out [*Disentangle* the yarn. We tried to *disentangle* the truth in his story from the lies.] **—dis′en·tan′gled,** *p.t. & p.p.;* **dis′en·tan′gling,** *pr.p.*

dis·fa·vor (dis fā′vər), *n.* **1.** a feeling against; disapproval; dislike [I view daylight-saving time with *disfavor.*] **2.** a being disliked or disapproved of [to fall into *disfavor*].

dis·fig·ure (dis fig′yər), *v.* to spoil the looks of as by marking up; deface; mar [Severe burns had *disfigured* his hands.] **—dis·fig′ured,** *p.t. & p.p.;* **dis·fig′ur·ing,** *pr.p.* **—dis·fig′ure·ment,** *n.*

dis·fran·chise (dis fran′chīz), *v.* to take away a right from someone, especially the right of a citizen to vote. **—dis·fran′chised,** *p.t. & p.p.;* **dis·fran′chis·ing,** *pr.p.* **—dis·fran·chise·ment** (dis fran′chiz mənt), *n.*

dis·gorge (dis gôrj′), *v.* to throw up something inside; vomit or discharge [The whale *disgorged* Jonah. The volcano *disgorged* lava.] **—dis·gorged′,** *p.t. & p.p.;* **dis·gorg′ing,** *pr.p.*

dis·grace (dis grās′), *n.* **1.** loss of favor, respect, or honor; dishonor; shame [He is in *disgrace* for cheating on the test.] **2.** a person or thing bringing shame [These slums are a *disgrace* to the city.] **—*v.* to bring shame upon; hurt the reputation of [His crime has *disgraced* the family.] **—dis·graced′,** *p.t. & p.p.;* **dis·grac′ing,** *pr.p.*

dis·grace·ful (dis grās′fəl), *adj.* causing disgrace; shameful. **—dis·grace′ful·ly,** *adv.*

dis·grun·tle (dis grun′t'l), *v.* to make dissatisfied and complaining [She was *disgruntled* when she didn't win a prize.] **—dis·grun′tled,** *p.t. & p.p.;* **dis·grun′tling,** *pr.p.*

dis·guise (dis gīz′), *v.* **1.** to make seem so different as not to be recognized [to *disguise* oneself with a false beard; to *disguise* one's voice]. **2.** to hide so as to keep from being known [She *disguised* her dislike of him by being very polite.] **—*n.* **1.** any clothes, make-up, way of acting, etc. used to hide who or what one is. **2.** a disguising or being disguised [Everyone came to the masquerade in *disguise.*] **—dis·guised′,** *p.t. & p.p.;* **dis·guis′ing,** *pr.p.*

dis·gust (dis gust′), *n.* a strong dislike that makes one feel sick [The smell of garbage filled her with *disgust.*] **—*v.* to cause disgust in. **—dis·gust′ing,** *adj.* **—dis·gust′ing·ly,** *adv.*

dish (dish), *n.* **1.** any of the plates, bowls, saucers, etc. used to serve food at the table. **2.** an amount of food served in a dish [He ate three *dishes* of ice cream.] **3.** a kind of food [Hash is his favorite *dish.*] **—*v.* to serve in a dish [*Dish* up the beans.] **—dish′ful,** *n.*

dish·cloth (dish′klôth), *n.* a cloth used for washing dishes.

dis·heart·en (dis här′t'n), *v.* to make lose hope; discourage. **—dis·heart′en·ing,** *adj.*

di·shev·eled or **di·shev·elled** (di shev′'ld), *adj.* not in neat order; mussed or rumpled; untidy [*disheveled* hair; a *disheveled* look].

dis·hon·est (dis än′ist), *adj.* not honest; lying, cheating, stealing, etc. **—dis·hon′est·ly,** *adv.* **—dis·hon′es·ty,** *n.*

dis·hon·or (dis än′ər), *n.* **1.** loss of honor or respect;

girl with disheveled hair

fat, āpe, cär, ten, ēven, hit, bīte, gō, hôrn, tool, book, up, fŭr; get, joy, yet, chin, she, thin, then; zh = s in pleasure; ′ as in able (ā′b'l); ə = a in ago, e in agent, i in sanity, o in confess, u in focus.

shame; disgrace [There is no *dishonor* in losing if you do your best.] **2.** a person or thing that causes dishonor; discredit. —*v.* to bring shame upon; disgrace or insult.

dis·hon·or·a·ble (dis än′ər ə b′l), *adj.* bringing dishonor; shameful; disgraceful. —**dis·hon′or·a·bly,** *adv.*

dis·il·lu·sion (dis′i lōō′zhən), *v.* to free from a false idea or an illusion [Janet *disillusioned* Timmy about Santa.] —*n.* a freeing from a false idea: also **dis′il·lu′sion·ment.**

dis·in·clined (dis in klīnd′), *adj.* not eager or willing; reluctant [to be *disinclined* to take risks]. —**dis·in·cli·na·tion** (dis′in klə nā′shən), *n.*

dis·in·fect (dis in fekt′), *v.* to kill disease germs in [to *disinfect* water with chlorine].

dis·in·fect·ant (dis′in fek′tənt), *n.* anything that disinfects, or kills disease germs [Alcohol is a common *disinfectant.*]

dis·in·her·it (dis′in her′it), *v.* to take away the right to inherit; keep from being an heir [She *disinherited* her son when he eloped.]

dis·in·te·grate (dis in′tə grāt), *v.* to break up into parts or pieces; separate entirely [The explosion *disintegrated* the airplane. The Roman Empire began to *disintegrate* in the 4th century.] —**dis·in′te·grat·ed,** *p.t. & p.p.;* **dis·in′te·grat·ing,** *pr.p.* —**dis·in′te·gra′tion,** *n.*

dis·in·ter (dis in tūr′), *v.* to dig up from a grave or take from a tomb. —**dis·in·terred′,** *p.t. & p.p.;* **dis·in·ter′ring,** *pr.p.*

dis·in·ter·est·ed (dis in′tər is tid *or* dis in′tris tid), *adj.* **1.** not having a selfish interest in the matter; impartial [A *disinterested* judge picked the winner.] **2.** not interested; uninterested: *used only in everyday talk.*

dis·joint (dis joint′), *v.* to cut or tear apart at the joints [to *disjoint* a duck].

dis·joint·ed (dis join′tid), *adj.* not connected in thought; not clear or orderly; broken up [She wrote in short, *disjointed* sentences.]

disk (disk), *n.* **1.** a thin, flat, round thing of any material. **2.** anything like this in form [the *disk* in the center of a daisy]. **3.** a phonograph record.

disk harrow, a harrow with sharp disks that turn to break up the soil.

disk jockey, a person who broadcasts a radio program of popular music on records.

dis·like (dis līk′), *v.* to have a feeling of not liking; be opposed to [I *dislike* people I can't trust.] —*n.* a feeling of not liking; distaste [She felt a strong *dislike* for toads.] —**dis·liked′,** *p.t. & p.p.;* **dis·lik′ing,** *pr.p.*

disk harrow

dis·lo·cate (dis′lō·kāt), *v.* **1.** to put a bone out of its proper place at a joint [to *dislocate* one's hip]. **2.** to put into disorder [to *dislocate* traffic]. —**dis′lo·cat·ed,** *p.t. & p.p.;* **dis′lo·cat·ing,** *pr.p.* —**dis′lo·ca′tion,** *n.*

dis·lodge (dis läj′), *v.* to force or push from its place [The landslide *dislodged* a big rock.] —**dis·lodged′,** *p.t. & p.p.;* **dis·lodg′ing,** *pr.p.*

dis·loy·al (dis loi′əl), *adj.* not loyal or true; faithless; false. —**dis·loy′al·ty,** *n.*

dis·mal (diz′m′l), *adj.* **1.** causing gloom or misery; sad [a *dismal* story]. **2.** dark and gloomy [a *dismal* cave]. —**dis′mal·ly,** *adv.*

dis·man·tle (dis man′t′l), *v.* **1.** to make bare by removing furniture, equipment, etc. [to *dismantle* an old ship]. **2.** to take apart [to *dismantle* heavy machinery in order to move it]. —**dis·man′tled,** *p.t. & p.p.;* **dis·man′tling,** *pr.p.*

dis·may (dis mā′), *v.* to fill with fear or dread so that one is not sure of what to do [We were *dismayed* at the sight of the destruction.] —*n.* loss of courage or confidence when faced with trouble or danger [The doctor's report filled her with *dismay.*]

dis·mem·ber (dis mem′bər), *v.* to tear or cut to pieces; divide up or mutilate [to *dismember* a body; to *dismember* a conquered country]. —**dis·mem′ber·ment,** *n.*

dis·miss (dis mis′), *v.* **1.** to send away; tell or allow to leave [The teacher *dismissed* the class at two o'clock.] **2.** to remove from a job or position; discharge; fire. **3.** to put out of one's mind [*Dismiss* your worries and enjoy your vacation.] **4.** to turn down a plea, claim, etc. in a law court. —**dis·miss′al,** *n.*

dis·mount (dis mount′), *v.* **1.** to get off or put off a horse, bicycle, motorcycle, etc. **2.** to take from its mounting or support [The mechanic *dismounted* the motor to work on it.]

dis·o·be·di·ence (dis′ə bē′di əns), *n.* a refusing to obey; lack of obedience. —**dis′o·be′di·ent,** *adj.* —**dis′o·be′di·ent·ly,** *adv.*

dis·o·bey (dis ə bā′), *v.* to fail to obey or refuse to obey.

dis·or·der (dis ôr′dər), *n.* **1.** lack of order; jumble; confusion [The troops retreated in *disorder.*] **2.** a riot or commotion. **3.** a sickness; ailment [a nervous *disorder*]. —*v.* to cause disorder in.

dis·or·der·ly (dis ôr′dər lē), *adj.* **1.** not orderly or neat; untidy; messy [a *disorderly* desk]. **2.** that disturbs peace and quiet [arrested for *disorderly* conduct]. —**dis·or′der·li·ness,** *n.*

dis·or·gan·ize (dis ôr′gə nīz), *v.* to make confused or disordered; break up the system of [Mother's illness *disorganized* the household.] —**dis·or′gan·ized,** *p.t. & p.p.;* **dis·or′gan·iz·ing,** *pr.p.* —**dis·or′gan·i·za′tion,** *n.*

dis·own (dis ōn′), *v.* to say that one will have nothing further to do with; refuse to accept as one's own [to *disown* one's family].

dis·par·age (dis par′ij), *v.* to speak of as having little importance or worth; belittle [Her envious brother *disparaged* her high grades.] —**dis·par′aged,** *p.t. & p.p.;* **dis·par′ag·ing,** *pr.p.* —**dis·par′age·ment,** *n.*

dis·par·i·ty (dis par′ə tē), *n.* a difference or unlikeness [a *disparity* between what one says and what one does]. —**dis·par′i·ties,** *pl.*

dis·pas·sion·ate (dis pash′ən it), *adj.* not filled with emotion or prejudice; calm and impartial [A judge should be *dispassionate*.] —**dis·pas′sion·ate·ly**, *adv.*

dis·patch (dis pach′), *v.* **1.** to send out promptly to a certain place or to do a certain job [We've *dispatched* a man to repair the break in the wire.] **2.** to kill or put to death. **3.** to finish quickly [to *dispatch* one's business]. —*n.* **1.** speed; haste [He carried out the orders with *dispatch*.] **2.** a message, especially an official one [a *dispatch* from the general ordering an attack]. **3.** a news story sent to a newspaper, radio station, etc. [A *dispatch* from Japan told of floods there.]

dis·patch·er (dis pach′ər), *n.* a person who sends out trains, buses, etc. on a schedule.

dis·pel (dis pel′), *v.* to scatter and drive away; make disappear [The wind *dispelled* the fog.] —**dis·pelled′**, *p.t. & p.p.*; **dis·pel′ling**, *pr.p.*

dis·pen·sa·ry (dis pen′sə rē), *n.* a room or place, as in a school, camp, or factory, where a person can get medicines or first-aid treatment. —**dis·pen′sa·ries**, *pl.*

dis·pen·sa·tion (dis′pən sā′shən), *n.* **1.** a dispensing or giving out; distribution. **2.** a managing or controlling of affairs [He believes in a divine *dispensation* of the universe.] **3.** a religious system [the Christian *dispensation*]. **4.** permission, as by a church, to ignore a rule.

dis·pense (dis pens′), *v.* **1.** to give out; distribute [The agency *dispensed* clothing to the refugees.] **2.** to prepare and give out [A pharmacist *dispenses* medicines.] —**dispense with**, to do without; get along without [to *dispense with* formality]. —**dis·pensed′**, *p.t. & p.p.*; **dis·pens′ing**, *pr.p.* —**dis·pens′er**, *n.*

dis·perse (dis pûrs′), *v.* to break up and scatter; spread in all directions [The crowd at the game began to *disperse*. The wind *dispersed* the clouds.] —**dis·persed′**, *p.t. & p.p.*; **dis·pers′ing**, *pr.p.* —**dis·per′sal** or **dis·per′sion**, *n.*

dis·pir·it (di spir′it), *v.* to make sad or discouraged; depress. —**dis·pir′it·ed**, *adj.*

dis·place (dis plās′), *v.* **1.** to move from its usual or proper place [The telephone wires were *displaced* by the storm.] **2.** to take the place of; replace [A ship *displaces* a certain amount of water.] —**dis·placed′**, *p.t. & p.p.*; **dis·plac′ing**, *pr.p.*

displaced person, a person forced from his country, as because of war, and left homeless in another country.

dis·place·ment (dis plās′mənt), *n.* **1.** a displacing or being displaced. **2.** the amount of water that a ship displaces.

dis·play (dis plā′), *v.* **1.** to put or spread out so as to be seen; exhibit [to *display* a collection of stamps]. **2.** to do something that is a sign or example of; show; reveal [to *display* one's courage]. —*n.* **1.** a displaying or showing; exhibition [a *display* of jewelry; a *display* of strength]. **2.** a mere show of something that is not genuine [a *display* of sympathy].

dis·please (dis plēz′), *v.* to make angry or not satisfied; annoy. —**dis·pleased′**, *p.t. & p.p.*; **dis·pleas′ing**, *pr.p.*

dis·pleas·ure (dis plezh′ər), *n.* the condition of being annoyed or not satisfied.

dis·port (dis pôrt′), *v.* to play or amuse oneself [puppies *disporting* themselves on the lawn].

dis·pos·a·ble (dis pō′zə b'l), *adj.* that can be thrown away after use [*disposable* bottles].

dis·pos·al (dis pō′z'l), *n.* the act of disposing; a getting rid of, arranging, settling, etc. [the *disposal* of garbage; the *disposal* of a lawsuit.] —**at one's disposal,** for one's use or service; as one wishes; at one's command.

dis·pose (dis pōz′), *v.* **1.** to put in a certain order; arrange [She *disposed* the children in a circle about her.] **2.** to make willing or ready [I am not *disposed* to agree.] **3.** to make likely to be or do [Hot weather *disposes* me to laziness.] —**dispose of, 1.** to get rid of, as by giving or throwing away, using up, or selling [We must *dispose of* these apples before they rot.] **2.** to take care of; settle [to *dispose of* a problem]. —**dis·posed′**, *p.t. & p.p.*; **dis·pos′ing**, *pr.p.*

dis·po·si·tion (dis′pə zish′ən), *n.* **1.** a disposing or being disposed; arrangement, willingness, likelihood, etc. [the *disposition* of chairs in a room; a *disposition* to be helpful]. **2.** the power to dispose or use as one wishes [All of us are at your *disposition*.] **3.** one's general nature or mood; temperament [a kind *disposition*].

dis·pos·sess (dis pə zes′), *v.* to force by law to give up property [The bank *dispossessed* them of their house.] —**dis′pos·ses′sion**, *n.*

dis·proof (dis prōōf′), *n.* **1.** a disproving. **2.** facts that disprove something.

dis·pro·por·tion (dis′prə pôr′shən), *n.* a being out of proportion, or unequal.

dis·pro·por·tion·ate (dis′prə pôr′shən it), *adj.* too great or too small in proportion to others.

dis·prove (dis prōōv′), *v.* to show to be false or incorrect [to *disprove* a theory]. —**dis·proved′**, *p.t. & p.p.*; **dis·prov′ing**, *pr.p.*

dis·pu·tant (dis′pyoo tant *or* dis pyōō′tənt), *n.* a person who disputes or argues.

dis·pu·ta·tion (dis′pyoo tā′shən), *n.* dispute.

dis·pute (dis pyōōt′), *v.* **1.** to argue or discuss a question; debate or quarrel. **2.** to question or deny the truth of [The U.S. *disputed* Spain's claim to Cuba.] **3.** to fight for; contest [The retreating army *disputed* every foot of ground.] —*n.* a disputing; argument, debate, etc. —**dis·put′ed**, *p.t. & p.p.*; **dis·put′ing**, *pr.p.*

dis·qual·i·fy (dis kwäl′ə fī), *v.* to make unfit or to say that someone is unfit, as for a position or to take part in some contest [The Constitution *disqualifies* a foreign-born person from becoming President.] —**dis·qual′i·fied**, *p.t. & p.p.*; **dis·qual′i·fy·ing**, *pr.p.*

---

fat, āpe, cär, ten, ēven, hit, bīte, gō, hôrn, tool, book, up, fûr; get, joy, yet, chin, she, thin, *then*; zh = s in pleasure; ′ as in able (ā′b'l); ə = a in ago, e in agent, i in sanity, o in confess, u in focus.

dis·qui·et (dis kwī′ət), *v.* to make uneasy or anxious; disturb [The deadly silence was *disquieting.*] —*n.* a disturbed or anxious feeling.

dis·qui·e·tude (dis kwī′ə tōōd), *n.* disquiet.

dis·qui·si·tion (dis′kwə zish′ən), *n.* a long, serious speech or writing on some subject.

dis·re·gard (dis ri gärd′), *v.* to pay no attention to; ignore [to *disregard* a warning]. —*n.* lack of attention; an ignoring [with total *disregard* for his safety].

dis·re·pair (dis ri per′), *n.* the condition of needing repairs [an old barn in *disrepair*].

dis·rep·u·ta·ble (dis rep′yoo tə b'l), *adj.* having or causing a bad reputation; not respectable [*disreputable* companions].

dis·re·pute (dis ri pyōōt′), *n.* the condition of no longer having a good reputation; disfavor.

dis·re·spect (dis ri spekt′), *n.* lack of respect or of politeness; rudeness. —**dis·re·spect′ful,** *adj.* —**dis·re·spect′ful·ly,** *adv.*

dis·robe (dis rōb′), *v.* to undress. —**dis·robed′,** *p.t. & p.p.;* **dis·rob′ing,** *pr.p.*

dis·rupt (dis rupt′), *v.* to break up; spoil the orderliness of [A few noisy members *disrupted* the meeting.] —**dis·rup′tion,** *n.*

dis·sat·is·fac·tion (dis′sat is fak′shən), *n.* a being dissatisfied; discontent.

dis·sat·is·fy (dis sat′is fī), *v.* to fail to satisfy; leave wanting something more or different; make discontented. —**dis·sat′is·fied,** *p.t. & p.p.;* **dis·sat′is·fy·ing,** *pr.p.*

dis·sect (di sekt′), *v.* **1.** to cut apart carefully, as in order to examine the parts [We *dissect* frogs in biology class.] **2.** to study carefully every part of; analyze [The senators *dissected* the budget report.] —**dis·sec′tion,** *n.*

dis·sem·ble (di sem′b'l), *v.* to hide one's real feelings or ideas by pretending to have different ones [to *dissemble* fear by smiling]. —**dis·sem′bled,** *p.t. & p.p.;* **dis·sem′bling,** *pr.p.*

dis·sem·i·nate (di sem′ə nāt), *v.* to scatter or spread far and wide [Books *disseminate* ideas.] —**dis·sem′i·nat·ed,** *p.t. & p.p.;* **dis·sem′i·nat·ing,** *pr.p.* —**dis·sem′i·na′tion,** *n.*

dis·sen·sion (di sen′shən), *n.* a dissenting; disagreement or quarreling.

dis·sent (di sent′), *v.* to differ in opinion or belief; disagree [Several of us *dissented* from the majority vote.] —*n.* a disagreement; difference of opinion. —**dis·sent′er,** *n.*

dis·ser·ta·tion (dis′ər tā′shən), *n.* a long, serious report on some subject, especially one written to get a degree from a university.

dis·ser·vice (dis sur′vis), *n.* an unkind or harmful act [I would be doing you a *disservice* if I solved the problem for you.]

dis·sev·er (di sev′ər), *v.* to cut off or cut apart; sever.

dis·sim·i·lar (dis sim′ə lər), *adj.* not alike; unlike; different. —**dis·sim·i·lar·i·ty** (dis sim′ə lar′ə tē), *n.*

dis·sim·u·late (di sim′yoo lāt), *v.* to hide one's real feelings by pretending to have different ones. —**dis·sim′u·lat·ed,** *p.t. & p.p.;* **dis·sim′u·lat·ing,** *pr.p.* —**dis·sim′u·la′tion,** *n.*

dis·si·pate (dis′ə pāt), *v.* **1.** to break up and disappear or make disappear [to *dissipate* smoke; to *dissipate* sorrow]. **2.** to spend or use foolishly; waste [to *dissipate* one's wealth]. **3.** to spend much time in wild or harmful pleasure. —**dis′si·pat·ed,** *p.t. & p.p.;* **dis′si·pat·ing,** *pr.p.* —**dis′si·pa′tion,** *n.*

dis·so·ci·ate (di sō′shi āt), *v.* to break the association between; separate [to *dissociate* two ideas]. —**dis·so·ci·at·ed,** *p.t. & p.p.;* **dis·so′ci·at·ing,** *pr.p.* —**dis·so′ci·a′tion,** *n.*

dis·so·lute (dis′ə lōōt), *adj.* living a wild, immoral life; dissipated.

dis·so·lu·tion (dis′ə lōō′shən), *n.* **1.** a dissolving or a breaking up; disintegration [the *dissolution* of the Roman Empire]. **2.** an ending; finish [the *dissolution* of a friendship].

dis·solve (di zälv′), *v.* **1.** to make or become liquid, as by melting in a liquid [to *dissolve* sugar in coffee]. **2.** to break up and disappear or make disappear [His courage *dissolved* in the face of danger.] **3.** to bring or come to an end; finish [They *dissolved* their partnership.] —**dis·solved′,** *p.t. & p.p.;* **dis·solv′ing,** *pr.p.*

dis·so·nance (dis′ə nəns), *n.* **1.** a sounding together of musical notes that do not harmonize; discord. **2.** any lack of harmony or agreement. —**dis′so·nant,** *adj.*

dis·suade (di swād′), *v.* to convince a person not to do something [Try to *dissuade* her from going.] —**dis·suad′ed,** *p.t. & p.p.;* **dis·suad′ing,** *pr.p.* —**dis·sua·sion** (di swā′zhən), *n.*

dis·taff (dis′taf), *n.* a stick from which flax or wool is unwound while it is being spun into thread on a spindle.

distaff side, the mother's side of a family.

dis·tance (dis′təns), *n.* **1.** the length of a line between two points [The *distance* between New York and Chicago is 713 miles.] **2.** a being far apart in space or time; remoteness ["*Distance* lends charm."] **3.** a place far away [We saw a ship in the *distance.*] —*v.* to leave behind; do better than; pass [He *distanced* all of his competition.] —**keep at a distance,** to be cool or unfriendly to. —**keep one's distance,** to stay aloof or be unfriendly. —**dis′tanced,** *p.t. & p.p.;* **dis′tanc·ing,** *pr.p.*

fibers being pulled from distaff (*above*) and twisted onto spindle (*below*)

dis·tant (dis′tənt), *adj.* **1.** far away in space or time; remote [a *distant* country; a *distant* age]. **2.** away [The next bus stop is a half mile *distant.*] **3.** aloof or unfriendly. **4.** not closely related [*distant* relatives]. —**dis′tant·ly,** *adv.*

dis·taste (dis tāst′), *n.* dislike.

dis·taste·ful (dis tāst′fəl), *adj.* not to one's taste or liking; disagreeable; unpleasant. —**dis·taste′ful·ly,** *adv.*

dis·tem·per (dis tem′pər), *n.* a disease of young dogs in which there is fever and weakness.

dis·tend (di stend′), v. to swell or expand [The pelican's pouch was *distended* with fish.]

dis·till or **dis·til** (di stil′), v. 1. to heat, especially a liquid, so that it gives off vapor which is then cooled so that it becomes a purer liquid [to *distill* ocean water for drinking]. 2. to get by distilling [to *distill* alcohol from fermented grain]. 3. to draw out the part that is basic, pure, etc. [to *distill* the meaning of a poem]. —**dis·tilled′**, *p.t. & p.p.;* **dis·till′ing**, *pr.p.*

dis·til·la·tion (dis′t'l ā′shən), n. 1. a distilling, as of crude oil to get gasoline, kerosene, etc. 2. anything gotten by distilling.

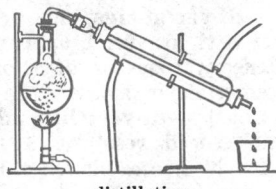
distillation

dis·till·er (di stil′ər), n. a person or company that distills alcoholic liquors.

dis·till·er·y (di stil′ər ē), n. a place where alcoholic liquors are distilled. —**dis·till′er·ies**, *pl.*

dis·tinct (di stingkt′), adj. 1. not alike; different [My twin brothers have *distinct* personalities.] 2. not the same; separate [His sermon was divided into four *distinct* parts.] 3. clearly seen, heard, felt, etc. [a *distinct* smell of perfume in the room]. 4. very definite; positive [a *distinct* improvement]. —**dis·tinct′ly**, *adv.* —**dis·tinct′ness**, *n.*

dis·tinc·tion (di stingk′shən), n. 1. the act of keeping distinct or separate [a school open to all, without *distinction* of race or creed]. 2. a way in which things differ [the *distinctions* between two breeds of dog]. 3. the condition of being better than average; excellence [He served with *distinction* in the war.] 4. the condition of being honored; fame; honor [to earn *distinction* as a scholar].

dis·tinc·tive (di stingk′tiv), adj. making distinct or different from others; characteristic [the *distinctive* markings of a skunk]. —**dis·tinc′tive·ly**, *adv.*

dis·tin·guish (di sting′gwish), v. 1. to set apart as different; be the difference in [What *distinguishes* man from the apes?] 2. to see the difference in [to *distinguish* right from wrong]. 3. to see, hear, taste, etc. clearly [I could *distinguish* no odor of gas in the room.] 4. to make famous or outstanding [Einstein *distinguished* himself as a scientist.] —**dis·tin′guish·a·ble**, *adj.*

dis·tin·guished (di sting′gwisht), adj. 1. famous; outstanding [a *distinguished* poet]. 2. having the look of a distinguished person [an old gentleman with a *distinguished* air].

dis·tort (di stôrt′), v. 1. to twist out of its usual shape or look [a face *distorted* with anger]. 2. to change so as to give a false idea [to *distort* facts]. —**dis·tor′tion**, *n.*

dis·tract (di strakt′), v. 1. to draw one's thoughts or attention to something else; divert [The show *distracted* him from his worries.] 2. to make unable to think clearly; confuse; bewilder [The three-ring circus *distracted* Jane.]

dis·trac·tion (di strak′shən), n. 1. a distracting or drawing away of one's attention. 2. anything that distracts in either a pleasant or an unpleasant way [The man's coughing was a *distraction* to the audience. Chess is his favorite *distraction* after work.] 3. a confused state of mind; bewilderment [Their shrieking is driving me to *distraction*.]

dis·trait (di strā′), adj. not paying attention; absent-minded.

dis·traught (di strôt′), adj. very confused or troubled, as by worry or grief.

dis·tress (di stres′), v. to cause pain, sorrow, or worry to; make suffer; trouble [The bad news *distressed* her.] —n. 1. pain, sorrow, or worry; suffering. 2. anything causing this. 3. a condition of danger or trouble [The Coast Guard helps ships in *distress*.] —**dis·tress′ful**, *adj.*

dis·trib·ute (di strib′yoot), v. 1. to give out in shares; deal out [The toys will be *distributed* among all the children.] 2. to spread out; scatter [The population is *distributed* unevenly over the continent.] 3. to sort out or arrange according to a plan [The flowers were *distributed* in neat rows in the garden.] —**dis·trib′ut·ed** *p.t. & p.p.;* **dis·trib′ut·ing**, *pr.p.*

dis·tri·bu·tion (dis′trə byōō′shən), n. the act or way of distributing something [a *distribution* of funds; a fair *distribution*]. —**dis·trib·u·tive** (di strib′yoo tiv), *adj.*

dis·trib·u·tor (di strib′yoo tər), n. 1. a person or company that distributes goods to customers. 2. a device for distributing electricity to the spark plugs of a gasoline engine.

dis·trict (dis′trikt), n. 1. any of the parts into which a country, city, etc. is divided for some special purpose [a school *district;* a Congressional *district*]. 2. any region; part of a country, city, etc. [the business *district* of Omaha].

district attorney, a lawyer who works for the government in some district by handling cases against those accused of breaking the law.

District of Columbia, a Federal district in the eastern United States on the Potomac River, occupied entirely by Washington, the capital: abbreviated **D.C.**

dis·trust (dis trust′), n. a lack of trust; doubt; suspicion. —v. to have no trust in; doubt. —**dis·trust′ful**, *adj.*

dis·turb (di stūrb′), v. 1. to break up the quiet or calm of [Croaking frogs *disturbed* the night.] 2. to make worried or uneasy; upset; trouble [He was *disturbed* by her strange behavior.] 3. to put into disorder; mix up [Who has *disturbed* the books on this shelf?] 4. to break in on; bother or interrupt [Don't *disturb* me while I'm working.]

---

fat, āpe, cär, ten, ēven, hit, bīte, gō, hôrn, tōol, book, up, fũr; get, joy, yet, chin, she, thin, *th*en; zh = s in pleasure; ′ as in able (ā′b'l); ə = a in ago, e in agent, i in sanity, o in confess, u in focus.

dis·turb·ance (di stŭr′bəns), *n.* **1.** a disturbing or being disturbed. **2.** anything that disturbs. **3.** noisy confusion; uproar; disorder.

dis·un·ion (dis yōōn′yən), *n.* **1.** a breaking up; separation. **2.** a failing to work together in harmony; disagreement.

dis·u·nite (dis yoo nīt′), *v.* to break up; separate or divide. —**dis·u·nit′ed,** *p.t. & p.p.;* **dis·u·nit′ing,** *pr.p.*

dis·use (dis yōōs′), *n.* lack of use [Skills can be forgotten through *disuse.*]

ditch (dich), *n.* a long, narrow opening dug in the earth, as for carrying off water; trench [There is often a *ditch* along a road.] —*v.* **1.** to dig a ditch in or around. **2.** to throw into a ditch. **3.** to get rid of: *slang in this meaning.*

dith·er (di*th*′ər), *n.* an excited and confused condition; fluster.

dit·to (dit′ō), *n.* **1.** the same as what was just said or written. **2.** the mark ″, used to show that what is written above it is to be repeated.
Example: 2 pairs of shoes at $10.00 a pair
      5   ″   ″ socks ″ $1.00 ″ ″
—*adv.* as said before. —**dit′tos,** *pl.*

dit·ty (dit′ē), *n.* a short and simple song. —**dit′ties,** *pl.*

di·ur·nal (dī ûr′n'l), *adj.* **1.** happening every day; daily. **2.** of the daytime.

di·van (dī′van *or* di van′), *n.* a large, low couch, usually without arm rests or back.

dive (dīv), *v.* **1.** to plunge into water, usually headfirst. **2.** to plunge into anything, as with the hand, body, or mind [The soldiers *dived* into their foxholes. I *dived* into my homework right after dinner.] **3.** to make a steep plunge downward, as an airplane. —*n.* **1.** the act of diving into water. **2.** any sudden plunge [an airplane *dive*]. **3.** a low, cheap restaurant or saloon: *used only in everyday talk.* —**dived** or **dove,** *p.t.;* **dived,** *p.p.;* **div′ing,** *pr.p.*

div·er (dīv′ər), *n.* **1.** a person who dives. **2.** a person who works under water, usually wearing a special suit and a helmet through which he gets air. **3.** a bird that dives into water for its food, as the kingfisher.

di·verge (də vûrj′), *v.* **1.** to branch off and move further away from one another [The light passing through the lens broke up into rays which *diverged.*] **2.** to differ, as in opinion. —**di·verged′,** *p.t. & p.p.;* **di·verg′ing,** *pr.p.*

di·ver·gence (də vûr′jəns), *n.* **1.** a diverging or branching off. **2.** a difference, as in opinion. —**di·ver′gent,** *adj.*

diver

di·vers (dī′vərz), *adj.* various or several: *no longer much used.*

di·verse (də vûrs′ *or* dī′vûrs), *adj.* not alike; plainly different [The customs of France and Italy are quite *diverse.*] —**di·verse′ly,** *adv.*

di·ver·si·fy (də vûr′sə fī), *v.* to make different or keep changing; vary [Farmers *diversify* crops to keep soil healthy.] —**di·ver′si·fied,** *p.t. & p.p.;* **di·ver′si·fy·ing,** *pr.p.*

di·ver·sion (də vûr′zhən), *n.* **1.** a diverting or turning aside [The dam caused a *diversion* of the stream.] **2.** anything to which one turns for fun or relaxation; pastime [In a small town, the circus is a welcome *diversion.*]

di·ver·si·ty (də vûr′sə tē), *n.* **1.** a being different or varied; difference [The male and female cardinal show a *diversity* in plumage.] **2.** variety. —**di·ver′si·ties,** *pl.*

di·vert (də vûrt′), *v.* **1.** to turn aside [to *divert* enemy troops; to *divert* one's attention]. **2.** to entertain or amuse [The fiddlers *diverted* King Cole.] —**di·vert′ing,** *adj.*

di·vest (də vest′), *v.* **1.** to take off; strip [The knight *divested* himself of his armor.] **2.** to take away from; make give up; deprive [The officer was *divested* of his rank.]

di·vide (də vīd′), *v.* **1.** to separate into parts; split up [Korea was *divided* by the armistice of 1953.] **2.** to separate into equal parts by arithmetic [If you *divide* 12 by 3, you get 4.] **3.** to put into separate groups; classify [Trees are *divided* into two classes: those that shed their leaves and those that do not.] **4.** to make separate or keep apart [A stone wall *divides* their farms.] **5.** to give out in shares; portion out [*Divide* the cake among the children.] **6.** to disagree or cause to disagree [The Senate *divided* on the issue of taxes.] —*n.* a ridge that separates two areas drained by rivers flowing in opposite directions. —**di·vid′ed,** *p.t. & p.p.;* **di·vid′ing,** *pr.p.*

div·i·dend (div′ə dend), *n.* **1.** the number into which another number is divided [In 6 ÷ 3 = 2, the number 6 is the *dividend.*] **2.** an amount of money from profits that a company divides especially among those who own stock in it; also, a single share of this.

di·vid·ers (də vīd′ərz), *n.pl.* same as **compass** (*meaning* 2).

div·i·na·tion (div′ə nā′shən), *n.* **1.** a trying or pretending to tell the future by means of magic spells, the stars, or other mysterious means. **2.** something told in this way; prophecy.

di·vine (də vīn′), *adj.* **1.** of or like God or a god [a *divine* power]. **2.** coming from God; holy [*divine* scripture]. **3.** devoted to God; religious [*divine* worship]. **4.** most excellent; extremely good or great [the *divine* poetry of Shakespeare]. —*n.* a clergyman or other person trained in theology. —*v.* **1.** to try or pretend to tell the future; prophesy. **2.** to guess or sense what another is thinking or feeling [I *divined* the purpose of her visit from the way she looked.] —**di·vined′,** *p.t. & p.p.;* **di·vin′ing,** *pr.p.* —**di·vine′ly,** *adv.* —**di·vin′er,** *n.*

div·ing board (dīv′ing), a springboard from which swimmers can dive into a pool or lake.

di·vin·i·ty (də vin′ə tē), *n.* **1.** the condition of being a god or like a god. **2.** a god or goddess. **3.** the study of religion; theology. —**the Divinity,** God. —**di·vin′i·ties,** *pl.*

di·vis·i·ble (də viz′ə b'l), *adj.* that can be divided; especially, that can be divided without having anything left over [The number 6 is *divisible* by 2 and 3.] —**di·vis′i·bil′i·ty,** *n.*

di·vi·sion (də vizh′ən), *n.* **1.** a dividing or being divided. **2.** the process in arithmetic of finding out how many times one number is contained in another. **3.** a sharing or giving out in portions; distribution [the *division* of profits among partners]. **4.** a difference in opinion; disagreement. **5.** anything that divides, as a line or wall. **6.** a section, department, or part [the sales *division* of a company; the children's *division* of a library]. **7.** a large section of an army, made up of several regiments. —**di·vi′sion·al,** *adj.*

di·vi·sor (də vī′zər), *n.* the number by which another number is divided [In 6 ÷ 3 = 2, the number 3 is the *divisor.*]

di·vorce (də vôrs′), *n.* **1.** the ending of a marriage by an act of law. **2.** complete separation [to favor the *divorce* of Church and State]. —*v.* **1.** to end one's marriage by an act of law. **2.** to separate; keep apart [He *divorced* himself from the pleasures of life.] —**di·vorced′,** *p.t. & p.p.;* **di·vorc′ing,** *pr.p.*

di·vor·cee (də vôr′sē′), *n.* a person, especially a woman, who is divorced.

di·vulge (də vulj′), *v.* to make known; reveal [to *divulge* a secret]. —**di·vulged′,** *p.t. & p.p.;* **di·vulg′ing,** *pr.p.*

Dix·ie (dik′sē), *n.* the Southern States of the United States; the South.

diz·zy (diz′ē), *adj.* **1.** having a whirling or spinning feeling that makes one lose his balance; giddy; unsteady [Riding on the merry-go-round made him *dizzy.*] **2.** that makes one feel dizzy [a *dizzy* height]. —**diz′zi·er,** *compar.;* **diz′zi·est,** *superl.* —**diz′zi·ly,** *adv.* —**diz′zi·ness,** *n.*

DNA, an essential part of all living matter: it is a basic material in chromosomes and it carries the inherited characteristics.

Dnie·per or **Dne·pr** (nē′pər), *n.* a river in the western Soviet Union, flowing into the Black Sea.

do (dōō), *v.* **1.** to work at or carry out an action; perform [I'll *do* the job. *Do* your duty.] **2.** to finish [Dinner has been *done* for an hour.] **3.** to bring about; cause [The storm *did* a lot of damage.] **4.** to put forth; exert [I'll *do* my best.] **5.** to take care of; attend to [Who will *do* the dishes?] **6.** to be right for the purpose; fit [This color will never *do.*] **7.** to get along; fare [The patient is *doing* well.] **8.** to give [to *do* honor to a famous person]. *Do* is also used to ask a question [*Do* you want some candy?], to give force to what one is saying [I *do* have to go. *Do* stay for dinner. I *do* not believe you.], and to take the place of another verb [He will vote as I *do.*] —**do away with, 1.** to get rid of. **2.** to kill. —**do up, 1.** to make ready; arrange. **2.** to wrap up. —**have to do with,** to be related to; have connection with. —**make do,** to manage or get along with what one has. —**did,** *p.t.;* **done,** *p.p.;* **do′ing,** *pr.p.*

do (dō), *n.* the first and last note of a musical scale.

do., abbreviation for **ditto.**

D.O., abbreviation for **Doctor of Osteopathy.**

dob·bin (däb′in), *n.* a gentle, plodding horse.

doc (däk), *n.* doctor: *a slang word.*

doc·ile (däs′'l), *adj.* easy to handle or train; tame; obedient [a *docile* horse]. —**doc′ile·ly,** *adv.* —**do·cil·i·ty** (dä sil′ə tē), *n.*

dock (däk), *n.* **1.** a long platform built out over water as a landing place for ships; pier; wharf. **2.** the water between two docks. **3.** same as **dry dock. 4.** a platform at which trucks or freight cars are loaded or unloaded. —*v.* **1.** to bring a ship to a dock [Tugs help to *dock* ocean liners.] **2.** to come into a dock [The ship *docks* at Pier 9.]

dock

dock (däk), *n.* the place in a court of law where the prisoner stands or sits.

dock (däk), *n.* a common weed with small, green flowers and large, smooth leaves.

dock (däk), *n.* the solid part of an animal's tail. —*v.* **1.** to cut off the end of; bob [to *dock* a horse's tail]. **2.** to cut or take some part from [They will *dock* your wages if you are absent.]

dock·et (däk′it), *n.* **1.** a list of the cases to be tried by a law court. **2.** any list of things to be done or considered; agenda. —*v.* to put on a docket.

dock·yard (däk′yärd), *n.* a place along a water front where ships are built or repaired.

doc·tor (däk′tər), *n.* **1.** a person trained to heal the sick; especially, a physician or surgeon. **2.** a person who has received the highest degree given by a university [*Doctor* of Philosophy]. —*v.* **1.** to try to heal [to *doctor* oneself]. **2.** to change secretly; tamper with [The dishonest lawyer tried to *doctor* the evidence.] *The verb is used only in everyday talk.*

doc·trine (däk′trin), *n.* something that is taught as a belief or principle of a religion, political party, scientific group, etc. —**doc′trin·al,** *adj.*

doc·u·ment (däk′yoo mənt), *n.* **1.** any printed or written record used to prove something, as a birth certificate or a deed to property. **2.** anything used as proof [Brady's photographs are useful *documents* of the Civil War.] —*v.* (däk′yoo ment′), to furnish or prove with documents.

doc·u·men·ta·ry (däk′yoo men′tə rē), *adj.* made up of documents [*documentary* proof of age].

doc·u·men·ta·tion (däk´yoo men tā´shən), *n.* the use of documents as proof, or such documents.

dod·der (däd´ər), *v.* to tremble or move in an unsteady way, as a very old person does.

dodge (däj), *v.* **1.** to move quickly to one side, as to get out of the way of a person or thing [to *dodge* a blow]. **2.** to get away from or avoid by tricks or cleverness [to *dodge* a question]. —*n.* **1.** the act of dodging. **2.** a trick used in cheating or in avoiding something. —**dodged,** *p.t. & p.p.;* **dodg´ing,** *pr.p.* —**dodg´er,** *n.*

do·do (dō´dō), *n.* a large bird that had small wings useless for flying. Dodos lived on an island in the Indian Ocean and were all killed off by the year 1700. —**do´dos** or **do´does,** *pl.*

dodo (2 ft. high)

doe (dō), *n.* the female of the deer, antelope, rabbit, etc. —**does** or **doe,** *pl.*

do·er (dōō´ər), *n.* **1.** a person who does something [a *doer* of good]. **2.** a person who gets things done [a *doer*, not a talker].

does (duz), the form of **do** showing the present time with singular nouns and *he, she,* or *it.*

doe·skin (dō´skin), *n.* **1.** a soft leather made from the skin of a female deer or a female sheep. **2.** a soft, smooth woolen cloth.

does·n't (duz´nt), does not.

doff (däf), *v.* to take off, as one's hat or coat.

dog (dôg), *n.* **1.** a flesh-eating animal related to the fox and wolf, that is raised as a pet or for use in hunting or herding. **2.** a device for holding or gripping something. **3. dogs,** *pl.* feet: *slang in this meaning.* —*v.* to follow or hunt like a dog [The child *dogged* his father's footsteps.] —**dogged,** *p.t. & p.p.;* **dog´ging,** *pr.p.*

dog days, the uncomfortably hot part of summer.

doge (dōj), *n.* the chief official in the former republics of Venice and Genoa.

dog-ear (dôg´ir´), *n.* a turned-down corner of the leaf of a book. —**dog´-eared´,** *adj.*

dog·fish (dôg´fish), *n.* a small kind of shark.

dog-eared pages

dog·ged (dôg´id), *adj.* refusing to give up; steady and determined [Lincoln's *dogged* efforts to get an education]. —**dog´ged·ly,** *adv.*

dog·ger·el (dôg´ər əl), *n.* poetry of a poor kind; also, light or comic verses with a regular rhythm and simple ideas.

dog·gy or **dog·gie** (dôg´ē), *n.* a little dog: *a child's word.* —**dog´gies,** *pl.*

do·gie or **do·gy** (dō´gē), *n.* a stray or motherless calf: *used in the western U.S.* —**do´gies,** *pl.*

dog·ma (dôg´mə), *n.* **1.** a belief that a church holds and teaches to be truth, not to be doubted; also, all such beliefs of any particular church. **2.** any belief held as a truth not to be questioned [a matter of scientific *dogma*].

dog·mat·ic (dôg mat´ik), *adj.* **1.** having to do with dogma. **2.** giving an opinion in a too positive or self-assured way, but without proof [a *dogmatic* person]. —**dog·mat´i·cal·ly,** *adv.*

dog·ma·tism (dôg´mə tiz'm), *n.* the giving of an opinion in a dogmatic way.

dog·trot (dôg´trät), *n.* a slow, easy trot.

dog·wood (dôg´wood), *n.* a tree whose blossom is surrounded by four white or pink leaves that look like petals.

doi·ly (doi´lē), *n.* a small mat, as of lace or paper, often placed under a vase, dish, etc. as a decoration or to protect the top of the table. —**doi´lies,** *pl.*

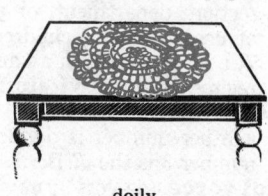
doily

do·ings (dōō´ingz), *n.pl.* things done; actions or activities.

dol·drums (däl´drəmz), *n.pl.* **1.** parts of the ocean near the equator where the winds are light or do not blow at all. **2.** a condition of feeling sad, bored, etc.

dole (dōl), *n.* **1.** the giving of money, food, etc. to people in great need; relief. **2.** anything given out in this way. —*v.* to give out in small amounts [Father *doled* out our allowance a nickel at a time.] —**doled,** *p.t. & p.p.;* **dol´ing,** *pr.p.*

dole·ful (dōl´fəl), *adj.* very sad; sorrowful; mournful. —**dole´ful·ly,** *adv.*

doll (däl), *n.* **1.** a toy that is a small figure of a person, especially of a baby or child. **2.** a pretty child or young woman. —*v.* to dress in a showy or stylish way: *this verb is slang* [She's all *dolled* up for the party.]

dol·lar (däl´ər), *n.* **1.** a United States silver coin or piece of paper money, equal to 100 cents. The dollar is our basic unit of money. Its symbol is $. **2.** a unit of money in certain other countries, as Canada.

dol·ly (däl´ē), *n.* **1.** a doll: *a child's word.* **2.** a low frame on wheels, for moving heavy things around, as in a factory. —**dol´lies,** *pl.*

do·lor (dō´lər), *n.* deep sorrow or sadness; grief: *used mainly in poetry.*

dol·or·ous (däl´ər əs), *adj.* very sorrowful or sad; mournful [*dolorous* weeping; the *dolorous* news of the shipwreck]. —**dol´or·ous·ly,** *adv.*

dol·phin (däl´fin), *n.* a water animal related to the whale but smaller. The common dolphin has a long snout with many teeth in it.

dolphin (5 to 9 ft. long)

dolt (dōlt), *n.* a stupid, slow-thinking person. —**dolt´ish,** *adj.*

-dom (dəm), a suffix meaning: **1.** the position or domain of [A *kingdom* is the domain of a king.] **2.** the condition of being [*Wisdom* is the condition of being wise.] **3.** the whole group of [*Officialdom* is the whole group of officials.]

do·main (dō mān′), *n.* **1.** all the land controlled by a certain government or ruler [the king's *domain*]. **2.** a field of activity or thought [the *domain* of science].

dome (dōm), *n.* **1.** a round roof shaped more or less like half a globe. **2.** anything shaped like a dome [the *dome* of a mountain].

dome

do·mes·tic (də mes′tik), *adj.* **1.** of the home or family [*domestic* joys; *domestic* chores]. **2.** of or made in one's own country [*domestic* olives grown in California]. **3.** not wild; tame; used to living with people [Dogs, horses, cows, etc. are *domestic* animals.] **4.** enjoying the home and family life [a girl with *domestic* tastes]. —*n.* a maid, cook, butler, or other house servant. —**do·mes′ti·cal·ly,** *adv.*

do·mes·ti·cate (də mes′tə kāt), *v.* **1.** to tame an animal or cultivate a plant for man's use. **2.** to make happy or content with the home and family life [Marriage has *domesticated* Jim.] —**do·mes′ti·cat·ed,** *p.t. & p.p.;* **do·mes′ti·cat·ing,** *pr.p.* —**do·mes′ti·ca′tion,** *n.*

do·mes·tic·i·ty (dō′mes tis′ə tē), *n.* **1.** life with one's family around the home. **2.** a liking for home life.

dom·i·cile (däm′ə sil), *n.* one's house or home; residence. —*v.* to put in a domicile. —**dom′i·ciled,** *p.t. & p.p.;* **dom′i·cil·ing,** *pr.p.*

dom·i·nant (däm′ə nənt), *adj.* most important or most powerful; ruling, controlling, etc. [a nation *dominant* in the world; the *dominant* idea of a speech]. —**dom′i·nance,** *n.*

dom·i·nate (däm′ə nāt), *v.* **1.** to control or rule; be most important or powerful [Greed *dominates* his actions. The small country was *dominated* by its big neighbors.] **2.** to tower over; rise high above [That building *dominates* the city.] —**dom′i·nat·ed,** *p.t. & p.p.;* **dom′i·nat·ing,** *pr.p.* —**dom′i·na′tion,** *n.*

dom·i·neer (däm ə nir′), *v.* to rule over in a harsh or bullying way [She *domineered* over the servants.] —**dom·i·neer′ing,** *adj.*

Dom·in·ic, Saint, (däm′ə nik), 1170–1221; a Spanish priest who started the Dominican order.

Do·min·i·can (də min′i kən), *adj.* **1.** having to do with the religious order founded by Saint Dominic. **2.** of the Dominican Republic. —*n.* **1.** a Dominican friar or nun. **2.** a person born or living in the Dominican Republic.

Dominican Republic, a country in the eastern part of Hispaniola, in the West Indies.

dom·i·nie (däm′ə nē), *n.* **1.** in Scotland, a schoolmaster. **2.** a clergyman.

do·min·ion (də min′yən), *n.* **1.** the power of governing; rule. **2.** a territory or country ruled over. **3. Dominion,** any of the self-governing countries of the British Commonwealth: *no longer much used.*

dom·i·no (däm′ə nō), *n.* **1.** any of a set of small tiles that are divided into halves and marked with spots on one face. These halves are matched in playing the game called **dominoes.** **2.** a mask for the eyes; also, a masquerade costume consisting of a loose, hooded cloak and such a mask. —**dom′i·noes,** *pl.*

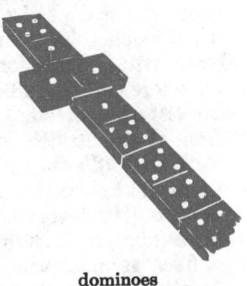
dominoes

Don (dän), *n.* a Spanish title of respect used before the first name of a man [*Don* Juan].

don (dän), *v.* to put on, as one's hat or coat. —**donned,** *p.t. & p.p.;* **don′ning,** *pr.p.*

do·nate (dō′nāt), *v.* to give to some cause, fund, etc.; contribute [to *donate* clothes to charity]. —**do′nat·ed,** *p.t. & p.p.;* **do′nat·ing,** *pr.p.* —**do·na′tion,** *n.*

done (dun), past participle of **do.** —*adj.* **1.** finished; completed. **2.** cooked.

Don Ju·an (dän wän′ *or* dän jōō′ən), a nobleman of Spanish legend, who had many love affairs.

don·key (däng′kē *or* dung′kē), *n.* an animal like a horse but smaller and with longer ears. —**don′keys,** *pl.*

do·nor (dō′nər), *n.* a person who donates or gives something [a blood *donor*].

DonQuix·ote (dän ki hō′tē *or* kwik′sət), the mad but harmless hero of a book by the Spanish writer Cervantes. In his desire to help those in need and to fight evil, he does foolish things.

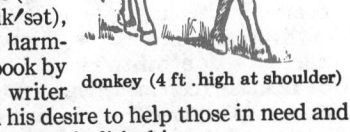
donkey (4 ft. high at shoulder)

don't (dōnt), do not.

doo·dle (dōō′d'l), *v.* to scribble in an aimless way, especially when thinking about something else. —*n.* a design, mark, etc. made in this way. —**doo′dled,** *p.t. & p.p.;* **doo′dling,** *pr.p.* —**doo′dler,** *n.*

doom (dōōm), *n.* **1.** one's fate or destiny, especially when bad or tragic; ruin or death [The first time our dog chased a car, its *doom* was sealed.] **2.** a judgment that someone is guilty and must be punished [She gasped when the judge pronounced her *doom.*] —*v.* to mark or sentence to some bad or tragic end [*doomed* to die].

dooms·day (dōōmz′dā), *n.* Judgment Day.

door (dôr), *n.* **1.** a frame, as of boards or panels, for closing or opening an entrance to a building, room, cupboard, etc. Doors usually swing on hinges or slide in grooves. **2.** the room or building into which a door leads [I live two *doors* down the hall.] **3.** a doorway. **—out of doors,** same as **outdoors.**

door·man (dôr′man), *n.* a man whose work is guarding the door of a public building, or opening it for people going in and out. **—door′men,** *pl.*

door mat, a mat for people to wipe their shoes on before entering a building.

door·step (dôr′step), *n.* the step or steps in front of an outside door.

door·way (dôr′wā), *n.* **1.** an opening in a wall that can be closed by a door. **2.** a way of getting in or to [Hard work is a *doorway* to success.]

dope (dōp), *n.* **1.** a thick liquid used as a varnish or filler, as on airplane wings. **2.** a narcotic drug. **3.** a stupid person. **4.** information. *Slang in meanings 2, 3, and 4.* **—v.** to give a narcotic drug to. **—doped,** *p.t. & p.p.;* **dop′ing,** *pr.p.* **—dope′y,** *adj.*

Dor·ic (dôr′ik), *adj.* describing the oldest and plainest style of Greek architecture. The columns have no fancy carving at the top.

dor·mant (dôr′mənt), *adj.* **1.** not moving or growing, as if asleep [Many trees are *dormant* in winter.] **2.** not active; quiet [a *dormant* volcano.]

dor·mer (dôr′mər), *n.* **1.** a part that is built out from a sloping roof, containing an upright window. **2.** such a window: also **dormer window.**

dormer

dor·mi·to·ry (dôr′mə tôr′ē), *n.* **1.** a large room with beds for a number of people. **2.** a building with many rooms for sleeping and living in, as at a college. **—dor′mi·to′ries,** *pl.*

dor·mouse (dôr′mous), *n.* a European animal like a small squirrel. **—dor·mice** (dôr′mīs), *pl.*

dor·sal (dôr′s'l), *adj.* of, on, or near the back.

do·ry (dôr′ē), *n.* a small fishing boat with a flat bottom and high sides. **—do′ries,** *pl.*

dos·age (dōs′ij), *n.* **1.** the system that is to be followed in taking doses [The recommended *dosage* is ½ teaspoon every 4 hours.] **2.** a dose of a medicine.

dorsal fin of a sailfish

dose (dōs), *n.* the amount of a medicine to be taken at one time. **—v.** to give a dose of medicine to. **—dosed,** *p.t. & p.p.;* **dos′ing,** *pr.p.*

dost (dust), older form of **do,** used with thou; *now used only in poetry, prayers, etc.*

dot (dät), *n.* **1.** a tiny mark or spot, as made by a pencil [Put a *dot* over every "i" and "j."] **2.** a small, round spot [a tie with polka *dots*]. **3.** a mark like a period that stands for the short click used in forming letters in the Morse code. **—v.** to mark with a dot or cover as with dots [Islands

dotted the bay.] **—on the dot,** at the exact time: *used only in everyday talk.* **—dot′ted,** *p.t. & p.p.;* **dot′ting,** *pr.p.*

dot·age (dōt′ij), *n.* the condition of a very old person who is childish and weak in mind.

do·tard (dō′tərd), *n.* a person in his dotage.

dote (dōt), *v.* **1.** to be childish or weak-minded because of very old age. **2.** to be fond or loving in a blind, foolish way [to *dote* on one's children]. **—dot′ed,** *p.t. & p.p.;* **dot′ing,** *pr.p.*

doth (duth), older form of **does:** *now used only in poetry, prayers, etc.*

dou·ble (dub′'l), *adj.* **1.** having two parts that are alike [a *double* house; a *double* door; gun with a *double* barrel]. **2.** being of two kinds [a *double* standard]. **3.** twice as much, as many, as great, as fast, etc. [a *double* portion; *double* time]. **4.** made for two [a *double* bed; a *double* garage]. **5.** having more than the usual number of petals [a *double* daffodil]. **—adv. 1.** with twice the amount, size, speed, etc.; doubly. **2.** two at one time; in a pair [to ride *double* on a horse]. **—n. 1.** an amount twice as great. **2.** a person or thing that looks very much like another; duplicate [The boy is a *double* of his father.] **3.** a hit in baseball on which the batter gets to second base. **4. doubles,** *pl.* a game of tennis, badminton, etc. with two players on each side. **—v. 1.** to make or become twice as large, as strong, as fast, etc. [*Double* the recipe. The population of the city has *doubled*.] **2.** to fold over or up [She *doubled* over the edge of the cloth to make a hem. He *doubled* his fist.] **3.** to make a sharp turn and go back [to *double* on one's tracks]. **4.** to be used for more than one purpose [The living room *doubles* as a dining area.] **5.** to sail around [The ship *doubled* the Cape.] **—double up, 1.** to fold or bend over [to *double up* with laughter]. **2.** to share a room, etc. with someone else. **—on the double,** quickly: *used only in everyday talk.* **—dou′bled,** *p.t. & p.p.;* **dou′bling,** *pr.p.*

double bass, same as **bass viol.**

double boiler, two pots, one set on top of the other. Water is boiled in the bottom pot in order to cook food placed in the top one.

dou·ble-breast·ed (dub′'l bres′tid), *adj.* overlapping across the breast, as a style of coat.

double boiler

dou·ble-cross (dub′'l krôs′), *v.* to trick or betray by doing the opposite of what one has promised: *a slang word.* **—dou′ble-cross′er,** *n.*

dou·ble-deal·ing (dub′'l dēl′ing), *n.* a dealing with others in a tricky or dishonest way.

dou·ble-head·er (dub′'l hed′ər), *n.* two games, especially baseball games, played one right after the other on the same playing field.

dou·ble-joint·ed (dub′'l join′tid), *adj.* having joints that let the fingers, legs, etc. bend at unusual angles.

double play, in baseball, a single play in which two players are put out.

dou·ble-quick (dub′'l kwik′), *adj.* very quick. —*n.* a very quick marching pace, almost a run.

dou·blet (dub′lit), *n.* a short jacket worn by men from the 14th to the 16th centuries.

double talk, meaningless talk or sounds intended to confuse someone.

dou·bloon (du bloōn′), *n.* an old Spanish coin that was made of gold.

dou·bly (dub′lē), *adv.* 1. twice or twice as much [*doubly* cautious]. 2. two at a time.

doubt (dout), *v.* to think that something may not be true or right; be unsure of; question [I *doubt* if this is the right road. Never *doubt* my love.] —*n.* 1. a doubting; being unsure of something [I have no *doubt* that it will rain.] 2. a condition of being uncertain or not yet decided [The time of the dance is still in *doubt*.] —**beyond doubt** or **without doubt,** surely. —**no doubt, 1.** surely. 2. probably. —**doubt′er,** *n.*

doubt·ful (dout′fəl), *adj.* feeling or causing doubt; not sure; not decided [I'm *doubtful* about our chances of winning.] —**doubt′ful·ly,** *adv.*

doubt·less (dout′lis), *adv.* 1. without doubt; certainly. 2. probably.

dough (dō), *n.* 1. a mixture of flour, liquid, etc. worked into a soft, thick mass for baking into bread, etc. 2. money: *slang in this meaning.*

dough·nut (dō′nut), *n.* a small, sweet cake fried in deep fat, usually shaped like a ring.

dough·ty (dou′tē), *adj.* bold and strong: *no longer much used.* —**dough′ti·er,** *compar.;* **dough′ti·est,** *superl.*

dough·y (dō′ē), *adj.* of or like dough; pasty. —**dough′i·er,** *compar.;* **dough′i·est,** *superl.*

dour (door *or* dour), *adj.* unfriendly or gloomy in looks or manner; glum; sullen.

douse (dous), *v.* 1. to plunge quickly into a liquid [The blacksmith *doused* the hot metal in water.] 2. to pour liquid over; drench. 3. to put out a light or a fire: *used only in everyday talk.* —**doused,** *p.t. & p.p.;* **dous′ing,** *pr.p.*

dove (duv), *n.* a pigeon, especially any of the smaller kinds. The dove is often used as a symbol of peace.

dove (dōv), a past tense of **dive.**

dove·cote (duv′-kōt) or **dove·cot** (duv′kät), *n.* a small box for pigeons to build their nests in. It is usually set on a pole.

doves (10 in. long)

doublet

Do·ver (dō′vər), *n.* 1. the capital of Delaware. 2. a strait between England and France. 3. an English seaport on this strait.

dove·tail (duv′tāl), *v.* 1. to fasten two pieces together by fitting parts cut out in one piece into notches cut out of the other. 2. to fit facts, plans, etc. together in a sensible way. —*n.* a joint made by dovetailing.

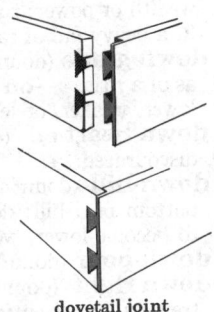

dow·a·ger (dou′ə jər), *n.* 1. a widow holding a title or property from her dead husband. 2. any elderly woman who is rich and dignified: *used only in everyday talk.*

dovetail joint

dow·dy (dou′dē), *adj.* not neat or not stylish in looks or dress. —**dow′di·er,** *compar.;* **dow′di·est,** *superl.*

dow·el (doul), *n.* a peg that fits into opposite holes in two pieces to join them together.

dow·er (dou′ər), *n.* 1. that part of a man's property which his widow inherits for life. 2. a dowry. 3. a natural skill, gift, or talent. —*v.* to give a dower to.

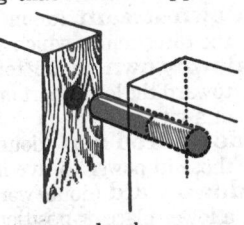
dowel

down (doun), *adv.* 1. to, in, or on a lower place [to tumble *down;* to lie *down*]. 2. in or to a place thought of as lower [The sun goes *down* in the evening. He has gone *down* in the world.] 3. from an earlier to a later time [*down* through the years; passed *down* from father to son]. 4. in or to a worse condition [to break *down* in body or mind]. 5. to a smaller amount, size, etc. [to come *down* in price; to boil *down* maple sirup]. 6. to a more quiet or serious condition [to settle *down* to work]. 7. completely; to the greatest amount [loaded *down*]. 8. in cash [Pay $5 *down* and $5 a week.] 9. in writing [Take *down* her name.] —*adj.* 1. put, brought, going, or gone down [There is no *down* payment. The boxer is *down.* The sun is *down.* The piston rattles on the *down* stroke.] 2. ill [He is *down* with the flu.] 3. sad or discouraged. —*prep.* down to, toward, along, through, into, among, or upon [The bus rolled *down* the hill. I live *down* this street.] —*v.* to put, throw, or swallow down [The fighter *downed* his opponent. She *downed* a glass of milk.] —*n.* 1. bad luck [to have one's ups and *downs*]. 2. in football, one of a series of plays by which a team tries to move the ball forward. —**down and out,** without money, friends, health, etc. —**down on,** angry with: *only in everyday talk.* —**down with!** away with! get rid of!

down (doun), *n.* 1. soft, fluffy feathers, as on a young bird. 2. soft, fuzzy hair.

down·cast (doun′kast), *adj.* **1.** looking down toward the ground [*downcast* eyes]. **2.** very unhappy; sad [a *downcast* expression].

down·fall (doun′fôl), *n.* **1.** a sudden loss of wealth or power; ruin [the *downfall* of a tyrant]. **2.** a heavy fall of rain or snow.

down·grade (doun′grād), *n.* a downward slope, as of a road. **—on the downgrade,** becoming lower, weaker, or less important.

down·heart·ed (doun′här′tid), *adj.* sad or discouraged.

down·hill (doun′hil), *adv. & adj.* toward the bottom of a hill; downward. **—go downhill,** to become lower, weaker, or less important.

down·pour (doun′pôr), *n.* a heavy rainfall.

down·right (doun′rīt), *adv.* very; really; extremely [a *downright* good book]. **—adj.** absolute; complete [He's a *downright* fool.]

down·stairs (doun′sterz′), *adv. & adj.* to or on a lower floor [to go *downstairs*; a *downstairs* room]. **—n.** a lower floor or floors.

down·stream (doun′strēm′), *adv. & adj.* in the direction in which a stream is flowing.

down·town (doun′toun′), *adj. & adv.* in or toward the lower part or the main business section of a city.

down·trod·den (doun′träd″n), *adj.* forced by those in power to live in poverty or slavery.

down·ward (doun′wərd), *adv. & adj.* **1.** toward a lower place or position. **2.** from an earlier to a later time. Also **down′wards,** *adv.*

down·y (doun′ē), *adj.* of or like down, or covered with down; soft and fuzzy. **—down′i·er,** *compar.;* **down′i·est,** *superl.*

dow·ry (dou′rē), *n.* the property that a bride brings to her husband when she is married. **—dow′ries,** *pl.*

dox·ol·o·gy (däks äl′ə jē), *n.* a hymn of praise to God. **—dox·ol′o·gies,** *pl.*

doz., abbreviation for **dozen** or **dozens.**

doze (dōz), *v.* to sleep lightly; nap. **—n.** a nap. **—doze off,** to fall into a light sleep. **—dozed,** *p.t. & p.p.;* **doz′ing,** *pr.p.*

doz·en (duz′′n), *n.* a group of twelve. **—doz′ens** or, *especially after a number,* **doz′en,** *pl.*

DP (dē′pē′), *n.* a displaced person. **—DP's,** *pl.*

Dr., abbreviation for **doctor, drive.**

drab (drab), *n.* a dull, light-brown color. **—adj.** **1.** dull light-brown. **2.** dull; not bright or attractive. **—drab′ber,** *compar.;* **drab′best,** *superl.*

draft (draft), *n.* **1.** a movement of air, as in a room or chimney. **2.** a part for controlling the movement of air, as in a furnace. **3.** a drink. **4.** a choosing of persons who must serve in the armed forces; also, the persons chosen. **5.** a plan or drawing of a work to be done. **6.** an outline or trial copy of a piece of writing [the first *draft* of a speech]. **7.** a written order for the payment of money by a bank; check [a *draft* for $50]. **8.** a drawing or hauling, as of a load. **9.** the depth to which a ship sinks when it is loaded. **—v.** **1.** to order persons chosen from a group to serve in the armed forces. **2.** to choose for some special work or position [They *drafted* him to act as chairman.] **3.** to make a plan, outline, etc.

[to *draft* a speech]. Also spelled **draught.**

draf·tee (draf tē′), *n.* a person drafted to serve in the armed forces.

drafts·man (drafts′mən), *n.* a person who prepares drawings or sketches for buildings, machinery, etc. **—drafts′men,** *pl.*

draft·y (draf′tē), *adj.* letting in or having a draft of air [a *drafty* room]. **—draft′i·er,** *compar.;* **draft′i·est,** *superl.*

drag (drag), *v.* **1.** to pull in a slow, hard way, especially along the ground; haul [He *dragged* the sled up the hill.] **2.** to be pulled along the ground; trail [Her skirt *dragged* in the mud.] **3.** to move or pass too slowly [Time *dragged* as he waited for his turn.] **4.** to search for something in a river, lake, etc. by dragging a net or hooks along the bottom. **—n.** **1.** something that works by being dragged along, as a harrow, grapnel, or dragnet. **2.** anything that holds back or slows down [Poor training is a *drag* on any career.] **—dragged,** *p.t. & p.p.;* **drag′ging,** *pr.p.*

drag·gle (drag′′l), *v.* to make or become wet and dirty by dragging in mud or water. **—drag′-gled,** *p.t. & p.p.;* **drag′gling,** *pr.p.*

drag·net (drag′net), *n.* **1.** a net dragged along the bottom of a river, lake, etc. or along the ground, to catch something. **2.** any system set up for catching people wanted by the police.

drag·on (drag′ən), *n.* a make-believe monster in stories, that looked like a giant lizard with wings and claws, breathing out fire.

dragon

drag·on·fly (drag′ən flī), *n.* an insect with a long, slender body and four delicate wings. It does not sting. **—drag′-on·flies,** *pl.*

dra·goon (drə gōōn′), *n.* in earlier times, a soldier who fought on horseback. **—v.** to force to do something [The peasants were *dragooned* into building a fort.]

dragonfly (about 2½ in. long)

drain (drān), *v.* **1.** to make flow away [*Drain* the water from the potatoes.] **2.** to draw off water or other liquid from; make empty [to *drain* a swimming pool; to *drain* one's glass]. **3.** to flow off [The water won't *drain* from our flat roof.] **4.** to become empty or dry [Our bathtub *drains* slowly.] **5.** to flow into [The Ohio River *drains* into the Mississippi.] **6.** to use up slowly; exhaust [The hard work *drained* his energy.] **—n.** **1.** a pipe or channel for carrying off water, sewage, etc. [a bathtub *drain*]. **2.** something that drains or uses up slowly [War is a *drain* on a nation's youth.]

drain·age (drān′ij), *n.* **1.** a draining, or the way in which something is drained off. **2.** liquid that is drained off.

drake (drāk), *n.* a male duck.

dram (dram), *n.* **1.** a small weight, equal to $1/8$ ounce in apothecaries' weight or $1/16$ ounce in avoirdupois weight. **2.** a small drink.

dra·ma (drä′mə *or* dram′ə), *n.* **1.** a story that is written to be acted out, as on a stage; play. **2.** the art of writing or performing plays. **3.** a series of interesting or exciting events [the *drama* of the American Revolution].

dra·mat·ic (drə mat′ik), *adj.* **1.** of or having to do with drama or the theater. **2.** like a drama or play; interesting and exciting [a *dramatic* baseball game]. **—dra·mat′i·cal·ly,** *adv.*

dra·mat·ics (drə mat′iks), *n.pl.* the art of acting in or producing plays: *used with a singular verb.*

dram·a·tist (dram′ə tist), *n.* a person who writes plays; playwright.

dram·a·tize (dram′ə tīz), *v.* **1.** to make into a drama, or play [The life of Edison was *dramatized* in a movie.] **2.** to be very dramatic about; make seem very exciting or tense [She *dramatizes* all her illnesses.] **—dram′a·tized,** *p.t. & p.p.;* **dram′a·tiz·ing,** *pr.p.***—dram′a·ti·za′tion,** *n.*

drank (drangk), past tense of **drink.**

drape (drāp), *v.* **1.** to cover or decorate with cloth hanging in loose folds [The windows were *draped* with red velvet.] **2.** to arrange or hang in graceful folds [She *draped* the shawl about her shoulders.] **—***n.* cloth hanging in loose folds; especially, a curtain; drapery. **—draped,** *p.t. & p.p.;* **drap′ing,** *pr.p.*

dra·per·y (drā′pər ē), *n.* a curtain or other cloth hanging in loose folds. **—dra′per·ies,** *pl.*

dras·tic (dras′tik), *adj.* acting with force; having a strong effect; harsh [*drastic* punishment]. **—dras′ti·cal·ly,** *adv.*

draught (draft), *n. & v.,* same as **draft.**

draped toga

draughts (drafts), *n.pl.* the game of checkers: *the British name.*

draw (drô), *v.* **1.** to make move toward one or along with one; pull; haul [The mules *drew* the wagon.] **2.** to pull up, down, back, in, or out [to *draw* the drapes; *draw* a cork from a bottle]. **3.** to take out; get [to *draw* money from the bank; to *draw* a conclusion]. **4.** to get the attention of; attract [to *draw* a large audience]. **5.** to come or move [We *drew* near the town. The train *drew* away from the station.] **6.** to bring about; result in [His question *drew* no reply.] **7.** to make a picture, design, etc., as with a pencil or pen. **8.** to describe [He *drew* a glowing picture of the future.] **9.** to write a check or bank draft.

10. to stretch or pull out of shape [to *draw* a rope tight; a face *drawn* with fear]. **11.** to inhale [*Draw* a deep breath.] **12.** to allow air or smoke to move through [This chimney *draws* well.] **13.** to sink to a certain depth in water [This ship *draws* 30 feet.] **—***n.* **1.** a drawing or being drawn. **2.** something drawn. **3.** a contest in which the final scores are the same; tie. **4.** a gully or ravine. **—draw out, 1.** to make longer; lengthen [He always *draws out* his stories.] **2.** to get a person to talk. **—draw up, 1.** to put in the proper written form [to *draw up* a contract]. **2.** to stop [The car *drew up* in front of the house.] **—drew,** *p.t.;* **drawn,** *p.p.;* **draw′ing,** *pr.p.*

draw·back (drô′bak), *n.* a condition that acts against one; hindrance; disadvantage.

draw·bridge (drô′brij), *n.* a bridge that can be raised or moved to one side, as to allow ships to pass or to keep someone from crossing.

draw·er (drô′ər), *n.* **1.** a person or thing that draws. **2.** (drôr), a box that slides in and out of a table, chest, desk, etc.

drawbridge

draw·ers (drôrz), *n.pl.* a piece of underwear with legs, for the lower part of the body. Drawers can be short or long.

draw·ing (drô′ing), *n.* **1.** the making of pictures, designs, etc., as with a pencil or pen. **2.** such a picture, design, etc. **3.** a lottery.

drawing room, a room where guests are received and entertained; parlor.

drawl (drôl), *v.* to speak in a slow way, drawing out the syllables. **—***n.* drawling speech.

drawn (drôn), past participle of **draw. —***adj.* having a worn-out look, as from pain.

dray (drā), *n.* a wagon for heavy loads, having sides that can be taken off.

dray·man (drā′mən), *n.* a man who drives a dray. **—dray′men,** *pl.*

dread (dred), *v.* to look forward to with great fear or worry [I *dread* having to give a speech.] **—***n.* great fear, especially of something about to happen [to live in *dread* of the future]. **—***adj.* causing great fear [a *dread* plague].

dread·ful (dred′fəl), *adj.* **1.** causing dread; fearful [the *dreadful* threat of war]. **2.** very bad, unpleasant, unhappy, etc.: *used only in everyday talk.* **—dread′ful·ly,** *adv.*

dread·nought *or* **dread·naught** (dred′nôt), *n.* a large battleship with many big guns.

dream (drēm), *n.* **1.** a series of thoughts, pictures, or feelings that passes through the mind of a sleeping person. **2.** a pleasant idea that one imagines or hopes for; daydream [to have *dreams* of glory]. **—v. 1.** to have a dream or dreams. **2.** to have daydreams. **3.** to imagine as possible; have any idea of [I wouldn't *dream* of going without you.] **—dreamed** or **dreamt** (dremt), *p.t. & p.p.;* **dream′ing,** *pr.p.* **—dream′er,** *n.*

dream·y (drēm′ē), *adj.* **1.** fond of daydreaming or of imagining things; not practical. **2.** like something in a dream; not clear; misty, soft, etc. [*dreamy* music]. **—dream′i·er,** *compar.;* **dream′i·est,** *superl.* **—dream′i·ly,** *adv.*

drear (drir), *adj.* dreary: *used in poetry.*

drear·y (drir′ē), *adj.* without happiness or cheer; gloomy, sad, or dull [a long, *dreary* tale]. **—drear′i·er,** *compar.;* **drear′i·est,** *superl.* **—drear′i·ly,** *adv.* **—drear′i·ness,** *n.*

dredge (drej), *n.* **1.** a machine for scooping or sucking up mud, sand, etc. as from a harbor or river bed. **2.** a kind of net dragged along the bottom of a river, bay, etc. to gather shellfish. **—v.** to clear, gather, etc. with a dredge. **—dredged,** *p.t. & p.p.;* **dredg′ing,** *pr.p.*

dredge

dredge (drej), *v.* to sprinkle or sift [*Dredge* the chicken with flour before frying.] **—dredged,** *p.t. & p.p.;* **dredg′ing,** *pr.p.*

dregs (dregz), *n.pl.* **1.** solid bits that settle to the bottom in a liquid; grounds [coffee *dregs*]. **2.** a worthless thing or part [the *dregs* of society].

drench (drench), *v.* to make wet all over; soak [The garden was *drenched* by the rain.]

Dres·den (drez′dən), *n.* a city in eastern Germany, famous for its chinaware.

dress (dres), *n.* **1.** the common outer garment worn by girls and women. It is usually of one piece, including the skirt. **2.** clothes in general [native *dress;* formal *dress*]. **—v. 1.** to put clothes on; clothe. **2.** to arrange the hair in a certain way. **3.** to put medicine and bandages on a wound or sore. **4.** to make ready for use; prepare [to *dress* a chicken; to *dress* leather]. **5.** to arrange in an attractive way [to *dress* a store window]. **6.** to get or put in a straight line, as soldiers.

dress·er (dres′ər), *n.* **1.** a person or thing that dresses. **2.** a chest of drawers for a bedroom, often with a mirror.

dress·ing (dres′ing), *n.* **1.** a bandage or medicine for a wound or sore. **2.** a sauce, as of oil, vinegar, and seasoning, added to salads, etc. **3.** a stuffing, as of bread and seasoning, for roast chicken, turkey, etc.

dressing gown, a loose robe or coat worn by a person who is not fully dressed.

dresser

dress·mak·er (dres′māk′ər), *n.* a person whose work is making dresses and other clothes for girls and women. **—dress′mak′ing,** *n.*

dress·y (dres′ē), *adj.* **1.** fancy or showy in dress or looks [Those shoes are too *dressy* for school.] **2.** in the latest fashion; stylish; smart. *This word is used only in everyday talk.* **—dress′i·er,** *compar.;* **dress′i·est,** *superl.*

drew (drōō), past tense of **draw.**

drib·ble (drib′'l), *v.* **1.** to flow or let flow in drops or in a trickle [Water *dribbled* from the pipe. Contributions *dribbled* in.] **2.** to let saliva, etc. drip from the mouth; drool. **3.** in basketball, soccer, etc., to control the ball while moving, by using short bounces or short, light kicks. **—n. 1.** a dribbling flow or driblet. **2.** the act of dribbling a ball. **—drib′bled,** *p.t. & p.p.;* **drib′bling,** *pr.p.*

drib·let (drib′lit), *n.* a small amount; bit.

dried (drīd), past tense and past participle of **dry.**

dri·er (drī′ər), *adj.* more dry. *Drier* is the comparative of **dry. 1.** a liquid put in paint or varnish to make it dry fast. **2.** same as **dryer.**

dries (drīz), the form of **dry** showing the present time with singular nouns and *he, she,* or *it.*

dri·est (drī′ist), *adj.* most dry. *Driest* is the superlative of **dry.**

drift (drift), *v.* **1.** to be carried along by a current of water or air [The log *drifted* downstream. The leaves *drifted* to the ground.] **2.** to go along in an aimless way [He *drifted* from job to job.] **3.** to pile up in heaps by the force of wind [The snow *drifted* against the door.] **—n. 1.** a drifting; also, the direction or amount of drifting. **2.** a pile formed by the force of wind or water [a *drift* of sand along the shore]. **3.** general meaning [I got the *drift* of his speech.] **—drift′er,** *n.*

drift·wood (drift′wood), *n.* wood drifting in the water or washed ashore.

drill (dril), *n.* **1.** a tool with a sharp point that is turned in wood, metal, etc. to make holes. **2.** the training of soldiers in marching, handling guns, etc. **3.** a practicing of something over and over in order to learn it. **—v. 1.** to make a hole with a drill. **2.** to teach or train by having practice the same thing over and over [Will you help *drill* them in spelling?] **3.** to train soldiers in marching and other exercises.

electric drill

drill (dril), *n.* a machine for making holes or furrows and planting seeds in them.

dri·ly (drī′lē), *adv.* same as **dryly.**

drink (dringk), *v.* **1.** to swallow a liquid [to *drink* water]. **2.** to soak up or draw in [The dry soil quickly *drank* up the rain.] **3.** to take in eagerly with the mind or senses [to *drink* in knowledge]. **4.** to drink alcoholic liquor. **—n. 1.** any liquid that one drinks. **2.** alcoholic liquor. **—drink to,** to drink a toast to. **—drank,** *p.t.;* **drunk,** *p.p.;* **drink′ing,** *pr.p.*

drip (drip), *v.* **1.** to fall in drops [Sweat *dripped* from his brow.] **2.** to let drops of liquid fall [The faucet *dripped* all night.] —*n.* **1.** a falling in drops. **2.** liquid falling in drops. —**dripped,** *p.t. & p.p.;* **drip′ping,** *pr.p.*

drip·pings (drip′ingz), *n.pl.* the melted fat that drips from roasting meat.

drive (drīv), *v.* **1.** to control the movement of an automobile, bus, carriage, etc. **2.** to move or go [The truck *drove* slowly up the hill.] **3.** to go or take in an automobile, etc. [Shall we *drive* to New York? Mother *drives* the children to school.] **4.** to make move or go [They *drove* the cattle along the trail. This engine is *driven* by steam.] **5.** to move by hitting [to *drive* a nail]. **6.** to force into a certain condition or act [They're *driving* her mad.] **7.** to force to work hard. **8.** to use effort in bringing about [to *drive* a bargain]. —*n.* **1.** a trip in an automobile, etc. **2.** a street, road, or driveway. **3.** a hard, swift blow, hit, thrust, etc. [The golfer hit a 250-yard *drive*.] **4.** the working parts that make something go [This car has an automatic *drive*.] **5.** a group effort to get something done; campaign [a *drive* to collect money for charity]. **6.** the power or energy to get things done [His *drive* made him a success.] —**drive at,** to have in mind; mean. —**let drive,** to hit or aim. —**drove,** *p.t.;* **driv′en,** *p.p.;* **driv′ing,** *pr.p.*

drive-in (drīv′in′), *adj.* describing a restaurant, bank, movie theater, or the like where persons drive up and remain in their automobiles while they are served, watch the movie, etc.

driv·el (driv′'l), *v.* **1.** to talk in a foolish, childish way. **2.** to let saliva drip from the mouth. *n.* foolish talk; nonsense. —**driv′eled** or **driv′elled,** *p.t. & p.p.;* **driv′el·ing** or **driv′el·ling,** *pr.p.* —**driv′el·er** or **driv′el·ler,** *n.*

driv·en (driv′'n), past participle of **drive.**

driv·er (drīv′ər), *n.* **1.** a person or thing that drives. **2.** a golf club with a wooden head, used in hitting the ball from the tee.

drive·way (drīv′wā), *n.* a path for cars, leading from a street or road to a garage, etc.

driz·zle (driz′'l), *v.* to rain lightly in fine drops. —*n.* such a rain. —**driz′zled,** *p.t. & p.p.;* **driz′zling,** *pr.p.* —**driz′zly,** *adj.*

droll (drōl), *adj.* comical in a strange or odd way [a *droll* clown]. —**drol′ly,** *adv.*

drom·e·dar·y (dräm′ə der′ē), *n.* a camel trained for fast riding; especially, the Arabian camel, with one hump. —**drom′e·dar′ies,** *pl.*

drone (drōn), *n.* **1.** a male honeybee. It has no sting and does no work. **2.** an idle person who lives by the work of others. **3.** a humming or buzzing. —*v.* **1.** to make a humming or buzzing sound [The planes *droned* overhead.] **2.** to talk on and on in a dull way. —**droned,** *p.t. & p.p.;* **dron′ing,** *pr.p.*

drool (drōōl), *v.* to drip saliva, etc. from the mouth; drivel.

droop (drōōp), *v.* **1.** to sink, hang, or bend down [The heavy snow made the branches *droop*.] **2.** to become weak, tired, sad, etc. [The team's spirit *drooped* after the defeat.] —*n.* a drooping or hanging down [the *droop* of his shoulders]. —**droop′y,** *adj.*

drop (dräp), *n.* **1.** a bit of liquid that is rounded in shape, as when falling [*drops* of rain]. **2.** anything like this in shape [a chocolate *drop*]. **3.** a very small amount [He hasn't a *drop* of courage.] **4.** a sudden fall or decrease [a *drop* in attendance]. **5.** the distance down [a *drop* of five feet to the ground]. —*v.* **1.** to fall or let fall in drops [Tears *dropped* from her eyes.] **2.** to fall or let fall [Ripe fruit *dropped* from the trees. He *dropped* his lunch in the mud.] **3.** to fall dead or wounded; also, to kill or wound. **4.** to pass into a certain condition [She *dropped* off to sleep.] **5.** to stop, end, or let go [Let's *drop* this argument. He was *dropped* from his job last week.] **6.** to make or become lower; sink [The temperature *dropped* 20 degrees.] **7.** to send or say in an offhand way [to *drop* someone a note; to *drop* a hint]. **8.** to leave out [He *dropped* a line when he rewrote the poem.] **9.** to leave at a certain place: *used only in everyday talk* [The taxi *dropped* him at his hotel.] —**drop back** or **drop behind,** to fall behind; lag. —**drop in,** to make an unexpected or informal visit. —**drop out,** to stop taking part; stop being a member. —**dropped** or *sometimes* **dropt** (dräpt), *p.t. & p.p.;* **drop′ping,** *pr.p.*

drop·let (dräp′lit), *n.* a very small drop.

drop·out (dräp′out), *n.* a student who leaves school before graduating.

drop·per (dräp′ər), *n.* a small glass tube with a hollow rubber bulb on one end, used to measure out a liquid in drops.

drop·sy (dräp′sē), *n.* a condition, as in heart disease, in which a liquid gathers in parts of the body, causing swelling. —**drop′si·cal,** *adj.*

dropper

dross (drôs), *n.* **1.** a scum on top of molten metal. **2.** worthless stuff.

drought (drout) or **drouth** (drouth), *n.* a long period of dry weather, with little or no rain.

drove (drōv), *n.* **1.** a group of cattle, sheep, etc. driven along together. **2.** a moving crowd of people.

drove (drōv), past tense of **drive.**

dro·ver (drō′vər), *n.* **1.** a man who drives animals to market. **2.** a cattle dealer.

drown (droun), *v.* **1.** to die or kill by keeping under water, where the lungs can get no air to breathe. **2.** to be so loud as to overcome some other sound [Cheers *drowned* out the speaker.]

drowse (drouz), *v.* to be half asleep; doze. —**drowsed,** *p.t. & p.p.;* **drows′ing,** *pr.p.*

drow·sy (drou′zē), *adj.* **1.** sleepy or half asleep. **2.** making one feel sleepy [*drowsy* music]. **—drow′si·er,** *compar.;* **drow′si·est,** *superl.* **—drow′si·ly,** *adv.* **—drow′si·ness,** *n.*

drub (drub), *v.* to beat as with a stick or club. **—drubbed,** *p.t. & p.p.;* **drub′bing,** *pr.p.*

drudge (druj), *n.* a person who does hard and tiresome work. **—v.** to work as a drudge does. **—drudged,** *p.t. & p.p.;* **drudg′ing,** *pr.p.*

drudg·er·y (druj′ər ē), *n.* hard and tiresome work. **—drudg′er·ies,** *pl.*

drug (drug), *n.* **1.** any substance used as or in a medicine. **2.** a substance used to make one sleep or to lessen pain; narcotic. **—v. 1.** to give drugs to, especially so as to put to sleep or make unconscious. **2.** to put harmful drugs in [They had *drugged* his coffee.] **3.** to make feel dull or dazed. **—drug on the market,** a product which few or none want to buy. **—drugged,** *p.t. & p.p.;* **drug′ging,** *pr.p.*

drug·gist (drug′ist), *n.* a person who sells drugs, medical supplies, etc., especially one who has a license to fill doctors' prescriptions; pharmacist.

drug·store (drug′stôr), *n.* a store where medicines are sold and often prepared. Most drugstores today also sell a variety of other things.

dru·id or **Dru·id** (drōō′id), *n.* one of the priests of the Celtic religion in ancient Britain, Ireland, and France.

drum (drum), *n.* **1.** a rhythm instrument that is usually a hollow cylinder with skin stretched tightly over one or both ends. It is played by beating. **2.** a sound like that made by beating a drum. **3.** a container or other object shaped like a drum [an oil *drum*]. **—v. 1.** to beat or play on a drum. **2.** to keep on beating or tapping, as with the fingers. **—drum into,** to make remember by repeating again and again. **—drum up,** to get by trying [to *drum up* new business]. **—drummed,** *p.t. & p.p.;* **drum′ming,** *pr.p.*

drum

drum major, a person who twirls a baton at the head of a marching band. **—drum ma·jor·ette** (mā′jər et′), *fem.*

drum·mer (drum′ər), *n.* **1.** a person who plays a drum. **2.** a traveling salesman: *used only in everyday talk.*

drum·stick (drum′stik), *n.* **1.** a stick used in playing a drum. **2.** the leg of a cooked chicken, turkey, etc., next to the thigh.

drumstick of a turkey

drunk (drungk), past participle of **drink. —adj.** having lost control of oneself from drinking alcoholic liquor; intoxicated. **—n.** a drunkard: *slang in this meaning.*

drunk·ard (drung′kərd), *n.* a person who is often drunk.

drunk·en (drung′kən), an old past participle of

drink. —adj. 1. drunk; intoxicated [a *drunken* man]. **2.** brought on by being drunk [a *drunken* sleep]. **—drunk′en·ly,** *adv.* **—drunk′en·ness,** *n.*

dry (drī), *adj.* **1.** not wet or damp; without moisture. **2.** not under water [*dry* land]. **3.** having little or no water or rain [a *dry* desert]. **4.** with all its water or other liquid gone [a *dry* fountain pen; *dry* bread; a *dry* well]. **5.** not giving milk [a *dry* cow]. **6.** not shedding tears [*dry* eyes]. **7.** thirsty. **8.** not having butter, margarine, etc. spread on it [*dry* toast]. **9.** not bringing up mucus [a *dry* cough]. **10.** funny in a quiet but sharp way [*dry* humor]. **11.** not interesting; dull; boring [a *dry* lecture]. **12.** plain or bare [the *dry* facts]. **13.** not sweet [a *dry* wine]. **14.** not allowing alcoholic liquor to be sold [a *dry* State]. **—v.** to make or become dry. **—dry up,** to make or become completely dry. **—dri′er,** *compar.;* **dri′est,** *superl.* **—dried,** *p.t. & p.p.;* **dry′ing,** *pr.p.* **—dry′ly,** *adv.* **—dry′ness,** *n.*

dry·ad or **Dry·ad** (drī′əd), *n.* a nymph of the woods in Greek myths.

dry cell, an electric battery cell packed with a material to soak up the chemicals that would otherwise spill.

dry-clean (drī′klēn′), *v.* to clean clothing or fabrics with some liquid other than water, as naphtha. **—dry cleaner —dry cleaning.**

dry dock, a dock from which the water can be emptied, used in building or repairing ships.

dry·er (drī′ər), *n.* **1.** a machine for drying things by heating or blowing air [clothes *dryer;* hair *dryer*]. **2.** same as **drier.**

dry goods, cloth, clothing, thread, etc.

dry ice, carbon dioxide in a solid form, used for cooling things or keeping them cold. It evaporates instead of melting.

dry measure, a system of measuring the volume of dry things, as grain, coal, vegetables, etc. In dry measure, one pint = 33.6 cubic inches, 2 pints = 1 quart, 8 quarts = 1 peck, and 4 pecks = 1 bushel.

du·al (dōō′əl), *adj.* of, having, or being two; double [The actor played a *dual* role.]

dub (dub), *v.* **1.** to make a man a knight by tapping him on the shoulder with a sword. **2.** to give a name, nickname, or title to [Tom's friends *dubbed* him "Slim."] **3.** to make smooth by hammering, scraping, or rubbing. **—dubbed,** *p.t. & p.p.;* **dub′bing,** *pr.p.*

du·bi·ous (dōō′bi əs), *adj.* **1.** full of doubt; not sure [I feel *dubious* about trusting him.] **2.** causing doubt; not clear in meaning [a *dubious* answer]. **3.** probably not good, right, moral, etc.; questionable [a man of *dubious* character]. **—du′bi·ous·ly,** *adv.*

Dub·lin (dub′lin), *n.* the capital of Ireland.

du·cal (dōō′k'l), *adj.* of a duke or dukedom.

duc·at (duk′ət), *n.* any of several gold or silver coins once used in countries of Europe.

duch·ess (duch′is), *n.* **1.** the wife or widow of a duke. **2.** a woman who has the rank of a duke and rules a duchy.

duch·y (duch′ē), *n.* the land ruled by a duke or a duchess. —**duch′ies,** *pl.*

duck (duk), *n.* **1.** a swimming bird with a flat bill, short legs, and webbed feet; especially, the female of this bird. The male is called a *drake.* **2.** the flesh of a duck eaten as food. **3.** a military truck that can move on both land and water.

duck (duk), *v.* **1.** to dive or dip under water for a very short time. **2.** to lower or move the head or body quickly, as in getting away from a blow or in hiding. —*n.* the act of ducking.

duck (2 ft. long)

duck (duk), *n.* a linen or cotton cloth like canvas but finer and lighter in weight [Doctors' uniforms are often made of white *duck.*]

duck·bill (duk′bil), *n.* same as **platypus.**

duck·ling (duk′ling), *n.* a young duck.

duct (dukt), *n.* **1.** a tube or channel through which a gas or liquid moves [air *ducts* from a furnace]. **2.** a tube in the body through which a liquid flows [tear *ducts* of the eyes]. **3.** a pipe through which electric wires are run.

duc·tile (duk′t'l), *adj.* **1.** that can be drawn out into wire or hammered thin [Copper is a *ductile* metal.] **2.** that can be molded or shaped, as clay. —**duc·til·i·ty** (duk til′ə tē), *n.*

duct·less gland (dukt′lis), a gland, as the thyroid, that has no ducts but sends its fluid directly into the blood or lymph.

dud (dud), *n.* **1.** a bomb or shell that fails to explode. **2.** a person or thing that fails to do what is expected. *A slang word.*

dude (dōōd *or* dyōōd), *n.* **1.** a man who is very fussy about his clothes and looks; dandy. **2.** a person from the city, especially one from the East who is vacationing on a ranch: *a Western slang meaning.*

dudg·eon (duj′ən), *n.* anger; hurt feeling: *used mainly in the phrase* **in high dudgeon,** very angry.

due (dōō *or* dyōō), *adj.* **1.** owed as a debt; payable [Your gas bill of $5 is *due* today.] **2.** that is right and fitting; proper; suitable [to act with all *due* respect; to use *due* care]. **3.** expected to come or be done at a certain time [The plane is *due* at 7:15.] —*adv.* in a straight line; exactly [a town *due* west of Detroit]. —*n.* **1.** anything due [to give a man his *due*]. **2. dues,** *pl.* money paid regularly for being a member in a club, etc. —**due to, 1.** caused by [losses *due to* carelessness]. **2.** because of: *used only in everyday talk* [The train is late *due to* the storm.]

du·el (dōō′əl *or* dyōō′əl), *n.* **1.** a fight according to set rules between two people armed with weapons and watched by witnesses. **2.** any contest like this, as a debate. —*v.* to fight a duel.

—**du′eled** *or* **du′elled,** *p.t. & p.p.;* **du′el·ing** *or* **du′el·ling,** *pr.p.* —**du′el·ist** *or* **du′el·list,** *n.*

du·et (dōō et′ *or* dyōō et′), *n.* **1.** a piece of music for two voices or two instruments. **2.** the two people who sing or play it.

dug (dug), past tense and past participle of **dig.**

dug·out (dug′out), *n.* **1.** a boat made by hollowing out a log. **2.** a shelter dug in the ground or in a hillside. **3.** a covered shelter near a baseball diamond, where the players of a team sit when not at bat or in the field.

duke (dōōk *or* dyōōk), *n.* **1.** a prince who is the ruler of a duchy. **2.** a nobleman of the highest rank, just below a prince. —**duke′dom,** *n.*

dul·cet (dul′sit), *adj.* pleasant to hear; sweet-sounding; melodious [a *dulcet* voice].

dul·ci·mer (dul′sə mər), *n.* a musical instrument with metal strings. It is played by striking the strings with two small hammers.

dulcimer

dull (dul), *adj.* **1.** not having a sharp edge or point; blunt [a *dull* knife]. **2.** not feeling or felt in a sharp way; weak [a *dull* sense of smell; a *dull* pain]. **3.** slow in thinking or learning; stupid. **4.** not active or lively; sluggish or listless [Business is *dull*]. **5.** not interesting; boring [a long, *dull* book]. **6.** not bright; dim [a *dull* sky]. **7.** not clear; muffled [a *dull* thud]. —*v.* to make or become dull. —**dull′ness,** *n.* —**dul′ly,** *adv.*

dull·ard (dul′ərd), *n.* a stupid person.

Du·luth (də lōōth′), *n.* a city in eastern Minnesota, on Lake Superior.

du·ly (dōō′lē *or* dyōō′lē), *adv.* as due; in a way or at a time that is right or fitting [Are you *duly* grateful? Their rent was *duly* paid.]

dumb (dum), *adj.* **1.** not having the power to speak; mute [a *dumb* beast]. **2.** not speaking for a time; speechless [struck *dumb* with fear]. **3.** stupid: *used only in everyday talk.* —**dumb′ly,** *adv.* —**dumb′ness,** *n.*

dumb·bell (dum′bel), *n.* a short bar with round weights at the ends, usually used in pairs to exercise the muscles.

dumb-wait·er (dum′wāt′ər), *n.* a small elevator for sending food, etc. from one floor to another.

dum·found *or* **dumb·found** (dum′found′), *v.* to make unable to speak, as by shocking.

dumbbells

dum·my (dum′ē), *n.* **1.** an imitation of something, as a figure made to look like a person and

fat,   āpe,   cär,   ten,   ēven,   hit,   bīte,   gō,   hôrn,   tōōl,   book,   up,   fŭr;
get,   joy,   yet,   chin,   she,   thin,   *th*en;   zh = s in pleasure;   ′ as in able (ā′b'l);
ə = a in ago,   e in agent,   i in sanity,   o in confess,   u in focus.

used to display clothing. **2.** a player in some card games, as bridge, whose cards are laid face up on the table and played by his partner. **3.** a stupid person: *slang in this meaning.* —*adj.* **1.** imitation or substitute [a *dummy* gun]. **2.** secretly acting for another or controlled by another [a *dummy* corporation]. —**dum′mies,** *pl.*

dump (dump), *v.* **1.** to unload in a pile or heap, as sand. **2.** to throw away; get rid of. —*n.* **1.** a place where rubbish is dumped. **2.** a place where military supplies are stored. **3.** a place that is dirty, run-down, etc.: *slang in this meaning.* —**in the dumps,** feeling sad.

dump·ling (dump′ling), *n.* **1.** a small ball of dough, cooked and served with meat or soup. **2.** a crust of baked dough filled with fruit.

dump truck, a truck with a back end that can be tilted to dump a load.

dump·y (dump′ē), *adj.* short and fat; plump. —**dump′i·er,** *compar.;* **dump′i·est,** *superl.*

dun (dun), *adj. & n.* dull grayish brown.

dun (dun), *v.* to ask again and again for money owed. —*n.* a demand that a debt be paid. —**dunned,** *p.t. & p.p.;* **dun′ning,** *pr.p.*

dunce (duns), *n.* a stupid person or one who learns slowly.

dune (dōōn *or* dyōōn), *n.* a rounded hill or ridge of sand piled up by the wind.

dung (dung), *n.* the waste matter dropped by animals; manure.

dun·ga·ree (dung gə rē′), *n.* denim, the cotton cloth, especially as used in making work pants or overalls, which are called **dungarees.**

dun·geon (dun′jən), *n.* a dark room underground, used as a prison.

dunk (dungk), *v.* to dip bread, cake, etc. into coffee or other liquid before eating it.

dupe (dōōp *or* dyōōp), *n.* a person who is easily fooled or cheated. —*v.* to fool or cheat. —**duped,** *p.t. & p.p.;* **dup′ing,** *pr.p.*

du·plex (dōō′pleks *or* dyōō′pleks), *adj.* having two parts or units; double [a *duplex* house].

du·pli·cate (dōō′plə kit *or* dyōō′plə kit), *adj.* **1.** exactly like another or like each other [*duplicate* keys]. **2.** double. —*n.* a thing exactly like another; an exact copy [She made a *duplicate* of the letter.] —*v.* (dōō′plə kāt *or* dyōō′plə kāt), to make an exact copy or copies of; repeat. —**in duplicate,** in two copies that are exactly alike. —**du′pli·cat·ed,** *p.t. & p.p.;* **du′pli·cat·ing,** *pr.p.* —**du′pli·ca′tion,** *n.*

du·plic·i·ty (dōō plis′ə tē *or* dyōō plis′ə tē), *n.* a dealing with others in a tricky or dishonest way. —**du·plic′i·ties,** *pl.*

du·ra·ble (door′ə b′l *or* dyoor′ə b′l), *adj.* lasting in spite of hard wear or much use. —**du′ra·bil′i·ty,** *n.* —**du′ra·bly,** *adv.*

dur·ance (door′əns *or* dyoor′əns), *n.* imprisonment: *now seen mainly in the phrase* **in durance vile,** *meaning* "imprisoned."

du·ra·tion (doo rā′shən *or* dyoo rā′shən), *n.* the time that something lasts or continues [He lived here for the *duration* of his life.]

du·ress (doo res′ *or* dyoo res′), *n.* the use of force or threats to make someone do something

[Anything signed or agreed to under *duress* is not binding in law.]

dur·ing (door′ing *or* dyoor′ing), *prep.* **1.** through the whole time of; throughout [The lake is frozen *during* the winter.] **2.** at some time in the course of [He left *during* the night.]

durst (dŭrst), an old past tense of **dare.**

dusk (dusk), *n.* the dim part of twilight that comes before the dark of night.

dusk·y (dus′kē), *adj.* dim, dark, or gloomy; shadowy. —**dusk′i·er,** *compar.;* **dusk′i·est,** *superl.* —**dusk′i·ness,** *n.*

dust (dust), *n.* **1.** fine, powdery earth or other material that floats in the air and settles on surfaces. **2.** the human body after death. —*v.* **1.** to wipe the dust from [*Dust* the table.] **2.** to sprinkle with a dust or fine powder [*Dust* the cake with powdered sugar.] —**bite the dust,** to be killed or wounded in battle. —**shake the dust off one's feet,** to leave in anger or scorn. —**throw dust in someone's eyes,** to fool or mislead someone.

dust·er (dust′ər), *n.* **1.** a cloth or brush used for getting dust off. **2.** a kind of light coat worn to protect the clothes from dust.

dust·pan (dust′pan), *n.* a pan like a small shovel, into which dirt from the floor is swept.

dustpan

dust·y (dus′tē), *adj.* **1.** covered or filled with dust [*dusty* furniture]. **2.** like dust or powder [the *dusty* scales of a moth's wing]. **3.** of the color of dust; grayish. —**dust′i·er,** *compar.;* **dust′i·est,** *superl.* —**dust′i·ness,** *n.*

Dutch (duch), *adj.* of the Netherlands, its people, language, etc. —*n.* **1.** the language of the Netherlands. **2.** the people of the Netherlands: *used with a plural verb.* See also **Pennsylvania Dutch.** —**go Dutch,** to have each person pay for himself: *used only in everyday talk.* —**in Dutch,** in trouble: *a slang phrase.*

Dutch·man (duch′mən), *n.* **1.** a person born or living in the Netherlands. **2.** a German: *slang in this meaning.* —**Dutch′men,** *pl.*

Dutch treat, a dinner, party, or other entertainment at which each person pays for himself: *used only in everyday talk.*

du·te·ous (dōō′ti əs *or* dyōō′ti əs), *adj.* dutiful or obedient. —**du′te·ous·ly,** *adv.*

du·ti·ful (dōō′ti fəl *or* dyōō′ti fəl), *adj.* doing or ready to do one's duty; having a proper sense of duty [a *dutiful* son]. —**du′ti·ful·ly,** *adv.*

du·ty (dōō′tē *or* dyōō′tē), *n.* **1.** what a person should do because it is thought to be right, just, or moral [It is the *duty* of every citizen to vote.] **2.** any of the things a person is supposed to do as part of his work [the *duties* of a secretary]. **3.** the obedience or respect that one should show toward one's parents, older people, etc. **4.** a tax paid to the government, especially on goods brought in from other countries. —**du′ties,** *pl.*

dwarf (dwôrf), *n.* **1.** a person, animal, or plant that is much smaller than most others of its kind. **2.** a little man in fairy tales who is supposed to have magic powers. —*v.* **1.** to make something seem small in comparison; tower over [The redwood *dwarfs* other trees.] **2.** to keep small; stunt the growth of [Poor diet *dwarfed* the children.] —*adj.* smaller than others of its kind [The Japanese raise *dwarf* trees for gardens.] —**dwarf′ish,** *adj.*

dwell (dwel), *v.* to make one's home; live: *no longer used in everyday talk.* —**dwell on** or **dwell upon,** to go on thinking or talking about for a long time. —**dwelt** (dwelt) or **dwelled,** *p.t. & p.p.;* **dwell′ing,** *pr.p.* —**dwell′er,** *n.*

dwell·ing (dwel′ing), *n.* a house or home.

dwin·dle (dwin′d'l), *v.* to keep on becoming smaller or less; diminish [His fortune had *dwindled* away.] —**dwin′dled,** *p.t. & p.p.;* **dwin′dling,** *pr.p.*

dye (dī), *n.* **1.** a substance dissolved in water and used to color cloth, hair, leather, etc. **2.** the color produced in cloth, etc. by dyeing. —*v.* to color as with a dye. —**dyed,** *p.t. & p.p.;* **dye′ing,** *pr.p.* —**dy′er,** *n.*

dye·stuff (dī′stuf), *n.* any substance used as a dye or from which a dye is gotten.

dy·ing (dī′ing), present participle of **die.**

dyke (dīk), *n. & v.* same as **dike.**

dy·nam·ic (dī nam′ik), *adj.* **1.** having to do with energy or force in action. **2.** full of energy or power; forceful [a *dynamic* person]. —**dy·nam′i·cal·ly,** *adv.*

dy·nam·ics (dī nam′iks), *n.pl.* **1.** the science that has to do with the action of force on bodies in motion or at rest. **2.** all the forces that are at work in any activity [the *dynamics* of politics].

dy·na·mite (dī′nə mīt), *n.* an explosive made of nitroglycerine and used in mining, etc. —*v.* to blow up with dynamite. —**dy′na·mit·ed,** *p.t. & p.p.;* **dy′na·mit·ing,** *pr.p.*

dy·na·mo (dī′nə mō), *n.* a machine for changing mechanical energy into electricity. —**dy′na·mos,** *pl.*

dy·nas·ty (dī′nəs tē), *n.* **1.** a family of rulers following one after another. **2.** the period of time during which such a family rules. —**dy′nas·ties,** *pl.* —**dy·nas·tic** (dī nas′tik), *adj.*

dys·en·ter·y (dis′ən ter′ē), *n.* a disease of the intestines, in which there are loose bowel movements containing blood and mucus.

dys·pep·sia (dis pep′shə *or* dis pep′si ə), *n.* indigestion.

dys·pep·tic (dis pep′tik), *adj.* **1.** having indigestion. **2.** grouchy or gloomy.

dz., abbreviation for **dozen** or **dozens.**

E

E, e (ē), *n.* the fifth letter of the English alphabet. —**E's, e's** (ēz), *pl.*

E., E, e., e, abbreviations for **east** or **eastern.**

each (ēch), *adj. & pron.* every one of two or more, thought of separately [*Each* pupil will receive a book. *Each* of the books is numbered.] —*adv.* for each; apiece [These balls cost 50 cents *each.*] —**each other,** each one the other [You and I should help *each other.*]

ea·ger (ē′gər), *adj.* wanting very much; anxious to do or get [*eager* to please; *eager* for success]. —**ea′ger·ly,** *adv.* —**ea′ger·ness,** *n.*

ea·gle (ē′g'l), *n.* a large, strong bird that captures and eats other birds and animals and has sharp eyesight. See also **bald eagle.**

ea·glet (ē′glit), *n.* a young eagle.

ear (ir), *n.* **1.** either of two organs in the head through which sound is heard. **2.** the part of the ear that sticks out from the head. **3.** anything like an ear [the *ear* of a pitcher]. **4.** the sense of

bald eagle (wingspread 6 ft.)

hearing [He has a good *ear* for speech sounds.] **5.** attention or heed [They lent *ear* to his plea.] —**be all ears,** to listen in an eager way. —**fall on deaf ears,** to be unheeded. —**keep an ear to the ground,** to pay close attention to what people are thinking. —**play by ear,** to play music without reading notes. —**turn a deaf ear,** to refuse to listen or heed.

ear (ir), *n.* the part of a cereal plant on which the grain grows [an *ear* of corn].

ear·ache (ir′āk), *n.* a pain in the ear.

ear·drum (ir′drum), *n.* the thin, tight skin inside the ear that vibrates when sound waves strike it.

earl (url), *n.* a British nobleman ranking just below a marquis. —**earl′dom,** *n.*

ear·ly (ur′lē), *adv. & adj.* **1.** near the beginning; soon after the start [in the *early* afternoon; *early* in his career]. **2.** before the usual or expected time [The train arrived *early.*] —**ear′li·er,** *compar.;* **ear′li·est,** *superl.* —**ear′li·ness,** *n.*

ear·mark (ir′märk), *n.* **1.** a notch or other mark made on the ear of a cow, horse, etc. to show who owns it. **2.** a trait or quality that tells what a person or thing is or can be [He has all the *earmarks* of a good salesman.] —*v.* **1.** to put an earmark on [to *earmark* cattle]. **2.** to set

fat, āpe, cär, ten, ēven, hit, bīte, gō, hôrn, tōōl, book, up, fur;
get, joy, yet, chin, she, thin, *then;* zh = s in pleasure; ' as in able (ā′b'l)
ə = a in ago, e in agent, i in sanity, o in confess, u in focus.

aside for a special purpose [supplies *earmarked* for the army].

ear·muffs (ir′mufs), *n.pl.* cloth or fur coverings worn over the ears to keep them warm in cold weather.

earn (ûrn), *v.* **1.** to get as pay for work done [He *earns* $90 a week.] **2.** to get or deserve because of something one has done [His bravery has *earned* him a medal.] **3.** to get as profit [a bond *earning* 3% interest].

ear·nest (ûr′nist), *adj.* not light or joking; serious or sincere [an *earnest* wish]. —**in earnest,** serious or determined [We began again, this time *in earnest.*] —**ear′·nest·ly,** *adv.* —**ear′nest·ness,** *n.*

earn·ings (ûr′ningz), *n.pl.* money earned; wages, salary, or profits.

ear·phone (ir′fōn), *n.* a receiver held to the ear, for listening to a telephone, radio, etc.

ear·ring (ir′ring), *n.* an ornament fastened to the lobe of the ear.

ear·shot (ir′shät), *n.* the distance within which a person's voice or other sound can be heard; range of hearing.

earth (ûrth), *n.* **1.** the planet on which we live. It is the fifth largest planet and the third in distance away from the sun. **2.** the dry part of the earth's surface, that is not the sea. **3.** soil or ground [two acres of good, rich *earth*]. —**down to earth,** practical or realistic. —**move heaven and earth,** to do everything one can. —**run to earth,** to hunt down.

earth·en (ûrth′ən), *adj.* **1.** made of earth [an *earthen* floor]. **2.** made of baked clay [*earthen* jars].

earth·en·ware (ûrth′ən wer), *n.* dishes, vases, jars, etc. made of baked clay.

earth·ly (ûrth′lē), *adj.* **1.** having to do with the earth, or this world, and not with heaven [*earthly* possessions]. **2.** possible [This advice was of no *earthly* use.]

earth·quake (ûrth′kwāk), *n.* a shaking or trembling of the ground caused by the shifting of underground rock or by the action of a volcano.

earth·work (ûrth′wûrk), *n.* a wall made by piling up earth, as around a fort.

earth·worm (ûrth′wûrm), *n.* a round worm that lives in the earth and helps keep the soil loose.

earth·y (ûr′thē), *adj.* **1.** of or like earth or soil [an *earthy* smell]. **2.** simple, or coarse, and natural; not refined [*earthy* humor]. —**earth′i·er,** *compar.;* **earth′i·est,** *superl.*

earthworm
(6 to 10 in. long)

ease (ēz), *n.* **1.** the condition of not needing to try too hard [He worked the puzzle with *ease.*] **2.** a calm condition or relaxed position [to put a person at *ease;* to stand at *ease*]. **3.** a being without worry, pain, or trouble; comfort or luxury [a life of *ease*]. —*v.* **1.** to make feel less worry,

pain, or trouble; comfort [Her father's kind words *eased* the upset girl.] **2.** to make less painful [The pills *eased* his headache.] **3.** to take away some of the strain or pressure on; loosen: *often used with* up [*Ease* up on that rope.] **4.** to move slowly and carefully [The big ship *eased* into the dock.] —**eased,** *p.t. & p.p.;* **eas′ing,** *pr.p.*

ea·sel (ē′z'l), *n.* a standing frame for holding an artist's canvas, a blackboard, etc.

eas·i·ly (ē′z'l ē), *adv.* **1.** without trying too hard; with no trouble [I can do that problem *easily.*] **2.** without a doubt; by far [Our team is *easily* the best.] **3.** very likely; probably [The train may *easily* be an hour late.]

easel

eas·i·ness (ēz′ē nis), *n.* the fact or condition of being easy.

east (ēst), *n.* **1.** the direction toward the point where the sun rises. **2.** a place or region in or toward this direction. In the United States, **the East** usually means the northern part east of the Alleghenies. **3. East,** Asia or the Orient: see **Near East, Middle East, Far East.** —*adj.* **1.** in, of, to, or toward the east [the *east* bank of the river]. **2.** from the east [an *east* wind]. **3. East,** that is the eastern part of [*East* Pakistan]. —*adv.* in or toward the east [Follow that road *east.*]

East·er (ēs′tər), *n.* a Christian festival held on a Sunday early in spring to celebrate the resurrection of Jesus.

east·er·ly (ēs′tər lē), *adj. & adv.* **1.** in or toward the east. **2.** from the east.

east·ern (ēs′tərn), *adj.* **1.** in, of, or toward the east [the *eastern* sky]. **2.** from the east [an *eastern* wind]. **3. Eastern,** of the East.

Eastern Church, same as **Orthodox Eastern Church.**

east·ern·er (ēs′tər nər), *n.* a person born or living in the east [A native of New England is called an *Easterner.*]

Eastern Hemisphere, the half of the earth that includes Europe, Africa, Asia, and Australia.

east·ern·most (ēs′tərn mōst), *adj.* farthest east.

Eastern Standard Time, see **Standard Time.**

East Indies, 1. the islands of Indonesia and the Philippines. **2.** these islands along with southeast Asia.

east·ward (ēst′wərd), *adv. & adj.* toward the east: also **east′wards,** *adv.* —*n.* an eastward direction or place.

eas·y (ēz′ē), *adj.* **1.** not hard to do, learn, get, etc. [an *easy* job; an *easy* book]. **2.** without worry, pain, or trouble [an *easy* life]. **3.** restful or comfortable [an *easy* chair]. **4.** not stiff or awkward; relaxed and pleasant [an *easy* manner]. **5.** not hard to put up with; not strict [*easy* punishment; an *easy* master]. **6.** not rushed [an *easy* pace]. —*adv.* easily: *used only in everyday talk.* —**take it easy,** to keep from being rushed, hasty, angry, etc.: *used only in everyday talk.* —**eas′i·er,** *compar.;* **eas′i·est,** *superl.*

eas·y·go·ing or **eas·y-go·ing** (ēz′ē gō′ing), *adj.* not worried, rushed, or strict about things.

eat (ēt), *v.* **1.** to take food into the mouth and swallow it. **2.** to have a meal [Who is *eating* here today?] **3.** to use up; consume [High prices *ate* up his savings.] **4.** to destroy by wearing away [hinges *eaten* away by rust]. **5.** to make as by eating [The acid *ate* holes in the cloth.] —**eat one's words,** to admit that what one said was wrong. —**ate,** *p.t.;* **eat·en** (ēt′'n), *p.p.;* **eat′ing,** *pr.p.* —**eat′er,** *n.*

eat·a·ble (ēt′ə b'l), *adj.* fit to be eaten. —*n.* **eatables,** *pl.* things to be eaten; food.

eaves (ēvz), *n.pl.* the edge or edges of a roof hanging over the side of a building.

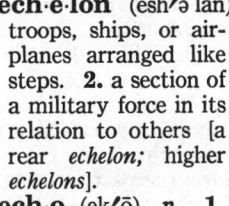
eaves

eaves·drop (ēvz′dräp), *v.* to listen to others talking when they do not know they are being overheard. —**eaves′-dropped,** *p.t. & p.p.;* **eaves′drop·ping,** *pr.p.* —**eaves′drop·per,** *n.*

ebb (eb), *n.* **1.** the flow of water back toward the sea as the tide falls. **2.** a becoming weaker or less [the *ebb* of one's hopes]. —*v.* **1.** to fall, as the tide. **2.** to become weaker or less [Our hopes for victory *ebbed.*]

ebb tide, the tide flowing back toward the sea.

eb·on (eb′ən), *adj. & n.* ebony: *used in poetry.*

eb·on·y (eb′ən ē), *n.* the black, hard wood of certain tropical trees. —*adj.* **1.** made of ebony. **2.** black or dark.

e·bul·lient (i bul′yənt), *adj.* bubbling or overflowing, as with joy or enthusiasm.

ec·cen·tric (ik sen′trik), *adj.* **1.** not usual or normal in the way one behaves; odd or queer [an *eccentric* old hermit]. **2.** not having the same center, as two circles one inside the other. **3.** having its axis not in the center [*Eccentric* wheels are used to change circular motion into back-and-forth motion.] —*n.* an eccentric person. —**ec·cen′-tri·cal·ly,** *adv.*

ec·cen·tric·i·ty (ek′sən tris′ə tē), *n.* unusual or odd behavior, or a queer habit or action. —**ec′cen-tric′i·ties,** *pl.*

upper: eccentric circles
lower: eccentric wheel

Ec·cle·si·as·tes (i klē′zi as′tēz), *n.* a book of the Old Testament.

ec·cle·si·as·tic (i klē′zi as′tik), *n.* a clergyman. —*adj.* same as **ecclesiastical.**

ec·cle·si·as·ti·cal (i klē′zi as′ti k'l), *adj.* having to do with the church or clergy.

ech·e·lon (esh′ə län), *n.* **1.** a formation of troops, ships, or airplanes arranged like steps. **2.** a section of a military force in its relation to others [a rear *echelon;* higher *echelons*].

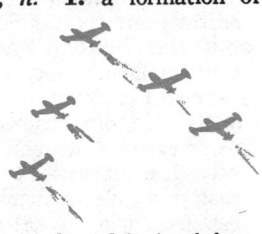
airplanes flying in echelon

ech·o (ek′ō), *n.* **1.** sound heard again when sound waves bounce back from a surface. **2. Echo,** a nymph of Greek myths who pined away for Narcissus until only her voice was left. —*v.* **1.** to be filled with echoes [The long hall *echoed.*] **2.** to be repeated as an echo [His words *echoed* in the valley.] **3.** to repeat the words or actions of another person. —**ech′oes,** *pl.* —**ech′oed,** *p.t. & p.p.;* **ech′o·ing,** *pr.p.*

é·clair (ā kler′ or i kler′), *n.* an oblong shell of pastry filled with custard or whipped cream.

e·clipse (i klips′), *n.* **1.** a hiding of all or part of the sun by the moon when it passes between the sun and the earth (called a **solar eclipse**); also, a hiding of the moon by the earth's shadow (called a **lunar eclipse**). **2.** a becoming dim or less brilliant [His fame has suffered an *eclipse.*] —*v.* **1.** to cause an eclipse of; darken. **2.** to make seem less brilliant by outshining [His latest book has *eclipsed* all his earlier ones.] —**e·clipsed′,** *p.t. & p.p.;* **e·clips′ing,** *pr.p.*

e·col·o·gy (ē käl′ə jē), *n.* the science that deals with the relations between all living things and the conditions that surround them.

e·co·nom·ic (ē′kə näm′ik or ek′ə näm′ik), *adj.* **1.** having to do with the managing of money in a home, business, or government [the President's *economic* advisers]. **2.** having to do with economics [the *economic* development of a country].

e·co·nom·i·cal (ē′kə näm′i k'l or ek′ə näm′i-k'l), *adj.* not wasting money, time, material, etc.; thrifty [an *economical* person; an *economical* car]. —**e′co·nom′i·cal·ly,** *adv.*

e·co·nom·ics (ē′kə näm′iks or ek′ə näm′iks), *n.pl.* the science that deals with the way in which goods and wealth are produced, distributed, and used: *used with a singular verb.* —**e·con·o·mist** (i kän′ə mist), *n.*

e·con·o·mize (i kän′ə mīz), *v.* to be economical or to cut down on expenses. —**e·con′o·mized,** *p.t. & p.p.;* **e·con′o·miz·ing,** *pr.p.*

e·con·o·my (i kän′ə mē), *n.* **1.** the managing of money earned and spent in a home, business, etc. **2.** a careful managing of money, etc. so that there is no waste. —**e·con′o·mies,** *pl.*

ec·ru (ek′rōo), *adj. & n.* light tan.

ec·sta·sy (ek′stə sē), *n.* a strong feeling of joy or delight; rapture. —**ec′sta·sies,** *pl.*

ec·stat·ic (ek stat′ik), *adj.* **1.** full of ecstasy [an *ecstatic* mood]. **2.** causing ecstasy; thrilling [*ecstatic* music]. —**ec·stat′i·cal·ly,** *adv.*

fat, āpe, cär, ten, ēven, hit, bīte, gō, hôrn, tool, book, up, fũr;
get, joy, yet, chin, she, thin, then; zh = s in pleasure; ′ as in able (ā′b'l);
ə = a in ago, e in agent, i in sanity, o in confess, u in focus.

Ec·ua·dor (ek′wə dôr), *n.* a country on the northwestern coast of South America.

ec·u·men·i·cal (ek′yoo men′i k′l), *adj.* promoting religious unity among Christian churches.

ec·ze·ma (ek′sə mə *or* eg zē′mə), *n.* a condition of the skin, often caused by allergy, in which it becomes red, scaly, and very itchy.

-ed, 1. a suffix used to form the past tense and past participle of many verbs, as *walked*. The past participle may often be an adjective as well [*boiled* meat]. **2.** a suffix meaning "having" [A *moneyed* man is one having money.]

ed·dy (ed′ē), *n.* a little current of air, water, etc. moving in circles against the main current. —*v.* to move in an eddy. —**ed′dies,** *pl.* —**ed′died,** *p.t. & p.p.;* **ed′dy·ing,** *pr.p.*

E·den (ē′d′n), *n.* **1.** in the Bible, the garden where Adam and Eve lived. **2.** any place of great happiness or delight.

edge (ej), *n.* **1.** the sharp, cutting part [the *edge* of a knife]. **2.** the line or part where something begins or ends; border or margin [the *edge* of a plate; the *edge* of the forest]. **3.** the brink, as of a cliff. —*v.* **1.** to form or put an edge on [She *edged* the dress with lace.] **2.** to move with the side forward, as through a crowd. **3.** to move in a slow and careful way [He *edged* away from the dog.] —**on edge, 1.** very tense or nervous. **2.** impatient. —**edged,** *p.t. & p.p.;* **edg′ing,** *pr.p.*

edge·ways (ej′wāz) *or* **edge·wise** (ej′wīz), *adv.* with the edge forward.

edg·ing (ej′ing), *n.* something that forms an edge or is placed along the edge; border.

edg·y (ej′ē), *adj.* very nervous and tense; on edge. —**edg′i·er,** *compar.;* **edg′i·est,** *superl.*

ed·i·ble (ed′ə b′l), *adj.* fit to be eaten.

e·dict (ē′dikt), *n.* an order or law put forth by a ruler or other high official; decree.

ed·i·fice (ed′ə fis), *n.* a building, especially one that is large or looks important.

ed·i·fy (ed′ə fī), *v.* to teach, especially so as to improve in morals or character [an *edifying* sermon]. —**ed′i·fied,** *p.t. & p.p.;* **ed′i·fy·ing,** *pr.p.* —**ed′i·fi·ca′tion,** *n.*

Ed·in·burgh (ed′′n bûr′ō), *n.* the capital of Scotland, in the southeastern part.

Ed·i·son, Thomas A. (ed′i s′n), 1847–1931; U.S. inventor of many things.

ed·it (ed′it), *v.* **1.** to get a piece of writing ready to be published, by arranging, correcting, or changing the material. **2.** to be in charge of a newspaper, magazine, etc. and decide what is to be printed in it.

e·di·tion (i dish′ən), *n.* **1.** the size or form in which a book is published [a pocket *edition* of a novel]. **2.** all the copies of a book, newspaper, etc. printed at about the same time; also, any one of these copies [the first *edition* of a book].

ed·i·tor (ed′i tər), *n.* **1.** a person who edits. **2.** a person who writes editorials.

ed·i·to·ri·al (ed′ə tôr′i əl), *adj.* of or by an editor [*editorial* offices]. —*n.* an article, as in a newspaper or magazine, that openly states the opinion of the editor or publisher. —**ed′i·to′ri·al·ly,** *adv.*

ed·u·cate (ej′oo kāt′), *v.* to teach or train a person, especially in a school or college; develop the mind of. —**ed′u·cat′ed,** *p.t. & p.p.;* **ed′u·cat′ing,** *pr.p.*

ed·u·ca·tion (ej′oo kā′shən), *n.* **1.** the act or work of educating or training people; teaching [He is seeking a career in *education*.] **2.** the things a person learns by being taught; schooling or training [a high-school *education*].

ed·u·ca·tion·al (ej′oo kā′shən ′l), *adj.* **1.** having to do with education [an *educational* society]. **2.** that teaches something worth-while [an *educational* television program]. —**ed′u·ca′tion·al·ly,** *adv.*

ed·u·ca·tor (ej′oo kā′tər), *n.* **1.** a teacher. **2.** a person who trains others to be teachers.

-ee (ē), a suffix meaning: **1.** a person to whom something is given or done [An *appointee* is a person who is appointed.] **2.** a person in a particular condition [An *employee* is a person in the employ of another.] **3.** a person or thing connected in some way [A *goatee* is connected with a goat's beard in looks.]

eel (ēl), *n.* a fish that has a long, slippery body and looks like a snake.

e'en (ēn), *adv.* even: *used in poetry.*

e'er (er), *adv.* ever: *used in poetry.*

-eer (ir), a suffix meaning: **1.** a person who has something to do with [An *auctioneer* is in charge of auctions. A *profiteer* makes unfair profits.] **2.** to do something in connection with [To *electioneer* is to campaign in an election.]

eel (2 ft. long)

ee·rie *or* **ee·ry** (ir′ē), *adj.* giving one a feeling of fear or mystery; weird [*eerie* sounds in the dark]. —**ee′ri·er,** *compar.;* **ee′ri·est,** *superl.*

ef·face (i fās′), *v.* **1.** to get rid of, as by marking off or rubbing out; erase; wipe out [The date on the old coin was *effaced*. Time *effaces* many memories.] **2.** to keep oneself from being noticed; stay in the background. —**ef·faced′,** *p.t. & p.p.;* **ef·fac′ing,** *pr.p.*

ef·fect (ə fekt′), *n.* **1.** anything that is caused by some other thing; result [Late hours have a bad *effect* on children.] **2.** the power to bring about results; influence [What is the *effect* of aspirin on a headache? Scolding has no *effect* on him.] **3.** an impression made on the mind [The artist created a clever *effect* through his use of color.] **4. effects,** *pl.* goods or belongings [All his personal *effects* were in a single trunk.] —*v.* to make happen; bring about [The new manager *effected* many changes in the office.] —**give effect to,** to put into action. —**in effect, 1.** really; in fact. **2.** in force or operation, as a law. —**of no effect,** having no results. —**take effect,** to begin to have results.

ef·fec·tive (ə fek′tiv), *adj.* **1.** making a certain thing happen; especially, bringing about the result wanted [an *effective* remedy]. **2.** in force or operation; active [The law becomes *effective* Monday.] **3.** making a strong impression on the mind; impressive [an *effective* speaker]. —**ef·fec′tive·ly,** *adv.* —**ef·fec′tive·ness,** *n.*

ef·fec·tu·al (ə fek′chōo əl), *adj.* that brings or can bring the result that is wanted [an *effectual* cure; an *effectual* plan]. —**ef·fec′tu·al·ly,** *adv.*

ef·fem·i·nate (ə fem′ə nit), *adj.* having the looks or ways of a woman; not manly; weak, soft, etc. —**ef·fem·i·na·cy** (ə fem′ə nə sē), *n.*

ef·fer·vesce (ef ər ves′), *v.* **1.** to give off bubbles as soda water does; bubble up. **2.** to be lively, sparkling, and gay. —**ef·fer·vesced′,** *p.t. & p.p.;* **ef·fer·vesc′ing,** *pr.p.* —**ef·fer·ves′cence,** *n.* —**ef·fer·ves′cent,** *adj.*

ef·fete (e fēt′), *adj.* no longer strong and vigorous; exhausted; worn out [the *effete* culture of Rome in Nero's time].

ef·fi·ca·cious (ef′ə kā′shəs), *adj.* that brings about the result wanted; effective. —**ef·fi·ca′cious·ly,** *adv.*

ef·fi·ca·cy (ef′i kə sē), *n.* the power to bring about the result wanted; effectiveness.

ef·fi·cient (i fish′ənt), *adj.* bringing about the result wanted with the least waste of time, effort, or materials [an *efficient* method of production; an *efficient* secretary]. —**ef·fi′cien·cy,** *n.* —**ef·fi′cient·ly,** *adv.*

ef·fi·gy (ef′ə jē), *n.* a statue or other image of a person; often, a crude figure of a person who is hated [The angry crowd burned the king in *effigy*.] —**ef′fi·gies,** *pl.*

ef·fort (ef′ərt), *n.* **1.** the using of energy to get something done; a trying hard with the mind or body [It took great *effort* to row to shore.] **2.** a try or attempt [He made no *effort* to be friendly.] **3.** something done with effort [Her early *efforts* at poetry were never published.]

ef·fort·less (ef′ərt lis), *adj.* using or seeming to use very little effort [an *effortless* swing at the ball]. —**ef′fort·less·ly,** *adv.*

ef·fron·ter·y (e frun′tər ē), *n.* boldness that shows no shame; audacity [After losing my baseball, Jack had the *effrontery* to ask me for another.]

ef·ful·gence (e ful′jəns), *n.* shining brightness; radiance; brilliance. —**ef·ful′gent,** *adj.*

ef·fu·sion (e fyōo′zhən), *n.* **1.** a pouring forth of a liquid. **2.** a pouring out of feeling, words, etc. [an *effusion* of joy].

ef·fu·sive (e fyōo′siv), *adj.* overflowing with words or feeling; gushing [*Effusive* praise seldom seems sincere.] —**ef·fu′sive·ly,** *adv.*

eft (eft), *n.* a newt or small lizard.

e.g., for example: *e.g.* is the abbreviation of *exempli gratia,* Latin for "for example."

egg (eg), *n.* **1.** the oval or round body that is laid by a female bird, fish, reptile, insect, etc.

effervescing soda water

and from which a young bird, fish, etc. is later hatched. It is covered by a brittle shell or tough skin. **2.** the cell formed by a female, that will make a new plant or animal of the same kind if it is fertilized; ovum. **3.** a hen's egg, raw or cooked.

egg (eg), *v.* to urge to do something; incite [The boys *egged* Fred on to climb the tree.]

egg·nog (eg′näg), *n.* a drink made of beaten eggs, milk, sugar, and, often, whisky or wine.

egg·plant (eg′plant), *n.* **1.** a large vegetable shaped like a pear and covered with a purple skin. **2.** the plant that it grows on.

egg·shell (eg′shel), *n.* the thin shell covering a bird's egg. —*adj.* yellowish-white.

e·gis (ē′jis), *n.* same as **aegis.**

eg·lan·tine (eg′lən tīn), *n.* a wild rose that has pink flowers and a prickly stem; sweetbrier.

eggplant

e·go (ē′gō), *n.* a person as he is aware of himself; the self. —**e′gos,** *pl.*

e·go·ism (ē′gō iz′m), *n.* **1.** a thinking mainly of oneself and of one's own interests; selfishness. **2.** same as **egotism.** —**e′go·ist,** *n.*

e·go·tism (ē′gə tiz′m), *n.* **1.** a thinking or talking about oneself too much; also, too high an opinion of oneself; conceit. **2.** same as **egoism.** —**e′go·tist,** *n.* —**e′go·tis′tic** or **e′go·tis′ti·cal,** *adj.*

e·gre·gious (i grē′jəs), *adj.* standing out sharply as wrong or bad [*egregious* errors].

e·gress (ē′gres), *n.* **1.** a going out [The blockade prevented the *egress* of ships from the harbor.] **2.** a way to go out; exit.

e·gret (ē′gret), *n.* **1.** a kind of heron that has long white plumes. **2.** such a plume, often used in women's hats: usually **aigrette.**

E·gypt (ē′jipt), *n.* a country in northeastern Africa on the Mediterranean and Red seas: now officially called **United Arab Republic.**

E·gyp·tian (i jip′shən), *adj.* of Egypt, its people, or their culture. —*n.* **1.** a person born or living in Egypt. **2.** the language of the ancient Egyptians: modern Egyptians speak Arabic.

egret (2 ft. high)

eh (ā), *interj.* a sound made to show doubt or surprise. It often means "What did you say?" or "Don't you agree?"

ei·der (ī′dər), *n.* **1.** a large sea duck of the northern regions. **2.** short for **eider down.**

eider down, 1. the soft breast feathers, or down, of eiders, used for stuffing quilts and pillows. **2.** a quilt stuffed with this.

eight (āt), *n. & adj.* one more than seven; the number 8.

eight·een (ā'tēn'), *n. & adj.* eight more than ten; the number 18.

eight·eenth (ā'tēnth'), *adj.* coming after seventeen others; 18th in order. —*n.* **1.** the eighteenth one. **2.** one of eighteen equal parts of something; 1/18.

eighth (ātth), *adj.* coming after seven others; 8th in order. —*n.* **1.** the eighth one. **2.** one of eight equal parts of something; 1/8.

eighth note, a note in music that is held for one eighth as long a time as a whole note.

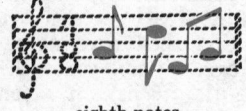

eighth notes

eight·i·eth (ā'tē ith), *adj.* coming after seventy-nine others; 80th in order. —*n.* **1.** the eightieth one. **2.** one of eighty equal parts of something; 1/80.

eight·y (ā'tē), *n. & adj.* **1.** eight times ten; the number 80. **2. eighties,** *n.pl.* the numbers or years from 80 to 89.

Ein·stein, Albert (īn'stīn), 1879–1955; famous scientist who was born in Germany and became a U.S. citizen.

Eir·e (er'ə), *n.* an earlier name of the Republic of Ireland: see **Ireland.**

Ei·sen·how·er, Dwight D. (dwīt ī'z'n hou'-ər), 1890–1969; 34th president of the United States, from 1953 to 1961.

ei·ther (ē'thər or ī'thər), *adj.* **1.** one or the other of the two [I can paint with *either* hand.] **2.** both one and the other; each [He had a tool in *either* hand.] —*pron.* one or the other of two [*Either* of the suits will fit you.] —*conj.* according to the first of two choices: *a word used to show a choice between two things joined by* or [*Either* come with me or stay home.] —*adv.* any more than the other; also [If she doesn't go, he won't *either*.]

e·jac·u·late (i jak'yoo lāt), *v.* to say suddenly and loudly; cry out; exclaim. —**e·jac'u·lat·ed,** *p.t. & p.p.;* **e·jac'u·lat·ing,** *pr.p.* —**e·jac'u·la'tion,** *n.*

e·ject (i jekt'), *v.* to force out; throw out; expel [The chimney *ejects* smoke. The heckler was *ejected* from the meeting.] —**e·jec'tion,** *n.*

eke (ēk), *v.* **1.** to be barely able to get or make: *used with* out [to *eke* out a living]. **2.** to add to so as to have enough: *used with* out [She *eked* out her income by taking in washing.] —**eked,** *p.t. & p.p.;* **ek'ing,** *pr.p.*

e·lab·o·rate (i lab'ər it), *adj.* worked out in a very careful way, with many details; complicated [an *elaborate* plan; an *elaborate* costume]. —*v.* (i lab'ə rāt), **1.** to work out in a very careful and detailed way [to *elaborate* a theory]. **2.** to give more details [The reporters asked the President to *elaborate* on his statement.]—**e·lab'-o·rat·ed,** *p.t. & p.p.;* **e·lab'o·rat·ing,** *pr.p.* —**e·lab'o·ra'tion,** *n.*

e·lapse (i laps'), *v.* to slip by; pass by, as time does [An hour *elapsed* before his return.] —**e·lapsed',** *p.t. & p.p.;* **e·laps'ing,** *pr.p.*

e·las·tic (i las'tik), *adj.* **1.** able to spring back into shape or position after being stretched or squeezed; springy [Rubber, coil springs, etc. are *elastic*.] **2.** that can be easily changed to fit conditions; adaptable [*elastic* rules]. —*n.* any cloth or tape with rubber threads running through it to make it elastic. —**e·las'ti·cal·ly,** *adv.*

e·las·tic·i·ty (i las'tis'ə tē), *n.* the condition of being elastic.

e·late (i lāt'), *v.* to make very proud, happy, or joyful [We're all *elated* by her success.] —**e·lat'-ed,** *p.t. & p.p.;* **e·lat'ing,** *pr.p.*

e·la·tion (i lā'shən), *n.* a feeling of great joy or pride; high spirits.

El·ba (el'bə), *n.* an Italian island between Corsica and Italy. Napoleon was exiled on it from 1814 to 1815.

El·be (el'bə), *n.* a river flowing from Czechoslovakia through Germany into the North Sea.

el·bow (el'bō), *n.* **1.** the joint where the forearm and upper arm meet; the outer part of the angle made by bending the arm. **2.** anything bent like an elbow, as a pipe used in plumbing. —*v.* to push or shove as with the elbows.

elbow grease, hard work or effort: *used only in everyday talk.*

el·bow·room (el'bō rōōm'), *n.* enough room to move around in or work in.

eld·er (el'dər), *adj.* older [Which of you is the *elder* son?] —*n.* **1.** an older person [We can learn much from our *elders*.] **2.** any of certain church officials.

el·der (el'dər), *n.* elderberry (*in meaning 1*).

el·der·ber·ry (el'dər ber'ē), *n.* **1.** a shrub or small tree with white flowers and black or red berries. **2.** its berry. —**el'der·ber'ries,** *pl.*

eld·er·ly (el'dər lē), *adj.* rather old.

eld·est (el'dist), *adj. & n.* oldest.

El Do·ra·do or **El·do·ra·do** (el'də rä'dō), *n.* an imaginary place that is supposed to be filled with wealth. Early Spanish explorers in America were seeking such a place.

e·lect (i lekt'), *v.* **1.** to choose for some office by voting [to *elect* a student council]. **2.** to choose or decide [He *elected* to go.] —*adj.* elected but not yet holding office [the president-*elect*]. —**the elect,** persons belonging to a group that has special privileges.

e·lec·tion (i lek'shən), *n.* a choosing or being chosen, especially by voting.

e·lec·tion·eer (i lek'shən ir'), *v.* to try to get people to vote for a candidate, etc.

e·lec·tive (i lek'tiv), *adj.* **1.** filled by election [The presidency is an *elective* office.] **2.** chosen by vote; elected [Some judges are *elective* officials and some are appointed.] **3.** that may be chosen but need not be [Music and art are usually *elective* subjects in high school.] —*n.* an elective subject in a school or college.

e·lec·tor (i lek'tər), *n.* **1.** a person who has the right to vote in an election. **2.** a member of the electoral college. —**e·lec'tor·al,** *adj.*

electoral college, a group of persons elected by the voters to choose the president and vice-president of the United States. Each elector is expected to vote for the candidates who won the election in his State.

e·lec·tor·ate (i lek′tər it), *n.* all the persons who have the right to vote in an election.

e·lec·tric (i lek′trik), *adj.* **1.** of or having to do with electricity [*electric* current; *electric* wire]. **2.** making or made by electricity [an *electric* generator; *electric* lighting]. **3.** worked by electricity [an *electric* iron]. **4.** very tense or exciting [an *electric* situation].

e·lec·tri·cal (i lek′tri k′l), *adj.* **1.** same as **electric. 2.** having to do with the science of electricity [an *electrical* engineer].

e·lec·tri·cal·ly (i lek′tri k′l ē), *adv.* by the use of electricity.

electric eye, a device that sends out an electric current as long as light falls on it. When the light is cut off, some action takes place, such as the opening of a door or the sounding of a burglar alarm.

e·lec·tri·cian (i lek′trish′ən), *n.* a person whose work is setting up or repairing electrical equipment or electrical machinery.

e·lec·tric·i·ty (i lek′tris′ə tē), *n.* a form of energy produced by friction (as by rubbing wax with wool), by chemical action (as in a storage battery), or by induction (as in a dynamo or generator). Electricity is used to produce light, heat, power, etc. When electricity moves in a stream, as through a wire, it is also called **electric current.**

e·lec·tri·fy (i lek′trə fī), *v.* **1.** to charge with electricity. **2.** to bring the use of electric power into [Most farms have now been *electrified.*] **3.** to give a shock of excitement to; thrill [The good news *electrified* the students.] —**e·lec′tri·fied,** *p.t. & p.p.;* **e·lec′tri·fy·ing,** *prp.* —**e·lec′tri·fi·ca′tion,** *n.*

electro-, a prefix meaning: **1.** electric [An *electro*magnet is an electric magnet.] **2.** electricity [To *electro*cute is to execute by electricity.]

e·lec·tro·cute (i lek′trə kyoot), *v.* to kill by electricity, as through accident or in carrying out a death sentence by law. —**e·lec′tro·cut·ed,** *p.t. & p.p.;* **e·lec′tro·cut·ing,** *prp.* —**e·lec′tro·cu′tion,** *n.*

e·lec·trode (i lek′trōd), *n.* either of the two terminals (one positive, the other negative) in an electric battery, electron tube, etc. Some electron tubes have extra electrodes called grids.

e·lec·trol·y·sis (i lek′träl′ə sis), *n.* the breaking up of a dissolved chemical compound into its parts by passing an electric current through it [When copper sulfate is broken up by *electrolysis,* the copper is deposited on a piece of metal, which becomes copper-plated.]

e·lec·tro·lyte (i lek′trə līt), *n.* any dissolved compound that can carry an electric current and be broken up into its parts by the current.

e·lec·tro·lyt·ic (i lek′trə lit′ik), *adj.*

e·lec·tro·mag·net (i lek′trō mag′nit), *n.* a piece of soft iron with a coil of wire around it, that becomes a magnet when an electric current passes through the wire. —**e·lec·tro·mag·net·ic** (i lek′trō mag net′ik), *adj.*

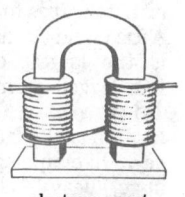
electromagnet

e·lec·tro·mo·tive (i lek′trə mō′tiv), *adj.* producing an electric current.

e·lec·tron (i lek′trän), *n.* any of the particles with a negative electric charge that move around the nucleus of an atom. See also **proton.**

e·lec·tron·ic (i lek′trän′ik), *adj.* **1.** of electrons. **2.** working or produced by the action of electrons.

e·lec·tron·ics (i lek′trän′iks), *n.pl.* the science dealing with the action of electrons and with the uses of electronic devices in radio, television, radar, etc.: *used with a singular verb.*

electron tube, a sealed glass or metal container with two or more electrodes and a gas or a vacuum inside through which electrons can flow: also called **vacuum tube** or **tube.** Electron tubes are used in radio and television sets and in electronic equipment.

e·lec·tro·plate (i lek′trə plāt), *v.* to put a coating of silver, copper, nickel, etc. on by electrolysis. —**e·lec′tro·plat·ed,** *p.t. & p.p.;* **e·lec′tro·plat·ing,** *prp.*

e·lec·tro·type (i lek′trə tīp), *n.* a printing plate made by electroplating a wax mold of the original page of type, of an engraving, etc.

el·e·gant (el′ə gənt), *adj.* **1.** rich-looking and attractive in a dignified or refined way [an *elegant* dress]. **2.** showing good taste, politeness, etc. [*elegant* manners]. —**el′e·gance,** *n.*

el·e·gy (el′ə jē), *n.* a serious or sad poem, usually honoring a dead person. —**el′e·gies,** *pl.*

el·e·ment (el′ə mənt), *n.* **1.** any of the parts or qualities of a thing, especially a necessary or basic part [The story has an *element* of suspense. Have you learned the *elements* of grammar?] **2.** any substance that cannot be broken down into different substances except by splitting its atom. All matter is made up of such chemical elements, of which there are more than 100, including carbon, oxygen, iron, sulfur, uranium, etc. **3.** the part of an electrical device that does the work [the heating *element* of an iron]. —**in one's element,** in a condition or situation that fits or pleases one. —**the elements,** wind, rain, and the other forces of nature that make the weather. —**el·e·men·tal** (el′ə men′t′l), *adj.*

el·e·men·ta·ry (el′ə men′tər ē), *adj.* having to do with the first or simplest things to be learned about something; basic [*elementary* arithmetic].

elementary school, a school of the first six grades (sometimes, first eight grades), where basic subjects are taught.

fat, āpe, cär, ten, ēven, hit, bīte, gō, hôrn, tool, book, up, fûr; get, joy, yet, chin, she, thin, *th*en; zh = s in pleasure; ′ as in able (ā′b′l); ə = a in ago, e in agent, i in sanity, o in confess, u in focus.

el·e·phant (el'ə fənt), *n.* a huge animal with a thick skin, two ivory tusks, and a long snout, or trunk. It is found in Africa and India and is the largest of the four-legged animals.

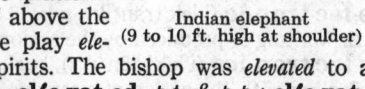

Indian elephant
(9 to 10 ft. high at shoulder)

el·e·phan·tine (el'ə-fan'tēn *or* el'ə fan'tīn), *adj.* like an elephant; huge, heavy, clumsy, etc.

el·e·vate (el'ə vāt), *v.* to lift up; raise; make higher [The platform was *elevated* above the ground. The play *elevated* our spirits. The bishop was *elevated* to a cardinal.] —**el'e·vat·ed**, *p.t. & p.p.*; **el'e·vat·ing**, *pr.p.*

el·e·va·tion (el'ə vā'shən), *n.* **1.** an elevating or being elevated. **2.** a high place or position [We set up our tent on an *elevation* of the ground.] **3.** height above the surface of the earth or above sea level [Mt. McKinley has an *elevation* of 20,300 ft.]

el·e·va·tor (el'ə vā'tər), *n.* **1.** a platform or cage for carrying people and things up and down in a building, mine, etc. It is attached by cables to a machine that moves it. **2.** a building for storing grain. **3.** a part of the tail of an airplane that can be moved to make the airplane go up or down.

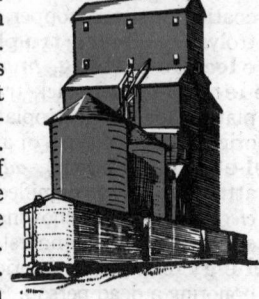

grain elevator

e·lev·en (i lev'n), *n. & adj.* one more than ten; the number 11.

e·lev·enth (i lev'nth), *adj.* coming after ten others; 11th in order. —*n.* **1.** the eleventh one. **2.** one of the eleven equal parts of something; 1/11.

elf (elf), *n.* a small fairy in folk tales, often one that is full of mischief; sprite. —**elves**, *pl.*

elf·in (el'fin), *adj.* of or like an elf; full of strange charm [*elfin* laughter]. —*n.* an elf.

elf·ish (el'fish), *adj.* like an elf; full of mischief; impish [*elfish* pranks].

e·lic·it (i lis'it), *v.* to draw out; bring forth [His jokes *elicited* laughter.]

el·i·gi·ble (el'i jə b'l), *adj.* having the proper qualities; considered fit to be chosen; qualified [Only juniors and seniors are *eligible* to hold office in student council.] —**el'i·gi·bil'i·ty**, *n.*

E·li·jah (i lī'jə), *n.* in the Bible, a Hebrew prophet of the 9th century B.C.

e·lim·i·nate (i lim'ə nāt), *v.* to get rid of; take out or leave out; remove or omit [a building program to *eliminate* slums; to *eliminate* waste matter from the body]. —**e·lim'i·nat·ed**, *p.t. & p.p.*; **e·lim'i·nat·ing**, *pr.p.* —**e·lim'i·na'·tion**, *n.*

e·lite or **é·lite** (i lēt' *or* ā lēt'), *n.* the group thought of as being the finest or best [the *elite* of society].

e·lix·ir (i lik'sər), *n.* **1.** a substance for turning cheap metals into gold, or one for keeping people alive forever, that alchemists of the Middle Ages kept trying to find. **2.** a medicine made of drugs mixed with alcohol and usually sweetened.

E·liz·a·beth I (i liz'ə bəth), 1533–1603; queen of England from 1558 to 1603.

Elizabeth II, born in 1926; queen of England since 1952.

E·liz·a·be·than (i liz'ə bē'thən), *adj.* of the time when Elizabeth I was queen of England. —*n.* an English person, especially a writer, of this time.

elk (elk), *n.* **1.** a large deer of North America with branching antlers; the wapiti. **2.** a large deer of northern Europe and Asia that looks like a moose. —**elk** or **elks,** *pl.*

elk (5 ft. high at shoulder)

ell (el), *n.* an old measure of length that was equal to 45 inches in England.

el·lipse (i lips'), *n.* a closed curve that is shaped like an egg, but with equal ends; perfect oval.

el·lip·ti·cal (i lip'ti k'l) or **el·lip·tic** (i lip'tik), *adj.* shaped like an ellipse; oval.

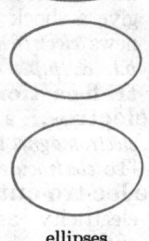

ellipses

elm (elm), *n.* **1.** a tall shade tree with spreading branches. **2.** its hard wood.

el·o·cu·tion (el'ə kyōo'shən), *n.* a style of giving talks or readings in public, especially an older style now thought of as showy and not natural. —**el'o·cu'tion·ist,** *n.*

e·lon·gate (i lông'gāt), *v.* to make or become longer; lengthen. —**e·lon'gat·ed,** *p.t. & p.p.*; **e·lon'gat·ing,** *pr.p.* —**e·lon'ga'tion,** *n.*

e·lope (i lōp'), *v.* to run away secretly in order to get married. —**e·loped',** *p.t. & p.p.*; **e·lop'ing,** *pr.p.* —**e·lope'ment,** *n.*

el·o·quence (el'ə kwəns), *n.* strong, graceful speech or writing that can stir people's feelings or influence their thinking.

el·o·quent (el'ə kwənt), *adj.* **1.** having eloquence; stirring people's feelings or influencing their thinking [an *eloquent* plea to a jury]. **2.** expressing much feeling [He gave an *eloquent* sigh.] —**el'o·quent·ly,** *adv.*

El Pas·o (el pas'ō), a city in northwestern Texas, on the Rio Grande.

El Sal·va·dor (el sal'və dôr), a country in western Central America.

else (els), *adj.* **1.** not the same; different; other [I thought you were someone *else*.] **2.** that may be added; more [Do you want anything *else*?] *The adjective* else *comes after the word it describes.* —*adv.* **1.** in a different time, place, or way [Where *else* did you go?] **2.** if not; otherwise [You tell him or *else* I will.]

else·where (els′hwer), *adv.* in, at, or to some other place; somewhere else.

e·lu·ci·date (i lōō′sə dāt), *v.* to make clear; explain. —**e·lu′ci·dat·ed,** *p.t.* & *p.p.;* **e·lu′ci·dat·ing,** *pr.p.* —**e·lu′ci·da′tion,** *n.*

e·lude (i lōōd′), *v.* **1.** to escape or get away from by being quick or clever; evade [The convict *eluded* the police for a week.] **2.** to keep from being seen or understood by; puzzle [The point you are trying to make *eludes* me.] —**e·lud′ed,** *p.t.* & *p.p.;* **e·lud′ing,** *pr.p.*

e·lu·sive (i lōō′siv), *adj.* **1.** that keeps eluding or escaping [an *elusive* criminal]. **2.** hard to understand or keep clearly in mind; puzzling [a strange, *elusive* tune].

elves (elvz), *n.* the plural of **elf.**

E·ly·sian (i lizh′ən), *adj.* of or like Elysium; happy; blissful; delightful.

E·ly·si·um (i lizh′i əm *or* i liz′i əm), *n.* **1.** the place in Greek myths where good people went after death. **2.** any place or condition of complete happiness.

'em (əm), *pron.* them: *used only in everyday talk.*

em-, the same as the prefix **en-:** used before *p, b,* or *m,* as in *empower* or *embrace.*

e·ma·ci·ate (i mā′shi āt), *v.* to make very thin; make lose much weight [He was *emaciated* after his long illness.] —**e·ma′ci·at·ed,** *p.t.* & *p.p.;* **e·ma′ci·at·ing,** *pr.p.* —**e·ma′ci·a′tion,** *n.*

em·a·nate (em′ə nāt), *v.* to come out; proceed; issue [A faint smell *emanated* from the kitchen. The order *emanated* from headquarters.] —**em′a·nat·ed,** *p.t.* & *p.p.;* **em′a·nat·ing,** *pr.p.* —**em′a·na′tion,** *n.*

e·man·ci·pate (i man′sə pāt), *v.* to set free from slavery or strict control [Lincoln *emancipated* the Negro slaves.] —**e·man′ci·pat·ed,** *p.t.* & *p.p.;* **e·man′ci·pat·ing,** *pr.p.* —**e·man′ci·pa′tion,** *n.* —**e·man′ci·pa·tor,** *n.*

e·mas·cu·late (i mas′kyoo lāt), *v.* **1.** to remove the male sex glands of. **2.** to take out the force or strength of [The law against gambling was *emasculated* by lowering the fine.] —**e·mas′cu·lat·ed,** *p.t.* & *p.p.;* **e·mas′cu·lat·ing,** *pr.p.* —**e·mas′cu·la′tion,** *n.*

em·balm (im bäm′), *v.* to treat a dead body with chemicals in order to keep it from decaying rapidly.

em·bank·ment (im bangk′mənt), *n.* a long mound or wall of earth, stone, etc. used to keep back water, hold up a roadway, etc.

em·bar·go (im bär′gō), *n.* **1.** a government order that forbids certain ships to leave or enter its ports. **2.** any government order that stops or hinders trade. —*v.* to put an embargo on.

—**em·bar′goes,** *pl.* —**em·bar′goed,** *p.t.* & *p.p.;* **em·bar′go·ing,** *pr.p.*

em·bark (im bärk′), *v.* **1.** to go on board a ship or put on a ship [We *embarked* at San Francisco for Japan.] **2.** to start out; begin [to *embark* on an adventure]. —**em·bar·ka·tion** (em′bär kā′shən), *n.*

em·bar·rass (im bar′əs), *v.* **1.** to make feel uncomfortable, confused, or self-conscious [Nancy is always *embarrassed* when someone pays her a compliment.] **2.** to bring into trouble; hinder or worry [to be financially *embarrassed*].

em·bar·rass·ment (im bar′əs mənt), *n.* **1.** an embarrassing or being embarrassed. **2.** something that embarrasses.

em·bas·sy (em′bə sē), *n.* **1.** the building where an ambassador lives and works. **2.** an ambassador together with his staff. **3.** the work or mission of an ambassador, or any important mission or errand. —**em′bas·sies,** *pl.*

em·bat·tled (em bat′'ld), *adj.* in position for battle; ready to fight.

em·bed (im bed′), *v.* to set firmly in some substance [to *embed* tiles in cement]. —**em·bed′ded,** *p.t.* & *p.p.;* **em·bed′ding,** *pr.p.*

em·bel·lish (im bel′ish), *v.* to decorate or improve by adding something [to *embellish* a talk with details]. —**em·bel′lish·ment,** *n.*

em·ber (em′bər), *n.* a piece of coal, wood, etc. still glowing in the ashes of a fire.

em·bez·zle (im bez′'l), *v.* to steal money that has been placed in one's care [The bank teller *embezzled* $20,000.] —**em·bez′zled,** *p.t.* & *p.p.;* **em·bez′zling,** *pr.p.* —**em·bez′zle·ment,** *n.* —**em·bez′zler,** *n.*

em·bit·ter (im bit′ər), *v.* to make bitter; make feel angry or hurt [*embittered* by his failure].

em·bla·zon (em blā′z'n), *v.* **1.** to decorate with bright colors or in a rich, showy way [The bandstand was *emblazoned* with flags and bunting.] **2.** to mark with an emblem [His shield was *emblazoned* with a golden lion.] **3.** to praise widely; celebrate [deeds *emblazoned* in legend].

em·blem (em′bləm), *n.* a thing that stands for another thing or for an idea; sign or symbol [The bald eagle is the *emblem* of the U.S.]

em·blem·at·ic (em′blə mat′ik), *adj.* being an emblem; symbolic [The color green is *emblematic* of Irish nationalism.]

em·bod·y (im bäd′ē), *v.* **1.** to put an idea or quality into a definite form that can be seen; make real in any way [The Constitution *embodies* Jefferson's ideas on government.] **2.** to bring together in a single thing or system [The laws of a State are *embodied* in its legal code.] **3.** to make part of some thing or system; incorporate [The latest findings are *embodied* in his new book.] —**em·bod′ied,** *p.t.* & *p.p.;* **em·bod′y·ing,** *pr.p.* —**em·bod′i·ment,** *n.*

em·bold·en (im bōl′d'n), *v.* to make bold or bolder; give courage to.

---

fat, āpe, cär, ten, ēven, hit, bīte, gō, hôrn, tool, book, up, fur; get, joy, yet, chin, she, thin, *th*en; zh = s in pleasure; ′ as in able (ā′b'l); ə = a in ago, e in agent, i in sanity, o in confess, u in focus.

em·bo·lism (em′bə liz′m), *n.* the stopping up of a vein or artery, as by a blood clot.

em·bos·om (em booz′əm), *v.* **1.** to take to one's bosom; cherish. **2.** to surround and shelter.

em·boss (im bôs′), *v.* **1.** to decorate with patterns that stand out from the surface [wallpaper *embossed* with a leaf design]. **2.** to make stand out from the surface [Lincoln's head is *embossed* on the penny.]

em·bow·er (em bou′ər), *v.* to shelter or cover with leafy boughs or vines.

em·brace (im brās′), *v.* **1.** to hold closely in one's arms in showing fondness or love; hug [The groom *embraced* his bride.] **2.** to take up in an eager or serious way [to *embrace* a religion, an idea, a career, etc.]. **3.** to surround or close in [a coral isle *embraced* by the sea]. **4.** to include or contain [Biology *embraces* both botany and zoology.] —*n.* an embracing; a hug. —**em·braced′,** *p.t. & p.p.;* **em·brac′ing,** *pr.p.*

em·broi·der (im broi′dər), *v.* **1.** to make fancy designs on cloth with needlework [She *embroidered* roses on her blouse.] **2.** to add imaginary details to a story to make it more interesting.

em·broi·der·y (im broi′dər ē), *n.* **1.** the art or work of embroidering. **2.** an embroidered decoration. —**em·broi′der·ies,** *pl.*

em·broil (em broil′), *v.* to draw into a quarrel or fight; involve [The slavery question soon *embroiled* the States in a civil war.]

embroidery

em·bry·o (em′bri ō), *n.* **1.** an animal in the first stages of its growth, while it is in the egg or in the womb. **2.** the part of a seed from which a plant develops. **3.** an early stage of development [Our vacation plans are still in *embryo.*] —**em′bry·os,** *pl.*

em·bry·on·ic (em′bri än′ik), *adj.* **1.** of an embryo. **2.** not fully developed [*embryonic* ideas].

e·mend (i mend′), *v.* to correct an error or fault, as in a piece of writing. —**e·men·da·tion** (ē′men dā′shən), *n.*

em·er·ald (em′ər əld), *n.* **1.** a clear, bright-green jewel. **2.** bright green.

e·merge (i mürj′), *v.* **1.** to come out so as to be seen; appear [A bear *emerged* from the woods.] **2.** to become known [The true story of his life *emerged* after his death.] —**e·merged′,** *p.t. & p.p.;* **e·merg′ing,** *pr.p.* —**e·mer·gence** (i mür′jəns), *n.*

e·mer·gen·cy (i mür′jən sē), *n.* a sudden happening that needs action or attention right away [the *emergency* created by a hurricane]. —**e·mer′gen·cies,** *pl.*

e·mer·i·tus (i mer′ə təs), *adj.* retired from work, but keeping one's rank as a special honor [professor *emeritus*]

Em·er·son, Ralph Wal·do (wôl′dō em′ər-s'n), 1803–1882; U.S. writer and philosopher.

em·er·y (em′ər ē), *n.* a dark, very hard mineral, crushed to a powder which is used on grinding wheels, polishing cloths, etc.

e·met·ic (i met′ik), *adj.* that makes one vomit. —*n.* a medicine that makes one vomit.

em·i·grant (em′ə grənt), *n.* one who emigrates.

em·i·grate (em′ə grāt), *v.* to leave one country or region to settle in another [Many people have *emigrated* from Ireland to the U.S.] —**em′i·grat·ed,** *p.t. & p.p.;* **em′i·grat·ing,** *pr.p.* —**em′i·gra′tion,** *n.*

em·i·nence (em′ə nəns), *n.* **1.** a place above most others in rank, worth, fame, etc.; greatness [Shakespeare's *eminence* in literature]. **2.** a high place, as a hill. **3. Eminence,** a title of honor for a cardinal in the Roman Catholic Church.

em·i·nent (em′ə nənt), *adj.* standing above most others in rank, worth, fame, etc.; very famous [an *eminent* poet]. —**em′i·nent·ly,** *adv.*

e·mir (ə mir′), *n.* **1.** an Arabian ruler or chieftain. **2.** a Moslem or Turkish title of honor.

em·is·sar·y (em′ə ser′ē), *n.* a person sent on some special errand; often, a secret agent. —**em′is·sar′ies,** *pl.*

e·mis·sion (i mish′ən), *n.* **1.** the act of emitting. **2.** something emitted; discharge.

e·mit (i mit′), *v.* to send out or give forth [The kettle *emitted* steam. The owl *emitted* a screech.] —**e·mit′ted,** *p.t. & p.p.;* **e·mit′-ting,** *pr.p.*

e·mol·u·ment (i mäl′yoo mənt), *n.* money received for work; salary, wages, or fees.

e·mo·tion (i mō′shən), *n.* **1.** strong feeling [a voice choked with *emotion*]. **2.** any particular feeling, such as love, hate, joy, or fear.

e·mo·tion·al (i mō′shən 'l), *adj.* **1.** of the emotions or feelings [*emotional* problems]. **2.** full of emotion or strong feeling [an *emotional* look; an *emotional* speech]. **3.** having feelings that are easily stirred; quick to cry, be angry, etc. [an *emotional* person]. —**e·mo′tion·al·ly,** *adv.*

em·pan·el (im pan′'l), *v.* same as **impanel.**

em·per·or (em′pər ər), *n.* a man who rules an empire.

em·pha·sis (em′fə sis), *n.* **1.** special attention given to something so as to make it stand out; importance; stress [That college puts too much *emphasis* on athletics.] **2.** special force given to certain syllables or words in speaking. —**em·pha·ses** (em′fə sēz), *pl.*

em·pha·size (em′fə sīz), *v.* to give special force or attention to; stress [I want to *emphasize* the importance of honesty.] —**em′pha·sized,** *p.t. & p.p.;* **em′pha·siz·ing,** *pr.p.*

em·phat·ic (im fat′ik), *adj.* **1.** said or done with emphasis, or special force [She agreed with an *emphatic* nod.] **2.** without doubt; definite [an *emphatic* defeat]. —**em·phat′i·cal·ly,** *adv.*

em·pire (em′pir), *n.* **1.** a government whose ruler has the title of emperor or empress. **2.** a group of countries or territories under the control of one government or ruler [Much of Europe was once a part of the Roman *Empire.*] **3.** complete power or rule.

em·pir·i·cal (em pir′i k′l), *adj.* based mainly on practical experience or on experiment and not on theory [*empirical* knowledge].

em·place·ment (im plās′mənt), *n.* the platform from which a heavy gun or cannon is fired.

em·ploy (im ploi′), *v.* **1.** to pay for the work or services of; have working for one; hire [This company *employs* fifty people.] **2.** to use [He *employed* clever tactics in his rise to power.] **3.** to keep busy; occupy [She needs something to *employ* her mind.] —*n.* the condition of being employed; a working for pay [He is no longer in our *employ*.]

em·ploy·ee or **em·ploy·e** (im ploi′ē or em′-ploi ē′), *n.* a person who works for another in return for pay.

em·ploy·er (im ploi′ər), *n.* a person or company for whom other people work for pay.

em·ploy·ment (im ploi′mənt), *n.* **1.** the condition of being employed; work. **2.** one's work, trade, or profession.

em·po·ri·um (em pôr′i əm), *n.* a large store that has many different things for sale. —**em·po′ri·ums** or **em·po·ri·a** (em pôr′i ə), *pl.*

em·pow·er (im pou′ər), *v.* to give certain power or rights to; authorize [The warrant *empowered* the police to search the house.]

em·press (em′pris), *n.* **1.** the wife of an emperor. **2.** a woman who rules an empire.

emp·ty (emp′tē), *adj.* **1.** having nothing or no one in it; not occupied; vacant [an *empty* jar; an *empty* house]. **2.** without real meaning or worth; vain [*empty* pleasures; *empty* promises]. —*v.* **1.** to make or become empty [The auditorium was *emptied* in ten minutes.] **2.** to take out or pour out [*Empty* the dirty water into the sink.] **3.** to flow out; discharge [The Nile *empties* into the Mediterranean.] —*n.* an empty bottle, box, freight car, etc. —**emp′ti·er,** *compar.*; **emp′-ti·est,** *superl.* —**emp′ties,** *pl.* —**emp′ti·ly,** *adv.* —**emp′ti·ness,** *n.*

em·pyr·e·al (em pir′i əl or em′pə rē′əl), *adj.* heavenly; celestial.

em·py·re·an (em′pə rē′ən), *n.* **1.** the highest heaven. **2.** the sky. —*adj.* empyreal.

e·mu (ē′myōō), *n.* a large Australian bird like the ostrich but smaller. Emus cannot fly.

em·u·late (em′yoo-lāt), *v.* to try to be as good as or better than [He will do well if he *emulates* his father.] —**em′u·lat·ed,** *p.t. & p.p.*; **em′u·lat·ing,** *pr.p.* —**em′u·la′tion,** *n.*

em·u·lous (em′yoo-ləs), *adj.* wanting to be as good as or better than another.

emu (6 ft. high)

e·mul·si·fy (i mul′sə fī), *v.* to form into an emulsion. —**e·mul′si·fied,** *p.t. & p.p.*; **e·mul′-si·fy·ing,** *pr.p.*

e·mul·sion (i mul′shən), *n.* a mixture of liquids, as oil and water, in which very fine drops of one stay evenly scattered throughout the other [Homogenized milk is an *emulsion*.]

en-, a prefix meaning: **1.** to put into or on [*Enthrone* means to put on a throne.] **2.** to make [*Enable* means to make able.] **3.** in or into [*Enclose* means to close in.] *En-* is often added to a word to make it stronger in meaning [*Enliven* means to liven very much.] Many words beginning with *en-* are also spelled *in-*.

-en (ən), a suffix meaning: **1.** to make or become [*Darken* means to make or become dark.] **2.** to get or give [*Strengthen* means to get or give strength.] **3.** made of [*Wooden* means made of wood.] The suffix *-en* is also used to form the past participle of some verbs (as *fallen*) and the plural of some nouns (as *oxen*).

en·a·ble (in ā′b′l), *v.* to make able; give the means or power to [A loan from his uncle *enabled* George to finish college.] —**en·a′bled,** *p.t. & p.p.*; **en·a′bling,** *pr.p.*

en·act (in akt′), *v.* **1.** to make into a law [Congress *enacted* a bill raising tariffs.] **2.** to act out, as in a play [to *enact* the part of a judge].

en·act·ment (in akt′mənt), *n.* **1.** an enacting of a law. **2.** a law.

en·am·el (i nam′′l), *n.* **1.** a glassy substance baked onto metal, etc., as in pans, sinks, stoves, or jewelry, to form a coating that protects or decorates. **2.** the hard, glossy coating of the teeth. **3.** a paint that leaves a hard, glossy surface when it dries. —*v.* to coat or decorate with enamel. —**en·am′eled** or **en·am′elled,** *p.t. & p.p.*; **en·am′el·ing** or **en·am′el·ling,** *pr.p.*

en·am·or or **en·am·our** (in am′ər), *v.* to fill with love; charm; captivate.

en·camp (in kamp′), *v.* to set up a camp [The army *encamped* in the valley.] —**en·camp′-ment,** *n.*

en·case (in kās′), *v.* **1.** to put into a case or cases. **2.** to cover completely [a turtle *encased* in its shell]. Also spelled **incase.** —**en·cased′,** *p.t. & p.p.*; **en·cas′ing,** *pr.p.*

-ence (əns), a suffix meaning "act," "condition," or "quality" [*Indulgence* is the act of indulging. *Excellence* is the condition or quality of being excellent.]

en·chant (in chant′), *v.* **1.** to cast a magic spell over; bewitch. **2.** to delight; charm greatly [I'm *enchanted* by his garden.] —**en·chant′er,** *n.* —**en·chant′ress,** *n.fem.* —**en·chant′-ing,** *adj.*

en·chant·ment (in chant′mənt), *n.* **1.** the act of enchanting, as by a magic spell. **2.** something that enchants. **3.** great delight or pleasure.

en·cir·cle (in sur′k′l), *v.* **1.** to form a circle around; surround [Hills *encircle* the valley.]

2. to move around, as in a circle [The earth *encircles* the sun.] **—en·cir′cled,** *p.t. & p.p.;* **en·cir′cling,** *pr.p.* **—en·cir′cle·ment,** *n.*

en·close (in klōz′), *v.* **1.** to shut in all around; surround [High walls *enclose* the garden.] **2.** to put inside a container, often along with something else [I *enclosed* a check in the envelope with my order.] Also spelled **inclose. —en·closed′,** *p.t. & p.p.;* **en·clos′ing,** *pr.p.*

en·clo·sure (in klō′zhər), *n.* **1.** the act of enclosing. **2.** a space that is enclosed. **3.** anything put into an envelope along with a letter. **4.** something that encloses, as a fence. Also spelled **inclosure.**

en·co·mi·um (en kō′mi əm), *n.* high praise, especially when given in a formal way.

en·com·pass (in kum′pəs), *v.* to surround on all sides; enclose or encircle.

en·core (äng′kôr), *interj.* again! once more!: a call by an audience to repeat a song, recitation, etc. or give an extra one. **—n.** a song, etc. added in answer to applause by an audience.

en·coun·ter (in koun′tər), *v.* **1.** to meet by chance or unexpectedly [He *encountered* a former classmate on his vacation.] **2.** to come up against [to *encounter* trouble]. **3.** to meet in battle. **—n. 1.** a meeting by chance. **2.** a battle or fight.

en·cour·age (in kur′ij), *v.* **1.** to give courage or hope to; make feel more confident [His praise *encouraged* me to go on with the project.] **2.** to give help to; aid; promote [Warm weather *encourages* the sale of ice cream.] **—en·cour′-aged,** *p.t. & p.p.;* **en·cour′ag·ing,** *pr.p.* **—en·cour′age·ment,** *n.*

en·croach (in krōch′), *v.* **1.** to go beyond the usual limits [The lake has *encroached* upon the shore line.] **2.** to push into the property or rights of another; trespass, especially in a gradual or sneaking way [Over the years, campers had been *encroaching* on the farmer's land.] **—en·croach′ment,** *n.*

en·crust (in krust′), *v.* **1.** to set into all parts of the surface of [a bracelet *encrusted* with diamonds]. **2.** to cover with a crust or layer [His shoes were *encrusted* with mud.] Also spelled **incrust. —en′crus·ta′tion,** *n.*

en·cum·ber (in kum′bər), *v.* **1.** to load down or burden so as to make it hard to move or act [a hiker *encumbered* with a heavy knapsack; a business *encumbered* with debt]. **2.** to fill up so as to block; obstruct [a hallway *encumbered* with furniture]. **—en·cum′brance,** *n.*

-en·cy (ən sē), a suffix, like **-ence,** meaning "act," "condition," or "quality" [*Efficiency* is the quality or condition of being efficient.]

en·cy·cli·cal (en sik′li k'l), *n.* a letter from the Pope to the bishops of the Roman Catholic Church.

en·cy·clo·pe·di·a or **en·cy·clo·pae·di·a** (in-sī′klə pē′di ə), *n.* a book or set of books that gives information on all branches of knowledge or, sometimes, on just one branch of knowledge. It is made up of articles in alphabetical order.

en·cy·clo·pe·dic or **en·cy·clo·pae·dic** (in-sī′klə pē′dik), *adj.* of or like an encyclopedia; having information on many subjects.

end (end), *n.* **1.** the last part; finish; conclusion [the *end* of a day; the *end* of a story]. **2.** the place where something begins or stops; farthest part [the north *end* of the town; the *end* of a rope]. **3.** death or destruction [He met his *end* in battle.] **4.** what one hopes to get or do; aim; goal [to achieve one's *ends*]. **5.** a piece left over; remnant [a sale of odds and *ends*]. **6.** the player at either end of a line in certain games, as in football. **—v.** to bring or come to an end; finish; stop. **—adj.** at the end; final [an *end* product]. **—at loose ends,** in an unsettled condition. **—end up,** to come to an end. **—make both ends meet,** to just manage to live on one's income.

en·dan·ger (in dān′jər), *v.* to put in danger; lay open to harm [to *endanger* one's life].

en·dear (in dir′), *v.* to make beloved or well liked [Her smile *endeared* her to us.]

en·dear·ment (in dir′mənt), *n.* **1.** an endearing. **2.** a word or act showing love or affection.

en·deav·or (in dev′ər), *v.* to try hard; make an effort; strive. **—n.** an effort or try.

en·dem·ic (en dem′ik), *adj.* widespread in a certain place or among a certain group of people [an *endemic* disease].

end·ing (en′ding), *n.* the last part; end; finish [The story had a happy *ending*.]

en·dive (en′dīv *or* än′dēv), *n.* a plant with ragged, curly leaves that are used in salads.

end·less (end′lis), *adj.* **1.** having no end; going on forever [*endless* space]. **2.** lasting too long; seeming never to end [her *endless* chatter]. **3.** with the ends joined to form a closed ring [an *endless* chain]. **—end′less·ly,** *adv.*

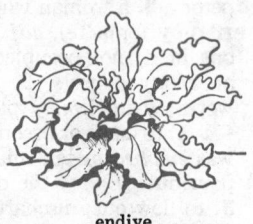
endive

en·do·crine gland (en′də krin), a gland whose secretion goes straight into the blood or lymph, which carries it to some part of the body where it has its effect [The thyroid, adrenal, and pituitary glands are *endocrine glands*.]

en·dorse (in dôrs′), *v.* **1.** to sign one's name on the back of a check, note, etc., as in order to cash it or pass it on to another person. **2.** to give support to; approve of; favor [The newspaper *endorsed* our candidate.] Also spelled **indorse. —en·dorsed′,** *p.t. & p.p.;* **en·dors′ing,** *pr.p.* **—en·dorse′ment,** *n.* **—en·dors′er,** *n.*

en·dow (in dou′), *v.* **1.** to provide with some quality or thing [a girl *endowed* with musical talent; a land *endowed* with natural resources]. **2.** to provide a gift of money to a college, hospital, museum, etc., that will bring a regular income to help support it. **—en·dow′ment,** *n.*

en·due (in dōō′ *or* in dyōō′), *v.* to give to someone, especially as a quality; endow [His fear *endued* him with strength.] Also spelled **indue. —en·dued′,** *p.t. & p.p.;* **en·du′ing,** *pr.p.*

en·dur·ance (in door′əns *or* in dyoor′əns), *n.* a being able to endure, last, or hold up under strain or suffering [Boxing takes *endurance*.]

en·dure (in door′ *or* in dyoor′), *v.* **1.** to hold

up under suffering; put up with; bear; stand [to *endure* pain; to *endure* insults]. **2.** to go on for a long time; last; remain [His fame will *endure* for ages.] —**en·dured′**, *p.t.* & *p.p.*; **en·dur′ing**, *pr.p.* —**en·dur′a·ble**, *adj.*

end·ways (end′wāz) or **end·wise** (end′wīz), *adv.* **1.** standing on end; upright. **2.** with the end forward [The boat came into the dock *endways.*] **3.** with the ends meeting; end to end.

en·e·ma (en′ə mə), *n.* a method of making the bowels move by bringing water or other liquid into the colon through a tube.

en·e·my (en′ə mē), *n.* **1.** a person, group, or country that hates another or fights against another; foe [Germany was our *enemy* in World Wars I and II.] **2.** one who hates or fights against an idea, cause, conditions, etc. [John Brown was an *enemy* of slavery.] **3.** anything that harms [He is his own greatest *enemy.*] —**en′e·mies,** *pl.*

en·er·get·ic (en′ər jet′ik), *adj.* full of energy; active or ready to act; forceful [an *energetic* athlete]. —**en′er·get′i·cal·ly,** *adv.*

en·er·gize (en′ər jīz), *v.* to put energy into; make active [The fresh air *energized* us.] —**en′er·gized,** *p.t.* & *p.p.*; **en′er·giz·ing,** *pr.p.*

en·er·gy (en′ər jē), *n.* **1.** power to work or be active; force; vigor [Theodore Roosevelt was a man of great *energy.*] **2.** the power of certain forces in nature to do work [Electricity and heat are forms of *energy.*] —**en′er·gies,** *pl.*

en·er·vate (en′ər vāt), *v.* to take away the strength or energy of; weaken [Lack of exercise had *enervated* Fred.] —**en′er·vat·ed,** *p.t.* & *p.p.*; **en′er·vat·ing,** *pr.p.* **en′er·va′tion,** *n.*

en·fee·ble (in fē′b'l), *v.* to make feeble. —**en·fee′bled,** *p.t.* & *p.p.*; **en·fee′bling,** *pr.p.*

en·fold (in fōld′), *v.* **1.** to wrap up; cover with folds of something [*enfolded* in layers of clothes]. **2.** to hold closely; embrace [The nurse *enfolded* the baby in her arms.] Also spelled **infold.**

en·force (in fôrs′), *v.* **1.** to force people to pay attention to; make people obey [to *enforce* traffic laws]. **2.** to bring about by being strict [The teacher *enforced* complete silence.] —**en·forced′,** *p.t.* & *p.p.*; **en·forc′ing,** *pr.p.* —**en·force′a·ble,** *adj.* —**en·force′ment,** *n.*

en·fran·chise (en fran′chīz), *v.* **1.** to free, as from slavery. **2.** to give the right to vote to [Women in the U.S. were *enfranchised* in 1920.] —**en·fran′chised,** *p.t.* & *p.p.*; **en·fran′chis·ing,** *pr.p.* —**en·fran′chise·ment,** *n.*

Eng., abbreviation for **England** or **English.**

en·gage (in gāj′), *v.* **1.** to promise to marry [He is *engaged* to his childhood sweetheart.] **2.** to promise or undertake something [She *engaged* to tutor the child after school.] **3.** to arrange for the services or use of; hire [He *engaged* Smith as his lawyer. I *engaged* a hotel room.] **4.** to keep busy or active [I have no time to *engage* in dramatics. Tennis *engages* all his spare time.] **5.** to draw into; involve [She *engaged* him in conversa-

tion.] **6.** to get and hold [I'm trying to *engage* his attention.] **7.** to meet in battle with [to *engage* enemy forces]. **8.** to fit or lock together, as the teeth of gears. —**en·gaged′,** *p.t.* & *p.p.*; **en·gag′ing,** *pr.p.*

en·gage·ment (in gāj′mənt), *n.* **1.** the act of engaging. **2.** a promise or arranging to marry. **3.** an appointment to meet someone or go somewhere. **4.** a being hired for some job, especially in show business. **5.** a battle.

en·gag·ing (in gāj′ing), *adj.* charming or attractive [an *engaging* manner].

en·gen·der (in jen′dər), *v.* to bring into being; produce [Friction *engenders* heat.]

en·gine (en′jən), *n.* **1.** a machine that uses energy of some kind to create motion and do work [An automobile *engine* uses the energy of hot gases formed by exploding gasoline.] **2.** a railroad locomotive. **3.** any machine or mechanical device [*engines* of warfare].

en·gi·neer (en jə nir′), *n.* **1.** a person who is trained in some branch of engineering. **2.** a person who runs an engine, as the driver of a railroad locomotive. **3.** a soldier whose special work is the building or wrecking of roads, bridges, etc. —*v.* **1.** to plan, direct, or build as an engineer. **2.** to plan or manage skillfully [to *engineer* a merger of companies].

en·gi·neer·ing (en′jə nir′ing), *n.* the science or work of planning and building machinery, roads, bridges, buildings, etc. There are many different branches of engineering, as civil, electrical, mechanical, and chemical engineering.

Eng·land (ing′glənd), *n.* the largest part of Great Britain, south of Scotland.

Eng·lish (ing′glish), *adj.* of England, its people, language, etc. —*n.* **1.** the people of England. **2.** the language spoken in England, and also in the United States, Canada, Australia, etc. **3.** a course in school for studying the English language or English literature. **4.** *sometimes* **english,** a spinning motion given to a ball, as in bowling.

English Channel, the part of the Atlantic Ocean between England and France.

English horn, a wood-wind instrument with a double reed, that is like an oboe but a little larger and lower in pitch.

Eng·lish·man (ing′glish mən), *n.* a person, especially a man, born or living in England. —**Eng′lish·men,** *pl.*

Eng·lish·wom·an (ing′glish woom′ən), *n.* a woman born or living in England. —**Eng′lish·wom′en,** *pl.*

en·graft (en graft′), *v.* **1.** to graft a shoot of one plant onto another. **2.** to fix firmly as in the mind.

English horn

fat, āpe, cär, ten, ēven, hit, bīte, gō, hôrn, tool, book, up, fur;
get, joy, yet, chin, she, thin, *th*en; zh = s in pleasure; ′ as in able (ā′b'l);
ə = a in ago, e in agent, i in sanity, o in confess, u in focus.

en·grave (in grāv´), *v.* **1.** to carve or etch letters, designs, etc. on [a date *engraved* on a cornerstone]. **2.** to cut or etch a picture, lettering, etc. into a metal plate, wooden block, etc. to be used for printing; also, to print from such a plate, block, etc. [an *engraved* invitation]. **3.** to fix in the mind [This poem is *engraved* in my memory.] —**en·graved´,** *p.t. & p.p.;* **en·grav´ing,** *pr.p.* —**en·grav´er,** *n.*

en·grav·ing (in grāv´ing), *n.* **1.** the act or art of making metal plates, wooden blocks, etc. for printing. **2.** a picture, design, etc. printed from such a plate or block.

en·gross (in grōs´), *v.* to interest so much that other things are forgotten or not noticed; absorb [to be *engrossed* in a book].

en·gulf (in gulf´), *v.* to cover completely; swallow up [A huge wave *engulfed* the swimmer.]

en·hance (in hans´), *v.* to make better, greater, etc. [The soft music *enhanced* the scene.] —**en·hanced´,** *p.t. & p.p.;* **en·hanc´ing,** *pr.p.*

e·nig·ma (i nig´mə), *n.* anything or anyone that is hard to understand or explain; puzzle.

en·ig·mat·ic (en´ig mat´ik) or **en·ig·mat·i·cal** (en´ig mat´i k'l), *adj.* of or like an enigma; puzzling; mysterious [an *enigmatic* smile]. —**en´ig·mat´i·cal·ly,** *adv.*

en·join (in join´), *v.* **1.** to order or command [The judge *enjoined* the jury not to talk about the case.] **2.** to forbid or prohibit [The court *enjoined* the union from picketing.]

en·joy (in joi´), *v.* **1.** to get joy or pleasure from [Did you *enjoy* the baseball game?] **2.** to have the use of or have as a benefit [The book *enjoyed* large sales.] —**enjoy oneself,** to have a good time; have fun. —**en·joy´ment,** *n.*

en·joy·a·ble (in joi´ə b'l), *adj.* giving joy or pleasure; delightful.

en·large (in lärj´), *v.* to make or become larger, more, etc. —**enlarge on** or **enlarge upon,** to give more details about. —**en·larged´,** *p.t. & p.p.;* **en·larg´ing,** *pr.p.*

en·large·ment (in lärj´mənt), *n.* **1.** a making or becoming larger. **2.** something that has been made larger; especially, an enlarged copy of a photograph.

en·light·en (in līt´'n), *v.* to give knowledge or truth to; get rid of ignorance or false beliefs; inform. —**en·light´en·ment,** *n.*

en·list (in list´), *v.* **1.** to join or get someone to join; especially, to join some branch of the armed forces [He *enlisted* in the navy. This office *enlisted* ten new recruits.] **2.** to get the support of [Try to *enlist* your father's help.] —**en·list´ment,** *n.*

enlisted man, any member of the armed forces who is not a commissioned officer or a warrant officer.

en·liv·en (in līv´ən), *v.* to make lively, gay, bright, etc.; liven up [He *enlivened* the party by telling funny stories.]

en·mesh (in mesh´), *v.* to tangle up, as if in a net [*enmeshed* in troubles].

en·mi·ty (en´mə tē), *n.* the bitter feeling that enemies have; hatred. —**en´mi·ties,** *pl.*

en·no·ble (i nō´b'l), *v.* to make noble; make a person better or finer; uplift. —**en·no´bled,** *p.t. & p.p.;* **en·no´bling,** *pr.p.*

en·nui (än´wē), *n.* a feeling of being very bored and tired of everything.

e·nor·mi·ty (i nôr´mə tē), *n.* **1.** great wickedness [the *enormity* of his crime]. **2.** a very wicked crime. —**e·nor´mi·ties,** *pl.*

e·nor·mous (i nôr´məs), *adj.* much larger than usual; huge [an *enormous* house]. —**e·nor´mous·ly,** *adv.* —**e·nor´mous·ness,** *n.*

e·nough (i nuf´), *adj.* as much or as many as needed or wanted; sufficient [There is *enough* food for all.] —*n.* the amount needed or wanted [I have had *enough* of that pudding.] —*adv.* **1.** as much as needed; to the right amount [The steak is not cooked *enough*.] **2.** fully; quite [Oddly *enough*, I wasn't even there.]

en·quire (in kwīr´), *v.* same as **inquire.** —**en·quired´,** *p.t. & p.p.;* **en·quir´ing,** *pr.p.*

en·quir·y (in kwīr´ē *or* in´kwə rē), *n.* same as **inquiry.** —**en·quir´ies,** *pl.*

en·rage (in rāj´), *v.* to make very angry; put into a rage; infuriate. —**en·raged´,** *p.t. & p.p.;* **en·rag´ing,** *pr.p.*

en·rap·ture (in rap´chər), *v.* to fill with great delight; enchant. —**en·rap´tured,** *p.t. & p.p.;* **en·rap´tur·ing,** *pr.p.*

en·rich (in rich´), *v.* to make richer in value, quality, etc. [Music *enriches* one's life. This bread is *enriched* with vitamins.] —**en·rich´ment,** *n.*

en·roll or **en·rol** (in rōl´), *v.* **1.** to write one's name in a list, as in becoming a member; register [New students must *enroll* Monday.] **2.** to make someone a member [I'd like to *enroll* you in our art class.] —**en·rolled´,** *p.t. & p.p.;* **en·roll´ing,** *pr.p.*

en·roll·ment or **en·rol·ment** (in rōl´mənt), *n.* **1.** the act of enrolling. **2.** the number of people enrolled.

en route (än rōōt´), on the way [Will you stop in New York *en route* to Europe?]

en·sconce (en skäns´), *v.* to settle in a snug, safe, or hidden place [Father was *ensconced* in his favorite easy chair.] —**en·sconced´,** *p.t. & p.p.;* **en·sconc´ing,** *pr.p.*

en·sem·ble (än säm´b'l), *n.* **1.** all the parts taken as a whole; whole effect. **2.** a complete costume; articles of clothing that match and are worn together [Gray shoes and gloves completed her *ensemble*.] **3.** a small group of musicians playing or singing together [a string *ensemble*].

en·shrine (in shrīn´), *v.* **1.** to put in a shrine [Washington's body is *enshrined* at Mount Vernon.] **2.** to keep with love and respect; cherish [His memory is *enshrined* in our hearts.] —**en·shrined´,** *p.t. & p.p.;* **en·shrin´ing,** *pr.p.*

en·shroud (en shroud´), *v.* to cover so as to hide [towers *enshrouded* in mist].

en·sign (en´sīn), *n.* **1.** a flag or banner, especially a national flag. **2.** (en´s'n), a navy officer of the lowest rank.

en·si·lage (en´s'l ij), *n.* green or fresh fodder for cattle, etc., stored in a silo.

en·slave (in slāv'), *v.* **1.** to make a slave of; put into slavery. **2.** to keep complete control over, as though by force [She was *enslaved* by her work.] —**en·slaved'**, *p.t. & p.p.;* **en·slav'-ing,** *pr.p.* —**en·slave'ment,** *n.*

en·snare (en sner'), *v.* to catch in a snare or trap; trap. —**en·snared'**, *p.t. & p.p.;* **en·snar'ing,** *pr.p.*

en·sue (en sōō' *or* en syōō'), *v.* **1.** to come after; follow [We met in school and a long friendship *ensued.*] **2.** to happen as a result; result [the damage that *ensued* from the flood]. —**en·sued'**, *p.t. & p.p.;* **en·su'ing,** *pr.p.*

en·sure (in shoor'), *v.* same as **insure.** —**en·sured'**, *p.t. & p.p.;* **en·sur'ing,** *pr.p.*

-ent (ənt), a suffix meaning: **1.** that is or acts a certain way [A *persistent* person is one who persists.] **2.** a person or thing that [A *president* is a person who presides.]

en·tail (in tāl'), *v.* **1.** to make necessary; require; involve [This plan will *entail* much work.] **2.** to leave property to a certain line of heirs, so that none of them may sell it or give it away. —*n.* property entailed or the line of heirs to which it must go.

en·tan·gle (in tang'g'l), *v.* **1.** to catch or trap in a tangle [Our fishing lines became *entangled.* Flies get *entangled* in a spider's web.] **2.** to get mixed up, as in some trouble [They *entangled* him in a dishonest business deal.] —**en·tan'-gled,** *p.t. & p.p.;* **en·tan'gling,** *pr.p.* —**en·tan'gle·ment,** *n.*

en·tente (än tänt'), *n.* **1.** an understanding or agreement between nations or persons. **2.** the nations, etc. having such an understanding.

en·ter (en'tər), *v.* **1.** to come or go in or into [to *enter* a room]. **2.** to force a way into; pierce [The bullet *entered* his leg.] **3.** to join; become a member of [to *enter* the navy]. **4.** to start or begin [to *enter* a career]. **5.** to cause to join or be let in [to *enter* a horse in a race]. **6.** to write down in a list [His name was *entered* on the honor roll.] **7.** to put on record before a law court [He *entered* a plea of guilty.] —**enter on** or **enter upon,** to start; begin.

en·ter·prise (en'tər prīz), *n.* **1.** any business or undertaking, especially one that takes daring and energy. **2.** a being ready to undertake new or risky projects [He's lost his *enterprise.*]

en·ter·pris·ing (en'tər prīz'ing), *adj.* ready to start or try new things; bold and active.

en·ter·tain (en tər tān'), *v.* **1.** to keep interested and give pleasure to [He *entertained* us by playing the violin.] **2.** to have as a guest; be a host to [to *entertain* friends at dinner]. **3.** to have guests [It's expensive to *entertain* these days.] **4.** to have in mind; consider [He *entertained* the idea of going to Europe.] —**en·ter·tain'ing,** *adj.*

en·ter·tain·er (en tər tān'ər), *n.* a person who entertains, especially one whose work is singing,

dancing, etc., as on television or in night clubs.

en·ter·tain·ment (en tər tān'mənt), *n.* **1.** the act of entertaining. **2.** something that entertains, as a show or a concert.

en·thrall or **en·thral** (in thrôl'), *v.* **1.** to hold as if in a spell; fascinate; charm [We were *enthralled* by his exciting story.] **2.** to make a slave of. —**en·thralled'**, *p.t. & p.p.;* **en·thrall'-ing,** *pr.p.*

en·throne (in thrōn'), *v.* **1.** to seat on a throne. **2.** to place in a high position; exalt. —**en·throned'**, *p.t. & p.p.;* **en·thron'ing,** *pr.p.*

en·thuse (in thōōz'), *v.* to show or fill with enthusiasm: *used only in everyday talk.* —**en·thused'**, *p.t. & p.p.;* **en·thus'ing,** *pr.p.*

en·thu·si·asm (in thōō'zi az'm), *n.* a strong liking or interest [an *enthusiasm* for golf].

en·thu·si·ast (in thōō'zi ast), *n.* a person who is full of enthusiasm.

en·thu·si·as·tic (in thōō'zi as'tik), *adj.* full of enthusiasm; showing great interest or liking [an *enthusiastic* follower; *enthusiastic* applause]. —**en·thu'si·as'ti·cal·ly,** *adv.*

en·tice (in tīs'), *v.* to tempt by offering something that is wanted [He *enticed* the bird to eat from his hand.] —**en·ticed'**, *p.t. & p.p.;* **en·tic'ing,** *pr.p.* —**en·tice'ment,** *n.*

en·tire (in tīr'), *adj.* **1.** including all the parts; whole; complete [The *entire* class is here.] **2.** not broken, not lessened, not weakened, etc. —**en·tire'ly,** *adv.*

en·tire·ty (in tīr'tē), *n.* wholeness; completeness. —**in its entirety,** as a whole.

en·ti·tle (in tī't'l), *v.* **1.** to give a right or claim to [This ticket *entitles* you to be admitted free.] **2.** to give a name or title to [Shakespeare's first comedy was *entitled* "A Comedy of Errors."] —**en·ti'tled,** *p.t. & p.p.;* **en·ti'tling,** *pr.p.*

en·ti·ty (en'tə tē), *n.* **1.** a real being or real thing, not just an idea, quality, etc. [A person is an *entity.* A law firm is an *entity.*] **2.** being or existence. —**en'ti·ties,** *pl.*

en·tomb (in tōōm'), *v.* to put in a tomb; bury.

en·to·mol·o·gy (en'tə mäl'ə jē), *n.* the science that studies insects. —**en·to·mo·log·i·cal** [en'tə mə läj'i k'l], *adj.* —**en'to·mol'o·gist,** *n.*

en·trails (en'trālz), *n.pl.* the parts inside an animal's body, especially the intestines.

en·train (in trān'), *v.* to get on a train or put on a train.

en·trance (en'trəns), *n.* **1.** the act of entering. **2.** a place for entering; door, gate, etc. **3.** the right or liberty to enter; admission.

en·trance (in trans'), *v.* **1.** to put into a trance. **2.** to fill with joy or delight; enchant [We were *entranced* by the sunset.] —**en·tranced'**, *p.t. & p.p.;* **en·tranc'ing,** *pr.p.*

en·trant (en'trənt), *n.* a person who enters, especially one who enters a contest.

en·trap (in trap'), *v.* **1.** to catch in a trap. **2.** to get someone into trouble by tricking him

fat, āpe, cär, ten, ēven, hit, bīte, gō, hôrn, tōōl, book, up, fũr; get, joy, yet, chin, she, thin, *th*en; zh = s in pleasure; ' as in able (ā'b'l); ə = a in ago, e in agent, i in sanity, o in confess, u in focus.

[to *entrap* a man into telling a lie]. **—en·trapped′**, *p.t. & p.p.;* **en·trap′ping,** *pr.p.*

en·treat (in trēt′), *v.* to plead with or beg [I *entreat* you to heed his warning.]

en·treat·y (in trēt′ē), *n.* a pleading or begging; strong request. **—en·treat′ies,** *pl.*

en·tree or **en·trée** (än′trā), *n.* **1.** the right to enter [Everyone has *entree* into a public library.] **2.** the main dish of a meal [For the *entree*, we had a choice of chicken or steak.]

en·trench (in trench′), *v.* **1.** to surround or protect with trenches [Enemy troops were *entrenched* across the river.] **2.** to fix firmly and deeply [an official *entrenched* in office]. Also spelled **intrench. —en·trench′ment,** *n.*

en·trust (in trust′), *v.* **1.** to put in charge of; give a duty to [I will *entrust* you with my records.] **2.** to turn over for safekeeping [*Entrust* your key to me.] Also spelled **intrust.**

en·try (en′trē), *n.* **1.** the act of entering. **2.** a way or passage by which to enter. **3.** each separate thing or part put down in a list, diary, etc. [Each word printed in heavy type in this dictionary is an *entry*.] **4.** a person or thing entered in a contest. **—en′tries,** *pl.*

en·twine (in twīn′), *v.* to twine together or around [a fence *entwined* with ivy]. **—en·twined′,** *p.t. & p.p.;* **en·twin′ing,** *pr.p.*

e·nu·mer·ate (i nōō′mə·rāt *or* i nyōō′mə rāt), *v.* to count or name one by one; list [He *enumerated* all his cousins for me.] **—e·nu′mer·at·ed,** *p.t. & p.p.;* **e·nu′mer·at·ing,** *pr.p.* **—e·nu′mer·a′tion,** *n.*

e·nun·ci·ate (i nun′si āt), *v.* **1.** to speak or pronounce words [A telephone operator must *enunciate* clearly.] **2.** to state clearly; announce [to *enunciate* a theory]. **—e·nun′·ci·at·ed,** *p.t. & p.p.;* **e·nun′ci·at·ing,** *pr.p.* **—e·nun′ci·a′tion,** *n.*

vine entwined on a trellis

en·vel·op (in vel′əp), *v.* to cover on all sides; wrap up or wrap in [Darkness *enveloped* the camp.] **—en·vel′oped,** *p.t. & p.p.;* **en·vel′op·ing,** *pr.p.* **—en·vel′op·ment,** *n.*

en·ve·lope (en′və lōp *or* än′və lōp), *n.* **1.** a folded paper cover in which letters are sealed for mailing [The address and stamp go on the front of the *envelope*.] **2.** any wrapper or covering [a seed *envelope*].

en·ven·om (en ven′əm), *v.* **1.** to put poison in [The air was *envenomed* by a deadly gas.] **2.** to fill with hate or bitterness [He was *envenomed* by his master's cruelty.]

en·vi·a·ble (en′vi ə b'l), *adj.* good enough to be envied or wished for [with *enviable* skill].

en·vi·ous (en′vi əs), *adj.* full of envy or showing envy. **—en′vi·ous·ly,** *adv.*

en·vi·ron (in vī′rən), *v.* to form a circle around; surround; encircle.

en·vi·ron·ment (in vī′rən mənt), *n.* the things that surround anything; especially, all the conditions that surround a person, animal, or plant and affect growth, actions, character, etc. [He blamed his life of crime on his early *environment*.] **—en·vi·ron·men′tal,** *adj.*

en·vi·rons (in vī′rənz), *n.pl.* the districts that surround a place; suburbs or outskirts.

en·vis·age (en viz′ij), *v.* to form a picture of in the mind; imagine [The scientist *envisaged* the happiness his invention would bring.] **—en·vis′aged,** *p.t. & p.p.;* **en·vis′ag·ing,** *pr.p.*

en·voy (en′voi), *n.* **1.** a messenger. **2.** a person sent to represent his government in a foreign country. He ranks just below an ambassador.

en·vy (en′vē), *n.* **1.** jealousy and dislike felt toward another because he has some thing, quality, etc. that one would like to have [He stared at the winner with a look of *envy*.] **2.** the person or thing one has such feelings about [Their new car is the *envy* of the neighborhood.] **—v.** to feel envy toward or because of [to *envy* a person for his wealth]. **—en′vies,** *pl.* **—en′·vied,** *p.t. & p.p.;* **en′vy·ing,** *pr.p.*

en·wrap (en rap′), *v.* to wrap up. **—en·wrapped′,** *p.t. & p.p.;* **en·wrap′ping,** *pr.p.*

en·zyme (en′zīm), *n.* a substance produced in plant and animal cells that causes a chemical change in other substances but is not changed itself [Pepsin is an *enzyme* in the stomach that helps to digest food.]

e·on (ē′ən *or* ē′än), *n.* a very long period of time; thousands and thousands of years [The first men lived *eons* ago.] Also spelled **aeon.**

ep·au·let or **ep·au·lette** (ep′ə let), *n.* a decoration worn on the shoulder of a uniform.

e·phem·er·al (ə fem′ər əl), *adj.* lasting only one day or a very short time; short-lived [*ephemeral* insects; *ephemeral* pleasures].

E·phe·sians (i fē′zhənz), *n.* a book of the New Testament, believed to be written by Paul.

epaulets

epi-, a prefix meaning "on," "over," or "outside" [The *epidermis* is the outside layer of skin.]

ep·ic (ep′ik), *n.* **1.** a long, serious poem that tells the story of a hero or heroes [Homer's "Odyssey" is an *epic* about the wanderings of Ulysses.] **2.** a story, play, etc. thought of as having the greatness and splendor of an epic. **—adj.** of or like an epic; heroic, grand, etc. [the *epic* western march of the pioneers].

ep·i·cure (ep′i kyoor), *n.* a person who knows and cares much about fine foods, wines, etc.

ep·i·cu·re·an (ep′i kyoo rē′ən), *adj.* fond of eating and drinking good things and having pleasures. **—n.** an epicurean person.

ep·i·dem·ic (ep ə dem′ik), *n.* the rapid spreading of a disease, etc. to many people at the same time [an *epidemic* of flu in the city]. **—adj.** widespread, as a disease.

ep·i·der·mis (ep ə dûr′mis), *n.* the outer layer of skin, that has no blood vessels.

ep·i·glot·tis (ep ə glät′is), *n.* a little piece of cartilage that covers the windpipe when a person swallows. It keeps food from getting into the lungs.

ep·i·gram (ep′ə gram), *n.* a short saying that makes its point in a witty or clever way ["Experience is the name everyone gives to his mistakes" is an *epigram.*] —**ep·i·gram·mat·ic** (ep′i grə mat′ik), *adj.*

ep·i·lep·sy (ep′ə lep′sē), *n.* a sickness of the nervous system that causes fits from time to time, in which there is tightening of the muscles, fainting etc.

ep·i·lep·tic (ep′ə lep′tik), *adj.* of or having epilepsy. —*n.* a person who has epilepsy.

ep·i·logue or **ep·i·log** (ep′ə lôg), *n.* a part added at the end of a play or novel, in which the author makes some comment; especially, a closing speech to the audience by one of the actors.

E·piph·a·ny (i pif′ə nē), *n.* a church festival on January 6 celebrating the visit of the Wise Men to worship the infant Jesus.

e·pis·co·pal (i pis′kə p'l), *adj.* of or governed by bishops. The word *Episcopal* is sometimes used in the names of Protestant churches that are governed by bishops, as the Protestant Episcopal Church.

E·pis·co·pa·li·an (i pis′kə pā′li ən), *adj.* Episcopal. —*n.* a member of the Protestant Episcopal Church, the church in the U.S. that follows the practice of the Church of England.

ep·i·sode (ep′ə sōd), *n.* any happening or incident that forms a part of a whole story, life, history, etc. [The capture of Guadalcanal was an *episode* in World War II.]

e·pis·tle (i pis′'l), *n.* 1. a letter. 2. **Epistle,** any of the letters written by the Apostles and included as books of the New Testament.

ep·i·taph (ep′ə taf), *n.* words carved on a tomb in memory of the person buried there.

ep·i·thet (ep′ə thet), *n.* a word or phrase that describes a person or thing by naming some quality or feature, as Jack, *the Giant-Killer.*

e·pit·o·me (i pit′ə mē), *n.* 1. a person or thing that shows all the typical qualities of something [She is the *epitome* of motherhood.] 2. a short report of the main points of a book, etc.; summary.

e·pit·o·mize (i pit′ə mīz), *v.* to make or be an epitome, or typical example, of [Daniel Boone *epitomizes* the frontiersman.] —**e·pit′o·mized,** *p.t. & p.p.;* **e·pit′o·miz·ing,** *pr.p.*

e plu·ri·bus u·num (ē ploor′ə bəs yoo′nəm), out of many, one: *a Latin phrase* that is the motto of the United States.

ep·och (ep′ək), *n.* 1. the beginning of an important period in history [The first earth satellite marked a new *epoch* in the study of the universe.] 2. a period of time thought of in connection with the important happenings, changes, etc. in it [the *epoch* of discovery in the 15th and 16th centuries]. 3. a period in the history of the earth [The recent *epoch* in geology began about 50,000 years ago.] —**ep′och·al,** *adj.*

ep·ox·y (e päk′sē), *adj.* that contains a resin which gives it a strong, hard, sticking quality [an *epoxy* glue, an *epoxy* enamel].

Ep·som salts or **Ep·som salt** (ep′səm), a white powder in the form of crystals, that is dissolved in water for use in industry and medicine.

eq·ua·ble (ek′wə b'l), *adj.* 1. changing very little or not at all; steady; even [an *equable* climate]. 2. not easily stirred up or troubled; calm [an *equable* temper]. —**eq′ua·bly,** *adv.*

e·qual (ē′kwəl), *adj.* 1. of the same amount, size, or value [The horses were of *equal* height.] 2. having the same rights, ability, or position [A captain in the navy is *equal* to a colonel in the army.] —*n.* any person or thing that is equal [As a pitcher, Lefty has few *equals.*] —*v.* 1. to be equal to; match [His broad jump *equals* the record. Six minus two *equals* four.] 2. to do or make something equal to [You can *equal* my score easily.] —**equal to,** having enough power, skill, or courage for [I'm not *equal to* climbing that hill.] —**e′qualed** or **e′qualled,** *p.t. & p.p.;* **e′qual·ing** or **e′qual·ling,** *pr.p.* —**e′qual·ly,** *adv.*

e·qual·i·ty (i kwäl′ə tē), *n.* the condition of being equal, especially of having the same political and social rights.

e·qual·ize (ē′kwəl īz), *v.* to make equal or even. —**e′qual·ized,** *p.t. & p.p.;* **e′qual·iz·ing,** *pr.p.* —**e′qual·i·za′tion,** *n.* —**e′qual·iz·er,** *n.*

equal mark or **equal sign,** the mark or sign =, used in arithmetic to show that amounts or figures are equal, as $2 + 2 = 4$.

e·qua·nim·i·ty (ē′kwə nim′ə tē *or* ek′wə nim′ə tē), *n.* a being calm and not easily troubled or made angry; evenness of temper.

e·quate (i kwāt′), *v.* to think of or deal with as being equal or the same [Many people *equate* wealth with happiness.] —**e·quat′ed,** *p.t. & p.p.;* **e·quat′ing,** *pr.p.*

e·qua·tion (i kwā′zhən), *n.* 1. a statement showing that two quantities are equal by putting an equal mark (=) between them [$4 + 8 = 6 \times 2$ is an *equation.*] 2. the act of equating things, or making them equal.

e·qua·tor (i kwā′tər), *n.* an imaginary circle around the middle of the earth, at an equal distance from the North Pole and South Pole.

e·qua·to·ri·al (ē′kwə tôr′i əl), *adj.* 1. of or near the equator [*equatorial* regions]. 2. like the conditions near the equator [*equatorial* heat].

fat,   āpe,   cär,   ten,   ēven,   hit,   bīte,   gō,   hôrn,   tool,   book,   up,   fûr;
get,   joy,   yet,   chin,   she,   thin,   then;   zh = s in pleasure;   ' as in able (ā′b'l);
ə = a in ago,   e in agent,   i in sanity,   o in confess,   u in focus.

Equatorial Guinea, a country in western Africa, on the Atlantic Ocean.

eq·uer·ry (ek′wər ē), *n.* an officer in the court of a king or noble, originally one who had charge of the horses. —**eq′uer·ries,** *pl.*

e·ques·tri·an (i kwes′tri ən), *adj.* **1.** of horses or horseback riding. **2.** on horseback [an *equestrian* statue of Napoleon]. —*n.* a rider or circus performer on horseback. —**e·ques·tri·enne** (i kwes′tri en′), *n.fem.*

equi-, a prefix meaning "equal" or "equally" [An *equilateral* triangle has all sides equal.]

e·qui·dis·tant (ē′kwə dis′tənt), *adj.* at an equal distance from [Parallel lines are *equidistant* from each other at all points.]

e·qui·lat·er·al (ē′kwə lat′ər əl), *adj.* having all sides equal in length.

e·qui·lib·ri·um (ē′kwə lib′ri əm), *n.* the condition in which opposite weights, forces, etc. are in balance.

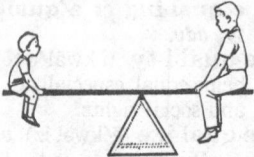
equilateral triangle

e·quine (ē′kwīn), *adj.* of or like a horse.

e·qui·noc·tial (ē′kwə näk′shəl), *adj.* of, or happening at the time of, an equinox.

e·qui·nox (ē′kwə näks), *n.* either of the two times of the year when the sun crosses the equator, about March 21 and September 23. At these times night and day are equal in length all over the earth.

weights in equilibrium

e·quip (i kwip′), *v.* to provide with what is needed; outfit [The soldiers were *equipped* for battle. The truck was *equipped* with air brakes.] —**e·quipped′,** *p.t. & p.p.;* **e·quip′ping,** *pr.p.*

eq·ui·page (ek′wə pij), *n.* **1.** equipment. **2.** a carriage, especially one with its horses, coachmen, and other servants.

equip·ment (i kwip′mənt), *n.* **1.** the special things needed for some purpose; outfit, supplies, etc. [fishing *equipment*]. **2.** the act of equipping.

e·qui·poise (ek′wə poiz), *n.* **1.** perfect balance of weights or forces. **2.** a weight or force that balances another.

eq·ui·ta·ble (ek′wi tə b′l), *adj.* fair or just [an *equitable* share]. —**eq′ui·ta·bly,** *adv.*

eq·ui·ty (ek′wə tē), *n.* fairness or justice.

equiv·a·lent (i kwiv′ə lənt), *adj.* equal or the same in amount, value, meaning, etc. —*n.* something that is equal or the same [Three teaspoonfuls are the *equivalent* of one tablespoonful in cooking.] —**e·quiv′a·lence,** *n.*

equiv·o·cal (i kwiv′ə k′l), *adj.* **1.** having more than one meaning so as to be confusing or misleading [An *equivocal* answer is one that evades the question.] **2.** undecided or doubtful [an *equivocal* outcome]. **3.** that can be questioned; suspicious [*equivocal* conduct in politics]. —**e·quiv′o·cal·ly,** *adv.*

e·quiv·o·cate (i kwiv′ə kāt), *v.* to say things that have more than one meaning so as to confuse or mislead. —**e·quiv′o·cat·ed,** *p.t. & p.p.;* **e·quiv′o·cat·ing,** *pr.p.* —**e·quiv′o·ca′tion,** *n.*

-er (ər), a suffix meaning: **1.** a person or thing that [A *catcher* is a person or thing that catches.] **2.** a person living in [A *Vermonter* is a person living in Vermont.] **3.** a person having to do with [A *hatter* is a person who makes hats.] **4.** more [A *pleasanter* day is a day that is more pleasant.]

e·ra (ir′ə), *n.* **1.** a period of time measured from some important event [The Christian *Era* is dated from the birth of Jesus.] **2.** a period of history having some special characteristic [We have entered the *era* of space travel.]

e·rad·i·cate (i rad′i kāt), *v.* to uproot or remove completely; get rid of; wipe out [to *eradicate* crime]. —**e·rad′i·cat·ed,** *p.t. & p.p.;* **e·rad′i·cat·ing,** *pr.p.* —**e·rad′i·ca′tion,** *n.*

e·rase (i rās′), *v.* **1.** to rub out; scrape away or wipe clean [to *erase* writing; to *erase* a blackboard]. **2.** to remove from the mind or memory. —**e·rased′,** *p.t. & p.p.;* **e·ras′ing,** *pr.p.*

e·ras·er (i rās′ər), *n.* a thing that erases, as a piece of rubber used to rub out pencil or ink marks or a felt pad used to wipe chalk marks from a blackboard.

e·ra·sure (i rā′shər), *n.* **1.** an erasing or rubbing out. **2.** an erased word, mark, etc.

ere (er), *prep. & conj.* before: *now seldom used except in poetry* [Nor shall I leave *ere* sundown.]

Er·e·bus (er′ə bəs), *n.* a place of darkness in Greek myths, through which the dead passed before entering Hades.

e·rect (i rekt′), *adj.* straight up; not bending or leaning; upright [The sentries stood *erect* at the gate.] —*v.* **1.** to put up or put together; build; construct [to *erect* a house]. **2.** to set in an upright position [to *erect* a telephone pole]. —**e·rec′tion,** *n.*

erg (ûrg), *n.* a unit of work or energy in physics.

er·go (ûr′gō), *conj. & adv.* therefore: *a Latin word.*

Er·ic·son, Leif (lēf *or* lāv er′ik s′n), Norwegian explorer who lived about 1000 A.D. and is thought to have discovered America.

Er·ie (ir′ē), *n.* **1.** one of the Greak Lakes, between Lake Huron and Lake Ontario: *usually* **Lake Erie. 2.** a city in northwestern Pennsylvania, on Lake Erie.

Erie Canal, a former canal between Buffalo on Lake Erie and Albany on the Hudson River.

Er·in (er′in), *n.* Ireland: *used mainly in poetry.*

er·mine (ûr′min), *n.* **1.** a weasel that lives in northern regions. Its fur is brown in summer, but turns white with a black-tipped tail in winter. **2.** the white fur of this animal, used especially on royal robes and on the robes of some European judges.

ermine (about 1 ft. long)

e·rode (i rōd′), *v.* to wear away; eat away or into [Rust *eroded* the iron fence. The hillside was *eroded* by wind and rain.] —**e·rod′ed,** *p.t. & p.p.;* **e·rod′ing,** *pr.p.*

E·ros (ir′äs *or* er′äs), *n.* the Greek god of love. The Romans called this god *Cupid.*

e·ro·sion (i rō′zhən), *n.* an eroding or wearing away [the *erosion* of soil by water and wind].

err (ŭr), *v.* **1.** to be wrong; make a mistake [The speaker *erred* in calling Columbus a Spaniard.] **2.** to do wrong; sin ["To *err* is human, to forgive divine."]

er·rand (er′ənd), *n.* **1.** a short trip to do a thing, often for someone else [I'm going downtown on an *errand* for mother.] **2.** the thing to be done on such a trip [What is your *errand*?]

er·rant (er′ənt), *adj.* **1.** roaming about in search of adventure [a knight-*errant*]. **2.** turning from what is right; erring.

er·rat·ic (ə rat′ik), *adj.* **1.** not regular in action; likely to change and, therefore, not to be depended on [an *erratic* motor]. **2.** queer or odd [*erratic* notions]. **—er·rat′i·cal·ly,** *adv.*

er·ro·ne·ous (ə rō′ni əs), *adj.* not correct; mistaken; wrong [an *erroneous* idea]. **—er·ro′ne·ous·ly,** *adv.*

er·ror (er′ər), *n.* **1.** a belief, answer, act, etc. that is untrue, incorrect, or wrong; mistake [an *error* in multiplication]. **2.** the condition of being wrong or incorrect [He is in *error* if he believes Balboa discovered America.] **3.** a play by a baseball fielder which is poorly made, but which would have resulted in an out if it had been properly made.

erst·while (ŭrst′hwīl), *adj.* former; of an earlier time [my *erstwhile* friend].

er·u·dite (er′yoo dīt *or* er′oo dīt), *adj.* having or showing much knowledge; learned or scholarly. **—er′u·dite·ly,** *adv.*

er·u·di·tion (er′yoo dish′ən *or* er′oo dish′ən), *n.* wide knowledge gained by reading and study; scholarship; learning.

e·rupt (i rupt′), *v.* **1.** to burst forth, as lava from a volcano. **2.** to throw forth lava, water, etc., as a volcano. **3.** to break out in a rash.

e·rup·tion (i rup′shən), *n.* **1.** a bursting or throwing forth, as of lava from a volcano. **2.** a breaking out in a rash; also, a rash [Measles causes an *eruption*.]

e·rup·tive (i rup′tiv), *adj.* causing a skin eruption [Chicken pox is an *eruptive* disease.]

-er·y (ər ē), a suffix meaning: **1.** a place to [A *brewery* is a place to brew.] **2.** a place for [A *nunnery* is a place for nuns.] **3.** the practice or work of [*Surgery* is the work of a surgeon.] **4.** the product of [*Pottery* is the product of a potter.] **5.** a collection of [*Crockery* is a collection of crocks and earthenware.] **6.** the condition of [*Slavery* is the condition of a slave.]

E·sau (ē′sô), *n.* in the Bible, Isaac's older son, who sold his birthright to his brother, Jacob.

es·ca·late (es′kə lāt), *v.* **1.** to rise as on an escalator. **2.** to make or grow larger in scope or size, higher in cost, etc. **—es′ca·lat·ed,** *p.t. & p.p.;* **es′ca·lat·ing,** *pr.p.*

es·ca·la·tor (es′kə lā′tər), *n.* a stairway whose steps are part of an endless moving belt, for carrying people up or down.

es·cal·op or **es·cal·lop** (e skäl′əp *or* e skal′əp), *n. & v.* same as **scallop.**

es·ca·pade (es′kə pād), *n.* a daring or mischievous adventure or prank.

escalator

es·cape (ə skāp′), *v.* **1.** to break loose; get free, as from prison. **2.** to keep from getting hurt, killed, etc.; keep safe from; avoid [Very few people *escaped* the plague.] **3.** to leak out; flow or drain away [Gas was *escaping* from the pipe.] **4.** to slip away from; be forgotten or not noticed by [Her name *escaped* me.] **5.** to come from without being intended [A scream *escaped* her lips.] **—n. 1.** the act of escaping [The prisoners made their plans for an *escape*.] **2.** a way of escaping [a fire *escape*]. **3.** a leaking out [an *escape* in the gas line]. **4.** any way of putting problems out of the mind for a while [Movies are her *escape*.] **—es·caped′,** *p.t. & p.p.;* **es·cap′ing,** *pr.p.*

es·cape·ment (ə skāp′mənt), *n.* **1.** the part of a watch or clock that keeps the action regular. It consists of a notched wheel that turns as it is released, one notch at a time, by a catch. **2.** the part of a typewriter that keeps the movement of the carriage regular.

es·carp·ment (ə skärp′mənt), *n.* **1.** a high, steep cliff. **2.** a bank of earth with a steep slope, made as part of a fortification.

escapement of a clock

es·chew (es choō′), *v.* to stay away from; shun; avoid [to *eschew* all evil].

es·cort (es′kôrt), *n.* **1.** one or more persons, ships, automobiles, etc. that go along with another or others in order to give protection or pay honor. **2.** a man who accompanies a woman, as to a party. **—v.** (i skôrt′), to go along with or accompany as an escort.

es·crow (es′krō), *n.* the state of a deed, bond, etc. held by a third person until certain conditions are carried out [A bank may hold a deed in *escrow* until a property sale is completed.]

es·cutch·eon (i skuch′ən), *n.* a shield on which a coat of arms is shown.

-ese (ēz), a suffix meaning "of a certain country or place" [*Chinese* is the language of China.]

Es·ki·mo (es′kə mō), *n.* **1.** any member of a race of people who live mainly in the Arctic regions of the Western Hemisphere. **2.** the language of the Eskimos. **—adj.** of the Eskimos. **—Es′ki·mos** or **Es′ki·mo,** *pl.*

escutcheon

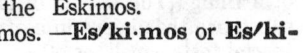
fat,   āpe,   cär,   ten,   ēven,   hit,   bīte,   gō,   hôrn,   tōōl,   book,   up,   fŭr;
get,   joy,   yet,   chin,   she,   thin,   *th*en;   zh = s in pleasure;   ′ as in able (ā′b'l).
ə = a in ago,   e in agent,   i in sanity,   o in confess,   u in focus.

Eskimo dog, a strong dog with a bushy tail and gray shaggy fur, used for pulling sleds in the Arctic.

e·soph·a·gus (i säf′ə gəs), *n.* the tube through which food passes from the throat to the stomach.

es·o·ter·ic (es′ə ter′ik), *adj.* understood or known by only a few people; of a secret kind that has been taught only to certain chosen persons [the *esoteric* rites of some religions].

Eskimo dogs (2 ft. high at shoulder)

esp., abbreviation for **especially.**

es·pe·cial (ə spesh′əl), *adj.* more than ordinary; outstanding; special [of *especial* interest to you].

es·pe·cial·ly (ə spesh′ə lē), *adv.* mainly; in particular; specially [I like all fruit, but I am *especially* fond of pears.]

es·pi·o·nage (es′pi ə näzh′ *or* es′pi ə nij), *n.* the act of spying on the secrets of others; especially, the use of spies by a government to learn the military secrets of other nations.

es·pous·al (i spou′z′l), *n.* **1.** the act of espousing or supporting a cause, plan, or idea; advocacy. **2.** *usually* **espousals,** *pl.* an engagement to marry, or a wedding.

es·pouse (i spouz′), *v.* **1.** to take up and support a cause, plan, or idea; advocate [Grandmother *espoused* the cause of women's rights.] **2.** to marry; take for a wife. —**es·poused′,** *p.t. & p.p.;* **es·pous′ing,** *pr.p.*

es·prit (es prē′), *n.* spirit or bright wit: *a French word.*

es·prit de corps (es prē′ də kôr′), a feeling of pride and honor in the group to which one belongs: *a French phrase.*

es·py (ə spī′), *v.* to manage to get a look at; catch sight of; see suddenly [Alex *espied* the snake half hidden in the tall grass.] —**es·pied′,** *p.t. & p.p.;* **es·py′ing,** *pr.p.*

es·quire (ə skwīr′ *or* es′kwīr), *n.* **1.** in England, a man who ranks just below a knight. **2.** **Esquire,** a polite title used instead of *Mr.:* it is more commonly used in England than in the U.S., and is usually abbreviated **Esq.** and placed after the name [Samuel Johnson, *Esq.*].

-ess (is *or* əs), a suffix meaning "female" [A *lioness* is a female lion.]

es·say (es′ā), *n.* **1.** a short piece of writing on a single subject, in which the writer gives his personal ideas. **2.** (*also* e sā′), an attempt to do something; a try. —*v.* (ə sā′), to try; attempt [to *essay* a task].

es·say·ist (es′ā ist), *n.* a writer of essays.

es·sence (es′'ns), *n.* **1.** that which makes something what it is; most important or basic quality of a thing [The *essence* of law is justice.] **2.** a substance that keeps in a strong, pure form the special taste, smell, or other quality of the plant, drug, etc. from which it is taken [*essence* of wintergreen]. **3.** a perfume.

es·sen·tial (ə sen′shəl), *adj.* **1.** that is a most typical or basic part [Kindness was an *essential* part of his character.] **2.** most important or necessary; vital [It is *essential* for guards on duty to stay awake.] —*n.* something that is most important or necessary [Love is the one *essential* of a happy marriage.] —**es·sen′tial·ly,** *adv.*

-est (ist *or* əst), **1.** a suffix meaning "most" that is used for the superlative form of many adjectives and adverbs [*Greatest* means "most great."] **2.** an old-fashioned ending for the present tense of verbs used with *thou* ["Thou *goest*" is an older way of saying "you go."]

E.S.T., abbreviation for **Eastern Standard Time.**

es·tab·lish (ə stab′lish), *v.* **1.** to put in a condition that is not easily changed; settle; fix [to *establish* a habit]. **2.** to put into an office, position, etc. [King Charles II was *established* on the throne of England in 1660.] **3.** to begin or found a government, nation, company, etc. [Ghana was *established* in 1957.] **4.** to show to be true; prove [The suspect was released when he *established* his alibi.]

es·tab·lish·ment (ə stab′lish mənt), *n.* **1.** the act of establishing or the fact of being established. **2.** something established, as a business, household, army, church, etc. —**the Establishment,** the exclusive group of powerful people who control the affairs of a nation or institution.

es·tate (ə stāt′), *n.* **1.** everything a person owns, including money, land, and other property [He left his entire *estate* to his niece.] **2.** a large piece of land with a large home on it [They have a city house and a country *estate*.] —**man's estate,** the time when a boy becomes a man.

es·teem (ə stēm′), *v.* **1.** to have a good opinion of; regard as valuable; respect [I *esteem* his praise above all other.] **2.** to think of; consider; deem [We *esteem* it an honor to be your hosts.] —*n.* good opinion; high regard; respect [to hold someone in high *esteem*].

es·ter (es′tər), *n.* an organic chemical substance containing carbon that is formed by combining an acid and an alcohol.

Es·ther (es′tər), *n.* **1.** in the Bible, the Jewish wife of a Persian king: she saved her people from slaughter. **2.** the book of the Old Testament that tells her story.

es·thet·ic (es thet′ik), *adj.* same as **aesthetic.**

es·ti·ma·ble (es′tə mə b′l), *adj.* worthy of esteem or respect; fine [an *estimable* book].

es·ti·mate (es′tə māt), *v.* to make a general but careful guess about the size, value, cost, etc. of [He *estimated* the size of the audience to be 500.] —*n.* (es′tə mit), **1.** a general guess about size, value, cost, etc. [an *estimate* of $50 to repair your car]. **2.** opinion or judgment [Was this a good book in your *estimate?*] —**es′ti·mat·ed,** *p.t. & p.p.;* **es′ti·mat·ing,** *pr.p.*

es·ti·ma·tion (es′tə mā′shən), *n.* **1.** the act of making an estimate. **2.** opinion or judgment; estimate. **3.** good opinion; esteem; respect [He is held in *estimation* by his fellow workers.]

Es·to·ni·a (es tō′ni ə), *n.* a former country in northeastern Europe, since 1940 a republic of the Soviet Union. —**Es·to′ni·an,** *adj. & n.*

es·trange (ə strānj′), *v.* to make no longer friendly; make stay away [She has *estranged* her friends by gossiping.] —**es·tranged′,** *p.t.* & *p.p.;* **es·trang′ing,** *pr.p.* —**es·trange′-ment,** *n.*

es·tu·ar·y (es′chōō er′ē), *n.* an arm of the sea; especially, a wide mouth of a river where the tide flows in. —**es′tu·ar′ies,** *pl.*

-et (it), a suffix meaning "small" [An *eaglet* is a small eagle.]

etc., abbreviation for **et cetera.**

et cet·er·a (et set′ər ə), and others; and so forth: *a Latin phrase.* It is usually abbreviated **etc.** and is used after a list of things to show that other similar things not mentioned could be included [Vitamin C is in oranges, lemons, *etc.*]

etch (ech), *v.* to engrave a design on metal or glass by coating the surface with a substance such as wax, on which the design is drawn with a sharp needle. Acid is then used to eat into the open parts of the surface. A metal plate prepared in this way can be used to print the design.

etch·ing (ech′ing), *n.* **1.** a plate or design that is etched. **2.** a print made from an etched plate. **3.** the art of making such designs or prints.

e·ter·nal (i tūr′n'l), *adj.* **1.** lasting forever; without a beginning or end. **2.** seeming to have no end; continual [Stop your *eternal* arguments!] **3.** always the same [*eternal* truth]. —**the Eternal,** God. —**e·ter′nal·ly,** *adv.*

e·ter·ni·ty (i tūr′nə tē), *n.* **1.** all time that ever has been or ever will be; time without beginning or end. **2.** a long period of time that seems to have no end [It seemed an *eternity* before they arrived.] **3.** the time after death.

-eth, see **-th.**

-eth (əth), an old-fashioned ending for the present tense of verbs used with *he, she,* or *it* ["He *asketh*" is an older way of saying "he asks."]

e·ther (ē′thər), *n.* **1.** a colorless liquid used to make a person unconscious, as during a surgical operation. **2.** an invisible substance that was once supposed to fill all space not filled by a solid, liquid, or gas, as the space between stars or between molecules. **3.** the clear sky above the clouds: *used mainly in poetry.*

e·the·re·al (i thir′i əl), *adj.* **1.** like the clear sky; light; airy; delicate [*ethereal* music]. **2.** not of the earth; heavenly.

eth·i·cal (eth′i k'l), *adj.* **1.** having to do with ethics or morals [*ethical* standards]. **2.** that is right according to some system of morals [*ethical* behavior]. —**eth′i·cal·ly,** *adv.*

eth·ics (eth′iks), *n.pl.* **1.** the study of right and wrong in human conduct; science of morals: *used with a singular verb.* **2.** rules of right and wrong behavior [According to legal *ethics,* a lawyer must not reveal his client's secrets.]

E·thi·o·pi·a (ē′thi ō′pi ə), *n.* a country in eastern Africa, south of Egypt: a former name was *Abyssinia.* —**E·thi·o′pi·an,** *adj.* & *n.*

eth·nic (eth′nik), *adj.* having to do with any of the different groups of mankind as set apart by their customs, languages, or cultures [Hawaii is a State with many *ethnic* groups.]

eth·nol·o·gy (eth näl′ə jē), *n.* the science that studies the different groups of mankind, their origins, cultures, etc. —**eth·no·log·i·cal** (eth′-nə läj′i k'l), *adj.* —**eth·nol′o·gist,** *n.*

et·i·quette (et′i ket), *n.* rules that society has set up for the proper way to behave in dealing with other people; good manners [It is *etiquette* to say "How do you do?" when being introduced. A book of *etiquette* tells how the bride should dress.]

Et·na (et′nə), *n.* a volcano in eastern Sicily.

E·tru·ri·a (i troor′i ə), *n.* an ancient country in what is now western Italy.

E·trus·can (i trus′kən), *adj.* of ancient Etruria, its people, or their culture. —*n.* **1.** a person who was born in or lived in Etruria. **2.** the ancient language of Etruria.

-ette (et), a suffix meaning: **1.** small [A *kitchenette* is a small kitchen.] **2.** girl or woman [A drum *majorette* is a girl drum major.] **3.** used in place of [*Leatherette* is used in place of leather.]

é·tude (ā′tōōd *or* ā tyōōd′), *n.* a piece of music written to give practice in developing certain skills on some instrument [piano *études*].

et·y·mol·o·gy (et′ə mäl′ə jē), *n.* **1.** the history of a word, which shows where it came from and how it has changed into its present form and meaning [The *etymology* of the word "nice" shows that in earlier English use it meant "foolish," and that it came from an old French word which came from the Latin word *nescius,* meaning "ignorant."] **2.** the science that studies such word histories. —**et′y·mol′o·gies,** *pl.* —**et·y·mo·log·i·cal** (et′ə mə läj′i k'l), *adj.*

eu-, a prefix meaning "good," "well," or "pleasant" [*Euphony* is pleasant sound.]

eu·ca·lyp·tus (yōō′kə lip′təs), *n.* an evergreen tree that grows in hot, moist regions near the tropics. It is valuable for its gum, oil, and wood. At one time these trees grew mainly in Australia. —**eu′ca·lyp′tus·es** or **eu·ca·lyp′ti** (yōō′kə lip′tī), *pl.*

Eu·cha·rist (yōō′kə rist), *n.* **1.** Holy Communion. **2.** the sacred bread and wine used in this rite. —**Eu′-cha·ris′tic,** *adj.*

eucalyptus tree and leaves

Eu·clid (yōō′klid), *n.* a Greek mathematician of about 300 B.C. who wrote a famous book on geometry.

eu·gen·ics (yoo jen′iks), *n.pl.* the science that has to do with improving the human race, especially by trying to match parents who should produce healthy, intelligent children: *used with a singular verb.* —**eu·gen′ic,** *adj.*

---

fat, āpe, cär, ten, ēven, hit, bīte, gō, hôrn, tōōl, book, up, fūr; get, joy, yet, chin, she, thin, *th*en; zh = s in pleasure; ' as in able (ā′b'l); ə = a in ago, e in agent, i in sanity, o in confess, u in focus.

eu·lo·gize (yōō′lə jīz), *v.* to say very good things about; praise highly; extol. —**eu′lo·gized,** *p.t. & p.p.;* **eu′lo·giz·ing,** *pr.p.* —**eu′·lo·gis′tic,** *adj.*

eu·lo·gy (yōō′lə jē), *n.* a speech or writing praising a person or thing; often, a formal speech praising a person who has just died. —**eu′lo·gies,** *pl.*

eu·nuch (yōō′nək), *n.* a man whose sex glands have been removed; castrated man [*Eunuchs* once served as guards in a sultan's harem.]

eu·phe·mism (yōō′fə miz′m), *n.* **1.** a word or phrase that is used in place of another that is thought to be too strong or unpleasant ["Remains" is a *euphemism* for "corpse."] **2.** the use of such words or phrases. —**eu′phe·mis′tic,** *adj.*

eu·pho·ny (yōō′fə nē), *n.* pleasant sound; especially, a pleasant combining of sounds in music or speaking. —**eu′pho·nies,** *pl.* —**eu·pho·ni·ous** (yoo fō′ni əs), *adj.*

Eu·phra·tes (yoo frā′tēz), *n.* a river that flows southward through eastern Turkey, Syria, and Iraq, into the Persian Gulf.

Eur·a·sia (yoo rā′zhə), *n.* Europe and Asia, thought of as a unit.

Eur·a·sian (yoo rā′zhən), *n.* a person who has one European parent and one Asian parent.

eu·re·ka (yoo rē′kə), *interj.* I have found it!: a shout of surprise or pleasure upon finding something one is looking for.

Eu·rip·i·des (yoo rip′ə dēz), *n.* a Greek writer of tragic plays, in the 5th century B.C.

Eu·rope (yoor′əp), *n.* the continent east of the Atlantic Ocean and west of Asia.

Eu·ro·pe·an (yoor′ə pē′ən), *adj.* of Europe, its people, or their culture. —*n.* a person born or living in Europe.

Eu·sta·chi·an tube (yoo stā′ki ən *or* yoo stā′shən), a thin tube leading into the middle ear, that makes the air pressure equal on both sides of the eardrum.

e·vac·u·ate (i vak′yōō āt), *v.* **1.** to remove; empty out; take away [to *evacuate* troops from a region; to *evacuate* air from a jar]. **2.** to move out of; leave [*Evacuate* the building in case of fire.] **3.** to make empty; take out the contents of [to *evacuate* the stomach]. —**e·vac′u·at·ed,** *p.t. & p.p.;* **e·vac′u·at·ing,** *pr.p.* —**e·vac′u·a′tion,** *n.*

e·vade (i vād′), *v.* to keep away from or avoid by using tricks or cleverness; elude [The fullback *evaded* the tackler by dodging. Jones was fined for *evading* the payment of his taxes.] —**e·vad′ed,** *p.t. & p.p.;* **e·vad′ing,** *pr.p.*

e·val·u·ate (i val′yōō āt), *v.* to find or try to find the value or amount of; judge the worth of [Critics *evaluate* the new books as they are published.] —**e·val′u·at·ed,** *p.t. & p.p.;* **e·val′·u·at·ing,** *pr.p.* —**e·val′u·a′tion,** *n.*

ev·a·nes·cent (ev′ə nes′′nt), *adj.* disappearing quickly; lasting only a short time [His fame was *evanescent.*] —**ev′a·nes′cence,** *n.*

e·van·gel·i·cal (ē′van jel′i k′l *or* ev′ən jel′i k′l), *adj.* **1.** having to do with the four Gospels or the New Testament. **2.** of those Protestant churches which believe that the soul is saved only through faith in Jesus.

e·van·gel·ism (i van′jə liz′m), *n.* a preaching of the gospel, as at revival meetings.

e·van·gel·ist (i van′jə list), *n.* **1.** anyone who preaches the gospel, especially, a preacher who travels about from place to place holding religious meetings. **2. Evangelist,** any of the four writers of the Gospels; Matthew, Mark, Luke, or John. —**e·van′gel·is′tic,** *adj.*

e·vap·o·rate (i vap′ə rāt), *v.* **1.** to change into vapor [Heat *evaporates* water. The perfume in the bottle has *evaporated.*] **2.** to disappear like vapor; vanish [His courage *evaporated* when he saw the lion.] **3.** to make thicker by heating so as to take some of the water from [to *evaporate* milk]. —**e·vap′o·rat·ed,** *p.t. & p.p.;* **e·vap′o·rat·ing,** *pr.p.* —**e·vap′o·ra′tion,** *n.*

evaporated milk, milk that is made thick by evaporation and then put in cans.

e·va·sion (i vā′zhən), *n.* the act of evading; especially, an avoiding of a duty, question, etc. by using tricks or cleverness [His wordy answer was really an *evasion* of my charge.]

e·va·sive (i vā′siv), *adj.* trying to evade; not direct or frank [an *evasive* answer to a question]. —**e·va′sive·ly,** *adv.*

Eve (ēv), *n.* in the Bible, Adam's wife, the first woman.

eve (ēv), *n.* **1.** the evening or day before a holiday [Christmas *Eve*]. **2.** the period just before something [on the *eve* of victory]. **3.** evening: *used in poetry.*

e·ven (ē′vən), *adj.* **1.** flat, level, or smooth [an *even* surface]. **2.** regular or steady; not changing [an *even* flow of air]. **3.** on the same level; to the same height [The water was *even* with the rim.] **4.** that can be divided by two without leaving a remainder [The *even* numbers are 2, 4, 6, 8, etc.] **5.** the same in number or amount; equal [Divide the candy in *even* shares.] **6.** owing nothing and being owed nothing [We owe each other a dollar and so we're *even.*] **7.** calm; not easily excited [an *even* temper]. **8.** exact [It cost an *even* $9.00.] —*adv.* **1.** though it may seem unlikely; indeed: *used to give force to what is being said* [*Even* a child could do it. He didn't *even* look.] **2.** by comparison; still [an *even* better meal]. **3.** exactly; just [He hurt himself *even* as I had said he would.] **4.** at the same time; while [*Even* as he spoke, the bell rang.] —*v.* to make or become even or level [*Even* off the ends of the logs.] —**even if,** in spite of the fact that; though. —**get even with,** to have revenge upon. —**e′ven·ly,** *adv.* —**e′ven·ness,** *n.*

e·ven (ē′vən), *n.* evening: *used in poetry.*

eve·ning (ēv′ning), *n.* the close of the day and early part of the night, or the time from sunset to bedtime.

evening star, a bright planet, usually Venus, seen in the western sky soon after sunset.

e·vent (i vent′), *n.* **1.** a happening; especially, an important happening [The annual circus was a great *event* in our lives.] **2.** any of the contests in a sports program [The final *event* in the track meet was the pole vault.] **3.** a result; outcome. **—in any event,** no matter what happens. **—in the event of,** in case of.

e·vent·ful (i vent′fəl), *adj.* **1.** full of important happenings [an *eventful* life]. **2.** having an important result [an *eventful* talk].

e·ven·tide (ē′vən tīd), *n.* evening: *used mainly in poetry.*

e·ven·tu·al (i ven′choo əl), *adj.* coming at the end or as a result [Quarrels led to *eventual* war.]

e·ven·tu·al·i·ty (i vench′oo al′ə tē), *n.* a possible happening [Be prepared for any *eventuality*.] **—e·ven′tu·al′i·ties,** *pl.*

e·ven·tu·al·ly (i ven′choo əl ē), *adv.* in the end; finally [We *eventually* became friends.]

ev·er (ev′ər), *adv.* **1.** at any time [Have you *ever* seen a falling star?] **2.** at all times; always [They lived happily *ever* after.] *Ever* is also used in everyday talk to give force to what is being said [How *ever* did you cut yourself?] **—ever so,** very; extremely: *used only in everyday talk.*

Ev·er·est, Mount (ev′ər ist), a mountain in southeastern Asia, between Tibet and Nepal. It is the highest mountain in the world, a little over 29,000 feet.

ev·er·glade (ev′ər glād), *n.* a large swamp. **—the Everglades,** a large area of swampland in southern Florida.

ev·er·green (ev′ər grēn), *adj.* having green leaves all through the year. **—n.** an evergreen tree or bush [Pines and spruces are *evergreens*.]

ev·er·last·ing (ev′ər las′ting), *adj.* **1.** lasting forever; never ending; eternal. **2.** going on too long; seeming as though it will never end [I'm tired of your *everlasting* complaints.] **—the Everlasting,** God.

ev·er·more (ev′ər môr′), *adv.* forever; always [Promise that you will *evermore* be true.] **—for evermore,** always.

eve·ry (ev′rē), *adj.* **1.** all the group of which the thing named is one; each [*Every* student must do his best. I've read *every* book on the list.] **2.** all that there could be [He's been given *every* chance.] **3.** each time after a certain period has passed [Take a pill *every* three hours.] **—every other,** with one between; skipping one, as the first, third, fifth, etc. in a series, or the second, fourth, sixth, etc. **—every now and then** or **every so often,** from time to time; once in a while: *used only in everyday talk.*

eve·ry·bod·y (ev′rē bäd′ē), *pron.* every person; everyone [*Everybody* loves a good story.]

eve·ry·day (ev′rē dā), *adj.* **1.** happening each day; daily. **2.** fit for usual or common use [*Everyday* talk is ordinary common speech, often different from formal talk or writing.]

eve·ry·one (ev′rē wun), *pron.* every person.

every one, every person or thing of those named [I told *every one* of the boys.]

eve·ry·thing (ev′rē thing), *pron.* **1.** every thing that there is; all things [Did you remember to bring *everything* for the picnic?] **2.** the most important thing [Money is *everything* to him.]

eve·ry·where (ev′rē hwer), *adv.* in all places; in every place [I see happy faces *everywhere*.]

e·vict (i vikt′), *v.* to force a person by law to move from a rental building, as for not paying his rent. **—e·vic′tion,** *n.*

ev·i·dence (ev′ə dəns), *n.* something that shows or proves, or that gives reason for believing; proof or indication [His footprint near the window was *evidence* that he had been there. Her clear skin gave *evidence* of a good diet.] **—v.** to show clearly; make plain. **—in evidence,** easily seen; in plain sight. **—ev′i·denced,** *p.t. & p.p.;* **ev′i·denc·ing,** *pr.p.*

ev·i·dent (ev′ə dənt), *adj.* easy to see or understand; clear; plain [It was *evident* that she had been crying.] **—ev′i·dent·ly,** *adv.*

e·vil (ē′vəl), *adj.* **1.** bad or wrong on purpose; wicked [to lead an *evil* life]. **2.** causing pain or trouble; harmful [Those were *evil* years.] **—n.** **1.** something bad or wrong done on purpose; wickedness; sin ["The *evil* that men do lives after them."] **2.** anything that causes harm, pain, or suffering [War is a great *evil*.] **—e′vil·ly,** *adv.*

e·vil·do·er (ē′v'l doo′ər), *n.* a person who does evil; wicked person.

e·vil-mind·ed (ē′v'l mīn′did), *adj.* having evil thoughts or plans.

e·vince (i vins′), *v.* to show plainly; make clear [His smile *evinced* his pleasure.] **—e·vinced′,** *p.t. & p.p.;* **e·vinc′ing,** *pr.p.*

e·voke (i vōk′), *v.* to bring forth or produce [Those cookies *evoke* memories of my childhood.] **—e·voked′,** *p.t. & p.p.;* **e·vok′ing,** *pr.p.*

ev·o·lu·tion (ev′ə loo′shən), *n.* **1.** the gradual changes that take place as something develops into its final form [the *evolution* of the automobile from the buggy; the *evolution* of the frog from the tadpole]. **2.** the theory that every plant and animal has developed from an earlier form, by a series of changes that took place over periods of many years and were passed on from one generation to the next. This theory is now commonly believed. **3.** a movement that is part of a series, as in dancing. **—ev′o·lu·tion·ar·y,** *adj.*

e·volve (i välv′), *v.* to develop by gradual changes; unfold [to *evolve* a new theory]. **—e·volved′,** *p.t. & p.p.;* **e·volv′ing,** *pr.p.*

ewe (yoo), *n.* a female sheep.

ew·er (yoo′ər), *n.* a large water pitcher that has a wide mouth.

ex-, 1. a prefix seen in words that come from Latin or Greek, meaning "out," "from," "out of," "beyond" [To *exhale* is to breathe out. To *exceed* is to go beyond a limit.] **2.** a prefix meaning "former" or "earlier," written with a hyphen [An *ex-judge* is a former judge.]

ewer

---

fat,   āpe,   cär,   ten,   ēven,   hit,   bīte,   gō,   hôrn,   tool,   book,   up,   fur;
get,   joy,   yet,   chin,   she,   thin,   *then;*   zh = s in pleasure;   ' as in able (ā′b'l);
    ə = a in ago,   e in agent,   i in sanity,   o in confess,   u in focus.

ex·act (ig zakt'), *adj.* **1.** not having any mistakes; strictly correct; accurate [*exact* measurements; his *exact* words]. **2.** very strict [He was *exact* in enforcing the rules.] —*v.* to demand and get [to *exact* a high fee; to *exact* obedience]. —**ex·act'ness,** *n.*

ex·act·ing (ig zak'ting), *adj.* **1.** demanding much; strict [an *exacting* employer]. **2.** that needs great skill and care [an *exacting* job].

ex·ac·tion (ig zak'shən), *n.* **1.** an exacting, or demanding. **2.** something that is exacted.

ex·act·i·tude (ig zak'tə tōōd *or* ig zak'tə tyōōd), *n.* a being exact; exactness.

ex·act·ly (ig zakt'lē), *adv.* **1.** in an exact way; precisely [Do *exactly* as I say.] **2.** quite true; I agree: *used as an answer to something said by another.*

ex·ag·ger·ate (ig zaj'ə rāt), *v.* to make seem larger or greater than it really is [He *exaggerated* his illness in order to get sympathy.] —**ex·ag'ger·at·ed,** *p.t. & p.p.;* **ex·ag'ger·at·ing,** *pr.p.* —**ex·ag'ger·a'tion,** *n.*

ex·alt (ig zôlt'), *v.* **1.** to praise or worship [to *exalt* God]. **2.** to make higher in rank, power, dignity, etc. **3.** to fill with happiness, pride, etc. [They were *exalted* by the music.]

ex·al·ta·tion (eg'zôl tā'shən), *n.* **1.** the act of exalting. **2.** a feeling of great joy or pride.

ex·am (ig zam'), *n.* an examination: *used only in everyday talk.*

ex·am·i·na·tion (ig zam'ə nā'shən), *n.* **1.** an examining or being examined. **2.** a test to find out how much someone knows or what he has learned.

ex·am·ine (ig zam'in), *v.* **1.** to look at closely in order to find out the facts about or the condition of; inspect [to *examine* the sky for signs of rain; to *examine* a sick patient]. **2.** to ask questions in order to find out how much someone knows or has learned [to *examine* a witness in court]. —**ex·am'ined,** *p.t. & p.p.;* **ex·am'in·ing,** *pr.p.* —**ex·am'in·er,** *n.*

ex·am·ple (ig zam'p'l), *n.* **1.** something chosen to show what others are like or to explain a general rule; sample; instance [This sentence is an *example* of how the word "example" is used.] **2.** a model or pattern that is to be copied [Sally's generous act set a good *example* for the others.] **3.** a warning or caution [The judge fined the speeder as an *example* to others.] —**set an example,** to behave in such a way as to be a model for others.

ex·as·per·ate (ig zas'pə rāt), *v.* to make angry; annoy very much; irritate [Such carelessness is enough to *exasperate* anyone.] —**ex·as'per·at·ed,** *p.t. & p.p.;* **ex·as'per·at·ing,** *pr.p.* —**ex·as'per·a'tion,** *n.*

ex·ca·vate (eks'kə vāt), *v.* **1.** to dig a hole or opening in [to *excavate* a hill in building a tunnel]. **2.** to make by digging; dig [to *excavate* the basement for a house]. **3.** to take out by digging; dig out [to *excavate* a ton of earth]. **4.** to uncover by digging [to *excavate* the ruins of a temple]. —**ex'ca·vat·ed,** *p.t. & p.p.;* **ex'ca·vat·ing,** *pr.p.* —**ex'ca·va·tor,** *n.*

ex·ca·va·tion (eks'kə vā'shən), *n.* **1.** the act of excavating. **2.** a hole made by digging.

excavation

ex·ceed (ik sēd'), *v.* **1.** to go beyond a limit or measure [You have *exceeded* your authority.] **2.** to be more or better than [The scenery of Alaska *exceeded* our hopes.]

ex·ceed·ing (ik sēd'ing), *adj.* more than usual; extreme [Avoid *exceeding* pride.]

ex·ceed·ing·ly (ik sēd'ing lē), *adv.* very; extremely [He is *exceedingly* rich.]

ex·cel (ik sel'), *v.* to be better or greater in a certain way [Rudy *excels* us all at chess.] —**ex·celled',** *p.t. & p.p.;* **ex·cel'ling,** *pr.p.*

ex·cel·lence (ek's'l əns), *n.* the fact of being better or greater; extra goodness [We all praised the *excellence* of her cooking.]

Ex·cel·len·cy (ek's'l ən sē), *n.* a title of honor given to certain persons of high position, as ambassadors, bishops, or governors [An ambassador is addressed as "Your *Excellency*."] —**Ex'cel·len·cies,** *pl.*

ex·cel·lent (ek's'l ənt), *adj.* better than others of its kind; very good [Mother makes fairly good cakes, but her pies are *excellent*.] —**ex'cel·lent·ly,** *adv.*

ex·cel·si·or (ek sel'si ôr'), *adj. & interj.* always upward; higher: *a Latin word used as a motto or as an exclamation.* —*n.* thin, curly shavings of wood used for packing breakable things or for stuffing some furniture.

ex·cept (ik sept'), *prep.* leaving out; other than; but [Everyone *except* Anne went home.] —*v.* to leave out; omit [He *excepted* Jones from his criticism.] —*conj.* unless: *now seldom used.*

ex·cept·ing (ik sep'ting), *prep.* except.

ex·cep·tion (ik sep'shən), *n.* **1.** an excepting, or leaving out [Everyone must attend, with the *exception* of Dan.] **2.** a person or thing that is different from others of its kind; case to which certain rules or principles do not apply [Most animals do not lay eggs, but the platypus is an *exception*.] —**take exception,** to object; argue against or resent.

ex·cep·tion·al (ik sep'shən 'l), *adj.* that is an exception; different or unusual; also, unusually good [He is an *exceptional* pianist.] —**ex·cep'tion·al·ly,** *adv.*

ex·cerpt (ek'sərpt), *n.* a section copied or quoted from a book or other writing; extract. —*v.* (ik sûrpt'), to take out and quote from a piece of writing; extract.

ex·cess (ik ses'), *n.* **1.** more than what is needed or proper; too much [His teeth were harmed by an *excess* of candy and gum.] **2.** the amount that is larger or more than that which is needed or kept; extra amount [He bought a bicycle with some of the money and put the *excess* in the bank.] —*adj.* (*usually* ek'ses), more than the usual limit; extra [Airlines charge for *excess* luggage.] —**in excess of,** more than. —**to excess,** too much [to eat *to excess*].

ex·ces·sive (ik ses′iv), *adj.* that is too much or too great [her *excessive* laughter]. —**ex·ces′sive·ly,** *adv.*

ex·change (iks chānj′), *v.* **1.** to give in return for something else; trade [He *exchanged* the bicycle for a larger one.] **2.** to give each other similar things [Jane and I always *exchange* birthday cards.] —*n.* **1.** a giving of one thing in return for another; trade [I'll give you my pen in *exchange* for that book.] **2.** a giving to one another of similar things [Our class has a gift *exchange* at Christmas time.] **3.** a place where business or trading is carried on [a stock *exchange*]. **4.** a central office in a telephone system, serving a certain area [In the telephone number Erie 7255, "Erie" is the name of the *exchange.*] —**ex·changed′,** *p.t. & p.p.;* **ex·chang′ing,** *pr.p.*

ex·cheq·uer (iks chek′ər), *n.* **1.** the treasury of a country. **2. Exchequer,** the department of the British government that is in charge of the national funds.

ex·cise (ek′sīz *or* ik sīz′), *n.* a tax on the making, selling, or using of certain goods, as tobacco, within a country: also **excise tax.**

ex·cise (ik sīz′), *v.* to cut out; remove [The surgeon *excised* the tumor with no difficulty.] —**ex·cised′,** *p.t. & p.p.;* **ex·cis′ing,** *pr.p.* —**ex·ci·sion** (ik sizh′ən), *n.*

ex·cit·a·ble (ik sī′tə b'l), *adj.* easily excited. —**ex·cit′a·bil′i·ty,** *n.*

ex·cite (ik sīt′), *v.* **1.** to stir into motion; make active; stimulate [Tapping on the hive *excited* the bees.] **2.** to call forth; bring out [The child's tears *excited* our pity.] **3.** to cause strong feeling in; stir up; arouse [The news of Lindbergh's flight *excited* the country.] —**ex·cit′ed,** *p.t. & p.p.;* **ex·cit′ing,** *pr.p.*

ex·cit·ed (ik sīt′id), *adj.* having strong feelings; stirred up. —**ex·cit′ed·ly,** *adv.*

ex·cite·ment (ik sīt′mənt), *n.* **1.** an exciting or being excited [The fox caused *excitement* in the hen house.] **2.** anything that excites.

ex·cit·ing (ik sīt′ing), *adj.* causing excitement; stirring; thrilling [an *exciting* story].

ex·claim (iks klām′), *v.* to speak out suddenly and with strong feeling, as in surprise, anger, etc. ["She's falling!" he *exclaimed.*]

ex·cla·ma·tion (eks′klə mā′shən), *n.* **1.** the act of exclaiming. **2.** a word or phrase that is exclaimed to show strong feeling; interjection ["Oh!" and "Help!" are *exclamations.*]

exclamation mark or **exclamation point,** the mark ! used after a word or sentence to show surprise, anger, or other strong feeling.

ex·clam·a·to·ry (iks klam′ə tôr′ē), *adj.* showing or using exclamation [an *exclamatory* style].

ex·clude (iks klōōd′), *v.* to keep out or shut out; refuse to let in, think about, include, etc.; bar [They *excluded* John from their club. Don't *exclude* the possibility of an error in the date.] —**ex·clud′ed,** *p.t. & p.p.;* **ex·clud′ing,** *pr.p.*

ex·clu·sion (iks klōō′zhən), *n.* the act of excluding or the fact of being excluded.

ex·clu·sive (iks klōō′siv), *adj.* **1.** given or belonging to no other; not shared; sole [He has the *exclusive* right to dig for oil on this land.] **2.** keeping out certain people, especially those who are not wealthy or who are not wanted for other reasons; not open to the public [an *exclusive* club]. **3.** shutting out all other interests, thoughts, activities, etc. [an *exclusive* interest in sports]. —**exclusive of,** not including; leaving out [How long is the school year, *exclusive of* holidays?] —**ex·clu′sive·ly,** *adv.*

ex·com·mu·ni·cate (eks′kə myōō′nə kāt), *v.* to make no longer a member of a church; punish by putting out of a church. —**ex′com·mu′ni·cat·ed,** *p.t. & p.p.;* **ex′com·mu′ni·cat·ing,** *pr.p.* —**ex′com·mu′ni·ca′tion,** *n.*

ex·cre·ment (eks′krə mənt), *n.* waste matter from the bowels.

ex·cres·cence (iks kres′'ns), *n.* a thing growing out of something else in a way that is not normal, as a wart.

ex·crete (iks krēt′), *v.* to get rid of waste matter from the body. —**ex·cret′ed,** *p.t. & p.p.;* **ex·cret′ing,** *pr.p.*

ex·cre·tion (iks krē′shən), *n.* **1.** an excreting. **2.** waste matter excreted; sweat, urine, etc.

ex·cru·ci·at·ing (iks krōō′shi āt′ing), *adj.* causing great pain; torturing; agonizing.

ex·cur·sion (ik skur′zhən), *n.* **1.** a short trip taken for pleasure. **2.** a round trip on a bus, train, etc. at a special lower rate.

ex·cus·a·ble (ik skyōōz′ə b'l), *adj.* that can or should be excused [an *excusable* error].

ex·cuse (ik skyōōz′), *v.* **1.** to be a proper reason or explanation for [That was a selfish act that nothing will *excuse.*] **2.** to think of a fault or wrongdoing as not important; overlook; forgive; pardon [Please *excuse* my interrupting you.] **3.** to set free from some duty or promise; release [The busy teacher was *excused* from serving on the jury.] **4.** to allow to leave or go [You may be *excused* from the table.] —*n.* (ik skyōōs′), **1.** a reason given to explain some action or behavior; apology [Ignorance of the law is no *excuse* for wrongdoing.] **2.** a freeing from a duty or promise [May I have an *excuse* from gym class?] **3.** anything that serves as an excuse [Her lame ankle was Flo's *excuse* for staying home.] **4.** a reason that one has made up to explain his actions; pretext [I shall invent some *excuse* for not going.] —**ex·cused′,** *p.t. & p.p.;* **ex·cus′ing,** *pr.p.*

ex·e·cra·ble (ek′si krə b'l), *adj.* that deserves to be hated; very bad. —**ex′e·cra·bly,** *adv.*

ex·e·crate (ek′si krāt), *v.* **1.** to call down a curse on; curse. **2.** to dislike very much; hate. —**ex′e·crat·ed,** *p.t. & p.p.;* **ex′e·crat·ing,** *pr.p.* —**ex′e·cra′tion,** *n.*

ex·e·cute (ek′si kyōōt), *v.* **1.** to carry out; do; perform [to *execute* a plan; to *execute* a difficult

---

fat,　āpe,　cär,　ten,　ēven,　hit,　bīte,　gō,　hôrn,　tōol,　book,　up,　fūr;
get,　joy,　yet,　chin,　she,　thin,　*th*en;　zh = s in pleasure;　′ as in able (ā′b'l);
ə = a in ago,　e in agent,　i in sanity,　o in confess,　u in focus.

piece of music on the piano]. **2.** to put a law or order into operation; administer [The President promises to *execute* the laws passed by Congress.] **3.** to put to death in a way that is ordered by law [to *execute* a criminal]. **4.** to make a work of art according to a plan or design [to *execute* a statue]. —**ex·e·cut·ed,** *p.t.* & *p.p.*; **ex·e·cut·ing,** *pr.p.*

ex·e·cu·tion (ek′si kyōō′shən), *n.* **1.** the act of executing, or carrying out something [The patrol put the captain's plan into *execution*.] **2.** a putting to death as ordered by law. **3.** the way in which something is done or performed [the *execution* of a painting; the *execution* of a solo passage on a violin]. **4.** the act of making legal, as by signing one's name [the *execution* of a contract].

ex·e·cu·tion·er (ek′si kyōō′shən ər), *n.* a person who kills those sentenced by law to die.

ex·ec·u·tive (ig zek′yoo tiv), *n.* **1.** any of the persons who manage the affairs of an organization, as the officers and managers of a business. **2.** any of the persons who see that the laws of a nation are carried out [The Constitution makes the President our chief *executive*.] —*adj.* **1.** having to do with managing; of or like an executive [A police chief must have *executive* ability.] **2.** having the power and the duty to see that the laws of a nation are carried out [the *executive* branch of a government].

ex·ec·u·tor (ig zek′yoo tər), *n.* a person who has been named to carry out the directions of another person's will.

ex·em·pla·ry (ig zem′plə rē), *adj.* **1.** that is a model or example; worth imitating [Mary had an *exemplary* record at school.] **2.** meant to be a warning [*exemplary* punishment].

ex·em·pli·fy (ig zem′plə fī), *v.* to show by giving or being an example of [My mother *exemplified* kindness and generosity.] —**ex·em′pli·fied,** *p.t.* & *p.p.*; **ex·em′pli·fy·ing,** *pr.p.* —**ex·em·pli·fi·ca·tion** (ig zem′plə fi kā′shən), *n.*

ex·empt (ig zempt′), *v.* to set free from a rule or duty that others must follow; excuse [He was *exempted* from military service because of his age.] —*adj.* freed from a usual rule or duty [goods that are *exempt* from payment of tax].

ex·emp·tion (ig zemp′shən), *n.* **1.** the act of exempting. **2.** a certain sum of money earned, on which income tax is not paid [An *exemption* is given for each person supported, for old age, etc.]

ex·er·cise (ek′sər siz), *n.* **1.** the act of using; use [the *exercise* of a skill]. **2.** active use of the body in order to make it stronger or healthier [Long walks are good outdoor *exercise*.] **3.** *usually* **exercises,** *pl.* a series of movements done regularly to make some part of the body stronger or to develop some skill [These *exercises* will strengthen your legs.] **4.** a problem to be studied and worked on by a student in order to develop certain skills [piano *exercises*]. **5. exercises,** *pl.* a program of speeches, songs, etc. at some ceremony [Our graduation *exercises* opened with a prayer.] —*v.* **1.** to put into action; use [*Exercise* caution in driving.] **2.** to put into action or do certain regular movements, in order to develop

or train [*Exercise* your weak ankle. I *exercise* every morning.] —**ex′er·cised,** *p.t.* & *p.p.*; **ex′er·cis·ing,** *pr.p.*

ex·ert (ig zūrt′), *v.* to put into use; use [*Exert* your will.] —**exert oneself,** to try hard.

ex·er·tion (ig zūr′shən), *n.* **1.** the act of exerting, or using [the *exertion* of skill]. **2.** the use of power and strength; effort [The swimmer was worn out by his *exertions*.]

ex·hale (eks hāl′), *v.* **1.** to breathe out [Take a deep breath, then *exhale*.] **2.** to give off a gas or vapor, or pass off as a vapor. —**ex·haled′,** *p.t.* & *p.p.*; **ex·hal′ing,** *pr.p.* —**ex·ha·la·tion** (eks′hə lā′shən), *n.*

ex·haust (ig zôst′), *v.* **1.** to use up completely [I've *exhausted* my patience.] **2.** to let out the contents of; make completely empty [The leak *exhausted* the gas tank.] **3.** to use up the strength of; to tire out; weaken [Tennis *exhausts* her.] **4.** to study or deal with in a complete or thorough way [to *exhaust* a subject]. —*n.* **1.** the used steam or gas that comes from the cylinders of an engine; especially, the fumes from the gasoline engine in an automobile. **2.** the forcing out of such steam or gas. **3.** a pipe through which such steam or gas is forced out: also **exhaust pipe.**

ex·haus·tion (ig zôs′chən), *n.* **1.** the act of exhausting, or using up. **2.** the condition of being very tired or weakened; great weariness.

ex·haus·tive (ig zôs′tiv), *adj.* leaving nothing out; complete; thorough [an *exhaustive* search].

ex·hib·it (ig zib′it), *v.* **1.** to show or display to the public [to *exhibit* a stamp collection]. **2.** to show or reveal [Such an act *exhibits* great courage.] —*n.* **1.** something exhibited to the public [an art *exhibit*]. **2.** something shown as evidence in a court of law.

ex·hi·bi·tion (ek′sə bish′ən), *n.* **1.** the act of exhibiting, or showing. **2.** a public showing, as of a collection of things.

ex·hi·bi·tion·ist (ek′sə bish′ən ist), *n.* a person who shows off to make people look at him.

ex·hib·i·tor or **ex·hib·i·ter** (ig zib′ə tər), *n.* a person who exhibits at a public showing.

ex·hil·a·rate (ig zil′ə rāt), *v.* to make feel lively and gay. —**ex·hil′a·rat·ed,** *p.t.* & *p.p.*; **ex·hil′a·rat·ing,** *pr.p.* —**ex·hil′a·ra′tion,** *n.*

ex·hort (ig zôrt′), *v.* to urge or advise strongly [He *exhorted* us to try harder.] —**ex′hor·ta′tion,** *n.*

ex·hume (ig zyōōm′), *v.* to remove from a grave. —**ex·humed′,** *p.t.* & *p.p.*; **ex·hum′ing,** *pr.p.*

ex·i·gen·cy (ek′sə jən sē), *n.* something that calls for quick action, or the need created by such a situation; emergency. —**ex′i·gen·cies,** *pl.*

ex·ile (eg′zīl *or* ek′sīl), *v.* to force a person to leave his own country and live somewhere else; banish. —*n.* **1.** the condition of being exiled; banishment. **2.** a person who is exiled. —**ex′·iled,** *p.t.* & *p.p.*; **ex′il·ing,** *pr.p.*

ex·ist (ig zist′), *v.* **1.** to be; have actual being [The unicorn never really *existed*.] **2.** to occur or be found [the qualities that *exist* in a person]. **3.** to live [Fish cannot *exist* long out of water.]

ex·ist·ence (ig zis′təns), *n.* **1.** the condition of being; an existing. **2.** an occurring. **3.** life [a happy *existence*]. —**ex·ist′ent,** *adj.*

ex·it (eg′zit *or* ek′sit), *n.* **1.** a place for going out; door or passage out. **2.** a going out [He made a quick *exit*.] *Exit* is a Latin word meaning "he (or she) goes out": originally a direction to an actor to go off the stage [*Exit* Hamlet.]

Ex·o·dus (ek′sə dəs), *n.* **1.** the going out of the Israelites from Egypt, as told in the Bible. **2.** the second book of the Old Testament, telling of this. **3.** exodus, any going out; departure [the *exodus* to the suburbs].

ex of·fi·ci·o (eks ə fish′i ō), because of the position that one holds: *a Latin phrase* [The president of the company was, *ex officio*, on the board of directors.]

ex·on·er·ate (ig zän′ə rāt), *v.* to prove to be not guilty; declare to be innocent [The prisoner was *exonerated* by the testimony of two witnesses.] —**ex·on′er·at·ed,** *p.t. & p.p.;* **ex·on′er·at·ing,** *prp.* —**ex·on′er·a′tion,** *n.*

ex·or·bi·tant (ig zôr′bə tənt), *adj.* too much or too great; not reasonable or not fair [an *exorbitant* price]. —**ex·or′bi·tance,** *n.*

ex·or·cise or **ex·or·cize** (ek′sôr sīz), *v.* to drive out a supposed evil spirit by saying a charm or making a magic sign. —**ex′or·cised** or **ex′or·cized,** *p.t. & p.p.;* **ex′or·cis·ing** or **ex′or·ciz·ing,** *prp.*

ex·ot·ic (ig zät′ik), *adj.* strange, different, or foreign, especially in a fascinating way [*exotic* foods]. —**ex·ot′i·cal·ly,** *adv.*

ex·pand (ik spand′), *v.* **1.** to make or grow bigger or wider, as by unfolding, puffing out, or spreading; enlarge [Take a deep breath to *expand* your chest. The peacock *expanded* his tail.] **2.** to tell or develop the details of [to *expand* an idea into a short story].

ex·panse (ik spans′), *n.* a large, open area or surface [an *expanse* of desert].

ex·pan·sion (ik span′shən), *n.* **1.** the act of expanding or the fact of being expanded [the *expansion* of a country by conquest]. **2.** the amount or part that is expanded [Plans for the school include a six-room *expansion*.]

ex·pan·sive (ik span′siv), *adj.* **1.** that can expand [Gases are *expansive*.] **2.** spread over a wide area; broad [the *expansive* area of the wheat fields]. **3.** showing a frank and open manner, especially in a warm and friendly way [Father grew *expansive* as he talked of his childhood.]

ex·pa·ti·ate (ik spā′shi āt), *v.* to speak or write in great detail [to *expatiate* on a subject]. —**ex·pa′ti·at·ed,** *p.t. & p.p.;* **ex·pa′ti·at·ing,** *prp.*

ex·pa·tri·ate (eks pā′tri āt), *v.* to force a person to leave his own country; exile. —*n.* (eks pā′tri·it), an expatriated person or one who leaves his own country to live in another. —**ex·pa′tri·at·ed,** *p.t. & p.p.;* **ex·pa′tri·at·ing,** *prp.* —**ex·pa′tri·a′tion,** *n.*

ex·pect (ik spekt′), *v.* **1.** to think that something will happen or come; look forward to [I *expect* to hear from Mary soon.] **2.** to look for as proper or due [Some parents *expect* too much of their children.] **3.** to guess or suppose: *used only in everyday talk.*

ex·pect·an·cy (ik spek′tən sē), *n.* **1.** the act of expecting; expectation [The children awaited the party in happy *expectancy*.] **2.** that which is expected [Babies today have an *expectancy* of longer life than those born a hundred years ago.] —**ex·pect′an·cies,** *pl.*

ex·pect·ant (ik spek′tənt), *adj.* waiting for something to happen; expecting [The children went to bed on Christmas Eve with happy, *expectant* faces.] —**ex·pect′ant·ly,** *adv.*

ex·pec·ta·tion (ek′spek tā′shən), *n.* **1.** an expecting, or looking forward to something [He sat on the edge of his seat in *expectation*.] **2.** *often* **expectations,** *pl.* something expected, or looked forward to, especially with good reason [He has *expectations* of inheriting his father's wealth.]

ex·pec·to·rate (ik spek′tə rāt), *v.* to spit. —**ex·pec′to·rat·ed,** *p.t. & p.p.;* **ex·pec′to·rat·ing,** *prp.* —**ex·pec′to·ra′tion,** *n.*

ex·pe·di·en·cy (ik spē′di ən sē), *n.* **1.** the condition of being right or useful for some purpose; fitness [I sent the order by air mail as a matter of *expediency*.] **2.** the doing of something that is selfish rather than right [The decision was made more for his own *expediency* than for the general good.] Also **ex·pe′di·ence.** —**ex·pe′di·en·cies,** *pl.*

ex·pe·di·ent (ik spē′di ənt), *adj.* **1.** wise or useful for some purpose; convenient [The telephone is an *expedient* way to deliver messages.] **2.** helpful to oneself, but not really right or proper. —*n.* something useful for a certain purpose [The watchman kept awake by the *expedient* of hot coffee.] —**ex·pe′di·ent·ly,** *adv.*

ex·pe·dite (ek′spi dīt), *v.* to make move or act in an easier or faster way; speed up; hasten [We can *expedite* the loading by adding two men to the crew.] —**ex′pe·dit·ed,** *p.t. & p.p.;* **ex′pe·dit·ing,** *prp.* —**ex′pe·dit·er,** *n.*

ex·pe·di·tion (ek′spi dish′ən), *n.* **1.** a long journey or voyage by a group of people, as for exploring a region or to take part in a battle. **2.** the people, ships, etc. making such a trip. **3.** speed or quickness with little effort or waste [He finished the task with *expedition*.]

ex·pe·di·tion·ar·y (ek′spi dish′ən er′ē), *adj.* going on an expedition [the American *Expeditionary* Force sent to Europe in World War I].

ex·pe·di·tious (ek′spi dish′əs), *adj.* with great speed; quick and efficient [to work in an *expeditious* manner].

ex·pel (ik spel′), *v.* **1.** to drive out or throw out with force; eject [This gun automatically *expels* the cartridges.] **2.** to send away or make leave as a punishment [Bruce was *expelled* from school for stealing.] —**ex·pelled′**, *p.t. & p.p.*; **ex·pel′ling**, *pr.p.*

ex·pend (ik spend′), *v.* to spend; use up.

ex·pend·a·ble (ik spen′də b'l), *adj.* that can be spent or used up; especially, in warfare, worth sacrificing in order to gain some end.

ex·pend·i·ture (ik spen′di chər), *n.* **1.** a spending or using up of money, time, energy, etc. **2.** the amount spent or used up.

ex·pense (ik spens′), *n.* **1.** the act of spending money, time, etc. **2.** *also* **expenses**, *pl.* the amount of money spent; often, money spent or needed for carrying out a job [Many salesmen are paid a salary, plus traveling *expenses*.] **3.** something that causes spending [Going to college is a great *expense* today.] **4.** loss or sacrifice [The battle was won at terrible *expense*.]

ex·pen·sive (ik spen′siv), *adj.* costing much [*expensive* clothes]. —**ex·pen′sive·ly**, *adv.*

ex·pe·ri·ence (ik spir′i əns), *n.* **1.** the act of living through a happening or happenings [*Experience* teaches us many things.] **2.** something that one has done or lived through [This trip was an *experience* that I'll never forget.] **3.** skill gotten by training, practice, and work [an actor with much *experience*]. —*v.* to have the experience of [to *experience* success]. —**ex·pe′ri·enced**, *p.t. & p.p.*; **ex·pe′ri·enc·ing**, *pr.p.*

ex·pe·ri·enced (ik spir′i ənst), *adj.* having had experience or having learned from experience.

ex·per·i·ment (ik sper′ə mənt), *n.* a test or tests to find out something or to see whether a theory is correct [Television is used in some schools as an *experiment* in teaching.] —*v.* to make experiments. —**ex·per′i·men·ta′tion** (ik sper′ə men tā′shən), *n.*

ex·per·i·men·tal (ik sper′ə men′t'l), *adj.* **1.** based on or having to do with experiment [an *experimental* science]. **2.** being an experiment; testing; trial [a baby's first, *experimental* steps]. —**ex·per′i·men′tal·ly**, *adv.*

ex·pert (ek′spərt *or* ik spûrt′), *adj.* **1.** having much special knowledge and experience; very skillful [an *expert* golfer]. **2.** of or from an expert [*expert* advice]. —*n.* (ek′spərt), an expert person; authority [an *expert* in art].

ex·per·tise (ek′spər tēz′), *n.* the special skill or knowledge that an expert has [an architect's *expertise* in building materials].

ex·pi·ate (ek′spi āt), *v.* to make up for some wrongdoing; make amends for [He *expiated* his sins by doing good works.] —**ex′pi·at·ed**, *p.t. & p.p.*; **ex′pi·at·ing**, *pr.p.* —**ex′pi·a′tion**, *n.*

ex·pi·ra·tion (ek′spə rā′shən), *n.* **1.** a coming to an end; close [the *expiration* of a term of office]. **2.** a breathing out.

ex·pire (ik spīr′), *v.* **1.** to come to an end; stop [Our lease *expires* next month.] **2.** to die. **3.** to breathe out. —**ex·pired′**, *p.t. & p.p.*; **ex·pir′ing**, *pr.p.*

ex·plain (iks plān′), *v.* **1.** to make clear or plain; give details of [The coach will *explain* the new play.] **2.** to give the meaning of [The teacher *explained* the story.] **3.** to give reasons for [Can you *explain* your absence?]

ex·pla·na·tion (eks′plə nā′shən), *n.* **1.** the act of explaining [This plan needs *explanation*.] **2.** something that explains [The leak in the roof is the *explanation* for that puddle.] **3.** a meaning given in explaining [different *explanations* of the same event].

ex·plan·a·to·ry (iks plan′ə tôr′ē), *adj.* that explains; explaining [an *explanatory* letter].

ex·ple·tive (eks′pli tiv), *n.* **1.** an oath or exclamation ["Gosh" and "oh" are *expletives*.] **2.** a word that has no particular meaning but is used to fill out a phrase [In the phrase "it is raining," the word "it" is an *expletive*.]

ex·plic·it (iks plis′it), *adj.* so clear and plain that there can be no doubt as to the meaning; definite [He gave us his *explicit* approval.] —**ex·plic′it·ly**, *adv.*

ex·plode (iks plōd′), *v.* **1.** to blow up or burst with a loud noise and force [The firecracker *exploded*. The engineer *exploded* the dynamite.] **2.** to show to be false or foolish [Science has helped to *explode* many superstitions.] **3.** to burst forth noisily [He *exploded* with anger.] —**ex·plod′ed**, *p.t. & p.p.*; **ex·plod′ing**, *pr.p.*

ex·ploit (eks′ploit), *n.* a daring act or bold deed [the *exploits* of Robin Hood]. —*v.* (iks ploit′), **1.** to make full and proper use of [to *exploit* the water power of a river]. **2.** to use in a selfish way; take unfair advantage of [Talented children are sometimes *exploited* by their parents.] —**ex′ploi·ta′tion**, *n.*

ex·plore (iks plôr′), *v.* **1.** to travel in a region that is unknown or not well known, in order to find out more about it [to *explore* a wild jungle]. **2.** to look into or examine carefully [to *explore* a problem]. —**ex·plored′**, *p.t. & p.p.*; **ex·plor′ing**, *pr.p.* —**ex′plo·ra′tion**, *n.* —**ex·plor′er**, *n.*

ex·plo·sion (iks plō′zhən), *n.* **1.** an exploding, or blowing up with a loud noise [the *explosion* of a bomb]. **2.** any noisy outburst [an angry *explosion* of temper].

ex·plo·sive (iks plō′siv), *adj.* **1.** that can cause an explosion [an *explosive* substance]. **2.** like an explosion [an *explosive* clap of thunder]. **3.** that might explode suddenly [Riots had caused an *explosive* situation.] —*n.* a substance that can explode [dynamite and other *explosives*].

ex·po·nent (ik spō′nənt), *n.* **1.** a person who explains and interprets [an *exponent* of modern music]. **2.** a person or thing that is an example or symbol of something [Washington was an *exponent* of honesty.]

ex·port (ik spôrt′ *or* ek′spôrt), *v.* to send goods from one country for sale in another [Germany *exports* many automobiles.] —*n.* (ek′spôrt), **1.** the act of exporting [Ceylon raises tea for *export*.] **2.** something exported [Oil is Venezuela's chief *export*.] —**ex′por·ta′tion**, *n.* —**ex·port′er**, *n.*

ex·pose (ik spōz′), *v.* **1.** to put in a position of danger; leave unprotected [By playing with Billy, the children had all been *exposed* to the measles.] **2.** to put something where it can be worked on or changed by outside action [Copper that is *exposed* to the weather will turn green.]

3. to let be seen; display [He removed the bandage and *exposed* the wound.] **4.** to make known; reveal [to *expose* a crime]. **5.** to let light fall on the film or plate in a camera, and in this way cause a picture to be recorded. —**ex·posed′**, *p.t. & p.p.;* **ex·pos′ing**, *pr.p.*

ex·po·si·tion (ek′spə zish′ən), *n.* **1.** a large show or fair that is open to the public [Chicago held a great *exposition* in 1893.] **2.** explanation, or some writing or speaking that explains something [His *exposition* of *Hamlet* was helpful.]

ex·pos·i·tor (ik späz′ə tər), *n.* a person, piece of writing, etc. that explains something.

ex·pos·i·to·ry (ik späz′ə tôr′ē), *adj.* that serves to explain; explanatory.

ex·pos·tu·late (ik späs′chə lāt), *v.* to argue with a person seriously against something he has done or means to do [The players *expostulated* in vain with the umpire.] —**ex·pos′tu·lat·ed**, *p.t. & p.p.;* **ex·pos′tu·lat·ing**, *pr.p.* —**ex·pos′tu·la′tion**, *n.*

ex·po·sure (ik spō′zhər), *n.* **1.** the act of exposing [the *exposure* of a plot]. **2.** the fact of being exposed [tanned by *exposure* to the sun]. **3.** the position of a house, etc., described by the direction from which it is exposed to sun and wind [Our kitchen has a southern *exposure*.] **4.** the time during which a photographic film, etc. is exposed to light; also, a section of film that can be made into one picture [Give this film a short *exposure*. There are eight *exposures* on this film.]

ex·pound (ik spound′), *v.* to explain, especially by giving many details [to *expound* a theory].

ex·press (iks pres′), *v.* **1.** to put into words; state [It is hard to *express* my meaning.] **2.** to give or be a sign of; show [His frown *expressed* doubt.] **3.** to send goods by a fast way. —*adj.* **1.** clearly said or meant; definite; explicit [I came for the *express* purpose of seeing Frank.] **2.** taking the shortest and fastest route; not making many stops [an *express* train or bus]. **3.** for fast driving [an *express* highway]. —*n.* **1.** a train, bus, etc. that takes the shortest and fastest route, not making many stops. **2.** a way of sending goods or packages that is faster than the usual ways. Express usually costs more. **3.** goods sent by express. —*adv.* by express [The package came *express*.] —**express oneself,** to tell in words what one thinks or how one feels.

ex·pres·sion (iks presh′ən), *n.* **1.** an expressing, or putting into words [This note is an *expression* of my gratitude.] **2.** a way of speaking, singing, or playing something that gives it real meaning or feeling [She sang with such *expression* that the audience wept.] **3.** a word or phrase ["You bet" is an everyday *expression* meaning "certainly."] **4.** a showing of the way one thinks or feels [Applause is an *expression* of pleasure.] **5.** a look that shows how one thinks or feels [She had a sad *expression*.]

ex·pres·sive (iks pres′iv), *adj.* **1.** that expresses or shows [a smile *expressive* of joy]. **2.** full of meaning or feeling [an *expressive* nod].

ex·press·ly (iks pres′lē), *adv.* **1.** in a plain and definite way [I told you *expressly* not to go.] **2.** for the purpose; especially [Sarah went to college *expressly* to become a nurse.]

ex·press·way (iks pres′wā), *n.* a divided highway for high-speed traffic; freeway.

ex·pul·sion (ik spul′shən), *n.* an expelling, or forcing out, or the condition of being expelled [the *expulsion* of hot gases from a rocket].

ex·punge (ik spunj′), *v.* to erase or remove completely [to *expunge* a word from a sentence]. —**ex·punged′**, *p.t. & p.p.;* **ex·pung′ing**, *pr.p.*

ex·pur·gate (ek′spər gāt), *v.* to clean up by taking out words or sentences thought to be indecent [to *expurgate* a book]. —**ex′pur·gat·ed**, *p.t. & p.p.;* **ex′pur·gat·ing**, *pr.p.*

ex·qui·site (eks′kwi zit *or* ik skwiz′it), *adj.* **1.** done with great care and skill [*exquisite* carvings]. **2.** very beautiful [an *exquisite* sunset]. **3.** of the best quality; excellent [an *exquisite* performance]. **4.** very great or sharp [*exquisite* joy or pain]. —**ex′qui·site·ly**, *adv.*

ex·tant (ek′stənt *or* ik stant′), *adj.* still existing [None of his letters are *extant*.]

ex·tem·po·ra·ne·ous (ik stem′pə rā′ni əs), *adj.* done or spoken without much planning, especially without being written down [an *extemporaneous* speech].

ex·tem·po·re (ik stem′pə rē), *adv.* without much planning; offhand [The mayor spoke *extempore* in favor of the plan.]

ex·tend (ik stend′), *v.* **1.** to make longer; stretch out [Careful cleaning *extends* the life of a rug.] **2.** to lie or stretch [The fence *extends* along the meadow.] **3.** to make larger or more complete; enlarge; increase [to *extend* one's power]. **4.** to offer or give [May I *extend* congratulations to the bride?] **5.** to straighten or stretch out [*Extend* your arm for the vaccination.] —**ex·tend′ed**, *adj.*

ex·ten·sion (ik sten′shən), *n.* **1.** the act of extending; a stretching out, enlarging, increasing, etc. **2.** something that extends, or makes larger; addition [We are building an *extension* on our school library.] **3.** an extra telephone on the same line as the main telephone.

ex·ten·sive (ik sten′siv), *adj.* **1.** covering a large area; widespread [the *extensive* jungles of Brazil]. **2.** applying to many things; on a large scale; far-reaching [to make *extensive* changes in a program]. —**ex·ten′sive·ly**, *adv.*

ex·tent (ik stent′), *n.* **1.** the size, amount, length, etc. to which something extends [The *extent* of knowledge has increased since Aristotle's day.] **2.** degree or limit [To a certain *extent*, I agree with you.] **3.** a large area [He owns a vast *extent* of woodland.]

ex·ten·u·ate (ik sten′yoo āt), *v.* to make a wrongdoing seem less serious by being a partial excuse [His great anger will *extenuate* his rude remarks.] —**ex·ten'u·at·ed,** *p.t.* & *p.p.;* **ex·ten'u·at·ing,** *pr.p.* —**ex·ten'u·a'tion,** *n.*

ex·te·ri·or (ik stir'i ər), *adj.* **1.** of or on the outside; outer [The *exterior* trim of the house is gray.] **2.** coming from the outside [*exterior* forces]. —*n.* the outside or outer part.

ex·ter·mi·nate (ik stūr'mə nāt), *v.* to kill or destroy completely; wipe out [His work is to *exterminate* rats.] —**ex·ter'mi·nat·ed,** *p.t.* & *p.p.;* **ex·ter'mi·nat·ing,** *pr.p.* —**ex·ter'mi·na'tion,** *n.* —**ex·ter'mi·na·tor,** *n.*

ex·ter·nal (ik stūr'n'l), *adj.* **1.** on the outside; outer [Red spots are an *external* sign of measles.] **2.** on the outside of the body [a medicine for *external* use only]. **3.** that comes from the outside [an *external* force]. **4.** merely seeming to be so [*external* politeness]. **5.** having to do with foreign relations [a nation's *external* affairs]. —*n.* an external thing or appearance. —**ex·ter'nal·ly,** *adv.*

ex·tinct (ik stingkt'), *adj.* **1.** no longer living; having died out [Dinosaurs are *extinct.*] **2.** no longer burning or active [an *extinct* volcano].

ex·tinc·tion (ik stingk'shən), *n.* **1.** the fact of becoming extinct, or dying out [The California condor faces *extinction.*] **2.** a putting an end to or wiping out [the *extinction* of all debts]. **3.** an extinguishing, or putting out.

ex·tin·guish (ik sting'gwish), *v.* **1.** to put out; quench [to *extinguish* a fire or light]. **2.** to put an end to; destroy [to *extinguish* all hope].

ex·tin·guish·er (ik sting'gwish ər), *n.* a person or thing that extinguishes; especially, a device for putting out a fire by spraying a liquid or gas on it.

fire extinguisher

ex·tir·pate (ek'stər pāt), *v.* **1.** to pull up a plant by the roots. **2.** to get rid of altogether; destroy completely; abolish [to *extirpate* prejudice]. —**ex'tir·pat·ed,** *p.t.* & *p.p.;* **ex'tir·pat·ing,** *pr.p.* —**ex'tir·pa'tion,** *n.*

ex·tol or **ex·toll** (ik stōl'), *v.* to say very good things about; praise highly. —**ex·tolled',** *p.t.* & *p.p.;* **ex·tol'ling,** *pr.p.*

ex·tort (ik stôrt'), *v.* to get money, a confession, etc. from someone by using force or threats.

ex·tor·tion (ik stôr'shən), *n.* **1.** the act of extorting. **2.** something that has been extorted. —**ex·tor'tion·ist,** *n.*

ex·tor·tion·ate (ik stôr'shən it), *adj.* like extortion; too great [an *extortionate* fee].

ex·tra (eks'trə), *adj.* more than is usual, expected, or necessary; in addition [You must pay an *extra* charge for this service.] —*n.* **1.** an extra person, thing, charge, etc. [The grocer hires *extras* to work on Saturday.] **2.** a special edition of a newspaper to tell an important news story. **3.** an actor in a motion picture who is hired from day to day to play a small part, as a member of a crowd. —*adv.* more than it usually is; especially [Today's meeting was an *extra* long one.]

ex·tract (iks trakt'), *v.* **1.** to pull out something by trying hard [to *extract* a tooth; *extract* a promise]. **2.** to get by squeezing, pressing, etc. [to *extract* orange juice]. **3.** to manage to get [to *extract* the meaning of a remark]. **4.** to take or choose a section from a piece of writing, as in order to quote it. —*n.* (eks'trakt), **1.** a strong substance that has been extracted from something, for use as a flavoring or food [vanilla *extract*]. **2.** a section of a book, etc. that has been chosen as for quoting.

ex·trac·tion (ik strak'shən), *n.* **1.** the act of extracting. **2.** the people from whom a person is descended; origin; descent [a man of Scottish *extraction*].

ex·tra·cur·ric·u·lar (eks'trə kə rik'yoo lər), *adj.* not part of the regular course of study in a school or college [Football and student council are *extracurricular* activities.]

ex·tra·dite (eks'trə dīt), *v.* to hand over a person accused of a crime or an escaped prisoner to another country or state that claims him. —**ex'tra·dit·ed,** *p.t.* & *p.p.;* **ex'tra·dit·ing,** *pr.p.* —**ex·tra·di·tion** (eks'trə dish'ən), *n.*

ex·tra·ne·ous (iks trā'ni əs), *adj.* coming from outside; not really belonging; foreign [The milk is strained to remove *extraneous* material.]

ex·traor·di·nar·y (iks trôr'd'n er'ē), *adj.* much different from the ordinary; very unusual; remarkable [What *extraordinary* clothes clowns wear!] —**ex·tra·or'di·nar'i·ly,** *adv.*

ex·trav·a·gant (iks trav'ə gənt), *adj.* **1.** spending more than one can afford or more than is necessary; wasteful [My *extravagant* sister bought four dresses.] **2.** going beyond what is proper; too much [*extravagant* praise]. —**ex·trav'a·gance,** *n.* —**ex·trav'a·gant·ly,** *adv.*

ex·treme (iks trēm'), *adj.* **1.** to the greatest degree; very great; excessive [*extreme* pain]. **2.** farthest away; most remote [the *extreme* limits of outer space]. **3.** far from what is usual; very advanced [He holds *extreme* political views.] —*n.* either of two things that are as different or as far from each other as possible [the *extremes* of laughter and tears]. —**go to extremes,** to do or say more than is necessary or proper. —**ex·treme'ly,** *adv.*

ex·trem·ist (iks trēm'ist), *n.* a person who goes to extremes or who holds extreme ideas.

ex·trem·i·ty (iks trem'ə tē), *n.* **1.** the farthest point or part; end [the eastern *extremity* of the turnpike]. **2. extremities,** *pl.* the hands and feet. **3.** the greatest degree [an *extremity* of grief]. **4.** great need, danger, etc. [The surrounded troops realized the *extremity* of their position.] **5.** a strong or severe action [a country driven to the *extremity* of declaring war]. —**ex·trem'i·ties,** *pl.*

ex·tri·cate (eks'tri kāt), *v.* to set free from some danger or difficulty; release [The boy tried to *extricate* his foot from the crevice.] —**ex'tri·cat·ed,** *p.t.* & *p.p.;* **ex'tri·cat·ing,** *pr.p.* —**ex'tri·ca'tion,** *n.*

ex·trin·sic (eks trin′sik), *adj.* not really belonging to the thing with which it is connected; external [the *extrinsic* advantages of wealth].

ex·tro·vert (eks′trō vŭrt), *n.* a person who is interested in other people and things rather than just in his own thoughts and feelings.

ex·u·ber·ant (ig zōō′bər ənt), *adj.* **1.** healthy and lively; full of good humor [I always feel *exuberant* in the spring.] **2.** growing thickly and in great quantity; luxuriant [an *exuberant* growth of trees]. —**ex·u′ber·ance,** *n.*

ex·ude (ig zōōd′ *or* ik syōōd′), *v.* to come or pass out in drops, as through the pores or a cut; ooze [Maple trees *exude* sap in the spring.] —**ex·ud′ed,** *p.t. & p.p.;* **ex·ud′ing,** *pr.p.*

ex·ult (ig zult′), *v.* to be very proud and happy; rejoice [to *exult* in victory].

ex·ult·ant (ig zul′t′nt), *adj.* exulting; full of happiness and pride [an *exultant* smile].

ex·ul·ta·tion (eg′zul tā′shən), *n.* an exulting; a feeling of great joy and pride.

eye (ī), *n.* **1.** the part of the body with which a man or animal sees. **2.** the iris of the eye [a baby with blue *eyes*]. **3.** the ability to see; sight; vision [weak *eyes*]. **4.** a look; glance [Cast an *eye* over here.] **5.** the ability to judge by looking [a good *eye* for distances]. **6.** *often* **eyes,** *pl.* judgment; opinion [In my *eyes*, she is not guilty.] **7.** something that reminds one of an eye, as a bud of a potato or the hole in a needle. —*v.* to look at; observe [She *eyed* the stranger suspiciously.] —**catch one's eye,** to get one's attention. —**feast one's eyes on,** to look at with pleasure. —**have an eye for,** to be able to notice and appreciate. —**keep an eye on,** to take care of; watch carefully. —**lay eyes on** *or* **set eyes on,** to see; look at. —**make eyes at,** to flirt with. —**open one's eyes,** to make one aware of the real facts. —**see eye to eye,** to agree completely. —**shut one's eyes to,** to refuse

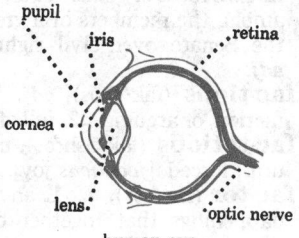
pupil · iris · retina · cornea · lens · optic nerve
human eye

to see or think about. —**eyed,** *p.t. & p.p.;* **ey′ing,** *pr.p.*

eye·ball (ī′bôl), *n.* the whole part of the eye inside the socket.

eye·brow (ī′brou), *n.* the curved, bony part over each eye, or the hair growing on it.

eye·glass (ī′glas), *n.* **1.** a lens to help one see better. **2. eyeglasses,** *pl.* a pair of such lenses fitted together in a frame.

eye·lash (ī′lash), *n.* **1.** any of the hairs that grow along the edge of the eyelid. **2.** a fringe of these hairs.

eye·less (ī′lis), *adj.* without eyes; blind.

eye·let (ī′lit), *n.* **1.** a small hole for a cord, lace, or hook to go through. **2.** a metal ring placed in such a hole to make it stronger.

eye·lid (ī′lid), *n.* either of the two folds of skin that cover and uncover the eyeball.

eye·piece (ī′pēs), *n.* the lens in a microscope or telescope that is held nearest the eye.

eyelets of a shoe

eye·sight (ī′sīt), *n.* **1.** the ability to see; sight; vision [keen *eyesight*]. **2.** the distance a person can see [Keep within *eyesight*!]

eye·sore (ī′sôr), *n.* an unpleasant thing to look at [A lawn full of weeds is an *eyesore*.]

eye·strain (ī′strān), *n.* a tired condition of the eye muscles, caused by too much use or an incorrect use of the eyes.

eye·tooth (ī′tōōth), *n.* either of the two canine teeth in the upper jaw, the third tooth from the center on each side. —**eye′teeth,** *pl.*

eye·wit·ness (ī′wit′nis), *n.* a person who actually saw something happen, not one who was told of it by someone else.

ey·rie *or* **ey·ry** (er′ē *or* ir′ē), *n.* same as **aerie.** —**ey′ries,** *pl.*

E·zek·i·el (i zē′ki əl), *n.* **1.** a Hebrew prophet in the Bible. **2.** a book of the Old Testament with his teachings.

Ez·ra (ez′rə), *n.* **1.** a Hebrew prophet in the Bible. **2.** a book of the Old Testament about him.

F

F, f (ef), *n.* the sixth letter of the English alphabet. —**F's, f's** (efs), *pl.*

F, the symbol for the chemical element *fluorine.*

F., abbreviation for **Fahrenheit.**

fa (fä), *n.* the fourth note of a musical scale.

fa·ble (fā′b'l), *n.* **1.** a very short story that teaches a lesson. It is usually about animals who act and talk like people [Aesop's *fable* "The

Grasshopper and the Ant" teaches the need to work hard and be thrifty.] **2.** a story that is not true.

fa·bled (fā′b'ld), *adj.* told about in fables or legends [the *fabled* wealth of El Dorado].

fab·ric (fab′rik), *n.* **1.** a material made from fibers or threads by weaving, knitting, etc., as any cloth, felt, lace, or the like. **2.** anything made of

fat, āpe, cär, ten, ēven, hĭt, bīte, gō, hôrn, tōōl, book, up, fŭr; get, joy, yet, chin, she, thin, *th*en; zh = s in pleasure; ′ as in able (ā′b'l); ə = a in ago, e in agent, i in sanity, o in confess, u in focus.

parts put together, or the way in which it is put together; structure [the *fabric* of a poet's writing].

fab·ri·cate (fab′ri kāt), *v.* **1.** to make or build by putting parts together; manufacture. **2.** to make up; invent [He *fabricated* an excuse for being late.] —**fab′ri·cat·ed**, *p.t. & p.p.;* **fab′-ri·cat·ing**, *pr.p.* —**fab′ri·ca′tion**, *n.* —**fab′-ri·ca′tor**, *n.*

fab·u·lous (fab′yoo ləs), *adj.* **1.** of or like a fable; made up; imaginary [The griffin is a *fabulous* monster.] **2.** hard to believe; astounding; very unusual [They spent a *fabulous* amount of money.] —**fab′u·lous·ly**, *adv.*

fa·çade or **fa·cade** (fə säd′), *n.* the front of a building, especially a front meant to be grander or more attractive than the sides or back.

face (fās), *n.* **1.** the front part of the head, including the eyes, nose, and mouth. **2.** a look that shows meaning or feeling [a sad *face*]. **3.** surface or

façade of a temple

side; especially, the main, top, or front side [the *face* of the earth; the *face* of a playing card]. **4.** dignity or reputation [to lose *face*]. —*v.* **1.** to turn toward or have the face turned toward [Please *face* the class. Our house *faces* a park.] **2.** to meet or oppose with boldness or courage [to *face* danger]. **3.** to put another material on the surface of [The courthouse is *faced* with marble.] —**face to face, 1.** with each facing the other. **2.** very close. —**in the face of, 1.** in the presence of. **2.** in spite of. —**make a face,** to twist the face; make a grimace. —**on the face of it,** as far as can be seen. —**to one's face,** openly; in front of one. —**faced,** *p.t. & p.p.;* **fac′ing,** *pr.p.*

fac·et (fas′it), *n.* **1.** any of the many polished sides of a cut gem, as a diamond. **2.** any of the various sides or appearances [the many *facets* of her personality].

fa·ce·tious (fə sē′shəs), *adj.* joking or trying to be funny, especially at the wrong time. —**fa·ce′tious·ly**, *adv.* —**fa·ce′tious·ness**, *n.*

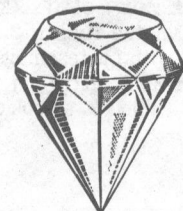

facets of a gem

fa·cial (fā′shəl), *adj.* of or for the face. —*n.* a massage or other treatment for the face.

fac·ile (fas′'l), *adj.* **1.** easy [a *facile* job]. **2.** acting, working, or done easily, or in a quick, smooth way [a *facile* mind; a *facile* style of writing]. —**fac′ile·ly**, *adv.*

fa·cil·i·tate (fə sil′ə tāt), *v.* to make easier; help [This new machine will *facilitate* your work.] —**fa·cil′i·tat·ed**, *p.t. & p.p.;* **fa·cil′i·tat·ing**, *pr.p.* —**fa·cil′i·ta′tion**, *n.*

fa·cil·i·ty (fə sil′ə tē), *n.* **1.** ease or skill in working or acting [She types with great *facility.*]

2. a thing that helps one do something more easily [The apartment has its own laundry *facilities*.] —**fa·cil′i·ties**, *pl.*

fac·ing (fās′ing), *n.* **1.** a trimming on the edge of a dress, coat, etc. [a velvet *facing* on the collar]. **2.** a covering of another material, used to decorate or protect a surface [a marble *facing* on a building].

fac·sim·i·le (fak sim′ə lē), *n.* something made to look just like another thing; exact copy [You may send a label or a *facsimile* of it.]

fact (fakt), *n.* **1.** a thing that has actually happened or that is really true [I can't deny the *fact* that I was late.] **2.** realness or truth [Can you separate *fact* from fiction in his story?] **3.** something said to have happened or supposed to be true [Have you checked the accuracy of your *facts*?] —**as a matter of fact** or **in fact,** really; actually.

fac·tion (fak′shən), *n.* **1.** a group of people inside a political party, club, government, etc. working together against other such groups for its own ideas or goals. **2.** an arguing or quarreling among the members of a group [bitter *faction* in the Senate over civil rights]. —**fac′tion·al,** *adj.*

fac·tious (fak′shəs), *adj.* **1.** tending to cause faction, or arguing. **2.** full of or caused by faction.

fac·ti·tious (fak tish′əs), *adj.* not real or natural; forced [*factitious* joy].

fac·tor (fak′tər), *n.* **1.** any one of the causes or happenings that together bring about a result [Good study habits are an important *factor* of good grades.] **2.** any of the numbers or symbols that are multiplied together to form a product [2, 5, and 10 are *factors* of 100.] **3.** a person who acts for another in a business deal; agent.

fac·to·ry (fak′tə rē), *n.* a building or group of buildings where goods are made, especially by machinery. —**fac′to·ries,** *pl.*

fac·to·tum (fak tō′təm), *n.* a person hired to do all sorts of odd jobs.

fac·tu·al (fak′chōō əl), *adj.* containing or based on facts; real; true [a *factual* account]. —**fac′tu-al·ly,** *adv.*

fac·ul·ty (fak′'l tē), *n.* **1.** any of the natural powers of the body; sense [the *faculties* of tasting and smelling]. **2.** a special skill or talent; knack [the *faculty* of remembering names]. **3.** all the teachers of a school or college [our high-school *faculty*]. **4.** all the teachers in a certain department of a college or university [the medical *faculty*]. —**fac′ul·ties,** *pl.*

fad (fad), *n.* a hobby style, etc. that many people are interested in for a short time; passing fashion [Raccoon coats were once a *fad* among college students.]

fade (fād), *v.* **1.** to make or become less bright; lose or take away color [Sunlight may *fade* your curtains. The painting had *faded* with age.] **2.** to become less fresh or strong; wither [The roses *faded* and their petals fell.] **3.** to become weaker and pass slowly out of sight or hearing [The music *faded* away.] —**fad′ed,** *p.t. & p.p.;* **fad′ing,** *pr.p.*

fag (fag), *v.* to make tired by hard work [I was *fagged* after cutting the grass.] —**fagged,** *p.t. & p.p.;* **fag′ging,** *pr.p.*

fag end, 1. the worn-out or untwisted end of a piece of rope or cloth. **2.** the last and worst part [tired at the *fag end* of the day].

fag·ot or **fag·got** (fag′ət), *n.* a bundle of sticks or twigs tied together for use as fuel.

Fahr·en·heit (far′ən hīt), *adj.* of or describing a thermometer on which the boiling point of pure water is 212 degrees and the freezing point is 32 degrees above zero.

fail (fāl), *v.* **1.** to not do what one tried to do or what one should have done; not succeed; miss or neglect [I'm afraid I'd *fail* as an artist. He *failed* to meet me at six o'clock.] **2.** to give or get a grade that shows one has not passed a test, a school course, etc. **3.** to be of no help to; disappoint [Do not *fail* me in my hour of need.] **4.** to not be present when needed or called upon; leave [His courage *failed* him when he saw the policeman.] **5.** to lose strength; weaken [The wounded knight was *failing* fast.] **6.** to become bankrupt [Many banks *failed* in 1933.] —**without fail,** surely; positively.

fail·ing (fāl′ing), *n.* **1.** a fault or weakness [His worst *failing* is that he talks too much.] **2.** failure. —*prep.* without; lacking [*Failing* some rain soon, the crops will wither.]

fail·ure (fāl′yər), *n.* **1.** the act of failing, or not succeeding [the *failure* of a plan]. **2.** a weakening [the *failure* of eyesight in old age]. **3.** a not doing; neglect [Her *failure* to answer my letter worried me]. **4.** a becoming bankrupt. **5.** a failing to pass to a higher grade in school. **6.** a person or thing that has failed.

fain (fān), *adj.* glad or willing. —*adv.* gladly or willingly [I *fain* would go with you.] *This word is now seldom used except in poetry.*

faint (fānt), *adj.* **1.** weak; not strong or clear; dim or feeble [a *faint* whisper; a *faint* odor; *faint* shadows; a *faint* chance]. **2.** weak and dizzy, as if about to swoon. —*n.* a condition in which one becomes unconscious because not enough blood reaches the brain, as in sudden shock. —*v.* to fall into a faint; swoon.

faint·heart·ed (fānt′här′tid), *adj.* cowardly or timid.

fair (fer), *adj.* **1.** beautiful [a *fair* maiden]. **2.** clean, spotless, without error, etc. [a *fair* copy of a letter; a *fair* name]. **3.** light in color; blond [*fair* hair; *fair* skin]. **4.** clear and sunny [*fair* weather]. **5.** just and honest; according to what is right [a *fair* price; *fair* play]. **6.** neither very bad nor very good; average [He plays a *fair* game of golf.] **7.** pleasant and polite [*fair* words]. **8.** that may be hunted [*fair* game]. **9.** in baseball, describing a batted ball that is not foul. —*adv.* **1.** in a fair manner [Play *fair.*] **2.** straight; squarely [The ball struck him *fair* in the face.] —**bid fair,** to seem likely. —**fair′ness,** *n.*

fair (fer), *n.* **1.** a gathering of people held every so often for the buying and selling of goods, the showing of things made, work done, animals and crops raised, etc. Prizes are often awarded and amusements and side shows are often found at a fair [a county *fair;* a world *fair*]. **2.** a carnival where there is entertainment and things are sold in order to raise money, as for a church.

fair·ly (fer′lē), *adv.* **1.** in a just and honest way. **2.** to a fair degree; neither very much nor very little; somewhat [It is *fairly* hot.] **3.** completely; really [His voice *fairly* rang.]

fair·way (fer′wā), *n.* that part of a golf course where the grass is cut short, but not including the putting greens.

fair·y (fer′ē), *n.* a tiny, graceful being in folk tales and legends. Fairies were supposed to have magic powers and to look like little people with wings. —*adj.* **1.** of fairies. **2.** like a fairy; graceful; delicate. —**fair′ies,** *pl.*

fair·y·land (fer′ē land), *n.* **1.** the imaginary land where fairies live. **2.** a lovely and enchanting place.

fairy

fairy tale, 1. a story about fairies and their magic deeds. **2.** any untrue story or lie.

faith (fāth), *n.* **1.** belief or trust that does not question or ask for proof [They have great *faith* in their doctor.] **2.** belief in God and religion [Job kept his *faith* in spite of his troubles.] **3.** a particular religion [the Jewish *faith;* the Christian *faith*]. **4.** a being loyal; allegiance [The knights pledged their *faith* to the king.] **5.** a promise [to keep, or break, one's *faith*]. —*interj.* indeed; really. —**bad faith,** a being dishonest and not sincere. —**good faith,** a being honest and sincere.

faith·ful (fāth′fəl), *adj.* **1.** deserving trust; loyal and honest [a *faithful* employee]. **2.** accurate; exact [a *faithful* account of the accident]. —**the faithful,** the true believers or loyal followers of some religion, cause, etc. —**faith′ful·ly,** *adv.* —**faith′ful·ness,** *n.*

faith·less (fāth′lis), *adj.* not deserving trust; disloyal or dishonest. —**faith′less·ly,** *adv.*

fake (fāk), *v.* to make something seem real or genuine in order to fool or deceive [The quarterback *faked* a pass and then ran with the ball.] —*n.* a person or thing that is not really what it is supposed to be; fraud [He's no doctor; he's a *fake.*] —*adj.* not genuine or real; false; sham [to cry *fake* tears]. —**faked,** *p.t. & p.p.;* **fak′ing,** *pr.p.* —**fak′er,** *n.*

fa·kir (fə kir′ *or* fā′kər), *n.* a Moslem or Hindu holy man who makes his living by begging.

fal·chion (fôl′chən), *n.* a sword used in the Middle Ages, with a broad, curved blade.

fal·con (fôl′k'n *or* fô′k'n), *n.* any of various hawks with long, pointed wings and a short, curved beak, especially one trained to hunt and kill small birds or animals.

falcon (16 in. long)

fal·con·ry (fôl′k'n rē *or* fô′k'n rē), *n.* the training of falcons to hunt, or the sport of hunting with them. **—fal′con·er,** *n.*

fall (fôl), *v.* **1.** to drop to a lower place; come down [Rain is *falling*. Apples *fell* from the tree.] **2.** to come down suddenly from an upright position; tumble or collapse [The runner stumbled and *fell*. The old building *fell* to the ground.] **3.** to take a downward direction [Her glance *fell*. The land *falls* away to the river.] **4.** to become lower, less, weaker, etc. [Prices are *falling*. Her voice *fell*.] **5.** to hit or land [The arrow *fell* wide of its mark.] **6.** to be wounded or killed in battle [Thousands *fell* at Gettysburg.] **7.** to be conquered [Berlin *fell* to the Allies.] **8.** to lose power, position, etc. [The government *fell*.] **9.** to pass into a certain condition; become [to *fall* asleep; to *fall* into a rage.] **10.** to take on a sad look [His face *fell*.] **11.** to take place; happen [My birthday *falls* on a Friday.] **12.** to come as by chance, inheritance, etc. [The estate *falls* to the son.] **13.** to come at a certain place [The accent *falls* on the first syllable.] **14.** to be divided into [These poems *fall* into two classes.] **—n. 1.** a dropping or coming down [a steady *fall* of rain; a *fall* on the ice]. **2.** a downward direction or slope. **3.** *usually* **falls,** *pl.* a waterfall. **4.** something that has fallen, or the amount that has fallen [a six-inch *fall* of snow]. **5.** the distance that something falls [a *fall* of 50 feet]. **6.** the time of year when leaves fall from the trees, between summer and winter; autumn. **7.** overthrow or ruin; downfall [the *fall* of Rome]. **8.** a becoming less; decrease [a *fall* in the temperature]. **—fall back,** to retreat or withdraw. **—fall back on,** to turn, or return, to for help. **—fall behind, 1.** to drop back. **2.** to not pay in time. **—fall flat,** to be a complete failure. **—fall for, 1.** to fall in love with. **2.** to be fooled by. *A slang phrase.* **—fall in, 1.** to get into line, as soldiers. **2.** to meet or join with others. **3.** to agree. **—fall off, 1.** to drop. **2.** to become smaller, less, worse, etc. **—fall on** or **fall upon,** to attack. **—fall out, 1.** to drop out of line. **2.** to quarrel. **—fall through,** to fail; come to nothing. **—fall to, 1.** to begin. **2.** to start eating. **—fall under,** to come under. **—fell,** *p.t.;* **fall′en,** *p.p.;* **fall′ing,** *pr.p.*

fal·la·cious (fə lā′shəs), *adj.* mistaken or misleading in ideas, opinion, etc. **—fal·la′cious·ly,** *adv.*

fal·la·cy (fal′ə sē), *n.* **1.** a false or mistaken idea, etc. **2.** false reasoning. **—fal′la·cies,** *pl.*

fall·en (fôl′'n), *adj.* **1.** thrown or dropped down; lying on the ground [*fallen* apples]. **2.** overthrown or ruined [the *fallen* city]. **3.** dead.

fal·li·ble (fal′ə b'l), *adj.* liable to be wrong or make mistakes. **—fal′li·bil′i·ty,** *n.*

falling star, a meteor.

fall·out (fôl′out′), *n.* **1.** the falling to earth of radioactive particles after an atomic explosion. **2.** these particles.

fal·low (fal′ō), *adj.* plowed but left unplanted during the growing season [Farmers let land lie *fallow* at times to kill weeds, make the soil richer, etc.] **—n.** land that lies fallow.

fallow deer, a small European deer that has a yellowish coat spotted with white in summer.

false (fôls), *adj.* **1.** not true or right; wrong [a *false* idea]. **2.** not honest; lying [The witness gave *false* testimony.] **3.** not loyal or faithful [a *false* friend]. **4.** not real or genuine; often, meant to fool or mislead [a *false* clue; *false* alarm; *false* teeth]. **5.** based on wrong or foolish ideas [*false* modesty]. **—adv.** in a false way. **—to play a person false,** to fool, cheat, or betray a person. **—fals′er,** *compar.;* **fals′est,** *superl.* **—false′ly,** *adv.* **—false′ness,** *n.*

false·hood (fôls′hood), *n.* a lie or lying.

fal·set·to (fôl set′ō), *n.* a way of singing in a voice that is much higher than the usual voice. It is used mainly by tenors. **—adj.** of or singing in falsetto. **—adv.** in falsetto. **—fal·set′tos,** *pl.*

fal·si·fy (fôl′sə fī), *v.* **1.** to make false by giving an untrue idea of or by changing [to *falsify* one's feelings; to *falsify* records]. **2.** to tell lies. **—fal′si·fied,** *p.t. & p.p.;* **fal′si·fy·ing,** *pr.p.* **—fal′si·fi·ca′tion,** *n.*

fal·si·ty (fôl′sə tē), *n.* **1.** the fact of being false; a being wrong, dishonest, disloyal, etc. **2.** a lie or error. **—fal′si·ties,** *pl.*

fal·ter (fôl′tər), *v.* **1.** to move in a shaky or unsteady way; stumble. **2.** to speak in a broken or stumbling way; stammer [He *faltered* as he told of his tragedy.] **3.** to act in an unsure way; hesitate; waver [The army *faltered* under enemy fire.] **—n.** a faltering.

fame (fām), *n.* the condition of being well-known or much talked about; great reputation [Edison's inventions brought him much *fame*.]

famed (fāmd), *adj.* well-known; famous.

fa·mil·iar (fə mil′yər), *adj.* **1.** friendly; well-acquainted; intimate [a *familiar* face in the crowd]. **2.** too friendly; intimate in a bold way [She was annoyed by his *familiar* manner.] **3.** knowing about; acquainted with [Are you *familiar* with this book?] **4.** well-known; common; ordinary [Accidents are a *familiar* sight.] **—n.** a close friend.

fa·mil·i·ar·i·ty (fə mil′yar′ə tē), *n.* **1.** very close friendship or acquaintance; intimacy. **2.** friendliness or intimacy that is too bold or not wanted. **3.** the fact of having close knowledge of or experience with [*familiarity* with poverty]. **—fa·mil′i·ar′i·ties,** *pl.*

fa·mil·iar·ize (fə mil′yə rīz), *v.* **1.** to make familiar, or well acquainted [to *familiarize* oneself with a city]. **2.** to make widely known [a song *familiarized* by much playing]. **—fa·mil'-iar·ized,** *p.t. & p.p.;* **fa·mil'iar·iz·ing,** *pr.p.* **—fa·mil'iar·i·za'tion,** *n.*

fam·i·ly (fam'ə lē), *n.* **1.** all the people living together in a house. **2.** a group made up of parents and all of their children. **3.** the children alone [a widow who raised a large *family*]. **4.** a group of people who are related by blood or marriage; relatives; clan. **5.** a large group of related plants or animals [The robin is a member of the thrush *family*.] **6.** a group of related things [a *family* of languages]. **—fam'i·lies,** *pl.*

fam·ine (fam'in), *n.* **1.** a great lack of food that causes starving throughout a wide region. **2.** starvation. **3.** a great lack of anything [the steel *famine* during the war].

fam·ish (fam'ish), *v.* **1.** to be or make very hungry [We were *famished* after the hard day's work.] **2.** to starve.

fa·mous (fā'məs), *adj.* much talked about as being outstanding; very well known.

fan (fan), *n.* **1.** a thing used to stir up the air so as to cool, freshen, etc. Simple fans are waved in the hand and some can be folded together when not in use. Electric fans have blades that are turned by a motor. **2.** anything shaped like an open fan: *see upper picture* [The turkey spread its tail into a *fan*.] **—v. 1.** to stir up the air as with a fan. **2.** to blow air toward as with a fan [She *fanned* herself with the program. The wind *fanned* the flames.] **3.** to spread out like an open fan [The police *fanned* out to search the field.] **—fanned,** *p.t. & p.p.;* **fan'ning,** *pr.p.*

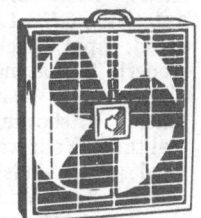

upper: hand fan
lower: electric fan

fan (fan), *n.* a person who is greatly interested in some sport or hobby, or is a great admirer of some famous person [a football *fan*].

fa·nat·ic (fə nat'ik), *n.* a person who carries his interest or belief in something to a point that is no longer reasonable [a religious *fanatic* who spends all his time in prayer]. **—fa·nat'i·cal** or **fa·nat'ic,** *adj.* **—fa·nat'i·cal·ly,** *adv.*

fa·nat·i·cism (fə nat'ə siz'm), *n.* the eagerness or interest of a fanatic.

fan·ci·er (fan'si ər), *n.* a person with a strong interest in something, especially in the breeding of some plant or animal [a cat *fancier*].

fan·ci·ful (fan'si fəl), *adj.* **1.** full of fancy; having or showing a quick and playful imagination [*fanciful* costumes for the Hallowe'en ball]. **2.** not real, practical, etc.; imaginary [a *fanciful* idea that horseshoes bring luck].

fan·cy (fan'sē), *n.* **1.** the power of picturing things in the mind that are not real, especially in a light and playful way; imagination ["Alice in Wonderland" is the product of Lewis Carroll's *fancy*.] **2.** anything imagined; an idea, notion, whim, etc. [She had a sudden *fancy* that no one would come.] **3.** a liking [to take a *fancy* to someone]. **—adj. 1.** having much design and decoration; not plain; elaborate [a *fancy* tie]. **2.** of better quality than the usual; special [a *fancy* grade of canned goods]. **3.** needing more skill or grace than usual [*fancy* diving]. **4.** very high or too high; extravagant [*fancy* prices for new cars]. **—v. 1.** to form an idea of; imagine [I can't *fancy* you as a dancer.] **2.** to have a liking for [He *fancies* Swiss chocolate.] **3.** to believe something without being sure; suppose [I *fancy* that I saw her there.] **—fan'cies,** *pl.* **—fan'-ci·er,** *compar.;* **fan'ci·est,** *superl.* **—fan'cied,** *p.t. & p.p.;* **fan'cy·ing,** *pr.p.*

fan·fare (fan'fer), *n.* **1.** a loud, showy musical phrase played on trumpets or bugles [A *fanfare* announced the entrance of the queen.] **2.** any showy display [to do one's duty with no *fanfare*].

fang (fang), *n.* **1.** one of the long, pointed teeth with which meat-eating animals seize and tear their prey. **2.** one of the long, hollow teeth through which poisonous snakes shoot their poison.

fangs

fan·tail (fan'tāl), *n.* **1.** a tail that spreads out like an open fan. **2.** a pigeon, goldfish, etc. with such a tail.

fan·tas·tic (fan tas'tik), *adj.* **1.** very strange and unreal; fanciful in a wild way; weird [the *fantastic* costumes in the Mardi Gras parade]. **2.** seeming to be beyond belief [the *fantastic* strides made in the study of space travel]. Also **fan·tas'ti·cal.** **—fan·tas'ti·cal·ly,** *adv.*

fan·ta·sy (fan'tə sē), *n.* **1.** imagination or fancy. **2.** a play, story, daydream, etc. that is full of imagination and very unreal ["Peter Pan" is a *fantasy*.] **—fan'ta·sies,** *pl.*

far (fär), *adj.* **1.** not near or close; a long way off; distant [a *far* land; the *far* past]. **2.** more distant [Go to the *far* side of the room.] **—adv. 1.** to or from a great distance [He has traveled *far*.] **2.** to a certain distance or degree [How *far* have you read in this book?] **3.** a great deal; very much [He is *far* taller than I am.] **—as far as** or **so far as,** to the distance or degree that. **—by far** or **far and away,** very much. **—from far,** from a distant place. **—so far,** up to this place, time, or degree. **—so far, so good,** up to this point everything is all right. **—far'ther,** *compar.;* **far'thest,** *superl.*

far·a·way (fär'ə wā), *adj.* **1.** distant; far [a *faraway* place]. **2.** seeming to be distant or away; withdrawn [a *faraway* look on his face].

farce (färs), *n.* **1.** a humorous play with ridiculous things in it that are meant to make people

fat, āpe, cär, ten, ēven, hit, bīte, gō, hôrn, tōōl, book, up, fûr;
get, joy, yet, chin, she, thin, *th*en; zh = s in pleasure; ' as in able (ā'b'l);
ə = a in ago, e in agent, i in sanity, o in confess, u in focus.

laugh. **2.** any ridiculous action; especially, a pretending that is ridiculous because no one is fooled by it [His concern for us was a *farce*.]

far·ci·cal (fär′si k′l), *adj.* of or like a farce; ridiculous; absurd.

fare (fer), *v.* **1.** to get along; do or be [He *fared* well on his trip.] **2.** to happen or result [How did it *fare* with him?] —*n.* **1.** money paid for a trip in a train, bus, etc. [How much is the airplane *fare* to Boston?] **2.** a passenger who has paid a fare. **3.** food [to live on simple *fare*]. —**fared**, *p.t. & p.p.;* **far′ing**, *pr.p.*

Far East, eastern Asia, including China, Japan, etc.

fare·well (fer′wel′), *interj.* good-by. —*n.* a leaving or going away; also, good wishes said when leaving. —*adj.* last; final [a *farewell* wave].

far·fetched (fär′fecht′), *adj.* not natural; forced [a *farfetched* example].

far-flung (fär′flung′), *adj.* covering a wide area [Rome controlled a *far-flung* empire.]

farm (färm), *n.* **1.** a piece of land used to raise crops or animals; also, the house, barns, orchards, etc. on such land. **2.** any place where certain things are raised [An area of water for raising fish is a fish *farm*.] —*v.* to use land to raise crops or animals [He *farmed* ten acres.] —**farm out, 1.** to rent land, a business, etc. for a fee. **2.** to send out work from a shop or office to workers on the outside.

farm·er (färm′ər), *n.* a person who owns or works on a farm.

farm·house (färm′hous), *n.* a house on a farm.

farm·ing (fär′ming), *n.* the work of running a farm; the raising of crops, animals, etc.

farm·stead (färm′sted), *n.* the land and buildings of a farm.

farm·yard (färm′yärd), *n.* the yard around the buildings of a farm.

far-off (fär′ôf′), *adj.* distant; faraway.

far-reach·ing (fär′rēch′ing), *adj.* having a wide influence on many people [The invention of radio had *far-reaching* effects.]

far·ri·er (far′i ər), *n.* a man who shoes horses; blacksmith.

far·row (far′ō), *n.* a litter of pigs. —*v.* to give birth to a litter of pigs.

far·see·ing (fär′sē′ing), *adj.* **1.** able to see far. **2.** farsighted (*in meaning* 2).

far·sight·ed (fär′sīt′id), *adj.* **1.** able to see things that are far away more clearly than those that are close. **2.** able to look ahead and plan for the future. —**far′sight′ed·ness**, *n.*

far·ther (fär′thər), comparative of **far.** —*adj.* **1.** more distant [My home is *farther* from school than yours.] **2.** more; added: *see the note at the end.* —*adv.* **1.** at or to a greater distance [I can swim *farther* than you can.] **2.** to a greater extent; more. **3.** in addition; moreover; besides. In meaning 2 of the adjective, and meanings 2 and 3 of the adverb, *further* is more commonly used.

far·ther·most (fär′thər mōst), *adj.* farthest.

far·thest (fär′thist), superlative of **far.** —*adj.* **1.** most distant [the *farthest* parts of the State]. **2.** longest [That road is the best but it is also the farthest.] —*adv.* at or to the greatest distance [Who threw the ball *farthest*?]

far·thing (fär′thing), *n.* a small British coin worth less than a cent, and no longer in use.

fas·ci·nate (fas′′n āt), *v.* **1.** to hold the attention of by being interesting or delightful; charm [The puppet show *fascinated* the children.] **2.** to hold still without the power to move or act, as by terrifying. —**fas′ci·nat·ed**, *p.t. & p.p.;* **fas′ci·nat·ing**, *pr.p.* —**fas′ci·na′tion**, *n.*

fas·cism or **Fas·cism** (fash′iz′m), *n.* a system of government in which the country is ruled by a dictator, and in which minority groups have no rights, war is glorified, etc. Fascism came to power in Italy under Mussolini and in Germany under Hitler. —**fas′cist** or **Fas′cist**, *adj. & n.*

fash·ion (fash′ən), *n.* **1.** the popular or up-to-date way of dressing, speaking, or behaving; style [It was once the *fashion* to wear powdered wigs.] **2.** the way in which a thing is made, done, or formed [tea served in the Japanese *fashion*]. —*v.* to make, form, or shape [Bees *fashion* honeycombs out of wax.] —**after a fashion** or **in a fashion,** in some way; to some extent.

fash·ion·a·ble (fash′ən ə b′l), *adj.* following the latest fashions or styles; stylish [a *fashionable* hat]. —**fash′ion·a·bly**, *adv.*

fast (fast), *adj.* **1.** moving, working, etc. at high speed; rapid; quick; swift [a *fast* current; a *fast* reader]. **2.** that makes high speed possible [a *fast* highway]. **3.** that takes a short time [a *fast* lunch]. **4.** showing a time that is ahead of the real time [Your watch is *fast*.] **5.** close and true; loyal [*fast* friends]. **6.** that will not fade [*fast* colors]. **7.** fastened in a firm way; fixed [Make that rope *fast* before you leave the boat.] **8.** wild and reckless [a *fast* life]. —*adv.* **1.** at a high speed; swiftly; rapidly [Don't eat so *fast*.] **2.** in a firm or fixed way; firmly [The boat was stuck *fast* on the sand bar.] **3.** in a complete way; soundly; thoroughly [*fast* asleep].

fast (fast), *v.* to go without any food or certain foods, as in observing a religion. —*n.* **1.** a fasting. **2.** a day or period of fasting.

fas·ten (fas′′n), *v.* **1.** to join or become joined; attach [The collar is *fastened* to the shirt.] **2.** to make stay closed or in place, as by locking or shutting [*Fasten* the door.] **3.** to direct and hold; fix [*Fasten* your attention on this experiment.] —**fas′ten·er**, *n.*

fas·ten·ing (fas′′n ing), *n.* anything used to fasten, as a bolt, lock, button, etc.

fas·tid·i·ous (fas tid′i əs), *adj.* not easy to please; very particular [a *fastidious* taste in music]. —**fas·tid′i·ous·ly**, *adv.*

fast·ness (fast′nis), *n.* **1.** the quality of being fast. **2.** a strong, safe place; stronghold.

fat (fat), *n.* **1.** an oily, yellow or white substance found in animal bodies. **2.** any oily substance, as from plants, used in cooking and frying. **3.** the richest or best part [to live off the *fat* of the land]. —*adj.* **1.** covered with much fat or flesh; plump, or too plump [*fat* cheeks; a *fat* chicken]. **2.** full of fat; oily or greasy [Butter is a *fat* food.] **3.** thick or broad [a *fat* book]. **4.** bringing much profit; fruitful [a *fat* contract]. **5.** well supplied; plentiful [a *fat* purse]. —*v.* to make or become fat. —**fat′ter,** *compar.;* **fat′test,** *superl.* —**fat′ted,** *p.t. & p.p.;* **fat′ting,** *pr.p.*

fa·tal (fā′t'l), *adj.* **1.** causing death [a *fatal* disease]. **2.** causing ruin; disastrous [a *fatal* blow to their hopes]. **3.** important in its outcome; decisive [the *fatal* day]. —**fa′tal·ly,** *adv.*

fa·tal·ist (fā′t'l ist), *n.* a person who believes that fate decides everything and that no one can control his fate. —**fa′tal·is′tic,** *adj.*

fa·tal·i·ty (fə tal′ə tē), *n.* **1.** death caused by a disaster, as in an accident, war, etc. [The earthquake caused many *fatalities*.] **2.** a tendency to cause death; deadliness [The *fatality* of polio has been reduced.] —**fa·tal′i·ties,** *pl.*

fate (fāt), *n.* **1.** a power that is supposed to settle ahead of time how things will happen [He believed that *fate* had destined him to be famous.] **2.** the things that happen as though controlled by this power; one's lot or fortune [Was it his *fate* to be President?] **3.** the way things turn out in the end; outcome [What was the *fate* of the ship in the storm?] —**the Fates,** the three goddesses in Greek and Roman myths who control human life.

fat·ed (fāt′id), *adj.* fixed by fate; destined or doomed [the *fated* day].

fate·ful (fāt′fəl), *adj.* **1.** telling what is to come; prophetic [the *fateful* words of the oracle]. **2.** having most important results [a *fateful* decision]. **3.** controlled as if by fate. **4.** bringing death or destruction [the *fateful* explosion]. —**fate′ful·ly,** *adv.*

fa·ther (fä′thər), *n.* **1.** a man as he is related to his child or children; a male parent. **2. Father,** God. **3.** an ancestor. **4.** a person important to the beginning of something; founder; creator [Hippocrates is called the *Father* of Medicine.] **5. fathers,** *pl.* the leaders of a city, country, etc. **6.** a priest. —*v.* **1.** to become the father of [He *fathered* three sons.] **2.** to care for as a father does. **3.** to bring into being; create; invent [to *father* an idea]. —**fa′ther·hood,** *n.* —**fa′ther·less,** *adj.*

fa·ther-in-law (fä′thər 'n lô′), *n.* the father of one's wife or husband. —**fa′thers-in-law′,** *pl.*

fa·ther·land (fä′thər land), *n.* one's country; especially, the country where one was born.

fa·ther·ly (fä′thər lē), *adj.* of or like a father [*fatherly* care]. —**fa′ther·li·ness,** *n.*

fath·om (fath′əm), *n.* a length of six feet, used as a unit of measure for the depth of water. —*v.* **1.** to measure the depth of. **2.** to understand completely [I can't *fathom* the mystery.]

fath·om·less (fath′əm lis), *adj.* **1.** too deep to measure. **2.** too mysterious to understand.

fa·tigue (fə tēg′), *n.* a tired feeling, as from hard work or not enough rest; weariness. —*v.* to tire out; make weary; exhaust. —**fa·tigued′,** *p.t. & p.p.;* **fa·ti′guing,** *pr.p.*

fat·ten (fat′'n), *v.* to make or become fat.

fat·ty (fat′ē), *adj.* **1.** containing or made of fat [*fatty* tissue]. **2.** like fat; greasy; oily. —**fat′ti·er,** *compar.;* **fat′ti·est,** *superl.*

fat·u·ous (fach′oo əs), *adj.* stupid or foolish in a smug way. —**fat′u·ous·ly,** *adv.*

fau·cet (fô′sit), *n.* a device with a valve which can be turned on or off to control the flow of a liquid, as from a pipe; tap; cock.

faucet

fault (fôlt), *n.* **1.** a thing that keeps something from being perfect; defect; flaw [Every person has his *faults*.] **2.** an error; mistake. **3.** blame; responsibility [It isn't my *fault* that we were late.] —**at fault,** deserving blame. —**find fault,** to look for faults; complain. —**find fault with,** to criticize.

fault·less (fôlt′lis), *adj.* not having a fault; perfect. —**fault′less·ly,** *adv.*

fault·y (fôl′tē), *adj.* having a fault or faults; imperfect. —**fault′i·er,** *compar.;* **fault′i·est,** *superl.* —**fault′i·ly,** *adv.*

faun (fôn), *n.* in Roman myths, a minor god who had the head and body of a man, and the horns, legs, and tail of a goat: *see the picture of* **Pan.**

fau·na (fô′nə), *n.* all the animals of a particular place and time [the *fauna* of Iceland].

Faust (foust), *n.* a man in an old legend who sold his soul to the devil in return for knowledge and power.

fa·vor (fā′vər), *n.* **1.** a helpful and kind action [Will you do me the *favor* of visiting my mother?] **2.** liking or approval [He tried to win his teacher's *favor*.] **3.** a small gift or souvenir [Everyone at the party received a pen as a *favor*.] —*v.* **1.** to like or approve of [I *favor* his plan for lower taxes.] **2.** to help or aid [The dark night *favored* his escape.] **3.** to prefer or help in an unfair way [Some parents *favor* their youngest child.] **4.** to look like [The baby *favors* his father.] **5.** to use gently so as to keep from hurting [He *favors* his injured leg.] —**in favor of, 1.** supporting or approving. **2.** to the advantage of. —**in one's favor,** to one's advantage.

fa·vor·a·ble (fā′vər ə b'l), *adj.* **1.** helpful [*favorable* winds]. **2.** supporting or approving [a *favorable* opinion]. —**fa′vor·a·bly,** *adv.*

fa·vor·ite (fā′vər it), *n.* **1.** the person or thing liked better than others. **2.** the one who is thought most likely to win a contest. —*adj.* best liked; preferred [Pie is my *favorite* food.]

fa·vor·it·ism (fā′vər it iz'm), *n.* the act of showing unfair liking for one over others.

fa·vour (fā′vər), *n. & v.* British spelling of **favor.**

fawn (fôn), *v.* **1.** to show pleasure by wagging its tail, licking hands, etc. [Dogs *fawn*.] **2.** to try to gain favor by acting humble, flattering, etc. [to *fawn* on a rich person].

fawn (fôn), *n.* **1.** a young deer, less than a year old. **2.** its yellowish-brown color.

fay (fā), *n.* a fairy.

faze (fāz), *v.* to confuse or disturb: *used only in everyday talk.* —**fazed,** *p.t. & p.p.;* **faz′ing,** *pr.p.*

FBI or **F.B.I.,** abbreviation for **Federal Bureau of Investigation,** which is a branch of the U.S. Department of Justice whose duty is to investigate crimes against Federal law.

fawn

Fe, symbol for the chemical element *iron.*

fe·al·ty (fē′əl tē), *n.* loyalty; especially, the loyalty owed by a vassal to his feudal lord.

fear (fir), *n.* **1.** the feeling one has when danger, pain, or trouble is near; feeling of being worried or excited or of wanting to run and hide [Jungle animals have a natural *fear* of lions.] **2.** a feeling of being uneasy [I have no *fear* that it will rain.] **3.** something that causes fear [What is your greatest *fear*?] —*v.* **1.** to feel fear of; be afraid of; dread [Shepherds *fear* wolves.] **2.** to feel uneasy or anxious [I *fear* that she'll be angry.]

fear·ful (fir′fəl), *adj.* **1.** causing fear; dreadful [a *fearful* danger]. **2.** feeling fear; afraid [*fearful* of the dark]. **3.** caused by fear [a *fearful* cry]. **4.** very bad, great, etc.: *used only in everyday talk* [a *fearful* liar]. —**fear′ful·ly,** *adv.*

fear·less (fir′lis), *adj.* having no fear; not afraid; brave. —**fear′less·ly,** *adv.*

fear·some (fir′səm), *adj.* causing fear; frightful.

feas·i·ble (fē′zə b'l), *adj.* **1.** that can be done with conditions as they are; possible [Your plan is not *feasible* because it is too costly.] **2.** that is likely or within reason; probable [Is it *feasible* that John is wrong?] —**fea′si·bil′i·ty,** *n.*

feast (fēst), *n.* **1.** a large meal with many courses; banquet. **2.** a happy religious celebration; festival. —*v.* **1.** to eat a big or rich meal. **2.** to make a feast for. **3.** to cause delight or pleasure to [She *feasted* her eyes on the jewels.]

feat (fēt), *n.* something done that shows great courage, skill, or strength; remarkable deed.

feath·er (feth′ər), *n.* **1.** any of the parts that grow out of the skin of birds, covering the body and filling out the wings and tail. Feathers are soft and light. **2.** anything like a feather in looks, lightness, etc. **3.** the same class or kind [birds of a *feather*]. —*v.* **1.** to cover or become covered with feathers. **2.** to turn the blade of an oar or propeller so that the edge is foremost. —**feather in one's cap,** something one can be proud of having done or gotten. —**in fine feather,** in good humor or health. —**feath′er·y,** *adj.*

feather

feather bed, a thick quilt stuffed with feathers or down and used as a mattress.

fea·ture (fē′chər), *n.* **1.** any part of the face, as the nose, eyes, mouth, chin, etc. [a girl with fine *features*]. **2.** a separate or special part or quality [Geysers are a *feature* of Yellowstone National Park. Your plan has some bad *features.*] **3.** a main attraction at a show, sale, etc.; especially, a full-length movie. **4.** a special article or column in a newspaper or magazine. —*v.* to be or make a feature of [Acrobats are *featured* on the program.] —**fea′tured,** *p.t. & p.p.;* **fea′tur·ing,** *pr.p.*

Feb·ru·ar·y (feb′roo er′ē *or* feb′yoo er′ē), *n.* the second month of the year. It usually has 28 days but in leap year it has 29 days. Abbreviated **Feb.**

fe·cund (fē′kənd *or* fek′ənd), *adj.* bringing much or many into being; fruitful or fertile. —**fe·cund·i·ty** (fi kun′də tē), *n.*

fed (fed), past tense and past participle of **feed.** —**fed up,** disgusted or bored: *a slang phrase.*

fed·er·al (fed′ər əl), *adj.* **1.** of or describing a union of states having a central government. **2.** *often* **Federal,** of such a central government; especially, of the central government of the United States [a *federal* constitution; the *Federal* courts]. **3. Federal,** of or supporting an early American political party (**Federalist Party**) that was in favor of strong federal power. **4. Federal,** of or supporting the Union in the Civil War. —*n.* **Federal,** a supporter of the Union in the Civil War. —**fed′er·al·ist,** *adj. & n.*

fed·er·ate (fed′ər āt), *v.* to join in a federation. —**fed′er·at·ed,** *p.t. & p.p.;* **fed′er·at·ing,** *pr.p.*

fed·er·a·tion (fed′ə rā′shən), *n.* a union of states or groups under a central power [the *federation* of German states under Bismarck; the *Federation* of Women's Clubs].

fee (fē), *n.* **1.** a charge for some service or special right [a doctor's *fee;* admission *fees;* a license *fee*]. **2.** ownership of land or property. A person holding land in **fee simple** has the right to sell or give it to anyone.

fee·ble (fē′b'l), *adj.* weak; not strong [a *feeble* old man; a *feeble* excuse]. —**fee′ble·ness,** *n.* —**fee′bly,** *adv.*

fee·ble-mind·ed (fē′b'l mīn′did), *adj.* having a very slow mind that can learn much less than the ordinary person's.

feed (fēd), *v.* **1.** to give food to [*Feed* the children first.] **2.** to serve as food [to *feed* oats to horses]. **3.** to eat [The cattle are *feeding.*] **4.** to supply something that is needed for the working or growth of [We *fed* the stove with wood. Their insults *fed* his anger.] —*n.* **1.** food for animals; fodder. **2.** a meal: *used only in everyday talk.* —**feed on** or **feed upon, 1.** to eat. **2.** to get satisfaction from. —**fed,** *p.t. & p.p.;* **feed′ing,** *pr.p.* —**feed′er,** *n.*

feed·back (fēd′bak), *n.* a process in which factors that produce a result are themselves changed, corrected, etc. by that result.

feel (fēl), *v.* **1.** to touch in order to find out something [Mother *felt* the baby's bottle to see if the milk was warm.] **2.** to be aware of through the senses or the mind [He *felt* rain on his face. Do you *feel* pain in this tooth?] **3.** to be aware of being; be [I *feel* sad.] **4.** to have grief, pity, etc. because of [He *felt* her death deeply.] **5.** to be or seem to the sense of touch [The water *feels* warm.] **6.** to think or believe [I *feel* that you are wrong.] **7.** to try to find by touching; grope [He *felt* his way down the dark hall.] —*n.* **1.** the act of feeling **2.** the way a thing seems to the touch [You can tell it's good material by the *feel* of it.] —**feel like,** to have a desire for: *used only in everyday talk* [I don't *feel like* talking.] —**feel up to,** to feel able to: *used only in everyday talk.* —**felt,** *p.t. & p.p.;* **feel′ing,** *pr.p.*

feel·er (fēl′ər), *n.* **1.** a person or thing that feels. **2.** a slender part growing out from an animal or insect, by which it can touch or feel; antenna. **3.** something said or asked to find out what a person thinks.

feelers

feel·ing (fēl′ing), *n.* **1.** the sense of touch, by which one can tell whether something is rough or smooth, hot or cold, etc. **2.** the condition of being aware; consciousness [a *feeling* of pain]. **3.** what is felt deeply inside one, as love, hate, joy, anger, or fear; emotion [to control one's *feelings*]. **4.** sympathy or pity [He spoke with *feeling* about their suffering.] **5.** an opinion or belief [I have a *feeling* that Jack is right.] —*adj.* sensitive and full of sympathy [He spoke *feeling* words.] —**to hurt one's feelings,** to make one unhappy or angry; offend. —**feel′ing·ly,** *adv.*

feet (fēt), *n.* plural of **foot.**

feign (fān), *v.* **1.** to make up something that is not true [to *feign* an excuse]. **2.** to pretend [to *feign* illness].

feint (fānt), *n.* **1.** a pretended blow or attack meant to put one's opponent off guard against the real one that follows. **2.** a false show; pretense; sham [to make a *feint* of working]. —*v.* to make a feint, as in boxing.

feld·spar (feld′spär), *n.* a hard, glassy kind of rock, containing aluminum.

fe·lic·i·tate (fə lis′ə tāt), *v.* to wish joy to; congratulate. —**fe·lic′i·tat·ed,** *p.t. & p.p.;* **fe·lic′i·tat·ing,** *pr.p.* —**fe·lic′i·ta′tion,** *n.*

fe·lic·i·tous (fə lis′ə təs), *adj.* just right for the occasion; fitting; apt [a *felicitous* remark].

fe·lic·i·ty (fə lis′ə tē), *n.* **1.** great happiness; bliss. **2.** a way of writing or speaking, or a remark, that is pleasing and just right for the occasion [He expressed his thanks with *felicity*.] —**fe·lic′i·ties,** *pl.*

fe·line (fē′lin), *adj.* **1.** of a cat or the cat family. **2.** like a cat. —*n.* any member of the cat family, as the leopard, lion, tiger, etc.

fell (fel), past tense of **fall.**

fell (fel), *v.* **1.** to make fall; knock down [The boxer *felled* his opponent with a blow.] **2.** to cut down [to *fell* a tree].

fell (tel), *adj.* fierce; cruel [a *fell* blow].

fell (fel), *n.* an animal's skin; hide.

fel·low (fel′ō), *n.* **1.** a man or boy ["He's a jolly good *fellow*!"] **2.** a partner, helper, or associate [*fellows* in crime]. **3.** either one of two things that go together [I can't find the *fellow* to this shoe.] **4.** a student who has a fellowship. **5.** a member of any of various scholarly societies. —*adj.* in the same situation; associated [my *fellow* students].

fel·low·ship (fel′ō ship′), *n.* **1.** friendship; companionship. **2.** a group of people having the same activities or interests. **3.** money given to a student at a university or college to help him study for a higher degree.

fel·on (fel′ən), *n.* a person who commits a serious crime, such as murder; criminal.

fel·on (tel′ən), *n.* a painful infection near a fingernail or toenail.

fel·o·ny (fel′ə nē), *n.* a serious crime, such as murder or kidnaping, that brings severe punishment. —**fe·lo·ni·ous** (fə lō′ni əs), *adj.*

felt (felt), *n.* a heavy material made of wool, fur, or hair pressed together under heat. —*adj.* made of felt [a *felt* hat].

felt (felt), past tense and past participle of **feel.**

fe·male (fē′māl), *adj.* **1.** belonging to the sex that bears the young or produces eggs [A *female* fox is called a "vixen."] **2.** of or for women or girls [*female* clothing]. —*n.* a female person, animal, or plant.

fem·i·nine (fem′ə nin), *adj.* **1.** of or having to do with women or girls [*feminine* traits]. **2.** like women or girls; gentle, weak, soft, etc. **3.** of a class of words in grammar that refer to females or to things thought of as female. —**fem·i·nin·i·ty** (fem′ə nin′ə tē), *n.*

fe·mur (fē′mər), *n.* the bone in the thigh; thighbone: it is the largest bone in the body.

fen (fen), *n.* a swamp; marsh.

fence (fens), *n.* **1.** a railing or wall, as of posts, rails, or wire, put around a field or yard to keep something in or out or to mark a boundary. **2.** a person who buys and sells stolen goods. —*v.* **1.** to close in or hem in as with a fence. **2.** to fight with foils or other swords. —**on the fence,** not decided about some question; neither on one side nor on the other. —**fenced,** *p.t. & p.p.;* **fenc′ing,** *pr.p.* —**fenc′er,** *n.*

fenc·ing (fen′sing), *n.* **1.** the art or sport of fighting with foils or other swords; swordplay. **2.** material for making fences.

fend (fend), *v.* to keep off or turn aside [to *fend* off danger, a blow, etc.]. —**fend for oneself,** to get along without help from others.

boys fencing

fend·er (fen′dər), *n.* **1.** a metal piece over the wheels of cars, etc. or at the front of locomotives, etc. to throw off splashing mud or things that are hit. **2.** a low screen or frame in front of an open fireplace.

fen·nel (fen′′l), *n.* a tall herb that has yellow flowers and seeds that are used as a seasoning and in medicine.

fer·ment (fər ment′), *v.* **1.** to cause a slow chemical change to take place in a substance by means of yeast, bacteria, etc. Fermenting changes apple juice to vinegar, grape juice to wine, starch to sugar, and malt to beer. **2.** to undergo this change [The milk *fermented* and became sour.] **3.** to make or become excited or stirred up. —*n.* (fûr′mənt), **1.** a substance that causes fermenting. **2.** fermentation. **3.** a state of excitement; commotion [the *ferment* of war].

fer·men·ta·tion (fûr′mən tā′shən), *n.* the chemical change in a substance that is caused by a ferment, as yeast or bacteria.

fern (fûrn), *n.* a plant that does not bear flowers but instead has special seeds (called **spores**) that grow on the backs of its feathery leaves. Ferns grow in shady and moist places.

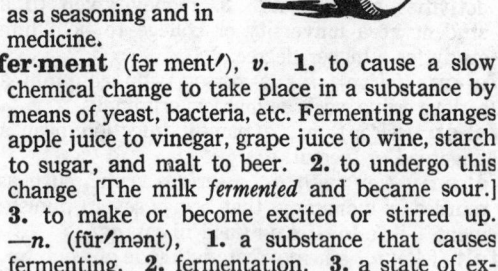

fern

fe·ro·cious (fi rō′shəs), *adj.* **1.** cruel or fierce in a wild way; savage. **2.** very great: *used only in everyday talk* [a *ferocious* appetite]. —**fe·ro′cious·ly**, *adv.*

fe·roc·i·ty (fi räs′ə tē), *n.* wild force or cruelty; fierceness.

fer·ret (fer′it), *n.* a small animal like a weasel, that can be tamed for use in hunting rabbits, rats, etc. —*v.* **1.** to force out of a hiding place by using a ferret. **2.** to search for and force out [to *ferret* out the truth].

fer·ric (fer′ik) or **fer·rous** (fer′əs), *adj.* having to do with or containing iron.

Fer·ris wheel (fer′əs), a very large wheel that turns in an upright position and has seats hanging from the rim. It is used as an amusement ride.

fer·rule (fer′əl), *n.* a metal ring or cap put on the end of a handle, cane, etc. to keep it from splitting or to make it stronger.

Ferris wheel

fer·ry (fer′ē), *v.* **1.** to take or go across a river, bay, etc. in a boat or, sometimes, in an airplane. **2.** to deliver an airplane by flying it to the place where it will be used. —*n.* **1.** a boat used in ferrying: also **fer′ry·boat.** **2.** the place where ferrying is done. **3.** the regular ferrying of people, cars, etc. as across a river. —**fer′ried,** *p.t. & p.p.;* **fer′ry·ing,** *pr.p.* —**fer′ries,** *pl.*

fer·tile (fûr′t′l), *adj.* **1.** producing much fruit or large crops; rich [*fertile* soil]. **2.** able to produce offspring, seeds, or fruit [a *fertile* orchard; *fertile* cattle]. **3.** able to develop into a new plant or animal [*fertile* seeds; *fertile* eggs]. **4.** bringing forth many ideas; inventive [a *fertile* imagination]. —**fer·til·i·ty** (fər til′ə tē), *n.*

fer·ti·lize (fûr′t′l īz), *v.* **1.** to make fertile, especially by adding fertilizer to [*Fertilize* your lawn in the spring and in the fall.] **2.** to bring a male germ cell to a female egg cell so as to cause a new animal or plant to develop [Bees *fertilize* flowers by carrying pollen from one to another.] —**fer′ti·lized,** *p.t. & p.p.;* **fer′ti·liz·ing,** *pr.p.* —**fer′ti·li·za′tion,** *n.*

fer·ti·liz·er (fûr′t′l īz′ər), *n.* manure or certain chemicals put in the soil as a food for plants.

fer·ule (fer′əl *or* fer′ool), *n.* a flat stick or ruler used for punishing children.

fer·vent (fûr′vənt), *adj.* **1.** showing very warm or strong feeling; intense; ardent [a *fervent* appeal for help]. **2.** hot; glowing [*fervent* rays of the sun]. —**fer′ven·cy,** *n.* —**fer′vent·ly,** *adv.*

fer·vid (fûr′vid), *adj.* full of fervor or passion [*fervid* hatred].

fer·vor (fûr′vər), *n.* great heat or strength of feeling; passion.

fes·tal (fes′t′l), *adj.* of or like a festival or holiday; gay [His graduation was a *festal* event.]

fes·ter (fes′tər), *v.* **1.** to become filled with pus [The cut on his arm *festered*.] **2.** to cause angry or bitter feelings [His envy *festered* in him.] —*n.* a sore that fills up with pus.

fes·ti·val (fes′tə v′l), *n.* **1.** a day or time of feasting or celebrating; happy holiday [The Mardi Gras in New Orleans is a colorful *festival*.] **2.** a time of special celebration or entertainment [Our town holds a maple sugar *festival* every spring.]

fes·tive (fes′tiv), *adj.* of or for a festival; merry; gay [*festive* decorations].

fes·tiv·i·ty (fes tiv′ə tē), *n.* **1.** merrymaking and celebrating [a time of *festivity*]. **2. festivities,** *pl.* things done as part of a happy celebration [the *festivities* of graduation week]. —**fes·tiv′i·ties,** *pl.*

fes·toon (fes tōōn′), *n.* a decoration of flowers, leaves, paper, etc. arranged to hang in loops. —*v.* to form into festoons or decorate with festoons.

festoon

fetch (fech), *v.* **1.** to go after and bring back; get [The dog *fetched* my slippers.] **2.** to bring forth; draw [She *fetched* a sigh.] **3.** to sell for [The sofa should *fetch* $50.]

fetch·ing (fech′ing), *adj.* attractive or charming [She has a *fetching* smile.]

fete or **fête** (fāt), *n.* a festival or party, especially one held outdoors. —*v.* to honor with a fete; entertain [The poet was *feted* many times on his lecture tour.] —**fet′ed** or **fêt′ed**, *p.t. & p.p.;* **fet′ing** or **fêt′ing**, *pr.p.*

fet·id (fet′id *or* fē′tid), *adj.* having a bad smell; stinking.

fe·tish (fē′tish *or* fet′ish), *n.* **1.** any object that is believed to have magic power [Primitive people wear *fetishes* to protect themselves from harm.] **2.** anything to which a person is devoted in a way that is too strong [He makes a *fetish* of sports.]

fet·lock (fet′läk), *n.* a tuft of hair on the back of a horse's leg just above the hoof; also, this part of the horse's leg.

.fetlock

fet·ter (fet′ər), *n.* **1.** a shackle or chain for the feet. **2.** anything that keeps one from moving or acting in a free way. —*v.* to bind as with fetters [*fettered* by debts].

fet·tle (fet′'l), *n.* condition of body and mind [Our team is in fine *fettle* for the game.]

fe·tus (fē′təs), *n.* an animal in the later stages of its growth inside the womb. —**fe′tus·es**, *pl.*

feud (fyōōd), *n.* a bitter quarrel, especially one between two families. —*v.* to carry on a feud.

feu·dal (fyōō′d'l), *adj.* of or having to do with feudalism.

feu·dal·ism (fyōō′d'l iz'm), *n.* the way of life in Europe during the Middle Ages, when land was owned by the king or lords, but held by vassals in return for help in war and other services. The land was worked by serfs.

feu·da·to·ry (fyōō′də tôr′ē), *n.* **1.** a person who held land under feudalism as the vassal of a lord. **2.** land held in this way. —**feu′da·to′ries**, *pl.*

fe·ver (fē′vər), *n.* **1.** a body temperature that is higher than normal, as in some sicknesses. **2.** a sickness in which there is a high fever [yellow *fever;* scarlet *fever*]. **3.** a condition of nervousness or excitement [the *fever* of city life].

fe·vered (fē′vərd), *adj.* **1.** having a fever. **2.** excited or nervous.

fe·ver·ish (fē′vər ish), *adj.* **1.** having a fever, especially a slight fever. **2.** caused by fever [*feverish* raving]. **3.** causing fever [a *feverish* climate]. **4.** excited or nervous [*feverish* plans for escape]. —**fe′ver·ish·ly**, *adv.*

few (fyōō), *adj.* not many; a small number of [Christmas comes a *few* days before New Year's.] —*n. & pron.* not many; a small number [John ate most of the cookies, saving us only a *few*.] —**quite a few**, a rather large number: *used only in everyday talk.*

fez (fez), *n.* a felt cap with no brim that was once worn by Turkish men. It was usually red and had a black tassel. —**fez′zes**, *pl.*

ff., and the following pages ["The article is found on pages 39 *ff.*" means that it begins on page 39 and continues on the following pages.]

fi·an·cé (fē′än sā′), *n.* the man who is engaged to marry a certain woman.

fi·an·cée (fē′än sā′), *n.* the woman who is engaged to marry a certain man.

fi·as·co (fi as′kō), *n.* something that ends as a complete or foolish failure [His scheme to get rich ended in a *fiasco*.] —**fi·as′coes** or **fi·as′cos**, *pl.*

fi·at (fi′ət), *n.* an order given by a person who has authority; decree.

fib (fib), *n.* a lie about something not very important. —*v.* to tell such a lie. —**fibbed**, *p.t. & p.p.;* **fib′bing**, *pr.p.* —**fib′ber**, *n.*

fi·ber or **fi·bre** (fi′bər), *n.* **1.** any of the thin parts like threads that form the tissue of animals and plants [Cotton *fibers* are spun into yarn.] **2.** the tissue formed of such fibers [muscle *fiber*]. **3.** the way a person thinks and acts; character; nature [a girl of delicate *fiber*].

fi·brin (fi′brin), *n.* a substance formed in blood clots that helps the action of clotting.

fi·broid (fi′broid), *adj.* formed of tissue that is made up of fibers [a *fibroid* tumor].

fi·brous (fi′brəs), *adj.* **1.** made up of fibers. **2.** like fibers.

fib·u·la (fib′yoo lə), *n.* the long, thin outer bone of the human leg, between the knee and the ankle. —**fib·u·lae** (fib′yoo lē) or **fib′u·las**, *pl.*

-fi·ca·tion (fi kā′shən), a suffix used to form nouns from many verbs that end with the suffix *-fy*. It means "the act or condition of" [*Glorification* is the act or condition of glorifying.]

fick·le (fik′'l), *adj.* changing often in one's feelings or interests; inconstant [a *fickle* sweetheart]. —**fick′le·ness**, *n.*

fic·tion (fik′shən), *n.* **1.** a piece of writing about imaginary people and happenings, as a novel, play, or story; also, such writings as a group. **2.** the writing of novels and stories. **3.** something made up or imagined [Truth is often stranger than *fiction*.] —**fic′tion·al**, *adj.*

fic·ti·tious (fik tish′əs), *adj.* of or like fiction; not real; made-up [a *fictitious* character in a play].

fid·dle (fid′'l), *n.* a violin: *now used mainly in everyday talk.* —*v.* **1.** to play on the violin: *used only in everyday talk.* **2.** to move the fingers in a nervous or restless way; toy or play [Stop *fiddling* with your tie.] —**fit as a fiddle**, in excellent health. —**fid′dled**, *p.t. & p.p.;* **fid′dling**, *pr.p.* —**fid′dler** (fid′lər), *n.*

fiddler crab, a small crab of the Atlantic coast, having one claw larger than the other.

fid·dle·stick (fid′'l stik), *n.* a bow for playing a violin: *used only in everyday talk.*

fid·dle·sticks (fid′'l·stiks), *interj.* nonsense!

fi·del·i·ty (fi del′ə tē *or* fə del′ə tē), *n.* **1.** a being

fiddler crab
(1 in. across body)

true to one's promise, duty, etc.; loyalty; faithfulness. **2.** exactness in copying or translating.

fidg·et (fij′it), *v.* to move about in a nervous or restless way [to *fidget* in one's seat]. —**the fidgets,** restless or nervous feelings or movements. —**fidg′et·y,** *adj.*

fie (fī), *interj.* for shame! shame on you!: *now often used in a joking way.*

fief (fēf), *n.* land held from a feudal lord in return for help in war and other services.

field (fēld), *n.* **1.** a wide piece of open land without many trees; especially, a piece of land for growing crops, grazing animals, etc. **2.** a piece of land having a special use or producing a certain thing [a baseball *field*; an oil *field*]. **3.** a battle-field. **4.** a wide, flat space [a *field* of ice]. **5.** the space within which something is active, can be seen, etc. [*field* of vision; magnetic *field*]. **6.** a branch of learning or of special work [the *field* of industry; the *field* of science]. **7.** the surface or background on which something is shown [The U.S. flag has 50 white stars on a blue *field*.] **8.** such events in a track meet as jumping, pole vault, shot-put, etc.; also, the place where these events are held: see also **track. 9.** all the people entered in a contest. —*adj.* of, in, or on a field. —*v.* **1.** to stop or catch and return a batted baseball. **2.** to put a player or team into active play. —**to take the field,** to go into action at the start of a game, battle, etc.

field·er (fēl′dər), *n.* a player in the field in baseball, cricket, etc.

field glasses, a pair of powerful binoculars.

field goal, a goal scored in football by a place kick. It counts three points.

field marshal, an officer ranking just below the commander in chief in some armies.

fiend (fēnd), *n.* **1.** an evil spirit; devil; demon. **2.** a very evil or cruel person. **3.** a person who is too strongly devoted to a habit or interest [a fresh-air *fiend*]. —**fiend′ish,** *adj.*

fierce (firs), *adj.* **1.** wild or cruel; violent; raging [a *fierce* dog; a *fierce* wind]. **2.** very strong or eager [a *fierce* effort]. —**fierc′er,** *compar.*; **fierc′est,** *superl.* —**fierce′ly,** *adv.* —**fierce′ness,** *n.*

fi·er·y (fī′rē *or* fī′ər ē), *adj.* **1.** of or filled with fire; flaming [the dragon's *fiery* breath]. **2.** like fire; very hot [the *fiery* sun]. **3.** full of strong feeling; excited [*fiery* words; a *fiery* nature]. —**fi′er·i·er,** *compar.*; **fi′er·i·est,** *superl.*

fi·es·ta (fī es′tə), *n.* a holiday or time of feasting and merrymaking; festival.

fife (fīf), *n.* a small flute that has a high, shrill tone. It is used with drums in marching music. —*v.* to play on a fife. —**fifed,** *p.t. & p.p.;* **fif′ing,** *pr.p.*

fif·teen (fif′tēn′), *n. & adj.* five more than ten; the number 15.

fif·teenth (fif′tēnth′), *adj.* coming after fourteen others; 15th in order. —*n.* **1.** the fifteenth one. **2.** one of fifteen equal parts of something; 1/15.

fife

fifth (fifth), *adj.* coming after four others; 5th in order. —*n.* **1.** the fifth one. **2.** one of five equal parts of something; 1/5.

fifth column, a group of people within a country who secretly help its enemy.

fif·ti·eth (fif′tē ith), *adj.* coming after forty-nine others; 50th in order. —*n.* **1.** the fiftieth one. **2.** one of fifty equal parts of something; 1/50.

fif·ty (fif′tē), *n. & adj.* **1.** five times ten; the number 50. **2. fifties,** *n.pl.* the numbers or years from 50 to 59.

fif·ty-fif·ty (fif′tē fif′tē), *adj. & adv.* in two equal shares: *used only in everyday talk.*

fig (fig), *n.* **1.** a sweet fruit shaped like a small pear and filled with a soft pulp containing many seeds. Figs are often dried for eating. **2.** the tree on which this fruit grows. **3.** the smallest amount [not worth a *fig*].

fig., abbreviation for **figure.**

fig tree and fruit

fight (fīt), *v.* **1.** to use fists, weapons, or other force in trying to beat or overcome someone or something; battle; struggle [to *fight* hand to hand; to *fight* a war]. **2.** to work hard in trying to overcome [to *fight* against fear]. —*n.* **1.** the use of force to beat or overcome someone or something; battle. **2.** any contest or struggle [the *fight* against disease]. **3.** strength or desire for fighting [He still has some *fight* left in him.] —**fought,** *p.t. & p.p.;* **fight′ing,** *pr.p.* —**fight′er,** *n.*

fig·ment (fig′mənt), *n.* something imagined or made up in the mind.

fig·ur·a·tive (fig′yoor ə tiv), *adj.* giving a meaning that is different from the exact meaning, but that forms a sharp picture in the mind [In "screaming headlines," the word "screaming" is a *figurative* use.] —**fig′ur·a·tive·ly,** *adv.*

fig·ure (fig′yoor), *n.* **1.** shape, outline, or form [A triangle is a *figure* with three sides. Exercise to keep a slim *figure*.] **2.** a picture or diagram, as in a book of instructions. **3.** a design or pattern, as in cloth or wallpaper. **4.** a person thought of in a certain way [an important *figure* in world affairs; a sorry *figure* of a man]. **5.** a number [the *figures* from 1 to 10]. **6. figures,** *pl.* arithmetic [He is very good at *figures*.] **7.** a sum of money [to sell a thing at a high *figure*]. **8.** a set of movements in dancing or skating. **9.** a form of speech in which words are used out of their usual meaning to form a sharp picture in the mind: also called **figure of speech** ["Cool as a cucumber" is a *figure of speech*.] —*v.* **1.** to find out by using arithmetic [Please *figure* how much I owe you.] **2.** to think or believe: *used only in everyday talk* [I *figure* it will rain today.] **3.** to decorate with a design. **4.** to have something to do with [Lack of education *figured* in his failure.] —**figure on,** to plan or depend on. —**figure out,** find the answer to; solve; understand. —**fig′ured**, *p.t.* & *p.p.*; **fig′ur·ing**, *pr.p.*

fig·ured (fig′yoord), *adj.* decorated with figures or designs [a *figured* necktie].

fig·ure·head (fig′yoor hed′), *n.* **1.** a carved figure placed at the bow of a ship for decoration. **2.** a person who holds a high position but has no real power.

fig·u·rine (fig′yoo rēn′), *n.* a small statue made of china, metal, etc.; statuette.

Fi·ji (fē′jē), *n.* a country on a group of islands in the South Pacific.

figurehead

fil·a·ment (fil′ə mənt), *n.* a very slender thread, fiber, or wire [the *filaments* of a spider's web or inside an electric light bulb].

fil·bert (fil′bərt), *n.* a hazelnut.

filch (filch), *v.* to steal something small and of little value; pilfer.

file (fīl), *n.* **1.** a folder, box, or cabinet for keeping papers in order. **2.** a number of papers, cards, magazines, etc. kept in an orderly way. **3.** an orderly line of persons or things. —*v.* **1.** to arrange papers, cards, etc. in order [*File* these letters according to date.] **2.** to put into official records [to *file* a claim for a piece of land]. **3.** to move in a line [The children *filed* out of the school.] —**in file**, in line, one behind another. —**on file**, kept in order so that it can be referred to. —**filed**, *p.t.* & *p.p.*; **fil′ing**, *pr.p.*

file (fīl), *n.* a steel tool with rough ridges for smoothing or grinding down. —*v.* to smooth or grind down with a file [to *file* one's toenails]. —**filed**, *p.t.* & *p.p*; **fil′ing**, *pr.p.*

file

fi·let (fi lā′ *or* fil′ā), *n.* **1.** a kind of net or lace. **2.** a fillet of fish or meat.

fil·i·al (fil′i əl), *adj.* that should be expected from a son or daughter [*filial* devotion].

fil·i·bus·ter (fil′ə bus′tər), *v.* to try to keep a bill from being passed in a legislature, by making long speeches or talking about other things. —*n.* **1.** a filibustering. **2.** a member of a legislature who filibusters.

fil·i·gree (fil′ə grē), *n.* delicate, lacy work, as of gold or silver wire, used for decoration. —*adj.* like or made of filigree. —*v.* to decorate with filigree. —**fil′i·greed**, *p.t.* & *p.p.*; **fil′i·gree·ing**, *pr.p.*

filigree earrings

fil·ing (fīl′ing), *n.* any of the tiny bits scraped off with a file [metal *filings*].

Fi·li·pi·no (fil′ə pē′nō), *n.* a native of the Philippines. —*adj.* Philippine. —**Fil′i·pi′nos**, *pl.*

fill (fil), *v.* **1.** to put as much as possible into; make full [to *fill* a pail with water]. **2.** to take up all the space in; occupy all of [The crowd *filled* the hall.] **3.** to become full [Her eyes *filled* with tears.] **4.** to hold, or put someone into, a certain job or office; occupy [Can he *fill* the position of treasurer?] **5.** to supply the things needed in [to *fill* an order; to *fill* a prescription]. **6.** to close up by stuffing something in [to *fill* holes or cracks with putty]. **7.** to satisfy the hunger of [The cookies *filled* them.] **8.** to swell out, as the sail of a boat. —*n.* **1.** all that is needed to make full or satisfy [to drink one's *fill*]. **2.** anything used to fill a space or hole [The gravel will be used as *fill* in the driveway.] —**fill in, 1.** to make complete by adding something. **2.** to be a substitute. —**fill out, 1.** to make or become larger, rounder, etc. **2.** to write the information asked for, as in a form. —**fill up**, to make or become completely full.

fil·er (fil′ər), *n.* **1.** a person or thing that fills. **2.** something used for filling, as a substance used for cracks or paper for a loose-leaf notebook.

fil·let (fil′it), *n.* **1.** a narrow band worn around the head as a decoration, etc. **2.** (fil′ā *or* fi lā′), a lean piece of fish or meat without bones.

fill·ing (fil′ing), *n.* a thing used to fill something, as metal that a dentist puts into a tooth cavity.

filling station, same as **gas station.**

fil·lip (fil′əp), *n.* **1.** a sharp tap made by snapping a finger from the end of the thumb. **2.** anything that stirs or livens up; stimulus [Salads give a *fillip* to meals.] —*v.* to toss with a fillip.

fillip

Fill·more, Mill·ard (mil′ərd fil′môr), 1800–1874; 13th president of the United States, from 1850 to 1853.

fil·ly (fil′ē), *n.* a young female horse; young mare. —**fil′lies**, *pl.*

film (film), *n.* **1.** a thin skin or coating [a *film* of ice on the pond]. **2.** a sheet or roll of material covered with a chemical substance that is changed by light, and used for taking photographs. **3.** a haze or blur [a *film* over the eyes]. **4.** a motion picture. —*v.* **1.** to cover or become covered with a film. **2.** to make a motion picture of [to *film* a stage play].

film·strip (film′strip), *n.* a strip of film having still photographs, often of charts, diagrams, etc., which can be shown one after another on a screen and used as an aid in teaching.

film·y (fil′mē), *adj.* like a film, or covered with a film. —**film′i·er**, *compar.*; **film′i·est**, *superl.*

fil·ter (fil′tər), *n.* **1.** a device for making water, air, or other fluid clean or pure by passing it through sand, charcoal, cloth, etc. **2.** the sand, charcoal, etc. used in this device. **3.** anything that acts like a filter [A color *filter* for a camera lens lets only certain light rays through.] *—v.* **1.** to pass or put through a filter [to *filter* smoke; water *filtering* through gravel]. **2.** to act as a filter for. **3.** to remove with a filter. **4.** to pass slowly [The news *filtered* through town.]

filth (filth), *n.* **1.** dirt that is disgusting [Sewers carry away *filth*.] **2.** anything that is very mean, disgusting, not decent, etc.

filth·y (fil′thē), *adj.* full of filth; disgusting. **—filth′i·er,** *compar.;* **filth′i·est,** *superl.* **—filth′i·ly,** *adv.* **—filth′i·ness,** *n.*

fil·tra·tion (fil trā′shən), *n.* a filtering or being filtered.

fin (fin), *n.* **1.** any of the parts like a blade or fan that stick out from the body of a fish and are used in swimming and balancing. **2.** anything like a fin, as certain parts for balancing an airplane or rocket.

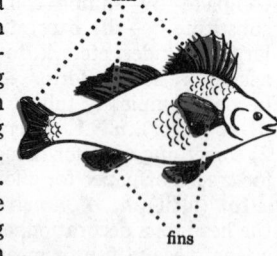

fins

fins

fi·nal (fī′n′l), *adj.* **1.** coming at the end; last; concluding [the *final* chapter in a book]. **2.** allowing no further change; deciding [The decision of the judges is *final*.] *—n.* **1.** anything final. **2.** **finals,** *pl.* the last set in a series of games, tests, etc. **—fi′nal·ly,** *adv.*

fi·na·le (fi nä′lē), *n.* **1.** the closing part of a piece of music, a musical show, etc. **2.** the close or end, as of a career.

fi·nal·ist (fī′n′l ist), *n.* a person taking part in the final, deciding contest of a series.

fi·nal·i·ty (fī nal′ə tē), *n.* **1.** the fact of being final [the *finality* of a court decision]. **2.** a final action, remark, etc. **—fi·nal′i·ties,** *pl.*

fi·nal·ize (fī′n′l īz), *v.* to make final; complete [Businessmen talk of *finalizing* agreements.] **—fi′nal·ized,** *p.t. & p.p.;* **fi′nal·iz·ing,** *pr.p.*

fi·nance (fə nans′ *or* fī′nans), *n.* **1. finances,** *pl.* all the money or income that a government, company, etc. has ready for use. **2.** the managing of money, credit, etc. in large amounts [Bankers are experts in *finance*.] *—v.* to give or get money for [loans to *finance* new business]. **—fi·nanced′,** *p.t. & p.p.;* **fi·nanc′ing,** *pr.p.*

fi·nan·cial (fə nan′shəl), *adj.* having to do with money matters [to have *financial* problems]. **—fi·nan′cial·ly,** *adv.*

fin·an·cier (fin ən sir′), *n.* an expert in money matters, as a banker or stockbroker.

finch (finch), *n.* a songbird that has a short beak and eats seeds, as the sparrow and canary.

find (fīnd), *v.* **1.** to come upon by chance; discover [I sometimes *find* violets in the woods.] **2.** to get or see by searching [The prospectors

purple finch (6 in. long)

found gold in 1849.] **3.** to get back something that has been lost; recover [Have you *found* the missing book yet?] **4.** to learn about; come to know [I *find* that I was wrong.] **5.** to decide [The jury *found* him guilty.] **6.** to get to; reach [The arrow *found* its mark.] *—n.* something found, especially something of value. **—find out,** to learn; discover [to *find out* a secret]. **—found,** *p.t. & p.p.;* **find′ing,** *pr.p.*

find·er (fīn′dər), *n.* **1.** a person or thing that finds. **2.** a camera lens that shows just what will appear in the picture.

find·ing (fīn′ding), *n.* **1.** the act of one who finds; discovery. **2.** something found. **3.** a decision reached by a judge, jury, etc. after thinking carefully about the facts.

fine (fīn), *adj.* **1.** very good; better than average; excellent [a *fine* report card]. **2.** not having impurities; refined [*fine* gold]. **3.** clear and bright [a *fine* fall day]. **4.** having small particles or grains [*fine* sand]. **5.** very thin; not thick or heavy [*fine* hairs]. **6.** delicate; carefully made [*fine* china]. **7.** sharp; keen [a *fine* edge on the razor]. **8.** hard to see or understand; subtle [the *fine* distinction between pity and sympathy]. *—adv.* very well: *used only in everyday talk.* **—fin′er,** *compar.;* **fin′est,** *superl.* **—fine′ly,** *adv.* **—fine′ness,** *n.*

fine (fīn), *n.* money paid as punishment for breaking a law or rule [a traffic *fine;* a library *fine*]. *—v.* to order to pay a fine [He was *fined* five dollars for speeding.] **—fined,** *p.t. & p.p.;* **fin′ing,** *pr.p.*

fine arts, such arts as drawing, painting, sculpture, etc., and also, sometimes, music, literature, dancing, etc.

fin·er·y (fīn′ər ē), *n.* showy or fancy clothes and jewelry. **—fin′er·ies,** *pl.*

fi·nesse (fi nes′), *n.* **1.** skill in taking care of difficult or touchy problems without causing anger [to show *finesse* in dealing with customers]. **2.** delicate or skillful work [the *finesse* with which the artist drew a portrait].

fin·ger (fing′gər), *n.* **1.** any of the five parts at the end of the hand, especially any of these besides the thumb. **2.** the part of a glove that covers a finger. **3.** anything shaped or used like a finger. *—v.* **1.** to touch with the fingers [Don't *finger* the toys on the counter.] **2.** to play by using certain fingers on the strings or keys of a musical instrument [How would you *finger* this chord?]

fin·ger·nail (fing′gər nāl), *n.* the hard, tough cover at the top of each finger tip.

fin·ger·print (fing′gər print), *n.* the mark made by pressing the tip of a finger against a flat surface. The fine lines and circles form a pattern that can be used to identify a person.

fin·i·cal (fin′i k′l) or **fin·ick·y** (fin′i kē), *adj.* too particular; fussy [He is *finical* about his food.]

fi·nis (fī′nis *or* fin′is), *n.* the end; finish.

fingerprint

fin·ish (fin′ish), *v.* **1.** to bring or come to an end; complete or become completed [Did you *finish* your homework? The games *finished* ahead of time.] **2.** to give a certain surface to, as by polishing or painting. **3.** to polish or perfect. **4.** to use up; consume [*Finish* what's on your plate.] —*n.* **1.** the last part; end [The audience stayed to the *finish*.] **2.** polish or perfection, as in one's manners. **3.** the kind of surface a thing has [an oil *finish* on wood]. —**finish off, 1.** to end. **2.** to kill or destroy. —**finish up, 1.** to end. **2.** to use all of. —**finish with, 1.** to end. **2.** to stop dealing with. —**fin′ished,** *adj.*

fi·nite (fī′nīt), *adj.* having definite limits; that can be measured [*finite* distances].

Fin·land (fin′lənd), *n.* a country in northern Europe, east of Sweden.

Finn (fin), *n.* a person born or living in Finland.

fin·nan had·die (fin′ən had′ē), smoked haddock.

Finn·ish (fin′ish), *adj.* of Finland, its people, etc. —*n.* the language of the Finns.

fin·ny (fin′ē), *adj.* **1.** having fins. **2.** like a fin. **3.** of or full of fish.

fiord (fyôrd), *n.* a narrow inlet of the sea between steep cliffs, especially in Norway.

fir (fûr), *n.* **1.** an evergreen tree of the pine family, with leaves shaped like flat needles. **2.** its wood.

fire (fīr), *n.* **1.** the heat and light of something burning; flame. **2.** something burning, as in a stove or furnace.

fiord

3. a burning that destroys things [a forest *fire*]. **4.** great warmth of feeling; excitement; fervor [a speech full of *fire*]. **5.** the shooting of guns [under enemy *fire*]. **6.** a great number of questions, complaints, etc. [He resigned under the *fire* of criticism.] —*v.* **1.** to set fire to; make burn: *now seldom used except in connection with the stirring up of feeling, thought, or action* [to *fire* one's imagination; to *fire* a revolt]. **2.** to keep burning; tend the fire of [to *fire* a furnace]. **3.** to bake in a kiln [to *fire* bricks]. **4.** to shoot, as a gun or a bullet. **5.** to throw or direct with great force: *used only in everyday talk* [The shortstop *fired* the ball to first base.] **6.** to send away from a job or position; discharge: *used only in everyday talk.* —**between two fires,** shot at, criticized, etc. from both sides. —**catch fire,** to begin burning. —**fire up,** to start a fire, as in a boiler. —**hang fire,** to delay or be delayed. —**miss fire, 1.** to fail to fire, as a gun. **2.** to fail in a try. —**on fire, 1.** burning. **2.** very excited. —**open fire,** to begin to shoot. —**set fire to,** to make burn. —**take fire, 1.** to begin to burn. **2.** to become excited. —**under fire,** under attack or criticism. —**fired,** *p.t. & p.p.;* **fir′ing,** *pr.p.*

fire·arm (fīr′ärm), *n.* any weapon that shoots bullets or shells and that is small enough to carry, as a rifle or pistol.

fire·brand (fīr′brand), *n.* **1.** a piece of burning wood. **2.** a person who stirs up a revolt.

fire·crack·er (fīr′krak ər), *n.* a roll of paper with gunpowder inside. It is exploded with a loud noise by lighting a fuse.

fire·damp (fīr′damp), *n.* a gas in coal mines that can explode when mixed with air.

fire engine, 1. a machine, usually on a motor truck, for spraying water to put out a fire. **2.** any motor truck for carrying firemen to a fire.

fire escape, a ladder, stairway, etc. by which one can escape from a burning building.

fire extinguisher, a device for putting out a fire by spraying liquid or gas on it. *See the picture for* **extinguisher.**

fire·fly (fīr′flī), *n.* a small, flying beetle whose lower body glows with a light that goes off and on at night. —**fire′-flies,** *pl.*

fire·light (fīr′līt), *n.* light from an open fire.

fire·man (fīr′mən), *n.* **1.** a member of a company of men whose work is putting out fires. **2.** a man who tends the fire in a furnace or a steam locomotive. —**fire′men,** *pl.*

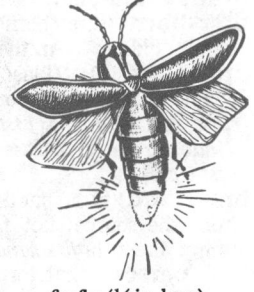

firefly (½ in. long)

fire·place (fīr′plās), *n.* an open place for a fire, especially one inside a house, built of brick or stone and connected to a chimney.

fire·plug (fīr′plug), *n.* same as **hydrant.**

fire·proof (fīr′prōof), *adj.* that does not burn or is not easily destroyed by fire [a *fireproof* hotel]. —*v.* to make fireproof, as by treating with chemicals.

fire·side (fīr′sīd), *n.* **1.** the part of a room near a fireplace; hearth. **2.** home or home life.

fire station, a place where fire engines are kept and where firemen stay when on duty.

fire·trap (fīr′trap), *n.* a building that would not be safe if it caught on fire.

fire·wood (fīr′wood), *n.* wood for burning in a fireplace, campfire, etc.

fire·works (fīr′wûrks), *n.pl.* things made with gunpowder, etc. that are burned or exploded to make loud noises or a fancy show of lights at night, often used in celebrations [Rockets, sparklers, and firecrackers are *fireworks*.] *Sometimes used in the singular,* **firework.**

firm (fûrm), *adj.* **1.** that does not easily give way when pressed; solid [*firm* muscles]. **2.** that cannot be moved easily; fixed; stable [He stood as *firm* as a rock.] **3.** that stays the same; not changing; constant [a *firm* friendship]. **4.** strong and steady; not weak; determined [a *firm* command].

firm (fŭrm), *n.* a business company in which there are two or more partners.

fir·ma·ment (fŭr/mə mənt), *n.* the sky, written of by poets as if it were a solid blue arch.

first (fŭrst), *adj.* **1.** before another or before all others in time, order, quality, etc.; earliest, foremost, etc. [the *first* snow of winter; the *first* door to the right; *first* prize; fruit of the *first* quality]. **2.** playing or singing the highest part [*first* violin; *first* tenor]. —*adv.* **1.** before anything or anyone else [*First* we had soup. The guests will be served *first.*] **2.** for the first time [When did you *first* meet her?] **3.** more willingly; rather [When told to beg, he said he'd starve *first.*] —*n.* **1.** the one that is first [to be the *first* to succeed]. **2.** the beginning; start [At *first*, I believed him.] **3.** the first day of the month [He left on the *first.*].

first aid, the help given to an injured or sick person while waiting for regular medical help. —**first/-aid/,** *adj.*

first-born (fŭrst/bôrn/), *adj.* born first in a family; oldest. —*n.* the first-born child.

first-class (fŭrst/klas/), *adj.* best of its kind; of the highest quality or most expensive [a *first-class* restaurant; a *first-class* cabin on a ship]. —*adv.* in a first-class cabin, etc. [to travel *first-class*].

first·hand (fŭrst/hand/), *adj. & adv.* straight from the source; not from a second person or thing; direct [a *firsthand* report].

first person, that form of a pronoun or verb which refers to the speaker or speakers ["I," "me," "we," "us," etc. are in the *first person.*]

first-rate (fŭrst/rāt/), *adj.* of the highest class or quality; very good; excellent [a *first-rate* novel]. —*adv.* very well: *used only in everyday talk* [I feel *first-rate.*]

firth (fŭrth), *n.* a narrow inlet of the sea, especially in Scotland.

fis·cal (fis/kəl), *adj.* having to do with money matters; financial. A **fiscal year** is any period of twelve months used for figuring financial accounts [Our *fiscal year* begins July 1.]

fish (fish), *n.* **1.** an animal that lives in water and has a backbone, fins, and gills for breathing. Most fish are covered with scales. **2.** the flesh of a fish used as food. —*v.* **1.** to catch or try to catch fish. **2.** to grope for, find, and pull out [He *fished* a dime out of his pocket.] **3.** to try to get or find out something in a roundabout way [to *fish* for a compliment]. —**fish** (or when different kinds are meant, **fishes**), *pl.* [He caught three *fish.* The aquarium exhibits many *fishes.*]

fish·er (fish/ər), *n.* a person or animal that fishes; especially, a kind of marten.

fish·er·man (fish/ər mən), *n.* a person who fishes either for sport or for a living. —**fish/er·men,** *pl.*

fish·er·y (fish/ər ē), *n.* **1.** the business of catching fish. **2.** a place where fish are caught. **3.** a place for breeding fish. —**fish/er·ies,** *pl.*

fish·hook (fish/hook), *n.* a hook with a barb or barbs for catching fish.

fish·ing (fish/ing), *n.* the catching of fish for sport or for a living.

fishing rod, a long pole with a line, hook, and sometimes a reel, used in fishing.

fish·mon·ger (fish/mung-gər), *n.* a person who buys and sells fish.

fishing rod

fish·y (fish/ē), *adj.* **1.** full of fish. **2.** tasting or smelling of fish. **3.** dull; without expression [a *fishy* stare]. **4.** that makes one feel doubt; not likely; suspicious: *used only in everyday talk* [a *fishy* story]. —**fish/i·er,** *compar.*; **fish/i·est,** *superl.*

fis·sion (fish/ən), *n.* a splitting apart; dividing into parts: see also **nuclear fission.**

fis·sure (fish/ər), *n.* a crack or split, as in a rock.

fist (fist), *n.* a hand with the fingers closed tightly into the palm [*Fists* are used in boxing.]

fis·ti·cuffs (fis/ti kufs/), *n.pl.* the act or skill of fighting with the fists; boxing.

fis·tu·la (fis/choo lə), *n.* **1.** a pipe or tube. **2.** an unnatural opening, like a pipe, caused by an abscess or other illness in some part of the body. —**fis/tu·las** or **fis·tu·lae** (fis/choo lē), *pl.*

fit (fit), *v.* **1.** to be the right size or shape for [Does this coat *fit* you?] **2.** to make or change so as to be the right size or shape [His new suit has to be *fitted.*] **3.** to be right or suitable to [Let the punishment *fit* the crime.] **4.** to make right or suitable [to *fit* words to music]. **5.** to furnish with what is needed or wanted; outfit: *often used with* out [to *fit* out a ship for a voyage]. —*adj.* **1.** suitable or suited to someone or something [a meal *fit* for a king]. **2.** proper or right [It is not *fit* for you to show fear.] **3.** healthy; in good physical condition [He looks *fit* again after his illness.] —*n.* the way something fits [This coat is a tight *fit.*] —**fit/ted** or **fit,** *p.t. & p.p.*; **fit/ting,** *pr.p.* —**fit/ter,** *compar.*; **fit/test,** *superl.* —**fit/ly,** *adv.* —**fit/ness,** *n.*

fit (fit), *n.* **1.** a sudden attack or outburst that is hard to control [a *fit* of coughing; a *fit* of anger]. **2.** a sudden attack of some disease; especially, a convulsion. —**by fits and starts,** from time to time; not in a regular way.

fit·ful (fit/fəl), *adj.* happening or done only from time to time; not regular or steady [a *fitful* sleep]. —**fit/ful·ly,** *adv.*

fit·ting (fit/ing), *adj.* right, proper, or suitable [a *fitting* tribute to a great man]. —*n.* **1.** a trying on of clothes, etc. to see that they fit. **2. fittings,** *pl.* the necessary fixtures, furnishings, etc., as of a house.

five (fīv), *n. & adj.* one more than four; the number 5.

fix (fiks), *v.* **1.** to make stay in place; fasten firmly [a flagpole *fixed* in concrete; an idea *fixed* in the mind]. **2.** to direct and hold [to *fix* one's eyes on something]. **3.** to make stiff or rigid [a jaw *fixed* in determination]. **4.** to decide on; settle; set definitely [to *fix* the date of a wedding]. **5.** to set right or set in order; adjust [to *fix* one's hair]. **6.** to make whole again; repair or mend

[He *fixed* the broken chair.] **7.** to get ready; prepare [to *fix* dinner]. **8.** to treat with a chemical so as to keep from fading [to *fix* photographic film]. **9.** to get the result wanted by bribery, trickery, etc.: *used only in everyday talk* [to *fix* an election]. **10.** to get even with; punish: *used only in everyday talk.* —*n.* an unpleasant or difficult situation; predicament: *used only in everyday talk.* —**fix on** or **fix upon,** to choose. —**fix up, 1.** to repair; mend. **2.** to arrange properly. **3.** to take care of. *This phrase is used only in everyday talk.* —**fixed,** *adj.* —**fix·ed·ly** (fik′sid lē), *adv.*

fix·a·tion (fik sā′shən), *n.* a fixing or being fixed into some special or lasting form.

fixed star, any star, as distinct from a planet. All stars really move, but they are so far from the earth that they seem to keep the same position with respect to each other.

fix·ings (fik′singz), *n.pl.* all the things that go with the main thing; trimmings: *used only in everyday talk* [a turkey and all the *fixings*].

fix·ture (fiks′chər), *n.* **1.** any of the fittings that are fastened to a building in such a way as to be considered a part of it [bathroom *fixtures;* a light *fixture*]. **2.** any person or thing that has been in some position or place so long as to seem fixed there [Dr. Lander is a *fixture* at the hospital.]

fizz (fiz), *n.* a hissing or sputtering sound, as of soda water. —*v.* to make this sound.

fiz·zle (fiz′'l), *v.* **1.** to make a hissing or sputtering sound. **2.** to fail, especially after a good start: *used only in everyday talk.* —*n.* **1.** a hissing or sputtering sound. **2.** a thing that ends in failure: *used only in everyday talk.* —**fiz′zled,** *p.t. & p.p.;* **fiz′zling,** *pr.p.*

fjord (fyôrd), *n.* same as **fiord.**

Fl, symbol for the chemical element *fluorine.*

fl., abbreviation for **fluid.**

Fla., abbreviation for **Florida.**

flab·ber·gast (flab′ər gast), *v.* to surprise so greatly that one is speechless; amaze.

flab·by (flab′ē), *adj.* soft and limp; not firm and strong [*flabby* muscles]. —**flab′bi·er,** *compar.;* **flab′bi·est,** *superl.* —**flab′bi·ness,** *n.*

flac·cid (flak′sid), *adj.* soft and limp; flabby.

flag (flag), *n.* a piece of cloth with certain colors and designs, used as a symbol of a country, State, etc. or as a signal. —*v.* to signal with a flag. —**flag down,** to stop by waving a flag. —**flagged,** *p.t. & p.p.;* **flag′ging,** *pr.p.*

flag (flag), *n.* the iris, a plant with sword-shaped leaves and showy flowers.

flag (flag), *v.* to become limp, weak, or tired; droop [The hikers began to *flag* after the tenth mile.] —**flagged,** *p.t. & p.p.;* **flag′ging,** *pr.p.*

Flag Day, June 14, the anniversary of the day in 1777 when the United States flag was adopted.

flag·el·late (flaj′ə lāt), *v.* to whip or flog. —**flag′el·lat·ed,** *p.t. & p.p.;* **flag′el·lat·ing,** *pr.p.* —**flag′el·la′tion,** *n.*

flag·eo·let (flaj ə let′), *n.* an old musical instrument like the recorder.

fla·gi·tious (flə jish′əs), *adj.* so wrong or wicked as to cause shame.

flag·on (flag′ən), *n.* a kind of pitcher with a handle, a spout, and, usually, a lid.

flag·pole (flag′pōl), *n.* a pole on which a flag is raised and flown: also **flag·staff** (flag′staf).

fla·grant (flā′grənt), *adj.* clearly bad or wicked; outrageous [a *flagrant* crime].

flag·ship (flag′ship), *n.* the main ship of a fleet, on which the commander stays.

flag·stone (flag′stōn), *n.* any of the flat stones used in making a walk or terrace.

flail (flāl), *n.* a farm tool used to beat grain in order to separate it from its husk. It has a long handle, with a shorter stick attached so that it will swing freely. —*v.* to beat, as with a flail.

flair (fler), *n.* natural skill; talent [He has a *flair* for music.]

flake (flāk), *n.* a small, thin piece or chip [a *flake* of snow; a *flake* of dried paint]. —*v.* to come off in flakes [The plaster had *flaked* from the walls.]

harvesters using flails

—**flaked,** *p.t. & p.p.;* **flak′ing,** *pr.p.*

flak·y (flāk′ē), *adj.* **1.** of or made up of flakes. **2.** breaking easily into flakes. —**flak′i·er,** *compar.;* **flak′i·est,** *superl.*

flam·boy·ant (flam boi′ənt), *adj.* **1.** as brilliant and showy as a flame [*flamboyant* autumn leaves]. **2.** too showy or fancy [a *flamboyant* costume].

flame (flām), *n.* **1.** the burning gas of a fire seen as a flickering light; blaze. **2.** the condition of burning with a blaze [to burst into *flame*]. **3.** anything as hot or as brilliant as a flame. —*v.* **1.** to burn with a flame; blaze. **2.** to burst out like a flame [to *flame* with anger]. —**flamed,** *p.t. & p.p.;* **flam′ing,** *pr.p.*

fla·min·go (flə ming′gō), *n.* a wading bird that has a very long neck and legs, and pink or red feathers. It lives in tropical regions. —**fla·min′gos** or **fla·min′goes,** *pl.*

flam·ma·ble (flam′ə b'l), *adj.* quick to catch on fire; inflammable [Gasoline is *flammable*.] —**flam′ma·bil′i·ty,** *n.*

Flan·ders (flan′dərz), *n.* a region in Europe in western Belgium and northern France. It was once a country.

flamingo (3¾ ft. long, shoulder to tail)

flange (flanj), *n.* a flat edge that stands out from the rim of a wheel, pipe, etc. to hold it in place.

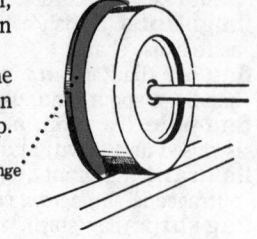

flange

flank (flangk), *n.* **1.** the side of an animal between the ribs and the hip. **2.** the side of anything [the right flank of an army]. —*v.* **1.** to be at the side of [Fountains *flank* the statue on either side.] **2.** to go around the side of enemy troops, etc.

flan·nel (flan′'l), *n.* **1.** a soft cloth with a nap, made usually of wool or cotton. **2. flannels**, *pl.* trousers, etc. made of flannel.

flan·nel·ette (flan 'l et′), *n.* cotton flannel.

flap (flap), *n.* **1.** anything flat and broad that hangs loose or covers an opening [the *flap* of a pocket; the *flap* of an envelope]. **2.** the motion or slapping sound of a swinging flap [the *flap* of an awning]. —*v.* **1.** to move with a slapping sound [The flag *flapped* in the wind.] **2.** to move up and down or back and forth [The bird *flapped* its wings.] —**flapped**, *p.t. & p.p.;* **flap′ping**, *pr.p.*

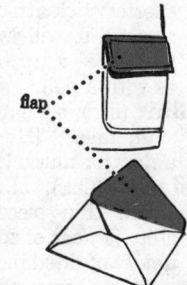

flap

flap·jack (flap′jak), *n.* a pancake.

flare (fler), *v.* **1.** to blaze up with a bright flame or burn with a flame that is whipped about [The torch *flared* in the wind.] **2.** to spread outward like a bell [The lower end of a clarinet *flares* out.] —*n.* **1.** a short burst of bright light. **2.** a very bright light used as a distress signal, to light up a landing field, etc. **3.** a sudden, short outburst [a *flare* of temper]. **4.** a spreading outward like a bell, or the part that spreads out [the *flares* in a skirt]. —**flare up, 1.** to burst into flame. **2.** to become suddenly angry, excited, etc. —**flared**, *p.t. & p.p.;* **flar′ing**, *pr.p.*

flash (flash), *v.* **1.** to send out a short and bright burst of light [Electric signs *flashed* all along the street.] **2.** to sparkle or gleam [Her eyes *flashed* with anger.] **3.** to come, move, or send swiftly or suddenly [The train *flashed* by. The news was *flashed* to Paris by radio.] —*n.* **1.** a short burst of light or of something bright [a *flash* of lightning; a *flash* of wit, hope, etc.]. **2.** a very short time; moment [I'll be there in a *flash.*] **3.** a bit of late news sent by telegraph, radio, etc.

flash·bulb (flash′bulb), *n.* a light bulb on a camera that flashes a bright light when the shutter is opened.

flash·cube (flash′kyoob), *n.* a cube with a flashbulb in each one of four sides: it rotates after each bulb flashes, placing the next one in a position ready for flashing.

flash·ing (flash′ing), *n.* sheets of metal, etc. used to seal joints or edges, as of a roof.

flash·light (flash′līt), *n.* **1.** an electric light that uses batteries and is small enough to carry. **2.** the light of a flashbulb.

flash·y (flash′ē), *adj.* too showy or fancy [*flashy* clothes]. —**flash′i·er**, *compar.;* **flash′i·est**, *superl.*

flask (flask), *n.* a small bottle with a narrow neck, used by chemists, etc.

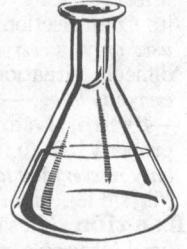

flask

flat (flat), *adj.* **1.** smooth and level [a *flat* stretch of land]. **2.** lying spread out; horizontal [to lie *flat* on the floor]. **3.** not very thick or deep [A penny is round and *flat.*] **4.** definite; positive [a *flat* refusal]. **5.** not changing; always the same [a *flat* rate]. **6.** without much taste or sparkle [This ginger ale is *flat.*] **7.** having lost air [a *flat* tire]. **8.** not shiny or glossy [a *flat* paint]. **9.** in music, below the true pitch; also, lower in pitch by a half tone. —*adv.* **1.** in a flat way; flatly [to fall *flat* on the floor; to sing *flat*]. **2.** exactly [He ran the race in 10 seconds *flat.*] —*n.* **1.** a flat part [the *flat* of the hand]. **2.** a stretch of flat land. **3.** a shallow box, as for carrying seedlings. **4.** a musical tone or note one half step below another; also, the sign ♭, used to mark such a note. —*v.* to make or become flat [to *flat* a note]. —**fall flat**, to fail to have the effect that is wanted [His joke *fell flat.*] —**flat′ter**, *compar.;* **flat′test**, *superl.* —**flat′ted**, *p.t. & p.p.;* **flat′ting**, *pr.p.* —**flat′ly**, *adv.* —**flat′ness**, *n.*

flat (flat), *n.* an apartment of rooms on one floor.

flat·boat (flat′bōt), *n.* a boat with a flat bottom, for carrying heavy loads, especially on rivers.

flat·car (flat′kär), *n.* a railroad car without sides or a top, for carrying certain freight.

flat·fish (flat′fish), *n.* a fish with a flat body and both eyes on the top side, as the flounder and halibut.

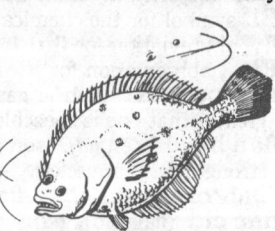

flatfish

flat·foot (flat′foot), *n.* a condition in which the bottom of the foot is flat instead of being curved by the arch. —**flat′-foot′ed**, *adj.*

flat·i·ron (flat′ī′ərn), *n.* an iron (*in meaning 3*).

flat·ten (flat′'n), *v.* to make or become flat.

flat·ter (flat′ər), *v.* **1.** to praise too much or without meaning it, as in order to win favor. **2.** to make seem better or more attractive than is really so [This picture *flatters* me.] **3.** to make feel pleased and honored [I'm *flattered* that you remember me.] —**flatter oneself**, to hold the pleasing belief that [Don't *flatter yourself* that he will forgive you.] —**flat′ter·er**, *n.*

flat·ter·y (flat′ər ē), *n.* too much praise, or praise that is not really meant. —**flat′ter·ies**, *pl.*

flaunt (flônt), *v.* **1.** to show off in a bold way [to *flaunt* one's wealth]. **2.** to wave proudly, as banners.

fla·vor (flā′vər), *n.* **1.** the special quality of something that is a mixing of its taste and smell [the *flavor* of chocolate; the *flavor* of lemon]. **2.** taste in general [This soup has no *flavor*.] —*v.* to give flavor to; season.

fla·vor·ing (flā′vər ing), *n.* something added to give a certain flavor [vanilla *flavoring*].

fla·vour (flā′vər), *n. & v.* flavor: *the British spelling*.

flaw (flô), *n.* **1.** a break, scratch, crack, etc. that spoils something; blemish [There is a *flaw* in this diamond.] **2.** any fault or error [a *flaw* in one's reasoning]. —**flaw′less,** *adj.*

flax (flaks), *n.* **1.** a slender plant with blue flowers and narrow leaves. The fibers from its stem are spun into linen thread and its seeds are used to make linseed oil. **2.** the thin fibers of this plant.

flax·en (flak′s'n), *adj.* **1.** of flax. **2.** like flax in color; pale-yellow [*flaxen* hair].

flay (flā), *v.* **1.** to strip off the skin of, as by whipping. **2.** to scold in a harsh way.

flea (flē), *n.* a small jumping insect that has no wings. It bites animals and people and feeds on their blood.

fleck (flek), *n.* a spot of color, dirt, etc.; speck.—*v.* to cover or sprinkle with flecks; speckle [brown cloth *flecked* with green].

flea (¼ in. long)

fled (fled), past tense and past participle of **flee.**

fledged (flejd), *adj.* of or describing a young bird that has already grown the feathers it needs for flying.

fledg·ling or **fledge·ling** (flej′ling), *n.* **1.** a young bird that has grown the feathers it needs for flying. **2.** a young person who has had little or no experience.

flee (flē), *v.* **1.** to run away from danger or from something unpleasant; escape [The farmers *fled* when they heard the flood warnings.] **2.** to move swiftly away [The years *flee* by.] —**fled,** *p.t. & p.p.;* **flee′ing,** *pr.p.*

fleece (flēs), *n.* the coat of wool on a sheep or on a goat, llama, etc. —*v.* **1.** to clip the fleece from. **2.** to take money from by trickery; swindle. —**fleeced,** *p.t. & p.p.;* **fleec′ing,** *pr.p.*

fleec·y (flēs′ē), *adj.* of or like fleece; soft, light, and fluffy [*fleecy* clouds]. —**fleec′i·er,** *compar.;* **fleec′i·est,** *superl.*

fleet (flēt), *n.* **1.** a group of warships under one command [our Pacific *fleet*]. **2.** the entire navy of a country [the British *fleet*]. **3.** any group of ships, buses, trucks, etc. moving together or under one control.

fleet (flēt), *adj.* moving swiftly; swift.

fleet·ing (flēt′ing), *adj.* passing swiftly; not lasting [a *fleeting* glimpse].

Flem·ing (flem′ing), *n.* **1.** a person born in Flanders. **2.** a Belgian who speaks Flemish.

Flem·ish (flem′ish), *adj.* of Flanders, its people, etc. —*n.* **1.** the people of Flanders: *used with*

a plural verb. **2.** their language, which is a kind of German.

flesh (flesh), *n.* **1.** the soft parts of the body, especially the parts between the skin and the bones. **2.** these parts of an animal used as food; meat. **3.** man's body; also, mankind [more than *flesh* can bear; the way of all *flesh*]. **4.** the pulpy part of fruits and vegetables. —**in the flesh, 1.** in person; really present. **2.** alive. —**one's own flesh and blood,** one's close relatives.

flesh·ly (flesh′lē), *adj.* having to do with the body, its weaknesses, appetites, etc. —**flesh′li·er,** *compar.;* **flesh′li·est,** *superl.*

flesh·y (flesh′ē), *adj.* having much flesh; plump. —**flesh′i·er,** *compar.;* **flesh′i·est,** *superl.*

fleur-de-lis (flûr′də lē′), *n.* a design that looks a little like a lily or iris. It was an emblem of French kings. —**fleurs-de-lis** (flûr′də lēz′), *pl.*

fleur-de-lis

flew (flōō), past tense of **fly.**

flex (fleks), *v.* **1.** to bend [to *flex* an arm]. **2.** to make tighter and harder; contract [to *flex* a muscle].

flex·i·ble (flek′sə b'l), *adj.* **1.** that bends easily without breaking [a *flexible* rubber hose]. **2.** easily changed or managed [Our doctor has *flexible* office hours.] —**flex′i·bil′i·ty,** *n.*

flick (flik), *n.* **1.** a light, quick stroke, as with a whip; snap. **2.** a light, snapping sound. —*v.* to give a light, quick stroke to, as with a whip or the fingernail [He *flicked* the ant off the table.]

flick·er (flik′ər), *v.* **1.** to burn or shine in a way that is not clear or steady; waver [The candles *flickered* in the wind.] **2.** to move in a quick, light, unsteady way [*flickering* shadows]. —*n.* **1.** a flickering light or flame. **2.** a look or feeling that comes and goes quickly [A *flicker* of pleasure crossed his face.]

flick·er (flik′ər), *n.* a brown woodpecker of North America with a red mark on the back of the head and wings colored golden on the underside.

flied (flīd), a past tense and past participle of **fly,** in its meaning in baseball.

fli·er (flī′ər), *n.* **1.** a thing that flies. **2.** a person who flies an airplane; aviator. **3.** a bus or train that travels very fast.

flicker (1 ft. long)

flies (flīz), **1.** the form of the verb **fly** used in the present with *he, she,* or *it.* **2.** the plural of the noun **fly.**

flight (flīt), *n.* **1.** the act or way of flying. **2.** a trip through the air, as by an airplane, bird, bullet, etc. [a 500-mile *flight*]. **3.** a group of things flying together [a *flight* of wild swans]. **4.** a going above or beyond the usual limits [a *flight* of the imagination]. **5.** a set of stairs, as between landings or floors.

flight (flīt), *n.* a fleeing or running away. —**put to flight,** to make run away.

flight·y (flīt′ē), *adj.* not taking things seriously; unsettled; frivolous. —**flight′i·er,** *compar.;* **flight′i·est,** *superl.*

flim·sy (flim′zē), *adj.* easily broken or damaged; not solid or strong; weak [a *flimsy* cardboard box; a *flimsy* excuse]. —**flim′si·er,** *compar.;* **flim′si·est,** *superl.* —**flim′si·ness,** *n.*

flinch (flinch), *v.* to draw back from a blow or from anything difficult or painful [The soldier never *flinched* from duty.] —*n.* a flinching.

fling (fling), *v.* to throw or hurl; put or move suddenly and with force [He *flung* the spear at the tiger. The lost child was *flung* into a panic. He *flung* himself into his work. She *flung* out of the room in a rage.] —*n.* **1.** the act of flinging; a throw. **2.** a short time when one throws oneself into a life of fun and pleasure [He had his *fling* before he went into the army.] **3.** a fast, lively dance of the Scottish Highlands. **4.** a try: *used only in everyday talk* [Have a *fling* at it.] —**flung,** *p.t. & p.p.;* **fling′ing,** *pr.p.*

Flint (flint), *n.* a city in eastern Michigan.

flint (flint), *n.* a very hard stone, a kind of quartz, that makes sparks when it is struck against steel. —**flint′y,** *adj.*

flint·lock (flint′läk), *n.* an old-fashioned gun in which a flint in the hammer strikes a steel plate, making sparks that set off the powder.

flip (flip), *v.* **1.** to toss or move with a quick jerk [The acrobat *flipped* over twice in the air.] **2.** to snap a coin into the air, with the thumb, as in betting on which side will land uppermost. —*n.* a flipping; toss. —**flipped,** *p.t. & p.p.;* **flip′ping,** *pr.p.*

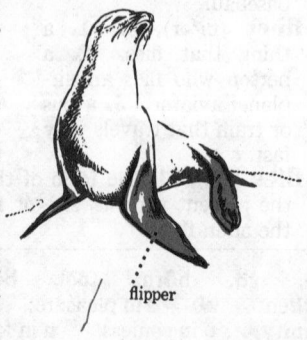
firing part of a flintlock

flip·pant (flip′ənt), *adj.* joking or trying to be funny when one should be more serious or show more respect. —**flip′pan·cy,** *n.*

flip·per (flip′ər), *n.* any of the broad, flat limbs on seals, whales, etc., used for swimming.

flirt (flŭrt), *v.* **1.** to pretend to be making love without being serious about it. **2.** to think about or have to do with, but not in a serious way; toy [Jim *flirted* with the idea of studying law.] **3.**

flipper

to move back and forth quickly [The sparrow *flirted* its tail.] —*n.* **1.** a person who flirts with others. **2.** a flirting motion.

flir·ta·tion (flŭr tā′shən), *n.* the act of flirting, or making love in a way that is not serious. —**flir·ta′tious,** *adj.*

flit (flit), *v.* to fly or move in a quick and light way; dart [butterflies *flitting* from blossom to blossom; memories *flitting* through the mind]. —**flit′ted,** *p.t. & p.p.;* **flit′ting,** *pr.p.*

flitch (flich), *n.* a side of bacon.

float (flōt), *v.* **1.** to rest on top of water or other liquid and not sink [Ice *floats*.] **2.** to move or drift slowly, as on a liquid or through the air [Clouds *floated* overhead.] **3.** to cause to float [You may *float* your boats in this pond.] **4.** to get started; set going; launch [to *float* a loan]. —*n.*

float in a parade

1. something that floats on a liquid or keeps something else afloat, as a raft, a cork on a fishing line, or a hollow tank on an airplane wing to allow landing on water. **2.** a hollow metal ball that floats on the liquid in a tank and shuts off the valve controlling the liquid when it reaches a certain level. **3.** a platform on wheels that carries a display or exhibit in a parade. —**float′er,** *n.*

flock (fläk), *n.* **1.** a group of animals or birds that feed or travel together [a *flock* of sheep; a *flock* of geese]. **2.** any group of people or things, as the members of a church. —*v.* to come or travel together in a group ["Birds of a feather *flock* together."]

floe (flō), *n.* a large sheet of floating ice.

flog (fläg *or* flôg), *v.* to beat, as with a whip or stick; thrash. —**flogged,** *p.t. & p.p.;* **flog′ging,** *pr.p.*

flood (flud), *n.* **1.** an overflowing of water on land next to a river, lake, etc. **2.** the flowing in of the tide. **3.** any great flow or outburst [a *flood* of tears, words, etc.]. —*v.* **1.** to flow over its banks onto near-by land. **2.** to flow, cover, or fill like a flood [The sound of trumpets *flooded* the air.]

flood·gate (flud′gāt), *n.* a gate that controls the flow of water, as in a canal.

flood·light (flud′līt), *n.* **1.** a lamp that sends out a broad beam of bright light. **2.** such a beam of light. —*v.* to light by such a lamp.

floor (flôr), *n.* **1.** the bottom part of a room, hall, etc., on which to walk. **2.** the bottom surface of anything [the ocean *floor*]. **3.** a story of a building [Our office is on the fifth *floor*.] **4.** permission to speak at a meeting ["Mr. Chairman, may I have the *floor?*"] —*v.* **1.** to cover with a floor. **2.** to knock down to the floor. **3.** to puzzle or confuse: *used only in everyday talk* [His answer *floored* me.]

floor·ing (flôr′ing), *n.* **1.** a floor or floors. **2.** material for making floors.

flop (fläp), *v.* **1.** to move or flap about in a loose or clumsy way [a beagle with ears *flopping*]. **2.** to fall or drop in this way [He *flopped* into a chair.] **3.** to fail: *used only in everyday talk* [Our school play *flopped*.] —*n.* **1.** the act or sound of flopping. **2.** a failure: *used only in everyday talk*. —**flopped,** *p.t. & p.p.*; **flop′ping,** *pr.p.*

flo·ra (flôr′ə), *n.* all the plants of a particular place or time [the *flora* of Alaska].

flo·ral (flôr′əl), *adj.* of or like flowers [a *floral* design on cloth].

Flor·ence (flôr′əns), *n.* a city in central Italy. —**Flor·en·tine** (flôr′ən tēn), *adj. & n.*

flor·id (flôr′id), *adj.* **1.** flushed with color; ruddy [a *florid* face]. **2.** too full of decoration; very showy [a *florid* piece of music]. —**flor′id·ly,** *adv.* —**flor′id·ness,** *n.*

Flor·i·da (flôr′i də), *n.* a State in the southeastern part of the United States: abbreviated **Fla.**

flor·in (flôr′in), *n.* any of certain gold or silver coins used at various times in some European countries.

flo·rist (flôr′ist), *n.* a person who grows or sells flowers.

floss (flôs), *n.* **1.** soft and light bits of silky fiber. **2.** loosely twisted thread of soft silk, used in embroidery. **3.** waxed thread of this kind, used for cleaning between the teeth: *its full name is* **dental floss.** —**floss′y,** *adj.*

flo·til·la (flō til′ə), *n.* **1.** a small fleet. **2.** a fleet of boats or small ships.

flot·sam (flät′səm), *n.* parts of a wrecked ship or its cargo found floating on the sea: see also **jetsam.**

flounce (flouns), *v.* to move or turn quickly, flinging the arms or body about, as in anger [She *flounced* out of the room.] —*n.* a flouncing. —**flounced,** *p.t. & p.p.*; **flounc′ing,** *pr.p.*

flounce (flouns), *n.* a wide ruffle sewed on by its upper edge to a skirt, sleeve, etc. —*v.* to trim with a flounce or flounces. —**flounced,** *p.t. & p.p.*; **flounc′ing,** *pr.p.*

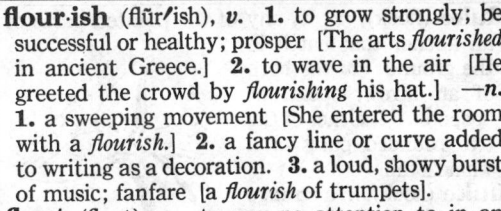

flounce

floun·der (floun′dər), *v.* **1.** to struggle in a clumsy way in moving through mud, snow, etc. **2.** to speak or act in a clumsy or confused way [to *flounder* through a speech].

floun·der (floun′dər), *n.* a kind of flatfish valuable as food.

flour (flour), *n.* wheat or other grain that has been ground into a fine powder, or meal. It is used for making bread, cakes, etc. —*v.* to put flour on or in. —**flour′y,** *adj.*

flour·ish (flûr′ish), *v.* **1.** to grow strongly; be successful or healthy; prosper [The arts *flourished* in ancient Greece.] **2.** to wave in the air [He greeted the crowd by *flourishing* his hat.] —*n.* **1.** a sweeping movement [She entered the room with a *flourish*.] **2.** a fancy line or curve added to writing as a decoration. **3.** a loud, showy burst of music; fanfare [a *flourish* of trumpets].

flout (flout), *v.* to pay no attention to in an insulting or mocking way; treat with scorn [to *flout* someone's advice].

flow (flō), *v.* **1.** to move in a stream as water does [Oil *flows* through the pipeline.] **2.** to move in a smooth and easy way [The crowds *flowed* by. The talk *flowed* on for hours.] **3.** to come from as a source; spring ["Praise God from whom all blessings *flow*."] **4.** to hang loose [Her hair *flowed* down her back.] —*n.* **1.** the act, way, or amount of flowing. **2.** anything that moves along in a steady way; stream or current [a *flow* of mail]. **3.** the rising of the tide.

flow·er (flou′ər), *n.* **1.** the part of a plant that bears the seed and usually has brightly colored petals; blossom or bloom. **2.** a plant grown for its blossoms. **3.** the best or finest part [King Arthur's knights were the *flower* of chivalry.] **4.** the best time or finest period [in the *flower* of his life]. —*v.* **1.** to come into bloom; bear flowers. **2.** to reach its best or finest period [As a poet he *flowered* early.]

flow·ered (flou′ərd), *adj.* decorated with flowers or a design like flowers [a *flowered* dress].

flow·er·pot (flou′ər pät), *n.* a pot to hold earth for a plant to grow in.

flow·er·y (flou′ər ē), *adj.* **1.** covered or decorated with flowers [a *flowery* field; a *flowery* design]. **2.** full of fine words or fancy language [a *flowery* speech]. —**flow′er·i·ness,** *n.*

flown (flōn), past participle of **fly.**

flu (flōō), *n.* influenza.

fluc·tu·ate (fluk′chōō āt), *v.* to rise and fall; keep changing or wavering [The price of eggs *fluctuates*.] —**fluc′tu·at·ed,** *p.t. & p.p.*; **fluc′tu·at·ing,** *pr.p.* —**fluc′tu·a′tion,** *n.*

flue (flōō), *n.* a tube for allowing smoke, hot air, etc. to go out, as in a chimney.

flu·en·cy (flōō′ən sē), *n.* the quality of being fluent, especially in writing or speaking.

flu·ent (flōō′ənt), *adj.* **1.** moving easily and smoothly [*fluent* verse]. **2.** able to write or speak easily and clearly. —**flu′ent·ly,** *adv.*

fluff (fluf), *n.* downy bits of feathers, cotton, fur, etc., or a soft mass of such bits. —*v.* to shake or pat until soft and fluffy [to *fluff* a pillow].

fluff·y (fluf′ē), *adj.* **1.** soft, loose, and light like fluff. **2.** covered with fluff. —**fluff′i·er,** *compar.*; **fluff′i·est,** *superl.*

flu·id (flōō′id), *n.* any substance that flows, as water, air, molten metal, etc.; any liquid or gas. —*adj.* **1.** that can flow. **2.** like a fluid; moving or changing; not fixed [*fluid* beliefs].

fat,   āpe,   cär,   ten,   ēven,   hit,   bīte,   gō,   hôrn,   tōōl,   book,   up,   fur;
get,   joy,   yet,   chin,   she,   thin,   *th*en;   zh = s in pleasure;   ′ as in able (ā′b'l);
ə = a in ago,   e in agent,   i in sanity,   o in confess,   u in focus.

fluke (flook), *n.* **1.** any of the pointed parts of an anchor that catch in the ground. **2.** the barb of an arrow, spear, or harpoon. **3.** either of the two rounded parts of a whale's tail.

fluke (flook), *n.* a strange bit of luck, good or bad: *used mainly in everyday talk.*

flukes of a whale

flume (floom), *n.* **1.** a sloping chute in which water is run down, as for moving logs, supplying power, etc. **2.** a deep, narrow ravine with a stream at the bottom.

flung (flung), past tense and past participle of **fling.**

flunk (flungk), *v.* to fail, as in schoolwork: *used only in everyday talk.*

flunk·y or **flunk·ey** (flungk/ē), *n.* **1.** a footman or other man servant: *no longer used in this meaning.* **2.** a person who obeys the orders of another as if he were a servant. —**flunk/ies** or **flunk/eys,** *pl.*

flu·o·res·cent (floo/ə res/'nt *or* floor es/'nt), *adj.* that gives off cool light while being acted on by some form of energy, such as certain rays. —**flu/o·res/cence,** *n.*

fluorescent lamp, a glass tube coated on the inside with a substance that gives off cool light when mercury vapor in the tube is acted on by an electric current.

flu·o·ri·date (floo/ə ri dāt/ *or* floor/ə dāt), *v.* to add fluorides to drinking water in trying to prevent tooth decay. —**flu/o·ri·dat/ed,** *p.t.* & *p.p.;* **flu/o·ri·dat/ing,** *pr.p.* —**flu/o·ri·da/tion,** *n.*

flu·o·ride (floo/ə rīd), *n.* a salt containing fluorine.

flu·o·rine (floo/ə rēn), *n.* a greenish-yellow, poisonous gas that is a chemical element. It is very active chemically.

flu·o·ro·scope (floor/ə skōp), *n.* a machine for examining the bones or organs of the body. X rays are passed through the body, casting shadows of the parts on a fluorescent screen.

flur·ry (flūr/ē), *n* **1.** a sudden short rush of wind, or a sudden, light fall of rain or snow. **2.** a sudden, brief excitement or confusion. —*v.* to confuse or excite [The heavy traffic *flurried* the new driver.] —**flur/ries,** *pl.* —**flur/ried,** *p.t.* & *p.p.;* **flur/ry·ing,** *pr.p.*

flush (flush), *v.* **1.** to make or become red in the face; blush [Fever had *flushed* his cheeks. Grace *flushed* with anger.] **2.** to make happy or excited [Our team was *flushed* with victory.] **3.** to empty out with a sudden flow of water [to *flush* a toilet]. **4.** to rise or make rise suddenly from a hiding place [The dog *flushed* a pheasant in the tall grass.] —*n.* **1.** a sudden flow, as of water. **2.** a blush. **3.** a sudden, strong feeling [the *flush* of pleasure]. **4.** a sudden, strong growth [the first *flush* of youth]. —*adj.* **1.** having plenty of something, especially of money. **2.** being even or on the same line or plane with; making an even line or surface [a door that is *flush* with the wall]. **3.** direct or exact; straight [The blow was *flush* on his chin.] —*adv.* so as to form an even surface or line [Storm doors close *flush* with the door frame.]

flus·ter (flus/tər), *v.* to make or become excited and confused. *n.* a flustered condition.

flute (floot), *n.* **1.** a musical wind instrument with a high pitch. It is a long, thin tube that is played by blowing across a hole at one end and opening or closing a series of holes along the side with the fingers or with keys. **2.** a long, rounded groove, as in a column. —*v.* **1.** to play on a flute, or to sound like a flute. **2.** to make long, rounded grooves in a column. —**flut/ed,** *p.t.* & *p.p.;* **flut/ing,** *pr.p.*

flut·ing (floot/ing), *n.* a series of long, rounded grooves, as in a column.

flut·ist (floot/ist), *n.* a flute player.

flut·ter (flut/ər), *v.* **1.** to flap the wings without flying [The sick bird *fluttered* helplessly.] **2.** to wave rapidly [The flag *fluttered* in the breeze.] **3.** to move about in a restless way. **4.** to tremble; quiver [His heart *fluttered* when the car skidded.] **5.** to excite or confuse. —*n.* **1.** a fluttering. **2.** a state of excitement or confusion [women in a *flutter* over a wedding].

flux (fluks), *n.* **1.** a flowing or flow. **2.** constant changing [Women's fashions are always in a state of *flux.*] **3.** a passing of fluid from the body in a way that is not normal. **4.** a substance, such as borax or rosin, used to help metals melt together, as in soldering.

fly (flī), *n.* **1.** a flying insect having one pair of wings, as the gnat, mosquito, or, especially, the common housefly. Some insects with two pairs of wings are called flies, as the dragonfly. **2.** an object used in fishing, made of bright feathers, silk, etc. tied to a fishhook to look like a fly. —**flies,** *pl.*

fly (flī), *v.* **1.** to move through the air by using wings, as a bird. **2.** to travel or carry through the air, as in an aircraft. **3.** to pilot an aircraft. **4.** to wave or float in the air, as a flag or kite. **5.** to move swiftly [The door *flew* open. Time *flies.*] **6.** to run away from danger or evil; flee. **7.** to hit a fly in baseball. —*n.* **1.** a flap of cloth

upper: **fishing fly**
lower: **housefly** (⅜ in. long)

flute
fluting

covering buttons, a zipper, etc. in a garment. **2.** a baseball batted high in the air inside the foul lines. **—let fly,** to hurl or attack. **—on the fly, 1.** while flying. **2.** while in a hurry: *slang in this meaning.* **—flew,** *p.t.;* **flown,** *p.p.* (**flied** *is p.t. & p.p. for meaning 7*); **fly′ing,** *pr.p.* **—flies,** *pl.*

fly·catch·er (flī′kach′ər), *n.* a small bird that catches insects while flying.

fly·er (flī′ər), *n.* same as **flier.**

flying fish, a fish of warm seas that has a pair of fins like wings. It can leap out of the water and glide through the air with these.

flying saucer, any of the mysterious objects that people now and then claim to have seen in the sky flying very high and very fast.

flying fish (15 in. long)

fly·leaf (flī′lēf), *n.* an extra leaf, usually blank, at the very beginning or end of a book. **—fly·leaves** (flī′lēvz), *pl.*

fly·speck (flī′spek), *n.* **1.** a tiny spot made by a fly. **2.** any tiny spot.

fly·wheel (flī′hwēl), *n.* a heavy wheel on a machine, for keeping its motion smooth and steady.

FM or **F.M.,** frequency modulation, a method of radio broadcasting in which the number of vibrations per second of the radio wave changes according to the sound being broadcast: see also **AM.**

foal (fōl), *n.* a very young horse, mule, donkey, etc. **—v.** to give birth to a foal.

foam (fōm), *n.* a white mass of bubbles formed on liquids, as when they are shaken. **—v.** to form or collect foam; froth [The mad dog *foamed* at the mouth.]

foam rubber, rubber made in the form of firm sponge, used in chair seats, mattresses, etc.

foam·y (fōm′ē), *adj.* foaming, full of foam, or like foam [the *foamy* water in the rapids]. **—foam′i·er,** *compar.;* **foam′i·est,** *superl.* **—foam′i·ness,** *n.*

fob (fäb), *n.* **1.** a small pocket in the front of trousers, for carrying a watch. **2.** a short chain or ribbon attached to a watch and hanging out of such a pocket, often with an ornament at the end.

F.O.B. or **f.o.b.,** free on board: this abbreviation after a price means that it includes free delivery from the factory to the train, ship, etc., but that the buyer must pay all further transportation costs.

fo·cal (fō′k'l), *adj.* of or at a focus.

fo·cus (fō′kəs), *n.* **1.** a point where rays of light, heat, etc. come together or from which they spread; especially, the point where rays of light meet after being reflected by a mirror or refracted by a lens: see picture in next column.

2. the distance from the center of a lens to the point where light rays passing through it meet. **3.** an adjustment of this distance to make a clear image [He brought the camera into *focus.*] **4.** any center of activity or interest [The baby was a *focus* of attention.]**—v.** **1.** to bring to a focus [to *focus* light rays]. **2.** to adjust the eye or a lens in order to make a clear image [Glasses help him to *focus* his eyes on small print.] **3.** to fix or settle on some one thing; center [He couldn't *focus* his attention on his homework.] **—in focus,** clear; distinct. **—out of focus,** not clear; blurred. **—fo′cus·es** or **fo·ci** (fō′sī), *pl.* **—fo′cused** or **fo′cussed,** *p.t. & p.p.;* **fo′-cus·ing** or **fo′cus·sing,** *pr.p.*

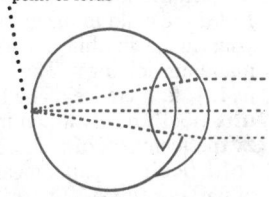

point of focus

focus of light through lens of an eye

fod·der (fäd′ər), *n.* coarse food for cattle, horses, etc., such as cornstalks, hay, and straw.

foe (fō), *n.* an enemy or opponent.

foe·tus (fē′təs), *n.* same as **fetus.**

fog (fôg *or* fäg), *n.* **1.** a large mass of tiny drops of water, near the earth's surface; thick mist that makes it hard to see. **2.** a condition of being confused or bewildered. **—v.** **1.** to cover with fog. **2.** to make or become blurred; confuse [a *fogged* photograph; a *fogged* mind]. **—fogged,** *p.t. & p.p.;* **fog′ging,** *pr.p.*

fog·gy (fôg′ē *or* fäg′ē), *adj.* **1.** having fog [a *foggy* day]. **2.** mixed up; confused [a *foggy* idea]. **—fog′gi·er,** *compar.;* **fog′gi·est,** *superl.* **—fog′gi·ly,** *adv.* **—fog′gi·ness,** *n.*

fog·horn (fôg′hôrn *or* fäg′hôrn), *n.* a horn blown during a fog to warn ships of danger.

fo·gy (fō′gē), *n.* a person who sticks to old-fashioned ideas or ways. **—fo′gies,** *pl.*

foi·ble (foi′b'l), *n.* a small fault or weakness in a person's character.

foil (foil), *v.* to keep from doing something; thwart; stop [He was *foiled* in his plot.] **—n.** a long, thin sword used in fencing, with a button on the point to prevent injury.

foil (foil), *n.* **1.** a very thin sheet of metal [Aluminum *foil* is used for wrapping foods.] **2.** something that makes another thing seem better by contrast [Bill's dull answers served as a *foil* for Ann's wit.]

foil

foist (foist), *v.* to cheat or use tricks in passing something off as a fine or genuine thing [to *foist* a false diamond on someone].

fold (fōld), *v.* **1.** to bend something over upon itself so that one part is on top of another [You *fold* a letter before putting it in an envelope.] **2.** to bring together and twist around one another [to *fold* the arms]. **3.** to clasp or embrace [He *folded* the child in his arms.] **4.** to wrap up [Fold your lunch in this newspaper.] —*n.* **1.** a layer made in folding [The handkerchief has eight *folds*.] **2.** a crease made by folding.

fold (fōld), *n.* **1.** a pen in which sheep are kept. **2.** the members of a church.

-fold (fōld), a suffix meaning "a certain number of parts or times" [A *tenfold* division is a division into ten parts or a dividing ten times.]

fold·er (fōl'dər), *n.* **1.** a folded piece of heavy paper or cardboard, for holding papers. **2.** a booklet made of folded sheets. **3.** a person or thing that folds.

fo·li·age (fō'li ij), *n.* the leaves of a tree or plant, or of many trees or plants.

fo·li·o (fō'li ō), *n.* **1.** a sheet of paper folded once so that it forms four pages of a book. **2.** a book of the largest size, originally made of sheets folded in this way. **3.** the number of a page in a book. —**fo'li·os**, *pl.*

folk (fōk), *n.* **1.** a people or nation. **2.** **folk** or **folks**, *pl.* people or persons [The farmer disliked city *folk. Folks* differ in their tastes.] —*adj.* of the common people [a *folk* saying]. —**one's folks**, one's family or relatives: *used only in everyday talk.* —**folk** or **folks**, *pl.*

folk dance, folk song, folk tale, a dance, song, or story that has been handed down among the common people of a country for a long time.

folk·lore (fōk'lôr), *n.* the stories, beliefs, customs, etc. handed down among a people.

fol·li·cle (fäl'i k'l), *n.* a tiny opening or sac, as in the skin [Hairs grow from *follicles.*]

fol·low (fäl'ō), *v.* **1.** to come or go after [The lamb *followed* Mary to school. Monroe *followed* Madison as President.] **2.** to result; come as a result [He worked hard, and success *followed.*] **3.** to travel along [*Follow* this road for two miles.] **4.** to watch or listen to closely. **5.** to understand [I can't *follow* your reasoning.] **6.** to take as one's work [He *followed* the plumber's trade.] **7.** to be guided or led by; obey [to *follow* rules, a leader, advice, etc.]. —**as follows,** as will next be told or explained. —**follow out** or **follow up,** to carry out fully. —**follow through,** to continue a stroke after hitting a ball, as in golf.

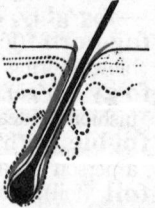

hair follicle

fol·low·er (fäl'ō ər), *n.* **1.** a person or thing that follows, especially one who follows another's teachings. **2.** a servant or other attendant.

fol·low·ing (fäl'ō ing), *adj.* going or coming after; next after [the *following* week]. —*n.* people who follow; followers. —**the following,** the persons or things to be mentioned next.

fol·ly (fäl'ē), *n.* **1.** the condition of being foolish. **2.** any foolish action, belief, etc. —**fol'lies,** *pl.*

fo·ment (fō ment'), *v.* to excite or stir up trouble of some sort [to *foment* a riot].

fond (fänd), *adj.* **1.** loving and tender [*fond* parents; *fond* words]. **2.** held dear; cherished [a *fond* hope]. —**fond of,** having a liking for. —**fond'ly,** *adv.* —**fond'ness,** *n.*

fon·dle (fän'd'l), *v.* to stroke or handle in a tender and loving way; caress [to *fondle* a doll]. —**fon'dled,** *p.t. & p.p.;* **fon'dling,** *pr.p.*

font (fänt), *n.* **1.** a basin for holding holy water or water for baptizing. **2.** a spring or source.

food (fōōd), *n.* **1.** anything that is taken in by a plant or animal to keep up its life and growth; what is eaten or drunk by an animal or absorbed by a plant. **2.** such a thing in solid form [*food* and drink]. **3.** anything that helps another thing to develop [*food* for thought].

food·stuff (fōōd'stuf), *n.* any material that is used as food.

fool (fōōl), *n.* **1.** a person who does silly or senseless things or who is easily tricked. **2.** a man kept by a nobleman or king in olden times to amuse by joking and clowning; jester. —*v.* **1.** to get someone to believe something that is not true; trick; deceive [He *fooled* his mother by pretending to be asleep.] **2.** to act like a fool; to joke or clown. —**fool with,** to meddle with or toy with: *used only in everyday talk.*

fool·har·dy (fōōl'här dē), *adj.* bold or daring in a foolish way; rash [a *foolhardy* attempt to climb a mountain alone]. —**fool'har·di·ness,** *n.*

fool·ish (fōōl'ish), *adj.* without good sense; silly. —**fool'ish·ly,** *adv.* —**fool'ish·ness,** *n.*

fool·proof (fōōl'prōōf), *adj.* so simple, safe, etc. that nothing can go wrong [a *foolproof* plan].

fools·cap (fōōlz'kap), *n.* a large size of writing paper, about 13 by 16 inches.

foot (foot), *n.* **1.** the end part of the leg, on which a person or animal stands or moves. **2.** the lowest part; base or bottom [the *foot* of a page; the *foot* of a mountain]. **3.** the part farthest from the head or beginning [the *foot* of a bed; the *foot* of the line]. **4.** the part that covers the foot [the *foot* of a stocking]. **5.** a measure of length, equal to 12 inches. **6.** one of the parts into which a line of poetry is divided by the rhythm ["Jack/and Jill/went up/the hill" contains four *feet*.] —*v.* to pay: *used only in everyday talk* [to *foot* the bill]. —**foot it,** to dance, walk, or run: *used only in everyday talk.* —**on foot,** walking or running. —**put one's foot down,** to be firm: *used only in everyday talk.* —**under foot,** in the way. —**feet,** *pl.*

foot·ball (foot'bôl), *n.* **1.** a leather ball with a bladder inside blown up with air, used in certain games. The American football is oval in shape. **2.** a game played with such a ball by two teams on a long field with goals at each end.

foot·fall (foot'fôl), *n.* the sound of a step.

foot·hill (foot'hil), *n.* a low hill at or near the bottom of a mountain or mountain range.

football

foot·hold (foot'hōld), *n.* **1.** a place to put a foot down securely [He climbed the cliff by finding *footholds*.] **2.** a secure place from which one cannot easily be moved.

foot·ing (foot'ing), *n.* **1.** a firm placing of the feet [He lost his *footing* on the muddy path.] **2.** a foothold [There's no *footing* on that ice.] **3.** the way things are set, arranged, etc.; condition or relationship [to put a business on a sound *footing;* to be on a friendly *footing* with one's neighbors].

foot·lights (foot'līts), *n.pl.* a row of lights along the front of a stage floor.

foot·man (foot'mən), *n.* a man servant who helps the butler in a large household. —**foot'·men,** *pl.*

foot·note (foot'nōt), *n.* a note at the bottom of a page that explains something on the page.

foot·pad (foot'pad), *n.* a robber who attacks people on streets or highways.

foot·path (foot'path), *n.* a narrow path for use only by people walking.

foot·print (foot'print), *n.* a mark made by a foot or shoe, as in sand.

foot·sore (foot'sôr), *adj.* having sore or tired feet, as from much walking.

foot·step (foot'step), *n.* **1.** a step in walking, or the distance covered by this. **2.** the sound of a step. **3.** a footprint. —**follow in someone's footsteps,** to be or try to be like someone who has gone before.

foot·stool (foot'stool), *n.* a low stool used as a rest for the feet when sitting.

foot·wear (foot'wer), *n.* shoes, boots, etc.

foot·work (foot'wûrk), *n.* the way of moving or using the feet, as in dancing or sports.

fop (fäp), *n.* a man who is very fussy about his clothes and looks; dandy. —**fop'·pish,** *adj.*

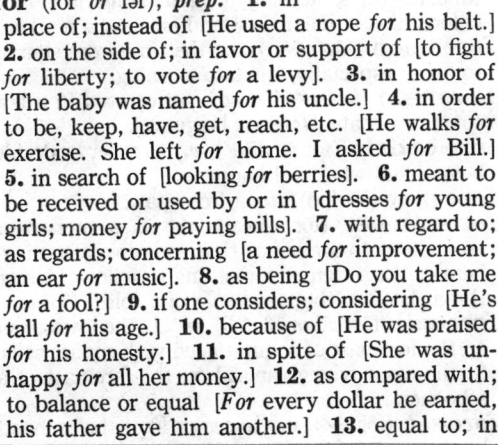
footstool

for (fôr *or* fər), *prep.* **1.** in place of; instead of [He used a rope *for* his belt.] **2.** on the side of; in favor or support of [to fight *for* liberty; to vote *for* a levy]. **3.** in honor of [The baby was named *for* his uncle.] **4.** in order to be, keep, have, get, reach, etc. [He walks *for* exercise. She left *for* home. I asked *for* Bill.] **5.** in search of [looking *for* berries]. **6.** meant to be received or used by or in [dresses *for* young girls; money *for* paying bills]. **7.** with regard to; as regards; concerning [a need *for* improvement; an ear *for* music]. **8.** as being [Do you take me *for* a fool?] **9.** if one considers; considering [He's tall *for* his age.] **10.** because of [He was praised *for* his honesty.] **11.** in spite of [She was unhappy *for* all her money.] **12.** as compared with; to balance or equal [*For* every dollar he earned, his father gave him another.] **13.** equal to; in

the amount of [a bill *for* $60.00]. **14.** at the price of [Joe sold his bicycle *for* $10.] **15.** to the distance of; as far as [I walked with him *for* two miles.] **16.** through the time of; as long as [The movie lasts *for* an hour.] —*conj.* because; since [Comfort her, *for* she is sad.] —O! **for,** I wish that I had [O! *for* a glass of cold water.]

for·age (fôr'ij), *n.* food for cows, horses, etc.; fodder. —*v.* **1.** to go about looking for food [The sheep were *foraging* in the meadow.] **2.** to look about for what one needs or wants [I *foraged* in the attic for some old magazines.] **3.** to steal or take food or supplies from by force; plunder, as armies do in war. —**for'aged,** *p.t. & p.p.;* **for'ag·ing,** *pr.p.* —**for'ag·er,** *n.*

for·ay (fôr'ā), *n.* a sudden attack or raid in order to seize or steal things. —*v.* to make a foray; plunder; raid.

for·bade *or* **for·bad** (fər bad'), past tense of **forbid.**

for·bear (fôr ber'), *v.* **1.** to hold back from doing or saying something [The other children were teasing the dog, but Jim *forbore*.] **2.** to keep one's feelings under control. —**for·bore',** *p.t.;* **for·borne',** *p.p.;* **for·bear'ing,** *pr.p.*

for·bear (fôr'ber), *n.* same as **forebear.**

for·bear·ance (fôr ber'əns), *n.* the act of forbearing; especially, a showing self-control or patience [He listened to the insults with *forbearance.*]

for·bid (fər bid'), *v.* to order that something not be done; not allow; prohibit [Did she *forbid* you to leave the house? Talking is *forbidden* in the halls.] —**for·bade'** *or* **for·bad',** *p.t.;* **for·bid'den,** *p.p.;* **for·bid'ding,** *pr.p.*

for·bid·ding (fər bid'ing), *adj.* looking as if it may be harmful or unpleasant; frightening [the *forbidding* storm clouds].

force (fôrs), *n.* **1.** power or energy that can do or make something [Electricity is a powerful natural *force*. The *force* of the wind broke the windows.] **2.** power or strength used against a person or thing [The police used *force* to scatter the crowd.] **3.** the power to make someone think or act in a certain way [the *force* of logic; the *force* of threats]. **4.** the power to cause motion or to stop or change motion [the *force* of gravity]. **5.** a group of people working together for some special purpose [a sales *force;* a military *force*]. —*v.* **1.** to make do something by using strength or power of some kind [You can't *force* a child to eat. Hunger *forced* him to steal.] **2.** to break open or through by using strength [He *forced* the lock with a pick.] **3.** to get or put by using strength [I *forced* the gun from his hand. He *forced* another book into the box.] **4.** to produce by trying hard or straining [Marcia *forced* a smile, through her tears.] **5.** to make a plant, fruit, etc. grow faster than is natural [Gardeners *force* tomatoes in a greenhouse by giving them extra heat and light.] **6.** in baseball, to cause a base runner to run to the

fat, āpe, cär, ten, ēven, hit, bīte, gō, hôrn, tool, book, up, fûr;
get, joy, yet, chin, she, thin, *th*en;   zh = s in pleasure;   ' as in able (ā'b'l);
ə = a in ago,   e in agent,   i in sanity,   o in confess,   u in focus.

next base, where he is put out. **—in force,** **1.** having effect; operating [Is this law still *in force*?] **2.** with full strength. **—forced,** *p.t.* & *p.p.*; **forc′ing,** *pr.p.*

force·ful (fôrs′fəl), *adj.* having much force; strong; powerful; vigorous [a *forceful* reason]. **—force′ful·ly,** *adv.*

for·ceps (fôr′səps), *n.* small tongs or pincers for pulling or grasping, used by dentists, surgeons, etc. **—for′ceps,** *pl.*

for·ci·ble (fôr′sə b'l), *adj.* **1.** done or made by force [The robbers made a *forcible* entry into the bank.] **2.** having force; forceful [*forcible* arguments]. **—for′-ci·bly,** *adv.*

forceps

ford (fôrd), *n.* a shallow place in a river or stream where one can walk or ride across. **—v.** to cross a stream or river in this way.

fore (fôr), *adv.* & *adj.* at, in, or toward the front part, as of a ship; forward. **—n.** the front part. **—interj.** a warning shouted by someone about to drive a golf ball. **—to the fore,** to the front; into view.

fore-, a prefix meaning: **1.** before [*Forenoon* is the time before noon.] **2.** the front or front part [A *foreleg* is a front leg.]

fore and aft, from the bow to the stern of a ship; lengthwise [sails rigged *fore and aft*]. **—fore′-and-aft′,** *adj.*

fore·arm (fôr′ärm), *n.* the part of the arm between the elbow and the wrist.

fore·arm (fôr ärm′), *v.* to arm beforehand; get ready for trouble before it comes.

fore·bear (fôr′ber), *n.* an ancestor.

fore·bode (fôr bōd′), *v.* to be a sign of something bad about to happen; warn of [His angry looks *forbode* a quarrel.] **—fore·bod′ed,** *p.t.* & *p.p.*; **fore·bod′ing,** *pr.p.*

fore·bod·ing (fôr bōd′ing), *n.* a warning or a feeling of something bad about to happen.

fore·cast (fôr′kast), *v.* to tell or try to tell how something will turn out; predict [Rain is *forecast* for this evening.] **—n.** a telling of what will happen; prediction [a weather *forecast*]. **—fore′cast** or **fore′cast·ed,** *p.t.* & *p.p.*; **fore′cast·ing,** *pr.p.* **—fore′cast·er,** *n.*

fore·cas·tle (fōk′s'l *or* fôr′kas 'l), *n.* **1.** the upper deck of a ship in front of the foremast. **2.** the front part of a merchant ship, where the sailors eat and sleep.

fore·close (fôr klōz′), *v.* to end a mortgage and become the owner of the mortgaged property [A bank can *foreclose* a mortgage if payments on its loan are not made in time.] **—fore·closed′,** *p.t.* & *p.p.*; **fore·clos′ing,** *pr.p.* **—fore·clo-sure** (fôr klō′zhər), *n.*

fore·fa·ther (fôr′fä thər), *n.* an ancestor.

fore·fin·ger (fôr′fing gər), *n.* the finger nearest the thumb; index finger.

fore·foot (fôr′foot), *n.* either of the front feet of an animal. **—fore′feet,** *pl.*

fore·front (fôr′frunt), *n.* **1.** the part at the very front. **2.** the most active or important position [in the *forefront* of a campaign].

fore·gath·er (fôr gath′ər), *v.* same as **for-gather.**

fore·go (fôr gō′), *v.* **1.** to go before; precede. **2.** to forgo; do without. **—fore·went′,** *p.t.*; **fore·gone′,** *p.p.*; **fore·go′ing,** *pr.p.*

fore·go·ing (fôr′gō ing), *adj.* going or coming before; just mentioned. **—the foregoing,** the persons or things mentioned just before.

fore·gone (fôr gôn′), *adj.* that could be known before or foretold [a *foregone* conclusion].

fore·ground (fôr′ground), *n.* the part of a scene or picture that is or seems to be nearest to the one looking at it.

fore·hand (fôr′hand), *n.* a kind of stroke as in tennis, made with the palm of the hand turned forward. **—adj.** done with such a stroke [a *forehand* swing]. **—adv.** with a forehand swing.

fore·head (fôr′id), *n.* the part of the face above the eyebrows.

for·eign (fôr′in), *adj.* **1.** that is outside one's own country, region, etc. [a *foreign* land]. **2.** of, from, or dealing with other countries [*foreign* trade; *foreign* languages; *foreign* policy]. **3.** not belonging; not a natural or usual part [conduct *foreign* to one's nature; *foreign* matter in the eye].

for·eign·er (fôr′in ər), *n.* a person from another country, thought of as an outsider.

fore·knowl·edge (fôr′näl′ij), *n.* knowledge of something before it happens.

fore·leg (fôr′leg), *n.* either of the front legs of an animal.

fore·lock (fôr′läk), *n.* a lock of hair growing just above the forehead.

fore·man (fôr′mən), *n.* **1.** a man in charge of a group of workers, as in a factory. **2.** the chairman and spokesman of a jury. **—fore′men,** *pl.*

fore·mast (fôr′mast), *n.* the mast nearest the front or bow of a ship.

fore·most (fôr′mōst), *adj.* first, as in place, time, importance, etc. [the *foremost* writer of his time; to keep something *foremost* in mind]. **—adv.** before all else [He is first and *foremost* a teacher.]

fore·noon (fôr′nōon), *n.* the time from sunrise to noon; especially, the late morning.

fo·ren·sic (fə ren′sik), *adj.* of or used in a law court or debate [*forensic* language].

fore·or·dain (fôr′ôr dān′), *v.* to order or decide beforehand what will happen.

fore·paw (fôr′pô), *n.* a front paw.

fore·run·ner (fôr run′ər), *n.* **1.** a messenger sent ahead to announce that someone is coming; herald. **2.** a sign of something to follow [A sore throat is often the *forerunner* of a cold.]

fore·sail (fôr′sāl *or* fôr′s'l), *n.* **1.** the lowest sail on the foremast of a ship rigged with square sails. **2.** the main triangular sail on the foremast of a schooner.

fore·see (fôr sē′), *v.* to see or know beforehand [to *foresee* the future]. **—fore·saw′,** *p.t.*; **fore-seen′,** *p.p.*; **fore·see′ing,** *pr.p.*

fore·shad·ow (fôr shad′ō), *v.* to be a sign of something to come.

fore·short·en (fôr shôr/t'n), *v.* to shorten some lines in drawing something so as to make some parts seem farther from the eye than others.

fore·sight (fôr/sīt), *n.* **1.** a foreseeing. **2.** the power to foresee. **3.** a looking forward. **4.** a looking ahead and planning for the future.

foreshortened arm

fore·skin (fôr/skin), *n.* the fold of skin that covers the end of the penis.

for·est (fôr/ist), *n.* many trees growing closely together over a large piece of land; large woods. —*v.* to cover with trees.

fore·stall (fôr stôl/), *v.* to get ahead of or keep from happening by doing something first [to *forestall* an argument by changing the subject].

for·est·er (fôr/is tər), *n.* a person who takes care of forests, fights forest fires, etc.

for·est·ry (fôr/is trē), *n.* the science and work of planting and taking care of forests.

fore·taste (fôr/tāst), *n.* a taste or sample of what can be expected [The private school had given Dick a *foretaste* of college life.]

fore·tell (fôr tel/), *v.* to tell or show what will take place in the future; predict. —**fore·told/,** *p.t. & p.p.;* **fore·tell/ing,** *pr.p.*

fore·thought (fôr/thôt), *n.* a thinking or planning ahead of time.

for·ev·er (fər ev/ər), *adv.* **1.** for all time; without ever coming to an end [No man lives *forever*.] **2.** always; at all times [The child is *forever* interrupting us.]

for·ev·er·more (fər ev/ər môr/), *adv.* forever (*in meaning 1*).

fore·warn (fôr wôrn/), *v.* to warn ahead of time ["*Forewarned* is forearmed."]

fore·went (fôr went/), past tense of **forego.**

fore·word (fôr/wərd), *n.* a piece of writing at the beginning of a book that tells something about it; introduction or preface.

for·feit (fôr/fit), *v.* to give up or lose something because of what one has done or has failed to do [Because our team was late in arriving, we had to *forfeit* the game.] —*n.* **1.** the thing that is forfeited; penalty. **2.** the act of forfeiting [the *forfeit* of a right].

for·fei·ture (fôr/fi chər), *n.* **1.** the act of forfeiting. **2.** the thing forfeited.

for·gath·er (fôr gath/ər), *v.* to come together; assemble; meet.

for·gave (fər gāv/), past tense of **forgive.**

forge (fôrj), *n.* **1.** a furnace for heating metal

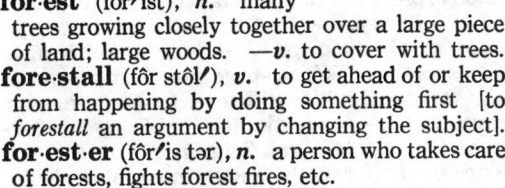

forge

so that it can be pounded into the shape wanted. **2.** a place where such work with metal is done, as a blacksmith's shop. —*v.* **1.** to shape on a forge by heating and pounding. **2.** to make something false to be passed off as true or real; especially, to commit the crime of copying another's signature on a bank check. —**forged,** *p.t. & p.p.;* **forg/ing,** *pr.p.*

forge (fôrj), *v.* to move with difficulty [They *forged* ahead through the snow.] —**forged,** *p.t. & p.p.;* **forg/ing,** *pr.p.*

forg·er (fôr/jər), *n.* **1.** a person who forges metal. **2.** a person guilty of forgery.

forg·er·y (fôr/jər ē), *n.* **1.** the crime of copying another's signature, or of making a false piece of writing, in order to pass it off as the real thing. **2.** something that has been forged [This letter, supposedly written by Lincoln, is a *forgery*.]

for·get (fər get/), *v.* **1.** to be unable to remember; lose from the mind [I have *forgotten* Henry's address.] **2.** to fail to do, bring, etc., as because of carelessness; neglect [You *forgot* to lock the door. I *forgot* my books again.] —**to forget oneself,** to behave in a way that is not proper. —**for·got/,** *p.t.;* **for·got/ten** or **for·got/,** *p.p.;* **for·get/ting,** *pr.p.*

for·get·ful (fər get/fəl), *adj.* **1.** always forgetting things; having a poor memory. **2.** careless or neglectful. —**for·get/ful·ness,** *n.*

for·get-me-not (fər get/mē nät/), *n.* a low-growing plant bearing small blue flowers.

for·give (fər giv/), *v.* to give up feeling angry or wanting to punish; show mercy to; excuse or pardon [She *forgave* him for his rudeness.] —**for·gave/,** *p.t.;* **for·giv/en,** *p.p.;* **for·giv/ing,** *pr.p.* —**for·giv/a·ble,** *adj.*

forget-me-not

for·give·ness (fər giv/nis), *n.* **1.** a forgiving or being forgiven; pardon. **2.** a being ready to forgive.

for·go (fôr gō/), *v.* to do without; give up [I'll *forgo* dessert today.] —**for·went/,** *p.t.;* **for·gone/,** *p.p.;* **for·go/ing,** *pr.p.*

fork (fôrk), *n.* **1.** a tool with a handle at one end and two or more points or prongs at the other, used to pick up something. Small forks are used in eating. Large forks, as pitchforks, are used for tossing hay and manure on a farm. **2.** anything with points like a fork's [a *fork* of lightning]. **3.** a dividing of something into two or more branches [the *fork* of a road or of a tree]. **4.** any of these branches [Follow the left *fork* into town.] —*v.* **1.** to divide into branches [Go left where the road *forks*.] **2.** to pick up with a fork [*Fork* some hay into the stalls.] —**fork over** or **fork out,** to hand over or pay out: *only in everyday talk.*

forked (fôrkt), *adj.* shaped like a fork; divided into branches.

fat, āpe, cär, ten, ēven, hit, bīte, gō, hôrn, tōōl, book, up, fũr;
get, joy, yet, chin, she, thin, *th*en; zh = s in pleasure; ' as in able (ā/b'l)
ə = a in ago, e in agent, i in sanity, o in confess, u in focus.

for·lorn (fôr lôrn'), *adj.* sad or unhappy, as because of loneliness or being uncared for; pitiful; wretched [a *forlorn*, lost child].

form (fôrm), *n.* **1.** a shape or outline; figure [I saw a dark *form* against the sky.] **2.** a mold used to give a certain shape to something [Cement is poured in wooden *forms* to make slabs for sidewalks.] **3.** the way in which something is put together to make it what it is; kind; sort [a *form* of government; a *form* of poetry]. **4.** a way of doing something [His *form* in golf is awkward.] **5.** a way of acting or behaving [It is good *form* to write your hostess a thank-you note.] **6.** a printed paper that has blank spaces to be filled in [an order *form;* an employment *form*]. **7.** the condition of one's health, spirits, etc. [The speaker was in good *form* and kept us all amused.] **8.** any of the ways in which a word is changed for different uses ["Am" is a *form* of "be."] **9.** a long bench once used in schoolrooms. —*v.* **1.** to give a certain shape to [Bill *formed* the wet sand into a castle.] **2.** to train [to *form* the character of a child]. **3.** to build up or develop [He has *formed* good habits.] **4.** to come together in order to make [Let's *form* a club!] **5.** to make up out of separate parts [The U.S. is *formed* of 50 States.]

for·mal (fôr'm'l), *adj.* **1.** following the rules or customs in an exact way [*formal* manners; a *formal* wedding]. **2.** not relaxed or familiar; stiff [a *formal* welcome]. **3.** made for wear at ceremonies and fancy parties [*formal* dress]. **4.** arranged in a regular, orderly way [*formal* gardens]. —*n.* a woman's long, evening dress: *used only in everyday talk.* —**for'mal·ly,** *adv.*

form·al·de·hyde (fôr mal'də hīd'), *n.* a colorless gas with a strong smell. It is usually dissolved in water for killing germs and for preserving animal parts in a laboratory.

for·mal·i·ty (fôr mal'ə tē), *n.* **1.** the condition of being formal; especially, the following of rules or customs in an exact way. **2.** a formal act or ceremony [the *formalities* of graduation exercises]. —**for·mal'i·ties,** *pl.*

for·ma·tion (fôr mā'shən), *n.* **1.** a forming or being formed [the *formation* of coal beds in the earth]. **2.** the way something is formed or put together; arrangement [the *formation* of rock ledges; soldiers lined up in close *formation*].

for·ma·tive (fôr'mə tiv), *adj.* of formation, growth, or development [one's *formative* years].

for·mer (fôr'mər), *adj.* **1.** coming before; earlier; past [in *former* times; a *former* senator]. **2.** being the first of two just mentioned: *often used as a noun with* the [In the contest between Jefferson and Burr, the *former* was elected.]

for·mer·ly (fôr'mər lē), *adv.* at an earlier time; in the past [Iran, *formerly* called Persia].

for·mi·da·ble (fôr'mi də b'l), *adj.* **1.** causing great fear [the *formidable* appearance of the tiger]. **2.** hard to do or take care of [a *formidable* task]. —**for'mi·da·bly,** *adv.*

form·less (fôrm'lis), *adj.* having no definite form or plan; shapeless.

For·mo·sa (fôr mō'sə), *n.* a large island in the Pacific Ocean, off the southeastern coast of China. The Chinese name is *Taiwan.*

for·mu·la (fôr'myoo lə), *n.* **1.** a phrase that is used over and over in a certain way so that its actual meaning is nearly lost ["Very truly yours" is a common *formula* for ending a letter.] **2.** a set of directions for doing or making something [a *formula* for the baby's milk]. **3.** a group of symbols or figures that show some rule or fact in mathematics [The *formula* A = πr^2 shows how to find the area of a circle.] **4.** a group of symbols and figures showing the elements in a chemical compound [The *formula* for water is H_2O.]

for·mu·late (fôr'myoo lāt), *v.* to put together and express in a clear and orderly way [to *formulate* a theory]. —**for'mu·lat·ed,** *p.t. & p.p.;* **for'mu·lat·ing,** *pr.p.* —**for'mu·la'tion,** *n.*

for·sake (fər sāk'), *v.* to go away from or give up; leave; abandon [He will never *forsake* a friend in trouble.] —**for·sook** (fôr sook'), *p.t.;* **for·sak'en,** *p.p.;* **for·sak'ing,** *pr.p.*

for·sooth (fôr sooth'), *adv.* in truth; no doubt; indeed: *no longer used.*

for·swear (fôr swer'), *v.* **1.** to swear or promise to give up something [to *forswear* smoking]. **2.** to swear falsely that something is true; perjure oneself. —**for·swore** (fôr swôr'), *p.t.;* **for·sworn** (fôr swôrn'), *p.p.;* **for·swear'ing,** *pr.p.*

for·syth·i·a (fôr sith'i ə), *n.* a shrub with yellow flowers that bloom in early spring.

fort (fôrt), *n.* a building with strong walls, guns, etc., for defending against an enemy.

forte (fôrt), *n.* a thing that one does especially well [Reciting poetry is his *forte.*]

forsythia shrub and flowers

for·te (fôr'tē *or* fôr'tā), *adj. & adv.* loud: an Italian word used as a direction in music.

forth (fôrth), *adv.* **1.** forward or onward [He never said a word from that day *forth.*] **2.** out; into view [The bears came *forth* from their den.] —**and so forth,** and others: see *et cetera.*

forth·com·ing (fôrth'kum'ing), *adj.* **1.** about to take place, come out, etc. [the author's *forthcoming* novel]. **2.** ready when needed [The help they had promised was not *forthcoming.*]

forth·right (fôrth'rīt'), *adj.* frank and open; direct, not hinted at [a *forthright* criticism].

forth·with (fôrth with'), *adv.* immediately; at once [Give us your answer *forthwith.*]

for·ti·eth (fôr'tē ith), *adj.* coming after thirty-nine others; 40th in order. —*n.* **1.** the fortieth one. **2.** one of forty equal parts of something; 1/40.

for·ti·fi·ca·tion (fôr'tə fi kā'shən), *n.* **1.** a fortifying or making strong. **2.** a tower, wall, etc. for fortifying. **3.** a fortified place.

for·ti·fy (fôr'tə fī), *v.* **1.** to make stronger; strengthen [to *fortify* concrete with steel wire; to *fortify* an argument with many facts]. **2.** to strengthen against attack, as by building forts, walls, etc. **3.** to add vitamins or minerals to [milk *fortified* with vitamin D]. **—for′ti·fied,** *p.t.* & *p.p.;* **for′ti·fy·ing,** *pr.p.*

for·tis·si·mo (fôr tis′ə mō), *adj.* & *adv.* very loud: an Italian word used as a direction in music.

for·ti·tude (fôr′tə tōod *or* fôr′tə tyōod), *n.* courage to bear up calmly under pain or trouble.

fort·night (fôrt′nīt), *n.* two weeks: *used mainly in Great Britain.* **—fort′night·ly,** *adj.* & *adv.*

for·tress (fôr′tris), *n.* a fort.

for·tu·i·tous (fôr tōo′ə təs *or* fôr tyōo′ə təs), *adj.* happening by chance; accidental [a *fortuitous* meeting].

for·tu·nate (fôr′chə nit), *adj.* lucky; having, bringing, or coming by good luck [a *fortunate* man]. **—for′tu·nate·ly,** *adv.*

for·tune (fôr′chən), *n.* **1.** the supposed power that brings good or bad to people; luck; chance. **2.** what is going to happen to a person; one's future [The gypsy said she would tell his *fortune*.] **3.** good luck; success. **4.** a large sum of money; wealth [to inherit a *fortune*].

for·tune-tell·er (fôr′chən tel′ər), *n.* a person who pretends to tell what is going to happen in people's lives, as by reading cards.

Fort Wayne (fôrt′ wān′), a city in northeastern Indiana.

Fort Worth (fôrt′ wûrth′), a city in northern Texas.

for·ty (fôr′tē), *n.* & *adj.* **1.** four times ten; the number 40. **2. forties,** *n.pl.* the numbers or years from 40 to 49.

fo·rum (fôr′əm), *n.* **1.** the public square of an ancient Roman city, where the lawmakers and courts met. **2.** a meeting of people to discuss public matters, problems, etc.

for·ward (fôr′wərd), *adj.* **1.** at, toward, or of the front. **2.** ahead of others in ideas, growth, progress, etc.; advanced. **3.** ready or eager; prompt [He was *forward* in helping.] **4.** too free or bold in manners; rude or impudent. **—adv. 1.** to the front; ahead [He moved slowly *forward* on the ledge.] **2.** toward the future [He looks *forward* to old age.] **—n.** any of certain players in a front position, as in basketball or football. **—v. 1.** to help move forward; advance; promote [to *forward* the interests of education]. **2.** to send on, as to a new address [*Forward* her mail to Paris.] **—for′-ward·ness,** *n.*

for·wards (fôr′wərdz), *adv.* forward.

fos·sil (fäs′'l), *n.* **1.** any hardened remains or prints, as in rocks or bogs, of plants or animals who lived many ages ago. **2.** a person who is very set or old-fashioned in his ideas or ways: *used only in everyday talk.*

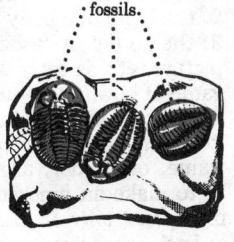
·fossils·

fos·ter (fôs′tər), *v.* **1.** to bring up with care; nourish. **2.** to help grow or develop; promote [Dirty hands *foster* disease.] **3.** to cling to in one's mind; cherish [to *foster* a hope]. **—adj.** having the standing of a certain member of the family, but not by birth or adoption [a *foster* father; a *foster* child; a *foster* sister].

Fos·ter, Stephen Col·lins (käl′inz fôs′tər), 1826–1864; American song composer.

fought (fôt), past tense and past participle of **fight.**

foul (foul), *adj.* **1.** dirty; smelly, rotten, etc.; disgusting [a *foul* pigsty]. **2.** blocked up, as with dirt [Water barely trickled through the *foul* pipes.] **3.** very wicked; evil [a *foul* crime]. **4.** stormy; not clear [*foul* weather]. **5.** not decent; coarse or profane [*foul* language]. **6.** tangled or snarled [*foul* rope]. **7.** not fair [A *foul* play, blow, etc. in sports is one that is against the rules. A *foul* ball in baseball is a batted ball that falls outside the base lines.] **8.** unpleasant; not good: *used only in everyday talk* [We had a *foul* time at the picnic.] **—n. 1.** an act that is against the rules of a game [Pushing is a *foul* in basketball.] **2.** a foul ball in baseball. **—v. 1.** to make or become dirty, smelly, etc. [The city sewers have *fouled* the lake.] **2.** to make or become blocked up; clog [Rust has *fouled* the pipes.] **3.** to make or become tangled [*fouled* yarn]. **4.** to make a foul against, as in a game [The boxer *fouled* his opponent by hitting below the belt.] **5.** to bat a baseball foul. **—run foul of,** to get in trouble with. **—foul′ly,** *adv.* **—foul′ness,** *n.*

fou·lard (fōo lärd′), *n.* **1.** a thin, light material of silk, rayon, etc., usually printed with small figures. **2.** a necktie, scarf, etc. made of this material.

found (found), past tense and past participle of **find.**

found (found), *v.* **1.** to set up; establish [to *found* a new college]. **2.** to set for support; base [an argument *founded* on facts].

found (found), *v.* to make by pouring molten metal into a mold; cast.

foun·da·tion (foun dā′shən), *n.* **1.** the part at the bottom that supports a wall, house, etc.; base. **2.** the basis on which an idea, belief, etc. rests. **3.** a founding or being founded; establishment. **4.** a fund set up by gifts of money for helping others, paying for research, etc.

found·er (foun′dər), *n.* **1.** a person who founds, or establishes [the *founder* of a city]. **2.** a person who founds, or casts, metals.

foun·der (foun′dər), *v.* **1.** to fill with water and sink [The ship struck a reef and *foundered.*] **2.** to stumble, fall, or break down.

found·ling (found′ling), *n.* a baby found after its parents have abandoned it.

found·ry (foun′drē), *n.* a place where molten metal is cast in molds. **—found′ries,** *pl.*

fount (fount), *n.* **1.** a fountain; spring. **2.** a source.

foun·tain (foun′t'n), *n.* **1.** a place from which water flows; spring. **2.** a thing built for a stream of water to rise and fall in [a drinking *fountain;* a decorative *fountain* in a garden]. **3.** a source [A library is a *fountain* of knowledge.] **4.** a counter for making and serving soft drinks, sodas, etc.: *the full name is* **soda fountain.**

fountain

foun·tain·head (foun′-t'n hed), *n.* the main source of something.

fountain pen, a pen that carries a supply of ink which flows to the writing point.

four (fôr), *n. & adj.* one more than three; the number 4. **—on all fours, 1.** on all four feet. **2.** on hands and knees.

four-foot·ed (fôr′foot′-id), *adj.* having four feet [The bear is a *four-footed* animal.]

baby on all fours

Four-H club or **4-H club** (fôr′āch′), a national club for young people living in farm areas. It gives training in farming and home economics.

four·score (fôr′skôr′), *adj. & n.* four times twenty; 80 ["*Fourscore* and seven years ago . . ."]

four·some (fôr′səm), *n.* a group of four people, as four people playing golf together.

four·square (fôr′skwer′), *adj.* **1.** perfectly square. **2.** frank; honest [a *foursquare* answer].

four·teen (fôr′tēn′), *n. & adj.* four more than ten; the number 14.

four·teenth (fôr′tēnth′), *adj.* coming after thirteen others; 14th in order. **—n. 1.** the four-teenth one. **2.** one of fourteen equal parts of something; 1/14.

fourth (fôrth), *adj.* coming after three others; 4th in order. **—n. 1.** the fourth one. **2.** one of four equal parts of something; 1/4.

Fourth of July, see **Independence Day.**

fowl (foul), *n.* **1.** any bird [wild *fowl*]. **2.** any of the larger birds raised for food, as the chicken, turkey, or duck. **3.** the flesh of such a bird.

fowl·er (foul′ər), *n.* one who hunts wild birds.

fowl·ing piece (foul′ing), a kind of shotgun used in hunting birds.

fox (fäks), *n.* **1.** a small, wild animal of the dog family, with pointed ears, a bushy tail, and, usually, reddish-brown fur. **2.** its fur. **3.** a foxy person.

fox·glove (fäks′gluv), *n.* a tall plant with clusters of flowers shaped like thimbles.

fox·hole (fäks′hōl), *n.* a hole dug in the ground as protection for one or two soldiers.

fox (14 in. high at the shoulder)

fox·hound (fäks′hound), *n.* a strong, fast hound trained to hunt foxes.

fox terrier, a small, lively dog with a smooth or wire-haired coat.

fox trot, 1. a popular dance for couples, with some fast steps and some slow steps. **2.** the music for this dance.

fox·y (fäk′sē), *adj.* sly and cunning; tricky. **—fox′i·er,** *compar.;* **fox′i·est,** *superl.*

foy·er (foi′ər *or* foi′ā), *n.* a lobby or entrance hall, as in a theater or hotel.

Fr., abbreviation for **French.**

fr., abbreviation for **franc** or **francs.**

fra·cas (frā′kəs), *n.* a noisy fight or loud quarrel; brawl.

frac·tion (frak′shən), *n.* **1.** a quantity less than a whole, or one; one or more equal parts of a whole [Some *fractions* are 1/2, 3/4, and 19/25.] **2.** any quantity written with a numerator and denominator [5/4 is a *fraction.*] **3.** a small part or amount [He saves only a *fraction* of the money he earns.] **—frac′tion·al,** *adj.*

frac·tious (frak′shəs), *adj.* hard to manage; unruly, cross, fretful, etc.

frac·ture (frak′chər), *n.* **1.** a breaking or being broken. **2.** a break or crack, especially in a bone. **—v.** to break or crack [an arm *fractured* in a fall]. **—frac′tured,** *p.t. & p.p.;* **frac′tur·ing,** *pr.p.*

frag·ile (fraj′əl), *adj.* easily broken or damaged; delicate [a *fragile* teacup; *fragile* health]. **—fra·gil·i·ty** (frə jil′ə tē), *n.*

frag·ment (frag′mənt), *n.* **1.** a piece of something that has broken; a part broken away [*fragments* of a broken cup]. **2.** a part taken from a whole [a *fragment* of a song].

frag·men·tar·y (frag′mən ter′ē), *adj.* made up of fragments; incomplete [a *fragmentary* report].

fra·grance (frā′grəns), *n.* a sweet or pleasant smell.

fra·grant (frā′grənt), *adj.* having a sweet or pleasant smell.

frail (frāl), *adj.* **1.** easily broken or damaged; fragile; weak [a *frail* ladder; a *frail,* sickly child]. **2.** easily led to do wrong; morally weak.

frail·ty (frāl′tē), *n.* **1.** the condition of being frail. **2.** a weakness in health, character, etc.; fault or flaw. **—frail′ties,** *pl.*

frame (frām), *n.* **1.** the support or skeleton around which a thing is built and that gives the thing its shape; framework [the *frame* of a house]. **2.** the build of a body [a man with a large *frame*]. **3.** the border or case into which a window, door, picture, etc. is set. **4.** any of the divisions of a game of bowling. **—v. 1.** to put together according to some plan; make, form, build, compose, etc. [to *frame* laws; to *frame* an excuse]. **2.** to put a frame, or border, around [to *frame* a picture]. **3.** to make an innocent person seem guilty by a plot: *used only in everyday talk.* **—frame of mind,** the way one thinks or feels; mood. **—framed,** *p.t. & p.p.;* **fram′ing,** *pr.p.*

frame-up (frām′up′), *n.* a secret plot to make an innocent person seem guilty: *used only in everyday talk.*

frame·work (frām'wûrk), *n.* the structure or support that holds together the thing built around it [the *framework* of a house or of society].

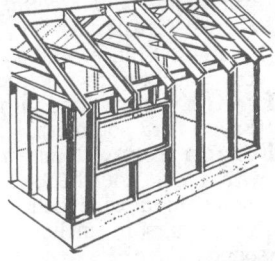
framework of a house

franc (frangk), *n.* the basic unit of money in France, and also in Belgium, Switzerland, etc.

France (frans), *n.* a country in western Europe.

fran·chise (fran'chīz), *n.* **1.** a special right or permission given by a government [One must get a *franchise* from the Federal government to operate a TV station.] **2.** the right to vote; suffrage. **3.** the right given to a dealer to sell the products of a certain company.

Fran·cis·can (fran sis'kən), *adj.* of the religious order founded by St. Francis of Assisi in 1209. —*n.* a member of this order.

Fran·cis of As·si·si, Saint (fran'sis əv ə sē'zē), 1182–1226; Italian friar.

Frank (frangk), *n.* a member of the German tribes who, by the 9th century, ruled over what is now France, Germany, and Italy.

frank (frangk), *adj.* open and honest about what one is thinking and feeling; speaking one's mind freely. —*v.* to send mail free of postage [Senators may *frank* official mail.] —*n.* the right to send mail free; also, a mark on the envelope showing this right. —**frank'ly,** *adv.* —**frank'ness,** *n.*

Frank·en·stein (frangk'ən stīn), *n.* the man in a famous novel who builds a monster that destroys him. By mistake, some people call the monster itself "Frankenstein."

Frank·fort (frangk'fərt), *n.* the capital of Kentucky.

Frank·furt am Main (frängk'foort äm mīn'), a city in western Germany.

frank·furt·er (frangk'fər tər), *n.* a smoked sausage of beef or of beef and pork; wiener.

frank·in·cense (frangk'in sens'), *n.* a resin from certain trees of Asia and East Africa. It gives off a spicy smell when burned.

Frank·ish (frangk'ish), *adj.* of the Franks, their language, or culture.

Frank·lin, Benjamin (frangk'lin), 1706–1790; U.S. statesman, scientist, and writer.

fran·tic (fran'tik), *adj.* wild with anger, pain, worry, etc. —**fran'ti·cal·ly,** *adv.*

fra·ter·nal (frə tur'n'l), *adj.* of or like brothers; brotherly.

fra·ter·ni·ty (frə tur'nə tē), *n.* **1.** the close tie among brothers; brotherly feeling. **2.** a club of men or boys, especially a social club, as in a college. Fraternities usually have letters of the Greek alphabet for their name. **3.** a group of people with the same work, interests, beliefs, etc.

[Doctors are often called the medical *fraternity.*] —**fra·ter'ni·ties,** *pl.*

frat·er·nize (frat'ər nīz), *v.* to act like brothers to one another; be friendly. —**frat'er·nized,** *p.t. & p.p.;* **frat'er·niz·ing,** *pr.p.*

Frau (frou), *n.* a married woman; wife: a German word also used as a title meaning "Mrs."

fraud (frôd), *n.* **1.** a cheating, tricking, or lying; dishonesty. **2.** something used to cheat or trick. **3.** a person who cheats or is not what he pretends to be: *used only in everyday talk.*

fraud·u·lent (frô'jə lənt), *adj.* **1.** using fraud; cheating, tricking, or lying [a *fraudulent* scheme]. **2.** gotten by means of fraud [*fraudulent* wealth].

fraught (frôt), *adj.* filled or loaded [A pioneer's life is *fraught* with hardships.]

Frau·lein (froi'līn), *n.* an unmarried woman; young woman or girl: a German word also used as a title meaning "Miss."

fray (frā), *n.* a noisy quarrel or fight.

fray (frā), *v.* to wear down so as to become ragged and have loose threads showing [a coat *frayed* at the elbows].

fraz·zle (fraz'l), *v.* **1.** to wear out until in shreds. **2.** to tire out. —*n.* the condition of being frazzled. *This word is used only in everyday talk.* —**fraz'zled,** *p.t. & p.p.;* **fraz'zling,** *pr.p.*

freak (frēk), *n.* **1.** an animal or plant that is very much different from what is normal [A two-headed calf is a *freak.*] **2.** an odd or unusual idea or happening. —*adj.* very different from what is normal; unusual. —**freak'ish,** *adj.*

freck·le (frek'l), *n.* a small brownish spot on the skin. Freckles are brought out on the face, arms, etc. by the sun. —*v.* to make or become spotted with freckles. —**freck'led,** *p.t. & p.p.;* **freck'ling,** *pr.p.*

freckles

Fred·er·ick the Great (fred'ər ik), 1712–1786; king of Prussia from 1740 to 1786.

free (frē), *adj.* **1.** not under the control of another; not a slave or not in prison. **2.** able to vote and to speak, write, meet, and worship as one pleases; having political and civil liberty. **3.** not tied up, fastened, or shut in; loose [As soon as the bird was *free,* it flew away. Grab the *free* end of the rope.] **4.** not bothered or held down, as by duty, work, worry, etc. [*free* from pain; *free* of debt]. **5.** not following the usual rules or patterns [*free* verse]. **6.** giving readily; generous [He is *free* with his money.] **7.** with no charge; without cost [*free* tickets to the play]. **8.** not needing to pay the usual taxes, etc.; exempt [a package from England *free* of duty]. **9.** with no blocking; open or clear [The harbor is *free* of ice all winter.] —*adv.* **1.** without cost [He let us in *free.*] **2.** in a free manner; without being held back [The wind blows *free.*] —*v.* to make free

fat, āpe, cär, ten, ēven, hit, bīte, gō, hôrn, tōol, book, up, fûr;
get, joy, yet, chin, she, thin, *th*en; zh = s in pleasure; ' as in able (ā'b'l)
ə = a in ago, e in agent, i in sanity, o in confess, u in focus.

[The sailors worked to *free* the tangled ropes.]
—**free from** or **free of, 1.** not having; without.
2. let go from. —**fre·er** (frē′ər), *compar.*;
fre·est (frē′ist), *superl.* —**freed** (frēd), *p.t.* &
p.p.; **free′ing**, *pr.p.* —**free′ly**, *adv.*

free·boot·er (frē′boot′ər), *n.* a pirate.

freed·man (frēd′mən), *n.* a man who has been
set free from slavery. —**freed′men**, *pl.*

free·dom (frē′dəm), *n.* **1.** the condition of being
free; liberty; independence. **2.** a being able to
use or go in as one wishes [Has your dog been
given *freedom* of the house?] **3.** easiness, as of
action [The tight coat hindered his *freedom* of
movement.] **4.** frankness or easiness of manner;
often, too great frankness, or a being too familiar
[The clerk was warned about the *freedom* of his
manner with customers.]

free·hand (frē′hand), *adj.* drawn by hand,
without using a ruler, compasses, etc.

free lance, a writer, actor, or artist who sells
his work to different buyers at different times.
—**free′-lance′**, *adj.*

free·man (frē′mən), *n.* a person who is not a
slave; person free to work for himself, to own
land, etc. —**free′men**, *pl.*

Free·ma·son (frē′mā′s'n), *n.* a member of a
secret social society that has branches throughout
the world.

free·stone (frē′stōn), *adj.* having a pit that
does not cling to the fruit [a *freestone* peach].

free·think·er (frē′thingk′ər), *n.* a person who
forms his own ideas about religion without following established religious teachings.

free·way (frē′wā), *n.* a highway with many
lanes and few, if any, traffic lights, stop signs, etc.,
so that traffic can move swiftly.

free will, freedom to act, give, etc. as one wishes.
—**free′will′**, *adj.*

freeze (frēz), *v.* **1.** to harden into ice; make or
become solid because of cold [Water *freezes* at
32° F.] **2.** to make or become filled or covered
with ice [The river *froze* over.] **3.** to make or
become very cold; especially, to kill, die, spoil, etc.
with cold [The sudden cold spell *froze* our peaches.]
4. to stick by freezing [The wheels *froze* to the
ground.] **5.** to stick or become tight because of
overheating, as a piston in a cylinder. **6.** to make
or become motionless or stunned [to *freeze* with
terror]. **7.** to make or become unfriendly. **8.** to
set limits on prices, wages, etc. —*n.* **1.** a freezing
or being frozen. **2.** a spell of freezing weather.
—**froze**, *p.t.*; **fro′zen**, *p.p.*; **freez′ing**, *pr.p.*

freeze-dry (frēz′drī′), *v.* to freeze something
quickly and then dry it in a vacuum: freeze-dried
foods can be kept for a long time at room temperature. *For principal parts see* **dry.**

freez·er (frēz′ər), *n.* **1.** a machine for making
ice cream. **2.** a refrigerator for freezing foods or
storing frozen foods.

freight (frāt), *n.* **1.** a load of goods shipped by
train, ship, truck, airplane, etc. **2.** the cost of
shipping such goods. **3.** the shipping of goods in
this way [Send it by *freight.*] —*v.* **1.** to load with
freight. **2.** to send by freight.

freight·er (frāt′ər), *n.* a ship for freight.

French (french), *adj.* of France, its people, etc.
—*n.* **1.** the language of France. **2.** the people of
France: *used with a plural verb.*

French Community, a group of countries,
including France, Gabon, Malagasy Republic,
etc., joined together politically.

French fried, fried in hot, deep fat until crisp
[*French fried* potatoes].

French horn, a brass-wind musical instrument
with a long, coiled tube
ending in a wide bell.
It has a soft, mellow
sound.

French·man (french′-
mən), *n.* a person,
especially a man, born
or living in France.
—**French′men**, *pl.*

French Revolution,
the revolution in France
from 1789 to 1799, which
replaced the king with
France's first republic.

French horn

French toast, bread
slices fried after being dipped in an egg batter.

French·wom·an (french′woom′ən), *n.* a
woman born or living in France. —**French′-**
wom′en, *pl.*

fren·zy (fren′zē), *n.* a wild or mad outburst of
feeling or action [a *frenzy* of joy, fear, work, etc.].
—**fren′zies**, *pl.* —**fren′zied**, *adj.*

fre·quen·cy (frē′kwən sē), *n.* **1.** the fact of
being frequent, or happening often. **2.** the
number of times something is repeated in a
certain period [a *frequency* of 1,000 vibrations
per second]. —**fre′quen·cies**, *pl.*

fre·quent (frē′kwənt), *adj.* happening often or
time after time [This bus makes *frequent* trips.]
—*v.* (fri kwent′), to go to again and again; be
found in often [She *frequents* movie theaters.]
—**fre′quent·ly**, *adv.*

fres·co (fres′kō), *n.* **1.** the art of painting with
water colors on wet plaster. **2.** a painting so
made. —**fres′coes** or **fres′cos**, *pl.*

fresh (fresh), *adj.* **1.** newly made, got, or grown;
not spoiled, stale, etc. [*fresh* coffee; *fresh* eggs].
2. not pickled, canned, etc. [*fresh* meat]. **3.** not
tired; lively [He felt *fresh* after a short nap.]
4. not worn or dirty [*fresh* clothes]. **5.** looking
youthful or healthy [a *fresh* complexion]. **6.** new
or different [a *fresh* approach to a problem].
7. having just arrived [a youth *fresh* from a
farm]. **8.** cool and clean [*fresh* air]. **9.** not salty
[Most lakes are *fresh* water.] —**fresh′ly**, *adv.*
—**fresh′ness**, *n.*

fresh (fresh), *adj.* acting too bold; rude or
impudent: *a slang word.*

fresh·en (fresh′ən), *v.* to make or become
fresh.

fresh·et (fresh′it), *n.* **1.** a flooding of a stream
because of melting snow or heavy rain. **2.** a flow
of fresh water into the sea.

fresh·man (fresh′mən), *n.* a student in the
ninth grade in high school, or one in the first year
of college. —**fresh′men**, *pl.*

fret (fret), *v.* **1.** to make or become annoyed or worried [Don't *fret* about things you can't change. Small troubles *fretted* her all the time.] **2.** to wear away by gnawing, rubbing, etc. —*n.* annoyance or worry [Vacations help us forget our *frets* and cares.] —**fret′ted,** *p.t. & p.p.;* **fret′ting,** *pr.p.*

fret (fret), *n.* a design made up of short, straight bars or lines put together in various ways. —*v.* to decorate with fretwork. —**fret′ted,** *p.t. & p.p.;* **fret′ting,** *pr.p.*

fret (fret), *n.* any of the ridges across the finger board of a banjo, guitar, etc.

fret·ful (fret′fəl), *adj.* annoyed or worried.

fret·work (fret′wûrk), *n.* a carving or other decoration of frets.

Fri., abbreviation for **Friday.**

fri·a·ble (frī′ə b′l), *adj.* easily crumbled or broken into bits [*friable* soil].

fri·ar (frī′ər), *n.* a member of certain religious orders of the Roman Catholic Church.

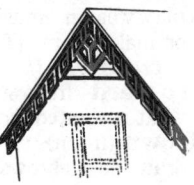
fretwork

fric·as·see (frik′ə sē′), *n.* meat cut into pieces, cooked and served in a sauce of its own gravy. —*v.* to cook meat in this way. —**fric′as·seed′,** *p.t. & p.p.;* **fric′as·see·ing,** *pr.p.*

fric·tion (frik′shən), *n.* **1.** a rubbing of one thing against another. **2.** arguments or quarrels caused by differences of opinions. **3.** the force that slows down the motion of surfaces that touch [Ball bearings lessen *friction* in machines.]

Fri·day (frī′dē), *n.* the sixth day of the week.

fried (frīd), past tense and past participle of **fry.** —*adj.* cooked by frying.

friend (frend), *n.* **1.** a person whom one knows well and likes. **2.** a person on the same side in a struggle; ally. **3.** a person who helps or supports something [a *friend* of liberty]. **4. Friend,** a member of the Society of Friends; Quaker. —**make friends with,** to become a friend of.

friend·ly (frend′lē), *adj.* **1.** of, like, to, or from a friend; kindly [some *friendly* advice]. **2.** showing good and peaceful feelings; ready to be a friend [a *friendly* nation]. —*adv.* in a friendly way [to act *friendly*]. —**friend′li·er,** *compar.;* **friend′li·est,** *superl.* —**friend′li·ness,** *n.*

friend·ship (frend′ship), *n.* **1.** the condition of being friends. **2.** friendly feeling.

frieze (frēz), *n.* a band of designs, drawings, or carvings used as a decoration along a wall or around a room.

frig·ate (frig′it), *n.* a fast, sailing warship of the 18th and early 19th centuries.

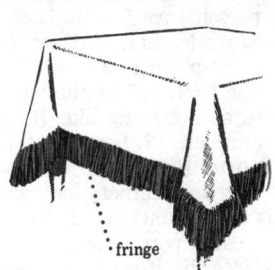
part of a frieze

fright (frīt), *n.* **1.** sudden fear; alarm. **2.** something that looks so strange or ugly as to startle one: *used only in everyday talk* [Her hat was a perfect *fright.*]

fright·en (frīt′'n), *v.* **1.** to make or become suddenly afraid; scare. **2.** to force to do something by making afraid [I'll *frighten* him away.]

fright·ful (frīt′fəl), *adj.* **1.** causing fright; making afraid [a *frightful* groan]. **2.** terrible; shocking [victory won at a *frightful* cost]. **3.** great: *used only in everyday talk* [a *frightful* nuisance]. —**fright′ful·ly,** *adv.*

frig·id (frij′id), *adj.* **1.** very cold; freezing [a *frigid* day in January]. **2.** not warm or friendly; stiff [a *frigid* welcome]. —**fri·gid·i·ty** (fri-jid′ə tē), *n.*

frill (fril), *n.* **1.** a piece of cloth or lace used as trimming; ruffle. **2.** something useless added just for ornament [a speech full of *frills*]. —**frill′y,** *adj.*

fringe (frinj), *n.* **1.** a border of threads for decoration, either hanging loose or tied in bunches. **2.** an outside edge; border [He stood at the *fringe* of the crowd.] —*v.* to be or make a fringe for; border [Trees *fringe* the lake.] —**fringed,** *p.t. & p.p.;* **fring′ing,** *pr.p.*

frip·per·y (frip′ər ē), *n.* **1.** cheap, showy clothes or decorations. **2.** any silly showing off, as in speech or manners. —**frip′per·ies,** *pl.*

frisk (frisk), *v.* **1.** to move or jump about in a lively, playful way; frolic. **2.** to search a person quickly, as for hidden weapons: *slang in this meaning.*

frisk·y (fris′kē), *adj.* lively or playful. —**frisk′i·er,** *compar.;* **frisk′i·est,** *superl.* —**frisk′i·ly,** *adv.* —**frisk′i·ness,** *n.*

frit·ter (frit′ər), *v.* to waste bit by bit [to *fritter* away money or time].

frit·ter (frit′ər), *n.* a small cake of fried batter filled with fruit, corn, etc.

fri·vol·i·ty (fri väl′ə tē), *n.* **1.** the condition of being frivolous. **2.** a frivolous act or thing. —**fri·vol′i·ties,** *pl.*

friv·o·lous (friv′ə ləs), *adj.* not at all serious or important; flighty, silly, etc. [a *frivolous* objection; a *frivolous* person].

friz·zle (friz′'l), *v.* to make a sputtering noise, as in frying; sizzle. —**friz′zled,** *p.t. & p.p.;* **friz′zling,** *pr.p.*

friz·zle (friz′'l), *v.* to arrange hair in small, tight curls. —**friz′zled,** *p.t. & p.p.;* **friz′zling,** *pr.p.* —**friz′zly** or **friz′zy,** *adj.*

fro (frō), *adv.* back: *now used only in the phrase* **to and fro,** meaning "back and forth."

frock (fräk), *n.* **1.** a girl's or woman's dress. **2.** the robe worn by friars, monks, etc.

fat, āpe, cär, ten, ēven, hit, bīte, gō, hôrn, to͞ol, book, up, fûr;
get, joy, yet, chin, she, thin, *then;* zh = s in pleasure; ′ as in able (ā′b'l);
ə = a in ago, e in agent, i in sanity, o in confess, u in focus.

frog (frôg), *n.* **1.** a small, cold-blooded animal that can live on land and in water. It has long, strong hind legs with which it leaps. **2.** a fancy loop made of braid and used to fasten clothing. —**frog in the throat,** a hoarseness.

frog (8 in. long)

frol·ic (fräl′ik), *n.* a lively game or party; merry play. —*v.* to play or romp about in a happy and carefree way —**frol′icked,** *p.t. & p.p.;* **frol·ick·ing,** *pr.p.*

frol·ic·some (fräl′ik səm), *adj.* lively and full of fun; playful.

from (frum *or* främ), *prep.* **1.** starting at [*from* Erie to Buffalo; *from* noon to midnight]. **2.** out of [to take clothes *from* a closet; to release a person *from* jail; to keep a child *from* mischief]. **3.** made, sent, said, etc. by [a letter *from* Mary]. **4.** at a place not near to [Keep away *from* the dog.] **5.** out of the whole of [Take 2 *from* 4.] **6.** as not being like [I can't tell one baby *from* another.] **7.** because of [He trembled *from* fear.]

frond (fränd), *n.* **1.** the leaf of a fern. **2.** any long and feathery leaf, as of a palm tree.

front (frunt), *n.* **1.** the part that faces forward; most important side [The *front* of a house usually faces the street.] **2.** the part ahead of the rest; first part; beginning [That chapter is toward the *front* of the book.] **3.** outward look or behavior [He put on a bold *front* in spite of his fear.] **4.** the land alongside a lake, ocean, street, etc. [docks on the water *front*]. **5.** in a war, the part where the actual fighting is going on. **6.** a person or thing used as a cover to hide the actions of others. **7.** the boundary between two large masses of air [a cold *front* advancing from the west]. —*adj.* at, to, in, on, or of the front. —*v.* to face toward [The house *fronts* the lake.]

front·age (frun′tij), *n.* **1.** the front part of a building or of a lot. **2.** the length of the front of a lot. **3.** land bordering a street, lake, etc.

fron·tal (frun′t'l), *adj.* of, on, or at the front [The bones of the forehead are called *frontal* bones.]

fron·tier (frun tir′), *n.* **1.** the line or border between two countries. **2.** the part of a settled country that lies next to a region that is still a wilderness. **3.** any new field of learning or any part of it still to be explored [the *frontiers* of medicine].

fron·tiers·man (frun tirz′mən), *n.* a man who lives on the frontier. —**fron·tiers′men,** *pl.*

fron·tis·piece (frun′tis pēs), *n.* a picture that faces the title page of a book.

front·let (frunt′lit), *n.* **1.** a band or other object worn on the forehead. **2.** the forehead, especially of an animal.

frost (frôst), *n.* **1.** frozen dew or vapor in the form of white crystals [the *frost* on the coils of a refrigerator]. **2.** cold weather that can freeze things [*Frost* late in the spring may damage fruit trees.] —*v.* to cover with frost or with frosting.

frost·bite (frôst′bīt), *n.* damage to a part of the body, as the ears or toes, from being out in great cold.

frost·bit·ten (frôst′bit″n), *adj.* hurt by having been frozen [*frostbitten* toes].

frost·ing (frôs′ting), *n.* **1.** a mixture of sugar, butter, flavoring, etc. for covering cakes; icing. **2.** a dull finish on glass that looks like frost.

frost·y (frôs′tē), *adj.* **1.** cold enough to have frost [a *frosty* day]. **2.** covered with frost [the *frosty* ground]. **3.** not friendly or cordial [a *frosty* greeting]. —**frost′i·er,** *compar.;* **frost′i·est,** *superl.*

froth (frôth), *n.* **1.** a white mass of bubbles; foam. **2.** anything light and unimportant [The play was an amusing bit of *froth*.] —*v.* to foam or make foam [The dog *frothed* at the mouth.] —**froth′y,** *adj.* —**froth′i·ness,** *n.*

fro·ward (frō′wərd), *adj.* always going against what is wanted; contrary; stubborn.

frown (froun), *v.* **1.** to wrinkle the forehead and draw the eyebrows together in anger, worry, or deep thought. **2.** to show that one dislikes or does not approve [Father *frowns* upon such waste of food.] —*n.* a frowning or the look one has in frowning.

frow·zy (frou′zē), *adj.* dirty and untidy; slovenly. —**frow′zi·er,** *compar.;* **frow′zi·est,** *superl.* —**frow′zi·ness,** *n.*

girl frowning

froze (frōz), past tense of **freeze.**

fro·zen (frō′z'n), past participle of **freeze.** —*adj.* **1.** turned into or covered with ice [a *frozen* pond]. **2.** hurt or killed by freezing [*frozen* blossoms]. **3.** kept fresh by freezing [*frozen* foods]. **4.** stunned or shocked [*frozen* with terror].

fru·gal (frōō′g'l), *adj.* **1.** not wasteful; thrifty or saving [a *frugal* housewife]. **2.** costing little and very plain [a *frugal* meal]. —**fru·gal·i·ty** (frōō gal′ə tē), *n.* —**fru′gal·ly,** *adv.*

fruit (frōōt), *n.* **1.** the parts of certain plants or trees that can be eaten, containing the seeds inside a sweet and juicy pulp, as apples, pears, or grapes. In botany, the seed-bearing part of any plant is called its *fruit*, as a nut, ear of corn, pea pod, tomato, etc. **2.** the product of any plant, as grain, flax, cotton, etc. [to harvest the *fruits* of the field]. **3.** the result or product of any action [His success was the *fruit* of hard work.] —*v.* to bear fruit.

fruit·age (frōōt′ij), *n.* **1.** the bearing of fruit. **2.** a crop of fruit. **3.** a result; product.

fruit·ful (frōōt′fəl), *adj.* **1.** bearing much fruit [a *fruitful* tree]. **2.** producing a great deal [Mozart was a *fruitful* composer.] **3.** bringing about results; profitable [a *fruitful* scheme]. —**fruit′ful·ly,** *adv.* —**fruit′ful·ness,** *n.*

fru·i·tion (frōō ish′ən), *n.* **1.** the bearing of fruit. **2.** a reaching or getting what was planned or worked for; fulfillment [His book is the *fruition* of years of research.]

fruit·less (frōōt′lis), *adj.* **1.** having no results; not successful [*fruitless* efforts]. **2.** bearing no fruit; barren.

fruit·y (frōōt′ē), *adj.* having the taste or smell of fruit. —**fruit′i·er**, *compar.*; **fruit′i·est**, *superl.*

frus·trate (frus′trāt), *v.* to keep a person from getting or doing what he wants or a thing from being carried out; block; thwart [The rain *frustrated* our plans for a picnic. He is constantly *frustrated* by his lack of skill in sports.] —**frus′trat·ed**, *p.t. & p.p.*; **frus′trat·ing**, *pr.p.* **frus·tra′tion**, *n.*

fry (frī), *v.* to cook in hot fat over direct heat. —*n.* **1.** a kind of picnic at which food is fried and eaten [a fish *fry*]. **2. fries**, *pl.* things fried, as potatoes. —**fried**, *p.t. & p.p.*; **fry′ing**, *pr.p.* —**fries** (frīz), *pl.*

fry (frī), *n. sing. & pl.* a young fish or young fishes. —**small fry**, **1.** children or a child. **2.** a person or people who are not important.

ft., abbreviation for **foot** and **feet**.

fuch·sia (fyōō′shə), *n.* **1.** a shrub with pink, red, or purple flowers. **2.** a purplish red.

fud·dle (fud′'l), *v.* to make stupid or confused, as from drinking alcoholic liquor. —**fud′dled**, *p.t. & p.p.*; **fud′dling**, *pr.p.*

fudge (fuj), *n.* **1.** a soft candy made of butter, sugar, milk, and chocolate or other flavoring. **2.** nonsense; foolish talk.

fuchsia flowers and leaves

fu·el (fyōō′l), *n.* **1.** anything that is burned to give heat or power [Coal, gas, oil, and wood are *fuels*.] **2.** anything that makes a strong feeling even stronger [Their teasing added *fuel* to his anger.] —*v.* **1.** to supply with fuel. **2.** to get fuel. —**fu′eled** or **fu′elled**, *p.t. & p.p.*; **fu′el·ing** or **fu′el·ling**, *pr.p.*

fu·gi·tive (fyōō′jə tiv), *adj.* **1.** running away, as from danger or capture [a *fugitive* criminal]. **2.** not lasting long; passing away quickly [*fugitive* pleasures]. —*n.* a person who is running away, as from the law.

fugue (fyōōg), *n.* a piece of music in which one part after another takes up a melody and all parts stay in harmony as the melody is repeated in various ways.

Füh·rer (fyoor′ər), *n.* leader: a German word, the title of Adolf Hitler in Nazi Germany.

Fu·ji·ya·ma (fōō′jē yä′mä), *n.* a mountain near Tokyo, Japan. It is a volcano.

-ful (fəl), a suffix meaning: **1.** full of [*Joyful* means full of joy.] **2.** likely to [*Forgetful* means likely to forget.] **3.** the amount that will fill [A *teaspoonful* is the amount that will fill a teaspoon.] **4.** having the ways of [*Masterful* means having the ways of a master.]

ful·crum (ful′krəm), *n.* the support or point that a lever rests on when it is lifting something. —**ful′crums** or **ful·cra** (ful′krə), *pl.*

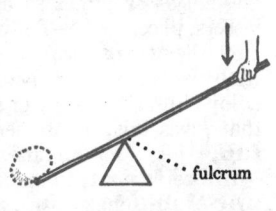

fulcrum

ful·fill or **ful·fil** (fool fil′), *v.* to make happen; carry out, perform, do, complete, etc. [to *fulfill* a promise, a duty, a purpose, a mission.] —**ful·filled′**, *p.t. & p.p.*; **ful·fill′ing**, *pr.p.* —**ful·fill′ment** or **ful·fil′ment**, *n.*

full (fool), *adj.* **1.** having in it all there is space for; filled [a *full* jar]. **2.** having much or many in it [a pond *full* of fish; to lead a *full* life]. **3.** having eaten all that one wants. **4.** whole or complete [a *full* dozen; a *full* load]. **5.** clear and strong [the *full* tones of an organ]. **6.** filled out; plump; round [a *full* face]. **7.** with loose, wide folds [a *full* skirt]. —*n.* the greatest amount or degree [to enjoy life to the *full*]. —*adv.* **1.** completely [a *full*-grown boy]. **2.** straight; directly [The ball hit him *full* in the face.] —**full many**, very many: *used mainly in poetry.* —**full of**, filled with. —**full well**, very well. —**in full**, **1.** to the complete amount [paid *in full*]. **2.** not abbreviated [Write your name *in full*.] —**full′ness**, *n.*

full·back (fool′bak), *n.* a football player who is a member of the backfield.

full·er (fool′ər), *n.* a person who cleans, shrinks, and thickens newly woven cloth.

full-fledged (fool′flejd′), *adj.* completely developed or trained [a *full-fledged* pilot].

full-grown (fool′grōn′), *adj.* fully grown.

full moon, the moon seen as a full circle.

full·y (fool′ē), *adv.* in a way that is complete, plentiful, exact, etc.; thoroughly; quite [to understand *fully*; to be *fully* ripe].

ful·mi·nate (ful′mə nāt), *v.* **1.** to explode. **2.** to protest, argue, or blame in a loud or strong way. —*n.* an explosive. —**ful′mi·nat·ed**, *p.t. & p.p.*; **ful′mi·nat·ing**, *pr.p.* —**ful′mi·na′tion**, *n.*

ful·some (fool′səm), *adj.* so full of praise, sweetness, etc. as to be sickening; annoying because not sincere [*fulsome* flattery].

Ful·ton, Robert (fool′t'n), 1765–1815; U.S. engineer who invented a steamboat.

fum·ble (fum′b'l), *v.* **1.** to handle or grope about in a clumsy way [He *fumbled* for the keys in his pocket.] **2.** to lose one's grasp on something while trying to catch or hold it [to *fumble* a football]. —*n.* the act of fumbling. —**fum′bled**, *p.t. & p.p.*; **fum′bling**, *pr.p.*

fume (fyōōm), *n.* a gas, smoke, or vapor, especially if harmful or bad-smelling. —*v.* **1.** to give off fumes. **2.** to show that one is angry or irritated [He *fumed* at the long delay.] —**fumed**, *p.t. & p.p.*; **fum′ing**, *pr.p.*

fu·mi·gate (fyoo'mə gāt), *v.* to fill a place with poison gas or fumes so as to get rid of germs, insects, mice, etc. —**fu'mi·gat·ed**, *p.t. & p.p.;* **fu'mi·gat·ing**, *pr.p.* —**fu'mi·ga'tion**, *n.*

fun (fun), *n.* lively play or joking that makes one enjoy himself; a happy or gay time, or something that gives this; amusement. —**for fun** or **in fun**, just for amusement; not seriously. —**make fun of**, to make jokes about; ridicule.

func·tion (fungk'shən), *n.* **1.** special or typical work or purpose of a thing or person [The *function* of the brakes is to stop the car.] **2.** a formal party or an important ceremony. —*v.* to do its work; act [The motor is not *functioning* properly.] —**func'tion·al**, *adj.* —**func'tion·al·ly**, *adv.*

func·tion·ar·y (fungk'shən er'ē), *n.* an official. —**func'tion·ar'ies**, *pl.*

fund (fund), *n.* **1.** an amount of money to be used for a particular purpose [a scholarship *fund*]. **2. funds**, *pl.* money on hand, ready for use. **3.** a supply; stock [a *fund* of good will].

fun·da·men·tal (fun'də men't'l), *adj.* of or forming a basis or foundation; basic [Freedom of speech is a *fundamental* right in our country.] —*n.* a fundamental or basic thing; very necessary part [Mathematics is one of the *fundamentals* of science.] —**fun'da·men'tal·ly**, *adv.*

Fun·dy, Bay of (fun'dē), a bay of the Atlantic between New Brunswick and Nova Scotia.

fu·ner·al (fyoo'nər əl), *n.* the services held when a dead person is buried or cremated. —*adj.* of or for a funeral [a *funeral* march].

fu·ne·re·al (fyoo nir'i əl), *adj.* fit for a funeral; sad or gloomy; mournful.

fun·gous (fung'gəs), *adj.* of or like a fungus.

fun·gus (fung'gəs), *n.* a plant that has no leaves, flowers, or green color. Mildews, molds, mushrooms, and toad-stools are forms of fungus. —**fun·gi** (fun'jī) or **fun'gus·es**, *pl.*

fungi

funk (fungk), *n.* the condition of being afraid or in a panic, because of cowardliness: *used only in everyday talk.*

fun·nel (fun'l), *n.* **1.** a tube with a wide cone at one end, used for pouring liquids, powders, etc. into narrow openings. **2.** the smoke-stack of a steamship. —*v.* to move or pour as through a funnel. —**fun'neled** or **fun'nelled**, *p.t. & p.p.;* **fun'nel·ing** or **fun'nel·ling**, *pr.p.*

fun·ny (fun'ē), *adj.* **1.** causing smiles or laughter; amusing; comical. **2.** odd or unusual: *used only in everyday talk.* —*n.* *usually* **funnies**, *pl.* comic strips: *used only in everyday talk.* —**fun'ni·er**, *compar.;* **fun'ni·est**, *superl.* —**fun'ni·ly**, *adv.*

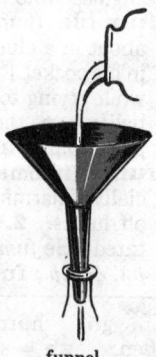
funnel

fur (fûr), *n.* **1.** the soft, thick hair that covers many animals. **2.** an animal's skin with such hair on it [Indians traded *furs* for guns.] **3.** a coat, scarf, etc. made of such skins. **4.** a fuzzy coating, as on the tongue during illness. —*adj.* of fur [a *fur* coat]. —*v.* to make, cover, or trim with fur. —**furred**, *p.t. & p.p.;* **fur'ring**, *pr.p.*

fur·be·low (fûr'bə lō), *n.* a fancy but useless trimming [frills and *furbelows*].

fur·bish (fûr'bish), *v.* **1.** to brighten by rubbing; polish. **2.** to put into better condition; clean or freshen up [to *furbish* up an old sofa].

fu·ri·ous (fyoor'i əs), *adj.* **1.** full of fury or wild anger. **2.** very fierce, strong, wild, etc. [*furious* activity]. —**fu'ri·ous·ly**, *adv.*

furl (fûrl), *v.* to roll up tightly around a staff or mast, as a flag or sail.

fur·long (fûr'lông), *n.* a measure of distance equal to 1/8 of a mile, or 220 yards.

fur·lough (fûr'lō), *n.* a vacation given to a soldier or sailor. —*v.* to give a furlough to.

furled sail

fur·nace (fûr'nis), *n.* an enclosed place in which heat is produced, as by burning fuel, for warming a building, melting ores and metals, etc.

fur·nish (fûr'nish), *v.* **1.** to give whatever is needed; supply [to *furnish* a lawyer with facts]. **2.** to put furniture in [to *furnish* a home].

fur·nish·ings (fûr'nish ingz), *n.pl.* **1.** furniture, carpets, etc., as for a house. **2.** things to wear; clothing [men's *furnishings*].

fur·ni·ture (fûr'ni chər), *n.* the things needed for living in a house, as chairs, beds, tables, chests, etc.

fu·ror (fyoor'ôr), *n.* **1.** great excitement or enthusiasm [His new book has caused quite a *furor*.] **2.** wild anger; rage [the *furor* of the mob].

fur·ri·er (fûr'i ər), *n.* a person who deals in furs, especially one who prepares furs for use or who makes and repairs fur garments.

fur·row (fûr'ō), *n.* **1.** a long groove made in the ground by a plow. **2.** anything like this, as a deep wrinkle. —*v.* to make furrows in [Trouble had *furrowed* his brow.]

furrows

fur·ry (fûr'ē), *adj.* **1.** covered with fur [a *furry* kitten]. **2.** of or like fur [*furry* cloth]. —**fur'ri·er**, *compar.;* **fur'ri·est**, *superl.*

fur·ther (fûr'thər), *adj.* **1.** more; added [I have no *further* news.] **2.** more distant. —*adv.* **1.** to a greater extent; more [We must investigate *further*.] **2.** in addition; moreover; besides [*Further*, I want you to leave at once.] **3.** at or to a greater distance. In meaning 2 of the adjective and meaning 3 of the adverb, *farther* is more commonly used. —*v.* to help onward; promote [to *further* the cause of education].

fur·ther·ance (fūr′thər əns), *n.* a furthering, or helping onward [the *furtherance* of a plan].

fur·ther·more (fūr′thər môr), *adv.* besides; also; moreover.

fur·ther·most (fūr′thər mōst), *adj.* furthest.

fur·thest (fūr′thist), *adj.* most distant; farthest. —*adv.* at or to the greatest distance [His ideas were the *furthest* removed from mine.]

fur·tive (fūr′tiv), *adj.* done or acting in a sly, sneaky way; stealthy [a *furtive* glance]. —**fur′tive·ly**, *adv.* —**fur′tive·ness**, *n.*

fu·ry (fyoor′ē), *n.* 1. wild anger; great rage [He is in a *fury* over his wrecked car.] 2. rough or wild force; fierceness [The wave beat the shore with *fury*.] 3. a wild or raging person. —**fu′ries**, *pl.*

furze (fūrz), *n.* a prickly evergreen shrub with yellow flowers, growing wild in Europe.

fuse (fyooz), *v.* 1. to melt or to join by melting, as metals. 2. to join together completely; unite. —**fused**, *p.t. & p.p.*; **fus′ing**, *pr.p.*

fuse (fyooz), *n.* 1. a wick on a bomb, firecracker, etc. that is lighted to set off the explosion. 2. a strip of metal that melts easily, usually set in a plug that is made part of an electric circuit as a safety device. If the current becomes too strong, the fuse melts and breaks the circuit.

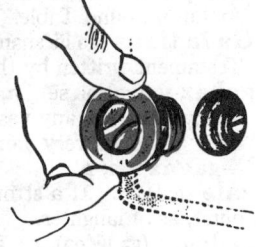

electric fuse

fu·se·lage (fyoo′z'l ij *or* fyoo′zə läzh′), *n.* the body of an airplane, not including the wings and tail.

fu·si·ble (fyoo′zə b'l), *adj.* that can be fused, or melted. —**fu′si·bil′i·ty**, *n.*

fu·sil·ier *or* **fu·sil·eer** (fyoo′zə lir′), *n.* a soldier of earlier times armed with a light flintlock musket. The name *Fusiliers* is still given to some British regiments.

fu·sil·lade (fyoo′z'l ād′), *n.* 1. a shooting of many guns at the same time. 2. something like this [a *fusillade* of questions].

fu·sion (fyoo′zhən), *n.* a fusing, melting, or joining together: see also **nuclear fusion.**

fuss (fus), *n.* too much bother or worry; nervous or excited action over a small thing [She made a great *fuss* over the spilled glass of water.] —*v.* to bustle about or bother with small things.

fuss·y (fus′ē), *adj.* 1. always fussing; too nervous or too particular about things [a *fussy* mother; to be *fussy* about one's food]. 2. full of small, fancy details that are not necessary [a *fussy* painting]. —**fuss′i·er**, *compar.*; **fuss′i·est**, *superl.* —**fuss′i·ness**, *n.*

fus·tian (fus′chən), *n.* 1. a thick, strong cotton cloth, as corduroy or velveteen. 2. talk or writing that sounds more important than it actually is.

fust·y (fus′tē), *adj.* 1. smelling stale or moldy; musty. 2. old-fashioned; not up-to-date. —**fust′i·er**, *compar.*; **fust′i·est**, *superl.*

fu·tile (fyoo′t'l), *adj.* 1. that could not succeed; hopeless; useless [He made a *futile* attempt to climb the wall.] 2. not important because not likely to have results [a *futile* discussion]. —**fu·til·i·ty** (fyoo til′ə tē), *n.*

fu·ture (fyoo′chər), *adj.* 1. in the time to come; after the present time [a *future* date; my *future* happiness]. 2. showing time to come ["Shall" and "will" are used with a verb to express *future* tense.] —*n.* 1. the time that is to come [I'll buy it sometime in the *future*.] 2. what is going to be [We all have some control over the *future*.] 3. chance to succeed [Mary's *future* as a singer seems bright.]

fu·tur·i·ty (fyoo toor′ə tē *or* fyoo tyoor′ə tē), *n.* the future. —**fu·tur′i·ties**, *pl.*

fuze (fyooz), *n. & v.* same as **fuse.**

fuzz (fuz), *n.* soft, light hairs or fibers [the *fuzz* on a cheek or on a peach].

fuzz·y (fuz′ē), *adj.* 1. of, like, or covered with fuzz [a *fuzzy* sweater]. 2. not clear or distinct; blurred [a *fuzzy* picture on TV]. —**fuzz′i·er**, *compar.*; **fuzz′i·est**, *superl.*

-fy (fī), a suffix meaning: 1. to make or become [To *purify* is to make pure. To *putrefy* is to become putrid.] 2. to make have or feel [To *terrify* is to make feel terror.]

G

G, g (jē), *n.* the seventh letter of the English alphabet. —**G's, g's** (jēz), *pl.*

G. *or* **g.,** abbreviation for **gram** or **grams.**

Ga., abbreviation for **Georgia.**

gab (gab), *v.* to talk a great deal or in an idle way; chatter. —*n.* idle talk; chatter. *This word is used only in everyday talk.* —**gabbed**, *p.t. & p.p.*; **gab′bing**, *pr.p.*

gab·ar·dine *or* **gab·er·dine** (gab′ər dēn), *n.* 1. a closely woven cloth with fine, slanting ribs, used in suits, coats, etc. 2. a loose coat made of coarse cloth, worn in the Middle Ages.

gab·ble (gab′'l), *v.* to talk rapidly without making any sense; jabber. —*n.* rapid talk that does not make sense [the *gabble* of the crowd leaving the theater]. —**gab′bled**, *p.t. & p.p.*; **gab′bling**, *pr.p.*

gab·by (gab′ē), *adj.* talking too much: *used only in everyday talk.* —**gab′bi·er**, *compar.*; **gab′bi·est**, *superl.*

fat, āpe, cär, ten, ēven, hit, bīte, gō, hôrn, tool, book, up, fūr;
get, joy, yet, chin, she, thin, *th*en; zh = s in pleasure; ′ as in able (ā′b'l);
ə = a in ago, e in agent, i in sanity, o in confess, u in focus,

ga·ble (gā′b'l), *n.* the triangle formed in a wall of a building by the sloping ends of a ridged roof.

ga·bled (gā′b'ld), *adj.* having or forming a gable or gables [a *gabled* roof].

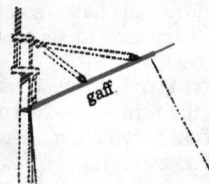

gable

Ga·bon (gä bôn′), *n.* a country in western Africa, on the Atlantic Ocean.

Ga·bri·el (gā′bri əl), *n.* an angel in the Bible who acts as God's messenger.

gad (gad), *v.* to wander about in an idle or restless way, as in looking for excitement. —**gad′-ded,** *p.t. & p.p.;* **gad′ding,** *pr.p.*

gad·a·bout (gad′ə bout), *n.* a person who goes about looking for fun and excitement.

gad·fly (gad′flī), *n.* **1.** a large fly that stings cattle and horses. **2.** a person who annoys or irritates others. —**gad′flies,** *pl.*

gadg·et (gaj′it), *n.* **1.** a small, mechanical thing having some special use [a *gadget* for opening cans]. **2.** any interesting but unnecessary device.

Gael·ic (gāl′ik), *n.* the Celtic language of the Scottish Highlands and of Ireland. —*adj.* of this language or of the people who speak it.

gaff (gaf), *n.* **1.** a large hook or spear, used in lifting large fish out of the water. **2.** a spar or pole holding up the upper edge of a fore-and-aft sail. —*v.* to hook or pull in a fish with a gaff. —**stand the gaff,** to bear up well under trouble: *a slang phrase.*

gaff

gaff (meaning 2)

gag (gag), *v.* **1.** to strain or choke as in vomiting; retch or make retch. **2.** to keep from talking or crying out, as by covering the mouth. —*n.* **1.** a thing that gags, or keeps one from talking. **2.** a joke: *a slang meaning.* —**gagged,** *p.t. & p.p.;* **gag′ging,** *pr.p.*

gage (gāj), *n.* **1.** a glove thrown down by a knight challenging another to fight. **2.** a challenge. **3.** something given as a pledge.

gage (gāj), *n. & v.* same as **gauge.**

gai·e·ty (gā′ə tē), *n.* **1.** the condition of being gay; cheerfulness. **2.** lively fun; merrymaking. **3.** showy brightness. —**gai′e·ties,** *pl.*

gai·ly (gā′lē), *adv.* **1.** in a gay manner; happily; merrily. **2.** brightly [a *gaily* decorated hall].

gain (gān), *n.* **1.** a thing or amount added; increase or addition [a *gain* in weight]. **2.** profit or winnings: *often used in the plural,* **gains** [the *gains* from his business]. **3.** the act of getting something, especially money [His love of *gain* made him greedy.] —*v.* **1.** to get by trying hard or as a reward; win; earn [to *gain* a living; *gain* first prize]. **2.** to get as an increase or advantage [He *gained* ten pounds in two months.] **3.** to get to; reach [We drove all day, hoping to *gain* our destination.] **4.** to become better; improve. —**gain on, 1.** to draw nearer to, as in a race. **2.** to do better than. —**gain′er,** *n.*

gain·ful (gān′fəl), *adj.* bringing gain or profit [*gainful* employment]. —**gain′ful·ly,** *adv.*

gain·say (gān sā′), *v.* to deny or contradict. —**gain·said** (gān sed′), *p.t. & p.p.;* **gain·say′ing,** *pr.p.*

'gainst or **gainst** (genst), *prep.* against: *used mainly in poetry.*

gait (gāt), *n.* a way of walking or running [The old man had a shuffling *gait.* Pacing and trotting are two different *gaits* used by horses.]

gai·ter (gā′tər), *n.* a cloth or leather covering for the lower part of the leg; spat or legging.

gaiters

gal (gal), *n.* a girl: *a slang word.*

gal., abbreviation for **gallon** or **gallons.**

ga·la (gā′lə *or* gal′ə), *adj.* of, for, or like a gay celebration; festive [a *gala* costume]. —*n.* a gay celebration; festival.

Gal·a·had (gal′ə had), *n.* the purest knight of King Arthur's Round Table.

Ga·la·tians (gə lā′shənz), *n.* a book of the New Testament written by the Apostle Paul.

gal·ax·y (gal′ək sē), *n.* **1.** *often* **Galaxy,** the Milky Way. **2.** any vast group of stars like this. **3.** a group of very famous or brilliant people. —**gal′ax·ies,** *pl.*

gale (gāl), *n.* **1.** a strong wind. **2.** a loud outburst, as of laughter.

ga·le·na (gə lē′nə), *n.* a gray mineral that is the chief ore of lead.

Gal·i·le·an (gal′ə lē′ən), *adj.* of Galilee or its people. —*n.* a person born or living in Galilee. —**the Galilean,** Jesus.

Gal·i·lee (gal′ə lē), *n.* a region in the northern part of ancient Palestine.

Galilee, Sea of, a small, fresh-water lake in northeastern Palestine.

Gal·i·le·o (gal′ə lē′ō), *n.* 1564–1642; Italian astronomer who proved that the earth moves around the sun.

gall (gôl), *n.* **1.** bile, the bitter liquid made by the liver. **2.** bitter feeling. **3.** rude boldness; impudence: *used only in everyday talk.*

gall (gôl), *n.* a sore made by rubbing, especially on a horse's back. —*v.* **1.** to make sore by rubbing. **2.** to annoy or irritate [The thought of losing *galled* Jim.] —**gall′ing,** *adj.*

gall (gôl), *n.* a lump that grows on the parts of a plant hurt by insects, bacteria, etc.

gal·lant (gal′ənt), *adj.* **1.** brave and noble; daring. **2.** (*sometimes* gə länt′), very polite and respectful, especially to ladies. **3.** fine and showy; brilliant [knights in *gallant* attire]. —*n.* **1.** a brave, noble man.

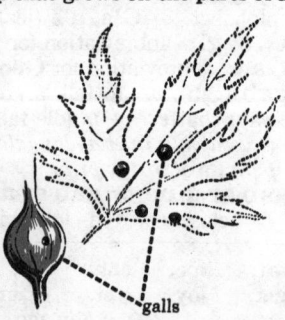

galls

2. a man who pays much polite attention to women. —**gal′lant·ly,** *adv.*

gal·lant·ry (gal′ən trē), *n.* **1.** great courage. **2.** very polite behavior, especially toward women. **3.** a polite act or remark. —**gal′lant·ries,** *pl.*

gall bladder, a small sac attached to the liver: the gall, or bile, is stored in it.

gal·le·on (gal′i ən), *n.* a large Spanish sailing ship of olden times, having three or four decks.

gal·ler·y (gal′ər ē), *n.* **1.** a balcony, especially the highest balcony in a theater, etc.: it usually has the cheapest seats. **2.** the people who sit in these seats. **3.** the public in general; ordinary people. **4.** a long hall or corridor, often open or with windows at one side. **5.** a room or group of rooms, as in a museum, in which works of art are shown. **6.** any room used for a special purpose, as for shooting at targets. —**gal′ler·ies,** *pl.*

gal·ley (gal′ē), *n.* **1.** a large, low ship of long ago, having both sails and many oars. The oars were usually rowed by slaves or prisoners in chains. **2.** the kitchen of a ship. —**gal′leys,** *pl.*

galley

Gal·lic (gal′ik), *adj.* **1.** of ancient Gaul or its people. **2.** French [a *Gallic* expression].

gal·li·vant (gal′ə vant), *v.* to wander about looking for fun or excitement; gad about.

gal·lon (gal′ən), *n.* a measure of liquids, equal to four quarts or eight pints.

gal·lop (gal′əp), *n.* **1.** the fastest gait of a horse, etc. In a gallop, all four feet are off the ground at the same time in each stride. **2.** a ride on a galloping animal. —*v.* **1.** to go or ride at a gallop. **2.** to move very fast; hurry.

galloping horse

gal·lows (gal′ōz), *n.* **1.** a wooden framework with a rope by which people are hanged as a punishment. **2.** the punishment of death by hanging. —**gal·lows·es** (gal′ō zəz) or **gal′lows,** *pl.*

ga·lore (gə lôr′), *adv.* in great plenty [to have fun *galore;* to attract crowds *galore*].

ga·losh (gə läsh′), *n.* a high overshoe worn in wet weather or snow.

gal·van·ic (gal van′ik), *adj.* **1.** of or describing an electric current produced by chemical action, as in a battery. **2.** startling; shocking.

gal·va·nize (gal′və nīz), *v.* **1.** to apply an electric current to. **2.** to make someone do something by startling or shocking him. **3.** to coat with a layer of zinc [Iron is often *galvanized* to keep it from

galosh

rusting.] —**gal′va·nized,** *p.t. & p.p.;* **gal′va·niz·ing,** *pr.p.*

Gam·bi·a (gam′bi ə), *n.* a country in western Africa, on the Atlantic Ocean.

gam·bit (gam′bit), *n.* **1.** an opening move in chess in which a pawn is risked to get some advantage. **2.** any action used to get an advantage.

gam·ble (gam′b'l), *v.* **1.** to take part in games in which the players bet, as poker or dice. **2.** to bet or wager. **3.** to risk losing something in trying to gain something else [By giving up school for a job, Bill is *gambling* with his future.] —*n.* an act by which one gambles or risks something [Starting a new business is usually a *gamble.*] —**gamble away,** to lose in gambling. —**gam′bled,** *p.t. & p.p.;* **gam′bling,** *pr.p.* —**gam′bler,** *n.*

gam·bol (gam′bəl), *v.* to jump and skip about in play, as lambs do; frolic. —*n.* the act of frolicking. —**gam′boled** or **gam′bolled,** *p.t. & p.p.;* **gam′bol·ing** or **gam′bol·ling,** *pr.p.*

gam·brel roof (gam′brəl), a roof with two slopes on each side, as in this picture.

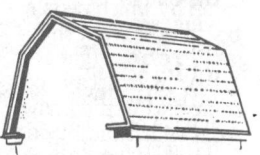
gambrel roof

game (gām), *n.* **1.** a sport or kind of contest carried on according to rules by persons or teams playing against each other [Baseball and chess are *games.*] **2.** any form of play; amusement [He thinks of life as a *game.*] **3.** the set of things used in playing a game [Helen received some books and *games* for her birthday.] **4.** wild animals or birds hunted for sport or food; also, their flesh used as food. **5.** a scheme or plan [I saw through his *game.*] —*adj.* **1.** describing or having to do with wild animals or birds that are hunted [a *game* bird; a *game* warden]. **2.** brave in a stubborn way; plucky: *used only in everyday talk* [a *game* fighter]. —*v.* to gamble. —**make game of,** to make fun of; ridicule. —**gam′er,** *compar.;* **gam′est,** *superl.* —**gamed,** *p.t. & p.p.;* **gam′ing,** *pr.p.* —**game′ly,** *adv.* —**game′ness,** *n.*

game (gām), *adj.* lame [a *game* leg].

game·cock (gām′käk), *n.* a rooster bred and trained for fighting other roosters.

game·some (gām′səm), *adj.* playful; full of fun [in a *gamesome* mood]. —**game′some·ness,** *n.*

game·ster (gām′stər), *n.* a person who gambles.

gamecock

gam·in (gam′in), *n.* a child who roams the streets because he has no home.

gam·ing (gām′ing), *n.* gambling.

gam·ma (gam′ə), *n.* the third letter of the Greek alphabet.

---

gam·ut (gam′ət), *n.* **1.** the whole musical scale. **2.** the full range of anything [the *gamut* of emotions, from joy to grief].

gam·y (gām′ē), *adj.* **1.** having a strong flavor like that of cooked game. **2.** plucky. **—gam′-i·er,** *compar.;* **gam′i·est,** *superl.*

gan·der (gan′dər), *n.* a male goose.

Gan·dhi, Mo·han·das K. (mō′hən däs′ gän′dē), 1869–1948; political leader and reformer in India: often called *Mahatma Gandhi.* See **mahatma.**

gang (gang), *n.* **1.** a group of people who work together or spend much time together [a railroad *gang;* a neighborhood *gang*]. **2.** a group of criminals. **3.** a set of tools or machines fixed in place to work together [a *gang* of saws]. **—gang up** or **gang up on,** to attack or oppose as a group: *used only in everyday talk.*

Gan·ges (gan′jēz), *n.* a river in northern India.

gan·gling (gang′gling), *adj.* tall, thin, and awkward; lanky [a *gangling* teen-ager].

gang·plank (gang′plangk), *n.* a movable ramp by which people board or leave a ship.

gan·grene (gang′-grēn), *n.* decay of some part of the body from which the blood is blocked by injury or disease [Frostbite can cause *gangrene* in a toe.] **—gan·gre·nous** (gang′gri nəs), *adj.*

gangplank

gang·ster (gang′stər), *n.* a member of a gang of criminals.

gang·way (gang′wā), *n.* **1.** a passageway. **2.** a gangplank. **—***interj.* move out of the way!

gan·net (gan′it), *n.* a large sea bird that looks a little like the pelican.

gant·let (gônt′lit *or* gant′lit), *n.* same as **gauntlet** (punishment).

gaol (jāl), *n.* a jail: *a British spelling.* **—gaol′er,** *n.*

gap (gap), *n.* **1.** an opening made by breaking, tearing, etc. [a *gap* in a wall]. **2.** a mountain pass. **3.** an empty space; break or blank [a *gap* in one's memory].

gape (gāp), *v.* **1.** to open the mouth wide, as in yawning. **2.** to stare with the mouth open [The child *gaped* at the elephants.] **3.** to be wide open [a *gaping* wound]. **—***n.* the act of gaping. **—gaped,** *p.t. & p.p.;* **gap′ing,** *pr.p.*

child gaping

ga·rage (gə räzh′), *n.* **1.** a closed place where automobiles are sheltered. **2.** a place where automobiles are repaired.

garb (gärb), *n.* clothing; style of dress [the *garb* of a priest]. **—***v.* to dress or clothe.

gar·bage (gär′bij), *n.* spoiled or waste food that is thrown away.

gar·ble (gär′b'l), *v.* to mix up or leave out parts of a story or report, so that what is told is false or not clear. **—gar′bled,** *p.t. & p.p.;* **gar′bling,** *pr.p.*

gar·den (gär′d'n), *n.* a piece of ground where flowers, vegetables, etc. are grown. **—***v.* to take care of a garden. **—gar·den·er** (gärd′nər), *n.*

gar·de·ni·a (gär dēn′yə), *n.* a flower with waxy, white petals and a very sweet odor.

Gar·field, James A. (gär′fēld), 1831–1881; twentieth president of the United States, in 1881. He was assassinated.

gar·gle (gär′g'l), *v.* to rinse the throat with a liquid that is moved about by forcing the breath out with the head held back. **—***n.* a liquid used for gargling. **—gar′gled,** *p.t. & p.p.;* **gar′gling,** *pr.p.*

gar·goyle (gär′goil), *n.* a decoration on a building in the form of a strange, imaginary creature. It often has a channel to let rain water run off through its mouth.

gargoyle

gar·ish (ger′ish), *adj.* bright and showy in an unpleasant way; gaudy. **—gar′ish·ly,** *adv.* **—gar′ish·ness,** *n.*

gar·land (gär′lənd), *n.* a wreath of leaves or flowers. **—***v.* to decorate with garlands.

gar·lic (gär′lik), *n.* a plant of the onion family with a strong-smelling bulb used as a seasoning.

gar·ment (gär′mənt), *n.* any piece of clothing.

gar·ner (gär′nər), *v.* to gather and store up, as grain. **—***n.* a storehouse for grain.

gar·net (gär′nit), *n.* **1.** a clear, deep-red stone that is used as a jewel. **2.** deep red.

gar·nish (gär′nish), *v.* to decorate; especially, to decorate food to make it look or taste better [to *garnish* potatoes with parsley]. **—***n.* something used in garnishing.

gar·nish·ee (gär′ni shē′), *v.* to hold back wages from someone who owes a debt, so that the money can be used to pay the debt. **—gar′nish·eed′,** *p.t. & p.p.;* **gar′nish·ee′ing,** *pr.p.*

gar·ret (gar′it), *n.* the room or space just below the slanting roof of a house; attic.

gar·ri·son (gar′i s'n), *n.* **1.** soldiers stationed in a fort or town to protect it. **2.** such a place with its soldiers, guns, etc.; military post. **—***v.* to put soldiers in a fort, town, etc. to defend it.

gar·ru·lous (gar′oo ləs *or* gar′yoo ləs), *adj.* talking too much, especially about unimportant things; talkative. **—gar′ru·lous·ly,** *adv.*

gar·ter (gär′tər), *n.* an elastic band or strap worn to hold up a stocking or sock.

garter snake, a small, striped snake of North America that is not poisonous.

Gar·y (ger′ē), *n.* a city in northwestern Indiana.

gas (gas), *n.* **1.** a substance that has the same form as air and can spread out so as to take up all the space open to it; form of matter that is neither liquid nor solid [Oxygen and

garter

carbon dioxide are *gases*.] **2.** any mixture of gases that will burn easily, used for lighting and heating. **3.** any gas used as an anesthetic. **4.** any substance used, as in war, to make the air poisonous or very irritating. **5.** *a short form of* **gasoline.** —*v.* **1.** to attack, hurt, or kill with poison gas. **2.** to talk in an idle or boastful way: *a slang meaning.* —**gas′es,** *pl.* —**gassed,** *p.t. & p.p.;* **gas′sing,** *pr.p.*

gas·e·ous (gas′i əs *or* gas′yəs), *adj.* of, like, or in the form of, gas.

gash (gash), *v.* to make a long, deep cut in. —*n.* a long, deep cut.

gas·ket (gas′kit), *n.* a ring or other piece of rubber, metal, etc. fitted tightly around a joint to keep it from leaking

gas mask, a mask with a filter, worn over the face to protect against poisonous gases.

gas·o·line or **gas·o·lene** (gas′′l ēn), *n.* a pale liquid that burns very easily and is used mainly as a fuel in motor engines. It is made from petroleum.

gasp (gasp), *v.* **1.** to catch the breath suddenly or with effort, as in surprise or in choking. **2.** to say or tell with gasps [He *gasped* out his story.] —*n.* the act of gasping [a *gasp* of horror].

gas mask

gas station, a place where gasoline, oil, and other things for motor cars, trucks, etc. are sold.

gas·tric (gas′trik), *adj.* of, in, or near the stomach [*gastric* juices; *gastric* pains].

gate (gāt), *n.* **1.** a door in a fence or outside wall, especially one that swings on hinges. **2.** a gateway. **3.** a door, valve, etc. that controls the flow of water, as in a canal or pipe. **4.** the number of people who have paid to see a certain sports contest, exhibition, etc.

gate·way (gāt′wā), *n.* **1.** an opening in a wall or fence with a gate fitted into it. **2.** a way of getting in, out, or at [the *gateway* to the West; the *gateway* to knowledge].

gath·er (gath′ər), *v.* **1.** to bring or come together in one place or group [The child *gathered* her toys together. The families *gathered* for a reunion.] **2.** to get or collect gradually; accumulate [to *gather* wealth; to *gather* one's strength; to *gather* news for a paper]. **3.** to pick or glean [to *gather* crops]. **4.** to get as an idea; conclude [I *gather* that he is rich.] **5.** to pull together so as to make folds or pleats [to *gather* cloth]. **6.** to fill with pus and come to a head, as a boil. —*n.* a single pleat or fold in cloth. —**gath′er·er,** *n.*

gath·er·ing (gath′ər ing), *n.* **1.** a coming together of people; meeting. **2.** a boil or abscess.

gau·cho (gou′chō), *n.* a cowboy of the South American pampas. —**gau′chos,** *pl.*

gaud (gôd), *n.* a cheap, showy ornament.

gaud·y (gôd′ē), *adj.* bright and showy in a cheap way; not in good taste. —**gaud′i·er,** *compar.;* **gaud′i·est,** *superl.* —**gaud′i·ly,** *adv.* —**gaud′i·ness,** *n.*

gauge (gāj), *n.* **1.** a standard for measuring size, thickness, etc.; also, a measure according to such a standard [The *gauge* of a railway tells how far apart the rails are. The *gauge* of a wire tells how thick it is.] **2.** any device for measuring something, as steam or air pressure, the thickness of wire, etc. —*v.* **1.** to measure exactly the size or amount of. **2.** to judge or estimate [to *gauge* a man's honesty]. —**gauged,** *p.t. & p.p.;* **gaug′ing,** *pr.p.* —**gaug′er,** *n.*

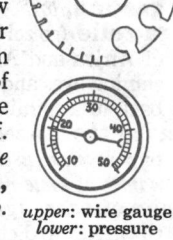

upper: wire gauge
lower: pressure gauge

Gaul (gôl), *n.* **1.** a part of the empire of ancient Rome, including mainly what is now France and some regions around it. **2.** any of the people who lived in Gaul.

gaunt (gônt), *adj.* **1.** so thin that the bones show; worn and lean, as from hunger or illness. **2.** looking gloomy and deserted [the *gaunt*, rocky coast of the island]. —**gaunt′ly,** *adv.* —**gaunt′ness,** *n.*

gaunt·let (gônt′lit), *n.* **1.** a glove worn by knights in armor. It was usually made of leather covered with metal plates. **2.** a heavy glove with a long cuff flaring up from the wrist. —**throw down the gauntlet,** to challenge, as to a fight.

gaunt·let (gônt′lit), *n.* a punishment in which a person was made to run between two lines of men who struck him with clubs or switches as he ran past.

gauze (gôz), *n.* any thin, light cloth so loosely woven that one can see through it [Cotton *gauze* is used for bandages.]

gauz·y (gôz′ē), *adj.* thin, light, and easy to see through, like gauze. —**gauz′i·er,** *compar.;* **gauz′i·est,** *superl.* —**gauz′i·ness,** *n.*

gave (gāv), past tense of **give.**

gav·el (gav′'l), *n.* a small wooden hammer that a chairman, judge, etc. raps on the table to call for attention or silence.

ga·votte or **ga·vot** (gə vät′), *n.* a 17th-century dance like the minuet, but livelier.

Ga·wain (gä′win), *n.* a knight of the Round Table, nephew of King Arthur.

gavel

gawk (gôk), *v.* to stare in a stupid way: *used only in everyday talk.*

gawk·y (gôk′ē), *adj.* tall and awkward or clumsy [a *gawky* youth]. —**gawk′i·er,** *compar.;* **gawk′i·est,** *superl.* —**gawk′i·ness,** *n.*

---

fat, āpe, cär, ten, ēven, hit, bīte, gō, hôrn, tōōl, book, up, fûr; get, joy, yet, chin, she, thin, *th*en; zh = s in pleasure; ′ as in able (ā′b'l); ə = a in ago, e in agent, i in sanity, o in confess, u in focus.

gay (gā), *adj.* **1.** lively and full of joy; merry; happy. **2.** bright and showy [*gay* colors]. —**gay′ness,** *n.*

gay·e·ty (gā′ə tē), *n.* same as **gaiety.** —**gay′-e·ties,** *pl.*

gay·ly (gā′lē), *adv.* same as **gaily.**

gaze (gāz), *v.* to look in a steady way; stare, as in wonder [The crowd *gazed* at the strange aircraft.] —*n.* a steady look. —**gazed,** *p.t. & p.p.;* **gaz′ing,** *pr.p.* —**gaz′er,** *n.*

ga·zelle (gə zel′), *n.* a small, graceful antelope of Africa and Asia. It has large, shining eyes and horns that twist back in a spiral.

ga·zette (gə zet′), *n.* a newspaper: *now used mainly in the names of some newspapers.*

gaz·et·teer (gaz ə tir′), *n.* a dictionary of geographical names, as of cities, countries, mountains, rivers, etc.

gazelles (2½ ft. high)

gear (gir), *n.* **1.** a part of a machine consisting of two or more wheels having teeth that fit together so that when one wheel moves the others are made to move [the steering *gear* of an automobile]. **2.** same as **gearwheel.** **3.** a certain arrangement of such wheels [He shifted into low *gear* to get more power.] **4.** tools and equipment needed for doing something [A fisherman's *gear* consists of rods, lines, flies, etc.] —*v.* **1.** to furnish with gear; equip. **2.** to connect by gears [The pedals of the bicycle are *geared* to the wheels.] **3.** to adjust or make fit [Our new cafeteria is *geared* to handle more students.] —**high gear,** the arrangement of gears that gives the greatest speed but little power. —**in gear,** connected to the motor. —**low gear,** the arrangement of gears that gives little speed but great power. —**out of gear,** not connected to the motor. —**shift gears,** to change from one gear arrangement to another.

gear·ing (gir′ing), *n.* a system of gears or other parts for passing on motion.

gear·shift (gir′shift), *n.* a part for connecting any of several sets of gears to a motor, or for disconnecting them.

gear·wheel (gir′hwēl), *n.* any of the toothed wheels in a gear: also written **gear wheel.**

geck·o (gek′ō), *n.* a small lizard that has a soft skin and suction pads on its feet. It eats insects. —**geck′os** or **geck′oes,** *pl.*

gearwheels

gee (jē), *interj.* a word of command to a horse or ox meaning "turn to the right!"

gee (jē), *interj.* a slang exclamation showing surprise, wonder, etc.

geese (gēs), *n.* plural of **goose.**

Gei·ger counter (gī′gər), a device used for checking radioactivity and for measuring the amount of it.

gei·sha (gā′shə), *n.* a Japanese woman whose work is to entertain by singing and dancing. —**gei′sha** or **gei′shas,** *pl.*

Geiger counter

gel·a·tin or **gel·a·tine** (jel′ə t'n), *n.* a substance boiled from the bones, hoofs, etc. of animals; also, a vegetable substance like this. Gelatin dissolves in hot water and makes a sort of jelly when it cools. It is used as a food, in photographic film, etc.

ge·lat·i·nous (ji lat′'n əs), *adj.* of or like gelatin or jelly.

geld·ing (gel′ding), *n.* a male horse whose sex glands have been removed.

gem (jem), *n.* **1.** a precious stone, cut and polished for use as a jewel. **2.** a person or thing that is very precious or valuable.

Gen., abbreviation for **General** and **Genesis.**

gen·darme (zhän′därm), *n.* a policeman in France and some other countries. —**gen′-darmes,** *pl.*

gen·der (jen′dər), *n.* any of the three classes that nouns, pronouns, and, often, adjectives belong to. These classes are called *masculine, feminine,* and *neuter,* and are more important in the grammars of other languages than in English. In English, such words as *boy, rooster,* and *he* are of the masculine gender; *girl, ship,* and *she* are of the feminine gender; and *baby, ball,* and *it* are of the neuter gender.

gene (jēn), *n.* any of the units of heredity that are carried by chromosomes: see **chromosome.**

ge·ne·al·o·gy (jē′ni al′ə jē *or* jen′i äl′ə jē), *n.* **1.** a list of a person's ancestors, that shows how they are related to one another; family tree. **2.** the study of families and how they have descended. —**ge′ne·al′o·gies,** *pl.* —**ge·ne·a·log·i·cal** (jē′ni ə läj′i k'l *or* jen′i ə läj′i k'l), *adj.*

gen·er·a (jen′ər ə), *n.* plural of **genus.**

gen·er·al (jen′ər əl), *adj.* **1.** of, for, or from the whole or all, not just a part or some [to act in the interest of the *general* welfare]. **2.** widespread or common [a *general* unrest among the people]. **3.** having to do with main parts but not with details [the *general* features of a plan]. **4.** not special or specialized [*general* science; a *general* store]. **5.** highest in rank; most important [the attorney *general*]. —*n.* any of various military officers ranking above a colonel; especially, such an officer who wears four stars and is called a *full general.* —**in general,** in the main; usually.

General Assembly, 1. the lawmaking body of some States. **2.** the main body of the United

Nations, in which all member nations are represented.

gen·er·al·i·ty (jen′ər al′ə tē), *n.* **1.** a statement that is general or vague rather than definite or with details [She offered no exact plan, but spoke only in *generalities*.] **2.** the greater number or part; majority [The *generality* of people are friendly.] **3.** the fact of being general or widespread. —**gen′er·al′i·ties,** *pl.*

gen·er·al·ize (jen′ər əl īz), *v.* **1.** to form a general rule or idea from particular facts or cases [To *generalize* from my experience with Tabby, I would say that cats make clean, friendly pets.] **2.** to make more general or widely used [The doctors hope to *generalize* the use of the new vaccine.] **3.** to talk or write in a general way, without being definite or giving details. —**gen′er·al·ized,** *p.t. & p.p.;* **gen′er·al·iz·ing,** *pr.p.* —**gen′er·al·i·za′tion,** *n.*

gen·er·al·ly (jen′ər əl ē), *adv.* **1.** to or by most people; widely [Is it *generally* known that the prisoner escaped?] **2.** in most cases; usually [I *generally* go straight home from school.] **3.** in a general way; without details [Speaking *generally,* I think he's right.]

gen·er·al·ship (jen′ər əl ship), *n.* **1.** the rank, power, or term of office of a general. **2.** the skill of a general in military affairs. **3.** skill in directing others; leadership.

gen·er·ate (jen′ə rāt), *v.* to bring into being; cause to be; produce [A dynamo *generates* electricity. Faith can *generate* hope.] —**gen′er·at·ed,** *p.t. & p.p.;* **gen′er·at·ing,** *pr.p.*

gen·er·a·tion (jen′ər ā′shən), *n.* **1.** a single stage in the history of a family [Grandfather, father, and son are three *generations*.] **2.** all the people born at about the same time [Children of grandfather's *generation* knew nothing of television.] **3.** the average time between the birth of one generation and the birth of the next, about 30 years. **4.** a generating, or producing [the *generation* of electricity from steam power].

gen·er·a·tive (jen′ə rā′tiv), *adj.* of, or having the power of, producing.

gen·er·a·tor (jen′ə rā′tər), *n.* **1.** a machine for changing mechanical energy into electricity. **2.** any person or thing that generates [The gift was a *generator* of much good will.]

ge·ner·ic (jə ner′ik), *adj.* of a whole genus, kind, class, etc.; general; inclusive [The word "ship" is a *generic* term for many kinds of large water craft.] —**ge·ner′i·cal·ly,** *adv.*

gen·er·os·i·ty (jen′ə räs′ə tē), *n.* **1.** the quality of being generous. **2.** a generous or unselfish act. —**gen′er·os′i·ties,** *pl.*

gen·er·ous (jen′ər əs), *adj.* **1.** willing to give or share; not selfish or stingy; openhanded. **2.** large; great in amount [*generous* helpings of dessert]. **3.** noble and forgiving; not mean [To forgive your enemy is a *generous* act.] —**gen′er·ous·ly,** *adv.* —**gen′er·ous·ness,** *n.*

Gen·e·sis (jen′ə sis), *n.* **1.** the first book of the Old Testament, telling a story of how the world was created by God. **2. genesis,** a beginning or origin.

ge·net·ics (jə net′iks), *n.pl.* the study of the way animals and plants pass on to their offspring such characteristics as size, color, etc.; science of heredity: *used with a singular verb.* —**ge·net′ic,** *adj.*

Ge·ne·va (jə nē′və), *n.* **1.** a city in Switzerland. **2.** a lake between Switzerland and France.

gen·ial (jēn′yəl), *adj.* **1.** friendly and cheerful. **2.** pleasant and healthful [a *genial* climate]. —**ge·ni·al·i·ty** (jē′ni al′ə tē), *n.* —**gen′ial·ly,** *adv.*

ge·nie (jē′nē), *n.* an imaginary being in Arabian tales, having great magic power.

ge·ni·i (jē′ni ī′), *n.* plural of **genius** in meanings 4 and 5.

gen·i·tals (jen′ə t′lz), *n.pl.* the sex organs. —**gen′i·tal,** *adj.*

gen·i·tive (jen′ə tiv), *adj.* describing the form of words that shows ownership, origin, etc. In Latin and some other languages, nouns, pronouns, and adjectives have certain endings to show that they are in the genitive case. In English the possessive case is sometimes called the genitive case. —*n.* the genitive case.

gen·ius (jēn′yəs), *n.* **1.** the special power of mind or the special ability that shows itself in the greatest artists, writers, scientists, etc. **2.** a person who has such ability [Leonardo da Vinci was a *genius* in both science and art]. **3.** any special ability [a *genius* for making friends]. **4.** a spirit that was believed by the ancient Romans to watch over a person or place. **5.** a person who has great power over another for good or evil. **6.** the special nature or spirit of a nation, time, etc. —**gen′ius·es,** *pl. for meanings 1, 2, 3, and 6;* **gen′i·i″,** *pl. for meanings 4 and 5.*

Gen·o·a (jen′ō ə), *n.* a seaport in northwestern Italy. —**Gen·o·ese** (jen′ō ēz′), *adj. & n.*

gent (jent), *n.* a gentleman: *a slang word.*

gen·teel (jen tēl′), *adj.* polite or well-bred; now, especially, trying too hard to seem refined or well-bred.

gen·tian (jen′shən), *n.* a plant with flowers that are usually blue, sometimes with fringed edges.

gen·tile or **Gen·tile** (jen′tīl), *n.* a person who is not a Jew. —*adj.* not Jewish.

gen·til·i·ty (jen til′ə tē), *n.* **1.** the condition of being born into the upper classes. **2.** good manners; politeness; refinement.

gen·tle (jen′t′l), *adj.* **1.** mild, soft, or easy; not rough [a *gentle* touch; a *gentle* scolding]. **2.** tame; easy to handle [a *gentle* dog]. **3.** gradual; not sudden [a *gentle* slope]. **4.** of or like the upper

gentian

---

fat,   āpe,   cär,   ten,   ēven,   hit,   bīte,   gō,   hôrn,   tōōl,   book,   up,   fûr;
get,   joy,   yet,   chin,   she,   thin,   *th*en;   zh = s in pleasure;   ′ as in able (ā′b′l);
ə = a in ago,   e in agent,   i in sanity,   o in confess,   u in focus.

classes. **5.** kindly or patient [a *gentle* nature]. —**gen′tler**, *compar.*; **gen′tlest**, *superl.* —**gen′tle·ness,** *n.*

gen·tle·folk (jen′t'l fōk), *n.pl.* people of high social standing.

gen·tle·man (jen′t'l mən), *n.* **1.** a man who is polite and cultured and has a sense of honor. **2.** a man belonging to a family of high social standing. **3.** any man: *a polite form.* —**gen′tle·men,** *pl.* —**gen′tle·man·ly,** *adj.*

gen·tle·wom·an (jen′t'l woom′ən), *n.* a lady: *now seldom used.* —**gen′tle·wom′en,** *pl.*

gen·tly (jen′tlē), *adv.* in a gentle manner; mildly, softly, easily, etc.

gen·try (jen′trē), *n.* **1.** people of high social standing, but not including nobles. **2.** people of any group or class [the newspaper *gentry*].

gen·u·ine (jen′yoo in), *adj.* **1.** really being what it seems to be; not false; true [a *genuine* diamond]. **2.** sincere or honest [*genuine* praise]. —**gen′u·ine·ly,** *adv.* —**gen′u·ine·ness,** *n.*

ge·nus (jē′nəs), *n.* a kind, sort, or class. In biology, a genus is a large group of plants or animals. divided into species, that are much alike in certain ways. —**gen′er·a** or **ge′nus·es,** *pl.*

geo-, a prefix meaning "the earth" [*Geometry* originally meant "the measurement of the earth."]

ge·o·graph·i·cal (jē′ə graf′i k'l) or **ge·o·graph·ic** (jē′ə graf′ik), *adj.* having to do with geography. —**ge′o·graph′i·cal·ly,** *adv.*

ge·og·ra·phy (jē äg′rə fē), *n.* **1.** the study of the surface of the earth and how it is divided into continents, countries, seas, etc. Geography also studies the climates, plants, animals, minerals, etc. of the earth. **2.** the natural features of a certain part of the earth. —**ge·og′ra·pher,** *n.*

ge·o·log·i·cal (jē′ə läj′i k'l) or **ge·o·log·ic** (jē′ə läj′ik), *adj.* having to do with geology. —**ge′o·log′i·cal·ly,** *adv.*

ge·ol·o·gy (jē äl′ə jē), *n.* the study of the earth's crust and of the way in which its layers were formed. It includes the study of rocks and fossils. —**ge·ol′o·gist,** *n.*

ge·o·met·ric (jē′ə met′rik) or **ge·o·met·ri·cal** (jē′ə met′ri k'l), *adj.* **1.** having to do with geometry. **2.** formed of straight lines, triangles, circles, etc. [a *geometric* pattern].

ge·om·e·try (jē äm′ə trē), *n.* the branch of mathematics that deals with lines, angles, surfaces, and solids, and with their measurement.

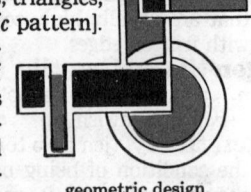
geometric design

George III (jôrj), 1738–1820; king of England at the time of the American Revolution. He ruled from 1760 to 1820.

George, Saint, the patron saint of England, who died about 303 A.D.

Geor·gia (jôr′jə), *n.* **1.** a State in the southeastern part of the United States: abbreviated **Ga. 2.** a republic in the southwestern part of the Soviet Union. —**Geor′gian,** *adj. & n.*

Ger., abbreviation for **German.**

ge·ra·ni·um (jə rā′ni əm), *n.* **1.** a common garden plant with showy pink, red, or white flowers. **2.** a wild plant like this, with pink or purple flowers.

geranium
(*meaning 1*)

germ (jûrm), *n.* **1.** a living thing that can cause disease and is too small to be seen except with a microscope; especially, one of the bacteria. **2.** a seed, bud, etc. from which a plant or animal develops. **3.** that from which something can grow; origin [the *germ* of an idea].

Ger·man (jûr′mən), *adj.* of Germany, its people, etc. —*n.* **1.** a person born or living in Germany. **2.** the language of the Germans.

Ger·man·ic (jər man′ik), *adj.* **1.** of Germany or the Germans; German. **2.** describing any of a group of languages that are related to German, as Norwegian, Danish, Dutch, and English.

Ger·ma·ny (jûr′mə nē), *n.* a country in north central Europe. Since 1949, it has been divided into East Germany and West Germany, each with a separate government.

ger·mi·cide (jûr′mə sīd), *n.* anything used to kill disease germs. —**ger′mi·cid′al,** *adj.*

ger·mi·nate (jûr′mə nāt), *v.* to start growing or developing; sprout or make sprout, as from a seed. —**ger′mi·nat·ed,** *p.t. & p.p.*; **ger′mi·nat·ing,** *pr.p.* —**ger′mi·na′tion,** *n.*

ger·und (jer′ənd), *n.* a verb ending in *-ing* that is used as a noun. A gerund sometimes takes an object [In "Playing golf is his only exercise," the word "playing" is a *gerund.*]

ges·tic·u·late (jes tik′yoo lāt), *v.* to make motions, especially with the hands or arms, as in showing feeling or adding force to one's speech. —**ges·tic′u·lat·ed,** *p.t. & p.p.*; **ges·tic′u·lat·ing,** *pr.p.* —**ges·tic′u·la′tion,** *n.*

ges·ture (jes′chər), *n.* **1.** a motion made with some part of the body, especially the hands or arms, to show some idea or feeling. **2.** anything said or done to show one's feelings; often, something done just for effect, and not really meant [Their gift was a *gesture* of friendship. He made a *gesture* of welcoming us.] —*v.* to make a gesture or gestures. —**ges′tured,** *p.t. & p.p.*; **ges′tur·ing,** *pr.p.*

get (get), *v.* **1.** to become the owner of by receiving, buying, earning, etc.; gain; obtain [We *got* a new car. He *got* a raise in salary.] **2.** to arrive at; reach [They *got* home late.] **3.** to reach by telephone, radio, television, etc. **4.** to go and bring [*Get* my slippers for me.] **5.** to catch [John often *gets* colds.] **6.** to make willing; persuade [*Get* her to sing for us.] **7.** to cause to be [We can't *get* the door shut. He *got* his hands dirty.] **8.** to be or become [He *got* caught in the rain. Don't *get* angry.] **9.** to make ready; prepare [She's *getting* dinner.] **10.** to be forced or obliged: *used only in everyday talk, with* have *or* has [He's *got* to pass this test.] **11.** to own or possess: *used only in everyday talk, with* have *or* has [He's *got* ten dollars.] **12.** to become the master of;

overpower; strike, kill, puzzle, master, etc.: *used only in everyday talk* [The blow *got* him in the eye. The hunter *got* two birds. This problem *gets* me. Did you *get* the point of the joke?] **13.** to notice: *a slang use* [*Get* the look on his face!] —**get along, 1.** to go on or go away. **2.** to manage or succeed. **3.** to agree. —**get around, 1.** to move from place to place. **2.** to become known, as news. **3.** to avoid or overcome, as a difficulty. **4.** to flatter in order to gain something. —**get away, 1.** to go away. **2.** to escape. **3.** to start. —**get away with,** to manage to do without being found out or punished: *a slang phrase.* —**get by,** to manage or succeed. —**get down to,** to begin. —**get in, 1.** to enter. **2.** to arrive. **3.** to put in. —**get off, 1.** to come off or out of. **2.** to go away. **3.** to take off. **4.** to escape or to help to escape. **5.** to start. —**get on, 1.** to go on or into. **2.** to put on. **3.** to grow older. **4.** to agree. **5.** to manage or succeed. —**get out, 1.** to go out. **2.** to go away. **3.** to become known. **4.** to publish. —**get out of,** to escape or avoid. —**get over, 1.** to recover from, as an illness. **2.** to forget about. —**get through,** to finish. —**get together,** to bring or come together. —**get up, 1.** to rise, as from a chair or from sleep. **2.** to organize. —**got,** *p.t.;* **got** or **got′ten,** *p.p.;* **get′ting,** *pr.p.* —**get′ter,** *n.*

get·a·way (get′ə wā), *n.* **1.** the act of starting, as in a race. **2.** an escape.

Geth·sem·a·ne (geth sem′ə nē), *n.* the garden near Jerusalem where, according to the Bible, Jesus was betrayed and arrested.

get-to·geth·er (get′tə geth′ər), *n.* a small meeting or party.

Get·tys·burg (get′iz bûrg′), *n.* a town in southern Pennsylvania. An important battle of the Civil War was fought there in 1863.

get-up (get′up′), *n.* **1.** costume or dress [Her old-fashioned *get-up* amused the crowd.] **2.** the energy to get things done. *Used only in everyday talk.*

gew·gaw (gyōō′gô), *n.* something showy but useless and of little value; trinket.

gey·ser (gī′zər), *n.* a spring that shoots streams of boiling water and steam up into the air from time to time.

Gha·na (gä′nə), *n.* a country in western Africa that is a member of the British Commonwealth of Nations.

ghast·ly (gast′lē), *adj.* **1.** horrible or frightening [a *ghastly* sight]. **2.** like a ghost; pale and wan [The prisoner looked *ghastly.*]. **3.** very bad: *used only in everyday talk* [a *ghastly* mistake]. —**ghast′li·er,** *compar.;* **ghast′li·est,** *superl.* —**ghast′li·ness,** *n.*

geyser

gher·kin (gûr′kin), *n.* a small pickled cucumber.

ghet·to (get′ō), *n.* **1.** the section of some European cities where Jews were once forced to live. **2.** any section of a city in which a particular group of people live or are forced to live. —**ghet′tos,** *pl.*

ghost (gōst), *n.* **1.** the spirit of a dead person, supposedly seen as a pale and shadowy form that can pass through solid walls [an old house haunted by *ghosts*]. **2.** a mere shadow or slight trace [not a *ghost* of a chance]. —**give up the ghost,** to die.

ghost·ly (gōst′lē), *adj.* of or like a ghost [a *ghostly* paleness; *ghostly* tales]. —**ghost′li·er,** *compar.;* **ghost′li·est,** *superl.*

ghoul (gōōl), *n.* **1.** a supposed evil spirit that robs graves and feeds on the dead. **2.** a person who robs graves. **3.** a person who enjoys things that trouble or disgust most people. —**ghoul′ish,** *adj.* —**ghoul′ish·ness,** *n.*

GI or **G.I.** (jē′ī′), *n.* an enlisted person in the United States Army. —*adj.* of or having to do with the army or army life. This term is an abbreviation for *government issue* (clothing or supplies passed out to soldiers). *Used only in everyday talk.*

gi·ant (jī′ənt), *n.* **1.** an imaginary being that looks like a man but is many times larger and stronger. **2.** a person or thing that is especially large, strong, etc. [Our teacher is a mental *giant*.] —*adj.* very great in size or power [*giant* strides]. —**gi′ant·ess,** *n.fem.*

gib·ber (jib′ər), *v.* to talk or chatter in a confused or meaningless way [Monkeys *gibber.*]

gib·ber·ish (jib′ər ish), *n.* confused or meaningless talk or chatter.

gib·bet (jib′it), *n.* a kind of gallows on which the bodies of criminals were hung after they had been put to death. —*v.* to hang on a gibbet.

gib·bon (gib′ən), *n.* a small ape of the East Indies and southeastern Asia, with very long arms and no tail.

gibe (jīb), *v.* to make fun of; scoff; taunt; jeer. —*n.* a jeering remark; taunt. —**gibed,** *p.t. & p.p.;* **gib′ing,** *pr.p.*

gib·lets (jib′lits), *n.pl.* the parts inside a fowl that can be used as food, as the gizzard, heart, and liver.

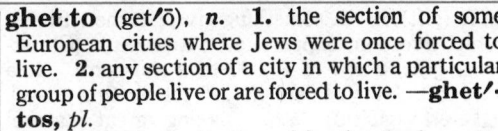

gibbon (3 ft. high)

Gi·bral·tar (ji brôl′tər), *n.* a British colony and fortress on a huge rock in southern Spain at the entrance to the Mediterranean.

gid·dy (gid′ē), *adj.* **1.** feeling as though things were whirling about; dizzy [Climbing ladders makes her *giddy.*] **2.** making one dizzy [a *giddy* ride on a roller coaster]. **3.** turning from one thing to another in a light and silly way; not serious about things; flighty [a *giddy* young girl]. —**gid′di·er,** *compar.;* **gid′di·est,** *superl.* —**gid′di·ly,** *adv.* —**gid′di·ness,** *n.*

---

fat, āpe, cär, ten, ēven, hit, bīte, gō, hôrn, tōōl, book, up, fûr;
get, joy, yet, chin, she, thin, *th*en; zh = s in pleasure; ′ as in able (ā′b'l);
ə = a in ago, e in agent, i in sanity, o in confess, u in focus.

gift (gift), *n.* **1.** something given to show friendship, affection, support, etc.; a present [Christmas *gifts;* a *gift* of $5,000 to a museum]. **2.** a natural ability; talent [a *gift* for writing plays].

gift·ed (gif′tid), *adj.* having great natural ability; talented [a *gifted* child violinist].

gig (gig), *n.* **1.** a light, open carriage with two wheels, pulled by one horse. **2.** a ship's small boat, used to carry the captain to and from the ship.

gi·gan·tic (jī gan′tik), *adj.* like a giant in size; very big; huge; enormous [a *gigantic* building].

gig·gle (gig′'l), *v.* to laugh with high, quick sounds in a silly or nervous way, as if trying to hold back. —*n.* such a laugh. —**gig′gled,** *p.t. & p.p.;* **gig′gling,** *pr.p.* —**gig′gly,** *adj.*

Gi·la monster (hē′lə), a poisonous lizard of the Southwest. It has a thick body covered by beady scales that are black and orange.

Gil·bert and Sul·li·van (gil′bərt 'n sul′ə-vən), English writers of many comic operettas in the last part of the 19th century. Gilbert wrote the words and Sullivan wrote the music.

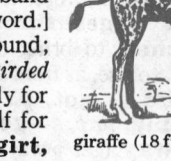
Gila monster (1½ ft. long)

gild (gild), *v.* **1.** to cover with a thin layer of gold. **2.** to make something seem better than it really is. —**gild′ed** or **gilt,** *p.t. & p.p.;* **gild′ing,** *pr.p.*

gild (gild), *n.* same as **guild.**

Gil·e·ad (gil′i əd), *n.* a mountainous region in ancient Palestine, east of the Jordan River.

gill (gil), *n.* the organ for breathing of most animals that live in water, as fish, lobsters, etc. As water passes through them, the gills remove oxygen from it.

gill (jil), *n.* a measure of liquids, equal to 1/4 pint. A gill is half a cup.

gilt (gilt), a past tense and past participle of **gild.** —*n.* a thin layer of gold or a gold-colored paint, used to cover a surface. —*adj.* covered with gilt.

gim·crack (jim′krak), *n.* a thing that is bright and showy but of little or no use.

gim·let (gim′lət), *n.* a small tool used to bore holes. *See the picture.*

gim·mick (gim′ik), *n.* a clever gadget, trick, or idea: *a slang word.*

gin (jin), *n.* a strong alcoholic liquor that is flavored with juniper berries.

gin (jin), *n.* a machine for taking the seeds out of cotton: *its full name is* **cotton gin.** —*v.* to put cotton through a gin. —**ginned,** *p.t. & p.p.;* **gin′ning,** *pr.p.*

gimlet

gin·ger (jin′jər), *n.* **1.** a spice made from the root of a tropical plant. **2.** this root. **3.** energy or vigor: *used only in everyday talk.*

ginger ale, a sweet drink made of soda water flavored with ginger.

gin·ger·bread (jin′jər bred), *n.* **1.** a dark cake flavored with ginger and molasses, often baked in fancy shapes. **2.** fancy decoration.

gin·ger·ly (jin′jər lē), *adv.* in a timid and very careful way [She lifted the trap *gingerly.*] —*adj.* very careful; timid [a *gingerly* step forward].

gin·ger·snap (jin′jər snap), *n.* a crisp cooky flavored with ginger and molasses.

ging·ham (ging′əm), *n.* a light cotton cloth, woven in colored checks, plaids, or stripes.

gin rummy (jin), a form of the card game rummy, for two players.

gin·seng (jin′seng), *n.* the root of a plant found in China and North America, used in medicine by the Chinese.

gip·sy (jip′sē), *n.* same as **gypsy.**

gi·raffe (jə raf′), *n.* a large animal of Africa, that chews its cud. It has a very long neck and legs and a spotted coat, and is the tallest animal alive.

gird (gŭrd), *v.* **1.** to put a belt or band around. **2.** to fasten with a belt or band [Lancelot *girded* on his sword.] **3.** to form a circle around; surround [Farmlands *girded* the castle.] **4.** to get ready for action [He *girded* himself for battle.] —**gird′ed** or **girt,** *p.t. & p.p.;* **gird′ing,** *pr.p.*

giraffe (18 ft. high)

gird·er (gŭr′dər), *n.* a long beam of steel or wood used to support some part in a building, bridge, etc.

gir·dle (gŭr′d'l), *n.* **1.** a belt. **2.** a light, elastic corset worn to support the waist and hips. **3.** anything that surrounds like a belt. —*v.* to surround; encircle. —**gir′dled,** *p.t. & p.p.;* **gir′dling,** *pr.p.*

girders

girl (gŭrl), *n.* **1.** a female child or a young, unmarried woman. **2.** any woman: *used only in everyday talk.* **3.** a man's sweetheart: *used only in everyday talk.*

girl·hood (gŭrl′hood), *n.* the time of being a girl.

girl·ish (gŭr′lish), *adj.* of, like, or fit for a girl. —**girl′ish·ly,** *adv.* —**girl′ish·ness,** *n.*

girl scout, a member of the **Girl Scouts,** a club for girls that trains them in outdoor skills and in citizenship.

girt (gŭrt), a past tense and past participle of **gird.**

girth (gŭrth), *n.* **1.** the distance around a waist, tree trunk, etc. **2.** a band put around the middle of a horse to hold the saddle in place.

gist (jist), *n.* the main point or idea of a story, speech, article, etc.

give (giv), *v.* **1.** to pass or hand over to another [*Give* me your coat and I'll hang it up.] **2.** to hand over to another to keep; make a gift of [Uncle Joe *gave* me this book for my birthday.]

3. to cause to have [Music *gives* most people pleasure.] **4.** to be the source of; supply [Cows *give* milk.] **5.** to part with; sacrifice [He *gave* his life for his country.] **6.** to say or state; utter [Please *give* me your answer.] **7.** to perform; present [to *give* a concert]. **8.** to yield or move because of pressure or force [He tugged so hard that the drawer suddenly *gave*.] —*n.* the quality of yielding, bending, or moving because of pressure; a being elastic [This mattress doesn't have much *give*.] —**give away, 1.** to hand over as a present. **2.** to make known; reveal; tell, as a secret: *used only in everyday talk.* —**give back,** to return. —**give in,** to stop fighting or resisting; surrender; yield. —**give off** or **give forth,** to send out; emit, as a smell. —**give out, 1.** to make known. **2.** to hand out; distribute. **3.** to become worn out or used up. —**give up, 1.** to hand over; yield. **2.** to stop doing something [to *give up* smoking]. **3.** to stop trying; admit that one has failed. **4.** to lose hope for. —**gave,** *p.t.*; **giv′en,** *p.p.*; **giv′ing,** *pr.p.* —**giv′er,** *n.*

give·a·way (giv′ə wā), *n.* **1.** something made known or revealed, as a secret. **2.** something given free or sold cheap in order to try to get customers. *Used only in everyday talk.*

giv·en (giv′′n), past participle of **give.** —*adj.* **1.** in the h abit of; accustomed; inclined [He is *given* to walking after dinner.] **2.** that has been mentioned or decided upon [He did not finish within the *given* period.]

given name, a person's first name [John Brown's *given name* is John.]

giz·zard (giz′ərd), *n.* the second stomach of a bird, where the food is ground up again.

gla·cial (glā′shəl), *adj.* of or like ice or glaciers [a *glacial* period].

gla·cier (glā′shər), *n.* a large mass of snow and ice that moves slowly down a mountain or across land until it melts. Icebergs are pieces of a glacier that have broken away into the sea.

glad (glad), *adj.* **1.** feeling or showing joy; happy; pleased [the *glad* winners]. **2.** causing joy; pleasing [*glad* news]. **3.** very willing [I'm *glad* to help.] **4.** bright or beautiful [a *glad* summer day]. —**glad′er,** *compar.*; **glad′dest,** *superl.* —**glad′ly,** *adv.* —**glad′ness,** *n.*

glad·den (glad′′n), *v.* to make or become glad.

glade (glād), *n.* an open space in a forest.

glad·i·a·tor (glad′i ā′tər), *n.* **1.** a man, usually a slave or captive, who fought against animals or other men in the arenas of ancient Rome, for the entertainment of the public. **2.** any person taking part in a dispute.

glad·i·a·to·ri·al (glad′i ə tôr′i əl), *adj.* of gladiators or their fights.

glad·i·o·la (glad′i ō′lə), *n.* a gladiolus.

gladiators

glad·i·o·lus (glad′i ō′ləs), *n.* a plant related to the iris, with sword-shaped leaves and tall spikes of showy flowers. —**glad′i·o′lus·es** or **glad·i·o·li** (glad′i ō′lī), *pl.*

glad·some (glad′səm), *adj.* full of joy or giving joy; joyful; cheerful.

glam·our or **glam·or** (glam′ər), *n.* mysterious beauty or charm; strange attraction [the *glamour* of faraway lands]. —**glam′or·ous,** *adj.*

gladiolus

glance (glans), *v.* **1.** to strike at a slant and go off at an angle [The hail *glanced* off the roof.] **2.** to give a quick look [She *glanced* in my direction.] **3.** to flash or gleam [The sunlight *glanced* off their shields.] —*n.* **1.** a glancing off. **2.** a flash or gleam. **3.** a quick look. —**glanced,** *p.t. & p.p.*; **glanc′ing,** *pr.p.*

gland (gland), *n.* a part of the body that takes certain things from the blood and changes them into a substance that the body can use or throw off [The liver, kidneys, and thyroid are *glands*. Bile, milk, and sweat are produced by *glands*.]

glan·du·lar (glan′joo lər), *adj.* of, like, or containing glands.

glare (gler), *v.* **1.** to shine with a light so bright that it hurts the eyes. **2.** to stare in an angry way. —*n.* **1.** a strong, blinding light. **2.** an angry stare. **3.** a smooth, glassy surface [The streets are a *glare* of ice.] —**glared,** *p.t. & p.p.*; **glar′ing,** *pr.p.*

glar·ing (gler′ing), *adj.* **1.** shining so brightly that it hurts the eyes [*glaring* headlights]. **2.** too bright and showy [*glaring* colors]. **3.** staring in an angry way [*glaring* eyes]. **4.** standing out so that it cannot be overlooked [a *glaring* mistake]. —**glar′ing·ly,** *adv.*

Glas·gow (glas′gō), *n.* a city in west central Scotland.

glass (glas), *n.* **1.** a hard substance that breaks easily and that lets light through. It is made by melting together sand, soda or potash, lime, etc. **2.** an article made of glass, as a container for drinking, a mirror, or a windowpane. **3. glasses,** *pl.* eyeglasses or binoculars. **4.** the amount that a drinking glass holds [He drank two *glasses* of milk.] —*v.* to enclose or cover with glass. —*adj.* made of glass.

glass·ful (glas′fool), *n.* the amount that will fill a drinking glass. —**glass′fuls,** *pl.*

glass·ware (glas′wer), *n.* things made of glass.

glass·y (glas′ē), *adj.* **1.** like glass; smooth, clear, etc. **2.** having a dull or lifeless look [a *glassy* stare]. —**glass′i·er,** *compar.*; **glass′i·est,** *superl.* —**glass′i·ness,** *n.*

glaze (glāz), *v.* **1.** to give a hard, shiny finish to [to *glaze* pottery]. **2.** to cover with a sugar coating [to *glaze* doughnuts]. **3.** to make or become glassy [His eyes were *glazed* from lack

of sleep.] **4.** to fit with glass, as a window. —*n.*
1. a glassy coating, as on pottery. **2.** anything
used to form such a coating. —**glazed,** *p.t. &*
p.p.; **glaz′ing,** *pr.p.*

gla·zier (glā′zhər), *n.* a person whose work is
fitting glass in window frames, etc.

gleam (glēm), *n.* **1.** a faint light or one that
lasts only a short time [the *gleam* of dying embers].
2. a shining of brightness, as from a polished
surface. **3.** a faint show or sign [a *gleam* of hope].
—*v.* to shine with a gleam [We polished the car
until it *gleamed.*]

glean (glēn), *v.* **1.** to gather the grain left on a
field after the reapers are through. **2.** to collect
facts, information, etc. bit by bit. —**glean′er,**
n.

glee (glē), *n.* **1.** lively joy; merriment [to laugh
in *glee*]. **2.** a song for three or more voices singing
in harmony, usually without accompaniment.

glee club, a group formed to sing part songs.
glee·ful (glē′fəl), *adj.* full of glee; merry.

glen (glen), *n.* a small, narrow valley in a lonely
place in the hills.

glib (glib), *adj.* speaking or spoken in a smooth,
easy way, often in a way that cannot easily be
believed [a *glib* lawyer; *glib* flattery]. —**glib′-**
ber, *compar.;* **glib′best,** *superl.* —**glib′ly,**
adv. —**glib′ness,** *n.*

glide (glīd), *v.* **1.** to move along in a smooth and
easy way, as in skating. **2.** to go on from one
thing to another without a break [Time *glides*
by.] —*n.* the act of gliding; smooth, easy motion.
—**glid′ed,** *p.t. & p.p.;* **glid′ing,** *pr.p.*

glid·er (glīd′ər), *n.* **1.** a person or thing that
glides. **2.** an aircraft like an airplane except that
it has no engine and is carried along by air currents. **3.** a porch seat hung in a frame so that it
can swing back and forth.

glim·mer (glim′ər), *v.* to give a faint and unsteady light [The stars *glimmered* in the sky.]
—*n.* **1.** a faint and unsteady light. **2.** a faint
show or sign, as of hope.

glimpse (glimps), *v.* **1.** to get a quick look at
[We *glimpsed* the President as his car sped by.]
2. to look quickly; glance [to *glimpse* at a book].
—*n.* **1.** a quick look; passing glance. **2.** a faint
trace or notion [I can see *glimpses* of your mother
in you.] —**glimpsed,** *p.t. & p.p.;* **glimps′-**
ing, *pr.p.*

glint (glint), *n.* a gleam or flash [a *glint* of mischief in his eyes]. —*v.* to gleam or flash.

glis·ten (glis′'n), *v.* to shine or sparkle, as fresh
snow or a well-polished surface.

glis·ter (glis′tər), *v. & n.* same as **glitter:**
now seldom used.

glit·ter (glit′ər), *v.* **1.** to shine with a sparkling
light [The Christmas tree *glittered* with tinsel.]
2. to be showy and bright [His speech *glittered*
with wit.] —*n.* **1.** a sparkling light [the *glitter*
of gold]. **2.** showiness or brightness; splendor.
—**glit′ter·y,** *adj.*

gloam·ing (glōm′ing), *n.* the dusk of evening.
gloat (glōt), *v.* to feel a mean or greedy kind of
pleasure [to *gloat* over another's misfortunes; to
gloat over one's jewels].

glo·bal (glō′b'l), *adj.* **1.** having the shape of a
globe. **2.** involving the whole world; world-wide
[*global* warfare].

globe (glōb), *n.* **1.** anything shaped like a ball;
sphere. **2.** the earth. **3.** a
round model of the earth
showing the continents, oceans,
etc.

glob·u·lar (gläb′yoo lər), *adj.*
1. shaped like a globe; round.
2. made up of many globules
[Caviar is a *globular* mass of
fish eggs.]

glob·ule (gläb′yool), *n.* a
tiny globe or ball, as a small
drop of liquid.

globe

glock·en·spiel (gläk′ən spēl), *n.* a musical instrument with tuned
metal bars in a frame,
played with one or two
hammers.

gloom (gloom), *n.* **1.**
dimness of light; gray
darkness, as in a cave or
forest. **2.** deep sadness
or hopelessness.

gloom·y (gloom′ē), *adj.*
1. dark, dim, or dusky
[a *gloomy* dungeon]. **2.** having or giving a feeling
of deep sadness [a *gloomy* mood; a *gloomy* story].
—**gloom′i·er,** *compar.;* **gloom′i·est,** *superl.*
—**gloom′i·ly,** *adv.* —**gloom′i·ness,** *n.*

glockenspiel

glo·ri·fy (glôr′ə fī), *v.* **1.** to give glory to; make
splendid [His deeds have *glorified* his name.]
2. to praise in worship [to *glorify* God]. **3.** to
make seem better or more beautiful [Old soldiers
often *glorify* war.] —**glo′ri·fied,** *p.t. & p.p.;*
glo′ri·fy·ing, *pr.p.* —**glo′ri·fi·ca′tion,** *n.*

glo·ri·ous (glôr′i əs), *adj.* **1.** giving, having, or
deserving glory or honor [a *glorious* act of brav-
ery]. **2.** beautiful in a rich and splendid way;
magnificent [a *glorious* symphony]. **3.** very
pleasant or enjoyable: *only in everyday talk.*

glo·ry (glôr′ē), *n.* **1.** great praise or fame for
doing something fine [Edison's inventions brought
him *glory*.] **2.** worship or praise [*Glory* be to
God.] **3.** the condition of being very famous and
successful. **4.** great beauty, power, or splendor
[the *glory* that was ancient Greece]. —*v.* to be
very proud or joyful [to *glory* in one's victory].
—**gone to glory,** dead. —**in one's glory,**
at one's best, happiest, most successful, etc.
—**glo′ries,** *pl.* —**glo′ried,** *p.t. & p.p.;* **glo′ry-**
ing, *pr.p.*

gloss (glôs), *n.* **1.** a polish or shine on the surface.
2. a smooth and pleasant look that hides something bad or wrong. —*v.* **1.** to put a shine on.
2. to pass over, cover, or hide something bad or
wrong [to *gloss* over a mistake with a joke.]

glos·sa·ry (gläs′ər ē), *n.* a list of hard words
with their meanings, often printed at the end of a
book. —**glos′sa·ries,** *pl.*

gloss·y (glôs′ē), *adj.* smooth and shining.
—**glos′si·er,** *compar.;* **glos′si·est,** *superl.*
—**glos′si·ness,** *n.*

glot·tis (glät′is), *n.* the opening between the vocal cords in the larynx.

Glou·ces·ter (gläs′tər), *n.* **1.** a city in southwestern England. **2.** a fishing port in northeastern Massachusetts.

glove (gluv), *n.* **1.** a covering to protect the hand, with a separate part for each finger and the thumb [Surgeons wear rubber *gloves*. Padded *gloves* are worn in playing baseball.] **2.** a padded mitt worn in boxing. —*v.* to put gloves on. —**gloved**, *p.t. & p.p.;* **glov′ing**, *pr.p.*

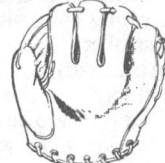

baseball glove

glow (glō), *v.* **1.** to give off light because of great heat; be red-hot or white-hot. **2.** to give out light without flame or heat [Fireflies *glowed* in the dark.] **3.** to show a warm or rosy color [cheeks *glowing* with health]. **4.** to show eagerness or excitement [His face *glowed* with delight.] —*n.* **1.** light given off as a result of great heat [the *glow* of a blast furnace]. **2.** light without flame or heat. **3.** warmth or brightness of color. **4.** warm or rosy look of the skin. **5.** a good or pleasant feeling.

glow·er (glou′ər), *v.* to stare in a fierce or angry way; scowl. —*n.* an angry stare.

glow·worm (glō′wurm), *n.* an insect without wings, or an insect larva, that glows in the dark, as the wingless female or the larva of the firefly.

glu·cose (glōō′kōs), *n.* **1.** a kind of sugar found in plants and animals; dextrose. **2.** a sweet sirup containing glucose, made from starch.

glue (glōō), *n.* **1.** a thick, sticky substance made by boiling animal hoofs and bones, used for sticking things together. **2.** any sticky substance like this. —*v.* **1.** to stick together with glue. **2.** to keep or hold without moving [The exciting movie kept us *glued* to our seats.] —**glued**, *p.t. & p.p.;* **glu′ing**, *pr.p.* —**glue′y**, *adj.*

glum (glum), *adj.* silent in a gloomy or sullen way. —**glum′mer**, *compar.;* **glum′mest**, *superl.* —**glum′ly**, *adv.* —**glum′ness**, *n.*

glut (glut), *v.* **1.** to stuff oneself with food. **2.** to supply with much more than is needed or wanted [The market was *glutted* with used cars.] —*n.* a supply that is greater than is needed. —**glut′ted**, *p.t. & p.p.;* **glut′ting**, *pr.p.*

glu·ten (glōō′t′n), *n.* a gray, sticky protein substance found in wheat flour.

glu·tin·ous (glōō′ti nəs), *adj.* sticky.

glut·ton (glut′′n), *n.* **1.** a person who stuffs himself with food in a greedy way. **2.** a person who is ready and willing to do or receive something [a *glutton* for hard work]. —**glut′ton·ous**, *adj.* —**glut′ton·y**, *n.*

glyc·er·in or **glyc·er·ine** (glis′ər in), *n.* a clear, sirupy liquid made from fats and oils and used in skin lotions, explosives, etc.

gnarl (närl), *n.* a knot or lump on the trunk or branch of a tree.

gnarled (närld), *adj.* full of gnarls or knobs; twisted and knotty [*gnarled* hands].

gnash (nash), *v.* to grind or strike the teeth together, as in anger or pain.

gnat (nat), *n.* a small insect with two wings, that bites or stings.

gnaw (nô), *v.* **1.** to bite and wear away bit by bit with the teeth [The rat *gnawed* the rope in two. The dog *gnawed* on the bone.] **2.** to make by gnawing [to *gnaw* a hole]. **3.** to keep on troubling for a long time [Jealousy *gnawed* at his heart.] —**gnawed**, *p.t.;* **gnawed** or **gnawn** (nôn), *p.p.;* **gnaw′ing**, *pr.p.*

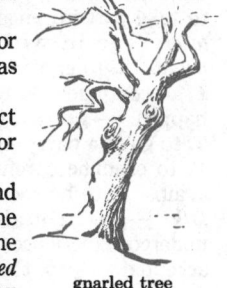

gnarled tree

gneiss (nīs), *n.* a rock that has a coarse grain and looks like granite.

gnome (nōm), *n.* a dwarf in folk tales who lives inside the earth and guards the treasures there.

gnu (nōō *or* nyōō), *n.* a large African antelope with a head like an ox's and a long tail.

go (gō), *v.* **1.** to move along from one place, point, or person to another; pass or proceed [*Go* ten miles down the road. Time *goes* fast. The rumor *went* all over town.] **2.** to move away; leave; pass away; depart [The years come and *go*. Has the pain *gone?*] **3.** to fail; become worse [His hearing is *going*.] **4.** to be given or sold [The prize *goes* to Jean. The chair *went* for $30.] **5.** to turn out; result [Our plans *went* wrong.] **6.** to be or become [to *go* hungry for days; to *go* mad]. **7.** to work or run, as a clock, machine, etc. does. **8.** to be worded, told, sung, etc. [How does that poem *go?*] **9.** to make a certain motion, sound, etc. [The gun *went* "bang."] **10.** to put oneself [He *went* to a lot of trouble.] **11.** to begin or take part in a certain activity [Will you *go* to college? Let's *go* swimming.] **12.** to belong in a certain place [The brooms *go* in that closet.] **13.** to fit or suit [Does this belt *go* well with my dress?] —*n.* **1.** a success [He made a *go* of his business.] **2.** energy or liveliness: *used only in everyday talk* [He has plenty of *go*.] **3.** a try: *used only in everyday talk* [Let me have a *go* at it.] —**go along, 1.** to continue. **2.** to agree. **3.** to accompany. —**go at,** to attack or work at. —**go back on, 1.** to betray. **2.** to break, as a promise. *Used only in everyday talk.* —**go beyond,** to do more than; exceed. —**go by, 1.** to pass. **2.** to be overlooked. **3.** to be guided by. **4.** to be known by a certain name. —**go for, 1.** to try to get. **2.** to support. **3.** to

gnu (4½ ft. high at shoulder)

attack: *used only in everyday talk.* **4.** to be attracted by: *slang in this meaning.* —**go in for,** to take part in; engage in: *used only in everyday talk.* —**go in with,** to join. —**go off, 1.** to leave. **2.** to explode. **3.** to happen. —**go on, 1.** to continue. **2.** to behave. **3.** to take place; happen. —**go out, 1.** to come to an end; stop. **2.** to go to a party, the theater, etc. —**go over, 1.** to examine carefully. **2.** to do or look over again. **3.** to be successful: *used only in everyday talk.* —**go through, 1.** to do thoroughly. **2.** to undergo; experience. **3.** to search. **4.** to become accepted. —**go through with,** to complete. —**go together, 1.** to suit or fit one another. **2.** to be sweethearts: *used only in everyday talk.* —**go without,** to do without. —**let go, 1.** to let escape. **2.** to stop holding. **3.** to give up; abandon. —**let oneself go,** to stop holding back in one's feelings or actions. —**no go,** not possible; no use: *used only in everyday talk.* —**on the go,** always moving about or doing something: *used only in everyday talk.* —**went,** *p.t.;* **gone,** *p.p.;* **go′ing,** *pr.p.*

goad (gōd), *n.* **1.** a stick with a sharp point, used in driving oxen. **2.** anything that drives a person to do something; spur. —*v.* to drive with a goad; urge on [*goaded* into a rage by insults].

goal (gōl), *n.* **1.** the place at which a race or trip is ended. **2.** an end that one tries to reach; aim or purpose [Her *goal* was to be a nurse.] **3.** the line, net, etc. in certain games over or into which the ball or puck must go to score; also, a score made in this way.

goal·ie (gōl′ē), *n.* a goalkeeper.

goal·keep·er (gōl′kēp′ər), *n.* a player who defends the goal for his team in a game.

goal post, either of a pair of posts with a crossbar, used as the goal in football, soccer, etc.

goalkeeper in ice hockey

goat (gōt), *n.* **1.** an animal that chews its cud and is related to the sheep. It has horns that curve backward, a lean body, and straight hair. **2.** short for **scapegoat.**

goat·ee (gō tē′), *n.* a pointed beard on a man's chin.

goat·herd (gōt′hŭrd), *n.* a person who herds or tends goats.

goat·skin (gōt′skin), *n.* **1.** the skin of a goat. **2.** leather made from this. **3.** a container for wine or water made from this leather.

gob·ble (gäb′'l), *n.* the throaty sound made by a male turkey. —*v.* to make this sound. —**gob′bled,** *p.t. & p.p.;* **gob′bling,** *pr.p.*

gob·ble (gäb′'l), *v.* to eat quickly and greedily. —**gob′bled,** *p.t. & p.p.;* **gob′bling,** *pr.p.*

gob·bler (gäb′lər), *n.* a male turkey.

go-be·tween (gō′bi twēn′), *n.* a person who deals with each of two sides in making arrangements between them.

Go·bi (gō′bē), *n.* a large desert in Mongolia.

gob·let (gäb′lət), *n.* a drinking glass with a base and stem.

gob·lin (gäb′lin), *n.* an ugly little elf or spirit in folk tales, that is full of mischief.

goblet

go·cart (gō′kärt), *n.* a small carriage pushed by hand, in which a young child sits to be taken about; stroller.

god (gäd), *n.* **1.** a being that is worshiped for the special powers he is supposed to have over people and the world [Odin was the chief *god* of the Norsemen. Neptune was the Roman *god* of the sea.] **2. God,** in the Christian, Jewish, and Moslem religions, the all-powerful Being who made and rules the universe and is worshiped by man. **3.** any image or thing that is worshiped as a god; idol. **4.** any person or thing that one thinks of as being most important [Money is his *god*.]

god·child (gäd′chīld), *n.* a godson or goddaughter. —**god′chil′dren,** *pl.*

god·daugh·ter (gäd′dô′tər), *n.* a girl for whom a man or woman acts as godparent.

god·dess (gäd′is), *n.* **1.** a female god. **2.** a very beautiful or charming woman.

god·fa·ther (gäd′fä′thər), *n.* a man who pledges, as at the baptism of a child, that he will be responsible for its religious upbringing.

god·head (gäd′hed), *n.* **1.** the condition of being a god; divinity: also **god·hood** (gäd′hood). **2. Godhead,** God.

god·less (gäd′lis), *adj.* **1.** not believing in God. **2.** wicked; evil.

god·like (gäd′līk), *adj.* like or fit for God or a god; very noble or powerful; divine.

god·ly (gäd′lē), *adj.* serious and faithful in worshiping God; religious. —**god′li·er,** *compar.;* **god′li·est,** *superl.* —**god′li·ness,** *n.*

god·moth·er (gäd′muth′ər), *n.* a woman who serves in the same way as a godfather does.

god·par·ent (gäd′per′ənt), *n.* a godfather or godmother.

god·send (gäd′send), *n.* something that comes when needed the most, as if sent by God.

god·son (gäd′sun), *n.* a boy for whom a man or woman acts as godparent.

God·speed (gäd′spēd′), *n.* success; good luck. In olden days, one said "May God speed you" to a person starting a trip.

Goe·the, Jo·hann von (yō′hän fôn gŭr′tə), 1749–1832; German author.

gog·gle (gäg′'l), *v.* to stare with the eyes very wide open [He *goggled* at the odd sight.] —*adj.* bulging [*goggle* eyes]. —*n.* **goggles,** *pl.* large eyeglasses that fit tightly around the eyes to protect them from wind, dust, etc. —**gog′gled,** *p.t. & p.p.;* **gog′gling,** *pr.p.*

goggles

go·ing (gō′ing), *n.* **1.** the act or time of leaving; departure [the *goings* and comings of trains]. **2.** the condition of a road or path for traveling [The *going* was difficult through the mountain pass.] —*adj.* doing its work or business successfully [a *going* concern]. —be **going to,** to be planning to; will or shall.

goi·ter or **goi·tre** (goi′tər), *n.* **1.** a disease of the thyroid gland that causes a swelling in the front of the neck. **2.** this swelling.

gold (gōld), *n.* **1.** a heavy, yellow metal that is a chemical element. Gold is a precious metal and is used in coins and jewelry. It is easily beaten or stretched into different shapes. **2.** gold coins; also, money or wealth. **3.** a bright or shining yellow. —*adj.* **1.** of or containing gold [*gold* coins; a *gold* watch]. **2.** having the color of gold.

gold·en (gōl′d'n), *adj.* **1.** made of or containing gold [*golden* earrings]. **2.** bright-yellow [*golden* autumn leaves]. **3.** very good or valuable; excellent [a *golden* opportunity]. **4.** happy and flourishing [the *Golden* Age of Greece].

Golden Fleece, the magic fleece of gold in a Greek myth, that Jason captured from a dragon.

Golden Gate, the water passage between San Francisco Bay and the Pacific.

gold·en·rod (gōl′d'n räd), *n.* a common wild plant with small, yellow flowers on long stalks. It blooms at the end of the summer.

golden rule, the rule that a person should treat others in the same way that he wants them to treat him.

goldenrod

gold-filled (gōld′fild′), *adj.* covered with a thin layer of gold [a *gold-filled* ring].

gold·finch (gōld′finch), *n.* a small songbird related to the canary. The male has a yellow body with black markings.

gold·fish (gōld′fish), *n.* a small, yellow or orange fish, often kept in ponds or fish bowls.

gold·smith (gōld′smith), *n.* a skilled worker who makes things of gold.

golf (gôlf *or* gälf), *n.* a game played with a small, hard ball and a set of clubs on an outdoor course with 9 or 18 holes. The player tries to hit the ball into each of the holes in turn with the fewest possible strokes. —*v.* to play this game —**golf′-er,** *n.*

Gol·go·tha (gäl′gə thə), *n.* the place where Jesus was crucified; Calvary.

Go·li·ath (gə lī′əth), *n.* in the Bible, a giant killed by David using a sling.

man playing golf

gol·ly (gäl′ē), *interj.* an exclamation showing pleasure, surprise, wonder, etc.

Go·mor·rah or **Go·mor·rha** (gə môr′ə), *n.* a city told about in the Bible as being destroyed by fire from heaven because the people were wicked.

gon·do·la (gän′də lə), *n.* **1.** a long, narrow boat with high, pointed ends, used on the canals of Venice. **2.** a railroad freight car with low sides and no top. **3.** the cabin fastened to the underside of a balloon or blimp.

gon·do·lier (gän-də lir′), *n.* a man who rows or poles a gondola.

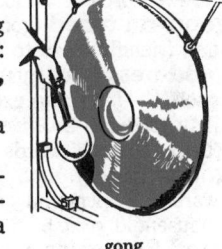
gondola

gone (gôn), past participle of **go.** —*adj.* **1.** moved away; departed. **2.** ruined, lost, dead, etc. **3.** used up.

gong (gông), *n.* a big metal disk that gives a loud, booming sound when struck.

goo (gōō), *n.* anything sticky, or sticky and sweet: *a slang word.* —**goo′ey,** *adj.*

goo·ber (gōō′bər), *n.* a peanut.

gong

good (good), *adj.* **1.** better than the usual or average kind [*good* work; a *good* writer; a *good* grade]. **2.** right for the purpose; satisfactory [a cloth *good* for polishing]. **3.** pleasing or satisfying; enjoyable or happy [*good* news; a *good* time]. **4.** helpful; that benefits [Exercise is *good* for the health.] **5.** doing what is right or proper; well-behaved [a *good* child]. **6.** kind or friendly [a *good* neighbor]. **7.** in good condition; sound, fresh, etc. [*good* health; *good* eggs]. **8.** honorable or respected [a *good* name]. **9.** full or thorough [a *good* scolding]. **10.** great or large [a *good* many people]. **11.** at least; a little more than [She lost a *good* ten pounds.] —*n.* **1.** that which is good [to know *good* from evil]. **2.** benefit [for the *good* of all]. See also **goods.** —*interj.* a word spoken to show that one agrees or that one is pleased or satisfied. —**as good as,** nearly; practically. —**for good,** for all time or for the last time. —**good and,** very: *used only in everyday talk* [He's *good and* angry.] —**good for, 1.** able to last for. **2.** able to pay or give. —**make good, 1.** to repay or replace. **2.** to succeed. **3.** to carry out, as a promise or boast. —**no good,** useless or worthless. —**to the good,** as a profit or advantage. —**bet′ter,** *compar.;* **best,** *superl.*

good-by or **good·by** (good bī′), *interj. & n.* a word said when leaving someone; farewell [We said our *good-bys* quickly and left.] —**good-bys′** or **good·bys′,** *pl.*

fat,   āpe,   cär,   ten,   ēven,   hit,   bīte,   gō,   hôrn,   tōōl,   book,   up,   fŭr;
get,   joy,   yet,   chin,   she,   thin,   *then;*   zh = s in pleasure;   ′ as in able (ā′b'l).
ə = a in ago,   e in agent,   i in sanity,   o in confess,   u in focus.

good-bye or good·bye (good bī′), *interj.* & *n.* same as good-by. —good-byes′ or good·byes′, *pl.*

Good Friday, the Friday before Easter, observed as the anniversary of the Crucifixion.

good-heart·ed (good′här′tid), *adj.* kind and generous.

Good Hope, Cape of, a cape at the southern tip of Africa.

good-hu·mored (good′hyoo′mərd), *adj.* cheerful and agreeable [a *good-humored* mood].

good-look·ing (good′look′ing), *adj.* pleasing to look at; handsome.

good·ly (good′lē), *adj.* 1. rather large [a *goodly* sum of money]. 2. pleasing or handsome [a *goodly* lad]. —good′li·er, *compar.*; good′li·est, *superl.* —good′li·ness, *n.*

good·man (good′mən), *n.* a husband or master of a household; also, a title like "Mr.": *no longer used.* —good′men, *pl.*

good morning, good afternoon, good evening, good day, words of greeting or farewell used at various times of the day.

good-na·tured (good′nā′chərd), *adj.* pleasant and friendly; easy to get along with.

good·ness (good′nis), *n.* the condition of being good. —*interj.* an exclamation showing surprise [My *goodness! Goodness* me!]

good night, words of farewell at night.

goods (goodz), *n.pl.* 1. things made to be sold; wares. 2. personal property that can be moved [household *goods*]. 3. cloth; fabric [dress *goods*].

good Samaritan, any person who pities and helps others in an unselfish way.

good-sized (good′sīzd′), *adj.* big or fairly big; ample [a *good-sized* house].

good-tempered (good′tem′pərd), *adj.* cheerful and patient; not easily made angry.

good turn, a friendly and helpful act; favor.

good·wife (good′wīf), *n.* a wife or mistress of a household; also, a title like "Mrs.": *no longer used.* —good′wives, *pl.*

good will or good·will (good′wil′), *n.* 1. a feeling of kindness and friendliness. 2. the extra amount that a business is worth because of its good name and the trade it has built up.

good·y (good′ē), *n.* a candy, cake, or other sweet thing to eat. —*interj.* a child's exclamation showing delight. *This word is used only in everyday talk.* —good′ies, *pl.*

goose (goos), *n.* 1. a swimming bird that is like a duck but has a larger body and a longer neck; especially, the female. The male is called a *gander.* 2. the flesh of the goose, used as food. 3. a silly person. —cook one's goose, to spoil one's chances: *used only in everyday talk.* —geese, *pl.*

Canada geese (3 ft. long)

goose·ber·ry (goos′ber′ē), *n.* a small, round, sour berry used in making pies, jam, etc. It grows on a prickly shrub. —goose′ber′ries, *pl.*

goose flesh or goose pimples, a bumpy condition of the skin caused by cold or fear.

G.O.P., the Grand Old Party: *a name for the* Republican Party.

go·pher (gō′fər), *n.* 1. a furry animal like a large rat, with pouches in its cheeks. It lives in tunnels which it digs underground. 2. a striped ground squirrel of the prairies.

gopher (9 in. long)

gore (gôr), *n.* clotted blood from a wound.

gore (gôr), *v.* to stab or wound with a horn or tusk. —gored, *p.t.* & *p.p.*; gor′ing, *pr.p.*

gore (gôr), *n.* a piece of cloth shaped like a triangle, that is sewed into a skirt, sail, etc. to make it wider or fuller. —*v.* to put or sew a gore in. —gored, *p.t.* & *p.p.*; gor′ing, *pr.p*

gorge (gôrj), *n.* 1. a narrow pass or valley between steep cliffs or walls. 2. the throat or gullet. —*v.* to stuff with food in a greedy way [to *gorge* oneself with cake]. —make one's gorge rise, to make one disgusted or angry —gorged, *p.t.* & *p.p.*; gorg′ing, *pr.p.*

gor·geous (gôr′jəs), *adj.* bright and richly colored; splendid; magnificent [the *gorgeous* tail of a peacock]. —gor′geous·ly, *adv.*

Gor·gon (gôr′gən), *n.* in Greek myths, any of three sisters who had snakes instead of hair and were so horrible that anyone who looked at them turned to stone.

go·ril·la (gə ril′ə), *n.* the largest and strongest of the apes, found in African jungles.

gorse (gôrs), *n.* same as furze.

gor·y (gôr′ē), *adj.* 1. covered with gore; bloody. 2. full of bloodshed or killing [a *gory* mystery story]. —gor′i·er, *compar.*; gor′i·est, *superl.* —gor′i·ness, *n.*

gorilla (5 ft. high)

gosh (gäsh), *interj.* an exclamation showing surprise, wonder, etc.

gos·hawk (gäs′hôk), *n.* a large, swift hawk with short wings.

gos·ling (gäz′ling), *n.* a young goose.

gos·pel (gäs′p'l), *n.* 1. the teachings of Jesus and the Apostles. 2. Gospel, any of the first four books of the New Testament: *Matthew, Mark, Luke,* or *John.* 3. anything that is believed to be absolutely true [We accepted her story as *gospel.*]

gos·sa·mer (gäs′ə mər), *n.* 1. a fine cobweb or a thin thread from one. 2. a very thin, delicate cloth. —*adj.* light as a cobweb [*gossamer* wings].

gos·sip (gäs′əp), *n.* 1. small talk or chatter about someone, often about things heard from others but not known to be facts. 2. a person who spends much time in such talk. —*v.* to spread gossip. —gos′siped, *p.t.* & *p.p.*; gos′-sip·ing, *pr.p.* —gos′sip·y, *adj.*

got (gät), past tense and a past participle of **get.**

Goth (gäth), *n.* a member of the German tribes that conquered most of the Western Roman Empire in the 3d, 4th, and 5th centuries A.D.

Goth·ic (gäth′ik), *adj.* **1.** of the Goths or their language. **2.** of or describing a style of architecture common in western Europe from the 12th to the 16th centuries. *See the picture.* —*n.* **1.** the language of the Goths. **2.** Gothic architecture.

Gothic architecture

got·ten (gät′n), past participle of **get.**

gouge (gouj), *n.* a rounded chisel for scooping a groove or hollow in wood. —*v.* **1.** to scoop out with a gouge, the fingers, etc. **2.** to cheat out of money; also, to charge too high a price: *only in everyday talk.* —**gouged,** *p.t. & p.p.;* **goug′ing,** *pr.p.*

gou·lash (gōō′läsh), *n.* a beef or veal stew seasoned with paprika.

gourd (gôrd *or* goord), *n.* **1.** a vine with large fruit containing many seeds. Gourds belong to the same family as the squash and pumpkin. **2.** the fruit of this vine, not fit for eating but often dried and used for cups, bowls, etc.

gourds

gour·mand (goor′mənd *or* goor mȯn′), *n.* a person who is very fond of eating.

gour·met (goor′mā *or* goor mā′), *n.* a person who likes fine food and is a good judge of it.

gout (gout), *n.* a sickness in which there is swelling and pain in the joints, especially in the big toe. —**gout′y,** *adj.*

gov. or **Gov.,** abbreviations for **government** or **governor.**

gov·ern (guv′ərn), *v.* **1.** to have control over; rule; direct or manage [to *govern* a nation; to *govern* one's feelings]. **2.** to guide in action or thought; influence; determine [Newspapers help *govern* public opinion.] —**gov′ern·a·ble,** *adj.*

gov·ern·ess (guv′ər nis), *n.* a woman who is hired to teach and train a child or children in a private home.

gov·ern·ment (guv′ərn mənt *or* guv′ər mənt), *n.* **1.** control or rule, as over a country, city, etc. **2.** a system of ruling or controlling [a centralized *government;* republican *governments*]. **3.** all the people who control the affairs of a country, city, etc. [The French *government* moved to Vichy during World War II.] —**gov′ern·men′tal,** *adj.*

gov·er·nor (guv′ər nər), *n.* **1.** the person elected to be the head of a State of the United States. **2.** a person appointed to govern a province, territory, etc. **3.** any of the persons who direct some organization [the board of *governors* of a hospital]. **4.** a device in an engine, etc. that automatically controls its speed. —**gov′er·nor·ship′,** *n.*

govt. or **Govt.,** abbreviations for **government.**

gown (goun), *n.* **1.** a woman's dress. **2.** a nightgown. **3.** a dressing gown. **4.** a long, flowing robe worn by judges, ministers, college graduates, etc. —*v.* to dress in a gown.

gown worn by a college graduate

Gr., abbreviation for **Greece** or **Greek.**

gr., abbreviation for **grain** (or **grains**), **gram** (or **grams**), **gross,** or **grade.**

grab (grab), *v.* to seize or snatch suddenly; often, to take by force or in a selfish way. —*n.* **1.** the act of grabbing [He made a *grab* for the handle.] **2.** something grabbed. —**grabbed,** *p.t. & p.p.;* **grab′bing,** *pr.p.*

grab bag, any one of a number of closed bags containing some merchandise. Buyers pay a fixed price for each bag without knowing what is in it.

grace (grās), *n.* **1.** beauty or charm of form or in the way one moves [the *grace* of a statue; to dance with *grace*]. **2.** a pleasing quality or manner [She has all the social *graces.*] **3.** a sense of what is right and proper; decency [She had the *grace* to make her visit brief.] **4.** an extra period allowed for doing or paying something [We have a week of *grace* to pay the rent.] **5.** a short prayer asking a blessing or giving thanks for a meal. **6.** **Grace,** a title of respect in speaking to or about an archbishop, duke, or duchess. **7.** the love and favor that God shows toward man. **8.** **Graces,** *pl.* three sister goddesses in Greek myths who brought pleasure and beauty to life. —*v.* **1.** to bring honor to [The mayor *graced* our banquet with his presence.] **2.** to add grace or charm to; adorn [Paintings *graced* the walls.] —**fall from grace,** to do wrong; sin. —**in the bad graces of,** disliked by. —**in the good graces of,** liked by. —**with bad grace,** in an unwilling or sullen way. —**with good grace,** in a willing way. —**graced,** *p.t. & p.p.;* **grac′ing,** *pr.p.*

grace·ful (grās′fəl), *adj.* having grace, or beauty of form or movement. —**grace′ful·ly,** *adv.* —**grace′ful·ness,** *n.*

grace·less (grās′lis), *adj.* **1.** not showing any sense of what is right [a *graceless* thief]. **2.** without grace; not elegant; clumsy. —**grace′less·ly,** *adv.* —**grace′less·ness,** *n.*

gra·cious (grā′shəs), *adj.* **1.** kind, polite, and charming [a *gracious* hostess]. **2.** full of grace,

fat, āpe, cär, ten, ēven, hit, bīte, gō, hôrn, tōōl, book, up, fūr;
get, joy, yet, chin, she, thin, *th*en; zh = s in pleasure; ′ as in able (ā′b'l)
ə = a in ago, e in agent, i in sanity, o in confess, u in focus.

comfort, and charm [*gracious* living]. —*interj.* an expression showing surprise. —**gra′cious·ly,** *adv.* —**gra′cious·ness,** *n.*

grack·le (grak′'l), *n.* a kind of blackbird that is a little smaller than a crow.

gra·da·tion (grā dā′shən), *n.* **1.** a gradual change by steps or stages [a *gradation* of color from pink to deep red]. **2.** any of the steps or stages in a series.

grade (grād), *n.* **1.** any of the stages or steps in a series [Civil service jobs are usually arranged in *grades.*] **2.** a degree in a scale of rank or quality

purple grackle (1 ft. long)

[Which is the best *grade* of oranges?] **3.** any of the divisions of a school course, usually equal to one year [Jim is twelve years old and in the seventh *grade.*] **4.** a mark or score on a test or in a school course [His *grades* are mostly B's.] **5.** a group of people or class of things that are of the same grade, class, rank, etc. **6.** amount of slope, as in a road; also, a sloping part [The train went up a steep *grade.*] —*v.* **1.** to arrange in grades; sort [to *grade* apples]. **2.** to give a grade to, as on a test. **3.** to make ground level or slope it evenly. **4.** to change gradually [green *grading* into blue]. —**make the grade,** to succeed. —**grad′ed,** *p.t. & p.p.*; **grad′ing,** *pr.p.*

grade crossing, the place where railroad tracks cross other tracks or a road on the same level.

grade school, an elementary school.

grad·u·al (graj′oo əl), *adj.* taking place by degrees or changes that are so small that they can hardly be seen; little by little [a *gradual* return to health]. —**grad′u·al·ly,** *adv.*

grad·u·ate (graj′oo it), *n.* a person who has finished a course of study at a school or college and has been given a diploma or degree. —*adj.* **1.** that is a graduate [*Graduate* students work for degrees above the bachelor's.] **2.** of or for graduates [*graduate* courses]. —*v.* (graj′oo āt), **1.** to make or become a graduate of a school or college. **2.** to mark off with small lines for measuring [A thermometer is a tube *graduated* in degrees.] —**grad′u·at·ed,** *p.t. & p.p.*; **grad′u·at·ing,** *pr.p.* —**grad′u·a′tion,** *n.*

graft (graft), *n.* **1.** a shoot or bud of one plant or tree set into a cut made in another so as to grow there. **2.** the setting in of such a bud or shoot. **3.** a piece of skin, bone, etc. taken from one body or from a part of a body and set into another so as to grow there. **4.** the dishonest use of one's job, especially by a

types of plant graft

public official, to get money; also, money gotten in this way. —*v.* **1.** to set a graft into a plant or animal [to *graft* skin from the thigh onto the chest]. **2.** to get money by graft.

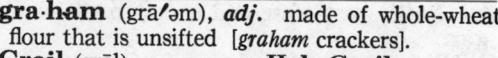

gra·ham (grā′əm), *adj.* made of whole-wheat flour that is unsifted [*graham* crackers].

Grail (grāl), *n.* same as **Holy Grail.**

grain (grān), *n.* **1.** the small, hard seed of any cereal plant, as wheat, corn, or rye. **2.** such cereal plants [fields of *grain*]. **3.** a single, tiny piece of salt, sugar, sand, or the like. **4.** a tiny bit [a *grain* of sense]. **5.** a very small unit of weight: one pound equals 7000 grains. **6.** the markings or pattern formed

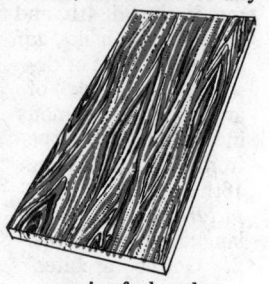

grain of a board

by the way the layers or fibers are arranged in a piece of wood, stone, etc. **7.** the way one thinks and feels; one's nature [The thought of stealing goes against my *grain.*] —*v.* to paint with marks that imitate the grain of wood, etc.

gram (gram), *n.* the basic unit of weight in the metric system. It equals about 1/28 of an ounce.

-gram (gram), a suffix meaning "something written or drawn" [A *cablegram* is a message written for sending by electric cable.]

gram·mar (gram′ər), *n.* **1.** the study of the forms of words and of the way they are arranged in sentences. **2.** a system of rules for speaking and writing a particular language. **3.** a book containing such rules. **4.** the way a person speaks or writes, as judged by these rules [His *grammar* is poor.]

gram·mar·i·an (grə mer′i ən), *n.* a person who has made a special study of grammar.

grammar school, 1. an elementary school: *an earlier term.* **2.** in England, a kind of high school.

gram·mat·i·cal (grə mat′i k'l), *adj.* of or according to the rules of grammar ["Between you and I" is a *grammatical* mistake.] —**gram·mat′i·cal·ly,** *adv.*

gramme (gram), *n.* gram: *a British spelling.*

gram·pus (gram′pəs), *n.* **1.** a small, fierce whale, called the killer whale. **2.** a kind of porpoise. —**gram′pus·es,** *pl.*

Gra·na·da (grə nä′də), *n.* a city in southern Spain.

gran·a·ry (gran′ə rē), *n.* a place or building for storing grain. —**gran′a·ries,** *pl.*

grand (grand), *adj.* **1.** standing out because of its great size and beauty [a *grand* mansion]. **2.** splendid and costly; luxurious [a *grand* banquet]. **3.** more important or higher in rank than others [a *grand* duke]. **4.** most important; main [the *grand* ballroom of the palace]. **5.** very dignified and noble; distinguished [the *grand* old statesman]. **6.** complete; full [a *grand* total of $200]. **7.** acting too important; haughty [She dismissed us with a *grand* wave of her hand.] **8.** very satisfying or pleasing: *used only in everyday talk.* —*n.* a thousand dollars: *a slang word.* —**grand′ly,** *adv.* —**grand′ness,** *n.*

gran·dam (gran′dam), *n.* a grandmother or other old woman: *a word no longer used.*

grand·aunt (grand'ant *or* grand'änt), *n.* an aunt of one's father or mother; great-aunt.

Grand Canyon, the deep gorge of the Colorado River, in northern Arizona.

grand·child (gran'chīld *or* grand'chīld), *n.* a grandson or granddaughter. **—grand'chil'dren,** *pl.*

grand·daugh·ter (gran'dô'tər *or* grand'dô'tər), *n.* a daughter of one's son or daughter.

gran·dee (gran dē'), *n.* **1.** a nobleman of the highest rank in Spain or Portugal. **2.** any person of high social rank.

gran·deur (gran'jər), *n.* **1.** great size, beauty, dignity, etc.; splendor [the *grandeur* of the Swiss Alps]. **2.** great power or high position.

grand·fa·ther (gran'fä'thər *or* grand'fä'thər), *n.* **1.** the father of one's father or mother. **2.** a forefather.

gran·dil·o·quent (gran dil'ə kwənt), *adj.* using long words and fancy language that sounds more important than it is. **—gran·dil'o·quence,** *n.*

gran·di·ose (gran'di ōs), *adj.* **1.** very grand in size, beauty, etc.; magnificent. **2.** seeming or trying to seem very grand or important without really being so.

grand jury, a jury of from 12 to 23 members that looks into cases of crime and suspected crime, and decides whether there is enough evidence to hold a trial before a regular jury.

grand·ma (gran'mä *or* grand'mä *or* gram'mä), *n.* grandmother: *used only in everyday talk.*

grand·moth·er (gran'muth'ər *or* grand'muth'ər), *n.* the mother of one's father or mother.

grand·neph·ew (gran'nef'yoo *or* grand'nef'yoo), *n.* a son of one's nephew or niece.

grand·niece (gran'nēs *or* grand'nēs), *n.* a daughter of one's nephew or niece.

grand·pa (gran'pä *or* grand'pä *or* gram'pä), *n.* grandfather: *used only in everyday talk.*

grand·par·ent (gran'per'ənt *or* grand'per'ənt), *n.* a grandfather or grandmother.

grand piano, a large piano with its strings lying flat in a case shaped like a harp.

Grand Rapids, a city in southwestern Michigan.

grand·sire (gran'sir *or* grand'sir), *n.* **1.** a grandfather or other old man. **2.** a forefather. *A word no longer used.*

grand·son (gran'sun *or* grand'sun), *n.* a son of one's son or daughter.

grand piano

grand·stand (gran'stand *or* grand'stand), *n.* the main seating place for people watching an outdoor sports event, as at a race track.

grand·un·cle (grand'ung'k'l), *n.* an uncle of one's father or mother; great-uncle.

grange (grānj), *n.* **1.** a farm with all its buildings. **2. Grange,** an association of farmers.

gran·ite (gran'it), *n.* a very hard rock used for buildings and monuments. It is usually gray or pink and can be polished like marble.

gran·ny *or* **gran·nie** (gran'ē), *n.* **1.** a grandmother. **2.** an old woman. *Used only in everyday talk.* **—gran'nies,** *pl.*

grant (grant), *v.* **1.** to give what is asked or wanted; let have; agree to [He *granted* permission for us to go.] **2.** to admit as true [I *grant* that you have reason to be angry.] **—n. 1.** the act of granting. **2.** something granted or given [a *grant* of $5,000 for study; land *grants* given by Congress for building railroads.] **—take for granted,** to think of as already proved or settled.

Grant, Ulysses S. (grant), 1822–1885; 18th president of the United States, from 1869 to 1877; commander in chief of the Union Army in the Civil War.

gran·u·lar (gran'yoo lər), *adj.* of, like, or containing grains or granules [*granular* sugar].

gran·u·late (gran'yoo lāt), *v.* to form into grains or granules [to *granulate* sugar]. **—gran'u·lat·ed,** *p.t. & p.p.;* **gran'u·lat·ing,** *pr.p.*

gran·ule (gran'yool), *n.* a small grain or tiny particle.

grape (grāp), *n.* **1.** a small fruit with a smooth skin, usually purple, red, or green, that grows in bunches on a woody vine. Grapes are eaten raw and are used to make wine and raisins. **2.** a grapevine. **3.** grapeshot.

grape·fruit (grāp'froot), *n.* a large, round citrus fruit with a yellow rind and a juicy, somewhat sour pulp.

grape·shot (grāp'shät), *n.* a bunch of small iron balls fired from a cannon in olden times.

grape·vine (grāp'vīn), *n.* **1.** a woody vine that grapes grow on. **2.** rumor or gossip [I hear by the *grapevine* that he's leaving town.]

graph (graf), *n.* a chart or diagram that shows the changes taking place in something, by the use of connected lines [a *graph* showing how sales figures vary during the year].

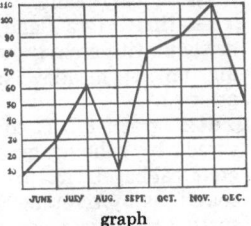

graph

-graph (graf), a suffix meaning: **1.** something written or recorded [A *photograph* is a picture recorded by a camera.] **2.** something that writes or records [A *seismograph* records earthquakes.]

graph·ic (graf'ik), *adj.* **1.** shown by a graph [a *graphic* record of the rainfall for a month]. **2.** told in a way that makes a sharp picture in the mind; vivid [The announcer gave a *graphic* account of the fire.] **3.** having to do with drawing, painting, engraving, etc. [the *graphic* arts]. **4.** of or shown in handwriting; written. **—graph'i·cal·ly,** *adv.*

fat,   āpe,   cär,   ten,   ēven,   hit,   bīte,   gō,   hôrn,   tool,   book,   up,   fūr;

get,   joy,   yet,   chin,   she,   thin,   *then;*   zh = s in pleasure;   ' as in able (ā'b'l);

ə = a in ago,   e in agent,   i in sanity,   o in confess,   u in focus.

graph·ite (graf′īt), *n.* a soft, black carbon used as the writing part of a pencil, as a lubricating powder, etc.

grap·nel (grap′n'l), *n.* **1.** a small anchor with several hooks. **2.** an iron piece with claws at one end for grasping and holding things.

grap·ple (grap′'l), *v.* **1.** to fight or struggle in a close or hard way [to *grapple* with a burglar; to *grapple* with a problem]. **2.** to grip or seize. —*n.* **1.** the act of grappling. **2.** a grapnel (*meaning* 2): also called **grappling iron. —grap′-pled,** *p.t. & p.p.;* **grap′-pling,** *pr.p.*

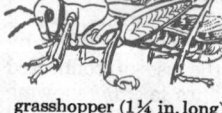
grapnel

grasp (grasp), *v.* **1.** to seize firmly with the hand; grip. **2.** to take hold of with the mind; understand [Did you *grasp* what he was trying to say?] —*n.* **1.** a grasping; grip of the hand [The fish squirmed from his *grasp* and fell into the water.] **2.** control or possession [land in the *grasp* of the enemy]. **3.** the ability to seize or reach [It is on the top shelf, beyond the baby's *grasp*.] **4.** understanding or knowledge [a good *grasp* of the subject]. —**grasp at, 1.** to try to seize. **2.** to take eagerly [I would *grasp* at the chance to go.]

grasp·ing (gras′ping), *adj.* eager to get more money, power, etc.; greedy.

grass (gras), *n.* **1.** the common green plants with narrow, pointed leaves that cover lawns and meadows [Grazing animals feed on *grass*.] **2.** a plant with narrow leaves, jointed stems, and clusters of seeds [Wheat, oats, bamboo, and sugar cane are *grasses*.] —**grass′y,** *adj.*

grass·hop·per (gras′häp′ər), *n.* a leaping insect with two pairs of wings and strong hind legs. It feeds on leafy plants.

grass·land (gras′land), *n.* land with grass growing on it; meadow or prairie.

grasshopper (1¼ in. long)

grate (grāt), *v.* **1.** to grind into small bits or shreds by rubbing against a rough surface [to *grate* cabbage]. **2.** to make a harsh or rasping sound, as by scraping [The wheel *grated* on the rusty axle. His voice *grated*.] **3.** to annoy or irritate [His boasting *grated* on us all.] —**grat′-ed,** *p.t. & p.p.;* **grat′ing,** *pr.p.*

grate (grāt), *n.* **1.** a frame of metal bars for holding fuel, as in a fireplace or furnace. **2.** a fireplace. **3.** a framework of bars set in a window or door. —*v.* to furnish with a grate. —**grat′-ed,** *p.t. & p.p.;* **grat′ing,** *pr.p.*

grate·ful (grāt′fəl), *adj.* **1.** feeling thankful or showing thanks. **2.** pleasing or welcome [a *grateful* blessing]. —**grate′ful·ly,** *adv.*

grat·er (grāt′ər), *n.* **1.** a person or thing that grates. **2.** a kitchen tool with a rough surface for grating vegetables, cheese, etc.

grat·i·fy (grat′ə fī), *v.* **1.** to make pleased or satisfied [Actors are *gratified* by applause.]

2. to give in to; indulge; humor [to spoil a child by *gratifying* his every wish]. —**grat′i·fied,** *p.t. & p.p.;* **grat′i·fy·ing,** *pr.p.* —**grat′i·fi·ca′tion,** *n.*

grat·ing (grāt′ing), *n.* a framework of bars set in a window or door; grate.

grat·ing (grāt′ing), *adj.* **1.** harsh and rasping in sound. **2.** irritating or annoying.

gra·tis (grā′tis *or* grat′is), *adv. & adj.* free of charge [This ticket will admit you *gratis*.]

grat·i·tude (grat′ə tōōd *or* grat′ə tyōōd), *n.* a being grateful for some favor; thankfulness.

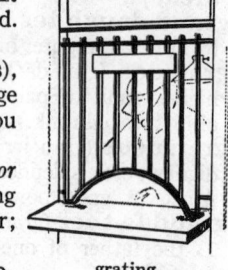
grating

gra·tu·i·tous (grə tōō′ə-təs), *adj.* **1.** given or gotten free [*gratuitous* lessons]. **2.** done without any good reason; unnecessary [He told a *gratuitous* lie.] —**gra·tu′i·tous·ly,** *adv.*

gra·tu·i·ty (grə tōō′ə tē), *n.* a gift of money in return for some service; tip [He left a *gratuity* for the waiter.] —**gra·tu′i·ties,** *pl.*

grave (grāv), *adj.* **1.** important or serious [*grave* doubts]. **2.** full of danger; threatening [a *grave* illness]. **3.** not gay; slow and dignified [a *grave* dance]. —**grav′er,** *compar.;* **grav′est,** *superl.* —**grave′ly,** *adv.* —**grave′ness,** *n.*

grave (grāv), *n.* **1.** a place in the ground where a dead body is buried. It is often marked with a tombstone. **2.** any place where a dead body is laid to rest [The sea becomes the *grave* for many sailors.] **3.** death. —*v.* to carve out or engrave. —**graved,** *p.t.;* **grav′en** or **graved,** *p.p.;* **grav′ing,** *pr.p.*

grav·el (grav′'l), *n.* a mixture of small stones and pebbles, used for paving roads, etc. —*v.* to cover with gravel. —**grav′eled** or **grav′-elled,** *p.t. & p.p.;* **grav′el·ing** or **grav′el-ling,** *pr.p.*

grav·en (grāv′'n), a past participle of **grave.** —*adj.* engraved; carved [a *graven* image].

grave·stone (grāv′stōn), *n.* a carved stone placed at a grave, telling who is buried there.

grave·yard (grāv′yärd), *n.* a cemetery.

grav·i·tate (grav′ə tāt), *v.* **1.** to move or be pulled by the force of gravity [The moon *gravitates* toward the earth.] **2.** to sink or settle down to the bottom of a liquid. **3.** to be attracted and move [The crowd *gravitated* toward the main tent of the circus.] —**grav′i·tat·ed,** *p.t. & p.p.;* **grav′i·tat·ing,** *pr.p.*

grav·i·ta·tion (grav′ə tā′shən), *n.* **1.** the act of gravitating. **2.** the force by which every particle or mass of matter attracts and is attracted by every other particle or mass. Gravitation keeps all the planets moving around the sun and prevents them from moving off into space. —**grav′i·ta′tion·al,** *adj.*

grav·i·ty (grav′ə tē), *n.* **1.** the condition of being grave, or serious. **2.** danger or threat [the *gravity* of his illness]. **3.** gravitation, especially the force that tends to draw objects toward the center of the earth [Things fall to the ground because of *gravity*.] **4.** weight; heaviness: see **center of gravity, specific gravity.**

gra·vy (grā'vē), *n.* **1.** the juice given off by meat in cooking. **2.** a sauce made by mixing this juice with flour and seasoning. —**gra'vies,** *pl.*

gray (grā), *n.* **1.** a color made by mixing black and white. **2.** a person dressed in a gray uniform. —*adj.* **1.** of the color gray. **2.** somewhat dark; dull or dismal [a *gray* day]. **3.** having hair that is gray. —*v.* to make or become gray.

gray·beard (grā'bird), *n.* an old man.

gray·ish (grā'ish), *adj.* somewhat gray.

gray·ling (grā'ling), *n.* a fish of the trout family, that lives in fresh water.

gray matter, 1. the grayish nerve tissue of the brain and spinal cord. **2.** brains; intelligence: *used only in everyday talk.*

graze (grāz), *v.* **1.** to feed on growing grass or other plants in pastures [Cows are *grazing* in the meadow.] **2.** to put into a pasture to feed [to *graze* livestock]. —**grazed,** *p.t. & p.p.;* **graz'ing,** *pr.p.*

graze (grāz), *v.* to rub lightly or scrape in passing [The car swerved and *grazed* the tree. The bullet *grazed* his arm.] —*n.* **1.** a grazing. **2.** a scratch or scrape caused by grazing. —**grazed,** *p.t. & p.p.;* **graz'ing,** *pr.p.*

grease (grēs), *n.* **1.** soft or melted animal fat. **2.** any soft, oily substance. —*v.* (grēs *or* grēz), to smear with grease, as in order to make slippery or smooth [to *grease* machine parts; to *grease* a cake pan]. —**greased,** *p.t. & p.p.;* **greas'ing,** *pr.p.*

greas·y (grēs'ē *or* grēz'ē), *adj.* **1.** smeared with grease [*greasy* hands]. **2.** full of grease [*greasy* food]. **3.** like grease; oily [a *greasy* salve]. —**greas'i·er,** *compar.;* **greas'i·est,** *superl.* —**greas'i·ly,** *adv.* —**greas'i·ness,** *n.*

great (grāt), *adj.* **1.** much above the average in size, degree, power, etc.; big or very big; much or very much [the *Great* Lakes; a *great* distance; *great* pain]. **2.** very much of a [a *great* reader]. **3.** very important; noted; remarkable [a *great* composer; a *great* day in history]. **4.** older or younger by a generation: *used in words formed with a hyphen* [One's *great*-grandmother is the daughter of one's *great-great*-grandparents.] **5.** very able or skillful: *used only in everyday talk* [He's *great* at tennis.] **6.** fine or excellent: *used only in everyday talk* [a *great* party]. —**great'ly,** *adv.* —**great'ness,** *n.*

great-aunt (grāt'ant' *or* grāt'änt'), *n.* an aunt of one's father or mother; grandaunt.

Great Bear, a constellation whose brightest stars form the Big Dipper.

Great Britain, England, Wales, and Scotland. Great Britain is the largest of the British Isles. See also **British Commonwealth of Nations.**

great·coat (grāt'kōt), *n.* a heavy overcoat.

great Dane or **Great Dane,** a very large dog with short, smooth hair.

great Dane (30 in. high at shoulder)

Great Divide, the Rocky Mountains, which divide the rivers flowing toward the Atlantic from those flowing toward the Pacific.

great-grand·child (grāt'gran'child *or* grāt'grand'child), *n.* a child of one's grandchild (**great'-grand'daugh'ter** or **great'-grand'son**). —**great'-grand'chil'dren,** *pl.*

great-grand·par·ent (grāt'gran'per'ənt *or* grāt'grand'per'ənt), *n.* a parent of one's grandparent (**great'-grand'fa'ther** or **great'-grand'moth'er**).

great-heart·ed (grāt'här'tid), *adj.* **1.** brave; fearless. **2.** noble and unselfish.

Great Lakes, a chain of lakes in Canada and the United States. They are Lakes Superior, Michigan, Huron, Erie, and Ontario.

Great Salt Lake, a shallow salt lake in northern Utah.

great-un·cle (grāt'ung'k'l), *n.* an uncle of one's father or mother; granduncle.

grebe (grēb), *n.* a water bird about the size of a duck, with partly webbed feet and a sharp bill.

Gre·cian (grē'shən), *adj. & n.* Greek.

Greece (grēs), *n.* a country in southeastern Europe, on the Mediterranean.

grebes (14 in. long)

greed (grēd), *n.* the condition of being greedy [the miser's *greed* for money].

greed·y (grēd'ē), *adj.* wanting or taking all that one can get with no thought of what others need [The *greedy* boy ate all the cookies.] —**greed'i·er,** *compar.;* **greed'i·est,** *superl.* —**greed'i·ly,** *adv.* —**greed'i·ness,** *n.*

Greek (grēk), *adj.* of Greece, its people, etc. —*n.* **1.** a person born or living in Greece. **2.** the language of the Greeks.

green (grēn), *adj.* **1.** having the color of grass [*green* peas]. **2.** not ripe [*green* bananas]. **3.** not having had training or experience [a *green* camper]. **4.** not yet dried or cured for use [*green* lumber]. **5.** fresh; not faded [to keep someone's memory *green*]. —*n.* **1.** the color of grass [*Green* is produced by mixing blue and yellow.] **2.** a grassy piece of ground, especially the smooth, grassy area around each of the holes on a golf course. **3.** **greens,** *pl.* green, leafy

fat,   āpe,   cär,   ten,   ēven,   hit,   bīte,   gō,   hôrn,   tōōl,   book,   up,   fur,
get,   joy,   yet,   chin,   she,   thin,   *th*en;   zh = s in pleasure;   ' as in able (ā'b'l)
ə = a in ago,   e in agent,   i in sanity,   o in confess,   u in focus.

vegetables, as spinach, turnip leaves, etc. —**green′ness,** *n.*

green·back (grēn′bak), *n.* a piece of United States paper money printed green on the back.

green·er·y (grēn′ər ē), *n.* green leaves, plants, branches, etc.

green·horn (grēn′hôrn), *n.* a person who is new to a country, job, etc.; beginner.

green·house (grēn′hous), *n.* a heated building with glass roof and sides, for growing plants.

green·ish (grēn′-ish), *adj.* somewhat green.

Green·land (grēn′-lənd), *n.* a Danish island northeast of North America. It is the largest island in the world.

greenhouse

green pepper, the green, unripe fruit of the sweet red pepper. It is eaten as a vegetable.

green·sward (grēn′swôrd), *n.* ground covered with grass.

Green·wich (gren′ich; *the usual British pronun. is* grin′ij), *n.* a section of London, England. Degrees of longitude and zones of time are measured east and west from Greenwich.

green·wood (grēn′wood), *n.* a green forest.

greet (grēt), *v.* **1.** to meet and speak to with polite or friendly words; hail or welcome [Our host *greeted* us with a warm "Hello!"] **2.** to meet or receive in a particular way [He *greeted* her with a wave of the hand.] **3.** to come or appear to [A roaring sound *greeted* his ears.]

greet·ing (grēt′ing), *n.* **1.** the act or words of one who greets. **2.** *often* **greetings,** *pl.* a message of regards from someone not present.

gre·gar·i·ous (gri ger′i əs), *adj.* **1.** liking to be with other people; sociable. **2.** living in herds or flocks [Seals are *gregarious* animals.]

Gre·gor·i·an (gri gôr′i ən), *adj.* **1.** of or describing the calendar in common use today. It was established in 1582 by Pope **Greg·o·ry XIII** (greg′ə rē). **2.** describing a kind of chant used in Roman Catholic churches, introduced by Pope Gregory I in the 6th century.

gre·nade (gri nād′), *n.* a small bomb set off by a fuse and usually thrown by hand.

gren·a·dier (gren ə dir′), *n.* **1.** a soldier in earlier days who threw grenades. **2.** a member of a special regiment, as in the British army.

grew (grōō), past tense of **grow.**

grey (grā), *n., adj. & v.* same as **gray:** *mainly British spelling.*

grey·hound (grā′hound), *n.* a tall, slender dog with a narrow head. It is a swift runner.

grid (grid), *n.* **1.** a framework of parallel bars; gridiron or grating. **2.** a lead plate in a

greyhound (28 in. high at shoulder)

storage battery. **3.** a network of fine wires in an electron tube: it controls the flow of electrons through the tube.

grid·dle (grid′'l), *n.* a heavy, flat, metal pan for cooking pancakes (**grid′dle·cakes**), etc.

grid·i·ron (grid′ī′ərn), *n.* **1.** a framework of metal bars or wires for broiling meat or fish; grill. **2.** any framework that looks like this. **3.** a football field.

grief (grēf), *n.* **1.** deep and painful sorrow, as that caused by someone's death. **2.** something that causes such sorrow. —**come to grief,** to fail or be ruined.

gridiron

Grieg, Ed·vard (ed′värt grēg), 1843–1907; Norwegian composer of music.

griev·ance (grēv′əns), *n.* something that one thinks is unjust and feels hurt and angry about; a real or supposed wrong [The men stated their *grievances* about working conditions.]

grieve (grēv), *v.* **1.** to fill with grief; sadden deeply [His death *grieved* the whole nation.] **2.** to feel grief; be sad [It is useless to *grieve* over a lost opportunity.] —**grieved,** *p.t. & p.p.;* **griev′ing,** *pr.p.*

griev·ous (grēv′əs), *adj.* **1.** causing grief or deep sorrow [a *grievous* loss]. **2.** showing grief [a *grievous* cry]. **3.** hard to bear; severe [*grievous* pain]. **4.** very cruel or very bad [a *grievous* crime]. —**griev′ous·ly,** *adv.*

grif·fin or **grif·fon** (grif′ən), *n.* an imaginary animal with the body and hind legs of a lion and the head and wings of an eagle.

grill (gril), *n.* **1.** a gridiron (*in meaning* 1) or a griddle. **2.** food that has been broiled, as on a grill. **3.** a restaurant that specializes in such food: also called **grill′room.** —*v.* **1.** to broil, as on a grill. **2.** to torture with heat. **3.** to keep firing questions at, as about a crime [The police *grilled* the suspect.]

griffin

grille (gril), *n.* a framework of bars forming a screen in a window or door; grating.

grim (grim), *adj.* **1.** fierce or cruel; savage [War is *grim*]. **2.** not giving in; unyielding [*grim* courage]. **3.** looking stern or harsh [a *grim* face]. **4.** frightful or shocking; ghastly [The gravedigger made *grim* jokes about his *grim* task.] —**grim′mer,** *compar.;* **grim′mest,** *superl.* —**grim′ly,** *adv.* —**grim′ness,** *n.*

gri·mace (gri mās′ *or* grim′əs), *n.* a twisting of the face in fun or in a look of pain, disgust, etc. —*v.* to make grimaces. —**gri·maced′,** *p.t. & p.p.;* **gri·mac′ing,** *pr.p.*

grime (grīm), *n.* dirt or soot rubbed into a surface, as of the skin. —*v.* to soil with grime. —**grimed,** *p.t. & p.p.;* **grim′ing,** *pr.p.*

Grimm, Ja·kob and **Wil·helm** (yä′kôp grim, vil′helm), brothers in 19th-century Germany who collected and wrote fairy tales.

grim·y (grīm′ē), *adj.* covered with grime; very dirty. —**grim′i·er**, *compar.*; **grim′i·est**, *superl.* —**grim′i·ness**, *n.*

grin (grin), *v.* to draw back the lips and show the teeth, as in a big or foolish smile. —*n.* the look on the face when grinning [a broad *grin*]. —**grinned**, *p.t. & p.p.*; **grin′ning**, *pr.p.*

grind (grīnd), *v.* **1.** to crush into tiny bits or into powder [The farmer *grinds* his grain between millstones.] **2.** to sharpen or smooth by rubbing against a rough surface [to *grind* a knife]. **3.** to press down or rub together harshly or with a grating sound [She *ground* her teeth in anger.] **4.** to treat in a harsh or cruel way [a people *ground* by tyranny]. **5.** to work by turning the crank of [to *grind* a pepper mill]. **6.** to work or study hard: *used only in everyday talk.* —*n.* **1.** the act of grinding. **2.** the fineness of the particles ground [We sell three *grinds* of coffee.] **3.** long, hard work or study; drudgery. **4.** a student who studies very hard: *used only in everyday talk.* —**grind out**, to produce by hard, steady work [to *grind out* a novel]. —**ground**, *p.t. & p.p.*; **grind′ing**, *pr.p.*

grind·er (grīn′dər), *n.* a person or thing that grinds, as any of the back teeth, or molars.

grind·stone (grīnd′stōn), *n.* a flat, round stone that is turned on an axle for sharpening or polishing things.

grip (grip), *v.* **1.** to grasp and hold fast, as with the hand or the teeth. **2.** to get and hold the attention of; have control over [The tale of terror *gripped* them.] —*n.* **1.** a grasping and holding fast, as with the hand or the teeth. **2.** any special way of clasping hands [Some fraternities have secret *grips*.] **3.** the way one holds a bat, golf club, etc. **4.** the ability to understand or deal with something [He has a good *grip* on the situation.] **5.** a handle, as of a tool. **6.** a small handbag for travelers. —**come to grips**, to fight or struggle. —**gripped** or **gript** (gript), *p.t. & p.p.*; **grip′ping**, *pr.p.*

grindstone

gripe (grīp), *v.* **1.** to cause sharp pains in the bowels. **2.** to annoy or irritate. **3.** to complain. —*n.* **1. gripes**, *pl.* sharp pains in the bowels. **2.** a complaint. *Slang in meanings 2 and 3 of the verb and meaning 2 of the noun.* —**griped**, *p.t. & p.p.*; **grip′ing**, *pr.p.*

grippe (grip), *n.* influenza; flu: *this word is not used much now.*

gris·ly (griz′lē), *adj.* very frightening; horrible [a *grisly* tale of ghosts]. —**gris′li·er**, *compar.*; **gris′li·est**, *superl.*

grist (grist), *n.* grain that is ready to be ground or that has been ground.

gris·tle (gris′'l), *n.* a tough, flexible tissue, like soft bone, found in meat; cartilage.

gris·tly (gris′lē), *adj.* **1.** full of gristle. **2.** like gristle.

grist·mill (grist′mil), *n.* a mill for grinding grain.

grit (grit), *n.* **1.** small bits of stone or sand. **2.** a coarse kind of sandstone. **3.** stubborn courage; pluck. —*v.* to clench or grind together [to *grit* one's teeth in anger]. —**grit′ted**, *p.t. & p.p.*; **grit′ting**, *pr.p.*

grits (grits), *n.pl.* coarsely ground grain, especially corn.

grit·ty (grit′ē), *adj.* **1.** full of or like grit. **2.** brave or plucky: *used only in everyday talk.* —**grit′ti·er**, *compar.*; **grit′ti·est**, *superl.*

griz·zled (griz′'ld), *adj.* gray or streaked with gray [a *grizzled* beard].

griz·zly (griz′lē), *adj.* grayish; grizzled. —*n.* a grizzly bear. —**griz′zli·er**, *compar.*; **griz′zli·est**, *superl.* —**griz′zlies**, *pl.*

grizzly bear, a large, fierce, grayish-brown bear found in western North America.

groan (grōn), *v.* **1.** to make a deep sound showing sorrow, pain, etc. [We *groaned* when our team lost.] **2.** to make a creaking sound, as from great strain [The heavy gate *groaned* on its hinges.] **3.** to be loaded down [The table *groaned* with food.] —*n.* a groaning sound.

grizzly bear (3½ ft. high at shoulder)

gro·cer (grō′sər), *n.* a storekeeper who sells food and certain household supplies.

gro·cer·y (grō′sər ē), *n.* **1.** a store selling food and household supplies. **2. groceries**, *pl.* the goods sold by a grocer. —**gro′cer·ies**, *pl.*

grog (gräg), *n.* **1.** rum or whisky mixed with water. **2.** any alcoholic liquor.

grog·gy (gräg′ē), *adj.* shaky or dizzy, as from being sleepy or drunk. —**grog′gi·er**, *compar.*; **grog′gi·est**, *superl.* —**grog′gi·ly**, *adv.*

groin (groin), *n.* **1.** the hollow or fold where the leg joins the body. **2.** the curved line where two ceiling vaults meet. —*v.* to build with groins [a *groined* vault].

groined vault

groom (grōōm), *n.* **1.** a man or boy whose work is taking care of horses. **2.** a bridegroom. —*v.* **1.** to brush and clean a horse. **2.** to make neat and tidy [to *groom* one's hair]. **3.** to train for a particular purpose [He was *groomed* to take over the manager's job.]

groove (grōōv), *n.* **1.** a long and narrow hollow, cut or worn into a surface. **2.** the track cut in a

---

fat, āpe, cär, ten, ēven, hit, bīte, gō, hôrn, tōol, book, up, fur;
get, joy, yet, chin, she, thin, *th*en; zh = s in pleasure; ′ as in able (ā′b'l)
ə = a in ago, e in agent, i in sanity, o in confess, u in focus.

phonograph record for the needle to follow. **3.** a regular way of doing something, as by habit [After our vacation, we slipped back into our everyday *groove.*] —*v.* to make a groove in. —**grooved,** *p.t.* & *p.p.;* **groov'ing,** *pr.p.*

grope (grōp), *v.* **1.** to feel or search about in a blind or fumbling way [to *grope* for the keys in one's pocket; to *grope* for knowledge]. **2.** to seek or find by feeling about [to *grope* one's way in the dark]. —**groped,** *p.t.* & *p.p.;* **grop'-ing,** *pr.p.*

gros·beak (grōs'bēk), *n.* a small songbird with a thick beak shaped like a cone.

gross (grōs), *adj.* **1.** very bad; glaring [a *gross* error; a *gross* lie]. **2.** vulgar; not refined; coarse [*gross* language; *gross* manners]. **3.** big or fat, and coarse-looking [*gross* features]. **4.** with nothing taken away; total; entire [What is your *gross* income before you pay taxes?] —*n.* **1.** the whole amount; total [We earned a *gross* of $30, but we owed $10 for supplies.] **2.** twelve dozen; 144. —*v.* to earn a certain amount before expenses are subtracted: *used only in everyday talk.* —**gross'es,** *pl. for meaning 1;* **gross,** *pl. for meaning 2.* —**gross'ly,** *adv.* —**gross'ness,** *n.*

gro·tesque (grō tesk'), *adj.* **1.** looking strange and unreal in a wild way [*grotesque* drawings of imaginary creatures on Mars]. **2.** so strange, twisted, different, etc. as to be funny; absurd [People often have *grotesque* adventures in their dreams.] —*n.* a grotesque person or thing. —**gro·tesque'ly,** *adv.*

grot·to (grät'ō), *n.* **1.** a cave. **2.** any shaded or sheltered place or shrine that is like a cave. —**grot'toes** or **grot'tos,** *pl.*

grouch (grouch), *v.* to be in a bad mood and keep finding fault with things. —*n.* **1.** a person who grouches. **2.** a bad or grumbling mood. *This word is used only in everyday talk.*

grouch·y (grouch'ē), *adj.* in a grouch; cross and complaining: *used only in everyday talk.* —**grouch'i·er,** *compar.;* **grouch'i·est,** *superl.* —**grouch'i·ly,** *adv.* —**grouch'i·ness,** *n.*

ground (ground), *n.* **1.** the solid part of the earth's surface; land; earth. **2.** a piece of land of a particular kind [a hunting *ground;* a battle-*ground*]. **3. grounds,** *pl.* the lands around a house, that belong to it. **4.** a reason, cause, or basis [He hasn't much *ground* for complaint. On what *grounds* are you refusing?] **5. grounds,** *pl.* solid bits that settle to the bottom of a liquid [coffee *grounds*]. **6.** the background, as of a painting, flag, etc. **7.** the connection of an electrical conductor with the ground. —*adj.* of, on, or near the ground [the *ground* floor of a building]. —*v.* **1.** to put on the ground. **2.** to run aground [The ship *grounded* on the reef.] **3.** to base or establish [On what do you *ground* your argument?] **4.** to give good, sound training in some subject to [to *ground* students in science]. **5.** to keep from flying [The airplanes were *grounded* by the storm.] **6.** to connect an electrical conductor with the ground. —**break ground, 1.** to dig or plow. **2.** to start building. —**cover ground, 1.** to go some distance; travel.

2. to get some amount done. —**gain ground,** to move ahead; make progress; advance. —**give ground,** to yield or retreat. —**lose ground,** to drop back; fall behind. —**ground out,** to be put out by a grounder in baseball.

ground (ground), past tense and past participle of **grind.**

ground·er (groun'dər), *n.* a batted ball in baseball that rolls or bounces along the ground.

ground hog, a woodchuck: also **ground'hog.**

ground-hog day or **groundhog day** (ground'hôg'), February 2. There is a legend that the ground hog comes out of his winter hole on this day. If he sees his shadow, he returns to his hole for six more weeks of winter weather.

ground·less (ground'lis), *adj.* without good cause or reason [a *groundless* rumor].

ground·work (ground'wŭrk), *n.* a foundation or basis [the *groundwork* of a good education].

group (grōōp), *n.* **1.** a number of persons or things gathered together. **2.** a number of related things that form a class [the wood-wind *group* of instruments].—*v.* to gather together into a group [*Group* yourselves in a circle.]

grouse (grous), *n.* a wild bird, like a plump chicken, that is hunted as game. —**grouse,** *pl.*

grove (grōv), *n.* a small group of trees.

grov·el (gruv''l *or* gräv''l), *v.* **1.** to lie or crawl on the ground with the face down. **2.** to act in a very humble or cringing way. —**grov'-eled** or **grov'elled,** *p.t.* & *p.p.;* **grov'el·ing** or **grov'el·ling,** *pr.p.* —**grov'el·er** or **grov'el·ler,** *n.*

grouse (1½ ft. long)

grow (grō), *v.* **1.** to become larger; increase [Our business has *grown* rapidly.] **2.** to become older; develop; mature [to *grow* from childhood to adulthood]. **3.** to be found; exist [Oranges *grow* in warm regions.] **4.** to make grow; raise [They *grow* wheat on their farm.] **5.** to come to be; become [He *grew* tired after the long drive.] —**grow on,** to become gradually more likable or desirable to. —**grow out of, 1.** to develop from. **2.** to grow too large for. —**grow together,** to become joined by growing. —**grow up,** to become an adult. —**grew,** *p.t.;* **grown,** *p.p.;* **grow'ing,** *pr.p.*—**grow'er,** *n.*

growl (groul), *v.* **1.** to make a low, rumbling sound in the throat, as an angry dog does. **2.** to grumble. —*n.* the act or sound of growling.

grown (grōn), past participle of **grow.** —*adj.* finished growing; fully mature [a *grown* man].

grown-up or **grown·up** (grōn'up'), *adj.* **1.** fully grown. **2.** of or for adults. —*n.* an adult.

growth (grōth), *n.* **1.** the act of growing; a becoming larger or a developing. **2.** the amount grown; increase [a *growth* of two inches over the summer]. **3.** something that grows or has grown [He has a *growth* of hair on his arms. A tumor is an abnormal *growth* in the body.]

grub (grub), *v.* **1.** to dig or dig up; uproot. **2.** to work hard; drudge or plod. —*n.* **1.** a larva, as of the beetle, that looks like a short, fat worm. **2.** food: *slang in this meaning.* —**grubbed,** *p.t. & p.p.;* **grub′bing,** *pr.p.*

grub·by (grub′ē), *adj.* dirty or untidy. —**grub′bi·er,** *compar.;* **grub′bi·est,** *superl.*

grub·stake (grub′stāk), *n.* money or supplies loaned to a prospector in return for a share of whatever he finds: *used only in everyday talk.*

grudge (gruj), *v.* **1.** to envy someone because of something he has; begrudge [They *grudged* him his success.] **2.** to give without wanting to [The miser *grudges* his dog its food.] —*n.* bad feeling against a person because of some wrong he is supposed to have done [She bore a *grudge* against me all her life.] —**grudged,** *p.t. & p.p.;* **grudg′ing,** *pr.p.* —**grudg′ing·ly,** *adv.*

gru·el (grōō′əl), *n.* a thin, watery food made by cooking oatmeal or the like in milk or water. It is often fed to sick people.

gru·el·ing or **gru·el·ling** (grōō′əl ing), *adj.* very tiring; exhausting [*grueling* work].

grue·some (grōō′səm), *adj.* causing fear and disgust; horrible [a *gruesome* murder].

gruff (gruf), *adj.* **1.** rough or unfriendly; rude [a *gruff* reply]. **2.** harsh; hoarse [*gruff* voices].

grum·ble (grum′b′l), *v.* **1.** to make a low, growling or rumbling sound. **2.** to complain in an angry or sullen way [The soldiers *grumbled* about the food.] —*n.* the act of grumbling. —**grum′bled,** *p.t. & p.p.;* **grum′bling,** *pr.p.* —**grum′bler,** *n.*

grump·y (grum′pē), *adj.* grouchy; peevish. —**grump′i·er,** *compar.;* **grump′i·est,** *superl.*

grunt (grunt), *v.* **1.** to make the short, deep, hoarse sound of a hog. **2.** to make a sound like this [Tom *grunted* as he picked up the heavy load.] **3.** to say by grunting ["No!" he *grunted.*] —*n.* the sound made in grunting.

Guam (gwäm), *n.* an island in the western Pacific, belonging to the United States.

guar·an·tee (gar ən tē′), *n.* **1.** a promise to replace something sold if it does not work or last as it should [a thirty-day *guarantee* on the clock]. **2.** a promise or assurance that something will happen [You have my *guarantee* that we'll be on time.] **3.** same as **guaranty** (*meanings 1 and 2*). **4.** a person who gives a guarantee; guarantor. —*v.* **1.** to give a guarantee or guaranty for. **2.** to promise or assure [I cannot *guarantee* that he'll be there.] —**guar·an·teed′,** *p.t. & p.p.;* **guar·an·tee′ing,** *pr.p.*

guar·an·tor (gar′ən tər *or* gar′ən tôr), *n.* a person who gives a guaranty or guarantee.

guar·an·ty (gar′ən tē), *n.* **1.** a promise to pay another person's debt or to do something else he has agreed to do, if he is not able to do it himself. **2.** something given or kept as security. **3.** same as **guarantee** (*meanings 1 and 2*). —**guar′an·ties,** *pl.*

guard (gärd), *v.* **1.** to watch over; protect; defend [Shepherds *guard* their flocks by night.] **2.** to keep from escaping [Two sentries *guarded* the prisoners.] **3.** to be watchful; take care [Lock the door to *guard* against prowlers.] —*n.* **1.** the act of guarding; careful watch; protection [Keep a *guard* against suspicious strangers.] **2.** anything that protects against injury or loss [The hilt on a sword usually has a *guard* for the hand.] **3.** any person or group that guards or protects [a museum *guard*]. **4.** either of two basketball players who defend their own goal. **5.** either of two football players who are placed at each side of the center. —**on one's guard,** careful and watchful.

guard·ed (gär′did), *adj.* **1.** watched over and protected. **2.** kept from escaping. **3.** cautious; careful [a *guarded* reply]. —**guard′ed·ly,** *adv.*

guard·house (gärd′hous), *n.* a building used by guards for resting. In the army, the guardhouse is also used as a jail for holding soldiers who have broken some rules.

guard·i·an (gär′di ən), *n.* **1.** a person chosen by a court to take charge of a child or of someone else who cannot take care of his own affairs. **2.** a person who guards or protects; custodian [A sexton is a *guardian* of church property.] —**guard′i·an·ship,** *n.*

guard·room (gärd′rōōm), *n.* a room used as a guardhouse.

guards·man (gärdz′mən), *n.* **1.** a guard. **2.** a member of any military group called a guard, as of the National Guard. —**guards′men,** *pl.*

Gua·te·ma·la (gwä′tə mäl′ə), *n.* a country in Central America, south and east of Mexico.

gua·va (gwä′və), *n.* the yellowish, pear-shaped fruit of a tropical American tree or shrub. It is used for making jelly.

Guern·sey (gûrn′zē), *n.* **1.** a British island in the English Channel. **2.** a breed of dairy cattle first raised on this island: it is usually light brown with white markings. —**Guern′seys,** *pl.*

Guernsey cow
(4 ft. high at shoulder)

guer·ril·la or **gue·ril·la** (gə ril′ə), *n.* a member of a small group of fighters who are not part of a regular army. They usually make surprise raids behind the enemy's lines.

guess (ges), *v.* **1.** to judge or decide about something without having enough facts to know for certain [Can you *guess* how old she is?] **2.** to judge correctly by doing this [He *guessed* the exact number of beans in the jar.] **3.** to think or suppose [I *guess* you're right.] —*n.* a judgment formed by guessing; surmise [Your *guess* is as good as mine.]

guess·work (ges′wûrk), *n.* the act of guessing, or a judgment formed by guessing.

---

fat, āpe, cär, ten, ēven, hit, bīte, gō, hôrn, tōōl, book, up, fûr; get, joy, yet, chin, she, thin, *then;* zh = s in pleasure; ' as in able (ā′b'l); ə = a in ago, e in agent, i in sanity, o in confess, u in focus.

guest (gest), *n.* **1.** a person who is visiting another's home, or who is being treated to a meal, etc. by another. **2.** any paying customer of a hotel or restaurant. —*adj.* **1.** for guests. **2.** that has been invited [a *guest* speaker].

guf·faw (gə fô′), *n.* a loud and rough laugh. —*v.* to laugh in this way.

Gui·a·na (gi an′ə *or* gi ä′nə), *n.* a region in northern South America.

guid·ance (gīd′′ns), *n.* **1.** a guiding, or directing; leadership [Our school clubs are all under the *guidance* of teachers.] **2.** something that guides.

guide (gīd), *v.* **1.** to show the way to; conduct or lead [Can you *guide* me through the museum?] **2.** to manage or control; steer [to *guide* the affairs of state]. —*n.* **1.** a person who leads others on a trip or tour. **2.** something that controls, directs, or instructs [The *guide* on a typewriter keeps the paper straight. A dictionary is a *guide* to the use of words.] **3.** a guidebook. —**guid′ed,** *p.t. & p.p.;* **guid′ing,** *pr.p.*

guide·book (gīd′book), *n.* a book that has directions and information for tourists.

guided missile, a war missile or rocket that is guided to its target by radio signals or radar.

guide·line (gīd′līn), *n.* a rule or principle set forth as a guide for those who must choose a policy or course of action.

guide·post (gīd′pōst), *n.* a post along a road, with a sign giving directions to places.

guild (gild), *n.* **1.** in the Middle Ages, a union of men in the same craft or trade to keep the quality of work high and to protect the members. **2.** any group of people joined together in some work or for some purpose [The Ladies' *Guild* of our church makes hospital bandages.]

guil·der (gil′dər), *n.* the basic unit of money in the Netherlands. It is a silver coin.

guild·hall (gild′hôl), *n.* **1.** a hall where a guild meets. **2.** a town hall.

guile (gīl), *n.* slyness and cunning in dealing with others; craftiness. —**guile′ful,** *adj.*

guile·less (gīl′lis), *adj.* not having or using guile; honest; frank. —**guile′less·ly,** *adv.*

guil·lo·tine (gil′ə tēn), *n.* an instrument for cutting off a person's head by means of a heavy blade that drops in a framework. The guillotine was introduced in France during the French Revolution. —*v.* (gil ə tēn′), to kill as a punishment with a guillotine. —**guil·lo·tined′,** *p.t. & p.p.;* **guil·lo·tin′ing,** *pr.p.*

guillotine

guilt (gilt), *n.* **1.** the fact of having done a wrong or committed a crime; a being guilty [We have no proof of his *guilt*.] **2.** a wrong act; crime; sin.

guilt·less (gilt′lis), *adj.* not guilty; innocent.

guilt·y (gil′tē), *adj.* **1.** having done something wrong; being to blame for something [He is often *guilty* of losing his temper.] **2.** judged in court to be a wrongdoer [The jury found him *guilty* of robbery.] **3.** caused by a feeling of guilt [a *guilty* look]. —**guilt′i·er,** *compar.;* **guilt′i·est,** *superl.* —**guilt′i·ly,** *adv.* —**guilt′i·ness,** *n.*

Guin·ea (gin′ē), *n.* a country on the western coast of Africa.

guin·ea (gin′ē), *n.* **1.** a gold coin used in England in earlier times. The word is still used to mean the sum of 21 shillings. **2.** a guinea fowl.

guinea fowl, a bird like a chicken, having a rounded body and dark feathers with white spots. It is hunted and also raised for food.

guinea fowl (16 in. long)

guinea hen, a guinea fowl, especially a female.

guinea pig, 1. a small, fat animal like a rat, with short ears and a short tail. It is used in experiments in biology. **2.** any person or thing used in an experiment.

guinea pig (7 in. long)

Guin·e·vere (gwin′ə vir), *n.* the wife of King Arthur in the legends about him.

guise (gīz), *n.* **1.** a way or style of dressing; costume. **2.** the way something looks; appearance; often, a false appearance [Under the *guise* of friendship he betrayed us.]

gui·tar (gi tär′), *n.* a musical instrument with six strings. It is played by plucking the strings with the fingers or with a plectrum.

gulch (gulch), *n.* a narrow valley with steep walls, cut by a swift stream.

gul·den (gool′dən), *n.* same as **guilder.**

guitar

gulf (gulf), *n.* **1.** a large area of ocean reaching into land. It is larger than a bay. **2.** a wide, deep cut in the earth; large chasm. **3.** a wide gap or separation [There is a *gulf* between our beliefs.]

Gulf Stream, a warm ocean current, about 50 miles wide, that flows from the Gulf of Mexico northward across the Atlantic toward Europe.

gull (gul), *n.* a sea bird with large wings, webbed feet, and feathers of gray and white.

gull (gul), *n.* a person who is easily cheated or tricked. —*v.* to cheat or trick.

gul·let (gul′it), *n.* **1.** the tube through which food passes from the mouth to the stomach; esophagus. **2.** the throat or neck.

gulls (18 in. long)

gul·li·ble (gul′ə b'l), *adj.* that is easily cheated or tricked. —**gul′li·bil′i·ty,** *n.*

gul·ly (gul′ē), *n.* a channel worn by water; small, narrow ravine. —**gul′lies,** *pl.*

gulp (gulp), *v.* **1.** to swallow in a hurried or greedy way [He *gulped* his breakfast and ran to school.] **2.** to choke back as if swallowing [She *gulped* down her sobs.] **3.** to catch one's breath; gasp [The swimmer came up *gulping* for air.] —*n.* **1.** the act of gulping. **2.** the amount swallowed at one time [He took two *gulps* of milk.]

gum (gum), *n.* **1.** a sticky substance given off by certain trees and plants. It is used in pastes, jellies, varnishes, etc. **2.** short for **gum tree. 3.** rubber. **4.** short for **chewing gum.** —*v.* **1.** to stick together or cover with gum. **2.** to become sticky or clogged [The drain in the sink is *gummed* up.] —**gummed,** *p.t. & p.p.;* **gum′ming,** *pr.p.*

gum (gum), *n.* the firm flesh around the teeth: *often used in the plural,* **gums.**

gum·bo (gum′bō), *n.* **1.** the okra plant or its sticky pods. **2.** a soup made thick with okra pods. —**gum′bos,** *pl.*

gum·drop (gum′dräp), *n.* a small candy that is like firm and chewy jelly.

gum·my (gum′ē), *adj.* **1.** full of or covered with gum [a *gummy* plant]. **2.** thick and sticky. —**gum′mi·er,** *compar.;* **gum′mi·est,** *superl.*

gump·tion (gump′shən), *n.* courage or boldness: *used only in everyday talk.*

gum tree, any of the trees that give gum.

gun (gun), *n.* **1.** a weapon that has a metal tube from which a bullet, shell, etc. is shot by exploding gunpowder. In technical use, a gun is only a large, heavy weapon such as a cannon or machine gun, but in common talk, it is also a rifle or pistol. **2.** anything like this that shoots or squirts something [an air *gun;* a spray *gun*]. **3.** a shooting of a gun to signal or salute someone [The President receives a salute of 21 *guns.*] —*v.* to shoot or hunt with a gun. —**stick to one's guns,** to refuse to give in or to change one's opinion. —**gunned,** *p.t. & p.p.;* **gun′ning,** *pr.p.*

gun·boat (gun′bōt), *n.* a small armed ship used in guarding rivers, harbors, etc.

gun·cot·ton (gun′kät′'n), *n.* an explosive made of cotton treated with nitric and sulfuric acids.

gun·fire (gun′fīr), *n.* the shooting of a gun or guns [the sound of *gunfire* far away].

gun·lock (gun′läk), *n.* the part by which the charge was fired in early guns.

gun·man (gun′mən), *n.* a gangster, robber, etc. who carries a gun. —**gun′men,** *pl.*

gun·ner (gun′ər), *n.* **1.** a soldier, sailor, etc. who helps to fire large guns. **2.** a naval officer in charge of a ship's guns.

gun·ner·y (gun′ər ē), *n.* the science of making or firing cannon or other large guns.

gun·ny (gun′ē), *n.* **1.** a coarse, thick material, as of jute, used for making sacks. **2.** a sack of this: also **gunny sack.** —**gun′nies,** *pl.*

gun·pow·der (gun′pou′dər), *n.* an explosive powder used in firing guns, for blasting, etc.

gun·shot (gun′shät), *n.* **1.** shot fired from a gun. **2.** the distance a bullet, shell, etc. can be fired; range of a gun [a duck within *gunshot*].

gun·smith (gun′smith), *n.* a man who makes or repairs small guns.

gun·stock (gun′stäk), *n.* the wooden handle of a gun to which the barrel is attached.

gun·wale (gun′'l), *n.* the upper edge of the side of a boat or ship.

gup·py (gup′ē), *n.* a tiny tropical fish that lives in fresh water and is kept in home aquariums. —**gup′pies,** *pl.*

gur·gle (gur′g'l), *v.* **1.** to flow with a bubbling sound, as water out of a bottle. **2.** to make a bubbling sound in the throat [Babies *gurgle* when they are pleased.] —*n.* a gurgling sound. —**gur′gled,** *p.t. & p.p.;* **gur′gling,** *pr.p.*

gush (gush), *v.* **1.** to flow out with force and in large amounts; spout [Water *gushed* from the broken pipe.] **2.** to talk with too much feeling or enthusiasm in a silly way: *used only in everyday talk.* —*n.* **1.** a gushing; sudden, heavy flow [a *gush* of water]. **2.** gushing talk: *used only in everyday talk.* —**gush′y,** *adj.*

gush·er (gush′ər), *n.* an oil well from which oil gushes without being pumped

gus·set (gus′it), *n.* a small piece shaped like a triangle or diamond, set into a skirt, glove, etc. to make it stronger or roomier.

gust (gust), *n.* **1.** a strong and sudden rush of air or of something carried by the air [a *gust* of wind; *gusts* of smoke]. **2.** a sudden outburst of laughter, rage, etc. —**gust′y,** *adj.*

gus·to (gus′tō), *n.* much relish or enjoyment [to eat with *gusto;* to sing with *gusto*].

gusset

gut (gut), *n.* **1.** often **guts,** *pl.* the intestines or bowels: *now considered by some people to be not a polite use.* **2.** tough cord made from the intestines of sheep, goats, etc. It is used for violin strings, in tennis rackets, etc. **3.** **guts,** *pl.* courage: *a slang meaning.* —*v.* **1.** to take out the intestines, etc. from [to *gut* a fish]. **2.** to destroy the inside of [The building had been *gutted* by fire.] —**gut′ted,** *p.t. & p.p.;* **gut′ting,** *pr.p.*

Gu·ten·berg, Jo·hann (yō′hän gōō′t'n bərg), 1398?–1468; German printer thought to be the first European to use separate pieces of type.

gut·ta-per·cha (gut′ə pur′chə), *n.* a substance like rubber, made from the milky juice of certain tropical trees.

---

fat, āpe, cär, ten, ēven, hit, bīte, gō, hôrn, tōōl, book, up, fur; get, joy, yet, chin, she, thin, *th*en; zh = s in pleasure; ′ as in able (ā′b'l); ə = a in ago, e in agent, i in sanity, o in confess, u in focus.

gut·ter (gut'ər), *n.* **1.** a narrow channel along the edge of a road or street to carry water, as to a sewer. **2.** a narrow channel of metal or tile along the edge of a roof, to carry off rain water. **3.** a channel or groove like a gutter, as the groove on either side of a bowling alley. —*v.* to melt quickly so that the wax runs off in channels [The wind made the candle *gutter*.]

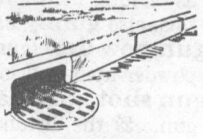

street gutter

gut·tur·al (gut'ər 'l), *adj.* **1.** of or made in the throat [The g in "go" is a *guttural* sound.] **2.** harsh or growling [a *guttural* voice].

guy (gī), *n.* a rope, chain, wire, etc. fastened to something to keep it steady.

guy (gī), *n.* a boy or man: *a slang word.* —*v.* to make fun of; tease: *used only in everyday talk.*

Guy·a·na (gī an'ə *or* gī än'ə), *n.* a country in northeastern South America.

guz·zle (guz''l), *v.* to drink, or sometimes eat, in a greedy way and in large amounts. —**guz'-zled,** *p.t. & p.p.;* **guz'zling,** *pr.p.*

gym (jim), *n.* **1.** a gymnasium. **2.** a course in athletic exercises in a school or college. *This word is used only in everyday talk.*

gym·na·si·um (jim nā'zi əm), *n.* a building or room with equipment for doing athletic exercises and for playing certain games.

gym·nast (jim'nast), *n.* a person who is trained in doing athletic exercises.

gym·nas·tics (jim nas'tiks), *n.pl.* exercises that develop and train the body and the muscles. —**gym·nas'tic,** *adj.*

gyp (jip), *v. & n.* cheat or swindle: *a slang word.* —**gypped,** *p.t. & p.p.;* **gyp'ping,** *pr.p.*

gyp·sum (jip'səm), *n.* a calcium mineral in crystal or chalky form, used for making plaster of Paris and as a fertilizer.

gyp·sy (jip'sē), *n.* **1.** often **Gypsy,** a member of a wandering people with dark skin and black hair, found throughout the world. They are thought to have come from India many centuries ago. **2.** a person who looks like a gypsy, or who lives a wandering life. —**gyp'sies,** *pl.*

gypsy moth, a brownish or white moth whose larvae feed on leaves, damaging trees and plants.

gy·rate (jī'rāt), *v.* to move in a circle or spiral; revolve; whirl. —**gy'rat·ed,** *p.t. & p.p.;* **gy'-rat·ing,** *pr.p.* —**gy·ra'tion,** *n.*

gy·ro·scope (jī'rə skōp), *n.* a wheel set in a ring so that the shaft on which it spins can turn in any direction. When the wheel is spun rapidly, the shaft stays at a tilt as if free from the law of gravity. The gyroscope is used to help keep boats, airplanes, etc. steady.

gyve (jīv), *n.* a shackle: *now seldom used.*

gyroscope

H

H, h (āch), *n.* the eighth letter of the English alphabet. —**H's, h's** (āch'iz), *pl.*

H, symbol for the chemical element *hydrogen.*

ha (hä), *interj.* a sound made in showing surprise, triumph, etc., or in laughing.

ha·be·as cor·pus (hā'bi əs kôr'pəs), a writ from a court of law ordering officials either to prove that they have a lawful reason for keeping a person in jail or to release him.

hab·er·dash·er (hab'ər dash'ər), *n.* a person who sells small articles of men's clothing, as hats, shirts, gloves, neckties, etc.

hab·er·dash·er·y (hab'ər dash'ər ē), *n.* **1.** a haberdasher's store. **2.** the articles sold in such a store. —**hab'er·dash'er·ies,** *pl.*

ha·bil·i·ments (hə bil'ə mənts), *n.pl.* clothing.

hab·it (hab'it), *n.* **1.** a thing that a person has done so often without thinking about it that he finds it hard to stop [the *habit* of biting, one's nails]. **2.** a usual or typical way of doing, being, etc.; practice [It is the *habit* of bears to sleep through the winter.] **3.** special clothes, as a religious costume, or clothing for a certain occasion [a nun's *habit;* a riding *habit*].

riding habit

hab·it·a·ble (hab'i tə b'l), *adj.* fit to be lived in [a *habitable* cottage].

hab·i·tat (hab'ə tat), *n.* the place where an animal or plant is normally found [Woodland streams are the *habitat* of beavers.]

hab·i·ta·tion (hab'ə tā'shən), *n.* **1.** a place in which to live; dwelling or home. **2.** the act of living in [a slum unfit for *habitation*].

ha·bit·u·al (hə bich'oo əl), *adj.* **1.** done by habit; fixed as a habit [*habitual* kindness]. **2.** doing something by habit [a *habitual* smoker]. **3.** often used, seen, done, etc.; usual [That easy chair is grandfather's *habitual* seat.] —**ha·bit'u·al·ly,** *adv.*

ha·bit·u·ate (hə bich'oo āt), *v.* to make or get used to something; accustom [to *habituate* oneself to a cold climate]. —**ha·bit'u·at·ed,** *p.t. & p.p.;* **ha·bit'u·at·ing,** *pr.p.*

ha·ci·en·da (hä'si en'də), *n.* a large ranch or country home in those parts of the Americas where Spanish is spoken.

hack (hak), *v.* **1.** to chop or cut roughly, as with an ax. **2.** to give harsh and dry coughs. —*n.* **1.** a chopping cut. **2.** a dry cough.

hack (hak), *n.* **1.** a horse, or horse and carriage, that can be hired. **2.** an old, worn-out horse. **3.** a taxicab. **4.** a person, especially a writer, who does dull, ordinary work. —*adj.* **1.** working as a hack [a *hack* writer]. **2.** done by a hack [a *hack* job].

hack·le (hak′'l), *n.* **1.** any of the feathers at the neck of a rooster, pigeon, etc. **2. hackles,** *pl.* the hairs on a dog's neck and back that bristle, as when the dog is ready to fight.

hack·ney (hak′nē), *n.* **1.** a horse for driving or riding. **2.** a carriage that can be hired. **—hack′neys,** *pl.*

hack·neyed (hak′nēd), *adj.* used so often that it has become stale and dull ["Last but not least" is a *hackneyed* phrase.]

hack saw, a saw with a narrow blade and fine teeth, used for cutting metal.

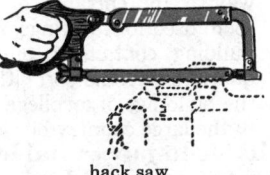
hack saw

had (had), past tense and past participle of **have.** *Had* is also used with certain words of comparison, as *better, rather, sooner,* etc. [You *had* better leave now.]

had·dock (had′ək), *n.* a small ocean fish used as food. It is related to the cod. **—had′dock** or **had′docks,** *pl.*

Ha·des (hā′dēz), *n.* **1.** in Greek myths, the place where the spirits of the dead go, beneath the earth. **2.** hell: *used only in everyday talk.*

had·n't (had′'nt), had not.

hadst (hadst), an older form of **had,** used with *thou,* as in the Bible.

hae·mo·glo·bin (hē′mə glō′bin), *n.* same as **hemoglobin.**

haft (haft), *n.* the handle of a knife, ax, etc.

hag (hag), *n.* an ugly old woman, especially one who is wicked [Witches were called *hags.*]

hag·gard (hag′ərd), *adj.* having a wild but tired look, as from illness, hunger, or grief.

hag·gle (hag′'l), *v.* to argue about the price of something or the terms of an agreement. **—hag′gled,** *p.t. & p.p.;* **hag′gling,** *pr.p.*

Hague, The (hāg), one of the two capitals of the Netherlands. The lawmakers meet there.

haggard face

hah (hä), *interj.* same as **ha.**

hail (hāl), *v.* **1.** to welcome or greet with a shout; cheer [The Romans *hailed* Caesar as emperor.] **2.** to try to get the attention of, as by shouting [He *hailed* a cab.] **—n. 1.** the act of hailing or greeting. **2.** the distance that a shout can be heard [The boat approached within *hail* of shore.] **—interj.** a shout of greeting or welcome. **—hail from,** to come from [My family *hails from* Iowa.]

hail (hāl), *n.* **1.** small, round pieces of ice that sometimes fall during a thunderstorm; frozen raindrops. **2.** anything that comes in large numbers and with force [a *hail* of bullets; a *hail* of curses]. **—v. 1.** to pour down hail [It *hailed* last night.] **2.** to come down or throw down in large numbers and with force [Arrows *hailed* down on them from the castle walls.]

hail·stone (hāl′stōn), *n.* a piece of hail.

hair (her), *n.* **1.** any of the thin growths, like threads, that come from the skin of animals and human beings. **2.** the whole number of these growths that cover a person's head, the skin of an animal, etc. [I must comb my *hair*.] **3.** a tiny space or amount [You missed the bull's-eye by a *hair*.] **4.** a growth like a fine thread on the leaves or stems of some plants. **—split hairs,** to pay too much attention to small differences that are not important.

hair·breadth (her′bredth) or **hairs·breadth** (herz′bredth), *n.* a tiny space or amount [Our team won by a *hairsbreadth*.] **—adj.** very close; narrow [a *hairbreadth* escape].

hair·cloth (her′klôth), *n.* cloth woven from the hair of a horse or camel. It is used mainly for covering furniture.

hair·cut (her′kut), *n.* the act or style of cutting the hair of the head.

hair·do (her′dōō′), *n.* the style in which a woman's hair is arranged.

hair·dress·er (her′dres ər), *n.* a person whose work is cutting and arranging women's hair.

hair·less (her′lis), *adj.* without hair; bald.

hair·line (her′līn), *n.* **1.** a very thin line. **2.** the line just above the forehead where the hair begins to grow.

hair·pin (her′pin), *n.* a small, curved piece of wire, plastic, etc. that is used by women to keep the hair in place. **—adj.** shaped like a hairpin [a *hairpin* curve].

hair-rais·ing (her′rāz′ing), *adj.* very frightening or shocking: *used only in everyday talk.*

hair·spring (her′spring), *n.* a very slender spring that controls the movement of the balance wheel in a watch or clock.

hair·y (her′ē), *adj.* **1.** covered with hair [*hairy* arms]. **2.** of or like hair. **—hair′i·er,** *compar.;* **hair′i·est,** *superl.* **—hair′i·ness,** *n.*

Hai·ti (hā′tē), *n.* a country in the western part of Hispaniola, in the West Indies. **—Hai·ti·an** (hā′ti ən *or* hā′shən), *adj. & n.*

hake (hāk), *n.* a sea fish that looks like the cod and is used for food.

hal·berd (hal′bərd) or **hal·bert** (hal′bərt), *n.* a weapon of the 15th and 16th centuries that is like a spear and battle-ax combined.

halberd

fat, āpe, cär, ten, ēven, hit, bīte, gō, hôrn, tōol, book, up, fūr;
get, joy, yet, chin, she, thin, *th*en; zh = s in pleasure; ' as in able (ā′b'l).
ə = a in ago, e in agent, i in sanity, o in confess, u in focus.

hal·cy·on (hal′si ən), *adj.* happy and peaceful [*halcyon* days].

hale (hāl), *adj.* healthy and strong [Grandfather is still *hale* and hearty.] —**hal′er**, *compar.*; **hal′est**, *superl.*

hale (hāl), *v.* to drag, pull, or force along [He was *haled* into court.] —**haled**, *p.t. & p.p.*; **hal′ing**, *pr.p.*

Hale, Na·than (nā′thən hāl), 1755–1776; American soldier in the Revolutionary War, who was hanged by the British as a spy.

half (haf), *n.* **1.** either of the two equal parts of something [Five is *half* of ten.] **2.** either of two almost equal parts: *a loose use* [He took the smaller *half* of the pie.] —*adj.* **1.** being either of the two equal parts [a *half* share; a *half* gallon]. **2.** being about a half [A *half* mask covered his eyes.] **3.** not complete or perfect; partial [I could barely see him in the *half* light.] —*adv.* **1.** to half or about half of the whole amount [*half* full; *half* baked]. **2.** to some degree; partly [I was *half* convinced.] —**in half**, into halves. —**not half bad**, rather good. —**halves**, *pl.*

half·back (haf′bak), *n.* either of two football players whose position is behind the line.

half-baked (haf′bākt′), *adj.* **1.** only partly baked. **2.** not having enough thought, planning, experience, etc.; foolish [a *half-baked* idea].

half-breed (haf′brēd′), *n.* a person whose parents are of different races.

half brother, a brother through one parent only.

half-caste (haf′kast′), *n.* **1.** a half-breed. **2.** a person who has one European parent and one Asiatic parent.

half crown, a British silver coin equal to two and a half shillings.

half dollar, a silver coin of the United States and Canada, worth 50 cents.

half·heart·ed (haf′här′tid), *adj.* with little enthusiasm or interest [a *halfhearted* attempt]. —**half′heart′ed·ly**, *adv.*

half-hour (haf′our′), *n.* **1.** half of an hour; thirty minutes. **2.** the point thirty minutes after any given hour [Take your medicine on the *half-hour*.] —*adj.* lasting for thirty minutes [a *half-hour* program].

half-mast (haf′mast′), *n.* the position of a flag lowered about halfway down its staff, as in mourning someone who has died.

half note, a note in music that is held half as long as a whole note.

half·pen·ny (hā′pən ē *or* hāp′nē), *n.* a British bronze coin equal to half a penny. —**half′pence** (hā′pəns) *or* **half′pennies**, *pl.*

half notes

half sister, a sister through one parent only.

half·way (haf′wā′), *adj.* **1.** at the middle between two points or limits [to reach the *halfway* mark]. **2.** not complete; partial [to take *halfway* measures]. —*adv.* **1.** to the midway point [They had gone *halfway* home.] **2.** partially [The house is *halfway* built.] —**meet halfway**, to try to

reach an agreement by having each side give up something.

half-wit (haf′wit′), *n.* **1.** a person who is feeble-minded. **2.** a stupid or silly person; fool. —**half′-wit′ted**, *adj.*

hal·i·but (hal′ə bət), *n.* a very large flatfish of the northern seas, used for food. —**hal′i·but** *or* **hal′i·buts**, *pl.*

Hal·i·fax (hal′ə faks), *n.* the capital of Nova Scotia, Canada.

hal·ite (hā′līt *or* hal′īt), *n.* rock salt.

hall (hôl), *n.* **1.** a passageway from which doors open into various rooms. **2.** a room or passageway at the entrance of a building. **3.** a large room used for meetings, shows, dances, etc. **4.** a building containing public offices or a headquarters of some sort [the city *hall*]. **5.** any of the buildings of a college, especially a dormitory. **6.** the large country house of a baron, squire, etc.

hal·le·lu·jah *or* **hal·le·lu·iah** (hal′ə lōō′yə), *interj.* praise the Lord! —*n.* a hymn of praise to God.

hall·mark (hôl′märk), *n.* **1.** a mark stamped on gold and silver articles to show where they were made, how pure they are, etc. **2.** anything that shows how genuine something is [Bravery is the *hallmark* of a good soldier.] Also **hall mark.** —*v.* to put a hallmark on.

hal·lo *or* **hal·loa** (hə lō′), *interj., n. & v.* shout or call, as to get attention or urge on hounds in hunting. —**hal′los** *or* **hal′loas**, *pl.* —**hal′loed** *or* **hal′loaed**, *p.t. & p.p.*; **hal′lo·ing** *or* **hal′loa·ing**, *pr.p.*

hal·loo (hə lōō′), *interj., n. & v.* same as **hallo.**

hal·low (hal′ō), *v.* to make or keep holy or sacred [to *hallow* the name of God].

Hal·low·een *or* **Hal·low·e′en** (hal′ō ēn′ *or* häl′ə wēn′), *n.* the evening of October 31, celebrated nowadays with fun-making and masquerades.

hal·lu·ci·na·tion (hə lōō′sə nā′shən), *n.* **1.** the seeing or hearing of things around one that are not really there at all [People with very sick minds sometimes have *hallucinations*.] **2.** the thing seen or heard in this way.

hal·lu·ci·no·gen (hə lōō′sə nə jen *or* hal′yoo-sin′ə jen), *n.* a drug that causes hallucinations. —**hal·lu′ci·no·gen′ic**, *adj.*

hall·way (hôl′wā), *n.* a passageway, as between rooms; corridor.

ha·lo (hā′lō), *n.* **1.** a ring of light around the sun, the moon, a street light, etc. **2.** a ring of light shown around the head of a saint, angel, etc., as in a painting. It is a symbol of holiness. —**ha′los** *or* **ha′loes**, *pl.*

halo (*meaning 2*)

halt (hôlt), *n. & v.* stop [He worked all morning without a *halt*. Rain *halted* the game.] —**call a halt**, to order a stop.

halt (hôlt), *v.* **1.** to walk in a lame way; limp. **2.** to hesitate [to be *halting* in one's speech]. —*adj.* lame or crippled.

hal·ter (hôl'tər), *n.* **1.** a rope or strap for leading or tying an animal. **2.** an upper garment without a back, worn by a woman or girl. It is held up by a loop around the neck. **3.** a rope for hanging a person.

halve (hav), *v.* **1.** to divide into two equal parts. **2.** to make only half as much, half as large, etc. [This new process will *halve* our costs.] —**halved,** *p.t. & p.p.;* **halv'ing,** *pr.p.*

halves (havz), *n.* plural of **half.** —**go halves,** to share expenses equally.

hal·yard (hal'yərd), *n.* a rope used to raise or lower a flag, sail, etc.

halter

ham (ham), *n.* **1.** the upper part of a hog's hind leg, salted, smoked, etc. for eating. **2.** the back part of the thigh and the buttock. **3.** an actor who acts in an awkward or exaggerated way: *slang in this meaning.* **4.** an amateur radio operator: *slang in this meaning.*

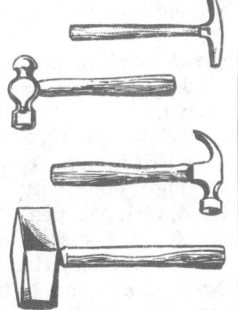

Ham·burg (ham'bərg), *n.* a city in northwestern Germany.

ham·burg·er (ham'bər gər) or **ham·burg** (ham'bərg), *n.* **1.** ground beef. **2.** a small, flat cake of ground beef, fried or broiled. It is often eaten as a sandwich in a round bun.

Ham·il·ton, Alexander (ham'il t'n), 1757–1804; first secretary of the United States treasury, from 1789 to 1795.

Ham·let (ham'lit), *n.* **1.** a tragic play by Shakespeare. **2.** the hero of this play.

ham·let (ham'lit), *n.* a very small village.

ham·mer (ham'ər), *n.* **1.** a tool for driving in nails, breaking stones, shaping metal, etc. It usually has a metal head and a handle. **2.** a thing like this in shape or use, as the part that strikes against the firing pin of a gun or any of the parts that strike the strings of a piano. —*v.* **1.** to hit with many blows [He *hammered* on the door with his fists.] **2.** to make or fasten with a hammer and, often, nails [to *hammer* together a box]. **3.** to drive or force [to *hammer* an idea into someone's head]. —**hammer away at, 1.** to work hard and steadily at. **2.** to keep talking about. —**hammer out, 1.** to shape by hammering. **2.** to work out with thought or effort [to *hammer out* a plan].

types of hammer

ham·mock (ham'ək), *n.* a long piece of canvas that is hung from ropes at each end and is used as a bed or couch.

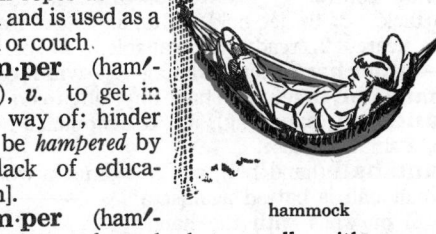

hammock

ham·per (ham'pər), *v.* to get in the way of; hinder [to be *hampered* by a lack of education].

ham·per (ham'pər), *n.* a large basket, usually with a cover [Put your soiled shirt in the clothes *hamper*.]

ham·ster (ham'stər), *n.* a small animal like a mouse, with large cheek pouches. It is often used in scientific experiments, or kept as a pet.

ham·string (ham'string), *n.* **1.** one of the tendons at the back of a person's knee. **2.** the large tendon at the back of the hock of a horse, ox, etc. —*v.* to make lame, as by cutting the hamstring. —**ham·strung** (ham'strung), *p.t. & p.p.;* **ham'string·ing,** *pr.p.*

Han·cock, John (han'käk), 1737–1793; American statesman. He was the first to sign the Declaration of Independence.

hand (hand), *n.* **1.** the end of the arm beyond the wrist, including the fingers and thumb. **2.** any of the pointers on a clock or watch. **3.** side [The guest of honor sat at the host's right *hand*.] **4.** a person hired to work with his hands [a farm *hand;* dock *hand*]. **5.** skill or ability [These sketches show the *hand* of a master.] **6.** control or power [He rules with an iron *hand*. This matter is now in the *hands* of my lawyer.] **7.** a part or share in some action [Take a *hand* in the work.] **8.** help [Give me a *hand* with this job.] **9.** a clapping of hands; applause [Give the dancer a big *hand*.] **10.** handwriting [He writes a poor *hand*.] **11.** the place from which something comes; source [I got the news at first *hand*.] **12.** a promise to marry [He asked Mary's father for her *hand*.] **13.** the breadth of a hand, about four inches [This horse is 15 *hands* high.] **14.** the cards held by each player in a card game. **15.** a single round of play in a card game. —*adj.* of, for, or worked by the hand or hands [*hand* lotion; a *hand* saw]. —*v.* **1.** to give with the hand; pass [*Hand* me the book, please.] **2.** to help or lead with the hand. —**at hand,** near; close by. —**at the hand of,** through the action of. —**by hand,** with the hands, not by machines. —**change hands,** to pass from one owner to another. —**from hand to mouth,** with nothing left over for future needs. —**hand down, 1.** to pass along, as from generation to generation. **2.** to give a verdict, as in a court. —**hand in glove** or **hand and glove,** very close, as in friendship or in working together. —**hand in hand, 1.** holding hands. **2.** together. —**hands down,** easily [to win *hands* *down*]. —**hand to hand,** very close to the opponent [to fight *hand to hand*]. —**in hand,** under control. —**lay hands on, 1.** to hurt or attack. **2.** to get hold of; take. —**on hand, 1.** near. **2.** ready or available. **3.** present. —**upper hand,** the advantage. —**wash one's hands of,** to refuse to have anything to do with.

hand·bag (hand'bag), *n.* **1.** a woman's purse. **2.** a small suitcase.

hand·ball (hand'bôl), *n.* **1.** a game in which a small ball is batted against a wall or walls with the hand. **2.** the small rubber ball used in this game.

hand·bill (hand'-bil), *n.* a small, printed advertisement that is passed out by hand.

hand·book (hand'-book), *n.* a small book of facts or instructions; manual.

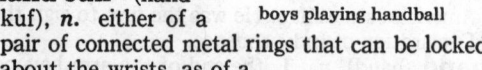
boys playing handball

hand·cuff (hand'-kuf), *n.* either of a pair of connected metal rings that can be locked about the wrists, as of a prisoner. —*v.* to put handcuffs on.

Han·del, George Frederick (han'd'l), 1685–1759; English composer, born in Germany.

hand·ful (hand'fool), *n.* **1.** as much or as many as the hand can hold [a *handful* of popcorn]. **2.** a small number; few [a *handful* of people]. **3.** a person or thing that is hard to manage: *used only in everyday talk.* —**hand'fuls,** *pl.*

handcuffs

hand·i·cap (han'dē kap), *n.* **1.** a race or other contest in which things are made harder for some or easier for others so that all have an equal chance. **2.** the harder or easier condition given in such a contest [a *handicap* of extra weight in a horse race or of a shorter distance in running]. **3.** anything that holds a person back or gives him less chance than others have; hindrance [Lack of education can be a great *handicap*.] —*v.* to be or give a handicap; make things harder for. —**hand'i·capped,** *p.t. & p.p.;* **hand'i·cap·ping,** *pr.p.*

hand·i·craft (han'dē kraft), *n.* **1.** skill in working with the hands. **2.** work that takes this kind of skill, as weaving.

hand·i·ly (han'd'l ē), *adv.* in a handy way; without difficulty; easily.

hand·i·ness (han'dē nis), *n.* the quality of being handy; skill in working with the hands.

hand·i·work (han'dē wûrk), *n.* **1.** work done by hand. **2.** anything made or done by someone [Is this poem your *handiwork?*]

hand·ker·chief (hang'kər chif), *n.* a small piece of soft cloth for wiping the nose, eyes, or face, or worn as a decoration.

han·dle (han'd'l), *n.* the part by which a tool, door, cup, etc. can be held, lifted, or turned with the hand. —*v.* **1.** to hold or touch with the hand [*Handle* that china cup with care.] **2.** to take care of, manage, or control [This restaurant can *handle* hundreds of customers during the lunch hour.] **3.** to deal with; treat [There are various ways of *handling* this problem.] **4.** to work or act in a certain way [My new bicycle *handles* well.] **5.** to buy or sell as a business; deal in [Most drugstores *handle* a variety of items.] —**han'dled,** *p.t. & p.p.;* **han'dling,** *pr.p.* —**hand'ler,** *n.*

handle bar, a curved metal bar on a bicycle or motorcycle, used for steering.

hand·made (hand'mād'), *adj.* made by hand instead of by machine.

hand·maid (hand'mād) or **hand·maid·en** (hand'-mād 'n), *n.* a woman or girl servant. *These words are now seldom used.*

handle bar

hand organ, same as **barrel organ.**

hand·out (hand'out), *n.* a gift of food, clothing, etc., as to a beggar or tramp.

hand·rail (hand'rāl), *n.* a rail that can be used for support, as along a stairway.

hand·shake (hand'shāk), *n.* a holding and shaking of another's hand, as in greeting.

hand·some (han'səm), *adj.* **1.** pleasant to look at; good-looking, especially in a manly or dignified way. **2.** large in amount or size [a *handsome* sum of money]. **3.** proper or fitting [He treated us all in a *handsome* way.] —**hand'some·ly,** *adv.* —**hand'some·ness,** *n.*

hand·spring (hand'spring), *n.* a kind of somersault in which only the hands or a hand touches the ground: *see the picture.*

hand·work (hand'-wûrk), *n.* work done by hand.

hand·writ·ing (hand'rīt ing), *n.* **1.** writing done by hand, with pen, pencil, etc. **2.** a person's way of forming letters and words in writing [His *handwriting* slants to the left.]

handspring

hand·y (han'dē), *adj.* **1.** easily reached; near-by [The bus stop is *handy*.] **2.** easily used; saving time or work [a *handy* device for opening cans]. **3.** clever in using one's hands; deft [He is *handy* with tools.] —**hand'i·er,** *compar.;* **hand'i·est,** *superl.*

hang (hang), *v.* **1.** to fasten or be fastened to something above, as by pins, hooks, nails, etc. [to *hang* laundry on a clothesline; to *hang* a picture]. **2.** to put to death or to die by hanging from a rope tied around the neck. **3.** to fasten or be fastened so as to swing freely [The shutters are *hung* on hinges.] **4.** to fasten to walls and ceilings with paste [to *hang* wallpaper]. **5.** to decorate by hanging pictures, drapes, etc. [The room was *hung* with oil paintings.] **6.** to bend or lean down; droop [He *hung* his head in shame.] **7.** to keep from coming to a decision [The jury was *hung* because its members couldn't agree on a verdict.] —*n.* **1.** the way a thing hangs [the *hang* of the curtains]. **2.** the way a thing is done or used [He can't get the *hang* of driving a car.] **3.** general idea; meaning [I don't get the *hang* of this story.] —**hang around** or **hang about,** to loiter or linger in some place: *used only in everyday talk.* —**hang back,** to be unwilling to go forward, as because of shyness. —**hang fire,** to stay undecided. —**hang on, 1.** to keep hold. **2.** to depend on. **3.** to lean on. **4.** to listen closely to. —**hang out, 1.** to lean out. **2.** to dwell or spend time at: *a slang phrase.* —**hang over, 1.** to stick out over; overhang. **2.** to hover over. **3.** to be a threat to. —**hang together, 1.** to stick together. **2.** to make sense, as a story. —**hang up, 1.** to put on a hanger or hook, as a coat. **2.** to put a telephone receiver back in place in ending a call. **3.** to delay. —**hung,** *p.t. & p.p.* (**hanged** *for* meaning 2); **hang'ing,** *pr.p.*

hang·ar (hang'ər), *n.* a shed in which aircraft are kept when not in use.

hang·dog (hang'- dôg), *adj.* ashamed and cringing [a *hangdog* look].

hangar

hang·er (hang'- ər), *n.* **1.** a person who hangs things [a paper *hanger*]. **2.** a thing on which another thing is hung [a clothes *hanger*].

hang·er-on (hang'ər än'), *n.* a supporter of someone, especially one who hopes to gain something in this way. —**hang'ers-on',** *pl.*

hang·ing (hang'ing), *adj.* that hangs [a *hanging* lamp; *hanging* cliffs]. —*n.* **1.** the act of putting to death by hanging. **2.** something hung on a wall, window, etc., as a drapery.

hang·man (hang'mən), *n.* a man who hangs persons sentenced by law to die. —**hang'-men,** *pl.*

hang·nail (hang'nāl), *n.* a bit of torn skin hanging next to a fingernail.

hang-up (hang'up'), *n.* a problem that involves a person's feelings or private affairs and is one that he cannot seem to work out: *a slang word.*

hank (hangk), *n.* a loop or coil of hair or yarn.

hank·er (hang'kər), *v.* to have a strong wish or longing; crave [to *hanker* after fame].

Han·ni·bal (han'ə b'l), *n.* 247 B.C.–183 B.C.; a general of Carthage who invaded Italy.

Han·o·ver (han'ō vər), *n.* **1.** a city in northern Germany. **2.** the ruling family of England from 1714 to 1901.

han·som (han'səm), *n.* a covered carriage with two wheels, drawn by one horse. The driver's seat is above and behind the cab. Also **hansom cab.**

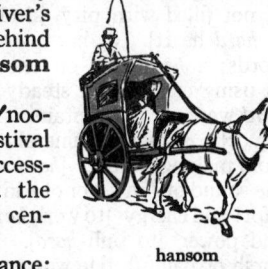

hansom

Ha·nuk·kah (hä'noo- kä), *n.* a Jewish festival celebrating the successful revolt against the Syrians in the 2nd century B.C.

hap (hap), *n.* chance; luck. —*v.* to happen. *This word is now seldom used.* —**happed,** *p.t. & p.p.;* **hap'ping,** *pr.p.*

hap·haz·ard (hap'haz'ərd), *adj.* not planned; accidental [*haphazard* events]. —*adv.* by chance; in a haphazard way [toys scattered *haphazard* on the floor]. —**hap'haz'ard·ly,** *adv.*

hap·less (hap'lis), *adj.* unlucky; unfortunate.

hap·ly (hap'lē), *adv.* by chance; perhaps: *now seldom used.*

hap·pen (hap''n), *v.* **1.** to take place, especially by chance; occur [When did the accident *happen*? It *happened* to rain that day.] **2.** to have the luck, good or bad; chance [I *happened* to meet him.] —**happen along** or **happen by,** to come by chance: *used only in everyday talk.* —**happen on,** to meet or find by chance.

hap·pen·ing (hap''n ing), *n.* something that happens; event [the day's *happenings*].

hap·py (hap'ē), *adj.* **1.** feeling or showing pleasure or joy; glad; contented [a *happy* child; a *happy* song]. **2.** lucky; fortunate [The story has a *happy* ending.] **3.** suitable and clever [He paid her a *happy* compliment.] —**hap'pi·er,** *compar.;* **hap'pi·est,** *superl.* —**hap'pi·ly,** *adv.* —**hap'pi·ness,** *n.*

hap·py-go-luck·y (hap'ē gō luk'ē), *adj.* trusting to luck; not worrying; carefree.

Haps·burg (haps'bərg), *n.* a former ruling family in Austria and Spain.

ha·rangue (hə rang'), *n.* a long speech made in a loud or scolding way. —*v.* to give a harangue or talk to in a harangue. —**ha·rangued',** *p.t. & p.p.;* **ha·rangu'ing,** *pr.p.*

har·ass (har'əs *or* hə ras'), *v.* **1.** to worry or trouble [He was *harassed* with many debts.] **2.** to trouble by attacking again and again [Flies *harassed* the horse.] —**har'ass·ment,** *n.*

har·bin·ger (här'bin jər), *n.* a person or thing that comes to show what will follow [The first frost is a *harbinger* of winter.]

har·bor (här'bər), *n.* **1.** a place where ships may anchor and be safe from storms; port; haven. **2.** any place where one is safe; shelter. —*v.* **1.** to shelter or hide [to *harbor* an outlaw]. **2.** to hold in the mind [to *harbor* ill will].

hard (härd), *adj.* **1.** firm to the touch; not easy to cut, bend, or crush; not soft; solid [a *hard* rock]. **2.** not easy to do, understand, or deal

fat, āpe, cär, ten, ēven, hit, bīte, gō, hôrn, tool, book, up, fūr;
get, joy, yet, chin, she, thin, *th*en; zh = s in pleasure; ' as in able (ā'b'l)
ə = a in ago, e in agent, i in sanity, o in confess, u in focus.

with; difficult [a *hard* job; a *hard* problem].
3. strong or powerful; violent [a *hard* wind].
4. not filled with pity, kindness, etc.; unfeeling
[a *hard* heart]. **5.** harsh or severe; stern [*hard*
words; a *hard* look on one's face; a *hard* life].
6. using energy and steady effort; energetic [a
hard worker]. **7.** containing much alcohol [*hard*
liquor]. **8.** having minerals in it that keep soap
from making a lather [*hard* water]. **9.** describing
the sound of *g* in *get* or of *c* in *can.* —*adv.* **1.** with
effort and energy [to work *hard*]. **2.** with strength
and power [to pull *hard*]. **3.** in a way that is
harsh or painful [He was *hard* hit by her death.]
4. in a firm way [to hold on *hard*]. **5.** so as to be
solid [to freeze *hard*]. **6.** close or near [We
lived *hard* by the woods.] —**hard and fast,**
strict; that cannot be changed. —**hard of
hearing,** not able to hear well. —**hard up,**
in great need of money: *only in everyday talk.*
hard-boiled (härd'boild'), *adj.* **1.** boiled until
the inside is solid [*hard-boiled* eggs]. **2.** without
gentle feelings or sympathy; tough: *used only in
everyday talk.*
hard·en (här'd'n), *v.* to make or become hard.
hard·head·ed (härd'hed'id), *adj.* **1.** stubborn.
2. having only practical thoughts and not moved
by feeling [a *hardheaded* businessman].
hard·heart·ed (härd'här'tid), *adj.* without
pity or sympathy; cruel or unfeeling.
har·di·hood (här'dē hood), *n.* boldness; daring.
Har·ding, Warren G. (här'ding), 1865–
1923; 29th president of the United States, from
1921 to 1923.
hard·ly (härd'lē), *adv.* **1.** only just; almost not;
scarcely [I can *hardly* tell them apart. There is
hardly any time left.] **2.** probably not; not likely
[That can *hardly* be the case.] **3.** in a hard way;
with harshness, difficulty, etc.
hard·ness (härd'nis), *n.* a being hard.
hard·ship (härd'ship), *n.* something that is
hard to bear; trouble, pain, suffering, etc.
hard·tack (härd'tak), *n.* a kind of unraised
bread in the form of hard biscuits, much used by
sailors and soldiers in earlier days.
hard·ware (härd'wer), *n.* things made of
metal, as tools, nails, pots and pans, etc.
hard·wood (härd'wood), *n.* any wood that is
hard and has a close grain, as oak, walnut, maple,
ebony, etc.
har·dy (här'dē), *adj.* **1.** strong and sturdy; able
to hold up under bad conditions [*Hardy* plants
can live through frosts.] **2.** bold or daring [a
hardy adventurer]. —**har'di·er,** *compar.;* **har'-
di·est,** *superl.* —**har'di·ly,** *adv.* —**har'di-
ness,** *n.*
hare (her), *n.* a swift animal with long ears, a
split upper lip, large
front teeth used for
gnawing, and long
hind legs; a rabbit,
especially any of the
larger kind.
hare·bell (her'bel).
n. the bluebell, a   hare (1½ ft. long)
plant with blue flowers shaped like bells.

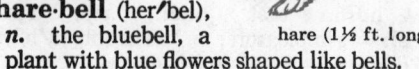

hare·brained (her'brānd), *adj.* having or
showing little sense; silly [a *harebrained* idea].
hare·lip (her'lip), *n.* a split upper lip that some
people are born with.
ha·rem (her'əm), *n.* **1.** the part of a Moslem's
house in which the women live. **2.** the women
who live in a harem.
hark (härk), *v.* to listen carefully: *now seldom
used except in poetry* ["*Hark!* the herald angels
sing"]. —**hark back,** to go back, as in thought
[to *hark back* to one's childhood].
hark·en (här'k'n), *v.* same as **hearken.**
Har·lem (här'ləm), *n.* a part of New York City
in which many Negroes and Puerto Ricans live.
Har·le·quin (här'lə kwin), *n.* **1.** a comic character in pantomime, who wears
tights of many colors and a
mask. **2. harlequin,** a
clown.
har·lot (här'lət), *n.* a prostitute.
harm (härm), *n.* **1.** damage
or hurt [Too much rain can do
harm to crops.] **2.** wrong [He
meant no *harm* by his remark.]
—*v.* to do harm to; hurt or
damage.
harm·ful (härm'fəl), *adj.* do-   Harlequin
ing harm or able to do harm. —**harm'ful·ly,**
adv.
harm·less (härm'lis), *adj.* that cannot harm;
doing no harm. —**harm'less·ly,** *adv.*
har·mon·ic (här män'ik), *adj.* of or in harmony
in music. —*n.* same as **overtone.**
har·mon·i·ca (här män'i kə), *n.* a small musical instrument with
a row of reeds that
sound tones when the
breath is blown out or
sucked in across them;
mouth organ.
har·mo·ni·ous (här-
mō'ni əs), *adj.* **1.** fitting or blending to-
gether in an orderly or
pleasing way [a *har-*   harmonica
monious group of statues]. **2.** friendly; getting
along well together [*harmonious* partners].

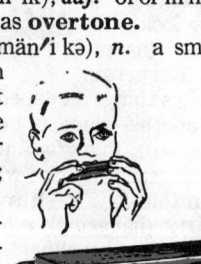

har·mo·nize (här'mə nīz), *v.* **1.** to be, sing,
or play in harmony [Brown *harmonizes* with
green. The voices *harmonized* in a quartet.] **2.** to
bring into harmony [to *harmonize* the colors in a
room; to *harmonize* a melody]. —**har'mo-
nized,** *p.t. & p.p.;* **har'mo·niz·ing,** *pr.p.*
har·mo·ny (här'mə nē), *n.* **1.** pleasing arrangement of things, parts, colors, etc. **2.** peace and
friendship; agreement in ideas, feelings, etc.
[We work in perfect *harmony*.] **3.** the sound of
music. **4.** the sounding together of tones in a
way that is pleasing to hear. **5.** the study of
chords and their use in music. —**har'mo·nies,**
pl.
har·ness (här'nis), *n.* **1.** the leather straps and
metal pieces by which a horse, mule, etc. is
fastened to a wagon, plow, or the like. **2.** any

arrangement of straps like this [the *harness* that fastens a parachute to a person]. —*v.* **1.** to put a harness on. **2.** to control so as to use the power of [to *harness* one's energies].

harp (härp), *n.* a musical instrument having many strings stretched on a large, upright frame. The strings are plucked with the fingers. —*v.* **1.** to talk or write about something so much that it becomes boring [He's always *harping* on his illness.] **2.** to play on a harp.

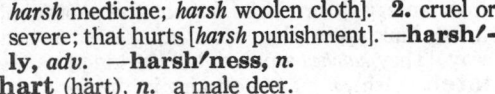

harp

harp·ist (här′pist), *n.* a harp player.

har·poon (här poon′), *n.* a spear with a barb at one end and a line attached to the shaft. It is used for spearing whales or other sea animals. —*v.* to strike or catch with a harpoon.

harp·si·chord (härp′si kôrd), *n.* an early musical instrument like a piano, except that the strings are plucked by points instead of being struck by hammers.

Har·py (här′pē), *n.* **1.** an ugly monster in Greek myths with the head and body of a woman and the wings, tail, and claws of a bird. **2. harpy,** a greedy or grasping person. —**Har′pies** or **har′pies,** *pl.*

har·que·bus (här′kwi bəs), *n.* an arquebus.

har·ri·er (har′i ər), *n.* a breed of dog used for hunting rabbits and hares.

Har·ris·burg (har′is bürg), *n.* the capital of Pennsylvania.

Har·ri·son, Benjamin (har′ə s′n), 1833–1901; 23rd president of the United States, from 1889 to 1893.

Harrison, William Henry, 1773–1841; ninth president of the United States, in 1841. He was the grandfather of Benjamin Harrison.

har·row (har′ō), *n.* a heavy frame with metal spikes or sharp disks: it is pulled over plowed ground for breaking up the soil and for covering seeds. —*v.* to pull a harrow over.

har·row·ing (har′ō ing), *adj.* causing pain, fear, or discomfort [The fire was a *harrowing* experience.]

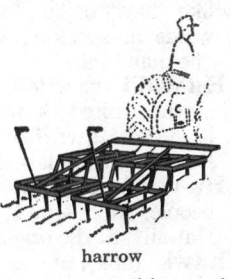

harrow

har·ry (har′ē), *v.* **1.** to keep on attacking and raiding; plunder [Invaders from Denmark *harried* the early British tribes.] **2.** to worry or trouble; harass [*harried* by debts]. —**har′ried,** *p.t. & p.p.*; **har′ry·ing,** *pr.p.*

harsh (härsh), *adj.* **1.** rough and not pleasing to one's hearing, sight, taste, or touch; grating, glaring, coarse, etc. [*harsh* music; a *harsh* light;

harsh medicine; *harsh* woolen cloth]. **2.** cruel or severe; that hurts [*harsh* punishment]. —**harsh′ly,** *adv.* —**harsh′ness,** *n.*

hart (härt), *n.* a male deer.

Hart·ford (härt′fərd), *n.* the capital of Connecticut.

har·um-scar·um (her′əm sker′əm), *adj.* acting or done without thinking; reckless; rash. —*n.* a reckless or rash person.

har·vest (här′vist), *n.* **1.** the act of gathering a crop of grain, fruit, etc. when it becomes ripe. **2.** the time of the year when a crop is gathered. **3.** all the grain, fruit, etc. gathered in one season; crop [a large *harvest*]. —*v.* **1.** to gather in a crop [to *harvest* peaches]. **2.** to gather a crop from [to *harvest* a field].

har·vest·er (här′vis tər), *n.* **1.** a person who harvests a crop. **2.** a machine for harvesting.

has (haz), the form of the verb **have** used to show the present time with *he, she,* and *it,* and with singular nouns [The boy *has* his book. *Has* he gone? She *has* a new dress.]

hash (hash), *n.* **1.** a dish made of meat and vegetables chopped up into small pieces, mixed together, and baked or fried. **2.** a careless or jumbled mixture; mess [He made a *hash* of the job.] —*v.* to chop up into small pieces.

has·n't (haz′nt), has not.

hasp (hasp), *n.* a metal piece that swings on a hinge and fits over a staple through which a pin or lock is passed to keep a door, window, or lid closed.

has·sle or **has·sel** (has′'l), *n.* an angry or excited argument; squabble: *a slang word.*

has·sock (has′ək), *n.* a firm cushion used as a footstool or low seat.

hasp

hast (hast), an older form of **have,** used with *thou,* as in the Bible.

haste (hāst), *n.* **1.** the act of hurrying; quick movement or action [He left in *haste*.] **2.** a hurrying in a careless way [*Haste* makes waste.] —**make haste,** to hurry.

has·ten (hās′'n), *v.* **1.** to go or act quickly; hurry [*Hasten* to call the doctor.] **2.** to send or bring faster [to *hasten* one's departure].

hast·y (hās′tē), *adj.* **1.** done or made with haste; hurried [a *hasty* lunch]. **2.** done or made too quickly, without enough thought; rash [a *hasty* decision]. —**hast′i·er,** *compar.*; **hast′i·est,** *superl.* —**hast′i·ly,** *adv.* —**hast′i·ness,** *n.*

hat (hat), *n.* a covering for the head, usually with a brim and a crown. —**pass the hat,** to take up a collection, as for charity. —**take one's hat off to,** to congratulate.

hatch (hach), *v.* **1.** to bring forth young birds, fish, turtles, etc. from eggs [Birds *hatch* their eggs by keeping them warm.] **2.** to come forth from an egg [Our chicks *hatched* this morning.] **3.** to think up or plan, often in a secret or bad way [They *hatched* a plot to kill the king.]

hatch (hach), *n.* **1.** an opening in the deck of a ship, as one through which cargo is moved into and out of the hold. **2.** any opening in a floor, or the trap door covering this.

hatch·er·y (hach/ər ē), *n.* a place for hatching eggs, as of fish or hens. —**hatch/er·ies,** *pl.*

hatch·et (hach/it), *n.* a small ax with a short handle. —**bury the hatch- et,** to stop fighting.

hatchet

hatch·way (hach/wā), *n.* an opening in the deck of a ship or in a floor; hatch.

hate (hāt), *v.* to have very bad feeling against; dislike very much [to *hate* an enemy; to *hate* to wash dishes]. —*n.* a very strong dislike; hatred [eyes full of *hate*]. —**hat/ed,** *p.t. & p.p.;* **hat/ing,** *pr.p.* —**hat/er,** *n.*

hate·ful (hāt/fəl), *adj.* **1.** deserving to be hated [a *hateful* lie; a *hateful* person]. **2.** feeling or showing hate: *now seldom used.* —**hate/ful·ly,** *adv.* —**hate/ful·ness,** *n.*

hath (hath), the older form of **has,** as in the Bible.

ha·tred (hā/trid), *n.* a strong dislike; hate.

hat·ter (hat/ər), *n.* a person who makes or sells men's hats.

Hat·ter·as, Cape (hat/ər əs), a cape on an island off the coast of North Carolina.

hau·berk (hô/bərk), *n.* a long coat of chain mail worn as armor in the Middle Ages.

haugh·ty (hô/tē), *adj.* having or showing too much pride in oneself and scorn for others. —**haugh/ti·er,** *compar.;* **haugh/ti·est,** *superl.* —**haugh/ti·ly,** *adv.* —**haugh/ti·ness,** *n.*

hauberk

haul (hôl), *v.* **1.** to move by pulling; drag or tug [We *hauled* the boat up on the beach.] **2.** to carry by wagon, truck, etc. [He *hauls* coal.] **3.** to change the course of a ship by setting the sails. —*n.* **1.** the act of hauling; pull [Give a *haul* on the rope.] **2.** the amount caught, taken, etc. at one time; catch [a good *haul* of fish]. **3.** the distance that something is hauled [It's a long *haul* to town.] **4.** the load hauled. —**haul off,** to draw the arm back before hitting: *used only in everyday talk.*

haunch (hônch), *n.* **1.** the hip, buttock, and upper part of the thigh. **2.** an animal's loin and leg together [a *haunch* of mutton].

haunt (hônt), *v.* **1.** to spend much time at; visit often [The boys *haunted* the drugstore. A *haunted* house is one that is supposed to be visited by a ghost.] **2.** to keep coming back to the mind [Memories *haunt* her.] —*n.* a place often visited [He made the library his *haunt*.]

hau·teur (hō tür/), *n.* haughty manner.

Ha·van·a (hə van/ə), *n.* the capital of Cuba.

have (hav), *v.* **1.** to be the owner of; possess [He *has* money. She *has* red hair.] **2.** to contain within itself [A week *has* seven days.] **3.** to hold in the mind, as an idea or a memory. **4.** to undergo or experience [to *have* the measles; to *have* a good time]. **5.** to get or take [*Have* a piece of candy.] **6.** to be the parent of [Mrs. Smith *has* twins.] **7.** to cause to do, go, be, etc. [*Have* the plumber fix the leak. He *had* his shoes shined.] **8.** to put up with; allow [I won't *have* any foolishness here.] **9.** to be forced or obliged [I *have* to go now.] **10.** to claim or say [Rumor *has* it that he's rich.] **11.** to hold an advantage over: *only in everyday talk* [He *had* me on that point.] *Have* is used as a helping verb with past participles [He *has* won. He *had* won. He will *have* won.] *Have got* is sometimes used in place of *have* [I *have* got to go. I've got new shoes.] In the present tense *have* has these forms: I, we, you, or they *have;* he, she, or it *has.* —**have on,** to be wearing. —**have to do with,** to be connected with. —**had,** *p.t. & p.p.;* **hav/ing,** *pr.p.*

ha·ven (hā/v'n), *n.* **1.** a port or harbor. **2.** any place of shelter or safety; refuge.

have·n't (hav/'nt), have not.

hav·er·sack (hav/ər sak), *n.* a canvas bag for carrying food, etc., worn on the back or over the shoulder by soldiers and hikers.

hav·oc (hav/ək), *n.* great damage or destruction [The hurricane caused much *hav- oc.*] —**play havoc with,** to destroy or ruin.

haw (hô), *n.* **1.** the reddish berry of the hawthorn. **2.** the hawthorn.

haw (hô), *interj.* a word of command to a horse or ox meaning "turn to the left!"

boy wearing a haversack

haw (hô), *v.* to make sounds like "haw" or "uh" while searching for the right words in speaking: *usually used in the phrase* "hem and haw."

Ha·wai·i (hə wī/ē *or* hə wä/yə), *n.* **1.** a State of the United States, consisting of a group of islands (**Hawaiian Islands**) in the North Pacific. **2.** the largest of these islands.

Ha·wai·ian (hə wī/yən), *adj.* of Hawaii, its people, etc. —*n.* **1.** a person born or living in Hawaii. **2.** the original language of Hawaii.

hawk (hôk), *n.* a large bird with a strong, hooked beak and claws, and keen sight. It captures and eats smaller birds and animals. —*v.* to hunt birds with the help of trained hawks.

hawk (hôk), *v.* to advertise or offer things for sale in the street by shouting. —**hawk/- er,** *n.*

hawk (hôk), *v.* to clear the throat noisily.

hawk (1½ ft. long)

hawk-eyed (hôk′īd′), *adj.* having keen sight.

hawse (hôz), *n.* **1.** the part at the front of a ship with holes through which the hawsers and cables go. **2.** any of these holes.

haw·ser (hô′zər), *n.* a large rope or small cable used in anchoring or towing a ship.

haw·thorn (hô′thôrn), *n.* a shrub or small tree with white or pink, sweet-smelling flowers and red berries.

Haw·thorne, Na·than·iel (nə than′yəl hô′thôrn), 1804-1864; U.S. writer of novels and stories.

hay (hā), *n.* grass, clover, etc. cut and dried for use as food for animals. —*v.* to cut down grass, etc. and spread it out to dry.

hay·cock (hā′käk), *n.* a small heap of hay drying in a field.

Hay·dn, Franz Jo·seph (fränts yō′zef hī′d'n, 1732-1809; Austrian composer of music.

Hayes, Ruth·er·ford B. (ruth′ər fərd hāz), 1822-1893; 19th president of the United States, from 1877 to 1881.

hay fever, an illness like a cold that makes the eyes water and causes sneezing and coughing. It is caused in people who are sensitive to the pollen of ragweed and other plants.

hay·field (hā′fēld), *n.* a field of grass, clover, etc. grown to make hay.

hay·loft (hā′lôft), *n.* a loft in a barn or stable, used for storing hay.

hay·mow (hā′mou), *n.* same as **hayloft.**

hay·rick (hā′rik), *n.* same as **haystack.**

hay·ride (hā′rīd), *n.* a pleasure ride taken by people in a wagon partly filled with hay.

hay·stack (hā′stak), *n.* a large heap of hay piled up outdoors.

hay·wire (hā′wīr), *n.* wire for tying up bales of hay or straw. —*adj.* mixed up, confused, crazy, etc.: *this meaning is slang.*

haz·ard (haz′ərd), *n.* **1.** danger or something dangerous; risk; peril [the *hazards* of icy streets]. **2.** anything on a golf course that makes it harder to play, as a pond. —*v.* to take a chance on; risk [to *hazard* a guess].

haystack

haz·ard·ous (haz′ər dəs), *adj.* dangerous; risky.

haze (hāz), *n.* **1.** thin mist, smoke, or dust in the air, that makes it harder to see. **2.** the condition of being confused in the mind; daze.

haze (hāz), *v.* to play tricks on or make do dangerous or silly things [It is forbidden to *haze* freshmen at our school.] —**hazed,** *p.t. & p.p.;* **haz′ing,** *pr.p.*

ha·zel (hā′z'l), *n.* a shrub or small tree related to the birch. —*adj.* light brown [*Hazel* eyes usually have green or gray flecks.]

haz·el·nut (hā′z'l nut), *n.* the small, round nut of the hazel, used as food.

ha·zy (hā′zē), *adj.* **1.** covered by or full of haze; somewhat misty or smoky [a *hazy* autumn day]. **2.** not certain; confused [His future plans are *hazy.*] —**ha′zi·er,** *compar.;* **ha′zi·est,** *superl.* —**ha′zi·ly,** *adv.* —**ha′zi·ness,** *n.*

H-bomb (āch′bäm′), *n.* same as **hydrogen bomb.**

hazelnuts

he (hē), *pron.* **1.** the man, boy, or male animal being talked about [John knew *he* was late.] **2.** a person; anyone [*He* who hesitates is lost.] —*n.* a man, boy, or male animal [This cat is a *he.*] —**they,** *pl.*

He, the symbol for the chemical element *helium.*

head (hed), *n.* **1.** the top part or front part of the body, which contains the brain, eyes, ears, nose, and mouth. **2.** a person's mind or intelligence [Use your *head.*] **3.** a single person or animal of a group: *for animals, the plural is* **head** [dinner at $2.00 a *head;* fifty *head* of cattle]. **4.** *often* **heads,** *pl.* the main side of a coin, usually showing a head. **5.** the top part of a thing [the *head* of a page; the *head* of a nail]. **6.** the front part of a thing [the *head* of a bed; the *head* of a line of people]. **7.** the part of something used to hit other things [the *head* of a hammer]. **8.** the skin stretched across the end of a drum. **9.** the place where a stream or river begins; source [The *head* of the Mississippi is in Minnesota.] **10.** the person who is in charge; leader, ruler, etc. [the *head* of a committee]. **11.** the highest position or rank [She's at the *head* of the class.] **12.** the part of a boil where pus is gathered. **13.** a turning point or crisis [Their quarrels have come to a *head.*] **14.** a topic or title [to deal with a subject under several *heads*]. —*adj.* **1.** most important; of highest rank; chief [the *head* coach]. **2.** at the front or coming from in front [*head* winds]. —*v.* **1.** to be the leader of; command [A colonel *heads* a regiment.] **2.** to be at the front or top of; lead [Marcia *heads* the class in spelling.] **3.** to turn or go in a certain direction [*Head* the horses home. Are you *heading* toward town?] —**go to one's head, 1.** to make one dizzy or drunk. **2.** to make one feel too proud or vain. —**head off,** to get ahead of and force to stop. —**keep one's head,** to keep control over oneself. —**lose one's head,** to lose control over oneself. —**out of one's head,** crazy, mad, or enraged. *This phrase is used only in everyday talk.* —**over one's head,** too hard for one to understand. —**put heads together,** to talk over plans or a plot together. —**turn one's head,** to make one feel too proud or vain. —**head′less,** *adj.*

fat, āpe, car, ten, ēven, hit, bīte, gō, hôrn, tōol, book, up, fur;
get, joy, yet, chin, she, thin, then; zh = s in pleasure; ' as in able (ā′b'l)
ə = a in ago, e in agent, i in sanity, o in confess, u in focus.

head·ache (hed′āk), *n.* **1.** a pain in the head. **2.** a worry; trouble: *used only in everyday talk.*

head·dress (hed′dres), *n.* a fancy covering or decoration for the head.

head·er (hed′ər), *n.* a fall or dive with the head first: *used only in everyday talk.*

head·first (hed′fûrst′) or **head·fore·most** (hed′fôr′mōst), *adv.* with the head first; head-long [to dive *headfirst* into water].

head·gear (hed′gir), *n.* a hat, cap, helmet, or other covering for the head.

head·ing (hed′ing), *n.* **1.** something at the head, top, or front. **2.** a title at the top of a paragraph, chapter, etc. **3.** a topic or subject

head·land (hed′lənd), *n.* a piece or point of land reaching out into the water; cape.

head·light (hed′līt), *n.* any of the lamps at the front of an automobile, train, etc., for throwing a bright light ahead at night.

head·line (hed′līn), *n.* a line or lines in large print at the top of a newspaper article, telling about it in a few words. —*v.* to list as the main attraction in a show. —**head′lined,** *p.t. & p.p.;* **head′lin·ing,** *pr.p.*

head·long (hed′lông), *adv. & adj.* **1.** with the head first [to fall *headlong;* a *headlong* dive]. **2.** with wild speed or force; reckless or recklessly [to rush *headlong* into a fight; a *headlong* plunge into the stock market].

head·mas·ter (hed′mas′tər), *n.* a principal, especially of a private school for boys.

head·mis·tress (hed′mis′tris), *n.* a woman principal of a private school for girls.

head·on (hed′än′), *adj. & adv.* with the head or front first [a *head-on* crash; to hit *head-on*].

head·phone (hed′fōn), *n.* **1.** a telephone or radio receiver held to the ear by a band over the head. **2.** *usually* **head-phones,** *pl.* a pair of such receivers: also called **head′set.**

head·piece (hed′pēs), *n.* a helmet, cap, or other covering for the head.

headphone

head·quar·ters (hed′-kwôr′tərz), *n.pl.* **1.** the main office or center of work of those in command of an army, police force, etc. **2.** any main office. *Sometimes used with a singular verb.*

heads·man (hedz′mən), *n.* a man who beheads persons sentenced by law to die. —**heads′-men,** *pl.*

head·stone (hed′stōn), *n.* same as **gravestone.**

head·strong (hed′strông), *adj.* doing just as one pleases, without listening to others; hard to control; stubborn.

head·wa·ters (hed′wô′tərz), *n.pl.* the small streams that come together to form a river.

head·way (hed′wā), *n.* **1.** motion ahead or forward [The boat made slow *headway* against the wind.] **2.** advance or progress [The club made little *headway* in raising funds.] **3.** clear space overhead, as in a tunnel or doorway.

head·y (hed′ē), *adj.* **1.** reckless or headstrong. **2.** going to one's head; intoxicating [a *heady* wine]. —**head′i·er,** *compar.;* **head′i·est,** *superl.*

heal (hēl), *v.* to get or bring back to good health or a sound condition; cure or mend [The wound *healed* slowly. Time *heals* grief.] —**heal′er,** *n.*

health (helth), *n.* **1.** the condition of being well in body and mind; freedom from sickness. **2.** condition of body or mind [good *health;* bad *health*]. **3.** a wish for one's health and happiness, as in drinking a toast.

health·ful (helth′fəl), *adj.* good for one's health; wholesome [*healthful* food].

health·y (hel′thē), *adj.* **1.** having good health; well [a *healthy* child]. **2.** showing good health [a *healthy* appetite]. **3.** good for one's health [a *healthy* climate]. —**health′i·er,** *compar.;* **health′i·est,** *superl.* —**health′i·ness,** *n.*

heap (hēp), *n.* **1.** a group of things lying together in a pile [The leaves were raked into *heaps.*] **2.** a large amount: *used only in everyday talk* [a *heap* of money]. —*v.* **1.** to pile up in a heap [toys *heaped* in the corner]. **2.** to give in large amounts [He *heaped* gifts upon me.] **3.** to fill very full; load up [a plate *heaped* with food].

hear (hir), *v.* **1.** to receive sound through the ears [I *hear* music. He doesn't *hear* well.] **2.** to listen to; pay attention [*Hear* what I tell you.] **3.** to hold a hearing, as of a law case. **4.** to give what is asked for; grant, as a prayer. **5.** to learn about; be told [I *hear* prices are going up.] —**hear from,** to get a letter, telephone call, etc. from. —**not hear of,** not allow or permit. —**heard** (hûrd), *p.t. & p.p.;* **hear′ing,** *pr.p.*

hear·ing (hir′ing), *n.* **1.** the act of receiving sound through the ears. **2.** the power to hear; sense by which sound is received [His *hearing* is poor.] **3.** a chance to be heard [The king granted us a *hearing.*] **4.** the distance that a sound can be heard [He is within *hearing* of my voice.]

heark·en (här′k'n), *v.* to listen carefully; pay attention: *no longer much used.*

hear·say (hir′sā), *n.* something one has heard but does not know to be true; gossip or rumor.

hearse (hûrs), *n.* a car or carriage for carrying a dead body to a grave.

heart (härt), *n.* **1.** the hollow muscle that gets blood from the veins and sends it through the arteries by squeezing together and ex-panding. **2.** the part at the center [*hearts* of celery; the *heart* of the jungle]. **3.** the main or most important part [Get to the *heart* of the matter.] **4.** the heart thought of as the part that feels love, kind-ness, pity, sadness, etc. [a tender *heart;* a heavy *heart*]. **5.** courage or spirit [to lose *heart*]. **6.** a person who is liked or admired [He's a brave *heart.*] **7.** a figure or design shaped a little like the heart: *see the top picture.* **8.** a playing card of a suit

upper: heart (meaning 7)
lower: diagram of human heart

marked with this figure in red. —**after one's own heart,** that pleases one perfectly. —**at heart,** in one's truest feelings. —**by heart, 1.** by memorizing. **2.** from memory. —**change of heart,** a change of mind or feeling. —**set one's heart on,** to want very much. —**take heart,** to get courage or confidence; cheer up. —**take to heart,** to be very serious or troubled about. —**with all one's heart, 1.** very sincerely. **2.** very willingly; gladly.

heart·ache (härt′āk), *n.* sorrow or grief.

heart·break·ing (härt′brāk′ing), *adj.* that causes very great disappointment or sadness.

heart·bro·ken (härt′brō′k'n), *adj.* very disappointed or unhappy; filled with grief.

heart·burn (härt′bûrn), *n.* a burning feeling in or near the stomach caused by too much acid in the stomach.

heart·ed (här′tid), *adj.* having a certain kind of heart: *used mainly in words formed with a hyphen* [good-*hearted*].

heart·en (här′t'n), *v.* to cheer up; encourage.

heart·felt (härt′felt), *adj.* with deep feeling; sincere [*heartfelt* gratitude].

hearth (härth), *n.* **1.** the stone or brick floor of a fireplace. **2.** the home, or life in the home. **3.** the lowest part of a blast furnace, where the melted metal and slag settle.

hearth·stone (härth′stōn), *n.* **1.** a flat stone forming a hearth. **2.** the home.

heart·i·ly (här′t'l ē), *adv.* **1.** in a friendly way; sincerely [to welcome *heartily*]. **2.** with eagerness or zest [to work *heartily;* to eat *heartily*]. **3.** completely; very [*heartily* sorry for lying].

heart·less (härt′lis), *adj.* without pity; unkind or cruel [a *heartless* tyrant]. —**heart′less·ly,** *adv.* —**heart′less·ness,** *n.*

heart-rend·ing (härt′ren′ding), *adj.* causing much grief; very sad [a *heart-rending* story].

heart·sick (härt′sik), *adj.* very sad or unhappy; in low spirits.

heart·strings (härt′stringz), *n.pl.* deep feelings of pity or sympathy [His sad tale tugged at my *heartstrings*.]

heart·y (här′tē), *adj.* **1.** friendly or sincere [a *hearty* welcome]. **2.** deeply felt; strong [a *hearty* dislike]. **3.** healthy, lively, strong, etc. [a *hearty* laugh; a *hearty* appetite]. **4.** large and satisfying [a *hearty* meal]. —**heart′i·er,** *compar.;* **heart′i·est,** *superl.* —**heart′i·ness,** *n.*

heat (hēt), *n.* **1.** the condition of being hot; great warmth [the *heat* of the sun]. **2.** hot weather or climate [the *heat* of the tropics]. **3.** the warming of a room, house, etc. [We get our *heat* from a gas furnace.] **4.** strong feeling or emotion; excitement [to argue with *heat;* in the *heat* of battle]. **5.** a single round, trial, etc.; especially, any of the early trials of a race: the winners race in the final round. —*v.* **1.** to make or become warm or hot [to *heat* water]. **2.** to make or become excited [a *heated* argument].

heat·er (hēt′ər), *n.* a stove, furnace, or the like for heating a room, car, water, etc.

heath (hēth), *n.* **1.** an open stretch of land covered with heather, low shrubs, etc., mainly in Great Britain. **2.** heather or a plant like it.

hea·then (hē′thən), *n.* **1.** a person who does not believe in the God of the Bible; one who is not a Jew, Christian, or Moslem. **2.** a person thought of as uncivilized or as worshiping false gods. —*adj.* of or having to do with heathens; pagan. —**hea′thens** or **hea′then,** *pl.* —**hea′then·ish,** *adj.*

heath·er (he*th*′ər), *n.* a low plant with tiny, purple flowers, found mainly in Great Britain.

heat wave, a period of very hot weather.

heave (hēv), *v.* **1.** to lift or to lift and throw, with much effort [We *heaved* the sofa onto the truck.] **2.** to make a sound, as if with effort or pain [to *heave* a sigh or groan]. **3.** to rise and fall in a regular rhythm [His chest *heaved* with sobs.] **4.** to breathe hard; pant. **5.** to vomit. **6.** to lift or pull with a rope or cable [*Heave* in the anchor!] **7.** to move or come [We saw a ship *heave* into view.] —*n.* the act or strain of heaving. —**heave ho!** pull hard! —**heave to,** to stop going forward, as a ship. —**heaved** or **hove,** *p.t. & p.p.;* **heav′ing,** *pr.p.*

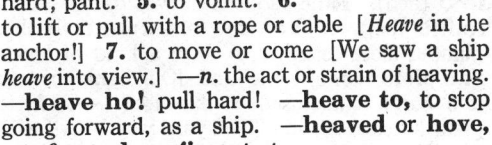

heather

heav·en (hev′'n), *n.* **1.** *usually* **heavens,** *pl.* the space in which the sun, moon, and stars move; the sky. **2.** the place where God, the angels, and saints are thought to be. **3. Heaven,** God [May *Heaven* help her!] **4.** any place or condition of great happiness [It's *heaven* to be home again.]

heav·en·ly (hev′'n lē), *adj.* **1.** of or in the heavens or sky [The sun is a *heavenly* body.] **2.** of or in heaven [God is called our *heavenly* Father.] **3.** very delightful or pleasing [a *heavenly* mood; *heavenly* music].

heav·en·ward (hev′'n wərd), *adj. & adv.* to or toward heaven [a *heavenward* glance].

heav·y (hev′ē), *adj.* **1.** hard to lift or move because of its weight; weighing very much [a *heavy* load]. **2.** weighing more than is usual for its kind [Lead is a *heavy* metal.] **3.** larger, greater, deeper, etc. than usual [a *heavy* vote; a *heavy* sleep; a *heavy* blow]. **4.** full of sorrow; sad [a *heavy* heart]. **5.** hard to do, bear, etc.; difficult [*heavy* work; *heavy* sorrow]. **6.** dark and gloomy [*heavy* skies]. **7.** hard to digest [a *heavy* meal]. **8.** almost closed, as if weighed down [*heavy* eyelids]. **9.** clumsy or awkward [a *heavy* way of walking]. —*adv.* in a heavy manner [Time hangs *heavy* on his hands.] —**heav′i·er,** *compar.;* **heav′i·est,** *superl.* —**heav′i·ly,** *adv.* —**heav′i·ness,** *n.*

heav·y·weight (hev′ē wāt′), *n.* **1.** a boxer or wrestler who weighs 176 pounds or more. One weighing between 161 and 175 is called a light heavyweight. **2.** a person or animal that weighs more than average.

He·brew (hē′brōō), *n.* **1.** a member of the ancient people of the Bible who settled in Canaan; Israelite. In modern use this word means the same as *Jew*. **2.** the ancient language of the Israelites or the modern form of this language, used in Israel today. —*adj.* of the Hebrews or the Hebrew language.

He·brews (hē′brōōz), *n.* a book of the New Testament.

Heb·ri·des (heb′rə dēz), *n.pl.* a group of Scottish islands west of northern Scotland.

heck·le (hek′'l), *v.* to annoy by asking many questions, shouting insults, etc. [The speaker was *heckled* by the audience.] —**heck′led,** *p.t. & p.p.;* **heck′ling,** *pr.p.* —**heck′ler,** *n.*

hec·tic (hek′tik), *adj.* **1.** having a fever; flushed, as in an illness. **2.** full of rush and confusion [the *hectic* life of an actor].

Hec·tor (hek′tər), *n.* a Trojan hero in Homer's *Iliad,* who was killed by Achilles.

hec·tor (hek′tər), *v.* to bully or tease.

he'd (hēd), **1.** he had. **2.** he would.

hedge (hej), *n.* **1.** a row of shrubs or bushes planted close together to form a kind of fence. **2.** a protection of some kind [Our bank account is a *hedge* against sudden expense.] —*v.* **1.** to plant a hedge around [The yard was *hedged* with roses.] **2.** to shut in on all sides; hem in [Switzerland is *hedged* in by mountains.] **3.** to get out of giving a straight answer [Phil *hedged* when I asked him for a loan.] —**hedged,** *p.t. & p.p.;* **hedg′ing,** *pr.p.*

hedge·hog (hej′hôg), *n.* **1.** a small animal of Europe, with sharp spines on its back, which bristle when the animal curls up to protect itself. **2.** the porcupine.

hedgehog (1 ft. long)

hedge·row (hej′rō), *n.* a row of bushes, shrubs, or small trees forming a hedge.

heed (hēd), *v.* to pay careful attention to [*Heed* my advice.] —*n.* careful attention [He paid no *heed* to our warning.] —**heed′ful, adj.** —**heed′ful·ly, adv.**

heed·less (hēd′lis), *adj.* not paying any attention; careless. —**heed′less·ly, adv.** —**heed′less·ness,** *n.*

hee·haw (hē′hô), *n.* **1.** the sound a donkey makes. **2.** a loud or silly laugh.

heel (hēl), *v.* to lean to one side; list [The ship *heeled* to port under the strong wind.]

heel (hēl), *n.* **1.** the back part of the foot, below the ankle and behind the arch. **2.** that part of a stocking or sock which covers the heel. **3.** the part of a shoe that is built up to support the heel. **4.** anything like a heel in shape, position, etc., as the end of a loaf of bread. —*v.* **1.** to put heels on [to *heel* shoes]. **2.** to follow closely [Did you teach your dog to *heel?*] —**down at the heels,**

shabby or run-down. —**take to one's heels,** to run away.

heft (heft), *v.* **1.** to lift or heave. **2.** to try to guess the weight of by lifting. —*n.* heaviness; weight. *This word is used only in everyday talk.*

heft·y (hef′tē), *adj.* **1.** heavy. **2.** large and strong [the *hefty* wrestler]. *This word is used only in everyday talk.* —**heft′i·er,** *compar.;* **heft′i·est,** *superl.*

Hei·del·berg (hī′d'l berg), *n.* a city in southwestern Germany, home of an old university.

heif·er (hef′ər), *n.* a young cow that has not given birth to a calf.

heigh-ho (hī′hō′), *interj.* an exclamation showing that one is bored, tired, surprised, etc.

height (hīt), *n.* **1.** the distance from the bottom to the top; tallness [the *height* of a building; a man six feet in *height*]. **2.** the highest point or degree [the *height* of the tide; the *height* of prosperity]. **3.** the distance above the surface of the earth [The plane flew at a *height* of 20,000 feet.] **4.** a high place or point [Alpine *heights*].

height·en (hīt′'n), *v.* to make or become higher, greater, or stronger; increase.

hei·nous (hā′nəs), *adj.* very evil or wicked [a *heinous* crime]. —**hei′nous·ly, adv.**

heir (er), *n.* a person who gets or has the right by law to get property or a title when the person holding it dies.

heir apparent, the person who is sure to be the heir to some property or title if he outlives the person holding it [The king's *heir apparent* was the oldest prince.]

heir·ess (er′is), *n.* a woman or girl who has inherited or will inherit much wealth.

heir·loom (er′lōōm), *n.* a valuable or valued article handed down in a family over the years.

held (held), past tense and past participle of **hold.**

Hel·e·na (hel′i nə), *n.* the capital of Montana.

Hel·en of Troy (hel′ən), a beautiful queen of Sparta in Greek legends. The Trojan War began because she was taken away by a prince of Troy.

hel·i·cop·ter (hel′i käp′tər), *n.* a kind of airplane that has a large propeller fixed above in a horizontal way, but no wings. It can be flown backward or forward or straight up and down.

helicopter

he·li·o·trope (hē′li ə trōp′), *n.* **1.** a plant having small, bright-purple or white flowers. **2.** bright purple.

he·li·um (hē′li əm), *n.* a very light gas that will not burn or explode. It is used to inflate balloons and dirigibles.

hell (hel), *n.* **1.** the place where Christians believe that devils live and wicked people go to be punished after they die. **2.** the place where the ancient Greeks, Hebrews, etc. believed that the spirits of people go after they die: see **Hades, Sheol. 3.** any place or condition of evil, pain, or misery ["War is *hell.*"]

he'll (hēl *or* hil), **1.** he will. **2.** he shall.

Hel·las (hel′əs), *n.* Greece: *the Greek name.*

hel·le·bore (hel′ə bôr), *n.* **1.** a plant that blooms in winter with flowers like buttercups. Its dried root has been used as a medicine. **2.** a plant related to the lily. A powder that kills insects is made from its roots.

Hel·len·ic (he len′ik *or* he lē′nik), *adj.* having to do with the Greeks, especially the ancient Greeks.

Hel·les·pont (hel′əs pänt), *n.* the Dardanelles: *the name used in ancient times.*

hell·ish (hel′ish), *adj.* as if from hell; horrible; devilish [a *hellish* plot].

hel·lo (he lō′ *or* hə lō′), *interj.* **1.** a word used in greeting someone or in answering the telephone. **2.** a word called out to get attention or to show surprise [*Hello!* what's this?] —*n.* a saying or calling of "hello." —*v.* to say or call "hello." —**hel·los′,** *pl.* —**hel·loed′,** *p.t. & p.p.;* **hel·lo′ing,** *pr.p.*

helm (helm), *n.* **1.** the wheel or tiller by which a ship is steered. **2.** the position of leading or controlling a government, business, etc. [The president has taken the *helm*.]

helm (helm), *n.* a helmet: *a word no longer used.*

hel·met (hel′mit), *n.* a hard covering for the head to protect it in war, in some sports, etc.

helms·man (helmz′mən), *n.* the man who steers a ship. —**helms′men,** *pl.*

Hel·ot (hel′ət *or* hē′lət), *n.* **1.** a serf in ancient Sparta. **2. helot,** any serf or slave.

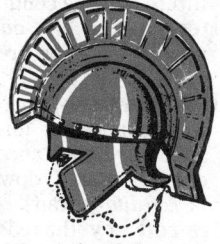
ancient helmet

help (help), *v.* **1.** to give or do something that is needed or useful; make things easier for; aid; assist [He *helped* his poor relatives. *Help* me lift this.] **2.** to make better; give relief to; remedy [This medicine will *help* your cold.] **3.** to stop or keep from; prevent or avoid [I can't *help* feeling sad.] —*n.* **1.** the act of helping or being helped [He is beyond *help*.] **2.** something that helps; aid; assistance [*help* for the needy]. **3.** a person or persons hired to help, as in housework or farming. —**help oneself to, 1.** to serve oneself with [*Help yourself to* some food.] **2.** to take without asking. —**help out,** to help in getting or doing something. —**help′-er,** *n.*

help·ful (help′fəl), *adj.* giving help; useful. —**help′ful·ly,** *adv.* —**help′ful·ness,** *n.*

help·ing (hel′ping), *n.* **1.** a giving of help. **2.** the amount of a food served to one person at a time.

help·less (help′lis), *adj.* **1.** not able to help oneself or do what is necessary [a *helpless* child]. **2.** without help or protection. —**help′less·ly,** *adv.* —**help′less·ness,** *n.*

help·mate (help′māt), *n.* a wife or husband.

Hel·sin·ki (hel′sing kē), *n.* the capital of Finland.

hel·ter-skel·ter (hel′tər skel′tər), *adv. & adj.* in a wild rush or confusion [He threw his clothes *helter-skelter* around the room. She worked in a *helter-skelter* way.]

helve (helv), *n.* the handle of an ax, hatchet, etc.

hem (hem), *n.* the border on a skirt, curtain, towel, etc., made by folding the edge over and sewing it down. —*v.* **1.** to fold back the edge of and sew down [to *hem* a skirt]. **2.** to close in on all sides; surround or confine [troops *hemmed* in by the enemy]. —**hemmed,** *p.t. & p.p.;* **hem′ming,** *pr.p.*

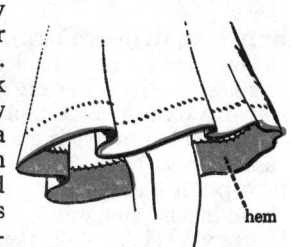
hem

hem (hem), *interj. & n.* the sound made in clearing one's throat, or a sound like this. —*v.* **1.** to make this sound, as in trying to get attention or in showing doubt. **2.** to make this sound while searching for the right words: *usually used in the phrase* "to hem and haw." —**hemmed,** *p.t. & p.p.;* **hem′ming,** *pr.p.*

hemi-, a prefix meaning "half" [A *hemisphere* is half of a sphere.]

hem·i·sphere (hem′ə sfir), *n.* **1.** half of a sphere or globe [The church dome was in the shape of a *hemisphere*.] **2.** any of the halves into which the earth's surface is divided in geography: see **Eastern Hemisphere, Western Hemisphere, Northern Hemisphere, Southern Hemisphere.**

hem·lock (hem′läk), *n.* **1.** an evergreen tree of the pine family, with drooping branches and short, flat needles. **2.** a poisonous weed of the carrot family, or a poison made from it.

he·mo·glo·bin (hē′mə glō′bin), *n.* the red coloring matter in red blood corpuscles.

hem·or·rhage (hem′ər ij), *n.* bleeding; especially, heavy bleeding. —*v.* to bleed heavily. —**hem′or·rhaged,** *p.t. & p.p.;* **hem′or·rhag·ing,** *pr.p.*

hemp (hemp), *n.* **1.** a tall plant having tough fibers in its stalk. **2.** this fiber, used for making rope, heavy cloth, etc. —**hemp′en,** *adj.*

hem·stitch (hem′stich), *n.* a fancy stitch made by pulling out several threads in a piece of cloth and tying the cross threads together in small groups. This stitch is often used to decorate a hem. —*v.* to put hemstitches in.

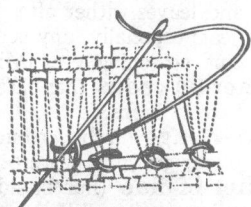
hemstitching

hen (hen), *n.* the female of the chicken, or of certain other birds, as the pheasant.

fat,   āpe,   cär,   ten,   ēven,   hit,   bīte,   gō,   hôrn,   tōol,   book,   up,   fûr;

get,   joy,   yet,   chin,   she,   thin,   *then;*   zh = s in pleasure;   ' as in able (ā′b'l);

ə = a in ago,   e in agent,   i in sanity,   o in confess,   u in focus.

hence (hens), *adv.* **1.** for this reason; as a result; therefore [He eats too much and is, *hence*, overweight.] **2.** from here; away [We shall be ten miles *hence* by dusk.] **3.** from this time; after now [A year *hence* things may be different.]

hence·forth (hens′fôrth′), *adv.* from this time on [We shall *henceforth* be friends.]

hence·for·ward (hens′fôr′wərd), *adv.* henceforth.

hench·man (hench′mən), *n.* a man who blindly follows and supports his leader [a gangster and his *henchmen*]. —**hench′men,** *pl.*

hen·na (hen′ə), *n.* **1.** a plant from whose leaves a reddish-brown dye is made. **2.** this dye, often used to color hair. **3.** reddish brown.

hen·peck (hen′pek), *v.* to rule over one's husband in a nagging way. —**hen′pecked,** *adj.*

Hen·ry VIII (hen′rē), 1491–1547; king of England from 1509 to 1547. He founded the Church of England.

Henry, O., pen name of William Sydney Porter; a United States short-story writer who lived from 1862 to 1910.

Henry, Patrick, 1736–1799; one of the leaders of the American Revolution.

he·pat·i·ca (hi pat′i kə), *n.* a plant with broad leaves and small white, pink, or purple flowers that bloom early in the spring.

her (hur), *pron.* **1.** the form of *she* that is used as the object of a verb or preposition [I saw *her*. Give it to *her*.] **2.** of her or done by her: the possessive form of *she*, used before a noun and thought of as an adjective [*her* dress; *her* work]. See also **hers.**

He·ra (hir′ə), *n.* the Greek goddess who was the wife of Zeus, and the goddess of marriage. The Romans called this goddess *Juno.*

her·ald (her′əld), *n.* **1.** an official in earlier times who made public announcements, carried messages for kings or lords, etc. **2.** a person or thing that comes to show or tell what will follow [Dark clouds are *heralds* of storms.] —*v.* to be a sign of; announce [The crocus *heralds* spring.]

he·ral·dic (he ral′dik), *adj.* having to do with heraldry or heralds.

her·ald·ry (her′əld rē), *n.* **1.** the science in which coats of arms are studied or designed, families are traced back, etc. **2.** a coat of arms. **3.** formal behavior; pomp. —**her′ald·ries,** *pl.*

herb (urb *or* hurb), *n.* any plant whose stems and leaves wither after the growing season each year; especially, any such plant used as a medicine, seasoning, etc. [Mint and sage are *herbs.*]

her·ba·ceous (hər bā′shəs), *adj.* of or like an herb or herbs.

herb·age (ur′bij *or* hur′bij), *n.* grass or green plants grown in pastures as food for cattle.

her·bi·cide (hur′bə sīd *or* ur′bə sīd), *n.* any poison used to kill plants, especially weeds.

her·biv·o·rous (hər biv′ər əs), *adj.* that eats mainly grass or other plants.

Her·cu·le·an (hər kyoo′li ən *or* hur′kyoo lē′ən), *adj.* **1.** of Hercules. **2.** *usually* **herculean,** very strong, large, and brave; also, needing great strength or courage [a *herculean* task].

Her·cu·les (hur′kyoo lēz), *n.* **1.** a very strong and powerful hero in Greek and Roman myths. **2. hercules,** any very large, strong man.

herd (hurd), *n.* **1.** a number of cattle or other large animals feeding or living together [a *herd* of cows; a *herd* of elephants]. **2.** a herdsman: *now used only in combined words, as* **goatherd. 3.** the common people; a crowd: *a scornful word.* —*v.* **1.** to form into a herd, group, or crowd. **2.** to take care of a herd of animals.

herds·man (hurdz′mən), *n.* a person who takes care of a herd of animals. —**herds′men,** *pl.*

here (hir), *adv.* **1.** at or in this place [Who lives *here?*] **2.** to, toward, or into this place [Come *here.*] **3.** at this point; now [*Here* everyone applauded.] **4.** on earth; among the living [No one is *here* forever.] —*interj.* a word called out to get attention, answer a roll call, etc. —*n.* **1.** this place [Let's get out of *here.*] **2.** the present; this life or time [He cares more about the *here* than the hereafter.] —**here and there,** in or to various places. —**neither here nor there,** without real purpose or meaning; beside the point.

here·a·bout (hir′ə bout′) *or* **here·a·bouts** (hir′ə bouts′), *adv.* in or near this place.

here·af·ter (hir af′tər), *adv.* after this; from now on [*Hereafter* I'll be careful.] —*n.* **1.** the future. **2.** the condition after death.

here·by (hir bī′), *adv.* by means of this message, paper, etc. [You are *hereby* ordered to appear in court.]

he·red·i·tar·y (hə red′ə ter′ē), *adj.* **1.** inherited from an ancestor [his *hereditary* home]. **2.** having a title by inheritance [a *hereditary* king]. **3.** that can be passed down to offspring by heredity [a *hereditary* trait].

he·red·i·ty (hə red′ə tē), *n.* **1.** the passing on of certain characteristics from parent to offspring, by means of the chromosomes [The color of one's hair is determined by *heredity.*] **2.** the characteristics passed on in this way [one's *heredity*].

Her·e·ford (hur′fərd *or* her′ə fərd), *n.* a breed of beef cattle with a white face and a red body.

here·in (hir in′), *adv.* **1.** in this place, writing, etc. [His name is listed *herein.*] **2.** in this matter or detail [*Herein* you are wrong.]

here·of (hir uv′), *adv.* of this or about this.

here's (hirz), here is.

her·e·sy (her′ə sē), *n.* **1.** a religious belief that a particular church considers to be false. **2.** any belief that is against a belief held by most people, as in politics, science, etc. **3.** the holding of such a belief [guilty of *heresy*]. —**her′e·sies,** *pl.*

her·e·tic (her′ə tik), *n.* a person who believes in something that is regarded by a church or other group as a heresy.

he·ret·i·cal (hə ret′i k'l), *adj.* **1.** of heresy or heretics. **2.** that is or contains a heresy [*heretical* writings].

here·to·fore (hir′too fôr′), *adv.* until this time; up to now.

here·up·on (hir ə pän′), *adv.* just after this; at this point.

here·with (hir with′), *adv.* along with this [You will find my check enclosed *herewith.*]

her·it·a·ble (her′i tə b′l), *adj.* that can be inherited.

her·it·age (her′ə tij), *n.* something handed down from one's ancestors or the past, as certain skills or rights, or a way of life [Free speech is an American *heritage.*]

Her·mes (hur′mēz), *n.* a Greek god who was the messenger of the other gods. The Romans called him *Mercury.*

her·met·ic (hər met′ik) or **her·met·i·cal** (hər met′i k′l), *adj.* closed so tightly that air cannot get in or out; airtight. **—her·met·i·cal·ly,** *adv.*

her·mit (hur′mit), *n.* a person who lives by himself away from others, often for religious reasons.

her·mit·age (hur′mə tij), *n.* a hermit's home.

hermit crab, a small crab with a soft body, that lives in empty shells, as of snails.

her·ni·a (hur′ni ə), *n.* a rupture in the body.

he·ro (hir′ō), *n.* **1.** a man or boy who is looked up to for the brave or noble things he has done [He became a *hero* when he saved his brother from drowning. Washington was the *hero* of the American Revolution.] **2.** the most important man in the story of a novel, play, etc., especially if he is good or noble. **—he′roes,** *pl.*

Her·od (her′əd), *n.* 73?–4 B.C.; king of Judea at the time Jesus was born.

He·rod·o·tus (hi räd′ə təs), *n.* Greek historian who lived in the 5th century B.C.

he·ro·ic (hi rō′ik), *adj.* **1.** of or like a hero [a *heroic* life; a *heroic* woman]. **2.** showing great bravery or daring [*heroic* deeds]. **3.** of or about heroes and their deeds [a *heroic* poem]. Also **he·ro′i·cal. —he·ro′i·cal·ly,** *adv.*

he·ro·ics (hi rō′iks), *n.pl.* talk or action that seems grand or noble but is really false or foolish.

her·o·in (her′ō in), *n.* a drug like morphine that is habit-forming and is illegal in the U.S.

her·o·ine (her′ō in), *n.* a woman or girl hero [Joan of Arc is one of the great *heroines* of history. Evangeline is the *heroine* of Longfellow's poem.]

her·o·ism (her′ō iz'm), *n.* the actions and qualities of a hero or heroine; bravery, nobility, etc. [Our soldiers fought with *heroism.*]

her·on (her′ən), *n.* a wading bird with long legs, a long neck, and a long, pointed bill. Herons live in marshes or along river banks.

Herr (her), *n.* a man; gentleman: a German word also used as a title meaning "Mr."

her·ring (her′ing), *n.* a small fish of the North Atlantic. The full-grown fish are eaten cooked, dried, salted, or smoked, and the young of some kinds are canned as sardines.

heron (4 ft. long)

her·ring·bone (her′ing bōn′), *n.* a woven pattern in cloth. **—adj.** having this pattern.

herringbone jacket

hers (hurz), *pron.* the one or the ones that belong to her: the form of *her* used when it is not followed by a noun [This book is *hers. Hers* are larger than ours.]

her·self (hər self′), *pron.* **1.** her own self: the form of *she* that makes the subject also the object of the verb [She cut *herself.*] **2.** her usual or true self [She's not *herself* today.] *Herself* is also used to give force to the subject [She *herself* told me so.]

hertz (hurts), *n.* a unit for measuring frequency, as of radio waves. **—hertz,** *pl.*

he's (hēz), **1.** he is. **2.** he has.

hes·i·tan·cy (hez′ə tən sē), *n.* hesitation.

hes·i·tant (hez′ə tənt), *adj.* hesitating; having doubt [She was *hesitant* to speak of his faults.]

hes·i·tate (hez′ə tāt), *v.* **1.** to stop or hold back, as because of feeling unsure [He never *hesitated* to speak the truth. She *hesitated* at the door before entering.] **2.** to feel rather unwilling [I *hesitate* to ask you for money.] **—hes′i·tat·ed,** *p.t. & p.p.;* **hes′i·tat·ing,** *pr.p.* **—hes′i·tat·ing·ly,** *adv.*

hes·i·ta·tion (hez′ə tā′shən), *n.* **1.** a hesitating, as because of doubt, fear, etc.; unsure or unwilling feeling [She agreed without *hesitation.*] **2.** a pausing for a moment [talk filled with *hesitations*].

Hes·per·i·des (hes per′ə dēz), *n.pl.* the nymphs in Greek myths guarding Hera's golden apples.

Hes·per·us (hes′pər əs), *n.* the evening star.

Hesse (hes), *n.* a state in West Germany.

Hes·sian (hesh′ən), *adj.* of Hesse or its people. **—n. 1.** a person born or living in Hesse. **2.** any of the Hessian soldiers hired to fight for the British in the Revolutionary War.

het·er·o·dox (het′ər ə däks′), *adj.* differing from the ideas, opinions, etc. that are usually held or taught; not orthodox [*heterodox* beliefs in religion]. **—het′er·o·dox′y,** *n.*

het·er·o·ge·ne·ous (het′ər ō jē′ni əs), *adj.* different in kind; not alike or made up of parts that are not alike [a *heterogeneous* group of people].

hew (hyōō), *v.* **1.** to chop or cut with an ax, knife, etc. [to *hew* wood for a fire]. **2.** to make or shape by chopping or cutting [a statue *hewn* from wood]. **—hewed,** *p.t.;* **hewed** or **hewn** (hyōōn), *p.p.;* **hew′ing,** *pr.p.* **—hew′er,** *n.*

HEW, abbreviation for the Department of **Health, Education, and Welfare** in the U.S. government.

hex (heks), *n.* something supposed to bring bad luck; jinx, **—v.** to cause bad luck to. *This word is used only in everyday talk.*

fat,   āpe,   cär,   ten,   ēven,   hit,   bīte,   gō,   hôrn,   tōōl,   book,   up,   fur;
get,   joy,   yet,   chin,   she,   thin,   *th*en;   zh = s in pleasure;   ′ as in able (ā′b'l).
ə = a in ago,   e in agent,   i in sanity,   o in confess,   u in focus.

hex·a·gon (heks′ə gän), *n.* a flat figure having six angles and six sides.

hex·ag·o·nal (hek sag′ə n'l), *adj.* having the shape of a hexagon.

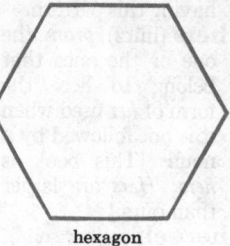
hexagon

hex·am·e·ter (hek sam′ə tər), *n.* **1.** a line of verse having six measures or feet. **2.** poetry made up of hexameters.

hey (hā), *interj.* a word called out to get attention or to show surprise, wonder, etc. [*Hey*, watch out! Quite a show tonight, *hey*?]

hey·day (hā′dā), *n.* the time of greatest success, strength, etc.; prime [He reached his *heyday* as a boxer when he was only twenty-two.]

Hg, symbol for the chemical element *mercury*.

hi (hī), *interj.* an everyday word of greeting.

H.I., abbreviation for **Hawaiian Islands.**

hi·a·tus (hī ā′təs), *n.* a blank space where a part is missing; gap [a *hiatus* in an old manuscript]. —**hi·a′tus·es** or **hi·a′tus,** *pl.*

Hi·a·wa·tha (hī′ə wô′thə), *n.* the Indian hero of Longfellow's poem *The Song of Hiawatha.*

hi·ber·nate (hī′bər nāt), *v.* to spend the winter in a kind of sleep [Bears *hibernate* in caves, holes, etc.] —**hi′ber·nat·ed,** *p.t. & p.p.;* **hi′ber·nat·ing,** *pr.p.* —**hi′ber·na′tion,** *n.*

hic·cup or **hic·cough** (hik′əp), *n.* a sudden stopping of the breath with a sharp gulping sound. Hiccups are caused by spasms of the muscles used in breathing and are hard to stop. —*v.* to have hiccups.

hick·o·ry (hik′ər ē), *n.* **1.** a tree related to the walnut, with smooth-shelled nuts that can be eaten. **2.** its hard wood. —**hick′o·ries,** *pl.*

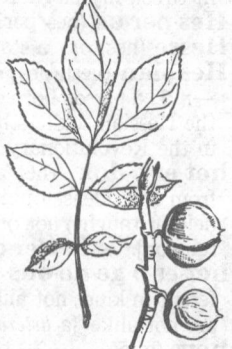
hickory leaves and nuts

hid (hid), past tense and a past participle of **hide.**

hid·den (hid′'n), a past participle of **hide.** —*adj.* concealed; secret.

hide (hīd), *v.* **1.** to put or keep out of sight; conceal [He *hid* the present in his pocket.] **2.** to keep others from knowing about; keep secret [She tried to *hide* her sorrow.] **3.** to keep from being seen; cover up [The billboard *hides* the view.] **4.** to keep oneself out of sight [I *hid* in the closet.] —**hid,** *p.t.;* **hid′den** or **hid,** *p.p.;* **hid′ing,** *pr.p.*

hide (hīd), *n.* **1.** the skin of an animal, either raw or tanned. **2.** a person's skin: *used in a joking or scornful way* [To tan a person's *hide* means to give him a beating.]

hide-and-seek (hīd′ən sēk′), *n.* a children's game in which some players hide and others then try to find them: also **hide-and-go-seek.**

hide·bound (hīd′bound), *adj.* keeping to one's old ideas and opinions; narrow-minded.

hid·e·ous (hid′i əs), *adj.* horrible to see, hear, etc.; very ugly or disgusting. —**hid′e·ous·ly,** *adv.* —**hid′e·ous·ness,** *n.*

hide-out (hīd′out′), *n.* a hiding place, as for gangsters: *used only in everyday talk.*

hid·ing (hīd′ing), *n.* a beating or whipping: *used only in everyday talk.*

hie (hī), *v.* to hurry or hasten [You'd better *hie* yourself to school.] —**hied,** *p.t. & p.p.;* **hie′ing** or **hy′ing,** *pr.p.*

hi·er·arch·y (hī′ər är′kē), *n.* **1.** a system in which a church is ruled by priests of different ranks or grades [a *hierarchy* of priests, bishops, archbishops, etc.]. **2.** all the priests in such a system. **3.** any group in which there are higher and lower positions of power. —**hi′er·arch′ies,** *pl.* —**hi′er·ar′chi·cal,** *adj.*

hi·er·o·glyph·ic (hī′ər ə glif′ik), *n.* **1.** a picture or symbol that stands for a word, syllable, or sound. The ancient Egyptians and others used such pictures instead of an alphabet. **2.** *usually* **hieroglyphics,** *pl.* a method of writing that uses such pictures. **3. hieroglyphics,** *pl.* any writing that is hard to read. —*adj.* of or like hieroglyphics.

hieroglyphics

hi-fi (hī′fī′), *n. & adj.* a shortened form of **high fidelity.**

high (hī), *adj.* **1.** reaching a long distance up; tall; lofty [a *high* building]. **2.** as measured from top to bottom [a fence four feet *high*]. **3.** far above the ground [The plane was *high* in the clouds.] **4.** upward to or downward from a height [a *high* jump; a *high* dive]. **5.** above others, as in rank or position; superior [a *high* official; *high* marks in school]. **6.** good; favorable [He has a *high* opinion of you.] **7.** main or chief [the *high* priest]. **8.** very serious [*high* treason]. **9.** greater than usual in amount, cost, power, etc. [*high* prices; *high* voltage]. **10.** raised in pitch [a *high* note]. **11.** slightly spoiled, as meat. **12.** joyful or merry [*high* spirits]. **13.** drunk or under the influence of a drug: *slang in this meaning.* —*adv.* in or to a high level, place, degree, etc. [Throw the ball *high*.] —*n.* **1.** a high level, place, or degree [Prices reached a new *high*.] **2.** an arrangement of gears that gives the greatest speed [He shifted into *high*.] —**high and dry,** alone and helpless, as a boat stranded on the shore. —**high and low,** everywhere [to look *high and low*]. —**on high,** in heaven.

high·ball (hī′bôl), *n.* a drink of whisky or brandy mixed with soda water or ginger ale.

high·born (hī′bôrn), *adj.* born into a family of the upper class.

high·brow (hī′brou′), *n.* a person who knows or pretends to know more about literature, music, etc. than most people do: *a slang word.*

high fidelity, the reproducing of music or speech on a radio, phonograph, etc. so that it sounds very much like a live performance. This is done by using the full range of sound waves that can be heard by the human ear.

high-flown (hī′flōn′), *adj.* that tries to be grand or elegant instead of simple [*high-flown* speech].

high-grade (hī′grād′), *adj.* of the very best.

high·hand·ed (hī′han′did), *adj.* acting just as one pleases, with no regard for what others want or think; arrogant.

high jump, an athletic contest to see who can jump the highest over a bar that is raised higher and higher: see also **broad jump.**

high jump

high·land (hī′lənd), *n.* a region of many hills or mountains, that is higher than the land around it. —**the Highlands,** the region of high mountains in northern Scotland. —**high′land·er** or **High′land·er,** *n.*

high·light (hī′līt), *v.* **1.** to give high lights to [Her cheeks are *highlighted* in the picture.] **2.** to give an important place to [*Highlight* these books in your display.]

high light, 1. the part on which there is the brightest light; also, the part of a painting that is made lighter or brighter [Rembrandt painted *high lights* on the metal helmet for contrast.] **2.** an interesting or important part [Yellowstone Park was a *high light* of our trip.]

high·ly (hī′lē), *adv.* **1.** to a high degree; very much [*highly* pleased]. **2.** in a kind or friendly way; favorably [He speaks *highly* of you.] **3.** in a high position [a *highly* placed official]. **4.** at a high price [*highly* paid].

high-mind·ed (hī′mīn′did), *adj.* having or showing high ideals or noble feelings [a *high-minded* attitude].

High·ness (hī′nis), *n.* **1.** a title of respect used in speaking to or about a member of a royal family. **2. highness,** height; elevation.

high-pres·sure (hī′presh′ər), *adj.* **1.** that has, or that can resist, a strong pressure [a *high-pressure* steam boiler]. **2.** using strong arguments in order to convince [a *high-pressure* salesman].

high-rise (hī′rīz′), *n.* a tall apartment house or office building that has many stories.

high·road (hī′rōd), *n.* a main road; highway.

high school, a school that includes grades 10, 11, and 12, and sometimes grade 9. It prepares students for college or trains them for business or a trade. See also **junior high school.**

high seas, the open parts of the ocean that do not belong to any country.

high-sound·ing (hī′soun′ding), *adj.* sounding important or dignified, often in a false way.

high-spir·it·ed (hī′spir′it id), *adj.* **1.** full of energy; lively [a *high-spirited* horse]. **2.** full of courage or daring [a *high-spirited* lad].

high-strung (hī′strung′), *adj.* very nervous or tense; easily excited.

high tide, 1. the time when the tide rises highest. **2.** the highest level of the tide.

high time, time after the proper time, but before it is too late.

high·way (hī′wā), *n.* a main road.

high·way·man (hī′wā mən), *n.* a man who robs travelers on a highway. —**high′way-men,** *pl.*

hi·jack (hī′jak), *v.* to take over by force and direct to a place not originally intended [to *hijack* an airplane; to *hijack* a truckload of goods]: *used only in everyday talk.*

hike (hīk), *n.* a long walk, especially in the country or in woods. —*v.* **1.** to take a hike. **2.** to pull up or raise: *used only in everyday talk* [to *hike* up one's socks; to *hike* prices]. —**hiked,** *p.t. & p.p.;* **hik′ing,** *pr.p.*

hi·lar·i·ous (hi ler′i əs), *adj.* noisy and full of fun and laughter; very gay.

hi·lar·i·ty (hi lar′ə tē), *n.* noisy fun; gaiety.

hill (hil), *n.* **1.** a piece of ground that is heaped up higher than the land around it, but not so high as a mountain. **2.** any small heap or mound [an ant *hill*]. **3.** a small heap of soil piled up around plant roots [a *hill* of potatoes].

hill·ock (hil′ək), *n.* a small hill; mound.

hill·side (hil′sīd), *n.* the slope of a hill.

hill·top (hil′täp), *n.* the top of a hill.

hill·y (hil′ē), *adj.* full of hills; rolling and uneven [*hilly* country]. —**hill′i·er,** *compar.;* **hill′i·est,** *superl.* —**hill′i·ness,** *n.*

hilt (hilt), *n.* a handle of a sword or dagger.

him (him), *pron.* the form of *he* that is used as the object of a verb or preposition [Call *him* back. The dog jumped on *him.*]

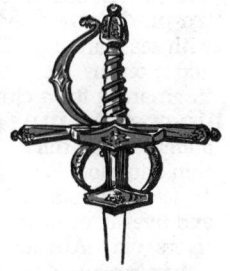
hilt of a sword

Hi·ma·la·yas (him′ə lā′əz *or* hi mäl′yəz), *n.pl.* a group of very high mountains between India and Tibet. —**Hi′ma·la′yan,** *adj.*

him·self (him self′), *pron.* **1.** his own self: the form of *he* that makes the subject also the object of the verb [He hurt *himself.*] **2.** his usual or true self [He isn't *himself* today.] *Himself* is also used to give force to the subject [He *himself* told us so.]

hind (hīnd), *adj.* back; rear [a *hind* leg].

hind (hīnd), *n.* a full-grown, female red deer.

hin·der (hin′dər), *v.* to keep back; get in the way of; obstruct; prevent [Poor eyesight *hindered* Tim in his schoolwork.]

hind·er (hīn′dər), *adj.* hind; back; rear.

hind·most (hīnd′mōst) or **hind·er·most** (hīn′dər mōst), *adj.* farthest back; last.

hin·drance (hin′drəns), *n.* **1.** any person or thing that hinders; obstacle [A poor education can be a *hindrance* to success.] **2.** the act of hindering [to come and go without *hindrance*].

hind·sight (hīnd′sīt), *n.* a recognizing of what one should have done, after it is too late.

Hin·du (hin′dōō), *n.* **1.** a member of the largest native group of India. **2.** any person whose religion is Hinduism. —*adj.* of the Hindus.

Hin·du·ism (hin′dōō iz′m), *n.* the main religion of India.

hinge (hinj), *n.* a joint on which a door, lid, etc. swings open and shut. —*v.* **1.** to put a hinge or hinges on. **2.** to swing on a hinge. **3.** to depend on in an important way [Our chances of winning *hinge* on whether or not you play.] —**hinged,** *p.t. & p.p.;* **hing′-ing,** *pr.p.*

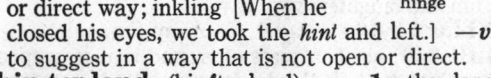

hinge

hint (hint), *n.* a slight suggestion that is not made in an open or direct way; inkling [When he closed his eyes, we took the *hint* and left.] —*v.* to suggest in a way that is not open or direct.

hin·ter·land (hin′tər land), *n.* **1.** the land lying behind the land along a coast or river. **2.** land that is far from cities or towns.

hip (hip), *n.* the part between the upper thigh and the waist on either side of the body.

hip·pie (hip′ē), *n.* a young person who does not want to follow the usual customs and beliefs of society and, as a result, dresses in unusual ways, shows a fondness for unconventional art, takes drugs, etc.: *a slang word.*

Hip·poc·ra·tes (hi päk′rə tēz), *n.* 460?–377? B.C.; Greek doctor: called the *Father of Medicine.*

hip·po·drome (hip′ə drōm), *n.* **1.** an oval track with seats around it, used by the ancient Greeks and Romans for horse races and chariot races. **2.** an arena for a circus, games, etc.

hip·po·pot·a·mus (hip′ə pät′ə məs), *n.* a large animal with a thick skin and short legs. It feeds on plants and lives in or near rivers in Africa. —**hip′po·pot′a·mus·es** or **hip·po·pot·a·mi** (hip′-ə pät′ə mī′), *pl.*

hippopotamus (12 ft. long)

hire (hīr), *v.* **1.** to agree to pay wages to in return for work; employ [He has *hired* a new secretary.] **2.** to pay money for the use of; rent [We *hired* a hall for the dance.] **3.** to allow to be used in return for pay [The farmer *hires* out his horses.] —*n.* the amount of money paid to get the services of a person or the use of a thing [not worth his *hire*]. —**for hire,** available for work or use in return for pay. —**hired,** *p.t. & p.p.;* **hir′ing,** *pr.p.*

hire·ling (hīr′ling), *n.* a person who will do almost anything for pay.

Hi·ro·shi·ma (hir′ō shē′mə), *n.* a seaport in southwest Japan. On August 6, 1945, it was largely destroyed by an American atomic bomb, the first ever used in warfare.

his (hiz), *pron.* the one or the ones that belong to him [This book is *his. His* cost more than hers.] *His* is the possessive form of *he* and is also used as an adjective meaning "of him or done by him" [*his* hat; *his* work].

His·pan·io·la (his′pən yō′lə), *n.* an island in the West Indies, between Cuba and Puerto Rico.

hiss (his), *v.* **1.** to make a sound like the sound of an *s* held for a long time [The snake *hissed.* Gas *hissed* from the stove burner.] **2.** to make such a sound in showing dislike [They *hissed* the speaker.] —*n.* the act or sound of hissing.

hist (st *or* hist), *interj.* a hissing sound made to mean "Be quiet! Listen!"

his·to·ri·an (his tôr′i ən), *n.* a writer of histories or an expert in history.

his·tor·ic (his tôr′ik), *adj.* famous in history; historical [a *historic* invention].

his·tor·i·cal (his tôr′i k′l), *adj.* **1.** of or having to do with history as a science. **2.** that actually existed or happened in history; not imaginary or fictional [*historical* persons and events]. **3.** based on real people or events of the past [a *historical* novel]. **4.** historic. —**his·tor′i·cal·ly,** *adv.*

his·to·ry (his′tə rē), *n.* **1.** what has happened in the life of a people, country, science, art, etc.; also, an account of this [the *history* of medicine; a *history* of England]. **2.** the record of everything that has happened in the past [Nero was one of the worst tyrants in *history*.] **3.** the science or study that keeps a record of past events [How will *history* treat our times?] **4.** a story or tale [He told us the *history* of his life.] —**his′to·ries,** *pl.*

his·tri·on·ics (his′tri än′iks), *n.pl.* the art of acting in plays. —**his′tri·on′ic,** *adj.*

hit (hit), *v.* **1.** to come against with force; bump or knock [The car *hit* the tree. I *hit* my head on the door.] **2.** to give a blow to; strike [The boxer was *hit* on the jaw.] **3.** to strike by throwing or shooting something at [He *hit* the target with his next shot.] **4.** to make suffer; distress [Sally was hard *hit* by the loss of her cat.] **5.** to find by chance or after searching [He *hit* upon the right answer.] **6.** to get as a hit in baseball [to *hit* a home run.] —*n.* **1.** a blow or stroke, especially one that strikes its mark. **2.** a song, play, etc. that is a great success. **3.** the successful hitting of a baseball, which lets the batter get on base safely: also called **base hit.** —**hit it off,** to get along well together. —**hit out at, 1.** to aim blows at. **2.** to attack in words. —**hit,** *p.t. & p.p.;* **hit′ting,** *pr.p.* —**hit′ter,** *n.*

hit-and-run (hit′n run′), *adj.* speeding away to escape after causing an accident with one's car: also **hit′-skip′** [a *hit-and-run* driver].

hitch (hich), *v.* **1.** to move with jerks [He *hitched* his chair forward.] **2.** to fasten with a hook, knot, strap, etc. [to *hitch* a horse to a fence]. **3.** to become fastened or caught, as on a nail or hook. **4.** to get a ride by hitchhiking: *slang in this meaning.* —*n.* **1.** a quick pull; tug or jerk [He gave a *hitch* to his pants.] **2.** something that gets in the way; hindrance [The parade went off without a *hitch*.] **3.** a fastening or catching; also, a part that catches [The *hitch* holding the trailer broke.] **4.** a kind of knot that cán be untied easily.

hitch·hike (hich′hīk), *v.* to travel by asking for rides from motorists along the way. —**hitch′-hiked**, *p.t. & p.p.;* **hitch′hik·ing**, *pr.p.* —**hitch′hik·er**, *n.*

hith·er (hi*th*′ər), *adv.* to this place; here: *no longer much used.*

hith·er·to (hi*th*′ər tōō′), *adv.* until this time; till now [a *hitherto* unknown writer].

Hit·ler, A·dolf (ä′dôlf hit′lər), 1889–1945; dictator of Nazi Germany from 1933 to 1945.

Hit·tite (hit′īt), *n.* a member of a people who lived in Asia Minor and Syria from about 2000 B.C. to about 700 B.C.

hive (hīv), *n.* **1.** a box or other shelter for a colony of bees: see **beehive. 2.** a colony of bees living in a hive. **3.** a place where there are many people busy doing something. —*v.* to gather into a hive, as bees. —**hived**, *p.t. & p.p.;* **hiv′ing**, *pr.p.*

hives (hīvz), *n.* a skin disease caused by an allergy, in which smooth, raised patches form and there is itching.

ho (hō), *interj.* a word called out to get attention or to show surprise, wonder, etc.

hoar (hôr), *adj.* hoary. —*n.* hoarfrost.

hoard (hôrd), *v.* to collect and store away, often secretly [A miser *hoards* money.] —*n.* anything that is hoarded. —**hoard′er**, *n.*

hoar·frost (hôr′frôst), *n.* white, frozen dew on the ground, leaves, etc.

hoarse (hôrs), *adj.* sounding rough and husky [the *hoarse* call of a crow; to become *hoarse* from shouting]. —**hoars′er**, *compar.;* **hoars′est**, *superl.* —**hoarse′ly**, *adv.* —**hoarse′ness**, *n.*

hoar·y (hôr′ē), *adj.* **1.** white or gray [ground *hoary* with frost]. **2.** having white or gray hair because of old age [*hoary* grandfathers]. **3.** very old; ancient [*hoary* laws]. —**hoar′i·er**, *compar.;* **hoar′i·est**, *superl.* —**hoar′i·ness**, *n.*

hoax (hōks), *n.* something that is meant to trick or fool others, especially a practical joke. —*v.* to play a trick on; fool.

hob (häb), *n.* an elf or goblin. —**play hob** or **raise hob**, to do mischief.

hob·ble (häb′'l), *v.* **1.** to walk in a lame or clumsy way. **2.** to keep from moving by tying the legs together [to *hobble* a horse]. **3.** to hinder in any way. —*n.* **1.** a limping walk. **2.** a rope or strap used to hobble a horse. —**hob′bled**, *p.t. & p.p.;* **hob′bling**, *pr.p.*

hob·by (häb′ē), *n.* some work, play, etc. that a person carries on in his spare time for pleasure [Music is his *hobby*.] —**hob′bies**, *pl.*

hob·by·horse (häb′ē hôrs), *n.* **1.** a stick with a horse's head at one end, used as a child's toy. **2.** a rocking horse.

hob·gob·lin (häb′gäb′lin), *n.* **1.** an elf or goblin. **2.** an imaginary being that scares one.

hob·nail (häb′nāl), *n.* a short nail with a large head, put on the soles of heavy shoes to keep them from slipping or wearing out.

hob·nob (häb′näb), *v.* to get together with as friends [The reporter *hobnobbed* with politicians and prize fighters.] —**hob′nobbed**, *p.t. & p.p.;* **hob′nob-bing**, *pr.p.*

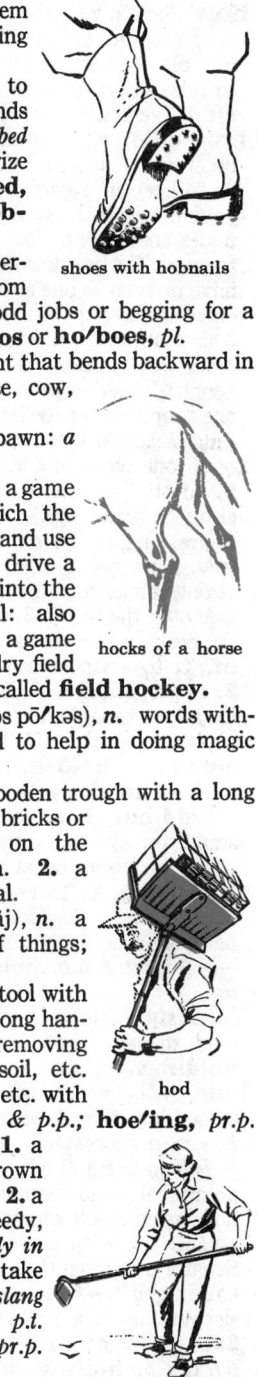
shoes with hobnails

ho·bo (hō′bō), *n.* a person who wanders from place to place, doing odd jobs or begging for a living; tramp. —**ho′bos** or **ho′boes**, *pl.*

hock (häk), *n.* the joint that bends backward in the hind leg of a horse, cow, dog, etc.

hock (häk), *v. & n.* pawn: *a slang word.*

hock·ey (häk′ē), *n.* **1.** a game played on ice, in which the players wear ice skates and use curved sticks to try to drive a rubber disk (the *puck*) into the opposing team's goal: also called **ice hockey. 2.** a game like this played on a dry field with a small ball: also called **field hockey.**

hocks of a horse

ho·cus-po·cus (hō′kəs pō′kəs), *n.* words without meaning, supposed to help in doing magic tricks.

hod (häd), *n.* **1.** a wooden trough with a long handle: it is filled with bricks or cement and carried on the shoulder by workmen. **2.** a bucket for carrying coal.

hodge·podge (häj′päj), *n.* a jumbled-up mixture of things; mess.

hod

hoe (hō), *n.* a garden tool with a thin, flat blade on a long handle. It is used for removing weeds, loosening the soil, etc. —*v.* to dig, loosen soil, etc. with a hoe. —**hoed**, *p.t. & p.p.;* **hoe′ing**, *pr.p.*

hog (hôg *or* häg), *n.* **1.** a pig, especially a full-grown pig raised for its meat. **2.** a person who is selfish, greedy, or very dirty: *used only in everyday talk.* —*v.* to take all of or too much of: *a slang meaning.* —**hogged**, *p.t. & p.p.;* **hog′ging**, *pr.p.* —**hog′gish**, *adj.*

woman hoeing

hogs·head (hôgz′hed *or* hägz′hed), *n.* **1.** a large barrel, especially one that holds from 100 to 140 gallons. **2.** a measure of liquids, equal to 63 gallons.

Hoh·en·zol·lern (hō′ən zäl′ərn), *n.* the former ruling family of Prussia and Germany.

hoist (hoist), *v.* to lift or pull up; raise, especially with a crane, pulley, or rope [to *hoist* a statue into place]. —*n.* **1.** an elevator, pulley, etc. used to raise heavy things. **2.** the act of hoisting; a lift [Give Bill a *hoist* over the fence.]

hold (hōld), *v.* **1.** to take and keep in the hands or arms [Will you *hold* the baby for a while?] **2.** to keep in a certain place or position [*Hold* your head up. He was *held* in jail.] **3.** to keep under control; not lose or let go of [*Hold* your temper. The speaker *held* our attention.] **4.** to have or keep as one's own; occupy [He *holds* the office of mayor.] **5.** to have or carry on; conduct [Our club *held* a meeting Tuesday.] **6.** to have room for; contain [The elevator will *hold* ten people. This can *holds* one pint.] **7.** to have as one's opinion or belief; decide; consider [The judge *held* that I was at fault.] **8.** to stay together or in one piece; not give way [Will that *hold*?] **9.** to stay the same or be true [This rule of etiquette still *holds*.] —*n.* **1.** the act of holding or grasping, or the way this is done [Take a firm *hold*. I learned a new *hold* in wrestling.] **2.** a strong influence or power [Religion had a great *hold* over the boy.] **3.** the inside of a ship, below the decks, where the cargo is stored. —**get hold of, 1.** to grasp or seize: also **catch hold of. 2.** to get; acquire. —**hold forth, 1.** to speak for a long time; lecture or preach. **2.** to offer, as a plan. —**hold off,** to keep away; keep at a distance. —**hold on, 1.** to keep on holding. **2.** to keep on doing something. **3.** wait! stop! —**hold out, 1.** to go on; continue; last. **2.** to stand up against without giving in. —**hold over,** to keep or stay longer than planned. —**hold up, 1.** to keep from falling; prop up. **2.** to show or display. **3.** to continue or last. **4.** to stop or delay. **5.** to rob by using force. —**held,** *p.t. & p.p.;* **hold′ing,** *pr.p.* —**hold′er,** *n.*

hold·ing (hōld′ing), *n.* something owned, as land, stocks, or bonds: *usually used in the plural,* **holdings.**

hole (hōl), *n.* **1.** an opening in or through something; a break or tear [a *hole* in the fence; a *hole* in my sweater]. **2.** a hollow place; cavity [a *hole* in the ground]. **3.** the burrow or den of an animal [a gopher's *hole*]. **4.** any of the small hollows on a golf course, into which the ball is to be hit. **5.** a weak point; fault [a *hole* in the Senator's argument]. —*v.* to put into a hole, as a ball in golf. —**hole up, 1.** to spend the winter sleeping, as in a hole [Bears *hole up* in caves.] **2.** to stay some place for a long time. —**holed,** *p.t. & p.p.;* **hol′ing,** *pr.p.*

hol·i·day (häl′ə dā), *n.* **1.** a day on which most people do not have to work; often, one set aside by law [Which *holiday* celebrates the Declaration of Independence?] **2.** a religious festival; holy day [Easter is a Christian *holiday*.]

ho·li·ness (hō′lē nis), *n.* **1.** the condition of being holy. **2. Holiness,** a title of the Pope: *used with* His *or* Your.

Hol·land (häl′ənd), *n.* the Netherlands. —**Hol′land·er,** *n.*

hol·ler (häl′ər), *v.* to shout or yell: *used only in everyday talk.*

hol·lo (häl′ō *or* hə lō′), *interj., n. & v.* same as **hallo.**

hol·low (häl′ō), *adj.* **1.** having an empty space on the inside; not solid [a *hollow* log]. **2.** shaped like a bowl; concave [The top of the birdbath is *hollow.*] **3.** sunken in [*hollow* cheeks]. **4.** with no real meaning; empty or false [*hollow* praise]. **5.** having a deep and dull sound [a *hollow* voice]. —*n.* **1.** a hollow place; hole or cavity. **2.** a small valley. —*v.* to make or become hollow. —**hollow out, 1.** to make a hollow in. **2.** to make by hollowing. —**hol′low·ness,** *n.*

hol·ly (häl′ē), *n.* a small tree or shrub with glossy leaves and red berries. Its branches are used as Christmas decoration. —**hol′lies,** *pl.*

hol·ly·hock (häl′ē häk), *n.* a tall plant with a hairy stem and large, showy flowers.

Hol·ly·wood (häl′ē wood), *n.* a part of Los Angeles where many movie studios were once located.

holly leaves and berries

Holmes, Ol·i·ver Wen·dell (äl′ə vər wen′d'l hōmz), **1.** 1809–1894; U.S. writer. **2.** 1841–1935; his son, who was a Supreme Court justice from 1902 to 1932.

Holmes, Sher·lock (shur′läk hōmz), an expert detective in stories by A. Conan Doyle (1859–1930) of England.

hol·o·caust (häl′ə kôst), *n.* **1.** the destroying of many people or animals by fire. **2.** any terrible destruction.

Hol·stein (hōl′stīn), *n.* a breed of large, black-and-white dairy cattle.

hol·ster (hōl′stər), *n.* a leather case for holding a pistol, usually fastened to a belt.

ho·ly (hō′lē), *adj.* **1.** set apart for religious use; connected with religion or God; sacred [a *holy* festival; the *Holy* Bible]. **2.** very good or very religious; saintly [a *holy* man]. **3.** thought of with very deep feeling [The fight for freedom was a *holy* cause to him.] —**ho′li·er,** *compar.;* **ho′li·est,** *superl.*

Holstein cow
(4½ ft. high at shoulder)

Holy Communion, a ritual in Christian churches during which bread and wine are blessed and received as the body and blood of Jesus or as symbols of them.

Holy Ghost or **Holy Spirit,** the third person of the Trinity; spirit of God.

Holy Grail, in medieval legend, the lost cup from which Jesus had drunk at the Last Supper. It was sought for by the knights of King Arthur.

Holy Land, Palestine.

Holy Roman Empire, the empire in central Europe that lasted from 800 A.D. to 1806.

Holy See, the office or authority of the Pope.

ho·ly·stone (hō′lē stōn), *n.* a flat piece of sandstone used for scrubbing a ship's decks.

Holy Week, the week before Easter.

Holy Writ, the Bible.

hom·age (häm′ij *or* äm′ij), *n.* **1.** anything done to show honor or respect [Lincoln's speech paid *homage* to the men who fought at Gettysburg.] **2.** a pledge of allegiance made by a vassal to his lord in the Middle Ages.

hom·bre (ôm′brā *or* äm′brē), *n.* a man; fellow: *a Spanish word used as slang in English.*

home (hōm), *n.* **1.** the place where one lives; one's house, apartment, etc. **2.** the city, country, etc. where one was born or brought up. **3.** a family or family life [Some *homes* are broken up by divorce.] **4.** a place where orphans or people who are old or helpless are taken care of. **5.** the place where a certain plant or animal is normally found [Australia is the *home* of the kangaroo.] **6.** the place where something began or where it developed [Detroit is the *home* of the auto industry.] **7.** in many games, the base or goal; especially, the home plate in baseball. —*adj.* **1.** of one's home or country; domestic [*home* management]. **2.** that is the headquarters; main or central [the *home* office of a company]. —*adv.* **1.** at, to, or toward home [Go *home!*] **2.** to the point aimed at [He drove the nail *home*. The speaker drove his argument *home*.] —*v.* **1.** to go home. **2.** to have a home [Where does the eagle *home?*] —**at home, 1.** in one's home. **2.** at ease; comfortable. **3.** willing to receive visitors. —**bring home to,** to make clear to. —**homed,** *p.t. & p.p.;* **hom′ing,** *pr.p.* —**home′less,** *adj.*

home economics, the science of managing a home, including budgeting, cooking, etc.

home·land (hōm′land), *n.* the country where one was born or where one makes his home.

home·like (hōm′līk), *adj.* like one's home; comfortable, cozy, and familiar.

home·ly (hōm′lē), *adj.* **1.** plain or simple [*homely* food; *homely* virtues]. **2.** not good-looking; not handsome [a *homely* face]. —**home′li·er,** *compar.;* **home′li·est,** *superl.* —**home′li·ness,** *n.*

home·made (hōm′mād′), *adj.* made at home.

home·mak·er (hōm′māk′ər), *n.* a woman who manages a home; housewife.

home plate, in baseball, the slab that a player stands beside when at bat. It is the last base that must be touched in scoring a run.

Ho·mer (hō′mər), *n.* a Greek poet who lived about the 9th century B.C. He wrote the *Iliad* and the *Odyssey.* —**Ho·mer·ic** (hō mer′ik), *adj.*

home run, a safe hit in baseball that allows the batter to touch all bases and score a run.

home·sick (hōm′sik), *adj.* unhappy at being away from home. —**home′sick·ness,** *n.*

home·spun (hōm′spun), *n.* **1.** cloth made of yarn spun at home. **2.** coarse, loosely woven cloth like this. —*adj.* **1.** spun at home or made of homespun. **2.** plain or simple [*homespun* humor].

home·stead (hōm′sted), *n.* **1.** a place where a family makes its home, including the house and land around it. **2.** a piece of public land given by the United States government to a settler to develop as a farm. —*v.* to become a settler on a homestead. —**home′stead·er,** *n.*

home·stretch (hōm′strech′), *n.* **1.** the part of a race track from the last turn to the finish line. **2.** the last part of an undertaking.

home·ward (hōm′wərd), *adj. & adv.* toward home: also **home′wards,** *adv.*

home·work (hōm′wûrk), *n.* **1.** work done at home. **2.** lessons to be studied or schoolwork to be done outside the classroom.

home·y (hōm′ē), *adj.* like home; comfortable, cozy, etc.: *used only in everyday talk.* —**hom′i·er,** *compar.;* **hom′i·est,** *superl.*

hom·i·cide (häm′ə sīd), *n.* **1.** any killing of one human being by another. **2.** a person who kills another. —**hom′i·cid′al,** *adj.*

hom·i·ly (häm′ə lē), *n.* **1.** a sermon about something in the Bible. **2.** a long, dull talk on what is right and wrong. —**hom′i·lies,** *pl.*

homing pigeon, a pigeon trained to find its way home from far-off places, and used to carry a written message fastened to its leg.

hom·i·ny (häm′ə nē), *n.* dry corn kernels that have had the hulls removed and have been broken into coarse bits, which are boiled for food.

ho·mo (hō′mō), *n.* man: *a Latin word.*

ho·mo·ge·ne·ous (hō′mə jē′ni əs *or* häm′ə jē′ni əs), *adj.* alike or made up of parts that are alike [a *homogeneous* group of people].

ho·mo·gen·ize (hə mäj′ə nīz), *v.* to make something the same throughout [Milk is *homogenized* by breaking down and blending the fat particles so that the cream does not separate and go to the top.] —**ho·mo′gen·ized,** *p.t. & p.p.;* **ho·mo′gen·iz·ing,** *pr.p.*

hom·o·nym (häm′ə nim), *n.* a word that is pronounced like another word but that has a different meaning and is usually spelled differently ["Bore" and "boar" are *homonyms*.]

hom·y (hōm′ē), *adj.* same as **homey.** —**hom′i·er,** *compar.;* **hom′i·est,** *superl.*

Hon., abbreviation for **Honorable.**

Hon·du·ras (hän door′əs *or* hän dyoor′əs), *n.* a country in Central America.

hone (hōn), *n.* a hard stone used to sharpen razors, knives, etc. —*v.* to sharpen on a hone. —**honed,** *p.t. & p.p.;* **hon′ing,** *pr.p.*

hon·est (än′ist), *adj.* **1.** that does not steal, cheat, or lie; upright or trustworthy [an *honest* man]. **2.** got by fair means, not by stealing, cheating, or lying [to earn an *honest* living]. **3.**

sincere or genuine [He made an *honest* effort to help.] **4.** frank and open [an *honest* face].

hon·est·ly (än/ist lē), *adv.* **1.** in an honest way. **2.** really; truly [*Honestly*, it is so.]

hon·es·ty (än/is tē), *n.* the quality or fact of being honest; uprightness; sincerity.

hon·ey (hun/ē), *n.* **1.** a thick, sweet, yellow sirup that bees make from the nectar of flowers and store in honeycombs. **2.** anything like honey; sweetness. **3.** sweet one; darling; dear. —*v.* **1.** to make sweet, as with honey. **2.** to speak sweetly to or flatter. —**hon/eys,** *pl.* —**hon/eyed** or **hon/ied,** *p.t. & p.p.;* **hon/ey·ing,** *pr.p.*

hon·ey·bee (hun/ē bē), *n.* a bee that makes honey.

hon·ey·comb (hun/ē kōm), *n.* **1.** a cluster of wax cells made by bees to hold their honey, eggs, etc. Each cell has six sides. **2.** anything like this. —*v.* to fill with holes like a honeycomb [The hill is *honeycombed* with caves.] —*adj.* of or like a honeycomb [a *honeycomb* design].

honeycombs

hon·ey·dew (hun/ē dōō *or* hun/ē dyōō), *n.* **1.** a sweet liquid that comes from the leaves of some plants in summer. **2.** a sweet substance made by aphids and other insects that suck juice from plants. **3.** a kind of muskmelon with a smooth, light-green skin: *its full name is* **honeydew melon.**

hon·eyed (hun/ēd), *adj.* **1.** sweetened, as with honey. **2.** flattering; loving [*honeyed* words].

hon·ey·moon (hun/ē mōōn), *n.* the vacation spent together by a couple after their wedding. —*v.* to have a honeymoon. —**hon/ey·moon/er,** *n.*

hon·ey·suck·le (hun/ē suk/'l), *n.* a climbing vine with small flowers having a sweet smell.

Hong Kong (hông/ kông/), a British colony in southeastern China.

honk (hôngk), *n.* **1.** the call of a wild goose. **2.** a sound like this. —*v.* to make this sound.

Hon·o·lu·lu (hän/ə lōō/lōō), *n.* the capital of Hawaii.

honeysuckle

hon·or (än/ər), *n.* **1.** great respect given because of worth, noble deeds, high rank, etc. [to pay *honor* to the heroes of science]. **2.** glory or credit, or a person or thing that brings this to others [to have the *honor* of dining with the Queen; to be an *honor* to one's profession]. **3.** something done or given as a sign of respect [Madame Curie received many *honors* for her work.] **4.** **Honor,** a title of respect given to a judge, mayor, etc. [His *Honor*, the Mayor]. **5.** good name or reputation [You must uphold the *honor* of your family.] **6.** a being true to what is right, honest, etc. [His sense of *honor* kept him from cheating.]

7. honors, *pl.* special praise given to a student with very high grades [to graduate with *honors*]. —*v.* **1.** to have or show great respect for [America *honors* the memory of Lincoln. *Honor* your father and your mother.] **2.** to do or give something in honor of [We *honored* our track team with a banquet.] **3.** to accept as good for payment, credit, etc. [Will the bank *honor* your check?] —**do the honors,** to act as a host or hostess.

hon·or·a·ble (än/ər ə b'l), *adj.* **1.** worthy of being honored or respected [an *honorable* trade; an *honorable* name]. **2.** honest, upright, and sincere [*honorable* intentions]. **3.** bringing honor [*honorable* mention]. **4.** **Honorable,** a title of respect used before the name of some officials, etc. —**hon/or·a·bly,** *adv.*

hon·or·ar·y (än/ə rer/ē), *adj.* **1.** done or given as an honor [an *honorary* degree]. **2.** holding the office only as an honor, without duties or pay [The President is often made *honorary* chairman of various groups.]

hon·our (än/ər), *n.* British spelling of **honor.**

Hon·shu (hän/shōō/), *n.* the largest of the islands that form Japan.

hood (hood), *n.* **1.** a covering for the head and neck, often part of a coat or cloak. **2.** anything like a hood, as the metal cover over the engine of an automobile. —*v.* to cover with a hood. —**hood/ed,** *adj.*

-hood (hood), a suffix meaning: **1.** the condition or time of being [*Childhood* is the time of being a child.] **2.** all the members in a group [The *priesthood* is the whole group of priests.]

hood

hood·lum (hōōd/ləm), *n.* a person who is cruel and wild, and has no respect for the law: *used only in everyday talk.*

hoo·doo (hōō/dōō), *n.* **1.** same as **voodoo. 2.** bad luck or a person or thing that causes it: *used only in everyday talk.*

hood·wink (hood/wingk), *v.* to trick or fool; mislead [Don't be *hoodwinked* by his promises.]

hoof (hoof *or* hōōf), *n.* **1.** the horny covering on the feet of cows, horses, deer, pigs, etc. **2.** the whole foot of such an animal. —*v.* to dance: *slang in this meaning.* —**on the hoof,** not butchered; alive. —**hoofs,** *pl.*

hook (hook), *n.* **1.** a piece of metal, plastic, etc. that is curved or bent so that it will catch or hold something [a fish*hook;* a coat *hook*]. **2.** something shaped like a hook, as the bend in a river. **3.** a stroke, blow, etc. with a curving motion. —*v.* **1.** to curve as a hook does. **2.** to catch, fasten, throw, hit, etc. with a hook [*Hook* the screen door. I *hooked* a fish.] **3.** to cheat, trick, or steal: *used only in*

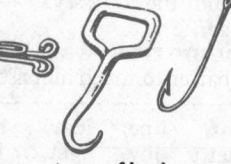
types of hook

hoofs

everyday talk. —**by hook or by crook,** in any way at all, fair or foul. —**hook up,** to set up and connect the parts, as of a radio. —**on one's own hook,** without getting help, advice, etc.

hooked (hookt), *adj.* **1.** curved like a hook. **2.** having a hook or hooks. **3.** made by drawing strips of cloth or yarn back and forth with a hook through canvas or burlap [a *hooked* rug].

hook·up (hook′up), *n.* the way the parts or circuits are connected, as in radio.

hook·worm (hook′wûrm), *n.* a small worm with hooks around the mouth, that can live in the intestines and cause fever, weakness, and pain.

hoop (hoop), *n.* **1.** a round band of metal that holds together the staves of a barrel. **2.** anything like this, as a ring in a hoop skirt, a wicket in croquet, or a large ring used as a toy. —*v.* to bind together with a hoop or hoops.

hoop skirt, a woman's skirt worn over a framework of hoops to make it spread out.

hoo·ray (hoo rā′), *interj.,* *n. & v.* hurrah.

hoot (hoot), *n.* **1.** the sound that an owl makes, or a sound like this. **2.** a loud shout or boo of anger or scorn. —*v.* **1.** to make the sound that an owl makes or a sound like this [The train whistle *hooted.*] **2.** to show anger or scorn, as by hooting or booing. **3.** to chase away by hooting [The actors were *hooted* off the stage.]

hoop skirt

Hoo·ver, Herbert C. (hoo′vər), 1874–1964; 31st president of the United States, from 1929 to 1933.

Hoover Dam, a dam on the Colorado River, between Nevada and Arizona.

hop (häp), *v.* **1.** to make a short leap or leaps on one foot. **2.** to jump onto or over [to *hop* on a bus; to *hop* a fence]. **3.** to move by jumps, as a bird or frog. **4.** to go or move briskly: *slang in this meaning.* —*n.* **1.** the act of hopping. **2.** a party at which people dance: *used only in everyday talk.* —**hopped,** *p.t. & p.p.;* **hop′ping,** *pr.p.*

hop (häp), *n.* **1.** a climbing vine with small yellow flowers shaped like cones. **2. hops,** *pl.* these dried flowers, used to flavor beer and ale.

hope (hōp), *n.* **1.** a feeling that what one wants will happen [We gave up *hope* of being rescued.] **2.** the thing that one wants [It is her *hope* to go to college.] **3.** a person or thing on which one may base some hope [Bill is the great *hope* of his family.] —*v.* to have hope; expect and wish [I *hope* to see you again soon.] —**hoped,** *p.t. & p.p.;* **hop′ing,** *pr.p.*

hope·ful (hōp′fəl), *adj.* **1.** feeling or showing hope. **2.** causing or giving hope [a *hopeful* sign]. —**hope′ful·ly,** *adv.* —**hope′ful·ness,** *n.*

hope·less (hōp′lis), *adj.* **1.** without hope [a *hopeless* prisoner]. **2.** causing one to lose hope [a *hopeless* situation]. —**hope′less·ly,** *adv.* —**hope′less·ness,** *n.*

hop·per (häp′ər), *n.* **1.** a person or thing that hops. **2.** a hopping insect. **3.** a container, often shaped like a funnel, from which the contents can be emptied slowly and evenly.

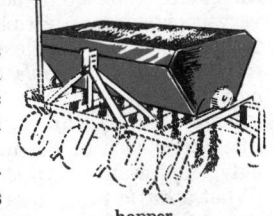

hopper

hop·scotch (häp′-skäch), *n.* a children's game in which the players hop from one section to another of a figure drawn on the ground.

Hor·ace (hôr′is), *n.* 65–8 B.C.; Roman poet.

horde (hôrd), *n.* **1.** a wandering tribe, as of early Mongols. **2.** a large group or crowd [a *horde* of picnickers].

ho·ri·zon (hə rī′z′n), *n.* **1.** the line where the sky seems to meet the earth [A ship appeared over the *horizon.*] **2.** the limit of one's experience, knowledge, etc. [Travel widens our *horizons.*]

hor·i·zon·tal (hôr′ə zän′t′l), *adj.* parallel to the horizon; not vertical; level; flat [A table top is *horizontal;* its legs are vertical.] —*n.* a horizontal line, plane, etc. —**hor′i·zon′tal·ly,** *adv.*

hor·mone (hôr′mōn), *n.* a substance formed in an organ of the body and carried in the blood to some other part, where it has an effect [The pituitary gland makes *hormones* controlling growth.]

horn (hôrn), *n.* **1.** a hard, pointed growth on the head of some animals, as cattle and goats. Horns usually grow in pairs. **2.** the substance that horns are made of [*Horn* is used to make the frames of some eyeglasses.] **3.** anything that sticks out or is curved like a horn, as each end of a crescent. **4.** a container made by hollowing out a horn [a powder *horn*]. **5.** any brass-wind instrument, especially the *French horn.* The *English horn* is not truly a horn. **6.** a device that makes a loud noise as a warning or a signal [a fog*horn*]. —**horn in,** to interfere or meddle: *a slang phrase.* —**horn′less,** *adj.*

Horn, Cape, a cape on an island at the southern tip of South America.

horned (hôrnd), *adj.* having a horn or horns.

horned toad, a small lizard with a short tail and spines like horns.

hor·net (hôr′nit), *n.* a large wasp with a very painful sting.

horn of plenty, same as **cornucopia.**

horn·pipe (hôrn′pīp), *n.* **1.** a lively dance that sailors used to do. **2.** music for this.

horn·y (hôr′nē), *adj.* **1.** hard like horn; tough and callous [the carpenter's *horny* hands]. **2.** made of horn. **3.** having horns. —**horn′i·er,** *compar.;* **horn′i·est,** *superl.*

hor·o·scope (hôr′ə skōp), *n.* a chart showing the signs of the zodiac and the positions of the stars and planets. Astrologers believe that such a chart shows how the stars influence a person's life and fate.

hor·ri·ble (hôr′ə b'l), *adj.* **1.** causing horror; very frightening or terrible [a *horrible* accident]. **2.** very bad, ugly, unpleasant, etc.: *used only in everyday talk* [a *horrible* color]. —**hor′ri·bly,** *adv.*

hor·rid (hôr′id), *adj.* **1.** causing horror; terrible [the *horrid* face of the monster]. **2.** very bad, ugly, unpleasant, etc.: *used only in everyday talk* [What a *horrid* thing to say!]

hor·ri·fy (hôr′ə fī), *v.* **1.** to fill with horror. **2.** to shock or disgust: *used only in everyday talk* [We were *horrified* by his bad manners.] —**hor′ri·fied** *p.t. & p.p.;* **hor′ri·fy·ing,** *pr.p.*

hor·ror (hôr′ər), *n.* **1.** strong fear and disgust that makes one shudder. **2.** strong dislike; loathing [She has a *horror* of being photographed.] **3.** the fact of being horrible [the *horror* of starvation]. **4.** something that causes horror [the *horrors* of war].

horse (hôrs), *n.* **1.** a large animal with four legs, solid hoofs, and a flowing mane and tail. People have been riding horses and using them to pull loads since ancient times. **2.** a frame on legs for supporting something, as a saw-horse. **3.** a padded block on legs, used in doing exercises in a gymnasium. —*v.* to supply with a horse or horses. —**horse around,**

horse *(meaning 3)*

to take part in horseplay: *a slang phrase.* —**horsed,** *p.t. & p.p.;* **hors′ing,** *pr.p.*

horse·back (hôrs′bak), *n.* the back of a horse. —*adv.* on horseback [to ride *horseback*].

horse chestnut, **1.** a tree with large leaves, clusters of white flowers, and glossy brown, bitter nuts growing inside burs. **2.** this nut.

horse·fly (hôrs′flī), *n.* a large fly that bites horses and cattle. —**horse′flies,** *pl.*

horse·hair (hôrs′her), *n.* **1.** hair from the mane or tail of a horse. **2.** a stiff cloth made from this hair. —*adj.* made of or stuffed with horsehair [a *horsehair* sofa].

horse chestnuts

horse·hide (hôrs′hīd), *n.* **1.** the hide of a horse. **2.** leather made from this.

horse·man (hôrs′mən), *n.* **1.** a man who rides on horseback. **2.** a man skilled in managing horses. —**horse′men,** *pl.* —**horse′man·ship,** *n.*

horse·play (hôrs′plā), *n.* rough play in fun.

horse·pow·er (hôrs′pou′ər), *n.* a unit for measuring the power of motors or engines. One horsepower equals the force needed to raise 33,000 pounds at the rate of one foot per minute.

horse·rad·ish (hôrs′rad′ish), *n.* **1.** a plant with a long white root. **2.** a relish that has a burning taste, made from this root.

horse sense, plain common sense: *used only in everyday talk.*

horse·shoe (hôrs′shōō), *n.* **1.** a flat metal plate shaped like a U, nailed to a horse's hoof to protect it. **2.** anything shaped like this. **3.** **horseshoes,** *pl.* a game in which players toss horseshoes at a stake in the ground. —*v.* to fit with a horseshoe or horseshoes. —**horse′-shoed,** *p.t. & p.p.;* **horse′shoe·ing,** *pr.p.*

horseshoe

horse·whip (hôrs′hwip), *n.* a whip for driving horses. —*v.* to lash with a horsewhip —**horse′-whipped,** *p.t. & p.p.;* **horse′whip·ping,** *pr.p.*

horse·wom·an (hôrs′woom′ən), *n.* a woman who rides on horseback, especially in a skillful way. —**horse′wom′en,** *pl.*

hors·y (hôr′sē), *adj.* **1.** of or like a horse [a *horsy* face]. **2.** fond of horses, horse racing, etc.

hor·ti·cul·ture (hôr′ti kul′chər), *n.* the science of growing flowers, fruits, and vegetables. —**hor′ti·cul′tur·al,** *adj.* —**hor′ti·cul′tur·ist,** *n.*

ho·san·na (hō zan′ə), *n. & interj.* a shout of praise to God.

hose (hōz), *n.* **1.** a stocking or sock: *usually used in the plural,* **hose.** **2.** a tube of rubber, plastic, etc., through which water or other liquid is sent [a garden *hose* for sprinkling]. **3.** an outer garment once worn by men, that fitted tightly about the hips, legs, and feet. —*v.* to water with a hose. —**hose,** *pl. for meanings 1 & 3;* **hos′es,** *pl. for meaning 2.* —**hosed,** *p.t. & p.p.;* **hos′-ing,** *pr.p.*

fireman's hose

ho·sier·y (hō′zhər ē), *n.* stockings and socks.

hos·pice (häs′pis), *n.* a place where travelers can stop for rest and food, especially one run by monks of St. Bernard in the Alps.

hos·pi·ta·ble (häs′pi tə b'l *or* häs pit′ə b'l), *adj.* **1.** liking to have guests in one's home and treating them in a warm and generous way. **2.** having an open mind [*hospitable* to new ideas]. —**hos′pi·ta·bly,** *adv.*

hos·pi·tal (häs′pi t'l), *n.* a place where doctors, nurses, etc. take care of those who are sick or hurt.

hos·pi·tal·i·ty (häs′pi tal·i·tē), *n.* a generous and friendly way of treating guests.

hos·pi·tal·ize (häs′pi t'l īz′), *v.* to put in a hospital [I was *hospitalized* for my broken leg.] —**hos′pi·tal·ized′,** *p.t. & p.p.;* **hos′pi·tal·iz′ing,** *pr.p.* —**hos′pi·tal·i·za′tion,** *n.*

Host or **host** (hōst), *n.* the bread eaten at Holy Communion. It is often a wafer.

host (hōst), *n.* **1.** a man who has guests in his own home, or who pays for their entertainment away from home. **2.** a man who runs a hotel or inn. **3.** an animal or plant on or in which another animal or plant (called a *parasite*) lives.

host (hōst), *n.* **1.** a great number [a *host* of tourists in Europe]. **2.** an army.

hos·tage (häs'tij), *n.* a person given to or taken by an enemy and held prisoner until certain things are done.

hos·tel (häs't'l), *n.* an inn or other place for staying overnight; now often, a shelter for use by hikers.

hos·tel·ry (häs't'l rē), *n.* a hotel, inn, or other lodging place. —**hos'tel·ries,** *pl.*

hos·tess (hōs'tis), *n.* **1.** a woman who acts as host; also, the wife of a host. **2.** a woman hired by a restaurant to show people to their tables.

hos·tile (häs't'l), *adj.* **1.** of or like an enemy; warlike [surrounded by *hostile* tribes]. **2.** having or showing hate or dislike; unfriendly [a *hostile* gesture]. —**hos'tile·ly,** *adv.*

hos·til·i·ty (häs til'ə tē), *n.* **1.** a feeling of hate or dislike; enmity. **2. hostilities,** *pl.* acts of war; warfare. —**hos·til'i·ties,** *pl.*

hos·tler (häs'lər *or* äs'lər), *n.* a person who takes care of horses at an inn or a stable.

hot (hät), *adj.* **1.** having a high temperature, especially one that is higher than that of the human body; very warm [a *hot* day; a *hot* bath]. **2.** that causes a burning feeling in the mouth [*hot* pepper]. **3.** full of strong feeling or great activity; angry, violent, eager, etc. [a *hot* temper; a *hot* argument]. **4.** close behind [We're *hot* on his trail.] **5.** fresh or new: *slang in this meaning* [*hot* news; a *hot* tip]. —*adv.* in a hot way [The fire burns *hot*.] —**hot'ter,** *compar.;* **hot'test,** *superl.* —**hot'ly,** *adv.* —**hot'ness,** *n.*

hot·bed (hät'bed), *n.* **1.** a warm bed of earth in a frame covered with glass, in which plants can be grown quickly. **2.** any place where something develops quickly [a *hotbed* of crime].

hot dog, a wiener: *used only in everyday talk.*

ho·tel (hō tel'), *n.* a building where travelers may rent rooms, buy meals, etc.

hotbed

hot·head·ed (hät'hed'id), *adj.* very easily excited or made angry; hasty; rash.

hot·house (hät'hous), *n.* same as **greenhouse.**

hot plate, a small stove or burner for cooking.

hot rod, an automobile, usually an old one, in which the power of the engine has been increased to produce greater speed: *a slang term.*

Hot·ten·tot (hät''n tät), *n.* **1.** a member of a Negro people living in South Africa. **2.** their language.

hound (hound), *n.* **1.** a hunting dog with long, drooping ears, short hair, and a keen sense of smell. **2.** any dog. —*v.* to chase or keep after closely [He was *hounded* by reporters.]

hour (our), *n.* **1.** any of the 24 equal parts of a day; 60 minutes. **2.** a particular time [At what *hour* shall we meet?] **3.** *often* **hours,** *pl.* a particular period of time [the dinner *hour;* the doctor's office *hours*]. **4.** distance measured by the time it takes to travel it [He lives two *hours* away from us.] —**after hours,** after the regular hours for business, school, etc.

hour·glass (our'glas), *n.* a device for measuring time, made up of two glass bulbs with a small opening between them through which sand trickles. It takes one hour for the sand to go from one bulb to the other.

hou·ri (hoo'rē *or* hou'rē), *n.* a maiden of the Moslem paradise, thought of as always young and beautiful. —**hou'ris,** *pl.*

hour·ly (our'lē), *adj.* **1.** done, taken, etc. every hour [an *hourly* cup of tea]. **2.** for every hour [an *hourly* wage of $2.00]. **3.** continual [to live in *hourly* dread of disaster]. —*adv.* **1.** every hour [Bells ring *hourly*.] **2.** soon [We expect him *hourly*.]

hourglass

house (hous), *n.* **1.** a building for people to live in. **2.** a family or household, especially a royal family [the head of the *house;* the *House* of Stuart]. **3.** any building, especially one for sheltering or storing something [the elephant *house* at the zoo; a ware*house;* a court*house*]. **4.** a place of business, or a business firm. **5.** an audience [The actors played to a large *house*.] **6.** a group of persons who make the laws, or the place where it meets [the *House* of Representatives]. —*v.* (houz), **1.** to give shelter or lodging to [The cottage *housed* a family of five.] **2.** to store or shelter [We *housed* their furniture in our attic.] —**keep house,** to take care of a home; do housework. —**hous·es** (houz'iz), *pl.* —**housed,** *p.t. & p.p.;* **hous'ing,** *pr.p.*

house·boat (hous'bōt), *n.* a large boat used as a home.

house·break·ing (hous'brāk'ing), *n.* the act of forcing one's way into another's house in order to rob or commit some other crime.

house·fly (hous'flī), *n.* a fly with two wings, found about houses. It feeds on garbage, etc. and can spread disease. —**house'flies,** *pl.*

house·hold (hous'hōld), *n.* **1.** all the persons who live in one house, especially a family. **2.** the home and its affairs [to manage a *household*].

house·hold·er (hous'hōl'dər), *n.* **1.** a person who owns or occupies a house. **2.** the head of a household.

fat,   āpe,   cär,   ten,   ēven,   hit,   bīte,   gō,   hôrn,   tool,   book,   up,   fŭr;
get,   joy,   yet,   chin,   she,   thin,   then;   zh = s in pleasure;   ' as in able (ā'b'l);
ə = a in ago,   e in agent,   i in sanity,   o in confess,   u in focus.

house·keep·er (hous′kēp′ər), *n.* a woman who manages a home, often one who is hired to do so.

house·maid (hous′mād), *n.* a girl or woman servant who does housework.

House of Representatives, the lower branch of the United States Congress or of the lawmaking body of most States.

house·top (hous′täp), *n.* the roof of a house.

house·warm·ing (hous′wôr′ming), *n.* a party given by or for someone moving into a new home.

house·wife (hous′wīf), *n.* a woman who keeps house for her family. —**house′wives,** *pl.*

house·work (hous′wûrk), *n.* the work done in keeping house, such as cleaning and cooking.

hous·ing (houz′ing), *n.* 1. the providing of a home or lodging. 2. houses or lodgings [new *housing* in the area]. 3. a frame or box in which something is protected [the *housing* of an engine].

Hous·ton (hyōōs′tən), *n.* a city in southeastern Texas.

Hous·ton, Samuel (hyōōs′tən), 1793–1863; U.S. statesman who was president of the Republic of Texas before it became a State.

hove (hōv), a past tense and past participle of **heave.**

hov·el (huv′′l *or* häv′′l), *n.* a small house or hut that is old and broken down.

hov·er (huv′ər *or* häv′ər), *v.* 1. to stay fluttering in the air near one place [The butterfly *hovered* over the flower.] 2. to stay or wait very close by [The courtiers *hovered* about the queen.] 3. to be uncertain; waver [to *hover* between hope and despair].

how (hou), *adv.* 1. in what way [*How* do you start the motor? He taught her *how* to act.] 2. in what condition [*How* is your mother today?] 3. for what reason; why [*How* is it that you don't know?] 4. to what degree or amount [*How* high will it fly?] *How* is also used to make an exclamation stronger [*How* nice!] —**how so?** why?

how·be·it (hou bē′it), *adv.* however; nevertheless: *now seldom used.*

how·dah (hou′də), *n.* a seat for riding on the back of an elephant. It is sometimes covered.

how·e′er (hou er′), *adv. & conj.* however.

how·ev·er (hou ev′ər), *adv.* 1. in whatever way; by whatever means [*However* did you find the place?] 2. no matter how; to whatever degree [*However* hard the task, he succeeded.] —*conj.* nevertheless; but [I'll go; *however,* I don't want to.]

how·itz·er (hou′it sər),

howdah

n. a short cannon that fires shells in a high curve.

howl (houl), *v.* 1. to make the long wailing cry of wolves, dogs, etc. 2. to make a sound like this [The boy *howled* in pain.] 3. to shout or laugh in scorn, glee, etc. 4. to drive by howling [The audience *howled* the actor off the stage.] —*n.* the sound of howling.

how·so·ev·er (hou′sō ev′ər), *adv.* no matter how; in whatever way; however.

hoy·den (hoi′d′n), *n.* a bold girl who acts like a rough boy; tomboy.

H.P., HP, h.p., or **hp,** abbreviation for **horsepower.**

H.Q. or **Hq.,** abbreviation for **Headquarters.**

hr., abbreviation for **hour** or **hours.** —**hrs.,** *pl.*

H.R.H., abbreviation for **His Royal Highness** or **Her Royal Highness.**

hub (hub), *n.* 1. the center part of a wheel: it is the part fastened to the axle, or turning on it. 2. a center of activity or interest [Detroit is the *hub* of the auto industry.]

hub·bub (hub′ub), *n.* the noise of many voices mixed together; uproar, as of a crowd.

huck·le·ber·ry (huk′- ′l ber′ē), *n.* 1. a dark-blue berry that looks like the blueberry. 2. the shrub it grows on. —**huck′le·ber′ries,** *pl.*

huck·ster (huk′stər), *n.* a peddler, especially of fruits and vegetables.

HUD, abbreviation for the Department of **Housing and Urban Development** in the U.S. government.

hud·dle (hud′′l), *v.* 1. to crowd or push close together [Cows often *huddle* together in a storm. We *huddled* the children into the car.] 2. to draw or hunch oneself up [The child *huddled* under the blanket.] —*n.* 1. a confused crowd of people or heap of things [His clothes lay in a *huddle* on the floor.]

football huddle

2. a huddling together of a football team to get the signals for the next play. 3. a private talk: *a slang meaning.* —**hud′dled,** *p.t. & p.p.;* **hud′dling,** *pr.p.*

Hud·son (hud′s′n), *n.* a river in eastern New York. Its mouth is at New York City.

Hudson Bay, a bay of the Atlantic that reaches into central Canada.

hue (hyōō), *n.* color, especially a shade of color; tint [orange of a reddish *hue*].

hue and cry, a loud outcry of alarm or anger.

huff (huf), *n.* a fit of anger, as because of hurt feelings. —**huff′y,** *adj.*

hug (hug), *v.* 1. to clasp in the arms and hold close to one in a loving way. 2. to keep close to [The car *hugged* the curb.] —*n.* close embrace. —**hugged,** *p.t. & p.p.;* **hug′ging,** *pr.p.*

huge (hyōōj), *adj.* very large; immense [the *huge* trunk of the redwood tree]. —**huge′ly,** *adv.* —**huge′ness,** *n.*

Hu·go, Vic·tor (vik′tər hyōō′gō), 1802–1885; French writer.

Hu·gue·not (hyōō′gə nät), *n.* a French Protestant of the 16th and 17th centuries.

huh (hu), *interj.* a sound made in showing surprise, scorn, etc. or in questioning.

hu·la-hu·la (hōō′lə hōō′lə) or **hu·la** (hōō′lə), *n.* a Hawaiian dance performed by women.

hulk (hulk), *n.* **1.** an old ship that is no longer sailed on voyages. **2.** a big, clumsy person or a big thing that is hard to handle.

hulk·ing (hul′king), *adj.* big and clumsy.

hull (hul), *n.* **1.** the outer covering of a seed or fruit, as the shell of nuts, the pod of peas, or the husk of grain. **2.** the tiny leaves at the base of some berries, as the strawberry. **3.** the main body of a ship or seaplane. —*v.* to take the hulls from [to *hull* peanuts].

hul·la·ba·loo (hul′ə bə lōō′), *n.* a loud noise of many voices and sounds; uproar.

hum (hum), *v.* **1.** to make a low, steady, buzzing sound like that of a bee or a motor. **2.** to sing with the lips closed, not saying the words. **3.** to be very busy or active: *used only in everyday talk* [Business is *humming*.] —*n.* the act or sound of humming. —**hummed,** *p.t. & p.p.;* **hum′-ming,** *pr.p.*

hu·man (hyōō′mən), *adj.* **1.** that is a person or that has to do with people or mankind in general [a *human* being; *human* affairs]. **2.** that is typical of or like people in general ["To err is *human.*"] —*n.* a person: usually called **human being.**

hu·mane (hyoo mān′), *adj.* kind, gentle, and generous [*humane* treatment of prisoners].

hu·man·ist (hyōō′mən ist), *n.* a person whose main interest is human ideals and needs, rather than religion.

hu·man·i·tar·i·an (hyoo man′ə ter′i ən), *n.* a person who spends much time in doing good for others; philanthropist. —*adj.* that helps mankind; philanthropic [a *humanitarian* plan to eliminate famines].

hu·man·i·ty (hyoo man′ə tē), *n.* **1.** all human beings; mankind; the human race [Atomic warfare threatens *humanity.*] **2.** kindness or sympathy [She showed her *humanity* by helping the sick.] **3.** the special qualities of all human beings; human nature [It is our common *humanity* to be both greedy and unselfish.] —**the humanities,** studies that deal with human thought and human relations, as literature, philosophy, the fine arts, etc., but not the sciences.

hu·man·ize (hyōō′mə nīz), *v.* to make or become human or humane; make kind, gentle, generous, etc.; civilize. —**hu′man·ized,** *p.t. & p.p.;* **hu′man·iz·ing,** *pr.p.*

hu·man·kind (hyōō′mən kīnd′), *n.* mankind; the human race; humanity.

hu·man·ly (hyōō′mən lē), *adv.* by human means or in a human way [Do all that is *humanly* possible to help him.]

hum·ble (hum′b'l), *adj.* **1.** knowing one's own weaknesses and faults; not proud or bold; modest or meek [His failure did not make him *humble.*] **2.** low in rank or position; plain and simple; lowly ["Be it ever so *humble*, there's no place like home."] —*v.* to make humble; take away the pride, fame, or power of [John Paul Jones *humbled* the British Navy.] —**hum′bler,** *compar.;* **hum′blest,** *superl.* —**hum′bled,** *p.t. & p.p.;* **hum′bling,** *pr.p.* —**hum′ble·ness,** *n.* —**hum′bly,** *adv.*

hum·bug (hum′bug), *n.* **1.** something said or done to cheat or trick; fraud. **2.** a person who is not what he pretends to be; imposter. —*v.* to cheat; trick. —**hum′bugged,** *p.t. & p.p.;* **hum′bug·ging,** *pr.p.*

hum·drum (hum′drum), *adj.* dull or boring because always the same [to lead a *humdrum* life].

hu·mid (hyōō′mid), *adj.* full of water vapor; damp; moist [the *humid* jungles of Africa].

hu·mid·i·fy (hyoo mid′ə fī), *v.* to make humid; moisten. —**hu·mid′i·fied,** *p.t. & p.p.;* **hu·mid′i·fy·ing,** *pr.p.* —**hu·mid′i·fi·er,** *n.*

hu·mid·i·ty (hyoo mid′ə tē), *n.* dampness; especially, the amount of moisture in the air.

hu·mil·i·ate (hyoo mil′i āt), *v.* to take away the pride or dignity of; make feel ashamed [It *humiliated* Mary that no one asked her to dance.] —**hu·mil′i·at·ed,** *p.t. & p.p.;* **hu·mil′i·at·ing,** *pr.p.* —**hu·mil′i·a′tion,** *n.*

hu·mil·i·ty (hyoo mil′ə tē), *n.* the condition of being humble, or not proud; meekness.

hum·ming·bird (hum′ing bûrd′), *n.* a tiny bird that has a long, thin bill, with which it sucks nectar from flowers. It can fly backward as well as forward, or can hover in the air.

hummingbird (about 3½ in. long)

hum·mock (hum′ək), *n.* **1.** a low, rounded hill; mound. **2.** a raised mound in a field of ice.

hu·mor (hyōō′mər), *n.* **1.** the quality of being funny or amusing [a play full of *humor*]. **2.** the ability to see or express what is funny or amusing [He has no sense of *humor* and rarely laughs.] **3.** a state of mind; mood [He was in a bad *humor* and wouldn't answer.] **4.** whim or fancy [He ate when it pleased his *humor*.] —*v.* to give in to; give whatever another wishes; indulge [Susan whines if people don't *humor* her.] —**out of humor,** in a bad mood; cross.

hu·mor·ist (hyōō′mər ist), *n.* a person who says amusing things or tells funny stories well.

hu·mor·ous (hyōō′mər əs), *adj.* funny or amusing; comical. —**hu′mor·ous·ly,** *adv.*

hu·mour (hyōō′mər), *n. & v.* British spelling of **humor.**

hump (hump), *n.* **1.** a round lump on the back, as of a camel. **2.** a mound; hummock. —*v.* to form into a hump; arch; hunch [A cat often *humps* its back.]

fat, āpe, cär, ten, ēven, hit, bīte, gō, hôrn, tōōl, book, up, fûr;
get, joy, yet, chin, she, thin, *th*en; zh = s in pleasure; ' as in able (ā′b'l);
ə = a in ago, e in agent, i in sanity, o in confess, u in focus.

hump·back (hump′bak), *n.* **1.** a person with a hump on his back; hunchback. **2.** a back with such a hump. —**hump′backed,** *adj.*

humph (humf), *interj. & n.* a snorting sound made to show doubt, surprise, disgust, etc.

hu·mus (hyōō′məs), *n.* brown or black soil made up of decayed leaves, plants, etc.

Hun (hun), *n.* **1.** a member of an Asiatic people who invaded Europe in the 4th and 5th centuries A.D. **2. hun,** any savage or cruel person.

hunch (hunch), *v.* **1.** to draw one's body up so as to form a hump [He *hunched* himself over his desk.] **2.** to push forward by jerks [He *hunched* his way through the crowd.] —*n.* **1.** a hump on the back. **2.** a feeling about something not based on known facts: *used only in everyday talk* [I have a *hunch* that nobody is there.]

hunch·back (hunch′bak), *n.* same as **hump-back.**

hun·dred (hun′drid), *n. & adj.* ten times ten; the number 100.

hun·dred·fold (hun′drid fōld′), *adj., adv. & n.* a hundred times as much or as many.

hun·dredth (hun′dridth), *adj.* coming after ninety-nine others; 100th in order. —*n.* **1.** the hundredth one. **2.** one of 100 equal parts of something; 1/100.

hun·dred·weight (hun′drid wāt′), *n.* a unit of weight, equal to 100 pounds in the United States and 112 pounds in England.

hung (hung), past tense and past participle of **hang.**

Hun·ga·ry (hung′gər ē), *n.* a country in central Europe. —**Hun·gar·i·an** (hung ger′i ən), *adj. & n.*

hun·ger (hung′gər), *n.* **1.** the discomfort caused by having nothing or not enough to eat. **2.** an appetite or need for food [The meal satisfied their *hunger*.] **3.** any strong desire; craving [a *hunger* for knowledge]. —*v.* **1.** to be hungry; need food. **2.** to have a strong desire; crave; long [to *hunger* for love].

hun·gry (hung′grē), *adj.* **1.** wanting or needing food [Cold weather makes me *hungry*.] **2.** having a strong desire; eager [*hungry* for praise]. —**hun′gri·er,** *compar.;* **hun′gri·est,** *superl.* —**hun′gri·ly,** *adv.* —**hun′gri·ness,** *n.*

hunk (hungk), *n.* a large piece or lump: *used only in everyday talk* [a *hunk* of chocolate].

hunt (hunt), *v.* **1.** to set out to kill wild animals or birds, for food or as a sport. **2.** to try to find; search; seek [to *hunt* for buried treasure]. **3.** to chase or drive [The mob *hunted* him out of town.] —*n.* **1.** the act of hunting; a chase or search [a fox *hunt;* a treasure *hunt*]. **2.** a group of people hunting together.

hunt·er (hun′tər), *n.* **1.** a person who hunts. **2.** a horse or dog trained for use in hunting.

hunt·ing (hun′ting), *n.* the act of a person or animal that hunts. —*adj.* of or for hunting.

hunt·ress (hun′tris), *n.* a woman who hunts.

hunts·man (hunts′mən), *n.* **1.** a man who hunts. **2.** the manager of a hunt, especially a fox hunt. *This word is mainly British.* —**hunts′-men,** *pl.*

hur·dle (hur′d'l), *n.* **1.** any of the small fences or frames that runners or horses must jump over in a special race, called **the hurdles. 2.** a frame made of twigs woven together, used as a movable fence. **3.** something difficult that has to be overcome [Passing the final exams is our last *hurdle*.] —*v.* **1.** to jump over, as a hurdle. **2.** to overcome something difficult. —**hur′dled,** *p.t. & p.p.;* **hur′dling,** *pr.p.*

boy running the hurdles

hur·dy-gur·dy (hur′dē gur′dē), *n.* a barrel organ. —**hur′dy-gur′dies,** *pl.*

hurl (hurl), *v.* **1.** to throw with great force [to *hurl* a javelin]. **2.** to say in a strong or angry way [to *hurl* insults]. —**hurl′er,** *n.*

hurl·y-burl·y (hur′lē bur′lē), *n.* an uproar or confusion; hubbub.

Hu·ron, Lake (hyoor′ən), one of the Great Lakes, between Lake Michigan and Lake Erie.

hur·rah (hoo rô′ *or* hə rä′), *interj. & n.* a word called out to show joy, approval, etc. —*v.* to shout "hurrah"; cheer. Also **hur·ray** (hoo rā′).

hur·ri·cane (hur′i kān), *n.* a very strong wind-storm, often with heavy rain, in which the wind blows in a circle at 73 or more miles per hour. Hurricanes usually start in the West Indies and move slowly northward.

hur·ried (hur′ēd), *adj.* done or acting in a hurry; hasty. —**hur′ried·ly,** *adv.*

hur·ry (hur′ē), *v.* **1.** to move, send, or carry quickly or too quickly [You fell because you *hurried*. A taxi *hurried* us home.] **2.** to make happen or be done more quickly [Please try to *hurry* dinner.] **3.** to try to make move or act faster [Don't *hurry* me when I'm eating.] —*n.* **1.** the act of hurrying; rush or haste [In his *hurry* John left the door open.] **2.** need for hurrying [There's no *hurry* about repaying me.] —**hur′ried,** *p.t. & p.p.;* **hur′ry·ing,** *pr.p.*

hurt (hurt), *v.* **1.** to cause pain or injury to; wound [The fall *hurt* my leg.] **2.** to have pain [My head *hurts*.] **3.** to harm or damage in some way [Water won't *hurt* this table top.] **4.** to offend or make unhappy [His criticism *hurt* my feelings.] —*n.* pain, injury, or harm. —**hurt,** *p.t. & p.p.;* **hurt′ing,** *pr.p.*

hurt·ful (hurt′fəl), *adj.* causing hurt; harmful.

hur·tle (hur′t'l), *v.* to move or throw with great speed or much force [The racing cars *hurtled* through the town.] —**hur′tled,** *p.t. & p.p.;* **hur′tling,** *pr.p.*

hus·band (huz′bənd), *n.* the man to whom a woman is married. —*v.* to manage carefully so that nothing is wasted [to *husband* one's money].

hus·band·man (huz′bənd mən), *n.* a farmer: *now seldom used.* —**hus′band·men,** *pl.*

hus·band·ry (huz′bənd rē), *n.* **1.** a careful managing so that nothing is wasted; thrift. **2.** the business of running a farm; farming [Animal *husbandry* is the raising of farm animals.]

hush (hush), *v.* to make or become quiet [I hushed the baby. *Hush*, or you will wake her.] —*n.* silence; quiet [the *hush* of a cathedral].

husk (husk), *n.* the dry covering of certain fruits and seeds, as of an ear of corn. —*v.* to remove the husk from [to *husk* corn].

Hus·ky or **hus·ky** (hus/kē), *n.* a strong dog closely related to the Eskimo dog, used for pulling sleds in the Arctic. —**Hus/kies** or **hus/kies,** *pl.*

hus·ky (hus/kē), *adj.* **1.** sounding deep and hoarse; rough [a *husky* voice]. **2.** big and strong. —**hus/ki·er,** *compar.*; **hus/ki·est,** *superl.* —**hus/ki·ly,** *adv.* —**hus/ki·ness,** *n.*

husk of an ear of corn

hus·sar (hoo zär/), *n.* a member of certain European cavalry troops with showy uniforms.

hus·sy (huz/ē *or* hus/ē), *n.* **1.** a woman of low morals. **2.** a girl who is bold and lively in a way that is not thought proper.

hus·tle (hus/'l), *v.* **1.** to push or force one's way [to *hustle* through a crowd]. **2.** to force in a rough and hurried way [The waiter *hustled* the rowdy customer out the door.] **3.** to go, do, etc. quickly or with much energy. —*n.* a hustling [the *hustle* and bustle of the city]. —**hus/tled,** *p.t. & p.p.*; **hus/tling,** *pr.p.* —**hus/tler,** *n.*

hut (hut), *n.* a little house or cabin of the plainest kind.

hutch (huch), *n.* **1.** a pen or coop for small animals. **2.** a chest for storing things; especially, a kind of movable cupboard.

rabbit hutches

huz·za (hə zä/), *interj., n. & v.* same as **hurrah:** *now seldom used.*

Hwang Ho (hwäng/ hō/), a river in China, flowing into the Yellow Sea: also called **Yellow River.**

hy·a·cinth (hī/ə sinth), *n.* a plant of the lily family, with long, narrow leaves and a spike of sweet-smelling flowers shaped like bells.

hy·brid (hī/brid), *n.* **1.** the offspring of two animals or plants of different species or varieties [The mule is a *hybrid*, being the offspring of a donkey and a horse.] **2.** anything of mixed background [The word "hydroplane" is a *hybrid* because "hydro-" comes from Greek and "plane" comes from Latin.] —*adj.* being a hybrid.

hyacinth

hy·brid·ize (hī/bri dīz), *v.* to breed or produce hybrids; crossbreed [to *hybridize* corn]. —**hy/-brid·ized,** *p.t. & p.p.*; **hy/brid·iz·ing,** *pr.p.* —**hy/brid·i·za/tion,** *n.*

hy·dra (hī/drə), *n.* **1. Hydra,** a serpent with nine heads in Greek myths, who was killed by Hercules. When one of its heads was cut off, two others grew in its place. **2.** a tiny water animal with a body shaped like a tube. Any part that is cut off will grow into a whole new animal. —**hy/dras** or **hy·drae** (hī/drē), *pl.*

hy·dran·ge·a (hī drān/jə), *n.* a shrub with large balls of white, blue, or pink flowers.

hy·drant (hī/drənt), *n.* a closed pipe at a street curb, with a spout for drawing water from a main water line; fireplug.

hy·drate (hī/drāt), *n.* a chemical compound in which each molecule has some water in it [Plaster of Paris is a *hydrate*.]

hy·drau·lic (hī drô/lik), *adj.* **1.** worked by the force of a moving liquid [*hydraulic* brakes]. **2.** hardening under water [*hydraulic* cement]. **3.** having to do with hydraulics. —**hy·drau/li·cal·ly,** *adv.*

hy·drau·lics (hī drô/liks), *n.pl.* the study of how water and other liquids act at rest or in motion and how the force of moving liquids can be used to run machines: *used with a singular verb.*

hy·dro·car·bon (hī/drə kär/bən), *n.* any compound made up of only hydrogen and carbon [Benzene is a *hydrocarbon*.]

hy·dro·chlo·ric acid (hī/drə klôr/ik), an acid formed of hydrogen and chlorine.

hy·dro·e·lec·tric (hī/drō i lek/trik), *adj.* producing electricity by water power or having to do with such production of electricity [*hydroelectric* power from Niagara Falls].

hy·dro·gen (hī/drə jən), *n.* a gas that has no color or smell and burns very easily. It is a chemical element and the lightest of all known substances.

hy·dro·gen·ate (hī/drə jə nāt), *v.* to treat with hydrogen [Vegetable oils are often *hydrogenated* in making margarine.] —**hy/dro·gen·at·ed,** *p.t. & p.p.*; **hy/dro·gen·at·ing,** *pr.p.*

hydrogen bomb, the most destructive kind of bomb. Its great force comes from the energy given off when atoms of a heavy form of hydrogen combine under the great heat and pressure of an atomic bomb explosion to form molecules of helium. Also **H-bomb.**

hy·drom·e·ter (hī dräm/ə tər), *n.* an instrument for finding out the weight of any liquid as compared with that of water.

hy·dro·pho·bi·a (hī/drə fō/bi ə), *n.* a disease that can kill dogs, or people bitten by dogs that have this disease; rabies. A person who has this disease is unable to swallow water.

hy·dro·plane (hī/drə plān), *n.* **1.** a small motorboat with a flat bottom, that skims along the water at high speeds. **2.** a seaplane.

fat,   āpe,   cär,   ten,   ēven,   hit,   bīte,   gō,   hôrn,   tool,   book,   up,   fûr;
get,   joy,   yet,   chin,   she,   thin,   *then*;   zh = s in pleasure;   ' as in able (ā/b'l);
ə = a in ago,   e in agent,   i in sanity,   o in confess,   u in focus.

hy·e·na (hī ē′nə), *n.* a wild animal of Africa and Asia that looks like a large dog. It eats the remains of dead animals and has a shrill cry.

hyena (4 ft. long)

hy·giene (hī′jēn), *n.* the science that has to do with keeping people healthy; also, a system of rules for keeping healthy.

hy·gi·en·ic (hī′ji en′ik), *adj.* **1.** free from dirt and germs that might cause disease; sanitary [This farm has *hygienic* dairy equipment.] **2.** having to do with hygiene or health. —**hy′gi·en′i·cal·ly,** *adv.*

hy·gi·en·ist (hī′ji ən ist), *n.* an expert in hygiene, or the rules of health.

hy·ing (hī′ing), a present participle of **hie.**

Hy·men (hī′mən), *n.* the Greek god of marriage.

hymn (him), *n.* **1.** a song praising or honoring God. **2.** any song of praise.

hym·nal (him′nəl), *n.* a book of hymns: also **hymn′book.**

hyper-, a prefix meaning "over," "more than normal," "too," "too much" [A *hypercritical* person is one who is too critical.]

hy·per·bo·le (hī pûr′bə lē), *n.* a way of speaking or writing to make something seem greater or better than it is; exaggeration [It is *hyperbole* to say "John is as strong as an ox."] —**hy·per·bol·ic** (hī′pər bäl′ik), *adj.*

hy·per·crit·i·cal (hī′pər krit′i k'l), *adj.* too critical; too hard to please.

hy·per·son·ic (hī′pər sän′ik), *adj.* moving at a speed greater than five times the speed of sound, or over 3,700 miles per hour.

hy·per·ten·sion (hī′pər ten′shən), *n.* blood pressure that is much higher than normal.

hy·phen (hī′f'n), *n.* the mark -, used between the parts of a compound word (as *court-martial*), or between the parts of a word divided at the end of a line. —*v.* to hyphenate.

hy·phen·ate (hī′f'n āt), *v.* to join or write with a hyphen. —**hy′phen·at·ed,** *p.t. & p.p.;* **hy′phen·at·ing,** *pr.p.* —**hy′phen·a′tion,** *n.*

hyp·no·sis (hip nō′sis), *n.* the condition of being hypnotized.

hyp·not·ic (hip nät′ik), *adj.* **1.** causing sleep [*hypnotic* drugs]. **2.** of, like, or causing hypnosis [*hypnotic* suggestion; a *hypnotic* trance]. —*n.* **1.** any drug that causes sleep. **2.** a hypnotized person or one who is easily hypnotized. —**hyp·not′i·cal·ly,** *adv.*

hyp·no·tism (hip′nə tiz′m), *n.* the act or practice of hypnotizing, or the condition of being hypnotized.

hyp·no·tist (hip′nə tist), *n.* a person who hypnotizes others.

hyp·no·tize (hip′nə tīz), *v.* to put someone into a condition like sleep, in which he will do or say the things suggested by the person who has put him into this condition. —**hyp′no·tized,** *p.t. & p.p.;* **hyp′no·tiz·ing,** *pr.p.*

hy·po (hī′pō), *n.* a chemical used to wash camera film that has just been developed, to keep it from fading.

hy·po·chon·dri·a (hī′pə kän′dri ə), *n.* a condition in which one keeps worrying about his health and imagining that he has some sickness.

hy·po·chon·dri·ac (hī′pə kän′dri ak), *n.* a person who has hypochondria.

hy·poc·ri·sy (hi päk′rə sē), *n.* the condition of being a hypocrite, or the action of a hypocrite. —**hy·poc′ri·sies,** *pl.*

hyp·o·crite (hip′ə krit), *n.* a person who pretends to have feelings, a goodness, etc. that he does not really have [I would be a *hypocrite* if I said I enjoyed his speech.]

hyp·o·crit·i·cal (hip′ə krit′i k'l), *adj.* of or like a hypocrite; not sincere. —**hyp′o·crit′i·cal·ly,** *adv.*

hy·po·der·mic (hī′pə dûr′mik), *n.* **1.** a glass tube with a hollow needle at one end and a plunger, used for forcing a medicine under the skin: its full name is **hypodermic syringe. 2.** a dose of medicine given in this way. —*adj.* under the skin [a *hypodermic* injection].

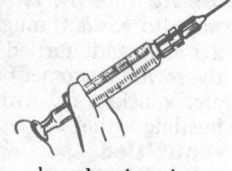

hypodermic syringe

hy·pot·e·nuse (hī pät′'n ōōs *or* hī pät′'n yōōs), *n.* in a triangle having a right angle, the side that is opposite the right angle.

hy·poth·e·sis (hi päth′ə sis), *n.* an unproved idea taken for granted for the time being because it may explain certain facts or can be used as the basis for reasoning, study, etc. [the *hypothesis* that sunspots affect our weather].

hy·po·thet·i·cal (hī′pə thet′i k'l), *adj.* based on a hypothesis; supposed. —**hy′po·thet′i·cal·ly,** *adv.*

hys·sop (his′əp), *n.* **1.** a low shrub with blue flowers. Its leaves are used in medicine and for flavoring. **2.** in the Bible, a plant used in ancient Jewish religious ceremonies.

hys·ter·i·a (his tir′i ə), *n.* **1.** a sickness of the mind in which a person may become blind or paralyzed, suffer from imaginary pains, etc. without any real, physical cause. **2.** a wild fit of laughing or crying that gets out of control.

hys·ter·i·cal (his ter′i k'l), *adj.* **1.** of or like hysteria. **2.** having or likely to have wild fits of laughing, crying, etc. Also **hys·ter′ic.**

hys·ter·ics (his ter′iks), *n.pl.* a wild fit of laughing, crying, etc. that is out of control.

Hz or **hz,** abbreviation for **hertz.**

I

I, i (ī), *n.* the ninth letter of the English alphabet. **—I's, i's** (īz), *pl.*

I (ī), *n.* **1.** the Roman numeral for the figure 1. **2.** symbol for the chemical element *iodine.*

I (ī), *pron.* the person speaking or writing [*I* like candy. It is *I*.] **—we,** *pl.*

Ia., abbreviation for **Iowa.**

i·am·bic (ī am′bik), *adj.* describing poetry made up of measures of two syllables each, with the accent on the second syllable ["Whose woods′/ these are′/ I think′/ I know′" is an *iambic* line.]

-i·an (i ən *or* yən), a suffix meaning: **1.** of or having to do with [*Reptilian* fossils are the fossils of reptiles.] **2.** born or living in [An *Italian* is a person born or living in Italy.]

I·be·ri·a (ī bir′i ə), *n.* the peninsula in southwestern Europe that includes Spain and Portugal: *a Latin name.* **—I·be′ri·an,** *adj.*

i·bex (ī′beks), *n.* a wild goat that lives in the mountains of Europe, Asia, and Africa. The male has large horns that curve backward.

i·bis (ī′bis), *n.* a large wading bird with long legs and a long, curved bill, usually found in warm regions. The ibis was sacred to the ancient Egyptians.

ibex (3 ft. high at shoulder)

-i·ble (i b'l), a suffix meaning: **1.** that can be [A *divisible* number can be divided.] **2.** tending to [A *sensible* idea tends to make sense.]

-ic (ik), a suffix meaning: **1.** of or like [An *angelic* voice is like that of an angel.] **2.** made by or caused by [A *photographic* reproduction is made by taking a photograph.] **3.** made up of or containing [An *alcoholic* drink is one containing alcohol.]

-i·cal (i k'l), a suffix meaning the same as **-ic.** Some words have a different meaning if the suffix is *-ical* instead of *-ic* [*Economical* means "thrifty," but *economic* does not.]

ICBM, intercontinental ballistic missile.

ice (īs), *n.* **1.** water frozen solid by cold [Water turns to *ice* at 32° F.] **2.** anything that looks like frozen water [Dry *ice* is carbon dioxide made solid.] **3.** a frozen dessert, usually made of water, fruit juice, egg white, and sugar. **4.** icing, or frosting. **—v. 1.** to change into ice; freeze [The lake *iced* over.] **2.** to cover or fill with ice, especially to cool [to *ice* a drink]. **3.** to cover with icing, or frosting [to *ice* a cake]. **—iced,** *p.t. & p.p.;* **ic′ing,** *pr.p.*

ice age, any period of time when a large part of the earth was covered with glaciers.

ice·berg (īs′bŭrg), *n.* a mass of ice broken off from a glacier and floating in the sea. The larger part of an iceberg is under water.

ice·boat (īs′bōt), *n.* **1.** a light frame or boat on runners, with sails for moving over ice. **2.** an icebreaker.

ice·box (īs′bäks), *n.* a box or cabinet with ice in it for keeping food cold.

ice·break·er (īs′brāk′ər), *n.*
iceberg
a sturdy boat for breaking a channel through ice.

ice cream, a frozen food made of cream or milk, sugar, flavoring, etc.

Ice·land (īs′lənd), *n.* a country on a large island in the North Atlantic, between Norway and Greenland. **—Ice′land·er,** *n.*

Ice·lan·dic (īs lan′dik), *adj.* of Iceland or its people. **—n.** the language of Iceland.

ice pick, a metal tool with a sharp point for breaking up ice into pieces.

ich·neu·mon (ik nyōō′mən *or* ik nōō′mən), *n.* **1.** a variety of mongoose found in Egypt. **2.** an insect that looks like a wasp but has no sting: *its full name is* **ichneumon fly.**

i·ci·cle (ī′si k'l), *n.* a hanging stick of ice formed by water freezing as it drips down.

ic·ing (īs′ing), *n.* a mixture of sugar, butter, flavoring, etc. for covering cakes; frosting.

i·con (ī′kän), *n.* **1.** an image or picture. **2.** in some churches, a sacred image or picture of Jesus, Mary, a saint, etc.

i·con·o·clast (ī kän′ə klast), *n.* **1.** a person who is against the worship of images. **2.** a person who attacks or makes fun of the things most people believe in or accept without questioning. **—i·con′o·clas′tic,** *adj.*

-ics (iks), a suffix meaning: **1.** a study or science [*Dietetics* is the study of proper diets.] **2.** practice or system [*Athletics* is the practice or system of athletic sports.]

i·cy (ī′sē), *adj.* **1.** full of or covered with ice [*icy* streets]. **2.** like ice; slippery or very cold [*icy* fingers]. **3.** cold in feeling; unfriendly [an *icy* look]. **—i′ci·er,** *compar.;* **i′ci·est,** *superl.* **—i′ci·ly,** *adv.* **—i′ci·ness,** *n.*

I'd (īd), **1.** I had. **2.** I would. **3.** I should.

I·da·ho (ī′də hō), *n.* a State in the northwestern part of the United States: abbreviated **Ida.** or **Id.**

i·de·a (ī dē′ə), *n.* **1.** a thing that comes to the mind; something one thinks, knows, imagines, feels, etc.; belief or thought [Einstein set forth

fat, āpe, cär, ten, ēven, hit, bīte, gō, hôrn, tōōl, book, up, fŭr;
get, joy, yet, chin, she, thin, *th*en; zh = s in pleasure; ' as in able (ā′b'l);
ə = a in ago, e in agent, i in sanity, o in confess, u in focus.

the *idea* that matter can be changed into energy. Their *idea* of beauty is quite different from ours.] **2.** a plan or purpose [The *idea* of the new system is to speed up the work.]

i·de·al (ī dē′əl *or* ī dēl′), *adj.* **1.** exactly as one would wish; perfect [His farm is *ideal* for a vacation.] **2.** that is only in the mind; not real; imaginary [A utopia is an *ideal* society.] —*n.* **1.** an idea of something perfect, used as a standard [Our Bill of Rights is based on *ideals* of freedom.] **2.** a person or thing thought of as perfect; perfect model [Their house is the *ideal* of a comfortable home.] —**i·de′al·ly,** *adv.*

i·de·al·ism (ī dē′əl iz′m), *n.* **1.** the setting up of ideals or the practice of living according to ideals that one has set up [His *idealism* kept him from being selfish.] **2.** any theory of philosophy which holds that things exist only as ideas in the mind.

i·de·al·ist (ī dē′əl ist), *n.* **1.** a person who tries to live according to ideals; often, one who follows his ideals to the point of not being practical. **2.** a person who believes in a philosophy of idealism. —**i′de·al·is′tic,** *adj.* —**i′de·al·is′ti·cal·ly,** *adv.*

i·de·al·ize (ī dē′ə līz), *v.* to think of or make seem ideal or perfect [Some people *idealize* their childhood.] —**i·de′al·ized,** *p.t. & p.p.;* **i·de′al·iz·ing,** *pr.p.* —**i·de′al·i·za′tion,** *n.*

i·den·ti·cal (ī den′ti k'l), *adj.* **1.** the very same [This is the *identical* house where I was born.] **2.** exactly alike [These two pictures are *identical.*] —**i·den′ti·cal·ly,** *adv.*

i·den·ti·fi·ca·tion (ī den′tə fi kā′shən), *n.* **1.** an identifying or being identified. **2.** anything that identifies a person or thing [Fingerprints are used as *identification.*]

i·den·ti·fy (ī den′tə fī), *v.* **1.** to think of or treat as the same [The Roman god Jupiter is *identified* with the Greek god Zeus.] **2.** to show or prove to be a certain person or thing [He was *identified* by the scar on his chin.] **3.** to connect closely [He is now *identified* with the new party.] —**i·den′ti·fied,** *p.t. & p.p.;* **i·den′ti·fy·ing,** *pr.p.*

i·den·ti·ty (ī den′tə tē), *n.* **1.** a being the same or exactly alike; sameness [groups united by *identity* of interests.] **2.** who or what a person or thing is; the fact of being oneself or itself and none other [The thief wore a mask to hide his *identity.*] —**i·den′ti·ties,** *pl.*

i·de·ol·o·gy (ī′di äl′ə jē), *n.* the teachings, beliefs, or ideas of a person, group, etc. [a political *ideology*]. —**id′e·ol′o·gies,** *pl.*

ides (īdz), *n.pl.* in the ancient Roman calendar, the fifteenth day of March, May, July, or October, or the thirteenth of the other months.

id·i·o·cy (id′i ə sē), *n.* **1.** the condition of being an idiot. **2.** great foolishness or stupidity. —**id′i·o·cies,** *pl.*

id·i·om (id′i əm), *n.* **1.** a phrase or expression that has a meaning different from what the words suggest in their usual meaning ["To catch one's eye," meaning "to get one's attention," is an *idiom.*] **2.** the way in which a certain people, writer, group, etc. put words together to express meaning [the Italian *idiom;* the *idiom* of Shake-

speare]. —**id·i·o·mat·ic** (id′i ə mat′ik), *adj.* —**id′i·o·mat′i·cal·ly,** *adv.*

id·i·o·syn·cra·sy (id′i ə sing′krə sē), *n.* a different or unusual way of acting, being, etc. that is special to some person, thing, or group [Wearing only black ties is an *idiosyncrasy* of his.] —**id′i·o·syn′cra·sies,** *pl.*

id·i·ot (id′i ət), *n.* **1.** a person whose mind is so slow that he can never learn more than a two-year-old child can. **2.** a very foolish or stupid person.

id·i·ot·ic (id′i ät′ik), *adj.* of or like an idiot; very foolish or stupid. —**id′i·ot′i·cal·ly,** *adv.*

i·dle (ī′d'l), *adj.* **1.** not working; not busy [*idle* machines]. **2.** not wanting to work; lazy [The *idle* girl wouldn't help her mother.] **3.** having no use or value; worthless; useless [*idle* talk; *idle* rumors]. —*v.* **1.** to spend time doing nothing or doing useless things [He *idled* away the summer.] **2.** to run slowly and out of gear [Let the motor *idle* to warm it up.] —**i′dled,** *p.t. & p.p.;* **i′dling,** *pr.p.* —**i′dle·ness,** *n.* —**i′dly,** *adv.*

i·dler (ī′dlər), *n.* a lazy person.

i·dol (ī′d'l), *n.* **1.** an image of a god, that is worshiped. **2.** a person or thing that is greatly admired or loved [Money is his *idol.*]

i·dol·a·ter (ī däl′ə tər), *n.* a person who worships idols. —**i·dol′a·tress,** *n.fem.*

i·dol·a·trous (ī däl′ə trəs), *adj.* **1.** worshiping idols. **2.** having to do with idolatry.

i·dol·a·try (ī däl′ə trē), *n.* **1.** the worship of idols. **2.** too great love or admiration for some person or thing. —**i·dol′a·tries,** *pl.*

i·dol·ize (ī′d'l īz), *v.* **1.** to love or admire very much or too much [Baseball players are often *idolized* by young people.] **2.** to make an idol of for worshiping [The Aztecs *idolized* a sun god.] —**i′dol·ized,** *p.t. & p.p.;* **i′dol·iz·ing,** *pr.p.*

i·dyl *or* **i·dyll** (ī′d'l), *n.* **1.** a short poem or story describing a simple, pleasant scene of country life. **2.** any scene or happening about which such a story or poem could be written.

i·dyl·lic (ī dil′ik), *adj.* simple and pleasant, as a scene of country life [an *idyllic* vacation]. —**i·dyl′li·cal·ly,** *adv.*

i.e., an abbreviation for the Latin phrase *id est*, meaning "that is" or "namely."

if (if), *conj.* **1.** in case that; supposing that [*If* I write, will you answer?] **2.** whether [I wonder *if* it will rain.] **3.** although; even though [*If* he made a mistake, at least he meant well.] **4.** I wish that [*If* I could only have another chance!]

ig·loo (ig′loo), *n.* a hut built by Eskimos using blocks of packed snow. —**ig′loos,** *pl.*

ig·ne·ous (ig′ni əs), *adj.* formed by fire or great heat, especially by the action of volcanoes [Granite is an *igneous* rock.]

ig·nite (ig nīt′), *v.* **1.** to set fire to; make burn [the glowing

igloo

cigarette *ignited* the dry leaves.] **2.** to catch fire; burn [Paper *ignites* easily.] **—ig·nit′ed,** *p.t. & p.p.;* **ig·nit′ing,** *pr.p.*

ig·ni·tion (ig nish′ən), *n.* **1.** the act of setting on fire or catching fire. **2.** the switch, spark plugs, etc. that set fire to the mixture of gases in the cylinders of a gasoline engine.

ig·no·ble (ig nō′b'l), *adj.* not honorable or respectable: shameful [To betray one's country is an *ignoble* act.] **—ig·no′bly,** *adv.*

ig·no·min·i·ous (ig′nə min′i əs), *adj.* of or causing shame or disgrace; dishonorable [an *ignominious* defeat]. **—ig′no·min′i·ous·ly,** *adv.*

ig·no·min·y (ig′nə min′ē), *n.* shame and disgrace; dishonor. **—ig′no·min′ies,** *pl.*

ig·no·ra·mus (ig′nə rā′məs *or* ig′nə ram′əs), *n.* an ignorant person. **—ig′no·ra′mus·es,** *pl.*

ig·no·rance (ig′nər əns), *n.* the condition of being ignorant; lack of knowledge or education.

ig·no·rant (ig′nər ənt), *adj.* **1.** having little or no knowledge or education [an intelligent, but *ignorant*, peasant]. **2.** showing a lack of knowledge [an *ignorant* suggestion]. **3.** not knowing about; not aware of [*ignorant* of the rules]. **—ig′no·rant·ly,** *adv.*

ig·nore (ig nôr′), *v.* to pay no attention to; take no notice of [Try to *ignore* their laughter.] **—ig·nored′,** *p.t. & p.p.;* **ig·nor′ing,** *pr.p.*

i·gua·na (i gwä′nə), *n.* a large lizard of the tropical parts of the Americas. It is green and brown and lives in trees.

il-, a form of the prefix **in-,** meaning "not," used before words beginning with *l* [*Illogical* means "not logical."]

Il·i·ad (il′i əd), *n.* a long Greek poem about the Trojan War, written by Homer.

-il·i·ty (il′ə tē), a suffix used to form nouns from adjectives ending in *-ile, -il, -able, -ible* [*Capability* is a noun formed from "capable."]

iguana (5 ft. long)

ilk (ilk), *n.* family; kind; sort: *usually used in the phrase* **of that ilk,** meaning "of the same kind or sort."

ill (il), *adj.* **1.** not healthy; having a disease; sick. **2.** harmful or evil; bad; wrong [the *ill* effects of smoking; *ill* fortune]. **3.** not proper or right [*ill* manners]. **—***adv.* **1.** in a bad or wrong way; improperly [*ill*-gotten]. **2.** in an unkind way; harshly [to speak *ill* of someone]. **3.** not easily; hardly [He can *ill* afford to refuse.] **—***n.* harm, trouble, pain, sickness, etc. [the *ills* of old age]. **—ill at ease,** not comfortable; uneasy. **—worse,** *compar.;* **worst,** *superl.*

I'll (īl), **1.** I shall. **2.** I will.

Ill., abbreviation for **Illinois.**

ill-bred (il′bred′), *adj.* not having been taught good manners; not polite; rude.

il·le·gal (i lē′gəl), *adj.* not legal; not allowed by law; against the law. **—il·le′gal·ly,** *adv.*

il·leg·i·ble (i lej′ə b'l), *adj.* hard to read or impossible to read, as because badly written or printed. **—il·leg′i·bly,** *adv.*

il·le·git·i·mate (il′i jit′ə mit), *adj.* **1.** against the law or rules [the dictator's *illegitimate* seizure of power]. **2.** born of parents not married to each other. **—il′le·git′i·mate·ly,** *adv.*

ill-fat·ed (il′fāt′id), *adj.* sure to come to a bad or unhappy end; unlucky [The *ill-fated* liner struck an iceberg and sank.]

ill-fa·vored (il′fā′vərd), *adj.* not pleasant to look at; ugly [an *ill-favored* man].

ill-got·ten (il′gät′'n), *adj.* gotten in an evil or dishonest way [*ill-gotten* gains].

il·lib·er·al (i lib′ər əl), *adj.* **1.** not liberal; narrow-minded. **2.** not generous; stingy.

il·lic·it (i lis′it), *adj.* not allowed; improper or unlawful.

il·lim·it·a·ble (i lim′i tə b'l), *adj.* without limit or boundary; endless [an *illimitable* supply].

Il·li·nois (il ə noi′ *or* il ə noiz′), *n.* a State in the north central part of the United States: abbreviated **Ill.**

il·lit·er·ate (i lit′ər it), *adj.* **1.** not educated; especially, not knowing how to read or write. **2.** showing a lack of education [an *illiterate* letter]. **—***n.* a person who does not know how to read or write. **—il·lit′er·a·cy,** *n.*

ill-man·nered (il′man′ərd), *adj.* having bad manners; rude; impolite.

ill-na·tured (il′nā′chərd), *adj.* having or showing a bad temper; cross; disagreeable.

ill·ness (il′nis), *n.* the condition of being ill or in poor health; sickness; disease.

il·log·i·cal (i läj′i k'l), *adj.* not logical; showing poor reasoning. **—il·log′i·cal·ly,** *adv.*

ill-tem·pered (il′tem′pərd), *adj.* having or showing a bad temper; cross; irritable.

ill-treat (il′trēt′), *v.* to treat in a cruel or unkind way; abuse. **—ill′-treat′ment,** *n.*

il·lu·mi·nate (i lōō′mə nāt), *v.* **1.** to give light to; light up [Candles *illuminated* the room.] **2.** to make clear; explain [He *illuminated* his meaning by giving examples.] **3.** to decorate, as letters on a page, with fancy designs, colors, etc. **—il·lu′-mi·nat·ed,** *p.t. & p.p.;* **il·lu′mi·nat·ing,** *pr.p.* **—il·lu′mi·na′tion,** *n.*

il·lu·mine (i lōō′min), *v.* to illuminate; light up. **—il·lu′mined,** *p.t. & p.p.;* **il·lu′min·ing,** *pr.p.*

ill-use (il′yōōz′), *v.* to treat in an unkind or cruel way; abuse. **—ill′-used′,** *p.t. & p.p.;* **ill′-us′ing,** *pr.p.*

il·lu·sion (i lōō′zhən), *n.* **1.** a false idea or mistaken belief [Her harsh words destroyed any *illusion* he had about her kind nature.] **2.** the appearance of something that makes one see it in a false way [This wallpaper gives the *illusion* of a brick wall.]

fat, āpe, cär, ten, ēven, hit, bīte, gō, hôrn, tōol, book, up, fŭr; get, joy, yet, chin, she, thin, *th*en; zh = s in pleasure; ′ as in able (ā′b'l); ə = a in ago, e in agent, i in sanity, o in confess, u in focus.

il·lu·sive (i loo'siv), *adj.* caused by an illusion; not real; false; deceiving.

il·lu·so·ry (i loo'sər ē), *adj.* illusive.

il·lus·trate (il'əs trāt *or* i lus'trāt), *v.* **1.** to make clear or explain by giving examples, making comparisons, etc. [The census figures *illustrate* how the nation has grown.] **2.** to put drawings or pictures in that explain or decorate [an *illustrated* book]. —**il'lus·trat·ed,** *p.t. & p.p.;* **il'lus·trat·ing,** *pr.p.*

il·lus·tra·tion (il'əs trā'shən), *n.* **1.** a picture or drawing used to explain or decorate something. **2.** an example, comparison, etc. that helps explain [He gave many *illustrations* of the way the law works.] **3.** the act of illustrating.

il·lus·tra·tive (i lus'trə tiv *or* il'əs trā'tiv), *adj.* that illustrates or explains [The speaker used *illustrative* slides in his talk.]

il·lus·tra·tor (il'əs trā'tər), *n.* an artist who makes illustrations for books and magazines.

il·lus·tri·ous (i lus'tri əs), *adj.* very famous; outstanding [an *illustrious* scientist].

ill will, unfriendly feeling; hate; dislike.

I'm (īm), I am.

im-, a prefix meaning: **1.** not [An *imperfect* copy is not perfect.] **2.** in or into [An *immigrant* is a person who moves into a country.] **Im-** is the form of **in-** used before words beginning with *m, b,* and *p.*

im·age (im'ij), *n.* **1.** a drawing, picture, or especially a statue, of some person or thing [to worship *images*]. **2.** that which is seen in a mirror, through a lens, etc. [He saw his own *image* reflected in the pool.] **3.** a close likeness or copy [Joan is the *image* of her aunt.] **4.** a picture in the mind; idea; impression [*Images* of what might happen frightened her.] **5.** a picture in words, especially a simile or metaphor [Homer uses often the *image* of "rosy-fingered dawn."] —*v.* **1.** to reflect as in a mirror. **2.** to present in images; describe or portray. —**im'aged,** *p.t. & p.p.;* **im'ag·ing,** *pr.p.*

im·age·ry (im'ij rē), *n.* **1.** images, especially statues. **2.** pictures in words, especially similes and metaphors [the *imagery* in poems].

im·ag·i·na·ble (i maj'i nə b'l), *adj.* that can be imagined [the worst crime *imaginable*].

im·ag·i·nar·y (i maj'i ner'ē), *adj.* that is only in the imagination; not real [unicorns, griffins, and other *imaginary* beasts].

im·ag·i·na·tion (i maj'i nā'shən), *n.* **1.** the act or power of making up pictures or ideas in the mind of what is not present or of how things might be [It takes great *imagination* to write a play. The airplane you thought you saw was just in your *imagination.*] **2.** the ability to understand and appreciate what others imagine [He lacks *imagination* and has no interest in art.]

im·ag·i·na·tive (i maj'i nā'tiv *or* i maj'i nə tiv), *adj.* having or showing imagination.

im·ag·ine (i maj'in), *v.* **1.** to make up a picture or idea in the mind; form an idea of [*Imagine* that you are on Mars.] **2.** to suppose; guess; think [I *imagine* he'll be there.] —**im·ag'-ined,** *p.t. & p.p.;* **im·ag'in·ing,** *pr.p.*

im·be·cile (im'bə s'l), *n.* **1.** a person whose mind is so slow that he cannot learn more than an eight-year-old child can. **2.** a very foolish or stupid person. —*adj.* of or like an imbecile.

im·be·cil·i·ty (im'bə sil'ə tē), *n.* **1.** the condition of being an imbecile. **2.** great foolishness or stupidity. —**im'be·cil'i·ties,** *pl.*

im·bed (im bed'), *v.* same as **embed.** —**im·bed'ded,** *p.t. & p.p.;* **im·bed'ding,** *pr.p.*

im·bibe (im bīb'), *v.* **1.** to drink, especially alcoholic liquor. **2.** to absorb [The desert sands *imbibed* the rain water.] **3.** to take into the mind and keep [to *imbibe* new ideas]. —**im·bibed',** *p.t. & p.p.;* **im·bib'ing,** *pr.p.*

im·bro·glio (im brōl'yō), *n.* **1.** a confused situation that is hard to clear up [a hopeless *imbroglio* over national boundaries]. **2.** any mix-up in which there is much misunderstanding or disagreement. —**im·bro'glios,** *pl.*

im·bue (im byoo'), *v.* **1.** to fill with ideas or feelings; inspire [Patrick Henry was *imbued* with ideals of liberty.] **2.** to fill with a liquid or color [a cloak *imbued* with scarlet dye]. —**im·bued',** *p.t. & p.p.;* **im·bu'ing,** *pr.p.*

im·i·tate (im'ə tāt), *v.* **1.** to copy the way someone looks, acts, sounds, etc. [Children often try to *imitate* the people they respect. Some birds can *imitate* human speech.] **2.** to act like in fun; mimic [The comedian *imitated* famous movie stars.] **3.** to look like; resemble [Rhinestones are glass cut to *imitate* diamonds.] —**im'i·tat·ed,** *p.t. & p.p.;* **im'i·tat·ing,** *pr.p.* —**im'i·ta·tor,** *n.*

im·i·ta·tion (im'ə tā'shən), *n.* **1.** an imitating or copying [The children danced in *imitation* of swaying trees.] **2.** a copy or likeness [These jewels are merely clever *imitations.*] —*adj.* made to look like something better; not real [a suitcase of *imitation* leather].

im·i·ta·tive (im'ə tā'tiv), *adj.* imitating or copying [the *imitative* sounds of a parrot].

im·mac·u·late (i mak'yoo lit), *adj.* **1.** perfectly clean; spotless [*immaculate* hospital rooms]. **2.** without sin; pure [the *immaculate* life of a saint]. —**im·mac'u·late·ly,** *adv.*

im·ma·te·ri·al (im'ə tir'i əl), *adj.* **1.** of no importance [The cost is *immaterial* to him, if the quality is good.] **2.** not made of matter; spiritual.

im·ma·ture (im ə tyoor'), *adj.* not mature; not fully grown or developed [*immature* fruit; *immature* judgment]. —**im·ma·tu'ri·ty,** *n.*

im·meas·ur·a·ble (i mezh'ər ə b'l), *adj.* too large or too much to be measured; very great [the *immeasurable* space of the universe; an *immeasurable* love]. —**im·meas'ur·a·bly,** *adv.*

im·me·di·ate (i mē'di it), *adj.* **1.** without delay; happening at once [The medicine had an *immediate* effect.] **2.** closest; with nothing coming between [the *immediate* past; one's *immediate* family]. **3.** acting in a direct way; direct [What was the *immediate* cause of their quarrel?] —**im·me'di·ate·ly,** *adv.*

im·me·mo·ri·al (im'ə môr'i əl), *adj.* reaching back further than all memory or records [customs handed down from time *immemorial*].

im·mense (i mens′), *adj.* very large; huge; vast [an *immense* territory]. —**im·mense′ly**, *adv.*

im·men·si·ty (i men′sə tē), *n.* the fact of being immense; great size; vastness.

im·merse (i mûrs′). *v.* **1.** to plunge or dip into a liquid. **2.** to baptize a person by dipping him under water. **3.** to get or be deeply in; absorb [*immersed* in study; *immersed* in despair]. —**im·mersed′**, *p.t.* & *p.p.*; **im·mers′ing**, *pr.p.* —**im·mer·sion** (i mûr′shən), *n.*

im·mi·grant (im′ə grənt), *n.* a person who comes into a foreign country to make his home.

im·mi·grate (im′ə grāt), *v.* to come into a foreign country to make one's home [Over 15 million persons *immigrated* into the U.S. from 1900 to 1955.] —**im′mi·grat·ed**, *p.t.* & *p.p.*; **im′mi·grat·ing**, *pr.p.* —**im′mi·gra′tion**, *n.*

im·mi·nent (im′ə nənt), *adj.* likely to take place soon; about to happen [By 1938, many people knew war was *imminent*.] —**im′mi·nence**, *n.* —**im′mi·nent·ly**, *adv.*

im·mo·bile (i mō′b'l), *adj.* not moving or changing; without motion [The frightened deer stood *immobile*.] —**im′mo·bil′i·ty**, *n.*

im·mo·bi·lize (i mō′b'l īz), *v.* to make immobile; keep from moving. —**im·mo′bi·lized**, *p.t.* & *p.p.*; **im·mo′bi·liz·ing**, *pr.p.*

im·mod·er·ate (i mäd′ər it), *adj.* not moderate; too much; too great [an *immoderate* thirst].

im·mod·est (i mäd′ist), *adj.* **1.** not modest or decent. **2.** not shy or humble; bold; forward.

im·mor·al (i môr′əl), *adj.* against what is right or moral; not good or decent; corrupt, wicked, lewd, etc. —**im·mo·ral·i·ty** (im′ə ral′ə tē), *n.* —**im·mor′al·ly**, *adv.*

im·mor·tal (i môr′t'l), *adj.* **1.** never dying; living forever [The gods of ancient Greece were *immortal* beings.] **2.** having fame that will last a long time [Milton is an *immortal* poet.] —*n.* **1.** a being that lives forever. **2.** a person having lasting fame. —**im·mor·tal·i·ty** (im′ôr tal′ə tē), *n.* —**im·mor′tal·ly**, *adv.*

im·mor·ta·lize (i môr′t'l īz), *v.* to make immortal; especially, to make famous for a long time [Whistler *immortalized* his mother in a painting.] —**im·mor′ta·lized**, *p.t.* & *p.p.*; **im·mor′ta·liz·ing**, *pr.p.*

im·mov·a·ble (i mōōv′ə b'l), *adj.* **1.** that cannot be moved; firmly fixed [The ancients thought the earth was *immovable*.] **2.** not changing; steadfast [an *immovable* purpose].

im·mune (i myōōn′), *adj.* protected against a bad or unpleasant thing, especially against a disease, as by a vaccine [*immune* to smallpox; *immune* from punishment]. —**im·mu′ni·ty**, *n.*

im·mu·nize (im′yoo nīz), *v.* to make immune, as by vaccination. —**im′mu·nized**, *p.t.* & *p.p.*; **im′mu·niz′ing**, *pr.p.*

im·mure (i myoor′), *v.* to shut up within walls, as in a prison; confine. —**im·mured′**, *p.t.* & *p.p.*; **im·mur′ing**, *pr.p.*

im·mu·ta·ble (i myōō′tə b'l), *adj.* never changing; always the same.

imp (imp), *n.* **1.** a child of a devil; a young, small demon. **2.** a naughty, mischievous child.

im·pact (im′pakt), *n.* a hitting together with force; collision [The *impact* of the two cars broke both windshields.]

im·pair (im per′), *v.* to make worse, less, weaker, etc.; damage [The disease *impaired* his hearing.] —**im·pair′ment**, *n.*

im·pale (im pāl′), *v.* to pierce through with [to *impale* a dead moth on a pin]. —**im·paled′**, *p.t.* & *p.p.*; **im·pal′ing**, *pr.p.*

im·pal·pa·ble (im pal′pə b'l), *adj.* **1.** that cannot be felt by touching [an *impalpable* shadow]. **2.** not plain and clear to the mind; not easily understood [an *impalpable* change].

im·pan·el (im pan′'l), *v.* **1.** to add to a list of those who may be called to serve on a jury. **2.** to choose from such a list [to *impanel* a jury]. Also spelled **empanel**. —**im·pan′eled** or **im·pan′elled**, *p.t.* & *p.p.*; **im·pan′el·ing** or **im·pan′el·ling**, *pr.p.*

im·part (im pärt′), *v.* **1.** to give a part or share of; give [The onion *imparted* its smell to the soup.] **2.** to tell; reveal [to *impart* news].

im·par·tial (im pär′shəl), *adj.* not favoring one side more than another; fair; just [an *impartial* referee]. —**im·par·ti·al·i·ty** (im′pär shi al′ə tē), *n.* —**im·par′tial·ly**, *adv.*

im·pass·a·ble (im pas′ə b'l), *adj.* that cannot be traveled on or across [*impassable* icy roads].

im·passe (im′pas *or* im pas′), *n.* a difficulty that cannot be solved or an argument where no agreement is possible.

im·pas·sioned (im pash′ənd), *adj.* having or showing strong feelings or emotions; passionate [an *impassioned* plea for mercy].

im·pas·sive (im pas′iv), *adj.* not showing any feelings or emotions; calm [John's *impassive* face hid his anger.] —**im·pas′sive·ly**, *adv.*

im·pa·tience (im pā′shəns), *n.* the condition of being impatient; lack of patience.

im·pa·tient (im pā′shənt), *adj.* **1.** not patient; not willing to put up with delay, annoyance, etc. [Mother becomes *impatient* when Amy whines.] **2.** eager to do something or for something to happen [He is *impatient* to go swimming.] —**im·pa′tient·ly**, *adv.*

im·peach (im pēch′), *v.* **1.** to accuse of doing wrong; especially, to try a public official on a charge of wrongdoing [President Andrew Johnson was *impeached* in the U.S. Senate, but was found innocent.] **2.** to raise questions or doubts about [This gossip *impeaches* his honor.] —**im·peach′ment**, *n.*

im·pec·ca·ble (im pek′ə b'l), *adj.* without faults or errors; perfect [His manners were *impeccable*.] —**im·pec′ca·bly**, *adv.*

im·pe·cu·ni·ous (im′pi kyōō′ni əs), *adj.* having no money; poor.

---

fat, āpe, cär, ten, ēven, hit, bīte, gō, hôrn, tōōl, book, up, fûr;
get, joy, yet, chin, she, thin, *th*en; zh = s in pleasure; ′ as in able (ā′b'l);
ə = a in ago, e in agent, i in sanity, o in confess, u in focus.

im·pede (im pēd′), *v.* to get in the way of; delay or obstruct [The accident *impeded* traffic.] —**im·ped′ed**, *p.t. & p.p.;* **im·ped′ing**, *pr.p.*

im·ped·i·ment (im ped′ə mənt), *n.* anything that impedes or gets in the way; obstacle [Bad roads are *impediments* to travel. A lisp is an *impediment* in speaking.]

im·pel (im pel′), *v.* **1.** to push or move forward. **2.** to force or drive [What *impels* her to lie?] —**im·pelled′**, *p.t. & p.p.;* **im·pel′ling**, *pr.p.*

im·pend (im pend′), *v.* **1.** to be about to happen; threaten [Disaster seemed to be *impending*.] **2.** to hang over [*impending* cliffs].

im·pen·e·tra·ble (im pen′i trə b′l), *adj.* **1.** that cannot be penetrated or passed through [an *impenetrable* jungle]. **2.** that cannot be understood [the *impenetrable* mystery of death].

im·pen·i·tent (im pen′i tənt), *adj.* not feeling shame or regret; not sorry for what one has done. —**im·pen′i·tent·ly**, *adv.*

im·per·a·tive (im per′ə tiv), *adj.* **1.** that must be done; necessary; urgent [Quick action is *imperative*.] **2.** showing power or authority; commanding [The policeman stopped traffic with an *imperative* gesture.] **3.** describing the mood of a verb used in giving commands or orders [In "Be careful!", "be" is in the *imperative* mood.] —*n.* an order or command.

im·per·cep·ti·ble (im′pər sep′tə b′l), *adj.* so small or slight that it is not noticed [an *imperceptible* scar]. —**im′per·cep′ti·bly**, *adv.*

im·per·fect (im pur′fikt), *adj.* **1.** not perfect; having some fault or flaw. **2.** lacking in something; not complete; unfinished [an *imperfect* knowledge of Russian]. —**im·per′fect·ly**, *adv.*

im·per·fec·tion (im′pər fek′shən), *n.* **1.** the condition of being imperfect. **2.** a flaw.

im·pe·ri·al (im pir′i əl), *adj.* of an empire, emperor, or empress [an *imperial* army]. —*n.* a small, pointed beard on the chin.

im·pe·ri·al·ism (im pir′i əl iz′m), *n.* the idea or practice of setting up an empire by conquering other countries, forming colonies in other lands, etc. —**im·pe′ri·al·ist**, *n.* —**im·pe′ri·al·is′tic**, *adj.*

im·per·il (im per′əl), *v.* to put in peril, or danger [Their lives were *imperiled* by the fire.] —**im·per′iled** or **im·per′illed**, *p.t. & p.p.;* **im·per′il·ing** or **im·per′il·ling**, *pr.p.*

im·pe·ri·ous (im pir′i əs), *adj.* **1.** like a dictator or dictator's; arrogant; haughty [In an *imperious* voice he ordered us away.] **2.** necessary or urgent [an *imperious* duty]. —**im·pe′ri·ous·ly**, *adv.*

im·per·ish·a·ble (im per′ish ə b′l), *adj.* that will not perish or die; lasting a long time or forever [the *imperishable* fame of a hero].

im·per·son·al (im pur′s'n əl), *adj.* **1.** not referring to any particular person [Miss Brown's remarks about cheating were *impersonal* and meant for all the students.] **2.** not existing as a person [Nature is an *impersonal* force.] **3.** describing a verb that is used only in the third person singular, usually with *it* as the subject [In the sentence "It is cold in here," "is" is an *impersonal* verb.] —**im·per′son·al·ly**, *adv.*

im·per·son·ate (im pur′sə nāt), *v.* **1.** to act the part of [Who *impersonated* Tom Sawyer in the play?] **2.** to imitate or mimic in fun. **3.** to pretend to be [He was arrested for *impersonating* an officer.] —**im·per′son·at·ed**, *p.t. & p.p.;* **im·per′son·at·ing**, *pr.p.* —**im·per′son·a′tion**, *n.* —**im·per′son·a′tor**, *n.*

im·per·ti·nent (im pur′t'n ənt), *adj.* **1.** not showing the right respect; impudent or rude [The *impertinent* boy turned his back on the teacher and left the room.] **2.** not suitable or fitting [He wasted our time by making *impertinent* remarks.] —**im·per′ti·nence**, *n.*

im·per·turb·a·ble (im′pər tûr′bə b′l), *adj.* not easily excited or disturbed; calm.

im·per·vi·ous (im pur′vi əs), *adj.* **1.** not letting something come through it [These tiles are *impervious* to water.] **2.** not affected by [a man *impervious* to criticism].

im·pet·u·ous (im pech′oo əs), *adj.* **1.** moving with great or wild force; rushing [*impetuous* winds]. **2.** rushing into action with little thought; rash. —**im·pet·u·os·i·ty** (im pech′oo äs′ə tē), *n.* —**im·pet′u·ous·ly**, *adv.*

im·pe·tus (im′pə təs), *n.* **1.** the force with which a body moves; momentum. **2.** any force that helps something along; stimulus [The new loans gave fresh *impetus* to the building program.]

im·pi·e·ty (im pī′ə tē), *n.* **1.** a lack of respect or reverence for sacred things. **2.** an impious act or remark. —**im·pi′e·ties**, *pl.*

im·pinge (im pinj′), *v.* **1.** to come in contact with; touch or strike [The sound of trumpets *impinged* on their eardrums.] **2.** to break in on; encroach or infringe [Censorship *impinges* on our freedoms.] —**im·pinged′**, *p.t. & p.p.;* **im·ping′ing**, *pr.p.* —**im·pinge′ment**, *n.*

im·pi·ous (im′pi əs), *adj.* not pious; lacking respect for what one should honor or worship.

imp·ish (imp′ish), *adj.* like an imp; mischievous. —**imp′ish·ly**, *adv.* —**imp′ish·ness**, *n.*

im·pla·ca·ble (im plā′kə b′l *or* im plak′ə b′l), *adj.* that cannot be made calm or peaceful; relentless [*implacable* anger; *implacable* enemies]. —**im·pla′ca·bly**, *adv.*

im·plant (im plant′), *v.* **1.** to plant firmly [to *implant* seeds]. **2.** to fix firmly in the mind [Respect for the law was *implanted* in them.]

im·ple·ment (im′plə mənt), *n.* something used in doing some work; tool or instrument [A plow is a farm *implement*.] —*v.*(im′plə ment), to carry out; put into effect [to *implement* a plan].

im·pli·cate (im′pli kāt), *v.* to show that someone has had a part, especially in something bad [His reply *implicated* Jones in the crime.] —**im′pli·cat·ed**, *p.t. & p.p.;* **im′pli·cat·ing**, *pr.p.*

im·pli·ca·tion (im′pli kā′shən), *n.* **1.** an implicating or being implicated. **2.** an implying, or suggesting. **3.** the thing implied [Do you understand the *implications* of his offer?]

im·plic·it (im plis′it), *adj.* **1.** implied or suggested but not actually said [He gave *implicit* approval by his silence.] **2.** without doubting or holding back; absolute [to have *implicit* faith in another]. —**im·plic′it·ly**, *adv.*

im·plore (im plôr′), *v.* to plead for or beg with much feeling; beseech [The woman *implored* Lincoln to spare her son's life.] —**im·plored′**, *p.t. & p.p.;* **im·plor′ing**, *pr.p.*

im·ply (im plī′), *v.* to mean or suggest without openly saying [His frown *implied* disapproval.] —**im·plied′**, *p.t. & p.p.;* **im·ply′ing**, *pr.p.*

im·po·lite (im pə lit′), *adj.* not polite; rude. —**im·po·lite′ly**, *adv.* —**im·po·lite′ness**, *n.*

im·pol·i·tic (im päl′ə tik), *adj.* not wise or careful; showing poor judgment [It was *impolitic* of him to insult his superior.]

im·port (im′pôrt), *v.* **1.** to bring goods into one country from another [England *imports* much of her food.] **2.** to have as its meaning; mean [Some say a red sunset *imports* a fair day on the morrow.] —*n.* **1.** something imported from another country. **2.** meaning [the *import* of a remark]. **3.** importance [a matter of no *import*].

im·por·tance (im pôr′t'ns), *n.* the fact of being important [news of little *importance*].

im·por·tant (im pôr′tənt), *adj.* **1.** having much meaning or value [July 4, 1776, is an *important* date in American history.] **2.** having power or authority, or acting as if one had power [an *important* official]. —**im·por′tant·ly**, *adv.*

im·por·ta·tion (im′pôr tā′shən), *n.* **1.** something that has been imported into a country. **2.** the importing of goods into a country.

im·port·er (im pôr′tər), *n.* a person or company in the business of importing goods.

im·por·tu·nate (im pôr′chə nit), *adj.* asking or asked again and again in a pressing way [an *importunate* job seeker; *importunate* pleas].

im·por·tune (im′pôr toon′ *or* im′pôr tyoon′ *or* im pôr′choon), *v.* to plead for or beg again and again in a pestering way [Tim kept *importuning* his father to take him to the circus.] —**im′por·tuned′**, *p.t. & p.p.;* **im′por·tun′ing**, *pr.p.*

im·por·tu·ni·ty (im′pôr too′nə tē *or* im′pôr tyoo′nə tē), *n.* a pleading or begging in a pestering way. —**im′por·tu′ni·ties**, *pl.*

im·pose (im pōz′), *v.* **1.** to put on as a duty, burden, penalty, etc. [to *impose* a tax on furs; to *impose* a fine on speeders]. **2.** to force one's company on another or put another to some trouble [Can I *impose* on you to drive me home?] **3.** to cheat or trick [to *impose* on the public]. —**im·posed′**, *p.t. & p.p.;* **im·pos′ing**, *pr.p.*

im·pos·ing (im pōz′ing), *adj.* grand in size, manner, looks, etc. [an *imposing* statue].

im·po·si·tion (im′pə zish′ən), *n.* **1.** an imposing or imposing on [Staying for a meal when you were not invited is an *imposition*.] **2.** something imposed, as a tax, fine, or burden.

im·pos·si·ble (im päs′ə b'l), *adj.* **1.** that cannot be, be done, or happen; not possible [He found it *impossible* to lift the crate.] **2.** very unpleasant or hard to put up with: *used only in everyday talk* [an *impossible* child]. —**im·pos′·si·bil′i·ty**, *n.* —**im·pos′si·bly**, *adv.*

im·post (im′pōst), *n.* a tax; especially, a tax on imported goods.

im·pos·tor (im päs′tər), *n.* a person who tricks people into believing that he is someone or something he is not.

im·pos·ture (im päs′chər), *n.* the act of tricking as an impostor; deception.

im·po·tent (im′pə tənt), *adj.* not having the strength or power to act; helpless [We were *impotent* against the storm.] —**im′po·tence**, *n.*

im·pound (im pound′), *v.* **1.** to shut up in a pound or enclosure [Stray dogs will be *impounded*.] **2.** to take and hold in the care of the law [The police *impounded* his car.]

im·pov·er·ish (im päv′ər ish), *v.* **1.** to make poor [Gambling had *impoverished* him.] **2.** to make lose strength or richness [Planting the same crops every year *impoverishes* the soil.] —**im·pov′er·ish·ment**, *n.*

im·prac·ti·ca·ble (im prak′ti kə b'l), *adj.* that cannot be put into practice or used [*impracticable* plans]. —**im·prac′ti·ca·bly**, *adv.*

im·prac·ti·cal (im prak′ti k'l), *adj.* not practical; not useful, efficient, etc.

im·pre·ca·tion (im′pri kā′shən), *n.* a curse.

im·preg·na·ble (im preg′nə b'l), *adj.* that cannot be conquered or overcome; unyielding [an *impregnable* faith]. —**im·preg′na·bil′i·ty**, *n.*

im·preg·nate (im preg′nāt), *v.* **1.** to fill full or mix throughout [Their clothing was *impregnated* with smoke.] **2.** to make pregnant; fertilize. —**im·preg′nat·ed**, *p.t. & p.p.;* **im·preg′nat·ing**, *pr.p.* —**im′preg·na′tion**, *n.*

im·pre·sa·ri·o (im′pri sä′ri ō), *n.* the organizer or manager of an opera company, a series of concerts, etc. —**im′pre·sa′ri·os**, *pl.*

im·press (im pres′), *v.* **1.** to seize and force to serve in a navy or an army [The British used to *impress* men into their navy.] **2.** to seize for public use [The general *impressed* the house for his headquarters.]

im·press (im pres′), *v.* **1.** to affect the thinking or feelings of [His quick answers *impressed* us all greatly.] **2.** to fix firmly in the mind [Let me *impress* on you the importance of fire drills.] **3.** to mark by pressing on; stamp [The envelopes were *impressed* with her name.] —*n.* **1.** (im′pres), any mark or imprint made by pressing [All letters carry the *impress* of a postmark.] **2.** a strong effect made on the mind; impression.

im·pres·sion (im presh′ən), *n.* **1.** the act of impressing. **2.** a mark or imprint made by pressing [The police took an *impression* of his fingerprints.] **3.** an effect produced on the mind [The play made a great *impression* on her.] **4.** the effect produced by some action [Hard scrubbing made little *impression* on the stain.] **5.** a vague feeling [I have the *impression* that he was there.]

im·pres·sion·a·ble (im presh′ən ə b'l), *adj.* with a mind or feelings that are easily impressed; sensitive.

---

fat,   āpe,   cär,   ten,   ēven,   hit,   bīte,   gō,   hôrn,   tool,   book,   up,   fur;
get,   joy,   yet,   chin,   she,   thin,   *th*en;   zh = s in pleasure;   ′ as in able (ā′b'l);
ə = a in ago,   e in agent,   i in sanity,   o in confess,   u in focus.

im·pres·sive (im pres′iv), *adj.* that impresses or has a strong effect on the mind [an *impressive* display]. —**im·pres′sive·ly,** *adv.*

im·print (im print′), *v.* **1.** to mark by pressing or stamping [The paper was *imprinted* with the state seal.] **2.** to fix firmly [Her face is *imprinted* in my memory.] —*n.* (im′print), **1.** a mark made by pressing; print [the *imprint* of a dirty hand on the wall]. **2.** an impression or effect [the *imprint* of starvation on his body]. **3.** a note, as on the title page of a book, giving the publisher's name and telling where and when the book was published.

im·pris·on (im priz′'n), *v.* **1.** to put or keep in prison. **2.** to shut up or confine [a bird *imprisoned* in a cage]. —**im·pris′on·ment,** *n.*

im·prob·a·ble (im präb′ə b'l), *adj.* not probable; not likely to happen or be true [It is *improbable* that he will win again.] —**im·prob′-a·bil′i·ty,** *n.* —**im·prob′a·bly,** *adv.*

im·promp·tu (im prämp′tōō *or* im prämp′tyōō), *adj. & adv.* without preparation or thought ahead of time; offhand [The governor gave an *impromptu* speech at the airport.]

im·prop·er (im präp′ər), *adj.* **1.** not proper or suitable; unfit [Sandals are *improper* shoes for tennis.] **2.** not true; wrong; incorrect [an *improper* street address]. **3.** not decent; in bad taste [*improper* jokes]. —**im·prop′er·ly,** *adv.*

improper fraction, a fraction in which the denominator is less than the numerator [4/3, 8/5, and 9/7 are *improper fractions*.]

im·pro·pri·e·ty (im′prə prī′ə tē), *n.* **1.** the fact of being improper, or something that is not proper. **2.** an incorrect use of a word or phrase [The use of "its" for "it's" is an *impropriety*.] —**im·pro·pri′e·ties,** *pl.*

im·prove (im prōōv′), *v.* **1.** to make or become better [Business has *improved*.] **2.** to make good use of [He *improved* his spare time by reading.] —**im·proved′,** *p.t. & p.p.;* **im·prov′ing,** *pr.p.*

im·prove·ment (im prōōv′mənt), *n.* **1.** a making or becoming better [Your playing shows *improvement*.] **2.** an addition or change that makes something worth more [His taxes rose because of *improvements* to the house.] **3.** a person or thing that is better than another [The new choir is an *improvement* over the old one.]

im·prov·i·dent (im präv′ə dənt), *adj.* not planning carefully for the future; not thrifty. —**im·prov′i·dence,** *n.*

im·pro·vise (im′prə vīz), *v.* **1.** to compose and perform at the same time, without preparing [Calypso singers often *improvise* verses as they sing.] **2.** to make quickly with whatever is at hand [We *improvised* a bed by putting some chairs together.] —**im′pro·vised,** *p.t. & p.p.;* **im′pro·vis·ing,** *pr.p.* —**im·pro·vi·sa·tion** (im präv′ə zā′shən), *n.*

im·pru·dent (im prōō′d'nt), *adj.* not prudent or cautious; rash or indiscreet. —**im·pru′-dence,** *n.* —**im·pru′dent·ly,** *adv.*

im·pu·dent (im′pyoo dənt), *adj.* not showing respect; shamelessly rude [an *impudent* sneer]. —**im′pu·dence,** *n.* —**im′pu·dent·ly,** *adv.*

im·pugn (im pyōōn′), *v.* to doubt or question [Do you *impugn* my sincerity?]

im·pulse (im′puls), *n.* **1.** a sudden feeling that makes one want to do something [She had an *impulse* to scream.] **2.** the force that starts some action; push or thrust [The *impulse* of the propeller drives the ship through the water.]

im·pul·sion (im pul′shən), *n.* an impulse.

im·pul·sive (im pul′siv), *adj.* **1.** acting or likely to act suddenly and without thinking [The *impulsive* child dashed into the street.] **2.** done or made on a sudden impulse [an *impulsive* statement]. —**im·pul′sive·ly,** *adv.*

im·pu·ni·ty (im pyōō′nə tē), *n.* freedom from the danger of being punished or harmed [You can't ignore the rules of health with *impunity*.]

im·pure (im pyoor′), *adj.* **1.** not clean; dirty [Smoke made the air *impure*.] **2.** mixed with things that do not belong [*impure* gold]. **3.** not decent or proper [*impure* thoughts].

im·pu·ri·ty (im pyoor′ə tē), *n.* **1.** the condition of being impure. **2.** something mixed in that makes another thing impure [Strain the oil to remove *impurities*.] —**im·pu′ri·ties,** *pl.*

im·pute (im pyōōt′), *v.* to consider to be guilty of; blame; charge [to *impute* a crime to someone]. —**im·put′ed,** *p.t. & p.p.;* **im·put′ing,** *pr.p.* —**im·pu·ta·tion** (im′pyoo tā′shən), *n.*

in (in), *prep.* **1.** contained by, covered by, or surrounded by [to live *in* town; to dress *in* furs; caught *in* a storm]. **2.** during or after [to do *in* a second; to leave *in* an hour]. **3.** not beyond [still *in* sight]. **4.** having or showing [*in* trouble; *in* tears]. **5.** having to do with; with regard to [*in* business; *in* my opinion; the best *in* the school]. **6.** by means of; using [written *in* ink]. **7.** because of [to shout *in* anger]. **8.** into [Go *in* the house.] —*adv.* **1.** inside or toward the inside [He walked *in* slowly.] **2.** within a certain place [Keep the cat *in*.] —*adj.* **1.** that has power or control [the *in* group]. **2.** that is inside or leads inside [Use the *in* door.] —*n.* **1.** *usually* **ins,** *pl.* those who are in power or in office. **2.** a way to get special favor: *used only in everyday talk* [Do you have an *in* with him?] —**in for,** certain to have [He's *in for* a big surprise.] —**ins and outs,** all the parts or details. —**in that,** for this reason; because. —**in with,** being friends or partners with.

in-, a prefix meaning "in," "into," "within," "on," or "toward": it is usually seen in words coming from Latin, such as *induct* and *infer*.

in-, a prefix meaning "not" [*Incorrect* means not correct.]

in., abbreviation for **inch** or **inches.**

in·a·bil·i·ty (in′ə bil′ə tē), *n.* the condition of being unable; lack of ability or power.

in·ac·ces·si·ble (in′ak ses′ə b'l), *adj.* impossible or hard to reach or get to [Their cottage is *inaccessible* except by boat.] —**in′ac·ces′-si·bil′i·ty,** *n.*

in·ac·cu·ra·cy (in ak′yoo rə sē), *n.* **1.** the condition of being inaccurate, or wrong; incorrectness. **2.** an error or mistake [This map has many *inaccuracies*.] —**in·ac′cu·ra·cies,** *pl.*

in·ac·cu·rate (in ak′yoo rit), *adj.* not accurate or exact; in error; wrong [an *inaccurate* clock]. —**in·ac′cu·rate·ly**, *adv.*

in·ac·tion (in ak′shən), *n.* the condition of not moving or acting; lack of action; idleness.

in·ac·tive (in ak′tiv), *adj.* not active; idle. —**in·ac′tive·ly**, *adv.* —**in·ac·tiv′i·ty**, *n.*

in·ad·e·quate (in ad′ə kwit), *adj.* not adequate; less than is needed. —**in·ad·e·qua·cy** (in ad′ə kwə sē), *n.* —**in·ad′e·quate·ly**, *adv.*

in·ad·mis·si·ble (in′əd mis′ə b'l), *adj.* that cannot be admitted or allowed; unacceptable [an *inadmissible* excuse].

in·ad·vert·ent (in′əd vŭr′t'nt), *adj.* not meant; not on purpose; accidental [an *inadvertent* insult]. —**in′ad·vert′ence**, *n.* —**in′ad·vert′ent·ly**, *adv.*

in·ad·vis·a·ble (in′əd vīz′ə b'l), *adj.* not advisable; not wise or sensible.

in·al·ien·a·ble (in āl′yən ə b'l), *adj.* that cannot be taken away or given away [Liberty is an *inalienable* right.]

in·ane (in ān′), *adj.* foolish or silly [an *inane* smile]. —**in·ane′ly**, *adv.*

in·an·i·mate (in an′ə mit), *adj.* **1.** without life [A rock is an *inanimate* object.] **2.** not lively; dull [an *inanimate* style of writing].

in·an·i·ty (in an′ə tē), *n.* **1.** the condition of being foolish or silly. **2.** a foolish or silly act or remark. —**in·an′i·ties**, *pl.*

in·ap·pli·ca·ble (in ap′li kə b'l), *adj.* that does not apply or is not suitable.

in·ap·pro·pri·ate (in′ə prō′pri it), *adj.* not appropriate; not suitable or proper.

in·apt (in apt′), *adj.* **1.** not apt; not suitable or fitting [an *inapt* remark]. **2.** not skillful; awkward; inept. —**in·apt′ly**, *adv.*

in·ar·tic·u·late (in′är tik′yoo lit), *adj.* **1.** not in speech that can be understood [an *inarticulate* cry]. **2.** not able to speak or not able to speak clearly [*inarticulate* with rage].

in·ar·tis·tic (in′är tis′tik), *adj.* not artistic; without good taste. —**in′ar·tis′ti·cal·ly**, *adv.*

in·as·much (in əz much′), *conj.* because; since; seeing that: *followed by* as [I couldn't have seen him, *inasmuch* as he wasn't there.]

in·at·ten·tion (in′ə ten′shən), *n.* a failing to pay attention; carelessness; negligence.

in·at·ten·tive (in′ə ten′tiv), *adj.* not attentive; not paying attention; careless; negligent.

in·au·di·ble (in ô′də b'l), *adj.* not audible; that cannot be heard. —**in·au′di·bly**, *adv.*

in·au·gu·ral (in ô′gyoo rəl), *adj.* of an inauguration [an *inaugural* ceremony]. —*n.* a speech made by a person at his inauguration.

in·au·gu·rate (in ô′gyoo rāt), *v.* **1.** to place in office with a ceremony; install [The new President will be *inaugurated* on January 20.] **2.** to begin or start [to *inaugurate* a new school year]. **3.** to mark the first public use of with a ceremony [to *inaugurate* a new bridge]. —**in·au′gu·rat·ed**,

p.t. & p.p.; **in·au′gu·rat·ing**, *pr.p.* —**in·au′gu·ra′tion**, *n.*

in·aus·pi·cious (in′ôs pish′əs), *adj.* not auspicious; not favorable to plans or hopes; unlucky [an *inauspicious* beginning].

in·board (in′bôrd), *adj.* inside the hull of a ship or boat [an *inboard* motor].

in·born (in′bôrn), *adj.* that seems to have been born in one; natural [an *inborn* talent].

in·bred (in′bred), *adj.* **1.** bred from animals that are closely related. **2.** inborn; natural.

in·breed·ing (in′brēd′ing), *n.* breeding from animals that are closely related.

inc., abbreviation for **incorporated.**

In·ca (ing′kə), *n.* a member of the highly civilized Indian people of ancient Peru, who were conquered by the Spanish.

Inca

in·cal·cu·la·ble (in kal′kyoo lə b'l), *adj.* **1.** too great to be calculated [*incalculable* damage]. **2.** too uncertain to be predicted [the *incalculable* future]. —**in·cal′cu·la·bly**, *adv.*

in·can·des·cent (in′kən des′'nt), *adj.* **1.** glowing with heat. An **incandescent lamp** has a metal filament that gives off light when it is made hot by an electric current. **2.** very bright; gleaming. —**in′can·des′cence**, *n.*

incandescent lamp

in·can·ta·tion (in′kan tā′shən), *n.* **1.** the chanting of special words that are supposed to have magic power [an *incantation* to drive away demons]. **2.** such words.

in·ca·pa·ble (in kā′pə b'l), *adj.* **1.** not capable; not having the ability or power needed [*incapable* of helping]. **2.** not able to undergo; not open to [*incapable* of change]. —**in′ca·pa·bil′i·ty**, *n.*

in·ca·pac·i·tate (in′kə pas′ə tāt), *v.* to make unable or unfit; disable [*incapacitated* by a broken leg]. —**in′ca·pac′i·tat·ed**, *p.t. & p.p.*; **in′ca·pac′i·tat·ing**, *pr.p.*

in·ca·pac·i·ty (in′kə pas′ə tē), *n.* lack of ability or fitness; a being unable or unfit.

in·car·cer·ate (in kär′sə rāt), *v.* to put in prison. —**in·car′cer·at·ed**, *p.t. & p.p.*; **in·car′cer·at·ing**, *pr.p.* —**in·car′cer·a′tion**, *n.*

in·car·nate (in kär′nit *or* in kär′nāt), *adj.* in human form; being a living example of [He is evil *incarnate*.] —*v.* (in kär′nāt), **1.** to give solid form to; make real. **2.** to be a living example of; typify [He *incarnates* the courage of the nation.] —**in·car′nat·ed**, *p.t. & p.p.*; **in·car′nat·ing**, *pr.p.*

in·car·na·tion (in′kär nā′shən), *n.* **1.** a taking on of human form. In Christian belief, **the Incarnation** is the taking on of human form by Jesus as the Son of God. **2.** a living example or symbol of a quality [She is the *incarnation* of evil.]

in·case (in kās′), *v.* same as **encase.** —**incased′,** *p.t. & p.p.;* **in·cas′ing,** *pr.p.*

in·cau·tious (in kô′shəs), *adj.* not cautious; not careful; reckless [an *incautious* driver].

in·cen·di·ar·y (in sen′di er′ē), *adj.* **1.** having to do with the destroying of property on purpose by setting fire to it. **2.** causing fires [an *incendiary* bomb]. **3.** stirring up riots, trouble, etc. [*incendiary* speeches]. —*n.* a person who sets fire to property on purpose. —**in·cen′di·ar′ies,** *pl.*

in·cense (in′sens), *n.* **1.** a substance made of gums, spices, etc., that is burned for the sweet smell it gives off. **2.** the smoke or sweet smell from it. **3.** any pleasant smell.

in·cense (in sens′), *v.* to make very angry; fill with rage [He was *incensed* at her lies.] —**incensed′,** *p.t. & p.p.;* **in·cens′ing,** *pr.p.*

in·cen·tive (in sen′tiv), *n.* the thing that makes one want to work, try, etc.; motive or stimulus [The scholarship award was an *incentive* for George to study harder.]

in·cep·tion (in sep′shən), *n.* a beginning; start [the *inception* of a new project].

in·ces·sant (in ses′′nt), *adj.* going on without stopping or in a way that seems endless [*incessant* chatter]. —**in·ces′sant·ly,** *adv.*

in·cest (in′sest), *n.* sexual intercourse between persons too closely related to marry legally.

inch (inch), *n.* a unit for measuring length, equal to 1/12 foot. —*v.* to move a little at a time [He *inched* along the narrow ledge.] —**by inches,** slowly or gradually: also **inch by inch.** —**within an inch of,** very close to.

in·ci·dence (in′si dəns), *n.* the range within which something falls or has an effect [The *incidence* of flu was widespread that year.]

in·ci·dent (in′si dənt), *n.* something that happens in real life or in a story; often, an event of little importance [He told an *incident* of his childhood.] —*adj.* likely to happen as a part of [the problems *incident* to teaching].

in·ci·den·tal (in′si den′t′l), *adj.* **1.** likely to happen along with something else [the duties *incidental* to a job]. **2.** minor or of lesser importance [the *incidental* costs of education]. —*n.* **1.** something incidental. **2. incidentals,** *pl.* various small items or expenses.

in·ci·den·tal·ly (in′si den′t′l ē), *adv.* **1.** in an incidental way; along with something else. **2.** by the way [*Incidentally,* what time is it?]

in·cin·er·ate (in sin′ə rāt), *v.* to burn to ashes; burn up. —**in·cin′er·at·ed,** *p.t. & p.p.;* **in·cin′er·at·ing,** *pr.p.* —**in·cin·er·a′tion,** *n.*

in·cin·er·a·tor (in sin′ə rā′tər), *n.* a furnace for burning trash.

in·cip·i·ent (in sip′i ənt), *adj.* just starting; in the first stage [an *incipient* illness].

in·cise (in sīz′), *v.* to cut into with a sharp tool; carve; engrave [letters *incised* in stone]. —**incised′,** *p.t. & p.p.;* **in·cis′ing,** *pr.p.*

in·ci·sion (in sizh′ən), *n.* **1.** an incising. **2.** a cut or gash, as one made in surgery.

in·ci·sive (in sī′siv), *adj.* sharp and clear; keen [an *incisive* mind]. —**in·ci′sive·ly,** *adv.* —**in·ci′sive·ness,** *n.*

in·ci·sor (in sī′zər), *n.* any of the front teeth with a cutting edge, between the canine teeth. A human being has eight incisors.

incisors

in·cite (in sīt′), *v.* to stir up; rouse; urge [to *incite* a mob to riot]. —**in·cit′ed,** *p.t. & p.p.;* **in·cit′ing,** *pr.p.* —**in·cite′ment,** *n.*

in·ci·vil·i·ty (in′si vil′ə-tē), *n.* impoliteness or an impolite act. —**in′ci·vil′i·ties,** *pl.*

in·clem·ent (in klem′ənt), *adj.* **1.** rough or stormy [*inclement* weather]. **2.** lacking mercy; harsh [an *inclement* king]. —**in·clem′en·cy,** *n.*

in·cli·na·tion (in′klə nā′shən), *n.* **1.** a natural liking for or leaning toward something; tendency [an *inclination* to talk]. **2.** a bending, leaning, or sloping [the *inclination* of the head in prayer; the *inclination* of a roof].

in·cline (in klīn′), *v.* **1.** to lean, slope, or slant [The chimney *inclines* toward the left.] **2.** to bend or bow, as the head. **3.** to have a liking for or leaning toward; tend [John *inclines* to be lazy.] —*n.* (in′klīn), a sloping surface; slope or slant [a road with a steep *incline*]. —**in·clined′,** *p.t. & p.p.;* **in·clin′ing,** *pr.p.*

in·close (in klōz′), *v.* same as **enclose.** —**in·closed′,** *p.t. & p.p.;* **in·clos′ing,** *pr.p.*

in·clo·sure (in klō′zhər), *n.* same as **enclosure.**

in·clude (in klōōd′), *v.* to have or take in as part of a whole; contain [Prices *include* taxes.] —**in·clud′ed,** *p.t. & p.p.;* **in·clud′ing,** *pr.p.*

in·clu·sion (in klōō′zhən), *n.* **1.** the act of including. **2.** something included.

in·clu·sive (in klōō′siv), *adj.* including; especially, including both limits mentioned [A vacation from the first to the tenth *inclusive* is a vacation of ten days.] —**in·clu′sive·ly,** *adv.*

in·cog·ni·to (in käg′ni tō *or* in′kəg nē′tō), *adv. & adj.* hiding under a false name [The king toured the country *incognito.*]

in·co·her·ent (in′kō hir′ənt), *adj.* not coherent; not clearly connected; confused; rambling [an *incoherent* story]. —**in′co·her′ence,** *n.* —**in′co·her′ent·ly,** *adv.*

in·com·bus·ti·ble (in′kəm bus′tə b′l), *adj.* that cannot be burned; fireproof.

in·come (in′kum), *n.* the money that one gets as wages, salary, rent, interest, profit, etc.

in·com·ing (in′kum′ing), *adj.* coming in or about to come in [the *incoming* traffic]. —*n.* a coming in [the *incoming* of the flood waters].

in·com·men·su·rate (in′kə men′shoor it), *adj.* **1.** not adequate; not enough [a supply *incommensurate* to the demand]. **2.** that cannot be compared.

in·com·mode (in kə mōd′), *v.* to cause trouble or annoyance to; bother [It will *incommode* us if you are late.] **—in·com·mod′ed**, *p.t. & p.p.;* **in·com·mod′ing**, *pr.p.*

in·com·mu·ni·ca·ble (in′kə myōō′ni kə b′l), *adj.* that cannot be told to others.

in·com·mu·ni·ca·do (in′kə myōō′ni kä′dō), *adj.* not able to send messages to others [The prisoners were held *incommunicado*.]

in·com·pa·ra·ble (in käm′pər ə b′l), *adj.* so much greater or better that it cannot be compared with any other; without an equal; matchless [the *incomparable* genius of Shakespeare]. **—in·com′pa·ra·bly**, *adv.*

in·com·pat·i·ble (in′kəm pat′ə b′l), *adj.* **1.** not getting along in a friendly or peaceful way; not in agreement [*incompatible* partners]. **2.** not going well together; not in harmony [*incompatible* colors]. **—in′com·pat′i·bil′i·ty**, *n.*

in·com·pe·tent (in käm′pə tənt), *adj.* **1.** not able to do what is needed; without enough skill or knowledge [an *incompetent* typist]. **2.** not fit according to the law [The old woman was judged *incompetent* to make a will.] **—n.** an incompetent person. **—in·com′pe·tence**, *n.* **—in·com′pe·tent·ly**, *adv.*

in·com·plete (in kəm plēt′), *adj.* not complete; without all its parts; not whole or finished. **—in·com·plete′ly**, *adv.*

in·com·pre·hen·si·ble (in′kam pri hen′sə b′l), *adj.* that cannot be understood; not clear; obscure. **—in′com·pre·hen′si·bly**, *adv.*

in·con·ceiv·a·ble (in′kən sēv′ə b′l), *adj.* that cannot be thought of, imagined, or believed; unthinkable [It is *inconceivable* that he would lie.] **—in′con·ceiv′a·bly**, *adv.*

in·con·clu·sive (in′kən klōō′siv), *adj.* not conclusive or final; not leading to a definite result [The experiments were *inconclusive*.] **—in′con·clu′sive·ly**, *adv.*

in·con·gru·i·ty (in′kən grōō′ə tē), *n.* **1.** the condition of being incongruous. **2.** something that is incongruous. **—in′con·gru′i·ties**, *pl.*

in·con·gru·ous (in käng′grōō əs), *adj.* not going well together; out of place; not fitting or proper. **—in′con·gru·ous·ly**, *adv.*

in·con·se·quen·tial (in′kän si kwen′shəl), *adj.* of no importance; too small or ordinary to matter; trivial [It cost an *inconsequential* sum.] **—in′con·se·quen′tial·ly**, *adv.*

in·con·sid·er·a·ble (in′kən sid′ər ə b′l), *adj.* not worth considering; trivial; small.

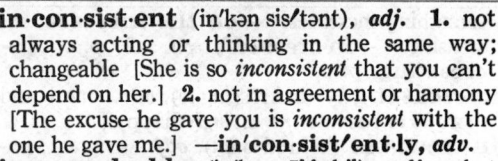

an incongruous combination

in·con·sid·er·ate (in′kən sid′ər it), *adj.* not thoughtful of other people; thoughtless.

in·con·sist·en·cy (in′kən sis′tən sē), *n.* **1.** the condition of being inconsistent. **2.** an inconsistent thing. **—in′con·sist′en·cies**, *pl.*

in·con·sist·ent (in′kən sis′tənt), *adj.* **1.** not always acting or thinking in the same way; changeable [She is so *inconsistent* that you can't depend on her.] **2.** not in agreement or harmony [The excuse he gave you is *inconsistent* with the one he gave me.] **—in′con·sist′ent·ly**, *adv.*

in·con·sol·a·ble (in′kən sōl′ə b′l), *adj.* that cannot be comforted or cheered; very sad or unhappy [She was *inconsolable* for weeks when her parakeet died.] **—in′con·sol′a·bly**, *adv.*

in·con·spic·u·ous (in′kən spik′yōō əs), *adj.* hard to see or notice; attracting little attention [an *inconspicuous* stain]. **—in′con·spic′u·ous·ly**, *adv.* **—in′con·spic′u·ous·ness**, *n.*

in·con·stant (in kän′stənt), *adj.* not constant or steady; changing often; changeable; fickle [an *inconstant* friend]. **—in·con′stan·cy**, *n.*

in·con·test·a·ble (in′kən tes′tə b′l), *adj.* that cannot be argued about or questioned [an *incontestable* decision].

in·con·ti·nent (in kän′tə nənt), *adj.* not able to control one's feelings, desires, etc.; lacking self-control. **—in·con′ti·nence**, *n.*

in·con·tro·vert·i·ble (in′kän trə vūr′tə b′l), *adj.* that cannot be argued against or questioned; undeniable [an *incontrovertible* fact].

in·con·ven·ience (in′kən vēn′yəns), *n.* **1.** the condition of being inconvenient; trouble or bother. **2.** anything that causes this. **—v.** to cause trouble or bother to. **—in′con·ven′ienced**, *p.t. & p.p.;* **in′con·ven′ienc·ing**, *pr.p.*

in·con·ven·ient (in′kən vēn′yənt), *adj.* not convenient; causing trouble or bother.

in·cor·po·rate (in kôr′pə rāt), *v.* **1.** to make part of another thing; combine with something else [*Incorporate* these new facts into your report.] **2.** to bring together into a single whole; merge [The two churches have been *incorporated* into one.] **3.** to form into a corporation [The owner of a store may *incorporate* his business.] **—in·cor′po·rat·ed**, *p.t. & p.p.;* **in·cor′po·rat·ing**, *pr.p.* **—in·cor·po·ra′tion**, *n.*

in·cor·po·re·al (in′kôr pôr′i əl), *adj.* not made of matter; not material; spiritual.

in·cor·rect (in kə rekt′), *adj.* not correct; not right, true, proper, etc.; wrong [*incorrect* answer; *incorrect* conduct]. **—in·cor·rect′ly**, *adv.* **—in·cor·rect′ness**, *n.*

in·cor·ri·gi·ble (in kôr′i jə b′l), *adj.* that cannot be made better or cured because so bad or so deeply fixed [an *incorrigible* liar; an *incorrigible* habit]. **—n.** an incorrigible person.

in·cor·rupt·i·ble (in′kə rup′tə b′l), *adj.* **1.** that cannot be bribed into doing wrong [an *incorruptible* official]. **2.** that will not decay or be destroyed [*incorruptible* ideals].

in·crease (in krēs′), *v.* to make or become greater, larger, etc.; add to or grow [When he *increased* his wealth, his power *increased*.] **—n.** (in′krēs), **1.** an increasing; addition; growth [an *increase* in population]. **2.** the amount by which something increases. **—on the increase,** increasing. **—in·creased',** *p.t.* & *p.p.;* **in·creas'ing,** *pr.p.*

in·creas·ing·ly (in krēs'ing lē), *adv.* more and more [He became *increasingly* happy.]

in·cred·i·ble (in kred'ə b'l), *adj.* so great, unusual, etc. that it is hard or impossible to believe [an *incredible* story; *incredible* speed]. **—in·cred'i·bly,** *adv.*

in·cre·du·li·ty (in'krə dōō'lə tē), *n.* a being unwilling or unable to believe something; doubt.

in·cred·u·lous (in krej'oo ləs), *adj.* **1.** not willing or able to believe; doubting. **2.** showing doubt or disbelief [an *incredulous* look]. **—in·cred'u·lous·ly,** *adv.*

in·cre·ment (in'krə mənt), *n.* **1.** the amount by which something increases [a yearly *increment* of $300 in wages]. **2.** a growing greater or larger; increase.

in·crim·i·nate (in krim'ə nāt), *v.* to say or show that someone is guilty [His fingerprints on the window tend to *incriminate* him.] **—in·crim'i·nat·ed,** *p.t.* & *p.p.;* **in·crim'i·nat·ing,** *pr.p.;* **in·crim'i·na'tion,** *n.*

in·crust (in krust'), *v.* **1.** to set into all parts of the surface of [a bracelet *incrusted* with diamonds]. **2.** to cover with a crust or layer [His shoes were *incrusted* with mud.] Also spelled **encrust.** **—in'crus·ta'tion,** *n.*

in·cu·bate (in'kyoo bāt), *v.* **1.** to hatch eggs by sitting on them or otherwise keeping them warm. **2.** to develop or mature gradually [An idea was *incubating* in my mind.] **—in'cu·bat·ed,** *p.t.* & *p.p.;* **in'cu·bat·ing,** *pr.p.* **—in'cu·ba'tion,** *n.*

in·cu·ba·tor (in'kyoo bā'tər), *n.* **1.** a container that is kept warm for hatching eggs. **2.** a container in which babies who are born too soon are kept warm and protected for a time.

in·cu·bus (in'kyoo bəs), *n.* **1.** a nightmare, or the evil spirit that was once supposed to weigh a person down in a nightmare. **2.** anything that weighs one down; burden.

incubator for hatching chicks

in·cul·cate (in kul'kāt *or* in'kul kāt), *v.* to fix in a person's mind by teaching over and over again [to *inculcate* obedience in children]. **—in·cul'cat·ed,** *p.t.* & *p.p.;* **in·cul'cat·ing,** *pr.p.* **—in'cul·ca'tion,** *n.*

in·cum·bent (in kum'bənt), *n.* the person holding a certain office or position. **—adj.** resting upon as a duty [It is *incumbent* on us to help them.] **—in·cum'ben·cy,** *n.*

in·cum·ber (in kum'bər), *v.* same as **encumber. —in·cum'brance,** *n.*

in·cur (in kur'), *v.* to bring something bad or unpleasant upon oneself [He *incurred* debts because of his illness.] **—in·curred',** *p.t.* & *p.p.;* **in·cur'ring,** *pr.p.*

in·cur·a·ble (in kyoor'ə b'l), *adj.* that cannot be cured [an *incurable* disease]. **—n.** a person with an incurable disease. **—in·cur'a·bly,** *adv.*

in·cur·sion (in kur'zhən), *n.* a sudden, brief invasion or raid [the *incursions* of armed bands at a border].

Ind., abbreviation for **India, Indian,** or **Indiana.**

in·debt·ed (in det'id), *adj.* owing money, thanks, etc.; in debt; obliged [I will always be *indebted* to him for saving my life.]

in·debt·ed·ness (in det'id nis), *n.* **1.** the condition of being indebted. **2.** the amount owed.

in·de·cen·cy (in dē's'n sē), *n.* **1.** the condition of being indecent. **2.** an indecent act or remark. **—in·de'cen·cies,** *pl.*

in·de·cent (in dē's'nt), *adj.* **1.** not decent, proper, or fitting [*indecent* vanity]. **2.** not moral or modest; nasty [to call someone an *indecent* name]. **—in·de'cent·ly,** *adv.*

in·de·ci·sion (in'di sizh'ən), *n.* a being unable to decide or make up one's mind.

in·de·ci·sive (in'di sī'siv), *adj.* **1.** not able to decide or make up one's mind; hesitating. **2.** not deciding or settling anything [an *indecisive* reply]. **—in'de·ci'sive·ly,** *adv.*

in·dec·o·rous (in dek'ə rəs), *adj.* not proper or fitting; lacking good taste; unbecoming.

in·deed (in dēd'), *adv.* in fact; truly; really [It is *indeed* warm.] **—interj.** a word said to show surprise, doubt, scorn, etc.

in·de·fat·i·ga·ble (in'di fat'i gə b'l), *adj.* that cannot be tired out; untiring.

in·de·fen·si·ble (in'di fen'sə b'l), *adj.* **1.** that cannot be defended or protected [an *indefensible* bridge]. **2.** that cannot be excused or proved right [an *indefensible* act].

in·de·fin·a·ble (in'di fīn'ə b'l), *adj.* that cannot be defined [an *indefinable* feeling].

in·def·i·nite (in def'ə nit), *adj.* **1.** having no exact limits [an *indefinite* area]. **2.** not clear or exact in meaning; vague [*indefinite* instructions]. **3.** not sure or positive; uncertain [*indefinite* plans]. **—in·def'i·nite·ly,** *adv.*

indefinite article, either of the words "a" or "an."

in·del·i·ble (in del'ə b'l), *adj.* that cannot be erased or rubbed out; permanent [*indelible* ink; an *indelible* impression]. **—in·del'i·bly,** *adv.*

in·del·i·ca·cy (in del'i kə sē), *n.* **1.** the quality of being indelicate. **2.** an indelicate act, remark, etc. **—in·del'i·ca·cies,** *pl.*

in·del·i·cate (in del'i kit), *adj.* not refined or polite; improper; coarse [*indelicate* jokes].

in·dem·ni·fy (in dem'nə fī), *v.* **1.** to pay back for some loss or injury [We were *indemnified* for our stolen car.] **2.** to protect against loss or damage; insure. **—in·dem'ni·fied,** *p.t.* & *p.p.;* **in·dem'ni·fy·ing,** *pr.p.* **—in·dem'ni·fi·ca'tion,** *n.*

in·dem·ni·ty (in dem'nə tē), *n.* **1.** protection or insurance against loss or damage. **2.** payment for loss or damage. **—in·dem'ni·ties,** *pl.*

in·dent (in dent′), *v.* **1.** to cut notches into the edge of something; make jagged or uneven [The shore line is *indented* with bays.] **2.** to begin the first line of a paragraph, etc. farther in from the margin than the other lines.

in·den·ta·tion (in′den tā′shən), *n.* **1.** the act of indenting. **2.** an indented part; notch, bay, dent, etc.

in·den·ture (in den′chər), *n.* an agreement in writing; especially, a contract that binds a person to work for another for a certain length of time. —*v.* to put under such a contract [an *indentured* servant]. —**in·den′tured**, *p.t. & p.p.;* **in·den′tur·ing**, *pr.p.*

in·de·pend·ence (in′di pen′dəns), *n.* the condition of being independent; freedom from the control of another or others.

Independence Day, the Fourth of July, a national holiday. The Declaration of Independence was adopted on July 4, 1776.

in·de·pend·ent (in′di pen′dənt), *adj.* **1.** not ruled or controlled by another; self-governing [Many colonies became *independent* countries after World War II.] **2.** not connected with others; separate [an *independent* grocery]. **3.** not influenced by others; thinking for oneself [an *independent* voter]. **4.** not depending on another for money to live on; supporting oneself. **5.** that gives one enough to live on without working [an *independent* income]. —*n.* an independent person, especially one who is not a member of any political party. —**in′de·pend′ent·ly,** *adv.*

independent clause, same as **main clause.**

in·de·scrib·a·ble (in′di skrīb′ə b'l), *adj.* that cannot be described; too beautiful, horrible, etc. to describe. —**in′de·scrib′a·bly,** *adv.*

in·de·struct·i·ble (in′di struk′tə b'l), *adj.* that cannot be destroyed; very strong. —**in′de·struct′i·bil′i·ty,** *n.* —**in′de·struct′i·bly,** *adv.*

in·de·ter·mi·nate (in′di tûr′mə nit), *adj.* not having exact limits; not definite; vague.

in·dex (in′deks), *n.* **1.** a list of names, subjects, etc. in alphabetical order at the end of a book. It shows on what pages these names, etc. are mentioned. **2.** a thing that points out something else; indication; sign [High wages are an *index* of prosperity.] **3.** a pointer, as the needle on a dial. **4.** the finger next to the thumb; forefinger: *its full name is* **index finger.** —*v.* to make an index for [to *index* a book]. —**in′dex·es** or **in′di·ces,** *pl.*

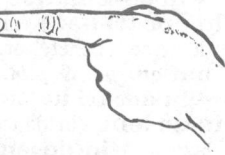

index finger

In·di·a (in′di ə), *n.* **1.** a large peninsula of southern Asia. **2.** a country that takes up most of this peninsula: it is a member of the British Commonwealth of Nations.

In·di·an (in′di ən), *n.* **1.** a member of any of the peoples living in America when it was discovered by Europeans: also called **American Indian. 2.** a native person of India or the East Indies. **3.** any of the languages of the American Indians. —*adj.* **1.** of the American Indians. **2.** of India or the East Indies or their people.

In·di·an·a (in′di an′ə), *n.* a State in the north central part of the United States: abbreviated **Ind.**

In·di·an·ap·o·lis (in′di ən ap′'l is), *n.* the capital of Indiana.

Indian club, a wooden club swung in the hand for exercise.

Indian corn, same as **corn** (the grain, *meaning* 1).

Indian Ocean, an ocean south of Asia, between Africa and Australia.

Indian summer, a period of warm, hazy weather after the first frosts of late fall.

India paper, a thin, strong printing paper.

Indian clubs

in·di·cate (in′də kāt), *v.* **1.** to point out; make known; point to; show [*Indicate* with a pointer where India is on the map.] **2.** to be or give a sign of [Smoke *indicates* fire.] —**in′di·cat·ed,** *p.t. & p.p.;* **in′di·cat·ing,** *pr.p.*

in·di·ca·tion (in′də kā′shən), *n.* **1.** an indicating. **2.** something that indicates, or shows; sign [His smile was an *indication* of pleasure.]

in·dic·a·tive (in dik′ə tiv), *adj.* **1.** that shows or is a sign of [Her questions are *indicative* of a keen mind.] **2.** describing the mood of a verb used in making a statement of actual fact, rather than in stating a wish or possibility or a command [In the sentences "I went home" and "Is he here?", "went" and "is" are in the *indicative* mood.]

in·di·ca·tor (in′də kā′tər), *n.* a pointer, dial, gauge, etc. that measures or shows something.

in·di·ces (in′də sēz), *n.* a plural of **index.**

in·dict (in dīt′), *v.* to accuse of having committed a crime; especially, to order that a suspect be put on trial after charging him with some crime [A grand jury can *indict* a person if it decides there is enough evidence to do so.] —**in·dict′ment,** *n.*

In·dies (in′dēz), *n.pl.* **1.** the East Indies. **2.** the West Indies.

in·dif·fer·ence (in dif′ər əns *or* in dif′rəns), *n.* **1.** lack of interest or concern [the crowd's *indifference* to his speech]. **2.** no importance [His problems are a matter of *indifference* to me.]

in·dif·fer·ent (in dif′ər ənt *or* in dif′rənt), *adj.* **1.** having or showing no interest or concern; unmoved [He remained *indifferent* to my pleas for help.] **2.** neither very good nor very bad; mediocre [an *indifferent* singer]. **3.** having no choice; not caring [to remain *indifferent* in a dispute]. **—in·dif'fer·ent·ly,** *adv.*

in·dig·e·nous (in dij'ə nəs), *adj.* growing or living naturally in a certain place; native [The kangaroo is *indigenous* to Australia.]

in·di·gent (in'di jənt), *adj.* very poor or needy. **—in'di·gence,** *n.*

in·di·gest·i·ble (in'də jes'tə b'l), *adj.* that cannot be digested, or hard to digest.

in·di·ges·tion (in'də jes'chən), *n.* difficulty in digesting food, or discomfort caused by this.

in·dig·nant (in dig'nənt), *adj.* angry about something that seems unjust, unfair, mean, etc. [to become *indignant* at a bully]. **—in·dig'-nant·ly,** *adv.*

in·dig·na·tion (in'dig nā'shən), *n.* anger at something that seems unjust, unfair, mean, etc.

in·dig·ni·ty (in dig'nə tē), *n.* something that insults or hurts one's pride [The porter objected to the *indignity* of being called "boy."] **—in·dig'ni·ties,** *pl.*

in·di·go (in'di gō), *n.* **1.** a blue dye that comes from a certain plant of the pea family or is now made artificially. **2.** deep violet-blue.

in·di·rect (in də rekt'), *adj.* **1.** not direct or straight; by a longer way; roundabout [an *indirect* route]. **2.** not the main one; secondary [an *indirect* benefit]. **3.** not honest or frank [an *indirect* reply]. **—in·di·rect'ly,** *adv.*

indirect object, the word in a sentence that names the person or thing that something is given to or done for: see also **direct object** [In "Bill gave me a dime," "dime" is the direct object and "me" is the *indirect object*.]

in·dis·creet (in dis krēt'), *adj.* not discreet; not careful about what one says or does; unwise. **—in·dis·creet'ly,** *adv.*

in·dis·cre·tion (in'dis kresh'ən), *n.* **1.** lack of good judgment or care in what one says or does. **2.** an indiscreet act or remark.

in·dis·crim·i·nate (in'dis krim'ə nit), *adj.* not paying attention to differences; not showing care in choosing; making no distinctions [*indiscriminate* praise for everyone; an *indiscriminate* buyer of books]. **—in'dis·crim'i·nate·ly,** *adv.*

in·dis·pen·sa·ble (in'dis pen'sə b'l), *adj.* that cannot be done without; absolutely necessary [Good brakes are *indispensable* to a car.]

in·dis·posed (in dis pōzd'), *adj.* **1.** not well; slightly sick. **2.** not willing; unwilling.

in·dis·po·si·tion (in'dis pə zish'ən), *n.* **1.** a slight sickness. **2.** unwillingness.

in·dis·pu·ta·ble (in'dis pyoo'tə b'l *or* in dis'-pyoo tə b'l), *adj.* that cannot be argued against or doubted; certain [an *indisputable* truth]. **—in'dis·pu'ta·bly,** *adv.*

in·dis·sol·u·ble (in'di säl'yoo b'l), *adj.* that cannot be dissolved, broken up, etc.; lasting; durable [an *indissoluble* partnership].

in·dis·tinct (in di stingkt'), *adj.* not clearly heard, seen, or understood; dim or confused [an *indistinct* signature; an *indistinct* murmur of voices]. **—in·dis·tinct'ly,** *adv.*

in·dis·tin·guish·a·ble (in'di sting'gwish ə b'l), *adj.* that cannot be told apart because very much alike [The twins are *indistinguishable*.]

in·dite (in dīt'), *v.* to write or compose [to *indite* a poem]. **—in·dit'ed,** *p.t. & p.p.;* **in·dit'ing,** *pr.p.*

in·di·vid·u·al (in'də vij'ōō əl), *adj.* **1.** that is one separate being or thing; single [presents for each *individual* child]. **2.** for or from each single person or thing [a dormitory with *individual* rooms; *individual* reports]. **3.** different from others; personal or unusual [Jane's *individual* way of signing her name]. **—n. 1.** a single being or thing [to fight for the rights of the *individual*]. **2.** a person [He's a clever *individual*.]

in·di·vid·u·al·ism (in'də vij'ōō əl iz'm), *n.* **1.** the practice of living as one wants to, without paying attention to others. **2.** the idea that the individual is more important than the state or nation. **—in'di·vid·u·al·ist,** *n.* **—in'di·vid·u·al·is'tic,** *adj.*

in·di·vid·u·al·i·ty (in'də vij'ōō al'ə tē), *n.* **1.** the qualities that make a person different from all others [Her cheerful smile is part of her *individuality*.] **2.** the condition of being individual, or different from others [Houses in the suburbs often have no *individuality*.] **—in'di·vid·u·al'i·ties,** *pl.*

in·di·vid·u·al·ize (in'də vij'ōō ə līz), *v.* to make individual, or different from all others [to *individualize* one's writing]. **—in'di·vid·u·al·ized,** *p.t. & p.p.;* **in'di·vid·u·al·iz·ing,** *pr.p.*

in·di·vid·u·al·ly (in'də vij'ōō əl ē), *adv.* in an individual way; one at a time; as individuals [I shall answer you *individually*.]

in·di·vis·i·ble (in'də viz'ə b'l), *adj.* **1.** that cannot be divided or broken up ["one nation under God, *indivisible*"]. **2.** that cannot be divided by another number without leaving a remainder [The number 17 is *indivisible*.] **—in'di·vis'i·bly,** *adv.*

In·do-Chi·na (in'dō chī'nə), *n.* **1.** a large peninsula in Asia, south of China. **2.** a part of this peninsula that once belonged to France. **—In·do-Chi·nese** (in'dō chī nēz'), *adj.*

in·doc·tri·nate (in däk'tri nāt), *v.* to teach a doctrine, belief, or idea to. **—in·doc'tri·nat·ed,** *p.t. & p.p.;* **in·doc'tri·nat·ing,** *pr.p.* **—in·doc'tri·na'tion,** *n.*

in·do·lent (in'də lənt), *adj.* not liking work; lazy. **—in'do·lence,** *n.* **—in'do·lent·ly,** *adv.*

in·dom·i·ta·ble (in däm'i tə b'l), *adj.* that cannot be conquered or overcome; not yielding [*indomitable* courage].

In·do·ne·si·a (in'dō nē'zhə), *n.* a country in the Malay Archipelago made up of Java, Sumatra, most of Borneo, and other islands.

In·do·ne·sian (in'dō nē'zhən), *adj.* of Indonesia, its people, etc. **—n. 1.** a person born or living in Indonesia. **2.** any of the languages spoken in Indonesia.

in·door (in'dôr), *adj.* being, belonging, done, etc. inside a house or other building [*indoor* lighting; *indoor* games].

in·doors (in′dôrz′), *adv.* in or into a house or other building [Let's go *indoors*.]

in·dorse (in dôrs′), *v.* **1.** to sign one's name on the back of a check, etc., as in order to cash it. **2.** to give support to; favor. Also spelled **endorse. —in·dorsed′,** *p.t. & p.p.;* **in·dors′-ing,** *pr.p.* **—in·dorse′ment,** *n.* **—in·dors′er,** *n.*

in·du·bi·ta·ble (in dōō′bi tə b'l *or* in dyōō′bi-tə b'l), *adj.* that cannot be doubted; certain [*indubitable* evidence]. **—in·du′bi·ta·bly,** *adv.*

in·duce (in dōōs′ *or* in dyōōs′), *v.* **1.** to lead a person into doing something; persuade [Can't we *induce* you to stay another week?] **2.** to cause; bring on [Indigestion may be *induced* by over-eating.] **3.** to come to a general rule or conclusion by studying particular facts. **4.** to produce an electric or magnetic effect by induction. **—in·duced′,** *p.t. & p.p.;* **in·duc′ing,** *pr.p.*

in·duce·ment (in dōōs′mənt *or* in dyōōs′mənt), *n.* **1.** the act of inducing. **2.** anything that induces [Your mother's cooking is *inducement* enough for me to stay.]

in·duct (in dukt′), *v.* **1.** to place in office with a ceremony; install [The new councilmen were *inducted* this morning.] **2.** to enroll in the armed forces, a society, etc.

in·duc·tion (in duk′shən), *n.* **1.** an inducting or being inducted, as into office, the armed forces, a society, etc. **2.** the act of coming to a general conclusion from particular facts; also, the conclusion reached. **3.** the creating of magnetism or electricity in a body, as by bringing it near to a magnet or a conductor carrying an electrical current. **—in·duc′tive,** *adj.*

in·due (in dōō′ *or* in dyōō′), *v.* same as **endue. —in·dued′,** *p.t. & p.p.;* **in·du′ing,** *pr.p.*

in·dulge (in dulj′), *v.* **1.** to give in to something one wants or wants to do; let oneself have some pleasure [to *indulge* a craving for sweets; to *indulge* in sports]. **2.** to give in to the wishes of; humor [He *indulges* his son too much.] **—in·dulged′,** *p.t. & p.p.;* **in·dul′ging,** *pr.p.*

in·dul·gence (in dul′jəns), *n.* **1.** an indulging. **2.** a thing indulged in [Golf is my one *indulgence*.] **3.** a favor or right granted; permission. **4.** in the Roman Catholic Church, a freeing from all or part of the punishment due in purgatory for a sin.

in·dul·gent (in dul′jənt), *adj.* indulging; kind or too kind; not at all strict [*indulgent* parents]. **—in·dul′gent·ly,** *adv.*

in·dus·tri·al (in dus′tri əl), *adj.* having to do with industries or with the people working in industries [an *industrial* city; *industrial* unions]. **—in·dus′tri·al·ly,** *adv.*

in·dus·tri·al·ist (in dus′tri əl ist), *n.* an owner or manager of a large industry.

in·dus·tri·al·ize (in dus′tri əl īz′), *v.* to build up industries in [to *industrialize* a backward country]. **—in·dus′tri·al·ized′,** *p.t. & p.p.;* **in·dus′tri·al·iz′ing,** *pr.p.*

in·dus·tri·ous (in dus′tri əs), *adj.* working hard and steadily. **—in·dus′tri·ous·ly,** *adv.*

in·dus·try (in′dəs trē), *n.* **1.** any branch of business or manufacturing [the steel *industry;* the motion-picture *industry*]. **2.** all business and manufacturing [Leaders of *industry* met in Chicago.] **3.** hard, steady work; diligence. **—in′dus·tries,** *pl.*

-ine (in), a suffix meaning: **1.** of or like [A *crystalline* compound is made up of crystals.] **2.** female; woman [A *heroine* is a woman hero.]

in·e·bri·ate (in ē′bri āt′), *v.* to make drunk. **—n.** (in ē′bri it), a drunkard. **—in·e′bri·at·ed,** *p.t. & p.p.;* **in·e′bri·at·ing,** *pr.p.*

in·ed·i·ble (in ed′ə b'l), *adj.* not fit to be eaten.

in·ef·fa·ble (in ef′ə b'l), *adj.* **1.** too great to be described [*ineffable* beauty]. **2.** too holy to be spoken [the *ineffable* name of God].

in·ef·fec·tive (in′ə fek′tiv), *adj.* not having the result that is wanted; not effective [an *ineffective* punishment]. **—in′ef·fec′tive·ly,** *adv.*

in·ef·fec·tu·al (in′ə fek′chōō əl), *adj.* not having or not able to bring the result wanted [an *ineffectual* plan]. **—in′ef·fec′tu·al·ly,** *adv.*

in·ef·fi·cient (in′ə fish′ənt), *adj.* **1.** not having the skill to do what is needed; incapable [an *inefficient* worker]. **2.** not bringing the result wanted without wasting time, energy, or material [an *inefficient* motor]. **—in′ef·fi′cien·cy,** *n.* **—in′ef·fi′cient·ly,** *adv.*

in·e·las·tic (in′ə las′tik), *adj.* not elastic; stiff; rigid; not yielding.

in·el·e·gant (in el′ə gənt), *adj.* not elegant or refined; in poor taste; crude [*inelegant* manners]. **—in·el′e·gance,** *n.* **—in·el′e·gant·ly,** *adv.*

in·el·i·gi·ble (in el′i jə b'l), *adj.* not fit to be chosen according to rules; not qualified [Poor grades made him *ineligible* for football.] **—in·el′i·gi·bil′i·ty,** *n.*

in·ept (in ept′), *adj.* **1.** not right or suitable; wrong in a foolish and awkward way [*inept* praise]. **2.** clumsy or bungling [an *inept* mechanic]. **—in·ept′ly,** *adv.* **—in·ept′ness,** *n.*

in·e·qual·i·ty (in′i kwäl′ə tē), *n.* **1.** the fact of not being equal in size, amount, position, etc. **2.** the condition of not being even or regular; unevenness. **—in′e·qual′i·ties,** *pl.*

in·eq·ui·ta·ble (in ek′wi tə b'l), *adj.* not fair or just; unfair. **—in·eq′ui·ta·bly,** *adv.*

in·ert (in ûrt′), *adj.* **1.** not having the power to move or act [*inert* matter]. **2.** very slow in action; sluggish [Cold weather made the snake lie *inert* in its cage.] **3.** having no chemical action on other substances [*Inert* gases, as neon and helium, do not combine with other elements.]

in·er·tia (in ûr′shə), *n.* **1.** the natural force in matter that makes it stay at rest or keep on moving in a fixed direction unless it is acted on by an outside force. **2.** a feeling that keeps one from wanting to do things, make changes, etc. [*Inertia* kept him from seeking a new job.]

fat, āpe, cär, ten, ēven, hit, bīte, gō, hôrn, tōōl, book, up, fūr; get, joy, yet, chin, she, thin, *then*; zh = s in pleasure; ′ as in able (ā′b'l); ə = a in ago, e in agent, i in sanity, o in confess, u in focus.

in·es·cap·a·ble (in′ə skāp′ə b′l), *adj.* that cannot be escaped or avoided; inevitable [an *inescapable* conclusion]. **—in′es·cap′a·bly,** *adv.*

in·es·ti·ma·ble (in es′ti mə b′l), *adj.* too great to be measured [treasure of *inestimable* value].

in·ev·i·ta·ble (in ev′i tə b′l), *adj.* that must happen; unavoidable. **—in·ev′i·ta·bly,** *adv.*

in·ex·act (in′ig zakt′), *adj.* not exact or accurate; not strictly correct.

in·ex·cus·a·ble (in′ik skyōōz′ə b′l), *adj.* that cannot or should not be excused or forgiven; unpardonable. **—in′ex·cus′a·bly,** *adv.*

in·ex·haust·i·ble (in′ig zôs′tə b′l), *adj.* **1.** too much to be used up or emptied [an *inexhaustible* water supply]. **2.** that cannot be tired out; tireless [an *inexhaustible* worker].

in·ex·or·a·ble (in ek′sər ə b′l), *adj.* that cannot be stopped or turned aside by arguing or pleading; relentless [the *inexorable* passing of time]. **—in·ex′or·a·bly,** *adv.*

in·ex·pe·di·ent (in′ik spē′di ənt), *adj.* not expedient; not right or suitable; unwise.

in·ex·pen·sive (in′ik spen′siv), *adj.* not expensive; low-priced. **—in′ex·pen′sive·ly,** *adv.*

in·ex·pe·ri·ence (in′ik spir′i əns), *n.* lack of experience or of the skill that it brings.

in·ex·pe·ri·enced (in′ik spir′i ənst), *adj.* without experience or the skill that it brings.

in·ex·pert (in ek′spərt *or* in′ik spûrt′), *adj.* not expert; unskilled.

in·ex·pi·a·ble (in ek′spi ə b′l), *adj.* that cannot be atoned for or made up for, as a sin.

in·ex·pli·ca·ble (in eks′pli kə b′l *or* in′ik splik′ə b′l), *adj.* that cannot be explained or understood. **—in·ex′pli·ca·bly,** *adv.*

in·ex·press·i·ble (in′iks pres′ə b′l), *adj.* that cannot be expressed or described.

in·ex·tin·guish·a·ble (in′ik sting′gwish ə b′l), *adj.* that cannot be put out, as a fire or hope.

in·ex·tri·ca·ble (in eks′tri kə b′l), *adj.* **1.** that one cannot get himself out of [an *inextricable* difficulty]. **2.** that cannot be cleared up or straightened out [*inextricable* confusion].

in·fal·li·ble (in fal′ə b′l), *adj.* **1.** that cannot make a mistake; never wrong. **2.** not likely to fail or go wrong; sure [*infallible* proof]. **—in·fal′li·bil′i·ty,** *n.* **—in·fal′li·bly,** *adv.*

in·fa·mous (in′fə məs), *adj.* **1.** having a very bad reputation; notorious [an *infamous* thief]. **2.** very bad or wicked [an *infamous* crime]. **—in′fa·mous·ly,** *adv.*

in·fa·my (in′fə mē), *n.* **1.** very bad reputation; disgrace [He brought *infamy* on himself by his crime.] **2.** great wickedness, or a wicked act. **—in′fa·mies,** *pl.*

in·fan·cy (in′fən sē), *n.* **1.** the time of being an infant; babyhood. **2.** the earliest stage of anything [In 1900 the automobile industry was in its *infancy*.] **—in′fan·cies,** *pl.*

in·fant (in′fənt), *n.* a baby. —*adj.* **1.** of or for infants [a book on *infant* care]. **2.** in a very early stage [an *infant* nation].

in·fan·tile (in′fən tīl), *adj.* **1.** of infants or infancy [*infantile* diseases]. **2.** like an infant; babyish [*infantile* behavior].

infantile paralysis, same as **poliomyelitis.**

in·fan·try (in′fən trē), *n.* soldiers who are trained and armed for fighting on foot.

in·fan·try·man (in′fən trē mən), *n.* a soldier in the infantry. **—in′fan·try·men,** *pl.*

in·fat·u·ate (in fach′ōō āt), *v.* to make fall in love in a foolish or shallow way [He is *infatuated* with each pretty girl he meets.] **—in·fat′u·at·ed,** *p.t. & p.p.;* **in·fat′u·at·ing,** *pr.p.* **—in·fat′u·a′tion,** *n.*

in·fect (in fekt′), *v.* **1.** to make diseased with a germ or virus that enters the body [The dirty bandage *infected* his wound.] **2.** to spread to others, as one's feelings, ideas, etc. [Her gaiety *infected* the whole group.]

in·fec·tion (in fek′shən), *n.* **1.** an infecting or being infected. **2.** a disease caused by a germ or virus. **3.** anything that infects.

in·fec·tious (in fek′shəs), *adj.* **1.** caused by infection [Shingles is an *infectious* disease, but not contagious.] **2.** likely to spread to others [*infectious* laughter]. **—in·fec′tious·ly,** *adv.*

in·fer (in fûr′), *v.* to arrive at a conclusion or opinion by reasoning [I *infer* from your smile that you're happy.] *Infer* is sometimes confused with **imply. —in·ferred′,** *p.t. & p.p.;* **in·fer′ring,** *pr.p.*

in·fer·ence (in′fər əns), *n.* **1.** the act of inferring. **2.** a conclusion or opinion arrived at by inferring.

in·fe·ri·or (in fir′i ər), *adj.* **1.** not so good as someone or something else [My plan is *inferior* to yours.] **2.** not very good; below average [*inferior* merchandise]. **3.** lower in position, rank, etc. [an *inferior* official of the bank]. —*n.* an inferior person or thing.

in·fe·ri·or·i·ty (in fir′i ôr′ə tē), *n.* the condition of being inferior.

in·fer·nal (in fûr′n′l), *adj.* of hell or as if from hell; hellish; horrible [*infernal* torture].

in·fer·no (in fûr′nō), *n.* **1.** hell. **2.** any place that seems like hell [The desert was an *inferno* in the noonday sun.] **—in·fer′nos,** *pl.*

in·fest (in fest′), *v.* to swarm in or over, so as to harm or bother [Mice *infested* the house.]

in·fi·del (in′fə d′l), *n.* **1.** a person who has no religion. **2.** a person who does not believe in a certain religion, especially in the main religion of his land; among Christians, a non-Christian. —*adj.* that is an infidel or has to do with infidels.

in·fi·del·i·ty (in′fə del′ə tē), *n.* **1.** a being untrue to one's promise, duty, etc.; unfaithfulness. **2.** lack of belief in religion or in a certain religion. **—in′fi·del′i·ties,** *pl.*

in·field (in′fēld), *n.* **1.** the part of a baseball field enclosed by the four base lines; diamond. **2.** all the infielders.

in·field·er (in′fēl′dər), *n.* a baseball player whose position is in the infield; any of the basemen or the shortstop.

in·fil·trate (in fil′trāt *or* in′fil trāt), *v.* to pass through or into, as if being filtered [Our troops *infiltrated* the enemy lines.] **—in·fil′trat·ed,** *p.t. & p.p.;* **in·fil′trat·ing,** *pr.p.* **—in′fil·tra′tion,** *n.*

in·fi·nite (in'fə nit), *adj.* **1.** that has no limits; without beginning or end [Is the universe *infinite?*] **2.** very great; vast [*infinite* love]. —*n.* something infinite. —**in'fi·nite·ly,** *adv.*

in·fin·i·tes·i·mal (in'fin ə tes'ə m'l), *adj.* too small to be measured. —**in'fin·i·tes'i·mal·ly,** *adv.*

in·fin·i·tive (in fin'ə tiv), *n.* a form of a verb that does not show person, number, or tense, and is usually used with "to" [In "I need to eat" and "I must eat," "eat" is an *infinitive.*]

in·fin·i·tude (in fin'ə tood *or* in fin'ə tyood), *n.* **1.** the fact of being infinite. **2.** a vast number, extent, etc. [an *infinitude* of details].

in·fin·i·ty (in fin'ə tē), *n.* **1.** the fact of being infinite. **2.** space, time, or number without beginning or end. **3.** a very great number, extent, etc. —**in·fin'i·ties,** *pl.*

in·firm (in fũrm'), *adj.* not strong; weak or feeble [*infirm* from old age; *infirm* of purpose].

in·fir·ma·ry (in fũr'mə rē), *n.* a room or building for the care of people who are sick or injured, especially at a school or other institution. —**in·fir'ma·ries,** *pl.*

in·fir·mi·ty (in fũr'mə tē), *n.* weakness or sickness. —**in·fir'mi·ties,** *pl.*

in·flame (in flām'), *v.* **1.** to make excited or angry. **2.** to make greater or stronger [Our remarks just *inflamed* his rage.] **3.** to make or become hot, swollen, red, and sore [a wound *inflamed* by infection]. —**in·flamed',** *p.t. & p.p.*; **in·flam'ing,** *pr.p.*

in·flam·ma·ble (in flam'ə b'l), *adj.* **1.** quick to catch on fire; flammable [Oil is *inflammable.*] **2.** easily excited. —**in·flam'ma·bly,** *adv.*

in·flam·ma·tion (in'flə mā'shən), *n.* **1.** a hot, red, sore swelling in some part of the body, caused by disease or injury. **2.** an inflaming or being inflamed.

in·flam·ma·to·ry (in flam'ə tôr'ē), *adj.* **1.** likely to stir up anger or trouble [an *inflammatory* speech]. **2.** of or caused by inflammation.

in·flate (in flāt'), *v.* **1.** to swell out by putting in air or gas; expand [to *inflate* a balloon]. **2.** to make proud or happy [He is *inflated* by his victory.] **3.** to make greater or higher than normal [War *inflates* prices.] —**in·flat'ed,** *p.t. & p.p.*; **in·flat'ing,** *pr.p.*

in·fla·tion (in flā'shən), *n.* **1.** an inflating or being inflated. **2.** an increase in the amount of money in circulation. It makes the money less valuable and brings prices up.

in·fla·tion·ar·y (in flā'shən er'ē), *adj.* causing or caused by inflation.

in·flect (in flekt'), *v.* **1.** to change the tone or pitch of the voice. **2.** to change the form of a word by inflection.

in·flec·tion (in flek'shən), *n.* **1.** a change in the tone or pitch of the voice [A rising *inflection* at the end of a sentence often means a question.] **2.** a change in the form of a word to show case, number, gender, tense, comparison, etc. [The word "he" is changed by *inflection* to "him" or "his," depending on what case is needed.] —**in·flec'tion·al,** *adj.*

in·flex·i·ble (in flek'sə b'l), *adj.* not flexible; stiff, rigid, fixed, unyielding, etc. [*inflexible* steel rods; *inflexible* rules]. —**in·flex'i·bil'i·ty,** *n.* —**in·flex'i·bly,** *adv.*

in·flict (in flikt'), *v.* **1.** to cause as by striking; make suffer [to *inflict* a wound; to *inflict* pain]. **2.** to impose, or put on, as a penalty or tax. —**in·flic'tion,** *n.*

in·flow (in'flō), *n.* **1.** the act of flowing in. **2.** anything that flows in.

in·flu·ence (in'floo əns), *n.* **1.** the power to act on or affect persons or things [under the *influence* of a drug]. **2.** a person or thing that has this power [He's a good *influence* on the children.] **3.** power that comes from being rich or having a high position [man of *influence*]. —*v.* to have influence or power over [His advice *influenced* my decision.] —**in'flu·enced,** *p.t. & p.p.*; **in'flu·enc·ing,** *pr.p.*

in·flu·en·tial (in'floo en'shəl), *adj.* having or using influence, especially great influence.

in·flu·en·za (in'floo en'zə), *n.* a disease caused by a virus, like a bad cold only more serious.

in·flux (in'fluks), *n.* a coming in or pouring in without stopping [an *influx* of tourists].

in·fold (in fōld'), *v.* **1.** to wrap up; cover [to *infold* a baby in a blanket]. **2.** to hold close in the arms; embrace or hug. Also spelled **enfold.**

in·form (in fôrm'), *v.* **1.** to give facts to; tell [*Inform* us of your plans.] **2.** to give information or tell secrets that harm another; tattle [The spy *informed* against his friends.]

in·for·mal (in fôr'm'l), *adj.* **1.** not following fixed rules or forms; relaxed or familiar [an *informal* letter; an *informal* dinner]. **2.** of or in everyday talk; colloquial [*informal* speech]. —**in·for'mal·ly,** *adv.*

in·for·mal·i·ty (in'fôr mal'ə tē), *n.* **1.** the condition of being informal. **2.** an informal act. —**in'for·mal'i·ties,** *pl.*

in·form·ant (in fôr'mənt), *n.* a person who gives information or facts about something.

in·for·ma·tion (in'fər mā'shən), *n.* **1.** an informing or being informed [This is for your *information* only.] **2.** something told or facts learned; news or knowledge [An encyclopedia gives *information* about many things.] **3.** a person or service that answers certain questions [Call *information* for that phone number.]

in·form·a·tive (in fôr'mə tiv), *adj.* that gives information or facts [an *informative* talk].

in·form·er (in fôr'mər), *n.* a person who secretly accuses another, often for a reward.

in·frac·tion (in frak'shən), *n.* a breaking of a law, rule, or agreement; violation.

in·fra·red (in'frə red'), *adj.* describing rays of light that are just beyond red in the spectrum.

---

fat, āpe, cär, ten, ēven, hit, bīte, gō, hôrn, tool, book, up, fũr;
get, joy, yet, chin, she, thin, *th*en; zh = s in pleasure; ' as in able (ā'b'l);
ə = a in ago, e in agent, i in sanity, o in confess, u in focus.

They cannot be seen and they can go deep inside an object to produce heat.

in·fre·quent (in frē′kwənt), *adj.* not frequent; rare; uncommon. —**in·fre′quent·ly,** *adv.*

in·fringe (in frinj′), *v.* 1. to fail to obey; break or violate [to *infringe* a law]. 2. to break in; encroach [to *infringe* on the rights of others]. —**in·fringed′,** *p.t. & p.p.;* **in·fring′ing,** *pr.p.* —**in·fringe′ment,** *n.*

in·fu·ri·ate (in fyoor′i āt), *v.* to make very angry; enrage. —**in·fu′ri·at·ed,** *p.t. & p.p.;* **in·fu′ri·at·ing,** *pr.p.*

in·fuse (in fyooz′), *v.* 1. to put or pour in; instill [The teacher *infused* a desire to learn into the students.] 2. to fill or inspire [He *infused* us with hope.] 3. to soak or steep [Tea is made by *infusing* tea leaves in hot water.] —**in·fused′,** *p.t. & p.p.;* **in·fus′ing,** *pr.p.* —**in·fu·sion** (in fyoo′zhən), *n.*

-ing (ing), a suffix used to form the present participle of many verbs, as *flying.* It is also used as a suffix meaning: 1. the act of [A *washing* is the act of one who washes.] 2. something made by or used for [A *painting* is something made by a painter. *Carpeting* is material used for carpets.] 3. something that [A *covering* is something that covers.]

in·gen·ious (in jēn′yəs), *adj.* 1. clever or skillful, as at inventing things [an *ingenious* designer]. 2. made or done in a clever way [an *ingenious* plan]. —**in·gen′ious·ly,** *adv.*

in·ge·nu·i·ty (in′jə noo′ə tē *or* in′jə nyoo′ə tē), *n.* the quality of being ingenious; cleverness.

in·gen·u·ous (in jen′yoo əs), *adj.* frank or innocent in an open or natural way [The *ingenuous* girl believed that everyone loved her.] —**in·gen′u·ous·ly,** *adv.*

in·glo·ri·ous (in glôr′i əs), *adj.* 1. bringing shame; disgraceful [an *inglorious* defeat]. 2. without glory; not famous.

in·got (ing′gət), *n.* gold, steel, or other metal cast into a bar or other solid shape.

in·graft (in graft′), *v.* same as **engraft.**

in·grained (in grānd′), *adj.* that cannot be changed; firmly fixed [an *ingrained* habit].

in·grate (in′grāt), *n.* an ungrateful person.

in·gra·ti·ate (in grā′shi āt), *v.* to make oneself liked by doing things that please [He *ingratiated* himself by flattering her.] —**in·gra′ti·at·ed,** *p.t. & p.p.;* **in·gra′ti·at·ing,** *pr.p.*

ingot

in·grat·i·tude (in grat′ə tood *or* in grat′ə tyood), *n.* a lack of gratitude; ungratefulness.

in·gre·di·ent (in grē′di ənt), *n.* any of the things that a mixture is made of [Sugar is a basic *ingredient* of candy.]

in·gress (in′gres), *n.* 1. the act of entering or the right to enter [The guard refused us *ingress.*] 2. a place for entering; entrance.

in·grown (in′grōn), *adj.* that has grown inward, as a toenail that curves under at the sides.

in·hab·it (in hab′it), *v.* to live in or on; occupy [The island is not *inhabited.*]

in·hab·it·a·ble (in hab′i tə b'l), *adj.* that can be inhabited; fit to live in.

in·hab·it·ant (in hab′i tənt), *n.* a person or animal that lives in a certain place.

in·hal·ant (in hāl′ənt), *n.* a medicine that is breathed in.

in·hale (in hāl′), *v.* to breathe in; draw into the lungs, as air or tobacco smoke. —**in·haled′,** *p.t. & p.p.;* **in·hal′ing,** *pr.p.* —**in·ha·la·tion** (in′hə lā′shən), *n.* —**in·hal′er,** *n.*

in·har·mo·ni·ous (in′här mō′ni əs), *adj.* not harmonious; not blending well or getting along well together [*inharmonious* relations].

in·her·ent (in hir′ənt *or* in her′ənt), *adj.* being a natural part of someone or something; characteristic [Mary's *inherent* shyness kept her from speaking.] —**in·her′ent·ly,** *adv.*

in·her·it (in her′it), *v.* 1. to get from another when he dies; receive as an heir [John *inherited* his uncle's fortune.] 2. to have or get certain characteristics because one's parents or ancestors had them [Paul *inherited* his father's good looks.] —**in·her′i·tor,** *n.*

in·her·it·ance (in her′i təns), *n.* 1. the act or right of inheriting. 2. something inherited.

in·hib·it (in hib′it), *v.* to hold back or keep from some action, feeling, etc.; check [a boy *inhibited* by fear; drugs that *inhibit* sweating].

in·hi·bi·tion (in′hi bish′ən), *n.* 1. an inhibiting or being inhibited. 2. anything that inhibits; especially, some process in the mind that holds one back from some action, feeling, etc. [His *inhibitions* kept him from laughing.]

in·hos·pi·ta·ble (in häs′pi tə b'l), *adj.* not hospitable; not kind or generous to visitors.

in·hu·man (in hyoo′mən), *adj.* cruel or heartless. —**in·hu·man·i·ty** (in′hyoo man′ə tē), *n.*

in·im·i·cal (in im′i k'l), *adj.* 1. unfriendly; showing hate [*Inimical* acts led to war.] 2. acting against a thing; harmful [laws *inimical* to freedom; a climate *inimical* to health].

in·im·i·ta·ble (in im′i tə b'l), *adj.* that cannot be imitated or copied [Mark Twain's *inimitable* humor].

in·iq·ui·tous (in ik′wə təs), *adj.* very wicked or unjust.

in·iq·ui·ty (in ik′wə tē), *n.* 1. great wickedness or injustice. 2. a very wicked or unjust act. —**in·iq′ui·ties,** *pl.*

in·i·tial (i nish′əl), *adj.* of or at the beginning; first [the *initial* stage of a disease]. —*n.* the first letter of a name [John Paul Jones' *initials* were J.P.J.] —*v.* to mark with one's initials [He *initialed* the letter to show he had read it.] —**in·i′tialed** or **in·i′tialled,** *p.t. & p.p.;* **in·i′tial·ing** or **in·i′tial·ling,** *pr.p.*

in·i·tial·ly (i nish′əl ē), *adv.* at first; at the beginning.

in·i·ti·ate (i nish′i āt), *v.* 1. to begin to use, do, etc.; start [to *initiate* a new course of studies]. 2. to give the first knowledge or experience of something to [Father *initiated* me into the study of Latin.] 3. to take in as a member of a fraternity or club, with a special or secret ceremony. —*n.* (i nish′i it), a person who has just been initiated. —**in·i′ti·at·ed,** *p.t. & p.p.;* **in·i′ti·at·ing,** *pr.p.* —**in·i′ti·a′tion,** *n.* —**in·i′ti·a′tor,** *n.*

in·i·ti·a·tive (i nish′i ə tiv *or* i nish′ə tiv), *n.* **1.** the first step in bringing something about [John took the *initiative* in forming our club.] **2.** the ability to get things started or done without needing to be told what to do. **3.** the right of citizens to get a new law voted on by means of petitions calling for such a vote.

in·ject (in jekt′), *v.* **1.** to force a fluid in; especially, to force a liquid into some part of the body [The doctor *injected* the serum in Bob's arm with a hypodermic syringe.] **2.** to break in with [to *inject* a note of humor in a serious story]. —**in·jec′tion,** *n.* —**in·jec′tor,** *n.*

in·ju·di·cious (in′jōō dish′əs), *adj.* showing poor judgment; unwise.

in·junc·tion (in jungk′shən), *n.* an order or command; especially, an order from a court of law forbidding something or ordering something to be done.

in·jure (in′jər), *v.* to do harm to; hurt or damage [to *injure* a leg; to *injure* one's pride]. —**in′jured,** *p.t. & p.p.;* **in′jur·ing,** *pr.p.*

in·ju·ri·ous (in joor′i əs), *adj.* harmful or damaging [Lack of sleep is *injurious* to health.]

in·ju·ry (in′jər ē), *n.* harm or damage done to a person or thing [*injuries* received in a fall; *injury* to one's good name]. —**in′ju·ries,** *pl.*

in·jus·tice (in jus′tis), *n.* **1.** lack of justice or fairness [the *injustice* of imprisonment without a trial]. **2.** an unjust act; a wrong.

ink (ingk), *n.* a black or colored liquid or paste used for writing, printing, etc. —*v.* to cover, mark, or color with ink.

ink·horn (ingk′hôrn), *n.* an old kind of inkwell made of horn.

ink·ling (ingk′ling), *n.* a slight hint or suggestion; vague idea [I had no *inkling* of the facts.]

ink·well (ingk′wel), *n.* a container for holding ink, usually set into a desk.

ink·y (ing′kē), *adj.* **1.** like ink in color; black or dark. **2.** covered or marked with ink. —**ink′i·er,** *compar.;* **ink′i·est,** *superl.*

in·laid (in′lād *or* in lād′), *adj.* **1.** set into the surface in small pieces that form a smooth surface [a cherry table top with an *inlaid* walnut design]. **2.** having a surface made in this way [an *inlaid* floor].

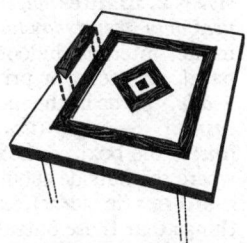
inlaid surface showing separate piece of inlay

in·land (in′lənd), *adj.* not on or near the coast or border; inside a country or region [*inland* waterways; *inland* commerce]. —*adv.* into or toward an inland area.

in-law (in′lô), *n.* a relative by marriage: *used only in everyday talk.*

in·lay (in lā′ *or* in′lā), *v.* **1.** to set into a surface to form a decoration. **2.** to decorate in this way [to *inlay* a wood panel with mother-of-pearl]. —*n.* (in′lā), **1.** inlaid decoration. **2.** a filling of gold, etc. for a tooth, made from a mold and cemented into place. —**in·laid′,** *p.t. & p.p.;* **in·lay′ing,** *pr.p.* —**in′lays,** *pl.*

in·let (in′let), *n.* **1.** a narrow strip of water running into land, as from a river, lake, or ocean. **2.** an opening or entrance.

in·mate (in′māt), *n.* a person kept in a prison, hospital, etc.

in·most (in′mōst), *adj.* same as **innermost.**

inn (in), *n.* a small hotel that has a tavern or restaurant. The word *inn* is now usually used only in the names of such places.

in·nate (i nāt′ *or* in′āt), *adj.* that seems to have been born in one; natural [an *innate* sense of humor].

in·ner (in′ər), *adj.* **1.** farther in; interior [the *inner* rooms of the palace]. **2.** more secret or private [one's *inner* feelings].

in·ner·most (in′ər mōst), *adj.* **1.** farthest in [the *innermost* chamber]. **2.** most secret or private [one's *innermost* thoughts].

in·ning (in′ing), *n.* **1.** a round of play in which both teams have a turn at bat. In baseball, there are usually nine innings, each team's turn being ended by three outs. **2.** a turn at bat. **3.** *often* **innings,** *pl.* the time a person or political party is in power.

inn·keep·er (in′kē′pər), *n.* a person who owns or manages an inn.

in·no·cence (in′ə s'ns), *n.* the condition of being innocent; freedom from guilt, trickery, harmfulness, etc.

in·no·cent (in′ə s'nt), *adj.* **1.** not guilty of some crime or sin; blameless [Another's confession proved him *innocent* of the robbery.] **2.** that knows no evil; simple [an *innocent* child]. **3.** that does no harm [*innocent* entertainment]. —*n.* an innocent person. —**in′no·cent·ly,** *adv.*

in·noc·u·ous (i näk′yōō əs), *adj.* that cannot harm or hurt; harmless. —**in·noc′u·ous·ly,** *adv.*

in·no·va·tion (in′ə vā′shən), *n.* a new device or a new way of doing something; change [Lighting by electricity was an *innovation* in 1890.]

in·no·va·tor (in′ə vā′tər), *n.* a person who makes changes or thinks of new ways to do things.

in·nu·en·do (in′yōō en′dō), *n.* a hint or sly remark, especially one that suggests something bad about someone. —**in′nu·en′does,** *pl.*

in·nu·mer·a·ble (i nōō′mər ə b'l *or* i nyōō′mər ə b'l), *adj.* more than can be counted; countless.

in·oc·u·late (in äk′yoo lāt), *v.* to inject into the body a serum or vaccine that will cause a mild form of a disease. In this way the body is able to build up its ability to fight off that disease later. —**in·oc′u·lat·ed,** *p.t. & p.p.;* **in·oc′u·lat·ing,** *pr.p.* —**in·oc′u·la′tion,** *n.*

in·of·fen·sive (in′ə fen′siv), *adj.* not offensive; causing no trouble; harmless.

in·op·er·a·tive (in äp′ə rā′tiv), *adj.* not working; not in effect [an *inoperative* law].

in·op·por·tune (in äp′ər tōōn′ *or* in′äp ər-tyōōn′), *adj.* happening at the wrong time; not suitable [an *inopportune* time to call].

in·or·di·nate (in ôr′d'n it), *adj.* too great or too many; excessive. —**in·or′di·nate·ly,** *adv.*

in·or·gan·ic (in′ôr gan′ik), *adj.* made up of matter that is not animal or vegetable; not living [Minerals are *inorganic*.]

in·put (in′poot), *n.* what is put in, as electric power put into a machine to make it work, information fed into a computer to be stored, etc.

in·quest (in′kwest), *n.* an investigation made by a jury or coroner in order to decide whether or not someone's death was the result of a crime.

in·quire (in kwīr′), *v.* to ask a question; ask about in order to learn [The student *inquired* about his grade. He *inquired* where we were going.] —**in·quired′,** *p.t. & p.p.;* **in·quir′-ing,** *pr.p.* —**in·quir′er,** *n.*

in·quir·y (in kwīr′ē *or* in′kwə rē), *n.* **1.** the act of inquiring. **2.** an investigation or examination. **3.** a question; query. —**in·quir′ies,** *pl.*

in·qui·si·tion (in′kwə zish′ən), *n.* **1.** the act of inquiring; investigation. **2. Inquisition,** a court for finding and punishing heretics, set up by the Roman Catholic Church in the 13th century and lasting until 1820. **3.** strict control by those in power over the beliefs of others.

in·quis·i·tive (in kwiz′ə tiv), *adj.* asking many questions; curious; especially, too curious about others' affairs. —**in·quis′i·tive·ly,** *adv.*

in·quis·i·tor (in kwiz′ə tər), *n.* **1.** a person who makes an investigation; investigator. **2. In-quisitor,** a member of the Inquisition.

in·road (in′rōd), *n.* **1.** a sudden raid or attack. **2.** harm or damage [Eating too much will make *inroads* on your health.]

in·sane (in sān′), *adj.* **1.** mentally ill; not sane: *no longer much used except as a term in law.* **2.** of insane people. **3.** very foolish; senseless. —**in-sane′ly,** *adv.*

in·san·i·ty (in san′ə tē), *n.* **1.** the condition of being insane, or mentally ill. **2.** a very foolish action or belief. —**in·san′i·ties,** *pl.*

in·sa·ti·a·ble (in sā′shə b'l), *adj.* always wanting more; never satisfied; greedy [*insatiable* hunger]. —**in·sa′ti·a·bly,** *adv.*

in·scribe (in skrīb′), *v.* **1.** to write, print, or engrave [an old tombstone *inscribed* with a verse]. **2.** to add to a list [Harold's name was *inscribed* on the Honor Roll.] **3.** to fix firmly in the mind. —**in·scribed′,** *p.t. & p.p.;* **in·scrib′ing,** *pr.p.*

in·scrip·tion (in skrip′shən), *n.* **1.** the act of inscribing. **2.** something printed, written, or engraved, as on a coin or monument.

in·scru·ta·ble (in skrōō′tə b'l), *adj.* that cannot be understood; strange; mysterious [an *in-scrutable* expression]. —**in·scru′ta·bly,** *adv.*

in·sect (in′sekt), *n.* **1.** a small animal with six legs, usually two pairs of wings, and a head, thorax, and abdomen [Flies, ants, wasps, and mosquitoes are *insects*.] **2.** any small animal somewhat like this, as the spider, centipede, and louse: *this is a popular but not a scientific use.*

in·sec·ti·cide (in sek′tə sīd), *n.* any poison used to kill insects.

in·se·cure (in′si kyoor′), *adj.* **1.** not secure or safe; dangerous; not dependable [an *insecure* mountain ledge; an *insecure* partnership]. **2.** not feeling safe or confident; anxious [She was *inse-cure* in her new job.] —**in′se·cure′ly,** *adv.* —**in·se·cur·i·ty** (in′si kyoor′ə tē), *n.*

in·sen·sate (in sen′sāt), *adj.* **1.** not having feelings, because not living; inanimate [*insensate* rocks]. **2.** without reason or good sense; stupid [*insensate* fury]. **3.** without feeling for others; cold; unmoved [an *insensate* judge].

in·sen·si·ble (in sen′sə b'l), *adj.* **1.** not able to notice or feel [His frozen fingers were *insensible* to pain.] **2.** unconscious [She fainted and lay *insensible*.] **3.** not noticing or not concerned about; indifferent [Factory workers become *in-sensible* to noise.] **4.** so small or slight that it is not easily seen or felt [the *insensible* movement of the hour hand]. —**in·sen′si·bil′i·ty,** *n.* —**in-sen′si·bly,** *adv.*

in·sen·si·tive (in sen′sə tiv), *adj.* not sensitive; not affected by [*insensitive* to music].

in·sep·a·ra·ble (in sep′ər ə b'l), *adj.* that cannot be separated or parted [*inseparable* friends]. —**in·sep′a·ra·bly,** *adv.*

in·sert (in sûrt′), *v.* to put or fit something into something else [to *insert* a hand in the pocket]. —*n.* (in′sərt), something inserted or to be inserted [an *insert* of lace in a dress].

in·ser·tion (in sûr′shən), *n.* **1.** the act of inserting. **2.** something inserted, as an advertisement in a newspaper.

in·set (in′set), *n.* something inserted or set in, as a small map set inside the border of a larger one. —*v.* (in set′), to insert; set in. —**in·set′,** *p.t. & p.p.;* **in·set′ting,** *pr.p.*

in·shore (in′shôr *or* in shôr′), *adv. & adj.* toward the shore or near the shore.

in·side (in′sīd′), *n.* **1.** the side or part that is within; interior [Wash the windows on the *in-side*.] **2. insides,** *pl.* the organs within the body: *used only in everyday talk.* —*adj.* **1.** on or in the inside; internal; indoor [*inside* work; an *inside* page]. **2.** secret or private [*inside* information]. —*adv.* on or in the inside; within [They played *inside*.] —*prep.* (*usually* in sīd′), within; in [*inside* the box]. —**inside out,** with the inside where the outside should be.

in·sid·er (in sīd′ər), *n.* a person who knows things that those outside his group cannot know.

in·sid·i·ous (in sid′i əs), *adj.* **1.** dishonest, sly, or tricky [an *insidious* plot]. **2.** more dangerous than it seems to be [an *insidious* disease]. —**in-sid′i·ous·ly,** *adv.*

in·sight (in′sīt), *n.* **1.** the ability to understand people and things as they really are. **2.** a clear understanding of some problem or idea.

in·sig·ni·a (in sig′ni ə), *n.pl.* the special marks or badges of some organization, rank, etc. [A general wears stars as *insignia* of his rank.]

in·sig·nif·i·cant (in′sig nif′ə kənt), *adj.* not important; of little value [*insignificant* details]. **—in′sig·nif′i·cance,** *n.*

in·sin·cere (in′sin sir′), *adj.* not sincere; not meaning what one says or does. **—in′sin·cere′ly,** *adv.* **—in·sin·cer·i·ty** (in′sin ser′ə tē), *n.*

in·sin·u·ate (in sin′yoo āt), *v.* **1.** to get in slowly and in an indirect way, so as to be hardly noticed [to *insinuate* oneself into a group]. **2.** to hint at something without actually saying it [Are you *insinuating* that I lied?] **—in·sin′u·at·ed,** *p.t. & p.p.;* **in·sin′u·at·ing,** *pr.p.* **—in·sin′u·a′tion,** *n.*

in·sip·id (in sip′id), *adj.* **1.** having no flavor; tasteless. **2.** not interesting; dull [*insipid* talk].

in·sist (in sist′), *v.* **1.** to stick strongly to a belief [I *insist* that I saw her there.] **2.** to demand strongly [I *insist* that you come.]

in·sist·ent (in sis′tənt), *adj.* **1.** insisting or demanding [*insistent* pleas]. **2.** that forces and keeps one's attention [an *insistent* pain]. **—in·sist′ence,** *n.* **—in·sist′ent·ly,** *adv.*

in·snare (in sner′), *v.* same as **ensnare.**

in·sole (in′sōl), *n.* the inside sole of a shoe, especially an extra one put in for comfort.

in·so·lent (in′sə lənt), *adj.* not having or showing the proper respect; rude. **—in′so·lence,** *n.* **—in′so·lent·ly,** *adv.*

in·sol·u·ble (in säl′yoob′l), *adj.* **1.** that cannot be solved [an *insoluble* problem]. **2.** that cannot be dissolved [an *insoluble* powder].

in·sol·vent (in säl′vənt), *adj.* not able to pay one's debts; bankrupt. **—in·sol′ven·cy,** *n.*

in·som·ni·a (in säm′ni ə), *n.* the condition of being unable to sleep; sleeplessness.

in·so·much (in′sō much′), *adv.* **1.** to such a degree; so [He worked fast, *insomuch* that he finished first.] **2.** inasmuch; because.

in·spect (in spekt′), *v.* **1.** to look at carefully; examine [*Inspect* the house before buying it.] **2.** to examine officially; review [The major will *inspect* Company B.] **—in·spec′tion,** *n.*

in·spec·tor (in spek′tər), *n.* **1.** a person who inspects, as in a factory. **2.** a police officer who ranks next below a superintendent.

in·spi·ra·tion (in′spə rā′shən), *n.* **1.** an inspiring or being inspired [Our cheers gave *inspiration* to the team.] **2.** something that inspires thought or action [The ocean was an *inspiration* to the artist.] **3.** an inspired idea, action, etc. [He has an *inspiration* for a novel.] **4.** a breathing in; inhaling. **—in′spi·ra′tion·al,** *adj.*

in·spire (in spīr′), *v.* **1.** to cause, urge, or influence to do something [The sunset *inspired* her to write a poem.] **2.** to cause to have a certain feeling or thought [Praise *inspires* us with confidence.] **3.** to arouse or bring about [Her kindness *inspired* our love.] **4.** to do or make as if guided by some higher power [The Bible is an *inspired* book.] **5.** to breathe in; inhale. **—inspired′,** *p.t. & p.p.;* **in·spir′ing,** *pr.p.*

in·spir·it (in spir′it), *v.* to give spirit or courage to; cheer [*inspiriting* news].

in·sta·bil·i·ty (in′stə bil′ə tē), *n.* the condition of being unstable; lack of firmness or steadiness.

in·stall (in stôl′), *v.* **1.** to place in an office or position with a ceremony [We saw the new governor *installed*.] **2.** to fix in position for use [to *install* a gas stove]. **3.** to put or settle in a place [John *installed* himself in the hammock and fell asleep.] **—in·stal·la·tion** (in′stə lā′shən), *n.*

in·stall·ment or **in·stal·ment** (in stôl′mənt), *n.* **1.** a sum of money that a person pays at regular times until he has paid the total amount that he owes [I paid the debt in nine monthly *installments*.] **2.** one of several parts that appear at different times, as of a serial story in a magazine. **3.** an installing or being installed.

in·stance (in′stəns), *n.* **1.** an example; something that shows or proves [This gift is another *instance* of his generosity.] **2.** an occasion or case [The fine in the first *instance* is $10.]

in·stant (in′stənt), *n.* **1.** a very short time; moment [Wait just an *instant*.] **2.** a particular moment [At that *instant* the bell rang.] **—adj.** **1.** with no delay; immediate [an *instant* response]. **2.** calling for fast action; urgent [an *instant* need for a new law]. **3.** that can be prepared quickly, as by adding water [*instant* coffee]. **4.** of the present month [your letter of the 8th *instant*].

in·stan·ta·ne·ous (in′stən tā′ni əs), *adj.* done or happening in an instant [an *instantaneous* effect]. **—in′stan·ta′ne·ous·ly,** *adv.*

in·stant·ly (in′stənt lē), *adv.* with no delay.

in·stead (in sted′), *adv.* in place of the other; as a substitute [If you have no cream, use milk *instead*.] **—instead of,** in place of.

in·step (in′step), *n.* **1.** the upper part of the foot at the arch. **2.** the part of a shoe or stocking that covers this.

in·sti·gate (in′stə gāt), *v.* to stir up or urge on, or bring about by urging [to *instigate* a plot]. **—in′sti·gat·ed,** *p.t. & p.p.;* **in′sti·gat·ing,** *pr.p.* **—in′sti·ga′tion,** *n.* **—in′sti·ga′tor,** *n.*

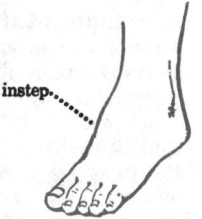

in·still or **in·stil** (in stil′), *v.* **1.** to put in drop by drop. **2.** to put an idea or feeling into someone's mind in a slow but sure way [He *instilled* honesty in his children.] —**in·stilled′**, *p.t. & p.p.*; **in·still′ing**, *pr.p.*

in·stinct (in′stingkt), *n.* **1.** a way of acting, feeling, etc. that is natural to an animal from birth [the *instinct* of birds for building nests]. **2.** a natural ability or knack; talent [an *instinct* for saying the right thing]. —*adj.* filled with [a look *instinct* with pity].

in·stinc·tive (in stingk′tiv), *adj.* caused or done by instinct; seeming to be natural to one since birth [an *instinctive* fear of the dark]. —**in·stinc′tive·ly**, *adv.*

in·sti·tute (in′stə tōōt *or* in′stə tyōōt), *v.* **1.** to set up; bring into being; establish [The modern Olympic games were *instituted* in 1896.] **2.** to start; enter upon [The police *instituted* a search.] —*n.* a school or organization for some special study or work, as in education, science, art, etc. —**in′sti·tut·ed**, *p.t. & p.p.*; **in′sti·tut·ing**, *pr.p.*

in·sti·tu·tion (in′stə tōō′shən *or* in′stə tyōō′shən), *n.* **1.** an instituting or being instituted. **2.** an established law, custom, practice, etc. [the *institution* of marriage]. **3.** a school, church, hospital, prison, or other organization for doing some special work. —**in′sti·tu′tion·al**, *adj.*

in·struct (in strukt′), *v.* **1.** to teach or train [Mother *instructed* me in algebra.] **2.** to order or direct [Father *instructed* me to be quiet.] **3.** to give certain facts, rules, etc. to; inform [The judge *instructed* the jury.]

in·struc·tion (in struk′shən), *n.* **1.** the act of teaching; education [Socrates spent his life in the *instruction* of others.] **2.** something taught; lesson [swimming *instruction*]. **3. instructions,** *pl.* orders or directions [*instructions* for a test].

in·struc·tive (in struk′tiv), *adj.* instructing; giving knowledge [an *instructive* book].

in·struc·tor (in struk′tər), *n.* **1.** a teacher. **2.** a college teacher of the lowest rank.

in·stru·ment (in′stroo mənt), *n.* **1.** a person or thing used to get something done; means [People once believed in witches as *instruments* of the Devil.] **2.** a tool or other device for doing very exact work, for scientific purposes, etc. [surgical *instruments*]. **3.** a device used in making musical sound, as a flute, violin, piano, etc. **4.** a legal paper by means of which some action is carried out, as a deed or will.

in·stru·men·tal (in′stroo men′t'l), *adj.* **1.** serving as a means; helpful [The librarian was *instrumental* in finding this book for me.] **2.** played on or written for musical instruments [Bach wrote both *instrumental* and vocal music.]

in·stru·men·tal·i·ty (in′stroo men tal′ə tē), *n.* the thing by which something is done; means; agency. —**in′stru·men·tal′i·ties**, *pl.*

in·sub·or·di·nate (in′sə bôr′d'n it), *adj.* refusing to obey. —**in′sub·or′di·na′tion**, *n.*

in·sub·stan·tial (in′səb stan′shəl), *adj.* **1.** not solid or firm; flimsy. **2.** not real; imaginary [the *insubstantial* dream world].

in·suf·fer·a·ble (in suf′ər ə b'l), *adj.* hard to put up with; unbearable [an *insufferable* bore]. —**in·suf′fer·a·bly**, *adv.*

in·suf·fi·cien·cy (in′sə fish′ən sē), *n.* a lack of something needed; inadequacy.

in·suf·fi·cient (in′sə fish′ənt), *adj.* not enough; inadequate. —**in′suf·fi′cient·ly**, *adv.*

in·su·lar (in′sə lər *or* in′syoo lər), *adj.* **1.** of or like an island or people living on an island. **2.** narrow-minded; prejudiced [*insular* thinking].

in·su·late (in′sə lāt), *v.* **1.** to separate or cover with a material that keeps electricity, heat, or sound from escaping [electric wire *insulated* with rubber; a furnace *insulated* with asbestos]. **2.** to set apart; keep away from others. —**in′su·lat·ed**, *p.t. & p.p.*; **in′su·lat·ing**, *pr.p.*

in·su·la·tion (in′sə lā′shən), *n.* **1.** an insulating or being insulated. **2.** any material used to insulate.

in·su·la·tor (in′sə lā′tər), *n.* anything that insulates; especially, a device as of glass or porcelain, for insulating electric wires.

insulators

in·su·lin (in′sə lin), *n.* a hormone of the pancreas that helps the body use sugars and starches. People who have diabetes get regular injections of insulin taken from animals.

in·sult (in sult′), *v.* to say or do something on purpose that hurts a person's feelings or pride [He *insulted* me by ignoring my question.] —*n.* (in′sult), an insulting act or remark.

in·su·per·a·ble (in sōō′pər ə b'l *or* in syoo′pər ə b'l), *adj.* that cannot be overcome [*insuperable* difficulties].

in·sup·port·a·ble (in′sə pôr′tə b'l), *adj.* that cannot be borne or put up with.

in·sur·ance (in shoor′əns), *n.* **1.** an insuring against loss by fire, death, accident, etc. **2.** a contract by which a company guarantees a person that a certain sum of money will be paid in case of loss by fire, death, etc. The insured person makes regular payments for this guarantee. **3.** the regular sum paid for insurance; premium. **4.** the amount for which something is insured [How much *insurance* does he have on his car?] **5.** the business of insuring against loss.

in·sure (in shoor′), *v.* **1.** to make sure; guarantee [He went early to *insure* getting a good seat.] **2.** to make safe; protect [Care *insures* one against error.] **3.** to get or give insurance on [She *insured* her jewels against theft. Will your company *insure* my house against storms?] —**in·sured′**, *p.t. & p.p.*; **in·sur′ing**, *pr.p.*

in·sur·gent (in sur′jənt), *adj.* rising up in revolt; rebelling. —*n.* a rebel. —**in·sur′gence**, *n.*

in·sur·mount·a·ble (in′sər moun′tə b'l), *adj.* that cannot be overcome [*insurmountable* tasks].

in·sur·rec·tion (in′sə rek′shən), *n.* a revolt or rebellion. —**in′sur·rec′tion·ist**, *n.*

in·tact (in takt′), *adj.* kept or left whole; with nothing missing or injured; in one piece [He inherited the stamp collection *intact*.]

in·take (in′tāk), *n.* **1.** a taking in [A gasp is a sharp *intake* of breath.] **2.** the place in a pipe or channel where water, air, or gas is taken in. **3.** the amount or thing that is taken in [Old Mr. Jones' *intake* of food is small.]

in·tan·gi·ble (in tan′jə b'l), *adj.* that cannot be touched or grasped [Good will is an *intangible* asset in a business.]

in·te·ger (in′tə jər), *n.* a whole number; a number that is not a fraction [2, 83, and 145 are *integers*.]

in·te·gral (in′tə grəl), *adj.* **1.** necessary to something to make it complete; essential [Wheels are *integral* parts of automobiles.] **2.** having to do with integers.

in·te·grate (in′tə grāt), *v.* **1.** to bring together into a whole; unite or unify [to *integrate* the study of history with the study of English]. **2.** to do away with the segregation of races, as in schools. —**in′te·grat·ed,** *p.t. & p.p.;* **in′te·grat·ing,** *pr.p.* —**in′te·gra′tion,** *n.*

in·teg·ri·ty (in teg′rə tē), *n.* **1.** the quality of being honest and trustworthy; honesty or uprightness [A man of *integrity* never takes a bribe.] **2.** the condition of being whole, not broken into parts [Wars destroyed the territorial *integrity* of Germany.]

in·teg·u·ment (in teg′yoo mənt), *n.* an outer covering, as a skin, shell, or rind.

in·tel·lect (in′tə lekt), *n.* **1.** the ability to understand ideas and to think; understanding. **2.** high intelligence; great mental power. **3.** a person of high intelligence.

in·tel·lec·tu·al (in′tə lek′choo əl), *adj.* **1.** of the intellect or understanding [one's *intellectual* powers]. **2.** needing intelligence and clear thinking [Chess is an *intellectual* game.] **3.** having or showing high intelligence. —*n.* a person who does intellectual work or has intellectual interests. —**in′tel·lec′tu·al·ly,** *adv.*

in·tel·li·gence (in tel′ə jəns), *n.* **1.** the ability to learn and understand, or to solve problems [Man has much greater *intelligence* than any other animal.] **2.** news or information [secret *intelligence* about the enemy's plans]. **3.** the gathering of secret information [He works in *intelligence* for the State Department.]

in·tel·li·gent (in tel′ə jənt), *adj.* having or showing intelligence, especially high intelligence. —**in·tel′li·gent·ly,** *adv.*

in·tel·li·gi·ble (in tel′i jə b'l), *adj.* that can be understood; clear [an *intelligible* explanation]. —**in·tel′li·gi·bly,** *adv.*

in·tem·per·ance (in tem′pər əns), *n.* **1.** a lack of control or of self-control. **2.** the drinking of too much alcoholic liquor.

in·tem·per·ate (in tem′pər it), *adj.* **1.** having or showing a lack of self-control; not moderate; excessive [*intemperate* language]. **2.** harsh or severe [the *intemperate* climate of Antarctica]. **3.** drinking too much alcoholic liquor.

in·tend (in tend′), *v.* **1.** to have in mind; plan [I *intend* to leave tomorrow.] **2.** to set apart; mean [The cake is *intended* for the party.]

in·tend·ed (in ten′did), *adj.* **1.** meant or planned [We set off on our *intended* trip.] **2.** expected or future [his *intended* bride]. —*n.* the person whom one has agreed to marry: *used only in everyday talk.*

in·tense (in tens′), *adj.* **1.** very strong or deep; very great; extreme [an *intense* light; *intense* joy]. **2.** feeling things strongly and acting with force [an *intense* person]. —**in·tense′ly,** *adv.*

in·ten·si·fy (in ten′sə fī), *v.* to make or become more intense; increase [to *intensify* one's efforts]. —**in·ten′si·fied,** *p.t. & p.p.;* **in·ten′si·fy·ing,** *pr.p.* —**in·ten′si·fi·ca′tion,** *n.*

in·ten·si·ty (in ten′sə tē), *n.* **1.** the quality of being intense; great strength or force [the *intensity* of the battle; to speak with *intensity*]. **2.** the amount of a force, as of heat, light, or sound per unit of area, volume, etc.

in·ten·sive (in ten′siv), *adj.* **1.** complete and in great detail; deep and thorough [an *intensive* study of a problem]. **2.** giving force; emphasizing [In "I myself saw him," "myself" is an *intensive* pronoun.] —**in·ten′sive·ly,** *adv.*

in·tent (in tent′), *adj.* **1.** having the mind or attention fixed; concentrating [He was *intent* on the book before him.] **2.** firmly fixed or directed [an *intent* look]. **3.** firmly decided; determined [He is *intent* on saving money.] —*n.* something intended; purpose; intention [It was not my *intent* to harm you.] —**in·tent′ly,** *adv.*

in·ten·tion (in ten′shən), *n.* anything intended or planned; purpose [She borrowed the chair with the *intention* of returning it.]

in·ten·tion·al (in ten′shən 'l), *adj.* done on purpose; intended. —**in·ten′tion·al·ly,** *adv.*

in·ter (in tur′), *v.* to put into a grave; bury. —**in·terred′,** *p.t. & p.p.;* **in·ter′ring,** *pr.p.*

inter-, a prefix meaning: **1.** between or among [An *intercontinental* missile can be fired between continents.] **2.** with or on each other; together [*Interacting* parts act on each other.]

in·ter·act (in tər akt′), *v.* to act on each other. —**in′ter·ac′tion,** *n.*

in·ter·breed (in tər brēd′), *v.* to breed together different kinds of animals or plants [to *interbreed* a lion with a tiger]. *For principal parts see* **breed.**

in·ter·cede (in tər sēd′), *v.* **1.** to ask or plead in behalf of another [The prisoner's wife *interceded* with the king for his release.] **2.** to interfere in order to bring about an agreement [to *intercede* in another's quarrel]. —**in·ter·ced′ed,** *p.t. & p.p.;* **in·ter·ced′ing,** *pr.p.*

in·ter·cept (in tər sept′), *v.* **1.** to stop or seize on the way; cut off [to *intercept* a message]. **2.** to

fat,   āpe,   cär,   ten,   ēven,   hit,   bīte,   gō,   hôrn,   tōōl,   book,   up,   fur;
get,   joy,   yet,   chin,   she,   thin,   then;   zh = s in pleasure;   ′ as in able (ā′b'l);
ə = a in ago,   e in agent.   i in sanity,   o in confess,   u in focus.

stop or prevent [to *intercept* the escape of a thief].
—**in·ter·cep·tion,** *n.*

in·ter·ces·sion (in'tər sesh'ən), *n.* the act of interceding. —**in·ter·ces·sor,** *n.*

in·ter·change (in tər chānj'), *v.* **1.** to put two things in one another's place; change about [If you *interchange* the middle letters of "clam," you get "calm."] **2.** to give and receive in exchange [to *interchange* ideas]. —*n.* (in'tər-chānj), **1.** the act of interchanging. **2.** a place on a freeway where traffic can come in or go out. —**in·ter·changed',** *p.t. & p.p.;* **in·ter·chang'·ing,** *pr.p.*

in·ter·change·a·ble (in'tər chān'jə b'l), *adj.* that can be put or used in place of one another [The tires on an automobile are *interchangeable.*]

in·ter·col·le·gi·ate (in'tər kə lē'jit), *adj.* between colleges [*intercollegiate* sports].

in·ter·com·mu·ni·cate (in'tər kə myōō'ni-kāt), *v.* to communicate with each other. —**in·ter·com·mu·ni·cat·ed,** *p.t. & p.p.;* **in'·ter·com·mu·ni·cat·ing,** *pr.p.* —**in'·ter·com·mu·ni·ca'·tion,** *n.*

in·ter·con·nect (in'tər kə nekt'), *v.* to connect with each other. —**in'·ter·con·nec'·tion,** *n.*

in·ter·con·ti·nen·tal (in'tər kän'tə nen't'l), *adj.* between or among continents.

in·ter·course (in'tər kôrs), *n.* **1.** dealings between people or countries; exchange of products, ideas, etc. [Airplanes have made *intercourse* between nations more rapid.] **2.** sexual union.

in·ter·de·pend·ent (in'tər di pen'dənt), *adj.* depending on each other. —**in'·ter·de·pend'·ence,** *n.*

in·ter·dict (in tər dikt'), *v.* **1.** to forbid or prohibit. **2.** in the Roman Catholic Church, to refuse to allow to take part in certain church services. —*n.* (in'tər dikt), the act of interdicting; prohibition.

in·ter·est (in'tər ist *or* in'trist), *n.* **1.** a feeling of wanting to know, learn, see, or take part in something; curiosity or concern [an *interest* in mathematics; an *interest* in seeing justice done]. **2.** the power of causing this feeling [The movie held no *interest* for me.] **3.** something that causes this feeling [Her main *interest* is dancing.] **4.** a share in something [to buy an *interest* in a business]. **5.** what is good for one; benefit; advantage [He has our best *interests* at heart.] **6.** a group of people taking part or having a share in the same business or industry [the steel *interest*]. **7.** money paid for the use of money; also, the rate at which it is paid [He had to pay 5% *interest* on the loan.] —*v.* **1.** to stir up the interest or curiosity of [His new novel *interests* me.] **2.** to cause to have an interest or take part in; involve [Can I *interest* you in a game of tennis?] —**in the interest of,** for the sake of.

in·ter·est·ing (in'tər is ting *or* in'tris ting), *adj.* stirring up one's interest; exciting attention. —**in'·ter·est·ing·ly,** *adv.*

in·ter·fere (in tər fir'), *v.* **1.** to meddle in another's affairs [His parents seldom *interfere* in his plans.] **2.** to come between for some purpose

[The teacher *interfered* in the boys' fight.] **3.** to come against; get in the way of; conflict [Noise *interferes* with his work.] —**in·ter·fered',** *p.t. & p.p.;* **in·ter·fer'·ing,** *pr.p.*

in·ter·fer·ence (in'tər fir'əns), *n.* an interfering, as the act of blocking players in football to clear the way for the ball carrier, or the act of illegally keeping an opponent from catching the ball.

illegal interference

in·ter·im (in'tər im), *n.* the time between; meantime [It took a month to get the book, and in the *interim* he lost interest.] —*adj.* during an interim; temporary [an *interim* mayor].

in·te·ri·or (in tir'i ər), *n.* **1.** the inside or inner part [an old building with a modern *interior*]. **2.** the inland part of a country. **3.** the internal affairs of a country [The U.S. Department of the *Interior* has charge of national parks, public lands, conservation, etc.] —*adj.* of the interior; inside; inner [an *interior* wall].

interj., abbreviation for **interjection.**

in·ter·ject (in tər jekt'), *v.* to interrupt with; throw in; insert [to *interject* a question].

in·ter·jec·tion (in'tər jek'shən), *n.* **1.** the act of interjecting. **2.** a word or phrase that is exclaimed to show strong feeling; exclamation ["Oh!" and "Well!" are *interjections.*] **3.** a remark, question, etc. interjected.

in·ter·lace (in tər lās'), *v.* to join or become joined as by weaving or lacing together [a chair seat made by *interlacing* strips of cane]. —**in·ter·laced',** *p.t. & p.p.;* **in·ter·lac'·ing,** *pr.p.*

interlaced hands

in·ter·line (in tər līn'), *v.* to write between the lines of a book, letter, etc. —**in·ter·lined',** *p.t. & p.p.;* **in·ter·lin'·ing,** *pr.p.*

in·ter·line (in'tər līn), *v.* to put another lining inside the regular lining, as of a coat. —**in'·ter·lined,** *p.t. & p.p.;* **in'·ter·lin·ing,** *pr.p.*

in·ter·lock (in tər läk'), *v.* to lock or fit tightly together [an *interlocking* jigsaw puzzle].

in·ter·lop·er (in'tər lōp'ər), *n.* a person who meddles in others' affairs; intruder.

in·ter·lude (in'tər lōōd), *n.* **1.** anything that fills time between two happenings [Recess is an *interlude* between classes.] **2.** a short scene or skit put on between the acts of a play. **3.** a piece of music played between the parts of a song, the acts of a play, etc.

in·ter·mar·ry (in'tər mar'ē), *v.* to marry a person of a different tribe, race, religion, etc. —**in'·ter·mar'·ried,** *p.t. & p.p.;* **in'·ter·mar'·ry·ing,** *pr.p.* —**in·ter·mar·riage** (in'tər-mar'ij), *n.*

in·ter·me·di·ar·y (in'tər mē'di er'ē), *n.* a person who deals with each of two sides in making arrangements between them; go-between. —*adj.*

1. intermediate. **2.** acting as an intermediary. —in·ter·me′di·ar′ies, *pl.*

in·ter·me·di·ate (in′tər mē′di it), *adj.* coming between two other things or happenings; in the middle [an *intermediate* stage of development]. —*n.* anything intermediate.

in·ter·ment (in tŭr′mənt), *n.* a burial.

in·ter·mez·zo (in′tər met′sō), *n.* a short piece of music; especially, one played between scenes or acts of an opera. —in′tər·mez′zos or in·ter·mez·zi (in′tər met′sē), *pl.*

in·ter·mi·na·ble (in tŭr′mi nə b'l), *adj.* that lasts or seems to last forever; endless [an *interminable* talk]. —in·ter′mi·na·bly, *adv.*

in·ter·min·gle (in′tər ming′g'l), *v.* to mix together; blend; mingle. —in′ter·min′gled, *p.t. & p.p.;* in′ter·min′gling, *pr.p.*

in·ter·mis·sion (in′tər mish′ən), *n.* a stopping for a time; rest or pause [a ten-minute *intermission* between the first two acts of the play; to work all day without *intermission*.]

in·ter·mit·tent (in′tər mit′'nt), *adj.* stopping and starting again from time to time; recurring [Malaria causes an *intermittent* fever.] —in′ter·mit′tent·ly, *adv.*

in·ter·mix (in tər miks′), *v.* to mix together; blend. —in′ter·mix′ture, *n.*

in·tern or in·terne (in′tərn), *n.* a doctor who is finishing his training, after graduation from medical school, by assisting other doctors in a hospital. —*v.* to serve as an intern.

in·tern (in tŭrn′), *v.* to keep from leaving a country, as by putting in special camps [to *intern* aliens in time of war].

in·ter·nal (in tŭr′n'l), *adj.* **1.** of or on the inside; inner [*internal* bleeding]. **2.** within a country; domestic [*Internal* revenue is money that a government gets by taxing income, luxuries, etc.] —in·ter′nal·ly, *adv.*

in·ter·nal-com·bus·tion engine (in tŭr′n'l kəm bus′chən), an engine used in automobiles, airplanes, etc. in which the power is built up inside the cylinders by exploding a mixture of air and some fuel, such as gasoline or oil.

in·ter·na·tion·al (in′tər nash′ən 'l), *adj.* **1.** between or among nations [*international* trade]. **2.** having to do with the relations between nations [an *international* court]. **3.** for the use of all nations [*international* waters]. —in′ter·na′tion·al·ly, *adv.*

in·ter·na·tion·al·ize (in′tər nash′ən 'l īz), *v.* to put under the control of a number of nations, or open for the use of all nations [The Suez Canal was *internationalized* in 1888.] —in′ter·na′tion·al·ized, *p.t. & p.p.;* in′ter·na′tion·al·iz·ing, *pr.p.*

in·ter·ne·cine (in′tər nē′sin), *adj.* causing many deaths, especially on both sides in a conflict; destructive [*internecine* warfare].

in·ter·plan·e·tar·y (in′tər plan′ə ter′ē), *adj.* between planets [*interplanetary* travel].

in·ter·play (in′tər plā), *n.* action of things on each other; interaction.

in·ter·po·late (in tŭr′pə lāt), *v.* to add words or sections in a book or other piece of writing, usually so as to change the meaning. —in·ter′po·lat·ed, *p.t. & p.p.;* in·ter′po·lat·ing, *pr.p.* —in·ter′po·la′tion, *n.*

in·ter·pose (in tər pōz′), *v.* **1.** to interrupt with [to *interpose* a question]. **2.** to place between or come between [Our view is cut off by an *interposing* wall.] **3.** to come between in order to settle an argument; intervene. —in·ter·posed′, *p.t. & p.p.;* in·ter·pos′ing, *pr.p.* —in·ter·po·si·tion (in′tər pə zish′ən), *n.*

in·ter·pret (in tŭr′prit), *v.* **1.** to explain the meaning of; make clear [to *interpret* a poem]. **2.** to translate [Our guide *interpreted* for us what the natives said.] **3.** to understand in one's own way; construe; take [I *interpreted* his smile as a sign of approval.] **4.** to show one's own understanding of a piece of music, a role in a play, etc. by the way one performs it. —in·ter′pre·tive, *adj.*

in·ter·pre·ta·tion (in tŭr′pri tā′shən), *n.* the act or way of interpreting; explanation; meaning [the *interpretation* of dreams; a pianist's *interpretation* of a sonata].

in·ter·pret·er (in tŭr′pri tər), *n.* a person who interprets, especially one whose work is translating things said in another language.

in·ter·ra·cial (in′tər rā′shəl), *adj.* between, among, or for persons of different races.

in·ter·reg·num (in′tər reg′nəm), *n.* **1.** the time between two reigns, when a country has no ruler. **2.** any break or pause; interval.

in·ter·re·lat·ed (in′tər ri lā′tid), *adj.* closely connected with each other or one another. —in′ter·re·la′tion, *n.*

in·ter·ro·gate (in ter′ə gāt), *v.* to ask questions of in examining [to *interrogate* a witness]. —in·ter′ro·gat·ed, *p.t. & p.p.;* in·ter′ro·gat·ing, *pr.p.* —in·ter′ro·ga′tion, *n.* —in·ter′ro·ga′tor, *n.*

interrogation mark, same as question mark.

in·ter·rog·a·tive (in′tə räg′ə tiv), *adj.* that asks or seems to ask a question [an *interrogative* glance]. —*n.* a word used in asking questions [“When?” and “where?” are *interrogatives*.]

in·ter·rupt (in tə rupt′), *v.* **1.** to break in on talk, action, etc. or on a person talking, working, etc. [We *interrupt* this program with a news bulletin. Don't *interrupt* your mother!] **2.** to get in the way of [to *interrupt* a view].

in·ter·rup·tion (in′tə rup′shən), *n.* **1.** an interrupting or being interrupted. **2.** anything that interrupts. **3.** a break, pause, or halt.

in·ter·scho·las·tic (in′tər skə las′tik), *adj.* between or among schools [*interscholastic* sports].

in·ter·sect (in tər sekt′), *v.* **1.** to divide into parts by passing through or across [A river *intersects* the plain.] **2.** to cross each other [The lines *intersect* to form right angles.]

in·ter·sec·tion (in'tər sek'shən), *n.* **1.** an intersecting. **2.** the place where two lines, streets, etc. meet or cross.

in·ter·sperse (in-tər spŭrs'), *v.* **1.** to put here and there; scatter [Sprigs of mistletoe were *interspersed* in the holly wreath.] **2.** to

intersection of two streets

vary with things scattered here and there [black hair *interspersed* with gray]. —**in·ter·spersed'**, *p.t. & p.p.;* **in·ter·spers·ing**, *pr.p.*

in·ter·state (in'tər stāt), *adj.* between or among the states of a federal government [*interstate* commerce].

in·ter·stice (in tŭr'stis), *n.* a small space between things; crevice; crack [the *interstices* in wickerwork].

in·ter·twine (in tər twīn'), *v.* to twist together [Strands of hemp are *intertwined* to make rope.] —**in·ter·twined'**, *p.t. & p.p.;* **in·ter·twin·ing**, *pr.p.*

in·ter·ur·ban (in'tər ŭr'bən), *adj.* between cities or towns [an *interurban* bus].

in·ter·val (in'tər v'l), *n.* **1.** space or time between things [an *interval* of three feet between desks]. **2.** the difference in pitch between two musical tones. —**at intervals, 1.** once in a while. **2.** here and there.

in·ter·vene (in tər vēn'), *v.* **1.** to come or be between [Two days *intervened* between semesters.] **2.** to come in so as to help settle, stop, etc. [to *intervene* in a dispute, a war, etc.]. **3.** to get in the way [If nothing *intervenes*, I'll arrive on Monday.] —**in·ter·vened'**, *p.t. & p.p.;* **in·ter·ven·ing**, *pr.p.*

in·ter·ven·tion (in'tər ven'shən), *n.* **1.** an intervening. **2.** interference, as by one country in the affairs of another.

in·ter·view (in'tər vyōō), *n.* **1.** a meeting of one person with another to talk about something [an *interview* with an employer for a job]. **2.** a meeting between a reporter and a person from whom he wants to get news, opinions, etc. for a newspaper story. —*v.* to have an interview with.

in·ter·weave (in tər wēv'), *v.* **1.** to weave together. **2.** to mingle or mix together. *For principal parts see* **weave.**

in·tes·tate (in tes'tāt), *adj.* not having made a will [He died *intestate*.]

in·tes·ti·nal (in tes'ti n'l), *adj.* of or in the intestines [*intestinal* flu].

in·tes·tine (in tes'tin), *n.* usually **intestines**, *pl.* the tube through which food passes from the stomach. The long, narrow part with

intestines

many coils is called the **small intestine.** The shorter and thicker part is called the **large intestine.** Food is digested in the intestines as well as in the stomach.

in·thrall (in thrôl'), *v.* same as **enthrall.**

in·ti·ma·cy (in'tə mə sē), *n.* the condition of being intimate; closeness, as in friendship.

in·ti·mate (in'tə mit), *adj.* **1.** most private or personal [one's *intimate* thoughts]. **2.** very close or familiar [an *intimate* friend]. **3.** deep and thorough [an *intimate* knowledge of physics]. —*n.* an intimate friend. —**in'ti·mate·ly**, *adv.*

in·ti·mate (in'tə māt), *v.* **1.** to hint; suggest without openly saying [He only *intimated* what he felt.] **2.** to make known; announce. —**in'ti·mat·ed**, *p.t. & p.p.;* **in'ti·mat·ing**, *pr.p.* —**in'ti·ma'tion**, *n.*

in·tim·i·date (in tim'ə dāt), *v.* to make afraid; force to do something by frightening. —**in·tim'i·dat·ed**, *p.t. & p.p.;* **in·tim'i·dat·ing**, *pr.p.* —**in·tim'i·da'tion**, *n.*

in·to (in'tōō *or* in'tə), *prep.* **1.** to the inside of [to go *into* a house]. **2.** to the form, condition, etc. of [He got *into* trouble. The land was turned *into* a park.]

in·tol·er·a·ble (in täl'ər ə b'l), *adj.* too painful, cruel, etc. to bear. —**in·tol'er·a·bly**, *adv.*

in·tol·er·ant (in täl'ər ənt), *adj.* not tolerant; especially, not willing to put up with ideas, beliefs, etc. that are different from one's own. —**intolerant of,** not willing or able to bear. —**in·tol'er·ance**, *n.*

in·to·na·tion (in'tō nā'shən), *n.* **1.** an intoning. **2.** the way the voice rises and falls in pitch in speaking.

in·tone (in tōn'), *v.* to speak or recite in a singing tone or chant [to *intone* a prayer]. —**in·toned'**, *p.t. & p.p.;* **in·ton·ing**, *pr.p.*

in·tox·i·cant (in täk'sə kənt), *n.* something that intoxicates, as alcoholic liquor.

in·tox·i·cate (in täk'sə kāt), *v.* **1.** to make drunk as alcoholic liquor does. **2.** to make wild with excitement or happiness [He was *intoxicated* by his new wealth.] —**in·tox'i·cat·ed**, *p.t. & p.p.;* **in·tox'i·cat·ing**, *pr.p.*

in·tox·i·ca·tion (in täk'sə kā'shən), *n.* **1.** drunkenness. **2.** wild excitement of the mind. **3.** poisoning of the body, as by a drug.

in·trac·ta·ble (in trak'tə b'l), *adj.* hard to control; stubborn [an *intractable* prisoner].

in·tra·mu·ral (in'trə myoor'əl), *adj.* between or among members of the same school, college, etc. [*intramural* games].

in·tran·si·tive (in tran'sə tiv), *adj.* not transitive; describing a verb that does not take a direct object [In "He seems to be better," "seems" and "be" are *intransitive* verbs.]

in·tra·ve·nous (in'trə vē'nəs), *adj.* directly into a vein [an *intravenous* injection].

in·treat (in trēt'), *v.* same as **entreat.**

in·trench (in trench'), *v.* same as **entrench.**

in·trep·id (in trep'id), *adj.* not afraid; very brave. —**in·tre·pid·i·ty** (in'trə pid'ə tē), *n.*

in·tri·ca·cy (in'tri kə sē), *n.* **1.** the quality of being intricate [the *intricacy* of a design]. **2.**

something that is intricate [a plot full of *intrica-cies*]. —**in'tri·ca·cies,** *pl.*

in·tri·cate (in'tri kit), *adj.* hard to follow or understand because full of details and complicated [an *intricate* pattern]. —**in'tri·cate·ly,** *adv.*

in·trigue (in trēg'), *v.* **1.** to plot or plan in a secret or sneaky way; scheme [The nobles *intrigued* against the king.] **2.** to stir up the interest of; make curious; fascinate [Her beauty *intrigued* me.] *n.* **1.** a sneaky plot; scheme. **2.** a secret love affair. —**in·trigued',** *p.t. & p.p.;* **in·tri'guing,** *pr.p.*

in·trin·sic (in trin'sik), *adj.* that has to do with what a thing really is; real; essential [The *intrinsic* worth of a man cannot be measured by his wealth.] —**in·trin'si·cal·ly,** *adv.*

in·tro·duce (in trə dōos' *or* in trə dyōos'), *v.* **1.** to make known; make acquainted; present [Please *introduce* me to your friend.] **2.** to bring into use; make popular or common [The war *introduced* the jeep.] **3.** to make familiar with something; give an experience to [Jane's father *introduced* her to the fun of swimming.] **4.** to add or bring in [The clown *introduces* humor into the play.] **5.** to present or bring forward [to *introduce* a bill into Congress]. **6.** to put in; insert [to *introduce* a cotton swab in the outer ear]. —**in·tro·duced',** *p.t. & p.p.;* **in·tro·duc'ing,** *pr.p.*

in·tro·duc·tion (in'trə duk'shən), *n.* **1.** the act of introducing, especially of making one person known to another or others. **2.** the part at the beginning of a book, speech, etc. leading up to or explaining what follows. **3.** anything that has been introduced, or brought into use [Television is a fairly recent *introduction*.]

in·tro·duc·to·ry (in'trə duk'tər ē), *adj.* that introduces or begins something; preliminary [an *introductory* course in science].

in·tro·spec·tion (in'trə spek'shən), *n.* a looking into and examining one's own thoughts or feelings. —**in'tro·spec'tive,** *adj.*

in·tro·vert (in'trə vûrt), *n.* a person who has a greater interest in himself and his own thoughts than in the people and things around him. —**in'tro·vert·ed,** *adj.*

in·trude (in trōōd'), *v.* to force oneself or one's thoughts upon others without being asked or wanted. —**in·trud'ed,** *p.t. & p.p.;* **in·trud'ing,** *pr.p.* —**in·trud'er,** *n.*

in·tru·sion (in trōō'zhən), *n.* the act of intruding. —**in·tru·sive** (in trōō'siv), *adj.*

in·trust (in trust'), *v.* same as **entrust.**

in·tu·i·tion (in'tōō ish'ən *or* in'tyōō ish'ən), *n.* a knowing of something without actually thinking it out or studying; instant understanding [to sense danger by a flash of *intuition*].

in·tu·i·tive (in tōō'i tiv *or* in tyōō'i tiv), *adj.* knowing or known by intuition [an *intuitive* person; an *intuitive* sense of right and wrong]. —**in·tu'i·tive·ly,** *adv.*

in·un·date (in'ən dāt), *v.* to cover as with an overflow of water; flood or overwhelm [Creek water *inundated* the road. Angry letters *inundated* the newspaper.] —**in'un·dat·ed,** *p.t. & p.p.;* **in'un·dat·ing,** *pr.p.* —**in'un·da'tion,** *n.*

in·ure (in yoor'), *v.* to make used to something hard or painful; accustom [His term as mayor has *inured* him to criticism.] —**in·ured',** *p.t. & p.p.;* **in·ur'ing,** *pr.p.*

in·vade (in vād'), *v.* **1.** to enter with an army in order to conquer [Caesar *invaded* Gaul.] **2.** to crowd into; throng [Crowds *invaded* the new hotel.] **3.** to break in on; intrude upon; violate [Reporters *invaded* his privacy by asking personal questions.] —**in·vad'ed,** *p.t. & p.p.;* **in·vad'ing,** *pr.p.* —**in·vad'er,** *n.*

in·va·lid (in'və lid), *n.* a person who is sick or injured, especially one who is likely to be so for some time. —*adj.* **1.** not well; weak and sick [an *invalid* parent]. **2.** of or for invalids [an *invalid* home]. —*v.* to send back from military service because of an injury or illness [The major was *invalided* home from Japan.]

in·val·id (in val'id), *adj.* not valid; having no force or value [an *invalid* reason].

in·val·i·date (in val'ə dāt), *v.* to make invalid; take away the force or value of; void [The new will *invalidates* the old one.] —**in·val'i·dat·ed,** *p.t. & p.p.;* **in·val'i·dat·ing,** *pr.p.*

in·val·u·a·ble (in val'yōō ə b'l), *adj.* having value too great to measure; priceless; precious.

in·var·i·a·ble (in ver'i ə b'l), *adj.* not changing; always the same; constant; uniform [an *invariable* rule]. —**in·var'i·a·bly,** *adv.*

in·va·sion (in vā'zhən), *n.* the act of invading; an attacking, intruding, etc.

in·vec·tive (in vek'tiv), *n.* an attacking in words; strong criticism, insults, curses, etc.

in·veigh (in vā'), *v.* to attack strongly in words; talk or write bitterly against.

in·vei·gle (in vē'g'l *or* in vā'g'l), *v.* to trick or lure into doing something [Tom Sawyer *inveigled* his friends into painting the fence.] —**in·vei'gled,** *p.t. & p.p.;* **in·vei'gling,** *pr.p.*

in·vent (in vent'), *v.* **1.** to think out or make something that did not exist before; be the first to do or make [Bell *invented* the telephone.] **2.** to plan in the mind; think up [to *invent* excuses].

in·ven·tion (in ven'shən), *n.* **1.** the act of inventing [the *invention* of television]. **2.** something invented [the many *inventions* of Edison]. **3.** the ability to invent [This novelist shows much *invention* in telling his story.] **4.** a false story.

in·ven·tive (in ven'tiv), *adj.* **1.** skilled in inventing [an *inventive* genius]. **2.** of invention [*inventive* powers].

in·ven·tor (in ven'tər), *n.* a person who invents.

in·ven·to·ry (in'vən tôr'ē), *n.* **1.** a complete list of goods or property [The store takes *inventory* of its stock twice a year.] **2.** the stock of goods on hand [Because of fewer sales this year, dealers

---

fat, āpe, cär, ten, ēven, hit, bīte, gō, hôrn, tōol, book, up, fûr;
get, joy, yet, chin, she, thin, *th*en; zh = s in pleasure; ' as in able (ā'b'l);
ə = a in ago, e in agent, i in sanity, o in confess, u in focus.

have high *inventories*.] —*v.* to make an inventory or list of. —**in′ven·to′ries,** *pl.* —**in′ven·to′ried,** *p.t. & p.p.;* **in′ven·to′ry·ing,** *pr.p.*

in·verse (in vûrs′ *or* in′vûrs), *adj.* exactly opposite in order, direction, etc.; reversed [The number 237 in *inverse* order becomes 732.] —*n.* the exact opposite; reverse.

in·ver·sion (in vûr′zhən), *n.* **1.** an inverting or being inverted ["Said he" is an *inversion* of "he said."] **2.** something inverted.

in·vert (in vûrt′), *v.* **1.** to turn upside down [The image that falls on the film in a camera is *inverted*.] **2.** to change the order of; turn around.

in·ver·te·brate (in vûr′tə brit *or* in vûr′tə·brāt), *adj.* having no backbone. —*n.* an animal that has no backbone, or spinal column [Worms, insects, clams, crabs, etc. are *invertebrates*.]

in·vest (in vest′), *v.* **1.** to use or lend money for some business, property, stocks, etc. in order to get a profit. **2.** to spend in order to get something in return [to *invest* much time in a project]. **3.** to put in office with a ceremony; install. **4.** to give some power or right to [a regent *invested* with the power to rule]. **5.** to cover or surround. —**in·ves′tor,** *n.*

in·ves·ti·gate (in ves′tə gāt), *v.* to search into so as to learn the facts; examine in detail [to *investigate* an accident]. —**in·ves′ti·gat·ed,** *p.t. & p.p.;* **in·ves′ti·gat·ing,** *pr.p.* —**in·ves′ti·ga′tion,** *n.* —**in·ves′ti·ga·tor,** *n.*

in·vest·ment (in vest′mənt), *n.* **1.** an investing of money, time, etc. to get something in return. **2.** the amount of money invested. **3.** something in which money is invested.

in·vet·er·ate (in vet′ər it), *adj.* **1.** firmly fixed over a long period of time [an *inveterate* habit]. **2.** doing a certain thing by habit; habitual [an *inveterate* liar].

in·vid·i·ous (in vid′i əs), *adj.* likely to cause bad feeling, as an unfair comparison between things that are not really equal.

in·vig·or·ate (in vig′ə rāt), *v.* to fill with vigor or energy. —**in·vig′or·at·ed,** *p.t. & p.p.;* **in·vig′or·at·ing,** *pr.p.* —**in·vig′or·a′tion,** *n.*

in·vin·ci·ble (in vin′sə b′l), *adj.* that cannot be beaten or overcome [an *invincible* army]. —**in·vin′ci·bil′i·ty,** *n.* —**in·vin′ci·bly,** *adv.*

in·vi·o·la·ble (in vī′ə lə b′l), *adj.* that should not be violated or broken; sacred [an *inviolable* promise]. —**in·vi′o·la·bil′i·ty,** *n.*

in·vi·o·late (in vī′ə lit *or* in vī′ə lāt), *adj.* not violated or broken; kept sacred.

in·vis·i·ble (in viz′ə b′l), *adj.* that cannot be seen; not visible [Clouds made the moon *invisible*. Oxygen is *invisible*. Most body cells are *invisible* except under a microscope.] —**in·vis′i·bil′i·ty,** *n.* —**in·vis′i·bly,** *adv.*

in·vi·ta·tion (in′və tā′shən), *n.* **1.** the act of inviting. **2.** the spoken or written form by which a person is invited.

in·vite (in vīt′), *v.* **1.** to ask in a polite way to come somewhere or do something; ask to be one's guest [They *invited* her to dine with them.] **2.** to ask for [After his talk he *invited* questions from the audience.] **3.** to bring on; give the chance for;

attract [His sudden wealth *invited* gossip.] —**in·vit′ed,** *p.t. & p.p.;* **in·vit′ing,** *pr.p.*

in·vit·ing (in vīt′ing), *adj.* tempting or attractive [an *inviting* display of goods].

in·vo·ca·tion (in′və kā′shən), *n.* **1.** a prayer calling on God, a god, etc. for blessing or help. **2.** magic words used in calling up evil spirits.

in·voice (in′vois), *n.* a list of the goods shipped to a buyer, giving the prices and amounts of the goods sent. —*v.* to list in an invoice. —**in′voiced,** *p.t. & p.p.;* **in′voic·ing,** *pr.p.*

in·voke (in vōk′), *v.* **1.** to call on for blessing or help, as in a prayer [to *invoke* God; to *invoke* the muse of poetry; to *invoke* the power of the law]. **2.** to plead for or demand [to *invoke* aid]. **3.** to call forth by magic [to *invoke* evil spirits]. —**in·voked′,** *p.t. & p.p.;* **in·vok′ing,** *pr.p.*

in·vol·un·tar·y (in väl′ən ter′ē), *adj.* **1.** not done by choice; unwilling [the *involuntary* labor of prisoners]. **2.** done or doing without thinking about it [Sneezing is *involuntary*.] —**in·vol′un·tar′i·ly,** *adv.*

in·volve (in välv′), *v.* **1.** to have as a part of it; include or require [Becoming a doctor *involves* years of study.] **2.** to take up the attention of; absorb [*involved* in work]. **3.** to draw into trouble or difficulty [Repairs on his house *involved* him in debt.] **4.** to make difficult or mixed-up; complicate [The more he spoke, the more *involved* his plan became.] —**in·volved′,** *p.t. & p.p.;* **in·volv′ing,** *pr.p.*

in·vul·ner·a·ble (in vul′nər ə b′l), *adj.* that cannot be hurt, destroyed, etc. [Is any place *invulnerable* to modern missiles?]

in·ward (in′wərd), *adj.* **1.** being on the inside; inner. **2.** toward the inside [an *inward* push on the door]. **3.** of the mind or feelings [He felt an *inward* calm.] —*adv.* toward the inside. —**in′ward·ly,** *adv.*

in·wrought (in′rôt), *adj.* having a design worked in [a silver plate *inwrought* with gold].

i·o·dine (ī′ə dīn *or* ī′ə din), *n.* a mineral that is a chemical element, in the form of dark crystals. The crystals are dissolved in alcohol and used as an antiseptic.

i·on (ī′ən), *n.* an atom or a group of atoms that has an electrical charge. A salt dissolved in water breaks down into ions.

-ion, a suffix meaning: **1.** the act or condition of [*Translation* is the act of translating.] **2.** the result of [A *correction* is the result of correcting.]

I·on·ic (ī än′ik), *adj.* describing a style of Greek architecture in which the columns have decorations like scrolls at the top.

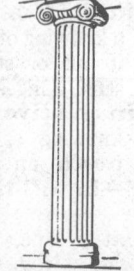

i·o·ta (ī ō′tə), *n.* **1.** the ninth letter of the Greek alphabet, like our letter "i". **2.** a very small amount; bit [The story hasn't an *iota* of truth in it.]

IOU or **I.O.U.** (ī′ō yoo′), **1.** I owe you. **2.** a paper with these letters on it, signed by someone to show that he owes money to someone else.

Ionic column

I·o·wa (ī′ə wə), *n.* a State in the north central part of the United States: abbreviated **Ia.**

IQ or **I.Q.,** abbreviation for **intelligence quotient,** a number that is supposed to show whether a person's intelligence is average, below average, or above average, according to a test he is given.

ir-, a prefix meaning "not." It is the form of **in-** used before words beginning with *r*, as *irrational.*

I·ran (ē rän′ *or* i ran′), *n.* a country in south-western Asia: its older name is **Persia.** —**I·ra·ni·an** (ī rā′ni ən), *adj. & n.*

I·raq (ē räk′ *or* i rak′), *n.* a country in south-western Asia: its older name is **Mesopotamia.** —**I·ra·qi** (ē rä′kē), *adj. & n.*

i·ras·ci·ble (i ras′ə b'l), *adj.* easily made angry; quick-tempered; irritable.

i·rate (ī′rāt *or* ī rāt′), *adj.* angry. —**i′rate·ly,** *adv.*

IRBM, intermediate range ballistic missile.

ire (īr), *n.* anger; wrath. —**ire′ful,** *adj.*

Ire·land (īr′lənd), *n.* a large island west of Great Britain. An independent country, the Republic of Ireland, takes up most of the island, but a small part in the north (**Northern Ireland**) is in the United Kingdom.

ir·i·des·cent (ir′ə des′'nt), *adj.* showing many colors that are constantly changing [Soap bubbles are often *iridescent.*] —**ir′i·des′cence,** *n.*

i·ris (ī′ris), *n.* **1.** the colored part of the eye, around the pupil. *See the picture for* eye. **2.** a plant with long leaves like blades and showy flowers: also called **flag. 3.** a rainbow.

I·rish (ī′rish), *adj.* of Ireland, its people, etc. —*n.* **1.** the people of Ireland: *used with a plural verb.* **2.** the Celtic language used by some of the Irish. **3.** the English dialect of Ireland.

iris

I·rish·man (ī′rish mən), *n.* a person, especially a man, born or living in Ireland. —**I′rish·men,** *pl.*

Irish potato, the common white potato.

Irish Sea, the part of the Atlantic Ocean between Ireland and England.

I·rish·wom·an (ī′rish woom′ən), *n.* a woman born or living in Ireland. —**I′rish·wom′en,** *pl.*

irk (ũrk), *v.* to annoy or tire out.

irk·some (ũrk′səm), *adj.* tiresome or annoying [*irksome* duties].

i·ron (ī′ərn), *n.* **1.** a strong metal that is a chemical element. Iron can be molded or stretched into various shapes after being heated. It is much used in the form of steel in buildings, automobiles, etc. **2.** something made of iron. **3.** a device made of iron or other metal and having a flat, smooth bottom. It is heated and used for pressing clothes, etc. **4. irons,** *pl.* iron shackles or chains. **5.** great strength or power [a will of *iron*]. —*adj.* **1.** of or made of iron [*iron* bars]. **2.** like iron; strong [*iron* determination]. —*v.* to press clothes, etc. with a hot iron. —**iron out,** to smooth out; get rid of [to *iron out* a problem]. —**strike while the iron is hot,** to act while there is a good opportunity to do so.

i·ron·clad (ī′ərn klad), *adj.* **1.** covered or protected with iron. **2.** hard to change or break [an *ironclad* agreement].

iron curtain, secrecy and censorship that keep a country cut off from the rest of the world.

i·ron·i·cal (ī rän′i k'l) or **i·ron·ic** (ī rän′ik), *adj.* **1.** meaning just the opposite of what is said [He was *ironical* when he called their mansion "a humble home."] **2.** opposite to what is or might be expected [It was *ironical* that the lifeguard drowned.] —**i·ron′i·cal·ly,** *adv.*

ironing board, see the picture for **board.**

iron lung, a large machine used to force air into and out of the lungs, as of a person who has had polio and cannot breathe by himself.

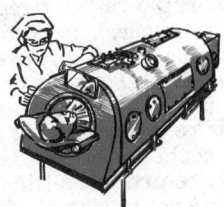
iron lung

i·ro·ny (ī′rə nē), *n.* **1.** a way of being amusing or sarcastic by saying exactly the opposite of what one means [Using *irony*, she called the stupid plan "very clever."] **2.** an event or a result that is the opposite of what might be expected [That the fire station burned down was an *irony*.] —**i′ro·nies,** *pl.*

Ir·o·quois (ir′ə kwoi *or* ir′ə kwoiz), *n.* a member of a group of Indian tribes that lived in western and northern New York. —**Ir′o·quois,** *pl.*

ir·ra·di·ate (i rā′di āt), *v.* **1.** to send X rays, ultraviolet rays, etc. on, as in treating a disease. **2.** to give out; spread [to *irradiate* joy]. **3.** to shine or shine upon; make or be bright [Stars *irradiate* the night.] —**ir·ra′di·at·ed,** *p.t. & p.p.;* **ir·ra′di·at·ing,** *pr.p.*

ir·ra·tion·al (i rash′ən 'l), *adj.* that does not make sense; not rational; absurd [an *irrational* fear of the dark]. —**ir·ra′tion·al·ly,** *adv.*

ir·re·claim·a·ble (ir′i klām′ə b'l), *adj.* that cannot be reclaimed [an *irreclaimable* swamp].

ir·rec·on·cil·a·ble (i rek′ən sīl′ə b'l), *adj.* that cannot be reconciled or made to agree; incompatible [*irreconcilable* foes].

ir·re·cov·er·a·ble (ir′i kuv′ər ə b'l), *adj.* that cannot be recovered, regained, or got back [an *irrecoverable* loss].

ir·re·deem·a·ble (ir′i dēm′ə b'l), *adj.* that cannot be redeemed, saved, exchanged, made better, etc. [*irredeemable* Confederate money; an *irredeemable* sinner].

ir·re·duc·i·ble (ir′i dōōs′ə b'l *or* ir′i dyōōs′ə b'l), *adj.* that cannot be reduced or made smaller.

ir·ref·u·ta·ble (i ref′yoo tə b′l *or* ir′ri fyōō′tə-b′l), *adj.* that cannot be denied or proved wrong [an *irrefutable* claim].

ir·reg·u·lar (i reg′yoo lər), *adj.* **1.** not regular; not like the usual rule, way, or custom [an *irregular* diet]. **2.** not straight, even, or the same throughout [an *irregular* design]. **3.** not changing its forms in the usual way ["Go" is an *irregular* verb.] —**ir·reg′u·lar·ly,** *adv.*

ir·reg·u·lar·i·ty (i reg′yoo lar′ə tē), *n.* **1.** the condition of being irregular. **2.** something irregular. —**ir·reg′u·lar′i·ties,** *pl.*

ir·rel·e·vant (i rel′ə vənt), *adj.* having nothing to do with the subject; not to the point [His remark about the candidate's religion was *irrelevant* to the issues of the campaign.] —**ir·rel′e·vance,** *n.* —**ir·rel′e·vant·ly,** *adv.*

ir·re·li·gious (ir′i lij′əs), *adj.* not religious.

ir·re·me·di·a·ble (ir′i mē′di ə b′l), *adj.* that cannot be remedied, cured, or corrected.

ir·rep·a·ra·ble (i rep′ər ə b′l), *adj.* that cannot be repaired, mended, or put right [*irreparable* damage]. —**ir·rep′a·ra·bly,** *adv.*

ir·re·place·a·ble (ir′i plās′ə b′l), *adj.* that cannot be replaced [an *irreplaceable* friend].

ir·re·press·i·ble (ir′i pres′ə b′l), *adj.* that cannot be held back or controlled [*irrepressible* tears].

ir·re·proach·a·ble (ir′i prōch′ə b′l), *adj.* that cannot be blamed or criticized; blameless.

ir·re·sist·i·ble (ir′i zis′tə b′l), *adj.* that cannot be resisted; too strong to fight against [an *irresistible* force]. —**ir′re·sist′i·bly,** *adv.*

ir·res·o·lute (i rez′ə lōōt), *adj.* not able to decide or make up one's mind; hesitating. —**ir·res·o·lu·tion** (i rez′ə lōō′shən), *n.*

ir·re·spec·tive (ir′i spek′tiv), *adj.* regardless [All citizens may vote, *irrespective* of sex.]

ir·re·spon·si·ble (ir′i spän′sə b′l), *adj.* not responsible; not showing a sense of duty; doing as one pleases. —**ir′re·spon′si·bly,** *adv.*

ir·re·triev·a·ble (ir′i trēv′ə b′l), *adj.* that cannot be recovered or brought back.

ir·rev·er·ent (i rev′ər ənt), *adj.* not reverent; not showing respect for religion or for things that deserve respect. —**ir·rev′er·ence,** *n.*

ir·re·vers·i·ble (ir′i vûr′sə b′l), *adj.* that cannot be reversed or changed [the *irreversible* decision of the judge].

ir·rev·o·ca·ble (i rev′ə kə b′l), *adj.* that cannot be called back, undone, or changed [the *irrevocable* past]. —**ir·rev′o·ca·bly,** *adv.*

ir·ri·gate (ir′ə gāt), *v.* **1.** to water by means of canals, ditches, or pipes [to *irrigate* desert land so it can bear crops]. **2.** to wash out with a flow of water or other liquid [The doctor *irrigated* the wound.] —**ir′ri·gat·ed,** *p.t. & p.p.;* **ir′ri·gat·ing,** *pr.p.* —**ir′ri·ga′tion,** *n.*

irrigation ditch

ir·ri·ta·ble (ir′ə tə b′l), *adj.* easily annoyed or made angry. —**ir·ri·ta·bil·i·ty** (ir′ə tə bil′ə tē), *n.* —**ir′ri·ta·bly,** *adv.*

ir·ri·tant (ir′ə tənt), *adj.* that irritates. —*n.* something that irritates.

ir·ri·tate (ir′ə tāt), *v.* **1.** to bother or annoy; make impatient or angry [Jack's bragging *irritates* his schoolmates.] **2.** to make red, raw, sore, etc. [Harsh soap *irritates* her skin.] —**ir′ri·tat·ed,** *p.t. & p.p.;* **ir′ri·tat·ing,** *pr.p.* —**ir′ri·ta′tion,** *n.*

ir·rup·tion (i rup′shən), *n.* a bursting in or rushing in with wild force [the *irruption* of flood waters into the valley].

Ir·ving, Washington (ûr′ving), 1783–1859; United States writer.

is (iz), the form of **be** showing the present time with singular nouns and with *he, she,* or *it.* —**as is,** as it is now; without change.

is., abbreviation for **island.**

I·saac (ī′zək), *n.* in the Bible, the son of Abraham and the father of Jacob and Esau.

I·sa·iah (ī zā′ə), *n.* **1.** a Hebrew prophet in the Bible. **2.** a book of the Old Testament with his teachings.

Iscariot, *n.* see **Judas Iscariot.**

-ise (īz), same as **-ize,** mainly in British use.

-ish (ish), a suffix meaning: **1.** of or belonging to [A *Swedish* citizen is a citizen of Sweden.] **2.** like or like that of [A *boyish* man is like a boy.] **3.** somewhat; rather [*Warmish* weather is rather warm weather.]

i·sin·glass (ī′z′n glas′), *n.* **1.** a jelly made from fish bladders. It is used in glues, etc. **2.** mica, especially in thin sheets.

I·sis (ī′sis), *n.* a goddess of ancient Egypt.

Is·lam (is′ləm *or* is läm′), *n.* **1.** the Moslem religion, founded by Mohammed, in which God is called Allah. **2.** all the Moslems, or all the countries in which mostly Moslems live. —**Is·lam·ic** (is lam′ik *or* is läm′ik), *adj.*

is·land (ī′lənd), *n.* **1.** a piece of land smaller than a continent and surrounded by water. **2.** any place set apart from what surrounds it [The oasis was an *island* of green in the desert.]

is·land·er (ī′lən dər), *n.* a person born or living on an island.

isle (īl), *n.* an island, usually a small island.

is·let (ī′lit), *n.* a very small island.

-ism (iz′m), a suffix meaning: **1.** doctrine, theory, or belief [*Liberalism* is a belief in liberal ideas.] **2.** the act or result of [*Criticism* is the act of or result of criticizing.] **3.** the condition, conduct, or qualities of [*Patriotism* is the conduct of a patriot.] **4.** an example of [A *witticism* is an example of a witty saying.]

is·n't (iz′'nt), is not.

i·so·bar (ī′sə bär), *n.* a line on a weather map connecting places where the air pressure is the same.

i·so·late (ī′sə lāt), *v.* to set apart from others; place alone; seclude [The snowstorm *isolated* the village.] —**i′so·lat·ed,** *p.t. & p.p.;* **i′so·lat·ing,** *pr.p.* —**i′so·la′tion,** *n.*

isobars

i·so·la·tion·ist (ī′sə lā′shən ist), *n.* a person who believes his country should not take part in international affairs. —**i′so·la′tion·ism,** *n.*

i·sos·ce·les triangle (ī säs′ə lēz), a triangle that has two equal sides.

i·so·therm (ī′sə thûrm), *n.* a line on a map connecting places where the average temperature is the same.

isosceles triangle

i·so·tope (ī′sə tōp), *n.* any of two or more forms of a chemical element having the same atomic number but different atomic weights.

Is·ra·el (iz′ri əl), *n.* **1.** a country at the eastern end of the Mediterranean. **2.** an ancient Hebrew kingdom in Palestine. **3.** in the Bible, the name given to Jacob after he wrestled with the angel. **4.** the Jewish people, as descendants of Jacob.

Is·rae·li (iz rā′lē), *adj.* of modern Israel or its people. —*n.* a person born or living in modern Israel.

Is·ra·el·ite (iz′ri əl īt′), *n.* any of the people of ancient Israel; also, any Jew.

is·su·ance (ish′ōō əns), *n.* the act of issuing.

is·sue (ish′ōō), *n.* **1.** a sending out or giving out [the army *issue* of clothing to the soldiers]. **2.** a thing or group of things sent or given out [the July *issue* of a magazine]. **3.** a problem to be talked over [New paving is an *issue* in our town.] **4.** a flowing out; outflow [*issue* of water from a pipe]. **5.** a result; outcome [The *issue* of the battle was in doubt.] **6.** a child or children; offspring [Elizabeth I died without *issue.*] —*v.* **1.** to put forth or send out [The city *issues* bonds. The general *issued* an order.] **2.** to give or deal out; distribute [The teacher *issued* new books.] **3.** to go forth or flow out [Blood *issued* from the wound.] **4.** to come about as a result [Victory *issued* from our efforts.] —**at issue,** to be decided. —**take issue,** to disagree. —**is′sued,** *p.t. & p.p.;* **is′su·ing,** *pr.p.*

-ist (ist), a suffix meaning: **1.** a person who [A *moralist* is one who moralizes.] **2.** a person who is skilled in or who works at [An *artist* is one skilled in art.] **3.** a person who believes in [A *socialist* is one who believes in socialism.]

Is·tan·bul (is′tän bool′), *n.* a city in the European part of Turkey: see **Constantinople.**

isth·mus (is′məs), *n.* a narrow strip of land with water on each side, that joins two larger bodies of land [the *Isthmus* of Panama].

it (it), *pron.* the animal or thing being talked about [I read that book and liked *it.*] *It* is also used as: **1.** the subject of a clause to refer to another clause that comes later [*It* is settled that he will go.] **2.** a word referring to the condition of the weather or to things in general [*It* is snowing. *It's* all right; no harm was done.] —*n.* in some children's games, such as tag, the player who must try to catch another. —**they,** *pl.*

i/t/a or **I.T.A.,** abbreviation for **Initial Teaching Alphabet,** an alphabet of 44 letters, each having a single sound: it is used for teaching beginning students to read English.

I·tal·ian (i tal′yən), *adj.* of Italy, its people, etc. —*n.* **1.** a person born or living in Italy. **2.** the language of Italy.

i·tal·ic (i tal′ik), *adj.* describing printing type in which the letters slant upward to the right: it is used to call attention to words [*This is italic type.*] —*n.* **italics,** *pl.* italic type: sometimes used with a singular verb.

i·tal·i·cize (i tal′ə sīz), *v.* **1.** to print in italic type. **2.** to underline something written, to show that it is to be printed in italics. —**i·tal′i·cized,** *p.t. & p.p.;* **i·tal′i·ciz·ing,** *pr.p.*

It·a·ly (it′ə lē), *n.* a country in southern Europe, including the islands of Sicily and Sardinia.

itch (ich), *v.* **1.** to have a tickling feeling on the skin, that makes one want to scratch. **2.** to have a restless desire [He's *itching* to leave.] —*n.* **1.** an itching feeling on the skin. **2.** a skin disease in which this feeling is very strong. **3.** a restless desire [an *itch* to buy a car]. —**itch′y,** *adj.*

-ite (īt), a suffix meaning: **1.** a person born in [A *Canaanite* was one born in Canaan.] **2.** a person who believes in or supports [A *laborite* is a supporter of a labor party.]

i·tem (ī′təm), *n.* **1.** a separate thing; one of a group of things; unit [Check each *item* on this list.] **2.** a piece of news or information.

i·tem·ize (ī′təm īz), *v.* to list the items of, one by one [Please *itemize* my purchases.] —**i′tem·ized,** *p.t. & p.p.;* **i′tem·iz·ing,** *pr.p.*

it·er·ate (it′ə rāt), *v.* to say or do over again; repeat. —**it′er·at·ed,** *p.t. & p.p.;* **it′er·at·ing,** *pr.p.* —**it′er·a′tion,** *n.*

Ith·a·ca (ith′ə kə), *n.* an island off the west coast of Greece: said to be the home of Odysseus.

i·tin·er·ant (ī tin′ər ənt), *adj.* traveling from place to place [an *itinerant* preacher]. —*n.* a person who travels from place to place, especially in connection with his work [Farm work in some parts of the country is done by *itinerants.*]

i·tin·er·ar·y (ī tin′ə rer′ē), *n.* **1.** the route that one travels or plans to travel on a journey. **2.** a record of a journey. —**i·tin′er·ar′ies,** *pl.*

it'll (it′'l), **1.** it will. **2.** it shall.

its (its), *pron.* of it or done by it: the possessive form of *it,* thought of as an adjective [Give the cat *its* dinner. The frost had done *its* damage.]

it's (its), **1.** it is. **2.** it has.

it·self (it self′), *pron.* its own self: the form of *it* that makes the subject also the object of the verb [The dog scratched *itself.*] *Itself* is also used to give force to a noun [Life *itself* was not dearer to him than freedom.]

-i·ty (ə tē), a suffix meaning "condition" or "quality" [*Acidity* is the condition or quality of being acid.]

I've (īv), I have.

---

fat,   āpe,   cär,   ten,   ēven,   hit,   bīte,   gō,   hôrn,   tool,   book,   up,   fûr;
get,   joy,   yet,   chin,   she,   thin,   *th*en;   zh = s in pleasure;   ′ as in able (ā′b'l);
ə = a in ago,   e in agent,   i in sanity,   o in confess,   u in focus.

-ive (iv), a suffix meaning: **1.** of or having to do with [*Instinctive* feelings are feelings having to do with instinct.] **2.** likely to; given to [An *instructive* story is a story that is likely to instruct.]

i·vied (ī′vēd), *adj.* with ivy growing over it [an *ivied* wall].

i·vo·ry (ī′vər ē), *n.* **1.** the hard, white substance that forms the tusks of the elephant, walrus, etc. **2.** any substance like ivory, as the white plastic used on piano keys. **3.** the color of ivory; creamy white. —*adj.* **1.** made of ivory. **2.** having the color of ivory; creamy-white. —**i′vo·ries,** *pl.*

Ivory Coast, a country in western Africa, on the Atlantic Ocean.

i·vy (ī′vē), *n.* **1.** a climbing vine with a woody stem and shiny, evergreen leaves: *its full name is* **English ivy.** **2.** any of various plants like this.

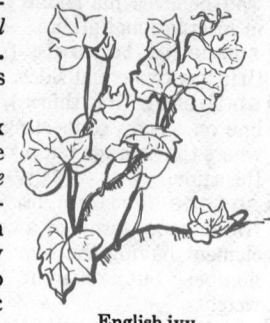
English ivy

-ize (īz), a suffix meaning: **1.** to make or become [*Sterilize* means to make sterile.] **2.** to engage in or act in a certain way [*Sympathize* means to act in a sympathetic way.] **3.** to treat or unite with [*Oxidize* means to unite with oxygen.]

J

J, j (jā), *n.* the tenth letter of the English alphabet. —**J's, j's** (jāz), *pl.*

jab (jab), *v.* **1.** to poke with something hard or sharp [He *jabbed* his elbow into my ribs.] **2.** to punch with short blows. —*n.* a poke or punch. —**jabbed,** *p.t. & p.p.;* **jab′bing,** *pr.p.*

jab·ber (jab′ər), *v.* to talk fast in a silly, rambling way, or without making sense; chatter. —*n.* talk of this kind. —**jab′ber·er,** *n.*

ja·bot (zha bō′), *n.* a broad ruffle or frill worn on the front of a blouse or dress and fastened at the neck. —**ja·bots** (zha bōz′), *pl.*

jack (jak), *n.* **1.** a machine or tool used to lift or move something heavy a short distance [an automobile *jack*]. **2.** the male of some animals. **3.** a playing card with the picture of a page or servant on it. **4.** a man or boy: *no longer much used.* **5.** a jackstone. **6. jacks,** the game of jackstones. **7.** a small flag flown at the front of a ship as a signal: see also **union jack. 8.** money: *slang in this meaning.* —**jack up, 1.** to lift by means of a jack. **2.** to raise, as prices: *only in everyday talk.*

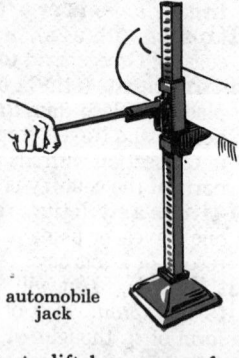
automobile jack

jack·al (jak′əl), *n.* a wild dog of Asia and Africa, smaller than a wolf. Jackals hunt in packs, often feeding on flesh left uneaten by other animals.

jack·a·napes (jak′ə nāps), *n.* an impudent young person who is full of mischief; pert or saucy rascal.

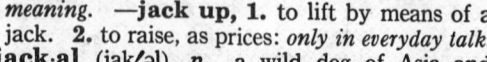
jackal (15 in. high at shoulder)

jack·ass (jak′as), *n.* **1.** a male donkey. **2.** a stupid or foolish person.

jack·boot (jak′boot), *n.* a heavy boot reaching above the knee: also **jack boot.**

jack·daw (jak′dô), *n.* a European black bird like the crow, but smaller.

jack·et (jak′it), *n.* **1.** a short coat. **2.** an outer covering, as the paper wrapper of a book, or the skin of a potato.

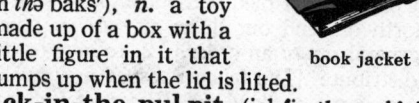
book jacket

jack-in-the-box (jak′-in *th*ə bäks′), *n.* a toy made up of a box with a little figure in it that jumps up when the lid is lifted.

jack-in-the-pul·pit (jak′in *th*ə pool′pit), *n.* a wild flower that grows in the woods. Its blossom is covered by a kind of hood.

jack·knife (jak′nīf), *n.* **1.** a large pocketknife. **2.** a dive in which the diver touches his feet with his hands while in the air. —**jack′knives,** *pl.*

jack-of-all-trades (jak′əv ôl′trādz′), *n.* a person who can do many kinds of work; handy man.

jack-in-the-pulpit

jack-o'-lan·tern (jak′ə lan′tərn), *n.* a lantern made of a hollow pumpkin cut to look like a face. It is used as a decoration at Halloween.

jack rabbit, a large hare of western North America, with long ears and strong hind legs.

Jack·son (jak′s'n), *n.* the capital of Mississippi.

Jack·son, Andrew (jak′s'n), 1767–1845; seventh president of the United States, from 1829 to 1837.

Jackson, Thomas J., 1824–1863; Confederate general in the Civil War: called **Stonewall Jackson.**

Jack·son·ville (jak′s'n vil), *n.* a city in northeastern Florida.

jack·stone (jak′stōn), *n.* any of the small six-pointed metal pieces that are tossed and picked up in a children's game called **jack-stones.**

jack·straw (jak′strô), *n.* any of the narrow strips of wood, plastic, etc. used in a children's game called **jack-straws.**  The strips are tossed in a jumbled heap from which the players try to remove them one at a time without moving the others.

jackstones

Ja·cob (jā′kəb), *n.* in the Bible, a son of Isaac and father of the founders of the tribes of Israel.

jade (jād), *n.* **1.** a hard, green stone used in jewelry and artistic carvings. **2.** its green color.

jade (jād), *n.* **1.** an old worn-out horse. **2.** a woman of low morals. —*v.* to make tired or worn out. —**jad′ed,** *p.t. & p.p.;* **jad′ing,** *pr.p.*

jag (jag), *n.* a sharp, rough point, as of rock, or a sharp tear, as in cloth.

jag·ged (jag′id), *adj.* having sharp points and notches, as the edge of a saw.

jag·uar (jag′wär), *n.* a wild animal of the cat family, that looks like a large leopard. It is found from northern Mexico to southern Brazil.

jaguar (2½ ft. high at shoulder)

jail (jāl), *n.* a building where people are locked up who are waiting for a trial or who are serving a short sentence for breaking a law. —*v.* to put or keep in jail.

jail·er or **jail·or** (jāl′ər), *n.* a person in charge of a jail or of prisoners in a jail.

Ja·kar·ta (jä kär′tə), *n.* the capital of Indonesia, on the island of Java.

ja·lop·y (jə läp′ē), *n.* an old, worn-out automobile: *only in everyday talk.* —**ja·lop′ies,** *pl.*

jal·ou·sie (jal′oo sē), *n.* a window, door, or shade made of metal, wood, or glass slats fixed as in a Venetian blind. The slats can be moved to control the amount of air or light coming in.

jam (jam), *v.* **1.** to squeeze or force tightly [to *jam* one's hands into one's pockets]. **2.** to injure or crush [His hand was *jammed* in the car door.] **3.** to fill or block up by crowding in [Cars *jammed* the parking lot.] **4.** to push or shove hard [to *jam* on the brakes]. **5.** to wedge in or stick tight so that it cannot move [The door was *jammed* shut.] **6.** to keep radio signals from being clearly heard, by sending out others on the same

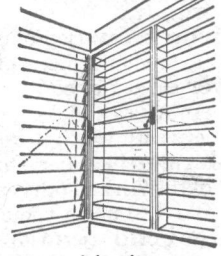

jalousies

wave length. —*n.* **1.** a jamming or being jammed, or many things jammed together [a traffic *jam*]. **2.** a difficult situation: *only in everyday talk.* —**jammed,** *p.t. & p.p.;* **jam′ming,** *pr.p.*

jam (jam), *n.* a sweet food made by boiling fruit and sugar until it forms a thick paste.

Ja·mai·ca (jə mā′kə), *n.* a country on an island in the West Indies. —**Ja·mai′can,** *adj. & n.*

jamb or **jambe** (jam), *n.* a side post in the frame of a doorway or window.

jam·bo·ree (jam bə rē′), *n.* **1.** a large gathering of boy scouts from many places. **2.** a gay, noisy party: *used only in everyday talk.*

James·town (jāmz′toun), *n.* the first successful English colony in America, set up in 1607 in what is now Virginia.

jan·gle (jang′g'l), *v.* **1.** to make or cause to make a harsh, jarring sound [keys *jangling* together]. **2.** to argue loudly. —*n.* a harsh sound. —**jan′gled,** *p.t. & p.p.;* **jan′gling,** *pr.p.*

jan·i·tor (jan′i tər), *n.* a person who takes care of cleaning and repairing a building.

Jan·u·ar·y (jan′yoo er′ē), *n.* the first month of the year. It has 31 days. Abbreviated **Jan.**

Ja·nus (jā′nəs), *n.* the Roman god of gates and doors who kept special watch over beginnings and endings. He is shown as having two faces, one in front and the other at the back of his head.

Jap., abbreviation for **Japan** or **Japanese.**

Ja·pan (jə pan′), *n.* a country east of Korea, made up of many islands.

ja·pan (jə pan′), *n.* a hard lacquer that gives a shiny finish. —*v.* to cover with japan. —**ja·panned′,** *p.t. & p.p.;* **ja·pan′ning,** *pr.p.*

Jap·a·nese (jap ə nēz′), *adj.* of Japan, its people, language, or culture. —*n.* **1.** a member of a people whose native country is Japan. **2.** the language of Japan. —**Jap·a·nese′,** *pl.*

Japanese beetle, a small, green-and-brown beetle that is harmful to crops.

jar (jär), *v.* **1.** to shake up; rattle; jolt [The explosion *jarred* our windows.] **2.** to make a harsh sound; grate. **3.** to be harsh on the ears, eyes, nerves, etc. [a *jarring* noise; *jarring* news]. **4.** to clash; disagree sharply [Her rude remark *jarred* with her refined manners.] —*n.* **1.** a shaking or rattling; jolt. **2.** a harsh or grating sound. —**jarred,** *p.t. & p.p.;* **jar′ring,** *pr.p.*

jar (jär), *n.* **1.** a container made of glass, pottery, etc., having a broad mouth. **2.** as much as a jar will hold.

jar·di·niere (jär′d'n ir′), *n.* a fancy pot or stand for flowers or plants.

jars

jar·gon (jär′gən), *n.* **1.** the special words and phrases used by people of the same class or in the same kind of work [Sports writers have a *jargon* of their own, and so do scientists.] **2.** talk that makes no sense; gibberish.

---

fat,   āpe,   cär,   ten,   ēven,   hit,   bīte,   gō,   hôrn,   tōōl,   book,   up,   fûr;
get,   joy,   yet,   chin,   she,   thin,   then;   zh = s in pleasure;   ′ as in able (ā′b'l);
ə = a in ago,   e in agent,   i in sanity,   o in confess,   u in focus.

jas·mine (jaz′min), *n.* a shrub of warm regions that has sweet-smelling flowers of red, yellow, or white.

Ja·son (jā′s'n), *n.* the prince in a Greek legend who searched for the Golden Fleece.

jas·per (jas′pər), *n.* a dull kind of quartz, usually yellow, red, or brown.

jaun·dice (jôn′dis), *n.* **1.** a condition caused by various diseases, in which bile gets into the blood and makes the skin, eyeballs, etc. very yellow. **2.** a bitterness of mind or outlook, as because of jealousy or hate. —*v.* **1.** to cause jaundice in. **2.** to make bitter or prejudiced, as from envy. —**jaun′diced,** *p.t. & p.p.;* **jaun′dic·ing,** *pr.p.*

jaunt (jônt), *n.* a short trip for pleasure.

jaun·ty (jôn′tē), *adj.* gay and carefree; showing an easy confidence [a cap worn at a *jaunty* angle]. —**jaun′ti·er,** *compar.;* **jaun′ti·est,** *superl.* —**jaun′ti·ly,** *adv.* —**jaun′ti·ness,** *n.*

Ja·va (jä′və *or* jav′ə), *n.* **1.** a large, important island of Indonesia. **2.** a kind of coffee grown there. **3.** java, any coffee: *slang in this meaning.* —**Jav·a·nese** (jav ə nēz′), *adj. & n.*

jave·lin (jav′lin *or* jav′ə lin), *n.* a light spear; nowadays, one used in an athletic contest to see who can throw it farthest.

man throwing the javelin

jaw (jô), *n.* **1.** either of the two bony parts that form the frame of the mouth and that hold the teeth. **2.** either of two parts that close to grip or crush something [A vise and a pair of pliers have *jaws.*] **3.** jaws, *pl.* the narrow entrance of a canyon, valley, etc. —*v.* to talk, especially in a dull, steady way: *slang in this meaning.*

jaw·bone (jô′bōn), *n.* a bone of the jaw, especially of the lower jaw.

jay (jā), *n.* **1.** any of several brightly colored birds of the crow family. **2.** a bluejay.

jay·walk (jā′wôk), *v.* to walk in or across a street carelessly, without obeying traffic rules and signals. —**jay′walk·er,** *n.*

jazz (jaz), *n.* a kind of popular American music that originated with Southern Negroes and is usually played by small groups. It has strong rhythms and the players or singers often make up parts as they go along.

jeal·ous (jel′əs), *adj.* **1.** worried or afraid that someone is taking the love or attention one has or wants [a *jealous* husband]. **2.** resulting from such a feeling [a *jealous* rage]. **3.** unhappy because another has something one would like; envious [to be *jealous* of another person's good fortune]. **4.** careful in guarding; watchful [The new nation was *jealous* of its hard-won liberty.] —**jeal′ous·ly,** *adv.*

jeal·ous·y (jel′əs ē), *n.* the condition of being jealous, or a jealous feeling.

Jeanne d'Arc (zhän′därk′), Joan of Arc.

jeans (jēnz), *n.pl.* trousers or overalls made of a heavy, cotton cloth, usually blue.

jeep (jēp), *n.* a small, powerful automobile first made in World War II for army use.

jeep

jeer (jir), *v.* to make fun of in a rude or mocking way [The audience *jeered* at the awkward dancer.] —*n.* a jeering cry or remark.

Jef·fer·son, Thomas (jef′ər s'n), 1743–1826; third president of the United States, from 1801 to 1809.

Jefferson City, the capital of Missouri.

Je·ho·vah (ji hō′və), *n.* God.

je·june (ji jōōn′), *adj.* not interesting or satisfying; dull or empty [a *jejune* philosophy].

jell (jel), *v.* **1.** to become, or make into, jelly [The mixture will *jell* when it cools.] **2.** to take on or give a definite form [Plans for the dance have *jelled.*] *Used only in everyday talk.*

jel·ly (jel′ē), *n.* **1.** a soft, firm food that looks smooth and glassy, and is easily cut, spread, etc. Jelly is made from cooked fruit sirup, meat juice, or gelatin. **2.** any substance like this. —*v.* to become, or make into, jelly. —**jel′lies,** *pl.* —**jel′lied,** *p.t. & p.p.;* **jel′ly·ing,** *pr.p.*

jel·ly·bean (jel′ē bēn′), *n.* a small, gummy candy shaped like a bean.

jel·ly·fish (jel′ē fish), *n.* a sea animal with a body that feels like jelly.

jen·ny (jen′ē), *n.* **1.** a machine that can spin a number of threads at one time: also called **spinning jenny. 2.** the female of some animals [a *jenny* wren]. —**jen′nies,** *pl.*

jeop·ard·ize (jep′ər dīz), *v.* to put in danger; risk; endanger [He *jeopardized* his career by supporting his friend.] —**jeop′ard·ized,** *p.t. & p.p.;* **jeop′ard·iz·ing,** *pr.p.*

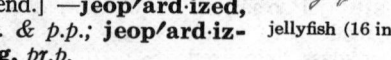

jellyfish (16 in. long)

jeop·ard·y (jep′ər dē), *n.* great danger or risk [A fireman's life is often in *jeopardy*.]

jer·bo·a (jər bō′ə), *n.* a small animal of northern Africa and Asia, like a mouse: it has long hind legs with which it can jump far.

Jer·e·mi·ah (jer′ə mī′ə), *n.* **1.** a Hebrew prophet of the 7th and 6th centuries B.C. **2.** a book of the Old Testament containing his warnings.

Jer·i·cho (jer′ə kō), *n.* a village in Jordan, where an ancient city stood whose walls, according to the Bible, were destroyed by a miracle when trumpets were blown.

jerk (jurk), *n.* **1.** a sudden, sharp pull, lift, twist, or push [The train started with a *jerk* that threw our heads back.] **2.** a sudden twitch of a muscle. —*v.* **1.** to move or pull with a jerk or jerks [He *jerked* the book from my hand.] **2.** to twitch.

jerk (jurk), *v.* to slice meat into strips and dry it in the sun or over a fire [*jerked* beef].

jer·kin (jŭr′kin), *n.* a short, tight jacket often with no sleeves, worn by men in the 16th and 17th centuries.

jerk·y (jŭr′kē), *adj.* making sudden, sharp movements; moving by jerks. —**jerk′i·er,** *compar.*; **jerk′i·est,** *superl.*

Jer·ome, Saint (jə rōm′), 340?-420 A.D.; a monk who translated the Bible into Latin.

Jer·sey (jŭr′zē), *n.* **1.** a British island in the English Channel. **2.** a breed of small, reddish-brown dairy cattle first raised there. **3. jersey,** a soft, knitted cloth; also, a blouse, shirt, etc. made of this. —**Jer′seys** or **jer′seys,** *pl.*

jerkin

Jersey City, a city in New Jersey: it is across the Hudson River from New York City.

Je·ru·sa·lem (jə rōō′sə ləm), *n.* the capital of Israel: the city is partly in Jordan.

jes·sa·mine (jes′ə min), *n.* same as **jasmine.**

jest (jest), *n.* **1.** a joke or joking remark. **2.** the act of joking or having fun [I spoke only in *jest,* but I hurt her feelings.] **3.** something to be made fun of or laughed at. —*v.* **1.** to say something funny; joke. **2.** to make fun of; mock or jeer.

jest·er (jes′tər), *n.* a person who jests; especially, a clown hired by a ruler in the Middle Ages to do tricks and tell jokes.

Jes·u·it (jezh′ōō it *or* jez′yōō it), *n.* a member of the **Society of Jesus,** a Roman Catholic religious group begun in 1534. —**Jes′u·it′ic** or **Jes′u·it′i·cal,** *adj.*

Je·sus (jē′zəs), *n.* the founder of the Christian religion: also called **Jesus Christ.**

jester

jet (jet), *n.* **1.** a stream of liquid or gas forced from a nozzle or spout. **2.** a nozzle or spout for shooting out a jet. **3.** a jet-propelled airplane. —*v.* to spout or shoot out in a stream. —*adj.* **1.** jet-propelled [a *jet* plane]. **2.** of a jet-propelled airplane [a *jet* flight]. —**jet′ted,** *p.t.* & *p.p.*; **jet′ting,** *pr.p.*

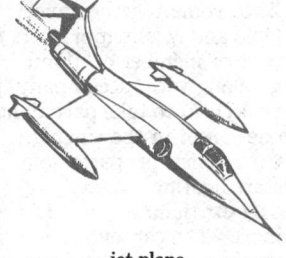

jet plane

jet (jet), *n.* **1.** a hard, black mineral that is polished and used in jewelry. **2.** a bright, shiny black. —*adj.* of or like jet.

jet-pro·pelled (jet′prə peld′), *adj.* driven by jet propulsion.

jet propulsion, a method of driving an airplane, rocket, or bomb forward by forcing a jet of hot gases under pressure through a rear opening.

jet·sam (jet′səm), *n.* **1.** part of a cargo that is thrown overboard to lighten a ship in danger. **2.** such cargo that is washed ashore. See **flotsam.**

jet·ti·son (jet′ə s'n), *v.* **1.** to throw goods overboard to lighten a ship or aircraft in danger. **2.** to throw away; get rid of.

jet·ty (jet′ē), *n.* **1.** a kind of wall built out into the water to protect a harbor, pier, etc. from the force of currents or waves. **2.** a landing pier. —**jet′ties,** *pl.*

Jew (jōō), *n.* **1.** a person whose ancestors were the ancient Hebrews. **2.** a person whose religion is Judaism.

jew·el (jōō′əl), *n.* **1.** a precious stone, as a diamond or ruby; gem. **2.** a valuable ring, pin, necklace, etc., often set with such stones or gems. **3.** a person or thing that is very precious or valuable. —*v.* to decorate with jewels [a *jeweled* dagger]. —**jew′eled** or **jew′elled,** *p.t.* & *p.p.*; **jew′el·ing** or **jew′el·ling,** *pr.p.*

jew·el·er or **jew·el·ler** (jōō′əl ər), *n.* a person who makes or sells jewelry, watches, etc.

jew·el·ry (jōō′əl rē), *n.* jewels or ornaments made with jewels.

Jew·ish (jōō′ish), *adj.* of or having to do with Jews.

Jew·ry (jōō′rē), *n.* the Jewish people; Jews as a group [American *Jewry*].

jew's-harp or **jews'-harp** (jōōz′härp′), *n.* a small musical instrument made of metal: it is held between the teeth, and a thin, bent piece is plucked with the finger, making twanging sounds.

Jez·e·bel (jez′ə b'l), *n.* **1.** a very wicked woman in the Bible, who married a king of Israel. **2.** any wicked woman who shows no shame.

jib (jib), *n.* a sail shaped like a triangle, set ahead of the foremast.

jibe (jīb), *v.* **1.** to shift suddenly to the other side of the boat: said of a fore-and-aft sail or its boom. **2.** to change the course of a boat so that the sails jibe. **3.** to agree; fit together: *used only in everyday talk* [Their stories don't *jibe*.] —**jibed,** *p.t.* & *p.p.*; **jib′ing,** *pr.p.*

jib

jibe (jīb), *v.* same as **gibe.**

jif·fy (jif′ē), *n.* a very short time: *used only in everyday talk* [I'll be done in a *jiffy*.]

jig (jig), *n.* **1.** a fast, lively dance. **2.** the music for it. **3.** a fishhook with a part that twirls. **4.** a device used to guide a tool. —*v.* to dance a jig. —**jigged,** *p.t.* & *p.p.*; **jig′ging,** *pr.p.*

jig·gle (jig′'l), *v.* to move quickly up and down or back and forth. —*n.* a jiggling. —**jig′gled,** *p.t.* & *p.p.*; **jig′gling,** *pr.p.*

fat, āpe, cär, ten, ēven, hit, bīte, gō, hôrn, tōol, book, up, fŭr;
get, joy, yet, chin, she, thin, *th*en; zh = s in pleasure; ′ as in able (ā′b'l);
ə = a in ago, e in agent, i in sanity, o in confess, u in focus.

jig·saw (jig′sô), *n.* a saw with a narrow blade set in a frame. The blade moves up and down and is used for cutting along irregular lines. Also **jig saw.**

jigsaw

jigsaw puzzle, a puzzle made by cutting up a picture into pieces of uneven shapes, which must be put together again.

jilt (jilt), *v.* to turn away a lover or sweetheart that one no longer wants. —*n.* a woman who jilts her lover or sweetheart.

jim·my (jim′ē), *n.* a short metal bar used by burglars to pry open windows, etc. —*v.* to pry open, as with a jimmy. —**jim′mies,** *pl.* —**jim′mied,** *p.t. & p.p.;* **jim′my·ing,** *pr.p.*

jin·gle (jing′g'l), *v.* 1. to make ringing, tinkling sounds, as bits of metal striking together [The pennies *jingled* in his pocket.] 2. to make jingle [He *jingled* his keys.] 3. to have simple rhymes and a regular rhythm, as some poetry and music. —*n.* 1. a jingling sound. 2. a verse that jingles [advertising *jingles* on the radio]. —**jin′gled,** *p.t. & p.p.;* **jin′gling,** *pr.p.*

jin·ni (ji nē′), *n.* genie. —**jinn** (jin), *pl.*

jin·rik·i·sha or **jin·rick·sha** (jin rik′shô), *n.* a small carriage with two wheels, used in oriental countries. It is pulled by one or two men.

jinx (jingks), *v.* to cause bad luck to. —*n.* something that brings bad luck. *A slang word.*

jit·ney (jit′nē), *n.* a bus or taxicab that charges a small fare: *a slang word.* —**jit′neys,** *pl.*

jit·ter·y (jit′ər ē), *adj.* nervous or restless. —**the jitters,** a nervous feeling. *Slang terms.*

jiu·jit·su (jōō jit′sōō), *n.* same as **jujitsu.**

Joan of Arc, Saint (jōn′əv ärk′), 1412–1431; French heroine who led the French army to victory over the English. She was burned as a witch.

Job (jōb), *n.* 1. a man in the Bible who kept his faith in God in spite of his many troubles. 2. a book of the Old Testament telling of him.

job (jäb), *n.* 1. a piece of work done for pay [We let Brown have the *job* of painting the house.] 2. anything one has to do; task or duty [It is my *job* to do the dishes.] 3. a place or kind of work; employment [to look for a new *job*]. —*adj.* done by the job or piece [*job* work].

job·ber (jäb′ər), *n.* a person who buys goods wholesale and sells to dealers.

jock·ey (jäk′ē), *n.* a person whose work is riding horses in races. —*v.* 1. to trick into or cheat out of something. 2. to manage things in a skillful way so as to get some advantage [to *jockey* for position in a race]. —**jock′eys,** *pl.* —**jock′eyed,** *p.t. & p.p.;* **jock′ey·ing,** *pr.p.*

jo·cose (jō kōs′), *adj.* joking or playful [a *jocose* talk]. —**jo·cose′ly,** *adv.*

jockey

joc·u·lar (jäk′yoo lər), *adj.* full of fun; joking [a *jocular* suggestion]. —**joc·u·lar·i·ty** (jäk′yoo lar′ə tē), *n.* —**joc′u·lar·ly,** *adv.*

joc·und (jäk′ənd *or* jō′kənd), *adj.* cheerful; gay and friendly.

jodh·purs (jäd′pərz), *n.pl.* trousers for horseback riding made loose and full above the knees and tight from the knees to the ankles.

jog (jäg), *v.* 1. to give a little shake to; jostle or nudge [*Jog* him to see if he's awake.] 2. to shake up or rouse, as the memory or mind. 3. to move along slowly and steadily, but with a jolting motion. —*n.* 1. a little shake or nudge. 2. a jogging pace. —**jogged,** *p.t. & p.p.;* **jog′ging,** *pr.p.*

jog (jäg), *n.* a part, as in a wall or road, that changes direction sharply.

jog·gle (jäg′'l), *v.* to jolt slightly. —*n.* a slight jolt. —**jog′gled,** *p.t. & p.p.;* **jog′gling,** *pr.p.*

Jo·han·nes·burg (jō han′is bûrg *or* yō hän′isbûrg), *n.* a city in South Africa.

John (jän), *n.* 1. one of the twelve Apostles of Jesus. 2. the fourth book of the New Testament. John is believed to have written this book and several others in the New Testament. 3. John the Baptist. 4. a king of England who reigned from 1199 to 1216. He was forced by his barons to sign the Magna Charta in 1215.

John Bull (bool), a name that stands for England or for an Englishman.

John Doe (dō), a name used in legal papers for any person whose name is not known.

john·ny·cake (jän′ē kāk), *n.* a kind of corn bread, originally baked on a griddle.

John·son, Andrew (jän′s'n), 1808–1875; 17th president of the United States, from 1865 to 1869.

Johnson, Lyn·don B. (lin′dən), 1908– ; 36th president of the United States, from 1963 to 1969.

Johnson, Samuel, 1709–1784; English writer and dictionary maker.

John the Baptist, in the Bible, the cousin and baptizer of Jesus.

join (join), *v.* 1. to bring together; connect; fasten [We *joined* hands and stood in a circle.] 2. to come together; meet; unite [Where do the Ohio and Mississippi rivers *join?*] 3. to become a part or member of [Paul *joined* our club.] 4. to go along with; accompany [Will you *join* us in a walk?] 5. to take part along with others [Everyone *joined* in the singing.] —*n.* the place where two things or parts join. —**join battle,** to start fighting.

join·er (join′ər), *n.* 1. a person or thing that joins. 2. a carpenter, especially one who finishes inside woodwork, as doors, molding, etc.

joint (joint), *n.* 1. a place where two things or parts are joined [Water leaked from the *joint* in the pipe.] 2. a place or part where two bones are joined, usually so that they can move [the elbow *joint*]. 3. any of the parts that are connected by joints [the *joints* of a finger]. 4. a large cut of meat with the bone still in it. 5. a cheap restaurant or drinking place; also, any house, building, etc.: *slang in this meaning.* —*v.* 1. to connect by a joint or joints [Bamboo is *jointed.*] 2. to cut at the joints [The butcher *jointed* the chicken for me.] **—adj. 1.** done or owned by two or more [a *joint* appeal by several colleges for money; the *joint* property of husband and wife]. **2.** sharing with someone else [a *joint* owner]. **—out of joint, 1.** not in place at the joint; dislocated. **2.** out of order. **—joint′ly,** *adv.*

joist (joist), *n.* any of the parallel pieces that hold up the boards of a floor or the laths of a ceiling.

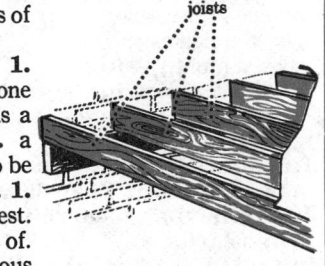

joists

joke (jōk), *n.* **1.** anything said or done to get a laugh, as a funny story. **2.** a person or thing to be laughed at. **—v. 1.** to make jokes; jest. **2.** to make fun of. **—no joke,** a serious matter. **—joked,** *p.t. & p.p.;* **jok′ing,** *pr.p.* **—jok′ing·ly,** *adv.*

jok·er (jōk′ər), *n.* **1.** a person who jokes. **2.** an extra card in a deck of playing cards, used in some games. **3.** a tricky section put into a law, contract, etc. to make it different from what it seems to be.

jol·li·ty (jäl′ə tē), *n.* fun or merriment.

jol·ly (jäl′ē), *adj.* **1.** full of fun; merry; gay [a *jolly* old man]. **2.** pleasant or enjoyable: *used only in everyday talk* [a *jolly* party]. **—adv.** very: *mainly in British everyday talk.* **—jol′li·er,** *compar.;* **jol′li·est,** *superl.* **—jol′li·ness,** *n.*

Jol·ly Rog·er (jäl′ē räj′ər), a black flag of pirates, with white skull and crossbones on it.

jolt (jōlt), *v.* **1.** to shake up; jar [We were *jolted* along over the bumpy road.] **2.** to move along in a bumpy, jerky manner [The cart *jolted* over the cobblestones.] **—n. 1.** a sudden bump or jerk. **2.** a shock [The news gave us a *jolt.*]

Jo·nah (jō′nə), *n.* **1.** a Hebrew prophet in the Bible. He was swallowed by a big fish but later was cast up on shore unharmed. **2.** a book of the Old Testament telling of him. **3.** any person said to bring bad luck by being present.

Jon·a·than (jän′ə thən), *n.* a son of Saul in the Bible, and a close friend of David.

Jones, John Paul (jōnz), 1747–1792; American naval officer in the Revolutionary War.

jon·quil (jäng′kwil), *n.* a narcissus with a yellow or white flower and long, slender leaves.

Jor·dan (jôr′d'n), *n.* **1.** a country in the Middle East, east of Israel. **2.** a river that flows through Jordan and Israel into the Dead Sea.

Jo·seph (jō′zəf), *n.* **1.** one of Jacob's sons in the Bible. He was sold into slavery in Egypt but became a high official there. **2.** the husband of Mary, mother of Jesus.

josh (jäsh), *v.* to make fun of or tease in a joking way; banter: *a slang word.*

Josh·u·a (jäsh′oo ə), *n.* **1.** in the Bible, the man who led the Israelites into the Promised Land after Moses died. **2.** a book of the Old Testament telling about him.

jos·tle (jäs′'l), *v.* to shove or push in a rough way. **—n.** a rough push or shove. **—jos′tled,** *p.t. & p.p.;* **jos′tling,** *pr.p.*

jot (jät), *n.* the smallest bit [There's not a *jot* of truth in it.] **—v.** to make a brief note of [He *jotted* down the address.] **—jot′ted,** *p.t. & p.p.;* **jot′ting,** *pr.p.*

jounce (jouns), *v. & n.* jolt or bounce. **—jounced,** *p.t. & p.p.;* **jounc′ing,** *pr.p.*

jour·nal (jur′n'l), *n.* **1.** a daily record of what happens, such as a diary [He kept a *journal* of his trip to Europe.] **2.** a written record of what happens at the meetings of a club, legislature, etc. **3.** a newspaper or magazine. **4.** a book in which business accounts are kept. **5.** the part of an axle or shaft that turns in a bearing.

jour·nal·ism (jur′n'l iz'm), *n.* the work of gathering news for, writing for, or editing a newspaper or magazine.

jour·nal·ist (jur′n'l ist), *n.* a person who writes for or edits a newspaper or magazine; reporter or editor. **—jour′nal·is′tic,** *adj.*

jour·ney (jur′ni), *n.* a traveling from one place to another; trip. **—v.** to go on a trip; travel. **—jour′neys,** *pl.* **—jour′neyed,** *p.t. & p.p.;* **jour′ney·ing,** *pr.p.*

jour·ney·man (jur′nē mən), *n.* a worker who is skilled at his trade. **—jour′ney·men,** *pl.*

joust (joust *or* just), *n.* a fight between two knights on horseback using lances. **—v.** to take part in a joust, as for sport.

Jove (jōv), *n.* Jupiter, the Roman god.

jo·vi·al (jō′vi əl), *adj.* friendly and cheerful; playful and jolly. **—jo·vi·al·i·ty** (jō′vi al′ə tē), *n.* **—jo′vi·al·ly,** *adv.*

jowl (joul), *n.* **1.** a jaw, especially the lower jaw with the chin. **2.** the cheek. **3.** *often* **jowls,** *pl.* fleshy parts hanging under the lower jaw.

joy (joi), *n.* **1.** a very happy feeling; great pleasure; delight [The new baby brought them *joy.*] **2.** anything that causes this feeling [This book is a *joy* to read.]

..... jowls

joy·ful (joi′fəl), *adj.* feeling, showing, or causing joy; glad; happy. **—joy′ful·ly,** *adv.*

joy·less (joi′lis), *adj.* without joy; unhappy; sad. **—joy′less·ly,** *adv.*

joy·ous (joi′əs), *adj.* full of joy; happy. **—joy′ous·ly,** *adv.*

Jr. or **jr.,** abbreviation for **junior.**

ju·bi·lant (jōō′b'l ənt), *adj.* joyful and proud; rejoicing [*Jubilant* crowds celebrated the victory.] **—ju′bi·lant·ly,** *adv.*

fat,   āpe,   cär,   ten,   ēven,   hit,   bīte,   gō,   hôrn,   tōōl,   book,   up,   fŭr;
get,   joy,   yet,   chin,   she,   thin,   *then;*   zh = s in pleasure;   ′ as in able (ā′b'l);
ə = a in ago,   e in agent,   i in sanity,   o in confess,   u in focus.

ju·bi·la·tion (jōo′b'l ā′shən), *n.* the act of rejoicing, as in celebrating a victory.

ju·bi·lee (jōo′b'l ē), *n.* **1.** a celebration of an anniversary, especially of a 50th or 25th anniversary. **2.** a time or condition of great joy.

Ju·dah (jōo′də), *n.* **1.** in the Bible, one of Jacob's sons, or the tribe descended from him. **2.** an ancient kingdom in Palestine formed by the tribes of Judah and Benjamin.

Ju·da·ism (jōo′di iz′m), *n.* the religion of the Jewish people, which is based on a belief in one God and on the teachings of the Old Testament.

Ju·das Is·car·i·ot (jōo′dəs is kar′i ət), **1.** the disciple who betrayed Jesus for money. **2.** anyone who betrays another person; informer.

Ju·de·a or **Ju·dae·a** (jōo dē′ə), *n.* a part of southern Palestine that was ruled by Rome.

judge (juj), *n.* **1.** a public official with power to hear cases in a law court and decide what laws apply to them. **2.** a person chosen to decide the winner in a contest or to settle an argument. **3.** a person who has enough knowledge to give an opinion on something [a good *judge* of music]. —*v.* **1.** to hear cases and make decisions in a law court. **2.** to act as a judge in a contest or argument [to *judge* a beauty contest]. **3.** to form an opinion on something [Don't *judge* by first impressions.] **4.** to blame or criticize [Try not to *judge* me too harshly.] **5.** to think or suppose [How tall do you *judge* him to be?] —**judged,** *p.t. & p.p.;* **judg′ing,** *pr.p.*

Judg·es (juj′iz), *n.* a book of the Old Testament, telling the history of the Jews from the death of Joshua to the birth of Samuel.

judg·ment (juj′mənt), *n.* **1.** a judging or deciding. **2.** a decision given by a judge or a law court [The *judgment* was for the defendant.] **3.** an opinion; the way one feels or thinks about something [In my *judgment,* he will win the election.] **4.** criticism or blame [to pass *judgment* on another]. **5.** a being able to decide what is right, good, practical, etc.; good sense [a man of clear *judgment*]. Sometimes also **judgement.**

Judgment Day, in certain religions, the day on which God gives his final rewards and punishments to all people; doomsday.

ju·di·cial (jōo dish′əl), *adj.* **1.** of judges, law courts, or their duties [*judicial* robes; *judicial* power]. **2.** ordered or allowed by a court [a *judicial* decree]. **3.** careful in forming opinions or making decisions; fair [a *judicial* mind]. —**ju·di′cial·ly,** *adv.*

ju·di·ci·ar·y (jōo dish′i er′ē), *adj.* of judges, law courts, or their duties; judicial. —*n.* **1.** the part of a government whose work is to see that justice is carried out according to the laws; system of law courts. **2.** judges as a group.

ju·di·cious (jōo dish′əs), *adj.* having or showing good judgment. —**ju·di′cious·ly,** *adv.*

ju·do (jōo′dō), *n.* a kind of wrestling used for self-defense, in which the opponent's strength and weight are used against him. Judo was developed from the Japanese sport *jujitsu.*

jug (jug), *n.* a container for holding liquids, with a small opening and a handle.

jug·gle (jug′'l), *v.* **1.** to do skillful tricks with the hands; especially, to keep tossing a number of things up in the air one by one and keep them all moving. **2.** to handle in a tricky way so as to cheat or fool others [The cashier *juggled* the figures so as to show a profit.] —**jug′gled,** *p.t. & p.p.;* **jug′gling,** *pr.p.* —**jug′gler,** *n.*

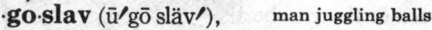
man juggling balls

Ju·go·slav (ū′gō släv′), *n. & adj.* same as **Yugoslav.**

Ju·go·sla·vi·a (ū′gō slä′vi ə), *n.* same as **Yugoslavia.**

jug·u·lar (jug′yoo lər), *adj.* of the neck or throat. The **jugular veins** are the two large veins in the neck carrying blood from the head back to the heart.

juice (jōos), *n.* **1.** the liquid part of a plant or animal [orange *juice;* gastric *juice;* meat *juices*]. **2.** electricity: *slang in this meaning.* —*v.* to squeeze juice from [to *juice* lemons]. —**juiced,** *p.t. & p.p.;* **juic′ing,** *pr.p.*

juic·y (jōo′sē), *adj.* **1.** full of juice [a *juicy* plum]. **2.** full of interest [a *juicy* story]. —**juic′i·er,** *compar.;* **juic′i·est,** *superl.*

ju·jit·su or **jiu·jit·su** (jōo jit′sōo), *n.* a Japanese form of wrestling: see **judo.**

juke box (jōok), an electric phonograph worked by dropping a coin in a slot. *Used only in everyday talk.*

ju·lep (jōo′lip), *n.* an iced drink made with whisky, sugar, and mint: also called **mint julep.**

Ju·li·et (jōol′yət *or* jōo′li ət), *n.* the heroine of Shakespeare's tragedy *Romeo and Juliet.*

jujitsu

Ju·ly (jōo lī′), *n.* the seventh month of the year. It has 31 days.

jum·ble (jum′b'l), *v.* to mix up or put into disorder [The file cards were *jumbled* together on the desk.] —*n.* a jumbled heap or mix-up; confused mess [a *jumble* of words]. —**jum′bled,** *p.t. & p.p.;* **jum′bling,** *pr.p.*

jum·bo (jum′bō), *n.* a large thing or animal. —*adj.* larger than usual [a *jumbo* lemon soda].

jump (jump), *v.* **1.** to move oneself suddenly from the ground or some other surface by using the leg muscles; spring or leap [to *jump* up and touch a branch; to *jump* from a plane; to *jump* on a train]. **2.** to leap over [The boy *jumped* the creek.] **3.** to make leap or spring [He *jumped* his horse over the fence.] **4.** to jerk or bounce; bob [The line *jumped* when the fish took the bait.] **5.** to move suddenly, as from fright; start [She *jumped* when the door banged shut.] **6.** to rise or make rise suddenly [The price of milk *jumped* two cents last week.] **7.** to move or change suddenly in thinking, talking, etc. [to *jump* to conclusions; to *jump* to a new subject]. **8.** to attack suddenly: *slang in this meaning.* —*n.* **1.** a jumping; leap. **2.** a distance jumped [a *jump* of ten feet]. **3.** a sudden rise, as in prices. **4.** a sudden, nervous start; twitch. **5.** a contest in jumping [the high *jump;* the broad *jump*]. —**get the jump on,** to get an advantage over: *a slang phrase.* —**jump a claim,** to seize land claimed by someone else. —**jump at,** to take eagerly [She *jumped at* the chance to go.] —**jump the gun,** to begin something before the right time: *a slang phrase.* —**jump′er,** *n.*

jump·er (jum′pər), *n.* **1.** a dress without sleeves, worn over a blouse or sweater. **2.** a smock, sailor's blouse, child's rompers, etc.

jump·y (jum′pē), *adj.* **1.** moving in jumps or jerks. **2.** nervous; easily startled [Ghost stories make me *jumpy.*] —**jump′i·er,** *compar.;* **jump′- i·est,** *superl.* —**jump′i- ness,** *n.*

jumper

jun·co (jung′kō), *n.* an American finch with a white breast; snowbird.

junc·tion (jungk′shən), *n.* **1.** a joining or being joined. **2.** a place where things join or cross [a railroad *junction*].

junc·ture (jungk′chər), *n.* **1.** a joining or being joined. **2.** a point or line where things join or connect; joint. **3.** a point of time or a state of affairs [At this *juncture,* we changed our plans.]

June (jōōn), *n.* the sixth month of the year. It has 30 days.

Ju·neau (jōō′nō), *n.* the capital of Alaska.

June bug, any of various large beetles found in the United States.

jun·gle (jung′g'l), *n.* land thickly covered with trees, vines, etc., as in the tropics. Jungles are usually filled with animals that prey on one another.

jun·ior (jōōn′yər), *adj.* **1.** the younger: a word written after the name of a son who has exactly the same name as his father: abbreviated **Jr. 2.** lower in position or rank [a *junior* executive]. **3.** of juniors in a high school or college [the *junior* class]. —*n.* **1.** a person who is younger or has a lower rank than another [His wife is his *junior* by five years.] **2.** a student in the next to last year of a high school or college.

junior high school, a school between elementary school and high school. It usually has the 7th, 8th, and 9th grades.

ju·ni·per (jōō′nə pər), *n.* a small evergreen shrub or tree with cones that look like berries.

junk (jungk), *n.* old metal, glass, paper, rags, etc.; things of little value; rubbish; trash. —*v.* to get rid of as worthless: *used only in everyday talk* [I *junked* my old car.]

junk (jungk), *n.* a Chinese sailing ship with a flat bottom.

jun·ket (jung′kit), *n.* **1.** milk that has been sweetened, flavored, and thickened into curd. **2.** a pleasure trip, especially one paid for out of public funds. **3.** a picnic. —*v.* to go on a junket, or pleasure trip.

junk

junk·man (jungk′man), *n.* a man who buys and sells old metal, glass, paper, rags, etc.

Ju·no (jōō′nō), *n.* the Roman goddess of marriage and the wife of Jupiter. The Greeks called this goddess *Hera.*

jun·to (jun′tō), *n.* a small group of politicians plotting to get more power. —**jun′tos,** *pl.*

Ju·pi·ter (jōō′pə tər), *n.* **1.** the chief Roman god, ruling over all other gods. The Greeks called this god *Zeus.* **2.** the largest planet. It is the fifth in distance away from the sun.

ju·ris·dic·tion (joor′is dik′shən), *n.* **1.** power and authority, as of a judge, court, or official [The juvenile court has *jurisdiction* over children.] **2.** the limits or territory over which one's power or authority reaches [This area is outside the *jurisdiction* of the city police.]

ju·ris·pru·dence (joor′is prōō′d'ns), *n.* **1.** the science that deals with the principles on which law is based. **2.** a system of laws [American *jurisprudence;* criminal *jurisprudence*].

ju·rist (joor′ist), *n.* an expert in law; scholar in the field of law.

ju·ror (joor′ər), *n.* a member of a jury.

ju·ry (joor′ē), *n.* **1.** a group of people chosen to listen to the evidence in a law trial, and then to reach a decision, or verdict: see also **grand jury. 2.** a group of people chosen to decide the winners in a contest. —**ju′ries,** *pl.*

ju·ry·man (joor′ē mən), *n.* a juror. —**ju′ry·men,** *pl.*

just (just), *n. & v.* same as **joust.**

just (just), *adj.* **1.** that is right or fair [a *just* decision; *just* praise]. **2.** doing what is right or honest; righteous [a *just* man]. **3.** based on good reasons [*just* suspicions]. **4.** true or correct; exact [a *just* measurement]. —*adv.* **1.** neither more nor less than; exactly [You are *just* on time.] **2.** almost at the point of; nearly [I was *just* leaving.] **3.** no more than; only [He is *just* teasing you.] **4.** by a very small amount; barely [The arrow *just* missed the bull's-eye.] **5.** now or a very short time ago [The plane *just* took off.] **6.** truly; really; quite: *used only in everyday talk* [I feel *just* fine.] —**just now,** a very short time ago. —**just the same,** nevertheless; notwithstanding: *used only in everyday talk.* —**just′- ness,** *n.*

jus·tice (jus′tis), *n.* **1.** the fact or condition of being just or fair [There is *justice* in his demand.] **2.** reward or punishment as deserved [The prisoner asked only for *justice*.] **3.** the upholding of what is just or lawful [a court of *justice*]. **4.** a judge [a *justice* of the Supreme Court]. —**bring to justice,** to bring a person who has done wrong into a law court to be tried. —**do justice to, 1.** to treat in a fair or proper way. **2.** to enjoy fully [to *do justice to* a meal].

justice of the peace, a public official with power to decide law cases that are less serious than crimes, send persons to trial in a higher court, perform marriages, etc.

jus·ti·fi·a·ble (jus′tə fī′ə b'l), *adj.* that can be shown to be just, right, or free from blame. —**jus′ti·fi′a·bly,** *adv.*

jus·ti·fi·ca·tion (jus′tə fi kā′shən), *n.* **1.** a justifying or being justified. **2.** a fact that frees one from blame or guilt [There is no *justification* for such a mistake.]

jus·ti·fy (jus′tə fī), *v.* **1.** to show to be right or fair [His higher pay is *justified* by the extra work he does.] **2.** to free from blame or guilt; absolve [He tried to *justify* himself before the court.] —**jus′ti·fied,** *p.t. & p.p.;* **jus′ti·fy·ing,** *pr.p.*

just·ly (just′lē), *adv.* **1.** in a just way; rightly. **2.** in a way that is deserved [*justly* rewarded].

jut (jut), *v.* to stick out; project [a *jutting* cliff]. —**jut′ted,** *p.t. & p.p.;* **jut′ting,** *pr.p.*

jute (joot), *n.* a strong fiber gotten from a plant of India and Pakistan. It is used for making burlap, rope, etc.

ju·ven·ile (jōō′və n'l *or* jōō′və nīl), *adj.* **1.** young or youthful. **2.** of, like, or for children or young people [*juvenile* ideas; *juvenile* books]. —*n.* **1.** a child or young person. **2.** a book for children.

jux·ta·po·si·tion (juks′tə pə zish′ən), *n.* the act of putting or the condition of being side by side or close together.

K

K, k (kā), *n.* the eleventh letter of the English alphabet. —**K's, k's** (kāz), *pl.*

K, symbol for the chemical element *potassium.*

K. or **k.,** abbreviation for **karat, kilogram.**

Kai·ser (kī′zər), *n.* an emperor, especially of Germany or Austria before 1918.

kale (kāl), *n.* a kind of cabbage with loose, curled leaves instead of a head.

ka·lei·do·scope (kə lī′də skōp), *n.* **1.** a small tube with mirrors and loose bits of colored glass in it. When the tube is held to the eye and turned, the bits of glass form one pattern after another. **2.** anything that is always changing. —**ka·lei·do·scop·ic** (kə lī′də skäp′ik), *adj.*

kan·ga·roo (kang gə rōō′), *n.* an animal of Australia with short fore-legs and strong, large hind legs, with which it makes long leaps. The female carries her young in a pouch in front.

Kan·sas (kan′zəs), *n.* a State in the central part of the United States: abbreviated **Kan.** or **Kans.** —**Kan′san,** *adj. & n.*

Kansas City, 1. a city in western Missouri. **2.** a city next to it in eastern Kansas.

kangaroo (5 ft. high)

ka·o·lin (kā′ə lin), *n.* a fine white clay used in making porcelain.

Ka·ra·chi (kə rä′chē), *n.* a city in West Pakistan, on the Arabian Sea.

kar·a·kul (kar′ə kəl), *n.* same as **caracul.**

kar·at (kar′ət), *n.* same as **carat.**

ka·ra·te (kä rä′tē), *n.* a Japanese form of self-defense, in which chopping blows are given with the side of the open hand.

Kash·mir (kash mir′), *n.* a region north of India, claimed by both India and Pakistan.

ka·ty·did (kā′tē did), *n.* a large, green insect that looks like a grass-hopper. The male ka-tydid makes a shrill sound with its wings.

kay·ak (kī′ak), *n.* an Eskimo canoe made of a wooden frame covered with skins all around, except for an opening for the pad-dler.

katydid (1½ in. long)

kc., abbreviation for **kilocycle** or **kilocycles.**

Keats, John (kēts), 1795–1821; English poet.

keel (kēl), *n.* **1.** the center timber or steel plate that runs along the lowest part of a ship's bottom. **2.** anything like this, as beams or girders along the bottom of an airship. —**keel over, 1.** to turn over; upset. **2.** to fall over suddenly, as in a faint. —**on an even keel,** in an even, steady way; without being upset.

kayak

keel·son (kel′s'n *or* kēl′s'n), *n.* a set of timbers or metal plates fastened along a ship's keel to make it stronger.

keen (kēn), *adj.* **1.** having a sharp edge or point [a *keen* knife]. **2.** sharp or cutting in force [a *keen* wind; a *keen* appetite]. **3.** sharp and quick in seeing, hearing, thinking, etc.; acute [*keen* eyesight; a *keen* mind]. **4.** eager or enthusiastic [Is he *keen* about going?] **5.** strong or intense [*keen* enjoyment; *keen* competition]. **6.** good,

fine, excellent, etc.: *slang in this meaning.*
—keen′ly, *adv.* **—keen′ness,** *n.*

keep (kēp), *v.* **1.** to have or hold and not let go [He was *kept* after school. She *kept* her trim figure. Can you *keep* a secret?] **2.** to hold for a later time; save [I *kept* the cake to eat later.] **3.** to hold back; restrain [I can't *keep* her from talking.] **4.** to take care of; look after [She *keeps* house for her father.] **5.** to guard or protect [Tighten the cap to *keep* the bottle from spilling.] **6.** to write down a regular record in [to *keep* a diary; to *keep* the books]. **7.** to have in stock for sale [Our grocer *keeps* meat.] **8.** to have in one's service or for one's use [to *keep* servants]. **9.** to stay or make stay as it is; last; continue [The fruit will *keep* in the refrigerator. *Keep* your engine running. *Keep* on dancing.] **10.** to carry out; fulfill; observe [to *keep* a promise; to *keep* the Sabbath]. **—***n.* **1.** food and shelter; support [George earned his *keep* by doing odd jobs.] **2.** a castle or the stronghold of a castle. **—for keeps, 1.** with the winner keeping what he wins. **2.** for always; permanently. *This phrase is used only in everyday talk.* **—keep to oneself, 1.** to avoid being with other people. **2.** to hold back from telling. **—keep up, 1.** to make stay in good condition. **2.** to continue; go on. **3.** to stay informed about something. **—keep up with,** to go or do as fast as; stay even with. **—kept,** *p.t. & p.p.;* **keep′ing,** *pr.p.*

keep·er (kēp′ər), *n.* a person or thing that keeps, guards, or takes care of something.

keep·ing (kēp′ing), *n.* **1.** care or protection [She left her money in his *keeping.*] **2.** the observing of a rule, holiday, etc. **—in keeping with,** in agreement or harmony with.

keep·sake (kēp′sāk), *n.* something kept in memory of the person who gave it.

keg (keg), *n.* a small barrel.

kelp (kelp), *n.* **1.** a brown seaweed that is large and coarse. **2.** the ashes of burned seaweed.

ken (ken), *n.* knowledge or understanding [Nuclear physics is beyond his *ken.*] **—***v.* to know: *used mainly in Scotland.* **—kenned,** *p.t. & p.p.;* **ken′ning,** *pr.p.*

kelp

Ken·ne·dy, John F. (ken′ə dē), 1917–1963; 35th president of the United States, from 1961 to 1963.

Kennedy, Cape, a cape on the eastern coast of Florida: site for launching spacecraft.

ken·nel (ken′'l), *n.* **1.** a doghouse. **2.** *often* **kennels,** *pl.* a place where dogs are raised or kept. **—***v.* to put or keep in a kennel. **—ken′neled** or **ken′nelled,** *p.t. & p.p.;* **ken′nel·ing** or **ken′nel·ling,** *pr.p.*

Ken·tuck·y (kən tuk′ē), *n.* a State in the eastern central part of the United States: abbreviated **Ky.** or **Ken.**

Ken·ya (ken′yə *or* kēn′yə), *n.* a country in east central Africa, on the Indian Ocean.

kept (kept), past tense and past participle of **keep.**

ker·chief (kûr′chif), *n.* **1.** a piece of cloth, usually square, worn over the head or around the neck. **2.** a handkerchief.

ker·nel (kûr′n'l), *n.* **1.** a grain or seed, as of corn or wheat. **2.** the soft, inner part of a nut or fruit pit. **3.** the most important part; gist.

ker·o·sene or **ker·o·sine** (ker′ə sēn), *n.* a thin oil made from coal or petroleum and used in some lamps, stoves, etc.: also called **coal oil.**

ketch (kech), *n.* a small sailing ship with two masts: *see the picture.*

ketch·up (kech′əp), *n.* a thick sauce made of tomatoes, onion, spices, etc. and used as a flavoring on foods: also called **catchup, catsup.**

ketch

ket·tle (ket′'l), *n.* **1.** a metal container for boiling or cooking things. **2.** a teakettle.

ket·tle·drum (ket′'l drum), *n.* a drum that is half a hollow, metal globe with a parchment top that can be loosened or tightened to change the pitch.

kettledrum

key (kē), *n.* **1.** a small metal device that one puts into a lock and turns so as to lock or unlock a door, drawer, etc. **2.** anything like this, as a device for winding a clock. **3.** any one of the flat parts that are pressed down in playing a piano, clarinet, etc. or in using a typewriter, adding machine, etc. **4.** a thing that explains something else, as a book of answers to problems or a set of symbols for pronouncing words. **5.** a person or thing that controls something else [The steel industry is the *key* to our nation's economy.] **6.** a group of related musical notes based on and named after a certain keynote: these notes form a scale whose lowest note is the keynote [a sonata in the *key* of F]. **7.** a certain manner, tone, or style [He answered my letter in a mournful *key.*] **—***adj.* that controls or is important [a *key* man in the government]. **—***v.* **1.** to furnish notes or answers that explain something else. **2.** to make agree; bring into harmony [The colors in the drapes are *keyed* to the red and blue carpet.] **—key up,** to make nervous or excited. **—keyed,** *p.t. & p.p.;* **key′ing,** *pr.p.*

fat,   āpe,   cär,   ten,   ēven,   hit,   bīte,   gō,   hôrn,   tōōl,   book,   up,   fūr;
get,   joy,   yet,   chin,   she,   thin,   *th*en;   zh = s in pleasure;   ′ as in able (ā′b'l)
ə = a in ago,   e in agent,   i in sanity,   o in confess,   u in focus.

key (kē), *n.* an island or reef that does not stick up very far above the water.

key·board (kē'bôrd), *n.* the row or rows of keys of a piano, organ, typewriter, etc.

key·hole (kē'hōl), *n.* the opening in a lock in which a key is put to lock or unlock it.

key·note (kē'nōt), *n.* **1.** the note on which a musical key is based. **2.** the main idea or principle of a speech, policy, etc.

key ring, a metal ring for holding keys.

key·stone (kē'stōn), *n.* **1.** the central stone of an arch at its very top. It holds the other stones in place. **2.** the main idea or most important part [Free speech is the *keystone* of our liberties.]

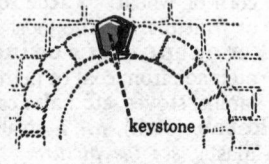

keystone

kg., abbreviation for **kilogram** or **kilograms.**

kha·ki (kak'ē), *n.* **1.** yellowish brown. **2.** a strong, heavy cotton cloth of this color. **3.** *often* **khakis,** *pl.* a uniform made of khaki.

khan (kän), *n.* **1.** a title once used by the Mongol rulers of Asia. **2.** now, a title given to certain officials in Afghanistan, Iran, Pakistan, etc.

Khar·kov (kär'kôf), *n.* a city in the Ukraine, in the Soviet Union.

Khar·toum or **Khar·tum** (kär tōōm'), *n.* the capital of Sudan.

khe·dive (kə dēv'), *n.* the title of the Turkish rulers of Egypt from 1867 to 1914.

Khrush·chev, Ni·ki·ta (ni kē'tä krōōs'chôf), 1894– ; premier of the Soviet Union from 1958 to 1964.

kib·itz·er (kib'it sər), *n.* a person who watches others do something and gives advice that is not wanted: *used only in everyday talk.*

kick (kik), *v.* **1.** to swing the foot or feet with force, as in striking something [to *kick* a door]. **2.** to move by striking with the foot [to *kick* a football]. **3.** to spring back suddenly, as a gun does when fired. **4.** to complain or grumble: *used only in everyday talk.* —*n.* **1.** a blow with the foot. **2.** the act of kicking. **3.** a springing back suddenly, as a gun does when fired; recoil. **4.** a complaint or protest: *used only in everyday talk.* **5.** a thrill, or excited feeling: *used only in everyday talk.* —**kick out,** to get rid of or put out: *used only in everyday talk.* —**kick'er,** *n.*

kick·off (kik'ôf), *n.* a kick in football that begins play, as at the beginning of each half.

kid (kid), *n.* **1.** a young goat. **2.** leather from the skin of young goats. It is used for gloves, shoes, etc. **3.** a child: *used only in everyday talk.* —*v.* to tease, fool, etc.: *used only in everyday talk.* —**kid'ded,** *p.t. & p.p.;* **kid'ding,** *pr.p.*

Kidd, Captain (kid), 1645?–1701; Scottish pirate, whose full name was *William Kidd.*

kid·dy or **kid·die** (kid'ē), *n.* a child: *used only in everyday talk.* —**kid'dies,** *pl.*

kid·nap (kid'nap), *v.* to carry off a person by force or trickery, often in order to get a ransom. —**kid'naped** or **kid'napped,** *p.t. & p.p.;* **kid'nap·ing** or **kid'nap·ping,** *pr.p.* —**kid'·nap·er** or **kid'nap·per,** *n.*

kid·ney (kid'nē), *n.* **1.** either of a pair of organs in the body that take water and waste products out of the blood and pass them through the bladder as urine. **2.** the kidney of an animal, used as food. **3.** nature or kind [a man of the right *kidney* for the deed]. —**kid'neys,** *pl.*

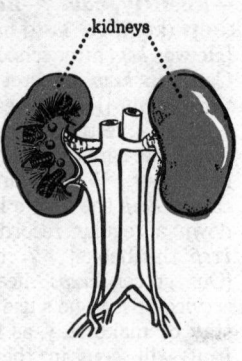

kidneys

kid·skin (kid'skin), *n.* kid (*meaning 2*).

Ki·ev (kē'yef), *n.* the capital of the Ukraine, in the Soviet Union.

kill (kil), *v.* **1.** to cause the death of; make die; slay. **2.** to put an end to; destroy or ruin [His defeat *killed* all our hopes.] **3.** to defeat or veto, as a bill before a lawmaking body. **4.** to make time pass in doing unimportant things [an hour to *kill* before my train leaves]. **5.** to overcome, as with laughter, surprise, dismay, etc.: *used only in everyday talk.* —*n.* **1.** the act of killing [to be in at the *kill*]. **2.** an animal or animals killed [a lion's *kill*]. —**kill'er,** *n.*

kill·deer (kil'dir), *n.* a small wading bird that has a shrill cry.

kill·joy (kil'joi'), *n.* a person who spoils other people's fun or enjoyment.

kiln (kil *or* kiln), *n.* a furnace or oven for drying or baking bricks, pottery, lime, etc.

ki·lo (kē'lō *or* kil'ō), *n.* **1.** a kilogram. **2.** a kilometer. —**ki'los,** *pl.*

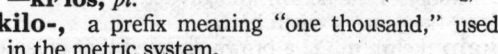

killdeer (9 in. long)

kilo-, a prefix meaning "one thousand," used in the metric system.

kil·o·cy·cle (kil'ə sī'k'l), *n.* same as **kilohertz.**

kil·o·gram or **kil·o·gramme** (kil'ə gram), *n.* a unit of weight, equal to 1,000 grams or about 2.2 pounds.

kil·o·hertz (kil'ə hūrts), *n.* 1,000 hertz: the frequency of radio waves is measured in kilohertz.

kil·o·me·ter or **kil·o·me·tre** (kil'ə mē'tər *or* ki läm'ə tər), *n.* a unit of measure, equal to 1,000 meters or about ⅝ mile.

kil·o·watt (kil'ə wät), *n.* a unit of electrical power, equal to 1,000 watts.

kilt (kilt), *n.* a short skirt with pleats worn by men of the Scottish Highlands.

kil·ter (kil'tər), *n.* working order: *only in everyday talk* [Our TV set is out of *kilter*.]

ki·mo·no (kə mō'nə), *n.* **1.** a loose robe with wide sleeves and a sash, that used to be the common outer garment of Japanese men and women and is still sometimes worn: *see picture on next page.* **2.** a woman's dressing gown like this. —**ki·mo'nos,** *pl.*

kilt

kin (kin), *n.* relatives or family. One's **next of kin** is one's nearest relative or relatives. —*adj.* related, as by birth [Is he *kin* to you?]

-kin (kin), a suffix meaning "little" [A *lambkin* is a little lamb.]

kind (kīnd), *n.* **1.** sort or variety [He reads all *kinds* of books.] **2.** a natural grouping, as of plants or animals [a bird of the parrot *kind*]. —**in kind, 1.** in the same way. **2.** with goods instead of money [payment *in kind*]. —**kind of,** somewhat: *used only in everyday talk* [It's *kind of* cold here.] —**of a kind,** of the same kind; alike [The twins are two *of a kind*.]

kimono

kind (kīnd), *adj.* **1.** always ready to help others and do good; friendly, gentle, generous, sympathetic, etc. **2.** showing goodness, generosity, sympathy, etc. [*kind* deeds; *kind* regards].

kin·der·gar·ten (kin'dər gär't'n), *n.* a school or class for young children about five years old, to get them ready for regular school work by games, exercises, simple handicraft, etc.

kind·heart·ed (kīnd'här'tid), *adj.* kind.

kin·dle (kin'd'l), *v.* **1.** to set on fire; light [to *kindle* logs in a fireplace.] **2.** to catch fire; start burning [The logs *kindled* quickly.] **3.** to stir up or excite [Insults *kindled* her anger.] **4.** to light up; brighten [Her eyes *kindled* with joy.] —**kin'dled,** *p.t. & p.p.;* **kin'dling,** *pr.p.*

kin·dling (kin'dling), *n.* bits of dry wood or the like, for starting a fire.

kind·ly (kīnd'lē), *adj.* **1.** kind, gentle, sympathetic, etc. **2.** agreeable or pleasant [a *kindly* climate]. —*adv.* **1.** in a kind and pleasant way [Please treat my cousins *kindly*.] **2.** please [*Kindly* shut the door.] —**take kindly to,** to be attracted to. —**kind'li·er,** *compar.;* **kind'li·est,** *superl.* —**kind'li·ness,** *n.*

kind·ness (kīnd'nis), *n.* **1.** the condition or habit of being kind. **2.** a kind act.

kin·dred (kin'drid), *n.* **1.** relatives or family; kin [He and all his *kindred* lived in the same town.] **2.** family relationship; kinship. —*adj.* **1.** related, as by birth. **2.** alike or similar [They are *kindred* spirits.]

kine (kīn), *n.pl.* *an old word for* cattle *or* cows.

ki·net·ic (ki net'ik *or* kī net'ik), *adj.* of or caused by motion [*kinetic* energy].

kin·folks (kin'fōks) or **kin·folk** (kin'fōk), *n.pl.* family or relatives; kin.

king (king), *n.* **1.** a man who rules a country and whose position is handed down from father to son. Kings today usually have little power to rule. **2.** an important or powerful man in some field [an oil *king*]. **3.** a playing card with a picture of a king on it. **4.** the piece in chess whose capture ends the game. **5.** a piece in checkers that has moved the length of the board.

king·dom (king'dəm), *n.* **1.** a country ruled by a king or queen; monarchy. **2.** a region or place of spiritual rule [the *kingdom* of heaven]. **3.** any of the three groupings into which all things are placed [the animal, vegetable, and mineral *kingdoms*].

king·fish·er (king'fish'ər), *n.* a bright-colored bird with a short tail, a large head, and a strong beak. Many kingfishers eat fish.

king·ly (king'lē), *adj.* of, like, or fit for a king; royal; regal [*kingly* splendor]. —**king'li·er,** *compar.;* **king'li·est,** *superl.*

Kings (kingz), *n.* either of two books of the Old Testament, or in the Roman Catholic Bible, any of four books.

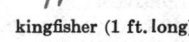

kingfisher (1 ft. long)

king·ship (king'ship), *n.* **1.** the position or power of a king. **2.** rule by a king; monarchy.

king-size (king'sīz') or **king-sized** (king'sīzd'), *adj.* larger than the regular kind: *used only in everyday talk* [*king-size* cigarettes].

kink (kingk), *n.* **1.** a short twist or curl, as in a hair or thread. **2.** a painful cramp in some muscle. **3.** an odd idea or queer notion. —*v.* to form a kink or kinks.

kink·y (king'kē), *adj.* full of kinks; tightly curled [*kinky* hair]. —**kink'i·er,** *compar.;* **kink'i·est,** *superl.* —**kink'i·ness,** *n.*

kin·ship (kin'ship), *n.* the condition of being related or connected; especially, a family relationship.

kins·man (kinz'mən), *n.* a relative; especially, a man who is a relative. —**kins'men,** *pl.*

kins·wom·an (kinz'woom'ən), *n.* a woman who is a relative. —**kins'wom'en,** *pl.*

ki·osk (ki äsk'), *n.* a small, open building used as a newsstand, bandstand, etc.

Kip·ling, Rud·yard (rud'yərd kip'ling), 1865–1936; English writer and poet, born in India.

kip·per (kip'ər), *v.* to clean and salt a fish, and then dry or smoke it. —*n.* a kippered fish, especially a herring.

kirk (kûrk), *n.* a church: *a Scottish word.*

kiosk

kis·met (kiz'met *or* kis'met), *n.* fate; destiny.

kiss (kis), *v.* **1.** to touch with the lips as a way of showing love, respect, etc. or as a greeting. **2.** to touch lightly [His bowling ball just *kissed* the last pin.] —*n.* **1.** an act of kissing. **2.** a light touch. **3.** any of various candies.

kit (kit), *n.* a set of tools or other articles for some special use, a number of parts to be put

fat,   āpe,   cär,   ten,   ēven,   hit,   bīte,   gō,   hôrn,   tool,   book,   up,   fûr;
get,   joy,   yet,   chin,   she,   thin,   *th*en;   zh = s in pleasure;   ' as in able (ā'b'l);
ə = a in ago,   e in agent,   i in sanity,   o in confess,   u in focus.

together, etc.; also, a box or bag for carrying these [a carpenter's *kit;* a model airplane *kit*].

kitch·en (kich′ən), *n.* a room or place for preparing and cooking food.

kitch·en·ette (kich ən et′), *n.* a small kitchen or the corner of a room with kitchen equipment.

kitch·en·ware (kich′ən wer), *n.* pots, pans, ladles, etc. used in the kitchen.

kite (kīt), *n.* **1.** a light frame, as of wood, covered with paper or cloth. It is tied to a string and flown in the air when the wind is blowing. **2.** a hawk with long, pointed wings.

kith (kith), *n.* friends: *now only in the phrase* **kith and kin,** meaning "friends and relatives."

kit·ten (kit′'n), *n.* a young cat.

kite

kit·ty (kit′ē), *n.* a pet name for a kitten or cat. **—kit′ties,** *pl.*

Klon·dike (klän′dīk), *n.* a region in northwestern Canada where gold was found in 1896.

km., abbreviation for **kilometer** or **kilometers.**

knack (nak), *n.* a special ability or skill [He has the *knack* of making friends.]

knap·sack (nap′sak), *n.* a leather or canvas bag worn on the back, as by hikers, for carrying supplies.

knave (nāv), *n.* **1.** a dishonest or tricky person; rascal or scoundrel. **2.** same as **jack,** the playing card.

knav·er·y (nāv′ər ē), *n.* an act or way of acting that is dishonest or tricky. **—knav′er·ies,** *pl.*

knav·ish (nāv′ish), *adj.* like a knave; dishonest or tricky. **—knav′ish·ly,** *adv.*

knapsack

knead (nēd), *v.* **1.** to keep pressing and squeezing dough, clay, etc. to make it ready for use. **2.** to rub or press with the hands; massage [to *knead* a sore muscle].

knee (nē), *n.* **1.** the joint between the thigh and the lower leg. **2.** anything shaped like a knee, especially like a bent knee. **3.** the part of a trouser leg, etc. that covers the knee.

knee·cap (nē′kap), *n.* the flat, movable bone that forms the front of a person's knee.

kneel (nēl), *v.* to rest on a knee or knees [Some people *kneel* when they pray.] **—knelt** or **kneeled,** *p.t.* & *p.p.;* **kneel′ing,** *pr.p.*

knell (nel), *n.* **1.** the sound of a bell rung slowly, as at a funeral. **2.** a warning that something will end or pass away [The invention of the automobile sounded the *knell* of the horse and buggy.] **—v. 1.** to ring a bell slowly; toll. **2.** to announce or warn as by a knell [The judge's sentence *knelled* his death.]

knelt (nelt), a past tense and past participle of **kneel.**

knew (nōō *or* nyōō), past tense of **know.**

knick·er·bock·ers (nik′ər bäk′ərz), *n.pl.* short, loose trousers gathered in just below the knees. The early Dutch settlers of New York, who were called **Knickerbockers,** wore them. Also called **knick·ers** (nik′ərz).

knickerbockers

knick·knack (nik′nak), *n.* a small, showy, but not valuable, article [Her shelves were loaded with china figures and other *knickknacks*.]

knife (nīf), *n.* **1.** a tool having a flat, sharp blade set in a handle, used for cutting. **2.** a cutting blade that is part of a machine. **—v.** to cut or stab with a knife. **—knives,** *pl.* **—knifed,** *p.t.* & *p.p.;* **knif′ing,** *pr.p.*

knight (nīt), *n.* **1.** a man in the Middle Ages who was given a military rank of honor after serving as a page and squire. Knights were supposed to be gallant, brave, etc. **2.** in Great Britain, a man who has been honored with a high social rank that allows him to use *Sir* before his first name. **3.** a chess piece shaped like a horse's head. **—v.** to give the rank of knight to.

knight-er·rant (nīt′er′ənt), *n.* a knight of the Middle Ages who wandered about seeking adventure. **—knights′-er′rant,** *pl.* **—knight′-er′rant·ry,** *n.*

knight·hood (nīt′hood), *n.* **1.** the rank of a knight. **2.** politeness and bravery, as of a knight; chivalry. **3.** knights as a group.

knight·ly (nīt′lē), *adj.* of or like a knight; brave, polite, etc. **—knight′li·ness,** *n.*

knit (nit), *v.* **1.** to make by looping yarn or thread together with special needles [to *knit* a scarf]. **2.** to join or grow together in a close and firm way; unite [My broken leg *knit* slowly. Our family is close *knit*.] **3.** to draw together in wrinkles; frown [to *knit* the brows]. **—knit′ted** or **knit,** *p.t.* & *p.p.;* **knit′ting,** *pr.p.*

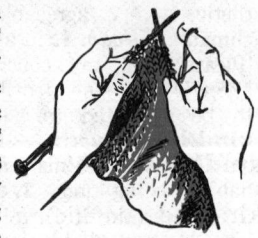
knitting

knives (nīvz), *n.* plural of **knife.**

knob (näb), *n.* **1.** a handle that is more or less round, as on a door or drawer, or on a radio set for working some control. **2.** a round part that sticks out [a *knob* at the end of a cane]. **3.** a hill or mountain with a round top. **—knob′by,** *adj.*

knock (näk), *v.* **1.** to hit, as with the fist; especially, to rap on a door [Who is *knocking?*] **2.** to hit and cause to fall [The dog *knocked* down Billy.] **3.** to make by hitting [to *knock* a hole in a wall]. **4.** to make a pounding or tapping noise [An engine *knocks* when the combustion is faulty.] **5.** to find fault with; criticize: *used only in everyday talk.* **—n. 1.** a hard, loud blow, as with the fist; rap, as on a door. **2.** a pounding or tapping noise, as in an engine. **—knock about** or **knock around,** to wander about; roam: *used only in everyday talk.* **—knock off, 1.** to stop working. **2.** to take away; deduct. *This phrase is used only in everyday talk.* —**knock out, 1.** to score a knockout over in boxing. **2.** to make unconscious or very tired. —**knock together,** to make or put together quickly or crudely.

knock·er (näk′ər), *n.* a person or thing that knocks, especially a ring or knob fastened to a door by a hinge and used for knocking.

knock-kneed (näk′nēd′), *adj.* having legs that bend inward at the knee.

knock·out (näk′out), *n.* a blow that knocks a boxer down so that he cannot get up and go on fighting before the referee counts to ten.

knock-kneed
girl

knoll (nōl), *n.* a little rounded hill; mound.

knot (nät), *n.* **1.** a lump, as in a string or ribbon, formed by a loop or tangle drawn tight. **2.** a fastening made by tying together parts or pieces of string, rope, etc. [Sailors make a variety of *knots.*] **3.** a small group [a *knot* of people]. **4.** something that joins closely, as the bond of marriage. **5.** a problem or difficulty. **6.** a hard lump on a tree where a branch grows out, or a cross section of such a lump in a board. **7.** a unit of speed of one nautical mile (6,076.1 feet) an hour [The ship averaged 20 *knots.*] —*v.* **1.** to tie or fasten with a knot; make a knot in. **2.** to become tangled. —**knot′ted,** *p.t. & p.p.;* **knot′ting,** *pr.p.*

knot·hole (nät′hōl), *n.* a hole in a board or tree trunk where a knot has fallen out.

knot·ty (nät′ē), *adj.* **1.** full of knots [*knotty* pine]. **2.** hard to deal with [a *knotty* problem]. —**knot′ti·er,** *compar.;* **knot′ti·est,** *superl.*

know (nō), *v.* **1.** to be sure of or have the facts about [Do you *know* why grass is green? He *knows* the law.] **2.** to be aware of; realize [He suddenly *knew* that she wouldn't stay.] **3.** to have in one's mind [The actor *knows* his lines.] **4.** to be acquainted with [I *know* your brother well.] **5.** to recognize [I'd *know* that face anywhere.] **6.** to be able to tell the difference in [It's not always easy to *know* right from wrong.] —**knew,** *p.t.;* **known,** *p.p.;* **know′ing,** *pr.p.*

know·ing (nō′ing), *adj.* **1.** having the facts; well-informed. **2.** clever or shrewd. **3.** showing shrewd or secret understanding [a *knowing* look].

know·ing·ly (nō′ing lē), *adv.* **1.** in a knowing way. **2.** on purpose; knowing clearly what one is doing [He would not *knowingly* lie.]

knowl·edge (näl′ij), *n.* **1.** the fact or condition of knowing [*Knowledge* of the murder spread through the town.] **2.** what is known or learned, as through study or experience [a man of great *knowledge*]. **3.** all that is known by man. —**to one's knowledge,** as far as one knows.

known (nōn), past participle of **know.**

Knox·ville (näks′vil), *n.* a city in eastern Tennessee.

knuck·le (nuk′'l), *n.* **1.** a joint of the finger; especially, a joint connecting a finger to the rest of the hand. **2.** the knee or hock joint of a pig, calf, etc., used as food. —**knuckle down, 1.** to work hard. **2.** *also* **knuckle under,** to give in; surrender. —**knuck′led,** *p.t. & p.p.;* **knuck′ling,** *pr.p.*

ko·a·la (kō ä′lə), *n.* an Australian animal that lives in trees and looks like a very small bear. The mother carries its young in a pouch in front.

kohl·ra·bi (kōl′rä bē *or* kōl rä′bē), *n.* a kind of cabbage whose leaves grow from a rounded stem that looks like a turnip.

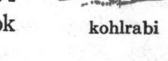
kohlrabi

kook·a·bur·ra (kook′ə bur′ə), *n.* an Australian bird of the kingfisher family. Its cry sounds like someone laughing loudly.

ko·peck or **ko·pek** (kō′pek), *n.* a small Russian coin. One ruble equals 100 kopecks.

Ko·ran (kô rän′ *or* kô′ran), *n.* the sacred book of the Moslems.

Ko·re·a (kō rē′ə *or* kô rē′ə), *n.* a country southeast of Manchuria, divided into two republics, North Korea and South Korea. —**Ko·re′an,** *adj. & n.*

ko·sher (kō′shər), *adj.* clean or fit to eat according to the Jewish laws of diet.

kow·tow (kou′tou′), *v.* to be very humble or like a slave in showing obedience [The Chinese used to *kowtow* to their lords by kneeling and bringing the forehead to the ground.]

woman kowtowing

Krem·lin (krem′lin), *n.* a large fortress in the center of Moscow, where the government offices of the Soviet Union used to be.

Kriss Krin·gle (kris kring′g'l), Santa Claus.

kt., abbreviation for **karat** or **carat.**

ku·chen (kōō′kən), *n.* a cake that is like a sweet bread, often covered or filled with sugar and spices, raisins, nuts, etc.

ku·du (kōō′dōō), *n.* a large, gray-brown antelope of Africa.

kum·quat (kum′kwät), *n.* a fruit like a small orange, used for preserves.

Ku·wait (koo wāt′), *n.* a country in eastern Arabia.

kw., abbreviation for **kilowatt.**

Ky., abbreviation for **Kentucky.**

Kyo·to (kyō′tō′), *n.* a city in Honshu, Japan.

Kyu·shu (kyōō′shōō′), *n.* one of the islands of Japan.

kumquats

fat,   āpe,   cär,   ten,   ēven,   hit,   bīte,   gō,   hôrn,   tōōl,   book,   up,   fur;
get,   joy,   yet,   chin,   she,   thin,   then;   zh = s in pleasure;   ' as in able (ā′b'l)
ə = a in ago,   e in agent,   i in sanity,   o in confess,   u in focus

L

L, l (el), *n.* the twelfth letter of the English alphabet. —**L's, l's** (elz), *pl.*

L (el), *n.* **1.** something shaped like an L. **2.** the Roman numeral for 50.

L., l., abbreviation for **lake, latitude, left, length, line, liter** or **liters.**

L., abbreviation for **Latin.**

la (lä *or* lô), *interj.* a sound made to show surprise: *now seldom used.*

la (lä), *n.* the sixth note of a musical scale.

La., abbreviation for **Louisiana.**

lab (lab), *n.* a laboratory: *only in everyday talk.*

la·bel (lā′b'l), *n.* a piece of paper, cloth, etc. that is marked and attached to an object to show what it is, what it contains, who owns it, etc. [a *label* on a can or in a suit; a mailing *label* on a package]. —*v.* **1.** to attach a label to [to *label* a package]. **2.** to name or describe as; call [No one wants to be *labeled* a "coward."] —**la′beled** or **la′belled,** *p.t. & p.p.;* **la′bel·ing** or **la′bel·ling,** *pr.p.*

label

la·bi·al (lā′bi əl), *adj.* **1.** of the lips. **2.** formed with the lips in speaking, as the sounds of *b, m,* and *p.* —*n.* a sound formed by the lips.

la·bor (lā′bər), *n.* **1.** work. **2.** a piece of work; task [the twelve *labors* of Hercules]. **3.** workers as a group [Both *labor* and management contribute to this fund.] **4.** the act of giving birth to a child. —*v.* **1.** to work or toil [Coal miners *labor* underground.] **2.** to move slowly and with effort [Grandpa *labored* up the steps.]

lab·o·ra·to·ry (lab′rə tôr′ē *or* lab′ər ə tôr′ē), *n.* a room or building where scientific work or tests are carried on, or where chemicals, drugs, etc. are prepared. —**lab′o·ra′to·ries,** *pl.*

Labor Day, the first Monday in September, a legal holiday honoring labor.

la·bored (lā′bərd), *adj.* done with great effort; strained [a *labored* attempt to be funny].

la·bor·er (lā′bər ər), *n.* a worker; especially, one doing rough work that takes little skill.

la·bo·ri·ous (lə bôr′i əs), *adj.* **1.** taking much work or effort [*laborious* tasks]. **2.** hard-working.

labor union, a group of workers joined together to protect and further their interests.

la·bour (lā′bər), *n. & v.* labor: *British spelling.*

Lab·ra·dor (lab′rə dôr), *n.* **1.** a large peninsula in northeastern North America, between the Atlantic Ocean and Hudson Bay. **2.** the eastern part of this peninsula, a part of Newfoundland.

la·bur·num (lə būr′nəm), *n.* a small tree or shrub with drooping yellow flowers.

lab·y·rinth (lab′ə rinth), *n.* a place with winding passages, blind alleys, etc. that make it hard to find one's way through; maze.

lab·y·rin·thine (lab′ə rin′thin), *adj.* like a labyrinth; complicated; hard to follow.

lace (lās), *n.* **1.** a string, ribbon, etc. put through holes or around hooks in a shoe, bodice, etc. for pulling the edges together and fastening them. **2.** a fabric of thread woven into fancy designs with many openings like those in a net. —*v.* **1.** to pull together and fasten with a lace. **2.** to trim with lace. **3.** to weave together; intertwine. **4.** to beat or whip. —**laced,** *p.t. & p.p.;* **lac′ing,** *pr.p.*

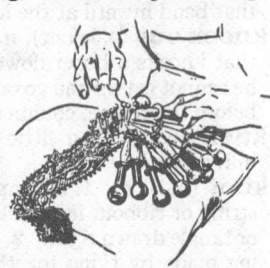

making lace

lac·er·ate (las′ə rāt), *v.* **1.** to tear in a jagged way [He *lacerated* his arm on the barbed wire.] **2.** to hurt deeply [Her cruel words *lacerated* his feelings.] —**lac′er·at·ed,** *p.t. & p.p.;* **lac′er·at·ing,** *pr.p.* —**lac′er·a′tion,** *n.*

lach·ry·mal (lak′rə m'l), *adj.* of or producing tears [The *lachrymal* glands produce tears.]

lack (lak), *n.* **1.** a need for something that is missing; shortage [*Lack* of money forced him to return home.] **2.** the thing that is needed [Our most serious *lack* was fresh water.] —*v.* **1.** to be without or not have enough; need [The soil *lacks* nitrogen.] **2.** to be missing or not enough [Money is *lacking* to buy new band uniforms.]

lack·a·dai·si·cal (lak′ə dā′zi k'l), *adj.* showing little or no interest or spirit; listless.

lack·ey (lak′ē), *n.* **1.** a man servant of low rank. **2.** a person who carries out another's orders like a servant. —**lack′eys,** *pl.*

lack·lus·ter (lak′lus′tər), *adj.* lacking brightness; dull [*lackluster* eyes].

la·con·ic (lə kän′ik), *adj.* saying much in a few words; brief; concise [a *laconic* reply].

lac·quer (lak′ər), *n.* **1.** a varnish made of shellac, natural or artificial resins, etc. dissolved in alcohol or some other liquid. Coloring matter can be added to lacquer to form a **lacquer enamel. 2.** a natural varnish obtained from certain trees in Asia. —*v.* to coat with lacquer.

la·crosse (lə krôs′), *n.* a ball game played by two teams on a field with a goal at each end. The players use webbed rackets with long handles.

lac·te·al (lak′ti əl), *adj.* of or like milk.

lac·tic (lak′tik), *adj.* of or gotten from milk [*Lactic* acid is formed when milk sours.]

lacrosse

lac·tose (lak′tōs), *n.* a kind of sugar found in milk: also called **milk sugar.**

lac·y (lās′ē), *adj.* of or like lace. —**lac′i·er, compar.; lac′i·est, superl.**

lad (lad), *n.* a boy or youth.

lad·der (lad′ər), *n.* 1. a framework of two side-pieces connected by a series of rungs or cross-pieces on which one can climb up or down. 2. anything that helps a person to go higher [to rise on the *ladder* of fame].

lad·die (lad′ē), *n.* a lad: *a Scottish word.*

lade (lād), *v.* to load. —**lad′ed,** *p.t.;* **lad′en** or **lad′ed,** *p.p.;* **lad′ing,** *pr.p.*

lad·en (lād′′n), *adj.* having or carrying a load; burdened [a mule *laden* with packs].

lad·ing (lād′ing), *n.* a load; cargo: *usually used in* **bill of lading,** a receipt, as from a shipping company, that lists the goods received for shipping.

la·dle (lā′d′l), *n.* a cuplike spoon with a long handle, used for dipping liquids out of a container. —*v.* to dip out, as with a ladle. —**la′dled,** *p.t. & p.p.;* **la′dling,** *pr.p.*

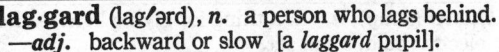

ladle

la·dy (lā′dē), *n.* 1. a woman, especially one who is polite and refined and has a sense of honor. 2. a woman belonging to a family of high social standing, as the wife of a lord. 3. **Lady,** a British title given to some women of high rank, as countesses. —*adj.* that is a woman; female [a *lady* barber]. —**Our Lady,** the Virgin Mary. —**la′dies,** *pl.*

la·dy·bug (lā′dē bug), or **la·dy·bird** (lā′dē-bûrd), *n.* a small, round, flying beetle, brightly colored with dark spots on its back.

lady in waiting, a woman who waits upon, or serves, a queen or princess.

la·dy·like (lā′dē līk), *adj.* like or fit for a lady; polite, cultured, or refined.

ladybug (⅜ in. long)

La·dy·ship (lā′dē ship), *n.* a title of respect used in speaking to or of a Lady.

la·dy's-slip·per (lā′dēz slip′ər) or **la·dy·slip·per** (lā′dē slip′ər), *n.* a wild orchid with a flower shaped like a slipper.

La·fa·yette, Marquis **de** (də lä′fi yet′), 1757–1834; French general who served in the American Revolutionary army.

lag (lag), *v.* to move so slowly as to fall behind; loiter [The tired hikers *lagged* behind.] —*n.* 1. the act of lagging. 2. the amount by which one thing lags behind another [There is a great *lag* between our social behavior and our scientific knowledge.] —**lagged,** *p.t. & p.p.;* **lag′ging,** *pr.p.*

lag·gard (lag′ərd), *n.* a person who lags behind. —*adj.* backward or slow [a *laggard* pupil].

la·goon (lə gōōn′), *n.* 1. a shallow lake or pond, especially one that joins a larger body of water. 2. the water that is surrounded by an atoll. 3. shallow salt water cut off from the sea by sand dunes.

laid (lād), past tense and past participle of **lay.**

lain (lān), past participle of **lie** (stretch out).

lair (ler), *n.* the bed or resting place of a wild animal; den.

laird (lerd), *n.* a landowner: *a Scottish word.*

la·i·ty (lā′ə tē), *n.* all laymen, as a group.

lake (lāk), *n.* 1. a large body of water, usually fresh water, surrounded by land. 2. a pool of liquid, as of oil.

la·ma (lä′mə), *n.* a Buddhist priest or monk in Tibet and Mongolia.

la·ma·ser·y (lä′mə ser′ē), *n.* a monastery of lamas. —**la′ma·ser′ies,** *pl.*

lamb (lam), *n.* 1. a young sheep. 2. its flesh, used as food. 3. lambskin. 4. a gentle or innocent person, especially a child.

Lamb, Charles (lam), 1775–1834; English writer of essays and, with his sister Mary, of *Tales from Shakespeare.*

lam·baste (lam bāst′), *v.* 1. to beat or thrash. 2. to scold harshly. *A slang word.* —**lambast′ed,** *p.t. & p.p.;* **lam·bast′ing,** *pr.p.*

lam·bent (lam′bənt), *adj.* 1. moving lightly about on a surface, as a flame. 2. glowing softly [the *lambent* sky]. 3. light and graceful [*lambent* wit].

lamb·kin (lam′kin), *n.* a little lamb.

lamb·skin (lam′skin), *n.* 1. the skin of a lamb, especially with the wool left on it. 2. leather or parchment made from this skin.

lame (lām), *adj.* 1. having a hurt leg or foot that makes one limp. 2. crippled, or stiff and painful [a *lame* leg; a *lame* back]. 3. not good enough; poor [a *lame* excuse]. —*v.* to make lame. —**lamed,** *p.t. & p.p.;* **lam′ing,** *pr.p.* —**lame′ly,** *adv.* —**lame′ness,** *n.*

la·mé (la mā′), *n.* a cloth made of or with metal threads, especially of gold or silver.

la·ment (lə ment′), *v.* to feel or show deep sorrow over something; mourn [to *lament* the death of someone]. —*n.* 1. weeping or crying that shows sorrow; wail. 2. a poem, song, etc. that mourns some loss or death.

lam·en·ta·ble (lam′ən tə b′l), *adj.* 1. that should be lamented; regrettable [a *lamentable* accident]. 2. so bad as to be pitiful [a *lamentable* piece of acting]. —**lam′en·ta·bly,** *adv.*

lam·en·ta·tion (lam′ən tā′shən), *n.* the act of lamenting; a wailing because of grief.

lam·i·nate (lam′ə nāt), *v.* 1. to form into or cover with a thin layer. 2. to make by putting together thin layers, as plywood. —**lam′i·nat·ed,** *p.t. & p.p.;* **lam′i·nat·ing,** *pr.p.* —**lam′i·na′tion,** *n.*

---

fat, āpe, cär, ten, ēven, hit, bīte, gō, hôrn, tōōl, book, up, fûr; get, joy, yet, chin, she, thin, *th*en; zh = s in pleasure; ′ as in able (ā′b′l); ə = a in ago, e in agent, i in sanity, o in confess, u in focus.

lamp (lamp), *n.* **1.** a thing for giving light, as an electric bulb, a gas jet, a wick soaked in oil, a fluorescent tube, etc. **2.** such a thing with the support or stand that it is set in [a table *lamp;* a floor *lamp*].

lamp·black (lamp'-blak), *n.* fine soot formed by burning oils, tars, etc. It is used in making black paints and inks.

lam·poon (lam pōōn'), *n.* a piece of writing

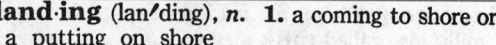

types of lamps

that attacks someone by making fun of him. —*v.* to make fun of in a lampoon.

lamp·post (lamp'pōst), *n.* a post that holds a street lamp.

lam·prey (lam'prē), *n.* a water animal like an eel, with a mouth shaped like a funnel, by which it clings to fishes it feeds on. —**lam'preys,** *pl.*

lance (lans), *n.* **1.** a weapon made of a long pole with a pointed metal head. **2.** a soldier armed with a lance; lancer. **3.** anything that stabs or cuts like a lance, as a fish spear, a surgeon's lancet, etc. —*v.* **1.** to stab with a lance. **2.** to cut open with a lancet [to *lance* a boil]. —**lanced,** *p.t. & p.p.;* **lanc'ing,** *pr.p.*

Lan·ce·lot (lan'sə lät), *n.* the bravest knight of King Arthur's Round Table.

horseman with a lance

lan·cer (lan'sər), *n.* a cavalry soldier armed with a lance.

lan·cet (lan'sit), *n.* a small, pointed knife with two cutting edges, used by surgeons.

land (land), *n.* **1.** the solid part of the earth's surface [by *land* or by sea]. **2.** a country, region, etc. [a distant *land;* one's native *land*]. **3.** ground or soil [high *land;* fertile *land*]. **4.** ground thought of as property [to invest money in *land*]. —*v.* **1.** to put or go on shore from a ship [The ship *landed* its cargo. The Marines *landed.*] **2.** to come to a port or to shore [The Mayflower *landed* in America in 1620.] **3.** to bring an aircraft down to the ground or on water. **4.** to come down after flying, jumping, or falling [The cat *landed* on its feet.] **5.** to bring to or end up at a place [This bus *lands* you in Reno at 3 A.M. He stole the money and *landed* in jail.] **6.** to catch [to *land* a fish]. **7.** to get or win [to *land* a job]. **8.** to strike [to *land* a blow to the jaw]. *Meanings 7 and 8 are used only in everyday talk.*

land·ed (lan'did), *adj.* **1.** owning land [a *landed* family]. **2.** consisting of land [a *landed* estate].

land·hold·er (land'hōl'dər), *n.* a person who owns or holds land. —**land'hold'ing,** *adj. & n.*

land·ing (lan'ding), *n.* **1.** a coming to shore or a putting on shore [the *landing* of troops]. **2.** a place where a ship can land; pier or dock. **3.** a platform at the end of a flight of stairs. **4.** a coming down after flying, jumping, or falling.

landing field, a field with a smooth surface, used by airplanes for landing and taking off.

landing

land·la·dy (land'lā'dē), *n.* a woman landlord. —**land'la'dies,** *pl.*

land·locked (land'läkt), *adj.* **1.** shut in on all sides or nearly all sides by land, as a bay or country. **2.** living in fresh water, cut off from the sea [*landlocked* salmon].

land·lord (land'lôrd), *n.* **1.** a person, especially a man, who owns land, houses, etc. that he rents to others. **2.** a man who keeps a rooming house, inn, etc.

land·lub·ber (land'lub'ər), *n.* a person who has not spent much time on ships and is clumsy when sailing: *a sailor's word.*

land·mark (land'märk), *n.* **1.** a building, tree, etc. that helps one to find or recognize a place because it is easily seen [The Eiffel Tower is a Paris *landmark.*] **2.** a very important happening in the development of something [The invention of the microscope is a *landmark* in science.] **3.** a post, rock, etc. that marks the boundary of a piece of land.

land·own·er (land'ōn'ər), *n.* a person who owns land.

land·scape (land'skāp), *n.* **1.** a stretch of scenery that can be seen in one view [the dull *landscape* of the desert]. **2.** a picture of such scenery [to paint a mountain *landscape*]. —*v.* to make a piece of ground more attractive by adding trees, shrubs, gardens, etc. —**land'-scaped,** *p.t. & p.p.;* **land'scap·ing,** *pr.p.* —**land'scap·er,** *n.*

land·slide (land'slīd), *n.* **1.** the sliding of a great mass of rocks and earth down the side of a hill; also, the mass itself. **2.** the winning of an election by a great majority of the votes.

lands·man (landz'mən), *n.* any person who is not a sailor. —**lands'men,** *pl.*

land·ward (land'wərd), *adj. & adv.* toward the land: also **land'wards,** *adv.*

lane (lān), *n.* **1.** a narrow path between hedges, walls, etc.; narrow country road or city street. **2.** any narrow way through [The police formed a *lane* through the crowd.] **3.** a path or route for ships, autos, or airplanes going in the same direction [a highway with three *lanes* on either side]. **4.** the long stretch of polished wood along which the balls are rolled in bowling; alley.

lan·guage (lang'gwij), *n.* **1.** human speech or writing that stands for speech [How did man come to invent *language?*] **2.** the speech of a particular nation, tribe, etc. [the Greek *language*]. **3.** any means of passing on one's thoughts or feelings to others [sign *language*]. **4.** the special words, phrases, or style of a particular group, writer, etc. [technical *language;* the *language* of teen-agers; the *language* of Lewis Carroll]. **5.** the study of language or languages; linguistics.

lan·guid (lang′gwid), *adj.* without energy or spirit; weak, sluggish, listless, etc. **—lan′- guid·ly,** *adv.*

lan·guish (lang′gwish), *v.* **1.** to become weak; lose energy or spirit; droop. **2.** to keep on suffering [to *languish* in poverty]. **3.** to pretend to be filled with tender feelings or sadness. **—lan′- guish·ing,** *adj.*

lan·guor (lang′gər), *n.* **1.** a feeling of being weak or tired; weakness [The hot sun filled her with *languor*.] **2.** a tender feeling or mood [the *languor* of a love song]. **3.** the condition of being still and sluggish [the *languor* of the steaming jungle]. **—lan′guor·ous,** *adj.*

lank (langk), *adj.* **1.** tall and slender; lean [a *lank* youth]. **2.** straight; not curly [*lank* hair].

lank·y (lang′kē), *adj.* tall and slender in an awkward way [a *lanky* cowboy]. **—lank′i·er,** *compar.;* **lank′i·est,** *superl.* **—lank′i·ness,** *n.*

lan·o·lin (lan′ə lin), *n.* a fat gotten from wool and used in hair oils, face creams, etc.

Lan·sing (lan′sing), *n.* the capital of Michigan.

lan·tern (lan′tərn), *n.* a case of glass, paper, etc. holding a light and protect- ing it from wind and rain.

lan·yard (lan′yərd), *n.* **1.** a short rope or cord used by sailors for holding or fastening something. **2.** a cord used in firing some cannons.

La·os (lä′ōs), *n.* a country in a large peninsula south of central China.

lap (lap), *n.* **1.** the front part

lantern

of a person sitting down, from the waist to the knees; also, the part of the clothing covering this [She caught the spool in her *lap*.] **2.** a place where something is held and protected like a baby in a lap [raised in the *lap* of luxury]. **3.** a part that overlaps or hangs loose [The rug had a three-inch *lap* on one side.] **4.** one complete trip around a race track [He fell behind in the third *lap* of the race.] **—v. 1.** to fold or wrap. **2.** to put something so that it lies partly on something else [*Lap* each row of shingles over the next row.] **3.** to reach beyond, into, or onto something else [The English class *lapped* over into the next period.] **—lapped,** *p.t. & p.p.;* **lap′ping,** *pr.p.*

lap (lap), *v.* **1.** to drink by dipping up with the tongue as a dog does. **2.** to hit against with a gentle splash [Waves *lapped* the boat.] **—n.** the act or sound of lapping. **—lap up,** to take in or receive eagerly: *used only in everyday talk.* **—lapped,** *p.t. & p.p.;* **lap′ping,** *pr.p.*

la·pel (lə pel′), *n.* either of the front parts of a coat that are folded back. *See the picture.*

lap·i·dar·y (lap′ə der′ē), *n.* a person who cuts and polishes precious stones, either as his work or as a hobby. **—lap′i·dar′ies,** *pl.*

lapel

lap·is laz·u·li (lap′is laz′- yoo lī), **1.** a bright-blue stone used as a jewel. **2.** bright blue.

Lap·land (lap′land), *n.* a region in northern Norway, Sweden, Finland, and the Soviet Union.

Lapp (lap), *n.* **1.** any of a short people who live in Lapland and herd reindeer. **2.** their language.

lap·pet (lap′it), *n.* a small fold or flap, as of a garment or as of flesh.

lapse (laps), *n.* **1.** a small mistake or slip; fault [a *lapse* of memory]. **2.** a going by of time [a *lapse* of five years]. **3.** a slipping into a worse condition [a *lapse* of health; the store's *lapse* into bankruptcy]. **4.** the ending of some right or claim because it was not used, renewed, etc. [the *lapse* of an insurance policy because premiums were not paid]. **—v. 1.** to fall or slip into some condition [He *lapsed* into his old life of crime.] **2.** to come to an end; stop [His insurance *lapsed*.] **—lapsed,** *p.t. & p.p.;* **laps′ing,** *pr.p.*

lap·wing (lap′wing), *n.* a shore bird of Europe and Asia, with a shrill cry.

lar·board (lär′bərd), *n.* the left side of a ship as one faces forward; port. **—adj. & adv.** on or toward this side.

lar·ce·ny (lär′sə nē), *n.* the stealing of another's property; theft. **—lar′- ce·nous,** *adj.*

larch (lärch), *n.* **1.** a kind of pine tree having leaves shaped like nee- dles and shed yearly. **2.** its tough wood.

lapwing (10 in. long)

lard (lärd), *n.* the fat of pigs or hogs, melted down for use in cooking. **—v. 1.** to cover or smear with lard or other fat. **2.** to scatter throughout; sprinkle [a talk *larded* with puns].

lard·er (lär′dər), *n.* **1.** a place in a home where food is kept; pantry. **2.** a supply of food.

large (lärj), *adj.* of great size or amount; big [a *large* house; a *large* sum of money]. **—adv.** in a large way [Do not write so *large*.] **—at large, 1.** free; not locked up [Bandits roamed *at large* in the countryside.] **2.** representing the whole State or district rather than one of its divisions [a congressman *at large*]. **—larg′er,** *compar.;* **larg′est,** *superl.* **—large′ness,** *n.*

large·ly (lärj′lē), *adv.* for the most part; mainly [Jim is *largely* to blame for the fight.]

fat, āpe, cär, ten, ēven, hit, bīte, gō, hôrn, tōol, book, up, fûr;
get, joy, yet, chin, she, thin, *th*en; zh = s in pleasure; ′ as in able (ā′b'l);
ə = a in ago, e in agent, i in sanity, o in confess, u in focus.

lar·gess or **lar·gesse** (lär′jis), *n.* generous giving or a generous gift.

lar·go (lär′gō), *adj.* & *adv.* slow and dignified: an Italian word used in music to tell how fast a piece should be played.

lar·i·at (lar′i ət), *n.* in the Southwest, a rope, especially a lasso.

lark (lärk), *n.* 1. any of a group of songbirds of Europe, especially the skylark. 2. a bird somewhat like this, as the meadow lark.

lark (lärk), *n.* a happy or gay time; bit of fun. —*v.* to play about or have fun.

lark·spur (lärk′spŭr), *n.* a plant with long spikes of flowers, usually blue, that have spurs.

lar·va (lär′və), *n.* an insect in the stage after it has hatched from the egg and before it becomes a pupa [A caterpillar is the *larva* of a butterfly.] —**lar·vae** (lär′vē), *pl.* —**lar′val**, *adj.*

lar·yn·gi·tis (lar′in jī′tis), *n.* a condition, as during a cold, in which the larynx is inflamed and the voice becomes hoarse or lost.

lar·ynx (lar′ingks), *n.* the upper end of the windpipe, that contains the vocal cords.

larynx

La Salle, Robert (lə sal′), 1643–1687; French explorer of the Mississippi.

las·civ·i·ous (lə siv′i əs), *adj.* showing too much interest in sex; lustful. —**las·civ′i·ous·ly**, *adv.*

la·ser (lā′zər), *n.* a device that emits a very intense beam of light.

lash (lash), *n.* 1. a whip, especially the part that strikes the blow. 2. a blow or stroke as with a whip [forty *lashes* as punishment]. 3. an eyelash. —*v.* 1. to strike or make move as with a whip; flog [The driver *lashed* the horses onward.] 2. to strike with force; beat [Waves *lashed* against the rocks.] 3. to swing back and forth in a quick or angry way; switch [The tiger *lashed* his tail in fury.] 4. to attack or stir up with harsh, bitter words [to *lash* out at critics]. 5. to tie or fasten to something with a rope.

lass (las), *n.* a girl.

las·sie (las′ē), *n.* a girl: *a Scottish word.*

las·si·tude (las′ə tōōd), *n.* a feeling of being tired, weak, and without interest in doing things.

las·so (las′ō), *n.* a long rope with a sliding loop at one end, used to catch horses or cattle. —*v.* to catch with a lasso. —**las′sos** or **las′soes**, *pl.* —**las′soed**, *p.t.* & *p.p.*; **las′so·ing**, *pr.p.*

last (last), *adj.* 1. being or coming after all others; final [December is the *last* month. Tom had the *last* word in the argument.] 2. that is the only one left [I ate the *last* cooky.] 3.

cowboy with lasso

that is the one just before this one; most recent [I was ill *last* week.] 4. that is least likely or expected [He is the *last* person I would suspect of lying.] —*adv.* 1. after all others [Our team came in *last*.] 2. most recently [I *last* heard from him in May.] —*n.* 1. the one that is last ["The *Last* of the Mohicans"]. 2. the end [friends to the *last*]. —**at last,** after a long time.

last (last), *v.* 1. to go on; continue [The play *lasts* only an hour.] 2. to stay in good condition; wear well [Stone *lasts* longer than wood.]

last (last), *n.* 1. a wooden or metal block shaped like a foot, used in making or mending shoes. 2. a particular shape of shoe.

last·ly (last′lē), *adv.* at the end; finally [*Lastly*, the speaker discussed the future.]

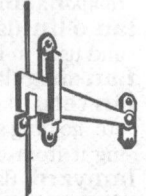
lasts

Last Supper, the last meal eaten by Jesus with the Apostles before the Crucifixion; Lord's Supper.

Lat., abbreviation for **Latin.**

lat., abbreviation for **latitude.**

latch (lach), *n.* a simple fastening for a door, gate, or window. It usually has a lever which moves a bar in or out of a notch fixed to the jamb. —*v.* to fasten with a latch.

latch·key (lach′kē), *n.* a key for drawing back or unfastening the latch of a door.

latch·string (lach′string), *n.* a cord fastened to a latch so that it can be raised from the outside.

latch

late (lāt), *adj.* 1. happening or coming after the usual or expected time; tardy [*late* for school; a *late* train]. 2. coming toward the end of some period [the *late* Middle Ages]. 3. happening or appearing just before now; recent [a *late* issue of the magazine]. 4. that died or left some office not long ago [her *late* father; our *late* mayor's new job]. —*adv.* 1. after the usual or expected time [Roses bloomed *late* last year.] 2. toward the end of some period [He came *late* in the day.] 3. lately; recently [I saw him as *late* as yesterday.] —**of late,** lately; recently. —**lat′er** or **lat′ter**, *compar. for adj.;* **lat′er**, *compar. for adv.;* **lat′est** or **last**, *superl. for adj. & adv.*

la·teen sail (la tēn′), a sail shaped like a triangle and fastened to a long yard that sticks out from a short mast.

late·ly (lāt′lē), *adv.* just before this time; not long ago; recently.

la·tent (lā′t'nt), *adj.* present but hidden or not active [*latent* talents].

lat·er·al (lat′ər əl), *adj.* of, at, from, or toward the side; sideways [a *lateral* pass in football]. —**lat′er·al·ly**, *adv.*

lateen sails

la·tex (lā'teks), *n.* a milky liquid in certain plants and trees, as the rubber tree.

lath (lath), *n.* **1.** any of the thin, narrow strips of wood used to build lattices or as the framework on which plaster is put. **2.** any framework for plaster, as wire screening. —**laths** (la*th*z), *pl.*

lathe (lā*th*), *n.* a machine for shaping a piece of wood, metal, etc. by holding and turning it rapidly against the edge of a cutting tool.

lath·er (la*th*'ər), *n.* **1.** foam made by mixing soap and water. **2.** foamy sweat, as on a horse after a race. —*v.* **1.** to cover with lather [He *lathered* his face and shaved.] **2.** to form lather [Few soaps *lather* in salt water.]

lathe

Lat·in (lat'n), *n.* **1.** the language of the ancient Romans. **2.** a person whose language developed from Latin, as a Spaniard or Italian. —*adj.* **1.** of or in the language of the ancient Romans. **2.** having to do with the languages that developed from Latin or with the peoples who speak them, their countries, etc.

Latin America, all of the Western Hemisphere south of the United States where Spanish, Portuguese, and French are spoken.

lat·i·tude (lat'ə tōōd *or* lat'ə tyōōd), *n.* **1.** freedom from strict rules; freedom to do as one wishes [Our school allows some *latitude* in choosing courses.] **2.** distance north or south of the equator, measured in degrees [Minneapolis is at 45 degrees north *latitude*.] **3.** a region in relation to its distance from the equator [cold northern *latitudes*].

parallels of latitude

lat·ter (lat'ər), a comparative of **late.** —*adj.* **1.** nearer the end or last part; later [the *latter* part of May]. **2.** being the second of two just mentioned: *often used as a noun with* the [He likes football and baseball but prefers the *latter*.]

lat·tice (lat'is), *n.* a framework made of thin strips of wood or metal crossed and fastened together, and used as a screen or as a support for climbing plants. —*v.* to form into or furnish with a lattice. —**lat'ticed,** *p.t. & p.p.;* **lat'tic·ing,** *pr.p.*

lat·tice·work (lat'is-wûrk'), *n.* a lattice or lattices [The old house has *latticework* on all the windows.]

lattice

Lat·vi·a (lat'vi ə), *n.* a former country in northeastern Europe, since 1940 a republic of the Soviet Union. —**Lat'vi·an,** *adj. & n.*

laud (lôd), *v.* to praise highly; extol.

laud·a·ble (lôd'ə b'l), *adj.* deserving praise [*laudable* work]. —**laud'a·bly,** *adv.*

laud·a·num (lôd'n əm), *n.* opium in alcohol.

laud·a·to·ry (lôd'ə tôr'ē), *adj.* that praises.

laugh (laf), *v.* **1.** to make a series of quick sounds with the voice that show one is amused or happy or, sometimes, that show scorn. One usually smiles or grins when laughing. **2.** to bring about, get rid of, etc. by means of laughter [*Laugh* your fears away.] —*n.* the act or sound of laughing. —**have the last laugh,** to win after seeming to have lost. —**laugh at, 1.** to be amused by. **2.** to make fun of. —**laugh off,** to ignore or get rid of by laughing [You can't *laugh off* that mistake.]

laugh·a·ble (laf'ə b'l), *adj.* causing laughter; funny; ridiculous [a *laughable* costume].

laugh·ing·stock (laf'ing stäk'), *n.* a person or thing laughed at or made fun of by all.

laugh·ter (laf'tər), *n.* the act or sound of laughing [He shook with *laughter*.]

launch (lônch), *v.* **1.** to throw, hurl, or send off into space [to *launch* a rocket]. **2.** to cause to slide into the water; set afloat [to *launch* a new ship]. **3.** to start or begin [to *launch* an attack]. —*n.* **1.** the largest boat carried by a warship. **2.** a large, open motorboat.

launching pad, the platform from which a rocket, guided missile, etc. is fired.

laun·der (lôn'dər), *v.* to wash, or to wash and iron, clothes, linens, etc.

laun·dress (lôn'dris), *n.* a woman whose work is washing and ironing clothes, etc.

laun·dry (lôn'drē), *n.* **1.** a place where laundering is done. **2.** clothes, linens, etc. that have been, or are about to be, washed and ironed. —**laun'dries,** *pl.*

laun·dry·man (lôn'drē mən), *n.* a man who works for a laundry, especially one who picks up and delivers laundry. —**laun'dry·men,** *pl.*

lau·re·ate (lô'ri it), *adj.* **1.** crowned with a wreath of laurel leaves as a sign of honor. **2.** famous and honored. See also **poet laureate.**

lau·rel (lô'rəl), *n.* **1.** an evergreen tree or shrub of Europe, with large, glossy leaves. The ancient Greeks crowned heroes and winners of contests with wreaths of laurel leaves. **2.** a plant similar to this, as the mountain laurel. **3. laurels,** *pl.* honor or victory. —**rest on one's laurels,** to be satisfied with what one has already done.

wreath of laurel leaves

la·va (lä'və *or* lav'ə), *n.* **1.** hot, melted rock pouring out of a volcano. **2.** such rock when cooled and solid.

fat, āpe, cär, ten, ēven, hit, bīte, gō, hôrn, tōōl, book, up, fûr;
get, joy, yet, chin, she, thin, *th*en; zh = s in pleasure; ' as in able (ā'b'l);
ə = a in ago, e in agent, i in sanity, o in confess, u in focus.

lav·a·to·ry (lav′ə tôr′ē), *n.* **1.** a bowl or basin for washing the face and hands. **2.** a room with such a basin and a toilet. —**lav′a·to′ries,** *pl.*

lave (lāv), *v.* to wash or bathe: *used mainly in poetry.* —**laved,** *p.t. & p.p.;* **lav′ing,** *pr.p.*

lav·en·der (lav′ən dər), *n.* **1.** a sweet-smelling plant of the mint family, having pale-purple flowers. **2.** the dried flowers and leaves of this plant, placed with stored clothes or linens to make them smell sweet. **3.** pale purple.

lav·ish (lav′ish), *adj.* **1.** very generous or too generous in giving or spending. **2.** more than enough; very great or costly [a *lavish* allowance; *lavish* decorations]. —*v.* to give or spend generously [She *lavished* time and money on her dogs.]

law (lô), *n.* **1.** all the rules that tell people what they must or must not do, made by the government of a city, state, nation, etc. [the *law* of the land]. **2.** any one of these rules; a statute, ordinance, etc. [a *law* against jaywalking]. **3.** the condition that exists when these rules are obeyed [to keep *law* and order on the frontier]. **4.** the courts that enforce these rules [to go to *law*]. **5.** all such rules that have to do with a particular activity [criminal *law;* maritime *law*]. **6.** the profession of lawyers and judges [a career in *law*]. **7.** a series of events that will happen in the same way every time conditions are the same [the *law* of gravitation]. **8.** any rule that people are expected to obey [the *laws* of health].

law-a·bid·ing (lô′ə bīd′ing), *adj.* obeying the law [*law-abiding* citizens].

law·break·er (lô′brāk′ər), *n.* a person who breaks the law. —**law′break′ing,** *n. & adj.*

law·ful (lô′fəl), *adj.* in keeping with the law; permitted or recognized by law; legal [a *lawful* act; a *lawful* heir]. —**law′ful·ly,** *adv.*

law·giv·er (lô′giv′ər), *n.* a person who draws up a code of laws for a people, as Moses.

law·less (lô′lis), *adj.* **1.** not controlled by law; having no laws [a *lawless* town]. **2.** not obeying the law; disorderly or wild [*lawless* bandits].

law·mak·er (lô′māk′ər), *n.* a person who helps to make laws; especially, a member of a legislature. —**law′mak′ing,** *n. & adj.*

lawn (lôn), *n.* ground covered with grass that is cut short, as around a house.

lawn (lôn), *n.* a very thin linen or cotton cloth used for handkerchiefs, blouses, etc.

lawn mower, a machine with steel blades that turn for cutting the grass of a lawn. It is pushed by hand or driven by a motor.

lawn tennis, same as **tennis.**

law·suit (lô′sōōt *or* lô′syōōt), *n.* a case which a person brings before a law court in order to get something that he claims a right to.

lawn mower

law·yer (lô′yər), *n.* a person whose profession is giving advice on law or acting for others in lawsuits.

lax (laks), *adj.* **1.** not strict or exact; careless [a *lax* parent; *lax* morals]. **2.** not tight or firm; loose; slack [a *lax* rope].

lax·a·tive (lak′sə tiv), *adj.* making the bowels move. —*n.* a medicine that does this.

lax·i·ty (lak′sə tē), *n.* the condition of being lax; looseness.

lay (lā), *v.* **1.** to put down so as to rest on, in, or against something [*Lay* your books on the shelf.] **2.** to knock down [One blow *laid* him low.] **3.** to put down in a special way; set in place [to *lay* floor tiles; to *lay* a carpet]. **4.** to put or place; set [He *lays* great emphasis on diet. The scene is *laid* in France.] **5.** to bring forth an egg, as a hen does. **6.** to settle or quiet down; still [Sprinkle water to *lay* the dust. Hamlet sought revenge to *lay* the ghost of his father.] **7.** to work out; prepare [to *lay* plans]. **8.** to present; put forth [He *laid* claim to the property.] **9.** to work or act with energy [*Lay* to your oars, men!] **10.** to bet [to *lay* a wager]. —*n.* the way in which a thing lies or is arranged [the *lay* of the land]. —**lay aside, lay away,** or **lay by,** to put away for future use; save. —**lay for,** to be waiting to attack: *used only in everyday talk.* —**lay in,** to get and store away for future use. —**lay into,** to attack with blows or words: *a slang phrase.* —**lay off,** to discharge a worker from his job, usually for only a short time. —**lay open, 1.** to cut open. **2.** to leave unprotected, as from attack or blame. —**lay out, 1.** to set out clothes, equipment, etc. ready for wear or use. **2.** to get a dead body ready for burial. **3.** to plan or arrange [to *lay out* a flower garden]. **4.** to spend. —**lay over,** to stop for a while in a place before going on with a journey. —**lay up, 1.** to store for future use. **2.** to make unable to get about because of illness or injury. —**laid,** *p.t. & p.p.;* **lay′ing,** *pr.p.*

lay (lā), past tense of **lie** (to stretch out).

lay (lā), *adj.* **1.** having to do with people who are not clergymen. **2.** of or for people who are not in a certain profession [a medical handbook for *lay* readers].

lay (lā), *n.* a short poem or song, especially one that tells a story.

lay·er (lā′ər), *n.* **1.** a single thickness, fold, coating, etc. [a cake in two *layers*]. **2.** a person or animal that lays [These hens are poor *layers.*]

lay·ette (lā et′), *n.* a complete outfit of clothes, bedding, etc. for a newborn baby.

lay·man (lā′mən), *n.* a person who is not a clergyman, or one who does not belong to a certain profession. —**lay′men,** *pl.*

lay·out (lā′out), *n.* **1.** the way in which something is laid out or arranged; plan [the *layout* of a factory]. **2.** the thing arranged in this way.

lay·o·ver (lā′ō′vər), *n.* a stop for a short time before going on with one's journey.

Laz·a·rus (laz′ə rəs), *n.* in the Bible, a man raised from the dead by Jesus.

la·zy (lā′zē), *adj.* **1.** not eager or willing to work or busy oneself [a *lazy* man]. **2.** slow and sluggish [a *lazy* river]. —**la′zi·er,** *compar.;* **la′zi·est,** *superl.* —**la′zi·ly,** *adv.* —**la′zi·ness,** *n.*

lb., pound: *lb.* is the abbreviation for *libra*, the Latin word for "pound." **—lbs.,** *pl.*

lea (lē), *n.* a meadow: *used in poetry.*

leach (lēch), *v.* **1.** to wash with water that filters through and removes something [*Leach* wood ashes to get lye.] **2.** to dissolve and wash away [The minerals in this soil have *leached* out.]

lead (lēd), *v.* **1.** to show the way for; guide [He *led* us along the path. The lights *led* me to the house.] **2.** to cause to do something as by teaching or setting an example [His advice *led* me to change jobs.] **3.** to go or make go in some direction [This path *leads* to the lake. Drainpipes *lead* the water away.] **4.** to be at the head of or be first [to *lead* a band; to *lead* in a game]. **5.** to live or spend time [They *lead* a hard life.] **6.** to bring one as a result [A bad cold may *lead* to pneumonia.] **7.** to go or do first; begin [He *led* with a left jab to the jaw.] **—***n.* **1.** position or example of a leader [Let us follow his *lead.*] **2.** the first place or position [The bay horse is in the *lead.*] **3.** the amount or distance that one is ahead [Our team has a *lead* of six points.] **4.** a clue [The police followed up every *lead.*] **5.** a going first or the right to go first, as in a game. **6.** the most important role in a play. **7.** the opening paragraph in a newspaper story. **—lead off** or **lead out,** to begin. **—lead on, 1.** to guide further. **2.** to lure or tempt. **—lead up to,** to prepare the way for. **—led,** *p.t. & p.p.;* **lead′ing,** *pr.p.*

lead (led), *n.* **1.** a heavy, soft, gray metal that is a chemical element. Lead is easily shaped and is used in making pipe and in many alloys. **2.** anything made of this metal, as a weight lowered on a line to find out how deep water is. **3.** bullets. **4.** a thin stick of graphite or other substance, used in pencils. **—***adj.* made of lead. **—***v.* **1.** to fasten in place with lead [to *lead* windowpanes]. **2.** to make heavier by adding lead.

lead·en (led′n), *adj.* **1.** made of lead. **2.** hard to move or lift [a *leaden* weight]. **3.** dull gray or gloomy [a *leaden* sky; *leaden* spirits].

lead·er (lēd′ər), *n.* a person or thing that leads, or guides. **—lead′er·ship,** *n.*

lead·ing (lēd′ing), *adj.* **1.** that leads; guiding [A *leading* question guides one toward a certain answer.] **2.** most important; playing a chief role [the *leading* man in a play].

leaf (lēf), *n.* **1.** any of the flat, green parts growing from the stem of a plant or tree. **2.** a petal [a rose *leaf*]. **3.** a sheet of paper in a book [Each side of a *leaf* is a page.] **4.** metal in very thin sheets [a frame covered with gold *leaf*]. **5.** a board hinged to a table, or put into a table top, to make it larger. **—***v.* **1.** to grow leaves, as a tree. **2.**

leaves of a table

to turn the pages of [to *leaf* through a book]. **—turn over a new leaf,** to make a new start. **—leaves,** *pl.* **—leaf′less,** *adj.*

leaf·let (lēf′lit), *n.* **1.** a small or young leaf. **2.** a sheet of printed matter, folded once or twice [advertising *leaflets*].

leaf·y (lēf′ē), *adj.* made up of many leaves or having many leaves [a *leafy* vegetable; a *leafy* tree]. **—leaf′i·er,** *compar.;* **leaf′i·est,** *superl.*

league (lēg), *n.* a number of persons, groups, or nations joined together for some purpose, as to help one another. **—***v.* to join in a league. **—in league,** united for a common purpose. **—leagued,** *p.t. & p.p.;* **lea′guing,** *pr.p.*

league (lēg), *n.* an old measure of distance, usually equal to about 3 miles.

League of Nations, a union of nations that was formed in 1920 to help keep world peace. It was replaced by the United Nations.

Le·ah (lē′ə), *n.* in the Bible, Jacob's first wife, the older sister of Rachel.

leak (lēk), *v.* **1.** to let water, air, or other fluid in or out by accident [The roof *leaks* when it rains. The oven is *leaking* gas.] **2.** to go in or come out by accident [The air in the tire *leaked* out through the valve.] **3.** to become known little by little or by accident [The truth *leaked* out.] **—***n.* **1.** a hole, crack, etc. that lets something in or out by accident [Sand spilled from the *leak* in the bag.] **2.** any way by which something gets out, becomes known, etc. [They learned of the plans through a *leak* in the government.] **3.** a leaking in or out; leakage [a slow *leak* in one of the tires]. **—leak′y,** *adj.*

leak·age (lēk′ij), *n.* **1.** a leaking in or out. **2.** the thing or the amount that leaks.

lean (lēn), *v.* **1.** to bend or slant so as to rest upon something [John *leaned* against the desk. *Lean* the ladder against the house.] **2.** to bend to one side; stand at a slant [The old tree *leans* toward the barn.] **3.** to depend on for advice, support, etc. [Jack still *leans* on his parents.] **4.** to favor a little; tend [to *lean* toward an opposite opinion]. **—leaned** (lēnd) or **leant** (lent), *p.t. & p.p.;* **lean′ing,** *pr.p.*

lean (lēn), *adj.* **1.** having little or no fat [a *lean* athlete; *lean* meat]. **2.** producing very little; meager [a *lean* year for business]. **—***n.* meat with little or no fat. **—lean′ness,** *n.*

lean-to (lēn′tōō′), *n.* a shed with a roof that slopes up and rests against another building, etc. **—lean′-tos′,** *pl.*

leap (lēp), *v.* **1.** to move oneself suddenly from the ground by using the leg muscles; jump; spring [The cat *leaped* onto my lap.] **2.** to move in jumps; bound [The deer were *leaping* across the meadow.] **3.** to jump over [to *leap* a brook]. **—***n.* a leaping;

lean-to

jump [over the fence in one *leap*]. —**leap at,** to take advantage of eagerly [I'd *leap at* a chance to go to Europe.] —**leaped** (lēpt) or **leapt** (lept *or* lēpt), *p.t. & p.p.;* **leap′ing,** *pr.p.*

leap·frog (lēp′frôg), *n.* a game in which each player in turn jumps over the the backs of the other players, who are bending over.

leap year, a year of 366 days, in which February has 29 days. Every fourth year is a leap year.

leapfrog

learn (lūrn), *v.* **1.** to get some knowledge or skill, as by studying or being taught [I have *learned* to knit. He never *learns* from experience.] **2.** to find out about something; come to know [When did you *learn* of her illness?] **3.** to fix in one's mind; memorize [*Learn* this poem by tomorrow.] —**learned** (lūrnd) or **learnt** (lūrnt), *p.t. & p.p.;* **learn′ing,** *pr.p.*

learn·ed (lūr′nid), *adj.* full of knowledge or learning; scholarly [a *learned* professor; a *learned* book].

learn·ing (lūr′ning), *n.* **1.** the getting of some knowledge or skill [A few tumbles are part of a baby's *learning* to walk.] **2.** knowledge [a man of great *learning*].

lease (lēs), *n.* **1.** an agreement by which an owner rents his property for a certain period of time and for a certain price. **2.** the period of time that this lasts [a three-year *lease*]. —*v.* to get or give by means of a lease; rent [I *leased* this car for a week. The owner will not *lease* the apartment to noisy tenants.] —**leased,** *p.t. & p.p.;* **leas′ing,** *pr.p.*

leash (lēsh), *n.* a strap or chain by which a dog, etc. is led or held. —*v.* **1.** to lead or hold with a leash. **2.** to keep under control; check [to *leash* the energy of a river with a dam]. —**hold in leash,** to control.

least (lēst), *adj.* smallest in size, amount, or importance [I haven't the *least* interest in the matter.] *Least* is a superlative of **little.** —*adv.* in the smallest amount or degree [I was *least* impressed by the music.] —*n.* the smallest in amount, degree, etc. [The *least* you can do is apologize. I'm not in the *least* interested.] —**at least,** in any case [*At least* I tried.]

dog on a leash

least·wise (lēst′wīz), *adv.* at least; anyway: *used only in everyday talk.*

leath·er (leth′ər), *n.* a material made from the skin of cows, horses, goats, etc. by cleaning and tanning it. —*adj.* made of leather.

leath·ern (leth′ərn), *adj.* made of leather.

leath·er·y (leth′ər ē), *adj.* like leather; tough, tan, etc. [a *leathery* skin].

leave (lēv), *v.* **1.** to go away or go from [Ted *left* early. Anne *leaves* the house at 8:00.] **2.** to stop living in or being in [The boy *left* home when he was 16. Ten members *left* the club last year.] **3.** to let stay or be [*Leave* the door open.] **4.** to cause to remain behind one [The invaders *left* a trail of destruction. His heavy boots *left* footprints.] **5.** to let be in the care of [He *leaves* such decisions to me.] **6.** to have remaining after one or more are gone [Five minus two *leaves* three.] **7.** to give at one's death; give by a will [Mr. Hall *left* all his money to charity.] —**leave off, 1.** to stop. **2.** to stop doing or using. —**leave one alone,** not to bother one. —**leave out,** not to include; omit. —**left,** *p.t. & p.p.;* **leav′ing,** *pr.p.*

leave (lēv), *n.* **1.** permission [May I have your *leave* to go?] **2.** permission to be away, as from work, school, the army, navy, etc.: also **leave of absence. 3.** the length of time for which this is given [a three-day *leave*]. —**take leave of,** to say good-by to. —**take one's leave,** to depart.

leave (lēv), *v.* to grow leaves; leaf. —**leaved,** *p.t. & p.p.;* **leav′ing,** *pr.p.*

leav·en (lev′'n), *n.* **1.** yeast or another substance that is used to make dough rise. **2.** anything that works on something else to make it more active, lighter, etc. [Humor is a welcome *leaven* to conversation.] —*v.* **1.** to make rise with a leaven, as dough. **2.** to spread through, slowly working a change.

leav·en·ing (lev′'n ing), *n.* a leaven.

leaves (lēvz), *n.* plural of **leaf.**

leave-tak·ing (lēv′tāk′ing), *n.* the act of taking leave, or saying good-by.

leav·ings (lēv′ingz), *n.pl.* things left over, as from a meal; leftovers.

Leb·a·non (leb′ə nən), *n.* a country at the eastern end of the Mediterranean, north of Israel. —**Leb·a·nese** (leb ə nēz′), *adj. & n.*

lec·i·thin (les′ə thin), *n.* a fatty substance found in egg yolk and in the cells of animals, and used in medicine, foods, etc.

lec·tern (lek′tərn), *n.* a stand with a sloping top on which to rest a book that is being read from, as in a church.

lec·ture (lek′chər), *n.* **1.** a talk on some subject to an audience or class. **2.** a long or tiresome scolding. —*v.* **1.** to give a lecture. **2.** to scold. —**lec′tured,** *p.t. & p.p.;* **lec′tur·ing,** *pr.p.* —**lec′tur·er,** *n.*

led (led), past tense and past participle of **lead** (to guide).

ledge (lej), *n.* a flat part like a narrow shelf that comes out from a cliff, a wall, etc. [a *ledge* of rock; a window *ledge*].

ledg·er (lej′ər), *n.* a book in which a business keeps a record of all its accounts.

lee (lē), *n.* **1.** the sheltered side, away from the wind [The cows stood in the *lee* of the barn.] **2.** the side of a ship farther from the direction from which the wind is blowing. —*adj.* of or on the lee [Parachutists jump from the *lee* side of a plane.]

Lee, Robert E. (lē), 1807–1870; commander of the Confederate army in the Civil War.

leech (lēch), *n.* **1.** a worm that lives in water and sucks blood from animals. Leeches are sometimes used in medicine to draw blood from bruises, etc. **2.** a person who stays close to another to get what he can from him.

leek (lēk), *n.* a vegetable like a thick green onion, but with a milder taste.

leer (lir), *n.* a sly look out of the corner of the eye, often together with a wicked or hinting smile. —*v.* to look with a leer.

leech
(3 in. long)

leer·y (lir′ē), *adj.* suspicious or doubting: *used only in everyday talk* [I am *leery* of anyone who promises me something for nothing.]

lees (lēz), *n.pl.* dregs, as of wine.

lee·ward (lē′wərd *or* lōō′ərd), *adj.* in the same direction as the wind is blowing [the *leeward* drift of a boat]. —*n.* the lee side [The canoes approached the ship from *leeward*.] —*adv.* toward the lee.

Lee·ward Islands (lē′wərd), a group of small islands in the West Indies.

leek

lee·way (lē′wā), *n.* **1.** the leeward drift of a ship or plane from its course. **2.** more time, money, etc. than might be needed: *used only in everyday talk* [He gives himself a *leeway* of ten minutes when he goes to school in bad weather.]

left (left), *adj.* **1.** on or to the side that is toward the west when one faces north [the *left* hand; a *left* turn]. **2.** closer to the left side of one facing the thing mentioned [the top *left* drawer of the desk]. **3.** liberal or radical in politics. —*n.* the left side [Forks are placed at the *left* of the plate.] —*adv.* on or toward the left hand or side.

left

left (left), past tense and past participle of **leave** (to go away).

left-hand (left′hand′), *adj.* **1.** on or to the left [a *left-hand* turn]. **2.** left-handed (*meaning* 2).

left-hand·ed (left′han′did), *adj.* **1.** using the left hand more easily than the right. **2.** done with or made for the left hand [a *left-handed* throw; *left-handed* scissors]. **3.** not sincere; doubtful [a *left-handed* compliment]. —*adv.* with the left hand [He writes *left-handed*.]

left·ist (lef′tist), *n.* a liberal or radical in politics. —*adj.* liberal or radical.

left·o·ver (left′ō′vər), *n.* something left over, as food not eaten at a meal.

left·y (lef′tē), *n.* a left-handed person: *a slang word.* —**left′ies,** *pl.*

leg (leg), *n.* **1.** one of the parts of the body used for standing and walking. **2.** the part of a garment that covers a leg. **3.** anything like a leg in looks or use [the *legs* of a chair]. **4.** a stage, as of a trip. —**on one's last legs,** nearly dead, exhausted, etc. —**pull one's leg,** to fool one. *These phrases are used only in everyday talk.*

leg·a·cy (leg′ə sē), *n.* **1.** money or other property left to someone by a will. **2.** anything handed down from an ancestor. —**leg′a·cies,** *pl.*

le·gal (lē′g′l), *adj.* **1.** of or based on law [*legal* knowledge; *legal* rights]. **2.** allowed by law; lawful [Is it *legal* to park the car here?] **3.** of or for lawyers [*legal* ethics]. —**le′gal·ly,** *adv.*

le·gal·i·ty (li gal′ə tē), *n.* the condition of being legal or lawful.

le·gal·ize (lē′g′l īz), *v.* to make legal or lawful [Some States have *legalized* gambling.] —**le′-gal·ized,** *p.t. & p.p.;* **le′gal·iz·ing,** *pr.p.*

legal tender, money that a person must by law accept in payment of a debt owed him.

leg·ate (leg′it), *n.* an ambassador or envoy, especially one who represents the Pope.

leg·a·tee (leg ə tē′), *n.* a person to whom money or property is left by a will.

le·ga·tion (li gā′shən), *n.* **1.** an official of lower rank than an ambassador, together with his assistants, representing their government in a foreign country. **2.** their headquarters.

le·ga·to (li gä′tō), *adj. & adv.* in a smooth, even style, with no pauses between notes: an Italian word used as a direction in music.

leg·end (lej′ənd), *n.* **1.** a story handed down through the years and connected with some real events, but probably not true in itself [The story of Paul Bunyan is an American *legend*.] **2.** all such stories as a group [a tale from Irish *legend*]. **3.** the writing on a coin, medal, etc. **4.** a title or description under a picture, map, etc.

leg·end·ar·y (lej′ən der′ē), *adj.* of, in, or like a legend [a *legendary* hero].

leg·er·de·main (lej′ər di mān′), *n.* **1.** the clever tricks of a stage magician. **2.** trickery.

leg·gings (leg′ingz), *n.pl.* **1.** coverings of canvas, leather, etc. worn by soldiers, etc. to protect the leg below the knee. **2.** a child's outer garment with legs, worn in cold weather.

leg·horn or **Leg·horn** (leg′hôrn *or* leg′ərn), *n.* a breed of small chicken.

leg·i·ble (lej′ə b′l), *adj.* clear enough to be read easily [*legible* handwriting]. —**leg·i·bil-i·ty** (lej′ə bil′ə tē), *n.* —**leg′i·bly,** *adv.*

le·gion (lē′jən), *n.* **1.** a division of the ancient Roman army, with from 3,000 to 6,000 soldiers. **2.** any large group of soldiers, or army. **3.** a large number [a *legion* of followers].

le·gion·ar·y (lē′jən er′ē), *adj.* of or forming a legion. —*n.* a member of a legion. —**le′gion-ar′ies,** *pl.*

leg·is·late (lej′is lāt), *v.* to make or pass laws. —**leg′is·lat·ed,** *p.t. & p.p.;* **leg′is·lat·ing,** *pr.p.*

fat, āpe, cär, ten, ēven, hit, bīte, gō, hôrn, tōōl, book, up, fûr;
get, joy, yet, chin, she, thin, *th*en; zh = s in pleasure; ' as in able (ā′b'l);
ə = a in ago, e in agent, i in sanity, o in confess, u in focus.

leg·is·la·tion (lej′is lā′shən), *n.* **1.** the making of laws. **2.** the laws made.

leg·is·la·tive (lej′is lā′tiv), *adj.* **1.** having to do with making laws [*legislative* powers]. **2.** having the power to make laws [a *legislative* assembly].

leg·is·la·tor (lej′is lā′tər), *n.* a lawmaker; member of a congress, parliament, etc.

leg·is·la·ture (lej′is lā′chər), *n.* a group of persons who make laws; congress, parliament, etc.

le·git·i·mate (li jit′ə mit), *adj.* **1.** allowed by law or custom; lawful or right [a *legitimate* claim]. **2.** reasonable; to be expected [a *legitimate* complaint]. **3.** born of parents married to each other [a *legitimate* child]. —**le·git·i·ma·cy** (li jit′ə mə sē), *n.*

leg·ume (leg′yo̅o̅m *or* li gyo̅o̅m′), *n.* any plant of the pea family, with seeds growing in pods, as peas, beans, and lentils. Because they store up nitrates, legumes are often plowed under to fertilize the soil.

le·gu·mi·nous (li gyo̅o̅′mi nəs), *adj.* of or belonging to the group of legumes.

le·i (lā *or* lā′ē), *n.* a wreath of flowers, often worn about the neck in Hawaii. —**le′is,** *pl.*

Leip·zig (līp′sig), *n.* a city in eastern Germany.

lei·sure (lē′zhər *or* lezh′-ər), *n.* free time not taken up with work or duty, when a person may rest, or do what he wants to do. —*adj.* free and not busy; spare [*leisure* time]. —**at one's leisure,** when one has time.

girl wearing lei

lei·sure·ly (lē′zhər lē *or* lezh′ər lē), *adj.* slow; without hurrying [a *leisurely* walk]. —*adv.* in a slow, unhurried way [We talked *leisurely.*]

lem·on (lem′ən), *n.* **1.** a small citrus fruit with a yellow skin and a juicy, sour pulp, used to make drinks or to flavor foods. **2.** the tree it grows on. **3.** pale yellow.

lem·on·ade (lem′ən ād′), *n.* a drink made of lemon juice, sugar, and water.

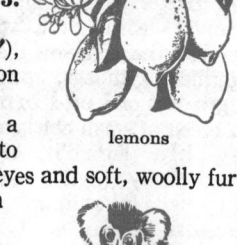

lemons

le·mur (lē′mər), *n.* a small animal related to the monkey, with large eyes and soft, woolly fur. It is found mainly in Madagascar.

lend (lend), *v.* **1.** to let someone use something for a while: opposite of **borrow** [Will you *lend* me your umbrella until tomorrow?] **2.** to give something to someone who must later give back an equal thing, sometimes with interest [to *lend* $100 at 6% interest; to *lend* a cup of sugar].

lemur (2 ft. long)

3. to give help of some kind [The flowers *lend* gaiety to the room. *Lend* us your support.] —**lend itself** or **lend oneself to,** to be useful for or open to. —**lent,** *p.t. & p.p.;* **lend′ing,** *pr.p.* —**lend′er,** *n.*

length (length), *n.* **1.** the measure of how long a thing is; distance from end to end or time from beginning to end [a rope 20 feet in *length;* a movie 90 minutes in *length*]. **2.** the longest side of a thing [*length*, width, and breadth]. **3.** the fact of being long or too long [I object mainly to the *length* of the car.] **4.** a piece of a certain length [a *length* of pipe]. **5.** the time taken to pronounce a certain vowel or syllable. —**at full length,** stretched out. —**at length, 1.** after a long time; finally. **2.** in full. —**go to any length,** to do whatever is necessary.

length·en (leng′thən), *v.* to make or become longer.

length·wise (length′wīz) or **length·ways** (length′wāz), *adj. & adv.* in the direction of the length [Carry the box in *lengthwise.*]

length·y (leng′thē), *adj.* long or too long [a *lengthy* speech]. —**length′i·er,** *compar.;* **length′i·est,** *superl.* —**length′i·ly,** *adv.*

len·ient (lēn′yənt), *adj.* not harsh or strict in dealing with others; gentle, merciful, etc. [a *lenient* judge]. —**len′ien·cy** or **len′ience,** *n.* —**len′ient·ly,** *adv.*

Len·in, V. I. (len′in), 1870–1924; leader of the Russian Revolution of 1917; first premier of the Soviet Union: also called **Nikolai Lenin.**

Len·in·grad (len′in grad), *n.* a Baltic seaport in the northwestern Soviet Union.

len·i·ty (len′ə tē), *n.* mildness; gentleness.

lens (lenz), *n.* **1.** a piece of clear glass, plastic, etc. curved on one or both sides so as to bring together or spread rays of light that pass through it. Lenses are used in eyeglasses, cameras, microscopes, telescopes, etc. **2.** a clear part of the eye that focuses light rays on the retina. *See the picture for* **eye.**

Lent (lent), *n.* the forty weekdays from Ash Wednesday to Easter, a time of fasting and repenting in Christian churches. —**Lent·en** or **lent·en** (lent′ən), *adj.*

lent (lent), past tense and past participle of **lend.**

len·til (len′t'l), *n.* **1.** a plant of the pea family, with small, rather flat seeds that grow in pods and are used as food. **2.** the seed itself.

le·o·nine (lē′ə nīn), *adj.* of or like a lion.

leop·ard (lep′ərd), *n.* **1.** a large, fierce animal of the cat family, having a tan coat with black spots. It is found in Africa and Asia. Also called *panther.* **2.** the jaguar: also called **American leopard.**

leopard (7 ft. long, including tail)

lep·er (lep′ər), *n.* a person who has leprosy.

lep·re·chaun (lep′rə kôn), *n.* an elf in Irish legends who knows of hidden treasure.

lep·ro·sy (lep′rə sē), *n.* a disease that causes open sores and white scabs, and slowly wastes away parts of the body. —**lep′rous,** *adj.*

lese majesty (lēz), a crime against a ruler or an offense against his dignity.

le·sion (lē′zhən), *n.* a hurt or injury, especially a sore or wound in some part of the body.

Le·so·tho (le sut′hō *or* le sō′thō), *n.* a country in southern Africa, surrounded by South Africa.

less (les), *adj.* not so much, so many, so great, etc.; smaller, fewer, of lower degree, etc. [6 is *less* than 8.] —*adv.* not so much; to a smaller or lower degree [Please talk *less* and work more.] *Less* is the comparative form of **little.** —*n.* a smaller amount [She ate *less* than I did.] —*prep.* minus [She earned $5,000 *less* taxes.]

-less (lis), a suffix meaning: **1.** without [A *worthless* thing is without worth.] **2.** that does not or cannot be [A *ceaseless* effort does not cease. A *dauntless* man cannot be daunted.]

les·see (les ē′), *n.* a person to whom property is leased; tenant.

less·en (les′'n), *v.* to make or become less [Your help *lessens* my work. The rain *lessened.*]

less·er (les′ər), *adj.* smaller, less, or less important [a *lesser* evil].

les·son (les′'n), *n.* **1.** something to be learned, as by a student; teaching done during one class period [Did you study today's history *lesson?*] **2.** something that needs to be learned for one's safety, etc. [My narrow escape taught me a *lesson.*] **3.** a part of the Bible, read during a church service.

les·sor (les′ôr), *n.* a person who gives a lease on some property; landlord.

lest (lest), *conj.* **1.** for fear that [We spoke low *lest* we be overheard.] **2.** that: used after words that show fear [I was afraid *lest* he should fall.]

let (let), *v.* **1.** to not keep from doing something; allow; permit [She *let* me help her.] **2.** to allow to go, pass, etc. [*Let* him by.] **3.** to rent [We *let* our spare room.] **4.** to cause to flow out [to *let* blood]. *Let may be used as a helping verb with other verbs in order to give commands or suggestions* [*Let* us go to the movies.] —**let alone, 1.** to keep away from; not disturb. **2.** not to mention; much less [He can't walk, *let alone* run.] —**let down, 1.** to put down; lower. **2.** to disappoint. —**let off, 1.** to give forth [to *let off* steam]. **2.** to treat in a mild or gentle way. —**let on, 1.** to pretend. **2.** to show that one is aware of something. *This phrase is used only in everyday talk.* —**let out, 1.** to allow to flow or run away; release. **2.** to make a garment larger. —**let up,** to become slower or to stop. —**let,** *p.t. & p.p.;* **let′ting,** *pr.p.*

let (let), *n.* an obstacle: *now used only in the phrase* **without let or hindrance,** meaning "without anything standing in the way."

-let (lit), a suffix meaning "small" [An *islet* is a small isle.]

le·thal (lē′thəl), *adj.* causing death; deadly; fatal [a *lethal* blow].

leth·ar·gy (leth′ər jē), *n.* the condition of being very tired or sleepy; lack of energy. —**le·thar·gic** (li thär′jik), *adj.*

Le·the (lē′thē), *n.* in Greek and Roman myths, a river in Hades that made those who drank from it forget everything.

let's (lets), let us.

let·ter (let′ər), *n.* **1.** any of the marks used in writing or printing to stand for a sound of speech; character of an alphabet. **2.** a written message, usually sent by mail. **3.** the exact or strict meaning, as different from the purpose or spirit [The judge enforced the *letter* of the law.] **4.** the first letter of the name of a school or college, given as a prize in sports, etc. **5. letters,** *pl.* the work of a writer; literature. —*v.* to print letters by hand [Will you *letter* this poster?] —**to the letter,** exactly as written or ordered.

let·ter·head (let′ər hed), *n.* **1.** a printed name and address at the top of a sheet of letter paper. **2.** a sheet of such paper.

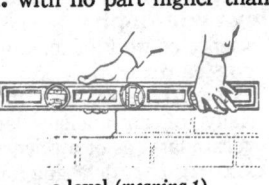
letterhead

let·ter·ing (let′ər ing), *n.* **1.** the act of printing, stamping, or carving letters. **2.** letters made in this way.

let·ter-per·fect (let′ər-pūr′fikt), *adj.* correct in every detail; perfect.

let·tuce (let′is), *n.* a plant with crisp, green leaves, much used in salads.

let·up (let′up), *n.* a becoming slower or less, or a stopping: *used only in everyday talk.*

leu·co·cyte (lōō′kə sīt), *n.* any of the small, white cells in the blood that kill germs; white corpuscle.

types of lettuce

leu·ke·mi·a (lōō kē′mi ə), *n.* a disease in which too many leucocytes are formed.

lev·ee (lev′ē), *n.* **1.** a bank built along a river to keep it from overflowing. **2.** a landing place for ships, along a river.

lev·el (lev′'l), *adj.* **1.** with no part higher than any other; flat and even [a *level* plain]. **2.** as high as something else; even [Make this pile *level* with the other.] **3.** even with the top or rim; not heaping

a level (*meaning 1*)

[a *level* cup of sugar]. **4.** not excited or confused; steady or sensible [Keep a *level* head on your shoulders.] —*n.* **1.** a small tube of liquid in a frame that is placed on a surface to see if it is level. A bubble in the liquid moves to the center when the frame is level. **2.** height [The water in the tank rose to a *level* of five feet.] See also **sea level. 3.** the same even line or surface [The tops of the pictures are on a *level* with each other.] **4.** a stage or degree, as of position or rank [the reading *level* of sixth graders]. —*v.* **1.** to make level or flat [to *level* ground with a bulldozer]. **2.** to knock to the ground [The storm *leveled* the tree.] **3.** to raise and aim a gun. —**level off, 1.** to give a flat, even surface to. **2.** to come or bring into a level position [Airplanes *level off* just before landing.] —**on the level,** honest and fair: *a slang phrase.* —**lev′eled** or **lev′elled,** *p.t. & p.p.;* **lev′el·ing** or **lev′el·ling,** *pr.p.* —**lev′el·er** or **lev′el·ler,** *n.* —**lev′el·ness,** *n.*

lev·er (lev′ər *or* lē′vər), *n.* **1.** a bar that can be rested on a support (the *fulcrum*) and pushed down at one end to lift a weight at the other. *See the picture for* **fulcrum. 2.** any bar that can be turned or moved to work something joined to it [a gearshift *lever*].

lev·er·age (lev′ər ij *or* lē′vər ij), *n.* **1.** the working of a lever. **2.** the extra power that comes from using a lever [We put a wedge under the crowbar to get *leverage*.]

Le·vi (lē′vī), *n.* in the Bible, one of Jacob's sons, or the tribe descended from him.

le·vi·a·than (lə vī′ə thən), *n.* **1.** a large water animal mentioned in the Bible. **2.** anything huge or powerful, as a huge ship.

Le·vite (lē′vīt), *n.* in the Bible, a member of the tribe of Levi. The Levites were chosen to assist the Jewish priests.

Le·vit·i·cus (lə vit′i kəs), *n.* the third book of the Old Testament.

lev·i·ty (lev′ə tē), *n.* gaiety or joking, especially when it is out of place; lack of seriousness. —**lev′i·ties,** *pl.*

lev·y (lev′ē), *v.* **1.** to order the payment of [to *levy* a tax]. **2.** to force into military service; enlist [to *levy* troops]. **3.** to wage; carry on [to *levy* war]. —*n.* **1.** a levying of a tax, of troops, etc. **2.** the money, troops, etc. collected by levying. —**lev′ied,** *p.t. & p.p.;* **lev′y·ing,** *pr.p.* —**lev′ies,** *pl.*

lewd (lood), *adj.* having to do with sex in a way that is wrong or immoral. —**lewd′ness,** *n.*

lex·i·cog·ra·phy (lek′sə käg′rə fē), *n.* the science or work of making dictionaries. —**lex′i·cog′ra·pher,** *n.*

lex·i·con (lek′si kən), *n.* **1.** a dictionary, especially of an ancient language. **2.** a special vocabulary, as of a science.

Lex·ing·ton (lek′sing tən), *n.* a town in eastern Massachusetts, where the first battle of the American Revolution was fought on April 19, 1775.

li·a·bil·i·ty (lī′ə bil′ə tē), *n.* **1.** the condition of being liable [*liability* to error; *liability* for dam-

ages]. **2.** *usually* **liabilities,** *pl.* money owed; a debt. **3.** a condition that acts against one; disadvantage [Small hands can be a *liability* to a pianist.] —**li′a·bil′i·ties,** *pl.*

li·a·ble (lī′ə b'l), *adj.* **1.** obliged by law to pay; responsible [He caused the accident and is *liable* for the damage done.] **2.** likely to have, get, or do something that is unpleasant or not wanted [The boxes are *liable* to fall. He is especially *liable* to colds. It's *liable* to rain.]

li·ai·son (lē′ā zän′ *or* lē′ə zän *or* li ā′z'n), *n.* a linking up of groups or parts, as of an army, so that they can work together effectively.

li·ar (lī′ər), *n.* a person who tells lies.

li·ba·tion (lī bā′shən), *n.* **1.** the ceremony of pouring out wine or oil in honor of a god. **2.** the wine or oil poured out.

li·bel (lī′b'l), *n.* **1.** anything written or printed that harms a person's reputation in an unfair way and makes others laugh at him or hate him. **2.** the act or crime of publishing such a thing. —*v.* to publish a libel against. —**li′beled** or **li′belled,** *p.t. & p.p.;* **li′bel·ing** or **li′bel·ling,** *pr.p.* —**li′bel·er** or **li′bel·ler,** *n.*

li·bel·ous or **li·bel·lous** (lī′b'l əs), *adj.* containing or making a libel against someone.

lib·er·al (lib′ər əl), *adj.* **1.** giving freely; generous [a *liberal* contributor to charity]. **2.** more than enough or than might be expected [a *liberal* reward]. **3.** open to new ideas; broad-minded; tolerant. **4.** broad in range; not limited [a *liberal* education]. **5.** in favor of reform or progress in politics, religion, etc. —*n.* a person who is in favor of reform and progress. —**lib′er·al·ly,** *adv.*

liberal arts, literature, philosophy, languages, history, etc. as courses of study.

lib·er·al·ism (lib′ər əl iz'm), *n.* the quality of being liberal, as in politics; liberal beliefs.

lib·er·al·i·ty (lib′ə ral′ə tē), *n.* the quality of being liberal; generosity, broad-mindedness, tolerance, etc.

lib·er·al·ize (lib′ər ə līz′), *v.* to make or become liberal. —**lib′er·al·ized′,** *p.t. & p.p.;* **lib′er·al·iz′ing,** *pr.p.* —**lib′er·al·i·za′tion,** *n.*

lib·er·ate (lib′ə rāt), *v.* to free as from slavery [to *liberate* prisoners of war]. —**lib′er·at·ed,** *p.t. & p.p.;* **lib′er·at·ing,** *pr.p.* —**lib′er·a′tion,** *n.* —**lib′er·a·tor,** *n.*

Li·ber·i·a (lī bir′i ə), *n.* a country on the western coast of Africa.

lib·er·tine (lib′ər tēn), *n.* a man of loose morals, who makes love to many women.

lib·er·ty (lib′ər tē), *n.* **1.** the condition of being free from control by others [The slaves fought for their *liberty*.] **2.** the power or right of a person to believe and act as he thinks right ["sweet land of *liberty*"]. **3.** the area in which one is free to move or go [They gave us the *liberty* of the whole house.] **4.** permission given to a sailor to go ashore. —**at liberty, 1.** not shut in or confined; free. **2.** allowed; permitted [I am not *at liberty* to say.] **3.** not busy or in use. —**take liberties,** to be too free, bold, or friendly. —**lib′er·ties,** *pl.*

Liberty Bell, the bell of Independence Hall in Philadelphia. It was rung on July 4, 1776, to announce the independence of the United States.

li·brar·i·an (lī brer′i ən), *n.* a person who is in charge in a library.

li·brar·y (lī′brer ē), *n.* **1.** a place where a collection of books is kept for reading or borrowing. **2.** a collection of books. —**li′brar·ies,** *pl.*

li·bret·to (li bret′ō), *n.* **1.** the words of an opera, oratorio, etc. **2.** a book containing these words. —**li·bret′tos** or **li·bret·ti** (li bret′ē), *pl.*

Lib·y·a (lib′i ə), *n.* a country in northern Africa. —**Lib′y·an,** *adj. & n.*

lice (līs), *n.* plural of **louse.**

li·cence (lī′s'ns), *n.* British spelling of **license.**

li·cense (lī′s'ns), *n.* **1.** a paper, card, etc. showing that one is permitted by law to do something [a marriage *license;* driver's *license*]. **2.** freedom to ignore the usual rules [To take poetic *license* is to ignore the usual rules of meter, grammar, etc., as in a poem, in order to gain some effect.] **3.** freedom of action or speech that goes beyond what is right or proper [She showed *license* in calling her teacher by her first name.] —*v.* to give a license to; permit by law [Is he *licensed* to hunt?] —**li′censed,** *p.t. & p.p.;* **li′cens·ing,** *pr.p.*

li·cen·tious (lī sen′shəs), *adj.* not controlled by moral laws or rules; immoral. —**li·cen′tious·ly,** *adv.* —**li·cen′tious·ness,** *n.*

li·chen (lī′kən), *n.* a plant that looks like dry moss and grows in patches on rocks and trees.

lick (lik), *v.* **1.** to rub the tongue over [to *lick* one's lips]. **2.** to remove by lapping up with the tongue [The dog *licked* the gravy from the floor.] **3.** to pass lightly over like a tongue [Flames were *licking* the roof of the house.] **4.** to whip or thrash: *used only in everyday talk.* —*n.*

types of lichen

1. the act of licking with the tongue. **2.** a place where animals go to lick salt that comes naturally from the earth: *its full name is* **salt lick. 3.** a sharp blow; also, a short, quick burst of action: *used only in everyday talk.*

lic·o·rice (lik′ər is *or* lik′ər ish), *n.* **1.** a black, sweet flavoring made from the root of a European plant. **2.** candy flavored with this.

lid (lid), *n.* **1.** a movable cover for a pot, box, trunk, etc. **2.** an eyelid.

lie (lī), *v.* **1.** to stretch one's body in a flat position along the ground, a bed, etc. **2.** to be in a flat position; rest [The book is *lying* on the table.] **3.** to be or stay in some condition [The treasure *lay* hidden for years.] **4.** to be placed or situated [Ohio *lies* east of Indiana.] **5.** to be or exist [Help for the farmer *lies* in new laws.] **6.** to be dead and buried [He *lies* in the graveyard.] —**lie over,** to stay and wait until later. —**take**

something lying down, to take punishment, a wrong, etc. without fighting or protesting. —**lay,** *p.t.;* **lain,** *p.p.;* **ly′ing,** *pr.p.*

lie (lī), *n.* something said that is not true, especially if it is said on purpose to deceive. —*v.* **1.** to tell a lie; say what is not true. **2.** to give a false idea [Your camera *lied;* she isn't that stout.] —**give the lie to, 1.** to accuse of telling a lie. **2.** to prove to be false. —**lied,** *p.t. & p.p.;* **ly′ing,** *pr.p.*

Liech·ten·stein (lēk′tən shtīn), *n.* a small country in Europe, west of Austria.

lief (lēf), *adv.* willingly; gladly [He would as *lief* die as tell the secret.]

liege (lēj), *adj.* in the Middle Ages, having a right to the loyal service of one's vassals [a *liege* lord]; also, owing such service [*liege* subjects]. —*n.* a liege lord or his vassal.

liege·man (lēj′mən), *n.* **1.** a vassal. **2.** a loyal follower. —**liege′men,** *pl.*

li·en (lēn *or* lē′ən), *n.* a legal claim that one has on the property of a person who owes one money [The bank has a *lien* on my house until I pay back my loan.]

lieu (lōō), *n.* place: *used only in the phrase* **in lieu of,** meaning "instead of" or "in place of."

Lieut., abbreviation for **Lieutenant.**

lieu·ten·ant (lōō ten′ənt), *n.* **1.** an army or air force officer ranking below a captain: a **second lieutenant** is the lowest ranking officer and a **first lieutenant** is next above him. **2.** a navy officer ranking above an ensign. **3.** a person who assists someone of higher rank, and acts in his place when he is away.

lieutenant colonel, a military officer ranking just above a major.

lieutenant commander, a navy officer ranking just above a lieutenant.

lieutenant general, a military officer ranking just above a major general.

lieutenant governor, the official of a State who ranks just below the governor and takes his place if the governor dies or is away.

life (līf), *n.* **1.** the quality of plants and animals that makes it possible for them to take in food, grow, produce others of their kind, etc. and that makes them different from rocks, water, etc. [Death is the loss of *life.*] **2.** a living thing; especially, a human being [The crash took six *lives.*] **3.** living things as a group [the plant *life* in the pond]. **4.** the time that a person or thing is alive or lasts [Your *life* has just begun. What is the *life* of a battery?] **5.** the story of a person's life; biography [Johnson wrote a *life* of Milton.] **6.** the way that a person or group lives [a *life* of wealth; the military *life*]. **7.** gaiety or liveliness [His jokes put *life* in the party.] —**lives,** *pl.*

life belt, a life preserver in the form of a belt.

life·blood (līf′blud), *n.* **1.** the blood that one needs to live. **2.** the necessary part of anything [Oil is the *lifeblood* of their economy.]

life·boat (līf′bōt), *n.* **1.** any of the small boats carried by a ship for use in case of trouble. **2.** a sturdy boat kept on a shore, for use in rescuing people in danger of drowning.

lifeboat

life·guard (līf′gärd), *n.* an expert swimmer hired to keep people from drowning, as at a beach.

life insurance, insurance by which a person arranges to have a certain sum of money paid to his family or others when he dies.

life·less (līf′lis), *adj.* **1.** no longer living; dead [the *lifeless* body of the accident victim]. **2.** that never had life [a *lifeless* statue]. **3.** not lively or active; dull [a *lifeless* expression].

life·like (līf′līk), *adj.* like real life; that looks alive [a *lifelike* photograph].

life·line (līf′līn), *n.* **1.** the rope used to raise and lower a diver in the water. **2.** a route for trade, supplies, etc. that is very important.

life·long (līf′lông′), *adj.* lasting or not changing during one's life [a *lifelong* love].

life preserver, a belt, jacket, or large ring that can keep a person afloat in water.

life·sav·er (līf′sāv′ər), *n.* a person or thing that saves people from drowning. —**life′-sav′ing,** *n. & adj.*

life-size (līf′sīz′) or **life-sized** (līf′sīzd′), *adj.* as big as the person or thing that it represents [a *life-size* statue of the king].

life preserver

life·time (līf′tīm), *n.* the length of time that someone or something lives or lasts.

lift (lift), *v.* **1.** to bring up to a higher place; raise [I can't *lift* that heavy box onto the truck.] **2.** to make higher or better in rank, condition, value, etc. [to *lift* oneself up from poverty]. **3.** to rise or go up [His spirits *lifted* when he heard the news.] **4.** to disappear; go away [The fog is beginning to *lift*.] **5.** to steal: *used only in everyday talk.* —*n.* **1.** the act of lifting. **2.** the amount lifted, or the distance that something is lifted. **3.** a raising of one's spirits; a making one feel good [His kind words gave me a *lift*.] **4.** a ride in the direction one is going. **5.** help of any kind. **6.** an elevator: *a British meaning.* —**lift one's voice,** to speak or sing loudly.

lift·off (lift′ôf), *n.* **1.** the sudden upward movement of a spacecraft, missile, etc. as it is launched. **2.** the time when this takes place.

lig·a·ment (lig′ə mənt), *n.* a band of strong, tough tissue that joins bones or holds organs of the body in place.

lig·a·ture (lig′ə chər), *n.* **1.** something used for tying or binding; especially, a thread used by a doctor to tie up the end of a bleeding artery or

vein. **2.** two or more letters joined together as one character in printing [fl and æ are *ligatures*.]

light (līt), *n.* **1.** the form of energy that acts on the eyes so that one can see [*Light* travels at a speed of 186,000 miles per second.] **2.** brightness or radiance [the *light* of a candle; the *light* of love in her face]. **3.** something that gives light, as a lamp [Turn off the *light*.] **4.** a flame or spark to start something burning [a *light* for a cigarette]. **5.** helpful information or knowledge [Can you shed *light* on the problem?] **6.** public notice or attention [New facts have been brought to *light*.] **7.** the way something is seen; aspect [This report puts you in an unfavorable *light*.] **8.** an outstanding person [one of the shining *lights* of our school]. —*adj.* **1.** having light; not dark [It was just getting *light* outside.] **2.** having a pale color; fair [a *light* skin]. —*adv.* not brightly; in a pale way [a *light* green dress]. —*v.* **1.** to set on fire or catch fire; burn [to *light* a match; wood that *lights* easily]. **2.** to cause to give off light [to *light* a lamp]. **3.** to cast light on or in [Lamps *light* the streets.] **4.** to guide by giving light [The servant *lighted* their way with a torch.] **5.** to become light, bright, or lively [Her face *lighted* up with joy.] —**in the light of,** knowing that; considering. —**shed light on** or **throw light on,** to make clear; explain. —**light′ed** or **lit,** *p.t. & p.p.;* **light′-ing,** *pr.p.* —**light′ness,** *n.*

light (līt), *adj.* **1.** having little weight, especially for its size; not heavy [a *light* cargo; a *light* summer suit]. **2.** little or less than usual in force, quantity, etc. [a *light* blow; a *light* rain; a *light* meal]. **3.** not serious or important [*light* conversation; *light* reading]. **4.** not sad; gay; happy [*light* spirits]. **5.** easy to do, put up with, etc.; not hard or severe [*light* work; a *light* tax]. **6.** dizzy or silly [to feel *light* in the head]. **7.** soft and spongy; not soggy [a *light* cake]. **8.** moving in a quick, easy way; nimble [*light* on her feet]. **9.** having small weapons or thin armor [*light* cruiser; *light* tank]. —*v.* **1.** to get down, as from a horse. **2.** to come to rest after traveling through the air; land [birds *lighting* on the roof]. **3.** to come by chance; happen [He *lighted* on the right answer.] —**light out,** to leave suddenly: *a slang phrase.* —**make light of,** to treat as silly or unimportant. —**light′ed** or **lit,** *p.t. & p.p.;* **light′ing,** *pr.p.* —**light′ness,** *n.*

light·en (līt′'n), *v.* **1.** to make or become light or brighter; brighten. **2.** to shine brightly; flash.

light·en (līt′'n), *v.* **1.** to make or become less heavy [to *lighten* a load]. **2.** to make or become more cheerful [His jokes *lightened* our spirits.]

light·er (līt′ər), *n.* a thing that starts something burning [a cigarette *lighter*].

light·er (līt′ər), *n.* a large, open barge used for loading and unloading ships offshore.

light-foot·ed (līt′foot′id), *adj.* moving lightly on one's feet; nimble.

light·head·ed (līt′hed′id), *adj.* **1.** feeling dizzy. **2.** not serious; silly or flighty.

light·heart·ed (līt′här′tid), *adj.* gay or cheerful; not sad or worried.

light·house (līt′hous), *n.* a tower with a bright light on top to guide ships at night or in fog.

light·ly (līt′lē), *adv.* **1.** with little weight or force; gently [The leaves brushed *lightly* against his face.] **2.** to a small degree; very little [to eat *lightly*]. **3.** with grace and skill; nimbly [skipping *lightly* along]. **4.** in a gay or cheerful way. **5.** in a careless way; without being concerned [taking her responsibility *lightly*].

lighthouse

light·ning (līt′ning), *n.* a flash of light in the sky caused by the passing of electricity from one cloud to another or to the earth.

lightning bug, a firefly.

lightning rod, a metal rod placed high on a building, ship, etc. and connected to the ground or water, to carry off lightning that might otherwise strike the building, etc.

lightning

light·ship (līt′ship), *n.* a ship with a bright light, anchored for use as a lighthouse.

light·some (līt′səm), *adj.* **1.** lighthearted or gay. **2.** graceful, lively, or nimble.

light·weight (līt′wāt), *n.* **1.** a boxer or wrestler who weighs between 127 and 135 pounds. **2.** a person or animal that weighs less than normal.

light-year (līt′yir′), *n.* the distance that light travels in a year, about 6 trillion miles. Distance between stars is measured in light-years.

lig·nite (lig′nīt), *n.* soft, dark-brown coal in which the grain of the original wood is seen.

lik·a·ble or **like·a·ble** (līk′ə b'l), *adj.* easy to like because pleasing, friendly, etc.

like (līk), *prep.* **1.** somewhat the same as; similar to [muscles *like* iron]. **2.** in the same way as [crying *like* a baby]. **3.** as one would expect of; typical of [It is not *like* him to be late.] **4.** in the mood for [I feel *like* eating.] **5.** as if there will be [It looks *like* rain.] —*adj.* the same or nearly the same; equal or similar [a cup of sugar and a *like* amount of flour]. —*n.* a person or thing equal or similar to another [Did you ever see the *like* of this rain?] —*conj. used only in everyday talk* **1.** the same as [It's *like* you said.] **2.** as if [It looks *like* you'll win.] —**and the like,** and others of the same kind. —**like anything, like crazy, like mad, etc.,** with wild energy, great speed, etc.: *slang phrases.* —**like as not,** likely; probably: *used only in everyday talk.*

like (līk), *v.* **1.** to be fond of or pleased with; enjoy [I *like* to travel. Tom *likes* cats.] **2.** to

want to have, do, be, etc.; wish [Would you *like* more milk? You may go whenever you *like*.] —*n.* **likes,** *pl.* the things one enjoys or prefers [a list of his *likes* and dislikes]. —**liked,** *p.t. & p.p.*; **lik′ing,** *pr.p.*

-like (līk), a suffix meaning "like," "like that of," or "typical of" [A *childlike* smile is like the smile of a child.]

like·li·hood (līk′lē hood), *n.* the fact of being likely to happen; probability [There is little *likelihood* that he will win.]

like·ly (līk′lē), *adj.* **1.** apt to be, happen, do etc.; to be expected [A storm is *likely* before morning.] **2.** seeming to be true; probable [a *likely* explanation]. **3.** seeming to be good, suitable, etc.; promising [a *likely* man for the job]. —*adv.* probably [I will very *likely* go.] —**like′li·er,** *compar.*; **like′li·est,** *superl.*

lik·en (līk′'n), *v.* to describe as being like something else; compare [The poet *likened* her eyes to cornflowers.]

like·ness (līk′nis), *n.* **1.** the fact of being like or similar [his *likeness* to his brother]. **2.** shape or form [a cloud in the *likeness* of a camel]. **3.** something that is like; copy; picture [The photograph is a good *likeness* of you.]

like·wise (līk′wīz), *adv.* **1.** in the same way [He gave generously and we must do *likewise*.] **2.** also; too [Jim will sing and Mary *likewise*.]

lik·ing (līk′ing), *n.* the fact of enjoying or being fond of something; preference [a *liking* for sweets].

li·lac (lī′lək), *n.* **1.** a shrub with clusters of tiny, sweet-smelling flowers, ranging in color from white to purple. **2.** pale purple.

lilac flowers and leaves

lilt (lilt), *v.* to sing or play with a light, swinging rhythm. —*n.* **1.** a light, swinging rhythm or movement. **2.** a tune or song with such a rhythm.

lil·y (lil′ē), *n.* **1.** a plant that grows from a bulb and has white or colored flowers shaped like a trumpet. **2.** any plant somewhat like this [the water *lily*]. —*adj.* like a lily; white, pure, etc. [her *lily* hands]. —**lil′ies,** *pl.*

lily of the valley, a low plant with tiny, sweet-smelling, white flowers growing along a single stem. *See the picture on the next page.* —**lilies of the valley,** *pl.*

lily

Li·ma (lē′mə), *n.* the capital of Peru.

Li·ma bean (lī′mə), a large, flat bean that grows in pods and is used for food.

---

fat,   āpe,   cär,   ten,   ēven,   hit,   bīte,   gō,   hôrn,   tōōl,   book,   up,   fûr;
get,   joy,   yet,   chin,   she,   thin,   *then;*   zh = s in pleasure;   ′ as in able (ā′b'l);
ə = a in ago,   e in agent,   i in sanity,   o in confess,   u in focus.

limb (lim), *n.* **1.** an arm, leg, or wing. **2.** a large branch of a tree.

lim·ber (lim′bər), *adj.* bending easily; not stiff; flexible; supple [the *limber* branches of a young tree; the *limber* body of an athlete]. —*v.* to make or become limber [Exercise *limbers* the fingers.]

lim·bo (lim′bō), *n.* **1.** *often* **Limbo,** a place near the borders of hell that some Christians believe in. The souls of unbaptized infants and of good people who lived before Jesus are thought to go there after death. **2.** a place or condition of those who are forgotten or neglected [the *limbo* of defeated politicians].

lily of the valley

Lim·burg·er cheese (lim′bər gər), a soft, white cheese with a strong smell.

lime (līm), *n.* a white substance gotten by burning limestone, shells, etc. It is used in making cement, mortar, and fertilizers. —*v.* to put lime on; treat with lime [to *lime* the soil]. —**limed,** *p.t. & p.p.;* **lim′ing,** *pr.p.*

lime (līm), *n.* **1.** a fruit like a lemon, with a green skin and a sour, juicy pulp, used to make drinks or flavor foods. **2.** the tree it grows on.

lime (līm), *n.* the linden tree.

lime·light (līm′līt), *n.* **1.** a very bright light used at one time in theaters to throw a beam of light on a part of the stage. **2.** the condition of getting much attention from the public [Movie stars are often in the *limelight*.]

lim·er·ick (lim′ər ik), *n.* a funny poem of five lines, with this kind of rhyme and rhythm:
"A flea and a fly in a flue
Were imprisoned, so what could they do?
Said the flea, 'Let us fly!'
Said the fly, 'Let us flee!'
So they flew through a flaw in the flue."

lime·stone (līm′stōn), *n.* rock containing calcium carbonate, used to make building stones, lime, etc. Marble is a kind of limestone.

lim·it (lim′it), *n.* **1.** the point or line where something ends or that cannot be passed [There is a *limit* to my patience.] **2. limits,** *pl.* boundary lines; bounds [the city *limits*]. **3.** the greatest amount allowed [A catch of ten trout is the *limit*.] —*v.* to set a limit to; restrict [*Limit* your talk to ten minutes.]

lim·i·ta·tion (lim′ə tā′shən), *n.* **1.** a limiting or being limited. **2.** something that limits; restriction [His chief *limitation* as a student is his slowness in reading.]

lim·it·ed (lim′it id), *adj.* **1.** having a limit or limits; restricted in some way [This offer is good for a *limited* time only.] **2.** making only a few stops [a *limited* bus].

lim·it·less (lim′it lis), *adj.* without limits or without an end; vast; infinite.

limn (lim), *v.* **1.** to paint or draw, as a picture. **2.** to describe in words.

lim·ou·sine (lim′ə zēn), *n.* a large automobile driven by a chauffeur, who is usually separated from the passengers by a glass window.

limp (limp), *v.* to walk in an uneven way because of a lame leg. —*n.* a lameness in walking.

limp (limp), *adj.* not stiff or firm; flexible [as *limp* as a wet rag].

limp·et (lim′pit), *n.* a shellfish that clings to rocks and timbers with its thick foot.

lim·pid (lim′pid), *adj.* so clear that one can see through it [a *limpid* pool of water].

Lin·coln (ling′kən), *n.* the capital of Nebraska.

Lincoln, Abraham, 1809–1865; 16th president of the United States, from 1861 to 1865.

lin·den (lin′dən), *n.* a tree with heart-shaped leaves and sweet-smelling yellowish flowers.

line (līn), *n.* **1.** a cord, rope, string, etc. [a fishing *line*]. **2.** a wire or pipe or a system of wires or pipes for carrying water, gas, electricity, etc. **3.** a long, thin mark [*lines* made by a pen, pencil, etc.; *lines* formed in the face by wrinkles]. **4.** a border or boundary [to cross a State *line*]. **5. lines,** *pl.* outline or form in general [This car has good *lines*. The house is built along modern *lines*.] **6.** a row of persons or things [a long *line* of people waiting to get in; a *line* of words across a page]. **7.** a series of persons or things following each other [a *line* of Democratic presidents]. **8.** a company that carries people or goods by bus, ship, airplane, etc. **9.** one of the routes followed by such a company [the main *line* of a railroad]. **10.** the path of something that moves [in the *line* of cannon fire]. **11.** a way of thinking, acting, etc. [the *line* of an argument]. **12.** a person's business, work, etc. [He's in the hardware *line*.] **13.** a supply of goods of a certain kind [This store carries a fine *line* of shoes.] **14.** a short letter or note [Drop me a *line*.] **15. lines,** *pl.* all the speeches of a single actor in a play. **16.** the football players who are arranged in a row in front of the backs. **17.** any of the imaginary circles that divide the earth into zones or parts [the date *line;* the *line* of the equator]. **18.** in mathematics, the path of a moving point; especially, a straight line. —*v.* **1.** to mark with lines [Age has *lined* his face.] **2.** to form a line along [Elms *line* the street.] —**all along the line,** at all points; everywhere. —**draw a line,** to set a limit. —**get a line on,** to find out about: *used only in everyday talk.* —**hold the line,** to keep anyone or anything from getting through; stand firm. —**in line,** in a straight row or in agreement. —**into line,** into a straight row or into agreement [to bring or come *into line*]. —**line of duty,** the work or duties that one is expected to do [above and beyond the *line of duty*]. —**line up,** to bring or come into a line, or row. —**on a line,** even or level. —**out of line,** not in a straight line, or not in agreement. —**read between the lines,** to find hidden meanings in something written, said, or done. —**toe the line,** to do just as one

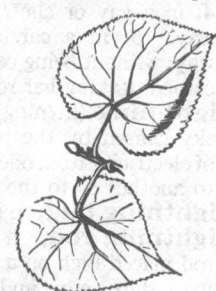

linden leaves

has been told. **—lined,** *p.t. & p.p.;* **lin′ing,** *pr.p.*

line (līn), *v.* to cover on the inside with a layer or lining [The coat is *lined* with fur. Canvas *lined* the trunk.] **—lined,** *p.t. & p.p.;* **lin′ing,** *pr.p.*

lin·e·age (lin′i ij), *n.* line of descent; ancestry.

lin·e·al (lin′i əl), *adj.* **1.** in the direct line of descent, as from father to son to grandson [George Washington has no *lineal* descendants.] **2.** of a line or lines; linear.

lin·e·a·ment (lin′i ə mənt), *n.* a special feature or part, especially of the face.

lin·e·ar (lin′i ər), *adj.* **1.** of, made of, or using a line or lines [*linear* boundaries]. **2.** of length [*linear* measure].

line·man (līn′mən), *n.* **1.** a man whose work is putting up and repairing telephone, telegraph, or electric wires. **2.** a football player in the line; center, guard, tackle, or end. **—line′men,** *pl.*

lin·en (lin′ən), *n.* **1.** thread or cloth made of flax. **2.** things made of linen, or of cotton, etc., as tablecloths, sheets, shirts, etc.

lin·er (līn′ər), *n.* **1.** a ship or airplane used in a transportation line. **2.** a batted baseball that moves in a line not far above the ground.

lineman

lines·man (līnz′mən), *n.* **1.** a lineman (*in meaning 1*). **2.** a football official who keeps track of the yards gained or lost. **—lines′men,** *pl.*

line-up or **line·up** (līn′up′), *n.* **1.** a number of persons or things in a line, especially a row of persons lined up by police to be identified. **2.** a list of the players on a team, arranged in a certain order.

-ling (ling), a suffix meaning: **1.** small [A *duckling* is a small duck.] **2.** low in rank or respect [A *hireling*, who can be hired to do almost anything for pay, is held low in respect.]

lin·ger (ling′gər), *v.* to keep on staying, as if not wanting to leave; loiter [The last guest *lingered.*]

lin·ge·rie (län′zhə rē *or* lan′zhə rē′), *n.* women's underwear.

lin·go (ling′gō), *n.* a language or dialect that sounds strange to one: *used in a joking or mocking way* [the *lingo* of lawyers]. **—lin′goes,** *pl.*

lin·guist (ling′gwist), *n.* **1.** a person who can speak, read, and write several languages. **2.** an expert in linguistics.

lin·guis·tics (ling gwis′tiks), *n.pl.* the general study of language, including the sounds of speech, forms and meanings of words, grammar, etc.: *used with a singular verb.* **—lin·guis′tic,** *adj.*

lin·i·ment (lin′ə mənt), *n.* a liquid rubbed on the skin to soothe sores, sprains, etc.

lin·ing (līn′ing), *n.* material that covers an inside surface [the *lining* of a hat].

link (lingk), *n.* **1.** any of the rings or loops that form a chain. **2.** any of the joined sections of something like a chain [a *link* of sausage]. **3.** anything that joins or connects [Books are a *link* with the past.] **—v.** to join or connect [We *linked* arms.]

upper: links of sausage
lower: links of a chain

linking verb, a verb showing a state of being, used to connect a subject and the word or words that tell about the subject ["Am" is a *linking verb* in the sentence "I am happy."]

links (lingks), *n.pl.* a golf course.

lin·net (lin′it), *n.* a small songbird found in Europe, Asia, and Africa.

li·no·le·um (li nō′li əm), *n.* a hard, smooth floor covering made of a mixture of ground cork and linseed oil on a backing, as of canvas.

lin·seed (lin′sēd), *n.* the seed of flax.

linseed oil, a yellowish oil pressed from linseed and used in oil paints, printer's ink, linoleum, etc.

lint (lint), *n.* **1.** fine bits of thread, fluff, etc. from cloth or yarn. **2.** linen scraped and made soft, once used to cover wounds. **—lint′y,** *adj.*

lin·tel (lin′t'l), *n.* the piece set lengthwise across the top of a door or window to support the wall above the opening.

lintel

li·on (lī′ən), *n.* **1.** a large, strong animal of the cat family, living in Africa and southwest Asia. Lions have a brownish-yellow coat, and the males have a heavy mane. **2.** a person who is very strong and brave. **3.** a man who is famous.

li·on·ess (lī′ən is), *n.* a female lion.

lip (lip), *n.* **1.** either the upper or the lower edge of the mouth. **2.** anything like a lip, as the edge of a wound or the rim of a cup. **—adj.** spoken, but not sincere or honest; false [to pay *lip* service to an idea one does not really believe]. **—keep a stiff upper lip,** to remain unafraid and not give up hope.

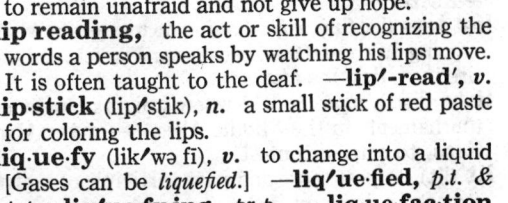
lion and lioness
(9 to 11 ft. long, including tail)

lip reading, the act or skill of recognizing the words a person speaks by watching his lips move. It is often taught to the deaf. **—lip′-read′,** *v.*

lip·stick (lip′stik), *n.* a small stick of red paste for coloring the lips.

liq·ue·fy (lik′wə fī), *v.* to change into a liquid [Gases can be *liquefied.*] **—liq′ue·fied,** *p.t. & p.p.;* **liq′ue·fy·ing,** *pr.p.* **—liq·ue·fac·tion** (lik′wə fak′shən), *n.*

fat,   āpe,   cär,   ten,   ēven,   hit,   bīte,   gō,   hôrn,   tool,   book,   up,   fûr;
get,   joy,   yet,   chin,   she,   thin,   then;   zh = s in pleasure;   ′ as in able (ā′b'l);
ə = a in ago,   e in agent,   i in sanity,   o in confess,   u in focus.

li·queur (li kūr′), *n.* a strong, sweet alcoholic liquor, often with a fruit flavor.

liq·uid (lik′wid), *n.* a substance that flows easily; matter that is neither a solid nor a gas [Water is a *liquid* when it is not ice or steam.] —*adj.* **1.** flowing easily; fluid [Oil is a *liquid* fuel.] **2.** moving or flowing in a smooth, musical way [dancing with *liquid* grace]. **3.** easily changed into cash [Bonds and stocks are *liquid* assets.]

liq·ui·date (lik′wi dāt), *v.* **1.** to settle the affairs of a business that is closing, usually because it is bankrupt. **2.** to pay a debt in full. **3.** to get rid of, as by killing [The dictator *liquidated* his enemies.] —**liq′ui·dat·ed,** *p.t.* & *p.p.;* **liq′ui·dat·ing,** *pr.p.* —**liq′ui·da′tion,** *n.*

liq·uor (lik′ər), *n.* **1.** a drink that contains alcohol, as whisky, gin, or rum. **2.** any liquid, as sap from trees or juice from meat.

li·ra (lir′ə), *n.* the basic unit of money in Italy. —**li·re** (lir′ā) or **li′ras,** *pl.*

Lis·bon (liz′bən), *n.* the capital of Portugal.

lisle (līl), *n.* a thin, hard, very strong cotton thread. —*adj.* made of lisle [*lisle* socks].

lisp (lisp), *v.* **1.** to use the sounds "th" and "*th*" in place of the sounds "s" and "z" ["Yeth," he *lisped,* trying to say "yes."] **2.** to speak in a way that is childish or not clear. —*n.* the act or sound of lisping.

lis·some or **lis·som** (lis′əm), *adj.* bending or moving easily and gracefully; supple.

list (list), *n.* a series of names, words, or numbers set down in order [a grocery *list*]. —*v.* to make a list of; put into a list [Is your name *listed* in the phone book?] See also **lists.**

list (list), *v.* to wish; choose: *now seldom used* [Let them think what they *list.*]

list (list), *v.* to tilt to one side [The ship *listed* in the storm.] —*n.* the act of listing.

list (list), *v.* to listen: *now seldom used.*

lis·ten (lis′n), *v.* to pay attention in order to hear; try to hear [*Listen* to the rain. Please *listen* when I speak to you.] —**listen in,** to listen to others talking, as on the telephone or radio. —**lis′ten·er,** *n.*

a listing ship

list·less (list′lis), *adj.* having no interest in what is going on around one, because one is sick, sad, or tired. —**list′less·ly,** *adv.*

lists (lists), *n.pl.* a field where knights fought in tournaments in the Middle Ages. —**enter the lists,** to enter a contest.

lit (lit), a past tense and past participle of **light** (to set on fire) and **light** (to get down).

lit., abbreviation for **liter** or **liters, literature.**

lit·a·ny (lit′n ē), *n.* a prayer in which the clergyman and the congregation take turns in reciting the parts. —**lit′a·nies,** *pl.*

li·ter (lē′tər), *n.* a measure of volume in the metric system that is equal to a little more than a quart in liquid measure, and to a little less than a quart in dry measure.

lit·er·a·cy (lit′ər ə sē), *n.* the ability to read and write.

lit·er·al (lit′ər əl), *adj.* **1.** following the original, word for word [a *literal* translation of a French poem]. **2.** based on the actual words in their usual meaning; not allowing for idiom or exaggeration [The *literal* meaning of "lend an ear" is to let another borrow one's ear]. **3.** according to the facts; real; correct [the *literal* truth]. —**lit′er·al·ly,** *adv.*

lit·er·ar·y (lit′ə rer′ē), *adj.* having to do with literature [*literary* studies; *literary* men].

lit·er·ate (lit′ər it), *adj.* educated; especially, able to read and write. —*n.* a literate person.

lit·er·a·ture (lit′ər ə chər), *n.* **1.** all the writings of a certain time, country, etc.; especially, those that have lasting value because of their beauty, imagination, etc., as fine novels, plays, and poems. **2.** the work or profession of writing such things; also, the study of such writings. **3.** all the writings on some subject [medical *literature*].

lithe (līth), *adj.* bending easily; limber or supple [a *lithe* dancer; *lithe* willow branches].

lith·o·graph (lith′ə graf), *n.* a picture or print made by lithography. —*v.* to make by lithography.

li·thog·ra·phy (li thäg′rə fē), *n.* the process of printing from a flat stone or metal plate whose surface is treated so that only the parts having the design will hold ink. —**li·thog′ra·pher,** *n.*

Lith·u·a·ni·a (lith′oo wā′ni ə), *n.* a former country in northeastern Europe, since 1940 a republic of the Soviet Union. —**Lith′u·a′ni·an,** *adj. & n.*

lit·i·gant (lit′ə gənt), *n.* any of the persons taking part in a lawsuit.

lit·i·ga·tion (lit′ə gā′shən), *n.* **1.** the act of carrying on a lawsuit. **2.** a lawsuit.

lit·mus (lit′məs), *n.* a purple coloring matter got from a certain plant: paper treated with this (called **litmus paper**) turns red in an acid and blue in an alkali.

li·tre (lē′tər), *n.* same as **liter.**

lit·ter (lit′ər), *n.* **1.** a stretcher for carrying a sick or injured person. **2.** a couch joined to long poles by which it can be carried, as on men's shoulders. **3.** straw or hay for animals to lie on. **4.** odd bits or scraps lying around in disorder [Pick up your *litter* after a picnic.] **5.** all the puppies, kittens, etc. born at one time to a dog, cat, etc. —*v.* **1.** to make messy or untidy with things scattered about [The lawn was *littered* with leaves.] **2.** to give birth to a number of young animals at one time.

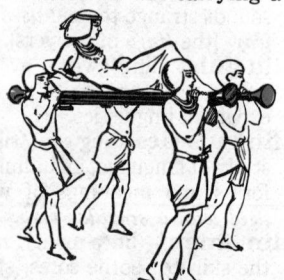
litter *(meaning 2)*

lit·tle (lit′'l), *adj.* **1.** small in size; not large [a *little* house]. **2.** small in amount or degree; not much [*little* sugar; *little* danger]. **3.** short or brief [Wait a *little* while. Go a *little* distance.] **4.** not important; trivial [just a *little* error]. **5.** not open to new ideas; not liberal [a *little* mind]. —*adv.* **1.** to a small degree; not very much [He is a *little* better.] **2.** not at all [He *little* knew what lay ahead.] —*n.* **1.** a small amount [Have a *little* of this cake.] **2.** a short time [Sit a *little* with me.] —**little by little,** in a slow way; in small amounts; gradually. —**not a little,** very much; very. —**think little of,** to think of or treat as not very important. —**lit′tler** or **less** or **less′er,** *compar. of adj.;* **lit′tlest** or **least,** *superl. of adj.* —**less,** *compar. of adv.;* **least,** *superl. of adv.* —**lit′tle·ness,** *n.*

Little Rock, the capital of Arkansas.

lit·ur·gy (lit′ər jē), *n.* the form or order of worship in a religious service. —**lit′ur·gies,** *pl.* —**li·tur·gi·cal** (li tûr′ji k′l), *adj.*

liv·a·ble (liv′ə b'l), *adj.* **1.** fit or pleasant to live in [a *livable* house]. **2.** that can be lived through or endured [He found life on the island quite *livable*.]

live (liv), *v.* **1.** to have life; be alive [No one *lives* forever.] **2.** to stay alive; last or endure [He *lived* to be 100 years old.] **3.** to pass one's life in a certain way [They *lived* happily. She *lived* a useful life.] **4.** to have a full, exciting life [That man has really *lived*.] **5.** to support oneself [She *lives* on a small pension.] **6.** to feed [Bats *live* on insects and fruit.] **7.** to make one's home; reside [We *live* on a farm.] —**live down,** to live in a way that makes people forget something wrong that one has done. —**live up to,** to act in keeping with one's ideals, promises, etc. —**lived,** *p.t. & p.p.;* **liv′ing,** *pr.p.*

live (līv), *adj.* **1.** having life; not dead. **2.** full of life or energy; active [a *live* person]. **3.** of interest now [a *live* topic]. **4.** still burning or glowing [*live* coals]. **5.** that has not exploded [a *live* bomb]. **6.** carrying electrical current [a *live* wire]. **7.** that is broadcast while it is taking place; not photographed or recorded [a *live* television or radio program].

live·li·hood (līv′lē hood), *n.* the means of living, or of supporting oneself [He earned his *livelihood* by repairing radios.]

live·long (liv′lông), *adj.* through the whole length of; entire [the *livelong* day].

live·ly (līv′lē), *adj.* **1.** full of life or energy; active [a *lively* puppy]. **2.** full of excitement [a *lively* meeting]. **3.** gay, cheerful, or bright [a *lively* voice; *lively* colors]. **4.** with quick, light movements [a *lively* dance]. **5.** having much bounce [a *lively* ball]. —*adv.* in a lively way. —**live′li·er,** *compar.;* **live′li·est,** *superl.* —**live′li·ness,** *n.*

liv·en (liv′ən), *v.* to make or become lively, gay, bright, etc. [Games *liven* up a party.]

liv·er (liv′ər), *n.* **1.** a large organ of the body, near the stomach. It makes bile and helps break down food into parts that the body can absorb. **2.** the liver of some animals, used as food.

liv·er (liv′ər), *n.* a person who lives in a certain way [a clean *liver*].

liv·er·ied (liv′ər ēd), *adj.* wearing livery.

Liv·er·pool (liv′ər pool), *n.* a seaport in northwestern England.

liv·er·wort (liv′ər wûrt), *n.* **1.** a small plant that looks like moss. **2.** same as **hepatica.**

liv·er·y (liv′ər ē), *n.* **1.** a uniform worn by servants or by people doing a certain kind of work [the *livery* of a butler]. **2.** the work of keeping and feeding horses for pay; also, the business of renting horses and carriages. **3.** a stable where horses are kept for these purposes: also **livery stable.** —**liv′er·ies,** *pl.*

lives (līvz), *n.* plural of **life.**

live·stock (līv′stäk), *n.* animals kept or raised on farms, as cattle, horses, pigs, or sheep.

liv·id (liv′id), *adj.* **1.** black-and-blue from a bruise. **2.** grayish-blue; ashen [His face was *livid* with rage.]

liv·ing (liv′ing), *adj.* **1.** having life; alive; not dead. **2.** still active or in common use among people [a *living* tradition; a *living* language]. **3.** of people alive [within *living* memory]. **4.** exact in every detail [He is the *living* image of his brother.] **5.** of life or of keeping alive [poor *living* conditions]. **6.** enough to live on [a *living* wage]. —*n.* **1.** the fact of being alive. **2.** the means of supporting oneself or one's family [He works hard for a *living*.] **3.** the way in which one lives [the standard of *living*].

living room, a room in a home, with soft chairs, sofas, etc., used by the family for reading, playing, entertaining guests, etc.

liz·ard (liz′ərd), *n.* a reptile with a long slender body and tail, a scaly skin, and four legs, as the chameleon, gecko, and iguana.

lla·ma (lä′mə), *n.* a South American animal like the camel, but smaller and without a hump. It is used as a beast of burden, and its wool is made into cloth.

lla·no (lä′nō), *n.* any of the flat, grassy plains of Spanish America. —**lla′nos,** *pl.*

lo (lō), *interj.* look! see! *Now seldom used.*

load (lōd), *n.* **1.** something that is carried or is to be

llama (3 ft. high at shoulder)

fat,   āpe,   cär,   ten,   ēven,   hit,   bīte,   gō,   hôrn,   tool,   book,   up,   fûr;
get,   joy,   yet,   chin,   she,   thin,   *th*en;   zh = s in pleasure;   ′ as in able (ā′b'l);
ə = a in ago,   e in agent,   i in sanity,   o in confess,   u in focus.

carried at one time [a heavy *load* on his back].
2. the usual amount carried at one time [We
used up six *loads* of coal.] **3.** something that
makes one worried or anxious [Her safe arrival
took a *load* off my mind.] **4.** the amount of current or power supplied by a dynamo, engine, etc.
5. a single charge for a gun [a *load* of shot].
6. *often* **loads,** *pl.* a great amount or number:
used only in everyday talk [She has *loads* of friends.]
—*v.* **1.** to put something to be carried into or
upon a carrier [to *load* a bus with passengers; to
load coal]. **2.** to weigh down with a burden
[She is *loaded* with troubles.] **3.** to supply in
great amounts [He was *loaded* with medals.]
4. to fill with what is needed to make something
work [to *load* a gun with bullets; to *load* a camera
with film]. **5.** to take on a load [The truck is
loading at the platform.] **6.** to ask in such a way
that it is hard not to give the answer that is
wanted [a *loaded* question]. —**load′er,** *n.*

load·stone (lōd′stōn′), *n.* **1.** an iron mineral
that is a natural magnet. **2.** anything that
attracts strongly.

loaf (lōf), *n.* **1.** a portion of bread baked in one
piece. **2.** any food baked in this shape. **3.** a
mass of sugar shaped like a cone. —**loaves,** *pl.*

loaf (lōf), *v.* to spend time doing little or nothing; idle [to *loaf* on the job].

loaf·er (lōf′ər), *n.* **1.** a person who loafs; idler.
2. a sport shoe somewhat like a moccasin.

loam (lōm), *n.* a rich, dark soil with rotting plant
matter in it.

loan (lōn), *n.* **1.** the act of lending [Thanks for
the *loan* of your pen.] **2.** something lent, especially a sum of money. —*v.* to lend.

loath (lōth), *adj.* not willing; reluctant [They
were *loath* to go home.]

loathe (lō*th*), *v.* to feel hate or disgust for.
—**loathed,** *p.t. & p.p.;* **loath′ing,** *pr.p.*

loath·ing (lō*th*′ing), *n.* hatred or disgust.

loath·some (lō*th*′səm), *adj.* very disgusting.

loaves (lōvz), *n.* plural of **loaf.**

lob (läb), *v.* to hit or throw a ball, etc. so that it
goes high in the air. —*n.* the act of lobbing.
—**lobbed,** *p.t. & p.p.;* **lob′bing,** *pr.p.*

lob·by (läb′ē), *n.* **1.** an entrance hall or waiting
room, as in a hotel or theater. **2.** a person or
persons who try to get lawmakers to pass certain
laws, etc., often to benefit a special group. —*v.*
to try to get lawmakers to pass certain laws, etc.
—**lob′bies,** *pl.* —**lob′bied,** *p.t. & p.p.;* **lob′-**
by·ing, *pr.p.* —**lob′by·ist,** *n.*

lobe (lōb), *n.* a rounded part that sticks out, as
the fleshy lower end of the human
ear.

lo·be·li·a (lō bē′li ə), *n.* a plant
with long clusters of blue, red, or
white flowers.

lob·lol·ly (läb′läl′ē), *n.* a pine
tree with thick bark, that grows
in the southern United States.
—**lob·lol′lies,** *pl.*

lob·ster (läb′stər), *n.* **1.** a large
sea shellfish with five pairs of legs,
of which the first pair are large,

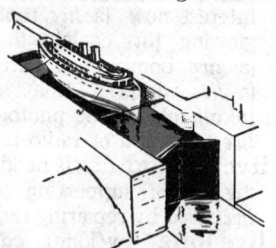
lobe

powerful pincers. Lobsters' shells turn red when
boiled. **2.** the flesh of this
animal used as food.

lo·cal (lō′k'l), *adj.* **1.**
having to do with a par-
ticular place; not general
[*local* customs]. **2.** having
an effect on just a certain
part of the body [a *local*
anesthetic]. **3.** making
many stops; not limited
[a *local* train]. —*n.* **1.** a local train, bus, etc.
2. a branch or chapter of a larger organization,
as of a labor union.

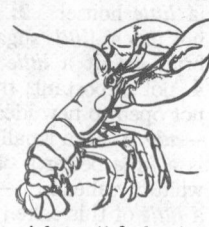
lobster (1 ft. long)

lo·cal·ism (lō′k'l iz'm), *n.* a word, custom,
pronunciation, etc. used only in a certain region
["Butter bean" is a Southern *localism* for "Lima
bean."]

lo·cal·i·ty (lō kal′ə tē), *n.* a place, district, or
neighborhood. —**lo·cal′i·ties,** *pl.*

lo·cal·ize (lō′k'l īz), *v.* to keep or make stay
in a particular part or place [The pain is *localized*
in his hand.] —**lo′cal·ized,** *p.t. & p.p.;* **lo′cal·**
iz·ing, *pr.p.*

lo·cal·ly (lō′k'l ē), *adv.* within a particular place
[The storm did much damage *locally*.]

lo·cate (lō′kāt *or* lō kāt′), *v.* **1.** to set up or
place; situate [His shop is *located* downtown.]
2. to show where something is [*Locate* Alaska on
this map.] **3.** to find out where something is
[He finally *located* the gloves he had lost.] **4.** to
settle: *used only in everyday talk* [The family
located in Boston.] —**lo′cat·ed,** *p.t. & p.p.;*
lo′cat·ing, *pr.p.*

lo·ca·tion (lō kā′shən), *n.* **1.** the act of locating.
2. the place where something is or will be; site
[a fine *location* for a gas station].

loch (läk), *n.* a lake; also, a long narrow bay,
nearly cut off from the sea: *a Scottish word.*

lock (läk), *n.* **1.** a device for fastening a door,
safe, etc. by means of
a bolt. A lock can usu-
ally be opened only by
a special key, etc. **2.**
an enclosed part of a
canal, river, etc. with
gates at each end.
Water can be let in or
out of it to raise or
lower ships from one
level to another. **3.**
anything that holds something in place or keeps
it from moving [an oar*lock;* an arm *lock* in
wrestling]. **4.** the part of a firearm that fires
the charge. —*v.* **1.** to fasten or become fastened
with a lock. **2.** to shut in or out [*Lock* the money
in the box. *Lock* the cat out of the house.] **3.** to
join or become joined together firmly; interlock
[The two elks *locked* horns while fighting.] **4.** to
jam together so that no movement is possible
[The gears are *locked*.]

lock in a canal

lock (läk), *n.* **1.** a curl of hair. **2.** a tuft of wool,
cotton, etc.

lock·er (läk′ər), *n.* a closet, chest, etc., usually
of metal, that can be locked.

lock·et (läk′it), *n.* a small metal case for holding a picture, lock of hair, etc., usually worn around the neck on a chain or ribbon.

lock·jaw (läk′jô), *n.* a disease in which the jaws become tightly closed: also called **tetanus.**

lock·out (läk′out), *n.* the refusal by an employer to allow his employees to work until they agree to his terms.

lock·smith (läk′smith), *n.* a person whose work is making or repairing locks and keys.

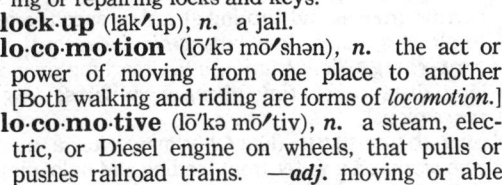

locket

lock·up (läk′up), *n.* a jail.

lo·co·mo·tion (lō′kə mō′shən), *n.* the act or power of moving from one place to another [Both walking and riding are forms of *locomotion.*]

lo·co·mo·tive (lō′kə mō′tiv), *n.* a steam, electric, or Diesel engine on wheels, that pulls or pushes railroad trains. —*adj.* moving or able to move from one place to another.

lo·cust (lō′kəst), *n.* 1. a large insect like a grasshopper, that often travels in great swarms and destroys crops. 2. the cicada. 3. a tree with a number of leaflets growing from each stem and clusters of sweet-smelling, white flowers.

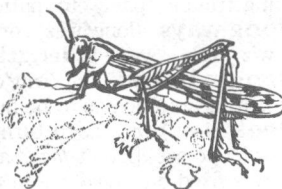

locust (3 in. long)

lode (lōd), *n.* a deposit of the ore of some metal which fills a crack or seam in rock.

lode·star (lōd′stär), *n.* a star to be guided by; especially, the North Star.

lode·stone (lōd′stōn), *n.* same as **loadstone.**

lodge (läj), *n.* 1. a place to live in; especially, a small house for some special use [a hunting *lodge*]. 2. the local branch of certain societies or clubs, or its meeting place. 3. a beaver's den. —*v.* 1. to provide with a place to live or sleep in for a time [She agreed to *lodge* the strangers overnight.] 2. to live in a place for a time; be a lodger [John *lodged* with the Smith family while attending college.] 3. to put, drive, shoot, etc. firmly [The archer *lodged* the arrow in the center of the target.] 4. to come to rest and stick firmly [The fish bone *lodged* in her throat.] 5. to bring before an official [to *lodge* a protest with the mayor]. —**lodged,** *p.t. & p.p.;* **lodg′ing,** *pr.p.*

lodg·er (läj′ər), *n.* a person who rents a room in another person's home.

lodg·ing (läj′ing), *n.* 1. a place to live in, especially for a short time. 2. **lodgings,** *pl.* a room or rooms rented in another's home.

lodg·ment (läj′mənt), *n.* 1. a lodging or being lodged. 2. a lodging place. 3. a pile of something that has become lodged in a place.

loft (lôft), *n.* 1. the space just below the roof of a house, barn, etc. [a hay*loft*]. 2. an upper story of a warehouse or factory. 3. a gallery or balcony [a choir *loft*]. —*v.* to send high into the air [The golfer *lofted* the ball over the bunker.]

loft·y (lôf′tē), *adj.* 1. very high [a *lofty* skyscraper]. 2. high in ideals or noble in feelings [the *lofty* teachings of Socrates]. 3. too proud; haughty [the king's *lofty* manner]. —**loft′i·er,** *compar.;* **loft′i·est,** *superl.* —**loft′i·ness,** *n.*

log (lôg), *n.* 1. a part of a tree that has been cut down [Cut the trunk into *logs* for the fireplace.] 2. a device floated at the end of a line to measure the speed of a ship. 3. a daily record of a ship's voyage, giving speed, position, weather, and other important happenings. 4. any record of a trip [the flight *log* of an airplane]. —*adj.* made of logs [a *log* cabin]. —*v.* 1. to cut down trees and take the logs to a sawmill. 2. to write in a ship's log. —**logged,** *p.t. & p.p.;* **log′ging,** *pr.p.*

lo·gan·ber·ry (lō′gən ber′ē), *n.* a purplish-red berry that is a cross between the blackberry and the red raspberry. —**lo′gan·ber′ries,** *pl.*

log·a·rithm (lôg′ə rith′m), *n.* 1. the figure that tells to what power a certain fixed number, as ten, must be raised to equal a given number [The *logarithm* of 100 is 2, and of 1000 is 3, when 10 is taken as the fixed number ($10^2 = 100$; $10^3 = 1000$).] 2. any of a system of such numbers listed in tables to shorten the working of problems in mathematics.

log·book (lôg′book), *n.* a book in which the log of a ship or airplane is kept.

log·ger·head (lôg′ər hed), *n.* 1. a stupid person; blockhead. 2. a sea turtle with a large head, that lives in warm seas. —**at loggerheads,** in a quarrel; arguing; disagreeing.

log·ging (lôg′ing), *n.* the work of cutting down trees and taking the logs to a sawmill. —**log′ger,** *n.*

log·ic (läj′ik), *n.* 1. correct reasoning; sound thinking. 2. the science that deals with the rules of correct reasoning and with proof by reasoning. 3. way of reasoning [poor *logic*].

log·i·cal (läj′i k'l), *adj.* 1. based on logic or using logic [a *logical* explanation]. 2. that is to be expected because of what has gone before [the *logical* result of one's acts]. —**log′i·cal·ly,** *adv.*

lo·gi·cian (lō jish′ən), *n.* a person who is skilled in logic.

-lo·gy (lə jē), a suffix meaning "the science or study of" [*Zoology* is the science of animal life.]

loin (loin), *n.* 1. the part of an animal between the hip and the ribs; lower back. 2. **loins,** *pl.* the hips and lower part of the abdomen. —**gird up the loins,** to get ready to do something difficult.

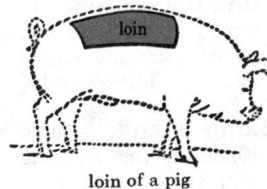

loin of a pig

fat,   āpe,   cär,   ten,   ēven,   hit,   bīte,   gō,   hôrn,   tōōl,   book,   up,   fŭr;
get,   joy,   yet,   chin,   she,   thin,   *th*en;   zh = s in pleasure;   ′ as in able (ā′b'l);
ə = a in ago,   e in agent,   i in sanity,   o in confess,   u in focus.

loin·cloth (loin′klôth), *n.* a cloth worn about the loins by some tribes in warm climates.

loi·ter (loi′tər), *v.* **1.** to spend time in an idle way; linger [Do not *loiter* in the halls.] **2.** to walk in a slow, lazy way. —**loi′ter·er,** *n.*

loll (läl), *v.* **1.** to sit or lean back in a lazy way. **2.** to hang down [The dog's tongue *lolled* out.]

lol·li·pop or **lol·ly·pop** (läl′ē päp), *n.* a piece of hard candy on a small stick; sucker.

Lom·bar·dy (läm′bər dē or lum′bər dē), *n.* a region of northern Italy.

Lo·mond, Loch (lō′mənd), a lake in western Scotland.

Lon·don (lun′dən), *n.* the capital of the United Kingdom, in southeastern England.

lone (lōn), *adj.* by itself or by oneself; solitary.

lone·ly (lōn′lē), *adj.* **1.** unhappy because one is alone or away from friends or family [Billy was *lonely* his first day at camp.] **2.** without others near-by; alone [a *lonely* cottage]. **3.** with few or no people [a *lonely* island]. —**lone′li·er,** *compar.;* **lone′li·est,** *superl.* —**lone′li·ness,** *n.*

lone·some (lōn′səm), *adj.* **1.** having a lonely feeling [a *lonesome* sentry]. **2.** causing a lonely feeling [a *lonesome* whistle]. —**lone′some·ness,** *n.*

long (lông), *adj.* **1.** measuring much from end to end or from beginning to end; not short [a *long* board; a *long* trip; a *long* wait]. **2.** reaching over a certain distance; in length [a rope six feet *long*]. **3.** large; big [He took a *long* chance.] **4.** taking a longer time to say than other sounds [The "a" in "cave" and the "i" in "hide" are *long.*] —*adv.* **1.** for a long time [Don't be gone *long.*] **2.** from the beginning to the end [all summer *long*]. **3.** at a far distant time [He died *long* ago.] —**as long as** or **so long as, 1.** during the time that. **2.** seeing that; since. **3.** on the condition that. —**before long,** soon.

long (lông), *v.* to want very much; feel a strong desire for [We *long* to go home.]

long., abbreviation for **longitude.**

long·boat (lông′bōt), *n.* the largest boat carried on a merchant sailing ship.

long distance, a system by which telephone calls can be made between distant places.

lon·gev·i·ty (län jev′ə tē), *n.* long life.

Long·fel·low, Henry Wads·worth (wädz′wərth lông′fel′ō), 1807–1882; U.S. poet.

long·hand (lông′hand), *n.* ordinary handwriting, with the words written out in full.

long·horn (lông′hôrn), *n.* a breed of cattle with long horns, raised in the Southwest.

long·ing (lông′ing), *n.* strong desire; yearning. —*adj.* showing strong desire. —**long′ing·ly,** *adv.*

Long Island, a large island in the Atlantic that is partly in New York City.

lon·gi·tude (län′jə-tōōd or län′jə tyōōd), *n.* distance measured in

longhorn (4½ ft. high at shoulder)

degrees east or west of a line running north and south through Greenwich, England. See also **me·ridian** [Chicago is at 87 degrees west *longitude.*]

lon·gi·tu·di·nal (län′jə-tōō′di n′l or län′jə tyōō′-di n′l), *adj.* **1.** of or in length. **2.** running lengthwise; placed lengthwise. **3.** of longitude. —**lon′gi-tu′di·nal·ly,** *adv.*

lines of longitude

long-lived (lông′līvd′ or lông′livd′), *adj.* living or lasting for a long time.

long-playing (lông′plā′ing), *adj.* having very narrow grooves and turning at a slow speed so as to play for a long time [a *long-playing* record].

long-range (lông′rānj′), *adj.* reaching over a long distance or time [*long-range* guns; *long-range* plans].

long·shore·man (lông′shôr′mən), *n.* a man who works on a water front loading and unloading ships. —**long′shore′men,** *pl.*

long-suf·fer·ing (lông′suf′ər ing), *adj.* bearing trouble, pain, etc. patiently for a long time.

long·ways (lông′wāz) or **long·wise** (lông′-wīz), *adv.* same as **lengthwise.**

long-wind·ed (lông′win′did), *adj.* speaking or writing so much as to be boring.

look (look), *v.* **1.** to turn or aim one's eyes in order to see [Don't *look* back.] **2.** to keep one's eyes fixed on [*Look* me in the face.] **3.** to bring one's attention [Just *look* at the trouble you've caused.] **4.** to search or hunt [Did you *look* in every pocket for the letter?] **5.** to seem or appear [Jane *looks* sad.] **6.** to face in a certain direction [The hotel *looks* to the lake.] —*n.* **1.** the act of looking; glance [an angry *look*]. **2.** the way someone or something seems; appearance [He has the *look* of a beggar.] **3. looks,** *pl.* appearance: *used only in everyday talk* [I don't like the *looks* of this place.] —**look after,** to take care of. —**look alive!** be alert! act quickly! —**look back,** to think about the past. —**look down on,** to think of as bad or worthless; despise. —**look for, 1.** to search or hunt for. **2.** to expect. —**look forward to,** to wait eagerly for. —**look in on,** to pay a brief visit to. —**look into** or **look over,** to examine; inspect. —**look on, 1.** to watch what is going on. **2.** to consider; regard. —**look out,** to be careful. —**look to, 1.** to take care of. **2.** to rely upon. **3.** to expect. —**look up, 1.** to search for, as in a dictionary. **2.** to pay a visit to: *used only in everyday talk.* —**look up to,** to respect; admire. —**look′er,** *n.*

look·er-on (look′ər än′), *n.* an onlooker; spectator. —**look′ers-on′,** *pl.*

looking glass, a mirror.

look·out (look′out), *n.* **1.** a careful watching for someone or something [He's on the *lookout* for a new job.] **2.** a person who is supposed to keep watch; guard; sentry. **3.** a place, especially a high place, from which to watch. **4.** concern or worry: *used only in everyday talk.*

loom (lōōm), *n.* a machine for weaving thread or yarn into cloth.

loom (lōōm), *v.* to come into sight in a sudden or frightening way [A ship *loomed* out of the fog.]

loon (lōōn), *n.* a diving bird that looks like a duck but has a pointed bill and a weird cry.

loon (lōōn), *n.* a clumsy, stupid person.

loom

loop (lōōp), *n.* **1.** the figure made by a line, string, wire, etc. that curves back to cross itself. **2.** anything having or forming a figure like this or like a ring [The letter *g* has a *loop.* The belt goes through *loops* at the waist.] —*v.* **1.** to make a loop of or in [to *loop* a rope]. **2.** to form a loop or loops [The airplane *looped.*] **3.** to fasten with a loop [The curtain was *looped* to one side.]

loons (2¼ ft. long)

loop·hole (lōōp/hōl), *n.* **1.** a hole in a wall for looking or shooting through. **2.** a way of getting around some law or escaping some trouble.

loose (lōōs), *adj.* **1.** not tied or held back; free [a *loose* end of wire]. **2.** not tight or firmly fastened [a *loose* table leg; *loose* clothing]. **3.** not packed down [*loose* soil]. **4.** not put up in a special package or box [*loose* salt]. **5.** not careful or exact [*loose* talk; a *loose* translation]. **6.** not moral [to lead a *loose* life]. —*adv.* in a loose way [The coat hung *loose.*] —*v.* **1.** to make loose, or set free; release [We *loosed* the wild horse. He *loosed* an arrow from the bow.] **2.** to make less tight; loosen [He *loosed* his collar.] —**break loose,** to free oneself; escape. —**cast loose,** to unfasten or untie. —**set loose** or **turn loose,** to make free; release. —**loosed,** *p.t. & p.p.*; **loos'ing,** *pr.p.* —**loose'ly,** *adv.* —**loose'ness,** *n.*

loose-leaf (lōōs/lēf'), *adj.* having leaves that can be taken out or put in easily [a *loose-leaf* notebook].

loos·en (lōōs/'n), *v.* to make or become loose or looser.

loot (lōōt), *n.* something stolen or robbed; plunder; booty. —*v.* to rob or plunder.

lop (läp), *v.* **1.** to cut off or chop off [to *lop* a branch]. **2.** to trim by cutting off branches. —**lopped,** *p.t. & p.p.*; **lop'ping,** *pr.p.*

lop (läp), *v.* to hang down loosely [the *lopping* ears of a spaniel]. —**lopped,** *p.t. & p.p.*; **lop'ping,** *pr.p.*

lope (lōp), *v.* to move along easily with long, jumping steps. —*n.* the act of loping. —**loped,** *p.t. & p.p.*; **lop'ing,** *pr.p.*

lop·sid·ed (läp/sīd/id), *adj.* larger, heavier, or lower on one side than the other.

lo·qua·cious (lō kwā/shəs), *adj.* talking very much; talkative. —**lo·quac·i·ty** (lō kwas/ə tē), *n.*

lord (lôrd), *n.* **1.** a person with much power or authority; ruler or master. **2.** the owner of an estate in the Middle Ages. **3. Lord,** God; also, Jesus Christ. **4. Lords,** *pl.* the upper house in the British Parliament: usually called the **House of Lords. 5. Lord,** a British title given to some men of high rank [The Earl of Russell is called *Lord* Russell.] **6.** a man with this title. —**lord it over,** to order about in a bullying way.

lord·ly (lôrd/lē), *adj.* **1.** of or fit for a lord; grand. **2.** too proud; scornful; haughty. —**lord'li·er,** *compar.*; **lord'li·est,** *superl.*

Lord·ship (lôrd/ship), *n.* a title of respect used in speaking to or of a Lord.

Lord's Prayer, the prayer beginning "Our Father," which Jesus taught his disciples.

Lord's Supper, 1. same as **Last Supper. 2.** same as **Holy Communion.**

lore (lôr), *n.* knowledge or learning, especially that handed down from earlier times.

lor·gnette (lôr nyet'), *n.* a pair of eyeglasses, or opera glasses, with a handle.

lorn (lôrn), *adj.* forlorn: *now seldom used.*

Lor·raine (lô rān'), *n.* a region in France: see **Alsace-Lorraine.**

lor·ry (lôr/ē), *n.* **1.** a flat wagon without sides. **2.** a motor truck: *a British meaning.* —**lor'ries,** *pl.*

lorgnette

Los An·gel·es (lôs an/j'l əs *or* lôs ang/gəl əs), a city on the southwestern coast of California.

lose (lōōz), *v.* **1.** to put, leave, or drop, so as to be unable to find; mislay [He *lost* a glove in the library.] **2.** to have taken from one by death, accident, etc. [He *lost* a brother in the war.] **3.** to fail to keep [to *lose* one's temper]. **4.** to fail to win; be defeated in [We *lost* the football game.] **5.** to fail to have or make use of; miss or waste [He *lost* his chance. Don't *lose* any time.] **6.** to fail to see, hear, or understand [I did not *lose* a word of the lecture.] **7.** to destroy or ruin [The ship was *lost* in a storm.] **8.** to cause the loss of [His bad manners *lost* him friends.] **9.** to wander from and not be able to find [He *lost* his way in the woods.] —**lose oneself, 1.** to lose one's way; become confused. **2.** to become so interested in something as to notice nothing else. —**lost,** *p.t. & p.p.*; **los'ing,** *pr.p.* —**los'er,** *n.*

fat,   āpe,   cär,   ten,   ēven,   hit,   bīte,   gō,   hôrn,   tōōl,   book,   up,   fūr;
get,   joy,   yet,   chin,   she,   thin,   *th*en;   zh = s in pleasure;   ' as in able (ā/b'l);
ə = a in ago,   e in agent,   i in sanity,   o in confess,   u in focus.

los·ing (lōōz′ing), *adj.* that loses [the *losing* team]. —*n.* **losings,** *pl.* money lost, as in gambling.

loss (lôs), *n.* **1.** a losing or being lost [a *loss* of weight]. **2.** the amount, thing, or person that is lost [The company's *loss* was great.] **3.** trouble, damage, etc. caused by losing something [His absence was no *loss*.] —**at a loss,** puzzled; not certain.

lost (lôst), past tense and past participle of **lose.** —*adj.* that is mislaid, missing, destroyed, defeated, wasted, etc. [a *lost* hat; a *lost* child; a *lost* ship; a *lost* cause; *lost* time]. —**lost in,** very much interested in; absorbed by [*lost in* thought]. —**lost on,** having no effect on [My advice was *lost on* her.]

Lot (lät), *n.* in the Bible, Abraham's nephew, who escaped from the doomed city of Sodom. When his wife stopped to look back, she was turned into a pillar of salt.

lot (lät), *n.* **1.** any of a number of slips of paper, counters, etc. that people draw from without looking, in deciding something by chance [Draw *lots* to see who goes first.] **2.** the use of such a method in deciding [Ten men were chosen by *lot*.] **3.** the decision reached in this way. **4.** what comes to a person in this way; one's share by lot. **5.** the fate of a person in life [his unhappy *lot*]. **6.** a small piece of land [a *lot* to build a house on]. **7.** a number of persons or things thought of as a group [the only one in the *lot* that you can trust]. **8.** *often* **lots,** *pl.* a great amount: *used only in everyday talk* [He drinks a *lot* (or *lots*) of milk.] —*adv.* very much [He is a *lot* happier.] —**cast in one's lot with,** to take one's chances with.

loth (lōth), *adj.* same as **loath.**

lo·tion (lō′shən), *n.* a liquid rubbed on the skin to keep it soft, to heal it, etc.

lot·ter·y (lät′ər ē), *n.* a form of gambling in which people buy numbered tickets, and prizes are given to those whose numbers are drawn by lot. —**lot′ter·ies,** *pl.*

lo·tus (lō′təs), *n.* **1.** a kind of water lily found in Egypt and other warm places. **2.** a plant in old Greek legends that made those who ate it dreamy and forgetful.

lotus

loud (loud), *adj.* **1.** strong in sound; not soft or quiet [a *loud* noise; a *loud* bell]. **2.** noisy [*loud* boys]. **3.** so strong as to force attention; forceful [*loud* demands]. **4.** too bright or showy: *used only in everyday talk* [a *loud* tie]. —*adv.* in a loud way. —**loud′ly,** *adv.* —**loud′ness,** *n.*

loud·speak·er or **loud-speak·er** (loud′spēk′ər), *n.* a part, as in a radio, that changes electric waves into sound loud enough to be heard by everyone listening.

Louis XVI, 1754–1793; king of France from 1774 to 1792. He was executed during the French Revolution.

Lou·i·si·an·a (loo wē′zi an′ə), *n.* a State in the south central part of the United States: abbreviated **La.**

Lou·is·ville (lōō′i vil), *n.* a city in northern Kentucky, on the Ohio River.

lounge (lounj), *v.* to move, sit, or lie in an easy or lazy way; loll. —*n.* **1.** a room with comfortable furniture where people can lounge. **2.** a sofa. —**lounged,** *p.t. & p.p.;* **loung′ing,** *pr.p.*

lour (lour), *v.* same as **lower** (to frown).

louse (lous), *n.* **1.** a small insect pest that lives in the hair or on the skin of man and other animals and sucks their blood. **2.** an insect like this that lives on plants. —**lice,** *pl.*

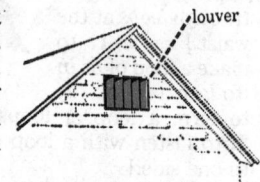
louse (1/16 in. long)

lous·y (louz′ē), *adj.* **1.** covered with lice. **2.** dirty, disgusting, poor, bad, etc.: *a slang use.* —**lous′i·er,** *compar.;* **lous′i·est,** *superl.*

lout (lout), *n.* a clumsy, stupid person; boor. —**lout′ish,** *adj.*

lou·ver (lōō′vər), *n.* **1.** an opening in a wall, with sloping boards that let in air and light but keep out rain. **2.** any one of these boards.

Lou·vre (lōō′vrə *or* lōōv), *n.* a large and famous art museum in Paris.

lov·a·ble or **love·a·ble** (luv′ə b'l), *adj.* that deserves to be loved; easily loved.

love (luv), *n.* **1.** a deep and tender feeling of fondness and devotion [a father's *love* for his child; the *love* that sweethearts share]. **2.** a strong liking [a *love* of books]. **3.** a sweetheart [his own true *love*]. **4.** in tennis, a score of zero. —*v.* **1.** to feel love for [to *love* one's parents; to *love* all mankind]. **2.** to take great pleasure in [He *loves* to eat.] —**fall in love,** to begin to love. —**for the love of,** for the sake of. —**in love,** feeling love. —**make love,** to hug and kiss as lovers do. —**loved,** *p.t. & p.p.;* **lov′ing,** *pr.p.* —**love′less,** *adj.*

love·bird (luv′bʉrd), *n.* a small parrot that is often kept as a cage bird. The mates seem to show great fondness for each other.

love·lorn (luv′lôrn), *adj.* sad or lonely because the person one loves does not love in return.

love·ly (luv′lē), *adj.* **1.** very pleasing in looks or character; beautiful [a *lovely* girl]. **2.** very enjoyable: *used only in everyday talk* [We had a *lovely* time.] —**love′li·er,** *compar.;* **love′li·est,** *superl.* —**love′li·ness,** *n.*

lov·er (luv′ər), *n.* **1.** the person who is in love with one; sweetheart. **2.** a person who likes something very much [a music *lover*].

love seat, a small sofa that seats two people.

love·sick (luv′sik), *adj.* so much in love that one cannot act in a normal way.

lov·ing (luv′ing), *adj.* feeling or showing love [a *loving* father]. —**lov′ing·ly,** *adv.*

loving cup, a large drinking cup with two handles, given as a prize in contests.

lov·ing-kind·ness (luv'ing kīnd'nis), *n.* kind or tender actions that show love.

low (lō), *adj.* **1.** reaching only a short distance up; not high or tall [a *low* building]. **2.** close to the earth; not far above the ground [*low* clouds]. **3.** below the usual surface or level [*low* land]. **4.** below others, as in rank or position; inferior or humble [*low* marks in school; of *low* birth]. **5.** less than usual in amount, cost, power, strength, etc. [*low* prices; *low* voltage]. **6.** deep in pitch [the *low* notes of a bass]. **7.** not loud; soft [Speak in a *low* voice.] **8.** not good or favorable; poor [a *low* opinion of the book]. **9.** sad or gloomy [*low* spirits]. **10.** rude or vulgar [*low* jokes]. **11.** having only a little of [The soldiers were *low* on ammunition.] —*adv.* in or to a low level, place, degree, etc. [Pitch the ball *low*. Speak *low*.] —*n.* **1.** a low level, place, or degree [The temperature hit a new *low*.] **2.** an arrangement of gears that gives the lowest speed and greatest power [Shift into *low* on steep hills.] —**lay low,** to overcome or kill. —**lie low,** to stay hidden. —**low'ness,** *n.*

low (lō), *n.* the sound that a cow makes; moo. —*v.* to make this sound.

low-brow or **low·brow** (lō'brou'), *n.* a person who has little or no interest in literature, music, art, etc. *A slang word.*

Low Countries, the Netherlands, Belgium, and Luxemburg.

low-down (lō'doun'), *n.* the important facts; especially, secret information. *A slang word.*

low·er (lō'ər), *adj.* **1.** below another [a *lower* berth; a *lower* price]. **2.** of less importance, rank, etc. [the *Lower* House of Congress]. —*v.* **1.** to let down or put down [*Lower* the window.] **2.** to make or become less in amount, cost, value, etc. [He will *lower* the price. His voice *lowered* to a whisper.] **3.** to make lose respect [His cowardly acts *lowered* him in our eyes.]

low·er (lou'ər), *v.* **1.** to frown or scowl. **2.** to look dark and threatening [a *lowering* sky].

low·er·most (lō'ər mōst), *adj.* lowest.

low-grade (lō'grād'), *adj.* of poorer quality.

low·land (lō'lənd), *n.* land that is lower than the land around it. —**the Lowlands,** the region of low land in southern and eastern Scotland. —**low'land·er** or **Low'land·er,** *n.*

low·ly (lō'lē), *adj.* **1.** of a low position or rank [a *lowly* job]. **2.** not proud; humble or meek [the *lowly* manner of the slave]. —*adv.* in a humble, meek, or modest way. —**low'li·er,** *compar.;* **low'li·est,** *superl.* —**low'li·ness,** *n.*

low-spir·it·ed (lō'spir'i tid), *adj.* full of sadness, doubts, and fears; unhappy.

low tide, 1. the time when the tide sinks lowest. **2.** the lowest level of the tide.

loy·al (loi'əl), *adj.* **1.** faithful to one's country [a *loyal* citizen]. **2.** faithful to one's family, duty, beliefs, etc. [a *loyal* son; a *loyal* friend]. —**loy'al·ly,** *adv.*

loy·al·ist (loi'əl ist), *n.* a person who supports the government during a revolt.

loy·al·ty (loi'əl tē), *n.* the condition of being loyal; faithfulness. —**loy'al·ties,** *pl.*

loz·enge (läz'inj), *n.* **1.** a figure in the shape of a diamond. **2.** a cough drop or hard piece of candy, at one time made in this shape.

LSD, a chemical substance used as a drug to cause hallucinations.

Lt., abbreviation for **Lieutenant.**

Ltd. or **ltd.,** abbreviation for **limited.**

lu·au (lōō cu' *or* lōō'ou), *n.* a Hawaiian feast.

lozenge
(meaning 1)

lub·ber (lub'ər), *n.* **1.** a big, clumsy person. **2.** a clumsy sailor aboard a ship.

lu·bri·cant (lōō'bri kənt), *n.* an oil, grease, etc. put on parts, as of a machine, to let them move more smoothly against each other.

lu·bri·cate (lōō'bri kāt), *v.* to put a lubricant in or on so as to make the parts more slippery [to *lubricate* a motor]. —**lu'bri·cat·ed,** *p.t. & p.p.;* **lu'bri·cat·ing,** *pr.p.* —**lu'bri·ca'tion,** *n.* —**lu'bri·ca'tor,** *n.*

lu·cid (lōō'sid), *adj.* **1.** clear to the mind; easily understood; not vague or confused [a *lucid* explanation]. **2.** that can be seen through; clear [*lucid* water]. **3.** sane; sound in mind. **4.** bright; shining: *used in poetry.* —**lu·cid·i·ty** (lōō sid'ə tē), *n.* —**lu'cid·ly,** *adv.*

Lu·ci·fer (lōō'sə fər), *n.* Satan; the Devil.

luck (luk), *n.* **1.** the things that seem to happen to a person by chance, good or bad; fortune [He started a new business, hoping for a change in *luck*.] **2.** good fortune [I had the *luck* to get there first.] —**in luck,** lucky. —**out of luck,** unlucky.

luck·less (luk'lis), *adj.* having no good luck; unlucky. —**luck'less·ly,** *adv.*

luck·y (luk'ē), *adj.* **1.** having good luck [He is *lucky* in games.] **2.** having a good result by chance [A *lucky* accident led to the discovery of penicillin.] **3.** thought to bring good luck [a *lucky* rabbit's foot]. —**luck'i·er,** *compar.;* **luck'i·est,** *superl.* —**luck'i·ly,** *adv.*

lu·cra·tive (lōō'krə tiv), *adj.* bringing wealth or profit; profitable [a *lucrative* business].

lu·cre (lōō'kər), *n.* riches or money. *Usually a joking or scornful word.*

lu·di·crous (lōō'di krəs), *adj.* so out of place or silly as to be funny; ridiculous [a *ludicrous* costume—derby, sneakers, and swimming trunks].

luff (luf), *v.* to turn the bow of a ship toward the wind. —*n.* a sailing close to the wind.

lug (lug), *v.* to carry or drag with effort [We *lugged* the heavy box upstairs.] —*n.* a part that sticks out, by which something is held or supported. —**lugged,** *p.t. & p.p.;* **lug'ging,** *pr.p.*

lug·gage (lug′ij), *n.* the suitcases, trunks, etc. of a traveler; baggage.

lug·ger (lug′ər), *n.* a boat with lugsails.

lug·sail (lug′s'l *or* lug′sāl), *n.* a four-cornered sail attached to a yard that hangs on the mast in a slanting position.

lugger

lu·gu·bri·ous (loo goo′bri-əs), *adj.* very sad or mournful, especially in a way that seems exaggerated or ridiculous.

Luke (look), *n.* **1.** an early Christian who was a companion of Paul the Apostle. **2.** the third book of the New Testament, probably written by Luke.

luke·warm (look′wôrm′), *adj.* **1.** just barely warm [*lukewarm* water]. **2.** not very eager or enthusiastic [*lukewarm* praise].

lugubrious expression

lull (lul), *v.* **1.** to calm by gentle sound or motion [She *lulled* her baby to sleep.] **2.** to make or become calm; quiet [The good news *lulled* her fears. The storm *lulled.*] —*n.* a short period when things are quiet or less active [a *lull* in business].

lull·a·by (lul′ə bī), *n.* a song for lulling a baby to sleep. —**lull′a·bies,** *pl.*

lum·ba·go (lum bā′gō), *n.* a backache in the lower part of the back.

lum·bar (lum′bər), *adj.* of or near the loins, or lower part of the back.

lum·ber (lum′bər), *n.* **1.** wood that has been sawed into beams, planks, and boards. **2.** furniture and other household things that are stored away because they are no longer used.

lum·ber (lum′bər), *v.* to move in a heavy and clumsy way [The truck *lumbered* up the hill.]

lum·ber·ing (lum′bər ing), *n.* the work of cutting down trees and sawing them into lumber.

lum·ber·jack (lum′bər jak), *n.* a man whose work is cutting down trees and getting them ready for the sawmill.

lum·ber·man (lum′bər mən), *n.* **1.** a lumberjack. **2.** a person whose business is buying and selling lumber. —**lum′ber·men,** *pl.*

lu·mi·nar·y (loo′mə ner′ē), *n.* **1.** the sun, the moon, and any like body that gives off light. **2.** a famous person. —**lu′mi·nar′ies,** *pl.*

lu·mi·nous (loo′mə nəs), *adj.* **1.** giving off light; bright [*luminous* paint]. **2.** filled with light [a *luminous* room]. **3.** making something especially clear [a *luminous* explanation]. —**lu·mi·nos·i·ty** (loo′mə näs′ə tē), *n.*

lump (lump), *n.* **1.** a small, solid mass, with no special shape; hunk [a *lump* of clay]. **2.** raised place; swelling [The bee sting made a *lump* on his neck.] —*adj.* **1.** in a lump or lumps [*lump* sugar]. **2.** in a single total [He was paid for his work in one *lump* sum.] —*v.* **1.** to form into a lump or lumps. **2.** to put or group together.

3. to put up with anyhow: *used only in everyday talk* [If you don't like it, you can *lump* it.]

lump·ish (lump′ish), *adj.* **1.** like a lump; heavy. **2.** dull or stupid.

lump·y (lump′ē), *adj.* full of lumps [*lumpy* pudding; a *lumpy* bed]. —**lump′i·er,** *compar.;* **lump′i·est,** *superl.* —**lump′i·ness,** *n.*

Lu·na (loo′nə), *n.* the Roman goddess of the moon.

lu·na·cy (loo′nə sē), *n.* **1.** the condition of being unsound of mind; insanity; madness. **2.** great foolishness.

lu·nar (loo′nər), *adj.* **1.** of or like the moon [a *lunar* eclipse]. **2.** measured by the revolution of the moon around the earth [A *lunar* month is equal to about 29 1/2 days.]

lu·na·tic (loo′nə tik), *adj.* **1.** mentally ill; insane. **2.** of or for insane persons. **3.** very foolish. —*n.* a person who is mentally ill. *This word is no longer much used.*

lunch (lunch), *n.* **1.** the meal eaten in the middle of the day, between breakfast and dinner. **2.** any light meal. —*v.* to eat lunch.

lunch·eon (lun′chən), *n.* a lunch; especially, a formal lunch.

lunch·room (lunch′room), *n.* a restaurant where lunches are served.

lung (lung), *n.* either of the two organs in the chest that are used in breathing. They are like sponges that put oxygen into the blood and take carbon dioxide from it.

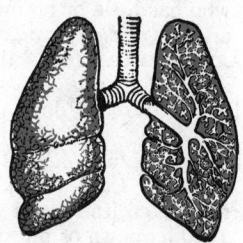
lungs, showing blood vessels within

lunge (lunj), *n.* a sudden, sharp move forward; thrust, as with a sword. —*v.* to make a lunge. —**lunged,** *p.t. & p.p.;* **lung′ing,** *pr.p.*

lu·pine (loo′pin), *n.* a plant with long spikes of white, yellow, rose, or blue flowers and pods that contain white seeds like beans.

lurch (lûrch), *v.* to lean or roll suddenly forward or to one side. —*n.* a lurching movement [The bus started with a *lurch.*]

lurch (lûrch), *n.* danger or trouble: *used only in the phrase* **leave in the lurch,** meaning "to leave in trouble and needing help."

lure (loor), *v.* to attract or lead by offering something that seems pleasant; entice [The witch *lured* Hansel and Gretel to her house.] —*n.* **1.** anything that lures [the *lure* of the sea]. **2.** an artificial bait used in fishing. —**lured,** *p.t. & p.p.;* **lur′ing,** *pr.p.*

lu·rid (loor′id), *adj.* **1.** so terrible as to shock or startle; sensational [the *lurid* details of the murder]. **2.** glowing in a strange or frightening way [the *lurid* sky before a storm].

lurk (lûrk), *v.* to stay or be hidden, usually ready to attack or spring out suddenly.

lus·cious (lush′əs), *adj.* **1.** having a delicious taste or smell; full of flavor. **2.** pleasing to see, hear, etc.

lush (lush), *adj.* growing thick and healthy, or covered with thick, healthy growth [*lush* jungle plants; *lush* fields].

lust (lust), *n.* **1.** a strong desire [a *lust* for success]. **2.** a strong sexual desire. —*v.* to feel a strong desire [The tyrant *lusted* for more power.] —**lust'ful,** *adj.*

lus·ter (lus'tər), *n.* **1.** the brightness of things that reflect light; gloss; brilliance [the *luster* of polished brass]. **2.** great fame or glory [His brave deeds gave new *luster* to his name.]

lus·trous (lus'trəs), *adj.* having luster; shining; bright [*lustrous* silken robes].

lust·y (lus'tē), *adj.* strong and full of energy and spirit; robust. —**lust'i·er,** *compar.*; **lust'i·est,** *superl.* —**lust'i·ly,** *adv.* —**lust'i·ness,** *n.*

lute (lōōt), *n.* an early musical instrument played like a guitar.

Lu·ther, Martin (lōō'thər), 1483–1546; German Protestant leader.

Lu·ther·an (lōō'thər-ən), *n.* a member of the Protestant church founded by Martin Luther. —*adj.* having to do with this church or its doctrines.

lute

Lux·em·burg (luk'səm bûrg), *n.* **1.** a small country in western Europe, surrounded by Belgium, Germany, and France. **2.** its capital.

lux·u·ri·ant (lug zhoor'i ənt *or* luk shoor'i ənt), *adj.* **1.** growing thick and healthy; lush [*luxuriant* vines]. **2.** full or too full of fancy decorations or ideas; flowery. —**lux·u'ri·ance,** *n.* —**lux·u'ri·ant·ly,** *adv.*

lux·u·ri·ate (lug zhoor'i āt *or* luk shoor'i āt), *v.* **1.** to live in great luxury. **2.** to take much pleasure; delight [He *luxuriated* in a hot bath.] —**lux·u'ri·at·ed,** *p.t. & p.p.*; **lux·u'ri·at·ing,** *pr.p.*

lux·u·ri·ous (lug zhoor'i əs *or* luk shoor'i əs), *adj.* **1.** giving a feeling of luxury; rich, comfortable, etc. [a big, soft, *luxurious* chair]. **2.** fond of luxury [*luxurious* tastes]. —**lux·u'ri·ous·ly,** *adv.*

lux·u·ry (luk'shə rē *or* lug'zhə rē), *n.* **1.** the use and enjoyment of the best and most costly things that give one the most comfort and pleasure [a life of *luxury*]. **2.** anything that gives one such comfort, usually something one does not need for life or health [Jewels and furs are *luxuries*.] —**lux'u·ries,** *pl.*

Lu·zon (lōō zän'), *n.* the main island of the Philippine Islands.

-ly (lē), a suffix used to form adjectives and adverbs, meaning: **1.** of, like, or suitable to [*Fatherly* advice is advice like a father's.] **2.** every or each [A *weekly* newspaper appears every week.] **3.** in a certain way, or at a certain time or place [To sing *harshly* is to sing in a harsh way.] **4.** in or from a certain direction [A *westerly* wind blows from the west.] **5.** in a certain order [*Secondly* means second in order.]

ly·ce·um (lī sē'əm), *n.* **1.** a large hall where lectures are given. **2.** an organization that gives public lectures, concerts, etc.

lye (lī), *n.* any strong alkaline substance, used in cleaning and in making soap. At one time lye was gotten from wood ashes.

ly·ing (lī'ing), present participle of **lie** (either verb). —*adj.* not telling the truth [a *lying* witness]. —*n.* the telling of a lie.

lymph (limf), *n.* a clear, slightly yellow liquid that flows through the body in a system of tubes. Lymph is like blood, but without red cells.

lym·phat·ic (lim fat'ik), *adj.* **1.** of or carrying lymph [The *lymphatic* vessels carry lymph to the various parts of the body.] **2.** sluggish; without energy.

lynch (linch), *v.* to kill by the action of a mob, without a lawful trial.

lynx (lingks), *n.* a wildcat of North America, that has long legs, a short tail, and long, silky, yellow fur.

lynx (3 ft. long)

Lyon (lyōn), *n.* a city in southeastern France: *the British spelling is* **Ly·ons** (lī'ənz).

lyre (līr), *n.* an old instrument like a small harp, used by the ancient Greeks to accompany singers or poets.

lyre·bird (līr'bûrd), *n.* an Australian songbird. The long tail feathers of the male spread out to look like a lyre.

lyre

lyr·ic (lir'ik), *adj.* **1.** of or having to do with poetry that describes the poet's feelings and thoughts [Sonnets and odes are *lyric* poems.] **2.** like a song or suitable for singing. **3.** of or having a high voice that moves lightly and easily from note to note [a *lyric* soprano]. —*n.* **1.** a lyric poem. **2.** *usually* **lyrics,** *pl.* the words of a song.

lyr·i·cal (lir'i k'l), *adj.* **1.** lyric. **2.** very excited, emotional, enthusiastic, etc. [She gave a *lyrical* account of her trip.] —**lyr'i·cal·ly,** *adv.*

M

M, m (em), *n.* the thirteenth letter of the English alphabet. —**M's, m's** (emz), *pl.*

M, *n.* the Roman numeral for 1,000.

M., abbreviation for **Monsieur.** —**MM.,** *pl.*

M., m., abbreviation for **male, meter** or **meters, mile** or **miles, minute** or **minutes.**

ma (mä), *n.* mother: *used only in everyday talk.*

M.A., Master of Arts: also **A.M.**

ma'am (mam), *n.* madam.

mac·ad·am (mə kad′əm), *n.* **1.** small broken stones, used in making roads. **2.** a road made with layers of such stones.

mac·ad·am·ize (mə kad′əm iz), *v.* to make or cover a road with layers of macadam, often mixed with tar, rolled until smooth. —**mac·ad′am·ized,** *p.t. & p.p.;* **mac·ad′am·iz·ing,** *pr.p.*

mac·a·ro·ni (mak′ə rō′nē), *n.* long, hollow tubes of dried flour paste, cooked for food.

mac·a·roon (mak ə rōōn′), *n.* a small, sweet cooky made with crushed almonds or coconut.

ma·caw (mə kô′), *n.* a large, bright-colored parrot of Central and South America.

Mac·beth (mək beth′), *n.* **1.** a tragic play by Shakespeare. **2.** its main character. With the help of his wife, he kills the king so that he himself may become king.

mace (mās), *n.* **1.** a heavy club with a metal head, usually with spikes, used as a weapon in the Middle Ages. **2.** a staff carried by or before an official as a symbol of his power.

mace (mās), *n.* a spice made from the dried outer covering of the nutmeg.

Mac·e·don (mas′ə dän), *n.* ancient Macedonia.

Mac·e·do·ni·a (mas′ə dō′ni ə), *n.* an ancient kingdom north of Greece. It is now part of Greece, Bulgaria, and Yugoslavia. —**Mac′e·do′ni·an,** *adj. & n.*

maces
left: weapon
right: staff

mach or **Mach number** (mäk), a number that represents the ratio of the speed of an airplane or missile to the speed of sound [A plane with a speed of *mach* 1 travels as fast as sound, or about 750 miles per hour.]

ma·che·te (mə shet′ē *or* mə shet′), *n.* a large knife with a heavy blade, used in parts of Spanish America, as for cutting sugar cane, peeling bark from trees, etc.

Mach·i·a·vel·li·an (mak′i ə vel′i ən), *adj.* of or like Machiavelli, an Italian statesman of the 16th century, who believed it was right for rulers to use tricky and dishonest methods to keep power; deceitful; crafty.

machete

mach·i·na·tion (mak′ə nā′shən), *n.* a secret plot or scheming, especially of a kind meant to cause trouble: *usually used in the plural,* **machinations.**

ma·chine (mə shēn′), *n.* **1.** a thing made up of fixed and moving parts, for doing some kind of work [a sewing *machine*]. **2.** an automobile, airplane, etc. **3.** a thing that works in a simple way to get the most force from the energy used [Levers, screws, and pulleys are simple *machines.*] **4.** a person or group thought of as acting like a machine, without thought. **5.** the group of people who control a political party. —*adj.* **1.** of machines. **2.** made or done by machinery [a *machine* product]. —*v.* to make or shape by machinery. —**ma·chined′,** *p.t. & p.p.;* **ma·chin′ing,** *pr.p.*

machine gun, an automatic gun that fires many bullets, one right after the other.

ma·chin·er·y (mə shēn′ər ē), *n.* **1.** machines in general [the *machinery* of a factory]. **2.** the working parts of a machine [the *machinery* of a printing press]. **3.** the means or system by which something is kept in action [the *machinery* of government]. —**ma·chin′er·ies,** *pl.*

machine shop, a factory for making or repairing machines or parts for machines.

machine tool, a tool worked by electricity, steam, etc., as a lathe, drill, or saw.

ma·chin·ist (mə shēn′ist), *n.* **1.** a person who is skilled in working with machine tools. **2.** a person who makes, repairs, or runs machinery.

mack·er·el (mak′ər əl), *n.* a fish of the North Atlantic, used for food. —**mack′er·el** or **mack′er·els,** *pl.*

Mack·i·nac (mak′ə nô′), *n.* a strait joining Lake Huron and Lake Michigan.

mack·i·naw (mak′ə nô′), *n.* **1.** a short coat of heavy woolen cloth, often with a plaid design. **2.** a thick woolen blanket, often woven in bars of bright colors.

mackerel (1 ft. long)

mack·in·tosh (mak′in täsh), *n.* a raincoat of waterproof, rubberized cloth.

ma·cron (mā′krən *or* mak′rän), *n.* the mark ⁻, used over a vowel to show how it is pronounced, as in *came* (kām).

mad (mad), *adj.* **1.** very sick in the mind; insane. **2.** excited in a wild way; frantic [*mad* with fear]. **3.** foolish and reckless; unwise [a *mad* scheme]. **4.** fond or enthusiastic in a way that is foolish [She's *mad* about hats.] **5.**

mackinaw

having rabies [a *mad* dog]. **6.** angry: *used only in everyday talk* [He's *mad* at us.] —**mad′der,** *compar.;* **mad′dest,** *superl.*

Mad·a·gas·car (mad′ə gas′kər), *n.* a large island off the southeastern coast of Africa. See **Malagasy.**

mad·am (mad′əm), *n.* a woman: *a polite form used in speaking to or of a woman* [May I serve you, *madam? Madam* is not in.] —**mes·dames** (mā däm′) or **mad′ams,** *pl.*

mad·ame (mad′əm *or* mə däm′), *n.* a French word used, like "Mrs.," as a title for a married woman: abbreviated **Mme.** or **Mdme.** —**mes·dames** (mā däm′), *pl.*

mad·cap (mad′kap), *n.* a gay, reckless person. —*adj.* gay and reckless [*madcap* pranks].

mad·den (mad′'n), *v.* to make or become insane, angry, or wildly excited.

made (mād), past tense and past participle of **make.** —*adj.* built; put together; formed [a well-*made* house].

Ma·dei·ra (mə dir′ə), *n.* **1.** the main island in a group of Portuguese islands (called **Madeira Islands**), off the coast of Morocco. **2.** a white wine made on this island.

ma·de·moi·selle (mad′ə mə zel′ *or* mam′zel′ *or* mäd mwä zel′), *n.* a French word used, like "Miss," as a title for an unmarried woman or girl: abbreviated **Mlle.** or **Mdlle.** —**mes·de·moi·selles** (mäd mwä zel′), *French pl.*

made-to-or·der (mād′tə ôr′dər), *adj.* made just as the customer ordered; not ready-made.

made-up (mād′up′), *adj.* **1.** invented; false; not true [a *made-up* story]. **2.** with powder, lipstick, etc. on.

mad·house (mad′hous), *n.* **1.** a place for keeping insane people: *this word is no longer used.* **2.** a place of noise and confusion [The stores are *madhouses* during the Christmas rush.]

Mad·i·son (mad′i s'n), *n.* the capital of Wisconsin.

Madison, James, 1751–1836; fourth president of the United States, from 1809 to 1817.

mad·ly (mad′lē), *adv.* in a way that is insane, wild, foolish, etc.

mad·man (mad′man *or* mad′mən), *n.* a person who is insane; maniac. —**mad′men,** *pl.*

mad·ness (mad′nis), *n.* **1.** the condition of being mad, or insane. **2.** great anger; fury. **3.** great foolishness.

Ma·don·na (mə dän′ə), *n.* **1.** Mary, the mother of Jesus. **2.** a picture or statue of her.

ma·dras (mad′rəs *or* mə dras′), *n.* a fine cotton cloth, used for shirts, dresses, etc.

Ma·drid (mə drid′), *n.* the capital of Spain.

mad·ri·gal (mad′ri g'l), *n.* **1.** a short poem, usually about love, which can be set to music. **2.** a song with parts for several voices, sung without accompaniment.

mael·strom (māl′strəm), *n.* **1.** a large or violent whirlpool; especially, **the Maelstrom,**

a dangerous whirlpool off the west coast of Norway. **2.** a condition in which things are very confused or upset.

ma·es·tro (mīs′trō *or* mä es′trō), *n.* a master: an Italian word, especially for a great composer, conductor, or teacher of music.

mag·a·zine (mag ə zēn′ *or* mag′ə zēn), *n.* **1.** a publication that comes out regularly, as weekly or monthly, and contains articles, stories, pictures, etc. **2.** a place for storing things, as military supplies. **3.** a space, as in a warship, for storing explosives. **4.** the space in a gun from which the cartridges are fed. **5.** the space in a camera from which the film is fed.

Ma·gel·lan, Ferdinand (mə jel′ən), 1480?–1521; Portuguese explorer who led a voyage that became the first around the world. He died on the way.

ma·gen·ta (mə jen′tə), *n.* **1.** a purplish-red dye. **2.** purplish red.

mag·got (mag′ət), *n.* an insect in an early stage, when it looks like a worm, as the larva of the housefly. Maggots are usually found in rotting matter.

Ma·gi (mā′jī), *n.pl.* the wise men in the Bible who brought gifts to the baby Jesus.

mag·ic (maj′ik), *n.* **1.** the use of charms, spells, etc. that are supposed to make maggots (½ in. long) things happen in an unnatural way [In fairy tales, *magic* is used to work miracles.] **2.** any power or force that seems mysterious or hard to explain [the *magic* of love]. **3.** the skill of doing puzzling tricks by moving the hands so fast as to fool those watching and by using boxes with false bottoms, hidden strings, etc.; sleight of hand. —*adj.* of or as if by magic.

mag·i·cal (maj′i k'l), *adj.* of or like magic. —**mag′i·cal·ly,** *adv.*

ma·gi·cian (mə jish′ən), *n.* **1.** a person, as in fairy tales, who works magic. **2.** a person who does magic tricks, or sleight of hand.

magic lantern, an old name for a picture projector.

mag·is·te·ri·al (maj′is tir′i əl), *adj.* **1.** of or fit for a magistrate [*magisterial* robes]. **2.** that shows authority [a *magisterial* manner].

mag·is·tra·cy (maj′is trə sē), *n.* **1.** the rank of a magistrate. **2.** magistrates as a group.

mag·is·trate (maj′is trāt), *n.* **1.** an official with the power to put laws into effect, as the president of a republic. **2.** a minor official, as a judge in a police court.

Mag·na Char·ta or **Mag·na Car·ta** (mag′nə kär′tə), **1.** the paper that King John was forced by the English barons to sign in 1215, guaranteeing certain rights to them. **2.** any constitution that guarantees civil and political rights.

mag·na·nim·i·ty (mag'nə nim'ə tē), *n.* the condition of being magnanimous.

mag·nan·i·mous (mag nan'ə məs), *adj.* generous in forgiving; not mean or full of revenge.

mag·nate (mag'nāt), *n.* a very important or powerful person [a business *magnate*].

mag·ne·sia (mag nē'shə *or* mag nē'zhə), *n.* a white powder with no taste, mixed with water and used as a medicine.

mag·ne·si·um (mag nē'shi əm *or* mag nē'zhi əm), *n.* a silvery, very light metal that is a chemical element. It burns with a bright light, and is used in flash bulbs for taking photographs.

mag·net (mag'nit), *n.* **1.** any piece of iron, steel, or loadstone that has the natural power to draw iron and steel to it. This power may also be given by passing an electric current through wire wrapped around the metal. **2.** a person or thing that attracts.

magnet holding pins

mag·net·ic (mag net'ik), *adj.* **1.** working like a magnet [a *magnetic* needle]. **2.** that can be magnetized. **3.** that attracts strongly [*magnetic* eyes].

magnetic north, the direction toward which the needle of a compass points, usually not true north.

mag·net·ism (mag'nə tiz'm), *n.* **1.** the power that a magnet has. **2.** the branch of physics dealing with magnets and their power. **3.** the power to attract or charm.

mag·net·ize (mag'nə tīz), *v.* **1.** to make magnetic, as iron or steel. **2.** to charm or attract [We were *magnetized* by his personality.] —**mag'net·ized**, *p.t. & p.p.;* **mag'net·iz·ing**, *pr.p.*

mag·ne·to (mag nē'tō), *n.* a small kind of electric generator used with some gasoline engines to make the electric spark for the ignition. —**mag·ne'tos**, *pl.*

mag·nif·i·cence (mag nif'ə s'ns), *n.* grand or rich beauty; grandeur or splendor.

mag·nif·i·cent (mag nif'ə s'nt), *adj.* rich, fine, noble, beautiful, etc. in a grand way; splendid [a *magnificent* castle; a *magnificent* idea].

mag·ni·fy (mag'nə fī), *v.* to make look or seem larger or greater than is really so [This lens *magnifies* an object to twice its size. He *magnified* the seriousness of his illness.] —**mag'ni·fied**, *p.t. & p.p.;* **mag'ni·fy·ing**, *pr.p.*

magnifying glass, a lens that makes the things seen through it look larger.

mag·nil·o·quent (mag nil'ə kwənt), *adj.* **1.** too grand or pompous in talking or writing. **2.** boastful or vain. —**mag·nil'o·quence**, *n.*

magnifying glass

mag·ni·tude (mag'nə tōōd *or* mag'nə tyōōd), *n.* **1.** greatness, as of size, importance, power, etc. [the *magnitude* of his invention]. **2.** size or importance [a country of lesser *magnitude*].

mag·no·li·a (mag nō'li ə), *n.* a tree or shrub with large, sweet-smelling flowers of white, pink, or purple.

mag·pie (mag'pī), *n.* **1.** a black-and-white bird of the crow family, that chatters noisily. **2.** a person who chatters.

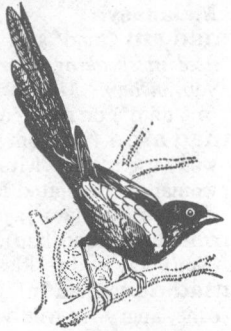

Mag·yar (mag'yär), *n.* **1.** a member of the main group of people of Hungary. **2.** their language; Hungarian. —*adj.* of the Magyars, their language, customs, etc.

ma·ha·ra·jah or **ma·ha·ra·ja** (mä'hə rä'jə), *n.* a prince of India, especially one who in earlier times was a ruler of one of its states.

magpie (20 in. long, including tail)

ma·hat·ma (mə hät'mə *or* mə hät'mə), *n.* a very wise and holy person in India [Mohandas Gandhi was called *Mahatma*.]

mah-jongg or **mah·jong** (mä'jông'), *n.* a game that came from China, played with many small tiles.

ma·hog·a·ny (mə häg'ə nē), *n.* **1.** the hard, reddish-brown wood of a tropical American tree, used in making furniture. **2.** this tree. **3.** reddish brown. —**ma·hog'a·nies**, *pl.*

Ma·hom·et (mə häm'it), *n.* same as **Mohammed.** —**Ma·hom'et·an**, *adj. & n.*

maid (mād), *n.* **1.** a maiden. **2.** a girl or woman servant.

maid·en (mād''n), *n.* a girl or young woman who is not married. —*adj.* **1.** of, like, or fit for a maiden. **2.** unmarried [a *maiden* aunt]. **3.** first or earliest [the ship's *maiden* voyage]. —**maid'en·ly**, *adj.*

maid·en·hair (mād''n her), *n.* a kind of fern with very thin stalks and delicate leaflike parts: *its full name is* **maidenhair fern.**

maid·en·hood (mād''n hood), *n.* the time or condition of being a maiden.

maiden name, the family name that a woman had before she was married.

maid of honor, an unmarried woman who is the chief bridesmaid at a wedding.

maid·ser·vant (mād'sūr'vənt), *n.* a girl or woman servant.

mail (māl), *n.* **1.** letters, packages, etc. carried and delivered by a post office. **2.** the system of picking up and delivering letters, etc.; postal system [Send it by *mail*.] —*adj.* having to do with or carrying mail [a *mail* truck]. —*v.* to send by mail; place in a mailbox.

mail (māl), *n.* armor for the body, made of small metal rings or overlapping plates so that it will bend easily.

mail·box (māl'bäks), *n.* **1.** a box into which mail is delivered

soldier wearing mail

to a home. **2.** a box, as on a street, into which mail is put to be collected by the post office for delivery.

mail·man (māl'man), *n.* a man whose work is delivering mail; postman. —**mail'men,** *pl.*

mail order, an order sent by mail for goods to be delivered by mail.

maim (mām), *v.* to hurt a person so that he loses an arm, leg, etc., or its use; cripple.

main (mān), *adj.* first in size or importance; chief; principal [the *main* office of a company; the *main* characters in a play]. —*n* **1.** any of the larger pipes from which smaller pipes carry water, gas, etc. to a building. **2.** the ocean or sea: *used in poetry.* —**by main force** or **by main strength,** by great force or strength alone. —**in the main,** mostly; chiefly. —**with might and main,** with all one's strength.

main clause, a clause that can stand alone in a sentence.

Maine (mān), *n.* a New England State of the United States: abbreviated **Me.**

main·land (mān'land *or* mān'lənd), *n.* the main part of a country or continent, as apart from its peninsulas or near-by islands.

main·ly (mān'lē), *adv.* most of all; chiefly.

main·mast (mān'məst *or* mān'mast), *n.* the highest and most important mast on a ship.

main·sail (mān's'l *or* mān'sāl), *n* the largest sail of a ship, as that set from the mainmast.

main·spring (mān'spring), *n.* **1.** the most important spring in a clock, watch, etc., that keeps it going. **2.** the chief cause, purpose, etc.

mainspring

main·stay (mān'stā) *n.* **1.** the rope that is run from the upper part of the mainmast to hold it in place. **2.** the main or chief support [She was the *mainstay* of her family.]

main·tain (mān tān'), *v.* **1.** to keep or keep up; continue in the same condition; carry on [Try to *maintain* this speed. Food *maintains* life.] **2.** to support by supplying what is needed [Father *maintains* a family of six.] **3.** to protect against attack; defend. **4.** to say in a positive way; declare to be true [He still *maintains* that he's innocent.]

main·te·nance (mān'tə nəns), *n.* **1.** a maintaining or being maintained; upkeep or support [Taxes pay for the *maintenance* of schools.] **2.** a means of support; livelihood [His job barely provides a *maintenance* for the family.]

maize (māz), *n.* corn; Indian corn: *now mainly a British word.*

Maj., abbreviation for **Major.**

ma·jes·tic (mə jes'tik) or **ma·jes·ti·cal** (mə-jes'ti k'l), *adj.* having majesty; grand, stately, dignified, etc. [a *majestic* mountain peak]. —**ma·jes'ti·cal·ly,** *adv.*

maj·es·ty (maj'is tē), *n.* **1.** the dignity or power of a king, queen, etc. **2. Majesty,** a title used in speaking to or of a king, queen, etc. [His *Majesty*, the Emperor]. **3.** grandeur or stateliness [the *majesty* of the Alps]. —**maj'es·ties,** *pl.*

ma·jor (mā'jər), *adj.* **1.** greater in size, importance, amount, etc. [the *major* part of his wealth; a *major* poet]. **2.** in music, that is separated from the next tone by a full step instead of a half step [a *major* interval]; also, that is or has to do with a musical scale with half steps after the third and seventh tones: see also **minor.** —*n.* **1.** a military officer ranking just above a captain. **2.** the main subject that a student is studying [His *major* is history.] —*v.* to have as one's major subject [to *major* in English].

ma·jor-do·mo (mā'jər dō'mō), *n.* a servant in charge of a royal household. —**ma'jor-do'-mos,** *pl.*

major general a military officer ranking above a brigadier general. —**major generals,** *pl.*

ma·jor·i·ty (mə jôr'ə tē), *n.* **1.** the greater part or number; more than half [A *majority* of the class wanted no party.] **2.** the amount by which the greater or greatest number of votes is more than all the rest [To get 50 votes of a total of 90 is to have a *majority* of 10.] **3.** the age at which a young person is said by law to become an adult [One ordinarily reaches his *majority* on his 21st birthday.] —**ma·jor'i·ties,** *pl.*

make (māk), *v.* **1.** to bring into being; build, create, produce, put together, etc. [to *make* a dress; to *make* a fire; to *make* plans; to *make* a sound]. **2.** to cause to be or become [Her giggling *makes* me nervous. Lincoln *made* Grant a general.] **3.** to turn out to be; become [He will *make* a good doctor.] **4.** to do, perform, carry on, etc. [to *make* a right turn; to *make* a speech]. **5.** to get or gain, as by working; earn; acquire [to *make* money; to *make* friends]. **6.** to prepare for use; arrange [to *make* the bed]. **7.** to equal; amount to [Two pints *make* a quart.] **8.** to cause or force to [Who *made* her cry?] **9.** to cause to be successful [Good pitching can *make* a baseball team.] **10.** to understand [What do you *make* of his strange behavior?] **11.** to arrive at; reach [The ship *makes* port today.] **12.** to travel at a certain speed [The ship can *make* 35 knots.] **13.** to succeed in becoming a member of, being mentioned in, etc.: *used only in everyday talk* [Jack *made* the honor roll.] —*n.* **1.** the way something is made or put together [Do you like the *make* of this suit?] **2.** a brand or type of product, as showing where or by whom it is made [a foreign *make* of car]. —**make after,**

to chase or follow. —**make away with, 1.** to steal. **2.** to get rid of. **3.** to kill. —**make believe,** to pretend. —**make for, 1.** to go toward; head for. **2.** to help bring about [Respect for the rights of others *makes for* a happy home.] —**make it,** to manage to do a certain thing: *used only in everyday talk.* —**make off with,** to steal. —**make out, 1.** to see or distinguish. **2.** to understand. **3.** to fill out, as a blank form. **4.** to prove or try to prove to be [She *makes* me *out* to be a coward.] **5.** to get along; succeed. —**make over, 1.** to change; cause to be different. **2.** to hand over the ownership of [He *made over* the house to his son.] —**make up, 1.** to put together. **2.** to form; be the parts of. **3.** to invent. **4.** to supply what is missing. **5.** to give or do in place of; compensate [How can I *make up* for your loss?] **6.** to become friendly again after a quarrel. **7.** to put on powder, lipstick, etc. **8.** to decide [He *made up* his mind to go.] —**made,** *p.t. & p.p.;* **mak′ing,** *pr.p.* —**mak′er,** *n.*

make-be·lieve (māk′bə lēv′), *n.* a pretending or imagining, as in a game. —*adj.* pretended; imagined [a *make-believe* toy].

make·shift (māk′shift), *n.* something used for a time in place of the usual thing [He slept on the sofa as a *make-shift* for a bed.]

make-up (māk′up′), *n.* **1.** the way in which a thing is put together; composition [the *make-up* of the atom]. **2.** one's nature or disposition [a cheerful *make-up*]. **3.** cosmetics; lipstick, powder, etc. **4.** the paint, wigs, costumes, etc. put on by an actor in a play.

a makeshift for a cuff link

mal-, a prefix meaning "bad" or "badly" [*Maladjustment* is bad adjustment.]

mal·ad·just·ed (mal′ə jus′tid), *adj.* badly adjusted; especially, not able to fit happily into the life around one. —**mal′ad·just′ment,** *n.*

mal·a·droit (mal ə droit′), *adj.* awkward.

mal·a·dy (mal′ə dē), *n.* a sickness or disease. —**mal′a·dies,** *pl.*

Mal·a·gas·y (mal′ə gas′ē), *n.* a country whose land consists of the island of Madagascar.

ma·lar·i·a (mə ler′i ə), *n.* a disease in which a person keeps having chills and fever. It is carried to man by the bite of a certain kind of mosquito. —**ma·lar′i·al,** *adj.*

Mal·a·wi (mäl′ə wē), *n.* a country in southeastern Africa.

Ma·lay (mā′lā), *n.* **1.** a member of a brown-skinned people of the Malay Peninsula and Archipelago. **2.** their language. —*adj.* of the Malays, their language, etc. Also **Ma·lay·an** (mə lā′ən).

Ma·lay·a (mə lā′ə), *n.* the Malay Peninsula.

Malay Archipelago, a chain of islands between the Malay Peninsula and Australia.

Malay Peninsula, a long, narrow peninsula in southeastern Asia, north of Sumatra.

Ma·lay·sia (mə lā′zhə), **Federation of,** a country in southeastern Asia, mostly on the Malay Peninsula. —**Ma·lay′sian,** *adj. & n.*

mal·con·tent (mal′kən tent), *adj.* not satisfied with the way things are; ready to rebel. —*n.* a person who is malcontent.

Mal·dive Islands (mal′dīv), a country on a group of islands in the Indian Ocean.

male (māl), *adj.* **1.** of or belonging to the sex that can make the egg of the female fertile [A *male* goose is called a "gander."] **2.** of or for men or boys [a *male* chorus]. —*n.* a male person, animal, or plant.

mal·e·dic·tion (mal′ə dik′shən), *n.* a calling on God or a god to bring harm to someone; curse.

mal·e·fac·tor (mal′ə fak′tər), *n.* a person who does evil or wrong; criminal.

ma·lev·o·lent (mə lev′ə lənt), *adj.* wishing harm or evil to others; malicious. —**ma·lev′o·lence,** *n.* —**ma·lev′o·lent·ly,** *adv.*

mal·fea·sance (mal fē′z′ns), *n.* wrongdoing by someone holding a public office, as the taking of graft.

mal·for·ma·tion (mal′fôr mā′shən), *n.* a wrong or unusual formation, as of some part of the body. —**mal·formed′,** *adj.*

mal·func·tion (mal fungk′shən), *v.* to fail to work as it should [*Malfunctioning* brakes caused the car to swerve.] —*n.* a time when this happens.

Ma·li (mä′li), *n.* a country in western Africa.

mal·ice (mal′is), *n.* a feeling of wanting to hurt or harm someone; ill will; spite.

ma·li·cious (mə lish′əs), *adj.* having or showing malice; spiteful [The jealous girl started *malicious* rumors.] —**ma·li′cious·ly,** *adv.*

ma·lign (mə līn′), *v.* to say bad or unfair things about; slander. —*adj.* bad, evil, harmful, etc. [*malign* forces]. —**ma·lign′er,** *n.*

ma·lig·nant (mə lig′nənt), *adj.* **1.** causing or wishing harm to others; evil [a *malignant* person]. **2.** causing or likely to cause death [a *malignant* tumor]. —**ma·lig′nan·cy,** *n.*

ma·lig·ni·ty (mə lig′nə tē), *n.* **1.** a very strong desire to harm others; great malice. **2.** great harmfulness; deadliness.

ma·lin·ger (mə ling′gər), *v.* to pretend to be sick in order to keep from working or doing one's duty. —**ma·lin′ger·er,** *n.*

mall (môl), *n.* a broad, often shaded place for the public to walk, as in the center of a city.

mal·lard (mal′ərd), *n.* a common wild duck. The male has a dark-green head and a white ring around the neck.

mal·le·a·ble (mal′i ə b'l), *adj.* **1.** that can be hammered or pressed into a new shape without breaking, as gold and silver. **2.** that can be changed, formed, trained, etc. [a *malleable* mind]. —**mal′le·a·bil′i·ty,** *n.*

mallard (1½ ft. long)

mal·let (mal′it), *n.* a wooden hammer made with either a short handle for use as a tool, or with a long handle for playing croquet and polo.

mal·low (mal′ō), *n.* a plant with purplish, pink, or white flowers and hairy leaves.

mallet

mal·nu·tri·tion (mal′nōō trish′ən *or* mal′nyōō-trish′ən), *n.* an unhealthy condition of the body caused by not getting enough food, or enough of the right foods; faulty nutrition.

mal·prac·tice (mal prak′tis), *n.* **1.** medical treatment that harms a patient because the doctor has done something wrong or has failed to do the right thing. **2.** any wrong practice by a professional person or by an official.

malt (môlt), *n.* barley or other grain soaked in water until it sprouts, and then dried. It is used in brewing beer, ale, etc. —*v.* **1.** to change into malt. **2.** to add malt to [A *malted* milk is made with milk, ice cream, and malt.]

Mal·ta (môl′tə), *n.* a country on an island in the Mediterranean, south of Sicily. It was a British colony. **Mal·tese** (môl tēz′), *adj. & n.*

Maltese cat, a type of cat with blue-gray fur.

Maltese cross, a type of cross: *see the picture.*

mal·treat (mal trēt′), *v.* to treat in a rough, unkind, or cruel way; abuse. —**mal·treat′-ment,** *n.*

Maltese cross

mam·ma or **ma·ma** (mä′mə *or now seldom* mə mä′), *n.* mother: *mainly a child's word.*

mam·mal (mam′əl), *n.* any animal with glands in the female that produce milk for feeding its young. —**mam·ma·li·an** (mə mā′li ən), *adj.*

mam·mon (mam′ən), *n.* wealth thought of as an evil that makes people selfish and greedy.

mam·moth (mam′əth), *n.* a type of huge elephant that lived a long time ago. Mammoths had a hairy skin and long tusks that curved upward. —*adj.* very big; huge.

mam·my (mam′ē), *n.* **1.** mother: *a child's word.* **2.** a Negro woman in the South who takes care of white children. —**mam′-mies,** *pl.*

mammoth (15 ft. high)

man (man), *n.* **1.** an adult, male human being. **2.** any human being; person ["that all *men* are created equal"]. **3.** the human race; mankind [*man's* conquest of space]. **4.** a male servant, employee, follower, etc. [giving orders to his *men*]. **5.** a husband [*man* and wife]. **6.** any of the pieces used in playing chess, checkers, etc. —*v.* **1.** to supply with men for work, defense,

etc. [to *man* a ship]. **2.** to take one's place at, on, or in [to *man* a gun]. —**man oneself,** to make oneself stronger or braver; brace oneself. —**to a man,** with all taking part. —**men,** *pl.* —**manned,** *p.t. & p.p.;* **man′ning,** *pr.p.*

-man (mən *or* man), a suffix meaning: **1.** a person of a certain country [A *Frenchman* is a person born or living in France.] **2.** a person doing a certain kind of work [A *laundryman* works for a laundry.] **3.** a person who uses or works some device [A *plowman* uses a plow.]

Man., abbreviation for **Manitoba.**

man·a·cle (man′ə k'l), *n.* a handcuff. —*v.* **1.** to put handcuffs on. **2.** to keep from acting freely; hamper; hinder. —**man′a·cled,** *p.t. & p.p.;* **man′a·cling,** *pr.p.*

man·age (man′ij), *v.* **1.** to have charge of; direct the work of [to *manage* a factory]. **2.** to control the movement or behavior of; handle; guide [Grandmother knows how to *manage* the children.] **3.** to succeed in getting something done [We *managed* to reach shelter.] —**man′-aged,** *p.t. & p.p.;* **man′ag·ing,** *pr.p.*

man·age·a·ble (man′ij ə b'l), *adj.* that can be managed, controlled, or done.

man·age·ment (man′ij mənt), *n.* **1.** the act or skill of managing; a controlling or directing [A successful business needs careful *management.*] **2.** the persons who manage a certain business; also, managers of businesses as a group [the problems of labor and *management*].

man·ag·er (man′ij ər), *n.* a person who manages a business, baseball team, etc.

man·a·ge·ri·al (man′ə jir′i əl), *adj.* having to do with a manager or management.

man-at-arms (man′ət ärmz′), *n.* **1.** a soldier. **2.** a soldier of the Middle Ages who rode on a horse and carried powerful weapons. —**men′-at-arms′,** *pl.*

man·a·tee (man ə tē′), *n.* a large animal that lives in shallow tropical waters and feeds on plants: it has flippers and a broad, flat tail.

Man·ches·ter (man′ches′-tər), *n.* a city in northwestern England.

manatee (10 ft. long)

Man·chu or **Man·choo** (man′chōō *or* man chōō′), *n.* **1.** a member of a people of Manchuria who ruled China from 1644 to 1912. **2.** their language.

Man·chu·ri·a (man choor′i ə), *n.* a large region in northeastern China. —**Man·chu′ri·an,** *adj. & n.*

man·da·rin (man′də rin), *n.* **1.** a high public official of China under the emperors, before 1911. **2. Mandarin,** the most widespread form of the Chinese language. It is the official language of China. **3.** a kind of tangerine.

man·date (man′dāt), *n.* **1.** an order or command, especially one in writing. **2.** the will of the

fat, āpe, cär, ten, ēven, hit, bīte, gō, hôrn, tōōl, book, up, fûr;
get, joy, yet, chin, she, thin, *th*en; zh = s in pleasure; ′ as in able (ā′b'l);
ə = a in ago, e in agent, i in sanity, o in confess, u in focus.

people as made known by their votes in elections. **3.** control over a territory as given by the League of Nations to one of its member nations; also, the territory so controlled. Territories controlled in this way by United Nations members are called **trust territories.**

man·da·to·ry (man′də tôr′ē), *adj.* ordered or demanded by someone in power; required.

man·di·ble (man′də b′l), *n.* **1.** the jaw; especially, the lower jaw. **2.** a part like this, as either part of a bird's beak or of an insect's biting parts.

man·do·lin (man′də lin), *n.* a musical instrument with four or five pairs of strings, played with a pick. *See the picture.*

man·drake (man′drāk), *n.* a poisonous plant with purple or white flowers. Its thick, often forked root is used in medicine.

mandibles

man·drill (man′dril), *n.* a large, strong baboon of western Africa. The male has blue and red patches on the face and rump.

mane (mān), *n.* the long hair growing along the neck of a horse, male lion, etc.

ma·neu·ver (mə-nōō′vər or mə-nyōō′vər), *n.* **1.** a carefully directed
mandolin
movement of troops, warships, etc., as in a battle or for practice. **2.** a skillful move or clever trick [a *maneuver* to get control of the business]. *—v.* **1.** to carry out maneuvers with [The major *maneuvered* his troops on the left flank.] **2.** to plan or manage in a skillful or clever way [Who *maneuvered* this plot?] **3.** to move, get, make, etc. by some trick or scheme [I *maneuvered* Bill into asking the question for me.]

man·ful (man′fəl), *adj.* brave, determined, etc.; manly. **—man′ful·ly,** *adv.* **—man′ful·ness,** *n.*

man·ga·nese (mang′gə nēs or mang′gə nēz), *n.* a grayish, brittle metal that is a chemical element. It is used in making alloys.

mange (mānj), *n.* a skin disease of animals that makes the hair fall out.

man·ger (mān′jər), *n.* a box or trough in a barn, from which horses or cattle eat.

man·gle (mang′g′l), *v.* **1.** to tear, cut, or crush badly [The toy was *mangled* in the lawn mower.] **2.** to botch or spoil [to *mangle* a piano solo]. **—man′gled,** *p.t. & p.p.;* **man′gling,** *pr.p.*

man·gle (mang′g′l), *n.* a machine for pressing and smoothing sheets, tablecloths, etc. between rollers. *—v.* to press in a mangle. **—man′gled,** *p.t. & p.p.;* **man′gling,** *pr.p.*

mangle

man·go (mang′gō), *n.* **1.** a slightly sour fruit with a thick, orange rind and a hard stone. **2.** the tropical tree that it grows on. **—man′goes** or **man′gos,** *pl.*

man·grove (mang′grōv), *n.* a tropical tree with branches that spread and send down roots, which then form new trunks.

man·gy (mān′jē), *adj.* **1.** having mange [a *mangy* dog]. **2.** dirty and poor; shabby [*mangy* clothing]. **3.** mean and low [to play a *mangy* trick]. **—man′gi·er,** *compar.;* **man′gi·est,** *superl.* **—man′gi·ness,** *n.*

man·han·dle (man′han′d′l), *v.* to handle in a rough way. **—man′han′dled,** *p.t. & p.p.;* **man′han′dling,** *pr.p.*

Man·hat·tan (man hat′ən), *n.* an island at the mouth of the Hudson River, that is a borough of New York City.

man·hole (man′hōl), *n.* an opening through which a man can get into a sewer, large pipe, etc., as in order to do repair work.

man·hood (man′hood), *n.* **1.** the time of being a man. **2.** the qualities a man is supposed to have, as strength and courage [a test of one's *manhood*]. **3.** men as a group [the *manhood* of the nation].

manhole

ma·ni·a (mā′ni ə), *n.* **1.** mental illness in which a person acts or talks in a wild way. **2.** too much enthusiasm or fondness for something; craze [a *mania* for dancing].

ma·ni·ac (mā′ni ak), *n.* a mentally ill person who behaves in a wild way. *—adj.* maniacal.

ma·ni·a·cal (mə nī′ə k′l), *adj.* having or showing mania; wildly insane [*maniacal* laughter].

man·i·cure (man′ə kyoor), *n.* the care of the hands; especially, the trimming and cleaning of the fingernails. *—v.* to give a manicure to. **—man′i·cured,** *p.t. & p.p.;* **man′i·cur·ing,** *pr.p.* **—man′i·cur′ist,** *n.*

man·i·fest (man′ə fest), *adj.* plain to see or understand; clear; evident [a *manifest* lie]. *—v.* **1.** to make clear; show plainly; reveal [When did your illness *manifest* itself?] **2.** to prove or show [Her kindness to them *manifested* her love.] *—n.* a list of all the things in a ship's cargo. **—man′i·fest·ly,** *adv.*

man·i·fes·ta·tion (man′ə fes tā′shən), *n.* **1.** the act of showing, making clear, or proving. **2.** something that shows, proves, etc. [Her smile was a *manifestation* of happiness.]

man·i·fes·to (man′ə fes′tō), *n.* a public statement by a government, political party, etc., giving its views, plans, etc. **—man′i·fes′toes,** *pl.*

man·i·fold (man′ə fōld), *adj.* **1.** having many parts or forms [*manifold* wisdom]. **2.** of many kinds; many and varied [his *manifold* duties]. *—n.* a pipe with several openings for connecting it to other pipes, as for carrying away exhaust from an engine. *—v.* to make many copies of [to *manifold* a letter with carbon paper].

man·i·kin or **man·ni·kin** (man′ə kin), *n.* **1.** same as **mannequin.** **2.** a little man; dwarf.

Ma·nil·a (mə nil/ə), *n.* the largest city of the Philippines. See **Quezon City.**

Manila hemp, a strong fiber from the leafstalks of a Philippine tree. It is used for making rope, paper, etc.

Manila paper, a strong, light brown paper, used for envelopes, wrapping paper, etc.

ma·nip·u·late (mə nip/yoo lāt), *v.* **1.** to work or operate with the hands; use with skill [to *manipulate* the controls of an airplane]. **2.** to manage or control in a clever or unfair way [to *manipulate* an election by bribing the voters]. **3.** to change figures, as in bookkeeping, for some dishonest reason. —**ma·nip/u·lat·ed,** *p.t.* & *p.p.;* **ma·nip/u·lat·ing,** *pr.p.* —**ma·nip/u·la/tion,** *n.* —**ma·nip/u·la/tor,** *n.*

Man·i·to·ba (man/ə tō/bə), *n.* a province in the south central part of Canada.

man·kind (man kīnd/ *or* man/kīnd), *n.* **1.** all human beings; the human race. **2.** (*always* man/kīnd), all human males; men in general.

man·ly (man/lē), *adj.* **1.** having the qualities that a man is supposed to have; strong, brave, honest, etc. **2.** fit for a man; masculine [*manly* sports]. —**man/li·er,** *compar.;* **man/li·est,** *superl.* —**man/li·ness,** *n.*

man-made (man/mād/), *adj.* made by man; artificial.

man·na (man/ə), *n.* **1.** in the Bible, the food provided by a miracle for the Israelites in the wilderness. **2.** anything needed badly that comes as a surprise [Your praise was *manna* to me.]

man·ne·quin (man/ə kin), *n.* **1.** a woman whose work is modeling clothes in stores, etc. for customers to see. **2.** a model of the human body, used by dressmakers, tailors, artists, etc.

man·ner (man/ər), *n.* **1.** a way in which something happens or is done; style [He sang in an amusing *manner*.] **2.** a way of acting; behavior [His *manner* showed anger.] **3. manners,** *pl.* ways of behaving or living, especially polite ways of behaving [It is good *manners* to say "Thank you."] **4.** kind; sort [What *manner* of man is he?]

mannequin

man·ner·ism (man/ər iz'm), *n.* a special manner or way of doing something that has become a habit [She had a *mannerism* of scratching her ear.]

man·ner·ly (man/ər lē), *adj.* showing good manners; polite; well-behaved. —*adv.* politely.

man·nish (man/ish), *adj.* like or fit for a man [She walks with a *mannish* stride.]

ma·noeu·vre (mə nōō/vər *or* mə nyōō/vər), *n.* & *v.* same as **maneuver.** —**ma·noeu/vred,** *p.t.* & *p.p.;* **ma·noeu/vring,** *pr.p.*

man-of-war (man/əv wôr/), *n.* a ship used in war; warship. —**men'-of-war',** *pl.*

man·or (man/ər), *n.* **1.** land belonging to a lord in the Middle Ages, that was partly divided among peasants who paid rent. **2.** any large estate.

ma·no·ri·al (mə nôr/i əl), *adj.* of, like, or forming a manor.

man·sard or **man·sard roof** (man/särd), *n.* a roof having four sides with two slopes on each side: *see the picture.*

manse (mans), *n.* the house that a church provides for its minister, especially in Scotland.

mansard roof

man·sion (man/shən), *n.* a large, stately house.

man·slaugh·ter (man/slô/tər), *n.* the killing of one person by another, especially when it is unlawful but not done on purpose [A driver who is responsible for a traffic death may be charged with *manslaughter*.]

man·tel (man/t'l), *n.* **1.** the shelf above a fireplace: also **man/tel·piece. 2.** the material around a fireplace, usually stone, brick, etc.

man·tis (man/tis), *n.* an insect that holds its front pair of legs as if praying, and eats other insects: often called **praying mantis.**

man·tle (man/t'l), *n.* **1.** a loose cloak without sleeves; cape. **2.** anything that covers or hides as a cloak [the night's *mantle* of darkness]. **3.** a small tube or hood made of a fine screen that is placed over a flame so that it glows and gives off light. —*v.* **1.** to cover or hide as with a mantle. **2.** to blush. —**man/tled,** *p.t.* & *p.p.;* **man/tling,** *pr.p.*

mantis (3 in. long)

man·u·al (man/yōō əl), *adj.* made, done, or worked with the hands [*manual* labor; *manual* controls]. —*n.* a small book of facts or instructions; handbook [a stamp collectors' *manual*].

manual training, training in work that is done with the hands, as woodwork or metalworking.

man·u·fac·ture (man/yoo fak/chər), *n.* **1.** the making of goods or articles, especially in large amounts and by machinery. **2.** the making of something in any way [the *manufacture* of bile by the liver]. —*v.* **1.** to make goods, especially in large amounts. **2.** to make or make up in any way [to *manufacture* an excuse]. —**man'u·fac/tured,** *p.t.* & *p.p.;* **man'u·fac/tur·ing,** *pr.p.*

man·u·fac·tur·er (man/yoo fak/chər ər), *n.* a person or company that manufactures.

ma·nure (mə nyoor/), *n.* any substance used to fertilize soil; especially, the waste matter of animals. —*v.* to put manure on or into. —**ma·nured/,** *p.t.* & *p.p.;* **ma·nur/ing,** *pr.p.*

fat, āpe, cär, ten, ēven, hit, bīte, gō, hôrn, tōōl, book, up, fûr; get, joy, yet, chin, she, thin, *th*en; zh = s in pleasure; ' as in able (ā/b'l); ə = a in ago, e in agent, i in sanity, o in confess, u in focus.

man·u·script (man′yoo skript), *n.* a book, article, etc. that is typewritten or in handwriting; especially, the copy of an author's work that is sent to a publisher or printer.

man·y (men′ē), *adj.* a large number of; not few [*many* men; *many* times]. —*n.* a large number [*Many* of us plan to go.] —*pron.* many persons or things [*Many* came to see our play.] The phrases *many a*, *many an*, and *many another* followed by a singular noun mean the same as *many* followed by the plural form ["*Many a* man has tried" means the same as "*Many* men have tried."] —**a good many,** quite a large number: *used with a plural verb.* —**more,** *compar.;* **most,** *superl.*

Ma·o·ri (mä′ō rē *or* mou′rē), *n.* **1.** a member of a brown-skinned people who live in New Zealand. **2.** their language. — **Ma′o·ris,** *pl.*

Mao Tse-tung (mou′ dzu′doong′), 1893– ; Chinese Communist leader.

map (map), *n.* **1.** a drawing or chart of all or part of the earth's surface, showing where countries, oceans, rivers, cities, etc. are. **2.** a drawing of part of the sky, showing where the stars, planets, etc. are. —*v.* **1.** to make a map of [Lewis and Clark *mapped* western America.] **2.** to plan in a careful way, step by step [to *map* out one's work]. —**mapped,** *p.t. & p.p.;* **map′ping,** *pr.p.*

ma·ple (mā′p'l), *n.* **1.** a tree of the Northern Hemisphere, grown for its wood or sap, or as a shade tree. **2.** its hard, light-colored wood. **3.** the flavor of the sirup (**maple sirup**) or sugar (**maple sugar**) made from its sap.

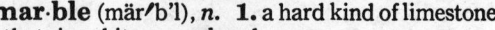

maple leaves and winged fruits

mar (mär), *v.* to hurt or spoil the looks, value, etc. of; damage [The kitten's claws *marred* the table top.] —**marred,** *p.t. & p.p.;* **mar′ring,** *pr.p.*

Mar., abbreviation for **March.**

ma·ra·ca (mə rä′kə), *n.* a musical instrument made of a gourd or rattle, with loose pebbles in it. It is shaken to beat out a rhythm.

mar·a·schi·no cherry (mar′ə skē′nō), a cherry preserved in a sweet sirup and used to decorate sundaes, salads, drinks, etc.

Mar·a·thon (mar′ə thän), *n.* **1.** a plain near Athens where the Athenians defeated the Persians in a battle in 490 B.C. An Athenian runner carried the news to Athens. **2. marathon,** a foot race of 26 miles, 385 yards, run through open country; also, any contest to test endurance.

maracas

ma·raud·er (mə rôd′ər), *n.* a person or animal that roams about, attacking or plundering. —**ma·raud′ing,** *adj.*

mar·ble (mär′b'l), *n.* **1.** a hard kind of limestone that is white or colored, sometimes with streaks. It takes a high polish and is used as a building material and in statues. **2.** a little ball of stone, glass, or clay, used in a children's game called **marbles.** —*adj.* made of or like marble. —*v.* to make look like marble that is streaked [to *marble* the edges of a book]. —**mar′bled,** *p.t. & p.p.;* **mar′bling,** *pr.p.*

boy playing marbles

March (märch), *n.* the third month of the year. It has 31 days. Abbreviated **Mar.**

march (märch), *v.* **1.** to walk with regular, steady steps, as soldiers do. **2.** to move or go on in a steady way [Time *marches* on.] **3.** to cause to march [He *marched* the children up to bed.] —*n.* **1.** a marching [the army's *march* to the sea]. **2.** steady movement forward; progress [the *march* of history]. **3.** a piece of music with a steady rhythm, to be played while people march. **4.** the distance traveled in marching [The enemy was camped two days' *march* away.] —**on the march,** marching. —**steal a march on,** to get a secret advantage over. —**march′er,** *n.*

march (märch), *n.* a border or frontier.

mar·chion·ess (mär′shən is), *n.* **1.** the wife or widow of a British marquis. **2.** a lady with the rank of a British marquis.

Mar·co·ni, Gu·gliel·mo (gōō lyel′mō mär- kō′nē), 1874–1937; Italian inventor who developed the wireless telegraph.

Mar·di gras (mär′di grä′), the last day before Lent, celebrated with parties and parades.

mare (mer), *n.* a female horse, donkey, etc.

mar·ga·rine (mär′jə rin), *n.* a spread like butter, made of vegetable oils and skim milk.

mar·gin (mär′jin), *n.* **1.** a border or edge [the *margin* of a pond]. **2.** the blank space around the writing or printing on a page. **3.** an extra amount of time, money, etc. that can be used if needed [Budgets must allow a *margin* for emergencies.]

mar·gin·al (mär′ji n'l), *adj.* **1.** written in the margin of a page. **2.** of, at, or near a margin.

mar·i·gold (mar′i gōld), *n.* a plant with yellow or orange flowers.

mar·i·jua·na (mar′ə wä′nə), *n.* the dried leaves and flowers of a hemp plant, smoked in cigarettes: it can cause the user to lose control of himself, as by giving him a false feeling of well-being.

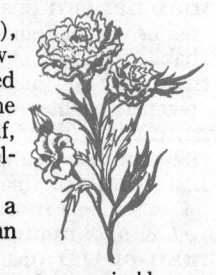

ma·ri·na (mə rē′nə), *n.* a small harbor where boats can dock, pick up supplies, etc.

mar·i·nate (mar′ə nāt), *v.* to soak meat or fish in spiced vinegar, wine, salt water, etc. —**mar′i·nat·ed,** *p.t. & p.p.;* **mar′i·nat·ing,** *pr.p.*

marigold

ma·rine (mə rēn′), *adj.* **1.** of the sea [Seaweeds

are *marine* plants.] **2.** having to do with sailing or shipping [*Marine* insurance protects cargo ships.] **3.** for use on a ship [a *marine* engine]. —*n. usually* **Marine**, a member of the Marine Corps. See also **merchant marine.**

Marine Corps, a branch of the U.S. armed forces, trained to fight on land, at sea, and in the air. It is a part of the Navy.

mar·i·ner (mar′ə nər), *n.* a sailor: *now seldom used.*

mar·i·o·nette (mar′i ə net′), *n.* a small doll, or puppet, moved by strings or wires, and used in putting on shows on a small stage.

mar·i·tal (mar′ə t'l), *adj.* of or having to do with marriage [*marital* bliss].

mar·i·time (mar′ə tīm), *adj.* **1.** on, near, or living near the sea [California is a *maritime* state.] **2.** having to do with sailing or shipping on the sea [*maritime* laws].

marionette

Maritime Provinces, the Canadian provinces of Nova Scotia, New Brunswick, and Prince Edward Island.

Mark (märk), *n.* **1.** an early follower of Jesus. **2.** the second book of the New Testament, believed to have been written by Mark.

mark (märk), *n.* **1.** a spot, stain, scratch, dent, etc. made on a surface. **2.** a printed or written sign or label [punctuation *marks;* a trade*mark*]. **3.** a sign of some quality [Politeness is the *mark* of good training.] **4.** a grade or rating [a *mark* of A in English]. **5.** a cross or other sign made by a person who is not able to sign his name. **6.** influence or effect [Gandhi left his *mark* on many people.] **7.** a line, dot, or notch that shows a certain position [Fill the cup to this *mark.*] **8.** the starting line of a race [On your *mark*, get set, and go!] **9.** something aimed at; target [The arrow fell short of the *mark.*] **10.** something that acts as a sign or guide; landmark. **11.** importance or fame [a person of *mark*]. —*v.* **1.** to make a mark or marks on. **2.** to name or show; make clear [His answers *marked* him as a good student.] **3.** to draw or write [He *marked* his name on his gym shoes.] **4.** to show by a mark or marks [*Mark* the capitals on the map.] **5.** to set off; make different [the qualities that *mark* a scholar]. **6.** to pay attention to; note [*Mark* what I say.] **7.** to give a grade to [to *mark* a test]. —**beside the mark, 1.** not hitting what was aimed at. **2.** not to the point; not relevant. —**hit the mark, 1.** to reach one's goal; succeed. **2.** to be right. —**make one's mark,** to become famous. —**mark down, 1.** to make a note of; record. **2.** to mark for sale at a lower price. —**mark off** or **mark out,** to mark the limits of. —**mark time, 1.** to keep time by lifting the feet as if marching,

but not going forward. **2.** to make no progress for a while. —**mark up, 1.** to cover with marks. **2.** to mark for sale at a higher price. —**miss the mark, 1.** to fail to reach one's goal. **2.** to be wrong. —**mark′er,** *n.*

mark (märk), *n.* the basic unit of money in Germany. Its full official name is **Deut·sche·mark** (doi′chə märk).

marked (märkt), *adj.* **1.** having a mark or marks on it. **2.** very easily noticed; obvious [a *marked* change]. **3.** picked out as a suspicious person to be watched [a *marked* man].

mark·ed·ly (mär′kid lē), *adv.* in a marked way; noticeably; obviously.

mar·ket (mär′kit), *n.* **1.** a gathering of people for buying and selling things; also, the people gathered in this way. **2.** an open place, or a building, with stalls where goods are sold. **3.** any store where food is sold [a meat *market*]. **4.** a place where goods can be sold [England is a good *market* for tea.] **5.** a desire by many people to buy; demand [Is there a *market* for used cars?] —*v.* **1.** to take to market to sell. **2.** to buy food [Mother *markets* on Saturday.] —**be in the market for,** to want to buy. —**put on the market,** to offer to sell. —**mar′ket·a·ble,** *adj.*

market place, a market (*meaning 2*).

mark·ing (mär′king), *n.* **1.** a mark or marks. **2.** the special way marks or colorings are arranged, as on fur or feathers.

marks·man (märks′mən), *n.* a person who shoots well at targets. —**marks′men,** *pl.* —**marks′man·ship,** *n.*

mar·lin (mär′lin), *n.* a large deep-sea fish whose upper jaw sticks out like a spear.

mar·line·spike or **mar·lin·spike** (mär′lin spīk), *n.* a pointed iron tool used to separate the strands of a rope, as for splicing.

mar·ma·lade (mär′mə lād), *n.* a sweet food like jam, made from oranges or other fruit.

Mar·ma·ra, Sea of (mär′mə rə), a sea between the part of Turkey in Europe and the part in Asia.

mar·mo·set (mär′mə zet), *n.* a very small monkey of South and Central America, with a long tail and thick, silky fur.

mar·mot (mär′mət), *n.* any of a group of small animals with a thick body and a short, bushy tail, related to rabbits, rats, etc. [The woodchuck is a *marmot.*] See the picture on the next page.

marmoset (about 8 in. long, not including tail)

ma·roon (mə rōōn′), *n. & adj.* dark brownish red.

ma·roon (mə rōōn′), *v.* **1.** to put someone ashore in a lonely place and leave him. **2.** to leave helpless and alone [The storm *marooned* us.]

mar·quee (mär kē′), *n.* a small roof built out over an entrance to a theater, store, etc.

marmot (1½ ft. long, including tail)

mar·quess (mär′kwis), *n.* same as **marquis.**

Mar·quette (mär ket′), *n.* 1637–1675; French Jesuit missionary who explored part of the Mississippi River: called *Père* (Father) *Marquette.*

mar·quis (mär′kwis), *n.* a nobleman ranking above an earl or count, and below a duke.

mar·quise (mär kēz′), *n.* **1.** the wife or widow of a marquis. **2.** a lady with the rank of a marquis. See also **marchioness.**

mar·qui·sette (mär′ki zet′ *or* mär′kwi zet′), *n.* a thin cloth, like net, used for curtains.

marquee

mar·riage (mar′ij), *n.* **1.** the condition of being married; married life. **2.** the act of marrying; wedding.

mar·riage·a·ble (mar′ij ə b′l), *adj.* old enough for marriage [a *marriageable* girl].

mar·ried (mar′ēd), *adj.* **1.** being husband and wife [a *married* couple]. **2.** having a husband or wife. **3.** of marriage [*married* life].

mar·row (mar′ō), *n.* **1.** the soft, fatty substance that fills the hollow centers of most bones. **2.** the central or most important part [The lawyer got to the *marrow* of the facts.]

mar·ry (mar′ē), *v.* **1.** to join a man and a woman as husband and wife [A ship's captain may *marry* people at sea.] **2.** to take as one's husband or wife [John Alden *married* Priscilla.] **3.** to give in marriage [Mrs. Bennet was anxious to *marry* off her daughters.] **4.** to join closely [Strength and tenderness are *married* in her.] —**mar′ried,** *p.t.* & *p.p.;* **mar′ry·ing,** *pr.p.*

mar·ry (mar′ē), *interj.* indeed! really!: *now seldom used.*

Mars (märz), *n.* **1.** the Roman god of war. The Greeks called this god *Ares.* **2.** the seventh largest planet, known for its reddish color. It is the fourth in distance away from the sun.

Mar·seil·laise (mär sə lāz′), *n.* the national song of France, composed in 1792.

Mar·seilles (mär sālz′), *n.* a seaport in southeastern France, on the Mediterranean.

marsh (märsh), *n.* low land that is wet and soft; swamp; bog. —**marsh′y,** *adj.*

mar·shal (mär′shəl), *n.* **1.** an officer of a U.S. Federal court, with duties like those of a sheriff. **2.** the head of some police or fire departments. **3.** a person in charge of a parade or of certain ceremonies. **4.** a general of the highest rank in certain foreign armies. —*v.* **1.** to arrange in order, as troops, ideas, etc. **2.** to lead or guide.

—**mar′shaled** or **mar′shalled,** *p.t.* & *p.p.;* **mar′shal·ing** or **mar′shal·ling,** *pr.p.*

Mar·shall, John (mär′shəl), 1755–1835; chief justice of the United States from 1801 to 1835.

marsh·mal·low (märsh′mal′ō *or* märsh′mel ō), *n.* a soft, white, spongy candy made of sugar, gelatin, etc. and covered with powdered sugar.

marsh mallow, a hairy plant with large, pink flowers, growing in marshes.

mar·su·pi·al (mär soo′pi əl *or* mär syoo′pi əl), *n.* an animal that carries its newly born young in a pouch on the front of the female. Kangaroos are marsupials.

mart (märt), *n.* a market; place where goods are bought and sold.

mar·ten (mär′t'n), *n.* **1.** an animal like a large weasel, with soft, thick, valuable fur. **2.** this fur, which is like sable.

mar·tial (mär′shəl), *adj.* **1.** having to do with war or armies [*martial* music]. **2.** showing a readiness or eagerness to fight [*martial* spirit].

marten (2½ ft. long, including tail)

martial law, rule by an army over civilians, as during war or riots.

Mar·tian (mär′shən), *n.* a creature that might be living on the planet Mars. —*adj.* of Mars.

mar·tin (mär′t'n), *n.* a bird of the swallow family; especially, the **purple martin,** a large, dark-blue swallow of North America.

mar·ti·net (mär t'net′), *n.* a person who believes in very strict discipline; one who forces others to follow rules exactly.

Mar·ti·nique (mär t'n ēk′), *n.* a French island in the southern part of the West Indies.

purple martin (6 in. long)

mar·tyr (mär′tər), *n.* **1.** a person who chooses to suffer or die rather than give up his religion, beliefs, etc. **2.** a person who suffers silently for a long time. —*v.* to kill or make suffer for not giving up one's religion, beliefs, etc. —**mar′tyr·dom,** *n.*

mar·tyr·ize (mär′tər īz), *v.* to make a martyr of, as by killing. —**mar′tyr·ized,** *p.t.* & *p.p.;* **mar′tyr·iz·ing,** *pr.p.*

mar·vel (mär′v'l), *n.* a wonderful or astonishing thing [the natural *marvels* of Yellowstone Park]. —*v.* to wonder; be amazed [We *marveled* at her skill.] —**mar′veled** or **mar′velled,** *p.t.* & *p.p.;* **mar′vel·ing** or **mar′vel·ling,** *pr.p.*

mar·vel·ous or **mar·vel·lous** (mär′v'l əs), *adj.* **1.** causing wonder; astonishing [the *marvelous* structure of the human body]. **2.** very good; fine; splendid: *used only in everyday talk.* —**mar′vel·ous·ly** or **mar′vel·lous·ly,** *adv.*

Marx, Karl (kärl märks), 1818–1883; German socialist leader and writer.

Mar·y (mer′ē), *n.* the mother of Jesus: often called the **Virgin Mary.**

Mar·y·land (mer′i lənd), *n.* a State on the eastern coast of the United States: abbreviated **Md.**

Mary, Queen of Scots, 1542–1587; queen of Scotland from 1542 to 1567.

mas·ca·ra (mas kar′ə), *n.* a dark paste for coloring the eyelashes and eyebrows.

mas·cot (mas′kät *or* mas′kət), *n.* a person, animal, or thing thought to bring good luck [A goat is the *mascot* of the U.S. Naval Academy.]

mas·cu·line (mas′kyoo lin), *adj.* **1.** of or fit for men or boys [Football and boxing are *masculine* sports.] **2.** like a man; strong, brave, etc.; manly. **3.** of a class of words in grammar that refer to males or to things thought of as male. —**mas·cu·lin·i·ty** (mas′kyoo lin′ə tē), *n.*

ma·ser (mā′zər), *n.* a device that emits a very intense beam of radio waves.

mash (mash), *n.* **1.** a mixture of bran, meal, etc. for feeding horses, cattle, and poultry. **2.** crushed malt or meal soaked in hot water and used in brewing beer. **3.** any soft mass. —*v.* to beat or crush into a soft mass [to *mash* potatoes]. —**mash′er,** *n.*

mask (mask), *n.* **1.** something worn over the face to hide or protect it [a Halloween *mask;* a baseball catcher's *mask*]. **2.** anything that hides or disguises [His smile was a *mask* to hide his disappointment.] **3.** a masquerade. **4.** a copy of a person's face, made of clay, wax, etc. [a death *mask*]. —*v.* **1.** to cover or hide with a mask [to *mask* one's face]. **2.** to hide or disguise [to *mask* one's fear]. —**mask′er,** *n.*

upper: Halloween mask
lower: nurse's protective mask

ma·son (mā′s'n), *n.* **1.** a person whose work is building with stone, brick, etc. **2. Mason,** a Freemason.

Ma·son-Dix·on line (mā′s'n dik′s'n), **1.** an old name for the boundary between Pennsylvania and Maryland. **2.** an imaginary line thought of as separating the North from the South.

Ma·son·ic or **ma·son·ic** (mə sän′ik), *adj.* of Freemasons or their society.

ma·son·ry (mā′s'n rē), *n.* **1.** something built of stone, brick, etc. by a mason. **2.** the work or skill of a mason. —**ma′son·ries,** *pl.*

masque (mask), *n.* **1.** a masquerade (*meaning 1*). **2.** a kind of play in verse put on for kings and nobles in the 16th and 17th centuries, using fancy costumes, music, dancing, etc.

mas·quer·ade (mas kə rād′), *n.* **1.** a party or dance where masks and fancy costumes are worn. **2.** a costume for such a party. **3.** the act of hiding who one is, how one feels, etc.; disguise. —*v.* **1.** to take part in a masquerade. **2.** to hide who one is by pretending to be someone else. —**mas·quer·ad′ed,** *p.t. & p.p.;* **mas·quer·ad′ing,** *pr.p.* —**mas·quer·ad′er,** *n.*

Mass or **mass** (mas), *n.* **1.** the service in the Roman Catholic Church and some other churches in which Holy Communion takes place. **2.** music set to certain parts of this service.

mass (mas), *n.* **1.** a piece or amount of no definite shape or size [a *mass* of clay; a *mass* of cold air]. **2.** a large amount or number [a *mass* of bruises]. **3.** bulk or size [He couldn't move the piano because of its *mass.*] **4.** the main part; majority [The *mass* of opinion is against the plan.] **5.** in physics, the amount of matter in a body. —*adj.* of a large number of persons or things [a *mass* meeting; *mass* production]. —*v.* to gather or form into a mass [Crowds were *massing* along the curbs.] —**in the mass,** as a whole; taken together. —**the masses,** working people as a class, or the public generally.

Mas·sa·chu·setts (mas′ə chŏŏ′sits), *n.* a New England State of the United States: abbreviated **Mass.**

mas·sa·cre (mas′ə kər), *n.* the cruel and violent killing of a large number of people; wholesale slaughter. —*v.* to kill in large numbers. —**mas′sa·cred,** *p.t. & p.p.;* **mas′sa·cring,** *pr.p.*

mas·sage (mə säzh′), *n.* a rubbing and kneading of part of the body to loosen up muscles and improve the circulation. —*v.* to give a massage to. —**mas·saged′,** *p.t. & p.p.;* **mas·sag′ing,** *pr.p.*

mas·sive (mas′iv), *adj.* large, solid, heavy, etc. [a *massive* statue]. —**mas′sive·ness,** *n.*

mast (mast), *n.* **1.** a tall pole set upright on a ship or boat, for supporting the sails, yards, etc. **2.** any upright pole like this [the *mast* of a derrick]. —**sail before the mast,** to be a common sailor.

. masts

mas·ter (mas′tər), *n.* **1.** a man who rules others or has control over something, as an owner of an animal or slave, the head of a household, or the captain of a merchant ship. **2.** a man teacher: *used only in Great Britain.* **3.** an expert in some work, as a skilled craftsman or great artist. **4.** a painting by a great artist. **5. Master,** a title used before the name of a boy too young to be called *Mr.* **6.** a person who holds a college degree beyond that of a bachelor [He is a *Master* of Arts in music.] —*adj.* **1.** being or of a master [a *master* workman]. **2.** chief; main; controlling

[A *master* switch controls a number of other switches.] —*v.* **1.** to become master of; control or conquer [He *mastered* his fear.] **2.** to become expert in [Rubens *mastered* the art of painting.]

mas·ter·ful (mas/tər fəl), *adj.* **1.** acting like a master; liking to be in control. **2.** very skillful; expert [a *masterful* pianist].

mas·ter·ly (mas/tər lē), *adj.* showing the skill of a master; expert [He did a *masterly* job of repair work.] —*adv.* in an expert way.

mas·ter·mind (mas/tər mīnd), *n.* a very intelligent person, especially one who plans and directs the work of a group. —*v.* to be the mastermind of.

master of ceremonies, a person in charge of an entertainment, who introduces the people on the program, tells jokes, etc.

mas·ter·piece (mas/tər pēs), *n.* **1.** a thing made or done with very great skill; great work of art. **2.** the best thing one has ever made or done ["The Divine Comedy" was Dante's *masterpiece.*]

mas·ter·work (mas/tər wûrk), *n.* a masterpiece.

mas·ter·y (mas/tər ē), *n.* **1.** control or power that a master has. **2.** victory over another or others. **3.** expert skill or knowledge [his *mastery* of tennis].

mast·head (mast/hed), *n.* **1.** the top part of a ship's mast. **2.** that part of a newspaper or magazine that tells who its publisher and editors are, where its offices are, etc.

mas·ti·cate (mas/tə kāt), *v.* to chew or chew up. —**mas/ti·cat·ed,** *p.t. & p.p.;* **mas/ti·cat·ing,** *pr.p.* —**mas/ti·ca/tion,** *n.*

mas·tiff (mas/tif), *n.* a large, strong dog with a smooth coat and powerful jaws.

mas·to·don (mas/tə dän), *n.* a large animal like an elephant, that lived a long time ago.

mas·toid (mas/toid), *n.* a small bone at the back of the ear.

mas·tur·bate (mas/tər bāt), *v.* to excite oneself in a sexual way. —**mas/tur·bat·ed,** *p.t. & p.p.;* **mas/tur·bat·ing,** *pr.p.*

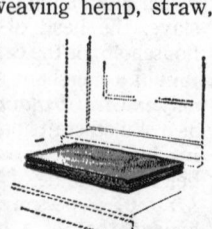

mastodon
(10 ft. high at shoulder)

mat (mat), *n.* **1.** a flat, rough material made by weaving hemp, straw, rope, etc., often used as a floor covering. **2.** a piece of this, or of a material like this, as for wiping the shoes on. **3.** a flat piece of cloth, woven straw, etc., put under a vase, hot dish, etc. **4.** a thickly padded floor covering, as for wrestling or tumbling on. **5.** anything tangled or woven together in a thick mass [a *mat* of hair]. —*v.* **1.** to cover with a mat. **2.** to weave together or tangle into a thick mass. —**mat/ted,** *p.t. & p.p.;* **mat/ting,** *pr.p.*

mat (*meaning 2*)

mat (mat), *n.* a piece of cardboard used to form a border around a picture.

mat·a·dor (mat/ə dôr), *n.* the bullfighter who kills the bull with a sword thrust.

match (mach), *n.* **1.** a slender piece of wood or cardboard having a tip coated with a chemical that catches fire when rubbed on a certain surface. **2.** a slowly burning cord or wick once used for firing a gun or cannon.

match (mach), *n.* **1.** any person or thing equal to or like another in some way [Tom met his *match* in chess when he played Bill.] **2.** two or more people or things that go well together [His suit and tie were a good *match.*] **3.** a game or contest between two persons or teams [a tennis *match*]. **4.** a marriage [A *match*maker arranges marriages for others.] **5.** a person thought of as a future husband or wife [Would Dan be a good *match* for their daughter?] —*v.* **1.** to go well together [Do your socks and suit *match?*] **2.** to make or get something like or equal to [Can you *match* this cloth?] **3.** to be equal to [I could never *match* father in an argument.] **4.** to pit against one another [to *match* two boxers.]

match·less (mach/lis), *adj.* having no equal; best of its kind; peerless.

match·lock (mach/läk), *n.* **1.** an old-fashioned gunlock in which the gunpowder was set off by a burning wick. **2.** a musket with such a gunlock.

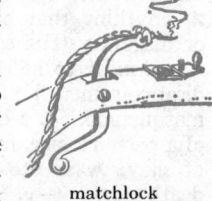

matchlock

mate (māt), *n.* **1.** one of a pair [Where is the *mate* to this sock?] **2.** a husband or wife. **3.** the male or female of a pair of animals. **4.** a friend or companion [a school*mate*]. **5.** an officer of a merchant ship ranking next below the captain; also, any of various petty officers in the navy. —*v.* **1.** to join as a pair. **2.** to join in marriage. —**mat/ed,** *p.t. & p.p.;* **mat/ing,** *pr.p.*

ma·te·ri·al (mə tir/i əl), *adj.* **1.** of or having to do with matter; physical [a *material* object]. **2.** having to do with the body and its needs [*material* comforts]. **3.** important or necessary [a *material* witness; a fact *material* to the debate]. —*n.* **1.** what a thing is made up of [raw *material*]. **2.** cloth or other fabric. **3.** ideas, notes, etc. that can be worked up [*material* for a story]. **4. materials,** *pl.* things or tools needed to do something [writing *materials*].

ma·te·ri·al·ism (mə tir/i əl iz'm), *n.* **1.** a tendency to be concerned only with material things and pleasures. **2.** the belief that nothing exists except matter and that everything can be explained in terms of physical matter. —**ma·te/ri·al·ist,** *n.*

ma·te·ri·al·ize (mə tir/i ə līz), *v.* **1.** to become fact; develop into something real [His plan never *materialized.*] **2.** to give a physical form to, or take on a physical form [to *materialize* an idea by drawing a sketch of it]. —**ma·te/ri·al·ized,** *p.t. & p.p.;* **ma·te/ri·al·iz·ing,** *pr.p.* —**ma·te/ri·al·i·za/tion,** *n.*

ma·te·ri·al·ly (mə tir′i əl ē), *adv.* **1.** as regards the matter or content of something and not its form or spirit; physically. **2.** to a great extent; considerably [He is *materially* improved.]

ma·te·ri·el or **ma·té·ri·el** (mə tir′i el′), *n.* the weapons, supplies, etc. of an army.

ma·ter·nal (mə tŭr′n'l), *adj.* **1.** of or like a mother; motherly. **2.** related to one on one's mother's side [my *maternal* aunt]. —**ma·ter′nal·ly,** *adv.*

ma·ter·ni·ty (mə tŭr′nə tē), *n.* the condition or quality of being a mother; motherhood or motherliness. —*adj.* for women who are about to become mothers [a *maternity* dress].

math·e·mat·i·cal (math′ə mat′i k'l), *adj.* **1.** having to do with mathematics. **2.** accurate; exact; precise. —**math′e·mat′i·cal·ly,** *adv.*

math·e·ma·ti·cian (math′ə mə tish′ən), *n.* an expert in mathematics.

math·e·mat·ics (math′ə mat′iks), *n.pl.* the group of sciences using numbers and symbols in dealing with the relationships and measurements of amounts and forms: *used with a singular verb* [*Mathematics* includes arithmetic, geometry, algebra, and calculus.]

mat·i·nee or **mat·i·née** (mat″n ā′), *n.* a performance of a play, movie, etc. in the afternoon.

mat·ins (mat′inz), *n.pl.* **1.** in the Roman Catholic Church, a daily service held at midnight or at daybreak. **2.** in the Church of England, the morning prayer service.

ma·tri·arch (mā′tri ärk), *n.* a woman who is the head or ruler of her family or tribe.

ma·tric·u·late (mə trik′yoo lāt), *v.* to enroll as a student, especially in a college or university. —**ma·tric′u·lat·ed,** *p.t. & p.p.;* **ma·tric′u·lat·ing,** *pr.p.* —**ma·tric′u·la′tion,** *n.*

mat·ri·mo·ny (mat′rə mō′nē), *n.* the condition of being married; marriage. —**mat′ri·mo′ni·al,** *adj.*

ma·trix (mā′triks), *n.* something within which or from which a thing develops or is formed [A mold for casting is called a *matrix.* Boston was the *matrix* of the Revolution.] —**ma′trix·es** or **ma·tri·ces** (mā′trə sēz), *pl.*

ma·tron (mā′trən), *n.* **1.** a wife or a widow, especially one who is not young. **2.** a woman who has charge of others, as in a prison.

ma·tron·ly (mā′trən lē), *adj.* of, like, or fit for a matron; serious and dignified.

mat·ted (mat′id), *adj.* **1.** tangled together in a thick mass [*matted* hair]. **2.** covered with a mat or mats.

mat·ter (mat′ər), *n.* **1.** what all things are made of; anything that takes up space. Science has now shown that matter can be changed into energy, and energy into matter [Solids, liquids, and gases are *matter.*] **2.** what a particular thing is made of; material [The hard *matter* of bones is mainly calcium salts.] **3.** things sent by mail;

mail [first-class *matter*]. **4.** something to be talked about, acted upon, etc.; affair [business *matters*]. **5.** the contents or meaning of something written or spoken, as apart from its style or form [the subject *matter* of an essay]. **6.** an amount or number [We waited a *matter* of hours.] **7.** importance [It's of no *matter.*] **8.** an unpleasant happening; trouble [What's the *matter?*] **9.** pus. —*v.* **1.** to be important or have meaning [Getting good grades really *matters* to me.] **2.** to form pus. —**as a matter of fact,** really; to tell the truth. —**for that matter,** as far as that is concerned. —**matter of course,** a thing that can be expected to happen. —**no matter, 1.** it is not important. **2.** in spite of.

mat·ter-of-fact (mat′ər əv fakt′), *adj.* keeping to the facts; showing no strong feeling or imagination.

Mat·thew (math′yoo), *n.* **1.** one of the twelve Apostles of Jesus. **2.** the first book of the New Testament. Matthew is believed to have written this book.

mat·ting (mat′ing), *n.* a fabric woven of straw, hemp, or other fiber, used for mats, rugs, etc.

mat·tock (mat′ək), *n.* a tool for loosening soil, digging up roots, etc. See *the picture.*

mat·tress (mat′ris), *n.* a casing of strong cloth filled with cotton, foam rubber, coiled springs, etc. and used on a bed.

mattock

ma·ture (mə tyoor′ *or* mə-choor′), *adj.* **1.** fully grown or developed [a *mature* plant; a *mature* person; a *mature* mind]. **2.** completely or carefully worked out [a *mature* plan]. **3.** due or payable [This note is now *mature.*] —*v.* to make or become mature. —**ma·tured′,** *p.t. & p.p.;* **ma·tur·ing,** *pr.p.*

ma·tu·ri·ty (mə tyoor′ə tē *or* mə choor′ə tē), *n.* **1.** the condition of being fully grown or developed. **2.** the time when a bond, insurance policy, etc. becomes due or reaches its full value.

mattress (cut open to show a spring)

matz·o (mät′sô), *n.* a thin, crisp bread without leavening, eaten during Passover. —**matz·oth** (mät′sōth *or* mät′sōs), *pl.*

maud·lin (môd′lin), *adj.* showing sorrow, pity, etc. in a foolish, tearful way; too sentimental, as because of being drunk.

maul (môl), *v.* to handle roughly or injure by being rough [The lion *mauled* its victim.]

Mau·na Lo·a (mou′nä lō′ä), an active volcano on the island of Hawaii.

maun·der (môn′dər), *v.* **1.** to talk in a confused or rambling way. **2.** to move or act in a confused or dreamy way.

Mau·ri·ta·ni·a (môr′ə tā′ni ə), *n.* a country in western Africa, on the Atlantic Ocean.

Mau·ri·ti·us (mô rish′i əs), *n.* a country on a group of islands in the Indian Ocean.

mau·so·le·um (mô′sə lē′əm), *n.* a large tomb.

mauve (mōv), *adj. & n.* pale purple.

mav·er·ick (mav′ər ik), *n.* **1.** an animal, especially a lost calf, that has not been branded. **2.** a person who is independent of any political party or group: *used only in everyday talk.*

maw (mô), *n.* **1.** the crop of a bird. **2.** the throat, gullet, jaws, etc. of some animals, as of the alligator.

mawk·ish (môk′ish), *adj.* **1.** showing love, pity, etc. in a foolish or tearful way; so sentimental as to be sickening. **2.** having a sweet, weak, sickening taste. —**mawk′ish·ly,** *adv.*

max·im (mak′sim), *n.* a short saying that has become a rule of conduct ["Better late than never" is a *maxim.*]

max·i·mum (mak′sə məm), *n.* **1.** the greatest amount or number that is possible or allowed [Forty pounds of luggage is the *maximum* that you can take.] **2.** the highest degree or point reached [Today's *maximum* was 95° F.] —*adj.* greatest possible or allowed [*maximum* speed]. —**max′i·mums** or **max·i·ma** (mak′sə mə), *pl.*

May (mā), *n.* the fifth month of the year. It has 31 days.

may (mā), *a helping verb used with other verbs and meaning:* **1.** to be possible or likely [It *may* rain.] **2.** to be allowed or have permission [You *may* go.] **3.** to be able to as a result [Be quiet so that we *may* hear.] *May* is also used in exclamations to mean "I or we hope or wish" [*May* you win!] —**might,** *p.t.*

Ma·ya (mä′yə), *n.* **1.** a member of a highly civilized Indian people of southern Mexico and Central America who were conquered by the Spanish in the 16th century. **2.** their language. —*adj.* of the Mayas. —**Ma′yan,** *n. & adj.*

may·be (mā′bē), *adv.* it may be; perhaps.

May·day (mā′dā), *n.* a call for help, used by ships and aircraft in trouble.

May Day, May 1, celebrated in honor of spring by dancing, crowning a May queen, etc. May Day is also sometimes celebrated as an international labor holiday.

May·flow·er (mā′flou ər), *n.* **1.** any of various early spring flowers, especially the arbutus. **2.** the ship on which the Pilgrims sailed to America in 1620.

May·fly, a slender insect with large front wings and small back wings. The adult lives only a few days.

may·hap (mā′hap *or* mā hap′), *adv.* maybe; perhaps: *now seldom used.*

May fly (1 in. long)

may·hem (mā′hem *or* mā′əm), *n.* the crime of crippling or maiming a person on purpose.

may·on·naise (mā ə nāz′), *n.* a thick, creamy salad dressing made of egg yolks, olive oil, seasoning, etc.

may·or (mā′ər *or* mer), *n.* the head of the government of a city or town.

may·or·al·ty (mā′ər əl tē *or* mer′əl tē), *n.* the position of a mayor or the time of being a mayor. —**may′or·al·ties,** *pl.*

May·pole (mā′pōl), *n.* a decorated pole around which people dance on May Day.

mayst (māst), an older form of **may,** used with *thou,* as in the Bible.

maze (māz), *n.* **1.** a series of winding passages, blind alleys, etc. that make it hard to find one's way through. **2.** a condition of confusion.

Maypole

M.C., abbreviation for **master of ceremonies.**

Mc·Kin·ley, William (mə kin′lē), 1843–1901; 25th president of the United States, from 1897 to 1901.

maze for testing rats

McKinley, Mount, a mountain in Alaska that is the highest peak in North America.

Md., abbreviation for **Maryland.**

M.D., abbreviation for **Doctor of Medicine,** used after the doctor's name.

Mdlle., an abbreviation for **Mademoiselle.** —**Mdlles.,** *pl.*

Mdme., an abbreviation for **Madame.** —**Mdmes.,** *pl.*

mdse., abbreviation for **merchandise.**

me (mē), *pron.* the form of *I* that is used as the object of a verb or preposition [She helped *me.* Send it to *me.*] *Me* is also used in everyday talk after the verb *be* [It's *me.*]

Me., abbreviation for **Maine.**

mead (mēd), *n.* an alcoholic drink made from honey.

mead (mēd), *n.* a meadow: *used in poetry.*

mead·ow (med′ō), *n.* **1.** a piece of level land where grass is grown for hay. **2.** any field of grass, wildflowers, etc.

meadow lark, a North American songbird about the size of a robin. It has a yellow breast and builds its nest on the ground.

mea·ger or **mea·gre** (mē′gər), *adj.* **1.** of poor quality or small amount; scanty [a *meager* lunch]. **2.** thin or lean; gaunt.

meal (mēl), *n.* **1.** any of the regular times at which food is eaten, as breakfast, lunch, or dinner. **2.** the food eaten at such a time [a good *meal.*]

meadow lark (11 in. long)

meal (mēl), *n.* **1.** grain ground up, but not so fine as flour [corn *meal*]. **2.** anything ground up like this.

meal·time (mēl′tīm), *n.* the usual time for serving or eating a meal.

meal·y (mēl/ē), *adj.* **1.** like meal; dry, crumbly, pale, etc. **2.** of or covered with meal. **—meal'-i·er,** *compar.;* **meal'i·est,** *superl.*

meal·y-mouthed (mēl/ē mouthd/), *adj.* not willing to speak frankly or plainly; not sincere.

mean (mēn), *v.* **1.** to have in mind as a purpose; intend [She *meant* to go, but she changed her mind.] **2.** to want to make known or understood [He says exactly what he *means*.] **3.** to be a sign of; signify or indicate [Falling leaves *mean* winter is near. What does this word *mean*?] **4.** to have a certain importance, effect, etc. [Good grades *mean* a lot if you plan to enter college.] **—mean well,** to have a good purpose in mind. **—meant,** *p.t. & p.p.;* **mean'ing,** *pr.p.*

mean (mēn), *adj.* **1.** poor in looks, quality, etc.; shabby [a shack in a *mean* part of town]. **2.** low in rank; humble or poor [the *meanest* subject of the king]. **3.** not noble or honorable; petty [Revenge is a *mean* motive.] **4.** not generous; stingy [A miser is *mean* with his money.] **5.** dangerous or bad-tempered; hard to control [a *mean* dog]. **6.** selfish, unkind, rude, etc. in a shameful way: *used only in everyday talk.*

mean (mēn), *adj.* halfway between two limits or extremes [If the highest temperature in May was 85 and the lowest 55, then the *mean* temperature was 70.] **—n. 1.** a point halfway between extremes [The *mean* between 2 and 10 is 6. She wore her blue dress as a happy *mean* between her black one and her bright red one.] **2. means,** *pl.* a way of getting or doing something [Flying is the fastest *means* of travel.] **3. means,** *pl.* wealth; riches [a man of *means*]. **—by all means,** certainly; of course. **—by means of,** by using. **—by no means,** certainly not.

me·an·der (mi an/dər), *v.* **1.** to go winding back and forth [a *meandering* creek]. **2.** to wander in an idle or aimless way.

mean·ing (mēn/ing), *n.* what is meant; what is supposed to be understood; significance [He repeated his words to make his *meaning* clear. What is the *meaning* of this poem?] **—adj.** that has some meaning [a *meaning* smile].

mean·ing·ful (mēn/ing f'l), *adj.* full of meaning [She gave me a *meaningful* look.]

mean·ing·less (mēn/ing lis), *adj.* having no meaning; senseless [a *meaningless* scribble].

mean·ness (mēn/nis), *n.* the condition of being mean, low, poor, selfish, unkind, etc.

meant (ment), past tense and past participle of **mean.**

mean·time (mēn/tīm), *adv.* **1** during the time between [She came back in an hour; *meantime,* I had eaten.] **2.** at the same time [She ironed some shirts; *meantime,* dinner was cooking.] **—n.** the time between [in the *meantime*].

mean·while (mēn/hwīl), *adv. & n.* meantime.

mea·sles (mē/z'lz), *n.pl.* **1.** a disease in which there is a fever and red spots form on the skin. It is more common among children than adults.

2. a disease like this but milder, usually called **German measles.** *This word is used with a singular verb* [*Measles* is catching.]

meas·ur·a·ble (mezh/ər ə b'l), *adj.* large enough to be measured. **—meas/ur·a·bly,** *adv.*

meas·ure (mezh/ər), *v.* **1.** to find out the size, amount, etc. of, as by comparing with something else [*Measure* the boy's height with a yardstick. How do you *measure* a man's worth?]

measure

2. to set apart or mark off a certain amount or length of [*Measure* out three pounds of sugar.] **3.** to be of a certain size, amount, etc. [The table *measures* five feet on each side.] **4.** to be a thing for measuring [Clocks *measure* time.] **5.** to compare [*Measure* her score against the class average.] **—n. 1.** the size, amount, etc. of something, found out by measuring [The *measure* of the bucket is four gallons.] **2.** a unit or standard for use in measuring [The inch is a *measure* of length. Are grades a true *measure* of learning?] **3.** a system of measuring [Liquid *measure* is a system of measuring liquids.] **4.** anything used to measure with [This milk bottle will serve as a quart *measure*.] **5.** a certain amount, extent, or degree [His success is due in large *measure* to hard work.] **6.** an action meant to bring something about [recent *measures* taken to safeguard swimmers]. **7.** a law [Congress passed a *measure* for flood control.] **8.** the notes or rests between two bars on a staff of music. **9.** rhythm or meter, as of a poem or song. **—beyond measure,** so much that it cannot be measured; extremely. **—measure up to,** to be as good, satisfying, etc. as. **—meas/ured,** *p.t. & p.p.;* **meas/ur·ing,** *pr.p.*

meas·ured (mezh/ərd), *adj.* **1.** set or marked off according to a standard [a *measured* mile]. **2.** regular or steady [*measured* steps]. **3.** planned with care [*measured* words].

meas·ure·less (mezh/ər lis), *adj.* too large or great to be measured; huge; vast.

meas·ure·ment (mezh/ər mənt), *n.* **1.** a measuring or being measured. **2.** size, amount, etc. found by measuring [His waist *measurement* is 32 inches.] **3.** a system of measuring [liquid *measurement*].

meat (mēt), *n.* **1.** the flesh of animals used as food: meat usually does not include fish and often does not include poultry. **2.** the part that can be eaten [the *meat* of a nut]. **3.** the main part [the *meat* of an argument]. **4.** food in general: *now used only in the phrase* "meat and drink."

meat·y (mēt/ē), *adj.* **1.** of, like, or full of meat [a rich, *meaty* broth]. **2.** full of ideas or meaning [a *meaty* speech]. **—meat/i·er,** *compar.;* **meat/i·est,** *superl.* **—meat/i·ness,** *n.*

Mec·ca (mek′ə), *n.* **1.** a capital of Saudi Arabia. It is a holy city of Moslems because Mohammed was born there. **2.** *often* **mecca,** any place that many people visit or want to visit [a *mecca* for tourists].

me·chan·ic (mə kan′ik), *n.* a worker skilled in using tools or in making, repairing, and using machinery.

me·chan·i·cal (mə kan′i k′l), *adj.* **1.** having to do with machinery. **2.** made or run by machinery [a *mechanical* toy]. **3.** acting or done as if by a machine and without thought; automatic [to greet someone in a *mechanical* way]. **—me·chan′i·cal·ly,** *adv.*

me·chan·ics (mə kan′iks), *n.pl.* **1.** the science that deals with motion and the effect of forces on bodies. **2.** knowledge of how to make, run, and repair machinery. **3.** the technical part or skills [Spelling and punctuation form part of the *mechanics* of writing.] *This word is used with a singular verb.*

mech·a·nism (mek′ə niz′m), *n.* **1.** the working parts of a machine. **2.** any system whose parts work together like the parts of a machine [The human body is an efficient *mechanism.*]

mech·a·nize (mek′ə nīz), *v.* **1.** to bring about the use of machinery in [Henry Ford *mechanized* the production of automobiles.] **2.** to supply with tanks, trucks, etc. [to *mechanize* an army]. **3.** to make mechanical, or like a machine. **—mech′a·nized,** *p.t. & p.p.;* **mech′a·niz·ing,** *pr.p.*

med·al (med′l), *n.* a small, flat piece of metal with words or a design on it, given as an honor or reward for some great action or service.

me·dal·lion (mə dal′yən), *n.* **1.** a round design, decoration, etc. that looks like a medal. **2.** a large medal.

med·dle (med′l), *v.* to touch another's things or take part in another's affairs without being asked or wanted; interfere. **—med′dled,** *p.t. & p.p.;* **med′dling,** *pr.p.* **—med′dler,** *n.*

soldier wearing a medal

med·dle·some (med′l səm), *adj.* in the habit of meddling; interfering.

Mede (mēd), *n.* a person of ancient Media.

Me·de·a (mi dē′ə), *n.* a witch in a Greek myth, who helped Jason get the Golden Fleece.

Me·di·a (mē′di ə), *n.* an ancient country in what is now northwestern Iran.

me·di·a (mē′di ə), *n.* a plural of **medium.**

me·di·ae·val (mē′di ē′v′l *or* med′i ē′v′l), *adj.* same as **medieval.**

me·di·al (mē′di əl), *adj.* **1.** of or in the middle; median. **2.** average or ordinary.

me·di·an (mē′di ən), *adj.* in the middle; halfway between the two ends [7 is the *median* number in the series 1, 4, 7, 25, 48.] **—n.** a median number, point, or line.

me·di·ate (mē′di āt), *v.* **1.** to act as a judge or go-between in trying to settle a quarrel between others. **2.** to bring about an agreement by acting as a go-between. **—me′di·at·ed,** *p.t. & p.p.;* **me′di·at·ing,** *pr.p.* **—me′di·a·tor,** *n.*

me·di·a·tion (mē′di ā′shən), *n.* a mediating, or working to bring about an agreement.

med·ic (med′ik), *n.* **1.** a medical doctor. **2.** a soldier whose work is giving first aid in battle. *Used only in everyday talk.*

med·i·cal (med′i k′l), *adj.* having to do with the practice or study of medicine [*medical* care; a *medical* school]. **—med′i·cal·ly,** *adv.*

me·dic·a·ment (mə dik′ə mənt), *n.* a medicine.

med·i·care (med′i ker), *n.* a system of government insurance for providing medical and hospital care for the aged.

med·i·cate (med′i kāt), *v.* **1.** to put medicine in or on [These cough drops are *medicated.*] **2.** to treat with medicine [It is often dangerous to *medicate* oneself without a doctor's advice.] **—med′i·cat·ed,** *p.t. & p.p.;* **med′i·cat·ing,** *pr.p.*

med·i·ca·tion (med′i kā′shən), *n.* **1.** the act of medicating. **2.** a medicine.

me·dic·i·nal (mə dis′'n 'l), *adj.* that is or acts as a medicine; curing or healing [a *medicinal* substance].

med·i·cine (med′ə s'n), *n.* **1.** any substance used in or on the body to treat disease, lessen pain, heal, etc. **2.** the science of treating and preventing disease. **3.** the branch of this science that makes use of drugs, diet, etc., especially as separate from surgery. **4.** any thing or action once supposed to have magic power to cure illness, ward off evil, etc.; also, such magic power.

medicine man, a man supposed by primitive peoples to have magic power in curing disease, warding off evil, etc.

me·di·e·val (mē′di ē′v'l *or* med′i ē′v'l), *adj.* of, like, or belonging to the Middle Ages.

me·di·o·cre (mē′di ō′kər), *adj.* neither very good nor very bad; just ordinary; not good enough. **—me·di·oc·ri·ty** (mē′di äk′rə tē), *n.*

med·i·tate (med′ə tāt), *v.* **1.** to pass some time thinking in a quiet way; reflect. **2.** to plan or consider [to *meditate* making a change]. **—med′i·tat·ed,** *p.t. & p.p.;* **med′i·tat·ing,** *pr.p.* **—med′i·ta′tion,** *n.* **—med′i·ta′tive,** *adj.*

Med·i·ter·ra·ne·an (med′ə tə rā′ni ən), *n.* a large sea surrounded by Europe, Africa, and Asia: also **Mediterranean Sea. —adj.** of this sea or the regions around it.

me·di·um (mē′di əm), *adj.* in the middle in amount, degree, etc.; average [a *medium* price]. **—n. 1.** a thing or condition in the middle; something that is not an extreme [A temperature of 70° is a happy *medium.*] **2.** a thing through which a force acts or an effect is made [Copper is a good *medium* for conducting heat.] **3.** any means by which something is done [Television can be a *medium* for education.] **4.** the substance, condition, etc. in which something lives. **5.** a person through whom messages are supposedly sent from the dead, as at a séance. **—me′di·ums** *or* **me·di·a** (mē′di ə), *pl.*

med·ley (med′lē), *n.* **1.** a mixture of unlike things. **2.** a selection of songs or tunes played as a single piece. —**med′leys,** *pl.*

Me·du·sa (mə doo′sə *or* mə dyoo′zə), *n.* in Greek myths, one of the Gorgons: see **Gorgon.**

meek (mēk), *adj.* **1.** patient and mild; not showing anger. **2.** very humble or too humble in one's feelings, actions, etc.; not showing spirit. —**meek′ly,** *adv.* —**meek′ness,** *n.*

meer·schaum (mir′shəm), *n.* **1.** a soft, white mineral, like clay. **2.** a tobacco pipe made of this.

meet (mēt), *v.* **1.** to come upon; come face to face with [We *met* two friends walking down the street.] **2.** to be introduced to [I *met* her at your party.] **3.** to become acquainted [Have you two *met?*] **4.** to be present at the arrival of [He *met* the bus.] **5.** to keep an appointment with [I'll *meet* you at noon.] **6.** to come into contact [The cars *met* with a crash.] **7.** to come together; assemble [The school board *meets* today.] **8.** to be joined [The rivers *meet* below the mill.] **9.** to face or deal with [He *met* our questions with frank answers.] **10.** to undergo; experience [Their plan will *meet* disaster.] **11.** to satisfy, as a demand or a need. **12.** to pay [to *meet* one's bills]. —*n.* a meeting, as for some sport [a track *meet*]. —**meet with, 1.** to experience; have [to *meet with* an accident]. **2.** to come upon. —**met,** *p.t.* & *p.p.;* **meet′ing,** *pr.p.*

meet (mēt), *adj.* fitting or proper: *no longer much used.*

meet·ing (mēt′ing), *n.* **1.** a coming together of persons or things. **2.** a gathering of people for some purpose; assembly.

meet·ing·house (mēt′ing hous′), *n.* a building used for religious services; church.

meg·a·lop·o·lis (meg′ə läp′'l is), *n.* a very large, crowded area made up of several cities.

meg·a·phone (meg′ə fōn), *n.* a large tube shaped like a funnel, through which a person speaks or shouts. It sends the voice farther.

megaphone

mel·an·chol·y (mel′- ən käl′ē), *n.* sadness or a tendency to be sad and gloomy. —*adj.* **1.** sad and gloomy. **2.** causing sadness or gloom [a *melancholy* drizzle].

Mel·a·ne·sia (mel′ə nē′zhə), *n.* a group of islands in the South Pacific, northeast of Australia. —**Mel′a·ne′sian,** *adj.* & *n.*

Mel·bourne (mel′bərn), *n.* a seaport in southeastern Australia.

me·lee or **mê·lée** (mā lā′ *or* mā′lā), *n.* a noisy, confused fight or struggle among a number of people; brawl; riot.

mel·lif·lu·ous (mə lif′loo əs), *adj.* sounding sweet and smooth [a *mellifluous* voice].

mel·low (mel′ō), *adj.* **1.** soft, sweet, and juicy; ripe [a *mellow* apple]. **2.** having a good flavor from being aged [a *mellow* wine]. **3.** rich, soft, and pure; not harsh [the *mellow* tone of a cello]. **4.** made gentle and kind by age and experience [a *mellow* old man]. —*v.* to make or become mellow. —**mel′low·ness,** *n.*

me·lod·ic (mə läd′ik), *adj.* **1.** of or like melody [the *melodic* pattern]. **2.** melodious.

me·lo·di·ous (mə lō′di əs), *adj.* **1.** making pleasant music. **2.** pleasing to hear; tuneful.

mel·o·dra·ma (mel′ə drä′mə *or* mel′ə dram′ə), *n.* **1.** a play in which there is so much violence, strong feeling, and exaggeration of good and evil that it does not seem true. **2.** any exciting action or talk like that in such a play.

mel·o·dra·mat·ic (mel′ə drə mat′ik), *adj.* of, like, or fit for melodrama; violent, emotional, etc. —**mel′o·dra·mat′i·cal·ly,** *adv.*

mel·o·dy (mel′ə dē), *n.* **1.** an arrangement of musical tones in a series so as to form a tune; often, the main tune in the harmony of a musical piece [The *melody* is played by the oboes.] **2.** any pleasing series of sounds [a *melody* sung by birds]. —**mel′o·dies,** *pl.*

mel·on (mel′ən), *n.* a large, juicy fruit that grows on a vine and is full of seeds [Watermelons, muskmelons, and cantaloupes are *melons.*]

melt (melt), *v.* **1.** to change from a solid to a liquid, as by heat [The butter *melted* in the sunlight.] **2.** to dissolve [The candy *melted* in his mouth.] **3.** to disappear or go away [His fear *melted* away.] **4.** to blend in slowly [The blue sky seemed to *melt* into the sea.] **5.** to make gentle or full of pity [Tears *melt* my heart.] —**melt′ed,** *p.t.* & *p.p.;* **melt′ing,** *pr.p.*

mem·ber (mem′bər), *n.* **1.** any of the persons who make up a church, club, political party, etc. **2.** a leg, arm, or other part of the body. **3.** a single part of a thing, as a word in a sentence or a column of a building.

mem·ber·ship (mem′bər ship), *n.* **1.** the condition of being a member. **2.** all the members of a group. **3.** the number of members.

mem·brane (mem′brān), *n.* a thin, soft layer of tissue that covers a part of an animal or plant.

mem·bra·nous (mem′brə nəs), *adj.* of or like membrane.

me·men·to (mi men′tō), *n.* an object kept to remind one of something; souvenir [This doll is a *memento* of my childhood.] —**me·men′tos** or **me·men′toes,** *pl.*

mem·o (mem′ō), *n.* a memorandum: *used only in everyday talk.* —**mem′os,** *pl.*

mem·oir (mem′wär), *n.* **1. memoirs,** *pl.* the story of one's own life written by oneself; autobiography; also, a written report based on the writer's own experience and knowledge. **2.** a written story of someone's life; biography.

mem·o·ra·ble (mem′ər ə b'l), *adj.* worth remembering; not easily forgotten; remarkable.

mem·o·ran·dum (mem′ə ran′dəm), *n.* **1.** a short note written to help one remember something. **2.** an informal note, as from one part of a business office to another. —**mem′o·ran′dums** or **mem·o·ran·da** (mem′ə ran′də), *pl.*

me·mo·ri·al (mə môr′i əl), *adj.* held or done in memory of some person or event [a *memorial* service for the dead]. —*n.* anything meant to remind people of some event or person, as a holiday or statue.

Memorial Day, the last Monday in May, a legal holiday for honoring dead soldiers and sailors by decorating their graves.

mem·o·rize (mem′ə rīz), *v.* to fix in one's memory exactly or word for word; learn by heart. —**mem′o·rized,** *p.t. & p.p.;* **mem′o·riz·ing,** *pr.p.*

mem·o·ry (mem′ər ē), *n.* **1.** the act or power of remembering [to have a good *memory*]. **2.** all that one remembers. **3.** something remembered [The music brought back many *memories*.] **4.** the time over which one can remember [It had never happened before within my *memory*.] —**in memory of,** to keep alive in one's memory [a statue *in memory of* the President]. —**mem′o·ries,** *pl.*

Mem·phis (mem′fis), *n.* **1.** a city in southwestern Tennessee. **2.** a city in ancient Egypt.

men (men), *n.* plural of **man.**

men·ace (men′is), *n.* a threat or danger; thing likely to cause harm. —*v.* to threaten with harm; be a danger to [Snow *menaced* the crops.] —**men′aced,** *p.t. & p.p.;* **men′ac·ing,** *pr.p.*

me·nag·er·ie (mə naj′ər ē), *n.* a collection of wild animals kept in cages; often, such a collection taken from place to place for public showing.

mend (mend), *v.* **1.** to put back in good condition; repair; fix [to *mend* a broken lamp; to *mend* a torn shirt]. **2.** to make or become better; improve [He *mended* his ways. Her health *mended*.] —*n.* a part that has been mended. —**on the mend,** becoming better, as in health.

men·da·cious (men dā′shəs), *adj.* not truthful; lying or false. —**men·dac·i·ty** (men das′ə tē), *n.*

Men·dels·sohn, Fe·lix (fā′liks men′d'l s'n), 1809–1847; German composer of music.

men·di·cant (men′di kənt), *adj.* begging; asking for charity [*mendicant* friars]. —*n.* a beggar.

men·folk (men′fōk) or **men·folks** (men′fōks), *n.pl.* men: *used mainly in the South.*

men·ha·den (men hā′d'n), *n.* a fish of the herring family, found along the Atlantic coast. It is important for its oil and for its use as fertilizer.

me·ni·al (mē′ni əl *or* mēn′yəl), *adj.* of or fit for servants; low or humble. —*n.* a servant.

men·in·gi·tis (men′in jī′tis), *n.* a disease in which the membranes surrounding the brain or spinal cord become inflamed by infection.

Men·non·ite (men′ən īt), *n.* a member of a Christian church that is against military service, the taking of oaths, etc. Mennonites dress and live in a very plain way.

men·stru·ate (men′strōō āt), *v.* to have the normal flow of blood from the uterus, about every four weeks [Women *menstruate* from the time they become sexually mature until some time in middle age.] —**men′stru·a′tion,** *n.*

men·su·ra·tion (men′shə rā′shən), *n.* the act or mathematics of measuring.

-ment (mənt), a suffix meaning: **1.** the act or result of [*Improvement* is the act or result of improving.] **2.** a means or thing for [An *adornment* is a thing for adorning.] **3.** the condition or fact of being [*Disappointment* is the condition or fact of being disappointed.]

men·tal (men′t'l), *adj.* **1.** of, for, by, or in the mind [*mental* ability; *mental* arithmetic]. **2.** sick in mind [a *mental* patient]. **3.** for the sick in mind [a *mental* hospital].

men·tal·i·ty (men tal′ə tē), *n.* the ability to think and reason; mind. —**men·tal′i·ties,** *pl.*

men·tal·ly (men′tə lē), *adv.* in, with, or by the mind [*mentally* ill; *mentally* alert].

men·thol (men′thôl), *n.* a substance gotten from oil of peppermint in the form of white crystals that give a cool taste or feeling. It is used in salves, cough drops, etc.

men·tion (men′shən), *v.* to speak about or name briefly. —*n.* something said or named briefly, without going into detail. —**make mention of,** to mention; remark about.

men·tor (men′tər), *n.* a wise, loyal adviser.

men·u (men′yōō), *n.* a list of the foods served at a meal [a restaurant's dinner *menu*].

me·ow (mi ou′), *n.* the sound made by a cat. —*v.* to make this sound.

mer·can·tile (mūr′kən til *or* mūr′kən tīl), *adj.* having to do with merchants, trade, or commerce.

mer·ce·nar·y (mūr′sə ner′ē), *adj.* working or done just for money; greedy [her *mercenary* reasons for helping the rich man]. —*n.* a soldier who fights for any country that will pay him. —**mer′ce·nar′ies,** *pl.*

mer·cer·ize (mūr′sə rīz), *v.* to treat cotton thread with a chemical that makes it strong and silky. —**mer′cer·ized,** *p.t. & p.p.;* **mer′cer·iz·ing,** *pr.p.*

mer·chan·dise (mūr′chən dīz *or* mūr′chən dīs), *n.* things bought and sold; goods. —*v.* (mūr′chən dīz), to buy and sell; deal in [to *merchandise* hardware]. —**mer′chan·dised,** *p.t. & p.p.;* **mer′chan·dis·ing,** *pr.p.*

mer·chant (mūr′chənt), *n.* a person who buys and sells goods for profit, either wholesale or as a storekeeper. —*adj.* of or used in buying and selling goods; commercial [a *merchant* ship].

mer·chant·man (mūr′chənt mən), *n.* a ship for carrying cargo. —**mer′chant·men,** *pl.*

merchant marine, all the ships of a nation that carry cargo, or their crews.

mer·ci·ful (mūr′si fəl), *adj.* having or showing mercy; kind; forgiving. —**mer′ci·ful·ly,** *adv.*

mer·ci·less (mūr′si lis), *adj.* having or showing no mercy; cruel. —**mer′ci·less·ly,** *adv.*

mer·cu·ri·al (mər kyoor′i əl), *adj.* **1.** like mercury; quick, lively, changeable, etc. [a *mercurial* person]. **2.** of or having to do with mercury.

Mer·cu·ry (mũr′kyoo rē), *n.* **1.** the Roman messenger of the gods, who was also the god of trade and cleverness. The Greeks called this god *Hermes.* **2.** the smallest planet. It is also the one nearest the sun. **3.** mercury, a heavy, silvery metal that is a chemical element. It is ordinarily a liquid and is used in thermometers, medicines, etc.

Mercury

mer·cy (mũr′sē), *n.* **1.** kindness, especially to a wrongdoer or enemy, that is greater than might be expected. **2.** the power to forgive or be kind [Throw yourself on the *mercy* of the court.] **3.** a lucky thing; blessing [It's a *mercy* he wasn't killed.] —*interj.* a word showing surprise, annoyance, etc. —**at the mercy of,** in the power of. —**mer′cies,** *pl.*

mere (mir), *adj.* nothing more than; only [He's a *mere* child.] —**mer′est,** *superl.*

mere·ly (mir′lē), *adv.* no more than; only.

mer·e·tri·cious (mer′ə trish′əs), *adj.* attractive in a false, showy way; flashy, but cheap.

mer·gan·ser (mər gan′sər), *n.* a large duck with a long, slender beak.

merge (mũrj), *v.* to combine or unite into one larger thing so as to lose separate character [The two companies *merged.*] —**merged,** *p.t.* & *p.p.;* **merg′ing,** *pr.p.*

mergansers (2 ft. long)

merg·er (mũr′jər), *n.* a merging; especially, a combining of several companies into one.

me·rid·i·an (mə rid′i ən), *n.* **1.** the half circle made by a line passing north and south across the surface of the earth, from one pole to the other. The lines of longitude on a map or globe are a series of such half circles. **2.** the highest point that the sun or a star seems to reach in its daily movement. **3.** the highest point; apex.

me·ringue (mə rang′), *n.* egg whites mixed with sugar, beaten stiff and baked as a covering for pies, or as separate small cakes.

me·ri·no (mə rē′nō), *n.* **1.** a sheep with long, silky wool. **2.** its wool, or a soft yarn made from it. **3.** a soft, thin, woolen cloth. —**me·ri′nos,** *pl.*

mer·it (mer′it), *n.* **1.** good quality; worth; goodness [a plan of great *merit*]. **2.** merits, *pl.* actual facts or qualities [to decide a case on its *merits*]. —*v.* to be worthy of; deserve [to *merit* praise].

merino (2½ ft. high at shoulder)

mer·i·to·ri·ous (mer′ə tôr′i əs), *adj.* deserving reward, praise, etc.

Mer·lin (mũr′lin), *n.* a magician in the legends about King Arthur.

mer·maid (mũr′mād), *n.* an imaginary sea creature with the head and upper body of a woman and the tail of a fish.

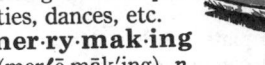

mer·man (mũr′man), *n.* an imaginary sea creature with the head and upper body of a man and the tail of a fish. —**mer′men,** *pl.*

mermaid

mer·ri·ment (mer′i mənt), *n.* gay laughter and fun; merrymaking; mirth.

mer·ry (mer′ē), *adj.* filled with fun and laughter; gay; lively [a *merry* party]. —**make merry,** to be gay; have fun. —**mer′ri·er,** *compar.;* **mer′ri·est,** *superl.* —**mer′ri·ly,** *adv.* —**mer′ri·ness,** *n.*

mer·ry-go-round (mer′ē gō round′), *n.* **1.** a platform that is turned round and round by machinery and that has wooden animals and seats on which people ride for amusement; carrousel. **2.** an exciting series of parties, dances, etc.

merry-go-round

mer·ry·mak·ing (mer′ē māk′ing), *n.* **1.** the act of making merry and having fun. **2.** a gay party or amusement. —**mer′ry·mak′er,** *n.*

me·sa (mā′sə), *n.* a large, high rock having steep walls and a flat top.

mes·dames (mā·däm′), *n.* plural of **madame, madam,** or **Mrs.** Abbreviated **Mmes.**

mes·de·moi·selles (mād mwä zel′), *n.* plural of **mademoiselle:** abbreviated **Mlles.**

mesa

mesh (mesh), *n.* **1.** any of the open spaces of a net, screen, or sieve. **2.** meshes, *pl.* the threads, cords, or wires that form a network [to repair the *meshes* of a fishing net]. —*v.* **1.** to catch or trap as in a net. **2.** to fit together; interlock. —**in mesh,** with the gears engaged.

mes·mer·ize (mes′mə rīz *or* mez′mə rīz), *v.* to hypnotize. —**mes′mer·ized,** *p.t.* & *p.p.;* **mes′mer·iz·ing,** *pr.p.* —**mes′mer·ism,** *n.*

Mes·o·po·ta·mi·a (mes′ə pə tā′mi ə), *n.* an ancient country in southwestern Asia, between the Tigris and Euphrates rivers.

---

fat,   āpe,   cär,   ten,   ēven,   hit,   bīte,   gō,   hôrn,   tōol,   book,   up,   fũr;
get,   joy,   yet,   chin,   she,   thin,   *th*en;   zh = s in pleasure;   ′ as in able (ā′b'l);
ə = a in ago,   e in agent,   i in sanity,   o in confess,   u in focus.

mes·quite or **mes·quit** (mes kēt′ or mes′kēt), *n.* a spiny tree or shrub of the southwestern United States and Mexico.

mess (mes), *n.* **1.** a serving of soft or mushy food [a *mess* of porridge]. **2.** a heap or mass of things thrown together or mixed up; jumble [clothes in a *mess* on the bed]. **3.** a condition of being dirty, untidy, etc. [Your room is in a *mess.*] **4.** a person or thing in such a condition. **5.** a condition of trouble or difficulty [He's in a real *mess* for failing to finish the assignment.] **6.** a group of people who regularly eat together, as in the army or navy. **7.** a meal eaten by such a group, or the place where they eat. —*v.* **1.** to make a mess of; make dirty, confused, etc. **2.** to putter or meddle [Don't *mess* around with my books.] **3.** to eat as one of a mess (*meaning 6*).

mes·sage (mes′ij), *n.* **1.** a piece of news, a request, facts, etc. sent from one person to another, either by speaking or writing. **2.** an important idea that a writer, artist, etc. is trying to bring to people.

mes·sen·ger (mes′'n jər), *n.* a person who carries a message or goes on an errand.

Mes·si·ah (mə sī′ə), *n.* **1.** in Jewish belief, the person that God will send to save the Jewish people. **2.** in Christian belief, Jesus. **3.** **messiah**, any person expected to save others.

Mes·si·an·ic (mes′i an′ik), *adj.* **1.** of the Messiah. **2.** **messianic**, of or like a messiah.

mes·sieurs (mes′ərz or mā syūr′), *n.* plural of **monsieur.** See also **Messrs.**

mess kit, a set of plates, forks, spoons, etc. carried by a soldier or camper for eating.

mess·mate (mes′māt), *n.* a person with whom one regularly has meals, as in the army.

Messrs. (mes′ərz), abbreviation for **Messieurs:** *commonly used as the plural of* **Mr.**

mess·y (mes′ē), *adj.* in or like a mess; untidy, dirty, etc. —**mess′i·er**, *compar.;* **mess′i·est**, *superl.* —**mess′i·ly**, *adv.* —**mess′i·ness**, *n.*

met (met), past tense and past participle of **meet.**

me·tab·o·lism (mə tab′ə liz′m), *n.* the process in all plants and animals by which food is changed into energy, new cells, waste products, etc. —**met·a·bol·ic** (met′ə bäl′ik), *adj.*

met·al (met′'l), *n.* **1.** a chemical element that is more or less shiny, can be hammered or stretched, and can conduct heat and electricity [Iron, gold, aluminum, lead, and magnesium are some of the *metals.*] **2.** a substance of some metal [made of either plastic or *metal*]. **3.** material; stuff [He is made of stronger *metal* than his brother.] —*adj.* made of metal.

me·tal·lic (mə tal′ik), *adj.* **1.** of or like metal [*metallic* ore]. **2.** like that of metal [a *metallic* sound].

met·al·lur·gy (met′'l ûr′jē), *n.* the science of getting metals from their ores and making them ready for use, by smelting, refining, etc. —**met′al·lur′gi·cal**, *adj.* —**met′al·lur′gist**, *n.*

met·al·work (met′'l wûrk), *n.* **1.** things made of metal. **2.** the making of such things: also **met′al·work′ing.** —**met′al·work′er**, *n.*

met·a·mor·phose (met′ə môr′fōz), *v.* to change completely in form; transform [The caterpillar *metamorphosed* into a butterfly.] —**met′a·mor′phosed**, *p.t.* & *p.p.;* **met′a·mor′phos·ing**, *pr.p.*

met·a·mor·pho·sis (met′ə môr′fə sis), *n.* **1.** a change in form; especially, the change that some animals go through in developing, as of tadpole to frog or larva to moth. **2.** a complete change in the way someone or something looks or acts. —**met·a·mor·pho·ses** (met′ə môr′fə sēz′), *pl.*

metamorphosis of a frog

met·a·phor (met′ə fôr), *n.* the use of a word or phrase in a way that is different from its usual use, to show a likeness to something else ["The curtain of night" is a *metaphor* that likens "night" to a "curtain" that conceals.]

met·a·phor·i·cal (met′ə fôr′i k'l), *adj.* of or using metaphors [*metaphorical* language].

met·a·phys·i·cal (met′ə fiz′i k'l), *adj.* **1.** of or like metaphysics. **2.** hard to understand because dealing with abstract, not real, things.

met·a·phys·ics (met′ə fiz′iks), *n.pl.* a philosophy that tries to answer questions about what really exists and what can really be known: *used with a singular verb.*

mete (mēt), *v.* to deal out in shares or according to what is deserved [The king *meted* out punishments.] —**met′ed**, *p.t.* & *p.p.;* **met′ing**, *pr.p.*

me·te·or (mē′ti ər), *n.* a small solid body that moves with great speed from outer space into the air around the earth, where it is made white-hot by friction and usually burned up; shooting star.

me·te·or·ic (mē′ti ôr′ik), *adj.* **1.** of a meteor or meteors. **2.** bright and swift like a meteor [the actor's *meteoric* rise to fame].

me·te·or·ite (mē′ti ər īt′), *n.* a mass of metal or stone remaining from a meteor that has fallen upon the earth.

me·te·or·o·log·i·cal (mē′ti ər ə läj′i k'l), *adj.* **1.** of weather or climate [*meteorological* conditions]. **2.** of meteorology.

me·te·or·ol·o·gy (mē′ti ər äl′ə jē), *n.* the science that studies weather, climate, and the earth's atmosphere. —**me′te·or·ol′o·gist**, *n.*

me·ter (mē′tər), *n.* **1.** a measure of length that is the basic unit in the metric system. One meter is equal to 39.37 inches. **2.** rhythm in poetry; regular arrangement of accented syllables in each line. **3.** rhythm in music; arrangement of beats in each measure [Marches are often in 4/4 *meter*, with four equal beats in each measure.]

me·ter (mē′tər), *n.* an instrument for measuring and keeping a record of the amount of gas, electricity, water, etc. that passes through it.

meth·ane (meth′ān), *n.* a gas that has neither color nor smell and burns easily. It is formed by decaying plants, as in marshes and swamps, or can be made artificially.

me·thinks (mi thingks′), *v.* it seems to me: *now seldom used* [*Methinks* thou art brave.]

meth·od (meth′əd), *n.* **1.** a way of doing anything; process [Broiling is a common *method* of cooking meat.] **2.** a way of thinking or of doing things that is regular and orderly [There is *method* in his madness.]

me·thod·i·cal (mə thäd′i k′l), *adj.* working, acting, etc. by a method or system; doing or done in an orderly way. —**me·thod′i·cal·ly,** *adv.*

Meth·od·ist (meth′əd ist), *n.* a member of a Protestant church that follows the teachings of John Wesley. —*adj.* of the Methodists.

me·thought (mi thôt′), past tense of **methinks**: *now seldom used.*

Me·thu·se·lah (mə thoō′z′l ə *or* mə thyoō′z′l ə), *n.* **1.** in the Bible, a man who lived 969 years. **2.** any very old man.

me·tic·u·lous (mə tik′yoo ləs), *adj.* very careful or too careful about details; fussy.

me·tre (mē′tər), *n.* meter: British spelling.

met·ric (met′rik), *adj.* **1.** of or in the metric system: see **metric system** [The liter is a *metric* unit.] **2.** same as **metrical.**

met·ri·cal (met′ri k′l), *adj.* **1.** of or written in meter or verse [*metrical* lines]. **2.** of or used in measuring [*metrical* systems].

metric system, a system of weights and measures in which units go up or down by tens, hundreds, etc. The basic unit of length in this system is the meter (39.37 inches). The unit of weight is the gram (.0022 pound). The unit of volume is the liter (61.025 cubic inches).

met·ro·nome (met′rə nōm), *n.* an instrument that can be set to make a clicking sound at different rates of speed. It is used to set the tempo for playing a musical piece.

me·trop·o·lis (mə träp′′l is), *n.* **1.** the main city of a state, country, or region. **2.** any large or important city. —**me·trop′o·lis·es,** *pl.*

met·ro·pol·i·tan (met′rə päl′ə t′n), *adj.* of or making up a metropolis [a *metropolitan* park; *metropolitan* Chicago]. —*n.* **1.** a person who lives in, or is at home in, a big city. **2.** an archbishop.

metronome

met·tle (met′′l), *n.* spirit or courage. —**on one's mettle,** prepared to do one's best.

mew (myoo), *n. & v.* same as **meow.**

mewl (myool), *v.* to cry or whimper like a baby.

Mex., abbreviation for **Mexican** or **Mexico.**

Mex·i·can (mek′si kən), *adj.* of Mexico, its people, etc. —*n.* a person born or living in Mexico.

Mexican War, a war between the United States and Mexico, from 1846 to 1848.

Mex·i·co (mek′si kō), *n.* a country in North America, south of the United States.

Mexico, Gulf of, a gulf of the Atlantic, east of Mexico and south of the United States.

Mexico City, the capital of Mexico.

mez·za·nine (mez′ə nēn), *n.* **1.** a low story between two main stories of a building. It is usually just above the ground floor and sometimes sticks out over it like a balcony. **2.** in some theaters, the first few rows of the balcony.

mez·zo·so·pra·no (met′sō sə pran′ō), *n.* **1.** a woman's singing voice between soprano and contralto. **2.** a woman singer with such a voice. —**mez′zo·so·pra′nos,** *pl.*

mfg., abbreviation for **manufacturing.**

Mg, symbol for the chemical element *magnesium.*

mg., abbreviation for **milligram** or **milligrams.**

Mgr., abbreviation for **Manager.**

mi (mē), *n.* the third note of a musical scale.

mi., abbreviation for **mile** or **miles, minute.**

Mi·am·i (mī am′ē), *n.* a city on the southeastern coast of Florida.

mi·ca (mī′kə), *n.* a mineral that forms thin layers that are easily separated and are not affected by heat or electricity. When these layers can be seen through, mica is called *isinglass.*

mice (mīs), *n.* plural of **mouse.**

Mi·chael (mī′k′l), *n.* an archangel in the Bible.

Mich·ael·mas (mik′′l məs), *n.* a church feast on September 29, honoring the archangel Michael.

Mi·chel·an·ge·lo (mī′k′l an′jə lō), *n.* 1475–1564; Italian artist, architect, and poet.

Mich·i·gan (mish′ə gən), *n.* **1.** a State in the north central part of the United States: abbreviated **Mich. 2.** one of the Great Lakes, west of Lake Huron: *usually* **Lake Michigan.**

mick·le (mik′′l), *adj., adv. & n.,* much: *now only a Scottish word.*

micro-, a prefix meaning "little, small, tiny, etc." or "making small things larger" [A *microscope* makes small things look larger.]

mi·crobe (mī′krōb), *n.* any living thing too tiny to be seen without a microscope; now, especially, a disease germ.

mi·cro·film (mī′krə film), *n.* film on which written or printed pages, pictures, etc. are photographed in a very small size, so that they can be stored in a small space.

mi·crom·e·ter (mī kräm′ə tər), *n.* a tool for measuring very small distances, angles, etc.

Mi·cro·ne·sia (mī′krə nē′zhə), *n.* a group of islands in the Pacific, east of the Philippines.

mi·cro·or·gan·ism (mī′krō ôr′gən iz′m), *n.* any living thing too tiny to be seen without a microscope; especially, any of the bacteria, viruses, protozoans, etc. Also written **microörganism, micro-organism.**

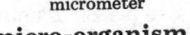
micrometer

fat,   āpe,   cär,   ten,   ēven,   hit,   bīte,   gō,   hôrn,   tool,   book,   up,   fŭr;

get,   joy,   yet,   chin,   she,   thin,   *th*en;   zh = s in pleasure;   ′ as in able (ā′b′l).

ə = a in ago,   e in agent,   i in sanity,   o in confess,   u in focus.

mi·cro·phone (mī′krə fōn), *n.* a device for catching sound that is to be made stronger, as in a theater, or sent over long distances, as in radio. Microphones change sound into electric waves, which are picked up and strengthened by electron tubes and changed back into sound by loudspeakers.

mi·cro·scope (mī′krə skōp), *n.* a device with a lens or group of lenses for making tiny things look larger so that they can be seen and studied.

mi·cro·scop·ic (mī′krə skäp′-ik), *adj.* **1.** so tiny that it cannot be seen without a microscope. **2.** of, with, or like a microscope [*microscopic* examination]. **—mi′cro·scop′i·cal·ly,** *adv.*

microscope

mid (mid), *adj.* middle.

mid or **'mid** (mid), *prep.* amid: *used in poetry.*

mid-, a prefix meaning "middle" or "middle part of" [*Midweek* means the middle of the week.]

Mi·das (mī′dəs), *n.* a king in a Greek legend who was given the power of turning everything he touched into gold.

mid·day (mid′dā), *n. & adj.* noon.

mid·dle (mid′′l), *n.* the point or part that is halfway between the ends or that is in the center [the *middle* of the afternoon; an island in the *middle* of the lake]. **—adj.** being in the middle or center [the *middle* toe on a foot].

middle age, the time of life when a person is neither young nor old, usually the years from about 40 to about 60. **—mid′dle-aged′,** *adj.*

Middle Ages, the period of history in Europe between ancient and modern times: the time from about 500 A.D. to about 1450 A.D.

middle class, 1. a social class, especially in earlier times, between the nobles or very wealthy and the working class. It included storekeepers, professional people, etc. **2.** the class of people with an income close to the average. **—mid′dle-class′,** *adj.*

middle ear, the hollow part of the ear just inside the eardrum, containing three small bones.

Middle East, the part of southwestern Asia around the eastern end of the Mediterranean, including Israel, Jordan, Iran, Iraq, the United Arab Republic, etc.

Middle English, the English language as spoken and written between about 1125 and 1475.

mid·dle·man (mid′′l man), *n.* **1.** a merchant who buys goods from the producer and sells them to storekeepers or directly to the public. **2.** a go-between. **—mid′dle·men,** *pl.*

mid·dle·weight (mid′′l wāt), *n.* **1.** a boxer or wrestler who weighs between 148 and 160 pounds. **2.** a person or animal of average weight.

Middle West or **middle west,** that part of the United States between the Rocky Mountains and the Allegheny Mountains, north of the Ohio River and the southern borders of Kansas and Missouri. **—Middle Western.**

mid·dling (mid′ling), *adj.* of medium size, quality, grade, etc.; average; ordinary. **—n.**

middlings, *pl.* **1.** goods that are middling. **2.** coarse bits of ground wheat mixed with bran.

mid·dy (mid′ē), *n.* **1.** a loose blouse with a large, wide collar, worn by women or children: also **middy blouse. 2.** a midshipman: *used only in everyday talk.* **—mid′-dies,** *pl.*

middy blouse

midge (mij), *n.* a tiny gnat, fly, etc.

midg·et (mij′it), *n.* **1.** a very small person. **2.** anything very small of its kind.

mid·land (mid′lənd), *n.* the middle part of a country, away from its coasts or borders. **—adj.** in or of the midland; inland [*midland* lakes].

mid·most (mid′mōst), *adj.* exactly in the middle, or nearest to the middle.

mid·night (mid′nīt), *n.* twelve o'clock at night; the middle of the night. **—adj. 1.** of or at midnight [a *midnight* ride]. **2.** like midnight; very dark [*midnight* blue].

mid·rib (mid′rib), *n.* the middle vein of a leaf.

mid·riff (mid′rif), *n.* the middle part of the body, between the belly and the chest.

mid·ship·man (mid′ship mən), *n.* a student at the U.S. Naval Academy. **—mid′ship′-men,** *pl.*

midst (midst), *n.* the middle; part in the center. **—in the midst of, 1.** in the middle of; surrounded by. **2.** in the course of; during.

midst or **'midst** (midst), *prep.* in the middle of; amid: *used in poetry.*

mid·stream (mid′strēm), *n.* the middle of a stream or flow of water.

mid·sum·mer (mid′sum′ər), *n.* **1.** the middle of summer. **2.** the period around June 21.

mid·way (mid′wā), *adj. & adv.* in the middle; halfway. **—n.** the part of a fair, circus, etc. where side shows, rides, etc. are located.

Mid·west (mid′west′), *n.* the Middle West.

Mid·west·ern (mid′wes′tərn), *adj.* of, in, or having to do with the Middle West.

mid·wife (mid′wīf), *n.* a woman who takes care of women in childbirth. **—mid′wives,** *pl.*

mid·win·ter (mid′win′tər), *n.* **1.** the middle of winter. **2.** the period around December 22.

mien (mēn), *n.* the way a person looks or carries himself; manner; bearing.

might (mīt), past tense of **may.** *Might* is also used as a helping verb with about the same meaning as *may*, but often showing a bit of doubt [It *might* be raining there. I *might* go.]

might (mīt), *n.* great strength, force, or power [Pull with all your *might*.] **—with might and main,** using one's full strength.

might·y (mīt′ē), *adj.* **1.** very strong; powerful [a *mighty* blow]. **2.** great; very large [a *mighty* forest]. **—adv.** very; extremely: *used only in everyday talk* [*mighty* tired]. **—might′i·er,** *compar.;* **might′i·est,** *superl.* **—might′i·ly,** *adv.* **—might′i·ness,** *n.*

mi·gnon·ette (min yə net′), *n.* a plant with small, sweet-smelling, pale green flowers.

mi·graine (mī′grān), *n.* a very painful kind of headache, usually on only one side of the head.

mi·grant (mī′grənt), *adj.* migrating; migratory. —*n.* a person, bird, or animal that migrates.

mignonette

mi·grate (mī′grāt), *v.* **1.** to move from one place or country to another, especially in order to make a new home. **2.** to move from one region to another when the season changes, as some birds do in the spring and fall. —**mi′grat·ed,** *p.t. & p.p.;* **mi′grat·ing,** *pr.p.* —**mi·gra′tion,** *n.*

mi·gra·to·ry (mī′grə tôr′ē), *adj.* that migrates, or moves from one place to another [*Migratory* workers travel about from one job to another.]

mi·ka·do or **Mi·ka·do** (mi kä′dō), *n.* a title for the emperor of Japan, used by foreigners but not the Japanese. —**mi·ka′dos,** *pl.*

mike (mīk), *n.* a microphone: *a slang word.*

mi·la·dy or **mi·la·di** (mi lā′dē), *n.* a polite title used in speaking to or of an English woman of the upper classes.

Mi·lan (mi lan′), *n.* a city in northern Italy.

milch (milch), *adj.* that gives milk; raised for its milk [a *milch* cow].

mild (mīld), *adj.* **1.** gentle; not harsh or severe [a *mild* winter; a *mild* punishment]. **2.** having a weak taste; not strong or sharp [a *mild* cheese]. —**mild′ly,** *adv.* —**mild′ness,** *n.*

mil·dew (mil′dōō *or* mil′dyōō), *n.* a fungus that appears as a furry, white coating on plants or on damp, warm paper, cloth, etc. —*v.* to become coated with mildew.

mile (mīl), *n.* a measure of length, equal to 5,280 feet. A **nautical mile, air mile,** or **geographical mile** is about 6,076 feet.

mile·age (mīl′ij), *n.* **1.** total number of miles [What is the *mileage* from Boston to Chicago?] **2.** money given for traveling expenses, at the rate of a certain amount for each mile. **3.** the average number of miles an automobile, etc. will go on a gallon of fuel.

mile·post (mīl′pōst), *n.* a signpost showing the distance in miles to some place or places.

mile·stone (mīl′stōn), *n.* **1.** a stone showing the distance in miles to some place or places. **2.** an important happening in history, in someone's life, etc.

mil·i·tant (mil′i tənt), *adj.* ready to fight,

milepost

especially for some cause or idea [a *militant* defender of freedom]. —*n.* a militant person. —**mil′i·tan·cy,** *n.* —**mil′i·tant·ly,** *adv.*

mil·i·ta·rism (mil′i tə riz′m), *n.* the policy of keeping strong armed forces and preparing for war; warlike spirit. —**mil′i·ta·rist,** *n.*

mil·i·ta·ris·tic (mil′i tə ris′tik), *adj.* fond of war or preparing for war; warlike.

mil·i·ta·rize (mil′i tə rīz′), *v.* **1.** to build up the armed forces of in preparing for war. **2.** to fill with warlike spirit. —**mil′i·ta·rized′,** *p.t. & p.p.;* **mil′i·ta·riz′ing,** *pr.p.* —**mil′i·ta·ri·za′tion,** *n.*

mil·i·tar·y (mil′ə ter′ē), *adj.* **1.** of, for, or by soldiers, an army, etc. [a *military* band; *military* law]. **2.** of or for war. —*n.* soldiers; the army [The *military* took charge.]

mil·i·tate (mil′ə tāt), *v.* to have an effect; work; operate [Careless habits *militate* against chances of success.] —**mil′i·tat·ed,** *p.t. & p.p.;* **mil′i·tat·ing,** *pr.p.*

mi·li·tia (mə lish′ə), *n.* a group of citizens who are not regular soldiers, but who get some military training for service in an emergency.

milk (milk), *n.* **1.** a white liquid formed in special glands of female mammals for suckling their young. The milk that is a common food comes from cows. **2.** any liquid or juice like this [*Milk* of magnesia is a white liquid, made of magnesia in water.] —*v.* **1.** to squeeze milk out from a cow, goat, etc. **2.** to get money, ideas, etc. from, as if by milking. —**milk′er,** *n.* —**milk′ing,** *n.*

milk·maid (milk′mād), *n.* a girl or woman who milks cows or who works in a dairy.

milk·man (milk′man), *n.* a man who sells or delivers milk. —**milk′men,** *pl.*

milk shake, a drink of milk, flavoring, and ice cream, mixed until frothy.

milk·sop (milk′säp), *n.* a man or boy who is weak and timid; sissy.

milk·weed (milk′wēd), *n.* a plant with a milky juice in the stems and leaves and large pods holding many seeds with silky fibers on them.

milk·y (mil′kē), *adj.* **1.** like milk; white as milk. **2.** of or containing milk. —**milk′i·er,** *compar.;* **milk′i·est,** *superl.* —**milk′i·ness,** *n.*

Milky Way, a broad band of cloudy light seen across the sky at night. It is made up of billions of stars that are very far away.

milkweed pods and seeds

mill (mil), *n.* **1.** a building with machinery for grinding grain into flour or meal. **2.** a machine for grinding, crushing, cutting, etc. [a coffee *mill*]. **3.** a factory [a steel *mill*]. —*v.* **1.** to grind, make, form, etc. in or as in a mill. **2.** to put ridges in the edge of [to *mill* a coin]. **3.** to move slowly in a confused way [The crowd was *milling* around outside the stadium.]

mill (mil), *n.* one tenth of a cent; $.001. A mill is not a coin but it is used in figuring, especially for taxes.

mil·len·ni·um (mi len′i əm), *n.* **1.** a thousand years. **2.** in the belief of many Christians, the period of a thousand years during which Christ is expected to return and reign on earth. **3.** a period of peace and happiness for everyone. —**mil·len′ni·ums** or **mil·len·ni·a** (mi len′i ə), *pl.* —**mil·len′ni·al,** *adj.*

mill·er (mil′ər), *n.* **1.** a person who owns or works in a mill where grain is ground. **2.** a moth with wings that look dusty like the clothes of a miller.

mil·let (mil′it), *n.* **1.** a cereal grass grown for hay. **2.** its small seeds, or grain, used for food in Asia and Europe.

mil·li·gram or **mil·li·gramme** (mil′ə gram), *n.* a weight equal to one thousandth of a gram.

mil·li·me·ter or **mil·li·me·tre** (mil′ə mē′tər), *n.* one thousandth of a meter, or .03937 inch.

mil·li·ner (mil′ə nər), *n.* a person who designs, makes, or sells women's hats.

mil·li·ner·y (mil′ə ner′ē), *n.* **1.** women's hats. **2.** the work or business of a milliner.

mil·lion (mil′yən), *n. & adj.* a thousand thousands; the number 1,000,000.

mil·lion·aire (mil yən er′), *n.* a person who has at least a million dollars, pounds, etc.; very wealthy person.

mil·lionth (mil′yənth), *adj.* last in a series of a million. —*n.* **1.** the millionth one. **2.** one of the million equal parts of something.

mill·pond (mil′pänd), *n.* a pond from which water flows for driving a mill wheel.

mill·race (mil′rās), *n.* **1.** the stream of water that drives a mill wheel. **2.** the channel in which it runs.

mill·stone (mil′stōn), *n.* **1.** either of a pair of flat, round stones between which grain is ground. **2.** a heavy burden.

mill wheel, the wheel that drives the machinery in a mill, usually a water wheel.

Mil·ton, John (mil′t'n), 1608-1674; English poet and political writer.

Mil·wau·kee (mil wô′kē), *n.* a city in southeastern Wisconsin.

man turning a millstone

mime (mīm), *n.* a clown or mimic. —*v.* to act as a mime; imitate, usually without speaking. —**mimed,** *p.t. & p.p.;* **mim′ing,** *pr.p.*

mim·e·o·graph (mim′i ə graf), *n.* a machine for making copies of written or typewritten matter by using a stencil. —*v.* to make copies of on such a machine.

mim·ic (mim′ik), *v.* **1.** to imitate someone so as to make fun of him. **2.** to copy closely; imitate [Parakeets *mimic* human voices.] —*n.* a person, especially an actor, who mimics; imitator. —*adj.* **1.** that mimics; imitative. **2.** make-believe; not real; mock [*mimic* tears]. —**mim′icked,** *p.t. & p.p.;* **mim′icking,** *pr.p.*

boy mimicking a monkey

mim·ic·ry (mim′ik rē), *n.* **1.** the art of imitating, or an example of this. **2.** the way in which some living thing looks like another or like some natural object. —**mim′ic·ries,** *pl.*

mi·mo·sa (mi mō′sə), *n.* a tree of warm climates, with white, yellow, or pink flowers.

min., abbreviation for **minimum, minute** or **minutes.**

min·a·ret (min ə ret′), *n.* a high tower on a mosque with a balcony from which a crier calls Moslems to prayer.

mince (mins), *v.* **1.** to cut into small pieces; hash [to *mince* onions]. **2.** to make weaker or less direct [He *minced* no words.] **3.** to act, move, or say in a way that is too careful or dainty. —*n.* mincemeat. —**not mince matters,** to speak frankly. —**minced,** *p.t. & p.p.;* **minc′ing,** *pr.p.*

minaret

mince·meat (mins′mēt), *n.* a mixture of chopped apples, raisins, suet, spices, and, at one time, meat, used as a filling for a pie (called a **mince pie**).

minc·ing (min′sing), *adj.* elegant or dainty in an unnatural way; affected [a *mincing* smile].

mind (mīnd), *n.* **1.** the part of a person that thinks, reasons, feels, decides, etc.; intellect [The *mind* was once thought of as apart from the body.] **2.** what one thinks or intends; opinion, desire, purpose, etc. [I've changed my *mind* about going.] **3.** the ability to think or reason; intelligence [Have you lost your *mind?*] **4.** the act of remembering; memory [That brings to *mind* a funny story.] **5.** a very intelligent person [Who are the great *minds* of our day?] —*v.* **1.** to pay attention to; heed [*Mind* your manners.] **2.** to obey [The dog *minds* its master.] **3.** to take care of; look after [Will you *mind* the store while I'm out?] **4.** to care about; object to [I don't *mind* the noise.] **5.** to remember: *now seldom used.* —**bear in mind** or **keep in mind,** to remember. —**be of one mind,** to agree about something. —**give a person a piece of one's mind,** to scold a person. —**have a mind to,** to be inclined to; intend to.

—have half a mind to, to be a little inclined to. **—have in mind,** to think of. **—keep one's mind on,** to pay attention to. **—make up one's mind,** to decide. **—never mind,** don't be concerned. **—on one's mind,** filling one's thoughts. **—out of one's mind, 1.** mentally ill. **2.** wildly excited, as with worry.

mind·ed (mīn′did), *adj.* having a certain kind of mind: *used mainly in words formed with a hyphen* [strong-*minded*].

mind·ful (mīnd′fəl), *adj.* keeping something in mind; careful [Be *mindful* of the danger.]

mind·less (mīnd′lis), *adj.* **1.** having a poor mind; stupid or foolish. **2.** careless or heedless.

mine (mīn), *pron.* the one or the ones that belong to me: the form of *my* used when it is not followed by a noun [This book is *mine*. *Mine* are the red ones.] *Mine* is sometimes used, especially in poetry, as an adjective meaning "my" ["*Mine* eyes have seen the glory"].

mine (mīn), *n.* **1.** a large hole made in the earth from which to dig out coal, ores, etc. **2.** a large supply or store [a *mine* of information]. **3.** an explosive hidden in the ground or in water to blow up enemy troops, ships, etc. **—v. 1.** to dig a mine for ores, coal, etc. **2.** to get from a mine [to *mine* copper]. **3.** to work in a mine. **4.** to place explosive mines under or in [to *mine* a harbor]. **—mined,** *p.t. & p.p.;* **min′ing,** *pr.p.*

min·er (mīn′ər), *n.* a person whose work is digging ore, coal, etc. in a mine.

min·er·al (min′ər əl), *n.* a substance that has been formed in the earth by nature; especially, a solid substance that was never animal or vegetable [Iron, granite, and salt are *minerals*. Oil and coal are sometimes called *minerals*.] **—adj.** of or full of minerals [*mineral* water].

min·er·al·o·gy (min′ər al′ə jē), *n.* the science of minerals. **—min′er·al′o·gist,** *n.*

Mi·ner·va (mi nûr′və), *n.* the Roman goddess of wisdom and of arts and crafts. The Greeks called this goddess *Athena*.

min·gle (ming′g'l), *v.* **1.** to mix or be mixed together; blend [*mingled* feelings of pleasure and disappointment]. **2.** to join with others [We *mingled* with the crowd to watch the parade.] **—min′gled,** *p.t. & p.p.;* **min′gling,** *pr.p.*

min·i-, a prefix meaning "very small," "very short," etc. [A *miniskirt* is a very short skirt.]

min·i·a·ture (min′i ə chər *or* min′i chər), *n.* **1.** a very small copy or model [We bought a *miniature* of the Liberty Bell as a souvenir.] **2.** a very small painting, especially a portrait. **—adj.** that is a miniature [a *miniature* railroad].

min·i·mize (min′ə mīz), *v.* **1.** to make as small as possible [Proper care will *minimize* the danger of fire.] **2.** to make seem small or unimportant [He *minimized* his act of bravery.] **—min′i·mized,** *p.t. & p.p.;* **min′i·miz·ing,** *pr.p.*

min·i·mum (min′ə məm), *n.* **1.** the smallest amount or number that is possible or allowed [The patient must have a *minimum* of excitement.] **2.** the lowest degree or point reached [The temperature dropped to a *minimum* of 14°.] **—adj.** smallest or least possible or allowed [a law on *minimum* wages]. **—min′i·mums** or **min·i·ma** (min′ə mə), *pl.*

min·ing (mīn′ing), *n.* the work of digging ore, coal, etc. from mines.

min·ion (min′yən), *n.* a trusted or faithful follower, often one who serves in a slavish way [Policemen are often called "*minions* of the law."]

min·is·ter (min′is tər), *n.* **1.** a person who is the spiritual head of a church, especially a Protestant church; pastor. **2.** a person in charge of some department of government, as in Great Britain [the *Minister* of Education]. **3.** an official who represents his government in a foreign country. He ranks below an ambassador. **—v.** to give help; serve or attend [to *minister* to the poor]. **—min·is·te·ri·al** (min′is tir′i əl), *adj.*

min·is·trant (min′is trənt), *adj.* ministering. **—n.** a person who ministers.

min·is·tra·tion (min′is trā′shən), *n.* the act of helping others; service.

min·is·try (min′is trē), *n.* **1.** the office or duties of a minister, or the time that he serves. **2.** church ministers or government ministers as a group. **3.** a department of government that has a minister as its head. **4.** the act of ministering, or helping others. **—min′is·tries,** *pl.*

mink (mingk), *n.* **1.** an animal somewhat like a large weasel, that lives on land and in the water. **2.** its costly thick, brown fur.

Min·ne·ap·o·lis (min′i ap′'l is), *n.* a city in eastern Minnesota.

Min·ne·so·ta (min′i sō′tə), *n.* a State

mink (2 ft. long)

in the north central part of the United States: abbreviated **Minn.**

min·now (min′ō), *n.* **1.** a very small fish of the carp family, found in fresh water and used as bait. **2.** any very small fish like this.

mi·nor (mī′nər), *adj.* **1.** smaller in size, importance, amount, etc.; lesser [a *minor* part of one's time; a *minor* traffic accident]. **2.** in music, that is separated from the next tone by a half step instead of a full step [a *minor* interval]; also, that is or has to do with either of two musical scales, especially one with half steps after the second and seventh tones going up and after the sixth and third tones going down: see also **major.** **—n.** a person under the age at which he is said by law to become an adult, usually the age of 21.

mi·nor·i·ty (mə nôr′ə tē), *n.* **1.** the smaller part or number; less than half [A *minority* of the Senate voted for the law.] **2.** a small group of people of a different race, religion, etc. from the main group of which it is a part. **3.** the time of being a minor, or not yet an adult. —**mi·nor'i·ties,** *pl.*

Min·o·taur (min'ə tôr), *n.* a monster in a Greek myth, with the head of a bull and the body of a man. It was kept in a labyrinth in Crete, where it was killed by Theseus.

min·strel (min'strəl), *n.* **1.** an entertainer during the Middle Ages, as at the court of a lord, or one who traveled from place to place singing and reciting poems. **2.** a performer in a minstrel show. *See next entry.*

minstrel show, an earlier type of stage show put on by performers with faces painted black, telling jokes, singing songs, etc.

Minotaur

min·strel·sy (min'strəl sē), *n.* **1.** the art or work of a minstrel. **2.** a group of minstrels. **3.** a collection of their songs.

mint (mint), *n.* **1.** a place where a government makes coins. **2.** a large amount [He made a *mint* of money.] —*adj.* new; not used [a book in *mint* condition]. *v.* to make into coins, as silver.

mint (mint), *n.* **1.** a plant with a pleasant smell whose leaves are used for flavoring, as peppermint and spearmint. **2.** a piece of candy flavored with mint.

min·u·end (min'yoo end), *n.* the number from which another number is to be subtracted [In the problem 9 − 5 = 4, 9 is the *minuend*.]

min·u·et (min yoo et'), *n.* **1.** a slow, graceful dance, popular in the 18th century. **2.** music for such a dance.

mi·nus (mī'nəs), *prep.* **1.** less; made smaller by subtracting [Four *minus* two equals two (4 − 2 = 2).] **2.** without: *used only in everyday talk* [This cup is *minus* a handle.] —*adj.* **1.** less than zero; negative [The temperature is *minus* 5°, or five degrees below zero.] **2.** a little less than [a rating of A *minus*]. —*n.* the sign −, put before a number or quantity that is to be subtracted or one that is less than zero: *its full name is the* **minus sign.**

min·ute (min'it), *n.* **1.** any of the 60 equal parts of an hour; 60 seconds. **2.** any of the sixty equal parts of a degree of an arc. **3.** a short period of time; moment [He'll be done in a *minute*.] **4.** a particular time [Come home this *minute*!] **5.** minutes, *pl.* a written record of what happened during a meeting [The club's secretary writes the *minutes*.]

mi·nute (mī noot' *or* mī nyoot'), *adj.* **1.** very small; tiny. **2.** paying attention to small details; exact [She keeps a *minute* account of expenses.] —**mi·nute'ly,** *adv.* —**mi·nute'ness,** *n.*

min·ute·man (min'it man), *n.* a member of the American citizen army at the time of the Revolutionary War, who volunteered to be ready to fight at a minute's notice. —**min'ute·men,** *pl.*

mi·nu·ti·ae (mi nyoo'shi ē), *n.pl.* small or unimportant details.

minx (mingks), *n.* a bold or saucy girl.

mir·a·cle (mir'ə k'l), *n.* **1.** a happening that seems to be against the known laws of nature or science, thought of as caused by God or a god [the *miracles* in the Bible]. **2.** an amazing or remarkable thing; marvel [It will be a *miracle* if we win the game.]

mi·rac·u·lous (mi rak'yoo ləs), *adj.* **1.** of or having to do with miracles. **2.** very remarkable or amazing. —**mi·rac'u·lous·ly,** *adv.*

mi·rage (mi räzh'), *n.* an image caused by the reflection of light in such a way that something far away seems to be near and often looks like something else [The pool of water often seen up ahead on a hot highway is a *mirage* caused by the reflection of the sky.]

mire (mīr), *n.* **1.** an area of wet, soft ground; bog. **2.** deep mud. —*v.* to sink or get stuck in mire. —**mired,** *p.t. & p.p.;* **mir'ing,** *pr.p.*

mir·ror (mir'ər), *n.* **1.** a smooth surface that reflects light; especially, a piece of glass coated with silver on the back; looking glass. **2.** anything that gives a true description [A good novel is a *mirror* of life.] —*v.* to reflect as in a mirror [The moon was *mirrored* in the lake.]

mirth (mûrth), *n.* joyfulness or gay fun, usually shown by laughter. —**mirth'less,** *adj.*

mirth·ful (mûrth'fəl), *adj.* full of mirth or showing mirth; merry; gay.

mis-, a prefix meaning "wrong," "wrongly," "bad," "badly" [To *misplace* is to place wrongly. *Misconduct* is bad conduct.]

mis·ad·ven·ture (mis'əd ven'chər), *n.* an unlucky accident; bad luck; mishap.

mis·an·thrope (mis'ən thrōp), *n.* a person who hates people or does not trust anybody. —**mis·an·throp·ic** (mis'ən thräp'ik), *adj.*

mis·ap·ply (mis ə plī'), *v.* to use in a wrong or wasteful way [to *misapply* one's energy]. —**mis·ap·plied',** *p.t. & p.p.;* **mis·ap·ply'ing,** *pr.p.* —**mis·ap·pli·ca·tion** (mis'ap lə kā'shən), *n.*

mis·ap·pre·hend (mis'ap ri hend'), *v.* to misunderstand. —**mis'ap·pre·hen'sion,** *n.*

mis·ap·pro·pri·ate (mis'ə prō'pri āt), *v.* to use in a wrong or dishonest way [The lawyer *misappropriated* his client's money.] —**mis'-ap·pro'pri·at·ed,** *p.t. & p.p.;* **mis'ap·pro'-pri·at·ing,** *pr.p.* —**mis'ap·pro'pri·a'tion,** *n.*

mis·be·have (mis'bi hāv'), *v.* to behave in a bad way; do what one is not supposed to do. —**mis'be·haved',** *p.t. & p.p.;* **mis'be·hav'-ing,** *pr.p.* —**mis·be·hav·ior** (mis'bi hāv'yər), *n.*

misc., abbreviation for **miscellaneous.**

mis·cal·cu·late (mis kal'kyoo lāt), *v.* to make a mistake in figuring or planning; misjudge. —**mis·cal·cu·lat·ed,** *p.t. & p.p.;* **mis·cal'-cu·lat·ing,** *pr.p.* —**mis'cal·cu·la'tion,** *n.*

mis·call (mis kôl'), *v.* to call by a wrong name.

mis·car·riage (mis kar'ij), *n.* **1.** failure to carry out what was intended [Putting an innocent man in prison is a *miscarriage* of justice.] **2.** the birth of a baby before it has developed enough to live.

mis·car·ry (mis kar′ē), *v.* **1.** to go wrong; fail [Our careful plans *miscarried*.] **2.** to fail to arrive, as mail that is lost. **3.** to have a miscarriage. **—mis·car′ried**, *p.t. & p.p.;* **mis·car′ry·ing**, *pr.p.*

mis·cel·la·ne·ous (mis′′l ā′ni əs), *adj.* of many different kinds; mixed; varied [On this shelf is a *miscellaneous* assortment of books.]

mis·cel·la·ny (mis′′l ā′nē), *n.* a mixed collection; especially, a book containing various writings. **—mis′cel·la′nies**, *pl.*

mis·chance (mis chans′), *n.* an unlucky accident; bad luck; misfortune.

mis·chief (mis′chif), *n.* **1.** harm or damage [Gossip can cause great *mischief*.] **2.** action that causes harm, damage, or trouble. **3.** a person, especially a child, who annoys or teases. **4.** a playful trick; prank. **5.** gay, harmless teasing; playful spirits [a child full of *mischief*].

mis·chie·vous (mis′chi vəs), *adj.* **1.** causing some slight harm, or annoying, often in fun; naughty. **2.** full of playful tricks and teasing; prankish. **3.** causing harm or damage; harmful [*mischievous* slander].

mis·con·ceive (mis kən sēv′), *v.* to get a wrong idea about; misunderstand. **—mis·con·ceived′**, *p.t. & p.p.;* **mis·con·ceiv′ing**, *pr.p.*

mis·con·cep·tion (mis′kən sep′shən), *n.* a misunderstanding; wrong idea.

mis·con·duct (mis kän′dukt), *n.* bad or wrong conduct or behavior. **—v.** (mis kən dukt′), **1.** to behave badly. **2.** to manage badly or dishonestly.

mis·con·struc·tion (mis′kən struk′shən), *n.* the act of judging or explaining in a wrong way; misunderstanding.

mis·con·strue (mis kən strōō′), *v.* to think of or explain in a wrong way; misunderstand [He *misconstrued* her silence as approval.] **—mis·con·strued′**, *p.t. & p.p.;* **mis·con·stru′ing**, *pr.p.*

mis·cre·ant (mis′kri ənt), *n.* a person who does wrong or commits a crime; villain; criminal. **—adj.** doing wrong; evil and wicked.

mis·deed (mis dēd′), *n.* a wrong or wicked act; crime, sin, etc.

mis·de·mean·or (mis′di mēn′ər), *n.* a breaking of the law that is less serious than a crime and brings a lesser punishment [It is a *misdemeanor* to throw litter in the streets.]

mis·di·rect (mis də rekt′), *v.* to direct wrongly or badly [to *misdirect* a letter].

mis·do·ing (mis dōō′ing), *n.* wrongdoing.

mi·ser (mī′zər), *n.* a greedy, stingy person who saves up money without ever using it. **—mi′ser·ly**, *adj.*

mis·er·a·ble (miz′ər ə b′l), *adj.* **1.** very unhappy; sad; wretched. **2.** causing pain, unhappiness, etc. [a *miserable* headache]. **3.** bad, poor, unpleasant, etc. [a *miserable* performance]. **—mis′er·a·bly**, *adv.*

mis·er·y (miz′ər ē), *n.* **1.** a condition in which one suffers or is very unhappy. **2.** something that causes such suffering, as illness or poverty. **—mis′er·ies**, *pl.*

mis·fire (mis fir′), *v.* to fail to go off; fail to work right [The rocket *misfired*.] **—mis·fired′**, *p.t. & p.p.;* **mis·fir′ing**, *pr.p.*

mis·fit (mis′fit), *n.* **1.** anything that does not fit right, as a suit that is too small. **2.** a person who does not get along well in his job, with certain people, etc. **—v.** (mis fit′), to fit badly. *For principal parts see* **fit.**

mis·for·tune (mis fôr′chən), *n.* **1.** bad luck; trouble. **2.** an accident that brings trouble.

mis·give (mis giv′), *v.* to cause fear, doubt, or worry in [His heart *misgave* him.] *For principal parts see* **give.**

mis·giv·ing (mis giv′ing), *n.* a feeling of fear, doubt, worry, etc. [He had *misgivings* about whether he could do the job.]

mis·gov·ern (mis guv′ərn), *v.* to govern or rule badly. **—mis·gov′ern·ment**, *n.*

mis·guid·ed (mis gīd′id), *adj.* led into making mistakes or doing wrong [The *misguided* boy had run away from home.]

mis·han·dle (mis han′d′l), *v.* to handle or manage badly or roughly; abuse. **—mis·han′dled**, *p.t. & p.p.;* **mis·han·dling**, *pr.p.*

mis·hap (mis′hap), *n.* an accident that brings trouble; bad luck; misfortune.

mis·in·form (mis in fôrm′), *v.* to give wrong facts or ideas to. **—mis·in·for·ma′tion**, *n.*

mis·in·ter·pret (mis′in tûr′prit), *v.* to give a wrong meaning to; explain or understand in a wrong way. **—mis·in·ter′pre·ta′tion**, *n.*

mis·judge (mis juj′), *v.* to judge unfairly or wrongly. **—mis·judged′**, *p.t. & p.p.;* **mis·judg′ing**, *pr.p.*

mis·lay (mis lā′), *v.* to put something in a place and then forget where it is. **—mis·laid** (mis·lād′), *p.t. & p.p.;* **mis·lay′ing**, *pr.p.*

mis·lead (mis lēd′), *v.* **1.** to lead in a wrong direction [That old map will *mislead* you.] **2.** to cause to believe what is not true; deceive [He tried to *mislead* us into thinking he would help.] **3.** to lead into wrongdoing [He was *misled* by criminals who taught him to steal.] **—mis·led** (mis led′), *p.t. & p.p.;* **mis·lead′ing**, *pr.p.*

mis·man·age (mis man′ij), *v.* to manage in a bad or dishonest way. **—mis·man′aged**, *p.t. & p.p.;* **mis·man′ag·ing**, *pr.p.* **—mis·man′age·ment**, *n.*

mis·name (mis nām′), *v.* to call by a wrong name. **—mis·named′**, *p.t. & p.p.;* **mis·nam′ing**, *pr.p.*

mis·no·mer (mis nō′mər), *n.* a wrong name or one that does not fit ["Fish" is a *misnomer* for a whale.]

mis·place (mis plās′), *v.* **1.** to put in a wrong place [He *misplaced* the book of poems in the science section.] **2.** to give trust, love, etc. to one who does not deserve it [I *misplaced* my confidence in you.] **3.** to mislay: *used only in everyday talk.* —**mis·placed′,** *p.t. & p.p.;* **mis·plac′ing,** *pr.p.*

mis·play (mis plā′), *v.* to play wrongly or badly, as in a game. —*n.* a wrong or bad play.

mis·print (mis′print), *n.* a mistake in printing.

mis·pro·nounce (mis prə nouns′), *v.* to pronounce in a wrong way [Some people *mispronounce* "cavalry" as "calvary."] —**mis·pro·nounced′,** *p.t. & p.p.;* **mis·pro·nounc′ing,** *pr.p.* —**mis·pro·nun·ci·a·tion** (mis′prə nun′si ā′shən), *n.*

mis·quote (mis kwōt′), *v.* to quote wrongly. —**mis·quot′ed,** *p.t. & p.p.;* **mis·quot′ing,** *pr.p.*

mis·read (mis rēd′), *v.* to read in the wrong way, especially so that one gets the wrong meaning [to *misread* directions]. —**mis·read** (mis-red′), *p.t. & p.p.;* **mis·read′ing,** *pr.p.*

mis·rep·re·sent (mis′rep ri zent′), *v.* to give a wrong or false idea of, on purpose. —**mis′-rep·re·sen·ta′tion,** *n.*

mis·rule (mis rōōl′), *v.* to rule in a bad or unfair way. —*n.* **1.** bad or unfair government. **2.** disorder or riot. —**mis·ruled′,** *p.t. & p.p.;* **mis·rul′ing,** *pr.p.*

miss (mis), *v.* **1.** to fail to hit, meet, reach, get, catch, see, hear, etc. [The arrow *missed* the target. We *missed* our train. I *missed* the last line of the joke.] **2.** to let go by; fail to take [You *missed* your turn.] **3.** to escape or avoid [He just *missed* being hit.] **4.** to fail to do, keep, have, attend, etc. [She *missed* a class yesterday.] **5.** to notice or feel the absence or loss of [I suddenly *missed* my watch. Do you *miss* your friends back home?] —*n.* a failure to hit, meet, get, etc.

miss (mis), *n.* **1. Miss,** a title used before the name of a girl or unmarried woman [*Miss* Smith]. **2.** a young unmarried woman or girl [coats in *misses′* sizes]. —**miss′es,** *pl.*

Miss., abbreviation for **Mississippi.**

mis·sal (mis′'l), *n.* a book of prayers used in celebrating Mass in the Roman Catholic Church.

mis·shap·en (mis shāp′'n), *adj.* badly shaped or formed; deformed.

mis·sile (mis′'l), *n.* a weapon or other object made to be thrown or shot through the air [Bullets, arrows, some rockets, etc. are *missiles*.]

miss·ing (mis′ing), *adj.* absent, lost, gone, lacking, etc. [Tim found the *missing* book.]

mis·sion (mish′ən), *n.* **1.** the special duty or errand that a person or group is sent out to do, as by a church, government, air force, etc. [a *mission* to make a treaty; a *mission* to convert people to Christianity; a *mission* to bomb a factory]. **2.** a group of missionaries, or the place where they live, preach, etc. [the foreign *missions* of a church]. **3.** a group of persons sent to a foreign government to carry on dealings, as for trade, a treaty, etc. **4.** a special task to which a person devotes his life; calling [Joan of Arc's *mission* was to set France free.]

mis·sion·ar·y (mish′ər er′ē), *n.* a person sent out by a church to spread its religion in a foreign country. —*adj.* having to do with religious missions. —**mis′sion·ar′ies,** *pl.*

Mis·sis·sip·pi (mis′ə sip′ē), *n.* **1.** a river in the United States, flowing from Minnesota to the Gulf of Mexico. **2.** a State in the southeastern part of the United States: abbreviated **Miss.**

mis·sive (mis′iv), *n.* a letter or note.

Mis·sour·i (mi zoor′ē *or* mi zoor′ə), *n.* **1.** a river in the United States, flowing from Montana into the Mississippi River. **2.** a State in the central part of the United States: abbreviated **Mo.**

mis·spell (mis spel′), *v.* to spell wrongly. *For principal parts see* **spell.** —**mis·spell′ing,** *n.*

mis·spent (mis spent′), *adj.* spent in a wrong or wasteful way [a *misspent* life].

mis·state (mis stāt′), *v.* to state wrongly or falsely. —**mis·stat′ed,** *p.t. & p.p.;* **mis·stat′ing,** *pr.p.* —**mis·state′ment,** *n.*

mis·step (mis step′), *n.* **1.** a wrong or clumsy step. **2.** a mistake in one's behavior.

mist (mist), *n.* **1.** a large mass of tiny drops of water in the air, like a fog but not so thick [the morning *mist* along the river bank]. **2.** anything that blurs or makes it hard to see or understand something; haze or film [through a *mist* of tears; lost in the *mists* of the past]. —*v.* to cover by a mist; blur or dim [windows *misted* by steam].

mis·take (mis tāk′), *n.* an idea, answer, act, etc. that is wrong; error or blunder. —*v.* **1.** to get a wrong idea of; misunderstand [You *mistake* his real purpose.] **2.** to think that someone or something is some other person or thing [to *mistake* John for his brother]. —**mis·took′,** *p.t.;* **mis·tak′en,** *p.p.;* **mis·tak′ing,** *pr.p.*

mis·tak·en (mis tāk′'n), *adj.* wrong; making or showing a mistake [a *mistaken* idea]. —**mis·tak′en·ly,** *adv.*

Mis·ter (mis′tər), *n.* a title used before the name of a man or his office, and usually written *Mr.* [*Mr.* Brown; *Mr.* President].

mis·tle·toe (mis′'l tō), *n.* an evergreen plant with waxy, white berries, growing as a parasite on certain trees. Sprigs of mistletoe are used as a Christmas decoration.

mistletoe

mis·took (mis took′) past tense of **mistake.**

mis·treat (mis trēt′), *v.* to treat badly; abuse.

mis·tress (mis′tris), *n.* **1.** a woman who rules others or has control over something, as the owner of an animal or slave, the head of a household or school, etc. Also, a country or thing thought of as a female ruler [England was once called *Mistress* of the seas.] **2.** a woman who lives with a man without being married to him. **3.** a sweetheart: *now seldom used.* **4. Mistress,** a title used in earlier times before the name of a woman: now replaced by *Mrs.* or *Miss.*

mis·trust (mis trust′), *n.* a lack of trust or confidence; suspicion; doubt [He felt *mistrust* of the stranger.] —*v.* to have no trust or confidence in; doubt. —**mis·trust′ful,** *adj.*

mist·y (mis'tē), *adj.* **1.** of, like, or covered by mist. **2.** blurred, as if by mist; vague [a *misty* idea]. —**mist'i·er,** *compar.;* **mist'i·est,** *superl.* —**mist'i·ness,** *n.*

mis·un·der·stand (mis'un dər stand'), *v.* to understand in a way that is wrong; give a wrong meaning to. —**mis·un·der·stood** (mis'un-dər stood'), *p.t. & p.p.;* **mis'un·der·stand'-ing,** *pr.p.*

mis·un·der·stand·ing (mis'un dər stan'ding), *n.* **1.** a failure to understand correctly; wrong idea of the meaning or purpose of something. **2.** a quarrel or disagreement.

mis·use (mis yōōz'), *v.* **1.** to treat badly; abuse. **2.** to use in a wrong way [to *misuse* one's time]. —*n.* (mis yōōs'), the use of something in a way that is wrong [the *misuse* of an adverb for an adjective]. —**mis·used',** *p.t. & p.p.;* **mis·us'ing,** *pr.p.*

mite (mīt), *n.* **1.** a tiny animal of the spider family that lives as a parasite on plants or animals. **2.** a very small sum of money **3.** a tiny thing, amount, etc.; bit.

mi·ter (mī'tər), *n.* **1.** a tall cap worn by bishops during certain ceremonies. **2.** a corner joint formed by fitting together two pieces cut at an angle. —*v.* to fit together in a miter.

miter (*meaning 1*)

mit·i·gate (mit'ə gāt), *v.* to make or become milder or less severe [The aspirin helped to *mitigate* her pain.] —**mit'i·gat·ed,** *p.t. & p.p.;* **mit'i·gat·ing,** *pr.p.* —**mit'i·ga'-tion,** *n.*

mi·tre (mī'tər), *n. & v.* same as **miter.** —**mi'tred,** *p.t. & p.p.;* **mi'tring,** *pr.p.*

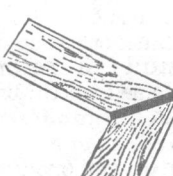
miter (*meaning 2*)

mitt (mit), *n.* **1.** a glove covering the forearm, but only part of the fingers. **2.** a mitten. **3.** a large, padded glove worn by baseball players, especially one without separate pouches for all the fingers [a catcher's *mitt*]. **4.** a padded mitten worn by boxers. **5.** a hand: *slang in this meaning.*

mit·ten (mit''n), *n.* a glove with a separate pouch for the thumb and another, larger pouch for the four fingers.

catcher's mitt

mix (miks), *v.* **1.** to put, stir, or come together to form a single, blended thing [*Mix* red and yellow paint to get orange. Oil and water won't *mix*.] **2.** to make by stirring together the necessary things [to *mix* a cake]. **3.** to join or combine [We try to *mix* work and play.] **4.** to get along in a friendly way; associate [He *mixes* well with all kinds of people.] —*n.* a mixture, or a group of things that are to be mixed together [a cake *mix*]. —**mix up, 1.** to mix thoroughly. **2.** to confuse. **3.** to involve [The mayor is *mixed up* in the scandal.] —**mixed** or **mixt** (mikst), *p.t. & p.p.;* **mix'ing,** *pr.p.*

mixed (mikst), *adj.* **1.** put or stirred together in a single blend. **2.** of different kinds [*mixed* nuts]. **3.** made up of both sexes [*mixed* company]. **4.** confused [He got his dates *mixed*.]

mixed number, a number that is a whole number and a fraction, as 6 7/8.

mix·er (mik'sər), *n.* **1.** a device for mixing things, as foods. **2.** a person thought of in the way he gets along with people [a poor *mixer*].

mix·ture (miks'chər), *n.* **1.** a mixing. **2.** something made by mixing [Punch is a *mixture* of fruit juices.]

mix-up (miks'up'), *n.* confusion or tangle.

miz·zen (miz''n), *n.* **1.** a fore-and-aft sail set on the mizzenmast. **2.** a mizzenmast.

miz·zen·mast (miz''n mast *or* miz''n məst), *n.* the mast closest to the stern of a ship with two or three masts.

Mlle., abbreviation for **Mademoiselle.** —**Mlles.,** *pl.*

MM., abbreviation for **Messieurs.**

mm., abbreviation for **millimeter** or **millimeters.**

Mme., abbreviation for **Madame.** —**Mmes.,** *pl.*

Mn, symbol for the chemical element *manganese.*

Mo, symbol for the chemical element *molybdenum.*

Mo., abbreviation for **Missouri.**

mo., abbreviation for **month.** —**mos.,** *pl.*

Mo·ab (mō'ab), *n.* an ancient kingdom mentioned in the Bible, east of the Dead Sea.

moan (mōn), *n.* **1.** a low, long sound of sorrow or pain. **2.** any sound like this [the *moan* of the wind]. —*v.* **1.** to make a moan or moans. **2.** to say with a moan. **3.** to complain.

moat (mōt), *n.* a deep, wide ditch dug around a castle, to keep enemies out. Moats were often filled with water.

moat

mob (mäb), *n.* **1.** a large crowd; especially, an excited crowd that pays no attention to law and order. **2.** the common people: *an unfriendly use.* **3.** a gang of criminals: *slang in this meaning.* —*v.* to crowd around and annoy, attack, admire, etc. —**mobbed,** *p.t. & p.p.;* **mob'bing,** *pr.p.*

mo·bile (mō'b'l *or* mō'bēl), *adj.* **1.** that can be moved quickly and easily [A house trailer is a *mobile* home.] **2.** showing changes in one's feelings by changes in looks [She has *mobile* features.]

---

fat, **ape,** **car,** **ten,** **ēven,** **hit,** **bīte,** **gō,** **hôrn,** **tōōl,** **book,** **up,** **fūr;**
get, **joy,** **yet,** **chin,** **she,** **thin,** **then;** **zh** = s in pleasure; **'** as in able (ā'b'l);
ə = a in ago, e in agent, i in sanity, o in confess, u in focus.

—*n.* (mō′bēl), a kind of sculpture made of flat pieces, rods, etc. that hang balanced from wires so as to move about easily. —**mo·bil·i·ty** (mō-bil′ə ti), *n.*

mo·bil·ize (mō′b'l īz), *v.* to make or become organized and ready, as for war [to *mobilize* the armed forces]. —**mo′bil·ized,** *p.t. & p.p.;* **mo′bil·iz·ing,** *pr.p.* —**mo′bil·i·za′tion,** *n.*

moc·ca·sin (mäk′ə s'n), *n.* **1.** a slipper made of soft leather, without a heel, as those once worn by American Indians. **2.** a poisonous snake found in the southeastern United States: *its full name is* **water moccasin.**

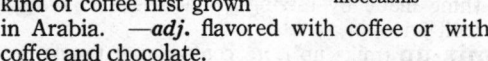
moccasins

mo·cha (mō′kə), *n.* a kind of coffee first grown in Arabia. —*adj.* flavored with coffee or with coffee and chocolate.

mock (mäk), *v.* **1.** to make fun of or scoff at; ridicule [Many scientists *mocked* Darwin's theories.] **2.** to make fun of by imitating or mimicking [It is cruel to *mock* a limping person.] **3.** to lead on and then disappoint [The weather *mocked* them by changing suddenly.] **4.** to defeat or make useless [The high wall *mocked* his hopes of escaping.] —*adj.* not genuine; false; pretended [a *mock* battle]. —**make a mock of,** to scoff at. —**mock′er,** *n.* —**mock′ing·ly,** *adv.*

mock·er·y (mäk′ər ē), *n.* **1.** the act of mocking, or making fun. **2.** a person or thing that deserves to be made fun of. **3.** a poor imitation or copy [The movie is a *mockery* of the novel.] **4.** a useless or disappointing effort [Rain made a *mockery* of our picnic.] —**mock′er·ies,** *pl.*

mock·ing·bird (mäk′ing būrd), *n.* a small bird of the southern United States that imitates the calls of other birds.

mod (mäd), *adj.* very fashionable, especially in a showy way: *used of young people or their clothes.*

mockingbird (10 in. long)

mode (mōd), *n.* **1.** a way of acting or doing something; method [a new *mode* of transportation]. **2.** style or fashion [girls dressed in the latest *mode*]. **3.** same as **mood** (of verbs).

mod·el (mäd′'l), *n.* **1.** a small copy of something [a *model* of the ship in a bottle]. **2.** a small figure made to serve as the plan for the final, larger thing [a clay *model* for a marble sculpture]. **3.** a person or thing that ought to be imitated [He is a very *model* of honesty.] **4.** a style or design [Our new car is a two-door *model*.] **5.** a person who poses for an artist or photographer. **6.** a

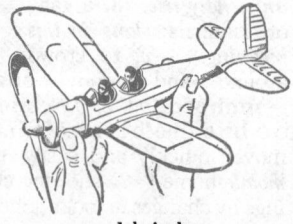
model airplane

person whose work is wearing clothes that are for sale, so that customers can see how they look when worn. —*adj.* **1.** that is a model [a *model* airplane]. **2.** that ought to be imitated; perfect [a *model* wife]. —*v.* **1.** to plan, form, or make, using a model as a guide [a church *modeled* after a Greek temple]. **2.** to make a piece of sculpture [to *model* a figure in clay]. **3.** to show how an article of clothing looks by wearing it [Will you *model* this coat for me?] **4.** to work as a model (*in meaning 5 or 6*). —**mod′eled** or **mod′-elled,** *p.t. & p.p.;* **mod′el·ing** or **mod′el·ling,** *pr.p.*

mod·er·ate (mäd′ər it), *adj.* **1.** neither very great, good, strong, etc. nor very small, bad, weak, etc.; reasonable or ordinary [a *moderate* fee; a *moderate* wind]. **2.** mild or gentle [a *moderate* reply to an angry letter]. —*n.* a person whose opinions, as in politics or religion, are not strong or extreme. —*v.* (mäd′ə rāt), **1.** to make or become less strong or extreme. **2.** to serve as chairman of a discussion or debate. —**mod′-er·at·ed,** *p.t. & p.p.;* **mod′er·at·ing,** *pr.p.* —**mod′er·ate·ly,** *adv.*

mod·er·a·tion (mäd′ə rā′shən), *n.* the act or condition of being moderate, or within limits; a keeping away from extremes [Watching television in *moderation* can be fun.]

mod·er·a·tor (mäd′ə rā′tər), *n.* the chairman of a discussion or debate.

mod·ern (mäd′ərn), *adj.* **1.** of or having to do with the present time or the period we live in [a *modern* poet]. **2.** of the period after about 1450 [the *modern* history of Europe]. **3.** of or having to do with the latest styles, methods, or ideas; up-to-date [He travels the *modern* way, by jet airplane.] —*n.* a person who lives in modern times or has up-to-date ideas.

mod·ern·ize (mäd′ərn īz), *v.* to make or become modern; bring up to date in style, design, etc. —**mod′ern·ized,** *p.t. & p.p.;* **mod′ern·iz·ing,** *pr.p.* —**mod′ern·i·za′tion,** *n.*

mod·est (mäd′ist), *adj.* **1.** not vain or boastful about one's worth, skills, deeds, etc.; humble [a *modest* hero]. **2.** not bold or forward; shy. **3.** behaving, dressing, speaking, etc. in a way that is considered proper or moral; decent [*Modest* ladies in 1900 wore shoes and stockings as part of their swimming costume.] **4.** reasonable; not extreme [a *modest* home; a *modest* request].

mod·es·ty (mäd′is tē), *n.* the quality of being modest; humble or proper behavior.

mod·i·cum (mäd′i kəm), *n.* a small amount; bit [a *modicum* of common sense].

mod·i·fy (mäd′ə fī), *v.* **1.** to make a small or partial change in [Modern exploration has *modified* our maps of Antarctica.] **2.** to make less harsh, strong, etc. [to *modify* a jail sentence]. **3.** to limit the meaning of; describe or qualify [In the phrase "old man" the adjective "old" *modifies* the noun "man."] —**mod′i·fied,** *p.t. & p.p.;* **mod′i·fy·ing,** *pr.p.* —**mod′i·fi·ca′-tion,** *n.* —**mod′i·fi′er,** *n.*

mod·ish (mōd′ish), *adj.* in the latest style; fashionable.

mod·u·late (mäj′oo lāt), *v.* **1.** to make a slight change in; adjust [to *modulate* the light in a room]. **2.** to change the pitch or loudness of the voice in speaking. **3.** to vary a radio wave in some way according to the sound being broadcast: see **AM, FM.** —**mod′u·lat·ed,** *p.t. & p.p.;* **mod′u·lat·ing,** *pr.p.* —**mod′u·la′tion,** *n.*

mod·ule (mäj′ool), *n.* a section of a machine or device that can be detached for some special use [the landing *module* of a spacecraft].

Mo·gul (mō′gul), *n.* **1.** a Mongolian; especially, any of the Mongolian conquerors of India. **2. mogul,** a powerful or important person.

mo·hair (mō′her), *n.* **1.** the hair of the Angora goat. **2.** a fabric made of this, especially an upholstery fabric with a mohair pile.

Mo·ham·med (mō ham′id), *n.* 570–632 A.D.; Arabian founder of the Moslem religion.

Mo·ham·med·an (mō ham′ə dən), *adj.* of Mohammed or the Moslem religion. —*n.* a Moslem. —**Mo·ham′med·an·ism,** *n.*

Mo·hawk (mō′hôk), *n.* a member of an Indian tribe that lived in central New York State.

Mo·hi·can (mō hē′kən) or **Mo·he·gan** (mō-hē′gən), *n.* a member of an Indian tribe that lived along the upper Hudson River.

moi·e·ty (moi′ə tē), *n.* **1.** a half. **2.** some part or share. —**moi′e·ties,** *pl.*

moist (moist), *adj.* damp or slightly wet.

mois·ten (mois′'n), *v.* to make or become moist.

mois·ture (mois′chər), *n.* liquid causing a dampness, as fine drops of water in the air.

mo·lar (mō′lər), *n.* any of the back teeth used for grinding food [An adult person has twelve *molars,* three on each side of each jaw.]

mo·las·ses (mə las′iz), *n.* a thick, dark sirup that remains after sugar is refined.

upper molars

lower molars

mold (mōld), *n.* **1.** a hollow form used to give shape to something soft or melted [Candles are made of wax poured into *molds.*] **2.** something shaped in a mold [a *mold* of gelatin]. **3.** a special character or kind [The college needs men of his *mold.*] —*v.* **1.** to make or shape in a mold. **2.** to give a certain shape or form to [He *molded* the soft clay into a figure. Education *molds* character.]

mold of gelatin

mold (mōld), *n.* a fuzzy growth caused by a fungus on vegetable or animal matter that is damp or decaying. —*v.* to become moldy.

mold (mōld), *n.* loose, soft soil, especially when it is rich and good for growing plants.

mold·er (mōl′dər), *v.* to crumble into dust; decay slowly [Even iron in time *molders* away.]

mold·ing (mōl′ding), *n.* **1.** the act of giving shape or form to [the *molding* of metals; the *molding* of a child's personality]. **2.** something molded. **3.** a shaped strip of wood, etc. fastened along the upper part of a wall, around the frame of a door, etc.

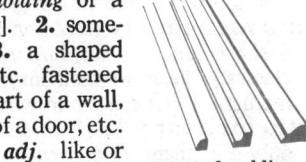
types of molding

mold·y (mōl′dē), *adj.* like or covered with a fuzzy growth of mold; stale or musty [a *moldy* smell; *moldy* bread]. —**mold′i·er,** *compar.;* **mold′iest,** *superl.*

mole (mōl), *n.* a small, brownish spot on the skin, often one that is there at birth.

mole (mōl), *n.* a small animal with tiny, weak eyes and soft fur, that lives mainly underground.

mole (mōl), *n.* a break-water.

mol·e·cule (mäl′ə kyool), *n.* **1.** the smallest particle of a substance that can exist alone without losing its chemical form. A molecule consists of one or more atoms. **2.** a very small piece. —**mo·lec·u·lar** (mə lek′yoo lər), *adj.*

mole (7 in. long)

mole·hill (mōl′hil), *n.* a small ridge of earth formed by a mole burrowing under the ground. —**make a mountain out of a molehill,** to treat a small problem as a large, important one.

mo·lest (mə lest′), *v.* to meddle with so as to trouble or hurt; bother. —**mo·les·ta·tion** (mō′les tā′shən), *n.*

mol·li·fy (mäl′ə fī), *v.* to soothe; make calm or less violent [She *mollified* the crying child.] —**mol′li·fied,** *p.t. & p.p.;* **mol′li·fy·ing,** *pr.p.*

mol·lusk or **mol·lusc** (mäl′əsk), *n.* an animal with a soft body that is usually protected by a shell, as the oyster, clam, snail, etc.

mol·ly·cod·dle (mäl′ē käd′'l), *n.* a man or boy who is too much pampered or taken care of; sissy. —*v.* to pamper; coddle. —**mol′ly·cod′dled,** *p.t. & p.p.;* **mol′ly·cod′dling,** *pr.p.*

molt (mōlt), *v.* to shed skin, feathers, etc. before getting a new growth, as snakes, birds, etc.

mol·ten (mōl′t'n), *adj.* **1.** melted by heat [*molten* iron]. **2.** made by being melted and put in a mold [a *molten* statue]. *Molten* was once used as a past participle of **melt.**

Mo·luc·ca Islands (mō luk′-ə), a group of islands of Indonesia.

mo·lyb·de·num (mə lib′də-nəm), *n.* a silver-white metal that is a chemical element, used in alloys.

cicada molting

fat, āpe, cär, ten, ēven, hit, bīte, gō, hôrn, tool, book, up, fūr;
get, joy, yet, chin, she, thin, then; zh = s in pleasure; ′ as in able (ā′b'l);
ə = a in ago, e in agent, i in sanity, o in confess, u in focus.

mom (mäm), *n.* mother: *only in everyday talk.*

mo·ment (mō′mənt), *n.* **1.** a very short period of time; instant [to pause for a *moment*]. **2.** a particular time [At that *moment* the bell rang.] **3.** importance [matters of great *moment*].

mo·men·tar·i·ly (mō′mən ter′ə lē), *adv.* **1.** for a short time [I saw him *momentarily* between classes.] **2.** from moment to moment; at any moment [We expect him *momentarily*.]

mo·men·tar·y (mō′mən ter′ē), *adj.* lasting for only a moment [a *momentary* pain].

mo·men·tous (mō men′təs), *adj.* very important [a *momentous* date in history].

mo·men·tum (mō men′təm), *n.* **1.** the force with which a body moves, equal to its mass multiplied by its speed [His sled gained *momentum* as it coasted downhill.] **2.** strength or force that keeps growing [The campaign to make him president gained *momentum*.]

Mon., abbreviation for **Monday.**

Mon·a·co (män′ə kō), *n.* a small country on the Mediterranean, mostly surrounded by France.

mon·arch (män′ərk), *n.* **1.** a ruler; king, queen, emperor, etc. **2.** a large North American butterfly, with reddish-brown wings.

mo·nar·chi·cal (mə när′ki k'l), *adj.* of or like a monarch or monarchy.

mon·arch·ist (män′ər kist), *n.* a person who is in favor of government by a monarch.

mon·arch·y (män′ər kē), *n.* government by a monarch, or a country with such government. —**mon′arch·ies,** *pl.*

mon·as·ter·y (män′əs ter′ē), *n.* a place where a group of monks live. —**mon′as·ter′ies,** *pl.*

mo·nas·tic (mə nas′tik), *adj.* of or having to do with monks or their way of life. —*n.* a monk.

Mon·day (mun′dē), *n.* second day of the week.

mon·e·tar·y (män′ə ter′ē), *adj.* **1.** in money; pecuniary [That old car has little *monetary* value.] **2.** of the money used in a country [The *monetary* unit of France is the franc.]

mon·ey (mun′ē), *n.* **1.** coins of gold, silver, or other metal, or paper bills to take the place of these, issued by a government for use in buying and selling. **2.** anything regularly used as money [Shells were the *money* of some Indian tribes.] **3.** wealth, property, etc. [a man of *money*]. —**make money,** to earn or get wealth; become wealthy. —**mon′eys** or **mon′ies,** *pl.*

mon·eyed (mun′ēd), *adj.* very rich; wealthy.

money order, a written order that a certain sum of money be paid to a certain person. It can be bought at a bank or post office as a safe way of sending money to another person, who can cash it at his bank or post office.

Mon·gol (mäng′gəl), *n. & adj.* Mongolian.

Mon·go·li·a (mäng gō′li ə), *n.* a country in central Asia, north of China.

Mon·go·li·an (mäng gō′li ən), *adj.* **1.** having to do with or belonging to the division of mankind that is loosely called the "yellow race." Most of the peoples of Asia are Mongolian. **2.** of Mongolia, its people, etc. —*n.* **1.** a member of the Mongolian group of mankind. **2.** a native of Mongolia. **3.** the language of Mongolia.

mon·goose or **mon·goos** (mäng′gōōs *or* mung′gōōs), *n.* an animal of India that looks like a ferret: it kills rats, snakes, etc. —**mon′goos·es,** *pl.*

mongoose (2½ ft. long, including tail)

mon·grel (mung′grəl *or* mäng′grəl), *n.* an animal or plant produced by crossing different kinds or breeds; especially, a dog of this kind. —*adj.* of mixed breed or origin.

mon·i·tor (män′ə tər), *n.* **1.** in some schools, a student chosen to help keep order, take attendance, etc. **2.** something that reminds or warns. **3.** a former kind of armored warship with a low deck and heavy guns mounted in turrets. **4.** in a radio or television studio, a receiver for checking on programs in order to tell how they are coming through. —*v.* to listen to or watch in order to check up on [to *monitor* a broadcast].

mon·i·to·ry (män′ə tôr′ē), *adj.* warning or cautioning [a *monitory* letter].

monk (mungk), *n.* a man who has joined a religious order whose members live together in a monastery according to certain rules, after vowing to give up worldly goods, never to marry, etc.

mon·key (mung′kē), *n.* **1.** any animal of the group that is closest to man in form; especially, any small animal of this group having a long tail and distinguished from the apes. **2.** a playful child who is full of mischief. —*v.* to meddle or trifle: *used only in everyday talk* [Don't *monkey* with the radio dial.] —**mon′keys,** *pl.*

spider monkey (3 ft. long, including tail)

monkey wrench, a tool with a kind of vise at one end that can be tightened, used for grasping and turning pipes, nuts, etc.

monk·ish (mungk′ish), *adj.* of or like monks: *often used scornfully.*

monks·hood (mungks′hood), *n.* the aconite plant.

mono-, a prefix meaning "one," "single" [A *monoplane* is an airplane with one pair of wings.]

mon·o·cle (män′ə k'l), *n.* an eyeglass for one eye only.

mo·nog·a·my (mə näg′ə mē), *n.* the practice of being married to only one person at a time.

mon·o·gram (män′ə gram), *n.* initials, especially of a person's name, put together in a design and used on clothing, stationery, etc.

mon·o·graph (män′ə graf), *n.* a book or a long article on one particular subject.

mon·o·lith (män′ə lith), *n.* a large block of stone, or a statue, monument, etc. carved of a single, large stone. —**mon′o·lith′ic,** *adj.*

monogram

mon·o·logue or **mon·o·log** (män′ə lôg), *n.*
1. a long speech by one person during a conversation. **2.** a poem, part of a play, etc. in which one person speaks alone. **3.** a play, skit, etc. performed by one actor.

mon·o·ma·ni·a (män′ə mā′ni ə), *n.* too great an interest in something; especially, an interest or concern that is beyond the point of reason. —**mon·o·ma·ni·ac** (män′ə mā′ni ak), *n.*

mon·o·plane (män′ə plān), *n.* an airplane with only one pair of wings.

mo·nop·o·list (mə näp′ə list), *n.* a person who has a monopoly or is in favor of monopolies.

mo·nop·o·lis·tic (mə näp′ə lis′tik), *adj.* that is a monopoly or that has a monopoly.

mo·nop·o·lize (mə näp′ə līz), *v.* **1.** to get or have a monopoly of some product or service. **2.** to get or take up all of [to *monopolize* a conversation]. —**mo·nop′o·lized,** *p.t. & p.p.;* **mo·nop′o·liz·ing,** *pr.p.*

mo·nop·o·ly (mə näp′ə lē), *n.* **1.** complete control of a product or service in some place by a single person or group. A company with a monopoly has no competition and can set prices as it wishes. **2.** such control given and regulated by a government [The city gave the bus company a *monopoly* for ten years.] **3.** a company that has a monopoly. **4.** the thing that is controlled by a monopoly. **5.** the condition of having something all by oneself [No one has a *monopoly* on brains.] —**mo·nop′o·lies,** *pl.*

mon·o·rail (män′ə rāl), *n.* **1.** a railway having cars that run on a single rail, or track, and are usually hung from it. **2.** this track.

mon·o·syl·la·ble (män′ə sil′ə b′l), *n.* a word of one syllable, as *he* or *thought.* —**mon·o·syl·lab·ic** (män′ə si lab′ik), *adj.*

mon·o·the·ism (män′ə thē iz′m), *n.* the belief that there is only one God. —**mon′o·the·ist,** *n.* —**mon′o·the·is′tic,** *adj.*

mon·o·tone (män′ə tōn), *n.* **1.** a keeping of the same tone or pitch without change, as in talking or singing. **2.** a person who sings with few if any changes of tone. **3.** sameness of color, style, etc. [The room was done in gray *monotones.*]

mo·not·o·nous (mə nät′ə nəs), *adj.* **1.** going on and on in the same tone [a *monotonous* voice]. **2.** having little or no change; boring or tiresome [a *monotonous* trip; *monotonous* work].

mo·not·o·ny (mə nät′ə nē), *n.* **1.** sameness of tone or pitch. **2.** lack of change or variety; tiresome sameness.

mon·ox·ide (män äk′sīd), *n.* an oxide with one atom of oxygen in each molecule.

Mon·roe, James (mən rō′), 1758–1831; fifth president of the United States, from 1817 to 1825.

Monroe Doctrine, President Monroe's statement that the United States would regard as an unfriendly act any move by a European nation to mix into the affairs of American countries or to get more territory in this hemisphere.

mon·sieur (mə syür′ *or* mə syoo′), *n.* a French word used, like "Mr.," as a title for a man. —**mes·sieurs** (mes′ərz *or* mā syür′), *pl.*

Mon·si·gnor or **mon·si·gnor** (män sēn′yər), *n.* **1.** a title given to certain clergymen of high rank in the Roman Catholic Church. **2.** a person who has this title.

mon·soon (män soon′), *n.* **1.** a wind of the Indian Ocean and southern Asia, blowing from the southwest from April to October, and from the northeast the rest of the year. **2.** the rainy season when this wind blows from the southwest.

mon·ster (män′stər), *n.* **1.** any plant or animal that is not normal in shape or form, as a fish with two heads. **2.** an imaginary creature in stories, as a dragon or unicorn; often, one that is partly human, as a mermaid or centaur. **3.** a very cruel or wicked person. **4.** a huge animal or thing [a *monster* of a house]. —*adj.* huge; enormous.

mon·stros·i·ty (män strä′sə tē), *n.* **1.** the condition of being monstrous. **2.** a monster. —**mon·stros′i·ties,** *pl.*

mon·strous (män′strəs), *adj.* **1.** very large; huge. **2.** very different from the normal in looks or shape [a *monstrous* face]. **3.** very wicked; shocking; horrible [a *monstrous* crime].

Mon·tan·a (män tan′ə), *n.* a State in the northwestern part of the United States: abbreviated **Mont.**

Mont Blanc (mōn blän′), the highest mountain in the Alps, in eastern France on the Italian border.

Mon·te Car·lo (män′tē kär′lō), a town in Monaco that is a gambling resort.

Mon·te·vi·de·o (män′tə vi dā′ō), *n.* the capital of Uruguay.

Mon·te·zu·ma II (män′tə zoo′mə), 1480?–1520; the last Aztec emperor of Mexico, from 1502 to 1520. He was conquered by Cortés.

Mont·gom·er·y (mänt gum′ər ē *or* mən gum′rē), *n.* the capital of Alabama.

month (munth), *n.* **1.** any of the twelve parts into which the year is divided. **2.** the period of one complete revolution of the moon, about 29½ days. **3.** any period of four weeks or of 30 days.

month·ly (munth′lē), *adj.* **1.** happening, done, being due, etc. once a month [*monthly* payments]. **2.** lasting for a month. —*n.* a magazine that comes out once a month. —*adv.* once a month; every month. —**month′lies,** *pl.*

Mont·pel·ier (mänt pēl′yər), *n.* the capital of Vermont.

Mont·re·al (mänt′ri ôl′), *n.* a city in southern Quebec, Canada, on the St. Lawrence River.

mon·u·ment (män′yoo mənt), *n.* **1.** something put up in memory of a person or happening, as a statue, building, etc. **2.** something great or famous, especially from long ago [Homer's works are *monuments* of Greek culture.]

---

fat, āpe, cär, ten, ēven, hit, bīte, gō, hôrn, tool, book, up, fur;
get, joy, yet, chin, she, thin, *th*en; zh = s in pleasure; ′ as in able (ā′b′l);
ə = a in ago, e in agent, i in sanity, o in confess, u in focus.

mon·u·men·tal (män′yoo men′t'l), *adj.* **1.** that is or has to do with a monument. **2.** large, important, and likely to last for a long time [the *monumental* symphonies of Beethoven]. **3.** very great; colossal [a *monumental* liar]. —**mon′u·men′tal·ly**, *adv.*

moo (mōō), *n.* the sound made by a cow. —*v.* to make this sound. —**moos**, *pl.* —**mooed**, *p.t. & p.p.;* **moo′ing**, *pr.p.*

mooch (mōōch), *v.* to get by begging or asking, without paying: *a slang word.*

mood (mōōd), *n.* the way one feels; frame of mind [I'm in no *mood* for joking. She's in a happy *mood* today.]

mood (mōōd), *n.* the form of a verb that shows whether it is expressing a fact (*indicative mood*), a wish or possibility (*subjunctive mood*), or a command (*imperative mood*).

mood·y (mōōd′ē), *adj.* having or showing sad, gloomy moods or changes of mood [a *moody* boy; a *moody* face]. —**mood′i·er**, *compar.;* **mood′i·est**, *superl.* —**mood′i·ly**, *adv.* —**mood′i·ness**, *n.*

moon (mōōn), *n.* **1.** the heavenly body that revolves around the earth once about every 29½ days and shines at night by reflecting the light of the sun. **2.** any small body that spins around a planet. Moons may be natural or man-made. **3.** moonlight [the *moon* on the water]. **4.** anything shaped like the moon. **5.** a month [Hiawatha returned in five *moons*.] —*v.* to wander or look about in a dreamy or aimless way.

phases of the moon

moon·beam (mōōn′bēm), *n.* a ray of moonlight.

moon·light (mōōn′līt). *n.* the light of the moon. —*adj.* **1.** lighted by moonlight; moonlit. **2.** done or happening by moonlight, or at night [a *moonlight* ride].

moon·lit (mōōn′līt), *adj.* lighted by the moon.

moon·shine (mōōn′shīn), *n.* **1.** moonlight. **2.** foolish or useless talk, ideas, etc. **3.** whisky made secretly and sold without paying a government tax: *used only in everyday talk.*

moon·stone (mōōn′stōn), *n.* a milky-white, glassy mineral that is used as a gem.

moon·struck (mōōn′struk), *adj.* insane, dazed, or confused.

Moor (moor), *n.* a member of a Moslem people who live in northwestern Africa. Moors invaded Spain and settled there in the 8th century, but were driven out in the late 15th century. —**Moor′ish**, *adj.*

moor (moor), *n.* an area of open wasteland, usually covered with heather and often swampy: *mainly a British word.*

moor (moor), *v.* **1.** to hold a ship in place by means of cables to the shore or by anchors. **2.** to hold or fix in place [a tent firmly *moored* by strong ropes].

moor·ings (moor′ingz), *n.pl.* **1.** the lines, cables, or anchors by which a ship is moored. **2.** a place where a ship is moored.

moose (mōōs), *n.* a large animal of the deer family, of North America. The male has broad antlers with many points. —**moose**, *pl.*

moose (7 ft. high at shoulder)

moot (mōōt), *adj.* that can be discussed or argued about; debatable [a *moot* point]. —*v.* to debate; argue.

mop (mäp), *n.* **1.** a bundle of rags or yarn, or a sponge, fastened to the end of a stick for washing floors. **2.** anything like a mop, as a thick head of hair. —*v.* to wash or wipe as with a mop. —**mopped**, *p.t. & p.p.;* **mop′ping**, *pr.p.*

mope (mōp), *v.* to be gloomy and dull, without spirit. —**moped**, *p.t. & p.p.;* **mop′ing**, *pr.p.*

mo·raine (mə rān′), *n.* a mass of rocks, gravel, sand, etc. pushed along or left by a glacier.

mor·al (môr′əl), *adj.* **1.** having to do with right and wrong in conduct [a *moral* question]. **2.** good or right according to the accepted standards of behavior [a *moral* person]. **3.** teaching or showing ideas of right and wrong [a *moral* story]. **4.** able to tell the difference between right and wrong [Man is the *moral* being.] **5.** that shows sympathy but gives no active help [*moral* support]. —*n.* **1.** a lesson about what is right and wrong, taught by a story or event [the *moral* of a fable]. **2. morals**, *pl.* standards of behavior having to do with right and wrong; ethics. —**moral victory**, a defeat that is thought of as a victory because of its general results.

mop

mo·rale (mə ral′), *n.* the courage, self-control, and confidence that help one to keep up his spirits in facing hardship or danger [The army was defeated because of its low *morale*.]

mor·al·ist (môr′əl ist), *n.* a person who moralizes.

mo·ral·i·ty (mô ral′ə tē), *n.* **1.** rightness or wrongness of an action [The students discussed the *morality* of getting help with their homework.] **2.** good or proper conduct. **3.** rules of right and wrong; ethics. —**mo·ral′i·ties**, *pl.*

mor·al·ize (môr′ə līz), *v.* **1.** to talk or write about matters of right and wrong. **2.** to make morally better. —**mor′al·ized**, *p.t. & p.p.;* **mor′al·iz·ing**, *pr.p.*

mor·al·ly (môr′əl ē), *adv.* **1.** in a way that is moral, good, honest, etc. **2.** with regard to morals [a *morally* admirable man]. **3.** practically [I am *morally* certain that we shall win].

mo·rass (mə ras′), *n.* a piece of marshy ground; bog or swamp.

mor·a·to·ri·um (môr′ə tôr′i əm), *n.* **1.** a time during which a delay is granted, as by law, for paying debts. **2.** the granting of such a delay.

Mo·ra·vi·a (mô rā′vi ə), *n.* a region in Czechoslovakia. —**Mo·ra′vi·an**, *adj. & n.*

mor·bid (môr′bid), *adj.* **1.** having or showing an interest in gloomy or unpleasant things [a *morbid* imagination]. **2.** horrible or disgusting [*morbid* details of a murder]. **3.** of or caused by disease; unhealthy [a *morbid* growth in the body]. —**mor·bid′i·ty**, *n.* —**mor′bid·ly**, *adv.*

mor·dant (môr′d'nt), *adj.* sharp and cutting with words; sarcastic [His *mordant* wit made him unpopular.] —*n.* a substance used in dyeing to fix the colors so that they will not fade.

more (môr), *adj.* **1.** greater in amount or degree: *the comparative of* **much** [He has *more* time than I do.] **2.** greater in number: *the comparative of* **many** [We need *more* helpers.] **3.** additional; further [There will be *more* news later.] —*n.* **1.** a greater amount or degree [He spends *more* of his time playing than working.] **2.** a greater number: *used with a plural verb* [*More* of us are going.] **3.** something extra or further [I shall have *more* to say later.] —*adv.* **1.** in or to a greater degree or extent [He laughs *more* than he used to.] *Also used before many adjectives and adverbs to form comparatives* [*more* horrible; *more* quickly]. **2.** in addition; again [Do it once *more*.] —**more and more, 1.** to an ever greater degree. **2.** an amount that keeps on growing. —**more or less, 1.** to some extent; somewhat. **2.** about; nearly. —**most,** *superl.*

more·o·ver (môr ō′vər), *adv.* in addition to what has been said; besides; also.

morgue (môrg), *n.* **1.** a place where the bodies of unknown dead and those dead of unknown causes are kept to be examined, identified, etc. **2.** a newspaper office's library of back copies, etc.

Mor·mon (môr′mən), *n.* a member of a church founded in the United States in 1830 by Joseph Smith. The official name of this church is **Church of Jesus Christ of Latter-day Saints.**

morn (môrn), *n.* morning: *used in poetry.*

morn·ing (môr′ning), *n.* the early part of the day, from midnight to noon or, especially, from dawn to noon.

morn·ing-glo·ry (môr′ning glôr′ē), *n.* a climbing plant with flowers of blue, pink, or white, shaped like trumpets. —**morn′ing-glo′ries,** *pl.*

morning star, a planet seen in the eastern sky before sunrise, usually Venus.

morning-glory

Mo·roc·co (mə räk′ō), *n.* **1.** a country in north-western Africa. **2. morocco,** a fine, soft leather made from goatskins and used for binding books. —**Mo·roc′can,** *adj. & n.*

mo·ron (môr′än), *n.* **1.** a person whose mind is so slow that he cannot learn more than a twelve-year-old child can. **2.** a very foolish or stupid person. —**mo·ron′ic,** *adj.*

mo·rose (mə rōs′), *adj.* gloomy, bad-tempered, sullen, etc. —**mo·rose′ly,** *adv.*

Mor·pheus (môr′fi əs *or* môr′fyoos), *n.* the Greek god of dreams.

mor·phine (môr′fēn), *n.* a drug gotten from opium, used in medicine to lessen pain.

mor·ris dance (môr′is), an old English folk dance.

mor·row (mär′ō *or* môr′ō), *n.* **1.** morning. **2.** the next day. *Now seldom used except in poetry.*

Morse, Samuel F. B. (môrs), 1791–1872; United States inventor of the telegraph.

Morse code, a code or alphabet made up of a system of dots and dashes (or short and long clicks, flashes, etc.) that stand for letters and numbers. It is used in sending messages by telegraph, or in signaling.

mor·sel (môr′s'l), *n.* **1.** a small bite or bit of food. **2.** any small piece or amount.

mor·tal (môr′t'l), *adj.* **1.** that must die at some time [All men are *mortal*.] **2.** of man as a being who must die; human [*mortal* weakness]. **3.** causing death of the body or soul [a *mortal* wound; *mortal* sin]. **4.** lasting until death [*mortal* combat; *mortal* enemies]. **5.** very great; extreme [*mortal* terror]. —*n.* a human being.

mor·tal·i·ty (môr tal′ə tē), *n.* **1.** the condition of being mortal or sure to die. **2.** the death of a large number of people, as from war or disease. **3.** the number of deaths in relation to the number of people, as in a certain place; death rate.

mor·tal·ly (môr′t'l ē), *adv.* **1.** so as to cause death; fatally [*mortally* wounded]. **2.** very; greatly [*mortally* embarrassed].

mor·tar (môr′tər), *n.* **1.** a mixture of cement or lime with sand and water, used to hold bricks or stones together. **2.** a small cannon that shoots shells in a high curve. **3.** a hard bowl in which materials are ground to a powder with a pestle.

mortar and pestle

mort·gage (môr′gij), *n.* **1.** an agreement in which a person borrowing money gives the lender a claim to property as a pledge that the debt will be paid [The bank holds a *mortgage* of $5,000 on our house.] **2.** the legal paper by which such a claim is given. —*v.* **1.** to pledge by a mortgage in order to borrow money [to *mortgage* a home]. **2.** to put a claim on; make risky [He *mortgaged* his future by piling up debts.] —**mort′gaged,** *p.t. & p.p.;* **mort′gag·ing,** *pr.p.*

mort·ga·gee (môr′gi jē′), *n.* the lender to whom property is mortgaged.

mort·ga·gor or **mort·gag·er** (môr′gi jər), *n.* the borrower who mortgages his property.

mor·ti·fy (môr′tə fī), *v.* **1.** to make ashamed or embarrassed [He was *mortified* when he forgot his speech.] **2.** to control one's desires or feelings as by fasting or otherwise giving oneself pain

fat,   āpe,   cär,   ten,   ēven,   hit,   bīte,   gō,   hôrn,   tool,   book,   up,   fur;
get,   joy,   yet,   chin,   she,   thin,   then;   zh = s in pleasure;   ′ as in able (ā′b'l);
ə = a in ago,   e in agent,   i in sanity,   o in confess,   u in focus.

[to *mortify* one's body]. **3.** to decay with gangrene. —**mor'ti·fied,** *p.t. & p.p.;* **mor'ti·fy·ing,** *pr.p.* —**mor'ti·fi·ca'tion,** *n.*

mor·tise or **mor·tice** (môr'tis), *n.* a hole cut in a piece of wood, etc. so that a part (called a **tenon**) coming out from another piece will fit into it to form a joint. —*v.* to fasten with a mortise. —**mor'tised** or **mor'ticed,** *p.t. & p.p.;* **mor'tis·ing** or **mor'tic·ing,** *pr.p.*

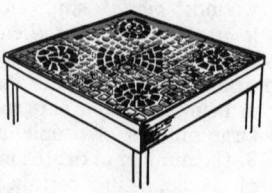
tenon
mortise

mor·tu·ar·y (môr'choo-er'ē), *n.* a place where dead bodies are kept before the funeral. —*adj.* of death or funerals. —**mor'tu·ar'ies,** *pl.*

Mo·sa·ic (mō zā'ik), *adj.* of Moses [The code of laws in the Pentateuch, supposedly written down by Moses, is called the *Mosaic* law.]

mo·sa·ic (mō zā'ik), *n.* **1.** a picture or design made by putting together small bits of colored stone, glass, etc. **2.** the art of making such pictures and designs. **3.** anything like a mosaic. —*adj.* of, like, or forming a mosaic.

mosaic table top

Mos·cow (mäs'kou *or* mäs'kō), *n.* the capital of the Soviet Union, in the western part.

Mo·ses (mō'ziz), *n.* in the Bible, the man who led the Israelites out of slavery in Egypt and passed on to them laws from God.

Mos·lem (mäz'ləm), *n.* a believer in the religion of Islam. —*adj.* of Islam or the Moslems.

mosque (mäsk), *n.* a Moslem place of worship.

mos·qui·to (mə skē'tō), *n.* a small insect with two wings. The female bites animals to suck their blood. Some mosquitoes spread diseases, as malaria. —**mos·qui'toes** or **mos·qui'tos,** *pl.*

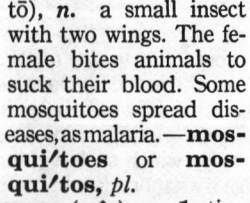
mosque

moss (môs), *n.* **1.** tiny green plants growing in clumps like velvet, on rocks, trees, etc. **2.** one of these plants.

moss·y (môs'ē), *adj.* **1.** covered with moss [a *mossy* rock]. **2.** like moss [*mossy* green]. —**moss'i·er,** *compar.;* **moss'i·est,** *superl.*

most (mōst), *adj.* **1.** greatest in amount or degree: *the superlative of* **much** [This is the *most* snow we have ever had.] **2.** greatest in number; almost all: *the superlative of* **many** [*Most* children like

mosquito

candy.] —*n.* **1.** the greatest amount or degree [He spent *most* of his money.] **2.** the greatest number: *used with a plural verb* [*Most* of us have read the book.] —*adv.* **1.** in or to the greatest degree or extent [The music pleased me *most.*] *Also used before many adjectives and adverbs to form superlatives* [*most* horrible; *most* quickly]. **2.** very [a *most* beautiful dress]. —**at most** or **at the most,** not more than. —**for the most part,** usually; mainly. —**make the most of,** to use in the best way. —**more,** *compar.*

-most (mōst), a suffix used in forming superlatives [The *topmost* branch is the highest one.]

most·ly (mōst'lē), *adv.* mainly; chiefly.

mote (mōt), *n.* a speck, as of dust.

mo·tel (mō tel'), *n.* a hotel for automobile travelers, usually arranged so that each room or suite has an outside entrance.

moth (môth), *n.* an insect like a butterfly, but usually smaller and less brightly colored. Moths fly mostly at night. One kind has larvae that eat holes in woolen cloth, fur, etc. —**moths** (mô*th*z *or* môths), *pl.*

moth

moth ball, a small ball of a substance that gives off fumes which keep moths away from woolen clothes, furs, etc.

moth-eat·en (môth'ēt'n), *adj.* **1.** having holes where moths have eaten in it [a *moth-eaten* coat]. **2.** worn out or out-of-date.

moth·er (mu*th*'ər), *n.* **1.** a woman as she is related to her child or children; a female parent. **2.** the origin, source, or cause of something [Which State is the *mother* of Presidents?] **3.** a nun who is the head of a convent: *the full name is* **mother superior.** —*adj.* of, like, or as if from a mother [*mother* love; one's *mother* tongue]. *v.* to care for as a mother does. —**moth'er·hood,** *n.* —**moth'er·less,** *adj.*

moth·er (mu*th*'ər), *n.* a stringy, slimy substance formed by bacteria in vinegar.

moth·er-in-law (mu*th*'ər 'n lô'), *n.* the mother of one's wife or husband. —**moth'ers-in-law',** *pl.*

moth·er·land (mu*th*'ər land), *n.* **1.** the country where one was born. **2.** the country that one's ancestors came from.

moth·er·ly (mu*th*'ər lē), *adj.* of or like a mother [*motherly* care]. —**moth'er·li·ness,** *n.*

moth·er-of-pearl (mu*th*'ər əv pûrl'), *n.* the hard, pearly layer on the inside of some sea shells. It is used in making buttons, jewelry, etc.

mo·tif (mō tēf'), *n.* a main theme or idea that is developed, or a figure that is repeated, in a work of art, music, or literature.

mo·tion (mō'shən), *n.* **1.** a moving from one place to another; movement [the car's forward *motion*]. **2.** a moving of the head, a hand, etc., especially in a way that has meaning [He made a beckoning *motion.*] **3.** a suggestion made at a meeting for the group to discuss and vote on [a *motion* to adjourn]. —*v.* to move the hand, head, etc. so as to show what one means or wants [He *motioned* me forward.] —**in motion,** moving, working, etc.

mo·tion·less (mō'shən lis), *adj.* not moving.

motion picture, 1. a series of pictures flashed on a screen quickly, one after another, so that the persons and things in them seem to move. **2.** a story told in such pictures.

mo·ti·vate (mō'tə vāt), *v.* to give a motive to or be a motive for [Love *motivated* his actions.] —**mo'ti·vat·ed,** *p.t. & p.p.;* **mo'ti·vat·ing,** *pr.p.* —**mo'ti·va'tion,** *n.*

mo·tive (mō'tiv), *n.* **1.** a desire, feeling, etc. that makes one do something [What was his *motive* for inviting us?] **2.** a motif. —*adj.* of or causing motion [Engines supply *motive* power.]

mot·ley (mät'lē), *adj.* **1.** of many colors [The clown wore a *motley* costume.] **2.** made up of many different kinds or parts [a *motley* group]. —*n.* a garment of many colors [a clown in *motley*].

mo·tor (mō'tər), *n.* **1.** a machine that uses electricity to make something move or work [the *motor* of an electric fan]. **2.** an engine, especially a gasoline engine, as in an automobile. —*adj.* **1.** of or run by a motor [a *motor* vehicle]. **2.** of, by, or for motor vehicles [a *motor* trip]. **3.** causing motion [*Motor* nerves cause the muscles to move.] —*v.* to travel by automobile.

mo·tor·boat (mō'tər bōt), *n.* a boat run by a motor (gasoline engine).

mo·tor·car (mō'tər kär), *n.* an automobile.

mo·tor·cy·cle (mō'tər sī'k'l), *n.* a kind of very heavy bicycle that is run by a gasoline engine. —*v.* to ride a motorcycle. —**mo'-tor·cy'cled,** *p.t. & p.p.;* **mo'tor·cy'-cling,** *pr.p.* —**mo'-tor·cy'clist,** *n.*

mo·tor·ist (mō'tər ist), *n.* a person who drives an automobile or travels by automobile.

motorcycle

mo·tor·man (mō'-tər mən), *n.* a person who drives an electric railway car. —**mo'tor·men,** *pl.*

mot·tle (mät''l), *v.* to mark with spots or blotches of different colors. —**mot'tled,** *p.t. & p.p.;* **mot'tling,** *pr.p.*

mot·to (mät'ō), *n.* **1.** a brief saying used as a rule to live by ["Honesty is the best policy" was his *motto*.] **2.** a word or phrase chosen to show the goals or ideals of a nation, club, etc. and marked or written on a seal, flag, coin, etc. —**mot'toes** or **mot'tos,** *pl.*

mould (mōld), **mould·er** (mōl'dər), **mould-ing** (mōl'ding), **mould·y** (mōl'dē), same as **mold, molder, molding, moldy.**

moult (mōlt), *v.* same as **molt.**

mound (mound), *n.* **1.** a heap or bank of earth, sand, etc.; little hill. **2.** the slightly raised place from which a baseball pitcher throws.

mount (mount), *n.* a mountain or hill: used in poetry or as part of a name [*Mount* Etna].

mount (mount), *v.* **1.** to climb or go up [to *mount* stairs]. **2.** to get up on [to *mount* a bicycle]. **3.** to provide with a horse or horses [Troops that are *mounted* are called cavalry.] **4.** to increase or rise [The flood waters are *mounting*. Profits *mounted*.] **5.** to place, fix, or arrange on or in a support, backing, etc., as a gem in a setting, a picture in a scrapbook, or a cannon on a carriage. **6.** to furnish the costumes, settings, etc. for [to *mount* a play]. **7.** to be armed with [This ship *mounts* six cannon.] —*n.* **1.** a horse for riding. **2.** the support, setting, etc. on or in which something is mounted.

moun·tain (moun't'n), *n.* **1.** a part of the earth's surface that rises high into the air; very high hill. **2. mountains,** *pl.* a chain or group of such high hills: also **mountain chain, mountain range. 3.** a large heap [a *mountain* of trash]. —*adj.* of, on, or in mountains.

moun·tain·eer (moun t'n ir'), *n.* **1.** a person who lives in a region of mountains. **2.** a person who climbs mountains, as for sport.

mountain goat, an antelope of the Rocky Mountains that looks like a goat and has long hair.

mountain laurel, an evergreen shrub with pink and white flowers and shiny leaves, growing in the eastern United States.

mountain lion, a common name for the **cougar** of the Rocky Mountains.

mountain goat (3½ ft. high at shoulder)

moun·tain·ous (moun't'n əs), *adj.* **1.** full of mountains [a *mountainous* region]. **2.** very large [a *mountainous* debt].

Mountain Standard Time, see **Standard Time.**

moun·te·bank (moun'tə bangk), *n.* a person who cheats or tricks people by telling lies about himself or the thing he is selling; charlatan. The word *mountebank* was first used of men who sold quack medicines in public.

Mount Ver·non (vûr'nən), the home of George Washington, in Virginia, near Washington, D.C.

mourn (môrn), *v.* to be sad or show sorrow over someone's death, a loss, etc. —**mourn'er,** *n.*

mourn·ful (môrn'fəl), *adj.* showing or causing sorrow or grief; sad. —**mourn'ful·ly,** *adv.*

mourn·ing (môr'ning), *n.* **1.** the showing of sorrow or grief, as when someone dies. **2.** black clothes, a black arm band, etc. worn to show sorrow at someone's death

mourning dove, a wild dove of the United States whose cooing sounds mournful.

---

fat,   āpe,   cär,   ten,   ēven,   hit,   bīte,   gō,   hôrn,   tool,   book,   up,   fûr;
get,   joy,   yet,   chin,   she,   thin,   *th*en;   zh = s in pleasure;   ' as in able (ā'b'l);
ə = a in ago,   e in agent,   i in sanity,   o in confess,   u in focus.

mouse (mous), *n.* **1.** a small, gnawing animal found in houses and fields throughout the world. **2.** a timid person. —*v.* (mouz), to hunt for mice. —**mice** (mīs), *pl.* —**moused,** *p.t.* & *p.p.;* **mous'ing,** *pr.p.*

mouse
(6 in. long, including tail)

mouse·trap (mous'-trap), *n.* a trap for mice.

mousse (mōōs), *n.* a sweet frozen dessert, made of whipped cream, gelatin, etc.

mous·tache (məs tash' *or* mus'tash), *n.* same as **mustache.**

mous·y or **mous·ey** (mou'sē), *adj.* quiet, timid, shy, etc. —**mous'i·er,** *compar.;* **mous'i·est,** *superl.*

mouth (mouth), *n.* **1.** the opening in an animal's head through which food is taken in and sounds are made; also, the space behind this opening, which contains the tongue and teeth. **2.** any opening thought of as like the mouth [the *mouth* of a river; the *mouth* of a jar]. —*v.* (mouth), **1.** to say in a showy, unnatural way [to *mouth* speeches in a play]. **2.** to hold or rub with the mouth. —**mouths** (mouthz), *pl.*

mouth·ful (mouth'fool), *n.* **1.** as much as the mouth can hold. **2.** as much as is usually put into the mouth at one time. —**mouth'fuls,** *pl.*

mouth organ, same as **harmonica.**

mouth·piece (mouth'pēs), *n.* **1.** a part held in or near the mouth [the *mouthpiece* of a trumpet, pipe, or telephone]. **2.** a person, newspaper, etc. that is used by some other person or persons to express their ideas; spokesman.

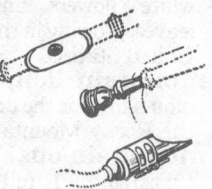
mouthpieces of
musical instruments

mov·a·ble or **move·a·ble** (mōōv'ə b'l), *adj.* **1.** that can be moved; not fixed [*movable* shelves]. **2.** changing in date from one year to the next [Thanksgiving is a *movable* holiday.] —*n.* **mov·ables,** *pl.* movable things, especially furniture.

move (mōōv), *v.* **1.** to change the place or position of [*Move* the lamp closer. Can you *move* your legs?] **2.** to change place or position [Please *move* to the left. Your head *moved* a little.] **3.** to turn, work, revolve, stir, etc. [The steering wheel *moves* the front wheels of the car.] **4.** to change the place where one lives [We *moved* three times in the last year.] **5.** to cause; give a reason for [What *moved* you to buy a car?] **6.** to cause to have strong feelings [His plea *moved* me deeply.] **7.** to go forward; make progress [This book *moves* slowly.] **8.** to begin to act or cause to act [Fresh troops *moved* against the enemy. Laxatives *move* the bowels.] **9.** to suggest or propose, as in a meeting [I *move* that we accept his offer.] **10.** to change the position of a piece in chess, checkers, etc. —*n.* **1.** the act of moving; movement [Don't make a *move!*] **2.** an action toward getting something done [the city's latest *move* in its housing program]. **3.** the act of moving a piece in checkers, chess, etc.; also, a player's turn to move. —**on the move,** moving about from place to place: *used only in everyday talk.* —**moved,** *p.t.* & *p.p.;* **mov'ing,** *pr.p.*

move·ment (mōōv'mənt), *n.* **1.** a moving or a way of moving [a *movement* of the branches; the regular *movement* of the stars]. **2.** a working together to bring about some result [the *movement* for world peace]. **3.** a getting rid of waste matter in the bowels. **4.** the moving parts of a watch, clock, etc. **5.** the rhythm of a piece of music. **6.** one of the main sections of a long piece of music, as of a symphony.

mov·er (mōōv'ər), *n.* a person or thing that moves; especially, one whose work is moving people's furniture from one home to another.

mov·ie (mōōv'ē), *n.* **1.** a motion picture. **2.** a theater where motion pictures are shown.

mov·ing (mōōv'ing), *adj.* **1.** that moves or causes movement [a *moving* car; the *moving* spirit behind the revolt]. **2.** that makes one feel sad or full of pity [a *moving* plea for help].

moving picture, same as **motion picture.**

mow (mō), *v.* **1.** to cut down grass or grain with a lawn mower, sickle, etc. **2.** to cut grass or grain from [to *mow* a lawn]. **3.** to cause to fall like cut grass; knock down [to *mow* down pins in bowling]. —**mowed,** *p.t.;* **mowed** or **mown** (mōn), *p.p.;* **mow'ing,** *pr.p.*

mow (mou), *n.* **1.** a pile of hay, grain, etc., especially in a barn. **2.** the part of a barn where hay, grain, etc. is stored.

mow·er (mō'ər), *n.* a person or machine that mows [a lawn *mower*].

Mo·zam·bique (mō zəm bēk'), *n.* a Portuguese colony in southeastern Africa.

Mo·zart, Wolf·gang (vôlf'gäng mō'tsärt), 1756–1791; Austrian composer of music.

MP or **M.P.,** abbreviation for **Military Police.**

M.P., abbreviation for **Member of Parliament.**

mph or **m.p.h.,** abbreviation for **miles per hour.**

Mr. (mis'tər), mister: *used before the name of a man or of his title* [*Mr.* Johnson; *Mr.* Secretary]. —**Messrs.,** *pl.*

Mrs. (mis'iz), mistress: *used before the name of a married woman.* —**Mmes.,** *pl.*

MS. or **ms.,** abbreviation for **manuscript.** —**MSS.** or **mss.,** *pl.*

Msgr., abbreviation for **Monsignor.**

Mt. or **mt.,** abbreviation for **mount, mountain.** —**Mts.** or **mts.,** *pl.*

much (much), *adj.* great in amount or degree [*much* applause; *much* joy]. —*n.* **1.** a great amount [We learned *much* from her.] **2.** something great or important [He's not *much* of an acrobat.] —*adv.* **1.** to a great extent [I feel *much* better.] **2.** just about; almost [The patient is *much* the same.] —**more,** *compar.;* **most,** *superl.*

mu·ci·lage (myōō's'l ij), *n.* a sticky substance, such as glue, for making things stick together.

muck (muk), *n.* **1.** moist manure from animals. **2.** black earth with rotting leaves, etc. in it, used as fertilizer. **3.** any dirt or filth.

muck·rake (muk′rāk), *v.* to search for and make known dishonest practices in politics or business. —**muck′raked,** *p.t. & p.p.;* **muck′-rak·ing,** *pr.p.* —**muck′rak·er,** *n.*

mu·cous (myoo′kəs), *adj.* **1.** of, having, or giving off mucus. **2.** like mucus; slimy.

mucous membrane, the moist skin that lines body cavities that open to the surface, as the nose, throat, etc.

mu·cus (myoo′kəs), *n.* the thick, slimy substance given off by mucous membranes. Mucus protects the membranes by keeping them moist.

mud (mud), *n.* wet earth that is soft and sticky.

mud·dle (mud′'l), *v.* **1.** to mix up; confuse [to *muddle* a discussion]. **2.** to act or think in a confused way [to *muddle* through a hard day at work]. —*n.* a confused or mixed-up condition. —**mud′dled,** *p.t. & p.p.;* **mud′dling,** *pr.p.*

mud·dy (mud′ē), *adj.* **1.** full of mud or smeared with mud [a *muddy* yard; *muddy* boots]. **2.** not clear: cloudy [*muddy* coffee]. **3.** confused [*muddy* thinking]. —*v.* to make or become muddy. —**mud′di·er,** *compar.;* **mud′di·est,** *superl.* —**mud′died,** *p.t. & p.p.;* **mud′dy·ing,** *pr.p.*

muff (muf), *n.* **1.** a covering, as of fur, into which the hands are placed from either end for keeping them warm. **2.** in baseball, a failure to hold a ball when trying to catch it. **3.** any clumsy or bungling act. —*v.* **1.** to handle in a clumsy or bungling way. **2.** in baseball, to miss a catch.

muff

muf·fin (muf′in), *n.* a kind of bread baked in small cups and usually eaten hot.

muf·fle (muf′'l), *v.* **1.** to wrap up or cover closely so as to keep warm, hide, protect, etc. [*muffled* up in a scarf against the cold]. **2.** to cover so as to deaden sound [rowing with *muffled* oars to surprise the enemy]. **3.** to make less loud or less clear [Heavy shutters *muffled* the sounds from the street.] —**muf′fled,** *p.t. & p.p.;* **muf′fling,** *pr.p.*

muf·fler (muf′lər), *n.* **1.** a scarf worn around the throat for warmth. **2.** a thing used to deaden noise, as a part fastened to the exhaust pipe of an automobile engine.

muffler

upper: in place beneath car
lower: cut to show inside parts

muf·ti (muf′tē), *n.* ordinary clothes, especially when worn by one who usually wears a uniform.

mug (mug), *n.* **1.** a heavy drinking cup, usually with a handle. **2.** as much as a mug will hold [a *mug* of milk]. **3.** the face: *a slang meaning.*

mug

mug·gy (mug′ē), *adj.* hot and damp, with little or no stirring of the air; close [*muggy* weather]. —**mug′-gi·er,** *compar.;* **mug′gi·est,** *superl.*

mu·lat·to (mə lat′ō *or* myoo lat′ō), *n.* a person who has one Negro parent and one white parent.

mul·ber·ry (mul′ber ē), *n.* **1.** a tree whose leaves are used as food for silkworms. **2.** its purplish-red fruit, that is like a berry. **3.** purplish red. —**mul′ber·ries,** *pl.*

mulch (mulch), *n.* leaves, straw, peat, etc. spread on the ground around plants to keep the moisture in the soil or to keep the roots from freezing. —*v.* to spread mulch around.

mulct (mulkt), *v.* **1.** to take away from, as by cheating or tricking [The scoundrel *mulcted* the poor woman out of her life savings.] **2.** to fine. —*n.* a fine or penalty.

mule (myool), *n.* **1.** the offspring of a donkey and a horse. **2.** a stubborn person: *used only in everyday talk.* **3.** a machine that spins cotton fibers into yarn and winds the yarn.

mule (myool), *n.* a slipper that leaves the heel uncovered, for wearing around the house.

mule (5 ft. high at shoulder)

mu·le·teer (myoo′lə tir′), *n.* a mule driver.

mul·ish (myool′ish), *adj.* like a mule; stubborn.

mull (mul), *v.* to think over; ponder: *used only in everyday talk* [to *mull* over the plan].

mull (mul), *v.* to heat cider, wine, etc. and add sugar and spices to it.

mul·lein *or* **mul·len** (mul′in), *n.* a tall weed with fuzzy leaves and flower spikes of various colors.

mul·let (mul′it), *n.* a fish found both in the sea and in fresh water, used as food. Some kinds have silvery scales and others reddish scales.

multi-, a prefix meaning "of, by, or having many or several" [A *multicolored* scarf has many colors in it. A *multilateral* agreement is one entered into by several nations.]

mul·ti·col·ored (mul′ti kul′ərd), *adj.* having many colors.

mul·ti·far·i·ous (mul′tə fer′ē əs), *adj.* of many kinds; taking many forms; varied.

mul·ti·form (mul′tə fôrm), *adj.* having many forms, shapes, etc.

mul·ti·lat·er·al (mul′ti lat′ər əl), *adj.* **1.** having many sides. **2.** among more than two nations [a *multilateral* treaty].

fat,   āpe,   cär,   ten,   ēven,   hit,   bīte,   gō,   hôrn,   tool,   book,   up,   fur;
get,   joy,   yet,   chin,   she,   thin,   *th*en;   zh = s in pleasure;   ′ as in able (ā′b'l).
ə = a in ago,   e in agent,   i in sanity,   o in confess,   u in focus.

mul·ti·mil·lion·aire (mul'ti mil'yən er'), *n.* a person who has at least several million dollars, pounds, etc.; extremely wealthy person.

mul·ti·ple (mul'tə p'l), *adj.* of or made up of a number of parts, elements, etc. [Twins, triplets, etc. are *multiple* births.] —*n.* a number that contains another number an exact number of times, with no remainder [18 is a *multiple* of 9, and also of 2, 3, and 6.]

mul·ti·pli·cand (mul'tə pli kand'), *n.* the number that is to be multiplied by another; number that stands above the multiplier.

mul·ti·pli·ca·tion (mul'tə pli kā'shən), *n.* a multiplying or being multiplied; especially, a method used to find the result of adding a certain figure repeated a certain number of times.

mul·ti·plic·i·ty (mul'tə plis'ə tē), *n.* a great number or variety [a *multiplicity* of plans].

mul·ti·pli·er (mul'tə pli'ər), *n.* **1.** the number by which another number is multiplied; number that stands below the multiplicand. **2.** a person or thing that multiplies, or increases.

mul·ti·ply (mul'tə plī), *v.* **1.** to become more, greater, etc.; increase [His troubles *multiplied*.] **2.** to repeat a certain figure a certain number of times [If you *multiply* 10 by 4, or repeat 10 four times, you get the product 40.] —**mul'ti·plied,** *p.t. & p.p.;* **mul'ti·ply·ing,** *pr.p.*

mul·ti·tude (mul'tə tōōd *or* mul'tə tyōōd), *n.* a large number of persons or things; crowd.

mul·ti·tu·di·nous (mul'tə tōō'd'n əs *or* mul'tə-tyōō'd'n əs), *adj.* very many; numerous.

mum (mum), *n.* a chrysanthemum: *used only in everyday talk.*

mum (mum), *adj.* not speaking; silent [Keep *mum*.] —**mum's the word,** say nothing.

mum·ble (mum'b'l), *v.* to speak or say in a way hard to hear, as with the mouth partly closed. —*n.* a mumbling, or something mumbled. —**mum'bled,** *p.t. & p.p.;* **mum'bling,** *pr.p.*

mum·ble·ty·peg (mum'b'l tē peg'), *n.* a game in which a jackknife is tossed in various ways to make it land with the blade in the ground.

mum·mer (mum'ər), *n.* **1.** a person who wears a mask or costume for fun, as for acting out pantomimes. **2.** any actor.

mum·mer·y (mum'ər ē), *n.* **1.** the acting done by mummers. **2.** any foolish ritual that cannot be taken seriously. —**mum'mer·ies,** *pl.*

mum·mi·fy (mum'ə fī), *v.* **1.** to make into a mummy. **2.** to shrivel up. —**mum'mi·fied,** *p.t. & p.p.;* **mum'mi·fy·ing,** *pr.p.*

mum·my (mum'ē), *n.* a dead body kept from decaying by being treated with chemicals, as was done by the ancient Egyptians. —**mum'-mies,** *pl.*

mumps (mumps), *n.pl.* a disease that causes the swelling of certain glands, especially in the jaw below each ear: *used with a singular verb* [*Mumps* is catching.]

mummy case, open to show wrapped mummy

munch (munch), *v.* to chew in a noisy, steady way [Rabbits *munch* carrots.]

mun·dane (mun'dān), *adj.* of the world, not of heaven, the spirit, etc.; worldly; earthly [the *mundane* affairs of business].

Mu·nich (myōō'nik), *n.* a city in southwestern Germany.

mu·nic·i·pal (myōō nis'ə p'l), *adj.* of or having to do with a city or town, or its government.

mu·nic·i·pal·i·ty (myōō nis'ə pal'ə tē), *n.* a city or town that has self-government in local matters. —**mu·nic'i·pal'i·ties,** *pl.*

mu·nif·i·cent (myōō nif'ə s'nt), *adj.* very generous; lavish [a *munificent* reward]. —**mu·nif'i·cence,** *n.*

mu·ni·tions (myōō nish'ənz), *n.pl.* war supplies; especially, weapons and ammunition.

mu·ral (myoor'əl), *n.* a picture painted on a wall. —*adj.* of or on a wall [a *mural* painting].

mur·der (mūr'dər), *n.* the unlawful killing of one person by another, especially when done on purpose or while committing another crime. —*v.* **1.** to kill in an unlawful way. **2.** to spoil something as by doing it badly [to *murder* a poem in reading it aloud].

mur·der·er (mūr'dər ər), *n.* a person who is guilty of murder. —**mur'der·ess,** *n.fem.*

mur·der·ous (mūr'dər əs), *adj.* **1.** of or like murder; brutal [a *murderous* act]. **2.** guilty of murder or ready to murder [a *murderous* brute].

murk (mūrk), *n.* darkness; gloom.

murk·y (mūr'kē), *adj.* dark or gloomy [a *murky* cave]. —**murk'i·er,** *compar.;* **murk'i·est,** *superl.*

mur·mur (mūr'mər), *n.* **1.** a low, steady sound, as of voices far away. **2.** a complaint made in a very low voice. —*v.* **1.** to make a low, steady sound [The wind *murmured* through the trees.] **2.** to speak or complain in a very low voice.

mur·rain (mūr'in), *n.* **1.** a disease of cattle that is catching. **2.** a plague: *an old word.*

Mus·cat and O·man (mus kat' 'n ō män'), a country in southeastern Arabia.

mus·cle (mus''l), *n.* **1.** the tissue in an animal's body that makes up the fleshy parts. Muscle can be stretched or tightened to move the parts of the body. **2.** any single part or band of this tissue [The biceps is a *muscle* in the upper arm.] **3.** strength that comes from muscles that are developed; brawn.

muscles of the back and arms

mus·cu·lar (mus'kyoo-lər), *adj.* **1.** of, made up of, or done by a muscle or muscles [*muscular* effort]. **2.** with muscles that are well developed; strong [*muscular* legs].

Muse (myōōz), *n.* **1.** any one of the nine Greek goddesses of the arts and sciences. **2. muse,** the spirit that is thought to give ideas and feelings to a poet or other artist.

muse (myōōz), *v.* to think seriously; meditate. —**mused,** *p.t. & p.p.;* **mus'ing,** *pr.p.*

mu·se·um (myoo zē'əm), *n.* a building or room for keeping and showing objects that are important in history, art, or science, as paintings, tools, stuffed animals, machines, etc.

mush (mush), *n.* **1.** corn meal boiled in water or milk. **2.** any thick, soft mass.

mush (mush), *interj.* in Canada and Alaska, a shout urging sled dogs to start or to move faster. —*v.* to travel over snow, as with a dog sled.

mush·room (mush'room), *n.* a small, fleshy fungus that grows very fast and has a stalk topped with a cap of various shapes. Some kinds can be eaten; poisonous ones are often called *toadstools.* —*adj.* of or like a mushroom [the *mushroom* cloud of an atom bomb]. —*v.* to grow and spread out rapidly like a mushroom.

types of mushroom

mush·y (mush'ē), *adj.* **1.** thick and soft, like mush. **2.** showing love or affection in a silly way: *only in everyday talk.* —**mush'i·er,** *compar.;* **mush'i·est,** *superl.*

mu·sic (myoo'zik), *n.* **1.** the art of putting tones together in various melodies, rhythms, and harmonies to form compositions for singing or playing on instruments [She teaches *music.*] **2.** such a composition or compositions, especially as written down in notes [Did you remember to bring your *music?*] **3.** any series of pleasing sounds [the *music* of birds]. —**face the music,** to accept the results, no matter how unpleasant. —**set to music,** to compose music for, as a poem.

mu·si·cal (myoo'zi k'l), *adj.* **1.** of music or for making music [a *musical* score; a *musical* instrument]. **2.** like music; full of melody, harmony, etc. [The waterfall had a *musical* sound.] **3.** fond of music or skilled in music. **4.** containing songs, dances, etc. [a *musical* comedy]. —*n.* a musical comedy. —**mu'si·cal·ly,** *adv.*

mu·si·cale (myoo zi kal'), *n.* a party where the guests listen to music.

music box, a box that contains a bar with a row of steel teeth that produce a series of tones. These teeth are struck by pins arranged on a roller to produce a certain tune when the roller is turned, as by a clockwork.

mu·si·cian (myoozish'ən), *n.* a person skilled in music, as a composer or one who plays a musical instrument or sings, especially for a living.

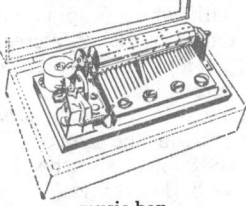

music box

musk (musk), *n.* **1.** a substance got from a gland of the male musk deer. It has a strong smell and is used in making perfumes. **2.** the smell of this substance.

musk deer, a small deer without horns found in central Asia.

mus·kel·lunge (mus'kə lunj), *n.* a very large fish of the pike family, found especially in the Great Lakes. —**mus'kel·lunge,** *pl.*

mus·ket (mus'kit), *n.* a gun with a long barrel, used before the rifle was invented.

mus·ket·eer (mus kə tir'), *n.* in earlier times, a soldier armed with a musket.

mus·ket·ry (mus'kit rē), *n.* **1.** the firing of muskets. **2.** muskets or musketeers as a group.

musk·mel·on (musk'mel'ən), *n.* a round melon with a thick, rough rind and sweet, juicy flesh: also called **cantaloupe.**

musk ox, an animal that lives in the arctic and is related to cattle and sheep. It has long hair and long, curved horns.

musk·rat (musk'rat), *n.* **1.** a North American animal, like a large rat, that lives in water and has glossy brown fur. **2.** its fur.

musk·y (mus'kē), *adj.* of or like musk [a *musky* odor]. —**musk'i·er,** *compar.;* **musk'i·est,** *superl.*

muskrat (20 in. long, not including tail)

mus·lin (muz'lin), *n.* a strong, often thin, cotton cloth used for curtains, dresses, sheets, etc.

muss (mus), *v.* to make untidy, messy, etc. [The wind *mussed* her hair.] —*n.* a mess; disorder. *Used only in everyday talk.* —**muss'y,** *adj.*

mus·sel (mus'l), *n.* a water animal having a soft body enclosed in two shells hinged together. The shells of fresh-water mussels are made into buttons. Salt-water mussels are used as food.

Mus·so·li·ni, Be·ni·to (be nē'tō moos'ə lē'nē), 1883–1945; Fascist dictator of Italy from 1922 to 1943.

Mus·sul·man (mus''l mən), *n.* a Moslem: an *earlier name.* —**Mus'sul·mans,** *pl.*

must (must), *a helping verb used with other verbs and meaning:* **1.** to be obliged to; to have to [I *must* pay the bill.] **2.** to be likely or certain to [It *must* be five o'clock. You *must* have seen him.] —*n.* something that must be done, read, seen, etc. [This book is a *must.*] —**must,** *p.t.*

mus·tache (məs tash' *or* mus'tash), *n.* **1.** the hair that a man has let grow out on his upper lip. **2.** the hair or bristles growing around an animal's mouth.

mus·ta·chio (məs tä'shō), *n.* a man's mustache.—**mus·ta'chios,** *pl.*

mus·tang (mus'tang), *n.* a small wild or half-wild horse of the Southwest plains.

types of mustache

mus·tard (mus′tərd), *n.* **1.** a plant with yellow flowers and slender seed pods. **2.** a dark yellow powder or paste made from its hot-tasting seeds and used as seasoning for food.

mus·ter (mus′tər), *v.* **1.** to bring or come together; gather [to *muster* troops for a roll call]. **2.** to gather up; summon [He *mustered* up his strength.] —*n.* **1.** a gathering together, as of troops for inspection. **2.** the persons or things gathered together. **3.** the list of soldiers, sailors, etc. in a unit. —**muster out,** to discharge from military service. —**pass muster,** to be approved after being inspected.

must·n't (mus′′nt), must not.

mus·ty (mus′tē), *adj.* **1.** having a stale, moldy smell or taste [a *musty* attic; *musty* bread]. **2.** worn-out or out-of-date [*musty* ideas]. —**mus′-ti·er,** *compar.;* **mus′ti·est,** *superl.* —**mus′-ti·ness,** *n.*

mu·ta·ble (myōō′tə b′l), *adj.* that can be changed; liable to change [*mutable* laws]. —**mu′-ta·bil′i·ty,** *n.*

mu·ta·tion (myōō tā′shən), *n.* **1.** a change, as in form. **2.** the appearance in a plant or animal of a characteristic that is not normal for its species, and that may be passed on by heredity.

mute (myōōt), *adj.* **1.** not able to speak. **2.** not speaking or making any sound; silent [He sat there *mute* and unmoving. The frozen waterfall was *mute.*] **3.** not pronounced; silent [The *e* in "mouse" is *mute.*] —*n.* **1.** a person who cannot speak; especially, a deaf-mute. **2.** a device used to soften or muffle the tone of a musical instrument, as a block placed in the bell of a trumpet. —*v.* to soften or muffle the sound of, as with a mute. —**mut′ed,** *p.t. & p.p.;* **mut′ing,** *pr.p.* —**mute′ly,** *adv.*

mute on a trumpet

mu·ti·late (myōō′t′l āt), *v.* to hurt or damage seriously by cutting or breaking off a necessary part or parts [to *mutilate* a hand by removing a finger; to *mutilate* a book by tearing out pages]. —**mu′ti·lat·ed,** *p.t. & p.p.;* **mu′ti·lat·ing,** *pr.p.* —**mu′ti·la′tion,** *n.*

mu·ti·neer (myōō t′n ir′), *n.* a person who takes part in a mutiny.

mu·ti·nous (myōō′t′n əs), *adj.* taking part or likely to take part in a mutiny; rebellious.

mu·ti·ny (myōō′t′n ē), *n.* a resisting or fighting against the leaders of a group; especially, a rebellion by sailors or soldiers against their officers. —*v.* to take part in a mutiny; revolt. —**mu′-ti·nies,** *pl.* —**mu′ti·nied,** *p.t. & p.p.;* **mu′-ti·ny·ing,** *pr.p.*

mutt (mut), *n.* a mongrel dog: *a slang word.*

mut·ter (mut′ər), *v.* **1.** to speak or say in low tones, with the lips almost closed, as in talking to oneself. **2.** to complain or grumble [The people *muttered* about the high taxes.] —*n.* a muttering or something muttered.

mut·ton (mut′′n), *n.* the flesh of a sheep, especially a grown sheep, used as food.

mu·tu·al (myōō′choo əl), *adj.* **1.** done, felt, etc. by two or more for or toward the other or others [*mutual* admiration]. **2.** of each other [*mutual* enemies]. **3.** shared together [We have *mutual* friends.] —**mu′tu·al·ly,** *adv.*

muz·zle (muz′′l), *n.* **1.** the mouth, nose, and jaws of a dog, horse, etc.; snout. **2.** a device made of wire, leather, etc. fastened over the mouth of an animal to keep it from biting. **3.** the front end of the barrel of a rifle, pistol, etc. —*v.* **1.** to put a muzzle on an animal. **2.** to keep a person from talking or giving an opinion [The writer was *muzzled* by censorship.] —**muz′-zled,** *p.t. & p.p.;* **muz′zling,** *pr.p.*

muzzle

my (mī), *pron.* of me or done by me: the possessive form of *I,* used before a noun and thought of as an adjective [*my* car; *my* work]. See also **mine.** —*interj.* a word said to show surprise, distress, pity, etc. [Oh, *my!* What a mess!]

my·na or **my·nah** (mī′nə), *n.* a starling of southeastern Asia that is often kept as a pet.

my·o·pi·a (mī ō′pi ə), *n.* the condition of being nearsighted. —**my·op·ic** (mī äp′ik), *adj.*

myr·i·ad (mir′i əd), *n.* **1.** ten thousand. **2.** any very large number [a *myriad* of locusts].

myna (10 in. long)

Myr·mi·don (mur′mi dän), *n.* **1.** in Greek legend, any of the warriors who fought under Achilles, their king, in the Trojan War. **2. myrmidon,** a follower who carries out orders without question.

myrrh (mur), *n.* a sticky substance with a sweet smell, got from certain shrubs of Arabia and Africa, and used in incense or perfume.

myr·tle (mur′t′l), *n.* **1.** an evergreen shrub with white or pink flowers and dark berries. **2.** a creeping evergreen plant with blue flowers; the periwinkle.

my·self (mī self′), *pron.* **1.** my own self: the form of *I* that makes the subject also the object of the verb [I hurt *myself.*] **2.** my usual or true self [I'm not *myself* today.] *Myself* is also used to give force to the subject [I'll do it *myself.*]

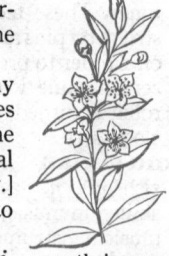

myrtle leaves and flowers (meaning 1)

mys·te·ri·ous (mis tir′i əs), *adj.* full of or suggesting mystery; hard to explain or solve [*mysterious* crimes]. —**mys·te′ri·ous·ly,** *adv.*

mys·ter·y (mis′tər ē), *n.* **1.** something that is not known or explained, or that is kept secret [the *mystery* of life]. **2.** anything that remains unexplained or is so secret that it makes people curious [a murder *mystery*]. **3.** a story or play about such a happening. **4.** the quality of being secret, hard to explain, etc. [She has an air of *mystery*.] **5.** a kind of play that was popular in the Middle Ages, about some happening in the Bible. —**mys′ter·ies**, *pl.*

mys·tic (mis′tik), *n.* a person who claims to have visions and mysterious experiences by which he can learn truths not known by ordinary people. —*adj.* **1.** of mystics or mysticism. **2.** secret, hidden, or mysterious [*mystic* powers].

mys·ti·cal (mis′ti k'l), *adj.* **1.** that is a symbol of some spiritual thing [The *mystical* rose is a symbol of the Virgin Mary.] **2.** mystic.

mys·ti·cism (mis′tə siz′m), *n.* **1.** the theories or beliefs of mystics; especially, the belief that certain people can know God directly or understand mysteries through visions. **2.** confused thinking, or beliefs.

mys·ti·fy (mis′tə fī), *v.* to puzzle or bewilder [I was completely *mystified* by his answer.] —**mys′ti·fied**, *p.t. & p.p.*; **mys′ti·fy·ing**, *pr.p.* —**mys′ti·fi·ca′tion**, *n.*

myth (mith), *n.* **1.** an old story handed down through the years, usually meant to explain how something came to be [The *myth* of Prometheus explains how men got fire.] **2.** any story that was made up and did not really happen. **3.** any imaginary person or thing [His large stamp collection was just a *myth*.]

myth·i·cal (mith′i k'l), *adj.* **1.** of, in, or like a myth [a *mythical* tale; *mythical* creatures]. **2.** imaginary; not real [a *mythical* friend].

my·thol·o·gy (mi thäl′ə jē), *n.* **1.** myths as a group; especially, all the myths of a certain people [Roman *mythology*]. **2.** the study of myths. —**my·thol′o·gies**, *pl.* —**myth·o·log·i·cal** (mith′ə läj′i k'l), *adj.*

N

N, n (en), *n.* the fourteenth letter of the English alphabet. —**N's, n's** (enz), *pl.*

N, symbol for the chemical element *nitrogen*.

N., N, n., n, abbreviations for **north** or **northern.**

n., abbreviation for **noun.**

Na, symbol for the chemical element *sodium*.

nab (nab), *v.* **1.** to arrest or catch [The police *nabbed* the robber.] **2.** to grab or snatch. *This word is used only in everyday talk.* —**nabbed**, *p.t. & p.p.*; **nab′bing**, *pr.p.*

na·dir (nā′dər), *n.* **1.** the point in the heavens directly opposite the zenith; the point directly beneath one. **2.** the lowest point [He had reached the *nadir* of his hopes.]

nag (nag), *v.* to annoy or disturb by constantly scolding, complaining, or urging. —**nagged**, *p.t. & p.p.*; **nag′ging**, *pr.p.*

nag (nag), *n.* a horse, especially an old one.

Na·ga·sa·ki (nä′gə sä′kē), *n.* a seaport in southwest Japan. On August 9, 1945, was largely destroyed by an American atomic bomb.

nai·ad (nā′ad *or* nī′ad), *n.* in Greek and Roman myths, a nymph living in a river, lake, etc.

nail (nāl), *n.* **1.** a narrow, pointed piece of metal, often with a flat head. It is hammered into pieces of wood, etc. to hold them together. **2.** the hard, thin substance that grows out from the ends of the fingers and toes. —*v.* **1.** to fasten or attach

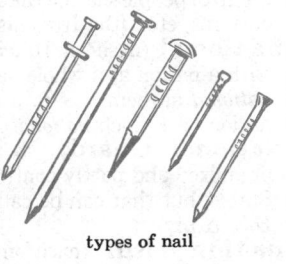

types of nail

with nails [*Nail* the box shut. *Nail* the sign on the wall.] **2.** to catch or capture: *used only in everyday talk.* —**hit the nail on the head,** to do or say whatever is exactly right or to the point.

na·ive *or* **na·ïve** (nä ēv′), *adj.* simple in a childlike or, sometimes, foolish way; innocent; not experienced. —**na·ive′ly**, *adv.* —**na·ive·té** *or* **na·ïve·te** (nä ēv′tā), *n.*

na·ked (nā′kid), *adj.* **1.** without any clothes on; bare; nude. **2.** without its usual covering [a *naked* sword]. **3.** without anything added that hides, changes, decorates, etc.; plain [the *naked* truth; the *naked* eye]. —**na′ked·ness**, *n.*

nam·by-pam·by (nam′bē pam′bē), *adj.* weak, foolish, without force, etc. —*n.* a namby-pamby person.

name (nām), *n.* **1.** a word or words by which a person, thing, or place is known; title [Ruth, Jones, North Dakota, and terrier are *names*.] **2.** a descriptive word or words used instead of the real name, sometimes in order to insult [They called him "Chubby," "Fatty," and other unkind *names*.] **3.** reputation [Guard your good *name*.] —*v.* **1.** to give a name to [She *named* the child after his father.] **2.** to tell the name or names of [Can you *name* all the Presidents?] **3.** to refer to; mention [to *name* an example]. **4.** to choose for a certain position; appoint [He was *named* Secretary of State.] **5.** to fix or set, as a date for meeting, a price, etc. —**in the name of, 1.** in appeal to [*in the name of* good sense]. **2.** by the authority of [Open *in the name of* the law!] —**to one's name,** belonging to one. —**named**, *p.t. & p.p.*; **nam′ing**, *pr.p.*

name·less (nām′lis), *adj.* **1.** not having a name. **2.** having a name that is not known or not given

fat, āpe, cär, ten, ēven, hit, bīte, gō, hôrn, tool, book, up, fūr;
get, joy, yet, chin, she, thin, then; zh = s in pleasure; ' as in able (ā′b'l);
ə = a in ago, e in agent, i in sanity, o in confess, u in focus.

[the *nameless* author of this article]. **3.** that cannot be described [*nameless* horror].

name·ly (nām′lē), *adv.* that is to say; to wit [a choice of two desserts, *namely*, cake or pie].

name·sake (nām′sāk), *n.* a person with the same name as another; especially, a person named after another.

Nan·king (nan′king′), *n.* a city in eastern China, on the Yangtze River.

Na·o·mi (nā ō′mē), *n.* in the Bible, the mother-in-law of Ruth: see **Ruth.**

nap (nap), *v.* **1.** to sleep for a short time; doze. **2.** to be careless or not ready [to be caught *napping*]. —*n.* a short sleep. —**napped,** *p.t.* & *p.p.*; **nap′ping,** *pr.p.*

nap (nap), *n.* the fuzzy or hairy surface of cloth formed by very short fibers.

na·palm (nā′päm), *n.* a jellylike substance shot in flaming streams from special weapons: it sticks to the skin of victims, causing severe burns.

nape (nāp), *n.* the back of the neck.

naph·tha (naf′thə), *n.* an oily liquid got from petroleum, used as a fuel or cleaning fluid.

nap·kin (nap′kin), *n.* **1.** a small piece of cloth or paper used while eating to protect the clothes or to wipe the fingers or lips. **2.** any small cloth or towel.

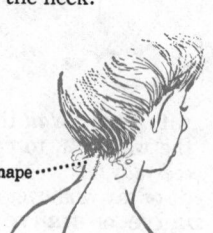

Na·ples (nā′p'lz), *n.* a city on the southwestern coast of Italy.

Na·po·le·on Bo·na·parte (nə pō′li ən bō′nə pärt), 1769–1821; French general; emperor of France from 1804 to 1815. —**Na·po·le·on·ic** (nə pō′li än′ik), *adj.*

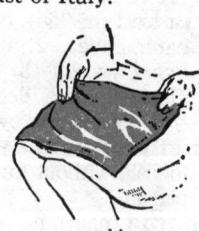

napkin

Nar·cis·sus (när sis′əs), *n.* **1.** a beautiful youth in a Greek legend, who fell in love with his own reflection in a pool and was changed into the narcissus. **2. narcissus,** a plant that grows from a bulb and has white, yellow, or orange flowers.

nar·cot·ic (när kät′ik), *n.* a drug, as morphine, that causes deep sleep and lessens pain. —*adj.* of, or having the effect of, a narcotic.

nar·rate (na rāt′ or nar′āt), *v.* to give the story of in writing or speech; tell what has happened. —**nar·rat′ed,** *p.t.* & *p.p.*; **nar·rat′ing,** *pr.p.* —**nar′ra·tor,** *n.*

narcissus

nar·ra·tion (na rā′shən), *n.* **1.** a narrating, or telling of a story or of happenings. **2.** a story or report; narrative.

nar·ra·tive (nar′ə tiv), *n.* **1.** a story; a report of happenings; tale. **2.** the telling of stories or events; narration. —*adj.* in the form of a story [a *narrative* history of England].

nar·row (nar′ō), *adj.* **1.** small in width; less wide than usual [a *narrow* road]. **2.** small or limited in size, amount, or degree [winner by a *narrow* majority]. **3.** not having an open mind; not broad-minded; prejudiced. **4.** with barely enough space, time, means, etc.; close [a *narrow* escape]. —*v.* to lessen in size, width, or degree [The road *narrows* at the bend.] —*n. usually* **narrows,** *pl.* a narrow passage, as the narrow part of a valley or of a river. —**nar′row·ly,** *adv.* —**nar′row·ness,** *n.*

nar·row-mind·ed (nar′ō mīn′did), *adj.* not keeping one's mind open to the beliefs, ways of life, etc. of others; not liberal; prejudiced.

nar·whal (när′wəl *or* när′hwəl), *n.* a small whale of the arctic. The male has a long tusk.

nar·y (ner′ē), *adj.* not any; no: *used only in everyday talk* [He had *nary* a doubt.]

na·sal (nā′z'l), *adj.* **1.** of the nose [*nasal* passages]. **2.** produced by letting air pass through the nose [The *nasal* sounds are "m," "n," and "ng." He spoke with a *nasal* twang.]

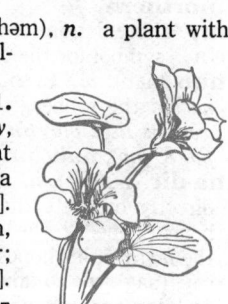

narwhal (16 ft. long, not including tusk)

Nash·ville (nash′vil), *n.* the capital of Tennessee.

na·stur·tium (nə stûr′shəm), *n.* a plant with a sharp smell and red, yellow, or orange flowers.

nas·ty (nas′tē), *adj.* **1.** very dirty; filthy [a *nasty*, smelly room]. **2.** not decent or proper; disgusting [a *nasty* word; a *nasty* mind]. **3.** very unpleasant; mean, painful, etc. [*nasty* weather; a *nasty* temper; a *nasty* fall]. —**nas′ti·er,** *compar.*; **nas′ti·est,** *superl.* —**nas′ti·ly,** *adv.* —**nas′ti·ness,** *n.*

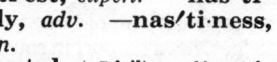

nasturtium

na·tal (nā′t'l), *adj.* of or from one's birth [One's *natal* day is the day of one's birth.]

na·tion (nā′shən), *n.* **1.** a group of people living together in a certain region under the same government; state; country [the Swiss *nation*]. **2.** a group of people sharing the same history, language, customs, etc. [the Iroquois *nation*].

na·tion·al (nash′ən 'l), *adj.* of or having to do with a nation as a whole [a *national* election; the *national* anthem]. —*n.* a citizen of a particular nation [a French *national*].

National Guard, a militia force that is organized and partly controlled by the individual States, but that can be called to service with the U.S. Army.

na·tion·al·ism (nash′ən 'l iz'm), *n.* **1.** love of one's nation or country; patriotism. **2.** the desire to make one's nation free of control by another country. —**na′tion·al·ist,** *n.* & *adj.* —**na′tion·al·is′tic,** *adj.*

na·tion·al·i·ty (nash′ə nal′ə tē), *n.* **1.** the nation in which a person was born, or of which he is a citizen. **2.** the condition of being a citizen of a certain nation; citizenship. **3.** the condition of being a nation [Israel won *nationality* in 1948.] —**na′tion·al′i·ties,** *pl.*

na·tion·al·ize (nash′ən ′l īz), *v.* **1.** to put under the ownership or control of the national government [Coal mines in England were *nation-alized* in 1947.] **2.** to make national in character [Mark Twain *nationalized* the American novel.] **3.** to make into a nation. —**na′tion·al·ized,** *p.t. & p.p.;* **na′tion·al·iz·ing,** *pr.p.* —**na′-tion·al·i·za′tion,** *n.*

na·tion·al·ly (nash′ən ′l ē), *adv.* throughout the nation; by the whole nation.

na·tion-wide (nā′shən wīd′), *adj.* by or through the whole nation [*nation-wide* effort].

na·tive (nā′tiv), *adj.* **1.** that is or has to do with the place where one was born [his *native* land; her *native* language]. **2.** born in or belonging naturally in a certain place or country [a plant *native* to China; a *native* New Yorker]. **3.** of or having to do with the natives of a place [a *native* custom; *native* dances]. **4.** that is part of one from birth; not learned; natural [his *native* ability to make friends]. **5.** as found in nature; pure or unchanged [*native* ores]. —*n.* **1.** a person born in a certain region, especially one whose ancestors were also born there [a *native* of Ohio; the Indian *natives* of America]. **2.** an animal or plant that lives or grows naturally in a certain region.

na·tive-born (nā′tiv bôrn′), *adj.* born in a certain region [a *native-born* Canadian].

na·tiv·i·ty (nə tiv′ə tē), *n.* birth. —**the Na-tivity, 1.** the birth of Jesus. **2.** Christmas Day.

natl., abbreviation for **national.**

nat·ty (nat′ē), *adj.* neat and in style [a *natty* suit; a *natty* dresser]. —**nat′ti·er,** *compar.;* **nat′ti·est,** *superl.* —**nat′ti·ly,** *adv.*

nat·u·ral (nach′ər əl), *adj.* **1.** produced by nature; not made by man [*natural* resources; *natural* curls]. **2.** of or dealing with nature [Biology and chemistry are *natural* sciences.] **3.** that is part of one from birth; native [a *natural* ability]. **4.** of or for all people at all times [*natural* rights]. **5.** true to nature; lifelike [The portrait of him is *natural.*] **6.** normal or usual; to be expected [It is *natural* for rivers to flood in the spring.] **7.** free and easy; not forced or artificial [a *natural* laugh]. **8.** in music, that is neither flat nor sharp [Play B *natural.*] —*n.* **1.** a musical note that is neither a sharp nor a flat; also, the sign ♮, used to mark a note that would otherwise be played as a sharp or a flat. **2.** a person who seems just right for something: *used only in everyday talk* [He's a *natural* for the job.] —**nat′u·ral·ness,** *n.*

nat·u·ral·ist (nach′ər əl ist), *n.* a person who makes a special study of plants and animals.

nat·u·ral·ize (nach′ər ə līz), *v.* **1.** to make a citizen of [Aliens in the United States can be *naturalized* after living here a certain time and passing certain tests.] **2.** to take over from some other place and make one's own; adopt [The French word "menu" has been *naturalized* in English.] **3.** to make used to new surroundings; adapt [Hawaiian farmers *naturalized* the South American pineapple.] —**nat′u·ral·ized,** *p.t. & p.p.;* **nat′u·ral·iz·ing,** *pr.p.* —**nat′u·ral·i·za′-tion,** *n.*

nat·u·ral·ly (nach′ər əl ē), *adv.* **1.** in a natural way [to behave *naturally*]. **2.** by nature; according to the way one happens to be [He is *naturally* shy.] **3.** as one might expect; of course [*Naturally* he caught cold from being chilled.]

na·ture (nā′chər), *n.* **1.** all things in the universe; the physical world and everything in it that is not made by man. **2.** sometimes **Nature,** the power or force that seems to control these things [*Nature* heals an animal's wounds.] **3.** scenery that is not artificial, and the plants and animals in it [a *nature* lover]. **4.** the special character that makes a thing what it is [the *nature* of light; human *nature*]. **5.** the qualities one seems to be born with [a man of a happy *nature*]. **6.** kind or type [books, magazines, and other things of that *nature*]. **7.** the primitive way people lived before they became civilized [a return to *nature*].

naught (nôt), *n.* **1.** nothing. **2.** the figure zero (0).

naugh·ty (nô′tē), *adj.* **1.** not behaving; bad, disobedient, mischievous, etc. [*naughty* children]. **2.** not nice or proper [*naughty* words]. —**naugh′ti·er,** *compar.;* **naugh′ti·est,** *superl.* —**naugh′ti·ly,** *adv.* —**naugh′ti·ness,** *n.*

nau·se·a (nô′shə *or* nô′zi ə), *n.* **1.** a feeling of sickness that makes one want to vomit. **2.** great disgust; loathing.

nau·se·ate (nô′shi āt *or* nô′zi āt), *v.* to make feel like vomiting; cause nausea or disgust in. —**nau′se·at·ed,** *p.t. & p.p.;* **nau′se·at·ing,** *pr.p.*

nau·seous (nô′shəs *or* nô′zi əs), *adj.* causing nausea; sickening; disgusting.

nau·ti·cal (nô′ti k′l), *adj.* having to do with sailors, ships, or sailing. —**nau′ti·cal·ly,** *adv.*

nau·ti·lus (nô′t′l əs), *n.* a small sea animal found in warm seas. The **pearly nautilus** has a spiral shell divided into many chambers. The **paper nautilus** has eight arms and, in the female, a thin shell like paper.

Nav·a·ho *or* **Nav·a·jo** (nav′ə hō), *n.* a member of a tribe of American Indians now mainly in Arizona, New Mexico, and Utah. —**Nav′a·hos** *or* **Nav′a·jos;** also **Nav′a·hoes** *or* **Nav′a·joes,** *pl.*

na·val (nā′v′l), *adj.* **1.** of or for a navy, its ships, men, etc. [*naval* vessels]. **2.** having a navy [England is a great *naval* power.]

---

nave (nāv), *n.* the main part of a church, in the middle, where the seats are.

na·vel (nā′v'l), *n.* the small scar left in the middle of the belly, where the umbilical cord was separated after birth.

navel orange, an orange without seeds, having a mark at one end that looks like a navel.

navel orange

nav·i·ga·ble (nav′i gə b'l), *adj.* 1. wide enough or deep enough for ships to travel on [a *navigable* river]. 2. that can be steered [a *navigable* balloon]. —**nav′·i·ga·bil′i·ty,** *n.*

nav·i·gate (nav′ə gāt), *v.* 1. to steer, or control the course of, as a ship or aircraft. 2. to travel by ship. 3. to travel through, on, or over [to *navigate* the Nile]. —**nav′·i·gat·ed,** *p.t.* & *p.p.;* **nav′i·gat·ing,** *pr.p.*

nav·i·ga·tion (nav′ə gā′shən), *n.* the act or skill of navigating; especially, the science of figuring the course of a ship or aircraft.

nav·i·ga·tor (nav′ə gā′tər), *n.* a person who navigates; especially, one skilled in figuring the course of a ship or aircraft.

na·vy (nā′vē), *n.* 1. all the warships of a nation, with their men, supplies, shipyards, offices, etc. 2. navy blue. 3. a fleet of ships: *now seldom used.* —**na′vies,** *pl.*

navy blue, very dark blue.

nay (nā), *adv.* 1. not only that, but beyond that [He is well-off, *nay,* rich.] 2. no: *no longer so used.* —*n.* a vote of "no" [The count was 57 *nays* and 41 ayes.]

Naz·a·rene (naz ə rēn′ *or* naz′ə rēn), *n.* a person born or living in Nazareth; especially, Jesus, who grew up there.

Naz·a·reth (naz′ə rəth), *n.* a town in northern Israel.

Na·zi (nä′tsē), *adj.* describing or having to do with the fascist political party that ruled Germany under Hitler from 1933 to 1945. —*n.* a member or supporter of this party. —**Na′zism,** *n.*

N.B., abbreviation for **New Brunswick.**

N.B. or **n.b.,** note well: the abbreviation for *nota bene,* Latin for "note well."

N.C., abbreviation for **North Carolina.**

N. Dak., or **N.D.** abbreviation for **North Dakota.**

Ne, the symbol for the chemical element *neon.*

NE or **N.E.** or **n.e.,** abbreviation for **northeast** or **northeastern.**

Ne·an·der·thal (ni an′dər täl *or* ni an′dər thôl), *adj.* describing or of an early race of man living in Europe during the Stone Age.

Ne·a·pol·i·tan (nē′ə päl′ə t'n), *adj.* of Naples. —*n.* a person born or living in Naples.

neap tide (nēp), a tide, occurring twice a month, when high tide is at its lowest level.

near (nir), *adv.* 1. at or to a short distance in space or time [Spring is drawing *near.*] 2. almost; nearly [You are *near* right.] —*adj.* 1. not distant; not far; close [a house *near* to the school; in the *near* past]. 2. close in relationship or in affection [a *near* cousin; his *nearest* friend]. 3. by a small degree; narrow [a *near* escape]. 4. short; direct [He took the *near* way home.] 5. stingy. —*prep.* close to; not far from [They sat *near* us.] —*v.* to come near to; approach [Slow down as you *near* the curve.] —**near at hand,** very close in time or space. —**near′ness,** *n.*

near-by or **near·by** (nir′bi′), *adj.* & *adv.* near; close at hand.

Near East, 1. same as **Middle East.** 2. the Balkans: *a British meaning.*

near·ly (nir′lē), *adv.* 1. almost; not quite [We are *nearly* ready.] 2. closely [They are *nearly* related.] —**not nearly,** not at all; far from [That's *not nearly* enough.]

near·sight·ed (nir′sīt′id), *adj.* seeing clearly only things that are near. —**near′sight′ed·ness,** *n.*

neat (nēt), *adj.* 1. clean and in good order; tidy [a *neat* room]. 2. careful and exact [a *neat* worker]. 3. pleasing in form or shape [a *neat* design]. 4. cleverly done or said [a *neat* trick]. —**neat′ly,** *adv.* —**neat′ness,** *n.*

'neath or **neath** (nēth), *prep.* beneath: *used in poetry.*

Ne·bras·ka (nə bras′kə), *n.* a State in the north central part of the United States: abbreviated **Neb.** or **Nebr.** —**Ne·bras′kan,** *adj.* & *n.*

Neb·u·chad·nez·zar (neb′yoo kəd nez′ər), *n.* king of Babylon from about 604 to about 562 B.C. He conquered Jerusalem.

neb·u·la (neb′yoo lə), *n.* a cloudlike patch seen in the sky at night. It is either burning gas or a group of stars too far away to be seen clearly. —**neb·u·lae** (neb′yoo lē) or **neb′u·las,** *pl.* —**neb′u·lar,** *adj.*

neb·u·lous (neb′yoo ləs), *adj.* 1. of or like a nebula. 2. cloudy; misty. 3. not clear; not definite; vague [*nebulous* plans].

nec·es·sar·i·ly (nes′ə ser′ə lē), *adv.* as a necessary result; of necessity; inevitably [She likes those shoes, but she will not *necessarily* buy them.]

nec·es·sar·y (nes′ə ser′ē), *adj.* 1. that is needed or must be done; required; essential [*necessary* repairs]. 2. that cannot be avoided; inevitable [a *necessary* result]. —*n.* something necessary. —**nec′es·sar′ies,** *pl.*

ne·ces·si·tate (nə ses′ə tāt), *v.* to make necessary; compel [The hard words in the article *necessitated* his use of a dictionary.] —**ne·ces′si·tat·ed,** *p.t.* & *p.p.;* **ne·ces′si·tat·ing,** *pr.p.*

ne·ces·si·ty (nə ses′ə tē), *n.* 1. that which is necessary or needed or cannot be done without [Food and shelter are *necessities.*] 2. great need [Call me in case of *necessity. Necessity* forced him to move.] 3. poverty; want [to live in great *necessity*]. —**of necessity,** as something that cannot be avoided; necessarily. —**ne·ces′si·ties,** *pl.*

neck (nek), *n.* 1. the part of a man or animal that joins the head to the body. 2. the part of a garment that goes around the neck. 3. the narrowest part of a bottle, peninsula, etc. —**neck and neck,** very close, or even, as in a race. —**risk one's neck,** to put oneself in danger.

neck·er·chief (nek'ər chif), *n.* a handkerchief or scarf worn around the neck.

neck·lace (nek'lis), *n.* a string of beads or a fine chain of gold, silver, etc. worn as an ornament around the neck.

neck·tie (nek'tī), *n.* a cloth band worn around the neck, usually under a collar and tied in a bow or knotted in front.

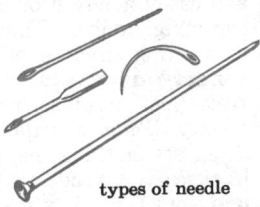
neckerchief

neck·wear (nek'wer), *n.* neckties, scarfs, etc.

nec·ro·man·cy (nek'rə man'sē), *n.* the act of trying to tell the future by supposedly getting messages from the dead. —**nec'ro·man'cer,** *n.*

nec·tar (nek'tər), *n.* **1.** the sweet liquid in many flowers, made into honey by bees. **2.** the drink of the gods in Greek myths. **3.** any delicious drink.

nec·tar·ine (nek tə rēn' *or* nek'tə rēn), *n.* a kind of peach that has a smooth skin.

nee or **née** (nā), *adj.* born: *used before the maiden name of a married woman* [Mrs. Paul Jones, *nee* Helen Hunt].

need (nēd), *n.* **1.** something that one wants or must have [New shoes are his greatest *need*.] **2.** a lack of something useful or wanted [He feels the *need* of companionship.] **3.** a condition that makes something necessary [no *need* to worry]. **4.** a time or condition when help is wanted [a friend in *need*]. **5.** the condition of being very poor; poverty [We gave food to those in *need*.] —*v.* to have need of; require; want [He *needs* new shoes.] *Need* is often used as a helping verb meaning "must" or "should" [She *needs* to take a rest. *Need* I tell you?] —**have need to,** to be required to; must. —**if need be,** if it is necessary.

need·ful (nēd'fəl), *adj.* necessary; needed.

nee·dle (nē'd'l), *n.* **1.** a small, slender piece of steel with a sharp point and a hole for thread, used for sewing. **2.** a slender rod of steel, bone, etc., used in knitting and crocheting. **3.** a short, slender piece of metal, often tipped with diamond, etc. that moves in the grooves of a phonograph record to pick up the vibrations. **4.** the pointer of a compass, gauge, meter, etc. **5.** the thin, pointed leaf of the pine, spruce, etc. **6.** the sharp, slender metal tube at the end of a hypodermic syringe. —*v.* to tease, annoy, or goad: *used only in everyday talk.* —**nee'dled,** *p.t. & p.p.;* **nee'dling,** *pr.p.*

types of needle

need·less (nēd'lis), *adj.* not needed; unnecessary. —**need'less·ly,** *adv.*

nee·dle·work (nē'd'l wūrk), *n.* work done with a needle; embroidery, sewing, etc.

need·n't (nēd'nt), need not.

need·y (nēd'ē), *adj.* very poor; not having enough to live on. —**need'i·er,** *compar.;* **need'i·est,** *superl.* —**need'i·ness,** *n.*

ne'er (ner), *adv.* never: *used only in poetry.*

ne'er-do-well (ner'dōō wel'), *n.* a lazy person who never does anything worth-while.

ne·far·i·ous (ni fer'i əs), *adj.* very bad or wicked; evil [a *nefarious* plot].

ne·ga·tion (ni gā'shən), *n.* **1.** the lack or the opposite of something thought of as positive or real [His wicked behavior was the complete *negation* of his moral preaching.] **2.** a saying "no" or a denying; negative answer; denial.

neg·a·tive (neg'ə tiv), *adj.* **1.** saying that something is not so or refusing; answering "no" [a *negative* reply]. **2.** that does not help, improve, etc. [*negative* criticism]. **3.** opposite to or lacking something thought of as positive or real [Ignorance, which is the lack of knowledge, is a *negative* condition.] **4.** showing that a certain disease, condition, etc. is not present [a *negative* reaction to an allergy test]. **5.** describing or of the kind of electricity that is made on rubber or wax by rubbing it with wool cloth. **6.** describing a quantity less than zero, or one that is to be subtracted. —*n.* **1.** a word, phrase, or action showing that one does not approve or agree ["No" and "not" are *negatives*.] **2.** the side that argues against the point being debated: see **affirmative. 3.** the film or plate from which a finished photograph is printed. The negative shows the light areas of the original subject as dark and the dark areas as light. —**in the negative,** refusing or denying something. —**neg'a·tive·ly,** *adv.*

negative of a photograph

neg·lect (ni glekt'), *v.* **1.** to fail to do what one should do as because of carelessness [In his hurry, Bob *neglected* to lock the door.] **2.** to fail to take care of as one should; give too little attention to [to *neglect* one's family]. —*n.* a neglecting or being neglected [The old house suffered from *neglect*.]

neg·lect·ful (ni glekt'fəl), *adj.* in the habit of neglecting things or people; careless [*neglectful* of her duty].

neg·li·gee (neg lə zhā' *or* neg'lə zhā), *n.* a woman's loosely fitting dressing gown.

neg·li·gent (neg'li jənt), *adj.* in the habit of neglecting things; not being careful; careless. —**neg'li·gence,** *n.* —**neg'li·gent·ly,** *adv.*

neg·li·gi·ble (neg'li jə b'l), *adj.* that can be ignored because it is small or not important; trifling [a *negligible* error].

ne·go·ti·a·ble (ni gō'shi ə b'l *or* ni gō'shə b'l), *adj.* that can be negotiated; especially, that can be sold or passed on to another without losing value [A check is *negotiable* if it is endorsed.]

ne·go·ti·ate (ni gō'shi āt), *v.* **1.** to talk over a problem, business deal, dispute, etc. in the hope of reaching an agreement [to *negotiate* with the enemy]. **2.** to arrange by talking about [to *negotiate* a loan]. **3.** to sell or transfer, as bonds, stocks, etc. **4.** to succeed in crossing, climbing, etc.: *used only in everyday talk* [to *negotiate* a flooded river]. **—ne·go'ti·at·ed,** *p.t. & p.p.;* **ne·go'ti·at·ing,** *pr.p.* **—ne·go'ti·a'tion,** *n.* **—ne·go'ti·a·tor,** *n.*

Ne·gro (nē'grō), *adj.* having to do with or belonging to the division of mankind that is loosely called the "black race." Most of the peoples of Africa are Negro. **—n. 1.** a member of the Negro group of mankind. **2.** any person who has some Negro ancestors. **—Ne'groes,** *pl.*

Ne·he·mi·ah (nē'ə mī'ə), *n.* **1.** a Hebrew leader of the 5th century B.C. **2.** a book of the Old Testament.

Neh·ru, Ja·wa·har·lal (jə wä'hər läl' nā'rōō), 1889–1964; prime minister of India from 1947 to 1964.

neigh (nā), *n.* the loud cry that a horse makes; whinny. **—v.** to make this cry.

neigh·bor (nā'bər), *n.* **1.** a person who lives near another. **2.** a person or thing that is near another [France and Spain are *neighbors*.] **3.** another human being; fellow man ["Love thy *neighbor*."] **—v.** to live or be situated near-by.

neigh·bor·hood (nā'bər hood), *n.* **1.** a small part or district of a city, town, etc. [an old *neighborhood*]. **2.** the people in such a district [The whole *neighborhood* helped.] **—in the neighborhood of, 1.** close to; near [*in the neighborhood of* the zoo]. **2.** about; nearly [*in the neighborhood of* $10].

neigh·bor·ing (nā'bər ing), *adj.* near or next to each other; adjacent [*neighboring* farms].

neigh·bor·ly (nā'bər lē), *adj.* friendly, kind, helpful, etc. **—neigh'bor·li·ness,** *n.*

nei·ther (nē'thər *or* nī'thər), *adj. & pron.* not one or the other of two; not either [*Neither* boy went. *Neither* of them was invited.] **—conj. 1.** not either: *a word used before the first of two other words or phrases that are separated by* nor [I could *neither* laugh nor cry.] **2.** nor yet; and not either [He doesn't sing, *neither* does he dance.]

nem·e·sis (nem'ə sis), *n.* **1.** punishment or a defeat that is deserved. **2.** one who brings about such punishment or defeat [In Greek myths, *Nemesis* was the goddess of revenge.]

ne·on (nē'än), *n.* a chemical element that is a gas without color or smell. It is found in the air in very small amounts.

neon lamp, a glass tube filled with neon, which glows when an electric current is sent through.

ne·o·phyte (nē'ə fīt), *n.* **1.** a person who has just been converted to a particular religion. **2.** a beginner in some work, art, etc.; novice.

Ne·pal (ni pôl'), *n.* a country in the Himalaya Mountains, between India and Tibet.

neph·ew (nef'yōō), *n.* **1.** the son of one's brother or sister. **2.** the son of one's brother-in-law or sister-in-law.

nep·o·tism (nep'ə tiz'm), *n.* the giving of jobs, or the showing of special favors, to one's relatives by a person in power.

Nep·tune (nep'tōōn *or* nep'tyōōn), *n.* **1.** the Roman god of the sea. The Greeks called this god *Poseidon.* **2.** the fourth largest planet. It is the eighth in distance away from the sun.

Ne·re·id (nir'i əd), *n.* any of the fifty sea nymphs in Greek myths.

Ne·ro (nir'ō), *n.* 37–68 A.D.; emperor of Rome from 54 to 68 A.D.: noted for his cruelty.

Neptune

nerve (nūrv), *n.* **1.** any of the fibers or bundles of fibers that connect the muscles, glands, organs, etc. with the brain and spinal cord. Nerves carry signals to and from the brain in controlling activity in the body. **2.** the power to control one's feelings in facing danger or risk [The acrobat is a man of *nerve*.] **3. nerves,** *pl.* a feeling of being nervous. **4.** a rib or vein in a leaf. **5.** boldness that knows no shame or respect; impudence: *used only in everyday talk.* **—v.** to give strength or courage to [He *nerved* himself for the ordeal.] **—get on one's nerves,** to make one annoyed or angry: *used only in everyday talk.* **—strain every nerve,** to try as hard as possible. **—nerved,** *p.t. & p.p.;* **nerv'ing,** *pr.p.*

nerve·less (nūrv'lis), *adj.* **1.** without strength, courage, etc.; weak [a *nerveless* coward]. **2.** without nerves [*nerveless* tissue].

nerve-rack·ing *or* **nerve-wrack·ing** (nūrv'-rak'ing), *adj.* very hard on one's patience.

nerv·ous (nur'vəs), *adj.* **1.** of the nerves [a *nervous* reaction; the *nervous* system]. **2.** restless and easily annoyed or upset. **3.** feeling fear or expecting trouble [Thunder makes me *nervous*.] **4.** showing strength or vigor [*nervous* energy]. **—nerv'ous·ly,** *adv.* **—nerv'ous·ness,** *n.*

-ness (nis), a suffix meaning: **1.** the condition or quality [*Sadness* is the condition of being sad.] **2.** an act or thing that is; an example of being [A *rudeness* is a rude act.]

nest (nest), *n.* **1.** a place built by a bird, as in a tree or field, for laying its eggs and caring for its young; also, a place like this where hornets, ants, etc. or squirrels, mice, etc. live and breed. **2.** the birds, insects, etc. in a nest. **3.** a cozy or snug place or shelter. **4.** a den or hideout, as of thieves, plotters, etc. **5.** a set of something in different sizes, each fitting into the one that is a little larger. **—v. 1.** to build a nest [Swallows often *nest* in chimneys.] **2.** to place as in a nest.

nest of tables

nest egg, money saved for the future; savings.

nes·tle (nes′'l), *v.* **1.** to lie or settle down in a comfortable and snug way [The baby *nestled* in his mother's arms.] **2.** to press or hold close for comfort or in fondness [She *nestled* the puppy in her lap.] **3.** to lie in a sheltered or partly hidden place [a house *nestled* in the hills]. —**nes′tled,** *p.t. & p.p.;* **nes′tling,** *pr.p.*

nest·ling (nest′ling *or* nes′ling), *n.* a young bird not yet ready to leave the nest.

net (net), *n.* **1.** a fabric of string, cord, etc. woven or knotted together so that open spaces are left between the strands. Nets are used to catch birds, fish, etc. **2.** a trap or snare [a thief trapped in the *net* of his own lies]. **3.** a piece of fine net used to hold, protect, or mark off something [hair *net;* mosquito *net;* tennis *net*]. **4.** a fine cloth like net, used to make curtains, trim dresses, etc. —*v.* **1.** to make into a net. **2.** to catch with a net. **3.** to cover or protect with a net. —**net′ted,** *p.t. & p.p.;* **net′- ting,** *pr.p.*

net

net (net), *adj.* left over after certain amounts have been subtracted [*Net* profit is the profit left after expenses. *Net* weight is the weight of an article without the weight of its container.] —*v.* to get or gain [to *net* a profit]. —**net′ted,** *p.t. & p.p.;* **net′ting,** *pr.p.*

neth·er (ne*th*′ər), *adj.* lower or under: *no longer much used* [Underwear was once called *nether* garments.]

Neth·er·lands (ne*th*′ər ləndz), *n.* a country in western Europe, on the North Sea; Holland.

neth·er·most (ne*th*′ər mōst), *adj.* lowest.

net·ting (net′ing), *n.* a netted fabric; net.

net·tle (net′'l), *n.* a weed with stinging hairs on its leaves. —*v.* to annoy or make angry. —**net′- tled,** *p.t. & p.p.;* **net′- tling,** *pr.p.*

net·work (net′wûrk), *n.* **1.** netting. **2.** any system of things that cross or are connected more or less like the strands in a net [*network* of roads; *network* of wires]. **3.** a chain of radio or television stations.

nettle

neu·ral·gia (noo ral′jə *or* nyoo ral′jə), *n.* sharp pain in or along a nerve.

neu·ri·tis (noo rī′tis *or* nyoo rī′tis), *n.* a condition in which a nerve or nerves are inflamed, causing pain and soreness.

neu·rol·o·gy (noo räl′ə jē *or* nyoo räl′ə jē), *n.* the branch of medicine that deals with the nervous system and its diseases. —**neu·rol′o·gist,** *n.*

neu·ro·sis (noo rō′sis *or* nyoo rō′sis), *n.* a mental condition in which a person is continually worried, fearful, etc. in a way that is not normal. —**neu·ro·ses** (noo rō′sēz *or* nyoo rō′sēz), *pl.*

neu·rot·ic (noo rät′ik *or* nyoo rät′ik), *adj.* like or having a neurosis; too nervous. —*n.* a person who has a neurosis. —**neu·rot′i·cal·ly,** *adv.*

neu·ter (noo′tər *or* nyoo′tər), *adj.* **1.** of a class of words in grammar that refer to things that are thought of as neither male nor female ["It" is a *neuter* pronoun.] **2.** having no sex organs, as the amoeba. **3.** having sex organs that never develop fully, as the worker ant.

neu·tral (noo′trəl *or* nyoo′trəl), *adj.* **1.** joining neither side in a quarrel or war. **2.** not one thing or the other; in the middle [A *neutral* solution in chemistry is neither acid nor alkaline.] **3.** not strong or definite [Gray and tan are *neutral* colors. The sound of (ə) is *neutral*.] —*n.* **1.** a person or nation not taking part in a quarrel or war. **2.** the position of gears when they are not meshed together and therefore cannot pass on power from the engine.

neu·tral·i·ty (noo tral′ə tē *or* nyoo tral′ə tē), *n.* the quality or condition of being neutral.

neu·tral·ize (noo′trə līz *or* nyoo′trə līz), *v.* **1.** to work against in an opposite way so as to make neutral or weaker [An alkali *neutralizes* an acid.] **2.** to declare to be neutral in war [to *neutralize* a seaport]. —**neu′tral·ized,** *p.t. & p.p.;* **neu′- tral·iz·ing,** *pr.p.* —**neu′tral·i·za′tion,** *n.*

neu·tron (noo′trän *or* nyoo′trän), *n.* one of the particles which make up the nucleus of an atom. A neutron has no electrical charge.

Ne·vad·a (nə vad′ə *or* nə vä′də), *n.* a State in the southwestern part of the United States: abbreviated **Nev.**

nev·er (nev′ər), *adv.* **1.** at no time; not ever [I *never* saw him again.] **2.** not at all; in no way [*Never* mind what he says.]

nev·er·more (nev′ər môr′), *adv.* never again.

nev·er·the·less (nev′ər *th*ə les′), *adv.* in spite of that; however; still [They were losing the game; *nevertheless,* they kept on trying.]

new (noo *or* nyoo), *adj.* **1.** seen, made, thought of, discovered, etc. for the first time [a *new* song; a *new* plan; a *new* star]. **2.** different from the earlier one [She's wearing her hair a *new* way.] **3.** that is the more recent or the most recent one [This is the *new* library. Bill is the *new* president of our club.] **4.** that has not been worn or used [*new* and used cars]. **5.** recently grown; fresh [*new* potatoes]. **6.** strange; not familiar [The idea is *new* to me.] **7.** more; additional [two *new* inches of snow]. **8.** beginning again; starting once more [the *new* year]. —*adv.* newly; recently: *used mainly in words formed with a hyphen* [the *new*-fallen snow]. —**new′ness,** *n.*

New·ark (noo′ərk *or* nyoo′ərk), *n.* a city in northeastern New Jersey.

new·born (noo′bôrn *or* nyoo′bôrn′), *adj.* **1.** just born; born not long ago [a *newborn* calf]. **2.** born again; revived [*newborn* courage].

New Bruns·wick (brunz′wik), a province of Canada, on the southeastern coast.

new·com·er (n⊙⊙′kum′ər or ny⊙⊙′kum′ər), *n.* a person who has come recently; new arrival.

New Del·hi (del′ē), the capital of India, right next to Delhi.

new·el (n⊙⊙′əl or ny⊙⊙′əl), *n.* a post at the bottom or top of a flight of stairs, used to support the railing: also called **newel post.**

New England, the six northeastern States of the United States: Maine, Vermont, New Hampshire, Massachusetts, Rhode Island, and Connecticut. **—New Englander.**

newel

new·fan·gled (n⊙⊙′fang′g′ld or ny⊙⊙′fang′g′ld), *adj.* new and strange; unusual, but not worthwhile [*newfangled* gadgets].

New·found·land (n⊙⊙ found′land′ or ny⊙⊙′fənd lənd), *n.* **1.** an island off the eastern coast of Canada. **2.** a province of Canada, made up of this island and Labrador.

New·found·land dog (n⊙⊙ found′lənd or ny⊙⊙found′lənd), a large dog with a thick coat of long hair, usually black.

New Guin·ea (gin′ē), a large island north of Australia, divided between Indonesia and Australia.

New Hamp·shire (hamp′shir), a New England State of the United States: abbreviated **N.H.**

New Ha·ven (hā′v′n), a city in southern Connecticut.

New Jer·sey (jur′zē), a State in the northeastern part of the United States: abbreviated **N.J.**

new·ly (n⊙⊙′lē or ny⊙⊙′lē), *adv.* a short time ago; recently [a *newly* paved road].

New Mexico, a State in the southwestern part of the United States: abbreviated **N.Mex.** or **N.M.**

New Or·le·ans (ôr′li ənz or ôr′lənz), a city in southeastern Louisiana, on the Mississippi.

news (n⊙⊙z or ny⊙⊙z), *n.pl.* **1.** happenings that have just taken place, especially as told about in a newspaper, over radio or television, etc. **2.** things told that a person has not heard of before; new information [This story about her childhood is *news* to me.] *This word is used with a singular verb.*

news·boy (n⊙⊙z′boi or ny⊙⊙z′boi), *n.* a boy who sells or delivers newspapers.

news·cast (n⊙⊙z′kast or ny⊙⊙z′kast), *n.* a program of news broadcast over radio or television. **—news′cast′er,** *n.*

New South Wales, a state of southeastern Australia.

news·pa·per (n⊙⊙z′pā′pər or ny⊙⊙z′pā′pər), *n.* a daily or weekly publication printed on large, folded sheets of paper and containing news, opinions, advertisements, etc.

news·reel (n⊙⊙z′rēl or ny⊙⊙z′rēl), *n.* a short motion picture of news events.

news·stand (n⊙⊙z′stand or ny⊙⊙z′stand), *n.* a stand or stall at which newspapers, magazines, etc. are sold.

news·y (n⊙⊙z′ē or ny⊙⊙z′ē), *adj.* full of news: *used only in everyday talk* [a *newsy* letter]. **—news′i·er,** *compar.*; **news′i·est,** *superl.*

newt (n⊙⊙t or ny⊙⊙t), *n.* a small salamander that lives on land and in water.

New Testament, the part of the Bible that tells of the life and teachings of Jesus and his followers.

New·ton, Sir **Isaac** (n⊙⊙′t′n or ny⊙⊙′t′n), 1642-1727; English mathematician and philosopher.

New World, the Western Hemisphere; the Americas.

newt (3 to 6 in. long)

New Year's Day or **New Year's,** January 1.

New York (yôrk), **1.** a State in the northeastern part of the United States: abbreviated **N.Y. 2.** a seaport in southeastern New York State; the largest city in the United States: often called **New York City.**

New Zea·land (zē′lənd), a country in the southern Pacific, made up of two large islands and some smaller ones. It is a member of the British Commonwealth of Nations.

next (nekst), *adj.* nearest or closest; coming just before or just after [the *next* boy in line; in the *next* room; *next* Monday]. **—adv. 1.** in the nearest place, time, etc. [He sits *next* to me in school. Please wait on me *next*.] **2.** at the first chance after this [when *next* we meet]. **—prep.** beside [He sat *next* the tree.] **—next door,** in or at the next house, building, etc.

next-door (neks′dôr′), *adj.* in or at the next house, building, etc. [a *next-door* neighbor].

Nfld., abbreviation for **Newfoundland.**

N.H., abbreviation for **New Hampshire.**

Ni, symbol for the chemical element *nickel.*

Ni·ag·a·ra Falls (nī ag′rə or nī ag′ə rə), the large waterfall of the Niagara River, which flows from Lake Erie into Lake Ontario.

nib (nib), *n.* **1.** a bird's beak. **2.** a point; especially, the point of a pen.

nib·ble (nib′′l), *v.* **1.** to eat with quick, small bites [The mouse *nibbled* the cheese.] **2.** to bite lightly or carefully [The fish *nibbled* at the bait.] **—n. 1.** a nibbling. **2.** a small bite. **—nib′bled,** *p.t. & p.p.*; **nib′bling,** *pr.p.*

Nic·a·ra·gua (nik′ə rä′gwə), *n.* a country in Central America. **—Nic′a·ra′guan,** *adj. & n.*

Nice (nēs), *n.* a seaport and resort in southeastern France, on the Mediterranean.

nice (nīs), *adj.* **1.** good, pleasant, agreeable, pretty, kind, polite, etc. [a *nice* time; a *nice* dress; a *nice* neighbor]. **2.** able to see, hear, or measure small differences [a *nice* ear for musical pitch]. **3.** slight and not easily seen; very fine [a *nice* difference]. **4.** calling for great care, exactness, tact, etc. [a *nice* problem]. **5.** not easy to please;

very particular [He shows *nice* taste in books.]
—**nic′er,** *compar.;* **nic′est,** *superl.* —**nice′ly,**
adv.

ni·ce·ty (nī′sə tē), *n.* **1.** accuracy or exactness
[a *nicety* in judgment]. **2.** the quality of being
very particular or hard to please. **3.** a small
detail or fine point [the *niceties* of grammar].
4. something choice, dainty, or elegant [the
niceties of life]. —**to a nicety,** to just the right
degree; exactly. —**ni′ce·ties,** *pl.*

niche (nich), *n.* **1.** a hollow place in a wall,
for a statue, vase, etc. **2.** a place
or position for which a person is
specially fitted [He found his
niche in teaching.]

Nich·o·las, Saint (nik′ə ləs), the
patron saint of Russia, who died
in 342 A.D. See **Santa Claus.**

nick (nik), *v.* **1.** to make a small
cut, chip, etc. on or in [to *nick* a
cup]. **2.** to barely touch [The
bat just *nicked* the ball.] —*n.* a
small cut, chip, etc. made in an
edge or surface. —**in the nick
of time,** just barely at the right
time.

statue in a niche

nick·el (nik′'l), *n.* **1.** a silver-
white metal that is a chemical element. Nickel
is used in alloys and as a plating for metals.
2. a coin of the United States or Canada, made of
copper and nickel and worth five cents.

nick·name (nik′nām), *n.* **1.** a name given to a
person or thing in fun or affection, often one that
describes in some way ["Shorty" and "Slim" are
common *nicknames*.] **2.** a common or familiar
form of a person's name ["Jim" is a *nickname*
for "James."] —*v.* to give a nickname to.
—**nick′named,** *p.t. & p.p.;* **nick′nam·ing,**
pr.p.

nic·o·tine (nik′ə tēn), *n.* a poisonous, oily
liquid taken from tobacco leaves and used for
killing insects.

niece (nēs), *n.* **1.** the daughter of one's brother
or sister. **2.** the daughter of one's brother-in-law
or sister-in-law.

Ni·ger (nī′jər), *n.* **1.** a river in western Africa.
2. a country in Africa, north of Nigeria.

Ni·ge·ri·a (nī jir′i ə), *n.* a country on the western
coast of Africa.

nig·gard (nig′ərd), *n.* a stingy person; miser.
—*adj.* stingy; miserly.

nig·gard·ly (nig′ərd lē), *adj.* **1.** stingy; miserly.
2. small or few [a *niggardly* sum]. —*adv.* in a
stingy way. —**nig′gard·li·ness,** *n.*

nigh (nī), *adv., adj. & prep.* near: *no longer in
common use, except in some regions.*

night (nīt), *n.* **1.** the time of darkness between
sunset and sunrise. **2.** the darkness of this time.
3. any period or condition of darkness or gloom,
as a time of sorrow, death, etc. —*adj.* of, for,
or at night [*night* school].

night·cap (nīt′kap), *n.* **1.** a cap worn in bed.
2. a drink taken just before go-
ing to bed.

night club, a place of entertainment open at night for eating, drinking, dancing, etc.

night·fall (nīt′fôl), *n.* the
day's end; dusk.

night·gown (nīt′goun), *n.* a
loose gown worn in bed by
women or small children.

night·hawk (nīt′hôk), *n.* **1.**
a bird related to the whippoorwill. It is active
mostly at night. **2.** same
as **night owl.**

night·in·gale (nīt′'n gāl),
n. a small European
thrush. The male is known
for its sweet singing, especially at night.

**Night·in·gale, Flor-
ence** (nīt′'n gāl), 1820–
1910; an English nurse,
thought of as the founder
of modern nursing.

night·ly (nīt′lē), *adj.*
done or happening every
night [his *nightly* bath]. —*adv.* at night or every
night [He reads a chap-
ter *nightly.*]

night·mare (nīt′mer),
n. **1.** a frightening
dream. **2.** any very
frightening experience.

night owl, a person
who works at night or
likes to stay up late.

night·shade (nīt′shād),
n. a flowering plant related to the potato and
tomato; especially, a poisonous kind, as the
belladonna.

night·shirt (nīt′shurt), *n.* a loose garment
like a long shirt, worn in bed by men or boys.

nil (nil), *n.* nothing [Our chances are *nil*.]

Nile (nīl), *n.* a river in eastern Africa, flowing
through Egypt into the Mediterranean.

nim·ble (nim′b'l), *adj.* **1.** moving quickly and
lightly; agile [the *nimble* fingers of the pianist].
2. having or showing mental quickness; clever
[a *nimble* mind]. —**nim′bler,** *compar.;* **nim′-
blest,** *superl.* —**nim′ble·ness,** *n.* —**nim′-
bly,** *adv.*

nim·bus (nim′bəs), *n.* **1.** a low, gray cloud that
covers the sky bringing rain or snow. **2.** a halo.

Nim·rod (nim′räd), *n.* **1.** a mighty hunter mentioned in the Bible. **2.** any hunter.

nin·com·poop (nin′kəm poop), *n.* a stupid,
silly person; fool.

nine (nīn), *n. & adj.* one more than eight; the
number 9.

nightcap

nighthawks (10 in. long)

nightingale (7 in. long)

nine·pins (nīn′pinz), *n.pl.* a game like bowling, in which only nine wooden pins are used.

nine·teen (nīn′tēn′), *n. & adj.* nine more than ten; the number 19.

nine·teenth (nīn′tēnth′), *adj.* coming after eighteen others; 19th in order. —*n.* **1.** the nineteenth one. **2.** one of nineteen equal parts of something; 1/19.

nine·ti·eth (nīn′tē ith), *adj.* coming after eighty-nine others; 90th in order. —*n.* **1.** the ninetieth one. **2.** one of ninety equal parts of something; 1/90.

nine·ty (nīn′tē), *n. & adj.* **1.** nine times ten; the number 90. **2.** **nineties,** *n.pl.* the numbers or years from 90 to 99.

Nin·e·veh (nin′ə və), *n.* a city in ancient Assyria.

nin·ny (nin′ē), *n.* a fool. —**nin′nies,** *pl.*

ninth (nīnth), *adj.* coming after eight others; 9th in order. —*n.* **1.** the ninth one. **2.** one of nine equal parts of something; 1/9.

nip (nip), *v.* **1.** to pinch, squeeze, or bite [He *nipped* his finger in the door.] **2.** to cut or pinch off; clip [to *nip* dead leaves from a plant]. **3.** to hurt or spoil [Frost *nipped* the buds.] —*n.* **1.** a pinch, squeeze, or bite. **2.** stinging cold; chill [There's a *nip* in the air.] —**nip and tuck,** so close or even that one cannot tell how it will turn out. —**nip in the bud,** to check or stop at the start. —**nipped,** *p.t. & p.p.;* **nip′ping,** *pr.p.*

nip (nip), *n.* a small drink or sip.

nip·per (nip′ər), *n.* **1.** anything that nips, or pinches. **2.** **nippers,** *pl.* a tool for grasping or cutting, as pliers or pincers. **3.** the claw of a crab or lobster.

nip·ple (nip′'l), *n.* **1.** the part of a breast or udder through which a baby or young animal sucks milk from its mother. **2.** anything like this, as a rubber cap for a baby's bottle.

nippers

Nip·pon (nip′än′), *n.* Japan: *the Japanese name.* —**Nip·pon·ese** (nip ə nēz′), *adj. & n.*

nip·py (nip′ē), *adj.* sharp; biting, as with cold. —**nip′pi·er,** *compar.;* **nip′pi·est,** *superl.*

nir·va·na (nər vän′ə *or* nir vä′nə), *n.* in Buddhism, perfect happiness in which the self becomes part of the supreme spirit of the universe.

nit (nit), *n.* the egg of a louse or similar insect.

ni·ter *or* **ni·tre** (nī′tər), *n.* potassium nitrate or sodium nitrate salts used in making gunpowder, fertilizers, etc.; saltpeter.

ni·trate (nī′trāt), *n.* a substance containing nitrogen, especially a salt of nitric acid used as a fertilizer.

ni·tric acid (nī′trik), a strong, colorless acid that contains nitrogen and eats into metal, cloth, etc.

ni·tro·gen (nī′trə jən), *n.* a gas that has no color, taste, or odor, and is a chemical element. It makes up nearly four fifths of the air around the earth, and is found in all living things. —**ni·trog·e·nous** (nī träj′ə nəs), *adj.*

ni·tro·glyc·er·in *or* **ni·tro·glyc·er·ine** (nī′trə glis′ər in), *n.* a thick, yellow oil that is a strong explosive. It is used in making dynamite, and also as a medicine.

ni·trous oxide (nī′trəs), a colorless gas used, as by dentists, to lessen pain.

Nix·on, Richard M. (nik′s'n), 1913– ; 37th president of the United States, from 1969.

N.J., abbreviation for **New Jersey.**

N.Mex. *or* **N.M.,** abbreviation for **New Mexico.**

no (nō), *adv.* **1.** not so; I won't, I can't, I refuse, it isn't, etc.: opposite of **yes.** **2.** not at all [He is *no* worse.] —*adj.* not in any way; not a [He is *no* student.] —*n.* **1.** the act of saying "no"; refusal or denial. **2.** a vote against something. —**noes,** *pl.*

No. *or* **no.,** abbreviation for **number.**

No·ah (nō′ə), *n.* a man in the Bible who was told by God to build an ark, so that he and his family and two of every kind of creature would be saved during a great flood.

No·bel prizes (nō bel′), five international prizes given every year for outstanding work in physics, chemistry, medicine, and literature, and for promoting peace

no·bil·i·ty (nō bil′ə tē), *n.* **1.** the quality of being noble. **2.** the class of people who have noble rank, as kings, princes, dukes, etc.

no·ble (nō′b'l), *adj.* **1.** having or showing a very good character or high morals; lofty [*noble* ideals]. **2.** of or having a high rank or title; aristocratic [a *noble* family]. **3.** grand; splendid; [a *noble* oak]. —*n.* a person who has noble rank or title. —**no′ble·ness,** *n.* —**no′bly,** *adv.*

no·ble·man (nō′b'l mən), *n.* a man who has a noble rank or title; peer. —**no′ble·men,** *pl.*

no·bod·y (nō′bəd ē *or* nō′bäd′ē), *pron.* not anybody; no one. —*n.* a person who is not important in any way. —**no′bod·ies,** *pl.*

noc·tur·nal (näk tūr′n'l), *adj.* **1.** of or during the night [a *nocturnal* ride]. **2.** active at night [The bat is a *nocturnal* animal.] —**noc·tur′nal·ly,** *adv.*

noc·turne (näk′tərn), *n.* a piece of music that is romantic or dreamy and is thought to suggest the evening or night.

nod (näd), *v.* **1.** to bend the head forward quickly, as in agreeing or in greeting someone. **2.** to let the head fall forward in falling asleep. **3.** to sway back and forth, as tree tops or flowers in the wind. —*n.* the act of nodding. —**nod′ded,** *p.t. & p.p.;* **nod′ding,** *pr.p.*

node (nōd), *n.* **1.** a swelling; knob. **2.** that part of a stem from which a leaf starts to grow.

nod·ule (näj′ool *or* näd′yool), *n.* a small node, especially on a stem or root. —**nod·u·lar** (näj′oo lər *or* näd′yoo lər), *adj.*

nodes

No·el *or* **No·ël** (nō el′), *n.* **1.** Christmas. **2.** noel *or* noël, a Christmas carol.

nog·gin (näg′in), *n.* **1.** a small cup or mug. **2.** the head: *used only in everyday talk.*

noise (noiz), *n.* sound, especially a loud, harsh, or confused sound [the *noise* of fireworks; *noises* of a city street]. —*v.* to make public by telling; spread, as news or a rumor. —**noised,** *p.t. & p.p.;* **nois'ing,** *pr.p.*

noise·less (noiz'lis), *adj.* with little or no noise; silent [a *noiseless* electric fan].

noi·some (noi'səm), *adj.* having a disgusting or sickening smell [a *noisome* swamp].

nois·y (noiz'ē), *adj.* **1.** making noise [a *noisy* bell]. **2.** full of noise [a *noisy* theater]. —**nois'·i·er,** *compar.;* **nois'i·est,** *superl.* —**nois'i·ly,** *adv.* —**nois'i·ness,** *n.*

no·mad (nō'mad), *n.* **1.** a member of a tribe or people that keeps moving about looking for pasture for its animals. **2.** any wanderer who has no fixed home. —**no·mad'ic,** *adj.*

Nome (nōm), *n.* a seaport in western Alaska.

no·men·cla·ture (nō'mən klā'chər), *n.* a system of names, as those used in studying a certain science [the *nomenclature* of botany].

nom·i·nal (näm'ə n'l), *adj.* **1.** in name only, not in fact [The queen is the *nominal* ruler of the country.] **2.** very small; slight [There is a *nominal* entrance fee.] —**nom'i·nal·ly,** *adv.*

nom·i·nate (näm'ə nāt), *v.* **1.** to name as a candidate for an election [Three students were *nominated* for chairman of the council.] **2.** to appoint to a position [The President *nominates* all postmasters.] —**nom'i·nat·ed,** *p.t. & p.p.;* **nom'i·nat·ing,** *pr.p.*

nom·i·na·tion (näm'ə nā'shən), *n.* the act of nominating or the fact of being nominated.

nom·i·na·tive (näm'i nə tiv), *adj.* showing the subject of a verb or the words that agree with the subject. In Latin and some other languages, nouns, pronouns, and adjectives have certain endings to show that they are in the nominative case. In English, only such forms of pronouns as *I, she,* and *he* are in the nominative case. —*n.* the nominative case.

nom·i·nee (näm ə nē'), *n.* a person who is nominated, especially as a candidate for an election.

non-, a prefix meaning "not." A hyphen is used after *non-* when it is put before a word beginning with a capital letter [A *non-English* word is a word that is not English. *Nonfiction* is writing that is not fiction.]

non·al·co·hol·ic (nän'al kə hôl'ik), *adj.* having no alcohol in it [Root beer is a *nonalcoholic* drink.]

non·break·a·ble (nän brāk'ə b'l), *adj.* not breakable; that cannot be broken.

nonce (näns), *n.* the present time; right now: *now used mainly in the phrase* **for the nonce,** meaning "for the time being."

non·cha·lant (nän'shə lənt *or* nän shə länt'), *adj.* not caring; not showing concern; casual [He is *nonchalant* about his debts.] —**non'·cha·lance,** *n.* —**non'cha·lant·ly,** *adv.*

non·com·bat·ant (nän käm'bə tənt *or* nän'kəm bat'ənt), *n.* a civilian in wartime, or a member of the armed forces who does not actually fight, as a nurse or chaplain. —*adj.* not fighting; of noncombatants.

non·com·mer·cial (nän'kə mūr'shəl), *adj.* not commercial.

non·com·mis·sioned officer (nän'kə mish'ənd), a person in the armed forces who holds a rank higher than private, but without a commission or warrant, as a sergeant or corporal.

non·com·mit·tal (nän'kə mit''l), *adj.* not having or showing a definite opinion or plan [He answered with a *noncommittal* smile, instead of a plain "yes" or "no."]

non·con·duc·tor (nän'kən duk'tər), *n.* something that does not easily conduct electricity, heat, or sound [Glass is a *nonconductor* of electricity.]

non·con·form·ist (nän'kən fôr'mist), *n.* **1.** a person whose beliefs and actions are not those of most people. **2.** a person who does not belong to the official church of a country. —**non'con·form'i·ty,** *n.*

non·con·ta·gious (nän'kən tā'jəs), *adj.* not contagious.

non·de·script (nän'di script), *adj.* hard to describe because not of a definite kind or class [a *nondescript* alley cat].

none (nun), *pron.* **1.** no one; not anyone [*None* of us is ready.] **2.** not any [*None* of the money is left. Many letters were received but *none* were answered.] —*adv.* in no way; not at all [He came *none* too soon.] —**none the less,** nevertheless.

non·en·ti·ty (nän en'tə tē), *n.* a person who is not at all important. —**non·en'ti·ties,** *pl.*

non·es·sen·tial (nän'i sen'shəl), *adj.* not essential; not absolutely necessary. —*n.* a person or thing that is not essential.

non·ex·ist·ent (nän'ig zis'tənt), *adj.* not existing; not real [worried over *nonexistent* dangers]. —**non'ex·ist'ence,** *n.*

non·pa·reil (nän pə rel'), *adj.* having no equal. —*n.* a person or thing that has no equal.

non·par·ti·san *or* **non·par·ti·zan** (nän pär'tə z'n), *adj.* not supporting or controlled by a political party or parties; not partisan [*nonpartisan* candidates for the office of judge].

non·pay·ment (nän pā'mənt), *n.* a refusing or failing to pay, as one's debts.

non·plus (nän plus'), *v.* to make so confused that one cannot speak or act; bewilder [The speaker was *nonplused* by the sudden interruption.] —**non·plused'** *or* **non·plussed',** *p.t. & p.p.;* **non·plus'ing** *or* **non·plus'sing,** *pr.p.*

non·pro·duc·tive (nän'prə duk'tiv), *adj.* not producing the goods or results wanted [*nonproductive* farmlands; a *nonproductive* plan].

non·prof·it (nän präf'it), *adj.* not intending to make a profit [a *nonprofit* hospital].

fat, āpe, cär, ten, ēven, hĭt, bīte, gō, hôrn, tōōl, book, up, fŭr;
get, joy, yet, chin, she, thin, *th*en; zh = s in pleasure; ' as in able (ā'b'l);
ə = a in ago, e in agent, i in sanity, o in confess, u in focus.

non·res·i·dent (nän rez/ə dənt), *adj.* not having one's home in the place, city, State, etc. where one works, goes to school, or the like [a *nonresident* doctor at the hospital]. —*n.* a nonresident person.

non·re·stric·tive (nän'ri strik/tiv), *adj.* describing a clause, phrase, or word that is not absolutely necessary to the meaning of a sentence and that is set off by commas. Example: John, *who is six feet tall*, is younger than Bill.

non·sec·tar·i·an (nän'sek ter/i ən), *adj.* not connected with or controlled by any church or religious sect [a *nonsectarian* college].

non·sense (nän/sens), *n.* words or actions that are foolish or have no meaning; silly talk or behavior [Let's have no more *nonsense* about your leaving. Stop that *nonsense*, Max!] —*interj.* how silly! how foolish! I disagree!

non·sen·si·cal (nän sen/si k'l), *adj.* not making sense; foolish; silly.

non·stop (nän/stäp/), *adj. & adv.* without a stop [a 2500-mile *nonstop* flight; to fly *nonstop* from New York to Paris].

non·un·ion (nän yoon/yən), *adj.* **1.** not belonging to a labor union. **2.** not made, done, etc. according to the rules of labor unions.

noo·dle (noo/d'l), *n.* a flat, narrow strip of dry dough, usually made with egg and served in soups, etc.

noodles in soup

nook (nook), *n.* **1.** a corner of a room, or a part cut off from the main part [breakfast *nook*]. **2.** a small, sheltered spot [a picnic in a shady *nook*].

noon (noon), *n.* twelve o'clock in the daytime: also **noon/day, noon/tide, noon/time.**

no-one (nō/wun), *pron.* same as **no one.**

no one, not anybody; no person; nobody.

noose (noos), *n.* **1.** a loop made by putting one end of a rope, etc. through a slipknot so the loop can be tightened. **2.** anything that snares, hampers, etc. —**the noose,** death by hanging.

nor (nôr *or* nər), *conj.* and not; and not either: *a word used to separate two other words or two groups of words introduced by* neither [Neither John *nor* Jane can go.] *Nor* is also used after other negative words, as *not* and *no* [They have no car, *nor* do they want one.]

noose

Nor·dic (nôr/dik), *adj.* describing or of a type of tall, blond people of northern Europe, as the Scandinavians. —*n.* a person of this type.

norm (nôrm), *n.* a standard for a certain group, usually based on the average for that group.

nor·mal (nôr/m'l), *adj.* agreeing with a standard or norm; natural; usual; regular; average [It is *normal* to make a mistake sometimes.] —*n.* what is normal; the usual condition, amount, level, etc. [His blood pressure is above *normal*.]

nor·mal·ly (nôr/m'l ē), *adv.* **1.** in a normal way [to behave *normally*]. **2.** under normal conditions; usually [*Normally* we eat at home.]

Nor·man (nôr/mən), *n.* **1.** a person born or living in Normandy. **2.** any of the people of Normandy who settled in England after the Norman Conquest. —*adj.* of Normandy or the Normans.

Norman Conquest, the conquest of England by the Normans in 1066, led by William the Conqueror.

Nor·man·dy (nôr/mən dē), *n.* a district in northern France, on the English Channel.

Norse (nôrs), *adj.* **1.** of or having to do with ancient Scandinavia. **2.** Norwegian. —*n.* the language of ancient Scandinavia. —**the Norse,** the people of ancient Scandinavia; Norsemen.

Norse·man (nôrs/mən), *n.* any of the people of ancient Scandinavia. —**Norse/men,** *pl.*

north (nôrth), *n.* **1.** the direction to the right of a person facing the sunset. **2.** a place or region in or toward this direction. In the United States, **the North** means the part north of Maryland, the Ohio River, and Missouri. **3.** *often* **North,** the northern part of the earth, especially the arctic regions. —*adj.* **1.** in, of, to, or toward the north [the *north* side of the house]. **2.** from the north [a *north* wind]. **3. North,** that is the northern part of [*North* Korea]. —*adv.* in or toward the north [Go *north* two miles.]

North America, the northern continent in the Western Hemisphere. Canada, the United States, Mexico, and Central America are in North America. —**North American.**

North Carolina, a State in the southeastern part of the United States: abbreviated **N.C.**

North Dakota, a State in the north central part of the United States: abbreviated **N.Dak.** or **N.D.**

north·east (nôrth ēst/), *n.* **1.** the direction halfway between north and east. **2.** a place or region in or toward this direction. —*adj.* **1.** in, of, or toward the northeast [the *northeast* part of town]. **2.** from the northeast [a *northeast* wind]. —*adv.* in or toward the northeast [to sail *northeast*].

north·east·er (nôrth ēs/tər), *n.* a storm or strong wind from the northeast.

north·east·er·ly (nôrth ēs/tər lē), *adj. & adv.* **1.** in or toward the northeast. **2.** from the northeast.

north·east·ern (nôrth ēs/tərn), *adj.* **1.** in, of, or toward the northeast [*northeastern* Ohio]. **2.** from the northeast [a *northeastern* wind].

north·er·ly (nôr/thər lē), *adj. & adv.* **1.** in or toward the north. **2.** from the north.

north·ern (nôr/thərn), *adj.* **1.** in, of, or toward the north [the *northern* sky]. **2.** from the north [a *northern* wind]. **3. Northern,** of the North.

North·ern·er (nôr/thər nər), *n.* a person born or living in the North.

Northern Hemisphere, the half of the earth that is north of the equator.

Northern Ireland, a part of the United Kingdom, in the north of the island of Ireland.

northern lights, same as **aurora borealis.**

north·ern·most (nôr/thərn mōst), *adj.* farthest north.

North Pole, the spot that is farthest north on the earth; northern end of the earth's axis.

North Sea, a part of the Atlantic, east of Great Britain and west of Norway and Denmark.

North Star, the bright star almost directly above the North Pole.

North·um·bri·a (nôr thum′bri ə), *n.* an Anglo-Saxon kingdom in northern England long ago.

north·ward (nôrth′wərd), *adj. & adv.* toward the north: also **north′wards,** *adv.* —*n.* a northward direction or place.

north·west (nôrth west′), *n.* **1.** the direction halfway between north and west. **2.** a place or region in or toward this direction. —*adj.* **1.** in, of, or toward the northwest [the *northwest* part of town]. **2.** from the northwest [a *northwest* wind]. —*adv.* in or toward the northwest [to sail *northwest*].

north·west·er (nôrth wes′tər), *n.* a storm or strong wind from the northwest.

north·west·er·ly (nôrth wes′tər lē), *adj. & adv.* **1.** in or toward the northwest. **2.** from the northwest.

north·west·ern (nôrth wes′tərn), *adj.* **1.** in, of, or toward the northwest. **2.** from the northwest [a *northwestern* wind].

Northwest Territories, a large division of northern Canada, north and west of Hudson Bay.

Nor·way (nôr′wā), *n.* a country in northern Europe, west of Sweden.

Nor·we·gian (nôr wē′jən), *adj.* of Norway, its people, etc. —*n.* **1.** a person born or living in Norway. **2.** the language of Norway.

nose (nōz), *n.* **1.** the part of the head that sticks out between the mouth and the eyes, and has two openings for breathing and smelling. The nose is part of the muzzle or snout in animals. **2.** the sense of smell [a dog with a good *nose*]. **3.** anything like a nose in shape or in the way it is placed, as the front of an airplane or the bow of a ship. —*v.* **1.** to move with the front end forward [The ship *nosed* into the harbor.] **2.** to meddle in another's affairs. **3.** to smell with the nose. **4.** to rub with the nose. —**look down one's nose at** or **turn up one's nose at,** to show dislike for: *used only in everyday talk.* —**nose out,** to defeat by a very small margin. —**pay through the nose,** to pay more than something is worth. —**nosed,** *p.t. & p.p.;* **nos′ing,** *pr.p.*

nose·bleed (nōz′blēd), *n.* a bleeding from the nose.

nose dive, 1. a fast, steep dive of an airplane, with the nose pointed down. **2.** any sudden, swift drop, as in profits or prices.

nose-dive (nōz′dīv′), *v.* to make a nose dive. —**nose′-dived′,** *p.t. & p.p.;* **nose′-div′ing,** *pr.p.*

nose·gay (nōz′gā), *n.* a bunch of flowers.

nos·tal·gia (näs tal′jə), *n.* a wishing for something that happened long ago or is now far away

[*nostalgia* for one's home town]. —**nos·tal′-gic,** *adj.*

nos·tril (näs′trəl), *n.* either of the two openings in the nose for breathing and smelling.

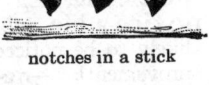

nostril

nos·trum (näs′trəm), *n.* **1.** a medicine that is sold to the public with exaggerated advertisement. **2.** a favorite scheme or plan for solving some problem: *a word used by those who dislike the plan.*

nos·y or **nos·ey** (nōz′ē), *adj.* too curious about others' affairs; prying: *used only in everyday talk.* —**nos′i·er,** *compar.;* **nos′i·est,** *superl.*

not (nät), *adv.* in no way or to no degree [Do *not* talk. She is *not* happy.]

no·ta·ble (nō′tə b'l), *adj.* worth noticing or paying attention to; remarkable; outstanding [a *notable* statesman; a *notable* success]. —*n.* a notable person. —**no′ta·bly,** *adv.*

no·ta·rize (nō′tə rīz), *v.* to sign and seal a legal paper in one's work as a notary. —**no′ta·rized,** *p.t. & p.p.;* **no′ta·riz·ing,** *pr.p.*

no·ta·ry (nō′tər ē), *n.* an official who has the power to witness the signing of a deed, will, contract, etc. and to declare that a person has sworn to the truth of something: the full name is **notary public.** —**no′ta·ries,** *pl.*

no·ta·tion (nō tā′shən), *n.* **1.** a brief note jotted down, as to remind one of something. **2.** a system of symbols or signs used in arithmetic, music, chemistry, etc., to stand for words, amounts, etc. [In chemical *notation*, H_2O stands for water.] **3.** the act of using such symbols or of noting something.

notch (näch), *n.* **1.** a cut in the form of a V, made in an edge or across a surface: *see the picture.* **2.** a narrow pass with steep sides. **3.** a step or degree: *used only in everyday talk* [His average dropped a *notch*.] —*v.* to cut a notch in.

notches in a stick

note (nōt), *n.* **1.** a word, phrase, etc. written down to help one remember something one has heard, read, thought, etc. [The students kept *notes* on the lecture.] **2.** a statement added to a book, as at the back or at the bottom of a page, to explain something or give more information. **3.** a short letter. **4.** an official letter from one government to another. **5.** a written promise to pay money. **6.** close attention; notice [Take *note* of what I say.] **7.** a musical tone, or the symbol for such a tone, showing how long it is to be sounded and how high or low it is. **8.** any of the keys of a piano, etc. **9.** a cry or call, as of a bird. **10.** importance

musical notes

or fame [a man of *note*]. **11.** a sign or hint [a *note* of sadness in her voice]. —*v.* **1.** to notice; observe. **2.** to mention. **3.** to set down in writing; make a note of. —**compare notes,** to exchange opinions. —**take notes,** to write down notes to remind one of something. —**not'-ed,** *p.t. & p.p.;* **not'ing,** *pr.p.*

note·book (nōt′book), *n.* a book in which notes are kept, as to help one remember things.

not·ed (nōt′əd), *adj.* famous; well-known.

note·wor·thy (nōt′wur′thē), *adj.* worth noticing or paying attention to; important.

noth·ing (nuth′ing), *n.* **1.** not anything; no thing [We saw *nothing* to frighten us.] **2.** a person or thing not important in any way [A few scratches are *nothing* to an animal trainer.] **3.** zero. —*adv.* in no way or degree [The adventure left him *nothing* wiser.] —**for nothing, 1.** free. **2.** with no effect. **3.** for no good reason. —**nothing but,** only; nothing other than. —**nothing less than,** no less than.

noth·ing·ness (nuth′ing nis), *n.* **1.** the condition of being nothing or not existing [The ancient scroll crumbled to *nothingness.*] **2.** the condition of having no value; uselessness.

no·tice (nō′tis), *n.* **1.** an announcement or warning [*notice* of a change in bus fares]. **2.** a written or printed sign announcing something or giving warning. **3.** attention; heed; regard [She paid him no *notice.*] **4.** an announcement that one plans to end a contract or agreement at a certain time [Did you give your landlord *notice* that you were moving?] **5.** a short review or other article about a book, play, etc. [The movie received good *notices.*] —*v.* to pay attention to; observe; take note of [He didn't *notice* his visitor.] —**serve notice,** to give information or a warning; announce. —**take notice,** to pay attention; look. —**no′ticed,** *p.t. & p.p.;* **no′tic·ing,** *pr.p.*

no·tice·a·ble (nō′tis ə b'l), *adj.* easily seen; likely to be noticed; remarkable [*noticeable* improvement]. —**no′tice·a·bly,** *adv.*

no·ti·fi·ca·tion (nō′tə fi kā′shən), *n.* **1.** a notifying or being notified. **2.** notice given or received [*notification* to appear in court].

no·ti·fy (nō′tə fī), *v.* to let know; inform; give notice to [Please *notify* me when he arrives.] —**no′ti·fied,** *p.t. & p.p.;* **no′ti·fy·ing,** *pr.p.*

no·tion (nō′shən), *n.* **1.** a general idea [Do you have any *notion* of what he meant?] **2.** a belief or opinion. **3.** a sudden fancy; whim [I had half a *notion* to call you.] **4.** a plan or intention [I have no *notion* of going.] **5.** **notions,** *pl.* small, useful things, as needles, thread, tape, etc., sold in a store.

no·to·ri·e·ty (nō′tə rī′ə tē), *n.* the condition of being notorious; bad reputation.

no·to·ri·ous (nō tôr′i əs), *adj.* well-known, especially for something bad [a *notorious* liar]. —**no·to′ri·ous·ly,** *adv.*

not·with·stand·ing (nät′with stan′ding), *prep.* in spite of [He drove on, *notwithstanding* the storm.] —*adv.* all the same; nevertheless [He must be told, *notwithstanding.*]

nou·gat (noo′gət), *n.* a candy made of a sugar paste with nuts in it.

nought (nôt), *n.* **1.** nothing [All his dreams came to *nought.*] **2.** the figure zero (0). Also spelled **naught.**

noun (noun), *n.* a word that is the name of a person, thing, action, quality, etc. A phrase or a clause can be used in a sentence as a noun ["Boy," "water," "truth," and "Cuba" are *nouns.*]

nour·ish (nur′ish), *v.* **1.** to feed; provide with the things needed for life and growth [Water and sunlight *nourished* the plants.] **2.** to keep up; make grow; foster; promote [Fair treatment *nourishes* good will.] —**nour′ish·ing,** *adj.*

nour·ish·ment (nur′ish mənt), *n.* **1.** a nourishing or being nourished. **2.** something that nourishes; food.

No·va Sco·tia (nō′və skō′shə), a province of Canada, on the southeastern coast.

nov·el (näv′'l), *adj.* new and strange [In 1920, flying was still a *novel* method of travel.] —*n.* a long story, usually a complete book about imaginary people and happenings.

nov·el·ette (näv′ə let′), *n.* a short novel.

nov·el·ist (näv′'l ist), *n.* a writer of novels.

nov·el·ty (näv′'l tē), *n.* **1.** newness and strangeness [The *novelty* of being alone had worn off and she was bored.] **2.** something new or unusual [It was a *novelty* for us to swim in the ocean.] **3.** a small, often cheap toy, decoration, souvenir, etc. —**nov′el·ties,** *pl.*

No·vem·ber (nō vem′bər), *n.* the eleventh month of the year. It has 30 days. Abbreviated **Nov.**

nov·ice (näv′is), *n.* **1.** a person new at something; beginner [a *novice* at photography]. **2.** a person who is going through a test period before being allowed to become a monk or nun.

no·vi·ti·ate or **no·vi·ci·ate** (nō vish′i it), *n.* the condition or time of being a novice, especially in a religious order.

now (nou), *adv.* **1.** at this moment; at the present time [He is sleeping *now.*] **2.** at that time; then; next [*Now* he started to climb the hill.] **3.** with things as they are [*Now* we'll never know what happened.] *Now* is often used without any definite meaning, as at the beginning of a sentence [*Now* where could it be? *Now, now,* don't cry.] —*conj.* since; seeing that [*Now* that you're here, we can leave.] —*n.* this time [That's all for *now.*] —**just now,** only a short while ago. —**now and then** or **now and again,** sometimes; occasionally.

now·a·days (nou′ə dāz), *adv.* in these days; at the present time. —*n.* the present time.

no·way (nō′wā) or **no·ways** (nō′wāz), *adv.* in no way; not at all; nowise.

no·where (nō′hwer), *adv.* not in, at, or to any place [He is *nowhere* to be found.] —*n.* a place that does not exist. —**nowhere near,** not nearly.

no·wise (nō′wīz), *adv.* in no way; not at all [I am *nowise* pleased about this.]

nox·ious (näk′shəs), *adj.* harmful or unhealthy [a *noxious* gas].

noz·zle (näz''l), *n.* a small spout at the end of a hose, pipe, etc., through which a stream of liquid or air comes out.

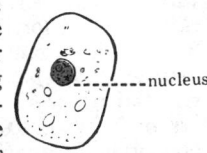

nozzle

N.S., abbreviation for **Nova Scotia.**

N.T., abbreviation for **New Testament.**

nu·ance (nōō äns' *or* nyōō'äns), *n.* a slight change in color, meaning, tone, etc. [His acting conveys every *nuance* of feeling in the part.]

nub (nub), *n.* **1.** a knob or lump. **2.** the point of a story, etc.; gist: *used only in everyday talk.*

nub·by (nub'ē), *adj.* having a rough, lumpy surface [a *nubby* cloth]. —**nub'bi·er,** *compar.;* **nub'bi·est,** *superl.*

nu·cle·ar (nōō'kli ər *or* nyōō'kli ər), *adj.* **1.** of or having to do with a nucleus or nuclei [*nuclear* physics]. **2.** of, involving, or using the nuclei of atoms, or atomic energy, atomic bombs, etc. [*nuclear* energy; *nuclear* warfare].

nuclear fission, the splitting of the nuclei of atoms, with the release of great amounts of energy, as in the atomic bomb.

nuclear fusion, the combining of the nuclei of atoms, with the release of great amounts of energy, as in the hydrogen bomb.

nu·cle·us (nōō'kli əs *or* nyōō'kli əs), *n.* **1.** the thing or part at the center, around which others are grouped. **2.** any center around which something grows [His few books became the *nucleus* of a large library.] **3.** the small mass at the center of most living cells. It is needed for the plant or animal to grow, reproduce itself, etc. **4.** the central part of an atom around which the electrons revolve. —**nu·cle·i** (nōō'kli ī *or* nyōō'kli ī), *pl.*

nucleus in a cell

nude (nōōd *or* nyōōd), *adj.* naked or bare. —*n.* a nude human figure in a work of art. —**in the nude,** in the condition of being nude; naked.

nudge (nuj), *v.* to push or poke gently, as with the elbow, especially so as to get the attention of. —*n.* a gentle push, as with the elbow. —**nudged,** *p.t. & p.p.;* **nudg'ing,** *pr.p.*

nug·get (nug'it), *n.* a lump or rough piece; especially, a lump of gold ore.

nui·sance (nōō's'ns *or* nyōō's'ns), *n.* an act, thing, or person that causes trouble or bother.

null (nul), *adj.* having no force or effect; invalid: *usually in the phrase* **null and void,** meaning "having no legal force; not binding."

nul·li·fy (nul'ə fī), *v.* **1.** to cause to have no effect as law; make void [to *nullify* a treaty by ignoring its terms]. **2.** to make useless; cancel [His losses *nullified* his profits.] —**nul'li·fied,**

p.t. & p.p.; **nul'li·fy·ing,** *pr.p.* —**nul'li·fi·ca'tion,** *n.*

numb (num), *adj.* not able to feel, or feeling very little; deadened [His toes were *numb* with cold. She sat *numb* with grief.] —*v.* to make numb. —**numb'ly,** *adv.* —**numb'ness,** *n.*

num·ber (num'bər), *n.* **1.** a symbol or word that is used in counting or that tells how many or which one in a series [Two, 7, 237, and tenth are all *numbers*.] **2.** the sum or total of persons or things [a small *number* of people]. **3.** *also* **numbers,** *pl.* a large group; many [*Numbers* of trees were cut down.] **4.** a single issue of a magazine [Was it in the June *number*?] **5.** one part of a program of dances, songs, etc. **6.** in grammar, the form of a word that shows whether one or more is meant [The word "he" shows singular *number*. The word "are" shows plural *number*.] —*v.* **1.** to give a number to [Dollar bills are *numbered*.] **2.** to include as one of a group or class [He is *numbered* among our friends.] **3.** to have or make up in number; total or contain [My books *number* almost eighty.] **4.** to limit the number of; make few [He is old and his years are *numbered*.] —**a number of,** several or many. —**beyond number** or **without number,** too many to be counted.

num·ber·less (num'bər lis), *adj.* too many to be counted [the *numberless* stars in the sky].

Num·bers (num'bərz), *n.* the fourth book of the Old Testament.

nu·mer·al (nōō'mər əl *or* nyōō'mər əl), *n.* **1.** a figure, letter, or word, or a group of these, standing for a number: see **Arabic numerals** and **Roman numerals. 2. numerals,** *pl.* numbers that show the year one will graduate from a school or college, given as a prize in sports, etc. and worn on a sweater or the like.

nu·mer·ate (nōō'mə rāt *or* nyōō'mə rāt), *v.* to count one by one; enumerate. —**nu'mer·at·ed,** *p.t. & p.p.;* **nu'mer·at·ing,** *pr.p.*

nu·mer·a·tor (nōō'mə rā'tər *or* nyōō'mə rā'tər), *n.* the number or quantity above the line in a fraction. It shows how many of the equal parts of a thing are taken [In the fraction 2/5, 2 is the *numerator*.]

nu·mer·i·cal (nōō mer'i k'l *or* nyōō mer'i k'l), *adj.* **1.** of or having to do with number or numbers; by numbers [to arrange in *numerical* order]. **2.** shown as a number, not as a letter [In the equation x + y = 10, 10 is the only *numerical* quantity.] —**nu·mer'i·cal·ly,** *adv.*

nu·mer·ous (nōō'mər əs *or* nyōō'mər əs), *adj.* **1.** very many [*numerous* friends]. **2.** made up of a large number [a *numerous* collection of animals].

nu·mis·mat·ics (nōō'miz mat'iks *or* nyōō'mis·mat'iks), *n.pl.* the study or collection of coins and medals: *used with a singular verb.* —**nu·mis·ma·tist** (nōō miz'mə tist *or* nyōō mis'mə·tist), *n.*

num·skull (num'skul), *n.* a stupid person.

---

fat,   āpe,   cär,   ten,   ēven,   hit,   bīte,   gō,   hôrn,   tōōl,   book,   up,   fur;
get,   joy,   yet,   chin,   she,   thin,   *th*en;   zh = s in pleasure;   ' as in able (ā'b'l);
ə = a in ago,   e in agent,   i in sanity,   o in confess,   u in focus.

nun (nun), *n.* a woman who has joined a religious order whose members live together in a convent according to certain rules, after taking vows to give up worldly goods, never to marry, etc.

nun·ci·o (nun'shi ō), *n.* the ambassador of the Pope to a foreign government. —**nun'ci·os,** *pl.*

nun·ner·y (nun'ər ē), *n.* a place where nuns live together: *this word has now been replaced by* convent. —**nun'ner·ies,** *pl.*

nup·tial (nup'shəl *or* nup'chəl), *adj.* of marriage or a wedding [a *nuptial* feast]. —*n.* **nuptials,** *pl.* a wedding; marriage ceremony.

nurse (nûrs), *n.* **1.** a person who has been trained to take care of sick people, help doctors, etc. **2.** a nursemaid. —*v.* **1.** to take care of sick people, as a nurse does. **2.** to try to cure; treat [He's *nursing* a cold.] **3.** to make grow or develop [to *nurse* revenge]. **4.** to give milk to from a breast; suckle. **5.** to suck milk from its mother. —**nursed,** *p.t. & p.p.;* **nurs'ing,** *pr.p.*

nurse·maid (nûrs'mād), *n.* a girl or woman hired to take care of a child or children.

nurs·er·y (nûr'sər ē), *n.* **1.** a room set aside for the special use of children or infants. **2.** a nursery school. **3.** a place where young trees or plants are raised for study or for sale. —**nurs'-er·ies,** *pl.*

nurs·er·y·man (nûr'sər ē mən), *n.* a person who owns or works in a nursery for growing trees, plants, etc. —**nurs'er·y·men,** *pl.*

nursery rhyme, a short poem for young children.

nursery school, a school for children who are too young for kindergarten.

nur·ture (nûr'chər), *n.* **1.** the training, care, or bringing up, as of a child. **2.** anything that nourishes; food. —*v.* **1.** to bring up with care; help grow or develop; train. **2.** to feed or nourish. —**nur'tured,** *p.t. & p.p.;* **nur'tur·ing,** *pr.p.*

nut (nut), *n.* **1.** a dry fruit that has a hard shell and a kernel inside that is often good to eat [Walnuts, pecans, and acorns are *nuts*.] **2.** the kernel of such a fruit. **3.** a small metal piece that is screwed onto a bolt to hold the bolt in place. **4.** a person who does silly or crazy things: *slang in this meaning.*

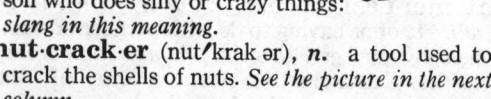
nut

nut·crack·er (nut'krak ər), *n.* a tool used to crack the shells of nuts. *See the picture in the next column.*

nut·hatch (nut'hach), *n.* a small bird that has a sharp beak and feeds on nuts, etc.

nut·meat (nut'mēt), *n.* the kernel of a nut.

nut·meg (nut'meg), *n.* the hard seed of a tropical tree. It is grated for use as a spice.

nutcracker

nu·tri·a (noo'tri ə *or* nyoo'tri ə), *n.* **1.** a South American animal somewhat like the beaver. **2.** its soft, brown fur.

nu·tri·ent (noo'tri ənt *or* nyoo'tri ənt), *adj.* nourishing. —*n.* anything that nourishes; food.

nu·tri·ment (noo'trə mənt *or* nyoo'trə mənt), *n.* anything that nourishes; food.

nu·tri·tion (noo trish'ən *or* nyoo trish'ən), *n.* **1.** the process by which an animal or plant takes in food and uses it in living and growing. **2.** food; nourishment. —**nu·tri'tion·al,** *adj.*

nu·tri·tious (noo trish'əs *or* nyoo trish'əs), *adj.* of value as food; nourishing.

nu·tri·tive (noo'trə tiv *or* nyoo'trə tiv), *adj.* **1.** nutritious. **2.** having to do with nutrition.

nut·shell (nut'shel), *n.* the shell of a nut. —**in a nutshell,** in a few words.

nut·ting (nut'ing), *n.* the gathering of nuts.

nut·ty (nut'ē), *adj.* **1.** having nuts in it [a *nutty* dessert]. **2.** that tastes like nuts. **3.** crazy, silly, enthusiastic, etc.: *slang in this meaning.* —**nut'ti·er,** *compar.;* **nut'ti·est,** *superl.*

nuz·zle (nuz'l), *v.* **1.** to push against or rub with the nose [The horse *nuzzled* my hand for the sugar.] **2.** to lie close; snuggle. —**nuz'zled,** *p.t. & p.p.;* **nuz'zling,** *pr.p.*

NW or **N.W.** or **n.w.,** abbreviation for **northwest** or **northwestern.**

N.W.T., abbreviation for **Northwest Territories.**

horse nuzzling child

N.Y., abbreviation for **New York.**

N.Y.C., abbreviation for **New York City.**

ny·lon (nī'län), *n.* **1.** a very strong, elastic material made by man and used for thread, bristles, etc. **2. nylons,** *pl.* women's stockings made of nylon thread.

nymph (nimf), *n.* **1.** any of the nature goddesses of Greek and Roman myths, who lived in trees, woods, rivers, etc. **2.** a beautiful young woman. **3.** the form of some insects before they become fully adult.

N.Z., abbreviation for **New Zealand.**

O

O, o (ō), *n.* the fifteenth letter of the English alphabet. —**O's, o's** (ōz), *pl.*

O (ō), *interj.* **1.** a word used before someone's name or title, in talking to him [*O* Lord, help us.] **2.** same as **oh.**

o' (ō *or* ə), *prep.* of [cat-*o*'-nine-tails].

O, symbol for the chemical element *oxygen.*

O., abbreviation for **Ohio.**

oaf (ōf), *n.* a stupid and clumsy fellow; dolt; lout. —**oaf'ish,** *adj.*

O·a·hu (ō ä'hoo), *n.* the main island of Hawaii. Honolulu is on this island.

oak (ōk), *n.* **1.** a large tree with hard wood and nuts called *acorns*. **2.** the wood of this tree.

oak·en (ōk'ən), *adj.* made of the wood of the oak [an *oaken* bucket].

Oak·land (ōk'lənd), *n.* a city in western California, across a bay from San Francisco.

Oak Ridge, a city in eastern Tennessee. It is a center for research in atomic energy.

oak·um (ōk'əm), *n.* loose, tough fiber got from old ropes. It is used to fill up cracks and seams in wooden boats.

oak leaf and acorn

oar (ôr), *n.* **1.** a long pole with a flat blade at one end, used in rowing a boat. **2.** a person who uses an oar; rower. **—put one's oar in,** to meddle in another's affairs. **—rest on one's oars,** to stop one's work in order to rest.

oar·lock (ôr'läk), *n.* a part for holding an oar in place while rowing: *see the picture.*

oarlock

oars·man (ôrz'mən), *n.* a man who rows; especially, an expert at rowing. **—oars'men,** *pl.*

o·a·sis (ō ā'sis), *n.* a fertile place with water in the desert. **—o·a·ses** (ō ā'sēz), *pl.*

oat (ōt), *n.* a cereal grass whose seed, or grain, is used as food; also, this grain. *Usually used in the plural,* **oats. —feel one's oats,** to feel or act frisky, lively, or important: *a slang phrase.*

oat·en (ōt''n), *adj.* of or made of oats.

oath (ōth), *n.* **1.** a serious promise in the name of God or of some revered person or thing, that one will speak the truth, keep a promise, etc. **2.** the use of the name of God or some other religious word to express anger or add force to one's words: such use shows a lack of respect for God. **3.** a curse or swearword. **—take oath,** to promise or state with an oath. **—under oath,** bound by an oath, or serious promise. **—oaths** (ōthz *or* ōths), *pl.*

oat·meal (ōt'mēl), *n.* **1.** oats that are ground or rolled into meal or flakes. **2.** a soft, thick food made by cooking such oats.

oats

ob·du·rate (äb'doo rit), *adj.* **1.** not giving in; stubborn; obstinate [The *obdurate* child would not answer.] **2.** not feeling sorry for what one has done; not repenting [an *obdurate* sinner]. **—ob·du·ra·cy** (äb'doo rə sē), *n.*

o·be·di·ence (ō bē'di əns), *n.* the act of obeying or a willingness to obey.

o·be·di·ent (ō bē'di ənt), *adj.* doing or willing to do what one is told; obeying orders. **—o·be'di·ent·ly,** *adv.*

o·bei·sance (ō bā's'ns *or* ō bē's'ns), *n.* **1.** a bow, curtsy, or other movement of the body to show respect. **2.** deep respect shown; homage.

ob·e·lisk (äb'ə lisk), *n.* a tall stone pillar with four sloping sides: *see the picture.*

O·ber·on (ō'bə rän), *n.* the king of fairyland in early folk tales.

o·bese (ō bēs'), *adj.* very fat; stout. **—o·bes·i·ty** (ō bēs'ə tē *or* ō bes'ə tē), *n.*

o·bey (ō bā'), *v.* **1.** to carry out the orders of [*Obey* your father.] **2.** to do as one is told [My dog always *obeys*.] **3.** to be ruled or guided by [to *obey* one's conscience; to *obey* the rules of a game].

obelisk

o·bit·u·ar·y (ō bich'oo er'ē), *n.* an announcement, as in a newspaper, of a person's death, often with a brief story of his life. **—o·bit'u·ar·ies,** *pl.*

ob·ject (äb'jikt), *n.* **1.** a thing that can be seen or touched; something that takes up space [That black *object* is her purse.] **2.** a person or thing toward which one turns his thoughts, feelings, or actions [the *object* of his affection]. **3.** what a person is trying to reach; goal; purpose [the *object* of this game; his *object* in life]. **4.** a word in a sentence that tells who or what is acted upon: see **direct object** and **indirect object.** Prepositions are often followed by a noun or pronoun called an *object* [In "the book on the table," "table" is the *object* of the preposition "on."] **—v.** (əb jekt'), **1.** to dislike or disapprove of something [Mother *objects* to my reading in bed.] **2.** to tell as a reason for not liking or not approving; protest [Jane *objected* that the prices were too high.] **—ob·jec'tor,** *n.*

ob·jec·tion (əb jek'shən), *n.* **1.** a feeling of dislike or disapproval; protest [I have no *objection* to that plan.] **2.** a reason for disliking or disapproving [My main *objection* to this climate is its dampness.]

ob·jec·tion·a·ble (əb jek'shən ə b'l), *adj.* likely to be objected to; not pleasant or agreeable [an *objectionable* smell].

ob·jec·tive (əb jek'tiv), *adj.* **1.** not having or showing a strong opinion for or against something; without bias [A judge must remain *objective*.] **2.** that is or has to do with something real, rather than ideas, feelings, etc.; actually existing [Is pain an *objective* experience?] **3.** that shows the object of a verb or of a preposition [In "I saw him," "him" is in the *objective* case.] **—n. 1.** something that one tries to reach; goal; purpose

[Good grades were his first *objective*.] **2.** the objective case. **—ob·jec′tive·ly,** *adv.* **—ob·jec·tiv·i·ty** (äb′jek tiv′ə tē), *n.*

ob·la·tion (äb lā′shən), *n.* **1.** an offering of something to God or a god, as a sacrifice. **2.** the thing offered; especially, the bread and wine of Holy Communion.

ob·li·gate (äb′lə gāt), *v.* to hold by means of a contract, promise, or feeling of duty [I am *obligated* to you for your help.] **—ob′li·gat·ed,** *p.t. & p.p.;* **ob′li·gat·ing,** *pr.p.*

ob·li·ga·tion (äb′lə gā′shən), *n.* **1.** the condition of being obligated as by duty or a promise [His kindness put me under *obligation* to him.] **2.** a contract, promise, or feeling of duty; also, something one must do because the law, his conscience, etc. demands it [a man's *obligation* to support his family].

ob·lig·a·to·ry (ə blig′ə tôr′ē *or* äb′li gə tôr′ē), *adj.* required by law or one's feeling of duty [Paying taxes is *obligatory*.]

o·blige (ə blīj′), *v.* **1.** to force to do something because the law, one's conscience, etc. demands it [His religion *obliges* him to fast on those days.] **2.** to make feel as if one owes something because of a favor or kindness received [I am much *obliged* for your help.] **3.** to do a favor for [Please *oblige* me by coming along.] **—o·bliged′,** *p.t. & p.p.;* **o·blig′ing,** *pr.p.*

o·blig·ing (ə blīj′ing), *adj.* ready to do favors; helpful, friendly, etc.

ob·lique (ə blēk′ *or* ō blīk′), *adj.* **1.** not level or not straight up and down; slanting [An *oblique* angle is any angle other than a right angle.] **2.** not going straight ahead; not direct [an *oblique* glance; an *oblique* remark]. **—ob·lique′ly,** *adv.*

ob·lit·er·ate (ə blit′ə rāt), *v.* to blot out or do away with, leaving no traces; erase or destroy [The spilled ink *obliterated* her signature. The bombs *obliterated* the bridge.] **—ob·lit′er·at·ed,** *p.t. & p.p.;* **ob·lit′er·at·ing,** *pr.p.* **—ob·lit′er·a′tion,** *n.*

ob·liv·i·on (ə bliv′i ən), *n.* **1.** the condition of being forgotten [Many old songs have passed into *oblivion*.] **2.** the condition of forgetting; forgetfulness [The *oblivion* of sleep eased her sorrow.]

ob·liv·i·ous (ə bliv′i əs), *adj.* **1.** forgetting or not noticing; not mindful [He kept on reading, *oblivious* of the noise.] **2.** causing one to be forgetful [*oblivious*, carefree days of vacation].

ob·long (äb′lông), *adj.* in the shape of a rectangle and longer than it is wide. **—n.** an oblong figure.

ob·lo·quy (äb′lə-kwē), *n.* **1.** loud and angry criticism, especially by many people [He continued to speak out, in spite of public *obloquy*.] **2.** disgrace or dishonor. **—ob′lo·quies,** *pl.*

oblongs

ob·nox·ious (əb näk′shəs), *adj.* very unpleasant; disgusting [an *obnoxious*, noisy neighbor].

o·boe (ō′bō), *n.* a wood-wind instrument whose mouthpiece has a double reed.

ob·scene (äb sēn′), *adj.* shocking to one's feelings of modesty or decency; disgusting. **—ob·scene′ly,** *adv.*

ob·scen·i·ty (äb sen′ə tē), *n.* **1.** the quality of being obscene. **2.** something that is obscene. **—ob·scen′i·ties,** *pl.*

oboe

ob·scure (äb skyoor′), *adj.* **1.** not easily seen, heard, or understood; not clear or distinct [an *obscure* figure in the fog; an *obscure* sound in the wall; an *obscure* remark]. **2.** dim or dark [the *obscure* night]. **3.** not easily noticed; hidden [an *obscure* mountain village]. **4.** not famous or well-known [an *obscure* poet]. **—v.** to make obscure; dim, hide, overshadow, confuse, etc. [In an eclipse, the moon *obscures* the sun. His arguments *obscured* the issue.] **—ob·scured′,** *p.t. & p.p.;* **ob·scur′ing,** *pr.p.* **—ob·scu′ri·ty,** *n.*

ob·se·quies (äb′si kwēz), *n.pl.* funeral services.

ob·se·qui·ous (əb sē′kwi əs), *adj.* too willing to serve or obey, as in trying to gain favor; servile; fawning. **—ob·se′qui·ous·ly,** *adv.*

ob·serv·a·ble (əb zʉr′və b'l), *adj.* **1.** easily observed, or seen; noticeable [an *observable* change]. **2.** that can or should be observed, or kept, as a holiday, rule, etc.

ob·serv·ance (əb zʉr′vəns), *n.* **1.** the observing, or keeping, of a law, custom, etc. **2.** an act, ceremony, etc. carried out by rule or custom.

ob·serv·ant (əb zʉr′vənt), *adj.* **1.** strict in observing, or keeping, a law, custom, etc. [He is *observant* of the rules of etiquette.] **2.** paying careful attention; alert [The *observant* girl noticed the wrong spelling.]

ob·ser·va·tion (äb′zər vā′shən), *n.* **1.** the act or power of seeing or noticing [It's a good night for *observation* of the stars.] **2.** the fact of being seen or noticed [We came in the back way to avoid *observation*.] **3.** the noting and writing down of some facts; also, the fact written down [The doctor published his *observations* on heart disease.] **4.** a remark or comment [the reviewer's *observations* on the novel].

ob·serv·a·to·ry (əb zʉr′və tôr′ē), *n.* a building with telescopes and other equipment in it for studying the stars, weather conditions, etc. **—ob·serv′a·to′ries,** *pl.*

ob·serve (əb zʉrv′), *v.* **1.** to keep or follow; be guided by [to *observe* the rules of a game]. **2.** to celebrate according to custom [We *observe* Memorial Day by putting flowers on graves.] **3.** to see, watch, or notice [He *observed* that she was smiling.] **4.** to remark or comment ["It may rain," he *observed*.] **5.** to examine and study carefully [to *observe* an experiment]. **—ob·served′,** *p.t. & p.p.;* **ob·serv′ing,** *pr.p.* **—ob·serv′er,** *n.*

observatory

ob·sess (əb ses′), *v.* to fill the thoughts of; haunt in the mind [*obsessed* with dreams of fame].

ob·ses·sion (əb sesh′ən), *n.* **1.** the condition of being obsessed with an idea, wish, etc. **2.** an idea, wish, etc. that fills one's thoughts and cannot be put out of the mind.

ob·sid·i·an (əb sid′i ən), *n.* a dark, glassy rock formed from the lava of volcanoes.

ob·so·les·cent (äb′sə les′'nt), *adj.* becoming obsolete; going out of use or fashion [*obsolescent* styles of dress]. —**ob′so·les′cence,** *n.*

ob·so·lete (äb′sə lēt), *adj.* no longer in use or fashion; out-of-date [an *obsolete* word; an *obsolete* airplane].

ob·sta·cle (äb′sti k'l), *n.* anything that gets in the way or keeps one from going ahead; obstruction [Lack of money was the main *obstacle* to his getting an education.]

ob·ste·tri·cian (äb′stə trish′ən), *n.* a doctor who is an expert in obstetrics.

ob·stet·rics (äb stet′riks), *n.pl.* the branch of medicine that deals with the care of women who are giving birth to children: *used with a singular verb.* —**ob·stet′ric** or **ob·stet′ri·cal,** *adj.*

ob·sti·na·cy (äb′sti nə sē), *n.* **1.** the quality of being obstinate; stubbornness. **2.** an obstinate act. —**ob′sti·na·cies,** *pl.*

ob·sti·nate (äb′sti nit), *adj.* **1.** not willing to give in or to change one's mind; stubborn [The *obstinate* child refused to answer.] **2.** hard to treat or cure [an *obstinate* fever]. —**ob′sti·nate·ly,** *adv.*

ob·strep·er·ous (əb strep′ər əs), *adj.* noisy or hard to manage; unruly [The *obstreperous* horse threw its rider.]

ob·struct (əb strukt′), *v.* **1.** to block or stop up; clog [Dirt *obstructed* the drain in the sink.] **2.** to hinder or hold back [to *obstruct* progress]. **3.** to get in the way of [The billboards *obstructed* our view.] —**ob·struc′tive,** *adj.*

ob·struc·tion (əb struk′shən), *n.* **1.** an obstructing or being obstructed [the *obstruction* of justice]. **2.** anything that obstructs or gets in the way [to remove an *obstruction* from a pipe].

ob·tain (əb tān′), *v.* **1.** to get by trying [to *obtain* a job; to *obtain* help]. **2.** to be in force or in use [That law no longer *obtains.*]

ob·tain·a·ble (əb tān′ə b'l), *adj.* that can be obtained; available.

ob·trude (əb trood′), *v.* **1.** to force oneself, one's opinions, etc. upon others without being asked or wanted [to *obtrude* upon another's privacy]. **2.** to push out. —**ob·trud′ed,** *p.t. & p.p.;* **ob·trud′ing,** *pr.p.*

ob·tru·sive (əb troo′siv), *adj.* tending to obtrude; forward; pushing.

ob·tuse (əb toos′ *or* äb tyoos′), *adj.* **1.** not quick to understand; dull or stupid. **2.** more than 90 degrees: said of angles. —**ob·tuse′ness,** *n.*

ob·verse (äb′vʉrs), *n.* the main side; front [The *obverse* of a U.S. coin has the date on it.]

ob·vi·ate (äb′vi āt), *v.* to prevent by acting ahead of time; get rid of; make unnecessary [Proper care of one's car can *obviate* the need for much repair.] —**ob′vi·at·ed,** *p.t. & p.p.;* **ob′vi·at·ing,** *pr.p.*

ob·vi·ous (äb′vi əs), *adj.* easy to see or understand; plain; clear [an *obvious* stain on his tie; an *obvious* danger]. —**ob′vi·ous·ly,** *adv.* —**ob′vi·ous·ness,** *n.*

oc·ca·sion (ə kā′zhən), *n.* **1.** a suitable time; good chance; opportunity [Did you have *occasion* to meet him?] **2.** a cause or reason [The attack on Pearl Harbor was the *occasion* for declaring war on Japan.] **3.** a particular time [We've met on several *occasions.*] **4.** a special time or happening [Independence Day is an *occasion* to celebrate.] —*v.* to cause; bring about [Jerry *occasioned* the quarrel by his impolite remarks.] —**on occasion,** once in a while.

oc·ca·sion·al (ə kā′zhən 'l), *adj.* **1.** happening only once in a while [an *occasional* trip to town]. **2.** of or for a special occasion [An *occasional* poem is one written for a birthday, anniversary, etc.] **3.** for use only now and then; extra [*occasional* chairs].

oc·ca·sion·al·ly (ə kā′zhən 'l ē), *adv.* now and then; once in a while.

Oc·ci·dent (äk′sə dənt), *n.* the part of the world west of Asia; especially, Europe and the Americas: opposite of *Orient.*

Oc·ci·den·tal (äk′sə den′t'l), *adj.* of the Occident; Western [*Occidental* music]. —*n.* a person born in or belonging to the Occident.

oc·cult (ə kult′ *or* äk′ult), *adj.* having to do with secret skills or powers that most people do not pretend to have [Magic and astrology are *occult* arts.]

oc·cu·pan·cy (äk′yoo pən sē), *n.* the act of occupying or holding in possession.

oc·cu·pant (äk′yoo pənt), *n.* a person who occupies land, a house, a position, etc. [the present *occupant* of the White House].

oc·cu·pa·tion (äk′yoo pā′shən), *n.* **1.** the work that a person does to earn a living; one's trade, profession, or business; vocation. **2.** an occupying or being occupied; possession [the Roman *occupation* of Britain]. —**oc′cu·pa′tion·al,** *adj.*

oc·cu·py (äk′yoo pī), *v.* **1.** to take possession of a place by capturing it or settling in it [The Germans *occupied* much of France during World War II. Pioneers *occupied* the wilderness of the West.] **2.** to have or hold [He *occupies* an important post in government.] **3.** to live in [to *occupy* a house]. **4.** to take up; fill [The store *occupies* the entire building.] **5.** to keep busy; employ [Many problems *occupy* his mind.] —**oc′cu·pied,** *p.t. & p.p.;* **oc′cu·py·ing,** *pr.p.*

oc·cur (ə kʉr′), *v.* **1.** to come into one's mind [The idea *occurred* to me before.] **2.** to happen; take place [The accident *occurred* last night.]

---

3. to be found; exist [Errors *occur* in his work.] **—oc·curred′,** *p.t. & p.p.;* **oc·cur′ring,** *pr.p.*

oc·cur·rence (ə kūr′əns), *n.* **1.** the act or fact of occurring [the *occurrence* of errors]. **2.** a happening or event [a strange *occurrence*].

o·cean (ō′shən), *n.* **1.** the whole body of salt water that covers more than two thirds of the earth's surface; the sea. **2.** any of the five main parts into which it is divided; the Atlantic, Pacific, Indian, Arctic, or Antarctic oceans.

O·ce·an·i·a (ō′shi an′i ə), *n.* the islands in the Pacific, especially Melanesia, Micronesia, and Polynesia.

o·ce·an·ic (ō′shi an′ik), *adj.* of, living in, or like the ocean.

o·ce·lot (ō′sə lät *or* äs′ə lət), *n.* a wildcat, like a small leopard, found in North and South America.

o·cher or **o·chre** (ō′kər), *n.* **1.** a dark-yellow or light-brown clay, used as a coloring matter in paints. **2.** dark yellow.

ocelot (3 ft. long)

o′clock (ə kläk′), of the clock; according to the clock [twelve *o'clock* midnight].

Oct., abbreviation for **October.**

oc·ta·gon (äk′tə gän), *n.* a flat figure having eight angles and eight sides.

oc·tag·o·nal (äk tag′ə n'l), *adj.* having the shape of an octagon.

oc·tave (äk′tiv *or* äk′tāv), *n.* **1.** a musical tone that is the eighth full tone above or below another tone. **2.** the difference in pitch between two such tones. **3.** the series of tones between two such tones; especially, the eight full steps of a musical scale. **4.** two tones an octave apart that are sounded together. **5.** a group of eight.

octagon

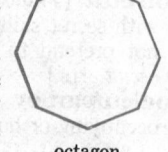

striking an octave (*meaning 4*)

oc·ta·vo (äk tā′vō), *n.* **1.** the page size of a book that is about 6 by 9 inches. **2.** a book of such pages. **—oc·ta′vos,** *pl.*

Oc·to·ber (äk tō′bər), *n.* the tenth month of the year. It has 31 days. Abbreviated **Oct.**

oc·to·pus (äk′tə pəs), *n.* **1.** a sea animal with a soft body and eight long arms covered with suckers. **2.** anything like an octopus, as a powerful organization that has many branches. **—oc′to·pus·es,** *pl.*

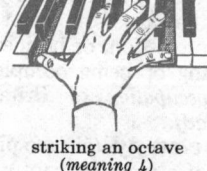

octopus (about 6 ft. across)

oc·u·lar (äk′yoo lər), *adj.* of or having to do with the eye or with eyesight [an *ocular* examination].

oc·u·list (äk′yoo list), *n.* a doctor who treats diseases of the eye.

odd (äd), *adj.* **1.** left over, as from what was once a pair, a set, etc. [an *odd* glove; a few *odd* volumes of an encyclopedia]. **2.** having a remainder of one when divided by two; not even [7, 11, and 43 are *odd* numbers.] **3.** having an odd number [the *odd* days of the month]. **4.** and a little more than what is mentioned; and some extra [forty *odd* years ago; five dollars and some *odd* change]. **5.** not regular; occasional [*odd* jobs]. **6.** strange or queer [What an *odd* thing to say!] **—odd′ly,** *adv.* **—odd′ness,** *n.*

odd·i·ty (äd′ə tē), *n.* **1.** strangeness or queerness [the *oddity* of his actions]. **2.** a strange or unusual person or thing. **—odd′i·ties,** *pl.*

odds (ädz), *n.pl.* **1.** a difference that favors one side over the other; advantage; superiority [a struggle against great *odds*]. **2.** advantage given to a bettor according to the chances that are thought to be against him [If a bettor gets *odds* of 10 to 1, he will receive 10 times as much as he has risked should he win.] **—at odds,** having a quarrel; disagreeing. **—by all odds,** by far. **—odds and ends,** scraps or small bits left over. **—the odds are,** it is likely.

ode (ōd), *n.* a serious poem in a noble and dignified style, usually honoring some person or event.

O·des·sa (ō des′ə), *n.* a city of the Ukraine in the Soviet Union, on the Black Sea.

O·din (ō′din), *n.* the chief god in Norse myths.

o·di·ous (ō′di əs), *adj.* very unpleasant; hateful; disgusting.

o·di·um (ō′di əm), *n.* **1.** hatred or the condition of being hated. **2.** the disgrace brought on by hateful or shameful action [Will he ever live down the *odium* of his crime?]

o·dom·e·ter (ō däm′ə tər), *n.* an instrument that measures how far a vehicle has traveled.

o·dor (ō′dər), *n.* any smell, either pleasant or unpleasant. **—be in bad odor,** to have a bad reputation. **—o′dor·less,** *adj.*

o·dor·if·er·ous (ō′də rif′ər əs), *adj.* giving off an odor, especially a pleasant odor.

o·dor·ous (ō′dər əs), *adj.* having an odor, especially a sweet odor; fragrant.

o·dour (ō′dər), *n.* British spelling of **odor.**

O·dys·se·us (ō dis′i əs *or* ō dis′yōōs), *n.* another name for **Ulysses.**

Od·ys·sey (äd′ə sē), *n.* **1.** a long Greek poem by Homer about the wanderings of Odysseus, or Ulysses, on his way home after the Trojan War. **2.** *sometimes* **odyssey,** any long journey with many adventures. **—Od′ys·seys** or **od′ys·seys,** *pl.*

Oed·i·pus (ed′ə pəs *or* ē′də pəs), *n.* a king in Greek legend who killed his father and married his mother, not knowing he was their son.

o′er (ôr), *prep. & adv.* over: *used in poetry.*

of (uv *or* äv *or* əv), *prep.* **1.** coming from [men *of* Ohio]. **2.** resulting from [She died *of* a fever.] **3.** at a distance from [a mile east *of* town]. **4.** by [the novels *of* Dickens]. **5.** separated from [robbed *of* his money]. **6.** from the whole that is or the total number that are [most *of* one's time; one *of* his brothers]. **7.** made from [a house *of* brick; a club *of* boys]. **8.** belonging to [the pages *of* a book]. **9.** having or owning [a man *of* wealth]. **10.** containing [a box *of* popcorn]. **11.** that is [a height *of* six feet; the State *of* Iowa]. **12.** with something mentioned as a goal, object, etc. [a reader *of* books; the education *of* children]. **13.** concerning; about [Think *of* me when I'm away.] **14.** during [He's been sick *of* recent months.] **15.** before: *used in telling time* [ten *of* four].

off (ôf), *adv.* **1.** away; to some other place [He moved *off* down the road.] **2.** so as to be no longer on or attached [Take your coat *off*. May I cut *off* the end?] **3.** at a later time [My birthday is only two weeks *off*.] **4.** so as to be no longer working, going on, etc. [Turn the motor *off*. They broke *off* their talk.] **5.** so as to be less, smaller, etc. [Sales dropped *off*.] **6.** away from one's work [Let's take the day *off*.] —*prep.* **1.** not on, not attached to, etc.; away from [The car is *off* the road.] **2.** branching out from [a lane *off* the main road]. **3.** free or released from [*off* duty]. **4.** below the usual level or standard of [He's *off* his game today. We sell it at 20% *off* list price.] **5.** no longer using, taking part in, etc.: *used only in everyday talk* [I'm *off* candy.] —*adj.* **1.** not on or attached [His hat is *off*.] **2.** not working, taking place, etc. [The motor is *off*. Our trip is *off*.] **3.** on the way [The children are *off* to school.] **4.** below the usual level or standard [Business is *off* a little.] **5.** slight; not very likely [an *off* chance]. **6.** taken care of, provided for, etc. [They are well *off*.] **7.** wrong; in error [Your guess is *off*.] —*interj.* go away! —**be off** or **take off,** to go away. —**off and on,** now and then. —**off with,** take off! remove!

of·fal (ôf′'l), *n.* **1.** the waste parts of an animal that has been cut up for meat, especially the intestines. **2.** rubbish; garbage; trash.

of·fence (ə fens′), *n.* British spelling of **offense.**

of·fend (ə fend′), *v.* **1.** to hurt the feelings of; make angry or upset; insult [His rude answer *offended* her.] **2.** to be unpleasant to; displease [The noise *offends* my ears.] **3.** to do wrong; commit a crime or sin. —**of·fend′er,** *n.*

of·fense (ə fens′), *n.* **1.** the act of doing wrong; crime or sin [a traffic *offense*]. **2.** a making or becoming angry, annoyed, etc. [I meant no *offense*.] **3.** something that causes anger, hurt feelings, etc. **4.** (*also* ôf′ens), the act of attacking; assault; also, a team or army that is attacking. —**give offense,** to offend; anger or annoy. —**take offense,** to become angry or annoyed.

of·fen·sive (ə fen′siv), *adj.* **1.** attacking or used for attacking [*offensive* battle; *offensive* weapons]. **2.** unpleasant; disgusting [an *offensive* odor]. **3.** making one angry, annoyed, etc.; insulting [*offensive* comments]. —*n.* an attack or a position for attacking [to take the *offensive*]. —**of·fen′-sive·ly,** *adv.*

of·fer (ôf′ər), *v.* **1.** to put forward for someone to take or refuse, as he wishes [to *offer* one's help; to *offer* an opinion]. **2.** to give in worship [to *offer* prayers]. **3.** to say that one is willing [I *offered* to go with him.] **4.** to suggest as a price one is willing to pay [to *offer* $3 for the book]. **5.** to show or give signs of [The rusty lock *offered* some resistance.] —*n.* an act of offering, or something that is offered [Will you accept a lower *offer*?]

of·fer·ing (ôf′ər ing), *n.* **1.** the act of one who offers. **2.** something offered, as money collected during a church service.

of·fer·to·ry (ôf′ər tôr′ē), *n.* **1.** the collection of money at a church service. **2.** prayers said or music sung while the collection is made. —**of′-fer·to′ries,** *pl.*

off·hand (ôf′hand′), *adv.* without thinking about it ahead of time [Can you tell us *offhand* how many you will need?] —*adj.* **1.** done or said offhand [an *offhand* reply]. **2.** sharp or rude; without politeness [an *offhand* refusal].

of·fice (ôf′is), *n.* **1.** the place where a certain kind of business or work is carried on [a lawyer's *office*; the main *office* of a company; a post *office*]. **2.** all the people working in such an office. **3.** an important position, job, or duty [elected to high *office*]. **4.** something done for another person; favor [He got the job through his uncle's good *offices*.] **5.** a religious ceremony.

of·fice·hold·er (ôf′is hōl′dər), *n.* a person holding some office, as a government official.

of·fi·cer (ôf′ə sər), *n.* **1.** a person holding some office, as in a business, club, or government. **2.** a policeman. **3.** a person who commands others in an army, navy, etc. [Generals and lieutenants are commissioned *officers*.] —*v.* **1.** to provide with officers. **2.** to command as an officer.

of·fi·cial (ə fish′əl), *n.* a person who holds an office, especially in government. —*adj.* **1.** of or having to do with an office [an *official* record; *official* duties]. **2.** coming from a person with authority [an *official* letter from the Secretary of State]. **3.** fit for an important officer; formal [an *official* reception at the White House]. —**of·fi′cial·ly,** *adv.*

of·fi·ci·ate (ə fish′i āt), *v.* **1.** to carry out the duties of an office [to *officiate* as secretary]. **2.** to be in charge of a religious service or a ceremony [to *officiate* at a wedding]. —**of·fi′ci·at·ed,** *p.t.* & *p.p.;* **of·fi′ci·at·ing,** *pr.p.*

of·fi·cious (ə fish′əs), *adj.* giving advice or help that is not wanted or needed; meddling.

of·fing (ôf′ing), *n.* distance or position far away: *now used only in the phrase* **in the offing,** meaning "far away but still in sight" or "at some time or other in the future."

off·set (ôf set′), *v.* to balance or make up for [The farmer's loss on corn was *offset* by his profit on wheat.] —*n.* (ôf′set), anything that offsets something else. —**off·set′**, *p.t.* & *p.p.;* **off-set′ting**, *pr.p.*

off·shoot (ôf′shoot), *n.* anything that branches off from a main line; especially, a shoot that grows from the main stem of a plant.

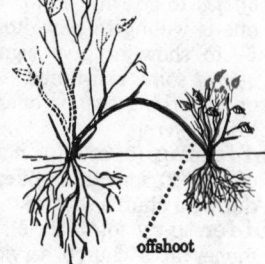

offshoot

off·shore (ôf′shôr′), *adj.* **1.** moving away from the shore [an *offshore* current]. **2.** at some distance from shore [an *offshore* island]. —*adv.* away from shore [to sail *offshore*].

off·side (ôf′sīd′), *adj.* not in the proper position for play, as a football player who is ahead of the ball before play begins.

off·spring (ôf′spring), *n.* a child or children; also, the young of animals.

oft (ôft), *adv.* often: *used mainly in poetry.*

of·ten (ôf′n), *adv.* many times; frequently.

of·ten·times (ôf′n tīmz), *adv.* often.

o·gle (ō′g′l), *v.* to keep looking at in a fond or loving way; flirt. —*n.* an ogling look. —**o′gled,** *p.t.* & *p.p.;* **o′gling,** *pr.p.*

o·gre (ō′gər), *n.* **1.** in fairy tales, a giant who eats people. **2.** a cruel or ugly man.

oh (ō), *interj.* a sound made in showing surprise, fear, wonder, pain, etc.

O. Henry, see **Henry, O.**

O·hi·o (ō hī′ō), *n.* **1.** a State in the north central part of the United States: abbreviated **O. 2.** a river that flows along the southern borders of Ohio, Indiana, and Illinois to the Mississippi. —**O·hi′o·an,** *adj.* & *n.*

ohm (ōm), *n.* a unit for measuring electrical resistance. It is the resistance of a conductor in which one volt produces a current of one ampere.

-oid (oid), a suffix meaning "like" [A *spheroid* is a form somewhat like a sphere.]

oil (oil), *n.* **1.** any of certain greasy liquids that come from animal, vegetable, or mineral matter, as whale oil, peanut oil, or petroleum. Oils can be burned and do not mix with water, but float on top. **2.** a paint made by mixing some coloring matter with oil: also **oil color. 3.** a picture painted with oil colors: *its full name is* **oil painting.** —*v.* to put oil on or in, as for lubricating [to *oil* the works of a clock]. —**strike oil, 1.** to discover oil by drilling in the earth. **2.** to become rich suddenly. —**oil′er,** *n.*

oil·cloth (oil′klôth), *n.* cloth made waterproof with oil or, now especially, with heavy coats of paint. It is used to cover tables, shelves, etc.

oil·skin (oil′skin), *n.* **1.** cloth made waterproof by being treated with oil. **2.** a garment made of this: *often used in the plural,* **oilskins.**

oil well, a well bored through layers of rock, etc. to get petroleum from the earth.

oil·y (oil′ē), *adj.* **1.** of or like oil [an *oily* liquid]. **2.** full of or covered with oil; greasy [*oily* hair]. **3.** too polite or flattering. —**oil′i·er,** *compar.;* **oil′i·est,** *superl.* —**oil′i·ness,** *n.*

oint·ment (oint′mənt), *n.* an oily cream rubbed on the skin to heal it or make it soft and smooth; salve.

O.K. or **OK** (ō′kā′), *adj., adv.* & *interj.* all right; correct. —*n.* approval. —*v.* to put an O.K. on; approve. —**O.K.'s** or **OK's,** *pl.* —**O.K.'d** or **OK'd,** *p.t.* & *p.p.;* **O.K.'ing** or **OK'ing,** *pr.p.*

o·kay (ō′kā′), *adj., adv., interj., n.* & *v.* same as **O.K.**

O·kla·ho·ma (ō′klə hō′mə), *n.* a State in the south central part of the United States: abbreviated **Okla.**

Oklahoma City, the capital of Oklahoma.

o·kra (ō′krə), *n.* a plant with green pods that become sticky when cooked, as in soups.

okra

old (ōld), *adj.* **1.** having lived or existed for a long time [an *old* man; an *old* building]. **2.** of a certain age; in age [He's ten years *old.*] **3.** made some time ago; not new [*old* books]. **4.** worn out by age or use [*old* shoes]. **5.** ancient [an *old* kingdom]. **6.** being the earlier or earliest [the *Old* Testament]. **7.** having much experience [He's an *old* hand at this work.] **8.** former; at one time [We moved from our *old* neighborhood.] **9.** of or like aged people [*old* at heart]. *Old* is sometimes used in everyday talk to show a warm or friendly feeling [Good *old* Jerry!] —*n.* time long past [days of *old*]. —**the old,** old people. —**old′er** or **eld′er,** *compar.;* **old′est** or **eld′est,** *superl.* —**old′ness,** *n.*

old country, the country from which an immigrant came, especially a country in Europe.

old·en (ōl′d′n), *adj.* of earlier times; old; ancient [in *olden* times].

Old English, the Anglo-Saxon language.

old-fash·ioned (ōld′fash′ənd), *adj.* suited to the past more than to the present; out-of-date [an *old-fashioned* dress; *old-fashioned* ideas].

Old Glory, the flag of the United States.

old·ish (ōld′ish), *adj.* somewhat old.

old maid, a woman, especially an older woman, who has never married. —**old′-maid′ish,** *adj.*

Old Testament, the Bible of Judaism or the first part of the Bible of Christianity. It contains the history of the Hebrews, the laws of Moses, the writings of the prophets, etc.

old-time (ōld′tīm′), *adj.* of or like past times.

old-tim·er (ōld′tīm′ər), *n.* a person who has lived or worked at the same place for a long time: *used only in everyday talk.*

old-world (ōld′wûrld′), *adj.* **1.** of or having to do with the ancient world or with former times. **2.** *often* **Old-World,** of the Old World.

Old World, the Eastern Hemisphere; Europe, Asia, and Africa.

o·le·an·der (ō′li an′dər), *n.* a poisonous evergreen shrub with sweet-smelling white or red flowers.

o·le·o·mar·ga·rine or **o·le·o·mar·ga·rin** (ō'li ō mär'jə rin), *n.* same as **margarine.**

ol·fac·to·ry (äl fak'tər ē), *adj.* of the sense of smell [*olfactory* nerves].

ol·i·garch (äl'i gärk), *n.* any of the rulers of an oligarchy.

ol·i·garch·y (äl'i gär'kē), *n.* **1.** government in which a few persons hold the ruling power. **2.** a country with such government. **3.** the persons ruling such a country. —**ol'i·garch'ies,** *pl.*

ol·ive (äl'iv), *n.* **1.** the small, oval fruit of an evergreen tree of southern Europe and the Middle East. Olives are eaten green or ripe, or are pressed for their oil. **2.** the tree that this fruit grows on, or its wood. **3.** the color of an unripe olive, dull yellowish green.

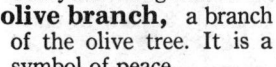
olive tree and branch with fruit

olive branch, a branch of the olive tree. It is a symbol of peace.

olive oil, a pale yellow oil pressed from ripe olives and used in cooking, soaps, etc.

O·lym·pi·a (ō lim'pi ə), *n.* **1.** the capital of the State of Washington. **2.** a plain in ancient Greece where the Olympic games were held.

O·lym·pi·an (ō lim'pi ən), *adj.* **1.** of Mount Olympus [the *Olympian* gods]. **2.** powerful and majestic, like a god [*Olympian* dignity]. —*n.* **1.** any of the Greek gods, on Mount Olympus. **2.** a person taking part in Olympic games.

O·lym·pic (ō lim'pik), *adj.* **1.** of or having to do with the Olympic games. **2.** Olympian. —*n.* **Olympics,** *pl.* the Olympic games.

Olympic games, 1. an ancient Greek festival that was held every four years, with contests in athletics, poetry, and music. **2.** a contest of modern times, held every four years, in which athletes from all over the world compete in many sports and games.

O·lym·pus (ō lim'pəs), *n.* a mountain in northern Greece. In Greek myths, it was the home of the gods.

O·ma·ha (ō'mə hô *or* ō'mə hä), *n.* a city in eastern Nebraska, on the Missouri River.

om·buds·man (äm'bədz mən), *n.* a public official who investigates complaints people have placed against their government. —**om'buds·men,** *pl.*

o·me·ga (ō mē'gə *or* ō mā'gə), *n.* **1.** the last letter of the Greek alphabet. **2.** the end.

om·e·let or **om·e·lette** (äm'lit *or* äm'ə let), *n.* eggs beaten up, often with milk or water, and cooked as a pancake in a frying pan.

o·men (ō'mən), *n.* anything that is supposed to be a sign of something to come, good or evil [A red sunset is an *omen* of good weather.]

om·i·nous (äm'ə nəs), *adj.* of or like an evil omen; threatening [An *ominous* silence filled the room.] —**om'i·nous·ly,** *adv.*

o·mis·sion (ō mish'ən), *n.* **1.** the act of omitting something. **2.** anything omitted.

o·mit (ō mit'), *v.* **1.** to leave out [You may *omit* the raisins.] **2.** to neglect; fail to do [Don't *omit* to cross your t's.] —**o·mit'ted,** *p.t.* & *p.p.;* **o·mit'ting,** *pr.p.*

om·ni·bus (äm'ni bus), *n.* a bus. —*adj.* that deals with many things at one time [An *omnibus* bill in the Senate contains many provisions.]

om·nip·o·tent (äm nip'ə tənt), *adj.* having power or authority without limit; all-powerful. —**om·nip'o·tence,** *n.*

om·ni·pres·ent (äm'ni prez''nt), *adj.* present in all places at the same time [an *omnipresent* fear of war]. —**om'ni·pres'ence,** *n.*

om·nis·cient (äm nish'ənt), *adj.* knowing all things. —**om·nis'cience,** *n.*

om·niv·o·rous (äm niv'ər əs), *adj.* **1.** eating all kinds of food, whether animal or vegetable [Bears are *omnivorous.*] **2.** liking all kinds; taking in everything [an *omnivorous* reader].

on (än), *prep.* **1.** held up by, covering, or attached to [a pack *on* his back; a cloth *on* the table; a picture *on* the wall]. **2.** in the surface of [a scratch *on* his arm]. **3.** near to; at the side of [the boy *on* my left]. **4.** at the time of [Pay your bill *on* leaving.] **5.** having to do with; concerning [a book *on* birds]. **6.** that is a part of [a pitcher *on* the team]. **7.** in the condition of [We bought it *on* sale. He is *on* vacation.] **8.** as a result of; from [We made $50 *on* the paper sale.] **9.** in the direction of; toward [Indians crept up *on* the fort.] **10.** by using; by means of [Most cars run *on* gasoline.] —*adv.* **1.** in a position of covering, touching, or being held up by something [Put your shoes *on.*] **2.** toward someone or something [He looked *on* while I worked.] **3.** in a forward direction; ahead [Move *on!*] **4.** without stopping [The band played *on.*] **5.** so that it is acting or working [Turn the light *on.*] —*adj.* in action; working or acting [The motor is *on.*] —**on and off,** stopping and starting; from time to time. —**on and on,** without stopping; continuously.

once (wuns), *adv.* **1.** one time [I see him only *once* a week.] **2.** at some time in the past; formerly [He *once* was rich.] **3.** ever; at any time [He'll succeed if *once* given a chance.] —*conj.* as soon as [*Once* he hears about it, he'll tell everyone.] —*n.* one time [I'll go this *once.*] —**all at once, 1.** all at the same time. **2.** suddenly. —**at once, 1.** immediately. **2.** at the same time. —**for once,** for at least one time. —**once and for all,** finally. —**once in a while,** now and then. —**once upon a time,** a long time ago.

on·com·ing (än'kum'ing), *adj.* coming nearer; approaching [an *oncoming* train]. —*n.* an approach [the *oncoming* of spring].

one (wun), *adj.* **1.** being a single thing [*one* man]. **2.** forming a whole; united [with *one* accord]. **3.** a certain, but not named; some

---

fat, āpe, cär, ten, ēven, hit, bīte, gō, hôrn, tool, book, up, fûr; get, joy, yet, chin, she, thin, *th*en; zh = s in pleasure; ' as in able (ā'b'l); ə = a in ago, e in agent, i in sanity, o in confess, u in focus.

[Choose *one* path or the other. I went *one* day last week.] **4.** single in kind; the same [We are all of *one* mind on the subject.] —*n.* **1.** the number that names a single unit; the number 1. **2.** a single person or thing [I'll take the blue *ones.*] —*pron.* **1.** a certain person or thing [*One* of us must go.] **2.** any person or thing; anyone or anything [What can *one* do at a time like this?] —**all one,** making no difference; of no matter. —**at one,** in agreement. —**one and all,** everybody. —**one another,** each person or thing the other. —**one by one,** one following the other.

one·ness (wun′nis), *n.* the condition of being one or being the same; unity, singleness, or sameness [a *oneness* of mind].

on·er·ous (än′ər əs), *adj.* hard to put up with; being a burden [*onerous* tasks].

one·self (wun self′), *pron.* one's own self [One cannot think only of *oneself.*] Also **one's self.**

one-sid·ed (wun′sīd′id), *adj.* **1.** favoring one side or one point of view; prejudiced; not fair [The newspaper gave a *one-sided* report of what happened.] **2.** unequal or uneven [A game between an expert and a beginner is *one-sided.*] **3.** larger, heavier, etc. on one side; lopsided. **4.** on or having only one side.

one-way (wun′wā′), *adj.* that moves or lets one move in one direction only [a *one-way* street].

on·ion (un′yən), *n.* **1.** a plant with a bulb that has a sharp smell and taste and is eaten as a vegetable. **2.** the bulb itself.

on·look·er (än′look′ər), *n.* a person who watches without taking part; spectator.

onion

on·ly (ōn′lē), *adj.* **1.** without any other or others of the same kind; sole [the *only* suit he owns; their *only* friends]. **2.** best; finest [This is the *only* soap to use on a baby's skin.] —*adv.* and no other; and no more; just; merely [I have *only* ten cents. Bite off *only* what you can chew.] —*conj.* except that; but: *used only in everyday talk* [I would have run, *only* I hurt my leg.] —**if only,** I wish that [*If only* he would leave!] —**only too,** very [I'll be *only too* glad to do it.]

on·rush (än′rush), *n.* a swift or strong rush forward.

on·set (än′set), *n.* **1.** an attack [The *onset* of enemy troops forced us to retreat.] **2.** a beginning; start [the *onset* of winter].

on·slaught (än′slôt), *n.* a fierce attack.

On·tar·i·o (än ter′i ō), *n.* **1.** the smallest of the Great Lakes, that is the one farthest east: *usually* **Lake Ontario. 2.** a province of south central Canada: abbreviated **Ont.**

on·to (än′tōō), *prep.* **1.** to a position on [He climbed *onto* the roof.] **2.** aware of: *slang in this meaning* [I'm *onto* your tricks.] Also **on to.**

on·ward (än′wərd), *adv.* toward or at a place ahead; forward [They marched *onward.*] Also **onwards.** —*adj.* moving ahead [an *onward* course].

on·yx (än′iks), *n.* a stone with layers of different colors, used in jewelry, etc.

ooze (ōōz), *v.* **1.** to leak out slowly [Oil *oozed* through the crack.] **2.** to disappear little by little [Her hope *oozed* away.] —*n.* **1.** an oozing or something that oozes [the *ooze* of sap from the tree]. **2.** soft, watery mud, as at the bottom of a lake or river. —**oozed,** *p.t. & p.p.;* **ooz′ing,** *pr.p.* —**oo′zy,** *adj.*

onyx

o·pal (ō′p'l), *n.* a stone of various colors, used as a jewel. Light passing through it seems to make the colors change and move about.

o·pal·es·cent (ō′pə les′'nt), *adj.* having colors that seem to change and move about, as in the opal. —**o′pal·es′cence,** *n.*

o·paque (ō pāk′), *adj.* **1.** that cannot be seen through; not letting light through; not transparent [an *opaque* screen]. **2.** not shiny; dull; dark [The desk had an *opaque* surface.] **3.** slow in understanding; stupid.

ope (ōp), *adj. & v.* open: *used only in poetry.* —**oped** (ōpt), *p.t. & p.p.;* **op′ing,** *pr.p.*

o·pen (ō′p'n), *adj.* **1.** not closed, shut, covered, or stopped up [*open* eyes; *open* doors; an *open* jar; an *open* drain]. **2.** not closed in, fenced in, protected, etc. [an *open* field; an *open* view; an *open* car; *open* to attack]. **3.** unfolded; spread out [an *open* book]. **4.** having spaces between parts [*open* ranks; cloth with an *open* weave]. **5.** that may be entered, taken part in, used, etc. by all [an *open* meeting]. **6.** not settled or decided [an *open* question]. **7.** not prejudiced; honest, fair, etc. [an *open* mind]. **8.** generous [Give with an *open* heart.] **9.** free from strict laws or limits [*open* season in deer hunting]. **10.** not already taken or filled; available [The job is still *open.*] **11.** not secret; public [an *open* quarrel]. —*v.* **1.** to make or become open, or no longer closed [Please *open* a window. The door suddenly *opened.*] **2.** to spread out; unfold [The soldiers *opened* their ranks. *Open* the book.] **3.** to begin or start [We *opened* the program with a song.] **4.** to start operating [He *opened* a new store.] **5.** to be an opening; lead [This door *opens* onto a porch.] —**open to,** willing to listen to or consider [*open to* suggestions]. —**the open, 1.** any open, clear space; the outdoors. **2.** the condition of being known to all. —**o′pen·ly,** *adv.* —**o′pen·ness,** *n.*

open air, the outdoors. —**o′pen-air′,** *adj.*

o·pen·er (ō′p'n ər), *n.* **1.** a person or thing that opens, as a tool for opening cans, bottles, etc. **2.** the first game in a series.

o·pen-eyed (ō′p'n īd′), *adj.* with the eyes wide open, as in surprise or in careful watching.

o·pen-faced (ō′p'n fāst′), *adj.* **1.** with the face uncovered. **2.** having a frank, honest face.

o·pen-hand·ed (ō′p'n han′did), *adj.* generous.

open house, 1. a house open to all visitors, who come and go as they wish. **2.** a time when a school, business, etc. is open to visitors.

o·pen·ing (ō′p'n ing), *n.* **1.** the act of making or becoming open. **2.** an open place; hole, clearing, etc. [an *opening* in the wall]. **3.** a beginning [the *opening* of a program; the *opening* of a new store]. **4.** a good chance; opportunity [At the first *opening* in the conversation, he made his suggestion.] **5.** a job that is not filled [The company has no *openings* now.]

o·pen-mind·ed (ō′p'n mīn′did), *adj.* willing to consider new ideas; not prejudiced.

o·pen·work (ō′p'n wûrk′), *n.* decorations, as in cloth, with openings that are part of the design.

op·er·a (äp′ər ə), *n.* a play in which all or most of the speeches are sung, usually with an orchestra accompanying the singers.

op·er·a (äp′ər ə), *n.* plural of **opus.**

opera glasses, a pair of binoculars, like small field glasses, for use in a theater, etc.

op·er·ate (äp′ə rāt), *v.* **1.** to keep or be in action; work; run [Can you *operate* a sewing machine? Our dishwasher *operates* automatically.] **2.** to have a certain result or effect [This drug *operates* on the heart.] **3.** to perform a surgical operation [to *operate* on diseased tonsils]. **4.** to control or manage [He *operates* a laundry.] —**op′er·at·ed,** *p.t. & p.p.;* **op′er·at·ing,** *pr.p.*

opera glasses

op·er·at·ic (äp′ə rat′ik), *adj.* of or like opera.

op·er·a·tion (äp′ə rā′shən), *n.* **1.** the act or way of operating [to explain the *operation* of a typewriter]. **2.** the condition of being in action or use [The new steel mill will be in *operation* soon.] **3.** any one of a series of actions or movements in some work or plan, as in manufacturing, warfare, etc. [Hundreds of *operations* are involved in making automobiles.] **4.** a surgical treatment to cure or correct an injury or illness.

op·er·a·tion·al (äp′ə rā′shən 'l), *adj.* **1.** of, or having to do with, the operation of a system, device, etc. [*operational* costs]. **2.** in use or able to be used [The new airplane will be *operational* within six months.]

op·er·a·tive (äp′ə rā′tiv *or* äp′ər ə tiv), *adj.* **1.** able to work; in effect; operating [The new contract will be *operative* in May.] **2.** having to do with the work of men or machines [low *operative* expenses]. —*n.* a skilled worker.

op·er·a·tor (äp′ə rā′tər), *n.* **1.** a person who operates some machine, etc. [a telephone *operator*]. **2.** an owner or manager of a factory, etc.

op·er·et·ta (äp′ə ret′ə), *n.* a short opera that is light and amusing.

oph·thal·mol·o·gy (äf′thal mäl′ə jē), *n.* the branch of medicine that deals with diseases of the eye. —**oph′thal·mol′o·gist,** *n.*

o·pi·ate (ō′pi it), *n.* **1.** any medicine containing opium or a drug made from opium, used to cause sleepiness or to lessen pain. **2.** anything that quiets or soothes.

o·pine (ō pīn′), *v.* to have or give an opinion; think; decide: *now seldom used, except in fun.* —**o·pined′,** *p.t. & p.p.;* **o·pin′ing,** *pr.p.*

o·pin·ion (ə pin′yən), *n.* **1.** a belief that is not based on what is certain, but on what one thinks to be true or likely [In my *opinion*, it will rain before dark.] **2.** a judgment or impression about something [He has a low *opinion* of her work.] **3.** a judgment made by an expert [The judge wrote his *opinion* on the case.]

o·pin·ion·at·ed (ə pin′yən ā′tid), *adj.* holding to one's own opinions in a stubborn way.

o·pi·um (ō′pi əm), *n.* a drug got from one kind of poppy, used to cause sleep and lessen pain.

o·pos·sum (ə päs′əm), *n.* a small American animal that lives in trees and moves about mostly at night. The female carries its newly born young in a pouch. When trapped, the opossum pretends to be dead.

opossum with young
(adult about 15 in. long)

op·po·nent (ə pō′nənt), *n.* a person against one in a fight, game, debate, etc.; foe; adversary.

op·por·tune (äp′ər tōōn′ *or* äp′ər tyōōn′), *adj.* just right for the purpose; suitable; timely [the *opportune* moment; an *opportune* remark].

op·por·tun·ist (äp′ər tōōn′ist *or* äp′ər tyōōn′ist), *n.* a person whose acts, opinions, etc. are guided by what will benefit him rather than by what is right or proper. —**op′por·tun′ism,** *n.*

op·por·tu·ni·ty (äp′ər tōō′nə tē *or* äp′ər tyōō′nə tē), *n.* a time or occasion that is right for doing something; good chance [You will have an *opportunity* to ask questions after the talk.] —**op′por·tu′ni·ties,** *pl.*

op·pose (ə pōz′), *v.* **1.** to act or be against; fight or resist [The mayor *opposes* raising taxes.] **2.** to put opposite or in contrast; set against [To each of my arguments Sue *opposed* one of her own. Black is *opposed* to white.] —**op·posed′,** *p.t. & p.p.;* **op·pos′ing,** *pr.p.*

op·po·site (äp′ə zit), *adj.* **1.** different in every way; exactly reverse or in contrast [Hot is *opposite* to cold.] **2.** at the other end or side; directly facing or back to back [the *opposite* end of a table; the *opposite* side of a coin]. —*n.* anything opposite [Love is the *opposite* of hate.] —*prep.* across from; facing [We sat *opposite* each other.] —**op′po·site·ly,** *adv.*

op·po·si·tion (äp′ə zish′ən), *n.* **1.** an opposing or being opposed; contrast. **2.** a fighting against or resisting [His plans met *opposition*.] **3.** anything that opposes; especially, a political party opposing the party in power.

op·press (ə pres′), *v.* **1.** to trouble the mind of; worry; weigh down [*oppressed* by a feeling of fear]. **2.** to keep down by the cruel use of power;

rule in a very harsh way [Pharaoh *oppressed* the Israelite slaves.]

op·pres·sion (ə presh/ən), *n.* **1.** an oppressing or being oppressed; harsh rule. **2.** a feeling of being weighed down with problems, worries, etc.

op·pres·sive (ə pres/iv), *adj.* **1.** hard to put up with; burdensome [*oppressive* tasks; the *oppressive* rain of the tropics]. **2.** cruel and unjust; harsh [the dictator's *oppressive* laws].

op·pro·bri·ous (ə prō/bri əs), *adj.* **1.** showing scorn or dislike; abusive [*opprobrious* remarks]. **2.** deserving scorn or dislike; disgraceful [*opprobrious* behavior].

op·pro·bri·um (ə prō/bri əm), *n.* disgrace or scorn brought on by shameful behavior.

op·tic (äp/tik), *adj.* of the eye or the sense of sight [the *optic* nerve].

op·ti·cal (äp/ti k'l), *adj.* **1.** of the sense of sight; visual [an *optical* illusion]. **2.** made to give help in seeing [Lenses are *optical* instruments.] **3.** of optics.

op·ti·cian (äp tish/ən), *n.* a person who makes or sells eyeglasses and other optical supplies.

op·tics (äp/tiks), *n.pl.* the science that deals with light and vision: *used with a singular verb* [*Optics* is a branch of physics.]

op·ti·mism (äp/tə miz'm), *n.* a bright and hopeful feeling about life, in which one expects things to turn out all right. —**op'ti·mis'tic,** *adj.* —**op'ti·mis'ti·cal·ly,** *adv.*

op·ti·mist (äp/tə mist), *n.* a person who is cheerful and hopeful, no matter what happens.

op·ti·mum (äp/tə mum), *n.* the condition, amount, etc. that is best or most favorable. —*adj.* best; most favorable [*optimum* conditions].

op·tion (äp/shən), *n.* **1.** the act of choosing; choice [He had no *option* but to go.] **2.** the right of choosing. **3.** the right to buy or sell something at a certain price within a certain period of time.

op·tion·al (äp/shən əl), *adj.* that one may choose to do or not do; not forced [a book list for *optional* reading].

op·tom·e·trist (äp täm/ə trist), *n.* a person specially trained to examine people's eyes and fit them with glasses to help them see better.

op·tom·e·try (äp täm/ə trē), *n.* the science or work of an optometrist.

op·u·lence (äp/yoo ləns), *n.* **1.** wealth; riches [a man of *opulence*]. **2.** a great amount; abundance [an *opulence* of hair]. —**op'u·lent,** *adj.*

o·pus (ō/pəs), *n.* a work or composition; especially, any of the musical works of a composer, numbered in the order in which they appeared. —**op·er·a** (äp/ər ə) or **o'pus·es,** *pl.*

or (ôr *or* ər), *conj.* a word used before: **1.** the second of two choices or possibilities [Do you want milk *or* cocoa? Answer, *or* he will be angry.] **2.** the last of a series of choices [Is the light red, yellow, *or* green?] **3.** a word or phrase of the same meaning [botany, *or* the study of plants]. **4.** the second of two choices when the first comes after *either* or *whether* [Take either this one *or* that one.]

-or (ər *or* ôr), a suffix meaning "a person or thing that" [An *inventor* is a person who invents.]

or·a·cle (ôr/ə k'l), *n.* **1.** a place or priest through which the ancient Greeks and Romans believed they could learn the will of the gods. **2.** a message coming from such a place or person. **3.** a very wise person whose opinions are greatly respected. —**o·rac·u·lar** (ô rak/yoo lər), *adj.*

o·ral (ôr/əl), *adj.* **1.** spoken, not written. **2.** of the mouth [*oral* surgery]. —**o'ral·ly,** *adv.*

or·ange (ôr/ənj), *n.* **1.** a round citrus fruit with a reddish-yellow skin and a sweet, juicy pulp. **2.** the tree it grows on, having shiny leaves and white, sweet-smelling blossoms. **3.** reddish yellow. —*adj.* reddish-yellow.

oranges

or·ange·ade (ôr/ənj ād/), *n.* a drink made of orange juice, water, and sugar.

o·rang·u·tan (ō rang/oo tan), *n.* a large ape with very long arms and shaggy, reddish hair, found in Borneo and Sumatra. Also **o·rang·ou·tang** (ō rang/oo tang).

o·ra·tion (ô rā/shən), *n.* a public speech of a serious kind, as at some ceremony.

or·a·tor (ôr/ə tər), *n.* **1.** a person who gives an oration. **2.** a skillful speaker.

or·a·to·ri·o (ôr/ə tôr/i ō), *n.* a long musical work for an orchestra, chorus, and solo singers. It is usually on

orangutan
(4 to 5 ft. high)

a religious subject and is like an opera except that the singers do not wear costumes or move about. —**or'a·to'ri·os,** *pl.*

or·a·to·ry (ôr/ə tôr/ē), *n.* the art or skill of speaking in public. —**or'a·tor'i·cal,** *adj.*

orb (ôrb), *n.* **1.** a ball or globe. **2.** a heavenly body, as the sun or moon. **3.** the eye or eyeball: *used in poetry.*

or·bit (ôr/bit), *n.* the path followed by a heavenly body going around another, as the path of a planet around the sun. —*v.* to put or go in an orbit, as an artificial satellite.

orbit of a planet

or·chard (ôr/chərd), *n.* **1.** a piece of land where fruit trees are grown. **2.** such trees.

or·ches·tra (ôr/kis trə), *n.* **1.** a group of musicians playing together, especially with some stringed instruments. **2.** the instruments of such a group. **3.** the space in front of the stage in a theater, where the musicians sit: also called **orchestra pit.** **4.** the main floor of a theater, especially the front part. —**or·ches·tral** (ôr·kes/trəl), *adj.*

or·ches·trate (ôr/kis trāt), *v.* to arrange a piece of music for the various instruments of an orchestra. —**or'ches·trat·ed,** *p.t. & p.p.;* **or'ches·trat·ing,** *pr.p.* —**or'ches·tra'tion,** *n.*

or·chid (ôr′kid), *n.* **1.** any of a large group of plants with flowers having three petals, of which the middle one is larger than the others and has an irregular shape. **2.** the pale purple color of some orchids.

orchid

or·dain (ôr dān′), *v.* **1.** to make happen; arrange beforehand; order; establish [to believe that fate *ordains* one's future]. **2.** to appoint as a minister, priest, etc., often by a special ceremony.

or·deal (ôr dēl′), *n.* **1.** a way used in earlier times to judge whether a person was guilty of some crime. The person was placed in great danger; if he was not hurt, he was supposed to be innocent. **2.** any difficult or painful experience [Reciting is an *ordeal* for him.]

or·der (ôr′dər), *n.* **1.** the way in which things are placed or follow one another; arrangement [names in alphabetical *order*]. **2.** a condition in which everything is in its right place or is working properly [The house is in *order*.] **3.** the way a thing is; condition [a motor in poor *order*]. **4.** a peaceful condition in which people obey the rules [Police help to keep law and *order*.] **5.** the rules by which a meeting, debate, etc. is carried out. **6.** a direction telling someone what to do, given by a person with authority; command [The general's *orders* were quickly obeyed.] **7.** a request for something that one wants to buy or receive [Mail your *order* for flower seeds today.] **8.** the things asked for [This store will deliver your *order*.] **9.** a group of related animals or plants, larger than a family [Whales and dolphins belong to the same *order* of mammals.] **10.** a class or kind [intelligence of a high *order*]. **11.** a group of people joined together because they share the same beliefs, interests, etc. [an *order* of monks; the Fraternal *Order* of Firemen]. **12.** a group of people who have been honored in some way, or a medal or ribbon worn by members of such a group [The *Order* of the Purple Heart is made up of soldiers wounded in action.] **13.** a style of ancient building shown by the kind of columns it has [the Doric *order*]. **14. orders,** *pl.* the position of a minister or priest [He took holy *orders*.] **15.** see **money order.** —*v.* **1.** to tell what to do; give an order to; command [The captain *ordered* his men to charge.] **2.** to put in order; arrange [I must *order* my affairs before I leave.] **3.** to ask for something one wants to buy or receive [Please *order* some art supplies for the class.] —**by order,** according to the command given [*by order* of the King]. —**call to order,** to ask to become quiet, as in order to start a meeting. —**in order, 1.** in its proper place. **2.** working as it should. **3.** according to the rules, as of a meeting. —**in order that,** so that. —**in order to,** for the purpose of. —**in short order,** in a short time; quickly. —**on order,**

asked for but not yet supplied. —**on the order of,** similar to; rather like. —**out of order, 1.** out of its proper place. **2.** not working. **3.** not according to rules, as of a meeting. —**to order,** in the way asked for by the buyer [a suit made *to order*].

or·der·ly (ôr′dər lē), *adj.* **1.** neatly arranged; tidy; in order [an *orderly* room]. **2.** behaving well; obeying the rules [an *orderly* crowd]. —*n.* **1.** a soldier who acts as a messenger or servant for an officer. **2.** a man who does general work in a hospital, helping the doctors and nurses. —**or′der·lies,** *pl.* —**or′der·li·ness,** *n.*

or·di·nal number (ôr′d'n əl), any number used to show where something comes in a series [First, sixth, and 10th are *ordinal numbers*.] See also **cardinal number.**

or·di·nance (ôr′di nəns), *n.* an order, command, or law; especially, a law made by a city government [an *ordinance* forbidding jaywalking].

or·di·nar·i·ly (ôr′d'n er′ə lē *or* ôr′də ner′ə lē), *adv.* usually; as a rule; generally.

or·di·nar·y (ôr′d'n er′ē), *adj.* **1.** usual; regular; normal [The *ordinary* price is $10.] **2.** not special in any way; common; average [a man of *ordinary* ability]. —**out of the ordinary,** unusual; extraordinary.

or·di·na·tion (ôr′də nā′shən), *n.* the act or ceremony of ordaining a minister, priest, etc.

ord·nance (ôrd′nəns), *n.* **1.** artillery and cannon. **2.** all military weapons and ammunition.

ore (ôr), *n.* a rock or mineral from which a metal can be got [iron *ore*].

Or·e·gon (ôr′i gän *or* ôr′i gən), *n.* a State in the northwestern part of the United States: abbreviated **Ore.** or **Oreg.**

or·gan (ôr′gən), *n.* **1.** a musical instrument having sets of pipes that make sounds when air is sent through them by pressing on keys or pedals: also called a **pipe organ. 2.** an instrument like this, but with reeds or electronic tubes instead of pipes. **3.** a part of an animal or plant that has some special purpose [The heart, liver, and eyes are *organs* of the body.] **4.** a means by which things are done [The city council is an *organ* of local government.] **5.** a means of passing on ideas or opinions, as a newspaper or magazine.

pipe organ

or·gan·dy or **or·gan·die** (ôr′gən dē), *n.* a very thin, stiff cotton cloth, used for blouses, etc.

or·gan·ic (ôr gan′ik), *adj.* **1.** of or having to do with an organ of the body [An *organic* disease causes some change in a body organ.] **2.** arranged according to a system [the *organic* structure of the U.S. government]. **3.** of, like, or produced by living matter [Coal is *organic* rather than mineral in origin.] **4.** having to do with chemical compounds containing carbon [*organic* chemistry]. —**or·gan′i·cal·ly,** *adv.*

or·gan·ism (ôr′gən iz′m), *n.* **1.** any living thing [Plants and animals are *organisms*.] **2.** anything made up of many complicated parts [A nation is a political *organism*.]

or·gan·ist (ôr′gən ist), *n.* a person who plays the organ.

or·gan·i·za·tion (ôr′gən i zā′shən), *n.* **1.** the act of organizing. **2.** the way in which the parts of something are organized or arranged [to study the *organization* of a beehive]. **3.** a group of persons organized for some purpose.

or·gan·ize (ôr′gən īz), *v.* **1.** to arrange or place according to a system [She *organized* her books according to their subjects.] **2.** to bring into being by working out the details; start [to *organize* a club; to *organize* a bank]. **3.** to make part of a group, union, etc. [The coal miners were *organized*.] —**or′gan·ized,** *p.t. & p.p.;* **or′gan·iz·ing,** *pr.p.* —**or′gan·iz′er,** *n.*

or·gy (ôr′jē), *n.* a wild, uncontrolled merrymaking. —**or′gies,** *pl.*

o·ri·el (ôr′i əl), *n.* a large window built out from a wall and resting on a bracket.

o·ri·ent (ôr′i ənt), *n.* **1.** the east: *used mainly in poetry.* **2. Orient,** the East, or Asia; especially, the Far East, or eastern Asia. —*v.* (ôr′i ent′), **1.** to put into the right position or direction with respect to something else [to *orient* a map with the directions of the compass]. **2.** to make or become used to a certain situation [The new boy has *oriented* himself to our school.]

O·ri·en·tal (ôr′i en′t'l), *adj.* **1.** of the Orient, its people, etc.; Eastern. **2. oriental,** eastern. —*n.* a member of a people whose native country is in the Orient.

o·ri·en·tate (ôr′i en tāt′), *v.* to orient. —**o′ri·en·tat′ed,** *p.t. & p.p.;* **o′ri·en·tat′ing,** *pr.p.*

o·ri·en·ta·tion (ôr′i en tā′shən), *n.* the condition or process of being oriented; especially, a making or becoming used to a certain situation.

or·i·fice (ôr′ə fis), *n.* an opening or mouth, as of a tube, cave, etc.

or·i·gin (ôr′ə jin), *n.* **1.** the place or point from which something comes; beginning [The word "rodeo" has its *origin* in Spanish.] **2.** parentage or ancestors [of French *origin*].

o·rig·i·nal (ə rij′ə n'l), *adj.* **1.** having to do with an origin; first or earliest [the *original* settlers of North America]. **2.** that has never been before; not copied; fresh; new [an *original* idea; *original* music]. **3.** able to think of new things; inventive [an *original* mind]. **4.** being the one of which there are copies [the *original* letter and three carbon copies]. —*n.* **1.** a painting, piece of writing, etc. that is not a copy, reproduction, or translation. **2.** the person or thing pictured in a painting, etc. **3.** the form from which others have developed [An animal the size of a fox was the *original* of the modern horse.] —**o·rig·i·nal·i·ty** (ə rij′ə nal′ə tē), *n.*

o·rig·i·nal·ly (ə rij′ə n'l ē), *adv.* **1.** at the start; at first [There were *originally* great herds of

bison in America.] **2.** in a way that is new, different, or fresh.

o·rig·i·nate (ə rij′ə nāt), *v.* **1.** to bring into being; create; invent [England *originated* the use of government postage stamps.] **2.** to begin; come from [Many TV programs *originate* in New York.] —**o·rig′i·nat·ed,** *p.t. & p.p.;* **o·rig′i·nat·ing,** *pr.p.* —**o·rig′i·na′tor,** *n.*

O·ri·no·co (ôr′ə nō′kō), *n.* a river in Venezuela, flowing into the Atlantic.

o·ri·ole (ôr′i ōl), *n.* any of a number of songbirds of Europe and America, having black and yellow, or orange, feathers.

O·ri·on (ō rī′ən), *n.* a constellation that is supposed to form the outline of a hunter's belt and sword. *See the picture for* **constellation.**

o·ri·son (ôr′i z'n), *n.* a prayer: *now seldom used except in poetry.*

Baltimore oriole
(8 in. long)

Ork·ney Islands (ôrk′nē), a group of islands north of Scotland.

or·na·ment (ôr′nə mənt), *n.* **1.** anything added or put on to make something look better; decoration [Christmas-tree *ornaments*]. **2.** a person whose character or talents makes his whole group seem better [He is an *ornament* to his profession.] —*v.* (ôr′nə ment′), to add ornaments to; decorate.

or·na·men·tal (ôr′nə men′t'l), *adj.* serving as an ornament; decorative [*ornamental* borders].

or·na·men·ta·tion (ôr′nə men tā′shən), *n.* **1.** an ornamenting or being ornamented. **2.** the things used as ornaments; decoration.

or·nate (ôr nāt′), *adj.* having much ornament or decoration; showy.

or·ni·thol·o·gy (ôr′ni thäl′ə jē), *n.* the scientific study of birds. —**or′ni·thol′o·gist,** *n.*

o·ro·tund (ôr′ə tund), *adj.* **1.** clear, strong, and deep [an *orotund* voice]. **2.** too solemn and dignified; pompous.

or·phan (ôr′fən), *n.* a child whose father or mother or, especially, both parents are dead. —*adj.* **1.** being an orphan [an *orphan* child]. **2.** of or for orphans [an *orphan* home]. —*v.* to cause to become an orphan [children *orphaned* by the war].

ornate chair

or·phan·age (ôr′fən ij), *n.* a home for taking care of a number of orphans.

Or·pheus (ôr′fi əs *or* ôr′fyōōs), *n.* a musician in a Greek myth, with such magical skill on the lyre that he could charm animals and things.

or·tho·don·tics (ôr′thə dän′tiks) *or* **or·tho·don·tia** (ôr′thə dän′shə), *n.* the branch of dentistry dealing with the straightening of teeth, especially in young people.

or·tho·dox (ôr′thə däks), *adj.* keeping to the usual or fixed beliefs, customs, etc., especially in religion; conventional [*orthodox* political views; *orthodox* Judaism]. —**or'tho·dox'y,** *n.*

Orthodox Eastern Church, the main Christian church in eastern Europe, western Asia, and northern Africa: also **Orthodox Church.**

or·thog·ra·phy (ôr thäg'rə fē), *n.* **1.** correct spelling. **2.** any style or way of spelling. —**or·tho·graph·ic** (ôr'thə graf'ik), *adj.*

-o·ry (ôr'ē), a suffix meaning: **1.** of or having the nature of [*Illusory* means of or having the nature of an illusion.] **2.** a place or thing for [An *observatory* is a place for observing the stars.]

o·ryx (ôr'iks), *n.* a large African antelope with long, straight horns that slant backward. —**o'ryx·es** or **o'ryx,** *pl.*

oryx (4 ft. high at shoulder)

O·sa·ka (ō sä'kə), *n.* a city and seaport of Japan.

os·cil·late (äs'ə lāt), *v.* **1.** to swing or move back and forth [an *oscillating* pendulum]. **2.** to shift back and forth, as in trying to decide something. —**os'cil·lat·ed,** *p.t. & p.p.;* **os'cil·lat·ing,** *pr.p.* —**os'cil·la'·tion,** *n.*

os·cu·late (äs'kyoo lāt), *v.* to kiss. —**os'cu·lat·ed,** *p.t. & p.p.;* **os'cu·lat·ing,** *pr.p.*

o·sier (ō'zhər), *n.* a willow tree whose twigs are used in making baskets and furniture.

O·si·ris (ō sī'ris), *n.* the ancient Egyptian god of the lower world and judge of the dead.

-os·i·ty (äs'ə tē), a suffix used to form nouns from adjectives ending in *-ous,* as *generosity* from *generous.*

Os·lo (äs'lō *or* äz'lō), *n.* the capital of Norway.

os·mo·sis (äz mō'sis *or* äs mō'sis), *n.* the tendency of liquids separated by a thin membrane, as the wall of a living cell, to pass through it, so as to become mixed and equal in strength on both sides.

os·prey (äs'prē), *n.* a large hawk that feeds mainly on fish. —**os'preys,** *pl.*

os·si·fy (äs'ə fī), *v.* **1.** to form or change into bone [The soft spots in a baby's skull *ossify* as he grows.] **2.** to make or become fixed or set, not likely to change [a mind *ossified* by prejudice]. —**os'si·fied,** *p.t. & p.p.;* **os'si·fy·ing,** *pr.p.* —**os'si·fi·ca'tion,** *n.*

osprey (wingspread 5½ ft.)

os·ten·si·ble (äs ten'sə b'l), *adj.* seeming, claimed, or pretended, but not real [his *ostensible* reason for calling]. —**os·ten'si·bly,** *adv.*

os·ten·ta·tion (äs'tən tā'shən), *n.* a showing off, as of one's wealth, knowledge, etc. [He spent money with great *ostentation.*]

os·ten·ta·tious (äs'tən tā'shəs), *adj.* showing off or done in order to get attention [an *ostentatious* monument]. —**os'ten·ta'tious·ly,** *adv.*

os·te·o·path (äs'ti ə path), *n.* a doctor of osteopathy.

os·te·op·a·thy (äs'ti äp'ə thē), *n.* a system of treating diseases by working on the joints and muscles with the hands, as well as by the use of medicine and surgery.

ost·ler (äs'lər), *n.* same as **hostler.**

os·tra·cism (äs'trə siz'm), *n.* **1.** a way of punishing someone in ancient Greece by voting to send him out of the country. **2.** the action of a group or of society in deciding to have nothing to do with someone who is disliked, etc.

os·tra·cize (äs'trə sīz), *v.* to refuse as a group to have anything to do with; banish or bar [The club *ostracized* him for his bad manners.] —**os'tra·cized,** *p.t. & p.p.;* **os'tra·ciz·ing,** *pr.p.*

os·trich (ôs'trich), *n.* a very large bird of Africa and southwestern Asia with a long neck and long legs. It cannot fly, but runs swiftly.

O·thel·lo (ə thel'ō), *n.* a play by Shakespeare in which the hero, Othello, is made jealous of his faithful wife and kills her.

ostrich (8 ft. high)

oth·er (uth'ər), *adj.* **1.** not this one or the one just mentioned, but a different one [Use your *other* foot. Not Jane but some *other* girl called.] **2.** being the one or ones remaining; in addition [Bill, Lou, and the *other* boys]. **3.** additional; extra [I have no *other* coat.] —*pron.* **1.** the other one [Each loved the *other.*] **2.** some other person or thing [How many *others* are coming?] —*adv.* in a different way; otherwise [He can't do *other* than go.] —**every other,** every second [*every other* day]. —**the other day,** not long ago; recently.

oth·er·wise (uth'ər wīz), *adv.* **1.** in some other way; differently [I believe *otherwise.*] **2.** in all other ways [He has a cough, but *otherwise* feels fine.] **3.** if things were different; or else [I'm tired; *otherwise,* I would play.] —*adj.* different [His answer could not be *otherwise.*]

Ot·ta·wa (ät'ə wə), *n.* the capital of Canada, in eastern Ontario.

ot·ter (ät'ər), *n.* **1.** a furry animal that swims. It has webbed feet and a long tail and eats small animals and fish. **2.** its soft, thick fur.

Ot·to·man (ät'ə mən), *n.* **1.** a Turk. **2. ottoman,** a low seat without back or arms; also, a padded footstool. —*adj.* Turkish. —**Ot'to·mans,** *pl.*

otter (3 ft. long)

ouch (ouch), *interj.* a sound made in showing sudden or sharp pain.

ought (ôt), *a helping verb used with infinitives and meaning:* **1.** to be forced by what is right, wise, or necessary [He *ought* to pay his debts. You *ought* to eat well-balanced meals.] **2.** to be expected or likely [He *ought* to have arrived by now.]

ounce (ouns), *n.* **1.** a unit of weight, equal to 1/16 pound in avoirdupois weight and 1/12 pound in troy weight. **2.** a measure of liquids, equal to 1/16 pint. **3.** any small amount.

our (our), *pron.* of us or done by us: the possessive form of *we*, used before a noun and thought of as an adjective [*our* car; *our* work]. See also **ours.**

ours (ourz), *pron.* the one or the ones that belong to us: the form of *our* used when no noun follows [This car is *ours. Ours* are larger.]

our·self (our self/), *pron.* myself: used by a king, queen, etc., as in a formal speech.

our·selves (our selvz/), *pron.* **1.** our own selves: the form of *we* that makes the subject also the object of the verb [We hurt *ourselves.*] **2.** our usual or true selves [We are not *ourselves* today.] *Ourselves* is also used to give force to the subject [We built it *ourselves.*]

-ous (əs), a suffix meaning "having," "full of," or "like" [A *courageous* person is full of courage.]

oust (oust), *v.* to force out; drive out [The usher *ousted* them from our seats.]

out (out), *adv.* **1.** away from the inside, center, etc. [Open the door and look *out.* Spit it *out.* Come *out* and play.] **2.** away from a certain place, as from one's home or office [Let's go *out* for dinner.] **3.** into being or action [A fire broke *out.*] **4.** to the end; completely; thoroughly [to argue it *out;* tired *out*]. **5.** so as to be no more [The fire died *out.*] **6.** beyond what is usual or normal [ears that stick *out*]. **7.** loudly [Sing *out!*] **8.** from among several [to pick *out* a new suit]. **9.** so as to make an out in baseball [He struck *out.*] **10.** into unconsciousness: *a slang meaning* [to pass *out*]. **—adj. 1.** away from work, school, etc. [He is *out* because of illness.] **2.** not in the inside, center, usual limits, etc. [Turn off the light after everyone is *out.*] **3.** not right; in error [He is *out* in his estimate.] **4.** known or made public [Her secret is *out.*] **5.** having lost [He is *out* ten dollars.] **6.** not working or in use [The lights are *out.*] **7.** having made an out in baseball. **—prep.** out of; through to the outside [He walked *out* the door.] **—n. 1.** in baseball, the act of failing to get on base or to the next base safely. **2.** a way of avoiding something; excuse: *slang in this meaning* [He has an *out* and won't have to go.] **—v.** to become known [Murder will *out.*] **—interj.** get out! **—all out,** with all effort; completely: *used only in everyday talk.* **—on the outs,** no longer friendly; quarreling: *used only in everyday talk.* **—out and away,** by far. **—out and out,** completely; thoroughly. **—out for,** trying hard to get or do. **—out of, 1.** from inside of [He went *out of* the room.] **2.** through to the outside [thrown *out of* the window]. **3.** from the number of [chosen *out of* a

crowd]. **4.** past the limits of; beyond [*out of* sight]. **5.** from; using [made *out of* bricks]. **6.** because of [done *out of* spite]. **7.** not having any [*out of* gas]. **8.** so as to take away or have taken away [cheated *out of* one's money]. **—out to,** trying hard to.

out-, a prefix meaning: **1.** away from; outside [An *outbuilding* is away from a main building.] **2.** going away or forth; outward [The *outbound* traffic goes away from the city.] **3.** better or more than [To *outdo* another means to do better than another.]

out-and-out (out/'n out/), *adj.* complete; thorough [an *out-and-out* rascal].

out·bid (out bid/), *v.* to bid more than another. *For principal parts, see* **bid.**

out·board motor (out/bôrd), a gasoline engine fixed to the outside of the stern of a boat.

out·bound (out/-bound/), *adj.* headed away from a place; outward bound [an *out-bound* ship].

out·break (out/brāk), *n.* a breaking out, as of disease or rioting among people.

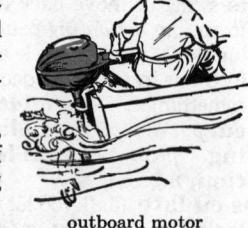

outboard motor

out·build·ing (out/-bil/ding), *n.* a shed, barn, garage, etc. separate from the main building.

out·burst (out/bûrst), *n.* a sudden show of strong feeling or energy.

out·cast (out/kast), *adj.* shunned by people; without home or friends. **—n.** an outcast person.

out·class (out klas/), *v.* to be better by far.

out·come (out/kum), *n.* the way something turns out; result [the *outcome* of the battle].

out·crop (out/kräp), *n.* a coming out at the surface of the earth [an *outcrop* of rock].

out·cry (out/krī), *n.* **1.** a crying out; a scream or shout. **2.** a strong protest or objection. **—out/cries,** *pl.*

out·dat·ed (out dāt/id), *adj.* out-of-date.

out·dis·tance (out dis/təns), *v.* to get far ahead of, as in a race. **—out·dis/tanced,** *p.t. & p.p.;* **out·dis/tanc·ing,** *pr.p.*

out·do (out dōō/), *v.* to do better or more than. **—outdo oneself,** to do one's best or better than expected. *For principal parts, see* **do.**

out·door (out/dôr), *adj.* being, belonging, done, etc outside a house or other building [an *outdoor* pool; *outdoor* exercise].

out·doors (out/dôrz), *adv.* in or into the open; outside [We went *outdoors* to play.] **—n.** (out-dôrz/), the world outside of buildings.

out·er (out/ər), *adj.* on or closer to the outside [the *outer* wall; an *outer* coating].

out·er·most (out/ər mōst), *adj.* farthest out.

out·field (out/fēld), *n.* **1.** the part of a baseball field beyond the infield. **2.** all the outfielders.

out·field·er (out/fēl/dər), *n.* a baseball player whose position is in the outfield.

out·fit (out/fit), *n.* **1.** the clothing or equipment used in some work, activity, etc. [a carpenter's *outfit;* a camping *outfit;* a new spring *outfit*]. **2.** a group of people working together; especially, a regiment, division, etc. in the armed forces. —*v.* to supply with what is needed [a store which *outfits* hunting parties]. —**out′·fit·ted,** *p.t.* & *p.p.;* **out′·fit·ting,** *pr.p.*

out·flank (out flangk′), *v.* to pass around the side or sides of enemy troops.

out·flow (out′flō), *n.* **1.** the act of flowing out. **2.** anything that flows out.

out·go (out′gō), *n.* that which goes out or is paid out; especially, money spent.

out·go·ing (out′gō′ing), *adj.* **1.** going out; departing [the *outgoing* mail]. **2.** friendly; sociable [a warm, *outgoing* person].

out·grow (out grō′), *v.* **1.** to grow bigger than [Tom *outgrew* his older brother.] **2.** to lose by growing older [to *outgrow* an interest in dolls]. **3.** to grow too large for [Jim has *outgrown* this suit.] *For principal parts, see* **grow.**

out·growth (out′grōth), *n.* **1.** something that develops from something else; result or offshoot [Astronomy was an *outgrowth* of astrology.] **2.** a growing out or that which grows out.

out·guess (out ges′), *v.* to outwit.

out·house (out′hous), *n.* an outbuilding; especially, an outdoor toilet.

outgrown clothing

out·ing (out′ing), *n.* a short pleasure trip or picnic out-of-doors.

out·land·ish (out lan′dish), *adj.* very strange or unusual [*outlandish* clothes or ideas].

out·last (out last′), *v.* to last longer than.

out·law (out′lô), *n.* **1.** originally, a person who had lost the rights and protection of the law. **2.** a criminal, especially one who is being hunted by police. —*v.* to pass a law against; rule out as not lawful [The city has *outlawed* gambling.]

out·lay (out′lā), *n.* a spending of money, or the amount spent.

out·let (out′let), *n.* **1.** a means or opening for letting something out [the *outlet* of a river; an electrical *outlet*]. **2.** a way of using up [Tennis is an *outlet* for his energy.] **3.** a market for goods.

out·line (out′līn), *n.* **1.** a line around the outer edges of an object, showing its shape [the dim *outline* of a ship in the fog]. **2.** a drawing that shows only the outer lines, or form, of a thing. **3.** a report or plan giving the main points, but not the details [an *outline* of history; an *outline* of a speech]. —*v.* to make an outline of. —**out′·lined,** *p.t.* & *p.p.;* **out′·lin·ing,** *pr.p.*

outline *(meaning 2)*

out·live (out liv′), *v.* to live longer than. —**out·lived′,** *p.t.* & *p.p.;* **out·liv′ing,** *pr.p.*

out·look (out′look), *n.* **1.** the view from a place. **2.** one's way of thinking; point of view;

attitude [an old-fashioned *outlook;* a cheerful *outlook*]. **3.** what is likely for the future; prospect [the weather *outlook;* the *outlook* for peace].

out·ly·ing (out′lī′ing), *adj.* quite far from the center; remote [*outlying* suburbs].

out·mod·ed (out mōd′id), *adj.* out-of-date.

out·num·ber (out num′bər), *v.* to be greater in number than [Girls *outnumber* boys here.]

out-of-date (out′əv dāt′), *adj.* no longer in style or use: old-fashioned.

out-of-doors (out′əv dôrz′), *adj.* outdoor: also **out-of-door.** —*n.* & *adv.* outdoors.

out-of-the-way (out′əv *th*ə wā′), *adj.* **1.** away from crowded centers, main roads, etc.; secluded [an *out-of-the-way* cabin]. **2.** unusual [an *out-of-the-way* experience].

out·play (out plā′), *v.* to play better than.

out·post (out′pōst), *n.* **1.** a small group of soldiers on guard some distance away from the main body of troops. **2.** the place where this group is. **3.** a small village on a frontier.

out·put (out′poot), *n.* **1.** the amount made or done [the daily *output* of one factory worker]. **2.** the information delivered by a computer. **3.** the electric current or power delivered by an electric circuit or by an electric machine, as a generator.

out·rage (out′rāj), *n.* **1.** a cruel or evil act that is shocking in its wickedness [War is an *outrage* against mankind.] **2.** an act, remark, etc. that deeply hurts or angers a person. —*v.* to be an outrage against or do something that is an outrage against. —**out′·raged,** *p.t.* & *p.p.;* **out′·rag·ing,** *pr.p.*

out·ra·geous (out rā′jəs), *adj.* **1.** doing great injury or wrong [*outrageous* crimes]. **2.** so wrong or bad that it hurts or shocks [an *outrageous* lie]. —**out·ra′geous·ly,** *adv.*

out·rank (out rangk′), *v.* to rank higher than.

out·rig·ger (out′rig′ər), *n.* **1.** a framework built out from the side of a canoe to keep it from tipping. **2.** a canoe of this type.

outrigger

out·right (out′rīt), *adj.* thorough, downright, complete, etc. [an *outright* fool; an *outright* denial]. —*adv.* **1.** entirely; wholly [The farm was sold *outright*.] **2.** without holding back; openly [to laugh *outright*]. **3.** at once [He was hired *outright*.]

out·run (out run′), *v.* **1.** to run faster or longer than. **2.** to go beyond the limits of; exceed [His expenses *outran* his income.] *For principal parts, see* **run.**

out·sell (out sel′), *v.* to sell in greater amounts than [This brand of tea *outsells* that.] —**out·sold′,** *p.t.* & *p.p.;* **out·sell′ing,** *pr.p.*

out·set (out′set), *n.* a setting out; beginning; start [We had trouble at the *outset*.]

out·shine (out shīn′), *v.* **1.** to shine brighter than. **2.** to be better than; surpass [Eddie

fat,   āpe,   cär,   ten,   ēven,   hit,   bīte,   gō,   hôrn,   tōōl,   book,   up,   fûr;
get,   joy,   yet,   chin,   she,   thin,   *th*en;   zh = s in pleasure;   ′ as in able (ā′b'l);
ə = a in ago,   e in agent,   i in sanity,   o in confess,   u in focus.

outshines the other players.] *For principal parts, see* **shine.**

out·side (out′sīd′), *n.* **1.** the side or part that faces out; exterior [Wash the windows on the *outside.*] **2.** any place not inside; the world beyond [The prisoners got little news from the *outside.*] —*adj.* **1.** of or on the outside; outer [the *outside* layer]. **2.** from some other person or place [He did it himself without *outside* help.] **3.** largest, highest, etc.; extreme [an *outside* estimate]. **4.** small; slight [He has an *outside* chance of winning.] —*adv.* on or to the outside [Let's play *outside.*] —*prep.* (*usually* out sīd′), on, to, or near the outside of [Leave it *outside* the door.] —**at the outside,** at the most. —**outside of, 1.** outside. **2.** except for: *used only in everyday talk.*

out·sid·er (out sīd′ər), *n.* a person who does not belong to a certain group.

out·skirts (out′skŭrts), *n.pl.* the districts or parts far from the center. as of a city.

out·spo·ken (out′spō′kən), *adj.* speaking or spoken in a frank or bold way.

out·spread (out′spred), *adj.* spread out [the *outspread* branches of the tree].

out·stand·ing (out′stan′ding), *adj.* **1.** that stands out as very good or important [an *outstanding* feat]. **2.** not paid [*outstanding* debts].

out·stretched (out′strecht), *adj.* stretched out; extended [with *outstretched* arms].

out·strip (out strip′), *v.* to get ahead of; leave behind or do better than; surpass or excel [to *outstrip* other runners]. —**out·stripped′,** *p.t. & p.p.;* **out·strip′-ping,** *pr.p.*

outspread fingers

out·ward (out′wərd), *adj.* **1.** being on the outside; outer. **2.** that can be seen or noticed; visible [He showed no *outward* sign of unhappiness.] **3.** toward the outside [an *outward* glance; *outward* traffic]. —*adv.* toward the outside [The door opens *outward.*] —**out′ward·ly,** *adv.*

outstretched arms

out·wards (out′wərdz), *adv.* same as **outward.**

out·wear (out wer′), *v.* **1.** to last longer than [These shoes will *outwear* any others.] **2.** to wear out or use up. *For principal parts, see* **wear.**

out·weigh (out wā′), *v.* **1.** to weigh more than. **2.** to be more important, valuable, etc. than [With him, honesty *outweighs* success.]

out·wit (out wit′), *v.* to win out over by being more clever or cunning [to *outwit* an opponent in chess]. —**out·wit′ted,** *p.t. & p.p.;* **out·wit′-ting,** *pr.p.*

out·worn (out′wôrn′), *adj.* **1.** worn out [*outworn* shoes]. **2.** out-of-date [*outworn* ideas].

ou·zel (ōō′z′l), *n.* the European blackbird.

o·va (ō′və), *n.* plural of **ovum.**

o·val (ō′v′l), *adj.* shaped like an egg or like an ellipse. —*n.* anything with such a shape.

oval

o·va·ry (ō′vər ē), *n.* **1.** the organ in a female in which the eggs are formed. **2.** the part of a flower in which the seeds are formed. —**o′va·ries,** *pl.*

o·va·tion (ō vā′shən), *n.* loud and long applause or cheering by a crowd to show welcome or approval.

ov·en (uv′ən), *n.* a container, or an enclosed space as in a stove, for baking or roasting food or for heating or drying things.

ov·en·bird (uv′ən bŭrd′), *n.* a bird that builds a nest on the ground, with a dome on top.

o·ver (ō′vər), *prep.* **1.** in, at, or to a place above [Hang the picture *over* the fireplace.] **2.** so as to cover [Put a blanket *over* his legs.] **3.** above in rank or power [A king ruled *over* them.] **4.** along the length of [I've driven *over* this road before.] **5.** to or on the other side of [Jump *over* the puddle.] **6.** above and beyond [He leaned *over* the edge.] **7.** through all parts of [*over* the whole country]. **8.** during; through [*over* the years]. **9.** more than [It cost *over* ten cents.] **10.** rather than [They chose him *over* me.] **11.** upon, so that it affects [He cast a spell *over* us.] **12.** concerning; about [Don't fight *over* it.] **13.** by means of [He told me *over* the telephone.] —*adv.* **1.** above or across [A plane flew *over.*] **2.** across the brim or edge [The soup boiled *over.*] **3.** more; beyond [He worked three hours or *over.*] **4.** so as to be covered [The wound healed *over.*] **5.** from a standing position; down [The tree fell *over.*] **6.** so that the other side is up [Turn the plate *over.*] **7.** again [Write the letter *over.*] **8.** at or to the other side of something [They live *over* in France.] **9.** from one side, opinion, etc. to another [We'll win him *over.*] —*adj.* **1.** finished; done with [The game is *over.*] **2.** having reached the other side [We were already *over* when the bridge collapsed.] —**all over, 1.** on or in every part. **2.** ended; finished: *also* **all over with.** —**over again,** another time; again. —**over against,** opposite to or in contrast with. —**over all,** from end to end. —**over and above,** in addition to; more than. —**over and over,** again and again.

over-, a prefix meaning: **1.** above or higher; superior [An *overhead* light is above one's head.] **2.** too much [To *overeat* is to eat too much.] **3.** across or beyond [To *overshoot* a target is to shoot beyond it.] Many words beginning with *over-* but not included here can be easily understood if *over-* is given the meaning "too" or "too much"; for example, **overanxious, overcook, overexposure.**

o·ver·all (ō′vər ôl), *adj.* **1.** from end to end [the *overall* length of a boat]. **2.** including everything; total [the *overall* cost].

o·ver·alls (ō′vər ôlz), *n.pl.* loose-fitting trousers, often with a part that comes up over the chest, worn over other clothes to keep them from getting dirty. *See picture on next page.*

o·ver·awe (ō'vər ô'), v. to overcome by filling with awe [The giant did not *overawe* Jack.] —**o'ver-awed'**, *p.t. & p.p.;* **o'ver-aw'ing,** *pr.p.*

o·ver·bal·ance (ō'vər bal'-əns), v. **1.** to be greater than, as in weight or importance. **2.** to throw off balance. —**o'ver·bal'anced,** *p.t. & p.p.;* **o'ver·bal'anc·ing,** *pr.p.*

o·ver·bear·ing (ō'vər ber'-ing), *adj.* ordering others about in a harsh, bullying way.

overalls

o·ver·board (ō'vər bôrd), *adv.* from a ship into the water [He fell *overboard*.]

o·ver·bur·den (ō'vər bûr'd'n), v. to be too great a burden for; weigh down.

o·ver·cast (ō'vər kast), *adj.* cloudy; dark [an *overcast* sky]. —v. **1.** to cover over with clouds or darkness. **2.** to sew over an edge with long, loose stitches to keep it from raveling. —**o'ver-cast,** *p.t. & p.p.;* **o'ver·cast·ing,** *pr.p.*

o·ver·charge (ō'vər chärj'), v. **1.** to charge too high a price. **2.** to fill too full. —n. (ō'vər-chärj), too high a charge. —**o'ver·charged',** *p.t. & p.p.;* **o'ver·charg'ing,** *pr.p.*

o·ver·cloud (ō'vər kloud'), v. **1.** to cover over with clouds; darken. **2.** to make or become gloomy [Grief *overclouded* his face.]

o·ver·coat (ō'vər kōt), n. a heavy coat worn outdoors in cold weather.

o·ver·come (ō'vər kum'), v. **1.** to get the better of; defeat; master [to *overcome* an enemy; to *overcome* a problem]. **2.** to make weak or helpless [He was *overcome* by laughter.] *For principal parts, see* **come.**

o·ver·crowd (ō'vər kroud'), v. to crowd with too many people or things.

o·ver·do (ō'vər dōō'), v. **1.** to tire oneself out by doing too much. **2.** to spoil by exaggerating [He *overdid* his praise.] **3.** to cook too long. *For principal parts, see* **do.**

o·ver·dose (ō'vər dōs), n. too large a dose. —v. (ō'vər dōs'), to give too large a dose to. —**o'ver·dosed',** *p.t. & p.p.;* **o'ver·dos'ing,** *pr.p.*

o·ver·draw (ō'vər drô'), v. **1.** to write checks for more money than one has in one's bank account. **2.** to exaggerate [Villains are *overdrawn* in melodramas.] *For principal parts, see* **draw.**

o·ver·dress (ō'vər dres'), v. to dress in a way that is too showy or too formal.

o·ver·drive (ō'vər drīv'), n. a gear that cuts down the power of an engine without lowering its speed.

o·ver·due (ō'vər dōō' *or* ō'vər dyōō'), *adj.* delayed past the time set for payment, arrival, etc. [an *overdue* bill; a train long *overdue*].

o·ver·eat (ō'vər ēt'), v. to eat too much. *For principal parts, see* **eat.**

o·ver·es·ti·mate (ō'vər es'tə māt), v. to put too high an estimate on or for; rate too highly. —n. (ō'vər es'tə mit), too high an estimate. —**o'ver·es'ti·mat·ed,** *p.t. & p.p.;* **o'ver·es'·ti·mat·ing,** *pr.p.*

o·ver·flow (ō'vər flō'), v. **1.** to flow across; flood [Water *overflowed* the streets.] **2.** to flow over the bounds of something [The river *overflowed* its banks. The crowd *overflowed* into the hall.] **3.** to have its contents flowing over [The sink is *overflowing*.] **4.** to be very full [She is *overflowing* with kindness.] —n. (ō'vər flō),

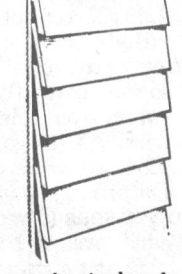
overflowing sink

1. an overflowing. **2.** an opening for draining off overflowing liquids, as at the top of a sink.

o·ver·grow (ō'vər grō'), v. **1.** to grow over so as to cover [The lawn is *overgrown* with weeds.] **2.** to grow too large or too fast [He is *overgrown* for his age.] *For principal parts, see* **grow.**

o·ver·hand (ō'vər hand), *adj. & adv.* with the hand held higher than the elbow [an *overhand* pitch; to throw a ball *overhand*].

o·ver·hang (ō'vər hang'), v. to hang over and beyond [The roof *overhangs* the house.] —n. (ō'vər hang), a part that overhangs. —**o'ver·hung',** *p.t. & p.p.;* **o'ver·hang'ing,** *pr.p.*

o·ver·haul (ō'vər hôl'), v. **1.** to check over carefully and make repairs or changes that are needed [to *overhaul* an engine]. **2.** to catch up with; overtake. —n. (ō'vər hôl), an overhauling.

o·ver·head (ō'vər hed), *adj.* **1.** above one's head [an *overhead* light]. **2.** in the sky [the clouds *overhead*]. —n. the regular expenses of running a business, as of rent, heat, light, taxes, etc. —*adv.* (ō'vər hed'), above the head; aloft.

o·ver·hear (ō'vər hir'), v. to hear something that one is not meant to hear [I *overheard* you arguing in the next room.] —**o·ver·heard** (ō'vər hûrd'), *p.t. & p.p.;* **o'ver·hear'ing,** *pr.p.*

o·ver·joy (ō'vər joi'), v. to give great joy to; delight. —**o'ver·joyed',** *adj.*

o·ver·land (ō'vər land), *adv. & adj.* by, on, or across land [an *overland* journey].

o·ver·lap (ō'vər lap'), v. to lap over part of something or part of each other [The scales on a fish *overlap* one another. The two events *overlapped* in time.] —n. (ō'vər-lap), **1.** an overlapping. **2.** a part that overlaps. —**o'ver-lapped',** *p.t. & p.p.;* **o'ver-lap'ping,** *pr.p.*

o·ver·lay (ō'vər lā'), v. to cover with a layer or coating of something that decorates [The box was *overlaid* with ivory.] —n. (ō'vər lā), a covering or

overlapping boards

layer of decoration. —**o′ver·laid′**, *p.t. & p.p.;* **o′ver·lay′ing**, *pr.p.*

o·ver·load (ō′vər lōd′), *v.* to put too great a load on or in [Don't *overload* the washing machine.] —*n.* (ō′vər lōd), too great a load.

o·ver·look (ō′vər look′), *v.* **1.** to give a view of from above; look down on [Our cottage *overlooks* the ocean.] **2.** to fail to notice [I *overlooked* that detail.] **3.** to ignore or neglect. **4.** to excuse [Can you *overlook* his rudeness?]

o·ver·lord (ō′vər lôrd′), *n.* a lord who ranks above other lords.

o·ver·ly (ō′vər lē), *adv.* too; too much [Macbeth was *overly* ambitious.]

o·ver·mas·ter (ō′vər mas′tər), *v.* to overcome.

o·ver·much (ō′vər much′), *adj., adv. & n.* too much.

o·ver·night (ō′vər nīt′), *adv.* through the night [to stop at a hotel *overnight*]. —*adj.* **1.** on or during the night [an *overnight* snow]. **2.** staying for the night [an *overnight* guest]. **3.** of or for a short trip [an *overnight* bag].

o·ver·pass (ō′vər pas), *n.* a bridge or road over a river, another road, etc.

o·ver·pow·er (ō′vər pou′ər), *v.* to get the better of; make helpless; overcome [Samson *overpowered* the lion. His rage *overpowered* him.]

o·ver·pro·duc·tion (ō′vər prə duk′shən), *n.* the production of more than is needed or wanted.

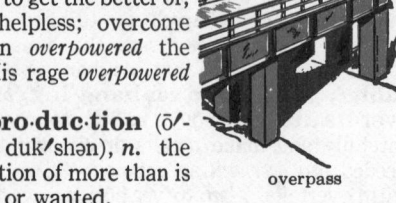

overpass

o·ver·rate (ō′vər rāt′), *v.* to rate too highly; think of as better or greater than it really is. —**o′ver·rat′ed**, *p.t. & p.p.;* **o′ver·rat′ing**, *pr.p.*

o·ver·reach (ō′vər rēch′), *v.* **1.** to reach beyond or above. **2.** to reach too far and miss. —**overreach oneself,** to fail because of trying too hard or being too clever.

o·ver·ride (ō′vər rīd′), *v.* **1.** to ignore in an unjust or impolite way [The tyrant *overrode* the wishes of the people.] **2.** to overrule; set aside [Congress *overrode* the president's veto.] *For principal parts, see* **ride.**

o·ver·rule (ō′vər rool′), *v.* **1.** to rule out or set aside a ruling by someone with less authority [The higher court *overruled* the judge's decision.] **2.** to gain control over; be too strong for. —**o′ver·ruled′**, *p.t. & p.p.;* **o′ver·rul′ing**, *pr.p.*

o·ver·run (ō′vər run′), *v.* **1.** to spread out over so as to cover [Weeds *overran* the garden.] **2.** to swarm over doing harm [a house *overrun* with mice]. **3.** to go over or beyond certain limits [Lou *overran* second base and was tagged out.] *For principal parts, see* **run.**

o·ver·seas (ō′vər sēz′) *or* **o·ver·sea** (ō′vər sē′), *adv.* over or beyond the sea; abroad [Troops were sent *overseas*.] —*adj.* **1.** over or across the sea [an *oversea* flight]. **2.** of, from, or to countries across the sea; foreign [an *overseas* visitor].

o·ver·see (ō′vər sē′), *v.* to watch over and direct; supervise [A teacher *oversees* our games at recess.] *For principal parts, see* **see.**

o·ver·se·er (ō′vər sē′ər), *n.* a person who watches over and directs the work of others.

o·ver·shad·ow (ō′vər shad′ō), *v.* **1.** to cast a shadow over. **2.** to make dark [Troubles *overshadowed* his life.] **3.** to seem more important than [Good times *overshadow* the bad ones.]

o·ver·shoe (ō′vər shoo), *n.* a shoe or boot, as of rubber, worn over the regular shoe in cold or wet weather.

o·ver·shoot (ō′vər shoot′), *v.* to shoot or go over or beyond [to *overshoot* a target or a turn in the road]. —**o′ver·shot′**, *p.t. & p.p.;* **o′ver·shoot′ing**, *pr.p.*

overshoes

o·ver·shot (ō′vər shät), *adj.* **1.** with the upper part sticking out over the lower part [an *overshot* jaw]. **2.** driven by water flowing over the top part [an *overshot* water wheel].

o·ver·sight (ō′vər sīt), *n.* **1.** a failure to notice or do something. **2.** an overseeing; supervision.

o·ver·size (ō′vər sīz′), *adj.* too large; larger than is usual or proper [*oversize* shoes].

o·ver·sleep (ō′vər slēp′), *v.* to sleep past the time for getting up; sleep too long. —**o′ver·slept′**, *p.t. & p.p.;* **o′ver·sleep′ing**, *pr.p.*

o·ver·spread (ō′vər spred′), *v.* to spread over [A faint blush *overspread* her face.] —**o′ver·spread′**, *p.t. & p.p.;* **o′ver·spread′ing**, *pr.p.*

o·ver·state (ō′vər stāt′), *v.* to state too strongly; say more than is true about; exaggerate. —**o′ver·stat′ed**, *p.t. & p.p.;* **o′ver·stat′ing**, *pr.p.* —**o′ver·state′ment**, *n.*

o·ver·stay (ō′vər stā′), *v.* to stay beyond the time of [The guest *overstayed* his welcome.]

o·ver·step (ō′vər step′), *v.* to go beyond the limits of; exceed [to *overstep* one's authority]. *For principal parts, see* **step.**

o·ver·stock (ō′vər stäk′), *v.* to stock more of than is needed or can be used. —*n.* (ō′vər stäk), too large a stock, or supply.

o·ver·sup·ply (ō′vər sə plī′), *v.* to supply with more than is needed. —*n.* too great a supply. —**o′ver·sup·plied′**, *p.t. & p.p.;* **o′ver·sup·ply′ing**, *pr.p.* —**o′ver·sup·plies′**, *pl.*

o·vert (ō′vərt *or* ō vūrt′), *adj.* not hidden; open; public [*overt* actions]. —**o′vert·ly**, *adv.*

o·ver·take (ō′vər tāk′), *v.* **1.** to catch up with [The tortoise *overtook* the hare.] **2.** to come upon suddenly or by surprise [A sudden storm *overtook* us.] *For principal parts, see* **take.**

o·ver·tax (ō′vər taks′), *v.* **1.** to tax too much [an *overtaxed* country]. **2.** to put too much of a strain on [The work *overtaxed* his strength.]

o·ver·throw (ō′vər thrō′), *v.* **1.** to put an end to; defeat; conquer [The rebels *overthrew* the government.] **2.** to throw or turn over; upset. **3.** to throw beyond [The catcher *overthrew* first base.] —*n.* (ō′vər thrō), an upset; defeat. *For principal parts, see* **throw.**

o·ver·time (ō′vər tīm), *n.* **1.** time beyond the regular time, as for working or playing a game; extra time. **2.** pay for working beyond the regular time. —*adj. & adv.* of, for, or during a period of overtime.

o·ver·tone (ō′vər tōn), *n.* a higher tone which sounds faintly along with a main tone made by a musical instrument.

o·ver·ture (ō′vər chər), *n.* **1.** a piece of music played at the beginning of an opera, musical play, etc.; introduction. **2.** an offer to talk over or do something; proposal.

o·ver·turn (ō′vər tûrn′), *v.* **1.** to turn or tip over; upset. **2.** to conquer; defeat; destroy.

o·ver·ween·ing (ō′vər wēn′ing), *adj.* too sure of oneself; conceited; too proud.

o·ver·weight (ō′vər wāt), *adj.* above the proper weight; too heavy. —*n.* more weight than is needed or allowed; extra weight.

o·ver·whelm (ō′vər hwelm′), *v.* **1.** to overcome completely; make helpless; crush [Our team *overwhelmed* theirs.] **2.** to cover over completely; bury [Floods *overwhelmed* the farm.]

o·ver·work (ō′vər wûrk′), *v.* to work too hard or too long [Pharaoh *overworked* his slaves. Don't *overwork* that excuse.] —*n.* too much work.

o·ver·wrought (ō′vər rôt′), *adj.* **1.** too nervous or excited; strained; tense. **2.** having too much decoration; showy [an *overwrought* design].

o·vule (ō′vyōōl), *n.* **1.** a small ovum. **2.** the part of a plant that develops into a seed.

o·vum (ō′vəm), *n.* an egg; a female cell that will develop into a new animal after it is fertilized. —*o′va*, *pl.*

owe (ō), *v.* **1.** to be in debt for a certain amount; have the duty to pay [He still *owes* $200 on his car.] **2.** to have or feel the need to do, give, etc., as because of being grateful [I *owe* my aunt a letter. We *owe* respect to our parents.] **3.** to be indebted for to someone [I *owe* my life to that doctor.] —**owed**, *p.t. & p.p.*; **ow′ing**, *pr.p.*

ow·ing (ō′ing), *adj.* **1.** that owes. **2.** due; not paid [There is $10 *owing* on your bill.] —**owing to,** on account of; as a result of.

owl (oul), *n.* a bird with a large head, large eyes, a short, hooked beak, and sharp claws. Owls fly mostly at night, hunting small animals and birds. —**owl′ish,** *adj.*

owl·et (oul′it), *n.* a young or small owl.

own (ōn), *adj.* belonging to or having to do with oneself or itself [He has his *own* pony.] —*n.* that which belongs to oneself [The car is his *own*.] —*v.* **1.** to have for oneself; possess [He *owns* three houses.] **2.** to admit; confess [He *owned* that he was wrong.] —**come into one's own,** to get what one deserves, especially fame and success. —**hold one's own,** to keep one's position in spite of difficulties, etc. —**of one's own,** belonging

owl (1½ ft. long)

strictly to oneself. —**on one's own,** by one's own efforts; without help: *only in everyday talk.*

own·er (ōn′ər), *n.* a person who owns.

own·er·ship (ōn′ər ship), *n.* the condition of being an owner; possession.

ox (äks), *n.* **1.** any of a group of animals that chew their cud and have cloven hoofs, including farm cattle, buffaloes, bison, etc. **2.** a castrated bull. —**ox·en** (äk′s'n), *pl.*

ox·bow (äks′bō), *n.* **1.** the U-shaped part of a yoke for oxen, which goes under the animal's neck. **2.** a U-shaped bend in a river.

Ox·ford (äks′fərd), *n.* a city in southern England, the home of Oxford University.

yoke with oxbows

ox·ford (äks′fərd), *n.* **1.** a low shoe that is laced over the instep: also **oxford shoe.** **2.** a cotton cloth with a loose weave, used for shirts, etc.: also **oxford cloth.**

ox·i·da·tion (äk′sə dā′shən), *n.* an oxidizing or being oxidized.

ox·ide (äk′sīd), *n.* a compound of oxygen with some other chemical element or with a radical.

ox·i·dize (äk′sə dīz), *v.* to unite with oxygen [When iron rusts or paper burns, it is *oxidized*.] —**ox′i·dized,** *p.t. & p.p.*; **ox′i·diz·ing,** *pr.p.*

ox·y·gen (äk′si jən), *n.* a gas that has no color, taste, or odor and is a chemical element. It makes up almost one fifth of the air and combines with nearly all other elements. All living things need oxygen.

oxygen tent, a small tent into which oxygen is fed, fitted around the bed of a patient to make breathing easier in certain conditions.

oys·ter (ois′tər), *n.* a shellfish with a soft body enclosed in two rough shells hinged together. Some are used as food, and pearls are formed inside others.

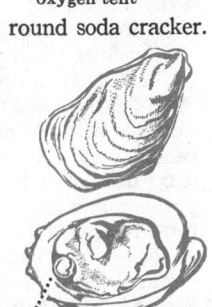

oxygen tent

oyster cracker, a small, round soda cracker.

oz., abbreviation for **ounce.** —**oz.** or **ozs.,** *pl.*

O·zark Mountains (ō′zärk), a low mountain range in southwestern Missouri, northwestern Arkansas, and northeastern Oklahoma: also **Ozarks.**

o·zone (ō′zōn), *n.* **1.** a form of oxygen with a sharp, clean smell, produced by an electrical discharge in the air. **2.** pure air: *a slang meaning.*

pearl

oysters (closed and open)

P

P, p (pē), *n.* the sixteenth letter of the English alphabet. —**mind one's p's and q's,** to be careful of what one does. —**P's, p's** (pēz), *pl.*

P, symbol for the chemical element *phosphorus.*

p., abbreviation for **page, participle.**

pa (pä), *n.* father: *used only in everyday talk.*

Pa., abbreviation for **Pennsylvania.**

pace (pās), *n.* **1.** a step in walking or running. **2.** the length of a step or stride, thought of as about 2½ to 3 feet. **3.** the rate of speed at which something moves or develops [The scoutmaster set the *pace* in the hike. Science goes forward at a rapid *pace.*] **4.** a certain way of walking or running [a halting *pace*]. **5.** a way of walking or running of some horses in which both legs on the same side are raised together. —*v.* **1.** to walk back and forth across [He *paced* the floor nervously.] **2.** to measure by paces [*Pace* off 30 yards.] **3.** to set the rate of speed for a runner. **4.** to move at a pace, as a horse does. —**keep pace with,** to keep up with in a race, progress, etc. —**put one through his paces,** to test one's abilities. —**paced,** *p.t. & p.p.;* **pac′ing,** *pr.p.* —**pac′er,** *n.*

a pacing horse

pach·y·derm (pak′ə dürm), *n.* any of various large animals with a thick skin, as the rhinoceros, hippopotamus, or, especially, the elephant.

Pa·cif·ic (pə sif′ik), *n.* the largest of the oceans, lying between the American continents and Asia. —*adj.* of, in, on, or near this ocean.

pa·cif·ic (pə sif′ik), *adj.* **1.** making or likely to make peace [a *pacific* agreement]. **2.** not warlike; peaceful; quiet. —**pa·cif′i·cal·ly,** *adv.*

Pacific Standard Time, see **Standard Time.**

pac·i·fi·er (pas′ə fī′ər), *n.* **1.** a person or thing that pacifies. **2.** a ring, nipple, etc., as of rubber, for babies to chew on while teething.

pac·i·fism (pas′ə fiz′m), *n.* the principle that quarrels between nations should be settled in a peaceful way, never by war.

pac·i·fist (pas′ə fist), *n.* a person who believes in pacifism and is opposed to war.

pac·i·fy (pas′ə fī), *v.* to make peaceful or calm; appease [Apologies *pacified* his neighbors.] —**pac′i·fied,** *p.t. & p.p.;* **pac′i·fy·ing,** *pr.p.* —**pac·i·fi·ca·tion** (pas′ə fi kā′shən), *n.*

pack (pak), *n.* **1.** a bundle of things tied or wrapped together for carrying [a hiker's *pack*]. **2.** a package holding a number of items [a *pack* of chewing gum]. **3.** a group or set of persons, animals, or things [a *pack* of thieves; a *pack* of wolves; a *pack* of lies]. **4.** a large mass of floating pieces of ice in the sea. —*v.* **1.** to tie or wrap together in a bundle. **2.** to put things together in a box, trunk, can, etc. for carrying or storing [to *pack* away summer clothes; to *pack* a suitcase]. **3.** to fill with more than it usually holds; crowd; cram [A huge crowd *packed* the stadium.] **4.** to fill or cover tightly in order to protect, keep from leaking, etc. [*Pack* the wheel bearings with grease.] —*adj.* used for carrying packs and loads [A camel is a *pack* animal.] —**pack off,** to send off [They *packed* him *off* to school.] —**send packing,** to send away or dismiss in a hurry.

pack (pak), *v.* to choose as members of a jury, committee, etc. people who will vote in one's favor [The chairman *packed* the committee so that it would approve his plan.]

pack·age (pak′ij), *n.* a thing or things wrapped or tied up, as in a box or in wrapping paper; parcel. —*v.* to make a package of. —**pack′aged,** *p.t. & p.p.;* **pack′ag·ing,** *pr.p.*

pack·er (pak′ər), *n.* a person or thing that packs, as one who works in a packing house.

pack·et (pak′it), *n.* **1.** a small package. **2.** a boat that travels a regular route, carrying passengers, freight, and mail: in full, **packet boat.**

packing house, a place where meats, vegetables, or fruits are prepared or packed for sale.

pact (pakt), *n.* an agreement between persons, groups, or nations; compact.

pad (pad), *n.* the dull sound of a footstep on a soft surface. —*v.* to walk with a soft step. —**pad′ded,** *p.t. & p.p.;* **pad′ding,** *pr.p.*

pad (pad), *n.* **1.** anything made of or stuffed with soft material, and used to protect against blows, to give comfort, etc.; cushion [a shoulder *pad*; seat *pad*]. **2.** the under part of the foot of some animals, as the wolf, lion, etc. **3.** the floating leaf of a water lily. **4.** a number of sheets of paper for writing or drawing, fastened together along one edge. **5.** a small cushion soaked with ink and used for inking a rubber stamp. —*v.* **1.** to stuff or cover with soft material [a *padded* chair]. **2.** to make larger or longer by putting in parts not needed [to *pad* a speech with jokes]. —**pad′ded,** *p.t. & p.p.;* **pad′ding,** *pr.p.*

pad·ding (pad′ing), *n.* **1.** a soft material, as cotton or felt, used to pad something. **2.** something added, as to a speech, to make it longer.

pad·dle (pad′'l), *n.* **1.** a short oar with a wide blade at one or both ends, pulled through the water with both hands to make a canoe go. **2.** something shaped like this and used for beating someone, for washing clothes, for playing table tennis, etc. **3.** any of the boards in a water wheel or in a paddle wheel. —*v.* **1.** to row

man paddling a canoe

with a paddle [to *paddle* a canoe]. **2.** to punish by beating with a paddle; spank. —**pad′dled,** *p.t.* & *p.p.;* **pad′dling,** *pr.p.* —**pad′dler,** *n.*

pad·dle (pad′'l), *v.* to move the hands or feet about in the water, as in playing; dabble. —**pad′-dled,** *p.t.* & *p.p.;* **pad′dling,** *pr.p.*

paddle wheel, a wheel with flat boards set around its rim, that turns for moving a steamboat through the water.

pad·dock (pad′ək), *n.* **1.** an enclosed place at a race track where horses are gathered before a race. **2.** a small field for exercising horses.

pad·dy (pad′ē), *n.* rice growing in a rice field. —**pad′dies,** *pl.*

pad·lock (pad′läk), *n.* a lock with a U-shaped arm that turns on a hinge at one end. The other end snaps into the body of the lock after the arm is passed through a staple, link, etc. —*v.* to fasten as with a padlock.

pa·dre (pä′drē), *n.* father: the title given to a priest in Italy, Spain, Portugal, etc.

pae·an (pē′ən), *n.* a song of joy or praise.

padlock

pa·gan (pā′gən), *n.* **1.** a person who is not a Christian, Jew, or Moslem; heathen. **2.** a person who has no religion. —*adj.* of or having to do with pagans. —**pa′gan·ism,** *n.*

page (pāj), *n.* **1.** one side of a leaf of paper in a book, newspaper, letter, etc. **2.** the printing or writing on such a leaf. **3.** an entire leaf in a book, etc. [This *page* is torn.] **4.** a record of events [the *pages* of history]. —*v.* to number the pages of. —**paged,** *p.t.* & *p.p.;* **pag′ing,** *pr.p.*

page (pāj), *n.* **1.** a person, especially a boy, who runs errands and carries messages in a hotel, office building, or legislature. **2.** a boy servant who waits upon a person of high rank. **3.** in the Middle Ages, a boy in training to become a knight. —*v.* to try to find a person by calling his name, as a hotel page does. —**paged,** *p.t.* & *p.p.;* **pag′ing,** *pr.p.*

pag·eant (paj′ənt), *n.* **1.** a large, elaborate public show, parade, etc. **2.** an elaborate play based on events in history, usually performed out-of-doors.

pag·eant·ry (paj′-ən trē), *n.* large, elaborate show; grand display or spectacle [the *pageantry* of the crowning of a king].

pa·go·da (pə gō′də), *n.* a temple in the form of a tower with several stories, as in China, India, Japan, etc.

pagoda

paid (pād), past tense and past participle of **pay.** —*adj.* receiving pay [a *paid* adviser].

pail (pāl), *n.* **1.** a round, deep container, usually with a handle, for holding and carrying liquids, etc.; bucket. **2.** a pailful.

pail·ful (pāl′fool), *n.* as much as a pail will hold. —**pail′fuls,** *pl.*

pain (pān), *n.* **1.** a feeling of hurting in some part of the body [a sharp *pain* in a tooth]. **2.** suffering of the mind; sorrow [The memory of that loss brought her *pain*.] **3.** **pains,** *pl.* very careful effort; special care [He took *pains* to do the work correctly.] —*v.* to give pain to; make suffer; hurt [His wound *pains* him. Her insult *pained* me.] —**on pain of** or **under pain of,** at the risk of bringing upon oneself punishment, death, etc.

Paine, Thomas (pān), 1737–1809; American Revolutionary patriot and writer.

pained (pānd), *adj.* showing hurt feelings [a *pained* expression].

pain·ful (pān′fəl), *adj.* causing pain; hurting; unpleasant [a *painful* wound; *painful* embarrassment]. —**pain′ful·ly,** *adv.*

pain·less (pān′lis), *adj.* causing no pain; without pain. —**pain′less·ly,** *adv.*

pains·tak·ing (pānz′tāk′ing), *adj.* taking or showing great care; very careful, diligent [a *painstaking* task].

paint (pānt), *n.* a mixture of coloring matter with oil, water, etc., used to coat a surface or to make a picture. —*v.* **1.** to make a picture of with paints [He *painted* the same scene twice.] **2.** to make pictures with paints [She *paints* as a hobby.] **3.** to cover or decorate with paint [to *paint* furniture]. **4.** to describe in a colorful way; picture in words. **5.** to spread medicine, etc. on, as with a brush or swab [The doctor *painted* his throat.]

paint·brush (pānt′brush), *n.* a brush used in putting on paint.

paint·er (pān′tər), *n.* **1.** an artist who paints pictures. **2.** a person whose work is painting walls, houses, etc.

paint·er (pān′tər), *n.* a rope fastened to the bow of a boat, used to tie it to a dock, etc.

paint·er (pān′tər), *n.* the mountain lion; panther: *a Western name.*

paint·ing (pān′ting), *n.* **1.** the work or art of one who paints. **2.** a picture made with paints.

pair (per), *n.* **1.** two things of the same kind that are used together; set of two [a *pair* of skates]. **2.** a single thing with two parts that are used together [a *pair* of scissors; a *pair* of pants]. **3.** two persons or animals that form a team [a *pair* of oxen; a newly married *pair*]. **4.** two legislators on opposite sides who agree not to vote on some question. **5.** two playing cards of the same value [a *pair* of aces]. —*v.* to arrange in or form a pair or pairs; match. —**pair off,** to join in or make a pair or pairs.

pa·ja·mas (pə jam′əz *or* pə jä′məz), *n.pl.* clothes for sleeping, usually a loosely fitting suit made up of a jacket and trousers.

Pa·ki·stan (pä′ki stän′ *or* pak′i stan′), *n.* a country northwest and northeast of India. It is a member of the British Commonwealth of Nations.

pajamas

pal (pal), *n.* a close friend; chum. —*v.* to go about together as close friends do. *This word is used only in everyday talk.* —**palled,** *p.t. & p.p.;* **pal′ling,** *pr.p.*

pal·ace (pal′is), *n.* **1.** the official house of a king, etc. **2.** any large, splendid building.

pal·an·quin (pal ən kēn′), *n.* a covered couch for one person, carried by poles on the shoulders of two or more men.

pal·at·a·ble (pal′i tə b'l), *adj.* pleasing to the taste or mind [a *palatable* meal or idea].

pal·ate (pal′it), *n.* **1.** the roof of the mouth. The bony front part is called the **hard palate;** the fleshy back part is called the **soft palate. 2.** taste [The food was delicious to his *palate.*]

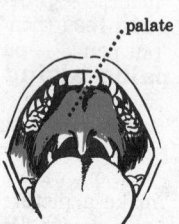
palate

pa·la·tial (pə lā′shəl), *adj.* of, like, or fit for a palace; large and splendid; grand.

pa·lav·er (pə lav′ər), *n.* **1.** talk; especially, idle chatter. **2.** smooth or flattering talk. —*v.* to talk in a smooth or flattering way.

pale (pāl), *adj.* **1.** having little color in the face; wan [*pale* with fright]. **2.** not bright; dim; faint [*pale* blue]. —*v.* **1.** to turn pale [Her face *paled* at the news.] **2.** to seem weaker or less important [My work *paled* beside his.] —**paled,** *p.t. & p.p.;* **pal′ing,** *pr.p.* —**pale′ness,** *n.*

pale (pāl), *n.* **1.** any of the pieces used in making a picket fence. *See the picture for* **picket fence. 2.** a boundary [outside the *pale* of the law].

pale·face (pāl′fās), *n.* a white person: a word that people suppose American Indians once used.

Pal·es·tine (pal′əs tīn), *n.* a region on the eastern coast of the Mediterranean. It was the country of the Jews in Biblical times and is now divided into Arab and Jewish states.

pal·ette (pal′it), *n.* **1.** a thin board with a hole for the thumb at one end, on which an artist mixes his paints: *see the picture.* **2.** the colors used by a particular artist.

pal·frey (pôl′frē), *n.* a riding horse, especially a gentle one for women: *this word is now seldom used.* —**pal′freys,** *pl.*

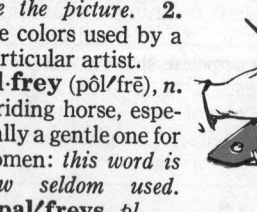
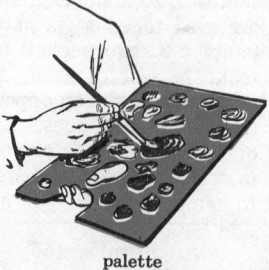
palette

pal·ing (pā′ling), *n.* **1.** a fence made of pales. **2.** a pale or pales.

pal·i·sade (pal ə sād′), *n.* **1.** a fence of large, pointed stakes, set firmly in the ground as a defense against attack. **2. palisades,** *pl.* a line of steep cliffs.

pall (pôl), *v.* to become dull, boring, tiresome, etc. [His jokes are beginning to *pall* on me.] —**palled,** *p.t. & p.p.;* **pall′ing,** *pr.p.*

pall (pôl), *n.* **1.** a piece of velvet or other heavy cloth used to cover a coffin, hearse, or tomb. **2.** a dark or gloomy covering [a heavy *pall* of smoke].

Pal·las (pal′əs), *n.* another name for **Athena.**

pall·bear·er (pôl′ber′ər), *n.* one of the men who carry or walk beside the coffin at a funeral.

pal·let (pal′it), *n.* a straw bed or mattress.

pal·li·ate (pal′i āt), *v.* **1.** to make less painful or severe without actually curing; ease [Aspirin *palliates* a fever.] **2.** to make seem less serious; excuse [to *palliate* an error]. —**pal′li·at·ed,** *p.t. & p.p.;* **pal′li·at·ing,** *pr.p.*

pal·li·a·tive (pal′i ā′tiv *or* pal′i ə tiv), *adj.* that palliates, eases, or excuses. —*n.* something that palliates, as a drug.

pal·lid (pal′id), *adj.* without much color; pale; wan [a *pallid* face].

pal·lor (pal′ər), *n.* paleness of the skin, especially of the face, that comes from being sick, tired, afraid, etc.

palm (päm), *n.* **1.** any of various trees that grow in warm climates and have a tall trunk with a bunch of large leaves at the top, but no branches. See **coconut** and **date. 2.** a leaf of this tree, used as a symbol of victory or joy. —**carry off the palm,** to have the victory; to win.

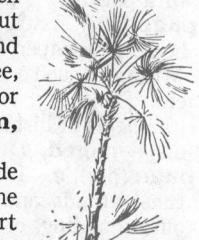
palm (60 ft. high)

palm (päm), *n.* **1.** the inside part of the hand between the fingers and wrist. **2.** the part of a glove, etc. that covers the palm. —*v.* to hide in the palm or between the fingers. —**palm off,** to get something sold, accepted, etc. by using trickery.

palm·er (päm′ər), *n.* a pilgrim who carried a palm leaf to show he had been to the Holy Land.

pal·met·to (pal met′ō), *n.* a small palm tree with leaves shaped like a fan. —**pal·met′tos** or **pal·met′toes,** *pl.*

palm·is·try (päm′is trē), *n.* the practice of pretending to tell a person's future from the lines on the palm of his hand. —**palm′ist,** *n.*

Palm Sunday, the Sunday before Easter.

palm·y (päm′ē), *adj.* **1.** having many palm trees. **2.** successful; prosperous [In his *palmy* days, he was the richest man in Chicago.] —**palm′i·er,** *compar.;* **palm′i·est,** *superl.*

pal·o·mi·no (pal′ə mē′nō), *n.* a horse having a pale-yellow coat and a white mane and tail.

pal·pa·ble (pal′pə b'l), *adj.* **1.** that can be touched or felt; tangible [a *palpable* object; *palpable* dampness]. **2.** easy to see, hear, recognize, etc.; clear; obvious [a *palpable* sound; *palpable* lies]. —**pal′pa·bly,** *adv.*

pal·pi·tate (pal′pə tāt), *v.* **1.** to beat rapidly, as the heart does after hard exercise. **2.** to shake or tremble. —**pal′pi·tat·ed**, *p.t. & p.p.*; **pal′pi·tat·ing**, *pr.p.* —**pal′pi·ta′tion**, *n.*

pal·sied (pôl′zēd), *adj.* **1.** having palsy; paralyzed. **2.** shaking; trembling [*palsied* hands].

pal·sy (pôl′zē), *n.* paralysis in some part of the body, often with a shaking or trembling that cannot be controlled.

pal·try (pôl′trē), *adj.* very small and almost worthless; trifling; petty [a *paltry* wage]. —**pal′tri·er**, *compar.*; **pal′tri·est**, *superl.*

pam·pas (pam′pəz), *n.pl.* the large plains, on which there are no trees, in Argentina and some other parts of South America.

pam·per (pam′pər), *v.* to give in easily to the wishes of; be too gentle with [to *pamper* a child].

pam·phlet (pam′flit), *n.* a thin booklet with a paper cover.

pam·phlet·eer (pam′fli tir′), *n.* a writer of pamphlets, especially political pamphlets.

Pan (pan), *n.* a Greek god of nature and of shepherds. He is shown as having a goat's body from the waist down, and often a goat's horns.

Pan

pan (pan), *n.* **1.** a wide, shallow dish used for cooking, etc., usually made of metal [a frying *pan*]. **2.** a thing or part like this [a *pan* for washing out gold from gravel in mining; the *pan* on either side of a pair of scales]. **3.** the part holding the powder in a flintlock. —*v.* **1.** in gold mining, to separate gold from gravel by washing in a pan. **2.** to find fault with; criticize: *used only in everyday talk* [to *pan* a new play]. —**pan out,** to turn out in some way; especially, to turn out well. —**panned**, *p.t. & p.p.*; **pan′ning**, *pr.p.*

pan-, a prefix meaning "of or for all" [*Pan-American* means of all the Americas or their people.]

pan·a·ce·a (pan′ə sē′ə), *n.* something that is supposed to cure all ills; cure-all.

Pan·a·ma (pan′ə mä *or* pan′ə mô), *n.* **1.** a country in Central America, on the narrow strip of land (**Isthmus of Panama**) that connects North America and South America. **2.** a fine hat woven from the leaves of a Central and South American tree: the full name is **Panama hat.**

Panama Canal, a ship canal built across Panama, joining the Atlantic and Pacific oceans.

Pan-A·mer·i·can (pan′ə mer′ə kən), *adj.* of all the Americas or their people.

pan·cake (pan′kāk), *n.* a thin, flat cake made by pouring batter onto a griddle or into a pan and frying it; griddlecake; flapjack.

pan·cre·as (pan′kri əs), *n.* a large gland behind the stomach that sends a juice into the small intestine to help digestion. —**pan·cre·at·ic** (pan′kri at′ik), *adj.*

pan·da (pan′də), *n.* **1.** a white-and-black animal of southeast Asia and the Himalaya Mountains, that looks like a bear: also called **giant panda. 2.** a small, reddish-brown animal of the same regions, that looks a little like a raccoon.

giant panda (6 ft. long)

pan·de·mo·ni·um (pan′di mō′ni əm), *n.* great disorder or confusion, or a place full of this.

Pan·do·ra (pan dôr′ə), *n.* in Greek myths, the first mortal woman, who let out all human troubles into the world when she became curious and opened a box she had been told not to open.

pane (pān), *n.* a single sheet of glass set in a frame, as in a window or door.

pan·e·gyr·ic (pan′ə jir′ik), *n.* **1.** a formal speech or writing in which a person or thing is highly praised. **2.** high praise.

pan·el (pan′'l), *n.* **1.** a flat section or part of a wall, door, etc., either raised above or sunk below the surfaces around it. **2.** a board or section containing dials, controls, etc. as for an airplane or a system of electric wiring. **3.** a picture or painting that is long and narrow. **4.** a strip of different material sewed lengthwise into a skirt or dress. **5.** a group of persons chosen for some purpose, as for serving on a jury or for discussing some subject. —*v.* to cover or decorate with panels [to *panel* a room with pine]. —**pan′eled** or **pan′elled**, *p.t. & p.p.*; **pan′el·ing** or **pan′el·ling**, *pr.p.*

pan·el·ing or **pan·el·ling** (pan′'l ing), *n.* a series of panels in a wall or other surface.

pan·el·ist (pan′'l ist), *n.* a member of a group of persons who join in discussing some subject, answering questions, etc., as on a radio or television program.

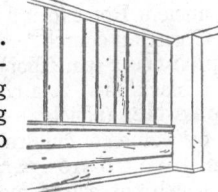
paneling

pang (pang), *n.* a sudden, sharp pain or feeling [hunger *pangs*; a *pang* of homesickness].

pan·ic (pan′ik), *n.* a sudden, wild fear that is not controlled and can spread quickly [The fire caused *panic* in the theater.] —*v.* to fill with panic [The loud noise *panicked* the hens.] —**pan′icked**, *p.t. & p.p.*; **pan′ick·ing**, *pr.p.*

pan·ick·y (pan′ik ē), *adj.* **1.** like, showing, or caused by panic [frightened soldiers in *panicky* retreat]. **2.** likely to be overcome with panic.

pan·nier (pan′yər *or* pan′i ər), *n.* a large basket for carrying loads, as either of a pair hung across the back of a donkey, horse, etc.

pan·o·plied (pan′ə plēd), *adj.* **1.** wearing a complete suit of armor. **2.** covered or decorated completely in a splendid or showy way.

---

fat,   āpe,   cär,   ten,   ēven,   hit,   bīte,   gō,   hôrn,   tool,   book,   up,   fur;
get,   joy,   yet,   chin,   she,   thin,   then;   zh = s in pleasure;   ′ as in able (ā′b'l)
ə = a in ago,   e in agent,   i in sanity,   o in confess,   u in focus.

pan·o·ply (pan′ə plē), *n.* **1.** a complete suit of armor. **2.** any complete, splendid covering or display. —**pan′o·plies,** *pl.*

pan·o·ra·ma (pan′ə ram′ə), *n.* **1.** a picture on a wide panel that is unrolled slowly to show a continuous scene. **2.** an open view in all directions [the *panorama* from the skyscraper]. **3.** a series of sights, events, etc. that keep changing [the *panorama* of the waterfront]. **4.** a full review of any subject. —**pan′o·ram′ic,** *adj.*

pan·sy (pan′zē), *n.* a small flower with flat, velvety petals of various colors. —**pan′sies,** *pl.*

pant (pant), *v.* **1.** to breathe with quick, deep breaths; gasp, as from running fast. **2.** to speak with quick, heavy breaths [A man rushed up and *panted* out the news.] **3.** to want very much; long [to *pant* after fame and fortune]. —*n.* any of a series of quick, heavy breaths; gasp.

pansies

pan·ta·lets or **pan·ta·lettes** (pan tə lets′), *n.pl.* long, loose underpants showing below the skirt, that were worn by women in the 19th century.

pan·ta·loon (pan tə lōōn′), *n.* **1.** a clown in old Italian comedies, dressed in tight trousers. **2. pantaloons,** *pl.* trousers: *usually used in a joking way.*

pan·the·ism (pan′thē iz′m), *n.* the belief that God is the sum of all beings, things, forces, etc. in the universe. —**pan′the·ist,** *n.* —**pan′the·is′tic,** *adj.*

Pan·the·on (pan′thē än), *n.* a temple built in ancient Rome for all the Roman gods. It is now a Christian church.

pan·ther (pan′thər), *n.* **1.** a leopard, especially a black one. **2.** a cougar. **3.** a jaguar.

pan·ties (pan′tēz), *n.pl.* short underpants worn by women or children.

pan·to·mime (pan′tə mīm), *n.* **1.** a play in which the actors move and gesture but do not speak. **2.** the use of gestures only, without words, to tell something. —*v.* to act or tell by pantomime. —**pan′to·mimed,** *p.t. & p.p.;* **pan′to·mim·ing,** *pr.p.*

pan·try (pan′trē), *n.* a small room near the kitchen, where food, dishes, pots, etc. are kept. —**pan′tries,** *pl.*

pants (pants), *n.pl.* **1.** a garment reaching from the waist to the ankles or the knees and covering each leg separately; trousers. **2.** drawers or panties.

pap (pap), *n.* soft food, as custard or cooked cereal, for babies or sick persons.

pa·pa (pä′pə *or, now seldom,* pə pä′), *n.* father: *mainly a child's word.*

pa·pa·cy (pā′pə sē), *n.* **1.** the position or power of the Pope. **2.** the period during which a pope rules. **3.** the list of all the popes. **4.** *also* **Pa·pacy,** the government of the Roman Catholic Church, headed by the Pope. —**pa′pa·cies,** *pl.*

pa·pal (pā′p'l), *adj.* **1.** of the Pope [a *papal* crown]. **2.** of the papacy [*papal* history]. **3.** of the Roman Catholic Church [*papal* rites].

pa·paw (pô′pô), *n.* **1.** a tree of the central and southern United States, with a yellowish fruit full of seeds. **2.** this fruit, used as food.

pa·pa·ya (pə pä′yə), *n.* **1.** a tropical tree a little like the palm, with a yellowish-orange fruit like a small melon. **2.** this fruit, used as food.

pa·per (pā′pər), *n.* **1.** a thin material in sheets, made from wood pulp, rags, etc. and used to write or print on, to wrap or decorate with, etc. **2.** a single sheet of this material. **3.** something written or printed on paper, as an essay, report, etc. [The teacher is grading a set of *papers.*] **4.** a newspaper. **5.** wallpaper. **6.** a small paper wrapper holding something [a *paper* of pins]. **7.** checks, written promises to pay, etc. that can be used as money in business dealings. **8.** an official document: *often used in the plural,* **papers** [Does he have his citizenship *papers* yet?] —*adj.* **1.** of, like, or made of paper [*paper* flowers]. **2.** written down on paper, but not really existing [*paper* profits]. —*v.* to cover with wallpaper.

pa·per·back (pā′pər bak), *n.* a book having a paper cover.

pa·per·boy (pā′pər boi), *n.* a boy who sells or delivers newspapers.

paper hanger, a person whose work is covering walls with wallpaper.

paper money, printed paper issued by a government to be used as money in place of metal coins.

pa·per·weight (pā′pər wāt), *n.* any small, heavy object placed on papers to keep them from being scattered.

pa·pier-mâ·ché (pā′pər mə shā′), *n.* a material made of paper pulp mixed with glue, oil, etc. It can be molded when wet and becomes hard when it dries.

pa·pil·la (pə pil′ə), *n.* a tiny bud of flesh, as on the tongue. —**pa·pil·lae** (pə pil′ē), *pl.*

pa·poose (pa pōōs′), *n.* a North American Indian baby.

pap·py (pap′ē), *n.* papa; father: *used only in some regions in everyday talk.*

pap·ri·ka (pa prē′kə *or* pap′ri kə), *n.* a mild, red seasoning made by grinding certain peppers.

pa·py·rus (pə pī′rəs), *n.* **1.** a tall plant growing in or near water, as in ancient Egypt. **2.** a kind of writing paper made from the pith of this plant by the ancient Egyptians, Greeks, and Romans. **3.** any ancient document on papyrus.

par (pär), *n.* **1.** the average or normal condition or quality [His work is above *par.*] **2.** the value that is written on stocks, bonds, etc.; face value. **3.** the number of strokes thought of as an expert score in golf for a particular hole or for a certain course. —*adj.* **1.** of or at par. **2.** average; normal. —**on a par,** equal in quality, rank, etc. [They are *on a par* in ability.]

par., abbreviation for **paragraph, parallel.**

par·a·ble (par′ə b'l), *n.* a short, simple story that teaches a moral lesson, as in the Bible.

pa·rab·o·la (pə rab′ə lə), *n.* a curve formed by cutting through a cone parallel to a sloping side; also, any curve having this shape.

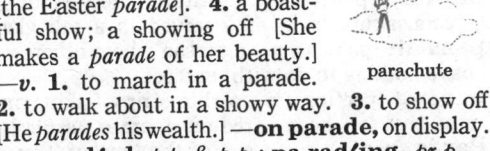
parabola

par·a·chute (par′ə shōōt), *n.* a large cloth device that opens up like an umbrella and is used for slowing down a person or thing dropping from an airplane. —*v.* to jump with or drop by a parachute. —**par′a·chut·ed,** *p.t. & p.p.;* **par′a·chut·ing,** *pr.p.* —**par′a·chut·ist,** *n.*

pa·rade (pə rād′), *n.* **1.** a ceremony of troops marching, as for review; also, a place for such a ceremony. **2.** any march or procession, as to celebrate a holiday [a Fourth of July *parade*]. **3.** a public walk; also, people walking along in a crowd [the Easter *parade*]. **4.** a boastful show; a showing off [She makes a *parade* of her beauty.] —*v.* **1.** to march in a parade. **2.** to walk about in a showy way. **3.** to show off [He *parades* his wealth.] —**on parade,** on display. —**pa·rad′ed,** *p.t. & p.p.;* **pa·rad′ing,** *pr.p.*

parachute

par·a·dise (par′ə dīs), *n.* **1. Paradise,** the garden of Eden. **2.** heaven. **3.** any place or condition of great beauty, happiness, etc.

par·a·dox (par′ə däks), *n.* **1.** a statement that seems to contradict itself or seems false, but that may be true in fact. Example: "Water, water, everywhere, and not a drop to drink." **2.** a statement that contradicts itself and is false. Example: "The sun was so hot we nearly froze." **3.** a person or thing that seems full of contradictions. —**par′a·dox′i·cal,** *adj.*

par·af·fin (par′ə fin), *n.* a white, waxy substance got from petroleum and used in candles, for sealing jars, etc.

par·a·gon (par′ə gän), *n.* a perfect or excellent person or thing that serves as an example.

par·a·graph (par′ə graf), *n.* **1.** a separate section of a piece of writing, that deals with a particular point and is made up of one or more sentences. Each paragraph begins on a new line that is usually moved in from the margin. **2.** a short note or item in a magazine or newspaper. —*v.* **1.** to write about in paragraphs. **2.** to arrange in paragraphs.

Par·a·guay (par′ə gwā *or* par′ə gwī), *n.* a country in central South America.–**Par′a·guay′an,** *adj. & n.*

par·a·keet (par′ə kēt), *n.* a small, slender parrot with a long tail. Parakeets are often kept as pets.

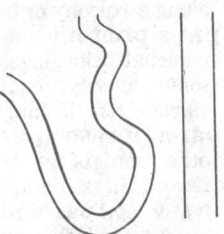

parakeet
(9 in. long)

par·al·lax (par′ə laks), *n.* **1.** the change that seems to occur in the position of an object when the person looking at it moves. **2.** the amount of such change, especially with regard to the stars as seen from different places.

par·al·lel (par′ə lel), *adj.* **1.** moving out in the same direction and always the same distance apart so as never to meet, as the tracks of a sled in the snow. **2.** similar or alike [Their lives followed *parallel* courses.] —*n.* **1.** a parallel line, plane, etc. **2.** something similar to or like something else [Your experience is a *parallel* to mine.] **3.** a comparison showing how things are alike [He drew a *parallel* between the two books.] **4.** any of the imaginary circles around the earth parallel to the equator that mark degrees of latitude [New Orleans is on the 30th *parallel* north of the equator.] —*v.* **1.** to be in a parallel line or plane with [The road *parallels* the river.] **2.** to be or find something that is like or similar to; match [Nothing can *parallel* that discovery.] **3.** to compare things in order to show likeness. —**par′al·leled** or **par′al·lelled,** *p.t. & p.p.;* **par′al·lel·ing** or **par′al·lel·ling,** *pr.p.*

two sets of parallel lines

parallel bars, two bars parallel to each other, set on upright posts about 15 inches apart and used in gymnastic exercises.

par·al·lel·ism (par′ə lel·iz'm), *n.* **1.** the condition of being parallel. **2.** close likeness or similarity.

par·al·lel·o·gram (par′ə lel′ə gram), *n.* a figure having four sides, with the opposite sides parallel and of equal length.

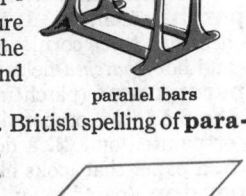
parallel bars

par·a·lyse (par′ə līz), *v.* British spelling of **paralyze.** —**par′a·lysed,** *p.t. & p.p.;* **par′a·lys·ing,** *pr.p.*

parallelogram

pa·ral·y·sis (pə ral′ə·sis), *n.* **1.** a loss of the power to move or feel in any part of the body, as because of injury to the brain. **2.** a condition of being powerless or helpless to act [a *paralysis* of industry].

par·a·lyt·ic (par′ə lit′ik), *adj.* of, having, or causing paralysis. —*n.* a person with paralysis.

par·a·lyze (par′ə līz), *v.* **1.** to cause paralysis in. **2.** to make powerless or helpless [Heavy snows *paralyzed* the city.] —**par′a·lyzed,** *p.t. & p.p.;* **par′a·lyz·ing,** *pr.p.*

par·a·me·ci·um (par′ə mē′shi əm), *n.* a tiny water animal made up of one cell, that moves by

fat, āpe, cär, ten, ēven, hit, bīte, gō, hôrn, tōōl, book, up, fűr; get, joy, yet, chin, she, thin, *then*; zh = s in pleasure; ′ as in able (ā′b'l). ə = a in ago, e in agent, i in sanity, o in confess, u in focus.

waving the fine hairs, or cilia, on its body. **—par·a·me·ci·a** (par′ə mē′shi ə), *pl.*

par·a·mount (par′ə mount), *adj.* most important; ranking highest; supreme; chief.

par·a·pet (par′ə pit), *n.* **1.** a wall for protecting soldiers from enemy fire. **2.** a wall or railing, as along a balcony or bridge.

par·a·pher·na·li·a (par′ə fər nāl′yə), *n.pl.* **1.** personal belongings. **2.** all the things used in some activity; equipment: *often used with a singular verb* [fishing *paraphernalia*].

par·a·phrase (par′ə frāz), *n.* a repeating in other words of the meaning of something. —*v.* to reword in a paraphrase. **—par′a·phrased,** *p.t. & p.p.;* **par′a·phras·ing,** *pr.p.*

par·a·site (par′ə sīt), *n.* **1.** a plant or animal that lives on or in another plant or animal and gets food from it [Mistletoe and fleas are *parasites*.] **2.** a person who lives at another's expense without paying him back in any way.

par·a·sit·ic (par′ə sit′ik) or **par·a·sit·i·cal** (par′ə sit′i k'l), *adj.* of, like, or caused by parasites.

par·a·sol (par′ə sôl), *n.* a light umbrella carried to shade oneself from the sun.

par·a·troops (par′ə trōōps), *n.pl.* a unit of soldiers trained to parachute from airplanes behind enemy lines. **—par′a·troop′er,** *n.*

par·boil (pär′boil), *v.* to boil until partly cooked, as before roasting.

par·cel (pär′s'l), *n.* **1.** a small, wrapped package; bundle. **2.** a piece of land [a *parcel* of ten acres]. —*v.* to divide into parts for giving away or selling [to *parcel* out land to settlers]. **—part and parcel,** a necessary part. **—par′celed** or **par′celled,** *p.t. & p.p.;* **par′cel·ing** or **par′cel·ling,** *pr.p.*

parcel post, the branch of the post office that carries and delivers parcels.

parch (pärch), *v.* **1.** to roast or dry with great heat [to *parch* corn]. **2.** to make or become dry and hot [*parched* fields]. **3.** to make thirsty.

parch·ment (pärch′mənt), *n.* **1.** the skin of a sheep or goat, prepared so that it can be written or painted on. **2.** a document written on this. **3.** a paper that looks like parchment.

par·don (pär′d'n), *v.* **1.** to free from further punishment [A governor may *pardon* a criminal.] **2.** to forgive [*Pardon* me for interrupting.] —*n.* the act of pardoning. **—par′don·er,** *n.*

par·don·a·ble (pär′d'n ə b'l), *adj.* that can be pardoned, forgiven, or excused.

pare (per), *v.* **1.** to cut or trim away the rind or covering of something; peel [to *pare* a potato; to *pare* the bark from a tree]. **2.** to make less, bit by bit [to *pare* expenses]. **—pared,** *p.t. & p.p.;* **par′ing,** *pr.p.*

par·e·gor·ic (par′ə gôr′ik), *n.* a medicine with opium in it, sometimes used for relieving stomach pains, etc.

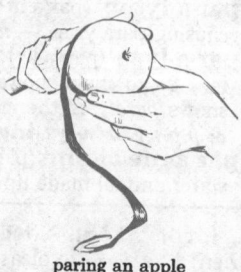

paring an apple

par·ent (per′ənt), *n.* **1.** a father or mother. **2.** any animal or plant as it is related to its offspring. **3.** anything from which other things come; source; origin [Latin is the *parent* of various languages.] **—par′ent·hood,** *n.*

par·ent·age (per′ənt ij), *n.* one's parents or ancestors; family line.

pa·ren·tal (pə ren′t'l), *adj.* of or like a parent.

pa·ren·the·sis (pə ren′thə sis), *n.* **1.** a word, phrase, etc. put into a sentence as an added note or explanation and set off, as between curved lines, from the rest of the sentence. **2.** either or both of the curved lines ( ) used in this way. **—pa·ren·the·ses** (pə ren′thə sēz), *pl.*

par·en·thet·i·cal (par′ən thet′i k'l) or **par·en·thet·ic** (par′ən thet′ik), *adj.* **1.** describing a word, phrase, etc. put in as an added note or explanation ["We'll win!" he shouted, adding a *parenthetical* "I hope."] **2.** marked off by parentheses. **—par′en·thet′i·cal·ly,** *adv.*

par·fait (pär fā′), *n.* a frozen dessert of ice cream, sirup, fruit, etc., served in a tall glass.

pa·ri·ah (pə rī′ə), *n.* a person whom others will have nothing to do with; outcast.

par·ing (per′ing), *n.* a thin strip of skin, rind, etc., that has been pared off [potato *parings*].

Par·is (par′is), *n.* a son of the king of Troy in Greek myths. His kidnaping of Helen, wife of the king of Sparta, started the Trojan War.

Par·is (par′is), *n.* the capital of France. **—Pa·ri·sian** (pə rizh′ən), *adj. & n.*

par·ish (par′ish), *n.* **1.** a church district under the charge of a priest or minister. **2.** the people living in such a district who go to its church. **3.** in Louisiana, a district like a county.

pa·rish·ion·er (pə rish′ən ər), *n.* a member of a parish.

par·i·ty (par′ə tē), *n.* the condition of being the same or equal, especially in value; equality.

park (pärk), *n.* **1.** a piece of land with trees, lawns, benches, etc., where people can come for rest or recreation. Some parks have playing fields, beaches, amusement rides, etc. **2.** a place known for its natural scenery, wild animals, etc., that is set apart by a State or country for the enjoyment of the public [Yellowstone National *Park*]. **3.** the lawns, pastures, woods, etc. belonging to a large house. —*v.* **1.** to leave an automobile, truck, etc. in a certain place for a time [You may not *park* here.] **2.** to steer an automobile, etc. into a space where it can be left for a time.

par·ka (pär′kə), *n.* a fur or woolen jacket with a hood on it for the head.

park·way (pärk′wā), *n.* a wide road with trees, grass, etc. along its edges.

par·lance (pär′ləns), *n.* a way of speaking or writing; language; talk [military *parlance*].

par·ley (pär′lē), *n.* a meeting to talk over or settle something [The opposing generals met in a *parley* to discuss a truce.] —*v.* to hold a parley, especially with an enemy. **—par′leys,** *pl.*

parka

Par·lia·ment (pär′lə mənt), *n.* **1.** the law-making body of Great Britain, that is like our Congress. It consists of the House of Commons and the House of Lords. **2. parliament,** any group like this.

par·lia·men·ta·ry (pär′lə men′tə rē), *adj.* **1.** of or like a parliament. **2.** of or following the rules of a group like this [*parliamentary* procedure]. **3.** governed by a parliament.

par·lor (pär′lər), *n.* **1.** a living room, especially one that in earlier times was for entertaining guests. **2.** any of certain places of business [a beauty *parlor*]. The British spelling is **parlour.**

par·lous (pär′ləs), *adj.* dangerous; perilous: *now seldom used.*

Par·nas·sus (pär nas′əs), *n.* a mountain in southern Greece. In ancient times it was sacred to Apollo and the Muses.

pa·ro·chi·al (pə rō′ki əl), *adj.* **1.** of, in, or run by a church parish [*parochial* schools]. **2.** limited; narrow [a *parochial* outlook].

par·o·dy (par′ə dē), *n.* a piece of writing or music that imitates another in such a way as to make fun of it. —*v.* to make fun of by imitating. —**par′o·dies,** *pl.* —**par′o·died,** *p.t. & p.p.;* **par′o·dy·ing,** *pr.p.*

pa·role (pə rōl′), *n.* **1.** the freeing of a prisoner before he has served his full sentence, on the condition that he will obey certain rules of good behavior. **2.** a promise made by a prisoner of war that if he is freed he will fight no further. —*v.* to free under the conditions of parole. —**on parole,** free under the conditions of parole. —**pa·roled′,** *p.t. & p.p.;* **pa·rol′ing,** *pr.p.*

par·ox·ysm (par′ək siz′m), *n.* a sudden, sharp outburst; fit, as of laughter, anger, etc.

par·quet (pär kā′), *n.* **1.** a flooring made of pieces of wood fitted together to form a pattern. **2.** the main floor in a theater; orchestra.

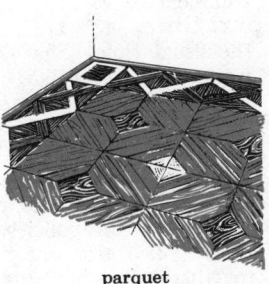

parquet

par·ra·keet (par′ə kēt), *n.* same as **parakeet.**

par·ri·cide (par′ə sīd), *n.* **1.** a person who murders his parent. **2.** the murder of a parent.

par·rot (par′ət), *n.* **1.** a bird with a hooked bill and brightly colored feathers. Some parrots can learn to imitate human speech. **2.** a person who just repeats or copies what others do or say without understanding. —*v.* to repeat or copy without full understanding.

parrot (1 ft. long)

par·ry (par′ē), *v.* **1.** to turn aside, as a blow or a lunge with a sword; ward off. **2.** to avoid answering, as a question; evade. —*n.* the act of parrying. —**par′ried,** *p.t. & p.p.;* **par′ry·ing,** *pr.p.* —**par′ries,** *pl.*

parse (pärs), *v.* **1.** to separate a sentence into its parts, explaining how each part is used. **2.** to describe a word in a sentence, telling its part of speech and how it is used. —**parsed,** *p.t. & p.p.;* **pars′ing,** *pr.p.*

par·si·mo·ni·ous (pär′sə mō′ni əs), *adj.* too careful in spending; too thrifty; miserly; stingy. —**par′si·mo′ni·ous·ly,** *adv.*

par·si·mo·ny (pär′sə mō′nē), *n.* the condition of being too thrifty; stinginess.

pars·ley (pärs′lē), *n.* a plant with small, often curly leaves used to flavor and decorate food.

pars·nip (pärs′nip), *n.* a plant with a long, thick, white root that is eaten as a vegetable.

par·son (pär′s′n), *n.* a minister or clergyman.

par·son·age (pär′s′n ij), *n.* the house provided by a church for its parson, or minister.

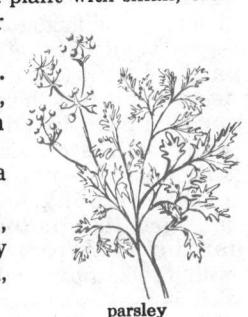

parsley

part (pärt), *n.* **1.** a section, piece, or portion of a whole [the newer *part* of town; *parts* of the body; *part* of our class]. **2.** a necessary piece that can be replaced [automobile *parts*]. **3.** any of the equal pieces or shares into which a thing can be divided [A cent is a 100th *part* of a dollar.] **4.** a share of work or duty [Everyone must do his *part*.] **5. parts,** *pl.* talents or abilities [a man of *parts*]. **6.** a role in a play; character [He plays the *part* of Hamlet.] **7.** the music for a certain voice or instrument in a musical piece [Ben will sing the tenor *part*.] **8.** *usually* **parts,** *pl.* a region or area [Are you from these *parts*?] **9.** a side in an argument, fight, etc. [I'll not take his *part* in the quarrel.] **10.** the dividing line formed by combing the hair in opposite directions. —*v.* **1.** to break or pull apart; separate [She *parted* the curtains to look out. The rope *parted* in the middle.] **2.** to go away from each other [They *parted* at the crossroads.] **3.** to comb the hair so as to form a part [He *parts* his hair in the middle.] —*adj.* less than a whole; not complete [*part* owner of a factory]. —*adv.* partly; to some extent [The house is *part* mine.] —**for one's part,** as far as one is concerned. —**for the most part,** mostly; usually. —**in good part,** in a good-natured way. —**in part,** partly; not completely. —**on one's part, 1.** as far as one is concerned. **2.** by or from one. —**part from,** to go away from; leave. —**part with,** to give up; let go. —**take part,** to have or take a share in something; participate.

par·take (pär tāk′), v. **1.** to eat or drink something. **2.** to take part; participate. —**partake of, 1.** to have or take a share of. **2.** to have a trace of; suggest. *For principal parts, see* **take.** —**par·tak′er,** n.

Par·the·non (pär′thə nän), n. the ancient Greek temple of Athena on the Acropolis in Athens.

par·tial (pär′shəl), adj. **1.** of or in only a part; not complete or total [a *partial* eclipse of the sun]. **2.** favoring one person or side more than another; biased [A judge should not be *partial*.] —**be partial to,** to have a special liking for; be fond of. —**par′tial·ly,** adv.

par·ti·al·i·ty (pär′shi al′ə tē), n. **1.** a being partial, or favoring one side unfairly. **2.** a strong liking; special fondness [a *partiality* for pickles]. —**par′ti·al′i·ties,** pl.

par·tic·i·pant (pär tis′ə pənt), n. a person who takes part in something.

par·tic·i·pate (pär tis′ə pāt), v. to take part with others; have a share [He *participated* in the school play.] —**par·tic′i·pat·ed,** p.t. & p.p.; **par·tic′i·pat·ing,** pr.p. —**par·tic′i·pa′tion,** n. —**par·tic′i·pa′tor,** n.

par·ti·cip·i·al (pär′tə sip′i əl), adj. of, formed with, or like a participle. —n. a form of a verb that is used as a noun or adjective. Examples: *Dancing* is fun. Wear your *dancing* shoes.

par·ti·ci·ple (pär′tə si p′l), n. a form of a verb used as both a verb and an adjective. Participles have tense and voice, and can take an object or be modified by adverbs [In "He is humming a tune." "humming" is a present *participle* used as a verb. In "a man dressed in gray," "dressed" is a past *participle* used as an adjective.]

par·ti·cle (pär′ti k′l), n. **1.** a very small piece; tiny bit; speck. **2.** a short part of speech, as a preposition or article. **3.** a prefix or suffix.

par·ti·col·ored (pär′tē kul′ərd), adj. having different colors in different parts [a *parti-colored* pansy].

par·tic·u·lar (pər tik′yoo lər), adj. **1.** of only one person, group, thing, etc.; individual; not general [What is your *particular* opinion?] **2.** apart from any other; specific [Do you have a *particular* color in mind?] **3.** more than ordinary; unusual; special [Pay *particular* attention.] **4.** hard to please; very careful [She is *particular* about what she wears.] —n. a detail; fact; item [Give full *particulars* to the police.] —**in particular,** particularly; especially.

par·tic·u·lar·i·ty (pər tik′yoo lar′ə tē), n. **1.** great care or special attention to small details. **2.** a particular trait; peculiarity. **3.** a small detail. —**par·tic′u·lar′i·ties,** pl.

par·tic·u·lar·ize (pər tik′yoo lər iz′), v. to tell or list in detail. —**par·tic′u·lar·ized′,** p.t. & p.p.; **par·tic′u·lar·iz′ing,** pr.p.

par·tic·u·lar·ly (pər tik′yoo lər lē), adv. **1.** especially; more than usually [a *particularly* hot day]. **2.** in a particular way; in detail.

part·ing (pär′ting), adj. **1.** said, given, etc. at the time of leaving [a *parting* remark]. **2.** departing or leaving. **3.** dividing or separating. —n.

1. the act of leaving or saying good-by ["*Parting* is such sweet sorrow."] **2.** a dividing or separating [the *parting* of a frayed rope].

par·ti·san or **par·ti·zan** (pär′tə z′n), n. **1.** a strong, often emotional supporter of some party, cause, or person. **2.** a guerrilla fighter. —adj. of or like a partisan. —**par′ti·san·ship′** or **par′ti·zan·ship′,** n.

par·ti·tion (pär tish′ən), n. **1.** a dividing into parts; separation [the *partition* of Ireland in 1925]. **2.** something that separates, as a wall between rooms. —v. to divide into parts [to *partition* a basement].

part·ly (pärt′lē), adv. in part; not completely.

part·ner (pärt′nər), n. **1.** a person who takes part in something with another or others; especially, one of the owners of a business who shares in its profits and risks. **2.** a player on the same team [my tennis *partner*]. **3.** either of two persons dancing together. **4.** a husband or wife.

part·ner·ship (pärt′nər ship), n. **1.** the condition or relationship of being a partner. **2.** a business firm made up of two or more partners.

part of speech, any of the classes in which words are placed according to the way they are used. The usual names for the parts of speech are: noun, verb, pronoun, adjective, adverb, preposition, conjunction, and interjection.

par·took (pär took′), past tense of **partake.**

par·tridge (pär′trij), n. any of several wild birds hunted as game, including the quail and ruffed grouse.

part song, a song for several voices singing in harmony, usually without accompaniment.

part time, a part of the usual time [She works *part time* in the library.] —**part′-time′,** adj.

European partridge (1 ft. long)

par·ty (pär′tē), n. **1.** a gathering of people to have a good time [a birthday *party*]. **2.** a group of people who share the same political opinions and work together to elect certain people, to further certain policies, etc. [the Republican *party*]. **3.** a group of people working or acting together [a hunting *party*]. **4.** a person connected in some way with an action, plan, lawsuit, etc. [a *party* to their crime]. **5.** a person: *used only in everyday talk.* —**par′ties,** pl.

Pas·a·de·na (pas′ə dē′nə), n. a city in southwestern California, near Los Angeles.

pa·sha (pə shä′ or pash′ə), n. a Turkish title of rank or honor, now no longer used.

pass (pas), n. a narrow opening or way through, especially between mountains.

pass (pas), v. **1.** to go by, beyond, over, or through [The mailman *passed* our house. The guards allowed no one to *pass*.] **2.** to go; move on [The crowd *passed* down the street. The days *passed* quickly.] **3.** to go or change from one place, form, condition, owner, etc. to another [The liquid *passed* into solid form when it froze.]

The property will *pass* to her son when she dies.] **4.** to come to an end or go away [The fever *passed*.] **5.** to get through a test, trial, course, etc. successfully [He *passed* the final exam. The bill *passed* Congress.] **6.** to approve; vote for [City Council *passed* the resolution.] **7.** to make or let go, move, advance, etc. [He *passed* a comb through his hair. *Pass* the bread to George. The teacher *passed* the entire class into the next grade.] **8.** to spend [He *passed* the night with friends.] **9.** to be taken as being; present oneself as being [They look so much alike that they could *pass* for brothers.] **10.** to give as a judgment, opinion, etc. [to *pass* sentence on a criminal]. **11.** to happen; take place [No one knows what *passed* behind those locked doors.] **12.** to make no bid when one's turn comes in certain card games. **13.** to throw or hit a ball, puck, etc. to another player. —*n.* **1.** an act of passing; passage. **2.** a ticket, note, etc. which allows a person to come and go freely or without charge [a movie *pass;* a *pass* to go through the halls of a school]. **3.** written permission given a soldier to be absent from duty for a short time [a weekend *pass*]. **4.** a state of affairs; condition [The company has come to a sorry *pass*.] **5.** a motion of the hand or hands [The magician made a quick *pass* and the rabbit disappeared.] **6.** a throwing or hitting of the ball, puck, etc. to another player. —**a pretty pass,** a bad situation: *used only in everyday talk.* —**bring to pass,** to make happen. —**come to pass,** to happen. —**pass away, 1.** to come to an end. **2.** to die. —**pass off, 1.** to come to an end. **2.** to take place. **3.** to cause to be accepted by trickery or fraud [to *pass* oneself *off* as a police officer]. —**pass out,** to faint: *a slang phrase.* —**pass over,** to ignore; leave out. —**pass up,** to refuse or let go, as an opportunity: *a slang phrase.* —**pass'er,** *n.*

pass·a·ble (pas'ə b'l), *adj.* **1.** that can be traveled over, crossed, etc. [a *passable* trail]. **2.** fairly good; adequate [a *passable* meal].

pas·sage (pas'ij), *n.* **1.** the act of passing [the *passage* of day into night; the *passage* of a bill into law]. **2.** permission or right to pass [He was given *passage* through the enemy lines.] **3.** a voyage [a *passage* to India]. **4.** passenger space on a ship, as a berth or cabin [He booked *passage* on the steamer.] **5.** a way through which to pass; road, opening, hall, etc. [a *passage* through the mountains]. **6.** a part of a speech or writing [to read a *passage* from the Bible]. **7.** an exchange, as of blows.

pas·sage·way (pas'ij wā'), *n.* a narrow passage or way, as a hall, corridor, or alley.

pas·sé (pa sā'), *adj.* old-fashioned; out-of-date.

pas·sen·ger (pas'n jər), *n.* a person, not the driver, traveling in a train, ship, bus, etc.

passenger pigeon, a North American wild pigeon, with a long, narrow tail. It is now extinct.

pass·er·by (pas'ər bī'), *n.* a person passing by. —**pass'ers·by',** *pl.*

pass·ing (pas'ing), *adj.* **1.** going by [a *passing* train]. **2.** that lasts only a short time; fleeting [a *passing* fancy]. **3.** done or made without careful thought; casual [a *passing* remark]. **4.** allowing one to pass a test, course, etc. [a *passing* grade]. —*adv.* very; extremely: *no longer much used* [She was *passing* fair.] —*n.* **1.** the act of one that passes. **2.** death. —**in passing,** without careful thought; casually.

pas·sion (pash'ən), *n.* **1.** any very strong feeling as of great joy, anger, etc.; especially, strong love between a man and woman. **2.** great liking; enthusiasm [his *passion* for books]. **3.** that for which one feels a strong desire or liking [Golf is his *passion*.] **4. Passion,** the suffering of Jesus on the cross or after the Last Supper.

pas·sion·ate (pash'ən it), *adj.* **1.** having or showing strong feelings [a *passionate* poet]. **2.** easily worked up, especially to anger. **3.** very strong; intense [a *passionate* rage]. —**pas'sion·ate·ly,** *adv.*

pas·sive (pas'iv), *adj.* **1.** not active, but acted upon [a *passive* interest in sports]. **2.** not resisting; yielding; submissive [the *passive* subjects of a tyrant]. **3.** having the verb in the form (called *voice*) that shows its subject as being acted upon: opposite of *active* [In the sentence "I was hit by the ball," "was hit" is in the *passive* voice.] —**pas'sive·ly,** *adv.*

pass·key (pas'kē), *n.* **1.** a key that fits a number of locks. **2.** one's own key to something.

Pass·o·ver (pas'ō'vər), *n.* a Jewish holiday in memory of the freeing of the ancient Hebrews from slavery in Egypt.

pass·port (pas'pôrt), *n.* **1.** a paper given by a government to a citizen traveling in foreign countries, stating who he is and giving him the right to protection. **2.** anything that makes it possible for a person to go somewhere, do something, etc. [Education was his *passport* to a job.]

pass·word (pas'wûrd), *n.* a secret word or signal that must be given to a guard or sentry in order to pass him.

past (past), *adj.* **1.** gone by; ended; over [What is *past* is finished.] **2.** of a former time [a *past* president]. **3.** that came just before this [the *past* week]. **4.** showing time gone by [The *past* tense of "walk" is "walked."] —*n.* **1.** the time that has gone by [That's all in the *past*.] **2.** the history or past life of a person, group, etc. [His *past* was exciting.] —*prep.* **1.** later than or farther than; beyond [ten minutes *past* two; *past* the city limits]. **2.** beyond the power or limits of [That story is *past* belief.] —*adv.* to and beyond; by [The band marched *past*.]

pas·ta (päs'tə), *n.* any food made of dried flour paste, as spaghetti, macaroni, etc.

paste (pāst), *n.* **1.** a mixture of flour, water, etc. used for sticking paper or other light things

fat, āpe, cär, ten, ēven, hit, bīte, gō, hôrn, tool, book, up, fûr; get, joy, yet, chin, she, thin, *th*en; zh = s in pleasure; ' as in able (ā'b'l); ə = a in ago, e in agent, i in sanity, o in confess, u in focus.

together. **2.** any soft, moist, smooth mixture [tooth *paste*]. **3.** a hard, shiny glass used for artificial gems. **4.** dough used in making pie crusts, noodles, etc. —*v.* to make stick, as with paste [to *paste* pictures in a book]. —**past′ed,** *p.t. & p.p.;* **past′ing,** *pr.p.*

paste·board (pāst′bôrd), *n.* a stiff material made by pasting layers of paper together or by pressing and drying paper pulp.

pas·tel (pas tel′), *n.* **1.** a soft, pale shade of some color. **2.** a kind of crayon made of ground coloring matter. **3.** a picture drawn with such crayons. —*adj.* soft and pale [*pastel* blue].

pas·tern (pas′tərn), *n.* the part of a horse's foot between the fetlock and the hoof.

Pas·teur, Louis (pas tür′), 1822–1895; French scientist who found a way of treating rabies and of killing bacteria in milk.

pastern

pas·teur·ize (pas′chər īz *or* pas′tər īz), *v.* to kill harmful bacteria in milk, beer, etc. by heating the liquid to 142°–145° F. for thirty minutes. —**pas′teur·ized,** *p.t. & p.p.;* **pas′teur·iz·ing,** *pr.p.* —**pas′teur·i·za′tion,** *n.*

pas·time (pas′tīm), *n.* a way of spending spare time pleasantly; amusement, recreation, etc.

pas·tor (pas′tər), *n.* a clergyman in charge of a church; minister or priest.

pas·to·ral (pas′tər əl), *adj.* **1.** of a pastor or his duties. **2.** of shepherds, their work, their way of life, etc. **3.** of life in the country, thought of as peaceful, simple, etc. —*n.* a poem, play, etc. about life in the country.

pas·tor·ate (pas′tər it), *n.* the position, duties, or time of service of a pastor.

past participle, a participle used to show time gone by or an action that took place in the past [In the sentence "He has given much to others," "given" is a *past participle.*]

pas·try (pās′trē), *n.* **1.** pies, tarts, and other baked goods that have a crust made from flour dough with shortening in it. **2.** such dough. **3.** all fancy baked goods. —**pas′tries,** *pl.*

pas·tur·age (pas′chər ij), *n.* pasture.

pas·ture (pas′chər), *n.* **1.** land where grass and other plants grow and where cattle, sheep, etc. can graze. **2.** grass and other plants eaten by grazing animals. —*v.* **1.** to put animals in a pasture to graze. **2.** to feed in a pasture; graze. —**pas′tured,** *p.t. & p.p.;* **pas′tur·ing,** *pr.p.*

past·y (pās′tē), *adj.* of or like paste; white, thick, or sticky [a *pasty* complexion]. —**past′i·er,** *compar.;* **past′i·est,** *superl.*

past·y (past′ē *or* pās′tē), *n.* a pie, especially a meat pie: *mainly a British word.* —**past′ies,** *pl.*

pat (pat), *n.* **1.** a quick, gentle tap or stroke with something flat, as the open hand. **2.** the sound made by this. **3.** a small lump, as of butter. —*v.* to touch or stroke with a pat or pats, as to show love, to encourage, etc. —*adj.* just right for the time or purpose; suitable; apt [a *pat* answer]. —**have down pat** *or* **know pat,** to know thoroughly: *used only in everyday talk.*

—**stand pat,** to refuse to change an opinion, way of acting, etc.: *used only in everyday talk.* —**pat′ted,** *p.t. & p.p.;* **pat′ting,** *pr.p.*

Pat·a·go·ni·a (pat′ə gō′ni·ə), *n.* a region in southern Argentina and Chile.

patch (pach), *n.* **1.** a piece of cloth, metal, etc. put on to mend a hole, tear, or worn spot. **2.** a bandage put on a wound, or a pad worn over an injured eye. **3.** an area or spot [*patches* of blue sky]. **4.** a small piece of ground [a cabbage *patch*]. **5.** a small piece; scrap; bit. —*v.* **1.** to put a patch or patches on [to *patch* a torn coat]. **2.** to make in a hurry as by putting bits together [He *patched* together a speech.] —**patch up,** to settle, as a quarrel.

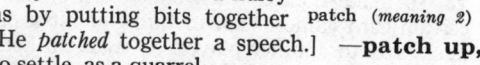

patch (meaning 2)

patch·work (pach′wûrk), *n.* **1.** a quilt, etc. sewed together from pieces of cloth of various colors and shapes. **2.** a design like this.

pate (pāt), *n.* the head, especially the top of the head: *used in a joking way.*

pat·ent (pat′'nt), *n.* **1.** the right given to someone by a government to

patchwork

be the only one who may make and sell a new invention, or use a new method, for a certain number of years. **2.** the paper giving such a right. **3.** the invention, etc. protected by such a right. —*v.* to get a patent for [to *patent* a new process]. —*adj.* **1.** protected by a patent. **2.** (pā′t′nt), easy to see or recognize; plain; evident [a *patent* lie].

pat·ent·ee (pat′'n tē′), *n.* a person who has been given a patent.

patent leather, leather with a hard, smooth, shiny surface: it is usually black.

pa·tent·ly (pā′t′nt lē), *adv.* in a patent or obvious way; plainly; clearly [*patently* false].

patent medicine, a medicine with a trademark, usually made by a secret process.

pa·ter·nal (pə tür′n'l), *adj.* **1.** of or like a father; fatherly. **2.** related to one on one's father's side [my *paternal* aunt]. —**pa·ter′nal·ly,** *adv.*

pa·ter·nal·ism (pə tür′n'l iz'm), *n.* a way of ruling a country, directing employees, etc. like that used by a father in dealing with his children. —**pa·ter′nal·is′tic,** *adj.*

pa·ter·ni·ty (pə tür′nə tē), *n.* **1.** the condition of being a father; fatherhood. **2.** the fact of who one's father is.

pa·ter·nos·ter (pā′tər näs′tər *or* pat′ər näs′tər), *n.* the Lord's Prayer, especially in Latin.

Pat·er·son (pat′ər s'n), *n.* a city in northeastern New Jersey.

path (path), *n.* **1.** a track worn by the footsteps of people or animals. **2.** a way made for people to walk on [a flagstone *path* in a garden]. **3.** a course along which something moves [the *path* of a rocket]. **4.** a way of behaving [to follow the *path* of duty]. —**path′less,** *adj.*

pa·thet·ic (pə thet′ik), *adj.* causing or deserving pity, sorrow, etc.; pitiful [a wounded bird's *pathetic* cries]. —**pa·thet′i·cal·ly,** *adv.*

path·o·log·i·cal (path′ə läj′i k'l) or **path·o·log·ic** (path′ə läj′ik), *adj.* **1.** of pathology [*pathological* research]. **2.** caused by or having to do with disease [a *pathological* thirst]. —**path′o·log′i·cal·ly,** *adv.*

pa·thol·o·gy (pə thäl′ə jē), *n.* the branch of medicine that deals with the causes, symptoms, and results of disease. —**pa·thol′o·gist,** *n.*

pa·thos (pā′thäs), *n.* the quality in some happening, story, speech, etc. that makes one feel pity, sadness, or sympathy [slow music, filled with *pathos*].

path·way (path′wā), *n.* a path.

pa·tience (pā′shəns), *n.* **1.** the fact of being patient or the ability to be patient. **2.** the card game solitaire.

pa·tient (pā′shənt), *adj.* **1.** able to put up with pain, trouble, delay, boredom, etc. without complaining [The *patient* children waited in line for the theater to open.] **2.** working steadily without giving up [It took five years of *patient* labor to perfect his invention.] **3.** showing that one is patient [a *patient* smile; a *patient* search for the needle]. —*n.* a person under the care of a doctor. —**pa′tient·ly,** *adv.*

pat·i·o (pat′i ō or pä′ti ō), *n.* **1.** in Spain and Spanish America, a court-yard around which a house is built. **2.** a paved area near a house, that overlooks a lawn or garden; terrace. —**pat′i·os,** *pl.*

patio *(meaning 2)*

pat·ois (pat′wä), *n.* a form of a language that is different from the standard form, as a dialect of a certain region [the *patois* of a French Canadian]. —**pat·ois** (pat′wäz), *pl.*

pat. pend., abbreviation for **patent pending** (patent applied for but not yet granted).

pa·tri·arch (pā′tri ärk), *n.* **1.** the father and head of a family or tribe, as Abraham, Isaac, or Jacob in the Bible. **2.** a man who is very old and dignified. **3.** a bishop of high rank, as in the Orthodox Eastern Church. —**pa′tri·ar′chal,** *adj.*

pa·tri·cian (pə trish′ən), *n.* **1.** a member of a noble family in ancient Rome. **2.** a person of high social rank; aristocrat. —*adj.* of, like, or fit for an aristocrat.

Pat·rick, Saint (pat′rik), British bishop of the 5th century, who is the patron saint of Ireland. His day is celebrated March 17.

pat·ri·mo·ny (pat′rə mō′nē), *n.* property inherited from one's father or ancestors.

pa·tri·ot (pā′tri ət), *n.* a person who shows great love for his country and is loyal to it.

pa·tri·ot·ic (pā′tri ät′ik), *adj.* showing great love for one's own country and loyalty to it. —**pa′tri·ot′i·cal·ly,** *adv.*

pa·tri·ot·ism (pā′tri ət iz'm), *n.* great love for one's own country and loyalty to it.

pa·trol (pə trōl′), *v.* to make regular trips around a place in order to guard it. —*n.* **1.** a patrolling, or the person or group that patrols. **2.** a group of ships, airplanes, or soldiers used to guard an area or to get information about the enemy. **3.** a group of about eight boy scouts or girl scouts, forming part of a troop. —**pa·trolled′,** *p.t. & p.p.;* **pa·trol′ling,** *pr.p.*

pa·trol·man (pə trōl′mən), *n.* a policeman who patrols a certain area. —**pa·trol′men,** *pl.*

pa·tron (pā′trən), *n.* **1.** a rich or important person who helps or supports another person, a group, etc. [the *patrons* of an orchestra]. **2.** a regular customer. —**pa′tron·ess,** *n.fem.*

pa·tron·age (pā′trən ij or pat′rən ij), *n.* **1.** the help or support given by a patron. **2.** customers; also, the regular business or trade of customers. **3.** the power to appoint persons to political office or give other political favors.

pa·tron·ize (pā′trə nīz or pat′rə nīz), *v.* **1.** to be a patron to; support or sponsor. **2.** to be kind to, but in a haughty or snobbish way. **3.** to be a regular customer of. —**pa′tron·ized,** *p.t. & p.p.;* **pa′tron·iz·ing,** *pr.p.*

patron saint, a saint looked on as the special protector of some person, group, or place.

pa·troon (pə trōōn′), *n.* a man who was given an estate that he could rent to others, in the old Dutch colonies of New York and New Jersey.

pat·ter (pat′ər), *n.* a series of light, quick taps [the *patter* of rain on the window]. —*v.* to make a patter.

pat·ter (pat′ər), *v.* to speak in a fast, easy way. —*n.* fast, easy talk, as that used by comedians.

pat·tern (pat′ərn), *n.* **1.** a plan or model used as a guide for making things [a dress *pattern*]. **2.** a person or thing taken as a model or example [Sir Galahad was the *pattern* of the noble knight.] **3.** a design or decoration [wallpaper *patterns*]. **4.** a habit or way of acting that does not change [the migration *pattern* of the swallow]. —*v.* to copy or model as from a pattern [She *patterned* her life on that of Florence Nightingale.]

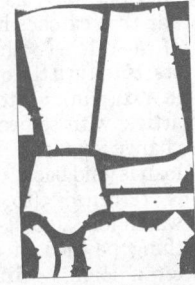

dress pattern

pat·ty (pat′ē), *n.* **1.** a small, flat cake of ground meat, fish, etc., usually fried. **2.** a small meat pie. —**pat′ties,** *pl.*

pau·ci·ty (pô′sə tē), *n.* smallness in number or amount; scarcity [a *paucity* of rain in July].

Paul, Saint (pôl), a Christian apostle who wrote many Epistles of the New Testament.

Paul Bun·yan (bun′yən), a giant lumberjack in American folk tales, who did amazing things.

paunch (pônch), *n.* the abdomen, or belly; also, a large, fat belly. —**paunch′y,** *adj.*

pau·per (pô′pər), *n.* a very poor person, especially one living on charity. —**pau′per·ism,** *n.*

pau·per·ize (pô′pər īz), *v.* to make a pauper of. —**pau′per·ized,** *p.t. & p.p.;* **pau′per·iz·ing,** *pr.p.*

pause (pôz), *n.* **1.** a short stop, as in speaking or working. **2.** a musical sign (⌣ or ⌢) placed below or above a note or rest that is to be held longer. —*v.* to make a pause; stop for a short time [He *paused* to catch his breath.] —**paused,** *p.t. & p.p.;* **paus′ing,** *pr.p.*

pave (pāv), *v.* to cover the surface of a road, walk, etc., as with concrete or asphalt. —**pave the way,** to make the way ready for something; prepare. —**paved,** *p.t. & p.p.;* **pav′ing,** *pr.p.*

pave·ment (pāv′mənt), *n.* a paved road, sidewalk, etc., or the material used in paving.

pa·vil·ion (pə vil′yən), *n.* **1.** a building or part of a building, often with open sides, used for exhibits, dancing, etc., as at a fair or park. **2.** a separate part of a group of buildings, as of a large hospital. **3.** a large tent, often with a pointed top.

pavilion

pav·ing (pāv′ing), *n.* pavement.

paw (pô), *n.* the foot of a four-footed animal that has claws [Dogs and cats have *paws*.] —*v.* **1.** to touch, dig, or hit with the paws or feet [The horse *pawed* the air.] **2.** to handle in a rough and clumsy way; maul [The angry man *pawed* through the papers on his desk.]

pawl (pôl), *n.* a device that lets a wheel turn only one way, as a hinged bar that catches in a notch of a ratchet wheel if it starts to turn the other way.

pawl

pawn (pôn), *v.* to leave an article with someone in exchange for a loan. When the loan is paid back, the article is returned [to *pawn* a watch for $20.00]. —*n.* anything pawned in exchange for a loan. —**in pawn,** being held as a pledge that a loan will be repaid.

pawn (pôn), *n.* **1.** a chess piece of the lowest value. **2.** a person used by another as his tool.

pawn·bro·ker (pôn′brō′kər), *n.* a person whose business is lending money at interest to people who pawn articles with him.

pawn·shop (pôn′shäp), *n.* a pawnbroker's shop.

paw·paw (pô′pô), *n.* same as **papaw.**

pay (pā), *v.* **1.** to give money to for goods or services [Did you *pay* the milkman?] **2.** to give in exchange [She *paid* ten dollars for the hat.] **3.** to settle or get rid of by giving money [to *pay* a debt]. **4.** to give or offer [to *pay* a compliment]. **5.** to make, as a visit. **6.** to bring as wages or salary [The job *pays* $100 a week.] **7.** to be worth-while to [It will *pay* you to listen.] —*n.* **1.** money paid for work or services [He gets his *pay* on Friday.] **2.** anything given or done in return [Your gratitude is my *pay*.] —*adj.* worked by putting in coins [a *pay* telephone]. —**in the pay of,** working for and paid by. —**pay back,** to repay. —**pay for, 1.** to be punished because of. **2.** to make up for. —**pay off,** to pay all that is owed. —**pay out, 1.** to give out, as money. **2.** to let out, as a rope. —**pay up,** to pay in full or on time. —**paid** or **payed** (*for meaning 2 of* **pay out**), *p.t. & p.p.;* **pay′ing,** *pr.p.* —**pay′er,** *n.*

pay·a·ble (pā′ə b'l), *adj.* **1.** due to be paid [This bill is *payable* today.] **2.** that can be paid.

pay·ee (pā ē′), *n.* the person to whom a check, money, etc. is to be paid.

pay·mas·ter (pā′mas tər), *n.* the person in charge of paying wages to employees.

pay·ment (pā′mənt), *n.* **1.** a paying or being paid [the *payment* of taxes]. **2.** something paid [a monthly car *payment* of $50].

pay roll, 1. a list of employees to be paid, with the amount due to each. **2.** the total amount needed for this.

Pb, symbol for the chemical element *lead.*

pd., abbreviation for **paid.**

pea (pē), *n.* **1.** a climbing plant having green pods with seeds in them. **2.** the small, round seed, eaten as a vegetable.

peace (pēs), *n.* **1.** freedom from war or fighting [to live in *peace* with all countries]. **2.** an agreement or treaty to end war. **3.** law and order [The rioters were disturbing the *peace*.] **4.** calm or quiet [to find *peace* of mind]. —**at peace,** free from war, fighting, etc. —**hold one's peace** or **keep one's peace,** to be silent. —**keep the peace,** to make sure that the law is not broken. —**make peace,** to end war, fighting, etc.

peas in a pod

peace·a·ble (pēs′ə b'l), *adj.* fond of peace; not fighting; peaceful. —**peace′a·bly,** *adv.*

Peace Corps, an agency of the U.S. Department of State that sends volunteer teachers, workers, etc. to help underdeveloped countries.

peace·ful (pēs′fəl), *adj.* **1.** free from noise or disorder; quiet; calm [the *peaceful* countryside]. **2.** fond of peace; not fighting [a *peaceful* people]. **3.** of or fit for a time of peace [*peaceful* trade between nations]. **—peace′ful·ly,** *adv.* **—peace′ful·ness,** *n.*

peace·mak·er (pēs′māk ər), *n.* a person who makes peace, as by stopping a fight or quarrel.

peach (pēch), *n.* **1.** a round, juicy, pinkish-yellow fruit, with a fuzzy skin and a rough pit. **2.** the tree that it grows on. **3.** pinkish yellow.

pea·cock (pē′käk), *n.* the male of a large bird, having long tail feathers of rich blue, green, bronze, etc. which it can spread out like a fan. The female is usually called a **pea·hen** (pē′hen).

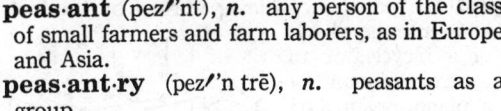
peacock (the body is 20 in. high)

pea jacket, a short, heavy coat worn by sailors.

peak (pēk), *n.* **1.** the pointed top of a hill or mountain. **2.** a hill or mountain with such a top. **3.** any pointed top or end, as of a roof or cap. **4.** the highest point or degree [The steel mills reached their *peak* of production in May.]

peaked (pēkt), *adj.* with a peak; pointed [a *peaked* roof].

peak·ed (pēk′id), *adj.* looking thin and tired, as from being ill [a *peaked* face].

peal (pēl), *n.* **1.** the loud ringing of a bell or bells. **2.** any loud sound that echoes, as of thunder or laughter. **3.** a set of bells, or chimes. **—v.** to ring out loud and long.

pea·nut (pē′nut), *n.* **1.** a vine like the pea plant, with dry pods that ripen underground and contain seeds like nuts that can be eaten. **2.** the pod or one of its seeds.

peanut butter, a food paste or spread made by grinding peanuts that have been roasted.

pear (per), *n.* **1.** a soft, juicy fruit, often yellow or green, that is round at one end and narrows toward the stem. **2.** the tree it grows on.

peanut plant

pearl (pûrl), *n.* **1.** a smooth, hard, roundish stone formed inside oysters and some other shellfish. It is usually white or bluish-gray and is used as a gem. **2.** mother-of-pearl. **3.** the color of pearl; bluish gray. **4.** anything like a pearl, as in shape, color, or value. **—adj. 1.** of or made with pearls [a *pearl* necklace]. **2.** made of mother-of-pearl [*pearl* buttons]. **—pearl′y,** *adj.*

pearl gray, pale bluish gray.

Pearl Harbor, a harbor in Hawaii, near Honolulu. The United States naval base there was attacked by Japan on December 7, 1941.

peas·ant (pez′′nt), *n.* any person of the class of small farmers and farm laborers, as in Europe and Asia.

peas·ant·ry (pez′′n trē), *n.* peasants as a group.

pease (pēz), *n.* an older plural of **pea.**

peat (pēt), *n.* a mass of partly rotted plants and grass, formed in marshes. It is dried for fuel.

peb·ble (peb′′l), *n.* a small stone worn smooth and round, as by water running over it.

peb·bly (peb′lē), *adj.* **1.** having many pebbles [a *pebbly* stream]. **2.** covered with little bumps; rough and uneven [*pebbly* leather].

pe·can (pi kan′ *or* pi kän′ *or* pē′kan), *n.* **1.** an oval nut with a thin, smooth shell. **2.** the tree it grows on, mainly in the southern United States.

pec·ca·dil·lo (pek′ə dil′ō), *n.* a slight fault or mistake that is not important. **—pec′ca·dil′loes** or **pec′ca·dil′los,** *pl.*

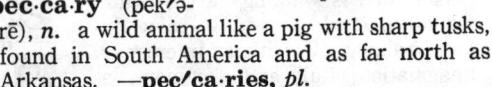
pecans

pec·ca·ry (pek′ə rē), *n.* a wild animal like a pig with sharp tusks, found in South America and as far north as Arkansas. **—pec′ca·ries,** *pl.*

peck (pek), *v.* **1.** to strike or strike at, as a bird does with its beak. **2.** to make by doing this [to *peck* a hole]. **3.** to pick up by pecking [Chickens *peck* corn.] **—n. 1.** a stroke or mark made by pecking. **2.** a quick, light kiss: *used only in everyday talk.* **—peck at, 1.** to eat very little of. **2.** to find fault with constantly. *This phrase is used only in everyday talk.*

peck (pek), *n.* **1.** a measure of volume for grain, fruit, vegetables, etc. It is equal to ¼ bushel or eight quarts. **2.** a basket, etc. that holds a peck. **3.** a large amount, as of trouble.

pec·to·ral (pek′tə rəl), *adj.* of, in, or on the breast or chest [a *pectoral* muscle].

pe·cul·iar (pi kyool′yər), *adj.* **1.** odd; strange; queer [Things look *peculiar* through these dark glasses.] **2.** of a particular person, thing, or group; special; distinctive [These markings are *peculiar* to this bird.] **—pe·cul′iar·ly,** *adv.*

pe·cu·li·ar·i·ty (pi kyoo′li ar′ə tē), *n.* **1.** the condition of being peculiar. **2.** something peculiar, unusual, or special [a *peculiarity* of speech]. **—pe·cu′li·ar′i·ties,** *pl.*

pe·cu·ni·ar·y (pi kyoo′ni er′ē), *adj.* of or having to do with money [*pecuniary* aid].

ped·a·gogue or **ped·a·gog** (ped′ə gäg), *n.* a teacher, especially one who pays more attention to details than to understanding.

ped·a·go·gy (ped′ə gō′jē), *n.* teaching, or the science of teaching. **—ped·a·gog′ic** (ped′ə gäj′ik) or **ped′a·gog′i·cal,** *adj.*

ped·al (ped′'l), *n.* a lever worked by the foot, as to turn the wheels of a bicycle, or to control the sound of a piano, organ, etc. —*v.* to move or work by pushing on a pedal or pedals [to *pedal* a bicycle]. —*adj.* **1.** of the foot

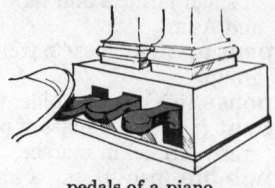
pedals of a piano

or feet. **2.** of or worked by a pedal. —**ped′aled** or **ped′alled**, *p.t. & p.p.;* **ped′al·ing** or **ped′-al·ling**, *pr.p.*

ped·ant (ped′'nt), *n.* a person who shows off his learning in a boring way, or one who pays too much attention to book learning. —**pe·dan·tic** (pi dan′tik), *adj.* —**ped′ant·ry**, *n.*

ped·dle (ped′'l), *v.* **1.** to go about from place to place selling small things [to *peddle* magazines]. **2.** to give out in small amounts [to *peddle* gossip]. —**ped′dled**, *p.t. & p.p.;* **ped′dling**, *pr.p.* —**ped′dler**, *n.*

ped·es·tal (ped′is t'l), *n.* **1.** the piece at the bottom that holds up a statue, column, etc. **2.** any base, especially a high one.

pe·des·tri·an (pə des′tri ən), *n.* a person who is walking [a crosswalk for *pedestrians*]. —*adj.* **1.** going on foot; walking. **2.** without interest or imagination; dull and common [a *pedestrian* lecture].

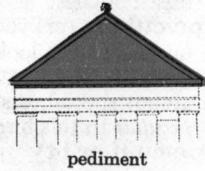
bust on a pedestal

pe·di·a·tri·cian (pē′di ə trish′ən), *n.* a doctor who takes care of babies and children.

pe·di·at·rics (pē′di at′riks), *n.pl.* the branch of medicine that has to do with the care and treatment of babies and children: *used with a singular verb.* —**pe′di·at′ric**, *adj.*

ped·i·gree (ped′ə grē), *n.* **1.** a list of one's ancestors. **2.** a record of the ancestors of a thoroughbred animal. —**ped′i·greed**, *adj.*

ped·i·ment (ped′ə mənt), *n.* **1.** a part in the shape of a low triangle on the front of an ancient Greek building. *See the picture.* **2.** a decoration like this, as over a doorway.

ped·lar (ped′lər), *n.* same as **peddler**.

pediment

peek (pēk), *v.* to take a quick, sly or secret look; peep [to *peek* through a hole in the fence]. —*n.* a quick, sly look.

peel (pēl), *v.* **1.** to cut away or pull off the skin or rind of [to *peel* a banana]. **2.** to shed skin, bark, etc. [My back is *peeling* from a sunburn.] **3.** to come off in flakes [The paint on the house is *peeling*.] —*n.* the rind or skin of fruit. —**keep one's eyes peeled**, to keep a close watch: *used only in everyday talk.*

peel·ing (pēl′ing), *n.* anything peeled off, as an apple skin.

peep (pēp), *n.* the short, high, thin sound made by a young bird or chicken; chirp. —*v.* to make this sound.

peep (pēp), *v.* **1.** to look through a small opening or from a hiding place; look secretly [to *peep* through a keyhole]. **2.** to show partly or briefly [Stars *peeped* through the clouds.] —*n.* **1.** a quick or secret look. **2.** the first showing [the *peep* of dawn]. —**peep′er**, *n.*

peep·hole (pēp′hōl), *n.* a hole to peep through.

peer (pir), *n.* **1.** a person or thing of the same value, rank, skill, etc.; an equal [As a poet, he has few *peers*.] **2.** a nobleman; especially, a British duke, marquis, earl, viscount, or baron. —**peer′ess**, *n.fem.*

peer (pir), *v.* **1.** to look closely or squint in order to see better [to *peer* into a dark room]. **2.** to come partly into sight [The moon *peered* over the hill.]

peer·age (pir′ij), *n.* **1.** all the peers, or nobles, of a country. **2.** the rank of a peer. **3.** a list of peers with their lines of ancestors.

peer·less (pir′lis), *adj.* having no equal; better than the rest [her *peerless* beauty].

peeve (pēv), *v.* to make or become cross or annoyed [Mother will be *peeved* if we are late.] —*n.* a thing that annoys one [a pet *peeve*]. *This word is used only in everyday talk.* —**peeved**, *p.t. & p.p.;* **peev′ing**, *pr.p.*

pee·vish (pēv′ish), *adj.* cross or irritable [Illness made her *peevish*.] —**pee′vish·ly**, *adv.* —**pee′vish·ness**, *n.*

pee·wee (pē′wē), *n.* a very small person or thing: *used only in everyday talk.*

peg (peg), *n.* **1.** a thick pin of wood, metal, etc. used to hold parts together, plug up an opening, hang things on, tighten the strings of a musical instrument, fasten ropes to, mark the score in a game, etc. **2.** a step or degree [The promotion moved me up a few

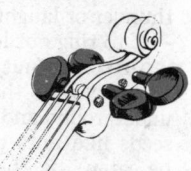
pegs of a violin

pegs.] —*v.* to fasten, fix, mark, etc. with pegs. —**peg away at,** to work hard at. —**take down a peg,** to make less proud or less vain; humble. —**pegged**, *p.t. & p.p.;* **peg′ging**, *pr.p.*

Peg·a·sus (peg′ə səs), *n.* a flying horse with wings in Greek myths. It is a symbol of the poet's inspiration.

P.E.I., abbreviation for **Prince Edward Island.**

Pei·ping (pā′ping′ *or* bā′-ping′), *n.* an earlier name for **Peking.**

Pe·king (pē′king′ *or* bā′-jing′), *n.* the capital of China, in the northeastern part.

Pegasus

Pe·king·ese *or* **Pe·kin·ese** (pē′kin ēz′), *n.* a small dog, with long hair, short legs, and a flat nose. —**Pe′king·ese′** *or* **Pe′kin·ese′**, *pl.*

pe·koe (pē′kō), *n.* a black tea grown in Ceylon and India.

pelf (pelf), *n.* money; wealth: *a scornful word.*

pel·i·can (pel′i kən), *n.* a large water bird with webbed feet and a pouch that hangs from the lower bill and is used for scooping in fish.

pelicans (5 ft. long)

pel·la·gra (pə lā′grə *or* pə-lag′rə), *n.* a disease in which there is a skin rash and nervous disorders, caused by a lack of vitamin B in the diet.

pel·let (pel′it), *n.* **1.** a little ball, as of clay, paper, etc. rolled between the fingers. **2.** a bullet or small lead shot.

pell-mell *or* **pell·mell** (pel′mel′), *adv.* **1.** in a jumbled mass; in a confused way [He tossed his clothes *pell-mell* into the suitcase.] **2.** with reckless speed [He ran *pell-mell* down the hill.]

pelt (pelt), *v.* **1.** to hit again and again; keep beating [Rain *pelted* the roof.] **2.** to throw things at [We *pelted* each other with snowballs.] —*n.* speed [We ran at full *pelt.*]

pelt (pelt), *n.* the skin of an animal with fur, especially when ready for tanning.

pel·vic (pel′vik), *adj.* of or near the pelvis.

pel·vis (pel′vis), *n.* the part of the skeleton formed by the bones of the hip and part of the backbone. It is shaped like a hollow basin.

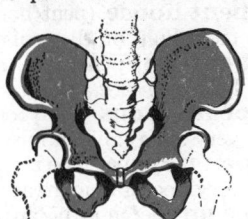

pelvis

pem·mi·can *or* **pem·i·can** (pem′i kən), *n.* dried meat pounded into a paste with fat and pressed into cakes: used by arctic explorers.

pen (pen), *n.* **1.** a small yard with a fence for keeping animals [a pig *pen*]. **2.** any small enclosed place [a play *pen* for a baby]. —*v.* to shut up as in a pen. —**penned** *or* **pent,** *p.t.* & *p.p.*; **pen′ning,** *pr.p.*

pen (pen), *n.* **1.** a device used for writing or drawing with ink, often having a split metal point: *see also* **ball point pen. 2.** the art, skill, or profession of writing ["The *pen* is mightier than the sword."] —*v.* to write. —**penned,** *p.t.* & *p.p.*; **pen′ning,** *pr.p.*

pe·nal (pē′n'l), *adj.* of, dealing with, or bringing punishment [*penal* laws; a *penal* offense].

pe·nal·ize (pē′n'l īz *or* pen′'l īz), *v.* **1.** to set a punishment or penalty for [How shall we *penalize* cheating?] **2.** to put a penalty on; punish [to *penalize* a boxer for a foul blow]. —**pe′nal·ized,** *p.t.* & *p.p.*; **pe′nal·iz·ing,** *pr.p.*

pen·al·ty (pen′'l tē), *n.* **1.** punishment for breaking a law. **2.** a disadvantage, fine, etc. put on one side in a contest for breaking a rule. **3.** any unfortunate result [Indigestion is often the *penalty* for eating fast.] —**pen′al·ties,** *pl.*

pen·ance (pen′əns), *n.* something that a person does, or a punishment that he bears, to show that he is sorry for his sins, wrongdoing, etc.

pence (pens), *n.* a British plural of **penny.**

pen·chant (pen′chənt), *n.* a strong liking or fondness [a *penchant* for baseball].

pen·cil (pen′s'l), *n.* a long, thin piece of wood, metal, etc. with a center stick of graphite or crayon that is sharpened to a point for writing or drawing. —*v.* to mark, write, or draw with a pencil. —**pen′ciled** *or* **pen′cilled,** *p.t.* & *p.p.*; **pen′cil·ing** *or* **pen′cil·ling,** *pr.p.*

pend·ant (pen′dənt), *n.* an ornament that hangs down, as a locket or earring.

pend·ent (pen′dənt), *adj.* **1.** hanging down or supported from above [a *pendent* lamp]. **2.** overhanging [a *pendent* cliff]. **3.** pending.

pend·ing (pen′ding), *adj.* **1.** not yet decided or settled [a lawsuit that is *pending*]. **2.** about to happen; threatening [*pending* dangers]. —*prep.* **1.** during [*pending* this discussion]. **2.** while awaiting; until [*pending* his arrival].

pen·du·lous (pen′joo ləs), *adj.* **1.** hanging loosely [*pendulous* jowls]. **2.** swinging [the *pendulous* movement of the willow branches].

pen·du·lum (pen′joo ləm *or* pen′d'l əm), *n.* a weight hung so that it swings freely back and forth, often used to control a clock's movement.

Pe·nel·o·pe (pə nel′ə pē), *n.* Ulysses' faithful wife, who waited many years for his return.

pen·e·tra·ble (pen′i trə b'l), *adj.* that can be penetrated [a *penetrable* wall].

pen·e·trate (pen′ə trāt), *v.* **1.** to pass into or through, as by piercing; enter [The needle *penetrated* her arm.] **2.** to spread through [Smoke *penetrated* the whole school.] **3.** to understand; find out [I finally *penetrated* the meaning of this riddle.] —**pen′e·trat·ed,** *p.t.* & *p.p.*; **pen′e·trat·ing,** *pr.p.*

pendulum of a clock

pen·e·trat·ing (pen′ə trāt′ing), *adj.* that can penetrate; keen or sharp [a *penetrating* mind].

pen·e·tra·tion (pen′ə trā′shən), *n.* **1.** the act of penetrating. **2.** keenness of mind; insight.

pen·guin (peng′gwin), *n.* a sea bird mainly of the antarctic region, with webbed feet and flippers for swimming and diving. Penguins cannot fly.

pen·i·cil·lin (pen′ə sil′in), *n.* a chemical substance gotten from a fungus growing as green mold. It is used in treating certain diseases because it can kill or weaken the germs that cause them.

penguins (3 ft. tall)

---

peninsula — 514 — pep

pen·in·su·la (pə nin′sə lə *or* pə nin′syoo lə), *n.* a long piece of land almost completely surrounded by water [Italy is a *peninsula.*] —pen·in′su·lar, *adj.*

pe·nis (pē′nis), *n.* the male sex organ. In male mammals, it is also the organ through which urine leaves the bladder.

pen·i·tence (pen′ə təns), *n.* a feeling of sorrow for having sinned or done wrong.

pen·i·tent (pen′ə tənt), *adj.* sorry for having sinned or done wrong. —*n.* a penitent person.

pen·i·ten·tial (pen′ə ten′shəl), *adj.* of or having to do with penitence or penance.

pen·i·ten·tia·ry (pen′ə ten′shə rē), *n.* a prison; especially, a State or Federal prison. —*adj.* 1. that can be punished by a term in a penitentiary [a *penitentiary* crime]. 2. of or for penance. —pen′i·ten′tia·ries, *pl.*

pen·knife (pen′nīf), *n.* a small pocketknife. —pen·knives (pen′nīvz), *pl.*

pen·man (pen′mən), *n.* 1. a person whose work is writing or copying; scribe or author. 2. a person whose handwriting is good. —pen′men, *pl.*

pen·man·ship (pen′mən ship), *n.* the art or skill of writing by hand; handwriting.

Penn, William (pen), 1644–1718; English Quaker who founded Pennsylvania.

pen name, a name used by an author in place of his real name; pseudonym.

pen·nant (pen′ənt), *n.* 1. a long, narrow flag or banner, usually in the shape of a triangle. 2. such a flag that is the symbol for a championship, as in baseball.

pen·ni·less (pen′i lis), *adj.* without even a penny; very poor.

pen·non (pen′ən), *n.* 1. a long, narrow flag once carried by a knight. 2. any flag or pennant.

pennants

Penn·syl·va·ni·a (pen′s'l vān′yə *or* pen′s'l vā′ni ə), *n.* a State in the northeastern part of the United States: abbreviated Pa., Penn., or Penna.

Pennsylvania Dutch, 1. people descended from Germans who settled in Pennsylvania. 2. their German dialect.

pen·ny (pen′ē), *n.* 1. a cent. 2. a British coin equal to 1/100 of a pound. —a pretty penny, a large sum of money: *used only in everyday talk.* —pen′nies, *pl.,* or also (*for meaning 2*), pence, *pl.*

pen·ny·weight (pen′ē wāt), *n.* a unit of weight equal to 1/20 of an ounce in troy weight.

pen·ny-wise (pen′ē wīz′), *adj.* thrifty in small matters. —penny-wise and pound-foolish, thrifty in small matters but wasteful in greater ones.

pen·sion (pen′shən), *n.* money paid regularly by a company or the government to a person who has retired from work, as because of old age, injuries, etc. —*v.* to pay a pension to.

pen·sion·er (pen′shən ər), *n.* a person who is getting a pension.

pen·sive (pen′siv), *adj.* thinking deeply in a serious or sad way; thoughtful. —pen′sive·ly, *adv.*

pent (pent), a past tense and past participle of pen (to shut in). —*adj.* shut in or kept in; penned [Children love the spring after being *pent* up all winter.]

pent·a·gon (pent′ə gän), *n.* 1. a flat figure having five sides and five angles. 2. Pentagon, the five-sided office building of the Defense Department, near Washington, D.C. —pen·tag·o·nal (pen tag′ə n'l), *adj.*

Pen·ta·teuch (pen′tə tōōk), *n.* the first five books of the Old Testament.

Pen·te·cost (pen′ti kôst), *n.* 1. a Christian festival on the seventh Sunday after Easter: also called Whitsunday. 2. a Jewish festival on the fiftieth day after Passover. —Pen′te·cost′al, *adj.*

pent·house (pent′hous), *n.* a house or apartment built on the roof of a building.

pent-up (pent′up′), *adj.* kept under control; held in [*pent-up* anger].

pe·nu·ri·ous (pə nyoor′i əs *or* pə noor′i əs), *adj.* very stingy; like a miser.

pen·u·ry (pen′yoo rē), *n.* the condition of being very poor and in great need.

pe·on (pē′ən *or* pē′än), *n.* in Spanish America, a person who works at hard labor; often, one who is forced to do this for a certain time to work off a debt. —pe′on·age, *n.*

pe·o·ny (pē′ə nē), *n.* 1. a plant with large, showy flowers of pink, white, red, or yellow. 2. the flower. —pe′o·nies, *pl.*

peo·ple (pē′p'l), *n.* 1. human beings; persons. 2. all the persons of a certain race, religion, nation, class, etc. [the French *people*]. 3. the persons of a certain place, group, or class [country *people*; the *people* of Oregon]. 4. one's family; relatives or ancestors [My *people* came to America from Italy.] 5. the public generally; persons without wealth, special position, etc. [Jones is the *people*'s choice for mayor.] —*v.* to fill with people; populate [The pioneers *peopled* the West.] —peo′ples, *pl. for meaning 2;* peo′ple, *pl. for other meanings.* —peo′pled, *p.t. & p.p.;* peo′pling, *pr.p.*

Pe·o·ri·a (pi ôr′i ə), *n.* a city in central Illinois.

pep (pep), *n.* energy or vigor. —pep up, to make or become livelier; fill with energy. *A slang word.* —pepped, *p.t. & p.p.;* pep′ping, *pr.p.* —pep′py, *adj.*

a pensive man

pentagon

peony

pep·per (pep′ər), *n.* **1.** a plant having green or red pods with many seeds. **2.** the sweet or hot pod, eaten as a vegetable or relish. **3.** a hot-tasting seasoning made from the berries of a tropical plant: *black pepper* is ground from the dried berries, and *white pepper* is ground from the dried seeds with the coatings removed. **4.** cayenne. —*v.* **1.** to sprinkle with ground pepper. **2.** to pelt or cover with many small things [Hailstones *peppered* the lawn.]

left: berries on a tropical pepper plant
right: pepper (*meaning 1*)

pep·per·corn (pep′ər kôrn), *n.* the dried berry from which black pepper is ground.

pep·per·mint (pep′ər mint), *n.* **1.** a plant of the mint family from which an oil with a sharp, cool taste is pressed. **2.** this oil, used for flavoring **3.** a candy flavored with this oil.

pep·per·y (pep′ər ē), *adj.* **1.** like or full of pepper; hot [*peppery* soup]. **2.** showing excitement or anger; fiery [a *peppery* speech].

pep·sin (pep′sin), *n.* **1.** a substance produced in the stomach, that helps to digest food. **2.** a medicine made of pepsin gotten from animals.

per (pər), *prep.* **1.** for each; for every [fifty cents *per* yard]. **2.** during each [50 miles *per* hour]. **3.** by means of [delivery *per* messenger].

per·ad·ven·ture (pūr′əd ven′chər), *adv.* possibly; maybe: *now seldom used.*

per·am·bu·late (pər am′byoo lāt), *v.* to walk around, through, or over. —**per·am′bu·lat·ed**, *p.t. & p.p.;* **per·am′bu·lat·ing**, *pr.p.* —**per·am′bu·la′tion**, *n.*

per·am·bu·la·tor (pər am′byoo lā′tər), *n.* a baby carriage: *mainly a British word.*

per an·num (pər an′əm), for each year; yearly [Tuition *per annum* is over $1,000.]

per·cale (pər kāl′ *or* pər kal′), *n.* a smooth, strong cotton cloth used for sheets, etc.

per cap·i·ta (pər kap′ə tə), for each person [the *per capita* cost of education].

per·ceive (pər sēv′), *v.* **1.** to become aware of through one of the senses, especially through seeing [to *perceive* the difference between two shades of red]. **2.** to take in through the mind; understand [I quickly *perceived* the joke.] —**per·ceived′**, *p.t. & p.p.;* **per·ceiv′ing**, *pr.p.*

per·cent (pər sent′), *n.* same as **per cent.**

per cent, out of or in every hundred [Ten *per cent* of the students read the book; that is, 20 out of the 200 students read the book.] *The symbol for per cent is %.*

per·cent·age (pər sent′ij), *n.* a part or portion of a whole thought of or shown as a certain rate per cent [A large *percentage* of the students won scholarships.]

per·cep·ti·ble (pər sep′tə b'l), *adj.* that can be perceived, or noticed [The sound was barely *perceptible.*] —**per·cep′ti·bly**, *adv.*

per·cep·tion (pər sep′shən), *n.* **1.** the act of perceiving or the ability to perceive [His *perception* of color is poor.] **2.** knowledge or understanding got by perceiving [He has a clear *perception* of his duty.]

per·cep·tive (pər sep′tiv), *adj.* able to perceive quickly and easily; intelligent.

perch (pūrch), *n.* **1.** a small, fresh-water fish used for food. **2.** a similar salt-water fish. —**perch** or **perch′es**, *pl.*

perch (pūrch), *n.* **1.** a branch on a tree, or a bar in a cage, for a bird to roost on. **2.** any resting place, especially a high one. **3.** a measure of length, equal to 5½ yards. —*v.* to rest or place as on a perch [Sparrows *perched* on the wires. He *perched* himself on the railing.]

per·chance (pər chans′), *adv.* possibly; maybe; perhaps: *now seldom used except in poetry.*

per·co·late (pūr′kə lāt), *v.* **1.** to prepare or be prepared in a percolator, as coffee. **2.** to pass slowly through something that has many tiny holes; filter. —**per′co·lat·ed**, *p.t. & p.p.;* **per′co·lat·ing**, *pr.p.*

per·co·la·tor (pūr′kə lā′tər), *n.* a coffeepot in which the water boils up through a tube and filters back down through the ground coffee.

percolator

per·cus·sion (pər kush′ən), *n.* the hitting of one thing against another; blow [A shot is fired by the *percussion* of the hammer against a powder cap.]

percussion instrument, a musical instrument in which the tone is made by striking some part of it, as a drum, cymbal, etc.

per·di·tion (pər dish′ən), *n.* **1.** hell. **2.** the loss of one's soul, or of the chance of going to heaven. **3.** complete loss.

per·e·gri·na·tion (per′ə gri nā′shən), *n.* a traveling about; journey.

per·emp·to·ry (pər emp′tər ē), *adj.* **1.** that may not be refused or questioned [a *peremptory* command]. **2.** forcing one's wishes or opinions on another in a bullying way [a *peremptory* tone]. **3.** not allowing delay; final [a *peremptory* order by a law court]. —**per·emp′to·ri·ly**, *adv.*

per·en·ni·al (pə ren′i əl), *adj.* **1.** that lives for more than two years: said of certain plants. **2.** lasting or active through the whole year [a *perennial* stream which does not freeze over]. **3.** lasting or going on for a long time [to seek *perennial* youth]. —*n.* a plant that lives for more than two years. —**per·en′ni·al·ly**, *adv.*

per·fect (pūr′fikt), *adj.* **1.** complete in every way and having no faults or errors [a *perfect* test paper]. **2.** being as good as is possible; most excellent [in *perfect* health]. **3.** correct or accu-

fat, āpe, cär, ten, ēven, hit, bīte, gō, hôrn, tool, book, up, fũr; get, joy, yet, chin, she, thin, *th*en; zh = s in pleasure; ' as in able (ā′b'l). ə = a in ago, e in agent, i in sanity, o in confess, u in focus.

rate; exact [a *perfect* copy of a drawing]. **4.** absolute or complete [*perfect* strangers]. **5.** showing that something is completed at the time of speaking or at the time spoken of ["They have eaten" is in the present *perfect* tense; "they had eaten" is in the past *perfect* tense.] —*v.* (pər fekt⁄), to make perfect or almost perfect [Practice to *perfect* your work.] —**per⁄fect·ly,** *adv.*

per·fect·i·ble (pər fek⁄tə b'l), *adj.* that can become, or be made, perfect [Is his idea *perfectible?*] —**per·fect⁄i·bil⁄i·ty,** *n.*

per·fec·tion (pər fek⁄shən), *n.* **1.** the act of perfecting [to work at the *perfection* of a skill]. **2.** the condition of being perfect [*Perfection* in spelling is her goal.] **3.** a person or thing that is perfect or excellent. —**to perfection,** completely; perfectly.

per·fec·tion·ist (pər fek⁄shən ist), *n.* a person who is always looking for perfection.

per·fid·i·ous (pər fid⁄i əs), *adj.* showing treachery; faithless; treacherous.

per·fi·dy (pŭr⁄fə dē), *n.* the act of betraying others or being false to one's promises; treachery. —**per⁄fi·dies,** *pl.*

per·fo·rate (pŭr⁄fə rāt), *v.* **1.** to make a hole or holes through [to *per-forate* the top of a can of cleaning powder]. **2.** to make a row of small holes in for easy tearing [Sheets of stamps are usually *perforated.*] —**per⁄fo·rat·ed,** *p.t.* & *p.p.;* **per⁄fo·rat·ing,** *pr.p.* —**per⁄fo·ra⁄tion,** *n.*

perforations between postage stamps

per·force (pər fôrs⁄), *adv.* because it must be; through necessity; necessarily.

per·form (pər fôrm⁄), *v.* **1.** to do or carry out [to *perform* a task; to *perform* a promise]. **2.** to do something to entertain an audience; act, play music, sing, etc. —**per·form⁄er,** *n.*

per·form·ance (pər fôr⁄məns), *n.* **1.** the act of performing; a doing [the *performance* of one's duty]. **2.** something done; deed. **3.** a showing of skill or talent before an audience, as in a play, on a musical instrument, etc.

per·fume (pŭr⁄fyōōm), *n.* **1.** a sweet smell; pleasing odor; fragrance [the *perfume* of roses]. **2.** a liquid with a pleasing smell, for use on the body, clothing, etc. —*v.* (pər fyōōm⁄), to give a pleasing smell to, as with perfume. —**per·fumed⁄,** *p.t.* & *p.p.;* **per·fum⁄ing,** *pr.p.*

per·fum·er·y (pər fyōōm⁄ər ē), *n.* **1.** a place where perfumes are made or sold. **2.** perfume or perfumes. —**per·fum⁄er·ies,** *pl.*

per·func·to·ry (pər fungk⁄tər ē), *adj.* done or acting without real care or interest; mechanical or careless [a *perfunctory* greeting; a *perfunctory* worker]. —**per·func⁄to·ri·ly,** *adv.*

per·haps (pər haps⁄), *adv.* possibly; maybe [*Perhaps* it will rain. Did you, *perhaps,* lose it?]

Per·i·cles (per⁄ə klēz), *n.* Greek statesman and general. He died in 429 B.C.

per·il (per⁄əl), *n.* the chance of being hurt, killed, destroyed, etc.; danger; risk [The pioneers faced many *perils.*] —*v.* to put in danger; risk; imperil. —**per⁄iled** or **per⁄illed,** *p.t.* & *p.p.;* **per⁄il·ing** or **per⁄il·ling,** *pr.p.*

per·il·ous (per⁄ə ləs), *adj.* dangerous; risky. —**per⁄il·ous·ly,** *adv.*

per·im·e·ter (pə rim⁄ə tər), *n.* **1.** the boundary or line around a figure or area. **2.** the total length of this; distance around an area.

pe·ri·od (pir⁄i əd), *n.* **1.** a space of time during which something goes on, a cycle is repeated, etc. [the medieval *period;* a *period* of hot weather]. **2.** any of the portions of time into which a game, a school day, etc. is divided. **3.** the mark of punctuation (.) used at the end of most sentences or after an abbreviation. **4.** an end; finish [Death put a *period* to his plans.]

pe·ri·od·ic (pir⁄i äd⁄ik), *adj.* happening or done from time to time, in a regular way [*periodic* tests to measure the students' progress].

pe·ri·od·i·cal (pir⁄i äd⁄i k'l), *n.* a magazine published every week, month, etc. —*adj.* **1.** same as **periodic. 2.** published every week, month, etc. **3.** of periodicals [a *periodical* index]. —**pe'ri·od⁄i·cal·ly,** *adv.*

per·i·pa·tet·ic (per⁄i pə tet⁄ik), *adj.* walking or moving about; not staying in one place.

pe·riph·er·y (pə rif⁄ər ē), *n.* **1.** an outer boundary, especially of something round [The rocket passed the *periphery* of the earth's atmosphere.] **2.** the space or area around something. —**pe·riph⁄er·ies,** *pl.* —**pe·riph⁄er·al,** *adj.*

per·i·scope (per⁄ə skōp), *n.* a tube with mirrors or prisms inside it so that a person can look in one end and see the reflection of an object at the other end. Periscopes are used on submarines so that the surface can be seen from under the water.

per·ish (per⁄ish), *v.* to be destroyed; die [Many animals *perished* in the forest fire.]

periscope

per·ish·a·ble (per⁄ish ə-b'l), *adj.* that is likely to perish, or spoil, as some foods. —*n.* a food, etc. that is likely to spoil.

per·i·wig (per⁄ə wig), *n.* same as **wig.**

per·i·win·kle (per⁄ə wing⁄k'l), *n.* a creeping, evergreen plant with blue flowers; myrtle.

per·i·win·kle (per⁄ə wing⁄k'l), *n.* a small, salt-water snail with a thick shell.

per·jure (pŭr⁄jər), *v.* to make oneself guilty of perjury; lie while under oath to tell the truth, as in a law court. —**per⁄jured,** *p.t.* & *p.p.;* **per⁄jur·ing,** *pr.p.* —**per⁄jur·er,** *n.*

periwinkle shell

per·ju·ry (pŭr⁄jər ē), *n.* the telling of a lie on purpose, after one has taken an oath to tell the truth. —**per⁄ju·ries,** *pl.*

perk (pŭrk), *v.* **1.** to raise in a quick and lively way [He *perked* up his head at the noise.] **2.** to make stylish or smart [all *perked* out in a new dress]. —**perk up,** to become lively.

perk·y (pŭr'kē), *adj.* gay or lively [a *perky* pup]. —**perk'i·er,** *compar.*; **perk'i·est,** *superl.*

per·ma·nent (pŭr'mə nənt), *adj.* lasting or meant to last for a very long time [One's *permanent* teeth should last as long as one lives.] —*n.* a permanent wave. —**per'ma·nence** or **per'ma·nen·cy,** *n.* —**per'ma·nent·ly,** *adv.*

permanent wave, a hair wave put in by means of chemicals or heat and lasting for months.

per·me·a·ble (pŭr'mi ə b'l), *adj.* that will let liquids or gases pass through [Blotting paper is a *permeable* material.] —**per'me·a·bil'i·ty,** *n.*

per·me·ate (pŭr'mi āt), *v.* to pass through or spread through every part of [The smells of cooking *permeated* the house.] —**per'me·at·ed,** *p.t. & p.p.*; **per'me·at·ing,** *pr.p.*

per·mis·si·ble (pər mis'ə b'l), *adj.* that can be permitted, or allowed; allowable.

per·mis·sion (pər mish'ən), *n.* the act of permitting; consent [He has my *permission* to go.]

per·mis·sive (pər mis'iv), *adj.* permitting or allowing certain things [*permissive* parents].

per·mit (pər mit'), *v.* **1.** to give consent to; let; allow [Will you *permit* me to help you?] **2.** to give a chance [We'll fly if the weather *permits.*] —*n.* (pŭr'mit), a paper, card, etc. showing permission; license [a *permit* to carry a gun]. —**per·mit'ted,** *p.t. & p.p.*; **per·mit'ting,** *pr.p.*

per·ni·cious (pər nish'əs), *adj.* causing great injury, harm, damage, etc. [a *pernicious* disease].

per·o·ra·tion (per'ə rā'shən), *n.* the last part of a speech, summing up the main ideas.

per·ox·ide (pər äk'sīd), *n.* a chemical compound containing a greater proportion of oxygen than the oxide of the same series [Hydrogen *peroxide* is used as a bleach and disinfectant.]

per·pen·dic·u·lar (pŭr'pən dik'yoo lər), *adj.* **1.** at right angles [The wall should be *perpendicular* to the floor.] **2.** straight up and down; exactly upright [a *perpendicular* flagpole]. —*n.* a line that is at right angles to the horizon, or to another line or plane [The tower of Pisa leans away from the *perpendicular.*]

perpendicular

per·pe·trate (pŭr'pə trāt), *v.* to do something bad; be guilty of [to *perpetrate* a crime]. —**per'pe·trat·ed,** *p.t. & p.p.*; **per'pe·trat·ing,** *pr.p.* —**per'pe·tra'tion,** *n.* —**per'pe·tra'tor,** *n.*

per·pet·u·al (pər pech'oo əl), *adj.* **1.** lasting forever or for a long time. **2.** continuing; constant [a *perpetual* nag]. —**per·pet'u·al·ly,** *adv.*

per·pet·u·ate (pər pech'oo āt), *v.* to cause to continue or be remembered [The Rhodes scholarships *perpetuate* the memory of Cecil Rhodes.] —**per·pet'u·at·ed,** *p.t. & p.p.*; **per·pet'u·at·ing,** *pr.p.* —**per·pet'u·a'tion,** *n.*

per·pe·tu·i·ty (pŭr'pə tōō'ə tē *or* pŭr'pə tyōō'ə-tē), *n.* the condition of being perpetual; existence forever. —**in perpetuity,** forever.

per·plex (pər pleks'), *v.* to make unsure of what to do; fill with doubt; confuse or puzzle [Her strange silence *perplexed* him.]

per·plex·i·ty (pər plek'sə tē), *n.* **1.** the condition of being perplexed or in great doubt. **2.** something that confuses or puzzles. —**per·plex'i·ties,** *pl. for meaning 2.*

per·qui·site (pŭr'kwə zit), *n.* something in addition to a worker's regular pay, as a tip.

per·se·cute (pŭr'sə kyōōt), *v.* to keep on treating in a cruel or harsh way, especially for holding certain beliefs or ideas; harass. —**per'se·cut·ed,** *p.t. & p.p.*; **per'se·cut·ing,** *pr.p.* —**per'se·cu'tion,** *n.* —**per'se·cu'tor,** *n.*

Per·seph·o·ne (pər sef'ə nē), *n.* the Greek name for **Proserpina.**

per·se·ver·ance (pŭr'sə vir'əns), *n.* the act of persevering, or the patience to persevere; persistence; continued efforts.

per·se·vere (pŭr sə vir'), *v.* to stick to a task or purpose, no matter how hard or troublesome; persist [Columbus *persevered* in sailing west, even though his crew was discouraged.] —**per·se·vered',** *p.t. & p.p.*; **per·se·ver'ing,** *pr.p.*

Per·sia (pŭr'zhə), *n.* the old name of **Iran.** —**Per'sian,** *adj. & n.*

Persian Gulf, the part of the Arabian Sea between Arabia and Iran.

per·si·flage (pŭr'si fläzh), *n.* playful or joking talk; banter.

per·sim·mon (pər sim'ən), *n.* **1.** an orange-colored fruit that looks like a plum and has several large seeds in it. It is very sour when green, but sweet when ripe. **2.** the tree this fruit grows on.

per·sist (pər sist'), *v.* **1.** to refuse to give up; go on in a stubborn way [He *persisted* in his courtship until she said "yes."] **2.** to say or do over and over again [He *persists* in calling me "Shorty."] **3.** to last for some time; continue [The pain *persisted* all day.]

persimmons

per·sist·ent (pər sis'tənt), *adj.* **1.** refusing to give up; steady and determined [a *persistent* job seeker]. **2.** lasting for some time; going on and on [a *persistent* rain]. —**per·sist'ence** or **per·sist'en·cy,** *n.* —**per·sist'ent·ly,** *adv.*

per·son (pŭr's'n), *n.* **1.** a human being; man, woman, or child [every *person* in this room]. **2.** the body or bodily appearance [She was neat and clean about her *person.*] **3.** any of the three classes of pronouns which show whether the person or thing referred to is speaking, being spoken to, or being spoken of. The **first person** (*I* or *we*) is used for the speaker; the **second person**

(*you*) for the one spoken to; the **third person** (*he*, *she*, *it* or *they*) for the one spoken of. Most verbs in English have a special form for the third person singular (he *has*, she *walks*, it *falls*); the verb *to be* has special forms for other persons (I *am*, you *are*, they *were*). —**in person**, actually present, not in a movie, on a record, etc.

per·son·a·ble (pŭr′s'n ə b'l), *adj.* pleasing in looks and manner; attractive.

per·son·age (pŭr′s'n ij), *n.* a person; especially, a famous or important person.

per·son·al (pŭr′s'n əl), *adj.* **1.** of or having to do with a certain person; private; individual [a *personal* opinion; a *personal* secretary]. **2.** done, made, learned, etc. by oneself, without the help of others [Do you have *personal* knowledge of this matter?] **3.** of the body [*personal* fitness]. **4.** having to do with the way a person looks, acts, etc. [a *personal* remark]. **5.** showing person in grammar ["I," "you," and "it" are *personal* pronouns.] **6.** describing property that can be moved or is not attached to, or a part of, the land [Furniture is *personal* property.] —*n.* a newspaper advertisement about a personal matter.

per·son·al·i·ty (pŭr′sə nal′ə tē), *n.* **1.** all the special qualities of a person which make him different from other people. **2.** personal qualities that attract others to one; charm, energy, cleverness, etc. [She is beautiful, but has no *personality*.] **3.** a person; especially, a very unusual or famous person. **4.** an impolite remark criticizing the way a certain person looks, acts, etc. [Let's avoid *personalities*.] —**per′son·al′i·ties,** *pl.*

per·son·al·ize (pŭr′s'n əl īz), *v.* to make personal; make for one person only [*Personalized* bank checks are printed with one's name.] —**per′son·al·ized,** *p.t. & p.p.;* **per′son·al·iz·ing,** *pr.p.*

per·son·al·ly (pŭr′s'n əl ē), *adv.* **1.** by oneself, without the help of others [I'll ask him *personally*.] **2.** as a person [I dislike the artist *personally*, but I respect his talent.] **3.** speaking for oneself [*Personally*, I think you're right.] **4.** as though aimed at oneself [She took his remark *personally*.]

per·son·i·fy (pər sän′ə fī), *v.* **1.** to think of or show some idea or thing as a person [A ship is *personified* when it is referred to as "she."] **2.** to be a good example of some quality, idea, etc. [Tom Sawyer *personifies* the spirit of boyhood.] —**per·son′i·fied,** *p.t. & p.p.;* **per·son′i·fy·ing,** *pr.p.* —**per·son′i·fi·ca′tion,** *n.*

per·son·nel (pŭr sə nel′), *n.* persons employed in any work, service, etc. [office *personnel*].

per·spec·tive (pər spek′tiv), *n.* **1.** the way things look from a given point according to their size, shape, distance, etc. [*Perspective* makes railroad tracks seem to come together in the distance.] **2.** the art of picturing things so that they seem close

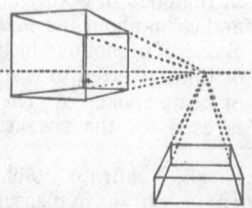

drawings showing perspective

or far away, big or small, etc., just as they look to the eye when viewed from a given point. **3.** a certain point of view in understanding or judging things or happenings, especially one that shows them in their true relations to one another [Working in a factory gave him a new *perspective* on labor problems.]

per·spi·ca·cious (pŭr′spi kā′shəs), *adj.* able to understand and judge things clearly; wise. —**per·spi·cac′i·ty** (pŭr′spi kas′ə tē), *n.*

per·spic·u·ous (pər spik′yōō əs), *adj.* easy to understand. —**per·spi·cu·i·ty** (pŭr′spi kyōō′- ə tē), *n.*

per·spi·ra·tion (pŭr′spə rā′shən), *n.* **1.** the act of perspiring, or sweating. **2.** sweat.

per·spire (pər spīr′), *v.* to sweat. —**per·spired′,** *p.t. & p.p.;* **per·spir′ing,** *pr.p.*

per·suade (pər swād′), *v.* to get someone to do or believe something, as by making it seem like a good idea; convince. —**per·suad′ed,** *p.t. & p.p.;* **per·suad′ing,** *pr.p.*

per·sua·sion (pər swā′zhən), *n.* **1.** a persuading or being persuaded. **2.** the ability to persuade. **3.** a belief; often, a particular religious belief [a man of the Moslem *persuasion*].

per·sua·sive (pər swā′siv), *adj.* able or likely to persuade [a *persuasive* argument]. —**per·sua′sive·ly,** *adv.* —**per·sua′sive·ness,** *n.*

pert (pŭrt), *adj.* lively in a way that is too bold; saucy [a *pert* child; a *pert* remark].

per·tain (pər tān′), *v.* **1.** to belong; be connected; be a part [lands *pertaining* to an estate]. **2.** to have to do with; be related in some way; have reference [laws that *pertain* to civil rights].

per·ti·na·cious (pŭr′tə nā′shəs), *adj.* continuing in a stubborn way to do, believe, or want something; persistent [a *pertinacious* salesman]. —**per·ti·nac′i·ty** (pŭr′tə nas′ə tē), *n.*

per·ti·nent (pŭr′t'n ənt), *adj.* having some connection with the subject that is being considered; to the point [a *pertinent* question]. —**per′ti·nence,** *n.*

per·turb (pər tŭrb′), *v.* to make worried or upset; trouble the mind of [I became *perturbed* when he failed to arrive.] —**per·tur·ba·tion** (pŭr′tər bā′shən), *n.*

Pe·ru (pə rōō′), *n.* a country on the western coast of South America. —**Pe·ru·vi·an** (pə- rōō′vi ən), *adj. & n.*

pe·rus·al (pə rōō′z'l), *n.* the act of perusing.

pe·ruse (pə rōōz′), *v.* to read; especially, to read through carefully. —**pe·rused′,** *p.t & p.p.;* **pe·rus′ing,** *pr.p.*

per·vade (pər vād′), *v.* to spread through every part of [Joy *pervades* his poems.] —**per·vad′ed,** *p.t. & p.p.;* **per·vad′ing,** *pr.p.*

per·va·sive (pər vā′siv), *adj.* tending to spread through every part [a *pervasive* odor].

per·verse (pər vŭrs′), *adj.* **1.** continuing in a stubborn way to do what is wrong or harmful [The *perverse* man continued to smoke, against his doctor's orders.] **2.** morally wrong; wicked [Cruelty to animals is a *perverse* act.] —**per·verse′ly,** *adv.* —**per·verse′ness,** *n.* —**per·ver′si·ty,** *n.*

per·ver·sion (pər vûr′zhən), *n.* **1.** a turning to what is wrong or harmful. **2.** a wrong or unhealthy form of something.

per·vert (pər vûrt′), *v.* **1.** to lead away from what is good or right [Too much candy can *pervert* one's appetite.] **2.** to give a wrong meaning to; distort. —*n.* (pûr′vərt), a perverted person.

pes·ky (pes′kē), *adj.* annoying or troublesome: *used only in everyday talk.* —**pes′ki·er,** *compar.;* **pes′ki·est,** *superl.*

pe·so (pā′sō), *n.* the basic unit of money in some countries where Spanish is spoken, as Mexico, Cuba, etc. —**pe′sos,** *pl.*

pes·si·mism (pes′ə miz′m), *n.* **1.** a gloomy feeling about life, in which one expects things to turn out badly. **2.** the belief that there is more evil than good in life. —**pes′si·mis′tic,** *adj.*

pes·si·mist (pes′ə mist), *n.* a person who expects things to turn out badly.

pest (pest), *n.* **1.** a person or thing that causes trouble; especially, a destructive insect or small animal. **2.** a plague: *an older use.*

pes·ter (pes′tər), *v.* to keep on bothering or annoying [to *pester* someone with questions].

pes·ti·cide (pes′tə sīd), *n.* any poison used to kill insects, weeds, etc.

pes·tif·er·ous (pes tif′ər əs), *adj.* **1.** carrying or having a disease that others can catch. **2.** annoying; pesky: *used only in everyday talk.*

pes·ti·lence (pes′tə ləns), *n.* a deadly disease that spreads rapidly from person to person; plague.

pes·ti·lent (pes′tə lənt), *adj.* **1.** likely to cause death; deadly [a *pestilent* disease]. **2.** dangerous to the peace and happiness of all people [the *pestilent* threat of war].

pes·tle (pes′'l *or* pes′t'l), *n.* a tool used to pound or grind something into a powder, as in a mortar. *See the picture for* **mortar.**

pet (pet), *n.* **1.** an animal that is tamed and kept as a companion or treated in a fond way. **2.** a person who is liked or treated better than others; favorite [Dick is his uncle's *pet*.] —*adj.* **1.** kept or treated as a pet [a *pet* turtle]. **2.** liked better than others; favorite [a *pet* project of his]. **3.** showing fondness ["Doll" is her *pet* name for Dorothy.] —*v.* to stroke or pat gently [to *pet* a dog]. —**pet′ted,** *p.t. & p.p.;* **pet′ting,** *pr.p.*

pet (pet), *n.* a sulky, cross mood.

pet·al (pet′'l), *n.* any of the brightly colored leaves that make up the flower of a plant.

pet·cock (pet′käk), *n.* a small faucet for draining water or air from pipes, etc.: *see picture in next column.*

petals

Pe·ter (pē′tər), *n.* **1.** one of the twelve Apostles of Jesus: also called **Simon Peter.** **2.** either of two books of the New Testament believed to have been written by him.

Peter I, 1672–1725; czar of Russia from 1682 to 1725: also called **Peter the Great.**

pet·i·ole (pet′i ōl), *n.* the stem by which a leaf is attached to a plant.

pe·tite (pə tēt′), *adj.* small and dainty: *said of a girl or woman.*

pe·ti·tion (pə tish′ən), *n.* **1.** a strong, serious request, as a prayer. **2.** a formal, written request to someone in authority, signed by a number of people. —*v.* to make a petition to or a request for [Our town has *petitioned* the Governor for flood relief.] —**pe·ti′tion·er,** *n.*

pet·rel (pet′rəl), *n.* a small, dark sea bird with long wings.

pet·ri·fy (pet′rə fī), *v.* **1.** to change into a substance like stone by replacing the normal cells with minerals [Trees buried under lava for a great many years can become *petrified*.] **2.** to make unable to move or act, as because of fear or surprise. —**pet′ri·fied,** *p.t. & p.p.;* **pet′ri·fy·ing,** *pr.p.*

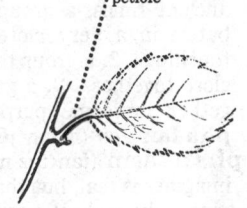
petcock

petiole

petrel (8 in. long)

pet·rol (pet′rəl), *n.* gasoline: *a British word.*

pe·tro·le·um (pə trō′li əm), *n.* an oily liquid found in the earth in certain layers of rock. We get gasoline, paraffin, fuel oil, etc. from it.

pet·ti·coat (pet′i kōt), *n.* a kind of skirt worn as an undergarment by women and girls.

pet·tish (pet′ish), *adj.* cross or peevish.

pet·ty (pet′ē), *adj.* **1.** of little importance; small; minor [*Petty* larceny is the stealing of a small thing or sum.] **2.** having or showing a narrow, mean character [full of *petty* spite]. **3.** of lower rank [a *petty* official]. —**pet′ti·er,** *compar.;* **pet′ti·est,** *superl.* —**pet′ti·ness,** *n.*

petty cash, a small sum of money kept on hand in a business to pay minor expenses.

petty officer, an enlisted man in the navy with the rank of a noncommissioned officer.

pet·u·lant (pech′oo lənt), *adj.* showing anger or annoyance over little things; peevish. —**pet′u·lance,** *n.* —**pet′u·lant·ly,** *adv.*

pe·tu·ni·a (pə tōōn′yə), *n.* a plant with flowers of various colors, shaped like funnels.

pew (pyōō), *n.* any of the benches with a back that are fixed in rows in a church: *see the picture at the top of the next page.*

pe·wee (pē′wē), *n.* the phoebe or any of several other small North American birds of the flycatcher kind.

pew·ter (pyŌŌ′tər), *n.* **1.** a grayish alloy of tin with lead, brass, or copper. **2.** things made of pewter, especially dishes, tableware, etc. —*adj.* made of pewter.

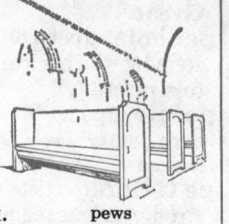
pews

pha·e·ton or **pha·ë·ton** (fā′ə t′n), *n.* a light carriage with four wheels, front and back seats, and a top that could be folded back.

pha·lanx (fā′langks *or* fal′angks), *n.* **1.** in ancient times, a group of soldiers arranged for battle in a very close formation, with shields touching. **2.** a group of persons or things massed close together. **3.** a group of persons joined together for some purpose. —**pha′lanx·es** or **pha·lan·ges** (fə lan′jēz), *pl.*

phan·tasm (fan′taz′m), *n.* something that one imagines is real, but that exists only in the mind; especially, a ghost or specter.

phan·ta·sy (fan′tə sē), *n.* same as **fantasy.** —**phan′ta·sies,** *pl.*

phan·tom (fan′təm), *n.* **1.** something that one seems to see although it is not really there [the *phantoms* of a dream]. **2.** any shadowy or ghostly image; ghost. **3.** a person or thing that is not really what it seems to be or should be [He is the mere *phantom* of a leader.] —*adj.* of or like a phantom; unreal [*phantom* ships in the fog].

Phar·aoh (fer′ō), *n.* the title of the rulers of ancient Egypt.

phar·ma·ceu·ti·cal (fär′mə sŌŌ′ti k′l), *adj.* **1.** of or by drugs. **2.** of pharmacy or pharmacists. Also **phar′ma·ceu′tic.**

phar·ma·cist (fär′mə sist), *n.* a person who is trained to prepare and sell drugs and medicine according to the orders of a doctor; druggist.

phar·ma·cy (fär′mə sē), *n.* **1.** the science or work of preparing drugs and medicines according to a doctor's orders. **2.** a place where this is done; drugstore. —**phar′ma·cies,** *pl.*

phar·yn·gi·tis (far′in jī′tis), *n.* a condition in which the pharynx is inflamed.

phar·ynx (far′ingks), *n.* the place at the back of the mouth where the larynx and esophagus begin. —**phar′ynx·es** or **pha·ryn·ges** (fə rin′jēz), *pl.*

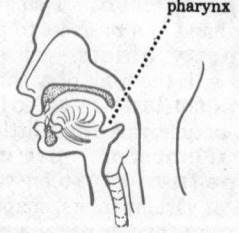
pharynx

phase (fāz), *n.* **1.** any of the sides or views of a subject by which it may be looked at, thought about, or shown; aspect [We discussed the many *phases* of the problem.] **2.** any stage in a series of changes [Adolescence is a *phase* we all go through. The moon is full in its third *phase*.] —*v.* to bring into use, or bring to an end, by stages [New equipment will be *phased* into our production line as we *phase* out old products.] —**phased,** *p.t. & p.p.;* **phas′ing,** *pr.p.*

Ph.D., abbreviation for **Doctor of Philosophy.**

pheas·ant (fez′′nt), *n.* a wild bird with a long, sweeping tail and brightly colored feathers. It is hunted as game.

pheasant (35 in. long, including tail)

phe·nix (fē′niks), *n.* same as **phoenix.**

phe·nom·e·nal (fi näm′ə n′l), *adj.* **1.** very unusual; extraordinary [a *phenomenal* success]. **2.** of or like a phenomenon or phenomena. —**phe·nom′e·nal·ly,** *adv.*

phe·nom·e·non (fi näm′ə nän), *n.* **1.** any fact, condition, or happening that can be seen, heard, etc. and described in a scientific way [A shooting star is a *phenomenon* of nature.] **2.** an unusual or remarkable person or thing [Rain is a *phenomenon* in the desert.] —**phe·nom·e·na** (fi näm′ə nə) or **phe·nom′e·nons,** *pl.*

phi·al (fī′əl), *n.* a small glass bottle; vial.

Phil·a·del·phi·a (fil′ə del′fi ə), *n.* a city in southeastern Pennsylvania.

phil·an·throp·ic (fil′ən thräp′ik), *adj.* of or showing philanthropy; generous; charitable.

phi·lan·thro·pist (fi lan′thrə pist), *n.* a person who shows his love of mankind by giving much time and money to help other people.

phi·lan·thro·py (fi lan′thrə pē), *n.* **1.** love of mankind shown by giving time and especially money to causes that help other people. **2.** something done or given by a philanthropist to help others. —**phi·lan′thro·pies,** *pl.*

phi·lat·e·ly (fi lat′′l ē), *n.* the collecting and studying of postage stamps, postmarks, etc., usually as a hobby. —**phi·lat′e·list,** *n.*

-phile (fīl *or* fil), a suffix meaning "liking" or "loving" [An *Anglophile* is a person who likes English people and their ways.]

phil·har·mon·ic (fil′här män′ik), *adj.* loving music [a *philharmonic* society]. —*n.* **Philharmonic,** a society that supports a symphony orchestra; also, such an orchestra.

Phil·ip·pines (fil′ə pēnz), *n.* a country in the Pacific, north of Indonesia, made up of more than 7,000 islands. —**Phil′ip·pine,** *adj.*

Phi·lis·tine (fə lis′tin *or* fil′əs tēn), *n.* **1.** a member of an ancient people in southwestern Palestine who were enemies of the Israelites. **2.** a person who is narrow-minded and has very ordinary tastes and ideas; one who does not have and does not want culture and learning.

phi·lol·o·gy (fi läl′ə jē), *n.* an earlier name for **linguistics.** —**phi·lol′o·gist,** *n.*

phi·los·o·pher (fi läs′ə fər), *n.* **1.** a person who studies philosophy. **2.** a person who lives by a certain philosophy. **3.** a person who meets everything that happens in a calm, brave way.

phil·o·soph·ic (fil′ə säf′ik) or **phil·o·soph·i·cal** (fil′ə säf′i k′l), *adj.* **1.** of philosophy or philosophers. **2.** calm and brave; reasonable [He was *philosophic* about losing his wallet.] —**phil′o·soph′i·cal·ly,** *adv.*

phi·los·o·phize (fi läs′ə fīz), *v.* to think or reason like a philosopher [to *philosophize* about the meanings of good and evil]. **—phi·los'o-phized,** *p.t. & p.p.;* **phi·los'o·phiz·ing,** *pr.p.*

phi·los·o·phy (fi läs'ə fē), *n.* **1.** the study of man's thinking about the meaning of life, the relationship of mind to matter, the problems of right and wrong, etc. [*Philosophy* includes ethics, logic, metaphysics, etc.] **2.** a system of principles that comes from such study [Plato's *philosophy*]. **3.** calmness and wisdom in meeting problems. **—phi·los'o·phies,** *pl.*

phil·ter or **phil·tre** (fil'tər), *n.* a magic drink that is supposed to make one fall in love.

phlegm (flem), *n.* the thick, stringy substance that is formed in the throat and nose and is coughed up, as during a cold.

phleg·mat·ic (fleg mat'ik), *adj.* hard to make excited or active; dull and sluggish, or calm and cool [The *phlegmatic* fellow showed no concern about the coming hurricane.]

phlox (fläks), *n.* a plant having clusters of small red, pink, blue, or white flowers.

-phobe (fōb), a suffix meaning "fearing" or "disliking" [An *Anglophobe* is a person who fears or dislikes the English people and their ways.]

pho·bi·a (fō'bi ə), *n.* a strong and unreasonable fear of something [She has a *phobia* about spiders.]

phlox

Phoe·be (fē'bē), *n.* **1.** another name for Artemis, the Greek goddess of the moon. **2.** the moon: *used in poetry.*

phoe·be (fē'bē), *n.* a small bird with a greenish-brown back, light-yellow breast, and a short tuft of feathers on its head.

Phoe·bus (fē'bəs), *n.* **1.** another name for Apollo, the Greek god of the sun. **2.** the sun: *used in poetry.*

Phoe·ni·ci·a (fə nish'ə *or* fə nē'shə), *n.* an ancient country on the eastern coast of the Mediterranean Sea. **—Phoe·ni'cian,** *adj. & n.*

Phoe·nix (fē'niks), *n.* the capital of Arizona.

phoe·nix (fē'niks), *n.* a beautiful bird of Arabia in ancient myths that lived about 500 years. Then it burned itself to death and rose out of its own ashes to start another long life. The phoenix is used as a symbol of life that goes on forever.

phone (fōn), *n. & v.* telephone: *used only in everyday talk.* **—phoned,** *p.t. & p.p.;* **phon'-ing,** *pr.p.*

pho·net·ic (fə net'ik), *adj.* **1.** of the sounds made in speaking [The letters and marks used to show pronunciations in this dictionary are called *phonetic* symbols.] **2.** of phonetics. **3.** according to the way something is pronounced ["Tuf" is a *phonetic* spelling of "tough."]

pho·net·ics (fə net'iks), *n.pl.* the study of speech sounds and of ways to represent them in writing: *used with a singular verb.*

phon·ics (fän'iks *or* fō'niks), *n.pl.* **1.** the science of sound. **2.** the use of a simple system of phonetics in teaching beginners to read. *This word is used with a singular verb.*

pho·no·graph (fō'nə graf), *n.* an instrument for playing records with sound grooves on them. **—pho'no·graph'ic,** *adj.*

pho·ny or **pho·ney** (fō'nē), *adj.* not real or genuine; fake; false. **—n.** a person or thing that is not really what it is supposed to be; a fake. *This is a slang word.* **—pho'ni·er,** *compar.;* **pho'ni·est,** *superl.* **—pho'nies,** *pl.*

phos·phate (fäs'fāt), *n.* **1.** a chemical salt having phosphorus in it. **2.** a fertilizer containing such salts. **3.** a soft drink made of soda water and flavored sirup.

phos·pho·res·cence (fäs'fə res''ns), *n.* **1.** the act or power of giving off light without heat or burning, as phosphorus does. **2.** such a light. **—phos'pho·res'cent,** *adj.*

phos·phor·ic (fäs fôr'ik) or **phos·pho·rous** (fäs'fər əs), *adj.* of, like, or containing phosphorus.

phos·pho·rus (fäs'fər əs), *n.* a chemical element that in its ordinary pure form is a white or yellow waxy solid. In this form it glows in the dark, starts burning at room temperature, and is very poisonous.

pho·to (fō'tō), *n.* a photograph: *used only in everyday talk.* **—pho'tos,** *pl.*

pho·to·e·lec·tric cell (fō'tō i lek'trik), same as **electric eye.**

pho·to·en·grav·ing (fō'tō in grāv'ing), *n.* **1.** a method of copying photographs onto printing plates. **2.** such a plate or a print made from it.

pho·to·flash (fō'tə flash), *n.* an electric bulb that burns out in one bright flash of light, used in taking photographs.

pho·to·gen·ic (fō'tə jen'ik), *adj.* that looks attractive in photographs [a *photogenic* person].

pho·to·graph (fō'tə graf), *n.* a picture made with a camera. **—v. 1.** to take a photograph of. **2.** to look a certain way in photographs [He always *photographs* taller than he is.]

pho·tog·ra·pher (fə täg'rə fər), *n.* a person who takes photographs, especially for a living.

pho·to·graph·ic (fō'tə graf'ik), *adj.* **1.** of or like photography [in *photographic* detail]. **2.** used in or made by photography [*photographic* equipment]. **—pho'to·graph'i·cal·ly,** *adv.*

pho·tog·ra·phy (fə täg'rə fē), *n.* the art or method of making pictures by means of a camera. See **camera.**

pho·to·syn·the·sis (fō'tə sin'thə sis), *n.* the forming of sugars and starches in plants from water and carbon dioxide, when sunlight acts upon the chlorophyll in the plant.

phrase (frāz), *n.* **1.** a group of words that is not a complete sentence, but that gives a single idea, usually as a separate part of a sentence ["Drinking fresh milk," "with meals," and "to be

fat, āpe, cär, ten, ēven, hit, bīte, gō, hôrn, tōōl, book, up, fũr;
get, joy, yet, chin, she, thin, *th*en; zh = s in pleasure; ' as in able (ā'b'l);
ə = a in ago, e in agent, i in sanity, o in confess, u in focus.

healthy" are *phrases*.] **2.** a short, forceful expression ["It's raining cats and dogs" is a well-known *phrase*.] **3.** a section of several measures of music, forming a separate musical idea. —*v.* to say or write in a certain way [He *phrased* his answer carefully.] —**phrased,** *p.t. & p.p.*; **phras′ing,** *pr.p.*

phra·se·ol·o·gy (frā′zi äl′ə jē), *n.* the words used and the way they are arranged; way of speaking or writing [legal *phraseology*].

Phryg·i·a (frij′i ə), *n.* an ancient country in central Asia Minor. —**Phryg′i·an,** *n. & adj.*

phys·ic (fiz′ik), *n.* **1.** a medicine for making the bowels move. **2.** the science of medicine: *an earlier name now seldom used.*

phys·i·cal (fiz′i k'l), *adj.* **1.** of nature or matter; material; natural [the *physical* universe]. **2.** of the body rather than the mind [*physical* exercise]. **3.** of or having to do with the natural sciences or the laws of nature [*physical* laws].

physical education, a course in schools that teaches the proper care of the body, as by means of games and sports.

phys·i·cal·ly (fiz′i k'l ē), *adv.* **1.** in regard to the laws of nature [It is *physically* impossible to be in two places at one time.] **2.** in regard to the body [Keep *physically* fit.]

phy·si·cian (fi zish′ən), *n.* a doctor of medicine, especially one who is not mainly a surgeon.

phys·i·cist (fiz′ə sist), *n.* an expert in physics.

phys·ics (fiz′iks), *n.pl.* the science that deals with energy and matter, and studies the ways that things are moved and work is done: *used with a singular verb* [*Physics* includes the study of electricity, light, heat, sound, and mechanics.]

phys·i·og·no·my (fiz′i äg′nə mē), *n.* the face; especially, the features of a person's face, as they make up his expression [the *physiognomy* of an honest man]. —**phys′i·og′no·mies,** *pl.*

phys·i·ol·o·gy (fiz′i äl′ə jē), *n.* the science that deals with living things and the ways in which their parts and organs work [the *physiology* of birds; plant *physiology*]. —**phys·i·o·log·i·cal** (fiz′i ə läj′i k'l), *adj.* —**phys′i·ol′o·gist,** *n.*

phy·sique (fi zēk′), *n.* the form or build of one's body.

pi (pī), *n.* the symbol π that stands for the ratio of the circumference of a circle to its diameter: π equals about 3.14159.

pi·a·nis·si·mo (pē′ə nis′ə mō), *adj. & adv.* very soft: an Italian word used as a direction in music.

pi·an·ist (pi an′ist *or* pē′ə nist), *n.* a person who plays the piano.

pi·an·o (pi än′ō), *adj. & adv.* soft: an Italian word used as a direction in music.

pi·an·o (pi an′ō), *n.* a large musical instrument with many wire strings in a case and a keyboard. When a key is struck, it makes a small hammer hit a string so that it gives out a tone. *See pictures for* **grand piano** *and* **upright.** —**pi·an′os,** *pl.*

pi·an·o·for·te (pi an′ə fôrt *or* pyan′ə fôr′tē), *n.* a piano.

pi·az·za (pi az′ə), *n.* **1.** a long porch with a roof, along the front or side of a building. **2.** a public square in Italian towns.

pi·broch (pē′bräk), *n.* a piece of music, as a march, for playing on the bagpipe.

Pic·ar·dy (pik′ər dē), *n.* a region in northern France.

Pi·cas·so, Pa·blo (pä′blō pē kä′sō), 1881– ; Spanish artist living in France.

pic·a·yune (pik′i yōōn′), *adj.* small and not very important; trivial or petty.

pic·ca·lil·li (pik′ə lil′ē), *n.* a relish made with chopped vegetables, vinegar, and hot spices.

pic·co·lo (pik′ə lō), *n.* a small flute that sounds notes an octave higher than an ordinary flute does. —**pic′co·los,** *pl.*

piccolo

pick (pik), *n.* **1.** a heavy metal tool with a pointed head, used for breaking up soil, rock, etc. **2.** any pointed tool for picking [an ice *pick*]. **3.** a plectrum.

pick (pik), *v.* **1.** to choose or select [The judges *picked* the winner.] **2.** to scratch or dig at with the fingers or with something pointed [to *pick* the teeth with a toothpick]. **3.** to pluck or gather with the fingers or hands [to *pick* flowers]. **4.** to clean or leave bare by taking away something [To *pick* a chicken means to remove its feathers.] **5.** to look for and find [to *pick* a fight; to *pick* flaws]. **6.** to pluck the strings of [to *pick* a guitar]. **7.** to open, as a lock, with a wire, etc. instead of a key. **8.** to steal from [to *pick* pockets]. —*n.* **1.** the act of choosing, or the thing chosen; choice [Take your *pick* of these books.] **2.** the one most wanted; best [This kitten is the *pick* of the litter.] —**pick at,** to take little bites of [to *pick at* one's food]. —**pick off,** to hit with a carefully aimed shot. —**pick on,** to criticize, tease, or annoy: *used only in everyday talk.* —**pick out, 1.** to choose. **2.** to single out; find [Can you *pick* her *out* in the crowd?] —**pick over,** to examine one by one; sort out. —**pick up, 1.** to take hold of and lift. **2.** to get, find, or learn without trying [He *picks up* languages quickly.] **3.** to stop for and take along. **4.** to go faster; gain speed. **5.** to make tidy, as a room. —**pick′er,** *n.*

pick·a·back (pik′ə bak), *adv. & adj.* same as **piggyback.**

pick·ax *or* **pick·axe** (pik′aks), *n.* a pick with a point at one end of the head and a blade like a chisel's at the other end.

pickax

pick·er·el (pik′ər əl), *n.* a fresh-water fish of the pike family, with a narrow, pointed head and sharp teeth. It is used for food. —**pick′er·el** *or* **pick′er·els,** *pl.*

pick·et (pik′it), *n.* **1.** a pointed stake used in a fence, as a post to tie animals to, as a marker, etc. **2.** a soldier or soldiers used to guard troops from surprise attack. **3.** a person, as a member of a labor union on strike, standing or walking outside a factory, store, etc. to show protest. —*v.* **1.** to place pickets, or act as a picket, at a factory, store, etc. **2.** to close in with a picket fence. **3.** to tie an animal to a picket.

picket fence, a fence made of pickets.

pick·ings (pik/- ingz), *n.pl.* something picked; especially, small scraps.

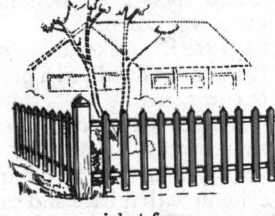
picket fence

pick·le (pik/'l), *n.* **1.** a cucumber or other vegetable pre- served in salt water, vinegar, or spicy liq- uid. **2.** a liquid of this kind used to preserve food. **3.** an unpleasant or difficult situation; trouble: *used only in everyday talk.* —*v.* to preserve in a pickle [*pickled* beets]. —**pick/led,** *p.t. & p.p.;* **pick/ling,** *pr.p.*

pick·pock·et (pik/päk'it), *n.* a person who steals from pockets or purses.

pick·up (pik/up), *n.* **1.** the act of picking up [The shortstop made a good *pickup* of the ball.] **2.** the act or power of gaining speed [Our old car still has good *pickup.*] **3.** a small truck, as one used for delivery. **4.** a device in a phonograph that changes the vibrations of the needle into electric current.

pic·nic (pik/nik), *n.* a pleasure outing during which a meal is eaten outdoors. —*v.* to have or go on a picnic. —**pic/nicked,** *p.t. & p.p.;* **pic/nick·ing,** *pr.p.* —**pic/nick·er,** *n.*

pi·cot (pē/kō), *n.* any one of the small loops forming a fancy edge on lace, ribbon, etc.

pic·to·ri·al (pik tôr/i əl), *adj.* **1.** of or having pictures [the *pictorial* page of a newspaper]. **2.** showing something by means of pictures [a *pictorial* graph]. **3.** that forms a picture in one's mind; vivid [a *pictorial* description]. —**pic·to/ri·al·ly,** *adv.*

pic·ture (pik/chər), *n.* **1.** a likeness of a person, thing, scene, etc. made by drawing, painting, or photography; also, a printed copy of this. **2.** any likeness, image, or good example [Hal is the *picture* of his father. That dog is the *picture* of laziness.] **3.** anything admired for its beauty [The garden in bloom was a *picture.*] **4.** an idea; image in the mind. **5.** a description [The book gives a clear *picture* of life in Peru.] **6.** a motion picture or an image on a television screen. —*v.* **1.** to make a picture of. **2.** to show; make clear [Joy was *pictured* in his face.] **3.** to describe or explain [Dickens *pictured* life in England.] **4.** to form an idea or picture in the mind; imagine [You can *picture* how pleased I was!] —**pic/- tured,** *p.t. & p.p.;* **pic/tur·ing,** *pr.p.*

pic·tur·esque (pik chər esk/), *adj.* **1.** like a picture; having natural beauty. **2.** pleasant and charming in a strange or unfamiliar way [a

picturesque village]. **3.** giving a clear picture in the mind; vivid [a *picturesque* description].

pidg·in English (pij/in), a form of English mixed with Chinese, used by Chinese traders, sailors, etc. in dealing with foreigners.

pie (pī), *n.* a dish made up of fruit, meat, etc. baked in a pastry crust.

pie (pī), *n.* a magpie.

pie·bald (pī/bôld), *adj.* covered with large patches of two colors, often white and black, as a horse. —*n.* a piebald animal.

piece (pēs), *n.* **1.** a part broken or separated from a whole thing [The glass shattered and I swept up the *pieces.*] **2.** a part or section of a whole, thought of as complete by itself [a *piece* of meat; a *piece* of land]. **3.** any one of a set or group of things [a dinner set of 52 *pieces;* a chess *piece*]. **4.** a work of music, writing, or art [a *piece* for the piano]. **5.** a firearm, as a rifle [an old shooting *piece*]. **6.** a coin [a fifty-cent *piece*]. **7.** a single item or example [a *piece* of informa- tion]. **8.** a thing or the amount of a thing made up as a unit [to sell cloth by the *piece*]. —*v.* **1.** to add a piece or pieces to, as in making larger or repairing [to *piece* a pair of trousers]. **2.** to join the pieces of, as in mending [to *piece* together a broken jug]. —**go to pieces, 1.** to fall apart. **2.** to lose control of oneself, as in crying. —**of a piece** or **of one piece,** of the same sort; alike.

piece·meal (pēs/mēl), *adv.* **1.** piece by piece; a part at a time. **2.** into pieces. —*adj.* made or done piecemeal.

piece of eight, the silver dollar of Spain and Spanish America in earlier times.

piece·work (pēs/wûrk), *n.* work paid for at a fixed rate for each piece of work done. —**piece/- work/er,** *n.*

pied (pīd), *adj.* covered with spots of two or more colors [The *Pied* Piper wore a suit of many colors].

Pied·mont (pēd/mänt), *n.* **1.** a plateau in the southeastern United States, between the Atlantic coast and the Appalachian Mountains. **2.** a district in northwestern Italy.

pier (pir), *n.* **1.** a structure built out over water on pillars and used as a landing place, a walk, etc. **2.** a strong support for the arch of a bridge or of a building. **3.** the part of a wall between windows or other openings.

pierce (pirs), *v.* **1.** to pass into or through; penetrate [The needle *pierced* her finger. A light *pierced* the darkness.] **2.** to have a sharp effect on the senses or feelings [*pierced* by the cold]. **3.** to make a hole through; perforate; bore [to *pierce* one's ears for earrings]. **4.** to force a way into; break through [The explorer *pierced* the jungle.] **5.** to understand [to *pierce* a mystery]. —**pierced,** *p.t. & p.p.;* **pierc/ing,** *pr.p.*

Pierce, Franklin (pirs), 1804–1869; 14th president of the U. S., from 1853 to 1857.

Pierre (pir), *n.* the capital of South Dakota.

---

fat, āpe, cär, ten, ēven, hit, bīte, gō, hôrn, tōol, book, up, fûr; get, joy, yet, chin, she, thin, *th*en; zh = s in pleasure; ' as in able (ā/b'l); ə = a in ago, e in agent, i in sanity, o in confess, u in focus.

pi·e·ty (pī'ə tē), *n.* **1.** the condition of being pious, or very strict in following one's religion. **2.** loyalty and a sense of duty toward one's parents, family, etc. **3.** a pious act, statement, etc. —**pi'e·ties,** *pl.*

pig (pig), *n.* **1.** an animal with a long, broad snout and a thick, fat body covered with coarse bristles; swine; hog. It is raised for its meat. **2.** a young hog. **3.** a person thought of as like a pig in being greedy, filthy, etc.: *used only in every-day talk.* **4.** a casting of metal that has been poured in a mold from the smelting furnace.

pig (2 ft. high)

pi·geon (pij'ən), *n.* a bird with a small head, plump body, and short legs; dove.

pi·geon·hole (pij'ən hōl), *n.* **1.** a small hole for pigeons to nest in; usually, one of a series of such holes. **2.** a small open box, as in a desk, for filing papers, etc.; usually, one of a series of such boxes. —*v.* **1.** to put in a pigeonhole of a desk, etc. **2.** to lay aside, where it is likely to be ignored or forgotten [The governor *pigeonholed* the plan for a new hospital.] **3.** to arrange according to a system; classify. —**pi'geon·holed,** *p.t. & p.p.;* **pi'geon·hol·ing,** *pr.p.*

pigeon (10 in. long)

pi·geon-toed (pij'ən tōd'), *adj.* having the feet turned in toward each other.

pig·gish (pig'ish), *adj.* like a pig; greedy; filthy. —**pig'gish·ly,** *adv.* —**pig'gish·ness,** *n.*

pig·gy·back (pig'ē·bak), *adv. & adj.* **1.** on the shoulders or back [to carry a child *piggyback*]. **2.** of or by a transportation system in which loaded truck trailers are carried on railroad flatcars: *usually written* **piggy-back.**

piggy bank, a small bank, often shaped like a pig, with a slot for putting coins into it.

pig·head·ed (pig'hed'id), *adj.* stubborn.

a piggyback ride

pig iron, crude iron, as it comes from the blast furnace.

pig·ment (pig'mənt), *n.* **1.** coloring matter, usually a powder, mixed with oil, water, etc. to make paints. **2.** the matter in the cells and tissues that gives color to plants and animals.

Pig·my (pig'mē), *adj. & n.* same as **Pygmy.** —**Pig'mies,** *pl.*

pig·pen (pig'pen), *n.* **1.** a pen where pigs are kept. **2.** any place that is very dirty.

pig·skin (pig'skin), *n.* **1.** the skin of a pig. **2.** leather made from this. **3.** a football: *used only in everyday talk.*

pig·sty (pig'stī), *n.* a pigpen. —**pig'sties,** *pl.*

pig·tail (pig'tāl), *n.* a long braid of hair hanging at the back of the head.

pike (pīk), *n.* a turnpike, or road with tollgates.

pike (pīk), *n.* a long wooden shaft with a sharp metal head, once used as a weapon by soldiers.

pike (pīk), *n.* a slender, fresh-water fish with a pointed snout and a lower jaw that sticks out.

Pikes Peak or **Pike's Peak** (pīks), a mountain in central Colorado.

pike·staff (pīk'staf), *n.* the wooden handle of a pike or spear.

pi·las·ter (pi las'tər), *n.* a support that is part of a wall and juts out a bit from it. It looks like a column with a base and capital.

pike (1 to 4 ft. long)

Pi·late, Pon·tius (pän'shəs *or* pän'ti əs pī'lət), the Roman governor of Judea when Jesus was crucified.

pile (pīl), *n.* **1.** a mass of things heaped together [a *pile* of leaves]. **2.** a heap of wood, etc. on which a corpse or sacrifice is burned. **3.** a large building or group of buildings. **4.** a large amount: *used only in everyday talk* [a *pile* of work]. **5.** in physics, same as **reactor.** —*v.* **1.** to put or set in a pile; heap up [to *pile* rubbish]. **2.** to gather or collect in heaps; accumulate [Letters *piled* up on his desk.] **3.** to cover with a heap or large amount [He *piled* the cart with hay.] **4.** to move together in a confused way; crowd [The football fans *piled* into the stadium.] —**piled,** *p.t. & p.p.;* **pil'ing,** *pr.p.*

pilaster

pile (pīl), *n.* **1.** the thick soft nap, as on a rug, made of loops of yarn that are either cut to make a velvety surface, or left uncut. **2.** soft, fine hair, as on fur or wool.

pile (pīl), *n.* a long, heavy beam or concrete column driven into the ground, sometimes under water, to support a bridge, dock, etc.

pile driver, a machine with a heavy weight that is raised and then dropped, used to drive piles.

pil·fer (pil'fər), *v.* to steal small sums or things of little value; filch.

pil·grim (pil'grim), *n.* **1.** a person who travels to a holy place or shrine. **2.** a person who travels about; wanderer. **3. Pilgrim,** any of the group of English Puritans who founded a colony in Plymouth, Massachusetts in 1620.

pil·grim·age (pil'grə mij), *n.* **1.** a journey made by a pilgrim to a holy place or shrine. **2.** any long journey.

pill (pil), *n.* a little ball of medicine to be swallowed whole.

pil·lage (pil'ij), *v.* to rob or plunder with wild force, as in war. —*n.* plunder; loot. —**pil'-laged,** *p.t. & p.p.;* **pil'lag·ing,** *pr.p.*

pil·lar (pil'ər), *n.* **1.** a long, slender, upright structure used as a support for a roof, etc. or as a monument; column. **2.** any person or thing thought of as like a pillar; a main support [a *pillar* of cloud; men who are *pillars* of society].

—from pillar to post, from one difficulty to another.

pil·lion (pil′yən), *n.* a seat behind the saddle on a horse or motorcycle, for an extra rider.

pil·lo·ry (pil′ə rē), *n.* a wooden board with holes in which the head and hands can be locked. At one time pillories were set up in public places and used to punish wrong-doers. —*v.* **1.** to punish by placing in a pillory. **2.** to present in such a way that people will be scornful or full of contempt [to *pillory* a man in a newspaper]. —**pil′lo·ries,** *pl.*

pillory

—**pil′lo·ried,** *p.t. & p.p.;* **pil′lo·ry·ing,** *pr.p.*

pil·low (pil′ō), *n.* a bag or case filled with feathers, foam rubber, air, etc., used to rest the head on, as in sleeping. —*v.* **1.** to rest as on a pillow. **2.** to be a pillow for [Roll up a blanket to *pillow* his head.]

pil·low·case (pil′ō kās′), *n.* a cloth covering for a pillow, that can be removed for washing.

pil·low·slip (pil′ō slip′), *n.* same as **pillow-case.**

pi·lot (pī′lət), *n.* **1.** a person who steers a ship; often, one whose job is steering ships in and out of harbors or through difficult waters. **2.** a person who flies an airplane, airship, etc. **3.** a guide or leader. **4.** a device that guides the action of a machine or machine part. —*v.* **1.** to act as a pilot of, on, in, or over. **2.** to guide or lead [to *pilot* a team to a championship].

pilot light, a small gas burner kept burning for use in lighting a main burner when needed.

pi·men·to (pi men′tō) or **pi·mien·to** (pi-myen′tō), *n.* a kind of garden pepper or its sweet, red fruit, used as a relish, for stuffing olives, etc. —**pi·men′tos** or **pi·mien′tos,** *pl.*

pim·per·nel (pim′pər nel), *n.* a plant with scarlet or blue flowers that close in bad weather.

pim·ple (pim′p'l), *n.* a small swelling of the skin that is red and sore. —**pim′ply,** *adj.*

pin (pin), *n.* **1.** a short piece of thin, stiff wire with a pointed end and a flat or round head, for fastening things together. **2.** a brooch or badge with a pin or clasp for fastening it to the clothing [a fraternity *pin*]. **3.** a small, thin rod of wood, metal, etc., used for fastening things together, hanging things on, etc. **4.** a clothespin, hairpin, rolling pin, safety pin, etc. **5.** any of the wooden clubs at which the ball is rolled in bowling. **6. pins,** *pl.* the legs: *used only in everyday talk.* —*v.* **1.** to fasten as with a pin. **2.** to hold firmly in one position [The wrestler *pinned* his opponent to the floor.] —**on pins and needles,** worried or anxious. —**pin one down,** to get one to tell what his real opinions, plans, etc. are. —**pin something on one,** to lay blame for something

on one. —**pinned,** *p.t. & p.p.;* **pin′ning,** *pr.p.*

pin·a·fore (pin′ə fôr), *n.* **1.** a garment without sleeves, like a kind of apron, worn by little girls over the dress. **2.** a house dress without sleeves, worn by women.

pinafore

pince-nez (pans′nā′ *or* pins′-nā′), *n.* eyeglasses kept in place by a spring that grips the bridge of the nose. —**pince′-nez′,** *pl.*

pin·cers (pin′sərz), *n.pl.* **1.** a tool used in gripping or nipping things. *See the picture.* **2.** the large claws of a crab, lobster, etc.

pinch (pinch), *v.* **1.** to squeeze between a finger and the thumb or between two surfaces [He gently *pinched* the baby's cheek. She *pinched* her finger in the door.] **2.** to press upon in a painful way [These new shoes *pinch* my toes.] **3.** to make look thin, gaunt, etc. [The illness had *pinched* his face.] **4.** to be stingy or thrifty [He *pinched* and saved for years to buy the car.] **5.** to steal: *slang in this meaning.* **6.** to arrest: *slang in this meaning.* —*n.* **1.** a pinching; squeeze; nip [a *pinch* on the arm]. **2.** the amount that can be picked up between the finger and thumb [a *pinch* of salt]. **3.** hardship; difficulty [the *pinch* of poverty]. **4.** an emergency [He will help us in a *pinch*.] **5.** an arrest: *slang in this meaning.*

pincers

pinch·ers (pin′chərz), *n.pl.* same as **pincers.**

pinch-hit (pinch′hit′), *v.* **1.** in baseball, to bat in place of the batter whose turn it is. **2.** to take the place of, in an emergency. —**pinch′-hit′,** *p.t. & p.p.;* **pinch′-hit′ting,** *pr.p.*

pin·cush·ion (pin′koosh ən), *n.* a small cushion in which pins and needles are stuck to keep them handy.

pine (pīn), *n.* **1.** an evergreen tree with cones and clusters of leaves shaped like needles. **2.** the wood of this tree, used in building.

pine (pīn), *v.* **1.** to become thin or weak through sorrow, longing, etc. [The jilted lover *pined* away.] **2.** to have a strong longing; yearn [to *pine* for the old days]. —**pined,** *p.t. & p.p.;* **pin′ing,** *pr.p.*

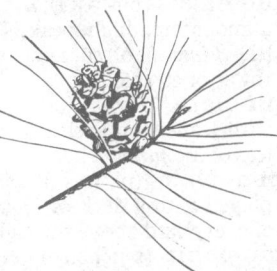

pine cone and leaves

pine·ap·ple (pīn/ap′'l), *n.* **1.** a juicy tropical fruit that looks a little like a large pine cone. **2.** the plant it grows on, having a short stem and curved leaves with prickly edges.

pineapple

pin·feath·er (pin/feth′ər), *n.* a feather that has just started to grow through the skin.

ping-pong (ping/pông′), *n.* same as **table tennis. Ping-Pong** is a trademark.

pin·hole (pin/hōl), *n.* a tiny hole of a kind that might be made by a pin.

pin·ion (pin/yən), *n.* a small gearwheel which meshes with a larger gearwheel or a rack.

pin·ion (pin/yən), *n.* **1.** the end joint of a bird's wing. **2.** a bird's wing. **3.** any wing feather. —*v.* **1.** to cut off a pinion of a bird or bind its wings, to keep it from flying. **2.** to bind a person's arms to keep him from moving them.

pink (pingk), *n.* **1.** a plant with pale-red flowers having five petals. **2.** pale red. —*adj.* pale-red. —**in the pink,** in very good condition; in fine form. —**pink/ish,** *adj.*

pink (pingk), *v.* **1.** to cut cloth with special shears (called **pinking shears**) so that it has a toothed edge, to keep it from unraveling or for decoration. **2.** to decorate with small holes in a pattern. **3.** to prick, as with a sword.

pinking shears

pink·eye (pingk/ī), *n.* a disease in which the lining of the eyelid becomes red and sore.

pink·ie or **pink·y** (pingk/ē), *n.* the smallest finger. — **pink/ies,** *pl.*

pin money, a small sum of money set aside for personal expenses, as by a housewife.

pin·nace (pin/is), *n.* **1.** a small sailing ship. **2.** a small boat carried by a ship.

pin·na·cle (pin/ə k'l), *n.* **1.** a pointed top, as of a mountain; high peak. **2.** the highest point [the *pinnacle* of success]. **3.** a slender, pointed tower or steeple.

pin·nate (pin/āt), *adj.* **1.** like a feather. **2.** with leaflets on each side of the stem [Hickory leaves are *pinnate*.]

pi·noch·le (pē/nuk′'l), *n.* a game of cards played with a deck of 48 cards, made up of two of every card above the eight.

pin·point (pin/point), *v.* to show the exact location of something, as on a map.

pint (pīnt), *n.* a measure of volume equal to ½ quart [a *pint* of milk; a *pint* of berries].

pin·to (pin/tō), *adj.* marked with spots of two or more colors. —*n.* a pinto horse. —**pin/tos,** *pl.*

pin-up (pin/up′), *adj.* that can be fastened to a wall [a *pin-up* lamp; a *pin-up* picture].

pin·wheel (pin/hwēl), *n.* **1.** a small wheel made of pieces of paper, plastic, etc., pinned to a stick so that it spins in the wind. **2.** a firework that spins and sends off colored lights.

pi·o·neer (pī ə nir′), *n.* a person who goes before, opening up the way for others to follow, as an early settler or a scientist doing original work [Daniel Boone was a *pioneer* in Kentucky. Franklin was a *pioneer* in the study of electricity.] —*v.* to act as a pioneer; open up the way for others [The Wright brothers *pioneered* in air travel.]

pinwheel
(*meaning* 1)

pi·ous (pī/əs), *adj.* very strict in following one's religion; devout.

pip (pip), *n.* a small seed, as of an apple.

pip (pip), *n.* a disease of chickens, etc.

pipe (pīp), *n.* **1.** a long tube of metal, concrete, etc. through which water, gas, oil, etc. can flow. **2.** a tube with a small bowl at one end in which tobacco is smoked. **3.** a wooden or metal tube through which air is blown for making musical sounds; often, one of a set of such tubes in an organ. **4. pipes,** *pl.* a bagpipe. **5.** the call or note of a bird. —*v.* **1.** to play on a pipe. **2.** to speak or sing in a high, shrill voice ["Good morning," *piped* the children.] **3.** to move from one place to another by means of pipes [to *pipe* water into a house]. **4.** to put pipes in. —**piped,** *p.t. & p.p.;* **pip/ing,** *pr.p.*

pipe line, a long line of pipes for moving water, gas, etc.

pip·er (pīp/ər), *n.* a person who plays on a pipe, especially on a bagpipe.

pip·ing (pīp/ing), *n.* **1.** music made by pipes [the *piping* of the band]. **2.** a high, shrill sound. **3.** a cord or a narrow fold of cloth used to trim edges or seams. **4.** pipes or the material for pipes. —*adj.* sounding high and shrill [a *piping* voice]. —*adv.* so as to sizzle [*piping* hot].

pip·pin (pip/in), *n.* any of several kinds of apple.

pi·quant (pē/kənt), *adj.* **1.** sharp or spicy in a pleasant way [a *piquant* sauce]. **2.** arousing interest or curiosity [a *piquant* remark]. —**pi·quan·cy** (pē/kən sē), *n.*

pique (pēk), *n.* hurt feelings caused by being insulted, ignored, etc.; resentment [her *pique* at not being invited]. —*v.* **1.** to hurt the feelings of or make resentful [His rudeness *piqued* her.] **2.** to arouse or excite [to *pique* one's curiosity]. —**pique oneself on,** to be proud of. —**piqued,** *p.t. & p.p.;* **pi/quing,** *pr.p.*

pi·qué (pi kā′), *n.* a stiff cotton cloth with ribs or cords along the length.

pi·ra·cy (pī/rə sē), *n.* **1.** the robbing of ships on the ocean. **2.** the use of a copyrighted or patented work without the right to use it. —**pi/ra·cies,** *pl.*

pi·rate (pī/rit), *n.* a person who attacks and robs ships on the ocean. —*v.* to use a copyrighted or patented work without having the right to do so. —**pi·rat·i·cal** (pī rat/i k'l), *adj.*

pir·ou·ette (pir′ōō et′), *n.* a whirling on the toes in dancing. —*v.* to do a pirouette. —**pir′ou·et′ted,** *p.t.* & *p.p.;* **pir′ou·et′ting,** *pr.p.*

Pi·sa (pē′zə), *n.* a city in northwestern Italy. It is famous for its Leaning Tower.

pis·ta·chi·o (pis tä′shi ō *or* pistash′i ō), *n.* **1.** a sweet, greenish nut. **2.** the tree it grows on. **3.** the flavor of this nut. **4.** a light yellowish green.

pis·til (pis′t'l), *n.* the part of a flower in which the seeds grow: a single pistil is made up of a stigma, style, and ovary. See **carpel.**

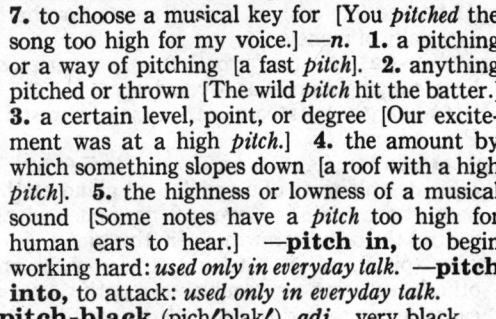

dancer doing a pirouette

pis·til·late (pis′tə lit), *adj.* having a pistil or pistils, but no stamen.

pis·tol (pis′t'l), *n.* a small gun held and fired in one hand, as a revolver.

pis·ton (pis′tən), *n.* a disk or short cylinder that moves back and forth in a hollow cylinder in which it fits closely. In a water pump, the piston pushes against the water; in a steam engine, the steam pushes against the piston.

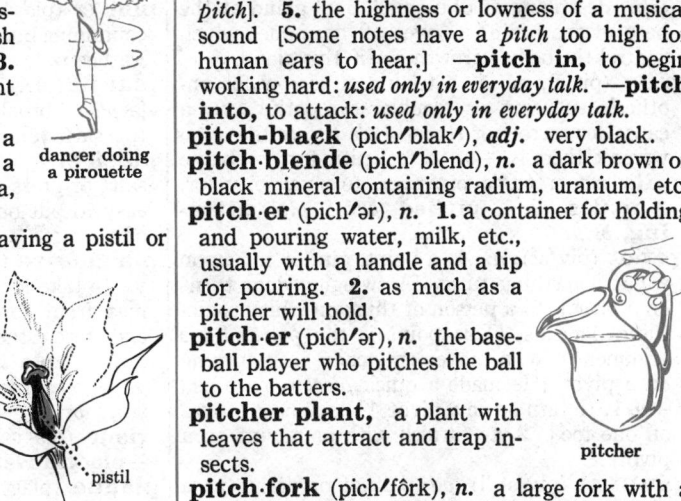

pistil

piston

piston ring, a metal ring around a piston to make it fit the cylinder closely.

piston rod, a rod fastened to a piston so as to move it or be moved by it.

pit (pit), *n.* the hard stone in the center of a peach, plum, cherry, etc., that holds the seed. —*v.* to take the pit from. —**pit′ted,** *p.t.* & *p.p.;* **pit′ting,** *pr.p.*

pit (pit), *n.* **1.** a hole in the ground, especially one dug deep, as the shaft of a coal mine. **2.** a small hollow on a surface, as a scar on the body. **3.** a hole covered lightly to catch wild animals that fall into it. **4.** a place in which animals are made to fight. **5.** the section where the orchestra sits in front of the stage. It is often lower than the main floor. —*v.* **1.** to make pits or scars in [iron *pitted* by rust]. **2.** to match or set up against [Which team is *pitted* against ours?] —**pit′ted,** *p.t.* & *p.p.;* **pit′ting,** *pr.p.*

pitch (pich), *n.* **1.** a black, sticky substance formed from coal tar, petroleum, etc. and used to cover roofs, pave streets, etc. **2.** a sticky substance found in certain evergreen trees.

pitch (pich), *v.* **1.** to throw or toss [*Pitch* the newspaper on the porch.] **2.** in baseball, to throw the ball to the batter. **3.** to set up; make ready for use [to *pitch* a tent]. **4.** to fall forward or head first. **5.** to slope downward; dip [The roof *pitches* sharply.] **6.** to be tossed so that the bow rises and falls rapidly, as a ship in a storm.

7. to choose a musical key for [You *pitched* the song too high for my voice.] —*n.* **1.** a pitching or a way of pitching [a fast *pitch*]. **2.** anything pitched or thrown [The wild *pitch* hit the batter.] **3.** a certain level, point, or degree [Our excitement was at a high *pitch*.] **4.** the amount by which something slopes down [a roof with a high *pitch*]. **5.** the highness or lowness of a musical sound [Some notes have a *pitch* too high for human ears to hear.] —**pitch in,** to begin working hard: *used only in everyday talk.* —**pitch into,** to attack: *used only in everyday talk.*

pitch-black (pich′blak′), *adj.* very black.

pitch·blende (pich′blend′), *n.* a dark brown or black mineral containing radium, uranium, etc.

pitch·er (pich′ər), *n.* **1.** a container for holding and pouring water, milk, etc., usually with a handle and a lip for pouring. **2.** as much as a pitcher will hold.

pitch·er (pich′ər), *n.* the baseball player who pitches the ball to the batters.

pitcher plant, a plant with leaves that attract and trap insects.

pitcher

pitch·fork (pich′fôrk′), *n.* a large fork with a long handle, for lifting and tossing hay, etc.

pitch pipe, a small metal pipe that sounds a fixed tone to help in tuning an instrument or in finding the right pitch.

pitch·y (pich′ē), *adj.* **1.** full of, covered with, or like pitch. **2.** black; very dark.

pitchfork

pit·e·ous (pit′i əs), *adj.* causing or deserving pity [*piteous* groans]. —**pit′e·ous·ly,** *adv.*

pit·fall (pit′fôl), *n.* **1.** a pit for trapping animals. **2.** any hidden danger.

pith (pith), *n.* **1.** the soft, spongy tissue in the center of some plant stems. **2.** the soft center of other things, as of a bone or feather. **3.** the important or necessary part [Get to the *pith* of your plan.]

pith·y (pith′ē), *adj.* **1.** of, like, or full of pith [*pithy* stems of reeds]. **2.** short and full of meaning or force [a *pithy* saying]. —**pith′i·er,** *compar.;* **pith′i·est,** *superl.* —**pith′i·ly,** *adv.*

pit·i·a·ble (pit′i ə b'l), *adj.* causing or deserving pity, sometimes mixed with scorn or contempt [his *pitiable* attempt to be witty]. —**pit′i·a·bly,** *adv.*

pit·i·ful (pit′i fəl), *adj.* **1.** causing or deserving pity [the *pitiful* sobs of the lost child]. **2.** causing or deserving contempt or scorn [What a *pitiful* repair job!] —**pit′i·ful·ly,** *adv.*

pit·i·less (pit′i lis), *adj.* having or showing no pity; cruel. —**pit′i·less·ly,** *adv.*

---

fat,   āpe,   cär,   ten,   ēven,   hit,   bīte,   gō,   hôrn,   tōōl,   book,   up,   fŭr;
get,   joy,   yet,   chin,   she,   thin,   *then;*   zh = s in pleasure;   ′ as in able (ā′b'l);
ə = a in ago,   e in agent,   i in sanity,   o in confess,   u in focus.

pit·tance (pit′əns), *n.* a small amount or share, especially of money.

pit·ter-pat·ter (pit′ər pat′ər), *n.* a series of light, tapping sounds, as of raindrops.

Pitts·burgh (pits′bərg), *n.* a city in western Pennsylvania.

pi·tu·i·tar·y (pi tōō′ə ter′ē *or* pi tyōō′ə ter′ē), *adj.* describing or of a small, oval gland at the base of the brain: it gives off hormones which control the body's growth. —*n.* this gland.

pit·y (pit′ē), *n.* **1.** a feeling of sorrow for another's suffering or trouble; sympathy. **2.** a cause for sorrow or regret [It's a *pity* that you weren't there.] —*v.* to feel pity for. —**have pity on** or **take pity on,** to show pity for. —**pit′ies,** *pl.* —**pit′ied,** *p.t. & p.p.;* **pit′y·ing,** *pr.p.*

piv·ot (piv′ət), *n.* **1.** a point, pin, or rod upon which something turns [A swinging door turns on a *pivot.*] **2.** a person or thing on which something depends [This point is the *pivot* of his argument.] **3.** a movement made as if turning on a pivot [He made a quick *pivot* to face us.] —*v.* **1.** to turn as on a pivot [The dancer *pivoted* on one toe.] **2.** to furnish with or mount on a pivot.

piv·ot·al (piv′ət 'l), *adj.* **1.** of or acting as a pivot. **2.** very important because much depends on it [a *pivotal* battle in the war].

pix·y or **pix·ie** (pik′sē), *n.* a fairy or elf. —**pix′ies,** *pl.*

piz·za (pēt′sə), *n.* an Italian dish made by baking a thin layer of dough covered with spices, tomatoes, cheese, etc.

pk., abbreviation for **peck.** —**pks.,** *pl.*

pkg., abbreviation for **package.** —**pkgs.,** *pl.*

pl., abbreviation for **plural.**

plac·ard (plak′ärd), *n.* a poster or sign put up in a public place. —*v.* to put placards on or in.

pla·cate (plā′kāt *or* plak′āt), *v.* to stop from being angry; make peaceful; soothe. —**pla′cat·ed,** *p.t. & p.p.;* **pla′cat·ing,** *pr.p.*

place (plās), *n.* **1.** a space taken up or used by a person or thing [Please take your *places.*] **2.** a city, town, or village. **3.** a house, apartment, etc. where one lives [Visit me at my *place.*] **4.** a building or space set aside for a certain purpose [a *place* of amusement]. **5.** a certain point, part, or position [a sore *place* on the leg; an important *place* in history]. **6.** rank or position, especially in a series [I finished the race in fifth *place.*] **7.** the usual or proper time or position [This is not the *place* for loud talking.] **8.** a position or job [Marie's new *place* in the bank]. **9.** the duties of any position or job [It is the judge's *place* to instruct the jury.] **10.** a short city street. —*v.* **1.** to put in a certain place, position, etc. [*Place* the pencil on the table.] **2.** to put or let rest [He *placed* his trust in God.] **3.** to recognize by connecting with some time, place, or happening [I can't *place* that man's face.] **4.** to finish in a certain position in a contest [He *placed* sixth in the race.] —**give place, 1.** to make room. **2.** to give in or yield. —**in place of,** instead of; rather than. —**take place,** to happen; occur.

—**take the place of,** to be a substitute for. —**placed,** *p.t. & p.p.;* **plac′ing,** *pr.p.*

place kick, a kick made in football while the ball is held in place on the ground, as in trying to make a field goal.

place mat, a small mat that serves as a separate table cover for each person at a meal.

plac·er (plas′ər), *n.* a deposit of sand or gravel containing bits of gold, platinum, etc., that can be washed out.

plac·id (plas′id), *adj.* calm and quiet; peaceful [a *placid* brook; a *placid* child]. —**pla·cid·i·ty** (plə sid′ə tē), *n.* —**plac′id·ly,** *adv.*

plack·et (plak′it), *n.* a slit at the waist of a skirt or dress to make it easy to put on and take off.

pla·gia·rize (plā′jə rīz), *v.* to take ideas or writings from someone else and present them as one's own. —**pla′gia·rized,** *p.t. & p.p.;* **pla′gia·riz·ing,** *pr.p.* —**pla·gia·rism** (plā′jə riz′m), *n.* —**pla′gia·rist,** *n.*

placket

plague (plāg), *n.* **1.** a deadly disease that spreads rapidly from person to person; especially, the bubonic plague. **2.** anything that causes suffering or trouble [a *plague* of mosquitoes]. —*v.* to trouble or make suffer [As a child he was *plagued* with illness.] —**plagued,** *p.t. & p.p.;* **pla′guing,** *pr.p.*

plaid (plad), *n.* **1.** a checkered pattern formed by colored bands and lines crossing each other. **2.** cloth with this pattern, especially a long woolen cloth worn over the shoulder in the Highlands of Scotland.

plain (plān), *adj.* **1.** open; clear; not blocked [a *plain* view]. **2.** easy to understand; clear to the mind [The meaning is *plain.*] **3.** without holding back what one thinks; frank [*plain* talk]. **4.** without luxury [a *plain* way of life]. **5.** simple; easy [I can do a little *plain* cooking.] **6.** not good-looking; homely. **7.** not fancy; not much decorated [a *plain* necktie]. **8.** common; ordinary [a *plain* workman]. —*n.* a large stretch of flat land. —*adv.* in a plain way; clearly. —**the Great Plains,** the broad, level land that stretches westward from the Mississippi. —**plain′ly,** *adv.* —**plain′ness,** *n.*

plaid

plains·man (plānz′mən), *n.* a person who lives on the plains. —**plains′men,** *pl.*

plain-spo·ken (plān′spō′k'n), *adj.* speaking or spoken in a plain or frank way.

plaint (plānt), *n.* **1.** a complaint. **2.** a wail of sorrow; lament: *used in poetry.*

plain·tiff (plān′tif), *n.* the person who starts a suit against another in a court of law.

plain·tive (plān′tiv), *adj.* sad or full of sorrow; mournful. —**plain′tive·ly,** *adv.*

plait (plāt *or* plat), *n.* **1.** a braid of hair, ribbon, etc. **2.** a pleat. —*v.* **1.** to braid. **2.** to pleat.

plan (plan), *n.* **1.** a method or way of doing something, that has been thought out ahead of time [vacation *plans*]. **2.** a drawing that shows how the parts of a building or piece of ground are arranged [floor *plans* of a house; a *plan* of the battlefield]. —*v.* **1.** to think out a way of making or doing something [He *planned* his escape carefully.] **2.** to make a drawing or diagram of beforehand [An architect is *planning* their new house.] **3.** to have in mind; intend [I *plan* to visit Hawaii soon.] —**planned,** *p.t. & p.p.;* **plan′ning,** *pr.p.*

plane (plān), *adj.* **1.** flat; level; even. **2.** of or having to do with flat surfaces or points, lines, etc. on them [*plane* geometry]. —*n.* **1.** a flat, level surface. **2.** a level or stage of growth or progress. **3.** an airplane.

plane (plān), *n.* a tool used by carpenters for shaving wood in order to make it smooth or level. —*v.* **1.** to make smooth or level with a plane. **2.** to take off part of, as with a plane [to *plane* off the top of a door]. —**planed,** *p.t. & p.p.;* **plan′ing,** *pr.p.*

plane

plan·et (plan′it), *n.* any of the large heavenly bodies that revolve around the sun and shine as they reflect the sun's light. The planets, in their order from the sun, are Mercury, Venus, Earth, Mars, Jupiter, Saturn, Uranus, Neptune, and Pluto. —**plan′e·tar′y,** *adj.*

plan·e·tar·i·um (plan′ə ter′i əm), *n.* a room with a large dome ceiling on which images of the heavens are cast by a special lantern. The natural movements of the sun, moon, planets, and stars can be shown in these images.

plank (plangk), *n.* **1.** a long, wide, thick board. **2.** any of the main points in the platform of a political party. —*v.* **1.** to cover with planks [to *plank* the deck of a sailboat]. **2.** to broil and serve on a plank, as steak. —**plank down, 1.** to set down with force. **2.** to pay. *This phrase is used only in everyday talk.* —**walk the plank,** to walk blindfold off a plank sticking out from the side of a ship, and be drowned. Pirates often made their victims do this.

plank·ton (plangk′tən), *n.* the mass of tiny plants and animal life found floating in a body of water, used as food by fishes.

plant (plant), *n.* **1.** any living thing that cannot move about by itself, has no sense organs, and usually makes its own food by photosynthesis [Trees, shrubs, and vegetables are *plants*.] **2.** a plant with a soft stem, as distinguished from a tree or a shrub [Ivy, grass, and mushrooms are *plants*.] **3.** the machinery, buildings, etc. of a factory or business. **4.** a factory. —*v.* **1.** to

put into the ground so that it will grow [to *plant* corn]. **2.** to place plants in a piece of land, or fish in a body of water; stock [to *plant* a garden; to *plant* trout in a pond]. **3.** to set firmly in place [*Plant* both feet squarely on the ground.] **4.** to put or fix in the mind; instill [to *plant* an idea]. **5.** to establish or found [to *plant* a colony].

plan·tain (plan′tin), *n.* a common weed with broad leaves and spikes of tiny, green flowers.

plan·tain (plan′tin), *n.* **1.** a tropical plant bearing a kind of banana. **2.** this fruit.

plan·ta·tion (plan tā′shən), *n.* **1.** a large estate, usually in a warm climate, on which crops are grown

plantain (weed)

by workers who live on the estate [a coffee *plantation* in Brazil]. **2.** a large group of trees planted for their product [a rubber *plantation*]. **3.** a colony.

plant·er (plan′tər), *n.* **1.** the owner of a plantation. **2.** a person or machine that plants. **3.** a decorated container in which plants are grown inside the house.

plaque (plak), *n.* a thin, flat piece of metal, wood, etc. with decoration or lettering on it. Plaques are hung on walls, set in monuments, etc.

plash (plash), *n. & v.* splash.

plas·ma (plaz′mə), *n.* the fluid part of blood or lymph, without the corpuscles.

plas·ter (plas′tər), *n.* **1.** a soft, sticky mixture of lime, sand, and water, used for coating walls, ceilings, etc. It becomes hard when it dries. **2.** a soft, sticky substance spread on cloth and put on the body as a medicine [a mustard *plaster*]. —*v.* **1.** to cover with or as with plaster [to *plaster* walls; to *plaster* one's hair down with hair oil]. **2.** to put on like a plaster [to *plaster* posters on a wall]. —**plas′ter·er,** *n.* —**plas′ter·ing,** *n.*

plas·ter·board (plas′tər bôrd), *n.* a board made of layers of plaster and paper, used for walls.

plaster of Paris, a thick paste of gypsum and water that hardens quickly. It is used to make statues, casts for broken bones, etc.

plas·tic (plas′tik), *adj.* **1.** that can be shaped or molded [Clay is a *plastic* material.] **2.** that gives form or shape to matter [Sculpture is a *plastic* art.] **3.** made of plastic [a *plastic* comb]. —*n.* a substance, made from various chemicals, that can be molded and hardened into many useful products. —**plas·tic·i·ty** (plas tis′ə tē), *n.*

plastic surgery, surgery in which injured parts of the body are repaired, usually by grafting on skin, bone, etc. from other places.

plat (plat), *n.* **1.** a map or plan. **2.** a small piece of ground. —*v.* to make a map or plan of. —**plat′ted,** *p.t. & p.p.;* **plat′ting,** *pr.p.*

plate (plāt), *n.* **1.** a shallow dish from which food is eaten. **2.** the food in a dish or course [Did you finish your *plate?*] **3.** a meal for one person [lunch at a dollar a *plate*]. **4.** dishes, knives, forks, spoons, etc. made of, or coated with, silver or gold. **5.** a flat, thin piece of metal, etc., especially one on which something is engraved. **6.** an illustration printed from such a plate. **7.** a solid cast of a page of type made from a mold of the set type. **8.** a sheet of metal used on boilers, as armor on ships, etc. **9.** in baseball, home plate. **10.** a set of false teeth. **11.** a sheet of glass, metal, etc. coated with a film sensitive to light. It is used in taking photographs. —*v.* **1.** to coat with gold, tin, silver, etc. **2.** to cover with metal plates, as for armor. —**plat′ed,** *p.t. & p.p.;* **plat′ing,** *pr.p.*

plate *(meaning 10)*

pla·teau (pla tō′), *n.* **1.** a broad stretch of high, level land. **2.** a period in which progress stops for a while [to reach a *plateau* in learning]. —**pla·teaus′,** *pl.*

plate·ful (plāt′fool), *n.* as much as a plate will hold. —**plate′fuls,** *pl.*

plate glass, polished, clear glass in thick sheets, used for store windows, mirrors, etc.

plat·form (plat′fôrm), *n.* **1.** a flat surface or stage higher than the ground or floor around it [a *platform* at a railroad station; a speaker's *platform*]. **2.** a statement of the principles or plans of a political party, etc.

plat·i·num (plat′n əm), *n.* a white precious metal that is a chemical element. Platinum is easily worked and does not rust much. It has many important uses in science and industry and is also much used in jewelry.

plat·i·tude (plat′ə tood *or* plat′ə tyood), *n.* a thought or saying that is stale and worn from use, especially one given as if it were new. Example: "Money doesn't always bring happiness."

Pla·to (plā′tō), *n.* 427-347 B.C.; Greek philosopher.

Pla·ton·ic (plə tän′ik), *adj.* of Plato or his philosophy.

pla·toon (plə toon′), *n.* **1.** a small group of soldiers, part of a company, usually led by a lieutenant. **2.** any small group [a *platoon* of police].

plat·ter (plat′ər), *n.* a large, shallow dish used for serving food.

plat·y·pus (plat′ə pəs), *n.* a small water animal of Australia that has webbed feet, a tail like a beaver's, and a bill like a duck's. It lays eggs, but suckles its young. Also called **duckbill** or **duck-billed platypus.** —**plat′y·pus·es** or **plat·y·pi** (plat′ə pī), *pl.*

platypus (1½ ft. long)

plau·dit (plô′dit), *n.* a strong show of approval or praise, as by a clapping of hands or cheering: *usually used in the plural,* **plaudits** [The hero received the *plaudits* of the crowd.]

plau·si·ble (plô′zə b'l), *adj.* that seems to be true, honest, fair, etc. but may not be; credible [a *plausible* excuse]. —**plau·si·bil·i·ty** (plô′zə bil′ə tē), *n.*

play (plā), *v.* **1.** to have fun; amuse oneself [to *play* with dolls]. **2.** to do in fun [to *play* a joke on one]. **3.** to take part in a game or sport [to *play* golf]. **4.** to take part in a game against [We *played* West High today.] **5.** to perform music on [She *plays* the piano.] **6.** to perform or be performed [The orchestra *played* brilliantly. What is *playing* at the movies tonight?] **7.** to act the part of [Who *played* Hamlet?] **8.** to handle in a light or careless way; trifle; toy [He merely *played* with his food.] **9.** to act in a certain way [to *play* fair]. **10.** to move quickly or lightly [A smile *played* across her face.] **11.** to make move or keep moving [to *play* a stream of water on a fire; to *play* a fish on a line]. **12.** to cause [to *play* havoc]. **13.** to bet or gamble on [to *play* the horses]. —*n.* **1.** something done just for fun or to amuse oneself; recreation [He has little time for *play*.] **2.** fun; joking [He said it in *play*.] **3.** the playing of a game [Rain halted *play*.] **4.** a move or act in a game [It's your *play*. The forward pass is an exciting *play*.] **5.** a story that is acted out, as on a stage, on radio or television, etc.; drama. **6.** movement or action, especially when quick and light [bringing his full strength into *play;* the *play* of sunlight on the waves]. **7.** freedom of movement or action [This steering wheel has too much *play*.] —**a play on words,** a pun or punning. —**play down,** to make seem not too important. —**played out, 1.** tired out. **2.** finished. —**play into someone's hands,** to let another get an advantage over one, by doing the wrong things. —**play off, 1.** to set one against another, as in a fight or contest. **2.** to break a tie by playing one more game. —**play on** or **play upon,** to make clever use of another's feelings in order to get what one wants. —**play out, 1.** to play to the finish; end. **2.** to let out little by little, as a rope; pay out. —**play up,** to give special attention to; emphasize: *used only in everyday talk.* —**play up to,** to flatter: *used only in everyday talk.*

play·er (plā′ər), *n.* **1.** a person who plays a game or a musical instrument [a baseball *player;* a trumpet *player*]. **2.** an actor.

play·ful (plā′fəl), *adj.* **1.** fond of play or fun; lively; frisky [a *playful* puppy]. **2.** said or done in fun; joking [a *playful* shove]. —**play′ful·ly,** *adv.* —**play′ful·ness,** *n.*

play·ground (plā′ground), *n.* a place, often near a school, for outdoor games and play.

play·house (plā′hous), *n.* **1.** a small house for children to play in. **2.** a theater.

playing cards, a set of cards used in playing a number of games. They are arranged in four suits: clubs, diamonds, hearts, and spades.

play·mate (plā′māt), *n.* a child who joins in fun and games with another; companion in play.

play-off (plā′ôf′), *n.* an extra game or match played to break a tie.

play·thing (plā′thing), *n.* a toy.

play·wright (plā′rīt), *n.* a person who writes plays; dramatist.

pla·za (plä′zə *or* plaz′ə), *n.* a public square or market place in a city or town.

plea (plē), *n.* **1.** an asking for help; appeal [a *plea* for mercy]. **2.** something said to defend oneself; excuse [Illness was his *plea* for being absent.] **3.** a statement made by a defendant in a law case, in answer to a charge against him [a *plea* of not guilty].

plead (plēd), *v.* **1.** to ask in a strong, serious way; beg [to *plead* for mercy]. **2.** to offer as an excuse [She *pleaded* her lack of experience.] **3.** to argue or make a plea in a law court [to *plead* guilty]. —**pleaded** or, sometimes, **plead** (pled) or **pled**, *p.t. & p.p.;* **plead′ing**, *pr.p.*

pleas·ant (plez′'nt), *adj.* **1.** that gives pleasure; bringing happiness [a *pleasant* day at the park]. **2.** having a look or manner that gives pleasure; agreeable [a *pleasant* person]. —**pleas′ant·ly**, *adv.* —**pleas′ant·ness**, *n.*

pleas·ant·ry (plez′'n trē), *n.* a pleasant joke or joking; jest. —**pleas′ant·ries**, *pl.*

please (plēz), *v.* **1.** to give pleasure to; satisfy [Nothing *pleased* him more than good music.] **2.** to be kind enough to: *used in asking for something politely* [*Please* pass the salt.] **3.** to wish or desire; like [Do as you *please*.] **4.** to be the wish of [It *pleased* the king to go.] —**pleased**, *p.t. & p.p.;* **pleas′ing**, *pr.p.*

pleas·ing (plēz′ing), *adj.* giving pleasure; enjoyable [a *pleasing* smile].

pleas·ur·a·ble (plezh′ər ə b'l), *adj.* pleasant; enjoyable.

pleas·ure (plezh′ər), *n.* **1.** a feeling of delight or satisfaction; enjoyment [He gets *pleasure* from taking long walks.] **2.** a thing that gives pleasure [It is a *pleasure* to hear her sing.] **3.** one's wish or choice [For dessert, what is your *pleasure*?]

pleat (plēt), *n.* a flat double fold in cloth, pressed or stitched in place. —*v.* to fold into pleats. —**pleat′ed**, *adj.*

ple·be·ian (pli bē′ən), *n.* **1.** a member of the lower class in ancient Rome. **2.** one of the common people. —*adj.* of or like plebeians; common.

pleb·i·scite (pleb′ə sīt), *n.* a direct vote of the people to settle some important political question.

plec·trum (plek′trəm), *n.* a small, thin piece of metal, bone, plastic, etc., used for plucking the strings of a guitar, mandolin, etc.

pled (pled), a past tense and past participle of **plead**.

pleated skirt

pledge (plej), *n.* **1.** a promise or agreement [the *pledge* of allegiance to the flag]. **2.** a thing given as a guarantee or token of something [He gave her a ring as a *pledge* of his love.] **3.** the condition of being held as a guarantee or token [She has his ring in *pledge*.] **4.** the drinking of a toast. —*v.* **1.** to promise to give [He *pledged* $100 to the building fund.] **2.** to bind by a promise [He is *pledged* to marry her.] **3.** to give as a guarantee; pawn. **4.** to drink a toast to. —**pledged**, *p.t. & p.p.;* **pledg′ing**, *pr.p.*

Ple·ia·des (plē′ə dēz), *n.pl.* a large group of stars in the constellation Taurus.

ple·na·ry (plē′nə rē *or* plen′ə rē), *adj.* **1.** full; complete; absolute [*plenary* power]. **2.** attended by all members [a *plenary* session].

plen·i·po·ten·ti·ar·y (plen′i pə ten′shi er′ē), *adj.* that has been given full power; absolute [an ambassador *plenipotentiary*]. —*n.* a person who has been given full power to act for his country in a foreign land. —**plen′i·po·ten′ti·ar′ies**, *pl.*

plen·i·tude (plen′ə tood *or* plen′ə tyood), *n.* fullness or plenty; completeness.

plen·te·ous (plen′ti əs), *adj.* plentiful.

plen·ti·ful (plen′ti fəl), *adj.* great in amount or number; plenty; more than enough [a *plentiful* food supply]. —**plen′ti·ful·ly**, *adv.*

plen·ty (plen′tē), *n.* a supply that is large enough; all that is needed [We have *plenty* of help.] —*adv.* very; quite: *used only in everyday talk* [It's *plenty* hot.]

pleth·o·ra (pleth′ə rə), *n.* too great an amount or number; excess [a *plethora* of words].

pleu·ri·sy (ploor′ə sē), *n.* a condition in which the membrane lining the chest and covering the lungs is inflamed. It causes a dry cough and painful breathing.

plex·us (plek′səs), *n.* a network, as of blood vessels, nerves, etc. See **solar plexus.**

pli·a·ble (plī′ə b'l), *adj.* **1.** easy to bend; flexible [Copper tubing is *pliable*.] **2.** easy to influence or persuade. —**pli′a·bil′i·ty**, *n.*

pli·ant (plī′ənt), *adj.* pliable.

pli·ers (plī′ərz), *n.pl.* a tool like a small pincers, used for handling small objects, for bending or cutting wire, etc.

plight (plīt), *n.* a condition or situation, especially a sad or dangerous one [the *plight* of the men trapped in the mine].

plight (plīt), *v.* to pledge or promise. —**plight one's troth,** to give one's word; especially, to promise to marry.

pliers

plinth (plinth), *n.* **1.** the square block at the base of a column, pedestal, etc. **2.** the base on which a statue is placed.

plod (pläd), *v.* **1.** to walk or move heavily or with effort [The old horse *plodded* along the street.] **2.** to work in a steady and dull way [to *plod* away at one's work]. —**plod′ded,** *p.t.* & *p.p.;* **plod′ding,** *pr.p.* —**plod′der,** *n.*

plop (pläp), *n.* the sound of something flat falling into water. —*v.* to drop with such a sound. —**plopped,** *p.t.* & *p.p.;* **plop′ping,** *pr.p.*

plot (plät), *n.* **1.** a secret plan, usually to do something bad or unlawful; conspiracy [a *plot* to overthrow the government]. **2.** the plan of action of a play, novel, etc. **3.** a small piece of ground [a *plot* for a garden]. **4.** a map or chart, as of an estate. —*v.* **1.** to plan together secretly; scheme [to *plot* against the king]. **2.** to make a map, plan, or outline of [to *plot* a ship's course]. —**plot′ted,** *p.t.* & *p.p.;* **plot′ting,** *pr.p.* —**plot′ter,** *n.*

plough (plou), *n.* & *v.* same as **plow.**

plov·er (pluv′ər *or* plō′vər), *n.* a shore bird with a short tail and long, pointed wings.

plow (plou), *n.* **1.** a tool used in farming to cut into the soil and turn it up. **2.** anything like this, as a snowplow for removing snow from a path. —*v.* **1.** to turn up the soil of with a plow [to *plow* a field]. **2.** to move, cut, etc. as if by plowing [He *plowed* his way through the crowd. Ships *plow* the waves.]

farmer plowing

plow·man (plou′mən), *n.* **1.** a man who guides a plow. **2.** a farm worker. —**plow′men,** *pl.*

plow·share (plou′sher), *n.* the cutting blade of a plow.

pluck (pluk), *v.* **1.** to pull off or out; pick [to *pluck* an apple from a tree]. **2.** to drag or snatch; grab [He *plucked* a burning stick from the fire.] **3.** to pull out the feathers of [to *pluck* a chicken]. **4.** to pull at and let go quickly [to *pluck* the strings of a guitar]. —*n.* **1.** a pulling; tug. **2.** courage to meet danger or difficulty. —**pluck up,** to become braver or more confident.

pluck·y (pluk′ē), *adj.* having or showing pluck; brave; courageous. —**pluck′i·er,** *compar.;* **pluck′i·est,** *superl.* —**pluck′i·ness,** *n.*

plug (plug), *n.* **1.** a piece of wood, rubber, etc. used to stop up a hole, drain, etc. **2.** a part with prongs or openings that connect an electrical circuit with a lamp, iron, radio, etc. **3.** a fireplug. **4.** a cake of tobacco pressed together for chewing. **5.** a worn-out horse: *slang in this meaning.* **6.** an advertisement or praising remark, especially one worked into the entertainment part of a radio or television program: *slang in this meaning.* —*v.* **1.** to stop up or close with a plug [to *plug* up a hole]. **2.** to work hard and steadily; plod: *used only in everyday talk.* **3.** to advertise with a plug: *slang in this meaning.* **4.** to hit with a bullet: *slang in this meaning.* —**plug in,** to connect to an electrical circuit. —**plugged,** *p.t.* & *p.p.;* **plug′ging,** *pr.p.*

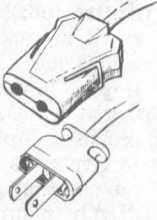
types of plug
(meaning 2)

plum (plum), *n.* **1.** a juicy fruit with a smooth skin and a smooth pit. **2.** the tree it grows on. **3.** the dark purple color of some plums. **4.** something worth getting [The new contract is a rich *plum* for the company.] **5.** a raisin: *now only in* **plum pudding,** a boiled or steamed pudding made with raisins, suet, etc.

plum·age (plōom′ij), *n.* a bird's feathers.

plumb (plum), *n.* a metal weight hung at the end of a line called a **plumb line.** It is used to find out how deep water is or whether a wall is straight up and down. —*adj.* straight up and down; vertical. —*adv.* **1.** straight down [to fall *plumb* to the ground]. **2.** completely: *used only in everyday talk* [*plumb* crazy]. —*v.* **1.** to test with a plumb. **2.** to get to the bottom of; solve [to *plumb* a mystery]. —**out of plumb** or **off plumb,** not straight up and down.

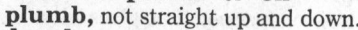

plumb

plumb·er (plum′ər), *n.* a workman who puts in and repairs the pipes and fixtures of water and gas systems in a building.

plumb·ing (plum′ing), *n.* **1.** the pipes and fixtures of water and gas systems in a building. **2.** the work of a plumber.

plume (plōom), *n.* **1.** a feather, especially a large, fluffy one. **2.** a group of these. **3.** a decoration of such a feather or feathers, worn on a hat or helmet. —*v.* **1.** to decorate with plumes. **2.** to smooth its feathers [The bird *plumed* itself.] —**plume oneself on,** to be proud because of; take credit for. —**plumed,** *p.t.* & *p.p.;* **plum′ing,** *pr.p.*

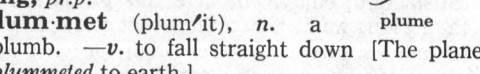
plume

plum·met (plum′it), *n.* a plumb. —*v.* to fall straight down [The plane *plummeted* to earth.]

plump (plump), *adj.* full and rounded in form; chubby [a *plump* girl]. —*v.* to fill out; puff up [to *plump* up a pillow]. —**plump′ness,** *n.*

plump (plump), *v.* to drop in a sudden or heavy way [He *plumped* himself down on the bed.] —*n.* a heavy or sudden fall, or the sound of this; thump. —*adv.* in a sudden or heavy way [He fell *plump* to the ground.] —**to plump for, 1.** to vote for. **2.** to support strongly.

plun·der (plun′dər), *v.* to rob or take from by force, as during war [The soldiers *plundered* the cities.] —*n.* **1.** the act of plundering. **2.** goods taken by force; loot; booty [the pirates' *plunder*]. —**plun′der·er,** *n.*

plunge (plunj), *v.* **1.** to throw or force suddenly [He *plunged* his hand into the water. The action *plunged* the country into war.] **2.** to dive or rush; throw oneself [She *plunged* into the pool. We *plunged* into our work.] **3.** to move in a rapid or reckless way; pitch [The car *plunged* over the cliff.] **4.** to gamble in large amounts: *used only* *in everyday talk.* —*n.* **1.** a dive or fall. **2.** a swim. **3.** a gamble; chance: *used only in everyday talk* [a *plunge* in the stock market]. —**plunged,** *p.t. & p.p.;* **plung'ing,** *pr.p.*

plung·er (plun'jər), *n.* **1.** a person who plunges. **2.** any device that works with a plunging, up-and-down motion, as a piston in an engine.

plunk (plungk), *v.* **1.** to put down or drop in a sudden or heavy way [He *plunked* down his money. The stone *plunked* into the water.] **2.** to pluck or strum, as on a banjo. **3.** to make a twanging sound, as a banjo. —*n.* a plunking or the sound made by plunking.

plu·ral (ploor'əl), *adj.* showing that more than one is meant [The *plural* form of "box" is "boxes."] —*n.* the form of a word which shows that more than one is meant. The plurals of most English words are formed by adding -*s* or -*es* (hat, hats; glass, glasses), but some plurals are formed in different ways (man, men; child, children). For some words there is no change for the plural (sheep, sheep).

plu·ral·i·ty (ploo ral'ə tē), *n.* **1.** the condition or fact of being plural. **2.** a great number; multitude. **3.** more than half of a total; majority. **4.** the number of votes that the winner of an election has over those received by the next highest candidate [If Smith gets 65 votes, Jones gets 40, and Brown gets 35, then Smith has a *plurality* of 25.] —**plu·ral'i·ties,** *pl.*

plus (plus), *prep.* **1.** added to [Two *plus* two equals four (2 + 2 = 4).] **2.** and in addition [It costs $10 *plus* tax.] —*adj.* **1.** more than zero; positive [a *plus* quantity]. **2.** a little more than [a grade of C *plus*]. **3.** having added or gained: *used only in everyday talk* [I'm *plus* a dollar.] —*n.* the sign +, put before a number or quantity that is to be added or one that is more than zero: *its full name is* **plus sign.**

plush (plush), *n.* a fabric like velvet, but with a deeper pile.

Plu·to (ploo'tō), *n.* **1.** the Greek and Roman god of Hades, the lower world of the dead. **2.** the planet farthest from the sun.

plu·to·crat (ploo'tə krat), *n.* a person who has power over others because he is rich.

plu·to·ni·um (ploo tō'ni əm), *n.* a radioactive chemical element, used in producing atomic energy.

ply (plī), *n.* **1.** a thickness or layer, as of plywood, cloth, etc. **2.** any of the strands twisted together to make rope, yarn, etc. —**plies,** *pl.*

ply (plī), *v.* **1.** to use with force or energy [to *ply* a chisel]. **2.** to work at [He *plied* his trade as a bricklayer.] **3.** to keep supplying [Our host *plied* us with food.] **4.** to travel back and forth, especially at regular times [Buses and trains *ply* between the two cities.] —**plied,** *p.t. & p.p.;* **ply'ing,** *pr.p.*

Plym·outh (plim'əth), *n.* **1.** a town on the coast of Massachusetts, settled by the Pilgrims in 1620. **2.** a seaport in southwestern England.

ply·wood (plī'wood), *n.* board made of thin layers of wood glued and pressed together.

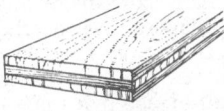

plywood

P.M. or **p.m.,** in the time from noon to midnight: *P.M.* is the abbreviation of *post meridiem,* Latin for "after noon" [Be home by 6:00 *P.M.*]

pneu·mat·ic (noo mat'ik *or* nyoo mat'ik), *adj.* **1.** filled with air [a *pneumatic* tire]. **2.** worked by air under pressure [a *pneumatic* hammer]. **3.** having to do with wind, air, or gases.

pneu·mo·nia (noo mō'nyə *or* nyoo mō'nyə), *n.* a disease in which the lungs become inflamed and a watery fluid collects in them.

Po (pō), *n.* a river in northern Italy.

P.O. or **p.o.,** abbreviation for **post office.**

poach (pōch), *v.* to cook an egg without its shell, in or over boiling water.

poach (pōch), *v.* to hunt or fish on another's land without the right to do so. —**poach'er,** *n.*

Po·ca·hon·tas (pō'kə hän'təs), *n.* 1595?–1617; an American Indian princess who is said to have saved Captain John Smith from being killed.

pock (päk), *n.* a pockmark.

pock·et (päk'it), *n.* **1.** a small bag or pouch sewed into a garment for carrying money and small articles. **2.** a hollow place, often one filled with something [the *pockets* of a pool table; *pockets* of ore in rock]. **3.** same as **air pocket.** —*adj.* that can be carried in a pocket [a *pocket* watch]. —*v.* **1.** to put into a pocket [He *pocketed* his change.] **2.** to enclose; shut in [The airport is *pocketed* in fog.] **3.** to take dishonestly [He *pocketed* some of the money he had collected for charity.] **4.** to put up with, as an insult, without showing anger. **5.** to cover up; hide [He *pocketed* his pride and begged for help.] —**line one's pockets,** to get much money.

pock·et·book (päk'it book), *n.* **1.** a woman's purse or handbag. **2.** a billfold or wallet.

pock·et·ful (päk'it fool), *n.* as much as a pocket will hold. —**pock'et·fuls,** *pl.*

pock·et·knife (päk'it nīf), *n.* a small knife with blades that fold into the handle. —**pock'et·knives,** *pl.*

pock·mark (päk'märk), *n.* a scar or pit left on the skin, as by smallpox, measles, etc.

pod (päd), *n.* the case or shell that holds the seeds of certain plants, as the pea and bean.

pocketknife

po·di·a·trist (pō dī'ə trist), *n.* the name now preferred for **chiropodist.**

po·di·um (pō'di əm), *n.* a raised platform where the conductor of an orchestra stands. —**po·di·a** (pō'di ə), *pl.*

Poe, Edgar Allan (pō), 1809–1849; U.S. poet and writer of short stories.

fat,   āpe,   cär,   ten,   ēven,   hit,   bīte,   gō,   hôrn,   tool,   book,   up,   fûr;
get,   joy,   yet,   chin,   she,   thin,   *th*en;   zh = s in pleasure;   ' as in able (ā'b'l);
ə = a in ago,   e in agent,   i in sanity,   o in confess,   u in focus.

po·em (pō′im), *n.* a piece of writing having rhythm and, often, rhyme, usually in language that shows more imagination and deep feeling than ordinary speech.

po·e·sy (pō′i sē), *n.* poetry: *now seldom used.*

po·et (pō′it), *n.* a person who writes poems.

po·et·ess (pō′it is), *n.* a woman poet: *no longer much used.*

po·et·ic (pō et′ik) or **po·et·i·cal** (pō et′i k′l), *adj.* 1. of, like, or fit for a poet or poetry [*poetic* talent; *poetic* language]. 2. written in verse [*poetic* drama]. —**po·et′i·cal·ly,** *adv.*

poetic justice, justice in which good is rewarded and evil is punished, as in some plays.

poet laureate, 1. the court poet of England, chosen by the king or queen to write poems about important events, etc. 2. any official poet. —**poets laureate** or **poet laureates,** *pl.*

po·et·ry (pō′it rē), *n.* 1. the writing of poems. 2. poems [the *poetry* of Keats]. 3. the rhythms, deep feelings, etc. of poems [There is *poetry* in her dancing.]

po·go stick (pō′gō), a stilt with pedals on a spring, used as a toy to bounce along on.

poign·ant (poin′yənt *or* poin′ənt), *adj.* 1. having a sharp and deep effect on the feelings; moving [a *poignant* memory]. 2. keen; sharp; piercing [*poignant* wit]. —**poign′an·cy,** *n.* —**poign′ant·ly,** *adv.*

poin·set·ti·a (poin set′i ə *or* poin set′ə), *n.* a tropical plant with small, yellow flowers and red leaves that look like petals.

poinsettia

point (point), *n.* 1. a position or place; location [the *point* where the roads meet]. 2. a dot in printing or writing [a decimal *point*]. 3. an exact time or moment [At that *point* the telephone rang.] 4. a stage or degree reached [the boiling *point* of water]. 5. a unit used in measuring or scoring [A touchdown is worth six *points.*] 6. any of the marks showing direction on a compass. 7. a part or detail; item [He explained the plan *point* by *point.*] 8. a special part or quality [Generosity is one of his good *points.*] 9. a sharp end [the *point* of a needle]. 10. a piece of land sticking out into the water; cape. 11. an important or main idea or fact [the *point* of a joke]. 12. a purpose; object [What's the *point* in crying?] —*v.* 1. to aim [Never *point* a gun at anyone.] 2. to aim one's finger [He *pointed* to the book he wanted.] 3. to be directed toward a certain place, condition, result, etc. [Our house *points* toward the park. Everything *points* to a happy outcome.] 4. to show or call attention to [to *point* the way; to *point* out mistakes]. 5. to show where game is by standing still and facing toward it, as some hunting dogs do. 6. to give extra force to; stress [He raised his voice to *point* up his meaning.] 7. to sharpen to a point, as a pencil. 8. to put a

period or decimal point in. —**at the point of,** very close to. —**beside the point,** not having to do with the subject at hand. —**make a point of,** to insist on. —**on the point of,** almost in the act of. —**stretch a point,** to make an exception. —**to the point** or **in point,** having much to do with the subject.

point-blank (point′blangk′), *adj.* 1. aimed straight at a mark, as a gun. 2. direct and plain [a *point-blank* answer]. —*adv.* in a way that is point-blank [to fire a gun *point-blank;* to refuse *point-blank*].

point·ed (poin′tid), *adj.* 1. having a point or sharp end. 2. sharp and to the point [a *pointed* saying]. 3. clearly aimed at someone [a *pointed* remark]. 4. easy to see or notice; obvious [He showed his regret in a very *pointed* way.] —**point′ed·ly,** *adv.*

point·er (poin′tər), *n.* 1. a long, thin rod used for pointing to things, as on a map. 2. a hand or needle on a clock, meter, scales, etc. 3. a large hunting dog with a smooth coat, trained to point game. 4. a hint or suggestion: *only in everyday talk* [*pointers* from the coach on how to hold a bat].

pointer (2 ft. high at shoulder)

point·less (point′lis), *adj.* 1. without a point. 2. without meaning or purpose; senseless [a *pointless* remark].

point of view, the way in which, or the place from which, something is viewed; standpoint [a liberal *point of view*].

poise (poiz), *n.* 1. balance, as in the way one carries oneself [the perfect *poise* of a tiger ready to spring]. 2. calmness and easiness of manner; self-control [He lost his *poise* when we laughed at him.] —*v.* to balance or be held balanced [The stork *poised* itself on one leg. The earth is *poised* in space.] —**poised,** *p.t. & p.p.;* **pois′ing,** *pr.p.*

poi·son (poi′z′n), *n.* 1. a substance that causes illness or death when taken into the body, even in small amounts. 2. anything that harms or destroys [the *poison* of his hate]. —*v.* 1. to harm or kill with poison [to *poison* rats]. 2. to put poison on or into [to *poison* bait]. 3. to harm or destroy [Fear *poisoned* his happiness.] —*adj.* poisonous [*poison* gas]. —**poi′son·er,** *n.*

poison ivy, a plant with grayish berries and leaves that grow in groups of three. It can cause a skin rash if touched.

poison oak, a poisonous shrub related to poison ivy.

poi·son·ous (poi′z′n əs), *adj.* that is or contains a poison; harming or killing by poison.

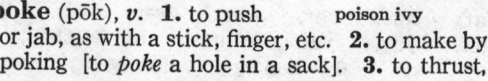
poison ivy

poke (pōk), *v.* 1. to push or jab, as with a stick, finger, etc. 2. to make by poking [to *poke* a hole in a sack]. 3. to thrust, push forward, pry, etc. [Don't *poke* your nose into my affairs.] **4.** to search [to *poke* around in the attic]. **5.** to move along in a slow or lazy way. **6.** to hit with the fist: *slang in this meaning.* —*n.* **1.** a poking; jab; push. **2.** a person who moves slowly; slowpoke. **3.** a bonnet with a wide front brim. —**poke fun at,** to make jokes about. —**poked,** *p.t. & p.p.;* **pok'ing,** *pr.p.*

poke (pōk), *n.* a sack; bag: *now used only in some regions.*

pok·er (pō'kər), *n.* a metal bar for stirring up a fire.

pok·er (pō'kər), *n.* a card game in which the players bet on the value of the cards they hold.

pok·y or **pok·ey** (pō'kē), *adj.* **1.** not lively; dull [a *poky* town]. **2.** small and stuffy [a *poky* room]. —**pok'i·er,** *compar.;* **pok'i·est,** *superl.*

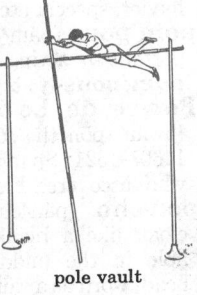
poker

Po·land (pō'lənd), *n.* a country in central Europe, on the Baltic Sea.

po·lar (pō'lər), *adj.* **1.** of or near the North or South Pole. **2.** of a pole or poles.

polar bear, a large white bear of arctic regions.

Po·lar·is (pō lar'is), *n.* the North Star.

Pole (pōl), *n.* a person born or living in Poland.

pole (pōl), *n.* a long, slender piece of wood, metal, etc. [a tent *pole*]. —*v.* to push along with a pole [to *pole* a raft down a river]. —**poled,** *p.t. & p.p.;* **pol'ing,** *pr.p.*

polar bear (8 ft. long)

pole (pōl), *n.* **1.** either end of an axis, especially of the earth's axis: see **North Pole** and **South Pole. 2.** either of two opposite forces, parts, etc., as the ends of a magnet or terminals of a battery.

pole·cat (pōl'kat), *n.* **1.** a skunk. **2.** a small animal of Europe that is like a weasel.

po·lem·ic (pō lem'ik), *adj.* of or having to do with argument or dispute: also **po·lem'i·cal.** —*n.* argument or dispute.

pole·star (pōl'stär), *n.* the North Star.

pole vault, an athletic contest to see who can jump highest over a crossbar, using a long pole to push oneself off the ground.

po·lice (pə lēs'), *n.* **1.** the department of a city, state, etc. that keeps order, prevents and discovers crimes, etc. **2.** the members of such a department: *used with a plural verb* [The *police* arrest lawbreakers.] **3.** the work of keeping an army camp clean and orderly; also, the soldiers

pole vault

who do this work. —*v.* **1.** to keep peaceful and orderly, as with police [to *police* a city]. **2.** to keep an army camp clean and orderly. —**po·liced',** *p.t. & p.p.;* **po·lic'ing,** *pr.p.*

po·lice·man (pə lēs'mən), *n.* a member of a police department. —**po·lice'men,** *pl.* —**po·lice'wom'an,** *n.fem.* —**po·lice'wom'en,** *pl.*

pol·i·cy (päl'ə sē), *n.* a plan, rule, or way of acting [It is a good *policy* to tell the truth. A country's foreign *policy* is its way of dealing with other countries.] —**pol'i·cies,** *pl.*

pol·i·cy (päl'ə sē), *n.* the written contract between an insurance company and one who is insured against some loss. —**pol'i·cies,** *pl.*

po·li·o (pō'li ō *or* päl'i ō), *n.* a shortened form of **poliomyelitis.**

po·li·o·my·e·li·tis (päl'i ō mī'ə lī'tis), *n.* a disease in which part of the spinal cord becomes inflamed and sometimes parts of the body are paralyzed: it is most common among young people. Also called **infantile paralysis.**

Pol·ish (pō'lish), *adj.* of Poland, its people, language, etc. —*n.* the language of Poland.

pol·ish (päl'ish), *v.* **1.** to make or become bright or shiny, as by rubbing with a wax or paste [to *polish* silverware]. **2.** to make less rough or crude; improve; perfect [to *polish* one's manners; to *polish* a speech one will give]. —*n.* **1.** brightness or shine on the surface [Your car has a nice *polish*.] **2.** a substance used to polish [fingernail *polish*; shoe *polish*]. **3.** the condition of being polite or refined, as in speech or manners.

po·lite (pə līt'), *adj.* **1.** having or showing good manners; thoughtful of others; courteous [It was *polite* of you to give me your seat.] **2.** having or showing good taste; cultured [*polite* literature]. —**po·lite'ly,** *adv.* —**po·lite'ness,** *n.*

pol·i·tic (päl'ə tik), *adj.* **1.** wise and clever; often, too clever or cunning; crafty [a *politic* answer to the reporter's questions]. **2.** worked out in a careful or crafty way to fit the situation.

po·lit·i·cal (pə lit'i k'l), *adj.* **1.** having to do with government, politics, etc. [*political* parties]. **2.** of or like political parties or politicians [a *political* speech]. —**po·lit'i·cal·ly,** *adv.*

political economy, same as **economics.**

political science, the study of the principles and methods of government.

pol·i·ti·cian (päl'ə tish'ən), *n.* a person who is active in politics, usually one holding or running for a political office: often used of a person who plans or works only for his own good.

pol·i·tics (päl'ə tiks), *n.pl.* **1.** the science of government; political science. **2.** the act of taking part in political affairs, often as a profession [to enter *politics*]. **3.** political beliefs, rules, etc. [What are your *politics*?] *Used with a singular verb in meanings 1 and 2.*

pol·i·ty (päl'ə tē), *n.* **1.** government, or a system for ruling. **2.** a group of people under one government; state. —**pol'i·ties,** *pl.*

Polk, James K. (pōk), 1795–1849; eleventh president of the United States, from 1845 to 1849.

pol·ka (pōl′kə), *n.* **1.** a fast dance for couples. **2.** music for this dance.

pol·ka dot (pō′kə), **1.** a pattern of small, round, evenly spaced dots. **2.** any of these dots.

poll (pōl), *n.* **1.** a voting or listing of opinions by persons; also, the counting of these votes or opinions [A *poll* of our class shows that most of us want a party.] **2.** the number of votes cast. **3.** a list of voters. **4.** *usually* **polls,** *pl.* a place where people vote. **5.** the head: *now seldom used.* —*v.* **1.** to take and count the votes or opinions of [to *poll* a county]. **2.** to get a certain number of votes [Jones *polled* a majority of the votes cast.] **3.** to cast one's vote. **4.** to cut off or trim the wool, hair, horns, or branches of.

pol·len (päl′ən), *n.* the yellow powder found on the stamens of flowers. It fertilizes a flower when it is carried to the pistil, as by bees or the wind.

pol·li·nate (päl′ə nāt), *v.* to place pollen on the pistil of a flower; fertilize. —**pol′li·nat·ed,** *p.t. & p.p.;* **pol′li·nat·ing,** *pr.p.* —**pol′li·na′tion,** *n.*

pol·li·wog (päl′i wäg), *n.* a tadpole.

poll tax, a tax, as in some States, that a person must pay in order to vote.

pol·lu·tant (pə lōō′tənt), *n.* something that pollutes; especially, a harmful chemical or waste material let into the water or air.

pol·lute (pə lōōt′), *v.* to make dirty or impure [Smoke from factories *polluted* the air.] —**pol·lut′ed,** *p.t. & p.p.;* **pol·lut′ing,** *pr.p.*

po·lo (pō′lō), *n.* a game played on horseback by two teams of four players each. The players try to drive a small wooden ball through the other team's goal, using mallets with long handles.

polo player

Po·lo, Mar·co (mär′kō pō′lō), 1254?–1324?; a Venetian traveler to Asia, who wrote a book about his travels.

po·lo·naise (päl ə nāz′ *or* pō lə nāz′), *n.* **1.** a slow, dignified Polish dance. **2.** music for this.

polo shirt, a knitted, pull-over sport shirt with short sleeves and a collar.

pol·troon (päl trōōn′), *n.* a great coward.

po·lyg·a·my (pə lig′ə mē), *n.* the practice of being married to more than one person at the same time. —**po·lyg′a·mous,** *adj.*

pol·y·glot (päl′i glät), *adj.* **1.** speaking or writing several languages. **2.** made up of or written in several languages [a *polyglot* book].

pol·y·gon (päl′i gän), *n.* a flat figure having more than four angles and sides. —**po·lyg·o·nal** (pə lig′ə n'l), *adj.*

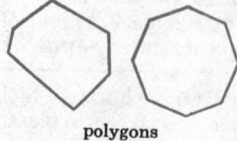
polygons

Pol·y·ne·sia (päl′ə nē′zhə), *n.* a scattered group of many islands in the central and south Pacific, including Hawaii and Tahiti. —**Pol′y·ne′sian,** *adj. & n.*

pol·yp (päl′ip), *n.* a small water animal having a body shaped like a tube with slender tentacles around a mouth at the top, for taking in food. The sea anemone and coral are polyps.

polyp (1 in. high)

pol·y·syl·la·ble (päl′i sil′ə b'l), *n.* a word of more than three syllables, such as "elementary." —**pol·y·syl·lab·ic** (päl′i si lab′ik), *adj.*

pol·y·tech·nic (päl′i tek′nik), *adj.* of or teaching many scientific and technical subjects [a *polytechnic* institute].

pol·y·the·ism (päl′i thē′iz′m), *n.* belief in more than one god [the *polytheism* of the ancient Greeks]. —**pol·y·the·is′tic,** *adj.*

po·made (pə mād′), *n.* a perfumed cream for keeping the hair in place.

pome·gran·ate (päm′gran′it *or* pum′gran′it), *n.* **1.** a round, red fruit with a hard skin, a red, juicy pulp, and many seeds. **2.** the tree that it grows on.

pom·mel (pum′'l), *n.* **1.** the rounded part that sticks up on the front of a saddle. **2.** a round knob at the end of the hilt of a sword. —*v.* to beat with the fists. —**pom′meled** *or* **pom′melled,** *p.t. & p.p.;* **pom′mel·ing** *or* **pom′mel·ling,** *pr.p.*

pomegranate (whole fruit and cross section)

pomp (pämp), *n.* dignified or showy display; splendor [the *pomp* of a coronation].

pom·pa·dour (päm′pə dôr), *n.* a hair style in which the hair is brushed straight up from the forehead so that it puffs up.

Pom·pe·ii (päm pā′ē *or* päm pā′), *n.* a city in Italy, destroyed when Mount Vesuvius erupted in 79 A.D. —**Pom·pe·i·an** (päm pā′ən), *adj.*

pom·pon (päm′pän), *n.* **1.** a ball of silk, wool, or feathers worn on clothing as an ornament. **2.** a chrysanthemum with small, round flowers.

pom·pos·i·ty (päm päs′ə tē), *n.* pompous behavior, speech, etc.; self-importance.

pom·pous (päm′pəs), *adj.* trying to seem important by acting in a way that is too dignified. **pom′pous·ly,** *adv.*

Pon·ce de Le·ón, Juan (hwän pōn′thə dā lā ōn′), 1460?–1521; Spanish explorer who discovered Florida.

pon·cho (pän′chō), *n.* a cloak like a blanket with a hole in the middle for the head, worn as a raincoat, etc., originally in South America. —**pon′chos,** *pl.*

poncho

pond (pänd), *n.* a small lake, often man-made.

pon·der (pän′dər), *v.* to think deeply about; consider carefully [to *ponder* an offer].

pon·der·ous (pän′dər əs), *adj.* **1.** large and heavy, often in a clumsy way; massive [The *ponderous* truck lumbered down the road.] **2.** dull or tiresome; without a light touch [a *ponderous* joke]. —**pon′der·ous·ly,** *adv.*

pone (pōn), *n.* bread made of corn meal: *this word is used mainly in the South.*

pon·gee (pän jē′), *n.* a soft, silk cloth, usually in its natural, light-brown color.

pon·iard (pän′yərd), *n.* a dagger.

pon·tiff (pän′tif), *n.* a bishop; especially, the Pope.

pon·tif·i·cal (pän tif′i k′l), *adj.* **1.** of or having to do with a bishop, especially with the Pope; papal. **2.** acting as if one had the dignity or power of a pontiff.

pon·tif·i·cate (pän tif′i kāt), *v.* **1.** to carry out the duties of a pontiff. **2.** to speak or act in a self-assured or pompous way [He *pontificates* on many subjects.] —*n.* (*usually* pän tif′i kit), the office of a pontiff. —**pon·tif′i·cat·ed,** *p.t.* & *p.p.*; **pon·tif′i·cat·ing,** *pr.p.*

pon·toon (pän tōōn′), *n.* **1.** a boat with a flat bottom. **2.** such a boat or other floating object, used with others like it to hold up a temporary bridge, called a **pontoon bridge. 3.** a float on an airplane to allow it to land on water.

pontoon bridge

po·ny (pō′nē), *n.* a type of small horse. —**po′nies,** *pl.*

pony express, a system of riders on swift ponies, once used to carry mail.

poo·dle (pōō′d′l), *n.* a breed of dog with black, white, gray, or brown hair that is sometimes trimmed in patterns.

pooh (pōō), *interj.* a sound made to show that one is annoyed or does not believe something.

pooh-pooh (pōō′pōō′), *v.* to show dislike for or treat as unimportant [to *pooh-pooh* an idea].

poodle (15 in. high at shoulder)

pool (pōōl), *n.* **1.** a small pond. **2.** a puddle. **3.** a swimming pool. **4.** a deep spot in a river.

pool (pōōl), *n.* **1.** a game of billiards played on a table having six pockets into which the balls are knocked. **2.** an amount of money or set of things collected or used by a group [The company owns a *pool* of cars for its employees.] **3.** a group of persons or companies working together for the benefit of each [a *pool* formed to buy an office building]. —*v.* to put together into a common fund [We *pooled* our money and rented a cottage.]

poop (pōōp), *n.* a deck at the stern of some ships, raised above the main deck and sometimes forming the roof of a cabin: also **poop deck.**

poor (poor), *adj.* **1.** having little or no money; not having enough to live on; needy. **2.** not good; not what it should be; below average; bad [*poor* health; *poor* grades; a *poor* wheat crop]. **3.** deserving pity; unfortunate [The *poor* bird had broken its wing.] —**the poor,** poor people. —**poor′ly,** *adv.* —**poor′ness,** *n.*

poor·house (poor′hous), *n.* a home for very poor people, supported by money from the public.

pop (päp), *n.* **1.** a sudden, short, bursting sound, as of a pistol shot. **2.** soda water that has been flavored and sweetened. —*v.* **1.** to make, or burst with, a pop. **2.** to make burst open [to *pop* corn]. **3.** to move, put, etc. in a quick, sudden way [She *popped* out of bed. He *popped* an unexpected question.] **4.** to open wide in a stare; bulge [eyes *popping* with curiosity]. **5.** to hit a baseball high in the air, but in the infield. —**popped,** *p.t.* & *p.p.*; **pop′ping,** *pr.p.*

pop (päp), *n.* father: *a slang word.*

pop·corn (päp′kôrn), *n.* **1.** a kind of corn with hard kernels which pop open into a white, puffy mass when heated. **2.** the popped kernels.

Pope or **pope** (pōp), *n.* the bishop who is the head of the Roman Catholic Church.

pop·gun (päp′gun), *n.* a toy gun that shoots little corks, etc. with a popping sound.

pop·in·jay (päp′in jā), *n.* a conceited person who talks a lot.

pop·lar (päp′lər), *n.* **1.** a tall tree that grows fast and has small leaves. **2.** its wood.

pop·lin (päp′lin), *n.* a cloth of silk, cotton, wool, etc. with fine ridges on the surface.

pop·o·ver (päp′ō′vər), *n.* a very light muffin that is puffy and hollow.

pop·py (päp′ē), *n.* a plant with a milky juice and flowers of various colors. Opium comes from the juice of one kind of poppy. —**pop′pies,** *pl.*

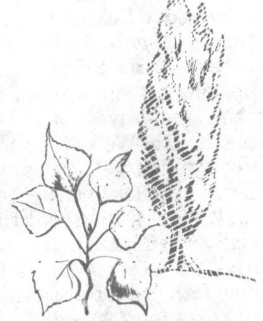

poplar tree and leaves

poppy seed, the small, dark seed of the poppy, used in baking, etc. as a flavoring.

pop·u·lace (päp′yoo lis), *n.* the public generally; the masses.

pop·u·lar (päp′yoo lər), *adj.* **1.** having many friends; very well liked [His quiet humor has made him *popular.*] **2.** liked by many people [a *popular* magazine]. **3.** of, for, or

poppy

by all the people or most people [election by *popular* vote]. **4.** that most people can afford [goods sold at *popular* prices]. —**pop·u·lar·i·ty** (päp′yoo lar′ə tē), *n.* —**pop′u·lar·ly,** *adv.*

pop·u·lar·ize (päp′yoo lə rīz), *v.* to make popular. —**pop′u·lar·ized,** *p.t.* & *p.p.;* **pop′u·lar·iz·ing,** *pr.p.* —**pop′u·lar·i·za′tion,** *n.*

pop·u·late (päp′yoo lāt), *v.* to fill with people; inhabit [New York is densely *populated.* The English *populated* Australia.] —**pop′u·lat·ed,** *p.t.* & *p.p.;* **pop′u·lat·ing,** *pr.p.*

pop·u·la·tion (päp′yoo lā′shən), *n.* **1.** the people living in a country, city, etc.; especially, the total number of these. **2.** a populating or being populated [The gold rush speeded the *population* of California.]

pop·u·lous (päp′yoo ləs), *adj.* full of people; thickly populated [a *populous* city].

por·ce·lain (pôr′s'l in), *n.* a fine, white, hard earthenware used in making bathtubs, sinks, tiles, etc. Porcelain used for dishes is called *china.*

porch (pôrch), *n.* **1.** a covered entrance to a building, usually with a roof that is held up by posts. **2.** a room on the outside of a building, either open or enclosed by screens, etc.

por·cu·pine (pôr′kyoo pīn), *n.* an animal having coarse hair mixed with long, sharp spines.

pore (pôr), *v.* to look, study, or read with close, steady attention [He *pored* over the book.] —**pored,** *p.t.* & *p.p.;* **por′ing,** *pr.p.*

porcupine (3 ft. long)

pore (pôr), *n.* a tiny opening as in the skin, the leaves of plants, etc. We sweat through pores in the skin.

por·gy (pôr′gē), *n.* any of several salt-water fishes used for food. —**por′gies** or **por′gy,** *pl.*

pork (pôrk), *n.* the flesh of a pig or hog, especially when not cured or salted.

pork·er (pôr′kər), *n.* a hog, especially a young one, fattened for use as food.

po·rous (pôr′əs), *adj.* full of pores or tiny holes through which water, air, etc. may pass [Leather is *porous.*] —**po·ros·i·ty** (pô räs′ə tē), *n.*

por·phy·ry (pôr′fə rē), *n.* a hard rock with red and white crystals in it. —**por′phy·ries,** *pl.*

por·poise (pôr′pəs), *n.* **1.** a water animal that is like a small whale. It is dark above and white below and has a blunt snout. **2.** a dolphin.

por·ridge (pôr′ij), *n.* a soft food made of oatmeal or some other cereal boiled in water or milk until thick: *mainly a British word.*

por·rin·ger (pôr′in jər), *n.* a small, shallow bowl for serving porridge, cereal, etc.

porpoise (5 ft. long)

port (pôrt), *n.* **1.** a harbor. **2.** a city with a harbor where ships can load and unload.

port (pôrt), *n.* a sweet, dark-red wine.

port (pôrt), *n.* the way one stands or walks; carriage [the stately *port* of the old gentleman].

port (pôrt), *n.* the left-hand side of a ship or airplane as one faces forward, toward the bow. —*adj.* of or on this side.

port (pôrt), *n.* **1.** a porthole. **2.** the covering for a porthole. **3.** an opening, as in an engine, for letting steam, gas, etc. in or out.

port·a·ble (pôr′tə b'l), *adj.* that can be carried; easily carried [a *portable* radio].

port·age (pôr′tij), *n.* **1.** a carrying of boats and supplies on land from one river or lake to another. **2.** any route over which this is done.

por·tal (pôr′t'l), *n.* a doorway, gate, or entrance, especially a large and splendid one.

port·cul·lis (pôrt kul′is), *n.* a large, heavy iron grating that was let down to close off the gateway of an ancient castle or walled town.

portcullis

por·tend (pôr tend′), *v.* to be a sign or warning of; foreshadow.

por·tent (pôr′tent), *n.* a sign that something bad is about to happen; omen [The Romans thought comets were *portents* of disaster.]

por·ten·tous (pôr ten′təs), *adj.* **1.** being a sign of something bad about to happen; ominous. **2.** amazing; marvelous [*portentous* ability].

por·ter (pôr′tər), *n.* a doorman or gatekeeper.

por·ter (pôr′tər), *n.* **1.** a man whose work is to carry luggage, as at a hotel or railroad station. **2.** a man who waits on passengers in a railroad sleeper or parlor car. **3.** a man who sweeps, cleans, does errands, etc., as in a bank or store. **4.** a dark-brown beer.

por·ter·house (pôr′tər hous), *n.* a choice cut of beef from between the tenderloin and the sirloin: *its full name is* **porterhouse steak.**

port·fo·li·o (pôrt fō′li ō), *n.* **1.** a flat case for carrying loose papers, drawings, etc.; brief case. **2.** things that may be carried in such a case, as a list of stocks, bonds, etc. that one owns. —**port·fo′li·os,** *pl.*

port·hole (pôrt′hōl), *n.* a small opening in a ship's side, as for letting in light and air.

por·ti·co (pôr′ti kō), *n.* a porch or covered walk, having a roof held up by columns. —**por′ti·coes** or **por′ti·cos,** *pl.*

por·tion (pôr′shən), *n.* **1.** a part given to a person or set aside for some purpose; share [a generous *portion* of cake for the guest; the *portion* of one's time spent in study]. **2.** a dowry [a marriage *portion*]. —*v.* to divide or give out in portions [She *portioned* out the food.]

portico

Port·land (pôrt/lənd), *n.* **1.** a city in southern Maine. **2.** a city in northwestern Oregon.

port·ly (pôrt/lē), *adj.* large and heavy in a dignified or stately way [a *portly* judge]. —**port/·li·er**, *compar.*; **port/li·est**, *superl.*

port·man·teau (pôrt man/tō), *n.* a stiff leather suitcase that opens like a book at the middle.

Por·to Ri·co (pôr/tə rē/kō), an earlier name of **Puerto Rico**. —**Por/to Ri/can**.

por·trait (pôr/trit *or* pôr/trāt), *n.* **1.** a drawing, painting, or photograph of a person, especially of his face. **2.** a description in a story or play.

por·trai·ture (pôr/tri chər), *n.* the art of making portraits.

por·tray (pôr trā/), *v.* **1.** to make a picture of, as in a painting. **2.** to make a picture of in words; describe [The writer *portrays* life in New York.] **3.** to play the part of on the stage [The actor *portrayed* a doctor.]

por·tray·al (pôr trā/əl), *n.* **1.** the act of portraying. **2.** a portrait or description.

Por·tu·gal (pôr/chə g'l), *n.* a country in southwestern Europe, west of Spain.

Por·tu·guese (pôr/chə gēz), *adj.* of Portugal, its people, etc. —*n.* **1.** a person born or living in Portugal. **2.** the language of Portugal and Brazil. —**Por/tu·guese**, *pl.*

pose (pōz), *v.* **1.** to hold oneself in a certain position for a time, as for a photograph. **2.** to put in a certain position [The artist *posed* the children around their mother.] **3.** to pretend to be what one is not; act [He *posed* as a war hero though he had never been in battle.] **4.** to introduce or present [The slums *pose* a problem for the city.] —*n.* **1.** a position of the body held for a picture by an artist, photographer, etc. **2.** a way of acting that is meant to fool people; pretense [His gruff manner is just a *pose.*] —**posed**, *p.t. & p.p.*; **pos/ing**, *pr.p.*

Po·sei·don (pō sī/d'n), *n.* the Greek god of the sea. The Romans called this god *Neptune*.

po·si·tion (pə zish/ən), *n.* **1.** the way in which a person or thing is placed or arranged [a sitting *position*]. **2.** the place where a person or thing is; location [The ship radioed its *position*.] **3.** one's opinion or attitude; stand [What is his *position* on foreign aid?] **4.** the usual or proper place; station [The players are in *position*.] **5.** a job or office; post [He has a *position* with the government.] **6.** a place of high rank in society, business, etc. —*v.* to put in a certain position.

pos·i·tive (päz/ə tiv), *adj.* **1.** that will not be changed and is not to be questioned; definite [He has *positive* orders not to leave.] **2.** perfectly sure; certain [I'm *positive* I locked the front door.] **3.** too sure or too confident in oneself. **4.** agreeing; saying "yes"; affirmative [a *positive* reply]. **5.** that does some good or helps in some way [*positive* criticism; a *positive* attitude toward life]. **6.** existing in itself, not just in the absence of other things [a *positive* good]. **7.** showing that a certain disease, condition, etc. is present [a *positive* reaction to the allergy test]. **8.** being the simple form of an adjective or adverb, not showing comparison ["Good" is the *positive* degree of which "better" and "best" are the comparative and superlative.] **9.** describing or of the kind of electricity that is made on glass by rubbing it with silk. **10.** describing a quantity that is greater than zero; plus. **11.** complete; downright: *used only in everyday talk* [a *positive* fool]. —*n.* **1.** something positive, as a degree, quality, quantity, etc. **2.** a photographic print, or a film for use in a projector, in which the light and dark areas are exactly as in the original subject. —**pos/i·tive·ly**, *adv.*

pos·se (päs/ē), *n.* a group of men called together by a sheriff to help him keep the peace.

pos·sess (pə zes/), *v.* **1.** to have as something that belongs to one; own [to *possess* great wealth]. **2.** to have as a part of one [to *possess* wisdom]. **3.** to get power over; control [Fear suddenly *possessed* her.] —**pos·ses/sor**, *n.*

pos·ses·sion (pə zesh/ən), *n.* **1.** the fact of possessing, holding, or owning; ownership [to have *possession* of secret information]. **2.** a thing possessed [This vase is her most prized *possession*.] **3.** territory ruled by an outside country [Guam is a *possession* of the U.S.] **4.** self-control.

pos·ses·sive (pə zes/iv), *adj.* **1.** having or showing a strong feeling for owning or keeping things [a *possessive* person]. **2.** in grammar, describing the case of words that shows ownership, origin, etc. [The *possessive* case of English nouns is formed by adding 's or ' (John's dog; Jesus' teachings). "My," "yours," "its," etc. are *possessive* pronouns.] —*n.* **1.** the possessive case. **2.** a word in this case. —**pos·ses/sive·ly**, *adv.* —**pos·ses/sive·ness**, *n.*

pos·si·bil·i·ty (päs/ə bil/ə tē), *n.* **1.** the fact of being possible; chance [There is a *possibility* of rain.] **2.** something that is possible [Failure is a *possibility* I must face.] —**pos/si·bil/i·ties**, *pl.*

pos·si·ble (päs/ə b'l), *adj.* **1.** that can be [The highest *possible* score in bowling is 300.] **2.** that may or may not happen [colder tomorrow, with *possible* showers]. **3.** that can be done, known, got, used, etc. [two *possible* routes to Denver].

pos·si·bly (päs/ə blē), *adv.* **1.** in any possible way [He can't *possibly* carry that load.] **2.** perhaps; maybe [*Possibly* it's true.]

pos·sum (päs/əm), *n.* an opossum. —**play possum**, to pretend to be asleep, ill, unaware, etc.

post (pōst), *n.* a long, thick piece of wood, metal, etc. set upright for holding something up, as a building, sign, fence, etc. —*v.* **1.** to put up on a wall, fence, post, etc. [to *post* a sign]. **2.** to announce as by posting signs [A reward is *posted* for his capture.] **3.** to put up signs warning strangers to stay out [The farmer *posted* his land during hunting season.]

post (pōst), *n.* **1.** the place where a soldier, guard, etc. is on duty [The sentry walked his *post.*] **2.** a place where soldiers are stationed [an army *post*]. **3.** the soldiers at such a place. **4.** a position or job [appointed to a *post* in the government]. **5.** same as **trading post.** —*v.* to place at a post [Guards were *posted* at every exit.]

post (pōst), *n.* **1.** mail, or the delivery of mail: *used especially in Great Britain* [The letter came in this morning's *post.*] **2.** in earlier times, any of the stations where riders, horses, etc. were kept as relays along a route. —*v.* **1.** to send by mail; place in a mailbox. **2.** to give news to; inform [I will keep you *posted* on my activities.] **3.** to travel fast; hurry.

post-, a prefix meaning "after" or "following" [A *postwar* period is a period after a war.]

post·age (pōs′tij), *n.* the amount charged for delivering a letter or package by mail.

postage stamp, a government stamp put on mail to show that postage has been paid.

post·al (pōs′t'l), *adj.* of mail or post offices [the *postal* service; a *postal* clerk].

postal card, a card with a postage stamp printed on it, used for sending messages by mail: *sometimes also called* **post card.**

post card, a picture card, etc. that can be sent through the mail when a postage stamp is stuck on it: *sometimes also called* **postal card.**

post chaise, a closed carriage with four wheels, that was pulled by fast horses.

post·er (pōs′tər), *n.* a large sign or notice put up in a public place [a circus *poster*].

pos·te·ri·or (päs tir′i ər), *adj.* **1.** at or toward the back; rear. **2.** coming after; later.

pos·ter·i·ty (päs ter′ə tē), *n.* **1.** the people of future times [His music will be admired by *posterity*.] **2.** all the descendants of a person.

post·grad·u·ate (pōst′graj′ōō it), *adj.* of or taking a course of study after graduation.

post·haste (pōst′hāst′), *adv.* in great haste.

post·hu·mous (päs′choo məs), *adj.* **1.** born after its father died [a *posthumous* child]. **2.** published after the author died [her *posthumous* poems]. **3.** coming after one has died [*posthumous* fame]. —**post′hu·mous·ly,** *adv.*

pos·til·ion or **pos·til·lion** (pōs til′yən or päs til′yən), *n.* the man who rides the front left-hand horse of a team pulling a carriage.

post·man (pōst′mən), *n.* a man whose work is delivering mail; mailman. —**post′men,** *pl.*

post·mark (pōst′märk), *n.* a mark stamped on mail at the post office of the sender, canceling the postage stamp and showing the place and date. —*v.* to stamp with a postmark.

post·mas·ter (pōst′mas′tər), *n.* a person in charge of a post office. —**post′mis′tress,** *n.fem.*

postmaster general, the person in charge of the entire postal system of a country. —**postmasters general,** *pl.*

post-mor·tem (pōst′môr′təm), *adj.* after death [a *post-mortem* examination of a body]. —*n.* an examination of a body after death; autopsy.

post office, 1. an office or building where mail is sorted, postage stamps are sold, etc. **2.** the department of a government that is in charge of the postal service. —**post′-of′fice,** *adj.*

post·paid (pōst′pād′), *adj.* with the sender or shipper paying the postage.

post·pone (pōst pōn′), *v.* to put off until later; delay [I *postponed* my trip because of illness.] —**post·poned′,** *p.t. & p.p.;* **post·pon′ing,** *pr.p.* —**post·pone′ment,** *n.*

post road, a road over which mail was carried or along which there were posts for relays of fresh horses, riders, etc.

post·script (pōst′skript), *n.* a note added below the signature of a letter.

pos·tu·late (päs′choo lāt), *v.* to suppose to be true or real as the first step in proving an argument; take for granted. —*n.* (päs′choo lit), an idea, etc. that is postulated. —**pos′tu·lat·ed,** *p.t. & p.p.;* **pos′tu·lat·ing,** *pr.p.*

pos·ture (päs′chər), *n.* **1.** the way one holds the body in sitting or standing; carriage [good *posture* with the back held straight]. **2.** a special way of holding the body or of acting, as in posing [He doubled up his fist in a *posture* of defiance.] —*v.* to take on a posture; pose. —**pos′tured,** *p.t. & p.p.;* **pos′tur·ing,** *pr.p.*

post·war (pōst′wôr′), *adj.* after the war.

po·sy (pō′zē), *n.* **1.** a flower. **2.** a bunch of flowers; bouquet. —**po′sies,** *pl.*

left: poor posture
right: good posture

pot (pät), *n.* **1.** a round container made of various materials and used for cooking or for certain other purposes [a tea*pot*; a flower *pot*]. **2.** as much as a pot will hold. **3.** marijuana: *slang in this meaning.* —*v.* **1.** to put into a pot [to *pot* a plant]. **2.** to preserve in a pot [*potted* meat]. **3.** to shoot, as game. —**go to pot,** to become ruined; fall apart. —**pot′ted,** *p.t. & p.p.;* **pot′ting,** *pr.p.* —**pot′ful,** *n.*

pot·ash (pät′ash), *n.* a white substance containing potassium, got from wood ashes and used in fertilizer, soap, etc.

po·tas·si·um (pə tas′i əm), *n.* a soft, silver-white metal that is a chemical element. Its salts are used in fertilizers, glass, etc.

po·ta·to (pə tā′tō), *n.* **1.** a plant whose tuber, or thick, starchy underground stem, is used as a vegetable. **2.** this tuber. **3.** a sweet potato. —**po·ta·toes,** *pl.*

potato chip, a very thin slice of potato, fried until crisp and then salted.

po·tent (pō′t'nt), *adj.* **1.** having great power; mighty [a *potent* monarch]. **2.** having a strong effect on the body or mind; very effective or forceful [a *potent* drug; a *potent* argument]. —**po·ten·cy** (pō′t'n sē), *n.*

potato plant

po·ten·tate (pō't'n tāt), *n.* a person having great power; ruler; monarch.

po·ten·tial (pə ten'shəl), *adj.* that can be, but is not yet; possible [a *potential* leader; a *potential* source of trouble]. —*n.* **1.** power or skill that may be developed [a baseball team with *potential*]. **2.** the amount of electrical force in a circuit as measured in volts. —**po·ten'tial·ly,** *adv.*

po·ten·ti·al·i·ty (pə ten'shi al'ə tē), *n.* a possibility of becoming, developing, etc. [a test that measures one's *potentiality* as a pilot]. —**po·ten'ti·al'i·ties,** *pl.*

poth·er (päth'ər), *n.* noisy confusion; fuss.

pot·hold·er (pät'hōl'dər), *n.* a thick pad of cloth for handling hot pots, pans, etc.

pot·hook (pät'hook), *n.* a hook shaped like the letter S, used to hang a pot over a fire.

po·tion (pō'shən), *n.* a drink that is supposed to heal, or to poison, do magic, etc.

pot·luck (pät'luk), *n.* whatever the family meal happens to be [Stay and take *potluck* with us.]

Po·to·mac (pə tō'mək), *n.* a river flowing between Virginia and Maryland into Chesapeake Bay.

pot·pie (pät'pī), *n.* **1.** a meat pie baked in a deep dish. **2.** a stew with dumplings.

pot·pour·ri (pō'poo rē'), *n.* **1.** a sweet-smelling mixture of dried flowers and spices. **2.** any mixture or medley [a *potpourri* of songs].

pot roast, a piece of beef, cooked slowly in a covered pan with a little liquid.

pot shot, 1. an easy shot, as one fired at close range. **2.** a shot or try at something without careful aim or planning.

pot·tage (pät'ij), *n.* a kind of thick soup.

pot·ter (pät'ər), *n.* a person who makes pots, dishes, etc. out of clay, shaping them on a wheel that keeps turning (called a **potter's wheel**).

pot·ter (pät'ər), *v.* to putter: *used mainly in Great Britain.*

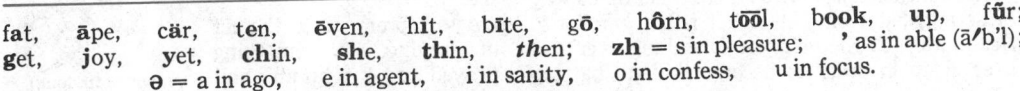

potter using
potter's wheel

potter's field, a burial ground for persons who die poor or unknown.

pot·ter·y (pät'ər ē), *n.* **1.** pots, dishes, etc. made of clay and hardened by baking. **2.** a place where such things are made. **3.** the art or work of a potter. —**pot'ter·ies,** *pl.*

pouch (pouch), *n.* **1.** a bag or sack [a tobacco *pouch;* a mail *pouch*]. **2.** a loose fold of skin, like a pocket, on the belly of certain female animals, as the kangaroo, in which they carry their newborn young. **3.** anything shaped like a pouch [the *pouch* of a pelican's bill]. —*v.* to form a pouch [His cheeks *pouched* out.]

poul·tice (pōl'tis), *n.* a soft, hot, wet mixture, as of flour or mustard and water, put on a sore or inflamed part of the body.

poul·try (pōl'trē), *n.* fowl raised for food; chickens, turkeys, ducks, geese, etc.

pounce (pouns), *v.* to spring or swoop down, as in order to attack or seize [The cat *pounced* at a bird. The catcher *pounced* on the bunted ball.] —*n.* a sudden spring or swoop. —**pounced,** *p.t. & p.p.;* **pounc'ing,** *pr.p.*

pound (pound), *n.* **1.** a unit of weight, equal to 16 ounces, or, in troy weight, 12 ounces. **2.** the basic unit of money in Great Britain, equal to 100 pennies; also, the basic unit of money in certain other countries, as Ireland, Israel, Sudan, etc. Its symbol is £.

pound (pound), *v.* **1.** to hit with many heavy blows; hit hard [to *pound* on a door]. **2.** to crush into a powder or pulp by beating [to *pound* corn into meal]. **3.** to move with loud, heavy steps [He *pounded* down the hall.] **4.** to beat in a heavy way; throb [His heart *pounded* from the exercise.] —*n.* a hard blow or the sound of it.

pound (pound), *n.* a closed-in place for keeping animals, especially stray ones [a dog *pound*].

pound-fool·ish (pound'fool'ish), *adj.* see **penny-wise.**

pour (pôr), *v.* **1.** to let flow in a steady stream [to *pour* milk into a glass; to *pour* money into a business]. **2.** to flow in a steady stream [Wet salt will not *pour.* Fans *poured* out of the stadium.] **3.** to rain heavily.

pout (pout), *v.* **1.** to push out the lips as in showing that one is annoyed or has hurt feelings; look sulky. **2.** to be silent and unfriendly; sulk. —*n.* the act of pouting.

girl pouting

pov·er·ty (päv'ər tē), *n.* **1.** the condition of being poor, or not having enough to live on. **2.** the condition of being poor in quality or lacking in something [the *poverty* of his imagination].

pov·er·ty-strick·en (päv'ər tē strik'′n), *adj.* very poor; suffering from great poverty.

pow·der (pou'dər), *n.* **1.** a dry substance in the form of fine particles like dust, made by crushing or grinding [bath *powder;* baking *powder;* gun*powder*]. **2.** talcum. —*v.* **1.** to sprinkle, dust, or cover as with powder [Snow *powdered* the rooftops.] **2.** to make into powder.

powder horn, a container made of an animal's horn, for carrying gunpowder.

powder horn

powder puff, a soft pad for putting talcum powder on the face or body.

powder room, a lavatory for women.

pow·der·y (pou'dər ē), *adj.* **1.** of, like, or in the form of powder [*powdery* snow]. **2.** easily crumbled into powder [soft, *powdery* rock]. **3.** covered with powder.

fat,   āpe,   cär,   ten,   ēven,   hit,   bīte,   gō,   hôrn,   tool,   book,   up,   fûr;
get,   joy,   yet,   chin,   she,   thin,   *then;*   zh = s in pleasure;   ' as in able (ā'b'l);
ə = a in ago,   e in agent,   i in sanity,   o in confess,   u in focus.

pow·er (pou′ər), *n.* **1.** ability to do or act [Lobsters have the *power* to grow new claws.] **2.** strength or force [the *power* of a boxer's blows]. **3.** force or energy that can be put to work [electric *power*]. **4.** the ability to control others; authority [the *power* of the law]. **5.** a person, thing, or nation that has control or influence over others. **6.** the number obtained by multiplying a number by itself a certain number of times [16 is the fourth *power* of 2, often written as 2^4, or 2 to the fourth *power*.] **7.** the degree to which a lens can magnify an object [A 300-*power* microscope makes things appear 300 times as large.] —*v.* to supply with power [The machine is *powered* by an engine.] —*adj.* worked by electricity or other kind of power [a *power* saw]. —**in power,** having control or authority.

pow·er·ful (pou′ər fəl), *adj.* having much power; strong or influential [a *powerful* hand; a *powerful* leader]. —**pow′er·ful·ly,** *adv.*

pow·er·house (pou′ər hous), *n.* a building where electric power is produced.

pow·er·less (pou′ər lis), *adj.* without power; weak or helpless [*powerless* against the storm].

pow·wow (pou′wou), *n.* **1.** a meeting of or with North American Indians. **2.** any meeting in order to discuss something: *used only in everyday talk.* —*v.* to hold a powwow.

pox (päks), *n.* a disease in which blisters form on the skin, as smallpox and chicken pox.

pp., abbreviation for **pages.**

p.p., abbreviation for **past participle.**

pr., abbreviation for **pair.** —**prs.,** *pl.*

P.R., abbreviation for **Puerto Rico.**

prac·ti·ca·ble (prak′ti kə b′l), *adj.* **1.** that can be done or put into use [a *practicable* plan]. **2.** that can be used; usable [Flat-bottomed boats are *practicable* in shallow water.] —**prac′ti·ca·bil′i·ty,** *n.* —**prac′ti·ca·bly,** *adv.*

prac·ti·cal (prak′ti k′l), *adj.* **1.** that can be put to use; useful and sensible [a *practical* idea; *practical* shoes]. **2.** dealing with things in a sensible and realistic way [It would be more *practical* to sell the boat and buy a car with the money.] **3.** learned through practice or experience [*practical* nursing]. **4.** really so, although not thought to be so; virtual [The *practical* head of England is the prime minister.]

practical joke, a trick played on one in fun.

prac·ti·cal·ly (prak′tik lē), *adv.* **1.** in a practical, useful, or sensible way [Let's look at the problem *practically*.] **2.** for practical purposes; virtually; as good as [The Civil War was *practically* over when Richmond fell.] **3.** almost; nearly: *used only in everyday talk.*

prac·tice (prak′tis), *v.* **1.** to do or carry out regularly; make a habit of [to *practice* what one preaches; to *practice* charity]. **2.** to do something over and over again in order to become skilled at it [He *practices* six hours a day on the piano.] **3.** to work at as a profession or occupation [to *practice* medicine]. —*n.* **1.** a usual action or way of acting; habit or custom [It is his *practice* to sleep late.] **2.** the doing of something over and over again in order to become skilled [batting

practice]. **3.** the skill one gets by doing this [I am out of *practice*.] **4.** the work of a profession or occupation [the *practice* of law]. **5.** the business built up by a doctor or lawyer [to have a large *practice*]. —**prac′ticed,** *p.t. & p.p.;* **prac′tic·ing,** *pr.p.*

prac·ticed (prak′tist), *adj.* skilled; expert [the *practiced* hand of the surgeon].

prac·tise (prak′tis), *v.* to practice: *used mainly in Great Britain.* —**prac′tised,** *p.t. & p.p.;* **prac′tis·ing,** *pr.p.*

prac·ti·tion·er (prak tish′ən ər), *n.* a person who practices a profession, art, etc.

prae·tor (prē′tər), *n.* an official of ancient Rome, ranking just below a consul.

prae·tor·i·an (pri tôr′i ən), *adj.* **1.** of a praetor. **2.** *often* **Praetorian,** naming or belonging to the bodyguard of a Roman emperor. —*n. often* **Praetorian,** a member of this guard.

Prague (präg), *n.* the capital of Czechoslovakia.

prai·rie (prer′ē), *n.* a large area of level or rolling grassy land without many trees.

prairie chicken, a large, brown and white grouse found on North American prairies.

prairie dog, a small animal of North America, a little like a squirrel. It has a barking cry.

prairie schooner, same as **covered wagon.**

praise (prāz), *v.* **1.** to say good things about; give a good opinion of [to *praise* someone's work]. **2.** to worship, as in song [to *praise* God]. —*n.* a praising

prairie dog (1 ft. long)

or being praised; words that show approval. —**sing one's praises,** to praise highly. —**praised,** *p.t. & p.p.;* **prais′ing,** *pr.p.*

praise·wor·thy (prāz′wûr thē), *adj.* deserving praise; that should be admired.

prance (prans), *v.* **1.** to rise up on the hind legs in a lively way, especially while moving along [*prancing* horses]. **2.** to move about with lively, strutting steps. —**pranced,** *p.t. & p.p.;* **pranc′ing,** *pr.p.*

prank (prangk), *n.* a playful trick, often one causing some mischief.

prate (prāt), *v.* to talk on and on, in a foolish way. —**prat′ed,** *p.t. & p.p.;* **prat′ing,** *pr.p.*

prat·tle (prat′'l), *v.* **1.** to talk in a childish way; babble. **2.** to prate; chatter foolishly. —*n.* chatter. —**prat′tled,** *p.t. & p.p.;* **prat′tling,** *pr.p.*

prawn (prôn), *n.* a shellfish like a large shrimp.

pray (prā), *v.* **1.** to talk or recite a set of words to God in worship or in asking for something. **2.** to beg or ask for seriously ["*Pray* tell me" means "I beg you to tell me."]

prawn (6 in. long)

prayer (prer), *n.* **1.** the act of praying. **2.** something prayed for. **3.** a humble and sincere request, as to God. **4.** a set of words used in praying to God [morning *prayer;* the Lord's *Prayer*].

prayer book, a book of prayers.

prayer·ful (prer′fəl), *adj.* **1.** praying often; devout [a *prayerful* monk]. **2.** of or like a prayer [a *prayerful* request]. —**prayer′ful·ly,** *adv.*

praying mantis, see **mantis.**

pre-, a prefix meaning "before" [A *prewar* period is a period before a war.]

preach (prēch), *v.* **1.** to speak to people on a religious subject, as in church; give a sermon. **2.** to urge or teach as by preaching [to *preach* the word of God; to *preach* peace]. **3.** to give moral or religious advice, often in a tiresome way.

preach·er (prēch′ər), *n.* a person who preaches; especially, a clergyman.

pre·am·ble (prē′am′b'l), *n.* the part at the beginning of a speech or piece of writing that tells its purpose [the *preamble* to a constitution].

pre·ar·range (prē ə ranj′), *v.* to arrange ahead of time [The meeting was *prearranged*.] —**pre·ar·ranged′,** *p.t. & p.p.;* **pre·ar·rang′ing,** *pr.p.*

pre·car·i·ous (pri ker′i əs), *adj.* not safe or sure; uncertain; risky [a *precarious* living; a *precarious* foothold]. —**pre·car′i·ous·ly,** *adv.*

pre·cau·tion (pri kô′shən), *n.* care taken ahead of time, as against danger, failure, etc. [He took the *precaution* of locking the door before he left.] —**pre·cau′tion·ar′y,** *adj.*

pre·cede (pri sēd′), *v.* to go or come before in time, order, rank, etc. [She *preceded* him into the room. A colonel *precedes* a major.] —**pre·ced′ed,** *p.t. & p.p.;* **pre·ced′ing,** *pr.p.*

pre·ced·ence (pres′ə dəns *or* pri sē′d'ns), *n.* the act, fact, or right of coming before in time, order, rank, etc. [The election of officers will take *precedence* at our next meeting.]

pre·ced·ent (pres′ə dənt), *n.* an act, ruling, etc. that may be used as an example or rule for one coming later. —*adj.* (pri sē′d'nt), going or coming before; preceding [a *precedent* event].

pre·ced·ing (pri sēd′ing), *adj.* going or coming before; previous [in the *preceding* paragraph].

pre·cept (prē′sept), *n.* a rule that tells how one should behave; maxim ["Look before you leap" is a well-known *precept*.]

pre·cep·tor (pri sep′tər), *n.* a teacher.

pre·cinct (prē′singkt), *n.* **1.** any of the districts into which a ward or city is divided [a voting *precinct;* a police *precinct*]. **2.** *usually* **precincts,** *pl.* the grounds inside the limits of a church, school, etc. **3.** a boundary or limit.

pre·cious (presh′əs), *adj.* **1.** having a high price or value [Diamonds are *precious* gems. Freedom is *precious*.] **2.** much loved; dear [her *precious* child]. **3.** too delicate or refined; not natural [a *precious* style of writing]. **4.** very great: *used only in everyday talk* [a *precious* liar]. —**pre′-cious·ly,** *adv.*

prec·i·pice (pres′ə pis), *n.* a steep cliff that goes almost straight down.

pre·cip·i·tant (pri sip′ə tənt), *adj.* acting or done in a sudden, hasty, or reckless way [He made a *precipitant* exit.] —*n.* a substance that causes another substance to separate out as a solid from the liquid in which it is dissolved.

pre·cip·i·tate (pri sip′ə tāt), *v.* **1.** to cause something to happen before one expects it or is ready for it [The floods *precipitated* a crisis.] **2.** to throw down or plunge headlong. **3.** to separate out as a solid from the liquid in which it is dissolved [Salt was *precipitated* from the solution when the acid was added.] **4.** to condense and cause to fall as rain, snow, etc. —*adj.* (*also* pri sip′ə tit), acting or done in a very hasty or reckless way [his *precipitate* departure]. —*n.* (*also* pri sip′ə tit), a substance precipitated from a solution. —**pre·cip′i·tat·ed,** *p.t. & p.p.;* **pre·cip′i·tat·ing,** *pr.p.*

pre·cip·i·ta·tion (pri sip′ə tā′shən), *n.* **1.** a sudden bringing about of something [the *precipitation* of a crisis]. **2.** a throwing or falling headlong. **3.** sudden or reckless haste. **4.** rain, snow, etc. or the amount of this. **5.** the separating out of a solid from the liquid in which it is dissolved.

pre·cip·i·tous (pri sip′ə təs), *adj.* **1.** steep like a precipice. **2.** hasty or reckless.

pre·cise (pri sīs′), *adj.* **1.** exact in every detail; definite; accurate [the *precise* sum of $11.29; *precise* pronunciation]. **2.** very careful or strict, especially in following rules. —**pre·cise′ly,** *adv.* —**pre·cise′ness,** *n.*

pre·ci·sion (pri sizh′ən), *n.* exactness; accuracy [the *precision* of a watch].

pre·clude (pri klōōd′), *v.* to make impossible; shut out; prevent [His care *precluded* any chance of failure.] —**pre·clud′ed,** *p.t. & p.p.;* **pre·clud′ing,** *pr.p.*

pre·co·cious (pri kō′shəs), *adj.* having or showing much more ability, knowledge, etc. than is usual at such a young age [The *precocious* boy entered college when he was fourteen.] —**pre·co′cious·ly,** *adv.* —**pre·coc·i·ty** (pri käs′ə tē), *n.*

pre·con·ceive (prē kən sēv′), *v.* to form an idea or opinion of beforehand [a *preconceived* notion]. —**pre·con·ceived′,** *p.t. & p.p.;* **pre·con·ceiv′ing,** *pr.p.*

pre·con·cep·tion (prē′kən sep′shən), *n.* an idea or opinion formed beforehand.

pre·con·cert·ed (prē′kən sur′tid), *adj.* arranged or agreed upon beforehand [a *preconcerted* attack].

pre·cur·sor (pri kur′sər), *n.* a person or thing that comes before and makes the way ready for what will follow; forerunner [The harpsichord was a *precursor* of the piano.]

pred·a·to·ry (pred′ə tôr′ē), *adj.* **1.** that lives by killing and eating other animals [Eagles are *predatory* birds.] **2.** that lives by robbing, stealing, etc. [a *predatory* band of thieves.]

---

fat, āpe, cär, ten, ēven, hit, bīte, gō, hôrn, tōōl, book, up, fur;
get, joy, yet, chin, she, thin, *th*en; zh = s in pleasure; ′ as in able (ā′b'l);
ə = a in ago, e in agent, i in sanity, o in confess, u in focus.

pred·e·ces·sor (pred′ə ses′ər), *n.* a person who held a job or position before another [Taft was the *predecessor* of Wilson as President.]

pre·des·ti·na·tion (pri des′tə nā′shən), *n.* **1.** the act by which God is believed to have decided beforehand upon everything that would happen. **2.** the belief that God decided beforehand which souls were to be saved and which to be condemned. **3.** one's fate in life; destiny.

pre·des·tine (pri des′tin), *v.* to order or decide beforehand; foreordain [He seemed *predestined* to be a poet.] —**pre·des′tined,** *p.t. & p.p.;* **pre·des′tin·ing,** *pr.p.*

pre·de·ter·mine (prē′di tūr′min), *v.* to determine or decide beforehand [a *predetermined* route]. —**pre′de·ter′mined,** *p.t. & p.p.;* **pre′de·ter′min·ing,** *pr.p.*

pre·dic·a·ment (pri dik′ə mənt), *n.* a bad situation which is hard to work one's way out of [Losing his keys put Tom in a *predicament.*]

pred·i·cate (pred′i kit), *n.* the word or words that say something about the subject of a sentence or clause. A predicate may be a verb, a verb and adverb, a verb and its object, etc. (The wind *blows.* The wind *blows hard.* The wind *blows the leaves down.*) —*adj.* of or in a predicate [In the sentence "John is ill," "ill" is a *predicate* adjective.] —*v.* (pred′i kāt), **1.** to base upon certain facts, conditions, etc. [The decisions of the courts are *predicated* upon the Constitution.] **2.** to say that something is a quality of something else [Let us *predicate* the honesty of his motives.] —**pred′i·cat·ed,** *p.t. & p.p.;* **pred′i·cat·ing,** *pr.p.*

pre·dict (pri dikt′), *v.* to tell what one thinks will happen in the future; foretell [I *predict* that you will win.] —**pre·dict′a·ble,** *adj.*

pre·dic·tion (pri dik′shən), *n.* **1.** the act of predicting. **2.** something predicted.

pre·di·lec·tion (prē′də lek′shən *or* pred″l ek′shən), *n.* a liking or taste; preference.

pre·dis·pose (prē′dis pōz′), *v.* to make more likely to accept, get, etc.; incline [Being tired *predisposes* a person to illness.] —**pre′dis·posed′,** *p.t. & p.p.;* **pre′dis·pos′ing,** *pr.p.* —**pre·dis·po·si·tion** (prē′dis pə zish′ən), *n.*

pre·dom·i·nant (pri däm′ə nənt), *adj.* **1.** having more power than others; dominating [The mayor had the *predominant* voice in the discussion.] **2.** most frequent; prevailing [Cotton is the *predominant* choice for summer dresses.] —**pre·dom′i·nance,** *n.* —**pre·dom′i·nant·ly,** *adv.*

pre·dom·i·nate (pri däm′ə nāt), *v.* to be greater in amount, power, etc.; prevail [Yellow *predominates* in this pattern.] —**pre·dom′i·nat·ed,** *p.t. & p.p.;* **pre·dom′i·nat·ing,** *pr.p.* —**pre·dom′i·na′tion,** *n.*

pre·em·i·nent *or* **pre·ëm·i·nent** (prē em′ə nənt), *adj.* most outstanding in worth, rank, fame, etc. [He is *pre-eminent* among modern painters.] —**pre·em′i·nence** *or* **pre·ëm′i·nence,** *n.* —**pre·em′i·nent·ly** *or* **pre·ëm′i·nent·ly,** *adv.*

pre·empt *or* **pre·ëmpt** (prē empt′), *v.* **1.** to get before anyone else can; appropriate [They came early and *pre-empted* the best seats.] **2.** to settle on in order to get the right to buy [Each settler *pre-empted* 160 acres of public land.] —**pre·emp′tion** *or* **pre·ëmp′tion,** *n.*

preen (prēn), *v.* **1.** to clean and smooth the feathers with the beak, as a bird does. **2.** to dress up or make oneself trim and neat.

pre·ex·ist *or* **pre·ëx·ist** (prē′ig zist′), *v.* to exist before, or at an earlier time. —**pre′-ex·ist′ence** *or* **pre′ëx·ist′ence,** *n.* —**pre′-ex·ist′ent** *or* **pre′ëx·ist′ent,** *adj.*

pre·fab·ri·cate (prē fab′ri kāt), *v.* to make at a factory in sections that can be put together quickly [a *prefabricated* house]. —**pre·fab′ri·cat·ed,** *p.t. & p.p.;* **pre·fab′ri·cat·ing,** *pr.p.*

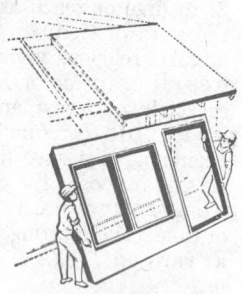
section of a prefabricated house

pref·ace (pref′is), *n.* an introduction to a book, article, or speech. —*v.* to give or be a preface to [He *prefaced* his talk with a joke.] —**pref′aced,** *p.t. & p.p.;* **pref′ac·ing,** *pr.p.*

pref·a·to·ry (pref′ə tôr′ē), *adj.* that is, or is like, a preface; introductory.

pre·fect (prē′fekt), *n.* an official of high rank, as in the government of ancient Rome or of local government in modern France.

pre·fec·ture (prē′fek chər), *n.* the office or area that a prefect is in charge of.

pre·fer (pri fūr′), *v.* **1.** to like better; choose first [He *prefers* baseball to football.] **2.** to bring before a law court [He *preferred* charges against the man who robbed him.] **3.** to put in a higher position or office; promote. —**pre·ferred′,** *p.t. & p.p.;* **pre·fer′ring,** *pr.p.*

pref·er·a·ble (pref′ər ə b'l), *adj.* that is to be preferred; more desirable. —**pref′er·a·bly,** *adv.*

pref·er·ence (pref′ər əns), *n.* **1.** the fact of preferring; greater liking [He has a *preference* for lively music.] **2.** something preferred; one's choice [What is your *preference* in sports?] **3.** favor shown to one over another; advantage [They show *preference* for younger men in hiring.]

pref·er·en·tial (pref′ə ren′shəl), *adj.* showing, giving, or getting preference [*preferential* treatment].

pre·fer·ment (pri fūr′mənt), *n.* the fact of being given a higher rank, office, etc.; promotion.

pre·fig·ure (prē fig′yər), *v.* **1.** to show ahead of time; be a foreshadowing of. **2.** to imagine ahead of time. —**pre·fig′ured,** *p.t. & p.p.;* **pre·fig′ur·ing,** *pr.p.*

pre·fix (prē′fiks), *n.* a syllable or group of syllables joined to the beginning of a word to change its meaning. Some common prefixes are *un-, non-, re-, anti-,* and *in-.* —*v.* (prē fiks′), to place before [*Prefix* a brief introduction to your talk.]

preg·nant (preg′nənt), *adj.* **1.** carrying an unborn child in the womb. **2.** filled; rich; loaded [a book *pregnant* with ideas]. **3.** full of meaning; significant [a *pregnant* silence]. —**preg·nan·cy** (preg′nən sē), *n.*

pre·his·tor·ic (prē′his tôr′ik) *or* **pre·his·tor·i·cal** (prē′his tôr′i k'l), *adj.* of the time before history was written [Dinosaurs were *prehistoric* creatures.] —**pre′his·tor′i·cal·ly,** *adv.*

pre·judge (prē juj′), *v.* to judge beforehand or before one knows enough to judge fairly. —**pre·judged′,** *p.t. & p.p.;* **pre·judg′ing,** *pr.p.*

prej·u·dice (prej′oo dis), *n.* **1.** an opinion formed without knowing the facts or by ignoring the facts; unfair or unreasonable opinion [Some people have a *prejudice* against modern art.] **2.** dislike or distrust of people just because they are of another race, religion, country, etc. **3.** harm or damage [He gave evidence to the *prejudice* of the defendant.] —*v.* **1.** to fill with prejudice [Joan *prejudiced* her sister against their aunt.] **2.** to harm or damage [One low grade *prejudiced* his chances for a scholarship.] —**prej′u·diced,** *p.t. & p.p.;* **prej′u·dic·ing,** *pr.p.*

prej·u·di·cial (prej′oo dish′əl), *adj.* causing prejudice, or harm; damaging.

prel·a·cy (prel′ə sē), *n.* **1.** the office or rank of a prelate. **2.** prelates as a group. **3.** church government by prelates. —**prel′a·cies,** *pl.*

prel·ate (prel′it), *n.* a member of the clergy who has a high rank, as a bishop.

pre·lim·i·nar·y (pri lim′ə ner′ē), *adj.* leading up to the main action; introductory [the *preliminary* matches before the main bout]. —*n.* something that is done first; preliminary step [When the *preliminaries* were over, the meeting began.] —**pre·lim′i·nar′ies,** *pl.*

prel·ude (prel′yŏŏd *or* prē′lŏŏd), *n.* **1.** a part that comes before or leads up to what follows [The calm was a *prelude* to the storm.] **2.** a part at the beginning of a piece of music, as of a fugue; also, a short, romantic piece of music.

pre·ma·ture (prē mə tyŏŏr′ *or* prē mə chŏŏr′), *adj.* before the usual or proper time; too early or too hasty. —**pre·ma·ture′ly,** *adv.*

pre·med·i·tate (prē med′ə tāt), *v.* to think out or plan ahead of time [a *premeditated* crime]. —**pre·med′i·tat·ed,** *p.t. & p.p.;* **pre·med′i·tat·ing,** *pr.p.* —**pre′med·i·ta′tion,** *n.*

pre·mier (pri mir′), *n.* a chief official; especially, a prime minister. —*adj.* (prē′mi ər), first in importance or position; chief.

pre·mière (pri mir′), *n.* the first performance of a play, motion picture, etc.

prem·ise (prem′is), *n.* **1.** a statement or belief that is taken for granted and is used as the basis for a theory, argument, etc. [the democratic *premise* that all citizens have equal rights]. **2.** premises, *pl.* a building and the land belonging to it [Keep off the *premises.*] —*v.* (pri mīz′), to state as a premise. —**pre·mised′,** *p.t. & p.p.;* **pre·mis′ing,** *pr.p.*

pre·mi·um (prē′mi əm), *n.* **1.** a reward or prize offered to give an added reason for buying or doing something [a valuable *premium* inside the box; extra pay as a *premium* for good work]. **2.** an extra amount added to the regular charge. **3.** any of the payments made for an insurance policy. **4.** very high value [She puts a *premium* on neatness.] —**at a premium,** very valuable because hard to get.

pre·mo·ni·tion (prē′mə nish′ən), *n.* a feeling that something bad will happen; forewarning.

pre·na·tal (prē nā′t'l), *adj.* before birth.

pre·oc·cu·py (prē äk′yoo pī), *v.* **1.** to take up one's attention so that other things are not noticed; absorb [He is *preoccupied* with vacation plans.] **2.** to take or occupy before someone else can. —**pre·oc′cu·pied,** *p.t. & p.p.;* **pre·oc′cu·py·ing,** *pr.p.* —**pre·oc′cu·pa′tion,** *n.*

pre·or·dain (prē′ôr dān′), *v.* to order or decide beforehand what will happen.

prep., abbreviation for **preposition.**

pre·paid (prē pād′), past tense and past participle of **prepay.**

prep·a·ra·tion (prep′ə rā′shən), *n.* **1.** a getting ready or being ready. **2.** something done to prepare, or get ready. **3.** something made or put together for some purpose, as a medicine, cosmetic, etc.

pre·par·a·to·ry (pri par′ə tôr′ē), *adj.* **1.** that prepares or helps to prepare [A *preparatory* school prepares students for college.] **2.** being prepared.

pre·pare (pri per′), *v.* **1.** to make or get ready [to *prepare* for a test; to *prepare* ground for planting]. **2.** to furnish with what is needed; equip [to *prepare* an expedition]. **3.** to make or put together out of parts or materials [to *prepare* a medicine]. —**pre·pared′,** *p.t. & p.p.;* **pre·par′ing,** *pr.p.*

pre·pay (prē pā′), *v.* to pay for ahead of time [Postage is normally *prepaid.*] —**pre·paid′,** *p.t. & p.p.;* **pre·pay′ing,** *pr.p.*

pre·pon·der·ant (pri pän′dər ənt), *adj.* greater in amount, power, importance, etc. [the *preponderant* religion of a country]. —**pre·pon′der·ance,** *n.*

pre·pon·der·ate (pri pän′də rāt), *v.* to be greater in amount, power, importance, etc. —**pre·pon′der·at·ed,** *p.t. & p.p.;* **pre·pon′der·at·ing,** *pr.p.*

prep·o·si·tion (prep′ə zish′ən), *n.* a word that connects a noun or pronoun to something else in the sentence, as to a verb (he went *to* the store), to a noun (the sound *of* tramping feet), or to an adjective (old *in* years).

prep·o·si·tion·al (prep′ə zish′ən 'l), *adj.* of, used as, or formed with a preposition.

pre·pos·sess·ing (prē′pə zes′ing), *adj.* making a good impression; pleasing; attractive.

pre·pos·ter·ous (pri päs′tər əs), *adj.* so clearly wrong or against reason as to be laughable; absurd [a *preposterous* idea].

---

fat, āpe, cär, ten, ēven, hit, bīte, gō, hôrn, tōōl, book, up, fûr;
get, joy, yet, chin, she, thin, *then*; zh = s in pleasure; ′ as in able (ā′b'l);
ə = a in ago, e in agent, i in sanity, o in confess, u in focus.

pre·req·ui·site (prē rek′wə zit), *n.* something that is needed before something else can happen or be done [Mathematics is a *prerequisite* for a career in science.]

pre·rog·a·tive (pri räg′ə tiv), *n.* a special right of some group, office, etc. [Most governors have the *prerogative* of pardoning prisoners.]

pres·age (pri sāj′), *v.* to give a sign or warning of; foretell [dark clouds *presaging* a storm]. —*n.* (pres′ij), 1. a sign or warning of a future happening. 2. a feeling that something is going to happen, especially something bad. —**pres·aged′,** *p.t. & p.p.;* **pres·ag′ing,** *pr.p.*

Pres·by·ter·i·an (prez′bə tir′i ən), *n.* a member of a Protestant church that is governed by church officials called *elders.* —*adj.* of the Presbyterians. —**Pres′by·ter′i·an·ism.**

pres·by·ter·y (prez′bi tir′ē), *n.* 1. a Presbyterian church court made up of ministers and elders in a certain district. 2. such a district. 3. the part of a church where the clergy conduct the the services. —**pres′by·ter′ies,** *pl.*

pre·school (prē′skōōl′), *adj.* of or for children who do not yet go to school.

pre·sci·ence (prē′shi əns *or* presh′i əns), *n.* a knowing about things before they happen; foresight. —**pre′sci·ent,** *adj.*

pre·scribe (pri skrīb′), *v.* 1. to set up as a rule or direction to be followed; order [the penalty *prescribed* by law]. 2. to order or advise to take a certain medicine or treatment [The doctor *prescribed* aspirin and warm compresses.] —**pre·scribed′,** *p.t. & p.p.;* **pre·scrib′ing,** *pr.p.*

pre·scrip·tion (pri skrip′shən), *n.* 1. an order or direction. 2. a doctor's written instructions telling how to prepare and use a medicine; also, a medicine made by following such instructions.

pres·ence (prez′′ns), *n.* 1. the fact or condition of being present [his *presence* at the meeting]. 2. the very place where a certain person is [We were admitted to the king's *presence.*] 3. a person's looks, manner, etc. [a man of stately *presence*]. 4. a ghost, spirit, etc. felt to be present. —**presence of mind,** ability to think clearly and act quickly in an emergency.

pres·ent (prez′′nt), *adj.* 1. being here or at a certain place; not absent [Is everyone *present* today?] 2. of or at this time; for now; not past or future [My *present* needs are few.] 3. showing time now going on. The **present tense** of a verb shows action now taking place (he *goes*), a condition now existing (the plums *are* ripe), action that keeps taking place (he *speaks* with an accent), or action that is always true (living things *die*). —*n.* 1. this time; now [At *present,* I am in school.] 2. something presented, or given; gift [Christmas *presents*]. —*v.* (pri zent′), 1. to make known; introduce [John *presented* his friend to me.] 2. to put on view; display; show [to *present* a play on Broadway]. 3. to offer for others to think about [May I *present* my ideas at the meeting?] 4. to give as a gift [to *present* a book to someone]. 5. to give to [He *presented* the school with a piano.]

pre·sent·a·ble (pri zen′tə b′l), *adj.* 1. that can be presented; fit to be shown, given, etc. to others [He's putting his talk in *presentable* form.] 2. properly dressed for meeting people.

pres·en·ta·tion (prē′zen tā′shən *or* prez′′n-tā′shən), *n.* 1. the act of presenting, or introducing, giving, showing, etc. [a *presentation* of awards]. 2. something that is presented, as a show, gift, etc.

pres·ent-day (prez′′nt dā′), *adj.* of the present time [*present-day* styles in clothing].

pre·sen·ti·ment (pri zen′tə mənt), *n.* a feeling that something is going to happen, especially something bad; foreboding.

pres·ent·ly (prez′′nt lē), *adv.* 1. in a little while; soon [I'll join you *presently.*] 2. at this time; now [Bob is *presently* on vacation.]

pre·sent·ment (pri zent′mənt), *n.* presentation.

present participle, a participle used to show present time, or action still going on [In the sentence "I am leaving now," "leaving" is a *present participle.*]

pres·er·va·tion (prez′ər vā′shən), *n.* a preserving or being preserved [*preservation* of food].

pre·ser·va·tive (pri zūr′və tiv), *n.* anything that preserves; especially, a substance added to food to keep it from spoiling.

pre·serve (pri zūrv′), *v.* 1. to protect from harm or damage; save [to *preserve* our national forests]. 2. to keep from spoiling or rotting. 3. to prepare food for later use by canning, pickling, or salting it. 4. to keep in a certain condition; maintain [He tried to *preserve* his dignity.] —*n.* 1. *usually* **preserves,** *pl.* fruit preserved by cooking it with sugar and canning it. 2. a place where fish and wild animals are protected or are kept for controlled hunting and fishing. —**pre·served′,** *p.t. & p.p.;* **pre·serv′ing,** *pr.p.*

pre·side (pri zīd′), *v.* 1. to be in charge of a meeting; act as chairman [The Vice President *presides* over the U.S. Senate.] 2. to have charge of; control. —**pre·sid′ed,** *p.t. & p.p.* **pre·sid′-ing,** *pr.p.*

pres·i·den·cy (prez′i dən sē), *n.* 1. the office of president. 2. a president's term of office. —**pres′i·den·cies,** *pl.*

pres·i·dent (prez′i dənt), *n.* 1. the highest officer of a company, club, college, etc. 2. *often* **President,** the head of government in a republic.

pres·i·den·tial (prez′i den′shəl), *adj.* of or having to do with a president or the presidency.

press (pres), *v.* 1. to act on with steady force or weight; push against, weigh down, squeeze, etc. [to *press* a doorbell]. 2. to push closely together; crowd [Thousands *pressed* into the arena.] 3. to make clothes smooth by ironing; iron. 4. to squeeze out [to *press* oil from olives]. 5. to hold close; hug; embrace [He *pressed* the child in his arms.] 6. to keep moving forward [The soldiers *pressed* on through the night.] 7. to force [She *pressed* the gift on her friend.] 8. to trouble or worry by a lack of something [*pressed* for money]. 9. to keep on asking or urging [The store *pressed* her for the money she owed.] —*n.* **1.** a pressing or being pressed; pressure [The *press* of business kept him away for a time.] **2.** a crowd. **3.** a machine or tool by which something is pressed, smoothed, squeezed, etc. [a cider *press*]. **4.** short for **printing press.** **5.** a place where printing is done. **6.** newspapers, magazines, etc., or the people who work for them [The President meets the *press* on Tuesday.] **7.** a closet for storing clothes. —**go to press,** to start to be printed. —**press′er,** *n.*

press (pres), *v.* to force into some work or service, especially into an army or navy.

press agent, a person whose work is to get publicity for a person, group, etc.

press·ing (pres′ing), *adj.* needing quick action; urgent [a *pressing* problem].

pres·sure (presh′ər), *n.* **1.** a pressing or being pressed; force of pushing or of weight [the *pressure* of the foot on the brake]. **2.** a condition of trouble, strain, etc. that is hard to bear [overcome by the *pressure* of his grief]. **3.** influence or force to make someone do something [Bill's parents brought *pressure* to bear on him to return to college.] **4.** urgent demands; urgency [a news story written under *pressure* of time]. **5.** the force pressing against a surface, stated in weight per unit of area [Normal air *pressure* at sea level is about 14.7 pounds per square inch.] —*v.* to try to force to do something: *only in everyday talk.* —**pres′sured,** *p.t. & p.p.;* **pres′sur·ing,** *pr.p.*

pres·sur·ize (presh′ər īz), *v.* to keep the air pressure close to normal, as inside an airplane. —**pres′sur·ized,** *p.t. & p.p.;* **pres′sur·iz·ing,** *pr.p.*

pres·tige (pres tēzh′), *n.* fame or respect that comes from doing great things, having good character, etc.

pres·to (pres′tō), *adj. & adv.* fast: an Italian word used as a direction in music.

pre·sum·a·ble (pri zo͞om′ə b'l), *adj.* that can be taken to be true; probable. —**pre·sum′a·bly,** *adv.*

pre·sume (pri zo͞om′), *v.* **1.** to be so bold as to; dare [I wouldn't *presume* to tell you what to do.] **2.** to take as true; take for granted; suppose [I *presume* you know what you are doing.] **3.** to be too bold; take advantage of [Would I be *presuming* on our friendship if I asked a favor?] —**pre·sumed′,** *p.t. & p.p.;* **pre·sum′ing,** *pr.p.*

pre·sump·tion (pri zump′shən), *n.* **1.** the act of presuming. **2.** the thing that is presumed or taken for granted [Because of the dark clouds, the *presumption* is that it will rain.] **3.** a reason for presuming something. **4.** too great boldness [his *presumption* in ordering us to leave].

pre·sump·tive (pri zump′tiv), *adj.* **1.** giving reason for believing something [*presumptive* evidence]. **2.** based on what is probable [Since the king has no children, his brother is heir *presumptive*.] —**pre·sump′tive·ly,** *adv.*

pre·sump·tu·ous (pri zump′cho͞o əs), *adj.* too bold or daring; taking too much for granted [How *presumptuous* of her to offer advice without being asked!] —**pre·sump′tu·ous·ly,** *adv.*

pre·sup·pose (prē sə pōz′), *v.* **1.** to suppose beforehand; take for granted [Let's *presuppose* that we win the game.] **2.** to need or show as a reason [A healthy body *presupposes* a proper diet.] —**pre·sup·posed′,** *p.t. & p.p.;* **pre·sup·pos′ing,** *pr.p.* —**pre·sup·po·si·tion** (prē′sup ə zish′ən), *n.*

pre·tence (pri tens′ *or* prē′tens), *n.* British spelling of **pretense.**

pre·tend (pri tend′), *v.* **1.** to make believe, as in play [Let's *pretend* we're cowboys.] **2.** to claim or act in a false way [He *pretended* to be happy.] **3.** to lay claim [to *pretend* to a throne]. —**pre·tend′ed,** *adj.*

pre·tend·er (pri ten′dər), *n.* **1.** a person who pretends. **2.** a person who claims the right to a title, especially to be king.

pre·tense (pri tens′ *or* prē′tens), *n.* **1.** a claim [He made no *pretense* to being rich.] **2.** a false claim, excuse, or show [a *pretense* of being ill; a *pretense* of honesty]. **3.** a pretending, as in a game; make-believe. **4.** a showing off; display [a simple person, without *pretense*].

pre·ten·sion (pri ten′shən), *n.* **1.** a claim, as to some right or title [He has *pretensions* to the estate.] **2.** a false claim or excuse. **3.** a showing off; display.

pre·ten·tious (pri ten′shəs), *adj.* claiming or seeming to be very important, fine, etc.; showing off; flashy [a *pretentious* house]. —**pre·ten′tious·ly,** *adv.* —**pre·ten′tious·ness,** *n.*

pre·ter·nat·u·ral (prē′tər nach′ər əl), *adj.* different from or beyond what is natural; abnormal or supernatural. —**pre′ter·nat′u·ral·ly,** *adv.*

pre·text (prē′tekst), *n.* a false reason given to hide the real one [She was bored but left on the *pretext* of being ill.]

pret·ty (prit′ē *or* pur′tē), *adj.* **1.** pleasant to look at or hear, especially in a delicate, dainty, or graceful way [a *pretty* girl; a *pretty* voice; a *pretty* garden]. **2.** fine; good; nice: *often used to mean just the opposite* [You've made a *pretty* mess!] —*adv.* somewhat; rather [I'm *pretty* tired.] —*n.* a pretty person or thing. —**pret′ti·er,** *compar.;* **pret′ti·est,** *superl.* —**pret′ties,** *pl.* —**pret′ti·ly,** *adv.* —**pret′ti·ness,** *n.*

pret·zel (pret′s'l), *n.* a slender roll of dough, usually twisted in a knot, sprinkled with salt, and baked until hard.

pre·vail (pri vāl′), *v.* **1.** to be successful or win out [to *prevail* over an enemy]. **2.** to be or become more common or widespread, as a custom or practice. —**pre·vail upon** or **prevail on,** to get to do something; persuade.

pretzel

fat, āpe, cär, ten, ēven, hit, bīte, gō, hôrn, to͞ol, book, up, fûr;
get, joy, yet, chin, she, thin, *then*; zh = s in pleasure; ' as in able (ā′b'l);
ə = a in ago, e in agent, i in sanity, o in confess, u in focus.

pre·vail·ing (pri vāl/ing), *adj.* strongest, most common, or most frequent; leading all others [a *prevailing* wind; a *prevailing* style].

prev·a·lent (prev/ə lənt), *adj.* that exists, happens, etc. over a wide area; common; general [a *prevalent* belief]. —**prev/a·lence,** *n.*

pre·var·i·cate (pri var/ə kāt), *v.* to try to hide the truth; lie. —**pre·var/i·cat·ed,** *p.t. & p.p.;* **pre·var/i·cat·ing,** *pr.p.* —**pre·var/i·ca/tion,** *n.* —**pre·var/i·ca'tor,** *n.*

pre·vent (pri vent/), *v.* **1.** to stop or hinder [A storm *prevented* us from going.] **2.** to keep from happening [Careful driving *prevents* accidents.] —**pre·vent/a·ble** or **pre·vent/i·ble,** *adj.*

pre·ven·tion (pri ven/shən), *n.* **1.** the act of preventing. **2.** a means of preventing.

pre·ven·tive (pri ven/tiv), *adj.* that prevents; especially, that prevents disease [*preventive* medicine]. —*n.* anything that prevents disease, trouble, etc.

pre·view (prē/vyo͞o), *n.* a view or showing ahead of time; especially, a private showing of a movie before showing it to the public. —*v.* (prē vyo͞o/ *or* prē/vyo͞o), to give a preview of.

pre·vi·ous (prē/vi əs), *adj.* **1.** happening before in time or order; earlier [at a *previous* meeting; on the *previous* page]. **2.** too early or too quick: *used only in everyday talk.* —**previous to,** before. —**pre/vi·ous·ly,** *adv.*

pre·war (prē/wôr/). *adj.* before the war.

prey (prā), *n.* **1.** an animal hunted for food by another animal [Chickens often are the *prey* of hawks.] **2.** a person or thing that becomes the victim of someone or something [Many people fell *prey* to the plague.] **3.** the act of seizing other animals for food [The eagle is a bird of *prey*.] —*v.* **1.** to hunt other animals for food. **2.** to rob by force; plunder [The pirates *preyed* upon helpless ships.] **3.** to get money from, as by cheating [Gamblers *prey* on foolish people.] **4.** to harm or weigh down [Debts *prey* upon my mind.]

Pri·am (prī/əm), *n.* the king of Troy in Homer's *Iliad.* He was the father of Hector and Paris.

price (prīs), *n.* **1.** the amount of money asked or paid for something; cost [What is the *price* of that coat?] **2.** value or worth [a painting of great *price*]. **3.** a reward for the capture or killing as of a criminal [There's a *price* on his head.] **4.** what must be done or sacrificed in order to get something [He gained success at the *price* of his health.] —*v.* **1.** to set the price of [The rug was *priced* at $10.] **2.** to find out the price of: *used only in everyday talk* [I'll *price* all the models before I buy.] —**at any price,** no matter what the cost. —**beyond price,** very valuable; priceless. —**priced,** *p.t. & p.p.;* **pric/ing,** *pr.p.*

price·less (prīs/lis), *adj.* too valuable to be measured by price [a *priceless* painting].

prick (prik), *v.* **1.** to make a small hole in with a sharp point [I *pricked* my finger with the needle.] **2.** to cause or feel sharp pain in; sting [Guilt *pricked* his conscience.] **3.** to mark by dots or small holes [to *prick* a design in leather]. —*n.*

1. a tiny hole made by a sharp point. **2.** a pricking, or a sharp pain caused as by pricking [a *prick* of a pin]. —**prick up one's ears,** to raise the ears or listen closely.

prick·le (prik/'l), *n.* **1.** a small, sharp point, as a thorn. **2.** a stinging feeling; tingle. —*v.* **1.** to prick as with a thorn. **2.** to sting or tingle. —**prick/led,** *p.t. & p.p.;* **prick/ling,** *pr.p.*

prick·ly (prik/lē), *adj.* **1.** full of prickles, or sharp points. **2.** that stings or tingles. —**prick/li·er,** *compar.;* **prick/li·est,** *superl.*

prickly pear, 1. a kind of cactus with a flat stem. **2.** its fruit, which is shaped like a pear and can be eaten.

pride (prīd), *n.* **1.** an opinion of oneself that is too high; vanity [His *pride* blinded him to his own faults.] **2.** proper respect for oneself; dignity; self-respect [He has too much *pride* to go begging.] **3.** pleasure or satisfaction in something done, owned, etc. [He takes *pride* in his model airplanes.] **4.** a person or thing that makes one proud [He is his mother's *pride*.] —**pride oneself on,** to be proud of. —**prid/ed,** *p.t. & p.p.;* **prid/ing,** *pr.p.*

priest (prēst), *n.* **1.** a clergyman in certain Christian churches, especially in the Roman Catholic Church. **2.** a person of special rank who performs religious rites in a temple of God or a god. —**priest/ess,** *n. fem.* —**priest/hood,** *n.*

priest·ly (prēst/lē), *adj.* of, like, or fit for a priest.

prig (prig), *n.* an annoying person who acts as though he were better than others in manners, morals, etc. —**prig/gish,** *adj.*

prim (prim), *adj.* very proper in a stiff and narrow way. —**prim/mer,** *compar.;* **prim/mest,** *superl.* —**prim/ly,** *adv.* —**prim/ness,** *n.*

pri·ma·cy (prī/mə sē), *n.* **1.** the position of being first in time, rank, importance, etc. **2.** the rank or duties of a primate in a church. —**pri/ma·cies,** *pl.*

pri·ma don·na (prē/mə dän/ə), **1.** the most important woman singer in an opera. **2.** a very conceited, excitable person, especially a woman. —**pri/ma don/nas,** *pl.*

pri·mal (prī/m'l), *adj.* **1.** first in time; original. **2.** first in importance; chief.

pri·ma·ri·ly (prī mer/ə lē *or* prī/mer/ə lē), *adv.* **1.** at first; originally [The idea was *primarily* yours.] **2.** for the most part; mainly [a concert *primarily* for children].

pri·ma·ry (prī/mer/ē *or* prī/mər ē), *adj.* **1.** first in time or order [the *primary* grades in school]. **2.** from which others are taken or made; basic [Red, yellow, and blue are the *primary* colors.] **3.** first in importance; chief [a matter of *primary* interest]. —*n.* **1.** something first in order, importance, etc. **2.** *often* **primaries,** *pl.* an election in which candidates are chosen for a later election. —**pri/ma/ries,** *pl.*

pri·mate (prī/māt), *n.* **1.** an archbishop, or the bishop ranking highest in a region. **2.** any member of the most highly developed order of animals, including man, the apes, and monkeys.

prime (prīm), *adj.* **1.** first in rank or importance [his *prime* intention]. **2.** first in quality [*prime* beef]. **3.** that can be divided only by itself or by 1 without leaving a fraction [3, 5, 19, and 97 are *prime* numbers.] —*n.* **1.** the first or earliest part or stage. **2.** the best or most active period in the life of a person or thing [an athlete in his *prime*]. —*v.* to make ready by putting something in or on [to *prime* a gun by putting in gunpowder; to *prime* a pump by pouring in water; to *prime* a surface for painting by putting on sizing; to *prime* a student for a test by supplying him with facts]. —**primed,** *p.t. & p.p.;* **prim′ing,** *pr.p.*

prime minister, in some countries, the chief official of the government; premier.

prim·er (prim′ər), *n.* **1.** a simple book for first teaching children to read. **2.** a book that gives the first lessons of any subject.

prim·er (prīm′ər), *n.* a person or thing that primes, as a cap or tube with gunpowder for firing the main charge of a gun.

pri·me·val (prī mē′v'l), *adj.* of earliest times; primitive [a *primeval* grove of redwoods].

prim·ing (prīm′ing), *n.* **1.** the explosive used to fire a charge, as in a gun. **2.** a first coat of paint, sizing, etc.

prim·i·tive (prim′ə tiv), *adj.* **1.** of or living in earliest times; ancient [Some *primitive* peoples worshiped the sun.] **2.** like that of earliest times; crude; simple [*primitive* art]. —*n.* **1.** a primitive person or thing. **2.** an artist who does primitive work. —**prim′i·tive·ly,** *adv.*

pri·mo·gen·i·ture (prī′mə jen′i chər), *n.* **1.** the condition of being a first-born child. **2.** the right of the eldest son to inherit his father's estate.

primp (primp), *v.* to dress in a fussy way.

prim·rose (prim′rōz), *n.* **1.** a plant that has small, tubelike flowers of various colors. **2.** the light yellow of some primroses.

primrose

primrose path, a life of pleasure.

prince (prins), *n.* **1.** a ruler, especially of a principality. **2.** a man or boy of a royal family; especially, a son or grandson of a king or queen. **3.** a very important person [a merchant *prince*].

Prince Edward Island, an island province of Canada, north of Nova Scotia.

prince·ly (prins′lē), *adj.* **1.** of or like a prince; royal; noble. **2.** fit for a prince; magnificent.

prin·cess (prin′sis), *n.* **1.** a daughter or granddaughter of a king or queen. **2.** the wife of a prince. **3.** a woman ruler with the rank of a prince.

prin·ci·pal (prin′sə p'l), *adj.* most important; chief; main [the *principal* crop of a State]. —*n.*

1. a person or thing of first importance. **2.** the head of a school. **3.** the sum of money owed, invested, etc., not counting the interest.

prin·ci·pal·i·ty (prin′sə pal′ə tē), *n.* the land ruled by a prince [the *principality* of Monaco]. —**prin′ci·pal′i·ties,** *pl.*

prin·ci·pal·ly (prin′sə p'l ē), *adv.* mainly.

principal parts, the present infinitive, the past tense, the past participle, and, sometimes, the present participle of a verb [The *principal parts* of "drink" are "drink," "drank," "drunk," and, sometimes, "drinking."]

prin·ci·ple (prin′sə p'l), *n.* **1.** a rule, truth, etc. upon which others are based [the basic *principles* of law]. **2.** a rule used in deciding how to behave [It is against his *principles* to lie.] **3.** the following of the rules of right conduct; honesty and fairness [He is a man of *principle*.] **4.** a scientific law that explains how a thing works [Living things grow by the *principle* of cell division.] **5.** the way something works [the *principle* of the gasoline engine]. —**on principle,** because of a principle, or rule of conduct.

print (print), *n.* **1.** a mark made on a surface by pressing or stamping [a foot*print*]. **2.** cloth stamped with a design, or a dress made of this [She wore a flowered *print*.] **3.** letters or words stamped on paper by inked type [a book with small *print*]. **4.** a picture or design made from an inked plate or block. **5.** a picture made by developing a photographic negative. —*v.* **1.** to stamp letters, designs, etc. on a surface as with type or plates. **2.** to publish in print [The magazine *printed* his story.] **3.** to write in letters that look like printed ones. **4.** to make a photograph by passing light through a negative onto a specially treated paper. —**in print,** still for sale by the publisher.

print·ing (prin′ting), *n.* **1.** the act of one that prints. **2.** the making of printed material, as books, newspapers, etc. **3.** printed words. **4.** all the copies of a book, etc. printed at one time. —**print′er,** *n.*

printing press, a machine for printing from inked type, plates, etc.

pri·or (prī′ər), *adj.* coming before in time, order, importance, etc. [at some *prior* time; a *prior* claim to the land]. —**prior to,** before.

pri·or (prī′ər), *n.* the head of a priory. —**pri′or·ess,** *n.fem.*

printing press

pri·or·i·ty (prī ôr′ə tē), *n.* **1.** the fact of being prior [the *priority* of a claim to land]. **2.** the right to get, buy, or do something before others.

pri·or·y (prī′ər ē), *n.* a monastery headed by a prior, or a nunnery headed by a prioress. —**pri′or·ies,** *pl.*

fat, āpe, cär, ten, ēven, hit, bīte, gō, hôrn, tōol, book, up, fūr; get, joy, yet, chin, she, thin, *th*en; zh = s in pleasure; ′ as in able (ā′b'l); ə = a in ago, e in agent, i in sanity, o in confess, u in focus.

prism (priz'm), *n.* **1.** a solid figure whose ends are exactly equal and parallel and whose sides are parallelograms. **2.** an object of glass or clear plastic shaped like this, having ends that are triangles. It can break up light rays into the colors of the rainbow.

pris·mat·ic (priz mat'ik), *adj.* **1.** of or like a prism. **2.** formed by a prism [The *prismatic* colors are red, orange, yellow, green, blue, indigo, and violet.]

prism

pris·on (priz'n), *n.* a place where people are kept shut up, as while waiting for a trial or serving a sentence for breaking the law; jail.

pris·on·er (priz'n ər *or* priz'nər), *n.* a person who is kept shut up, as in a prison, or held as a captive, as in war.

pris·tine (pris'tēn), *adj.* of or like the earliest time or condition; also, fresh and untouched [the *pristine* look of newly fallen snow].

prith·ee (pri*th*'ē), *interj.* I pray thee; please: *now seldom used.*

pri·va·cy (prī'və sē), *n.* **1.** the condition of being away from the company of others; seclusion [He found *privacy* in the hills.] **2.** secrecy [I tell you this in strictest *privacy.*]

pri·vate (prī'vit), *adj.* **1.** of or for a particular person or group only; not public [*private* property; one's *private* affairs; a *private* school]. **2.** not holding public office [a *private* citizen]. **3.** secret; confidential [one's *private* opinion]. —*n.* a soldier of the lowest rank. —**in private,** secretly. —**pri'vate·ly,** *adv.*

pri·va·teer (prī və tir'), *n.* **1.** an armed ship owned by a private person, which is given permission by the government to attack enemy ships during war. **2.** the captain or a crew member of a privateer.

pri·va·tion (prī vā'shən), *n.* the lack of things needed to live or be comfortable [Washington's troops faced severe *privation* at Valley Forge.]

priv·et (priv'it), *n.* a shrub with small, shiny leaves, commonly used for hedges.

priv·i·lege (priv'l ij), *n.* a special right, favor, etc. given to some person or group [The children have the *privilege* of staying up late tonight.] —*v.* to give a privilege to [Nobles were *privileged* in many ways.] —**priv'i·leged,** *p.t. & p.p.;* **priv'i·leg·ing,** *pr.p.*

priv·y (priv'ē), *adj.* private or confidential: *now only in* **privy council,** a group appointed by a ruler to advise him. —*n.* a toilet, especially an outdoor one. —**privy to,** secretly informed about. —**priv'ies,** *pl.* —**priv'i·ly,** *adv.*

prize (prīz), *n.* **1.** something offered or given to a winner of a contest, lottery, etc. [The second *prize* is a green ribbon.] **2.** anything worth trying to get [His friendship would be a great *prize.*] **3.** something captured in a war, especially an enemy warship. —*adj.* **1.** that has won or should win a prize; outstanding [*prize* livestock]. **2.** given as a prize. —*v.* to think highly of; value [He *prizes* your friendship.] —**prized,** *p.t. & p.p.;* **priz'ing,** *pr.p.*

prize fight, a contest between prize fighters.

prize fighter, a man who takes part in boxing matches for money; professional boxer.

pro (prō), *adv.* in a way that is for [We discussed the subject *pro* and con.] —*n.* a reason or vote for. See **con.** —**pros,** *pl.*

pro (prō), *adj. & n.* professional: *used only in everyday talk* [*pro* golf; a golf *pro*]. —**pros,** *pl.*

pro- (prō), a prefix meaning "for" or "in favor of" [A *pro*-British speech is a speech in favor of Great Britain.]

prob·a·bil·i·ty (präb'ə bil'ə tē), *n.* **1.** the fact of being probable; likelihood; good chance [a *probability* of rain tomorrow]. **2.** something that is probable [His return is considered a *probability.*] —**in all probability,** very likely. —**prob'a·bil'i·ties,** *pl.*

prob·a·ble (präb'ə b'l), *adj.* likely to happen or to turn out to be [the *probable* winner of an election; the *probable* cause of a disease].

prob·a·bly (präb'ə blē), *adv.* very likely; without much doubt [It will *probably* rain.]

pro·bate (prō'bāt), *v.* to prove officially that the will of someone who has died is genuine and legal. —*adj.* having to do with such proving [a *probate* court]. —*n.* such official proof. —**pro'bat·ed,** *p.t. & p.p.;* **pro'bat·ing,** *pr.p.*

pro·ba·tion (prō bā'shən), *n.* **1.** a testing of a person's character or ability, or the time of this [As a new employee, you must pass six months' *probation.*] **2.** a system of dealing with certain lawbreakers, in which they are allowed to go free as long as they do nothing else wrong and report regularly to a probation officer.

pro·ba·tion·er (prō bā'shən ər), *n.* a person on probation.

probation officer, an officer of a court whose work is to watch over lawbreakers on probation.

probe (prōb), *n.* **1.** a slender instrument with a blunt end that a doctor uses in examining the inside of a wound or body opening. **2.** a complete investigation [The mayor demanded a *probe* of gambling in the city.] —*v.* **1.** to explore with a probe [to *probe* a wound]. **2.** to examine or investigate carefully [to *probe* space with rockets]. —**probed,** *p.t. & p.p.;* **prob'ing,** *pr.p.*

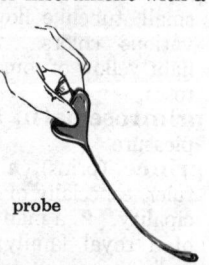

probe

prob·i·ty (prō'bə tē), *n.* the quality of being honest, upright, trustworthy, etc.

prob·lem (präb'ləm), *n.* **1.** a condition, person, etc. that is difficult to deal with or hard to understand [It's quite a *problem* to get that table through the small door.] **2.** a question to be solved or worked out [an arithmetic *problem;* the *problem* of crowded schools].

prob·lem·at·i·cal (präb'lə mat'i k'l) or **prob·lem·at·ic** (präb'lə mat'ik), *adj.* that is a problem; hard to figure out or deal with; not sure; uncertain [The future is *problematical.*]

pro·bos·cis (prō bäs'is), *n.* **1.** an elephant's trunk, or any long snout that bends easily. **2.** a tubelike part of some insects, used for sucking.

pro·ce·dure (prə sē′jər), *n.* a way or method of doing something [the correct *procedure* to follow during a fire drill].

pro·ceed (prə sēd′), *v.* **1.** to go on, especially after stopping for a while [After eating, we *proceeded* to the next town.] **2.** to begin and go on doing something [He *proceeded* to recite the poem.] **3.** to come out; issue [Smoke *proceeded* from the chimney.]

pro·ceed·ing (prə sēd′ing), *n.* **1.** an action or series of actions; activity or procedure. **2. proceedings,** *pl.* a record of the things done at a meeting. **3. proceedings,** *pl.* legal action; lawsuit [to start *proceedings* against someone].

pro·ceeds (prō′sēdz), *n.pl.* the money or profit from some business deal or other activity.

proc·ess (präs′es), *n.* **1.** a series of changes by which something develops [the *process* of growth in a plant]. **2.** a method of making or doing something, in which there are a number of steps [the refining *process* used in making gasoline from crude oil]. **3.** the act of doing something, or the time during which something is done [I was in the *process* of writing a report when you called.] **4.** a written order to appear in a court of law; court summons. A man who delivers such a summons is called a **process server. 5.** a part growing out [a bony *process* on his heel]. —*v.* to prepare by a special process [to *process* cheese].

pro·ces·sion (prə sesh′ən), *n.* **1.** a number of persons or things moving forward in an orderly way. **2.** the act of moving in this way.

pro·ces·sion·al (prə sesh′ən 'l), *adj.* of or having to do with a procession. —*n.* **1.** a hymn sung at the beginning of a church service when the clergy come in. **2.** any musical work played during a procession.

pro·claim (prō klām′), *v.* to make known publicly; announce [They *proclaimed* him a hero.]

proc·la·ma·tion (präk′lə mā′shən), *n.* a proclaiming or being proclaimed; public statement.

pro·con·sul (prō kän′s'l), *n.* the army commander or governor of an ancient Roman province.

pro·cras·ti·nate (prō kras′tə nāt), *v.* to put off doing something until later; delay. —**pro·cras′ti·nat·ed,** *p.t. & p.p.;* **pro·cras′ti·nat·ing,** *pr.p.* —**pro·cras′ti·na′tion,** *n.* —**pro·cras′ti·na′tor,** *n.*

pro·cre·a·tion (prō′kri ā′shən), *n.* the act of producing or bringing into being; especially, the begetting of offspring.

proc·tor (präk′tər), *n.* an official in a school or college who keeps order, watches over students taking tests, etc.

proc·u·ra·tor (präk′yoo rā′tər), *n.* an official in the Roman Empire who acted as governor of a territory, such as Judea.

pro·cure (prō kyoor′), *v.* to get or bring about by trying; obtain; secure [to *procure* money for one's education; to *procure* the settlement of a dispute]. —**pro·cured′,** *p.t. & p.p.;* **pro·cur′ing,** *pr.p.* —**pro·cur′a·ble,** *adj.*

prod (präd), *v.* **1.** to poke or jab with something pointed, as a stick. **2.** to urge or drive into action; goad [Ruth needed no *prodding* to practice on her violin.] —*n.* **1.** a poke or jab. **2.** something pointed used for prodding. —**prod′ded,** *p.t. & p.p.;* **prod′ding,** *pr.p.*

prod·i·gal (präd′i g'l), *adj.* **1.** wasteful in a reckless way [*prodigal* with his father's money]. **2.** very plentiful; generous or lavish [He was *prodigal* with his praise.] —*n.* a person who wastes his money, his skills, etc. in a reckless way. —**prod·i·gal·i·ty** (präd′i gal′ə tē), *n.*

pro·di·gious (prə dij′əs), *adj.* **1.** very great; huge; enormous [a *prodigious* appetite]. **2.** causing wonder; amazing [*prodigious* miracles].

prod·i·gy (präd′ə jē), *n.* a person or thing so remarkable as to cause wonder and admiration; marvel [The child *prodigy* gave concerts when he was six.] —**prod′i·gies,** *pl.*

pro·duce (prə dōōs′ *or* prə dyōōs′), *v.* **1.** to bring forth; bear; yield [trees *producing* apples; a well that *produces* oil]. **2.** to make or manufacture [a company that *produces* bicycles]. **3.** to bring out into view; show [*Produce* your fishing license.] **4.** to cause; bring about [The flood *produced* misery.] **5.** to get ready and bring to the public, as a play, movie, etc. —*n.* (präd′ōōs *or* prō′dyōōs), something that is produced, especially fruits and vegetables for marketing. —**pro·duced′,** *p.t. & p.p.;* **pro·duc′ing,** *pr.p.* —**pro·duc′er,** *n.*

prod·uct (präd′əkt), *n.* **1.** something produced by nature or by man [Wood is a natural *product.* A desk is a manufactured *product.*] **2.** result [The story is a *product* of his imagination.] **3.** a number that is the result of multiplying [28 is the *product* of 7 multiplied by 4.]

pro·duc·tion (prə duk′shən), *n.* **1.** the act of producing [The new steel plant began *production* last week.] **2.** something that is produced, as a play that is staged for the public.

pro·duc·tive (prə duk′tiv), *adj.* **1.** producing much; fertile [*productive* soil; a *productive* mind]. **2.** producing goods or wealth [*productive* labor]. **3.** causing [War is *productive* of much misery.] —**pro·duc·tiv·i·ty** (prō′duk tiv′ə tē), *n.*

Prof., abbreviation for **Professor.**

pro·fane (prə fān′), *adj.* **1.** showing disrespect or scorn for sacred things [*profane* language]. **2.** not connected with religion; not holy [Rembrandt painted both sacred and *profane* subjects.] —*v.* to treat something sacred with disrespect or scorn [to *profane* a Bible by ripping its pages]. —**pro·faned′,** *p.t. & p.p.;* **pro·fan′ing,** *pr.p.* —**pro·fane′ly,** *adv.* —**prof·a·na·tion** (präf′ə nā′shən), *n.*

pro·fan·i·ty (prə fan′ə tē), *n.* **1.** the quality of being profane. **2.** profane language; swearing. —**pro·fan′i·ties,** *pl.*

fat, āpe, cär, ten, ēven, hit, bīte, gō, hôrn, tōol, book, up, fûr; get, joy, yet, chin, she, thin, *th*en; zh = s in pleasure; ′ as in able (ā′b'l); ə = a in ago, e in agent, i in sanity, o in confess, u in focus.

pro·fess (prə fes′), *v.* **1.** to make clearly known; declare openly [He *professed* his love for her.] **2.** to claim to have or be [He *professed* a friendship which he did not really feel.] **3.** to declare one's belief in [to *profess* Christianity]. **4.** to follow as a profession [to *profess* medicine].

pro·fessed (prə fest′), *adj.* **1.** openly declared; admitted [a *professed* conservative]. **2.** falsely declared; pretended [his *professed* sympathy].

pro·fes·sion (prə fesh′ən), *n.* **1.** an occupation for which one must have special education and training [Medicine, law, and teaching are *professions.*] **2.** all the people in such an occupation [the legal *profession*]. **3.** the act of professing, or openly declaring [his *profession* of love].

pro·fes·sion·al (prə fesh′ən 'l), *adj.* **1.** of or in a profession [the *professional* ethics of a lawyer]. **2.** earning one's living from a sport or other activity not usually thought of as an occupation [a *professional* golfer]. **3.** engaged in by professional players [*professional* football]. —*n.* a person who is professional. —**pro·fes′sion·al·ism,** *n.* —**pro·fes′sion·al·ly,** *adv.*

pro·fes·sor (prə fes′ər), *n.* a teacher; especially, a college teacher of the highest rank. —**pro·fes·so·ri·al** (prō′fə sôr′i əl), *adj.* —**pro·fes′sor·ship,** *n.*

prof·fer (präf′ər), *v.* to offer [to *proffer* friendship to a new neighbor]. —*n.* an offer.

pro·fi·cient (prə fish′ənt), *adj.* able to do something very well; skilled; expert [a man *proficient* in many languages]. —**pro·fi′cien·cy,** *n.* —**pro·fi′cient·ly,** *adv.*

pro·file (prō′fil), *n.* **1.** a side view of a person's face. **2.** a drawing of this. **3.** an outline [the *profile* of the trees against the sky]. **4.** a short biography.

prof·it (präf′it), *n.* **1.** the amount of money gained in business deals after all expenses have been subtracted [They took in $500, of which $120 was *profit.*] **2.** gain of any kind; benefit; advantage [There's no *profit* in arguing about this.] —*v.* **1.** to be of advantage to [It will *profit* you to study hard.] **2.** to get a benefit; gain [He *profited* by the sale.]

profile

prof·it·a·ble (präf′it ə b'l), *adj.* that brings profit or benefit [a *profitable* sale; a *profitable* idea]. —**prof′it·a·bly,** *adv.*

prof·it·eer (präf ə tir′), *n.* a person who makes an unfair profit by charging very high prices when there is a short supply of something that people need. —*v.* to be a profiteer.

prof·li·gate (präf′lə git), *adj.* **1.** very wasteful; wildly extravagant [a *profligate* spender]. **2.** very wicked; immoral [a *profligate* life]. —*n.* a profligate person. —**prof′li·ga·cy,** *n.*

pro·found (prə found′), *adj.* **1.** showing great knowledge, thought, etc. [the *profound* remarks of the judge]. **2.** very deep or strong; intense [*profound* sleep; *profound* grief]. **3.** thorough [*profound* changes]. —**pro·found′ly,** *adv.*

pro·fun·di·ty (prə fun′də tē), *n.* **1.** the condi-

tion of being profound; great depth. **2.** something profound, as an idea. —**pro·fun′di·ties,** *pl.*

pro·fuse (prə fyōos′), *adj.* **1.** very plentiful; abundant [a *profuse* flow of water]. **2.** giving freely; generous [She was *profuse* in her praise.] —**pro·fuse′ly,** *adv.* —**pro·fuse′ness,** *n.*

pro·fu·sion (prə fyōo′zhən), *n.* a great or generous amount; abundance [lilies in *profusion*].

pro·gen·i·tor (prō jen′ə tər), *n.* an ancestor.

prog·e·ny (präj′ə nē), *n.* children or offspring.

prog·nos·tic (präg näs′tik), *adj.* that tells or warns of something to come; foretelling. —*n.* a sign of something to come.

prog·nos·ti·cate (präg näs′tə kāt), *v.* to tell what will happen; predict; foretell. —**prog·nos′ti·cat·ed,** *p.t. & p.p.;* **prog·nos′ti·cat·ing,** *pr.p.* —**prog·nos′ti·ca′tion,** *n.*

pro·gram (prō′gram), *n.* **1.** the acts, speeches, musical pieces, etc. that make up a ceremony or entertainment [a commencement *program;* a radio *program*]. **2.** a printed list of these [May I share your *program?*] **3.** a plan for doing something [a government *program* to help farmers]. —*v.* **1.** to place in a program; schedule. **2.** to set up as a plan or series of operations to be performed by an electronic computer [to *program* instructions]. **3.** to furnish with such a plan or series [to *program* a computer]. —**pro′grammed** or **pro′gramed,** *p.t. & p.p.;* **pro′gram·ming** or **pro′gram·ing,** *pr.p.*

prog·ress (präg′res), *n.* **1.** a moving forward [the boat's slow *progress* down the river]. **2.** a developing or improving [He shows *progress* in learning French]. —*v.* (prə gres′), **1.** to move forward; go ahead. **2.** to develop or improve; advance [Science has helped man *progress.*]

pro·gres·sion (prə gresh′ən), *n.* **1.** a moving forward or ahead; progress. **2.** a series, as of acts [A *progression* of events led to his downfall.] **3.** a series of numbers in which each is related to the next in the same way [The *progression* 1, 5, 9, 13, 17 has a difference of 4 between each two numbers. In the *progression* 1, 2, 4, 8, 16, each number is twice as large as the one before.]

pro·gres·sive (prə gres′iv), *adj.* **1.** moving forward; going ahead, as by a series of steps [the *progressive* improvement of the patient]. **2.** wanting, bringing, or showing progress or improvement, as through political reform [*progressive* laws; a *progressive* senator]. —*n.* a person who is in favor of progress or reform, especially in politics. —**pro·gres′sive·ly,** *adv.*

pro·hib·it (prō hib′it), *v.* **1.** to forbid by law or by an order [Smoking is *prohibited* in this building.] **2.** to stop or hold back; prevent [A high wall *prohibited* us from going farther.]

pro·hi·bi·tion (prō′ə bish′ən), *n.* **1.** a prohibiting or being prohibited. **2.** an order or law that prohibits, especially one that prohibits people from making or selling alcoholic liquors. **3. Prohibition,** the period from 1920 to 1933, when there was a Federal law of this kind. —**pro′hi·bi′tion·ist,** *n.*

pro·hib·i·tive (prō hib′ə tiv), *adj.* that prevents one from doing something [*Prohibitive* prices are prices so high that they prevent people from buying.] Also **pro·hib·i·to·ry** (prō hib′ə tôr′ē).

proj·ect (präj′ekt), *n.* a plan, scheme, or undertaking [Our next *project* is to build a raft.] —*v.* (prə jekt′), **1.** to plan or draw up, as a scheme; propose [our *projected* trip next summer]. **2.** to throw forward. **3.** to stick out [The shelf *projects* from the wall.] **4.** to cause a shadow or image to be seen on a surface [to *project* motion pictures on a screen].

pro·jec·tile (prə jek′t'l), *n.* an object made to be shot with force through the air, as a cannon shell, bullet, or rocket.

pro·jec·tion (prə jek′shən), *n.* **1.** a projecting or being projected. **2.** something that projects, or sticks out.

pro·jec·tor (prə jek′tər), *n.* a machine for projecting pictures or movies on a screen.

pro·le·tar·i·an (prō′lə ter′i ən), *adj.* of or belonging to the working class. —*n.* a member of the proletariat; worker.

pro·le·tar·i·at (prō′lə ter′i ət), *n.* the working class, especially those who work in industry.

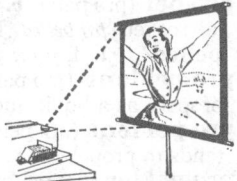
projector in use

pro·lif·ic (prə lif′ik), *adj.* **1.** producing many offspring [Mice are *prolific*.] **2.** producing much [a *prolific* song writer]. —**pro·lif′i·cal·ly,** *adv.*

pro·lix (prō liks′ *or* prō′liks), *adj.* too long and boring because of too many words; wordy [a *prolix* speech]. —**pro·lix′i·ty,** *n.*

pro·logue (prō′lôg), *n.* **1.** an introduction to a poem, play, etc.; especially, lines spoken by an actor before a play begins. **2.** any action or happening that serves as an introduction to another, more important happening.

pro·long (prə lông′), *v.* to make last longer; stretch out [We *prolonged* our visit by another day. Don't *prolong* the suspense.]

pro·lon·ga·tion (prō′lông gā′shən), *n.* **1.** the act of prolonging. **2.** a part added to make something longer.

prom (präm), *n.* a formal dance of a college or high-school class: *used only in everyday talk.*

prom·e·nade (präm′ə nād′ *or* präm′ə näd′), *n.* **1.** a walk taken for pleasure, to show off one's fine clothing, etc. **2.** a public place for such a walk, as an avenue or the deck of a ship. **3.** a march that begins a formal dance or comes between two parts of a square dance. —*v.* to take a promenade or walk. —**prom′e·nad′ed,** *p.t. & p.p.;* **prom′e·nad′ing,** *pr.p.*

Pro·me·theus (prə mē′thi əs *or* prə mē′thyŏŏs), *n.* a giant in a Greek myth who stole fire from heaven and taught man how to use it. He was punished by being chained to a rock.

prom·i·nence (präm′ə nəns), *n.* **1.** the condition of being prominent. **2.** something that is prominent or sticks out, as a hill.

prom·i·nent (präm′ə nənt), *adj.* **1.** standing out from a surface; projecting [*prominent* eyebrows]. **2.** widely known; famous; distinguished [a *prominent* artist]. **3.** sure to be seen; conspicuous [*prominent* markings]. —**prom′i·nent·ly,** *adv.*

prominent eyebrows

pro·mis·cu·ous (prə mis′kyŏŏ əs), *adj.* **1.** taking whatever comes along without care in choosing [the *promiscuous* reading of novels]. **2.** made up of different kinds [a *promiscuous* collection]. —**prom·is·cu·i·ty** (präm′is kyŏŏ′ə tē), *n.* —**pro·mis′cu·ous·ly,** *adv.*

prom·ise (präm′is), *n.* **1.** an agreement to do or not to do something; vow [to make and keep a *promise*]. **2.** a sign that gives reason for expecting success; cause for hope [She shows *promise* as a singer.] —*v.* **1.** to make a promise to [I *promised* Mother to be home by ten.] **2.** to make a promise of [I *promised* my help.] **3.** to give a reason to expect [Clear skies *promise* good weather.] —**prom′ised,** *p.t. & p.p.;* **prom′is·ing,** *pr.p.*

Promised Land, Canaan, the land promised to Abraham by God in the Bible.

prom·is·ing (präm′is ing), *adj.* likely to be successful; showing promise [a *promising* poet].

prom·is·so·ry (präm′ə sôr′ē), *adj.* containing a promise. A **promissory note** is a written promise to pay a certain sum of money on a certain date or when it is demanded.

prom·on·to·ry (präm′ən tôr′ē), *n.* a peak of high land that juts out into a sea, lake, etc.; headland. —**prom′on·to′ries,** *pl.*

pro·mote (prə mōt′), *v.* **1.** to raise to a higher rank, grade, or position [Corporal Brown was *promoted* to sergeant.] **2.** to help to grow, succeed, etc. [to *promote* the general welfare]. **3.** to help to organize, as a new company. —**pro·mot′ed,** *p.t. & p.p.;* **pro·mot′ing,** *pr.p.* —**pro·mot′er,** *n.* —**pro·mo′tion,** *n.*

prompt (prämpt), *adj.* **1.** quick in doing what should be done; on time [*prompt* in paying his bills]. **2.** done, spoken, etc. without waiting [a *prompt* reply]. —*v.* **1.** to urge or stir into action [Tyranny *prompted* them to revolt.] **2.** to remind of something that has been forgotten [to *prompt* an actor when he forgets a line]. **3.** to inspire [Gay music *prompts* happy thoughts.] —**prompt′ly,** *adv.* —**prompt′ness,** *n.*

prompt·er (prämp′tər), *n.* a person whose job is reminding actors, singers, etc. when they forget what they are supposed to say or do.

promp·ti·tude (prämp′tə tŏŏd *or* prämp′tə-tyŏŏd), *n.* the condition of being prompt; readiness.

pro·mul·gate (prō mul′gāt *or* präm′əl gāt), *v.* **1.** to make known in an official way; proclaim [to *promulgate* a law]. **2.** to spread over a wide

fat,   āpe,   cär,   ten,   ēven,   hit,   bīte,   gō,   hôrn,   tōōl,   book,   up,   fur;
get,   joy,   yet,   chin,   she,   thin,   *then;*   zh = s in pleasure;   ′ as in able (ā′b'l);
ə = a in ago,   e in agent,   i in sanity,   o in confess,   u in focus.

area [to *promulgate* a rumor]. —**pro·mul′·gat·ed**, *p.t.* & *p.p.*; **pro·mul′gat·ing**, *pr.p.* —**pro′mul·ga′tion**, *n.* —**pro·mul′ga·tor**, *n.*

pron., abbreviation for **pronoun, pronunciation.**

prone (prōn), *adj.* **1.** apt or likely; inclined [Billy is *prone* to daydream.] **2.** lying face downward. **3.** lying flat. —**prone′ness**, *n.*

prong (prông), *n.* **1.** any of the pointed ends of a fork. **2.** any pointed part that sticks out, as the tip of an antler. —**pronged**, *adj.*

prong·horn (prông′hôrn), *n.* a small antelope like a goat, found in the western United States.

pronghorn
(3 ft. high at shoulder)

pro·noun (prō′noun), *n.* a word used in the place of a noun. *I, us, you, they, he, her, it* are some pronouns.

pro·nounce (prə-nouns′), *v.* **1.** to say or make the sounds of [How do you *pronounce* "leisure"?] **2.** to say or declare in an official or solemn way [I now *pronounce* you man and wife.] —**pro·nounced′**, *p.t.* & *p.p.*; **pro·nounc′ing**, *pr.p.*

pro·nounced (prə nounst′), *adj.* clearly marked; definite [a *pronounced* change].

pro·nounce·ment (prə nouns′mənt), *n.* a formal statement of a fact, opinion, etc.

pro·nun·ci·a·tion (prə nun′si ā′shən), *n.* **1.** the act or way of forming sounds to say words [His *pronunciation* is clear.] **2.** the way a word is usually pronounced ["Either" has two *pronunciations*.]

proof (prōōf), *n.* **1.** anything that can be used to show that something is true or correct; evidence [Do they have *proof* of his guilt?] **2.** the act of showing that something is true [He is still working on the *proof* of his theory.] **3.** a test or trial [The *proof* of the pudding is in the eating.] **4.** a trial print from the negative of a photograph. **5.** a sheet printed from set type, used for checking errors. —*adj.* of tested strength in resisting [The fortress was *proof* against attack.]

-proof (prōōf), a suffix meaning "resisting" or "protected from" [*Waterproof* cloth resists wetting by water.]

proof·read (prōōf′rēd′), *v.* to read printer's proofs in order to correct errors in them.—**proofread** (prōōf′red′), *p.t.* & *p.p.*; **proof′read′ing**, *pr.p.* —**proof′read′er**, *n.*

prop (präp), *n.* **1.** a stake, pole, etc. used to hold something up. **2.** a person or thing that gives support or aid. —*v.* **1.** to support or hold up, as with a prop [to *prop* up a sagging roof; to *prop* up one's spirits]. **2.** to lean against a support [He *propped* his back against a pillow.]

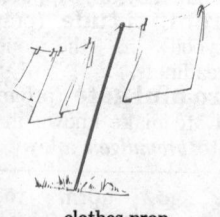
clothes prop

—**propped**, *p.t.* & *p.p.*; **prop′ping**, *pr.p.*

prop·a·gan·da (präp′ə gan′də), *n.* the spreading of information, ideas, etc. in a way meant to make others accept them; also, the ideas, etc. so spread. This word now often suggests that the ideas are false or misleading on purpose. —**prop′·a·gan′dist**, *n.*

prop·a·gan·dize (präp′ə gan′dīz), *v.* to spread ideas, etc. by propaganda. —**prop′a·gan′·dized**, *p.t.* & *p.p.*; **prop′a·gan′diz·ing**, *pr.p.*

prop·a·gate (präp′ə gāt), *v.* **1.** to increase by producing offspring [Animals and plants *propagate* their species.] **2.** to cause to reproduce; raise or breed [to *propagate* pine trees]. **3.** to spread from one person or place to another [to *propagate* ideas; to *propagate* light]. —**prop′·a·gat·ed**, *p.t.* & *p.p.*; **prop′a·gat·ing**, *pr.p.* —**prop′a·ga′tion**, *n.*

pro·pel (prə pel′), *v.* to push or drive forward [a rocket *propelled* by liquid fuel]. —**pro·pelled′**, *p.t.* & *p.p.*; **pro·pel′ling**, *pr.p.*

pro·pel·lant (prə pel′ənt), *n.* something that propels, as a liquid fuel used to fire rockets.

pro·pel·lent (prə pel′ənt), *adj.* that propels or tends to propel. —*n.* a propellant.

pro·pel·ler (prə pel′ər), *n.* a device made up of blades mounted on a shaft, which is turned by an engine for driving an airplane, ship, etc.

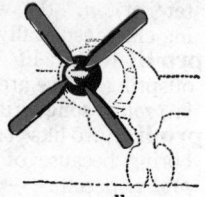
propeller

pro·pen·si·ty (prə pen′sə tē), *n.* a natural leaning or tendency; bent [He has a *propensity* for saving things.] —**pro·pen′si·ties**, *pl.*

prop·er (präp′ər), *adj.* **1.** right, correct, or suitable [the *proper* tool for this job; the *proper* clothes for a party]. **2.** not to be ashamed of; decent; respectable [*proper* manners]. **3.** in its strict sense; actual [Boston *proper*, not including its suburbs]. **4.** that naturally belongs to or goes with [weather *proper* to April]. —**prop′er·ly**, *adv.*

proper fraction, a fraction in which the numerator is less than the denominator, as 2/5.

proper noun, a noun that is the name of a particular person, thing, or place and is begun with a capital letter [Some *proper nouns* are "Jane," "Sunday," and "Paris."] See also **common noun.**

prop·er·ty (präp′ər tē), *n.* **1.** something owned, especially land or real estate [much loss of *property* during the fire; a fence around our *property*]. **2.** any of the special qualities by which a thing is known; characteristic [Oxygen has the *properties* of being colorless, odorless, and tasteless.] **3.** any of the articles used in a play, except costumes and scenery. —**prop′er·ties**, *pl.*

proph·e·cy (präf′ə sē), *n.* **1.** the act or power of prophesying. **2.** something told about the future, as by a prophet. —**proph′e·cies**, *pl.*

proph·e·sy (präf′ə sī), *v.* **1.** to tell what will happen; predict [to *prophesy* a change]. **2.** to speak or write as when inspired by God. —**proph′e·sied**, *p.t.* & *p.p.*; **proph′e·sy·ing**, *pr.p.*

proph·et (präf′it), *n.* **1.** a religious leader who is believed to speak for God or a god, as in giving messages or warnings [Isaiah was a *prophet.* The Greek oracles were *prophets.*] **2.** a person who tells what he thinks will happen.

proph·et·ess (präf′it is), *n.* a woman prophet.

pro·phet·ic (prə fet′ik), *adj.* **1.** of or like a prophet. **2.** like or containing a prophecy [a *prophetic* warning]. —**pro·phet′i·cal·ly,** *adv.*

pro·phy·lac·tic (prō′fə lak′tik), *adj.* that helps prevent disease [a *prophylactic* cleaning of the teeth]. —*n.* a medicine, device, etc. that helps prevent disease.

pro·pin·qui·ty (prō ping′kwə tē), *n.* the fact of being near or close; nearness.

pro·pi·ti·ate (prə pish′i āt), *v.* to stop or keep from being angry; win the good will of; appease [sacrifices made to *propitiate* the gods]. —**pro·pi′ti·at·ed,** *p.t. & p.p.;* **pro·pi′ti·at·ing,** *pr.p.* —**pro·pi′ti·a′tion,** *n.*

pro·pi·tious (prə pish′əs), *adj.* **1.** that helps in some way; favorable [*propitious* weather for golf]. **2.** in a mood to help; gracious [The gods were *propitious.*] —**pro·pi′tious·ly,** *adv.*

pro·po·nent (prə pō′nənt), *n.* a person who proposes or supports a certain idea [a *proponent* of lower taxes].

pro·por·tion (prə pôr′shən), *n.* **1.** the relation of one thing to another in size, amount, etc.; ratio [The *proportion* of girls to boys in our class is three to two; that is, there are three girls to every two boys.] **2.** a pleasing or proper arrangement or balance of parts [The small desk and large chair are not in *proportion.*] **3.** a part or portion [A large *proportion* of the earth is covered with water.] **4.** a relationship between four numbers, in which the first two are in the same relationship as the last two. Example: 2 is to 6 as 3 is to 9. **5. proportions,** *pl.* dimensions, as length, width, and height [a house of large *proportions*]. —*v.* **1.** to arrange the parts of in a pleasing or balanced way [a well-*proportioned* statue]. **2.** to put in proper relation; make fit [*Proportion* the punishment to the crime.]

pro·por·tion·al (prə pôr′shən 'l), *adj.* in proper proportion [The number of Congressmen from a State is *proportional* to its population.] —**pro·por′tion·al·ly,** *adv.*

pro·por·tion·ate (prə pôr′shən it), *adj.* in proper proportion; proportional. —**pro·por′-tion·ate·ly,** *adv.*

pro·pos·al (prə pō′z'l), *n.* **1.** the act of proposing. **2.** something proposed, as a plan or scheme [The council approved the mayor's *proposal.*] **3.** an offer of marriage.

pro·pose (prə pōz′), *v.* **1.** to suggest for others to think about, approve, etc. [We *propose* that the city build a zoo. I *propose* Tom for treasurer.] **2.** to plan or intend [He *proposes* to leave us.] **3.** to make an offer of marriage. —**pro·posed′,** *p.t. & p.p.;* **pro·pos′ing,** *pr.p.*

prop·o·si·tion (präp′ə zish′ən), *n.* **1.** something proposed; proposal; plan [I accepted his *proposition* to share expenses.] **2.** a subject or idea to be discussed, proved, etc., as in a debate. **3.** a problem in mathematics to be solved.

pro·pound (prə pound′), *v.* to put forth to be considered; propose [to *propound* a new theory].

pro·pri·e·tar·y (prə prī′ə ter′ē), *adj.* **1.** owned by a person or company, as under a patent, trademark, or copyright [A *proprietary* medicine is patented.] **2.** owning property [the *proprietary* classes]. **3.** of ownership [*proprietary* rights].

pro·pri·e·tor (prə prī′ə tər), *n.* an owner, as of a store or business. —**pro·pri′e·tress,** *n.fem.*

pro·pri·e·ty (prə prī′ə tē), *n.* **1.** the polite and correct way of behaving: *often used in the plural,* **proprieties** [He observed the *proprieties* and rose when a woman entered a room.] **2.** the fact of being proper or suitable; correctness [We questioned the *propriety* of letting her go alone.] —**pro·pri′e·ties,** *pl.*

pro·pul·sion (prə pul′shən), *n.* **1.** a propelling or being propelled. **2.** a force that propels.

pro·sa·ic (prō zā′ik), *adj.* **1.** of or like prose, not poetry. **2.** dull and ordinary [to lead a *prosaic* life]. —**pro·sa′i·cal·ly,** *adv.*

pro·scribe (prō skrīb′), *v.* **1.** to forbid or talk against as being wrong or harmful [Candy is *proscribed* for children by most dentists.] **2.** to take away legal rights or protection from; outlaw. —**pro·scribed′,** *p.t. & p.p.;* **pro·scrib′ing,** *pr.p.* —**pro·scrip·tion** (prō skrip′shən), *n.*

prose (prōz), *n.* speech or writing that is not poetry; ordinary language.

pros·e·cute (präs′i kyoot), *v.* **1.** to put on trial in a court of law on charges of crime or wrong-doing. **2.** to carry on; keep at [to *prosecute* one's studies]. —**pros′e·cut·ed,** *p.t. & p.p.;* **pros′-e·cut·ing,** *pr.p.*

pros·e·cu·tion (präs′i kyoo′shən), *n.* **1.** the carrying on of a case in a court of law. **2.** the one who starts and carries on such a case against another [a witness for the *prosecution*]. **3.** a prosecuting, or carrying on of something.

pros·e·cu·tor (präs′i kyoo′tər), *n.* a person who prosecutes; especially, a lawyer who works for the State in prosecuting persons charged with crime.

pros·e·lyte (präs′'l īt), *n.* a person who has changed from one religion, political party, etc. to another. —*v.* to proselytize. —**pros′e·lyt·ed,** *p.t. & p.p.;* **pros′e·lyt·ing,** *pr.p.*

pros·e·lyt·ize (präs′'l i tīz), *v.* to change or try to change a person from one religion, political party, etc. to another. —**pros′e·lyt·ized,** *p.t. & p.p.;* **pros′e·lyt·iz·ing,** *pr.p.*

Pro·ser·pi·na (prō sur′pi nə) or **Pro·ser·pi·ne** (prō sur′pi nē′), *n.* the daughter of the Roman goddess Ceres and wife of Pluto, who carried her off to the lower world. The Greeks called her *Persephone.*

pros·o·dy (präs'ə dē), *n.* the art or rules of poetry, especially of meter and rhythm.

pros·pect (präs'pekt), *n.* **1.** a looking forward to something; anticipation [the happy *prospect* of a party]. **2.** the likely chance of succeeding or getting something: *often used in the plural,* **prospects** [a team with no *prospects* of winning the pennant]. **3.** a person who is a likely customer, candidate, etc. **4.** a wide view that is seen, as from a tower. —*v.* to search for [*prospecting* for uranium]. —**in prospect,** expected.

pro·spec·tive (prə spek'tiv), *adj.* that is likely some day to be; expected [*prospective* parents; a *prospective* inheritance].

pros·pec·tor (präs'pek tər), *n.* a person who searches for deposits of valuable ores, oil, etc.

pro·spec·tus (prə spek'təs), *n.* a report describing a new business, project, etc.

pros·per (präs'pər), *v.* to succeed, thrive, grow, etc. in a vigorous way [The town *prospered* when oil was discovered nearby.]

pros·per·i·ty (präs per'ə tē), *n.* the condition of being prosperous, wealthy, successful, etc.

pros·per·ous (präs'pər əs), *adj.* successful, well-off, thriving, etc. [a *prosperous* business]. —**pros'per·ous·ly,** *adv.*

pros·ti·tute (präs'tə toot), *n.* a person who does immoral things for money; especially, a woman who offers herself to men for money. —*v.* to use in a wrongful way for money [to *prostitute* one's talent]. —**pros'ti·tut·ed,** *p.t. & p.p.;* **pros'ti·tut·ing,** *pr.p.* —**pros'ti·tu'tion,** *n.*

pros·trate (präs'trāt), *adj.* **1.** lying face downward [worshipers *prostrate* before an idol]. **2.** lying flat, either on one's face or on one's back [The boxer was laid *prostrate* by the blow.] **3.** completely overcome; weak and helpless [*prostrate* with terror]. —*v.* **1.** to lay in a prostrate position. **2.** to overcome; make helpless [*prostrated* by illness]. —**pros'trat·ed,** *p.t. & p.p.;* **pros'trat·ing,** *pr.p.* —**pros·tra'tion,** *n.*

pros·y (prō'zē), *adj.* dull and boring; not exciting. —**pros'i·er,** *compar.;* **pros'i·est,** *superl.*

pro·tect (prə tekt'), *v.* to guard or defend against harm or danger; shield [armor to *protect* the knight's body]. —**pro·tec·tor,** *n.*

pro·tec·tion (prə tek'shən), *n.* **1.** a protecting or being protected [The night watchman carried a gun for *protection*.] **2.** a person or thing that protects [Being careful is your best *protection* against accidents.]

pro·tec·tive (prə tek'tiv), *adj.* **1.** that protects or helps to protect [The *protective* coloring of the brown bird hides it from its enemies.] **2.** that is meant to protect industry against the competition of foreign products [a *protective* tariff]. —**pro·tec'tive·ly,** *adv.*

pro·tec·tor·ate (prə tek'tər it), *n.* **1.** a weak country or territory protected and controlled by a stronger country. **2.** the relationship of the ruling country to the weaker one.

pro·té·gé (prō'tə zhā), *n.* a person who is guided and helped in his career by another.

pro·te·in (prō'tēn *or* prō'tē in), *n.* a substance containing nitrogen and other elements, found in all living things and in such foods as cheese, meat, eggs, beans, etc. It is a necessary part of an animal's diet.

pro·test (prə test'), *v.* **1.** to speak out against; object [to *protest* against injustice]. **2.** to say in a positive way; insist [Bill *protested* that he was glad to help.] —*n.* (prō'test), the act of protesting; objection [They ignored his *protest* and continued hammering.] —**under protest,** without doing so willingly; while objecting.

Prot·es·tant (prät'is tənt), *n.* a member of any of the Christian churches that grew out of the Reformation or developed since then. —*adj.* of Protestants. —**Prot'es·tant·ism,** *n.*

prot·es·ta·tion (prät'əs tā'shən), *n.* a protest or protesting; especially, an insisting in a positive way [*protestations* of love].

pro·to·col (prō'tə käl), *n.* the manners and forms that are accepted as proper and polite in official dealings, as between the ministers of different countries.

pro·ton (prō'tän), *n.* one of the particles that make up the nucleus of an atom. A proton has a single positive electric charge.

pro·to·plasm (prō'tə plaz'm), *n.* the clear, thick, liquid substance that is the necessary part of all living animal and plant cells.

pro·to·type (prō'tə tīp), *n.* the first one of its kind; original or model [The U.S. Constitution was the *prototype* of other democratic constitutions.]

pro·tract (prō trakt'), *v.* **1.** to draw out in time; prolong [*protracted* arguments]. **2.** to thrust out; extend.

pro·trac·tor (prō trak'tər), *n.* an instrument used for drawing and measuring angles. It is in the form of a half-circle marked with degrees.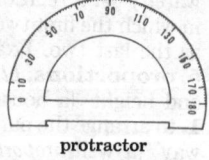

protractor

pro·trude (prō trood'), *v.* to stick out; project; extend [*protruding* front teeth]. —**pro·trud'ed,** *p.t. & p.p.;* **pro·trud'ing,** *pr.p.* —**pro·tru·sion** (prō troo'zhən), *n.*

pro·tu·ber·ance (prō too'bər əns *or* prō tyoo'bər əns), *n.* a part or thing that sticks out; bulge; swelling. —**pro·tu'ber·ant,** *adj.*

proud (proud), *adj.* **1.** having proper respect for oneself, one's work, one's family, etc. [He is too *proud* to ask for help.] **2.** thinking too highly of oneself; conceited; vain or haughty; arrogant [too *proud* to greet us]. **3.** feeling or causing pride or pleasure [his *proud* father; a *proud* moment]. **4.** splendid; magnificent [a *proud* castle]. —**proud of,** very pleased with; feeling pride about. —**proud'ly,** *adv.*

prove (proov), *v.* **1.** to show that something is true or correct [Your grades *prove* that you know how to study.] **2.** to put to a test or trial; find out about through experiments [A *proving* ground is a place for testing new equipment, as aircraft.] **3.** to turn out to be [Your guess *proved* right.] —**proved,** *p.t. & p.p.;* **prov'ing,** *pr.p.*

Pro·ven·çal (prō vən säl'), *n.* a common language of Provence and nearby regions in southern

France, much used in the writings of the Middle Ages.

Pro·vence (prō väns′), *n.* a region in southeastern France that was once a separate province.

prov·en·der (präv′ən dər), *n.* dry food for farm animals, as hay, corn, and oats.

prov·erb (präv′ərb), *n.* an old and familiar saying that tells something wise ["A penny saved is a penny earned" is a *proverb*.]

pro·ver·bi·al (prə vūr′bi əl), *adj.* **1.** of, like, or as in a proverb [*proverbial* wisdom]. **2.** well-known because often mentioned [the *proverbial* glamour of Paris]. —**pro·ver′bi·al·ly,** *adv.*

Prov·erbs (präv′ərbz), *n.* a book of the Old Testament containing many sayings supposed to have been said by Solomon and others.

pro·vide (prə vīd′), *v.* **1.** to get ready ahead of time; prepare [to *provide* for rain by taking umbrellas]. **2.** to give what is needed; supply; furnish [The school *provides* free books.] **3.** to set forth as a condition, as in a contract [Our lease *provides* that rent will be paid monthly.] —**pro·vid′ed,** *p.t. & p.p.;* **pro·vid′ing,** *pr.p.*

pro·vid·ed (prə vīd′id), *conj.* on the condition that; with the understanding; if [You may go swimming, *provided* you come home early.]

Prov·i·dence (präv′ə dəns), *n.* the capital of Rhode Island.

prov·i·dence (präv′ə dəns), *n.* **1.** a looking ahead to the future; careful preparation or management [the *providence* of a nation in saving its natural resources]. **2.** the care or help of God or fortune [A special *providence* seemed to guide the weary travelers.] **3.** **Providence,** God. —**prov′i·dent,** *adj.* —**prov·i·den·tial** (präv′ə den′shəl), *adj.*

pro·vid·ing (prə vīd′ing), *conj.* same as **provided.**

prov·ince (präv′əns), *n.* **1.** a region in or belonging to a country, having its own local government; especially, any of the divisions of Canada that are like the States. **2.** **provinces,** *pl.* the parts of a country away from the large cities. **3.** range of duties or work [Enforcing laws falls within the *province* of a police department.] **4.** a branch of learning [the *province* of medicine].

pro·vin·cial (prə vin′shəl), *adj.* **1.** of a province [a *provincial* capital]. **2.** having the ways, speech, etc. of a certain province [the *provincial* customs of Quebec]. **3.** of or like country people as apart from city people [*provincial* manners]. **4.** limited in one's point of view; thinking in narrow ways. —*n.* **1.** a person living in a province. **2.** a provincial person. —**pro·vin′cial·ism,** *n.*

pro·vi·sion (prə vizh′ən), *n.* **1.** a providing or supplying. **2.** something provided or arrangements made for the future [His savings are a *provision* for his old age.] **3.** **provisions,** *pl.* a supply or stock of food. **4.** a statement, as in a will, that makes a condition [He was left the money with the *provision* that it be for his educa-

tion.] —*v.* to supply with provisions, especially of food [to *provision* an army].

pro·vi·sion·al (prə vizh′ən 'l), *adj.* for the time being; until a permanent one can be set up; temporary [a *provisional* government]. —**pro·vi′sion·al·ly,** *adv.*

pro·vi·so (prə vī′zō), *n.* a statement that makes a condition; provision [You may borrow it, with the *proviso* that you return it promptly.] —**pro·vi′sos** or **pro·vi′soes,** *pl.*

prov·o·ca·tion (präv′ə kā′shən), *n.* **1.** the act of provoking. **2.** something that provokes or angers [His noisy parties are a *provocation* to the neighbors.]

pro·voc·a·tive (prə väk′ə tiv), *adj.* that arouses one to be angry, curious, amused, thoughtful, etc. [her *provocative* remark].

pro·voke (prə vōk′), *v.* **1.** to annoy or make angry [It *provoked* me to see such waste.] **2.** to arouse or call forth [His antics *provoked* a smile from the sick child.] —**pro·voked′,** *p.t. & p.p.;* **pro·vok′ing,** *pr.p.*

pro·vost marshal (prō′vō), an officer in charge of military police.

prow (prou), *n.* the forward part of a ship.

prow·ess (prou′is), *n.* **1.** very great skill or ability [his *prowess* in archery]. **2.** bravery or a brave act, especially in fighting or war.

prowl (proul), *v.* to roam about in a quiet, secret way, as an animal looking for prey. —**on the prowl,** prowling about. —**prowl′er,** *n.*

prow

prox·im·i·ty (präk sim′ə tē), *n.* the condition of being near; nearness; closeness.

prox·y (präk′sē), *n.* **1.** a person who is given the power to act for another, as in voting; deputy. **2.** a statement in writing giving such power. **3.** the power given in this way. **4.** the action of a proxy, or deputy [to vote by *proxy*]. —**prox′ies,** *pl.*

pr.p., abbreviation for **present participle.**

prude (prood), *n.* a person who is too modest or too proper in a way that annoys others.

pru·dent (prood′'nt), *adj.* careful or cautious in a sensible way; not taking chances; wise. —**pru′dence,** *n.* —**pru′dent·ly,** *adv.*

pru·den·tial (proo den′shəl), *adj.* of or showing prudence.

prud·er·y (prood′ər ē), *n.* **1.** the condition of being too proper or modest or of pretending to be so. **2.** a prudish act or comment. —**prud′er·ies,** *pl.*

prud·ish (prood′ish), *adj.* of or like a prude; too proper. —**prud′ish·ly,** *adv.* —**prud′ish·ness,** *n.*

prune (proon), *n.* a plum dried for eating.

---

fat, āpe, cär, ten, ēven, hit, bīte, gō, hôrn, tōōl, book, up, fûr; get, joy, yet, chin, she, thin, *th*en; zh = s in pleasure; ′ as in able (ā′b'l); ə = a in ago, e in agent, i in sanity, o in confess, u in focus.

prune (prōōn), *v.* **1.** to cut off or trim branches, twigs, etc. from [to *prune* hedges]. **2.** to make shorter by cutting out parts [to *prune* a novel]. —**pruned**, *p.t. & p.p.;* **prun'ing**, *pr.p.*

Prus·sia (prush'ə), *n.* a former state of northern Germany. —**Prus'sian**, *adj. & n.*

pry (prī), *v.* **1.** to raise or move with a lever or crowbar. **2.** to get by trying hard [to *pry* money from a miser]. —*n.* a lever or crowbar. —**pried**, *p.t. & p.p.;* **pry'ing**, *pr.p.* —**pries**, *pl.*

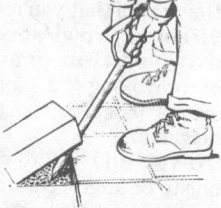

pry (prī), *v.* to look or search closely, often to satisfy one's curiosity [Don't *pry* into my affairs.] —**pried**, *p.t. & p.p.;* **pry'ing**, *pr.p.*

man prying up a stone

PS. or **P.S.,** abbreviation for **postscript.**

psalm (säm), *n.* a sacred song or hymn, especially one from the Book of Psalms.

psalm·ist (säm'ist), *n.* a person who writes psalms. —**the Psalmist,** King David, who is thought to have written the Book of Psalms.

Psalms (sämz), *n.* a book of the Old Testament, made up of 150 psalms.

Psal·ter (sôl'tər), *n.* the Book of Psalms, or a version of this for use in services.

psal·ter·y (sôl'tər ē), *n.* an ancient musical instrument, like a zither. —**psal'ter·ies,** *pl.*

psaltery

pseu·do (sōō'dō *or* syōō'dō), *adj.* not really so; false; pretended [a *pseudo* science].

pseu·do·nym (sōō'də nim *or* syōō'də nim), *n.* a name used by a writer or other person in place of his real name [O. Henry is the *pseudonym* of William Sydney Porter.]

pshaw (shô), *interj.* a sound made to show that one is impatient, disgusted, etc.

Psy·che (sī'kē), *n.* **1.** a maiden in Greek and Roman myths who was loved by Cupid and made immortal. **2. psyche,** the soul or the mind.

psy·che·del·ic (sī'kə del'ik), *adj.* **1.** causing one to have strange feelings, to see and hear things that are not there, and to have mistaken notions, like those in mental illness [LSD is a *psychedelic* drug.] **2.** having effects like those caused by a psychedelic drug [*psychedelic* art or music].

psy·chi·a·trist (sī kī'ə trist), *n.* a doctor who takes care of people who are mentally ill.

psy·chi·a·try (sī kī'ə trē), *n.* the branch of medicine that deals with the treatment of mental illness. —**psy·chi·at·ric** (sī'ki at'rik), *adj.*

psy·chic (sī'kik) or **psy·chi·cal** (sī'ki k'l), *adj.* **1.** that cannot be explained by natural or physical laws; supernatural [People used to think that an eclipse was due to *psychic* forces.] **2.** that seems to be sensitive to supernatural forces [a *psychic*

person who appears to read your mind]. **3.** of the mind; mental [*psychic* processes]. —**psy'chi·cal·ly,** *adv.*

psy·cho·log·i·cal (sī'kə läj'i k'l), *adj.* **1.** of or using psychology [*psychological* tests]. **2.** of the mind; mental [*psychological* development]. **3.** most suitable or most favorable; just right [the *psychological* moment]. —**psy'cho·log'i·cal·ly,** *adv.*

psy·chol·o·gy (sī käl'ə jē), *n.* **1.** the science that studies the mind and the reasons for the ways that people think and act. **2.** the ways of thinking and acting of a person or group [the *psychology* of the child; mob *psychology*]. —**psy·chol'o·gies,** *pl.* —**psy·chol'o·gist,** *n.*

psy·cho·sis (sī kō'sis), *n.* a severe mental illness. —**psy·cho·ses** (sī kō'sēz), *pl.*

psy·chot·ic (sī kät'ik), *adj.* like or having a psychosis; very ill mentally. —*n.* a person who has a psychosis. —**psy·chot'i·cal·ly,** *adv.*

Pt, symbol for the chemical element *platinum.*

pt., abbreviation for **part, pint, point.** —**pts.,** *pl.*

p.t. or **pt.,** abbreviation for **past tense.**

P.T.A., abbreviation for **Parent-Teacher Association.**

ptar·mi·gan (tär'mə gən), *n.* a grouse with feathers on its legs, found in northern regions.

pter·o·dac·tyl (ter'ə dak'til), *n.* a flying reptile that lived millions of years ago. It was somewhat like a lizard with huge wings.

ptarmigan (15 in. long)

Ptol·e·ma·ic (täl'ə mā'ik), *adj.* of Ptolemy or his theory that all heavenly bodies revolved around the earth.

Ptol·e·my (täl'ə mē), *n.* a Greek astronomer who lived in Egypt in the second century A.D.

pto·maine or **pto·main** (tō'mān), *n.* a substance found in spoiled food or decaying matter.

ptomaine poisoning, an illness caused by eating spoiled food containing poisonous bacteria: once thought to be caused by ptomaines.

Pu, symbol for the chemical element *plutonium.*

pub (pub), *n.* a bar or tavern in Great Britain: *the full name is* **public house.**

pu·ber·ty (pyōō'bər tē), *n.* the time of life at which boys and girls physically begin to be men and women.

pub·lic (pub'lik), *adj.* **1.** of or having to do with the people as a whole [*public* affairs; *public* opinion]. **2.** for the use or the good of everyone [a *public* park]. **3.** acting for the people as a whole [a *public* official]. **4.** known by all or most people; open [a *public* scandal]. —*n.* **1.** the people as a whole [what the *public* wants]. **2.** a particular part of the people [the driving *public*]. —**in public,** openly; where all can see.

pub·li·can (pub'li kən), *n.* **1.** a tax collector of ancient Rome. **2.** a person who keeps an inn or tavern: *used in Great Britain.*

pub·li·ca·tion (pub/li kā/shən), *n.* **1.** something published, as a book, magazine, etc. **2.** the printing and selling of books, magazines, newspapers, etc. **3.** a publishing or being published [the *publication* of the facts].

pub·li·cist (pub/li sist), *n.* **1.** a journalist who writes about public affairs. **2.** a person whose work is to bring some person, place, etc. to the attention of the public: also called **publicity agent.**

pub·lic·i·ty (pub lis/ə tē), *n.* **1.** information that brings a person, place, or thing to the attention of the public [The newspapers gave much *publicity* to our play.] **2.** the attention of the public [A politician seeks *publicity*.] **3.** things done or the business of doing things to get public attention [He hired an agent to handle his *publicity*.]

pub·li·cize (pub/li sīz), *v.* to give publicity to; get public attention for. —**pub/li·cized,** *p.t. & p.p.;* **pub/li·ciz·ing,** *pr.p.*

pub·lic·ly (pub/lik lē), *adv.* **1.** in a public or open manner [sold *publicly*, at an auction]. **2.** by the public [a *publicly* owned park].

public school, 1. in the United States, an elementary school or high school that is supported by public taxes. **2.** in England, a private boarding school where boys are prepared for college.

pub·lic-spir·it·ed (pub/lik spir/i tid), *adj.* interested in and working for the public welfare.

pub·lish (pub/lish), *v.* **1.** to prepare and bring out a book, magazine, newspaper, etc., as for sale. **2.** to make known to the public; announce [to *publish* a secret].

pub·lish·er (pub/lish ər), *n.* a person or business that publishes books, magazines, newspapers, printed music, etc.

puck (puk), *n.* the hard rubber disk used in ice hockey.

puck or **Puck** (puk), *n.* a mischievous elf or fairy in folk tales. —**puck/ish,** *adj.*

puck·er (puk/ər), *v.* **1.** to draw up into wrinkles or small folds [to *pucker* the brow in a frown; to *pucker* cloth by pulling a thread]. **2.** to push out the lips, as in kissing. —*n.* a wrinkle or small fold made by puckering.

pud·ding (pood/ing), *n.* a soft, sweet food, usually made with flour or some cereal and eggs, milk, fruit, etc.

puckered lips

pud·dle (pud/'l), *n.* a small pool of water, or water mixed with earth [*puddles* after the rain; a mud *puddle*].

pud·dling (pud/ling), *n.* the process of making wrought iron by heating and stirring melted pig iron with other substances.

pudg·y (puj/ē), *adj.* short and fat [*pudgy* fingers]. —**pudg/i·er,** *compar.;* **pudg/i·est,** *superl.*

pueb·lo (pweb/lō), *n.* **1.** a kind of Indian village in the southwestern United States, made up of stone or clay buildings built one above the other. **2. Pueblo,** an Indian of any of the tribes that live in such villages. —**pueb/los,** *pl. for meaning 1;* **Pueb/los** or **Pueb/lo,** *pl. for meaning 2.*

pueblo

pu·er·ile (pyoo/ər il), *adj.* acting like a child, not as a grown-up should; childish.

Puer·to Ri·co (pwer/tə rē/kō), an island in the West Indies that is a commonwealth joined to the United States. —**Puer/to Ri/can.**

puff (puf), *n.* **1.** a short, sudden burst, as of wind, breath, smoke, or steam [Try to blow out the candles in one *puff*.] **2.** a soft, light shell of pastry filled with a creamy mixture [cream *puffs*]. **3.** a soft roll of hair on the head. **4.** too great praise, as of a book. See also **powder puff.** —*v.* **1.** to blow in a puff or puffs [The wind *puffed* out the flame.] **2.** to give out puffs, as while moving [The steam engine *puffed* uphill.] **3.** to breathe hard and fast, as after running. **4.** to fill or swell as with air [The sails *puffed* out in the wind.] **5.** to praise too greatly. **6.** to smoke [to *puff* a cigar]. **7.** to set the hair in soft rolls. —**puff/er,** *n.*

puff adder, a large poisonous snake of Africa. It swells out its body when irritated.

puff·ball (puf/bôl), *n.* a round plant like a mushroom. When it is touched, it breaks and scatters a brown powder.

puf·fin (puf/in), *n.* a bird of northern seas, with a body like a duck's and a brightly colored beak shaped like a triangle.

puff·y (puf/ē), *adj.* **1.** puffed out like a roll; swollen [*puffy* clouds]. **2.** coming in puffs [*puffy* gusts of air]. —**puff/i·er,** *compar.;* **puff/i·est,** *superl.* —**puff/i·ness,** *n.*

puffin (13 in. long)

pug (pug), *n.* a small dog with short hair, a curled tail, and a short, turned-up nose.

Pu·get Sound (pyoo/jit), a narrow bay of the Pacific, reaching southward into the State of Washington.

pu·gil·ism (pyoo/jə liz'm), *n.* the skill or sport of fighting with the fists. —**pu/gil·ist,** *n.* —**pu/gil·is/tic,** *adj.*

pug·na·cious (pug nā/shəs), *adj.* eager and ready to fight; quarrelsome. —**pug·na/cious·ly,** *adv.* —**pug·nac·i·ty** (pug nas/ə tē) or **pug·na/cious·ness,** *n.*

pug nose, a short, thick, turned-up nose.

pu·is·sant (pyōo´i s'nt *or* pwis´'nt), *adj.* strong; powerful: *now seldom used.* —**pu´-is·sance,** *n.*

puke (pyōok), *n.* & *v.* same as **vomit.**

pul·chri·tude (pul´krə tōod), *n.* beauty.

pule (pyōol), *v.* to cry or whine, as a sick baby does. —**puled,** *p.t.* & *p.p.;* **pul´ing,** *pr.p.*

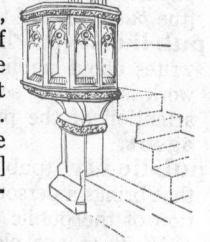

pug nose

pull (pool), *v.* **1.** to use force so as to move or draw something, usually closer or nearer [to *pull* a sled; to *pull* up a sock]. **2.** to draw or pluck out [to *pull* a tooth]. **3.** to tear or rip [The shutter *pulled* loose in the storm.] **4.** to stretch, especially to stretch so much as to hurt; strain [to *pull* a muscle]. **5.** to be able to be pulled [This wagon *pulls* easily.] **6.** to move or go [Tony *pulled* ahead of the other runners.] **7.** to perform; do: *used only in everyday talk* [to *pull* a trick]. —*n.* **1.** the act of pulling or the effort made in pulling [It's a long *pull* to the top. One more *pull* brought the car out of the ditch.] **2.** something by which to pull, as a handle [a drawer *pull*]. **3.** influence or an advantage: *a slang meaning.* —**pull for,** to hope for the success of: *used only in everyday talk.* —**pull off,** to manage to do: *used only in everyday talk.* —**pull oneself together,** to gather one's courage, self-control, etc. —**pull through,** to get safely through an illness or difficulty: *used only in everyday talk.* —**pull up, 1.** to take out by the roots. **2.** to bring or come to a stop. **3.** to move ahead. —**pull´er,** *n.*

pul·let (pool´it), *n.* a young hen, usually not more than one year old.

pul·ley (pool´ē), *n.* a small wheel with a groove in the rim in which a rope or belt moves. A pulley may be used to lift a thing fastened to one end of the rope by pulling down on the other end. —**pul´leys,** *pl.*

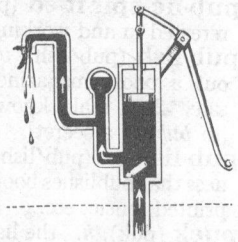

pulley

Pull·man car (pool´mən), a railroad car with small private rooms or seats that can be made into berths for sleeping.

pul·mo·nar·y (pul´mə ner´ē), *adj.* of or having to do with the lungs [The *pulmonary* artery carries blood to the lungs.]

pulp (pulp), *n.* **1.** the soft, juicy part of a fruit. **2.** the soft, center part of a tooth. It contains nerves and blood vessels. **3.** any soft, wet mass, as the mixture of ground-up wood, rags, etc. from which paper is made. —**pulp´y,** *adj.*

pul·pit (pool´pit), *n.* **1.** a platform in a church on which the clergyman stands when giving a sermon: *see the picture at the top of the next column.* **2.** preachers as a group; clergy.

pul·sate (pul´sāt), *v.* **1.** to beat or throb in a regular rhythm, as the heart. **2.** to shake;

vibrate; quiver. —**pul´sat·ed,** *p.t.* & *p.p.;* **pul´sat·ing,** *pr.p.* —**pul·sa´tion,** *n.*

pulse (puls), *n.* **1.** the regular beating in the arteries, caused by the movements of the heart in pumping the blood. **2.** any regular beat [the *pulse* of a radio signal]. —*v.* to beat or throb [The music *pulsed* in his ears.] —**pulsed,** *p.t.* & *p.p.;* **puls´-ing,** *pr.p.*

pulpit

pul·ver·ize (pul´və rīz), *v.* **1.** to crush or grind into a powder. **2.** to destroy completely [The bombs *pulverized* the city.] —**pul´ver·ized,** *p.t.* & *p.p.;* **pul´ver·iz·ing,** *pr.p.*

pu·ma (pyōo´mə), *n.* another name for the **cougar.**

pum·ice (pum´is), *n.* a light, spongy rock sometimes formed when lava from a volcano hardens. It is often ground into a powder, which is used for polishing things or taking out stains.

pum·mel (pum´'l), *n.* & *v.* same as **pommel.** —**pum´meled** or **pum´melled,** *p.t.* & *p.p.;* **pum´mel·ing** or **pum´mel·ling,** *pr.p.*

pump (pump), *n.* a machine that forces a liquid or gas into or out of something, as by pressure. —*v.* **1.** to raise, move, or force with a pump [to *pump* water from a well; to *pump* air into a tire]. **2.** to empty out with a pump [to *pump* out a flooded basement]. **3.** to move with the action of a pump [The heart *pumps* blood.] **4.** to move up and down like a pump handle [His legs kept *pumping* as the bicycle climbed the hill.] **5.** to keep on asking questions of in order to get information [The police *pumped* the suspect.]

pump

pump (pump), *n.* a kind of shoe with low sides and no straps or laces.

pump·er·nick·el (pum´pər nik´'l), *n.* a coarse, dark kind of rye bread.

pump·kin (pump´kin *or* pung´kin), *n.* a large, round, orange or yellow fruit that grows on a vine and has many seeds. The pulp is much used as a filling for pies.

pun (pun), *n.* the humorous use of words which have the same sound or spelling, but have different meanings; play on words [There is a *pun* in the name of a restaurant called "Dewdrop Inn."] —*v.* to make a pun or puns. —**punned,** *p.t.* & *p.p.;* **pun´ning,** *pr.p.*

pumpkin

punch (punch), *n.* **1.** a tool for making holes in something, or one for stamping or cutting designs on a surface. **2.** a hard blow with the fist. —*v.*

1. to hit with the fist. **2.** to make holes in, stamp, etc. with a punch. **3.** to herd or drive cattle.

punch (punch), *n.* a sweet drink made by mixing various fruit juices or other liquids together, sometimes with wine or liquor added.

Punch-and-Judy show (punch′'n joo̅′dē), a puppet show in which the humpbacked Punch is always fighting with his wife, Judy.

pun·cheon (pun′chən), *n.* a large barrel for beer or wine.

punc·til·i·ous (pungk til′i əs), *adj.* **1.** paying strict attention to the small details of good manners, conduct, etc. [a *punctilious* host]. **2.** very exact; careful of details [to keep *punctilious* records].

punc·tu·al (pungk′choo əl), *adj.* coming, or doing something, at the right time; prompt. —**punc′tu·al′i·ty,** *n.* —**punc′tu·al·ly,** *adv.*

punc·tu·ate (pungk′choo āt), *v.* **1.** to put in commas, periods, etc. to make the meaning clear [to *punctuate* a sentence]. **2.** to interrupt from time to time [a speech *punctuated* with applause]. —**punc′tu·at·ed,** *p.t. & p.p.;* **punc′tu·at·ing,** *pr.p.*

punc·tu·a·tion (pungk′choo ā′shən), *n.* **1.** the use of commas, periods, etc. in writing [rules of *punctuation*]. **2.** punctuation marks [What *punctuation* is used to end sentences?]

punctuation mark, any of the marks used in writing and printing to help make the meaning clear, as the comma, period, question mark, colon, semicolon, exclamation mark, dash, etc.

punc·ture (pungk′chər), *n.* a hole made by a sharp point or the act of making such a hole [a *puncture* in a tire caused by a nail]. —*v.* **1.** to make a hole with a sharp point; pierce [to *puncture* a balloon]. **2.** to put an end to or make smaller, as if by piercing [to *puncture* one's pride]. —**punc′tured,** *p.t. & p.p.;* **punc′tur·ing,** *pr.p.*

pun·dit (pun′dit), *n.* a person who knows a great deal; authority or expert.

pun·gent (pun′jənt), *adj.* **1.** having a sharp or stinging taste or smell [a *pungent* chili sauce]. **2.** very keen and direct, sometimes in a painful way; biting [*pungent* criticism; *pungent* wit]. —**pun′gen·cy,** *n.* —**pun′gent·ly,** *adv.*

pun·ish (pun′ish), *v.* **1.** to make suffer pain, loss, etc., for doing something wrong, bad, or against the law. **2.** to set as a penalty for [to *punish* murder with death]. **3.** to treat roughly or harshly: *used only in everyday talk* [The rough gravel *punished* his feet.]

pun·ish·a·ble (pun′ish ə b'l), *adj.* that can or should be punished [a *punishable* crime].

pun·ish·ment (pun′ish mənt), *n.* **1.** a punishing or being punished. **2.** what is done to a person because of his crime, wrongdoing, etc. [A ten-dollar fine was his *punishment* for speeding.]

pu·ni·tive (pyoo̅′nə tiv), *adj.* punishing or having to do with punishment [*punitive* laws].

Pun·jab (pun jäb′ *or* pun′jäb), *n.* a former province of British India, now divided between India and Pakistan.

punk (pungk), *n.* **1.** dry, rotted wood used for starting a fire. **2.** any substance that burns very slowly without a flame [A stick of *punk* is often used to light fireworks.]

punt (punt), *v.* to kick a football after letting it drop from the hands, but before it touches the ground. —*n.* such a kick.

punt (punt), *n.* a boat with a flat bottom and square ends. —*v.* to make a punt move by pushing against the bottom of the river or lake with a long pole.

pu·ny (pyoo̅′nē), *adj.* small or weak; feeble. —**pu′ni·er,** *compar.;* **pu′ni·est,** *superl.*

pup (pup), *n.* **1.** a young dog; puppy. **2.** a young seal.

pu·pa (pyoo̅′pə), *n.* an insect in the stage between a larva and an adult [The *pupa* of a moth is enclosed in a cocoon.] —**pu·pae** (pyoo̅′pē) or **pu′pas,** *pl.*

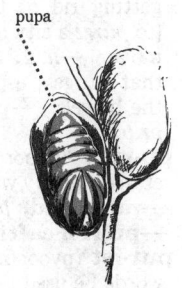

pupa

pu·pil (pyoo̅′p'l), *n.* **1.** a person being taught by a teacher, as in a school; student. **2.** the dark opening in the center of the eye that grows larger or smaller to let in more or less light.

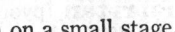

cocoons, left one cut open to show pupa

pup·pet (pup′it), *n.* **1.** a small figure in the form of a human being, moved by strings or the hands, as in acting out a play (called a **puppet show**) on a small stage. **2.** a person who does, says, and thinks what another tells him to.

pup·py (pup′ē), *n.* **1.** a young dog. **2.** a silly, vain young man. —**pup′pies,** *pl.*

pur·blind (pur′blīnd), *adj.* **1.** almost blind. **2.** slow in understanding.

puppets

pur·chase (pur′chis), *v.* **1.** to buy; get for money [to *purchase* a car]. **2.** to get by a sacrifice [The hero *purchased* fame with his life.] —*n.* **1.** anything that is bought [She carried her *purchases* home in a bag.] **2.** the act of buying [his *purchase* of a house]. **3.** a firm hold to keep from slipping or to move something heavy [The tires can't get a good *purchase* on ice.] —**pur′chased,** *p.t. & p.p.;* **pur′chas·ing,** *pr.p.* —**pur′chas·er,** *n.*

pure (pyoor), *adj.* **1.** not mixed with anything else [*pure* maple sirup]. **2.** not having anything dirty, unhealthful, etc. in it; clean [*pure* drinking water; *pure* country air]. **3.** not bad or evil; morally good; innocent ["Blessed are the *pure* in heart."] **4.** nothing else but; mere [*pure* luck].

---

fat,   āpe,   cär,   ten,   ēven,   hit,   bīte,   gō,   hôrn,   too̅l,   book,   up,   fur;
get,   joy,   yet,   chin,   she,   thin,   *th*en;   zh = s in pleasure;   ′ as in able (ā′b'l);
ə = a in ago,   e in agent,   i in sanity,   o in confess,   u in focus.

5. not for a certain practical use; dealing only with theory [*pure* science]. —**pur′er,** *compar.;* **pur′est,** *superl.* —**pure′ly,** *adv.* —**pure′-ness,** *n.*

pu·rée (pyoo rā′), *n.* **1.** food boiled and strained through a sieve to make a smooth paste. **2.** a thick soup. —*v.* to make a purée of. —**pu-réed′,** *p.t. & p.p.;* **pu·ré′ing,** *pr.p.*

pur·ga·tive (pur′gə tiv), *n.* a medicine that makes the bowels move; cathartic. —*adj.* causing the bowels to move [a *purgative* medicine].

pur·ga·to·ry (pur′gə tôr′ē), *n.* **1.** a condition or place in which some Christians believe that the souls of dead persons suffer until they have been cleansed of the minor sins of which they were guilty while alive. **2.** any place or condition in which people suffer or are punished. —**pur′-ga·to′ries,** *pl.* —**pur′ga·to′ri·al,** *adj.*

purge (purj), *v.* **1.** to make clean or pure by getting rid of things that are dirty or wrong [to *purge* a city of slums]. **2.** to make the bowels move. —*n.* **1.** the act of purging. **2.** anything that purges; especially, a medicine that moves the bowels. —**purged,** *p.t. & p.p.;* **purg′ing,** *pr.p.*

pu·ri·fy (pyoor′ə fī), *v.* to make pure, clean, etc. [to *purify* water by filtering it through sand]. —**pu′ri·fied,** *p.t. & p.p.;* **pu′ri·fy·ing,** *pr.p.* —**pu′ri·fi·ca′tion,** *n.*

pur·ist (pyoor′ist), *n.* a person who insists that words be used only in those ways that he thinks to be correct [A *purist* does not approve of "It's me."]

Pu·ri·tan (pyoor′ə t'n), *n.* **1.** a member of an English religious group in the 16th and 17th centuries, which wanted to make the Church of England simpler in its services and stricter about morals. Many Puritans came to New England in the 17th century. **2. puritan,** a person who is so strict in moral and religious matters that he thinks most pleasures are sinful. —**pu′ri·tan′i·cal** or **pu′ri·tan′ic,** *adj.* —**Pu′ri·tan·ism** or **pu′ri·tan·ism,** *n.*

pu·ri·ty (pyoor′ə tē), *n.* the condition of being pure; cleanness, goodness, etc.

purl (purl), *v.* to move in ripples or with a murmuring sound, as a shallow brook or small stream. —*n.* the sound of purling water.

purl (purl), *v.* to make stitches in knitting that are looped opposite to the usual stitches, so as to form ribbing.

pur·lieu (pur′loo), *n.* a part away from the center, as a suburb of a city.

pur·loin (pur loin′), *v.* to steal.

pur·ple (pur′p'l), *n.* **1.** a color that is a mixture of red and blue. **2.** crimson clothing worn long ago by kings and other high officials. —*adj.* of the color purple.

Purple Heart, a medal given to U.S. soldiers, sailors, etc. who were wounded in action.

pur·plish (pur′plish), *adj.* slightly purple.

pur·port (pur pôrt′), *v.* to seem or claim to be, mean, etc. [a book that *purports* to give the true facts]. —*n.* (pur′pôrt), meaning; main idea [What is the *purport* of his message?]

pur·pose (pur′pəs), *n.* **1.** what one plans to get or do; aim; goal [He came for the *purpose* of speaking to you.] **2.** the reason or use for something [a room with no *purpose*]. —*v.* to plan or intend: *not in common use.* —**on purpose,** not by accident; intentionally. —**to good purpose,** with a good result. —**to little or no purpose,** with little or no result. —**pur′-posed,** *p.t. & p.p.;* **pur′pos·ing,** *pr.p.* —**pur′-pose·ful,** *adj.* —**pur′pose·less,** *adj.*

pur·pose·ly (pur′pəs lē), *adv.* with a purpose; not by chance or by accident; intentionally; deliberately.

purr or **pur** (pur), *n.* the low, soft rumbling sound made by a cat when it seems to be pleased. —*v.* to make such a sound.

purse (purs), *n.* **1.** a small bag for carrying money. **2.** a larger bag of leather, etc., used by women for carrying money, cosmetics, keys, etc. **3.** a sum of money given as a prize or gift [a horse race with a $1000 *purse*]. —*v.* to draw together; pucker [He *pursed* his lips and began to whistle.] —**pursed,** *p.t. & p.p.;* **purs′ing,** *pr.p.*

purs·er (pur′sər), *n.* the officer on a ship who keeps the accounts, is in charge of the stores, checks passengers' tickets, etc.

purs·lane (purs′lin *or* purs′lān), *n.* a weed with pink, fleshy stems and small, round leaves.

pur·su·ance (pər soo′əns *or* pər syoo′əns), *n.* the act of pursuing, or carrying out, as a plan.

pur·su·ant (pər soo′ənt *or* pər syoo′ənt), *adj.* carrying out; following. —**pursuant to,** according to [He will leave now, *pursuant to* our plans.]

purslane

pur·sue (pər soo′ *or* pər-syoo′), *v.* **1.** to follow in order to catch or catch up to [to *pursue* a runaway horse]. **2.** to carry out or follow; go on with [She *pursued* a career in acting.] **3.** to try to find; seek [to *pursue* knowledge]. **4.** to continue to bother or trouble [Bad luck still *pursued* him.] —**pur·sued′,** *p.t. & p.p.;* **pur·su′ing,** *pr.p.* —**pur·su′er,** *n.*

pur·suit (pər soot′ *or* pər syoot′), *n.* **1.** the act of pursuing [the *pursuit* of truth]. **2.** an activity, job, sport, etc. [Golf is his favorite *pursuit*.]

pur·vey (pər vā′), *v.* to supply, as food or provisions. —**pur·vey′ance,** *n.* —**pur·vey′-or,** *n.*

pus (pus), *n.* the thick, yellowish matter that oozes from a sore or is found in a boil.

push (poosh), *v.* **1.** to press against so as to move; shove [to *push* a stalled car; to *push* a stake into the ground]. **2.** to move by using force [He *pushed* through the crowd.] **3.** to urge or press forward; force or drive [He *pushed* the men to work faster.] **4.** to urge the use, sale, etc. of [The company is *pushing* its new product.] —*n.* **1.** the act of pushing; a shove or thrust [One hard *push* and the door flew open.] **2.** the power or energy to get things done; drive: *used only in everyday talk* [a leader with plenty of *push*]. —**push on,** to go forward; proceed. —**push'-er,** *n.*

push-o·ver (poosh′ō′vər), *n.* **1.** anything that is very easy to do. **2.** a person who is very easy to fool, persuade, defeat, etc. *A slang word.*

push-up (poosh′up′), *n.* an exercise in which one lies face down on the floor and pushes the body up with the arms.

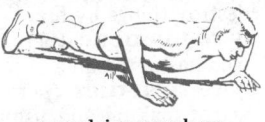

man doing a push-up

pu·sil·lan·i·mous (pyōō′s'l an′ə məs), *adj.* timid or cowardly; not brave. —**pu·sil·la·nim·i·ty** (pyōō′s'l ə nim′ə ti), *n.*

puss (poos), *n.* a pet name for a cat.

puss·y (poos′ē), *n.* a cat. —**puss′ies,** *pl.*

puss·y·foot (poos′ē foot), *v.* **1.** to move quickly and carefully, as a cat does. **2.** to keep from making one's feelings or opinions clear [The candidate *pussyfooted* on the subject of taxes.] *A slang word.*

pussy willow, a willow that bears soft, furry, grayish catkins.

put (poot), *v.* **1.** to make be in a certain place or position; place; set [*Put* soap in the water. *Put* the books side by side.] **2.** to make be in a certain condition [The sound of the waves *put* him to sleep.] **3.** to say or express; state [Can you *put* the problem in simple words?] **4.** to push with force; thrust [The tree has *put* down roots.] **5.** to give or assign; attach [He *put* a price of $10 on the rug. The government *put* a tax on luxuries.] **6.** to move or go [The fleet *put* out to sea.] **7.** to throw by pushing up and out from the shoulder [to *put* the shot]. —**put about,** to change a ship's direction. —**put across,** to succeed in making understood, accepted, successful, etc.: *a slang phrase.* —**put aside** or **put away** or **put by,** to save for later use. —**put down, 1.** to overcome with force; crush, as a revolt. **2.** to write down. **3.** to make feel ashamed or unimportant: *a slang meaning.* —**put forth,** to grow, as leaves or shoots. —**put off, 1.** to wait until later; postpone. **2.** to confuse, mislead, make wait, etc. —**put on, 1.** to dress oneself with. **2.** to pretend. **3.** to present, as a play on a stage. **4.** to fool or trick: *a slang meaning.* —**put out, 1.** to make leave; send away. **2.** to stop from burning; extinguish, as a fire. **3.** to annoy or bother. —**put over,** to do something by using tricks; also, to do something that is hard to do: *used only in everyday talk.* —**put through, 1.** to succeed in doing something; carry out [to *put through* a business deal]. **2.** to cause to do [He *put* the horse *through* its paces.]

catkins of a pussy willow

—**put up, 1.** to offer; show [to *put up* a house for sale]. **2.** to preserve or can, as fruits. **3.** to build; erect. **4.** to furnish with a place to live. **5.** to provide, as money. **6.** to get to do something, as by urging: *used only in everyday talk* [His friends *put* him *up* to it.] —**put upon,** to take advantage of. —**put up with,** to tolerate; bear. —**put,** *p.t. & p.p.;* **put′ting,** *pr.p.*

pu·tre·fy (pyōō′trə fī), *v.* to make or become rotten or decayed. —**pu′tre·fied,** *p.t. & p.p.;* **pu′tre·fy·ing,** *pr.p.* —**pu·tre·fac·tion** (pyōō′trə fak′shən), *n.*

pu·trid (pyōō′trid), *adj.* **1.** rotten and smelling bad [*putrid* garbage]. **2.** coming from decay or rottenness [a *putrid* smell].

putt (put), *n.* a light stroke made in golf in trying to roll the ball into the hole on a green. —*v.* to hit a golf ball with a putt.

put·tee (pu tē′ or put′ē), *n.* a covering for the leg from the ankle to the knee, once worn by soldiers, hikers, etc. It is either a long strip of cloth wound round the leg or a piece of leather or canvas buckled or laced in place.

putt·er (put′ər), *n.* **1.** a short golf club used in putting. **2.** a person who putts.

put·ter (put′ər), *v.* to busy oneself without getting anything worth-while done [He *puttered* around the house all day.]

put·ty (put′ē), *n.* a soft mixture of powdered chalk and linseed oil, used to hold panes of glass in windows, to fill cracks, etc. —*v.* to hold in place or fill with putty. —**put′tied,** *p.t. & p.p.;* **put′ty·ing,** *pr.p.*

putter

puz·zle (puz′'l), *n.* **1.** a question, problem, etc. that is hard to solve or understand [It's a *puzzle* to me how he got here so quickly.] **2.** a toy or problem that tests one's cleverness or skill [a jigsaw *puzzle;* a crossword *puzzle*]. —*v.* **1.** to make think hard or to confuse; perplex [Her strange behavior *puzzled* them.] **2.** to think hard or be perplexed [She *puzzled* a long time over his question.] —**puzzle out,** to find the answer to by serious thought, study, etc. —**puz′zled,** *p.t. & p.p.;* **puz′zling,** *pr.p.* —**puz′zle·ment,** *n.*

Pvt., abbreviation for **Private.**

Pyg·my (pig′mē), *n.* **1.** a member of any of several races of very short people living in Asia and Africa. **2. pygmy,** any very small person or thing; dwarf. —*adj.* **1.** of the Pygmies. **2. pygmy,** very small; dwarfish. —**Pyg′mies** or **pyg′mies,** *pl.*

py·ja·mas (pə jam′əz *or* pə jä′məz), *n.pl.* the usual British spelling of **pajamas.**

---

fat,   āpe,   cär,   ten,   ēven,   hit,   bīte,   gō,   hôrn,   tōōl,   book,   up,   fûr;
get,   joy,   yet,   chin,   she,   thin,   *th*en;   zh = s in pleasure;   ' as in able (ā′b'l);
ə = a in ago,   e in agent,   i in sanity,   o in confess,   u in focus.

py·lon (pī′län), *n.* **1.** a gateway, as of an Egyptian temple. **2.** any high tower, as for holding up electric lines, for marking a racecourse for airplanes, etc.

py·or·rhe·a or **py·or·rhoe·a** (pī′ə rē′ə), *n.* a disease of the gums and tooth sockets, in which pus forms and the teeth become loose.

pyr·a·mid (pir′ə mid), *n.* **1.** a solid figure whose sides are triangles that come together in a point at the top: *see the picture.* **2.** anything having this shape; especially, any of the huge structures with a square base and four sides in which ancient Egyptian rulers were buried. —*v.* to build up or heap up in the form of a pyramid. —**the Pyramids,** the three large pyramids near Cairo, Egypt.

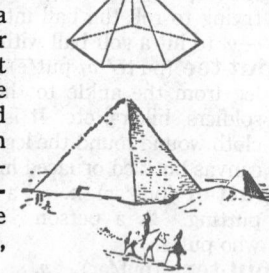

pylon marking a course for airplanes

upper: pyramid *(meaning 1)*
lower: Egyptian pyramids

py·ram·i·dal (pi-ram′ə d′l), *adj.* of a pyramid or shaped like a pyramid.

pyre (pīr), *n.* a pile of wood on which a dead body is burned; funeral pile.

Pyr·e·nees (pir′ə nēz), *n.pl.* a mountain range between France and Spain.

py·rite (pī′rīt), *n.* a shiny yellow mineral that is a compound of iron and sulfur. It is also called **iron pyrites** or **fool's gold.**

py·ri·tes (pī rī′tēz or pī′rīts), *n.* any mineral that is a compound of sulfur and a metal.

py·ro·ma·ni·a (pī′rə mā′ni ə), *n.* a sickness of the mind in which one has a strong desire to destroy things by fire.

py·ro·ma·ni·ac (pī′rə mā′ni ak), *n.* a person who has pyromania.

py·ro·tech·nics (pī′rə tek′niks), *n.pl.* **1.** the art of making and using fireworks: *used with a singular verb.* **2.** a display of fireworks. **3.** any brilliant display, as of skill in playing a musical instrument. —**py′ro·tech′nic** or **py′ro·tech′ni·cal,** *adj.*

Pyr·rhic victory (pir′ik), a victory that costs too much to win.

Py·thag·o·ras (pi thag′ər əs), *n.* Greek philosopher and mathematician who lived in the 6th century B.C.

Pythias, *n.* see **Damon and Pythias.**

py·thon (pī′thän or pī′thən), *n.* a very large snake found in Asia, Africa, and Australia. It is not poisonous, but twists around its prey and crushes it to death.

python (25 ft. long)

Q

Q, q (kyōō), *n.* the seventeenth letter of the English alphabet. —**Q's, q's** (kyōōz), *pl.*

q., abbreviation for **quart, queen, question.**

qt., abbreviation for **quart.** —**qts.,** *pl.*

quack (kwak), *n.* the sound that a duck makes. —*v.* to make this sound.

quack (kwak), *n.* **1.** a person without proper training or skill who pretends to be a doctor. **2.** any person who pretends to have knowledge or skill that he does not have; charlatan. —*adj.* that is or has to do with a quack; false; pretended [a *quack* medicine].

quack·er·y (kwak′ər ē), *n.* the actions or methods of a quack.

quad·ran·gle (kwäd′rang′g′l), *n.* **1.** a flat figure with four angles and four sides. **2.** a courtyard surrounded by buildings on all four sides. **3.** the buildings themselves. —**quad·ran·gu·lar** (kwäd rang′gyoo lər), *adj.*

quad·rant (kwäd′rənt), *n.* **1.** one quarter of a circle. *See the picture.* **2.** an instrument like the sextant, used for measuring angles and heights.

quad·ren·ni·al (kwäd ren′i əl), *adj.* **1.** happening once every four years. **2.** lasting four years. —**quad·ren′ni·al·ly,** *adv.*

quadrant

quad·ri·lat·er·al (kwäd′rə lat′ər əl), *adj.* having four sides. —*n.* a flat figure with four sides and four angles.

qua·drille (kwə dril′), *n.* **1.** a square dance for four couples. **2.** music for this dance.

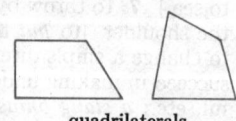

quadrilaterals

quad·ru·ped (kwäd′roo ped), *n.* an animal with four feet. —*adj.* having four feet.

quad·ru·ple (kwäd′roo p'l or kwäd rōō′p'l), *adj.* **1.** made up of four [a *quadruple* alliance of nations]. **2.** four times as much or as many. —*adv.* four times as much or as many. —*n.* an amount four times as much or as many [Forty is the *quadruple* of ten.] —*v.* to make or become four times as much or as many [The population of the city has *quadrupled.*] —**quad′ru·pled,** *p.t. & p.p.;* **quad′ru·pling,** *pr.p.*

quad·ru·plet (kwäd′roo plit or kwäd rōō′plit), *n.* any of four children born at a single birth.

quaff (kwäf or kwaf), *v.* to drink deeply in a thirsty way. —*n.* a quaffing.

quag·mire (kwag′mīr), *n.* **1.** soft, wet ground that sinks down under one's feet. **2.** a difficult or dangerous situation [He was stuck in a *quagmire* of debts.]

quail (kwāl), *v.* to shrink or draw back in fear; lose one's courage.

quail (kwāl), *n.* a small wild bird hunted for sport or for food; kind of partridge.

quaint (kwānt), *adj.* unusual or old-fashioned in a pleasing way [a *quaint* old inn]. —**quaint′ly,** *adv.* —**quaint′ness,** *n.*

quail (10 in. long)

quake (kwāk), *v.* **1.** to tremble or shake, as the ground does in an earthquake. **2.** to shudder or shiver, as with fear or cold. —*n.* **1.** an earthquake. **2.** a shaking or shivering. —**quaked,** *p.t. & p.p.;* **quak′ing,** *pr.p.*

Quak·er (kwāk′ər), *n.* a Friend: see **Society of Friends.**

qual·i·fi·ca·tion (kwäl′ə fi kā′shən), *n.* **1.** a qualifying or being qualified. **2.** a thing that changes, limits, or holds back [I can recommend the book without any *qualification.*] **3.** the skills and special training that fit a person for some work, office, etc.

qual·i·fied (kwäl′ə fīd), *adj.* **1.** having the qualities that are needed; fit [a man *qualified* to be a leader]. **2.** limited [*qualified* approval].

qual·i·fy (kwäl′ə fī), *v.* **1.** to make or be fit or suitable, as for some work or activity [His training *qualifies* him for the job. Does he *qualify* for the team?] **2.** to give or get the right to do something [His license *qualifies* him to drive a car.] **3.** to soften or limit; make less strong [to *qualify* a punishment; to *qualify* a statement by adding "perhaps"]. **4.** to limit the meaning of a word; modify [Adjectives *qualify* nouns.] —**qual′i·fied,** *p.t. & p.p.;* **qual′i·fy·ing,** *pr.p.*

qual·i·ta·tive (kwäl′ə tā′tiv), *adj.* having to do with quality or qualities, not quantity.

qualitative analysis, the branch of chemistry that tests substances to find out what elements or ingredients are in them.

qual·i·ty (kwäl′ə tē), *n.* **1.** any of the features that make a thing what it is; characteristic [Coldness is one *quality* of ice cream.] **2.** nature; character [soap with an oily *quality*]. **3.** degree of excellence [a poor *quality* of paper]. **4.** excellence [to look for *quality* in a product]. **5.** high position in society: *now seldom used* [a lady of *quality*]. —**qual′i·ties,** *pl.*

qualm (kwäm), *n.* **1.** a feeling of guilt; scruple [The thief had no *qualms* about taking the money.] **2.** a sudden anxious or uneasy feeling; misgiving [I felt *qualms* about sailing in rough weather.] **3.** a sudden, brief feeling of sickness or faintness.

quan·da·ry (kwän′drē *or* kwän′də rē), *n.* a condition of being doubtful or confused [in a *quandary* about going]. —**quan′da·ries,** *pl.*

quan·ti·ta·tive (kwän′tə tā′tiv), *adj.* **1.** having to do with quantity. **2.** that can be measured.

quantitative analysis, the branch of chemistry that tests substances to find out how much of certain elements or ingredients are in them.

quan·ti·ty (kwän′tə tē), *n.* **1.** an amount or portion [large *quantities* of food]. **2.** a large amount [The factory makes toys in *quantity.*] **3.** a number or symbol that stands for some amount in mathematics. —**quan′ti·ties,** *pl.*

quar·an·tine (kwôr′ən tēn), *n.* **1.** the act of keeping a diseased person, animal, or plant away from others so that the disease will not spread. **2.** a place where such persons, animals, or plants are kept. **3.** the time during which a ship is kept in port while the passengers, cargo, etc. are inspected for some disease. —*v.* **1.** to put in a place of quarantine. **2.** to cut off, as a country, from dealings with another or others. —**quar′an·tined,** *p.t. & p.p.;* **quar′an·tin·ing,** *pr.p.*

quar·rel (kwôr′əl), *n.* **1.** an argument or disagreement, especially an angry one; dispute. **2.** a reason for arguing [What is your *quarrel* with him?] —*v.* **1.** to argue or disagree in an angry way. **2.** to find fault; complain. —**quar′reled** or **quar′relled,** *p.t. & p.p.;* **quar′rel·ing** or **quar′rel·ling,** *pr.p.*

quar·rel·some (kwôr′əl səm), *adj.* likely to quarrel; fond of fighting or arguing.

quar·ry (kwôr′ē), *n.* an animal that is being chased or hunted down; prey. —**quar′ries,** *pl.*

quar·ry (kwôr′ē), *n.* a place where stone is cut or blasted out of the earth, to be used in building things. —*v.* to take from a quarry [to *quarry* marble]. —**quar′ries,** *pl.* —**quar′ried,** *p.t. & p.p.;* **quar′ry·ing,** *pr.p.*

quart (kwôrt), *n.* **1.** a measure of liquids, equal to two pints or ¼ gallon. **2.** a measure of volume for grain, fruit, vegetables, etc. It is equal to ⅛ peck. **3.** a bottle, box, etc. holding a quart.

quar·ter (kwôr′tər), *n.* **1.** any of the four equal parts of something; fourth [a *quarter* of a mile; the third *quarter* of a football game]. **2.** one fourth of a year; three months. **3.** the point fifteen minutes before or after any given hour [It's a *quarter* after five.] **4.** a silver coin of the United States or Canada, worth 25 cents; one fourth of a dollar. **5.** one leg of a four-legged animal with the parts connected to it [a *quarter* of beef]. **6.** any of the four main points of the compass; north, east, south, or west. **7.** a certain section of a town [the Chinese *quarter*]. **8.** **quarters,** *pl.* a place to live in, often just for a while. **9.** a source or origin [news from the highest *quarters*]. **10.** the time in which the moon makes one fourth of its circle around the earth, about 7 days. **11.** mercy shown to an enemy. —*v.* **1.** to divide into four equal parts. **2.** to furnish with a place to live or stay [to *quarter* soldiers in barracks]. —*adj.* that is equal to one fourth [a *quarter* share of the profits]. —**at close quarters,** very close together. —**cry quarter,** to beg for mercy.

---

fat, āpe, cär, ten, ēven, hit, bīte, gō, hôrn, tool, book, up, fûr; get, joy, yet, chin, she, thin, *then;* zh = s in pleasure; ′ as in able (ā′b'l); ə = a in ago, e in agent, i in sanity, o in confess, u in focus.

quar·ter·back (kwôr'tər bak), *n.* the player in football who usually calls the signals and receives the ball from the center.

quar·ter-deck or **quar·ter·deck** (kwôr'tər dek), *n.* the back part of the upper deck of a ship, usually for officers.

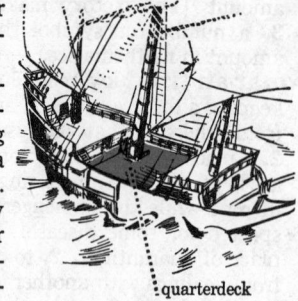
quarterdeck

quar·ter·ly (kwôr'tər lē), *adj.* happening or appearing four times a year [a *quarterly* magazine]. —*adv.* once every quarter of the year [to pay rent *quarterly*]. —*n.* a magazine that comes out four times a year. —**quar'ter·lies,** *pl.*

quar·ter·mas·ter (kwôr'tər mas'tər), *n.* **1.** a military officer who is in charge of supplies, quarters, etc. for troops. **2.** an officer on a ship in charge of the steering, signals, etc.

quarter note, a note in music that is held one fourth as long as a whole note.

quar·ter·staff (kwôr'tər staf), *n.* a long, wooden pole with an iron tip, once used in England as a weapon. —**quar·ter·staves** (kwôr'tər stāvz), *pl.*

quarter notes

quar·tet or **quar·tette** (kwôr tet'), *n.* **1.** a piece of music for four voices or four instruments. **2.** the four people who sing or play it. **3.** any group of four.

quar·to (kwôr'tō), *n.* **1.** a page size of a book, about 9 by 12 inches. **2.** a book with pages of this size. —**quar'tos,** *pl.*

quartz (kwôrts), *n.* a bright mineral, usually found in clear, glassy crystals, but also as colored stones which are used in jewelry [Agate, amethyst, and onyx are kinds of *quartz.*]

quash (kwäsh), *v.* to put an end to by law; annul or set aside [to *quash* an order].

quash (kwäsh), *v.* to put down or overcome by force; crush [to *quash* an uprising].

qua·si (kwā'sī or kwä'zī), *adv. & adj.* seeming as if it were; not real or not really. **Quasi** is usually used in words formed with a hyphen [a *quasi*-legal document].

qua·ver (kwā'vər), *v.* **1.** to tremble or shake, as the voice often does when one is afraid. **2.** to make a trill in singing or in playing an instrument. —*n.* a trembling or trilling tone.

quay (kē), *n.* a wharf for loading and unloading ships, usually one of stone or concrete.

quea·sy (kwē'zē), *adj.* **1.** causing or feeling sickness at one's stomach [Sailing makes her *queasy.*] **2.** easily made sick at the stomach; squeamish. **3.** uncomfortable; embarrassed. —**quea'si·er,** *compar.;* **quea'si·est,** *superl.* —**quea'si·ly,** *adv.* —**quea'si·ness,** *n.*

Que·bec (kwi bek'), *n.* **1.** a province of eastern Canada: abbreviated **Que. 2.** its capital.

queen (kwēn), *n.* **1.** the wife of a king. **2.** a woman who rules a country as a king does. **3.** a woman who is famous or honored for something [a beauty *queen*]. **4.** the female that lays all the eggs for a colony of bees or ants. **5.** a playing card with a picture of a queen on it. **6.** the most powerful piece in chess.

Queen Anne's lace, a wild plant of the carrot family, with white, lacy flowers.

queen·ly (kwēn'lē), *adj.* of, like, or fit for a queen [a *queenly* gown]. —**queen'li·er,** *compar.;* **queen'li·est,** *superl.*

Queens·land (kwēnz'lənd), *n.* a state of eastern Australia.

queer (kwir), *adj.* **1.** different from what is usual or normal; odd; strange [How *queer* to see snow in July!] **2.** slightly sick; faint. —*v.* to spoil the success of: *a slang use.* —**queer'ly,** *adv.* —**queer'ness,** *n.*

quell (kwel), *v.* **1.** to put an end to; crush [to *quell* a riot]. **2.** to quiet [to *quell* fears].

quench (kwench), *v.* **1.** to put out; extinguish [Water *quenched* the fire.] **2.** to satisfy or slake [to *quench* one's thirst.]

quer·u·lous (kwer'ə ləs or kwer'yoo ləs), *adj.* **1.** always complaining or finding fault [a *querulous* old man]. **2.** full of complaint [a *querulous* voice]. —**quer'u·lous·ly,** *adv.*

que·ry (kwir'ē), *n.* **1.** a question. **2.** a question mark (?). —*v.* **1.** to ask or ask about; question [He *queried* my reasons for leaving.] **2.** to show doubt about; question the correctness of [to *query* a date in an article]. —**que'ries,** *pl.* —**que'ried,** *p.t. & p.p.;* **que'ry·ing,** *pr.p.*

quest (kwest), *n.* **1.** a hunt or search [a student in *quest* of knowledge]. **2.** a journey in search of adventure, as those taken by knights in the Middle Ages. —*v.* to go in search: *now seldom used.*

ques·tion (kwes'chən), *n.* **1.** something that is asked in order to learn or know [He refused to answer the reporter's *questions.*] **2.** doubt [There is no *question* of his honesty.] **3.** a matter to be considered; problem [It's not a *question* of money.] **4.** a matter that is being talked over by a group; also, the putting of such a matter to a vote [The *question* is before the committee.] —*v.* **1.** to ask questions of [*Question* the prisoners.] **2.** to object to; have doubts about [The batter *questioned* the umpire's decision.] —**beyond question,** without any doubt. —**call in question,** to doubt or challenge. —**in question,** being considered or talked about. —**out of the question,** impossible. —**ques'tion·er,** *n.*

ques·tion·a·ble (kwes'chən ə b'l), *adj.* **1.** that can or should be doubted [a *questionable* story]. **2.** probably not moral, not honest, etc.; not well thought of [a man of *questionable* character].

question mark, the mark ?, used after a word or sentence to show that a question is being asked.

ques·tion·naire (kwes chən er'), *n.* a written or printed list of questions used in gathering information from persons.

quet·zal or **que·zal** (ket säl'), *n.* a bird of Central America with a crest and colorful feathers of green and red. The male has a very long tail.

queue (kyoo), *n.* **1.** a pigtail. **2.** a line of persons or things waiting for something. —*v.* to form in a line while waiting for something. *The v. and meaning 2 of the n. are used chiefly in Great Britain.* —**queued,** *p.t. & p.p.;* **queu'ing,** *pr.p.*

Que·zon City (kā'zän), the capital of the Philippines. It is a suburb of Manila.

quib·ble (kwib''l), *n.* a keeping away from the important point or from the truth, as by arguing about unimportant details or by using vague words. —*v.* to use quibbles. —**quib'bled,** *p.t. & p.p.;* **quib'bling,** *pr.p.*

quick (kwik), *adj.* **1.** done with speed; rapid; swift [a *quick* walk]. **2.** done or happening at once; prompt [a *quick* answer]. **3.** able to learn or understand easily [a *quick* mind]. **4.** easily excited; touchy [a *quick* temper]. —*adv.* with speed; fast; rapidly [Run *quick!*] —*n.* **1.** the tender flesh under a toenail or fingernail. **2.** a person's deepest feelings [hurt to the *quick*]. **3.** people who are alive; the living: *now used only in the phrase* "the quick and the dead." —**quick'ly,** *adv.* —**quick'ness,** *n.*

quick·en (kwik'ən), *v.* **1.** to move or make move faster; speed up [The horses *quickened* their pace. His pulse *quickens* at the thought of adventure.] **2.** to make or become active or more alive [The old trees *quickened* in the spring sun.]

quick·lime (kwik'līm), *n.* lime, the substance got from limestone.

quick·sand (kwik'sand), *n.* loose, wet, deep sand in which a person can be swallowed up because it will not hold up his weight.

quick·sil·ver (kwik'sil'vər), *n.* the metal mercury.

quick-tem·pered (kwik'tem'pərd), *adj.* becoming angry at the slightest thing.

quick-wit·ted (kwik'wit'id), *adj.* able to learn or understand quickly; alert.

quid (kwid), *n.* a piece of tobacco for chewing.

qui·es·cent (kwī es''nt), *adj.* quiet; not moving; inactive [The bear is *quiescent* during his winter hibernation.] —**qui·es'cence,** *n.*

qui·et (kwī'ət), *adj.* **1.** not making noise; hushed [a *quiet* motor]. **2.** not talking; silent [a *quiet* audience]. **3.** not moving; still; calm [a *quiet* sea]. **4.** not easily excited or upset; gentle [a *quiet* girl]. **5.** peaceful and relaxing [a *quiet* evening at home]. **6.** not bright or showy [*quiet* colors; a *quiet* tie]. —*n.* the condition of being quiet, hushed, calm, peaceful, etc. [the *quiet* of the night]. —*v.* to make or become quiet [Mother *quieted* the children. *Quiet* down and go to sleep.] —**qui'et·ly,** *adv.* —**qui'et·ness,** *n.*

qui·e·tude (kwī'ə tood *or* kwī'ə tyood), *n.* the condition of being quiet, still, calm, etc.

qui·e·tus (kwī ē'təs), *n.* **1.** the freeing of someone from a promise, debt, etc. **2.** death. **3.** anything that kills [to give the *quietus* to a rumor.]

quill (kwil), *n.* **1.** a large, stiff feather. **2.** something made from the hollow stem of such a feather, especially a pen for writing. **3.** any of the sharp, stiff spines that stick out on the body of a porcupine or hedgehog.

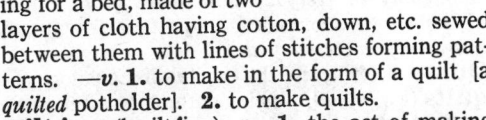

quill

quilt (kwilt), *n.* a covering for a bed, made of two layers of cloth having cotton, down, etc. sewed between them with lines of stitches forming patterns. —*v.* **1.** to make in the form of a quilt [a *quilted* potholder]. **2.** to make quilts.

quilt·ing (kwilt'ing), *n.* **1.** the act of making quilts. **2.** material for making quilts.

quince (kwins), *n.* **1.** a hard, yellow fruit shaped like an apple and used for jams and preserves. **2.** the tree that it grows on.

qui·nine (kwī'nīn), *n.* a bitter substance got from cinchona bark and used in treating malaria.

quinces

quin·sy (kwin'zē), *n.* a disease in which the throat is sore and pus forms in the tonsils.

quin·tes·sence (kwin tes''ns), *n.* **1.** the essence or most important part of something, in its purest form. **2.** the perfect type or example of something [the *quintessence* of beauty].

quin·tet *or* **quin·tette** (kwin tet'), *n.* **1.** a piece of music for five voices or five instruments. **2.** the five people who sing or play it. **3.** any group of five.

quin·tu·plet (kwin too'plit *or* kwin'too plit *or* kwin tup'lit), *n.* any of five children born at a single birth.

quip (kwip), *n.* a clever or witty remark; jest. —*v.* to make a quip or quips. —**quipped,** *p.t. & p.p.;* **quip'ping,** *pr.p.*

quire (kwīr), *n.* a set of 24 or 25 sheets of paper of the same size and kind.

quirk (kwûrk), *n.* **1.** a strange little habit; peculiarity. **2.** a twist or turn, as an extra curlicue in handwriting. **3.** a quibble. **4.** a jest.

quirt (kwûrt), *n.* a whip with a short handle and a lash of braided leather, carried by people who ride horseback.

quis·ling (kwiz'ling), *n.* a person who betrays his own country by helping an enemy to invade it.

quit (kwit), *v.* **1.** to stop doing something [We *quit* plowing when the sun goes down.] **2.** to give up [He *quit* his job.] **3.** to leave; go away from [The prince promised to *quit* England forever.] **4.** to pay off; repay,

quirt

fat, āpe, cär, ten, ēven, hit, bīte, gō, hôrn, tōōl, book, up, fûr;
get, joy, yet, chin, she, thin, *th*en; zh = s in pleasure; ' as in able (ā'b'l)
ə = a in ago, e in agent, i in sanity, o in confess, u in focus.

as a debt. —*adj.* free; clear [*quit* of all debts]. —**quit** or **quit′ted,** *p.t. & p.p.;* **quit′ting,** *pr.p.*

quit·claim (kwit′klām), *n.* a deed or other legal paper in which a person gives up his claim to a certain property or right.

quite (kwīt), *adv.* **1.** completely; entirely [I haven't *quite* finished eating.] **2.** really; truly [You are *quite* right.] **3.** very much or somewhat: *used only in everyday talk* [He's *quite* a man! It's *quite* warm outside.] —**quite a few,** many: *used only in everyday talk.*

Qui·to (kē′tō), *n.* the capital of Ecuador.

quits (kwits), *adj.* owing nothing, as after paying a debt or getting revenge; on even terms [Pay me a dollar, and we'll be *quits*.]

quit·tance (kwit′′ns), *n.* **1.** a freeing of someone from a debt, promise, or duty. **2.** a legal paper that states this; receipt. **3.** the act of paying back or getting revenge [to give him fair *quittance* for the injury].

quit·ter (kwit′ər), *n.* a person who quits or gives up easily.

quiv·er (kwiv′ər), *v.* to shake with little, trembling movements [leaves *quivering* in the breeze]. —*n.* the act of quivering.

quiv·er (kwiv′ər), *n.* a case for holding arrows.

Quixote, Don, see **Don Quixote.**

quix·ot·ic (kwik sät′ik), *adj.* kind, noble, and romantic, but in a way that is foolish, not practical. —**quix·ot′i·cal·ly,** *adv.*

quiver

quiz (kwiz), *n.* a questioning; especially, a short test given to find out how much one has learned. —*v.* to ask questions of; give a quiz to. —**quiz′zes,** *pl.* —**quizzed,** *p.t. & p.p.;* **quiz′zing,** *pr.p.*

quiz·zi·cal (kwiz′i k'l), *adj.* **1.** making fun of others; teasing [a *quizzical* smile]. **2.** that seems to ask a question [a *quizzical* look on his face]. **3.** funny or comical.

quoin (koin *or* kwoin), *n.* the outside corner of a building, or any of the stones in such a corner.

quoit (kwoit *or* koit), *n.* any of the metal or rope rings which are thrown to encircle a peg in the ground in a game called **quoits.**

quon·dam (kwän′dəm), *adj.* that was at one time; former [my *quondam* friends].

Quon·set hut (kwän′sit), a metal building with a curved roof: *see the picture.* Its sections are made ahead of time so that it can be put together quickly where needed.

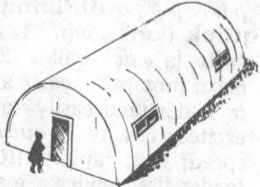
quoits

Quonset hut

quo·rum (kwôr′əm), *n.* the smallest number of members that must be present at a meeting of some group to carry on its business.

quo·ta (kwō′tə), *n.* the share or part of a total that each one of a certain group is asked to give or is allowed to get [There is a *quota* on immigrants from each country to the U.S.]

quot·a·ble (kwō′tə b'l), *adj.* that is worthwhile quoting [Lincoln's many *quotable* remarks].

quo·ta·tion (kwō tā′shən), *n.* **1.** the act of quoting. **2.** the words or section quoted [His talk is full of *quotations* from the Bible.] **3.** the present price as of a stock or bond.

quotation marks, the marks " ", placed before and after words that are quoted.

quote (kwōt), *v.* **1.** to repeat exactly the words of another person or words from a piece of writing [to *quote* my father; to *quote* from Shakespeare]. **2.** to give the price of [Cotton was *quoted* at 40 cents a pound.] —*n.* **1.** a quotation. **2. quotes,** *pl.* quotation marks. *The noun is used only in everyday talk.* —**quot′ed,** *p.t. & p.p.;* **quot′ing,** *pr.p.*

quoth (kwōth), *v.* said: *now seldom used* [*Quoth* the raven, "Nevermore."]

quo·tient (kwō′shənt), *n.* the number got by dividing one number into another [In 32 ÷ 8 = 4, the number 4 is the *quotient*.]

R

R, r (är), *n.* the eighteenth letter of the English alphabet. —**the three R's,** reading, writing, and arithmetic, thought of as the basic school subjects. —**R's, r's** (ärz), *pl.*

R. or **r.,** abbreviation for **radius, railroad, right, river.**

Ra, symbol for the chemical element *radium.*

Ra (rä), *n.* the ancient Egyptian sun god.

rab·bi (rab′ī), *n.* a teacher of the Jewish law, now usually the leader of a synagogue or temple. —**rab′bis** or **rab′bies,** *pl.*

rab·bin·i·cal (rə bin′i k'l), *adj.* of rabbis, their teachings, learning, etc.

rab·bit (rab′it), *n.* **1.** an animal having soft fur, long ears, and a very short tail. Rabbits are related to hares but are usually smaller and live in burrows. **2.** the fur of a rabbit.

rabbit (1 ft. long)

rab·ble (rab′'l), *n.* a noisy crowd of people that pays no attention to law and order; mob. —**the rabble,** the common people: *a scornful use.*

rab·id (rab′id), *adj.* **1.** holding certain ideas, opinions, etc. in a strong, unreasonable way;

fanatical. **2.** of or having rabies [a *rabid* dog].

ra·bies (rā′bēz), *n.* same as **hydrophobia.**

rac·coon (ra koon′), *n.* **1.** a furry animal having a long tail with black rings. It climbs trees and is active mostly at night. **2.** its fur.

raccoon (3 ft. long)

race (rās), *n.* **1.** a contest, as between runners, swimmers, cars, boats, etc., to see who can go fastest. **2.** any contest, as for election [the *race* for mayor]. **3.** a swift current of water, or the channel that it runs in. —*v.* **1.** to take part in a race [How many airplanes are *racing?*] **2.** to cause to take part in a race [Three owners are *racing* their horses.] **3.** to have a race with [I'll *race* you to the corner.] **4.** to go or make go swiftly. **5.** to go or make go too fast, as an engine, while the gears are not meshed. —**raced,** *p.t. & p.p.;* **rac′ing,** *pr.p.*

race (rās), *n.* **1.** any of the major groups into which mankind is divided on the basis of color of hair and skin, etc. [The Caucasian, Negroid, and Mongoloid *races* all belong to one species.] **2.** any large group of living creatures [the human *race*]. **3.** a group of people who have something in common [a *race* of heroes].

ra·ceme (rā sēm′), *n.* a flower stem on which single flowers grow from shorter stems along its length, as in a lily of the valley.

rac·er (rās′ər), *n.* **1.** a person, animal, car, etc. that takes part in races. **2.** the American blacksnake.

race track, a track laid out for racing, usually in a circle or oval.

Ra·chel (rā′chəl), *n.* in the Bible, Jacob's second wife, the younger sister of Leah.

raceme

ra·cial (rā′shəl), *adj.* of or having to do with a race of mankind. —**ra′cial·ly,** *adv.*

rack (rak), *n.* **1.** a framework, stand, etc. for holding or showing things [a clothes *rack;* a luggage *rack*]. **2.** a frame on a wagon for holding hay, straw, etc. **3.** a bar having teeth into which the teeth of a gearwheel fit as the wheel moves along. **4.** a device used at one time to torture people by stretching their limbs out of place. —*v.* to cause pain or suffering to [a body *racked* with disease]. —**on the rack,** in a difficult or painful condition. —**rack one's brains,** to try very hard to think of something.

clothes rack

rack (rak), *n.* destruction: *now used only in the phrase* **go to rack and ruin,** *meaning* "to become ruined."

rack·et (rak′it), *n.* **1.** loud, confused noise; clatter; din [She made a *racket* washing the pots and pans.] **2.** a scheme for getting money in a way that is not honest or legal: *slang in this meaning.*

rack·et or **rac·quet** (rak′it), *n.* a light bat for tennis, badminton, etc., having a network of catgut, nylon, etc. strung in a frame attached to a handle.

rack·et·eer (rak ə tir′), *n.* a person who gets money in a way that is not honest or legal, as by fraud or by threatening to harm. —*v.* to get money in such a way.

tennis racket

ra·coon (ra koon′), *n.* same as **raccoon.**

rac·y (rās′ē), *adj.* **1.** lively, or full of spirit [a *racy* style of writing]. **2.** not quite proper; slightly indecent [a *racy* story]. —**rac′i·er,** *compar.;* **rac′i·est,** *superl.* —**rac′i·ness,** *n.*

ra·dar (rā′där), *n.* a device that sends out radio waves and picks them up after they strike some object and bounce back. It is used for finding out the distance, direction, and speed of aircraft, ships, automobiles, etc.

ra·di·al (rā′di əl), *adj.* like a ray or rays; branching out in all directions from a center.

ra·di·ant (rā′di ənt), *adj.* **1.** shining brightly. **2.** showing joy, very good health, etc.; beaming [a *radiant* smile]. **3.** coming from a source in rays [the *radiant* heat of an electric stove]. —**ra′di·ance** or **ra′di·an·cy,** *n.* —**ra′di·ant·ly,** *adv.*

ra·di·ate (rā′di āt), *v.* **1.** to send out in rays [The hot water *radiated* heat.] **2.** to come forth in rays [Light *radiates* from the sun.] **3.** to give forth or show [Her face *radiates* happiness.] **4.** to branch out in lines from a center [The main streets *radiate* from a central square.] —*adj.* having rays or parts like rays [a *radiate* flower]. —**ra′di·at·ed,** *p.t. & p.p.;* **ra′di·at·ing,** *pr.p.*

ra·di·a·tion (rā′di ā′shən), *n.* **1.** the process in which energy is sent out in rays from atoms and molecules because of changes inside them. **2.** the energy or rays sent out. **3.** the treatment of disease by means of radioactive material.

ra·di·a·tor (rā′di ā′tər), *n.* **1.** a series of pipes through which hot water or steam moves in order to radiate heat into a room, etc. **2.** a system of pipes for cooling water that becomes hot when it passes through an engine. This helps keep the engine cool.

radiator

rad·i·cal (rad′i k'l), *adj.* **1.** getting at the root or source; basic; fundamental [Moving to the farm made a *radical* change in their lives.] **2.** in favor of basic changes or reforms [a *radical* political party]. —*n.* **1.** a person who favors basic changes or reforms. **2.** a group of two or more atoms that acts as a single atom during a

fat, āpe, cär, ten, ēven, hit, bīte, gō, hôrn, tool, book, up, fūr;
get, joy, yet, chin, she, thin, *then;* zh = s in pleasure; ′ as in able (ā′b'l).
ə = a in ago, e in agent, i in sanity, o in confess, u in focus.

chemical change [SO₄ is a *radical* in H₂SO₄.] —**rad′i·cal·ism,** *n.* —**rad′i·cal·ly,** *adv.*

ra·di·i (rā′dī ī), *n.* a plural of **radius.**

ra·di·o (rā′dī ō), *n.* **1.** a way of sending sounds through space without wires by changing them into electric waves which are picked up by a receiver that changes them back to sounds. **2.** such a receiver, usually in a cabinet. **3.** the act, business, etc. of broadcasting speech, music, etc. by radio. **4.** any system for sending and receiving signals of sound, light, etc. by electric waves without wires [Television images are sent by *radio.*] —*adj.* of, using, used in, or sent by radio [a *radio* program; a *radio* tube]. —*v.* to send a message by radio. —**ra′di·os,** *pl.* —**ra′di·oed,** *p.t.* & *p.p.*; **ra′di·o·ing,** *pr.p.*

ra·di·o·ac·tive (rā′dī ō ak′tiv), *adj.* giving off energy in the form of particles or rays as a result of the breaking up of nuclei of atoms [Radium and uranium are *radioactive* elements.] —**ra·di·o·ac·tiv·i·ty** (rā′dī ō ak tiv′ə tē), *n.*

ra·di·ol·o·gy (rā′dī äl′ə jē), *n.* the treatment or examination of disease by using X rays, radioactive drugs, etc. —**ra′di·ol′o·gist,** *n.*

rad·ish (rad′ish), *n.* **1.** a plant with a small, round or long root that has a red or white skin. **2.** this root, which has a sharp taste and is eaten raw as a relish.

radish

ra·di·um (rā′dī əm), *n.* a radioactive chemical element that is a metal. It is found in small amounts in pitchblende and other ores and is used in treating cancer.

ra·di·us (rā′dī əs), *n.* **1.** any straight line that goes from the center to the outside of a circle or sphere. **2.** a round area as measured by its radius [no houses within a *radius* of five miles]. **3.** the thicker of the two bones in the forearm. —**ra·di·i** (rā′dī ī) or **ra′di·us·es,** *pl.*

raf·fi·a (raf′ī ə), *n.* fiber from the leaves of certain palm trees, used for weaving.

raf·fle (raf′'l), *n.* a form of gambling in which a number of persons buy chances on getting prizes, which are given to winners picked by lot. —*v.* to sell chances on winning in a raffle [Their club made money by *raffling* off a new car.] —**raf′-fled,** *p.t.* & *p.p.*; **raf′fling,** *pr.p.*

raft (raft), *n.* a number of logs, boards, etc. fastened together and used as a flatboat.

raft (raft), *n.* a large number; much or many: *used only in everyday talk* [a *raft* of trouble].

raft·er (raf′tər), *n.* any of the sloping beams used to hold up a roof.

rag (rag), *n.* **1.** a waste piece of old or torn cloth. **2.** any small cloth used for dusting, washing, etc. **3.** **rags,** *pl.* old, worn clothing. **4.** anything as worthless as an old rag [A newspaper that is not respected is sometimes called a *rag*.] —*adj.* made of rags [a *rag* doll; *rag* paper].

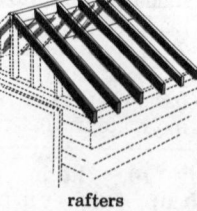
rafters

rag (rag), *v.* to tease or scold: *a slang word.* —**ragged,** *p.t.* & *p.p.*; **rag′ging,** *pr.p.*

rag·a·muf·fin (rag′ə muf′in), *n.* a dirty, ragged person; especially, a dirty, ragged child.

rage (rāj), *n.* **1.** a short period of great anger; raving fury [He flew into a *rage* and threw the papers to the floor.] **2.** great force or violence, as of the wind. **3.** anything that many people are eager to get or do; craze; fad [Short haircuts were the *rage* for a time.] —*v.* **1.** to show great anger. **2.** to be violent and out of control [a *raging* storm; a fire *raging* through the barn]. —**raged,** *p.t.* & *p.p.*; **rag′ing,** *pr.p.*

rag·ged (rag′id), *adj.* **1.** shabby or torn from being worn a great deal [*ragged* clothes]. **2.** wearing shabby or torn clothes [a *ragged* man]. **3.** rough and uneven [the *ragged* edge of a torn sheet of paper]. —**rag′ged·ness,** *n.*

rag·lan (rag′lən), *n.* a loose topcoat having sleeves that go straight to the collar with no seam at the shoulder. —*adj.* describing such a sleeve.

raglan sleeve

ra·gout (ra gōō′), *n.* a stew made of meat, vegetables, and much seasoning.

rag·time (rag′tīm), *n.* an early form of jazz music, first popular from about 1890 to 1915.

rag·weed (rag′wēd), *n.* a common weed with small, yellow-green flowers. Its pollen can cause hay fever.

rah (rä *or* rô), *interj.* same as **hurrah.**

raid (rād), *n.* **1.** a sudden attack, as by soldiers, bandits, etc. **2.** a sudden entering of a place, as by police to arrest people breaking the law. —*v.* to make a raid on, or take part in a raid. —**raid′er,** *n.*

rail (rāl), *n.* **1.** a bar of wood or metal placed crosswise between standing posts, as in a fence. **2.** either of the metal bars forming the track of a railroad. **3.** a railroad [Ship it by *rail*.]

rail (rāl), *v.* to keep on talking or shouting in an angry way; complain strongly [to *rail* at one's fate].

rail (rāl), *n.* a small wading bird that looks like a crane and lives in marshes.

rail·ing (rāl′ing), *n.* a fence made of a series of posts and rails [a porch *railing*].

rail·ler·y (rāl′ər ē), *n.* a joking or teasing in a friendly, playful way.

rail·road (rāl′rōd), *n.* **1.** a road on which there is a track made up of parallel steel rails on which the wheels of trains travel. **2.** a series of such roads managed as a unit, together

rail (14 in. long)

with the cars, engines, stations, etc. that belong to it. —**v. 1.** to work on a railroad. **2.** to rush through quickly in an unfair way: *only in everyday talk* [to *railroad* a bill through Congress].

rail·way (rāl′wā), *n.* **1.** a railroad: *the usual word in Great Britain.* **2.** any set of tracks for the wheels of a car [a street *railway*].

rai·ment (rā′mənt), *n.* clothing: *now seldom used except in poetry.*

rain (rān), *n.* **1.** water that falls to the earth in drops formed from the moisture in the air. **2.** the falling of such drops; a shower [Sunshine followed the *rain*.] **3.** a fast falling of many small things [a *rain* of ashes from the volcano]. —*v.* **1.** to fall as rain [It is *raining*.] **2.** to pour down like rain [Bullets *rained* about them.] **3.** to give in large amounts [They *rained* praises on him.]

rain·bow (rān′bō), *n.* a curved band of the colors of the spectrum seen in the sky when the sun's rays pass through falling rain or mist.

rain·coat (rān′kōt), *n.* a waterproof coat that protects a person from the rain.

rain·drop (rān′dräp), *n.* a single drop of rain.

rain·fall (rān′fôl), *n.* **1.** the amount of water falling as rain or snow over a certain area during a certain time [The annual *rainfall* in Louisiana is about 55 inches.] **2.** a falling of rain; shower.

Rai·nier, Mount (rā nir′), a mountain in the State of Washington.

rain·storm (rān′stôrm), *n.* a storm in which there is much rain.

rain·y (rān′ē), *adj.* having much rain [the *rainy* season]. —**a rainy day,** a future time when there may be great need. —**rain′i·er,** *compar.*; **rain′i·est,** *superl.* —**rain′i·ness,** *n.*

raise (rāz), *v.* **1.** to cause to rise; lift [*Raise* your hand if you have a question. *Raise* the window.] **2.** to build or put up; construct [to *raise* a monument to a hero]. **3.** to make larger, greater, higher, louder, etc. [to *raise* prices; to *raise* one's voice]. **4.** to bring up; take care of; support [to *raise* a family]. **5.** to cause to grow; produce [to *raise* cabbages]. **6.** to cause; bring about [Her joke *raised* a laugh.] **7.** to bring up for thinking about [to *raise* a question]. **8.** to bring together; collect [to *raise* money for flood victims]. **9.** to bring to an end; remove [to *raise* a blockade]. —*n.* a making or becoming larger; especially, an increase in pay. —**raised,** *p.t. & p.p.*; **rais′ing,** *pr.p.*

rai·sin (rā′z'n), *n.* a sweet grape dried for eating.

ra·jah or **ra·ja** (rä′jə), *n.* a prince or chief in India and some other Eastern countries.

rake (rāk), *n.* a tool with a long handle having a set of teeth or prongs at one end. It is used for gathering grass, leaves, etc. or for

smoothing broken ground. —*v.* **1.** to gather together or smooth as with a rake [to *rake* leaves; to *rake* a gravel path]. **2.** to look with great care; search carefully [He *raked* through the old papers looking for the letter.] **3.** to shoot guns along the whole length of [The deck of the ship was *raked* by cannon.] —**raked,** *p.t. & p.p.*; **rak′ing,** *pr.p.*

rake (rāk), *n.* a man who leads a wild life, drinking, gambling, etc.

rak·ish (rāk′ish), *adj.* **1.** having a gay, careless look; jaunty [a hat worn at a *rakish* angle]. **2.** looking as if it can move fast [a *rakish* ship].

Ra·leigh (rô′lē), *n.* the capital of North Carolina.

Ra·leigh, Sir Walter (rô′lē *or* rä′lē), 1552?–1618; English explorer, statesman, and poet.

ral·ly (ral′ē), *v.* **1.** to gather together so as to bring back into order [The troops retreated, then *rallied* for another charge.] **2.** to bring or come together for some purpose [The students *rallied* to cheer the football team.] **3.** to come in order to help [to *rally* to the side of a friend in trouble]. **4.** to get back health or strength; revive [As the fever left him, he began to *rally*.] —*n.* a rallying or being rallied; especially, a gathering of people for some purpose [a political *rally*]. —**ral′lied,** *p.t. & p.p.*; **ral′ly·ing,** *pr.p.* —**ral′lies,** *pl.*

ral·ly (ral′ē), *v.* to make fun of; tease playfully. —**ral′lied,** *p.t. & p.p.*; **ral′ly·ing,** *pr.p.*

ram (ram), *n.* **1.** a male sheep. **2.** a battering-ram. —*v.* **1.** to hit or drive with force [The car *rammed* into the fence.] **2.** to force into place by pressing down [to *ram* a charge into a gun]. —**rammed,** *p.t. & p.p.*; **ram′ming,** *pr.p.*

ram·ble (ram′b'l), *v.* **1.** to walk or stroll along without any special goal; roam. **2.** to talk or write on and on without sticking to any point or subject. **3.** to spread in all directions, as a vine. —*n.* a rambling; stroll. —**ram′bled,** *p.t. & p.p.*; **ram′bling,** *pr.p.*

ram·bler (ram′blər), *n.* a person or thing that rambles; especially, any climbing rose.

ram·i·fy (ram′ə fī), *v.* to divide or spread out into branches. —**ram′i·fied,** *p.t. & p.p.*; **ram′i·fy·ing,** *pr.p.* —**ram′i·fi·ca′tion,** *n.*

ramp (ramp), *n.* a sloping road, passage, plank, etc. going from a lower to a higher place.

ram·page (ram pāj′), *v.* to rush about in a wild, angry way; rage. —*n.* (ram′pāj), wild, angry action: *usually used in the phrase* "on the rampage" *or* "on a rampage." —**ram·paged′,** *p.t. & p.p.*; **ram·pag′ing,** *pr.p.*

ram·pant (ram′pənt), *adj.* **1.** spreading wildly, without control [The plague was *rampant* in Europe in the Middle Ages.] **2.** wild in action,

types of rake

ramp

speech, etc. **3.** standing up on the hind legs, as a lion on a shield: *see the picture for* **coat of arms.**

ram·part (ram′pärt), *n.* **1.** a bank of earth, often with a wall along the top, surrounding a place to defend it. **2.** anything that defends.

ram·rod (ram′räd), *n.* a metal rod for ramming a charge down the muzzle of a gun, or for cleaning the barrel of a rifle.

ram·shack·le (ram′shak″l), *adj.* ready to fall apart; shaky; rickety [a *ramshackle* old barn].

ran (ran), past tense of **run.**

ranch (ranch), *n.* **1.** a large farm, especially in Western States, where cattle, horses, or sheep are raised. **2.** any large farm [a fruit *ranch;* a turkey *ranch*]. —*v.* to work on or manage a ranch. —**ranch′er** or **ranch′man,** *n.*

ran·cid (ran′sid), *adj.* having the bad smell or taste of stale fats and oils; spoiled.

ran·cor (rang′kər), *n.* a strong hate or bitter, unfriendly feeling that lasts for a long time; deep spite. —**ran′cor·ous,** *adj.*

ran·dom (ran′dəm), *adj.* made, done, etc. in an aimless way, without planning; chance; haphazard [a *random* choice]. —**at random,** without careful choice, aim, plan, etc.; haphazardly.

rang (rang), past tense of **ring** (to sound).

range (rānj), *n.* **1.** a row or line, especially of connected mountains [the Appalachian *range*]. **2.** the distance that a gun can shoot, a missile can travel, a sound can carry, etc. [a cannon with a twenty-mile *range;* within *range* of my voice]. **3.** a place for practice in shooting [a rifle *range*]. **4.** the limits within which there are changes or differences of amount, degree, etc. [a *range* of prices from $20 to $100; a *range* of songs from sad ballads to comic jingles]. **5.** open land over which cattle graze. **6.** a cooking stove. —*v.* **1.** to wander about; roam [Bears *ranged* the forests.] **2.** to stretch or lie [Rocky cliffs *range* along the seashore.] **3.** to be within certain limits [The prices *range* from $5 to $15.] **4.** to place in a certain order; especially, to set in a row or rows [The tulips were *ranged* along the path.] **5.** to join with [He *ranged* himself with the rebels.] —**ranged,** *p.t. & p.p.;* **rang′ing,** *pr.p.*

rang·er (rān′jər), *n.* **1.** any of a group of special soldiers or policemen who patrol a certain region. **2.** a warden who patrols government forests.

Ran·goon (rang goon′), *n.* the capital of Burma.

rang·y (rān′jē), *adj.* tall and thin, and having long legs [a *rangy* boy]. —**rang′i·er,** *compar.;* **rang′i·est,** *superl.*

rank (rangk), *n.* **1.** a class or position of society [people from all *ranks* of life]. **2.** a high position [a man of *rank*]. **3.** a position or grade, as in the armed forces [the *rank* of captain]. **4.** a position as measured by quality [a poet of the first *rank*]. **5. ranks,** *pl.* all the soldiers, sailors, etc. who are not officers. **6.** a row or line, as of soldiers, placed side by side. —*v.* **1.** to place in a certain rank [I would *rank* this school among the best.] **2.** to hold a certain rank [South Africa *ranks* first in world gold production.] **3.** to hold a higher or the highest rank [one of our *ranking* scholars].

—**rank and file, 1.** all the soldiers, sailors, etc. who are not officers. **2.** the common people.

rank (rank), *adj.* **1.** growing in a wild, thick, coarse way [*rank* weeds]. **2.** having a strong, unpleasant smell or taste [*rank* fish]. **3.** of the worst or most extreme kind [*rank* injustice].

ran·kle (rang′k′l), *v.* to cause an angry or unfriendly feeling that lasts for a long time [Her harsh words *rankled* for days.] —**ran′kled,** *p.t. & p.p.;* **ran′kling,** *pr.p.*

ran·sack (ran′sak), *v.* **1.** to search through every part of [to *ransack* one's pockets for a key]. **2.** to search for loot [Bandits *ransacked* the town.]

ran·som (ran′səm), *n.* **1.** the price asked or paid for freeing a kidnaped person or other captive. **2.** the freeing of a captive by paying the price demanded. —*v.* to pay a price in order to free [to *ransom* a prisoner of war].

rant (rant), *v.* to talk in a loud, wild way; rave. —*n.* loud, wild speech.

rap (rap), *v.* **1.** to strike or knock sharply [to *rap* on a door]. **2.** to say in a sharp, quick way [The captain *rapped* out an order.] **3.** to find fault with; criticize: *used only in everyday talk* [The reviewer *rapped* the movie.] —*n.* **1.** a quick, sharp knock. **2.** blame or punishment: *slang in this meaning* [to take the *rap* for a crime]. —**rapped,** *p.t. & p.p.;* **rap′ping,** *pr.p.*

rap (rap), *n.* the least bit: *used only in everyday talk* [He doesn't care a *rap*.]

ra·pa·cious (rə pā′shəs), *adj.* **1.** taking by force; plundering [a *rapacious* army]. **2.** greedy or grasping. **3.** living on captured prey [a *rapacious* animal]. —**ra·pa′cious·ly,** *adv.*

ra·pac·i·ty (rə pas′ə tē), *n.* the fact or habit of being rapacious; greed.

rape (rāp), *n.* **1.** the act of seizing and carrying away by force. **2.** a sexual crime committed on a woman or girl by force. —*v.* to commit rape on; ravish. —**raped,** *p.t. & p.p.;* **rap′ing,** *pr.p.*

rape (rāp), *n.* a plant whose leaves are fed to sheep, etc. An oil is pressed from its seeds.

Raph·a·el (raf′i əl *or* rā′fi əl), *n.* 1483–1520; Italian painter.

rap·id (rap′id), *adj.* very swift or quick [a *rapid* journey]. —*n. usually* **rapids,** *pl.* a part of a river where the water moves swiftly. —**rap′id·ly,** *adv.*

rap·id-fire (rap′id fīr′), *adj.* **1.** that fires shots quickly one after the other [a *rapid-fire* gun]. **2.** done, made, etc. rapidly [a *rapid-fire* talk].

ra·pid·i·ty (rə pid′ə tē), *n.* speed or swiftness.

ra·pi·er (rā′pi ər), *n.* a light, slender sword used for thrusting.

rap·ine (rap′in), *n.* the act of seizing and carrying off things by force; plunder; pillage.

rap·scal·lion (rap skal′yən), *n.* a rascal.

rapt (rapt), *adj.* **1.** so completely interested as not to notice anything else; absorbed [*rapt* in a book]. **2.** full of or showing rapture, or deep pleasure [a *rapt* look on his face].

rapier

rap·ture (rap′chər), *n.* a deep feeling of joy, love, etc.; ecstasy [The music filled him with *rapture*.] —**rap′tur·ous,** *adj.*

rare (rer), *adj.* **1.** not often found; not common; scarce [Radium is a *rare* element.] **2.** very good; excellent [We had a *rare* time at the party.] **3.** not dense; thin [the *rare* air in the mountains]. —**rar′er,** *compar.;* **rar′est,** *superl.* —**rare′ly,** *adv.* —**rare′ness,** *n.*

rare (rer), *adj.* not completely cooked; partly raw [He likes *rare* beef.] —**rar′er,** *compar.;* **rar′est,** *superl.* —**rare′ness,** *n.*

rare·bit (rer′bit), *n.* same as **Welsh rabbit.**

rar·e·fy (rer′ə fī), *v.* **1.** to make or become thin, or less dense [The air at high altitudes is *rarefied*.] **2.** to make or become more refined or subtle [a *rarefied* sense of humor]. —**rar′e·fied,** *p.t. & p.p.;* **rar′e·fy·ing,** *pr.p.*

rar·i·ty (rer′ə tē), *n.* **1.** something rare or uncommon [This old coin is a *rarity*.] **2.** the condition of being rare; scarcity [the *rarity* of whooping cranes]. **3.** the condition of being not dense; thinness [the *rarity* of the air]. —**rar′i·ties,** *pl. for meaning 1.*

ras·cal (ras′k'l), *n.* **1.** a bad or dishonest person; scoundrel. **2.** a mischievous child. —**ras·cal·i·ty** (ras kal′ə tē), *n.* —**ras′cal·ly,** *adj.*

rash (rash), *adj.* too hasty or reckless; risky. —**rash′ly,** *adv.* —**rash′ness,** *n.*

rash (rash), *n.* a breaking out of red spots on the skin [The measles gave him a *rash*.]

rash·er (rash′ər), *n.* a thin slice of bacon or ham to be fried or broiled.

rasp (rasp), *v.* **1.** to scrape or rub as with a file. **2.** to say in a rough, harsh tone [The sergeant *rasped* out a command.] **3.** to make a rough, grating sound [The old hinges *rasped* as the door opened.] **4.** to annoy or irritate [Her giggling *rasped* his nerves.] —*n.* **1.** a rough file with sharp points instead of lines. **2.** a rough, grating sound.

rasp

rasp·ber·ry (raz′ber′ē), *n.* **1.** a small, juicy, red or black fruit with many tiny seeds. **2.** the shrub it grows on. —**rasp′ber′ries,** *pl.*

rat (rat), *n.* **1.** a gnawing animal like a mouse but larger, with a long tail and black, brown, or gray fur. **2.** a mean, sneaky person, especially one who deserts or betrays others: *slang in this meaning.* —*v.* **1.** to hunt for rats. **2.** to desert or betray others: *slang in this meaning.* —**smell**

rat (9 in. long, not including tail)

a rat, to suspect a trick or plot. —**rat′ed,** *p.t. & p.p.;* **rat′ting,** *pr.p.*

ra·tan (ra tan′), *n.* same as **rattan.**

ratch·et (rach′it), *n.* **1.** a wheel or bar with slanted teeth that catch on a pawl that keeps the wheel from going backward. **2.** the pawl. **3.** the wheel or bar together with the pawl.

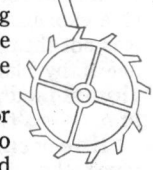
ratchet

rate (rāt), *n.* **1.** the amount or degree of anything in relation to something else [a *rate* of speed measured in miles per hour]. **2.** a price or charge, as for each unit [The *rate* for air mail is 7¢.] **3.** speed of moving or acting [He works at a fast *rate*.] **4.** class or rank [of the first *rate*]. —*v.* **1.** to set a value on; appraise [The dealer *rated* the diamond at $8,000.] **2.** to think of or be thought of as in a certain class or rank [Sid is *rated* among the best students.] **3.** to deserve: *used only in everyday talk* [She *rates* the best.] —**at any rate, 1.** in any event; anyhow. **2.** at least; anyway. —**rat′ed,** *p.t. & p.p.;* **rat′ing,** *pr.p.*

rate (rāt), *v.* to find fault; scold; blame. —**rat′ed,** *p.t. & p.p.;* **rat′ing,** *pr.p.*

rath·er (rath′ər), *adv.* **1.** in a more willing way; with greater liking; preferably [He would *rather* read than watch TV.] **2.** with more justice, reason, etc. [I, *rather* than you, should pay.] **3.** more accurately; more truly [a bad storm, or *rather*, a hurricane]. **4.** on the contrary [We won't go; *rather*, we'll stay.] **5.** to some degree; somewhat [I *rather* liked the play.] **6.** certainly; yes: *used as an answer in everyday talk, mainly in Great Britain.* —**had rather** or **would rather,** would prefer that [I *had rather* you went.]

rat·i·fy (rat′ə fī), *v.* to approve, especially in an official way [The Senate must *ratify* any treaty between the U.S. and another country.] —**rat′i·fied,** *p.t. & p.p.;* **rat′i·fy·ing,** *pr.p.* —**rat·i·fi·ca·tion** (rat′ə fi kā′shən), *n.*

rat·ing (rāt′ing), *n.* **1.** a rank or grade [a *rating* of sergeant in the army]. **2.** an estimating, as of the credit of a business, or of its ability to take on new debts.

ra·tio (rā′shō *or* rā′shi ō), *n.* **1.** the relation of one thing to another in size, amount, etc.; proportion [In our class there is a *ratio* of three girls to every two boys.] **2.** the quotient of one number divided by another, usually shown as a fraction [1/3 and 5/15 are equal *ratios*.] —**ra′tios,** *pl.*

ra·tion (rash′ən *or* rā′shən), *n.* a share or portion, especially a daily portion of food, as for a soldier. —*v.* **1.** to give out in rations, as food, clothing, etc. in wartime when these are scarce. **2.** to give rations to.

ra·tion·al (rash′ən 'l), *adj.* **1.** able to reason; thinking clearly [She was so upset that she wasn't *rational*.] **2.** of or based on reasoning;

reasonable; sensible [a *rational* argument]. —**ra′tion·al·ly**, *adv.*

ra·tion·al·i·ty (rash′ə nal′ə tē), *n.* the condition of being rational; clear thinking.

ra·tion·al·ize (rash′ən 'l īz′), *v.* to give a reasonable explanation without seeming to know that it is not the real one [We *rationalized* the team's defeat by blaming it on the weather.] —**ra′tion·al·ized′**, *p.t. & p.p.;* **ra′tion·al·iz′ing,** *pr.p.* —**ra′tion·al·i·za′tion**, *n.*

rat·line or **rat·lin** (rat′lin), *n.* any of the small ropes that join the shrouds of a ship and are used as a ladder by sailors.

rat·tan (ra tan′), *n.* **1.** the long, slender stems of a kind of palm tree, used in making wicker furniture, etc. **2.** a cane or switch made from one of these stems. **3.** this palm tree.

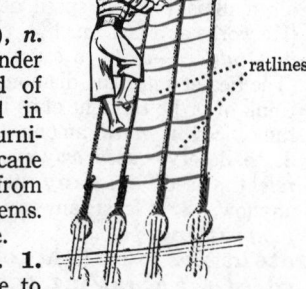
ratlines

rat·tle (rat′'l), *v.* **1.** to make or cause to make a series of sharp, short sounds [The shutter *rattled* in the wind. He *rattled* the door handle.] **2.** to move with such sounds [The wagon *rattled* over the stones.] **3.** to talk in a rapid and thoughtless way; chatter [Ann *rattled* on about her clothes.] **4.** to say or recite quickly [The actor *rattled* off his speech.] **5.** to confuse or upset: *used only in everyday talk* [The noisy audience *rattled* the speaker.] —*n.* **1.** a baby's toy or other device made to rattle when shaken. **2.** a series of sharp, short sounds [What is causing the *rattle* in your car?] **3.** a series of horny rings at the end of a rattlesnake's tail, used to make a rattling sound. —**rat′tled,** *p.t. & p.p.;* **rat′-tling,** *pr.p.*

rat·tler (rat′lər), *n.* a person or thing that rattles, especially a rattlesnake.

rat·tle·snake (rat′'l snāk), *n.* a poisonous American snake that has a series of horny rings on its tail, with which it makes a rattling sound.

rau·cous (rô′kəs), *adj.* having a rough, hoarse sound [*raucous* laughter]. —**rau′cous·ly,** *adv.*

rav·age (rav′ij), *v.* to destroy or ruin. —*n.*

raven (2 ft. long)

rattlesnake (2 to 8 ft. long)

violent destruction or ruin [the *ravages* of war]. —**rav′aged,** *p.t. & p.p.;* **rav′ag·ing,** *pr.p.*

rave (rāv), *v.* **1.** to talk in a wild way that does not make sense [The fever made him *rave*.] **2.** to praise greatly or too greatly [She *raved* about the movie.] —*n.* the act of raving. —**raved,** *p.t. & p.p.;* **rav′ing,** *pr.p.*

rav·el (rav′'l), *v.* to separate or undo the threads of something knitted or woven; unravel [The scarf has begun to *ravel* at one end.] The earlier

meaning was "to make or become tangled." —**rav′eled** or **rav′elled,** *p.t. & p.p.;* **rav′el·ing** or **rav′el·ling,** *pr.p.*

rav·el·ing or **rav·el·ling** (rav′'l ing), *n.* a thread raveled from a knitted or woven material.

rav·en (rā′vən), *n.* a crow of the largest kind, with shiny black feathers and a sharp beak. —*adj.* black and shiny [*raven* hair].

rav·en·ing (rav′ən ing), *adj.* searching for food or prey; very hungry or greedy.

rav·e·nous (rav′ən əs), *adj.* very hungry or greedy [a *ravenous* appetite]. —**rav′e-nous·ly,** *adv.*

ra·vine (rə vēn′), *n.* a long, deep hollow worn in the earth by a stream of water; gorge.

rav·ing (rāv′ing), *adj.* **1.** that raves; raging [a *raving* madman]. **2.** remarkable; outstanding: *used only in everyday talk* [She is a *raving* beauty.] —*adv.* so as to make one rave [*raving* mad].

rav·ish (rav′ish), *v.* **1.** to overcome with great joy; delight [We were *ravished* by the beautiful music.] **2.** to rape.

rav·ish·ing (rav′ish ing), *adj.* causing great pleasure or joy; enchanting [a *ravishing* voice].

raw (rô), *adj.* **1.** not cooked [*raw* vegetables]. **2.** in its natural condition; not manufactured [*raw* silk]. **3.** not yet trained; inexperienced [*raw* recruits]. **4.** with the skin rubbed off; sore [*raw* flesh]. **5.** cold and damp [a *raw* wind]. **6.** not fair or too harsh: *slang in this meaning* [*raw* treatment]. —**raw′ness,** *n.*

raw·boned (rô′bōnd), *adj.* very lean; gaunt.

raw·hide (rô′hīd), *n.* **1.** a cattle hide that is not tanned. **2.** a whip made of this.

ray (rā), *n.* **1.** a line or narrow beam of light [the *rays* of the lantern]. **2.** a tiny amount [a *ray* of hope]. **3.** a wave or stream of energy thought of as moving in a line [*rays* of heat; X *rays*]. **4.** any of a number of straight, thin parts that come out from a center, as the petals of a daisy. —*v.* to shine or send out in rays.

ray (rā), *n.* a fish with a broad, flat body, wide fins at each side, and a long, thin tail. *See the picture for* **sting ray.**

ray·on (rā′än), *n.* a fiber made from cellulose, or a fabric woven from such fibers.

raze (rāz), *v.* to tear down completely; destroy [The tower was *razed* by the earthquake.] —**razed,** *p.t. & p.p.;* **raz′ing,** *pr.p.*

ra·zor (rā′zər), *n.* a tool with a sharp edge or edges, for shaving off hair. See also **shaver.**

razz (raz), *v.* to make fun of: *a slang word.*

Rd. or **rd.,** abbreviation for **road** or **rod.**

R.D., abbreviation for **Rural Delivery.**

re (rā), *n.* the second note of a musical scale.

types of razor

re-, a prefix meaning: **1.** again [To *reappear* is to appear again.] A hyphen is used to separate this prefix from a root word beginning with *e* (*re-elect*), or to separate it from the root word when there is another word spelled the same that has a special meaning (*re-sound*, to sound again; *resound*, to echo). Words such as *re-elect* are also written **rēelect**. Many words beginning with *re-* that are not entered in this dictionary can be easily understood if *re-* is given the meaning "again." For example, **recheck** means "to check again." **2.** back [To *repay* is to pay back.]

reach (rēch), *v.* **1.** to stretch out one's hand, arm, etc. [He *reached* up and shook the branch.] **2.** to touch, as by stretching out [Can you *reach* the top shelf?] **3.** to stretch out in time, space, amount, etc. [His fame *reaches* into all parts of the world.] **4.** to get and hand over [Can you *reach* me the salt?] **5.** to try to seize or touch [He *reached* for his gun.] **6.** to go as far as; get to [The climbers *reached* the top of Mt. Everest. The news *reached* me this morning.] **7.** to get in touch with [You can *reach* me at this address.] **8.** to get the sympathy or understanding of; influence [Her sad face *reached* our hearts.] —*n.* **1.** the act or power of reaching [A long *reach* helps in playing basketball.] **2.** the distance or extent covered in reaching [We are out of the *reach* of danger.] **3.** a long stretch, as of water.

re·act (ri akt´), *v.* **1.** to act back on the thing that is acting; have a return effect [Do wages and prices *react* on each other in rising and falling?] **2.** to act as a result of some other action, influence, etc. [She *reacted* to the news by fainting.] **3.** to act in an opposite way; go back to an earlier condition [After wearing short skirts, women *reacted* by choosing longer ones.] **4.** to act with another substance in bringing about a chemical change.

re·ac·tion (ri ak´shən), *n.* **1.** an action, happening, etc. in return or in response to some other action, happening, force, etc. [What was his *reaction* to your suggestion? A rubber ball bounces as a *reaction* to hitting the ground.] **2.** a going back to an earlier or more backward stage or condition. **3.** a chemical change [Gas bubbles are formed by the *reaction* of yeast with starch and sugar.]

re·ac·tion·ar·y (ri ak´shən er´ē), *adj.* of, showing, or wanting a return to an earlier or more backward condition, as in politics. —*n.* a person who favors such reaction. —**re·ac´tion·ar´ies**, *pl.*

re·ac·tor (ri ak´tər), *n.* **1.** a person or thing that reacts. **2.** a device for releasing atomic energy by a chain reaction (see **chain reaction**). Layers of graphite are put between layers of uranium to control the reaction. Also called **atomic pile**.

read (rēd), *v.* **1.** to get the meaning of something written or printed by understanding its letters, signs, or numbers [I *read* the book. Can you *read* music?] **2.** to speak printed or written words

aloud [*Read* the story to me.] **3.** to learn the true meaning of, as if by reading [I *read* the answer in his face. We can *read* the history of a canyon in its rocks.] **4.** to tell ahead of time; predict [to *read* the future]. **5.** to study [to *read* law]. **6.** to measure and show [The thermometer *reads* 72 degrees.] **7.** to be put in certain words [The sentence *reads* as follows.] —**read into** or **read in,** to interpret or understand in a certain way. —**read** (red), *p.t. & p.p.;* **read´ing,** *pr.p.*

read (red), past tense and past participle of **read.** —*adj.* having knowledge got from reading; informed [He is well-*read*.]

read·a·ble (rēd´ə b'l), *adj.* **1.** that can be read; legible [Your handwriting is not *readable*.] **2.** interesting to read [a *readable* book].

read·er (rēd´ər), *n.* **1.** a person who reads. **2.** a schoolbook for learning reading.

read·ing (rēd´ing), *n.* **1.** the act of a person who reads. **2.** anything written or printed to be read [This novel is good *reading*.] **3.** the amount measured by a gauge [a thermometer *reading*]. **4.** the way something is written, read, performed, understood, etc. [I like his *reading* of Hamlet.]

re·ad·just (rē´ə just´), *v.* to adjust again; arrange differently. —**re´ad·just´ment,** *n.*

read·y (red´ē), *adj.* **1.** prepared to act or to be used at once [She is *ready* to sing. Your bath is *ready*.] **2.** willing [I am always *ready* to help.] **3.** about to; likely or liable; apt [She is so upset, she's *ready* to cry.] **4.** quick or prompt [a *ready* answer]. **5.** easy to get at and use [*ready* cash]. —*v.* to prepare [to *ready* the house for company]. —**read´i·er,** *compar.;* **read´i·est,** *superl.* —**read´ied,** *p.t. & p.p.;* **read´y·ing,** *pr.p.* —**read´i·ly,** *adv.* —**read´i·ness,** *n.*

read·y-made (red´ē mād´), *adj.* made so as to be ready for use or sale at once; not made-to-order [a *ready-made* suit].

re·al (rē´əl *or* rēl), *adj.* **1.** being such or happening so in fact; not imagined; true; actual [He could hardly believe that his good luck was *real*.] **2.** genuine [Are these *real* pearls?] —*adv.* very: *only in everyday talk* [Have a *real* nice time.]

re·al (rē´əl *or* re äl´), *n.* a Spanish silver coin of earlier times. —**re´als** or **re·a·les** (re ä´les), *pl.*

real estate, land and anything on it, as buildings, water, etc. —**re´al-es·tate´,** *adj.*

re·al·ism (rē´əl iz'm), *n.* **1.** the seeing of things as they really are, not as one might wish them to be [His *realism* told him he could never become a doctor.] **2.** in art and literature, the picturing of people and things as they really are.

re·al·ist (rē´əl ist), *n.* **1.** a person who faces facts with realism; practical person. **2.** an artist or writer who practices realism. —**re·al·is´tic,** *adj.* —**re·al·is´ti·cal·ly,** *adv.*

re·al·i·ty (ri al´ə tē), *n.* **1.** the condition of being real [to discuss the *reality* of flying saucers]. **2.** a person or thing that is real [His dream of fame became a *reality*.] **3.** trueness to life, as in art; realism. **—in reality,** in fact; actually. **—re·al'i·ties,** *pl.*

re·al·ize (rē'ə līz), *v.* **1.** to understand fully [I *realize* that good grades depend on careful work.] **2.** to make real; bring into being [to *realize* one's ambitions]. **3.** to change property, rights, etc. into money by selling [The company *realized* its assets.] **4.** to get as a profit or price. **—re'al·ized,** *p.t. & p.p.;* **re'al·iz·ing,** *pr.p.* **—re'al·i·za'tion,** *n.*

re·al·ly (rē'əl ē *or* rēl'ē), *adv.* **1.** in fact; truly [I am not *really* angry.] **2.** indeed [*Really*, you shouldn't do that.]

realm (relm), *n.* **1.** a kingdom. **2.** a region or area [the *realm* of the imagination].

re·al·ty (rē'əl tē), *n.* real estate.

ream (rēm), *n.* **1.** an amount of paper that varies from 480 to 516 sheets. **2. reams,** *pl.* a large amount: *used only in everyday talk.*

ream (rēm), *v.* to make a hole or opening larger [to *ream* out the barrel of a gun].

ream·er (rēm'ər), *n.* **1.** a sharp tool for making holes larger. **2.** a device for squeezing the juice from lemons, oranges, etc.

re·an·i·mate (rē an'ə-māt), *v.* to give new life, power, vigor, etc. to. **—re·an'i·mat·ed,** *p.t. & p.p.;* **re·an'i·mat·ing,** *pr.p.*

reamer *(meaning 1)*

reap (rēp), *v.* **1.** to cut down grain when it is ripe. **2.** to gather in after cutting [to *reap* a crop]. **3.** to get in return for work, effort, etc. [to *reap* a reward].

reap·er (rēp'ər), *n.* **1.** a person who reaps. **2.** a machine for reaping grain. **—the Reaper** or **the Grim Reaper,** death.

re·ap·pear (rē'ə pir'), *v.* to appear again. **—re'ap·pear'ance,** *n.*

rear (rir), *n.* **1.** the back part or place [the *rear* of a house]. **2.** the part of an army, navy, etc. farthest from the battle front. **—adj.** of, at, or in the rear [a *rear* entrance]. **—bring up the rear,** to come at the end, as of a parade.

rear (rir), *v.* **1.** to help grow up; bring up [to *rear* children]. **2.** to produce or breed [to *rear* sheep]. **3.** to set or bring upright; raise [to *rear* a flagpole]. **4.** to build [The barn was *reared* in a day.] **5.** to rise up on the hind legs, as a horse.

rear admiral, an officer in the navy who ranks just above a captain.

re·ar·range (rē'ə rānj'), *v.* to arrange again or in a different way. **—re'ar·ranged',** *p.t. & p.p.;* **re'ar·rang'ing,** *pr.p.* **—re'ar·range'ment,** *n.*

horse rearing

rear·ward (rir'wərd), *adj.* at, in, or toward the rear. **—adv.** toward the rear: also **rear'wards.**

rea·son (rē'z'n), *n.* **1.** something said to explain or try to explain an act, idea, etc. [Write the *reasons* for your answer.] **2.** a cause for some action, feeling, etc.; motive [Noisy neighbors were our *reason* for moving.] **3.** the power to think, get ideas, decide things, etc. [Man is the only animal that truly has *reason*.] **4.** good thinking or judgment [He won't listen to *reason*.] **—v. 1.** to think in a sensible way; come to a conclusion by considering facts [A lawyer learns to *reason* clearly.] **2.** to argue in a careful, sensible way [to *reason* with a child who is afraid of the dark]. **—by reason of,** because of. **—stand to reason,** to be logical or sensible.

rea·son·a·ble (rē'z'n ə b'l), *adj.* **1.** using or showing reason; sensible [a *reasonable* person; a *reasonable* decision]. **2.** not too high or too low; fair [a *reasonable* fee; a *reasonable* salary]. **—rea'son·a·bly,** *adv.*

rea·son·ing (rē'z'n ing), *n.* **1.** the act of coming to a conclusion based on facts. **2.** reasons or proofs got in this way.

re·as·sem·ble (rē'ə sem'b'l), *v.* to come or put together again. **—re'as·sem'bled,** *p.t. & p.p.;* **re'as·sem'bling,** *pr.p.*

re·as·sure (rē ə shoor'), *v.* to remove the doubts or fears of; make feel secure again. **—re·as·sured',** *p.t. & p.p.;* **re·as·sur'ing,** *pr.p.* **—re·as·sur'ance,** *n.*

re·bate (rē'bāt), *n.* a part given back from an amount paid [a *rebate* of an overpayment of income tax].

Re·bec·ca or **Re·bek·ah** (ri bek'ə), *n.* in the Bible, the wife of Isaac.

reb·el (reb'l), *n.* a person who fights or struggles against authority or any kind of control. **—adj.** fighting against authority; rebellious [a *rebel* army]. **—v.** (ri bel'), **1.** to fight or struggle against authority or control [The peasants *rebelled* against the king.] **2.** to have a strong dislike [My mind *rebels* at the idea of leaving.] **—re·belled',** *p.t. & p.p.;* **re·bel'ling,** *pr.p.*

re·bel·lion (ri bel'yən), *n.* **1.** an armed fight against the government; revolt. **2.** a fight or struggle against any kind of control.

re·bel·lious (ri bel'yəs), *adj.* fighting or struggling against authority or any kind of control [*rebellious* colonies]. **—re·bel'lious·ly,** *adv.*

re·birth (rē bûrth' *or* rē'bûrth), *n.* a coming back into use again, as if born again; revival [a *rebirth* of freedom].

re·born (rē bôrn'), *adj.* having new life, spirit, interests, etc., as if born again.

re·bound (ri bound'), *v.* to bounce back, as after hitting a surface [Stan caught the ball as it *rebounded* from the fence.] **—n.** (rē'bound), a bouncing or bounding back; recoil.

re·buff (ri buf'), *n.* the act of refusing advice, help, etc. in a sharp or rude way [Our offer met with a *rebuff*.] **—v.** to refuse in a sharp or rude way; snub [She *rebuffed* our friendship.]

re·build (ri bild'), *v.* to build again, especially something that was damaged, ruined, etc. **—re·built',** *p.t. & p.p.;* **re·build'ing,** *pr.p.*

re·buke (ri byook'), *v.* to blame or scold in a sharp way; reprimand. **—n.** a sharp scolding. **—re·buked',** *p.t. & p.p.;* **re·buk'ing,** *pr.p.*

re·bus (rē′bəs), *n.* a puzzle in which words or phrases are shown by means of pictures, signs, etc.

re·but (ri but′), *v.* to argue or prove that someone or something is wrong [to *rebut* a claim]. —**re·but′-ted,** *p.t. & p.p.;* **re·but′-ting,** *pr.p.* —**re·but′-tal,** *n.*

rebus

re·cal·ci·trant (ri kal′si trənt), *adj.* refusing to obey rules, follow orders, etc.; stubborn and disobedient. —**re·cal′ci·trance,** *n.*

re·call (ri kôl′), *v.* **1.** to bring back to mind; remember [Can you *recall* how you felt?] **2.** to call back; order to return [The ambassador was *recalled* to Washington.] **3.** to take back; withdraw or cancel [They *recalled* his license.] —*n.* (rē′kôl), **1.** the act of recalling. **2.** the right of citizens to vote an official out of office, using petitions to call for such a vote.

re·cant (ri kant′), *v.* to take back an opinion or belief; confess that one was wrong. —**re·can·ta·tion** (rē′kan tā′shən), *n.*

re·ca·pit·u·late (rē′kə pich′oo lāt), *v.* to tell again in a brief way, as in an outline; summarize. —**re·ca·pit′u·lat·ed,** *p.t. & p.p.;* **re·ca·pit′-u·lat·ing,** *pr.p.* —**re·ca·pit·u·la′tion,** *n.*

re·cap·ture (rē kap′chər), *v.* **1.** to capture again; retake. **2.** to bring back by remembering [You can't *recapture* your youth.] —**re·cap′-tured,** *p.t. & p.p.;* **re·cap′tur·ing,** *pr.p.*

re·cast (rē kast′), *v.* **1.** to cast, or shape, again [to *recast* a bronze statue]. **2.** to make better by doing over [to *recast* a sentence]. —**re·cast′,** *p.t. & p.p.;* **re·cast′ing,** *pr.p.*

recd. or **rec'd.,** abbreviation for **received.**

re·cede (ri sēd′), *v.* to go, move, or slope backward [The flood waters *receded.* Her chin *recedes.*] —**re·ced′ed,** *p.t. & p.p.;* **re·ced′ing,** *pr.p.*

re·ceipt (ri sēt′), *n.* **1.** a receiving or being received [Upon *receipt* of the telegram, she fainted.] **2.** a written statement that something has been received [The landlord gave me a *receipt* for the rent money.] **3. receipts,** *pl.* the amount of money taken in, as in a business. **4.** a recipe. —*v.* to mark "paid" as on a bill for goods.

re·ceiv·a·ble (ri sēv′ə b'l), *adj.* due; that must be paid, as a bill [The company will collect $5,000 from accounts *receivable.*]

re·ceive (ri sēv′), *v.* **1.** to take or get what has been given or sent to one [to *receive* gifts]. **2.** to meet with; be given; undergo [to *receive* punishment; *receive* applause]. **3.** to find out about; learn [He *received* the news calmly.] **4.** to greet guests and let them come in [Our host *received* us at the door.] **5.** to have room for or be able to bear [Each wheel *receives* an equal part of the weight.] **6.** to change electric waves or signals into sound or light [Our radio *receives* poorly.] —**re·ceived′,** *p.t. & p.p.;* **re·ceiv′ing,** *pr.p.*

re·ceiv·er (ri sēv′ər), *n.* **1.** a person who receives. **2.** a person appointed to take care of the property involved in a lawsuit. **3.** a device that receives electric waves or signals and changes them into sound or light [a television *receiver;* a telephone *receiver*].

re·ceiv·er·ship (ri sēv′ər ship), *n.* the condition of being taken care of by a receiver (*meaning* 2) [a bankrupt business in *receivership*].

re·cent (rē′sənt), *adj.* of a time just before now; made or happening a short time ago [*recent* news; a *recent* flood]. —**re′cent·ly,** *adv.*

re·cep·ta·cle (ri sep′tə k'l), *n.* anything used to keep something in [a trash *receptacle*].

re·cep·tion (ri sep′shən), *n.* **1.** a receiving or being received, or the way in which this is done [a friendly *reception*]. **2.** a party or gathering at which guests are received [a wedding *reception*]. **3.** the receiving of signals on radio or television [Storms affect the *reception.*]

re·cep·tive (ri sep′tiv), *adj.* able or ready to receive ideas, requests, etc.

re·cess (ri ses′ *or* rē′ses), *n.* **1.** a hollow place in a wall or other surface. **2.** a hidden or inner place [Fish darted through *recesses* in the coral.] **3.** (rē′ses), a stopping of work, study, etc. for a short time, to relax. —*v.* **1.** to set in a recess; set back [a *recessed* door]. **2.** to stop work, study, etc. for a while.

re·ces·sion (ri sesh′ən), *n.* **1.** a period when business is poor; mild depression. **2.** a going or moving back or backward; withdrawal.

re·ces·sion·al (ri sesh′ən 'l), *n.* a hymn sung at the end of a church service when the clergy and the choir march out.

re·ces·sive (ri ses′iv), *adj.* that recedes.

re·charge (rē chärj′), *v.* to charge again, as a battery. —*n.* (rē′chärj), a recharging. —**re·charged′,** *p.t. & p.p.;* **re·charg′ing,** *pr.p.*

rec·i·pe (res′ə pē), *n.* **1.** a list of things and directions for making something to eat or drink [a *recipe* for stew]. **2.** a way to get or do something [His *recipe* for success is hard work.]

re·cip·i·ent (ri sip′i ənt), *n.* a person or thing that receives.

re·cip·ro·cal (ri sip′rə k'l), *adj.* **1.** done, felt, or given in return [to lend a hand, hoping for a *reciprocal* favor]. **2.** on both sides; mutual [a *reciprocal* treaty]. **3.** acting or working together; complementary [*reciprocal* action of the parts of the machine]. —*n.* a number related to another number in such a way that the two numbers multiplied together equal 1 [The *reciprocal* of 1/7 is 7, because 1/7 × 7 = 1.] —**re·cip′ro·cal·ly,** *adv.*

re·cip·ro·cate (ri sip′rə kāt), *v.* **1.** to give and get in return; exchange [They *reciprocate* good wishes.] **2.** to give, do, or feel something in return for [He *reciprocated* her greeting with a cheerful "Hello!"] **3.** to move back and forth [*Reciprocating* pistons are used in steam engines.]

---

fat, āpe, cär, ten, ēven, hit, bīte, gō, hôrn, tōōl, book, up, fur; get, joy, yet, chin, she, thin, *th*en; zh = s in pleasure; ′ as in able (ā′b'l); ə = a in ago, e in agent, i in sanity, o in confess, u in focus.

—re·cip′ro·cat·ed, *p.t. & p.p.*; re·cip′ro·cat-ing, *pr.p.* —re·cip′ro·ca′tion, *n.*

rec·i·proc·i·ty (res′ə präs′ə tē), *n.* 1. the condition of being reciprocal. 2. the act of reciprocating, or of giving and getting equally [Two nations practice *reciprocity* when each lowers the duty on goods that the other wants to buy.]

re·cit·al (ri sī′t′l), *n.* 1. the act of reciting or telling with many details [a long *recital* of his troubles]. 2. the story or report told in this way. 3. a program of music or dances given by a soloist or soloists.

rec·i·ta·tion (res′ə tā′shən), *n.* 1. a recital (*meanings 1 and 2*). 2. the act of reciting before an audience a poem, story, etc. that one has memorized. 3. the poem, story, etc. recited. 4. a class meeting in which pupils answer aloud questions on the lesson.

rec·i·ta·tive (res′ə tə tēv′), *n.* a way of singing in which the singer sounds the words quickly, as in speaking, but with musical tones. Recitative is often used in opera for dialogue.

re·cite (ri sīt′), *v.* 1. to say aloud before an audience, as something that one has memorized [to *recite* the Gettysburg Address]. 2. to tell in detail; give an account of. 3. to answer questions about a lesson in class. —re·cit′ed, *p.t. & p.p.*; re·cit′ing, *pr.p.* —re·cit′er, *n.*

reck (rek), *v.* to care or heed: *now seldom used except in poetry* [I *reck* not what others think.]

reck·less (rek′lis), *adj.* not careful; taking chances; careless; rash [a *reckless* driver]. —reck′less·ly, *adv.* —reck′less·ness, *n.*

reck·on (rek′ən), *v.* 1. to count; figure up [to *reckon* one's hotel bill]. 2. to think of as being; consider or judge [I *reckon* him a real friend.] 3. to depend on; count on [I *reckoned* on his being early.] 4. to suppose: *only in everyday talk.* —reckon with, to think about; consider.

reck·on·ing (rek′ən ing), *n.* 1. the act of figuring up or finding out [the *reckoning* of a ship's position; a *reckoning* of costs]. 2. payment of an account. 3. a bill, as at an inn.

re·claim (rē klām′), *v.* 1. to make fit again for growing things or for living in [to *reclaim* a desert by irrigating it]. 2. to get something useful from waste products [to *reclaim* metal from wrecked cars]. 3. to bring back from a life of sin, crime, etc.; reform.

rec·la·ma·tion (rek′lə mā′shən), *n.* a reclaiming or being reclaimed.

re·cline (ri klīn′), *v.* to lie down or lean back. —re·clined′, *p.t. & p.p.*; re·clin′ing, *pr.p.*

re·cluse (rek′lōōs *or* ri klōōs′), *n.* a person who lives alone, away from others; hermit.

rec·og·ni·tion (rek′əg nish′ən), *n.* 1. a recognizing or being recognized; acknowledgment; acceptance. 2. the act of showing that one knows a person or thing; also, a greeting [He passed me without a sign of *recognition.*]

re·cog·ni·zance (ri käg′ni zəns), *n.* a sum of money, as a bond, which a person forfeits to a law court if he fails to keep a certain promise; also, the promise made [released on one's own *recognizance*].

rec·og·nize (rek′əg nīz), *v.* 1. to be aware of as something or someone seen, heard, etc. before; know again [to *recognize* a street; to *recognize* a tune]. 2. to know by a certain feature; identify [to *recognize* a giraffe by its long neck]. 3. to take notice of; show approval of [to *recognize* an employee for his years of service]. 4. to admit as true; acknowledge; accept [to *recognize* defeat]. 5. to accept as a new state or government, as by starting to do business with it [The U.S. *recognized* the U.S.S.R. in 1933.] 6. to give the right to speak at a meeting [The chair *recognizes* Mr. Jones.] —rec′og·nized, *p.t. & p.p.*; rec′og-niz·ing, *pr.p.*

re·coil (ri koil′), *v.* 1. to jump or shrink back suddenly, as because of fear, surprise, etc. [She *recoiled* in horror.] 2. to fly back when let go, as a spring; also, to jump back when fired, as a gun. —*n.* (also rē′koil), the act or fact of recoiling.

rec·ol·lect (rek ə lekt′), *v.* to remember; bring back to mind [to *recollect* an old song].

re-col·lect (rē′kə lekt′), *v.* 1. to gather together again [to *re-collect* scattered pearls]. 2. to make calm again [to *re-collect* oneself].

rec·ol·lec·tion (rek′ə lek′shən), *n.* 1. the act or power of recollecting, or remembering. 2. what is remembered.

rec·om·mend (rek ə mend′), *v.* 1. to speak of as being good for a certain use, job, etc.; praise [to *recommend* a good plumber; to *recommend* a book]. 2. to make pleasing or worth having [We found little to *recommend* that barren island.] 3. to give advice; advise [I *recommend* that you study harder.] 4. to turn over; entrust [I *recommend* him to your care.]

rec·om·men·da·tion (rek′ə men dā′shən), *n.* 1. the act of recommending. 2. anything that recommends, as a letter recommending a person for a job. 3. advice [My *recommendation* is that you return.]

rec·om·pense (rek′əm pens), *v.* 1. to pay or pay back; reward [The company *recompensed* him for his services.] 2. to make up for; compensate [Insurance *recompensed* his losses.] —*n.* payment for service, loss, etc. —rec′om-pensed, *p.t. & p.p.*; rec′om·pens·ing, *pr.p.*

rec·on·cile (rek′ən sīl), *v.* 1. to make friendly again [to *reconcile* feuding families]. 2. to settle [to *reconcile* a quarrel]. 3. to make agree or fit [I can't *reconcile* my memory of him with your description.] 4. to make ready to put up with something unpleasant [Time has *reconciled* him to his fate.] —rec′on·ciled, *p.t. & p.p.*; rec′-on·cil·ing, *pr.p.* —rec·on·cil·i·a·tion (rek′-ən sil′i ā′shən), *n.*

rec·on·dite (rek′ən dīt *or* ri kän′dīt), *adj.* very hard to understand [a *recondite* subject].

re·con·di·tion (rē′kən dish′ən), *v.* to put back in good condition by cleaning, repairing, etc.

re·con·nais·sance (ri kän′ə səns), *n.* the act of examining or spying on some area, as in a war, in order to get information.

rec·on·noi·ter (rek′ə noi′tər *or* rē′kə noi′tər), *v.* to examine or spy on an area, as one held by an enemy in a war, in order to get information.

rec·on·noi·tre (rek'ə noi'tər *or* rē'kə noi'tər), *v.* same as **reconnoiter.** —**rec'on·noi'tred,** *p.t. & p.p.;* **rec'on·noi'tring,** *pr.p.*

re·con·sid·er (rē'kən sid'ər), *v.* to think about again, as with the idea of changing one's mind.

re·con·struct (rē'kən strukt'), *v.* to build up again as it once was; remake.

re·con·struc·tion (rē'kən struk'shən), *n.* **1.** the act of reconstructing. **2.** something reconstructed. **3. Reconstruction,** the process of bringing the Southern States back into the Union after the Civil War, or the time when this took place (1867–1877).

re·cord (ri kôrd'), *v.* **1.** to write down for future use; keep an account of [to *record* an event in a diary]. **2.** to show, as on a dial [A thermometer *records* temperatures.] **3.** to put sound in a form in which it can be reproduced again, as on a disk with grooves or a magnetic tape [to *record* music]. —*n.* (rek'ərd), **1.** something written down and kept as a history; especially, an official account [secret government *records*]. **2.** the known facts about something or someone [his fine *record* as mayor]. **3.** a disk on which sound has been recorded, for playing on a phonograph. **4.** the best that has yet been done [The *record* for the high jump is over seven feet.] —*adj.* (rek'ərd), being the largest, fastest, etc. of its kind [a *record* wheat crop]. —**break a record,** to do better than the best that has been done. —**off the record,** not to be published. —**on record,** recorded for all to know.

re·cord·er (ri kôr'dər), *n.* **1.** a person or machine that records. **2.** a public officer who keeps records of deeds and other official papers. **3.** an early form of flute that is held straight up and down when played.

re·cord·ing (ri kôr'ding), *n.* **1.** what is recorded, as on a phonograph record. **2.** such a record.

re·count (ri kount'), *v.* to tell about in detail; narrate [He *recounted* his adventures.]

recorder

re·count (rē kount'), *v.* to count again. —*n.* (rē'kount), a second count, as of votes.

re·coup (ri kōōp'), *v.* **1.** to make up for [to *recoup* a loss]. **2.** to pay back; repay.

re·course (rē'kôrs *or* ri kôrs'), *n.* **1.** a turning for help, protection, etc. [As a last *recourse*, he called the police.] **2.** that to which one turns for help, etc. [He is our last *recourse*.]

re·cov·er (ri kuv'ər), *v.* **1.** to get back something lost; regain [to *recover* a stolen car; to *recover* consciousness]. **2.** to get well again; become normal [Has he *recovered* from the flu?] **3.** to save oneself from a fall, slip, etc. [She stumbled but was able to *recover* herself.] **4.** to make up for [to *recover* losses]. **5.** to bring to a useful condition; reclaim [to *recover* flooded land].

re·cov·er (rē kuv'ər), *v.* to put a new cover on.

re·cov·er·y (ri kuv'ər ē), *n.* **1.** a getting back of something lost, stolen, etc. **2.** a coming back to health, a normal condition, etc. —**re·cov'er·ies,** *pl.*

rec·re·ant (rek'ri ənt), *n.* **1.** a coward. **2.** a disloyal person. —*adj.* **1.** cowardly. **2.** disloyal.

re·cre·ate (rē'krē āt'), *v.* to create again or in a new way. —**re'-cre·at'ed,** *p.t. & p.p.;* **re'-cre·at'ing,** *pr.p.*

rec·re·a·tion (rek'ri ā'shən), *n.* **1.** the act of refreshing one's body or mind, as after work [He plays chess for *recreation*.] **2.** any sport, exercise, amusement, etc. by which one does this. —**rec're·a'tion·al,** *adj.*

re·crim·i·nate (ri krim'ə nāt), *v.* to answer an accuser by accusing him in return. —**re·crim'-i·nat·ed,** *p.t. & p.p.;* **re·crim'i·nat·ing,** *pr.p.* —**re·crim'i·na'tion,** *n.*

re·cru·des·cence (rē'krōō des''ns), *n.* a breaking out again, as of a disease, crime, etc. —**re'-cru·des'cent,** *adj.*

re·cruit (ri krōōt'), *n.* **1.** a soldier, sailor, etc. who recently joined the armed forces. **2.** a new member of any group. —*v.* **1.** to enlist new members in [to *recruit* an army]. **2.** to get to join [Our nature club *recruited* six new members.] **3.** to get an amount or supply of [We'll need to *recruit* some help.] —**re·cruit'ment,** *n.*

rec·tal (rek't'l), *adj.* of or for the rectum.

rec·tan·gle (rek'tang'g'l), *n.* any flat figure with four right angles and four sides.

rectangle

rec·tan·gu·lar (rek tang'gyoo lər), *adj.* shaped like a rectangle [a *rectangular* field].

rec·ti·fy (rek'tə fī), *v.* **1.** to put right; correct or adjust [to *rectify* an error]. **2.** to change an alternating current of electricity into a direct current. —**rec'ti·fied,** *p.t. & p.p.;* **rec'ti·fy·ing,** *pr.p.* —**rec'ti·fi·ca'tion,** *n.* —**rec'ti·fi·er,** *n.*

rec·ti·tude (rek'tə tōōd *or* rek'tə tyōōd), *n.* good moral character; honesty; trustworthiness.

rec·tor (rek'tər), *n.* **1.** in some churches, the head of a parish. **2.** the head of certain schools, colleges, etc.

rec·to·ry (rek'tər ē), *n.* the house in which a rector lives. —**rec'to·ries,** *pl.*

rec·tum (rek'təm), *n.* the lowest or end part of the large intestine.

re·cum·bent (ri kum'bənt), *adj.* lying down; reclining [a *recumbent* figure on the sofa].

re·cu·per·ate (ri kōō'pə rāt *or* ri kyōō'pə rāt), *v.* **1.** to get well again, as after being sick [He is *recuperating* from the flu.] **2.** to get back; recover [to *recuperate* one's losses]. —**re·cu'-per·at·ed,** *p.t. & p.p.;* **re·cu'per·at·ing,** *pr.p.* —**re·cu'per·a'tion,** *n.*

re·cur (ri kur'), *v.* **1.** to happen or come again or from time to time [His fever *recurs* every few months.] **2.** to go back in thought, talk, etc. [The speaker *recurred* to his first point.] —**re·curred′**, *p.t. & p.p.;* **re·cur′ring**, *pr.p.*

re·cur·rent (ri kŭr′ənt), *adj.* happening or coming again or from time to time [a *recurrent* dream]. —**re·cur′rence**, *n.*

red (red), *adj.* **1.** having the color of blood. **2.** *often* **Red,** radical in politics; especially, communist. —*n.* **1.** the color of blood. **2.** any red coloring matter. **3.** *often* **Red,** a person who is radical in politics; especially, a communist. —**in the red,** losing money. —**see red,** to become very angry: *used only in everyday talk.* —**red′der**, *compar.;* **red′dest**, *superl.* —**red′ness**, *n.*

red·bird (red′bŭrd), *n.* the cardinal bird.

red·breast (red′brest), *n.* the robin.

red·cap (red′kap), *n.* a porter in a railroad station, bus station, etc.

red·coat (red′kōt), *n.* a British soldier, as at the time of the American Revolution.

Red Cross, an international society with branches in different countries, set up to help people in time of war or during other disasters.

red deer, 1. a kind of deer that is found in Europe and Asia. **2.** the American deer, when it has its reddish summer coloring.

red·den (red′'n), *v.* to make or become red; especially, to blush [He *reddened* with anger.]

red·dish (red′ish), *adj.* somewhat red.

re·deem (ri dēm′), *v.* **1.** to get or buy back; recover [He *redeemed* his watch from the pawnshop.] **2.** to pay off, as a mortgage. **3.** to turn in for a prize, premium, etc. [She *redeemed* the coupon for a free box of soap.] **4.** to set free; rescue, as from sin. **5.** to carry out; fulfill, as a promise. **6.** to make up for [His brave act *redeemed* his faults.] —**re·deem′a·ble**, *adj.*

re·deem·er (ri dēm′ər), *n.* a person who redeems. —**the Redeemer,** Jesus Christ.

re·demp·tion (ri demp′shən), *n.* **1.** a redeeming or being redeemed; a buying back, paying off, etc. **2.** rescue or salvation.

red-hand·ed (red′han′did), *adj.* while committing a crime [a thief caught *redhanded*].

red·head (red′hed), *n.* a person with red hair. —**red′head·ed**, *adj.*

red herring, something used to take people's attention away from the important thing.

red-hot (red′hät′), *adj.* **1.** hot enough to glow [*red-hot* iron]. **2.** very excited, angry, eager, etc. **3.** very new, timely, etc. [*red-hot* news].

re·dis·cov·er (rē′dis kuv′ər), *v.* to discover again something that was lost or forgotten.

red-let·ter (red′let′ər), *adj.* worth remembering; important or happy [a *red-letter* day].

red·o·lent (red′ə lənt), *adj.* **1.** having a sweet smell; fragrant [*redolent* flowers]. **2.** giving off a smell [a harbor *redolent* of fish]. **3.** suggesting ideas or feelings [a song *redolent* of young love]. —**red′o·lence**, *n.*

re·dou·ble (rē dub′'l), *v.* **1.** to double again; make twice as much; make much greater [to *redouble* one's efforts]. **2.** to turn sharply backward [to *redouble* on one's tracks]. —**re·dou′bled**, *p.t. & p.p.;* **re·dou′bling**, *pr.p.*

re·doubt (ri dout′), *n.* a small fort away from the main fort, as for protecting a pass.

re·doubt·a·ble (ri dout′ə b'l), *adj.* that causes or should cause great fear [a *redoubtable* foe].

re·dound (ri dound′), *v.* to come back as a result; be reflected back [His honors *redound* to the nation's credit.]

red pepper, same as **cayenne.**

re·dress (ri dres′), *v.* to correct and make up for [to *redress* a wrong]. —*n.* (rē′dres), something done to make up for a fault, injury, etc. [The citizens petitioned the government for a *redress* of their grievances.]

Red Sea, a sea between Africa and Arabia. The Suez Canal connects it with the Mediterranean.

red·skin (red′skin), *n.* a North American Indian: *no longer used.*

red·start (red′stärt), *n.* **1.** a small European warbler with a reddish tail. **2.** an American warbler that catches flies for food.

red tape, too great attention to rules and details that slows things down in an annoying way.

re·duce (ri dōōs′ *or* ri dyōōs′), *v.* **1.** to make smaller, less, fewer, etc.; decrease [to *reduce* speed; to *reduce* taxes]. **2.** to lose weight, as by dieting. **3.** to make lower, as in rank or condition; bring down [to *reduce* a major to the rank of captain; a people *reduced* to poverty]. **4.** to change into a different form or condition [to *reduce* peanuts to a paste by grinding; to *reduce* the fraction 6/8 to 3/4]. **5.** to conquer [The army *reduced* the enemy fort.] —**re·duced′**, *p.t. & p.p.;* **re·duc′ing**, *pr.p.* —**re·duc′er**, *n.* —**re·duc′i·ble**, *adj.*

re·duc·tion (ri duk′shən), *n.* **1.** a reducing or being reduced. **2.** the amount by which a thing is reduced [a ten-pound *reduction* in weight]. **3.** anything reduced, as a lower price.

re·dun·dance (ri dun′dəns), *n.* redundancy.

re·dun·dan·cy (ri dun′dən sē), *n.* **1.** the condition of being redundant. **2.** something redundant. **3.** the use of more words than are needed to express an idea. —**re·dun′dan·cies**, *pl.*

re·dun·dant (ri dun′dənt), *adj.* **1.** more than enough; not needed. **2.** using more words than are needed; wordy [It is *redundant* to say "a sad tragedy."]

red·wing (red′wing), *n.* **1.** the red-winged blackbird. **2.** a European thrush with an orange-red patch on the underside of the wing.

red-winged blackbird (red′wingd′), a North American blackbird with a red patch on each wing.

red·wood (red′wood), *n.* **1.** a giant evergreen of California and Oregon; sequoia. **2.** the reddish wood of this tree.

re-ech·o (rē ek′ō), *v.* to echo back or again [The sound echoed and *re-echoed* through the valley.] —*n.* the echo of an echo. Also written **reëcho.** —**re-ech′oed**, *p.t. & p.p.;* **re-ech′o·ing**, *pr.p.* —**re-ech′oes**, *pl.*

red-winged blackbirds (9 in. long)

reed (rēd), *n.* **1.** a kind of grass having a hollow stem. **2.** a musical pipe made from such a stem. **3.** a thin strip of wood, plastic, or metal in some musical instruments, that vibrates when air is blown against it and produces a tone [The clarinet, oboe, bassoon, etc. have a *reed* or *reeds* in the mouthpiece.]

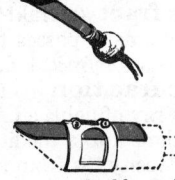

upper: **double reed** of oboe
lower: **single reed** of clarinet

reed organ, an organ with a set of metal reeds instead of pipes to make the tones.

reed·y (rēd′ē), *adj.* **1.** full of reeds. **2.** like a reed. **3.** sounding like a reed instrument; thin or shrill [the old man's high, *reedy* voice]. —**reed′i·er,** *compar.;* **reed′i·est,** *superl.*

reef (rēf), *n.* a ridge of sand or rock just about even with the surface of the water.

reef (rēf), *n.* a part of a sail that can be folded up and tied down so that the wind has less to push against. —*v.* to make a sail smaller by taking in part of it.

reef·er (rēf′ər), *n.* **1.** a short, thick coat worn especially by sailors. **2.** a person who reefs.

reek (rēk), *v.* to have a strong, bad smell; stink. —*n.* a strong, bad smell; stench.

reel (rēl), *v.* **1.** to sway or stagger, as from being struck; totter. **2.** to move in an unsteady way, as from dizziness. **3.** to spin or whirl [The room seemed to *reel* before his eyes.]

reel (rēl), *n.* a lively dance or the music for it.

reel (rēl), *n.* **1.** a frame or spool on which film, fishing line, wire, etc. is wound. **2.** the amount of motion-picture film, wire, etc. usually wound on one reel. —*v.* **1.** to wind on or off a reel [The firemen *reeled* out the hose.] **2.** to pull in by winding a fishing line on a reel [He *reeled* in a trout.] **3.** to tell or write easily and quickly [He *reeled* off a long list of names.]

reel for fishing line

re·e·lect (rē′i lekt′), *v.* to elect again: also written **reëlect.** —**re′-e·lec′tion,** *n.*

re·en·force (rē′in fôrs′), *v.* same as **reinforce:** also written **reënforce.** —**re′-en·force′-ment,** *n.*

re·en·list (rē′in list′), *v.* to enlist again: also written **reënlist.** —**re′-en·list′ment,** *n.*

re·en·ter (rē en′tər), *v.* to enter a second time or to come back in again: also written **reënter.** —**re·en′try,** *n.*

re·es·tab·lish (rē′ə stab′lish), *v.* to establish again: also written **reëstablish.** —**re′-es-tab′lish·ment,** *n.*

re·ex·am·ine (rē′ig zam′in), *v.* to examine again: also written **reëxamine.** —**re′-ex-am′i·na′tion,** *n.*

re·fec·to·ry (ri fek′tə rē), *n.* a dining hall, as in a monastery. —**re·fec′to·ries,** *pl.*

re·fer (ri fûr′), *v.* **1.** to speak of or call attention; mention [He seldom *refers* to his brother.] **2.** to go for facts, help, etc. [Columbus had no accurate maps to *refer* to.] **3.** to tell to go to a certain person or place for help, information, etc. [John *referred* me to his doctor.] **4.** to present to, as for help in settling [We *referred* our argument to the teacher.] —**re·ferred′,** *p.t. & p.p.;* **re·fer′ring,** *pr.p.*

ref·er·ee (ref′ə rē′), *n.* **1.** a person to whom something is presented to be settled [The judge was *referee* in the law suit.] **2.** a man whose duty is to see that the rules are followed in such sports as boxing, basketball, etc. —*v.* to act as referee in [to *referee* a game]. —**ref·er·eed′,** *p.t. & p.p.;* **ref·er·ee′ing,** *pr.p.*

ref·er·ence (ref′ər əns), *n.* **1.** the act or fact of referring; mention [She made no *reference* to the accident.] **2.** the fact of having to do with; relation; connection [in *reference* to his letter]. **3.** a mention, as in a book, of some other work where information can be found; also, the work so mentioned [Most of the author's *references* are useful.] **4.** something that gives information [He looked in the encyclopedia and other *references.*] **5.** a person who can give information about another; also, a statement about one's character, ability, etc. given by such a person [He gave three *references* when he applied for the job.]

ref·er·en·dum (ref′ə ren′dəm), *n.* **1.** the placing of a law before the people so that they can vote on it. **2.** the right of the people to vote directly on such a law.

re·fill (rē fil′), *v.* to fill again. —*n.* (rē′fil), something to refill a special container [a *refill* for a ball point pen].

re·fine (ri fīn′), *v.* **1.** to remove dirt, unwanted matter, etc. from; make pure [to *refine* sugar]. **2.** to make or become less coarse, crude, etc.; improve, polish, etc. [to *refine* one's style of writing]. —**re·fined′,** *p.t. & p.p.;* **re·fin′ing,** *pr.p.* —**re·fin′er,** *n.*

re·fined (ri fīnd′), *adj.* **1.** freed from dirt, unwanted matter, etc.; purified [*refined* sugar]. **2.** not crude or coarse; cultured, polished, etc. [*refined* manners].

re·fine·ment (ri fīn′mənt), *n.* **1.** the act or result of refining. **2.** fineness of manners, tastes, feelings, etc.; cultivation [a woman of *refinement*]. **3.** a change that improves the details [He made several *refinements* in his plan.]

re·fin·er·y (ri fīn′ər ē), *n.* a place where some raw material, such as oil or sugar, is refined or purified. —**re·fin′er·ies,** *pl.*

re·fit (rē fit′), *v.* to make fit for use again by repairing, adding new equipment, etc. [a passenger ship *refitted* for use as a freighter]. —**re·fit′ted,** *p.t. & p.p.;* **re·fit′ting,** *pr.p.*

re·flect (ri flekt′), *v.* **1.** to throw back or be thrown back, as light, heat, or sound [A polished metal surface *reflects* both light and heat.] **2.** to give back an image of [The calm lake *reflected* the trees on the shore.] **3.** to bring as a result [His success *reflects* credit on his teachers.] **4.** to bring blame, doubt, etc. [That act *reflects* on his honesty.] **5.** to think seriously [He *reflected* on his past errors.]

re·flec·tion (ri flek′shən), *n.* **1.** a reflecting of heat, light, sound, etc. **2.** anything reflected; image [one's *reflection* in a mirror]. **3.** serious thought; contemplation [After much *reflection*, he began to write.] **4.** an idea or remark that comes from such thought. **5.** a remark or an action that brings blame or doubt [That joke was not meant as a *reflection* on his skill.]

reflection

re·flec·tive (ri flek′tiv), *adj.* **1.** reflecting. **2.** thoughtful [a *reflective* poem].

re·flec·tor (ri flek′tər), *n.* a surface or part that reflects light, heat, sound, etc. [a *reflector* on a lamp].

re·flex (rē′fleks), *n.* an action of the muscles or glands caused by a stimulus sent through nerves

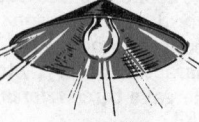

reflector

in an automatic way, without being controlled by the mind or by thinking [When a doctor strikes a person's knee to see if the lower leg will jerk, he is testing a *reflex*.] —*adj.* that is or has to do with such an action [A sneeze is a *reflex* action.]

re·flex·ive (ri flek′siv), *adj.* **1.** describing a verb whose subject and object refer to the same person or thing [In "He cut himself," "cut" is a *reflexive* verb.] **2.** describing a pronoun used as the object of a reflexive verb [In "I hurt myself," "myself" is a *reflexive* pronoun.]

re·for·est (rē fôr′ist), *v.* to plant trees where a forest once grew. —**re′for·est·a′tion,** *n.*

re·form (ri fôrm′), *v.* **1.** to make better by getting rid of faults, wrongs, etc.; improve [to *reform* working conditions in a factory; to *reform* a criminal]. **2.** to become better; give up one's ways [The outlaw *reformed* and became a useful citizen.] —*n.* correction of faults or evils, as in government.

re-form (rē fôrm′), *v.* to form again.

ref·or·ma·tion (ref′ər mā′shən), *n.* **1.** a reforming or being reformed. **2. Reformation,** the 16th-century religious movement that aimed at reforming the Roman Catholic Church and led to the formation of the Protestant sects.

re·form·a·to·ry (ri fôr′mə tôr′ē), *n.* a kind of prison, especially for young people or women, where training is given to try to reform the prisoners. —*adj.* aimed at reforming. —**re·form′a·to′ries,** *pl.*

re·form·er (ri fôr′mər), *n.* a person who tries to bring about reforms, as in government.

re·fract (ri frakt′), *v.* to bend a ray of light, etc. as it passes from one medium into another [Glass *refracts* light.]

re·frac·tion (ri frak′shən), *n.* the bending of a ray of light, etc. as it passes on a slant into a medium of a different density, as from air into water.

re·frac·to·ry (ri frak′tə rē), *adj.* **1.** hard to deal with or control; stubborn [a *refractory* horse; a *refractory* illness]. **2.** hard to melt or work, as certain ores or metals.

re·frain (ri frān′), *v.* to keep from doing something; hold back [Please *refrain* from talking.]

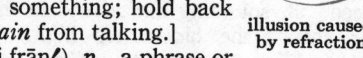

illusion caused by refraction

re·frain (ri frān′), *n.* a phrase or verse that is repeated from time to time in a song or poem.

re·fresh (ri fresh′), *v.* to make fresh again; bring back into good condition [A soft rain *refreshed* the wilted plants. He *refreshed* himself with a short nap. *Refresh* my memory by playing the piece again.]

re·fresh·ing (ri fresh′ing), *adj.* **1.** that refreshes [a *refreshing* sleep]. **2.** pleasant as a change from what is usual [It is *refreshing* to meet a person with new ideas.]

re·fresh·ment (ri fresh′mənt), *n.* **1.** a refreshing or being refreshed. **2.** something that refreshes. **3. refreshments,** *pl.* food or drink or both, especially when not a full meal.

re·frig·er·ate (ri frij′ə rāt), *v.* to make or keep cool or cold [Milk will sour if it is not *refrigerated*.] —**re·frig′er·at·ed,** *p.t. & p.p.;* **re·frig′er·at·ing,** *pr.p.* —**re·frig′er·a′tion,** *n.*

re·frig·er·a·tor (ri frij′ə rā′tər), *n.* a box or room in which the air is kept cool to keep food, etc. from spoiling.

reft (reft), *adj.* same as **bereft.**

ref·uge (ref′yōōj), *n.* **1.** shelter or protection, as from danger [He sought *refuge* from his enemies.] **2.** a safe place to stay.

ref·u·gee (ref yoo jē′ *or* ref′yoo jē), *n.* a person who flees from his home or country to seek refuge, as from persecution.

re·ful·gent (ri ful′jənt), *adj.* shining or glowing; brilliant. —**re·ful′gence,** *n.*

re·fund (ri fund′), *v.* to give back money, etc.; repay [We will *refund* the full price if you are not satisfied.] —*n.* (rē′fund), a refunding or the amount refunded.

re·fur·bish (ri fūr′bish), *v.* to freshen or polish up again; make like new; renovate.

re·fuse (ri fyōōz′), *v.* **1.** to say that one will not take something that is offered; reject [to *refuse* a gift; to *refuse* a suggestion]. **2.** to say that one will not give, do, or agree to something; turn down [to *refuse* a request; to *refuse* to go]. —**re·fused′,** *p.t. & p.p.;* **re·fus′ing,** *pr.p.* —**re·fus·al** (ri fyōō′z'l), *n.*

ref·use (ref′yōōs *or* ref′yōōz), *n.* worthless matter; waste; trash; rubbish.

re·fute (ri fyo͞ot/), v. to prove wrong or false; disprove [to *refute* an argument]. —**re·fut/ed,** *p.t. & p.p.;* **re·fut/ing,** *pr.p.* —**ref·u·ta·tion** (ref'yoo tā/shən), n.

re·gain (ri gān/), v. **1.** to get back again; recover [He *regained* his health slowly.] **2.** to get back to [The boat *regained* the harbor.]

re·gal (rē/g'l), adj. of, like, or fit for a king; royal; stately; splendid. —**re/gal·ly,** adv.

re·gale (ri gāl/), v. to entertain or delight; give pleasure to [to *regale* guests with a feast; to *regale* listeners with jokes]. —**re·galed/,** *p.t. & p.p.;* **re·gal/ing,** *pr.p.*

re·ga·li·a (ri gāl/yə *or* ri gā/li ə), *n.pl.* **1.** the symbols of an office or a special group [The crown, scepter, etc. are the *regalia* of a king.] **2.** splendid clothes; finery.

re·gard (ri gärd/), v. **1.** to think of in a certain way; consider [I *regard* him as a friend. He *regards* you highly.] **2.** to pay attention to; show respect for; heed [He never *regards* the feelings of others.] **3.** to look carefully at; gaze upon; observe. **4.** to have relation to; concern [This *regards* your welfare.] —*n.* **1.** attention; concern; care [Have some *regard* for your safety.] **2.** respect and liking; esteem [He has high *regard* for his teacher.] **3.** a steady look; gaze. **4. regards,** *pl.* good wishes; greetings [Give my *regards* to Bill.] —**as regards,** concerning. —**in regard to** or **with regard to,** in relation to; with respect to.

re·gard·ing (ri gär/ding), *prep.* having to do with; concerning; about [*regarding* your letter.]

re·gard·less (ri gärd/lis), adj. taking no heed; heedless [*Regardless* of the cost, I'll buy it.] —*adv.* anyway: *used only in everyday talk* [We objected, but he went *regardless.*]

re·gat·ta (ri gat/ə), n. a boat race or a series of boat races.

re·gen·cy (rē/jən sē), n. **1.** the position or power of a regent or group of regents. **2.** a group of regents ruling a country. **3.** government by a regent or group of regents [England was a *regency* from 1811 to 1820.] —**re/gen·cies,** *pl.*

re·gen·er·ate (ri jen/ə rāt), v. **1.** to give new life or force to; renew [to *regenerate* an old idea]. **2.** to open a new life to in a spiritual or religious way. **3.** to make better; improve or reform. **4.** to grow back anew [If a lizard loses its tail, it can *regenerate* a new one.] —*adj.* (ri jen/ər it), made better; renewed [*regenerate* spirits]. —**re·gen/-er·at·ed,** *p.t. & p.p.;* **re·gen/er·at·ing,** *pr.p.* —**re·gen/er·a/tion,** n. —**re·gen/er·a/tive,** adj.

re·gent (rē/jənt), n. **1.** a person chosen to rule while a king or queen is sick, absent, or too young. **2.** a member of a governing board, as of a university.

reg·i·cide (rej/ə sīd), n. **1.** a person who kills a king. **2.** the killing of a king.

re·gime or **ré·gime** (rā zhēm/ *or* ri zhēm/), n.

1. a system of rule or government [a democratic *regime*]. **2.** a regimen.

reg·i·men (rej/ə men), n. a system of diet, exercise, etc. for keeping healthy.

reg·i·ment (rej/ə mənt), n. a unit of soldiers, made up of several battalions. —*v.* (rej/ə ment), to organize in a strict system and with strict controls [Life in a prison is *regimented.*] —**reg/i·men/tal,** adj. —**reg/i·men·ta/tion,** n.

re·gion (rē/jən), n. **1.** a large stretch of land; area or district [an iron mining *region* of Minnesota]. **2.** any area, space, realm, etc. [the upper *regions* of the air; the *region* of the liver]. —**re·gion·al** (rē/jən 'l), adj.

reg·is·ter (rej/is tər), n. **1.** a record or list of names, events, or things; also, a book in which such a record is kept [a hotel *register; register* of accounts]. **2.** a device for counting and keeping a record of [a cash *register*]. **3.** an opening into a room, as from a furnace, that can be opened or closed to control the air passing through. **4.** the range, or part of the range, of a voice or musical instrument. —*v.* **1.** to keep a record of in a register [to *register* a birth]. **2.** to put one's name in a register, as of voters. **3.** to show on a gauge, scale, etc. [The thermometer *registers* 72°.] **4.** to show, as by a look on the face [to *register* surprise]. **5.** to protect important mail against loss by paying a fee to have it recorded at a post office.

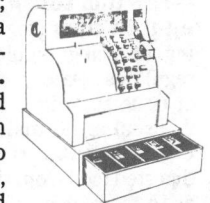

cash register

reg·is·trar (rej/i strär), n. a person who keeps records, as in a college.

reg·is·tra·tion (rej/i strā/shən), n. **1.** a registering or being registered. **2.** an entry in a register. **3.** the number of persons registered.

reg·is·try (rej/is trē), n. **1.** an office where records are kept. **2.** a register (*meaning 1*). **3.** the act of registering. —**reg/is·tries,** *pl.*

re·gress (ri gres/), v. to go back, as to an earlier condition. —**re·gres/sion,** n.

re·gret (ri gret/), v. to be sorry for something that has happened, that one has done, etc. [to *regret* the loss of a pet; to *regret* a mistake]. —*n.* a feeling of being sorry, as for something one has done or failed to do. —**regrets,** a polite way of saying that one is sorry, as at refusing an invitation. —**re·gret/ted,** *p.t. & p.p.;* **re·gret/-ting,** *pr.p.* —**re·gret/ful,** adj. —**re·gret/-ta·ble,** adj.

reg·u·lar (reg/yoo lər), adj. **1.** formed or arranged in an orderly way; balanced [a *regular* pattern; a face with *regular* features]. **2.** according to some rule or habit; usual; customary [He sat in his *regular* place.] **3.** steady and even; not changing [a *regular* rhythm]. **4.** in grammar, changing form in the usual way in showing tense, number, etc. ["Walk" is a *regular* verb, but "swim" is not.] **5.** describing or of an army that is kept up in peace as well as in war. **6.** qualified as by training; recognized [a *regular* nurse]. **7.** complete; thorough: *used only in everyday talk* [The game was a *regular* battle.] **8.** friendly and good-natured: *used only in everyday talk* [He's a *regular* fellow.] —*n.* a member of the regular army. —**reg′u·lar·ly,** *adv.* —**reg·u·lar·i·ty** (reg′yoo lar′ə tē), *n.*

reg·u·late (reg′yoo lāt), *v.* **1.** to control according to rules, a system, etc. [What forces *regulate* the weather?] **2.** to fix at a certain speed, amount, etc.; adjust to some standard [to *regulate* the heat; to *regulate* a fast clock]. —**reg′u·lat·ed,** *p.t.* & *p.p.;* **reg′u·lat·ing,** *pr.p.* —**reg′u·la′tor,** *n.*

reg·u·la·tion (reg′yoo lā′shən), *n.* **1.** a regulating or being regulated. **2.** a rule or law that regulates [safety *regulations*]. —*adj.* **1.** made or done according to rules [a *regulation* uniform]. **2.** usual or normal; ordinary.

re·gur·gi·tate (ri gūr′jə tāt), *v.* to bring partly digested food from the stomach back to the mouth, as a cow does. —**re·gur′gi·tat·ed,** *p.t.* & *p.p.;* **re·gur′gi·tat·ing,** *pr.p.* —**re·gur′gi·ta′tion,** *n.*

re·ha·bil·i·tate (rē′hə bil′ə tāt), *v.* **1.** to bring back to a normal or good condition [to *rehabilitate* a slum area]. **2.** to bring back to a former rank or reputation. —**re′ha·bil′i·tat·ed,** *p.t.* & *p.p.;* **re′ha·bil′i·tat·ing,** *pr.p.* —**re′ha·bil′i·ta′tion,** *n.*

re·hash (rē hash′), *v.* to work up again or go over again, with nothing new added [to *rehash* an argument]. —*n.* (rē′hash), the act or result of rehashing [a *rehash* of an earlier book].

re·hearse (ri hūrs′), *v.* **1.** to go through a play, speech, etc. for practice, before giving it in public. **2.** to repeat in detail [He *rehearsed* all his troubles to me.] —**re·hearsed′,** *p.t.* & *p.p.;* **re·hears′ing,** *pr.p.* —**re·hears′al,** *n.*

Reich (rīk), *n.* a former name for Germany or the German government.

reign (rān), *n.* **1.** the rule of a king, emperor, etc.; also, the time of ruling [laws made during the *reign* of Victoria]. **2.** influence or control [the *reign* of fashion]. —*v.* **1.** to rule as a king, etc. [Henry VIII *reigned* for 38 years.] **2.** to be widespread; prevail [when peace *reigns*].

re·im·burse (rē′im būrs′), *v.* to pay back money owed, as for services, loss, expenses, etc. [You will be *reimbursed* for your work.] —**re′im·bursed′,** *p.t.* & *p.p.;* **re′im·burs′ing,** *pr.p.* —**re′im·burse′ment,** *n.*

rein (rān), *n.* **1.** a narrow strap of leather attached to each end of a horse's bit. Reins are held by the rider or driver for guiding and controlling the horse. **2. reins,** *pl.* a means of guiding or controlling [to take up the *reins* of leadership]. —*v.* to guide,

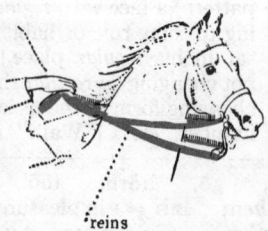

reins

control, or check as with reins. —**draw rein** or **draw in the reins,** to slow down or stop. —**give free rein to,** to allow to act freely.

re·in·car·nate (rē′in kär′nāt), *v.* to give a new body to after death [Souls are *reincarnated*, according to Hindu religious belief.] —**re′in·car′nat·ed,** *p.t.* & *p.p.;* **re′in·car′nat·ing,** *pr.p.* —**re′in·car·na′tion,** *n.*

rein·deer (rān′dir), *n.* a large deer found in northern regions, where it is tamed and used for work or as food. Both the male and female have antlers. —**rein′deer,** *pl.*

reindeer (3½ ft. high at shoulder)

re·in·force (rē′in fôrs′), *v.* to make stronger, as by adding something [to *reinforce* concrete with steel bars; to *reinforce* a theory with new evidence]. —**re′in·forced′,** *p.t.* & *p.p.;* **re′in·forc′ing,** *pr.p.*

re·in·force·ment (rē′in fôrs′mənt), *n.* **1.** a reinforcing or being reinforced. **2.** anything that reinforces. **3. reinforcements,** *pl.* extra troops, ships, etc. to help in a battle.

re·in·state (rē′in stāt′), *v.* to put back in a former position, rank, etc.; restore [to *reinstate* one as a member of a club]. —**re′in·stat′ed,** *p.t.* & *p.p.;* **re′in·stat′ing,** *pr.p.* —**re′in·state′ment,** *n.*

re·it·er·ate (rē it′ə rāt), *v.* to say over and over again; repeat [The prisoner *reiterated* his innocence.] —**re·it′er·at·ed,** *p.t.* & *p.p.;* **re·it′er·at·ing,** *pr.p.* —**re·it′er·a′tion,** *n.*

re·ject (ri jekt′), *v.* **1.** to refuse to take, agree to, use, etc. [to *reject* advice]. **2.** to throw away as worthless; discard. —*n.* (rē′jekt), something rejected, or thrown away. —**re·jec′tion,** *n.*

re·joice (ri jois′), *v.* to be or make glad or happy [We *rejoiced* at the news.] —**re·joiced′,** *p.t.* & *p.p.;* **re·joic′ing,** *pr.p.* —**re·joic′ing,** *n.*

re·join (rē join′), *v.* **1.** to join again; come or bring together again [to *rejoin* one's class after an illness; to *rejoin* the ends of a torn rope]. **2.** to answer ["That's not so!" he *rejoined*.]

re·join·der (ri join′dər), *n.* an answer, especially to another's reply.

re·ju·ve·nate (ri jōō′və nāt), *v.* to make feel or seem young or fresh again [The rest *rejuvenated* us.] —**re·ju′ve·nat·ed,** *p.t.* & *p.p.;* **re·ju′ve·nat·ing,** *pr.p.* —**re·ju′ve·na′tion,** *n.*

re·lapse (ri laps′), *v.* to fall back into an earlier condition, especially into illness after seeming to get better. —*n.* a relapsing. —**re·lapsed′,** *p.t.* & *p.p.;* **re·laps′ing,** *pr.p.*

re·late (ri lāt′), *v.* **1.** to tell about; give an account of [*Relate* to us what you did.] **2.** to connect, as in thought or meaning [to *relate* two events]. **3.** to have to do with; be connected with [Proper diet *relates* to good health.] —**re·lat′ed,** *p.t.* & *p.p.;* **re·lat′ing,** *pr.p.*

re·lat·ed (ri lāt′id), *adj.* of the same family or kind [oranges, lemons, and *related* fruits; a man *related* to the king].

re·la·tion (ri lā'shən), *n.* **1.** a telling, as of a story; account. **2.** connection, as in thought or meaning [His remark had no *relation* to the discussion.] **3.** connection by being of the same family; kinship. **4.** a member of the same family; relative. **5. relations,** *pl.* the dealings between people, countries, etc. [labor *relations;* foreign *relations*]. —**in relation to** or **with relation to,** concerning; about. —**re·la'tion·ship,** *n.*

rel·a·tive (rel'ə tiv), *adj.* **1.** having meaning only as related to something ["Cold" is a *relative* term.] **2.** as compared with something else; comparative [the *relative* importance of an idea.] **3.** having to do with; about [Is your question *relative* to this subject?] **4.** related each to the other [We ended in the same *relative* positions.] **5.** in grammar, referring to a person or thing mentioned or understood [In "the hat which you bought," "which" is a *relative* pronoun and "which you bought" is a *relative* clause.] —*n.* **1.** a relative word or thing. **2.** a person of the same family by origin or by marriage; relation. —**relative to, 1.** about; concerning. **2.** equal or similar to. —**rel'a·tive·ly,** *adv.*

rel·a·tiv·i·ty (rel'ə tiv'ə tē), *n.* **1.** the condition of being relative. **2.** a theory of the universe developed by Albert Einstein, dealing with the relationship of matter, energy, space, and time.

re·lax (ri laks'), *v.* **1.** to make or become less firm, tense, or strict; loosen up [The body *relaxes* in sleep. The guard never *relaxed* his watch.] **2.** to rest from work or effort [He *relaxes* by going fishing.] —**re'lax·a'tion,** *n.*

re·lay (rē'lā), *n.* **1.** a fresh group that takes over some work from another group; shift [The men worked in *relays* to finish the project on time.] **2.** a race in which each member of a team runs only a certain part of the whole distance: *its full name is* **relay race.** —*v.* (ri lā' or rē'lā), to get and pass on [to *relay* a message]. —**re·layed',** *p.t. & p.p.;* **re·lay'ing,** *pr.p.*

re-lay (rē lā'), *v.* to lay again [to *re-lay* a cable]. —**re-laid',** *p.t. & p.p.;* **re-lay'ing,** *pr.p.*

re·lease (ri lēs'), *v.* **1.** to set free [*Release* the bird from the cage. He was *released* from debt.] **2.** to let go; let loose [to *release* an arrow]. **3.** to allow to be shown, published, etc. [to *release* information to reporters]. —*n.* **1.** a setting free, as from prison, work, etc. **2.** a motion picture, news item, etc. released to the public. **3.** a giving up of a right, claim, etc.; also, the legal paper by which this is done. **4.** a device to release a catch, etc., as on a machine. —**re·leased',** *p.t. & p.p.;* **re·leas'ing,** *pr.p.*

rel·e·gate (rel'ə gāt), *v.* **1.** to put in a less important position [The manager of the team was *relegated* to the job of assistant coach.] **2.** to send away; banish; exile. **3.** to hand over; assign [He *relegated* the task to his assistant.] —**rel'e·gat·ed,** *p.t. & p.p.;* **rel'e·gat·ing,** *pr.p.*

re·lent (ri lent'), *v.* to become less harsh or stubborn; soften [Dad *relented* and let us go.]

re·lent·less (ri lent'lis), *adj.* **1.** not giving in; having no pity; harsh [a *relentless* foe]. **2.** going on without stopping; persistent [the *relentless* pounding of the waves on the beach].

rel·e·vant (rel'ə vənt), *adj.* having to do with the matter at hand; to the point [a *relevant* remark]. —**rel'e·vance** or **rel'e·van·cy,** *n.*

re·li·a·ble (ri lī'ə b'l), *adj.* that can be trusted; dependable [This barometer gives a *reliable* weather forecast.] —**re·li·a·bil·i·ty** (ri lī'ə bil'ə tē), *n.* —**re·li·a·bly,** *adv.*

re·li·ance (ri lī'əns), *n.* **1.** trust or confidence [Airplane travelers put complete *reliance* in the pilot.] **2.** a thing relied on.

re·li·ant (ri lī'ənt), *adj.* **1.** having or showing trust or confidence; depending. **2.** having or showing confidence in oneself; self-reliant.

rel·ic (rel'ik), *n.* **1.** a thing or part that remains from the past [This cannon is a *relic* of the Civil War.] **2.** something kept as sacred because it belonged to a saint.

re·lief (ri lēf'), *n.* **1.** a lessening of pain, discomfort, worry, etc. [This salve will give *relief* from itching.] **2.** anything that lessens pain, worry, etc. or gives a pleasing change [It's a *relief* to get out of that stuffy hall.] **3.** help given to poor people, to victims of a flood, etc. **4.** a rest from work or duty [Workers get a ten-minute *relief* every morning.] **5.** persons who bring such rest by taking over a post [The guard's *relief* arrived at midnight.] **6.** sculpture in which the figures stand out from a flat surface. —**in relief,** carved so as to stand out from a surface. —**on relief,** supported by payments from public funds, as when out of work.

relief
(*meaning 6*)

relief map, a map that shows the difference in height of hills, valleys, etc. by using special lines or colors, or by molding solid material.

re·lieve (ri lēv'), *v.* **1.** to make less or easier, as pain or worry [Cold water *relieves* a swelling.] **2.** to free from pain, worry, etc. [We were *relieved* when the danger passed.] **3.** to give or bring help to [to *relieve* a besieged city]. **4.** to set free from duty or work by replacing [The guard is *relieved* every four hours.] **5.** to bring a pleasant change to [a bare wall *relieved* by several pictures]. —**re·lieved',** *p.t. & p.p.;* **re·liev'ing,** *pr.p.*

re·li·gion (ri lij'ən), *n.* **1.** belief in, or the worship of, God or a group of gods. **2.** a particular system of belief or worship built around God, moral ideals, a philosophy of life, etc.

re·li·gious (ri lij'əs), *adj.* **1.** having or showing strong belief in a religion; devout; pious. **2.** having to do with religion [a *religious* service]. **3.** showing strict care or regard [paying *religious*

fat, āpe, cär, ten, ēven, hit, bīte, gō, hôrn, tool, book, up, fur;
get, joy, yet, chin, she, thin, *then;* zh = s in pleasure; ' as in able (ā'b'l);
ə = a in ago, e in agent, i in sanity, o in confess, u in focus.

attention to one's diet]. —*n.* a member of an order of monks, nuns, etc. —**re·li′gious·ly,** *adv.*

re·lin·quish (ri ling′kwish), *v.* to give up or let go, as a hold on something, a right or claim, etc. —**re·lin′quish·ment,** *n.*

rel·ish (rel′ish), *n.* **1.** a pleasing taste; appetizing flavor [Salt adds *relish* to the stew.] **2.** enjoyment; zest [He ate the pear with *relish*.] **3.** pickles, olives, etc. served with food, to add flavor. —*v.* to like or enjoy [to *relish* ice cream; to *relish* a joke].

re·luc·tant (ri luk′t'nt), *adj.* **1.** not wanting to do something; unwilling [He is *reluctant* to ask for help.] **2.** showing unwillingness [a *reluctant* agreement]. —**re·luc′tance,** *n.* —**re·luc′tant·ly,** *adv.*

re·ly (ri lī′), *v.* to trust or depend [You can *rely* on me to be on time.] —**re·lied′,** *p.t.* & *p.p.*; **re·ly′ing,** *pr.p.*

re·main (ri mān′), *v.* **1.** to stay while others go [He *remained* at home when they went in to town.] **2.** to be left over after a part is taken or destroyed [Only a few columns of the ancient temple *remain*.] **3.** to go on being; continue [He *remained* loyal to his friends.] **4.** to be left as not yet done, said, or taken care of [That *remains* to be seen.]

re·main·der (ri mān′dər), *n.* the part, number, etc. left over [I sold some of my books and gave the *remainder* away. When 3 is subtracted from 10 the *remainder* is 7.]

re·mains (ri mānz′), *n.pl.* **1.** what is left after part has been used, destroyed, etc. [the *remains* of last night's dinner]. **2.** a dead body.

re·make (rē māk′), *v.* to make again or in a new way [to *remake* a long coat into a jacket]. —**re·made′,** *p.t.* & *p.p.*; **re·mak′ing,** *pr.p.*

re·mand (ri mand′), *v.* to send back; especially, to send a prisoner back to jail to await trial.

re·mark (ri märk′), *v.* **1.** to say or comment; mention. **2.** to notice or observe [to *remark* a difference in quality]. —*n.* something said briefly; comment [an unkind *remark*].

re·mark·a·ble (ri mär′kə b'l), *adj.* worth noticing because it is very unusual [the *remarkable* strength of Samson]. —**re·mark′a·bly,** *adv.*

re·mar·ry (rē mar′ē), *v.* to marry again. —**re·mar′ried,** *p.t.* & *p.p.*; **re·mar′ry·ing,** *pr.p.* —**re·mar′riage,** *n.*

Rem·brandt (rem′brant), *n.* 1606–1669; Dutch painter of pictures.

re·me·di·a·ble (ri mē′di ə b'l), *adj.* that can be remedied, cured, or corrected.

re·me·di·al (rə mē′di əl), *adj.* that remedies, cures, or corrects [*remedial* treatment].

rem·e·dy (rem′ə dē), *n.* **1.** a medicine or treatment that cures, heals, or relieves [a *remedy* for sunburn]. **2.** anything that corrects a wrong or helps make things better [a *remedy* for unem-ployment]. —*v.* to cure, correct, make better, remedy a situation. —**rem′e·dies,** *pl.*lied, *p.t.* & *p.p.*; **rem′e·dy·ing,** *pr.p.*(ri mem′bər), *v.* **1.** to think ofenly *remembered* my first day at

school.] **2.** to bring back to mind by trying; recall [I just can't *remember* your name.] **3.** to be careful not to forget [*Remember* to look both ways before crossing.] **4.** to mention as sending greetings [*Remember* me to your family.] **5.** to keep in mind for a gift, inheritance, etc. [He always *remembers* me at Christmas.]

re·mem·brance (ri mem′brəns), *n.* **1.** the act of remembering; memory [He had no *remembrance* of what happened.] **2.** a souvenir or keepsake. **3. remembrances,** *pl.* greetings.

re·mind (ri mīnd′), *v.* to make remember or think of [*Remind* me to pay the gas bill.]

re·mind·er (ri mīn′dər), *n.* something that helps one remember.

rem·in·isce (rem ə nis′), *v.* to think, talk, or write about things in one's past. —**rem·in·isced′,** *p.t.* & *p.p.*; **rem·in·isc′ing,** *pr.p.*

rem·i·nis·cence (rem′ə nis′'ns), *n.* **1.** the act of remembering past experiences; recollection [The old soldier's eyes grew dim in *reminiscence*.] **2. reminiscences,** *pl.* a story telling about things remembered from one's past.

rem·i·nis·cent (rem′ə nis′'nt), *adj.* **1.** remembering past things [Old people often grow *reminiscent*.] **2.** causing one to remember [a perfume *reminiscent* of an old-fashioned garden]. —**rem′i·nis′cent·ly,** *adv.*

re·miss (ri mis′), *adj.* careless in doing one's work or duty; negligent [The waitress was *remiss* in forgetting our water.] —**re·miss′ness,** *n.*

re·mis·sion (ri mish′ən), *n.* **1.** forgiveness, as of a sin; pardon. **2.** a freeing or being freed from debt, tax, etc. **3.** a making or becoming less strong or active [the *remission* of a fever].

re·mit (ri mit′), *v.* **1.** to send in payment [*Remit* fifty cents in coin.] **2.** to make less or weaker; slacken [to keep working, without *remitting* one's efforts]. **3.** to forgive or pardon [to *remit* a sin]. **4.** to free someone from [to *remit* a prison sentence; to *remit* a debt]. —**re·mit′ted,** *p.t.* & *p.p.*; **re·mit′ting,** *pr.p.*

re·mit·tance (ri mit′'ns), *n.* **1.** money sent in payment. **2.** the sending of such money, as by mail.

rem·nant (rem′nənt), *n.* what is left over, as a piece of cloth at the end of a bolt.

re·mod·el (rē mäd′'l), *v.* to make over; rebuild [to *remodel* a kitchen]. —**re·mod′eled** or **re·mod′elled,** *p.t.* & *p.p.*; **re·mod′el·ing** or **re·mod′el·ling,** *pr.p.*

re·mon·strance (ri män′strəns), *n.* something said in objecting or complaining; protest.

re·mon·strate (ri män′strāt), *v.* to say or plead in objecting or protesting [Ella *remonstrated* with her naughty sister.] —**re·mon′strat·ed,** *p.t.* & *p.p.*; **re·mon′strat·ing,** *pr.p.*

re·morse (ri môrs′), *n.* a deep feeling of sorrow or guilt over a wrong one has done [Bill felt *remorse* at having lied to his father.] —**re·morse′ful,** *adj.* —**re·morse′less,** *adj.*

re·mote (ri mōt′), *adj.* **1.** far off or far away in space or time; distant [a *remote* valley in the Alps]. **2.** not closely related [a question *remote* from the subject; a *remote* cousin]. **3.** slight or faint [a *remote* chance]. —**re·mot′er,** *compar.;* **re·mot′est,** *superl.* —**re·mote′ly,** *adv.* —**re·mote′ness,** *n.*

re·mount (rē mount′), *v.* to mount again [to *remount* a horse]. —*n.* (rē′mount), a fresh horse to take the place of another.

re·mov·al (ri mōōv′'l), *n.* **1.** a taking away or being taken away. **2.** a dismissing or being dismissed [his *removal* from office]. **3.** the act of moving [the *removal* of a store to a new location].

re·move (ri mōōv′), *v.* **1.** to move to another place; take away or take off [*Remove* the rugs so we can dance. They *removed* their coats.] **2.** to put out from an office or position; dismiss. **3.** to get rid of [to *remove* a stain]. —*n.* a step, or short distance [a remark that was only one *remove* from an insult]. —**re·moved′,** *p.t. & p.p.;* **re·mov′ing,** *pr.p.* —**re·mov′a·ble,** *adj.* —**re·mov′er,** *n.*

re·mu·ner·ate (ri myōō′nə rāt), *v.* to pay for work done, a loss suffered, etc.; reward [You will be *remunerated* for your kindness.] —**re·mu′ner·at·ed,** *p.t. & p.p.;* **re·mu′ner·at·ing,** *pr.p.* —**re·mu·ner·a′tion,** *n.*

re·mu·ner·a·tive (ri myōō′nə rə tiv), *adj.* giving profit or reward [a *remunerative* business].

Re·mus (rē′məs), *n.* see **Romulus.**

Ren·ais·sance (ren ə säns′), *n.* **1.** the great rebirth of art, literature, and learning in Europe in the 14th, 15th, and 16th centuries. **2. renaissance,** any rebirth or revival like this.

re·name (rē nām′), *v.* to give a new or different name to [Siam was *renamed* Thailand.] —**re·named′,** *p.t. & p.p.;* **re·nam′ing,** *pr.p.*

re·nas·cence (ri nas′'ns *or* ri nā′s′ns), *n.* **1.** a rebirth or revival [a *renascence* of interest in folk songs]. **2. Renascence,** the Renaissance. —**re·nas′cent,** *adj.*

rend (rend), *v.* to tear, split, or pull apart with great force [The tree was *rent* by lightning.] —**rent,** *p.t. & p.p.;* **rend′ing,** *pr.p.*

rend·er (ren′dər), *v.* **1.** to give or present for someone to consider [to *render* a bill; to *render* an account of one's actions]. **2.** to give up; surrender [to *render* up a city to the enemy]. **3.** to give in return [to *render* good for evil]. **4.** to give or pay as something owed [to *render* thanks]. **5.** to cause to be; make [to *render* a contract invalid]. **6.** to do or perform [to *render* first aid; to *render* a tune on the piano]. **7.** to translate [to *render* a Spanish song into English]. **8.** to melt down, as fat.

ren·dez·vous (rän′də vōō), *n.* **1.** a meeting place [The ice-cream shop is our favorite *rendezvous.*] **2.** a place where troops, ships, etc. meet for battle maneuvers. **3.** an agreement to meet at a certain time and place. **4.** the meeting itself. —*v.* to come together at a rendezvous. —**ren·dez·vous** (rän′də vōōz), *pl.* —**ren·dez·voused** (rän′də vōōd), *p.t. & p.p.;* **ren·dez·vous·ing** (rän′də vōō ing), *pr.p.*

ren·di·tion (ren dish′ən), *n.* a rendering, as of a piece of music, a part in a play, etc.

ren·e·gade (ren′ə gād), *n.* a person who gives up his religion, political party, etc. and goes over to the opposite side; traitor.

re·nege (ri nig′), *v.* **1.** to break the rules in a card game by playing a card of the wrong suit. **2.** to break a promise: *used only in everyday talk.* —**re·neged′,** *p.t. & p.p.;* **re·neg′ing,** *pr.p.*

re·new (ri nōō′ *or* ri nyōō′), *v.* **1.** to make new or fresh again; restore [*Renew* your old car by painting it.] **2.** to begin again; start again after a break [The enemy *renewed* its attack.] **3.** to put in a fresh supply of [to *renew* provisions]. **4.** to give or get again for a new period of time [to *renew* a subscription]. —**re·new′al,** *n.*

ren·net (ren′it), *n.* a substance got from the stomach of a calf, etc., used to curdle milk, as in making cheese.

Re·no (rē′nō), *n.* a city in western Nevada.

re·nounce (ri nouns′), *v.* **1.** to give up, as a claim or right [The king *renounced* the throne.] **2.** to refuse to have anything more to do with; disown [He *renounced* his son.] —**re·nounced′,** *p.t. & p.p.;* **re·nounc′ing,** *pr.p.*

ren·o·vate (ren′ə vāt), *v.* to make new or like new; repair; restore [to *renovate* a sofa]. —**ren′o·vat·ed,** *p.t. & p.p.;* **ren′o·vat·ing,** *pr.p.* —**ren′o·va′tion,** *n.*

re·nown (ri noun′), *n.* fame. —**re·nowned′,** *adj.*

rent (rent), *n.* money paid at regular times for the use of a house, office, land, etc. —*v.* **1.** to get or give the use of a house, land, automobile, etc. in return for the regular payment of money. **2.** to be let for rent [This room *rents* for $7 a week.] —**for rent,** that may be rented. —**rent′er,** *n.*

rent (rent), past tense and past participle of **rend.** —*adj.* torn or split. —*n.* a tear, as in cloth; split.

rent·al (ren′t'l), *n.* **1.** an amount paid as rent. **2.** a house, automobile, etc. for rent. —*adj.* of or for rent.

re·nun·ci·a·tion (ri nun′si ā′shən), *n.* the act of renouncing a right, claim, etc.

re·or·gan·ize (rē ôr′gə nīz), *v.* to organize again or in a new way [to *reorganize* a company]. —**re·or′gan·ized,** *p.t. & p.p.;* **re·or′gan·iz·ing,** *pr.p.* —**re′or·gan·i·za′tion,** *n.*

Rep., abbreviation for **Representative** or **Republican.**

re·paid (ri pād′), past tense and past participle of **repay.**

re·pair (ri per′), *v.* **1.** to put into good condition again; fix; mend [to *repair* a broken toy]. **2.** to set right; correct [to *repair* a mistake; to *repair* an injustice]. —*n.* **1.** the act of repairing. **2.** *usually* **repairs,** *pl.* work done in repairing [to make *repairs* on a house]. **3.** the condition of being fit for use [The car was kept in good *repair.*] —**re·pair′a·ble,** *adj.*

---

fat,   āpe,   cär,   ten,   ēven,   hit,   bīte,   gō,   hôrn,   tōōl,   book,   up,   fũr;
get,   joy,   yet,   chin,   she,   thin,   *th*en;   zh = s in pleasure;   ′ as in able (ā′b'l);
     ə = a in ago,   e in agent,   i in sanity,   o in confess,   u in focus.

re·pair (ri per′), *v.* to go [After class, they *repaired* to the library.]

re·pair·man (ri per′mən), *n.* a man whose work is repairing things. —**re·pair′men**, *pl.*

rep·a·ra·tion (rep′ə rā′shən), *n.* 1. a making up for a wrong or injury. 2. something given or done to make up for damage done, especially by a defeated nation after a war.

rep·ar·tee (rep ər tē′), *n.* 1. a quick, witty reply. 2. skill in making quick, witty replies.

re·past (ri past′), *n.* a meal; food and drink.

re·pa·tri·ate (rē pā′tri āt), *v.* to send or bring back to one's native country [to *repatriate* prisoners of war]. —**re·pa′tri·at·ed**, *p.t.* & *p.p.*; **re·pa′tri·at·ing**, *pr.p.* —**re·pa·tri·a′-tion**, *n.*

re·pay (ri pā′), *v.* 1. to pay back [to *repay* a loan]. 2. to do or give something to someone in return for some favor, service, etc. received [to *repay* a kindness]. —**re·paid′**, *p.t.* & *p.p.*; **re·pay′ing**, *pr.p.* —**re·pay′ment**, *n.*

re·peal (ri pēl′), *v.* to do away with; put an end to; cancel [to *repeal* a law]. —*n.* the act of repealing.

re·peat (ri pēt′), *v.* 1. to say again [Will you *repeat* that question?] 2. to say or recite something learned by heart [to *repeat* a poem]. 3. to tell to others [to *repeat* a secret]. 4. to do or perform again [to *repeat* a success]. —*n.* 1. the act of repeating. 2. something repeated, as a part of a musical piece. —**repeat oneself**, to say again what one has already said.

re·peat·ed (ri pēt′id), *adj.* said, made, or done again or often [*repeated* warnings]. —**re·peat′-ed·ly**, *adv.*

re·pel (ri pel′), *v.* 1. to drive back [to *repel* an attack]. 2. to hold off; refuse [She *repelled* his attentions.] 3. to make feel disgusted [The odor *repelled* me.] 4. to keep out; resist [This raincoat *repels* water.] —**re·pelled′**, *p.t.* & *p.p.*; **re·pel′ling**, *pr.p.*

re·pel·lent (ri pel′ənt), *adj.* that repels in any of various ways [a *repellent* smell; a water-*repellent* jacket]. —*n.* something that repels, as a spray that keeps insects away.

re·pent (ri pent′), *v.* 1. to feel sorry for having done wrong [He *repented* and returned the stolen bicycle.] 2. to feel regret over something done and change one's mind [He gave away his books, but later *repented* his kindness.]

re·pent·ance (ri pen′təns), *n.* a repenting, or feeling sorry, especially for doing wrong. —**re·pent′ant**, *adj.*

re·per·cus·sion (rē′pər kush′ən), *n.* 1. a springing or bounding back, as of a gun on being fired; recoil. 2. the bounding back of sound from a surface; echo. 3. a reaction to some happening, often an indirect one [His death had *repercussions* all over the world.]

rep·er·toire (rep′ər twär), *n.* all the plays, songs, or other pieces that a company, actor, singer, etc. is ready to perform.

rep·er·to·ry (rep′ər tôr′ē), *n.* same as **repertoire**. —**rep′er·to′ries**, *pl.*

rep·e·ti·tion (rep′ə tish′ən), *n.* 1. the act of repeating, or of saying or doing something again. 2. something repeated.

rep·e·ti·tious (rep′ə tish′əs), *adj.* repeating, especially over and over again in a boring way.

re·pine (ri pīn′), *v.* to feel or show that one is not happy or satisfied; complain; fret. —**re·pined′**, *p.t.* & *p.p.*; **re·pin′ing**, *pr.p.*

re·place (ri plās′), *v.* 1. to put back in the right place [*Replace* the tools on my bench when you are through.] 2. to take the place of [The automobile has *replaced* the horse.] 3. to put another in the place of one used, lost, broken, etc. [to *replace* a worn tire]. —**re·placed′**, *p.t.* & *p.p.*; **re·plac′ing**, *pr.p.*

re·place·ment (ri plās′mənt), *n.* 1. a replacing or being replaced. 2. a person or thing that replaces another.

re·plen·ish (ri plen′ish), *v.* to make full or complete again; furnish a new supply for [to *replenish* a coal pile]. —**re·plen′ish·ment**, *n.*

re·plete (ri plēt′), *adj.* supplied with plenty of something; filled or stuffed [a play *replete* with jokes]. —**re·ple′tion**, *n.*

rep·li·ca (rep′li kə), *n.* an exact copy, as of a painting, statue, etc.

re·ply (ri plī′), *v.* to answer by saying or doing something [to *reply* to a question; to *reply* to the enemy's fire with a counterattack]. —*n.* an answer. —**re·plied′**, *p.t.* & *p.p.*; **re·ply′ing**, *pr.p.* —**re·plies′**, *pl.*

re·port (ri pôrt′), *v.* 1. to tell about; give an account of [We will *report* on our field trip today.] 2. to tell as news [The papers *reported* little damage as a result of the storm.] 3. to tell about in a formal way; announce [The committee *reported* on arrangements for the dance.] 4. to tell a person in charge about a wrongdoer, a wrongdoing, etc. [to *report* a theft to the police]. 5. to be present at a certain place; appear [*Report* for work at 8 o'clock.] —*n.* 1. a telling or account of something, often one in written or printed form [a financial *report*]. 2. rumor or gossip [*Reports* of victory filled the air.] 3. reputation [a man of good *report*]. 4. the noise made by an explosion [the *report* of a gun].

re·port·er (ri pôr′tər), *n.* a person who reports, especially for a newspaper.

re·pose (ri pōz′), *v.* 1. to lie at rest [to *repose* on a bed]. 2. to put to rest [to *repose* oneself on a sofa]. —*n.* 1. rest or sleep. 2. calm; peace [*repose* of mind or manner]. —**re·posed′**, *p.t.* & *p.p.*; **re·pos′ing**, *pr.p.*

re·pos·i·to·ry (ri päz′ə tôr′ē), *n.* a box, room, etc. in which things may be put for safekeeping. —**re·pos′i·to′ries**, *pl.*

re·pos·sess (rē pə zes′), *v.* to get possession of again [The loan company *repossessed* his car.]

rep·re·hend (rep′ri hend′), *v.* 1. to scold or rebuke. 2. to find fault with; blame.

rep·re·hen·si·ble (rep′ri hen′sə b'l), *adj.* deserving to be scolded, blamed, etc. [a *reprehensible* act or person].

rep·re·sent (rep′ri zent′), *v.* 1. to stand for; be a symbol of [Three dots *represent* "S" in the Morse code.] 2. to show or picture [The artist *represented* America as a woman holding a torch.] **3.** to act in place of [My lawyer will *represent* me in court.] **4.** to act the part of, as in a play. **5.** to serve as or be like [A cave *represented* home to them.] **6.** to be an example of [He *represents* the youth of America.] **7.** to describe or set forth [He *represented* himself as an authority.]

rep·re·sen·ta·tion (rep′ri zen tā′shən), *n.* **1.** a representing or being represented. **2.** a likeness, picture, image, etc. **3. representations,** *pl.* a list of facts, charges, etc. that are meant to convince someone or to protest something. **4.** representatives as a group [our *representation* in Congress]. **—rep′re·sen·ta′tion·al,** *adj.*

rep·re·sent·a·tive (rep′ri zen′tə tiv), *adj.* **1.** representing; standing for [a sculptured figure *representative* of Justice]. **2.** based on representation of the people by delegates [*representative* government]. **3.** being an example; typical [This building is *representative* of modern architecture.] **—n. 1.** a typical example. **2.** a person chosen to act or speak for others [Judy is our *representative* on the student council.] **3. Representative,** a member of the lower house of Congress or of a State legislature.

re·press (ri pres′), *v.* **1.** to hold back [to *repress* a sigh]. **2.** to put or hold down; subdue [to *repress* an uprising]. **3.** to force out of one's mind [to *repress* sad thoughts]. **—re·pres′sion,** *n.*

re·pres·sive (ri pres′iv), *adj.* that represses or tends to repress [a *repressive* law].

re·prieve (ri prēv′), *v.* **1.** to delay the execution of a person sentenced to die. **2.** to give relief to for a while, as from trouble or pain. **—n.** a reprieving or being reprieved; a delay, as in carrying out an execution. **—re·prieved′,** *p.t. & p.p.;* **re·priev′ing,** *pr.p.*

rep·ri·mand (rep′rə mand), *n.* a harsh or formal scolding, as by a person in authority. **—v.** to scold harshly or in a formal way.

re·print (rē print′), *v.* to publish again, as a new printing of a book, etc. **—n.** (rē′print), something reprinted.

re·pris·al (ri prī′z'l), *n.* a harmful thing done to another to get even for some wrong done to one as by nations at war.

re·proach (ri prōch′), *v.* to find fault with; blame; rebuke [She *reproached* me for spending too much.] **—n. 1.** shame or a cause of shame [Slums are a *reproach* to a city.] **2.** a scolding or blaming; rebuke. **—re·proach′ful,** *adj.*

rep·ro·bate (rep′rə bāt), *n.* a very bad or dishonest person; scoundrel.

rep·ro·ba·tion (rep′rə bā′shən), *n.* the act of finding fault; strong blame or disapproval.

re·pro·duce (rē prə dōōs′ *or* rē prə dyōōs′), *v.* **1.** to produce others of one's kind; have offspring [Most animals *reproduce* by fertilizing eggs.] **2.** to make a copy or imitation of [Tape recorders *reproduce* sound.] **3.** to produce again. **—re·pro·duced′,** *p.t. & p.p.;* **re·pro·duc′ing,** *pr.p.*

re·pro·duc·tion (rē′prə duk′shən), *n.* **1.** a reproducing or being reproduced. **2.** a copy or imitation [a *reproduction* of an ancient statue]. **3.** the process by which animals and plants produce offspring. **—re′pro·duc′tive,** *adj.*

re·proof (ri prōōf′), *n.* the act of reproving or something said in reproving; blame; rebuke.

re·prove (ri prōōv′), *v.* to find fault with; scold [She *reproved* him for being so rude.] **—re·proved′,** *p.t. & p.p.;* **re·prov′ing,** *pr.p.*

rep·tile (rep′til *or* rep′til), *n.* **1.** a cold-blooded animal that has a backbone and crawls on its belly or creeps on very short legs. Snakes, lizards, alligators, and turtles are reptiles. **2.** a mean, sneaky person.

re·pub·lic (ri pub′lik), *n.* a state or nation in which the voters elect officials to make the laws and run the government.

re·pub·li·can (ri pub′li kən), *adj.* **1.** of or having to do with a republic [a *republican* form of government]. **2. Republican,** of or belonging to the Republican Party. **—n. 1.** a person who believes in and supports a republic. **2. Republican,** a member of the Republican Party.

Republican Party, one of the two major political parties in the United States.

re·pu·di·ate (ri pyōō′di āt), *v.* **1.** to refuse to accept or support; reject [to *repudiate* a belief]. **2.** to refuse to pay, as a debt. **—re·pu′di·at·ed,** *p.t. & p.p.;* **re·pu′di·at·ing,** *pr.p.* **—re·pu′di·a′tion,** *n.*

re·pug·nant (ri pug′nant), *adj.* **1.** that makes one feel great dislike or distaste; disgusting [a *repugnant* odor]. **2.** opposed [conduct *repugnant* to his character]. **—re·pug′nance,** *n.*

re·pulse (ri puls′), *v.* **1.** to drive back; repel, as an attack. **2.** to act toward in an unfriendly or impolite way [He *repulsed* his former friends.] **—n. 1.** a repulsing or being repulsed. **2.** a refusal or rebuff. **—re·pulsed′,** *p.t. & p.p.;* **re·puls′ing,** *pr.p.*

re·pul·sion (ri pul′shən), *n.* **1.** the act of repulsing. **2.** strong dislike or disgust [The idea filled her with *repulsion*.]

re·pul·sive (ri pul′siv), *adj.* causing strong dislike; disgusting [*repulsive* manners].

rep·u·ta·ble (rep′yoo tə b'l), *adj.* having a good reputation; respected [a *reputable* lawyer].

rep·u·ta·tion (rep′yoo tā′shən), *n.* **1.** what people generally think about the character of a person or thing [He has a *reputation* for being lazy.] **2.** good character in the opinion of others; good name [Gossip ruined his *reputation*.] **3.** fame [His *reputation* as a writer has grown.]

re·pute (ri pyōōt′), *n.* reputation. **—v.** to think or consider generally; suppose [She is *reputed* to be very learned.] **—re·put′ed,** *p.t. & p.p.;* **re·put′ing,** *pr.p.*

re·put·ed (ri pyōōt′id), *adj.* generally thought of as such; supposed [the *reputed* owner of the house]. **—re·put′ed·ly,** *adv.*

fat, āpe, cär, ten, ēven, hit, bīte, gō, hôrn, tōōl, book, up, fûr; get, joy, yet, chin, she, thin, *then;* zh = s in pleasure; ′ as in able (ā′b'l); ə = a in ago, e in agent, i in sanity, o in confess, u in focus.

re·quest (ri kwest/), v. **1.** to ask for [to *request* a hearing]. **2.** to ask to do something [She *requested* him to shut the door.] —n. **1.** the act of requesting [a *request* for help]. **2.** what is asked for [Will he grant our *request?*] **3.** the condition of being wanted or asked for; demand [Is this song much in *request?*] —**by request**, in answer to a request [He sang *by request.*]

Re·qui·em or **re·qui·em** (rek/wi əm or rē/-kwi əm), n. **1.** a Roman Catholic Mass for a dead person or persons. **2.** the music for such a Mass.

re·quire (ri kwīr/), v. **1.** to be in need of [Most plants *require* sunlight.] **2.** to order, command, or insist upon [He *required* us to leave.] —**re·quired**/, p.t. & p.p.; **re·quir**/**ing**, pr.p.

re·quire·ment (ri kwīr/mənt), n. **1.** the act of requiring. **2.** something needed or demanded [Vitamins are a *requirement* in the diet. Does he meet the *requirements* for the job?]

req·ui·site (rek/wə zit), adj. needed for some purpose; required [Has she the training *requisite* for a nurse?] —n. something needed [a tent and other *requisites* for camping].

req·ui·si·tion (rek/wə zish/ən), n. **1.** an order or request, especially in writing [Do you have a *requisition* for these supplies?] **2.** the condition of being demanded or put to use [Horses were in *requisition.*] **3.** the act of requiring. —v. to demand or take, as by authority [The general *requisitioned* trucks for the troops.]

re·quit·al (ri kwīt/'l), n. something given or done in return; repayment.

re·quite (ri kwīt/), v. **1.** to pay back; reward [How can I *requite* him for his help?] **2.** to give the same in return for [She *requited* his love.] —**re·quit**/**ed**, p.t. & p.p.; **re·quit**/**ing**, pr.p.

re·route (rē rōōt/ or rē rout/), v. to send by a different route. —**re·rout**/**ed**, p.t. & p.p.; **re·rout**/**ing**, pr.p.

re·scind (ri sind/), v. to do away with; set aside; cancel; repeal [to *rescind* a law].

res·cue (res/kyōō), v. to free or save from danger, evil, etc. [to *rescue* a man from a fire]. —n. the act of rescuing. —**res**/**cued**, p.t. & p.p.; **res**/**cu·ing**, pr.p. —**res**/**cu·er**, n.

re·search (ri sûrch/ or rē/sûrch), n. careful, patient study in order to find out facts and principles about some subject [*research* into new uses for atomic power]. —v. to do research.

re·sem·blance (ri zem/bləns), n. the condition or fact of being or looking alike; likeness.

re·sem·ble (ri zem/b'l), v. to be or look like [Rabbits *resemble* hares but are smaller.] —**re·sem**/**bled**, p.t. & p.p.; **re·sem**/**bling**, pr.p.

re·sent (ri zent/), v. to feel a bitter hurt and anger about [He *resented* being called a coward.] —**re·sent**/**ful**, adj. —**re·sent**/**ful·ly**, adv.

re·sent·ment (ri zent/mənt), n. a feeling of bitter hurt and anger at being insulted, slighted, etc. [his great *resentment* at being left out].

res·er·va·tion (rez/ər vā/shən), n. **1.** the act of reserving or keeping back. **2.** an objection or thought that one does not tell [He signed the pledge without *reservation.*] **3.** public land set aside for some special use [an Indian *reservation*]. **4.** an arrangement by which a hotel room, train ticket, etc. is set aside until the buyer calls for it; also, anything set aside in this way.

re·serve (ri zûrv/), v. **1.** to keep back or set apart for later or special use [to *reserve* part of one's pay for emergencies]. **2.** to have set aside for oneself [Call the theater and *reserve* two seats.] **3.** to keep back for oneself [I *reserve* the right to refuse.] —n. **1.** something kept back or stored up, as for later use [a bank's cash *reserve*]. **2.** a keeping back, or staying within limits [He told us the plain facts, without *reserve.*] **3.** the habit of keeping one's thoughts to oneself; silent manner. **4.** **reserves**, pl. troops held out of action so that they can be used later; also, units in the armed forces whose members go on in civil life, getting part-time training so that they can be called up for duty when needed. **5.** land set apart for a special purpose [a forest *reserve*]. —**in reserve**, reserved for later use or for some person. —**re·served**/, p.t. & p.p.; **re·serv**/**ing**, pr.p.

re·served (ri zûrvd/), adj. **1.** set apart for some purpose, person, etc. [*reserved* seats]. **2.** keeping one's thoughts to oneself.

res·er·voir (rez/ər vwär or rez/ər vôr), n. **1.** a place where something, especially water, is collected and stored for use. **2.** a container for a liquid [the ink *reservoir* of a fountain pen]. **3.** a large supply [a *reservoir* of workers].

re·side (ri zīd/), v. **1.** to make one's home; dwell; live [to *reside* in the suburbs]. **2.** to be present or fixed [The power to tax *resides* in Congress.] —**re·sid**/**ed**, p.t. & p.p.; **re·sid**/**ing**, pr.p.

res·i·dence (rez/i dəns), n. **1.** the place where one resides; home. **2.** the fact or time of residing or living in some place.

res·i·dent (rez/i dənt), n. a person who lives in a place, not just a visitor. —adj. living or staying in a place, as while working [a *resident* physician in a hospital].

res·i·den·tial (rez/i den/shəl), adj. **1.** used for residences, or homes, not businesses [a *residential* area]. **2.** of or having to do with residence [a *residential* requirement for voting].

re·sid·u·al (ri zij/ōō əl), adj. of or being a residue; left over; remaining.

res·i·due (rez/ə dōō or rez/ə dyōō), n. what is left after part is taken away, burned, dried up, etc.; remainder [a *residue* of ashes].

re·sign (ri zīn/), v. to give up one's office, position, membership, etc. [He *resigned* from the club.] —**resign oneself**, to accept something without complaining; submit.

res·ig·na·tion (rez/ig nā/shən), n. **1.** the act of resigning. **2.** a written statement that one is resigning. **3.** calm or patient acceptance of something without complaining [to endure trouble with *resignation*].

re·signed (ri zīnd/), adj. feeling or showing resignation; accepting what happens patiently.

re·sil·i·ent (ri zil/i ənt), adj. **1.** springing back into shape, position, etc.; elastic. **2.** getting back strength, spirits, etc. quickly; buoyant. **—re·sil′i·ence** or **re·sil′i·en·cy,** *n.*

res·in (rez′′n), *n.* **1.** a sticky substance that comes out of certain plants and trees, as the pines. Resins are used in medicines, varnish, etc. **2.** rosin. **—res′in·ous,** *adj.*

re·sist (ri zist′), *v.* **1.** to fight or work against; oppose [to *resist* an invasion]. **2.** to hold off successfully; withstand [Gold *resists* rust. Try to *resist* temptation.]

re·sist·ance (ri zis′təns), *n.* **1.** the act of resisting. **2.** the power to resist or withstand [His *resistance* to colds is low.] **3.** the opposing of one force or thing to another [the fabric's *resistance* to wear; the electrical *resistance* in a coil of wire to a current passing through it].

re·sist·ant (ri zis′tənt), *adj.* that offers resistance; resisting [fire-*resistant* paint].

re·sist·less (ri zist′lis), *adj.* that cannot be resisted; irresistible [a *resistless* force].

res·o·lute (rez′ə loot), *adj.* fixed or firm; determined; not yielding. **—res′o·lute·ly,** *adv.*

res·o·lu·tion (rez′ə loo′shən), *n.* **1.** the act of resolving something. **2.** something decided upon [his *resolution* to work harder]. **3.** a formal statement, as by a club or assembly, giving its opinion, decision, etc. **4.** the quality of being resolute; determination [Don't hesitate—act with *resolution*.] **5.** the act of solving; answer or solution [the *resolution* of a problem].

re·solve (ri zälv′), *v.* **1.** to decide; make up one's mind [I *resolved* to tell him.] **2.** to make clear; solve or explain, as a problem. **3.** to decide by vote [It was *resolved* at the meeting to raise our club dues.] **4.** to change; turn into [The conversation *resolved* itself into an argument.] **5.** to break up into separate parts [to *resolve* water into hydrogen and oxygen]. **—n.** fixed purpose; intention or the thing intended [his *resolve* to be a teacher]. **—re·solved′,** *p.t.* & *p.p.;* **re·solv′ing,** *pr.p.*

re·solved (ri zälvd′), *adj.* determined.

res·o·nance (rez′ə nəns), *n.* **1.** the quality of being resonant. **2.** the strong, rich effect of a sound when it is reflected or when it causes some object to vibrate [The body of a violin gives the tones *resonance*.]

res·o·nant (rez′ə nənt), *adj.* **1.** rich, full, or deep [the *resonant* sound of a tuba]. **2.** making sounds richer or fuller [a *resonant* room].

re·sort (ri zôrt′), *v.* **1.** to turn for help [She *resorted* to tears when her pleas failed.] **2.** to go, especially often [People *resort* to parks in the summer.] **—n. 1.** a place where many people go, as for a vacation [a winter *resort* for skiing]. **2.** the act of turning for help [a *resort* to threats]. **3.** a person or thing that one turns to for help [Pawning his watch was his last *resort*.]

re·sound (ri zound′), *v.* **1.** to echo or be filled with sound [The hall *resounded* with music.] **2.** to make a loud, echoing sound; to be echoed [Her shout *resounded* throughout the cave.]

re·source (ri sôrs′ *or* rē′sôrs), *n.* **1.** a supply of something to take care of a need [His main *resource* during illness was his savings. Oil is one of our most valuable natural *resources*.] **2.** skill in solving problems or getting out of trouble [It takes great *resource* to survive a shipwreck.]

re·source·ful (ri sôrs′fəl), *adj.* skillful at solving problems or getting out of trouble.

re·spect (ri spekt′), *v.* **1.** to feel or show honor for; think highly of; look up to [We *respect* learned people.] **2.** to be thoughtful about; have regard for [to *respect* another's rights]. **—n. 1.** a feeling of honor or polite regard [He has great *respect* for his father.] **2.** concern; consideration [She had *respect* for our feelings.] **3. respects,** *pl.* a polite showing of respect; regards [He paid his *respects* to the hostess.] **4.** a particular point or detail [In this *respect* he's wrong.] **5.** relation or reference [a new solution with *respect* to this problem].

re·spect·a·ble (ri spek′tə b'l), *adj.* **1.** having a good reputation; decent, proper, correct, etc. **2.** fairly good, large, etc.; good enough [a *respectable* score for an amateur player]. **—re·spect′a·bil′i·ty,** *n.*

re·spect·ful (ri spekt′fəl), *adj.* feeling or showing respect; polite. **—re·spect′ful·ly,** *adv.*

re·spect·ing (ri spek′ting), *prep.* about; concerning [I know little *respecting* the plan.]

re·spec·tive (ri spek′tiv), *adj.* of or for each separately [We went our *respective* ways.]

re·spec·tive·ly (ri spek′tiv lē), *adv.* in regard to each in the order named [The first and second prizes went to Tim and Ina, *respectively*.]

res·pi·ra·tion (res′pə rā′shən), *n.* **1.** the act or process of breathing. **2.** the process by which a plant or animal takes in oxygen from the air, water, etc. and gives off carbon dioxide, etc.

res·pi·ra·tor (res′pə rā′tər), *n.* a device for helping one to breathe, as in giving artificial respiration.

res·pi·ra·to·ry (res′pər ə tôr′ē *or* ri spir′ə tôr′ē), *adj.* having to do with breathing.

re·spire (ri spir′), *v.* to breathe. **—re·spired′,** *p.t.* & *p.p.;* **re·spir′ing,** *pr.p.*

res·pite (res′pit), *n.* **1.** a period of relief or rest, as from pain, work, etc.; a pause [The men kept digging without *respite*.] **2.** a delay or postponement, especially of an execution.

re·splend·ent (ri splen′dənt), *adj.* shining brightly; dazzling. **—re·splend′ence,** *n.*

re·spond (ri spänd′), *v.* **1.** to answer; reply [He didn't *respond* to my question.] **2.** to act as if in answer; react [His infection hasn't *responded* to treatment.]

re·sponse (ri späns′), *n.* **1.** something said or done in answer; reply [We hailed the ship, but got no *response*. I came in *response* to your call.] **2.** words sung or spoken by the congregation or choir in answer to the clergyman during worship.

---

fat, āpe, cär, ten, ēven, hit, bīte, gō, hôrn, tool, book, up, fur; get, joy, yet, chin, she, thin, *th*en; zh = s in pleasure; ′ as in able (ā′b'l); ə = a in ago, e in agent, i in sanity, o in confess, u in focus.

re·spon·si·bil·i·ty (ri spän′sə bil′ə tē), *n.* **1.** the condition of being responsible [He accepted *responsibility* for the error.] **2.** a thing or person that one is supposed to look after, manage, etc. [Her education will be my *responsibility*.] —**re·spon′si·bil′i·ties,** *pl.*

re·spon·si·ble (ri spän′sə b'l), *adj.* **1.** supposed or expected to take care of something or do something [Harry is *responsible* for mowing the lawn.] **2.** that must get the credit or blame [Who was *responsible* for the accident?] **3.** having to do with important duties [a *responsible* job]. **4.** that can be trusted or depended upon; reliable [a *responsible* person].

re·spon·sive (ri spän′siv), *adj.* **1.** quick to respond; reacting quickly and easily, as to a suggestion [Actors appreciate a *responsive* audience.] **2.** containing responses [a *responsive* prayer]. **3.** answering [a *responsive* nod].

rest (rest), *n.* **1.** the act or period of taking one's ease after working or being active, as by sleeping, keeping still, etc. **2.** freedom from worry, trouble, pain, etc.; peace. **3.** the condition of being

rests (in music)

still, or not moving [His golf ball came to *rest* near the hole.] **4.** a device used to hold something up; a stand, as for a camera. **5.** a pause between musical notes; also, a symbol for such a pause. **6.** a resting place or shelter, as for travelers. —*v.* **1.** to take one's ease and become refreshed, as by sleeping, keeping still, etc. **2.** to give rest to; refresh with rest [He *rested* his horse.] **3.** to support or be supported; lie or lay; lean [*Rest* your head on the pillow. The hoe *rested* against a tree.] **4.** to be at ease; have peace of mind [He couldn't *rest* until he found it.] **5.** to be dead [to *rest* in one's grave]. **6.** to be or become still or quiet [Let the matter *rest*.] **7.** to be or lie [The fault *rests* with him.] **8.** to be fixed [His eyes *rested* on the picture.] **9.** to depend; rely [Success often *rests* on luck.] —**lay to rest,** to bury.

rest (rest), *n.* **1.** the part left over [Eat what you want and save the *rest* for later.] **2.** those that are left; the others: *used with a plural verb* [Some of you take this path; the *rest* follow me.] —*v.* to go on being [*Rest* assured that I'll be there.]

re·state (rē stāt′), *v.* to state again, especially in a new way [He *restated* the question as a riddle.] —**re·stat′ed,** *p.t. & p.p.;* **re·stat′ing,** *pr.p.* —**re·state′ment,** *n.*

res·tau·rant (res′tə rənt *or* res′tə ränt), *n.* a place where meals can be bought and eaten.

rest·ful (rest′fəl), *adj.* **1.** full of rest or letting one rest [a *restful* vacation]. **2.** quiet; peaceful [*restful* music].

res·ti·tu·tion (res′tə tōō′shən *or* res′tə tyōō′shən), *n.* the act of giving back or paying for what has been lost, taken away, damaged, etc. [The thief made *restitution* of the stolen goods.]

res·tive (res′tiv), *adj.* **1.** hard to control; unruly [a *restive* mob]. **2.** restless; nervous.

rest·less (rest′lis), *adj.* **1.** seldom at rest or quiet; unable or unwilling to rest [the *restless* winds; a *restless* child]. **2.** without rest; disturbed or disturbing [a *restless* sleep]. —**rest′less·ly,** *adv.* —**rest′less·ness,** *n.*

res·to·ra·tion (res′tə rā′shən), *n.* **1.** a restoring or being restored. **2.** something restored, as by rebuilding [Part of this old fort is a *restoration*.]

re·stor·a·tive (ri stôr′ə tiv), *adj.* able to restore health, strength, etc. [a *restorative* medicine]. —*n.* something that is restorative.

re·store (ri stôr′), *v.* **1.** to give back [He *restored* the lost dog to its owner.] **2.** to bring back to an earlier or normal condition, as by rebuilding [to *restore* an old house; to *restore* one's health]. **3.** to put back in a place, rank, etc. [to *restore* a king to power]. —**re·stored′,** *p.t. & p.p.;* **re·stor′ing,** *pr.p.* —**re·stor′er,** *n.*

re·strain (ri strān′), *v.* to hold back; keep under control; check [*Restrain* your temper.]

re·straint (ri strānt′), *n.* **1.** a restraining or being restrained [no *restraint* of action; kept in *restraint*]. **2.** something that restrains [The reins on a horse are used as a *restraint*.] **3.** control of oneself or one's feelings; reserve [It takes *restraint* to be calm in a crisis.]

re·strict (ri strikt′), *v.* to keep within certain limits; confine; limit [The use of the pool is *restricted* to members.] —**re·strict′ed,** *adj.*

re·stric·tion (ri strik′shən), *n.* **1.** a restricting or being restricted. **2.** something that restricts, as a rule or condition [to place *restrictions* on the sale of drugs].

re·stric·tive (ri strik′tiv), *adj.* **1.** that restricts; limiting [*restrictive* laws]. **2.** describing a clause, phrase, or word that is necessary to the meaning of a sentence and that is not set off by commas. Example: The man *who warned us* is here.

rest-room (rest′rōōm), *n.* a room in a public building, containing toilets and washbowls; lavatory: also **rest room.**

re·sult (ri zult′), *v.* to happen because of something else; follow as an outcome [Floods may *result* from heavy rains.] —*n.* **1.** anything caused by something else; effect; outcome [His skill is a *result* of practice.] **2.** the answer to a problem in mathematics. —**result in,** to have as a result; end in [The game *resulted in* a tie.]

re·sult·ant (ri zul′t'nt), *adj.* resulting; coming as a result [war and its *resultant* agony]. —*n.* a result.

re·sume (ri zōōm′ *or* ri zyōōm′), *v.* **1.** to take or occupy again [We *resumed* our seats after the intermission.] **2.** to begin again; continue [The game will be *resumed* when the rain stops.] —**re·sumed′,** *p.t. & p.p.;* **re·sum′ing,** *pr.p.*

ré·su·mé (rā zoo mā′ *or* rez′yoo mā), *n.* a short account of the main points; summary.

re·sump·tion (ri zump′shən), *n.* the act of resuming [*resumption* of classes after vacation].

res·ur·rect (rez ə rekt′), *v.* **1.** to bring back to life. **2.** to bring back into use [to *resurrect* an old custom].

res·ur·rec·tion (rez′ə rek′shən), *n.* **1.** a rising from the dead, or coming back to life. **2.** a

coming back into use; revival. —**the Resurrection,** the rising of Jesus from the dead.

re·sus·ci·tate (ri sus′ə tāt), *v.* to bring or
come back to life or consciousness; revive [The
fireman *resuscitated* the man overcome by smoke.]
—**re·sus′ci·tat·ed,** *p.t. & p.p.;* **re·sus′ci·tat·
ing,** *pr.p.* —**re·sus′ci·ta′tion,** *n.*

re·tail (rē′tāl), *n.* the sale of goods in small
amounts to actual users, not to those who will
resell them. —*adj.* of or having to do with such
sale of goods [a *retail* price; a *retail* store]. —*v.*
1. to sell or be sold in small amounts. **2.** (ri tāl′),
to repeat to others [to *retail* gossip]. —**re′-
tail·er,** *n.*

re·tain (ri tān′), *v.* **1.** to keep or hold [He
retained a firm grip on the rope. This oven *retains*
heat well.] **2.** to keep in mind; remember [He
retains what he reads.] **3.** to hire by paying a fee
to [to *retain* a lawyer].

re·tain·er (ri tān′ər), *n.* **1.** a fee paid to a
lawyer, etc. at the time he is hired. **2.** a servant
to a rich person or family. **3.** a person or thing
that retains.

re·take (rē tāk′), *v.* **1.** to take again; take back
or recapture. **2.** to photograph again. —*n.*
(rē′tāk), a scene in a movie, etc. photographed
again. *For principal parts see* **take.**

re·tal·i·ate (ri tal′i āt), *v.* to harm or do wrong
in return for harm or wrong done [If the bear is
hurt, he will *retaliate.*] —**re·tal′i·at·ed,** *p.t. &
p.p.;* **re·tal′i·at·ing,** *pr.p.* —**re·tal′i·a′tion,** *n.*

re·tal·i·a·to·ry (ri tal′i ə tôr′ē), *adj.* retaliating;
paying back one wrong with another.

re·tard (ri tärd′), *v.* to slow down or delay
[to *retard* a musical phrase; to *retard* development].
—**re·tar·da·tion** (rē′tär dā′shən), *n.*

retch (rech), *v.* to undergo the straining action
of vomiting, especially without bringing anything
up.

re·ten·tion (ri ten′shən), *n.* **1.** a retaining or
being retained. **2.** the ability to retain.

re·ten·tive (ri ten′tiv), *adj.* able to hold, keep,
or remember [a *retentive* mind].

ret·i·cent (ret′ə s'nt), *adj.* not saying much,
especially about one's thoughts. —**ret′i·
cence,** *n.*

ret·i·na (ret′'n ə), *n.* the part at the back of
the eyeball, made up of special cells that react to
light. The image picked up by the lens of the eye
is formed on the retina. *See the picture for* **eye.**

ret·i·nue (ret′'n ○○ *or* ret′i ny○○), *n.* the
servants or followers of an important person.

re·tire (ri tīr′), *v.* **1.** to give up one's work,
business, or career, especially because of age
[Dr. Held is 72 but refuses to *retire.*] **2.** to remove
from a position or office [to *retire* a general].
3. to go where it is quieter and more private
[He *retired* to the library after dinner.] **4.** to go
to bed. **5.** to retreat, as in battle. **6.** to take out
of circulation, as bonds. —**re·tired′,** *p.t. &
p.p.;* **re·tir′ing,** *pr.p.* —**re·tire′ment,** *n.*

re·tired (ri tīrd′), *adj.* **1.** that has given up
one's work, business, or career, especially because
of age [a *retired* fireman]. **2.** hidden or private
[a *retired* cabin].

re·tir·ing (ri tīr′ing), *adj.* drawing back from
being with others or attracting attention; shy.

re·tool (rē tool′), *v.* to change the machinery
of a factory for making a different product.

re·tort (ri tôrt′), *v.* to answer back, especially
in a sharp, quick, or clever way. —*n.* a sharp or
clever answer.

re·tort (ri tôrt′), *n.* a container with a long
tube, in which substances
are distilled or decom-
posed by heat.

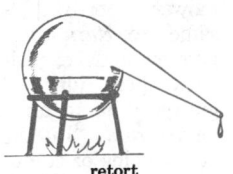

retort

re·touch (rē tuch′), *v.*
to change some of the
details, as in a painting
or photograph, in order
to make it look better.

re·trace (ri trās′), *v.* **1.** to go over again back
to the start [to *retrace* one's steps]. **2.** to trace
again the story of, from the beginning. **3.** (rē-
trās′), to trace over again, as the lines in a drawing: also written **re-trace.** —**re·traced′,** *p.t.
& p.p.;* **re·trac′ing,** *pr.p.*

re·tract (ri trakt′), *v.* **1.** to draw back or draw
in [The turtle can *retract* his head into his shell.]
2. to take back a statement, promise, offer, etc.
—**re·trac′tion,** *n.*

re·treat (ri trēt′), *v.* to go back; withdraw,
as because of attack [The bear *retreated* from the
honey when the bees began to swarm.] —*n.* **1.**
act of retreating [The enemy was in full *retreat.*]
2. a signal for a retreat [The bugle sounded the
retreat.] **3.** a safe, quiet place [the cabin that was
his *retreat* in the woods]. —**beat a retreat,** to
retreat in a hurry.

re·trench (ri trench′), *v.* to cut down; reduce,
as expenses. —**re·trench′ment,** *n.*

ret·ri·bu·tion (ret′rə byoo′shən), *n.* punishment that one deserves for a wrong he has done.
—**re·trib·u·tive** (ri trib′yoo tiv), *adj.*

re·trieve (ri trēv′), *v.* **1.** to get back; recover
[to *retrieve* a kite from a tree]. **2.** to find and
bring back [The spaniel *retrieved* the wounded
duck.] **3.** to win, find, or earn again; restore
[to *retrieve* a fortune; to *retrieve* one's temper].
4. to set right or make good, as a loss or error.
—**re·trieved′,** *p.t. & p.p.;* **re·triev′ing,** *pr.p.*

re·triev·er (ri trēv′ər), *n.* a dog that is trained
to retrieve game in hunting.

ret·ro·ac·tive (ret′rō ak′tiv), *adj.* acting upon
things that are already past [Your new salary
will be *retroactive* to last month.]

ret·ro·grade (ret′rə grād), *adj.* **1.** moving
backward. **2.** going back to an earlier or worse
condition.

ret·ro·gress (ret′rə gres), *v.* to move backward, especially into an earlier or worse condition.
—**ret′ro·gres′sion,** *n.*

---

fat,   āpe,   cär,   ten,   ēven,   hit,   bīte,   gō,   hôrn,   tool,   book,   up,   fŭr;
get,   joy,   yet,   chin,   she,   thin,   *th*en;   zh = s in pleasure;   ' as in able (ā′b'l);
ə = a in ago,   e in agent,   i in sanity,   o in confess,   u in focus.

ret·ro·rock·et (ret′rō räk′it), *n.* a small rocket on a spacecraft, that produces thrust in a direction opposite to the direction in which the spacecraft is flying, in order to reduce speed, as for landing.

ret·ro·spect (ret′rə spekt), *n.* the act of looking back on or thinking about the past [In *retrospect*, we decided that he had been right.] —**ret′ro·spec′tion,** *n.* —**ret′ro·spec′tive,** *adj.*

re·turn (ri tŭrn′), *v.* **1.** to go or come back [He *returned* home from his trip.] **2.** to bring, send, carry, or put back [I'll *return* your lawn mower tomorrow.] **3.** to pay back by doing the same [to *return* a visit; to *return* a favor]. **4.** to give or produce; yield, as a profit. **5.** to report back [The jury *returned* a verdict of "not guilty."] **6.** to answer; reply ["Never mind," he *returned*, "I'll do it myself."] —*n.* **1.** the act of going or coming back [the *return* of summer]. **2.** a bringing, sending, putting, or paying back [the *return* of a favor]. **3.** something returned. **4.** *often* **returns,** *pl.* an amount received as profit; yield. **5.** an official report; account [an income tax *return;* election *returns* from Hawaii]. —*adj.* **1.** of or for a return [a *return* ticket]. **2.** given, sent, or done in paying back [a *return* visit]. —**in return,** in exchange.

re·un·ion (rē yōōn′yən), *n.* the act of coming together again [a *reunion* of our former class].

re·u·nite (rē yoo nīt′), *v.* to bring or come together again; unite again [The States were *reunited* after the Civil War.] —**re·u·nit′ed,** *p.t.* & *p.p.;* **re·u·nit′ing,** *pr.p.*

Rev., abbreviation for **Reverend.** —**Revs.,** *pl.*

re·vamp (rē vamp′), *v.* to make over again; patch up [to *revamp* an old plot for a play].

re·veal (ri vēl′), *v.* **1.** to make known what was hidden or secret [The map *revealed* the spot where the treasure was buried.] **2.** to show [She took off her hat, *revealing* her golden hair.]

re·veil·le (rev′ə lē), *n.* a signal, usually on a bugle, calling soldiers or sailors to duty in the morning.

rev·el (rev′'l), *v.* **1.** to have fun in a noisy way; make merry. **2.** to take much pleasure; delight [He *reveled* in his new freedom.] —*n.* a time for reveling; merrymaking [holiday *revels*]. —**rev′eled** or **rev′elled,** *p.t.* & *p.p.;* **rev′el·ing** or **rev′el·ling,** *pr.p.* —**rev′el·er** or **rev′el·ler,** *n.*

rev·e·la·tion (rev′ə lā′shən), *n.* **1.** the act of revealing or making known [the *revelation* of a secret]. **2.** something revealed or made known, especially something that comes as a surprise [Her good cooking was a *revelation* to me.] **3. Revelation,** the last book of the New Testament.

rev·el·ry (rev′'l rē), *n.* the act of reveling; noisy merrymaking. —**rev′el·ries,** *pl.*

re·venge (ri venj′), *v.* to do harm or evil in return for a harm or evil received; get even for [Hamlet swore to *revenge* the murder of his father.] —*n.* **1.** the act of revenging; vengeance. **2.** a wanting to get even for some harm or evil. —**be revenged** or **revenge oneself,** to get even for some harm or evil. —**re·venged′,** *p.t.* & *p.p.;* **re·veng′ing,** *pr.p.* —**re·venge′ful,** *adj.*

rev·e·nue (rev′ə nōō or rev′ə nyōō), *n.* money got as rent, profit, etc.; income; especially, the money a government gets from taxes, duties, etc.

re·ver·ber·ate (ri vur′bə rāt), *v.* to bounce back, as sound; echo [His call *reverberated* in the cave.] —**re·ver′ber·at·ed,** *p.t.* & *p.p.;* **re·ver′ber·at·ing,** *pr.p.* —**re·ver′ber·a′tion,** *n.*

re·vere (ri vir′), *v.* to love and respect greatly [to *revere* the memory of one's grandparents]. —**re·vered′,** *p.t.* & *p.p.;* **re·ver′ing,** *pr.p.*

Re·vere, Paul (ri vir′), 1735–1818; American silversmith and patriot who rode at night to tell the colonists that British troops were coming.

rev·er·ence (rev′ər əns), *n.* **1.** great love and respect, as for something holy. **2. Reverence,** a title used in speaking to or of a clergyman: *no longer much used.* —*v.* to revere. —**rev′er·enced,** *p.t.* & *p.p.;* **rev′er·enc·ing,** *pr.p.*

rev·er·end (rev′ər ənd), *adj.* that deserves deep respect. **Reverend** is a title of respect used before the name of a clergyman.

rev·er·ent (rev′ər ənt), *adj.* feeling or showing reverence. —**rev′er·ent·ly,** *adv.*

rev·er·ie or **rev·er·y** (rev′ər ē), *n.* dreamy thinking, especially about pleasant things; daydreaming. —**rev′er·ies,** *pl.*

re·ver·sal (ri vur′s'l), *n.* a reversing or being reversed [the *reversal* of a decision].

re·verse (ri vurs′), *adj.* **1.** turned backward or upside down; opposite in position or direction [the *reverse* side of fabric; in *reverse* order]. **2.** causing something to move backward [a *reverse* gear]. —*n.* **1.** the opposite or contrary [He said "yes" but meant just the *reverse*.] **2.** the back side, as of a coin or rug. **3.** a change from good luck to bad; misfortune [Financial *reverses* ruined him.] **4.** a reverse gear [Shift into *reverse* and back out of the driveway.] —*v.* **1.** to turn backward, upside down, or inside out [*Reverse* the vest and wear the other side out.] **2.** to change so that it is opposite, or completely different [to *reverse* an opinion]. **3.** to do away with; revoke [The Supreme Court *reversed* the lower court's decision.] **4.** to go or make go in an opposite direction. —**re·versed′,** *p.t.* & *p.p.;* **re·vers′ing,** *pr.p.*

re·vers·i·ble (ri vur′sə b'l), *adj.* **1.** that can be reversed; made so that either side can be used as the outer side [a *reversible* raincoat]. **2.** that can reverse.

re·ver·sion (ri vur′zhən), *n.* the act of reverting; return to an earlier condition, owner, etc.

re·vert (ri vurt′), *v.* **1.** to go back to an earlier condition, way of acting, etc.; return [Without care, the lawn *reverted* to a field of weeds.] **2.** in law, to pass back to a former owner or his heirs.

reversible raincoat

re·view (ri vyōō′), *v.* **1.** to look at or study again [to *review* a subject before a test]. **2.** to think back on [He *reviewed* the events that led to their quarrel.] **3.** to inspect or examine in an official way [to *review* troops]. **4.** to tell what a book, play, etc. is about and give one's opinion of it. —*n.* **1.** the act of reviewing, or studying again, thinking back, etc. [a *review* of yesterday's lesson; a *review* of the week's events]. **2.** a talk or piece of writing in which a book, play, etc. is reviewed. **3.** an official inspection of soldiers, ships, etc. **4.** a revue.

re·view·er (ri vyoo′ər), *n.* a person who reviews books, plays, etc. as in a newspaper.

re·vile (ri vīl′), *v.* to say harsh or unkind things to or about; call bad names [The fisherman *reviled* the thieves who stole his nets.] —**re·viled′**, *p.t. & p.p.;* **re·vil′ing,** *pr.p.*

re·vise (ri vīz′), *v.* **1.** to change or amend [to *revise* one's opinion]. **2.** to read carefully and change where necessary in order to make better or bring up-to-date [to *revise* a history book]. —**re·vised′,** *p.t. & p.p.;* **re·vis′ing,** *pr.p.*

re·vi·sion (ri vizh′ən), *n.* **1.** the act or work of revising. **2.** something that has been revised [a *revision* of an earlier book].

re·viv·al (ri vī′v'l), *n.* **1.** the act of bringing or coming back to life, health, or activity. **2.** the act of bringing or coming back into use or popularity [a *revival* of a famous old play]. **3.** a meeting at which there is excited preaching for the purpose of stirring up religious feeling.

re·vive (ri vīv′), *v.* **1.** to bring or come back to life or consciousness [to *revive* a person who has fainted]. **2.** to bring or come back to a healthy, active condition [The warm bath *revived* him after the long journey.] **3.** to make or become popular again [to *revive* an old song]. —**re·vived′,** *p.t. & p.p.;* **re·viv′ing,** *pr.p.*

rev·o·ca·ble (rev′ə kə b'l), *adj.* that can be revoked.

rev·o·ca·tion (rev′ə kā′shən), *n.* the act of revoking; cancellation; repeal.

re·voke (ri vōk′), *v.* to put an end to, as a law, permit, etc.; cancel; repeal. —**re·voked′,** *p.t. & p.p.;* **re·vok′ing,** *pr.p.*

re·volt (ri vōlt′), *n.* **1.** a rebelling or rising up against the government; rebellion. **2.** any refusal to obey rules, customs, authority, etc. —*v.* **1.** to rebel or rise up against the government or other authority [The American Colonies *revolted* against England.] **2.** to disgust or be disgusted [The sight *revolted* her. His stomach *revolted* at the taste.] —**re·volt′ing,** *adj.*

rev·o·lu·tion (rev′ə loo′shən), *n.* **1.** overthrow of a government or a social system, with another taking its place [the American *Revolution;* the Industrial *Revolution*]. **2.** a complete change of any kind [The telephone caused a *revolution* in communication.] **3.** the act of revolving; movement in an orbit [the *revolution* of the moon around the earth]. **4.** a turning motion of a wheel, etc. around a center or axis; rotation. **5.** one complete turn [The wheel makes 100 *revolutions* per minute.]

rev·o·lu·tion·ar·y (rev′ə loo′shən er′ē), *adj.* **1.** of, in favor of, or causing a revolution, especially in a government. **2.** bringing about very great change [a *revolutionary* new way to make steel]. **3.** revolving or rotating. —*n.* a revolutionist. —**rev′o·lu′tion·ar′ies,** *pl.*

Revolutionary War, the war by which the American Colonies won their independence from England. It lasted from 1775 to 1783.

rev·o·lu·tion·ist (rev′ə loo′shən ist), *n.* a person who favors or takes part in a revolution.

rev·o·lu·tion·ize (rev′ə loo′shən īz), *v.* to make a complete change in [Automation has *revolutionized* industry.] —**rev′o·lu′tion·ized,** *p.t. & p.p.;* **rev′o·lu′tion·iz·ing,** *pr.p.*

re·volve (ri välv′), *v.* **1.** to move in an orbit or cycle [The earth *revolves* around the sun.] **2.** to turn around, as a wheel on its axis; rotate. **3.** to think about carefully, as a problem. —**re·volved′,** *p.t. & p.p.;* **re·volv′ing,** *pr.p.*

re·volv·er (ri väl′vər), *n.* a pistol with a revolving cylinder holding several bullets which can be fired without reloading.

revolving door, a door having several panels set upright around an axle. A person using the door turns it around by pushing on one of the panels.

revolver

re·vue (ri vyoo′), *n.* a musical show made up of songs, dances, and skits, often poking fun at recent events.

re·vul·sion (ri vul′shən), *n.* a sudden, strong change of feeling; especially, sudden disgust [filled with *revulsion* for the man she had loved].

re·ward (ri wôrd′), *n.* **1.** something given in return for something done, especially for something good [a hero's *reward* for bravery]. **2.** money offered, as for returning something lost. —*v.* to give a reward to or for.

re·word (rē wûrd′), *v.* to change the wording of; put into other words.

re·write (rē rīt′), *v.* to write again or in different words; revise [to *rewrite* a story]. *For principal parts see* **write.**

Rey·kja·vik (rā′kyä vēk), *n.* the capital of Iceland.

Reyn·ard (ren′ərd *or* rā′närd), *n.* a name for the fox in folk tales and poems.

rhap·so·dy (rap′sə dē), *n.* **1.** a speech or writing showing very great enthusiasm [She went into *rhapsodies* of delight over the gift.] **2.** a piece of music that has no fixed form and is full of feeling. —**rhap′so·dies,** *pl.* —**rhap·sod·i·cal** (rap säd′i k'l) *or* **rhap·sod′ic,** *adj.*

revolving door

---

fat, āpe, cär, ten, ēven, hit, bīte, gō, hôrn, tool, book, up, fûr; get, joy, yet, chin, she, thin, *th*en; zh = s in pleasure; ' as in able (ā′b'l) ə = a in ago, e in agent, i in sanity, o in confess, u in focus.

rhe·a (rē′ə), *n.* a large bird of South America that is like the ostrich, but smaller.

Rhen·ish (ren′ish), *adj.* of the Rhine River or the regions around it.

rhe·o·stat (rē′ə stat), *n.* a device for making an electric current stronger or weaker by changing the resistance in the circuit.

rhe·sus monkey (rē′səs), a small, brownish monkey of India, often used in medical experiments.

rhea (6 ft. high)

rhet·o·ric (ret′ə rik), *n.* **1.** the art of using words skillfully in speaking or writing. **2.** a book about this. **3.** showiness of language. —**rhe·tor·i·cal** (ri tôr′i k'l), *adj.* —**rhe·tor′i·cal·ly,** *adv.*

rhetorical question, a question asked only for effect, not because one expects an answer.

rhet·o·ri·cian (ret′ə rish′ən), *n.* **1.** a person skilled in rhetoric. **2.** a person who writes or speaks in a showy way.

rheum (rōōm), *n.* watery matter coming from the eyes, nose, etc., as in a cold. —**rheum′y,** *adj.*

rheu·mat·ic (rōō mat′ik), *adj.* **1.** of or caused by rheumatism [*rheumatic* pain]. **2.** having rheumatism. —*n.* a person who has rheumatism.

rheumatic fever, a disease in which there is fever, the joints ache and swell, and the heart valves sometimes become inflamed.

rheu·ma·tism (rōō′mə tiz'm), *n.* a general name for any disease in which the joints become stiff, sore, and swollen.

Rhine (rīn), *n.* a river flowing through Switzerland and Germany into the North Sea.

rhine·stone (rīn′stōn), *n.* an artificial gem of glass, etc., cut to look like a diamond.

rhi·no (rī′nō), *n.* a rhinoceros: *used only in everyday talk.* —**rhi′nos,** *pl.*

rhi·noc·er·os (rī näs′ər əs), *n.* a large animal with a thick skin, found in Africa and Asia. It has one or two horns on its snout.

rhinoceros (5½ ft. high at shoulder)

Rhode Island (rōd), a New England State of the United States: abbreviated **R.I.**

Rhodes (rōdz), *n.* an island in the Aegean Sea.

Rho·de·sia (rō dē′zhə), *n.* a country in southern Africa. —**Rho·de′sian,** *adj. & n.*

rho·do·den·dron (rō′də den′drən), *n.* a shrub or small tree, usually an evergreen, that bears flowers of pink, white, purple, etc.

Rhone or **Rhône** (rōn), *n.* a river flowing from Switzerland through France to the Mediterranean.

rhododendron flowers and leaves

rhu·barb (rōō′bärb), *n.* **1.** a plant with large leaves and thick sour stalks used as food: *see picture in next column.* **2.** the stalks, cooked as a sauce or baked in a pie. **3.** an argument: *slang in this meaning.*

rhyme (rīm), *n.* **1.** likeness of sounds at the ends of words or lines of verse. **2.** a word that has the same end sound as another ["Single" is a *rhyme* for "tingle."] **3.** poetry or a verse using such end sounds. —*v.* **1.** to have the same end sound; form a rhyme ["More" *rhymes* with "door."] **2.** to use as a rhyme [to *rhyme* "new" with "blue"]. **3.** to make verse, especially with rhymes. **4.** to have rhymes [Blank verse does not *rhyme.*] —**neither rhyme nor reason,** neither order nor sense. —**rhymed,** *p.t. & p.p.;* **rhym′ing,** *prp.* —**rhym′er,** *n.*

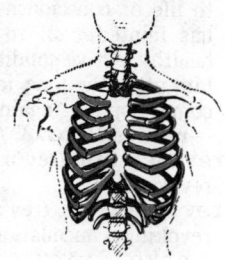
rhubarb

rhythm (rith′m), *n.* **1.** movement or flow in which the motions, sounds, etc. follow a regular pattern, with accents or beats coming at certain fixed times [the *rhythm* of the heart, of the waves, of dancing]. **2.** the form or pattern of this, as in music, speech, poetry, etc. [waltz *rhythm*].

rhyth·mi·cal (rith′mi k'l) or **rhyth·mic** (rith′mik), *adj.* of or having rhythm. —**rhyth′mi·cal·ly,** *adv.*

R.I., abbreviation for **Rhode Island.**

rib (rib), *n.* **1.** any of the curved bones that are attached to the backbone and reach around to form the chest. The human body has twelve pairs of such bones. **2.** a raised ridge in cloth or knitted material. **3.** a piece like a rib, used to form a frame of some kind [the *ribs* of an umbrella]. **4.** a large vein in a leaf. —*v.* **1.** to strengthen or form with ribs, or mark with ridges. **2.** to tease: *a slang meaning.* —**ribbed,** *p.t. & p.p.;* **rib′bing,** *prp.*

human ribs

rib·ald (rib′əld), *adj.* joking or funny in a coarse or vulgar way.

rib·ald·ry (rib′əld rē), *n.* ribald language.

rib·bon (rib′ən), *n.* **1.** a narrow strip of silk, velvet, rayon, etc., for tying things or for decoration. **2.** anything like such a strip [a *ribbon* of smoke]. **3.** ribbons, *pl.* torn strips or shreds; tatters [His shirt was in *ribbons.*] **4.** a narrow strip of cloth with ink on it, for use on a typewriter. —*v.* to decorate with a ribbon or ribbons.

rice (rīs), *n.* **1.** the small, starchy seeds or grains of a plant grown in warm climates. Rice is one of the main foods of China, Japan, India, etc. **2.** this plant, grown in flooded fields. —*v.* to cut into tiny bits like rice [to *rice* potatoes]. —**riced,** *p.t. & p.p.;* **ric′ing,** *prp.*

rice·bird (rīs′bûrd), *n.* the bobolink: *a name used in the South.*

rice plant

rich (rich), *adj.* **1.** having wealth; owning much money or property; wealthy. **2.** having much of something; well supplied [Oranges are *rich* in vitamin C.] **3.** worth much; valuable [a *rich* prize]. **4.** full of fats, or fats and sugar [*rich* foods]. **5.** full, deep, and brilliant [a *rich* voice; a *rich* blue color]. **6.** producing much [*rich* soil]. **7.** very funny or amusing: *used only in everyday talk* [a *rich* joke]. —**the rich,** wealthy people as a group. —**rich′ly,** *adv.* —**rich′ness,** *n.*

Rich·ard I (rich′ərd), 1157–1199; king of England from 1189 to 1199: called **Richard the Lion-Hearted.**

rich·es (rich′iz), *n.pl.* much money, property, etc.; wealth.

Rich·mond (rich′mənd), *n.* the capital of Virginia.

rick (rik), *n.* a stack of hay, straw, etc., especially one covered to protect it from rain.

rick·ets (rik′its), *n.* a children's disease in which the bones become soft, often bent. It is caused by a lack of vitamin D or sunlight.

rick·et·y (rik′i tē), *adj.* **1.** having rickets. **2.** weak and shaky; not firm [a *rickety* old barn].

rick·shaw or **rick·sha** (rik′shô), *n.* same as **jinrikisha.**

ric·o·chet (rik ə shā′), *n.* a quick bouncing or skipping, as of a flat stone thrown along the surface of a pond. —*v.* to bounce or skip in this way; rebound [The bullet *ricocheted* from the rock.] —**ric·o·cheted** (rik ə shād′), *p.t.* & *p.p.;* **ric·o·chet·ing** (rik ə shā′ing), *pr.p.*

rid (rid), *v.* to clear or free of something not wanted [to *rid* a garden of weeds]. —**be rid of,** to be made free from. —**get rid of, 1.** to get free from. **2.** to do away with. —**rid** or **rid′ded,** *p.t.* & *p.p.;* **rid′ding,** *pr.p.*

rid·dance (rid′'ns), *n.* a ridding or being rid of something not wanted. —**good riddance!** I am glad to be rid of this!

rid·den (rid′'n), past participle of **ride.** —*adj.* controlled or ruled over [*ridden* by fear].

rid·dle (rid′'l), *n.* **1.** a puzzle in the form of a question or statement with a tricky meaning or answer that is hard to guess. Example: "What has four wheels and flies?" "A garbage wagon." **2.** any person or thing that is hard to understand. —*v.* to solve or explain a riddle. —**rid′dled,** *p.t.* & *p.p.;* **rid′dling,** *pr.p.*

rid·dle (rid′'l), *v.* **1.** to make full of holes [Worms *riddled* our apples.] **2.** to show many weaknesses in, as an argument. **3.** to sift through a sieve. —*n.* a coarse sieve. —**rid′dled,** *p.t.* & *p.p.;* **rid′dling,** *pr.p.*

ride (rid), *v.* **1.** to sit on and make move along [to *ride* a horse; to *ride* a bicycle]. **2.** to move along, as in a car, train, etc. **3.** to be carried along on or by [Tanks *ride* on treads. The ship *rode* the waves.] **4.** to cause to ride; carry [I'll *ride* you in my wagon.] **5.** to control or rule over [Fear *rides* him.] **6.** to keep on teasing or nagging:

used only in everyday talk. **7.** to go on as is, with no action taken: *a slang meaning* [Let the matter *ride* for a while.] —*n.* a riding; especially, a trip by horseback, car, etc. [a *ride* in the park]. —**ride down, 1.** to knock down by riding against. **2.** to overtake or overcome. —**ride out,** to last or stay safe through a storm, time of trouble, etc. —**rode,** *p.t.;* **rid′den,** *p.p.;* **rid′ing,** *pr.p.*

rid·er (rid′ər), *n.* **1.** a person who rides. **2.** something added to an official paper, as a clause added to a proposed law before it is voted on.

ridge (rij), *n.* **1.** a top or high part that is long and narrow; crest [the *ridge* of a roof]. **2.** a range of hills or mountains. **3.** any narrow, raised strip [Waves made tiny *ridges* in the sand.] —*v.* to form into ridges or mark with ridges. —**ridged,** *p.t.* & *p.p.;* **ridg′ing,** *pr.p.*

ridge·pole (rij′pōl), *n.* the beam along the ridge of a roof: also called **ridge beam.**

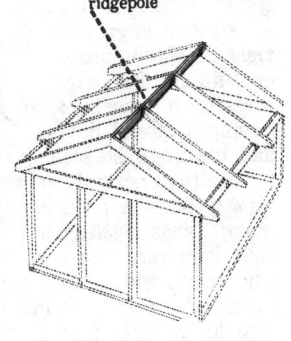

ridgepole

rid·i·cule (rid′i-kyōol′), *n.* **1.** the act of making a person or thing seem foolish, as by making fun, mocking, laughing, etc. **2.** words or actions used in doing this. —*v.* to make fun of or make others laugh at. —**rid′-i·culed′,** *p.t.* & *pp.;* **rid/i·cul′ing,** *pr.p.*

ri·dic·u·lous (ri dik′yoo ləs), *adj.* deserving ridicule; foolish; absurd. —**ri·dic′u·lous·ly,** *adv.*

rife (rīf), *adj.* **1.** happening often; common or widespread [Gossip is *rife* in our town.] **2.** filled [a jungle *rife* with insects].

riff·raff (rif′raf), *n.* those people thought of as being very low, common, etc.

ri·fle (rī′f'l), *n.* a gun having spiral grooves on the inside of the barrel to make the bullet spin. —*v.* to cut spiral grooves in. —**ri′fled,** *p.t.* & *p.p.;* **ri′fling,** *pr.p.*

ri·fle (rī′f'l), *v.* to go through wildly in searching and robbing; plunder [Soldiers *rifled* the city. Thieves *rifled* the safe.] —**ri′fled,** *p.t.* & *p.p.;* **ri′fling,** *pr.p.* —**ri′fler,** *n.*

rifle

ri·fle·man (rī′f'l mən), *n.* **1.** a soldier armed with a rifle. **2.** a man who can shoot well with a rifle. —**ri′fle·men,** *pl.*

rift (rift), *n.* an opening made as by splitting; crack; cleft [a *rift* in a tree hit by lightning; a *rift* in a friendship]. —*v.* to split.

---

fat, āpe, cär, ten, ēven, hit, bīte, gō, hôrn, tool, book, up, fŭr; get, joy, yet, chin, she, thin, *then*; zh = s in pleasure; ′ as in able (ā′b'l); ə = a in ago, e in agent, i in sanity, o in confess, u in focus.

rig (rig), *v.* **1.** to put the sails, braces, ropes, etc. of a ship in place [*Rig* the mainsail.] **2.** to supply or equip; outfit. **3.** to put together quickly for use [to *rig* up a table from boards and boxes]. **4.** to arrange in a dishonest way [to *rig* an election]. **5.** to dress: *used only in everyday talk* [He was *rigged* out in a cowboy suit.] —*n.* **1.** the way the sails and masts are arranged on a ship. **2.** a carriage with its horse or horses. **3.** costume: *only in everyday talk.* —**rigged**, *p.t. & p.p.*; **rig′ging**, *pr.p.* —**rig′ger**, *n.*

rig·ging (rig′ing), *n.* **1.** the chains and ropes used to hold up and work the masts, sails, etc. of a ship. **2.** equipment; tackle.

right (rīt), *adj.* **1.** that agrees with what is demanded by the law, one's conscience, etc.; just and good [Telling lies is not *right*.] **2.** that agrees with the facts; correct or true [a *right* answer; the *right* time]. **3.** proper or suitable [the *right* dress for a dance]. **4.** having a careful finish and meant to be seen [the *right* side of cloth]. **5.** healthy, normal, or well [He doesn't look *right*.] **6.** in a good condition or order [He'll make things *right* again.] **7.** on or to the side that is toward the east when one faces north [the *right* hand; a *right* turn]. **8.** closer to the right side of one facing the thing mentioned [the lower *right* drawer of the desk]. **9.** not curved; straight [a *right* line]. **10.** conservative in politics. —*n.* **1.** what is just, lawful, proper, etc. [to know *right* from wrong]. **2.** something to which a person has a just claim by law or nature [the *right* of all citizens to vote]. **3.** the right side [the first door on the *right*]. —*adv.* **1.** in a straight line; directly [Go *right* home.] **2.** in a correct, proper, or fair way; well [Do it *right*.] **3.** completely [The rain soaked *right* through his coat.] **4.** exactly [*right* here; *right* now]. **5.** on or toward the right hand or side. **6.** very: *used in certain titles* [the *Right* Honorable Earl of Essex]. —*v.* **1.** to put back in the proper or an upright position [We *righted* the boat.] **2.** to make right; correct [to *right* a wrong]. **3.** to put in order [The maid *righted* the room.] —**by right** or **by rights**, in justice; properly; rightly. —**in the right**, not wrong; correct. —**right away** or **right off**, at once; immediately. —**to rights**, in a good condition or order: *used only in everyday talk* [Set the room *to rights*.] —**right′ness**, *n.*

right

right angle, an angle of 90 degrees, formed by two lines perpendicular to each other.

right·eous (rī′chəs), *adj.* **1.** doing what is right; virtuous [a *righteous* man]. **2.** fair and just; right [a *right-eous* act]. —**right′eous·ly**, *adv.* —**right′eous·ness**, *n.*

right angle

right·ful (rīt′fəl), *adj.* **1.** fair and just. **2.** having or based on a just claim, or right [the

rightful owner; his *rightful* share]. —**right′-ful·ly**, *adv.* —**right′ful·ness**, *n.*

right-hand (rīt′hand′), *adj.* **1.** on or to the right [a *right-hand* turn]. **2.** same as **right-handed** (*in meaning 2*). **3.** most helpful [the president's *right-hand* man].

right-hand·ed (rīt′han′did), *adj.* **1.** using the right hand more easily than the left. **2.** done with or made for the right hand [a *right-handed* throw; *right-handed* golf clubs]. —*adv.* with the right hand [He eats *right-handed*.]

right·ist (rīt′ist), *n.* a conservative in politics. —*adj.* conservative.

right·ly (rīt′lē), *adv.* **1.** with justice; fairly. **2.** in a fitting or proper way. **3.** correctly.

right of way, **1.** the legal right to move in front of others, as at a traffic crossing. **2.** the legal right to use a certain route, as over another's land. Also **right′-of-way′**, *n.*

right triangle, a triangle with a right angle.

rig·id (rij′id), *adj.* **1.** not bending or moving; stiff and firm [a *rigid* steel bar]. **2.** strict; not changing [a *rigid* rule]. —**ri·gid·i·ty** (ri-jid′ə tē), *n.* —**rig′id·ly**, *adv.*

rig·ma·role (rig′mə rōl), *n.* confused talk that does not make much sense; nonsense.

rig·or (rig′ər), *n.* **1.** great strictness or harshness [laws enforced with *rigor*]. **2.** hardship [the *rigors* of pioneer life]. The British spelling is **rigour**.

rig·or·ous (rig′ər əs), *adj.* **1.** very strict or stern [a *rigorous* taskmaster]. **2.** severe or harsh [a *rigorous* climate]. **3.** very exact; precise [*rigorous* study]. —**rig′or·ous·ly**, *adv.*

rile (rīl), *v.* **1.** to make muddy, as water, by stirring up stuff from the bottom. **2.** to make angry; vex. *This word is used only in everyday talk.* —**riled**, *p.t. & p.p.*; **ril′ing**, *pr.p.*

Ri·ley, James Whit·comb (hwit′kəm rī′lē), 1853?–1916; American poet.

rill (ril), *n.* a little brook.

rim (rim), *n.* an edge or border, especially of something round [the *rim* of a bowl]. —*v.* to put or form a rim around. —**rimmed**, *p.t. & p.p.*; **rim′ming**, *pr.p.*

rime (rīm), *n. & v.* same as **rhyme**. —**rimed**, *p.t. & p.p.*; **rim′ing**, *pr.p.*

rime (rīm), *n.* white frost; hoarfrost.

rind (rīnd), *n.* a hard or firm outer layer or coating [the *rind* of cheese; orange *rind*].

ring (ring), *v.* **1.** to cause a bell to sound [*Ring* the doorbell.] **2.** to make the sound of a bell [The telephone *rang*.] **3.** to announce or call for as with a bell [*Ring* in the new year. *Ring* for the maid.] **4.** to sound loudly or clearly [The room *rang* with laughter.] **5.** to seem to be [Your story *rings* true.] **6.** to seem to be full of the sound of bells [The blow made his ears *ring*.] —*n.* **1.** the sound of a bell. **2.** any sound like this, especially when loud and long [the *ring* of applause]. **3.** a sound that shows a certain feeling [a *ring* of pride in his voice]. **4.** a telephone call [Give me a *ring* soon.] —**ring in**, to bring in or put in by a trick: *a slang phrase.* —**ring up**, to record, as a sale on a cash register. —**rang** or rarely **rung**, *p.t.*; **rung**, *p.p.*; **ring′ing**, *pr.p.* —**ring′er**, *n.*

ring (ring), *n.* **1.** a thin band of some material, shaped like a circle and worn on the finger or used to hold or fasten things [a wedding *ring*; a curtain *ring*]. **2.** a line or edge forming a circle [a *ring* around the moon]. **3.** a group in a circle [a *ring* of trees]. **4.** a group of people joined together, especially to do something wrong or bad [a spy *ring*]. **5.** an enclosed space for contests, shows, etc. [the *ring* of a circus; a boxing *ring*]. —*v.* **1.** to make a circle around or form in a ring. **2.** to fit with a ring [to *ring* a bull's nose]. —**run rings around,** to run much faster than, or do much better than: *used only in everyday talk.* —**ringed,** *p.t. & p.p.;* **ring′-ing,** *pr.p.* —**ringed,** *adj.* —**ring′er,** *n.*

ring·lead·er (ring′lēd′ər), *n.* a person who leads a group, as in breaking a law.

ring·let (ring′lit), *n.* **1.** a little ring. **2.** a curl of hair.

ring·side (ring′sīd), *n.* the place just outside the ring, as at a boxing match.

ring·worm (ring′würm), *n.* a skin disease caused by a fungus that forms round patches.

rink (ringk), *n.* a smooth area of ice for skating, or a smooth wooden floor for roller skating.

ringlets

rinse (rins), *v.* **1.** to wash lightly, as by running water over or into [to *rinse* out stockings; to *rinse* one's mouth]. **2.** to remove soap, scum, etc. from by washing in clear water. —*n.* **1.** the act of rinsing. **2.** the liquid used in rinsing. —**rinsed,** *p.t. & p.p.;* **rins′ing,** *pr.p.*

Ri·o de Ja·nei·ro (rē′ō dā zhə nā′rō), a seaport in Brazil, on the Atlantic.

Ri·o Grande (rē′ō grand′ *or* grän′dē), a river that flows from Colorado to the Gulf of Mexico. It forms the boundary between Texas and Mexico.

ri·ot (rī′ət), *n.* **1.** a wild outburst of disorder, especially by a crowd of people disturbing the peace. **2.** a very bright show or display [The sunset was a *riot* of color.] —*v.* **1.** to take part in a riot. **2.** to have a wild good time. —**read the riot act to,** to give very strict orders to so as to make obey; warn sternly. —**run riot, 1.** to act in a wild way. **2.** to grow wild [Roses *run riot* along the fence.] —**ri′ot·er,** *n.*

ri·ot·ous (rī′ət əs), *adj.* **1.** of or like a riot; wild; boisterous [a *riotous* celebration]. **2.** taking part in a riot. —**ri′ot·ous·ly,** *adv.*

rip (rip), *v.* **1.** to tear apart roughly [to *rip* the hem of a skirt]. **2.** to become torn or split apart [My sleeve *ripped* on the nail.] **3.** to remove as by tearing roughly [to *rip* a sheet of paper from a tablet]. **4.** to saw wood along the grain. **5.** to move or say quickly or roughly: *only in everyday talk.* —*n.* the act of ripping or a ripped place. —**ripped,** *p.t. & p.p.;* **rip′ping,** *pr.p.*

ripe (rīp), *adj.* **1.** ready to be gathered for eating, as fruit or grain. **2.** ready to be used [*ripe*

cheese]. **3.** fully developed; mature [*ripe* wisdom]. **4.** fully prepared; ready [a boy *ripe* for trouble]. —**rip′er,** *compar.;* **rip′est,** *superl.*

rip·en (rīp′'n), *v.* to get ripe; mature.

rip·ple (rip′'l), *v.* to form little waves on the surface, as water stirred by a breeze. —*n.* **1.** a small wave, or a movement like this [*ripples* in a field of grain]. **2.** a sound like that of water rippling [a *ripple* of applause]. —**rip′pled,** *p.t. & p.p.;* **rip′pling,** *pr.p.*

rip·saw (rip′sô), *n.* a saw with coarse teeth, for cutting wood along the grain.

rip·tide (rip′tīd), *n.* a tide that flows against another tide, causing rough waters.

Rip Van Winkle (rip′van wing′k'l), a man in a story by Washington Irving. He wakes from a twenty-year sleep to find everything changed.

rise (rīz), *v.* **1.** to stand up or get up from a lying or sitting position. **2.** to get up after sleeping. **3.** to move toward or reach a higher place or position [The sun is *rising.* He *rose* to be president of the company.] **4.** to slope upward [At the edge of the desert the hills begin to *rise.*] **5.** to become greater, higher, or stronger [The temperature *rose.* Prices are *rising.* Her voice *rose.*] **6.** to become larger and puffier, as dough with yeast in it. **7.** to rebel; revolt [The peasants *rose* against the king.] **8.** to come into being; begin [The Mississippi *rises* in northern Minnesota.] **9.** to return to life after dying [to *rise* from the grave]. —*n.* **1.** the act of moving to a higher place or position; climb [Lincoln's *rise* to the presidency; the *rise* of the flood waters]. **2.** an upward slope, as of land. **3.** a piece of ground higher than that around it [The fort was built on a *rise* for safety against attack.] **4.** the fact of becoming greater, higher, etc.; increase [a *rise* in prices]. **5.** a start or beginning; origin. —**give rise to,** to bring about; begin. —**rise to,** to prove oneself able to deal well with [to *rise* to an emergency]. —**rose,** *p.t.;* **ris·en** (riz′'n), *p.p.;* **ris′ing,** *pr.p.*

ris·er (rīz′ər), *n.* **1.** a person or thing that rises [I'm an early *riser*.] **2.** any of the upright pieces between the steps of a stairway.

risk (risk), *n.* the chance of getting hurt, or of losing, failing, etc.; danger [He ran into the burning house at the *risk* of his life.] —*v.* **1.** to lay open to risk; put in danger [He is *risking* his health by smoking.] **2.** to take the chance of [Are you willing to *risk* failure?]

risk·y (ris′kē), *adj.* full of risk; dangerous. —**risk′i·er,** *compar.;* **risk′i·est,** *superl.*

rite (rīt), *n.* a formal act or ceremony carried out according to fixed rules [marriage *rites*].

rit·u·al (rich′ōō əl), *adj.* of, like, or done as a rite [*ritual* sacrifices in ancient religions]. —*n.* a system or form of rites, as in a religion, etc. —**rit′u·al·ism,** *n.* —**rit′u·al·ly,** *adv.*

ri·val (rī′v'l), *n.* a person who tries to get the same thing as another, or one who tries to do something better than another; competitor [*rivals* for the championship]. —*adj.* acting as a rival or rivals; competing [*rival* businesses]. —*v.* **1.** to equal or be as good as [Her paintings soon *rivaled* her teacher's.] **2.** to be a rival of; compete with [They *rivaled* each other for her love.] —**ri′valed** or **ri′valled,** *p.t.* & *p.p.;* **ri′val·ing** or **ri′val·ling,** *pr.p.*

ri·val·ry (rī′v'l rē), *n.* the act of rivaling or the fact of being rivals. —**ri′val·ries,** *pl.*

riv·en (riv′'n), *adj.* torn or pulled apart; split [a giant oak *riven* by lightning].

riv·er (riv′ər), *n.* **1.** a large, natural stream of water flowing into an ocean, lake, etc. **2.** any large, flowing stream [a *river* of lava].

riv·er·side (riv′ər sīd), *n.* the bank of a river. —*adj.* on or near the bank of a river.

riv·et (riv′it), *n.* a metal bolt for holding metal beams or plates together. It is put through holes in the parts, and then the ends are hammered into heads. —*v.* **1.** to fasten together with rivets. **2.** to fix or hold firmly [He stood *riveted* to the spot with fear.]

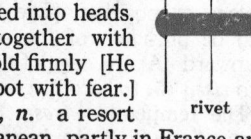

rivet

Riv·i·er·a (riv′i er′ə), *n.* a resort area on the Mediterranean, partly in France and partly in Italy.

riv·u·let (riv′yoo lit), *n.* a little stream.

rm., abbreviation for **ream, room.** —**rms.,** *pl.*

roach (rōch), *n.* same as **cockroach.**

roach (rōch), *n.* a fish like the carp, found in rivers of Europe. —**roach** or **roach′es,** *pl.*

road (rōd), *n.* **1.** a way made for cars, trucks, etc. to travel from place to place; highway. **2.** a way or course [the *road* to success]. **3.** a railroad. **4.** *usually* **roads,** *pl.* a protected place near the shore where ships can anchor. —**on the road,** traveling, as a salesman.

road·bed (rōd′bed), *n.* the foundation on which a road or railroad is built.

road·side (rōd′sīd), *n.* the side of a road. —*adj.* along the side of a road [a *roadside* park].

road·way (rōd′wā), *n.* a road, especially the part on which cars, trucks, etc. travel.

roam (rōm), *v.* to travel about with no special plan or purpose; wander [to *roam* the streets].

roan (rōn), *adj.* brown, yellow, etc. thickly sprinkled with gray or white. —*n.* a roan horse.

roar (rôr), *v.* **1.** to make a loud, deep, rumbling sound [A lion *roars*.] **2.** to talk or laugh in a loud, noisy way [The crowd *roared* at the clown.] —*n.* a loud, deep, rumbling sound, as of a motor.

roast (rōst), *v.* **1.** to cook with little or no liquid, as in an oven or over an open fire [to *roast* a chicken or a whole ox]. **2.** to dry or brown with great heat [to *roast* coffee]. **3.** to make or become very hot. —*n.* **1.** a piece of roasted meat. **2.** a piece of meat for roasting. **3.** a picnic at which food is roasted [a steak *roast*]. —*adj.* that has been roasted [*roast* beef].

roast·er (rōs′tər), *n.* **1.** a special oven or pan for roasting meat. **2.** a young chicken, pig, etc. fit for roasting.

rob (räb), *v.* **1.** to steal from by using force or threats [to *rob* a bank]. **2.** to take from in a

wrong way, as by cheating [to *rob* a person of his right to vote]. —**robbed,** *p.t.* & *p.p.;* **rob′bing,** *pr.p.* —**rob′ber,** *n.*

rob·ber·y (räb′ər ē), *n.* the act of robbing; theft. —**rob′ber·ies,** *pl.*

robe (rōb), *n.* **1.** a long, loose outer garment, as a bathrobe. **2.** a garment like this, worn to show one's rank, office, etc. [a judge's *robe*]. **3.** a covering or wrap [a lap *robe*]. —*v.* to dress in a robe. —**robed,** *p.t.* & *p.p.;* **rob′ing,** *pr.p.*

rob·in (räb′in), *n.* **1.** a large thrush of North America, with a dull-red breast. **2.** a small brown bird of Europe, with a reddish breast.

Robin Hood, an outlaw in English legend who robbed the rich in order to help the poor.

Robinson Crusoe, see **Crusoe.**

ro·bot (rō′bət), *n.* **1.** a machine made to look and work like a man. **2.** a person who acts or works automatically, like a machine.

ro·bust (rō bust′ *or* rō′bust), *adj.* strong and healthy; vigorous [a *robust* farmer].

roc (räk), *n.* a huge bird in Arabian and Persian legends, that could carry away large animals.

Roch·es·ter (rä′ches′tər *or* räch′is tər), *n.* a city in western New York.

rock (räk), *n.* **1.** a large mass of stone. **2.** broken pieces of stone [The glacier pushed *rock* and earth before it.] **3.** minerals formed into masses in the earth [Granite and salt occur as *rock*.] **4.** anything strong or hard like a rock. —**on the rocks,** in or into trouble or ruin: *used only in everyday talk.*

rock (räk), *v.* **1.** to move or swing back and forth or from side to side [to *rock* a cradle]. **2.** to sway strongly; shake [*rocked* by an explosion]. —*n.* **1.** a rocking movement. **2.** a form of popular music with a strong rhythm: it has developed from jazz, the music of folk songs, etc.

rock bottom, the lowest level; the very bottom. —**rock′-bot′tom,** *adj.*

rock candy, large, clear crystals of sugar.

rock·er (räk′ər), *n.* **1.** either of the curved pieces on the bottom of a cradle, rocking chair, etc. **2.** a rocking chair. **3.** anything that works with a rocking motion.

rock·et (räk′it), *n.* a device that is shot through the air as a weapon, aircraft, signal, firework, etc. When fuel is burned inside the rocket, gases escape in the rear, driving it forward. —*v.* to shoot ahead like a rocket.

rocket gun, a gun for firing rockets.

Rock·ies (räk′ēz), *n. pl.* the Rocky Mountains.

rocking chair, a chair set on rockers or springs, so that it can rock.

rocking horse, a toy horse set on rockers or springs, for a child to ride: *see picture on next page.*

rock salt, common salt in solid masses.

rock·y (räk′ē), *adj.* **1.** full of rocks [*rocky* soil]. **2.** made of rock. **3.** firm or hard like rock. —**rock′i·er,** *compar.;* **rock′i·est,** *superl.*

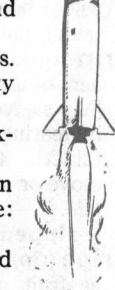

rocket

rock·y (räk'ē), *adj.* **1.** tending to rock or sway; not steady [a *rocky* desk]. **2.** weak or dizzy: *slang in this meaning.* —**rock'i·er,** *compar.*; **rock'i·est,** *superl.* —**rock'i·ness,** *n.*

rocking horse

Rocky Mountains, a mountain system in western North America. It stretches from Alaska to New Mexico. Also called *Rockies.*

ro·co·co (rə kō'kō), *adj.* having rich decoration and many fancy designs, such as leaves, scrolls, etc. [*Rococo* architecture was popular in the 18th century.]

rod (räd), *n.* **1.** a straight, thin bar of wood, metal, etc. [a fishing *rod*]. **2.** a stick for beating as punishment. **3.** punishment. **4.** a measure of length equal to 5½ yards. **5.** a staff carried as a symbol of position or rank, as by a king. —**spare the rod,** to keep from punishing.

rode (rōd), past tense of **ride.**

ro·dent (rō'd'nt), *n.* an animal having sharp front teeth for gnawing. Rats, mice, rabbits, and squirrels are rodents.

ro·de·o (rō'di ō *or* rō dā'ō), *n.* **1.** a contest or show in which cowboys match their skill in riding horses, roping and throwing cattle, etc. **2.** a roundup of cattle. —**ro'de·os,** *pl.*

roe (rō), *n.* fish eggs.

roe (rō), *n.* a small, graceful deer found in Asia and Europe. —**roe** or **roes,** *pl.*

roe·buck (rō'buk), *n.* the male of the roe.

Roent·gen rays (rent'gən), same as **X rays.**

rogue (rōg), *n.* **1.** a dishonest or tricky person; scoundrel; rascal. **2.** a person who likes to have fun and plays tricks. **3.** an elephant or other animal that wanders apart from the herd and is wild and fierce.

ro·guer·y (rō'gə rē), *n.* the actions of a rogue; trickery or playful mischief. —**ro'guer·ies,** *pl.*

ro·guish (rō'gish), *adj.* **1.** dishonest; tricky. **2.** playful; mischievous. —**ro'guish·ly,** *adv.*

roil (roil), *v.* **1.** to make muddy or cloudy, as by stirring up stuff at the bottom [to *roil* a pond]. **2.** to make angry; vex.

roist·er (rois'tər), *v.* **1.** to be noisy and lively; revel. **2.** to brag or show off. —**roist'er·er,** *n.*

role or **rôle** (rōl), *n.* **1.** the part that an actor takes in a play [the heroine's *role*]. **2.** a part that a person plays in life [his *role* as scoutmaster].

roll (rōl), *v.* **1.** to move by turning over and over [The dog *rolled* on the grass. Men *rolled* logs to the river.] **2.** to move on wheels or rollers [The wagons *rolled* by. *Roll* the cart over here.] **3.** to wrap up or wind into a ball or tube [*Roll* up the rug.] **4.** to move smoothly, one after the other [The waves *rolled* to the shore. The weeks *rolled* by.] **5.** to move or rock back and forth [The ship *rolled* in the heavy seas. Sally *rolled* her eyes.] **6.** to spread, make, or become flat under a

roller [to *roll* steel]. **7.** to say with a trill [He *rolls* his "r's".] **8.** to make a loud, echoing sound [The thunder *rolled*.] **9.** to beat with light, rapid blows [to *roll* a drum]. —*n.* **1.** the act of rolling [the *roll* of a ball]. **2.** a list of names for checking who is present. **3.** something rolled up into a ball or tube [a *roll* of wallpaper]. **4.** bread baked in a small, shaped piece. **5.** a roller. **6.** a rolling motion [the *roll* of a boat]. **7.** a loud, echoing sound [a *roll* of thunder]. **8.** a number of light, rapid blows on a drum. —**roll in, 1.** to arrive or come in large numbers. **2.** to have much of: *used only in everyday talk* [*rolling in* wealth]. —**roll out, 1.** to make flat by using a roller on. **2.** to spread out by unrolling. —**roll up,** to get or become more; increase [to *roll up* a big score].

roll call, the reading aloud of a list of names, as in a classroom, to find out who is absent.

roll·er (rōl'ər), *n.* **1.** a tube or cylinder on which something is rolled [the *roller* of a window shade]. **2.** a heavy rolling cylinder used to crush, smooth, or spread [A steam *roller* crushed the gravel on the road.] **3.** a long, heavy wave that breaks on the shore line. **4.** a canary that trills its notes. **5.** anything that rolls.

roller coaster, an amusement ride in which cars move on tracks that curve and dip sharply.

roller skate, a skate having wheels instead of a runner, for skating on floors, walks, etc.

roll·er-skate (rōl'ər-skāt'), *v.* to move on roller skates. —**roll'er-skat'ed,** *p.t.* & *p.p.*; **roll'er-skat'ing,** *pr.p.*

rol·lick (räl'ik), *v.* to play in a gay, lively way; romp; frolic. —**rol'lick·ing,** *adj.*

roller skates

rolling mill, a factory or machine for rolling metal into sheets and bars.

rolling pin, a heavy, smooth cylinder of wood, glass, etc., used to roll out dough.

rolling stock, all the locomotives and cars of a railroad.

ro·ly-po·ly (rō'lē pō'lē), *adj.* short and plump; pudgy [a *roly-poly* boy].

rolling pin

Rom., abbreviation for **Roman.**

Ro·man (rō'mən), *adj.* **1.** of ancient or modern Rome, its people, etc. **2.** of the Roman Catholic Church. **3.** *usually* **roman,** describing the ordinary style of printing type, in which the letters do not slant [This is roman type.] —*n.* **1.** a person born or living in ancient or modern Rome. **2.** *usually* **roman,** roman type. **3. Romans,** *pl.* a book of the New Testament written by the Apostle Paul.

Roman Catholic, 1. of or belonging to the Christian church that has the Pope as its head. **2.** a member of this church.

ro·mance (rō mans′ *or* rō′mans), *n.* **1.** a story or poem of love and adventure, originally one with knights as the heroes. **2.** love, adventure, or excitement of the kind found in such stories [a novel full of *romance*]. **3.** a love affair. —*v.* **1.** to write or tell romances. **2.** to think or talk about romantic things. —**ro·manced′,** *p.t.* & *p.p.*; **ro·manc′ing,** *pr.p.*

Romance language, any of the languages that spring from Latin, as French, Spanish, or Italian.

Roman Empire, the empire of ancient Rome, from 27 B.C. to 395 A.D., when it was divided into the **Western Roman Empire,** ending 476 A.D., and the **Eastern Roman Empire,** ending 1453.

Ro·man·esque (rō mə nesk′), *adj.* describing a style of architecture in Europe in the 11th and 12th centuries, using round arches and vaults.

Ro·ma·ni·a (rō mā′ni ə), *n.* a country in south central Europe, on the Black Sea: also **Rumania, Roumania. —Ro·ma′ni·an,** *adj. & n.*

Roman numerals, letters of the Roman alphabet used as numerals until the 10th century A.D. In this system, $I = 1$, $V = 5$, $X = 10$, $L = 50$, $C = 100$, $D = 500$, and $M = 1,000$.

ro·man·tic (rō man′tik), *adj.* **1.** of, like, or filled with romance [a *romantic* novel; a *romantic* life]. **2.** not practical or realistic; fanciful [a *romantic* scheme]. **3.** describing a kind of writing, music, etc., especially of the late 18th and 19th centuries, that shows much imagination, strong feeling, etc. [the *romantic* poetry of Lord Byron; the *romantic* music of Schubert]. **4.** suited for romance [a *romantic* night]. —*n.* a romantic writer, composer, etc. —**ro·man′ti·cal·ly,** *adv.*

ro·man·ti·cism (rō man′tə siz′m), *n.* the romantic style or outlook in writing, music, etc.

Rome (rōm), *n.* the capital of Italy. In ancient times it was the capital of the Roman Empire.

Ro·me·o (rō′mi ō), *n.* the hero of Shakespeare's tragedy *Romeo and Juliet.*

romp (rämp), *v.* to play in a lively, somewhat rough way; frolic. —*n.* **1.** rough, lively play. **2.** a child, especially a girl, who romps.

romp·ers (räm′pərz), *n.pl.* a loose, one-piece outer garment for a small child.

Rom·u·lus (räm′yoo ləs), *n.* in Roman myths, the founder and first king of Rome. He and his twin brother Remus were raised by a she-wolf.

rood (rōōd), *n.* **1.** a crucifix. **2.** a measure of land equal to ¼ acre.

roof (rōōf), *n.* **1.** the outside top covering of a building. **2.** anything like a roof in the way it is placed or used [the *roof* of the mouth; the *roof* of a car]. —*v.* to cover with a roof [a cottage *roofed* with straw]. —**roof′less,** *adj.*

roof·ing (rōōf′ing), *n.* materials used for roofs.

roof·tree (rōōf′trē), *n.* same as **ridgepole.**

rook (rook), *n.* **1.** a European crow that builds its nest in trees around buildings. **2.** a cheater,

especially in gambling. —*v.* to cheat; swindle.

rook (rook), *n.* same as **castle,** in chess.

rook·er·y (rook′ər ē), *n.* **1.** a place where rooks breed in large numbers. **2.** the breeding place of certain other birds or animals [a seal *rookery*]. **3.** a very crowded slum area. —**rook′er·ies,** *pl.*

rook·ie (rook′ē), *n.* **1.** a new recruit in the army. **2.** any beginner or novice. *A slang word.*

room (rōōm), *n.* **1.** a space inside a building, set off by walls, doors, etc. [the living *room*]. **2.** enough space [Is there *room* at the table for me?] **3.** a chance or opportunity [It leaves little *room* for doubt.] **4.** all the people in a room [The whole *room* was silent.] **5. rooms,** *pl.* a place to live in; apartment. —*v.* to live in a room or rooms; lodge [to *room* with friends].

room·er (rōōm′ər), *n.* a person who rents a room or rooms to live in; lodger.

room·ful (rōōm′fool), *n.* enough people or things to fill a room. —**room′fuls,** *pl.*

rooming house, a house with furnished rooms for people to rent.

room·mate (rōōm′māt), *n.* a person with whom one shares a room or rooms.

room·y (rōōm′ē), *adj.* having plenty of room or space; spacious [a *roomy* car]. —**room′i·er,** *compar.*; **room′i·est,** *superl.* —**room′i·ness,** *n.*

Roo·se·velt, Franklin D. (rō′zə velt), 1882–1945; 32nd president of the United States, from 1933 to 1945.

Roosevelt, Theodore, 1858–1919; 26th president of the United States, from 1901 to 1909.

roost (rōōst), *n.* **1.** a pole, shelf, etc. on which birds can rest or sleep; perch. **2.** a place with such roosts, as a hen house. **3.** a place to rest or sleep. —*v.* to rest or sleep as on a roost. —**come home to roost,** to have an effect back on the one who began the action; boomerang. —**rule the roost,** to be master.

roost·er (rōōs′tər), *n.* the male of the chicken.

root (rōōt), *n.* **1.** the part of a plant that grows into the ground, where it holds the plant in place and takes water and food from the soil. **2.** the part of a tooth, hair, etc. that is attached to the body. **3.** a source or cause [This mistake was the *root* of all our trouble.] **4.** a number which, when multiplied by itself a certain number of times, gives a certain result [4 is the square root of 16 ($4 \times 4 = 16$); 4 is the cube root of 64 ($4 \times 4 \times 4 = 64$).] **5.** a word or part of a word that is used as a base for making other words [The word "body" is the *root* for the words "bodily," "disembodied," etc.] —*v.* **1.** to start to grow

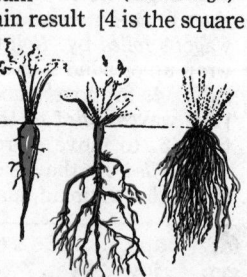
rooster (1½ ft. high)

types of root

by putting out roots [The new rosebush is *rooting* nicely.] **2.** to put firmly in place; settle [Her fear of him is deeply *rooted*.] —**root up** or **root out,** to pull out by the roots; destroy completely. —**take root, 1.** to start growing by putting out roots. **2.** to become settled.

root (root), *v.* **1.** to dig up with the snout [The wild pigs *rooted* up acorns in the forest.] **2.** to search by moving things about; rummage [to *root* through a closet. **3.** to support a team, etc. as by cheering: *a slang meaning.* —**root'er,** *n.*

root beer, a sweet drink made of soda water flavored with juices gotten from certain roots.

root·let (root'lit), *n.* a little root.

rope (rōp), *n.* **1.** a thick, strong cord made by twisting fibers or wires together. **2.** a number of things strung together on a line [a *rope* of pearls]. **3.** a sticky, stringy substance [a *rope* of taffy]. —*v.* **1.** to fasten or tie together with a rope. **2.** to set off or keep apart with a rope [*Rope* off the hole in the ice.] **3.** to catch with a lasso [The cowboy *roped* the steer.] —**know the ropes,** to know the details of a certain job: *used only in everyday talk.* —**rope in,** to get someone to do something, as by tricking him: *a slang phrase.* —**the end of one's rope,** the point where one can no longer do anything. —**roped,** *p.t. & p.p.;* **rop'ing,** *pr.p.*

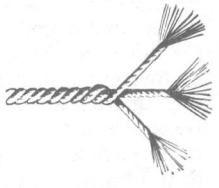
rope

rop·y (rōp'ē), *adj.* **1.** forming sticky, stringy masses, as some liquids. **2.** like a rope. —**rop'i·er,** *compar.;* **rop'i·est,** *superl.*

ro·sa·ry (rō'zə rē), *n.* **1.** a string of beads used as by Roman Catholics to keep count when saying prayers. **2.** the prayers said. —**ro'sa·ries,** *pl.*

rose (rōz), *n.* **1.** a bush with prickly stems and sweet-smelling flowers of red, pink, white, yellow, etc. **2.** its flower. **3.** a pinkish-red color.

rose (rōz), past tense of **rise.**

ro·se·ate (rō'zi it), *adj.* rose-colored; rosy.

rose·bud (rōz'bud), *n.* the bud of a rose.

rose·mar·y (rōz'mer ē), *n.* an evergreen shrub with sweet-smelling leaves that are used in perfume and as a seasoning in cooking.

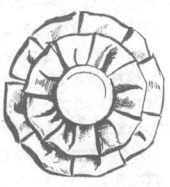
rose

ro·sette (rō zet'), *n.* a decoration, as of ribbon, made in the shape of a rose.

rose water, a mixture of water with an oil made from rose petals, used as a perfume.

rose·wood (rōz'wood), *n.* a hard, reddish wood from certain trees that grow in the tropics, used in making fine furniture.

rosette

Rosh Ha·sha·na (rōsh' hä shä'nə), the Jewish New Year. It comes in the fall.

ros·in (räz'n), *n.* a hard, yellowish resin made from crude turpentine. It is used in varnishes and is rubbed on violin bows, on athletes' hands and shoes to keep them from slipping, etc.

Ross, Betsy (rôs), 1752–1836; American woman who made the first American flag.

ros·ter (räs'tər), *n.* a list of names, as of soldiers or sailors, telling what work each is to do for a certain time.

ros·trum (räs'trəm), *n.* the platform on which a person stands while making a public speech. —**ros'trums** or **ros'tra** (räs'trə), *pl.*

ros·y (rōz'ē), *adj.* **1.** like a rose in color; red or pink [*rosy* cheeks]. **2.** bright, hopeful, etc. [a *rosy* outlook]. —**ros'i·er,** *compar.;* **ros'i·est,** *superl.* —**ros'i·ness,** *n.*

rot (rät), *v.* **1.** to fall apart or spoil, as by the action of bacteria, dampness, etc.; decay [A dead tree will *rot*.] **2.** to make this happen to [Water standing in the fields *rots* young plants.] —*n.* **1.** the act or result of rotting. **2.** any rotting disease of plants and animals. —**rot'ted,** *p.t. & p.p.;* **rot'ting,** *pr.p.*

ro·ta·ry (rō'tə rē), *adj.* **1.** turning around a point or axis in the middle; rotating [the *rotary* motion of a wheel]. **2.** having a part or parts that rotate [a *rotary* printing press].

ro·tate (rō'tāt), *v.* **1.** to turn around a center point or axis, as a wheel; revolve [The earth *rotates* on its axis.] **2.** to change by turns in regular order; alternate [Farmers *rotate* crops to keep soil fertile.] —**ro'tat·ed,** *p.t. & p.p.;* **ro'tat·ing,** *pr.p.* —**ro·ta'tion,** *n.* —**ro'ta·tor,** *n.*

R.O.T.C., abbreviation for **Reserve Officers Training Corps.**

rote (rōt), *n.* a fixed way of doing something: *now used only in the phrase* **by rote,** by memory alone, without thought or understanding [to answer *by rote*].

ro·tis·ser·ie (rō tis'ər ē), *n.* a broiler having a spit that is turned by electricity.

ro·tor (rō'tər), *n.* **1.** the rotating part of a motor, dynamo, etc. **2.** the system of rotating blades in a helicopter.

rot·ten (rät'n), *adj.* **1.** having rotted; decayed or spoiled [*rotten* apples; a *rotten* floor]. **2.** unpleasant or disgusting; putrid [a *rotten* odor]. **3.** wicked, dishonest, corrupt, etc. [*rotten* politics]. **4.** very bad; disagreeable: *a slang meaning.* —**rot'ten·ness,** *n.*

Rot·ter·dam (rät'ər dam), *n.* a seaport in the southwestern Netherlands.

ro·tund (rō tund'), *adj.* rounded out; plump or stout. —**ro·tun'di·ty,** *n.*

ro·tun·da (rō tun'də), *n.* a round building, hall, or room, especially one with a dome.

rou·é (roo ā'), *n.* a man who leads a wild life; rake.

rouge (rōozh), *n.* a red powder or paste used to color the cheeks and lips. —*v.* to put rouge on. —**rouged,** *p.t. & p.p.;* **roug'ing,** *pr.p.*

rough (ruf), *adj.* **1.** not smooth or level; uneven [a *rough* road; *rough* fur]. **2.** wild in force or motion [a *rough* sea]. **3.** stormy [*rough* weather]. **4.** full of noise and wild action; disorderly [*rough* play]. **5.** not gentle or mild, as in manners; rude, harsh, etc. [*rough* language]. **6.** having little comfort or luxury [the *rough* life of a pioneer]. **7.** not polished or refined; natural, crude, etc. [a *rough* diamond]. **8.** not finished; not worked out in detail [a *rough* sketch]. **9.** unpleasant or difficult: *used only in everyday talk* [a *rough* time]. —*n.* **1.** any part of a golf course where the grass, etc. grows uncut. **2.** a rough, disorderly person; a rowdy: *used mainly in Great Britain.* —*adv.* in a rough way. —*v.* **1.** to make rough; roughen [Use the file to *rough* up the metal.] **2.** to treat in a rough way [The gangsters *roughed* up their victim.] **3.** to make or shape in a rough way [He *roughed* in the windows and doors in the sketch of the house.] —**in the rough,** in a rough or crude condition. —**rough it,** to live without things that give comfort or luxury.

rough·age (ruf'ij), *n.* coarse, rough food, as bran and vegetable peel, that is only partly digested, but helps to move waste products through the intestines.

rough·en (ruf'n), *v.* to make or become rough.

rough-hew or **rough·hew** (ruf'hyōo'), *v.* to hew or form roughly, without the final smoothing. *For principal parts see* **hew.**

rough·ly (ruf'lē), *adv.* **1.** in a rough manner. **2.** more or less; about [*Roughly* 50 people came.]

rough·neck (ruf'nek), *n.* a rough person; rowdy: *a slang word.*

rough·shod (ruf'shäd'), *adj.* having horseshoes with metal points that keep the horse from slipping. —**ride roughshod over,** to show no pity or regard for; treat in a bullying way.

rou·lette (rōo let'), *n.* **1.** a gambling game in which players bet on where a ball rolling on a turning wheel will stop. **2.** a small wheel with sharp teeth for making rows of marks or holes, as between postage stamps.

roulette wheel
(meaning 1)

Rou·ma·ni·a (rōo mā'ni ə), *n.* same as **Romania.** —**Rou·ma'ni·an,** *adj. & n.*

round (round), *adj.* **1.** shaped like a ball, a circle, or a tube; having an outline that forms a circle or curve [The world is *round.* Wheels are *round.* The ship has a *round* smokestack.] **2.** plump; chubby [his *round* cheeks]. **3.** that moves in a circle [The polka is a *round* dance.] **4.** pronounced with the lips forming a circle [O is a *round* vowel.] **5.** mellow and rich; not harsh [full, *round* tones]. **6.** full; complete [a *round* dozen]. **7.** large [He paid a *round* price.] **8.** that is a whole number, or is given in even units, as tens, hundreds, thousands, etc. [500 is a *round* number for 498 or 503.] **9.** brisk;

lively [a *round* pace]. —*n.* **1.** something round, as a rung of a ladder. **2.** movement in a circle. **3.** a dance in which the dancers move in a circle. **4.** *often* **rounds,** *pl.* a course or route taken regularly; beat [The watchman made his *rounds.*] **5.** a series, as of actions or events [a *round* of parties]. **6.** a single shot from a gun, or from several guns fired together. **7.** bullets, shells, etc. for such a shot [He passed out one *round* of ammunition.] **8.** a single outburst [a *round* of applause]. **9.** a single period of action, as one complete game [a *round* of golf]. **10.** one of the timed periods in boxing [He was knocked out in the third *round.*] **11.** a short song for two or more persons or groups, in which the second starts when the first gets to the second phrase, and so on. **12.** the thigh of a beef animal: *the full name for this is* **round of beef. 13.** sculpture in which the figures are full, not coming out from a background. —*v.* **1.** to make or become round [*Round* the corners of the board.] **2.** to complete; finish [to *round* out the day]. **3.** to go around or pass by [The car *rounded* the corner.] **4.** to pronounce with the lips forming a circle [to *round* a vowel]. —*adv.* **1.** in a circle [The wheels turned *round.*] **2.** through a complete cycle of time [Summer will come *round* again. He works the whole year *round.*] **3.** from one place or person to another [The peddler went *round* from door to door.] **4.** for everyone [We have enough candy to go *round.*] **5.** in circumference; in distance around [His waist measures 28 inches *round.*] **6.** on all sides [The woods stretched *round.*] **7.** about; near [We'll visit all the people *round.*] **8.** in a roundabout way [We drove *round* by the river on our way home.] **9.** in the opposite direction [He turned *round.*] —*prep.* **1.** in a circle that surrounds [Tie the rope *round* the tree.] **2.** on all sides of [The crowd gathered *round* him.] **3.** near; in the area of [the farms *round* Cleveland]. **4.** to each part or person of [He passed the picture *round* the class.] **5.** here and there in; about [The boy played *round* the room.] **6.** so as to turn to the other side of [The water flowed *round* the rock.] *Round* and *around,* as adverbs and prepositions, are often used in place of each other in talk and writing that are not highly formal. —**round off** or **round out, 1.** to make or become round. **2.** to complete; finish. —**round up, 1.** to drive together into a group, as cattle. **2.** to gather or collect: *used only in everyday talk.* —**round'ish,** *adj.* —**round'ness,** *n.*

round·a·bout (round'ə bout), *adj.* not straight or direct [a *roundabout* trip; *roundabout* answers].

roun·de·lay (roun'də lā), *n.* a simple song in which some phrase is repeated over and over.

round·house (round'hous), *n.* **1.** a building for storing and repairing locomotives. It is usually round, with a turning platform in the center. **2.** a cabin at the rear of a ship's upper deck.

round·ly (round'lē), *adv.* **1.** in a round form; in a circle, curve, ball, etc. **2.** in a harsh or sharp manner [He was *roundly* scolded.] **3.** fully; completely.

round-shoul-dered (round′shōl′dərd), *adj.* stooped because the shoulders are not held straight.

Round Table, 1. the table around which King Arthur and his knights sat. **2.** King Arthur and his knights. **3. round table,** a group of persons gathered together to discuss something.

round trip, a trip to a place and back to the starting point. —**round′-trip′,** *adj.*

round-up (round′up), *n.* **1.** the act of driving cattle together into a group, as for branding. **2.** the cowboys, horses, etc. that drive the herd together. **3.** any act of collecting a group.

round-shouldered boy

rouse (rouz), *v.* **1.** to wake; come or bring out of sleep. **2.** to stir up; excite [to *rouse* anger]. —**roused,** *p.t. & p.p.;* **rous′ing,** *pr.p.*

Rous·seau, Jean Jacques (zhän zhäk rōō-sō′), 1712–1778; French philosopher and writer.

roust·a·bout (roust′ə bout), *n.* an unskilled worker on docks, in circuses, on ranches, etc.

rout (rout), *n.* **1.** a confused retreat, as of an army [The enemy was put to *rout*.] **2.** a complete, crushing defeat. —*v.* **1.** to make retreat in a confused way [to *rout* enemy troops]. **2.** to defeat completely.

rout (rout), *v.* **1.** to dig for food with the snout, as a pig does. **2.** to search for or get by poking and moving things. **3.** to force out. **4.** to scoop or gouge out.

route (rōōt *or* rout), *n.* **1.** a road or course traveled or to be traveled [We took the scenic *route* west.] **2.** a set of customers to whom one delivers something regularly [a milkman's *route*]. —*v.* to send by a certain route. —**rout′-ed,** *p.t. & p.p.;* **rout′ing,** *pr.p.*

rou·tine (rōō tēn′), *n.* a regular way of doing something, fixed by custom, habit, rules, etc. [the *routine* of preparing breakfast]. —*adj.* of, using, or done by routine [a *routine* task].

rove (rōv), *v.* to wander about; roam [He *roved* the woods.] —**roved,** *p.t. & p.p.;* **rov′ing,** *pr.p.*

rov·er (rōv′ər), *n.* **1.** a person who roves; wanderer. **2.** a pirate or pirate ship.

row (rō), *n.* a number of people or things in a line [a *row* of poplars; *rows* of seats]. —**a hard row to hoe,** a hard or tiring task or duty.

row (rō), *v.* **1.** to move a boat on water by using oars. **2.** to carry in a rowboat [I'll *row* you across the lake.] —*n.* a trip made by rowboat [to go for a *row*]. —**row′er,** *n.*

row (rou), *n.* **1.** a noisy quarrel; brawl. **2.** noise; uproar. *Used only in everyday talk.*

row·boat (rō′bōt), *n.* a boat made to be rowed.

row·dy (rou′dē), *n.* a rough, noisy person who starts fights; hoodlum. —*adj.* rough, noisy, etc. [a *rowdy* party]. —**row′dies,** *pl.* —**row′di·er,** *compar.;* **row′di·est,** *superl.* —**row′dy·ism,** *n.*

row·el (rou′əl), *n.* a small wheel with sharp points, forming the end of a spur. *See the picture for* **spur.**

row·lock (rō′läk), *n.* same as **oarlock.**

roy·al (roi′əl), *adj.* **1.** of or by a king or queen [a *royal* edict; *royal* power]. **2.** that is a king or queen [His *Royal* Highness]. **3.** of a kingdom, its government, etc. [the *royal* fleet]. **4.** like or fit for a king or queen; splendid, magnificent, etc. [a *royal* meal]. —**roy′al·ly,** *adv.*

roy·al·ist (roi′əl ist), *n.* a person who supports a king or a monarchy, as during a civil war or revolution. —*adj.* of royalists.

roy·al·ty (roi′əl tē), *n.* **1.** a royal person, or royal persons as a group [a member of English *royalty*]. **2.** the rank or power of a king or queen. **3.** royal quality or nature; nobility, splendor, etc. [the *royalty* of his manner] **4.** a share of the earnings as from an invention, book, or play, paid to the inventor, writer, etc. for the right to make, use, or publish it. —**roy′al·ties,** *pl.*

r.p.m., abbreviation for **revolutions per minute.**

R.R., an abbreviation for **railroad.**

R.S.V.P. or **r.s.v.p.,** abbreviation for French words meaning "please reply."

rub (rub), *v.* **1.** to move a hand, cloth, etc. back and forth over something firmly [Will you *rub* my sore leg? *Rub* the wood to make it shine.] **2.** to move with pressure and friction [The chair *rubbed* against the wall.] **3.** to spread on by rubbing [to *rub* wax on a car]. **4.** to make by rubbing [He *rubbed* himself dry with a towel.] **5.** to make sore by rubbing [These shoes *rub* my heel.] **6.** to remove or be removed by rubbing [You can *rub* out that mark with an eraser. This paint will not *rub* off easily.] —*n.* **1.** the act of rubbing. **2.** difficulty or trouble [He may not even know—there's the *rub*.] **3.** something that hurts the feelings, as a teasing remark. —**rub down,** to massage. —**rub it in,** to keep reminding someone of his failure or mistake: *a slang phrase.* —**rub the wrong way,** to annoy. —**rubbed,** *p.t. & p.p.;* **rub′bing,** *pr.p.*

rub·ber (rub′ər), *n.* **1.** a person or thing that rubs. **2.** a springy substance made from the milky sap of various tropical plants or from chemicals. It is used in making automobile tires, waterproof material, etc. **3.** something made of this substance, as an elastic band (**rubber band**), an eraser, an overshoe, etc. —*adj.* made of rubber [*rubber* gloves]. —**rub′ber·y,** *adj.*

rub·ber (rub′ər), *n.* **1.** a series of games in which two out of three or three out of five must be won to win the whole series. **2.** the deciding game in such a series.

rub·ber·ize (rub′ər īz), *v.* to coat or fill with rubber [to *rubberize* cloth]. —**rub′ber·ized,** *p.t. & p.p.;* **rub′ber·iz·ing,** *pr.p.*

rubber stamp, 1. a stamp made of rubber, inked on a pad and used for printing dates,

fat, āpe, cär, ten, ēven, hit, bīte, gō, hôrn, tōōl, book, up, fûr; get, joy, yet, chin, she, thin, *then;* zh = s in pleasure; ′ as in able (ā′b'l); ə = a in ago, e in agent, i in sanity, o in confess, u in focus.

signatures, etc. **2.** a person or group that approves another's plans, decisions, etc. in a routine way, never questioning or protesting.

rub·bish (rub/ish), *n.* **1.** anything thrown away as worthless; trash. **2.** nonsense.

rub·ble (rub/'l), *n.* **1.** rough, broken pieces of stone, brick, etc. **2.** masonry made up of such pieces [a fireplace made of *rubble*].

rub·down (rub/doun), *n.* a massage.

Ru·bens, Peter Paul (roo/bənz), 1577–1640; Flemish painter.

Ru·bi·con (roo/bi kän/), *n.* a small river in northern Italy. Julius Caesar crossed it in 49 B.C. and went on to seize power in Rome. **—cross the Rubicon,** to start on an action from which one cannot turn back.

ru·bi·cund (roo/bi kund/) *adj.* reddish; ruddy [*rubicund* cheeks].

ru·ble (roo/b'l), *n.* the basic unit of money in the Soviet Union.

ru·bric (roo/brik), *n.* **1.** a heading, title, first letter, etc. printed in red or in fancy lettering, as in early books or legal papers. **2.** a direction in a prayer book, usually printed in red.

ru·by (roo/bē), *n.* **1.** a clear, deep-red, costly jewel. **2.** deep red. **—ru/bies,** *pl.*

ruck·sack (ruk/sak), *n.* a kind of knapsack.

rud·der (rud/ər), *n.* **1.** a broad, flat piece of wood or metal attached by hinges to the rear of a boat or ship and used for steering. **2.** a piece like this on an airplane, etc.

~rudder

rud·dy (rud/ē), *adj.* **1.** red and healthy looking [a *ruddy* face]. **2.** red or reddish. **—rud/di·er,** *compar.;* **rud/di·est,** *superl.* **—rud/di·ness,** *n.*

rude (rood), *adj.* **1.** without respect for others; impolite [It was *rude* of him not to thank you.] **2.** rough or crude [a *rude* hut]. **3.** not civilized or educated. **4.** rough or violent; harsh [a *rude* awakening]. **—rud/er,** *compar.;* **rud/est,** *superl.* **—rude/ly,** *adv.* **—rude/ness,** *n.*

ru·di·ment (roo/də mənt), *n.* **1.** something to be learned first, as a basic principle [the *rudiments* of science]. **2.** a slight beginning or a part that is not fully developed [This animal has the *rudiment* of a tail.]

ru·di·men·ta·ry (roo/də men/tər ē), *adj.* **1.** to be learned first; elementary [*rudimentary* studies]. **2.** not fully developed; incomplete [A tadpole has *rudimentary* legs.]

rue (roo), *v.* to feel sorry because of something; regret [He *rued* his angry words.] **—rued,** *p.t. & p.p.;* **ru/ing,** *pr.p.*

rue (roo), *n.* a plant with yellow flowers and bitter leaves once used in medicine.

rue·ful (roo/fəl), *adj.* **1.** full of sorrow or regret; mournful [a *rueful* look]. **2.** causing sorrow or pity [*rueful* news]. **—rue/ful·ly,** *adv.*

ruff (ruf), *n.* **1.** a stiff, frilly collar worn by men and women in the 16th and 17th centuries. **2.** a ring of feathers or fur standing out about the neck of a bird or animal. **—ruffed,** *adj.*

ruff

ruffed grouse, a wild bird with a ruff, hunted as game.

ruf·fi·an (ruf/i ən), *n.* a rough, brutal person who does not obey the law.

ruf·fle (ruf/'l), *n.* **1.** a strip of cloth, lace, etc. gathered in pleats or puckers and used for trimming. **2.** something that disturbs or annoys. **—v. 1.** to put ruffles on. **2.** to fold into ruffles. **3.** to disturb the smoothness of; make rough [The wind *ruffled* the water. The bird *ruffled* its feathers.] **4.** to disturb or annoy [Their questions *ruffled* him.] **—ruf/fled,** *p.t. & p.p.;* **ruf/fling,** *pr.p.*

rug (rug), *n.* **1.** a piece of some thick, heavy material used to cover floors. **2.** a heavy blanket or lap robe: *mainly a British meaning.*

Rug·by (rug/bē), *n.* **1.** a private school for boys in England. **2.** a kind of football first played at this school.

rug·ged (rug/id), *adj.* **1.** having an uneven surface; rough [a *rugged* coast]. **2.** heavy and not regular [the *rugged* features of his face]. **3.** stormy or difficult; severe; hard [*rugged* weather; a *rugged* life]. **4.** strong; vigorous [a *rugged* man]. **5.** not refined [*rugged* manners].

Ruhr (roor), *n.* **1.** a river in western Germany. **2.** the industrial region along this river.

ru·in (roo/in), *n.* **1.** *often* **ruins,** *pl.* a building, city, etc. that has been destroyed or decayed [The bombed church was a *ruin*. We saw the *ruins* of the Roman Forum.] **2.** the condition of being destroyed, decayed, etc. [The mansion has fallen into *ruin*.] **3.** destruction, decay, or downfall [the *ruin* of his ambitions]. **4.** anything that causes downfall, destruction, etc. [Drinking was the *ruin* of him.] **—v. 1.** to destroy or damage greatly [The mud *ruined* her shoes.] **2.** to make bankrupt [*ruined* by gambling].

ru·in·a·tion (roo/ə nā/shən), *n.* **1.** a ruining or being ruined. **2.** anything that ruins.

ru·in·ous (roo/in əs), *adj.* **1.** causing ruin; very destructive [*ruinous* floods]. **2.** fallen into ruin [an old house in a *ruinous* state].

rule (rool), *n.* **1.** a statement or law that is meant to guide or control the way one acts or does something [the *rules* of grammar]. **2.** a usual way of doing, behaving, etc.; custom [It was his *rule* to rise early.] **3.** the usual or expected thing [Famine is the *rule* following war.] **4.** government or reign [the *rule* of Elizabeth I]. **5.** a ruler (*in meaning 2*). **—v. 1.** to have power or control over; govern; manage; guide [to *rule* as king; to be *ruled* by one's heart]. **2.** to decide in an official way [The judge *ruled* that Smith must pay the damages.] **3.** to mark straight lines on, as with a ruler [*ruled* paper]. **—as a rule,** usually. **—rule out,** to decide to ignore or omit. **—ruled,** *p.t. & p.p.;* **rul/ing,** *pr.p.*

rul·er (rool'ər), *n.* **1.** a person who rules, as a king. **2.** a straight, thin strip of wood, metal, etc. used in drawing lines, measuring, etc.

rul·ing (rool'ing), *adj.* that rules; having power or control; governing; chief [a *ruling* monarch; a *ruling* idea]. —*n.* **1.** an official decision [a *ruling* of the Supreme Court]. **2.** the act of governing or controlling.

rum (rum), *n.* **1.** an alcoholic liquor made from molasses or sugar cane. **2.** any strong liquor.

Ru·ma·ni·a (roo mā'ni ə), *n.* same as **Roma- nia.** —**Ru·ma'ni·an,** *adj. & n.*

rum·ble (rum'b'l), *v.* **1.** to make a deep, heavy, rolling sound [Thunder *rumbles.*] **2.** to move with such a sound [The truck *rumbled* across the bridge.] —*n.* **1.** a deep, heavy, rolling sound. **2.** a space for luggage or an open, extra seat (**rumble seat**) in the rear of some earlier automobiles. —**rum'bled,** *p.t. & p.p.;* **rum'- bling,** *pr.p.*

ru·mi·nant (roo'mə nənt), *n.* an animal that chews its cud [Cattle, sheep, goats, deer, and camels are *ruminants*.] —*adj.* **1.** of or like such animals. **2.** tending to think deeply; thoughtful.

ru·mi·nate (roo'mə nāt), *v.* **1.** to chew the cud, as a cow does. **2.** to think quietly; ponder. —**ru'mi·nat·ed,** *p.t. & p.p.;* **ru'mi·nat·ing,** *pr.p.* —**ru'mi·na'tion,** *n.*

rum·mage (rum'ij), *v.* to search in a thorough way by looking in all places and moving things about [She *rummaged* in the closet for a pair of shoes.] —*n.* odds and ends [A *rummage* sale is a sale of odds and ends.] —**rum'maged,** *p.t. & p.p.;* **rum'mag·ing,** *pr.p.*

rum·my (rum'ē), *n.* a card game in which one tries to match cards into sets or groups.

ru·mor (roo'mər), *n.* **1.** a story told as news, which may or may not be true [I heard a *rumor* that they were secretly married.] **2.** general talk about such stories [According to *rumor,* they're going to move.] —*v.* to tell as a rumor.

ru·mour (roo'mər), *n. & v.* rumor: *the British spelling.*

rump (rump), *n.* **1.** the hind part of an animal, where the legs and back join. **2.** a cut of beef from this part.

rum·ple (rum'p'l), *n.* a crease or wrinkle. —*v.* to make wrinkles in; crumple or muss, as clothes. —**rum'pled,** *p.t. & p.p.;* **rum'pling,** *pr.p.*

rum·pus (rum'pəs), *n.* noisy dis- turbance; uproar: *used only in every- day talk.*

run (run). *v.* **1.** to go by moving the legs faster than in walking. **2.** to move or go swiftly, easily, freely, etc. [A breeze *ran* through the trees.] **3.** to make a quick trip [Let's *run* up to Chicago.] **4.** to escape or flee [*Run* for your life!] **5.** to take part in or to place in a contest or race [John *ran*

rumpled clothing

in the 100-yard dash. Smith *ran* for mayor. The Democrats *ran* Jones.] **6.** to go back and forth; ply [This train *runs* between Detroit and Chi- cago.] **7.** to keep on going; continue; extend [The play *ran* for a year. This road *runs* to the lake. The lease *runs* for two more years.] **8.** to put or be in use or action; operate; work [What makes the engine *run?*] **9.** to climb or creep as a vine. **10.** to drive into or against something [He *ran* his car into a tree.] **11.** to flow or make flow [Hot water *runs* through this pipe.] **12.** to be in charge of; manage [He *runs* a small busi- ness.] **13.** to perform or do as by running [to *run* the mile; to *run* errands]. **14.** to bring, pass, force, etc. into a certain condition or position [His work *runs* him ragged. We *ran* into trouble.] **15.** to have a certain size, price, etc. [These shirts *run* $5 each.] **16.** to be told, written, etc. [The story *runs* that he is rich.] **17.** to spread into other parts [The dye in the design *ran* when the dress was washed.] **18.** to let out pus, saliva, etc. [The dog is *running* at the mouth.] **19.** to come apart or ravel [Her stocking *ran*.] **20.** to take upon oneself; incur [to *run* a risk]. **21.** to get past or through [The ship *ran* the blockade.] **22.** to be affected by; undergo [to *run* a fever]. **23.** to publish [All the newspapers *ran* the story.] **24.** to sew with continuous stitches. —*n.* **1.** the act of running [Take a *run* around the block.] **2.** a running pace [He went at a *run*.] **3.** a trip or route [The milkman finished his *run*.] **4.** a series of happenings, demands, performances, etc. without change or break [a *run* of good luck; a *run* on a bank; the *run* of a play]. **5.** a flow or rush [the *run* of the tide]. **6.** a small stream; brook. **7.** the time during which a machine is working; also, the work done. **8.** a kind or class [the ordinary *run* of students]. **9.** an enclosed place for animals or fowls to run about in [a chicken *run*]. **10.** freedom to move about as one pleases [We had the *run* of the house.] **11.** a large number of fish traveling in a group [a *run* of salmon]. **12.** a place in knitted material where the threads have raveled or become undone [a *run* in a stocking]. **13.** a point scored in baseball by touching all the bases in order. **14.** a series of musical notes played rapidly. —**a run for one's money, 1.** close competition. **2.** some satisfaction for the money or effort spent. —**in the long run,** in the end; finally. —**on the run,** running or running away. —**run across,** to come upon by chance. —**run away with,** to outdo all others in. —**run down, 1.** to stop working, as a clock. **2.** to hit so as to knock down. **3.** to chase and catch or kill. **4.** to say bad things about. **5.** to make or become run-down: see **run-down.** —**run for it,** to run to escape something. —**run in, 1.** to include or add to. **2.** to arrest: *slang in this meaning.* —**run into, 1.** to come upon by chance. **2.** to bump or crash into.

—**run off, 1.** to print, typewrite, etc. **2.** to cause to be run, played, etc. —**run on,** to go or talk on and on; continue without a break. —**run out,** to come to an end; become used up. —**run out of,** to have no more of; use up. —**run over, 1.** to ride over. **2.** to overflow. **3.** to look over or go through rapidly. —**run through, 1.** to use up or spend quickly. **2.** to pierce. —**run up,** to raise, rise, or make quickly. —**ran,** *p.t.;* **run,** *p.p.;* **run′ning,** *pr.p.*

run·a·way (run′ə wā), *n.* a person or animal that runs away. —*adj.* **1.** running away [a *runaway* horse]. **2.** easily won [a *runaway* race]. **3.** running out of control [A shortage of supplies caused *runaway* prices.]

run-down (run′doun′), *adj.* **1.** not working because not wound, as a clock. **2.** in poor health, as from overwork. **3.** in need of repair; falling apart [a *run-down* house]. —*n.* a quick report.

rune (rōōn), *n.* **1.** any of the letters in an alphabet used long ago in Northern Europe. **2.** something written in such letters. **3.** any mark whose meaning is mysterious. —**ru′nic,** *adj.*

rung (rung), *n.* a round stick forming a step of a ladder, a crosspiece on a chair, a spoke of a wheel, etc.

rung (rung), past participle of **ring** (to sound).

run·nel (run′'l) or **run·let** (run′lit), *n.* a small stream; brook.

run·ner (run′ər), *n.* **1.** a person who runs, as a racer or messenger. **2.** a long, narrow cloth or rug. **3.** a run, or ravel, in a stocking. **4.** a long, trailing stem of a plant, that puts out roots along the ground. **5.** the blade of a skate. **6.** either of the long, narrow pieces on which a sled or sleigh glides.

run·ner-up (run′ər-up′), *n.* a person or team that finishes second in a race or contest.

run·ning (run′ing), *n.* **1.** the act of one that runs. **2.** something that runs or flows. —*adj.* **1.** that runs or moves rapidly. **2.** flowing [*running* water]. **3.** letting out pus, mucus, etc. [a *running* nose]. **4.** in operation; working [a *running* motor]. **5.** going on without a break [a *running* account; for five days *running*]. **6.** done with a run [a *running* jump]. **7.** of the run of a train, bus, etc. [The *running* time is two hours.] —**in the running,** having a chance to win. —**out of the running,** having no chance to win.

running knot, a knot tied so that it will slide along the rope, forming a noose.

running mate, a candidate for a lesser office, as for the vice-presidency, running together with his party's candidate for the greater office.

run-of-the-mill (run′əv *th*ə mil′), *adj.* ordinary.

runt (runt), *n.* an animal or plant that is smaller than others of its kind.

run·way (run′wā), *n.* a track or path on which something moves, as a paved strip on an airfield used by airplanes in taking off and landing.

ru·pee (rōō pē′), *n.* the basic unit of money in India, and also in Pakistan and Ceylon.

rup·ture (rup′chər), *n.* **1.** a breaking apart or being broken apart [a *rupture* in a gas line]. **2.** an ending of friendly relations, as between nations. **3.** the pushing out of an organ of the body through a break in the membrane around it; hernia. —*v.* **1.** to break or burst [His appendix *ruptured.*] **2.** to cause to have a rupture, or hernia [to *rupture* oneself]. —**rup′tured,** *p.t.* & *p.p.;* **rup′tur·ing,** *pr.p.*

ru·ral (roor′əl), *adj.* having to do with the country or with people who live there, as on farms [*rural* schools; *rural* talk].

ruse (rōōz), *n.* a trick or plan for fooling someone [He pretended to be ill as a *ruse* to avoid work.]

rush (rush), *v.* **1.** to move, send, take, etc. with great speed [He *rushed* from the room. They *rushed* him to a hospital.] **2.** to act in haste, without careful thought [She *rushed* into marriage.] **3.** to do, make, etc. with great haste; hurry [to *rush* a job]. **4.** to attack suddenly [The troops *rushed* the fort.] —*n.* **1.** the act of rushing [the *rush* of the wind]. **2.** an eager movement of many people to get to a place [the *rush* to California for gold]. **3.** hurry; haste; bustle [the *rush* of modern life]. —*adj.* that must be done or sent in a hurry [a *rush* order].

rush (rush), *n.* a grassy plant that grows in wet places. It has a hollow stem that is used for weaving baskets, chair seats, etc.

rush hour, a time of day when business, traffic, etc. are very heavy.

rusk (rusk), *n.* **1.** a piece of sweet bread or cake toasted in an oven until brown and dry. **2.** a light, soft, sweet biscuit.

Russ., abbreviation for **Russian.**

rus·set (rus′it), *n.* **1.** yellowish brown or reddish brown. **2.** coarse, brownish, homemade cloth once used for clothing by country people.

Rus·sia (rush′ə), *n.* **1.** a former empire in eastern Europe and northern Asia, ruled by a czar. It is now the largest republic of the Soviet Union. **2.** the Union of Soviet Socialist Republics; Soviet Union: *a popular name.*

Rus·sian (rush′ən), *n.* **1.** a person born or living in Russia. **2.** the chief language of Russia and the Soviet Union. —*adj.* of Russia, its people, language, etc.

rust (rust), *n.* **1.** the reddish-brown coating formed on metal, especially iron, by the chemical action of oxygen in the air or in moisture. **2.** reddish brown. **3.** a disease of plants that makes brownish spots on stems and leaves. —*v.* **1.** to make or become coated with rust. **2.** to make or become weaker, slower, etc., as through not being used [His mind had *rusted*.]

rus·tic (rus'tik), *adj.* **1.** having to do with the country; rural. **2.** like country people; plain, simple, natural, etc. [a charming *rustic* scene]. **3.** not refined, polite, etc.; rough; awkward [*rustic* manners]. **4.** made of branches or roots covered with bark [*rustic* furniture]. —*n.* a country person, especially one thought of as simple, awkward, etc. —**rus·tic·i·ty** (rus tis'-ə tē), *n.*

rus·tle (rus''l), *v.* to make or move with soft, rubbing sounds [The wind *rustled* the leaves.] —*n.* soft, rubbing sounds [the *rustle* of her skirt as she walks]. —**rus'tled,** *p.t. & p.p.;* **rus'tling,** *pr.p.*

rus·tle (rus''l), *v.* to steal cattle, etc. —**rustle up,** to gather together, as by searching [I'll *rustle up* a meal from leftovers.] *This word is used only in everyday talk.* —**rus'tled,** *p.t. & p.p.;* **rus'tling,** *pr.p.* —**rus·tler** (rus'lər), *n.*

rust·y (rus'tē), *adj.* **1.** coated with rust [a *rusty* nail]. **2.** not working easily because of rust [a *rusty* lock]. **3.** not so good, strong, skillful, etc. as before, as from lack of practice. [My golf game is *rusty*.] **4.** reddish-brown [a *rusty* stain]. —**rust'i·er,** *compar.;* **rust'i·est,** *superl.* —**rust'i·ness,** *n.*

rut (rut), *n.* **1.** a groove made in the ground by the wheels of cars, wagons, etc. **2.** the act or fact of doing, thinking, etc. in the same way over and over [to get into a *rut*]. —*v.* to make ruts in. —**rut'ted,** *p.t. & p.p.;* **rut'ting,** *pr.p.*

ruts

ru·ta·ba·ga (rōō'tə bā'gə), *n.* a turnip with a large, yellow root.

Ruth (rōōth), *n.* **1.** a woman in the Bible who left her people and lived with the people of her mother-in-law, Naomi. **2.** a book of the Old Testament that tells of her.

ruth·less (rōōth'lis), *adj.* without pity; cruel; heartless. —**ruth'less·ly,** *adv.* —**ruth'less·ness,** *n.*

Rwan·da (ər wän' də), *n.* a country in east central Africa.

Rwy. or **Ry.,** abbreviation for **Railway.**

-ry (rē), a suffix having the same meanings as **-ery,** as in *dentistry*.

rye (rī), *n.* **1.** a cereal grass whose seed, or grain, is used in making flour and as feed for farm animals. **2.** this grain.

rye

S

S, s (es), *n.* the nineteenth letter of the English alphabet. —**S's, s's** (es'iz), *pl.*

S, symbol for the chemical element *sulfur.* —*n.* something shaped like an S.

-'s, an ending that is a short form of: **1.** is [*He's* here.] **2.** has [*She's* won.] **3.** us [*Let's* go.]

S., S, s., s, abbreviations for **south** or **southern.**

s., abbreviation for **second** or **seconds, shilling** or **shillings.**

S.A., abbreviation for **South America.**

Saar (sär), *n.* **1.** a river in northeastern France and western Germany. **2.** a state of West Germany, in the valley of the Saar River.

Sab·bath (sab'əth), *n.* **1.** the seventh day of the week, Saturday, set aside by Jews for rest and worship. **2.** Sunday, as a day for rest and worship by Christians: so called by most Protestants.

sa·ber or **sa·bre** (sā'bər), *n.* a heavy cavalry sword with a slightly curved blade.

saber

sa·ble (sā'b'l), *n.* **1.** an animal somewhat like a weasel, with dark, shiny fur. **2.** its costly fur. **3.** the color black.

sa·bot (sab'ō *or* sa bō'), *n.* **1.** a wooden shoe once worn by peasants in Europe. **2.** a heavy leather shoe with a wooden sole.

sab·o·tage (sab'ə täzh), *n.* **1.** the destroying of railroads, bridges, factories, etc., as by enemy agents or by civilians resisting an invader. **2.** the destroying of machines, tools, etc. by workers, as during a strike. —*v.* to damage or destroy by sabotage. —**sab'o·taged,** *p.t. & p.p.;* **sab'o·tag·ing,** *pr.p.*

sable (2½ ft. long, including tail)

sab·o·teur (sab ə tür'), *n.* a person who takes part in sabotage.

sac (sak), *n.* a part in a plant or animal that is shaped like a bag, often filled with fluid.

sac·cha·rin or **sac·cha·rine** (sak'ə rin), *n.* a very sweet, white substance made from coal tar and used in place of sugar.

sac·cha·rine (sak'ə rin), *adj.* **1.** of or like

fat, āpe, cär, ten, ēven, hit, bīte, gō, hôrn, tōōl, book, up, fūr;
get, joy, yet, chin, she, thin, *th*en; zh = s in pleasure; ' as in able (ā'b'l);
ə = a in ago, e in agent, i in sanity, o in confess, u in focus.

sugar; sweet. **2.** too sweet or sirupy [a *saccharine* voice].

sac·er·do·tal (sas'ər dō't'l), *adj.* having to do with priests; priestly.

sa·chem (sā'chəm), *n.* the chief in certain American Indian tribes.

sa·chet (sa shā'), *n.* **1.** a small bag filled with perfumed powder and stored with clothes to make them smell sweet. **2.** such powder.

sack (sak), *n.* **1.** a bag, especially a large one of coarse cloth used to hold grain, food, etc. **2.** as much as a sack will hold [a *sack* of potatoes]. **3.** a short, loose jacket. —*v.* to put into sacks [to *sack* grain].

sack (sak), *n.* the act of robbing or looting a city or town captured by an army. —*v.* to rob or loot a captured town, etc.; plunder.

sack (sak), *n.* a sort of dry white wine.

sack·cloth (sak'klôth), *n.* **1.** coarse cloth used to make sacks. **2.** rough, coarse cloth worn to show grief or sorrow.

sack·ful (sak'fool), *n.* as much as a sack will hold. —**sack'fuls,** *pl.*

sack·ing (sak'ing), *n.* a coarse cloth, as burlap, used for making sacks.

sac·ra·ment (sak'rə mənt), *n.* **1.** any of certain very sacred ceremonies in Christian churches, as baptism, Holy Communion, etc. **2.** something very sacred. —**the Sacrament,** Holy Communion. —**sac'ra·men'tal,** *adj.*

Sac·ra·men·to (sak'rə men'tō), *n.* the capital of California.

sa·cred (sā'krid), *adj.* **1.** having to do with religion, or set apart for some religious purpose; holy [a *sacred* shrine; a *sacred* song]. **2.** given or deserving the greatest respect; hallowed [a place *sacred* to his memory]. **3.** that must not be broken or ignored [a *sacred* oath].

sac·ri·fice (sak'ri fīs), *n.* **1.** the act of offering something, as the life of a person or animal, to God or a god; also, the thing offered. **2.** the act of giving up one thing for the sake of another; also, the thing given up [the *sacrifice* of principles to gain power]. **3.** a loss of profit [We are selling these cars at a *sacrifice*]. **4.** in baseball, a play in which the batter gets himself put out on purpose in order to move a runner up. —*v.* **1.** to make a sacrifice of. **2.** to sell at a loss. —**the supreme sacrifice,** the giving of one's life, as for a cause. —**sac'ri·ficed,** *p.t. & p.p.;* **sac'ri·fic·ing,** *pr.p.* —**sac·ri·fi·cial** (sak'rə fish'əl), *adj.*

sac·ri·lege (sak'ri lij), *n.* an act that shows disrespect for something sacred [Wrecking an altar is a *sacrilege*.] —**sac·ri·le·gious** (sak'ri-lē'jəs *or* sak'ri lij'əs), *adj.*

sac·ris·ty (sak'ris tē), *n.* the room in a church where the robes and sacred things are kept. —**sac'ris·ties,** *pl.*

sac·ro·sanct (sak'rō sangkt'), *adj.* very sacred or very holy [a *sacrosanct* shrine].

sad (sad), *adj.* **1.** feeling unhappy; having or showing sorrow or grief. **2.** causing sorrow [*sad* music]. —**sad'der,** *compar.;* **sad'dest,** *superl.* —**sad'ly,** *adv.* —**sad'ness,** *n.*

sad·den (sad''n), *v.* to make or become sad.

sad·dle (sad''l), *n.* **1.** a padded seat, usually of leather, for a rider on a horse, bicycle, etc. **2.** a part of a harness worn over an animal's back. **3.** anything shaped like a saddle. **4.** a cut of meat including part of the backbone and the two loins [a *saddle* of mutton]. —*v.* **1.** to put a saddle on. **2.** to weigh down, as with a burden or duty [*saddled* with debts]. —**in the saddle,** in control. —**sad'dled,** *p.t. & p.p.;* **sad'dling,** *pr.p.*

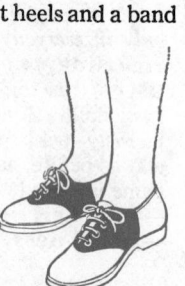
saddle

sad·dle·bag (sad''l bag), *n.* one of a pair of bags hung over a horse's back behind the saddle.

saddle horse, a horse trained to be ridden.

sad·dler (sad'lər), *n.* a person whose work is making, mending, or selling saddles.

saddle shoes, shoes having flat heels and a band of different-colored leather across the instep.

sad·ist (sad'ist), *n.* a person who gets pleasure from hurting others. —**sa·dis·tic** (sə-dis'tik), *adj.*

sa·fa·ri (sə fä'rē), *n.* a journey or hunting trip, especially in Africa. —**sa·fa·ris,** *pl.*

safe (sāf), *adj.* **1.** free from harm or danger; secure [Find a *safe* hiding place. He's *safe* in bed.] **2.** not hurt or harmed [He was *safe* after the battle.] **3.** that can be trusted [a *safe* adviser; a *safe* investment]. **4.** not able to cause trouble or harm; not dangerous [a *safe* toy; *safe* in jail]. **5.** taking no risks; careful [a *safe* driver]. **6.** in baseball, having reached a base without being put out. —*n.* a strong metal box with a lock, in which to keep money or valuables. —**saf'er,** *compar.;* **saf'est,** *superl.* —**safe'ly,** *adv.*

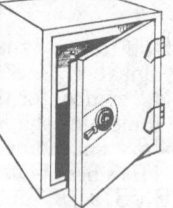
saddle shoes

safe

safe-con·duct (sāf'kän'dukt), *n.* **1.** permission to pass through a dangerous place, as in time of war, without being arrested or harmed. **2.** a written pass giving such permission.

safe·guard (sāf'gärd), *n.* a person or thing that keeps one safe from danger; protection. —*v.* to protect or guard.

safe·keep·ing (sāf'kēp'ing), *n.* a keeping or being kept safe; protection [Put your money in the bank for *safekeeping*.]

safe·ty (sāf'tē), *n.* **1.** the condition of being safe; freedom from danger or harm [Boats carried them to *safety*.] **2.** a device for preventing accident. —*adj.* that gives safety or makes something less dangerous [A *safety* match lights only when struck on a special surface. A *safety* pin has its point held inside a guard. A *safety* belt helps protect passengers in case of a crash.]

safety valve, a valve on a steam boiler, etc., that opens and lets out steam when the pressure gets too high.

saf·fron (saf′rən), *n.* **1.** a kind of crocus with purple flowers having bright orange center parts. **2.** a dye or a seasoning for food, made from the orange parts. **3.** a bright orange yellow: also **saffron yellow.**

sag (sag), *v.* **1.** to bend or sink, especially in the middle, as from weight [shelves that *sag*]. **2.** to hang down in a loose or uneven way [*sagging* flesh]. **3.** to lose strength; weaken [School spirit *sagged.*] —*n.* a place where something sags. —**sagged,** *p.t.* & *p.p.*; **sag′ging,** *pr.p.*

sagging roof

sa·ga (sä′gə), *n.* a long story of brave deeds; especially, such a story told in the Middle Ages about Norse heroes.

sa·ga·cious (sə gā′shəs), *adj.* very wise or shrewd. —**sa·gac·i·ty** (sə gas′ə tē), *n.*

sage (sāj), *adj.* wise; showing good judgment. —*n.* a very wise man. —**sag′er,** *compar.*; **sag′est,** *superl.* —**sage′ly,** *adv.*

sage (sāj), *n.* **1.** a plant related to the mint, with green leaves used as a seasoning in cooking. **2.** sagebrush.

sage·brush (sāj′brush), *n.* a shrub that smells like sage and has tiny, white or yellow flowers. It grows on the plains in the West.

sa·go (sā′gō), *n.* **1.** a starch made from the soft, inside part of the trunks of certain palm trees. **2.** any of these trees. —**sa′gos,** *pl.*

sagebrush

Sa·ha·ra (sə her′ə *or* sə hä′rə), *n.* a very large desert covering much of northern Africa.

sa·hib (sä′ib), *n.* master: a title once used by natives in India in speaking to a European man.

said (sed), past tense and past participle of **say.** —*adj.* named or mentioned before.

sail (sāl), *n.* **1.** a sheet of heavy cloth such as canvas, used on a ship or boat to move it by catching the wind. **2.** a trip in a ship or boat, especially one moved by sails. **3.** a sailing ship. **4.** anything like a sail, as an arm of a windmill. —*v.* **1.** to be moved forward by means of sails. **2.** to travel on water [This liner *sails* between France and Italy.] **3.** to begin a trip by water [We *sail* at noon for England.] **4.** to move upon in a boat or ship [to *sail* the seas]. **5.** to control or manage, especially a sailboat. **6.** to move smoothly [a hawk *sailing* in the sky]. **7.** to move or act quickly or with energy: *used only in everyday talk* [to *sail* through one's work]. —**sail into,** to attack or criticize with force: *used only in everyday talk.* —**set sail** or **make sail, 1.** to spread the sails and get ready to leave. **2.** to begin a trip by water. —**under sail,** with sails spread out.

sail·boat (sāl′bōt), *n.* a boat having a sail or sails to make it move.

sail·fish (sāl′fish), *n.* a large ocean fish that has a tall fin like a sail on its back.

sail·or (sāl′ər), *n.* **1.** a person who makes his living by sailing; seaman. **2.** an enlisted man in the navy. **3.** a person thought of in terms of whether or not he gets seasick [a good or bad *sailor*]. **4.** a straw hat with a flat crown and brim.

sailboat

saint (sānt), *n.* **1.** a holy person. **2.** a person who is very humble, unselfish, patient, etc. **3.** in certain churches, a person said officially to be in heaven as a result of having lived a very holy life. —*v.* to make a saint of; canonize. Saint **Peter,** Saint **Benedict,** etc. are listed in this dictionary under their given names. Place names beginning with **Saint** are listed among the words following **St.** —**saint′hood,** *n.*

Saint Ber·nard (bər närd′), a large, brown and white dog, at one time used in the Swiss Alps to rescue people lost in the snow.

saint·ed (sān′tid), *adj.* **1.** that has been declared a saint. **2.** of or fit for a saint. **3.** holy.

saint·ly (sānt′lē), *adj.* like or fit for a saint; very good or holy. —**saint′li·er,** *compar.*; **saint′li·est,** *superl.* —**saint′li·ness,** *n.*

Saint Bernard
(26 in. high at shoulder)

Saint Patrick's Day, see **Patrick,** Saint.
Saint Valentine's Day, see **Valentine,** Saint.

saith (seth), old form of **says,** as in the Bible.

sake (sāk), *n.* **1.** purpose or reason; motive [to cry for the *sake* of getting attention]. **2.** benefit or advantage; welfare [for my own *sake*].

sa·laam (sə läm′), *n.* **1.** an Arabic word meaning "peace," used as a greeting. **2.** a greeting in the Orient, made by bowing low with the right hand placed on the forehead. —*v.* to make a salaam.

sal·a·ble or **sale·a·ble** (sāl′ə b'l), *adj.* that can be sold; fit to buy [*salable* goods].

sal·ad (sal′əd), *n.* any mixture of vegetables, fruits, fish, eggs, etc., made with a dressing of oil, vinegar, spices, etc. It is usually served cold, often on lettuce leaves.

sal·a·man·der (sal′ə man′dər), *n.* **1.** a small animal that looks like a lizard but is related to the frog. It lives in damp, dark places. **2.** an animal in myths that was said to live in fire.

salamander (4 in. long)

sa·la·mi (sə lä′mē), *n.* a spicy, salted sausage.

sal·a·ried (sal′ə rēd), *adj.* getting a salary.

sal·a·ry (sal′ə rē), *n.* a fixed amount of money paid at regular times, as once a week, for work done. —**sal′a·ries,** *pl.*

sale (sāl), *n.* **1.** the act of selling, or exchanging something for money [The clerk made ten *sales* today.] **2.** an auction. **3.** a special selling of goods at prices lower than usual [a clearance *sale*]. —**for sale** or **on sale,** to be sold.

Sa·lem (sā′ləm), *n.* **1.** the capital of Oregon. **2.** a city on the coast of Massachusetts.

sales·man (sālz′mən), *n.* a man whose work is selling goods, either in a store or by traveling from place to place. —**sales′men,** *pl.*

sales·man·ship (sālz′mən ship), *n.* skill in selling goods.

sales tax, a tax on money received from sales. It is usually added to the price by the seller.

sales·wom·an (sālz′woom′ən), *n.* a woman whose work is selling goods, especially in a store. —**sales′wom′en,** *pl.*

sa·li·ent (sā′li ənt), *adj.* standing out; easily seen or noticed [the *salient* idea in a plan].

sa·line (sā′līn), *adj.* of, like, or containing common salt; salty [a *saline* solution]. —*n.* something salty.

sa·li·va (sə lī′və), *n.* the watery liquid produced in the mouth by certain glands; spit. It helps to digest food.

sal·i·var·y (sal′ə ver′ē), *adj.* of or producing saliva [*salivary* glands].

sal·low (sal′ō), *adj.* pale yellow in a way that looks unhealthy [a *sallow* complexion].

sal·ly (sal′ē), *n.* **1.** a sudden rush forward [The troops made a *sally* toward the enemy's lines.] **2.** a trip or jaunt. **3.** a short, witty remark. —*v.* to start out briskly, as on a trip. —**sal′lies,** *pl.* —**sal′lied,** *p.t. & p.p.;* **sal′ly·ing,** *pr.p.*

salm·on (sam′ən), *n.* a large food fish with silver scales and flesh that is orange pink when cooked. Salmon live in the ocean but swim up rivers to lay their eggs. —**salm′on** or **salm′ons,** *pl.*

salmon (3 ft. long)

sa·lon (sə län′), *n.* **1.** a large drawing room for entertaining guests. **2.** a regular meeting of artists, writers, etc., as at a wealthy person's home. **3.** a place where works of art are shown; gallery. **4.** a business for performing some service [beauty *salon*].

sa·loon (sə loon′), *n.* **1.** a place where alcoholic drinks are bought and drunk; bar. **2.** a large public room [the dining *saloon* on an ocean liner].

salt (sôlt), *n.* **1.** a white substance made up of crystals, used to flavor and preserve foods; sodium chloride. Salt is found in the earth and in ocean water. **2.** any chemical compound formed from an acid by replacing the hydrogen with a metal or a radical, such as ammonium. **3. salts,** *pl.* a medicine used to help move the bowels. **4.** a sailor: *used only in everyday talk.* —*adj.* **1.** containing salt [*salt* water]. **2.** preserved with salt [*salt* pork]. **3.** tasting or smelling of salt [*salt* breezes]. —*v.* to add salt to for flavoring, preserving, melting, etc. [to *salt* soup; to *salt* meat; to *salt* icy streets]. —**salt away,** **1.** to preserve with salt. **2.** to store away or save, as money: *used only in everyday talk.* —**salt of the earth,** a person or persons thought of as the finest or best. —**with a grain of salt,** with some doubt in believing. —**worth one's salt,** worth one's wages.

salt·cel·lar (sôlt′sel′ər), *n.* a small dish or holder for salt; also, a salt shaker.

Salt Lake City, the capital of Utah.

salt lick, same as **lick** (*meaning 2 of n.*).

salt·pe·ter or **salt·pe·tre** (sôlt′pē′tər), *n.* any of various minerals used in making gunpowder, fertilizers, etc.

salt shaker, a holder for salt, having holes in the top for shaking out the salt.

salt-wa·ter (sôlt′wô′tər), *adj.* of or living in salt water [*salt-water* fish].

salt water, water with much salt in it, as in the ocean or sea.

salt·y (sôl′tē), *adj.* **1.** tasting of salt or containing salt [*salty* soup]. **2.** witty and sharp [*salty* talk]. —**salt′i·er,** *compar.;* **salt′i·est,** *superl.* —**salt′i·ness,** *n.*

sa·lu·bri·ous (sə loo′bri əs), *adj.* good for one's health; wholesome [a *salubrious* climate].

sal·u·tar·y (sal′yoo ter′ē), *adj.* **1.** healthful; wholesome [Swimming is a *salutary* pastime.] **2.** useful or helpful [a *salutary* lesson].

sal·u·ta·tion (sal′yoo tā′shən), *n.* **1.** an act or words used in greeting or showing respect [Bill waved to us in *salutation*.] **2.** the words used at the beginning of a letter, as "Dear Sir."

sa·lute (sə loot′), *v.* **1.** to show honor and respect for, as by raising the hand to the forehead or by firing shots from a gun [A soldier *salutes* his superior officers. The battleship *saluted* the President when he arrived.] **2.** to greet in a friendly way, as by tipping the hat. —*n.* an act of saluting or greeting [a twenty-one gun *salute*; a *salute* to the flag]. —**sa·lut′ed,** *p.t. & p.p.;* **sa·lut′ing,** *pr.p.*

salute

sal·vage (sal′vij), *n.* **1.** the act of saving a ship and its cargo from fire, shipwreck, etc.; also, money paid for this. **2.** the act of saving any property or goods from damage or complete loss. **3.** the property or goods saved, as that brought up from a sunken ship. —*v.* **1.** to save from shipwreck, fire, destruction, etc. **2.** to use what can be saved from something damaged or destroyed [We *salvaged* two tires from the wreck.] —**sal′vaged,** *p.t. & p.p.;* **sal′vag·ing,** *pr.p.*

sal·va·tion (sal vā′shən), *n.* **1.** a saving or being saved from danger, evil, etc.; rescue. **2.** a person or thing that saves [The cellar was our *salvation* in the tornado.] **3.** in Christian belief, the saving of the soul from sin and death.

Salvation Army, a Christian organization that works to bring religion and help to the poor.

salve (sav), *n.* **1.** any greasy medicine put on wounds, burns, sores, etc. to soothe or heal them. **2.** anything that soothes or heals [Her smile was a *salve* to his anger.] —*v.* to soothe or make quiet; smooth over [We *salved* his wounded pride by praising his courage.] —**salved,** *p.t. & p.p.;* **salv'ing,** *pr.p.*

sal·ver (sal'vər), *n.* a small tray, as of metal.

sal·vo (sal'vō), *n.* **1.** the firing of a number of guns one after another or at the same time, in a salute or at a target. **2.** a burst of cheers or applause. —**sal'vos** or **sal'voes,** *pl.*

Sa·mar·i·a (sə mer'i ə), *n.* a region of ancient Palestine, or its main city.

Sa·mar·i·tan (sə mar'ə t'n), *n.* a person born or living in Samaria: see also **good Samaritan.**

same (sām), *adj.* **1.** being the very one, not another [He is the *same* man who spoke to me.] **2.** alike in some way; similar [Both rugs are of the *same* color.] **3.** without any change; not different [The weather is the *same* as it was yesterday.] —*pron.* the same person or thing [Bill wants chocolate, and I'll have the *same.*] —*adv.* in the same way [Treat her the *same* as us.] —**all the same, 1.** of no importance. **2.** in spite of that; however. —**just the same, 1.** in the same way. **2.** in spite of that; however.

same·ness (sām'nis), *n.* **1.** the condition of being the same or just alike. **2.** lack of change or variety; monotony.

Sa·mo·a (sə mō'ə), *n.* a group of islands in the South Pacific. Six of them (**American Samoa**) belong to the United States.

sam·o·var (sam'ə vär), *n.* a metal urn with a tube inside for heating water in making tea. Samovars are common in Russia.

sam·pan (sam'pan), *n.* a small boat used in China and Japan. It is rowed with an oar at the stern, and it often has a sail.

sam·ple (sam'p'l), *n.* a part or piece that shows what the whole group or thing is like; specimen or example [little pieces of wallpaper for *samples;* a *sample* of her typing]. —*adj.* that is a sample [a *sample* page of the book]. —*v.* to test by trying a sample [He *sampled* the basket of grapes.] —**sam'pled,** *p.t. & p.p.;* **sam'pling,** *pr.p.*

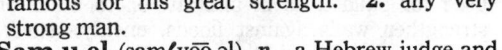
samovar

sam·pler (sam'plər), *n.* a piece of cloth with designs, mottoes, etc. sewn in fancy stitches.

Sam·son (sam's'n), *n.* **1.** an Israelite in the Bible

sampan

famous for his great strength. **2.** any very strong man.

Sam·u·el (sam'yōō əl), *n.* a Hebrew judge and prophet in the Bible. Two books of the Old Testament are named after him.

San An·to·ni·o (san ən tō'ni ō), a city in south central Texas.

san·a·to·ri·um (san'ə tôr'i əm), *n.* same as **sanitarium.**

sanc·ti·fy (sangk'tə fī), *v.* **1.** to set aside for religious use; consecrate [to *sanctify* a new altar]. **2.** to make holy or free from sin; purify. **3.** to make seem right; justify [a practice *sanctified* by custom]. —**sanc'ti·fied,** *p.t. & p.p.;* **sanc'ti·fy·ing,** *pr.p.* —**sanc'ti·fi·ca'tion,** *n.*

sanc·ti·mo·ni·ous (sangk'tə mō'ni əs), *adj.* pretending to be very holy or religious.

sanc·tion (sangk'shən), *n.* **1.** approval or permission given by someone in authority; authorization [The club was formed with the *sanction* of the principal.] **2.** an action taken by a group of nations against another nation considered to have broken international law [A blockade of shipping may be one of the *sanctions* imposed on a country.] —*v.* to approve or permit [I cannot *sanction* such rudeness.]

sanc·ti·ty (sangk'tə tē), *n.* **1.** the condition of being holy or saintly; holiness. **2.** the condition of being sacred, or set aside for religious purposes [the *sanctity* of a cathedral]. **3.** the condition of being binding and not to be broken [the *sanctity* of the marriage vows].

sanc·tu·ar·y (sangk'chōō er'ē), *n.* **1.** a place set aside for religious worship, as a church or temple. **2.** the main room for services in a house of worship. **3.** a place where one can find safety or shelter; also, the safety found there [The criminals found *sanctuary* in a church.] **4.** a place where birds and animals are protected from hunters [a wild-life *sanctuary*]. —**sanc'tu·ar'ies,** *pl.*

sanc·tum (sangk'təm), *n.* **1.** a sacred place. **2.** a private room where one is not to be disturbed.

sand (sand), *n.* **1.** tiny, loose grains worn away from rock and forming the ground of beaches, deserts, etc. **2.** *usually* **sands,** *pl.* an area of sand. —*v.* **1.** to make smooth with sand or sandpaper. **2.** to sprinkle, mix, or fill with sand. —**sand'er,** *n.*

san·dal (san'd'l), *n.* **1.** a kind of shoe that is just a flat sole fastened to the foot by straps. **2.** a kind of open slipper.

san·dal·wood (san'd'l-wood), *n.* the hard, sweet-smelling wood of certain trees of Asia, used for carvings, etc. and burned as incense.

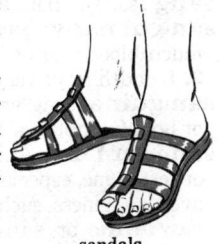
sandals

sand·bag (sand'bag), *n.* **1.** a bag filled with sand, used for ballast, as in aircraft, or to build or strengthen walls against floods, enemy attack, etc. **2.** a small bag of sand used as a weapon. —*v.* to put sandbags in or around. —**sand'-bagged,** *p.t. & p.p.;* **sand'bag·ging,** *pr.p.*

sand bar, a ridge of sand formed in a river or along a shore by currents or tides.

sand·blast (sand'blast), *n.* a strong stream of air carrying sand, used to etch glass, clean the surface of stone, etc. —*v.* to etch, clean, etc. with a sandblast.

sand·box (sand'bäks), *n.* a box filled with sand, as for children to play in.

San Di·e·go (san di ā'gō), a seaport in southern California.

sand-lot (sand'lät'), *adj.* having to do with, or played in, a sandy lot or empty field [*sand-lot* baseball].

sand·man (sand'man), *n.* a make-believe man who is supposed to make children sleepy by sprinkling sand in their eyes.

sand·pa·per (sand'pā'pər), *n.* strong paper with sand glued on one side, used for smoothing and polishing. —*v.* to rub with sandpaper.

sand·pip·er (sand'pĭp'ər), *n.* a shore bird having a long bill with a soft tip.

sand·stone (sand'stōn), *n.* a kind of rock formed of sand held together by silica, lime, etc. It is much used in building.

sand·storm (sand'stôrm), *n.* a windstorm in which sand is blown about in large clouds.

sandpiper
(about 8 in. long)

sand·wich (sand'wich *or* san'wich), *n.* slices of bread with a filling of meat, cheese, etc. between them. —*v.* to squeeze in [a shed *sandwiched* between two houses].

sand·y (san'dē), *adj.* **1.** of or full of sand [a *sandy* shore]. **2.** pale brown or dull yellow [*sandy* hair]. —**sand'i·er,** *compar.;* **sand'i·est,** *superl.*

sane (sān), *adj.* **1.** having a normal, healthy mind; rational. **2.** showing good sense; sensible [a *sane* policy]. —**san'er,** *compar.;* **san'est,** *superl.* —**sane'ly,** *adv.*

San Fran·cis·co (san frən sis'kō), a city on the coast of central California.

sang (sang), past tense of **sing.**

san·gui·nar·y (sang'gwi ner'ē), *adj.* **1.** with much bloodshed or killing [a *sanguinary* revolt]. **2.** bloodthirsty; very cruel.

san·guine (sang'gwin), *adj.* **1.** always cheerful or hopeful; optimistic. **2.** bright and red; ruddy.

san·i·tar·i·um (san'ə ter'i əm), *n.* a hospital or rest home, especially for people who are getting over an illness such as tuberculosis. —**san'i·tar'i·ums** or **san·i·tar·i·a** (san'ə ter'i ə), *pl.*

san·i·tar·y (san'ə ter'ē), *adj.* **1.** having to do with or bringing about health or healthful conditions [*sanitary* laws]. **2.** free from dirt that could bring disease; clean; hygienic [a *sanitary* meat market].

san·i·ta·tion (san'ə tā'shən), *n.* **1.** the science and work of bringing about healthful, sanitary conditions. **2.** the system of carrying away and getting rid of sewage.

san·i·tize (san'ə tīz), *v.* to make sanitary [a *sanitized* water glass in each hotel room]. —**san'-i·tized,** *p.t. & p.p.;* **san'i·tiz·ing,** *pr.p.*

san·i·ty (san'ə tē), *n.* **1.** the condition of being sane; soundness of mind; mental health. **2.** soundness of judgment; sensibleness.

San Juan (san hwän'), capital of Puerto Rico.

sank (sangk), a past tense of **sink.**

San Sal·va·dor (san sal'və dôr), **1.** an island in the Bahamas: the first land sighted by Columbus. **2.** the capital of El Salvador.

San·skrit or **San·scrit** (san'skrit), *n.* an ancient written language of India. It has given clues to language scholars about the origins of most European languages, which are related to it.

San·ta (san'tə), *n.* same as **Santa Claus.** —*adj.* holy or saint: *a Spanish or Italian word used in certain names,* as Santa Fe.

San·ta Claus (san'tə klôz'), a fat, jolly old man in popular legends, with a white beard and a red suit, who hands out gifts at Christmas.

San·ta Fe (san'tə fā'), the capital of New Mexico.

San·ti·a·go (sän'tē ä'gō), *n.* the capital of Chile.

San·to Do·min·go (san'tō də ming'gō), the old name of the **Dominican Republic.**

sap (sap), *n.* the juice that flows through a plant or tree, carrying food, water, etc. to all its parts.

sap (sap), *v.* **1.** to weaken or wear down by digging away at the foundations of; undermine [The flood waters *sapped* the wall of the canal.] **2.** to weaken or wear away slowly [A bad cold *sapped* his energy.] —**sapped,** *p.t. & p.p.;* **sap'ping,** *pr.p.*

sa·pi·ent (sā'pi ənt), *adj.* full of knowledge; wise. —**sa'pi·ence,** *n.*

sap·ling (sap'ling), *n.* a young tree.

sap·phire (saf'īr), *n.* **1.** a clear, deep-blue, costly jewel. **2.** deep blue.

sap·py (sap'ē), *adj.* **1.** full of sap; juicy. **2.** foolish; silly: *slang in this meaning.* —**sap'pi·er,** *compar.;* **sap'pi·est,** *superl.*

sap·suck·er (sap'suk'ər), *n.* a small American woodpecker that drills holes in trees and drinks the sap.

Sar·a·cen (sar'ə s'n), *n.* an Arab or Moslem, especially a Moslem at the time of the Crusades.

Sar·ah (ser'ə), *n.* in the Bible, the wife of Abraham and mother of Isaac.

sapsucker (9 in. long)

sar·casm (sär'kaz'm), *n.* **1.** a mocking or sneering remark meant to hurt someone or make him seem foolish. **2.** the act of making such a remark ["I only explained it five times," she replied in *sarcasm.*]

sar·cas·tic (sär kas'tik), *adj.* of, using, or showing sarcasm. —**sar·cas'ti·cal·ly,** *adv.*

sar·coph·a·gus (sär käf'ə gəs), *n.* a stone

coffin, especially a decorated one set in a tomb. **—sar·coph·a·gi** (sär käf′ə jī′) or **sar·coph′a·gus·es,** *pl.*

sar·dine (sär dēn′), *n.* a small fish, as a young herring, preserved in oil and packed in cans.

Sar·din·i·a (sär din′i ə), *n.* an Italian island in the Mediterranean, west of Italy.

sar·don·ic (sär dän′ik), *adj.* sneering or sarcastic in a bitter or scornful way [a *sardonic* smile]. **—sar·don′i·cal·ly,** *adv.*

sar·gas·so (sär gas′ō), *n.* a brownish seaweed floating over large warm areas of the ocean.

sa·ri (sä′rē), *n.* an outer garment of Hindu women, formed of a long cloth wrapped around the body, with one end over the head.

sa·rong (sə rông′), *n.* a kind of skirt worn by men and women in Indonesia, Ceylon, etc., formed of a long strip of cloth wrapped around the lower part of the body.

sari

sar·sa·pa·ril·la (sas′pə ril′ə or sär′sə pə ril′ə), *n.* **1.** a tropical American plant with sweet-smelling roots which are dried for use as a flavoring. **2.** soda water flavored with sarsaparilla.

sar·to·ri·al (sär tôr′i əl), *adj.* **1.** having to do with men's clothing [*sartorial* elegance]. **2.** of tailors or their work.

sash (sash), *n.* a band, ribbon, or scarf worn over the shoulder or around the waist.

sash (sash), *n.* a sliding frame that holds the glass pane or panes of a window or door.

Sas·katch·e·wan (sas kach′ə wän), *n.* a province of southwestern Canada: abbreviated **Sask.**

sas·sa·fras (sas′ə fras), *n.* **1.** a slender tree with yellow flowers. **2.** the dried bark of its root, used in medicine and for flavoring.

window sashes

sass·y (sas′ē), *adj.* talking back; impudent; saucy: *used only in everyday talk.* **—sass′i·er,** *compar.;* **sass′i·est,** *superl.*

sat (sat), past tense and past participle of **sit.**

Sat., abbreviation for **Saturday.**

Sa·tan (sā′t'n), *n.* the Devil.

sa·tan·ic (sā tan′ik), *adj.* like Satan; devilish.

satch·el (sach′əl), *n.* a small bag of leather, etc. for carrying clothes, books, or the like.

sassafras leaves and tree

sate (sāt), *v.* **1.** to satisfy completely [to *sate* a desire]. **2.** to supply with so much of something that it becomes unpleasant or disgusting; glut

[We were *sated* with all the rich food.] **—sat′ed,** *p.t. & p.p.;* **sat′ing,** *pr.p.*

sa·teen (sa tēn′), *n.* a smooth, glossy, cotton cloth, made to look like satin.

sat·el·lite (sat′ə lit), *n.* **1.** a heavenly body that revolves around another, larger one [The moon is a *satellite* of the earth.] **2.** a body put into space by man to revolve around the earth or the sun. **3.** a country that depends on and is controlled by a larger, more powerful one. **4.** a follower of an important person.

sa·ti·ate (sā′shi āt), *v.* **1.** to supply with so much of something that it becomes unpleasant or disgusting; glut [*satiated* with praise]. **2.** to satisfy fully: *seldom used.* **—sa′ti·at·ed,** *p.t. & p.p.;* **sa′ti·at·ing,** *pr.p.* **—sa′ti·a′tion,** *n.*

sa·ti·e·ty (sə tī′ə tē), *n.* the feeling of having had more than one wants.

sat·in (sat′n), *n.* a silk, rayon, or nylon cloth with a smooth, glossy finish on one side. **—adj.** of or like satin. **—sat′in·y,** *adj.*

sat·in·wood (sat′n wood), *n.* **1.** a smooth wood used in fine furniture. **2.** the tree of the East Indies that it comes from.

sat·ire (sat′īr), *n.* **1.** the use of irony, sarcasm, and humor to criticize or make fun of something bad or foolish. **2.** a novel, story, etc. in which this is done ["Gulliver's Travels" is a *satire* on England of the 18th century.]

sa·tir·i·cal (sə tir′i k'l) or **sa·tir·ic** (sə tir′ik), *adj.* of, like, full of, or using satire. **—sa·tir′i·cal·ly,** *adv.*

sat·i·rist (sat′ə rist), *n.* a person who writes satires or uses satire.

sat·i·rize (sat′ə rīz), *v.* to criticize or make fun of by using satire. **—sat′i·rized,** *p.t. & p.p.;* **sat′i·riz·ing,** *pr.p.*

sat·is·fac·tion (sat′is fak′shən), *n.* **1.** a satisfying or being satisfied. **2.** something that satisfies, especially anything that brings pleasure [It was a *satisfaction* to finish the work.] **—give satisfaction,** to satisfy.

sat·is·fac·to·ry (sat′is fak′tər ē), *adj.* good enough to satisfy, or meet the need or wish. **—sat′is·fac′to·ri·ly,** *adv.*

sat·is·fy (sat′is fī), *v.* **1.** to meet the needs or wishes of; content; please [Only first prize will *satisfy* him.] **2.** to make feel sure; convince [The jury was *satisfied* that he was innocent.] **3.** to pay off [to *satisfy* a debt]. **—sat′is·fied,** *p.t. & p.p.;* **sat′is·fy·ing,** *pr.p.*

sa·trap (sā′trap or sat′rap), *n.* **1.** the governor of a province in ancient Persia. **2.** a governor of a colony, etc. who is a tyrant.

sat·u·rate (sach′oo rāt), *v.* **1.** to soak through and through [The baby's bib was *saturated* with milk.] **2.** to fill so completely or dissolve so much of something in that no more can be taken up [to *saturate* water with salt]. **—sat′u·rat·ed,** *p.t. & p.p.;* **sat′u·rat·ing,** *pr.p.* **—sat′u·ra′tion,** *n.*

fat, āpe, cär, ten, ēven, hit, bīte, gō, hôrn, tool, book, up, fur; get, joy, yet, chin, she, thin, *th*en; zh = s in pleasure; ′ as in able (ā′b'l); ə = a in ago, e in agent, i in sanity, o in confess, u in focus.

Sat·ur·day (sat′ər dē), *n.* the seventh and last day of the week.

Sat·urn (sat′ərn), *n.* **1.** the Roman god of farming. **2.** the second largest planet, known for the rings seen around it. It is the sixth in distance away from the sun.

Saturn

sat·ur·nine (sat′ər nīn), *adj.* quiet and serious, often in a gloomy or solemn way.

sat·yr (sat′ər *or* sā′tər), *n.* in Greek myths, a minor god of the woods, with the head and body of a man and the legs, ears, and horns of a goat.

sauce (sôs), *n.* **1.** a liquid or soft dressing served with food to make it tastier [I'll make a tomato *sauce* for the spaghetti.] **2.** fruit that has been stewed and, often, mashed [apple*sauce*]. **3.** impudence: *used only in everyday talk.*

sauce·pan (sôs′pan), *n.* a small metal pot with a long handle, used for cooking.

sau·cer (sô′sər), *n.* **1.** a small, shallow dish, especially one for a cup to rest on. **2.** anything shaped like this.

saucepan

sau·cy (sô′sē), *adj.* **1.** rude; impudent. **2.** lively and bold [a *saucy* smile]. —**sau′ci·er,** *compar.;* **sau′ci·est,** *superl.* —**sau′ci·ness,** *n.*

Sa·u·di Arabia (sä ōō′dē), a kingdom in central Arabia.

sauer·kraut (sour′krout′), *n.* cabbage that has been chopped up, salted, and allowed to turn sour in its own juice.

Saul (sôl), *n.* in the Bible, first king of Israel.

saun·ter (sôn′tər), *v.* to walk about slowly, not in a hurry; stroll. —*n.* a walk taken in this way [to take a *saunter* through the park].

sau·sage (sô′sij), *n.* pork or other meat chopped up and seasoned and, usually, stuffed into a tube made of thin skin.

sau·té (sō tā′), *v.* to fry quickly in a pan with a little fat. —*adj.* fried in this way [chicken livers *sauté*]. —**sau·téed** (sō tād′), *p.t. & p.p.;* **sau·té′ing,** *pr.p.*

sav·age (sav′ij), *adj.* **1.** not civilized; primitive [a *savage* tribe]. **2.** not tamed; fierce; wild [a *savage* animal]. **3.** cruel; brutal [a *savage* pirate]. —*n.* **1.** a person living in a primitive or uncivilized way. **2.** a fierce, brutal person. —**sav′age·ly,** *adv.* —**sav′age·ness,** *n.*

sav·age·ry (sav′ij rē), *n.* **1.** the condition of being savage, wild, or uncivilized. **2.** a cruel or brutal act. —**sav′age·ries,** *pl.*

sa·van·na or **sa·van·nah** (sə van′ə), *n.* a flat, open region without trees; plain.

Sa·van·nah (sə van′ə), *n.* a seaport in Georgia.

sa·vant (sə vänt′ *or* sav′ənt), *n.* a scholar.

save (sāv), *v.* **1.** to rescue or keep from harm or danger [He was *saved* from drowning.] **2.** to keep or store up for future use [She *saved* her money for a vacation.] **3.** to keep from being lost or wasted [Traveling by plane *saved* many hours.] **4.** to prevent or make less [He *saved* the expense by doing it himself.] **5.** to keep from being worn out, damaged, etc. [*Save* your dress by wearing this apron.] **6.** to avoid expense, loss, waste, etc. [She *saves* on meat by buying cheaper cuts.] **7.** in religion, to free from sin, death, etc. —**saved,** *p.t. & p.p.;* **sav′ing,** *pr.p.* —**sav′er,** *n.*

save (sāv), *prep.* except; except for; but [I've asked everyone *save* you two.]

sav·ing (sāv′ing), *adj.* that saves, rescues, stores up, redeems, etc. [a time-*saving* device; a *saving* virtue]. —*n.* **1.** the act of one that saves. **2.** a thing, amount, sum of money, etc. saved [a *saving* of 20%; one's life's *savings*].

sav·ing (sāv′ing), *prep.* **1.** except; save. **2.** with due respect for [*Saving* your presence, this must be discussed.] *Now seldom used.*

sav·ior or **sav·iour** (sāv′yər), *n.* a person who saves, or rescues. —**the Saviour** or **the Savior,** Jesus Christ.

sa·vor (sā′vər), *n.* **1.** a special taste or smell; flavor [The salad has a *savor* of garlic.] **2.** a special, usually pleasing quality [Golf has lost all its *savor* for him.] —*v.* **1.** to taste, enjoy, etc. with relish [He *savored* his success as an actor.] **2.** to have a special taste, smell, or quality [His action *savors* of rudeness.]

sa·vor·y (sā′vər ē), *adj.* pleasing to the taste or smell [a *savory* stew].

sa·vor·y (sā′vər ē), *n.* a kind of herb with a mint flavor, used in cooking.

sa·vour (sā′vər), *n.* British spelling of **savor.**

saw (sô), *n.* a cutting tool that has a thin metal blade or disk with sharp teeth along the edge. Some saws are worked by hand and others by machinery. —*v.* **1.** to cut or form with a saw [to *saw* wood]. **2.** to move the arms through, as if sawing [He *sawed* the air as he argued.] **3.** to be sawed [This plank *saws* easily.] —**sawed,** *p.t.;* **sawed** or **sawn** (sôn), *p.p.;* **saw′ing,** *pr.p.*

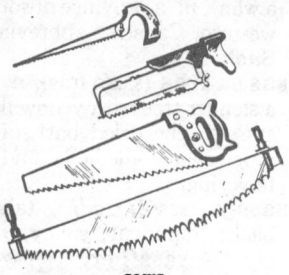

saws

saw (sô), *n.* an old saying, or proverb.

saw (sô), past tense of **see.**

saw·dust (sô′dust), *n.* tiny bits of wood formed in sawing wood.

saw·horse (sô′hôrs) or **saw·buck** (sô′buk), *n.* a rack on which wood is placed for sawing.

saw·mill (sô′mil), *n.* **1.** a place where logs are sawed into boards. **2.** a large sawing machine.

saw·yer (sô′yər), *n.* a person whose work is sawing wood.

sax (saks), *n.* a short form of **saxophone.**

sawhorse

sax·i·frage (sak′si frij), *n.* a plant with yellow, white, purple, or pink small flowers, and leaves growing in a clump at the base.

Sax·on (sak′s'n), *n.* a member of a people who lived in northern Germany long ago. Saxons invaded England in the 5th and 6th centuries A.D. —*adj.* of the Saxons, their language, etc.

Sax·o·ny (sak′sə nē), *n.* 1. a region in the southern part of East Germany. 2. a state in the northern part of West Germany: *the full name is* **Lower Saxony.**

sax·o·phone (sak′sə fōn), *n.* a musical instrument that is like a clarinet, but has a curved metal body. Its mouthpiece has a single reed.

saxophone

say (sā), *v.* 1. to speak or pronounce; utter ["Hello," he *said.*] 2. to put into words; tell; state [The newspaper *says* it will rain.] 3. to give as an opinion [I cannot *say* who will win.] 4. to recite or repeat [Did you *say* your prayers?] 5. to suppose or guess [He is, I'd *say,* forty.] —*n.* 1. what a person says. 2. a chance to speak [Not everyone has had his *say.*] 3. the power to decide [Father has the final *say* about that.] —**go without saying,** to be so clear that it needs no explaining. —**that is to say,** in other words; that means. —**said,** *p.t. & p.p.;* **say′ing,** *pr.p.* —**say′er,** *n.*

say·ing (sā′ing), *n.* something said, especially a proverb, such as "Waste not, want not."

says (sez), the form of **say** showing the present time with singular nouns and *he, she,* or *it.*

Sb, symbol for the chemical element *antimony.*

S.C., abbreviation for **South Carolina.**

scab (skab), *n.* 1. a crust that forms over a sore as it is healing. 2. mange, especially of sheep. 3. a plant disease caused by certain fungi. 4. a worker who keeps on working even though there is a strike. —*v.* 1. to become covered with a scab. 2. to act as a scab. —**scabbed,** *p.t. & p.p.;* **scab′bing,** *pr.p.*

scab·bard (skab′ərd), *n.* a case or sheath to hold the blade of a sword, dagger, etc.

scaf·fold (skaf′'ld), *n.* 1. a framework put up to support workmen while they are building, repairing, or painting something: *see the picture at the top of the next column.* 2. a raised platform on which criminals are hanged or beheaded.

scaf·fold·ing (skaf′'l ding), *n.* 1. the materials that make up a scaffold. 2. a scaffold.

scabbard

scald (skôld), *v.* 1. to burn with hot liquid or steam. 2. to use boiling liquid on, as to kill germs. 3. to heat until it almost boils [to *scald* milk for a custard]. —*n.* a burn caused by scalding.

scale (skāl), *n.* 1. a series of marks along a line, with regular spaces in between, used for measuring [My ruler has a *scale* for both centimeters and inches.] 2. the way that the size of a map, model, or drawing compares with the size of the thing that it stands for [One inch on a map of this *scale* equals 100 miles of real distance.] 3. a series of steps or degrees based on size, amount, etc. [The passing grade on this *scale* is 70.] 4. a series of musical tones arranged in order from the highest to the lowest or from the lowest to the highest. —*v.* 1. to climb up as by a ladder [to *scale* a wall]. 2. to set according to a scale [The pay is *scaled* according to skill.] —**on a large scale,** to a large extent. —**scaled,** *p.t. & p.p.;* **scal′ing,** *pr.p.*

scaffold

scale (skāl), *n.* 1. any of the thin, flat, hard plates that cover and protect certain fish and reptiles. 2. a thin piece or layer; flake [*scales* of rust in a water tank]. —*v.* 1. to scrape scales from [to *scale* a fish]. 2. to come off in scales [The old, dry paint *scaled* off in the hot sun.] —**scaled,** *p.t. & p.p.;* **scal′ing,** *pr.p.*

scale (skāl), *n.* 1. either of the shallow pans of a balance. *See the picture for* **balance.** 2. *usually* **scales,** *pl.* the balance itself; also, any device or machine for weighing. *See the picture.* —*v.* to weigh. —**turn the scales,** to decide or settle. —**scaled,** *p.t. & p.p.;* **scal′ing,** *pr.p.*

scal·lion (skal′yən), *n.* a kind of onion; especially, a young green onion or a leek.

scal·lop (skäl′əp *or* skal′əp), *n.* 1. a water animal with a soft body enclosed in two hard, ribbed shells hinged together. It has a large muscle, used as food. 2. any of a series of curves that form a fancy edge on cloth, lace, etc. —*v.* 1. to bake with a milk sauce and bread crumbs [*scalloped* potatoes]. 2. to cut in scallops [a *scalloped* neckline].

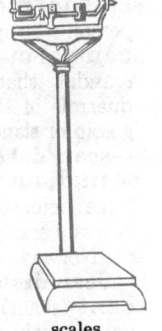
scales

scalp (skalp), *n.* 1. the part of the skin on the head that is usually

upper: scallop *(meaning 1)*
lower: scallops *(meaning 2)*

---

fat, āpe, cär, ten, ēven, hit, bīte, gō, hôrn, tōol, book, up, fûr;
get, joy, yet, chin, she, thin, *th*en; zh = s in pleasure; ′ as in able (ā′b'l);
ə = a in ago, e in agent, i in sanity, o in confess, u in focus.

covered with hair. **2.** a piece of this cut from the head of an enemy. Some American Indians kept scalps as trophies. —*v.* to cut the scalp from.

scal·pel (skal′pəl), *n.* a small, very sharp knife, used by surgeons in operations.

scal·y (skāl′ē), *adj.* covered with scales [a small, *scaly* lizard]. —**scal′i·er,** *compar.*; **scal′i·est,** *superl.* —**scal′i·ness,** *n.*

scamp (skamp), *n.* a person who often gets into trouble or mischief; rascal.

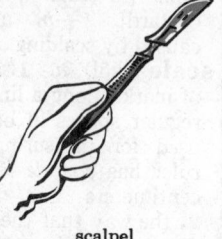
scalpel

scam·per (skam′pər), *v.* to move quickly or in a hurry [squirrels *scampering* through the trees]. —*n.* a quick run or dash.

scan (skan), *v.* **1.** to look at very carefully; examine [Columbus *scanned* the horizon for land.] **2.** to glance at or look over quickly [I *scanned* the list of names to find yours.] **3.** to show the pattern of rhythm in the lines of a poem [We can *scan* a line this way: Má rў/ Má rў/ quíte còn/trá rў.] —**scanned,** *p.t. & p.p.*; **scan′ning,** *pr.p.*

scan·dal (skan′d'l), *n.* **1.** someone or something that shocks people and causes shame or disgrace [Years ago, it was a *scandal* for a woman to wear lipstick.] **2.** the shame or disgrace caused by this. **3.** talk that harms a person's reputation; wicked gossip.

scan·dal·ize (skan′d'l īz), *v.* to shock by shameful words or acts [We were *scandalized* at the lies he told.] —**scan′dal·ized,** *p.t. & p.p.*; **scan′dal·iz·ing,** *pr.p.*

scan·dal·mon·ger (skan′d'l mung′gər), *n.* a person who spreads gossip.

scan·dal·ous (skan′d'l əs), *adj.* **1.** causing scandal; shameful; disgraceful [the *scandalous* quarrels of the noisy neighbors]. **2.** spreading gossip or slander [a *scandalous* newspaper story]. —**scan′dal·ous·ly,** *adv.*

Scan·di·na·vi·a (skan′də nā′vi ə), *n.* **1.** a large peninsula of northern Europe, on which Norway and Sweden are located. **2.** the countries of Norway, Sweden, Denmark, and Iceland. —**Scan′di·na′vi·an,** *adj. & n.*

scant (skant), *adj.* **1.** not as much as is needed; not enough; meager [a *scant* supply of food]. **2.** less than full; incomplete [Add a *scant* teaspoon of salt.] —*v.* to limit or make scant. —**scant of,** not having enough of; lacking.

scant·ling (skant′ling), *n.* **1.** a small beam or timber. **2.** small beams and timbers.

scant·y (skan′tē), *adj.* not enough or just barely enough; meager [a *scanty* harvest]. —**scant′i·ly,** *adv.* —**scant′i·ness,** *n.*

scape·goat (skāp′gōt), *n.* a person, group, or thing forced to take the blame for the mistakes or crimes of others.

scap·u·la (skap′yoo lə), *n.* the shoulder blade. —**scap·u·lae** (skap′yoo lē′) or **scap′u·las,** *pl.*

scar (skär), *n.* **1.** a mark left on the skin after a cut, burn, etc. has healed. **2.** any mark like this, as the mark on a plant where a leaf has

fallen off. **3.** the result left on the mind by suffering. —*v.* to mark with or form a scar. —**scarred,** *p.t. & p.p.*; **scar′ring,** *pr.p.*

scar·ab (skar′əb), *n.* **1.** a beetle of the kind that was sacred to the ancient Egyptians. **2.** a likeness of this beetle, once used as a charm.

scarab (meaning 2)

scarce (skers), *adj.* **1.** not common; rare [Horses are *scarce* on our streets today.] **2.** not plentiful; hard to get [Gasoline was *scarce* in wartime.] —**make oneself scarce,** to go or stay away: *used only in everyday talk.* —**scarc′er,** *compar.*; **scarc′est,** *superl.* —**scarce′ness,** *n.*

scarce·ly (skers′lē), *adv.* **1.** only just; barely; hardly [I can *scarcely* taste the pepper in it.] **2.** certainly not [You can *scarcely* expect us to believe that.]

scar·ci·ty (sker′sə tē), *n.* the condition of being scarce; lack, rareness, etc. —**scar′ci·ties,** *pl.*

scare (sker), *v.* **1.** to make or become afraid; frighten. **2.** to drive away by frightening [an alarm to *scare* off burglars]. —*n.* a sudden fear; fright [The loud noise gave me quite a *scare*.] —**scare up,** to produce or gather quickly: *used only in everyday talk.* —**scared,** *p.t. & p.p.*; **scar′ing,** *pr.p.*

scare·crow (sker′krō), *n.* a figure of a man made with sticks, old clothes, etc. and set up in a field to scare birds away from crops.

scarf (skärf), *n.* **1.** a long or broad piece of cloth worn about the head, neck, or shoulders for warmth or decoration. **2.** a long, narrow piece of cloth used as a covering for a table, piano, etc. —**scarfs** or **scarves** (skärvz), *pl.*

scarecrow

scar·la·ti·na (skär′lə tē′nə), *n.* scarlet fever, especially a mild form of the disease.

scar·let (skär′lit), *n.* very bright red with an orange tinge. —*adj.* of this color.

scarlet fever, a catching disease, especially of children. that causes a sore throat, fever, and a scarlet rash.

scarlet tanager, a songbird of the United States. The male has a scarlet body and black wings and tail.

scar·y (sker′ē), *adj.* **1.** causing fear; frightening. **2.** quick to frighten. *Used only in everyday talk.* —**scar′i·er,** *compar.*; **scar′i·est,** *superl.*

scath·ing (skā*th*′ing), *adj.* very harsh or bitter, as in showing dislike [a *scathing* reply]. —**scath′ing·ly,** *adv.*

scat·ter (skat′ər), *v.* **1.** to throw here and there; sprinkle [to *scatter* seed over a lawn]. **2.** to separate and send or go in many directions; disperse [The wind *scattered* the leaves. The crowd *scattered* after the game.]

scat·ter·brain (skat′ər brān), *n.* a person who cannot think seriously or pay attention; flighty person. —**scat′ter·brained,** *adj.*

scat·ter·ing (skat′ər ing), *n.* a few here and there [an audience of children with a *scattering* of adults].

scav·en·ger (skav′in jər), *n.* **1.** an animal that feeds on rotting meat or garbage [Vultures and hyenas are *scavengers*.] **2.** a person who gathers things that others have thrown away.

sce·na·ri·o (si ner′i ō), *n.* an older word for **screenplay.** —**sce·na′ri·os,** *pl.*

scene (sēn), *n.* **1.** the place where a thing happens [the *scene* of an accident]. **2.** the place and time of a story, play, etc. **3.** a division of a play, usually a separate part of an act. **4.** a certain event in a play, motion picture, or story [the *scene* in which the lovers meet]. **5.** the scenery of a play, motion picture, etc. **6.** a view, landscape, etc. [a pleasant autumn *scene*]. **7.** a show of anger, bad temper, etc. [She made quite a *scene* in court when she lost the case.]

scen·er·y (sēn′ər ē), *n.* **1.** the way a certain area looks; outdoor views [the *scenery* along the shore]. **2.** painted screens, hangings, etc. used on a stage for a play.

scen·ic (sē′nik *or* sen′ik), *adj.* **1.** having to do with scenery or landscapes [the *scenic* wonders of the Rockies]. **2.** having beautiful scenery [a *scenic* route]. **3.** of the stage and its scenery, lighting, etc. [The *scenic* effects included a pond.]

scent (sent), *n.* **1.** a smell; odor [the *scent* of new-mown hay]. **2.** the sense of smell [Lions hunt partly by *scent*.] **3.** a smell left by an animal [The dogs lost the fox's *scent* at the river.] **4.** a perfume. —*v.* **1.** to smell [Our dog *scented* a rat.] **2.** to get a hint of [to *scent* trouble]. **3.** to put perfume on or in [a *scented* handkerchief].

scep·ter *or* **scep·tre** (sep′tər), *n.* a rod or staff held by a ruler as a symbol of his power.

scep·tic (skep′tik), *n.* same as **skeptic.** —**scep′ti·cal,** *adj.* —**scep′ti·cism,** *n.*

sched·ule (skej′ool), *n.* **1.** a list of the times at which certain things are to happen; timetable [a *schedule* of the sailings of an ocean liner]. **2.** the time planned for something [He came ahead of *schedule*.] **3.** a list of details [a *schedule* of freight charges]. —*v.*

scepter

to make a schedule of; place in a schedule [to *schedule* a work program; to *schedule* a speech for 9:00 P.M.]. —**sched′uled,** *p.t. & p.p.;* **sched′-ul·ing,** *pr.p.*

scheme (skēm), *n.* **1.** a plan or system in which things are carefully put together [the color *scheme* of a painting]. **2.** a plan or program, often a secret or dishonest one [a *scheme* for getting control of a company]. —*v.* to make secret or dishonest plans; plot [He is always *scheming* to get out of work.] —**schemed,** *p.t. & p.p.;* **schem′ing,** *pr.p.* —**schem′er,** *n.*

schem·ing (skēm′ing), *adj.* forming schemes; sly; tricky.

Sche·nec·ta·dy (skə nek′tə dē), *n.* a city in eastern New York.

scher·zo (sker′tsō), *n.* a lively, playful piece of music, often a part of a symphony. —**scher′zos** or **scher·zi** (sker′tsē), *pl.*

schism (siz′m), *n.* a split or division between the members of a church or other group, when they no longer agree on what they believe.

schis·mat·ic (siz mat′ik), *adj.* **1.** of or like a schism. **2.** tending to cause a schism. —*n.* a person who takes part in a schism.

Schles·wig-Hol·stein (shles′wig hōl′stīn), *n.* a state in West Germany, bordering on Denmark.

schol·ar (skäl′ər), *n.* **1.** a person who has learned much through study. **2.** a student or pupil. **3.** a student who has a scholarship.

schol·ar·ly (skäl′ər lē), *adj.* **1.** of or like scholars. **2.** showing much learning [a *scholarly* book]. **3.** that likes to study and learn [a *scholarly* boy]. —**schol′ar·li·ness,** *n.*

schol·ar·ship (skäl′ər ship), *n.* **1.** the knowledge of a learned man; great learning. **2.** the kind of knowledge that a student shows [his faulty *scholarship*]. **3.** a gift of money to help a student continue his education.

scho·las·tic (skə las′tik), *adj.* having to do with schools, students, teachers, and studies [*scholastic* honors]. —**scho·las′ti·cal·ly,** *adv.*

school (skool), *n.* **1.** a place, usually a special building, for teaching and learning, as a public school, dancing school, college, etc. **2.** the students and teachers of a school [an assembly for the whole *school*]. **3.** the time during which students are in classes [*School* starts in September.] **4.** the full course of study in a school [He never finished *school*.] **5.** any time or situation during which a person learns [the *school* of experience]. **6.** a certain part of a college or university [the law *school*; the dental *school*]. **7.** a group of people who have the same ideas and opinions [a new *school* of writers]. —*v.* **1.** to teach or train; educate [He was *schooled* in the old methods.] **2.** to control; discipline [to *school* oneself to be patient]. —*adj.* of or for a school or schools [our *school* colors].

school (skool), *n.* a large group of fish or water animals swimming together [a *school* of porpoises]. —*v.* to swim together in a school.

school board, a group of people chosen to be in charge of local public schools.

school·book (skool′book), *n.* a book used for study in schools; textbook.

school·boy (skool′boi), *n.* a boy who goes to school.

school·fel·low (skool′fel′ō), *n.* a schoolmate.

school·girl (skool′gurl), *n.* a girl who goes to school.

school·house (skool′hous), *n.* a building used as a school.

---

fat, āpe, cär, ten, ēven, hit, bīte, gō, hôrn, tool, book, up, fur;
get, joy, yet, chin, she, thin, *th*en; zh = s in pleasure; ′ as in able (ā′b′l);
ə = a in ago, e in agent, i in sanity, o in confess, u in focus.

school·ing (skoōl/ing), *n.* teaching or training got at a school; education [How many years of *schooling* have you had?]

school·mas·ter (skoōl/mas/tər), *n.* a man who teaches in a school, or is its principal. **—school/-mis/tress,** *n.fem.*

school·mate (skoōl/māt), *n.* a person going to the same school at the same time as another.

school·room (skoōl/roōm), *n.* a room in which pupils are taught, as in a school.

school·teach·er (skoōl/tēch/ər), *n.* a person whose work is teaching in a school.

school·work (skoōl/wûrk), *n.* lessons worked on in classes at school or done as homework.

school·yard (skoōl/yärd), *n.* the ground around a school, often used as a playground.

school year, the part of a year during which school is held, usually from September to June.

schoon·er (skoōn/ər), *n.* a ship with two or more masts and sails that are set lengthwise.

schooner

Schu·bert, Franz (fränts shoō/bərt), 1797–1828; Austrian composer of music.

Schu·mann, Robert (shoō/män), 1810–1856; German composer of music.

schwa (shwä), *n.* the sound of a vowel in a syllable that is not accented, as the "a" in "ago"; also, the symbol ə used for this sound.

Schweit·zer, Albert (shwīt/sər), 1875–1965; European doctor and missionary in Africa.

sci·ence (sī/əns), *n.* **1.** knowledge made up of an orderly system of facts that have been learned from study, observation, and experiments [*Science* helps us to understand and control the world we live in.] **2.** a branch of this knowledge [the *science* of astronomy]. **3.** skill or ability [the *science* of boxing].

sci·en·tif·ic (sī/ən tif/ik), *adj.* **1.** having to do with, or used in, science [a *scientific* study; *scientific* equipment]. **2.** using the rules and methods of science [*scientific* procedure]. **3.** skillful or highly trained [a *scientific* boxer]. **—sci·en·tif/i·cal·ly,** *adv.*

sci·en·tist (sī/ən tist), *n.* an expert in science, such as a chemist, biologist, etc.

scim·i·tar or **scim·i·ter** (sim/ə tər), *n.* a curved sword used by Turks, Arabs, etc.

scin·til·la (sin til/ə), *n.* **1.** a spark. **2.** a tiny bit; trace [not a *scintilla* of hope].

scin·til·late (sin/tə lāt), *v.* **1.** to sparkle or twinkle. **2.** to be very clever and witty [to *scintillate* in conversation]. **—scin/til·lat·ed,** *p.t. & p.p.;* **scin/til·lat·ing,** *pr.p.* **—scin/til·la/tion,** *n.*

scimitar

sci·on (sī/ən), *n.* **1.** a bud or shoot of a plant, used for planting or grafting. **2.** an heir or descendant.

scis·sors (siz/ərz), *n.pl.* a tool for cutting, with two blades that are joined so that they slide over each other when their handles are moved: also called **pair of scissors.**

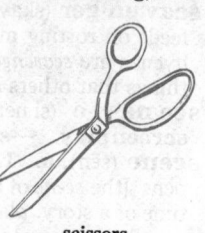
scissors

scoff (skôf *or* skäf), *v.* to mock or jeer at; make fun of [He *scoffed* at her foolish fears.] **—n. 1.** a rude or mocking remark; jeer. **2.** a person or thing scoffed at. **—scoff/er,** *n.*

scold (skōld), *v.* to find fault with someone in an angry way [A mother *scolds* a naughty child.] **—n.** a person who often scolds, nags, etc.

scol·lop (skäl/əp), *n. & v.* same as **scallop.**

sconce (skäns), *n.* a bracket attached to a wall, for holding a candle, etc.

scone (skōn), *n.* a small, flat cake, eaten as a biscuit with butter.

scoop (skoōp), *n.* **1.** a kitchen tool like a small shovel, used to take up sugar, flour, etc., or one with a small, round bowl for dishing up ice cream, etc. **2.** the part of a dredge or steam shovel which takes up the sand, dirt, etc. **3.** the act of taking up with a scoop [Every *scoop* of the shovel makes the hole deeper.] **4.** the amount taken up at one time by a scoop [three *scoops* of ice cream]. **5.** a hollowed-out place; hole. **6.** the printing of a news item before other newspapers can print it: *slang in this meaning.* **—v. 1.** to take up as with a scoop [We *scooped* up water with our hands.] **2.** to make a hole, etc. by scooping. **3.** to print a news item before others can: *slang in this meaning.*

types of scoop
(meaning 1)

scoot (skoōt), *v.* to go quickly; scamper: *used only in everyday talk.*

scoot·er (skoōt/ər), *n.* **1.** a child's toy for riding on, having a low board for the foot, with a wheel at each end, and a handle bar for steering. It is moved by pushing the other foot against the ground. **2.** a machine like this with a seat, run by a motor: *its full name is* **motor scooter.**

motor scooter

scope (skōp), *n.* **1.** the extent of one's ability to understand; range of understanding [The problem is beyond his *scope.*] **2.** the amount or kind of material that is covered or included [the *scope* of a school dictionary]. **3.** room for freedom of action or thought; opportunity [plenty of *scope* for new ideas].

-scope (skōp), a suffix meaning "an instrument for seeing or looking" [A *telescope* is an instrument for seeing things at a distance.]

scorch (skôrch), *v.* **1.** to burn or be burned slightly [I *scorched* the shirt with the iron.] **2.** to dry up by heat; parch [The sun *scorched* the plants.] —*n.* a slight burn on the surface.

score (skôr), *n.* **1.** the number of points made in a game or contest [The *score* is 2 to 1.] **2.** a grade or rating, as on a test [a *score* of 98%]. **3.** twenty people or things [a *score* of visitors]. **4. scores,** *pl.* very many [*scores* of soldiers]. **5.** a piece of music showing all the parts for the instruments or voices [the *score* of an opera]. **6.** a scratch or mark [the *scores* made on ice by skates]. **7.** an amount owed; debt [to settle a *score*]. **8.** an injury or wrong; grudge [to pay off an old *score*]. **9.** the real facts: *used only in everyday talk* [to know the *score*]. —*v.* **1.** to make points, runs, hits, etc. in a game [The hockey player *scored* two goals.] **2.** to mark or keep the score of [Will you *score* our game?] **3.** to give a grade or rating to [to *score* a test]. **4.** to mark with notches, lines, etc. [a face *scored* by age]. **5.** to win or achieve [to *score* a success]. **6.** to arrange a piece of music in a score. —**scored,** *p.t. & p.p.;* **scor′ing,** *pr.p.* —**scor′er,** *n.*

scorn (skôrn), *n.* **1.** a feeling that one has toward something low, mean, or evil; contempt [We have nothing but *scorn* for a cheater.] **2.** the showing of such feeling [the *scorn* in his smile]. **3.** a person or thing that meets with scorn. —*v.* **1.** to think of and treat as low, mean, etc.; show contempt for [to *scorn* a tattler]. **2.** to refuse as wrong or disgraceful [He *scorns* to fight with girls.]

scorn·ful (skôrn′fəl), *adj.* full of scorn or contempt [a *scornful* laugh]. —**scorn′ful·ly,** *adv.*

scor·pi·on (skôr′pi ən), *n.* a small animal related to the spider and having a long tail with a poisonous sting at the tip.

Scot (skät), *n.* a Scotsman.

Scotch (skäch), *adj.* Scottish. —*n.* the English spoken in Scotland. See **Scottish.**

scorpion (1 to 8 in. long)

scotch (skäch), *v.* **1.** to stop from causing trouble; put an end to [to *scotch* a rumor]. **2.** to wound without killing.

Scotch·man (skäch′mən), *n.* a Scot; Scotsman: see **Scotsman.** —**Scotch′men,** *pl.*

scot-free (skät′frē′), *adj.* without being punished or hurt; free from penalty; safe.

Scot·land (skät′lənd), *n.* a part of Great Britain, north of England.

Scotland Yard, the London police headquarters, especially its detective bureau.

Scots (skäts), *adj. & n.* Scottish.

Scots·man (skäts′mən), *n.* a person born or living in Scotland. —**Scots′men,** *pl.*

Scott, Sir Walter (skät), 1771–1832; Scottish writer of novels and poems.

Scot·tish (skät′ish), *adj.* of Scotland, its people, etc. —*n.* **1.** the people of Scotland:

used with a plural verb. **2.** the English dialect of Scotland. *Scottish* is now the preferred word in most cases, but *Scotch* is used with certain words, as "tweed" or "whisky."

scoun·drel (skoun′drəl), *n.* a bad or dishonest person; villain; rascal.

scour (skour), *v.* **1.** to clean by rubbing hard, especially with something rough or gritty [She *scoured* the greasy skillet with soap and steel wool.] **2.** to clear out or cleanse as by a flow of water. —*n.* the act of scouring.

scour (skour), *v.* to go about or through in a quick but thorough way, as in searching [Men *scoured* the town for the lost child.]

scourge (skūrj), *n.* **1.** a whip. **2.** something that causes great pain, suffering, etc., as war or a plague. —*v.* **1.** to whip or flog. **2.** to cause much pain or suffering to; punish; torment. —**scourged,** *p.t. & p.p.;* **scourg′ing,** *pr.p.*

scout (skout), *n.* **1.** a soldier, airplane, etc. sent to spy out the strength, movements, etc. of the enemy. **2.** a member of the Boy Scouts or Girl Scouts. **3.** a person sent out to get information about a competitor, find people with talent, etc. [a baseball *scout*]. **4.** fellow: *slang in this meaning* [He's a good *scout*.] —*v.* **1.** to go out looking for information, as about an enemy. **2.** to go in search of something; hunt [*Scout* around for some firewood.]

scout (skout), *v.* to scorn as ridiculous.

scout·mas·ter (skout′mas′tər), *n.* a man who leads a troop of Boy Scouts.

scow (skou), *n.* a large boat with a flat bottom and square ends, for carrying loads.

scowl (skoul), *v.* to look angry, mean, etc., as by lowering the eyebrows and the corners of the mouth. —*n.* a scowling look.

scrab·ble (skrab′'l), *v.* **1.** to scratch, scrape, etc. as in looking for a thing. **2.** to struggle. **3.** to scribble. —*n.* a scrabbling. —**scrab′bled,** *p.t. & p.p.;* **scrab′bling,** *pr.p.*

man scowling

scrag (skrag), *n.* **1.** a thin, scrawny person, animal, or plant. **2.** the neck: *a slang meaning.*

scrag·gly (skrag′lē), *adj.* rough, ragged, etc. —**scrag′gli·er,** *compar.;* **scrag′gli·est,** *superl.*

scrag·gy (skrag′ē), *adj.* **1.** scraggly. **2.** thin —**scrag′gi·er,** *compar.;* **scrag′gi·est,** *superl.*

scram·ble (skram′b'l), *v.* **1.** to climb, crawl, etc. in a quick, rough way [The children *scrambled* up the steep hill.] **2.** to struggle or scuffle for something [The puppies *scrambled* for the meat.] **3.** to cook eggs while stirring the mixed whites and yolks. **4.** to mix together in a disorderly way. —*n.* **1.** a climb or crawl over uneven ground. **2.** a rough, confused fight or struggle [a *scramble* for the scattered pennies]. —**scram′bled,** *p.t. & p.p.;* **scram′bling,** *pr.p.*

Scran·ton (skran′tən), *n.* a city in north-eastern Pennsylvania.

scrap (skrap), *n.* **1.** a small piece; bit [a *scrap* of paper; a *scrap* of information]. **2.** something thrown away because it is useless. **3. scraps,** *pl.* bits of leftover food. —*adj.* in the form of broken bits and pieces [*scrap* metal]. —*v.* **1.** to make into scrap or scraps. **2.** to get rid of as worthless; discard [He *scrapped* his old habits.] —**scrapped,** *p.t. & p.p.;* **scrap′ping,** *pr.p.*

scrap (skrap), *n. & v.* fight or quarrel: *a slang word.* —**scrapped,** *p.t. & p.p.;* **scrap′ping,** *pr.p.*

scrap·book (skrap′book), *n.* a book of blank pages in which pictures, clippings, etc. are kept.

scrape (skrāp), *v.* **1.** to make smooth or clean by rubbing with a tool or with something rough [to *scrape* the bottom of a ship]. **2.** to remove in this way [*Scrape* off the old paint.] **3.** to scratch or rub the skin from [He fell and *scraped* his knee.] **4.** to rub with a harsh or grating sound [The shovel *scraped* across the sidewalk.] **5.** to get together bit by bit, with some effort [They finally *scraped* up enough money to buy the stove.] **6.** to get along, but just barely [They *scrape* by on very little money.] —*n.* **1.** the act of scraping. **2.** a scraped place. **3.** a harsh, grating sound. **4.** an unpleasant situation that is hard to get out of [to get into a *scrape* by lying]. —**scraped,** *p.t. & p.p.;* **scrap′ing,** *pr.p.*

scrap·er (skrāp′ər), *n.* a tool for scraping.

scratch (skrach), *v.* **1.** to mark or cut the surface of slightly with something sharp [Thorns *scratched* his legs. Our cat *scratched* the chair with its claws.] **2.** to rub or scrape, as with the nails, to relieve itching [to *scratch* a mosquito bite]. **3.** to rub or scrape with a harsh, grating noise [The pen *scratched* when he wrote.] **4.** to cross out by drawing lines through [He *scratched* out what he had written.] **5.** to write carelessly or in a hurry [to *scratch* off a letter]. **6.** to take out of a contest; withdraw [Two horses were *scratched* from the race.] —*n.* **1.** a mark or cut made in a surface by something sharp. **2.** a slight wound. **3.** a harsh, grating sound [the *scratch* of chalk on a blackboard]. —*adj.* **1.** used for hasty notes, etc. [*scratch* paper]. **2.** done or made by chance; lucky [a *scratch* hit in baseball]. —**from scratch,** from little or nothing [He built up a good business *from scratch.*] —**up to scratch,** as good as was hoped or expected.

scratch·y (skrach′ē), *adj.* **1.** that scratches [a *scratchy* pen; a *scratchy* sweater]. **2.** made as if with scratches [*scratchy* handwriting]. —**scratch′i·er,** *compar.;* **scratch′i·est,** *superl.*

scrawl (skrôl), *v.* to write or draw in a hasty, careless way. —*n.* careless or poor handwriting that is hard to read.

scraw·ny (skrô′nē), *adj.* very thin; skinny. —**scraw′ni·er,** *compar.;* **scraw′ni·est,** *superl.*

scream (skrēm), *v.* **1.** to give a loud, shrill cry, as in fright or pain [She *screamed* when she saw the mouse.] **2.** to make a noise like this [The sirens *screamed.* The children *screamed* with laughter at the clown.] —*n.* **1.** a loud, shrill cry or sound; shriek. **2.** a very funny person or thing: *used only in everyday talk.*

screech (skrēch), *v.* to give a harsh, high shriek. —*n.* a harsh, high shriek.

screen (skrēn), *n.* **1.** a mesh woven loosely of wires so as to leave small openings between them. Screens are used in windows, doors, etc. to keep insects out. **2.** a covered frame or curtain used to hide, separate, or protect. **3.** anything that hides, separates, or protects [a smoke *screen;* a *screen* of bushes]. **4.** a sieve for separating smaller pieces of coal, stone, etc. from larger ones. **5.** a surface on which movies, television pictures, etc. are shown.

screen in a door

—*v.* **1.** to hide, shelter, or protect, as with a screen [A hedge *screens* the yard.] **2.** to sift coal, stones, etc. through a screen. **3.** to test and question in order to separate according to group [to *screen* people applying for jobs].

screen·play (skrēn′plā), *n.* the written script from which a motion picture is made.

screw (skrōō), *n.* **1.** a piece of metal like a nail with a groove winding around it in a spiral, and usually having a slot across its head. It is forced, by turning, into pieces of wood, etc. to hold them together. **2.** anything that looks or turns like a screw. **3.** a turn or twist, as of a screw. **4.** a propeller on a ship or airplane. —*v.* **1.** to turn or twist as or like a screw [*Screw* the lid on tight.] **2.** to fasten or be fastened with screws [He *screwed* the bookshelf to the wall. This hinge *screws* to the door.] **3.** to twist out of shape [to *screw* up one's face]. **4.** to force [He *screwed* up his courage.] —**put the screws on,** to use force on.

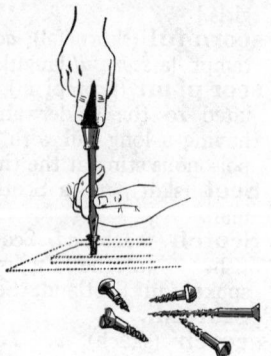
screws and screwdriver

screw·driv·er (skrōō′drīv′ər), *n.* a tool used to turn screws. It fits into the slot on the head of the screw. Also **screw driver.**

scrib·ble (skrib′'l), *v.* **1.** to write quickly or carelessly. **2.** to make marks that have no meaning [The baby *scribbled* on the wall.] —*n.* scribbled writing or marks. —**scrib′bled,** *p.t. & p.p.;* **scrib′bling,** *pr.p.* —**scrib′bler,** *n.*

scribe (skrīb), *n.* **1.** a person who wrote out copies of books, etc. before the invention of printing. **2.** a writer or author. **3.** in former times, a teacher of the Jewish law.

scrim·mage (skrim′ij), *n.* **1.** a rough, confused

fight or struggle. **2.** the play that follows the pass from center in a football game. —*v.* to take part in a scrimmage. —**line of scrimmage,** in football, the imaginary line along which the two teams line up before each play. —**scrim′maged,** *p.t. & p.p.;* **scrim′mag·ing,** *pr.p.*

scrimp (skrimp), *v.* to spend or use as little as possible; skimp [to *scrimp* on food; to *scrimp* to save money].

scrip (skrip), *n.* **1.** paper money in amounts of less than a dollar, once issued in the United States. **2.** a paper giving someone the right to receive something.

script (skript), *n.* **1.** handwriting. **2.** printing type that looks like handwriting. **3.** a copy of a play, radio or television show, etc., used by those putting it on.

Scrip·ture (skrip′chər), *n.* **1.** *usually* **Scriptures,** *pl.* the Bible: also **Holy Scripture** or **Holy Scriptures. 2. scripture,** any sacred writing [The Koran is Moslem *scripture.*] —**Scrip′tur·al** or **scrip′tur·al,** *adj.*

scriv·ner (skriv′nər), *n.* in earlier times, a person who hired himself out as a scribe or clerk.

scrof·u·la (skräf′yoo lə), *n.* a kind of tuberculosis that makes the lymph glands of the neck, etc. swell up. —**scrof′u·lous,** *adj.*

scroll (skrōl), *n.* **1.** a roll of parchment or paper, usually with writing on it. **2.** a decoration or design like a loosely rolled scroll.

scroll

Scrooge (skrōōj), *n.* the mean and miserly old man in Dickens' story *A Christmas Carol.*

scrounge (skrounj), *v.* to hunt around for and take without permission; pilfer: *a slang word.*

scrub (skrub), *n.* **1.** a growth of short, stubby trees or bushes. **2.** any person or thing of less than average size, quality, ability, etc. **3.** a football player, etc. not on the regular team. —*adj.* **1.** small, stunted, etc. **2.** of players that are scrubs [*scrub* practice]. —**scrub′by,** *adj.*

scrub (skrub), *v.* to clean or wash by rubbing hard [to *scrub* floors]. —*n.* the act of scrubbing. —**scrubbed,** *p.t. & p.p.;* **scrub′bing,** *pr.p.*

scruff (skruf), *n.* the back of the neck, or the loose skin there.

scru·ple (skrōō′p'l), *n.* **1.** a doubt or uneasy feeling that may keep one from doing something looked on as bad [He has *scruples* about telling even a small lie.] **2.** a very small unit of weight used by druggists. —*v.* to hesitate or hold back because of scruples [He *scrupled* at taking a bribe.] —**scru′pled,** *p.t. & p.p.;* **scru′pling,** *pr.p.*

kitten held by
its scruff

scru·pu·lous (skrōō′pyoo ləs), *adj.* **1.** paying strict attention to what is right or proper; very honest [*scrupulous* in his business dealings]. **2.** careful about details; exact [a *scrupulous* record of expenses]. —**scru′pu·lous·ly,** *adv.*

scru·ti·nize (skrōō′t'n īz), *v.* to look at very carefully; examine closely. —**scru′ti·nized,** *p.t. & p.p.;* **scru′ti·niz·ing,** *pr.p.*

scru·ti·ny (skrōō′t'n ē), *n.* a long, careful look; close examination. —**scru′ti·nies,** *pl.*

scu·ba or **Scu·ba** (skōō′bə), *n.* an apparatus with tanks of compressed air, worn by divers for breathing under water.

scud (skud), *v.* **1.** to move swiftly. **2.** to be driven by the wind, as clouds. —*n.* **1.** the act of scudding. **2.** clouds or spray driven by wind. —**scud′ded,** *p.t. & p.p.;* **scud′ding,** *pr.p.*

scuff (skuf), *v.* **1.** to wear a rough place on the surface of; scrape [He *scuffed* his new shoes.] **2.** to scrape or drag the feet along the ground in walking. —*n.* **1.** the act of scuffing. **2.** a worn or rough spot.

scuf·fle (skuf′'l), *v.* **1.** to fight or struggle in a rough, confused way. **2.** to drag the feet in walking; shuffle. —*n.* **1.** a rough, confused fight. **2.** the act or sound of feet shuffling. —**scuf′fled,** *p.t. & p.p.;* **scuf′fling,** *pr.p.*

scull (skul), *n.* **1.** an oar worked from side to side over the stern of a boat. **2.** either of a pair of short, light oars used in rowing. **3.** a light, narrow rowboat for racing. —*v.* to row with a scull or sculls. —**scull′er,** *n.*

scul·ler·y (skul′ər ē), *n.* a room next to a kitchen, where pots and pans are cleaned, etc. —**scul′ler·ies,** *pl.*

scul·lion (skul′yən), *n.* a servant who does rough kitchen work: *now seldom used.*

sculp·tor (skulp′tər), *n.* an artist in sculpture.

sculp·ture (skulp′chər), *n.* **1.** the art of cutting stone, wood, etc., or forming clay, into statues, figures, or the like. **2.** a statue, figure, etc. made in this way. —*v.* **1.** to cut, chisel, form, etc. in making sculptures. **2.** to decorate with sculpture. —**sculp′tured,** *p.t. & p.p.;* **sculp′tur·ing,** *pr.p.* —**sculp′tur·al,** *adj.*

sculpture

scum (skum), *n.* **1.** a thin layer of dirt or waste matter that forms on the top of a liquid [an oily *scum* on the lake]. **2.** people who are despised as bad or wicked.

scup·per (skup′ər), *n.* an opening in a ship's side to allow water to run off the deck.

scurf (skûrf), *n.* **1.** little dry scales shed by the skin, as dandruff. **2.** any scaly coating.

scur·ril·ous (skûr′i ləs), *adj.* attacking in a coarse or vulgar way [*scurrilous* language]. —**scur·ril·i·ty** (skə ril′ə tē), *n.*

---

fat,   āpe,   cär,   ten,   ēven,   hit,   bīte,   gō,   hôrn,   tōōl,   book,   up,   fûr;
get,   joy,   yet,   chin,   she,   thin,   *th*en;   zh = s in pleasure;   ′ as in able (ā′b'l);
ə = a in ago,   e in agent,   i in sanity,   o in confess,   u in focus.

scur·ry (skŭr'ē), *v.* to run quickly; scamper. —*n.* the act of scurrying, or scampering. —**scur'-ried,** *p.t. & p.p.;* **scur'ry·ing,** *pr.p.*

scur·vy (skŭr'vē), *n.* a disease that causes weakness and makes the gums swell and bleed. It comes from a lack of vitamin C in the diet. —*adj.* low; mean [a *scurvy* trick]. —**scur'vi·er,** *compar.;* **scur'vi·est,** *superl.* —**scur'vi·ly,** *adv.*

scutch·eon (skuch'ən), *n.* same as **escutcheon.**

scut·tle (skut''l), *n.* a bucket for holding or carrying coal.

scut·tle (skut'l), *v.* to run quickly; scamper; scurry. —*n.* the act of scuttling. —**scut'tled,** *p.t. & p.p.;* **scut'tling,** *pr.p.*

scuttle

scut·tle (skut'l), *v.* to sink by cutting holes in the lower hull [to *scuttle* a ship]. —*n.* an opening fitted with a cover, as in a roof, a ship's deck or hull, etc. —**scut'tled,** *p.t. & p.p.;* **scut'tling,** *pr.p.*

Scyl·la (sil'ə), *n.* a dangerous rock on the Italian coast: see **Charybdis.**

scythe (sīth), *n.* a tool with a long blade on a long, curved handle, for cutting grain, etc.

scythe

S.Dak. or **S.D.,** abbreviation for **South Dakota.**

SE or **S.E.** or **s.e.,** abbreviation for **southeast** or **southeastern.**

sea (sē), *n.* **1.** the whole body of salt water that covers much of the earth; ocean. **2.** a large body of salt water more or less enclosed by land [the Red *Sea*]. **3.** a large body of fresh water [the *Sea* of Galilee]. **4.** the condition of the ocean's surface [a calm *sea*]. **5.** a heavy wave [swamped by the *seas*]. **6.** a great amount or number [a *sea* of debt]. —**at sea, 1.** sailing on the sea. **2.** not sure; confused. —**follow the sea,** to be a sailor. —**go to sea,** to become a sailor. —**put to sea,** to sail away.

sea anemone, a water animal that looks like a flower. *See the picture for* **anemone.**

sea·board (sē'bôrd), *n.* land along the sea; seacoast [the Atlantic *seaboard*].

sea·coast (sē'kōst), *n.* land along the sea.

sea cow, a large mammal that lives in the sea, especially the manatee.

sea dog, a sailor, especially one with experience.

sea·far·er (sē'fer'ər), *n.* a person who travels on the sea; especially, a sailor.

sea·far·ing (sē'fer'ing), *n.* **1.** the work of a sailor. **2.** travel by sea. —*adj.* of or having to do with seafaring.

sea food, ocean fish or shellfish used as food.

sea·girt (sē'gûrt), *adj.* surrounded by the sea.

sea·go·ing (sē'gō'ing), *adj.* **1.** for use on the open sea [a *seagoing* ship]. **2.** seafaring.

sea gull, a sea bird with long wings and webbed feet. *See the picture for* **gull.**

sea horse, 1. a small fish with a slender tail and a head a little like that of a horse. **2.** a creature in myths, half fish and half horse. **3.** the walrus.

sea horse (3 to 10 in. long)

seal (sēl), *n.* **1.** a piece of paper, wax, etc. with a design pressed into it, fixed to an official document to show that it is genuine. Such wax designs were once also used to seal letters. **2.** a stamp or ring for pressing such a design into wax, on paper, etc. **3.** the design itself. **4.** something that closes or fastens tightly. **5.** a piece of metal, paper, etc. placed over a lid or cap, as of a box or bottle, which cannot be opened without breaking the metal or paper. **6.** a paper stamp used for decoration [a Christmas *seal*]. **7.** something that guarantees; pledge [His fear was a *seal* of secrecy.] **8.** a sign or token [Their handshake was a *seal* of friendship.] —*v.* **1.** to close or fasten tight [to *seal* cracks with putty; to *seal* a letter]. **2.** to settle definitely [His fate was *sealed*.] **3.** to mark with a seal, as a document, to make it official or genuine. —**seal'er,** *n.*

seal of the United States

seal (sēl), *n.* **1.** a sea animal with four flippers, that lives in cold waters and eats fish. **2.** its short fur. **3.** leather made from the skin of the seal. —*v.* to hunt seals. —**seal'er,** *n.*

sea legs, the ability to walk on a tossing ship without losing one's balance.

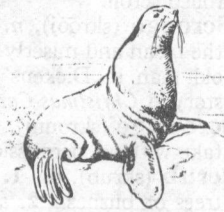
seal (6 ft. long)

sea level, the level of the surface of the sea, halfway between high and low tide. It is used as the point from which heights of land are measured.

sea lion, a large seal of the North Pacific.

seal·skin (sēl'skin), *n.* **1.** the skin or fur of the seal. **2.** a coat, etc. made of this.

seam (sēm), *n.* **1.** the line formed by sewing or joining together two pieces of material. **2.** a line like this, as a scar, wrinkle, etc. **3.** a layer of ore, coal, etc. in the ground. —*v.* **1.** to join together in a seam. **2.** to mark with a line like a seam [a face *seamed* with wrinkles].

sea·man (sē'mən), *n.* **1.** a sailor. **2.** a sailor in the navy, not an officer. —**sea'men,** *pl.*

sea·man·ship (sē'mən ship), *n.* skill as a sailor.

sea mew, same as **sea gull.**

seam·stress (sēm'stris), *n.* a woman who sews well or who makes her living by sewing.

seam·y (sēm'ē), *adj.* showing seams. —**the seamy side,** the unpleasant side, as of life. —**seam'i·er,** *compar.;* **seam'i·est,** *superl.*

sé·ance (sā'äns), *n.* a meeting at which people try to get messages from the dead.

sea·plane (sē'plān), *n.* any airplane designed to land on water and take off from water.

sea·port (sē'pôrt), *n.* a port or harbor for ocean ships, or a town or city with such a port.

sear (sir), *v.* **1.** to dry up; wither [The hot sun *seared* the crops.] **2.** to burn or scorch the surface of [The hot grease *seared* her arm.] **3.** to make hard and without feeling [a *seared* conscience]. —*adj.* withered; dried up.

search (sûrch), *v.* **1.** to look over or through in order to find something [We *searched* the house. The police *searched* him for a gun.] **2.** to try to find [to *search* for an answer]. —*n.* the act of searching. —**in search of,** trying to find. —**search out,** to seek or find by searching. —**search'er,** *n.*

search·ing (sûr'ching), *adj.* that searches or looks carefully or thoroughly [a *searching* test].

search·light (sûrch'līt), *n.* **1.** a lamp that can throw a strong beam of light in any direction. **2.** a strong beam of light.

search warrant, a written order from a court giving police the right to enter and search a place, as in looking for stolen goods.

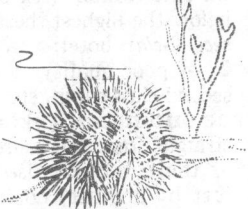
searchlight

sea shell, the shell of an oyster, clam, etc.

sea·shore (sē'shôr), *n.* land along the sea.

sea·sick (sē'sik), *adj.* made sick at the stomach and dizzy by the rolling of a ship at sea. —**sea'·sick·ness,** *n.*

sea·side (sē'sīd), *n.* land along the sea.

sea·son (sē'z'n), *n.* **1.** any of the four parts into which the year is divided: spring, summer, fall, or winter. **2.** a special time of the year [the Easter *season;* the hunting *season*]. **3.** a period of time [the busy *season* in a factory]. —*v.* **1.** to add to or change the flavor of [to *season* meat with herbs]. **2.** to make more fit for use by aging or treating [to *season* lumber]. **3.** to make more interesting [to *season* a speech with humor]. **4.** to make used to something; accustom [a *seasoned* traveler]. —**for a season,** for a while. —**in season, 1.** that can be had fresh for use as food [Corn is *in season* in late summer.] **2.** allowed to be hunted [Ducks are not *in season* now.] —**in good season,** early enough. —**out of season,** not in season.

sea·son·a·ble (sē'z'n ə b'l), *adj.* **1.** that fits the time of year [*seasonable* weather]. **2.** at the right time; timely [*seasonable* advice].

sea·son·al (sē'z'n əl), *adj.* of or depending on a season or the seasons [*seasonal* rains; *seasonal* work]. —**sea'son·al·ly,** *adv.*

sea·son·ing (sē'z'n ing), *n.* **1.** flavoring added to food. **2.** anything that adds interest.

seat (sēt), *n.* **1.** a thing to sit on, as a chair, bench, etc. **2.** a place to sit or the right to sit [to buy two *seats* for the opera; to win a *seat* in the Senate]. **3.** the part of the body or of a garment on which one sits [the *seat* of his pants]. **4.** the part of a chair, bench, etc. on which one sits. **5.** a way of sitting, as on a horse. **6.** the chief place; center [the *seat* of a government]. **7.** a residence; home [a rural *seat*]. —*v.* **1.** to cause to sit; put in or on a seat [*Seat* yourself quickly.] **2.** to have seats for [This car *seats* six people.] —**be seated, 1.** to sit down. **2.** to be sitting. **3.** to be located.

Se·at·tle (sē at''l), *n.* a city in Washington.

sea urchin, a small sea animal with a round body in a shell covered with sharp spines.

sea wall, a wall made to protect the shore from being washed away by waves.

sea·ward (sē'wərd), *adj.* **1.** toward the sea. **2.** from the sea [a *seaward* wind]. —*adv.* toward the sea. —*n.* the direction toward the sea.

sea urchin (3 in. wide)

sea·wards (sē'wərdz), *adv.* toward the sea.

sea·way (sē'wā), *n.* **1.** a route to the sea for large ships, through connected lakes, rivers, canals, etc. **2.** a route for travel on the sea.

sea·weed (sē'wēd), *n.* any plant or plants growing in the sea, especially algae.

sea·wor·thy (sē'wûr'thē), *adj.* fit or safe for travel on the sea [a *seaworthy* ship].

se·ba·ceous (si bā'shəs), *adj.* of or like fat; greasy; especially, naming certain glands of the skin that give out an oily liquid.

sec., abbreviation for **second** or **seconds, secretary, section.**

se·cede (si sēd'), *v.* to stop being a member of some group, as of a political union. —**se·ced'ed,** *p.t. & p.p.;* **se·ced'ing,** *pr.p.*

se·ces·sion (si sesh'ən), *n.* **1.** the act of seceding. **2. Secession,** the withdrawal of the Southern States from the Federal Union in 1860 and 1861. —**se·ces'sion·ist,** *n.*

se·clude (si klood'), *v.* **1.** to keep away from others; shut off [nuns *secluded* in a convent]. **2.** to make private or hidden [a *secluded* cabin]. —**se·clud'ed,** *p.t. & p.p.;* **se·clud'ing,** *pr.p.*

se·clu·sion (si kloo'zhən), *n.* a secluding or being secluded [to live in *seclusion*].

sec·ond (sek'ənd), *adj.* **1.** coming next after the first; 2d in order [the *second* seat; *second* prize]. **2.** another, like the first [He thinks he's a *second* Shakespeare.] **3.** playing or singing the lower part [*second* violin; *second* tenor]. —*n.* **1.** the second one [He was the *second* to arrive.] **2.** an article that is damaged or not of first quality [a sale on *seconds*]. **3.** a person who serves as an assistant or aid, as to a boxer. —*v.* **1.** to give help or support to; aid; assist [to *second* a cause by giving money]. **2.** to say that one

fat,   āpe,   cär,   ten,   ēven,   hit,   bīte,   gō,   hôrn,   tool,   book,   up,   fûr;
get,   joy,   yet,   chin,   she,   thin,   *th*en;   zh = s in pleasure;   ' as in able (ā'b'l);
ə = a in ago,   e in agent,   i in sanity,   o in confess,   u in focus.

supports a motion so that it can be voted on. —*adv.* in the second place, group, etc.

sec·ond (sek′ənd), *n.* **1.** any of the 60 equal parts of a minute, either of time or of an angle. **2.** a very short time; instant.

sec·ond·ar·y (sek′ən der′ē), *adj.* **1.** next after the first in time or order [*Secondary* schools are high schools.] **2.** less important; minor [a matter of *secondary* interest]. **3.** coming from something primary or basic; derived [A *secondary* color is made by mixing two primary colors.] —**sec′ond·ar′i·ly**, *adv.*

sec·ond-class (sek′ənd klas′), *adj.* **1.** next below the highest, best, most expensive, etc. [a *second-class* hotel; a *second-class* cabin on a ship]. **2.** of poor quality, standing, etc. —*adv.* in a second-class cabin, etc. [to go *second-class*].

sec·ond·hand (sek′ənd hand′), *adj.* **1.** not straight from the source; from a second person or thing; indirect [*secondhand* news]. **2.** used first by another; not new [a *secondhand* coat]. **3.** dealing in goods that are not new [a *secondhand* store].

sec·ond·ly (sek′ənd lē), *adv.* in the second place.

second nature, a habit that is fixed so deeply as to seem a part of one's nature [Being polite is *second nature* to her.]

second person, that form of a pronoun or verb which refers to the person or persons spoken to [*You, your,* and *yours* are in the *second person.*]

sec·ond-rate (sek′ənd rāt′), *adj.* second in quality; not among the best; inferior.

se·cre·cy (sē′krə sē), *n.* **1.** the condition of being secret. **2.** the practice of keeping things secret, or the ability to do this.

se·cret (sē′krit), *adj.* **1.** kept from being known or seen by others; hidden [a *secret* formula; a *secret* entrance]. **2.** acting without others knowing [a *secret* agent; a *secret* society]. —*n.* **1.** something hidden or to be kept hidden from the knowledge of others. **2.** something not understood or known [nature's *secrets*]. —**in secret,** without others knowing. —**se′cret·ly,** *adv.*

sec·re·tar·i·at (sek′rə ter′i it), *n.* a staff headed by a secretary.

sec·re·tar·y (sek′rə ter′ē), *n.* **1.** a person whose work is keeping records, writing letters, etc. for a person or organization. **2.** the head of a department of government [the *Secretary* of State]. **3.** a writing desk, with a bookcase built at the top. —**sec′re·tar′ies,** *pl.* —**sec·re·tar·i·al** (sek′rə ter′i əl), *adj.*

se·crete (si krēt′), *v.* **1.** to put in a secret place; hide. **2.** to make and give off into or out of the body [Glands in the skin *secrete* oil.] —**se·cret′ed,** *p.t. & p.p.;* **se·cret′ing,** *pr.p.*

secretary

se·cre·tion (si krē′shən), *n.* **1.** the act of secreting. **2.** something secreted by glands, etc. [Saliva is a *secretion.*]

se·cre·tive (si krē′tiv), *adj.* **1.** (*often* sē′krə-tiv), hiding one's feelings, thoughts, etc.; not frank or open. **2.** having to do with secretion by glands, etc.

secret service, a government office that does special detective work, as hunting down counterfeiters, guarding officials, etc.

sect (sekt), *n.* a group of people having the same leader, set of beliefs, etc., especially in religion.

sec·tar·i·an (sek ter′i ən), *adj.* **1.** of or like a sect. **2.** devoted to one's sect in a narrow-minded way. —*n.* a sectarian person.

sec·tion (sek′shən), *n.* **1.** a part cut off; separate part; division [a *section* of a tangerine; shelves sold in *sections*]. **2.** a part of a city, country, etc.; district or region [a hilly *section*; the business *section* of a city]. **3.** a division of a book, etc., as a numbered paragraph. **4.** a view or drawing of a thing as it looks or would look if cut straight through. —*v.* to cut into sections.

sec·tion·al (sek′shən 'l), *adj.* **1.** of a certain section or region; regional. **2.** made up of sections [a *sectional* sofa].

sec·tion·al·ism (sek′shən 'l iz'm), *n.* a narrow-minded interest in only one section or region at the expense of the whole.

sec·tor (sek′tər), *n.* **1.** a part of a circle formed by two radii and the arc between them [A slice of pie is a *sector.*] **2.** any of the areas into which a region is divided for military purposes. —*v.* to divide into sectors.

sector

sec·u·lar (sek′yoo lər), *adj.* **1.** not connected with a church or religion; not sacred [*secular* music; *secular* schools]. **2.** not living in a monastery, etc. [*secular* clergy].

se·cure (si kyoor′), *adj.* **1.** safe from harm, loss, attack, etc. [a *secure* hiding place]. **2.** free from fear, worry, etc. [He leads a *secure* life.] **3.** fastened or fixed in a firm way [a *secure* knot]. **4.** sure; certain [His success is now *secure.*] —*v.* **1.** to make safe; guard or protect [*Secure* your house against burglars.] **2.** to tie or fasten firmly [*Secure* the boat to the dock.] **3.** to make sure; guarantee [to *secure* a loan with a pledge]. **4.** to get; obtain [to *secure* an appointment]. —**se·cured′,** *p.t. & p.p.;* **se·cur′ing,** *pr.p.* —**se·cure′ly,** *adv.*

se·cu·ri·ty (si kyoor′ə tē), *n.* **1.** the condition or feeling of being safe or sure; freedom from danger, fear, doubt, etc. **2.** something that protects [Insurance is a *security* against loss.] **3.** something given or pledged as a guarantee [A car may be used as *security* for a loan.] **4.** **securities,** *pl.* stocks and bonds. —**se·cu′ri·ties,** *pl.*

secy. or **sec'y.,** abbreviation for **secretary.**

se·dan (si dan′), *n.* **1.** a closed automobile with front and rear seats and two or four doors. **2.** a sedan chair.

sedan chair, a box with a seat in it for one person,

sedan chair

carried on poles by two men. Sedan chairs were used in earlier times.

se·date (si dāt′), *adj.* quiet, serious, and without strong feeling. —**se·date′ly**, *adv.*

sed·a·tive (sed′ə tiv), *adj.* making one calmer and lessening pain. —*n.* a sedative medicine.

sed·en·tar·y (sed′′n ter′ē), *adj.* **1.** in the habit of sitting about and not going out [a *sedentary* old man]. **2.** keeping one seated much of the time [a *sedentary* job].

sedge (sej), *n.* a plant like coarse grass, usually growing in clumps in wet ground.

sed·i·ment (sed′ə mənt), *n.* **1.** matter that settles to the bottom of a liquid; dregs. **2.** any matter set down by wind or water, as sand or soil. —**sed′i·men′ta·ry**, *adj.*

se·di·tion (si dish′ən), *n.* a stirring up of rebellion against a government. —**se·di′tious**, *adj.*

se·duce (si dōōs′ *or* si dyōōs′), *v.* to get one to do something bad or wrong; tempt; lead astray. —**se·duced′**, *p.t.* & *p.p.*; **se·duc′ing**, *pr.p.* —**se·duc·tion** (si duk′shən), *n.*

se·duc·tive (si duk′tiv), *adj.* likely to seduce; very tempting or attractive.

sed·u·lous (sej′oo ləs), *adj.* working hard and with care; diligent. —**sed′u·lous·ly**, *adv.*

see (sē), *v.* **1.** to be aware of through the eyes; have or use the sense of sight [I *see* two birds. He doesn't *see* so well.] **2.** to get the meaning of; understand [Do you *see* the point of the joke?] **3.** to find out; learn [*See* what he wants.] **4.** to make sure [*See* that the door is locked.] **5.** to undergo or live through; experience [Our town has *seen* many changes.] **6.** to go along with; accompany [I'll *see* you to the door.] **7.** to visit with [We stopped to *see* a friend.] **8.** to go to for information or advice; consult [*See* a doctor about your cough.] **9.** to meet with or receive as a visitor [He's too ill to *see* you.] **10.** to think or try to remember [Let me *see*, where does he live?] —**see after**, to take care of. —**see off**, to go with to the train, ship, etc. to say good-by. —**see through, 1.** to understand the true meaning or nature of. **2.** to carry out to the end; finish. **3.** to help out during a hard time. —**see to**, to take care of; look after. —**saw**, *p.t.*; **seen**, *p.p.*; **see′ing**, *pr.p.*

see (sē), *n.* the office, authority, or district of a bishop.

seed (sēd), *n.* **1.** the part of a flowering plant that will grow into a new plant under the right conditions. **2.** a large number of seeds [to scatter grass *seed*]. **3.** a source or beginning [the *seeds* of knowledge]. **4.** children or descendants: *an earlier use, as in the Bible* [the *seed* of Jacob]. —*v.* **1.** to plant with

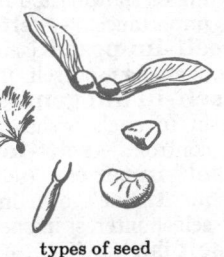
types of seed

seed [to *seed* a lawn]. **2.** to take the seeds from [to *seed* grapes]. **3.** to produce seeds. —**go to seed, 1.** to develop seeds from its flowers. **2.** to become weak, useless, etc. —**seeds** or **seed**, *pl.* —**seed′less**, *adj.*

seed·case (sēd′kās), *n.* a dry, hollow fruit with seeds in it, as the pod of a pea plant.

seed·ling (sēd′ling), *n.* a young plant grown from a seed, not from a cutting.

seed·y (sēd′ē), *adj.* **1.** full of seeds [a *seedy* grapefruit]. **2.** untidy and shabby; not neat. —**seed′i·er**, *compar.*; **seed′i·est**, *superl.*

see·ing (sē′ing), *conj.* in view of the fact; as; since [*Seeing* that he's here, let's begin eating.] —*n.* the sense of sight; vision. —*adj.* that sees.

seek (sēk), *v.* **1.** to try to find; search for [to *seek* gold]. **2.** to try to get; aim at [to *seek* a prize]. **3.** to try or attempt [He *seeks* to please us.] —**sought**, *p.t.* & *p.p.*; **seek′ing**, *pr.p.*

seem (sēm), *v.* **1.** to have the look of being; appear to be [He *seems* happy. The house *seems* empty.] **2.** to appear to one's own mind [Her voice *seemed* to falter.] **3.** to appear to be true [It *seems* I was right.]

seem·ing (sēm′ing), *adj.* that seems real, true, etc. but is not; pretended [her *seeming* anger]. —**seem′ing·ly**, *adv.*

seem·ly (sēm′lē), *adj.* as it should be; right; proper [*seemly* behavior]. —*adv.* in a right or proper way. —**seem′li·er**, *compar.*; **seem′li·est**, *superl.* —**seem′li·ness**, *n.*

seen (sēn), past participle of **see.**

seep (sēp), *v.* to leak through small openings; ooze [Rain *seeped* through the roof.]

seep·age (sēp′ij), *n.* **1.** the act of seeping. **2.** liquid that seeps through.

seer (sir), *n.* a person who tells what he thinks will happen; prophet.

seer·suck·er (sir′suk ər), *n.* a light, crinkled cloth of cotton or linen, usually striped.

see·saw (sē′sô), *n.* **1.** a board balanced on a support at the middle and used by children at play, who ride the ends so that when one goes up the other comes down. **2.** any movement back and forth or up and down. —*adj.* moving back and forth or up and down. —*v.* to move back and forth or up and down.

seesaw

seethe (sē*th*), *v.* **1.** to bubble or foam as a boiling liquid does [the *seething* waves]. **2.** to be very excited or upset [*seething* with rage]. —**seethed**, *p.t.* & *p.p.*; **seeth′ing**, *pr.p.*

seg·ment (seg′mənt), *n.* **1.** any of the parts into which something is divided or can be separated [the *segments* of an earthworm]. **2.** a part, as of a circle, cut off by a straight line.

seg·re·gate (seg′ri gāt), *v.* to set apart from others; especially, to keep people of different

fat, āpe, cär, ten, ēven, hit, bīte, gō, hôrn, tōōl, book, up, fûr; get, joy, yet, chin, she, thin, *then*; zh = s in pleasure; ′ as in able (ā′b'l) ə = a in ago, e in agent, i in sanity, o in confess, u in focus.

races separate, as in public schools. **—seg′re·gat·ed,** *p.t. & p.p.;* **seg′re·gat·ing,** *pr.p.* **—seg′re·ga′tion,** *n.* **—seg′re·ga′tion·ist,** *n.*

sei·gneur (sān′yər), *n.* a lord or noble, especially in the Middle Ages.

Seine (sān *or* sen), *n.* a river in France. It flows through Paris into the English Channel.

seine (sān), *n.* a large fishing net with floats along the top edge and weights along the bottom. **—v.** to fish or catch with a seine. **—seined,** *p.t. & p.p.;* **sein′ing,** *pr.p.*

seis·mic (sīz′mik), *adj.* of or caused by an earthquake.

seis·mo·graph (sīz′mə graf), *n.* an instrument that makes a record of the strength, time, and direction of earthquakes.

seize (sēz), *v.* **1.** to take hold of in a sudden, strong, or eager way; grasp [to *seize* a weapon and fight; to *seize* an opportunity]. **2.** to capture or arrest, as a criminal. **3.** to take over as by force [The troops *seized* the fort. The city *seized* the property for nonpayment of taxes.] **4.** to attack; strike [*seized* with a fit of sneezing]. **—seize on** or **seize upon,** to grasp or take eagerly. **—seized,** *p.t. & p.p;* **seiz′ing,** *pr.p.*

sei·zure (sē′zhər), *n.* **1.** a seizing or being seized. **2.** a sudden attack, as of illness.

sel·dom (sel′dəm), *adv.* not often; rarely [I *seldom* see my old friends since I've moved.]

se·lect (sə lekt′), *v.* to choose or pick out [He *selected* a tie to go with his suit.] **—adj.** **1.** chosen with care; specially picked as being best or choice [Our market sells only *select* cuts of meat.] **2.** allowing only certain people in; not open to all [a *select* club]. **—se·lec′tor,** *n.*

se·lec·tion (sə lek′shən), *n.* **1.** a selecting or being selected; choice. **2.** the thing or things chosen; also, things to choose from [a wide *selection* of colors].

se·lec·tive (sə lek′tiv), *adj.* **1.** of or set apart by selection. **2.** tending to select. **3.** having the power to select [A *selective* radio set brings in each station clearly.]

selective service, a system under which young men are drafted for military service.

se·lect·man (sə lekt′mən), *n.* in New England towns, a member of a board of officers that is like a city council. **—se·lect′men,** *pl.*

self (self), *n.* **1.** one's own person or being as apart from all others. **2.** one's own well-being or advantage [too much concern with *self*]. **—pron.** myself, himself, herself, or yourself: *used only in everyday talk* [tickets for *self* and wife]. **—selves,** *pl.*

self-, a prefix meaning: **1.** of oneself [*Self-restraint* is a restraining of oneself.] **2.** by oneself [A *self-appointed* leader is one appointed as such by himself.] **3.** to oneself [A *self-addressed* envelope is addressed to oneself.] **4.** in or with oneself [A *self-confident* person is confident in himself.] **5.** for oneself [*Self-pity* is pity for oneself.]

self-as·ser·tion (self′ə sur′shən), *n.* boldness in putting forward one's own claims, opinions, etc. **—self′-as·ser′tive,** *adj.*

self-as·sur·ance (self′ə shoor′əns), *n.* self-confidence. **—self′-as·sured′,** *adj.*

self-cen·tered (self′sen′tərd), *adj.* thinking mostly of oneself or one's own affairs; selfish.

self-com·mand (self′kə mand′), *n.* self-control.

self-con·ceit (self′kən sēt′), *n.* too high an opinion of oneself; conceit.

self-con·fi·dent (self′kän′fə dənt), *adj.* sure of oneself; confident of one's own ability. **—self′-con′fi·dent·ly,** *adv.* **—self′-con′fi·dence,** *n.*

self-con·scious (self′kän′shəs), *adj.* **1.** too conscious of oneself so that one feels or acts embarrassed when with others. **2.** showing that one is embarrassed [a *self-conscious* giggle]. **—self′-con′scious·ly,** *adv.* **—self′-con′scious·ness,** *n.*

self-con·tained (self′kən tānd′), *adj.* **1.** having within itself all that is needed [a *self-contained* radio transmitter]. **2.** keeping one's thoughts and feelings to oneself; reserved. **3.** showing self-control.

self-con·trol (self′kən trōl′), *n.* control of oneself or of one's feelings and actions.

self-de·fense (self′də fens′), *n.* defense of oneself or one's property, rights, etc.

self-de·ni·al (self′di nī′əl), *n.* the act of giving up what one wants or needs, often for the benefit of others. **—self′-de·ny′ing,** *adj.*

self-de·ter·mi·na·tion (self′di tûr′mə nā′shən), *n.* **1.** the act or power of making up one's own mind about what to think or do. **2.** the right of the people of a nation to choose their own form of government.

self-dis·ci·pline (self′dis′ə plin), *n.* the act or power of disciplining or controlling oneself.

self-ed·u·cat·ed (self′ej′oo kāt′id), *adj.* educated by oneself, with little or no schooling.

self-es·teem (self′ə stēm′), *n.* **1.** self-respect. **2.** self-conceit.

self-ev·i·dent (self′ev′i dənt), *adj.* plain to see or understand without proof or explanation.

self-ex·pres·sion (self′ik spresh′ən), *n.* a bringing out of one's feelings or personality, as through art, music, writing, etc.

self-gov·ern·ment (self′guv′ərn mənt), *n.* independence or democracy in government. **—self′-gov′ern·ing,** *adj.*

self-im·por·tant (self′im pôr′t'nt), *adj.* having or showing too high an opinion of one's own importance. **—self′-im·por′tance,** *n.*

self-im·posed (self′im pōzd′), *adj.* placed on oneself by oneself [*self-imposed* punishment].

self-in·dul·gent (self′in dul′jənt), *adj.* giving in to one's wishes, feelings, etc., without self-control. **—self′-in·dul′gence,** *n.*

self-in·ter·est (self′in′tər ist *or* self′in′trist), *n.* **1.** one's own interest or advantage. **2.** a selfish interest in one's own advantage.

self·ish (sel′fish), *adj.* caring too much about oneself, with little or no thought or care for others. **—self′ish·ly,** *adv.* **—self′ish·ness,** *n.*

self·less (self′lis), *adj.* caring more about others than about oneself; unselfish.

self-made (self′mād′), *adj.* **1.** successful, rich, etc. because of one's own efforts [a *self-made* man]. **2.** made by oneself or itself.

self-pit·y (self′pit′ē), *n.* pity for oneself.

self-pos·ses·sion (self′pə zesh′ən), *n.* full control over one's own actions and feelings; composure. —**self′-pos·sessed′**, *adj.*

self-pres·er·va·tion (self′prez ər vā′shən), *n.* the act or instinct of keeping oneself safe and alive.

self-pro·pelled (self′prə peld′), *adj.* moving by its own power.

self-re·li·ant (self′ri lī′ənt), *adj.* depending on one's own judgment, abilities, efforts, etc. —**self′-re·li′ance,** *n.*

self-re·proach (self′ri prōch′), *n.* a feeling of guilt; blame of oneself by oneself.

self-re·spect (self′rǐ spekt′), *n.* a proper respect for oneself. —**self′-re·spect′ing,** *adj.*

self-re·straint (self′ri strānt′), *n.* self-control. —**self′-re·strained′,** *adj.*

self-right·eous (self′rī′chəs), *adj.* thinking oneself more righteous or moral than others.

self-sac·ri·fice (self′sak′rə fīs), *n.* sacrifice of oneself or one's interests, usually for the benefit of others. —**self′-sac′ri·fic·ing,** *adj.*

self·same (self′sām), *adj.* the very same; identical [We two were born on the *selfsame* day.]

self-sat·is·fied (self′sat′is fīd), *adj.* satisfied or pleased with oneself or with what one has done. —**self′-sat·is·fac′tion,** *n.*

self-seek·ing (self′sēk′ing), *adj.* always seeking to benefit oneself; selfish.

self-serv·ice (self′sûr′vis), *n.* the practice of serving oneself in a cafeteria, store, etc.

self-styled (self′stīld′), *adj.* so called by oneself [He is a *self-styled* expert.]

self-suf·fi·cient (self′sə fish′ənt), *adj.* able to get along without help; independent.

self-sup·port·ing (self′sə pôr′ting), *adj.* supporting oneself by one's own effort or earnings.

self-taught (self′tôt′), *adj.* taught by oneself with little or no help from others.

self-willed (self′wild′), *adj.* stubborn about getting one's own way. —**self′-will′,** *n.*

self-wind·ing (self′wīn′ding), *adj.* wound automatically, as some wrist watches and clocks.

sell (sel), *v.* **1.** to give in return for money [Will you *sell* me your skates for $5.00?] **2.** to offer for sale; deal in [This store *sells* radios.] **3.** to be on sale [These belts *sell* for $2.00.] **4.** to help the sale of [TV *sells* many products.] **5.** to betray for money or other gain [to *sell* one's honor]. **6.** to win approval from or for: *used only in everyday talk* [to *sell* someone on an idea]. —**sell out, 1.** to get rid of completely by selling. **2.** to betray, as a cause: *used only in everyday talk.* —**sold,** *p.t.* & *p.p.;* **sell′ing,** *pr.p.*

sell·er (sel′ər), *n.* **1.** a person who sells. **2.** a thing sold, referring to its rate of sale [a good *seller*].

sel·vage or **sel·vedge** (sel′vij), *n.* a specially woven edge that keeps cloth from raveling.

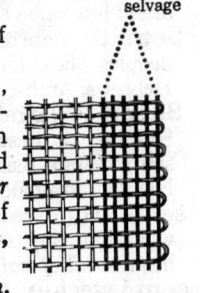
selvage

selves (selvz), *n.* plural of **self.**

se·man·tics (sə man′tiks), *n.pl.* the study of the meanings of words and ways in which the meanings change and develop: *used with a singular verb* [*Semantics* is a branch of linguistics.] —**se·man′tic,** *adj.*

sem·a·phore (sem′ə fôr), *n.* any device or system for signaling, as by lights, flags, etc. —*v.* to signal by semaphore. —**sem′-a·phored,** *p.t.* & *p.p.;* **sem′a·phor·ing,** *pr.p.*

sem·blance (sem′bləns), *n.* a seeming likeness; outward look or show [a *semblance* of order].

signaling by semaphore

se·mes·ter (sə mes′tər), *n.* either of the two terms which usually make up a school year.

semi-, a prefix meaning: **1.** half [A *semicircle* is a half circle.] **2.** partly; not fully [A *semiskilled* worker is only partly skilled.] **3.** twice in a certain period [A *semiannual* event takes place twice a year.]

sem·i·an·nu·al (sem′i an′yōō əl), *adj.* happening, coming, etc. twice a year [*semiannual* interest on savings]. —**sem′i·an′nu·al·ly,** *adv.*

sem·i·cir·cle (sem′i sûr′k′l), *n.* a half circle. —**sem·i·cir·cu·lar** (sem′i-sûr′kyoo lər), *adj.*

sem·i·co·lon (sem′i kō′lən), *n.* a punctuation mark (;) used to show a pause that is shorter than the pause at the end of a sentence, but longer than the pause marked by the comma [The *semicolon* is often used to separate closely related clauses, especially when they contain commas.]

children in a semicircle

sem·i·fi·nal (sem′i fī′n′l), *n.* a round, match, etc. that comes just before the final one in a contest or tournament.

sem·i·month·ly (sem′i munth′lē), *adj.* happening, coming, etc. twice a month. —*n.* a magazine that comes out twice a month. —*adv.* twice a month.

sem·i·nar·y (sem′ə ner′ē), *n.* **1.** a school, especially a private school for young women. **2.** a school or college where men are trained to be priests, ministers, etc. —**sem′i·nar′ies,** *pl.*

Sem·i·nole (sem′ə nōl), *n.* a member of a tribe of American Indians who settled in Florida.

---

fat,   āpe,   cär,   ten,   ēven,   hit,   bīte,   gō,   hôrn,   tōōl,   book,   up,   fūr;
get,   joy,   yet,   chin,   she,   thin,   *th*en;   zh = s in pleasure;   ′ as in able (ā′b′l);
ə = a in ago,   e in agent,   i in sanity,   o in confess,   u in focus.

sem·i·pre·cious (sem'i presh'əs), *adj.* describing gems, as the garnet or turquoise, that are of less value than the precious gems.

Sem·ite (sem'īt), *n.* a member of any of the peoples whose language is Semitic, including the Hebrews, Arabs, Phoenicians, etc.

Se·mit·ic (sə mit'ik), *adj.* **1.** of or like the Semites. **2.** describing a group of languages of southwestern Asia and northern Africa, including Hebrew, Aramaic, Arabic, etc.

sem·i·trop·i·cal (sem'i träp'i k'l), *adj.* somewhat like the tropics; nearly tropical [Florida has a *semitropical* climate.]

sem·i·week·ly (sem'i wēk'lē), *adj.* happening, coming, etc. twice a week. —*n.* a newspaper coming out twice a week. —*adv.* twice a week.

Sen., abbreviation for **Senate** or **Senator.**

sen·ate (sen'it), *n.* **1.** an assembly or council that makes laws [the *senate* of ancient Rome]. **2. Senate,** the upper and smaller branch of Congress or of a State legislature.

sen·a·tor (sen'ə tər), *n.* a member of a senate. —**sen·a·to·ri·al** (sen'ə tôr'i əl), *adj.*

send (send), *v.* **1.** to cause to go or be carried [*Send* him home for the book. Food was *sent* by plane.] **2.** to make happen, come, be, etc. [a crop *sent* to reward our toil]. **3.** to put into some condition [The noise *sent* him out of his mind.] —**send for, 1.** to call to come; summon. **2.** to place an order for. —**send forth,** to cause to appear; produce. —**sent,** *p.t. & p.p.;* **send'-ing,** *pr.p.* —**send'er,** *n.*

Sen·e·ca (sen'i kə), *n.* a member of a tribe of American Indians who lived in western New York.

Sen·e·gal (sen'i gôl'), *n.* a country in western Africa, on the Atlantic Ocean.

sen·es·chal (sen'ə shəl), *n.* an official who managed the estate of a noble in the Middle Ages and often acted as a judge.

se·nile (sē'nīl), *adj.* **1.** showing signs of old age; weak in mind and body. **2.** of or caused by old age.

se·nil·i·ty (sə nil'ə tē), *n.* **1.** old age. **2.** weakness of mind and body caused by old age.

sen·ior (sēn'yər), *adj.* **1.** the older: a word written after the name of a father whose son has exactly the same name: abbreviated **Sr. 2.** of higher rank or longer service [a *senior* partner]. **3.** of seniors in a high school or college [the *senior* class]. —*n.* **1.** a person who is older or has a higher rank than another [Ben is my *senior* by ten years.] **2.** a student in the last year of a high school or college.

senior high school, same as **high school.**

sen·ior·i·ty (sēn yôr'ə tē), *n.* the condition or fact of being older, higher in rank, or longer in service, which may carry with it some privileges.

sen·na (sen'ə), *n.* **1.** the dried leaves of some cassia plants, used as a medicine to make the bowels move. **2.** a cassia plant.

se·ñor (se nyôr'), *n.* a Spanish word used, like "Mr.," as a title for a man. —**se·ñor·es** (se-nyô'res), *pl.*

se·ño·ra (se nyô'rä), *n.* a Spanish word used, like "Mrs.," as a title for a married woman.

se·ño·ri·ta (se'nyô rē'tä), *n.* a Spanish word used, like "Miss," as a title for an unmarried woman or girl.

sen·sa·tion (sen sā'shən), *n.* **1.** a feeling that comes from the senses, the body, or the mind [a *sensation* of warmth, of dizziness, of joy, etc.]. **2.** a feeling of great excitement among people [The good news caused a *sensation* at home.] **3.** the thing that stirs up such feeling [His new book will be a *sensation.*]

sen·sa·tion·al (sen sā'shən 'l), *adj.* **1.** stirring up strong feeling or great excitement [a *sensational* new theory]. **2.** meant to shock, thrill, excite, etc. [a *sensational* novel]. —**sen·sa'-tion·al·ism,** *n.* —**sen·sa'tion·al·ly,** *adv.*

sense (sens), *n.* **1.** any of the special powers of the body and mind that let one see, hear, feel, taste, smell, etc. **2.** a feeling or sensation [a *sense* of warmth; a *sense* of guilt]. **3.** an understanding or appreciation; special awareness [a *sense* of honor; a *sense* of beauty; a *sense* of rhythm; a *sense* of humor]. **4.** judgment or intelligence; reasoning [He showed good *sense* in his decision. There's no *sense* in going there late.] **5. senses,** *pl.* normal ability to think or reason soundly [Come to your *senses*!] **6.** meaning, as of a word [Six common *senses* of this noun are listed here.] —*v.* to be or become aware of; feel [I *sensed* something wrong as soon as I saw them.] —**in a sense,** looking at it one way. —**make sense,** to have a meaning that can be understood; sensible. —**sensed,** *p.t. & p.p.;* **sens'ing,** *pr.p.*

sense·less (sens'lis), *adj.* **1.** unconscious [knocked *senseless* by a blow]. **2.** stupid, foolish, meaningless, etc. [a *senseless* answer].

sen·si·bil·i·ty (sen'sə bil'ə tē), *n.* **1.** the ability to feel or become aware of sensations; power of feeling [the *sensibility* of the skin to heat or cold]. **2.** *often* **sensibilities,** *pl.* delicate or refined feelings [That remark wounded her *sensibilities.*] —**sen'si·bil'i·ties,** *pl.*

sen·si·ble (sen'sə b'l), *adj.* **1.** having or showing good sense; reasonable; wise [*sensible* advice]. **2.** having understanding; aware [He was *sensible* of her unhappiness.] **3.** that can be felt or noticed by the senses [a *sensible* change in temperature]. **4.** that can receive a sensation [The eye is *sensible* to light rays.] —**sen'si·bly,** *adv.*

sen·si·tive (sen'sə tiv), *adj.* **1.** quick to feel, notice, appreciate, etc. [A dog's ear is *sensitive* to high tones we cannot hear. Poets are *sensitive* to beauty.] **2.** quick to change or react when acted on by something [Camera film is *sensitive* to light.] **3.** easily hurt, irritated, etc.; touchy [He is *sensitive* about having his manners corrected.] **4.** tender or sore [a *sensitive* bruise]. —**sen'si·tive·ly,** *adv.* —**sen'si·tive·ness,** *n.*

sen·si·tiv·i·ty (sen'sə tiv'ə tē), *n.* the condition or degree of being sensitive.

sen·so·ry (sen'sər ē), *adj.* of the senses or sensation [*sensory* impressions].

sen·su·al (sen'shoo əl), *adj.* **1.** of the body and the senses as apart from the mind or spirit [*sensual* pleasures]. **2.** giving oneself up to the pleasures of the senses or the body. —**sen·su·al·i·ty** (sen′shoo al′ə tē), *n.*

sen·su·ous (sen′shoo əs), *adj.* **1.** coming from the senses or acting on the senses [*sensuous* pleasures; *sensuous* music]. **2.** getting a special pleasure from sights, sounds, tastes, etc. —**sen′su·ous·ly,** *adv.*

sent (sent), past tense and past participle of **send.**

sen·tence (sen′təns), *n.* **1.** a group of words used to tell or ask something, usually having a subject and a predicate. A sentence begins with a capital letter and ends with a period, question mark, or exclamation point ["I saw John." is a *sentence.* "Whatever you do," is not a *sentence.*] **2.** the judgment of a court on the punishment to be given to a person found guilty. **3.** the punishment itself [He served his *sentence* at the State prison.] —*v.* to pass sentence on. —**sen′tenced,** *p.t. & p.p.;* **sen′tenc·ing,** *pr.p.*

sen·ten·tious (sen ten′shəs), *adj.* **1.** saying much in few words; pithy. **2.** using or full of old sayings or proverbs in a way that is high-sounding or boring [a *sententious* sermon].

sen·tient (sen′shənt), *adj.* having senses or feelings [The wind roared like a *sentient* beast.]

sen·ti·ment (sen′tə mənt), *n.* **1.** a feeling about something [Loyalty is a noble *sentiment.*] **2.** a thought, opinion, etc. mixed with feeling [What are your *sentiments* about the election?] **3.** feelings, especially tender feelings, as apart from reason or judgment [He claims that there is no room for *sentiment* in business.] **4.** gentle or tender feelings of a weak or foolish kind [a novel full of *sentiment*].

sen·ti·men·tal (sen′tə men′t'l), *adj.* **1.** having or showing tender, gentle feelings, sometimes in a weak or foolish way [a *sentimental* song]. **2.** of or caused by sentiment [I'll save this picture for *sentimental* reasons.] —**sen′ti·men′tal·ly,** *adv.* —**sen′ti·men·tal·ist,** *n.* —**sen·ti·men·tal·i·ty** (sen′tə men tal′ə tē), *n.*

sen·ti·nel (sen′ti n'l), *n.* a guard who keeps watch at a post to protect a group; sentry. —**stand sentinel,** to serve as a sentinel.

sen·try (sen′trē), *n.* a person, especially a soldier, who keeps watch as a sentinel. —**stand sentry,** to serve as a sentry. —**sen′tries,** *pl.*

se·pal (sē′p'l), *n.* any of the leaves that form the calyx at the base of a flower.

sep·a·ra·ble (sep′ər ə b'l), *adj.* that can be separated.

sep·a·rate (sep′ə rāt), *v.* **1.** to set apart; divide into parts or groups [*Separate* the good apples from the bad ones.] **2.** to keep apart or divide by being or putting between [A hedge *separates* his yard from ours.] **3.** to go apart; stop being together or

sepals

joined [The friends *separated* at the crossroads.] —*adj.* (sep′ər it *or* sep′rit), **1.** set apart from the rest or others; not joined [The garage is *separate* from the house.] **2.** not connected with others; distinct [The President has powers *separate* from those of Congress.] **3.** not shared; for one only [*separate* lockers]. **4.** single or individual [the body's *separate* parts]. —**sep′a·rat·ed,** *p.t. & p.p.;* **sep′a·rat·ing,** *pr.p.* —**sep′a·rate·ly,** *adv.* —**sep′a·ra′tion,** *n.*

sep·a·ra·tor (sep′ə rā′tər), *n.* a person or thing that separates, as a machine that separates cream from milk.

se·pi·a (sē′pi ə), *n.* **1.** a dark-brown coloring matter made from the inky fluid of cuttlefish. **2.** dark, reddish brown.

Sep·tem·ber (sep tem′bər), *n.* the ninth month of the year, having 30 days: abbreviated **Sept.**

sep·tic (sep′tik), *adj.* **1.** causing infection. **2.** caused by or having to do with infection.

septic tank, a tank, usually underground, into which waste matter from the drains in a house flows and is rotted away.

sep·ul·cher (sep′'l kər), *n.* a tomb or grave. The British spelling is **sepulchre.**

se·pul·chral (sə pul′krəl), *adj.* **1.** of tombs, death, or burial. **2.** sad, deep, gloomy, etc. [a *sepulchral* tone].

se·quel (sē′kwəl), *n.* **1.** something that follows something else, often as a result [Floods came as a *sequel* to the heavy rains.] **2.** a book that carries on a story started in another book ["Little Men" is a *sequel* to "Little Women."]

se·quence (sē′kwəns), *n.* **1.** the following of one thing after another; succession [the *sequence* of events in his life]. **2.** the order in which things follow one another [Line them up in *sequence* from shortest to tallest.] **3.** a series of things that are related [a *sequence* of misfortunes].

se·ques·ter (si kwes′tər), *v.* **1.** to hide, or keep away from others; withdraw [He *sequestered* himself in a lonely cabin.] **2.** to seize or hold, as until a debt is paid.

se·quin (sē′kwin), *n.* a small, shiny spangle or disk. Sequins are sewn on cloth as decoration.

se·quoi·a (si kwoi′ə), *n.* a giant evergreen tree of California, as the red-wood.

se·ra·pe (sə rä′pē), *n.* a brightly colored woolen blanket worn as a garment in Mexico and many countries of Central and South America. *See the picture on the next page.*

ser·aph (ser′əf), *n.* an angel of the highest rank. —**ser′aphs** or **ser·a·phim** (ser′ə fim), *pl.*

sequoia, showing branch with cone

se·raph·ic (sə raf′ik), *adj.* of or like a seraph, or angel; angelic.

Serb (sûrb), *n.* a member of a Slavic people living in southeastern Europe, especially in Serbia.

Ser·bi·a (sûr′bi ə), *n.* a former country in southeastern Europe, now a part of Yugoslavia. —**Ser′- bi·an,** *adj. & n.*

sere (sir), *adj.* dried up; withered: *seldom used except in poetry.*

ser·e·nade (ser ə nād′), *n.* **1.** the act of playing or singing music outdoors at night, as by a lover under his sweetheart's window. **2.** a piece of music that is right for this. —*v.* to play or sing a serenade to. —**ser·e- nad′ed,** *p.t. & p.p.;* **ser·e·nad′ing,** *pr.p.*

serape

se·rene (sə rēn′), *adj.* **1.** calm or peaceful [a *serene* look]. **2.** bright; clear; without clouds [a *serene* sky]. —**se·rene′ly,** *adv.*

se·ren·i·ty (sə ren′ə tē), *n.* the fact of being serene; calmness or clearness.

serf (sûrf), *n.* a farm worker who was almost like a slave and could be sold along with the land he worked on, as in the Middle Ages.

serge (sûrj), *n.* a hard, strong cloth, usually wool with slanting ribs woven in it. It is used for suits and coats.

ser·geant (sär′jənt), *n.* **1.** a noncommissioned officer in the armed forces above a corporal. **2.** a police officer of the lowest rank.

ser·geant-at-arms (sär′jənt ət ärmz′), *n.* an officer whose duty is to keep order at a meeting, in a law court, etc. —**ser′geants-at-arms′,** *pl.*

se·ri·al (sir′i əl), *adj.* **1.** of or arranged in a series [Dollar bills have *serial* numbers printed on them.] **2.** published in a series of parts, one at a time [a *serial* story]. —*n.* a long story published one part at a time in issues of a magazine or newspaper. —**se′ri·al·ly,** *adv.*

se·ri·al·ize (sir′i ə līz′), *v.* to publish as a serial. —**se′ri·al·ized′,** *p.t. & p.p.;* **se′ri·al·iz′ing,** *pr.p.*

se·ries (sir′ēz), *n.* **1.** a number of like things arranged in a row or coming one after another in regular order [a *series* of arches; a *series* of concerts]. **2.** a group of related things; set [a *series* of illustrations for a book]. —**se′ries,** *pl.*

se·ri·ous (sir′i əs), *adj.* **1.** thinking deeply in a solemn way; not frivolous; earnest [a *serious* interest in art]. **2.** not joking or fooling; sincere [Is he *serious* about wanting to help?] **3.** needing careful thought; important [a *serious* problem]. **4.** that can cause worry; dangerous [a *serious* illness]. —**se′ri·ous·ly,** *adv.* —**se′ri·ous- ness,** *n.*

ser·mon (sûr′mən), *n.* **1.** a speech, especially by a clergyman, on some religious topic or on morals. **2.** any serious or boring talk, as on what one should do.

se·rous (sir′əs), *adj.* **1.** of or containing serum [the *serous* part of the blood]. **2.** like serum; thin and watery [a *serous* fluid].

ser·pent (sûr′pənt), *n.* **1.** a snake, especially a large or poisonous one. **2.** a sneaky person.

ser·pen·tine (sûr′pən tēn *or* sûr′pən tīn), *adj.* **1.** of or like a serpent; twisted or winding [a *serpentine* path]. **2.** sly or sneaky. —*n.* (sûr′- pən tēn), a green or brownish-red mineral.

ser·rate (ser′āt) or **ser·rat·ed** (ser′āt id), *adj.* having notches like the teeth of a saw along the edge [a *serrate* leaf or knife].

ser·ried (ser′ēd), *adj.* placed close together [soldiers in *serried* ranks].

se·rum (sir′əm), *n.* **1.** any watery liquid formed in animals, especially the yellowish liquid that is left after blood clots. **2.** a liquid got from the blood of an animal that has been given a certain disease. It is used as an antitoxin against that disease.

a serrate leaf

ser·vant (sûr′vənt), *n.* **1.** a person who is hired to work in another's home as a maid, cook, chauffeur, etc. **2.** a person who works for a government [a civil *servant*]. **3.** a person who works eagerly for a cause [a *servant* of liberty].

serve (sûrv), *v.* **1.** to work for someone as a servant [She *served* in their household ten years.] **2.** to do services for; aid; help [He *served* his country well.] **3.** to hold a certain office [He *served* as mayor for two terms.] **4.** to worship [to *serve* God]. **5.** to be a member of the armed forces [He *served* in the navy during the war.] **6.** to pass or spend in a prison [He *served* six years for the robbery.] **7.** to offer or pass food, drink, etc. to [May I *serve* you some chicken?] **8.** to be useful to; provide with services or goods [One hospital *serves* the town.] **9.** to be suitable or enough for [One nail will *serve* to hang the picture. This recipe *serves* four.] **10.** to treat [She was cruelly *served* by fate.] **11.** to deliver or hand over [to *serve* a summons to appear in court]. **12.** to start play by hitting the ball, as in tennis. —*n.* **1.** the act or style of serving the ball in tennis, etc. **2.** one's turn at doing this. —**serve one right,** to be what one deserves. —**served,** *p.t. & p.p.;* **serv′ing,** *pr.p.*

serv·er (sûr′vər), *n.* **1.** a person who serves. **2.** a thing used in serving, as a tray.

serv·ice (sûr′vis), *n.* **1.** work done or duty performed for others [the *services* of a doctor; TV repair *service*]. **2.** helpful or friendly action; aid [They recognized his *services* to the cause of liberty.] **3.** work for the government, or the people who do it [a clerk in the civil *service*]. **4.** the armed forces; army, navy, etc. [He was in the *service* two years.] **5.** a religious ceremony, especially a meeting for prayer. **6.** a set of articles used in serving [a silver tea *service*]. **7.** the act or manner of providing people with something [telephone *service;* train *service*]. **8.** the act of serving a summons, writ, or other legal notice. **9.** the act or style of serving the ball in tennis, etc., or one's turn at this. **10.** the condition or work of being a servant [She was in *service* for many years.] —*adj.* **1.** of, for, or in service [the *service* trades]. **2.** used by servants or in making deliveries [a *service* entrance]. —*v.*

1. to put into good condition for use; repair or adjust [We *service* radios.] **2.** to furnish with a service; supply [One gas company *services* the whole region.] —**at one's service, 1.** ready to serve one. **2.** ready for one's use. —**of service,** helpful; useful. —**serv′iced,** *p.t.* & *p.p.*; **serv′ic·ing,** *pr.p.*

serv·ice·a·ble (sur′vis ə b'l), *adj.* **1.** that will give good or long service; durable [*serviceable* clothing]. **2.** that can be of service; useful [a *serviceable* fellow].

serv·ice·man (sur′vis man), *n.* **1.** a member of the armed forces. **2.** a person whose work is servicing or repairing something [a radio *serviceman*]. —**serv′ice·men,** *pl.*

service station, same as **gas station.**

ser·vile (sur′v'l), *adj.* **1.** like a slave; too humble; cringing [a *servile* flatterer]. **2.** of slaves or servants [*servile* employment]. —**ser·vil·i·ty** (sur vil′ə tē), *n.*

ser·vi·tor (sur′və tər), *n.* a servant: *now seldom used.*

ser·vi·tude (sur′və tood *or* sur′və tyood), *n.* **1.** the condition of a slave; slavery. **2.** work that a criminal is forced to do as punishment.

ses·a·me (ses′ə mē), *n.* **1.** an East Indian plant with flat seeds. **2.** its seeds, eaten as food. —**open sesame,** the magic words spoken by Ali Baba in *The Arabian Nights* to get the door to the robbers' cave open.

ses·sion (sesh′ən), *n.* **1.** the meeting of a court, legislature, class, etc. to do its work. **2.** a complete series of such meetings. **3.** the time during which such a meeting or meetings go on. **4.** any meeting with another [a *session* with one's lawyer]. —**in session,** meeting [Congress is *in session.*]

set (set), *v.* **1.** to put in a certain place or position [*Set* the book on the table.] **2.** to make be in a certain condition [The captives were *set* free.] **3.** to put in order or in the right condition, position, etc.; arrange; adjust [to *set* a trap; to *set* a thermostat; to *set* a broken bone; to *set* a table for a meal]. **4.** to start [My remark *set* him to thinking.] **5.** to make or become rigid, firm, or fixed [He *set* his jaw. Has the cement *set?*] **6.** to establish or fix, as a time for a meeting, a price, a rule, an example, a limit, etc. **7.** to sit or seat on eggs, as a hen, so as to hatch them. **8.** to mount in a ring, bracelet, etc., as a gem. **9.** to direct or turn [He *set* his face toward home.] **10.** to write or fit music to words or words to music [He *set* the poem to an old tune.] **11.** to furnish for copying [to *set* an example]. **12.** to sink below the horizon [The sun *sets* in the west.] —*adj.* **1.** that has been set; fixed, established, firm, rigid, etc. [a *set* time for the party; the *set* rules of a game; a *set* speech; a *set* look on one's face]. **2.** stubborn [He's *set* in his ways.] **3.** ready [On your mark! get *set!* go!] **4.** formed or

built [heavy-*set*]. —*n.* **1.** a setting or being set. **2.** the way in which a thing is set [the *set* of her head]. **3.** direction or course, as of the wind. **4.** something that is set, as a slip for planting, or the scenery for a play. **5.** a group of persons or things that go together [She belongs to the literary *set*. He bought a *set* of tools.] **6.** a number of parts put together, as in a cabinet [a radio or television *set*]. **7.** a group of six or more games of tennis won by a margin of at least two games. —**all set,** completely ready. —**set about,** to begin or start. —**set against, 1.** to balance or compare. **2.** to make an enemy of. —**set aside, 1.** to separate and keep for a purpose: also **set apart. 2.** to get rid of; dismiss, discard, or reject. —**set back,** to put behind, as by hindering. —**set down, 1.** to put down. **2.** to put in writing or print. —**set forth, 1.** to start out, as on a journey. **2.** to make known; state. —**set in,** to begin [Infection had *set in.*] —**set off, 1.** to start or start out. **2.** to make stand out; show off by contrast. **3.** to make explode. —**set on** or **set upon,** to attack or urge to attack. —**set out, 1.** to start out, as on a journey. **2.** to display, as for sale. **3.** to plant. —**set to, 1.** to get to work; begin. **2.** to begin fighting. —**set up, 1.** to raise to power, a high position, etc. **2.** to build; erect. **3.** to establish; found. **4.** to start. —**set,** *p.t.* & *p.p.*; **set′-ting,** *pr.p.*

set·back (set′bak), *n.* the condition of being set back, or put behind; also, something that sets one back, as by hindering.

set·tee (se tē′), *n.* **1.** a seat or bench with a back. **2.** a small or medium-sized sofa.

set·ter (set′ər), *n.* **1.** a person or thing that sets [a *setter* of rules; an automatic *setter* of bowling pins]. **2.** a hunting dog with long hair. Setters are trained to find birds and point them out by standing in a stiff position.

settee *(meaning 2)*

set·ting (set′ing), *n.* **1.** the act of one that sets. **2.** the thing in which something is set [the *setting* of a gem]. **3.** the time, place, etc. in which a story, poem, or play is set. **4.** surroundings, or scenery that surrounds. **5.** the music written for a set of words, as for a poem.

set·tle (set′'l), *n.* a long wooden bench with a back and arm rests.

set·tle (set′'l), *v.* **1.** to bring or come to an agreement or decision; decide [Did you *settle* on which route to take? We *settled* the argument by dividing our find.] **2.** to put in order; arrange, as one's affairs. **3.** to set in place firmly or comfortably [He *settled* himself in the chair to read.] **4.** to calm or quiet [This medicine will *settle* your stomach.] **5.** to come to rest [The bird

---

fat,   āpe,   cär,   ten,   ēven,   hit,   bīte,   gō,   hôrn,   tool,   book,   up,   fur;
get,   joy,   yet,   chin,   she,   thin,   *then;*   zh = s in pleasure;   ′ as in able (ā′b'l);
ə = a in ago,   e in agent,   i in sanity,   o in confess,   u in focus.

settled on the limb. The pain *settled* in his heart.] **6.** to make a home for or go to live in [Mr. Jones *settled* his family in the country. The Dutch *settled* New York.] **7.** to move downward; sink [The car *settled* in the mud. The rain *settled* the dust.] **8.** to clear as by having the dregs sink to the bottom [Let the coffee *settle* before you pour it.] **9.** to pay, as a bill or debt. **10.** to cast itself [Fog *settled* over the city. Gloom *settled* over him.] **—settle down, 1.** to become settled, as in a fixed place or regular way of life. **2.** to begin to work or act in a serious and steady way. **— settle upon** or **settle on,** to give to someone by law, as money or property. **—set′tled,** *p.t. & p.p.;* **set′tling,** *pr.p.*

set·tle·ment (set′′l mənt), *n.* **1.** a settling or being settled. **2.** the settling of people in a new land, a frontier region, etc. **3.** a place where people have gone to settle; colony [early English *settlements* in Virginia]. **4.** a small village or hamlet [A *settlement* grew up where the rivers met.] **5.** an agreement or understanding [to reach a *settlement* in a dispute]. **6.** payment, as of a claim. **7.** an amount that a person pays or agrees to pay to another, as at marriage, divorce, or death. **8.** a place in a poor, crowded neighborhood where people can go to get advice, take classes, play games, etc.

set·tler (set′lər), *n.* **1.** a person or thing that settles. **2.** one who settles in a new country.

sev·en (sev′′n), *n. & adj.* one more than six; the number 7.

seven seas, all the oceans of the world.

sev·en·teen (sev′′n tēn′), *n. & adj.* seven more than ten; the number 17.

sev·en·teenth (sev′′n tēnth′), *adj.* coming after sixteen others; 17th in order. **—n. 1.** the seventeenth one. **2.** one of seventeen equal parts of something; 1/17.

sev·enth (sev′′nth), *adj.* coming after six others; 7th in order. **—n. 1.** the seventh one. **2.** one of the seven equal parts of something; 1/7.

seventh heaven, complete happiness.

sev·en·ti·eth (sev′′n tē ith), *adj.* coming after sixty-nine others; 70th in order. **—n. 1.** the seventieth one. **2.** one of seventy equal parts of something; 1/70.

sev·en·ty (sev′′n tē), *n. & adj.* **1.** seven times ten; the number 70. **2. seventies,** *n.pl.* the numbers or years from 70 to 79.

sev·er (sev′ər), *v.* **1.** to cut off or break off [to *sever* a limb from a tree; to *sever* a friendship]. **2.** to separate or divide [A river *severs* Ohio from West Virginia.] **3.** to cut in two [to *sever* a cable]. **—sev′er·ance,** *n.*

sev·er·al (sev′ər əl *or* sev′rəl), *adj.* **1.** more than two but not many; a few [*Several* people called while you were out.] **2.** separate or different [We parted and went our *several* ways.] **—sev′er·al·ly,** *adv.*

se·vere (sə vir′), *adj.* **1.** strict or harsh; stern; not gentle or kind [*severe* punishment; a *severe* critic]. **2.** not gay; serious; grave. **3.** very plain and simple; with little or no decoration [a *severe* black dress]. **4.** causing great damage, pain, etc.; violent [a *severe* headache; a *severe* storm]. **5.** difficult; hard to bear [a *severe* test of his courage]. **—se·ver′er,** *compar.;* **se·ver′est,** *superl.* **—se·vere′ly,** *adv.* **—se·vere′ness,** *n.*

se·ver·i·ty (sə ver′ə tē), *n.* **1.** the condition of being severe; strictness, seriousness, plainness, etc. **2.** something severe, as a punishment. **—se·ver′i·ties,** *pl.*

Se·ville (sə vil′), *n.* a city in southern Spain.

sew (sō), *v.* **1.** to fasten with stitches made with needle and thread [to *sew* buttons on a coat]. **2.** to mend, make, etc. by sewing [She *sewed* me a fine shirt.] **3.** to work with needle and thread or at a sewing machine [Can you *sew?*] **—sew up, 1.** to fasten the edges together with stitches. **2.** to get or have complete control over: *used only in everyday talk.* **—sewed,** *p.t.;* **sewed** or **sewn,** *p.p.;* **sew′ing,** *pr.p.* **—sew′er,** *n.*

sew·age (soo′ij *or* syoo′ij), *n.* the waste matter carried off by sewers or drains.

sew·er (soo′ər *or* syoo′ər), *n.* an underground pipe or drain for carrying off water and waste matter.

sew·er·age (soo′ər ij *or* syoo′ər ij), *n.* **1.** the removal of water and waste matter by sewers. **2.** a system of sewers. **3.** sewage.

sew·ing (sō′ing), *n.* **1.** the act or skill of a person who sews [Her *sewing* is only fair.] **2.** something that is to be sewed.

sewing machine, a device for sewing with a needle that is worked by machinery.

sewn (sōn), a past participle of **sew.**

sex (seks), *n.* **1.** either of the two groups, male or female, into which persons, animals, or plants are divided. **2.** the character of being male or female.

sex·tant (seks′tənt), *n.* an instrument used to measure distance in degrees of an angle. It is used at sea to find out a ship's position by measuring the angle between a star, the sun, etc. and the horizon.

sex·tet or **sex·tette** (seks-tet′), *n.* **1.** a piece of music for six voices or six instruments. **2.** the six people who sing or play it. **3.** any group of six.

sextant

sex·ton (seks′tən), *n.* a man whose work is to clean and take care of a church, ring the church bells, etc.

sex·u·al (sek′shoo əl), *adj.* having to do with sex or the sexes. **—sex′u·al·ly,** *adv.*

Sgt., abbreviation for **Sergeant.**

shab·by (shab′ē), *adj.* **1.** that shows much wear; old and worn out [*shabby* clothing]. **2.** wearing shabby clothes. **3.** poorly taken care of; rundown [a *shabby* neighborhood]. **4.** not proper; disgraceful; mean [a *shabby* way to treat guests]. **—shab′bi·er,** *compar.;* **shab′bi·est,** *superl.* **—shab′bi·ly,** *adv.* **—shab′bi·ness,** *n.*

shack (shak), *n.* a small house or hut built in a rough, crude way; shanty.

shack·le (shak'l), *n.* **1.** a metal loop put around the wrist or ankle of a prisoner, usually in pairs joined by a chain; fetter. **2.** anything that keeps one from moving or acting in a free way [the *shackles* of ignorance]. **3.** any device used in fastening or connecting. —*v.* to bind or hinder as with a shackle or shackles. —**shack'led,** *p.t. & p.p.;* **shack'ling,** *pr.p.*

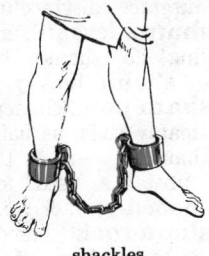
shackles

shad (shad), *n.* a food fish related to the herring. Shad live in the ocean, but swim up rivers to lay their eggs. —**shad** or **shads,** *pl.*

shade (shād), *n.* **1.** darkness caused by cutting off rays of light, as from the sun [the deep *shade* of the jungle]. **2.** an area with less light than other areas around it [in the *shade* of an awning]. **3.** a device used to cut off light [a window *shade;* a lamp *shade*]. **4.** degree of darkness of a color [light and dark *shades* of green]. **5.** a small amount or degree [a *shade* of anger in his voice]. **6.** a small difference [all *shades* of opinion]. **7. shades,** *pl.* the growing darkness after sunset. **8.** a ghost; spirit: *used mainly in poetry.* —*v.* **1.** to protect or screen from light or heat [The trees *shade* the house.] **2.** to change little by little [The drapes *shade* from purple to lavender.] **3.** to darken or dim [to *shade* the sun's rays]. **4.** to use lines or dark colors in a picture to show shade or shadow. —**shad'ed,** *p.t. & p.p.;* **shad'ing,** *pr.p.*

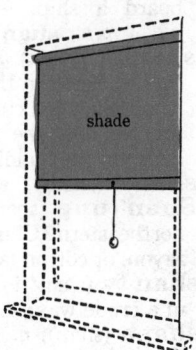
shade

shad·ing (shād'ing), *n.* **1.** protection against light and heat. **2.** the use of dark colors or of lines to give the effect of shade or shadow in a picture. **3.** any small difference, as in quality.

shad·ow (shad'ō), *n.* **1.** the darkness or the dark shape cast upon a surface by something cutting off light from it [Her large hat put her face in *shadow.* His hand cast a *shadow* on the wall.] **2. shadows,** *pl.* the growing darkness after sunset. **3.** gloom or sadness; also, something that causes gloom or sadness [the *shadow* of illness]. **4.** a small amount; trace; suggestion [a *shadow* of a frown]. **5.** something imagined, not real [Is fame a mere *shadow?*] **6.** a person who follows another person around, especially as a detective or spy. **7.** the shaded part in a picture. **8.** a ghost; spirit. —*v.* **1.** to make a shadow or shadows upon [Hills *shadowed* the valley.] **2.** to make dark or gloomy [A frown *shadowed* his face.] **3.** to follow closely in a secret way. —**in the shadow of,** very close to.

shad·ow·y (shad'ō ē), *adj.* **1.** shaded or full of shadow [a *shadowy* corner of the room]. **2.** not clear or real; dim [a *shadowy* figure in the fog; a *shadowy* hope].

shad·y (shād'ē), *adj.* **1.** giving shade [a *shady* tree]. **2.** shaded, as from the sun [a *shady* path]. **3.** not clearly honest, proper, etc.; doubtful: *used only in everyday talk* [a *shady* business deal]. —**shad'i·er,** *compar.;* **shad'i·est,** *superl.* —**shad'i·ness,** *n.*

shaft (shaft), *n.* **1.** the long, slender stem or handle of an arrow or spear. **2.** an arrow or spear. **3.** something that seems to be hurled like an arrow or spear [a *shaft* of light; *shafts* of wit]. **4.** a long, slender thing or part, as a column or a long handle [the *shaft* of a golf club]. **5.** either of the two poles between which an animal is harnessed to a wagon, etc. **6.** a bar that supports moving parts of a machine, or that makes them move [the drive *shaft* of an engine]. **7.** a long, narrow opening dug down into the earth [a mine *shaft*]. **8.** an opening going up through the floors of a building [an elevator *shaft*].

shaft

shag (shag), *n.* **1.** a heavy, rough nap on some cloth. **2.** cloth with such a nap.

shag·bark (shag'bärk), *n.* a hickory tree with gray bark that peels off in long shreds.

shag·gy (shag'ē), *adj.* **1.** having long, thick, rough hair or wool [a *shaggy* dog]. **2.** long, coarse, and uneven [*shaggy* eyebrows]. **3.** having a rough nap, as cloth. —**shag'gi·er,** *compar.;* **shag'gi·est,** *superl.* —**shag'gi·ness,** *n.*

shah (shä), *n.* the title of the ruler of certain Eastern countries, especially Iran.

shake (shāk), *v.* **1.** to move quickly up and down, back and forth, or from side to side [to *shake* one's head in approval]. **2.** to clasp another's hand, as in greeting. **3.** to bring, force, throw, stir up, etc. by short, quick movements [I'll *shake* salt on the popcorn. *Shake* the medicine well before taking it.] **4.** to tremble or make tremble [His voice *shook* with fear. Chills *shook* his body.] **5.** to weaken, disturb, upset, etc. [He was *shaken* by the news.] **6.** to get away from: *slang in this meaning* [He *shook* his pursuers.] —*n.* **1.** an act of shaking [a *shake* of the fist]. **2.** a trembling movement or sound [a *shake* in his voice]. —**no great shakes,** not outstanding or unusual: *used only in everyday talk.* —**shake down, 1.** to make fall by shaking, as fruit from a tree. **2.** to make settle by shaking. —**shake off,** to get away from or get rid of.

fat,   āpe,   cär,   ten,   ēven,   hit,   bīte,   gō,   hôrn,   tōol,   book,   up,   fũr;
get,   joy,   yet,   chin,   she,   thin,   *then*;   zh = s in pleasure;   ' as in able (ā'b'l);
ə = a in ago,   e in agent,   i in sanity,   o in confess,   u in focus.

—**shake out,** to empty or straighten out by shaking. —**shake up, 1.** to shake so as to mix up. **2.** to jar or shock. **3.** to change greatly. —**shook,** *p.t.;* **shak·en** (shāk/ən), *p.p.;* **shak/-ing,** *pr.p.*

shak·er (shāk/ər), *n.* **1.** a person or thing that shakes. **2.** a device used in shaking [a salt *shaker*]. **3. Shaker,** a person who belongs to a religious sect in which the members live and work together in their own communities.

Shake·speare, William (shāk/spir), 1564–1616; English poet and writer of plays. —**Shake-spear/e·an** or **Shake·spear/i·an,** *adj.*

shake-up (shāk/up/), *n.* a great and sudden change, as in an organization.

shak·y (shāk/ē), *adj.* **1.** not firm or steady; weak [a *shaky* bridge]. **2.** shaking; trembling [a *shaky* hand]. **3.** not to be trusted or relied on; not sound [*shaky* evidence]. —**shak/i·er,** *compar.;* **shak/i·est,** *superl.* —**shak/i·ly,** *adv.* —**shak/i·ness,** *n.*

shale (shāl), *n.* a rock formed of hardened clay. It splits into thin layers when broken.

shall (shal), *a helping verb used with other verbs in speaking of the future* [I *shall* leave tomorrow. *Shall* we eat?] *See the note following* **will.** *See also* **should.**

shal·lop (shal/əp), *n.* a small, open boat.

shal·low (shal/ō), *adj.* **1.** not deep [a *shallow* lake]. **2.** not serious in thinking or strong in feeling [a *shallow* mind]. —*n.* a shallow place, as in a river.

shalt (shalt), the older form of **shall,** used with *thou,* as in the Bible.

sham (sham), *n.* something false or fake; fraud [His bravery is just a *sham.*] —*adj.* not genuine or real; false; fake [a string of *sham* pearls]. —*v.* to fake; pretend [He's not asleep, he's only *shamming.*] —**shammed,** *p.t. & p.p.;* **sham/-ming,** *pr.p.*

sham·ble (sham/b'l), *v.* to walk in a lazy or clumsy way, barely lifting the feet; shuffle. —*n.* a shambling walk. —**sham/bled,** *p.t. & p.p.;* **sham/bling,** *pr.p.*

sham·bles (sham/b'lz), *n.* **1.** a slaughterhouse. **2.** a place of much bloodshed. **3.** a place where there is much destruction or disorder [The children left the room a *shambles.*]

shame (shām), *n.* **1.** a painful feeling of having lost respect because of something wrong done by oneself or another. **2.** loss of honor or respect; disgrace [to bring *shame* to one's family]. **3.** something that brings shame. **4.** a thing to feel sorry about [It's a *shame* that you missed the party.] —*v.* **1.** to give a feeling of shame to; make ashamed. **2.** to make lose honor or respect; disgrace [The actions of a few *shamed* the whole school.] **3.** to force into something because of a feeling of shame [Her pained look *shamed* him into apologizing.] —**for shame!** you ought to be ashamed! —**put to shame, 1.** to make ashamed. **2.** to do much better than; surpass. —**shamed,** *p.t. & p.p.;* **sham/ing,** *pr.p.*

shame·faced (shām/fāst), *adj.* **1.** showing shame; ashamed. **2.** bashful; shy.

shame·ful (shām/fəl), *adj.* bringing shame or disgrace; disgraceful. —**shame/ful·ly,** *adv.*

shame·less (shām/lis), *adj.* feeling or showing no shame; brazen [a *shameless* cheat]. —**shame/less·ly,** *adv.*

sham·poo (sham poo/), *v.* **1.** to wash with foamy suds, as hair or a rug. **2.** to wash the hair of. —*n.* **1.** the act of shampooing. **2.** a substance used for shampooing. —**sham-pooed/,** *p.t. & p.p.;* **sham·poo/ing,** *pr.p.*

sham·rock (sham/räk), *n.* a kind of clover that is the emblem of Ireland: *see the picture.*

Shang·hai (shang/hī/), *n.* a seaport in eastern China.

shang·hai (shang/hī), *v.* to kidnap and force to work as a sailor on board a ship. —**shang/haied,** *p.t. & p.p.;* **shang/hai·ing,** *pr.p.*

shamrock

shank (shangk), *n.* **1.** the part of the leg between the knee and the ankle. **2.** the whole leg. **3.** a cut of beef from the upper part of the leg. **4.** the part of a tool or instrument between the handle and the working part; shaft.

shan't (shant), shall not.

Shan·tung (shan/tung/), *n.* **1.** a province of northeastern China. **2. shantung,** a silk, rayon, or cotton fabric with an uneven surface.

shan·ty (shan/tē), *n.* a small house or hut built in a crude way; shack. —**shan/ties,** *pl.*

shape (shāp), *n.* **1.** the way a thing looks because of its outline; outer form; figure [The cloud had the *shape* of a lamb.] **2.** definite or regular form [He's getting his story into *shape.*] **3.** condition: *used only in everyday talk* [in bad *shape* financially]. —*v.* **1.** to give a certain shape to; form [He *shaped* the clay into a bowl.] **2.** to prepare or develop in a certain way [I am *shaping* an answer to his letter. The campaign is *shaping* up well.] —**take shape,** to develop or show a definite form. —**shaped,** *p.t. & p.p.;* **shap/-ing,** *pr.p.*

shape·less (shāp/lis), *adj.* without a definite or well-formed shape.

shape·ly (shāp/lē), *adj.* having a good shape or form; pleasing to look at. —**shape/li·er,** *compar.;* **shape/li·est,** *superl.*

share (sher), *n.* **1.** a part that each one of a group gets or has [your *share* of the cake; my *share* of the blame]. **2.** any of the equal parts into which the ownership of a company is divided, as by stock. —*v.* **1.** to divide and give out in shares [The owners *shared* the profits with their employees.] **2.** to have a share of with others; have or use together [The three of you will *share* the back seat.] **3.** to take part; have a share [We all *shared* in the gift for Miss Jones.] —**go shares,** to take part together; share. —**shared,** *p.t. & p.p.;* **shar/ing,** *pr.p.*

share·crop·per (sher/kräp/ər), *n.* a person who farms land owned by another and gets part of the crop in return for his work.

share·hold·er (sher/hōl/dər), *n.* a person who owns one or more shares of stock, as in a company.

shark (shärk), *n.* **1.** a large ocean fish that eats other fish and sometimes attacks people in the water. **2.** a dishonest person; swindler.

sharp (shärp), *adj.* **1.** having a thin edge for cutting, or a fine point for piercing [a *sharp* knife; a *sharp* needle]. **2.** having an edge or point; not round or blunt [a *sharp* ridge; a *sharp* nose]. **3.** not gradual; abrupt [a *sharp* turn]. **4.** easily seen; distinct; clear [a *sharp* contrast]. **5.** very clever or shrewd [a *sharp* mind]. **6.** keen in seeing or noticing; alert [*sharp* eyes; a *sharp* lookout]. **7.** harsh or severe [a *sharp* reply]. **8.** violent; sudden and forceful [a *sharp* attack]. **9.** very strong; intense; stinging [a *sharp* wind; *sharp* pain]. **10.** very active; brisk [a *sharp* run]. **11.** in music, above the true pitch; also, higher in pitch by a half tone. **12.** good-looking; attractive: *a slang meaning.* —*n.* a musical tone or note one half step above another; also, the sign ♯, used to mark such a note. —*adv.* **1.** exactly or promptly [He gets up at 6:30 *sharp.*] **2.** in a sharp manner; keenly, alertly, briskly, etc. [Look *sharp* when crossing streets.] **3.** in music, above the true pitch. —*v.* to make or become sharp [to *sharp* a note]. —**sharp′ly,** *adv.* —**sharp′ness,** *n.*

sharp·en (shär′p'n), *v.* to make or become sharp or sharper. —**sharp′en·er,** *n.*

sharp·shoot·er (shärp′shoot′ər), *n.* a person who shoots a gun with skill; good marksman.

sharp-tongued (shärp′tungd′), *adj.* using harsh or rude words [a *sharp-tongued* critic].

sharp-wit·ted (shärp′wit′id), *adj.* having or showing a quick and clever mind [a *sharp-witted* reply].

shat·ter (shat′ər), *v.* **1.** to break into many pieces; smash [Our ball *shattered* the window.] **2.** to ruin or destroy; damage badly [The storm *shattered* our plans.]

shave (shāv), *v.* **1.** to cut off hair with a razor, close to the skin. **2.** to cut off the hair of [He carefully *shaved* his chin.] **3.** to cut off the beard of [The barber will *shave* you.] **4.** to cut or scrape away a thin slice from [to *shave* ham]. **5.** to barely touch in passing; graze [The car *shaved* the side of the tree.] —*n.* the act of cutting off hair, especially the beard, with a razor. —**close shave,** a narrow escape: *used only in everyday talk.* —**shaved,** *p.t.;* **shaved** or **shav·en** (shāv′'n), *p.p.;* **shav′ing,** *pr.p.*

shav·er (shāv′ər), *n.* **1.** an instrument used in shaving [an electric *shaver*]. **2.** one who shaves. **3.** a young boy: *used only in everyday talk.*

shav·ing (shāv′ing), *n.* **1.** the act of one who shaves. **2.** a thin piece of wood, metal, etc. shaved off a larger piece.

Shaw, George Ber·nard (bŭr′nərd shô), 1856–1950; Irish writer of plays.

shawl (shôl), *n.* a large piece of cloth worn, especially by women, over the shoulders or head.

shay (shā), *n.* a light carriage; chaise.

she (shē), *pron.* the woman, girl, or female animal being talked about [Ellen thought *she* heard a noise.] —*n.* a woman, girl, or female animal [This dog is a *she.*] —**they,** *pl.*

shawl

sheaf (shēf), *n.* **1.** a bunch of cut stalks of wheat, rye, straw, etc. tied up together in a bundle. **2.** a number of things bound together [a *sheaf* of papers]. —**sheaves,** *pl.*

shear (shir), *v.* **1.** to cut as with shears or scissors [to *shear* one corner off a sheet of metal]. **2.** to clip the hair, wool, etc. from [to *shear* a sheep]. **3.** to move as if by cutting [The plane *sheared* through the clouds.] —**sheared,** *p.t.;* **sheared** or **shorn,** *p.p.;* **shear′ing,** *pr.p.*

shears (shirz), *n.pl.* any tool like large scissors, used to cut cloth, metal, etc. or to prune plants.

sheath (shēth), *n.* **1.** a case for the blade of a knife, sword, etc. **2.** any covering like this, as the membrane around a muscle. —**sheaths** (shēthz or shēths), *pl.*

sheathe (shēth), *v.* **1.** to put into a sheath [to *sheathe* a sword]. **2.** to cover with something that protects [wire *sheathed* with rubber insulation]. —**sheathed,** *p.t. & p.p.;* **sheath′ing,** *pr.p.*

knife in a sheath

sheave (shēv), *v.* to gather in sheaves, as grain. —**sheaved,** *p.t. & p.p.;* **sheav′ing,** *pr.p.*

sheaves (shēvz), *n.* plural of **sheaf.**

She·ba (shē′bə), *n.* an ancient country in southern Arabia [The Queen of *Sheba* visited King Solomon to find out how wise he was.]

shed (shed), *n.* a building or lean-to for storing and protecting things. Sheds are often small and crudely built, or open on one or more sides.

shed (shed), *v.* **1.** to let or make flow or fall; pour out [to *shed* tears; to *shed* blood]. **2.** to make flow off without going through [Raincoats *shed* water.] **3.** to lose or drop [Maples *shed* their leaves each year.] **4.** to send out or give forth [to *shed* confidence]. —**shed blood,** to kill in a violent way. —**shed light, 1.** to send out light; shine. **2.** to give information; explain. —**shed,** *p.t. & p.p.;* **shed′ding,** *pr.p.*

she'd (shēd), **1.** she had. **2.** she would.

sheen (shēn), *n.* brightness or shininess [the *sheen* of well-brushed hair].

---

fat, āpe, cär, ten, ēven, hit, bīte, gō, hôrn, tōōl, book, up, fûr;
get, joy, yet, chin, she, thin, *then;* zh = s in pleasure; ′ as in able (ā′b'l);
ə = a in ago, e in agent, i in sanity, o in confess, u in focus.

sheep (shēp), *n.* **1.** an animal that chews its cud and is related to the goat. Its body is covered with heavy wool and its flesh is used as food. **2.** a stupid or timid person. —**make sheep's eyes at,** to look at in a shy, loving way. —**sheep,** *pl.*

sheep (2½ ft. high at shoulder)

sheep dog, a dog trained to help herd sheep.

sheep·fold (shēp′fōld), *n.* a pen in which sheep are kept: also **sheep·cote** (shēp′kōt).

sheep·herd·er (shēp′hūr′dər), *n.* a person who herds a large flock of grazing sheep.

sheep·ish (shēp′ish), *adj.* shy or embarrassed in an awkward way [a *sheepish* grin]. —**sheep·ish·ly,** *adv.*

sheep·skin (shēp′skin), *n.* **1.** the skin of a sheep, especially with the wool left on it. **2.** a parchment or leather made from the skin of a sheep. **3.** a diploma: *used only in everyday talk.*

a sheepish look

sheer (shir), *v.* to turn aside; swerve.

sheer (shir), *adj.* **1.** very thin; fine enough to be seen through [*sheer* stockings]. **2.** absolute; utter [*sheer* love]. **3.** straight up or down, or almost so; very steep, as the face of a cliff. —*adv.* **1.** completely; utterly. **2.** very steeply.

sheet (shēt), *n.* **1.** a large piece of cloth, used on a bed, usually in pairs, one under and one over the body. **2.** a single piece of paper. **3.** a newspaper. **4.** a surface or piece that is broad and thin [a *sheet* of ice; a *sheet* of glass].

sheet·ing (shēt′ing), *n.* **1.** cloth, usually of cotton, used for bed sheets. **2.** material used to cover or line a surface [copper *sheeting*].

sheet metal, metal rolled in thin sheets.

sheet music, music printed and sold on separate sheets of paper, not in a book.

sheik or **sheikh** (shēk), *n.* a title of respect for an Arab chief or official.

shek·el (shek′'l), *n.* a gold or silver coin of the ancient Hebrews.

shel·drake (shel′drāk), *n.* **1.** a large wild duck of Europe. **2.** same as **merganser.**

shelf (shelf), *n.* **1.** a thin, flat length of wood, metal, etc. fastened against a wall or built into a frame so as to hold things [a book *shelf*]. **2.** something like a shelf, as a ledge of rock. —**on the shelf,** out of use. —**shelves,** *pl.*

shell (shel), *n.* **1.** a hard outer covering, as of eggs, nuts, certain animals, etc. **2.** material of or like animal shell, used in making or decorating things [eyeglasses with rims of *shell*]. **3.** something like a shell in being hollow, light, an outer part, etc. [the *shell* of a burned house; a pie *shell*]. **4.** a long, light racing

racing shell

boat, rowed by a team of men. **5.** a case or cartridge holding an explosive, shrapnel, shot, a bullet, etc., to be fired from a large or small gun. —*v.* **1.** to take off the shell from [to *shell* peas]. **2.** to separate from the ear or cob, as kernels of corn. **3.** to fire shells at from large guns. —**come out of one's shell,** to become less shy. —**shell out,** to pay out, as money: *used only in everyday talk.*

she'll (shēl), **1.** she will. **2.** she shall.

shel·lac (shə lak′), *n.* **1.** a kind of flaky resin. **2.** a thin varnish made from this resin and alcohol. —*v.* **1.** to coat with shellac. **2.** to beat or defeat soundly: *a slang meaning.* —**shel·lacked′,** *p.t.* & *p.p.*; **shel·lack′ing,** *pr.p.*

Shel·ley, Per·cy Bysshe (pūr′sē bish shel′ē), 1792–1822; English poet.

shell·fire (shel′fīr), *n.* the firing of large shells; an attack by artillery.

shell·fish (shel′fish), *n.* an animal that lives in water and has a shell, as the clam or lobster.

shel·ter (shel′tər), *n.* **1.** a place or thing that covers or protects, as from the weather, danger, etc. **2.** the condition of being covered or protected; protection [Give us *shelter*.] —*v.* **1.** to give shelter to [This barn will *shelter* us from the rain.] **2.** to find shelter.

shelve (shelv), *v.* **1.** to fit with shelves. **2.** to put on shelves [to *shelve* books]. **3.** to lay aside or stop discussing [to *shelve* a proposal]. —**shelved,** *p.t.* & *p.p.*; **shelv′ing,** *pr.p.*

shelves (shelvz), *n.* plural of **shelf.**

shelv·ing (shel′ving), *n.* **1.** material for shelves. **2.** shelves.

Shen·an·do·ah (shen′ən dō′ə), *n.* a river in Virginia flowing into the Potomac.

she·nan·i·gans (shə nan′i gənz), *n.pl.* mischief or trickery: *used only in everyday talk.*

She·ol (shē′ōl), *n.* a place mentioned in the Bible where the dead are supposed to go.

shep·herd (shep′ərd), *n.* **1.** a man who herds and takes care of sheep. **2.** a religious leader or minister. —*v.* to take care of, herd, lead, etc. like a shepherd. —**the Good Shepherd,** Jesus. —**shep′herd·ess,** *n.fem.*

sher·bet (shūr′bət), *n.* a frozen dessert of fruit juice, sugar, and water, milk, etc.

sher·iff (sher′if), *n.* the chief officer of the law in a county.

sher·ry (sher′ē), *n.* **1.** a strong, yellow or brownish wine from Spain. **2.** any wine like this.

Sher·wood Forest (shūr′wood), a forest in England, made famous in the Robin Hood stories.

she's (shēz), **1.** she is. **2.** she has.

Shet·land pony (shet′lənd), a breed of sturdy pony, with a rough coat and thick tail and mane.

shew (shō), *v.* & *n.* show. *This word is now seldom used.* —**shewed,** *p.t.*; **shewn,** *p.p.*; **shew′ing,** *pr.p.*

shib·bo·leth (shib′ə ləth), *n.* something said or done that is a sign or test of belonging to a certain group, party, or sect.

shied (shīd), past tense and past participle of **shy.**

shield (shēld), *n.* **1.** a piece of armor carried on the arm to ward off blows in battle. **2.** something that guards or protects, as a safety guard over machinery. **3.** anything shaped like a shield, as a coat of arms. —*v.* to guard or protect [Trees *shield* our house from the sun.]

shield

shift (shift), *v.* **1.** to move or change from one person, place, direction, etc. to another [Don't try to *shift* the responsibility. He *shifted* his feet. The wind is *shifting*. *Shift* into third gear.] **2.** to get along; manage [He *shifts* for himself.] —*n.* **1.** the act of shifting; change [a *shift* of public opinion; a *shift* in the wind]. **2.** a group of workers taking turns with other groups at the same jobs [The night *shift* will soon take over.] **3.** time or turn at work. **4.** something turned to in place of the usual means; especially, a scheme or trick [He invented a *shift* to keep him home from school.] —**make shift,** to manage or do the best one can with whatever means are at hand.

shift·less (shift/lis), *adj.* lazy or careless.

shift·y (shif/tē), *adj.* having or showing a nature that is not to be trusted; tricky. —**shift/i·er,** *compar.;* **shift/i·est,** *superl.*

shil·ling (shil/ing), *n.* a silver coin of Great Britain, equal to 1/20 of a pound. Shillings are no longer being made.

shil·ly-shal·ly (shil/ē shal/ē), *v.* to be unable to make up one's mind; hesitate. —*n.* the act of shilly-shallying. —**shil/ly-shal/lied,** *p.t. & p.p.;* **shil/ly-shal/ly·ing,** *pr.p.*

shim·mer (shim/ər), *v.* to shine with an unsteady or wavering light [a lake *shimmering* in the moonlight]. —*n.* a shimmering light. —**shim/mer·y,** *adj.*

shim·my (shim/ē), *n.* a shaking or wobbling, as in the wheels of a car. —*v.* to shake or wobble. —**shim/mied,** *p.t. & p.p.;* **shim/my·ing,** *pr.p.*

shin (shin), *n.* the front part of the leg between the knee and ankle. —*v.* to climb, as a pole or rope, by gripping with the hands and legs. —**shinned,** *p.t. & p.p.;* **shin/ning,** *pr.p.*

shin·bone (shin/bōn), *n.* the large bone of the lower leg; tibia: also **shin bone.**

shine (shīn), *v.* **1.** to give off light or reflect light; be bright [The sun *shines*. Her hair *shone*.] **2.** to make give off light [to *shine* a flashlight]. **3.** to do especially well; excel [He *shines* in arithmetic.] **4.** to show it-

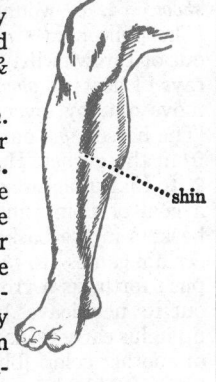
shin

self clearly or brightly [Love *shone* from her face.] **5.** to make bright by polishing [to *shine* shoes.] —*n.* **1.** the condition of being shiny. **2.** the act of polishing, as shoes. —**shone** or, *for meaning 5,* **shined,** *p.t. & p.p.;* **shin/ing,** *pr.p.*

shin·er (shīn/ər), *n.* **1.** a person or thing that shines. **2.** a black eye: *slang in this meaning.*

shin·gle (shing/g'l), *n.* pebbles and small stones lying on a beach. —**shin/gly,** *adj.*

shin·gle (shing/g'l), *n.* **1.** a thin piece of wood, slate, etc. shaped like a wedge and laid with others to form overlapping rows, as in covering a roof. **2.** a short haircut in which the hair in back is shaped close to the head. **3.** a small signboard, as of a doctor: *used only in everyday talk.* —*v.* **1.** to cover with shingles, as a roof. **2.** to cut hair in a shingle. —**shin/gled,** *p.t. & p.p.;* **shin/gling,** *pr.p.*

shingles

shin·gles (shing/g'lz), *n.* a virus disease causing pain and skin sores along the line of a nerve.

shin·ny (shin/ē), *v.* same as **shin**: *used only in everyday talk.* —**shin/nied,** *p.t. & p.p.;* **shin/ny·ing,** *pr.p.*

Shin·to (shin/tō), *n.* a religion of Japan, in which ancestors are worshiped.

shin·y (shīn/ē), *adj.* bright; shining. —**shin/i·er,** *compar.;* **shin/i·est,** *superl.* —**shin/i·ness,** *n.*

ship (ship), *n.* **1.** any vessel, larger than a boat, for traveling on deep water. **2.** the crew of a ship. **3.** an aircraft, spaceship, etc. —*v.* **1.** to put, take, go, or send in a ship or boat [to *ship* a cargo; to *ship* water during a storm]. **2.** to send by any means; transport [to *ship* coal by rail]. **3.** to fix in position for use on a ship or boat [to *ship* the rudder]. **4.** to hire or be hired for work on a ship. **5.** to send away; get rid of: *used only in everyday talk.* —**when one's ship comes in,** when one's fortune is made. —**shipped,** *p.t. & p.p.;* **ship/ping,** *pr.p.*

-ship (ship), a suffix meaning: **1.** the quality or condition of [*Friendship* is the condition of being friends.] **2.** the rank or office of [*Kingship* is the rank of a king.] **3.** skill as [*Statesmanship* is skill as a statesman.]

ship·board (ship/bôrd), *n.* a ship: *used only in the phrase* **on shipboard,** on or in a ship.

ship·build·er (ship/bil/dər), *n.* a person whose business or work is building ships. —**ship/build/ing,** *n. & adj.*

ship·load (ship/lōd), *n.* a full load of a ship.

ship·mate (ship/māt), *n.* a fellow sailor on the same ship.

ship·ment (ship/mənt), *n.* **1.** the shipping of goods by any means. **2.** the goods shipped.

ship·own·er (ship/ōn/ər), *n.* an owner of a ship or ships.

ship·per (ship/ər), *n.* one who ships goods.

fat,   āpe,   cär,   ten,   ēven,   hit,   bīte,   gō,   hôrn,   tōōl,   book,   up,   fūr;
get,   joy,   yet,   chin,   she,   thin,   *th*en;   zh = s in pleasure;   ' as in able (ā/b'l).
ə = a in ago,   e in agent,   i in sanity,   o in confess,   u in focus.

ship·ping (ship′ing), *n.* **1.** the sending or carrying of goods from place to place. **2.** all the ships of a nation or port, or their tonnage.

ship·shape (ship′shāp), *adj. & adv.* in good order; in a neat or trim condition or manner.

ship·wreck (ship′rek), *n.* **1.** the remains of a wrecked ship. **2.** the loss or ruin of a ship, as in a storm or crash. **3.** any ruin or destruction. —*v.* to wreck or destroy, especially a ship.

ship·yard (ship′yärd), *n.* a place where ships are built and repaired.

shire (shīr), *n.* a county of Great Britain: now used mainly in county names, as *Yorkshire*.

shirk (shûrk), *v.* to get out of doing or leave undone what should be done [to *shirk* homework]. —*n.* one who shirks: also called **shirk′er.**

shirr (shûr), *n.* a series of rows of stitches in cloth, pulled tight to form gathers between the rows. —*v.* **1.** to make shirrs in. **2.** to bake eggs with crumbs in small buttered dishes.

shirt (shûrt), *n.* **1.** the usual garment worn by a man on the upper part of the body, often with a necktie. **2.** an undershirt.

shirt·ing (shûr′ting), *n.* cloth for shirts.

shirt·waist (shûrt′wāst), *n.* a woman's blouse tailored more or less like a shirt.

shiv·er (shiv′ər), *v.* to shake or tremble, as from fear or cold. —*n.* the act of shivering. —**shiv′er·y,** *adj.*

shiv·er (shiv′ər), *n.* a thin, sharp, broken piece, as of glass; sliver. —*v.* to break into many thin, sharp pieces; shatter or splinter.

shirtwaist

shoal (shōl), *n.* a large group; especially, a school of fish.

shoal (shōl), *n.* **1.** a shallow place in a river, sea, etc. **2.** a sand bar, etc. causing a shallow place. —*v.* to become shallow.

shock (shäk), *n.* **1.** a sudden, powerful blow, shake, or jar [the *shock* of an earthquake]. **2.** a sudden and strong upsetting of the mind or feelings; also, the thing that causes this [Her accident was a *shock* to us.] **3.** the feeling or effect caused by an electric current passing through the body. **4.** a condition of the body caused by injury, loss of blood, a sudden nervous upset, etc., in which there is a drop in blood pressure, great weakness, and sometimes unconsciousness. —*v.* **1.** to upset the mind or feelings of with sudden force; astonish, horrify, disgust, etc. [His crime *shocked* us.] **2.** to give an electrical shock to. —**shock′er,** *n.*

shock (shäk), *n.* bundles of grain stacked in a pile to dry. —*v.* to gather in shocks.

shock (shäk), *n.* a thick, bushy mass, as of hair.

shock·ing (shäk′ing), *adj.* causing great surprise, horror, disgust, etc. [a *shocking* disaster]. —**shock′-ing·ly,** *adv.*

shod (shäd), past tense and past participle of **shoe.**

shocks of grain

shod·dy (shäd′ē), *n.* cloth made from used or waste wool. —*adj.* **1.** made of shoddy or other poor material. **2.** not as good as it seems or claims to be [a *shoddy* house]. **3.** low or mean [*shoddy* behavior]. —**shod′di·er,** *compar.;* **shod′di·est,** *superl.*

shoe (shoo), *n.* **1.** an outer covering for the foot, usually of leather. **2.** something like a shoe in shape or use, as a horseshoe or part of a brake that presses against a wheel. —*v.* to furnish with shoes; put shoes on [to *shoe* a horse]. —**fill one's shoes,** to take one's place. —**in another's shoes,** in another's position. —**where the shoe pinches,** what is really causing the trouble. —**shod,** *p.t. & p.p.;* **shoe′ing,** *pr.p.*

shoe·horn (shoo′hôrn), *n.* a small, curved piece of metal, plastic, etc. for helping to slip one's heel into a shoe.

shoe·lace (shoo′lās), *n.* a lace of cord, leather, etc. used for fastening a shoe.

shoe·mak·er (shoo′māk′-ər), *n.* a person whose work is making or repairing shoes.

shoe·string (shoo′-string), *n.* a shoelace. —**on a shoestring,** with very little money [to start a business *on a shoestring*].

shoehorn

shoe tree, a form put inside a shoe to stretch it or keep it in shape.

shone (shōn), past tense and past participle of **shine.**

shoo (shoo), *interj.* go away! get out! —*v.* to drive away, as by waving or crying "shoo" [to *shoo* flies away]. —**shooed,** *p.t. & p.p.;* **shoo′ing,** *pr.p.*

shoe tree

shook (shook), past tense of **shake.**

shoot (shoot), *v.* **1.** to send out with force from a gun, bow, etc. [to *shoot* bullets or arrows]. **2.** to send a bullet, arrow, etc. from [to *shoot* a gun]. **3.** to be fired or discharged [This gun won't *shoot*.] **4.** to wound or kill with a bullet, etc. [The policeman *shot* the mad dog.] **5.** to send out or throw swiftly and with force [to *shoot* out rays of heat; to *shoot* insults at someone]. **6.** to move up, by, over, etc. swiftly and with force [The horses *shot* out of the barn. The oil *shot* up from the gusher. He *shot* the rapids in a canoe.] **7.** to take a picture of with a camera. **8.** to score a goal or points in certain games [He *shot* six baskets in the basketball game.] **9.** to play, as certain games [to *shoot* nine holes of golf]. **10.** to push forth, as a growing part [The plant *shoots* out its new leaves.] **11.** to grow fast [He *shot* up in his early teens.] **12.** to scatter with streaks of another color [blue *shot* with orange]. **13.** to be felt suddenly and sharply [A pain *shot* across his back.] **14.** to stick out; project [A peninsula *shoots* out into the sea.] —*n.* **1.** a shooting trip, contest, etc. [a turkey *shoot*]. **2.** a new growth;

sprout. **3.** a chute. —**shot,** *p.t. & p.p.;* **shoot'ing,** *pr.p.* —**shoot'er,** *n.*

shooting star, a meteor.

shop (shäp), *n.* **1.** a place where things are sold; store [a book *shop*]. **2.** a place where a certain kind of work is done [a machine *shop*]. —*v.* to go to shops to look over and buy things. —**set up shop,** to start a business. —**talk shop,** to talk about one's work. —**shopped,** *p.t. & p.p.;* **shop'ping,** *pr.p.* —**shop'per,** *n.*

shop·keep·er (shäp'kēp'ər), *n.* a person who runs a shop, or store.

shop·lift·er (shäp'lif'tər), *n.* a person who steals things from counters in stores.

shop·worn (shäp'wôrn), *adj.* worn or dirty from having been displayed in a store.

shore (shôr), *n.* land at the edge of a sea, lake, etc. —**off shore,** in the water but close to shore. —**on shore, 1.** on the shore. **2.** on land.

shore (shôr), *n.* a beam, timber, etc. placed under or against something as a support. —*v.* to support with shores; prop [to *shore* up a sagging wall]. —**shored,** *p.t. & p.p.;* **shor'ing,** *pr.p.*

shore line, the edge of a body of water.

shore·ward (shôr'wərd), *adv. & adj.* toward the shore.

shorn (shôrn), a past participle of **shear.**

shores

short (shôrt), *adj.* **1.** not measuring much from end to end or from beginning to end; not long [a *short* stick; a *short* trip; a *short* throw]. **2.** not tall; low [a *short* tree]. **3.** brief and rude [a *short* answer]. **4.** less or having less than what is enough or correct [Our supply of food is *short*. We are *short* ten dollars.] **5.** that tends to break or crumble; flaky [*short* pastry]. **6.** taking a shorter time to say than other sounds [The "e" in "bed" and the "i" in "rib" are *short*.] —*n.* **1.** something short, especially a short movie. **2. shorts,** *pl.* short trousers reaching down part way to the knee; also, a garment like this worn by men as underwear. **3.** a short circuit. —*adv.* **1.** suddenly [The car stopped *short*.] **2.** in a brief or rude manner [to speak *short*]. **3.** so as to be short [Cut it off *short*. We fell *short* of our goal.] —*v.* to short-circuit. —**for short,** as a shorter form [Thomas is called Tom *for short*.] —**in short,** in a few words; briefly. —**short for,** being a shorter form of. —**short of, 1.** less than; not equal to or reaching. **2.** on the near side of. —**short'ness,** *n.*

short·age (shôr'tij), *n.* a lack in the amount that is needed or correct [a *shortage* of help].

short·cake (shôrt'kāk), *n.* a light biscuit or a sweet cake served with fruit as a dessert.

short-cir·cuit (shôrt'sur'kit), *v.* to make a short circuit in.

short circuit, a side circuit caused by faulty wiring, as when a bare wire touches some metal part, so that the electric current is turned aside from the main circuit, usually melting a fuse and breaking the circuit.

short·com·ing (shôrt'kum'ing), *n.* a fault or weakness, as in one's character.

short cut, 1. a shorter way of getting to a place. **2.** any way of saving time, money, etc.

short·en (shôr't'n), *v.* **1.** to make or become short or shorter [to *shorten* a skirt]. **2.** to add shortening to, as pastry.

short·en·ing (shôr't'n ing), *n.* **1.** the act of making or becoming short or shorter. **2.** butter or other fat used in pastry to make it flaky.

short·hand (shôrt'hand), *n.* **1.** any system for writing fast by using special symbols in place of letters, words, and phrases. **2.** such writing.

ß. ت ں ل ﻇ
"This is a sample of shorthand writing."

short·hand·ed (shôrt'han'did), *adj.* not having enough workers or helpers.

short·horn (shôrt'hôrn), *n.* a breed of cattle with short horns, raised for beef and milk.

short-lived (shôrt'līvd' *or* shôrt'livd'), *adj.* living or lasting only a short time.

short·ly (shôrt'lē), *adv.* **1.** in a short time; soon [I'll leave *shortly*.] **2.** in a few words; briefly [to put it *shortly*]. **3.** briefly and rudely; curtly [to answer *shortly*].

short·sight·ed (shôrt'sīt'id), *adj.* **1.** same as **nearsighted. 2.** not looking ahead or planning for the future. —**short'sight'ed·ness,** *n.*

short·stop (shôrt'stäp), *n.* a baseball player whose position is between second and third base.

short-tem·pered (shôrt'tem'pərd), *adj.* easily made angry; tending to lose one's temper.

short wave, a radio wave 60 meters or less in length. Overseas broadcasts, police calls, etc. are sent by short waves. —**short'-wave',** *adj.*

short-wind·ed (shôrt'win'did), *adj.* breathing hard or easily put out of breath [I am *shortwinded* from running.]

shot (shät), *n.* **1.** the act of shooting, as a gun [I heard a *shot*.] **2.** the distance that a sound, a bullet, etc. travels or can travel [to be within ear*shot*]. **3.** an attempt to hit something, as with a bullet [His first *shot* missed.] **4.** any attempt or try; also, a guess. **5.** an unkind remark [a parting *shot*]. **6.** a throw, drive, etc., as of a ball, in certain games. **7.** something to be fired from a gun, as a bullet or small metal ball; also, a number of such balls in a casing [gun*shot*]. **8.** a heavy metal ball to be thrown overhand in a contest, to see who can throw farthest. **9.** a person who shoots [He's a good *shot*.] **10.** a photograph. **11.** an injection, as of a vaccine. **—a long shot,** a try that will probably fail. **—like a shot,** quickly and suddenly. **—not by a long shot,** not likely or not at all.

shot (shät), past tense and past participle of **shoot.** *—adj.* **1.** streaked with another color [a green dress *shot* with blue]. **2.** worn out or ruined: *used only in everyday talk.*

shot·gun (shät′gun), *n.* a gun for firing cartridges filled with shot, or little metal balls.

shot-put (shät′poot), *n.* a contest in which athletes put, or throw, the shot.

man putting the shot

should (shood), past tense of **shall** [I thought I *should* never see him again.] *Should* is also used as a helping verb in speaking of something that is likely to happen or might happen [It *should* rain tomorrow. If I *should* go, would you care?] or of something that one ought to do [We *should* obey the law.] *Would* is sometimes used in place of *should.*

shoul·der (shōl′dər), *n.* **1.** the part of the body to which an arm or foreleg is connected. **2. shoulders,** *pl.* the two shoulders and the part of the back between them. **3.** a cut of meat including the upper part of an animal's foreleg and the parts near it. **4.** the part of a garment that covers the shoulder. **5.** a part that sticks out like a shoulder. **6.** the edge of a road. *—v.* **1.** to push with the shoulder [He *shouldered* his way into the room.] **2.** to carry on the shoulder. **3.** to take on the burden of [to *shoulder* a task]. **—give a cold shoulder to,** to snub or be unfriendly to. **—put one's shoulder to the wheel,** to start working hard; use extra effort. **—shoulder arms,** to rest a rifle against the shoulder, holding the butt with the hand. **—shoulder to shoulder, 1.** side by side and close together. **2.** working together. **—straight from the shoulder,** directly to the point; without holding back.

shoulder blade, either of two flat bones in the upper back.

shoulder strap, a strap worn over the shoulder as for holding up a garment.

should·n't (shood′'nt), should not.

shouldst (shoodst), the older form of **should,** used with *thou,* as in the Bible.

shout (shout), *n.* a loud, sudden cry or call. *—v.* to say or cry out in a loud voice. **—shout someone down,** to make someone be quiet by shouting at him. **—shout′er,** *n.*

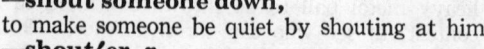

shoulder blade

shove (shuv), *v.* **1.** to push, as along a surface [*Shove* the chair across the room.] **2.** to push roughly [to *shove* others aside]. *—n.* a push. **—shove off, 1.** to push a boat away from shore.

2. to start off; leave: *used only in everyday talk.* **—shoved,** *p.t. & p.p.;* **shov′ing,** *pr.p.*

shov·el (shuv′'l), *n.* **1.** a tool with a broad scoop and a handle, for lifting and moving loose material. **2.** a shovelful. *—v.* **1.** to lift and move with a shovel [to *shovel* coal]. **2.** to dig out with a shovel, as a path. **3.** to put in large amounts [to *shovel* food into one's mouth]. **—shov′eled** or **shov′elled,** *p.t. & p.p.;* **shov′el·ing** or **shov′el·ling,** *pr.p.*

shov·el·ful (shuv′'l fool), *n.* as much as a shovel will hold. **—shov′el·fuls,** *pl.*

show (shō), *v.* **1.** to bring in sight; allow to be seen; display; reveal [*Show* us the new fashions. His red face *showed* his anger.] **2.** to be or become seen; appear [Daylight began to *show* in the sky.] **3.** to guide or lead [*Show* him to his room.] **4.** to point out [We *showed* them the sights of the city. A thermometer *shows* the temperature.] **5.** to be easily noticed [The stain won't *show.*] **6.** to make clear; explain, prove, or teach [He *showed* how it could be done.] **7.** to give or grant; bestow [She has *shown* many favors to us.] *—n.* **1.** the act of showing [a *show* of anger; a *show* of hands]. **2.** a collection of things shown publicly; display [an art *show*]. **3.** a performance of a play or movie, a radio or television program, etc. **4.** something false or pretended [Her sorrow is a mere *show.*] **5.** something meant to attract attention [a great *show* of wealth]. **—for show,** in order to attract attention. **—show off, 1.** to make a display of. **2.** to behave so as to get attention. **—show up, 1.** to make easily seen; expose, as faults. **2.** to be clearly seen; stand out. **3.** to come or arrive. **—showed,** *p.t.;* **shown** or **showed,** *p.p.;* **show′ing,** *pr.p.*

show·boat (shō′bōt), *n.* a boat with a theater and actors, giving shows in river towns.

show·case (shō′kās), *n.* a glass case in which things are put on display, as in a store.

show·down (shō′doun), *n.* the act of laying open all the true facts, so as to force a final settlement: *used only in everyday talk.*

show·er (shou′ər), *n.* **1.** a short fall of rain or hail. **2.** a sudden, very full fall or flow, as of sparks, praise, etc. **3.** a party at which gifts are given to the guest of honor [a *shower* for the bride]. **4.** a shower bath. *—v.* **1.** to spray or sprinkle as with water. **2.** to fall or come in a shower. **3.** to take a shower bath.

shower bath, 1. a bath in which the body is sprayed with fine streams of water. **2.** a device that sprays water for such a bath.

show·man (shō′mən), *n.* a person whose business is giving shows to entertain people. **—show′men,** *pl.* **—show′-man·ship,** *n.*

shower bath

shown (shōn), a past participle of **show.**

show-off (shō′ôf′), *n.* a person who shows off: *used only in everyday talk.*

show window, a store window in which things for sale are displayed.

show·y (shō′ē), *adj.* **1.** gay and colorful in an attractive way [a *showy* flower]. **2.** too bright or flashy; gaudy. —**show′i·er,** *compar.;* **show′i·est,** *superl.* —**show′i·ly,** *adv.* —**show′i·ness,** *n.*

shrank (shrangk), a past tense of **shrink.**

shrap·nel (shrap′nəl), *n.* **1.** an artillery shell filled with an explosive and with many small metal balls that scatter in the air when the shell explodes. **2.** such metal balls or fragments of a shell case scattered by an exploding shell.

shred (shred), *n.* **1.** a small strip or piece cut or torn off [His shirt was torn to *shreds.*] **2.** a tiny piece or amount; fragment [a story without a *shred* of truth]. —*v.* to cut or tear into shreds [*shredded* coconut]. —**shred′ded** or **shred,** *p.t.* & *p.p.;* **shred′ding,** *pr.p.*

shrew (shrōō), *n.* **1.** a small animal like a mouse, with soft, brown fur and a long snout. **2.** a woman who is always scolding and nagging. —**shrew′ish,** *adj.*

shrew (4 in. long, including tail)

shrewd (shrōōd), *adj.* clever or sharp in practical matters [a *shrewd* bargainer]. —**shrewd′ly,** *adv.* —**shrewd′ness,** *n.*

shriek (shrēk), *n.* a loud, sharp, shrill cry; screech; scream. —*v.* to cry out with a shriek [to *shriek* in terror].

shrift (shrift), *n.* the act of shriving. —**short shrift,** very little care, mercy, etc.

shrike (shrīk), *n.* a bird with a shrill cry and a hooked beak. Shrikes catch insects, small birds, frogs, etc., often hanging them on thorns or branches before eating them.

shrill (shril), *adj.* having or making a sharp, high sound [a *shrill* voice; a *shrill* whistle]. —*v.* to make a sharp, high sound. —**shrill′ness,** *n.* —**shril′ly,** *adv.*

shrimp (shrimp), *n.* **1.** a small shellfish with a long tail, used as food. **2.** a small or unimportant person: *used only in everyday talk.*

shrine (shrīn), *n.* **1.** something with sacred relics inside it, as the tomb of a saint. **2.** a sacred image that is prayed to, as in a church or along a roadside. **3.** a place or thing held in honor because of something or someone important connected with it [Mount Vernon is an American *shrine.*]

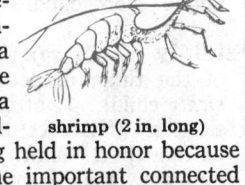
shrimp (2 in. long)

shrink (shringk), *v.* **1.** to make or become smaller by drawing the parts together [Wool often *shrinks* when washed.] **2.** to draw back, as from fear. —**shrank** or **shrunk,** *p.t.;* **shrunk** or **shrunk′en,** *p.p.;* **shrink′ing,** *pr.p.*

shrink·age (shringk′ij), *n.* **1.** the act or process of shrinking. **2.** the amount of shrinking.

shrive (shrīv), *v.* **1.** to listen to a confession and then give absolution, as a priest does. **2.** to confess sins. *This word is now seldom used.* —**shrived** or **shrove** (shrōv), *p.t.;* **shriv·en** (shriv′'n) or **shrived,** *p.p.;* **shriv·ing,** *pr.p.*

shriv·el (shriv′'l), *v.* to curl up and shrink or wither [Without water, the flowers *shriveled* up and died.] —**shriv′eled** or **shriv′elled,** *p.t.* & *p.p.;* **shriv′el·ing** or **shriv′el·ling,** *pr.p.*

shroud (shroud), *n.* **1.** a sheet in which a dead person is sometimes wrapped before burying. **2.** something that covers or hides; veil. **3.** any of the ropes stretched from a ship's side to the top of a mast to help keep it straight. —*v.* to wrap or cover as with a shroud [The town is *shrouded* in darkness.]

shriveled apple

shrouds

shrub (shrub), *n.* a woody plant that is smaller than a tree and has a number of stems instead of a single trunk; bush.

shrub·ber·y (shrub′ər ē), *n.* a group or heavy growth of shrubs, as around a house.

shrub·by (shrub′ē), *adj.* **1.** covered with shrubs [*shrubby* land]. **2.** like a shrub. —**shrub′bi·er,** *compar.;* **shrub′bi·est,** *superl.*

shrug (shrug), *v.* to draw up the shoulders, as in showing that one does not care or does not know. —*n.* the act of shrugging. —**shrugged,** *p.t.* & *p.p.;* **shrug′ging,** *pr.p.*

shrunk (shrungk), a past tense and past participle of **shrink.**

shrunk·en (shrungk′'n), a past participle of **shrink.**

shuck (shuk), *n.* a shell, pod, or husk. —*v.* **1.** to remove the shucks of [to *shuck* corn]. **2.** to remove like a shuck [He *shucked* his coat.]

shud·der (shud′ər), *v.* to shake or tremble in a sudden and violent way [He *shuddered* with fear.] —*n.* the act of shuddering; tremor.

shuf·fle (shuf′'l), *v.* **1.** to move the feet with a dragging motion, as in walking or dancing. **2.** to mix playing cards so as to change their order. **3.** to push or mix together in a jumbled way [He *shuffled* his clothes into a bag.] **4.** to keep shifting from one place to another [He *shuffled* the papers about on his desk.] —*n.* **1.** the act of shuffling, as playing cards. **2.** one's turn to shuffle playing cards. —**shuffle off,** to get rid of. —**shuf′fled,** *p.t.* & *p.p.;* **shuf′fling,** *pr.p.* —**shuf′fler,** *n.*

fat, āpe, cär, ten, ēven, hit, bīte, gō, hôrn, tōol, book, up, fûr;
get, joy, yet, chin, she, thin, *th*en; zh = s in pleasure; ′ as in able (ā′b'l);
ə = a in ago, e in agent, i in sanity, o in confess, u in focus.

shuf·fle·board (shuf′'l bôrd), *n.* a game in which the players make disks slide along a smooth lane, trying to get them on numbered sections.

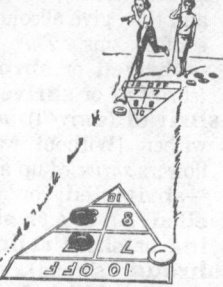

shuffleboard

shun (shun), *v.* to keep away from; avoid. —**shunned,** *p.t.* & *p.p.;* **shun′ning,** *pr.p.*

shunt (shunt), *v.* **1.** to move or turn to one side; turn out of the way. **2.** to switch from one track to another, as a train. —*n.* **1.** the act of shunting. **2.** a railroad switch. **3.** a wire connecting two points in an electric circuit and turning aside part of the current.

shush (shush), *interj.* hush! be quiet! —*v.* to tell to be quiet, as by saying "hush!"

shut (shut), *v.* **1.** to move so as to close an opening [to *shut* a door or window]. **2.** to fasten securely, as with a lock. **3.** to close the lid, doors, etc. of [to *shut* a chest]. **4.** to fold up or close the parts of [to *shut* an umbrella]. —*adj.* closed, fastened, locked up, etc. [Keep the lid *shut.*] —**shut down, 1.** to close by lowering. **2.** to stop work in, often just for a time [to *shut down* a factory]. —**shut in,** to surround or enclose; keep inside. —**shut off, 1.** to keep from moving, flowing, etc. [to *shut off* the water]. **2.** to stop movement into or out of [to *shut off* a street]. —**shut out, 1.** to keep out; exclude [The curtains *shut out* the light.] **2.** to keep from making even one score in a game. —**shut up, 1.** to enclose or lock up, as in a prison. **2.** to close all ways of getting in. **3.** to stop talking or make stop talking: *used only in everyday talk.* —**shut,** *p.t.* & *p.p.;* **shut′ting,** *pr.p.*

shut·down (shut′doun), *n.* a stopping of work or activity for a time, as in a factory.

shut-in (shut′in′), *n.* a person who is too ill, weak, etc. to go out. —*adj.* not able to go out.

shut·ter (shut′ər), *n.* **1.** a cover for a window, usually swinging on hinges. **2.** a part on a camera that opens and closes in front of the lens to control the light going in. **3.** a person or thing that shuts. —*v.* to close or cover with shutters.

shutters

shut·tle (shut′'l), *n.* **1.** a device in weaving that carries a thread back and forth between the threads that go up and down. **2.** a device on a sewing machine that carries the lower thread back and forth. **3.** a bus or train that makes regular trips back and forth over a short route. —*v.* to move rapidly to and fro. —**shut′tled,** *p.t.* & *p.p.;* **shut′tling,** *pr.p.*

shut·tle·cock (shut′'l käk), *n.* the cork with feathers in one end used in playing badminton.

shy (shī), *adj.* **1.** easily frightened; timid [a *shy* animal]. **2.** not at ease with other people;

bashful [a *shy* girl]. **3.** not having; lacking; short: *slang in this meaning* [It costs ten dollars, and he is two dollars *shy.*] —*v.* **1.** to move or pull back suddenly; start [The horse *shied* when the gun went off.] **2.** to be cautious or unwilling [John *shied* at going in the deep water.] —**fight shy of,** to keep away from; avoid. —**shi′er** or **shy′er,** *compar.;* **shi′est** or **shy′est,** *superl.* —**shied,** *p.t.* & *p.p.;* **shy′ing,** *pr.p.* —**shy′ly,** *adv.* —**shy′ness,** *n.*

shy (shī), *v.* to throw or toss with a jerk. —**shied,** *p.t.* & *p.p.;* **shy′ing,** *pr.p.*

Shy·lock (shī′läk), *n.* **1.** the lender of money in Shakespeare's *Merchant of Venice.* **2.** a person who is without pity in business dealings.

si (sē), *n.* the seventh note of a musical scale: also **ti.**

Si·am (sī am′), *n.* an earlier name for **Thailand.** —**Si·a·mese** (sī′ə mēz′), *adj.* & *n.*

Siamese twins, any pair of twins born joined to each other. A famous pair came from Siam.

Si·ber·i·a (sī bir′i ə), *n.* a part of the Soviet Union in northern Asia, from the Ural Mountains to the Pacific. —**Si·ber′i·an,** *adj.* & *n.*

sib·yl (sib′'l), *n.* any of certain women in ancient Greece and Rome who acted as prophets.

Sic·i·ly (sis′'l ē), *n.* a large Italian island off the southwestern tip of Italy. —**Si·cil·ian** (si sil′yən), *adj.* & *n.*

sick (sik), *adj.* **1.** suffering from disease or illness; not well; ill [a *sick* baby; *sick* with the flu]. **2.** having a feeling that makes one vomit or want to vomit; nauseated. **3.** of or for people who are ill [*sick* leave]. **4.** troubled by a feeling of sorrow or longing [*sick* over the loss of his dog]. **5.** disgusted by too much of something; tired [I'm *sick* of your excuses.] —**the sick,** sick people. —**sick′ness,** *n.*

sick (sik), *v.* to urge to attack [He *sicked* his dog on the burglar.] Also spelled **sic.**

sick·en (sik′'n), *v.* to make or become sick.

sick·en·ing (sik′'n ing), *adj.* causing sickness; making one want to vomit; disgusting.

sick·ish (sik′ish), *adj.* **1.** somewhat sick or nauseated. **2.** somewhat sick or sickening.

sick·le (sik′'l), *n.* a tool with a curved blade and a short handle, for cutting tall grasses.

sick·ly (sik′lē), *adj.* **1.** sick much of the time; in poor health [a *sickly* child]. **2.** of or caused by sickness [His face has a *sickly* paleness.] **3.** faint, weak, pale, dull, etc. [a *sickly* smile]. **4.** sickening [a *sickly* smell]. —**sick′li·er,** *compar.;* **sick′li·est,** *superl.*

sickle

side (sīd), *n.* **1.** the right or left half of the body [a pain in one's *side*]. **2.** the position beside one [He never left my *side.*] **3.** any of the lines or surfaces that bound something [A triangle has three *sides.* A cube has six *sides.*] **4.** a surface of an object that is not the back or front, nor the top or bottom [a door at the *side* of a house]. **5.** either of the two surfaces of paper, cloth, etc. **6.** a surface or part of a surface in a certain position [the inner *side* of a vase; the visible *side* of the moon]. **7.** the sloping part [a house on the *side* of a hill]. **8.** a place or direction as it is related in position to the person speaking [this *side* of the street; the other *side* of the lake]. **9.** a particular part or quality of a person or thing [his cruel *side;* the bright *side* of life]. **10.** any of the groups against each other in a fight, argument, contest, etc. [The judges voted for our *side* in the debate.] **11.** the ideas, opinions, or position of one person or group against another [My *side* of the quarrel is easy to explain.] **12.** all the relatives of either one's mother or one's father [an uncle on my mother's *side*]. —*adj.* **1.** of, at, or on a side [a *side* door]. **2.** to or from one side [a *side* glance]. **3.** not main or most important [a *side* issue]. —*v.* to take the same position or hold the same views in an argument or quarrel [The council *sided* with the mayor.] —**on the side,** as extra work, activity, etc.: *used only in everyday talk.* —**side by side,** beside one another; together. —**take sides,** to give help or support to one person or group in a fight or argument. —**sid′ed,** *p.t. & p.p.;* **sid′ing,** *pr.p.*

side·board (sīd′bôrd), *n.* a piece of furniture, as in a dining room, with drawers and shelves for holding dishes, silverware, linen, etc.

side·burns (sīd′bŭrnz), *n.pl.* the hair on the sides of a man's face, just in front of the ears.

sid·ed (sīd′id), *adj.* having sides: *used in words formed with a hyphen* [six-*sided*].

side line, 1. either of the lines that mark the side limits of a playing area, as in football. **2. side lines,** *pl.* the space just outside these lines [Reporters stood on the *side lines*.] **3.** an extra line of goods or work apart from the main one [He raises orchids as a *side line*.]

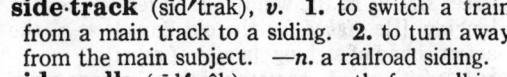

sideburns

side·long (sīd′lông), *adj. & adv.* toward or to the side [a *sidelong* glance].

si·de·re·al (sī dir′i əl), *adj.* **1.** of the stars or constellations. **2.** measured by what seems to be the motion of the stars [a *sidereal* day].

side show, a small, separate show in connection with a main show, as of a circus.

side-step (sīd′step′), *v.* to keep away from as by stepping aside. —**side′-stepped′,** *p.t. & p.p.;* **side′-step′ping,** *pr.p.*

sidelong glance

side·track (sīd′trak), *v.* **1.** to switch a train from a main track to a siding. **2.** to turn away from the main subject. —*n.* a railroad siding.

side·walk (sīd′wôk), *n.* a path for walking, usually paved, along the side of a street.

side·ways (sīd′wāz), *adv.* **1.** from the side [Seen *sideways*, it looks quite thin.] **2.** with one side toward the front [He turned his head *sideways* to show his profile.] —*adj.* toward one side [a *sideways* glance].

side·wise (sīd′wīz), *adj. & adv.* sideways.

sid·ing (sīd′ing), *n.* **1.** a covering, especially of overlapping boards, etc., for an outside wall. **2.** a short railroad track onto which cars can be switched from the main track.

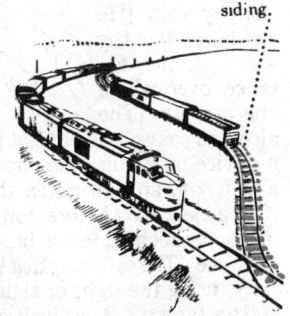

siding.

si·dle (sī′d'l), *v.* to move sideways in a shy or sneaky way [He *sidled* past the guard.] —**si′dled,** *p.t. & p.p.;* **si′- dling,** *pr.p.*

siege (sēj), *n.* **1.** the surrounding of a city, fort, etc. by an enemy army trying to capture it. **2.** any stubborn and continued effort to win or control something [After his long *siege*, she agreed to marry him.] **3.** any long, difficult period. —**lay siege to,** to force a siege on.

si·er·ra (si er′ə), *n.* a chain of mountains whose peaks look along the edge of a saw.

Si·er·ra Le·one (si er′ə lē ōn′), a country on the western coast of Africa.

Sierra Ne·va·da (nə vad′ə *or* nə vä′də), a mountain range in eastern California.

si·es·ta (si es′tə), *n.* a short nap or rest taken after the noon meal, as in Spain or Mexico.

sieve (siv), *n.* a strainer for separating liquids from solids or tiny pieces from large ones. —*v.* to sift. —**sieved,** *p.t. & p.p.;* **siev′ing,** *pr.p.*

sift (sift), *v.* **1.** to pass through a sieve so as to separate the large pieces from the tiny ones [to *sift* sand so as to remove pebbles]. **2.** to come down as if through a sieve [Rays of sunshine *sifted* through the clouds.]

sieve

3. to examine with care so as to separate the true from the false [The jury *sifted* the evidence.] **4.** to scatter or sprinkle as through a sieve [*Sift* flour over the bottom of the pan.] —**sift′er,** *n.*

sigh (sī), *v.* **1.** to let out a long, deep, sounded breath, usually to show that one is sad, tired, relieved, etc. **2.** to make a sound like a sigh [trees *sighing* in the wind]. **3.** to feel sadness or longing [He *sighed* for the old days.] —*n.* the act or sound of sighing [a *sigh* of relief].

sight (sīt), *n.* **1.** something that is seen; especially, something unusual worth seeing [The Grand Canyon is a *sight* you won't forget.] **2.** the act of seeing [our first *sight* of the town]. **3.** the ability to see; vision; eyesight [He lost his *sight* in the war.] **4.** the distance over which one can see [The airplane passed out of *sight*.] **5.** *often* **sights,** *pl.* a device on a gun, telescope, etc. that helps one aim it. **6.** an aim taken through such a device [Get a clear *sight* before you fire.] **7.** one's thinking or opinion [He's a hero in her eyes.] —*v.* **1.** to see [The sailor *sighted* land.] **2.** to aim carefully, using the sight or sights [to *sight* a rifle; to *sight* a target]. **3.** to look carefully [*Sight* along this line.] —**at sight** or **on sight,** as soon as seen. —**by sight,** by having seen, not by having known [I know her only *by sight*.] —**catch sight of,** to see, especially briefly; glimpse. —**not by a long sight,** not nearly or not at all.

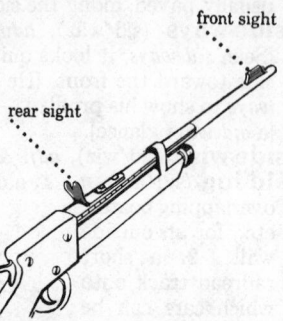

front sight

rear sight

sight·less (sīt′lis), *adj.* blind.
sight·ly (sīt′lē), *adj.* **1.** pleasing to look at; attractive. **2.** allowing a good view [a *sightly* hilltop]. —**sight′li·er,** *compar.;* **sight′li·est,** *superl.*
sight-see·ing (sīt′sē′ing), *n.* the act of going about to see places and things of interest. —**sight′-see′er,** *n.*
sign (sīn), *n.* **1.** a thing or act that stands for something else; symbol [Black is worn as a *sign* of grief. He bowed as a *sign* of respect. The *sign* + means "add."] **2.** a board, card, etc. put up in a public place, with information, warning, etc. on it [The *sign* said "No Smoking."] **3.** anything that tells of the existence or coming of something else [Red spots on the face may be a *sign* of measles.] —*v.* **1.** to write one's name on [to *sign* a contract to make it legal]. **2.** to hire by getting to sign a contract [The baseball club *signed* five new players.] —**sign off,** in radio and television, to stop broadcasting, especially for the night. —**sign up, 1.** to hire or be hired. **2.** to enlist, as in the army.
sig·nal (sig′n'l), *n.* **1.** a thing or happening that shows, warns, or points out [Birds flying south are a *signal* of coming winter.] **2.** something that tells when some action is to start or end [A loud bell is the *signal* for a fire drill. The traffic *signal* turned green, telling us to go.] **3.** the electrical waves sent out or received as sounds or pictures in radio and television. —*adj.* **1.** used as a signal [a *signal* light]. **2.** not ordinary; remarkable [The discovery of radium was a *signal* achievement.] —*v.* **1.** to make a signal

or signals to [The man in the car *signaled* for a turn. The policeman *signaled* us to drive on.] **2.** to make known by means of signals [The ship *signaled* it was sinking.] —**sig′naled** or **sig′-nalled,** *p.t. & p.p.;* **sig′nal·ing** or **sig′nal-ling,** *pr.p.*
sig·nal·ize (sig′n'l īz), *v.* to make known or worth noticing [His career was *signalized* by great achievements.] —**sig′nal·ized,** *p.t. & p.p.;* **sig′nal·iz·ing,** *pr.p.*
sig·nal·ly (sig′n'l ē), *adv.* in an unusual or outstanding way [He was *signally* honored.]
sig·na·ture (sig′nə chər), *n.* **1.** a person's name written by himself. **2.** a sign in music placed at the beginning of a staff to give the key or the time.
sign·board (sīn′bôrd), *n.* a board on which a sign with advertising has been painted or pasted.
sig·net (sig′nit), *n.* **1.** a seal or other mark stamped on a paper to make it official. **2.** a device used to make such a mark.
sig·nif·i·cance (sig nif′ə kəns), *n.* **1.** meaning or sense [I don't understand the *significance* of his remark.] **2.** importance [a battle of great *significance*].
sig·nif·i·cant (sig nif′ə kənt), *adj.* **1.** important; full of meaning [a *significant* speech]. **2.** having a meaning, especially a hidden one [a *significant* wink]. —**sig·nif′i·cant·ly,** *adv.*
sig·ni·fy (sig′nə fī), *v.* **1.** to be a sign of; mean [What does the sign ÷ *signify*?] **2.** to make known by a sign, words, etc. [*Signify* your approval by saying "aye."] —**sig′ni·fied,** *p.t. & p.p.;* **sig′ni·fy·ing,** *pr.p.*
si·gnor (sē nyôr′), *n.* an Italian word used, like "Mr.," as a title for a man.
si·gno·ra (sē nyô′rä), *n.* an Italian word used, like "Mrs.," as a title for a married woman.
si·gno·ri·na (sē′nyô rē′nä), *n.* an Italian word used, like "Miss," as a title for an unmarried woman or girl.
sign·post (sīn′pōst), *n.* a post with a sign on it, as for showing a route or direction.
Sikh (sēk), *n.* a member of a religious sect of India. The Sikhs are noted as fighters.
si·lage (sī′lij), *n.* green cornstalks, grasses, etc. stored in a silo as food for cattle.
si·lence (sī′ləns), *n.* **1.** the condition of keeping still and not speaking, making noise, etc. [His *silence* meant he agreed.] **2.** the condition of being without sound; stillness [the *silence* of a deep forest]. —*v.* **1.** to make silent; to still [*Silence* the dog's barking.] **2.** to put down; overcome [to *silence* a rebellion]. —*interj.* be silent! keep still! —**si′lenced,** *p.t. & p.p.;* **si′lenc·ing,** *pr.p.* —**si′lenc·er,** *n.*
si·lent (sī′lənt), *adj.* **1.** not speaking or not talking much. **2.** with no sound or noise; noiseless; quiet [Find a *silent* place to study.] **3.** not spoken or told [*silent* grief; the *silent* "b" in "comb"]. **4.** not active [a *silent* partner]. —**si′lent·ly,** *adv.*
Si·le·sia (sī lē′shə), *n.* a region of central Europe, now divided between Poland and Czechoslovakia. —**Si·le′sian,** *n. & adj.*

sil·hou·ette (sil′oo et′), *n.* **1.** an outline drawing, in black or some solid color, especially of a profile. **2.** any dark shape seen against a light background. —*v.* to show as a silhouette [birds *silhouetted* against the sky]. —**sil′hou·et′ted,** *p.t. & p.p.;* **sil′hou·et′ting,** *pr.p.*

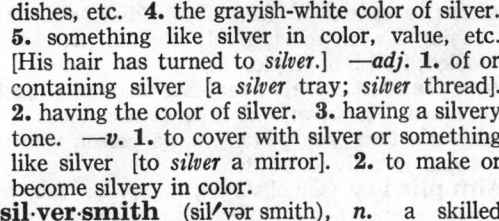
silhouette

sil·i·ca (sil′i kə), *n.* a glassy mineral found in various forms, as sand, quartz, etc.

sil·i·cate (sil′i kit), *n.* any of certain compounds containing silicon [Asbestos is a *silicate* of calcium and magnesium.]

sil·i·con (sil′i kən), *n.* a chemical element that is not a metal and is always found combined with something else, as oxygen. Silicon is one of the most common elements in the earth's crust.

sil·i·cone (sil′i kōn′), *n.* a substance containing silicon, used in polishes, oils, salves, etc.

silk (silk), *n.* **1.** the fine, soft fiber spun by silkworms to form their cocoons. **2.** thread or cloth made from this fiber. **3.** anything like silk, as the fibers in the tassels of corn. —*adj.* of or like silk; silken.

silk·en (sil′k'n), *adj.* **1.** made of silk [a *silken* gown]. **2.** like silk; shiny, soft, smooth, etc. [*silken* hair; *silken* words].

silk·worm (silk′wūrm), *n.* a moth caterpillar that spins silk fiber to make its cocoon.

silk·y (sil′kē), *adj.* of or like silk; soft, smooth, etc. [*silky* fur; a *silky* voice]. —**silk′i·er,** *compar.;* **silk′i·est,** *superl.* —**silk′i·ness,** *n.*

sill (sil), *n.* a board or a slab of stone that forms the bottom of the frame in a door or window.

sil·ly (sil′ē), *adj.* **1.** not having or showing good sense; foolish; unwise. **2.** having a weak mind. **3.** dazed or stunned: *used only in everyday talk* [The blow knocked him *silly*.] —*n.* a silly person: *used only in everyday talk.* —**sil′li·er,** *compar.;* **sil′li·est,** *superl.* —**sil′lies,** *pl.* —**sil′li·ness,** *n.*

si·lo (sī′lō), *n.* an airtight tower for storing silage, or green fodder. —**si′los,** *pl.*

silo

silt (silt), *n.* tiny particles of sand or soil, floating in or left by water. —*v.* to fill up or choke with silt, as a river bottom. —**silt′y,** *adj.*

sil·van (sil′vən), *adj.* same as **sylvan.**

sil·ver (sil′vər) *n.* **1.** a white precious metal that is a chemical element. Silver is soft and easy to mold and polish. **2.** silver coins [two dollars in *silver*]. **3.** tableware made of silver, as spoons, forks, dishes, etc. **4.** the grayish-white color of silver. **5.** something like silver in color, value, etc. [His hair has turned to *silver*.] —*adj.* **1.** of or containing silver [a *silver* tray; *silver* thread]. **2.** having the color of silver. **3.** having a silvery tone. —*v.* **1.** to cover with silver or something like silver [to *silver* a mirror]. **2.** to make or become silvery in color.

sil·ver·smith (sil′vər smith), *n.* a skilled worker who makes things of silver.

sil·ver·ware (sil′vər wer), *n.* things, especially tableware, made of or plated with silver.

sil·ver·y (sil′vər ē), *adj.* **1.** having the color of silver [the *silvery* moon]. **2.** soft and clear like the sound of a silver bell.

sim·i·an (sim′i ən), *adj.* of or like an ape or monkey. —*n.* an ape or monkey.

sim·i·lar (sim′ə lər), *adj.* almost but not exactly the same; alike [His ideas are *similar* to mine.] —**sim′i·lar·ly,** *adv.*

sim·i·lar·i·ty (sim′ə lar′ə tē), *n.* **1.** the condition of being similar; likeness. **2.** a similar point or feature. —**sim′i·lar′i·ties,** *pl.*

sim·i·le (sim′ə lē), *n.* a figure of speech in which two things that are different in most ways are said to be alike, by using either the word *as* or *like* ["He's as thin as a rail" and "She sings like a bird" are *similes*.] —**sim′i·les,** *pl.*

si·mil·i·tude (sə mil′ə tōōd *or* sə mil′ə tyōōd), *n.* likeness or similarity.

sim·mer (sim′ər), *v.* **1.** to boil gently with a murmuring sound. **2.** to keep close to the boiling point [*Simmer* the peas for ten minutes.] **3.** to be about to lose control of oneself [He *simmered* with rage.] —*n.* the condition of simmering [Keep the milk at a *simmer*.] —**simmer down, 1.** to simmer until little is left. **2.** to become calm; cool off.

Si·mon (sī′mən), *n.* same as **Peter,** the Apostle.

si·mo·ny (sī′mə nē *or* sim′ə nē), *n.* the buying or selling of sacred things, as an office in a church or pardon for a sin.

si·moom (si mōōm′) *or* **si·moon** (si mōōn′), *n.* a very strong, hot wind blowing sand in the deserts of Africa or Asia.

sim·per (sim′pər), *v.* **1.** to smile in a silly way that is not natural; smirk. **2.** to say with a simper. —*n.* a silly, unnatural smile.

sim·ple (sim′p'l), *adj.* **1.** having only one part or a few parts; not complicated [The amoeba is a *simple* animal.] **2.** easy to do or understand [a *simple* task; *simple* instructions]. **3.** without anything added; plain [the *simple* facts; a *simple* dress]. **4.** not showy or pretended; sincere; natural [his easy, *simple* ways]. **5.** of low rank; humble; common [*simple* peasants]. **6.** having a weak mind; foolish. —**sim′pler,** *compar.;* **sim′plest,** *superl.*

sim·ple-heart·ed (sim′p'l här′tid), *adj.* honest; sincere.

sim·ple-mind·ed (sim'p'l mīn'did), *adj.* **1.** having a weak mind; feeble-minded. **2.** easily fooled; foolish or stupid.

simple sentence, a sentence made up of just one main clause, with no dependent clauses.

sim·ple·ton (sim'p'l tən), *n.* a person who is stupid or easily fooled; fool.

sim·plic·i·ty (sim plis'ə tē), *n.* **1.** the fact of being simple, not complicated, not difficult, etc. **2.** a sincere or natural quality. **3.** the condition of being plain, not fancy, etc.

sim·pli·fy (sim'plə fī), *v.* to make more simple; make easier. —**sim'pli·fied,** *p.t. & p.p.;* **sim'pli·fy·ing,** *pr.p.* —**sim'pli·fi·ca'tion,** *n.*

sim·ply (sim'plē), *adv.* **1.** in a simple way; plainly [to speak *simply*]. **2.** merely; just [I'm *simply* trying to help.] **3.** completely; absolutely [I'm *simply* delighted to hear that.]

sim·u·late (sim'yoo lāt'), *v.* **1.** to pretend to have or feel [to *simulate* anger]. **2.** to look or act like; imitate [The insect *simulated* a twig.] —**sim'u·lat·ed,** *p.t. & p.p.;* **sim'u·lat·ing,** *pr.p.* —**sim'u·la'tion,** *n.*

si·mul·ta·ne·ous (sī'm'l tā'ni əs), *adj.* done or happening together or at the same time. —**si'·mul·ta'ne·ous·ly,** *adv.*

sin (sin), *n.* **1.** the breaking of a religious law, especially when done on purpose. **2.** a wrong or fault [a *sin* against good taste]. —*v.* to commit a sin. —**sinned,** *p.t. & p.p.;* **sin'ning,** *pr.p.*

Si·nai, Mount (sī'nī), in the Bible, the mountain where Moses received the law from God.

Sin·bad the Sailor (sin'bad), a merchant in *The Arabian Nights* who made seven voyages.

since (sins), *adv.* **1.** from then until now [He came Monday and has been here ever *since*.] **2.** at a time between then and now [He was ill last week but has *since* recovered.] **3.** before now; ago [It happened many years *since*.] —*prep.* from or during the time given until now [I've been up *since* dawn.] —*conj.* **1.** after the time that [It's been two years *since* I last saw him.] **2.** because [You may have these tools, *since* I no longer need them.]

sin·cere (sin sir'), *adj.* **1.** not pretending or fooling; honest; truthful [Are you *sincere* in wanting to help?] **2.** real; not pretended [*sincere* grief]. —**sin·cer'er,** *compar.;* **sin·cer'est,** *superl.* —**sin·cere'ly,** *adv.*

sin·cer·i·ty (sin ser'ə tē), *n.* the condition of being sincere; honesty; good faith.

si·ne·cure (sī'ni kyoor *or* sin'ə kyoor), *n.* a job or position for which one is paid well without having to do much work.

sin·ew (sin'yoo), *n.* **1.** a tendon. **2.** power of the muscles; strength [a man of *sinew*]. **3.** anything from which power or strength comes [Schools are the *sinews* of democracy.]

sin·ew·y (sin'yoo wē), *adj.* **1.** like or having sinews; tough [*sinewy* meat]. **2.** strong and powerful [*sinewy* arms].

sin·ful (sin'fəl), *adj.* full of sin; wicked. —**sin'·ful·ly,** *adv.* —**sin'ful·ness,** *n.*

sing (sing), *v.* **1.** to make musical sounds with the voice [She *sings* well.] **2.** to perform by singing [to *sing* a song; to *sing* an opera]. **3.** to make musical sounds, as a bird. **4.** to hum, buzz, whistle, etc., as an insect, the wind, etc. **5.** to tell or tell about in song or verse ["Of thee I *sing*." We *sing* his praises.] **6.** to bring or put by singing [*Sing* me to sleep.] —*n.* a gathering of people to sing songs: *used only in everyday talk.* —**sing out,** to call out loudly; shout: *used only in everyday talk.* —**sang** or **sung,** *p.t.;* **sung,** *p.p.;* **sing'ing,** *pr.p.*

sing., abbreviation for **singular.**

Sin·ga·pore (sing'gə pôr), *n.* **1.** a country on an island near the Malay Peninsula. **2.** its capital city.

singe (sinj), *v.* **1.** to burn slightly, especially at the ends [The moth *singed* its wings at the candle flame.] **2.** to hold in or near a flame so as to burn off feathers, etc. [to *singe* a chicken]. —*n.* a slight burn. —**singed,** *p.t. & p.p.;* **singe'ing,** *pr.p.*

sing·er (sing'ər), *n.* **1.** a person who sings. **2.** a bird that sings.

sin·gle (sing'g'l), *adj.* **1.** one only; one and no more [a carriage drawn by a *single* horse]. **2.** of or for one person, one family, etc. [a *single* bed; a *single* house]. **3.** not married [a *single* man]. **4.** having only one set of petals [a *single* daffodil]. **5.** between two persons only [*single* combat]. —*v.* **1.** to select from others [The teacher *singled* Tom out for praise.] **2.** to make a single in baseball. —*n.* **1.** a single person or thing. **2.** a hit in baseball by which the batter reaches first base only. **3. singles,** *pl.* a game, as in tennis, with only one player on each side. —**sin'gled,** *p.t. & p.p.;* **sin'gling,** *pr.p.* —**sin'gle·ness,** *n.*

sin·gle-breast·ed (sing'g'l bres'tid), *adj.* overlapping the front of the body just enough to fasten [a *single-breasted* coat].

single file, a single line of persons or things, one behind another.

sin·gle-hand·ed (sing'g'l han'did), *adj.* without help [He won the fight *single-handed*.]

sin·gle-heart·ed (sing'g'l här'tid), *adj.* honest; faithful; sincere.

sin·gle-mind·ed (sing'g'l mīn'did), *adj.* **1.** single-hearted. **2.** sticking to one purpose.

sin·gle·tree (sing'g'l trē), *n.* the crossbar at the front of a wagon or carriage, to which the traces of a horse's harness are hooked.

sin·gly (sing'glē), *adv.* **1.** as a single, separate person or thing; alone [We'll deal with each problem *singly*.] **2.** one at a time [They entered the hall *singly*.] **3.** single-handed.

sing·song (sing'sông), *n.* a rising and falling of the voice in a steady, boring rhythm. —*adj.* in or like a singsong.

sin·gu·lar (sing'gyoo lər), *adj.* **1.** more than ordinary; exceptional [the *singular* beauty of her voice]. **2.** strange; queer; unusual [a man of *singular* habits]. **3.** being the only one of its kind; unique [a *singular* specimen]. **4.** showing that only one is meant [The *singular* form of "geese" is "goose."] —*n.* the singular form of a word in grammar. —**sin·gu·lar·i·ty** (sing'gyoo lar'ə tē), *n.* —**sin'gu·lar·ly,** *adv.*

sin·is·ter (sin′is tər), *adj.* **1.** that threatens something bad [dark, *sinister* clouds]. **2.** wicked, evil, or dishonest [a *sinister* plot].

sink (singk), *v.* **1.** to go or put down below the surface, as of water, earth, etc. [The boat is *sinking.* He *sank* the spade into the ground.] **2.** to go down slowly; fall, settle, etc. [The balloon *sank* to the earth.] **3.** to seem to come down [The sun is *sinking* in the west.] **4.** to make or become lower in level,

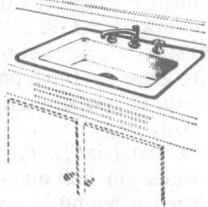

kitchen sink

value, amount, force, etc; drop [Her voice *sank* to a whisper. Prices *sank* to a new low.] **5.** to become hollow, as the cheeks. **6.** to go gradually into a certain condition [to *sink* into sleep]. **7.** to become weaker and closer to death [The patient is *sinking* rapidly.] **8.** to go into deeply and firmly [The experience *sank* into his memory.] **9.** to make by digging, drilling, etc. [to *sink* a well]. **10.** to lose by investing [He *sank* a fortune into that business.] **11.** to defeat or ruin [If they see us, we're *sunk.*] —*n.* **1.** a basin, as in a kitchen, with a drain and water faucets. **2.** a drain, sewer, or cesspool. **3.** a sunken place where water or filth collects. —**sank** or **sunk,** *p.t.;* **sunk,** *p.p.;* **sink′ing,** *pr.p.*

sink·er (singk′ər), *n.* something that sinks, as a lead weight put on the end of a fishing line.

sin·less (sin′lis), *adj.* without sin; innocent.

sin·ner (sin′ər), *n.* a person who sins.

sin·u·ous (sin′yōō əs), *adj.* **1.** twisting or winding in and out [a *sinuous* river]. **2.** not straightforward or honest; crooked. —**sin·u·os·i·ty** (sin′yōō os′ə tē), *n.*

si·nus (sī′nəs), *n.* a hollow place; especially, any of the cavities in the bones of the skull that open into the nose.

-sion (shən *or* zhən), a suffix meaning "the act, condition, or result of" [*Confusion* means the act, condition, or result of confusing.]

Sioux (sōō), *n.* a member of a group of Indian tribes living in the northern United States. —**Sioux** (sōō *or* sōōz), *pl.*

sip (sip), *v.* to drink a little at a time. —*n.* **1.** the act of sipping. **2.** a small amount sipped. —**sipped,** *p.t. & p.p.;* **sip′ping,** *pr.p.*

si·phon (sī′fən), *n.* **1.** a bent tube for carrying liquid out over the edge of a container down to a container below, by the force of air pressure. The tube must be filled, as by suction, before flow will start. **2.** a bottle for soda water with a tube inside. When a valve outside is opened, pressure forces the water out through the tube. —*v.* to draw off through a siphon [to *siphon* gasoline from a tank].

siphon

sir (sur), *n.* **1.** a word used to show respect in talking to a man [Thank you, *sir.* "Dear *Sir*" is often used to begin a letter.] **2. Sir,** a title used before the name of a knight or baronet [*Sir* Walter Raleigh].

sire (sīr), *n.* **1.** the male parent of a horse, dog, cow, etc. **2.** a father or male ancestor: *now seldom used.* **3.** a title of respect used in talking to a king. —*v.* to be the male parent of [This horse has *sired* three racing champions.] —**sired,** *p.t. & p.p.;* **sir′ing,** *pr.p.*

si·ren (sī′rən), *n.* **1.** a device that makes a wailing sound and is used as a warning signal, as on a fire engine. **2.** any of the sea nymphs in Greek and Roman myths, whose sweet singing lured sailors to their death on rocky coasts. **3.** any woman who attracts and tempts men. —*adj.* of or like a siren; tempting.

Sir·i·us (sir′i əs), *n.* the brightest star in the skies: also called *Dog Star.*

sir·loin (sur′loin), *n.* a fine cut of beef from the loin, next to the rump.

si·roc·co (sə räk′ō), *n.* any hot, stifling wind, especially one blowing from the deserts of northern Africa into southern Europe. —**si·roc′cos,** *pl.*

sir·rah (sir′ə), *n.* a title used in earlier times in talking to a man in an unfriendly way.

sir·up (sir′əp *or* sur′əp), *n.* **1.** a sweet, thick liquid made by boiling sugar with water, usually with some flavoring [chocolate *sirup*]. **2.** a sweet, thick liquid made by boiling the juice of certain plants [maple *sirup;* corn *sirup*]. Also spelled **syrup.** —**sir′up·y,** *adj.*

sis (sis), *n.* sister: *used only in everyday talk.*

si·sal (sī′s'l), *n.* **1.** a strong fiber obtained from the leaves of a tropical plant, used in making rope. **2.** this plant, a kind of agave.

sis·sy (sis′ē), *n.* a boy or man who acts in a way that is considered not manly: *used only in everyday talk.* —**sis′sies,** *pl.*

sis·ter (sis′tər), *n.* **1.** a girl or woman as she is related to the other children of her parents. **2.** a girl or woman who is close to one in some way, especially one who is a member of the same race, religion, club, etc. **3.** a nun.

sis·ter·hood (sis′tər hood), *n.* **1.** the tie between sisters or between women who feel a close relationship. **2.** a group of women joined together in some interest, work, belief, etc.

sis·ter-in-law (sis′tər in lô′), *n.* **1.** the sister of one's husband or wife. **2.** the wife of one's brother. —**sis′ters-in-law′,** *pl.*

sis·ter·ly (sis′tər lē), *adj.* **1.** of or like a sister. **2.** friendly, loyal, kindly, etc. [*sisterly* advice]. —**sis′ter·li·ness,** *n.*

sit (sit), *v.* **1.** to rest the weight of the body upon the buttocks or haunches [He is *sitting* on a bench. The dog *sat* still.] **2.** to make sit; seat [*Sit* yourself down.] **3.** to keep one's seat on [He *sits* his horse well.] **4.** to perch, rest, lie, etc.

---

fat,   āpe,   cär,   ten,   ēven,   hit,   bīte,   gō,   hôrn,   tōōl,   book,   up,   fûr;
get,   joy,   yet,   chin,   she,   thin,   *th*en;   zh = s in pleasure;   ′ as in able (ā′b'l);
ə = a in ago,   e in agent,   i in sanity,   o in confess,   u in focus.

[A bird *sat* on the fence. Worry *sits* on his brow.] **5.** to have a seat; be a member [to *sit* in the Senate]. **6.** to meet, as a court. **7.** to pose, as for a picture. **8.** to fit [This coat *sits* loosely.] **9.** to cover eggs with the body to hatch them [a *sitting* hen]. —**sit down,** to take a seat. —**sit in,** to take part. —**sit on** or **sit upon,** to be a member of, as a jury or committee. —**sit out, 1.** to stay until the end of. **2.** to stay out of for a while, as a dance or game. —**sit up, 1.** to rise to a sitting position. **2.** to sit with the back straight. **3.** to put off going to bed. **4.** to become suddenly alert: *used only in everyday talk.* —**sat,** *p.t. & p.p.;* **sit'ting,** *pr.p.* —**sit'ter,** *n.*

site (sīt), *n.* **1.** a piece of land for a special purpose [a good *site* for a factory]. **2.** the place where something is or was [Gettysburg was the *site* of a Civil War battle.]

sit·ting (sit'ing), *n.* **1.** the act or position of one that sits, as for a picture. **2.** a meeting, as of a court. **3.** a period of being seated [He read the book in one *sitting*.]

sitting room, a living room.

sit·u·ate (sich'oo āt), *v.* to put or place; locate [The cabin is *situated* in a wood.] —**sit'u·at·ed,** *p.t. & p.p.;* **sit'u·at·ing,** *pr.p.*

sit·u·a·tion (sich'oo ā'shən), *n.* **1.** place or position; location; site. **2.** condition or state, as caused by things that have happened [His election as mayor has created an interesting *situation.*] **3.** a job or place to work [He's looking for a *situation* as a clerk.]

six (siks), *n. & adj.* one more than five; the number 6. —**at sixes and sevens, 1.** confused. **2.** not in agreement.

six·pence (siks'pəns), *n.* **1.** the sum of six British pennies. **2.** a British coin worth six pence, or half a shilling.

six-shoot·er (siks'shoot'ər), *n.* a revolver that holds six shots: *used only in everyday talk.*

six·teen (siks'tēn'), *n. & adj.* six more than ten; the number 16.

six·teenth (siks'tēnth'), *adj.* coming after fifteen others; 16th in order. —*n.* **1.** the sixteenth one. **2.** one of the sixteen equal parts of something; 1/16.

sixteenth note, a note in music (♪) that is held one sixteenth as long as a whole note.

sixth (siksth), *adj.* coming after five others; 6th in order. —*n.* **1.** the sixth one. **2.** one of the six equal parts of something; 1/6.

six·ti·eth (siks'tē ith), *adj.* coming after fifty-nine others; 60th in order. —*n.* **1.** the sixtieth one. **2.** one of the sixty equal parts of something; 1/60.

six·ty (siks'tē), *n. & adj.* **1.** six times ten; the number 60. **2. sixties,** *n.pl.* the numbers or years from 60 to 69.

siz·a·ble or **size·a·ble** (sīz'ə b'l), *adj.* fairly large [a *sizable* fortune.]

size (sīz), *n.* **1.** the amount of space taken up by a thing; how large or how small a thing is [the *size* of a room; strong for his *size*]. **2.** any of a series of measures, often numbered, for grading things [a *size* 12 dress; jumbo *size* peanuts]. **3.** extent or amount [the *size* of his fortune]. —*v.* to arrange according to size. —**of a size,** of the same size. —**size up,** to form a judgment of: *used only in everyday talk.* —**sized,** *p.t. & p.p.;* **siz'ing,** *pr.p.*

size (sīz), *n.* a substance like a thin paste, used to glaze or stiffen paper, cloth, etc.: also **siz'ing.** —*v.* to put size on. —**sized,** *p.t. & p.p.;* **siz'-ing,** *pr.p.*

siz·zle (siz''l), *v.* to make a hissing sound, as water on hot metal or something frying. —*n.* such a sound. —**siz'zled,** *p.t. & p.p.;* **siz'-zling,** *pr.p.*

skate (skāt), *n.* **1.** a long, narrow metal blade, or runner, in a frame that can be fastened to a shoe for gliding on ice; also, a shoe with such a blade built onto it: also called **ice skate.** **2.** a frame or shoe like this with wheels instead of a blade, used for gliding on floors, walks, etc.: also called **roller skate.** —*v.* to move along on skates. —**skat'ed,** *p.t. & p.p.;* **skat'ing,** *pr.p.* —**skat'er,** *n.*

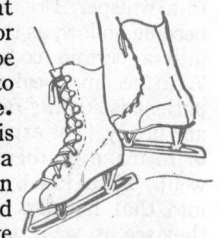
ice skates

skate (skāt), *n.* an ocean fish with a broad, flat body and a long, slender tail.

skeet (skēt), *n.* trapshooting in which the shooter fires from several different angles.

skein (skān), *n.* a loose, thick coil of yarn or thread.

skel·e·tal (skel'ə t'l), *adj.* of a skeleton or like a skeleton.

skel·e·ton (skel'ə t'n), *n.* **1.** the framework of bones of an animal body. **2.** anything like a skeleton, as the framework of a building or organization, an outline of a book, etc. —**skeleton in the closet,** some fact, as about one's family, kept secret because of shame.

skeleton key, a key that can open many simple locks.

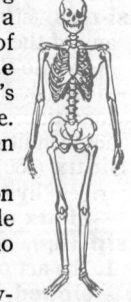
human skeleton

skep·tic (skep'tik), *n.* **1.** a person who questions things most people believe in; doubter. **2.** a person who doubts religious doctrines.

skep·ti·cal (skep'tə k'l), *adj.* having or showing doubt; not believing easily; questioning. —**skep'ti·cal·ly,** *adv.*

skep·ti·cism (skep'tə siz'm), *n.* a state of mind in which one doubts or questions things; disbelief.

sketch (skech), *n.* **1.** a simple, rough drawing or design, usually done quickly and with little detail. **2.** a short outline, giving the main points. **3.** a short, light story, scene in a show, etc. —*v.* to make a sketch of; draw sketches.

sketch·y (skech'ē), *adj.* like a sketch; not detailed; not complete [a *sketchy* report]. —**sketch'i·er,** *compar.;* **sketch'i·est,** *superl.*

skew (skyoo), *v.* to twist or slant. —*adj.* turned to one side; slanting.

skew·er (skyōō′ər), *n.* a long pin used to hold meat together while cooking. —*v.* to fasten or pierce with or as with a skewer or skewers.

skewer

ski (skē), *n.* one of a pair of long, wooden runners fastened to the shoes for gliding over snow. —*v.* to glide on skis, as down snow-covered hills. —**skied** (skēd), *p.t. & p.p.;* **ski′ing,** *pr.p.* —**ski′er,** *n.*

skid (skid), *n.* **1.** a plank, log, etc. used as a support or as a track on which to slide something heavy. **2.** a sliding wedge used as a brake on a wheel. **3.** the act of skidding. —*v.* **1.** to slide without turning, as a wheel does on ice when it is held by a brake. **2.** to slide sideways, as a car on ice. **3.** to slide on a skid or skids. —**on the skids,** losing one's power or influence, becoming a failure, etc.: *a slang phrase.* —**skid′ded,** *p.t. & p.p.;* **skid′ding,** *pr.p.*

man skiing

skies (skīz), *n.* plural of **sky.**

skiff (skif), *n.* a light rowboat, especially one with a small sail.

skill (skil), *n.* **1.** ability that comes from training, practice, etc. [He plays the violin with *skill.*] **2.** an art, craft, or science, especially one that calls for the use of the hands or body [Weaving is a *skill* often taught to the blind.]

skilled (skild), *adj.* **1.** having skill; skillful. **2.** needing a special skill got by training [Repairing watches is *skilled* work.]

skil·let (skil′it), *n.* a frying pan.

skill·ful or **skil·ful** (skil′fəl), *adj.* having or showing skill; expert [a *skillful* cook; her *skillful* performance on the piano]. —**skill′-ful·ly** or **skil′ful·ly,** *adv.*

skillet

skim (skim), *v.* **1.** to take off floating matter from the top of a liquid [to *skim* cream from milk; to *skim* molten lead]. **2.** to look through a book, magazine, etc. quickly without reading carefully. **3.** to glide lightly, as over a surface [bugs *skimming* over the water]. —**skimmed,** *p.t. & p.p.;* **skim′ming,** *pr.p.*

skim·mer (skim′ər), *n.* **1.** a person or thing that skims. **2.** any utensil for skimming liquids.

skim milk, milk from which cream is removed.

skimp (skimp), *v.* to spend or use as little as possible; allow less than enough; scrimp [They *skimped* on clothes to save for a new home.]

skimp·y (skim′pē), *adj.* barely or not quite enough; scanty [a *skimpy* meal]. —**skimp′-i·er,** *compar.;* **skimp′i·est,** *superl.*

skin (skin), *n.* **1.** the tissue covering the body of persons and animals. **2.** the hide or pelt of an animal [a coat made from beaver *skins*]. **3.** the outer covering of some fruits and vegetables [tomato *skin*]. **4.** something like skin, as the casing of a wiener. —*v.* **1.** to remove the skin from [to *skin* a rabbit; to *skin* one's elbow by falling]. **2.** to cheat or swindle: *used only in everyday talk.* —**by the skin of one's teeth,** by a very narrow margin. —**save one's skin,** to keep oneself from getting killed or hurt: *used only in everyday talk.* —**skinned,** *p.t. & p.p.;* **skin′ning,** *pr.p.* —**skin′less,** *adj.*

skin diving, the act or sport of swimming about under water, especially for a long time by breathing from a tank of air fastened to one.

skin·flint (skin′flint), *n.* a stingy person; miser.

skin·ny (skin′ē), *adj.* very thin or lean. —**skin′ni·er,** *compar.;* **skin′ni·est,** *superl.*

skin diving

skip (skip), *v.* **1.** to move along by hopping lightly on first one foot and then the other. **2.** to leap lightly over [to *skip* a brook]. **3.** to bound or make bounce across a surface [The boys *skipped* flat stones across the pond.] **4.** to pass from one point to another leaving out what is between; pass over; omit [*Skip* from page 56 to page 64. I *skipped* lunch.] **5.** to leave in a hurry: *used only in everyday talk* [to *skip* town]. —*n.* **1.** a light leap or jump. **2.** the act of passing over or omitting. —**skipped,** *p.t. & p.p.;* **skip′ping,** *pr.p.* —**skip′per,** *n.*

skip·per (skip′ər), *n.* **1.** the captain of a ship. **2.** any person who leads or manages.

skir·mish (skûr′mish), *n.* a brief fight between small groups, usually a part of a battle. —*v.* to take part in a skirmish.

skirt (skûrt), *n.* **1.** the part of a dress, coat, etc. that hangs below the waist. **2.** a woman's or girl's garment that hangs from the waist, worn with a blouse, sweater, etc. **3.** something hanging like a skirt [a *skirt* on a slip cover]. **4.** skirts, *pl.* the outer parts; outskirts. —*v.* to go along the edge of; pass around rather than through [The new highway will *skirt* our town.]

skit (skit), *n.* a short, usually funny sketch or scene, as in a show.

skit·tish (skit′ish), *adj.* **1.** easily frightened;

very nervous [a *skittish* horse]. **2.** lively or playful, especially in a coy way.

skit·tles (skit′'lz), *n.pl.* a game like ninepins, played with a wooden disk instead of a ball.

skul·dug·ger·y (skul dug′ər ē), *n.* sneaky, dishonest behavior: *used only in everyday talk.*

skulk (skulk), *v.* to move about or hide in a sneaky, cowardly, or threatening way [a hyena *skulking* in the shadows].

skull (skul), *n.* the bony framework of the head, that encloses and protects the brain.

skull and crossbones, a picture of a human skull with two crossed bones below. It was used on pirates' flags and is now used to label poisons.

skull·cap (skul′kap), *n.* a light, closefitting cap with no brim, usually worn indoors.

skunk (skungk), *n.* **1.** an animal having a bushy tail and black fur with white stripes down its back. It sprays out a very bad-smelling liquid when frightened or attacked. **2.** its fur. **3.** a nasty, mean person: *used only in everyday talk.*

skunk (2 ft. long)

sky (skī), *n.* **1.** *often* **skies,** *pl.* the upper part of the air around the earth; the dome that seems to cover the earth [a cloudy *sky;* blue *skies*]. **2.** heaven. —**out of a clear sky,** suddenly; without warning. —**skies,** *pl.*

sky blue, the blue color of a clear sky.

sky diving, the sport of jumping from an airplane and falling freely for some time before opening the parachute.

sky·lark (skī′lärk), *n.* the European lark, famous for the song it sings as it rises high into the air. —*v.* to play or frolic.

sky·light (skī′līt), *n.* a window in a roof or ceiling.

sky·line (skī′līn), *n.* **1.** the outline of a city, etc. seen against the sky. **2.** the line along which the earth and sky seem to meet; horizon.

sky·rock·et (skī′räk′it), *n.* a firework that explodes high in the air in a shower of colored sparks. —*v.* to rise rapidly: *used only in everyday talk* [Meat prices *skyrocketed.*]

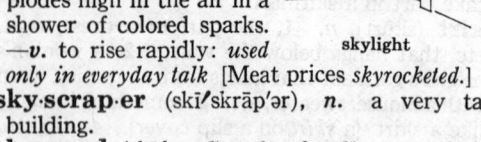
skylight

sky·scrap·er (skī′skrāp′ər), *n.* a very tall building.

sky·ward (skī′wərd), *adv. & adj.* toward the sky: also **sky′wards,** *adv.*

slab (slab), *n.* **1.** a piece that is flat, broad, and fairly thick [a *slab* of concrete]. **2.** a rough piece cut from the outside of a log.

slack (slak), *adj.* **1.** loose; not tight; relaxed [a *slack* tennis net; a *slack* jaw]. **2.** careless; lax [a *slack* workman]. **3.** not busy or active; dull [a *slack* season for business]. **4.** slow; sluggish; without energy or force. —*n.* **1.** a part that is

slack or hangs loose [Take in the *slack* of the rope!] **2.** a dull period; lull. **3. slacks,** *pl.* long trousers not made as part of a suit, worn by men or women. —**slack off,** to slacken. —**slack up,** to go or work more slowly. —**slack′ly,** *adv.* —**slack′ness,** *n.*

slack·en (slak′ən), *v.* **1.** to make or become slower or less full of energy [*Slacken* your pace so that I can keep up.] **2.** to loosen or relax; make or become less tight [to *slacken* one's grip].

slack·er (slak′ər), *n.* a person who tries to keep from doing his work or duty.

slag (slag), *n.* **1.** the waste matter that is left after metal has been melted down from ore. **2.** lava that looks like this.

slain (slān), past participle of **slay.**

slake (slāk), *v.* **1.** to satisfy or make less strong [to *slake* one's thirst with water]. **2.** to cause a chemical change in lime by adding water to it. Slaked lime is used in mortar, cement, etc. —**slaked,** *p.t. & p.p.;* **slak′ing,** *pr.p.*

slam (slam), *v.* **1.** to shut or close with force and noise [to *slam* a door]. **2.** to put, hit, or throw with force and noise [to *slam* a baseball over the fence]. —*n.* **1.** the act or sound of slamming. **2.** the winning of all the tricks in a hand of bridge (**grand slam**) or of all but one (**little slam**). —**slammed,** *p.t. & p.p.;* **slam′ming,** *pr.p.*

slan·der (slan′dər), *n.* **1.** anything spoken that harms a person's reputation in an unfair way and makes others laugh at him or hate him. **2.** the act or crime of saying such a thing. —*v.* to speak slander against.

slan·der·ous (slan′dər əs), *adj.* containing or speaking slander against someone.

slang (slang), *n.* words and phrases that are used in everyday talk but are out of place in fine or serious speech or writing. Slang words are usually popular for only a short time ["Hassle" is *slang,* and so is "rocky," when used to mean "weak or dizzy."]

slang·y (slang′ē), *adj.* of, like, or full of slang.

slant (slant), *v.* to turn or lie in a direction that is not straight up and down or straight across; slope [Straighten the picture; it *slants* to the left.] —*n.* **1.** a surface or line that slants; slope [The ramp goes up at a *slant.*] **2.** an attitude or opinion: *used only in everyday talk* [Your advice gave me a new *slant* on life.] —**slant′ing,** *adj.*

slant·wise (slant′wīz), *adv. & adj.* in a direction that slants: also **slant′ways,** *adv.*

slap (slap), *n.* a blow with something flat, as the palm of the hand. —*v.* **1.** to hit with something flat. **2.** to put or throw carelessly or with force [She *slapped* some butter into the pan.] —**slapped,** *p.t. & p.p.;* **slap′ping,** *pr.p.*

slash (slash), *v.* **1.** to cut by striking with something sharp [The knife slipped and he *slashed* his finger.] **2.** to whip or lash. **3.** to make cuts in cloth or a garment so as to show the material underneath. **4.** to make much less or much lower [to *slash* prices]. **5.** to speak or criticize harshly. —*n.* a sweeping blow or stroke, or a cut made with such a stroke.

slat (slat), *n.* a thin, narrow strip of wood or metal [the *slats* of a Venetian blind].

slate (slāt), *n.* **1.** a hard rock that splits easily into thin, smooth layers. **2.** the bluish-gray color of this rock. **3.** a thin piece of slate used in covering roofs or as something to write on with chalk. **4.** a list of candidates as in an election. —*v.* **1.** to cover with slate [to *slate* a roof]. **2.** to be among those chosen [John is *slated* to speak at the assembly.] —**a clean slate,** a record that shows no faults, mistakes, etc. —**slat′ed,** *p.t. & p.p.;* **slat′ing,** *pr.p.*

slat·tern (slat′ərn), *n.* a woman who is dirty and untidy in her looks, housework, etc. —**slat′tern·ly,** *adj. & adv.*

slaugh·ter (slô′tər), *n.* **1.** the killing of animals for food; butchering. **2.** the killing of people in a cruel way or in large numbers, as in a battle. —*v.* **1.** to kill for food; butcher [to *slaughter* a hog]. **2.** to kill people in a cruel way or in large numbers. —**slaugh′ter·er,** *n.*

slaugh·ter·house (slô′tər hous), *n.* a place where animals are killed for food.

Slav (släv), *n.* a member of a group of peoples of eastern Europe. Russians, Poles, Czechs, Slovaks, Serbs, etc. are Slavs. —*adj.* Slavic.

slave (slāv), *n.* **1.** a person who is owned by another person and has no freedom at all. **2.** a person who is completely controlled by a habit, an influence, etc. [a *slave* to fashion]. **3.** a person who works hard like a slave; drudge. —*v.* to work hard like a slave; toil. —**slaved,** *p.t. & p.p.;* **slav′ing,** *pr.p.*

slave·hold·er (slāv′hōl′dər), *n.* a person who owns slaves. —**slave′hold·ing,** *adj. & n.*

slav·er (slav′ər), *v.* to let saliva drip from the mouth. —*n.* saliva dripping from the mouth.

slav·er (slāv′ər), *n.* **1.** a ship in earlier times that carried people to another country to be sold as slaves. **2.** a person who deals in slaves.

slav·er·y (slāv′ər ē), *n.* **1.** the practice of owning slaves [The 13th Amendment abolished *slavery* in the U.S.] **2.** the condition of being a slave; bondage [Joseph was sold into *slavery.*] **3.** hard work like that of slaves; drudgery.

Slav·ic (släv′ik), *adj.* of the Slavs, their languages, etc. —*n.* the group of languages spoken by Slavs.

slav·ish (slāv′ish), *adj.* **1.** of or like a slave; too humble; cringing. **2.** of or like slavery [*slavish* work]. **3.** not free or independent [his *slavish* imitation of others]. —**slav′ish·ly,** *adv.* —**slav′ish·ness,** *n.*

slaw (slô), *n.* cabbage chopped into small shreds or pieces and served as a salad.

slay (slā), *v.* to kill in a violent way [Forty people were *slain* in traffic.] —**slew,** *p.t.;* **slain,** *p.p.;* **slay′ing,** *pr.p.* —**slay′er,** *n.*

slea·zy (slē′zē), *adj.* thin and easily torn; flimsy [*sleazy* cloth]. —**slea′zi·er,** *compar.;* **slea′zi·est,** *superl.* —**slea′zi·ness,** *n.*

sled (sled), *n.* a low platform on runners, used for riding or carrying things over snow or ice. —*v.* to carry, ride, or coast on a sled. —**sled′ded,** *p.t. & p.p.;* **sled′ding,** *pr.p.*

sledge (slej), *n.* a long, heavy hammer, usually used with both hands: also **sledge hammer.**

sledge (slej), *n.* **1.** a large, heavy sled for carrying loads over ice, snow, etc. **2.** a sleigh.

sled

sleek (slēk), *adj.* **1.** smooth and shiny; glossy [the *sleek* fur of a seal]. **2.** looking healthy and well-groomed [fat, *sleek* pigeons]. **3.** speaking or acting in a smooth but insincere way [a *sleek* villain]. —*v.* to make sleek; smooth down, as the hair. —**sleek′ly,** *adv.*

sleep (slēp), *n.* **1.** a condition of rest for the body and mind in which the eyes stay closed. In sleep, which comes at regular times, the mind does not control the body but may dream. **2.** any condition like this, as death, hibernation, etc. —*v.* **1.** to be in the condition of sleep [to *sleep* ten hours each night]. **2.** to be in a condition like sleep [Bears *sleep* through the winter.] —**sleep away,** to pass or spend in sleep [to *sleep away* the morning]. —**sleep off,** to get over the effects of by sleeping. —**slept,** *p.t. & p.p.;* **sleep′ing,** *pr.p.*

sledge

sleep·er (slēp′ər), *n.* **1.** one who sleeps, especially in a certain way [a light *sleeper*]. **2.** a railroad car that has berths for sleeping: also **sleeping car.** **3.** a heavy beam or timber laid flat for supporting something.

sleeping bag, a large bag with a warm lining, for sleeping in outdoors.

sleeping sickness, a disease that makes one weak and sleepy or unconscious. One type, as in Africa, is caused by the bite of a certain fly.

sleeping bag

sleep·less (slēp′lis), *adj.* with little or no sleep [a *sleepless* night].

sleep·walk·er (slēp′wôk′ər), *n.* a person who walks in his sleep. —**sleep′walk′ing,** *n.*

sleep·y (slēp′ē), *adj.* **1.** ready or likely to fall asleep; drowsy. **2.** not very active; dull; quiet [a *sleepy* little town]. —**sleep′i·er,** *compar.;* **sleep′i·est,** *superl.* —**sleep′i·ly,** *adv.* —**sleep′i·ness,** *n.*

sleet (slēt), *n.* **1.** rain that is partly frozen. **2.** a mixture of rain and snow. —*v.* to shower in the form of sleet. —**sleet′y,** *adj.*

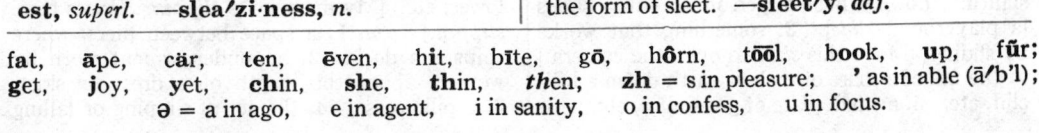

sleeve (slēv), *n.* the part of a garment that covers all or part of an arm. —**laugh up one's sleeve,** to be amused at something in a secret way. —**up one's sleeve,** hidden but ready at hand. —**sleeve′less,** *adj.*

sleigh (slā), *n.* a carriage with runners instead of wheels, for travel over snow or ice. —*v.* to ride in or drive a sleigh.

sleight of hand (slīt), **1.** the skill of doing puzzling tricks by moving the hands so fast as to fool those watching; magic. **2.** such tricks.

sleigh

slen·der (slen′dər), *adj.* **1.** small in width as compared with the length; thin; slim. **2.** small in amount, size, etc.; slight [a *slender* chance].

slept (slept), past tense and past participle of **sleep.**

sleuth (slooth), *n.* **1.** a bloodhound. **2.** a detective: *used only in everyday talk.*

slew (sloo), past tense of **slay.**

slew (sloo), *v. & n.* turn, twist, or swerve.

slew (sloo), *n.* a large number or amount; a lot: *used only in everyday talk.*

slice (slīs), *n.* a thin, broad piece cut from something [a *slice* of cheese; a *slice* of bread]. —*v.* **1.** to cut into slices [to *slice* a cake]. **2.** to cut off as a slice [*Slice* off the crust.] **3.** to cut as with a knife [The plow *sliced* through the soft earth.] **4.** to give a glancing stroke to, as a golf ball. —**sliced,** *p.t. & p.p.;* **slic′ing,** *pr.p.* —**slic′er,** *n.*

slick (slik), *adj.* **1.** smooth and shiny; sleek [*slick* hair]. **2.** slippery [a road *slick* with oil]. **3.** smooth in action, speech, etc. [*slick* flattery]. **4.** clever, sly, tricky, etc.: *used only in everyday talk* [a *slick* salesman]. **5.** excellent, fine, etc.: *a slang meaning.* —*v.* to make smooth and shiny [*Slick* down your hair with oil.] —*n.* a smooth area on water, as one caused by a film of oil.

slick·er (slik′ər), *n.* a person with smooth, tricky ways: *used only in everyday talk.*

slide (slīd), *v.* **1.** to move easily and smoothly along the length of a surface; glide [Children run and *slide* on the ice. The window won't *slide* up. *Slide* the note under the door.] **2.** to shift from a position; slip [The wet glass *slid* from his hand.] **3.** to pass, move, get, etc. gradually or without being noticed [to *slide* into bad habits]. —*n.* **1.** an act of sliding. **2.** a smooth surface, usually slanting, down which a person or thing slides [a playground *slide*]. **3.** something that works by sliding [Move this *slide* to open the camera.] **4.** the fall of a mass of rock or earth down a hill, cliff, etc. **5.** a small plate of glass, film, etc. with

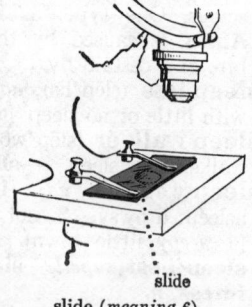
slide (meaning 6)

a picture on it that can be thrown on a screen by a projector. **6.** a small piece of glass on which things are placed for study under a microscope. —**slid** (slid), *p.t.;* **slid** or **slid·den** (slid′'n), *p.p.;* **slid′ing,** *pr.p.*

slide fastener, a device used to fasten and unfasten two edges of material by means of interlocking teeth worked by a sliding part.

slide rule, an instrument for quick figuring, made up of a ruler with a central sliding piece, both marked with scales.

slight (slīt), *adj.* **1.** small in amount or degree; not great, strong, important, etc. [a *slight* change in temperature; a *slight* advantage; a *slight* bruise]. **2.** light in build; slender [Most jockeys are short and *slight.*] —*v.* to pay little or no attention to; neglect, snub, etc. [to *slight* one's homework; to *slight* a neighbor]. —*n.* the act of slighting a person. —**slight′ly,** *adv.*

slim (slim), *adj.* **1.** slender or thin. **2.** small or slight [a *slim* crowd; *slim* hope]. —*v.* to make or become slim [She diets to *slim* down.] —**slim′mer,** *compar.;* **slim′mest,** *superl.* —**slimmed,** *p.t. & p.p.;* **slim′ming,** *pr.p.*

slime (slīm), *n.* any soft, moist, slippery matter that is often thought of as filthy or disgusting [*slime* in a cesspool].

slim·y (slīm′ē), *adj.* **1.** of, like, or covered with slime. **2.** filthy or disgusting. —**slim′i·er** *compar.;* **slim′i·est,** *superl.* —**slim′i·ness,** *n.*

sling (sling), *n.* **1.** a weapon of ancient times, made of a piece of leather tied to cords and used for hurling stones. **2.** a slingshot. **3.** a strap, rope, etc. used for holding or lifting a heavy object. **4.** a loop of cloth hanging down from around the neck, for holding an injured arm. —*v.* **1.** to throw as with a sling; cast, fling, hurl, etc. **2.** to carry, hold, or hang as in a sling.

sling (meaning 4)

—**slung,** *p.t. & p.p.;* **sling′ing,** *pr.p.*

sling·shot (sling′shät), *n.* a stick shaped like a Y with a rubber band tied to the upper tips. It is used for shooting stones.

slink (slingk), *v.* to move in a fearful or sneaky way, or as if ashamed. —**slunk,** *p.t. & p.p.;* **slink′ing,** *pr.p.*

slip (slip), *v.* **1.** to go or pass quietly or without being noticed; escape [He *slipped* out the door. It *slipped* my mind. Time *slipped* by.] **2.** to pass slowly into a certain condition [to *slip* into bad habits]. **3.** to move, shift, or drop, as by accident [The plate *slipped* from my hand.] **4.** to slide by accident [He *slipped* on the ice.] **5.** to make a mistake. **6.** to put or move smoothly, easily, or quickly [*Slip* the bolt through the hole. He *slipped* his shoes off.] **7.** to become worse, weaker, lower, etc. [My memory is *slipping.* Prices have *slipped.*] —*n.* **1.** a space between piers, where ships can dock. **2.** an undergarment worn by women, about the length of a dress or skirt. **3.** a pillowcase. **4.** the act of slipping or falling down. **5.** a mistake or accident [a *slip* of the tongue]. **—give one the slip,** to escape from one. **—let slip,** to say without meaning to. **—slip one over on,** to trick: *used only in everyday talk.* **—slip up,** to make a mistake: *used only in everyday talk.* **—slipped,** *p.t. & p.p.;* **slip′ping,** *pr.p.*

slip (slip), *n.* **1.** a stem, root, etc. cut off from a plant, used for starting a new plant. **2.** a young, slim person [a *slip* of a girl]. **3.** a small piece of paper, as for a special use [a sales *slip*].

slip cover, a fitted cover for a chair, sofa, etc., that can be taken off for washing.

slip·knot (slip′nät), *n.* a knot made so that it will slip along the rope around which it is tied: also **slip knot.**

slip·per (slip′ər), *n.* a light, low shoe that can be slipped on easily. **—slip′-pered,** *adj.*

slip·per·y (slip′ər ē), *adj.* **1.** that can cause slipping [Wet streets and waxed floors are *slippery*.] **2.** that might slip away, as from a hold [a *slippery* dish]. **3.** unreliable; tricky. **—slip′per·i·er,** *compar.;* **slip′per·i·est,** *superl.*

slip·shod (slip′shäd), *adj.* careless; not careful or neat [*slipshod* work].

slipknot

slit (slit), *v.* **1.** to cut or split open; make a long cut in [to *slit* an envelope]. **2.** to cut into long strips. **—n. 1.** a long, straight cut or tear. **2.** a long, narrow opening. **—slit,** *p.t. & p.p.;* **slit′ting,** *pr.p.*

slith·er (sli*th*′ər), *v.* to slide or glide, as a snake does. **—n.** a slithering motion.

sliv·er (sliv′ər), *n.* a thin, sharp piece that has been cut or split off; splinter [a *sliver* of glass]. **—v.** to cut or break into slivers.

slob·ber (släb′ər), *v.* **1.** to let saliva run from the mouth; drool. **2.** to show love, pity, etc. in a weak or foolish way. **—n.** saliva running from the mouth. **—slob′ber·y,** *adj.*

sloe (slō), *n.* **1.** a dark blue fruit like a small plum. **2.** the thorny bush it grows on.

slo·gan (slō′gən), *n.* a word or phrase used by a political party, business, etc. to get attention or to advertise a product.

sloop (slo͞op), *n.* a small sailboat with one mast, a mainsail, and a jib.

slop (släp), *n.* **1.** very wet snow or mud; slush. **2.** a puddle of spilled liquid. **3.** watery food that is thin and taste-less. **4.** *often* **slops,** *pl.* liquid waste or garbage. **—v. 1.** to spill or splash. **2.** to walk through slush. **—slop over,** to over-flow or spill; splash. **—slopped,** *p.t. & p.p.;* **slop′ping,** *pr.p.*

sloop

slope (slōp), *n.* **1.** land that slants up or down, as a hillside [to ski on a *slope*]. **2.** a surface, line, etc. that slants or the amount of this slant [The roof has a *slope* of 30 degrees.] **—v.** to have a slope; slant [The lawn *slopes* down to a lake.] **—sloped,** *p.t. & p.p.;* **slop′ing,** *pr.p.*

slop·py (släp′ē), *adj.* **1.** wet and likely to splash; slushy [a *sloppy* road]. **2.** not neat or careful; messy: *used only in everyday talk* [*sloppy* clothes]. **—slop′pi·er,** *compar.;* **slop′pi·est,** *superl.* **—slop′pi·ly,** *adv.* **—slop′pi·ness,** *n.*

slosh (släsh), *v.* to splash through mud, water, etc. in a clumsy way.

slot (slät), *n.* a narrow opening, as in a mailbox. **—v.** to make a slot in. **—slot′ted,** *p.t. & p.p.;* **slot′ting,** *pr.p.*

sloth (slôth *or* slōth), *n.* **1.** the condition of not liking to work or be ac-tive; laziness. **2.** an animal of South America that moves very slowly and lives in trees, often hanging upside down from the branches.

sloth·ful (slôth′fəl *or* slōth′fəl), *adj.* not lik-ing to work or act; lazy. **—sloth′ful·ly,** *adv.*

sloth (2 ft. long)

slouch (slouch), *v.* to sit, stand, or walk with the head drooping and the shoulders slumping. **—n. 1.** the act or position of slouching. **2.** a person who is awkward or lazy. **3.** a person who lacks skill: *used only in everyday talk* [He's no *slouch* at golf.] **—slouch′y,** *adj.*

slough (sluf), *v.* **1.** to shed or get rid of [Snakes *slough* their skins at least once a year. He has *sloughed* off his cold.] **2.** to fall off or become worse [Business has *sloughed* off.] **—n.** some-thing that is cast off, as a snake's skin.

slough (slou *or* slo͞o), *n.* a place full of soft, deep mud; swamp; bog.

girl slouching

Slo·va·ki·a (slō vä′ki ə *or* slō vak′i ə), *n.* one of the two main parts of Czechoslovakia. **—Slo′-vak** or **Slo·va′ki·an,** *adj. & n.*

slov·en (sluv′ən), *n.* a person who is careless and untidy about his looks, dress, work, etc.

Slo·ve·ni·a (slō vē′ni ə), *n.* a state in Yugo-slavia. **—Slo′vene** or **Slo·ve′ni·an,** *n. & adj.*

slov·en·ly (sluv′ən lē), *adj.* of or like a sloven; untidy, careless, etc. **—adv.** in a slovenly way. **—slov′en·li·ness,** *n.*

slow (slō), *adj.* **1.** not fast or quick in moving, working, etc. [a *slow* train; a *slow* reader]. **2.** that makes high speed difficult [a *slow* track]. **3.** taking a longer time than is usual [*slow* to learn]. **4.** not quick in understanding [a *slow* student]. **5.** not lively, active, or interesting; dull; sluggish [This book has a *slow* plot. Business is *slow*.] **6.** showing a time that is behind the real time [Your watch is *slow*.] —*v.* to make, become, or go slow or slower: *often used with* up *or* down. —*adv.* in a slow way; slowly. —**slow'-ly,** *adv.* —**slow'ness,** *n.*

slow-mo·tion (slō'mō'shən), *adj.* describing a motion picture in which the action is shown as much slower than the real action.

slow·poke (slō'pōk), *n.* a person who moves or acts slowly: *a slang word.*

sludge (sluj), *n.* soft mud or slush; also, any slimy waste, as thick, dirty oil. —**sludg'y,** *adj.*

slue (slōō), *v. & n.* turn, twist, or swerve.

slug (slug), *n.* **1.** a small, slow-moving animal like a snail, but having no outer shell. Slugs live in damp places and feed on plants. **2.** any smooth larva like this.

slug (3 in. long)

slug (slug), *n.* **1.** a small piece or lump of metal, as a bullet. **2.** a small, round piece of metal used in place of a coin in some machines.

slug (slug), *v.* to hit hard, as with the fist. —*n.* a hard blow. *This word is used only in everyday talk.* —**slugged,** *p.t. & p.p.;* **slug'-ging,** *pr.p.* —**slug'ger,** *n.*

slug·gard (slug'ərd), *n.* a lazy person.

slug·gish (slug'ish), *adj.* **1.** lacking energy or vigor; lazy; not active [a *sluggish* appetite]. **2.** slow or slow-moving [a *sluggish* engine]. —**slug'gish·ly,** *adv.* —**slug'gish·ness,** *n.*

sluice (slōōs), *n.* **1.** a channel for water with a gate to control the flow. **2.** the water held back by such a gate. **3.** such a gate; floodgate. **4.** any channel, as a trough for washing gold, carrying logs, etc. —*v.* **1.** to let out or flow out by means of a sluice. **2.** to wash with a flow of water [to *sluice* gravel for gold; to *sluice* a ship's deck with hoses]. —**sluiced,** *p.t. & p.p.;* **sluic'ing,** *pr.p.*

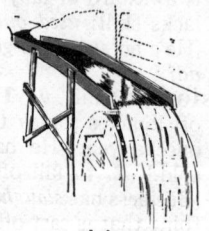

sluice

slum (slum), *n.* a part of a city which is very crowded, poor, and dirty. —*v.* to visit slums. —**slummed,** *p.t. & p.p.;* **slum'ming,** *pr.p.*

slum·ber (slum'bər), *v.* **1.** to sleep. **2.** to be quiet or inactive [trees *slumbering* in the winter]. —*n.* **1.** sleep. **2.** a quiet or inactive condition.

slum·ber·ous (slum'bər əs), *adj.* **1.** sleepy; drowsy. **2.** causing sleep [*slumberous* music]. Also **slum·brous** (slum'brəs).

slump (slump), *v.* **1.** to fall, sink, or drop suddenly or heavily [She *slumped* to the floor in a faint. Sales have *slumped*.] **2.** to have a drooping posture; slouch. —*n.* a fall or drop, as in value or amount.

slung (slung), past tense and past participle of **sling.**

slunk (slungk), past tense and past participle of **slink.**

slur (slur), *v.* **1.** to pass over quickly or carelessly [He *slurred* over this point in his talk.] **2.** to

pronounce in an unclear way, as by combining or dropping sounds [We *slur* "Gloucester" by pronouncing it (gläs'tər).] **3.** to sing or play two or more notes by gliding from one to another without a break. **4.** to speak badly of; insult. —*n.* **1.** the act of slurring. **2.** something slurred, as a pronunciation. **3.** a remark that hurts someone's reputation; insult. **4.** a group of slurred notes in music; also, a mark, (⌣) or (⌢), connecting such notes. —**slurred,** *p.t. & p.p.;* **slur'ring,** *pr.p.*

slush (slush), *n.* **1.** snow that is partly melted. **2.** soft mud. **3.** talk or writing that shows too much feeling in a weak or foolish way. —**slush'-i·ness,** *n.* —**slush'y,** *adj.*

slut (slut), *n.* a dirty or immoral woman.

sly (slī), *adj.* **1.** able to fool or trick others; cunning; crafty [the *sly* fox]. **2.** tricking or teasing in a playful way [*sly* humor]. —**on the sly,** secretly. —**sli'er** or **sly'er,** *compar.;* **sli'est** or **sly'est,** *superl.* —**sly'ly** or **sli'ly,** *adv.*

smack (smak), *n.* **1.** a slight taste or flavor. **2.** a small amount; trace. —*v.* to have a flavor or trace [a plan that *smacks* of injustice].

smack (smak), *n.* **1.** a sharp noise made by parting the lips suddenly, as in showing enjoyment of a taste. **2.** a loud kiss. **3.** a sharp slap. —*v.* **1.** to make a smack with [to *smack* one's lips]. **2.** to slap loudly. —*adv.* with a smack [He ran *smack* into the wall.]

smack (smak), *n.* **1.** a small sailboat. **2.** a fishing boat with a well for keeping fish alive.

small (smôl), *adj.* **1.** little in size; not large or great [a *small* city; a *small* business]. **2.** soft and weak [a *small* voice]. **3.** not important; trivial [a *small* matter; *small* talk]. **4.** mean or selfish [a *small* trick]. —*n.* the small or narrow part [the *small* of the back]. —**feel small,** to feel ashamed or humble. —**small'ness,** *n.*

small arms, firearms that are carried by hand, as pistols, rifles, shotguns, etc.

small fry, 1. small fish. **2.** small children.

small hours, the first hours after midnight.

small letter, a letter that is not a capital.

small-mind·ed (smôl'mīn'did), *adj.* selfish, mean, or narrow-minded.

small·pox (smôl'päks), *n.* a disease causing a high fever and sores on the skin that often leave pitted scars. It is very contagious.

smart (smärt), *adj.* **1.** intelligent or clever [a *smart* student]. **2.** neat, clean, and well-groomed. **3.** of the newest fashion; stylish [a *smart* new hat]. **4.** sharp; strong; intense [a *smart* pain]. **5.** causing sharp pain [a *smart* rap on the knuckles]. **6.** quick or lively; brisk [The horse trotted at a *smart* pace.] —*v.* **1.** to cause a sharp, stinging pain [A bee sting *smarts*.] **2.** to feel such a pain [Smoke makes my eyes *smart*.] **3.** to feel troubled or upset, as from sorrow, anger, etc. [His insult left her *smarting*.] —*n.* a sharp, stinging pain or feeling. —**smart'-ly,** *adv.* —**smart'ness,** *n.*

smart·en (smär't'n), *v.* to make smart, neat, brisk, etc.

smash (smash), *v.* **1.** to break into many pieces with noise or force [The plate *smashed* as it hit the ground. The fireman *smashed* the door with his ax.] **2.** to move or send with much force; crash [The car *smashed* into a tree.] **3.** to destroy completely [to *smash* one's hopes]. —*n.* **1.** the act or sound of smashing. **2.** a wreck or collision [Both drivers were hurt in the *smash*.] —*adj.* very successful: *used only in everyday talk* [The play is a *smash* hit.]

smash·up (smash′up), *n.* **1.** a very bad wreck or collision. **2.** complete failure; ruin [the *smashup* of his plans].

smat·ter·ing (smat′ər ing), *n.* a little knowledge [He has only a *smattering* of French.]

smear (smir), *v.* **1.** to cover with something greasy, sticky, etc. [She *smeared* her face with cold cream.] **2.** to rub or spread [*Smear* some grease on the wheel.] **3.** to make a mark or streak that is not wanted [He *smeared* the wet paint with his sleeve.] **4.** to harm the reputation of in an unfair way; slander [He claimed that the newspaper had *smeared* him.] —*n.* **1.** a mark or streak made by smearing. **2.** the act of smearing; especially, slander.

smell (smel), *v.* **1.** to be aware of something through a special sense in the nose; notice the odor or scent of [I *smell* something burning.] **2.** to breathe in the odor of [You'll know whether it's gasoline when you *smell* it.] **3.** to give off a certain scent [This perfume *smells* of violets.] **4.** to give off an unpleasant odor [Something in this basement *smells*.] —*n.* **1.** the power to smell; sense in the nose by which one becomes aware of things. **2.** that quality of a thing which is noticed by the nose; odor; scent; aroma [the *smell* of coffee]. **3.** an act of smelling [One *smell* told me she was baking.] —**smelled** or **smelt** (smelt), *p.t. & p.p.;* **smell′ing**, *pr.p.*

smelling salts, a compound of ammonia with a sharp smell, sniffed by people to relieve faintness, headaches, etc.

smell·y (smel′ē), *adj.* having a bad smell. —**smell′i·er**, *compar.;* **smell′i·est**, *superl.*

smelt (smelt), *n.* a small, silvery fish of northern seas, used as food.

smelt (smelt), *v.* **1.** to melt in order to get the pure metal away from the waste matter [to *smelt* iron ore]. **2.** to make pure by melting and removing the waste matter [to *smelt* tin].

smelt·er (smel′tər), *n.* **1.** a place, furnace, etc. in which smelting is done. **2.** a person whose work or business is smelting.

smidg·en (smij′in), *n.* a small amount; a bit: *used only in everyday talk.*

smile (smīl), *v.* **1.** to show that one is pleased, happy, amused, etc., or sarcastic or scornful, by making the corners of the mouth turn up. **2.** to show with a smile [He *smiled* his appreciation.] —*n.* **1.** the act of smiling or the look on one's face when one smiles. **2.** a cheerful, pleasant outlook [to face the future with a *smile*]. —**smile on,** to show approval of. —**smiled,** *p.t. & p.p.;* **smil′ing,** *pr.p.* —**smil′ing·ly,** *adv.*

smirch (smûrch), *v.* **1.** to stain or make dirty, as by smearing. **2.** to dishonor or disgrace [His name was *smirched* by ugly rumors.] —*n.* a smear, stain, or dirty spot.

smirk (smûrk), *v.* to smile in a silly, conceited way. —*n.* such a silly smile.

smite (smīt), *v.* **1.** to hit or strike hard, especially so as to kill or destroy: *no longer much used.* **2.** to affect in a sudden and strong way [He was *smitten* with love.] —**smote,** *p.t.;* **smit′ten,** *p.p.;* **smit′ing,** *pr.p.*

smith (smith), *n.* **1.** a person who makes or repairs metal objects [a silver*smith;* a lock*smith*]. **2.** a blacksmith.

man smirking

Smith, Captain John (smith), 1580–1631; English explorer who settled a colony in Virginia.

Smith, Joseph, 1805–1844; American who founded the Mormon Church.

smith·y (smith′ē), *n.* the workshop of a smith, especially a blacksmith. —**smith′ies,** *pl.*

smit·ten (smit′'n), past participle of **smite.**

smock (smäk), *n.* a loose outer garment worn over other clothes to protect them, as by an artist. —*v.* to decorate with smocking.

smock·ing (smäk′ing), *n.* fancy stitching used to gather cloth and make it hang in even folds.

smog (smäg), *n.* a mixture of fog and smoke.

smoke (smōk), *n.* **1.** the gas and bits of carbon that rise from something burning [*smoke* from a campfire]. **2.** any cloud or mist that looks like smoke. **3.** the act of smoking a cigarette, cigar, etc. **4.** a cigarette, cigar, etc. —*v.* **1.** to give off smoke [a *smoking* volcano]. **2.** to cause smoke to go in the wrong place [This fireplace *smokes*.] **3.** to breathe smoke from a cigar, cigarette, etc. into the mouth and blow it out again. **4.** to treat with smoke in order to flavor and keep from spoiling [to *smoke* a ham]. **5.** to force out as with smoke [We *smoked* the bees from the hollow tree.] —**smoked,** *p.t. & p.p.;* **smok′ing,** *pr.p.*

smock

smoke·house (smōk′hous), *n.* a place where meats, fish, etc. are cured or flavored with smoke.

smoke·less (smōk′lis), *adj.* making little or no smoke [*smokeless* gunpowder].

smok·er (smōk′ər), *n.* **1.** a person who smokes tobacco. **2.** a railroad car or section of a car where one may smoke. **3.** a party for men only.

smoke screen, a cloud of smoke spread to hide the movements of troops, ships, etc.

smoke·stack (smōk′stak), *n.* a pipe used as a chimney for carrying off smoke.

smok·y (smōk′ē), *adj.* **1.** giving off smoke, especially too much smoke [a *smoky* fireplace]. **2.** of, like, or having the color or taste of smoke [a *smoky* blue haze; *smoky* cheese]. **3.** filled with smoke [a *smoky* room]. **4.** made dirty by smoke [a *smoky* wall]. —**smok′i·er,** *compar.;* **smok′-i·est,** *superl.* —**smok′i·ness,** *n.*

smol·der (smōl′dər), *v.* **1.** to burn and smoke without flame. **2.** to be present but kept under control [a *smoldering* feeling of revenge].

smooth (smo͞oth), *adj.* **1.** having an even surface, with no bumps or rough spots [as *smooth* as marble; *smooth* water on the lake]. **2.** without lumps [a *smooth* paste]. **3.** even or gentle in movement; not jerky or rough [a *smooth* airplane flight; a *smooth* ride; *smooth* sailing]. **4.** with no trouble or difficulty [*smooth* progress]. **5.** pleasing in taste, sound, etc.; not harsh or sharp [a *smooth* flavor; *smooth* dance music]. **6.** speaking or spoken easily and politely, often in a way that seems false or not sincere [a *smooth* talker; *smooth* words]. —*v.* **1.** to make smooth or even [to *smooth* a board with sandpaper]. **2.** to make easy by taking away troubles, difficulties, etc. [to *smooth* one's way]. **3.** to make less crude; polish or refine. —*adv.* in a smooth way. —**smooth down,** to make calm; soothe. —**smooth over,** to make seem less serious or less bad. —**smooth′ly,** *adv.* —**smooth′-ness,** *n.*

smooth·bore (smo͞oth′bôr), *adj.* not grooved on the inside of the barrel [a *smoothbore* gun].

smor·gas·bord (smôr′gəs bôrd), *n.* a large variety of tasty foods, as cheeses, fishes, meats, etc., on a table where people help themselves.

smote (smōt), past tense of **smite.**

smoth·er (smu*th*′ər), *v.* **1.** to keep or be kept from getting enough air to breathe; often, to kill or die in this way; suffocate. **2.** to keep air from so as to stop burning [to *smother* a fire with sand]. **3.** to cover with a thick layer [liver *smothered* in onions]. **4.** to hold back or hide; suppress [to *smother* a yawn]. —*n.* a heavy, choking smoke or cloud.

smoul·der (smōl′dər), *v.* same as **smolder.**

smudge (smuj), *n.* **1.** a dirty spot; stain; smear. **2.** a fire made to give off a thick smoke, as for driving away insects or protecting plants from frost. —*v.* to streak with dirt; smear. —**smudged,** *p.t. & p.p.;* **smudg′ing,** *pr.p.* —**smudg′y,** *adj.*

smug (smug), *adj.* so pleased with oneself as to be annoying to others; too self-satisfied. —**smug′ger,** *compar.;* **smug′gest,** *superl.* —**smug′ly,** *adv.* —**smug′ness,** *n.*

smug·gle (smug′'l), *v.* **1.** to bring into or take out of a country in a way that is secret and against the law, as forbidden or taxable goods. **2.** to bring or take in a secret way [to *smuggle* a letter out of a jail]. —**smug′gled,** *p.t. & p.p.;* **smug′gling,** *pr.p.* —**smug′gler,** *n.*

smut (smut), *n.* **1.** soot or dirt, or a dirty mark or smear. **2.** disgusting or dirty talk or writing.

3. a fungus disease of grain, etc. in which the plant becomes covered with black dust.

smut·ty (smut′ē), *adj.* **1.** made dirty, as with soot. **2.** disgusting or indecent. —**smut′ti·er,** *compar.;* **smut′ti·est,** *superl.*

Sn, symbol for the chemical element *tin.*

snack (snak), *n.* something to eat or drink; often, a light meal eaten between regular meals.

snaf·fle (snaf′'l), *n.* a bit for a horse's mouth, having a joint in the middle.

snag (snag), *n.* **1.** an underwater tree stump or branch that is dangerous to boats. **2.** any sharp part that sticks out and may catch on things. **3.** a tear in cloth made by this [a *snag* in hose]. **4.** anything hidden or not expected that gets in the way [Our vacation plans hit a *snag* when I became sick.] —*v.* **1.** to tear or catch on a snag. **2.** to get in the way of; hinder. —**snagged,** *p.t. & p.p.;* **snag′ging,** *pr.p.*

snaffle

snail (snāl), *n.* a slow-moving animal with a soft body and a spiral shell into which it can draw back for protection. Snails live on land or in the water.

snail (1½in. long)

snake (snāk), *n.* **1.** a crawling reptile with a long, thin body and no legs. **2.** a person who is low, mean, disloyal, etc. **3.** a long, bending rod used by plumbers to clear blocked pipes. —*v.* to move, twist, or turn like a snake. —**snaked,** *p.t. & p.p.;* **snak′ing,** *pr.p.*

snak·y (snāk′ē), *adj.* **1.** of or like a snake or snakes [*snaky* hair]. **2.** winding or twisting [a *snaky* river]. —**snak′i·er,** *compar.;* **snak′-i·est,** *superl.*

snap (snap), *v.* **1.** to bite or grasp suddenly [The frog *snapped* at the fly. We *snapped* up his offer at once.] **2.** to speak or say in a short, sharp way [to *snap* out orders; to *snap* back at a person in anger]. **3.** to break suddenly with a sharp, cracking sound [The cord *snapped* when I pulled it tight.] **4.** to make or cause to make a sharp, cracking sound [He *snapped* his fingers.] **5.** to close, fasten, let go, etc. with a sound like this [The lock *snapped* shut.] **6.** to move in a quick, lively way [The soldiers *snapped* to attention.] **7.** to take a snapshot of. —*n.* **1.** a sudden bite, grasp, etc. **2.** a sharp, cracking or clicking sound [She closed her purse with a *snap.*] **3.** a fastening that closes with such a sound. **4.** a quick, sharp or lively way of speaking, moving, etc. **5.** a short period, as of cold weather. **6.** a hard, thin cooky [ginger*snaps*]. **7.** an easy job, problem, etc.: *a slang meaning.* —*adj.* **1.** made or done quickly, without much thought [a *snap* decision]. **2.** easy: *a slang meaning* [a *snap* problem]. —**not a snap,** not at all. —**snap out of it,** to recover suddenly, as one's normal ways, feelings, etc. —**snapped,** *p.t. & p.p.;* **snap′ping,** *pr.p.*

snap·drag·on (snap′drag′ ən), *n.* a plant with spikes of white, yellow, or red flowers.

snap·per (snap′ər), *n.* **1.** a food fish of warm oceans; especially, the **red snapper,** which has a reddish body. **2.** a snapping turtle.

snapping turtle, a large American turtle that lives in ponds and rivers. It has powerful jaws that snap with force.

snap·pish (snap′ish), *adj.* easily made angry; cross; irritable.

snapdragon

snap·py (snap′ē), *adj.* **1.** snappish; cross. **2.** lively or brisk: *used only in everyday talk.* —**snap′-pi·er,** *compar.;* **snap′pi·est,** *superl.*

snap·shot (snap′shät), *n.* a picture taken quickly with a hand camera.

snare (sner), *n.* **1.** a trap for catching animals, usually made of a noose that jerks tight about the animal's body. **2.** anything by which a person is caught or trapped. —*v.* to catch in a snare; trap. —**snared,** *p.t. & p.p.;* **snar′ing,** *pr.p.*

snare drum, a small drum with strings of wire or gut stretched across the bottom.

snarl (snärl), *v.* **1.** to growl in a fierce way, showing the teeth [a *snarling* wolf]. **2.** to speak or say in a harsh or angry tone ["Go away!" he *snarled.*] —*n.* the act or sound of snarling.

snare drum

snarl (snärl), *v.* to make or become tangled or confused [The cat *snarled* the ball of yarn. Traffic is *snarled.*] —*n.* **1.** a tangle or knot [hair full of *snarls*]. **2.** a confused condition.

snatch (snach), *v.* to reach for or seize suddenly; grab; grasp [The thief *snatched* her purse and ran.] —*n.* **1.** the act of snatching; a grab. **2.** a short time [to sleep in *snatches*]. **3.** a small amount; bit [I remember a *snatch* of the tune.] —**snatch at, 1.** to try to get. **2.** to be eager for.

sneak (snēk), *v.* **1.** to move or act in a quiet or secret way to keep from being noticed [He *sneaked* out of the room while we were talking.] **2.** to give, put, carry, etc. in this way. —*n.* a dishonest, cheating person.

sneak·ers (snēk′ərz), *n.pl.* canvas shoes with flat, rubber soles, worn for play and for sports: *used only in everyday talk.*

sneak·ing (snēk′ing), *adj.* **1.** moving or acting like a sneak [a *sneaking* thief]. **2.** secret or hidden [a *sneaking* desire for candy]. —**sneaking suspicion,** a suspicion that is getting stronger.

sneakers

sneak·y (snēk′ē), *adj.* of or like a sneak; dishonest; cheating. —**sneak′i·er,** *compar.;* **sneak′i·est,** *superl.* —**sneak′i·ly,** *adv.*

sneer (snir), *v.* **1.** to look scornful or sarcastic, as by curling the upper lip. **2.** to show scorn or sarcasm in speaking or writing [Many people *sneered* at the first automobiles.] —*n.* a sneering look or remark.

man sneering

sneeze (snēz), *v.* to blow out breath from the mouth and nose in a sudden, uncontrolled way, when one has a cold or something irritates the inside of the nose. —*n.* an act of sneezing. —**not to be sneezed at,** not to be thought of as unimportant. —**sneezed,** *p.t. & p.p.;* **sneez′ing,** *pr.p.*

snick·er (snik′ər), *v.* to give a silly laugh that is partly held back. —*n.* such a laugh.

sniff (snif), *v.* **1.** to make a noise in drawing air in through the nose, as when trying to smell something. **2.** to smell in this way [He *sniffed* the butter before tasting it.] **3.** to show dislike or doubt by sniffing [She just *sniffed* when I said hello.] —*n.* **1.** the act or sound of sniffing. **2.** something smelled by sniffing.

snif·fle (snif′'l), *v.* to sniff again and again as in trying to keep mucus from running out of the nose. —*n.* the act or sound of sniffling. —**the sniffles,** a cold in the head: *used only in everyday talk.* —**snif′fled,** *p.t. & p.p.;* **snif′fling,** *pr.p.*

snip (snip), *v.* to cut or cut off with a short, quick stroke, as of scissors [to *snip* a thread]. —*n.* **1.** a small cut made as with scissors. **2.** a small piece cut off by snipping. **3. snips,** *pl.* strong shears for cutting sheet metal. **4.** a young or small person: *used only in everyday talk.* —**snipped,** *p.t. & p.p.;* **snip′ping,** *pr.p.*

snipe (snīp), *n.* a wading bird with a long bill, that lives mainly in marshes. —*v.* **1.** to hunt for snipe. **2.** to shoot from a hidden place, as at enemy soldiers, one at a time. —**sniped,** *p.t. & p.p.;* **snip′ing,** *pr.p.* —**snip′-er,** *n.*

sniv·el (sniv′'l), *v.* **1.** to cry and sniffle. **2.** to cry or complain in a whining way. —**sniv′eled** or **sniv′elled,** *p.t. & p.p.;* **sniv′el·ing** or **sniv′-el·ling,** *pr.p.*

snipe (10 in. long)

snob (snäb), *n.* a person who thinks that money and rank are very important and who ignores or looks down on those who he thinks are not important. —**snob′bish,** *adj.* —**snob′bish·ly,** *adv.*

snob·ber·y (snäb′ər ē), *n.* the attitude or an act of a snob. —**snob′ber·ies,** *pl.*

fat, āpe, cär, ten, ēven, hit, bīte, gō, hôrn, tool, book, up, fûr;
get, joy, yet, chin, she, thin, then; zh = s in pleasure; ′ as in able (ā′b'l)
ə = a in ago, e in agent, i in sanity, o in confess, u in focus.

snood (sno͞od), *n.* **1.** a hair net worn on the back of a woman's head to hold the hair in place. **2.** a ribbon worn around the hair in earlier times by young women.

snoop (sno͞op), *v.* to look about or pry in a sneaking way; spy. —*n.* a person who snoops. *This word is used only in everyday talk.*

snooze (sno͞oz), *n.* a short sleep; nap. —*v.* to take a nap. *This word is used only in everyday talk.* —**snoozed,** *p.t. & p.p.;* **snooz'ing,** *pr.p.*

snore (snôr), *v.* to breathe with noisy, rough sounds while sleeping. —*n.* the act or sound of snoring. —**snored,** *p.t. & p.p.;* **snor'ing,** *pr.p.*

snor·kel (snôr'k'l), *n.* **1.** a device on a submarine for taking in air and removing exhaust. **2.** a short tube held in the mouth by swimmers for breathing under water.

snort (snôrt), *v.* **1.** to force breath from the nose in a sudden and noisy way [He *snorted* in disgust.] **2.** to make a noise like a snort. —*n.* the act or sound of snorting.

snout (snout), *n.* **1.** the nose and jaws of an animal when they stick out, as on a pig or dog. **2.** something that looks like this, as a nozzle.

snow (snō), *n.* **1.** soft, white flakes formed from drops of water that freeze in the upper air and fall to the earth. **2.** a fall of snow [We expect a heavy *snow* tonight.] —*v.* **1.** to shower down snow [It is *snowing*.] **2.** to cover or shut in with snow [The car was *snowed* under.]

snow·ball (snō'bôl), *n.* **1.** a mass of snow formed into a hard ball. **2.** a bush with large, round clusters of small white flowers. —*v.* **1.** to throw snowballs at. **2.** to grow larger rapidly like a rolling ball of snow [His debts *snowballed*.]

snow·bank (snō'bangk), *n.* a mound of snow.

snow·bird (snō'bûrd), *n.* **1.** an American finch with a white breast; junco. **2.** a small finch living in cold regions: also called **snow bunting.**

snow-blind (snō'blīnd'), *adj.* blinded for a short time by the glare of the sun shining on fallen snow. —**snow blindness.**

snow·bound (snō'bound), *adj.* shut in or blocked off by snow.

snow·drift (snō'drift), *n.* a bank or pile of snow heaped up by the wind.

snow·drop (snō'dräp), *n.* a small plant with drooping white flowers blooming in early spring.

snow·fall (snō'fôl), *n.* **1.** a fall of snow. **2.** the amount of snow that falls over a certain area during a certain time [a 3-inch *snowfall*].

snow·flake (snō'flāk), *n.* a flake of snow. Snowflakes are crystals. *See the picture.*

snow·mo·bile (snō'mō-bēl), *n.* a motor vehicle for traveling on snow: it has runners in front that move so that it can be steered.

snowflakes

snow·plow (snō'plou), *n.* a machine used to clear snow off a road, etc.

snow·shoe (snō'sho͞o), *n.* a wooden frame strung with leather strips, like a racket, and worn on the shoes to keep one from sinking in deep snow.

snow·storm (snō'stôrm), *n.* a storm with a heavy snowfall and a strong wind.

snow-white (snō'hwīt'), *adj.* white as snow.

snow·y (snō'ē), *adj.* **1.** having snow [a *snowy* day]. **2.** covered with snow [a *snowy* playground]. **3.** like snow. —**snow'i·er,** *compar.;* **snow'i·est,** *superl.*

snowshoes

snub (snub), *v.* **1.** to treat in an unfriendly or scornful way, as by ignoring; slight. **2.** to stop suddenly [to *snub* a rope by looping it around a post]. —*n.* scornful or unfriendly treatment. —*adj.* short and turned up [a *snub* nose]. —**snubbed,** *p.t. & p.p.;* **snub'bing,** *pr.p.*

snuff (snuf), *v.* **1.** to put out the flame of [to *snuff* a candle]. **2.** to trim off the burned end of a candle's wick. —**snuff out,** to end suddenly [The accident *snuffed out* three lives.]

snuff (snuf), *v.* **1.** to draw up into the nose by sniffing. **2.** to smell or sniff. —*n.* tobacco in powdered form snuffed up into the nose or put on the gums. —**up to snuff,** as good as might be expected: *used only in everyday talk.*

snuff·box (snuf'bäks), *n.* a small box for snuff.

snuf·fer (snuf'ər), *n.* or **snuf'fers,** *n.pl.* a device for snuffing candles.

snuf·fle (snuf'l), *v.* to breathe in a noisy way, as when the nose is stopped up with a cold. —*n.* the act or sound of snuffling. —**snuf'fled,** *p.t. & p.p.;* **snuf'fling,** *pr.p.*

snug (snug), *adj.* **1.** warm and comfortable; cozy [We lay *snug* in our beds.] **2.** small but well-arranged and neat [a *snug* kitchen]. **3.** fitting in a tight way [a *snug* vest]. —**snug'ger,** *compar.;* **snug'gest,** *superl.* —**snug'ly,** *adv.*

snug·gle (snug'l), *v.* to lie close or hold close in a warm, cozy way; cuddle [The kittens *snuggled* together. She *snuggled* her baby in her arms.] —**snug'gled,** *p.t. & p.p.;* **snug'gling,** *pr.p.*

so (sō), *adv.* **1.** to such a degree [He is not *so* tall as I. Why are you *so* late?] **2.** as a result; therefore [He couldn't swim and *so* was drowned.] **3.** very [They are *so* happy.] **4.** also; in the same way [I am hungry and *so* is he.] **5.** more or less; just about [I spent a dollar or *so* on candy.] **6.** after all; then [*So* you really don't care.] **7.** as shown, told, etc.; in such a way [Hold your pencil just *so*.] **8.** very much: *used only in everyday talk* [She loves her garden *so*.] —*conj.* **1.** for the reason that; in order that [Talk louder *so* that I may hear you.] **2.** with the result that: *used only in everyday talk* [He didn't study, *so* he failed the test.] —*pron.* the same [I am his friend and will remain *so*.] —*interj.* a word used to show surprise, dislike, approval, doubt, etc. [*So!* I caught you!] —**and so on** or **and so forth,** and the rest; and others. —**so as,** in order; for the purpose [He left early *so as* to be on time.]

soak (sōk), *v.* **1.** to make or become completely wet by keeping or staying in a liquid [He *soaked* his sore hand in hot water. Let the beans *soak* overnight to soften them.] **2.** to suck up or absorb [Use a sponge to *soak* up that water.] **3.** to take into the mind [to *soak* up information from books]. **4.** to pass or go through [The rain *soaked* through his coat.] —*n.* the act of soaking.

so-and-so (sō'n sō'), *n.* a certain person whose name is not mentioned or not remembered: *used only in everyday talk.* —**so'-and-sos'**, *pl.*

soap (sōp), *n.* a substance used with water to make suds for washing things. Soaps are usually made of an alkali, as potash, and a fat. —*v.* to rub or wash with soap.

soap·stone (sōp'stōn), *n.* a kind of rock that feels soft and smooth.

soap·suds (sōp'sudz), *n.pl.* water with soap stirred in until it is foamy.

soap·y (sōp'ē), *adj.* **1.** covered with soapsuds or full of soap [*soapy* water]. **2.** of or like soap or soapsuds [*soapy* foam on ocean waves]. —**soap'i·er**, *compar.*; **soap'i·est**, *superl.*

soar (sôr), *v.* **1.** to rise or fly high in the air [The plane *soared* out of sight.] **2.** to rise above what is usual [Prices *soared* after the war.]

sob (säb), *v.* **1.** to cry or weep with a break in the voice and short gasps. **2.** to bring or put by sobbing [to *sob* oneself to sleep]. **3.** to make a sound like that of a person sobbing [The wind *sobbed* in the trees.] —*n.* the act or sound of sobbing. —**sobbed**, *p.t. & p.p.*; **sob'bing**, *pr.p.*

so·ber (sō'bər), *adj.* **1.** showing self-control, especially in not drinking too much alcoholic liquor; temperate. **2.** not drunk. **3.** serious, quiet, plain, sensible, etc. [a *sober* look on one's face; the *sober* truth; *sober* colors]. —*v.* to make or become sober. —**so'ber·ly**, *adv.*

so·bri·e·ty (sō brī'ə tē), *n.* the condition of being sober.

so·bri·quet (sō'bri kā'), *n.* a nickname.

Soc. or **soc.,** abbreviation for **society.**

so-called (sō'kôld'), *adj.* called by this name, but usually not correctly so [His *so-called* friends tricked him.]

soc·cer (säk'ər), *n.* a football game in which a round ball is moved by kicking or by using any part of the body except the hands and arms.

so·cia·ble (sō'shə b'l), *adj.* **1.** enjoying the company of others; friendly [a *sociable* person]. **2.** full of pleasant talk and friendliness [a *sociable* evening]. —*n.* a social. —**so'cia·bil'·i·ty**, *n.* —**so'cia·bly**, *adv.*

so·cial (sō'shəl), *adj.* **1.** of or having to do with human beings as they live together in a group or groups [*social* problems; *social* forces]. **2.** living in groups or colonies [Ants are *social* insects.] **3.** liking to be with others; sociable [A hermit is not a *social* person.] **4.** of or having to do with society, especially with the upper classes [a *social* event]. **5.** of or for companionship [a *social* club]. —*n.* a friendly gathering; party [a church *social*]. —**so'cial·ly**, *adv.*

so·cial·ism (sō'shəl iz'm), *n.* any of various systems in which the means of producing goods are publicly owned, with all people sharing in the work and the goods produced.

so·cial·ist (sō'shəl ist), *n.* **1.** a person who is in favor of socialism. **2.** Socialist, a member of a political party that seeks to set up socialism. —**so'cial·is'tic,** *adj.*

so·cial·ize (sō'shə līz), *v.* **1.** to make fit for living and getting along in a group; make social. **2.** to set up or manage under a system of socialism [to *socialize* industry]. —**so'cial·ized,** *p.t. & p.p.*; **so'cial·iz·ing,** *pr.p.*

social science, the study of people living together in groups, their customs, activities, etc. Sociology, history, etc. are social sciences.

social security, a system of government insurance for making payments to the aged, people out of work, widows, etc.

social studies, social science, especially as studied in the lower schools.

social work, work for improving the condition of the people in a community, as by clinics, playgrounds, help for the needy or troubled, etc. —**social worker.**

so·ci·e·ty (sō sī'ə tē), *n.* **1.** people living together as a group, or forming a group, with the same way of life; also, their way of life [a primitive *society*; urban *society*]. **2.** all people [a law for the good of *society*]. **3.** company or companionship [to seek the *society* of others]. **4.** a group of people joined together for some purpose [a *society* of musicians]. **5.** the wealthy, upper class. —**so·ci'e·ties,** *pl.*

Society of Friends, a Christian religious sect that believes in a plain way of life and worship and is against violence of any kind, including war. Its members are often called **Quakers.**

so·ci·ol·o·gy (sō'si äl'ə jē), *n.* the study of people living together in groups; study of the history, problems, and forms of human society. —**so·ci·o·log·i·cal** (sō'si ə läj'i k'l), *adj.* —**so'·ci·ol'o·gist,** *n.*

sock (säk), *n.* a short stocking.

sock (säk), *v.* to hit hard. —*n.* a hard blow. *This is a slang word.*

sock·et (säk'it), *n.* a hollow part into which something fits [a *socket* for an electric bulb; the eye *socket*].

Soc·ra·tes (säk'rə tēz), *n.* Greek philosopher and teacher, who lived from about 470 to 399 B.C. —**So·crat·ic** (sō krat'ik), *adj. & n.*

sod (säd), *n.* **1.** a top layer of earth containing grass with its roots; turf. **2.** a piece of this layer. —*v.* to cover with sod or sods. —**sod'ded,** *p.t. & p.p.*; **sod'ding,** *pr.p.*

light socket

so·da (sō′də), *n.* **1.** any of certain substances containing sodium, as baking soda. **2.** soda water. **3.** a drink made of soda water, sirup, and, often, ice cream.

soda cracker, a light, crisp cracker made with baking soda. It is usually salted.

soda fountain, a counter for making and serving soft drinks, sodas, sundaes, etc.

so·dal·i·ty (sō dal′ə tē), *n.* a society of Roman Catholic Church members formed for religious or charitable purposes. —**so·dal′i·ties,** *pl.*

soda water, water filled with carbon dioxide gas to make it bubble.

sod·den (säd′'n), *adj.* **1.** completely wet; soaked through [a lawn *sodden* with rain]. **2.** heavy or soggy [*sodden* bread].

so·di·um (sō′di əm), *n.* a soft, silver-white metal that is a chemical element. It is found in nature only in compounds. Salt, baking soda, lye, etc. contain sodium.

sodium bicarbonate, baking soda.

sodium chloride, common salt.

Sod·om (säd′əm), *n.* a city told about in the Bible as being destroyed by fire from heaven because the people were wicked.

so·ev·er (sō ev′ər), *adv.* in any way or of any kind; at all. *Soever* is usually used as a suffix with certain words [who*soever*, what*soever*, where*soever*, how*soever*, when*soever*].

so·fa (sō′fə), *n.* an upholstered couch with a back and arms.

soft (sôft), *adj.* **1.** not hard or firm; easy to bend, crush, cut, etc. [This pillow is *soft*. Lead is a *soft* metal.] **2.** smooth to the touch; not rough [*soft* skin]. **3.** not bright or sharp [*soft* gray; a *soft* line]. **4.** weak; not strong or powerful [*soft* muscles; a *soft* wind]. **5.** not difficult; easy to do [a *soft* job]. **6.** filled with pity, kindness, etc. [a *soft* heart]. **7.** not harsh or severe [*soft* words; a *soft* life]. **8.** weak or low in sound [a *soft* chime]. **9.** containing no alcohol [a *soft* drink]. **10.** containing no minerals that keep soap from making a lather [*soft* water]. **11.** describing the sound of *c* in *cent* or of *g* in *germ*. —*adv.* in a soft or quiet way; gently. —*interj.* hush! quiet!: *now seldom used.* —**soft′ly,** *adv.* —**soft′ness,** *n.*

soft·ball (sôft′bôl), *n.* a form of baseball played on a smaller diamond with a ball that is larger and softer than an ordinary baseball.

soft-boiled (sôft′boild′), *adj.* boiled only a short time so that the yolk is still soft [*soft-boiled* eggs].

sof·ten (sôf′'n), *v.* to make or become soft or softer. —**sof′ten·er,** *n.*

soft·wood (sôft′wood), *n.* **1.** wood that is light and easy to cut. **2.** the wood of any tree with cones, as pine. **3.** a tree with soft wood.

sog·gy (säg′ē), *adj.* very wet and heavy; soaked. —**sog′gi·er,** *compar.*; **sog′gi·est,** *superl.*

soil (soil), *n.* **1.** the top layer of earth, in which plants grow; ground [fertile *soil*]. **2.** land; country [his native *soil*].

soil (soil), *v.* **1.** to make or become dirty; stain; spot. **2.** to disgrace [to *soil* one's honor].

—*n.* the act of soiling or a soiled spot; stain.

soi·ree or **soi·rée** (swä rā′), *n.* a party or gathering in the evening.

so·journ (sō′jürn), *v.* (*also* sō jürn′), to stay for a while, as on a visit [We *sojourned* in Italy.] —*n.* a short stay; visit. —**so′journ·er,** *n.*

Sol (säl), *n.* **1.** the sun. **2.** the sun god of the ancient Romans.

sol (sōl), *n.* the fifth note of a musical scale.

sol·ace (säl′is), *n.* comfort or relief [His kind words gave *solace* to my sorrow.] —*v.* to comfort or give solace to. —**sol′aced,** *p.t. & p.p.*; **sol′ac·ing,** *pr.p.*

so·lar (sō′lər), *adj.* **1.** of or having to do with the sun [a *solar* eclipse; *solar* energy]. **2.** depending on light or energy from the sun [*solar* heating]. **3.** measured by the motion of the earth around the sun [a *solar* day].

so·lar·i·um (sō ler′i əm), *n.* a room with glass walls, where people can sit in the sun; sunroom.

solar plexus, a network of nerves in the abdomen, behind the stomach.

solar system, the sun and all the planets, asteroids, comets, etc. that move around it.

sold (sōld), past tense and past participle of **sell.**

sol·der (säd′ər), *n.* a metal alloy that is melted and used to join or patch metal parts. —*v.* to join or patch as with solder.

soldering iron, a pointed metal tool heated so that it can be used in soldering.

sol·dier (sōl′jər), *n.* **1.** a person in an army, especially one who is not a commissioned officer. **2.** a person who works for a cause [a *soldier* for peace]. —*v.* **1.** to serve as a soldier. **2.** to pretend to work, without doing much. —**sol′dier·ly,** *adj.*

soldering iron

soldier of fortune, a man who will serve in any army for money or for adventure.

sole (sōl), *n.* **1.** the bottom surface of the foot. **2.** the bottom surface of a shoe, sock, etc. —*v.* to fasten a sole to, as a shoe. —**soled,** *p.t. & p.p.*; **sol′ing,** *pr.p.*

sole (sōl), *adj.* **1.** without others; one and only [the *sole* owner of a store]. **2.** of or having to do with only one person or group; only [They are the *sole* inhabitants of the town.]

sole (sōl), *n.* a kind of flatfish used as food.

sol·e·cism (säl′ə siz'm), *n.* **1.** a mistake in writing or speaking ["I seen him" is a *solecism*.] **2.** a mistake in etiquette.

sole·ly (sōl′lē), *adv.* **1.** alone; without others [We are *solely* to blame.] **2.** only; merely [He reads *solely* for pleasure.]

sole (1 ft. long)

sol·emn (säl′əm), *adj.* **1.** serious; grave; very earnest [a *solemn* face; a solemn oath]. **2.** according to strict rules; formal [a *solemn* ceremony]. **3.** set apart for religious reasons; sacred [a *solemn* holy day]. **4.** dark in color; somber. —**sol'emn·ly,** *adv.*

so·lem·ni·ty (sə lem'nə tē), *n.* **1.** a solemn ceremony or ritual. **2.** solemn feeling or quality; seriousness. —**so·lem'ni·ties,** *pl.*

sol·em·nize (säl'əm nīz), *v.* **1.** to celebrate in a formal way, as a holy day. **2.** to carry out the rites of [to *solemnize* a marriage]. **3.** to make solemn. —**sol'em·nized,** *p.t. & p.p.;* **sol'em·niz·ing,** *pr.p.*

so·lic·it (sə lis'it), *v.* to ask or plead in a serious way [to *solicit* money for charity; to *solicit* friends for help]. —**so·lic'i·ta'tion,** *n.*

so·lic·i·tor (sə lis'ə tər), *n.* **1.** a person who tries to get customers for a business, money for a fund, etc. **2.** a lawyer for a city, State, etc. **3.** in England, any lawyer who is not a barrister.

so·lic·i·tous (sə lis'ə təs), *adj.* **1.** showing care, interest, or worry; concerned [Mother is *solicitous* about your safety.] **2.** anxious or eager [*solicitous* to get praise]. —**so·lic'i·tous·ly,** *adv.*

so·lic·i·tude (sə lis'ə tood *or* sə lis'ə tyood), *n.* care, worry, or concern.

sol·id (säl'id), *adj.* **1.** keeping its shape instead of flowing or spreading out like a liquid or gas; quite firm or hard [Ice is water in a *solid* form.] **2.** filled with matter throughout; not hollow [a *solid* block of wood]. **3.** that has length, width, and thickness; cubic [A prism is a *solid* figure.] **4.** strong, firm, sound, dependable, etc. [*solid* thinking; a *solid* building]. **5.** serious or deep [*solid* reading]. **6.** with no breaks, stops, or rests; continuous [a *solid* wall around the castle; two *solid* hours of work]. **7.** of one color, material, etc. throughout [a tray of *solid* silver]. **8.** strongly united [The President had the *solid* support of Congress.] —*n.* **1.** something that is solid, not a liquid or gas [Iron and glass are *solids*.] **2.** anything that has length, width, and thickness [A cube is a *solid*.] —**sol'id·ly,** *adv.*

sol·i·dar·i·ty (säl'ə dar'ə tē), *n.* the condition of being strongly united, as in action or feeling.

so·lid·i·fy (sə lid'ə fī), *v.* to make or become solid or firm [Butter *solidifies* as it cools.] —**so·lid'i·fied,** *p.t. & p.p.;* **so·lid'i·fy·ing,** *pr.p.* —**so·lid'i·fi·ca'tion,** *n.*

so·lid·i·ty (sə lid'ə tē), *n.* the condition of being solid; firmness, hardness, etc.

sol·id-state (säl'id stāt'), *adj.* having electronic devices, as transistors, that control electric current without heated filaments.

so·lil·o·quize (sə lil'ə kwīz), *v.* to talk to oneself; speak a soliloquy. —**so·lil'o·quized,** *p.t. & p.p.;* **so·lil'o·quiz·ing,** *pr.p.*

so·lil·o·quy (sə lil'ə kwē), *n.* **1.** the act of talking to oneself. **2.** a speech in a play in which a character tells his thoughts by talking aloud, as if to himself. —**so·lil'o·quies,** *pl.*

sol·i·taire (säl'ə ter), *n.* **1.** a card game played by one person. **2.** a diamond or other gem set by itself, as in a ring.

sol·i·tar·y (säl'ə ter'ē), *adj.* **1.** living or being alone; lonely [a *solitary* hermit; a *solitary* lighthouse]. **2.** single; only [a *solitary* example].

sol·i·tude (säl'ə tood *or* säl'ə tyood), *n.* the condition of being solitary, or alone; loneliness.

so·lo (sō'lō), *n.* a piece of music that is sung or played by one person. —*adj.* **1.** for or by one singer or one instrument. **2.** made or done by one person [a *solo* flight in an airplane]. —*v.* to fly an airplane alone, especially for the first time. —**so'los,** *pl.* —**so'loed,** *p.t. & p.p.;* **so'lo·ing,** *pr.p.* —**so'lo·ist,** *n.*

Sol·o·mon (säl'ə mən), *n.* a king of Israel in the 10th century B.C., famous for his wisdom.

So·lon (sō'lən), *n.* **1.** a lawgiver of ancient Athens, who lived from about 638 to about 559 B.C. **2.** a wise man; especially, a lawmaker.

sol·stice (säl'stis), *n.* the time of year when the sun reaches either the point farthest north of the equator (June 21 or 22) or the point farthest south (December 21 or 22). In the Northern Hemisphere, the first is the **summer solstice** and the second, the **winter solstice.**

sol·u·ble (säl'yoo b'l), *adj.* **1.** that can be dissolved in a liquid [Iodine is *soluble* in alcohol.] **2.** that can be solved or explained [a *soluble* problem]. —**sol'u·bil'i·ty,** *n.*

so·lu·tion (sə loo'shən), *n.* **1.** the solving of a problem. **2.** an answer or explanation [to find the *solution* to a mystery]. **3.** the dissolving of something in a liquid. **4.** a mixture formed in this way [Make a *solution* of sugar and vinegar.]

solve (sälv), *v.* to find the answer to; make clear; explain [to *solve* a problem in arithmetic]. —**solved,** *p.t. & p.p.;* **solv'ing,** *pr.p.*

sol·vent (säl'vənt), *adj.* **1.** able to pay all one's debts [a *solvent* businessman]. **2.** able to dissolve a substance. —*n.* a substance that can dissolve another [Turpentine is used as a *solvent* to clean paint from brushes.] —**sol'ven·cy,** *n.*

So·ma·li·a (sə mäl'i ə), *n.* a country on the eastern coast of Africa.

som·ber (säm'bər), *adj.* **1.** dark and gloomy or dull [*somber* shadows]. **2.** sad or serious [*somber* thoughts on a rainy day]. —**som'ber·ly,** *adv.*

som·bre (säm'bər), *adj.* British spelling of **somber.** —**som'bre·ly,** *adv.*

som·bre·ro (säm brer'ō), *n.* a large hat with a wide brim, worn in Spain, Spanish America, and the southwestern United States. —**som·bre'ros,** *pl.*

sombrero

some (sum), *adj.* **1.** being a certain one or ones not named or not known [*Some* boys were playing ball.] **2.** being a certain but not a definite number or amount [Have *some* candy.] **3.** about [*Some* thirty of us came to the meeting.] **4.** outstanding or remarkable: *used only in everyday talk* [It was *some* party.] —*pron.* a certain number or amount, but not all [*Some* of the milk was spilled. There are *some* who know.]

-some (səm), a suffix meaning "tending to" or "tending to be" [A *tiresome* story tends to tire the listener.]

-some (səm), a suffix meaning "group of" [A *threesome* is a group of three.]

some·bod·y (sum′bud ē *or* sum′bäd ē), *pron.* a certain person not known or named; someone [*Somebody* left the door open.] —*n.* a person who is important. —**some′bod·ies,** *pl.*

some·day (sum′dā), *adv.* at some future time.

some·how (sum′hou), *adv.* in a way not known or explained; by some means [*Somehow* the pilot managed to land the plane.]

some·one (sum′wun), *pron.* somebody.

som·er·sault (sum′ər sôlt), *n.* a stunt in which one turns the body completely over in the air, landing on the feet. —*v.* to do a somersault.

boy turning a somersault

some·thing (sum′thing), *n.* **1.** a certain thing not named or known [I have *something* to tell you. I'd like *something* to eat.] **2.** a thing not definitely known or understood [*Something* is wrong with my car.] **3.** an important person or thing. —*adv.* somewhat; a little [He looks *something* like me.]

some·time (sum′tīm), *adv.* **1.** at some future time [Come see us *sometime* soon.] **2.** at some time not known or named [I saw her *sometime* last week.] —*adj.* former [my *sometime* friend].

some·times (sum′tīmz), *adv.* once in a while; occasionally [*Sometimes* she sings for us.]

some·what (sum′hwut), *adv.* to some degree; a little [I'm *somewhat* late.] —*n.* a certain part, amount, or degree [He is *somewhat* of a fool.]

some·where (sum′hwer), *adv.* **1.** in, to, or at some place not known or named [They live *somewhere* near here.] **2.** at some unknown point or stage [He is *somewhere* in his eighties.]

som·nam·bu·lism (säm nam′byoo liz′m), *n.* the habit or act of walking in one's sleep. —**som·nam′bu·list,** *n.*

som·no·lent (säm′nə lənt), *adj.* **1.** ready to sleep; sleepy; drowsy. **2.** making one sleepy [a *somnolent* summer afternoon].

son (sun), *n.* **1.** a boy or man as he is related to a parent or to both parents. **2.** a boy or man thought of as being related to someone or something [*sons* of France]. —**the Son,** Jesus Christ.

so·nar (sō′när), *n.* a device that sends sound waves through water and picks them up after they strike some object and bounce back. It is used to locate submarines, find depths of oceans, etc.

so·na·ta (sə nä′tə), *n.* a piece of music for one or two instruments, usually divided into three or four movements with different rhythms.

song (sông), *n.* **1.** a piece of music for singing. **2.** the act of singing. **3.** a poem that is or can be set to music, as a ballad. **4.** a musical sound like singing [the *song* of a canary]. —**for a song,** for very little money; cheap.

song·bird (sông′bʉrd), *n.* a bird that makes sounds that are like music.

song·ster (sông′stər), *n.* **1.** a singer. **2.** a writer of songs or poems. **3.** a songbird. —**song·stress** (sông′stris), *n.fem.*

son·ic (sän′ik), *adj.* of or having to do with sound or the speed of sound.

son-in-law (sun′n lô), *n.* the husband of one's daughter. —**sons′-in-law,** *pl.*

son·net (sän′it), *n.* a poem of fourteen lines that rhyme in a certain pattern.

son·ny (sun′ē), *n.* a pet name or friendly name used in talking to a young boy.

so·no·rous (sə nôr′əs *or* sän′ər əs), *adj.* **1.** making loud, deep, or mellow sounds; resonant [the *sonorous* bass viol]. **2.** loud, deep, or mellow [his *sonorous* voice]. **3.** sounding important [*sonorous* language].

soon (soon), *adv.* **1.** in a short time; before much time has passed [Spring will *soon* be here.] **2.** fast or quickly [as *soon* as possible]. **3.** ahead of time; early [He left too *soon*.] **4.** in a willing way; readily [I would as *soon* go as stay.]

soot (soot), *n.* a black powder formed when some things burn. It is mostly carbon and makes smoke gray or black.

sooth (sooth), *n.* truth; fact: *no longer used* [Dost thou love her in *sooth*?]

soothe (sooth), *v.* **1.** to make quiet or calm by being gentle or friendly [She *soothed* the angry man with her kind words.] **2.** to take away some of the pain, sorrow, etc. of; ease [This lotion will *soothe* your sunburn.] —**soothed,** *p.t. & p.p.;* **sooth′ing,** *pr.p.* —**sooth′ing·ly,** *adv.*

sooth·say·er (sooth′sā′ər), *n.* a person who pretends to tell what is going to happen.

soot·y (soot′ē), *adj.* covered or dirty with soot. —**soot′i·er,** *compar.;* **soot′i·est,** *superl.*

sop (säp), *n.* **1.** a piece of food soaked in milk, soup, etc. **2.** something given to keep someone calm or satisfied. —*v.* **1.** to suck up or absorb [He used bread to *sop* up the gravy.] **2.** to make very wet; soak [His clothes were *sopped* through.] —**sopped,** *p.t. & p.p.;* **sop′ping,** *pr.p.*

soph·ist (säf′ist), *n.* a person whose reasons seem clever and correct but are really false.

so·phis·ti·cate (sə fis′tə kit), *n.* a sophisticated person.

so·phis·ti·cat·ed (sə fis′tə kāt′id), *adj.* **1.** not simple, natural, or innocent; wise in the ways of the world. **2.** very complicated and based on the latest ideas, techniques, etc. [*sophisticated* electronic machinery]. —**so·phis′ti·ca′tion,** *n.*

soph·is·try (säf′is trē), *n.* reasoning or an argument that seems clever and correct but is really false or misleading. —**soph′is·tries,** *pl.*

Soph·o·cles (säf′ə klēz), *n.* Greek writer of tragedies who lived from about 496 to 406 B.C.

soph·o·more (säf′ə môr), *n.* a student in the tenth grade or in the second year of college.

sop·py (säp'ē), *adj.* very wet; soaked. —**sop'·pi·er**, *compar.;* **sop'pi·est**, *superl.*

so·pra·no (sə pran'ō), *n.* **1.** the highest kind of singing voice of women, girls, or young boys. **2.** a singer with such a voice, or an instrument with a range like this. —*adj.* of or for a soprano. —**so·pra'nos**, *pl.*

sor·cer·er (sôr'sər ər), *n.* a person who works magic or sorcery, as in fairy tales; magician; wizard. —**sor'cer·ess**, *n.fem.*

sor·cer·y (sôr'sər ē), *n.* the supposed use of magical power by means of charms, spells, etc., usually for a bad or harmful purpose; witchcraft. —**sor'cer·ies**, *pl.*

sor·did (sôr'did), *adj.* **1.** dirty, filthy, disgusting, etc. [*sordid* slums]. **2.** low, mean, selfish, etc. [a *sordid* scheme]. —**sor'did·ly**, *adv.*

sore (sôr), *adj.* **1.** giving pain; aching; painful [a *sore* toe]. **2.** feeling pain, as from bruises [He is *sore* all over.] **3.** filled with grief or sorrow; sad [*sore* at heart]. **4.** causing sadness, misery, etc. [a *sore* task]. **5.** making one angry or irritated [Her son's failure is a *sore* point with her.] **6.** angry or irritated: *used only in everyday talk.* —*n.* a place on the body where tissue is injured, as by a cut, burn, boil, etc. —*adv.* greatly; very: *no longer used* [*sore* afraid]. —**sor'er**, *compar.;* **sor'est**, *superl.* —**sore'ness**, *n.*

sore·ly (sôr'lē), *adv.* greatly or strongly [Help is *sorely* needed.]

sor·ghum (sôr'gəm), *n.* **1.** a tall grass with sweet, juicy stalks, grown for grain, fodder, sirup, etc. **2.** a sirup made from its juice.

so·ror·i·ty (sə rôr'ə tē), *n.* a club of women or girls, especially a social club, as in a college. —**so·ror'i·ties**, *pl.*

sorghum

sor·rel (sôr'əl), *n.* a plant with sour, fleshy leaves used in salads.

sor·rel (sôr'əl), *n.* **1.** reddish brown. **2.** a reddish-brown horse, etc.

sor·row (sär'ō), *n.* **1.** a sad or troubled feeling; sadness; grief. **2.** a loss, death, trouble, etc. causing such a feeling [Her illness is a great *sorrow* to us.] —*v.* to feel or show sorrow.

sor·row·ful (sär'ō fəl), *adj.* feeling, showing, or causing sorrow; sad [a *sorrowful* face; a *sorrowful* duty]. —**sor'row·ful·ly**, *adv.*

sor·ry (sär'ē), *adj.* **1.** full of sorrow, pity, etc. or often just mild regret [We were *sorry* to leave.] **2.** causing sorrow or pity; pitiful [a *sorry* sight].

sort (sôrt), *n.* **1.** a group of things that are alike in some way; kind; class [various *sorts* of toys]. **2.** quality or type [phrases of a noble *sort*]. —*v.* to separate or arrange according to class or kind [*Sort* out the clothes that need mending.] —**of sorts** or **of a sort**, of a kind that is not very good. —**out of sorts**, not in a good humor or not feeling well: *used only in everyday talk.* —**sort of**, somewhat: *used only in everyday talk.*

sor·tie (sôr'tē), *n.* **1.** a sudden attack made from a place surrounded by enemy troops. **2.** one battle flight by one military airplane.

SOS (es'ō es'), a signal calling for help, used by ships at sea, aircraft, etc.

so-so (sō'sō), *adj. & adv.* neither too good nor too bad; fair or fairly well.

sot (sät), *n.* a person who is often drunk.

sou (sōō), *n.* a French coin no longer in use. It was equal to 1/20 of a franc.

sou·bri·quet (sōō'bri kā'), *n.* same as **so·briquet.**

souf·flé (sōō flā'), *n.* a baked food made light and fluffy by adding beaten egg whites before baking [a cheese *soufflé*].

sough (suf *or* sou), *n.* a soft sighing or rustling sound. —*v.* to make a sough.

sought (sôt), past tense and past participle of **seek.**

soul (sōl), *n.* **1.** the part of one's being that is thought of as the center of feeling, thinking, will, etc. separate from the body. In some religions, the soul is believed to go on after death. **2.** warmth and force of feeling or spirit [His painting has no *soul.*] **3.** the most important part, quality, or thing ["Brevity is the *soul* of wit."] **4.** something or someone that is a perfect example of some quality [He is the *soul* of kindness.] **5.** a person [Not a *soul* left the room.]

soul·ful (sōl'fəl), *adj.* full of or showing deep feeling [a *soulful* look].

soul·less (sōl'lis), *adj.* without tender feelings.

sound (sound), *n.* **1.** the form of energy that acts on the ears so that one can hear. Sound consists of waves of vibrations carried in the air, water, etc. [In air, *sound* travels at a speed of about 1100 feet per second.] **2.** anything that can be heard; noise, tone, etc. [the *sound* of bells]. **3.** any of the noises made in speaking [a vowel *sound*]. **4.** the distance within which something may be heard [within *sound* of his voice]. —*v.* **1.** to make a sound [His voice *sounds* hoarse.] **2.** to cause to sound [*Sound* your horn.] **3.** to seem; appear [The plan *sounds* all right.] **4.** to make known or announce [*Sound* the alarm.] **5.** to pronounce [He doesn't *sound* his r's.]

sound (sound), *adj.* **1.** in good condition; not damaged or rotted [*sound* timber]. **2.** normal and healthy [a *sound* mind in a *sound* body]. **3.** firm, safe, secure, etc. [He kept his money in a *sound* bank.] **4.** full of good sense; sensible; wise [a *sound* plan]. **5.** deep and not disturbed [a *sound* sleep]. **6.** thorough; complete [a *sound* defeat]. —*adv.* in a sound way; completely; deeply [*sound* asleep]. —**sound'ly**, *adv.* —**sound'ness**, *n.*

sound (sound), *n.* **1.** a channel of water connecting two large bodies of water or separating an island from the mainland. **2.** a long arm of the sea. **3.** a bladder filled with air in a fish.

sound (sound), *v.* **1.** to measure the depth of water, as by lowering a weight fastened to a line. **2.** to try to find out the opinions of [Let's *sound* him out on the subject.] **3.** to dive suddenly downward through water, as a whale.

sound·ing (soun/ding), *n.* **1.** the act of measuring the depth of water by lowering a weighted line. **2.** depth as measured in this way.

sound·less (sound/lis), *adj.* without sound; quiet; noiseless. —**sound/less·ly,** *adv.*

sound·proof (sound/proof), *adj.* that keeps sound from coming through [*soundproof* walls]. —*v.* to make soundproof.

soup (soop), *n.* a liquid food made by cooking meat, vegetables, etc. as in water or milk.

sour (sour), *adj.* **1.** having the sharp, acid taste of lemon juice, vinegar, etc. **2.** made acid or spoiled by fermenting [*sour* milk]. **3.** having much acid [*sour* soil]. **4.** disagreeable or unpleasant [a *sour* attitude; a *sour* task]. —*v.* to make or become sour. —**sour/ly,** *adv.* —**sour/-ness,** *n.*

source (sôrs), *n.* **1.** a spring or fountain that is the starting point of a stream. **2.** a thing or place from which something comes or is gotten [The sun is our *source* of energy. This book was the *source* of my information.]

souse (sous), *v.* **1.** to make or become soaking wet. **2.** to plunge or dip in a liquid. **3.** to soak or pickle in vinegar, brine, etc. —*n.* **1.** the act of sousing. **2.** liquid for pickling; brine. **3.** food that has been pickled, as pigs' feet. —**soused,** *p.t. & p.p.;* **sous/ing,** *pr.p.*

south (south), *n.* **1.** the direction to the left of a person facing the sunset. **2.** a place or region in or toward this direction. In the United States, **the South** means the part south of Pennsylvania, the Ohio River, and Missouri. **3.** *often* **South.,** the southern part of the earth, especially the antarctic regions. —*adj.* **1.** in, of, to, or toward the south [the *south* end of town]. **2.** from the south [a *south* wind]. **3.** **South,** that is the southern part of [*South* Korea]. —*adv.* in or toward the south [Go two blocks *south*.]

South Africa, a country in southern Africa. —**South African.**

South America, the southern continent in the Western Hemisphere. —**South American.**

South·amp·ton (sou thamp/tən), *n.* a seaport in southern England.

South Carolina, a State in the southeastern part of the United States: abbreviated **S.C.**

South Dakota, a State in the north central part of the United States: abbreviated **S. Dak.** or **S.D.**

south·east (south ēst/), *n.* **1.** the direction halfway between south and east. **2.** a place or region in or toward this direction. —*adj.* **1.** in, of, or toward the southeast [the *southeast* part of town]. **2.** from the southeast [a *southeast* wind]. —*adv.* in or toward the southeast [The town lies *southeast* of here.]

south·east·er (south ēs/tər), *n.* a storm or strong wind from the southeast.

south·east·er·ly (south ēs/tər lē), *adj. & adv.* **1.** in or toward the southeast. **2.** from the southeast.

south·east·ern (south ēs/tərn), *adj.* **1.** in, of, or toward the southeast [*southeastern* Iowa]. **2.** from the southeast [a *southeastern* wind].

south·er·ly (su*th*/ər lē), *adj. & adv.* **1.** in or toward the south. **2.** from the south.

south·ern (su*th*/ərn), *adj.* **1.** in, of, or toward the south [the *southern* sky]. **2.** from the south [a *southern* wind]. **3.** **Southern,** of the South.

South·ern·er (su*th*/ər nər), *n.* a person born or living in the South.

Southern Hemisphere, the half of the earth that is south of the equator.

south·ern·most (su*th*/ərn mōst), *adj.* farthest south.

Southern Yemen, a country in southern Arabia.

South Pole, the spot that is farthest south on the earth; southern end of the earth's axis.

South Sea Islands, the islands in the South Pacific. —**South Sea Islander.**

south·ward (south/wərd), *adv. & adj.* toward the south: also **south/wards,** *adv.* —*n.* a southward direction or place.

south·west (south west/), *n.* **1.** the direction halfway between south and west. **2.** a place or region in or toward this direction. —*adj.* **1.** in, of, or toward the southwest [the *southwest* corner]. **2.** from the southwest [a *southwest* wind]. —*adv.* in or toward the southwest [to sail *southwest*].

south·west·er (south wes/tər), *n.* **1.** a storm or strong wind from the southwest. **2.** a sou'wester.

south·west·er·ly (south wes/tər lē), *adj. & adv.* **1.** in or toward the southwest. **2.** from the southwest.

south·west·ern (south wes/tərn), *adj.* **1.** in, of, or toward the southwest. **2.** from the southwest [a *southwestern* wind].

sou·ve·nir (soo və nir/), *n.* an object kept to remind one of something; memento [He saves programs as *souvenirs* of plays he's seen.]

sou'·west·er or **sou·west·er** (sou wes/tər), *n.* a sailor's waterproof hat, with a broad brim in the back to protect the neck.

sov·er·eign (säv/rən *or* säv/ər 'n), *adj.* **1.** highest in power or rank; supreme [a *sovereign* prince]. **2.** not controlled by others; independent [Indonesia became a *sovereign* republic in 1949.] **3.** greater than all others; highest; chief [a problem of *sovereign* importance]. —*n.* **1.** a ruler; king, queen, emperor, etc. **2.** a British gold coin of earlier times, worth 20 shillings, or one pound.

sou'wester

sov·er·eign·ty (säv/rən tē *or* säv/ər 'n tē), *n.* **1.** the rank or power of a sovereign. **2.** the condition of having independent political power [to respect the *sovereignty* of other nations].

so·vi·et (sō′vi it), *n.* any of the councils, or groups of people, chosen to govern a certain area in the Soviet Union, ranging from the small soviets of villages and towns to the **Supreme Soviet,** the national congress. —*adj.* **Soviet,** of or having to do with the Soviet Union.

Soviet Union, a shorter name for **Union of Soviet Socialist Republics.**

sow (sou), *n.* a full-grown female pig.

sow (sō), *v.* **1.** to scatter or plant seed for growing [to *sow* wheat]. **2.** to plant seed in or on [*Sow* the lawn with clover.] **3.** to spread or scatter [to *sow* hate]. —**sowed,** *p.t.;* **sown** (sōn) or **sowed,** *p.p.;* **sow′ing,** *pr.p.* —**sow′er,** *n.*

sox (säks), *n.pl.* same as **socks** (stockings).

soy (soi), *n.* a sauce made from soybeans, used on fish, meat, etc.: also called **soy sauce.**

soy·bean (soi′bēn), *n.* **1.** the seed, or bean, of a plant of Asia, now grown throughout the world. The beans are ground into flour, pressed for oil, etc. **2.** the plant itself.

soybean plant

spa (spä), *n.* a mineral spring, or a place that has such a spring, to which people go for their health.

space (spās), *n.* **1.** the area that stretches in all directions, has no limits, and contains all things in the universe [The earth, the sun, all stars, etc. exist in *space.*] **2.** the distance or area between things or inside of something, especially as used for some purpose; room [a closet with much *space;* parking *space* for cars]. **3.** a length of time; period [We visited there for the *space* of a week.] **4.** the area outside of the air around the earth: *its full name is* **outer space.** —*v.* to arrange with spaces in between [The trees are evenly *spaced.*] —**spaced,** *p.t. & p.p.;* **spac′ing,** *pr.p.*

space·craft (spās′kraft), *n. sing. & pl.* any spaceship or satellite for exploring or traveling in outer space.

space·ship (spās′ship), *n.* a vehicle for travel in outer space: its movement is controlled by rockets.

spac·ing (spās′ing), *n.* **1.** the way that something is spaced. **2.** space or spaces.

spa·cious (spā′shəs), *adj.* having much space or room; very large; vast [a *spacious* hall]. —**spa′cious·ly,** *adv.* —**spa′cious·ness,** *n.*

spade (spād), *n.* a tool for digging, like a shovel but with a flat blade. —*v.* to dig or break up with a spade. —**spad′ed,** *p.t. & p.p.;* **spad′ing,** *pr.p.*

spade

spade (spād), *n.* **1.** the mark ♠, used on a black suit of playing cards. **2.** a card of this suit.

spa·ghet·ti (spə get′ē), *n.* long, thin strings of dried flour paste, cooked for food.

Spain (spān), *n.* a country on a large peninsula in southwestern Europe.

spake (spāk), an old past tense of **speak.**

span (span), *n.* **1.** the distance between the tip of the thumb and the tip of the little finger when the hand is fully spread, thought of as equal to 9 inches. **2.** the part of a bridge, beam, arch, etc. between two supports. **3.** a certain period of time [the *span* of a man's life]. **4.** a team of two animals used together. —*v.* **1.** to stretch or reach across [The bridge *spans* the river.] **2.** to measure with the outspread hand or hands. —**spanned,** *p.t. & p.p.;* **span′ning,** *pr.p.*

span·gle (spang′g'l), *n.* a small, shiny piece of metal used for decoration, as on cloth or on a bracelet. —*v.* to cover or decorate as with spangles [the Star-*Spangled* Banner]. —**span′gled,** *p.t. & p.p.;* **span′gling,** *pr.p.*

Span·iard (span′yərd), *n.* a person born or living in Spain.

span·iel (span′yəl), *n.* a dog with long silky hair, large drooping ears, and short legs.

Span·ish (span′ish), *adj.* of Spain, its people, etc. —*n.* **1.** the language of Spain and Spanish America. **2.** the people of Spain.

spaniel (18 in. high at shoulder)

Spanish America, those countries and islands of America, south of the United States, where Spanish is the main language.

Span·ish-A·mer·i·can (span′ish ə mer′ə kən), *adj.* **1.** of both Spain and America. **2.** of Spanish America or its people. —*n.* a person born or living in Spanish America, especially one with Spanish ancestors.

Spanish-American War, the war between the United States and Spain in 1898.

Spanish Main, **1.** in earlier times, the northern coast of South America. **2.** the Caribbean Sea.

spank (spangk), *v.* to slap on the buttocks as a way of punishing. —*n.* the act of spanking.

spank·ing (spangk′ing), *adj.* strong and brisk [a *spanking* breeze]. —*adv.* very; completely: *used only in everyday talk* [*spanking* new].

spar (spär), *n.* a strong, heavy pole for holding up the sails on a ship. Masts, yards, and booms are spars.

spar (spär), *v.* **1.** to box in a skillful and careful way. **2.** to exchange remarks, as in arguing. —**sparred,** *p.t. & p.p.;* **spar′ring,** *pr.p.*

spare (sper), *v.* **1.** to save or free from something [*Spare* your mother the trouble of going to the store.] **2.** to keep from using, or use with care [*Spare* no effort to save the sinking ship.] **3.** to

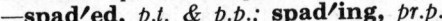

fat, āpe, cär, ten, ēven, hit, bīte, gō, hôrn, tōōl, book, up, fûr; get, joy, yet, chin, she, thin, *th*en; zh = s in pleasure; ′ as in able (ā′b'l); ə = a in ago, e in agent, i in sanity, o in confess, u in focus.

get along without; give up [I can't *spare* the money or the time.] **4.** to hold back from hurting or killing; show mercy to [Try to *spare* her feelings.] —*adj.* **1.** kept for use when needed; extra [a *spare* room; a *spare* tire]. **2.** not taken up by regular work or duties; free [*spare* time]. **3.** small in amount; meager; scanty [The explorers had to live on *spare* rations.] **4.** lean or thin; not fat [a *spare*, old horse]. —*n.* **1.** an extra part or thing. **2.** in bowling, the act of knocking down all ten pins with two rolls of the ball. —**spared,** *p.t.* & *p.p.*; **spar′ing,** *pr.p* —**spar′er,** *compar.*; **spar′est,** *superl.* —**spare′ly,** *adv.*

spare·rib (sper′rib), *n.* the thin end of a pork rib with most of the meat cut away.

spar·ing (sper′ing), *adj.* using or giving little; saving; frugal [He was *sparing* in his praise.] —**spar′ing·ly,** *adv.*

spark (spärk), *n.* **1.** a small bit of burning matter, as one thrown off by a fire. **2.** any flash of light like this [the *spark* of a firefly]. **3.** a bit or trace [to show a *spark* of enthusiasm]. **4.** the small flash of light that takes place when an electric current jumps across an open space, as in a spark plug. —*v.* **1.** to make or give off sparks. **2.** to stir into action [to *spark* one's interest].

spar·kle (spär′k'l), *v.* **1.** to give off sparks or flashes of light; glitter; glisten [A lake *sparkles* in sunlight.] **2.** to be lively and witty [talk that *sparkles*]. **3.** to bubble as ginger ale does. —*n.* **1.** a spark. **2.** glitter [the *sparkle* of sequins]. —**spar′kled,** *p.t.* & *p.p.*; **spar′kling,** *pr.p.*

spar·kler (spär′klər), *n.* a thing that sparkles, as a firework, gem, etc.

spark plug, a piece fitted into the cylinder of a gasoline engine to make sparks that explode the fuel mixture.

spar·row (spar′ō), *n.* a small gray and brown songbird with a short beak. The common sparrow seen on city streets is the **English sparrow.**

sparse (spärs), *adj.* thinly spread or scattered; not thick or crowded [a *sparse* crowd; *sparse* hair]. —**spar′si·ty,** *n.* —**sparse′ly,** *adv.*

Spar·ta (spär′tə), *n.* a rival city to Athens.

spark plug

Spar·tan (spär′t'n), *adj.* **1.** of Sparta. **2.** like the Spartans; brave, not complaining, not needing luxuries, etc. —*n.* **1.** a citizen of Sparta. **2.** a person who acts like a Spartan.

spasm (spaz′'m), *n.* **1.** any sudden tightening of a muscle or muscles, that cannot be controlled. **2.** any short, sudden burst of action or feeling [a *spasm* of coughing; a *spasm* of pity].

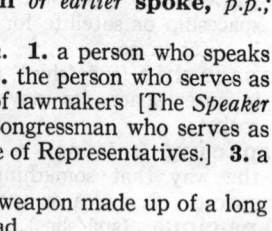
sparrow (6 in. long)

spas·mod·ic (spaz mäd′ik), *adj.* of or like spasms; sudden, sharp, and irregular [a *spasmodic* twitch, pain, etc.]. —**spas·mod′i·cal·ly,** *adv.*

spat (spat), *n.* a small quarrel or argument: *used only in everyday talk.*

spat (spat), *n.* a heavy cloth covering for the instep and ankle, like a short gaiter.

spat (spat), a past tense and past participle of **spit.**

spa·tial (spā′shəl), *adj.* **1.** of or in space. **2.** happening in space. —**spa′tial·ly,** *adv.*

spat·ter (spat′ər), *v.* **1.** to spot or splash with small drops [The hot fat *spattered* the stove.] **2.** to fall or strike in drops or in a shower [rain *spattering* on the sidewalk]. —*n.* **1.** the act of spattering. **2.** a mark made by spattering.

spat·u·la (spach′oo lə), *n.* a tool with a broad, flat blade that bends easily, used in various ways, as for spreading and mixing food, paint, etc.

spatula

spav·in (spav′in), *n.* a disease of horses that attacks the hock joint and causes lameness. —**spav′ined,** *adj.*

spawn (spôn), *n.* **1.** the eggs or newly hatched young of fish, clams, lobsters, frogs, etc. **2.** any offspring: *an unfriendly or sarcastic use.* —*v.* **1.** to produce eggs in large numbers as a fish does. **2.** to bring into being [This popular song *spawned* many imitations.]

speak (spēk), *v.* **1.** to say something with the voice; talk [I *spoke* to her over the telephone.] **2.** to tell or make known, as one's ideas or opinions [*Speak* your mind freely. He *speaks* well of Bob.] **3.** to make a speech [Who *speaks* first on the program?] **4.** to know how to talk in a certain language [Do you *speak* French?] —**so to speak,** that is to say; to put it in these words. —**speak for, 1.** to speak in behalf of. **2.** to ask for. —**speak out** or **speak up,** to speak loudly or openly. —**speak well for,** to show to be good, proper, etc. —**spoke** or *earlier* **spake,** *p.t.*; **spok′en** or *earlier* **spoke,** *p.p.*; **speak′ing,** *pr.p.*

speak·er (spēk′ər), *n.* **1.** a person who speaks or makes speeches. **2.** the person who serves as chairman of a group of lawmakers [The *Speaker* of the House is the Congressman who serves as chairman of the House of Representatives.] **3.** a loudspeaker.

spear (spir), *n.* **1.** a weapon made up of a long shaft with a sharp head. It is thrust or thrown by hand. **2.** a long blade or shoot, as of grass. —*v.* to pierce or stab as with a spear.

spear

spear·head (spir′hed), *n.* **1.** the head of a spear. **2.** the person, part, or group that leads, as in an attack. —*v.* to take the lead in.

spear·man (spir′mən), *n.* a fighting man armed with a spear. —**spear′men,** *pl.*

spear·mint (spir′mint), *n.* a common plant of the mint family, used for flavoring.

spe·cial (spesh′əl), *adj.* **1.** not like others; different; distinctive [She has a *special* recipe for cherry pie.] **2.** unusual; extraordinary [Your idea has *special* merit.] **3.** more than others; chief; main [her *special* friend]. **4.** of or for a particular use, purpose, or occasion [a *special* meeting of the club]. —*n.* a special person or thing, as a special train. —**spe′cial·ly,** *adv.*

special delivery, the delivery of mail quickly by a special messenger, for an extra fee.

spe·cial·ist (spesh′əl ist), *n.* a person who has made a special study of something or works in only one branch of some profession, etc. [Dr. Goode is a *specialist* in children's diseases.]

spe·cial·ize (spesh′ə līz), *v.* **1.** to make a special study of something or work only in a special branch of some profession, etc. [The doctor *specialized* in skin diseases.] **2.** to fit to a special use or purpose [The word "hound" has become *specialized* in meaning, though it once meant "any dog."] —**spe′cial·ized,** *p.t. & p.p.;* **spe′cial·iz·ing,** *pr.p.* —**spe′cial·i·za′tion,** *n.*

spe·cial·ty (spesh′əl tē), *n.* **1.** a special interest, study, work, etc. [Painting portraits is this artist's *specialty.*] **2.** a special article, product, etc. [Steaks are the *specialty* of this restaurant.] **3.** a special quality, feature, etc. —**spe′cial·ties,** *pl.*

spe·cie (spē′shē), *n.* money made of metal, not paper; coin [Dimes and quarters are *specie.*]

spe·cies (spē′shēz), *n.* **1.** a group of plants or animals that are alike in certain ways [The lion and the tiger are two different *species* of cat.] **2.** a kind or sort [a *species* of bravery]. —**the species,** the human race. —**spe′cies,** *pl.*

spe·cif·ic (spi sif′ik), *adj.* **1.** definite; exact [He made *specific* plans for the trip.] **2.** having to do with or like that of a particular thing [Streptomycin is a *specific* remedy for tuberculosis.] —*n.* a specific cure or remedy. —**spe·cif′i·cal·ly,** *adv.*

spec·i·fi·ca·tion (spes′ə fi kā′shən), *n.* **1.** the act of specifying. **2.** something specified; a specific item. **3.** *usually* **specifications,** *pl.* a statement or a description of all the necessary details, as of sizes, materials, etc. [the *specifications* for a new building].

specific gravity, the weight of a given volume of a substance compared with the weight of an equal volume of another substance used as a standard. Water is the standard for liquids and solids; air or hydrogen is the standard for gases [The *specific gravity* of silver is 10.5, which means it weighs 10.5 times as much as water.]

spec·i·fy (spes′ə fī), *v.* **1.** to mention or tell in detail; state definitely [He *specified* the time and place for the meeting.] **2.** to call for specifically [The architect *specified* hardwood floors for the house.] —**spec′i·fied,** *p.t. & p.p.;* **spec′i·fy·ing,** *pr.p.*

spec·i·men (spes′ə mən), *n.* a part of a whole, or one thing of a group, used as a sample of the rest [I need a *specimen* of his handwriting.]

spe·cious (spē′shəs), *adj.* seeming to be good, correct, etc. without really being so [His *specious* reasoning fooled us for a while.]

speck (spek), *n.* **1.** a small spot or mark [A few *specks* of paint got on the rug.] **2.** a very small bit; particle [not a *speck* of food in the house]. —*v.* to mark with specks; spot.

speck·le (spek′'l), *n.* a small mark; speck. —*v.* to mark with speckles [The walls are white *speckled* with red.] —**speck′led,** *p.t. & p.p.;* **speck′ling,** *pr.p.*

spec·ta·cle (spek′tə k'l), *n.* **1.** something to look at, especially an unusual sight or a grand public show [The fireworks display was quite a *spectacle.*] **2.** **spectacles,** *pl.* a pair of eyeglasses: *no longer much used.*

spec·tac·u·lar (spek tak′yoo lər), *adj.* of or like a spectacle; showy; striking [a *spectacular* display of roses]. —**spec·tac′u·lar·ly,** *adv.*

spec·ta·tor (spek′tā tər), *n.* a person who watches something without taking part; onlooker [*spectators* at a dance].

spec·ter (spek′tər), *n.* a ghost or phantom.

spec·tral (spek′trəl), *adj.* **1.** of or like a specter; ghostly. **2.** of or caused by a spectrum [*spectral* colors].

spec·tre (spek′tər), *n.* specter: *British spelling.*

spec·tro·scope (spek′trə skōp), *n.* an instrument for breaking up light into the colors of a spectrum so that they can be studied.

spec·trum (spek′trəm), *n.* a series of colored bands formed when light is broken up by being passed through a prism or in some other way. All the colors of the spectrum are found in a rainbow, ranging from red to violet. —**spec·tra** (spek′trə) or **spec′trums,** *pl.*

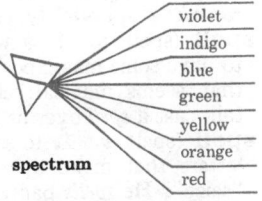

spectrum
violet
indigo
blue
green
yellow
orange
red

spec·u·late (spek′yoo lāt), *v.* **1.** to think about or make guesses; ponder; meditate [Scientists have *speculated* on the kinds of life there may be on Mars.] **2.** to make risky business deals with the hope of making large profits. —**spec′u·lat·ed,** *p.t. & p.p.;* **spec′u·lat·ing,** *pr.p.* —**spec′u·la′tion,** *n.* —**spec′u·la′tor,** *n.*

spec·u·la·tive (spek′yoo lā′tiv *or* spek′yoo lə tiv), *adj.* **1.** of, like, or taking part in speculation. **2.** having to do with theory only; not practical.

sped (sped), a past tense and past participle of **speed.**

speech (spēch), *n.* **1.** the act or way of speaking [We knew from his *speech* that he was British.] **2.** the power to speak [to lose one's *speech*]. **3.** something spoken; remark, utterance, etc.

fat,   āpe,   cär,   ten,   ēven,   hit,   bīte,   gō,   hôrn,   tool,   book,   up,   fûr;
get,   joy,   yet,   chin,   she,   thin,   *then*;   zh = s in pleasure;   ′ as in able (ā′b'l);
ə = a in ago,   e in agent,   i in sanity,   o in confess,   u in focus.

4. a talk given in public [political *speeches* on the radio]. **5.** the language of a certain people.

speech·less (spēch′lis), *adj.* **1.** not able to speak because of injury, shock, etc. [*speechless* with rage]. **2.** that cannot be put into words [*speechless* terror].

speed (spēd), *n.* **1.** fast motion; swiftness. **2.** rate of motion; velocity [a *speed* of 10 miles per hour]. **3.** an arrangement of gears for the drive of an engine [a truck with five forward *speeds*]. **4.** luck; success: *now seldom used* [He wished us good *speed*.] —*v.* **1.** to go or move fast or too fast [The arrow *sped* to its mark. He was arrested for *speeding*.] **2.** to make go or move fast [He *sped* the letter on its way.] **3.** to help to succeed; further; aid [Your gifts will *speed* the building program.] **4.** to wish good luck to [to *speed* the parting guest]. —**speed up,** to go or make go faster. —**sped** or **speed′ed,** *p.t. & p.p.;* **speed′ing,** *pr.p.*

speed·boat (spēd′bōt), *n.* a fast motorboat.

speed·er (spēd′ər), *n.* one who speeds, especially a person who drives a car, etc. faster than is safe or lawful.

speed·om·e·ter (spi däm′ə tər), *n.* a device in a car, etc. to show how fast it is going.

speed-up (spēd′up′), *n.* an increase in speed, as in the rate of work.

speed·way (spēd′wā), *n.* a track for racing cars.

speed·well (spēd′wel), *n.* a plant with tight clusters of white, blue, or violet flowers.

speed·y (spēd′ē), *adj.* **1.** fast; swift [*speedy* runners]. **2.** without delay; prompt [a *speedy* reply]. —**speed′i·er,** *compar.;* **speed′i·est,** *superl.* —**speed′i·ly,** *adv.* —**speed′i·ness,** *n.*

spell (spel), *n.* **1.** a word or words supposed to have some magic power. **2.** power or control that seems magical; charm; fascination [His talk cast a *spell* over us.]

spell (spel), *v.* **1.** to say or write in order the letters that make up a word [Can you *spell* "seize"? He *spells* badly.] **2.** to make up; form [What word do these letters *spell*?] **3.** to mean; signify [Hard work *spells* success.] —**spell out,** to read or make out with difficulty. —**spelled** or **spelt,** *p.t. & p.p.;* **spell′ing,** *pr.p.*

spell (spel), *v.* to work in place of another for a time; relieve [I'll *spell* you at mowing the lawn.] —*n.* **1.** a period of time during which something is done or happens [a *spell* of sickness; a hot *spell*]. **2.** a turn of working in place of another. —**spelled,** *p.t. & p.p.;* **spell′ing,** *pr.p.*

spell·bind·er (spel′bīn′dər), *n.* a speaker who holds his audience spellbound.

spell·bound (spel′bound), *adj.* held fast as if by a spell; fascinated; enchanted.

spell·er (spel′ər), *n.* **1.** a person who spells. **2.** a book with exercises to teach spelling.

spell·ing (spel′ing), *n.* **1.** the act of telling or writing the letters of a word in proper order. **2.** the way in which a word is spelled.

spelling bee, a contest in spelling words.

spelt (spelt), a past tense and past participle of **spell** (to say or write a word).

spend (spend), *v.* **1.** to pay out or give up, as money, time, or effort [He *spent* $10 for groceries. Try to *spend* some time with Grandma.] **2.** to pass [He *spent* the summer at the beach.] **3.** to use up; exhaust [His fury was *spent*.] —**spent,** *p.t. & p.p.;* **spend′ing,** *pr.p.* —**spend′er,** *n.*

spend·thrift (spend′thrift), *n.* a person who wastes money by spending carelessly; squanderer. —*adj.* wasteful with money; extravagant.

spent (spent), past tense and past participle of **spend.** —*adj.* tired out; used up.

sperm (spûrm), *n.* **1.** the fluid from the male sex glands that contains the cells for fertilizing the eggs of the female. **2.** any of these cells.

sperm whale, a large, toothed whale of warm seas, valuable for its oil.

spew (spyōō), *v.* to throw up from or as if from the mouth; vomit. —*n.* something spewed.

sp. gr., abbreviation for **specific gravity.**

sperm whale (60 ft. long)

sphere (sfir), *n.* **1.** any round object whose curved surface is the same distance from the center at all points; ball; globe. **2.** anything in the heavens shaped more or less like this, as a star, planet, moon, etc. **3.** the heavens seen as a dome or pictured as a globe. **4.** the place or range of action or being [our country's *sphere* of influence]. **5.** place in society; walk of life [He moves in a different *sphere* now that he's rich.]

spher·i·cal (sfer′i k'l), *adj.* of or shaped like a sphere; globular. —**spher′i·cal·ly,** *adv.*

sphe·roid (sfir′oid), *n.* an object shaped more or less like a sphere.

sphinx (sfingks), *n.* **1.** any ancient Egyptian statue having a lion's body and the head of a man, ram, or hawk [The famous *Sphinx* near Cairo, Egypt, has the head of a man.] **2.** a monster of Greek myths that asked riddles. It had a lion's body with wings, and a woman's head. **3.** a person who is hard to know or understand.

sphinx

spice (spīs), *n.* **1.** any of certain substances used to give a special flavor or smell to food [Cinnamon, nutmeg, and pepper are *spices*.] **2.** an interesting touch or detail [the humor that added *spice* to his talk]. —*v.* **1.** to season with spice. **2.** to add interest to. —**spiced,** *p.t. & p.p.;* **spic′ing,** *pr.p.*

Spice Islands, same as **Molucca Islands.**

spick-and-span (spik′'n span′), *adj.* **1.** new or fresh. **2.** neat and clean.

spic·y (spī′sē), *adj.* **1.** seasoned with spice or spices. **2.** having the flavor or smell of spices [a *spicy* flower]. **3.** interesting; lively [a *spicy* bit of gossip]. —**spic′i·er,** *compar.;* **spic′i·est,** *superl.* —**spic′i·ness,** *n.*

spi·der (spī'dər), *n.* **1.** a small animal with eight legs and a body made up of two parts. The back part has organs that spin silk threads into webs to trap insects. **2.** a frying pan, originally one with legs. —**spi'der·y,** *adj.*

spider (½ in. long)

spied (spīd), past tense and past participle of **spy.**

spies (spīz), *n.* plural of **spy.**

spig·ot (spig'ət), *n.* **1.** a plug used to stop up the hole in a cask. **2.** a faucet.

spike (spīk), *n.* **1.** a pointed piece of metal, etc., as any of the sharp pieces along the top of an iron fence or on the soles of shoes used in certain sports. **2.** a large, strong nail. —*v.* **1.** to fasten a spike or spikes to. **2.** to pierce or hurt with a spike or spikes. **3.** to stop or block, as a scheme. —**spiked,** *p.t.* & *p.p.;* **spik'ing,** *pr.p.* —**spik'y,** *adj.*

spike (spīk), *n.* **1.** a long cluster of flowers attached right to the stalk. **2.** an ear of grain.

spike·nard (spīk'närd), *n.* an ointment with a sweet smell, used in ancient times.

spill (spil), *v.* **1.** to let flow over or run out [Who *spilled* water on the floor? Try not to *spill* any sugar.] **2.** to flow over or run out [Tears *spilled* from her eyes.] **3.** to shed, as blood. **4.** to make fall; throw off [My horse *spilled* me.] **5.** to make known, as a secret: *used only in everyday talk.* —*n.* the condition of being spilled; a fall. —**spilled** or **spilt,** *p.t.* & *p.p.;* **spill'ing,** *pr.p.*

spike of flowers

spill (spil), *n.* a splinter of wood, thin roll of paper, etc. used to light a candle, pipe, etc.

spill·way (spil'wā), *n.* a channel to carry off an overflow of water, as from a dam.

spin (spin), *v.* **1.** to draw out the fibers of and twist into thread [to *spin* cotton, wool, flax, etc.]. **2.** to make in this way [to *spin* yarn]. **3.** to make from a thread given out by the body [Spiders *spin* webs.] **4.** to tell slowly, with many details [to *spin* out a story]. **5.** to whirl around swiftly [The earth *spins* in space. *Spin* the wheel.] **6.** to seem to be whirling [My head is *spinning.*] **7.** to move along swiftly and smoothly [Cars *spun* past us.] —*n.* **1.** a whirling movement. **2.** a fast ride or drive, as in a car. —**spun,** *p.t.* & *p.p.;* **spin'ning,** *pr.p.* —**spin'ner,** *n.*

spin·ach (spin'ich), *n.* a vegetable whose large, dark-green leaves are usually cooked before they are eaten.

spi·nal (spī'n'l), *adj.* of the spine.

spinal column, the long row of connected bones that form the backbone; spine.

spinal cord, the thick cord of nerve tissue inside the spinal column.

spin·dle (spin'd'l), *n.* **1.** a slender rod used to twist and hold the thread in spinning. **2.** something long and slender like a spindle. **3.** a rod or shaft that turns, or on which something turns, as an axle. —*v.* to grow long and thin, as a stalk or stem. —**spin'dled,** *p.t.* & *p.p.;* **spin'dling,** *pr.p.*

spinal column

spin·dle·legs (spin'd'l legz), *n.pl.* thin legs. —**spin'dle·legged,** *adj.*

spin·dling (spin'dling), *adj.* long and thin: also **spin·dly** (spin'dlē).

spin·drift (spin'drift), *n.* spray blown up from a rough sea.

spine (spīn), *n.* **1.** a thin, sharp, stiff part that sticks out on certain plants and animals, as the cactus or porcupine; thorn or quill. **2.** the backbone; spinal column. **3.** anything thought of as like a backbone, as the back of a book.

spine·less (spīn'lis), *adj.* **1.** having no backbone. **2.** having no courage or will power; weak. **3.** having no spines or thorns.

spin·et (spin'it), *n.* **1.** a type of small harpsichord. **2.** a short upright piano.

spin·na·ker (spin'ə kər), *n.* a large, extra sail shaped like a triangle, used on racing yachts.

spin·ner·et (spin'ər et), *n.* the organ in spiders, caterpillars, etc. with which they spin threads.

spinning wheel, a spinning machine with one spindle that is turned by a large wheel.

spin·ster (spin'stər), *n.* an unmarried woman, especially an older one; old maid.

spin·y (spīn'ē), *adj.* **1.** covered with spines or thorns. **2.** shaped like a spine. —**spin'i·er,** *compar.;* **spin'i·est,** *superl.*

spinning wheel

spi·ra·cle (spī'rə k'l), *n.* an opening for breathing, as on the sides of an insect's body or on top of a whale's head.

spi·ral (spī'rəl), *adj.* circling around a center in a flat or rising curve that keeps growing larger or smaller, as the thread of a screw, or that stays the same, as the thread of a bolt. —*n.* a spiral curve or coil [The mainspring of a watch is a *spiral.*] —*v.* to move in or form into a

spirals

fat, āpe, cär, ten, ēven, hit, bīte, gō, hôrn, tōol, book, up, fûr;
get, joy, yet, chin, she, thin, *th*en; zh = s in pleasure; ' as in able (ā'b'l);
ə = a in ago, e in agent, i in sanity, o in confess, u in focus.

spiral. —**spi′raled** or **spi′ralled,** *p.t. & p.p.;* **spi′ral·ing** or **spi′ral·ling,** *pr.p.* —**spi′-ral·ly,** *adv.*

spire (spīr), *n.* **1.** the tip of something that comes to a gradual point, as a mountain peak. **2.** anything that tapers to a point [the *spire* on a steeple].

…spire

spir·it (spir′it), *n.* **1.** the soul. **2.** a being that is not of this world, as a ghost, angel, fairy, etc. **3.** a person [He is a noble *spirit.*] **4.** *often* **spirits,** *pl.* state of mind; mood [He is in good *spirits.*] **5.** vigor, courage, liveliness, etc. [He answered with *spirit.*] **6.** enthusiasm and loyalty [school *spirit*]. **7.** the true meaning [He follows the *spirit* if not the letter of the law.] **8.** the main principle, quality, or influence [the *spirit* of the Western frontier]. **9. spirits,** *pl.* strong alcoholic liquor; also, a solution in alcohol, as of camphor. —*v.* to carry away secretly and swiftly [The fox *spirited* off two chickens.] —*adj.* **1.** of spirits or spiritualism [the *spirit* world]. **2.** that burns alcohol [a *spirit* lamp]. —**out of spirits,** sad; unhappy. —**spir′it·less,** *adj.*

spir·it·ed (spir′i tid), *adj.* **1.** having a certain nature or mood: *used in words formed with a hyphen* [high-*spirited*]. **2.** full of spirit; lively [a *spirited* argument; *spirited* horses].

spir·it·u·al (spir′i chōō əl), *adj.* **1.** of the spirit or soul as apart from the body or material things. **2.** having to do with religion or the church; sacred. —*n.* a religious folk song of the kind created by Negro Americans. —**spir·it·u·al·i·ty** (spir′i chōō al′ə tē), *n.* —**spir′it·u·al·ly,** *adv.*

spir·it·u·al·ism (spir′i chōō əl iz′m), *n.* **1.** the belief that the spirits of the dead can send messages to the living, especially with the help of a person called a "medium." **2.** the quality of being spiritual. —**spir′i·tu·al·ist,** *n.* —**spir′-it·u·al·is′tic,** *adj.*

spir·it·u·ous (spir′i chōō əs), *adj.* of, like, or containing distilled alcohol.

spirt (spurt), *n. & v.* same as **spurt.**

spit (spit), *n.* **1.** a thin, pointed rod on which meat is fixed for roasting over a fire. **2.** a narrow point of land stretching out into a body of water. —*v.* to fix on a spit; pierce. —**spit′ted,** *p.t. & p.p.;* **spit′ting,** *pr.p.*

spit (spit), *v.* **1.** to force out saliva or other matter from the mouth. **2.** to send out with sudden force [He *spat* out an oath. The radiator is *spitting* steam.] **3.** to make an angry, hissing noise, as a cat. —*n.* **1.** the act of spitting. **2.** saliva. —**spit and image** or **spitting image,** an exact likeness: *used only in everyday talk.* —**spat** or **spit,** *p.t. & p.p.;* **spit′ting,** *pr.p.*

spite (spīt), *n.* a mean feeling toward another that makes one want to hurt or annoy him; ill will; malice. —*v.* to hurt or annoy out of spite

[He built a high fence to *spite* his neighbors.] —**in spite of,** regardless of. —**spit′ed,** *p.t. & p.p.;* **spit′ing,** *pr.p.* —**spite′ful,** *adj.*

spit·fire (spit′fir), *n.* a person, especially a woman or girl, who has a quick temper.

spit·tle (spit′'l), *n.* spit; saliva.

spit·toon (spi tōōn′), *n.* a container to spit into.

splash (splash), *v.* **1.** to make a liquid scatter and fall in drops [to *splash* water or mud about]. **2.** to dash a liquid on, so as to wet or soil [The car *splashed* her dress.] **3.** to move, fall, or hit with a splash [He *splashed* through the swamp.] —*n.* **1.** the act or sound of splashing. **2.** water, mud, etc. splashed. **3.** a spot or mark made as if by splashing. —**make a splash,** to get much attention: *only in everyday talk.* —**splash′y,** *adj.*

splash·down (splash′doun), *n.* the landing of a spacecraft on water.

splat·ter (splat′ər), *n. & v.* spatter; splash.

splay (splā), *n.* a sloping surface or angle. —*adj.* flat and spreading out [*splay* feet]. —*v.* **1.** to spread outward. **2.** to make sloping.

spleen (splēn), *n.* **1.** an organ of the body, near the stomach, having something to do with the way the blood is made up. It was once thought of as the cause of bad temper and mean feelings. **2.** bad temper; spite; anger.

splen·did (splen′did), *adj.* **1.** very bright, brilliant, showy, magnificent, etc. [a *splendid* display; a *splendid* gown]. **2.** deserving high praise; glorious; grand [his *splendid* courage]. **3.** very good; excellent; fine: *used only in everyday talk* [a *splendid* trip]. —**splen′did·ly,** *adv.*

splen·dor (splen′dər), *n.* **1.** great brightness; brilliance [the *splendor* of a diamond]. **2.** glory or magnificence [the *splendor* of his reputation]. The usual British spelling is **splendour.**

sple·net·ic (spli net′ik), *adj.* easily made angry; bad-tempered; irritable; spiteful.

splice (splīs), *v.* **1.** to join ropes or cables by weaving together untwisted strands at the ends. **2.** to join pieces of wood by overlapping and fastening the ends. —*n.* the act or place of splicing. —**spliced,** *p.t. & p.p.;* **splic′ing,** *pr.p.*

…splice

splint (splint), *n.* **1.** a thin, stiff piece of wood or metal set along a broken bone to hold the parts in place. **2.** any of the thin strips of wood or cane used to weave baskets, chair seats, etc.

splin·ter (splin′tər), *v.* to break or split into thin, sharp pieces [Soft pine *splinters* easily.] —*n.* a thin, sharp piece of wood, bone, etc. broken off. —*adj.* describing a group that separates from a main group because of its different ideas.

split (split), *v.* **1.** to separate or divide along the length into two or more parts [to *split* a wiener bun]. **2.** to break apart by force; burst [The board *split* when I hammered in the nail.] **3.** to divide into parts or share [We *split* the cost of our trip.] —*n.* **1.** the act of splitting. **2.** a break, crack, or tear [a *split* in the seam of her dress]. **3.** a division in a group [The argument caused a *split* in our club.] **4.** *often* **splits,** *pl.* an acrobatic act in which the legs are spread flat on the floor in a straight line. —*adj.* broken into parts; divided. —**split,** *p.t. & p.p.;* **split'ting,** *pr.p.*

split·ting (split'ing), *adj.* very painful [a *splitting* headache].

splotch (spläch), *n.* a spot or stain. —*v.* to make a splotch on. —**splotch'y,** *adj.*

splurge (splŭrj), *v.* to spend much money or effort on something, often just to show off [to *splurge* on a big wedding]. —*n.* the act of splurging. *This word is used only in everyday talk.* —**splurged,** *p.t. & p.p.;* **splurg'ing,** *pr.p.*

splut·ter (splut'ər), *v.* **1.** to make hissing or spitting sounds [He fell into the pool and came up *spluttering*.] **2.** to talk in a fast, confused way, as when angry or embarrassed [He *spluttered* out an excuse.] —*n.* the act of spluttering.

spoil (spoil), *v.* **1.** to make or become useless, worthless, rotten, etc.; damage; ruin [Ink stains *spoiled* the paper. Illness *spoiled* his attendance record. Meat *spoils* fast in warm weather.] **2.** to cause a person to ask for or expect too much by giving in to all his wishes [to *spoil* a child]. —*n. usually* **spoils,** *pl.* **1.** goods taken by force in war; loot; booty. **2.** jobs or offices to which the political party that wins can appoint people. —**spoiled** or **spoilt** (spoilt), *p.t. & p.p.;* **spoil'ing,** *pr.p.* —**spoil'er,** *n.*

Spo·kane (spō kan'), *n.* a city in eastern Washington.

spoke (spōk), *n.* any of the braces reaching from the hub of a wheel to the rim.

spoke (spōk), past tense of **speak.**

spo·ken (spō'kən), past participle of **speak.** —*adj.* **1.** said aloud; oral [a *spoken* order]. **2.** speaking or said in a certain kind of voice [a soft-*spoken* man].

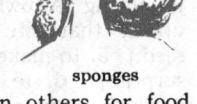
spokes

spokes·man (spōks'mən), *n.* a person who speaks for another or for a group. —**spokes'men,** *pl.*

sponge (spunj), *n.* **1.** a simple animal that lives in a mass with other such animals in warm seas. **2.** the light, elastic skeleton of such a mass of animals, that is full of holes and can soak up much water. Sponges are used for washing, bathing, etc. **3.** any artificial substance like this, as of plastic or rubber, used in the same way. —*v.* **1.** to wipe, clean, make wet, or soak up as with a sponge [to *sponge* up gravy with a crust of bread]. **2.** to depend on others for food,

sponges

money, etc. although able to support oneself: *used only in everyday talk.* —**sponged,** *p.t. & p.p.;* **spong'ing,** *pr.p.* —**spong'er,** *n.*

sponge bath, a bath taken by using a wet sponge or cloth without getting into water.

sponge·cake (spunj'kāk), *n.* a soft, light cake made with flour, eggs, sugar, etc., but no shortening: also **sponge cake.**

spon·gy (spun'jē), *adj.* light, elastic, full of holes, etc., like a sponge. —**spon'gi·er,** *compar.;* **spon'gi·est,** *superl.*

spon·sor (spän'sər), *n.* **1.** a person who agrees to be responsible for another person, as in paying his expenses. **2.** a person or business that pays the cost of a radio or television program on which it advertises something. **3.** a godparent. —*v.* to be a sponsor for. —**spon'sor·ship,** *n.*

spon·ta·ne·i·ty (spän'tə nē'ə tē), *n.* the condition of being spontaneous.

spon·ta·ne·ous (spän tā'ni əs), *adj.* **1.** acting or done in a free, natural way, without effort or much thought [We broke into a *spontaneous* song.] **2.** caused or brought about by its own force, without outside help [Chemical changes in the oily rags caused fire by *spontaneous* combustion.] —**spon·ta'ne·ous·ly,** *adv.*

spoof (spoof), *n. & v.* trick; joke: *a slang word.*

spook (spook), *n.* a ghost: *used only in everyday talk.*

spook·y (spook'ē), *adj.* of, like, or suggesting a ghost or ghosts; weird; eerie: *used only in everyday talk* [a *spooky* old house]. —**spook'i·er,** *compar.;* **spook'i·est,** *superl.*

spool (spool), *n.* a small roller on which thread, wire, etc. is wound.

spoon (spoon), *n.* a tool made up of a small, shallow bowl with a handle, used for eating or stirring food and drink. —*v.* to take up with a spoon.

spoon·bill (spoon'bil), *n.* a wading bird with a flat bill shaped like a spoon at the tip.

spool

spoon·ful (spoon'fool), *n.* the amount that a spoon will hold. —**spoon'-fuls,** *pl.*

spoor (spoor), *n.* the track, trail, or scent of a wild animal.

spo·rad·ic (spô rad'ik), *adj.* happening from time to time; not regular [*sporadic* gunfire]. —**spo·rad'i·cal·ly,** *adv.*

spore (spôr), *n.* a tiny cell produced by mosses, ferns, some one-celled animals, etc., that can grow into a new plant or animal.

spoonbill
(32 in. long)

sport (spôrt), *n.* **1.** active play, a game, etc. taken up for exercise or pleasure and, sometimes, as a profession [Football, golf, bowling, swimming, etc. are *sports*.] **2.** fun; play [It was great *sport* to make a snow man.] **3.** a person as regards his sense of fun and fair play: *used* *only in everyday talk* [Bill was a good *sport* about giving up his turn.] **4.** a person who is gay, lively, generous, willing to take chances, etc.: *used only in everyday talk.* **5.** a plant or animal different from the normal type [A white robin is a *sport*.] —*v.* **1.** to play or have fun [to *sport* on a beach]. **2.** to wear or display [to *sport* a new tie]. —*adj. also* **sports,** for play, relaxing, etc. [Sweaters and shorts are *sports* clothes.] —**in sport** or **for sport,** in fun or jest. —**make sport of,** to make fun of; ridicule.

sport·ing (spôr′ting), *adj.* **1.** of, for, or enjoying sports. **2.** like a sportsman; fair. **3.** bringing risk [a *sporting* chance].

spor·tive (spôr′tiv), *adj.* playful.

sports·man (spôrts′mən), *n.* **1.** a man who takes part or is interested in sports. **2.** a person who plays fair and does not complain when he loses or boast when he wins. —**sports′men,** *pl.* —**sports′man·like,** *adj.* —**sports′man·ship,** *n.*

spot (spät), *n.* **1.** a small part that is different in color, feeling, etc. from the parts around it [a leopard's *spots;* a sore *spot* on the skin]. **2.** a stain, mark, blemish, etc. [an ink *spot;* a *spot* on one's reputation]. **3.** a place [a quiet *spot* in the country]. —*v.* **1.** to mark or become marked with spots. **2.** to place [Let's *spot* two sentries on the hill.] **3.** to see or recognize: *used only in everyday talk* [I can *spot* our house from here.] **4.** to give the advantage of: *used only in everyday talk* [Dan *spotted* Ed fifty feet and still won the race.] —*adj.* **1.** ready; on hand [*spot* cash]. **2.** made at random [a *spot* check]. —**hit the spot,** to be exactly as wanted: *used only in everyday talk.* —**on the spot, 1.** at the very place and time. **2.** *also* **in a spot,** in trouble: *slang in this meaning.* —**spot′ted,** *p.t. & p.p.;* **spot′ting,** *pr.p.* —**spot′less,** *adj.*

spot·light (spät′līt), *n.* **1.** a strong beam of light shone on a particular person or thing, as on a stage. **2.** a lamp used to throw such a beam. **3.** public notice [The President is always in the *spotlight.*]

spot·ty (spät′ē), *adj.* **1.** marked with spots; spotted. **2.** not regular, even, or steady; not uniform [His attendance has been *spotty.*]

spouse (spous *or* spouz), *n.* a husband or wife.

spout (spout), *n.* **1.** a pipe, tube, or lip by which a liquid pours, as from a container. **2.** a stream or jet of liquid [Water shot up from the fountain in a high *spout.*] —*v.* **1.** to shoot out with force [The well began to *spout* oil. Water *spouted* from the cracked hose.] **2.** to talk on and on in a loud, forceful way [He kept *spouting* poems he had learned as a youth.]

spout

sprain (sprān), *v.* to twist a muscle or ligament in a joint without putting the bones out of place [to *sprain* one's wrist]. —*n.* an injury caused by this.

sprang (sprang), a past tense of **spring.**

sprat (sprat), *n.* a small kind of herring.

sprawl (sprôl), *v.* **1.** to sit or lie with the arms and legs spread out in a relaxed or awkward way. **2.** to spread out in an awkward or uneven way [His handwriting *sprawls* across the page.] —*n.* a sprawling position [His first attempt to ice skate ended in a *sprawl.*]

boy sprawling

spray (sprā), *n.* **1.** a mist of tiny drops, as of water thrown off from a waterfall. **2.** a stream of such tiny drops, as from a spray gun. **3.** something like this [a *spray* of buckshot]. **4.** a spray gun. —*v.* **1.** to put something on in a spray [to *spray* a car with paint]. **2.** to shoot out in a spray [She *sprayed* perfume on herself.] —**spray′er,** *n.*

spray (sprā), *n.* a small branch of a tree or plant with leaves, flowers, etc. on it.

spray gun, a device that shoots out a spray of liquid, as of paint or of an insect poison.

spread (spred), *v.* **1.** to open out or stretch out, in space or time [*Spread* out the tablecloth. The eagle *spread* its wings. Our trip *spread* out over two weeks.] **2.** to lay or place so as to cover, be seen, etc. [He *spread* his paintings on the floor.] **3.** to lie or extend [A beautiful valley *spread* out before us.] **4.** to go, pass, scatter, etc. [The rumors *spread* quickly.] **5.** to make go, pass, etc. [Flies *spread* disease.] **6.** to put or cover in a thin layer [to *spread* bread with jelly]. **7.** to set the things for a meal on [to *spread* a table]. —*n.* **1.** the act of spreading. **2.** the amount or distance something can be spread [The *spread* of its wings is six feet.] **3.** a cloth cover, as for a table or bed. **4.** any soft substance, as jam or butter, that can be spread in a layer. **5.** a meal, especially one with many kinds of food: *used only in everyday talk.* —**spread′er,** *n.*

spree (sprē), *n.* a lively, noisy time, especially with much drinking of alcoholic liquor.

sprig (sprig), *n.* a little twig or branch, with leaves, flowers, etc. on it.

spright·ly (sprīt′lē), *adj.* gay; lively; full of energy. —**spright′li·er,** *compar.;* **spright′li·est,** *superl.* —**spright′li·ness,** *n.*

spring (spring), *v.* **1.** to move suddenly and quickly; leap; jump up [The cowboy *sprang* to his horse.] **2.** to snap back into position or shape, as a rubber band that is stretched and then let go. **3.** to make snap shut [to *spring* a trap]. **4.** to come into being [A town *sprang* up at that site. The plant *springs* from a seed.] **5.** to make known suddenly [to *spring* a surprise]. **6.** to make or become split, bent, cracked, warped, etc. [The door has *sprung.*] —*n.* **1.** the act of springing; jump or leap. **2.** a device, as a coil of wire, that returns to its original shape when pressure on it is released. Springs are used in beds and automobiles to take

types of spring

up shock, or in clocks, etc. to make them go. **3.** the ability to snap back into position or shape [This elastic belt has no *spring* left.] **4.** water flowing up from the ground. **5.** a source or beginning. **6.** the season when plants begin to grow, between winter and summer. —*adj.* **1.** of the season spring [*spring* flowers]. **2.** having springs [a *spring* mattress]. **3.** coming from a spring [*spring* water]. —**spring a leak,** to begin to leak suddenly. —**sprang** or **sprung,** *p.t.;* **sprung,** *p.p.;* **spring'ing,** *pr.p.*

spring·board (spring'bôrd), *n.* a board that gives a springing motion to someone jumping from it, as a diving board.

spring·bok (spring'bäk), *n.* a South African gazelle that can jump high in the air. —**spring'bok** or **spring'boks,** *pl.*

Spring·field (spring'fēld), *n.* **1.** a city in Massachusetts. **2.** the capital of Illinois.

spring·time (spring'tīm) or **spring·tide** (spring'-tīd), *n.* the season of spring.

spring·y (spring'ē), *adj.* full of spring or bounce [*springy* wood for a bow]. —**spring'i·er,** *compar.;* **spring'i·est,** *superl.*

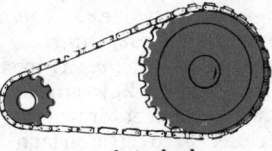

springbok
(2½ ft. high at shoulder)

sprin·kle (spring'k'l), *v.* **1.** to scatter in drops or bits [to *sprinkle* salt on an egg]. **2.** to scatter drops or bits on [to *sprinkle* a lawn with water]. **3.** to rain lightly. —*n.* **1.** the act of sprinkling. **2.** a light rain. —**sprin'kled,** *p.t. & p.p.;* **sprin'kling,** *pr.p.* —**sprin'kler,** *n.*

sprin·kling (spring'kling), *n.* a small number or amount [a *sprinkling* of people].

sprint (sprint), *v.* to run very fast, as in a short race. —*n.* a short run or race at full speed. —**sprint'er,** *n.*

sprit (sprit), *n.* a pole that stretches up at a slant from a mast to help hold a sail.

sprite (sprīt), *n.* an elf, pixie, fairy, etc.

sprit·sail (sprit'sāl *or* sprit's'l), *n.* a sail held up by a sprit.

sprock·et (spräk'it), *n.* **1.** any of a number of teeth, as on the rim of a wheel, that fit into the links of a chain, as on a bicycle. **2.** a wheel with such teeth: *its full name is* **sprocket wheel.**

sprocket wheels

sprout (sprout), *v.* **1.** to begin to grow [Buds are *sprouting* on the roses. Weeds began to *sprout* in the garden.] **2.** to grow or develop rapidly [Billy *sprouted* up this summer.] **3.** to make grow [Rain will *sprout* the grass.] —*n.* a young, new growth from a plant, bud, seed, etc.

spruce (sprōōs), *n.* **1.** an evergreen tree with leaves shaped like needles and drooping cones. **2.** the soft wood of this tree.

spruce (sprōōs), *adj.* neat and trim; smart. —*v.* to make or become neat, trim, etc. [New drapes will *spruce* up the room.] —**spruced,** *p.t. & p.p.;* **spruc'ing,** *pr.p.*

sprung (sprung), a past tense and the past participle of **spring.**

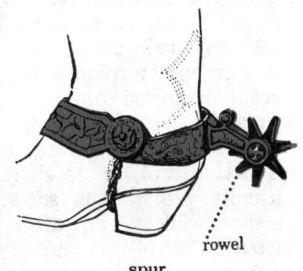

spruce tree, branch, and cone

spry (sprī), *adj.* moving with quickness and ease; lively; agile. —**spri'er** or **spry'er,** *compar.;* **spri'est** or **spry'est,** *superl.* —**spry'ly,** *adv.*

spud (spud), *n.* **1.** a sharp spade for digging out weeds. **2.** a potato: *only in everyday talk.*

spume (spyōōm), *n. & v.* foam; froth. —**spumed,** *p.t. & p.p.;* **spum'ing,** *pr.p.*

spun (spun), past tense and past participle of **spin.** —*adj.* formed by or as if by spinning.

spunk (spungk), *n.* courage or a brave spirit; pluck: *used only in everyday talk.*

spunk·y (spung'kē), *adj.* having spunk, or courage; brave: *used only in everyday talk.* —**spunk'i·er,** *compar.;* **spunk'i·est,** *superl.*

spur (spur), *n.* **1.** a metal piece with sharp points, worn on the heel by horsemen to urge the horse forward. **2.** something that sticks out like a point on a spur, as a ridge coming out from a mountain, or a sharp spine on the wing or leg of some birds. **3.** a short side track connected with the main track of a railroad. **4.** anything that urges one on [Fear was the *spur* that kept him going.] —*v.* **1.** to prick with spurs. **2.** to urge on [The prize money *spurred* him to greater efforts.] —**on the spur of the moment,** quickly, without planning. —**win one's spurs,** to gain honor. —**spurred,** *p.t. & p.p.;* **spur'ring,** *pr.p.*

rowel

spur

spu·ri·ous (spyoor'i əs), *adj.* not true or genuine; false [a *spurious* report].

spurn (spurn), *v.* **1.** to refuse in a scornful way [He *spurned* my friendship.] **2.** to drive away as with the foot [to *spurn* a cat].

spurt (spurt), *v.* **1.** to shoot forth suddenly in a stream; squirt [Juice *spurted* from the grapefruit.] **2.** to show a sudden, short burst of energy, as near the end of a race. —*n.* **1.** a sudden, short stream or jet [The ketchup came out in *spurts.*]

fat, āpe, cär, ten, ēven, hit, bīte, gō, hôrn, tōōl, book, up, fŭr;
get, joy, yet, chin, she, thin, *then;* zh = s in pleasure; ' as in able (ā'b'l);
ə = a in ago, e in agent, i in sanity, o in confess, u in focus.

2. a sudden, short burst of energy [to work in *spurts*].

sput·ter (sput′ər), *v.* **1.** to spit out drops, bits of food, etc. from the mouth, as when talking too fast. **2.** to talk in a fast, confused way [He *sputtered* out an excuse.] **3.** to make hissing or spitting sounds [The hamburgers *sputtered* over the fire.] —*n.* **1.** the act or sound of sputtering. **2.** confused talk, as in excitement.

spu·tum (spyoo′təm), *n.* saliva or spit, often mixed with matter coughed up from the lungs.

spy (spī), *n.* **1.** a person who watches others secretly and carefully. **2.** a person sent by a government to find out military secrets, etc. of another country, as in wartime. —*v.* **1.** to act as a spy. **2.** to see; catch sight of [Can you *spy* the ship yet?] **3.** to find out by watching carefully [She *spied* out our plans.] —**spies**, *pl.* —**spied**, *p.t. & p.p.*; **spy′ing**, *pr.p.*

spy·glass (spī′glas), *n.* a small telescope.

sq., abbreviation for **square**.

squab (skwäb), *n.* a very young pigeon.

squab·ble (skwäb′'l), *v.* to quarrel in a noisy way about something not important. —*n.* such a noisy quarrel. —**squab′bled**, *p.t. & p.p.*; **squab′bling**, *pr.p.*

squad (skwäd), *n.* **1.** a small group of soldiers, often part of a platoon. **2.** any small group of people [a football *squad*].

squad car, a police patrol car, with a special radio for talking to headquarters.

squad·ron (skwäd′rən), *n.* **1.** a group of warships on a special mission. **2.** a group of cavalry soldiers, made up of from two to four troops. **3.** a group of airplanes that fly together. **4.** any group organized to work together.

squal·id (skwäl′id), *adj.* **1.** dirty; filthy [a *squalid* house]. **2.** wretched [a *squalid* life].

squall (skwôl), *n.* a short, violent windstorm, usually with rain or snow. —*v.* to storm for a short while. —**squall′y**, *adj.*

squall (skwôl), *v.* to cry or scream loudly. —*n.* a loud, harsh cry or scream.

squal·or (skwäl′ər), *n.* a squalid condition; filth; misery; wretchedness.

squan·der (skwän′dər), *v.* to spend or use wastefully [to *squander* money or time].

square (skwer), *n.* **1.** a flat figure with four equal sides and four right angles. **2.** anything shaped like this [Arrange the chairs in a *square*.] **3.** an area in a city, with streets on four sides, often used as a public park, etc. **4.** a tool having two sides that form a right angle, used in drawing or testing right angles. **5.** the result gotten by multiplying a number by itself [The *square* of 3 is 9 (3 × 3 = 9).] —*adj.* **1.** having the shape of a square. **2.** forming a right angle [a *square* corner]. **3.** straight, level, or even. **4.** fair; honest [a *square* deal]. **5.** having measure in two

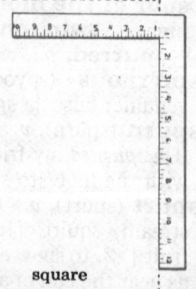

square
(meaning 4)

directions [A *square* foot is the area of a square that is one foot long and one foot wide.] **6.** satisfying; filling: *used only in everyday talk* [a *square* meal]. —*v.* **1.** to make square [to *square* a stone; to *square* a wall]. **2.** to make straight, level, or even [*Square* your shoulders.] **3.** to settle [to *square* accounts]. **4.** to mark off in squares [A checkerboard is *squared* off.] **5.** to multiply by itself [5 *squared* is 25.] **6.** to fit; agree [His story *squares* with mine.] —**on the square, 1.** at right angles. **2.** honestly; fairly: *used only in everyday talk.* —**square off,** to get into position for attacking or for defending. —**square oneself,** to make up for a wrong that one has done: *used only in everyday talk.* —**squared**, *p.t. & p.p.*; **squar′ing**, *pr.p.* —**square′ly**, *adv.* —**square′ness**, *n.*

square dance, a lively group dance for couples, with various steps, figures, etc.

square-rigged (skwer′rigd′), *adj.* having four-sided sails that are set straight across the masts: *see the picture of* **square-rigger**.

square-rig·ger (skwer′rig′ər), *n.* a sailing ship that is square-rigged.

square root, the number that is multiplied by itself to produce a given number [The *square root* of 9 is 3.]

square-rigger

squash (skwäsh), *v.* **1.** to crush or be crushed into a soft or flat mass [Grapes *squash* easily.] **2.** to put down or suppress, as a revolt. **3.** to press, crowd, or squeeze. —*n.* **1.** the act or sound of squashing [The tomatoes hit the floor with a *squash*.] **2.** something squashed. **3.** a game like handball, but played with rackets.

squash (skwäsh), *n.* a fleshy fruit that grows on a vine and is cooked as a vegetable. There are many kinds of squash, differing in color, size, and shape.

squash·y (skwäsh′ē), *adj.* **1.** soft and wet; mushy [*squashy* mud]. **2.** easy to squash or crush [a *squashy* fruit]. —**squash′i·er**, *compar.*; **squash′i·est**, *superl.*

kinds of squash

squat (skwät), *v.* **1.** to sit on the heels with the knees bent. **2.** to crouch with the feet drawn in close. **3.** to settle on land without any right or title to it. **4.** to settle on public land in order to get title to it from the government. —*adj.* **1.** crouching. **2.** short and heavy or thick [a *squat* man]. —*n.* the act or position of squatting. —**squat′ted** or **squat**, *p.t. & p.p.*; **squat′ting**, *pr.p.* —**squat′ter**, *n.*

catcher squatting

squaw (skwô), *n.* an American Indian woman.

squawk (skwôk), *n.* **1.** a loud, harsh cry such as a hen makes. **2.** a loud complaint: *slang in this meaning.* —*v.* **1.** to let out a squawk. **2.** to complain loudly: *slang in this meaning.*

squeak (skwēk), *n.* a short, high, thin cry or sound [the *squeak* of a mouse]. —*v.* to make a squeak [His new shoes *squeak.*] —**narrow squeak** or **close squeak,** a narrow escape. —**squeak′y,** *adj.*

squeal (skwēl), *n.* a long, high, shrill cry, as of a young pig. —*v.* **1.** to let out a squeal. **2.** to tell on someone; tattle: *slang in this meaning.*

squeam·ish (skwēm′ish), *adj.* **1.** easily made sick at the stomach; queasy [She is *squeamish* at the sight of blood.] **2.** easily shocked or too easily shocked; prudish. —**squeam′ish·ness,** *n.*

squee·gee (skwē′jē), *n.* a tool with a rubber blade set across a handle, for scraping water from a window, etc.

squeeze (skwēz), *v.* **1.** to press hard or force together [*Squeeze* the sponge to get rid of the water.] **2.** to get by pressing or by force [to *squeeze* juice from an orange; to *squeeze* money from poor people]. **3.** to force by pressing [He *squeezed* his hand into the jar.] **4.** to hug. **5.** to force one's way by pushing or pressing [He *squeezed* through the narrow window.] **6.** to give way to pressure [Foam rubber *squeezes* easily.] —*n.* a squeezing or being squeezed; hard press, etc. —**squeezed,** *p.t. & p.p.;* **squeez′ing,** *pr.p.* —**squeez′er,** *n.*

squelch (skwelch), *v.* to force to be silent; suppress [to *squelch* an unruly child].

squib (skwib), *n.* **1.** a kind of firecracker. **2.** a short, witty writing that criticizes; lampoon.

squid (skwid), *n.* a long, slender sea animal with ten arms, two of them longer than the rest.

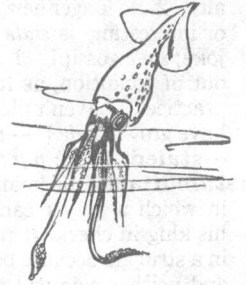

squid (9 in. long)

squint (skwint), *v.* **1.** to draw the eyelids closer together in order to see better. **2.** to look sideways. **3.** to be cross-eyed. —*n.* **1.** the act or condition of squinting. **2.** the condition of being cross-eyed. **3.** a quick glance: *only in everyday talk.* —*adj.* cross-eyed.

squire (skwīr), *n.* **1.** in England, a country gentleman who owns much land. **2.** a title of respect for a justice of the peace. **3.** a man who escorts a lady. **4.** a young man who attended a knight. —*v.* to escort a lady. —**squired,** *p.t. & p.p.;* **squir′ing,** *pr.p.*

girl squinting

squirm (skwûrm), *v.* **1.** to twist and turn the body as a snake does; wriggle;

writhe. **2.** to feel ashamed or embarrassed. —**squirm′y,** *adj.*

squir·rel (skwûr′əl), *n.* **1.** a small animal with a long, bushy tail, that lives in trees. **2.** its heavy fur, usually gray or red.

squirt (skwûrt), *v.* **1.** to shoot out in a jet; spurt. **2.** to wet with liquid shot out in a jet [He *squirted* us with the hose.] —*n.* **1.** the act of squirting. **2.** a small jet of liquid.

Sr, symbol for the chemical element *strontium.*

Sr., abbreviation for **Senior.**

S.S. or **SS,** abbreviation for **steamship.**

St., abbreviation for **Saint, Strait, Street.**

stab (stab), *v.* **1.** to pierce or wound with a knife, dagger, etc. **2.** to thrust into something [He *stabbed* the pitchfork into the hay.] **3.** to hurt very sharply [a *stabbing* pain; *stabbed* by insults]. —*n.* **1.** a wound made by stabbing. **2.** a thrust, as with a knife. **3.** a sharp hurt or pain. **4.** a try: *used only in everyday talk* [Let me take a *stab* at the problem.] —**stabbed,** *p.t. & p.p.;* **stab′bing,** *pr.p.* —**stab′ber,** *n.*

sta·bil·i·ty (stə bil′ə tē), *n.* the condition of being stable; steadiness; firmness.

sta·bi·lize (stā′bə līz), *v.* **1.** to make stable, or firm. **2.** to keep from changing [to *stabilize* prices]. —**sta′bi·lized,** *p.t. & p.p.;* **sta′bi·liz·ing,** *pr.p.* —**sta′bi·li·za′tion,** *n.*

sta·bi·liz·er (stā′bə līz′ər), *n.* a person or thing that stabilizes; especially, a device used to keep an airplane steady while flying.

sta·ble (stā′b'l), *adj.* **1.** not likely to break down, fall over, or give way; firm; steady [The chair is braced to make it *stable.*] **2.** not likely to change; lasting [a *stable* business].

sta·ble (stā′b'l), *n.* **1.** a building in which horses or cattle are sheltered and fed. **2.** all the race horses belonging to one owner. —*v.* to put or keep in a stable. —**sta′bled,** *p.t. & p.p.;* **sta′bling,** *pr.p.*

stac·ca·to (stə kä′tō), *adj. & adv.* in music, cut short, with sharp breaks between the tones.

stack (stak), *n.* **1.** a large pile of hay, straw, etc. stored outdoors. **2.** any neat pile [a *stack* of books]. **3.** a set of book shelves. **4.** a chimney or smokestack. **5.** a number of rifles leaned against each other on end to form a cone. —*v.* **1.** to arrange in a stack. **2.** to load with stacks of something [We *stacked* the truck with boxes.] **3.** to arrange in a secret and unfair way [to *stack* a deck of playing cards].

sta·di·um (stā′di əm), *n.* a place for outdoor games, meetings, etc., with rising rows of seats around the open field.

staff (staf), *n.* **1.** a stick, rod, or pole used for leaning on, or as a weapon, a sign of authority, etc. [a shepherd's *staff;* a bishop's *staff*]. **2.** something that serves

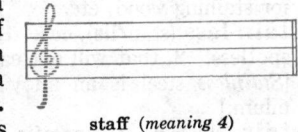

staff (meaning 4)

as a support. **3.** a group of people working together under a leader, manager, chief, etc. [the teaching *staff* of a school]. **4.** the five lines and the spaces between them on which music is written. —*v.* to supply with a staff, as of workers. —**staves,** *pl.; also, and for meaning 3 always,* **staffs,** *pl.*

stag (stag), *n.* **1.** a full-grown male deer. **2.** any male. —*adj.* for men only [a *stag* party].

stage (stāj), *n.* **1.** a raised platform or other area on which plays, speeches, etc. are given. **2.** the profession of acting; the theater [She left the *stage* to marry.] **3.** a platform or dock [a landing *stage*]. **4.** the place where something takes place; scene [Belgium has been the *stage* of many wars.] **5.** a place where a stop is made on a journey. **6.** the distance between two such stops. **7.** a stagecoach. **8.** a period or step in growth or development [He has reached a new *stage* in his career.] **9.** any of the separate systems that work one at a time in getting a rocket into outer space. —*v.* **1.** to present on a stage, as a play. **2.** to plan and carry out [to *stage* an attack]. —**by easy stages,** a little at a time, with many stops. —**staged,** *p.t. & p.p.;* **stag'-ing,** *pr.p.*

stage·coach (stāj'kōch), *n.* a coach pulled by horses that traveled a regular route, carrying passengers, mail, etc.

stag·ger (stag'ər), *v.* **1.** to walk or stand in an unsteady way, as if about to fall; sway; reel [The tired boxer *staggered* from the ring.] **2.** to make stagger [The blow *staggered* him.] **3.** to shock, confuse, etc. [*staggering* news]. **4.** to arrange in a zigzag way. **5.** to arrange so as to come at different times [to *stagger* vacations]. —*n.* the act of staggering. —**the staggers,** a nervous disease of horses, cattle, etc., causing them to stagger: *used with a singular verb.*

stag·nant (stag'nənt), *adj.* **1.** not flowing and therefore stale and dirty [*stagnant* water]. **2.** not active; sluggish [a *stagnant* mind].

stag·nate (stag'nāt), *v.* to become or make stagnant. —**stag'nat·ed,** *p.t. & p.p.;* **stag'-nat·ing,** *pr.p.* —**stag·na'tion,** *n.*

staid (stād), an earlier form of **stayed** (remained). —*adj.* steady and settled [a *staid* old man].

stain (stān), *v.* **1.** to spoil with dirt or a patch of color; soil or spot [a rug *stained* with ink]. **2.** to shame or disgrace [to *stain* one's reputation]. **3.** to change the color of; dye [to *stain* wood to look like walnut]. —*n.* **1.** a dirty or colored spot [grass *stains*]. **2.** a shame or disgrace. [without a *stain* on his character]. **3.** a dye for staining wood, etc.

stain·less (stān'lis), *adj.* **1.** that has no stains; spotless. **2.** that will not easily rust, stain, etc. [*Stainless* steel is an alloy of steel and chromium.]

stair (ster), *n.* **1.** one of a series of steps going up or down. **2.** *usually* **stairs,** *pl.* a flight of steps; staircase.

stair·case (ster'kās) or **stair·way** (ster'wā), *n.* a flight of steps, usually with a handrail.

stake (stāk), *n.* **1.** a pointed stick or metal rod for driving into the ground. **2.** the post to which a person was tied when being burned to death as a punishment. **3.** *often* **stakes,** *pl.* the money, etc. risked in a bet or game [They played cards for high *stakes.*] **4.** the winner's prize, as in a race. **5.** a share or interest [He has a *stake* in the business.] —*v.* **1.** to mark the boundaries of, as with stakes [to *stake* out a claim]. **2.** to support with a stake [to *stake* up a tomato plant]. **3.** to risk or bet. **4.** to give or lend money to for some reason: *used only in everyday talk* [He *staked* us to a meal.] —**at stake,** being risked. —**staked,** *p.t. & p.p.;* **stak'ing,** *pr.p.*

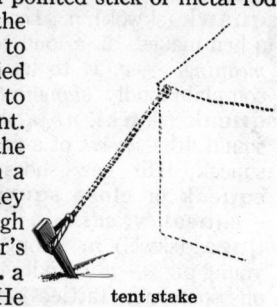
tent stake

sta·lac·tite (stə lak'tīt), *n.* a stick of lime shaped like an icicle and hanging from the roof of a cave. It is formed by water dropping down through the rocks above.

stalactites

sta·lag·mite (stə lag'mīt), *n.* a stick like a stalactite, but built up on the floor of a cave.

stale (stāl), *adj.* **1.** stalagmites no longer fresh; made bad by being kept too long [*stale* bread; *stale* air]. **2.** no longer new or interesting [a *stale* joke; *stale* gossip]. **3.** out of condition, as from too much or too little practice [I haven't played the piano for years and have grown *stale.*] —*v.* to make or become stale. —**staled,** *p.t. & p.p.;* **stal'ing,** *pr.p.*

stale·mate (stāl'māt), *n.* **1.** a position in chess in which a player cannot move without placing his king in check. It results in a draw. **2.** a halt in a struggle because both sides are equally strong and neither side will give in; deadlock. —*v.* to bring into a stalemate. —**stale'mat·ed,** *p.t. & p.p.;* **stale'mat·ing,** *pr.p.*

Sta·lin, Joseph (stä'lin), 1879–1953; Soviet dictator; premier of the U.S.S.R. from 1941 to 1953.

Sta·lin·grad (stä'lin grad), *n.* a city in the southeastern U.S.S.R.: now called *Volgograd.*

stalk (stôk), *v.* **1.** to walk in a stiff, haughty way; stride. **2.** to spread through [Terror *stalked* the streets.] **3.** to track secretly so as to catch or kill [to *stalk* game]. —*n.* the act of stalking.

stalk (stôk), *n.* **1.** the stem of a plant. **2.** any part like this.

stall (stôl), *n.* **1.** a small section for one animal in a stable. **2.** a booth, table, etc. at which goods are sold, as at a market. **3.** an enclosed seat in the choir of a church. —*v.* **1.** to put or keep in a stall. **2.** to bring or come to a stop without meaning to [The car *stalled* when the motor got wet.]

stall (stôl), *v.* to hold off by sly or clever means; delay by evading [to *stall* off one's creditors; to *stall* for time]. —*n.* anything said or done in order to stall.

stal·lion (stal′yən), *n.* a full-grown male horse that can be used for breeding.

stal·wart (stôl′wərt), *adj.* **1.** strong and well-built; robust; sturdy [a *stalwart* athlete]. **2.** brave; fearless [a *stalwart* soldier]. **3.** not giving in easily; firm [the *stalwart* defense of a cause]. —*n.* a stalwart person.

sta·men (stā′mən), *n.* the part of a flower in which the pollen grows, including the anther and its stem.

stam·i·na (stam′ə nə), *n.* the strength to carry on or endure; vigor; endurance.

stam·mer (stam′ər), *v.* to speak in a halting way, often repeating certain sounds, as in fear, embarrassment, etc. —*n.* stammering talk.

stamp (stamp), *v.* **1.** to bring one's foot down with force ["No!" she said, *stamping* on the floor.] **2.** to walk with loud, heavy steps [The angry boy *stamped* out of the room.] **3.** to beat, press, or crush as with the foot [to *stamp* out a fire; to *stamp* out a revolt]. **4.** to press or print marks, letters, a design, etc. on something [He *stamped* his initials on all his clothing.] **5.** to cut out by pressing with a sharp metal form [This machine can *stamp* out a hundred shoe soles every minute.] **6.** to mark with a certain quality [His face was *stamped* with fear.] **7.** to put a postage stamp, official seal, etc. on. —*n.* **1.** the act of stamping the foot. **2.** a machine, tool, or die used for stamping. **3.** a mark or form made by stamping. **4.** any official mark, seal, etc. put on papers. **5.** a small piece of paper printed and sold by a government for sticking on letters, packages, etc. as proof that the proper postage or taxes have been paid. **6.** any piece of paper like this, given to customers, who turn them in for premiums. **7.** a sign or mark [the *stamp* of truth]. **8.** kind or class [Men of his *stamp* are rare.]

stam·pede (stam pēd′), *n.* a sudden rush or flight, as of a herd of cattle or of a crowd of frightened or thoughtless people. —*v.* to move in or cause a stampede. —**stam·ped′ed,** *p.t. & p.p.;* **stam·ped′ing,** *pr.p.*

stance (stans), *n.* the way a person stands; position of one's feet [He bats with an open *stance,* keeping his feet far apart.]

stanch (stanch *or* stänch), *v.* to stop or slow down the flow of blood from a wound. —*adj.* same as **staunch.**

stan·chion (stan′shən), *n.* a post or bar placed upright and used as a support.

stand (stand), *v.* **1.** to be or get in an upright position on one's feet [*Stand* by your desk.] **2.** to be or place in an upright position on its base, bottom, etc. [The birdbath *stands* in the garden. *Stand* the broom in the corner.] **3.** to hold a certain opinion, belief, etc. [I *stand* with you in this matter.] **4.** to be placed or situated [Our house *stands* on a hill.] **5.** to be at a certain rank, degree, etc. [Where do you *stand* in your class?] **6.** to be in a certain condition [She *stands* convicted of cruelty.] **7.** to gather and stay [Sweat *stood* in drops on his forehead.] **8.** to stay without change [My orders *stand* until I cancel them.] **9.** to stop or halt. **10.** to try to fight off or hold back [One man *stood* alone against the enemy.] **11.** to put up with; endure; bear [She can't *stand* noise.] **12.** to withstand with little or no damage or change [This suitcase will *stand* years of hard use.] **13.** to be forced to go through; undergo [He must *stand* trial for his crime.] **14.** to pay for [Who will *stand* the cost?] —*n.* **1.** the act of standing. **2.** a stop or halt, as in making a defense [The retreating soldiers made one last *stand* at the bridge.] **3.** a place where a person stands [Take your *stand* at the door.] **4.** an opinion, belief, or attitude [What is the Senator's *stand* on higher taxes?] **5.** a platform to stand or sit on [a band*stand;* the witness *stand* in a courtroom]. **6.** *often* **stands,** *pl.* seats in rising rows, as in a stadium, from which to watch games, races, etc. **7.** a booth or counter where goods are sold [a cigar *stand*]. **8.** a rack, framework, etc. for holding something [a music *stand*]. **9.** a group of growing trees or plants [a *stand* of willows]. —**stand a chance,** to have a chance. —**stand by, 1.** to be near and ready if needed. **2.** to help or support. —**stand for, 1.** to be a sign for; represent [The mark & *stands for* the word "and."] **2.** to put up with; tolerate: *used only in everyday talk.* —**stand off,** to keep at a distance. —**stand out, 1.** to stick out; project. **2.** to be easily noticed because unusual or outstanding. —**stand up, 1.** to take a standing position. **2.** to prove to be true, good, lasting, etc. [His theory won't *stand up* under examination.] —**stand up for,** to support or defend. —**stood,** *p.t. & p.p.;* **stand′ing,** *pr.p.*

music stand

stand·ard (stan′dərd), *n.* **1.** something set up as a rule or model with which other things like it are to be compared [The government sets the *standards* for pure food and drugs.] **2.** a flag, banner, etc., as of a military group or a nation [The tricolor is the *standard* of France.] **3.** an upright support [Flagpoles are often called *standards.*] —*adj.* **1.** that is a standard, rule, or model [The *standard* Canadian gallon is larger

fat,   āpe,   cär,   ten,   ēven,   hit,   bīte,   gō,   hôrn,   tool,   book,   up,   fūr;
get,   joy,   yet,   chin,   she,   thin,   *th*en;   zh = s in pleasure;   ' as in able (ā′b'l);
ə = a in ago,   e in agent,   i in sanity,   o in confess,   u in focus.

than the *standard* American one.] **2.** not special or extra; ordinary [Headlights are *standard* equipment on all cars.] **3.** accepted as good or proper [Both "catalogue" and "catalog" are now *standard* spellings.]

stand·ard·ize (stan′dər dīz), *v.* to make according to a standard; make the same in all cases [Radio and television have begun to *standardize* American speech.] —**stand′ard·ized**, *p.t.* & *p.p.*; **stand′ard·iz·ing**, *pr.p.* —**stand′ard·i·za′tion**, *n.*

Standard Time, the official time for any of the twenty-four time zones in which the world is divided, starting at Greenwich, England. The four time zones of the mainland United States are Eastern, Central, Mountain, and Pacific.

stand-in (stand′in′), *n.* a person who takes the place of another for a short time; substitute.

stand·ing (stan′ding), *adj.* **1.** that stands; upright or erect. **2.** done from a standing position [a *standing* broad jump]. **3.** not flowing; stagnant [*standing* water in the fields]. **4.** going on regularly without change [a *standing* order for two quarts of milk each day]. —*n.* **1.** position, rank, or reputation [a man of high *standing*]. **2.** the time that something lasts; duration [a custom of long *standing*].

Stan·dish, Captain **Miles** (stan′dish), 1584?–1656; the English military leader of the Pilgrims at Plymouth, Massachusetts.

stand·point (stand′point), *n.* the point or position from which something is seen or judged; point of view.

stand·still (stand′stil), *n.* a stop or halt.

stank (stangk), a past tense of **stink.**

stan·za (stan′zə), *n.* a group of lines forming one of the sections of a poem; verse.

sta·ple (stā′p'l), *n.* **1.** the main product of a certain place [Coffee is the *staple* of Brazil.] **2.** any article of food that is regularly used and is kept in large amounts [We bought flour, sugar, and other *staples*.] **3.** the fiber of cotton, wool, flax, etc. [Egyptian cotton has a very long *staple*.] —*adj.* **1.** kept on hand because regularly used [*staple* foods]. **2.** most important; chief; main [Automobile manufacturing is a *staple* industry in our economy.]

sta·ple (stā′p'l), *n.* **1.** a piece of metal shaped like a U with sharp, pointed ends. It is driven into a surface to hold a wire, hook, etc. in place. **2.** a thin piece of wire like this, that is driven through papers or other materials so that the ends bend over as a binding. —*v.* to fasten with a staple or staples. —**sta′pled**, *p.t.* & *p.p.*; **sta′pling**, *pr.p.* —**sta′pler**, *n.*

star (stär), *n.* **1.** a heavenly body seen as a small point of light in the night sky; especially, such a body that is actually a far-off sun. **2.** a planet, etc. thought of in astrology as controlling one's life. **3.** a flat figure with five or more points, used as a symbol or decoration.

stars (*meaning 3*)

4. an asterisk (*). **5.** a person who is outstanding, as in some sport or in acting. —*v.* **1.** to play or be given an important part as an actor [She is *starred* in the new movie.] **2.** to decorate or mark with stars or asterisks [Some names on the list are *starred*.] **3.** to perform in an outstanding way [He *stars* at baseball.] —*adj.* showing great skill; outstanding [a *star* athlete]. —**starred**, *p.t.* & *p.p.*; **star′ring**, *pr.p.*

star·board (stär′bərd), *n.* the right-hand side of a ship or airplane as one faces forward, toward the bow. —*adj.* of or on this side.

starch (stärch), *n.* **1.** a white food substance with no taste, found in potatoes, beans, grain, etc. **2.** a powder made from this substance. It is mixed with water and used to make clothes stiff. **3.** a stiff, formal way of behaving. —*v.* to make stiff with starch [to *starch* a collar].

starch·y (stär′chē), *adj.* **1.** of, like, or full of starch. **2.** stiffened with starch. **3.** stiff or formal [a *starchy* manner]. —**starch′i·er,** *compar.*; **starch′i·est,** *superl.*

stare (ster), *v.* **1.** to look with a steady, fixed gaze, as in wonder, curiosity, dullness, etc. **2.** to stand out, as a bright color. —*n.* a long, steady look. —**stare down,** to stare back at another until he looks away. —**stared**, *p.t.* & *p.p.*; **star′ing**, *pr.p.*

star·fish (stär′fish), *n.* a small sea animal with a hard covering, shaped like a star.

stark (stärk), *adj.* **1.** lonely and bleak [a *stark* landscape]. **2.** complete; utter [*stark* terror]. **3.** stiff; rigid, as a dead body. —*adv.* completely; entirely [*stark* naked]. —**stark′ly,** *adv.*

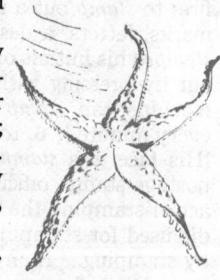
starfish (5 to 6 in. across)

star·light (stär′līt), *n.* light from the stars. —*adj.* lighted by the stars.

star·ling (stär′ling), *n.* a bird with black feathers that shine in a greenish or purplish way.

star·lit (stär′lit), *adj.* lighted by the stars.

star·ry (stär′ē), *adj.* **1.** of the stars [*starry* light]. **2.** full of stars [a *starry* sky]. **3.** shining like stars [*starry* eyes]. —**star′ri·er,** *compar.*; **star′ri·est,** *superl.*

starling (8½ in. long)

Stars and Stripes, the flag of the United States. It has thirteen stripes and fifty stars.

Star-Spangled Banner, 1. the United States flag. **2.** the national anthem of the United States.

start (stärt), *v.* **1.** to begin to go, do, act, be, etc. [We *start* for Boston today. The show *starts* at 2:30.] **2.** to cause to begin; set in motion or action [*Start* the car. Who *started* the fight?] **3.** to move suddenly, as when surprised; jump or jerk [The noise made her *start*.] **4.** to cause to move suddenly; rouse [We *started* a bird.] —*n.*

1. the act of starting, or beginning. **2.** a sudden jump or jerk, as in surprise. **3.** a lead or other advantage, as at the beginning of a race. **4.** the place or time that something begins [He was ahead from the *start*.] *See also the phrase* **fits and starts.** —**start in,** to begin to do something. —**start out,** to begin a trip, action, etc. —**start up, 1.** to spring up. **2.** to cause to begin running, as an engine.

start·er (stärt′ər), *n.* **1.** a person or thing that starts. **2.** the first in a series. **3.** one who gives the signal to start, as in a race.

star·tle (stär′t'l), *v.* to frighten suddenly or surprise; cause to move or jump [The ring of the telephone *startled* me.] —**star′tled,** *p.t. & p.p.;* **star′tling,** *pr.p.*

star·tling (stär′tling), *adj.* causing sudden fright or surprise [a *startling* sight].

starve (stärv), *v.* **1.** to die or suffer from lack of food. **2.** to kill or make suffer with hunger. **3.** to be very hungry: *used only in everyday talk.* —**starve for,** to need or want very much. —**starved,** *p.t. & p.p.;* **starv′ing,** *pr.p.* —**star·va·tion** (stär vā′shən), *n.*

starve·ling (stärv′ling), *adj.* starving; weak from hunger. —*n.* a starving person or animal.

stash (stash), *v.* to hide, as money, in a secret or safe place: *a slang word.*

state (stāt), *n.* **1.** the condition in which a person or thing is [He's in a nervous *state*. Things are in a *state* of change.] **2.** a wealthy and formal style or condition; pomp [We dined in *state*.] **3.** a group of people united under one government; nation. **4.** *usually* **State,** any of the political units that form a federal government, as in the United States [the *State* of Ohio]. **5.** the territory or government of a state. —*v.* **1.** to fix or settle [Let's *state* a time and place for meeting.] **2.** to tell in a definite or formal way [He *stated* his views.] —**the States,** the United States: *used only in everyday talk.* —**stat′ed,** *p.t. & p.p.;* **stat′ing,** *pr.p.* —**state′hood,** *n.*

state·craft (stāt′kraft), *n.* skill in government and politics; statesmanship.

stat·ed (stāt′id), *adj.* fixed; set [a *stated* schedule; his *stated* purpose].

State·house (stāt′hous), *n.* the capitol of a State, where its legislature meets.

state·ly (stāt′lē), *adj.* grand or dignified [a *stately* dance]. —**state′li·er,** *compar.;* **state′li·est,** *superl.* —**state′li·ness,** *n.*

state·ment (stāt′mənt), *n.* **1.** the act of stating. **2.** something stated or said [May we quote your *statement?*] **3.** a report or record, as of money owed [This store sends its customers monthly *statements*.]

state·room (stāt′rōōm), *n.* a private cabin or room on a ship or in a railroad car.

states·man (stāts′mən), *n.* a man who is wise and skillful in the business of government. —**states′men,** *pl.* —**states′man·ship,** *n.*

stat·ic (stat′ik), *adj.* **1.** at rest; not active; not moving or changing [A *static* mind produces no new ideas.] **2.** having to do with masses or forces at rest or in balance [*static* equilibrium]. **3.** acting through weight only, without motion [*static* pressure]. **4.** describing or of electrical charges produced by friction. —*n.* any of the electrical disturbances in the air that are picked up by a radio receiver.

sta·tion (stā′shən), *n.* **1.** the place where a person or thing stands or is located, as one's post when on duty, a building for a special purpose, etc. [a sentry's *station;* a police *station*]. **2.** a regular stopping place, as for a bus or train; also, a building at such a place. **3.** a place with equipment for sending out radio or television programs. **4.** social rank [A judge is a man of high *station*.] —*v.* to place at a station, or post.

sta·tion·ar·y (stā′shən er′ē), *adj.* **1.** not moving; fixed [*stationary* engines]. **2.** not changing in condition, value, etc. [Prices were kept *stationary* under wartime controls.]

sta·tion·er (stā′shən ər), *n.* a person who sells writing paper, pens, ink, etc.

sta·tion·er·y (stā′shən er′ē), *n.* paper, envelopes, etc. for writing letters.

station wagon, an automobile with a number of rear seats and a back end that opens for easy loading of luggage, etc.

sta·tis·ti·cal (stə tis′ti k'l), *adj.* having to do with statistics. —**sta·tis′ti·cal·ly,** *adv.*

stat·is·ti·cian (stat′is tish′ən), *n.* an expert in statistics; person who works with statistics.

sta·tis·tics (stə tis′tiks), *n.pl.* **1.** facts in the form of numbers, collected and arranged so as to show certain information [census *statistics*]. **2.** the science of collecting and arranging such facts: *used with a singular verb.*

stat·u·ar·y (stach′ōō er′ē), *n.* **1.** statues. **2.** the art of sculpture.

stat·ue (stach′ōō), *n.* the form or likeness of a person or animal carved in wood, stone, etc., modeled in clay, or cast in plaster or a metal.

stat·u·esque (stach′ōō esk′), *adj.* like a statue, as in size, grace, dignity, etc.

stat·u·ette (stach′ōō et′), *n.* a small statue.

stat·ure (stach′ər), *n.* **1.** the height of a person [a man of short *stature*]. **2.** development or growth [of high moral *stature*].

stat·us (stā′təs *or* stat′əs), *n.* **1.** position or rank; standing [A doctor has high *status* in our society.] **2.** state or condition, as of affairs.

status quo (kwō), the way things are at a particular time: *a Latin phrase.*

stat·ute (stach′oot), *n.* a rule or law, especially a law passed by a legislature.

stat·u·to·ry (stach′oo tôr′ē), *adj.* **1.** having to do with a statute. **2.** fixed by statute. **3.** that can be punished according to law.

St. Au·gus·tine (ô′gəs tēn), a seaport in northeastern Florida: oldest city in the U.S.

---

fat, āpe, cär, ten, ēven, hit, bīte, gō, hôrn, tōōl, book, up, fŭr;
get, joy, yet, chin, she, thin, *th*en; zh = s in pleasure; ′ as in able (ā′b'l);
ə = a in ago, e in agent, i in sanity, o in confess, u in focus.

staunch (stônch *or* stänch), *adj.* **1.** strong, firm, loyal, etc. [a *staunch* patriot; *staunch* friendship]. **2.** watertight [a *staunch* ship]. —*v.* same as **stanch.** —**staunch′ly,** *adv.*

stave (stāv), *n.* **1.** any of the curved strips of wood that form the wall of a barrel, cask, etc. **2.** a stick or staff. **3.** a set of lines of a poem or song; stanza. **4.** a musical staff. —*v.* **1.** to smash, especially by breaking in staves [to *stave* a hole in a boat]. **2.** to fit with staves. —**stave in,** to break a hole in.

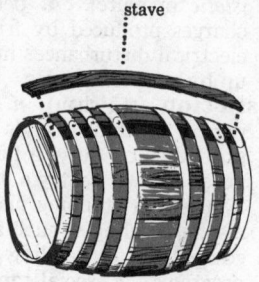

stave

—**stave off,** to hold off or put off, as by force, cleverness, etc. —**staved** *or* **stove,** *p.t. & p.p.;* **stav′ing,** *pr.p.*

staves (stāvz), *n.* **1.** a plural of **staff. 2.** the plural of **stave.**

stay (stā), *n.* a strong rope or cable used as a brace, as for a mast of a ship.

stay (stā), *n.* **1.** a support or prop. **2.** a thin strip of bone, plastic, etc. used to stiffen a corset, collar, etc. —*v.* to support; prop up.

stay (stā), *v.* **1.** to keep on being in some place or condition; remain [*Stay* at home today. The weather *stayed* bad for two weeks.] **2.** to live for a time; dwell [I am *staying* with friends.] **3.** to stop or halt; end [*Stay* your anger.] **4.** to hold back or put off for a time [A snack will *stay* your appetite.] **5.** to be able to last; hold out or keep up [This horse won't *stay* the distance in a long race.] —*n.* **1.** a stopping or being stopped; a halt, check, or delay [The prisoner won a *stay* of execution.] **2.** the act of remaining, or the time spent, in a place [a long *stay* in the hospital]. —**stayed** *or earlier* **staid,** *p.t. & p.p.;* **stay′ing,** *pr.p.*

staying power, power to last; endurance.

stay·sail (stā′sāl *or* stā′s′l), *n.* a sail fastened on a stay, or rope.

Ste., abbreviation for **Sainte,** the French word for a woman saint.

stead (sted), *n.* the place of a person or thing as filled by a substitute [If you can't come, send someone in your *stead.*] —**stand in good stead,** to give good use or service.

stead·fast (sted′fast), *adj.* firm or fixed; not changing [a *steadfast* friendship]. —**stead′fast·ly,** *adv.*

stead·y (sted′ē), *adj.* **1.** firm; not shaky [a *steady* table]. **2.** not changing or letting up; regular [a *steady* gaze; a *steady* worker]. **3.** not easily excited; calm [*steady* nerves]. **4.** serious and sensible; reliable [a *steady* young man]. —*v.* to make, keep, or become steady. —**go steady,** to be sweethearts: *only in everyday talk.* —**stead′i·er,** *compar.;* **stead′i·est,** *superl.* —**stead′ied,** *p.t. & p.p.;* **stead′y·ing,** *pr.p.* —**stead′i·ly,** *adv.* —**stead′i·ness,** *n.*

steak (stāk), *n.* a slice of meat or fish, especially beef, for broiling or frying.

steal (stēl), *v.* **1.** to take away secretly and without right something that does not belong to one. **2.** to take or do in a sly, secret way [to *steal* a look]. **3.** to get or win in a tricky or skillful way [He *stole* her heart.] **4.** to move in a quiet or secret way [He *stole* out of the house.] —*n.* **1.** an act of stealing. **2.** something gotten at an unusually low cost: *only in everyday talk.* —**stole,** *p.t.;* **stol′en,** *p.p.;* **steal′ing,** *pr.p.*

stealth (stealth), *n.* a secret, quiet way of moving or acting.

stealth·y (stel′thē), *adj.* done in a quiet or secret way, so as not to be seen or heard [the *stealthy* approach of a cat]. —**stealth′i·er,** *compar.;* **stealth′i·est,** *superl.* —**stealth′i·ly,** *adv.* —**stealth′i·ness,** *n.*

steam (stēm), *n.* **1.** water changed into a vapor or gas by being heated to the boiling point. Steam is used for heating, to give power in running engines, etc. **2.** such a vapor turned to mist by cooling [the *steam* on windows during cold weather]. **3.** energy; power: *used only in everyday talk* [He ran out of *steam* late in the afternoon.] —*adj.* **1.** using steam; heated, run, moved, etc. by the power of steam [a *steam* engine]. **2.** used for carrying steam [a *steam* pipe]. —*v.* **1.** to give off steam [a *steaming* teakettle]. **2.** to become covered with mist [His eyeglasses *steamed* up in the warm room.] **3.** to move by the power of steam under pressure [The ship *steamed* out of the harbor.] **4.** to cook, soften, or remove with steam [to *steam* asparagus; to *steam* labels off jars].

steam·boat (stēm′bōt), *n.* a steamship.

steam engine, an engine run by the power of steam under pressure.

steam·er (stēm′ər), *n.* something run by the power of steam under pressure, as a steamship.

steam fitter, a man whose work is putting in and repairing steam pipes, boilers, etc.

steam roller, 1. a machine run by steam power, with heavy rollers used to pack down and smooth the surface of roads. **2.** a power that crushes anything in its way.

steam·ship (stēm′ship), *n.* a ship driven by steam power.

steam shovel, a large machine run by steam power and used for digging.

steam·y (stēm′ē), *adj.* **1.** filled or covered with steam or mist [a *steamy* bathroom]. **2.** of or like steam [his *steamy* breath in the cold air]. —**steam′i·er,** *compar.;* **steam′i·est,** *superl.*

steed (stēd), *n.* a horse; especially, a lively riding horse: *seldom used except in poetry, etc.*

steel (stēl), *n.* **1.** a hard, tough metal made of iron mixed with a little carbon. **2.** something made of steel, as a sharp weapon. **3.** great strength or hardness [muscles of *steel*]. —*adj.* of or like steel. —*v.* to make strong or tough like steel [He *steeled* himself for the shock.]

steel wool, long, thin shavings of steel, used for cleaning, smoothing, and polishing.

steel·y (stēl′ē), *adj.* **1.** made of steel. **2.** like steel, as in hardness, color, etc. [a *steely* heart; *steely* blue eyes].

steel·yard (stēl′yärd), *n.* a scale made up of a metal bar hanging from a hook. The thing to be weighed is hung from the shorter end of the bar and a weight is moved along the longer end until the bar is level.

steelyard

steep (stēp), *adj.* **1.** slanting sharply up or down; having a sharp slope [a *steep* hill]. **2.** too high; above normal: *used only in everyday talk* [a *steep* price]. —**steep′ly,** *adv.* —**steep′ness,** *n.*

steep (stēp), *v.* to soak in liquid [to *steep* tea leaves]. —**steeped in,** completely filled with or absorbed in [*steeped in* a subject].

stee·ple (stē′p'l), *n.* **1.** a high tower, as on a church, usually having a spire. **2.** a spire.

stee·ple·chase (stē′p'l chās), *n.* a horse race in which hedges, ditches, etc. must be jumped.

stee·ple·jack (stē′p'l jak), *n.* a man who climbs steeples, smokestacks, etc. to paint or repair them.

steer (stir), *v.* **1.** to guide by means of a rudder or wheel; direct the movement of [A helmsman *steers* a ship. She *steered* the car into the driveway.] **2.** to be steered [This car *steers* smoothly.] **3.** to set and follow [He *steered* a straight course.] **4.** to direct or guide [The coach *steered* his team to victory.] —**steer clear of,** to avoid.

steer (stir), *n.* any male of cattle raised for its beef, especially a young ox with its sex glands removed.

steer·age (stir′ij), *n.* the part of a ship for passengers who pay the lowest fare.

steers·man (stirz′mən), *n.* a person who steers a ship or boat; helmsman. —**steers′men,** *pl.*

stein (stīn), *n.* a beer mug.

stel·lar (stel′ər), *adj.* **1.** of or like a star. **2.** by or for a star actor; most important; leading [a *stellar* role in a play].

stem (stem), *n.* **1.** the main part of a plant or tree that grows up from the ground and bears the leaves, flowers, etc.; trunk or stalk. **2.** any part that grows from this main part and has a flower, leaf, etc. at its end. **3.** any part like a stem [the *stem* of a goblet]. **4.** the front part of a ship; bow. **5.** the root or base of a word. —*v.* **1.** to remove the stem from [to *stem* cherries]. **2.** to move forward against [We rowed upstream, *stemming* the current.] **3.** to stop; check [to *stem* the bleeding]. **4.** to come or derive [Your troubles *stem* from past mistakes.] —**stemmed,** *p.t. & p.p.;* **stem′ming,** *pr.p.*

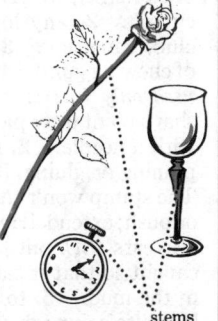

stems

stench (stench), *n.* a very bad smell; stink.

sten·cil (sten′s'l), *n.* **1.** a thin sheet of paper, metal, etc. with holes cut through in the shape of letters or designs. When ink or paint is spread over the stencil, the letters or designs are marked on the surface beneath. **2.** the design or letters marked in this way. —*v.* to mark with a stencil [He *stenciled* his name on the mailbox.] —**sten′ciled** or **sten′cilled,** *p.t. & p.p.;* **sten′cil·ing** or **sten′cil·ling,** *pr.p.*

ste·nog·ra·pher (stə näg′rə fər), *n.* a person whose work is stenography.

sten·o·graph·ic (sten′ə graf′ik), *adj.* of or made by stenography [a *stenographic* record of a conversation].

ste·nog·ra·phy (stə näg′rə fē), *n.* the work of taking down dictation, testimony, etc. in shorthand and then copying it out in full, as on a typewriter.

sten·to·ri·an (sten tôr′i ən), *adj.* very loud or strong in sound [a *stentorian* voice].

step (step), *n.* **1.** the act of moving and placing the foot forward, backward, sideways, up, or down, as in walking, dancing, or climbing. **2.** the distance covered by such a movement [They stood three *steps* apart.] **3.** a way of stepping; gait [light, skipping *steps*]. **4.** the sound of stepping; footfall [I hear *steps* outside.] **5.** a footprint. **6.** a place to rest the foot in going up or down, as a stair or the rung of a ladder. **7.** a degree, rank, grade, etc. [A major is one *step* above a captain.] **8.** an act or process in a series [After giving first aid, the next *step* is to call the doctor.] **9.** any pattern of movements in a dance [the waltz *step*]. —*v.* **1.** to move by taking a step or steps. **2.** to walk a short distance [*Step* outside.] **3.** to measure by taking steps [John *stepped* off 100 yards.] **4.** to press the foot down [to *step* on the brake.] **5.** to move quickly [That horse can really *step* along.] **6.** to enter or join [to *step* into an argument]. —**in step,** marching, dancing, etc. with the rhythm of others or of music. —**keep step,** to stay in step. —**out of step,** not in step. —**step by step,** gradually; slowly but surely. —**step down,** to resign, as from an office. —**step up, 1.** to move forward. **2.** to make greater or faster [Steel mills have *stepped up* production.] —**take steps,** to do the things needed. —**watch one's step,** to be careful: *used only in everyday talk.* —**stepped,** *p.t. & p.p.;* **step′ping,** *pr.p.*

step·broth·er (step′bruth′ər), *n.* one's stepparent's son by a former marriage.

step·child (step′chīld), *n.* a stepson or stepdaughter. —**step·chil·ren** (step′chil′drən), *pl.*

step·daugh·ter (step′dô′tər), *n.* one's husband's or wife's daughter by a former marriage.

step·fa·ther (step′fä′*th*ər), *n.* the man who has married one's mother after the death or divorce of one's father.

step·lad·der (step′lad′ər), *n.* a ladder with broad, flat steps: *see the picture.*

step·moth·er (step′mu*th*′ər), *n.* the woman who has married one's father after the death or divorce of one's mother.

step·par·ent (step′per′ənt), *n.* one's stepfather or stepmother.

steppe (step), *n.* one of the great plains of southeastern Europe and Asia, having few trees.

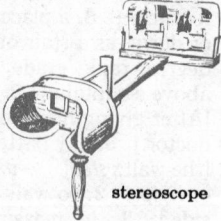
stepladder

step·ping·stone (step′ing stōn′), *n.* **1.** a stone used to step on, as in crossing a stream. **2.** a means of reaching some goal [Education is a *steppingstone* to success.] Also **stepping stone.**

step·sis·ter (step′sis′tər), *n.* one's stepparent's daughter by a former marriage.

step·son (step′sun), *n.* one's husband's or wife's son by a former marriage.

ster·e·o·phon·ic (ster′i ə fän′ik), *adj.* describing or having to do with a way of recording or broadcasting so that a listener, using several loudspeakers, hears the sounds from the directions in which they were picked up by several microphones.

ster·e·o·scope (ster′i ə skōp), *n.* a device with two eyepieces for looking at two slightly different pictures of the same scene placed side by side, so that one sees a single picture that seems to have depth instead of looking flat. —**ster·e·o·scop·ic** (ster′i ə skäp′ik), *adj.*

stereoscope

ster·e·o·type (ster′i ə tīp), *n.* **1.** a metal plate from which a page is printed. **2.** a way of thinking about a person, group, etc. that follows a fixed, common pattern, paying no attention to individual differences [the *stereotype* of a professor as a mild, absent-minded man].

ster·e·o·typed (ster′i ə tīpt), *adj.* following a fixed, common pattern, without change; not fresh or original [a *stereotyped* excuse].

ster·ile (ster′'l), *adj.* **1.** not able to produce offspring, fruit, plants, etc.; not fertile; barren [a *sterile* woman; *sterile* soil]. **2.** free from living germs [A dentist's tools must be kept clean and *sterile.*] —**ste·ril·i·ty** (stə ril′ə tē), *n.*

ster·i·lize (ster′ə līz), *v.* to make sterile [*Sterilize* the baby's bottles by putting them in boiling water.] —**ster′i·lized,** *p.t. & p.p.;* **ster′i·liz·ing,** *pr.p.* —**ster′i·li·za′tion,** *n.*

ster·ling (stur′ling), *adj.* **1.** describing or of silver that is at least 92.5% pure, until 1920 the standard of fineness in British silver coins. **2.** made of such silver [*sterling* candlesticks]. **3.** of British money [twenty pounds *sterling*]. **4.** very fine; excellent [a man of *sterling* character]. —*n.* **1.** sterling silver. **2.** British money.

stern (sturn), *adj.* **1.** strict or harsh; not gentle, tender, easy, etc. [*stern* parents; *stern* treatment]. **2.** firm or fixed; not giving in [*stern* reality]. —**stern′ly,** *adv.* —**stern′ness,** *n.*

stern (sturn), *n.* the rear end of a ship or boat.

ster·num (stur′nəm), *n.* the bone to which most of the ribs are joined in the front; breastbone.

steth·o·scope (steth′ə skōp), *n.* an instrument used by doctors for listening to sounds in the chest, as of the heart or lungs: *see the picture.*

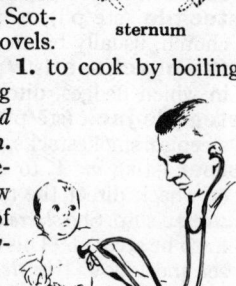
sternum

ste·ve·dore (stē′və dôr), *n.* a man who works on a dock, loading and unloading ships.

Ste·ven·son, Robert Louis (stē′vən s'n), 1850–1894; Scottish poet and writer of novels.

stew (stoo *or* styoo), *v.* **1.** to cook by boiling slowly, usually for a long time. **2.** to worry: *used only in everyday talk.* —*n.* **1.** a dish of meat and vegetables cooked by slow boiling. **2.** a condition of worry: *used only in everyday talk.*

stew·ard (stoo′ərd *or* styoo′ərd), *n.* **1.** a person hired to manage a large estate. **2.** a person put in charge of the affairs or property of another. **3.** a person in charge of the food supplies and kitchen, as in a dining car. **4.** a servant on a passenger ship. —**stew′ard·ship,** *n.*

stethoscope

stew·ard·ess (stoo′ər dis *or* styoo′ər dis), *n.* a woman whose job is to take care of the wants and needs of passengers on a ship or airplane.

St. He·le·na (he lē′nə), a British island in the southern Atlantic Ocean off the west coast of Africa. Napoleon was sent there in exile.

stick (stik), *n.* **1.** a twig or branch broken or cut off. **2.** any long, thin piece of wood, as a club, cane, etc. **3.** a long, thin piece [a *stick* of chewing gum]. **4.** a dull, stupid, or stiff person: *used only in everyday talk.* —*v.* **1.** to press a sharp point into; pierce; stab [She *stuck* her finger with a needle.] **2.** to fasten or be fastened as by pinning or gluing [He *stuck* a medal on his coat. The stamp won't *stick* to the paper.] **3.** to thrust or push; extend [He *stuck* his hands in his pockets. His ears *stick* out.] **4.** to hold back or become caught so that it cannot move [The wheels *stuck* in the mud.] **5.** to keep close or hold fast; cling [*Stick* to your job until you finish. Friends *stick* together.] **6.** to stop or hesitate because of fear, doubt, etc. [He'll *stick* at nothing to get what he wants.] **7.** to puzzle: *used only in everyday talk* [Here's a riddle that will *stick* you.] —**stick by,** to stay loyal to. —**stick up for,** to defend or support: *used only in everyday talk.* —**stuck,** *p.t. & p.p.;* **stick′ing,** *pr.p.*

stick·le·back (stik′'l bak), *n.* a small fish having sharp spines on its back and no scales.

The male builds a nest for the female's eggs.

stick·ler (stik′lər), *n.* a person who insists on having things done in a certain way [She is a *stickler* for following rules.]

stick·pin (stik′pin), *n.* a pin with a jewel, etc. at the head, for sticking in a necktie.

stick·y (stik′ē), *adj.* **1.** that sticks; gluey; clinging [His fingers were *sticky* with candy.] **2.** hot and damp; humid: *used only in everyday talk* [a *sticky* August day]. —**stick′i·er**, *compar.*; **stick′i·est**, *superl.* —**stick′i·ness**, *n.*

stiff (stif), *adj.* **1.** that does not bend easily; firm [*stiff* cardboard]. **2.** not able to move easily [*stiff* muscles]. **3.** not flowing easily; thick [Beat the egg whites until they are *stiff*.] **4.** strong; powerful [a *stiff* breeze]. **5.** not easy; difficult or hard [a *stiff* test; *stiff* punishment]. **6.** not relaxed; tense or formal [a *stiff* smile]. —**stiff′ly**, *adv.* —**stiff′ness**, *n.*

stiff·en (stif′'n), *v.* to make or become stiff or stiffer.

stiff-necked (stif′nekt′), *adj.* not giving in; stubborn.

sti·fle (stī′f'l), *v.* **1.** to kill by cutting off the supply of air; smother. **2.** to suffer or die from lack of air. **3.** to hold back; check [to *stifle* a sob]. —**sti′fled**, *p.t. & p.p.*; **sti′fling**, *pr.p.*

stig·ma (stig′mə), *n.* **1.** a bad mark on one's record; sign of disgrace [the *stigma* of having been in jail]. **2.** the upper tip of the pistil of a flower, where pollen settles to make seeds grow.

stig·ma·tize (stig′mə tīz), *v.* to give a bad name to; mark as disgraceful [His accident *stigmatized* him as a reckless driver.] —**stig′ma·tized**, *p.t. & p.p.*; **stig′ma·tiz·ing**, *pr.p.*

stile (stīl), *n.* **1.** one or more steps built beside a fence or wall for use in climbing over it. **2.** a turnstile.

sti·let·to (sti let′ō), *n.* a small, thin, sharp dagger. —**sti·let′tos** or **sti·let′toes**, *pl.*

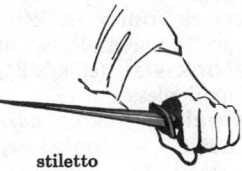

stiletto

still (stil), *adj.* **1.** without a sound or noise; quiet; silent [The empty house is *still*.] **2.** not moving or excited; calm [The air was *still* before the storm. Sit *still*!] —*n.* silence; quiet: *used mainly in poetry.* —*adv.* **1.** at or up to the time talked about; until then or now [Is he *still* living?] **2.** even; yet [It became *still* colder.] **3.** in spite of that; nevertheless [Mr. Jones, though rich, is *still* unhappy.] —*conj.* nevertheless; yet [I admire her bravery; *still* I think she was foolish.] —*v.* to make or become still, quiet, or calm [The audience *stilled* as he began to speak. The police *stilled* the outbreak.] —**still′ness**, *n.*

still (stil), *n.* a device used to distill liquids, especially alcoholic liquors.

still·born (stil′bôrn), *adj.* dead at birth.

stilt (stilt), *n.* **1.** a long pole with a support for the foot part way up it. One can walk high above the ground on a pair of stilts. **2.** any tall pole used as a support, as for a dock over water.

stilt·ed (stil′tid), *adj.* acting important or dignified in a way that is not natural.

stim·u·lant (stim′yoo lənt), *n.* something that stimulates or excites one, as coffee or any of certain drugs.

stim·u·late (stim′yoo lāt), *v.* to make more active; arouse; excite [Smells of cooking *stimulate* my appetite.] —**stim′u·lat·ed**, *p.t. & p.p.*; **stim′u·lat·ing**, *pr.p.* —**stim′u·la′tion**, *n.*

girl walking on stilts

stim·u·lus (stim′yoo ləs), *n.* anything that causes some action or activity [Under the *stimulus* of bright light, the pupil of the eye gets smaller. Advertising can be a *stimulus* to business.] —**stim·u·li** (stim′yoo lī), *pl.*

sting (sting), *v.* **1.** to hurt by pricking [Bees and wasps can *sting* you.] **2.** to cause or feel sharp pain [The cold wind *stung* her cheeks. My arm *stings* from the blow.] **3.** to make unhappy; pain [He was *stung* by her criticism.] **4.** to cheat: *a slang meaning.* —*n.* **1.** the act or power of stinging [The *sting* of some insects is dangerous.] **2.** a pain or wound caused by stinging. **3.** a pointed part with which some insects, etc. sting. —**stung**, *p.t. & p.p.*; **sting′ing**, *pr.p.*

sting ray, a large flat fish with a sharp spine or spines on its long, thin tail, that can cause serious wounds.

stin·gy (stin′jē), *adj.* not willing to give or spend money; like a miser; grudging. —**stin′gi·er**, *compar.*; **stin′gi·est**, *superl.* —**stin′gi·ly**, *adv.* —**stin′gi·ness**, *n.*

sting ray (20 in. long, not including tail)

stink (stingk), *v.* to give off a strong, bad smell. —*n.* a strong, bad smell; stench. —**stank** or **stunk**, *p.t.*; **stunk**, *p.p.*; **stink′ing**, *pr.p.*

stint (stint), *v.* to give only a small amount to; limit to a small share [He *stinted* himself on meals to buy an opera ticket.] —*n.* **1.** the act of stinting; limit [to help without *stint*]. **2.** a task or share of work to be done [Each child does his *stint* of housework.]

sti·pend (stī′pend), *n.* regular pay for work done; salary.

stip·ple (stip′'l), *v.* to paint or draw with small dots or spots. —**stip′pled**, *p.t. & p.p.*; **stip′pling**, *pr.p.*

stip·u·late (stip′yoo lāt), *v.* to tell or state as a necessary condition, as in a contract [He *stipulated* that the college use his gift for a new library.] —**stip′u·lat·ed,** *p.t. & p.p.;* **stip′-u·lat·ing,** *pr.p.* —**stip′u·la′tion,** *n.*

stip·ule (stip′yool), *n.* one of a pair of little leaves at the base of the stem of a leaf.

stir (stŭr), *v.* **1.** to move or shake slightly [Not a leaf *stirred* in the quiet air.] **2.** to move around or be active ["Not a creature was *stirring.*"] **3.** to make move or be active [He *stirred* himself to finish the work.] **4.** to mix by moving a spoon, fork, etc. around [*Stir* the paint well.] **5.** to cause strong feelings in; excite [His speech *stirred* the crowd.] —*n.* **1.** the act of stirring [Give the fire a *stir.*] **2.** the condition of being excited [The touchdown caused a *stir* in the crowd.] —**stirred,** *p.t. & p.p.;* **stir′ring,** *pr.p.*

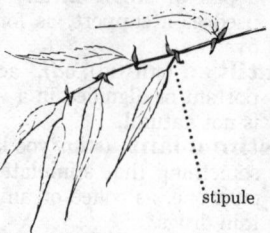
stipule

stir·ring (stŭr′ing), *adj.* that stirs one's feelings; exciting [*stirring* music].

stir·rup (stŭr′əp), *n.* either of two rings with a flat bottom, hung by straps from the sides of a saddle. The rider puts his feet in them.

stitch (stich), *n.* **1.** one complete movement of a needle and thread into and out of the material in sewing. **2.** one complete movement done in various ways in knitting, crocheting, etc. **3.** a loop made by stitching [Tight *stitches* pucker the cloth.] **4.** a sudden, sharp pain, as in the side. **5.** a bit: *used only in everyday talk* [I didn't do a *stitch* of work.] —*v.* to sew or fasten with stitches [to *stitch* a seam].

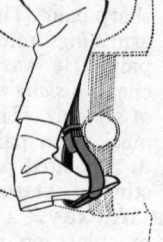
stirrup

St. Law·rence (lôr′əns), a river that flows from Lake Ontario into the Atlantic Ocean.

St. Lawrence Seaway, a waterway for large ships between the Great Lakes and the Atlantic Ocean, made up of the St. Lawrence River, canals, etc.

St. Lou·is (loo′is *or* loo′ē), a city in eastern Missouri, on the Mississippi River.

stock (stäk), *n.* **1.** a supply on hand for use or for sale [Our *stock* of food is low.] **2.** livestock; cattle, horses, sheep, pigs, etc. **3.** shares in a business [He bought *stock* in several companies.] **4.** ancestry or family [He is of French *stock.*] **5.** a particular breed of an animal or plant. **6.** water in which meat or fish has been boiled, used to make soup, gravy, etc. **7.** the part that serves as a handle or body for the working parts [The *stock* of a rifle holds the barrel in place.] **8.** a tree trunk or stump. **9. stocks,** *pl.* a wooden frame with holes for locking around a person's ankles and, sometimes, wrists, used in earlier times as a punishment. **10.** a stiff, close-fitting band once worn about the neck by men. —*v.* **1.** to furnish with stock or a supply [to *stock* a farm with cattle; to *stock* a store with new goods]. **2.** to put in or keep a supply of [This shop *stocks* the kind of shirt you want.] —*adj.* **1.** always kept on hand as for sale [The lumber-yard has *stock* sizes of door frames.] **2.** common or trite [a *stock* joke]. —**in stock,** on hand for sale or use. —**out of stock,** not on hand for sale or use. —**take stock, 1.** to make an inventory of stock. **2.** to examine the situation before deciding or acting. —**take stock in,** to believe in or have faith in: *used only in everyday talk.*

stock·ade (stä kād′), *n.* **1.** a wall of tall stakes built around a place for defense, as in early American forts. **2.** such a fort.

stock·bro·ker (stäk′brō′kər), *n.* a person in the business of buying and selling stocks and bonds for other people.

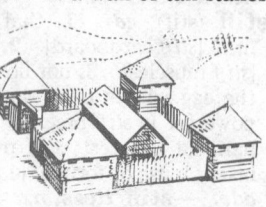
stockade (meaning 2)

stock company, a company of actors who put on a series of plays over a period of time.

stock exchange, 1. a place where stocks and bonds are bought and sold. **2.** the brokers who do business there.

stock·hold·er (stäk′hōl′dər), *n.* a person who owns stock or shares in a company.

Stock·holm (stäk′hōm *or* stäk′hōlm), *n.* the capital of Sweden, on the Baltic Sea.

stock·ing (stäk′ing), *n.* a knitted covering for the leg and foot, coming up to or over the knee.

stock market, 1. a place where stocks and bonds are bought and sold. **2.** the buying and selling done there, or the prices listed there.

stock·pile (stäk′pīl), *n.* a supply of goods, raw materials, etc. stored up for use when needed. —*v.* to collect a stockpile of [to *stockpile* steel]. —**stock′piled,** *p.t. & p.p.;* **stock′pil·ing,** *pr.p.*

stock·room (stäk′room), *n.* a room where goods, materials, etc. are stored.

stock-still (stäk′stil′), *adj.* not moving at all; motionless.

stock·y (stäk′ē), *adj.* having a short, heavy build. —**stock′i·er,** *compar.;* **stock′i·est,** *superl.*

stock·yard (stäk′yärd), *n.* a yard with pens where cattle, hogs, sheep, etc. are kept until they can be sent to market or slaughtered.

stodg·y (stäj′ē), *adj.* heavy and dull; stuffy, uninteresting, etc. [*stodgy* thinking]. —**stodg′-i·er,** *compar.;* **stodg′i·est,** *superl.*

sto·ic (stō′ik), *n.* a person who stays calm and patient under pain, suffering, trouble, etc. —**sto′i·cal** or **sto′ic,** *adj.* —**sto′i·cal·ly,** *adv.*

stoke (stōk), *v.* to stir up and add fuel to [to *stoke* a fire; to *stoke* a furnace]. —**stoked,** *p.t. & p.p.;* **stok′ing,** *pr.p.*

stoke·hold (stōk′hōld), *n.* the furnace and boiler room of a steamship.

stok·er (stōk′ər), *n.* **1.** a man who stokes a furnace, as of a boiler on a ship. **2.** a machine that puts fuel into a furnace as it is needed.

stole (stōl), *n.* **1.** a woman's long scarf of cloth or fur worn with the ends hanging down in front. **2.** a long strip of cloth worn like a scarf by clergymen in some churches.

stole (stōl), past tense of **steal.**

stol·en (stōl′ən), past participle of **steal.**

stol·id (stäl′id), *adj.* having or showing little feeling; not easily excited. **—sto·lid·i·ty** (stə lid′ə tē), *n.* **—stol′id·ly,** *adv.*

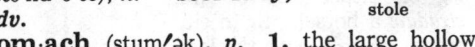
stole

stom·ach (stum′ək), *n.* **1.** the large hollow organ into which food goes after it is swallowed. Food is partly digested in the stomach. **2.** the belly, or abdomen [He was hit in the *stomach*.] **3.** appetite or desire [He has no *stomach* for fighting.] **—v.** to bear or put up with [She could not *stomach* such injustice.]

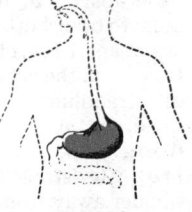
stomach

stom·ach·er (stum′ək ər), *n.* a decorated piece of cloth once worn by women over the front of the body.

stomp (stämp), *n. & v.* stamp: *used mainly in certain regions.*

stone (stōn), *n.* **1.** hard mineral matter that is found in the earth but is not metal; rock [a monument built of *stone*]. **2.** a small piece of this [Don't throw *stones*. Rubies are precious *stones*.] **3.** a piece of this shaped for some purpose, as a gravestone or grindstone. **4.** the hard seed of certain fruits [the *stone* of a peach]. **5.** a British unit of weight equal to 14 pounds. **6.** a small, hard mass that may form in the kidney or gall bladder and cause illness. **—v. 1.** to throw stones at or kill with stones. **2.** to remove the stone, or seed, from [to *stone* cherries]. **—adj.** of stone or stoneware. *The pl. for meaning 5 is* **stone.** **—stoned,** *p.t. & p.p.;* **ston′ing,** *pr.p.*

Stone Age, a very early period in the history of man when stone tools and weapons were used.

stone-blind (stōn′blīnd′), *adj.* completely blind.

stone·cut·ter (stōn′kut′ər), *n.* a person or machine that cuts stone and makes it smooth.

stone-deaf (stōn′def′), *adj.* completely deaf.

stone·ware (stōn′wer), *n.* a heavy kind of pottery with a thick glaze.

stone·work (stōn′wûrk), *n.* **1.** the work of building things of stone. **2.** something built of stone.

ston·y (stō′nē), *adj.* **1.** covered with stones [a *stony* road]. **2.** like stone; hard, cold, etc. [a *stony* heart; a *stony* look]. **—ston′i·er,** *compar.;* **ston′i·est,** *superl.* **—ston′i·ly,** *adv.*

stood (stood), past tense and past participle of **stand.**

stool (stōol), *n.* **1.** a single seat with no back or arms. **2.** a footstool.

stool pigeon, a person who acts as a spy for the police or who informs on others to the police: *used only in everyday talk.*

stool

stoop (stōop), *v.* **1.** to bend the body forward or in a crouch [He *stooped* to tie his shoes.] **2.** to stand or walk with the head and shoulders bent forward. **3.** to lower one's dignity or character [He *stooped* to taking bribes.] **—n.** the act or position of stooping.

stoop (stōop), *n.* a small porch or platform, usually with steps, at an entrance of a house.

stop (stäp), *v.* **1.** to halt or keep from going on, moving, acting, etc.; bring or come to an end [My watch *stopped*. The noise *stopped*. *Stop* the car. He *stopped* us from talking.] **2.** to close by filling, covering, etc. [to *stop* up cracks with putty]. **3.** to clog or block [The drain in the sink is *stopped* up.] **4.** to stay or visit [We *stopped* there overnight.] **—n. 1.** a place stopped at [a *stop* on a bus route]. **2.** something that stops [A *stop* for a door keeps it from opening or closing.] **3.** the act or fact of stopping; finish; end [Put a *stop* to this argument.] **4.** a stay or halt in a trip. **5.** a punctuation mark, especially a period. **6.** a hole, key, pull, etc. for making a certain tone or tones on a musical instrument. **—stop off,** to stop for a short visit on the way to a place. **—stop over, 1.** to stay for a while. **2.** to halt a journey, as for rest. **—stopped,** *p.t. & p.p.;* **stop′ping,** *pr.p.*

stop·gap (stäp′gap), *n.* something used for a time in place of the usual thing.

stop·o·ver (stäp′ō′vər), *n.* a stop for a time at a place while on a trip.

stop·page (stäp′ij), *n.* a stopping or being stopped or stopped up [a *stoppage* in the pipe].

stop·per (stäp′ər), *n.* something put into an opening to close it; plug [A cork is a bottle *stopper*.]

stop·ple (stäp′'l), *n.* same as **stopper.**

stop watch, a watch with a hand that can be started and stopped instantly so as to measure exactly the time that a race, etc. takes.

sink stopper

stor·age (stôr′ij), *n.* **1.** a storing or being stored. **2.** a place or space for storing things. **3.** the cost of keeping goods stored.

storage battery, a battery with cells in it in which electricity can be stored for use as needed.

store (stôr), *n.* **1.** a place of business where things are sold [a candy *store*; a department *store*]. **2.** a supply or stock for use as needed [a *store* of coal]. **3.** a storehouse. **4.** a great amount [a *store* of knowledge]. **—v. 1.** to put aside for safekeeping until needed [*Store* the extra chairs in the attic.] **2.** to fill with a supply or store [to *store* a cabin with provisions]. **—in store,** set aside; waiting to be used, to happen, etc. **—set store by,** to have a good opinion of; value. **—stored,** *p.t. & p.p.;* **stor′ing,** *pr.p.*

store·house (stôr′hous), *n.* a place where things are stored, especially a warehouse.

store·keep·er (stôr′kēp′ər), *n.* a person who owns or manages a store.

store·room (stôr′rōōm), *n.* a room where things are stored.

sto·rey (stôr′ē), *n.* a story of a building: *a British spelling.* **—sto′reys,** *pl.*

sto·ried (stôr′ēd), *adj.* famous in stories or in history [*storied* Rome].

sto·ried (stôr′ēd), *adj.* having a certain number of stories or floors [a ten-*storied* hotel].

stork (stôrk), *n.* a large wading bird with long legs and a long neck and bill.

storm (stôrm), *n.* **1.** a strong wind along with a heavy rain, snow, etc. and, often, thunder and lightning. **2.** any heavy fall of rain, snow, etc. **3.** any strong outburst or shower of objects [a *storm* of bullets; a *storm* of criticism].

storks (3½ ft. long)

4. a sudden, strong attack by soldiers [They took the city by *storm*.] **—v. 1.** to blow violently and rain, snow, etc. **2.** to be angry; rage; rant. **3.** to rush violently [He *stormed* out of the house.] **4.** to attack strongly [to *storm* a fort].

storm·y (stôr′mē), *adj.* **1.** of or having storms [*stormy* weather; a *stormy* day]. **2.** wild, rough, angry, etc. [a *stormy* debate]. **—storm′i·er,** *compar.;* **storm′i·est,** *superl.*

sto·ry (stôr′ē), *n.* **1.** a telling of some happening, whether true or made-up [the *story* of the first Thanksgiving]. **2.** a made-up tale, written down, that is shorter than a novel [the *stories* of Poe]. **3.** a lie or falsehood: *used only in everyday talk.* **—sto′ries,** *pl.*

sto·ry (stôr′ē), *n.* the space or rooms making up one level of a building, from a floor to the ceiling above it [a building with ten *stories*]. **—sto′ries,** *pl.*

stoup (stōōp), *n.* **1.** a large drinking cup: *now seldom used.* **2.** a basin for holy water inside the entrance of some churches.

stout (stout), *adj.* **1.** having a fat body. **2.** strong and firm; sturdy [a *stout* wall]. **3.** powerful [They put up a *stout* fight.] **4.** brave; full of courage [a *stout* heart]. *n.* a strong, dark beer. **—stout′ly,** *adv.* **—stout′ness,** *n.*

stout·heart·ed (stout′här′tid), *adj.* brave.

stove (stōv), *n.* a device for cooking or heating by the use of gas, oil, electricity, etc.

stove (stōv), a past tense and past participle of **stave.**

stove·pipe (stōv′pīp), *n.* **1.** a wide pipe used to carry off smoke from a stove. **2.** a man's tall silk hat: *used only in everyday talk.*

stow (stō), *v.* **1.** to pack in a close, orderly way [to *stow* luggage in a car trunk]. **2.** to fill by packing. **—stow away, 1.** to store or hide away. **2.** to be a stowaway.

stow·a·way (stō′ə wā), *n.* a person who hides aboard a ship, plane, etc. for a free or secret ride.

St. Paul, the capital of Minnesota, on the Mississippi River.

St. Pe·ters·burg (pē′tərz bŭrg), **1.** an old name for the city of Leningrad in the Soviet Union. **2.** a city in northern Florida.

strad·dle (strad′'l), *v.* **1.** to stand or sit with a leg on either side of [to *straddle* a horse]. **2.** to sit, stand, or walk with the legs wide apart. **3.** to take, or seem to take, both sides of an argument, issue, etc.; be neutral. **—n.** the act or position of straddling. **—strad′dled,** *p.t. & p.p.;* **strad′dling,** *pr.p.*

strag·gle (strag′'l), *v.* **1.** to wander away from the path, course, or main group. **2.** to be scattered or spread out in a careless or uneven way [old rambler roses *straggling* on a trellis]. **—strag′gled,** *p.t. & p.p.;* **strag′gling,** *pr.p.* **—strag′gler,** *n.* **—strag′gly,** *adj.*

boy straddling a fence

straight (strāt), *adj.* **1.** having the same direction all the way; not crooked, curved, wavy, etc. [a *straight* line; *straight* hair]. **2.** upright or erect [*straight* posture]. **3.** level or even [Put the picture *straight*.] **4.** direct; staying right to the point, direction, etc. [a *straight* course; a *straight* answer]. **5.** in order; not in confusion, error, etc. [Put your room *straight*. Is his figuring *straight*?] **6.** honest and sincere [*straight* dealing]. **7.** not mixed or divided [to vote a *straight* ticket]. **—adv. 1.** in a straight line. **2.** in a way that is straight, direct, right, etc. **—straight away** or **straight off,** at once; without delay.

straight·en (strāt′'n), *v.* **1.** to make or become straight [He *straightened* his tie.] **2.** to put in order [to *straighten* a room].

straight-faced (strāt′fāst′), *adj.* showing no amusement or other feeling.

straight·for·ward (strāt′fôr′wərd), *adj.* **1.** moving or leading straight ahead; direct. **2.** honest; frank. **—adv.** directly.

straight·way (strāt′wā), *adv.* at once.

strain (strān), *v.* **1.** to draw or stretch tight [Samson *strained* his chains and broke them.] **2.** to use or explain in a way that is forced and not right [He *strained* the rules to suit himself.] **3.** to use to the utmost [He *strained* every nerve to win.] **4.** to hurt or weaken by too much force, effort, etc. [to *strain* a muscle]. **5.** to try very hard [She *strained* to hear him.] **6.** to pull with force [The horse *strained* at the harness.] **7.** to put or pass through a screen, sieve, etc. [to *strain* soup]. **8.** to hug [to *strain* a child to one's bosom]. **—n. 1.** a straining or being strained. **2.** hard, tiring effort of the body or mind, or the hurt caused by this. **3.** great force or pressure

[The *strain* of the weight on the bridge made it collapse.] **4.** a sprain or wrench, as of a muscle.

strain (strān), *n.* **1.** family line; race, stock, breed, etc. **2.** a quality that seems to be inherited [There is a *strain* of genius in that family.] **3.** a trace or streak [There is a *strain* of sadness in his poems.] **4.** *often* **strains,** *pl.* a passage of music; tune.

strained (strānd), *adj.* not natural or relaxed; forced [a *strained* laugh].

strain·er (strān′ər), *n.* a thing used for straining, as a sieve, filter, etc.

strait (strāt), *n. often* **straits,** *pl.* **1.** a narrow body of water joining two larger ones. **2.** trouble or need [to be in desperate *straits*].

strait·en (strāt′n), *v.* to make narrow, limited, difficult, etc.: *now only in the phrase* **in straitened circumstances,** meaning "not having enough money to live on."

strait jacket, a kind of coat tied around one to keep the arms from being moved. It is sometimes used, as in hospitals, to keep people who are acting wild from doing harm.

strand (strand), *n.* a shore, especially along an ocean. —*v.* **1.** to run onto the ground [to *strand* a ship]. **2.** to put into a helpless position [*stranded* in a desert without water].

strand (strand), *n.* **1.** any of the threads, fibers, or wires that are twisted together to make a string, rope, or cable. **2.** anything like a string or rope [a *strand* of hair].

strange (strānj), *adj.* **1.** not known, seen, or heard before; not familiar [I saw a *strange* man at the door.] **2.** different from what is usual; peculiar; odd [wearing a *strange* costume]. **3.** not familiar; without experience [He is *strange* to this job.] —*adv.* in a strange way [He acts so *strange* lately.] —**stran′ger,** *compar.;* **stran′gest,** *superl.* —**strange′ly,** *adv.*

stran·ger (strān′jər), *n.* **1.** a person who is new to a place; outsider; foreigner. **2.** a person not known to one [The children were warned not to speak to *strangers*.] **3.** a person not used to something [He is a *stranger* to hate.]

stran·gle (strang′g'l), *v.* **1.** to kill by squeezing the throat so as to stop the breathing. **2.** to choke in any way; suffocate [*strangled* by the thick smoke]. **3.** to hold back; stop [He *strangled* a desire to scream.] —**stran′gled,** *p.t. & p.p.;* **stran′gling,** *pr.p.* —**stran′gler,** *n.*

strap (strap), *n.* **1.** a narrow strip of leather, canvas, etc., often with a buckle, for tying or holding things together. **2.** any narrow strip like a strap [a shoulder *strap*]. —*v.* **1.** to fasten with a strap [*Strap* the boxes together.] **2.** to beat with a strap. —**strapped,** *p.t. & p.p.;* **strap′ping,** *pr.p.* —**strap′less,** *adj.*

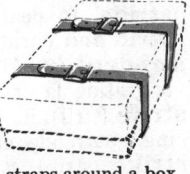
straps around a box

strap·ping (strap′ing), *adj.* tall and strong; robust: *used only in everyday talk.*

Stras·bourg (stras′bərg), *n.* a city in northeastern France, on the Rhine River.

stra·ta (strā′tə - *or* strat′ə), *n.* a plural of **stratum.**

strat·a·gem (strat′ə jəm), *n.* a trick or scheme, as one used in war to deceive an enemy.

stra·te·gic (strə tē′jik), *adj.* **1.** of or having to do with strategy [*strategic* problems]. **2.** showing sound planning; useful or important in strategy [a *strategic* retreat].

strat·e·gist (strat′ə jist), *n.* a person who is skilled in strategy.

strat·e·gy (strat′ə jē), *n.* **1.** the science of planning and directing military movements and operations. **2.** skill in managing any matter, especially by using tricks and schemes [It took *strategy* to get him to come with us.]

Strat·ford up·on A·von (strat′fərd ə pän′ ā′vən), a town in central England, where Shakespeare was born: also called **Stratford-on-Avon.**

strat·i·fy (strat′ə fī), *v.* to arrange in layers [*stratified* rock]. —**strat′i·fied,** *p.t. & p.p.;* **strat′i·fy·ing,** *pr.p.*

strat·o·sphere (strat′ə sfir), *n.* the upper part of the earth's atmosphere, beginning about seven miles above the earth.

stra·tum (strā′təm *or* strat′əm), *n.* **1.** a layer of matter, especially any of several layers, as of rock or earth, lying one upon another. **2.** a section or level of society [the upper *stratum*]. —**stra′ta** or **stra′tums,** *pl.*

rock strata

Strauss, Jo·han (yō′hän strous), 1825–1899; Austrian composer of waltzes.

straw (strô), *n.* **1.** hollow stalks, as of wheat or rye, after the grain has been threshed out. Straw is used as stuffing or is woven into hats, etc. **2.** a single one of such stalks. **3.** a tube, as of waxed paper, used for sucking a drink. —*adj.* **1.** of the color of straw; yellowish. **2.** made of straw [a *straw* hat].

straw·ber·ry (strô′ber′ē), *n.* **1.** the small, red, juicy fruit of a low plant of the rose family. **2.** this plant. —**straw′ber′ries,** *pl.*

straw vote, an unofficial poll to find out what people think about some matter.

stray (strā), *v.* **1.** to wander from a certain place, path, etc.; roam [Don't *stray* from the camp. His thoughts *strayed* from the test.] **2.** to go away from what is right [to *stray*

strawberry plant

from truth]. —*n.* a lost or wandering person or animal. —*adj.* **1.** that has strayed and is lost [a *stray* dog]. **2.** occasional; here and there [a few *stray* cars on the streets].

streak (strēk), *n.* **1.** a long, thin mark, stripe, or smear [a *streak* of dirt]. **2.** a layer, as of a mineral in the earth or of fat in meat. **3.** a certain amount of some quality [He has a mean *streak* in him.] **4.** a period or spell: *used only in everyday talk* [a *streak* of bad luck]. —*v.* **1.** to mark with streaks. **2.** to go fast; hurry [to *streak* down the road]. —**like a streak,** swiftly: *used only in everyday talk.*

stream (strēm), *n.* **1.** a flow of water; especially, a small river. **2.** a steady flow of anything [a *stream* of cold air; a *stream* of light; a *stream* of cars]. —*v.* **1.** to flow in a stream. **2.** to pour out or flow [eyes *streaming* with tears]. **3.** to move steadily or swiftly [The crowd *streamed* out of the stadium.] **4.** to float or fly [a flag *streaming* in the breeze].

stream·er (strēm/ər), *n.* **1.** a long, narrow flag. **2.** any narrow, flowing strip of material.

stream·line (strēm/līn), *v.* to make streamlined. —*adj.* streamlined. —**stream/lined,** *p.t. & p.p.;* **stream/lin·ing,** *pr.p.*

stream·lined (strēm/līnd), *adj.* **1.** having a shape that allows air, water, etc. to pass smoothly over it [a *streamlined* boat]. **2.** arranged so as to be more efficient [a *streamlined* program].

street (strēt), *n.* **1.** a road in a city or town; also, such a road with its sidewalks and buildings. **2.** the people who live or work on a certain street [Our whole *street* gave money to the fund.]

street·car (strēt/kär), *n.* a large car on rails for carrying people along the streets.

strength (strength), *n.* **1.** the quality of being strong; force, power, ability to last or resist, etc. [the *strength* of a blow, of a steel girder, or of a nation]. **2.** the degree to which something has an effect [the *strength* of a drug, or of a color, light, sound, taste, etc.]. **3.** force, as measured in numbers [an army at full *strength*]. **4.** something that gives strength. —**on the strength of,** depending on or relying on.

strength·en (streng/thən), *v.* to make or become stronger.

stren·u·ous (stren/yoo əs), *adj.* **1.** needing much energy [Chopping wood is a *strenuous* task.] **2.** very active or vigorous [a *strenuous* worker]. —**stren/u·ous·ly,** *adv.*

strep·to·coc·cus (strep/tə käk/əs), *n.* a kind of bacteria shaped like a ball. Some forms cause disease. —**strep·to·coc·ci** (strep/tə käk/sī), *pl.*

strep·to·my·cin (strep/tə mī/sin), *n.* a chemical substance gotten from a soil fungus. It is an antibiotic used in treating certain diseases, as tuberculosis.

stress (stres), *n.* **1.** strain or pressure [the *stress* on the wings of an airplane; under the *stress* of a crisis]. **2.** special attention; emphasis [Our doctor puts *stress* on good health habits.] **3.** special force given a syllable, word, or note in speaking or in music; accent. —*v.* **1.** to put pressure or strain on. **2.** to accent or emphasize.

stretch (strech), *v.* **1.** to reach out or hold out, as a hand, object, etc. **2.** to draw out to full length, to a greater size, to a certain distance, etc.; extend [He *stretched* out on the sofa. Will this material *stretch*? *Stretch* the rope between two trees. The road *stretches* for miles through the hills.] **3.** to pull or draw tight; strain [to *stretch* a muscle]. **4.** to draw out too far, as by exaggerating [to *stretch* a rule; to *stretch* the truth]. —*n.* **1.** a stretching or being stretched. **2.** the ability to be stretched [This elastic band has lost its *stretch*.] **3.** an unbroken space, as of time or land; extent [a *stretch* of two years; a long *stretch* of beach].

stretch·er (strech/ər), *n.* **1.** a person or thing that stretches, as a frame for stretching curtains. **2.** a light frame covered with canvas, etc., used for carrying people who are sick or hurt.

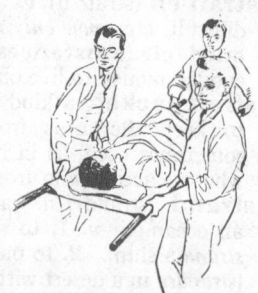
men carrying a stretcher

strew (stroo), *v.* **1.** to scatter; spread about here and there [clothes *strewn* on the floor]. **2.** to cover as by scattering [The street was *strewn* with litter.] —**strewed,** *p.t.;* **strewed** or **strewn** (stroon), *p.p.;* **strew/ing,** *pr.p.*

stri·at·ed (strī/āt id), *adj.* marked with parallel lines or bands; striped.

strick·en (strik/ən), a past participle of **strike.** —*adj.* **1.** struck or wounded. **2.** suffering, as from pain, trouble, etc.

strict (strikt), *adj.* **1.** keeping to rules in a careful, exact way. **2.** never changing; rigid [a *strict* rule]. **3.** perfect; exact or absolute [a *strict* translation; *strict* silence]. —**strict/ly,** *adv.* —**strict/ness,** *n.*

stric·ture (strik/chər), *n.* **1.** strong criticism. **2.** a narrowing of a tube, etc. in the body, as in a disease.

stride (strīd), *v.* **1.** to walk with long steps. **2.** to cross with one long step [He *strode* over the log.] **3.** to sit or stand with a leg on either side of; straddle [to *stride* a horse]. —*n.* **1.** a long step, or the distance covered by it. **2.** *usually* **strides,** *pl.* progress [great *strides* in industry]. —**hit one's stride,** to reach one's normal level of skill or speed. —**take in one's stride,** to deal with easily. —**strode,** *p.t.;* **strid·den** (strid/'n), *p.p.;* **strid/ing,** *pr.p.*

stri·dent (strī/d'nt), *adj.* harsh in sound; shrill or grating [a *strident* voice].

strife (strīf), *n.* **1.** the act or condition of fighting, quarreling, etc. **2.** a fight or quarrel.

strike (strīk), *v.* **1.** to hit by giving a blow, coming against with force, etc. [John *struck* him in anger. The car *struck* the curb.] **2.** to make a sound by hitting some part [The clock *struck* one. *Strike* middle C on the piano.] **3.** to set on fire as by rubbing [to *strike* a match]. **4.** to make by stamping, printing, etc. [The mint *strikes* coins.] **5.** to attack [A rattlesnake makes a noise before it *strikes.*] **6.** to come upon; reach or find [A sound of music *struck* my ear. They drilled and *struck* oil.] **7.** to hit one's mind or feelings [The idea just *struck* me. It *strikes* me as silly.] **8.** to bring about [The scream *struck* terror to my heart.] **9.** to overcome as by a blow [Flu *struck* the entire family.] **10.** to reach, as by planning [We *struck* a bargain.] **11.** to take down or take apart [We *struck* camp at noon. *Strike* the sails.] **12.** to go; proceed [We *struck* northward.] **13.** to take on; assume [to *strike* a pose]. **14.** to stop working until certain demands have been met [The workers are *striking* for shorter hours.] —*n.* **1.** the act of striking; a blow. **2.** the act of stopping work in order to get higher wages, better working conditions, etc. **3.** a sudden or lucky success, as the act of finding oil. **4.** in baseball, a fairly pitched ball which the batter does not hit into fair territory according to the rules of the game. Three strikes put the batter out. **5.** in bowling, the act of knocking down all ten pins with the first roll of the ball. —**on strike** or **out on strike,** striking; refusing to work. —**strike dumb,** to astonish. —**strike home,** to have an effect. —**strike it rich,** to have sudden success, as by discovering oil. —**strike off,** to remove as from a list. —**strike out, 1.** to cross out; erase. **2.** to start out. **3.** in baseball, to be put out by three strikes; also, to put out by pitching three strikes. —**strike up,** to begin, as a friendship. —**struck,** *p.t.;* **struck** or **strick'en,** *p.p.;* **strik'ing,** *pr.p.* —**strik'-er,** *n.*

strik·ing (strīk'ing), *adj.* getting attention because unusual or remarkable [She wore a *striking* hat.] —**strik'ing·ly,** *adv.*

string (string), *n.* **1.** a thick thread or thin strip of cloth, leather, etc., used for tying or pulling; cord. **2.** a number of objects on a string [a *string* of pearls]. **3.** a number of things in a row [a *string* of lights]. **4.** a thin cord of wire, gut, etc. that is bowed, plucked, or struck to make a musical sound, as on a violin or piano. **5. strings,** *pl.* stringed musical instruments played with a bow. **6.** a plant fiber like a thread, as along the seam in a pod of a string bean. **7.** a condition or limit: *used only in everyday talk* [an offer with no *strings* attached]. —*v.* **1.** to put strings on [to *string* a tennis racket]. **2.** to put on a string [to *string* beads]. **3.** to tie, hang, etc. with a string. **4.** to stretch like a string; extend [to *string* telephone wires on poles; to *string* out a speech]. **5.** to remove the strings from [to *string* beans]. —**pull strings,** to use influence to get what one wants or to control others. —**string along,** to fool; trick: *used only in everyday talk.* —**string along with,** to follow faithfully. —**strung,** *p.t. & p.p.;* **string'ing,** *pr.p.*

string bean, 1. a bean with thick pods eaten as a vegetable before they ripen. **2.** the pod.

stringed (stringd), *adj.* having strings [Harps, violins, etc. are *stringed* instruments.]

strin·gent (strin'jənt), *adj.* **1.** strict; severe [a *stringent* rule]. **2.** forceful; convincing [*stringent* reasons]. **3.** with little money for loans [a *stringent* market]. —**strin'gen·cy,** *n.* —**strin'gent·ly,** *adv.*

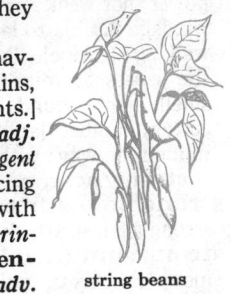
string beans

string·er (string'ər), *n.* a long piece of timber used as a support or to connect upright posts.

string·y (string'ē), *adj.* **1.** like string; long and thin. **2.** having tough fibers, as celery. **3.** forming strings [*stringy* honey]. —**string'i·er,** *compar.;* **string'i·est,** *superl.*

strip (strip), *v.* **1.** to take off one's clothes; undress. **2.** to take the covering from; skin, peel, etc. [to *strip* a tree of bark]. **3.** to take off; remove [to *strip* husks from corn]. **4.** to make bare by taking things away; clear or rob [to *strip* a room of furniture]. **5.** to take apart [to *strip* down a motor]. **6.** to break off, as the thread of a screw or the teeth of a gear. —**stripped,** *p.t. & p.p.;* **strip'ping,** *pr.p.* —**strip'per,** *n.*

strip (strip), *n.* a long, narrow piece, as of land, material, etc.

stripe (strīp), *n.* **1.** a narrow band of a different color or material from the part around it [The flag has red and white *stripes.*] **2.** a raised place on the skin, as from a whipping; welt. **3.** kind or sort [a man of his *stripe*]. —*v.* to mark with stripes. —**striped,** *p.t. & p.p.;* **strip'ing,** *pr.p.*

strip·ling (strip'ling), *n.* a grown boy; youth.

strive (strīv), *v.* **1.** to make great efforts; try very hard [We must *strive* to win.] **2.** to struggle or fight [We *strive* against disease.] —**strove,** *p.t.;* **striv·en** (striv'n), *p.p.;* **striv'ing,** *pr.p.*

strode (strōd), past tense of *stride.*

stroke (strōk), *n.* **1.** the act of striking; a blow [a tree felled with six *strokes; a stroke* of lightning]. **2.** the sound of striking, as of a clock. **3.** a single strong effort [He hasn't done a *stroke* of work.] **4.** a sudden action or event [a *stroke* of luck]. **5.** a sudden attack of illness, as of paralysis. **6.** a single movement, as with some tool [a *stroke* of a pen; a backhand *stroke* in tennis]. **7.** a mark made in writing, painting, etc. **8.** one of a series of repeated motions, as in swimming. **9.** the rower who sets the rate of rowing. —*v.* **1.** to rub gently with one's hand, a brush, etc. **2.** to set the rate of rowing for a crew. —**stroked,** *p.t. & p.p.;* **strok'ing,** *pr.p.*

stroll (strōl), *v.* **1.** to walk in a slow, easy way. **2.** to wander from place to place [a *strolling* musician]. —*n.* a slow, easy walk.

stroll·er (strōl'ər), *n.* **1.** a person who strolls. **2.** a small cart for babies learning to walk.

---

fat, āpe, cär, ten, ēven, hit, bīte, gō, hôrn, tool, book, up, fur; get, joy, yet, chin, she, thin, *th*en; zh = s in pleasure; ' as in able (ā'b'l); ə = a in ago, e in agent, i in sanity, o in confess, u in focus.

strong (strông), *adj.* **1.** having great force or power; not weak; powerful [a *strong* man; *strong* winds]. **2.** able to last; durable; tough [a *strong* wall; *strong* rope]. **3.** having a powerful effect on the senses or mind; not mild [a *strong* taste, smell, light, sound, liking, etc.]. **4.** having a certain number [an army 50,000 *strong*]. —*adv.* in a strong way; with force. —**strong′ly,** *adv.* —**strong′ness,** *n.*

strong·hold (strông′hōld), *n.* a place made strong against attack; fortress.

stron·ti·um (strän′shi əm), *n.* a chemical element that is a pale-yellow metal. A deadly radioactive form, **strontium 90,** occurs in the fallout of atomic explosions.

strop (sträp), *n.* a leather strap on which razors are sharpened. —*v.* to sharpen on a strop. —**stropped,** *p.t. & p.p.;* **strop′ping,** *pr.p.*

stro·phe (strō′fē), *n.* a stanza of a poem.

strove (strōv), past tense of **strive.**

struck (struk), past tense and a past participle of **strike.**

struc·tur·al (struk′chər əl), *adj.* **1.** used in building [*structural* steel]. **2.** of structure [*structural* design]. —**struc′tur·al·ly,** *adv.*

struc·ture (struk′chər), *n.* **1.** something built; a building, bridge, dam, etc. **2.** the way in which something is built or put together; construction, plan, design, etc. [the *structure* of a novel].

strug·gle (strug′'l), *v.* **1.** to fight hard [The wrestlers *struggled* with one another.] **2.** to try very hard; strive; labor [She *struggled* to learn French.] **3.** to make one's way with great effort [He *struggled* through the thicket.] —*n.* **1.** a great effort. **2.** a fight; conflict; strife. —**strug′gled,** *p.t. & p.p.;* **strug′gling,** *pr.p.*

strum (strum), *v.* to pluck or finger in a simple way, as a guitar. —*n.* the act or sound of strumming. —**strummed,** *p.t. & p.p.;* **strum′ming,** *pr.p.*

strung (strung), past tense and past participle of **string.**

strut (strut), *v.* to walk in a proud, swaggering way. —*n.* **1.** a strutting walk. **2.** a rod or brace set in a framework, often at an angle, as a support. —**strut′ted,** *p.t. & p.p.;* **strut′ting,** *pr.p.*

strych·nine (strik′nin), *n.* a poisonous drug given by doctors in small doses as a stimulant.

Stu·art (stōō′ərt *or* styōō′ərt), *n.* the ruling family of England from 1603 to 1714.

stub (stub), *n.* **1.** a short piece that is left after the main part has been used up or cut off [a pencil *stub*]. **2.** a short piece of a leaf in a checkbook, kept as a record. **3.** any part or thing that is short

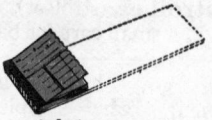

strut

stub (*meaning 2*)

and blunt. **4.** a tree stump. —*v.* to strike against something [He *stubbed* his toe on the rock.] —**stubbed,** *p.t. & p.p.;* **stub′bing,** *pr.p.*

stub·ble (stub′'l), *n.* **1.** the short stumps of grain left standing after the harvest. **2.** any short, uneven growth [a *stubble* of beard].

stub·born (stub′ərn), *adj.* **1.** set on having one's way; not willing to give in; obstinate. **2.** hard to treat or deal with [a *stubborn* rash]. —**stub′born·ly,** *adv.* —**stub′born·ness,** *n.*

stub·by (stub′ē), *adj.* **1.** covered with stubs or stubble [*stubby* land]. **2.** short and thick [*stubby* fingers]. —**stub′bi·er,** *compar.;* **stub′bi·est,** *superl.*

stuc·co (stuk′ō), *n.* a fine plaster for coating inside or outside walls, often in a rough or wavy finish. —*v.* to cover with stucco. —**stuc′coed,** *p.t. & p.p.;* **stuc′co·ing,** *pr.p.*

stuck (stuk), past tense and past participle of **stick.**

stuck-up (stuk′up′), *adj.* snobbish or conceited: *used only in everyday talk.*

stud (stud), *n.* **1.** a small knob or a nail with a round head, used to decorate a surface, as of leather. **2.** a kind of removable button used to fasten a collar, shirt, etc. **3.** one of the upright pieces to which boards or laths are nailed, as in making a wall. —*v.* **1.** to decorate as with studs [a crown *studded* with rubies]. **2.** to be set thickly on [Rocks *stud* the hillside.] —**stud′ded,** *p.t. & p.p.;* **stud′ding,** *pr.p.*

stud (stud), *n.* a number of horses kept especially for breeding.

stu·dent (stōō′d'nt *or* styōō′d'nt), *n.* a person who studies, as at a school or college.

stud·ied (stud′ēd), *adj.* carefully thought out or planned; done on purpose [Her clothes are simple in a *studied* way.]

stu·di·o (stōō′di ō *or* styōō′di ō), *n.* **1.** a room or building in which an artist does his work. **2.** a place where movies are made. **3.** a place from which radio or television programs are broadcast. —**stu′di·os,** *pl.*

studio couch, a kind of couch that can be opened up into a full bed.

stu·di·ous (stōō′di əs *or* styōō′di əs), *adj.* **1.** fond of studying [a *studious* pupil]. **2.** paying or showing careful attention [a *studious* look]. —**stu′di·ous·ly,** *adv.* —**stu′di·ous·ness,** *n.*

stud·y (stud′ē), *v.* **1.** to try to learn by reading, thinking, etc. [to *study* law]. **2.** to look at or into carefully; examine or investigate [He promised to *study* our problem.] **3.** to read so as to understand and remember [to *study* a lesson.] **4.** to give thought to [He *studies* to do right.] **5.** to take a course in [All seniors must *study* history.] —*n.* **1.** the act of reading, thinking, etc. in order to learn something. **2.** careful and serious examination [a *study* of traffic problems]. **3.** a branch of learning; subject [the *study* of medicine]. **4. studies,** *pl.* education; schooling [He continued his *studies* at college.] **5.** a piece of writing, a picture, etc. dealing with a subject in great detail. **6.** a piece of music for practice in certain skills; etude. **7.** deep thought [He is lost in *study*.] **8.** a room used for studying, reading, etc. —**stud'ied,** *p.t. & p.p.;* **stud'y·ing,** *pr.p.* —**stud'ies,** *pl.*

stuff (stuf), *n.* **1.** what anything is made of; material; substance. **2.** that which makes a thing what it is; character [He is made of sterner *stuff* than she is.] **3.** a collection of objects, belongings, etc. [She emptied the *stuff* from her purse.] **4.** foolish things or ideas; nonsense. —*v.* **1.** to fill or pack [pockets *stuffed* with candy]. **2.** to fill the skin of a dead animal to make it look alive [The bear was *stuffed* and put in a museum.] **3.** to fill with seasoning, bread crumbs, etc. before roasting [to *stuff* a chicken]. **4.** to eat too much food. **5.** to stop up or block [His nose is *stuffed* up.] **6.** to force; push [He *stuffed* the money in his wallet.]

stuff·ing (stuf'ing), *n.* something used to stuff, as the feathers in a pillow or the bread crumbs, etc. used to stuff a chicken.

stuff·y (stuf'ē) *adj.* **1.** having little fresh air; close [a *stuffy* room]. **2.** stopped up or stuffed full [Her head feels *stuffy*.] **3.** not interesting; dull: *used only in everyday talk* [a *stuffy* book]. —**stuff'i·er,** *compar.;* **stuff'i·est,** *superl.* —**stuff'i·ness,** *n.*

stul·ti·fy (stul'tə fī), *v.* to cause to seem or be foolish, useless, etc. —**stul'ti·fied,** *p.t. & p.p.;* **stul'ti·fy·ing,** *pr.p.*

stum·ble (stum'b'l), *v.* **1.** to trip or almost fall, as by stubbing the toe against something. **2.** to walk in an unsteady way [The tired boy *stumbled* off to bed.] **3.** to find or come by chance [We *stumbled* upon a clue to the mystery.] **4.** to speak or act in a confused way [He forgot his speech and began to *stumble*.] **5.** to do wrong or make mistakes. —*n.* **1.** the act of stumbling. **2.** a mistake or blunder. —**stum'bled,** *p.t. & p.p.;* **stum'bling,** *pr.p.*

stumbling block, something that gets in the way; obstacle or difficulty.

stump (stump), *n.* **1.** the part of a tree or plant left in the ground after cutting down the main part. **2.** the part of an arm, leg, etc. left after the rest has been removed. **3.** a butt; stub [the *stump* of a pencil]. **4.** a platform for making political speeches. —*v.* **1.** to travel about, making political speeches [The candidate *stumped* the West.] **2.** to puzzle; make unable to answer: *used only in everyday talk* [Her questions *stumped* the expert.] **3.** to walk in a heavy, clumsy way.

tree stump

stun (stun), *v.* **1.** to make unconscious or dazed, as by a blow. **2.** to shock deeply [The news *stunned* us.] —**stunned,** *p.t. & p.p.;* **stun'ning,** *pr.p.*

stung (stung), past tense and past participle of **sting.**

stunk (stungk), past participle and a past tense of **stink.**

stun·ning (stun'ing), *adj.* **1.** that stuns, as a blow. **2.** very attractive, beautiful, etc.: *used only in everyday talk.* —**stun'ning·ly,** *adv.*

stunt (stunt), *v.* to keep from growing or developing [Poor soil *stunted* the plants.]

stunt (stunt), *n.* something done for a thrill, to get attention, show off one's skill, etc. —*v.* to do a stunt. *Used only in everyday talk.*

stu·pe·fac·tion (stōō'pə fak'shən *or* styōō'pə-fak'shən), *n.* **1.** the condition of being stupefied or dazed. **2.** great amazement; astonishment.

stu·pe·fy (stōō'pə fī *or* styōō'pə fī), *v.* **1.** to make dull, senseless, or dazed [The drug *stupefied* her.] **2.** to amaze; astonish. —**stu'pe·fied,** *p.t. & p.p.;* **stu'pe·fy·ing,** *pr.p.*

stu·pen·dous (stōō pen'dəs *or* styōō pen'dəs), *adj.* amazing because very great or large; overwhelming. —**stu·pen'dous·ly,** *adv.*

stu·pid (stōō'pid *or* styōō'pid), *adj.* **1.** slow to learn or understand; not intelligent. **2.** foolish or silly [a *stupid* idea]. **3.** dull; boring [a *stupid* party]. —**stu'pid·ly,** *adv.*

stu·pid·i·ty (stōō pid'ə tē *or* styōō pid'ə tē), *n.* **1.** the condition of being stupid. **2.** a stupid remark or act. —**stu·pid'i·ties,** *pl.*

stu·por (stōō'pər *or* styōō'pər), *n.* a condition, as of shock, in which one can barely think, act, feel, etc.; dazed condition.

stur·dy (stūr'dē), *adj.* **1.** strong and hardy [a *sturdy* oak]. **2.** not giving in; firm [sturdy defiance]. —**stur'di·er,** *compar.;* **stur'di·est,** *superl.* —**stur'di·ly,** *adv.* —**stur'di·ness,** *n.*

stur·geon (stūr'jən), *n.* a large food fish with a long snout and rows of hard plates on the skin. Fine caviar is got from sturgeon.

stut·ter (stut'ər), *v.* to speak in a halting way, often repeating certain sounds, as in fear, embarrassment, etc.; stammer. —*n.* stuttering talk.

sturgeon (8 ft. long)

sty (stī), *n.* **1.** a pigpen. **2.** any filthy place. —**sties,** *pl.*

sty *or* **stye** (stī), *n.* a swollen, sore gland on the rim of the eyelid. —**sties,** *pl.*

Styg·i·an *or* **styg·i·an** (stij'i ən), *adj.* dark or gloomy, like the river Styx.

style (stīl), *n.* **1.** the way in which anything is made, done, written, spoken, etc.; manner; method [pointed arches in the Gothic *style*]. **2.** the way in which people generally dress, act, etc. at any particular period; fashion; mode [*Styles* in clothing keep changing.] **3.** a fine, original way of writing, painting, etc. **4.** the part of a flower's pistil between the stigma and the ovary. **5.** a stylus. —*v.* **1.** to name; call

[Lincoln was *styled* "Honest Abe."] **2.** to design the style of [Her gowns are *styled* in Paris.] **—styled,** *p.t. & p.p.;* **styl·ing,** *pr.p.*

styl·ish (stīl′ish), *adj.* in keeping with the latest style; fashionable; smart [a *stylish* hat]. **—styl′ish·ly,** *adv.* **—styl′ish·ness,** *n.*

sty·lus (stī′ləs), *n.* **1.** a phonograph needle. **2.** a pointed tool used long ago for writing on wax. **—sty′lus·es** or **sty·li** (stī′lī), *pl.*

styp·tic (stip′tik), *adj.* that stops bleeding by tightening the body tissues [A *styptic* pencil is a stick of alum, etc., used on small cuts.]

Styx (stiks), *n.* in Greek myths, a river crossed by dead souls before entering Hades.

suave (swäv), *adj.* polite or gracious in a smooth way. **—suave′ly,** *adv.* **—suav′i·ty,** *n.*

sub (sub), *n.* a short form of some words that begin with *sub-,* as **submarine, subscription,** and **substitute.** **—v.** to be a substitute for someone: *used only in everyday talk.* **—subbed,** *p.t. & p.p.;* **sub′bing,** *pr.p.*

sub-, a prefix meaning: **1.** under or below [*Subsoil* is soil under the topsoil.] **2.** not quite; somewhat [A *subtropical* region is somewhat tropical in climate.] **3.** forming or being a division [A *subcommittee* is one of the divisions of a main committee.]

sub·al·tern (səb ôl′tərn), *n.* any officer in the British army below the rank of captain.

sub·com·mit·tee (sub′kə mit′ē), *n.* any of the small committees chosen from the members of a main committee to carry out special tasks.

sub·con·scious (sub kän′shəs), *adj.* in or of the mind without one's being openly aware of it [a *subconscious* wish to be prettier than her sister]. **—n.** the part of one's mind where subconscious feelings, wishes, etc. are stored. **—sub·con′scious·ly,** *adv.*

sub·di·vide (sub də vīd′), *v.* **1.** to divide again the parts into which something is already divided. **2.** to divide land into small sections for sale. **—sub·di·vid′ed,** *p.t. & p.p.;* **sub·di·vid′ing,** *pr.p.* **—sub·di·vi·sion** (sub də vizh′ən), *n.*

sub·due (səb dōō′ *or* səb dyōō′), *v.* **1.** to conquer or overcome; get control over [Caesar *subdued* the tribes of Gaul.] **2.** to make less strong or harsh; soften [*subdued* anger; *subdued* light; *subdued* colors]. **—sub·dued′,** *p.t. & p.p.;* **sub·du′ing,** *pr.p.*

sub·ject (sub′jikt), *adj.* **1.** under the power or control of another [the *subject* peoples in colonies]. **2.** likely to have; liable [He is *subject* to fits of anger.] **3.** depending on some action or condition [Our treaties are *subject* to the approval of the Senate.] **—n. 1.** a person under the power or control of a ruler, government, etc. **2.** a person or thing being discussed, examined, dealt with, etc. [Lincoln has been the *subject* of many books. Mice have been made the *subject* of many experiments.] **3.** the word or group of words in a sentence about which something is said [In the sentence "Boys and girls enjoy sports," "boys and girls" is the *subject*.] **4.** a course of study, as in a school [What is your favorite *subject*?] **—v.** (səb jekt′), **1.** to bring under some power or

control. **2.** to lay open; make liable [His weakness *subjected* him to disease.] **3.** to make undergo [The suspect was *subjected* to a thorough questioning.] **—sub·jec′tion,** *n.*

sub·jec·tive (səb jek′tiv), *adj.* of or resulting from one's own feelings or thinking rather than from the plain facts [Most of our likes and dislikes are *subjective*.]

sub·ju·gate (sub′joo gāt), *v.* to bring under control; conquer or subdue. **—sub′ju·gat·ed,** *p.t. & p.p.;* **sub′ju·gat·ing,** *pr.p.*

sub·junc·tive (səb jungk′tiv), *adj.* describing the mood of a verb used in stating a wish, possibility, or condition [In the phrase "if I were king," "were" is in the *subjunctive* mood.]

sub·lease (sub′lēs), *n.* a lease for property given by a person who is himself leasing it from the owner. **—v.** (sub lēs′), to give or receive a sublease of. **—sub·leased′,** *p.t. & p.p.;* **sub·leas′ing,** *pr.p.*

sub·let (sub′let′), *v.* **1.** to sublease. **2.** to give someone part of the work that one has a contract to do [The builder of the house *sublet* the contract for the plumbing.] **—sub′let′,** *p.t. & p.p.;* **sub′let′ting,** *pr.p.*

sub·li·mate (sub′lə māt), *v.* **1.** to sublime a solid. **2.** to purify or refine. **—sub′li·mat·ed,** *p.t. & p.p.;* **sub′li·mat·ing,** *pr.p.* **—sub·li·ma′tion,** *n.*

sub·lime (sə blīm′), *adj.* of the highest kind; great, noble, lofty, etc. [*sublime* beauty]. **—v.** to make a solid substance pure by heating it until it becomes a gas, and then condensing the gas back to a solid form. **—sub·limed′,** *p.t. & p.p.;* **sub·lim′ing,** *pr.p.* **—sub·lim·i·ty** (sə blim′ə tē), *n.*

sub·ma·rine (sub′mə rēn), *n.* a kind of warship that can travel under the surface of water. **—adj.** (sub mə rēn′), that lives, grows, happens, etc. under the surface of the sea [Sponges are *submarine* animals.]

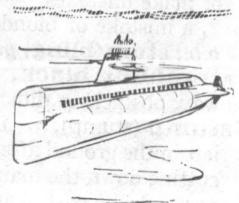

submarine

sub·merge (səb murj′), *v.* to put, go, or stay under water [Whales can *submerge* for as long as half an hour.] **—submerged′,** *p.t. & p.p.;* **sub·merg′ing,** *pr.p.* **—sub·mer′gence,** *n.*

sub·mer·sion (səb mur′shən *or* səb mur′zhən), *n.* the act of submerging.

sub·mis·sion (səb mish′ən), *n.* **1.** the act of submitting or giving up; surrender [He brought the rebels to *submission*.] **2.** the condition of being obedient or humble [The queen's subjects kneeled in *submission*.] **3.** the act of submitting something to someone [the *submission* of a petition to the mayor].

sub·mis·sive (səb mis′iv), *adj.* willing to give in to or obey another; humble; obedient.

sub·mit (səb mit′), *v.* **1.** to give or offer to someone for him to look over, decide about, etc.; refer [A new levy was *submitted* to the voters.] **2.** to give in to the power or control of another;

surrender [The enemy will never *submit*.] —**sub·mit′ted**, *p.t. & p.p.*; **sub·mit′ting**, *pr.p.*

sub·nor·mal (sub nôr′m'l), *adj.* below normal; less than normal, as in intelligence.

sub·or·di·nate (sə bôr′də nit), *adj.* **1.** low or lower in rank; less important; secondary [a *subordinate* job]. **2.** under the power or control of another [The firemen are *subordinate* to their chief.] —*n.* a subordinate person. —*v.* (sə·bôr′də nāt), to place in a lower position; treat as less important [We *subordinated* our wishes to his.] —**sub·or′di·nat·ed**, *p.t. & p.p.*; **sub·or′di·nat·ing**, *pr.p.* —**sub·or′di·na′tion**, *n.*

subordinate clause, a clause that cannot stand alone as a complete sentence [In "He told a story that he had read," the words "that he had read" form a *subordinate clause*.]

sub·poe·na or **sub·pe·na** (sə pē′nə), *n.* an official paper ordering a person to appear in a court of law. —*v.* to order with such a paper. —**sub·poe′naed** or **sub·pe′naed**, *p.t. & p.p.*; **sub·poe′na·ing** or **sub·pe′na·ing**, *pr.p.*

sub·scribe (səb skrīb′), *v.* **1.** to agree to take and pay for [to *subscribe* to a magazine for a year]. **2.** to promise to give [He *subscribed* $100 to the campaign for a new museum.] **3.** to agree with or approve of [I *subscribe* to the principles in the Constitution.] **4.** to sign one's name as to a petition. —**sub·scribed′**, *p.t. & p.p.*; **sub·scrib′ing**, *pr.p.* —**sub·scrib′er**, *n.*

sub·script (sub′skript), *n.* a figure or letter written underneath, as the 2 in H₂O.

sub·scrip·tion (səb skrip′shən), *n.* **1.** the act of subscribing or something that is subscribed. **2.** an agreement to take and pay for a magazine, newspaper, etc.

sub·se·quent (sub′sə kwənt), *adj.* coming after; later; following [He lost the first race but won a *subsequent* one.] —**sub′se·quent·ly**, *adv.*

sub·serve (səb sūrv′), *v.* to serve; help. —**sub·served′**, *p.t. & p.p.*; **sub·serv′ing**, *pr.p.*

sub·ser·vi·ent (səb sūr′vi ənt), *adj.* **1.** very obedient and eager to please; too polite; slavish [He is annoyed by *subservient* waiters.] **2.** useful as a means to something more important. —**sub·ser′vi·ence**, *n.*

sub·side (səb sīd′), *v.* **1.** to sink to a lower level; go down [In June, the river began to *subside*.] **2.** to become quiet or less active [The angry waves *subsided*. Her temper *subsided*.] —**sub·sid′ed**, *p.t. & p.p.*; **sub·sid′ing**, *pr.p.*

sub·sid·i·ar·y (səb sid′i er′ē), *adj.* **1.** helping or useful, especially in a lesser way. **2.** having to do with a subsidy. —*n.* **1.** a person or thing that helps or gives aid. **2.** a company that is controlled by another company [The bus company's *subsidiary* operates the lunchrooms in the stations.] —**sub·sid′i·ar′ies**, *pl.*

sub·si·dize (sub′sə dīz), *v.* to help by means of a subsidy. —**sub′si·dized**, *p.t. & p.p.*; **sub′si·diz·ing**, *pr.p.*

sub·si·dy (sub′sə dē), *n.* a grant or gift of money, as one made by a government to a private company [The airlines get a *subsidy* because they carry mail.] —**sub′si·dies**, *pl.*

sub·sist (səb sist′), *v.* **1.** to live or exist [The lost children *subsisted* on berries and roots.] **2.** to go on or continue to be.

sub·sist·ence (səb sis′təns), *n.* **1.** the act or fact of living or staying alive; existence. **2.** a way to stay alive and support oneself; livelihood [Hunting and a little farming gave the pioneers a fair *subsistence*.]

sub·soil (sub′soil), *n.* the layer of soil just beneath the surface layer of the earth.

sub·stance (sub′stəns), *n.* **1.** the material of which something is made; physical matter [He invented a plastic *substance* much like leather.] **2.** the real or important part [The movie is not changed in *substance* from the novel.] **3.** the main point or central meaning, as of a speech. **4.** wealth or property [a man of *substance*].

sub·stand·ard (sub stan′dərd), *adj.* below some standard or rule set by law or custom [a *substandard* dwelling].

sub·stan·tial (səb stan′shəl), *adj.* **1.** of or having substance; material; real or true [His fears turned out not to be *substantial*.] **2.** strong; solid; firm [The bridge didn't look very *substantial*.] **3.** more than average or usual; large [a *substantial* share]. **4.** wealthy or well-to-do [a *substantial* businessman]. **5.** with regard to the main or basic parts [We are in *substantial* agreement.] —**sub·stan′tial·ly**, *adv.*

sub·stan·ti·ate (səb stan′shi āt), *v.* to prove to be true or real [The experiments *substantiated* his theory.] —**sub·stan′ti·at·ed**, *p.t. & p.p.*; **sub·stan′ti·at·ing**, *pr.p.*

sub·stan·tive (sub′stən tiv), *n.* a noun, or any word or words used as a noun in a sentence. —*adj.* **1.** of or used as a substantive. **2.** substantial or large. —**sub′stan·tive·ly**, *adv.*

sub·sti·tute (sub′stə toot or sub′stə tyoot), *n.* a person or thing that takes the place of another [a *substitute* for the regular teacher]. —*v.* to use as or be a substitute [to *substitute* vinegar for lemon juice; to *substitute* for an injured player]. —**sub′sti·tut·ed**, *p.t. & p.p.*; **sub′sti·tut·ing**, *pr.p.* —**sub′sti·tu′tion**, *n.*

sub·stra·tum (sub strā′təm or sub′strat′əm), *n.* a layer, part, etc. that supports another above it [This land rests on a *substratum* of solid rock.] —**sub·stra·ta** (sub strā′tə or sub′strat′ə) or **sub·stra′tums**, *pl.*

sub·ter·fuge (sub′tər fyooj), *n.* any trick or scheme used to get out of something unpleasant.

sub·ter·ra·ne·an (sub′tə rā′ni ən), *adj.* underground [a *subterranean* river].

sub·tle (sut′'l), *adj.* **1.** having or showing a keenness about small differences in meaning, etc. [a *subtle* thinker; *subtle* reasoning]. **2.** hard to see or understand [a *subtle* problem]. **3.** not open or

---

fat, āpe, cär, ten, ēven, hit, bīte, gō, hôrn, to͞ol, book, up, fŭr; get, joy, yet, chin, she, thin, *then*; zh = s in pleasure; ′ as in able (ā′b'l); ə = a in ago, e in agent, i in sanity, o in confess, u in focus.

direct; sly, clever, crafty, etc. [a *subtle* hint; *subtle* criticism]. **4.** having or showing delicate skill [a *subtle* design in lace]. **5.** not sharp or strong; delicate [a *subtle* shade of red; a *subtle* perfume]. —**sub′tly,** *adv.*

sub·tle·ty (sut′'l tē), *n.* **1.** the quality of being subtle. **2.** a subtle thing. —**sub′tle·ties,** *pl.*

sub·tract (səb trakt′), *v.* to take away, as a part from a whole or one number from another [If 3 is *subtracted* from 5, the remainder is 2.]

sub·trac·tion (səb trak′shən), *n.* the act of subtracting one part, number, etc. from another.

sub·tra·hend (sub′trə hend), *n.* a number to be subtracted from another number [In the problem 5 − 3 = 2, the *subtrahend* is 3.]

sub·trop·i·cal (sub träp′i k'l), *adj.* near the tropics; nearly tropical in climate, features, etc.

sub·urb (sub′ərb), *n.* a district, town, etc. on the outskirts of a city.

sub·ur·ban (sə bûr′bən), *adj.* **1.** of or living in a suburb. **2.** typical of suburbs or of those who live in them [a *suburban* attitude].

sub·ur·ban·ite (sə bûr′bən īt), *n.* a person who lives in a suburb.

sub·ver·sive (səb vûr′siv), *adj.* tending to overthrow an established government, law, custom, belief, etc. —*n.* a subversive person.

sub·vert (səb vûrt′), *v.* **1.** to overthrow something established. **2.** to weaken or corrupt, as in morals. —**sub·ver·sion** (səb vûr′zhən), *n.*

sub·way (sub′wā), *n.* **1.** an underground electric railway in some large cities. **2.** any underground way or passage.

suc·ceed (sək sēd′), *v.* **1.** to manage to do or be what was planned; do or go well [I *succeeded* in convincing him.] **2.** to come next after; follow [Harding *succeeded* Wilson as President.]

suc·cess (sək ses′), *n.* **1.** the result that was hoped for; satisfactory outcome [Did you have *success* in training your dog?] **2.** the act of becoming rich, famous, etc. [Her *success* did not change her.] **3.** a successful person or thing [Our play was a *success*.]

suc·cess·ful (sək ses′fəl), *adj.* **1.** having success; turning out well. **2.** having become rich, famous, etc. —**suc·cess′ful·ly,** *adv.*

suc·ces·sion (sək sesh′ən), *n.* **1.** a number of persons or things coming one after another [a *succession* of cold, rainy days]. **2.** the act of coming after another [the *succession* of a new king to the throne]. **3.** the right to succeed to an office, rank, etc. **4.** the order in which persons succeed to an office [If the President dies, the first in *succession* to his office is the Vice President.] —**in succession,** one after another.

suc·ces·sive (sək ses′iv), *adj.* coming in regular order without a break; consecutive [I won six *successive* games.] —**suc·ces′sive·ly,** *adv.*

suc·ces·sor (sək ses′ər), *n.* a person who succeeds another to an office, rank, etc.

suc·cinct (sək singkt′), *adj.* said clearly in just a few words; concise [a *succinct* explanation]. —**suc·cinct′ly,** *adv.*

suc·cor (suk′ər), *v.* to give badly needed help to; aid. —*n.* help; relief.

suc·co·tash (suk′ə tash), *n.* beans and kernels of corn cooked together.

suc·cu·lent (suk′yoo lənt), *adj.* full of juice; juicy [a *succulent* peach]. —**suc′cu·lence,** *n.*

suc·cumb (sə kum′), *v.* **1.** to give in; yield [to *succumb* to curiosity]. **2.** to die.

such (such), *adj.* **1.** of this or that kind; like those mentioned or meant [*Such* rugs are quite expensive. It was on just *such* a night that she was born.] **2.** so much, so great, etc. [We had *such* fun that nobody left.] **3.** not named; some [at *such* time as you may decide to go]. —*pron.* **1.** such a person or thing [All *such* as need help will find it here.] **2.** that which has been mentioned or suggested [*Such* is the price of fame.] —**as such, 1.** as being what is mentioned or meant [He is the mayor and *as such* must be consulted.] **2.** in itself [A name, *as such*, means nothing.] —**such as, 1.** for example. **2.** like [I enjoy poets *such as* Keats.]

suck (suk), *v.* **1.** to draw into the mouth by pulling with the lips, etc. [to *suck* the juice from an orange]. **2.** to draw in as if by sucking; absorb, inhale, etc. [to *suck* air into one's lungs]. **3.** to suck liquid from [to *suck* a lemon]. **4.** to hold in the mouth and lick with the tongue [to *suck* a candy]. —*n.* the act of sucking.

suck·er (suk′ər), *n.* **1.** a person or thing that sucks. **2.** a fish like a carp with large, soft lips. **3.** a part or organ on a leech, octopus, etc. used for sucking or holding tight to something. **4.** a shoot growing from the roots or lower stem of a plant. **5.** a lollipop. **6.** a person easily fooled or cheated: *a slang meaning.*

suckers

suck·le (suk′'l), *v.* **1.** to give milk to from a breast; nurse. **2.** to suck milk from its mother. —**suck′led,** *p.t. & p.p.;* **suck′ling,** *pr.p.*

suck·ling (suk′ling), *n.* a baby or young animal that is still suckling.

su·crose (soo′krōs *or* syoo′krōs), *n.* a sugar found in sugar cane, sugar beets, etc.

suc·tion (suk′shən), *n.* **1.** the act of drawing air out of a space to make a vacuum that will suck in air or liquid surrounding it. **2.** the act of sucking. —*adj.* that works or is worked by means of suction [a *suction* pump].

Su·dan (soo dan′), *n.* a country in northeastern Africa.

sud·den (sud′'n), *adj.* **1.** happening or appearing without warning; not expected [A *sudden* storm came up.] **2.** done or taking place quickly; hasty [He made a *sudden* change in his plans.] —**all of a sudden,** without warning; quickly. —**sud′den·ly,** *adv.* —**sud′den·ness,** *n.*

suds (sudz), *n.pl.* soapy water or the foam on its surface. —**suds′y,** *adj.*

sue (soo *or* syoo), *v.* **1.** to begin a lawsuit in court against [to *sue* a person for damage caused by his carelessness]. **2.** to make an appeal; ask in a formal way [The weary enemy *sued* for peace.] —**sued**, *p.t. & p.p.*; **su'ing**, *pr.p.*

suede (swād), *n.* **1.** tanned leather with the flesh side rubbed until it is soft like velvet. **2.** cloth that looks like this.

su·et (sōō'it *or* syōō'it), *n.* hard fat from around the kidneys and loins of cattle and sheep. It is used in cooking.

Su·ez (sōō ez' *or* sōō'ez), *n.* **1.** a seaport in Egypt at the Suez Canal near the Red Sea. **2.** a strip of land in Egypt (**Isthmus of Suez**) connecting Asia and Africa.

Suez Canal, a ship canal in Egypt joining the Mediterranean and Red seas.

suf·fer (suf'ər), *v.* **1.** to feel or have pain, discomfort, etc. [Do you *suffer* in the heat?] **2.** to experience or undergo [The team *suffered* a great loss when Bill was injured.] **3.** to become worse or go from good to bad [Her grades *suffered* when she didn't study.] **4.** to put up with; tolerate [He won't *suffer* criticism.]

suf·fer·ance (suf'ər əns), *n.* consent given by not stopping or forbidding something. —**on sufferance,** allowed but not really supported.

suf·fer·ing (suf'ər ing), *n.* pain, sorrow, loss, etc. [War causes great *suffering*.]

suf·fice (sə fīs'), *v.* to be enough [One cake should *suffice* for serving the guests.] —**suf·ficed'**, *p.t. & p.p.*; **suf·fic'ing**, *pr.p.*

suf·fi·cien·cy (sə fish'ən sē), *n.* an amount that is enough [He has a *sufficiency* of funds.]

suf·fi·cient (sə fish'ənt), *adj.* as much as is needed; enough [*sufficient* supplies to last through the month]. —**suf·fi'cient·ly**, *adv.*

suf·fix (suf'iks), *n.* a syllable or group of syllables joined to the end of a word to change its meaning. Some common suffixes are *-ness, -ed, -ly, -ory,* and *-able.* —*v.* (sə fiks'), to add at the end.

suf·fo·cate (suf'ə kāt), *v.* **1.** to kill or die by stopping breathing; smother. **2.** to have trouble breathing. **3.** to hold back, suppress, etc. —**suf'fo·cat·ed**, *p.t. & p.p.*; **suf'fo·cat·ing**, *pr.p.* —**suf'fo·ca'tion**, *n.*

suf·fra·gan (suf'rə gən), *n.* a bishop who is an assistant to another bishop.

suf·frage (suf'rij), *n.* **1.** the right to vote in political elections. **2.** a vote or the act of voting.

suf·fra·gist (suf'rə jist), *n.* a person, especially a woman, who worked for women's right to vote.

suf·fuse (sə fyōōz'), *v.* to spread over [A blush *suffused* her cheek.] —**suf·fused'**, *p.t. & p.p.*; **suf·fus'ing**, *pr.p.* —**suf·fu'sion**, *n.*

sug·ar (shoog'ər), *n.* any of certain sweet substances in the form of crystals that dissolve in water. Glucose, lactose, and sucrose are different kinds of sugar. Sucrose is the common sugar used to sweeten food. —*v.* **1.** to sweeten or sprinkle with sugar [*sugared* cookies]. **2.** to make seem pleasant or less bad [*sugared* criticism]. **3.** to form crystals of sugar [The grape jelly *sugared*.]

sugar beet, a beet with a white root from which common sugar is gotten.

sugar cane, a tall grass grown in hot countries. Most of our common sugar comes from sugar cane.

sug·ar-coat (shoog'ər-kōt'), *v.* **1.** to cover or coat with sugar, as pills. **2.** to make seem more pleasant [to *sugar-coat* bad news].

sug·ar·plum (shoog'ər-plum'), *n.* a round or oval piece of sugary candy.

sug·ar·y (shoog'ər ē), *adj.* **1.** of, like, or full of sugar; very sweet. **2.** flattering in a sweet, but often false, way [*sugary* words].

man cutting sugar cane

sug·gest (səg jest'), *v.* **1.** to mention as something to think over, act on, etc. [I *suggest* we meet again.] **2.** to bring to mind as something similar or in some way connected [His poetry *suggests* that of Keats. Clouds *suggest* rain.]

sug·ges·tion (səg jes'chən), *n.* **1.** the act of suggesting [It was done at your *suggestion*.] **2.** something suggested. **3.** a faint hint; trace [A *suggestion* of a smile crossed his face.]

sug·ges·tive (səg jes'tiv), *adj.* suggesting or likely to suggest thoughts or ideas, especially of an indecent kind. —**sug·ges'tive·ly**, *adv.*

su·i·cide (sōō'i sīd *or* syōō'i sīd), *n.* **1.** the act of killing oneself on purpose. **2.** harm or ruin suffered through one's own actions. **3.** a person who commits suicide. —**su'i·cid'al**, *adj.*

suit (sōōt *or* syōōt), *n.* **1.** a set of clothes to be worn together, especially a coat and trousers or a coat and skirt. **2.** any of the four sets of playing cards in a deck; clubs, diamonds, hearts, or spades. **3.** a lawsuit. **4.** the act of suing, pleading, or wooing. —*v.* **1.** to meet the needs of; be right for [This color *suits* your complexion.] **2.** to make fit; adapt [a dance *suited* to the music]. —**follow suit, 1.** to play a card of the same suit as the card led. **2.** to follow the example set. —**suit oneself,** to do as one pleases.

suit·a·ble (sōōt'ə b'l *or* syōōt'ə b'l), *adj.* right for the purpose; fitting; proper. —**suit'a·bil·i·ty**, *n.* —**suit'a·bly**, *adv.*

suit·case (sōōt'kās *or* syōōt'kās), *n.* a traveling bag shaped like a long, narrow box.

suite (swēt), *n.* **1.** a group of connected rooms used together [a hotel *suite*]. **2.** (*sometimes* sōōt), a number of pieces of furniture forming a set [a bedroom *suite*]. **3.** a piece of music made up of several movements or, in earlier times, dances. **4.** a group of attendants or servants.

suit·or (sōō'tər *or* syōō'tər), *n.* **1.** a man who is wooing a woman. **2.** a person who sues.

sul·fa (sul'fə), *adj.* of or belonging to a group of drugs made from coal tar and used in treating certain infections.

sul·fate (sul′fāt), *n.* a salt of sulfuric acid.

sul·fide (sul′fīd), *n.* a chemical compound of sulfur and another element or elements.

sul·fur (sul′fər), *n.* a pale-yellow solid substance that is a chemical element. It burns with a blue flame, giving off choking fumes, and is used in making gunpowder, in medicine, etc.

sul·fu·ric (sul fyoor′ik), *adj.* of or containing sulfur.

sulfuric acid, an oily, colorless acid formed of hydrogen, sulfur, and oxygen.

sul·fu·rous (sul′fər əs *or* sul fyoor′əs), *adj.* **1.** of or containing sulfur. **2.** like sulfur in color, smell, etc. **3.** like the flames of hell; fiery.

sulk (sulk), *v.* to be sulky. —*n. often* **sulks,** *pl.* a sulky mood.

sulk·y (sul′kē), *adj.* sullen in a pouting or peevish way [a *sulky* child]. —*n.* a light, two-wheeled carriage for one person. —**sulk′i·er,** *compar.;* **sulk′i·est,** *superl.* —**sulk′ies,** *pl.*

sul·len (sul′ən), *adj.* **1.** silent and keeping to oneself because one feels angry, bitter, hurt, etc. **2.** gloomy or dismal [a *sullen* day]. —**sul′len·ly,** *adv.* —**sul′len·ness,** *n.*

sul·ly (sul′ē), *v.* to soil or damage; besmirch [to *sully* one's honor]. —**sul′lied,** *p.t. & p.p.;* **sul′ly·ing,** *pr.p.*

sul·phur (sul′fər), **sul·phu·rous** (sul′fər əs *or* sul fyoor′əs), etc., same as **sulfur, sulfurous,** etc.

sul·tan (sul′t'n), *n.* a ruler of a Moslem country, especially in earlier times.

sul·tan·a (sul tan′ə *or* sul tä′nə), *n.* the wife, mother, sister, or daughter of a sultan.

sul·tan·ate (sul′t'n āt), *n.* the territory, power, reign, etc. of a sultan.

sul·try (sul′trē), *adj.* **1.** hot and damp, without a breeze; sweltering [a *sultry* summer day]. **2.** very hot; fiery. —**sul′tri·er,** *compar.;* **sul′tri·est,** *superl.* —**sul′tri·ness,** *n.*

sum (sum), *n.* **1.** the result gotten by adding together two or more numbers or quantities; total [The *sum* of 7 and 9 is 16.] **2.** an amount of money [We paid the *sum* he asked for.] **3.** the whole amount [the *sum* of one's experiences]. **4.** a problem in arithmetic: *used only in everyday talk* [For our homework we did several *sums.*] —*v.* to add up and get the sum of. —**sum up,** to tell the main points of in a few words. —**summed,** *p.t. & p.p.;* **sum′ming,** *pr.p.*

su·mac *or* **su·mach** (shoo′mak *or* soo′mak), *n.* a bush with long, narrow leaves that turn red in the fall and clusters of hairy, red berries.

Su·ma·tra (soo mä′trə), *n.* a large island of Indonesia, south of the Malay Peninsula.

sum·ma·rize (sum′ə-rīz), *v.* to make a summary of; tell in a few words. —**sum′ma·rized,** *p.t. & p.p.;* **sum′ma·riz·ing,** *pr.p.*

sumac leaves and berries

sum·ma·ry (sum′ə rē), *n.* a brief report that tells the main points in a few words; digest. —*adj.* **1.** done quickly without attention to forms or details [*summary* justice]. **2.** brief; concise [a *summary* report]. —**sum′ma·ries,** *pl.* —**sum·ma·ri·ly** (su mer′ə lē), *adv.*

sum·mer (sum′ər), *n.* the warmest season of the year, following spring. —*adj.* of summer [a *summer* day]. —*v.* to spend the summer [We *summer* in Maine.]

sum·mer·time (sum′ər tīm), *n.* summer.

sum·mit (sum′it), *n.* the highest point; top [the *summit* of a hill; the *summit* of success]. —*adj.* of the heads of governments [a *summit* meeting].

sum·mon (sum′ən), *v.* **1.** to call together; call or send for [The President *summoned* his Cabinet.] **2.** to call forth; rouse; gather [*Summon* up your strength.] **3.** to order to appear in a court of law.

sum·mons (sum′ənz), *n.* **1.** a call or order to come or attend. **2.** an official order to appear in a law court [A traffic ticket is a *summons.*] —**sum′mons·es,** *pl.*

sump·tu·ous (sump′choo əs), *adj.* costing a great deal; costly; lavish [a *sumptuous* feast].

sun (sun), *n.* **1.** the very hot, bright star around which the earth and the other planets revolve. Our light, heat, and energy come from the sun. **2.** the heat or light of the sun [The *sun* is in my eyes.] **3.** any heavenly body like our sun. **4.** something bright or hot like the sun. —*v.* to warm, dry, tan, etc. in the sunlight [We *sunned* ourselves on the roof.] —**sunned,** *p.t. & p.p.;* **sun′ning,** *pr.p.*

Sun., abbreviation for **Sunday.**

sun·beam (sun′bēm), *n.* a beam of sunlight.

sun·bon·net (sun′bän′it), *n.* an old-fashioned bonnet with a large brim in front and a flap at the back that give shade to the face and neck.

sun·burn (sun′bûrn), *n.* a condition in which the skin is red and sore from too much sunlight. —*v.* to give or get sunburn. —**sun′burned** or **sun′burnt,** *p.t. & p.p.;* **sun′burn·ing,** *pr.p.*

sun·dae (sun′dē), *n.* a serving of ice cream covered with sirup, fruit, nuts, etc.

Sun·day (sun′dē), *n.* the first day of the week. Most Christians observe Sunday as a day of rest and worship.

Sunday school, a school held on Sunday for teaching religion.

sun·der (sun′dər), *v.* to break apart; separate; split [The ship *sundered* on the rock.] —**in sunder,** into pieces or parts; apart.

sun·di·al (sun′dī′əl), *n.* an instrument that shows time by the position of a shadow cast by a pointer across a dial marked in hours.

sun·down (sun′doun), *n.* sunset.

sun·dries (sun′drēz), *n.pl.* various things or articles; miscellaneous items [The drug store sells drugs and *sundries.*]

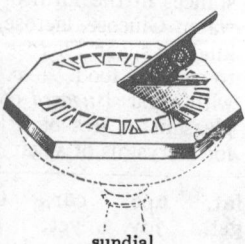
sundial

sun·dry (sun′drē), *adj.* various; of different kinds [He asked *sundry* questions.]

sun·fish (sun′fish), *n.* **1.** a small fresh-water fish of North America. **2.** a large ocean fish with a short, thick body and long fins.

sun·flow·er (sun′flou′ər), *n.* a tall plant with large, yellow flowers that look like daisies.

sung (sung), past participle and a past tense of **sing.**

sun·glass·es (sun′glas′iz), *n.pl.* eyeglasses with dark lenses to shade the eyes.

sunk (sungk), past participle and a past tense of **sink.**

sunk·en (sungk′ən), *adj.* **1.** sunk in water or other liquid [a *sunken* boat]. **2.** below the level of the surface around it [a *sunken* patio; a *sunken* room]. **3.** in or forming a hollow [*sunken* eyes].

sunflower

sun·less (sun′lis), *adj.* without sun or sunlight; dark [a *sunless* day].

sun·light (sun′līt), *n.* the light of the sun.

sun·lit (sun′lit), *adj.* lighted by the sun.

sun·ny (sun′ē), *adj.* **1.** bright with sunlight [a *sunny* day]. **2.** of, like, or from the sun [*sunny* beams]. **3.** cheerful; bright [a *sunny* face]. —**sun′ni·er,** *compar.;* **sun′ni·est,** *superl.*

sun·rise (sun′rīz), *n.* **1.** the daily rising of the sun in the eastern sky. **2.** the time when this happens. **3.** the color of the sky at this time.

sun·room (sun′rōōm), *n.* same as **solarium.**

sun·set (sun′set), *n.* **1.** the daily setting of the sun in the western sky. **2.** the time when this happens. **3.** the color of the sky at this time.

sun·shade (sun′shād), *n.* a parasol, awning, broad hat, etc. for giving shade.

sun·shine (sun′shīn), *n.* **1.** the shining of the sun. **2.** the light and heat from the sun. **3.** cheerfulness, happiness, etc. —**sun′shin·y,** *adj.*

sun·spot (sun′spät), *n.* any of the dark spots sometimes seen on the sun.

sun·stroke (sun′strōk), *n.* an illness caused by being out in the hot sun too long.

sun·up (sun′up), *n.* same as **sunrise.**

sup (sup), *v. & n.* sip. —**supped,** *p.t. & p.p.;* **sup′ping,** *pr.p.*

sup (sup), *v.* to eat the evening meal; have supper. —**supped,** *p.t. & p.p.;* **sup′ping,** *pr.p.*

su·per- (sōō′pər; syōō′pər *is also heard for words with this prefix*), a prefix meaning: **1.** over or above; on top of [A *superstructure* is a structure built on top of another.] **2.** very or very much; more than normal [A *supersensitive* person is more sensitive than the normal person.] **3.** greater than others of its kind [A *supermarket* is bigger than other markets.] **4.** extra; additional [A *supertax* is an extra tax.]

su·per·a·bun·dant (sōō′pər ə bun′dənt), *adj.* much more than is usual or needed [*superabundant* praise]. —**su′per·a·bun′dance,** *n.*

su·per·an·nu·at·ed (sōō′pər an′yōō āt id), *adj.* **1.** retired from work on a pension. **2.** too old to work or use.

su·perb (soo pŭrb′), *adj.* **1.** grand, majestic, splendid, etc. **2.** of the finest kind; excellent [*superb* cooking]. —**su·perb′ly,** *adv.*

su·per·car·go (sōō′pər kär′gō), *n.* an officer on a ship who has charge of the cargo and business matters connected with it. —**su′per·car′goes** or **su′per·car′gos,** *pl.*

su·per·charge (sōō′pər chärj), *v.* to increase the power of a gasoline engine by forcing more air into the cylinder with a device called a **su′per·charg·er.** —**su′per·charged,** *p.t. & p.p.;* **su′per·charg·ing,** *pr.p.*

su·per·cil·i·ous (sōō′pər sil′i əs), *adj.* proud and scornful; looking down on others; haughty [a *supercilious* snob].

su·per·fi·cial (sōō′pər fish′əl), *adj.* **1.** of or on the surface; not deep [a *superficial* cut; a *superficial* likeness]. **2.** with little attention, understanding, feeling, etc.; shallow, hasty, etc. [a *superficial* mind; a *superficial* reading of a book]. —**su·per·fi·ci·al·i·ty** (sōō′pər fish′i al′ə tē), *n.* —**su′per·fi′cial·ly,** *adv.*

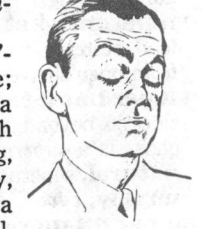

a supercilious look

su·per·fine (sōō′pər fīn′), *adj.* **1.** especially fine; extra fine [*superfine* sugar]. **2.** too fine, subtle, delicate, etc.

su·per·flu·i·ty (sōō′pər flōō′ə tē), *n.* **1.** an amount that is more than is needed; excess. **2.** something not needed. —**su′per·flu′i·ties,** *pl.*

su·per·flu·ous (soo pŭr′flōō əs), *adj.* more than is needed; unnecessary [*superfluous* motions; a *superfluous* remark]. —**su·per′flu·ous·ly,** *adv.*

su·per·high·way (sōō′pər hī′wā), *n.* a broad, divided highway for fast traffic, connecting with crossroads by means of cloverleafs.

su·per·hu·man (sōō′pər hyōō′mən), *adj.* **1.** thought of as having a nature above that of man; divine [a *superhuman* being]. **2.** greater than that of a normal person [*superhuman* strength].

su·per·im·pose (sōō′pər im pōz′), *v.* to put over or above something else. —**su′per·im·posed′,** *p.t. & p.p.;* **su′per·im·pos′ing,** *pr.p.*

su·per·in·tend (sōō′pər in tend′), *v.* to direct or manage; supervise.

su·per·in·tend·ent (sōō′pər in ten′dənt), *n.* a person in charge of something; director; manager. —**su′per·in·tend′ence** or **su′per·in·tend′en·cy,** *n.*

su·pe·ri·or (sə pir′i ər), *adj.* **1.** higher in rank, position, etc. [Soldiers salute their *superior* officers.] **2.** above the average in quality, value, skill, etc.; excellent [a *superior* grade of paper].

3. showing a feeling of being better than others; haughty. —*n.* **1.** a person of higher rank, greater skill, etc. **2.** the head of a monastery or convent. —**superior to, 1.** higher than. **2.** better or greater than. **3.** not affected by; not giving in to. —**su·pe·ri·or·i·ty** (sə pir′i ôr′ə tē), *n.*

Su·pe·ri·or, Lake (sə pir′i ər), the largest of the Great Lakes. It is the one farthest west.

superl., abbreviation for **superlative.**

su·per·la·tive (soo pûr′lə tiv), *adj.* **1.** of the highest sort; supreme. **2.** being the form of adjectives and adverbs that shows the greatest degree in meaning ["Worst" is the *superlative* degree of "bad."] —*n.* **1.** the highest degree; height. **2.** the superlative degree ["Hardest" and "most beautiful" are the *superlatives* of "hard" and "beautiful."] —**su·per′la·tive·ly,** *adv.*

su·per·man (soo′pər man), *n.* a man who seems to have powers beyond those of a normal human being. —**su′per·men,** *pl.*

su·per·mar·ket (soo′pər mär′kit), *n.* a large food store in which shoppers serve themselves from open shelves and pay at the exit.

su·per·nat·u·ral (soo′pər nach′ər əl), *adj.* outside or beyond the known laws of nature [A ghost is a *supernatural* being.] —**the supernatural,** supernatural things. —**su′per·nat′u·ral·ly,** *adv.*

su·per·nu·mer·ar·y (soo′pər noo′mər er′ē), *adj.* more than is usual or needed; extra. —*n.* an extra person or thing, as an actor with no lines to speak, usually part of a crowd. —**su′per·nu′mer·ar′ies,** *pl.*

su·per·script (soo′pər skript), *n.* a figure or letter written above, as the 2 in x².

su·per·scrip·tion (soo′pər skrip′shən), *n.* words written at the top, or on the outside, of something.

su·per·sede (soo pər sēd′), *v.* to take the place of; replace or succeed [The automobile *superseded* the horse and buggy. Mr. Smith *superseded* Mr. Fox as principal.] —**su·per·sed′ed,** *p.t.* & *p.p.;* **su·per·sed′ing,** *pr.p.*

su·per·son·ic (soo′pər sän′ik), *adj.* **1.** describing or having to do with sounds too high for human beings to hear. **2.** of or moving at a speed greater than the speed of sound.

su·per·sti·tion (soo′pər stish′ən), *n.* a belief or practice that is based on fear and ignorance and that is against the known laws of science [It is a *superstition* that breaking a mirror brings bad luck.]

su·per·sti·tious (soo′pər stish′əs), *adj.* of, caused by, or believing in superstitions. —**su′per·sti′tious·ly,** *adv.*

su·per·struc·ture (soo′pər struk′chər), *n.* **1.** a structure built on top of another. **2.** that part of a building above the foundation. **3.** that part of a ship above the main deck.

su·per·tax (soo′pər taks), *n.* an extra tax on something already taxed; surtax.

su·per·vene (soo pər vēn′), *v.* to come or happen as something added or not expected. —**su·per·vened′,** *p.t.* & *p.p.;* **su·per·ven′ing,** *pr.p.*

su·per·vise (soo′pər vīz), *v.* to direct or manage, as a group of workers; be in charge of. —**su′per·vised,** *p.t.* & *p.p.;* **su′per·vis·ing,** *pr.p.*

su·per·vi·sion (soo′pər vizh′ən), *n.* the act of supervising; direction; management.

su·per·vi·sor (soo′pər vī′zər), *n.* a person who supervises; director. —**su′per·vi′so·ry,** *adj.*

su·pine (soo pīn′ *or* syoo pīn′), *adj.* **1.** lying on the back, with the face up. **2.** not active; lazy; listless. —**su·pine′ly,** *adv.*

sup·per (sup′ər), *n.* the last meal of the day, eaten in the evening.

sup·plant (sə plant′), *v.* to take the place of, especially through force or plotting [Mary of Scotland schemed to *supplant* Elizabeth I.]

sup·ple (sup′′l), *adj.* **1.** bending easily; not stiff; flexible [*supple* leather; a *supple* body]. **2.** that can change easily to suit new conditions; adaptable [a *supple* mind].

sup·ple·ment (sup′lə mənt), *n.* **1.** something added, as to make up for something missing [Vitamin pills are a *supplement* for a poor diet.] **2.** a section added to a book or newspaper, to give extra or more up-to-date information, special articles, etc. —*v.* (sup′lə ment), to be or give a supplement to; add to.

sup·ple·men·ta·ry (sup′lə men′tər ē), *adj.* **1.** supplying what is missing; extra; additional [a *supplementary* income]. **2.** describing two angles that add up to exactly 180°. Also **sup′ple·men′tal.**

sup·pli·ant (sup′li ənt), *n.* a person who begs for something in a humble way, as in praying. —*adj.* asking in a humble way; beseeching; imploring [a *suppliant* look].

sup·pli·cant (sup′lə kənt), *adj.* & *n.* suppliant.

sup·pli·cate (sup′lə kāt), *v.* to ask or beg someone in a humble way to do or give something; pray; implore. —**sup′pli·cat·ed,** *p.t.* & *p.p.;* **sup′pli·cat·ing,** *pr.p.* —**sup′pli·ca′tion,** *n.*

sup·ply (sə plī′), *v.* **1.** to give what is needed; furnish; provide [The hotel *supplies* sheets and towels. This book *supplied* us with the facts.] **2.** to make up for; fill [Insurance will *supply* the loss.] —*n.* **1.** the amount at hand; store; stock [a small *supply* of money; a large *supply* of new cars]. **2.** supplies, *pl.* things needed; materials; provisions [school *supplies*]. **3.** the act of supplying. —**sup·plied′,** *p.t.* & *p.p.;* **sup·ply′ing,** *pr.p.* —**sup·plies′,** *pl.*

sup·port (sə pôrt′), *v.* **1.** to carry the weight or burden of; hold up [Will that old ladder *support* you?] **2.** to take the side of; uphold or help [to *support* a cause]. **3.** to earn a living for; provide for [He *supports* a large family.] **4.** to help prove [Use examples to *support* your argument.] **5.** to put up with; bear; endure. —*n.* **1.** a supporting or being supported [This wall needs *support*.] **2.** a person or thing that supports. —**sup·port′er,** *n.*

sup·pose (sə pōz′), *v.* **1.** to take to be true for the sake of argument; assume [Let's *suppose* that these two lines are equal.] **2.** to believe or guess; think [I *suppose* you're right.] **3.** to expect [It's *supposed* to rain today.] —**sup·posed/**, *p.t.* & *p.p.*; **sup·pos·ing**, *pr.p.*

sup·posed (sə pōzd/), *adj.* thought of as true or possible, without really being known [his *supposed* wealth]. —**sup·pos/ed·ly**, *adv.*

sup·po·si·tion (sup/ə zish/ən), *n.* **1.** the act of supposing. **2.** something supposed; theory.

sup·press (sə pres/), *v.* **1.** to put down by force or power; crush [to *suppress* a mutiny]. **2.** to keep back; hide; conceal [to *suppress* a laugh; to *suppress* the truth; to *suppress* a news story]. —**sup·pres·sion** (sə presh/ən), *n.*

sup·pu·rate (sup/yoo rāt/), *v.* to become filled with pus, as a wound. —**sup/pu·rat/ed**, *p.t.* & *p.p.*; **sup/pu·rat/ing**, *pr.p.* —**sup/pu·ra/tion**, *n.*

su·prem·a·cy (sə prem/ə sē), *n.* supreme power or rank.

su·preme (sə prēm/), *adj.* highest in power, rank, quality, or degree; greatest, strongest, etc. [The President is *supreme* commander of the Armed Forces. He won by a *supreme* effort.] —**su·preme/ly**, *adv.*

Supreme Being, God.

Supreme Court, **1.** the highest court in the United States, made up of a chief justice and eight associate justices. **2.** the highest court in any of the States.

Supt., abbreviation for **Superintendent.**

sur·charge (sur/chärj), *n.* **1.** an extra charge, as for some special service. **2.** an overcharge or overload. **3.** a new value or other mark printed over the face of a postage stamp. —*v.* (sur-chärj/), to put a surcharge on or in something. —**sur·charged/**, *p.t.* & *p.p.*; **sur·charg/ing**, *pr.p.*

sur·cin·gle (sur/sing'g'l), *n.* a strap around a horse's body to hold on a saddle, pack, etc.

sur·coat (sur/kōt), *n.* an outer coat; especially, a coat or cloak worn over a knight's armor.

sure (shoor), *adj.* **1.** that will not fail; safe, certain, reliable, etc. [a *sure* cure; a *sure* friend]. **2.** firm or steady [a *sure* footing]. **3.** without doubt; certain; positive [I'm *sure* he did it.] **4.** that cannot be avoided; bound to happen [The army moved on to *sure* defeat.] **5.** bound to do, be, etc. [He is *sure* to win the fight.] —*adv.* surely; certainly: *used only in everyday talk.* —**for sure** or **to be sure**, surely; certainly. —**sur/er**, *compar.*; **sur/est**, *superl.* —**sure/ness**, *n.*

surcoat

sure-foot·ed (shoor/foot/id), *adj.* not likely to stumble, slip, or fall.

sure·ly (shoor/lē), *adv.* **1.** in a sure way; firmly. **2.** certainly; without doubt.

sure·ty (shoor/ə tē), *n.* **1.** sureness or certainty. **2.** something that makes sure; security, as for a loan. **3.** a person who agrees to pay the debts of another, if the other fails to pay them.

surf (surf), *n.* the waves of the sea breaking on a shore or reef, or the foam of such waves.

sur·face (sur/fis), *n.* **1.** the outside or outer face of a thing [the *surface* of the earth]. **2.** any side of a thing having several sides [the *surfaces* of a box]. **3.** outward look or features [She was all smiles on the *surface* but angry within.] —*adj.* of, on, or at the surface. —*v.* **1.** to give a surface to, as in paving. **2.** to rise to the surface of water, as a submarine. —**sur/faced**, *p.t.* & *p.p.*; **sur/fac·ing**, *pr.p.*

surf·board (surf/bôrd), *n.* a long board used in the sport of surfing.

sur·feit (sur/fit), *n.* **1.** too much, especially of food, drink, etc. **2.** sickness or disgust from eating or drinking too much. —*v.* to give too much of something to [He was *surfeited* with idle pleasures.]

surfboard

surf·ing (sur/fing), *n.* the sport of riding in toward shore on the top of a wave, especially on a surfboard.

surge (surj), *n.* **1.** a large wave of water, or its violent rushing motion. **2.** any sudden, strong rush [a new *surge* of energy; the *surge* of immigrants to America]. —*v.* to move in a surge [The crowd *surged* over the football field.] —**surged**, *p.t.* & *p.p.*; **surg·ing**, *pr.p.*

sur·geon (sur/jən), *n.* a doctor who specializes in surgery.

sur·ger·y (sur/jər ē), *n.* **1.** the treating of disease or injury by operations with the hands or tools, as in setting broken bones, cutting out tonsils, etc. **2.** an operation of this kind. **3.** the room in a hospital where doctors do such operations. —**sur/ger·ies**, *pl.*

sur·gi·cal (sur/ji k'l), *adj.* of, in, or for surgery [*surgical* experience; *surgical* gauze].

sur·ly (sur/lē), *adj.* having or showing a bad temper; rude and unfriendly [The *surly* boy ignored our greeting.] —**sur/li·er**, *compar.*; **sur/li·est**, *superl.* —**sur/li·ness**, *n.*

sur·mise (sər mīz/), *n.* an idea or opinion that is only a guess, based on a few facts [My *surmise* is that they were delayed by the storm.] —*v.* to form such an idea; guess. —**sur·mised/**, *p.t.* & *p.p.*; **sur·mis/ing**, *pr.p.*

sur·mount (sər mount/), *v.* **1.** to get the better of; overcome; defeat [to *surmount* a difficulty]. **2.** to climb up and across [to *surmount* an obstacle]. **3.** to lie at the top of [A crown *surmounted* his head.]

sur·name (sur/nām), *n.* **1.** family name, or last name [Adams was the *surname* of two of our presidents.] **2.** a special name added to a person's name, often to describe him [The czar

Ivan IV of Russia had the *surname* "the Terrible."] —*v.* to give a surname to. —**sur′-named,** *p.t. & p.p.;* **sur′nam·ing,** *pr.p.*

sur·pass (sər pas′), *v.* **1.** to be better or greater than; excel [Shakespeare *surpasses* most other writers in the beauty of his poetry.] **2.** to go beyond the limit of [riches *surpassing* belief].

sur·plice (sur′plis), *n.* a loose, white gown with wide sleeves, worn over other garments by clergymen or members of a church choir.

surplice

sur·plus (sur′plus), *n.* an amount more than what is needed; that which is left over; excess [She made drapes with the cloth and used the *surplus* to cover a pillow.] —*adj.* that is a surplus; excess [*surplus* profits].

sur·prise (sər prīz′), *v.* **1.** to cause to feel wonder by being unexpected [Her sudden anger *surprised* us.] **2.** to come upon suddenly or unexpectedly [I *surprised* him in the act of stealing the watch.] **3.** to attack or capture suddenly. —*n.* **1.** the act of surprising [The news took them by *surprise.*] **2.** the condition of being surprised; amazement [Much to our *surprise*, it began to snow.] **3.** something that causes wonder because it is not expected [His answer was quite a *surprise.*] —**sur·prised′,** *p.t. & p.p.;* **sur·pris′ing,** *pr.p.*

sur·pris·ing (sər prīz′ing), *adj.* causing surprise; strange. —**sur·pris′ing·ly,** *adv.*

sur·ren·der (sə ren′dər), *v.* **1.** to give oneself up, especially as a prisoner; yield [The troops *surrendered.*] **2.** to give up; let go of; abandon [She never *surrendered* hope that her son would return.] —*n.* the act of surrendering.

sur·rep·ti·tious (sur′əp tish′əs), *adj.* done in a quiet or secret way; stealthy [a *surreptitious* wink]. —**sur′rep·ti′tious·ly,** *adv.*

sur·rey (sur′ē), *n.* a light carriage with two seats and a flat top. —**sur′-reys,** *pl.*

sur·ro·gate (sur′ə-gāt), *n.* **1.** a substitute or deputy, as for a bishop. **2.** a judge of a probate court in some States.

surrey

sur·round (sə round′), *v.* to form or arrange around on all or nearly all sides; enclose [The police *surrounded* the criminals. The house is *surrounded* with trees.]

sur·round·ings (sə roun′dingz), *n.pl.* the things or conditions around a place or person; environment [They work in fine *surroundings.*]

sur·tax (sur′taks), *n.* an extra tax on something that is already taxed.

sur·veil·lance (sər vā′ləns), *n.* close watch kept over someone [We kept the enemy patrol under *surveillance.*]

sur·vey (sər vā′), *v.* **1.** to look over in a careful way; examine; inspect [The lookout *surveyed*

the horizon.] **2.** to measure the size, shape, boundaries, etc. of a piece of land by the use of special instruments [to *survey* a farm]. —*n.* (sur′vā), **1.** a general study covering the main facts or points [The *survey* shows that we need more schools. This book is a *survey* of American poetry.] **2.** the act of surveying a piece of land, or a record of this [to make a *survey* of the lake shore]. —**sur′veys,** *pl.*

sur·vey·ing (sər vā′ing), *n.* the act, work, or science of one who surveys land.

sur·vey·or (sər vā′ər), *n.* a person whose work is surveying land.

sur·viv·al (sər vī′v′l), *n.* **1.** the act or fact of surviving, or continuing to exist [Atomic war threatens the *survival* of mankind.] **2.** something surviving from an earlier time, as a custom.

sur·vive (sər vīv′), *v.* **1.** to continue to live or exist [Thanksgiving is a Pilgrim custom that *survives* today.] **2.** to live or last longer than; outlive [He *survived* his brother.] **3.** to continue to live or exist in spite of [We *survived* the fire.] —**sur·vived′,** *p.t. & p.p.;* **sur·viv′ing,** *pr.p.*

sus·cep·ti·ble (sə sep′tə b'l), *adj.* having feelings that are easily affected; very sensitive [Sad stories make a *susceptible* child cry.] —**susceptible of,** that gives a chance for or allows [His answer is *susceptible of* being understood in two different ways.] —**susceptible to,** easily affected by; open to [*susceptible to* flattery; *susceptible to* colds]. —**sus·cep′ti·bil′i·ty,** *n.*

sus·pect (sə spekt′), *v.* **1.** to think of as probably guilty, although there is little proof [The detective *suspected* the butler of the murder.] **2.** to have no trust in; doubt; distrust [I *suspect* his honesty.] **3.** to guess or suppose [I *suspect* that you are right.] —*n.* (sus′pekt), a person suspected of wrongdoing [a *suspect* in the robbery]. —*adj.* (sus′pekt), that should be thought of with suspicion [His excuse remains *suspect.*]

sus·pend (sə spend′), *v.* **1.** to hang by a support from above [The keys were *suspended* by a chain from his belt.] **2.** to hold in place as though hanging [In homogenized milk, the fat particles are *suspended* in the milk.] **3.** to keep out for a while as a punishment [He was *suspended* from school for misbehaving.] **4.** to stop from operating for a time [to *suspend* train service; to *suspend* a rule]. **5.** to hold back or put off [The judge *suspended* his sentence.]

sus·pend·ers (sə spen′dərz), *n.pl.* bands worn over the shoulders to hold up the trousers.

sus·pense (sə spens′), *n.* **1.** the condition of being uncertain or hard to predict [a movie full of *suspense*]. **2.** the condition of being anxious and worried [He waited in *suspense* for the jury's verdict.]

suspenders

sus·pen·sion (sə spen′shən), *n.* **1.** a suspending or being suspended [the *suspension* of a policeman from the force; the *suspension* of dust in the air]. **2.** the springs, etc. that hold up the body of a car.

suspension bridge, a bridge held up by large cables that run between a series of towers.

suspension bridge

sus·pi·cion (sə spish′ən), *n.* **1.** a suspecting or being suspected [Everyone here is above *suspicion*.] **2.** the feeling or idea of one who suspects [I have a *suspicion* you are right.] **3.** a very small amount; trace; bit [a salad with just a *suspicion* of garlic].

sus·pi·cious (sə spish′əs), *adj.* **1.** causing or likely to cause suspicion [*suspicious* behavior]. **2.** feeling or showing suspicion [a *suspicious* look]. —**sus·pi′cious·ly,** *adv.*

Sus·que·han·na (sus′kwi han′ə), *n.* a river flowing through New York, Pennsylvania, and Maryland into Chesapeake Bay.

sus·tain (sə stān′), *v.* **1.** to hold up or support [Heavy piers *sustain* the bridge.] **2.** to keep up; maintain [The soft music *sustained* the mood.] **3.** to give courage or strength to [Hope of rescue *sustained* the shipwrecked sailors.] **4.** to undergo; suffer [He *sustained* injuries in the accident.] **5.** to uphold as true, right, etc. [The Supreme Court *sustained* the verdict.]

sus·te·nance (sus′ti nəns), *n.* that which sustains life; food or nourishment.

sut·ler (sut′lər), *n.* a person who followed an army to sell things to its soldiers.

su·ture (sōō′chər), *n.* **1.** the stitching together of the edges of a wound. **2.** any of the stitches of gut or thread used for this. **3.** the line where two parts, as the bones of the skull, grow together. —*v.* to join together as with sutures. —**su′tured,** *p.t. & p.p.;* **su′tur·ing,** *pr.p.*

su·ze·rain (sōō′zə rin), *n.* **1.** a feudal lord in the Middle Ages. **2.** a country having political control over another country.

su·ze·rain·ty (sōō′zə rin tē), *n.* the position or power of a suzerain.

SW or **S.W.** or **s.w.,** abbreviation for **southwest** or **southwestern.**

swab (swäb), *n.* **1.** a small piece of cotton, etc., often fixed to a small stick, used to clean a wound, the ears, etc. or to put medicine on. **2.** a mop. —*v.* **1.** to put medicine on, or clean, with a swab. **2.** to mop. —**swabbed,** *p.t. & p.p.;* **swab′bing,** *pr.p.*

swad·dle (swäd′'l), *v.* to wrap in long, narrow bands of cloth, bandages, etc. Newborn babies were once wrapped in such bands,

swab

called **swaddling clothes.** —**swad′dled,** *p.t. & p.p.;* **swad′dling,** *pr.p.*

swag (swag), *n.* stolen money or goods; loot; plunder: *a slang word.*

swag·ger (swag′ər), *v.* **1.** to walk in a showy, strutting way. **2.** to boast, brag, or show off. —*n.* a swaggering walk or manner.

swain (swān), *n.* a young man, especially a country fellow, who is courting or wooing: *now seldom used.*

swal·low (swäl′ō), *n.* a small, swift-flying bird with long, pointed wings and a forked tail.

swal·low (swäl′ō), *v.* **1.** to let food, drink, etc. go through the throat into the stomach. **2.** to work the muscle of the throat as in swallowing something [He *swallowed* hard to keep from crying.] **3.** to take in; engulf [The waters of the lake *swallowed* him up.] **4.** to put up with; bear with patience [to *swallow* the taunts of another]. **5.** to keep from showing; hold back [to *swallow* one's pride]. **6.** to take back, as one's own words. **7.** to believe without questioning: *used only in everyday talk* [Surely you won't *swallow* that story.] —*n.* **1.** the act of swallowing. **2.** the amount swallowed at one time.

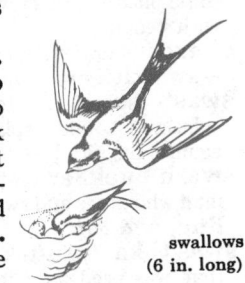
swallows
(6 in. long)

swal·low·tail (swäl′ō tāl′), *n.* a large butterfly with long points on the lower wings.

swallow-tailed coat, a man's formal suit coat that narrows down to two long tails at the back.

swam (swam), past tense of **swim.**

swamp (swämp), *n.* a piece of wet, spongy land; marsh; bog: also **swamp′land.** —*v.* **1.** to plunge as with a swamp, in deep water, etc. **2.** to flood as with water [The street was *swamped* in the flood.] **3.** to fill, or sink by filling, with water [High waves *swamped* the boat.] **4.** to overwhelm [*swamped* with debts]. —**swamp′y,** *adj.*

swan (swän), *n.* a large water bird with webbed feet, a long, graceful neck, and, usually, white feathers.

swank (swangk) or **swank·y** (swang′kē), *adj.* stylish in a showy way: *a slang word* [a *swank* hotel].—**swank′i·er,** *compar.;* **swank′i·est,** *superl.*

swans (5 ft. long)

swan's-down or **swans·down** (swänz′doun′), *n.* **1.** the soft, fine feathers, or down, of the swan, used for trimming clothes. **2.** a soft, thick fabric of cotton, wool, etc.

swan song, 1. the song supposed in old stories to be sung by a dying swan. **2.** the final piece of work of an artist, writer, etc.

fat, āpe, cär, ten, ēven, hit, bīte, gō, hôrn, tōōl, book, up, fŭr; get, joy, yet, chin, she, thin, *then;* zh = s in pleasure; ' as in able (ā′b'l); ə = a in ago, e in agent, i in sanity, o in confess, u in focus.

swap (swäp), *n. & v.* exchange, trade, or barter: *used only in everyday talk.* —**swapped,** *p.t. & p.p.;* **swap′ping,** *pr.p.*

sward (swôrd), *n.* grassy ground; turf.

swarm (swôrm), *n.* **1.** a large number of bees, led by a queen, leaving a hive to start a new colony. **2.** a colony of bees in a hive. **3.** any large, moving mass or crowd [a *swarm* of flies; a *swarm* of visitors]. —*v.* **1.** to fly off in a swarm, as bees do. **2.** to move, gather, etc. in large numbers [Shoppers *swarmed* into the store.] **3.** to be filled with a crowd [The beach is *swarming* with people.]

swarth·y (swôr′thē), *adj.* having a dark skin. —**swarth′i·er,** *compar.;* **swarth′i·est,** *superl.*

swash (swäsh), *v.* to strike, dash, etc. with a splashing sound; splash [The waves *swashed* against the pier.] —*n.* a splashing of water.

swash·buck·ler (swäsh′buk′lər), *n.* a fighting man who brags and swaggers. —**swash′buck′-ling,** *n. & adj.*

swas·ti·ka (swäs′ti kə), *n.* an ancient design that was used as a magic symbol in various parts of the world. One form was used as the symbol of the Nazis in Germany.

swastikas

swat (swät), *v.* to hit with a quick, sharp blow. —*n.* a quick, sharp blow. —**swat′ted,** *p.t. & p.p.;* **swat′ting,** *pr.p.* —**swat′ter,** *n.*

swatch (swäch), *n.* a small piece of cloth or other material used as a sample.

swath (swäth), *n.* **1.** the space or width covered by one cut of a scythe, etc. **2.** the strip or band of grass, wheat, etc. cut in a single trip across a field by a mower, etc.

swathe (swāth), *v.* to wrap around with a cloth or bandage [His head was *swathed* in a turban.] —**swathed,** *p.t. & p.p.;* **swath′ing,** *pr.p.*

sway (swā), *v.* **1.** to swing or bend back and forth or from side to side [The flowers *swayed* in the breeze.] **2.** to lean or go to one side; veer [The car *swayed* to the right on the curve.] **3.** to change the thinking or actions of; influence [His threats will not *sway* us.] —*n.* **1.** a swaying or being swayed. **2.** influence or control [under the *sway* of emotion.]

sway-backed (swā′bakt′), *adj.* having a spine that sags more than is normal.

Swa·zi·land (swä′zē land′), *n.* a country in southeastern Africa.

sway-backed horse

swear (swer), *v.* **1.** to make a serious statement, supporting it with an appeal to God or to something held sacred [He *swore* on his honor that it was true.] **2.** to say or promise in a serious way or with great feeling; vow [He *swore* that he would always love her.] **3.** to use bad or profane language; curse. **4.** to make take an oath, as when putting into office [The President was *sworn* in by the Chief Justice. The bailiff *swore* in the witness.] —**swear by, 1.** to name something sacred in taking an

oath. **2.** to have great faith in [The cook *swears by* this recipe.] —**swear off,** to promise to give up [to *swear off* smoking]. —**swear out,** to get by making a charge under oath [I *swore out* a warrant for his arrest.] —**swore,** *p.t.;* **sworn,** *p.p.;* **swear′ing,** *pr.p.* —**swear′er,** *n.*

swear·word (swer′wûrd), *n.* a word or phrase used in swearing or cursing.

sweat (swet), *v.* **1.** to give out a salty liquid through the pores of the skin; perspire [Running fast made him *sweat*.] **2.** to form little drops of water on its surface [A glass full of iced tea will *sweat* in a warm room.] **3.** to work so hard as to cause sweating. **4.** to make work long hours at low wages under bad conditions. —*n.* **1.** the salty liquid given out through the pores of the skin. **2.** the little drops of water that form on a cold surface. **3.** the act or condition of sweating [The long run left him in a *sweat*.] **4.** a condition of eagerness, great worry, etc. —**sweat out, 1.** to get rid of [to *sweat out* a cold]. **2.** to wait in an anxious way for: *a slang meaning.* —**sweat** or **sweat′ed,** *p.t. & p.p.;* **sweat′ing,** *pr.p.*

sweat·er (swet′ər), *n.* a knitted outer garment for the upper part of the body.

sweat shirt, a heavy cotton shirt like a T-shirt with long sleeves, worn to soak up sweat.

sweat·shop (swet′shäp), *n.* a shop or factory where workers are forced to work long hours at low wages under bad conditions.

sweat·y (swet′ē), *adj.* **1.** wet with sweat; sweating. **2.** of sweat [a *sweaty* odor]. **3.** causing sweat [*sweaty* work]. —**sweat′i·er,** *compar.;* **sweat′i·est,** *superl.*

Swede (swēd), *n.* a person born or living in Sweden.

Swe·den (swē′d′n), *n.* a country in northern Europe, east of Norway.

Swed·ish (swē′dish), *adj.* of Sweden or the Swedes. —*n.* the language of the Swedes.

sweep (swēp), *v.* **1.** to clean as by brushing with a broom [to *sweep* a floor]. **2.** to clear away as with a broom [*Sweep* the dirt from the porch.] **3.** to carry away or destroy with a quick, strong motion [The tornado *swept* the shed away.] **4.** to carry along with a sweeping movement [He *swept* the cards into a pile.] **5.** to touch in moving across [Her dress *sweeps* the ground.] **6.** to pass swiftly over [His glance *swept* the crowd.] **7.** to move in a quick, steady, important way [He *swept* down the aisle to the stage.] **8.** to reach in a long curve or line [The road *sweeps* up the hill.] —*n.* **1.** the act of sweeping, as with a broom. **2.** a steady, sweeping movement [the *sweep* of their oars]. **3.** the space covered; range [beyond the *sweep* of his flashlight]. **4.** an unbroken stretch [a *sweep* of flat country]. **5.** a line or curve [the *sweep* of his high forehead]. **6.** a person whose work is sweeping [a chimney *sweep*]. **7.** a long oar. **8.** a long pole with a bucket on one end, for raising water as from a well. —**swept,** *p.t. & p.p.;* **sweep′-ing,** *pr.p.* —**sweep′er,** *n.*

sweep·ing (swēp′ing), *adj.* **1.** that sweeps [a *sweeping* look]. **2.** including a great deal; very broad [The ad made *sweeping* claims.] —*n.* **1.** the act or work of a sweeper. **2. sweepings,** *pl.* things swept up, as dirt from the floor.

sweep·stakes (swēp′stāks) or **sweep·stake** (swēp′stāk), *n.* **1.** a lottery in which the prizes come from the money bet on a horse race, etc. **2.** such a race, etc. —**sweep′stakes,** *pl.*

sweet (swēt), *adj.* **1.** having the taste of sugar; having sugar in it [a *sweet* apple]. **2.** pleasant in taste, smell, sound, manner, etc. [*sweet* music; *sweet* perfume; a *sweet* girl]. **3.** not salty [*sweet* butter]. **4.** not spoiled, sour, etc. [*sweet* milk]. —*n.* **1.** something sweet, as a candy. **2.** a sweetheart. —*adv.* in a sweet manner. —**sweet′ish,** *adj.* —**sweet′ly,** *adv.* —**sweet′ness,** *n.*

sweet·bread (swēt′bred), *n.* the pancreas or thymus of a calf or other animal, used as food.

sweet·bri·er or **sweet·bri·ar** (swēt′brī ər), *n.* a rose with sharp thorns and single pink flowers.

sweet corn, a kind of corn with soft, sweet kernels, cooked for eating, often on the cob.

sweet·en (swē′t'n), *v.* to make or become sweet.

sweet·en·ing (swē′t'n ing), *n.* something used to make food sweeter, as sugar or honey.

sweet·heart (swēt′härt), *n.* a person with whom one is in love; lover.

sweet·meat (swēt′mēt), *n.* a bit of sweet food; especially, a candy, candied fruit, etc.

sweet pea, a climbing plant with sweet-smelling flowers of many colors.

sweet potato, 1. the sweet, yellow, thick root of a tropical vine, eaten as a vegetable. **2.** the vine itself.

sweet Wil·liam or **sweet wil·liam** (wil′yəm), a plant of the pink family, with clusters of small flowers of many colors.

swell (swel), *v.* **1.** to make or become larger, greater, stronger, etc. [buds *swelling* in the early spring; music *swelling* to a grand climax]. **2.** to bulge or make bulge; curve out [The wind *swelled* the sails.] **3.** to fill or be filled with pride, greed, anger, etc. —*n.* **1.** a part that swells, as a large, rolling wave or a piece of rising ground. **2.** a swelling or being swollen. **3.** an increase in size, force, loudness, etc. **4.** a man who dresses in a rich, stylish way: *used only in everyday talk.* —*adj.* fine, enjoyable, etc.: *slang in this meaning.* —**swelled,** *p.t.;* **swelled** or **swol′len,** *p.p.;* **swell′ing,** *pr.p.*

swell·ing (swel′ing), *n.* **1.** an increase in size, force, etc. [a *swelling* of profits]. **2.** a swollen

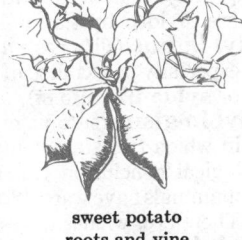

sweet pea

sweet potato
roots and vine

part, as on the body [a *swelling* from a bump].

swel·ter (swel′tər), *v.* to become sweaty, weak, etc. from great heat. —*n.* sweltering condition.

swel·ter·ing (swel′tər ing), *adj.* very hot, damp, sticky, etc.

swept (swept), past tense and past participle of **sweep.**

swerve (swūrv), *v.* to turn aside from a straight line or path [He *swerved* the car to avoid hitting a dog.] —*n.* a swerving motion. —**swerved,** *p.t. & p.p.;* **swerv′ing,** *pr.p.*

swift (swift), *adj.* **1.** moving or able to move very fast [a *swift* runner]. **2.** coming, happening, or done quickly [a *swift* reply]. **3.** acting quickly; prompt [He was *swift* to help us.] —*n.* a brown, swift bird that looks like the swallow. —**swift′ly,** *adv.* —**swift′ness,** *n.*

swig (swig), *v.* to drink in large gulps. —*n.* a large gulp of liquid. *Used only in everyday talk.* —**swigged,** *p.t. & p.p.;* **swig′ging,** *pr.p.*

swill (swil), *n.* garbage, often mixed with liquid and fed to pigs. —*v.* to drink or gulp greedily.

swim (swim), *v.* **1.** to move in water by working the arms, legs, fins, etc. **2.** to cross by swimming [to *swim* a river]. **3.** to move along smoothly; glide. **4.** to float or be dipped in a liquid [food *swimming* in butter]. **5.** to overflow [eyes *swimming* with tears]. **6.** to be dizzy [The ride made her head *swim*.] **7.** to seem to be whirling [The room *swam* before her eyes.] —*n.* **1.** an act, time, or distance of swimming. **2.** a dizzy feeling. —**in the swim,** taking part in what is popular at the moment. —**swam,** *p.t.;* **swum,** *p.p.;* **swim′ming,** *pr.p.* —**swim′mer,** *n.*

swim·ming·ly (swim′ing lē), *adv.* easily and with success [We got along *swimmingly.*]

swimming pool, a tank of water for swimming.

swin·dle (swin′d'l), *v.* to cheat or trick out of money or property. —*n.* an act of swindling; fraud. —**swin′dled,** *p.t. & p.p.;* **swin′dling,** *pr.p.* —**swin′dler,** *n.*

swine (swīn), *n.* **1.** a pig or hog. **2.** a mean or disgusting person. —**swine,** *pl.*

swine·herd (swīn′hŭrd), *n.* a person who looks after, or tends, swine.

swing (swing), *v.* **1.** to move or sway back and forth, as something hanging loosely [The pendulum *swings* in the clock.] **2.** to walk, trot, etc. with loose, swaying movements [They *swung* down the road.] **3.** to turn, as on a hinge or pivot [The door *swung* open. He *swung* the chair around to face the table.] **4.** to hang; sometimes, to be hanged in execution. **5.** to move with a sweeping motion [He *swung* the bat at the ball. I *swung* the bag onto my back.] **6.** to manage to get, do, win, etc. [to *swing* an election]. —*n.* **1.** the act of swinging. **2.** the curved path of something swinging [the *swing* of a pendulum]. **3.** a sweeping blow or stroke [He took a *swing* at the golf ball.] **4.** a strong, steady rhythm, as of poetry or music. **5.** a seat hanging from ropes or chains, on which one can sit and swing. **—in full swing,** in full, active operation. **—swung,** *p.t. & p.p.;* **swing'ing,** *pr.p.*

swin·ish (swīn'ish), *adj.* of, like, or fit for swine; beastly; disgusting.

swipe (swīp), *n.* a hard, sweeping blow. **—v. 1.** to hit with a hard, sweeping blow. **2.** to steal. *This word is used only in everyday talk.* **—swiped,** *p.t. & p.p.;* **swip'ing,** *pr.p.*

swirl (swŭrl), *v.* **1.** to move with a twisting or curving motion; whirl [The snow kept *swirling* down.] **2.** to be dizzy [The fever made my head *swirl.*] **—n. 1.** a swirling motion; whirl [a *swirl* of water down a drain]. **2.** a twist or curl.

swish (swish), *v.* **1.** to move with a sharp, hissing sound [He *swished* his cane through the air.] **2.** to rustle [Her skirts *swished* as she walked.] **—n.** a hissing or rustling sound, or a movement that makes such a sound.

Swiss (swis), *adj.* of Switzerland or its people. **—n.** a person born or living in Switzerland. **—Swiss,** *pl.*

Swiss cheese, a pale-yellow hard cheese with many large holes, first made in Switzerland.

switch (swich), *n.* **1.** a thin twig or stick used for whipping. **2.** a sharp stroke, as with a whip. **3.** a device used to open, close, or change the path of, an electric circuit. **4.** a section of railroad track that can be moved to shift a train from one track to another. **5.** a change; shift [a *switch* in attitude]. **—v. 1.** to whip as with a switch. **2.** to jerk or swing sharply [The horse *switched* its tail.] **3.** to shift; change [Let's *switch* the party to Friday.] **4.** to move a train from one track to another by means of a switch. **5.** to turn a light, radio, etc. on or off.

switch·board (swich'bôrd), *n.* a board with switches and other devices for controlling, connecting, etc. a number of electric circuits [a telephone *switchboard*].

switch·man (swich'mən), *n.* a man whose work is switching railroad cars. **—switch'-men,** *pl.*

Switz·er·land (swit'sər lənd), *n.* a country in western Europe, in the Alps.

swiv·el (swiv''l), *n.* a fastening that allows any part joined to it to turn freely, or a fastening in two parts, each of which can turn freely. **—v.** to turn as on a swivel [to *swivel* in one's seat]. **—swiv'eled** or **swiv'elled,** *p.t. & p.p.;* **swiv'-el·ing** or **swiv'el·ling,** *pr.p.*

swivel chair, a chair whose seat turns freely around on a swivel or pivot.

swol·len (swō'lən), a past participle of **swell.**

swoon (swoon), *n. & v.* faint.

swoop (swoop), *v.* **1.** to sweep down or pounce upon suddenly, as a bird in hunting. **2.** to snatch suddenly [He *swooped* up the change.] **—n.** the act of swooping.

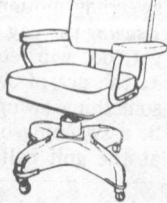
swivel chair

sword (sôrd), *n.* **1.** a weapon having a long, sharp blade with a handle, or hilt,

at one end. **2.** warfare, or the profession of a soldier ["The pen is mightier than the *sword.*"] **—at swords' points,** ready to quarrel or fight. **—cross swords,** to fight or argue.

sword·fish (sôrd'fish), *n.* a large ocean fish with an upper jawbone like a long, pointed sword.

swordfish (7 ft. long)

sword·play (sôrd'plā), *n.* the act or skill of using a sword, as in fighting or in sport.

swords·man (sôrdz'-mən), *n.* **1.** a person who uses a sword, as in fencing. **2.** a person skilled in using a sword. **—swords'men,** *pl.*

swore (swôr), past tense of **swear.**

sworn (swôrn), past participle of **swear.** **—adj.** bound as by an oath [*sworn* friends].

swum (swum), past participle of **swim.**

swung (swung), past tense and past participle of **swing.**

syc·a·more (sik'ə môr), *n.* **1.** an American shade tree with large leaves and bark that flakes off. **2.** a maple tree of Europe and Asia. **3.** a kind of fig tree of Egypt and Asia.

syc·o·phant (sik'ə fənt), *n.* a person who flatters others in order to get things from them.

Syd·ney (sid'nē), *n.* a seaport in southeastern Australia.

syl·lab·ic (si lab'ik), *adj.* that is or has to do with a syllable or syllables.

syl·lab·i·cate (si lab'i kāt), *v.* same as **syl-labify.** **—syl·lab'i·cat·ed,** *p.t. & p.p.;* **syl·lab'i·cat·ing,** *pr.p.* **—syl·lab'i·ca'tion,** *n.*

syl·lab·i·fy (si lab'ə fī), *v.* to divide into syllables. **—syl·lab'i·fied,** *p.t. & p.p.;* **syl·lab'-i·fy·ing,** *pr.p.* **—syl·lab'i·fi·ca'tion,** *n.*

syl·la·ble (sil'ə b'l), *n.* **1.** a word or part of a word spoken with a single sounding of the voice ["Sun" is a word of one *syllable.* "Sunshine" is a word of two *syllables.*] **2.** any of the parts into which a written word is divided to show where the word may be broken at the end of a line [The *syllables* of the entry words in this dictionary are divided by tiny dots.]

syl·la·bus (sil'ə bəs), *n.* an outline or summary, especially of a course of study. **—syl'la·bus·es** or **syl·la·bi** (sil'ə bī), *pl.*

syl·lo·gism (sil'ə jiz'm), *n.* a form of reasoning in which two statements are made from which a logical conclusion can be drawn. Example: All mammals have warm blood. Whales are mammals. Therefore, whales have warm blood.

sylph (silf), *n.* **1.** an imaginary being, or spirit, supposed to live in the air. **2.** a slender, graceful woman or girl.

syl·van (sil'vən), *adj.* **1.** of, like, or found in the woods [*sylvan* creatures]. **2.** covered with trees; wooded [a *sylvan* valley].

sym·bol (sim'b'l), *n.* an object, mark, sign, etc. that stands for another object, or for an idea, quality, etc. [The dove is a *symbol* of peace. The mark $ is a *symbol* for dollar or dollars.]

sym·bol·ic (sim bäl′ik) or **sym·bol·i·cal** (sim bäl′i k′l), *adj.* **1.** of or expressed by a symbol; using symbols [*symbolic* writings]. **2.** that is a symbol [White is *symbolic* of purity.] —**sym·bol′i·cal·ly**, *adv.*

sym·bol·ism (sim′b′l iz′m), *n.* **1.** the use of symbols to stand for things, especially in art or literature. **2.** a set of symbols, standing for a group of ideas.

sym·bol·ist (sim′b′l ist), *n.* a person who uses symbols, especially in art or literature.

sym·bol·ize (sim′b′l īz), *v.* **1.** to be a symbol of; stand for [A heart *symbolizes* love.] **2.** to represent by a symbol [How does this poet *symbolize* man's spirit?] —**sym′bol·ized**, *p.t. & p.p.*; **sym′bol·iz·ing**, *pr.p.*

sym·met·ri·cal (si met′ri k′l) or **sym·met·ric** (si met′rik), *adj.* having symmetry; balanced [a *symmetrical* design]. —**sym·met′ri·cal·ly**, *adv.*

sym·me·try (sim′ə trē), *n.* **1.** an arrangement in which the parts on opposite sides of a center line are alike in size, shape, and position [the *symmetry* of the human body]. **2.** balance or harmony that comes from such an arrangement.

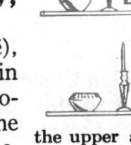
the upper arrangement is symmetrical

sym·pa·thet·ic (sim′pə thet′ik), *adj.* **1.** feeling, showing, or caused by sympathy; sympathizing [*sympathetic* words]. **2.** that suits one's tastes, mood, etc.; agreeable [*sympathetic* surroundings]. **3.** showing favor or approval [He's *sympathetic* to our plan.] —**sym′pa·thet′i·cal·ly**, *adv.*

sym·pa·thize (sim′pə thīz), *v.* to share the feelings or ideas of another; feel or show sympathy [to *sympathize* with a friend who has lost something]. —**sym′pa·thized**, *p.t. & p.p.*; **sym′pa·thiz·ing**, *pr.p.* —**sym′pa·thiz·er**, *n.*

sym·pa·thy (sim′pə thē), *n.* **1.** the sharing of another person's feelings, as by feeling sorry for his suffering [He wept out of *sympathy* for my loss.] **2.** a feeling or condition that is the same as another's; agreement [Our tastes in art are in *sympathy*.] **3.** favor; support [He is in *sympathy* with the strikers.] —**sym′pa·thies**, *pl.*

sym·pho·ny (sim′fə nē), *n.* **1.** a long piece of music for a full orchestra, usually divided into four movements with different rhythms and themes. **2.** a large orchestra for playing such works: *its full name is* **symphony orchestra**. **3.** harmony, as of sounds, color, etc. [The dance was a *symphony* in motion.] —**sym′pho·nies**, *pl.* —**sym·phon·ic** (sim fän′ik), *adj.* —**sym·phon′i·cal·ly**, *adv.*

sym·po·si·um (sim pō′zi əm), *n.* **1.** a meeting for discussing some subject. **2.** a group of writings or opinions on a particular subject. —**sym·po′si·ums** or **sym·po·si·a** (sim pō′zi ə), *pl.*

symp·tom (simp′təm), *n.* something showing that something else exists; sign [Spots on the skin may be a *symptom* of measles.] —**symp·to·mat·ic** (simp′tə mat′ik), *adj.*

syn·a·gogue (sin′ə gôg), *n.* a building where Jews gather for worship and religious study.

syn·chro·nize (sing′krə nīz), *v.* **1.** to move or happen at the same time or speed [The gears must *synchronize* when you shift.] **2.** to make agree in time or rate of speed [*Synchronize* your watch with mine.] —**syn′chro·nized**, *p.t. & p.p.*; **syn′chro·niz·ing**, *pr.p.*

syn·chro·nous (sing′krə nəs), *adj.* happening at the same time or moving at the same rate of speed [*synchronous* drum beats].

syn·co·pate (sing′kə pāt), *v.* in music, to shift the accent by putting the beat at a place that would normally not be accented and holding it into the next accented beat [Much jazz is *syncopated.*] —**syn′co·pat·ed**, *p.t. & p.p.*; **syn′co·pat·ing**, *pr.p.* —**syn′co·pa′tion**, *n.*

syn·di·cate (sin′di kit), *n.* **1.** a group of bankers, large companies, etc. formed to carry out some project that needs much money. **2.** an organization that sells articles, stories, comic strips, etc. to a number of newspapers. —*v.* (sin′di kāt), **1.** to form into a syndicate. **2.** to publish through a syndicate in a number of newspapers. —**syn′di·cat·ed**, *p.t. & p.p.*; **syn′di·cat·ing**, *pr.p.* —**syn′di·ca′tion**, *n.*

syn·od (sin′əd), *n.* a council of churches or church officials, acting as a governing body.

syn·o·nym (sin′ə nim), *n.* a word having the same or almost the same meaning as another ["Small" and "little" are *synonyms*.]

syn·on·y·mous (si nän′ə məs), *adj.* of the same or almost the same meaning.

syn·op·sis (si näp′sis), *n.* a short outline or review of the main points, as of a story; summary. —**syn·op·ses** (si näp′sēz), *pl.*

syn·tax (sin′taks), *n.* the way words are put together and related to one another in sentences; sentence structure. —**syn·tac′ti·cal** or **syn·tac′tic**, *adj.*

syn·the·sis (sin′thə sis), *n.* the putting together of parts or elements so as to make a whole [Plastics are made by chemical *synthesis*.] —**syn·the·ses** (sin′thə sēz), *pl.*

syn·thet·ic (sin thet′ik), *adj.* **1.** of, by, or using synthesis. **2.** made by putting together chemicals rather than by using natural products [*synthetic* rubber]. **3.** artificial; not real [a *synthetic* excuse]. —*n.* something synthetic [Nylon is a *synthetic*.] —**syn·thet′i·cal·ly**, *adv.*

syph·i·lis (sif′ə lis), *n.* a disease that can be passed on to another by the sex act. —**syph·i·lit·ic** (sif′ə lit′ik), *adj.*

sy·phon (sī′fən), *n. & v.* same as **siphon**.

Syr·a·cuse (sir′ə kyōōs), *n.* **1.** a city in central New York. **2.** a town in Sicily, once an important city of the ancient Greeks.

fat, āpe, cär, ten, ēven, hit, bīte, gō, hôrn, tōōl, book, up, fur; get, joy, yet, chin, she, thin, *then*; zh = s in pleasure; ′ as in able (ā′b′l); ə = a in ago, e in agent, i in sanity, o in confess, u in focus.

Syr·i·a (sir′i ə), *n.* a country in Asia on the Mediterranean, from 1958 to 1961 a part of the United Arab Republic. —**Syr′i·an,** *n. & adj.*

sy·rin·ga (sə ring′gə), *n.* a garden shrub with sweet-smelling white flowers.

syr·inge (sə rinj′ *or* sir′inj), *n.* a device made up of a narrow tube with a rubber bulb or a plunger at one end, for drawing in a liquid and then pushing it out in a stream. Syringes are used to inject fluids into the body, to wash out wounds, etc. See also **hypodermic.** —*v.* to wash with a syringe. —**syr·inged′,** *p.t. & p.p.;* **syr·ing′ing,** *pr.p.*

syringe

syr·up (sir′əp *or* sŭr′əp), *n.* same as **sirup.** —**syr′up·y,** *adj.*

sys·tem (sis′təm), *n.* **1.** a group of things or parts working together or connected in some way so as to form a whole [the solar *system;* a school *system;* a *system* of highways; the nervous *system*]. **2.** a set of facts, rules, ideas, etc. that make up an orderly plan [a democratic *system* of government]. **3.** an orderly way of doing things; method [He works with *system.*] **4.** the body as a whole [poison in his *system*].

sys·tem·at·ic (sis′tə mat′ik), *adj.* **1.** having or done by a system, method, or plan; orderly [a *systematic* search]. **2.** orderly in planning or doing things [a *systematic* person]. —**sys′tem·at′i·cal·ly,** *adv.*

sys·tem·a·tize (sis′təm ə tīz), *v.* to form into a system; arrange in a systematic way; make orderly. —**sys′tem·a·tized,** *p.t. & pp.;* **sys′tem·a·tizing,** *pr.p.*

T

T, t (tē), *n.* the twentieth letter of the English alphabet. —**T's, t's** (tēz), *pl.*

T (tē), *n.* something shaped like a T. —*adj.* shaped like T. —**to a T,** perfectly; exactly.

T., abbreviation for **tablespoon** or **tablespoons.**

T. or t., abbreviation for **ton** or **tons.**

t., abbreviation for **teaspoon** or **teaspoons.**

tab (tab), *n.* **1.** a small loop, flap, or tag fastened to something [He hung his jacket by the *tab.* Cards for dividing a filing box have *tabs* lettered from A to Z.] **2.** a record of money owed; bill: *used only in everyday talk.* —**keep tab on** or **keep tabs on,** to keep a check on.

tab·ard (tab′ərd), *n.* **1.** a short coat worn by a herald, decorated with his lord's coat of arms. **2.** a cloak with short sleeves worn by knights over their armor.

tab·by (tab′ē), *n.* **1.** a gray or brown cat with dark stripes. **2.** any pet cat, especially a female. —**tab′bies,** *pl.*

tab·er·nac·le (tab′ər nak′′l), *n.* **1.** a temporary shelter, as a tent. **2. Tabernacle,** the shelter which the Jews carried with them during their wanderings under Moses, for use as a place of worship; also, later, the Jewish Temple. **3.** any large place of worship. **4.** a container for something considered holy.

tabard

ta·ble (tā′b′l), *n.* **1.** a piece of furniture made up of a flat top set on legs. **2.** such a table set with food; also, the food served [His manners at the *table* have improved.] **3.** the people seated at a table [Our *table* played bridge.] **4.** an orderly list [a *table* of contents in a book]. **5.** an orderly arrangement of facts, figures, etc. [multiplication *tables*]. **6.** a tableland. **7.** a flat, thin piece of metal, stone, or wood, with words, etc. cut into it; tablet. —*v.* **1.** to put off discussing; set aside [to *table* a bill in Congress]. **2.** to put on a table. —**turn the tables,** to make a situation just the opposite of what it was. —**ta′bled,** *p.t. & p.p.;* **ta′bling,** *pr.p.*

tab·leau (tab′lō), *n.* a picture or scene, as of an event in history, made by persons posing in costume [a *tableau* of the landing of the Pilgrims]. —**tab·leaux** (tab′lōz) or **tab′leaus,** *pl.*

ta·ble·cloth (tā′b′l klôth), *n.* a cloth for covering a table, especially at meals.

ta·ble·land (tā′b′l land), *n.* a high, broad, usually flat region; plateau.

ta·ble·spoon (tā′b′l spoon), *n.* **1.** a large spoon for eating soup, for serving food, or for measuring things in cooking. **2.** a tablespoonful.

ta·ble·spoon·ful (tā′b′l spoon′fool), *n.* as much as a tablespoon will hold, usually 1/2 fluid ounce. —**ta′ble·spoon′fuls,** *pl.*

tab·let (tab′lit), *n.* **1.** sheets of writing paper fastened at one end to form a pad. **2.** a small, flat, hard cake, as of medicine [an aspirin *tablet*]. **3.** a flat, thin piece of metal, stone, etc. with words, etc. written on it or cut into it [A *tablet* on the museum wall lists the names of the founders.]

table tennis, a game like tennis, played on a table with a small, hollow ball and small, solid paddles with short handles.

tablet
(*meaning 3*)

ta·ble·ware (tā′b′l wer), *n.* dishes, forks, spoons, etc., used at the table for eating.

tab·loid (tab′loid), *n.* a newspaper on small sheets, with many pictures and short articles.

ta·boo (tə boo′ *or* ta boo′), *n.* **1.** the act or practice of making certain persons and things sacred so that they cannot be touched or talked about. **2.** any rule that makes something forbidden [There is a *taboo* against certain words in polite speech.] —*adj.* forbidden by taboo. —*v.*

to put under taboo; forbid. **—ta·boos′,** *pl.*
—ta·booed′, *p.t. & p.p.;* **ta·boo′ing,** *pr.p.*
ta·bu (tə bōō′ *or* ta bōō′) *n., adj. & v.* same as
taboo. —ta·bus′, *pl.* **—ta·bued′,** *p.t. &*
p.p.; **ta·bu′ing,** *pr.p.*
tab·u·lar (tab′yoo lər), *adj.* **1.** of or arranged
in columns in a table or list [*tabular* data]. **2.** flat
like a table.
tab·u·late (tab′yoo lāt), *v.* to arrange in tables
or columns [to *tabulate* facts]. **—tab′u·lat·ed,**
p.t. & p.p.; **tab′u·lat·ing,** *pr.p.* **—tab′u·la′-**
tion, *n.* **—tab′u·la′tor,** *n.*
tac·it (tas′it), *adj.* **1.** understood or meant,
but not openly said [His smile gave *tacit* approval.]
2. making no sound; silent. **—tac′it·ly,** *adv.*
tac·i·turn (tas′ə tûrn), *adj.* not liking to talk;
usually silent. **—tac′i·tur′ni·ty,** *n.*
tack (tak), *n.* **1.** a short nail with a sharp point
and a somewhat large, flat head.
2. the direction a ship goes in
relation to the position of the
sails. **3.** a change of a ship's
direction. **4.** a zigzag course.
5. a way of doing something;
course of action [He is on the
wrong *tack.*] **6.** a long, loose
stitch used in sewing, as to baste a hem. **—v. 1.**
to fasten with tacks [to *tack* down a carpet].
2. to add or attach as something extra [I'll *tack*
a new ending on to the story.] **3.** to change the
course of a ship. **4.** to sail in a zigzag course.
5. to sew together loosely with tacks.

types of tack

tack·le (tak′'l), *n.* **1.** the tools or equipment
needed for doing something; gear [fishing *tackle*].
2. a set of ropes and pulleys for moving heavy
things. **3.** the act of tackling, as in football.
4. either of two football players placed between
the guards and ends. **—v. 1.** to try to do or
solve; undertake [He *tackled* the job.] **2.** to
seize and stop or throw to the ground, as a player
carrying the ball in football. **3.** to fasten by
means of tackle. **—tack′led,** *p.t. & p.p.;*
tack′ling, *pr.p.* **—tack′ler,** *n.*
ta·co (tä′kō) *n.* a Mexican food made of a thin
fried cake, esp. of corn flour, which is folded over
chopped meat, lettuce, etc. **—ta′cos,** *pl.*
Ta·co·ma (tə kō′mə), *n.* a seaport in western
Washington.
tact (takt), *n.* a sense of what is the right thing
to do or say without causing anger or hurt feelings; skill in dealing with people.
tact·ful (takt′fəl), *adj.* having or showing tact.
—tact′ful·ly, *adv.* **—tact′ful·ness,** *n.*
tac·ti·cal (tak′ti k'l), *adj.* **1.** of tactics; especially, having to do with the movement of armed
troops in battle. **2.** skillful or clever in the tactics
used. **—tac′ti·cal·ly,** *adv.*
tac·ti·cian (tak tish′ən), *n.* a person who is
skilled in tactics.
tac·tics (tak′tiks), *n.pl.* **1.** the science of moving
armed troops about in battle in trying to get

the advantage: *used with a singular verb* [*Tactics*
is studied at West Point.] **2.** any skillful methods
used to bring something about [the *tactics* of a
political campaign].
tact·less (takt′lis), *adj.* not showing tact.
—tact′less·ly, *adv.* **—tact′less·ness,** *n.*
tad·pole (tad′pōl), *n.* a young toad or frog
when it still has a tail and lives only in water.
taf·fe·ta (taf′i tə), *n.* **1.** a stiff silk cloth with a
sheen. **2.** a cloth like this, of linen, rayon, etc.
taff·rail (taf′rāl), *n.* a rail around a ship's stern.
taf·fy (taf′ē), *n.* a chewy candy made of sugar
or molasses boiled down and pulled.
Taft, William Howard (taft), 1857–1930;
27th president of the United States, from 1909 to
1913, and Chief Justice, from 1921 to 1930.
tag (tag), *n.* **1.** a card, paper, etc. attached to
something as a label [price *tags* on merchandise].
2. any hanging part or loosely attached end
[Pull the *tag* to close the zipper.] **3.** a tip of
metal, etc. as on a string or lace. **4.** the last line
or lines of a speech, story, etc. **5.** a children's
game in which one player, called "it," chases the
others until he touches one of them, making him
"it." **—v. 1.** to put a tag on. **2.** to touch as in
the game of tag. **3.** to follow close behind: *only
in everyday talk* [Billy always *tags* along after us.]
—tagged, *p.t. & p.p.;* **tag′ging,** *pr.p.*
Ta·hi·ti (tä hē′tē), *n.* a French island in the
South Pacific, south of Hawaii.
tail (tāl), *n.* **1.** the part at the rear of an animal's
body that sticks out beyond the backbone. **2.** any
thing or part like this [the *tail* of a shirt; a pig*tail*].
3. the hind or last part [the *tail* of a parade].
4. *often* **tails,** *pl.* the side of a coin opposite the
head, or main side. **5. tails,** *pl.* a man's formal
evening suit having a swallow-tailed coat. **—v.**
to follow close behind: *used only in everyday talk*
[A detective was *tailing* us.] **—adj. 1.** at the rear;
hind [We saw the *tail* end of the movie.] **2.** from
the rear [a *tail* wind]. **—turn tail,** to run from
danger or trouble. **—tail′less,** *adj.*
tail·gate (tāl′gāt), *n.* a board at the back of a
truck, etc. that can be
taken off or lowered.
tail·light (tāl′līt), *n.* a
light at the back of an
automobile, truck, etc.
tai·lor (tā′lər), *n.* a person who makes or repairs
suits, coats, etc. **—v. 1.**
to work as a tailor or
make as a tailor does [suits *tailored* for stout
men]. **2.** to make or change so as to fit a certain
need [movies *tailored* for young people].
tail·spin (tāl′spin), *n.* a downward plunge of an
airplane out of control, with the tail up and spinning in circles.
taint (tānt), *n.* a trace of something that spoils,
rots, or poisons. **—v.** to spoil, rot, or poison
[The food is *tainted*.]

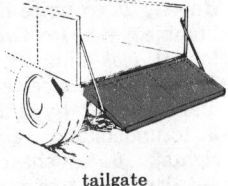

tailgate

fat, āpe, cär, ten, ēven, hit, bīte, gō, hôrn, tool, book, up, fûr;
get, joy, yet, chin, she, thin, *th*en; zh = s in pleasure; ′ as in able (ā′b'l);
ə = a in ago, e in agent, i in sanity, o in confess, u in focus.

Tai·wan (tī′wän′), *n.* the official name of **Formosa.**

take (tāk), *v.* **1.** to get hold of; grasp [*Take* my hand as we cross the street.] **2.** to get by force or skill; capture; seize; win [The soldiers *took* the town. Our team *took* two games.] **3.** to delight or charm [We were *taken* by her wit.] **4.** to get as one's own; obtain, select, assume, etc. [He *took* a wife. She *took* the job. When does the senator *take* office?] **5.** to eat, drink, etc. [He is so sick he can't *take* food.] **6.** to buy, rent, subscribe for, etc. [We *take* two daily papers.] **7.** to be used with [The verb "hit" *takes* an object.] **8.** to travel by or on [to *take* a bus; to *take* a short cut]. **9.** to deal with; consider [He *took* his studies seriously. *Take* this as an example.] **10.** to call for; require; need [It *took* courage to jump.] **11.** to get or draw from a source [He *took* this quotation from Shakespeare.] **12.** to get by observing, studying, etc. [to *take* a poll of opinion; to *take* Latin in school]. **13.** to write down; copy [to *take* notes on a lecture]. **14.** to photograph [She *took* our picture.] **15.** to receive or accept [She *took* my advice. He *took* his punishment.] **16.** to be affected by [He *took* cold. The cloth *took* the dye.] **17.** to understand [He *took* her remarks as praise.] **18.** to have or feel [to *take* pity]. **19.** to do, make, use, etc. [to *take* a walk; to *take* a look; to *take* care]. **20.** to remove from some person or place [Somebody *took* my purse.] **21.** to carry [*Take* your skates with you.] **22.** to subtract [*Take* two dollars off the price.] **23.** to lead or bring [This road *takes* us to the lake. I *took* her to a movie.] **24.** to catch [The fire *took* quickly.] **25.** to begin growing, taking effect, etc. [Roses won't *take* in this soil. His vaccination *took*.] **26.** to head for; go [They *took* to the hills.] **27.** to become: *used only in everyday talk* [He *took* sick.] **28.** to cheat or trick: *slang in this meaning.* —*n.* **1.** the act of taking. **2.** the amount taken or received [the day's *take* of money at the store]. —**take after,** to be, act, or look like. —**take back,** to withdraw something said, promised, etc. —**take down, 1.** to write down; record. **2.** to make humble. —**take for,** to think to be; mistake for [I *took* him *for* his father.] —**take in, 1.** to admit or receive [to *take in* lodgers]. **2.** to make smaller by drawing in cloth at a seam. **3.** to understand. **4.** to visit [to *take in* all the sights]. **5.** to cheat or fool. **6.** to include. —**take it, 1.** to suppose or believe. **2.** to stand up under trouble, criticism, etc.: *a slang phrase.* —**take off, 1.** to rise from the ground or water in an airplane. **2.** to imitate or mimic in fun: *used only in everyday talk.* —**take on, 1.** to get. **2.** to hire. **3.** to undertake. **4.** to play against, as in a game. **5.** to show strong feeling: *used only in everyday talk.* —**take one's time,** to be in no hurry. —**take over,** to begin managing. —**take to,** to become fond of. —**take up, 1.** to make tighter or shorter, as a rope. **2.** to absorb, as a liquid. **3.** to become interested in. **4.** to fill, as space or time. —**took,** *p.t.;* **tak′en,** *p.p.;* **tak′ing,** *pr.p.* —**tak′er,** *n.*

take-off (tāk′ôf′), *n.* **1.** the act of rising from the ground, as in an airplane or by jumping. **2.** an imitation of someone, as in making fun of him: *used only in everyday talk.*

tak·ing (tāk′ing), *adj.* attractive; charming [her *taking* smile]. —*n.* **1.** the act of one that takes [the *taking* of the census]. **2. takings,** *pl.* money earned; profits.

talc (talk), *n.* a soft mineral ground up to make talcum powder.

tal·cum (tal′kəm), *n.* **1.** talc. **2.** a powder for the face and body made of talc, often with perfume added: *its full name is* **talcum powder.**

tale (tāl), *n.* **1.** a story, especially about things that are imagined or made-up [folk *tales;* fairy *tales*]. **2.** a lie or false story. **3.** gossip, especially when it may do harm.

tale·bear·er (tāl′ber′ər), *n.* a person who gossips, tells secrets, informs on others, etc.

tal·ent (tal′ənt), *n.* **1.** a natural skill that is unusual [his *talent* as an artist]. **2.** people with talent [He helps young *talent* along.] **3.** a unit of weight or money used in ancient times.

tal·ent·ed (tal′ən tid), *adj.* having an unusually fine natural skill; gifted.

tal·is·man (tal′is mən), *n.* **1.** a ring, stone, etc. carved with designs supposed to bring good luck. **2.** anything supposed to have magic power; a charm. —**tal′is·mans,** *pl.*

talk (tôk), *v.* **1.** to say words or put ideas into words; speak [The baby is learning to *talk*. We *talked* of many things.] **2.** to make, bring about, etc. by talking [He *talked* himself hoarse. We *talked* him into going with us.] **3.** to pass on ideas in some way other than with spoken words [He *talked* in sign language.] **4.** to speak about; discuss [to *talk* business]. **5.** to chatter or gossip. **6.** to use in speaking [to *talk* Spanish]. —*n.* **1.** the act of talking; conversation [language used only in everyday *talk*]. **2.** a speech [He gave a *talk* on gardening.] **3.** a conference [*talks* between the company and the union]. **4.** gossip; a rumor [There is *talk* going around that they are engaged.] **5.** a person or thing that is being talked about [Her new play is the *talk* of the town.] —**talk back,** to answer in a way that is not respectful. —**talk down to,** to talk to in a simple way, as if to show that one does not expect to be understood. —**talk′er,** *n.*

talk·a·tive (tôk′ə tiv), *adj.* talking a great deal, or fond of talking.

tall (tôl), *adj.* **1.** reaching a long way up; not low or short [a *tall* building]. **2.** as measured from top to bottom; high [a man six feet *tall*]. **3.** hard to believe; exaggerated: *used only in everyday talk* [a *tall* tale].

Tal·la·has·see (tal′ə has′ē), *n.* the capital of Florida.

tal·low (tal′ō), *n.* the hard fat of cows, sheep, etc., melted for use in candles, soap, etc.

tal·ly (tal′ē), *n.* **1.** a record, account, score, etc. [Keep a *tally* of the money you spend.] **2.** a paper, pad, etc. on which such a record is kept. **3.** a tag or label. —*v.* **1.** to put on a tally; record; score [The team *tallied* two runs in the ninth inning.] **2.** to count; add [*Tally* up the score.] **3.** to match or agree [His story of what happened doesn't *tally* with hers.] —**tal′lies,** *pl.* —**tal′lied,** *p.t. & p.p.;* **tal′ly·ing,** *pr,p.*

tal·ly·ho (tal′ē hō′), *interj.* the cry of a fox hunter when he sees the fox. —*n.* a coach pulled by four horses. —**tal′ly·hos′,** *pl.*

Tal·mud (tal′mud *or* täl′mood), *n.* the collection of writings that make up the early Jewish civil and religious law.

tal·on (tal′ən), *n.* the claw of a bird that kills other animals for food, as the eagle.

tam (tam), *n.* a tam-o'-shanter.

ta·ma·le (tə mä′lē), *n.* a Mexican food of chopped meat and red peppers rolled in corn meal, wrapped in corn husks, and baked or steamed.

tam·a·rack (tam′ə rak), *n.* a kind of larch tree usually found in swamps.

tam·a·rind (tam′ə rind), *n.* **1.** a tropical tree with yellow flowers and brown fruit pods. **2.** its fruit, used in foods, medicine, etc.

tam·bou·rine (tam bə rēn′), *n.* a small, shallow drum with only one head and with jingling metal disks in the rim. It is shaken, struck with the hand, etc.

tambourine

tame (tām), *adj.* **1.** no longer wild, but trained for use by man or as a pet [Pat has a *tame* skunk.] **2.** gentle, easy to control, and not afraid of man [The bronco soon became quite *tame.*] **3.** not lively or forceful; dull [a *tame* boxing match]. —*v.* **1.** to make tame, or train to obey [to *tame* wild animals for a circus]. **2.** to make more gentle or easier to manage; subdue [Kind treatment helped *tame* the boy down.] —**tam′er,** *compar.;* **tam′est,** *superl.* —**tamed,** *p.t. & p.p.;* **tam′ing,** *pr.p.* —**tame′ly,** *adv.* —**tam′er,** *n.*

tam-o'-shan·ter (tam′ə shan′tər), *n.* a soft, round Scottish cap: *see the picture.*

tamp (tamp), *v.* to pack or pound down with blows or taps [to *tamp* down tobacco in a pipe].

Tam·pa (tam′pə), *n.* a city in western Florida.

tam-o'-shanter

tam·per (tam′pər), *v.* to meddle or interfere, especially in a way that is not right or honest or that makes things worse [He *tampered* with the clock, and now it's slow.]

tan (tan), *n.* **1.** tanbark. **2.** yellowish brown. **3.** the brown color the skin gets from being much in the sun. —*adj.* yellowish-brown. —*v.* **1.** to make into leather by soaking in tannic acid [to *tan* cowhides]. **2.** to make or become brown, as from being much in the sun [His skin *tans* quickly.] **3.** to whip or flog: *used only in everyday*

talk. —**tan′ner,** *compar.;* **tan′nest,** *superl.* —**tanned,** *p.t. & p.p.;* **tan′ning,** *pr.p.*

tan·a·ger (tan′ə jər), *n.* a small American songbird. The male is usually brightly colored.

tan·bark (tan′bärk), *n.* any tree bark that contains tannic acid. The acid is used to tan hides, and the bark with the acid removed is used to cover circus rings, race tracks, etc.

tan·dem (tan′dəm), *adv.* one behind another; in single file [five dogs hitched *tandem* to a sled]. —*n.* **1.** a team, as of horses, harnessed one behind the other. **2.** a carriage with two wheels, pulled by a tandem of horses. **3.** a bicycle with two seats, one behind the other: *its full name is* **tandem bicycle.**

tandem bicycle

tang (tang), *n.* **1.** a sharp, strong taste or smell [a spicy *tang*]. **2.** a point or prong on a chisel, file, etc. that fits into the handle.

tan·gent (tan′jənt), *adj.* touching a curved line or surface at only one point and not cutting across it [a line *tangent* to a circle]. —*n.* a tangent curve, line, or surface. —**go off at a tangent,** to change suddenly from one subject or line of action to another.

line tangent to a circle

tan·ge·rine (tan jə rēn′), *n.* a small orange with sections that come apart easily and a loose skin that peels off easily.

tan·gi·ble (tan′jə b'l), *adj.* **1.** that can be touched or felt; real or solid [A house is *tangible* property.] **2.** that can be understood; definite; not vague [I was frightened for no *tangible* reason.] —**tan′gi·bly,** *adv.*

Tan·gier (tan jir′), *n.* a seaport in Morocco.

tan·gle (tang′g'l), *v.* **1.** to make or become knotted, confused, etc. [Our fishing lines are *tangled*.] **2.** to catch or hold back, as in a snare [His feet became *tangled* in the garden hose.] —*n.* **1.** a mass of thread, branches, hair, etc. twisted or knotted together [a *tangle* of underbrush]. **2.** a confused or mixed-up condition; muddle [His affairs are in a *tangle*.] —**tan′gled,** *p.t. & p.p.;* **tan′gling,** *pr.p.*

tank (tangk), *n.* **1.** any large container for liquid or gas [a fuel *tank;* a swimming *tank*]. **2.** a military car covered with armor and carrying heavy guns. It moves on endless metal belts that let it travel over rough ground. —**tank′ful,** *n.*

tank

tank·ard (tangk′ərd), *n.* a large drinking cup with a handle, and a lid joined by a hinge.

tank·er (tangk′ər), *n.* a ship with large tanks in the hull for carrying oil or other liquids.

tan·ner (tan′ər), *n.* a person whose work is making leather by tanning hides.

tan·ner·y (tan′ər ē), *n.* a place where leather is made by tanning hides. —**tan′ner·ies**, *pl.*

tan·nic acid (tan′ik), an acid got from oak bark, used in tanning, dyeing, and medicine.

tan·nin (tan′in), *n.* tannic acid.

tan·sy (tan′zē), *n.* a plant with a strong smell and small, yellow flowers. —**tan′sies**, *pl.*

tan·ta·lize (tan′tə līz), *v.* to tease or disappoint by showing or promising something wanted and then holding it back [Dreams of food *tantalized* the hungry man.] —**tan′ta·lized**, *p.t. & p.p.*; **tan′ta·liz·ing**, *pr.p.*

tan·ta·mount (tan′tə mount), *adj.* almost the same as; equal [The king's wishes were *tantamount* to orders.]

tan·trum (tan′trəm), *n.* a fit of bad temper.

Tan·za·ni·a (tan zə nē′ə), *n.* a country on the eastern coast of Africa and on Zanzibar.

tap (tap), *v.* **1.** to hit lightly [He *tapped* my shoulder.] **2.** to hit something lightly with [He *tapped* the chalk against the blackboard.] **3.** to make or do by tapping [to *tap* out a rhythm]. —*n.* a light blow, or the sound made by it —**tapped**, *p.t. & p.p.*; **tap′ping**, *pr.p.*

tap (tap), *n.* **1.** a device for turning the flow of liquid on or off, as from a pipe; faucet. **2.** a plug or cork for stopping a hole in a cask. **3.** a place in a pipe, wire, etc. where a connection is made. —*v.* **1.** to drill a hole in, pull the plug from, etc., so as to draw off liquid [to *tap* a rubber tree; to *tap* a barrel]. **2.** to draw out, as from a container [to *tap* wine from a cask; to *tap* the wealth of a treasury]. **3.** to make a connection with [to *tap* a telephone line]. —**on tap**, ready for use, as liquid in a cask that has been tapped. —**tapped**, *p.t. & p.p.*; **tap′ping**, *pr.p.*

tap dance, a dance done by making sharp, loud taps with the foot, heel, or toe at each step.

tape (tāp), *n.* **1.** a strong, narrow strip of cloth, paper, etc. used for binding or tying [adhesive *tape*]. **2.** a narrow strip of paper, steel, etc. on which something is recorded [recording *tape*; a measuring *tape*]. **3.** a strip of cloth stretched above the finishing line of a race. —*v.* **1.** to tie or bind with tape. **2.** to record on tape. —**taped**, *p.t. & p.p.*; **tap′ing**, *pr.p.*

tape measure, a tape marked off in inches and feet for measuring: also **tape′line**, *n.*

ta·per (tā′pər), *v.* **1.** to make or become less wide or less thick little by little [A sword *tapers* to a point.] **2.** to lessen little by little [Her voice *tapered* off to a whisper.] —*n.* **1.** the fact or amount of tapering, or becoming gradually thinner. **2.** a slender candle.

tape recorder, a machine for recording sound on thin magnetic tape and for playing it back after it is recorded.

tap·es·try (tap′is trē), *n.* a heavy cloth with designs and pictures woven

shoe tapering at toe

into it, for hanging on walls, covering furniture, etc. —**tap′es·tries**, *pl.*

tape·worm (tāp′wûrm), *n.* a long, flat worm sometimes found in the intestines of man and animals.

tap·i·o·ca (tap′i ō′kə), *n.* a starchy substance from cassava roots, used in puddings, etc.

ta·pir (tā′pər), *n.* a large animal like a pig, with a long snout that can bend. It lives in the forests of Central and South America.

tapir (3 ft. high at shoulder)

tap·room (tap′room), *n.* a room where alcoholic liquor is sold; barroom.

tap·root (tap′root), *n.* a main root growing downward, from which small roots branch out.

taps (taps), *n.* a bugle call or drum signal to put out lights and go to bed, as in an army camp. It is also sounded at military burials.

tar (tär), *n.* a thick, black, sticky liquid distilled from wood or coal. —*v.* to cover or smear with tar. —**tarred**, *p.t. & p.p.*; **tar′ring**, *pr.p.*

tar (tär), *n.* a sailor: *only in everyday talk.*

tar·an·tel·la (tar′ən tel′ə), *n.* **1.** a fast, whirling Italian folk dance. **2.** music for this.

ta·ran·tu·la (tə ran′choo lə), *n.* a large, hairy spider of tropical regions, whose bite is slightly poisonous.

tar·dy (tär′dē), *adj.* **1.** not on time; late; delayed [to be *tardy* for class]. **2.** moving slowly. —**tar′di·er**, *compar.*; **tar′di·est**, *superl.* —**tar′di·ly**, *adv.* —**tar′di·ness**, *n.*

tarantula (1 to 3 in. long)

tare (ter), *n.* **1.** a kind of vetch grown as food for cattle. **2.** a weed mentioned in the Bible.

tare (ter), *n.* the weight of a container, wrapper, etc. taken from the total weight in figuring weight of the contents.

tar·get (tär′git), *n.* **1.** a thing aimed at, as in shooting a rifle or arrow; especially, a board with circles on it, one inside the other. **2.** a person or thing that is attacked, made fun of, etc. [to be the *target* of someone's hatred].

tar·iff (tar′if), *n.* **1.** a list of taxes on goods imported or, sometimes, on goods exported. **2.** such a tax or its rate. **3.** any list of prices or charges.

target

tarn (tärn), *n.* a small mountain lake.

tar·nish (tär′nish), *v.* to dull, stain, or discolor, as silver. —*n.* the condition of being tarnished; loss of brightness or polish.

ta·ro (tä′rō), *n.* a tropical plant with a starchy root that is eaten as food.

tar·pau·lin (tär pô′lin *or* tär′pə lin), *n.* **1.** canvas made waterproof with tar, paint, etc. **2.** a sheet of this for protecting something.

tar·pon (tär′pän), *n.* a large, silver-colored fish found in the western Atlantic.

tar·ry (tar′ē), *v.* **1.** to stay for a time [We *tarried* in the park till sundown.] **2.** to put off; delay [Don't *tarry*; mail the letter now.] —**tar′ried,** *p.t. & p.p.;* **tar′ry·ing,** *pr.p.*

tar·ry (tär′ē), *adj.* **1.** of or like tar. **2.** covered with tar. —**tar′ri·er,** *compar.;* **tar′ri·est,** *superl.* —**tar′ri·ness,** *n.*

tarpon (6 to 8 ft. long)

tart (tärt), *adj.* **1.** sharp in taste; sour; acid [*tart* grapes]. **2.** sharp in meaning; cutting [a *tart* answer]. —**tart′ly,** *adv.* —**tart′ness,** *n.*

tart (tärt), *n.* **1.** a small, open shell of pastry filled with jam, jelly, etc. **2.** any fruit pie: *a British meaning.*

tar·tan (tär′t'n), *n.* **1.** woolen cloth with a woven plaid pattern, worn in the Scottish Highlands. Each clan has its own pattern. **2.** any plaid cloth or pattern.

Tar·tar (tär′tər), *n.* **1.** a Tatar. **2. tartar,** a person who loses his temper easily.

tar·tar (tär′tər), *n.* **1.** a hard substance that forms on the teeth. **2.** a reddish, salty crust that forms inside wine casks. In a purified form it is the acid substance (**cream of tartar**) in baking powder.

task (task), *n.* a piece of work that one must do. —*v.* to put a strain on; be hard for; burden [Reading the small print *tasked* her eyesight.] —**take to task,** to find fault with; scold.

task·mas·ter (task′mas′tər), *n.* a person who gives tasks or hard work to others to do.

Tas·ma·ni·a (taz mā′ni ə), *n.* an Australian state that is an island southeast of Australia. —**Tas·ma′ni·an,** *adj. & n.*

tas·sel (tas′'l), *n.* **1.** a bunch of threads, cords, etc. hanging from a knob. **2.** something like this, as the silk that hangs from an ear of corn. —*v.* to put tassels on or have tassels. —**tas′-seled** or **tas′selled,** *p.t. & p.p.;* **tas′sel·ing** or **tas′-sel·ling,** *pr.p.*

tassel

taste (tāst), *v.* **1.** to be aware of something by a special sense in the mouth; notice the flavor of [I *taste* garlic in the salad.] **2.** to test the flavor of by putting some in one's mouth [*Taste* this sauce to see if it's too sweet.] **3.** to eat or drink very little of [He just *tasted* his food.] **4.** to have a certain flavor [The milk *tastes* sour.] **5.** to have the experience of [to *taste* success]. —*n.* **1.** the power to taste; the sense in the taste buds of the tongue by which one

can tell the flavor of things. **2.** that quality of a thing which is noticed by the tongue; flavor [Candy has a sweet *taste.*] **3.** a small amount, especially of food or drink; sample; bit [Give me a *taste* of the cake. He had a short *taste* of fame.] **4.** the ability to know and judge what is beautiful, proper, etc. [Her simple dress showed her good *taste.*] **5.** a style or way that shows such ability to judge what is beautiful, proper, etc. [That remark was in bad *taste.*] **6.** a liking; preference [He has no *taste* for sports.] —**tast′-ed,** *p.t. & p.p.;* **tast′ing,** *pr.p.* —**tast′er,** *n.*

taste bud, any of the cells in the tongue that tell whether something is sweet, sour, salty, or bitter.

taste·ful (tāst′fəl), *adj.* having or showing good taste (*in noun meaning 5*). —**taste′ful·ly,** *adv.*

taste·less (tāst′lis), *adj.* **1.** without taste or flavor [*tasteless* food]. **2.** lacking good taste (*in noun meaning 5*). —**taste′less·ly,** *adv.*

tast·y (tās′tē), *adj.* that tastes good; full of flavor [a *tasty* meal]. —**tast′i·er,** *compar.;* **tast′i·est,** *superl.* —**tast′i·ness,** *n.*

tat (tat), *v.* to do tatting or make by tatting. —**tat′ted,** *p.t. & p.p.;* **tat′ting,** *pr.p.*

Ta·tar (tä′tər), *n.* any of the Mongols or Turks who invaded western Asia and eastern Europe in the Middle Ages.

tat·ter (tat′ər), *n.* **1.** a torn and hanging piece or shred, as of cloth; rag. **2. tatters,** *pl.* torn, ragged clothes.

tat·tered (tat′ərd), *adj.* **1.** torn and ragged [*tattered* clothes]. **2.** wearing torn and ragged clothes [a *tattered* child].

tat·ting (tat′ing), *n.* **1.** the act of making lace by looping and knotting thread with a small shuttle held in the hand. **2.** this kind of lace.

tat·tle (tat′'l), *v.* **1.** to talk in a foolish way; chatter. **2.** to tell others' secrets; tell tales. —*n.* foolish talk; chatter. —**tat′tled,** *p.t. & p.p.;* **tat′tling,** *pr.p.* —**tat′tler,** *n.*

tat·tle·tale (tat′'l tāl), *n.* a person who tells the secrets of others; talebearer.

tat·too (ta tōō′), *v.* to make marks or designs on the skin by pricking it with needles and putting colors in. —*n.* a mark or design made in this way. —**tat·tooed′,** *p.t. & p.p.;* **tat·too′ing,** *pr.p.* —**tat·toos′,** *pl.*

tat·too (ta tōō′), *n.* **1.** a signal on a drum or bugle ordering soldiers or sailors to go to their quarters at night. **2.** a loud tapping or rapping [His fingers beat a *tattoo* on the table.] —**tat·toos′,** *pl.*

man being tattooed

taught (tôt), past tense and past participle of **teach.**

taunt (tônt *or* tänt), *v.* to jeer at; mock; tease. —*n.* a scornful or jeering remark.

taupe (tōp) *n. & adj.* dark, brownish gray.

Tau·rus (tôr′əs), *n.* a constellation of stars in the northern sky.

taut (tôt), *adj.* **1.** tightly stretched, as a rope. **2.** showing strain; tense [a *taut* smile].

tav·ern (tav′ərn), *n.* **1.** a place where beer, whisky, etc. are sold and drunk; bar. **2.** an inn.

taw (tô), *n.* **1.** a fancy marble used to shoot with in playing marbles. **2.** the game of marbles. **3.** the line that one shoots his marble from.

taw·dry (tô′drē), *adj.* cheap and showy; gaudy. —**taw′dri·er**, *compar.*; **taw′dri·est**, *superl.*

taw·ny (tô′nē), *adj. & n.* dark yellow or tan. —**taw′ni·er**, *compar.*; **taw′ni·est**, *superl.*

tax (taks), *n.* **1.** money that one must pay to help support a government. It is usually a percentage of one's income or of the value of something owned. **2.** a heavy burden or strain [The illness was a *tax* on his health.] —*v.* **1.** to put a tax on [to *tax* cigarettes]. **2.** to make pay a tax [Congress has the power to *tax* the people.] **3.** to put a burden or strain on [His pranks *tax* my patience.] **4.** to find fault with; accuse [They *taxed* him with being unfair.] —**tax′a·ble**, *adj.*

tax·a·tion (tak sā′shən), *n.* **1.** a taxing or being taxed. **2.** the amount collected in taxes.

tax·i (tak′sē), *n.* a taxicab. —*v.* **1.** to go in a taxicab. **2.** to move along the ground or water as an airplane does before taking off or after landing. —**tax′is**, *pl.* —**tax′ied**, *p.t. & p.p.*; **tax′i·ing** or **tax′y·ing**, *pr.p.*

tax·i·cab (tak′sē kab), *n.* an automobile in which passengers are carried for a fare. It usually has a meter that shows the amount owed.

tax·i·der·my (tak′si dûr′mē), *n.* the art of stuffing and mounting the skins of animals so that they look alive. —**tax′i·der′mist**, *n.*

tax·pay·er (taks′pā′ər), *n.* a person who pays a tax or taxes.

Tay·lor, Zach·a·ry (zak′ər ē tā′lər), 1784–1850; 12th president of the U.S., from 1849 to 1850.

TB or **T.B.,** abbreviation for **tuberculosis.**

T-bar (tē′bär′), *n.* a T-shaped bar hung from a moving endless cable: used to pull skiers up a slope as they hold it and stand on their skis.

Tchai·kov·sky, Peter Il·ich (il yēch′ chī kôf′skē), 1840–1893; Russian composer of music.

tea (tē), *n.* **1.** a plant grown in warm parts of Asia for its leaf buds and young leaves, which are prepared by drying, etc. for use in making a common drink. **2.** the dried leaves and leaf buds. **3.** the drink made by steeping these in hot water. **4.** a meal in the late afternoon, as in England, at which tea is the usual drink. **5.** an afternoon party at which tea, coffee, etc. are served. **6.** a drink like tea, made from some other plant or from meat [sassafras *tea*; beef *tea*].

left: tea leaves and flowers
right: tea plant

tea bag, a small bag of cloth or paper containing tea leaves.

teach (tēch), *v.* **1.** to show or help to learn how to do something; train [He *taught* us to skate.] **2.** to give lessons to or in [Who *teaches* your class? He *teaches* French.] **3.** to be a teacher [He wants to *teach*.] **4.** to make know or understand [The accident *taught* him to be careful.] —**taught**, *p.t. & p.p.*; **teach′ing**, *pr.p.* —**teach′a·ble**, *adj.*

teach·er (tēch′ər), *n.* a person who teaches; especially, a schoolteacher.

teach·ing (tēch′ing), *n.* **1.** the work of a teacher. **2.** *often* **teachings**, *pl.* something taught.

tea·cup (tē′kup), *n.* a cup for drinking tea.

teak (tēk), *n.* **1.** a large tree of the East Indies, with hard, golden-brown wood. **2.** this wood.

tea·ket·tle (tē′ket′'l), *n.* a kettle with a spout, used to heat water as for tea.

teal (tēl), *n.* **1.** a wild duck with a short neck. **2.** a dark grayish blue.

team (tēm), *n.* **1.** two or more horses, oxen, etc. harnessed together as for pulling a plow or wagon. **2.** a group of people working or playing together [a *team* of scientists; a baseball *team*]. —*v.* to join together in a team [Let's *team* up with them.]

teals (14 in. long)

team·mate (tēm′māt), *n.* a fellow member of a team.

team·ster (tēm′stər), *n.* a man whose work is hauling loads with a team or truck.

team·work (tēm′wûrk), *n.* the action or effort of people working together as a group.

tea·pot (tē′pät), *n.* a pot with a spout, handle, and lid, for making and pouring tea.

tear (ter), *v.* **1.** to pull apart by force; rip [Paper *tears* easily. The saw *tore* his skin.] **2.** to make by tearing [The nail *tore* a hole in her dress.] **3.** to pull up, down, out, at, etc. with force [The wind *tore* up trees by their roots.] **4.** to divide by struggle, fighting, etc. [The country was *torn* by civil war.] **5.** to make suffer very much [*torn* by grief]. **6.** to move with force or speed [He *tore* home.] —*n.* **1.** the act of tearing. **2.** a torn place; rip. —**tear down,** to take apart; wreck. —**tore**, *p.t.*; **torn**, *p.p.*; **tear′ing**, *pr.p.*

tear (tir), *n.* a drop of the salty liquid that flows from the eye, as in weeping: also **tear′drop.** —*v.* to shed tears —**in tears,** weeping.

tear·ful (tir′fəl), *adj.* **1.** weeping. **2.** full of or causing tears; sad. —**tear′ful·ly**, *adv.*

tear gas, a gas that makes the eyes sore and blinds them with tears.

tease (tēz), *v.* **1.** to bother or annoy by joking or mocking talk, playful fooling, etc. **2.** to beg in an annoying way [He keeps *teasing* for candy.] **3.** to comb out, as wool or flax. —*n.* a person who teases. —**teased**, *p.t. & p.p.*; **teas′ing**, *pr.p.*

tea·spoon (tē′spoon), *n.* **1.** a small spoon for stirring tea, coffee, etc., or for measuring things in cooking. **2.** a teaspoonful.

tea·spoon·ful (tē′spoon fool), *n.* as much as a teaspoon will hold [Three *teaspoonfuls* equal one tablespoonful.] —**tea′spoon·fuls,** *pl.*

teat (tēt), *n.* the nipple of a breast or udder.

tech·nic (tek′nik) *n.* technique: *seldom used.*

tech·ni·cal (tek′ni k'l), *adj.* **1.** having to do with the useful or industrial arts or skills [A *technical* school has courses in mechanics, welding, etc.] **2.** of or used in a particular science, art, profession, etc. [*technical* words; *technical* skill]. **3.** according to the rules of some science, art, sport, etc. [*technical* differences between football and Rugby]. —**tech′ni·cal·ly,** *adv.*

tech·ni·cal·i·ty (tek′ni kal′ə tē), *n.* **1.** a technical point, detail, etc. [the *technicalities* of radio repair]. **2.** a small point or detail related to a main issue [found guilty on a legal *technicality*]. **3.** the quality of being technical. —**tech′ni·cal′i·ties,** *pl.*

tech·ni·cian (tek nish′ən), *n.* a person skilled in the technique of some art, craft, etc.

tech·nique (tek nēk′), *n.* the way of using tools, materials, etc. and following rules in doing something artistic, carrying out a scientific experiment, etc. [Painting in water colors requires a sure and quick *technique*.]

tech·nol·o·gy (tek näl′ə jē), *n.* the study of the industrial arts or applied sciences, as engineering, mechanics, etc. —**tech·nol′o·gist,** *n.* —**tech·no·log·i·cal** (tek′nə läj′i k'l), *adj.* —**tech′no·log′i·cal·ly,** *adv*

te·di·ous (tē′di əs *or* tē′jəs), *adj.* long and boring [a *tedious* play]. —**te′di·ous·ly,** *adv.*

te·di·um (tē′di əm), *n.* the condition of being boring or tiresome; monotony.

tee (tē), *n.* **1.** a small holder of wood or plastic, on which a golf player places the ball before hitting it. **2.** the place from which a golf player makes the first stroke on each hole. **3.** a mark aimed at in some games, as quoits. —*v.* to place on a tee, as a golf ball. —**tee off,** to hit a golf ball from a tee. —**teed,** *p.t. & p.p.;* **tee′ing,** *pr.p.*

...tee

teem (tēm), *v.* to be very full; swarm; abound [a cabin *teeming* with flies].

teen-age (tēn′āj′), *adj.* **1.** in one's teens. **2.** of or for persons in their teens. —**teen′-ag′er,** *n.*

teens (tēnz), *n.pl.* the years of one's age from 13 to 19.

tee·pee (tē′pē), *n.* same as **tepee.**

tee·ter (tē′tər), *n. & v.* seesaw.

tee·ter-tot·ter (tē′tər tät′ər), *n. & v.* seesaw.

teeth (tēth), *n.* plural of **tooth.**

teethe (tē*th*), *v.* to grow teeth; cut one's teeth. —**teethed,** *p.t. & p.p.;* **teeth′ing,** *pr.p.*

tee·to·tal·er (tē tō′t'l ər), *n.* a person who never drinks alcoholic liquor.

Tef·lon (tef′län), *n.* a tough chemical substance used to coat surfaces, as of cooking utensils, so that things will not stick to the surfaces. **Teflon** is a trademark.

Te·hran (te′rän′), *n.* the capital of Iran.

Tel A·viv (tel′ə vēv′), a city in Israel.

tel·e·cast (tel′ə kast), *v.* to broadcast by television. —*n.* a television broadcast. —**tel′e·cast** or **tel′e·cast·ed,** *p.t. & p.p.;* **tel′e·cast·ing,** *pr.p.* —**tel′e·cast·er,** *n.*

tel·e·gram (tel′ə gram), *n.* a message sent by telegraph.

tel·e·graph (tel′ə graf), *n.* a device or system for sending messages by signals made by opening and closing an electric circuit with a lever or key. —*v.* **1.** to send by telegraph, as a message. **2.** to send a telegram to.

tel·e·graph·ic (tel′ə graf′ik), *adj.* of or sent by telegraph. —**tel′e·graph′i·cal·ly,** *adv.*

te·leg·ra·phy (tə leg′rə fē), *n.* the sending of messages by telegraph. —**te·leg′ra·pher,** *n.*

tel·e·me·ter (tel′ə mē′tər), *n.* an electronic device for recording and sending scientific data over great distances, as from a spaceship.

te·lep·a·thy (tə lep′ə thē), *n.* the supposed sending of messages from one mind to another, without the help of speech, sight, etc. —**tel·e·path·ic** (tel′ə path′ik), *adj.*

tel·e·phone (tel′ə fōn), *n.* **1.** a way of sending sounds over distances by changing them into electric signals which are sent through a wire and then changed back into sounds. **2.** a device for sending and receiving sounds in this way. —*v.* **1.** to talk over a telephone. **2.** to send by telephone, as a message. **3.** to speak to by telephone. —**tel′e·phoned,** *p.t. & p.p.;* **tel′e·phon·ing,** *pr.p.* —**tel·e·phon·ic** (tel′ə fän′ik), *adj.*

tel·e·scope (tel′ə skōp), *n.* a device for making far-off things seem closer and larger, used especially in astronomy. It consists of one or more tubes containing lenses and, often, mirrors. —*v.* **1.** to slide together, one part into another, as the tubes of some telescopes. **2.** to force or crush together in this way [The crash *telescoped* the whole front end of the car.] —**tel′e·scoped,** *p.t. & p.p.;* **tel′e·scop·ing,** *pr.p.*

tel·e·scop·ic (tel′ə skäp′ik), *adj.* **1.** of a telescope [*telescopic* lenses]. **2.** seen or gotten only by means of a telescope [*telescopic* photographs of the stars]. **3.** farseeing. **4.** having sections that slide one inside another [a *telescopic* drinking cup].

Tel·e·type (tel′ə tīp), *n.* a form of telegraph in which the message is typed on a keyboard that sends electric signals to a machine that prints the words. **Teletype** is a trademark.

telescopic
drinking cup

tel·e·vise (tel′ə vīz), *v.* to send pictures of by television [to *televise* a baseball game]. —**tel′e·vised**, *p.t. & p.p.;* **tel′e·vis-ing,** *pr.p.*

tel·e·vi·sion (tel′ə vizh′ən), *n.* **1.** a way of sending pictures through space by changing the light rays into electric waves which are picked up by a receiver that changes them back to light rays. The sound that goes with the picture is sent by radio at the same time. **2.** such a receiver, usually in a cabinet. **3.** the act, business, etc. of broadcasting by television. —*adj.* of, using, used in, or sent by television [a *television* program; a *television* tube].

tell (tel), *v.* **1.** to put into words; say [*Tell* the facts.] **2.** to give the story of; report; narrate [The book *tells* about his early adventures.] **3.** to make clear or make known; show [Her smile *told* her joy better than any words.] **4.** to let know; inform [*Tell* me how to get there.] **5.** to know by seeing, hearing, etc.; recognize [I can *tell* the difference between the twins.] **6.** to order or command [He *told* us to leave.] **7.** to have a definite effect [His hard efforts are beginning to *tell*.] **8.** to count off one by one [to *tell* one's beads in saying prayers with a rosary]. —**tell off,** to scold or criticize sharply: *used only in everyday talk.* —**tell on, 1.** to tire [The hard work is beginning to *tell on* him.] **2.** to inform against; carry tales about: *used only in everyday talk.* —**told,** *p.t. & p.p.;* **tell′ing,** *pr.p.*

Tell, William (tel), a hero in a Swiss legend, who was forced by a tyrant to shoot an apple off his son's head with an arrow.

tell·er (tel′ər), *n.* **1.** a person who tells a story, etc. **2.** a clerk in a bank who receives and pays out money.

tell·ing (tel′ing), *adj.* having a definite effect; forceful [a *telling* retort to an insult].

tell·tale (tel′tāl), *n.* a tattletale. —*adj.* telling what is meant to be kept secret or hidden [I knew he had been outside, by the *telltale* mud on his shoes.]

te·mer·i·ty (tə mer′ə tē), *n.* foolish or reckless boldness; rashness.

tem·per (tem′pər), *n.* **1.** state of mind; mood [She's in a bad *temper*.] **2.** calmness of mind; self-control [Keep your *temper*. He lost his *temper*.] **3.** anger or rage; also, quickness to anger [He flew into a *temper*. She has quite a *temper*.] **4.** hardness or toughness, as of a metal. —*v.* **1.** to make less strong by adding something else; moderate [to *temper* boldness with caution]. **2.** to bring to the right condition by treating in some way [Steel is *tempered* by heating and sudden cooling to make it hard and tough.]

tem·per·a·ment (tem′pər ə mənt), *n.* **1.** one's usual nature or mood; disposition [a person of calm *temperament*]. **2.** a nature or mood that makes one easily excited or upset [Some actors are noted for their *temperament*.]

tem·per·a·men·tal (tem′pər ə men′t'l), *adj.* **1.** of or caused by temperament [a *temperamental* burst of anger]. **2.** easily excited or upset; moody. —**tem′per·a·men′tal·ly,** *adv.*

tem·per·ance (tem′pər əns), *n.* **1.** care in keeping one's actions, appetites, feelings, etc.

under proper control; moderation [*Temperance* in eating would help him lose weight.] **2.** the drinking of little or no alcoholic liquor.

tem·per·ate (tem′pər it), *adj.* **1.** using or showing temperance in one's actions, appetites, etc.; moderate [Although I was angry, I made a *temperate* reply.] **2.** neither very hot nor very cold [a *temperate* climate; the *temperate* zones of the earth]. —**tem′per·ate·ly,** *adv.*

tem·per·a·ture (tem′pər ə chər), *n.* **1.** the degree of hotness or coldness, as of air, liquids, the body, etc., usually as measured by a thermometer. **2.** a body heat above the normal, which is about 98.6°; fever.

tem·pered (tem′pərd), *adj.* having a certain kind of temper: *used in words formed with a hyphen* [a sweet-*tempered* child].

tem·pest (tem′pist), *n.* **1.** a wild storm with high winds and, often, rain. **2.** a wild outburst of feeling, action, etc.

tem·pes·tu·ous (tem pes′chōō əs), *adj.* of or like a tempest; stormy, wild, raging, etc.

Tem·plar (tem′plər), *n.* a member of a military and religious group, the **Knights Templar,** founded by Crusaders in 1118.

tem·ple (tem′p'l), *n.* **1.** a building for the worship of God or a god. **2. Temple,** any of the three buildings for the worship of God built at different times by the Jews in ancient Jerusalem. Each was in turn destroyed. **3.** a building of great size, beauty, etc. for some special purpose [a *temple* of art].

tem·ple (tem′p'l), *n.* the flat area at either side of the forehead, above and behind the eye.

tem·po (tem′pō), *n.* the rate of speed for playing a piece of music ["America" has quite a slow *tempo*.] —**tem′pos** or **tem·pi** (tem′pē), *pl.*

tem·po·ral (tem′pər əl), *adj.* **1.** having to do with time. **2.** having to do with life on earth; earthly; not eternal. **3.** having to do with everyday life; worldly; not spiritual. **4.** having to do with the laws of a state rather than of a church or religion; civil.

tem·po·ral (tem′pər əl), *adj.* having to do with the temples of the head.

tem·po·rar·y (tem′pə rer′ē), *adj.* lasting only for a short time; not permanent [a *temporary* chairman]. —**tem′po·rar′i·ly,** *adv.*

tem·po·rize (tem′pə rīz), *v.* **1.** to talk or act in a way that one thinks will be popular or give an advantage, rather than in the right way. **2.** to put off making a decision, or to agree for a while, in order to gain time or avoid trouble. —**tem′po·rized,** *p.t. & p.p.;* **tem′po·riz-ing,** *pr.p.*

tempt (tempt), *v.* **1.** to try to get a person to do or want something that is wrong or forbidden [The old sailor's tales *tempted* the boy to run away from home.] **2.** to be attractive to; attract [The fish *tempted* the cat.] **3.** to provoke or risk provoking [to *tempt* fate by driving with a bad tire]. —**tempt′er,** *n.* —**tempt′ress,** *n.fem.*

temp·ta·tion (temp tā′shən), *n.* **1.** a tempting or being tempted. **2.** something that tempts [The cooling pie was a real *temptation* to the boys.]

tempt·ing (temp′ting), *adj.* that tempts; attractive [*tempting* odors of cooking].

ten (ten), *n. & adj.* one more than nine; the number 10.

ten·a·ble (ten′ə b'l), *adj.* that can be held, defended, or believed [The theory that the sun goes around the earth is no longer *tenable*.]

te·na·cious (ti nā′shəs), *adj.* **1.** that grips firmly or clings tightly [the *tenacious* ivy on the wall]. **2.** holding fast; stubborn [*tenacious* courage]. **3.** that keeps or retains something for a long time [a *tenacious* memory]. —**te·na′-cious·ly,** *adv.*

te·nac·i·ty (ti nas′ə tē), *n.* the condition of being tenacious.

ten·an·cy (ten′ən sē), *n.* **1.** the condition or fact of being a tenant. **2.** the length of time that one is a tenant.

ten·ant (ten′ənt), *n.* **1.** a person who pays rent to use land, live in a building, etc. **2.** one that lives in a certain place [These owls are *tenants* of barns.] —*v.* to live in as a tenant.

ten·ant·ry (ten′ənt rē), *n.* all the tenants of a place, especially of an estate.

Ten Commandments, in the Bible, the ten laws that God gave to Moses on Mount Sinai.

tend (tend), *v.* to take care of; watch over [to *tend* sheep; to *tend* a store].

tend (tend), *v.* **1.** to be likely or apt; have a tendency; incline [He *tends* to eat too much.] **2.** to move or go in a certain way; lead [a river *tending* east].

tend·en·cy (ten′dən sē), *n.* the fact of being likely or apt to move or act in a certain way [the *tendency* of prices to go up; Peggy's *tendency* to complain]. —**tend′en·cies,** *pl.*

ten·der (ten′dər), *adj.* **1.** soft or delicate and easily chewed, cut, etc. [*tender* meat; *tender* blades of grass]. **2.** that is hurt or feels pain easily; sensitive [a *tender* skin]. **3.** warm and gentle; loving [a *tender* smile]. **4.** young [at the *tender* age of five]. —**ten′der·ly,** *adv.* —**ten′der·ness,** *n.*

ten·der (ten′dər), *v.* **1.** to offer as payment for a debt. **2.** to give or offer for someone to take [to *tender* an invitation or an apology]. —*n.* **1.** an offer, especially a formal offer [a *tender* of marriage]. **2.** something offered, as in payment: see **legal tender.**

tend·er (ten′dər), *n.* **1.** a boat that carries people, supplies, etc. between a large ship and shore. **2.** the railroad car behind a locomotive for carrying its coal, water, etc. **3.** a person who tends, or takes care of, something.

ten·der·foot (ten′dər foot), *n.* **1.** a person who is not used to rough or outdoor life, as a newcomer to the West. **2.** a beginner in the Boy Scouts. **3.** any beginner or newcomer. —**ten′-der·foots** or **ten′der·feet,** *pl.*

ten·der·heart·ed (ten′dər här′tid), *adj.* having a tender heart; quick to feel pity.

ten·der·ize (ten′dər īz), *v.* to make tender [to *tenderize* a tough cut of meat]. —**ten′der-ized,** *p.t. & p.p.;* **ten′der·iz·ing,** *pr.p.*

ten·der·loin (ten′dər loin), *n.* the most tender part of the loin in beef and pork.

ten·don (ten′dən), *n.* the cord of tough fiber that fastens a muscle to a bone, etc.

ten·dril (ten′dril), *n.* any of the small, curly stems that hold up a climbing plant by coiling around something [Grapevines have *tendrils*.]

tendril

ten·e·ment (ten′ə mənt), *n.* **1.** a suite of rooms, or apartment, that is rented. **2.** an old, crowded apartment house, as in a city slum.

ten·et (ten′it), *n.* a principle or belief that is held as a truth, as by some group.

Ten·nes·see (ten ə sē′), *n.* **1.** a State in the southeastern part of the United States: abbreviated **Tenn. 2.** a river flowing through Tennessee, Alabama, and Kentucky, into the Ohio.

ten·nis (ten′is), *n.* a game in which players on each side of a net dividing a court hit a ball back and forth with rackets.

Ten·ny·son, Alfred (ten′ə s'n), 1809–1892; English poet: called **Alfred, Lord Tennyson.**

ten·on (ten′ən), *n.* a part of a piece of wood, etc. cut to stick out so that it will fit into a hole (called a **mortise**) in another piece to form a joint. —*v.* to fasten with a tenon.

ten·or (ten′ər), *n.* **1.** the highest kind of man's singing voice. **2.** a singer with such a voice, or an instrument with a range like this. **3.** general course [the even *tenor* of her happy life]. **4.** general meaning [What was the *tenor* of his remarks?] —*adj.* of or for a tenor.

ten·pins (ten′pinz), *n.pl.* **1.** the game of bowling: *used with a singular verb.* **2.** the pins used in bowling.

tense (tens), *adj.* **1.** stretched tight; taut [a *tense* rope; *tense* muscles]. **2.** feeling or showing nervous strain; anxious [a *tense* silence]. —*v.* to make or become tense; tighten, as muscles. —**tens′er,** *compar.;* **tens′est,** *superl.* —**tensed,** *p.t. & p.p.;* **tens′ing,** *pr.p.* —**tense′ly,** *adv.*

tense (tens), *n.* any of the forms of a verb that show the time of the action or condition [Present, past, and future *tenses* of "play" are "play," "played," and "will play."]

ten·sile (ten′s'l), *adj.* **1.** of or under tension [*tensile* strength]. **2.** that can be stretched.

ten·sion (ten′shən), *n.* **1.** a stretching or being stretched, so as to put or be under strain. **2.** nervous strain; tense or anxious feeling [The actress felt *tension* before the play.] **3.** voltage, or electric force [high-*tension* wire].

fat,   āpe,   cär,   ten,   ēven,   hit,   bīte,   gō,   hôrn,   tool,   book,   up,   fur;
get,   joy,   yet,   chin,   she,   thin,   then;   zh = s in pleasure;   ′ as in able (ā′b'l);
ə = a in ago,   e in agent,   i in sanity,   o in confess,   u in focus.

tent (tent), *n.* a shelter of canvas, etc. stretched over poles and fixed to stakes. —*v.* to live or camp out in a tent.

tent

ten·ta·cle (ten′tə k′l), *n.* **1.** a long, slender part growing around the head or mouth of some animals, used for feeling, gripping, or moving [The octopus has eight *tentacles.*] **2.** a sensitive hair on a plant.

ten·ta·tive (ten′tə tiv), *adj.* made or done as a test or for the time being; not definite or final [*tentative* plans]. —**ten′ta·tive·ly,** *adv.*

tenth (tenth), *adj.* coming after nine others; 10th in order. —*n.* **1.** the tenth one. **2.** one of ten equal parts of something; 1/10.

ten·u·ous (ten′yōō əs), *adj.* **1.** thin, slender, or fine [the *tenuous* threads of a cobweb]. **2.** not dense; thin, as air high up. **3.** not solid; flimsy [a *tenuous* argument]. —**ten′u·ous·ly,** *adv.*

ten·ure (ten′yər), *n.* **1.** the condition or right of holding property, a position, etc. **2.** the length of time something is held [A Senator's *tenure* of office is six years.]

te·pee or **tee·pee** (tē′pē), *n.* a tent used by some American Indians: *see the picture.*

tep·id (tep′id), *adj.* slightly warm; lukewarm.

term (tûrm), *n.* **1.** the time during which something lasts; time fixed by law, agreement, etc. [a school *term;* a *term* of office]. **2. terms,** *pl.* the conditions of a contract, agreement, will, etc. **3. terms,** *pl.* relations between persons [They are not on speaking *terms.*] **4.** a word or phrase, especially as used with a special meaning in some science, art, etc. ["Radical" is a chemical *term* for a cluster of atoms that act as a single atom.] **5. terms,** *pl.* language of a certain kind [He spoke of you in friendly *terms.*] **6. terms,** *pl.* agreement in dealings [to bring or come to *terms*]. **7.** a quantity in mathematics forming a part of a fraction, ratio, equation, etc. —*v.* to call by a term; name.

tepee

ter·mi·na·ble (tûr′mi nə b′l), *adj.* **1.** that can be ended [a *terminable* contract]. **2.** that ends after a certain time.

ter·mi·nal (tûr′mə n′l), *adj.* of, at, or forming the end [a *terminal* bud on a branch; the *terminal* game of the season]. —*n.* **1.** an end or end part. **2.** either end of an electric circuit. **3.** a main station of a railroad, bus line, or air line, where many trips begin or end.

ter·mi·nate (tûr′mə nāt), *v.* **1.** to bring or come to an end; stop; end [to *terminate* a contract]. **2.** to form the end or limit of. —**ter′mi·nat·ed,** *p.t. & p.p.;* **ter′mi·nat·ing,** *pr.p.* —**ter′mi·na′tion,** *n.*

ter·mi·nol·o·gy (tûr′mə näl′ə jē), *n.* the special words and phrases used in some art, science, work, etc. [legal *terminology*].

ter·mi·nus (tûr′mə nəs), *n.* **1.** either end of a railroad, bus line, or air line. **2.** an end, limit, goal, boundary, etc. —**ter′mi·ni** (tûr′mə nī) or **ter′mi·nus·es,** *pl.*

ter·mite (tûr′mīt), *n.* a small, pale insect like an ant, that eats wood and damages wooden buildings, furniture, etc.: also called **white ant.** Termites live in colonies.

termite (⅛ in. long)

tern (tûrn), *n.* a sea bird like a small gull. It has a slender body and beak, and a forked tail.

ter·race (ter′is), *n.* **1.** a flat platform of earth with sloping banks; also, any of a series of such platforms, rising one above the other, as on a hillside. **2.** a paved area near a house, that overlooks a lawn or garden; patio. **3.** a row of houses on ground raised from the street. **4.** a street in front of such houses. **5.** a flat roof on a house. —*v.* to form into a terrace or terraces. —**ter′raced,** *p.t. & p.p.;* **ter′rac·ing,** *pr.p.*

terrace (*meaning 2*)

ter·ra cot·ta (ter′ə kät′ə), **1.** a dull, brownish-red earthenware, usually not glazed. **2.** dull brownish red.

terra fir·ma (fûr′mə), solid ground.

ter·rain (tə rān′), *n.* ground or an area of land.

ter·ra·pin (ter′ə pin), *n.* **1.** an American turtle that lives in or near fresh water or tidewater. **2.** its flesh used as food.

ter·rar·i·um (tə rer′i əm), *n.* a glass container holding a garden of small plants, or one used for raising small land animals. —**ter·rar′i·ums** or **ter·rar·i·a** (tə rer′i ə), *pl.*

ter·res·tri·al (tə res′tri əl), *adj.* **1.** of the earth [a *terrestrial* globe]. **2.** made up of land, not water [the *terrestrial* parts of the world]. **3.** living on land [Man is *terrestrial;* fish are aquatic.] **4.** of this world; worldly [*terrestrial* pleasures].

ter·ri·ble (ter′ə b′l), *adj.* **1.** causing great fear or terror; dreadful [a *terrible* earthquake]. **2.** very bad or unpleasant: *used only in everyday talk* [*terrible* manners]. —**ter′ri·bly,** *adv.*

ter·ri·er (ter′i ər), *n.* any of several small, lively dogs, as the Scottish terrier, fox terrier, etc.

ter·rif·ic (tə rif′ik), *adj.* **1.** causing great fear; dreadful [a *terrific* hurricane]. **2.** very great or unusual: *used only in everyday talk* [a *terrific* play]. —**ter·rif′i·cal·ly,** *adv.*

ter·ri·fy (ter′ə fī), *v.* to fill with terror; frighten

terrier
(15 in. high at shoulder)

greatly. —**ter′ri·fied**, *p.t. & p.p.;* **ter′ri·fy-ing**, *pr.p.*

ter·ri·to·ri·al (ter′ə tôr′i əl), *adj.* **1.** of territory or land [*territorial* expansion]. **2.** of or limited to a certain territory [*territorial* waters]. —**ter′ri·to′ri·al·ly**, *adv.*

ter·ri·to·ry (ter′ə tôr′ē), *n.* **1.** the land ruled by a nation or state. **2.** a large division of a country or empire, that does not have the full rights of a Province or State, as in Canada or Australia [the Northwest *Territories*]. **3.** any large area of land; region. **4.** a particular area to travel or work in, as of a traveling salesman. —**ter′ri·to′ries**, *pl.*

ter·ror (ter′ər), *n.* **1.** great fear. **2.** a person or thing that causes great fear.

ter·ror·ism (ter′ər iz′m), *n.* the use of force and threats to frighten people into obeying completely. —**ter′ror·ist**, *n.*

ter·ror·ize (ter′ər īz), *v.* **1.** to fill with terror [The tiger *terrorized* the village.] **2.** to keep power over by force or threats. —**ter′ror·ized**, *p.t. & p.p.;* **ter′ror·iz·ing**, *pr.p.*

ter·ry cloth (ter′ē), a cotton cloth covered with loops of thread that have not been cut. It is used for towels, bathrobes, etc.

terse (tûrs), *adj.* using only a few words but clear and to the point [a *terse* reply]. —**ters′er**, *compar.;* **ters′est**, *superl.* —**terse′ly**, *adv.*

ter·ti·ar·y (tûr′shi er′ē *or* tûr′shə rē), *adj.* of the third rank, order, importance, etc.; third.

test (test), *n.* **1.** an examination or trial to find out what something is like, what it contains, how good it is, etc. [an eye *test;* a *test* of one's courage]. **2.** a set of questions, problems, etc. for finding out how much someone knows or how skilled he is [a spelling *test;* a driver's *test*]. —*v.* to put to a test, or examine by a test. —**test′er**, *n.*

tes·ta·ment (tes′tə mənt), *n.* **1. Testament,** either of the two parts of the Bible, the **Old Testament** and the **New Testament.** This word is sometimes used by itself to mean just the New Testament. **2.** in law, a will: *used mainly in the phrase* "last will and testament."

tes·ta·men·ta·ry (tes′tə men′tə rē), *adj.* having to do with a testament, or will.

tes·ta·tor (tes′tā tər), *n.* a person who has left a will after his death.

tes·ti·cle (tes′ti k′l), *n.* the gland in the male in which the sperm is formed.

tes·ti·fy (tes′tə fī), *v.* **1.** to tell or give as proof, especially under oath in a court [The witness *testified* that he saw the robbery.] **2.** to be or give a sign of; indicate [His words *testify* to his anger.] —**tes′ti·fied**, *p.t. & p.p.;* **tes′ti·fy-ing**, *pr.p.*

tes·ti·mo·ni·al (tes′tə mō′ni əl), *n.* **1.** a statement telling about or praising some person, product, etc. **2.** something given to show thanks or to honor someone.

tes·ti·mo·ny (tes′tə mō′nē), *n.* **1.** a statement made by one who testifies, especially under oath in a court. **2.** any declaration. **3.** a sign or indication [His smile was *testimony* of his joy.] —**tes′ti·mo′nies**, *pl.*

test tube, a tube of thin, clear glass closed at one end, used in chemical experiments, etc.

tes·ty (tes′tē), *adj.* easily angered; cross; touchy. —**tes′ti·er**, *compar.;* **tes′ti·est**, *superl.* —**tes′ti·ly**, *adv.* —**tes′ti·ness**, *n.*

tet·a·nus (tet′ə nəs), *n.* a disease that causes spasms of the body, stiffening of the muscles, as of the jaw, and often death. It is caused by a

test tubes

germ that gets into the blood stream through an open wound.

tête-à-tête (tāt′ə tāt′), *n.* a private talk between two people. —*adv.* two together and in private [to speak *tête-à-tête*]. —*adj.* of or for two people in private.

teth·er (teth′ər), *n.* a rope or chain tied to an animal to keep it from roaming. —*v.* to tie to a place with a tether. —**at the end of one's tether,** not able to bear or do any more.

Teu·ton (tōō′t′n *or* tyōō′t′n), *n.* **1.** a member of an ancient German people. **2.** a member of a group of northern Europeans, including the Germans, Swedes, Dutch, etc.; especially, a German. —**Teu·ton·ic** (tōō tän′ik *or* tyōō tän′ik), *adj.*

Tex·as (tek′səs), *n.* a State in the south central part of the United States: abbreviated **Tex.** —**Tex′an**, *adj. & n.*

text (tekst), *n.* **1.** the main part of the printed matter on a page, not including notes, pictures, etc. **2.** the actual words used by a writer in his book, speech, etc. **3.** a textbook. **4.** a line or sentence from the Bible used as the subject for a sermon. **5.** any topic or subject.

text·book (tekst′book), *n.* a book used in teaching a subject, especially one used in a school or college.

tex·tile (teks′t′l *or* teks′tīl), *n.* a fabric made by weaving; cloth. —*adj.* **1.** having to do with weaving or woven fabrics [the *textile* industry]. **2.** woven [a *textile* fabric].

tex·tu·al (teks′chōō əl), *adj.* of, found in, or based on a text [*textual* criticism].

tex·ture (teks′chər), *n.* **1.** the look and feel of a fabric as caused by the arrangement, size, and quality of its threads [Corduroy has a ribbed *texture*.] **2.** the general look and feel of any other kind of material; structure; make-up [Stucco has a rough *texture*.]

-th, a suffix used to form numbers showing order, or place in a series [*fourth, fifth, sixth,* etc.]. The suffix **-eth** is used after a vowel [*twentieth, thirtieth, fortieth,* etc.].

-th, an old-fashioned ending for the present tense of verbs used with *he, she,* or *it* ["He *hath*" is an older way of saying "he has."]

Thai (tī), *n.* **1.** a person born or living in Thailand. **2.** the language of Thailand. —*adj.* of Thailand, its people, etc.

Thai·land (tī′land), *n.* a country in southeastern Asia. Its older name is **Siam.**

thal·lus (thal′əs), *n.* any of a large group of plants, including algae, fungi, lichens, etc., that do not have the roots, stems, and leaves of higher plant life. —**thal·li** (thal′ī) or **thal′lus·es,** *pl.*

Thames (temz), *n.* a river in southern England, flowing through London to the North Sea.

than (than *or* thən), *conj.* **1.** compared to. *Than* is used before the second part of a comparison [I am older *than* you.] **2.** besides; except [What could I do other *than* leave?] —*prep.* compared to: as a preposition, used only in the phrases *than which* and *than whom* [a man *than whom* there is none finer].

thane (thān), *n.* a freeman in early England who got land from the king or a lord in return for military service.

thank (thangk), *v.* **1.** to say that one is grateful to another for a kindness [I *thanked* her for her help.] **2.** to blame [We have him to *thank* for this trouble.]

thank·ful (thangk′fəl), *adj.* feeling or showing thanks; grateful. —**thank′ful·ly,** *adv.*

thank·less (thangk′lis), *adj.* **1.** not feeling or showing thanks. **2.** not appreciated [a *thankless* task]. —**thank′less·ly,** *adv.*

thanks (thangks), *n.pl.* the act or fact of thanking someone for something [I owe you *thanks*.] —*interj.* I thank you. —**thanks to, 1.** because of. **2.** thanks be given to.

thanks·giv·ing (thangks′giv′ing), *n.* **1.** the act of giving thanks, especially a formal act of public thanks to God. **2. Thanksgiving,** a holiday in the United States, usually the fourth Thursday in November, for thanksgiving to God: *the full name is* **Thanksgiving Day.**

that (that *or* thət), *pron.* **1.** the person or thing mentioned [*That* is John.] **2.** the thing farther away or in some way different [This is larger than *that*.] **3.** who, whom, or which [He's the one *that* I saw. Here's the money *that* I owe you.] **4.** when [It rained the day *that* we left.] —*adj.* **1.** being the one mentioned [*That* boy is John.] **2.** being the one farther away or different in some way [This car costs more than *that* one.] —*conj. That* is used: **1.** before a noun clause [I know *that* he is right.] **2.** before a clause showing purpose [He died *that* we might live.] **3.** before a clause showing result [He left so late *that* he missed the train.] **4.** before a clause showing cause [I'm sorry *that* you're ill.] **5.** before an incomplete sentence showing surprise, desire, anger, etc. [Oh, *that* she were here!] —*adv.* to such a degree; so [I can't see *that* far.] —**at that, 1.** at that point. **2.** all things considered; even so. *Used only in everyday talk.* —**in that,** because. —**that's that!** that is done or settled! —**those,** *pl.*

thatch (thach), *n.* straw, rushes, leaves, etc. forming a roof. —*v.* to cover with thatch.

thatched roof

thaw (thô), *v.* **1.** to melt [The snow on the roof *thawed*.] **2.** to become warm enough to melt snow and ice [The weatherman says that it will *thaw* today.] **3.** to stop acting in a cold or formal way. —*n.* **1.** the act of thawing. **2.** weather that is warm enough to melt snow and ice.

the (thə *or* thi), *adj.* **1.** that one which is here or which has been mentioned [*The* day is hot. *The* story ended.] **2.** one and only [*the* universe]. **3.** that one of a number or group [Close *the* back door. Take *the* one you want.] **4.** that one thought of as best, outstanding, etc. [*the* baseball player of the year]. **5.** any one of a certain kind [*The* cow is a mammal.] *The* is also called the *definite article.* See also **a** and **an.** —*adv.* **1.** that much; to that degree [*the* better to see you with]. **2.** by that much [*the* sooner *the* better].

the·a·ter or **the·a·tre** (thē′ə tər), *n.* **1.** a place where plays, movies, etc. are shown. **2.** any place like this, with rows of seats. **3.** any place where certain things are happening [the Pacific *theater* of war]. **4.** the art of acting or of producing plays; drama. **5.** all the people who write, produce, or act in plays.

the·at·ri·cal (thi at′ri k'l), *adj.* **1.** having to do with the theater, plays, actors, etc. [a *theatrical* company]. **2.** like the theater; dramatic; artificial; not natural [She waved her arms around in a *theatrical* way.] Also **the·at′ric.** —**the·at′ri·cal·ly,** *adv.*

the·at·ri·cals (thi at′ri k'lz), *n.pl.* plays presented on a stage, especially by amateurs.

Thebes (thēbz), *n.* **1.** an ancient city in Egypt on the Nile. **2.** an ancient city in Greece. —**The·ban** (thē′bən), *adj. & n.*

thee (thē), *pron.* an older form of **you,** used as the object of a verb or preposition: *now used mainly in poetry, prayers, etc.*

theft (theft), *n.* the act of stealing another's property; larceny.

their (ther), *pron.* of them or done by them: the possessive form of *they,* used before a noun and thought of as an adjective [*their* house; *their* work]. See also **theirs.**

theirs (therz), *pron.* the one or the ones that belong to them: the form of *their* used when it is not followed by a noun [This house is *theirs. Theirs* are larger than ours.]

them (them), *pron.* the form of *they* that is used as the object of a verb or preposition [I saw *them.* Give it to *them.*]

theme (thēm), *n.* **1.** a topic or subject, as of an essay. **2.** a short essay or piece of writing on a single subject, written as a school exercise. **3.** a short melody that is the subject of a piece of music. **4.** the main tune or song of a musical play, movie, radio program, etc.: also **theme song. —the·mat·ic** (thē mat′ik), *adj.*

them·selves (thəm selvz′), *pron.* **1.** their own selves: the form of *they* that makes the subject also the object of the verb [They hurt *themselves*.] **2.** their usual or true selves [They are not *themselves* today.] *Themselves* is also used to give force to the subject [They built it *themselves*.]

then (then), *adv.* **1.** at that time [He was young *then*.] **2.** soon afterward; next in time [The party ended, and *then* we left.] **3.** next in order [Our house is on the corner and *then* comes Tom's.] **4.** in that case; therefore [If he read it, *then* he knows.] **5.** besides; also [I like to swim, and *then* it's good exercise.] **6.** at another time [Now he's serious, *then* he's joking.] —*adj.* being such at that time [the *then* mayor]. —*n.* that time [They were gone by *then*.] —**but then,** but on the other hand. —**then and there,** at once. —**what then?** what would happen in that case?

thence (thens), *adv.* from that place; from there [We flew to Boston and *thence* went by bus to Providence.]

thence·forth (thens′fôrth′), *adv.* from that time on [We were *thenceforth* friends.]

thence·for·ward (thens′fôr′wərd), *adv.* thenceforth.

the·oc·ra·cy (thē äk′rə sē), *n.* **1.** government of a country by a church. **2.** a country governed in this way. —**the·oc′ra·cies,** *pl.*

the·o·log·i·cal (thē′ə läj′i k'l), *adj.* of or having to do with theology [a *theological* school]. —**the·o·log′i·cal·ly,** *adv.*

the·ol·o·gy (thē äl′ə jē), *n.* **1.** the study of God and of religious beliefs. **2.** a system of religious beliefs. —**the·ol′o·gies,** *pl.* —**the·o·lo·gi·an** (thē′ə lō′jən), *n.*

the·o·rem (thē′ə rəm), *n.* **1.** something that can be proved from known facts and so is taken to be a law or principle, as of a science. **2.** something in mathematics that is to be proved or has been proved.

the·o·ret·i·cal (thē′ə ret′i k'l), *adj.* **1.** of or based on theory, not on practice or experience [a *theoretical* explanation]. **2.** forming theories [a *theoretical* mind]. Also **the′o·ret′ic. —the′o·ret′i·cal·ly,** *adv.*

the·o·rize (thē′ə rīz), *v.* to form a theory or theories; guess at causes, reasons, etc. —**the′o·rized,** *p.t. & p.p.;* **the′o·riz·ing,** *pr.p.* —**the′o·rist,** *n.*

the·o·ry (thē′ə rē), *n.* **1.** an explanation of how or why something happens, especially one based on scientific study and reasoning [Darwin's *theory* of evolution]. **2.** the general principles on which an art or science is based [music *theory*]. **3.** an idea, opinion, guess, etc. [My *theory* is that he's lying.] —**the′o·ries,** *pl.*

ther·a·peu·tic (ther′ə pyoo′tik), *adj.* having

to do with or used in treating or curing diseases. —**ther′a·peu′ti·cal·ly,** *adv.*

ther·a·peu·tics (ther′ə pyoo′tiks), *n.pl.* the branch of medicine that deals with the treating and curing of diseases: *used with a singular verb.*

ther·a·py (ther′ə pē), *n.* any method of treating disease [drug *therapy*; heat *therapy*]. —**ther′a·pies,** *pl.* —**ther′a·pist,** *n.*

there (ther), *adv.* **1.** at or in that place [Who lives *there*?] **2.** to, toward, or into that place [Go *there*.] **3.** at that point; then [He read to page 51, and *there* he stopped.] **4.** in that matter [*There* you are wrong.] **5.** right now [*There*'s the whistle.] *There* is also used to start sentences in which the real subject follows the verb [*There* are three men here.] —*interj.* a word used to show dismay, satisfaction, sympathy, etc. [*There!* see what you've done. *There, there!* don't worry.] —*n.* that place [We left from *there* at six.]

there·a·bouts (ther′ə bouts) or **there·a·bout** (ther′ə bout), *adv.* **1.** near that place. **2.** near that time. **3.** near that number or amount.

there·af·ter (ther af′tər), *adv.* after that; from then on.

there·at (ther at′), *adv.* **1.** at that place; there. **2.** at that time. **3.** for that reason. *This word is no longer in common use.*

there·by (ther bī′ or ther′bī), *adv.* **1.** by that means. **2.** connected with that [*Thereby* hangs a tale.] **3.** thereabouts.

there·for (ther fôr′), *adv.* for this or that; for it [I enclose a check and request a receipt *therefor*.]

there·fore (ther′fôr), *adv. & conj.* for this or that reason; as a result of this or that; hence [He missed the bus and *therefore* was late.]

there·from (ther frum′), *adv.* from this or that; from it.

there·in (ther in′), *adv.* **1.** in there; in that place [the box and all the contents *therein*]. **2.** in that matter or detail [*Therein* you are wrong.]

there·of (ther uv′), *adv.* **1.** of that; of it [He lifted the cup and drank *thereof*.] **2.** from that as a cause or reason.

there·on (ther än′), *adv.* **1.** on that. **2.** immediately following that.

there's (therz), there is.

there·to (ther too′), *adv.* **1.** to that place, thing, etc. **2.** in addition to that.

there·to·fore (ther′tə fôr′), *adv.* up to that time; until then; before that.

there·un·to (ther′ən too′ or ther un′too), *adv.* same as **thereto.**

there·up·on (ther′ə pän′), *adv.* **1.** just after that. **2.** because of that. **3.** upon or about that.

there·with (ther with′), *adv.* **1.** with that or this; with it. **2.** just after that.

there·with·al (ther′with ôl′), *adv.* **1.** in addition; besides. **2.** with that; with it.

ther·mal (thur′m'l), *adj.* **1.** having to do with heat. **2.** warm or hot.

ther·mom·e·ter (thər mäm'ə tər), *n.* a device for measuring temperature, as a glass tube, marked off in degrees, in which mercury rises or falls with changes in temperature: see also **centigrade, Fahrenheit.**

ther·mo·nu·cle·ar (thūr'mō noo'-kli ər *or* thūr'mō nyoo'kli ər), *adj.* describing, of, or using the heat energy set free in nuclear fission.

Ther·mop·y·lae (thər mäp'ə lē), *n.* a mountain pass in eastern Greece, where a small force of Spartans in 480 B.C. held off the Persian army, but were finally defeated.

ther·mos bottle (thūr'məs), a container for keeping liquids at almost the same temperature for a time. The name **Thermos** is a trademark.

thermometer

ther·mo·stat (thūr'mə stat), *n.* a device for keeping temperature even, especially one that automatically controls a furnace, etc. —**ther'-mo·stat'ic,** *adj.*

the·sau·rus (thi sô'rəs), *n.* a book containing lists of synonyms or related words. —**the·sau·ri** (thi sô'rī) *or* **the·sau'rus·es,** *pl.*

these (*thēz*), *pron. & adj.* plural of **this.**

The·seus (thē'sōōs *or* thē'si əs), *n.* a hero of Greek legend, who killed the Minotaur.

the·sis (thē'sis), *n.* **1.** a statement or idea to be defended in an argument. **2.** a long essay based on research, prepared by a candidate for a university degree. —**the·ses** (thē'sēz), *pl.*

Thes·pi·an (thes'pi ən), *adj.* having to do with the theater. —*n.* an actor: *now used humorously.*

Thes·sa·ly (thes'ə lē), *n.* an ancient region in northeastern Greece.

thews (thyoōz *or* thoōz), *n.pl.* **1.** muscles or sinews. **2.** bodily strength; muscular power.

they (*thā*), *pron.* **1.** the persons, animals, or things being talked about [The boys knew *they* had won. Put the keys back where *they* were.] **2.** people in general [*They* say it can't happen.] *They* is the plural of *he, she,* or *it.*

they'd (*thā*d), **1.** they had. **2.** they would.

they'll (*thā*l), **1.** they will. **2.** they shall.

they're (*ther*), they are.

they've (*thā*v), they have.

thick (thik), *adj.* **1.** great in width or depth from side to side; not thin [a *thick* board]. **2.** as measured from one side through to the other [a wall ten inches *thick*]. **3.** growing or set close together; dense; heavy [*thick* hair; a *thick* crowd]. **4.** flowing or pouring slowly; not watery [*thick* soup]. **5.** not clear [a *thick* voice; air *thick* with smoke]. **6.** stupid; dull. **7.** very friendly: *used only in everyday talk.* —*adv.* in a thick way. —*n.* the most active part [the *thick* of a fight]. —**through thick and thin,** in good times and hard times. —**thick'ly,** *adv.*

thick·en (thik'ən), *v.* **1.** to make or become thick or thicker. **2.** to make or become more complicated [The plot *thickens*.]

thick·et (thik'it), *n.* a place where shrubs, underbrush, or small trees grow close together.

thick-head·ed (thik'hed'id), *adj.* stupid.

thick·ness (thik'nis), *n.* **1.** the fact or condition of being thick. **2.** the distance from one side through to the other [a *thickness* of four inches]. **3.** a layer [three *thicknesses* of cloth].

thick·set (thik'set'), *adj.* **1.** planted closely [*thickset* trees]. **2.** thick in body; stocky.

thick-skinned (thik'skind'), *adj.* **1.** having a thick skin. **2.** not easily hurt by criticism, insults, etc.; unfeeling.

thief (thēf), *n.* a person who steals, especially secretly. —**thieves** (thēvz), *pl.*

thieve (thēv), *v.* to steal. —**thieved,** *p.t. & p.p.;* **thiev'ing,** *pr.p.* —**thiev'ish,** *adj.*

thiev·er·y (thēv'ər ē), *n.* the act of stealing; theft. —**thiev'er·ies,** *pl.*

thigh (thī), *n.* the part of the leg between the knee and the hip.

thim·ble (thim'b'l), *n.* a small cap of metal, plastic, etc. worn as a protection on the finger that pushes the needle in sewing.

thin (thin), *adj.* **1.** small in width or depth from side to side; not thick [a *thin* board]. **2.** having little fat or flesh; lean; slender. **3.** not growing or set close together; not dense; sparse [*thin* hair; a *thin* crowd]. **4.** flowing or pouring quickly; watery [*thin* soup]. **5.** not deep and strong; weak [*thin* colors; a *thin* voice]. **6.** seen through easily; flimsy [*thin* cloth; a *thin* excuse]. —*adv.* in a thin way. —*v.* to make or become thin or thinner. —**thin'ner,** *compar.;* **thin'nest,** *superl.* —**thinned,** *p.t. & p.p.;* **thin'ning,** *pr.p.* —**thin'ness,** *n.*

thimble

thine (*thīn*), *pron.* an older form of **yours:** *now used only in poetry, prayers, etc.* "Thine" is used as an adjective instead of "thy" before a vowel sound [*Thine* eyes are like stars.]

thing (thing), *n.* **1.** that which exists; a real object or substance, not a quality, idea, etc. [A stone is a *thing.* She likes pretty *things.*] **2.** a happening, act, event, step, etc. [What a *thing* to do! The next *thing* is to clean house.] **3.** any matter or affair [How are *things* with you?] **4. things,** *pl.* belongings, as clothes, equipment, etc. [Pick up your *things.*] **5.** a person or creature: *used only in everyday talk* [Poor *thing!*] —**the thing,** what one should have or do because it is needed, in style, etc.

think (thingk), *v.* **1.** to use the mind; reason [*Think* before you act.] **2.** to form or have in the mind [He was *thinking* happy thoughts.] **3.** to consider or judge [I *think* her charming.] **4.** to believe, expect, or imagine [They *think* they can come.] **5.** to work out, or solve, by reasoning [*Think* the problem through.] —**think better of, 1.** to form a new and better opinion of. **2.** to decide more wisely after thinking again. —**think nothing of,** to think of as easy or not important. —**think of, 1.** to remember. **2.** to have an opinion of. **3.** to invent. **4.** to consider.

—**think over,** to give thought to; consider. —**think twice,** to consider again. —**think up,** to invent by thinking. —**thought,** *p.t. & p.p.;* **think′ing,** *pr.p.* —**think′er,** *n.*

thin-skinned (thin′skind′), *adj.* **1.** having a thin skin. **2.** easily hurt by criticism or insults.

third (thûrd), *adj.* coming after two others; 3rd in order. —*n.* **1.** the third one. **2.** one of three equal parts of something; 1/3. —*adv.* in the third place, group, etc.

third degree, harsh questioning or torture by the police to make a prisoner confess.

third·ly (thûrd′lē), *adv.* in the third place.

third person, that form of a pronoun or verb which refers to the person or thing spoken of [*He, him, she, her, it, they, them,* etc. are in the *third person.*]

thirst (thûrst), *n.* **1.** the feeling of dryness and discomfort caused by a need for water; strong desire to drink. **2.** any strong desire; craving [a *thirst* for fame]. —*v.* **1.** to have a strong desire to drink; feel thirst. **2.** to have a strong desire.

thirst·y (thûrs′tē), *adj.* **1.** wanting to drink; feeling thirst [The spicy food made him *thirsty.*] **2.** needing water; dry [*thirsty* fields]. —**thirst′·i·er,** *compar.;* **thirst′i·est,** *superl.* —**thirst′·i·ly,** *adv.* —**thirst′i·ness,** *n.*

thir·teen (thûr′tēn′), *n. & adj.* three more than ten; the number 13.

thir·teenth (thûr′tēnth′), *adj.* coming after twelve others; 13th in order. —*n.* **1.** the thirteenth one. **2.** one of thirteen equal parts of something; 1/13.

thir·ti·eth (thûr′tē ith), *adj.* coming after twenty-nine others; 30th in order. —*n.* **1.** the thirtieth one. **2.** one of thirty equal parts of something; 1/30.

thir·ty (thûr′tē), *n. & adj.* **1.** three times ten; the number 30. **2. thirties,** *n.pl.* the numbers or years from 30 to 39.

this (*th*is), *pron.* **1.** the person or thing mentioned or understood [*This* is John. What is the meaning of *this?*] **2.** the thing that is present or nearer [*This* is prettier than that.] **3.** the fact, idea, etc. about to be told [Now hear *this!*] —*adj.* **1.** being the one that is mentioned or understood [Copy down *this* rule.] **2.** being the one that is present or nearer [*This* house is newer than that one.] —*adv.* to such a degree; so [It was *this* big.] —**these** (*th*ēz), *pl.*

this·tle (this′'l), *n.* a plant with prickly leaves and flower heads of purple, white, etc.

this·tle·down (this′'l-doun), *n.* the down or fluff from the flower of a thistle.

thith·er (thi*th*′ər *or* thi*th*′-ər), *adv.* to that place; there: *no longer much used.*

tho or **tho'** (*th*ō), *conj. & adv.* same as **though.**

thistle

thole (thōl) or **thole·pin** (thōl′pin), *n.* a pin, often one of a pair, set into the side of a boat for the oar to turn against in rowing.

Thom·as (täm′əs), *n.* in the Bible, the Apostle who at first doubted the resurrection of Jesus.

thong (thông), *n.* a narrow strip of leather, used as a lace, strap, rein, lash, etc.

Thor (thôr), *n.* the god of war and thunder in Norse myths.

tho·rac·ic (thô ras′ik), *adj.* of, in, or near the thorax.

tho·rax (thôr′aks), *n.* **1.** the part of the body between the neck and the abdomen, enclosed by the ribs; chest. **2.** the middle one of the three parts of an insect's body.

thorax

Tho·reau, Henry David (thôr′ō *or* thə rō′), 1817–1862; U.S. writer and philosopher.

thorn (thôrn), *n.* **1.** a short, sharp point growing out of a plant stem. **2.** a plant full of thorns. **3.** anything that keeps troubling or worrying one. —**thorn′y,** *adj.*

thor·ough (thûr′ō), *adj.* **1.** complete in every way; with nothing left out, undone, etc. [a *thorough* search; a *thorough* knowledge of the subject]. **2.** being wholly such; absolute [a *thorough* rascal]. **3.** very careful and exact [a *thorough* worker]. —**thor′ough·ly,** *adv.*

thor·ough·bred (thûr′ə bred), *adj.* of pure breed. —*n.* **1.** a thoroughbred animal. **2. Thoroughbred,** any of a breed of race horses. **3.** a cultured, well-bred person.

thor·ough·fare (thûr′ə fer), *n.* a public street open at both ends; especially, a main highway.

thor·ough·go·ing (thûr′ə gō′ing), *adj.* very thorough.

those (thōz), *adj. & pron.* plural of **that.**

thou (thou), *pron.* an older form of **you** (in the singular), used as the subject of a verb: *now used only in poetry, prayers, etc.*

though (*th*ō), *conj.* **1.** in spite of the fact that; although [*Though* he wasn't very tired, he fell asleep.] **2.** yet; still [She was kind, *though* not as generous as her sister.] **3.** even if [*Though* he may fail, he will have tried.] —*adv.* however; nevertheless [I must leave now; I'll be back, *though.*] —**as though,** as if.

thought (thôt), *n.* **1.** the act or process of thinking [When deep in *thought,* he doesn't hear.] **2.** what one thinks; opinion, plan, etc. [a penny for your *thoughts*]. **3.** the way of thinking of a particular group, time, etc. [ancient Greek *thought*]. **4.** attention or care [Give this matter some *thought.*] **5.** a little; trifle [Be a *thought* less hasty.]

---

fat,   āpe,   cär,   ten,   ēven,   hit,   bīte,   gō,   hôrn,   tōōl,   book,   up,   fūr;
get,   joy,   yet,   chin,   she,   thin,   *th*en;   zh = s in pleasure;   ′ as in able (ā′b'l);
ə = a in ago,   e in agent,   i in sanity,   o in confess,   u in focus.

thought (thôt), past tense and past participle of **think.**

thought·ful (thôt/fəl), *adj.* **1.** full of thought or showing thought; serious [a *thoughtful* book]. **2.** showing care or paying attention to others; considerate [It was *thoughtful* of you to remember her birthday.] —**thought/ful·ly,** *adv.*

thought·less (thôt/lis), *adj.* **1.** not stopping to think; careless [The *thoughtless* driver passed the red light.] **2.** showing little care for others; not considerate [Our *thoughtless* neighbors are very noisy.] —**thought/less·ly,** *adv.*

thou·sand (thou/z'nd), *n. & adj.* ten times one hundred; the number 1,000.

thou·sandth (thou/z'ndth), *adj.* coming after nine hundred and ninety-nine others; 1,000th in order. —*n.* **1.** the thousandth one. **2.** one of the thousand equal parts of something; 1/1000.

Thrace (thrās), *n.* an ancient region in the Balkan Peninsula.

thrall (thrôl), *n.* **1.** a slave. **2.** the condition of being enslaved; slavery; bondage.

thrall·dom or **thral·dom** (thrôl/dəm), *n.* slavery.

thrash (thrash), *v.* **1.** to beat severely, as with a stick or whip. **2.** to move about in a violent or jerky way [to *thrash* about in sleep]. **3.** to thresh. —**thrash out,** to discuss fully, as a problem, until it is settled. —**thrash/er,** *n.*

thrash·er (thrash/ər), *n.* an American songbird like the thrush, but with a long, stiff tail.

thread (thred), *n.* **1.** a very thin cord used in sewing and made of strands of spun cotton, silk, etc. twisted together. **2.** anything like a thread, as a slender strand of metal or glass, a fine line or vein, etc. **3.** the way that a number of ideas, events, etc. are joined together in a single line of thought [I can't follow the *thread* of his story.] **4.** the ridge that winds in a sloping way around a screw, in a nut, etc. —*v.* **1.** to put a thread through the eye of [to *thread* a needle]. **2.** to string on a thread [to *thread* beads]. **3.** to get through, following a winding course [We *threaded* our way through the crowd.] **4.** to make a thread, or ridge, on [to *thread* a screw]. —**thread/like,** *adj.*

types of thread (*meaning 4*)

thread·bare (thred/ber), *adj.* **1.** with the nap worn down so that the threads show [a *threadbare* rug]. **2.** wearing worn clothes; shabby. **3.** used so often that it is stale [a *threadbare* joke].

threat (thret), *n.* **1.** a warning that one plans to harm another, especially if a certain thing is done or not done [In spite of the bully's *threats* to beat him, Tom continued on his way.] **2.** a sign of something dangerous or harmful about to happen [the *threat* of war].

threat·en (thret/'n), *v.* **1.** to make a threat; say that one plans to harm [The umpire *threatened* to stop the game if we kept on arguing.] **2.** to be a sign of something dangerous or harmful about to happen [Those odd sounds *threaten* engine

trouble.] **3.** to be a possible danger to [A forest fire *threatened* the cabin.]

three (thrē), *n. & adj.* one more than two; the number 3.

three·fold (thrē/fōld), *adj.* **1.** having three parts. **2.** having three times as much or as many. —*adv.* three times as much or as many.

three·score (thrē/skôr/), *adj.* three times twenty; sixty.

three·some (thrē/səm), *n.* a group of three people, as three people playing golf together.

thresh (thresh), *v.* **1.** to separate the seed, or grain, from wheat, rye, etc. by beating. **2.** to move about in a violent or jerky way; thrash. —**thresh out,** same as **thrash out.**

thresh·er (thresh/ər), *n.* **1.** a person who threshes. **2.** a large machine used on farms for threshing: also **threshing machine. 3.** a large shark with a long tail.

thresh·old (thresh/ōld), *n.* **1.** the sill, or piece of wood, stone, etc., placed beneath a door. **2.** the point where something begins; entrance [at the *threshold* of a new career].

threw (thrōō), past tense of **throw.**

thrice (thrīs), *adv.* three times [The cock crowed *thrice.* He paid *thrice* what it is worth.]

thrift (thrift), *n.* a careful managing of money, etc. so that there is no waste; economy [By practicing *thrift,* we managed a long vacation.] —**thrift/less,** *adj.*

thrift·y (thrif/tē), *adj.* practicing or showing thrift; economical [a *thrifty* housewife; *thrifty* habits]. —**thrift/i·er,** *compar.;* **thrift/i·est,** *superl.* —**thrift/i·ly,** *adv.* —**thrift/i·ness,** *n.*

thrill (thril), *v.* **1.** to feel or make greatly excited; shiver or tingle with strong feeling [She *thrilled* at the praise. His playing *thrilled* us.] **2.** to quiver or tremble [a voice that *thrilled* with pleasure]. —*n.* **1.** a strong feeling of excitement that makes one shiver [Meeting the movie star gave her a *thrill.*] **2.** something that causes such a feeling [His first airplane ride was a real *thrill.*]

thrill·er (thril/ər), *n.* something that thrills, as an exciting book, movie, etc.

thrive (thrīv), *v.* **1.** to become successful, rich, etc.; prosper [a *thriving* business]. **2.** to grow in a strong, healthy way [Plants *thrive* under her care.] —**throve** or **thrived,** *p.t.;* **thrived** or **thriv·en** (thriv/'n), *p.p.;* **thriv/ing,** *pr.p.*

thro' or **thro** (thrōō), *prep., adv. & adj.* through.

throat (thrōt), *n.* **1.** the front part of the neck. **2.** the upper part of the passage from the mouth to the stomach or lungs [I have a sore *throat.*] **3.** any narrow passage [the *throat* of a bottle]. —**a lump in the throat,** a tight feeling in the throat, as when one tries to keep from crying.

throat·y (thrōt/ē), *adj.* **1.** describing sounds formed in the throat. **2.** that makes such sounds; husky [a deep, *throaty* voice]. —**throat/i·er,** *compar.;* **throat/i·est,** *superl.*

throb (thräb), *v.* to beat or vibrate hard or fast, as the heart does when one is excited. —*n.* the act of throbbing; a strong beat. —**throbbed,** *p.t. & p.p.;* **throb/bing,** *pr.p.*

throe (thrō), *n.* a sharp, sudden pain; pang. —**in the throes of,** in the act of struggling with some pain, trouble, etc.

throne (thrōn), *n.* **1.** the raised chair on which a king, bishop, etc. sits during ceremonies. **2.** the power or rank of a king, etc. [The king lost his *throne* in the revolution.]

throng (thrông), *n.* a great number gathered together; crowd. —*v.* to crowd together or into [The people *thronged* to see the parade.]

throt·tle (thrät′'l), *n.* **1.** a valve used to control the flow of steam or of air and gasoline into an engine [Opening the *throttle* makes a car go faster.] **2.** the handle or pedal that works this valve. —*v.* **1.** to cut down the flow of fuel or slow down by closing a throttle [to *throttle* an engine]. **2.** to choke, strangle, or suppress [to *throttle* freedom]. —**throt′tled,** *p.t. & p.p.;* **throt′tling,** *pr.p.*

through (thrōo), *prep.* **1.** in one side and out the other side of; from end to end of [The nail went *through* the board. We drove *through* the tunnel.] **2.** from one part of to another [Birds fly *through* the air.] **3.** by way of [a route to Boston *through* New York]. **4.** here and there in; to many places in; around [We toured *through* Utah.] **5.** from beginning to end of; throughout [We stayed in Maine *through* the summer.] **6.** by means of [We heard the news *through* friends.] **7.** as a result of; because of [He won out *through* sheer courage.] —*adv.* **1.** in one side and out the other [The target was pierced *through* by the arrow.] **2.** from the beginning to the end [to see a job *through*]. **3.** in a complete or thorough way; entirely [soaked *through* by the rain]. —*adj.* **1.** leading from one place to another; open [a *through* street]. **2.** going on to the end without a stop or change [a *through* plane to Seattle]. **3.** finished [Are you *through* with your homework?]

through·out (thrōo out′), *prep.* all the way through; in every part of [The fire spread *throughout* the barn. It rained *throughout* the day.] —*adv.* in every part; everywhere [painted white *throughout;* staying hopeful *throughout*].

throve (thrōv), a past tense of **thrive.**

throw (thrō), *v.* **1.** to send through the air by a fast motion of the arm; fling, hurl, toss, etc. [to *throw* a ball]. **2.** to make fall down; upset [to *throw* a man in wrestling]. **3.** to send or cast in a certain direction, as a glance, light, shadow, etc. **4.** to put suddenly into some condition or place [to *throw* into confusion; to *throw* into prison]. **5.** to move, as a switch, so as to connect or disconnect. **6.** to lose a contest, race, etc. on purpose: *used only in everyday talk.* —*n.* **1.** the act of throwing [The fast *throw* put the runner out at first base.] **2.** the distance that something is or can be thrown [It's a stone's *throw* from here.] —**throw away, 1.** to get rid of; discard. **2.** to waste. —**throw in,** to add extra or free. —**throw off, 1.** to rid oneself of [to *throw off*

a cold]. **2.** to send forth [to *throw off* sparks]. —**throw out, 1.** to get rid of. **2.** to offer; suggest [to *throw out* a hint]. **3.** to put out in baseball by throwing the ball to a base. —**throw over, 1.** to give up; abandon. **2.** to jilt. —**throw together,** to put together in a hurry. —**throw up, 1.** to give up; abandon. **2.** to vomit. —**threw,** *p.t.;* **thrown,** *p.p.;* **throw′ing,** *pr.p.*

throw·back (thrō′bak), *n.* a return to an earlier or more primitive type or condition.

thru (thrōo), *prep., adv. & adj.* through.

thrum (thrum), *v.* **1.** to pluck at the strings of; strum [to *thrum* a guitar]. **2.** to drum or tap with the fingers [to *thrum* on a table]. —**thrummed,** *p.t. & p.p.;* **thrum′ming,** *pr.p.*

thrush (thrush), *n.* any of a large group of songbirds, some plain in color, others having a spotted or bright breast. The wood thrush, robin, and bluebird are thrushes.

wood thrush
(8½ in. long)

thrust (thrust), *v.* **1.** to push with sudden force [He *thrust* the book into her hand. She *thrust* forward through the crowd.] **2.** to stab or pierce, as with a sword. —*n.* **1.** a sudden push or shove. **2.** a stab, as with a sword. **3.** the forward force produced by the propeller of an airplane or by the gases forced from a jet plane or rocket. —**thrust,** *p.t. & p.p.;* **thrust′ing,** *pr.p.*

thud (thud), *n.* a dull sound, as of something heavy dropping on the ground. —*v.* to hit with a thud. —**thud′ded,** *p.t. & p.p.;* **thud′ding,** *pr.p.*

thug (thug), *n.* a rough, violent criminal.

thumb (thum), *n.* **1.** the short, thick finger nearest the wrist. **2.** the part of a glove that covers a thumb. —*v.* **1.** to handle, turn, soil, etc. with the thumb [to *thumb* the pages of a book]. **2.** to ask for or get a ride in hitchhiking: *used only in everyday talk.* —**all thumbs,** clumsy; awkward. —**under one's thumb,** under one's power or influence.

thumb·nail (thum′nāl), *n.* the nail of the thumb. —*adj.* very small or brief [a *thumbnail* sketch of a man's life].

thumb·screw (thum′skrōo), *n.* a screw whose head can be turned by the thumb and forefinger.

thumb·tack (thum′tak), *n.* a tack with a wide, flat head, that can be pressed into a board, etc. with the thumb.

thumbscrew

thump (thump), *n.* **1.** a blow with something heavy and blunt. **2.** the dull sound made by such a blow. —*v.* to hit, fall, or pound with a thump.

fat,   āpe,   cär,   ten,   ēven,   hit,   bīte,   gō,   hôrn,   tōol,   book,   up,   fūr;
get,   joy,   yet,   chin,   she,   thin,   *th*en;   zh = s in pleasure;   ′ as in able (ā′b'l);
ə = a in ago,   e in agent,   i in sanity,   o in confess,   u in focus.

thun·der (thun′dər), *n.* **1.** the loud noise that comes after a flash of lightning. It is caused when the discharge of electricity disturbs the air. **2.** any loud, rumbling noise like this [the *thunder* of stampeding cattle]. —*v.* **1.** to cause thunder or a sound like thunder [The boys *thundered* down the steps.] **2.** to shout in a loud, forceful way.

thun·der·bolt (thun′dər bōlt), *n.* **1.** a flash of lightning with the thunder that follows it. **2.** something sudden and shocking, as bad news.

thun·der·clap (thun′dər klap), *n.* **1.** a loud crash of thunder. **2.** anything that happens in a sudden, shocking way.

thun·der·cloud (thun′dər kloud), *n.* a storm cloud that has electricity in it and makes lightning and thunder.

thun·der·ous (thun′dər əs), *adj.* making a loud, rumbling noise like thunder.

thun·der·show·er (thun′dər shou′ər), *n.* a shower along with thunder and lightning.

thun·der·storm (thun′dər stôrm), *n.* a storm along with thunder and lightning.

thun·der·struck (thun′dər struk), *adj.* amazed or shocked as if struck by a thunderbolt.

Thurs·day (thurz′dē), *n.* the fifth day of the week. Abbreviated **Thur.** or **Thurs.**

thus (*th*us), *adv.* **1.** in this way or in the following way [Do it *thus.*] **2.** to this or that degree; so [*Thus* far he has done well.] **3.** as a result; therefore [He is ill and *thus* absent.]

thwack (thwak), *v.* to hit with something flat; whack. —*n.* a blow with something flat.

thwart (thwôrt), *v.* to keep from doing or from being done; block; hinder [The guards *thwarted* his attempt to escape.] —*n.* a seat across a boat, for a rower. —*adj.* lying across.

thy (*th*ī), *pron.* an older form of **your:** *now used only in poetry, prayers, etc.* ["And crown *thy* good with brotherhood."]

thyme (tīm), *n.* a plant of the mint family, with sweet-smelling leaves used to flavor food.

thy·mus (thī′məs), *n.* a small gland near the lower part of the throat.

thy·roid (thī′roid), *n.* **1.** a large gland near the windpipe. It makes a hormone that controls the growth of the body. **2.** a substance made from the thyroid gland of certain animals, used in treating goiter. —*adj.* of this gland.

thy·self (*th*ī self′), *pron.* an older form of **yourself:** *now used only in poetry, prayers, etc.* ["Love thy neighbor as *thyself.*"]

ti (tē), *n.* the seventh note of a musical scale.

Ti, symbol for the chemical element *titanium.*

ti·ar·a (ti er′ə), *n.* **1.** an ornament for a woman's head, like a small crown with jewels, flowers, etc. **2.** the Pope's triple crown, worn at some special times.

Ti·ber (tī′bər), *n.* a river in Italy, flowing through Rome into the Mediterranean Sea.

Ti·bet (ti bet′), *n.* a country in central Asia under the control of China. —**Ti·bet′an,** *adj. & n.*

tiara

tib·i·a (tib′i ə), *n.* the long, thick inner bone of the leg, between the knee and the ankle. —**tib·i·ae** (tib′i ē) or **tib′i·as,** *pl.*

tic (tik), *n.* a twitch of a muscle, especially of the face, that cannot be controlled.

tick (tik), *n.* **1.** a light clicking sound, as that made by a clock. **2.** a mark made in checking off things, as the check mark √. —*v.* **1.** to make a tick or ticks, as a clock. **2.** to count by ticks [The watch *ticked* away the seconds.] **3.** to mark with a tick, or check [*Tick* off the names of those who are absent.]

tick (tik), *n.* any of various insects that suck the blood of man, cattle, etc.

tick (tik), *n.* the cloth case or cover of a mattress or pillow.

tick·et (tik′it), *n.* **1.** a printed card or piece of paper that one buys to get a certain right, as to a seat in a theater, train, etc. **2.** a label or tag on an article, giving its size, price, color, etc. **3.** the list of candidates of a political party in an election. **4.** a written order to appear in court for breaking a traffic law; traffic summons: *used only in everyday talk.* —*v.* to put a ticket on.

tick (¼ in. long)

tick·ing (tik′ing), *n.* a strong cotton or linen cloth for making mattress ticks, etc.

tick·le (tik′'l), *v.* **1.** to touch or stroke lightly, as with a finger or feather, causing a tingling, twitching, or laughing. **2.** to have such a tingling or twitching feeling [The dust made my nose *tickle.*] **3.** to give pleasure to; amuse; delight [The joke really *tickled* her.] —*n.* a tickling or a feeling of being tickled. —**tick′led,** *p.t. & p.p.;* **tick′ling,** *pr.p.* —**tick′ler,** *n.*

tick·lish (tik′lish), *adj.* **1.** easily made to laugh or squirm by tickling [He is *ticklish* under the arms.] **2.** easily upset; touchy [Jane is *ticklish* on the subject of her grades.] **3.** needing careful handling; delicate [a *ticklish* situation].

tick-tack-toe (tik′tak tō′ *or* ti′ta tō′), *n.* a game in which players take turns marking either crosses or circles in a block of nine squares, trying to get three of the same marks in a line.

tid·al (tī′d'l), *adj.* of, having, or caused by a tide [*tidal* current; *tidal* basin].

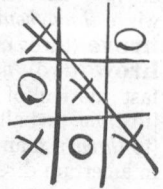

tick-tack-toe

tidal wave, a very large, damaging wave, caused by an earthquake or very strong wind.

tid·bit (tid′bit), *n.* a special, dainty bit of food, interesting piece of gossip, etc.

tid·dly·winks (tid′lē wingks′) or **tid·dle·dy·winks** (tid′'l dē wingks′), *n.* a game in which players try to snap little disks into a cup by pressing their edges with larger disks.

tide (tīd), *n.* **1.** the regular rise and fall of the ocean's surface, about every twelve hours, caused by the attraction of the moon and sun. **2.** something that rises and falls like the tide [His *tide* of popularity is ebbing.] **3.** a current, flow, trend, etc. [the *tide* of public opinion]. —*v.* to help in overcoming a time of trouble [Will ten dollars *tide* you over till Monday?] **—tid'ed,** *p.t. & p.p.;* **tid'ing,** *pr.p.*

tide·wa·ter (tīd'wô'tər), *n.* **1.** water, as in some streams along a seacoast, that rises and falls with the tide. **2.** a seacoast region with such streams, etc.

ti·dings (tī'dingz), *n.pl.* news; information.

ti·dy (tī'dē), *adj.* **1.** neat and orderly [a *tidy* person; a *tidy* cupboard]. **2.** quite large: *used only in everyday talk* [a *tidy* sum]. —*v.* to make tidy [*Tidy* up your room.] **—ti'di·er,** *compar.;* **ti'di·est,** *superl.* **—ti'died,** *p.t. & p.p.;* **ti'dy·ing,** *pr.p.* **—ti'di·ly,** *adv.* **—ti'di·ness,** *n.*

tie (tī), *v.* **1.** to bind together or fasten with string, rope, etc. [They *tied* his hands behind his back. *Tie* the boat to the pier.] **2.** to tighten and knot the laces, strings, etc. of [to *tie* one's shoes]. **3.** to make, as a knot or bow. **4.** to make a knot or bow in [to *tie* a necktie]. **5.** to bind in any way [He is *tied* to his work.] **6.** to equal, as in a score [Bill *tied* with Jim for first place.] —*n.* **1.** a string, lace, cord, etc. used for tying. **2.** something that joins, binds, etc. [family *ties*]. **3.** a necktie. **4.** a timber, beam, etc. holding parts together or in place [The rails of a railroad are fastened to wooden *ties*.] **5.** the fact of being equal, as in score; also, a contest in which scores are equal. **6.** a curved line joining two musical notes of the same pitch, and showing that the tone is to be held without a break. **—tie down,** to hold back or make less free; confine. **—tie up, 1.** to tie tightly. **2.** to wrap up and tie. **3.** to hinder; stop. **4.** to cause to be already in use, busy, etc. **—tied,** *p.t. & p.p.;* **ty'ing,** *pr.p.* **—ties,** *pl.*

Tien·tsin (tyen'tsin'), *n.* a city in northeastern China.

tier (tir), *n.* any of a series of rows, as of seats, set one above another.

Ti·er·ra del Fue·go (ti er'ə del fwā'gō), a group of islands, belonging to Chile and Argentina, at the southern tip of South America.

tie-up (tī'up'), *n.* **1.** a stopping of action or movement for a time [a traffic *tie-up*]. **2.** connection: *used only in everyday talk.*

tiff (tif), *n.* a slight quarrel; spat.

ti·ger (tī'gər), *n.* a large, fierce animal of the cat family, living in Asia. Tigers have a tawny coat with black stripes.

tiger lily, a kind of lily having orange flowers with dark purple spots.

tight (tīt), *adj.* **1.** made so that water, air, etc. cannot pass through [a *tight* boat]. **2.** put together firmly or closely [a *tight* knot]. **3.** fitting too closely [a

tiger (10 ft. long, including tail)

tight shirt; a *tight* door]. **4.** stretched to the point of strain; taut [a *tight* wire; *tight* nerves]. **5.** hard to manage, do, etc. [a *tight* situation]. **6.** almost even; close in score [a *tight* game]. **7.** hard to get; scarce [Money was *tight* in 1930.] **8.** stingy: *used only in everyday talk.* —*adv.* in a tight way; tightly. **—sit tight,** to keep one's place or position and not budge. **—tight'ly,** *adv.* **—tight'ness,** *n.*

tight·en (tīt''n), *v.* to make or become tight or tighter.

tight-fist·ed (tīt'fis'tid), *adj.* stingy.

tight-lipped (tīt'lipt'), *adj.* not saying much; keeping secrets.

tight·rope (tīt'rōp), *n.* a rope stretched tight, on which acrobats do balancing acts.

tights (tīts), *n.pl.* a garment that fits tightly over the legs and lower half of the body, worn by acrobats, dancers, etc.

ti·gress (tī'gris), *n.* a female tiger.

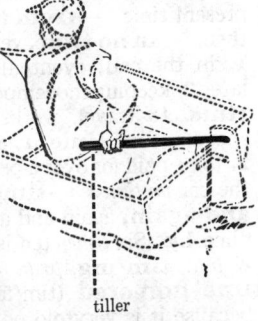

tightrope

Ti·gris (tī'gris), *n.* a river in southeastern Turkey and Iraq. It joins with the Euphrates.

tike (tīk), *n.* same as **tyke.**

til·de (til'də), *n.* in Spanish, the mark ~, used over an *n* to show that it has the sound of *ny*, as in "señor" (se nyôr'). This mark is also used in other ways to show pronunciation, as in this dictionary. *See the key at the bottom of this page.*

tile (tīl), *n.* **1.** a thin piece of baked clay, stone, plastic, etc., used for covering roofs, floors, walls, etc. **2.** a pipe of baked clay used for a drain. —*v.* to cover with tiles. **—tiled,** *p.t. & p.p.;* **til'ing,** *pr.p.*

till (til), *prep. & conj.* same as **until.**

till (til), *v.* to work land by plowing, planting, etc.; cultivate. **—till'er,** *n.*

till (til), *n.* a drawer for keeping money, as behind the counter in a store.

till·age (til'ij), *n.* the tilling of land.

till·er (til'ər), *n.* a bar or handle for turning the rudder of a boat.

tilt (tilt), *v.* **1.** to slope or tip [The deck *tilted* suddenly. He *tilted* his head to one side.] **2.** to fight with lances as knights did; joust. —*n.* **1.** a contest in which two knights on horseback tried to unseat each other by thrusting with lances. **2.** any lively contest. **3.** a tilting, or sloping; slant. **—at full tilt,** at full speed; with full force.

tiller

fat,   āpe,   cär,   ten,   ēven,   hit,   bīte,   gō,   hôrn,   tōōl,   book,   **up,**   fŭr;
get,   joy,   yet,   **chin,**   she,   thin,   *then*;   zh = s in pleasure;   ' as in able (ā'b'l);
ə = a in ago,   e in agent,   i in sanity,   o in confess,   u in focus.

tim·ber (tim′bər), *n.* **1.** wood for building houses, boats, etc. **2.** a large, thick piece of such wood; beam. **3.** trees or forests. —*v.* to provide, build, etc. with timbers.

tim·bered (tim′bərd), *adj.* **1.** made of timber. **2.** covered with trees or forests.

tim·ber·land (tim′bər land), *n.* land having trees on it fit for timber; wooded land.

tim·bre (tim′bər *or* tam′bər), *n.* the quality of sound, apart from pitch or loudness, that makes one voice or musical instrument different from others.

tim·brel (tim′brəl), *n.* a tambourine of ancient times.

time (tīm), *n.* **1.** the period between two events or during which something exists, happens, etc. [an hour's *time;* a *time* of joy; to serve *time* in prison]. **2.** the exact or proper instant, hour, day, year, etc. [The *time* is 5:17 P.M. It's *time* for bed.] **3.** the passing hours, days, years, etc.; every moment there has ever been or ever will be ["*Time* and tide wait for no man."] **4.** *often* **times,** *pl.* a period of history; age, era, etc. [in ancient *times*]. **5.** *usually* **times,** *pl.* conditions as they are; state of affairs [*Times* are getting better.] **6.** any one of a series of moments at which the same thing happens, is done, etc. [I read it three *times.*] **7.** a system of measuring the passing of hours [daylight-saving *time*]. **8.** the rate of speed for marching, playing a piece of music, etc.; tempo; rhythm [waltz *time;* double *time*]. **9.** the period that an employee works; also, the pay for this [He gets double *time* for working on holidays.] —*interj.* a signal during a game that play is to stop. —*v.* **1.** to arrange or choose a proper time, speed, etc. for [He *timed* his visit to find her at home. *Time* your marching to the music.] **2.** to measure or record the speed of [to *time* a racer]. —*adj.* **1.** having to do with time. **2.** set to work at a given time [a *time* lock]. —**against time,** trying to finish in a certain time. —**at one time, 1.** together. **2.** earlier; formerly. —**at the same time,** however. —**at times,** sometimes. —**behind the times,** out-of-date; old-fashioned. —**for the time being,** for the present time. —**from time to time,** now and then. —**in no time,** very quickly. —**in time, 1.** in the end; eventually. **2.** before it is too late. **3.** keeping the tempo, rhythm, etc. —**make time,** to travel, work, etc. at a fast rate of speed. —**on time, 1.** at the set time; not late. **2.** to be paid for over a period of time [He bought the car *on time.*] —**time after time** or **time and again,** again and again. —**times,** multiplied by [Six *times* ten is sixty.] —**timed,** *p.t. & p.p.;* **tim′ing,** *pr.p.* —**tim′er,** *n.*

time-hon·ored (tīm′än′ərd), *adj.* respected because it is very old or in use for a long time.

time·keep·er (tīm′kēp′ər), *n.* a person who keeps track of time, as in some games, or one who keeps a record of hours worked by employees.

time·less (tīm′lis), *adj.* **1.** never ending; eternal. **2.** not limited to a particular time.

time·ly (tīm′lē), *adj.* coming at the right time

[a *timely* remark]. —**time′li·er,** *compar.;* **time′li·est,** *superl.* —**time′li·ness,** *n.*

time·piece (tīm′pēs), *n.* a clock or watch.

time·ta·ble (tīm′tā′b'l), *n.* a schedule of the times when trains, planes, etc. arrive and leave.

tim·id (tim′id), *adj.* feeling or showing fright or shyness. —**ti·mid·i·ty** (ti mid′ə tē), *n.*

tim·ing (tīm′ing), *n.* the act of arranging or setting the speed or time of doing something so as to get the best results [A batter needs good *timing* to hit a home run.]

tim·or·ous (tim′ər əs), *adj.* full of fear or easily frightened; timid; shy.

tim·o·thy (tim′ə thē), *n.* a grass with long leaves and spikes, grown as food for cattle.

tim·pa·ni (tim′pə nē), *n.pl.* kettledrums. —**tim′pa·nist,** *n.*

tin (tin), *n.* **1.** a soft, silver-white metal that is a chemical element. Tin is easy to bend or shape. **2.** tin plate. **3.** a can in which food is sealed so that it will keep: *a British meaning.* —*v.* **1.** to cover with tin. **2.** to seal in tins; can: *a British meaning.* —**tinned,** *p.t. & p.p.;* **tin′ning,** *pr.p.*

tinc·ture (tingk′chər), *n.* **1.** a solution of a medicine in alcohol [*tincture* of quinine]. **2.** a slight trace, hint, or tint. —*v.* to give a slight trace or tint to. —**tinc′tured,** *p.t. & p.p.;* **tinc′tur·ing,** *pr.p.*

tin·der (tin′dər), *n.* any dry material that catches fire easily, used for starting a fire from the spark of a flint, etc.

tin·der·box (tin′dər bäks), *n.* **1.** a box for holding tinder, flint, and steel for starting a fire. **2.** anything that catches fire easily.

tine (tīn), *n.* a sharp point that sticks out; prong [the *tines* of a fork].

tin foil, a very thin sheet of tin, used to wrap food, tobacco, etc. to keep it fresh.

ting (ting), *n.* a light, ringing sound, as of a small bell. —*v.* to make such a sound.

tinge (tinj), *v.* **1.** to color slightly; tint [Northern lights *tinged* the sky.] **2.** to give a slight trace to [joy *tinged* with sorrow]. —*n.* **1.** a slight coloring; tint. **2.** a slight trace. —**tinged,** *p.t. & p.p.;* **tinge′ing** or **ting′ing,** *pr.p.*

tin·gle (ting′g'l), *v.* to have or give a prickling or stinging feeling, such as that caused by cold, excitement, etc. —*n.* such a feeling. —**tin′gled,** *p.t. & p.p.;* **tin′gling,** *pr.p.*

tink·er (ting′kər), *n.* a person who mends pots, pans, etc., often one who travels about doing this. —*v.* **1.** to work as a tinker. **2.** to mend or try to mend in a clumsy way. **3.** to fuss with something in a useless or careless way; putter.

tin·kle (ting′k'l), *v.* **1.** to make a series of light, ringing sounds, like those of a small bell. **2.** to cause to tinkle. —*n.* the act or sound of tinkling. —**tin′kled,** *p.t. & p.p.;* **tin′kling,** *pr.p.*

tin·ner (tin′ər), *n.* a man who works with tin, repairing roofs, gutters, etc.

tin·ny (tin′ē), *adj.* **1.** of or containing tin. **2.** like tin, as in looks, sound, value, etc. [*tinny* jewelry; *tinny* music]. —**tin′ni·er,** *compar.;* **tin′ni·est,** *superl.*

tin plate, thin sheets of iron or steel plated with tin.

tin·sel (tin's'l), *n.* **1.** thin, shiny strips or threads of tin, metal foil, etc., used for decoration, as on Christmas trees. **2.** anything that looks showy and fine but is really cheap and of little value. —*adj.* **1.** of or decorated with tinsel. **2.** showy; gaudy. —*v.* to decorate or make glitter as with tinsel. —**tin′seled** or **tin′selled,** *p.t. & p.p.;* **tin′sel·ing** or **tin′sel·ling,** *pr.p.*

tin·smith (tin′smith), *n.* a person who works with tin or tin plate; maker of tinware.

tint (tint), *n.* **1.** a light or pale color; tinge. **2.** a shading of a color [several *tints* of green]. —*v.* to give a tint to.

tin·ware (tin′wer), *n.* pots, pans, dishes, etc. made of tin plate.

ti·ny (ti′nē), *adj.* very small; minute. —**ti′ni·er,** *compar.;* **ti′ni·est,** *superl.*

-tion (shən), a suffix meaning: **1.** the act of [*Correction* is the act of correcting.] **2.** the condition of being [*Elation* is the condition of being elated.] **3.** a thing that is [A *creation* is a thing that is created.]

tip (tip), *n.* **1.** the rounded or pointed end of something [the *tip* of the nose; a spear *tip*]. **2.** something attached to the end [a rubber *tip* on a cane]. —*v.* to make or put a tip on. —**tipped,** *p.t. & p.p.;* **tip′ping,** *pr.p.*

tip (tip), *v.* **1.** to hit lightly and sharply; tap. **2.** to give a small gift of money to for some service [to *tip* a waitress]. **3.** to give secret information to: *used only in everyday talk* [He *tipped* off the police about the robbery.] —*n.* **1.** a light, sharp blow; tap. **2.** a piece of secret information. **3.** a suggestion, hint, warning, etc. **4.** a small gift of money given to a waiter, porter, etc. for some service. —**tipped,** *p.t. & p.p.;* **tip′ping,** *pr.p.* —**tip′per,** *n.*

tip (tip), *v.* **1.** to overturn; upset [He *tipped* over his glass.] **2.** to tilt or slant. **3.** to raise slightly in greeting, as one's hat. —*n.* a tipping or being tipped; tilt; slant. —**tipped,** *p.t. & p.p.;* **tip′ping,** *pr.p.*

tip·pet (tip′it), *n.* **1.** a long scarf for the neck and shoulders, with ends that hang down in front. **2.** formerly, a long, hanging part of a hood, cape, or sleeve.

tip·ple (tip′'l), *v.* to drink alcoholic liquor often. —*n.* alcoholic liquor. —**tip′pled,** *p.t. & p.p.;* **tip′pling,** *pr.p.* —**tip′pler,** *n.*

tip·sy (tip′sē), *adj.* **1.** that tips easily; not steady. **2.** somewhat drunk. —**tip′si·er,** *compar.;* **tip′si·est,** *superl.* —**tip′si·ly,** *adv.*

tippet

tip·toe (tip′tō), *n.* the tip of a toe. —*v.* to walk on one's tiptoes in a quiet or careful way. —**on tiptoe, 1.** on one's tiptoes. **2.** quietly or

carefully. —**tip′toed,** *p.t. & p.p.;* **tip′toe·ing,** *pr.p.*

tip·top (tip′täp′), *n.* the highest point; very top. —*adj. & adv.* **1.** at the highest point, or top. **2.** very best; excellent: *only in everyday talk.*

ti·rade (tī′rād *or* ti rād′), *n.* a long, angry or scolding speech; harangue.

tire (tīr), *v.* **1.** to make or become unable to go on because of a need for rest; exhaust [The hike *tired* me.] **2.** to make or become bored. —**tired,** *p.t. & p.p.;* **tir′ing,** *pr.p.*

tire (tīr), *n.* a hoop of iron or rubber, or a rubber tube filled with air, fixed around the rim of a wheel to serve as a tread.

tired (tīrd), *adj.* weary; exhausted.

tire·less (tīr′lis), *adj.* that does not become tired. —**tire′less·ly,** *adv.*

tire·some (tīr′səm), *adj.* tiring; boring.

'tis (tiz), it is.

tis·sue (tish′ōō), *n.* **1.** any material, made up of cells, that forms some part of a plant or animal [muscle *tissue;* nerve *tissue*]. **2.** any light, thin cloth, as gauze. **3.** a tangled mass or series; mesh [a *tissue* of lies]. **4.** a thin, soft paper used for handkerchiefs, for wrapping things, etc.: *its full name is* **tissue paper.**

tit (tit), *n.* a small bird, as a titmouse.

Ti·tan (tī′t'n), *n.* **1.** any one of a race of giant gods in Greek myths, who were overthrown by the gods of Olympus. **2. titan,** a person or thing that is very large or powerful; giant.

Ti·ta·ni·a (ti tā′ni ə), *n.* the queen of fairyland and wife of Oberon, in early folk tales.

ti·tan·ic (tī tan′ik), *adj.* very large, strong, or powerful.

ti·ta·ni·um (tī tā′ni əm), *n.* a dark-gray, shiny metal that is a chemical element. It is used in making steel.

tit·bit (tit′bit), *n.* same as **tidbit.**

tit for tat, blow for blow; this for that.

tithe (tīth), *n.* **1.** one tenth of one's income, paid as a tax to support a church. **2.** a tenth part or any small part. **3.** any tax. —*v.* to put a tithe on. —**tithed,** *p.t. & p.p.;* **tith′ing,** *pr.p.*

tit·il·late (tit′'l āt), *v.* to excite in a pleasant way. —**tit′il·lat·ed,** *p.t. & p.p.;* **tit′il·lat·ing,** *pr.p.* —**tit′il·la′tion,** *n.*

tit·lark (tit′lärk), *n.* a small bird like a lark.

ti·tle (tī′t'l), *n.* **1.** the name of a book, chapter, poem, picture, piece of music, etc. **2.** a word showing the rank, occupation, etc. of a person ["Baron," "Miss," and "Dr." are *titles*.] **3.** a claim or right; especially, a legal right to own something, or proof of such a right [Who has the *title* to this house?] **4.** a championship [Our team won the football *title*.] —*v.* to give a title to; name. —**ti′tled,** *p.t. & p.p.;* **ti′tling,** *pr.p.*

ti·tled (tī′t'ld), *adj.* having a title, especially the title of a knight, lord, etc.

tit·mouse (tit′mous), *n.* any of certain small

---

fat,   āpe,   cär,   ten,   ēven,   hit,   bīte,   gō,   hôrn,   tōol,   book,   up,   fūr;
get,   joy,   yet,   chin,   she,   thin,   *th*en;   zh = s in pleasure;   ' as in able (ā′b'l);
ə = a in ago,   e in agent,   i in sanity,   o in confess,   u in focus.

birds with dull-colored feathers, as the chickadee.
—**tit·mice** (tit′mīs), *pl.*

tit·ter (tit′ər), *v.* to laugh in a silly or nervous way, as if trying to hold back the sound; giggle. —*n.* such a laugh; giggle.

tit·tle (tit′′l), *n.* a very small bit; jot.

tit·tle-tat·tle (tit′′l tat′′l), *n. & v.* gossip or chatter. —**tit′tle-tat′tled,** *p.t. & p.p.;* **tit′tle-tat′tling,** *pr.p.*

tit·u·lar (tich′oo lər *or* tit′yoo lər), *adj.* 1. in name only, not in fact [The king is the *titular* head of their government.] 2. of a title. 3. having a title.

TNT *or* **T.N.T.,** a powerful explosive, used in blasting, in shells for large guns, etc.

to (too̅ *or* too *or* tə), *prep.* 1. in the direction of [Turn *to* the left.] 2. as far as [when we got *to* Boston; wet *to* the skin]. 3. until [from dawn *to* dark]. 4. on, onto, against, etc. [Tie it *to* the post. He put a hand *to* his eyes.] 5. for the purpose of [Go *to* their help.] 6. having to do with; involving [It's nothing *to* me.] 7. causing or resulting in [*to* my amazement; torn *to* pieces]. 8. with; along with [Add this *to* the rest.] 9. belonging with; fitting [the coat *to* this suit]. 10. compared with [a score of 7 *to* 0]. 11. in agreement with [not *to* my taste]. 12. in or for each [4 quarts *to* a gallon]. *To* is often used before an indirect object or before a person or thing receiving action [Give it *to* me. Listen *to* that noise.] *To* is also used as a sign of the infinitive form of verbs [I want *to* stay.] —*adv.* 1. forward [She has her dress on wrong side *to*.] 2. shut or closed [The door was blown *to*.] 3. to a conscious condition [He fainted, but a dash of cold water brought him *to*.] 4. to the matter at hand [They fell *to* and devoured the cake.] —**to and fro,** back and forth.

toad (tōd), *n.* a small animal that is much like a frog, but usually lives on land after an early stage in the water.

toad·stool (tōd′-stool), *n.* a mushroom, especially one that is poisonous.

toad·y (tōd′ē), *n.* a person who flatters others in order to get things from them. —*v.* to be a toady to; flatter. —**toad′ies,** *pl.* —**toad′ied,** *p.t. & p.p.;* **toad′y·ing,** *pr.p.*

toad (3 in. long)

toast (tōst), *v.* 1. to brown the surface of by heating, as bread. 2. to warm [*Toast* yourself by the fire.] —*n.* toasted bread. —**toast′er,** *n.*

toast (tōst), *n.* 1. a person, thing, idea, etc. in honor of which people raise their glasses and drink. 2. the act of suggesting or taking such a drink. —*v.* to suggest or drink a toast to.

toadstools

toast·mas·ter (tōst′mas′tər), *n.* the person at a banquet who offers toasts, introduces speakers, etc.

to·bac·co (tə bak′ō), *n.* 1. a plant with pink or white flowers and large leaves. 2. the dried leaves of this plant, prepared for smoking, chewing, or snuffing. —**to·bac′cos,** *pl.*

to·bog·gan (tə bäg′ən), *n.* a long, flat sled without runners, for coasting down hills. —*v.* 1. to coast down-hill on a toboggan. 2. to go down rapidly, as in value. —**to·bog′ganed,** *p.t. & p.p.;* **to·bog′-gan·ing,** *pr.p.*

toboggan

toc·sin (täk′sin), *n.* 1. a bell rung to give an alarm. 2. its sound. 3. any alarm.

to·day *or* **to-day** (tə dā′), *adv.* 1. on or during this day [Do it *today*.] 2. in these times; nowadays [We are making great strides in medicine *today*.] —*n.* 1. this day [*today's* game]. 2. the present time [the fashions of *today*].

tod·dle (täd′′l), *v.* to walk with short, unsteady steps, as a child does. —**tod′dled,** *p.t. & p.p.;* **tod′dling,** *pr.p.* —**tod′dler,** *n.*

to-do (tə doo̅′), *n.* a fuss: *only in everyday talk.*

toe (tō), *n.* 1. any of the five parts at the end of the foot. 2. the part of a shoe, stocking, etc. that covers the toes. 3. anything like a toe in position, shape, etc. —*v.* to touch with the toes [The runners *toed* the starting line.] —**on one's toes,** alert; ready: *only in everyday talk.* —**toe the line** *or* **toe the mark,** to follow orders strictly. —**toed,** *p.t. & p.p.;* **toe′ing,** *pr.p.*

toe·nail (tō′nāl), *n.* the hard, tough cover on the tip of each toe.

tof·fee *or* **tof·fy** (tôf′ē), *n.* a kind of taffy.

to·ga (tō′gə), *n.* a loose outer garment worn in public by citizens of ancient Rome.

to·geth·er (tə ge*th*′ər), *adv.* 1. in or into one gathering, group, or place [The reunion brought the whole family *together*.] 2. with one another [They arrived *together*.] 3. so as to hit, be joined, etc. [The cars skidded *together*.] 4. at the same time [The shots were fired *together*.] 5. in or into agreement [to get *together* on a deal].

toga

To·go (tō′gō), *n.* a country on the western coast of Africa.

togs (tägz), *n.pl.* clothes: *only in everyday talk.*

toil (toil), *v.* 1. to work hard; labor. 2. to go slowly with pain or effort [to *toil* up a hill]. —*n.* hard work. —**toil′er,** *n.*

toi·let (toi′lit), *n.* 1. the act of dressing or grooming oneself. 2. a fixture with a drain, used for ridding the body of waste. 3. a room with such a fixture; bathroom. —*adj.* of or for dressing or grooming oneself [*toilet* articles].

toilet water, a perfumed liquid, as cologne, for putting on the skin.

toils (toilz), *n.pl.* a net, snare, or trap [caught in the *toils* of the law].

toil·some (toil′səm), *adj.* that takes toil, or hard work; laborious [a *toilsome* task].

to·ken (tō′kən), *n.* **1.** a sign or symbol [This gift is a *token* of my love.] **2.** a keepsake or souvenir. **3.** a piece of stamped metal to be used in place of money, as for fare.

To·ky·o (tō′ki ō), *n.* the capital of Japan.

told (tōld), past tense and past participle of **tell.**

To·le·do (tə lē′dō), *n.* **1.** a city in northwestern Ohio. **2.** a city in central Spain.

tol·er·a·ble (täl′ər ə b'l), *adj.* **1.** that can be tolerated or put up with; bearable [a *tolerable* burden]. **2.** not too bad and not too good; fair [a *tolerable* dinner]. **—tol′er·a·bly,** *adv.*

tol·er·ance (täl′ər əns), *n.* **1.** willingness to let others have their own beliefs, ways, etc., even though these are not like one's own. **2.** the power of the body to keep a drug or poison from working [His body built up a *tolerance* for penicillin, so that it could no longer help him.]

tol·er·ant (täl′ər ənt), *adj.* having or showing tolerance; tolerating. **—tol′er·ant·ly,** *adv.*

tol·er·ate (täl′ə rāt), *v.* **1.** to let something be done or go on without trying to stop it [I won't *tolerate* such talk.] **2.** to put up with; endure; bear [She can't *tolerate* cats.] **3.** to have tolerance, as for a drug. **—tol′er·at·ed,** *p.t. & p.p.;* **tol′er·at·ing,** *pr.p.*

tol·er·a·tion (täl′ə rā′shən), *n.* tolerance; especially, willingness to let others worship as they please.

toll (tōl), *n.* **1.** a tax or charge paid for the use of a bridge, highway, etc. **2.** a charge made for some service, as for a long-distance telephone call. **3.** the number lost, taken, etc. [The storm took a heavy *toll* of lives.]

toll (tōl), *v.* **1.** to ring a bell with slow, regular strokes, as when someone dies. **2.** to announce by such ringing [The bell *tolled* ten o'clock.] **—n.** the sound of tolling a bell.

toll·gate (tōl′gāt), *n.* a gate that cannot be passed until a toll is paid.

tom·a·hawk (täm′ə hôk), *n.* a light ax used by North American Indians as a tool and a weapon. **—v.** to hit, cut, or kill with a tomahawk.

to·ma·to (tə mā′tō *or* tə mä′tō), *n.* **1.** a red or yellow, round fruit, with a juicy pulp, used as a vegetable. **2.** the plant it grows on. *See picture in next column.* **—to·ma′toes,** *pl.*

tomb (tōom), *n.* a grave, vault, etc. for the dead. **—the tomb,** death.

tomahawk

tom·boy (täm′boi), *n.* a girl who behaves or plays like an active boy.

tomb·stone (tōom′stōn), *n.* a stone put on a tomb telling who is buried there; gravestone.

tom·cat (täm′kat), *n.* a male cat.

tome (tōm), *n.* a book, especially a large one.

tom·fool·er·y (täm′fool′-ər ē), *n.* a foolish or silly way of acting. **—tom′fool′er·ies,** *pl.*

tomato leaves and fruit

to·mor·row or **to-mor·row** (tə mär′ō *or* too môr′ō), *adv.* on the day after today. **—n. 1.** the day after today. **2.** some future time.

tom·tit (täm′tit), *n.* any of certain small birds, as the titmouse or the wren.

tom-tom (täm′täm′), *n.* a simple kind of drum, usually beaten with the hands.

ton (tun), *n.* **1.** a measure of weight equal to 2,000 pounds, used in the United States, Canada, etc. It is often called the **short ton** to tell it from the **long ton,** which is equal to 2,240 pounds and is used in Great Britain. **2.** a metric ton, equal to 1,000 kilograms.

ton·al (tō′n'l), *adj.* of a tone or tones.

tone (tōn), *n.* **1.** a sound, especially one that is pleasant or musical [the clear *tones* of an oboe]. **2.** one of a series of such sounds arranged in a musical scale; note. **3.** the difference in pitch of one full step in the scale between musical notes [A is two *tones* below C.] **4.** a way of speaking or writing that shows a certain feeling [Her answer had a friendly *tone.*] **5.** the style, character, etc. of a place or period [Their many paintings gave the house a cultured *tone.*] **6.** a color, shade, or tint [Her dress has several *tones* of brown.] **7.** the normal, healthy condition of an organ, muscle, etc. [Exercise will improve the *tone* of your muscles.] **—v.** to give a certain tone to, as of color or sound. **—tone down,** to make or become less bright or sharp; soften. **—tone in with,** to blend or harmonize with [Her green hat *toned in with* her red hair.] **—tone up,** to make or become brighter or stronger. **—toned,** *p.t. & p.p.;* **ton′ing,** *pr.p.*

Ton·ga (täng′gə), *n.* a country on a group of islands in the South Pacific, east of Fiji.

tongs (tôngz), *n.pl.* a device for seizing or lifting things, usually made with two long arms hinged together.

tongue (tung), *n.* **1.** the movable muscle attached to the floor of the mouth. It is used in tasting, eating, and speaking. **2.** an animal's tongue used as food. **3.** the act or power of speaking [He lost his *tongue.*] **4.** a manner of speaking [He has a glib *tongue.*] **5.** a language [the French *tongue*].

tongs

6. something like a tongue in shape, motion, etc., as the flap under the laces of a shoe, a long, narrow flame, the clapper of a bell, or a narrow strip of land in a lake or sea. **—hold one's tongue,** to keep from speaking. **—on the tip of one's tongue,** almost said or remembered. **—tongue′less,** *adj.*

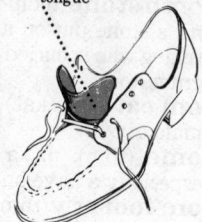
tongue

tongue-tied (tung′tīd′), *adj.* **1.** not able to move the tongue or speak properly, because the membrane fastening the tongue to the mouth is too short. **2.** not able to speak, because one is amazed, embarrassed, etc.

ton·ic (tän′ik), *adj.* **1.** giving strength or energy; stimulating [Swimming has a *tonic* effect.] **2.** of or having to do with a keynote in music [a *tonic* chord]. **—n. 1.** anything that stimulates or gives energy, as a tonic medicine. **2.** the keynote of a musical scale.

to·night or **to-night** (tə nīt′), *adv.* on or during this night or the night of today. **—n.** this night or the night of today.

ton·nage (tun′ij), *n.* **1.** the amount in tons that a ship can carry. **2.** the total amount of shipping of a country or port, figured in tons. **3.** a tax or duty on ships, based on tons carried. **4.** total weight in tons.

ton·sil (tän′s'l), *n.* either of two soft, oval masses of tissue at the back of the mouth.

ton·sil·lec·to·my (tän′s'l ek′tə mē), *n.* an operation by which a surgeon removes a person's tonsils. **—ton′sil·lec′to·mies,** *pl.*

ton·sil·li·tis (tän′s'l ī′tis), *n.* a diseased condition of a person's tonsils in which they become swollen and inflamed.

ton·so·ri·al (tän sôr′i əl), *adj.* of a barber or his work: *now used in a humorous way.*

ton·sure (tän′shər), *n.* **1.** the act of shaving a man's head, especially on top, when he becomes a priest or monk. **2.** the part of the head left bare by doing this.

tonsure

too (tōō), *adv.* **1.** in addition; besides; also [You come *too*.] **2.** more than enough [This hat is *too* big.] **3.** very [You are *too* kind.] *Too* is often used just to give force to what is said [I did *too* see him!]

took (took), past tense of **take.**

tool (tōōl), *n.* **1.** any instrument held in the hand or driven by a motor and used in doing some work [Knives, saws, drills, etc. are *tools*.] **2.** any person or thing used as a means to get something done [Books are *tools* of education.] **—v. 1.** to shape, work, or put designs on with a tool [to *tool* leather]. **2.** to furnish tools or machinery for [to *tool* a factory].

tool·mak·er (tōōl′māk′ər), *n.* a person who makes and repairs machine tools.

toot (tōōt), *n.* a short blast of a horn, whistle, etc. **—v.** to sound in short blasts, as a horn or whistle. **—toot′er,** *n.*

tooth (tōōth), *n.* **1.** any of the white, bony parts growing from the jaws and used for biting and chewing. **2.** any part more or less like a tooth, as on a saw, comb, gearwheel, etc. **3.** an appetite or taste for something [a sweet *tooth*]. **—in the teeth of,** going straight against the force of. **—tooth and nail,** with all one's strength. **—teeth,** *pl.* **—tooth′less,** *adj.*

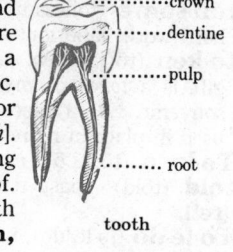
crown
dentine
pulp
root
tooth

tooth·ache (tōōth′āk), *n.* pain in a tooth or the teeth.

tooth·brush (tōōth′brush), *n.* a small brush for cleaning the teeth.

toothed (tōōtht *or* tōō*th*d), *adj.* **1.** having teeth, especially of a certain kind [sharp-*toothed*; buck*toothed*]. **2.** having notches [a *toothed* leaf].

tooth paste, a paste used in cleaning the teeth with a toothbrush.

tooth·pick (tōōth′pik), *n.* a small, pointed stick for getting bits of food free from between the teeth.

tooth·some (tōōth′səm), *adj.* pleasing to the taste; tasty.

top (täp), *n.* **1.** the highest part or point [the *top* of a hill; the *top* of a page]. **2.** the part of a plant growing above ground [carrot *tops*]. **3.** the head or the crown of the head [His hair is cut short on *top*.] **4.** a part that covers or is uppermost, as a lid or cover [a box *top*]. **5.** the highest degree or pitch [He shouted at the *top* of his voice.] **6.** the highest rank, position, etc. [Sue is at the *top* of her class.] **7.** the best part; pick [the *top* of the crop]. **8.** the platform around the head of the lowest section of a mast on a sailing ship. **—adj.** of or at the top; highest; uppermost [a *top* student]. **—v. 1.** to put a top on [to *top* a cake with icing]. **2.** to cut or trim the top of, as a plant or tree. **3.** to be at the top of [Snow *topped* the mountain.] **4.** to reach or go over the top of. **5.** to be more than in amount, height, etc. [The fish *topped* 75 pounds.] **6.** to do or be better than; surpass [He *tops* them all at golf.] **7.** to be at the top of; head; lead [Bill *topped* his class.] **—on top,** at the top; successful. **—on top of, 1.** resting upon. **2.** in addition to; besides. **—over the top,** beyond the goal set. **—top off,** to finish by adding a final touch. **—topped,** *p.t. & p.p.;* **top′ping,** *pr.p.*

top (täp), *n.* a child's toy shaped like a cone. It is spun on its pointed end.

to·paz (tō′paz), *n.* a clear, crystal stone, usually yellow, used as a gem.

top·coat (täp′kōt), *n.* a light overcoat.

To·pe·ka (tə pē′kə), *n.* the capital of Kansas.

top·gal·lant (tə gal′ənt *or* täp′gal′ənt), *adj.* next above the topmast on a sailing ship. **—n.** a topgallant mast or sail.

top hat, a tall, black hat with a flat top, worn by men in formal clothes.

top·heav·y (täp'hev'ē), *adj.* so heavy at the top that it may fall over.

top·ic (täp'ik), *n.* the subject of a talk, piece of writing, debate, etc.

top·i·cal (täp'i k'l), *adj.* **1.** dealing with topics of the day; of special interest because timely [The comedian told some *topical* jokes.] **2.** having to do with topics [a *topical* outline].

top hat

top·knot (täp'nät), *n.* a tuft of hair or feathers on the top of the head.

top·mast (täp'məst *or* täp'mast), *n.* the section of a mast next to the lowest section, on a sailing ship.

top·most (täp'mōst), *adj.* highest; uppermost.

to·pog·ra·phy (tə päg'rə fē), *n.* **1.** the surface features of a region, as hills, rivers, roads, etc. **2.** the science of showing these on maps and charts. **—to·pog'ra·pher,** *n.* **—top·o·graph·i·cal** (täp'ə graf'i k'l), *adj.*

top·ple (täp''l), *v.* **1.** to fall over; fall top forward [The tall pile of books *toppled* over.] **2.** to make topple; overturn. **—top'pled,** *p.t. & p.p.;* **top'pling,** *pr.p.*

top·sail (täp's'l *or* täp'sāl), *n.* the sail next above the lowest sail on a mast.

top·soil (täp'soil), *n.* the top layer of soil, usually richer than the soil underneath.

top·sy·tur·vy (täp'sē tur'vē), *adv. & adj.* upside down, or in confusion or disorder [The tornado left many houses *topsy-turvy.*]

torch (tôrch), *n.* **1.** a flaming light that can be carried in the hand, as a piece of burning wood with resin in it. **2.** something that inspires or sheds the light of truth, reason, etc. [the *torch* of science]. **3.** any device that makes a very hot flame, as a blowtorch. **4.** a flashlight: *a British meaning.*

torch·light (tôrch'līt), *n.* the light of a torch or torches.

tore (tôr), past tense of **tear** (to pull apart).

tor·e·a·dor (tôr'i ə dôr'), *n.* a bullfighter: *this term is no longer used in bullfighting.*

torch

tor·ment (tôr'ment), *n.* **1.** great pain or suffering of the body or mind. **2.** something that causes pain, worry, etc. **—v.** (tôr ment'), **1.** to make suffer in body or mind. **2.** to annoy or worry; harass. **—tor·men'tor** or **tor·ment'er,** *n.*

torn (tôrn), past participle of **tear** (to pull apart).

tor·na·do (tôr nā'dō), *n.* a wild, destroying wind that forms a whirling cloud shaped like a funnel and moving in a narrow path. **—tor·na'does** or **tor·na'dos,** *pl.*

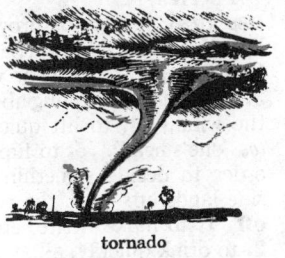

tornado

To·ron·to (tə rän'tō), *n.* the capital of Ontario, Canada, on Lake Ontario.

tor·pe·do (tôr pē'dō), *n.* a large, exploding missile shaped like a cigar. It is fired under water, where it moves under its own power to blow up enemy ships. **—v.** to attack or destroy with a torpedo. **—tor·pe'does,** *pl.* **—tor·pe'doed,** *p.t. & p.p.;* **tor·pe'do·ing,** *pr.p.*

torpedo boat, a small, fast warship used for firing torpedoes.

tor·pid (tôr'pid), *adj.* moving, feeling, thinking, etc. slowly or not at all; dull; sluggish [A hibernating animal is *torpid.*]

tor·por (tôr'pər), *n.* the condition of being torpid; dullness; sluggishness.

torque (tôrk), *n.* a force that gives a twisting or rotating motion.

tor·rent (tôr'ənt), *n.* **1.** a swift, rushing stream of water. **2.** any wild, rushing flow [a *torrent* of insults]. **3.** a heavy fall of rain.

tor·ren·tial (tô ren'shəl), *adj.* of or like a torrent; overwhelming [*torrential* rains].

tor·rid (tôr'id), *adj.* very hot and dry; scorching or scorched [a *torrid* desert].

tor·sion (tôr'shən), *n.* a twisting or being twisted, especially along the length of an axis.

tor·so (tôr'sō), *n.* **1.** the human body, not including the head, arms, and legs; trunk. **2.** a statue of the human trunk. **—tor'sos,** *pl.*

tor·toise (tôr'təs), *n.* a turtle, especially one that lives on land.

tortoise shell, the hard, yellow-and-brown shell of some turtles, used in making combs, frames, etc. **—tor'toise-shell',** *adj.*

tor·tu·ous (tôr'chōō əs), *adj.* full of twists, turns, etc.; winding; crooked [a *tortuous* river; *tortuous* thinking].

tor·ture (tôr'chər), *n.* **1.** the act of greatly hurting someone on purpose, as to punish him or make him confess. **2.** any great pain; agony [the *torture* of a toothache]. **—v. 1.** to use torture on. **2.** to cause great pain or agony to [He was *tortured* by doubts.] **3.** to twist the meaning, form, etc. of. **—tor'tured,** *p.t. & p.p.;* **tor'tur·ing,** *pr.p.* **—tor'tur·er,** *n.*

To·ry (tôr'ē), *n.* **1.** in former times, a member of one of the main political parties of England. This party is now called the *Conservative Party.* **2.** an American colonist who favored Great Britain during the American Revolution. **3.**

often tory, any very conservative person. **—To′ries,** *pl.*

toss (tôs), *v.* **1.** to throw from the hand in a light, easy way [to *toss* a ball]. **2.** to throw about; fling here and there [The waves *tossed* the boat.] **3.** to be thrown or flung about [The kite *tossed* in the wind.] **4.** to lift quickly; jerk upward [to *toss* one's head]. **5.** to flip a coin into the air in order to decide something according to which side lands up. **—***n.* the act of tossing. **—toss off, 1.** to make, write, etc. quickly and easily. **2.** to drink quickly, all at once.

tot (tät), *n.* a young child.

to·tal (tō′t'l), *n.* the whole amount; sum. **—***adj.* **1.** making up the whole amount; entire [The *total* amount of your bill is $3.50.] **2.** complete [a *total* eclipse of the moon]. **—***v.* **1.** to find the sum or total of; add [to *total* a column of figures]. **2.** to add up to; reach a total of [His golf score *totals* 89.] **—to′taled** or **to′talled,** *p.t. & p.p.;* **to′tal·ing** or **to′tal·ling,** *pr.p.* **—to′tal·ly,** *adv.*

to·tal·i·tar·i·an (tō tal′ə ter′i ən), *adj.* describing or having to do with a government in which one political party has complete control and outlaws all others. **—***n.* a person who is in favor of such a government.

to·tal·i·ty (tō tal′ə tē), *n.* total amount.

tote (tōt), *v.* to carry or haul: *used only in everyday talk.* **—tot′ed,** *p.t. & p.p.;* **tot′ing,** *pr.p.*

to·tem (tō′təm), *n.* **1.** an animal or other natural object, taken by a family, tribe, etc. as its symbol, especially among certain North American Indians. **2.** an image of this, often carved or painted on poles called **totem poles.**

tot·ter (tät′ər), *v.* **1.** to rock or sway back and forth as if about to fall. **2.** to walk in an unsteady way; stagger.

tou·can (tōō′kan *or* tookän′), *n.* a brightly colored bird of tropical America, with a very large beak that curves downward.

totem pole

touch (tuch), *v.* **1.** to put the hand, finger, etc. on something in order to feel it [He *touched* the fence to see if the paint was wet.] **2.** to tap lightly [to *touch* a horse with a whip]. **3.** to handle, use, or disturb [Don't *touch* the papers on my desk.] **4.** to eat or drink [He won't *touch* carrots.] **5.** to injure slightly [roses *touched* by the frost]. **6.** to bring or come into contact with something else [He *touched* a match to the candle. The bumpers of the cars *touched.*] **7.** to make feel pity, sympathy, gratefulness, etc. [Your kindness *touches* me.] **8.** to talk about briefly; mention [The speaker *touched* on many subjects.] **9.** to have to do with; con-

toucan (2 ft. long)

cern [a subject that *touches* our welfare]. **10.** to be a match for; equal; rival [His boat can't *touch* mine for speed.] **—***n.* **1.** a touching or being touched; light tap or stroke [I felt the *touch* of a hand on my arm.] **2.** the sense in the skin, especially of the fingers, by which one becomes aware of the size, shape, hardness, and smoothness of a thing; power to feel. **3.** the feeling one gets from touching something [The cloth has a soft, smooth *touch.*] **4.** a small, skillful change in a painting, story, etc. [With a few *touches* he made the joke really funny.] **5.** a very small amount or degree [Add a *touch* of salt.] **6.** a mild form [a *touch* of the flu.] **7.** the way in which a person strikes the keys or strings of a musical instrument. **—in touch with,** in contact with, as by meeting or talking with. **—out of touch with,** no longer in contact with. **—touch off, 1.** to make explode. **2.** to begin. **—touch up,** to improve by making small changes in.

touch·down (tuch′doun), *n.* **1.** a goal scored in football by putting the ball across the opponent's goal line. **2.** a score of six points made in this way.

touch·ing (tuch′ing), *adj.* that makes one feel pity, sympathy, etc. [a *touching* sight].

touch·stone (tuch′stōn), *n.* **1.** a black stone used at one time to test the purity of gold or silver by rubbing it with the metal and studying the streak made. **2.** any test or standard.

touch·y (tuch′ē), *adj.* **1.** easily hurt, annoyed, made angry, etc.; irritable. **2.** very risky; dangerous [a *touchy* situation]. **—touch′i·er,** *compar.;* **touch′i·est,** *superl.*

tough (tuf), *adj.* **1.** that will bend or twist without tearing or breaking [*tough* rubber]. **2.** that cannot be cut or chewed easily [*tough* meat]. **3.** strong and healthy; robust [a *tough* pioneer]. **4.** very difficult or hard [a *tough* job]. **5.** rough; brutal. **—***n.* a rough, brutal person; thug. **—tough′ness,** *n.*

tough·en (tuf′'n), *v.* to make or become tough or tougher.

tou·pee (tōō pā′), *n.* a small wig for covering a bald spot on the head.

tour (toor), *n.* **1.** a long trip, as for pleasure and sight-seeing. **2.** any round trip, as by actors going from city to city to perform. **—***v.* **1.** to go on a tour. **2.** to take a tour through [to *tour* New England].

tour·ism (toor′iz'm), *n.* the travel of tourists, especially when thought of as a business that brings income to a country.

tour·ist (toor′ist), *n.* a person who tours or travels for pleasure. **—***adj.* of or for tourists.

tour·ma·line (toor′mə lin *or* toor′mə lēn), *n.* a mineral of various colors. Some clear varieties are used as gems.

tour·na·ment (toor′nə mənt), *n.* **1.** a contest in which knights on horseback tried to knock each other off the horses with lances. **2.** a series of contests in some sport or game in which a number of people or teams take part, trying to win the championship. Also **tour·ney** (toor′nē), **tour′neys,** *pl.*

tour·ni·quet (toor′ni ket), *n.* anything used to stop bleeding from a wound by closing off a blood vessel, as a bandage twisted tight with a stick.

tou·sle (tou′z'l), *v.* to make untidy, or muss up; rumple [*tousled* hair]. —**tou′sled**, *p.t. & p.p.;* **tou′sling**, *pr.p.*

tow (tō), *v.* to pull by a rope or chain [A horse *towed* the canal boat.] —*n.* 1. a towing or being towed. 2. something towed. 3. a rope, etc. for towing. —**have in tow** or **take in tow,** to have or take under one's charge.

tow (tō), *n.* the coarse, broken fibers of flax, hemp, etc. before spinning.

toward (tôrd *or* twôrd), *prep.* 1. in the direction of [The house faces *toward* the park.] 2. leading to [steps *toward* peace]. 3. having to do with; about [What is his feeling *toward* you?] 4. just before; near [It became cold *toward* morning.] 5. for [to save *toward* a new car].

towards (tôrdz *or* twôrdz), *prep.* toward.

tow·el (tou′'l *or* toul), *n.* a piece of cloth or soft paper for drying things by wiping.

tow·el·ing or **tow·el·ling** (toul′ing *or* tou′- 'l ing), *n.* material for making towels.

tow·er (tou′ər), *n.* 1. a building that is much higher than it is wide or long, either standing alone or as part of another building [a water *tower;* the bell *tower* of a church]. 2. such a building, used as a fort or stronghold. —*v.* to stand or rise high above others [The giraffe *towers* over other animals.]

tow·er·ing (tou′ər ing), *adj.* very high, great, strong, etc. [a *towering* steeple; a *towering* rage].

tow·head (tō′hed), *n.* a person having very light yellow hair. —**tow′head·ed,** *adj.*

town (toun), *n.* 1. a place where there are a large number of houses and other buildings, larger than a village but smaller than a city. 2. a city. 3. the business center of a city or town [I'm going into *town.*] 4. the people of a town [a friendly *town*].

town hall, a building in which there are the offices of a town government.

town meeting, a meeting of the voters of a town, as in New England, to act on town business.

town·ship (toun′ship), *n.* 1. a part of a county having some powers of government, as control over its schools and roads. 2. in United States land surveys, a division six miles square.

towns·man (tounz′mən), *n.* 1. a person who lives in a town. 2. a person who lives in the same town with one. —**towns′men,** *pl.*

towns·peo·ple (tounz′pē′p'l), *n.pl.* the people of a town: also **towns·folk** (tounz′fōk).

tox·ic (täk′sik), *adj.* of or caused by a toxin, or poison [the *toxic* effects of some berries].

tox·in (täk′sin), *n.* 1. a poison produced by some bacteria, viruses, etc., causing certain diseases. 2. any poison produced by an animal or plant [Snake venom is a *toxin.*]

toy (toi), *n.* 1. a thing to play with; especially, a plaything for children. 2. anything small and of little value. —*adj.* 1. like a toy in size or use [a *toy* dog]. 2. made for use as a toy; especially, made as a small model [a *toy* train]. —*v.* to play or trifle [The boy just *toyed* with his food.]

trace (trās), *n.* 1. a mark, track, sign, etc. left by someone or something [no human *trace* on the island]. 2. a very small amount [a *trace* of garlic in the dressing]. —*v.* 1. to follow or move along, as a path or course. 2. to follow the trail of; track [to *trace* a lion to his den]. 3. to follow or study the course of [We *traced* the history of Rome back to Caesar.] 4. to copy a picture, drawing, etc. by following its lines on a thin piece of paper placed over it. 5. to draw, sketch, outline, etc. —**traced,** *p.t. & p.p.;* **trac′ing,** *pr.p.*

trace (trās), *n.* either of two straps, chains, etc. by which a horse is fastened to the wagon, cart, etc. that it pulls.

trac·er·y (trās′ər ē), *n.* any graceful design, as in carving, of lines that come together in various ways. —**trac′er·ies,** *pl.*

tra·che·a (trā′ki ə), *n.* the windpipe. —**tra·che·ae** (trā′ki ē), *pl.*

examples of tracery

trac·ing (trās′ing), *n.* 1. the action of one that traces. 2. something traced, as a copy of a picture or drawing.

track (trak), *n.* 1. a mark left in passing, as a footprint or wheel rut. 2. a path or trail. 3. steel rails, usually in pairs, on which the wheels of trains, etc. run. 4. a path or course, often in an oval, laid out for racing. 5. sports performed on such a track, as running or hurdling; also, such sports together with those held in the **field** (*meaning 8*). 6. a course of action; way of doing something [He's on the right *track* to solve the problem.] —*v.* 1. to follow the tracks of [We *tracked* the fox to its den.] 2. to make tracks or dirty marks [The boys *tracked* up the clean floor.] 3. to make tracks with [The dog *tracked* snow into the house.] —*adj.* of or having to do with sports held on a track [a *track* meet]. —**in one's tracks,** where one is at the moment. —**keep track of,** to go on knowing or being informed about. —**lose track of,** to stop knowing or being informed about. —**track′er,** *n.*

track·less (trak′lis), *adj.* 1. without a track or path [a *trackless* wilderness]. 2. not running on rails [a *trackless* trolley].

tract (trakt), *n.* 1. a large stretch of land, etc. 2. a number of parts or organs in the body that work together in carrying out some function [the digestive *tract*].

tract (trakt), *n.* a booklet or pamphlet, especially one on a religious subject.

trac·ta·ble (trak/tə b'l), *adj.* **1.** easy to control, train, etc.; not stubborn or disobedient [a *tractable* horse]. **2.** easy to shape or work with [a *tractable* metal].

trac·tion (trak/shən), *n.* **1.** the power to grip or hold to a surface while moving, without slipping [The tires lost *traction* on the icy hill, and the car slid backward.] **2.** the act of pulling or drawing a load over a surface. **3.** the pulling power of a locomotive, etc.

trac·tor (trak/tər), *n.* **1.** a powerful motor vehicle for pulling farm machinery, heavy loads, etc. **2.** a kind of truck with a driver's cab and no body, used to haul large trailers.

tractor

trade (trād), *n.* **1.** any work done with the hands that needs special skill got by training [the plumber's *trade*]. **2.** all those in a certain business or kind of work [the book *trade*]. **3.** buying and selling; commerce [Tariffs restrict *trade* between nations.] **4.** customers [This sale will bring in the *trade*.] **5.** the act of giving one thing for another; exchange [an even *trade* of his marbles for my jackknife]. **6.** **trades,** *pl.* the trade winds. —*v.* **1.** to carry on a business; buy and sell [This company *trades* in tea. Our country *trades* with other countries.] **2.** to exchange [I *traded* my stamp collection for John's camera.] **3.** to be a customer: *used only in everyday talk* [We *trade* at the corner grocery.] —**trade in,** to give an old or used thing as part of the payment for a new one. —**trade on** or **trade upon,** to take advantage of [He *traded on* his war record to get votes.] —**trad/ed,** *p.t. & p.p.;* **trad/ing,** *pr.p.*

trade·mark or **trade-mark** (trād/märk/), *n.* a special picture, mark, word, etc. placed on a product to show who its maker or dealer is. Trademarks are usually protected by law.

trade name, **1.** a name used as a trademark. **2.** the name used for a certain article by those who deal in it. **3.** the business name of a company.

trad·er (trād/ər), *n.* **1.** a person who trades; merchant. **2.** a ship used in trade.

trade school, a school where trades are taught.

trades·man (trādz/mən), *n.* a person in business; especially, a storekeeper. —**trades/men,** *pl.*

trade union, a labor union.

trade wind, a wind that blows without stopping from the northeast or southeast toward the equator.

trad·ing post (trād/ing), a store in a frontier town, etc., where trading is done.

tra·di·tion (trə dish/ən), *n.* **1.** the handing down of customs, beliefs, stories, etc. from generation to generation by word of mouth rather than in written records. **2.** a custom, belief, etc. handed down in this way [It's a *tradition* to eat turkey at Thanksgiving.]

tra·di·tion·al (trə dish/ən 'l), *adj.* of or handed down by tradition; customary [a *traditional* costume]. —**tra·di/tion·al·ly,** *adv.*

tra·duce (trə do͞os/ *or* trə dyo͞os/), *v.* to say false things so as to harm the reputation of; slander. —**tra·duced/,** *p.t. & p.p.;* **tra·duc/-ing,** *pr.p.* —**tra·duc/er,** *n.*

traf·fic (traf/ik), *n.* **1.** the movement or number of automobiles, persons, ships, etc. along a road or route of travel [to direct *traffic* on city streets; the heavy *traffic* on weekends]. **2.** the amount of business done by a railroad, air line, etc. **3.** buying and selling, often of a wrong or unlawful kind; trade; commerce [the 19th-century *traffic* in slaves.] **4.** dealings [I'll have no *traffic* with his kind.] —*adj.* of, for, or controlling traffic [a *traffic* light]. —*v.* to carry on traffic, or trade, often of an unlawful kind. —**traf/ficked,** *p.t. & p.p.;* **traf/fick·ing,** *pr.p.*

tra·ge·di·an (trə jē/di ən), *n.* an actor or writer of tragedy, mainly of earlier times.

trag·e·dy (traj/ə dē), *n.* **1.** a serious play with a sad ending. **2.** a very sad or tragic happening. —**trag/e·dies,** *pl.*

trag·ic (traj/ik), *adj.* **1.** of, like, or having to do with tragedy [a *tragic* actor; a *tragic* tale]. **2.** bringing great harm, suffering, etc.; dreadful [a *tragic* accident; a *tragic* misunderstanding]. —**trag/i·cal·ly,** *adv.*

trail (trāl), *v.* **1.** to drag or bring along behind [The bride's veil *trailed* on the floor. He *trailed* dirt into the house.] **2.** to flow or drift behind, as smoke. **3.** to follow or lag behind [The children *trailed* along after us. He is *trailing* in the race.] **4.** to follow the trail of, as in hunting; track. **5.** to grow along the ground, etc., as some plants. **6.** to become less or weaker [Her voice *trailed* off into a whisper.] —*n.* **1.** something that trails behind [a *trail* of dust]. **2.** a mark, scent, etc. left behind. **3.** a path through woods, etc.

trail·er (trāl/ər), *n.* **1.** a person or animal that trails another. **2.** a wagon, van, cart, etc. made to be pulled by an automobile, truck, or tractor. Some trailers are outfitted as homes.

train (trān), *n.* **1.** something that drags along behind, as a trailing skirt. **2.** a group of followers or attendants, as of a king. **3.** a group of persons, cars, etc. moving in a line; procession [a wagon *train* heading West]. **4.** a series of connected things [a *train* of thought; a gear *train*]. **5.** a line of connected railroad cars pulled by a locomotive. —*v.* **1.** to develop the mind, character, etc. of; rear [They *trained* their children to be kind.] **2.** to teach, or give practice in, some skill [to *train* airplane pilots; to *train* animals to do tricks]. **3.** to make or become fit for some sport, as by exercise, practice, etc. **4.** to make

dress with a train

grow in a certain direction [to *train* roses along a trellis]. **5.** to aim [Four guns were *trained* on the target.] —**train′er**, *n*.

train·ee (trān ē′), *n.* a person who is being trained in something.

train·ing (trān′ing), *n.* **1.** the practice, drills, etc. given by one who trains or received by one who is being trained. **2.** the condition of being trained for some sport, as by exercise, practice, etc.

train·man (trān′mən), *n.* a man who works on a railroad train. —**train′men**, *pl.*

traipse (trāps), *v.* to walk or wander in an aimless and lazy way: *used in some regions.* —**traipsed**, *p.t. & p.p.;* **traips′ing**, *pr.p.*

trait (trāt), *n.* a special quality, as of one's character [A sense of humor is his finest *trait*.]

trai·tor (trā′tər), *n.* a person who betrays his country, friends, a cause, etc.

trai·tor·ous (trā′tər əs), *adj.* of or like a traitor or treason; treacherous.

tra·jec·to·ry (trə jek′tər ē), *n.* the curved path followed by something thrown or shot through space, as a bullet. —**tra·jec′to·ries**, *pl.*

tram (tram), *n.* **1.** an open railway car used in mines for carrying loads. **2.** a streetcar: *a British meaning.*

tram·mel (tram′'l), *n.* **1.** anything that holds back, hinders, etc., as a shackle for a horse. **2.** a net for catching birds or fish. **3.** a pothook. —*v.* to keep from acting or moving freely; restrain, hinder, etc. [*trammeled* by harsh laws]. —**tram′meled** or **tram′melled**, *p.t. & p.p.;* **tram′mel·ing** or **tram′mel·ling**, *pr.p.*

tramp (tramp), *v.* **1.** to walk with heavy steps. **2.** to step heavily; stamp [The horse *tramped* on my foot.] **3.** to walk; roam about on foot [We *tramped* through the woods.] —*n.* **1.** a person who wanders from place to place, doing odd jobs or begging; vagrant. **2.** a journey on foot; hike [a *tramp* through the woods]. **3.** the sound of heavy steps. **4.** a freight ship that has no regular route, but picks up cargo wherever it can.

tram·ple (tram′p'l), *v.* **1.** to tread or step hard on. **2.** to crush, hurt, etc., as by stepping on [A herd of buffaloes *trampled* the crops.] —**tram′pled**, *p.t. & p.p.;* **tram′pling**, *pr.p.*

tram·po·line (tram′pə lin *or* tram′pə lēn), *n.* a strong net or piece of canvas stretched tightly on a frame, used as a kind of springboard in acrobatic tumbling.

tram·way (tram′-wā), *n.* a streetcar track: *a British word.*

trance (trans), *n.* **1.** a condition like sleep brought on by shock, hypnosis, etc., in which a person seems to be conscious but is unable to

trampoline

move or act of his own will. **2.** the condition of being completely lost in thought.

tran·quil (trang′kwil), *adj.* calm, quiet, peaceful, etc. [*tranquil* waters; a *tranquil* mood]. —**tran·quil′li·ty** or **tran·quil′i·ty**, *n.* —**tran′quil·ly**, *adv.*

tran·quil·ize or **tran·quil·lize** (trang′kwə līz), *v.* to make or become tranquil. —**tran′quil·ized** or **tran′quil·lized**, *p.t. & p.p.;* **tran′quil·iz·ing** or **tran′quil·liz·ing**, *pr.p.*

tran·quil·iz·er or **tran·quil·liz·er** (trang′-kwə līz ər), *n.* a drug used to calm the nerves.

trans-, a prefix meaning "over," "across," or "beyond" [A *transatlantic* cable is a cable that extends across the Atlantic.]

trans·act (tran sakt′ *or* tran zakt′), *v.* to carry on, do, complete, etc. [He has some business to *transact* in the city.]

trans·ac·tion (tran sak′shən *or* tran zak′shən), *n.* **1.** a transacting, as of business. **2.** something transacted, as a piece of business. **3.** **transactions**, *pl.* the minutes of a meeting.

trans·at·lan·tic (trans′ət lan′tik), *adj.* **1.** crossing the Atlantic [Lindbergh's *transatlantic* flight]. **2.** on the other side of the Atlantic.

tran·scend (tran send′), *v.* **1.** to go beyond the limits of; exceed [His story *transcends* belief.] **2.** to be better or greater than; surpass [Her beauty *transcends* that of others.]

tran·scend·ent (tran sen′dənt), *adj.* far beyond the usual or ordinary; superior; extraordinary [her *transcendent* wisdom].

tran·scen·den·tal (tran′sen den′t'l), *adj.* **1.** transcendent. **2.** supernatural.

trans·con·ti·nen·tal (trans′kän tə nen′t'l), *adj.* that goes from one side of a continent to the other [a *transcontinental* airplane flight].

tran·scribe (tran skrīb′), *v.* **1.** to write out or type out in full [She took down his speech in shorthand and then *transcribed* her notes.] **2.** to make a transcription of for radio. —**tran·scribed′**, *p.t. & p.p.;* **tran·scrib′ing**, *pr.p.*

tran·script (tran′skript), *n.* a copy, especially one made by writing or typing.

tran·scrip·tion (tran skrip′shən), *n.* **1.** the act of transcribing. **2.** something transcribed; copy. **3.** a recording made for broadcasting later on radio.

tran·sept (tran′sept), *n.* in a church shaped like a cross, the part that forms the arms across the long, main part.

trans·fer (trans fûr′ *or* trans′fər), *v.* **1.** to move, carry, send, or change from one person or place to another [He *transferred* his notes to another notebook. Jill has *transferred* to a new school.] **2.** to move a picture, design, etc. from one surface to another, as by making wet and pressing. **3.** to change from one bus, train, etc. to another. —*n.* (trans′fər), **1.** a transferring or being transferred. **2.** a thing or a person that is transferred [John is a *transfer* from another school.] **3.** a ticket that allows one to change from one bus, train, etc. to another. —**trans·ferred′**, *p.t.* & *p.p.*; **trans·fer′ing**, *pr.p.* —**trans·fer′a·ble**, *adj.*

trans·fer·ence (trans fûr′əns), *n.* a transferring or being transferred.

trans·fig·u·ra·tion (trans fig′yoo rā′shən), *n.* **1.** a change in form or looks. **2. Transfiguration,** in the Bible, the change that appeared in Jesus on the mountain.

trans·fig·ure (trans fig′yoor), *v.* **1.** to change the form or looks of; transform [A new dress and hair-do *transfigured* her.] **2.** to make seem splendid or glorious [He was *transfigured* by his deep love.] —**trans·fig′ured**, *p.t.* & *p.p.*; **trans·fig′ur·ing**, *pr.p.*

trans·fix (trans fiks′), *v.* **1.** to pierce through, as with an arrow. **2.** to make unable to move, as if pierced through [*transfixed* with horror].

trans·form (trans fôrm′), *v.* **1.** to change the form or looks of [A vase of roses *transformed* the drab room.] **2.** to change the nature or condition of [The barn has been *transformed* into a house.] —**trans′for·ma′tion**, *n.*

trans·form·er (trans fôr′mər), *n.* **1.** a person or thing that transforms. **2.** a device that changes the voltage of an electric current.

trans·fuse (trans fyooz′), *v.* **1.** to pass the blood of one person into a vein of another. **2.** to pour in or fill; instill [The victory *transfused* new courage into the team.] —**trans·fused′**, *p.t.* & *p.p.*; **trans·fus′ing**, *pr.p.* —**trans·fu′sion**, *n.*

trans·gress (trans gres′), *v.* **1.** to break a law or rule; do wrong; sin. **2.** to pass over or go beyond [His remark *transgressed* the limits of decency.] —**trans·gres′sor**, *n.*

trans·gres·sion (trans gresh′ən), *n.* the act of transgressing or breaking a law; a sin.

tran·sient (tran′shənt), *adj.* lasting or staying only a short time; temporary [*transient* guests at a hotel; *transient* pleasures]. —*n.* a person who stays for only a short time.

tran·sis·tor (tran zis′tər *or* tran sis′tər), *n.* a tiny electronic device used in place of an electron tube in hearing aids, small radios, etc.

tran·sis·tor·ize (tran zis′tər īz *or* tran sis′tər īz), *v.* to equip with transistors [a *transistorized* portable radio]. —**tran·sis′tor·ized**, *p.t.* & *p.p.*; **tran·sis′tor·iz·ing**, *pr.p.*

trans·it (tran′sit), *n.* **1.** travel or passage through or across. **2.** the act of carrying things from one place to another [The package was lost in *transit*.] **3.** an instrument used by surveyors to measure angles.

tran·si·tion (tran zish′ən *or* tran sish′ən), *n.* the act or process of passing from one condition, form, or place to another [the *transition* from war to peace]. —**tran·si′tion·al**, *adj.*

tran·si·tive (tran′sə tiv), *adj.* describing a

transit *(meaning 3)*

verb that takes a direct object [In the sentence "He saved money to buy a car," "saved" and "buy" are *transitive* verbs.]

tran·si·to·ry (tran′sə tôr′ē), *adj.* lasting only a short time; temporary [*transitory* fame].

trans·late (trans lāt′), *v.* **1.** to put into the words of a different language [to *translate* a Latin poem into English]. **2.** to change into another form [to *translate* ideas into action]. **3.** to change from one place or condition to another; especially, to carry up to heaven —**trans·lat′ed**, *p.t.* & *p.p.*; **trans·lat′ing**, *pr.p.*

trans·la·tion (trans lā′shən), *n.* **1.** the act of translating. **2.** writing or speech translated into a different language.

trans·la·tor (trans lā′tər), *n.* a person who translates from one language into another.

trans·lu·cent (trans loo′s'nt), *adj.* letting light pass through but not allowing things on the other side to be seen clearly [Tissue paper is *translucent*.]

trans·mi·gra·tion (trans′mī grā′shən), *n.* **1.** the act of moving from one region, country, etc. to another. **2.** in some religions, the passing of the soul into another body after one dies.

trans·mis·sion (trans mish′ən), *n.* **1.** the act of transmitting or passing something along [the *transmission* of messages by telegraph]. **2.** something transmitted. **3.** the part of a car that sends the power from the engine to the wheels. **4.** the moving of radio waves through space.

trans·mit (trans mit′), *v.* **1.** to send from one person or place to another; pass on; transfer [to *transmit* a disease; to *transmit* a letter; to *transmit* power from an engine by means of gears]. **2.** to hand down as by heredity [Color blindness may be *transmitted*.] **3.** to pass or let pass, as light, heat, etc. [Water *transmits* sound.] **4.** to send out radio or television signals. —**trans·mit′ted**, *p.t.* & *p.p.*; **trans·mit′ting**, *pr.p.*

trans·mit·ter (trans mit′ər), *n.* **1.** a person or thing that transmits. **2.** the part of a telegraph or telephone that sends out sounds or signals. **3.** the apparatus for sending out electric waves in radio and television.

trans·mute (trans myoot′), *v.* to change from one form, kind, thing, etc. into another [Alchemists tried to *transmute* lead into gold.] —**trans·mut′ed**, *p.t.* & *p.p.*; **trans·mut′ing**, *pr.p.* —**trans′mu·ta′tion**, *n.*

tran·som (tran′səm), *n.* **1.** a small window just above a door or other window. It is usually hinged to the crossbar below it, to allow it to be opened. **2.** this crossbar.

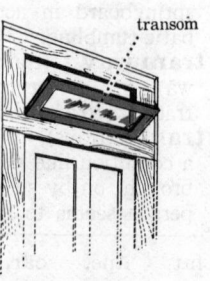

transom

tran·son·ic *or* **trans·son·ic** (tran sän′ik), *adj.* of or having to do with a range of speeds just above and below the speed of sound.

trans·par·ent (trans per′ənt), *adj.* **1.** so clear, or so fine, it can be seen through [*transparent* glass; a *transparent* veil]. **2.** plain to see or understand; clear [a *transparent* lie].

tran·spire (tran spīr/), *v.* **1.** to give off vapor, moisture, etc., as through pores. **2.** to become known. **3.** to take place; happen: *considered a loose or incorrect meaning by some people* [What *transpired* while I was gone?] —**tran·spired/**, *p.t. & p.p.*; **tran·spir/ing**, *pr.p.*

trans·plant (trans plant/), *v.* **1.** to dig up from one place and plant in another. **2.** to graft tissue in surgery.

trans·port (trans pôrt/), *v.* **1.** to carry from one place to another [to *transport* goods by train or truck]. **2.** to cause strong feelings in [*transported* with delight]. **3.** to send to a place far away as a punishment. —*n.* (trans/pôrt), **1.** a carrying from one place to another. **2.** a ship, airplane, etc. used for transporting freight, soldiers, etc. **3.** a strong feeling, as of delight.

trans·por·ta·tion (trans/pər tā/shən), *n.* **1.** a transporting or being transported. **2.** a system or business of transporting things. **3.** fare or a ticket for being transported.

trans·pose (trans pōz/), *v.* **1.** to change about in order or position; interchange [Don't *transpose* the *e* and the *i* in "weird."] **2.** to change the key of a piece of music. —**trans·posed/**, *p.t. & p.p.*; **trans·pos/ing**, *pr.p.* —**trans·po·si·tion** (trans/pə zish/ən), *n.*

trans·verse (trans vûrs/), *adj.* lying or placed across; set crosswise [*transverse* beams].

trap (trap), *n.* **1.** any device for catching animals, as one that snaps shut tightly when it is stepped on. **2.** a trick used to fool or catch someone [His question was a *trap* to make her tell the truth.] **3.** a bend in a drainpipe, shaped like a U, where some water stays to hold back bad-smelling gases coming from the sewer. **4.** a device for throwing targets into the air for trapshooting. **5.** a light carriage with two wheels. **6.** a trap door. **7. traps,** *pl.* the drums, cymbals, etc. in an orchestra or band. —*v.* **1.** to catch in a trap. **2.** to set traps to catch animals. —**trapped,** *p.t. & p.p.*; **trap/ping,** *pr.p.*

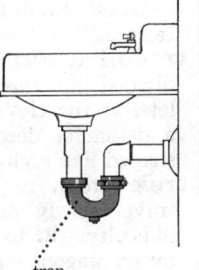

trap

trap door, a door in a roof or floor.

tra·peze (trə pēz/), *n.* a short crossbar hung by two ropes, on which acrobats do stunts.

trap·e·zoid (trap/ə zoid), *n.* a flat figure with four sides, two of which are parallel.

trap·per (trap/ər), *n.* a person who traps wild animals, especially for their furs.

trapezoid

trap·pings (trap/ingz), *n.pl.* **1.** highly decorated coverings for a horse. **2.** highly decorated clothing or ornaments.

trap·shoot·ing (trap/shoot/ing), *n.* the sport of shooting at clay targets tossed in the air.

trash (trash), *n.* **1.** anything thrown away as worthless; rubbish. **2.** nonsense. —**trash/y,** *adj.*

trav·ail (trav/āl *or* trə vāl/), *n.* **1.** very hard work; labor. **2.** the pains of childbirth. **3.** great pain; agony. —*v.* **1.** to toil or work hard. **2.** to suffer the pains of childbirth.

trav·el (trav/'l), *v.* **1.** to go from one place to another [a salesman who spends much time *traveling*]. **2.** to make a journey over or through [to *travel* a road]. **3.** to move or pass [A train *travels* on tracks. Light *travels* faster than sound.] —*n.* **1.** the act of traveling. **2. travels,** *pl.* trips, journeys, etc. —**trav/eled** *or* **trav/elled,** *p.t. & p.p.*; **trav/el·ing** *or* **trav/el·ling,** *pr.p.* —**trav/el·er** *or* **trav/el·ler,** *n.*

trav·eled *or* **trav·elled** (trav/'ld), *adj.* **1.** that has traveled much. **2.** much used by those who travel [a *traveled* road].

trav·e·logue *or* **trav·e·log** (trav/ə lôg), *n.* **1.** a lecture describing travels, usually given with pictures. **2.** a movie of travels.

trav·erse (trav/ərs *or* trə vûrs/), *v.* to pass over, across, or through; cross [Pioneers *traversed* the plains in covered wagons.] —*n.* something that traverses or crosses, as a crossbar. —*adj.* **1.** lying across. **2.** describing drapes hung in pairs so that they can be drawn by pulling cords. —**trav/ersed,** *p.t. & p.p.*; **trav/ers·ing** *pr.p.*

trav·es·ty (trav/is tē), *n.* **1.** an imitation of something done in such a way as to make it seem ridiculous; burlesque. **2.** a crude or ridiculous example of something [a *travesty* of justice]. —*v.* to imitate so as to make seem ridiculous. —**trav/es·ties,** *pl.* —**trav/es·tied,** *p.t. & p.p.*; **trav/es·ty·ing,** *pr.p.*

trawl (trôl), *n.* **1.** a large fishing net dragged by a boat along the bottom of a shallow part of the sea. **2.** a long line held up by buoys, from which baited fishing lines are hung. —*v.* to fish or catch with a trawl.

trawl

trawl·er (trôl/ər), *n.* a boat used in trawling.

tray (trā), *n.* a flat piece of wood, metal, etc., often with a low rim, for carrying food or other things.

treach·er·ous (trech/ər əs), *adj.* **1.** not loyal or faithful; betraying or likely to betray. **2.** seeming safe, reliable, etc. but not really so [*treacherous* rocks]. —**treach/er·ous·ly,** *adv.*

treach·er·y (trech/ər ē), *n.* **1.** the act of betraying those who have their trust or faith in one. **2.** treason. —**treach/er·ies,** *pl.*

---

fat, āpe, cär, ten, ēven, hit, bīte, gō, hôrn, tōōl, book, up, fûr; get, joy, yet, chin, she, thin, *th*en; zh = s in pleasure; ' as in able (ā/b'l); ə = a in ago, e in agent, i in sanity, o in confess, u in focus.

trea·cle (trē′k'l), *n.* molasses: *mainly a British word.*

tread (tred), *v.* **1.** to walk on, in, along, or over [We *trod* the dusty road for hours.] **2.** to beat or press with the feet; trample [to *tread* grapes in making wine]. **3.** to do or follow by walking, dancing, etc. [They *tread* the measures gaily.] —*n.* **1.** a way or sound of treading [We heard a heavy *tread* on the stairs.] **2.** the part on which a person or thing treads or moves, as the upper surface of a stair, or the outer part of the rim of a wheel. —**tread on air,** to be gay or happy. —**tread water,** to keep the body upright and the head above water by kicking the legs. —**trod** or, for *tread water,* **tread′ed,** *p.t.;* **trod′den** or **trod,** *p.p.;* **tread′ing,** *pr.p.*

trea·dle (tred′l), *n.* a lever worked by the foot, as to turn a wheel. —*v.* to work a treadle. —**trea′dled,** *p.t. & p.p.;* **trea′dling,** *pr.p.*

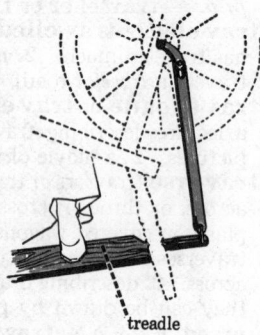
treadle

tread·mill (tred′mil), *n.* **1.** a mill or other device worked by persons or animals walking on steps about the rim of a wheel or treading on an endless belt. **2.** any monotonous series of tasks that never seems to end.

treas., abbreviation for **treasurer, treasury.**

trea·son (trē′z'n), *n.* the act of betraying one's country, especially by helping the enemy in time of war.

trea·son·a·ble (trē′z'n ə b'l) or **trea·son·ous** (trē′z'n əs), *adj.* having to do with treason.

treas·ure (trezh′ər), *n.* **1.** money, jewels, etc. collected and stored up. **2.** a person or thing that is loved or held dear. —*v.* **1.** to love or hold dear; cherish [I *treasure* their friendship.] **2.** to store away or save up, as money; hoard. —**treas′ured,** *p.t. & p.p.;* **treas′ur·ing,** *pr.p.*

treas·ur·er (trezh′ər ər), *n.* a person in charge of a treasury, as of a government, company, club, etc.

treas·ure-trove (trezh′ər trōv′), *n.* treasure found hidden, whose owner is not known.

treas·ur·y (trezh′ər ē), *n.* **1.** the money or funds of a country, company, club, etc. **2. Treasury,** the department of government in charge of issuing money, collecting taxes, etc. **3.** a place where money is kept. **4.** a collection of treasures in art, literature, etc. —**treas′ur·ies,** *pl.*

treat (trēt), *v.* **1.** to deal with or act toward in a certain way [He *treats* all people with respect. Don't *treat* this matter lightly.] **2.** to try to cure or heal, as with medicine [The doctor *treated* my cuts.] **3.** to act upon, as by adding something [The water is *treated* with chlorine.] **4.** to pay for the food, entertainment, etc. of [Uncle Ed *treated* us to the movies.] **5.** to discuss business or terms; negotiate. —*n.* **1.** the act of treating another, as to food or entertainment. **2.** the

food, entertainment, etc. paid for by another. **3.** anything that gives great pleasure [It was a *treat* to hear the children sing.] —**treat of,** to deal with in speaking or writing; discuss.

trea·tise (trē′tis), *n.* a book or long article dealing with some subject in a detailed way.

treat·ment (trēt′mənt), *n.* **1.** act or way of dealing with a person or thing [kind *treatment*]. **2.** the use of medicine, surgery, etc. to try to cure or heal.

treat·y (trē′tē), *n.* an agreement between two or more nations, having to do with peace, trade, etc. —**trea′ties,** *pl.*

tre·ble (treb′'l), *n.* **1.** the highest part in musical harmony; soprano. **2.** a singer or instrument that takes this part. **3.** a high-pitched voice or sound. —*adj.* **1.** of or for the treble. **2.** high-pitched; shrill. **3.** triple. —*v.* to make or become three times as much; triple. —**tre′bled,** *p.t. & p.p.;* **tre′bling,** *pr.p.*

treble clef, a sign on a musical staff showing that the notes on the staff are above middle C. *See the picture for* **clef.**

tre·bly (treb′lē), *adv.* three times; triply.

tree (trē), *n.* **1.** a large, woody plant with a long trunk having many branches from the upper part. **2.** a wooden beam, bar, post, etc. [a clothes *tree;* a single *tree* on a wagon]. **3.** anything like a tree, as in having many branches [A family *tree* is a diagram of a family line.] —*v.* to chase up a tree [The pack of dogs *treed* a possum.] —**up a tree,** in some trouble that is hard to get out of: *used only in everyday talk.* —**treed,** *p.t. & p.p.;* **tree′ing,** *pr.p.* —**tree′less,** *adj.*

tre·foil (trē′foil), *n.* **1.** a plant with leaves divided into three leaflets, as the clover. **2.** a design or decoration shaped like such a leaf.

trek (trek), *v.* **1.** to travel slowly or with difficulty. **2.** to travel by ox wagon: *an old meaning in South Africa.* —*n.* a long, slow journey. —**trekked,** *p.t. & p.p.;* **trek′king,** *pr.p.*

trefoils (*meaning 2*)

trel·lis (trel′is), *n.* a frame of crossed strips, as of wood, on which vines or other climbing plants are grown; lattice.

trem·ble (trem′b'l), *v.* **1.** to shake from cold, fear, weakness, excitement, etc. **2.** to quiver or quake [The earth *trembled*.] —*n.* the act or a fit of trembling. —**trem′bled,** *p.t. & p.p.;* **trem′bling,** *pr.p.* —**trem′bly,** *adj.*

tre·men·dous (tri men′dəs), *adj.* **1.** very large or great; enormous: the earlier meaning was "so great or dreadful as to make one tremble." **2.** wonderful, very fine, etc.: *used only in everyday talk.* —**tre·men′dous·ly,** *adv.*

trem·or (trem′ər *or* trē′mər), *n.* **1.** a shaking or trembling. **2.** a quivering or tingling feeling of excitement; nervous thrill.

trem·u·lous (trem′yoo ləs), *adj.* **1.** trembling or quivering [a *tremulous* voice]. **2.** fearful or timid. —**trem′u·lous·ly,** *adv.*

trench (trench), *n.* **1.** a ditch; deep furrow. **2.** a long ditch with earth banked in front, used to protect soldiers in battle. —*v.* to dig a trench in.

trench·ant (tren′chənt), *adj.* sharp and clear; keen; to the point [*trenchant* thinking].

trench·er (tren′chər), *n.* in earlier times, a wooden platter for carving and serving meat.

trench·er·man (tren′chər mən), *n.* an eater; especially, a heavy eater. —**trench′er·men,** *pl.*

trend (trend), *n.* the general direction or course; drift [the *trend* of public opinion]. —*v.* to take a certain direction or course; tend.

Tren·ton (tren′tən), *n.* the capital of New Jersey, on the Delaware River.

trep·i·da·tion (trep′ə dā′shən), *n.* **1.** a fearful feeling; dread. **2.** a trembling or tremor.

tres·pass (tres′pəs *or* tres′pas), *v.* **1.** to go on another's property without permission or right ["No *trespassing*" means "keep out."] **2.** to break in on; intrude [to *trespass* on one's privacy]. **3.** to do wrong; sin. —*n.* **1.** the act of trespassing. **2.** a sin or wrong. —**tres′pass·er,** *n.*

tress (tres), *n.* a long lock or braid of hair.

tres·tle (tres′'l), *n.* **1.** a frame like a sawhorse, used to support a table top, etc. **2.** a framework of uprights and crosspieces, supporting a bridge, etc.

tri-, a prefix meaning: **1.** having three [A *triangle* is a figure having three angles.] **2.** three times; into three [To *trisect* an angle is to divide it into three equal parts.] **3.** happening every three [A *triweekly* event takes place once every three weeks.]

tri·ad (trī′ad), *n.* a group of three.

tri·al (trī′əl), *n.* **1.** the act of hearing a case in a law court to decide whether the claim or charge is true [The *trial* proved him innocent.] **2.** the act of trying; effort; try [He was allowed two *trials* at the high jump.] **3.** the act of trying or testing; test [the *trial* of a new rocket.] **4.** a test of one's faith, patience, etc. [the *trial* of Job]. **5.** something that troubles or annoys one [His stubborn son is a great *trial* to him.] —*adj.* of or for a trial or test [a *trial* run; a *trial* sample]. —**on trial,** in the process of being tried.

trial and error, a trying or testing over and over again until the right result is found.

tri·an·gle (trī′ang′g'l), *n.* **1.** a flat figure with three sides and three angles. **2.** anything shaped like this. **3.** a musical instrument that is a steel rod bent in a triangle. It makes a high, tingling sound when struck with a metal rod.

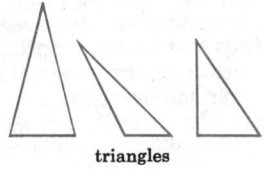
triangles

tri·an·gu·lar (trī ang′gyoo lər), *adj.* of or shaped like a triangle; having three corners.

tribe (trīb), *n.* **1.** a group of people or families living together under a leader or chief [the Indian *tribes* of North America]. **2.** any group of people having the same work or interests [the *tribe* of newspapermen]. **3.** any group or class, as of animals or plants. —**trib′al,** *adj.*

tribes·man (trībz′mən), *n.* a member of a tribe. —**tribes′men,** *pl.*

trib·u·la·tion (trib′yoo lā′shən), *n.* great misery or trouble [the *tribulations* of the poor].

tri·bu·nal (tri byoo′n'l *or* trī byoo′n'l), *n.* a court of justice.

trib·une (trib′yoon *or* tri byoon′), *n.* **1.** an official in ancient Rome whose duty was to protect the rights and interests of the lower classes. **2.** any person who defends the people.

trib·une (trib′yoon), *n.* a raised platform for speakers.

trib·u·tar·y (trib′yoo ter′ē), *n.* **1.** a stream or river that flows into a larger one. **2.** a nation that pays tribute or is under the power of another nation. —*adj.* **1.** flowing into a larger one [a *tributary* stream]. **2.** paying tribute to another, or under another's power [a *tributary* nation]. —**trib′u·tar·ies,** *pl.*

trib·ute (trib′yoot), *n.* **1.** something given, done, or said to show thanks or respect [He wrote a poem as a *tribute* to his mother.] **2.** money that one nation is forced to pay to another, more powerful nation. **3.** any forced payment.

trice (trīs), *n.* a moment: *now used only in the phrase* **in a trice,** *meaning* "in a very short time."

trick (trik), *n.* **1.** something that is done to fool, outwit, cheat, etc. [Her tears were just a *trick* to get sympathy.] **2.** a piece of playful mischief; prank. **3.** a clever or skillful act [Can you do any card *tricks?*] **4.** the right or skillful way; knack [the *trick* of making good gravy]. **5.** a personal habit [his *trick* of tugging at his ear.] **6.** a time or turn at work; shift [He's on the night *trick.*] **7.** the cards played in a single round of a card game. —*v.* to work a trick on; fool, outwit, cheat, etc. —*adj.* **1.** done by a trick [*trick* photography]. **2.** that tricks [a *trick* question]. —**do the trick,** to bring about what is wanted. —**trick out** or **trick up,** to dress up.

trick·er·y (trik′ər ē), *n.* the act of tricking or cheating. —**trick′er·ies,** *pl.*

trick·le (trik′'l), *v.* **1.** to flow slowly in a thin stream or fall in drops [Rain *trickled* down the window.] **2.** to move little by little [The crowd *trickled* away.] —*n.* a thin flow or drip. —**trick′led,** *p.t.* & *p.p.;* **trick′ling,** *pr.p.*

trick·ster (trik′stər), *n.* a person who tricks.

trick·y (trik′ē), *adj.* **1.** using tricks; fooling or cheating [a *tricky* scheme]. **2.** hard or difficult [a *tricky* problem]. —**trick′i·er,** *compar.;* **trick′i·est,** *superl.* —**trick′i·ness,** *n.*

tri·col·or (trī′kul ər), *n.* a flag having three colors, especially the flag of France. —*adj.* having three colors. —**tri′col·ored,** *adj.*

tri·cy·cle (trī/si k'l), *n.* a toy machine for children, like a bicycle, but with one wheel in front and two in back.

tri·dent (trī/d'nt), *n.* a spear with three prongs: *see the picture of* **Neptune.** —*adj.* having three prongs.

tricycle

tried (trīd), past tense and past participle of **try.** —*adj.* tested or trustworthy [a *tried* recipe; a friend, *tried* and true].

tri·en·ni·al (trī en/i əl), *adj.* **1.** happening once every three years [a *triennial* convention]. **2.** lasting for three years. —*n.* something that happens every three years. —**tri·en/ni·al·ly,** *adv.*

tri·er (trī/ər), *n.* a person who tries.

tries (trīz), **1.** the form of the verb **try** used in the present with *he, she,* or *it.* **2.** the plural of the noun **try.**

Tri·este (tri est/), *n.* a city in northeastern Italy, on the Adriatic.

tri·fle (trī/f'l), *n.* **1.** a thing of little value or importance. **2.** a small amount; bit. **3.** a small sum of money. —*v.* **1.** to talk or act in a joking way; deal lightly [He's not a person to *trifle* with.] **2.** to play or toy [Don't *trifle* with your food.] **3.** to spend in an idle way; waste [to *trifle* time away]. —**tri/fled,** *p.t. & p.p.;* **tri/fling,** *pr.p.* —**tri/fler,** *n.*

tri·fling (trī/fling), *adj.* **1.** of little value or importance; trivial. **2.** not at all serious; frivolous; fickle.

trig·ger (trig/ər), *n.* **1.** the lever that is pressed by the finger in firing a gun. **2.** any part like this that releases a catch or spring to set off some action, when it is pressed or pulled. —*v.* to set off: *used only in everyday talk* [The fight *triggered* a riot.]

trig·o·nom·e·try (trig/ə näm/ə trē), *n.* the branch of mathematics dealing with the relations between the sides and angles of triangles.

trill (tril), *n.* **1.** a wavering or trembling sound made by playing or singing two close notes back and forth rapidly. **2.** a speech sound made by vibrating the tongue or uvula rapidly, as *r* in some languages. **3.** a bird's warble. —*v.* to speak, sing, or play with a trill.

tril·lion (tril/yən), *n. & adj.* **1.** a thousand billions (1,000,000,000,000) in the United States and France. **2.** a million billion (1,000,000,000,-000,000,000) in Great Britain and Germany.

tril·li·um (tril/i əm), *n.* a wild flower with three leaves and a blossom of three petals.

tril·o·gy (tril/ə jē), *n.* a set of three plays, novels, etc. which form a related group, although each is a complete work. —**tril/-o·gies,** *pl.*

trim (trim), *v.* **1.** to make neat or tidy, especially by clipping, smoothing, etc.

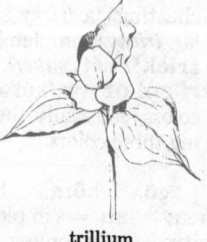
trillium

[to *trim* one's hair]. **2.** to cut, clip, etc. [He *trimmed* dead branches off the tree.] **3.** to decorate [to *trim* a store window]. **4.** to balance a ship, as by shifting cargo. **5.** to put in order for sailing [to *trim* the sails]. **6.** to take a middle position, as in trying to please both sides. **7.** to beat or defeat: *used only in everyday talk.* —*n.* **1.** good condition or order [An athlete must keep in *trim.*] **2.** the act of trimming, as by clipping or cutting. **3.** the decorative woodwork of a building, especially around windows and doors. **4.** the condition of being ready to sail; also, the position of a ship in the water. —*adj.* **1.** neat, tidy, in good condition, etc. **2.** well designed or put together [the *trim* lines of the boat]. —**trimmed,** *p.t. & p.p.;* **trim/ming,** *pr.p.* —**trim/mer,** *compar.;* **trim/mest,** *superl.*

trim·ming (trim/ing), *n.* **1.** something used to trim, as decorations. **2. trimmings,** *pl.* the side dishes of a meal [steak with all the *trimmings*]. **3. trimmings,** *pl.* parts trimmed off.

Trin·i·dad and To·ba·go (trin/ə dad 'n tō-bā/gō), a country on islands in the West Indies.

trin·i·ty (trin/ə tē), *n.* **1.** a set or union of three. **2. Trinity,** the three divine persons (Father, Son, and Holy Ghost) that in the belief of most Christians are united in one divine being. —**trin/i·ties,** *pl.*

trink·et (tring/kit), *n.* **1.** a small ornament, piece of jewelry, etc. **2.** a trifle or toy.

tri·o (trē/ō), *n.* **1.** a piece of music for three voices or three instruments. **2.** the three people who sing or play it. **3.** any group of three. —**tri/os,** *pl.*

trip (trip), *v.* **1.** to stumble or make stumble [I *tripped* over the rug. Bill put out his foot and *tripped* me.] **2.** to make or cause to make a mistake [He *tripped* on the spelling of "rhythm." That question *tripped* us all.] **3.** to walk, run, or dance with light, rapid steps [She *tripped* gaily about the room.] —*n.* **1.** a journey. **2.** a stumble. **3.** the act of tripping someone, as by catching his foot. **4.** a mistake. **5.** the strange, sometimes terrifying, feelings of a person who is under the effects of a psychedelic drug: *a slang meaning.* —**tripped,** *p.t. & p.p.;* **trip/ping,** *pr.p.*

tripe (trīp), *n.* **1.** part of the stomach of a cow, ox, etc., used as food. **2.** anything worthless, disgusting, etc.; nonsense: *slang in this meaning.*

trip·ham·mer (trip/ham/ər) *n.* a heavy hammer driven by power. It is lifted and then let fall over and over again.

tri·ple (trip/'l), *adj.* **1.** made up of three [a *triple* alliance of nations]. **2.** three times as much or as many. —*n.* **1.** an amount three times as much or as many. **2.** a hit in baseball on which the batter gets to third base. —*v.* to make or become three times as much or as many. —**tri/pled,** *p.t. & p.p.;* **tri/pling,** *pr.p.*

trip·let (trip/lit), *n.* **1.** any of three children born at a single birth. **2.** any group of three.

trip·li·cate (trip/lə kit), *adj.* made in three copies exactly alike [a *triplicate* receipt]. —**in triplicate,** in three copies exactly alike.

tri·pod (trī′päd), *n.* a stand, frame, etc. with three legs. Small telescopes are often held up by tripods.

Trip·o·li (trip′ə lē), *n.* a region in northern Africa, now a part of Libya.

trip·ping (trip′ing), *adj.* moving in a quick and easy way; nimble. —**trip′ping·ly,** *adv.*

tri·reme (trī′rēm), *n.* an ancient Greek or Roman warship with three rows of oars on each side, one above the other.

tripod for a telescope

tri·sect (trī sekt′), *v.* to divide into three parts.

trite (trīt), *adj.* used so much that it is no longer fresh or new; stale ["Happy as a lark" is a *trite* expression.] —**trit′er,** *compar.;* **trit′est,** *superl.*

Tri·ton (trī′t'n), *n.* an ancient Greek sea god with the head and body of a man and the tail of a fish.

tri·umph (trī′əmf), *n.* **1.** a victory, as in a battle; success [his *triumph* over illness]. **2.** great joy over a victory or success [He grinned in *triumph* when he won the race.] —*v.* **1.** to be the winner; win victory or success [to *triumph* over an enemy]. **2.** to rejoice over a victory or success. —**tri·um·phal** (trī um′fəl), *adj.*

tri·um·phant (trī um′fənt), *adj.* **1.** having won victory or success; victorious [the *triumphant* team]. **2.** happy or joyful over a victory [a *triumphant* laugh]. —**tri·um′phant·ly,** *adv.*

tri·um·vir (trī um′vər), *n.* in ancient Rome, any one of a ruling group of three officials.

tri·um·vi·rate (trī um′vər it), *n.* **1.** government by a group of three men, or the period of their rule. **2.** any group of three who hold control together.

triv·et (triv′it), *n.* **1.** a small stand with three legs, for holding pots or kettles over or near a fire. **2.** a small stand with short legs, for holding hot dishes on a table.

triv·i·a (triv′i ə), *n.pl.* small, unimportant matters [Her diary was filled with *trivia*.]

triv·i·al (triv′i əl), *adj.* not important; trifling; petty [a *trivial* sum].

triv·i·al·i·ty (triv′i al′ə tē), *n.* **1.** the condition of being trivial. **2.** something trivial; trifle. —**triv′i·al′i·ties,** *pl.*

trod (träd), the past tense and a past participle of **tread.**

trod·den (träd′'n), a past participle of **tread.**

Tro·jan (trō′jən), *adj.* of Troy or its people. —*n.* **1.** a person who was born or who lived in Troy. **2.** a person who is strong and hard-working.

Trojan horse, a huge, hollow wooden horse in a Greek myth, filled with Greek soldiers and left at the gates of Troy. When the Trojans brought it into the city, the soldiers crept out and opened the gates to the Greek army.

Trojan War, in Greek myths, the war that the Greeks fought with Troy to get back Helen, who had been kidnapped by Paris, a prince of Troy.

troll (trōl), *v.* **1.** to fish by pulling a line through the water, usually behind a moving boat. **2.** to sing loudly. **3.** to sing as a round: see **round** (*meaning 11*).

troll (trōl), *n.* in fairy stories, a giant or dwarf that lives in a cave or underground.

trol·ley (träl′ē), *n.* **1.** a device that sends electric current from a wire overhead to the motor of a streetcar, trolley bus, etc. **2.** an electric streetcar: also **trolley car. 3.** a carriage or basket hung from wheels that run on an overhead track. —**trol′leys,** *pl.*

trolley bus, a bus that is run by electricity from a trolley on an overhead wire.

trom·bone (träm′bōn *or* träm bōn′), *n.* a brasswind musical instrument with a long, bent tube that slides in and out to change the tones: also called **slide trombone.**

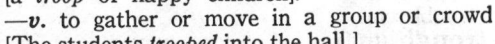

trombone

troop (tro͞op), *n.* **1.** a company of soldiers in the cavalry. **2. troops,** *pl.* soldiers. **3.** a group of from 16 to 32 boy scouts or girl scouts. **4.** any group of persons or animals [a *troop* of happy children]. —*v.* to gather or move in a group or crowd [The students *trooped* into the hall.]

troop·er (tro͞op′ər), *n.* **1.** a soldier in the cavalry. **2.** a mounted policeman.

troop·ship (tro͞op′ship), *n.* a ship used for carrying soldiers.

tro·phy (trō′fē), *n.* anything kept as a token of victory or success, as a deer's head from a hunting trip, a silver cup from a sports contest, or a sword from a battle. —**tro′phies,** *pl.*

trop·ic (träp′ik), *n.* **1.** either of two imaginary circles around the earth, parallel to the equator. The one about 23½ degrees north of the equator is called the **Tropic of Cancer;** the other, about 23½ degrees south, is called the **Tropic of Capricorn. 2. tropics** or **Tropics,** *pl.* the region of the earth that is between these two lines, noted for its hot climate. —*adj.* of the tropics; tropical.

trop·i·cal (träp′i k'l), *adj.* of, in, or like the tropics [*tropical* rains; the *tropical* air of the greenhouse].

trot (trät), *v.* **1.** to step along, as a horse sometimes does, by moving a front leg and the opposite hind leg at the same time. **2.** to ride at a trot. **3.** to run slowly, with a loose, easy motion [boys *trotting* to school]. —*n.* **1.** the movement of a trotting horse. **2.** a slow, jogging run. —**trot′ted,** *p.t. & p.p.;* **trot′ting,** *pr.p.*

troth (trôth), *n.* **1.** a promise, especially to marry; betrothal: see the verb **plight. 2.** truth. *This word is now seldom used.*

fat,   āpe,   cär,   ten,   ēven,   hit,   bīte,   gō,   hôrn,   to͞ol,   book,   up,   fŭr;
get,   joy,   yet,   chin,   she,   thin,   *th*en;   zh = s in pleasure;   ′ as in able (ā′b'l);
ə = a in ago,   e in agent,   i in sanity,   o in confess,   u in focus.

trot·ter (trät/ər), *n.* a horse that trots, especially one trained for special trotting races.

trou·ba·dour (troo/bə-dôr), *n.* any of the poets of the late Middle Ages in France and Italy who wrote and sang poems and ballads of love and knighthood.

trotter

trou·ble (trub/'l), *n.* **1.** worry, care, annoyance, suffering, etc. [a mind free from *trouble*]. **2.** a difficult or unhappy situation; disturbance [We've had no *trouble* with our neighbors.] **3.** a person or thing causing worry, annoyance, difficulty, etc. **4.** effort; bother; great care [He took the *trouble* to thank us.] **5.** a sick condition [heart *trouble*]. —*v.* **1.** to be or give trouble to; worry, annoy, pain, disturb, etc. [He was *troubled* by the bad news. Her back *troubles* her.] **2.** to put or go to extra work; bother [May I *trouble* you for a match? Don't *trouble* to return the pencil.] **3.** to stir up [The waters were *troubled*.] —**trou/·bled,** *p.t. & p.p.;* **trou/bling,** *pr.p.*

trou·ble·some (trub/'l səm), *adj.* giving, trouble; disturbing [a *troublesome* cough].

trou·blous (trub/ləs), *adj.* **1.** full of trouble, confusion or disorder: *no longer much used.* **2.** troublesome.

trough (trôf), *n.* **1.** a long, narrow, open container, especially one from which animals eat or drink. **2.** a gutter under the edges of a roof, for carrying off rain water. **3.** a long, narrow hollow, as between waves.

trounce (trouns), *v.* **1.** to beat or thrash. **2.** to defeat soundly: *used only in everyday talk.* —**trounced,** *p.t. & p.p.;* **trounc/ing,** *pr.p.*

troupe (troop), *n.* a band or company, especially of actors, singers, etc.

trou·sers (trou/zərz), *n.pl.* an outer garment with two legs, for men and boys, reaching from the waist usually to the ankles; pants.

trous·seau (troo/so *or* troo so/), *n.* a bride's outfit of clothes, linen, etc. —**trous·seaus** *or* **trous·seaux** (troo/soz *or* troo soz/), *pl.*

trout (trout), *n.* a small food fish of the salmon family, found mainly in fresh water.

trow (tro *or* trou), *v.* to think or suppose: *no longer used.*

trow·el (trou/əl), *n.* **1.** a tool with a flat blade for smoothing plaster, laying mortar between bricks, etc. **2.** a tool with a pointed scoop, used for digging in a garden.

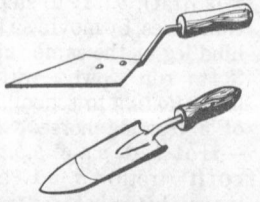

upper: brick trowel
lower: garden trowel

Troy (troi), *n.* **1.** an ancient city in Asia Minor. **2.** a city in eastern New York.

troy (troi), *n.* a system of weights used for gold, silver, jewels, etc. in which 12 ounces equal 1 pound: also called **troy weight.** See also **avoirdupois.**

tru·ant (troo/ənt), *n.* **1.** a pupil who stays away from school when he should be there. **2.** any person who fails to do what he should do. —*adj.* **1.** that is a truant [a *truant* boy]. **2.** having to do with truants [a *truant* officer]. **3.** shirking one's duty; idle or lazy.

truce (troos) *n.* a stop in warfare or fighting for a time, by agreement of both sides.

truck (truk), *n.* **1.** a large motor vehicle for carrying loads on highways, etc. Some large trucks are made up of a driver's cab and a trailer that can be taken off. **2.** a wagon or frame on wheels for moving heavy things. **3.** a frame with two or more pairs of wheels under each end of a railroad car. **4.** a small wheel. —*v.* **1.** to carry on a truck. **2.** to drive a truck.

truck *(meaning 2)*

truck (truk), *n.* **1.** vegetables raised for sale in markets. **2.** rubbish; trash: *used only in everyday talk.* —**have no truck with,** to have no dealings with: *used only in everyday talk.*

truck·ing (truk/ing), *n.* the business of carrying goods by truck. —**truck/er,** *n.*

truck·le (truk/'l), *v.* to give in or yield too easily; submit [to *truckle* to a tyrant]. —**truck/·led,** *p.t. & p.p.;* **truck/ling,** *pr.p.*

truckle bed, same as **trundle bed.**

truc·u·lent (truk/yoo lənt), *adj.* fierce, violent, and ready to fight. —**truc/u·lence,** *n.*

trudge (truj), *v.* to walk, especially in a tired way or with effort. —*n.* a long or tiring walk. —**trudged,** *p.t. & p.p.;* **trudg/ing,** *pr.p.*

true (troo), *adj.* **1.** that agrees with fact; not false [a *true* story]. **2.** as it should be; real; genuine [a *true* ruby; *true* love]. **3.** that can be trusted; faithful; loyal [a *true* friend]. **4.** exact or accurate [a *true* copy]. **5.** right in form, fit, etc. [The door is not *true* with the frame.] **6.** according to law; rightful [the *true* heirs]. —*adv.* truly; exactly [He shot *true* to the mark.] —*n.* **1.** that which is true [Can you tell the *true* from the false?] **2.** the condition of fitting properly [The door is out of *true*.] —**come true,** to happen as expected. —**tru/er,** *compar.;* **tru/est,** *superl.*

truf·fle (truf/'l), *n.* a fungus that grows underground and is used as food.

tru·ism (troo/iz'm), *n.* a statement so commonly known to be true that it seems unnecessary to say it, such as "You're young only once."

tru·ly (troo/le), *adv.* **1.** in a true way; exactly, faithfully, etc. [I love you *truly*.] **2.** in fact; really [Are you *truly* sorry?]

Tru·man, Harry S (troo/mən), 1884–; 33rd president of the U.S. from 1945 to 1953.

trump (trump), *n.* **1.** any playing card of a suit that ranks higher than any other suit during the playing of a hand. **2.** *sometimes* **trumps,** *pl.* this suit. —*v.* to take a trick in a card game by playing a trump. —**trump up,** to make up in order to deceive [to *trump up* an excuse].

trump·er·y (trum′pər ē), *n.* **1.** something showy but worthless. **2.** nonsense. —**trump′-er·ies,** *pl.*

trum·pet (trum′pit), *n.* **1.** a brass-wind musical instrument made of a long, looped metal tube that widens out like a funnel at the end. It has a loud, blaring sound. **2.** something shaped like this. **3.** a sound like that of a trumpet.

trumpet

—*v.* **1.** to blow on a trumpet or make a sound like a trumpet. **2.** to announce in a loud voice. —**trum′pet·er,** *n.*

trun·cheon (trun′chən), *n.* a short, thick club, as one carried by a policeman.

trun·dle (trun′d'l), *n.* **1.** a low cart with small wheels. **2.** a trundle bed. **3.** a small wheel or caster. —*v.* to roll along. —**trun′dled,** *p.t. & p.p.;* **trun′dling,** *pr.p.*

trundle bed, a low bed on small wheels, that can be rolled under another bed when not in use.

trunk (trungk), *n.* **1.** the main stem of a tree. **2.** a body, not including the head, arms, and legs. **3.** a long snout, as of an elephant. **4.** the main line, as of a blood vessel. **5.** a large, strong box for holding clothes, etc., as while traveling. **6.** a space in an automobile, usually at the rear, for carrying luggage, a spare tire, etc. **7. trunks,** *pl.* very short pants worn by men for sports, especially swimming.

trunk *(meaning 6)*

trunk line, a main line of a railroad, telephone system, etc.

truss (trus), *n.* **1.** a framework for holding up a roof, bridge, etc. **2.** a kind of belt worn to support a hernia or rupture. —*v.* to tie, fasten, or tighten; especially, to bind the arms or wings of to the sides.

trust (trust), *n.* **1.** strong belief that some person or thing is honest or can be depended on; faith [You can put your *trust* in that bank.] **2.** the one that is trusted [The Lord is our *trust.*] **3.** something that has been put in one's care or charge; duty [The children's welfare is his sacred *trust.*] **4.** confidence that a person will be able and willing to pay later; credit [to sell on *trust*]. **5.** property that is held and managed by a person, bank, etc. for the benefit of another. **6.** a group of businesses joined together to form a monopoly. —*v.* **1.** to have or put trust in; rely; depend [Can I *trust* you to be on time? I don't *trust* that rickety ladder.] **2.** to put something in the care of [His father *trusted* him with the car.] **3.** to expect; hope [I *trust* that you are well.] **4.** to believe [I *trust* his story.] **5.** to give credit to on something bought [The grocer refused to *trust* them for another week's supply.] —*adj.* **1.** of a trust or held in trust [a *trust* fund]. **2.** acting as trustee [a *trust* company]. —**in trust,** entrusted to another's care. —**trust to,** to rely on.

trus·tee (trus tē′), *n.* **1.** one who is put in charge of the property or affairs of another person. **2.** any of a group of people who manage the affairs of a college, hospital, etc.

trus·tee·ship (trus tē′ship), *n.* **1.** the position or work of a trustee. **2.** the right given by the United Nations to a country to manage the affairs of a certain territory, called a **trust territory.**

trust·ful (trust′fəl), *adj.* full of trust or confidence; trusting. —**trust′ful·ly,** *adv.*

trust·ing (trus′ting), *adj.* that trusts; trustful. —**trust′ing·ly,** *adv.*

trust·wor·thy (trust′wŭr′thē), *adj.* deserving to be trusted; reliable. —**trust′wor′thi·ness,** *n.*

trust·y (trus′tē), *adj.* that can be trusted; reliable [a *trusty* worker]. —*n.* a convict in a prison who is given special privileges because he has behaved well. —**trust′i·er,** *compar.;* **trust′i·est,** *superl.* —**trust′ies,** *pl.*

truth (trōōth), *n.* **1.** the quality or fact of being true, honest, sincere, accurate, etc. **2.** that which is true; the real facts [Did the newspaper print the *truth* about him?] **3.** a fact or principle that has been proved, as in science. —**in truth,** truly; in fact. —**truths** (trōōthz or trōōths), *pl.*

truth·ful (trōōth′fəl), *adj.* **1.** telling the truth; honest [a *truthful* boy]. **2.** that is the truth; accurate [a *truthful* account]. —**truth′ful·ly,** *adv.* —**truth′ful·ness,** *n.*

try (trī), *v.* **1.** to make an effort; attempt [to *try* to win]. **2.** to seek to find out about, as by experimenting; test [to *try* a recipe; *try* your luck]. **3.** to carry on the trial of in a law court [The judge *tried* the case. They *tried* him and found him guilty.] **4.** to test the faith, patience, etc. of [He was sorely *tried.*] **5.** to put to a severe test or strain [Such exercise *tried* his strength.] —*n.* an effort; attempt; trial. —**try on,** to put on, as a garment, to see how it fits and looks. —**try out, 1.** to test, as by putting into use. **2.** to test one's fitness, as for a place on a team, a part in a play, etc. —**tried,** *p.t. & p.p.;* **try′ing,** *pr.p.* —**tries,** *pl.*

try·ing (trī′ing), *adj.* hard to bear; annoying [That child has *trying* ways.]

try·out (trī′out), *n.* a test of one's fitness, as for a place on a team or a part in a play.

tryst (trist), *n.* **1.** an appointment to meet at a certain time and place, as one made by lovers. **2.** the place of meeting: also **tryst′ing place.**

tsar (tsär), *n.* same as **czar.**

tsa·ri·na (tsä rē′nə), *n.* same as **czarina.**

---

fat,   āpe,   cär,   ten,   ēven,   hit,   bīte,   gō,   hôrn,   tōōl,   book,   up,   fŭr;
get,   joy,   yet,   chin,   she,   thin,   then;   zh = s in pleasure;   ′ as in able (ā′b'l);
ə = a in ago,   e in agent,   i in sanity,   o in confess,   u in focus.

tset·se (tset′sē), *n.* a small fly found in central and southern Africa. One kind carries the germ that causes sleeping sickness. *Its full name is* **tsetse fly.**

T-shirt (tē′shûrt′), *n.* a knitted shirt or undershirt with short sleeves and no collar, pulled on over the head.

tsp., abbreviation for **teaspoon** or **teaspoons.**

T square, a T-shaped ruler for drawing parallel lines.

tub (tub), *n.* **1.** a round, open, wooden container, like a large bucket. **2.** any large, open container, as for washing clothes. **3.** as much as a tub will hold. **4.** a bathtub. **5.** a bath taken in a tub: *only in everyday talk, mainly in England.* —*v.* to wash or bathe in a tub. —**tubbed,** *p.t. & p.p.;* **tub′bing,** *pr.p.*

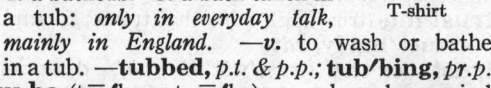
T-shirt

tu·ba (tōō′bə *or* tyōō′bə), *n.* a large brass-wind instrument with a full, deep tone.

tub·by (tub′ē), *adj.* **1.** shaped like a tub. **2.** short and fat. —**tub′bi·er,** *compar.;* **tub′bi·est,** *superl.*

tube (tōōb *or* tyōōb), *n.* **1.** a long, slender, hollow piece of material or tissue in which gases and liquids can flow or be kept [a fluorescent light *tube;* the bronchial *tubes*]. **2.** a long, slender container made of soft metal, etc., with a screw cap at one end, from which tooth paste, glue, etc. can be squeezed out. **3.** same as **electron tube. 4.** a hollow ring of rubber put inside some automobile tires and filled with air. **5.** an underground tunnel for an electric railroad.

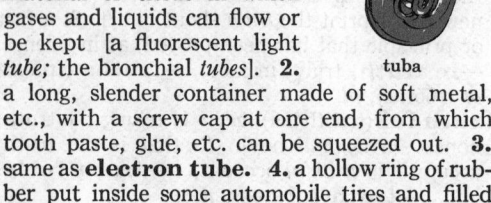
tuba

tu·ber (tōō′bər *or* tyōō′bər), *n.* a short, thick part of an underground stem, as a potato.

tu·ber·cle (tōō′bər k′l *or* tyōō′bər k′l) *n.* **1.** a small, rounded part growing out from a bone, a plant root, etc. **2.** a hard swelling that is not normal [Tuberculosis causes *tubercles* in the lungs.]

tu·ber·cu·lar (tōō bûr′kyoo lər *or* tyōō bûr′kyoo lər), *adj.* **1.** having tuberculosis. **2.** of, like, or having tubercles.

tu·ber·cu·lo·sis (tōō bûr′kyoo lō′sis *or* tyōō bûr′kyoo lō′sis), *n.* a disease caused by a germ, in which tubercles form in the body, especially in the lungs, and tissues waste away.

tu·ber·cu·lous (tōō bûr′kyoo ləs *or* tyōō bûr′kyoo ləs), *adj.* having tuberculosis.

tube·rose (tōōb′rōz *or* tyōōb′rōz), *n.* a plant with a tuberous root and a spike of sweet-smelling white flowers shaped like lilies.

tu·ber·ous (tōō′bər əs *or* tyōō′bər əs), *adj.* **1.** covered with rounded swellings; knobby. **2.** of, like, or having a tuber or tubers.

tub·ing (tōōb′ing *or* tyōōb′ing), *n.* **1.** tubes or a series of tubes. **2.** material in the form of a tube [glass *tubing*]. **3.** a piece of a tube.

tu·bu·lar (tōō′byoo lər *or* tyōō′byoo lər), *adj.* **1.** of or shaped like a tube [*tubular* steel]. **2.** made of or with tubes.

tuck (tuk), *v.* **1.** to gather up in folds, so as to make shorter [She *tucked* up her dress to wade the stream.] **2.** to push the edges of something in or under [*Tuck* in the sheets of the bed.] **3.** to cover or wrap snugly [to *tuck* a baby in bed]. **4.** to press snugly into a small space [to *tuck* shoes in a suitcase]. **5.** to make tucks in a garment. —*n.* a sewed fold in a garment.

tuck·er (tuk′ər), *n.* a piece of lace or fine cloth once worn by women to cover the neck and shoulders. —**one's best bib and tucker,** one's finest clothes: *used only in everyday talk.*

tuck·er (tuk′ər), *v.* to make tired: *used only in everyday talk* [I'm all *tuckered* out.]

Tuc·son (tōō sän′ *or* tōō′sän), *n.* a city in southern Arizona.

Tu·dor (tōō′dər *or* tyōō′dər), *n.* the ruling family of England from 1485 to 1603.

Tues., abbreviation for **Tuesday.**

Tues·day (tōōz′dē *or* tyōōz′dē), *n.* the third day of the week.

tuft (tuft), *n.* a bunch of hairs, feathers, grass, threads, etc. growing or tied closely together. —*v.* **1.** to put tufts on or decorate with tufts. **2.** to keep the padding of a quilt, mattress, etc. in place by putting tufts of threads through at various points.

tug (tug), *v.* **1.** to pull with force or effort; drag; haul [He *tugged* the trunk out of the locker.] **2.** to tow with a tugboat. —*n.* **1.** a hard pull [A *tug* on the old shoelace broke it.] **2.** a tugboat. —**tugged,** *p.t. & p.p.;* **tug′ging,** *pr.p.*

tug·boat (tug′bōt), *n.* a small, powerful boat used for towing or pushing ships and barges.

tug of war, a contest in which two teams pull at opposite ends of a rope. Each team tries to drag the other across a center line.

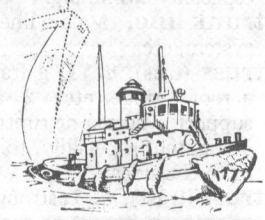
tugboat

tu·i·tion (tōō ish′ən *or* tyōō ish′ən), *n.* **1.** money paid for being taught in a private school or college. **2.** teaching; instruction.

tu·lip (tōō′lip *or* tyōō′ləp), *n.* a plant that grows from a bulb and has long, pointed leaves and a large flower shaped like a cup.

tulle (tōōl), *n.* a thin, fine, net cloth of silk, rayon, or nylon, used for veils.

Tul·sa (tul′sə), *n.* a city in Oklahoma.

tum·ble (tum′b'l), *v.* **1.** to do somersaults, handsprings, or other tricks of an acrobat. **2.** to fall in a sudden or clumsy way ["Jill came *tumbling* after."] **3.** to toss or roll about [The dryer *tumbles* the clothes.] **4.** to move in a

tulips

quick, disorderly way [The boys *tumbled* out of the house into the yard.] —*n.* **1.** a fall [to take a *tumble* down the stairs]. **2.** a messy or confused condition. —**tum′bled,** *p.t. & p.p.*; **tum′-bling,** *pr.p.*

tum·ble-down (tum′b'l doun′), *adj.* that looks ready to fall down; ramshackle [a *tumble-down* shack].

tum·bler (tum′blər), *n.* **1.** an ordinary drinking glass, without a stem. **2.** an acrobat. **3.** any of the parts of a lock that must be moved, as by a key, to open the lock.

tum·ble·weed (tum′b'l wēd), *n.* a plant that breaks off near the ground in the fall and is blown about by the wind.

tum·brel or **tum·bril** (tum′brəl), *n.* a cart, especially one that was used to carry prisoners to the guillotine during the French Revolution.

tu·mid (tōō′mid *or* tyōō′mid), *adj.* **1.** swollen; bulging. **2.** sounding important but not really so; pompous [a *tumid* style of writing].

tu·mor (tōō′mər *or* tyōō′mər), *n.* a growth of extra tissue on some part of the body. Tumors have no useful purpose and are sometimes harmful.

tu·mult (tōō′mult *or* tyōō′mult), *n.* **1.** loud noise or uproar, as from a crowd. **2.** an excited or confused condition; disturbance [The news left us in a *tumult*.]

tu·mul·tu·ous (tōō mul′chōō əs *or* tyōō mul′-chōō əs), *adj.* full of tumult; very noisy or confused [a *tumultuous* greeting for the hero].

tun (tun), *n.* **1.** a large cask, especially one for wine, beer, or ale. **2.** a former measure of volume equal to 252 gallons.

tu·na (tōō′nə), *n.* a large ocean fish whose oily flesh is used as food and is usually canned: also **tuna fish.** —**tu′na** or **tu′nas,** *pl.*

tun·dra (tun′drə *or* toon′drə), *n.* a large, flat plain without trees in the arctic regions.

tune (tōōn *or* tyōōn), *n.* **1.** a series of musical tones with a regular rhythm; melody; song [The music of "America" is a very old *tune*.] **2.** the condition of having correct musical pitch [Every instrument was in *tune*.] **3.** harmony; agreement [He is out of *tune* with the times.] —*v.* to put in the condition of correct musical pitch [to *tune* a piano]. —**to the tune of,** to the sum or amount of. —**tune in** or **tune in on,** to set a radio to receive a certain station or program. —**tune up, 1.** to put into good working condition by adjusting the parts [to *tune up* a motor]. **2.** to adjust musical instruments to the same pitch. —**tuned,** *p.t. & p.p.*; **tun′ing,** *pr.p.* —**tune′-less,** *adj.* —**tun′er,** *n.*

tune·ful (tōōn′fəl *or* tyōōn′fəl), *adj.* full of tunes or melody; pleasing to hear ["Carmen" is a *tuneful* opera.]

tung·sten (tung′stən), *n.* a hard, heavy metal that is a chemical element. It is used in steel alloys, the filaments of electric lights, etc.

tu·nic (tōō′nik *or* tyōō′nik), *n.* **1.** a garment like a loose gown worn by men and women in ancient Greece and Rome, or one like this worn in medieval Europe. **2.** a blouse or jacket that reaches to the hips, often worn with a belt.

tuning fork, a steel piece with two prongs, that sounds a certain fixed tone when it is struck. It is used as a guide in tuning instruments.

Tu·nis (tōō′nis *or* tyōō′nis), *n.* the capital of Tunisia, on the Mediterranean Sea.

medieval tunic

Tu·ni·si·a (tōō nish′i ə *or* tyōō nē′-shə), *n.* a country in northern Africa.

tun·nel (tun′'l), *n.* **1.** a passage under the ground for automobiles, trains, etc. **2.** a way or place in the ground like this, as the burrow of an animal. —*v.* to make a tunnel. —**tun′neled** or **tun′nelled,** *p.t. & p.p.*; **tun′nel·ing** or **tun′nel-ling,** *pr.p.*

tun·ny (tun′ē), *n.* the tuna. —**tun′-nies,** *pl.*

tu·pe·lo (tōō′pə lō *or* tyōō′pə lō), *n.* a tree with small, greenish flowers and blue or purple fruit, growing in wet soil. —**tu′pe·los,** *pl.*

tuning fork

tup·pence (tup′əns), *n.* twopence.

tur·ban (tur′bən), *n.* **1.** a covering for the head worn by Moslems, etc. and made up of a scarf wound around and around, sometimes over a cap. **2.** any head covering or hat like this.

tur·bid (tur′bid), *adj.* **1.** not clear; full of dirt or mud; cloudy [a *turbid* pond]. **2.** confused or muddled, as in thought.

turban

tur·bine (tur′bin *or* tur′bīn), *n.* an engine in which the driving shaft is made to turn by the pressure of steam, water, or air against the vanes of a wheel fixed to it.

tur·bo·jet (tur′bō jet′), *n.* a jet airplane engine in which the energy of the jet works a turbine which in turn works the air compressor.

tur·bo·prop (tur′bō präp′), *n.* a jet airplane engine in which the energy of the jet works a turbine which drives the propeller.

tur·bot (tur′bət), *n.* a kind of European flatfish, like a flounder.

tur·bu·lent (tur′byoo lənt), *adj.* **1.** very excited, upset, etc.; wild or disorderly [*turbulent* feelings; a *turbulent* crowd]. **2.** full of violent motion [*turbulent* rapids]. —**tur′bu·lence,** *n.* —**tur′bu·lent·ly,** *adv.*

tu·reen (too rēn′), *n.* a large deep dish with a lid, used for serving soup, etc.

---

fat,   āpe,   cär,   ten,   ēven,   hit,   bīte,   gō,   hôrn,   tōōl,   book,   up,   fur;
get,   joy,   yet,   chin,   she,   thin,   *th*en;   zh = s in pleasure;   ′ as in able (ā′b'l);
ə = a in ago,   e in agent,   i in sanity,   o in confess,   u in focus.

turf (tûrf), *n.* **1.** a top layer of earth containing grass with its roots; sod. **2.** a piece of this. **—the turf, 1.** a track for horse racing. **2.** horse racing. **—turfs,** *pl.*

tur·gid (tûr′jid), *adj.* **1.** swollen or puffed up. **2.** so full of long words and hard language that the meaning is not clear.

Turk (tûrk), *n.* a person born or living in Turkey.

Tur·key (tûr′kē), *n.* a country mostly in western Asia, but partly in southeastern Europe.

tur·key (tûr′kē), *n.* **1.** a large, wild or tame bird, originally of North America, with a small head and spreading tail. **2.** its flesh, used as food. **—tur′keys,** *pl.*

turkey buzzard, a dark-colored vulture of the Southwest and South America.

Turk·ish (tûr′kish), *adj.* of Turkey, its people, etc. **—n.** the language of Turkey.

tur·mer·ic (tûr′mər ik), *n.* the root of a plant of the East Indies ground into a spicy powder.

tur·moil (tûr′moil), *n.* a noisy, excited, or confused condition; commotion.

turn (tûrn), *v.* **1.** to move around a center point or axis; revolve; rotate [The wheels *turn*. *Turn* the key.] **2.** to do by moving in a circle [*Turn* a somersault.] **3.** to seem to be whirling [It made my head *turn*.] **4.** to move around or partly around [He tossed and *turned* in bed.] **5.** to change in position or direction [*Turn* your chair around. *Turn* to the left. The tide has *turned*.] **6.** to change so that the part that was underneath is on top; reverse [*Turn* the page. *Turn* over the soil.] **7.** to change in feelings, attitudes, etc. [The news *turned* his family against him. He *turned* against his friends.] **8.** to shift one's attention [He *turned* to music.] **9.** to change from one form or condition to another [Churning *turns* the cream to butter. The milk *turned* sour.] **10.** to drive, set, let go, etc. in some way [The cat was *turned* loose.] **11.** to depend [The outcome *turns* on whether he will agree.] **12.** to upset or unsettle [The smell *turned* his stomach.] **13.** to reach or pass [She has just *turned* 21.] **14.** to give a round shape to [to *turn* the legs of a table on a lathe]. **15.** to make [to *turn* a pretty phrase]. **—n. 1.** the act of turning around or revolving [a *turn* of the wheel]. **2.** a change in direction or position [a *turn* to the right; the *turn* of the tide]. **3.** a short walk, ride, etc. **4.** the place where there is a change in direction; bend [a *turn* in the road]. **5.** a twist, coil, etc. [Make one more *turn* with the rope.] **6.** the right, duty, or chance to do something in regular order [It's your *turn* to wash dishes.] **7.** an action or deed [to do someone a good *turn*]. **8.** a change in condition [a *turn* for the worse]. **9.** style, form, etc. [an odd *turn* of speech]. **10.** the time of change [the *turn* of the century]. **11.** a sudden surprise; shock: *used only in everyday talk* [His shout gave me quite a *turn*.] **—by turns,** one after the other. **—in turn,** in the proper order. **—out of turn,** not in the proper order. **—take turns,** to say or do something one after the other in a regular order.

—to a turn, perfectly. **—turn down,** to refuse or reject. **—turn in, 1.** to make a turn into; enter [*Turn in* that driveway.] **2.** to hand over [*Turn in* your homework.] **3.** to go to bed: *used only in everyday talk.* **—turn off, 1.** to leave, as a road. **2.** to shut off [*Turn off* the water.] **—turn on, 1.** to make go on, flow, etc. [*Turn on* the radio.] **2.** to attack suddenly. **—turn out, 1.** to shut off or put out, as a light. **2.** to put outside. **3.** to come or gather [Many people *turned out* for the picnic.] **4.** to make; produce [She *turns out* good pies.] **5.** to result or become [The trip *turned out* well. He *turned out* to be a good worker.] **—turn over, 1.** to hand over; give. **2.** to think about; ponder. **—turn to, 1.** to get to work. **2.** to go to for help. **—turn up,** to happen or arrive. **—turn′er,** *n.*

turn·coat (tûrn′kōt), *n.* a person who changes his party, opinions, etc. to join the other side.

tur·nip (tûr′nip), *n.* a plant with a round, white or yellow root that is eaten as a vegetable.

turn·key (tûrn′kē), *n.* a person in charge of the keys of a prison; jailer. **—turn′keys,** *pl.*

turn·out or **turn-out** (tûrn′out), *n.* a group or gathering of people, as at a meeting.

turnip

turn·o·ver (tûrn′ō vər), *n.* **1.** the act of turning over, or upsetting. **2.** a small pie made by turning one half of the crust back over the other half, with a filling in between. **3.** the amount of business done, shown by the rate at which goods are sold and replaced [The store had a high *turnover* in men's suits last year.] **4.** the rate at which workers in a company, patients in a hospital, etc. are replaced. **—adj.** that is turned over [a *turnover* collar].

turn·pike (tûrn′pīk), *n.* a large road, or highway, especially one having tollgates.

turn·stile (tûrn′stīl), *n.* a device in an entrance or exit, that turns to let through only one person at a time.

turn·ta·ble (tûrn′tā b'l), *n.* a round platform that turns, as for playing phonograph records.

tur·pen·tine (tûr′pən tīn), *n.* a light-colored oil made from the sap of pines and certain other trees, and used in paints and varnishes.

turnstile

tur·pi·tude (tûr′pə tōōd *or* tûr′pə tyōōd), *n.* the condition of being wicked or evil.

tur·quoise (tûr′koiz *or* tûr′kwoiz), *n.* **1.** a blue or greenish-blue stone used as a jewel. **2.** a greenish blue.

tur·ret (tûr′it), *n.* **1.** a small tower on a building, usually at a corner. **2.** a dome or low tower, often one that revolves, from which guns are fired, as on a warship, tank, or airplane. **3.** a part of a lathe that holds several cutting tools. It can be turned to change the tool in use. Such a lathe is called a **turret lathe. —tur′ret·ed,** *adj.*

tur·tle (tŭr′t'l), *n.* an animal with a soft body covered by a hard shell into which it can pull its head, tail, and four legs. Turtles live on land and in the water and some kinds are used as food: see also **tortoise.** —**turn turtle,** to turn upside down.

mud turtle (4 in. long)

tur·tle·dove (tŭr′t'l-duv), *n.* a wild dove known for its sad cooing and the love that the mates seem to show for each other.

turtle neck, a high collar that turns down and fits closely around the neck, as on some sweaters. —**tur′tle-neck′,** *adj.*

Tus·ca·ny (tus′kə nē), *n.* a region in western Italy.

tusk (tusk), *n.* a very long, pointed tooth, usually one of a pair, that sticks out of the mouth, as in elephants, wild boars, and walruses.

tus·sle (tus′'l), *v.* to struggle or wrestle; scuffle. —*n.* a short but rough struggle or fight. —**tus′-sled,** *p.t. & p.p.;* **tus′-sling,** *pr.p.*

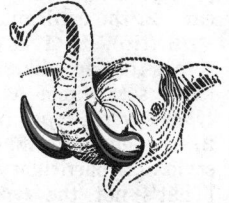

elephant tusks

tus·sock (tus′ək), *n.* a thick tuft or clump of grass, twigs, etc.

tut (tut), *interj.* a sound made to show that one is impatient, annoyed, angry, etc.

tu·te·lage (tōō′t'l ij *or* tyōō′t'l ij), *n.* 1. teaching; instruction. 2. care and protection, as of a guardian.

tu·te·lar·y (tōō′t'l er′ē *or* tyōō′t'l er′ē), *adj.* watching over or protecting a person or thing [Each Roman family had its *tutelary* gods.]

tu·tor (tōō′tər *or* tyōō′tər), *n.* a private teacher. —*v.* to teach or instruct, as a tutor does. —**tu·to·ri·al** (tōō tôr′i əl *or* tyōō tôr′i əl), *adj.*

tut·ti-frut·ti (tōō′tē frōō′tē), *adj.* made or flavored with mixed fruits, as ice cream.

tux·e·do (tuk sē′dō), *n.* 1. a man's suit coat worn at formal dinners, dances, etc. It is usually black, with satin lapels, but has no tails. 2. a suit with such a coat. —**tux′e·dos,** *pl.*

TV (tē′vē′), television.

twad·dle (twäd′'l), *n.* silly or foolish talk or writing; nonsense.

twain (twān), *n.* two: *now seldom used except in poetry* [broken in *twain*].

Twain, Mark (twān), 1835–1910; American writer. His real name was Samuel L. Clemens.

tuxedo

twang (twang), *n.* 1. a sharp, vibrating sound, as of a plucked string on a banjo. 2. a way of making speech sounds by letting air pass

through the nose. —*v.* 1. to make or cause to make a twang. 2. to speak with a twang.

'twas (twuz *or* twäz), it was.

tweak (twēk), *v.* to give a sudden, twisting pinch to [to *tweak* someone's cheek]. —*n.* a sudden, twisting pinch.

tweed (twēd), *n.* 1. a rough wool cloth in a weave of two or more colors. 2. **tweeds,** *pl.* clothes of tweed.

twee·dle·dum and twee·dle·dee (twē′d'l-dum′ 'n twē′d'l dē′), two persons or things so much alike that it is hard to tell them apart.

tweet (twēt), *n.* the high, chirping sound of a small bird. —*v.* to make this sound.

tweez·ers (twēz′ərz), *n.pl.* small pincers for plucking out hairs, handling small things, etc.

twelfth (twelfth), *adj.* coming after eleven others; 12th in order. —*n.* 1. the twelfth one. 2. one of twelve equal parts of something; 1/12.

Twelfth-night (twelfth′-nīt′), *n.* the evening of Epiphany. Epiphany is the twelfth day after Christmas.

twelve (twelv), *n. & adj.* two more than ten; the number 12.

twen·ti·eth (twen′tē ith), *adj.* coming after nineteen others; 20th in order. —*n.* 1. the twentieth one. 2. one of twenty equal parts of something; 1/20.

twen·ty (twen′tē), *n. & adj.* 1. two times ten; the number 20. 2. **twenties,** *n.pl.* the numbers or years from 20 to 29.

'twere (twŭr), it were.

twice (twīs), *adv.* 1. two times [Don't make me ask you *twice*.] 2. two times as much; doubly [Ed is *twice* the athlete Joe is.]

twid·dle (twid′'l), *v.* to twirl or play with lightly. —**twiddle one's thumbs, 1.** to twirl one's thumbs idly around one another. 2. to be idle. —**twid′dled,** *p.t. & p.p.;* **twid′dling,** *pr.p.*

twig (twig), *n.* a small branch or shoot of a tree or shrub.

twi·light (twī′līt), *n.* 1. the dim light just after sunset or, sometimes, just before sunrise. 2. the time between sunset and dark.

twill (twil), *n.* 1. a cloth woven with parallel slanting lines or ribs. 2. the pattern of this weave. —*v.* to weave with such a pattern.

'twill (twil), it will.

twin (twin), *n.* 1. either of two born at the same time to the same mother. 2. either of two persons or things very much alike or forming a pair. —*adj.* being a twin or twins [*twin* sisters; *twin* gables on the house].

twine (twīn), *n.* a strong string or cord made of two or more strands twisted together. —*v.* 1. to twist together. 2. to wind or grow in a

tweezers

winding way [The ivy *twined* around the post.]
—**twined,** *p.t. & p.p.;* **twin′ing,** *pr.p.*

twinge (twinj), *n.* **1.** a sudden, sharp pain.
2. a sudden, anxious feeling; qualm [a *twinge* of
conscience].   —*v.* to have or give a twinge.
—**twinged,** *p.t. & p.p.;* **twing′ing,** *pr.p.*

twin·kle (twing′k'l), *v.* **1.** to give off quick
flashes of light; sparkle ["*Twinkle, twinkle,*
little star."] **2.** to light up, as with laughter
[*twinkling* eyes]. **3.** to move rapidly, as a dancer's
feet. —*n.* **1.** a quick flash of light; sparkle.
2. a quick look of amusement in the eye. —**twin′-
kled,** *p.t. & p.p.;* **twin′kling,** *pr.p.*

twin·kling (twing′kling), *n.* **1.** a quick flash
of light; twinkle. **2.** a very short time; instant.

twirl (twûrl), *v.* to turn around rapidly; spin,
twist, whirl, etc. —*n.* **1.** a twirling or being
twirled. **2.** a twist, coil, curl, etc.

twist (twist), *v.* **1.** to wind or twine together
or around something [to *twist* wool fibers into
yarn]. **2.** to force out of its usual shape or
position [I tripped and *twisted* my ankle.] **3.**
to give the wrong meaning to on purpose [He
twisted my compliment into an insult.] **4.** to turn
around [*Twist* the lid to take it off.] **5.** to move
or turn in a spiral or curves [Dough is *twisted*
to make pretzels. The road *twists* up the hill.]
6. to break off by turning the end [to *twist* the
stem from an apple]. —*n.* **1.** something twisted,
as a bread roll made by twisting the dough.
2. a thread or cord of two or more strands
twisted together. **3.** a twisting or being twisted
[a *twist* to the left]. **4.** a special meaning or
slant [to give a new *twist* to an old joke].

twist·er (twis′tər), *n.* **1.** a person or thing that
twists. **2.** a tornado or cyclone.

twit (twit), *v.* to tease or taunt, as by pointing
out a fault or mistake. —**twit′ted,** *p.t. & p.p.;*
twit′ting, *pr.p.*

twitch (twich), *v.* to move or pull with a sudden
jerk [A rabbit's nose *twitches*.] —*n.* a sudden,
quick motion or pull, often one that cannot be
controlled [a *twitch* of the mouth].

twit·ter (twit′ər), *v.* **1.** to make a series of
chirping sounds, as birds do. **2.** to tremble with
excitement. —*n.* **1.** the act or sound of twitter-
ing. **2.** a condition of great excitement [She's
in a *twitter*.]

'twixt (twikst), *prep.* betwixt: *used mainly in
poetry.*

two (tōō), *n. & adj.* one more than one; the
number 2. —**in two,** in two parts.

two-edged (tōō′ejd′), *adj.* **1.** that has two
edges, as for cutting. **2.** that can have two
meanings [a *two-edged* remark].

two-faced (tōō′fāst′), *adj.* **1.** having two
faces. **2.** not sincere or honest; false.

two·fold (tōō′fōld′), *adj.* **1.** having two parts.
2. having two times as much or as many. —*adv.*
two times as much or as many.

two-leg·ged (tōō′leg′id), *adj.* having two legs.

two·pence (tup′'ns) *n.* two British pennies.

two·pen·ny (tup′ən ē), *adj.* **1.** worth or costing
twopence. **2.** cheap; worthless.

two·some (tōō′səm), *n.* two people; a couple.

two-step (tōō′step′), *n.* a popular dance for
couples, in march time.

two-way (tōō′wā′), *adj.* **1.** that moves or lets
one move in either direction [a *two-way* street].
2. used for both sending and receiving [a *two-
way* radio].

-ty (tē), a suffix meaning "the quality or condition of being" [*Safety* is the quality or condition
of being safe.]

-ty (tē), a suffix meaning "tens" or "times ten"
[Six times ten is *sixty*.]

ty·coon (tī kōōn′), *n.* a businessman with much
money and power: *used only in everyday talk.*

ty·ing (tī′ing), present participle of **tie.**

tyke (tīk), *n.* **1.** a small child: *used only in
everyday talk.* **2.** a mongrel dog; cur.

Ty·ler, John (tī′lər), 1790–1862; 10th president of the United States, from 1841 to 1845.

tym·pan·ic membrane (tim pan′ik), the
eardrum.

tym·pa·num (tim′pə nəm), *n.* **1.** the middle
ear. **2.** the eardrum. **3.** a drum.

type (tīp), *n.* **1.** a group or class of people or
things that are alike in some way;
kind; sort [men of the bravest
type; several *types* of insurance].
2. the general form, character, or
style of a particular kind or class
[That's not the *type* of shoe I
wanted.] **3.** a particular person or
thing pointed to as an example or
model [The Greek temple has been
the *type* for many public buildings.] **4.** a piece
of wood or metal with a raised letter or mark on
its top, used in printing. **5.** a set of such pieces.
6. the letters, etc. printed from such pieces
[Small *type* is hard to read.] —*v.* **1.** to find the
type or class of [to *type* a sample of blood]. **2.** to
typewrite. —**typed,** *p.t. & p.p.;* **typ′ing,** *pr.p.*

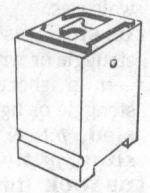
type

type·write (tīp′rīt), *v.* to write with a typewriter: *now usually shortened to* **type.** *For principal parts, see* **write.**

type·writ·er (tīp′rīt ər), *n.* **1.** a machine with
a keyboard, for making printed letters or figures
on paper. **2.** a typist: *an older use.*

ty·phoid (tī′foid), *n.* a serious disease spread
as by infected food or water, and causing fever,
sores in the intestines, etc.: *its full name is*
typhoid fever.

ty·phoon (tī fōōn′), *n.* a very strong wind-
storm in the China Sea and near-by regions, with
the wind blowing in a circle at hurricane force and
bringing very heavy rains.

ty·phus (tī′fəs), *n.* a serious disease whose
germ is carried to man by fleas, lice, etc. It causes
fever and red spots on the skin: *its full name is*
typhus fever.

typ·i·cal (tip′i k'l), *adj.* **1.** being a true example
of its kind [a church *typical* of Gothic style]. **2.**
of its type; characteristic [a snail moving with
typical slowness]. —**typ′i·cal·ly,** *adv.*

typ·i·fy (tip′ə fī), *v.* to have all the usual
qualities or features of; be a true example of
[Tom Sawyer *typified* the American boy.] —**typ′-
i·fied,** *p.t. & p.p.;* **typ′i·fy·ing,** *pr.p.*

typ·ist (tīp′ist), *n.* a person who uses a type-writer; especially, one whose work is typewriting.

ty·pog·ra·phy (tī päg′rə fē), *n.* **1.** the work or skill of setting type for printing. **2.** the style, design, etc. of material printed from type. —**ty·pog′ra·pher,** *n.* —**ty·po·graph·i·cal** (tī′pə graf′i k′l), *adj.*

ty·ran·ni·cal (ti ran′i k′l *or* tī ran′i k′l), *adj.* of or like a tyrant; harsh, cruel, unjust, etc.: also **ty·ran′nic.** —**ty·ran′ni·cal·ly,** *adv.*

tyr·an·nize (tir′ə nīz), *v.* to rule or act as a tyrant; use power in a harsh or cruel way. —**tyr′an·nized,** *p.t. & p.p.;* **tyr′an·niz·ing,** *pr.p.*

tyr·an·nous (tir′ə nəs), *adj.* tyrannical; cruel, harsh, unjust, etc.

tyr·an·ny (tir′ə nē), *n.* **1.** the government or power of a tyrant; harsh and unjust government. **2.** very cruel and unjust use of power. **3.** a tyrannical act. —**tyr′an·nies,** *pl.*

ty·rant (tī′rənt), *n.* **1.** a ruler having complete power, as in some ancient Greek cities. **2.** a ruler who is cruel and unjust. **3.** a person who uses his power in a cruel or unjust way.

Tyre (tīr), *n.* a seaport in ancient Phoenicia. —**Tyr·i·an** (tir′i ən), *adj. & n.*

ty·ro (tī′rō), *n.* a beginner in learning something; novice. —**ty′ros,** *pl.*

Tyr·ol (tir′äl *or* ti rōl′), *n.* a region in the Alps of western Austria and northern Italy. —**Tyr·o·lese** (tir′ə lēz′) or **Tyr·o·le·an** (ti rō′li ən), *adj. & n.*

tzar (tsär), *n.* same as **czar.**

tza·ri·na (tsä rē′nə), *n.* same as **czarina.**

U

U, u (yōō), *n.* the twenty-first letter of the English alphabet. —**U's, u's** (yōōz), *pl.*

U, symbol for the chemical element *uranium.*

U., abbreviation for **University.**

u·biq·ui·tous (yōō bik′wə təs), *adj.* being everywhere at the same time, or seeming to be so. —**u·biq′ui·ty,** *n.*

ud·der (ud′ər), *n.* the gland of a cow, goat, etc. from which milk comes.

UFO, unidentified flying object.

U·gan·da (yōō gan′də *or* ōō gän′dä), *n.* a country in east central Africa.

ugh, *interj.* a sound made in the throat to show disgust or horror.

ug·ly (ug′lē), *adj.* **1.** unpleasing to look at [an *ugly* shack]. **2.** bad, unpleasant, disgusting, etc. [an *ugly* lie; an *ugly* habit]. **3.** dangerous; threatening [a wolf with *ugly* fangs]. **4.** cross; in a bad temper: *used only in everyday talk.* —**ug′li·er,** *compar.;* **ug′li·est,** *superl.* —**ug′li·ness,** *n.*

U·kraine (yōō′krān *or* yōō krān′), *n.* a republic in the southwestern part of the Soviet Union. —**U·krain′i·an,** *adj. & n.*

u·ku·le·le (yōō′kə lā′lē), *n.* a musical instrument with four strings, like a small guitar.

ul·cer (ul′sər), *n.* **1.** an open sore with pus, as on the skin or stomach lining. **2.** any condition that is rotten or corrupting [Slums are the *ulcers* of our cities.] —**ul′cer·ous,** *adj.*

ul·cer·ate (ul′sə rāt), *v.* to have or cause to have an ulcer or

ukulele

ulcers [an *ulcerated* stomach]. —**ul′cer·at·ed,** *p.t. & p.p.;* **ul′cer·at·ing,** *pr.p.*

ul·na (ul′nə), *n.* the long bone that is the thinner of the two bones of the forearm. —**ul·nae** (ul′nē) or **ul′nas,** *pl.*

Ul·ster (ul′stər), *n.* **1.** a region in northern Ireland. **2. ulster,** a long, loose overcoat.

ul·te·ri·or (ul tir′i ər), *adj.* **1.** beyond what is openly said or made known [We suspect that he had an *ulterior* purpose in agreeing to help us.] **2.** lying beyond or on the farther side. **3.** later; future; further.

ul·ti·mate (ul′tə mit), *adj.* **1.** most distant; farthest [the *ultimate* limits of space]. **2.** final; last [an *ultimate* decision]. **3.** most basic; fundamental; primary [the *ultimate* goodness of man]. **4.** greatest possible; maximum [The flood water reached its *ultimate* level at noon.] —*n.* something ultimate [the *ultimate* in pleasure].

ul·ti·ma·tum (ul′tə mā′təm), *n.* a final offer or demand, especially in dealing with another in a dispute.

ul·tra (ul′trə), *adj.* going beyond the usual limits; extreme [He is an *ultra* liberal.]

ul·tra-, a prefix meaning: **1.** beyond [*Ultra-violet* rays lie beyond the violet end of the spectrum.] **2.** to an extreme; very [An *ultramodern* lamp is a very modern lamp.]

ul·tra·ma·rine (ul′trə mə rēn′), *adj.* deep-blue. —*n.* deep blue, or a deep-blue coloring matter.

ul·tra·son·ic (ul′trə sän′ik), *adj.* same as **supersonic** *(meaning 1).*

ul·tra·vi·o·let (ul′trə vī′ə lit), *adj.* lying just beyond the violet end of the spectrum [*Ultra-violet* rays are invisible rays of light that help to form vitamin D in plants and animals and can kill certain germs.]

---

fat, āpe, cär, ten, ēven, hit, bīte, gō, hôrn, tōōl, book, up, fur;
get, joy, yet, chin, she, thin, *th*en; zh = s in pleasure; ′ as in able (ā′b'l);
ə = a in ago, e in agent, i in sanity, o in confess, u in focus.

U·lys·ses (yoo lis′ēz), *n.* in Greek legends, a king of Ithaca and a leader of the Greeks in the Trojan War. He is the hero of the *Odyssey*.

um·bel (um′b'l), *n.* a cluster of flowers on stalks of about the same length that grow out from the end of the main stem.

um·ber (um′bər), *n.* **1.** a kind of earth used as a coloring matter. **2.** yellowish brown (**raw umber**) or reddish brown (**burnt umber**).

umbel

um·bil·i·cal cord (um-bil′i k'l), the cord that connects a pregnant woman with her unborn baby.

um·brage (um′brij), *n.* a feeling of hurt and anger over what one takes to be an insult or slight; offense [to take *umbrage* at a remark].

um·brel·la (um brel′ə), *n.* cloth stretched over a folding frame at the top of a stick, used to protect one from the rain or sun.

u·mi·ak (ōō′mi ak), *n.* a large open boat made of skins on a wooden frame, used by Eskimos.

um·pire (um′pīr), *n.* **1.** a person who rules on the plays of a game, as in baseball. **2.** a person chosen to settle an argument. —*v.* to be an umpire in a game or dispute. —**um′pired,** *p.t. & p.p.;* **um′pir·ing,** *pr.p.*

un-, **1.** a prefix meaning "not" or "the opposite of" [An *unhappy* man is not happy, but sad.] **2.** a prefix meaning "to reverse or undo the action of" [To *untie* a shoelace is to reverse the action of tying it.] This prefix can be put before a great many words to add the simple meaning "not." Some common words formed in this way will be found at the bottom of this page and the next few pages. Other words with special meanings are given in the regular listing.

UN or **U.N.,** abbreviation for **United Nations.**

un·a·ble (un ā′b'l), *adj.* not able; not having the means or power to do something.

un·ac·count·a·ble (un′ə koun′tə b'l), *adj.* **1.** that cannot be explained; strange [an *unaccountable* event]. **2.** not responsible [He is *unaccountable* to you.] —**un′ac·count′a·bly,** *adv.*

un·ac·cus·tomed (un′ə kus′təmd), *adj.* **1.** not accustomed or used [*unaccustomed* to wealth]. **2.** not usual; strange [*unaccustomed* action].

un·af·fect·ed (un′ə fek′tid), *adj.* **1.** not affected or influenced. **2.** sincere and natural; simple.

un-A·mer·i·can (un′ə mer′ə kən), *adj.* not American; especially, thought of as not conforming to the principles, policies, etc. of the United States.

u·na·nim·i·ty (yōō′nə nim′ə tē), *n.* the condition of being unanimous; complete agreement.

u·nan·i·mous (yoo nan′ə məs), *adj.* showing complete agreement; with no one opposed [a *unanimous* vote; *unanimous* in their decision]. —**u·nan′i·mous·ly,** *adv.*

un·ap·pe·tiz·ing (un ap′ə tīz ing), *adj.* looking, smelling, or tasting so bad as to spoil the appetite.

un·ap·proach·a·ble (un′ə prōch′ə b'l), *adj.* **1.** hard to be friendly with; aloof. **2.** having no equal; superior [*unapproachable* skill].

un·armed (un ärmd′), *adj.* having no weapon; especially, having no gun.

un·as·sum·ing (un′ə sōōm′ing *or* un′ə syōōm′-ing), *adj.* not bold or forward; modest.

un·at·tached (un ə tacht′), *adj.* **1.** not attached or fastened. **2.** not engaged or married.

un·a·vail·ing (un′ə vāl′ing), *adj.* not bringing success; useless; futile.

un·a·void·a·ble (un′ə void′ə b'l), *adj.* that cannot be avoided; inevitable [an *unavoidable* accident]. —**un′a·void′a·bly,** *adv.*

un·a·ware (un ə wer′), *adj.* not aware; not knowing or noticing [We were *unaware* that he was there.] —*adv.* unawares.

un·a·wares (un ə werz′), *adv.* by surprise; in a way not expected [to sneak up on someone *unawares*].

un·bal·anced (un bal′ənst), *adj.* **1.** not balanced or equal [an *unbalanced* budget]. **2.** not sane or normal in mind.

un·bar (un bär′), *v.* to open; unlock; unbolt. —**un·barred′,** *p.t. & p.p.;* **un·bar′ring,** *pr.p.*

un·be·com·ing (un′bi kum′ing), *adj.* not becoming; not fitting or proper [*unbecoming* behavior].

un·be·lief (un bə lēf′), *n.* a lack of belief, especially in matters of religion.

un·be·liev·er (un′bə lēv′ər), *n.* a person who does not believe, especially one who does not believe in the teachings of some religion.

un·be·liev·ing (un′bə lēv′ing), *adj.* not believing; doubting; skeptical.

un·bend (un bend′), *v.* **1.** to make or become straight again. **2.** to relax or become more natural [After his interview, the senator *unbent* and told some jokes.] —**un·bent** (un bent′), *p.t. & p.p.;* **un·bend′ing,** *pr.p.*

un·bend·ing (un ben′ding), *adj.* **1.** not bending; stiff. **2.** not giving in or yielding; firm.

un·bid·den (un bid′'n), *adj.* without being asked or ordered; uninvited [She walked in *unbidden*.]

un·bind (un bīnd′), *v.* to let loose or free; unfasten; untie [*Unbind* these prisoners!] —**un·bound′,** *p.t. & p.p.;* **un·bind′ing,** *pr.p.*

un·a·bashed′	un·ad·vis′a·ble	un′ap·pre′ci·at·ed	un′a·vail′a·ble
un′a·bat·ed	un·a·fraid′	un·ar′mored	un·baked′
un·a·bridged′	un·aid′ed	un·a·shamed′	un·bear′a·ble
un·ac′cent·ed	un·aimed′	un·asked′	un·beat′en
un·ac·cept′a·ble	un·al′ter·a·ble	un·as·signed′	un′be·liev′a·ble
un·ac·com′pa·nied	un·al′tered	un·as·sist′ed	un·bi′ased
un·ac·com′plished	un·am·big′u·ous	un·at·tained′	un·bi′assed
un·ac·quaint′ed	un·am·bi′tious	un·at·tend′ed	un·blamed′
un·ad·dressed′	un·an·nounced′	un·at·trac′tive	un·bleached′
un·a·dul′ter·at·ed	un·an′swer·a·ble	un·au′thor·ized	un·blem′ished

un·blessed or **un·blest** (un blest′), *adj.* **1.** not blessed. **2.** not happy; wretched.

un·blush·ing (un blush′ing), *adj.* **1.** not blushing. **2.** without any feeling of shame.

un·bolt (un bōlt′), *v.* to open by pulling back the bolt or bolts of; unbar.

un·born (un bôrn′), *adj.* **1.** not born. **2.** not yet born; yet to be; future [*unborn* generations].

un·bos·om (un booz′əm), *v.* to tell or make known, as a secret. —**unbosom oneself,** to tell or reveal one's feelings, etc.

un·bound (un bound′), past tense and past participle of **unbind.** —*adj.* **1.** unfastened or let loose. **2.** without a binding, as a book.

un·bri·dled (un brī′d'ld), *adj.* **1.** having no bridle on, as a horse. **2.** showing no control [an *unbridled* temper].

un·bro·ken (un brō′k'n), *adj.* **1.** not broken; all in one piece; whole. **2.** not tamed, as a wild horse. **3.** without any interruption; continuous [an *unbroken* silence].

un·buck·le (un buk′'l), *v.* to unfasten the buckle or buckles of. —**un·buck′led,** *p.t.* & *p.p.;* **un·buck′ling,** *pr.p.*

un·bur·den (un bûr′d'n), *v.* to free from a burden, guilt, anxious feeling, etc.

un·but·ton (un but′'n), *v.* to unfasten the button or buttons of.

un·called-for (un kôld′fôr′), *adj.* not needed or asked for; out of place [an *uncalled-for* act].

un·can·ny (un kan′ē), *adj.* **1.** mysterious and unnatural; weird [The empty house had an *uncanny* look.] **2.** so good, keen, etc. as to seem unnatural [an *uncanny* sense of hearing].

un·cap (un kap′), *v.* to remove the cap, as from a bottle. —**un·capped′,** *p.t.* & *p.p.;* **un·cap′- ping,** *pr.p.*

un·cer·tain (un sûr′t'n), *adj.* **1.** not certain or sure; full of doubt [He looked *uncertain* of what to do.] **2.** not definite; vague [an *uncertain* number]. **3.** not steady or constant; likely to change [*uncertain* weather].

un·cer·tain·ty (un sûr′t'n tē), *n.* **1.** lack of sureness; doubt. **2.** something uncertain. —**un·cer′tain·ties,** *pl.*

un·chain (un chān′), *v.* to free from chains; set loose.

un·chris·tian (un kris′chən), *adj.* **1.** not Christian. **2.** not worthy of a Christian or any decent, civilized person.

un·civ·il (un siv′'l), *adj.* not civil or polite; rude.

un·clasp (un klasp′), *v.* **1.** to open or loosen the clasp of [to *unclasp* a string of pearls]. **2.** to free from a clasp or grip.

un·cle (ung′k'l), *n.* **1.** the brother of one's father or mother. **2.** the husband of one's aunt.

un·clean (un klēn′), *adj.* **1.** dirty. **2.** not pure in a moral or religious way.

un·clean·ly (un klen′lē), *adj.* not clean; dirty.

Uncle Sam, the United States government, pictured as a tall man with whiskers.

Uncle Sam

un·coil (un koil′), *v.* to unwind.

un·com·fort·a·ble (un kum′fər tə b'l *or* un kumf′tər b'l), *adj.* not comfortable; having or giving an uneasy or unpleasant feeling. —**un·com′fort·a·bly,** *adv.*

un·com·mon (un käm′ən), *adj.* **1.** rare; unusual; not often seen, used, etc. **2.** remarkable; extraordinary. —**un·com′mon·ly,** *adv.*

un·com·pro·mis·ing (un käm′prə mīz′ing), *adj.* not giving in at all; firm or strict.

un·con·cern (un kən sûrn′), *n.* lack of interest or worry; indifference.

un·con·cerned (un kən sûrnd′), *adj.* not concerned, interested, worried, etc.; indifferent.

un·con·di·tion·al (un′kən dish′ən 'l), *adj.* not depending on any conditions; absolute [an *unconditional* guarantee]. —**un′con·di′tion·al·ly,** *adv.*

un·con·scious (un kän′shəs), *adj.* **1.** not conscious; not able to feel and think [*unconscious* from a blow on the head]. **2.** not aware [*unconscious* of his mistake]. **3.** not doing or done on purpose [an *unconscious* habit]. —**the unconscious,** the part of the mind in which are stored the feelings, desires, etc. that one is not aware of. —**un·con′scious·ly,** *adv.* —**un·con′scious·ness,** *n.*

un·con·sti·tu·tion·al (un′kän stə tōō′shən 'l *or* un′kän stə tyōō′shən 'l), *adj.* not allowed by the constitution of a nation, etc. [an *unconstitutional* law].

un·cork (un kôrk′), *v.* to pull the cork out of.

---

un·bound′ed
un·brand′ed
un·break′a·ble
un·brushed′
un·caught′
un·ceas′ing
un·cen′sored
un·chal′lenged
un·change′a·ble
un·changed′
un·chang′ing
un·char′i·ta·ble
un·chart′ed
un·char′tered
un·chaste′

un·checked′
un·chewed′
un·civ′i·lized
un·clad′
un·claimed′
un·clas′si·fied
un·cleaned′
un·clear′
un·clipped′
un·closed′
un·clothed′
un·cloud′ed
un′col·lect′ed
un·col′ored
un·combed′

un′com·mit′ted
un′com·mu′ni·ca′tive
un′com·plain′ing
un′com·plet′ed
un′com·pli·cat·ed
un′com·pli·men′ta·ry
un·con·cealed′
un′con·ced′ed
un′con·ceit′ed
un·con·densed′
un·con·fined′
un·con·firmed′
un·con·fused′
un·con·quer·a·ble

un′con′quered
un·con·soled′
un·con·strained′
un·con·sumed′
un′con·test′ed
un′con·trol′la·ble
un·con·trolled′
un′con·ven′tion·al
un′con·vert′ed
un′con·vinced′
un′con·vinc′ing
un·cooked′
un′-co-op′er·a·tive
un′-co-or′di·nat·ed
un′cor·rect′ed

---

un·count·ed (un koun′tid), *adj.* **1.** not counted. **2.** too many to be counted; innumerable.

un·cou·ple (un kup′′l), *v.* to disconnect or unfasten [to *uncouple* railroad cars]. —**un·cou′pled,** *p.t. & p.p.;* **un·cou′pling,** *pr.p.*

un·couth (un kōōth′), *adj.* clumsy, rough, or crude in manners, speech, etc.

un·cov·er (un kuv′ər), *v.* **1.** to remove the cover or covering from. **2.** to make known; disclose, as a hidden fact. **3.** to take off one's hat, as in respect.

unc·tion (ungk′shən), *n.* **1.** the act of putting oil, ointment, etc. on a person, as for a religious purpose. **2.** the oil, ointment, etc. used in this way. **3.** anything that soothes or comforts. **4.** the showing of deep or earnest feeling, often in a false way.

unc·tu·ous (ungk′chōō əs), *adj.* **1.** oily or greasy. **2.** making a false show of deep or earnest feeling; too smooth in speech, manners, etc.

un·curl (un kŭrl′), *v.* to straighten out, as something that has been curled up.

un·daunt·ed (un dôn′tid), *adj.* not afraid or discouraged [a team *undaunted* by its losses].

un·de·ceive (un di sēv′), *v.* to cause to be no longer mistaken or in error. —**un·de·ceived′,** *p.t. & p.p.;* **un·de·ceiv′ing,** *pr.p.*

un·de·cid·ed (un′di sīd′id), *adj.* **1.** not having made up one's mind [*undecided* whether to go or stay]. **2.** that is not decided or settled [The date for the dance is *undecided.*]

un·de·ni·a·ble (un′di nī′ə b′l), *adj.* so true, right, good, etc. that it cannot be questioned or doubted [an *undeniable* fact; of *undeniable* value]. —**un′de·ni′a·bly,** *adv.*

un·der (un′dər), *prep.* **1.** in or to a place, position, amount, value, etc. lower than; below [He sang *under* her window. It rolled *under* the table. It weighs *under* a pound.] **2.** below and to the other side of [We drove *under* the bridge.] **3.** beneath the surface of [oil wells *under* the sea]. **4.** covered or hidden by [I wore a sweater *under* my coat. He goes *under* an assumed name.] **5.** controlled, led, bound, etc. by [*under* orders from the President; *under* oath]. **6.** receiving the effect of [to work *under* a strain; a bridge *under* repair]. **7.** being the subject of [the question *under* discussion]. **8.** because of [*under* the circumstances]. **9.** in a certain class, group, section, etc.; with [List your rent *under* fixed expenses.] —*adv.* **1.** in or to a lower position or condition. **2.** so as to be covered, hidden, etc. [The car was snowed *under.*] —*adj.* lower in position, rank, amount, etc. —**go under,** to fail, as in business.

under-, a prefix meaning: **1.** lower than; below or beneath [*Underclothes* are worn beneath a suit, dress, etc. An *undersecretary* is lower in rank than the main secretary.] **2.** too little; less than usual or proper [An *underpaid* worker is paid too little.] Many words beginning with *under-* but not included here can be easily understood if *under-* is given the meaning of "below" or "less than usual."

un·der·age (un dər āj′), *adj.* below the age required, as by law.

un·der·arm (un′dər ärm), *adj.* under the arm; especially, in the armpit.

un·der·bid (un dər bid′), *v.* to bid lower than; offer to do or sell for less money than. —**un·der·bid′,** *p.t. & p.p.;* **un·der·bid′ding,** *pr.p.*

un·der·brush (un′dər brush), *n.* small trees, bushes, etc. under large trees, as in a forest.

un·der·clothes (un′dər klōz *or* un′dər klōthz), *n.pl.* clothes worn next to the skin, under a suit, dress, etc.; underwear.

un·der·cloth·ing (un′dər klōth′ing), *n.* same as **underclothes.**

un·der·cov·er (un′dər kuv′ər), *adj.* acting or done in secret [*undercover* work as a spy].

un·der·cur·rent (un′dər kŭr′ənt), *n.* **1.** a current beneath the surface current [a river with a strong *undercurrent*]. **2.** a feeling, opinion, etc. that is not out in the open [an *undercurrent* of anger about the policies].

un·der·de·vel·op (un′dər di vel′əp), *v.* to develop less than is needed or proper.

un·der·dog (un′dər dôg), *n.* a person, team, etc. that is losing or is expected to lose, as in a contest or struggle.

un·der·done (un′dər dun′), *adj.* not thoroughly cooked [*Underdone* pork may be harmful.]

un·der·es·ti·mate (un′dər es′tə māt), *v.* to make an estimate or guess that is too low about size, amount, cost, etc. —*n.* an estimate that is too low. —**un′der·es′ti·mat·ed,** *p.t. & p.p.;* **un′der·es′ti·mat·ing,** *pr.p.*

un·der·feed (un dər fēd′), *v.* to feed less than is needed; feed too little. —**un·der·fed** (un dər fed′), *p.t. & p.p.;* **un·der·feed′ing,** *pr.p.*

un·der·foot (un dər foot′), *adv. & adj.* **1.** under one's foot or feet [to trample young grass *underfoot*]. **2.** in the way.

un·der·gar·ment (un′dər gär′mənt), *n.* a piece of underwear.

un·der·go (un dər gō′), *v.* to go through; have happen to one; often, to suffer or endure [to *undergo* years of poverty]. *For principal parts see* **go.**

un·der·grad·u·ate (un′dər graj′ōō it), *n.* a college student who does not yet have a degree.

un·der·ground (un′dər ground′), *adj.* **1.** beneath the surface of the earth [an *underground* lake]. **2.** done in secret; undercover [an *underground* revolt]. —*adv.* **1.** beneath the surface of

un′cor·rupt′ed
un′count′a·ble
un·cred′it·ed
un·crit′i·cal
un·crowd′ed
un·crowned′
un·cul′ti·vat·ed
un·cul′tured
un·curbed′

un·cured′
un·cut′
un·dam′aged
un·dat′ed
un·daz′zled
un′de·bat′a·ble
un·de·cayed′
un′de·ci′pher·a·ble
un′de·clared′

un′dec·o·rat′ed
un′de·faced′
un′de·feat′a·ble
un′de·feat′ed
un·de·fend′ed
un′de·fen′si·ble
un·de·filed′
un′de·fin′a·ble
un·de·fined′

un′de·layed′
un′de·liv′ered
un′dem·o·crat′ic
un·de·mon′stra·ble
un′de·mon′stra·tive
un·de·nied′
un′de·pend′a·ble
un·de·posed′
un′de·praved′

the earth [Moles burrow *underground*.] **2.** in or into hiding [The hunted criminal went *underground*.] —**n.** (un'dər ground), **1.** the space beneath the surface of the earth. **2.** a group of people working secretly against the government or against an enemy occupying their country.

un·der·growth (un'dər grōth), *n.* underbrush.

un·der·hand (un'dər hand), *adj.* **1.** done with the hand kept lower than the elbow or shoulder [an *underhand* pitch in softball]. **2.** not honest, fair, etc.; secret; sly [*underhand* dealings in business]. —*adv.* **1.** with an underhand motion [to toss a ball *underhand*]. **2.** in a sly or secret way.

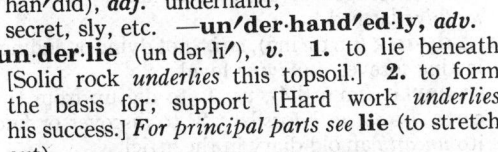
an underhand pitch

un·der·hand·ed (un'dər han'did), *adj.* underhand; secret, sly, etc. —**un'der·hand'ed·ly,** *adv.*

un·der·lie (un dər lī'), *v.* **1.** to lie beneath [Solid rock *underlies* this topsoil.] **2.** to form the basis for; support [Hard work *underlies* his success.] *For principal parts see* **lie** (to stretch out).

un·der·line (un'dər līn'), *v.* **1.** to draw a line under [He *underlined* the word "now."] **2.** to call attention to; emphasize [The speaker *underlined* his main points by repeating them.] —**un'·der·lined',** *p.t. & p.p.;* **un'der·lin'ing,** *pr.p.*

un·der·ling (un'dər ling), *n.* a person of low rank who must take orders from others.

un·der·ly·ing (un'dər lī'ing), *adj.* **1.** lying under; placed beneath. **2.** basic; fundamental [the *underlying* causes of the Civil War].

un·der·mine (un'dər mīn'), *v.* **1.** to dig or make a tunnel under. **2.** to wear away and weaken the supports of [to *undermine* a dock]. **3.** to injure or weaken in a slow or sneaky way [False rumors and gossip had *undermined* their confidence in him.] —**un'der·mined',** *p.t. & p.p.;* **un'der·min'ing,** *pr.p.*

un·der·most (un'dər mōst), *adj. & adv.* lowest in place, position, rank, etc.

un·der·neath (un dər nēth'), *prep. & adv.* under; below; beneath.

un·der·nour·ished (un'dər nūr'isht), *adj.* not getting the food needed to grow or stay healthy.

un·der·pants (un'dər pants), *n.pl.* short or long pants worn as an undergarment.

un·der·pass (un'dər pas), *n.* a passageway or road under a railway or highway.

un·der·pin·ning (un'dər pin'ing), *n.* supports placed under a wall, etc. to strengthen it.

un·der·priv·i·leged (un'dər priv'ə lijd), *adj.* kept from enjoying one's basic social rights, as because of being poor.

un·der·rate (un dər rāt'), *v.* to rate too low; underestimate. —**un·der·rat'ed,** *p.t. & p.p.;* **un·der·rat'ing,** *pr.p.*

un·der·score (un dər skôr'), *v.* to underline. —**un·der·scored',** *p.t. & p.p.;* **un·der·scor'-ing,** *pr.p.*

un·der·sea (un'dər sē'), *adj. & adv.* beneath the surface of the sea: also **un·der·seas',** *adv.*

un·der·sell (un dər sel'), *v.* to sell at a lower price than [to *undersell* a competitor]. —**un·der·sold** (un dər sōld'), *p.t. & p.p.;* **un·der·sell'ing,** *pr.p.*

un·der·shirt (un'dər shûrt), *n.* a shirt, often without sleeves, worn as an undergarment.

un·der·shot (un'dər shät), *adj.* **1.** having the lower front teeth sticking out beyond the upper teeth when the mouth is closed. **2.** turned by water passing beneath, as a water wheel.

un·der·side (un'dər sīd), *n.* the side or surface that is underneath; bottom side.

undershot wheel

un·der·signed (un'dər sīnd'), *n.* the person or persons who have signed a letter or document.

un·der·stand (un dər stand'), *v.* **1.** to get the meaning of; know what is meant by something or someone [Do you *understand* my question?] **2.** to get an idea or notion from what is heard, known, etc.; gather [I *understand* that you like to fish.] **3.** to take as the meaning; interpret [He *understood* my silence to be a refusal.] **4.** to take for granted; take as a fact [It is *understood* that no one is to leave.] **5.** to have knowledge of [Do you *understand* French?] **6.** to know the feelings of and have sympathy toward [Jane felt that no one *understood* her.] **7.** to fill in with the mind in order to make the grammar clear [In the sentence "She is taller than I," the word "am" is *understood* at the end.] —**un·der·stood',** *p.t. & p.p.;* **un·der·stand'ing,** *pr.p.* —**un·der·stand'a·ble,** *adj.*

un·der·stand·ing (un dər stan'ding), *n.* **1.** the fact of knowing what is meant; knowledge [a full *understanding* of the subject]. **2.** the ability to think, learn, judge, etc.; intelligence. **3.** a meaning or explanation [What is your *understanding* of this poem?] **4.** an agreement, especially one that settles a dispute [The feuding families have reached an *understanding*.] —*adj.* that understands; having sympathy and good judgment.

un·der·state (un dər stāt'), *v.* to say less or less strongly than the truth allows or demands. —**un·der·stat'ed,** *p.t. & p.p.;* **un·der·stat'-ing,** *pr.p.* —**un'der·state'ment,** *n.*

un·der·stood (un dər stood'), past tense and past participle of **understand.**

un·der·stud·y (un'dər stud'ē), *n.* an actor who stands ready to play the part of another when it becomes necessary. —*v.* to learn a part as an understudy. —**un'der·stud'ies,** *pl.* —**un'der·stud'ied,** *p.t. & p.p.;* **un'der·stud'y·ing,** *pr.p.*

---

fat, āpe, cär, ten, ēven, hit, bīte, gō, hôrn, tool, book, up, fûr;
get, joy, yet, chin, she, thin, then; zh = s in pleasure; ' as in able (ā'b'l)
    ə = a in ago, e in agent, i in sanity, o in confess, u in focus.

un·der·take (un dər tāk′), *v.* **1.** to enter into or upon, as a task, journey, etc. **2.** to agree, promise, pledge, etc. *For principal parts see* **take.**

un·der·tak·er (un′dər tāk′ər), *n.* a person whose business is taking care of funerals; funeral director. *This word is no longer much used.*

un·der·tak·ing (un′dər tāk′ing), *n.* **1.** something undertaken, as a task. **2.** a promise or pledge.

un·der·tone (un′dər tōn), *n.* **1.** a low tone of voice. **2.** a color, quality, etc. in the background [an *undertone* of blue in the rug; an *undertone* of worry in her letter].

un·der·took (un dər took′), past tense of **undertake.**

un·der·tow (un′dər tō), *n.* a strong current beneath the surface of water and in a different direction; especially, the flow of water back to the sea under the waves breaking on a shore.

un·der·val·ue (un′dər val′yōō), *v.* to value at less than the real worth. —**un′der·val′ued,** *p.t. & p.p.;* **un′der·val′u·ing,** *pr.p.*

un·der·wa·ter (un′dər wô′tər), *adj.* growing, moving, used, etc. under the surface of the water.

un·der·wear (un′dər wer), *n.* clothing worn under one's outer clothes, as undershirts, underpants, slips, etc.

un·der·weight (un′dər wāt), *adj.* not weighing enough; less than normal in weight.

un·der·went (un dər went′), past tense of **undergo.**

un·der·world (un′dər wûrld), *n.* **1.** the class of people who live by crime; criminals, gangsters, etc. as a group. **2.** Hades; hell.

un·der·write (un′dər rīt′), *v.* **1.** to agree to pay the cost of, as an undertaking. **2.** to agree to buy the unsold part of an issue of stocks, bonds, etc. **3.** to write an insurance policy for. *For principal parts see* **write.** —**un′der·writ′er,** *n.*

un·de·sir·a·ble (un′di zīr′ə b'l), *adj.* not desirable or pleasing; not wanted; unpleasant. —*n.* an undesirable person.

un·do (un dōō′), *v.* **1.** to open, untie, or unfasten [to *undo* a knot; to *undo* a package]. **2.** to get rid of the effect of; cancel; reverse [You cannot *undo* the damage done by your remark.] **3.** to ruin or destroy [*undone* by his own folly]. *For principal parts see* **do.**

un·do·ing (un dōō′ing), *n.* **1.** the act of reversing something that has been done. **2.** ruin or the cause of ruin [His ambition was his *undoing*.]

un·done (un dun′), past participle of **undo.** —*adj.* **1.** not done; not finished. **2.** ruined.

un·doubt·ed (un dout′id), *adj.* that cannot be doubted; certain [*undoubted* evidence].

un·doubt·ed·ly (un dout′id lē), *adv.* without doubt; certainly.

un·dreamed-of (un drēmd′əv), *adj.* not dreamed or thought of; never imagined [*undreamed-of* wealth]: also **un·dreamt-of** (un dremt′əv).

un·dress (un dres′), *v.* to take the clothes off; disrobe. —*n.* loose, informal clothes.

un·due (un dōō′ *or* un dyōō′), *adj.* more than is proper or right; too much [to pay *undue* attention to someone].

un·du·late (un′joo lāt *or* un′dyoo lāt), *v.* **1.** to move in waves. **2.** to have a wavy look [*undulating* fields of grain]. —**un′du·lat·ed,** *p.t. & p.p.;* **un′du·lat·ing,** *pr.p.*

un·du·la·tion (un′joo lā′shən *or* un′dyoo lā′shən), *n.* **1.** the act or motion of undulating. **2.** a wavy, curving line or form.

un·du·ly (un dōō′lē *or* un dyōō′lē), *adv.* beyond what is proper or right; too much [You are *unduly* alarmed.]

un·dy·ing (un dī′ing), *adj.* not dying or ending; lasting forever [*undying* love].

un·earth (un ûrth′), *v.* **1.** to dig up from the earth [to *unearth* fossils]. **2.** to discover or find [to *unearth* an old diary in the attic].

un·earth·ly (un ûrth′lē), *adj.* **1.** not of this world; supernatural. **2.** mysterious; weird [an *unearthly* shriek].

un·eas·y (un ē′zē), *adj.* **1.** having or giving no ease; not comfortable [an *uneasy* conscience; an *uneasy* position]. **2.** not natural or poised; awkward [an *uneasy* smile]. **3.** worried; anxious [Mother felt *uneasy* when he was late.] —**un·eas′i·er,** *compar.;* **un·eas′i·est,** *superl.* —**un·eas′i·ly,** *adv.* —**un·eas′i·ness,** *n.*

un·em·ployed (un im ploid′), *adj.* **1.** having no work; not employed. **2.** not being used; idle [*unemployed* wealth]. —**the unemployed,** people who are out of work.

un·em·ploy·ment (un′im ploi′mənt), *n.* **1.** the condition of being unemployed, or without work. **2.** the number of people out of work.

un·e·qual (un ē′kwəl), *adj.* not equal, as in amount, size, strength, value, or rank. —**unequal to,** not having enough power, skill, or courage for [*unequal to* the task of halting the fire]. —**un·e′qual·ly,** *adv.*

un·e·qualed *or* **un·e·qualled** (un ē′kwəld), *adj.* better than any other; without equal; unmatched; best.

un·e·quiv·o·cal (un′i kwiv′ə k'l), *adj.* very clear in meaning; plain [an *unequivocal* answer of "No!"]. —**un′e·quiv′o·cal·ly,** *adv.*

un·err·ing (un ûr′ing *or* un er′ing), *adj.* without error; making no mistake; certain; sure [He took *unerring* aim at the target.]

---

un′de·served′	un·dis′ci·plined	un′di·vid′ed	un′e·mo′tion·al
un′de·serv′ing	un·dis·closed′	un′do·mes′ti·cat·ed	un·end′ing
un′de·ter′mined	un′dis·cov′ered	un·du′ti·ful	un′en·dur′a·ble
un′de·vel′oped	un′dis·guised′	un·dyed′	un′en·force′a·ble
un′di·gest′ed	un′dis·mayed′	un·earned′	un′en·gaged′
un′dig′ni·fied	un′dis·put′ed	un·eat′a·ble	un′en·joy′a·ble
un′di·lut′ed	un·dis·solved′	un·eat′en	un′en·light′ened
un′di·min′ished	un′dis·tin′guish·a·ble	un′e·co·nom′i·cal	un′en·vi·a·ble
un·dimmed′	un′dis·tin′guished	un·ed′u·cat·ed	un·en′vied
un′dip·lo·mat′ic	un′dis·turbed′	un′em·bar′rassed	un·eth′i·cal

un·e·ven (un ē′vən), *adj.* **1.** not even, level, or smooth; irregular [an *uneven* hem on the skirt]. **2.** not equal in size, amount, etc. [pencils of *uneven* length]. **3.** that leaves a remainder when divided by two; odd [Five is an *uneven* number.] —**un·e′ven·ly,** *adv.* —**un·e′ven·ness,** *n.*

un·ex·am·pled (un′ig zam′p'ld), *adj.* with nothing like it before; with no other example [an *unexampled* achievement].

un·ex·cep·tion·a·ble (un′ik sep′shən ə b'l), *adj.* having no errors or faults; that cannot in any way be criticized.

un·ex·pect·ed (un′ik spek′tid), *adj.* not expected; unforeseen; sudden. —**un′ex·pect′-ed·ly,** *adv.*

un·fail·ing (un fāl′ing), *adj.* never failing or stopping; always dependable; certain [an *unfailing* source of water].

un·fair (un fer′), *adj.* not fair, just, or honest. —**un·fair′ly,** *adv.* —**un·fair′ness,** *n.*

un·faith·ful (un fāth′fəl), *adj.* **1.** not keeping a promise or doing a duty; faithless. **2.** not accurate or exact [an *unfaithful* translation]. —**un·faith′ful·ness,** *n.*

un·fa·mil·iar (un′fə mil′yər), *adj.* **1.** not familiar or well-known; strange [This street is *unfamiliar* to me.] **2.** not knowing about; ignorant about [I am *unfamiliar* with his poetry.]

un·fas·ten (un fas′'n), *v.* to open or make loose; untie, unlock, etc.

un·fa·vor·a·ble (un fā′vər ə b'l), *adj.* not favorable; opposed or harmful [an *unfavorable* review of a book]. —**un·fa′vor·a·bly,** *adv.*

un·feel·ing (un fēl′ing), *adj.* **1.** without pity; cruel; hardhearted [her *unfeeling* refusal to help]. **2.** that cannot feel.

un·feigned (un fānd′), *adj.* not false or imitated; real; genuine [*unfeigned* joy].

un·fin·ished (un fin′isht), *adj.* **1.** not finished or completed. **2.** having no finish, or final coat, as of paint.

un·fit (un fit′), *adj.* not fit or suitable [food *unfit* to eat]. —*v.* to make unfit. —**un·fit′ted,** *p.t. & p.p.;* **un·fit′ting,** *pr.p.* —**un·fit′ness,** *n.*

un·flinch·ing (un flin′ching), *adj.* not giving in or yielding; steadfast; firm.

un·fold (un fōld′), *v.* **1.** to open and spread out something that has been folded [to *unfold* a map]. **2.** to make or become known; disclose [to *unfold* one's plans].

un·for·get·ta·ble (un′fər get′ə b'l), *adj.* so important, beautiful, forceful, shocking, etc. that it cannot be forgotten.

un·for·tu·nate (un fôr′chə nit), *adj.* not fortunate; unlucky, unhappy, etc. —*n.* an unfortunate person. —**un·for′tu·nate·ly,** *adv.*

un·found·ed (un foun′did), *adj.* not based on fact or reason [*unfounded* rumors].

un·freeze (un frēz′), *v.* to melt or thaw something frozen. *For principal parts see* **freeze.**

un·furl (un fûrl′), *v.* to open or spread out, as a flag, sail, etc.; unfold.

un·gain·ly (un gān′lē), *adj.* clumsy; awkward.

un·god·ly (un gäd′lē), *adj.* not godly; wicked.

un·gov·ern·a·ble (un guv′ərn ə b'l), *adj.* that cannot be controlled; unruly.

un·guent (ung′gwənt), *n.* a salve or ointment.

un·hand (un hand′), *v.* to stop holding or grasping; let go of.

un·hap·py (un hap′ē), *adj.* **1.** not happy or glad; full of sorrow; sad. **2.** not lucky or fortunate [an *unhappy* result]. **3.** not suitable [an *unhappy* choice of words]. —**un·hap′pi·er,** *compar.;* **un·hap′pi·est,** *superl.* —**un·hap′pi·ly,** *adv.* —**un·hap′pi·ness,** *n.*

un·health·ful (un helth′fəl), *adj.* bad for one's health; unwholesome [*unhealthful* foods].

un·health·y (un hel′thē), *adj.* **1.** having or showing poor health; not well; sickly. **2.** bad for one's health [*unhealthy* habits]. —**un·health′i·er,** *compar.;* **un·health′i·est,** *superl.*

un·heard (un hûrd′), *adj.* not heard or listened to [My warning went *unheard.*]

un·heard-of (un hûrd′uv′), *adj.* not heard of before; never known or done before.

un·hinge (un hinj′), *v.* **1.** to remove from its hinges, as a door. **2.** to unfasten or detach. **3.** to unsettle, disorder, etc. [a mind *unhinged* with grief]. —**un·hinged′,** *p.t. & p.p.;* **un·hing′ing,** *pr.p.*

un·hitch (un hich′), *v.* **1.** to free from being hitched, as a horse. **2.** to unfasten; set loose.

un·ho·ly (un hō′lē), *adj.* **1.** not holy or sacred. **2.** wicked; sinful. —**un·ho′li·er,** *compar.;* **un·ho′li·est,** *superl.* —**un·ho′li·ness,** *n.*

un·hook (un hook′), *v.* **1.** to set loose from a hook [to *unhook* a fish]. **2.** to unfasten the hooks of [to *unhook* a dress].

un·horse (un hôrs′), *v.* to make fall from a horse. —**un·horsed′,** *p.t. & p.p.;* **un·hors′-ing,** *pr.p.*

---

un′e·vent′ful
un′ex·celled′
un′ex·cit′ing
un′ex·cused′
un′ex·per′i·enced
un′ex·pired′
un′ex·plained′
un′ex·plored′
un′ex·pressed′
un·fad′ed
un·fal′ter·ing
un·fash′ion·a·ble
un·fath′omed

un·fed′
un·felt′
un·fenced′
un·fer′ti·lized
un·fixed′
un·fla′vored
un·forced′
un·fore·seen′
un′for·giv′a·ble
un′for·giv′en
un′for·got′ten
un·formed′
un′fre·quent′ed

un·friend′ly
un·fruit′ful
un·ful·filled′
un·fur′nished
un·gen′er·ous
un·gen′tle
un·gen′tle·man·ly
un·gov′erned
un·grace′ful
un·gra′cious
un′gram·mat′i·cal
un·grate′ful
un·grudg′ing

un·guard′ed
un·hal′lowed
un·ham′pered
un·hard′ened
un·harmed′
un·har′nessed
un·heed′ed
un·her′ald·ed
un·hin′dered
un·hon′ored
un·hur′ried
un·hurt′
un′hy·gi·en′ic

---

fat, āpe, cär, ten, ēven, hit, bīte, gō, hôrn, tool, book, up, fûr; get, joy, yet, chin, she, thin, *th*en; zh = s in pleasure; ′ as in able (ā′b'l); ə = a in ago, e in agent, i in sanity, o in confess, u in focus.

uni-, a prefix meaning "of or having only one" [A *unicycle* is a vehicle having only one wheel.]

u·ni·cam·er·al (yōo'ni kam'ər əl), *adj.* having only one group in the lawmaking body [the *unicameral* State legislature of Nebraska].

UNICEF, abbreviation for **United Nations International Children's Emergency Fund.**

u·ni·corn (yōo'nə kôrn), *n.* an imaginary animal like a horse with one long horn in the center of its forehead.

unicorn

u·ni·fi·ca·tion (yōo'nə fi·kā'shən), *n.* the act of unifying or the condition of being unified.

u·ni·form (yōo'nə fôrm), *adj.* **1.** always the same; never changing [He drove at a *uniform* speed.] **2.** all alike; not different from one another [a row of *uniform* houses]. —*n.* the special clothes worn by the members of a particular group [a nurse's *uniform*]. —*v.* to dress in a uniform. —**u'ni·form·ly,** *adv.*

u·ni·form·i·ty (yōo'nə fôr'mə tē), *n.* the condition of being uniform; sameness.

u·ni·fy (yōo'nə fī), *v.* to make into one; unite. —**u'ni·fied,** *p.t. & p.p.;* **u'ni·fy·ing,** *pr.p.*

u·ni·lat·er·al (yōo'ni lat'ər əl), *adj.* **1.** of or on one side only. **2.** involving or done by only one of several persons, nations, etc.

un·im·peach·a·ble (un'im pēch'ə b'l), *adj.* that cannot be doubted or questioned; without fault [a man of *unimpeachable* honesty].

un·ion (yōon'yən), *n.* **1.** a uniting or being united; combination [A large corporation was formed by the *union* of several companies.] **2.** a group of nations, states, etc. united in a larger unit [the Soviet *Union*]. **3.** marriage. **4.** the place where two pipes, etc. are joined. **5.** a coupling, as for connecting pipes. **6.** same as **labor union.** —**the Union,** the United States of America; during the Civil War, the Federal government as opposed to the Confederacy.

un·ion·ist (yōon'yən ist), *n.* **1.** a person who believes in or supports union. **2.** a member of a labor union. **3.** Unionist, a supporter of the Union in the Civil War. —**un'ion·ism,** *n.*

un·ion·ize (yōon'yən īz), *v.* **1.** to organize into a labor union [to *unionize* miners]. **2.** to form labor unions in [to *unionize* shops]. —**un'ion·ized,** *p.t. & p.p.;* **un'ion·iz·ing,** *pr.p.*

union jack, 1. a flag bearing the symbol of national union, as an American naval flag that is a blue field with 50 white stars. **2. Union Jack,** the national flag of the United Kingdom.

Union of Soviet Socialist Republics, a country made up of 15 republics of eastern Europe and northern Asia, including Russia: also called **Soviet Union.**

u·nique (yōo nēk'), *adj.* **1.** that is the only one; having nothing like it [Man is *unique* among the animals in having language.] **2.** unusual; remarkable; rare: *thought of by some as an incorrect meaning* [We had a *unique* experience.]

u·ni·son (yōo'nə s'n *or* yōo'nə z'n), *n.* **1.** sameness of musical pitch, as of two or more voices or tones. **2.** agreement; harmony [The group shows a *unison* of spirit.] —**in unison,** singing or playing the same notes at the same time.

u·nit (yōo'nit), *n.* **1.** a single person or group, especially as a part of a whole [an army *unit*]. **2.** a single part with some special use [the lens *unit* of a camera]. **3.** a fixed quantity or measure used as a standard [The ounce is a *unit* of weight.] **4.** the smallest whole number; one.

U·ni·tar·i·an (yōo'nə ter'i ən), *n.* a member of a Christian church that does not accept the Trinity and that allows differing religious views.

u·nite (yoo nīt'), *v.* **1.** to put or join together so as to make one; combine [The two churches *united* to form a new church.] **2.** to bring or join together in doing something [The allied nations were *united* in their war effort.] —**u·nit'ed,** *p.t. & p.p.;* **u·nit'ing,** *pr.p.*

u·nit·ed (yoo nīt'id), *adj.* **1.** joined together in one; combined [*united* efforts]. **2.** in agreement [a group *united* in spirit].

United Arab Republic, same as **Egypt.**

United Kingdom, Great Britain and Northern Ireland.

United Nations, an organization set up in 1945 to work for world peace and security. Most of the nations of the world belong to it. Its headquarters are in New York City.

United States of America, a country, mostly in North America, made up of 50 States: also called **United States** or **America.**

u·ni·tize (yōo'nə tīz), *v.* to make into a single unit, all of one piece. —**u'ni·tized,** *p.t. & p.p.;* **u'ni·tiz·ing,** *pr.p.*

u·ni·ty (yōo'nə tē), *n.* **1.** the condition of being united or combined; oneness. **2.** the condition of being in agreement; harmony **3.** the single effect that a work of art or literature has because of the way it is put together. **4.** the number one. —**u'ni·ties,** *pl.*

u·ni·ver·sal (yōo'nə vūr's'l), *adj.* **1.** of, for, or by all people; concerning everyone [*universal* aid]. **2.** present everywhere [*universal* ruin]. —**u·ni·ver·sal·i·ty** (yōo'nə vər sal'ə tē), *n.*

universal joint, a joint that allows the parts joined to swing in any direction, as in the drive shaft of an automobile.

u·ni·ver·sal·ly (yōo'nə vūr's'l ē), *adv.* **1.** in every case [*universally* true]. **2.** in every part or place; everywhere [used *universally*].

u·ni·verse (yōo'nə vūrs), *n.* all space and everything in it; earth, the sun, stars, and all things that exist.

un'i·den'ti·fied	un'im·pres'sive	un·in'jured	un·in'ter·est·ed
un·il'lus·trat·ed	un'in·cor'po·rat·ed	un·in·spired'	un·in'ter·est·ing
un'im·ag'i·na·ble	un'in·dexed'	un'in·tel'li·gent	un·in'ter·rupt'ed
un'im·ag'i·na·tive	un'in·formed'	un'in·tel'li·gi·ble	un·in'ven·tive
un·im·paired'	un'in·hab'i·ta·ble	un·in·tend'ed	un·in·vit'ed
un'im·por'tant	un'in·hab'it·ed	un'in·ten'tion·al	un·in·vit'ing

u·ni·ver·si·ty (yoo'nə vŭr'sə tē), *n.* a school of higher education made up of a college or colleges and, usually, professional schools, as of law and medicine. —**u'ni·ver'si·ties,** *pl.*

un·just (un just'), *adj.* not just or right; unfair. —**un·just'ly,** *adv.*

un·kempt (un kempt'), *adj.* **1.** not combed [*unkempt* hair]. **2.** not tidy; messy.

un·kind (un kīnd'), *adj.* not kind; hurting the feelings of others; harsh; cruel. —**un·kind'ly,** *adv.* —**un·kind'ness,** *n.*

un·lace (un lās'), *v.* to unfasten the laces of. —**un·laced',** *p.t. & p.p.;* **un·lac'ing,** *pr.p.*

un·latch (un lach'), *v.* to open by releasing a latch.

un·law·ful (un lô'fəl), *adj.* against the law; illegal [an *unlawful* search of one's home]. —**un·law'ful·ly,** *adv.*

un·learn (un lŭrn'), *v.* to forget something learned [It is hard to *unlearn* a wrong method.]

un·learn·ed (un lŭr'nid), *adj.* **1.** not educated; ignorant. **2.** (un lŭrnd'), not learned by study; also, known without having been learned [Sneezing is an *unlearned* response.]

un·leash (un lēsh'), *v.* to let loose from being held back, as on a leash.

un·less (ən les'), *conj.* in any case other than; except if [Don't go *unless* you want to.]

un·let·tered (un let'ərd), *adj.* **1.** not educated; ignorant. **2.** not knowing how to read or write.

un·like (un līk'), *adj.* not alike; different. —*prep.* not like [It's *unlike* him to cry.] —**un·like'ness,** *n.*

un·lim·it·ed (un lim'it id), *adj.* without limits or bounds; indefinite [*unlimited* freedom; *unlimited* space].

un·load (un lōd'), *v.* **1.** to take a load or cargo from a ship, truck, etc. [to *unload* crates; to *unload* a freight car]. **2.** to take out the charge from, as a gun. **3.** to get rid of [to *unload* responsibilities].

un·lock (un läk'), *v.* **1.** to open by undoing a lock. **2.** to make known; reveal, as a secret.

un·looked-for (un lookt'fôr'), *adj.* unexpected.

un·loose (un loos'), *v.* to make or let loose; set free, unfasten, etc. —**un·loosed',** *p.t. & p.p.;* **un·loos'ing,** *pr.p.*

un·loos·en (un loos''n), *v.* to loosen; unloose.

un·luck·y (un luk'ē), *adj.* having or bringing bad luck; not lucky; unfortunate. —**un·luck'i·er,** *compar.;* **un·luck'i·est,** *superl.* —**un·luck'i·ly,** *adv.*

un·man (un man'), *v.* to make lose nerve, courage, or other qualities that a man should have. —**un·manned',** *p.t. & p.p.;* **un·man'ning,** *pr.p.*

un·man·ner·ly (un man'ər lē), *adj.* having bad manners; rude. —*adv.* rudely.

un·mask (un mask'), *v.* **1.** to take off a mask or disguise, as at a masquerade. **2.** to lay open the true nature, purpose, etc. of; expose.

un·mean·ing (un mēn'ing), *adj.* having no meaning or sense; meaningless.

un·meet (un mēt'), *adj.* not fitting or proper: *no longer much used.*

un·men·tion·a·ble (un men'shən ə b'l), *adj.* not fit to be mentioned; not proper or polite.

un·mis·tak·a·ble (un'mis tāk'ə b'l), *adj.* that cannot be mistaken or misunderstood; clear; plain. —**un'mis·tak'a·bly,** *adv.*

un·mit·i·gat·ed (un mit'ə gāt'id), *adj.* **1.** not lessened or eased [*unmitigated* suffering]. **2.** absolute; plain [an *unmitigated* fool].

un·mor·al (un môr'əl), *adj.* apart from morals or morality; neither moral nor immoral.

un·moved (un moovd'), *adj.* **1.** not moved from its place. **2.** firm or unchanged in purpose. **3.** not having one's feelings stirred; not affected [*unmoved* by their suffering].

un·nat·u·ral (un nach'ər əl), *adj.* **1.** not natural or normal; abnormal. **2.** artificial or affected. **3.** very evil or cruel. —**un·nat'u·ral·ly,** *adv.*

un·nec·es·sar·y (un nes'ə ser'ē), *adj.* not necessary; needless. —**un·nec'es·sar'i·ly,** *adv.*

un·nerve (un nŭrv'), *v.* to make lose nerve, courage, or control [The accident *unnerved* him.] —**un·nerved',** *p.t. & p.p.;* **un·nerv'ing,** *pr.p.*

un·num·bered (un num'bərd), *adj.* **1.** not numbered or counted. **2.** too many to count; countless.

un·pack (un pak'), *v.* **1.** to open and empty out, as a suitcase. **2.** to take from a crate, trunk, etc. [to *unpack* books].

un·par·al·leled (un par'ə leld), *adj.* that has no parallel or equal; matchless.

---

un·jus'ti·fi'a·ble	un·man'age·a·ble	un'mo·lest'ed	un'ob·tain'a·ble
un·kept'	un·man'ly	un·mount'ed	un'ob·tru'sive
un·know'a·ble	un·manned'	un·mourned'	un·oc'cu·pied
un·know'ing	un·marked'	un·mov'a·ble	un'of·fend'ing
un·known'	un·mar'ket·a·ble	un·mus'i·cal	un'of·fi'cial
un·la'beled	un·mar'ried	un·named'	un·o'pened
un·la'belled	un·mas'tered	un·nat'u·ral·ized	un·op·posed'
un·la'dy·like	un·matched'	un·nav'i·ga·ble	un'or·dained'
un·la·ment'ed	un·meas'ured	un·neigh'bor·ly	un'or·gan·ized
un·leav'ened	un'me·chan'i·cal	un·not'ed	un·o'rig'i·nal
un·li'censed	un·melt'ed	un·no'tice·a·ble	un·or'tho·dox
un·light'ed	un·men'tioned	un·no'ticed	un·owned'
un·like'ly	un·mer'ci·ful	un'ob·jec'tion·a·ble	un·paid'
un·lined'	un·mer'it·ed	un·o'blig'ing	un·paired'
un·lit'	un·mind'ful	un'ob·scured'	un·pal'a·ta·ble
un·lov'a·ble	un'mis·tak'en	un·ob·serv'ant	un·par'don·a·ble
un·loved'	un·mixed'	un·ob·served'	un·par'doned
un·love'ly	un·mod'i·fied	un'ob·struct'ed	un·pas'teur·ized

---

fat, āpe, cär, ten, ēven, hit, bīte, gō, hôrn, tool, book, up, fŭr; get, joy, yet, chin, she, thin, *th*en; zh = s in pleasure; ' as in able (ā'b'l) ə = a in ago, e in agent, i in sanity, o in confess, u in focus.

un·pin (un pin′), *v.* to unfasten by removing a pin or pins from. —**un·pinned′**, *p.t. & p.p.;* **un·pin′ning**, *pr.p.*

un·pleas·ant (un plez′'nt), *adj.* not pleasant or agreeable; offensive; disagreeable. —**un·pleas′ant·ly**, *adv.* —**un·pleas′ant·ness**, *n.*

un·pop·u·lar (un päp′yoo lər), *adj.* not popular; not liked by most people or by the public. —**un·pop·u·lar·i·ty** (un′päp yoo lar′ə tē), *n.*

un·prac·ticed or **un·prac·tised** (un prak′tist), *adj.* **1.** not done or used often or regularly. **2.** without skill or experience; not expert.

un·prec·e·dent·ed (un pres′ə den′tid), *adj.* without a precedent; not done or known before; novel [an *unprecedented* award].

un·prej·u·diced (un prej′oo dist), *adj.* not showing prejudice or bias; fair.

un·prin·ci·pled (un prin′sə p'ld), *adj.* without good morals or principles; unscrupulous.

un·print·a·ble (un print′ə b'l), *adj.* not fit to be printed.

un·pro·nounce·a·ble (un′prə nouns′ə b'l), *adj.* hard to pronounce.

un·quench·a·ble (un kwench′ə b'l), *adj.* that cannot be quenched, or stopped [an *unquenchable* fire; an *unquenchable* thirst].

un·ques·tion·a·ble (un kwes′chən ə b'l), *adj.* not to be questioned or doubted; certain. —**un·ques′tion·a·bly**, *adv.*

un·quote (un kwōt′), *interj.* that is the end of the quotation.

un·rav·el (un rav′'l), *v.* **1.** to separate or undo the threads of something woven, knitted, or tangled [to *unravel* a scarf]. **2.** to make clear; solve [to *unravel* a mystery]. *For principal parts see* **ravel**.

un·read (un red′), *adj.* **1.** not read, as a book. **2.** having read little [an *unread* person].

un·read·y (un red′ē), *adj.* **1.** not ready or prepared. **2.** not prompt or alert; slow. —**un·read′i·ly**, *adv.* —**un·read′i·ness**, *n.*

un·re·al (un rē′əl *or* un rēl′), *adj.* not real; imaginary. —**un·re·al·i·ty** (un′ri al′ə tē), *n.*

un·rea·son·a·ble (un rē′z'n ə b'l), *adj.* **1.** not showing reason; not reasonable [He is in an *unreasonable* mood.] **2.** beyond the limits of what is reasonable; not moderate [an *unreasonable* price]. —**un·rea′son·a·bly**, *adv.*

un·re·gen·er·ate (un′ri jen′ər it), *adj.* **1.** not reborn in spirit. **2.** wicked; sinful.

un·re·lent·ing (un′ri len′ting), *adj.* **1.** refusing to give in or relent. **2.** without mercy; cruel. **3.** not relaxing or slowing up, as in effort.

un·re·mit·ting (un′ri mit′ing), *adj.* not stopping or slowing down; continuing.

un·re·served (un ri zûrvd′), *adj.* **1.** not holding back one's thoughts, etc.; frank; open. **2.** not limited. —**un·re·serv·ed·ly** (un ri zûr′vid lē), *adv.*

un·rest (un rest′), *n.* a troubled or disturbed condition; restlessness.

un·right·eous (un rī′chəs), *adj.* wicked, sinful, unjust, etc. —**un·right′eous·ness**, *n.*

un·ri·valed or **un·ri·valled** (un rī′v'ld), *adj.* having no rival or equal; matchless.

un·roll (un rōl′), *v.* **1.** to open or spread out, as something rolled up. **2.** to show; display.

un·ruf·fled (un ruf′'ld), *adj.* not ruffled or disturbed; smooth; calm; serene.

un·rul·y (un rōō′lē), *adj.* hard to control or keep in order; not obedient or orderly. —**un·rul′i·er**, *compar.;* **un·rul′i·est**, *superl.*

un·sad·dle (un sad′'l), *v.* **1.** to take the saddle off, as a horse. **2.** to make fall from the saddle of a horse; unhorse. —**un·sad′dled**, *p.t. & p.p.;* **un·sad′dling**, *pr.p.*

un·sa·vor·y (un sā′vər ē), *adj.* **1.** having no flavor; tasteless. **2.** having a bad taste or smell [*unsavory* odors]. **3.** unpleasant or disgusting [an *unsavory* scandal].

un·say (un sā′), *v.* to take back something said; retract. —**un·said** (un sed′), *p.t. & p.p.;* **un·say′ing**, *pr.p.*

un·scathed (un skā*th*d′), *adj.* not hurt; unharmed [a warrior *unscathed* in battle].

un·screw (un skrōō′), *v.* **1.** to unfasten or loosen by taking out screws [to *unscrew* the hinges on a door]. **2.** to take out, off, etc. or loosen by turning [to *unscrew* a bolt, a jar lid, etc.].

---

un′pa·tri·ot′ic	un′pre·ten′tious	un·rea′son·ing	un′rep·re·sent′ed
un·paved′	un′pre·vent′a·ble	un′re·ceived′	un′re·pressed′
un·peo′pled	un·print′ed	un′re·claimed′	un′re·proved′
un′per·ceived′	un·priv′i·leged	un·rec′og·nized	un′re·quit′ed
un′per·plexed′	un′pro·duc′tive	un′rec·om·pensed′	un′re·signed′
un′per·suad′ed	un·prof′it·a·ble	un′rec·on·ciled′	un′re·sist′ing
un′per·sua′sive	un′pro·gres′sive	un′re·cord′ed	un′re·spon′sive
un′per·turbed′	un·prom′is·ing	un′re·deemed′	un′re·strained′
un·picked′	un·prompt′ed	un′re·fined′	un′re·strict′ed
un·pierced′	un·pro·nounced′	un′re·flect′ing	un′re·ten′tive
un·pit′ied	un′pro·pi′tious	un′re·formed′	un′re·vealed′
un·pit′y·ing	un′pro·tect′ed	un′re·gard′ed	un′re·venged′
un·planned′	un·proved′	un·reg′is·tered	un′re·voked′
un·plant′ed	un·prov′en	un·reg′u·lat·ed	un′re·ward′ed
un·played′	un′pro·vid′ed	un′re·lat′ed	un·rhymed′
un·pleas′ing	un′pro·voked′	un′re·laxed′	un·ripe′
un·pledged′	un·pruned′	un·re·li′a·ble	un′ro·man′tic
un·plowed′	un·pub′lished	un′re·lieved′	un·ruled′
un′po·et′ic	un·punc′tu·al	un′re·mem′bered	un·safe′
un′po·et′i·cal	un·pun′ished	un′re·moved′	un·said′
un·poised′	un·qual′i·fied	un′re·mu′ner·a·tive	un·salt′ed
un·pol′ished	un·ques′tioned	un′re·nowned′	un·sanc′ti·fied
un·pol·lut′ed	un·ques′tion·ing	un·rent′ed	un·san′i·tar′y
un′pre·dict′a·ble	un·qui′et	un′re·paired′	un·sat·is·fac′to·ry
un′pre·med′i·tat·ed	un·quot′a·ble	un′re·pealed′	un·scarred′
un·pre·pared′	un·raised′	un·re′pent′ant	un·scent′ed
un·pressed′	un·read′a·ble	un′re·port′ed	un·schol′ar·ly
un′pre·tend′ing	un′re·al·ized	un′rep·re·sen′ta·tive	un′sci·en·tif′ic

un·scru·pu·lous (un skrōō′pyoo ləs), *adj.* paying no attention to what is right or proper; not honest [*unscrupulous* business practices].

un·seal (un sēl′), *v.* to open by breaking a seal.

un·search·a·ble (un sürch′ə b'l), *adj.* that cannot be understood or searched into; mysterious.

un·seat (un sēt′), *v.* **1.** to make fall from one's seat, as from a saddle. **2.** to force out of office, as by an election.

un·seem·ly (un sēm′lē), *adj.* not proper, fitting, or decent; unbecoming [*unseemly* behavior]. —*adv.* in an unseemly way.

un·self·ish (un sel′fish), *adj.* not selfish; putting the good of others above one's own interests. —**un·self′ish·ly,** *adv.* —**un·self′ish·ness,** *n.*

un·set·tle (un set′'l), *v.* to make shaky, troubled, upset, etc. [The news *unsettled* her.] —**un·set′tled,** *p.t. & p.p.;* **un·set′tling,** *pr.p.*

un·set·tled (un set′'ld), *adj.* **1.** not fixed; changing or likely to change [*unsettled* weather]. **2.** not calm, quiet, or peaceful. **3.** not paid [an *unsettled* debt]. **4.** not decided or determined [an *unsettled* argument]. **5.** not lived in; having no settlers [*unsettled* lands].

un·sheathe (un shē*th*′), *v.* to take, as a sword or knife, from a sheath or case. —**un·sheathed′,** *p.t. & p.p.;* **un·sheath′ing,** *pr.p.*

un·shod (un shäd′), *adj.* not wearing shoes.

un·sight·ly (un sīt′lē), *adj.* not pleasant to look at; ugly.

un·skilled (un skild′), *adj.* not having or needing a special skill or training [Digging ditches is *unskilled* labor.]

un·skill·ful or **un·skil·ful** (un skil′fəl), *adj.* having little or no skill; clumsy; awkward.

un·snap (un snap′), *v.* to unfasten by opening the snaps of. —**un·snapped′,** *p.t. & p.p.;* **un·snap′ping,** *pr.p.*

un·snarl (un snärl′), *v.* to untangle.

un·so·phis·ti·cat·ed (un′sə fis′tə kāt′id), *adj.* simple, natural, or innocent; not wise in the ways of the world.

un·sound (un sound′), *adj.* **1.** not sound; not healthy, whole, safe, etc. [an *unsound* mind; an *unsound* ship]. **2.** not sensible [an *unsound* plan].

un·spar·ing (un sper′ing), *adj.* **1.** not sparing; generous in giving; lavish [*unsparing* charity].

2. without mercy; harsh [*unsparing* criticism]. —**un·spar′ing·ly,** *adv.*

un·speak·a·ble (un spēk′ə b'l), *adj.* hard to describe or speak about because so great, bad, etc. [*unspeakable* joy; *unspeakable* tortures]. —**un·speak′a·bly,** *adv.*

un·sta·ble (un stā′b'l), *adj.* **1.** not stable, firm, steady, etc. [an *unstable* foundation]. **2.** likely to change; changeable [the *unstable* weather of spring].

un·stead·y (un sted′ē), *adj.* **1.** not steady or firm; shaky. **2.** likely to change; changeable.

un·stop (un stäp′), *v.* **1.** to pull the stopper or cork from. **2.** to clear from being blocked. —**un·stopped′,** *p.t. & p.p.;* **un·stop′ping,** *pr.p.*

un·strung (un strung′), *adj.* **1.** nervous or upset. **2.** having the strings loosened or off.

un·sub·stan·tial (un′səb stan′shəl), *adj.* not substantial; not solid, firm, real, etc.; flimsy.

un·sung (un sung′), *adj.* **1.** not sung. **2.** not honored or praised, as in songs or poems [*unsung* heroes of the Revolutionary War].

un·tan·gle (un tang′g'l), *v.* to free from tangles, or confusion; straighten out [to *untangle* a knot; to *untangle* a mystery]. —**un·tan′-gled,** *p.t. & p.p.;* **un·tan′gling,** *pr.p.*

un·taught (un tôt′), *adj.* **1.** not taught or educated; ignorant. **2.** got without being taught; natural [an *untaught* skill].

un·think·a·ble (un thingk′ə b'l), *adj.* that cannot be thought about or imagined [It is *unthinkable* that anyone could be so cruel.]

un·think·ing (un thingk′ing), *adj.* showing no care or thought for others; thoughtless.

un·thought-of (un thôt′uv′), *adj.* not thought of or imagined before.

un·ti·dy (un tī′dē), *adj.* not tidy or neat; messy. —**un·ti′di·er,** *compar.;* **un·ti′di·est,** *superl.* —**un·ti′di·ly,** *adv.* —**un·ti′di·ness,** *n.*

un·tie (un tī′), *v.* to loosen or unfasten something that is tied or knotted. —**un·tied′,** *p.t. & p.p.;* **un·ty′ing,** *pr.p.*

un·til (un til′), *prep.* **1.** up to the time of; till [Wait *until* noon.] **2.** before [Don't leave *until* tomorrow.] —*conj.* **1.** up to the time when [He was lonely *until* he met her.] **2.** to the point,

---

un·sea′son·a·ble	un·slaked′	un·stamped′	un·sweet′ened
un·sea′soned	un·smil′ing	un·states′man·like	un·swept′
un·sea′worth·y	un·so′cia·ble	un·stint′ing	un·swerv′ing
un·see′ing	un·so′cial	un·stressed′	un′sym·met′ri·cal
un·seen′	un·soiled′	un·stud′ied	un′sym·pa·thet′ic
un′sen·ti·men′tal	un·sold′	un·sub·dued′	un·tact′ful
un·serv′ice·a·ble	un′so·lic′it·ed	un′sub·stan′ti·at·ed	un·taint′ed
un·shad′ed	un·solved′	un′suc·cess′ful	un·tal′ent·ed
un·shak′a·ble	un·sort′ed	un·suit′a·ble	un·tamed′
un·shak′en	un·sought′	un·suit′ed	un·tanned′
un·shaped′	un·spec′i·fied	un·sul′lied	un·tar′nished
un·shape′ly	un·spent′	un′sup·port′ed	un·tast′ed
un·shav′en	un·spoiled′	un′sup·pressed′	un·taxed′
un·shel′tered	un·spoilt′	un·sure′	un·ten′a·ble
un·shorn′	un·spo′ken	un′sur·passed′	un·ten′ant·ed
un·sift′ed	un·sports′man·like	un′sus·pect′ed	un·test′ed
un·signed′	un·spot′ted	un′sus·pect′ing	un·thank′ful
un·sized′	un·stained′	un′sus·pi′cious	un·thought′ful

---

fat, **āpe,** **cär,** **ten,** **ēven,** **hit,** **bīte,** **gō,** **hôrn,** **tōōl,** **book,** **up,** **fũr;** **get,** **joy,** **yet,** **chin,** **she,** **thin,** ***th*en;** **zh** = s in pleasure;   ′ as in able (ā′b'l);   ə = a in ago,   e in agent,   i in sanity,   o in confess,   u in focus.

degree, or place that [He ate *until* he was full.] **3.** before [Don't stop *until* I do.]

un·time·ly (un tīm/lē), *adj.* coming at the wrong time, especially too soon [his *untimely* death]. —*adv.* too soon or at the wrong time.

un·to (un/tŏŏ), *prep.* to: *now used only in poetry, prayers, etc.* [Give thanks *unto* the Lord.]

un·told (un tōld/), *adj.* **1.** not told or not known [He left, his story still *untold*.] **2.** too much to be counted; very great [*untold* wealth].

un·toward (un tôrd/), *adj.* **1.** causing trouble; unfortunate; unlucky [*Untoward* delays made us miss the bus.] **2.** hard to control; stubborn.

un·true (un trŏŏ/), *adj.* **1.** not correct; false. **2.** not faithful or loyal. —**un·tru/ly,** *adv.*

un·truth (un trŏŏth/), *n.* **1.** a statement that is not true; lie. **2.** the fact of being untrue or false; lack of truth.

un·truth·ful (un trŏŏth/fəl), *adj.* **1.** telling lies often [an *untruthful* boy]. **2.** that is not the truth [*untruthful* tales]. —**un·truth/ful·ly,** *adv.*

un·tu·tored (un tŏŏ/tərd *or* un tyŏŏ/tərd), *adj.* not educated; ignorant.

un·twist (un twist/), *v.* to undo something twisted or twined: also **un·twine** (un twīn/).

un·used (un yŏŏzd/), *adj.* **1.** not in use or never having been used [*unused* space; *unused* clothing]. **2.** not accustomed; not familiar with [He's *unused* to traveling.]

un·u·su·al (un yŏŏ/zhŏŏ əl), *adj.* not usual or common; rare; remarkable. —**un·u/su·al·ly,** *adv.*

un·ut·ter·a·ble (un ut/ər ə b'l), *adj.* that cannot be spoken, described, or talked about; unspeakable. —**un·ut/ter·a·bly,** *adv.*

un·veil (un vāl/), *v.* **1.** to take a veil or covering from so as to show or reveal [to *unveil* a statue]. **2.** to remove a veil that one is wearing.

un·war·y (un wer/ē), *adj.* not watchful or on one's guard [the *unwary* victims of a fraud].

un·well (un wel/), *adj.* not well; ill; sick.

un·wield·y (un wēl/dē), *adj.* hard to handle, use, or control because it is very large, heavy, etc. [an *unwieldy* crate]. —**un·wield/i·ness,** *n.*

un·will·ing (un wil/ing), *adj.* **1.** not willing or ready [*unwilling* to take the blame]. **2.** done, given, etc. against one's will [*unwilling* permission]. —**un·will/ing·ly,** *adv.*

un·wind (un wīnd/), *v.* to undo something wound by turning or rolling in the opposite direction; also, to become undone in this way [to *unwind* thread from a spool]. —**un·wound** (un wound/), *p.t. & p.p.;* **un·wind/ing,** *pr.p.*

un·wise (un wīz/), *adj.* not wise; not showing good sense; foolish. —**un·wise/ly,** *adv.*

un·wit·ting (un wit/ing), *adj.* **1.** not knowing or aware [*unwitting* of the danger around her]. **2.** not done on purpose; not intended [an *unwitting* insult]. —**un·wit/ting·ly,** *adv.*

un·wont·ed (un wun/tid), *adj.* not common or usual [His *unwonted* politeness surprised us.]

un·wor·thy (un wûr/thē), *adj.* **1.** not deserving [I am *unworthy* of such honors.] **2.** not fit or suitable [That remark is *unworthy* of a gentleman.] —**un·wor/thi·er,** *compar.;* **un·wor/-thi·est,** *superl.* —**un·wor/thi·ly,** *adv.* —**un·wor/thi·ness,** *n.*

un·wrap (un rap/), *v.* to open by taking off the wrapping; also, to become opened in this way. —**un·wrapped/,** *p.t. & p.p.;* **un·wrap/ping,** *pr.p.*

un·writ·ten (un rit/'n), *adj.* **1.** not in writing [an *unwritten* agreement]. **2.** practiced or observed because it is the custom, but not part of a written code [an *unwritten* law or rule].

un·yoke (un yōk/), *v.* **1.** to remove the yoke from, as oxen. **2.** to disconnect; separate. —**un·yoked/,** *p.t. & p.p.;* **un·yok/ing,** *pr.p.*

up (up), *adv.* **1.** to, in, or on a higher place [to climb *up;* to stay *up* in the air]. **2.** in or to a place thought of as higher [The sun comes *up* at dawn. He has come *up* in the world.] **3.** to a later time [from childhood *up*]. **4.** to a larger amount, size, etc. [to go *up* in price; to swell *up*]. **5.** in or into an upright position [to stand *up*]. **6.** into action, discussion, or view [Who brought *up* that question? I put *up* the new sign.] **7.** aside; away [to lay *up* wealth]. **8.** so as to be even with [Run to keep *up* with him!] **9.** completely [He ate *up* all our food. Don't use *up* the paste.] **10.** apiece; each [The score is six *up*.] The adverb *up* is used after many verbs in order to give special meaning to them. See the phrases following such verbs as *cut, catch, keep, look,* etc. —*adj.* **1.** put, brought, going, or gone up [His hand is *up*. The sun is *up*. Prices are *up*. Is the sign *up* yet?] **2.** out of bed [Aren't you *up* yet?] **3.** above the ground [The new grass is *up*.] **4.** at an end; over [Time's *up*.] **5.** at bat in baseball [You're *up* next.] **6.** going on; happening: *used only in everyday talk* [What's *up*?] —*prep.* up to, toward, along, through, into, or upon [We climbed *up* the hill. We rowed *up* the river.] —*v.* to get up, put up, lift up, raise, etc.: *used only in everyday talk* [The grocer *upped* his prices.] —*n.* good luck [to have one's *ups* and downs]. —**up against,** faced with: *used only in everyday talk.* —**up for, 1.** that is a candidate; nominated [*up for* class president]. **2.** before a court of law for trial [*up for* murder]. —**up to, 1.** doing or getting ready to do [That child is *up to* some mischief.]

un·tilled/   un·trod/   un·versed/   un·wel/come
un·tir/ing   un·trod/den   un·vexed/   un·whole/some
un·touched/   un·trou/bled   un·vis/it·ed   un·wom/an·ly
un·traced/   un·trust/wor/thy   un·want/ed   un·work/a·ble
un·trained/   un·turned/   un·war/rant·ed   un·world/ly
un·trans/fer·a·ble   un·ut/tered   un·washed/   un·wor/ried
un·trav/eled   un·var/ied   un·watched/   un·wound/ed
un·trav/elled   un·var/nished   un·wa/ver·ing   un·wov/en
un·tried/   un·var/y·ing   un·wea/ried   un·wrin/kled
un·trimmed/   un·ver/i·fied   un·wed/   un·yield/ing

2. capable of doing. **3.** to be decided by. **4.** resting upon as a duty. *This phrase is used only in everyday talk.* —**upped,** *p.t. & p.p.;* **up'ping,** *pr.p.*

up·braid (up brād'), *v.* to scold; find fault with in an angry way.

up·bring·ing (up'bring'ing), *n.* the care and training one gets while growing up.

up·coun·try (up'kun'trē), *adj. & adv.* in or toward the inner regions of a country.

up·date (up dāt'), *v.* to bring up to date; make agree with the latest facts, ideas, etc. —**up·dat'ed,** *p.t. & p.p.;* **up·dat'ing,** *pr.p.*

up·end (up end'), *v.* to set or stand on end.

up·grade (up'grād), *n.* an upward slope, as of a road. —**on the upgrade,** becoming higher, stronger, or more important.

up·heav·al (up hē'v'l), *n.* **1.** a forceful lifting up from beneath [the *upheaval* of ground in an earthquake]. **2.** a sudden, violent change [the *upheaval* begun by the French Revolution].

up·hill (up'hil'), *adj. & adv.* **1.** toward the top of a hill; upward. **2.** needing or using much effort; with difficulty [an *uphill* battle against illness].

up·hold (up hōld'), *v.* **1.** to hold up; keep from falling. **2.** to agree with and support against attack by others [to *uphold* the right of every citizen to vote]. —**up·held** (up held'), *p.t. & p.p.;* **up·hold'ing,** *pr.p.*

up·hol·ster (up hōl'stər), *v.* to put springs and padding in, and cover with material, as a chair, sofa, etc. —**up·hol'ster·er,** *n.*

up·hol·ster·y (up hōl'stər ē), *n.* the work of upholstering or materials used for this.

up·keep (up'kēp), *n.* the act of keeping something in good working condition, or the cost of this [the *upkeep* of a car].

up·land (up'land), *n.* land higher than the land around it. —*adj.* of or in such land.

up·lift (up lift'), *v.* **1.** to lift up; elevate [trees with *uplifted* branches]. **2.** to raise to a higher or better level [Her heart was *uplifted* by the good news.] —*n.* (up'lift), the act of uplifting, or of making better or more moral.

up·on (ə pän'), *prep. & adv.* on, or up and on [He climbed *upon* the fence. We were set *upon* by bandits.]

up·per (up'ər), *adj.* **1.** above another [the *upper* lip; an *upper* floor]. **2.** of greater importance, rank, etc. [the *upper* house of a legislature]. —*n.* the part of a shoe above the sole.

up·per·most (up'ər mōst), *adj.* **1.** highest. **2.** getting the most attention [The thought was *uppermost* in his mind.] —*adv.* in or to the highest place or position.

Upper Vol·ta (väl'tə), a country in western Africa, north of Ghana.

up·raise (up rāz'), *v.* to raise up; lift [marching with banners *upraised*]. —**up·raised',** *p.t. & p.p.;* **up·rais'ing,** *pr.p.*

up·right (up'rīt), *adj.* **1.** standing or pointing straight up; erect [*upright* pickets in a fence]. **2.** honest and just [an *upright* judge]. **3.** describing a piano in which the strings are mounted straight up and down in a rectangular box. —*adv.* in an upright position [to stand *upright*]. —*n.* **1.** an upright pole, beam, etc. [a lake house built on *uprights*]. **2.** an upright piano.

upright piano

up·ris·ing (up'rīz ing), *n.* the act of rising up, or rebelling; revolt.

up·roar (up'rôr), *n.* **1.** a noisy, confused condition; commotion [His remark threw the meeting into an *uproar*.] **2.** a loud, confused noise.

up·roar·i·ous (up rôr'i əs), *adj.* **1.** making an uproar. **2.** loud and noisy [*uproarious* laughter].

up·root (up rōōt'), *v.* **1.** to pull up by the roots [to *uproot* a dead shrub]. **2.** to get rid of completely [to *uproot* crime].

up·set (up set'), *v.* **1.** to turn or tip over; overturn [The frightened horse *upset* the wagon.] **2.** to disturb the order or working of [to *upset* a busy schedule]. **3.** to win a surprising victory over [Our swimming team *upset* the champions.] **4.** to make nervous or troubled [The news *upset* poor Dad.] —*n.* (up'set), **1.** the act of upsetting. **2.** a surprising victory. —*adj.* (up'set), **1.** tipped over; overturned [an *upset* bowl of flowers]. **2.** disturbed; out of order [*upset* plans]. —**up·set',** *p.t. & p.p.;* **up·set'ting,** *pr.p.*

up·shot (up'shät), *n.* the result; conclusion.

up·side down (up'sīd), **1.** with the top side or part underneath; with the wrong side up [Turn the glasses *upside down* to drain them.] **2.** in disorder or confusion [We turned the room *upside down* looking for the book.] —**up'side-down',** *adj.*

up·stairs (up'sterz'), *adv. & adj.* to or on an upper floor [to go *upstairs*; an *upstairs* room]. —*n.* an upper floor or floors.

up·stand·ing (up stan'ding), *adj.* honest; honorable [a fine, *upstanding* young man].

up·start (up'stärt), *n.* a person who has just become rich or important; especially, such a person who is very bold and conceited.

up·stream (up'strēm'), *adv. & adj.* against the current or flow of a stream.

up·tight (up'tīt'), *adj.* very nervous, anxious, or tense: *a slang word.*

up·to-date (up'tə dāt'), *adj.* **1.** having the latest facts, ideas, etc. [an *up-to-date* report]. **2.** of the newest or latest kind, as in style.

up·town (up'toun'), *adj. & adv.* in or toward the upper part of a city, or the part away from the main business section.

---

fat,   āpe,   **cär,**   ten,   ēven,   hit,   bīte,   gō,   hôrn,   tool,   book,   **up,**   fur;

get,   joy,   yet,   chin,   she,   thin,   *then;*   **zh** = s in pleasure;   ' as in able (ā'b'l);

ə = a in ago,   e in agent,   i in sanity,   o in confess,   u in focus.

up·turn (up/tûrn), *n.* a turn or move toward a higher place or better condition [Business took a sharp *upturn*.] —*v.* to turn up or over.

up·ward (up/wərd), *adv. & adj.* toward a higher place, position, degree, price, etc.: also **up/wards**, *adv.* —**upward of** or **upwards of**, more than.

Ur, symbol for the chemical element *uranium.*

U·ral (yoor/əl), *n.* **1.** a river flowing from the Ural Mountains into the Caspian Sea. **2. Urals,** *pl.* the Ural Mountains.

Ural Mountains, a mountain system in the Soviet Union, between Europe and Asia.

u·ra·ni·um (yoo rā/ni əm), *n.* a very hard, heavy metal that is a radioactive chemical element. It is used in producing atomic energy.

U·ra·nus (yoor/ə nəs), *n.* **1.** an early Greek god who was the symbol of heaven. **2.** the third largest planet. It is the seventh in distance away from the sun.

ur·ban (ûr/bən), *adj.* of, living in, or having to do with cities or towns [*urban* dwellers].

ur·bane (ûr bān/), *adj.* having smooth and polished manners; polite and refined. —**ur·bane/ly,** *adv.*

ur·ban·i·ty (ûr ban/ə tē), *n.* the quality of being urbane; refined politeness.

ur·chin (ûr/chin), *n.* a small boy or any young child, especially one who is full of mischief.

-ure (ər), a suffix meaning: **1.** act or result [An *enclosure* is the act or result of enclosing.] **2.** condition of being [*Exposure* is the condition of being exposed.] **3.** a thing or group that [A *legislature* is a group that legislates.]

u·re·a (yoo rē/ə), *n.* a substance found in urine or made artificially. It is used in making plastics, etc.

urge (ûrj), *v.* **1.** to plead with or encourage strongly to do something [We *urged* Ned to finish college.] **2.** to force forward; drive [He *urged* his mule up the hill.] **3.** to speak in favor of; recommend [to *urge* caution]. —*n.* a sudden feeling that makes one want to do something; impulse [an *urge* to sneeze; the *urge* to become a writer]. —**urged,** *p.t. & p.p.;* **urg/ing,** *pr.p.*

ur·gen·cy (ûr/jən sē), *n.* **1.** the condition of being urgent; need for quick action [the *urgency* of their need]. **2.** a strong demand; insistence [The *urgency* of public opinion forced him to resign.] —**ur/gen·cies,** *pl.*

ur·gent (ûr/jənt), *adj.* **1.** needing quick action [an *urgent* situation]. **2.** demanding in a strong and serious way; insistent [an *urgent* call for help]. —**ur/gent·ly,** *adv.*

u·ri·nal (yoor/ə n'l), *n.* a fixture with a drain, used for urinating.

u·ri·nar·y (yoor/ə ner/ē), *adj.* of the organs that make and carry off the urine.

u·ri·nate (yoor/ə nāt), *v.* to get rid of urine from the body. —**u/ri·nat·ed,** *p.t. & p.p.;* **u/ri·nat·ing,** *pr.p.*

u·rine (yoor/in), *n.* the liquid with waste products of the body that is passed by the kidneys into the bladder, from which it passes out of the body.

urn (ûrn), *n.* **1.** a vase with a flat base or pedestal. **2.** a vase like this for keeping the ashes of a cremated body. **3.** a metal container with a faucet, for making and serving coffee or tea.

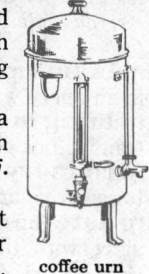
coffee urn

U·ru·guay (yoor/ə gwā), *n.* a country in southeastern South America. —**U/ru·guay/an,** *adj. & n.*

us (us), *pron.* the form of *we* that is used as the object of a verb or preposition [They warned *us.* Write a letter to *us.*]

U.S. or **US,** abbreviation for **United States.**

U.S.A. or **USA,** abbreviation for **United States of America, United States Army.**

us·a·ble or **use·a·ble** (yōoz/ə b'l), *adj.* that can be used; fit or ready for use.

USAF or **U.S.A.F.,** abbreviation for **United States Air Force.**

us·age (yōos/ij *or* yōoz/ij), *n.* **1.** the act or way of using; treatment [His shoes were scuffed from hard *usage*.] **2.** a practice followed for a long time; custom; habit. **3.** the way in which a word or phrase is used [The word "album" to mean "a single, long-playing record" is a recent *usage*.]

USCG or **U.S.C.G.,** abbreviation for **United States Coast Guard.**

use (yōoz), *v.* **1.** to put or bring into service or action [She *used* the vacuum cleaner. Don't *use* a singular verb with a plural subject.] **2.** to deal with; treat [He *used* us badly.] **3.** to do away with by using; consume [She *used* up all the soap. Don't *use* up your energy.] —*n.* (yōos), **1.** a using or being used [the *use* of atomic energy for power; old tools still in *use*]. **2.** the power to use [He lost the *use* of his hand.] **3.** the right or permission to use [May I have the *use* of your car?] **4.** the chance or need to use [Give away what you have no *use* for.] **5.** a way of using [to be taught the *use* of the typewriter]. **6.** benefit or advantage; usefulness [What's the *use* of your worrying?] —**make use of** or **put to use,** to use. —**used to, 1.** did in an earlier time; did once [I *used to* live in El Paso.] **2.** accustomed to; familiar with [He's *used to* hard work.] —**used,** *p.t. & p.p.;* **us/ing,** *pr.p.* —**us/er,** *n.*

used (yōozd), *adj.* that has been used; not new; secondhand [*used* cars].

use·ful (yōos/fəl), *adj.* that can be used; of service; helpful [*useful* advice]. —**use/ful·ly,** *adv.* —**use/ful·ness,** *n.*

use·less (yōos/lis), *adj.* having no use; worthless [It is *useless* for you to complain.] —**use/less·ly,** *adv.* —**use/less·ness,** *n.*

ush·er (ush/ər), *n.* a person who shows people to their seats in a church, theater, etc. —*v.* to show the way to or bring in [He *ushered* us to our seats. The atom bomb *ushered* in a new age.]

USMC or **U.S.M.C.,** abbreviation for **United States Marine Corps.**

USN or **U.S.N.,** abbreviation for **United States Navy.**

U.S.S.R. or USSR, abbreviation for **Union of Soviet Socialist Republics.**

u·su·al (yōo′zhōo əl), *adj.* such as is most often seen, heard, used, etc.; common; ordinary; normal. —**as usual,** in the usual way. —**u′su·al·ly,** *adv.*

u·surp (yōo zŭrp′ *or* yōo sŭrp′), *v.* to take and hold by force or without right [to *usurp* another's power or position]. —**u′sur·pa′tion,** *n.* —**u·surp′er,** *n.*

u·su·ry (yōo′zhoo rē), *n.* **1.** the act or practice of lending money at a rate of interest that is too high or against the law. **2.** such a rate of interest. —**u′su·rer,** *n.* —**u·su·ri·ous** (yōo zhoor′i əs), *adj.*

U·tah (yōo′tô *or* yōo′tä), *n.* a State in the southwestern part of the United States: abbreviated **Ut.**

u·ten·sil (yōo ten′s'l), *n.* a container, tool, etc. used for a special purpose [Pots, pans, egg beaters, can openers, etc. are kitchen *utensils.*]

u·ter·us (yōo′tər əs), *n.* a hollow organ of female mammals in which the young grow before birth; womb. —**u·ter·i** (yōo′tər ī), *pl.*

u·til·i·tar·i·an (yōo til′ə ter′i ən), *adj.* **1.** of or having utility; useful; practical. **2.** stressing usefulness over beauty, etc.

u·til·i·ty (yōo til′ə tē), *n.* **1.** the quality of being useful; usefulness. **2.** something useful to the public, as the service of gas, water, etc.; also, a company that provides such a service: also called **public utility.** —*adj.* containing laundry equipment, etc. [a *utility* room]. —**u·til′i·ties,** *pl.*

u·ti·lize (yōo′t'l īz), *v.* to put to use; make practical use of [to *utilize* atomic power for peaceful purposes]. —**u′ti·lized,** *p.t. & p.p.;* **u′ti·liz·ing,** *pr.p.* —**u′ti·li·za′tion,** *n.*

ut·most (ut′mōst), *adj.* **1.** most distant; farthest [the *utmost* regions of the earth]. **2.** greatest or highest [a meeting of the *utmost* importance]. —*n.* the most that is possible [He strained his muscles to the *utmost.*]

U·to·pi·a or **u·to·pi·a** (yōo tō′pi ə), *n.* **1.** any imaginary place where life is perfect and everyone is happy. **2.** any scheme for such a perfect society, that is not really practical or possible. —**U·to′pi·an** or **u·to′pi·an,** *adj. & n.*

ut·ter (ut′ər), *adj.* complete; total; absolute [*utter* joy; an *utter* fool]. —**ut′ter·ly,** *adv.*

ut·ter (ut′ər), *v.* to make or express with the voice [to *utter* a cry; to *utter* a thought].

ut·ter·ance (ut′ər əns), *n.* **1.** the act or way of uttering [to give *utterance* to an idea]. **2.** a word or words uttered; something said.

ut·ter·most (ut′ər mōst), *adj. & n.* same as **utmost.**

u·vu·la (yōo′vyoo lə), *n.* the small part of the soft palate hanging down above the back of the tongue. —**u′vu·las** or **u·vu·lae** (yōo′vyoo lē), *pl.*

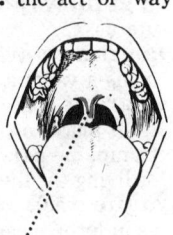

uvula

V

V, v (vē), *n.* the twenty-second letter of the English alphabet. —**V's, v's** (vēz), *pl.*

V (vē), *n.* **1.** the Roman numeral for five. **2.** symbol for the chemical element *vanadium.*

v., abbreviation for **verb, verse, versus.**

VA or **V.A.,** abbreviation for **Veterans Administration.**

Va., abbreviation for **Virginia.**

va·can·cy (vā′kən sē), *n.* **1.** a job or position for which someone is needed. **2.** a place to live in that is for rent. **3.** the condition of being vacant; emptiness. **4.** lack of interest or thought. —**va′can·cies,** *pl.*

va·cant (vā′kənt), *adj.* **1.** having nothing or no one in it; empty [a *vacant* lot; a *vacant* seat; a *vacant* house]. **2.** free from work; leisure [a *vacant* period in the day]. **3.** without interest or thought [a *vacant* stare]. —**va′cant·ly,** *adv.*

va·cate (vā′kāt), *v.* to make a place empty, as by leaving [You must *vacate* your room by noon.] —**va′cat·ed,** *p.t. & p.p.;* **va′cat·ing,** *pr.p.*

va·ca·tion (və kā′shən *or* vā kā′shən), *n.* a period of time when one stops working, going to school, etc. in order to rest and have recreation. —*v.* to take one's vacation.

vac·ci·nate (vak′sə nāt), *v.* to inject a vaccine into, in order to keep from getting a certain disease, especially smallpox. —**vac′ci·nat·ed,** *p.t. & p.p.;* **vac′ci·nat·ing,** *pr.p.*

vac·ci·na·tion (vak′sə nā′shən), *n.* **1.** the act of vaccinating. **2.** the scar on the skin where a vaccine has been injected.

vac·cine (vak′sēn), *n.* **1.** a substance with a mild virus of cowpox, that is injected to cause a mild form of smallpox. In this way the body builds up the ability to fight off the disease later. **2.** any substance with dead bacteria or a virus, used in this way to fight off some disease.

vac·il·late (vas′ə lāt), *v.* **1.** to be unable to decide; keep changing one's mind. **2.** to sway to and fro; waver. —**vac′il·lat·ed,** *p.t. & p.p.;* **vac′il·lat·ing,** *pr.p.* —**vac′il·la′tion,** *n.*

va·cu·i·ty (va kyōo′ə tē), *n.* **1.** the condition of being empty; emptiness. **2.** empty space; vacuum. **3.** emptiness of mind; stupidity. —**va·cu′i·ties,** *pl.*

vac·u·ous (vak′yōō əs), *adj.* **1.** showing little intelligence; stupid. **2.** with nothing in it; empty.

vac·u·um (vak′yōō əm *or* vak′yoom), *n.* **1.** a space, as in a bottle or tube, from which most of the air or gas has been taken. **2.** a space that has nothing at all in it. —*v.* to clean with a vacuum cleaner: *used only in everyday talk.*

vacuum bottle, a bottle with a vacuum between its inner and outer walls, keeping liquids at almost the same temperature for a time.

vacuum cleaner, a machine that cleans rugs, furniture, etc. by sucking up the dirt.

vacuum tube, same as **electron tube.**

vag·a·bond (vag′ə bänd), *n.* **1.** a person who wanders from place to place. **2.** a wandering beggar; tramp. —*adj.* **1.** wandering from place to place [a *vagabond* tribe]. **2.** of or like a vagabond or his life [*vagabond* habits].

va·gar·y (və ger′ē), *n.* an odd or unexpected idea or act; whim. —**va·gar′ies,** *pl.*

va·gi·na (və jī′nə), *n.* the canal leading into the uterus.

va·gran·cy (vā′grən sē), *n.* the condition of being a vagrant.

va·grant (vā′grənt), *n.* a person who wanders from place to place, doing odd jobs or begging; tramp. —*adj.* wandering from place to place, or living the life of a vagrant.

vague (vāg), *adj.* not clear, definite, or distinct, as in form, meaning, or purpose [*vague* figures in the fog; a *vague* answer]. —**va′guer,** *compar.;* **va′guest,** *superl.* —**vague′ly,** *adv.* —**vague′ness,** *n.*

vain (vān), *adj.* **1.** having too high an opinion of oneself; conceited [He is *vain* about his looks.] **2.** with little or no result; not successful [a *vain* attempt to climb the mountain]. **3.** worthless [*vain* promises]. —**in vain, 1.** without success [I pleaded *in vain* for help.] **2.** without the proper respect; in a profane way [to use the name of God *in vain*]. —**vain′ly,** *adv.*

vain·glo·ri·ous (vān′glôr′i əs), *adj.* feeling or showing pride in a boastful way.

vain·glo·ry (vān′glôr′ē), *n.* boastful pride.

val·ance (val′əns), *n.* a short curtain fitted across the top of a window or hanging from the edge of a bed, shelf, etc. to the floor.

vale (vāl), *n.* a valley: *used mainly in poetry.*

val·e·dic·to·ri·an (val′ə dik tôr′i ən), *n.* a student, usually the one with

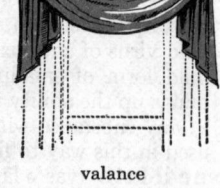
valance

the highest grades, who gives the farewell speech at a graduation.

val·e·dic·to·ry (val′ə dik′tə rē), *n.* a farewell speech, as at a graduation. —*adj.* saying farewell. —**val′e·dic′to·ries,** *pl.*

val·en·tine (val′ən tīn), *n.* **1.** a greeting card or gift sent on Saint Valentine's Day. **2.** a sweetheart to whom one sends a valentine.

Valentine, Saint, a Christian martyr of the 3rd century A.D., whose day is February 14. It is the custom to send valentines on this day.

val·et (val′it *or* val′ā), *n.* a man who works as a servant to another man, taking care of his clothes, helping him dress, etc. —*adj.* describing a service, as in a hotel, for cleaning and pressing clothes, etc.

Val·hal·la (val hal′ə), *n.* the great hall in Norse myths, where Odin feasts the souls of heroes killed in battle.

val·iant (val′yənt), *adj.* brave; full of courage. —**val′iant·ly,** *adv.*

val·id (val′id), *adj.* **1.** based on facts or good reasoning; true or sound [a *valid* argument]. **2.** binding under law; having legal force [a *valid* deed or will].

val·i·date (val′ə dāt), *v.* **1.** to make valid in law, as a will. **2.** to prove to be valid, or sound, true, etc.; confirm [A witness to the accident *validated* my story.] —**val′i·dat·ed,** *p.t. & p.p.;* **val′i·dat·ing,** *pr.p.*

va·lid·i·ty (və lid′ə tē), *n.* the quality or fact of being valid.

va·lise (və lēs′), *n.* a suitcase.

Val·kyr·ie (val kir′ē), *n.* any of the maidens in Norse myths who lead the souls of heroes killed in battle to Valhalla.

val·ley (val′ē), *n.* **1.** low land lying between hills or mountains. **2.** the land that is drained or watered by a large river and its branches [the Mississippi *valley*]. —**val′leys,** *pl.*

Valley Forge, a village in southeastern Pennsylvania, where Washington and his troops camped in the winter of 1777–1778.

val·or (val′ər), *n.* courage or bravery, as in battle. —**val′or·ous,** *adj.*

Val·pa·rai·so (val′pə rī′zō), *n.* a seaport in central Chile.

val·u·a·ble (val′yōō b'l *or* val′yōō ə b'l), *adj.* **1.** having value or worth; especially, worth much money [a *valuable* diamond]. **2.** thought of as precious, useful, worthy, etc. [*valuable* knowledge]. —*n.* something of value, as a piece of jewelry.

val·u·a·tion (val′yōō ā′shən), *n.* **1.** the act of deciding the value of something; appraisal [We took the pearls to a jeweler for a *valuation*.] **2.** the value set on something [He sold the car for less than its *valuation*.]

val·ue (val′yōō), *n.* **1.** the quality of a thing that makes it wanted or desirable; worth [the *value* of true friendship]. **2.** the worth of a thing in money or in other goods [The *value* of our house has gone up.] **3.** buying power [The *value* of the dollar falls with inflation.] **4.** a fair or proper exchange [I'm willing to pay for *value* received.] **5.** the meaning, force, special quality, etc., as of a piece of writing. **6.** **values,** *pl.* beliefs or ideals [the moral *values* of a nation]. —*v.* **1.** to set or estimate the value of [He *valued* the property at $2,000.] **2.** to think of or rate, as compared with other things [I *value* health above wealth.] **3.** to think highly of [I *value* his advice.] —**val′ued,** *p.t. & p.p.;* **val′u·ing,** *pr.p.* —**val′ue·less,** *adj.*

val·ued (val′yōōd), *adj.* **1.** having been given a price, value, etc. [a hat *valued* at $10]. **2.** highly thought of [a *valued* friend].

valve (valv), *n.* **1.** a device, as in a pipe, that controls the flow of a gas or liquid by means of a flap, lid, or plug that closes off the pipe. **2.** a membrane in the body that acts in this way [The *valves* of the heart let the blood flow in one direction only.] **3.** a device, as in a trumpet, that opens a branch to the main tube so as to change the pitch. **4.** either of the parts making up the shell of a clam, oyster, etc.

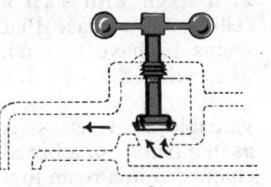

valve in a faucet

vamp (vamp), *n.* **1.** the top part of a shoe or boot covering the front of the foot. **2.** something patched up to look new. —*v.* to patch up or repair, as with a new vamp.

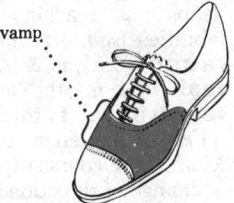

vamp

vam·pire (vam′pīr), *n.* **1.** in folk tales, a dead body that moves about at night and sucks the blood of sleeping persons. **2.** a person who gets things from others in a wicked or evil way. **3.** a tropical American bat that lives on the blood of other animals: in full, **vampire bat.**

van (van), *n.* same as **vanguard.**

van (van), *n.* a large closed truck, as for moving furniture, etc.

va·na·di·um (və nā′di əm), *n.* a silver-white metal that is a chemical element. It is used in making a steel alloy (**vanadium steel**) that is especially hard and tough.

Van Bu·ren, Martin (van byoor′ən), 1782–1862; eighth president of the United States, from 1837 to 1841.

Van·cou·ver (van koo′vər), *n.* **1.** a seaport in British Columbia, Canada. **2.** an island of British Columbia, off the southwestern coast.

Van·dal (van′d'l), *n.* **1.** a member of a Germanic tribe that invaded Italy and plundered Rome in 455 A.D. **2. vandal,** a person who destroys or damages things on purpose, especially works of art, public property, etc. —*adj.* **1.** of the Vandals. **2. vandal,** of or like a vandal; destroying in a brutal way.

van·dal·ism (van′d'l iz'm), *n.* the actions or attitudes of a vandal; brutal destruction.

van·dal·ize (van′d'l īz), *v.* to destroy or damage as a vandal does. —**van′dal·ized,** *p.t.* & *p.p.;* **van′dal·iz·ing,** *pr.p.*

Van·dyke beard (van dīk′), a closely trimmed beard that comes to a point.

vane (vān), *n.* **1.** a flat metal object on a pole, that swings with the wind to show which way it is blowing; weather vane. **2.** any of the blades of a windmill, electric fan, propeller, etc.

van·guard (van′gärd), *n.* **1.** the front part of an army going forward. **2.** the leaders of a movement, or the leading position in a movement.

va·nil·la (və nil′ə), *n.* **1.** a flavoring made from the pods of an orchid that twines around trees, etc. **2.** this plant, or any of its pods, called **vanilla beans.**

van·ish (van′ish), *v.* **1.** to go suddenly out of sight; disappear. **2.** to stop existing; become extinct [The dodo has *vanished.*]

van·i·ty (van′ə tē), *n.* **1.** the quality of being vain or conceited about oneself, one's looks, etc. **2.** the condition of being vain or worthless, or any worthless thing. —**van′i·ties,** *pl.*

vanilla plant and vanilla bean

van·quish (vang′kwish), *v.* to overcome or defeat; conquer.

van·tage (van′tij), *n.* a favorable position; advantage [Capturing the hill gave our troops a point of *vantage.*]

vap·id (vap′id), *adj.* **1.** having no taste or flavor; flat [a *vapid* drink]. **2.** not exciting; dull [*vapid* talk].

va·por (vā′pər), *n.* **1.** a thick mist or mass of tiny drops of water floating in the air, as steam or fog. **2.** the gas formed when a substance that is usually a liquid or solid is heated [Mercury *vapor* is used in some lamps.]

va·por·ize (vā′pər īz), *v.* to change into vapor, as by spraying or being heated [Atomizers are used to *vaporize* perfume. The water *vaporized* in the sun.] —**va′por·ized,** *p.t.* & *p.p.;* **va′por·iz·ing,** *pr.p.* —**va′por·iz·er,** *n.*

va·por·ous (vā′pər əs), *adj.* **1.** forming or full of vapor [a *vaporous* marsh]. **2.** like vapor. **3.** imaginary or fanciful [*vaporous* ideas].

va·pour (vā′pər), *n.* British spelling of **vapor.**

va·que·ro (vä ker′ō), *n.* a cowboy: *a Spanish word used in the Southwest.* —**va·que′ros,** *pl.*

var·i·a·ble (ver′i ə b'l), *adj.* **1.** likely to change or vary; changeable [in a *variable* mood]. **2.** that can be changed or varied [a *variable* price]. —*n.* anything that changes or varies, as a shifting wind. —**var·i·a·bil·i·ty** (ver′i ə bil′ə tē), *n.*

var·i·ance (ver′i əns), *n.* the act or amount of varying, or changing. —**at variance, 1.** disagreeing or quarreling. **2.** differing.

var·i·ant (ver′i ənt), *adj.* different in some way from others of the same kind ["Theatre" is a *variant* spelling of "theater."] —*n.* a variant form, spelling, etc.

var·i·a·tion (ver′i ā′shən), *n.* **1.** the act of varying, changing, or differing [a *variation* in style]. **2.** the amount of a change [a *variàtion* of ten feet]. **3.** the repeating of a tune or musical theme, with changes as in rhythm or key.

var·i·col·ored (ver′i kul′ərd), *adj.* of several or many colors.

---

fat, āpe, cär, ten, ēven, hit, bīte, gō, hôrn, tōōl, book, up, fûr; get, joy, yet, chin, she, thin, *th*en; zh = s in pleasure; ′ as in able (ā′b'l); ə = a in ago, e in agent, i in sanity, o in confess, u in focus.

var·i·cose (ver'i kōs), *adj.* swollen at irregular places [*varicose* veins].

var·ied (ver'ēd), *adj.* **1.** of different kinds [a program of *varied* entertainment]. **2.** showing differences, as of color. **3.** changed; altered.

var·i·e·gat·ed (ver'i ə gāt'id *or* ver'i gāt'id), *adj.* **1.** marked with different colors in spots, streaks, or patches [*variegated* tulips]. **2.** having variety; varied. —**var'i·e·ga'tion,** *n.*

va·ri·e·ty (və rī'ə tē), *n.* **1.** change; lack of sameness [to like *variety* in one's meals]. **2.** any of the various forms of something; sort; kind [many *varieties* of cloth; a cat of the striped *variety*]. **3.** a number of different kinds [a *variety* of fruits at the market]. **4.** vaudeville: also **variety show.** —**va·ri'e·ties,** *pl.*

var·i·ous (ver'i əs), *adj.* **1.** of several different kinds [We planted *various* seeds.] **2.** several or many [*Various* people have said so.] —**var'·i·ous·ly,** *adv.*

var·let (vär'lit), *n.* a rascal or knave; scoundrel: *now seldom used.*

var·nish (vär'nish), *n.* **1.** a liquid made of gums or resins mixed in oil, alcohol, or turpentine and spread over a surface to give it a hard and glossy coat. **2.** this hard and glossy coat. **3.** an outward show or look of smoothness or polish; gloss. —*v.* **1.** to cover with varnish. **2.** to smooth over in a false way [to *varnish* a lie with an innocent look].

var·si·ty (vär'sə tē), *n.* the team that represents a college or school in games or contests against others. —**var'si·ties,** *pl.*

var·y (ver'ē), *v.* **1.** to change; make or become different [She *varies* her hair style. The weather has *varied* from day to day.] **2.** to be different; differ [Opinions *vary* on this matter.] **3.** to give variety to [*Vary* your reading.] —**var'ied,** *p.t. & p.p.;* **var'y·ing,** *pr.p.*

vas·cu·lar (vas'kyoo lər), *adj.* of or having vessels for carrying blood, lymph, or sap.

vase (vās *or* vāz), *n.* an open container used for decoration or for holding flowers.

vas·e·line (vas'ə lēn), *n.* a white or yellow jelly made from petroleum and used as a salve or ointment: **Vaseline** is a trademark.

vas·sal (vas''l), *n.* **1.** a person in the feudal system who held land in return for military or other help to an overlord. **2.** a person or country that owes service or loyalty to another; servant, dependent, subject, etc. —*adj.* of or like a vassal. —**vas'sal·age,** *n.*

vast (vast), *adj.* very great or very large [a *vast* desert; a matter of *vast* importance]. —**vast'·ly,** *adv.* —**vast'ness,** *n.*

vat (vat), *n.* a large tank, tub, or cask for holding liquids.

Vat·i·can (vat'i kən), *n.* **1.** the palace of the Pope in Vatican City. **2.** the office, power, or government of the Pope.

Vatican City, a state inside the city of Rome, with the Pope as its head.

vau·de·ville (vô'də vil *or* vōd'vil), *n.* a stage show made up of different kinds of acts, as skits, songs, dances, etc.

vault (vôlt), *n.* **1.** an arched ceiling or roof. **2.** a room with such a ceiling, or a space that seems to have an arch [the *vault* of the sky]. **3.** a room for keeping money, valuable papers, etc. safe, as in a bank. **4.** a burial chamber. **5.** a room in a cellar for storing things. —*v.* **1.** to cover with a vault. **2.** to build in the form of a vault.

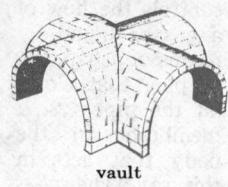
vault

vault (vôlt), *v.* to jump or leap over, as a fence or bar, by resting one's hands on the fence, etc. or by using a long pole to push oneself from the ground. *See also* **pole vault.**

vault·ing (vôl'ting), *adj.* **1.** that vaults or leaps. **2.** reaching too far or beyond one's abilities [*vaulting* ambition].

vaunt (vônt), *v. & n.* boast or brag.

veal (vēl), *n.* the flesh of a calf, used as meat.

veer (vir), *v.* **1.** to change direction; shift; turn [*Veer* to the left at the fork in the road.] **2.** to change the course of; turn [to *veer* a ship]. —*n.* a change of direction.

veg·e·ta·ble (vej'tə b'l *or* vej'i tə b'l), *n.* **1.** a plant or part of a plant that is eaten raw, as in a salad, or cooked and served with meat, etc. [Tomatoes, potatoes, peas, and lettuce are all *vegetables.*] **2.** any plant [Is seaweed an animal, *vegetable*, or mineral?] —*adj.* **1.** of, like, or from vegetables [*vegetable* oil]. **2.** having to do with plants in general [the *vegetable* kingdom].

veg·e·tar·i·an (vej'ə ter'i ən), *n.* a person who chooses to eat no meat and eats mainly vegetables. —*adj.* **1.** having to do with vegetarians or their ways of eating. **2.** made up only of vegetables. —**veg'e·tar'i·an·ism,** *n.*

veg·e·tate (vej'ə tāt), *v.* to live or grow as a plant does; especially, to lead a dull life with little action or thought. —**veg'e·tat·ed,** *p.t. & p.p.;* **veg'e·tat·ing,** *pr.p.*

veg·e·ta·tion (vej'ə tā'shən), *n.* **1.** things growing from the ground; plant life [thick *vegetation* in the jungle]. **2.** the act of vegetating.

veg·e·ta·tive (vej'ə tā'tiv), *adj.* **1.** having to do with plants, or growing as plants do [*vegetative* forms of life]. **2.** dull and not very active [a *vegetative* life].

ve·he·ment (vē'ə mənt), *adj.* **1.** full of deep, strong feeling; intense [a *vehement* argument]. **2.** acting or moving with great force; violent. —**ve'he·mence,** *n.* —**ve'he·ment·ly,** *adv.*

ve·hi·cle (vē'ə k'l), *n.* **1.** a device on wheels or runners for carrying persons or things, as an automobile, bicycle, or sled. **2.** a means of expressing [He uses poetry as the *vehicle* for his ideas.] **3.** oil, water, or other liquid in which colored pigments are mixed to make paint.

veil (vāl), *n.* **1.** a piece of thin cloth, as net or gauze, worn by women over the face or head to hide the features, as decoration, or as part of a uniform [a bride's *veil;* a nun's *veil*]. **2.** something that covers or hides [a *veil* of mist over the valley]. —*v.* **1.** to cover with a veil. **2.** to hide or disguise. —**take the veil,** to become a nun.

vein (vān), *n.* **1.** any blood vessel that carries blood back to the heart from some part of the body. **2.** any of the fine lines, or ribs, in a leaf or in an insect's wing. **3.** a crack in rock, or in the earth, filled with mineral [a *vein* of silver or of coal]. **4.** a streak of a different color or material, as in marble. **5.** a state of mind; mood [He spoke in a serious *vein*.] **6.** a trace or quality [His writing has a *vein* of humor.] —*v.* to mark as with veins.

veld or **veldt** (velt *or* felt), *n.* any grassy region in South Africa with few bushes or trees.

vel·lum (vel′əm), *n.* **1.** the best kind of parchment, used for writing on or for binding books. **2.** paper made to look like this.

veins of the arm and hand

ve·loc·i·pede (və läs′ə pēd), *n.* **1.** a child's tricycle. **2.** an early kind of bicycle.

ve·loc·i·ty (və läs′ə tē), *n.* **1.** rate of motion; speed [a wind *velocity* of 15 miles per hour]. **2.** fast motion; swiftness. —**ve·loc′i·ties,** *pl.*

ve·lours or **ve·lour** (və loor′), *n.* a cloth of wool, silk, or cotton, with a short, thick nap like velvet, used for upholstery, drapes, etc.

vel·vet (vel′vit), *n.* a cloth of silk, rayon, cotton, etc. with a soft, thick nap on one side. It is used for clothing, drapes, etc. —*adj.* **1.** made of velvet. **2.** soft or smooth like velvet. —**vel′vet·y,** *adj.*

vel·vet·een (vel və tēn′), *n.* a cotton cloth with a short, thick nap, like velvet.

ve·nal (vē′n'l), *adj.* **1.** that is easily bribed; willing to do wrong things for payment. **2.** marked or got by bribery; corrupt [a *venal* advantage]. —**ve·nal′i·ty** (vē nal′ə tē), *n.*

vend (vend), *v.* to sell: *used mainly in law.*

ven·det·ta (ven det′ə), *n.* a feud; war of revenge between families.

vending machine, a machine for selling small things, as candy, combs, cigarettes, etc. It is worked by putting coins in a slot.

ven·dor or **vend·er** (ven′dər), *n.* **1.** a person who sells; seller. **2.** a vending machine.

ve·neer (və nir′), *v.* to cover a common material with a thin layer of fine wood or costly material [piano keys *veneered* with ivory]. —*n.* **1.** a thin layer of fine wood or costly material put over a common material [a walnut *veneer* on a pine chest]. **2.** an outward look or show that hides what is below [a coarse man with a thin *veneer* of culture].

ven·er·a·ble (ven′ər ə b'l), *adj.* that should be respected or honored because of old age, fine character, etc. [a *venerable* scholar].

ven·er·ate (ven′ə rāt), *v.* to feel or show great respect for; honor; revere. —**ven′er·at·ed,** *p.t. & p.p.;* **ven′er·at·ing,** *pr.p.* —**ven′er·a′tion,** *n.*

ve·ne·re·al (və nir′i əl), *adj.* describing any of certain diseases that can be passed on by sexual intercourse, as syphilis.

Ve·ne·tian (və nē′shən), *adj.* of Venice. —*n.* a person born or living in Venice.

Venetian blind, a window blind made of a number of thin slats that can be set at any angle to control the amount of light or air passing through.

Ven·e·zue·la (ven′ə zwā′lə *or* ven′ə zwē′lə), *n.* a country in northern South America. —**Ven′-e·zue′lan,** *adj. & n.*

venge·ance (ven′jəns), *n.* the act of getting even for a wrong or injury; punishment in return for harm done; revenge. —**with a vengeance, 1.** with great force or fury. **2.** very much or too much.

Venetian blind

venge·ful (venj′fəl), *adj.* wanting or trying to get revenge. —**venge′ful·ly,** *adv.*

ve·ni·al (vē′ni əl *or* vēn′yəl), *adj.* that can be forgiven or excused, as a minor fault.

Ven·ice (ven′is), *n.* a seaport in northeastern Italy, built on many small islands, with canals running between them.

ven·i·son (ven′i z'n *or* ven′i s'n), *n.* the flesh of a deer, used as meat.

ven·om (ven′əm), *n.* **1.** the poison of some snakes, spiders, etc. **2.** bitter feeling; spite; malice [a look full of *venom*].

ven·om·ous (ven′əm əs), *adj.* **1.** full of venom; poisonous [a *venomous* snake]. **2.** full of spite or ill will; hurtful [a *venomous* reply].

vent (vent), *n.* **1.** an opening or passage for gas, air, etc. to pass through or escape. **2.** a way of letting something out; outlet [He gave *vent* to his good spirits by laughing.] —*v.* **1.** to make a vent in or for. **2.** to let out at an opening. **3.** to let out freely, as in words or action [to *vent* one's wrath].

ven·ti·late (ven′t'l āt), *v.* **1.** to get fresh air to move into or through [Open the windows to *ventilate* the room.] **2.** to bring into full and open discussion [to *ventilate* a problem]. —**ven′-ti·lat·ed,** *p.t. & p.p.;* **ven′ti·lat·ing,** *pr.p.* —**ven′ti·la′tion,** *n.*

ven·ti·la·tor (ven′t'l ā′tər), *n.* an opening or device for bringing in fresh air and driving out stale air.

ven·tral (ven′trəl), *adj.* of, on, or near the side of the body where the belly is.

ven·tri·cle (ven′tri k'l), *n.* either of the two lower sections of the heart. The blood flows from these into the arteries.

ven·tril·o·quist (ven tril′ə kwist), *n.* an entertainer who can speak in such a way that his voice seems to come from another point, as from a puppet he holds. —**ven·tril′o·quism,** *n.*

ven·ture (ven′chər), *n.* an activity or undertaking in which there is a risk of losing something

---

fat, āpe, cär, ten, ēven, hit, bīte, gō, hôrn, tōōl, book, up, fûr; get, joy, yet, chin, she, thin, *th*en; zh = s in pleasure; ′ as in able (ā′b'l); ə = a in ago, e in agent, i in sanity, o in confess, u in focus.

[a business *venture*]. —*v.* **1.** to place in danger; risk the loss of [to *venture* one's life, a fortune, etc.]. **2.** to dare to say, do, go, undertake, etc. [She *ventured* the opinion that we were wrong.] —**ven′tured**, *p.t. & p.p.;* **ven′tur·ing**, *pr.p.*

ven·ture·some (ven′chər səm), *adj.* **1.** ready to take chances; daring; bold; adventurous. **2.** full of risks or danger; risky.

ven·tur·ous (ven′chər əs), *adj.* venturesome.

Ve·nus (vē′nəs), *n.* **1.** the Roman goddess of love and beauty. **2.** a very beautiful woman. **3.** the sixth largest planet, that is the brightest in the skies. It is the second in distance away from the sun.

ve·ra·cious (və rā′shəs), *adj.* **1.** telling the truth; truthful; honest. **2.** true; accurate [a *veracious* report].

ve·rac·i·ty (və ras′ə tē), *n.* the quality of being veracious, or truthful, accurate, etc.

Ver·a·cruz (ver′ə krooz′), *n.* a city on the eastern coast of Mexico.

ve·ran·da or **ve·ran·dah** (və ran′də), *n.* an open porch, usually with a roof, along the side of a building.

veranda

verb (vûrb), *n.* a word that shows action or a condition of being [In the sentence "The children ate early and were asleep by seven o'clock," the words "ate" and "were" are *verbs*.]

ver·bal (vûr′b'l), *adj.* **1.** of, in, or by means of words [the author's great *verbal* skill]. **2.** in speech; oral, not written [a *verbal* agreement]. **3.** word for word; literal [a *verbal* translation]. **4.** of, having to do with, or formed from a verb [a *verbal* noun; a *verbal* ending]. —*n.* a word formed from a verb and often used as a noun or adjective [Gerunds, infinitives, and participles are *verbals*.] —**ver′bal·ly**, *adv.*

ver·ba·tim (vər bā′tim), *adv. & adj.* in exactly the same words, or word for word [to copy a speech *verbatim; a verbatim* report].

ver·be·na (vər bē′nə), *n.* a plant with clusters of red, white, or purplish flowers.

ver·bi·age (vûr′bi ij), *n.* the use of more words than are needed to be clear; wordiness.

ver·bose (vər bōs′), *adj.* using too many words; wordy. —**ver·bos·i·ty** (vər bäs′ə tē), *n.*

ver·dant (vûr′d'nt), *adj.* **1.** green [*verdant* grass]. **2.** covered with green plants [the *verdant* plain].

verbena

Verde, Cape (vûrd), a cape at the point farthest west on the African coast.

Ver·di, Gui·sep·pe (joo zep′i ver′dē), 1813–1901; Italian composer of operas.

ver·dict (vûr′dikt), *n.* **1.** the decision reached by a jury in a law case [a *verdict* of "not guilty"]. **2.** any decision or opinion.

ver·di·gris (vûr′di grēs-*or* vûr′di gris), *n.* a greenish coating that forms like rust on brass, bronze, or copper.

ver·dure (vûr′jər), *n.* a growth of green plants and trees, or their fresh green color.

verge (vûrj), *n.* the edge, border, or brink [the *verge* of a forest; on the *verge* of tears]. —*v.* to come close to the edge or border; tend [a comedy that *verges* on the serious]. —**verged**, *p.t. & p.p.;* **verg′ing**, *pr.p.*

Ver·gil (vûr′jil), *n.* same as **Virgil.**

ver·i·fi·ca·tion (ver′ə fi kā′shən), *n.* the act of verifying, or something that helps to verify [to seek *verification* of a theory].

ver·i·fy (ver′ə fī), *v.* **1.** to prove to be true; confirm [New research has *verified* his theory.] **2.** to test or check the accuracy of; make sure of [Will you please *verify* these figures?] —**ver′i·fied**, *p.t. & p.p.;* **ver′i·fy·ing**, *pr.p.*

ver·i·ly (ver′ə lē), *adv.* in fact; truly: *now seldom used* [*Verily* thou art wise.]

ver·i·ta·ble (ver′i tə b'l), *adj.* that is truly, or is very much like [He is a *veritable* hero.]

ver·i·ty (ver′ə tē), *n.* **1.** truth; reality [I doubt the *verity* of that rumor.] **2.** a belief, rule of conduct, etc. thought to be true and basic [the eternal *verities*]. —**ver′i·ties**, *pl.*

ver·mi·cel·li (vûr′mə sel′ē *or* vûr′mə chel′ē), *n.* a food like spaghetti but in thinner strings.

ver·mi·form (vûr′mə fôrm), *adj.* shaped more or less like a worm. The full name of the human appendix is the **vermiform appendix.**

ver·mil·ion (vər mil′yən), *n.* **1.** bright-red coloring matter. **2.** bright red.

ver·min (vûr′min), *n.sing. & pl.* **1.** small animals or insects, such as rats, lice, and flies, that cause harm or are troublesome to man. **2.** a very unpleasant or disgusting person.

Ver·mont (vər mänt′), *n.* a New England State of the United States: abbreviated **Vt.**

ver·nac·u·lar (vər nak′yoo lər), *n.* **1.** the native language of a country or place. **2.** the everyday language of ordinary people. **3.** the special words and phrases used in a particular work, by a particular class, etc. [In the *vernacular* of sailors, "deck" is the word for "floor."] —*adj.* of, using, or based on the everyday speech of ordinary people in a certain country or place [James Whitcomb Riley was a *vernacular* poet.]

ver·nal (vûr′n'l), *adj.* **1.** of, or happening in, the spring [the *vernal* equinox]. **2.** like that of spring; fresh, mild, etc. [a *vernal* breeze].

Ver·sailles (vər sālz′ *or* vər sī′), *n.* a city in France, near Paris.

ver·sa·tile (vûr′sə til), *adj.* able to do a number of things well [a *versatile* musician who plays five instruments]. —**ver·sa·til·i·ty** (vûr′sə til′ə tē), *n.*

verse (vûrs), *n.* **1.** poems or the form of writing found in poems [French *verse;* to write in *verse*]. **2.** a certain kind of poetry [free *verse*]. **3.** a group of lines forming one of the sections of a poem or song; stanza. **4.** a single line of poetry: *an older use.* **5.** any of the short, numbered divisions of a chapter in the Bible.

versed (vûrst), *adj.* knowing something because of training, study, etc.; skilled [He is well *versed* in languages.]

ver·si·fi·ca·tion (vur′sə fi kā′shən), *n.* **1.** the act or art of writing poems. **2.** the way in which a poem is written, in terms of rhythm, rhyme, etc. [the *versification* of a sonnet].

ver·si·fi·er (vur′sə fī′ər), *n.* a poet, especially one who writes light poems or not very good ones.

ver·si·fy (vur′sə fī), *v.* **1.** to write poetry. **2.** to tell in verse; make a poem about [to *versify* the story of Paul Bunyan]. —**ver′si·fied**, *p.t. & p.p.;* **ver′si·fy·ing**, *pr.p.*

ver·sion (vur′zhən), *n.* **1.** something translated from the original language [an English *version* of the Bible]. **2.** a report or description from one person's point of view [Give us your *version* of the argument.] **3.** a particular form of something [an abridged *version* of a novel].

ver·sus (vur′səs), *prep.* against [the law case of William Smith *versus* John Doe; Chicago *versus* Boston in the world series].

ver·te·bra (vur′tə brə), *n.* any of the bones that make up the spinal column, or backbone. —**ver′te·brae** (vur′tə brē) *or* **ver′te·bras**, *pl.* —**ver′te·bral**, *adj.*

ver·te·brate (vur′tə brāt *or* vur′tə brit), *adj.* having a backbone [Mammals, birds, reptiles, fishes, etc. are *vertebrate* animals.] —*n.* any vertebrate animal.

ver·tex (vur′teks), *n.* the highest point; top; especially, the point farthest from the base in a triangle, pyramid, etc. —**ver′tex·es** or **ver·ti·ces** (vur′tə sēz), *pl.*

upper: part of backbone
lower: a vertebra

ver·ti·cal (vur′ti k′l), *adj.* straight up and down; perpendicular to a horizontal line [The walls of a house are *vertical*.] —*n.* a vertical line, plane, etc.

ver·ti·go (vur′ti gō), *n.* a dizzy feeling.

verve (vurv), *n.* energy and enthusiasm.

ver·y (ver′ē), *adv.* **1.** in a high degree; to a great extent; extremely [*very* cold]. **2.** truly; really [This is the *very* same man.] —*adj.* **1.** in the fullest sense; complete; absolute [This is the *very* opposite of what I wanted.] **2.** the same; identical [That is the *very* hat I lost.] —**the very, 1.** even the [*The very* rafters shook with noise.] **2.** the actual [caught in *the very* act].

ves·i·cle (ves′i k′l), *n.* a small cavity, sac, or blister in or on the body.

ves·per (ves′pər), *n.* **1.** evening. **2.** Vesper, the evening star, Venus. **3.** vespers or Vespers, *pl.* a church service held in the evening. —*adj.* of vespers [*vesper* service].

Ves·puc·ci, A·me·ri·go (ä′me rē′gō ves pōō′chē), 1451-1512; Italian explorer after whom America is named.

ves·sel (ves′l), *n.* **1.** anything hollow for holding something; container [Bowls, kettles, tubs, etc. are *vessels*.] **2.** a ship or boat. **3.** any of the tubes in the body through which a fluid flows [a blood *vessel*].

vest (vest), *n.* **1.** a short garment without sleeves, worn especially by men and under a suit coat. **2.** an undershirt. —*v.* **1.** to clothe, as in the robes of a clergyman. **2.** to give some power or right to [The power to levy taxes is *vested* in Congress.] **3.** to put under the control of someone.

vest

Ves·ta (ves′tə), *n.* the Roman goddess of the hearth and the hearth fire.

ves·tal (ves′t′l), *n.* **1.** any of the virgins who kept the sacred fire burning in the temple of Vesta in ancient Rome: also **vestal virgin**. **2.** a virgin. **3.** a nun. —*adj.* chaste; pure.

vest·ed (ves′tid), *adj.* **1.** clothed, especially in church robes. **2.** held by law in an absolute or fixed′way; settled [to have a *vested* interest in an estate].

ves·ti·bule (ves′tə byōōl), *n.* **1.** a small hall through which one enters a building or a room. **2.** the enclosed passage between passenger cars of a train.

ves·tige (ves′tij), *n.* **1.** a trace or mark left of something that no longer exists as such [*Vestiges* of the ancient wall still stand. Not a *vestige* of hope is left.] **2.** a part of the body that is not so fully developed as it once was in the species, as the appendix in man. —**ves·tig·i·al** (ves tij′i əl), *adj.*

vest·ment (vest′mənt), *n.* a garment; especially, any of the garments worn by clergymen during religious services.

ves·try (ves′trē), *n.* **1.** a room in a church where vestments and articles for the altar are kept. **2.** a room in a church, where prayer meetings, Sunday school, etc. are held. **3.** a group of members who manage the business affairs of a church. —**ves′tries**, *pl.*

ves·try·man (ves′trē mən), *n.* a member of a vestry. —**ves′try·men**, *pl.*

ves·ture (ves′chər), *n.* **1.** clothing. **2.** a covering. *This word is now seldom used.*

Ve·su·vi·us (və sōō′vi əs *or* və syōō′vi əs), *n.* a live volcano near Naples, Italy. It destroyed Pompeii when it erupted in 79 A.D.

vet (vet), *n.* a short form in everyday talk of **veteran** or **veterinarian.**

vetch (vech), *n.* a plant related to the pea plant, grown as fodder for animals.

vet·er·an (vet′ər ən), *n.* **1.** a person who has served in the armed forces. **2.** a person with much experience in some kind of work. —*adj.* having had long experience in some work or service [*veteran* troops; a *veteran* diplomat].

Veterans Day, the fourth Monday in October, a legal holiday honoring veterans of the armed forces. It took the place of **Armistice Day,** which celebrated the armistice of World War I.

---

fat,   āpe,   cär,   ten,   ēven,   hit,   bīte,   gō,   hôrn,   tōōl,   book,   up,   fur;
get,   joy,   yet,   chin,   she,   thin,   *then;*   zh = s in pleasure;   ′ as in able (ā′b′l);
ə = a in ago,   e in agent,   i in sanity,   o in confess,   u in focus.

vet·er·i·nar·i·an (vet′ər ə ner′i ən), *n.* a doctor whose work is taking care of animals.

vet·er·i·nar·y (vet′ər ə ner′ē), *adj.* having to do with the medical care of animals. —*n.* a veterinarian. —**vet′er·i·nar′ies,** *pl.*

ve·to (vē′tō), *n.* **1.** the power of the President, a governor, etc. to keep a bill from becoming law by refusing to sign it after the lawmaking body has passed it. **2.** the use of this right [Congress can overrule the President's *veto* by a two-thirds vote.] **3.** the right or power to prevent a certain action from being taken. —*v.* to use the power of veto on [to *veto* a bill]. —**ve′toes,** *pl.* —**ve′toed,** *p.t. & p.p.;* **ve′to·ing,** *pr.p.*

vex (veks), *v.* to disturb, annoy, or trouble, often in little ways [I shall be *vexed* if you are late again.]

vex·a·tion (vek sā′shən), *n.* **1.** the condition of being vexed [Our *vexation* grew as we waited in line.] **2.** something that vexes [He was a great *vexation* to his sisters.]

vex·a·tious (vek sā′shəs), *adj.* that vexes or disturbs; annoying [his *vexatious* chatter.]

V.I., abbreviation for **Virgin Islands.**

vi·a (vī′ə *or* vē′ə), *prep.* by way of or passing through [from Rome to London *via* Paris.]

vi·a·ble (vī′ə b'l), *adj.* able to live or exist, especially after being born too soon.

vi·a·duct (vī′ə dukt), *n.* a bridge held up by a series of piers or towers, usually for carrying a road or railroad over a valley or gorge.

viaduct

vi·al (vī′əl), *n.* a small bottle, usually of glass, for holding medicine or other liquid.

vi·and (vī′ənd), *n.* **1.** an article of food. **2. viands,** *pl.* food, especially fine, costly food.

vi·brant (vī′brənt), *adj.* **1.** that vibrates or quivers [*vibrant* harp strings]. **2.** full and rich; resonant [*vibrant* tones]. **3.** full of energy [a *vibrant* person]. —**vi′bran·cy,** *n.*

vi·brate (vī′brāt), *v.* **1.** to move rapidly back and forth; quiver [A guitar string *vibrates* when plucked.] **2.** to echo; resound [The hall *vibrated* with their cheers.] **3.** to feel very excited; thrill. —**vi′brat·ed,** *p.t. & p.p.;* **vi′brat·ing,** *pr.p.*

vi·bra·tion (vī brā′shən), *n.* rapid motion back and forth; quivering [The *vibration* of the motor shook the bolts loose.] —**vi·bra·to·ry** (vī′brə tôr′ē), *adj.*

vi·bra·tor (vī′brā tər), *n.* something that vibrates or causes vibration, as an electrical machine that massages the body.

vi·bur·num (vī bûr′nəm), *n.* a shrub or small tree with large clusters of small white flowers, as the snowball.

vic·ar (vik′ər), *n.* **1.** a parish priest in the Church of England who is paid a salary from the tithes. **2.** a Roman Catholic official who serves as a substitute for another. **3.** a person who acts in place of another; substitute.

vic·ar·age (vik′ər ij), *n.* **1.** the house where a vicar lives. **2.** the salary of a vicar.

vi·car·i·ous (vī ker′i əs), *adj.* **1.** felt as if one were actually taking part in what is happening to another [She gets *vicarious* thrills from the movies.] **2.** done or undergone by one person in place of another [*vicarious* punishment]. **3.** taking the place of another [a *vicarious* ruler]. —**vi·car′i·ous·ly,** *adv.*

vice (vīs), *n.* **1.** bad or evil behavior; wickedness [He led a life of *vice*.] **2.** a bad or evil habit [Greed is his worst *vice*.]

vice (vīs), *n.* same as **vise.**

vice-, a prefix meaning "substitute" or "one who acts in the place of." It is usually written with a hyphen [A *vice-consul* is a substitute for a consul.]

vice-ad·mir·al (vīs′ad′mə rəl), *n.* an officer in the navy ranking just below an admiral.

vice-pres·i·den·cy (vīs′prez′i dən sē), *n.* the office or term of a vice-president.

vice-pres·i·dent (vīs′prez′i dənt), *n.* **1.** an officer next in rank to a president. He takes the place of the president if the president should die, be absent, etc. **2. Vice President,** such an officer in the United States government. He is also president of the Senate.

vice·roy (vīs′roi), *n.* a person sent by a king, etc. to rule a region or another country under the control of that king.

vi·ce ver·sa (vī′si vûr′sə *or* vīs′ vûr′sə), the other way around; turning the order around [We like him and *vice versa;* that is, he likes us.]

vi·cin·i·ty (və sin′ə tē), *n.* **1.** a near-by or surrounding region; neighborhood [suburbs in the *vicinity* of the city]. **2.** the condition of being close by [two theaters in close *vicinity*]. —**vicin′i·ties,** *pl.*

vi·cious (vish′əs), *adj.* **1.** wicked or evil [*vicious* habits]. **2.** likely to attack or bite one [a *vicious* dog]. **3.** meant to harm; spiteful; mean and cruel [a *vicious* rumor]. **4.** very severe, sharp, etc.: *used only in everyday talk* [a *vicious* pain]. —**vi′cious·ly,** *adv.* —**vi′cious·ness,** *n.*

vicious circle, a condition in which solving one problem brings on another, and solving that one brings back the first problem, etc.

vi·cis·si·tude (vi sis′ə tōōd *or* vi sis′ə tyōōd), *n.* any of the changes in conditions during a person's life, etc.; any of one's ups and downs [The *vicissitudes* of life brought Mozart both fame and poverty.]

vic·tim (vik′tim), *n.* **1.** someone or something killed, hurt, sacrificed, etc. [*victims* of disease; a *victim* of the storm]. **2.** a person who is cheated, tricked, bullied, etc. [a *victim* of swindlers].

vic·tim·ize (vik′tim īz), *v.* to make a victim of [*victimized* by blackmail]. —**vic′tim·ized,** *p.t. & p.p.;* **vic′tim·iz·ing,** *pr.p.*

vic·tor (vik′tər), *n.* the winner in a battle, struggle, or contest.

Vic·to·ri·a (vik tôr′i ə), *n.* **1.** 1819–1901; queen of England from 1837 to 1901. **2.** a state of southeastern Australia. **3.** a lake in east central Africa. **4.** the capital of British Columbia, in Canada.

vic·to·ri·a (vik tôr′i ə), *n.* a low carriage with four wheels and a single seat for passengers. It has a folding top and a high seat for the driver.

victoria

Vic·to·ri·an (vik tôr′i ən), *adj.* **1.** of or in the time when Victoria was queen of England. **2.** like the ideas, customs, styles, etc. of this time, thought of as being prudish, fussy, stuffy, etc. —*n.* a person, especially a writer, of the time of Queen Victoria.

vic·to·ri·ous (vik tôr′i əs), *adj.* having won a victory; winning or conquering.

vic·to·ry (vik′tə rē), *n.* the winning of a battle, struggle, or contest; success in defeating an enemy or rival. —**vic′to·ries,** *pl.*

vict·uals (vit′′lz), *n.pl.* food: *used only in everyday talk, mainly in some regions.*

vi·cu·ña (vī kōōn′yə *or* vī kyōō′nə), *n.* **1.** an animal related to the llama, found in the mountains of South America. Its soft, shaggy wool is made into costly cloth. **2.** this cloth.

vid·e·o (vid′i ō), *adj.* having to do with television, especially with the part of a broadcast that is seen: see also **audio.** —*n.* television.

vicuña (2 ft. high at shoulder)

video tape, a thin magnetic tape on which both the sound and picture signals of a television program are recorded by electronics, for broadcast at another time.

vie (vī), *v.* to be a rival or rivals; compete as in a contest [I *vied* with Bill for first place.] —**vied,** *p.t. & p.p.;* **vy′ing,** *pr.p.*

Vi·en·na (vi en′ə), *n.* the capital of Austria, on the Danube. —**Vi·en·nese** (vē′ə nēz′), *adj. & n. sing. & pl.*

Vi·et·nam (vē′ət näm′ *or* vyet′näm′), *n.* a country in southeastern Asia. Since 1954 it has been divided into two republics, North Vietnam and South Vietnam. Also written **Viet Nam.** —**Vi′et·nam·ese′,** *adj. & n.*

view (vyōō), *n.* **1.** the act of seeing or looking; examination [On closer *view,* I saw it was a robin.] **2.** the distance over which one can see; sight [The parade marched out of *view.*] **3.** that which is seen; scene [We admired the *view* from the bridge.] **4.** a picture of such a scene [He showed *views* of Niagara Falls.] **5.** an idea or thought [These facts will help you get a clear *view* of the situation.] **6.** a way of thinking about something; opinion [What are your *views* on this matter?] —*v.* **1.** to look at with great care; inspect [The landlord *viewed* the damage.] **2.** to see [A crowd gathered to *view* the fireworks.]

3. to think about; consider [His plan was *viewed* with scorn.] —**in view, 1.** in sight. **2.** being thought over, or considered. **3.** as a goal, hope, or wish. —**in view of,** because of; considering. —**on view,** placed where the public can see. —**with a view to,** with the purpose or hope of. —**view′less,** *adj.*

view·point (vyōō′point), *n.* **1.** a place from which something is looked at. **2.** a way of thinking about something; attitude; point of view.

vig·il (vij′əl), *n.* **1.** the act or a time of staying awake during the usual hours of sleep; watch [the nurse's *vigil* by the patient's bed]. **2.** the day or eve before a religious festival. **3.** **vigils,** *pl.* church services on such an eve.

vig·i·lant (vij′ə lənt), *adj.* wide-awake and ready for danger; watchful. —**vig′i·lance,** *n.*

vig·i·lan·te (vij′ə lan′tē), *n.* a member of a group that sets itself up without authority to seek out and punish crime.

vi·gnette (vin yet′), *n.* **1.** a photograph that fades away into the background, with no clear border. **2.** a short sketch or description written in a skillful way.

vig·or (vig′ər), *n.* strength and energy of the body or mind. The British spelling is **vigour.**

vig·or·ous (vig′ər əs), *adj.* full of vigor, or energy; energetic. —**vig′or·ous·ly,** *adv.*

vik·ing (vī′king), *n.* any of the Scandinavian pirates who raided the coasts of Europe during the 8th, 9th, and 10th centuries.

vile (vīl), *adj.* **1.** very evil or wicked [*vile* crimes]. **2.** very unpleasant or disgusting [*vile* language]. **3.** poor, lowly, mean, etc. [*vile* conditions in the prison].

viking ship

vil·i·fy (vil′ə fī), *v.* to speak to or about in a foul or insulting way; defame or slander. —**vil′i·fied,** *p.t. & p.p.;* **vil′i·fy·ing,** *pr.p.*

vil·la (vil′ə), *n.* a large, showy house in the country or on the outskirts of a city.

vil·lage (vil′ij), *n.* **1.** a group of houses and stores in the country, smaller than a town. **2.** the people of a village. —**vil′lag·er,** *n.*

vil·lain (vil′ən), *n.* an evil or wicked person, or such a character in a play, novel, etc.

vil·lain·ous (vil′ən əs), *adj.* of or like a villain; evil; wicked [*villainous* plots].

vil·lain·y (vil′ən ē), *n.* **1.** the quality of being a villain; wickedness. **2.** an act of a villain; crime. —**vil′lain·ies,** *pl.*

vil·lein (vil′ən), *n.* an English serf in the Middle Ages who was a freeman in some ways but still a slave to his lord.

vim (vim), *n.* energy; vigor.

Vin·ci, Le·o·nar·do da (lā′ə när′dō də vin′-chē), 1452–1519; Italian artist and scientist.

---

fat   āpe,   cär,   ten,   ēven,   hit,   bīte,   gō,   hôrn,   tōōl,   book,   up,   fʉr;

get,   joy,   yet,   chin,   she,   thin,   *th*en;   zh = s in pleasure;   ' as in able (ā′b'l);

ə = a in ago,   e in agent,   i in sanity,   o in confess,   u in focus.

vin·di·cate (vin'də kāt), *v.* **1.** to free from blame, guilt, suspicion, etc. [Smith's confession completely *vindicated* Brown.] **2.** to show to be true or right; justify [Can the company *vindicate* its claims for its product?] —**vin'di·cat·ed,** *p.t. & p.p.;* **vin'di·cat·ing,** *pr.p.*

vin·di·ca·tion (vin'də kā'shən), *n.* **1.** a vindicating or being vindicated. **2.** a fact or happening that shows something to be true or right [His success was the *vindication* of their faith.]

vin·dic·tive (vin dik'tiv), *adj.* **1.** wanting to get revenge; ready to do harm in return for harm [He was not *vindictive*, but readily forgave his enemies.] **2.** said or done in revenge [*vindictive* punishment]. —**vin·dic'tive·ly,** *adv.*

vine (vīn), *n.* **1.** a grapevine. **2.** any plant with a long, thin stem that grows along the ground or climbs walls, trees, etc. by fastening itself to them [Pumpkins, melons, etc. grow on *vines.*]

vin·e·gar (vin'i gər), *n.* a sour liquid made by fermenting cider, wine, malt, etc. It is used to flavor or preserve foods.

vine·yard (vin'yərd), *n.* a piece of land where grapevines are grown.

vi·nous (vī'nəs), *adj.* of, like, or having to do with wine.

vin·tage (vin'tij), *n.* **1.** the crop of grapes from a certain region in a single season, or the wine from such a crop. **2.** a model from an earlier time [an automobile of ancient *vintage*]. —*adj.* of a good vintage; choice [*vintage* wine].

vint·ner (vint'nər), *n.* a merchant who sells wine: *mainly a British word.*

vi·nyl (vī'nil), *adj.* having to do with a group of chemical compounds used in forming certain plastics that are made into phonograph records, tiles, etc.

vi·ol (vī'əl), *n.* any of a group of early stringed musical instruments that were replaced by the violin family.

vi·o·la (vi ō'lə), *n.* a stringed instrument like the violin, but a little larger and lower in pitch. —**vi·o'list,** *n.*

vi·o·late (vī'ə lāt), *v.* **1.** to break or fail to keep, as a law, rule, or promise [to *violate* a treaty]. **2.** to treat something sacred in a way that is not respectful [Robbers *violated* the grave by digging it up.] **3.** to break in upon; disturb [to *violate* one's privacy]. —**vi'o·lat·ed,** *p.t. & p.p.;* **vi'o·lat·ing,** *pr.p.* —**vi'o·la'tion,** *n.* —**vi'o·la·tor,** *n.*

vi·o·lence (vī'ə ləns), *n.* **1.** force used to cause injury or damage [The prisoners attacked their guards with *violence*.] **2.** great strength or force [the *violence* of the tornado; the *violence* of her tantrum]. **3.** the harm done by a lack of proper respect [His insults did *violence* to our sense of decency.]

vi·o·lent (vī'ə lənt), *adj.* **1.** showing or acting with great force that causes damage or injury [*violent* blows of the fists]. **2.** caused by such force [a *violent* death]. **3.** showing strong feelings [*violent* language]. **4.** very strong; severe [a *violent* headache]. —**vi'o·lent·ly,** *adv.*

vi·o·let (vī'ə lit), *n.* **1.** a small, short plant with white, blue, purple, or yellow flowers. **2.** bluish purple. —*adj.* bluish-purple.

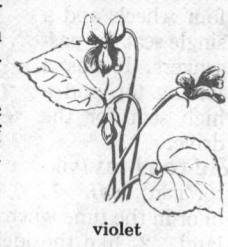
violet

vi·o·lin (vī'ə lin'), *n.* the smallest of a group of musical instruments having four strings played with a bow. The viola, cello, and bass viol belong to the same group, called the **violin family.** —**vi'o·lin'ist,** *n.*

vi·o·lon·cel·lo (vē'ə lən chel'ō), *n.* a cello.

vi·per (vī'pər), *n.* **1.** a poisonous snake, especially such a snake of Europe and Africa, as the adder. **2.** a mean person who cannot be trusted. —**vi'per·ous,** *adj.*

violin

vi·ra·go (vi rā'gō), *n.* a scolding, quarreling woman; shrew. —**vi·ra'goes** or **vi·ra'gos,** *pl.*

vir·e·o (vir'i ō), *n.* a small songbird with olive-green or gray feathers. It feeds on insects. —**vir'e·os,** *pl.*

Vir·gil (vur'jil), *n.* 70–19 B.C.; Roman poet who wrote the *Aeneid:* also spelled **Vergil.**

vireo (5 in. long)

vir·gin (vur'jin), *n.* **1.** a woman who has never had sexual intercourse; maiden. **2. Virgin,** Mary, the mother of Jesus: also called **Virgin Mary.** —*adj.* **1.** being a virgin. **2.** chaste or modest. **3.** pure and fresh; not touched, used, etc. [*virgin* snow; a *virgin* forest]. —**vir'gin·al,** *adj.*

vir·gin·al (vur'ji n'l), *n.* a small kind of harpsichord without legs, that was set on a table or held on the lap to be played.

Vir·gin·ia (vər jin'yə), *n.* a State on the eastern coast of the United States: abbreviated **Va.** —**Vir·gin'ian,** *adj. & n.*

Virginia reel, a lively kind of early American dance, or the music for it.

Virgin Islands, a group of islands in the West Indies, some of which belong to the United States and some to Great Britain.

vir·gin·i·ty (vər jin'ə tē), *n.* the condition or fact of being a virgin.

vir·ile (vir'əl), *adj.* **1.** of or having to do with a man; male. **2.** like a man is supposed to be; strong, forceful, etc.; manly. —**vi·ril·i·ty** (və ril'ə tē), *n.*

vir·tu·al (vur'choo əl), *adj.* being so in effect although not in name [Although we have met, he is a *virtual* stranger to me.]

vir·tu·al·ly (vur'choo əl ē), *adv.* in effect; really, practically, nearly, etc.

vir·tue (vur'choo), *n.* **1.** goodness; right action and thinking; morality. **2.** a particular moral quality thought of as good [Courage is his greatest *virtue*.] **3.** chastity; purity. **4.** a good quality or qualities; merit [Your plan has certain *virtues.*] **—by virtue of** or **in virtue of,** because of.

vir·tu·o·so (vŭr'chōō ō'sō), *n.* a person having great skill in the practice of some art, especially in the playing of music. **—vir'tu·o'sos** or **vir·tu·o·si** (vŭr'chōō ō'sē), *pl.* **—vir·tu·os·i·ty** (vŭr'chōō äs'ə tē), *n.*

vir·tu·ous (vŭr'chōō əs), *adj.* having virtue; good, moral, chaste, etc. **—vir'tu·ous·ly,** *adv.*

vir·u·lent (vir'yoo lənt *or* vir'oo lənt), *adj.* **1.** very harmful or poisonous; deadly [a *virulent* disease]. **2.** full of hate; very bitter or spiteful [a *virulent* enemy]. **—vir'u·lence,** *n.* **—vir'u·lent·ly,** *adv.*

vi·rus (vī'rəs), *n.* a form of matter smaller than any of the bacteria, that can multiply in living cells and cause disease in animals and plants. Smallpox, measles, the flu, polio, colds, etc. are caused by viruses.

vi·sa (vē'zə), *n.* something written or stamped on a passport by an official of a country to show that the passport holder has permission to enter that country.

vis·age (viz'ij), *n.* the face, especially as showing one's feelings [his stern *visage*].

vis·cer·a (vis'ər ə), *n.pl.* the organs inside the body, as the heart, lungs, intestines, etc.

vis·cid (vis'id), *adj.* thick and sticky, like sirup or glue; viscous.

vis·cos·i·ty (vis käs'ə tē), *n.* the condition or quality of being viscous.

vis·count (vī'kount), *n.* a nobleman ranking above a baron and below an earl or count.

vis·count·ess (vī'koun tis), *n.* **1.** the wife or widow of a viscount. **2.** a lady with the rank of a viscount.

vis·cous (vis'kəs), *adj.* thick and sticky, like sirup or glue; viscid.

vise (vīs), *n.* a device having two jaws opened and closed by a screw, used for holding an object firmly while it is being worked on.

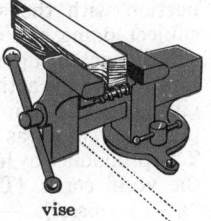
vise

vis·i·bil·i·ty (viz'ə bil'ə tē), *n.* **1.** the condition of being visible. **2.** the distance within which things can be seen [Fog reduced the *visibility* to 500 feet.]

vis·i·ble (viz'ə b'l), *adj.* that can be seen or noticed; evident [a barely *visible* scar; a *visible* increase in crime]. **—vis'i·bly,** *adv.*

Vis·i·goth (viz'i gäth), *n.* any of the western tribes of Goths who captured Rome in 410 A.D.

vi·sion (vizh'ən), *n.* **1.** the act or power of seeing; sight [She wears glasses to improve her *vision.*] **2.** something seen in the mind, or in a dream, trance, etc. ["while *visions* of sugarplums danced through their heads"]. **3.** the ability to

imagine or foresee what cannot actually be seen [a statesman of great *vision*]. **4.** a person or thing of unusual beauty.

vi·sion·ar·y (vizh'ən er'ē), *adj.* **1.** like or seen in a vision. **2.** imaginary or not practical [a *visionary* scheme]. **—n. 1.** a person who sees visions. **2.** a person whose ideas or ideals are not practical. **—vi'sion·ar'ies,** *pl.*

vis·it (viz'it), *v.* **1.** to go or come to see; call on out of friendship, for business, etc. **2.** to stay with as a guest. **3.** to come upon in a harmful way [The valley was *visited* by a drought.] **—n.** an act of visiting.

vis·it·ant (viz'ə tənt), *n.* a visitor.

vis·it·a·tion (viz'ə tā'shən), *n.* **1.** the act of visiting, especially an official visit as for inspecting or examining. **2.** trouble looked on as punishment sent by God.

vis·i·tor (viz'ə tər), *n.* a person making a visit; caller or guest.

vi·sor (vī'zər), *n.* **1.** a part of a helmet that can be pulled down to cover the face. **2.** the brim of a cap, sticking out in front to shade the eyes. **3.** any device, as over the windshield of a car, for shading the eyes.

visors

vis·ta (vis'tə), *n.* **1.** a view, especially one seen through a long passage, as between rows of houses [The tree-lined street gave us a *vista* of the river.] **2.** such a passage [a *vista* of oaks]. **3.** a view in the mind of happenings that one remembers or looks forward to.

Vis·tu·la (vis'choo lə), *n.* a river in Poland, flowing into the Baltic Sea.

vis·u·al (vizh'oo əl), *adj.* **1.** having to do with sight or used in seeing. **2.** that can be seen; visible. **—vis'u·al·ly,** *adv.*

vis·u·al·ize (vizh'oo əl īz), *v.* to form in the mind a picture of [Try to *visualize* your first home.] **—vis'u·al·ized,** *p.t. & p.p.;* **vis'u·al·iz·ing,** *pr.p.*

vi·tal (vī't'l), *adj.* **1.** of or having to do with life [*vital* energy]. **2.** necessary to life [the *vital* organs]. **3.** full of life and energy [a *vital* personality]. **4.** very important [a *vital* matter]. **5.** destroying life; fatal [a *vital* wound]. **—n. vitals,** *pl.* **1.** the vital organs of the body, as the brain, heart, and liver. **2.** the necessary parts of anything. **—vi'tal·ly,** *adv.*

vi·tal·i·ty (vī tal'ə tē), *n.* **1.** energy or strength of mind or body; vigor. **2.** the power to keep on living or existing.

vi·tal·ize (vī't'l īz), *v.* to make vital or lively; give life or energy to. **—vi'tal·ized,** *p.t. & p.p.;* **vi'tal·iz·ing,** *pr.p.*

vi·ta·min (vī′tə min), *n.* any of certain substances needed by the body to keep healthy. Vitamin A is found in fish-liver oil, yellow vegetables, egg yolk, etc. One kind of vitamin B, called vitamin B₁, is found in cereals, green peas, liver, etc. Vitamin C is found in citrus fruits, tomatoes, etc. Vitamin D is found in fish-liver oil, milk, eggs, etc. Lack of these vitamins or others can cause certain diseases.

vi·ti·ate (vish′i āt), *v.* **1.** to spoil the goodness of; make bad or faulty [Bad company has *vitiated* his character.] **2.** to take away the legal force of, as a contract. —**vi′ti·at·ed,** *p.t. & p.p.;* **vi′ti·at·ing,** *pr.p.* —**vi′ti·a′tion,** *n.*

vit·re·ous (vit′ri əs), *adj.* of or like glass; glassy [*vitreous* china].

vitreous humor, the clear substance like jelly that fills the eyeball behind the lens.

vit·ri·fy (vit′rə fī), *v.* to change into glass or a substance like glass, as by heating. —**vit′ri·fied,** *p.t. & p.p.;* **vit′ri·fy·ing,** *pr.p.*

vit·ri·ol (vit′ri əl), *n.* **1.** sulfuric acid. **2.** a salt formed by the action of sulfuric acid on certain metals [Green *vitriol* is iron sulfate.]

vit·ri·ol·ic (vit′ri äl′ik), *adj.* **1.** having to do with or like vitriol. **2.** very sharp, biting, or sarcastic [*vitriolic* talk].

vi·tu·per·ate (vī tōō′pə rāt *or* vī tyōō′pə rāt), *v.* to scold or talk about in a harsh way; berate. —**vi·tu′per·at·ed,** *p.t. & p.p.;* **vi·tu′per·at·ing,** *pr.p.* —**vi·tu′per·a′tion,** *n.* —**vi·tu′per·a·tive,** *adj.*

vi·va·cious (vi vā′shəs *or* vī vā′shəs), *adj.* full of life and energy; spirited; lively. —**vi·va′cious·ly,** *adv.* —**vi·va′cious·ness,** *n.*

vi·vac·i·ty (vi vas′ə tē *or* vī vas′ə tē), *n.* the quality of being vivacious; liveliness.

vive (vēv), *interj.* long may he live!: *a French word shouted in welcome or approval.*

viv·id (viv′id), *adj.* **1.** bright and strong [*vivid* colors]. **2.** forming or giving a clear picture in the mind [a *vivid* imagination; a *vivid* description]. **3.** full of life or energy; striking; lively [a *vivid* personality]. —**viv′id·ly,** *adv.* —**viv′id·ness,** *n.*

viv·i·fy (viv′ə fī), *v.* to give life to; make lively or active. —**viv′i·fied,** *p.t. & p.p.;* **viv′i·fy·ing,** *pr.p.*

viv·i·sec·tion (viv′ə sek′shən), *n.* medical experiments on living animals in studying diseases and trying to find cures for them.

vix·en (vik′s'n), *n.* **1.** a female fox. **2.** a spiteful, bad-tempered woman; shrew.

viz., that is; namely: *viz.* is the abbreviation of a Latin word, *videlicet* [You will need two things, *viz;* a pencil and a piece of paper.]

vi·zier or **vi·zir** (vi zir′), *n.* a title used in earlier times for a high official in Moslem states.

vi·zor (vī′zər), *n.* same as **visor.**

Vla·di·vos·tok (vlad′ə väs täk′), *n.* a seaport on the eastern coast of the Soviet Union.

vo·cab·u·lar·y (vō kab′yoo ler′ē), *n.* **1.** all the words of a language, or all those used by a certain person or group [Bob's *vocabulary* is large. The word "fracture" is part of the medical *vocabulary.*] **2.** a list of words, usually in alphabetical order with their meanings, as in a dictionary. —**vo·cab′u·lar′ies,** *pl.*

vo·cal (vō′k'l), *adj.* **1.** of or made by the voice; in or for singing or speech [the *vocal* cords; *vocal* music]. **2.** able to speak or make sounds. **3.** speaking often and openly [She was very *vocal* in the fight for women's rights.] —**vo′cal·ly,** *adv.*

vocal cords, the folds at the upper end of the windpipe that vibrate and make voice sounds when air from the lungs passes through.

vo·cal·ist (vō′k'l ist), *n.* a singer.

vo·cal·ize (vō′k'l īz), *v.* to make sounds with the voice; speak or sing. —**vo′cal·ized,** *p.t. & p.p.;* **vo′cal·iz·ing,** *pr.p.*

vo·ca·tion (vō kā′shən), *n.* one's profession, occupation, trade, or career [He found his *vocation* in social work.] —**vo·ca′tion·al,** *adj.*

vo·cif·er·ous (vō sif′ər əs), *adj.* loud and noisy in making one's feelings known; clamorous [a *vociferous* crowd; *vociferous* complaints].

vod·ka (väd′kə), *n.* a Russian alcoholic liquor made from grain. It is colorless.

vogue (vōg), *n.* **1.** the general fashion or style [Powdered wigs were in *vogue* in the 18th century.] **2.** popularity; popular approval [Folk singers have had a great *vogue* in recent years.]

voice (vois), *n.* **1.** sound made through the mouth, especially by human beings in talking, singing, etc. **2.** the ability to make such sound [She lost her *voice* in terror.] **3.** anything thought of as like speech or the human voice [the *voice* of the sea; the *voice* of one's conscience]. **4.** the right to say what one wants, thinks, or feels [Each voter has a *voice* in the government.] **5.** the act of putting into words what one thinks or feels [to give *voice* to one's opinion]. **6.** the quality of the sounds made in speaking or singing [He has a fine *voice* for radio. She has a soprano *voice.*] **7.** a form of a verb that shows its connection with the subject as active (with the subject doing the action) or passive (with the subject acted upon) ["Give" in "They give freely" is in the active *voice;* "am given" in "I am given presents" is in the passive *voice.*] —*v.* **1.** to put into words, as an idea, feeling, etc.; utter. **2.** to pronounce by letting the voice sound through the vocal cords [The sounds of "b," "v," and "z" are *voiced.*] —**voiced,** *p.t. & p.p.;* **voic′ing,** *pr.p.* —**voice′less,** *adj.*

void (void), *adj.* **1.** having nothing in it; empty; vacant [A vacuum is a *void* space.] **2.** being without; lacking [a heart *void* of kindness]. **3.** having no legal force; not valid [The contract is *void.*] —*n.* **1.** an empty space [The craters of the moon are huge *voids.*] **2.** a feeling of loss or emptiness [Bill's departure for the army left a *void* in our club.] —*v.* **1.** to make empty; empty out. **2.** to cause to be without legal force; cancel [to *void* an agreement]. —**void′a·ble,** *adj.*

voile (voil), *n.* a thin, fine cloth of cotton, silk, rayon, or wool.

vol., abbreviation for **volume.**

vol·a·tile (väl′ə t'l), *adj.* **1.** changing readily into a gas; evaporating quickly [Alcohol is a *volatile* liquid.] **2.** changing often in one's feelings or interests; fickle.

vol·can·ic (väl kan′ik), *adj.* **1.** of or from a volcano [*volcanic* rock]. **2.** like a volcano; violent; likely to explode [a *volcanic* temper].

vol·ca·no (väl kā′nō), *n.* **1.** an opening in the earth's surface through which molten rock from inside the earth is thrown up. **2.** a hill or mountain of ash and molten rock built up around such an opening. **—vol·ca′noes** or **vol·ca′nos,** *pl.*

volcano

vole (vōl), *n.* a small, burrowing animal like the mouse and rat.

Vol·ga (väl′gə), *n.* a river in the western Soviet Union, flowing into the Caspian Sea.

vo·li·tion (vō lish′ən), *n.* the act or power of using one's own will in deciding or making a choice [Of his own *volition* he apologized.]

vol·ley (väl′ē), *n.* **1.** the act of shooting a number of guns or other weapons at the same time. **2.** the bullets, arrows, etc. shot at one time. **3.** a sudden pouring out of a number of things [a *volley* of oaths]. **4.** the act of hitting a tennis ball back across the net before it touches the ground. **—v. 1.** to shoot or be shot in a volley. **2.** to hit a tennis ball back before it touches the ground. **—vol′leys,** *pl.*

vol·ley·ball (väl′ē bôl), *n.* **1.** a game played by two teams who hit a large, light ball back and forth over a high net with their hands. **2.** the ball used in this game.

volleyball

volt (vōlt), *n.* a unit for measuring the force of an electric current. One volt causes a current of one ampere to flow through a resistance of one ohm.

volt·age (vōl′tij), *n.* the force that produces electric current. It is measured in volts.

vol·ta·ic cell (väl tā′ik), a device for making an electric current by placing two plates of different metals in an electrolyte.

Vol·taire (väl ter′), *n.* 1694–1778; French writer and philosopher.

volt·me·ter (vōlt′mē′tər), *n.* a device for measuring the voltage of an electric current.

vol·u·ble (väl′yoo b'l), *adj.* talking very much and easily; talkative. **—vol′u·bil′i·ty,** *n.* **—vol′u·bly,** *adv.*

vol·ume (väl′yoom), *n.* **1.** a book [You may borrow four *volumes* at a time.] **2.** one of the books of a set [*Volume* III of the encyclopedia.] **3.** the amount of space inside something, measured in cubic inches, feet, etc. [The *volume* of this box is 4½ cubic feet.] **4.** an amount, bulk, or mass [a large *volume* of sales]. **5.** loudness of sound [Lower the *volume* of your radio.]

vo·lu·mi·nous (və loō′mə nəs), *adj.* **1.** writing, or made up of, enough to fill volumes [the *voluminous* works of Dickens]. **2.** large; bulky; full [a *voluminous* skirt].

vol·un·tar·y (väl′ən ter′ē), *adj.* **1.** acting, done, or given of one's own free will; by choice [*voluntary* workers; *voluntary* gifts]. **2.** controlled by one's mind or will [*voluntary* muscles]. **—vol′un·tar′i·ly,** *adv.*

vol·un·teer (väl ən tir′), *n.* a person who offers to do something of his own free will, as one who enlists in the armed forces by choice. **—adj.** of or done by volunteers [a *volunteer* regiment; *volunteer* help]. **—v. 1.** to offer to do or give of one's own free will [He *volunteered* some information. Sally *volunteered* to write the letter.] **2.** to enter into a service of one's own free will [The soldier *volunteered* for service overseas.]

vo·lup·tu·ar·y (və lup′choo er′ē), *n.* a person who is mainly interested in his own comforts and pleasures. **—vo·lup′tu·ar′ies,** *pl.*

vo·lup·tu·ous (və lup′choo əs), *adj.* having, giving, or seeking pleasure through the senses [a *voluptuous* feast; a *voluptuous* person]. **—vo·lup′tu·ous·ness,** *n.*

vom·it (väm′it), *v.* **1.** to be sick and have matter from the stomach come back up through the mouth; throw up. **2.** to throw out or be thrown out with force [The cannons *vomited* smoke and fire.] **—n.** the matter thrown up from the stomach.

voo·doo (voō′doō), *n.* **1.** a primitive religion based on a belief in magic, witchcraft, and charms, that began in Africa and is still practiced in the West Indies. **2.** a person who practices voodoo. **—voo′doos,** *pl.* **—voo′doo·ism,** *n.*

vo·ra·cious (vô rā′shəs), *adj.* **1.** eating large amounts of food rapidly; greedy. **2.** very eager for much of something [a *voracious* reader]. **—vo·ra′cious·ly,** *adv.* **—vo·rac·i·ty** (vô ras′ə tē), *n.*

vor·tex (vôr′teks), *n.* a whirling or spinning mass as of water or air; whirlpool or whirlwind. **—vor′tex·es** or **vor·ti·ces** (vôr′tə sēz), *pl.*

vo·ta·ry (vō′tə rē) or **vo·ta·rist** (vō′tə rist), *n.* **1.** a person who is bound by a vow, as a monk or nun. **2.** a person who is devoted to something, as to a cause or interest [a *votary* of music]. **—vo′ta·ries,** *pl.* **—vo′ta·ress,** *n.fem.*

vote (vōt), *n.* **1.** one's decision on some plan or idea, or one's choice between persons running for office, shown on a ballot, by raising one's hand, etc. **2.** the ballot, raised hand, etc. by which one shows his choice [to count the *votes*]. **3.** all the votes together [A heavy *vote* is expected.] **4.** the act of choosing by a vote [I call for a *vote*.] **5.** the right to take part in a vote [The 19th Amendment gave the *vote* to women.] **—v. 1.** to give or cast a vote [For whom did you *vote*?] **2.** to decide, elect, or bring about by vote [Congress *voted* new taxes.] **3.** to declare as a general opinion [We *voted* him our thanks.] **4.** to suggest: *used only in everyday talk* [I *vote* we leave now.] **—vot′ed,** *p.t. & p.p.;* **vot′ing,** *pr.p.*

vot·er (vōt′ər), *n.* a person who has the right to vote, especially one who votes.

vo·tive (vō′tiv), *adj.* given or done because of a promise or vow [*votive* offerings].

vouch (vouch), *v.* to give a guarantee; give one's word in backing [His friends *vouch* for his honesty.]

vouch·er (vouch′ər), *n.* **1.** a paper that serves as proof, as a receipt for the payment of a debt. **2.** a person who vouches for something, as for the truth of a statement.

vouch·safe (vouch sāf′), *v.* to be kind enough to give or grant [He did not *vouchsafe* an answer.] **—vouch·safed′,** *p.t. & p.p.;* **vouch·saf′ing,** *pr.p.*

vow (vou), *n.* a solemn promise, as one made to God, or with God as one's witness [marriage *vows*]. **—v. 1.** to make a vow or solemn promise [He *vowed* to love her always.] **2.** to say in a forceful or earnest way [He *vowed* that he had never heard such a racket.]

vow·el (vou′əl), *n.* **1.** any speech sound made by letting the voiced breath pass through without stopping it with the tongue, teeth, or lips. **2.** any of the letters used to show these sounds. The vowels are *a, e, i, o,* and *u,* and sometimes *y,* as in the word "my."

voy·age (voi′ij), *n.* **1.** a journey by water [an ocean *voyage*]. **2.** a journey through the air [a *voyage* by rocket into outer space]. **—v.** to make a voyage. **—voy′aged,** *p.t. & p.p.;* **voy′ag·ing,** *pr.p.* **—voy′ag·er,** *n.*

V.P. or **VP,** abbreviation for **Vice President.**

vs., abbreviation for **versus.**

Vt., abbreviation for **Vermont.**

Vul·can (vul′kən), *n.* the Roman god of fire and of metalworking.

vul·can·ize (vul′kən īz), *v.* to add sulfur to rubber and heat it in order to make it stronger and more elastic. **—vul′can·ized,** *p.t. & p.p.;* **vul′can·iz·ing,** *pr.p.* **—vul′can·i·za′tion,** *n.*

vul·gar (vul′gər), *adj.* **1.** showing bad taste or bad manners; crude; coarse [a *vulgar* joke]. **2.** of or common among people in general; of the common people [The Italian language developed from *Vulgar* Latin.] **—vul′gar·ly,** *adv.*

vul·gar·ism (vul′gər iz′m), *n.* a word or phrase heard in everyday talk, but regarded as improper or not standard ["He don't" is a *vulgarism*.]

vul·gar·i·ty (vul gar′ə tē), *n.* **1.** the condition of being vulgar or coarse. **2.** a vulgar act, habit, or remark. **—vul·gar′i·ties,** *pl.*

vul·gar·ize (vul′gər īz), *v.* to make vulgar. **—vul′gar·ized,** *p.t. & p.p.;* **vul′gar·iz·ing,** *pr.p.*

Vul·gate (vul′gāt), *n.* a translation of the Bible into Latin, made in the 4th century and used in the Roman Catholic Church.

vul·ner·a·ble (vul′nər ə b'l), *adj.* **1.** that can be hurt, destroyed, attacked, etc. [The wolf looked for a *vulnerable* spot into which to sink his fangs.] **2.** likely to be hurt; sensitive [A vain person is *vulnerable* to criticism.] **—vul′ner·a·bil′-i·ty,** *n.*

vul·ture (vul′chər), *n.* **1.** a large bird related to eagles and hawks, that eats the remains of dead animals. **2.** a greedy, ruthless person.

vy·ing (vī′ing), present participle of **vie.**

vulture (2½ ft. long)

W

W, w (dub′'l yōō), *n.* the twenty-third letter of the English alphabet. **—W's, w's** (dub′'l-yōōz), *pl.*

W., W, w., w, abbreviations for **watt** or **watts, west,** or **western.**

wab·ble (wäb′'l), *n. & v.* same as **wobble.** **—wab′bled,** *p.t. & p.p.;* **wab′bling,** *pr.p.*

Wac (wak), *n.* a member of the WAC.

WAC, abbreviation for the **Women's Army Corps.**

wad (wäd *or* wôd), *n.* **1.** a soft, small mass [a *wad* of cotton]. **2.** a lump or small, firm mass [a *wad* of chewing gum]. **3.** a plug stuffed into a gun to keep the charge in place. **—v. 1.** to roll up into a tight wad [to *wad* paper in a ball]. **2.** to stuff as with padding. **—wad′ded,** *p.t. & p.p.;* **wad′ding,** *pr.p.*

wad·dle (wäd′'l *or* wôd′'l), *v.* to walk with short steps, swaying from side to side, as a duck. **—n.** the act of waddling. **—wad′dled,** *p.t. & p.p.;* **wad′dling,** *pr.p.* **—wad′dler,** *n.*

wade (wād), *v.* **1.** to walk through water, mud, or anything that slows one down. **2.** to get through with difficulty [to *wade* through a long, dull report]. **3.** to cross by wading [to *wade* a stream]. **—wade in** or **wade into,** to begin or enter with force or energy: *used only in everyday talk.* **—wad′ed,** *p.t. & p.p.;* **wad′ing,** *pr.p.*

wad·er (wād′ər), *n.* **1.** one that wades, as a bird with long legs that wades in water for food. **2. waders,** *pl.* high waterproof boots.

wa·fer (wā′fər), *n.* **1.** a thin, flat, crisp cracker or cooky. **2.** a very thin, flat, crisp piece of bread used in Holy Communion. **3.** a thin, flat piece of candy. **4.** a small paper disk with glue, etc. on it, used to seal letters or papers.

waf·fle (wäf′'l *or* wôf′'l), *n.* a crisp cake with small, square hollows, baked in a waffle iron.

waffle iron, a device for baking waffles by pressing batter between its two heated plates.

waft (waft *or* wäft), *v.* to carry or move lightly over water or through the air [Cooking odors were *wafted* through the hallway.] —*n.* **1.** a smell, sound, etc. carried through the air. **2.** a gust of wind. **3.** a wafting movement.

waffle iron

wag (wag), *v.* to move rapidly back and forth or up and down [The dog *wagged* its tail.] —*n.* **1.** the act of wagging. **2.** a person who makes jokes. —**wagged,** *p.t. & p.p.;* **wag′ging,** *pr.p.*

wage (wāj), *v.* to take part in; carry on [to *wage* war]. —*n. usually* **wages,** *pl.* **1.** money paid to an employee for work done. **2.** what is given in return: *an older use, with a singular verb* ["The *wages* of sin is death."] —**waged,** *p.t. & p.p.;* **wag′ing,** *pr.p.*

wage earner, a person who works for wages.

wag·er (wā′jər), *n.* the act of betting or something bet. —*v.* to bet.

wag·ger·y (wag′ər ē), *n.* the act of joking, or a joke. —**wag′ger·ies,** *pl.*

wag·gish (wag′ish), *adj.* **1.** fond of joking. **2.** playful; joking [a *waggish* remark].

wag·gle (wag′'l), *v.* to wag with short, quick movements. —*n.* the act of waggling. —**wag′-gled,** *p.t. & p.p.;* **wag′gling,** *pr.p.*

Wag·ner, Richard (väg′nər), 1813–1883; German composer, especially of operas.

wag·on (wag′ən), *n.* a vehicle with four wheels, especially one for carrying heavy loads.

wag·on·er (wag′ən ər), *n.* a wagon driver.

waif (wāf), *n.* **1.** a person without a home or friends, especially a lost or deserted child. **2.** an animal that has strayed from its owner.

child's wagon

wail (wāl), *v.* **1.** to show that one is sad or hurt by making long, loud cries. **2.** to make a sad, crying sound [The wind *wailed* in the trees.] —*n.* a long cry of sadness or pain, or a sound like this. —**wail′er,** *n.*

wain·scot (wān′skət *or* wān′skät), *n.* **1.** panels of wood on the walls of a room, often only on the lower part. **2.** the lower part of the wall of a room when it is covered with a different material from the upper part. —*v.* to cover with a wainscot. —**wain′scot·ed** *or* **wain′scot·ted,** *p.t. & p.p.;* **wain′scot·ing** *or* **wain′scot·ting,** *pr.p.*

wain·scot·ing *or* **wain·scot·ting** (wān′-skət ing *or* wān′skät ing), *n.* wainscot.

waist (wāst), *n.* **1.** the part of the body between the ribs and the hips. **2.** the part of a garment that covers the upper part of the body to the waistline. **3.** a blouse. **4.** the waistline. **5.** the middle, narrow part of something [the *waist* of a violin].

waist·band (wāst′band), *n.* a band that fits around the waist, as at the top of a skirt or pair of trousers.

waist·coat (wāst′kōt *or* wes′kət), *n.* a man's vest: *the usual British word.*

waist·line (wāst′līn), *n.* **1.** an imaginary line around the middle of the waist. **2.** the narrow part of a woman's dress, etc., coming at the waist or above or below it, as styles change.

waistlines
(*meaning 2*)

wait (wāt), *v.* **1.** to stay in a place or do nothing while expecting a certain thing to happen [*Wait* for the signal. I *waited* until six o'clock, but he never arrived.] **2.** to remain undone for a time [Let it *wait* till next week.] **3.** to serve food at; be a waiter or waitress [She *waits* table at the inn.] **4.** to keep expecting, or look forward to; await [I'm *waiting* my chance.] **5.** to put off serving: *used only in everyday talk* [We'll *wait* dinner for you.] —*n.* the act or time of waiting [We had an hour's *wait* for the train.] —**lie in wait,** to keep hidden in order to make a surprise attack. —**wait on** *or* **wait upon, 1.** to act as a servant to. **2.** to serve as a clerk in a store [to *wait on* customers]. **3.** to visit a person of higher rank in order to pay one's respects, ask a favor, etc.

wait·er (wāt′ər), *n.* **1.** a man who serves food at table, as in a restaurant. **2.** one who waits.

wait·ing (wāt′ing), *adj.* that waits. —*n.* the act of one that waits, or the time that one waits. —**in waiting,** serving someone of high rank [a lady *in waiting* to the queen].

waiting room, a room where people wait, as in a railroad station, a dentist's office, etc.

wait·ress (wāt′ris), *n.* a woman who serves food at table, as in a restaurant.

waive (wāv), *v.* **1.** to give up, as a right, claim, or advantage. **2.** to put off; postpone [to *waive* a question]. —**waived,** *p.t. & p.p.;* **waiv′ing,** *pr.p.*

waiv·er (wāv′ər), *n.* the act of giving up a right or claim, or a paper showing this [to sign a *waiver* of all claims after an accident].

wake (wāk), *v.* **1.** to come or bring out of a sleep; awake [*Wake* up! Time to *wake* your sister!] **2.** to make or become active; stir up [His cruelty *woke* our anger.] **3.** to be alert or become aware of [to *wake* to a danger]. —*n.* a watch

fat,   āpe,   cär,   ten,   ēven,   hit,   bīte,   gō,   hôrn,   tool,   book,   up,   fur;
get,   joy,   yet,   chin,   she,   thin,   then;   zh = s in pleasure;   ' as in able (ā′b'l);
ə = a in ago,   e in agent,   i in sanity,   o in confess,   u in focus.

kept all night over a dead body before the funeral. **—waked** or **woke,** *p.t.;* **waked,** *p.p.;* **wak'ing,** *pr.p.*

wake (wāk), *n.* **1.** the trail left in water by a moving boat or ship. **2.** any track left behind [The storm left wreckage in its *wake.*] **—in the wake of,** following close behind.

wake of a boat

wake·ful (wāk'fəl), *adj.* **1.** not sleeping; watchful [*wakeful* guards]. **2.** not able to sleep. **3.** sleepless [a *wakeful* night]. **—wake'fulness,** *n.*

Wake Island (wāk), a small island in the northern Pacific, belonging to the United States.

wak·en (wāk''n), *v.* to wake.

wale (wāl), *n.* **1.** a raised line on the skin, as one made by a whip; welt. **2.** a ridge on the surface of cloth, as corduroy.

Wales (wālz), *n.* a part of Great Britain, west of England.

walk (wôk), *v.* **1.** to move along on foot at a normal speed [*Walk*, do not run, to the nearest exit.] **2.** to go through, over, or along by walking [I *walk* this path twice a day.] **3.** to cause a horse, dog, etc. to walk. **4.** to go along with on foot [I'll *walk* you home.] **5.** in baseball, to move to first base as a result of four pitched balls (*meaning 5*) [The pitcher *walked* three men. Smith *walked* his first time at bat.] **—***n.* **1.** the act of walking, often for pleasure or exercise; stroll; hike [an afternoon *walk*]. **2.** a way of walking [We knew her by her *walk.*] **3.** a sidewalk or path for walking on [The park has gravel *walks.*] **4.** a distance walked, often measured in time [a two-mile *walk;* an hour's *walk*]. **5.** in baseball, the act of walking a batter or of being walked. **—walk of life,** a way of living, a kind of work, a position in society, etc. [people of all *walks of life*]. **—walk'er,** *n.*

walk·ie-talk·ie (wôk'ē tôk'ē), *n.* a radio set for sending and receiving messages, that can be carried about by one person.

walking stick, 1. a cane. **2.** an insect that looks like a twig.

walk·out (wôk'out), *n.* a strike of workers: *used only in everyday talk.*

soldier using walkie-talkie

wall (wôl), *n.* **1.** a structure of wood, brick, plaster, etc. that forms the side of a building or shuts off a space [a stone *wall* around the town; a picture on the bedroom *wall*]. **2.** anything like a wall, as in shutting something in [a *wall* of secrecy; the *walls* of the chest]. **—***v.* **1.** to close in, divide, etc. with a wall [to *wall* off an unused room]. **2.** to close up with a wall [The windows have been *walled* up.] **—go to the wall,** to be defeated; yield or fail.

wal·la·by (wäl'ə bē), *n.* a small kind of kangaroo. **—wal'la·bies** or **wal'la·by,** *pl.*

wall·board (wôl'bôrd), *n.* a building material made of fibers, sawdust, etc. pressed together in thin sheets. It is used for making or covering walls and ceilings.

wal·let (wäl'it *or* wôl'it), *n.* a thin, flat case for carrying money, cards, etc. in the pocket.

wall·eye (wôl'ī), *n.* a fish with large, staring eyes, as the walleyed pike.

wall·eyed (wôl'īd), *adj.* **1.** having large, staring eyes. **2.** having the eyes turned outward, showing much white.

wall·flow·er (wôl'flou ər), *n.* **1.** a plant with clusters of red, yellow, or orange flowers. **2.** a shy or unpopular person who looks on, as at a dance, without taking part: *used only in everyday talk.*

wal·lop (wäl'əp *or* wôl'əp), *v.* **1.** to hit with a very hard blow. **2.** to defeat completely. **—***n.* a hard blow, or the power to strike a hard blow. *This word is used only in everyday talk.*

wal·low (wäl'ō *or* wôl'ō), *v.* **1.** to roll about in mud, dust, or filth, as pigs do. **2.** to live in a selfish or wicked way [to *wallow* in riches]. **—***n.* a place in which animals wallow.

wall·pa·per (wôl'pā pər), *n.* a kind of paper, usually printed with colored patterns, for covering walls or ceilings. **—***v.* to put wallpaper on.

wal·nut (wôl'nut), *n.* **1.** a round nut with a hard, crinkled shell and a seed that is eaten. **2.** the tree it grows on. **3.** the wood of this tree.

wal·rus (wôl'rus *or* wäl'rus), *n.* a large sea animal like a seal, found in northern oceans. It has two tusks and a thick layer of blubber.

upper: walnut
lower: half of its seed

waltz (wôlts *or* wôls), *n.* **1.** a dance for couples, with three beats to the measure. **2.** music for this dance. **—***v.* to dance a waltz.

wam·pum (wäm'pəm), *n.* small beads made of shells and used by North American Indians as money or in belts, bracelets, etc.

wan (wän *or* wôn), *adj.* **1.** having a pale, sickly color [a *wan* complexion]. **2.** weak, as when one is sick, sad, or tired [a *wan* smile].

wand (wänd *or* wônd), *n.* a slender rod, as one supposed to have magic power.

walrus (10 to 11 ft. long)

wan·der (wän'dər *or* wôn'dər), *v.* **1.** to go from place to place in an aimless way; ramble; roam [to *wander* about a city]. **2.** to go astray; stray [The ship *wandered* off course. The speaker *wandered* from his subject.] **—wan'der·er,** *n.*

wan·der·lust (wän'dər lust *or* wôn'dər lust), *n.* a strong feeling of wanting to travel.

wane (wān), *v.* **1.** to get smaller, weaker, dimmer, etc. [The moon waxes and *wanes.* The actor's fame *waned* as he grew older.] **2.** to draw near to the end [The day is *waning.*] **—***n.* the act of waning. **—on the wane,** waning; getting smaller, weaker, etc. **—waned,** *p.t. & p.p.;* **wan'ing,** *pr.p.*

wan·gle (wang′g'l), *v.* to get by sly or tricky means: *used only in everyday talk.* —**wan′gled,** *p.t. & p.p.;* **wan′gling,** *pr.p.*

want (wänt *or* wônt), *v.* **1.** to feel that one would like to have, do, get, etc.; wish or long for; desire [Do you *want* dessert? I *want* to visit Paris.] **2.** to have a need for; need [Your coat *wants* mending.] **3.** to wish to see or speak to [Your mother *wants* you.] **4.** to wish to seize, as for arrest [The man is *wanted* by the police.] **5.** to lack; be short of [It *wants* two minutes of noon.] **6.** to be poor ["Waste not, *want* not."] —*n.* **1.** a lack or need [to starve for *want* of food]. **2.** the condition of being very poor or needy [a family in *want*]. **3.** a wish or desire.

want ad, an advertisement, as in a newspaper, for something wanted, as a job, an employee, an apartment, etc.

want·ing (wän′ting *or* wôn′ting), *adj.* **1.** missing or lacking [Two forks are *wanting* in this set.] **2.** not up to what is needed or expected [given a chance and found *wanting*]. —*prep.* less; minus [The fund is *wanting* $500 of the goal set.]

wan·ton (wän′tən *or* wôn′tən), *adj.* **1.** without reason, sense, or mercy [the *wanton* killing by the Nazis]. **2.** paying no attention to what is right [*wanton* disregard of the law]. **3.** not decent or chaste; immoral [a *wanton* woman]. **4.** playful; lively; unruly [*wanton* breezes]. —*n.* an immoral woman. —**wan′ton·ly,** *adv.*

wap·i·ti (wäp′ə tē), *n.* the elk of North America.

war (wôr), *n.* **1.** fighting with weapons between countries or parts of a country. **2.** any fight or struggle [the *war* against disease and poverty]. **3.** the work or science of fighting a war [a general skilled in modern *war*]. —*v.* to carry on a war. —**warred,** *p.t. & p.p.;* **war′ring,** *pr.p.*

War between the States, the Civil War.

war·ble (wôr′b'l), *v.* to sing with trills, runs, etc. as some birds do. —*n.* the act or sound of warbling. —**war′bled,** *p.t. & p.p.;* **war′bling,** *pr.p.*

war·bler (wôr′blər), *n.* one that warbles, especially any of various songbirds.

war bonnet, a headdress with long feathers, worn by some North American Indians, as in war.

ward (wôrd), *n.* **1.** a person under the care of a guardian or a law court. **2.** a division of a hospital [the children's *ward*]. **3.** a district of a city or town, as for purposes of voting. —*v.* to keep watch over; guard: *now seldom used.* —**ward off,** to turn aside; fend off [to *ward off* a blow, a disaster, etc.].

-ward (wərd), a suffix meaning "in the direction of," "toward" [*Backward* means toward the back.]

ward·en (wôr′d'n), *n.* **1.** a person who guards or takes care of something [a game *warden*]. **2.** the chief official of a prison.

ward·er (wôr′dər), *n.* a watchman or guard.

ward·robe (wôrd′rōb), *n.* **1.** a closet or cabinet in which clothes are hung. **2.** one's supply of clothes [a spring *wardrobe*].

-wards, (wərdz), same as **-ward.**

ware (wer), *n.* **1.** a thing or things for sale; a piece or kind of goods for sale [the *wares* of a store; hard*ware*]. **2.** pottery or earthenware [dishes of fine white *ware*].

ware·house (wer′hous), *n.* a building where goods are stored; storehouse.

war·fare (wôr′fer), *n.* war or any conflict.

war·head (wôr′hed), *n.* the front part of a torpedo, rocket bomb, etc., carrying the explosive: also **war head.**

war·i·ly (wer′ə lē), *adv.* in a wary, or careful, way; cautiously.

war·i·ness (wer′ē nis), *n.* the condition of being wary; caution.

war·like (wôr′līk), *adj.* **1.** that likes to make war; ready to start a fight [a *warlike* general]. **2.** having to do with war [a *warlike* expedition]. **3.** threatening war [a *warlike* editorial].

warm (wôrm), *adj.* **1.** having or feeling a little heat; not cool but not hot [*warm* weather; exercise to keep *warm*]. **2.** making one heated [Chopping wood is *warm* work.] **3.** that keeps the body heat in [a *warm* coat]. **4.** showing strong feeling; lively or enthusiastic [a *warm* welcome; a *warm* argument]. **5.** full of love, kindness, etc. [*warm* friends; a *warm* heart]. **6.** that suggests warmth [Yellow and orange are *warm* colors.] **7.** close to guessing or finding out: *used only in everyday talk.* —*v.* **1.** to make or become warm [*Warm* yourself by the fire.] **2.** to make or become more interested, pleased, friendly, etc. [Your kind words *warmed* my heart.] —**warm up, 1.** to make or become warm; heat or reheat. **2.** to practice or exercise, as before playing in a game. —**warm′ly,** *adv.* —**warm′ness,** *n.*

warm-blood·ed (wôrm′blud′id), *adj.* **1.** having warm blood and a body heat that stays the same [Mammals and birds are *warm-blooded* animals; fish are not.] **2.** having strong feelings; ardent.

warm·heart·ed (wôrm′här′tid), *adj.* kind; loving.

warming pan, a covered pan for holding hot coals, used at one time to warm beds.

warmth (wôrmth), *n.* **1.** the condition of being warm [the sun's *warmth*]. **2.** strong feeling; ardor, anger, love, etc. [to reply with *warmth*].

warming pan

warn (wôrn), *v.* **1.** to tell of a danger; advise to be careful [I *warned* him not to play with matches.] **2.** to let know in advance [He signaled to *warn* us that he would turn.]

warn·ing (wôr′ning), *n.* something that warns [Pain in the body is a *warning* of trouble.]

War of 1812, the war from 1812 to 1815 between the United States and Great Britain.

War of American Independence, same as **Revolutionary War.**

warp (wôrp), *v.* **1.** to bend or twist out of shape [Rain and heat had *warped* the boards.] **2.** to turn from what is right, natural, etc.;

warped board

distort [Bad companions had *warped* his character.] —*n.* **1.** a twist or bend as in a piece of wood. **2.** a quirk or odd twist of the mind. **3.** the threads running lengthwise in a weaver's loom. They are crossed by the woof.

war·rant (wôr′ənt), *n.* **1.** a good reason for something; justification [He has no *warrant* for such a belief.] **2.** something that makes sure; guarantee [His wealth is no *warrant* of happiness.] **3.** an official paper that gives the right to do something [The police must have a *warrant* to search a house.] —*v.* **1.** to be a good reason for; justify [Her good work *warrants* our praise.] **2.** to give the right to do something [His arrest was not *warranted.*] **3.** to give a warranty for; guarantee [This appliance is *warranted.*] **4.** to say in a positive way; assure: *used only in everyday talk* [I *warrant* he'll be late.]

warrant officer, an officer in the armed forces ranking above an enlisted man but below a commissioned officer.

war·ran·ty (wôr′ən tē), *n.* same as **guarantee.** —**war′ran·ties,** *pl.*

war·ren (wôr′ən *or* wär′ən), *n.* an area in which rabbits breed or are raised.

war·ri·or (wôr′i ər), *n.* a soldier: *now used mainly in poetry, etc.*

War·saw (wôr′sô), *n.* the capital of Poland.

war·ship (wôr′ship), *n.* any ship for use in war; battleship, destroyer, etc.

wart (wôrt), *n.* **1.** a small, hard growth on the skin. **2.** a small growth on a plant.

wart hog, a wild African hog with curved tusks, and warts below the eyes.

war·time (wôr′tīm), *n.* any period of war.

war·y (wer′ē), *adj.* **1.** on one's guard; cautious [a *wary* patrol]. **2.** showing caution or suspicion [a

wart hog (3 ft. high at shoulder)

wary look]. —**wary of,** careful of. —**war′i·er,** *compar.;* **war′i·est,** *superl.*

was (wuz *or* wäz), the form of **be** showing the past time with singular nouns and with *I, he, she,* or *it.*

wash (wôsh *or* wäsh), *v.* **1.** to clean with water or other liquid, often with soap [to *wash* one's hands, a car, etc.]. **2.** to wash clothes [She *washes* on Monday.] **3.** to carry away by the action of water [*Wash* the dirt off your hands. The bridge was *washed* out.] **4.** to wear away by flowing over [The flood *washed* out the road.] **5.** to flow over or against [The sea *washed* the

shore.] **6.** to pass water through in order to get something out [The miners *washed* the gravel for gold.] **7.** to cover with a thin coating, as of paint or metal [silverware *washed* with gold]. **8.** to make clean in spirit [*washed* of all guilt]. **9.** to be washed without being damaged [Good muslin *washes* well.] —*n.* **1.** the act of washing [Your car needs a *wash.*] **2.** a load of clothes, etc. that has been washed or is to be washed [to hang out a *wash*]. **3.** the flow or sound of water rushing [the *wash* of the waves]. **4.** an eddy made in water by a propeller, oars, etc. **5.** the current of air pushed back by an airplane propeller. **6.** a special liquid for washing [a mouth *wash;* a hair *wash*]. **7.** a thin coating, as of paint or metal. **8.** watery garbage, as for feeding hogs. **9.** silt, mud, etc. carried and dropped by flowing water. —*adj.* that can be washed without damage [a *wash* dress]. —**wash down,** to take a drink along with food to help in swallowing.

Wash., abbreviation for **Washington.**

wash·a·ble (wôsh′ə b'l *or* wäsh′ə b'l), *adj.* that can be washed without being damaged.

wash·board (wôsh′bôrd *or* wäsh′bôrd), *n.* a board with ridges for scrubbing dirt out of clothes.

wash·bowl (wôsh′bōl *or* wäsh′bōl), *n.* a bowl or basin for washing the hands and face; often, a bathroom sink.

wash·cloth (wôsh′klôth *or* wäsh′klôth), *n.* a small cloth used in washing the face or body.

washed-out (wôsht′out′ *or* wäsht′out′), *adj.* **1.** faded in color. **2.** tired-looking; pale and wan: *only in everyday talk.*

washboard

wash·er (wôsh′ər *or* wäsh′ər), *n.* **1.** a machine for washing [an automatic clothes *washer*]. **2.** a disk or flat ring of metal, rubber, etc., used to help bolts, faucet valves, etc. fit more tightly. **3.** a person who washes [a car *washer*].

wash·er·wom·an (wôsh′ər woom′ən *or* wäsh′ər woom′ən), *n.* a woman whose work is washing clothes. —**wash′er·wom′en,** *pl.*

types of washer (meaning 2)

wash·ing (wôsh′ing *or* wäsh′ing), *n.* **1.** the act of one that washes. **2.** a load of clothes, etc. washed or to be washed. —*adj.* used for washing [a *washing* machine].

Wash·ing·ton (wôsh′ing tən *or* wäsh′ing tən), *n.* **1.** a State in the northwestern part of the United States: abbreviated **Wash. 2.** the capital of the United States, in the District of Columbia.

Washington, George, 1732–1799; first president of the United States, from 1789 to 1797. He was commander in chief of the American army in the Revolutionary War.

wash·out (wôsh′out *or* wäsh′out), *n.* **1.** the washing away of earth, a road, etc. as by a flood; also, the place washed away. **2.** a complete failure: *slang in this meaning.*

wash·room (wôsh′room *or* wäsh′room), *n.* **1.** a room in which washing is done. **2.** a rest-room.

wash·stand (wôsh′stand *or* wäsh′stand), *n.* **1.** a bathroom sink. **2.** a table holding a bowl and pitcher, for washing the face and hands.

wash·tub (wôsh′tub *or* wäsh′tub), *n.* a tub or deep sink for washing clothes.

was·n't (wuz′nt *or* wäz′nt), was not.

wasp (wäsp *or* wôsp), *n.* a flying insect with a slender body. Some wasps have a sharp sting.

wasp·ish (wäsp′ish *or* wôsp′ish), *adj.* **1.** of or like a wasp. **2.** bad-tempered; snappish.

was·sail (wäs′'l *or* wäs′āl), *n.* **1.** a toast of earlier times in drinking to a person's health. **2.** the liquor drunk when making this toast. **3.** a party where there is much drinking. —*v.* to drink wassails. —**was′sail·er,** *n.*

wasp (1 in. long)

wast (wäst *or* wəst), older form of **was,** used with thou: *now used only in poetry, prayers, etc.*

wast·age (wās′tij), *n.* what is wasted, as by spoiling, leaking out, etc.

waste (wāst), *v.* **1.** to use up or spend without real need or purpose; make bad use of [to *waste* money or time]. **2.** to fail to take advantage of [She *wasted* her chance for an education.] **3.** to wear away; use up [soil *wasted* away by erosion]. **4.** to lose or make lose strength, health, etc. [In her old age, she *wasted* away.] **5.** to destroy or ruin [Swarms of locusts *wasted* the fields.] —*n.* **1.** the act of wasting, or loss by wasting [Prevent *waste* by using less.] **2.** matter left over or thrown out as useless; refuse, scrap, etc. [Sewers carry away *waste.*] **3.** bits of cotton fiber or yarn, used to wipe machinery, etc. **4.** a desert or wilderness. —*adj.* **1.** barren or wild, as land. **2.** left over or thrown out as useless [*waste* paper]. **3.** used to carry off or hold waste [*waste* pipes]. —**go to waste,** to be wasted. —**lay waste,** to destroy or ruin. —**wast′ed,** *p.t. & p.p.;* **wast′ing,** *pr.p.* —**wast′er,** *n.*

waste·bas·ket (wāst′bas′kit), *n.* a container for waste paper, etc.

waste·ful (wāst′fəl), *adj.* using more than is needed; extravagant [a *wasteful* person; *wasteful* practices]. —**waste′ful·ly,** *adv.*

watch (wäch *or* wôch), *v.* **1.** to keep one's sight on; look at [We *watched* the sun setting.] **2.** to pay attention to; observe [I've *watched* his career with interest.] **3.** to take care of; look after; guard [The shepherd *watched* his flock.] **4.** to stay awake or keep vigil, as in tending a sick person. **5.** to be looking or waiting [*Watch* for the signal.] **6.** to be alert or on guard [*Watch* that you don't drop the plate.] —*n.* **1.** the act of watching, or guarding [The dog keeps *watch* over the house.] **2.** a person or group that guards.

3. the time that a guard is on duty [His *watch* is finished.] **4.** a device for telling time that is like a clock but small enough to be worn on the wrist or carried in the pocket. **5.** any of the periods of duty on shipboard, usually four hours. **6.** the part of a ship's crew on duty during such a period. —**on the watch,** watching. —**watch out,** to be careful or alert. —**watch′er,** *n.*

watch·dog (wäch′dôg *or* wôch′dôg), *n.* a dog kept to guard a building, grounds, etc.

watch·ful (wäch′fəl *or* wôch′fəl), *adj.* watching closely; alert. —**watch′ful·ly,** *adv.*

watch·mak·er (wäch′māk′ər *or* wôch′māk′ər), *n.* a person who makes or repairs watches.

watch·man (wäch′mən *or* wôch′mən), *n.* a person hired to guard a building, etc., especially at night. —**watch′men,** *pl.*

watch·tow·er (wäch′tou′ər *or* wôch′tou′ər), *n.* a high tower from which watch is kept, as for forest fires.

watch·word (wäch′würd *or* wôch′würd), *n.* **1.** a secret word that must be spoken to a guard in order to pass him; password. **2.** the slogan of some group.

wa·ter (wô′tər), *n.* **1.** the colorless liquid that falls as rain and is found in rivers, lakes, and oceans. **2.** **waters,** *pl.* the water in a spring, river, lake, or ocean. **3.** a liquid like or with water [*water* from a blister; soda *water*]. **4.** the degree of clearness or brightness [a diamond of the first *water*]. **5.** a wavy finish put on silk, linen, etc. or on metal. —*v.* **1.** to give water to [to *water* a horse]. **2.** to supply with water, as by sprinkling [to *water* a lawn]. **3.** to make weaker by adding water [to *water* milk]. **4.** to fill with tears [The onion made her eyes *water.*] **5.** to fill with saliva [The smell made his mouth *water.*] **6.** to put a wavy finish on [*watered* silk]. —*adj.* **1.** of or for water [*water* pipes]. **2.** in or on water [*water* sports]. **3.** found in or near water [*water* plants]. —**by water,** by ship or boat. —**wa′ter·less,** *adj.*

water bird, any bird that swims or that lives on or near water; waterfowl.

wa·ter·buck (wô′tər buk), *n.* an African antelope with long horns that lives near water. —**wa′ter·buck** or **wa′ter·bucks,** *pl.*

water buffalo, a slow, strong buffalo of Asia, Africa, and the Philippines, used for pulling loads. *See the picture for* **buffalo.**

water chestnut, 1. a water plant with white flowers and a fruit like a nut. **2.** this fruit.

water buck
(4 ft. high at shoulder)

water clock, a device for measuring time by the fall or flow of water.

water closet, a toilet (*meanings 2 and 3*).

---

fat,   āpe,   cär,   ten,   ēven,   hit,   bīte,   gō,   hôrn,   tool,   book,   **up,**   fŭr;
get,   joy,   yet,   chin,   she,   thin,   *th*en;   zh = s in pleasure;   ′ as in able (ā′b'l);
ə = a in ago,   e in agent,   i in sanity,   o in confess,   u in focus.

water color, 1. a paint made by mixing coloring matter with water instead of oil. **2.** a picture painted with water colors. **—wa′ter-col′or,** *adj.*

wa·ter·course (wô′tər kôrs), *n.* **1.** a stream of water; river, brook, etc. **2.** a channel for water, as a canal or a stream bed.

water cress, a plant with leaves that are used in salads, etc. It grows in water or wet soil.

wa·ter·fall (wô′tər fôl), *n.* a steep fall of water, as from a high cliff.

wa·ter·fowl (wô′tər foul), *n.* a water bird, especially one that swims.

water front, 1. land at the edge of a river, harbor, etc. **2.** an area of such land in a city, often with docks, wharves, etc.

watering place, 1. a place where animals come to drink. **2.** a resort with mineral springs or on a body of water: *mainly a British meaning.*

water lily, a water plant with large, flat, floating leaves and flowers in many colors.

water line, the line to which the surface of the water comes on the side of a ship or boat, depending on the weight of its load.

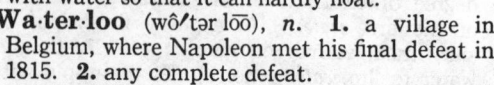
water lily

wa·ter·logged (wô′tər-lôgd′), *adj.* soaked or filled with water so that it can hardly float.

Wa·ter·loo (wô′tər lōō), *n.* **1.** a village in Belgium, where Napoleon met his final defeat in 1815. **2.** any complete defeat.

water main, a main pipe in a system of pipes which carry water.

wa·ter·man (wô′tər mən), *n.* **1.** a man who works on boats. **2.** a man who rows. **—wa′ter-men,** *pl.*

wa·ter·mark (wô′tər märk), *n.* **1.** a mark that shows the water level of a river, etc. **2.** a design pressed into paper while it is being made.

wa·ter·mel·on (wô′tər mel′ən), *n.* a large melon with a green rind and juicy, red pulp.

water moccasin, a large, brownish, poisonous snake of the southern United States; cottonmouth.

watermelons

water polo, a game played with a large ball by two teams of swimmers.

water power, the power of water falling or flowing, used to make machinery run.

wa·ter·proof (wô′tər prōōf), *adj.* treated with rubber, plastic, etc. so that water cannot come through. **—v.** to make waterproof.

water rat, 1. an animal like a mouse or rat that lives along the banks of streams and ponds in Europe. **2.** a muskrat.

wa·ter·shed (wô′tər shed), *n.* **1.** a ridge of high ground dividing one area whose streams flow into one river from another area whose streams flow into another river. **2.** one of these areas.

wa·ter·side (wô′tər sīd), *n.* land at the edge of a river, lake, or sea.

wa·ter·ski (wô′tər skē′), *v.* to be towed over water on boards like skis by a line from a speedboat. **—wa′ter-skied′,** *p.t.* & *p.p.;* **wa′ter-ski′ing,** *pr.p.*

girl water-skiing

wa·ter·spout (wô′tər-spout), *n.* **1.** a pipe or spout from which water runs. **2.** a whirling column of air, filled with water and reaching down from a storm cloud to a body of water.

wa·ter·tight (wô′tər tīt), *adj.* **1.** so tight that no water can get through [a *watertight* hatch on a ship]. **2.** perfectly thought out, with no weak points [a *watertight* plan].

wa·ter·way (wô′tər wā), *n.* **1.** a channel through which water runs. **2.** any body of water on which boats or ships can travel, as a canal or river.

water wheel, a wheel turned by flowing or falling water, used to give power.

wa·ter·works (wô′tər wŭrks), *n.pl.* **1.** a system of reservoirs, pumps, pipes, etc. for supplying a region with water. **2.** a building with machinery for pumping water in such a system. *Often used with a singular verb.*

wa·ter·y (wô′tər ē), *adj.* **1.** of water [the fish in his *watery* home]. **2.** full of water [*watery* soil; *watery* eyes]. **3.** like water. **4.** weak, tasteless, etc., as from too much water [*watery* soup].

watt (wät *or* wôt), *n.* a unit for measuring electric power. It is equal to a current of one ampere under one volt of pressure.

wat·tle (wät′'l *or* wôt′'l), *n.* **1.** the loose flap of skin hanging from the throat of a turkey, chicken, etc. **2.** sticks woven together with twigs or branches and used on walls, roofs, etc. **—v. 1.** to weave sticks, branches, etc. together. **2.** to build of wattle. **—wat′tled,** *p.t.* & *p.p.;* **wat′tling,** *pr.p.*

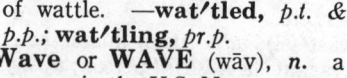
wattles

Wave or **WAVE** (wāv), *n.* a woman in the U.S. Navy.

wave (wāv), *v.* **1.** to move up and down or back and forth; flap or sway [The flag *waved* in the breeze.] **2.** to wave the hand, a handkerchief, etc., or to signal by doing this [The crowd *waved* as he drove past. She *waved* a good-by to us.] **3.** to arrange in curves [Her hair is *waved*.] **—n. 1.** a curving swell of water moving along the surface of an ocean, lake, etc. **2.** something with a motion like this [a light *wave;* a sound *wave*]. **3.** a curve or series of curves [Her hair has a natural *wave*.] **4.** a waving movement, as of the hand in signaling. **5.** a sudden increase or rise that builds up, then goes down [a crime *wave;* a *wave* of new settlers]. **—waved,** *p.t.* & *p.p.;* **wav′ing,** *pr.p.*

wa·ver (wā′vər), v. **1.** to show doubt or be uncertain [He never *wavered* in his decision to study law.] **2.** to flutter, quiver, tremble, flicker, etc. [His voice *wavered*. The candlelight *wavered*.] —n. the act of wavering.

wav·y (wāv′ē), adj. having or moving in waves [*wavy* hair; *wavy* shadows]. —**wav′i·er**, *compar.*; **wav′i·est**, *superl.* —**wav′i·ness**, n.

wax (waks), n. **1.** a yellow substance that bees make and use for building honeycombs; beeswax. **2.** any substance like this, as paraffin. Wax is used to make candles, polishes, etc. —v. to put wax or polish on.

wax (waks), v. **1.** to get larger, stronger, fuller, etc. [The moon *waxes* and wanes.] **2.** to become or grow [He began to *wax* angry.]

wax·en (wak′s'n), adj. **1.** made of wax [a *waxen* candle]. **2.** like wax [his *waxen* face].

wax·wing (waks′wing), n. a brown bird with a crest and with red, waxy tips on its wings.

wax·y (wak′sē), adj. **1.** covered with wax or made of wax. **2.** like wax. —**wax′-i·er**, *compar.*; **wax′i·est**, *superl.* —**wax′i·ness**, n.

way (wā), n. **1.** a road or path [an old Roman *way*; a high*way*]. **2.** room to pass through [Make *way* for the king!] **3.** a route or course [He took the long

cedar waxwing
(7 in. long)

way home.] **4.** movement forward [You lead the *way*. The wind died and the sailboat slowly lost *way*.] **5.** direction [Go that *way*.] **6.** distance [Come part of the *way* with me.] **7.** a method of doing something [the wrong *way* to shell peas]. **8.** manner; style [She smiled in a friendly *way*.] **9.** a usual or typical manner of living, behaving, etc. [to study the *ways* of ants]. **10.** wish; desire [He's happy when he gets his *way*.] **11.** a point or detail; particular [a bad idea in some *ways*]. **12. ways,** pl. a framework of timber on which a ship is built and down which it slides in launching. **13.** a condition: *used only in everyday talk* [He's in a bad *way*.] —adv. away; far: *used only in everyday talk* [*way* behind in the race]. —**by the way,** as a new but related point; incidentally. —**by way of, 1.** going through [to Rome *by way of* Paris]. **2.** as a way of [He did it *by way of* showing his thanks.] —**give way, 1.** to go back or give up; yield. **2.** to break down. —**in the way,** so as to keep from passing, going on, etc. —**make one's way, 1.** to move ahead. **2.** to be successful. —**out of the way, 1.** not in the way. **2.** taken care of; settled. **3.** by a longer or less common route. —**under way,** moving ahead; going on.

way·far·er (wā′fer′ər), n. one who travels, especially on foot; traveler. —**way′far′ing,** adj. & n.

way·lay (wā lā′), v. **1.** to lie in wait for and attack; ambush [Robbers *waylaid* the stagecoach at the pass.] **2.** to wait for and stop so as to speak with. —**way·laid** (wā lād′), p.t. & p.p.; **way·lay′ing,** pr.p.

-ways (wāz), a suffix meaning "in a certain direction, position, or manner" [To look *sideways* is to look in a direction to one side.]

way·side (wā′sīd), n. the edge of a road. —adj. on, near, or along the side of a road.

way·ward (wā′wərd), adj. **1.** insisting on having one's own way; willful or disobedient. **2.** not regular or steady; changeable; erratic.

we (wē), pron. the persons speaking or writing [Here *we* are!] *We* is also used by a person in speaking for himself and the person spoken to [Are *we* still friends?] or in speaking for a group. It is also used by a king, editor, etc. in speaking of himself ["*We* have so ordered," said Queen Victoria.]

weak (wēk), adj. **1.** having little strength, force, or power; not strong, firm, effective, etc. [*weak* from illness; a *weak* character; a *weak* team; a *weak* argument]. **2.** not able to last under strain, use, etc.; not sound [a *weak* railing]. **3.** lacking the usual or normal strength or power [*weak* tea; *weak* eyes]. **4.** lacking the needed skill [He is *weak* in arithmetic.] —**weak′ness,** n.

weak·en (wē′kən), v. to make or become weaker.

weak·fish (wēk′fish), n. an ocean fish used for food, found along the Atlantic coast.

weak-kneed (wēk′nēd′), adj. timid or cowardly.

weak·ling (wēk′ling), n. a person who is weak in body, will, character, etc.

weak·ly (wēk′lē), adj. weak or sickly; feeble. —adv. in a weak way. —**weak′li·er,** *compar.*; **weak′li·est,** *superl.*

weak·ness (wēk′nis), n. **1.** lack of strength, force, or power. **2.** a weak point; fault. **3.** a special liking that is hard to control [a *weakness* for pickles].

weal (wēl), n. a mark or ridge raised on the skin, as by a whip; welt.

weal (wēl), n. well-being; welfare: *no longer much used* [the common *weal* of the nation].

wealth (welth), n. **1.** much money or property; riches. **2.** a large amount [a *wealth* of ideas]. **3.** any valuable thing or things.

wealth·y (wel′thē), adj. having wealth; rich. —**wealthy in,** full of [a home *wealthy in* love]. —**wealth′i·er,** *compar.*; **wealth′i·est,** *superl.*

wean (wēn), v. **1.** to get a baby or young animal gradually trained away from suckling. **2.** to make draw away gradually, as from some habit.

weap·on (wep′ən), n. **1.** a thing used for fighting, as a club, sword, gun, bomb, etc. **2.** any means of attack or defense [A cat's claws are its *weapons*. His best *weapon* was silence.]

wear (wer), *v.* **1.** to have on the body, as clothes; carry, show, or arrange on the person [*Wear* your coat. He *wears* glasses. How do you *wear* your hair?] **2.** to have or show [He *wore* a frown.] **3.** to make or become damaged, used up, etc. by use or friction [He *wore* his jeans to rags. The water is *wearing* away the river bank.] **4.** to make by use or friction [to *wear* a hole in a sock]. **5.** to last in use [This cloth *wears* well.] **6.** to pass gradually [The year *wore* on.] —*n.* **1.** a wearing or being worn [a dress for holiday *wear*]. **2.** clothes; clothing [men's *wear*]. **3.** the damage or loss from use or friction [His shoes show a little *wear*.] **4.** the ability to last in use [There's much *wear* left in that coat.] —**wear down, 1.** to lessen in height or thickness by use or friction. **2.** to overcome by constant effort. —**wear off,** to pass away gradually. —**wear out, 1.** to make or become useless from much use or friction. **2.** to tire out; exhaust. —**wore,** *p.t.;* **worn,** *p.p.;* **wear′ing,** *pr.p.* —**wear′er,** *n.*

wear·ing (wer′ing), *adj.* that tires one out.

wea·ri·some (wir′ē səm), *adj.* tiring or tiresome.

wea·ry (wir′ē), *adj.* **1.** tired; worn out [*weary* after a day's work]. **2.** having little or no patience or interest left; bored [*weary* of reading]. **3.** tiring [a *weary* walk]. **4.** tiresome; boring [a *weary* speech]. —*v.* to make or become weary. —**wea′ri·er,** *compar.;* **wea′ri·est,** *superl.* —**wea′ried,** *p.t. & p.p.;* **wea′ry·ing,** *pr.p.* —**wea′ri·ly,** *adv.* —**wea′ri·ness,** *n.*

wea·sel (wē′z'l), *n.* a small animal with a long body and tail, and short legs. Weasels feed on rats, mice, birds, etc.

weasel (1½ ft. long, including tail)

weath·er (weth′ər), *n.* the conditions outside with regard to temperature, sunshine, rainfall, etc. [winter *weather;* good *weather* for a picnic]. —*v.* **1.** to pass through safely [to *weather* a storm]. **2.** to lay open to the weather; to season, dry, harden, etc. in the open air [his *weathered* face]. —*adj.* facing the wind; windward [the *weather* side of a ship]. —**keep one's weather eye open,** to be on the alert: *used only in everyday talk.* —**under the weather,** not feeling well; ill: *used only in everyday talk.*

weath·er-beat·en (weth′ər bē′t'n), *adj.* worn, damaged, or roughened by the weather.

weath·er·cock (weth′ər käk), *n.* a weather vane in the form of a cock, or rooster.

weath·er·glass (weth′ər glas), *n.* an instrument used to forecast the weather, as a barometer.

weather strip, a strip of metal, felt, etc., put along the edges of a door or window to keep out drafts, rain, etc.: also **weather stripping.**

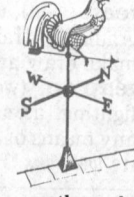

weathercock

weather vane, a device that swings in the wind to show in what direction it is blowing.

weave (wēv), *v.* **1.** to make by passing threads, strips, etc. over and under one another, as on a loom [to *weave* cloth; to *weave* a straw mat]. **2.** to form into a fabric or something woven [to *weave* grass into a basket]. **3.** to twist into or through [She *wove* flowers into her hair.] **4.** to put together; form [to *weave* events into a story]. **5.** to spin, as a spider does its web. **6.** to move from side to side or in and out [a car *weaving* through traffic]. —*n.* a method or pattern of weaving [Burlap has a rough *weave.*] —**wove,** *p.t.;* **wo′ven** or **wove,** *p.p.* (**weaved** *is a p.t. & p.p. for meaning 6);* **weav′ing,** *pr.p.* —**weav′er,** *n.*

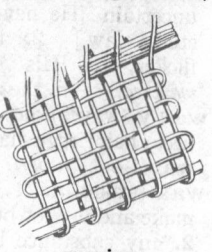

weaving

web (web), *n.* **1.** a woven fabric, especially one still on a loom or just taken off. **2.** the network of threads spun by a spider or other insect. **3.** anything put together in a careful or complicated way [a *web* of lies; the *web* of fate]. **4.** the skin joining the toes of a duck, frog, or other swimming animal.

webbed (webd), *adj.* **1.** having the toes joined by a web [*webbed* feet]. **2.** formed like a web or made of webbing.

web·bing (web′ing), *n.* **1.** a strong cloth woven in strips, used for belts, in the framework of furniture, etc. **2.** a web joining the toes.

web-foot·ed (web′foot'id), *adj.* having a web joining the toes.

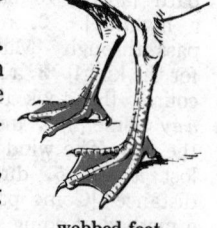

webbed feet

Web·ster, Daniel (web′stər), 1782–1852; U.S. statesman and orator.

Webster, Noah, 1758–1843; U.S. dictionary maker.

wed (wed), *v.* **1.** to marry. **2.** to join closely; unite [Science and art are *wedded* in this project.] —**wed′ded,** *p.t.;* **wed′ded** or **wed,** *p.p.;* **wed′ding,** *pr.p.*

we'd (wēd), **1.** we had. **2.** we should. **3.** we would.

Wed., abbreviation for **Wednesday.**

wed·ded (wed′id), *adj.* **1.** married. **2.** having to do with marriage [*wedded* bliss]. **3.** devoted [He's *wedded* to his work.] **4.** united [They are *wedded* by common interests.]

wed·ding (wed′ing), *n.* **1.** the act of becoming married; marriage or the marriage ceremony. **2.** an anniversary of a marriage [A silver *wedding* is the 25th wedding anniversary.]

wedge (wej), *n.* **1.** a piece of wood, metal, etc. narrowing to a thin edge that can be driven into a log or the like to split it. **2.** anything shaped like this [a *wedge* of pie]. **3.** anything that gradually opens the way for some action, change, etc. —*v.* **1.** to split or force apart as with

wedge

a wedge. **2.** to fix in place with a wedge [to *wedge* a door open]. **3.** to force or pack tightly [Ten people were *wedged* into the car.] —**wedged,** *p.t. & p.p.;* **wedg'ing,** *pr.p.*

wed·lock (wed'läk), *n.* marriage.

Wednes·day (wenz'dē), *n.* the fourth day of the week.

wee (wē), *adj.* very small; tiny. —**we'er,** *compar.;* **we'est,** *superl.*

weed (wēd), *n.* a plant that springs up where it is not wanted, as in a lawn. —*v.* **1.** to take out weeds, as from a garden. **2.** to pick out and get rid of as useless [to *weed* out faded pictures from an album]. —**weed'er,** *n.*

weeds (wēdz), *n.pl.* black clothes worn while in mourning, as by a widow.

weed·y (wēd'ē), *adj.* **1.** full of weeds. **2.** of or like a weed. **3.** thin, tall, and awkward. —**weed'i·er,** *compar.;* **weed'i·est,** *superl.*

week (wēk), *n.* **1.** a period of seven days, especially one beginning with Sunday and ending with Saturday. **2.** the hours or days one works each week [a 35-hour *week;* a five-day *week*].

week·day (wēk'dā), *n.* any day of the week except Sunday, or sometimes Saturday.

week·end or **week-end** (wēk'end'), *n.* Saturday and Sunday, as a time for rest and recreation. —*v.* to spend the weekend [to *weekend* at home].

week·ly (wēk'lē), *adj.* **1.** happening, done, being due, etc. once a week [*weekly* payments]. **2.** lasting for a week. —*adv.* once a week; every week. —*n.* a newspaper or magazine that comes out once a week. —**week'lies,** *pl.*

ween (wēn), *v.* to think; suppose: *now seldom used.*

weep (wēp), *v.* **1.** to shed tears, as in grief; cry. **2.** to let flow; shed [to *weep* bitter tears]. **3.** to shed tears for; mourn. —**wept,** *p.t. & p.p.;* **weep'ing,** *pr.p.* —**weep'er,** *n.* —**weep'y,** *adj.*

weep·ing (wēp'ing), *adj.* **1.** that weeps. **2.** having graceful, drooping branches [a *weeping* willow]. —*n.* the act of one that weeps.

wee·vil (wē'v'l), *n.* any of certain small beetles whose larvae destroy trees, cotton, grain, fruits, and nuts.

weft (weft), *n.* the threads woven across the warp in a loom; woof.

weigh (wā), *v.* **1.** to use a scales, balance, etc. to find out how heavy a thing is [to *weigh* oneself]. **2.** to have a certain weight [He *weighs* 126 pounds.] **3.** to have importance [His good behavior *weighs* in his favor.] **4.** to measure out as on scales [to *weigh* out two pounds of candy; to *weigh* out justice in a law court]. **5.** to think about carefully before choosing; ponder [to *weigh* one plan against another]. **6.** to bear down heavily upon, or be a burden [He is *weighed* down with worry. The theft *weighs* on his mind.] **7.** to lift up, as an anchor, before sailing.

weight (wāt), *n.* **1.** heaviness; the quality a thing has because of the pull of gravity on it. **2.** amount of heaviness [What is your *weight?*] **3.** a piece of metal used in weighing [Put the two-ounce *weight* on the balance.] **4.** any solid mass used for its heaviness [to lift *weights* for exercise; a paper *weight*]. **5.** any unit of heaviness, as an ounce,

man lifting weights *(meaning 4)*

pound, etc.; also, any system of such units: see **avoirdupois, troy. 6.** a burden, as of sorrow, worry, etc. **7.** importance or influence [a matter of great *weight*]. —*v.* **1.** to add weight to. **2.** to burden [He is *weighted* down with sorrow.] —**carry weight,** to be important, have influence, etc.

weight·less (wāt'lis), *adj.* seeming to have little or no weight, especially because of being beyond the pull of gravity [Astronauts are *weightless* on flights to the moon.]

weight·y (wāt'ē), *adj.* **1.** very heavy. **2.** hard to bear; being a burden [*weighty* responsibilities]. **3.** very important; serious [a *weighty* problem]. —**weight'i·er,** *compar.;* **weight'i·est,** *superl.*

weir (wir), *n.* **1.** a low dam built in a river. **2.** a fence built across a stream to catch fish.

weird (wird), *adj.* **1.** strange or mysterious in a ghostly way [*Weird* sounds came from the cave.] **2.** queer; unusual: *used only in everyday talk* [She wore a *weird* hat.] —**weird'ly,** *adv.*

wel·come (wel'kəm), *adj.* **1.** that one is glad to get [a *welcome* guest; *welcome* news]. **2.** gladly allowed or invited [You're *welcome* to use our library.] **3.** under no obligation for a favor given ["You're *welcome*" is the usual reply to "thank you."] —*n.* words or action used in greeting [We'll give him a hearty *welcome*.] —*v.* to greet or receive with pleasure [I *welcome* your advice.] —*interj.* I am glad you have come!: *a greeting.* —**wear out one's welcome,** to come too often or stay too long. —**wel'comed,** *p.t. & p.p.;* **wel'com·ing,** *pr.p.*

weld (weld), *v.* **1.** to join pieces of metal by heating until they melt together or can be hammered or pressed together. **2.** to join together; unite [The boys were *welded* in friendship.] **3.** to be capable of being welded [This metal *welds* easily.] —*n.* **1.** the act of welding. **2.** the joint formed by welding. —**weld'er,** *n.*

wel·fare (wel'fer'), *n.* health, happiness, etc.; well-being. —**on welfare,** getting help from the government because of being poor, out of work, etc.

wel·kin (wel'kin), *n.* the sky: *now seldom used except in the phrase* **to make the welkin ring,** meaning "to be very loud or noisy."

well (wel), *n.* **1.** a natural flow of water from the earth; spring. **2.** a deep hole dug in the earth to get water, gas, oil, etc. **3.** a supply

fat,   āpe,   cär,   ten,   ēven,   hit,   bīte,   gō,   hôrn,   tōol,   book,   up,   fűr;
get,   joy,   yet,   chin,   she,   thin,   *then;*   zh = s in pleasure;   ' as in able (ā'b'l);
ə = a in ago,   e in agent,   i in sanity,   o in confess,   u in focus.

or store [The book is a *well* of information.]
4. a shaft in a building, as for a staircase or elevator. **5.** a container for liquid, as an inkwell. —*v.* to flow or gush [Pity *welled* up in her.]

well (wel), *adv.* **1.** in a way that is pleasing, wanted, good, right, etc. [The work is going *well*. Treat him *well*. She sings *well*.] **2.** in comfort and plenty [to live *well*]. **3.** with good reason [You may *well* ask for mercy.] **4.** to a large degree; much [*well* advanced]. **5.** with certainty [You know perfectly *well* that he did it.] **6.** in a thorough way; completely [Stir it *well*.] **7.** in a familiar way; closely [I know him *well*.] **8.** properly, fully, etc.: *often used in words formed with a hyphen* [*well*-fed; *well*-worn]. —*adj.* **1.** in good health. **2.** comfortable, satisfactory, etc. [Things are *well* with us.] **3.** proper, fit, right, etc. [It is *well* that you came.] —*interj.* a word used to show surprise, relief, agreement, etc. —**as well, 1.** in addition. **2.** equally. —**as well as, 1.** just as good or as much as. **2.** in addition to. —**bet′ter,** *compar.;* **best,** *superl.*

we'll (wēl), **1.** we shall. **2.** we will.

well-bal·anced (wel′bal′ənst), *adj.* **1.** having the needed parts in the right amounts [a *well-balanced* meal]. **2.** showing good sense; reasonable.

well-be·ing (wel′bē′ing), *n.* the condition of being well, happy, wealthy, etc.; welfare.

well·born (wel′bôrn′), *adj.* coming from a family of high social position.

well-bred (wel′bred′), *adj.* having or showing good manners; polite.

well-done (wel′dun′), *adj.* **1.** done with skill. **2.** thoroughly cooked [a *well-done* steak].

well-fed (wel′fed′), *adj.* showing the results of eating much good food; plump; fat.

well-found·ed (wel′foun′did), *adj.* based on facts or good judgment [a *well-founded* belief].

well-groomed (wel′grōōmd′), *adj.* **1.** clean and neat. **2.** carefully cared for, as a horse.

well-ground·ed (wel′groun′did), *adj.* **1.** having good training in the basic facts of a subject. **2.** based on facts.

well-in·formed (wel′in fôrmd′), *adj.* **1.** knowing very much about a subject [*well-informed* on music]. **2.** knowing much about many subjects.

Wel·ling·ton, Duke of (wel′ing tən), 1769–1852; British general who defeated Napoleon at Waterloo.

well-known (wel′nōn′), *adj.* **1.** widely known; famous. **2.** fully known; familiar.

well-man·nered (wel′man′ərd), *adj.* having or showing good manners; polite; courteous.

well-mean·ing (wel′mēn′ing), *adj.* showing an intention to help or to do the right thing.

well-nigh (wel′nī′), *adv.* almost; very nearly.

well-off (wel′ôf′), *adj.* **1.** in a good or fortunate condition. **2.** wealthy.

well-pre·served (wel′pri zūrvd′), *adj.* in good condition or looking good, in spite of age.

well-read (wel′red′), *adj.* having read much.

well·spring (wel′spring), *n.* **1.** a spring or fountainhead. **2.** a supply that is always full.

well-thought-of (wel′thôt′uv), *adj.* having a good reputation.

well-to-do (wel′tə dōō′), *adj.* wealthy.

well-wish·er (wel′wish′ər), *n.* a person who wishes well to another, or to a cause, etc.

well-worn (wel′wôrn′), *adj.* **1.** much worn; much used [a *well-worn* sweater]. **2.** used too often; no longer fresh or new [a *well-worn* joke].

Welsh (welsh), *adj.* of Wales, its people, etc. —*n.* **1.** the people of Wales: *used with a plural verb.* **2.** the Celtic language used by some of the Welsh.

Welsh·man (welsh′mən), *n.* a person born or living in Wales. —**Welsh′men,** *pl.*

Welsh rabbit, a dish made with melted cheese, served on toast: also called **Welsh rarebit.**

welt (welt), *n.* **1.** a strip of leather used in a shoe to strengthen the seam where the sole and top part are joined. **2.** a mark or ridge raised on the skin, as by a whip. —*v.* **1.** to put a welt or welts on. **2.** to give a whipping to: *used only in everyday talk.*

welt·er (wel′tər), *v.* **1.** to roll about or wallow [The pigs *weltered* in the mud.] **2.** to be soaked, stained, etc. [to *welter* in blood]. —*n.* **1.** a tossing and tumbling. **2.** a confusion.

wel·ter·weight (wel′tər wāt), *n.* a boxer or wrestler who weighs between 136 and 147 pounds.

wen (wen), *n.* a harmless growth under the skin, especially of the scalp.

wench (wench), *n.* a girl or woman: *now seldom used except in a joking way.*

wend (wend), *v.* to go; travel: *now seldom used except in poetry* [to *wend* one's way].

went (went), past tense of **go.**

wept (wept), past tense and past participle of **weep.**

were (wūr *or* wər), the form of the verb **be** used to show the past time with *we, you,* and *they,* and with plural nouns [*Were* you pleased? We *were,* and our parents *were,* too.] *Were* is also used with all persons in supposing, wishing, etc. [If I *were* rich, I'd buy a boat.]

we're (wir), we are.

were·n't (wūrnt), were not.

were·wolf or **wer·wolf** (wir′woolf *or* wūr′-woolf), *n.* in folk tales, a person changed into a wolf, or one who can change into a wolf when he wants to. —**were′wolves** or **wer′wolves,** *pl.*

Wes·ley John (wes′lē), 1703–1791; English minister who founded the Methodist Church.

west (west), *n.* **1.** the direction toward the point where the sun sets. **2.** a place or region in or toward this direction. In the United States, **the West** usually means the part west of the Mississippi River. **3. West,** the Western Hemisphere, or the Western Hemisphere and Europe. —*adj.* **1.** in, of, to, or toward the west [the *west* side of the house]. **2.** from the west [a *west* wind]. **3. West,** that is the western part of [*West* Germany]. —*adv.* in or toward the west ["Go *west,* young man."]

west·er·ly (wes′tər lē), *adj. & adv.* **1.** toward the west. **2.** from the west.

west·ern (wes′tərn), *adj.* **1.** in, of, or toward the west [the *western* sky]. **2.** from the west [a *western* wind]. **3. Western,** of the West.

—n. a story, movie, etc. about cowboys or pioneers in the western United States.

west·ern·er (wes'tər nər), *n.* a person born in or living in the west [A native of the West is called a *Westerner.*]

Western Hemisphere, the half of the earth that includes North and South America.

west·ern·most (wes'tərn mōst), *adj.* farthest west.

West Indies, a large group of islands in the Atlantic between the United States and South America, including the Bahamas and the Antilles.

West·min·ster Abbey (west'min'stər), a church in London where English monarchs are crowned.

West Point, a military post in New York State on the Hudson. The United States Military Academy is located there.

West Virginia, a State in the northeastern part of the United States: abbreviated **W.Va.**

west·ward (west'wərd), *adj. & adv.* toward the west: also **west'wards,** *adv.*

wet (wet), *adj.* **1.** covered or soaked with water or some other liquid [Wipe it off with a *wet* rag.] **2.** rainy [a *wet* day]. **3.** not dry yet [*wet* paint]. **4.** allowing alcoholic liquors to be sold [a *wet* town]. —*n.* water, rain, moisture, etc. [He's out there working in the *wet.*] —*v.* to make or become wet [He *wet* his lips.] —**wet'-ter,** *compar.;* **wet'test,** *superl.* —**wet** or **wet'ted,** *p.t. & p.p.;* **wet'ting,** *pr.p.* —**wet'-ness,** *n.*

we've (wēv), we have.

wh-, these letters at the beginning of a word or syllable are pronounced (hw) or (w), although only the first pronunciation is shown for them. For example, **when** is pronounced either (hwen) or (wen).

whack (hwak), *v.* to hit or slap with a sharp sound. —*n.* a blow that makes a sharp sound; also, this sound. *Used only in everyday talk.*

whale (hwāl), *n.* a very large mammal that lives in the sea and looks like a fish. Whales are valued for their oil. —*v.* to hunt for whales. —**whaled,** *p.t. & p.p.;* **whal'ing,** *pr.p.*

whale (hwāl), *v.* to beat or thrash: *only in everyday talk.* —**whaled,** *p.t. & p.p.;* **whal'ing,** *pr.p.*

whale (60 ft. long)

whale·boat (hwāl'bōt), *n.* a long boat used in whaling, or a boat like this, as a ship's lifeboat.

whale·bone (hwāl'bōn), *n.* **1.** the tough, elastic substance that hangs in fringed sheets from the upper jaw of some whales. It strains out the tiny sea animals on which the whale feeds. **2.** something made of whalebone.

whal·er (hwāl'ər), *n.* **1.** a ship used in whaling. **2.** a man whose work is whaling.

whal·ing (hwāl'ing), *n.* the hunting and killing of whales for their blubber, whalebone, etc.

wharf (hwôrf), *n.* a long platform built out over water so that ships can dock beside it to load and unload. Some wharves have roofs. —**wharves** (hwôrvz) or **wharfs,** *pl.*

what (hwut *or* hwät), *pron.* **1.** which thing, happening, condition, etc.? [*What* is that object? *What* did he ask you? *What* is your address?] **2.** that which or those which [I heard *what* he said.] —*adj.* **1.** which or which kind of [*What* dog is your favorite? I know *what* cookies you like.] **2.** as much as or as many as [Borrow *what* books you need.] **3.** how great! so much! [*What* nonsense he's talking!] —*adv.* **1.** in what way; how [*What* does it help to complain?] **2.** in some way; partly [*What* with songs and games, the hours flew by.] —*conj.* that [Never doubt but *what* he loves you.] —*interj.* a word used to show surprise, anger, etc. ["*What!* Late again?"] —**and what not,** and other things of all sorts. —**what for?** for what reason? why? —**what if,** what would happen if; suppose. —**what's what,** the real facts of the matter: *used only in everyday talk.*

what·e'er (hwät er'), *pron. & adj.* whatever.

what·ev·er (hwät ev'ər), *pron.* **1.** anything that [Tell her *whatever* you wish.] **2.** no matter what [*Whatever* you do, don't hurry.] *Whatever* is also used in questions in place of *what* for extra force [*Whatever* can it be?] —*adj.* **1.** of any type or kind [I have no plans *whatever.*] **2.** no matter what [*Whatever* game we play, I never win.]

what·not (hwut'nät *or* hwät'nät), *n.* a set of open shelves for small art objects, books, etc.

what's (hwuts *or* hwäts), what is.

what·so·ev·er (hwut'sō ev'ər *or* hwät'sō ev'ər), *pron. & adj.* whatever.

wheat (hwēt), *n.* **1.** the cereal grass whose grain is used in making the most common type of flour. **2.** this grain.

wheat·en (hwēt''n), *adj.* made of wheat.

whee·dle (hwē'd'l), *v.* **1.** to coax or flatter into doing something. **2.** to get in this way [He tried to *wheedle* a promise out of me.] —**whee'dled,** *p.t. & p.p.;* **whee'dling,** *pr.p.*

wheel (hwēl), *n.* **1.** a round disk or frame that turns on an axle fixed at its center [a wagon *wheel*]. **2.** anything like a wheel or having a wheel as its main part [the steering *wheel* of a car; a spinning *wheel*]. **3.** a bicycle: *used only in everyday talk.* **4.** *usually* **wheels,** *pl.* the forces or machines that move or control something [the *wheels* of progress]. —*v.* **1.** to move on wheels or in a vehicle with wheels [to *wheel* a grocery cart]. **2.** to turn round; revolve, rotate, pivot, etc. [The deer *wheeled* to face the dogs.] —**at the wheel,** steering a car, ship, etc.

wheat

wheel·bar·row (hwēl′bar′ō), *n.* a small kind of cart pushed or pulled by hand and having a single wheel.

wheel chair, a chair on wheels, used by the sick or injured in moving about.

wheel·house (hwēl′hous), *n.* a shelter built around the steering wheel of a ship.

wheel·wright (hwēl′rīt), *n.* a person who makes and repairs wheels, wagons, etc.

wheelbarrow

wheeze (hwēz), *v.* **1.** to breathe hard with a whistling or rasping sound, as in asthma. **2.** to make a sound like this [The old organ *wheezed.*] —*n.* the act or sound of wheezing. —**wheezed,** *p.t. & p.p.;* **wheez′ing,** *pr.p.* —**wheez′y,** *adj.*

whelk (hwelk), *n.* a large sea snail with a spiral shell. Some kinds are used for food.

whelp (hwelp), *n.* the young of a dog, or of a lion, tiger, bear, etc.; puppy or cub. —*v.* to give birth to whelps.

whelk (3 in. long)

when (hwen), *adv.* at what time? [*When* did he leave?] —*conj.* **1.** at what time [They told us *when* to eat.] **2.** at which time [The rooster crowed at six, *when* the sun rose.] **3.** at or during the time that [*When* I was your age, I couldn't swim.] **4.** although [He's reading *when* he might be playing.] **5.** if [How can we finish, *when* you don't help?] —*pron.* what time; which time [Until *when* will you be here?]

whence (hwens), *adv.* from what place, person, or source; from where [*Whence* did he come? *Whence* does he get his strength?]

whence·so·ev·er (hwens′sō ev′ər), *adv. & conj.* from whatever place, person, or source.

when·e'er (hwen er′), *adv. & conj.* whenever.

when·ev·er (hwen ev′ər), *conj.* at whatever time; at any time that [Visit us *whenever* you can.] —*adv.* when?: *used in everyday talk for extra force* [*Whenever* will you stop teasing?]

when·so·ev·er (hwen′sō ev′ər), *adv. & conj.* whenever.

where (hwer), *adv.* **1.** in or at what place? [*Where* is my hat?] **2.** to what place? [*Where* did he go next?] **3.** in what way? how? [*Where* is he at fault?] **4.** from what place, person, or source? [*Where* did you find out?] —*conj.* **1.** at what place [I know *where* it is.] **2.** at the place in which [Stay home *where* you belong. Moss grows *where* there is shade.] **3.** to the place to which [We'll go *where* you go.] —*pron.* **1.** what place? [*Where* are you from?] **2.** the place at which [a mile to *where* I live.]

where·a·bouts (hwer′ə bouts), *n.* the place where a person or thing is [I don't know his *whereabouts.*] —*adv.* at what place? where? [*Whereabouts* are we?]

where·as (hwer az′), *conj.* **1.** in view of the fact that; because [*Whereas* the club needs more money, we hereby raise the dues.] **2.** while on the other hand [We had good luck, *whereas* they had none.]

where·at (hwer at′), *conj.* at which point: *no longer much used* [I scolded her, *whereat* she wept.]

where·by (hwer bī′), *adv.* with which; by which [a scheme *whereby* to make money].

where·fore (hwer′fôr), *adv.* for what reason? why? [*Wherefore* did you leave?] —*conj.* because of which; and so; therefore. —*n.* the reason [the *wherefores* of the plan].

where·in (hwer in′), *adv.* **1.** in what way? how? [*Wherein* was Tom wrong?] **2.** in which [the book *wherein* he read the story].

where·of (hwer uv′ *or* hwer äv′), *adv.* of what, which, or whom [the things *whereof* I spoke].

where·on (hwer än′), *adv.* on which [the rock *whereon* he stood].

where·so·ev·er (hwer′sō ev′ər), *adv. & conj.* wherever.

where·to (hwer tōō′), *adv.* to which [the place *whereto* they hurry].

where·up·on (hwer ə pän′), *conj.* at which; after which [He ended his speech, *whereupon* everyone cheered.] —*adv.* on what? whereon? [*Whereupon* does he base his argument?]

wher·ev·er (hwer ev′ər), *conj.* in, at, or to whatever place [I'll go *wherever* you tell me.] —*adv.* where?: *used in everyday talk for extra force* [*Wherever* have you been?]

where·with (hwer with′ *or* hwer with′), *adv.* with which [the money *wherewith* to pay].

where·with·al (hwer′with ôl′), *n.* what is needed to get something done, especially money [Do you have the *wherewithal* to travel?]

wher·ry (hwer′ē), *n.* a light rowboat. —**wher′ries,** *pl.*

whet (hwet), *v.* **1.** to sharpen by grinding or rubbing, as a knife or tool. **2.** to make stronger; stimulate [to *whet* the appetite]. —**whet′ted,** *p.t. & p.p.;* **whet′ting,** *pr.p.*

wheth·er (hweth′ər), *conj.* **1.** if it is true or likely that [I don't know *whether* I can leave.] **2.** in either case that [It makes no difference to me *whether* he comes or not.]

whet·stone (hwet′stōn), *n.* a stone with a rough surface, for sharpening knives and tools.

whew, *interj.* a sound made by forcing out breath through the half-open mouth, to show surprise, relief, disgust, etc.

whey (hwā), *n.* the thin, watery part of milk, that separates from the curd in cheesemaking.

which (hwich), *pron.* **1.** what one or what ones of those being considered [*Which* will you choose?] **2.** the one or the ones that [I know *which* I like best.] **3.** that [the story *which* we all know]. —*adj.* what one or ones [*Which* apples are best for baking?]

which·ev·er (hwich ev′ər), *pron. & adj.* **1.** any one [Choose *whichever* desk you like.] **2.** no matter which [*Whichever* you choose, I'll buy it.]

which·so·ev·er (hwich′sō ev′ər), *pron. & adj.* whichever.

whiff (hwif), *n.* **1.** a light puff of air or wind; breath. **2.** a faint smell [a *whiff* of garlic]. —*v.* to blow or move in puffs.

Whig (hwig), *n.* **1.** in former times, a member of one of the main political parties of England. **2.** an American colonist who favored the American Revolution against England. **3.** a member of an earlier political party in the United States, that opposed the Democratic Party.

while (hwīl), *n.* a period of time [I waited a short *while.*] —*conj.* **1.** during the time that [I read a book *while* I waited.] **2.** in spite of the fact that; although [*While* she isn't pretty, she has much charm.] **3.** and; on the other hand: *used only in everyday talk* [She likes concerts, *while* I like plays.] —*v.* to spend or pass in a pleasant way [to *while* away a few hours]. —**the while,** during the same time. —**worth one's while,** worth the time it takes one. —**whiled,** *p.t. & p.p.;* **whil′ing,** *pr.p.*

whi·lom (hwī′ləm), *adv.* at one time; formerly. —*adj.* former [their *whilom* friends]. *This word is now seldom used.*

whilst (hwīlst), *conj.* while: *mainly a British word.*

whim (hwim), *n.* a sudden thought or wish to do something, without any particular reason [On a *whim,* he climbed aboard the bus for Chicago.]

whim·per (hwim′pər), *v.* to make low, broken, crying sounds [The dog *whimpered* in fear of the bear.] —*n.* the act or sound of whimpering.

whim·sey (hwim′zē), *n.* whimsy. —**whim′-seys,** *pl.*

whim·si·cal (hwim′zi k'l), *adj.* **1.** full of whims or whimsy; having odd notions [a *whimsical* inventor of useless machines]. **2.** different in an odd way; fanciful [a *whimsical* costume for the party]. —**whim′si·cal·ly,** *adv.*

whim·sy (hwim′zē), *n.* **1.** an odd notion or wish that comes to one suddenly; whim. **2.** an odd or fanciful kind of humor [poems full of *whimsy*]. —**whim′sies,** *pl.*

whine (hwīn), *v.* **1.** to make a long, high, feeble sound or cry, as in complaining [a *whining* child]. **2.** to say or beg in a whining way [Susie kept *whining* to go home.] —*n.* the act or sound of whining. —**whined,** *p.t. & p.p.;* **whin′ing,** *pr.p.*

whin·ny (hwin′ē), *n.* the low, gentle neighing sound made by a horse when it is comfortable. —*v.* to make this sound. —**whin′nied,** *p.t. & p.p.;* **whin′ny·ing,** *pr.p.* —**whin′nies,** *pl.*

whip (hwip), *n.* **1.** a thing for striking or beating a person or animal, usually a rod with a lash at one end. **2.** a blow or stroke as with a whip. **3.** a dessert made of whipped cream or beaten egg whites, with fruit, sugar, etc. —*v.* **1.** to strike as with a whip, strap, etc.; beat; lash. **2.** to move, pull, throw, etc. suddenly [He *whipped* off his hat.] **3.** to beat into a froth [to *whip* cream]. **4.** to flap about [a sail *whipping* in the wind]. —**whipped** or **whipt,** (hwipt), *p.t. & p.p.;* **whip′ping,** *pr.p.*

whip·lash (hwip′lash), *n.* the lash of a whip.

whip·per·snap·per (hwip′ər snap′ər), *n.* a young or unimportant person who is thought to show lack of respect for those who are older or in a higher position.

whip·pet (hwip′it), *n.* a swift dog like a small greyhound, used in racing.

whip·ple·tree (hwip′'l-trē), *n.* the crossbar at the front of a wagon or carriage. Straps and chains fasten it to the harness.

whip·poor·will (hwip′-ər wil), *n.* a North American bird whose call sounds a little like its name. It is active only at night.

whippet (18 in. high at shoulder)

whir or **whirr** (hwur), *v.* to move swiftly with a sound like that of a wheel or propeller turning rapidly. —*n.* this sound. —**whirred,** *p.t. & p.p.;* **whir′ring,** *pr.p.*

whirl (hwurl), *v.* **1.** to turn rapidly round and round; spin fast [The dancers *whirled* around the room.] **2.** to move or carry rapidly [The car *whirled* up the hill.] **3.** to seem to be spinning; reel [My head is *whirling*.] —*n.* **1.** the act of whirling or a whirling motion [Give the crank a *whirl*.] **2.** a series of parties, etc. [in the social *whirl*]. **3.** a dizzy or confused condition [My head's in a *whirl*.]

whippoorwill (10 in. long)

whirl·i·gig (hwur′li gig), *n.* **1.** a child's toy that whirls or spins, as a pinwheel. **2.** a whirl.

whirl·pool (hwurl′pōōl), *n.* water whirling swiftly round and round. A whirlpool sucks floating things in toward its center.

whirl·wind (hwurl′wind), *n.* a current of air whirling violently round and round and moving forward, causing a storm.

whisk (hwisk), *v.* **1.** to move, brush, etc. with a quick, sweeping motion [He *whisked* the lint from his coat with his hand.] **2.** to move quickly [The cat *whisked* under the sofa.] —*n.* **1.** the act of whisking or a whisking motion. **2.** a small broom with a short handle, for brushing clothes, etc.: *its full name is* **whisk broom.**

whisk·er (hwis′kər), *n.* **1. whiskers,** *pl.* the hair growing on a man's face, especially the beard on his cheeks. **2.** a single hair of a man's beard. **3.** any of the long, stiff hairs on the upper lip of a cat, rat, etc. —**whisk′ered,** *adj.*

whis·key (hwis′kē), *n.* same as **whisky.** —**whis′keys,** *pl.*

whis·ky (hwis′kē), *n.* a strong alcoholic liquor made from certain kinds of grain, as wheat, corn, or rye. —**whis′kies,** *pl.*

whis·per (hwis′pər), *v.* **1.** to speak or say in a low, soft voice, especially without vibrating the vocal cords. **2.** to make a soft, rustling sound

---

fat,   āpe,   cär,   ten,   ēven,   hit,   bīte,   gō,   hôrn,   tōōl,   book,   up,   fur;
get,   joy,   yet,   chin,   she,   thin,   *then*;   zh = s in pleasure;   ′ as in able (ā′b'l);
ə = a in ago,   e in agent,   i in sanity,   o in confess,   u in focus.

[The breeze *whispered* in the tall grass.] **3.** to tell as a secret or gossip [It has been *whispered* that they will marry.] —*n.* **1.** soft, low tone of voice [to speak in a *whisper*]. **2.** something whispered, as a secret or rumor. **3.** a soft, rustling sound.

whist (hwist), *n.* a card game like bridge, usually for two pairs of players.

whis·tle (hwis/'l), *v.* **1.** to make a high, shrill sound as by forcing breath between the teeth or through puckered lips, or by sending steam through a small opening. **2.** to move with a high, shrill sound [The arrow *whistled* past his ear.] **3.** to blow a whistle. **4.** to produce by whistling [to *whistle* a tune]. —*n.* **1.** a device for making whistling sounds. **2.** the act or sound of whistling. —**whis'tled,** *p.t. & p.p.;* **whis'tling,** *pr.p.* —**whis'tler,** *n.*

whit (hwit), *n.* the least bit; jot [He hasn't changed a *whit.*]

white (hwīt), *adj.* **1.** of the color of pure snow or milk; opposite of black. Although we speak of white as a color, it is really the blending of all colors. A surface is white only when it reflects all the light rays that make color. **2.** of a light or pale color [*white* meat; *white* wine]. **3.** pale or wan [She turned *white* with fear.] **4.** pure or innocent; spotless. **5.** having a light-colored skin; Caucasian [the *white* race]. —*n.* **1.** white color, white paint, white dye, etc. **2.** white clothes [The bride wore *white.*] **3.** a person with a light-colored skin; Caucasian. **4.** a white or light-colored part or thing [the *white* of an egg; the *whites* of the eyes]. —**whit'er,** *compar.;* **whit'est,** *superl.* —**white'ness,** *n.*

white ant, a termite.

white·cap (hwīt/kap), *n.* a wave with its crest broken into white foam.

white-col·lar (hwīt/käl/ər), *adj.* describing or having to do with people who hold jobs as clerks, salesmen, professional workers, etc.

white elephant, something that is of little use or profit although it is expensive to keep up.

white feather, a symbol of being a coward.

white·fish (hwīt/fish), *n.* a white or silvery lake fish that is valued as food.

white flag, a white banner or cloth held up as a sign that one wants a truce or is willing to surrender.

white gold, gold alloy that looks like platinum.

White House, the, **1.** the building where the President of the United States lives, in Washington, D.C. The official name is the **Executive Mansion.** **2.** the executive branch of the United States government.

white lie, a lie about something unimportant, often one told to spare someone's feelings.

White Mountains, a mountain range in northern New Hampshire.

whit·en (hwīt/'n), *v.* to make or become white.

White Russia, same as **Byelorussia.**

white·wash (hwīt/wôsh *or* hwīt/wäsh), *n.* **1.** a white liquid made of lime, powdered chalk, and water, used to whiten walls. **2.** the act of covering up someone's faults or mistakes so that he will not be blamed. **3.** something said or done

for this purpose. —*v.* **1.** to cover with whitewash. **2.** to cover up the faults, etc. of. **3.** to defeat an opponent in a game, etc. without letting him score: *used only in everyday talk.*

whith·er (hwith/ər), *adv.* to what place, condition, etc.? where?: *used mainly in poetry, etc.*

whit·ing (hwīt/ing), *n.* any of various ocean fishes used for food. Two kinds of whiting are related to the cod.

whit·ing (hwīt/ing), *n.* powdered chalk, used in whitewash, silver polish, etc.

whit·ish (hwīt/ish), *adj.* somewhat white.

Whit·man, Walt (hwit/mən), 1819–1892; U.S. poet.

Whit·ney, E·li (ē/lī hwit/nē), 1765–1825; U.S. inventor of the cotton gin.

Whit·ney, Mount (hwit/nē), a mountain in eastern California, 14,501 ft. high.

Whit·sun·day (hwit/sun/dē), *n.* the seventh Sunday after Easter; Pentecost.

Whit·sun·tide (hwit/s'n tīd), *n.* the week beginning with Whitsunday, especially the first three days.

Whit·ti·er, John Green·leaf (grēn/lēf hwit/-i ər), 1807–1892; U. S. poet.

whit·tle (hwit/'l), *v.* **1.** to cut thin shavings from wood with a knife. **2.** to carve by doing this [to *whittle* a doll's head]. **3.** to make less bit by bit [to *whittle* down costs]. —**whit'tled,** *p.t. & p.p.;* **whit'tling,** *pr.p.* —**whit'tler,** *n.*

whiz *or* **whizz** (hwiz), *v.* **1.** to make the whirring or hissing sound of something rushing through the air. **2.** to rush with this sound [The bus *whizzed* by.] —*n.* a whizzing sound. —**whizzed,** *p.t. & p.p.;* **whiz'zing,** *pr.p.*

who (hoo), *pron.* **1.** what person or persons? [*Who* helped you?] **2.** which person or persons [I know *who* she is.] **3.** that [the girl *who* lives next door]. **4.** any person that ["*Who* steals my purse steals trash."]

whoa (hwō), *interj.* a word spoken to a horse, meaning "stop!"

who·ev·er (hoo ev/ər), *pron.* **1.** any person that [*Whoever* wins gets a prize.] **2.** no matter what person [*Whoever* told you that, it isn't true.] *Whoever* is also used in questions in place of *who* for extra force [*Whoever* is that knocking?]

whole (hōl), *adj.* **1.** not divided or cut up; in one piece [Put *whole* carrots in the stew.] **2.** having all its parts; complete; entire [The *whole* opera is on two records.] **3.** not broken or damaged [Not one dish was left *whole* when the shelf broke.] **4.** being the entire amount of; all of [He spent the *whole* $5.] **5.** not a fraction or a mixed number [7 and 12 are *whole* numbers; 4¾ is not.] —*n.* **1.** the total amount [He saved the *whole* of his allowance.] **2.** something complete in itself [Our 50 separate States form a *whole.*] —**on the whole,** considering everything; in general. —**whole'ness,** *n.*

whole·heart·ed (hōl/här/tid), *adj.* with all one's energy and interest [You have my *wholehearted* support.]

whole note, a note in music held four times as long as a quarter note.

whole·sale (hōl′sāl), *n.* the sale of goods in large amounts, especially to retail stores that resell them to actual users. —*adj.* **1.** of or having to do with such sale of goods [a *wholesale* dealer; a *wholesale* price]. **2.** widespread; general [*wholesale* destruction by the volcano]. —*v.* to sell or be sold in large amounts, usually at lower prices. —**whole′saled,** *p.t. & p.p.;* **whole′sal·ing,** *pr.p.* —**whole′sal·er,** *n.*

whole·some (hōl′səm), *adj.* **1.** good for one's health; healthful [a *wholesome* climate]. **2.** that tends to improve one's mind or character [a *wholesome* book]. **3.** suggesting good health of body and mind; healthy [There is a *wholesome* look about her.] —**whole′some·ness,** *n.*

whole-wheat (hōl′hwēt′), *adj.* made of the whole grain of wheat, including the husk [*whole-wheat* flour; *whole-wheat* bread].

who'll (hōōl), **1.** who shall. **2.** who will.

whol·ly (hō′lē), *adv.* to the whole amount or degree; altogether; completely [You are *wholly* right. The building was *wholly* destroyed.]

whom (hōōm), *pron.* the form of **who** that is used as the object of a verb or preposition [*Whom* did you see? He is the man to *whom* I wrote.] *Who* is often used for *whom* in everyday talk.

whoop (hōōp), *n.* **1.** a loud shout or cry, as of joy, surprise, etc. **2.** a long, loud, gasping breath after a fit of coughing in whooping cough. —*v.* to shout with whoops.

whooping cough, a children's disease in which there are fits of coughing that end in a whoop.

whop·per (hwäp′ər), *n.* **1.** anything very large. **2.** a great lie. *This word is used only in everyday talk.*

whore (hôr), *n.* a prostitute.

whorl (hwŭrl *or* hwôrl), *n.* anything arranged in a circle or circles, as the ridges that form a fingerprint or a group of leaves or petals at the same point on a stem.

who's (hōōz), who is.

whose (hōōz), *pron.* the one or the ones belonging to whom [*Whose* are these books?] *Whose* is the possessive form of *who* and is also used as an adjective meaning "of whom" or "of which" [the man *whose* car I bought; the tree *whose* branches shaded me.]

who·so·ev·er (hōō′sō ev′ər), *pron.* whoever.

why (hwī), *adv.* **1.** for what reason or purpose [*Why* are you angry?] **2.** because of which [There are good reasons *why* he left.] **3.** the reason for which [That is *why* I warned you.] —*n.* the reason, cause, etc. ["Never mind the *why* and wherefore."] —*interj.* a word used to show surprise, annoyance, etc., or when pausing to think [*Why*, I didn't know it was so late!] —**whys,** *pl.*

Wich·i·ta (wich′ə tô), *n.* a city in southern Kansas.

wick (wik), *n.* a piece of cord or a bundle of threads in a candle, oil lamp, etc. It soaks up the fuel and burns with a steady flame when it is lighted.

wick·ed (wik′id), *adj.* **1.** bad or harmful on purpose; evil [a *wicked* scheme]. **2.** causing pain or trouble [a *wicked* blow on the head]. **3.** naughty or full of mischief. —**wick′ed·ly,** *adv.* —**wick′ed·ness,** *n.*

wick·er (wik′ər), *n.* **1.** thin twigs or long, woody strips that bend easily and are woven together to make baskets or furniture. **2.** articles made in this way. —*adj.* made of wicker or covered with wicker.

wick of a candle

wick·er·work (wik′ər wŭrk), *n.* **1.** baskets, furniture, etc. made of wicker. **2.** wicker.

wick·et (wik′it), *n.* **1.** any of the small wire hoops through which the balls must be hit in croquet. **2.** a set of sticks at which the ball is thrown in cricket. **3.** a small window, as at a ticket office. **4.** a small door or gate, especially one in or near a larger one.

wicker chair

wide (wīd), *adj.* **1.** great in width; measuring much from side to side; broad [a *wide* road]. **2.** reaching over a certain distance from side to side [three feet *wide*]. **3.** large or not limited in size, amount, or degree [a *wide* variety of items]. **4.** opened as far as possible [eyes *wide* with surprise]. **5.** far from the point or goal aimed at [The arrow was *wide* of the mark.] —*adv.* **1.** over a large area [The news spread far and *wide*.] **2.** so as to be wide [Open your mouth *wide*. Their shots went *wide*.] —**wid′er,** *compar.;* **wid′est,** *superl.* —**wide′ly,** *adv.*

wide-a·wake (wīd′ə wāk′), *adj.* **1.** completely awake. **2.** watchful and ready; alert.

wide-eyed (wīd′īd′), *adj.* with the eyes opened wide, as in wonder or surprise.

wid·en (wīd′ən), *v.* to make or become wider.

wide·spread (wīd′spred′), *adj.* **1.** spread out widely [*widespread* wings]. **2.** spread, scattered, happening, etc. over a large area [*widespread* damage from the forest fire].

widg·eon (wij′ən), *n.* a duck found near rivers and lakes, having a head that is white on top.

wid·ow (wid′ō), *n.* a woman whose husband has died and who has not married again. —*v.* to make a widow of [*widowed* late in life].

wid·ow·er (wid′ō ər), *n.* a man whose wife has died and who has not married again.

width (width), *n.* **1.** distance or measure from side to side; breadth; wideness [a river 500 yards in *width*]. **2.** a piece of material of a certain width [Sew two *widths* of cloth together.]

fat, āpe, cär, ten, ēven, hĭt, bīte, gō, hôrn, tōōl, book, up, fŭr;
get, joy, yet, chin, she, thin, *th*en; zh = s in pleasure; ′ as in able (ā′b'l);
ə = a in ago, e in agent, i in sanity, o in confess, u in focus.

wield (wēld), *v.* **1.** to handle and use, especially with skill [to *wield* a scythe]. **2.** to have and use with effect; exercise [to *wield* power in a town].

wie·ner (wē'nər), *n.* a smoked sausage of beef or of beef and pork, stuffed into a narrow casing; frankfurter.

wife (wīf), *n.* the woman to whom a man is married; married woman. —**wives**, *pl.*

wife·ly (wīf'lē), *adj.* of, like, or fit for a wife.

wig (wig), *n.* a false covering of hair for the head, worn as part of a costume, to hide baldness, etc.

wig·gle (wig''l), *v.* to twist and turn from side to side [The pollywog moves by *wiggling* its tail.] —*n.* a wiggling motion. —**wig'gled**, *p.t. & p.p.;* **wig'gling**, *pr.p.*

wig·gly (wig'lē), *adj.* **1.** that wiggles [a *wiggly* worm]. **2.** wavy [a *wiggly* line]. —**wig'gli·er**, *compar.;* **wig'gli·est**, *superl.*

wight (wīt), *n.* a person: *now seldom used.*

wig·wag (wig'wag), *v.* to move back and forth; especially, to signal by waving flags, lights, etc. according to a code. —*n.* the sending of messages in this way. —**wig'wagged**, *p.t. & p.p.;* **wig'wag·ging**, *pr.p.*

wig·wam (wig'wäm), *n.* a kind of tent used by some American Indians, shaped in a dome or cone and covered with bark.

wigwam

wild (wīld), *adj.* **1.** living or growing in nature; not tamed or cultivated by man [*wild* animals; *wild* flowers]. **2.** not lived in or used for farming, etc. [*wild* land]. **3.** not civilized; savage [*wild* tribes]. **4.** not controlled; excited, unruly, rough, noisy, etc. [a *wild* boy; *wild* with delight]. **5.** violent or stormy [a *wild* seacoast]. **6.** reckless, fantastic, crazy, etc. [a *wild* plan to get rich]. **7.** missing the target [a *wild* shot]. —*adv.* in a wild way; without aim or control [to shoot *wild*; to run *wild*]. —*n. usually* **wilds**, *pl.* a wilderness or waste land [the *wilds* of Africa]. —**wild about,** liking very much. —**wild'ly**, *adv.* —**wild'ness**, *n.*

wild·cat (wīld'kat), *n.* **1.** a wild animal of the cat family, larger than a house cat, as the lynx. **2.** a person who is fierce in temper and always ready to fight. **3.** a successful oil well drilled in a region not known before to have oil. —*adj.* wild or reckless [a *wildcat* scheme].

wil·der·ness (wil'dər nis), *n.* a wild region; waste land or overgrown land with no settlers.

wild·fire (wīld'fīr), *n.* a fire that spreads fast and is hard to put out [The rumors spread like *wildfire.*]

Wild West or **wild west,** the western United States in its early frontier days.

wile (wīl), *n.* a clever trick used to fool or lure someone [using flattery and other *wiles* to gain his confidence]. —*v.* to use wiles on in order to lure. —**wiled**, *p.t. & p.p.;* **wil'ing**, *pr.p.*

will (wil), *n.* **1.** the power that the mind has to choose, decide, control one's own actions, etc. [a weak *will;* a strong *will;* free *will*]. **2.** something wished or ordered; wish; desire [What is your *will?*] **3.** strong and fixed purpose; determination ["Where there's a *will*, there's a way."] **4.** the way one feels about others [ill *will;* good *will*]. **5.** a legal paper in which a person tells what he wants done with his money and property after he dies. —*v.* **1.** to decide or choose [Let him do as he *wills.*] **2.** to control or bring about by the power of the will [He *willed* her to do as he wished.] **3.** to leave to someone by a will, as property. —**at will,** when one wishes.

will (wil), *a helping verb used with other verbs in speaking of the future* [He *will* be here soon. *Will* you ever learn?] It has been the rule to use *shall* with *I* and *we* and to use *will* with *you, he, she, it,* and *they,* but now *will* is ordinarily used with all of them, except in the most formal writing. *Will* sometimes means "can" [This jar *will* hold three pints.] or "am, is, or are willing to" [*Will* you open the door?] See also **would.**

will·ful or **wil·ful** (wil'fəl), *adj.* **1.** always wanting one's own way; doing as one pleases; stubborn [his *willful* son]. **2.** done or said on purpose [*willful* lies]. —**will'ful·ly** or **wil'ful·ly**, *adv.* —**will'ful·ness** or **wil'ful·ness,** *n.*

Wil·liam I (wil'yəm), 1027–1087; a Norman duke who conquered England in 1066 and was king of England from 1066 to 1087: called **William the Conqueror.**

will·ing (wil'ing), *adj.* **1.** ready or agreeing to do something [Are you *willing* to try?] **2.** doing, giving, etc. or done, given, etc. readily or gladly [a *willing* helper; *willing* service]. —**will'ing·ly**, *adv.* —**will'ing·ness**, *n.*

will-o'-the-wisp (wil'ə thə wisp'), *n.* **1.** a light seen at night moving over swamps or marshy places. **2.** any hope or goal that leads one on but is difficult or impossible to reach.

wil·low (wil'ō), *n.* **1.** a tree with narrow leaves and long spikes of flowers. Its twigs can be bent easily for weaving baskets, etc. **2.** the wood of this tree.

wil·low·y (wil'ō ē), *adj.* **1.** covered or shaded with willows [a *willowy* river bank]. **2.** slender, graceful, etc. [She has a *willowy* figure.]

weeping willow branch and tree

wil·ly-nil·ly (wil'ē nil'ē), *adv.* whether one wishes it or not [He will do his chores *willy-nilly.*]

Wil·son, Wood·row (wood'rō wil's'n), 1856–1924; 28th president of the U.S., from 1913 to 1921.

wilt (wilt), *v.* **1.** to become limp; wither; droop [Water the flowers so they won't *wilt.*] **2.** to lose strength or energy; become weak [We *wilted* under the tropical sun.]

wilt (wilt), an older form of **will,** used with *thou,* as in the Bible.

wi·ly (wī'lē), *adj.* full of sly tricks; cunning; crafty. —**wi'li·er**, *compar.;* **wi'li·est**, *superl.* —**wi'li·ness**, *n.*

wim·ble (wim′b'l), *n.* a tool used for boring.

wim·ple (wim′p'l), *n.* a cloth once worn by women for covering the head and neck, with just the face showing. It is now worn only by nuns.

wimple

win (win), *v.* **1.** to get by work, struggle, skill, etc. [to *win* a prize; to *win* applause]. **2.** to get the victory in a contest, debate, etc. [Our team *won.* You *win* the argument.] **3.** to get the approval or favor of; persuade [I *won* him over to our side. She *won* new friends.] **4.** to get to after some effort [The climbers *won* the top of the hill.] —*n.* an act of winning; victory: *used only in everyday talk.* —**won,** *p.t. & p.p.;* **win′ning,** *pr.p.*

wince (wins), *v.* to draw back suddenly, as in pain or fear; flinch. —*n.* the act of wincing. —**winced,** *p.t. & p.p.;* **winc′ing,** *pr.p.*

winch (winch), *n.* a machine for hoisting or pulling, having a drum turned by a crank or by a motor. A rope or chain tied to the load is wound on this drum.

wind (wīnd), *v.* **1.** to turn or coil something around itself or around something else [to *wind* yarn in a ball; to *wind* a bandage around one's hand]. **2.** to grow or pass by turning or coiling [The grapevine *wound* around the tree.] **3.** to cover by circling with something [*Wind* the armature with wire.] **4.** to tighten the spring of, as by turning a stem [Did you *wind* your watch?] **5.** to move or go in a twisting or curving course [The river *winds* through the valley.] —*n.* a turn or twist. —**wind up, 1.** to bring or come to an end; conclude. **2.** to excite very much. **3.** to swing the arm before pitching a baseball. —**wound,** *p.t. & p.p.;* **wind′ing,** *pr.p.*

wind (wind), *n.* **1.** air that is moving [Some seeds are carried by the *wind.*] **2.** a strong current of air; gale [A *wind* blew the tree down.] **3.** breath or the power of breathing [The blow knocked the *wind* out of him.] **4.** foolish or boastful talk. **5.** a smell or scent in the air [The dogs lost the *wind* of the fox.] **6. winds,** *pl.* the wind instruments of an orchestra. —*v.* to cause to be out of breath [The old man was *winded* from climbing.] —**get wind of,** to find out something about; get a hint of. —**in the wind,** about to happen.

wind (wīnd *or* wind), *v.* to blow, as a horn. —**wound** or **wind′ed,** *p.t. & p.p.;* **wind′ing,** *pr.p.*

wind·break (wind′brāk), *n.* a fence, hedge, or row of trees that shields a place from the wind.

wind·fall (wind′fôl), *n.* **1.** fruit blown down from a tree by the wind. **2.** money or gain that one gets without expecting it.

wind·flow·er (wind′flou′ər), *n.* a plant with flowers shaped like cups; anemone.

wind·ing (wīn′ding), *n.* **1.** a coiling, turning, turn, bend, etc. **2.** something that is wound around an object. —*adj.* that winds, turns, coils, etc. [a *winding* road].

wind instrument (wind), any musical instrument played by blowing air, especially breath, through it, as a flute, oboe, trombone, or tuba.

wind·jam·mer (wind′jam′ər), *n.* a sailing ship.

wind·lass (wind′ləs), *n.* a kind of winch, especially one for lifting up an anchor on a ship.

wind·mill (wind′mil), *n.* a machine getting its power from the wind turning a wheel of vanes at the top of a tower. Windmills are used to grind grain, pump water, etc.

types of windmill

win·dow (win′dō), *n.* **1.** an opening in a building, car, etc. for letting in light and air. **2.** a frame with a pane or panes of glass, set in such an opening.

window box, a long, narrow box set on or near a window ledge, for growing plants.

win·dow·pane (win′dō pān′), *n.* a pane of glass in a window.

win·dow-shop (win′dō shäp′), *v.* to look at things shown in store windows without going into the stores to buy. —**win′dow-shopped′,** *p.t. & p.p.;* **win′dow-shop′ping,** *pr.p.*

wind·pipe (wind′pīp), *n.* the tube from the back of the mouth to the lungs, through which the air passes in breathing; trachea.

wind·row (wind′rō *or* win′rō), *n.* hay raked into a low ridge to dry before being put into heaps.

wind·shield (wind′shēld), *n.* the window of glass, plastic, etc. in front of the driver's seat of a car, motorcycle, speedboat, etc.

Wind·sor (win′zər), *n.* the name of the ruling family of England since 1917.

Windsor Castle, a castle in southern England that is a residence of the English monarch.

wind·storm (wind′stôrm), *n.* a storm with a strong wind but little or no rain.

wind tunnel, a passage through which air is forced for testing models of airplanes, etc. against the effects of wind pressure.

wind·up (wīnd′up), *n.* **1.** the close or end. **2.** the swinging movements of a baseball pitcher's arm as he gets ready to throw the ball.

wind·ward (wind′wərd *or* win′dərd), *n.* the direction or side from which the wind is blowing. —*adv.* in the direction from which the wind is blowing. —*adj.* **1.** moving windward. **2.** on the side from which the wind is blowing.

Windward Islands, a group of islands in the West Indies, south of the Leeward Islands.

wind·y (win′dē), *adj.* **1.** with much wind [a *windy* day; a *windy* city]. **2.** talking too much. —**wind′i·er,** *compar.;* **wind′i·est,** *superl.* —**wind′i·ness,** *n.*

wine (wīn), *n.* **1.** the juice of grapes that has fermented and has alcohol in it. **2.** the juice of other fruits or plants fermented like this [dandelion *wine*]. —*v.* to drink wine, or serve wine to. —**wined,** *p.t. & p.p.;* **win'ing,** *pr.p.*

wine-col·ored (wīn'kul'ərd), *adj.* having the color of red wine; dark purplish-red.

wing (wing), *n.* **1.** either of the pair of feathered parts which a bird spreads out from its sides in flying. **2.** any of the paired parts used like this for flying, in other creatures [Bats' *wings* are formed of a webbing of skin. Most insects have two pairs of *wings*.] **3.** anything like a wing in shape or use [the *wings* of an airplane]. **4.** a part that sticks out from a main part [The *wing* of a building is often a part added later. The *wings* of a stage are at the sides out of sight of the audience.] **5.** the right or left section of an army, fleet, etc. **6.** a political group holding certain views, as of a leftist or rightist kind. —*v.* **1.** to fly, or make by flying [The bird *winged* its way across the lake.] **2.** to send swiftly [The archer *winged* his arrow at the target.] **3.** to wound in the wing or in the arm. —**on the wing,** in flight. —**take wing,** to fly away. —**under the wing of,** protected by. —**wing'less,** *adj.*

winged (wingd *or* wing'id), *adj.* **1.** having wings. **2.** moving as if on wings; swift; fast.

wing·spread (wing'spred), *n.* the distance between the ends of a pair of outspread wings.

wink (wingk), *v.* **1.** to close and open the eyes rapidly; especially, to do this with one eye, for a signal, etc. [He *winked* to show he was joking.] **2.** to give off quick flashes of light; twinkle [the *winking* stars]. —*n.* **1.** the act of winking. **2.** a very short time; instant [I'll be there in a *wink*.] **3.** a signal given by winking. —**wink at,** to pretend not to see [to *wink at* wrongdoing].

win·ner (win'ər), *n.* one that wins.

win·ning (win'ing), *adj.* **1.** that wins; having won a victory [the *winning* team]. **2.** attractive; charming [a *winning* smile]. —*n.* **1.** the act of one that wins. **2. winnings,** *pl.* something won, especially money won at gambling.

Win·ni·peg (win'ə peg), *n.* **1.** the capital of Manitoba, Canada. **2.** a large lake in Manitoba.

win·now (win'ō), *v.* **1.** to blow away the chaff from grain [to *winnow* barley after it is threshed]. **2.** to sort out or sift, as if by winnowing [to *winnow* useful facts from a report].

win·some (win'səm), *adj.* pleasant; charming; attractive [a *winsome* girl].

win·ter (win'tər), *n.* the coldest season of the year, following fall. —*adj.* of winter [*winter* weather]. —*v.* to spend or cause to spend winter [We *winter* in Florida.]

win·ter·green (win'tər grēn), *n.* **1.** an evergreen plant with leaves from which an oil with a sharp taste is pressed. **2.** this oil.

win·ter·ize (win'tər īz), *v.* to make ready for winter, as an automobile. —**win'ter·ized,** *p.t. & p.p.;* **win'ter·iz·ing,** *pr.p.*

win·ter·time (win'tər tīm), *n.* winter.

win·try (win'trē), *adj.* of or like winter; cold;

snowy, or gloomy [a *wintry* day]. —**win'tri·er,** *compar.;* **win'tri·est,** *superl.*

wipe (wīp), *v.* **1.** to clean or dry by rubbing, as with a cloth or on a mat [to *wipe* dishes; to *wipe* one's shoes]. **2.** to remove by rubbing, as with a cloth [to *wipe* dust off a table]. —*n.* the act of wiping. —**wipe out, 1.** to remove. **2.** to kill. —**wiped,** *p.t. & p.p.;* **wip'ing,** *pr.p.* —**wip'er,** *n.*

wire (wīr), *n.* **1.** metal that has been pulled into a very long, thin thread; also, a piece of this [*Wire* is used for carrying electric current, for making fences, for tying bales, etc.] **2.** telegraph [to send a message by *wire*]. **3.** a telegram: *used only in everyday talk.* —*v.* **1.** to fasten with wire [to *wire* a vine to a stake]. **2.** to furnish with wires for electric current [The cottage is *wired*.] **3.** to telegraph: *used only in everyday talk.* —**wired,** *p.t. & p.p.;* **wir'ing,** *pr.p.*

wire-haired (wīr'herd'), *adj.* having stiff, coarse hair.

wire·less (wīr'lis), *adj.* without wires; sending or sent by radio waves instead of by electric current in wires. —*n.* **1.** a wireless telegraph or telephone system. **2.** radio: *mainly a British use.* **3.** a message sent by wireless.

wire·tap (wīr'tap), *v.* to make a connection with a telephone line and secretly listen to a private conversation. —**wire'tapped,** *p.t. & p.p.;* **wire'tap·ping,** *pr.p.*

wir·ing (wīr'ing), *n.* a system of wires, as for carrying electric current.

wir·y (wīr'ē), *adj.* **1.** like wire; stiff [*wiry* hair]. **2.** slender and strong [a *wiry* young man]. —**wir'i·er,** *compar.;* **wir'i·est,** *superl.*

Wis·con·sin (wis kän's'n), *n.* a State in the north central part of the United States: abbreviated **Wis.** or **Wisc.**

wis·dom (wiz'dəm), *n.* **1.** the quality of being wise; good judgment, that comes from knowledge and experience in life [He had the *wisdom* to save money for his old age.] **2.** learning; knowledge [a book filled with the *wisdom* of India].

wisdom tooth, the back tooth on each side of each jaw. The wisdom teeth do not usually appear until the person is fully grown.

wise (wīz), *adj.* **1.** having or showing good judgment [a *wise* judge; a *wise* decision]. **2.** having knowledge or information; informed; learned [I was no *wiser* after reading that article.] —**wis'er,** *compar.;* **wis'est,** *superl.* —**wise'ly,** *adv.* —**wise'ness,** *n.*

wise (wīz), *n.* manner or way [She is in no *wise* at fault.]

-wise (wīz), a suffix meaning: **1.** in a certain way, position, etc. [*Likewise* means in a like way.] **2.** in the same way or direction as [To move *clockwise* is to move in the same direction as the hands of a clock.] **3.** with regard to [*Weatherwise* means with regard to the weather.]

wise·a·cre (wīz'ā kər), *n.* a person who acts as though he were much wiser than he really is.

wise·crack (wīz'krak), *n.* a joke or clever remark, often one that shows a lack of respect or of seriousness: *a slang word.*

wish (wish), *v.* **1.** to have a longing for; want; desire [You may have whatever you *wish*.] **2.** to have or express a desire about [I *wish* you were here. We *wished* him a happy birthday.] **3.** to ask or order [I *wish* you to leave now.] —*n.* **1.** a desire or longing [I have no *wish* to hear it.] **2.** something wanted or hoped for [He got his *wish*.] **3.** a request or order [We obeyed his *wishes*.] **4. wishes,** *pl.* a desire for another to have health and happiness [I send you my best *wishes*.] —**make a wish,** to think or tell what one wants.

wish·bone (wish′bōn), *n.* the bone in front of the breastbone of most birds: *see the picture.* There is a game in which two people make wishes and snap a wishbone in two. The one holding the longer piece is supposed to get his wish.

wishbone

wish·ful (wish′fəl), *adj.* having or showing a wish; longing or hopeful [a *wishful* look].

wish·y-wash·y (wish′ē wôsh′ē *or* wish′ē wäsh′ē), *adj.* not strong or definite; weak.

wisp (wisp), *n.* **1.** a small bunch or tuft [a *wisp* of hair]. **2.** a thin, hazy bit or puff [a *wisp* of smoke]. **3.** something thin or frail [a *wisp* of a girl]. —**wisp′y,** *adj.*

wist (wist), past tense and past participle of **wit** (to know): *no longer used.*

wis·te·ri·a (wis tir′i ə) or **wis·ta·ri·a** (wis ter′i ə), *n.* a shrub with clusters of blue, white, or purple flowers, that grows as a vine.

wist·ful (wist′fəl), *adj.* showing a wish or longing [With a *wistful* smile, he watched the others play ball.] —**wist′ful·ly,** *adv.*

wit (wit), *n.* **1.** the ability to say clever things in a sharp, amusing way. **2.** a person who says such things. **3. wits,** *pl.* the power to think and reason [frightened out of his *wits*].

wit (wit), *v.* to know: *now used only in the phrase* **to wit,** meaning "that is to say; namely" [Only one person knows; *to wit*, my father.]

witch (wich), *n.* **1.** a woman who is imagined to have magic power with the help of the devil. **2.** an ugly and mean old woman; hag.

witch·craft (wich′kraft), *n.* the magic power of a witch.

witch·er·y (wich′ər ē), *n.* **1.** witchcraft. **2.** fascination or charm. —**witch′er·ies,** *pl.*

witch hazel, 1. a shrub with yellow flowers and woody fruit. **2.** a lotion made from the bark and leaves of this shrub.

with (with *or* with), *prep.* **1.** in the care or company of [Did Mary leave *with* her father?] **2.** as part of; into [Mix blue *with* yellow to get green.] **3.** in the service of; as a member of [He has been *with* the company for years. She sings *with* the choir.] **4.** against; opposed to [Don't argue *with* him.] **5.** in regard to; concerning [Deal *with* that problem yourself.] **6.** in the opinion of [It's all right *with* me.] **7.** as a result of [pale *with* fear]. **8.** by means of [Paint *with* a large brush.] **9.** by [a pail filled *with* sand]. **10.** having gotten [*With* his help, we finished on time.] **11.** having or showing [She met him *with* a smile. She has a coat *with* a fur collar.] **12.** in spite of [*With* all her faults, I love her still.] **13.** at the same time as [*With* the coming of spring, the birds returned.] **14.** to or onto [Join this end *with* that one.] **15.** as well as [She can sew *with* the best.] **16.** from [I parted *with* him in June.] **17.** after [*With* that remark, he left.]

with·al (with ôl′ *or* with ôl′), *adv.* besides; as well: *now seldom used* [a handsome boy and brave *withal*].

with·draw (with drô′ *or* with drô′), *v.* **1.** to take or pull out; remove [to *withdraw* one's hand from a pocket]. **2.** to move back; go away; retreat [She *withdrew* behind the curtain.] **3.** to leave; retire or resign [to *withdraw* from school]. **4.** to take back; recall [I *withdraw* my statement.] —**with·drew** (-drōō′), *p.t.;* **with·drawn** (-drôn′), *p.p.;* **with·draw′ing,** *pr.p.*

with·draw·al (with drô′əl *or* with drô′əl), *n.* the act or fact of withdrawing, as money from the bank.

with·drawn (with drôn′ *or* with drôn′), past participle of **withdraw.** —*adj.* shy, or thinking quietly.

withe (with *or* with), *n.* a tough twig, as of willow, that is easily bent and is used for tying things.

with·er (with′ər), *v.* **1.** to dry up; shrivel [The hot sun *withered* the grass.] **2.** to lose strength [Our hopes soon *withered*.] **3.** to make lose courage or be ashamed [her *withering* scorn].

with·ers (with′ərz), *n.pl.* the highest part of a horse's back, between the shoulder blades.

withers

with·hold (with-hōld′), *v.* **1.** to keep from giving or granting; refuse [She *withheld* her approval of the plan.] **2.** to hold back; keep back; check [He *withheld* his anger.] —**with·held** (with held′), *p.t. & p.p.;* **with·hold′ing,** *pr.p.*

withholding tax, the amount of income tax that is held back from a person's pay by his employer, who then pays it to the government.

with·in (with in′ *or* with in′), *prep.* **1.** in the inner part of; inside [Stay *within* the house.] **2.** not more than; not beyond [They live *within* a mile of the school.] **3.** inside the limits of [to stay *within* the law]. —*adv.* in or to the inside [It is cold outdoors but warm *within*.]

with·out (wi*th* out′ *or* with out′), *prep.* **1.** free from; not having [a man *without* a worry; a cup *without* a saucer]. **2.** in a way that avoids [He passed by *without* speaking.] **3.** on or to the outside of [They stood *without* the gates.] —*adv.* on the outside [The apples were sound within but wrinkled *without*.]

with·stand (with stand′), *v.* to stand strongly against; resist or survive [These trees can *withstand* cold winters.] —**with·stood** (with stood′), *p.t. & p.p.;* **with·stand′ing,** *pr.p.*

wit·less (wit′lis), *adj.* without wit or intelligence; foolish; stupid.

wit·ness (wit′nis), *n.* **1.** a person who was present or saw something himself that he can tell about [A *witness* told how the fire started.] **2.** a person who gives evidence in a law court. **3.** a person who watches a contract, will, etc. being signed and then, as proof that he did, signs it himself. **4.** the statement made by a witness; testimony [to give false *witness*]. —*v.* **1.** to be present at; see [to *witness* a sports event]. **2.** to act as a witness of a contract, will, etc. **3.** to be or give proof of [Her tears *witnessed* her sadness.] —**bear witness,** to be or give proof, or evidence.

wit·ti·cism (wit′ə siz′m), *n.* a witty remark.

wit·ting·ly (wit′ing lē), *adv.* on purpose.

wit·ty (wit′ē), *adj.* showing wit; clever in an amusing way [a *witty* boy; a *witty* remark]. —**wit′ti·er,** *compar.;* **wit′ti·est,** *superl.* —**wit′ti·ly,** *adv.* —**wit′ti·ness,** *n.*

wive (wīv), *v.* to marry a woman. —**wived,** *p.t. & p.p.;* **wiv′ing,** *pr.p.*

wives (wīvz), *n.* plural of **wife.**

wiz·ard (wiz′ərd), *n.* a man who is thought to have magic power; magician.

wiz·ard·ry (wiz′ərd rē), *n.* magic.

wiz·ened (wiz′′nd), *adj.* dried up and wrinkled; shriveled [the old man's *wizened* face].

wk., abbreviation for **week.** —**wks.,** *pl.*

wob·ble (wäb′′l), *v.* **1.** to move from side to side in an unsteady way. **2.** to be uncertain, as in making up one's mind; waver. —*n.* a wobbling motion. —**wob′bled,** *p.t. & p.p.;* **wob′bling,** *pr.p.* —**wob′bly,** *adj.*

a wizened face

woe or **wo** (wō), *n.* **1.** great sorrow; grief. **2.** trouble. —*interj.* alas!

woe·be·gone or **wo·be·gone** (wō′bi gôn′), *adj.* showing woe; looking sad or mournful.

woe·ful or **wo·ful** (wō′fəl), *adj.* **1.** full of woe; mournful; sad. **2.** making one feel pity; pitiful. —**woe′ful·ly** or **wo′ful·ly,** *adv.*

woke (wōk), a past tense of **wake.**

wold (wōld), *n.* high, hilly land without trees.

wolf (woolf), *n.* **1.** a wild animal of the dog family. It kills other animals for food. **2.** a person who is fierce, cruel, greedy, etc. —*v.* to eat in a greedy way. —**cry wolf,** to give a false alarm. —**keep the wolf from the door,** to manage to have enough to live on. —**wolves,** *pl.* —**wolf′ish,** *adj.*

wolf·hound (woolf′hound), *n.* a large dog of a breed once used for hunting wolves.

wol·ver·ine or **wol·ver·ene** (wool′və rēn′), *n.* a strong, stocky animal of North America, related to the weasel.

wolfhound
(2½ ft. high at shoulder)

wolves (woolvz), *n.* plural of **wolf.**

wom·an (woom′ən), *n.* **1.** an adult, female human being. **2.** women as a group ["*Woman's* work is never done."] **3.** a female servant. —**wom′en,** *pl.*

wom·an·hood (woom′ən hood), *n.* **1.** the time or condition of being a woman. **2.** womanly qualities. **3.** women as a group.

wolverine (3 ft. long)

wom·an·ish (woom′ən ish), *adj.* like or fit for a woman [*womanish* frills].

wom·an·kind (woom′ən kīnd), *n.* all women; women in general.

wom·an·like (woom′ən līk), *adj.* womanly.

wom·an·ly (woom′ən lē), *adj.* like or fit for a woman [*womanly* modesty]. —**wom′an·li·ness,** *n.*

womb (woom), *n.* a hollow organ of female mammals in which the young grow before birth; uterus.

wom·bat (wäm′bat), *n.* a burrowing animal of Australia that looks like a small bear. The female carries her young in a pouch.

wom·en (wim′in), *n.* plural of **woman.**

wom·en·folk (wim′in fōk), *n.pl.* women: also **wom′en·folks.**

won (wun), past tense and past participle of **win.**

wombat (3 ft. long)

won·der (wun′dər), *n.* **1.** something so unusual that it causes surprise, amazement, etc.; marvel [The Colossus of Rhodes was one of the Seven *Wonders* of the ancient world.] **2.** the feeling caused by something strange and remarkable; awe [We gazed in *wonder* at the northern lights.] —*v.* **1.** to feel wonder or surprise; marvel [I *wonder* that you were able to do it.] **2.** to have doubt and curiosity about; want to know [I *wonder* why he came.]

won·der·ful (wun′dər fəl), *adj.* **1.** that causes wonder; marvelous; amazing. **2.** very good; excellent: *used only in everyday talk.* —**won′der·ful·ly,** *adv.*

won·der·land (wun′dər land), *n.* an imaginary land or place full of wonders, or a real place like this.

won·der·ment (wun′dər mənt), *n.* wonder or amazement.

won·drous (wun′drəs), *adj.* wonderful; marvelous. —*adv.* unusually [a maid *wondrous* fair]. *Now used only in poetry, etc.*

wont (wunt *or* wōnt), *adj.* having the habit; accustomed [He was *wont* to agree.] —*n.* usual practice; habit [It is his *wont* to dine late.]

won't (wōnt), will not.

wont·ed (wun′tid *or* wōn′tid), *adj.* usual; accustomed [in his *wonted* manner].

woo (wōō), *v.* **1.** to try to get the love of in order to marry; court [to *woo* a maid]. **2.** to try to get; seek [She *wooed* fame.] —**woo′er,** *n.*

wood (wood), *n.* **1.** the hard material of a tree or shrub, under the bark. **2.** trees cut and prepared for use; lumber or firewood. **3.** *often* **woods,** *pl.* a thick growth of trees; forest or grove. **4. woods,** *pl.* wood-wind musical instruments. —*adj.* **1.** of wood; wooden. **2.** growing or living in woods. —**out of the woods,** no longer in trouble or danger: *used only in everyday talk.*

wood alcohol, a poisonous alcohol distilled from wood and used in paints, as a fuel, etc.

wood·bine (wood′bīn), *n.* any of various climbing plants, as wild honeysuckle or a kind of American ivy.

wood·chuck (wood′chuk), *n.* a North American animal with a thick body and coarse fur, related to rabbits, rats, etc. It burrows in the ground and sleeps all winter. Also called **ground hog.**

wood·cock (wood′käk), *n.* a small game bird with short legs and a long bill.

woodchuck
(20 in. long)

wood·craft (wood′kraft), *n.* **1.** knowledge or skills that can help one in the woods, as in camping or hunting. **2.** woodworking.

wood·cut (wood′kut), *n.* **1.** a block of wood with a picture or design carved into it. **2.** a print made from this.

wood·cut·ter (wood′kut′ər), *n.* a man who chops down trees and cuts wood. —**wood′cut′ting,** *n.*

wood·ed (wood′id), *adj.* covered with trees.

wood·en (wood′'n), *adj.* **1.** made of wood. **2.** stiff, clumsy, or lifeless. **3.** dull; stupid.

wood·en·head·ed (wood′'n hed′id), *adj.* dull; stupid: *used only in everyday talk.*

wooden horse, same as **Trojan horse.**

wood·land (wood′lənd *or* wood′land), *n.* land covered with trees; forest. —*adj.* of or having to do with the woods [*woodland* creatures].

wood louse, a tiny animal with a flat, oval body and a hard shell, found in damp soil, under decaying wood, etc.

wood·man (wood′mən), *n.* **1.** a woodcutter. **2.** a person who lives in the woods. —**wood′men,** *pl.*

wood nymph, a nymph living in the woods.

wood·peck·er (wood′pek′ər), *n.* a bird having a strong, pointed bill, with which it pecks holes in bark to get insects.

wood·pile (wood′pīl), *n.* a pile of wood, especially of firewood.

wood·shed (wood′shed), *n.* a shed for storing wood, especially firewood.

woods·man (woodz′mən), *n.* a man who lives or works in the woods, as a hunter, trapper, or woodcutter. —**woods′men,** *pl.*

wood·sy (wood′zē), *adj.* of or like the woods, or forest. —**wood′si·er,** *compar.;* **wood′si·est,** *superl.*

redheaded
woodpecker
(9½ in. long)

wood thrush, a brown bird of eastern North America, having a strong, clear song.

wood winds, musical instruments made at one time of wood, but now often of metal, and having a mouthpiece into which the player blows [The clarinet, bassoon, oboe, and flute are *wood winds.*] —**wood′-wind′,** *adj.*

wood·work (wood′wûrk), *n.* **1.** things made of wood, especially the moldings, doors, stairs, etc. inside a house. **2.** woodworking.

wood·work·ing (wood′wûr′king), *n.* the art or work of making things out of wood.

wood·y (wood′ē), *adj.* **1.** covered with trees; wooded. **2.** made up of wood [the *woody* stem of a shrub]. **3.** like wood. —**wood′i·er,** *compar.;* **wood′i·est,** *superl.* —**wood′i·ness,** *n.*

woof (wōōf), *n.* **1.** the threads woven from side to side in a loom, crossing the warp. **2.** cloth; fabric.

wool (wool), *n.* **1.** the soft, curly hair of sheep, or the hair of some other animals, as the goat or llama. **2.** yarn, cloth, or clothing made from such hair. **3.** anything that looks or feels like wool. —*adj.* of wool. —**pull the wool over one's eyes,** to fool or trick one.

wool·en or **wool·len** (wool′ən), *adj.* **1.** made of wool. **2.** having to do with wool or woolen cloth. —*n.* **woolens** or **woollens,** *pl.* clothing or other goods made of wool.

wool·gath·er·ing (wool′gath′ər ing), *n.* the condition of being absent-minded or of daydreaming.

wool·ly (wool′ē), *adj.* **1.** of, like, or covered with wool. **2.** crude and uncivilized [wild and *woolly*]. —*n.* a woolen garment. —**wool′li·er,** *compar.;* **wool′li·est,** *superl.* —**wool′lies,** *pl.*

wool·y (wool′ē), *adj. & n.* same as **woolly.** —**wool′i·er,** *compar.;* **wool′i·est,** *superl.* —**wool′ies,** *pl.*

Worces·ter (woos′tər), *n.* a city in Massachusetts.

word (wûrd), *n.* **1.** a spoken sound or group of sounds having meaning and used as a single unit of speech. **2.** a letter or group of letters standing for such sounds and used in writing and printing. **3.** a brief statement [a *word* of advice]. **4.** news; information [Send *word* of yourself.]

---

5. a signal; order or password [We got the *word* to go ahead.] **6.** a promise [Give me your *word*.] **7. words,** *pl.* a quarrel. —*v.* to put into words [How shall I *word* this request?] —**by word of mouth,** by speech, not by writing. —**eat one's words,** to take back what one has said. —**have a word with,** to have a short talk with. —**in so many words,** exactly and plainly. —**man of his word,** one who keeps his promises. —**the Word** or **Word of God,** the Bible. —**upon my word!** indeed! really! —**word for word,** in exactly the same words.

word·book (wûrd′book), *n.* **1.** a dictionary or vocabulary. **2.** a book of words to songs.

word·ing (wûr′ding), *n.* the way something is put into words; choice and arrangement of words.

Words·worth, William (wûrdz′wərth), 1770–1850; English poet.

word·y (wûr′dē), *adj.* having or using too many words; not brief. —**word′i·er,** *compar.*; **word′-i·est,** *superl.* —**word′i·ness,** *n.*

wore (wôr), past tense of **wear.**

work (wûrk), *n.* **1.** the use of energy or skill in doing or making something; labor [Chopping wood is hard *work*.] **2.** what one does to earn a living; occupation, trade, profession, etc. [His *work* is teaching.] **3.** something to be done; task [to bring some *work* home from the office]. **4.** an act or deed [his good *works*]. **5.** something made, done, written, etc. [the *works* of Charles Dickens]. **6. works,** *pl.* a place where work is done; factory; plant: *used with a singular verb* [The steel *works* is shut down.] **7.** the moving parts of a machine [the *works* of a watch]. **8.** workmanship. —*v.* **1.** to use effort or energy to do or make something; labor; toil. **2.** to have a job for pay; be employed [He *works* in an office.] **3.** to cause to work [He *works* himself too hard.] **4.** to perform as it should; operate [My watch doesn't *work*.] **5.** to cause to operate; manage [Can you *work* this can opener?] **6.** to cause; bring about [His plan *worked* wonders.] **7.** to come or bring slowly to a certain condition [He *worked* up to a better job. He *worked* his tooth loose.] **8.** to make or shape [*Work* the clay into a ball.] **9.** to solve, as a problem. **10.** to do one's work in [This salesman *works* Ohio.] —**at work,** working. —**out of work,** without a job. —**work in,** to put in. —**work off,** to get rid of. —**work on,** to try to persuade. —**work out, 1.** to make its way out. **2.** to solve. **3.** to develop or come to some end. **4.** to have a workout: *used only in everyday talk.* —**work up, 1.** to advance; move up. **2.** to plan or develop. **3.** to excite or arouse. —**worked** *or,* now only for some meanings, **wrought,** *p.t. & p.p.;* **work′ing,** *pr.p.*

work·a·ble (wûr′kə b'l), *adj.* that can be worked, done, carried out, etc. [a machine in *workable* condition; a *workable* plan].

work·a·day (wûr′kə dā), *adj.* **1.** of or fit for workdays. **2.** ordinary; not interesting or unusual [a *workaday* style of writing].

work·bench (wûrk′bench), *n.* a table at which work is done, as by a machinist or carpenter.

work·book (wûrk′book), *n.* a book of problems, exercises, etc. to be worked out by students.

work·day (wûrk′dā), *n.* **1.** a day on which work is done, usually a weekday. **2.** the part of a day during which work is done [a 7-hour *workday*].

work·er (wûr′kər), *n.* **1.** a person who works for a living. **2.** any of the ants, bees, etc. that do the work for the colony.

work·house (wûrk′hous), *n.* a kind of jail where the prisoners are put to work while serving short sentences for minor crimes.

work·ing (wûr′king), *adj.* **1.** that works [a *working* girl]. **2.** of, for, or used in work [a *working* day; *working* clothes]. **3.** enough to get work done [a *working* majority]. —*n.* **1.** the act of one that works, or the way that a thing works. **2.** *usually* **workings,** *pl.* a part of a mine, quarry, etc. where work is or has been done.

work·ing·man (wûr′king man′), *n.* a man who works, especially one who works with his hands, as in industry. —**work′ing·men′,** *pl.*

work·man (wûrk′mən), *n.* a worker; laborer. —**work′men,** *pl.*

work·man·like (wûrk′mən līk), *adj.* done carefully and well [a *workmanlike* repair job].

work·man·ship (wûrk′mən ship), *n.* **1.** skill as a workman or artist; quality of work shown. **2.** something made [This lamp is my *workmanship*.]

work·out (wûrk′out), *n.* exercise or practice to develop one's body or improve one's skill in a sport, etc.: *used only in everyday talk.*

work·room (wûrk′room), *n.* a room in which work is done.

work·shop (wûrk′shäp), *n.* **1.** a room or building in which work is done. **2.** a group of people who meet for special study, work, etc. [a summer *workshop* in dramatics].

work·ta·ble (wûrk′tā′b'l), *n.* a table at which work is done.

world (wûrld), *n.* **1.** the earth [a cruise around the *world*]. **2.** the whole universe. **3.** any planet or place thought of as like the earth [Are there other *worlds* in space?] **4.** all people; mankind [He thinks the *world* is against him.] **5.** some part of the world, some period of history, some special group of people, things, etc. [the Old *World*; the *world* of ancient Rome; the business *world*; the plant *world*]. **6.** the everyday life of people, as apart from a life given over to religion and spiritual matters [She retired from the *world* to enter a convent.] **7.** *often* **worlds,** *pl.* a large amount; great deal [Your visit did me *worlds* of good.] —**for all the world,** in every way; exactly.

world·ly (wûrld′lē), *adj.* **1.** of this world; not heavenly or spiritual [his *worldly* cares]. **2.** worldly-wise. —**world′li·ness,** *n.*

world·ly-wise (wûrld′lē wīz′), *adj.* wise in the ways of the world; sophisticated.

world series, a series of baseball games played every autumn between the winning teams in the two major leagues to decide the championship.

World War I, a war from 1914 to 1918, between Great Britain, France, Russia, the United States, etc. on the one side and Germany, Austria-Hungary, etc. on the other.

World War II, a war from 1939 to 1945, between Great Britain, France, the Soviet Union, the United States, etc. on the one side and Germany, Italy, Japan, etc. on the other.

world-wea·ry (wûrld′wir′ē), *adj.* bored with the world; tired of living.

world-wide (wûrld′wīd′), *adj.* throughout the world [a *world-wide* reputation].

worm (wûrm), *n.* **1.** a small, creeping animal with a soft, slender body, usually jointed, and no legs. **2.** any small animal like this, as the larva of an insect. **3.** a person looked down on as being too meek, wretched, etc. **4.** something that suggests a worm, as the spiral thread of a screw. **5. worms,** *pl.* a disease caused by worms in the intestines, etc. —*v.* **1.** to move like a worm, in a winding or creeping way [The hunter *wormed* his way through the underbrush.] **2.** to get, bring, make, etc. in a sneaky or roundabout way [Delilah *wormed* the secret out of Samson.]

worm-eat·en (wûrm′ēt′'n), *adj.* **1.** eaten by worms, termites, etc. [*worm-eaten* wood]. **2.** worn-out, out-of-date, etc. [*worm-eaten* ideas].

worm·wood (wûrm′wood), *n.* **1.** a strong-smelling plant from which a bitter oil is gotten. **2.** any bitter, unpleasant experience.

worm·y (wûr′mē), *adj.* **1.** having worms; eaten into by worms [*wormy* apples]. **2.** like a worm. —**worm′i·er,** *compar.;* **worm′i·est,** *superl.* —**worm′i·ness,** *n.*

worn (wôrn), past participle of **wear.** —*adj.* **1.** showing signs of wear; damaged by use or wear. **2.** tired or looking tired.

worn-out (wôrn′out′), *adj.* **1.** used until it is no longer useful. **2.** very tired; tired out.

wor·ri·some (wûr′ē səm), *adj.* **1.** causing worry [a *worrisome* child]. **2.** always worrying.

wor·ry (wûr′ē), *v.* **1.** to be or make troubled in mind; feel or make uneasy or anxious [Don't *worry.* His absence *worried* us.] **2.** to annoy, bother, etc. **3.** to bite at and shake about with the teeth [The dog *worried* an old shoe.] —*n.* **1.** a troubled feeling; anxiety; care [sick with *worry*]. **2.** a cause of this [He has many *worries.*] —**wor′ried,** *p.t. & p.p.;* **wor′ry·ing,** *pr.p.* —**wor′ries,** *pl.* —**wor′ri·er,** *n.*

worse (wûrs), *adj.* **1.** more evil, harmful, bad, unpleasant, etc.; less good [an even *worse* crime]. **2.** in a less satisfactory condition; especially, in poorer health; sicker [The patient is *worse* today.] *Worse* is the comparative of **bad** and **ill.** —*adv.* in a worse way; to a worse degree [He acted *worse* than ever.] *Worse* is the comparative of **badly** and **ill.** —*n.* a person or thing that is worse [I have *worse* to report.] —**for the worse,** to a worse condition. —**worse off,** in a worse condition.

wors·en (wûr′s'n), *v.* to make or become worse.

wor·ship (wûr′ship), *n.* **1.** a prayer, church service, etc. showing reverence for God or a god. **2.** very great love or admiration [her *worship* of her older brother]. **3.** a title of respect given to certain officials, especially in England. —*v.* **1.** to show reverence for [to *worship* God]. **2.** to have very great love or admiration for [He *worships* his wife.] **3.** to take part in a religious service [Where do you *worship?*] —**wor′-shiped** or **wor′shipped,** *p.t. & p.p.;* **wor′ship·ing** or **wor′ship·ping,** *pr.p.* —**wor′ship·er** or **wor′ship·per,** *n.*

wor·ship·ful (wûr′ship fəl), *adj.* honorable: *used as a title* [*Worshipful* Sir].

worst (wûrst), *adj.* most evil, harmful, bad, unpleasant, etc.; least good [the *worst* cold I've ever had]. *Worst* is the superlative of **bad** and **ill.** —*adv.* in the worst way; to the worst degree [Of the three, he played *worst.*] *Worst* is the superlative of **badly** and **ill.** —*n.* **1.** that which is worst [The *worst* of it is that he never told me.] **2.** the most wrong that a person can do [The villain did his *worst.*] —*v.* to win out over; defeat [Our team was *worsted.*] —**at worst,** as the worst that can be expected. —**if worst comes to worst,** if the worst possible thing happens. —**in the worst way,** very much: *a slang phrase.*

wor·sted (woos′tid *or* woor′stid), *n.* **1.** a smooth thread or yarn made from wool. **2.** fabric made from this, with a smooth, hard surface.

worth (wûrth), *n.* **1.** the quality of a thing that makes it have value; merit [I know his *worth* as a friend.] **2.** the value of a thing in money or in other goods [What is its *worth* to you?] **3.** the amount to be had for a certain sum [a dime's *worth* of candy]. —*adj.* **1.** deserving or worthy of [a movie *worth* seeing]. **2.** equal in value to [It's not *worth* a nickel.] **3.** having wealth amounting to [He's *worth* a million dollars.]

worth·less (wûrth′lis), *adj.* having no worth, use, value, etc. —**worth′less·ly,** *adv.* —**worth′less·ness,** *n.*

worth-while (wûrth′hwīl′), *adj.* worth the time or effort needed for it [a *worth-while* book].

wor·thy (wûr′t͟hē), *adj.* **1.** having worth or merit [a *worthy* cause]. **2.** deserving; good enough for [not *worthy* of her love]. —*n.* a very important person: *often used in a joking way.* —**wor′thi·er,** *compar.;* **wor′thi·est,** *superl.* —**wor′thies,** *pl.* —**wor′thi·ly,** *adv.*

wot (wät), the form of **wit** (to know) that was used with *I, he, she, it,* and with nouns [God *wot.*]

would (wood), the past tense of **will** [He promised he *would* return.] *Would* is also used as a helping verb: **1.** in speaking of something that depends on something else [He *would* have helped if you had asked him.] **2.** in expressing a wish [*Would* that he were here!] **3.** in asking

fat,   āpe,   cär,   ten,   ēven,   hit,   bīte,   gō,   hôrn,   tool,   book,   up,   fûr;
get,   joy,   yet,   chin,   she,   thin,   t͟hen;   zh = s in pleasure;   ' as in able (ā′b'l);
ə = a in ago,   e in agent,   i in sanity,   o in confess,   u in focus.

something in a polite way [*Would* you please leave?] See also **should.**

would-be (wood'bē'), *adj.* **1.** wishing or pretending to be [a *would-be* actor]. **2.** meant to be [His *would-be* helpfulness was a bother.]

would·n't (wood'nt), would not.

wouldst (woodst), the older form of **would,** used with *thou,* as in the Bible.

wound (woond), *n.* **1.** an injury in which some part of the body is cut, torn, broken, etc. **2.** a scar. **3.** any hurt to the feelings, reputation, etc. —*v.* to give a wound to; injure; hurt [Her cruel words *wounded* him.]

wound (wound), **1.** past tense and past participle of **wind** (to turn). **2.** a past tense and past participle of **wind** (to blow).

wove (wōv), past tense and a past participle of **weave.**

wo·ven (wōv'n), a past participle of **weave.**

wrack (rak), *n.* **1.** ruin; destruction: *used mainly in the phrase* "wrack and ruin." **2.** seaweed, etc. washed up on shore.

wraith (rāth), *n.* a ghost.

wran·gle (rang'g'l), *v.* **1.** to quarrel in an angry, noisy way. **2.** to round up in a herd, as cattle. —*n.* an angry, noisy quarrel. —**wran'gled,** *p.t. & p.p.;* **wran'gling,** *pr.p.* —**wran'gler,** *n.*

wrap (rap), *v.* **1.** to wind or fold around something [She *wrapped* a scarf around her head.] **2.** to cover in this way [They *wrapped* the baby in a blanket.] **3.** to cover with paper, etc. [to *wrap* a present]. **4.** to hide; conceal [a town *wrapped* in fog.] —*n.* an outer garment [Put your *wraps* in the closet.] —**wrapped up in,** giving much time and attention to [*wrapped up in* his work]. —**wrapped** or **wrapt** (rapt), *p.t. & p.p.;* **wrap'ping,** *pr.p.*

wrap·per (rap'ər), *n.* **1.** a person or thing that wraps. **2.** a covering or cover [a newspaper mailed in a paper *wrapper*]. **3.** a woman's dressing gown.

wrap·ping (rap'ing), *n.* often **wrappings,** *pl.* the paper or other material in which something is wrapped.

wrath (rath), *n.* great anger; rage; fury.

wrath·ful (rath'fəl), *adj.* full of wrath; very angry. —**wrath'ful·ly,** *adv.*

wreak (rēk), *v.* **1.** to let out in words or acts [He *wreaked* his fury on the boy.] **2.** to put into effect [to *wreak* vengeance on someone].

wreath (rēth), *n.* **1.** a ring of leaves, flowers, etc. twisted together. **2.** something like this [*wreaths* of smoke]. —**wreaths** (rē*th*z), *pl.*

wreathe (rēth), *v.* **1.** to coil or twist into a wreath [to *wreathe* flowers and leaves]. **2.** to twist or wind around; encircle [Wrinkles *wreathed* his brow.] **3.** to decorate with or as if with wreaths [His face was *wreathed* in smiles.] —**wreathed,** *p.t. & p.p.;* **wreath'ing,** *pr.p.*

wreath

wreck (rek), *n.* **1.** the loss of a ship, or of a building, car, etc., through storm, accident, or the like. **2.** the remains of something that has been destroyed or badly damaged [an old *wreck* stranded on the reef]. **3.** a person in very poor health. **4.** the act of destroying or ruining [the *wreck* of all our hopes]. —*v.* **1.** to destroy or damage badly; ruin [to *wreck* a car in an accident; to *wreck* one's plans for a picnic]. **2.** to tear down; raze [to *wreck* an old house].

wreck·age (rek'ij), *n.* **1.** a wrecking or being wrecked. **2.** the remains of a wreck.

wreck·er (rek'ər), *n.* **1.** a person or thing that wrecks. **2.** a person, truck, etc. that clears away wrecks. **3.** a person whose work is tearing down old buildings, etc.

wreck·ing (rek'ing), *n.* the act or work of a wrecker. —*adj.* used in or taking part in the tearing down of old buildings, the removal of wrecks, etc. [a *wrecking* bar; a *wrecking* crew].

wren (ren), *n.* a small songbird with a long bill and a stubby tail that tilts up.

wren (5 in. long)

wrench (rench), *n.* **1.** a sudden, sharp twist or pull [With one *wrench,* he loosened the lid.] **2.** an injury, as to the back or an arm, caused by a twist. **3.** a sudden feeling of sadness, as at parting with someone. **4.** a tool for holding and turning nuts, bolts, pipes, etc. —*v.* **1.** to twist or pull sharply [He *wrenched* the keys from my grasp.] **2.** to injure with a twist [She *wrenched* her knee when she fell.] **3.** to twist or distort, as the meaning of a remark.

wrest (rest), *v.* **1.** to pull away with a sharp twist [He *wrested* the pistol from the robber's hand.] **2.** to get by struggle [Rebels *wrested* control of the government from the king.]

wrench (*meaning 4*)

wres·tle (res''l), *v.* **1.** to struggle with an opponent, trying to throw or force him to the ground without striking blows with the fists. **2.** to struggle hard, as with a problem. —*n.* **1.** the action or a bout of wrestling. **2.** a struggle. —**wres'tled,** *p.t. & p.p.;* **wres'tling,** *pr.p.* —**wres'tler,** *n.*

wres·tling (res'ling), *n.* a sport in which two people wrestle with each other.

wretch (rech), *n.* **1.** a person in great misery. **2.** a person looked down on as bad or wicked.

wretch·ed (rech'id), *adj.* **1.** very unhappy or troubled; miserable. **2.** causing misery [*wretched* slums]. **3.** hateful; vile [a *wretched* tyrant]. **4.** bad in quality; very poor; unsatisfactory [a *wretched* meal]. —**wretch'ed·ly,** *adv.* —**wretch'ed-ness,** *n.*

wrig·gle (rig''l), *v.* **1.** to twist and turn; squirm [to *wriggle* in one's seat]. **2.** to move along with such a motion, as a worm does. **3.** to manage by shifty or tricky means [He *wriggled* out of his promise.] —*n.* a wriggling motion. —**wrig′gled,** *p.t. & p.p.;* **wrig′gling,** *pr.p.* —**wrig′gler,** *n.*

wright (rīt), *n.* a person who makes or builds something: *now used mainly as a suffix* [A ship*wright* is one who builds ships.]

Wright, Orville (rīt), 1871–1948; U.S. inventor who, with his brother **Wilbur** (1867–1912), built the first airplane to have a successful flight.

wring (ring), *v.* **1.** to squeeze and twist with force [to *wring* out wet clothes]. **2.** to force out by squeezing, twisting, etc. [to *wring* water from a wet towel]. **3.** to get by force, threats, etc. [to *wring* a confession from someone]. **4.** to bring painful feelings of pity, distress, etc. to [Her sad story *wrung* our hearts.] —*n.* the act of wringing. —**wrung,** *p.t. & p.p.;* **wring′ing,** *pr.p.*

wring·er (ring′ər), *n.* a machine with rollers that squeeze water from wet clothes.

wrin·kle (ring′k′l), *n.* **1.** a small or uneven crease or fold [*wrinkles* in a coat; *wrinkles* in skin]. **2.** a clever trick, idea, etc.: *used only in everyday talk.* —*v.* **1.** to make wrinkles in [a brow *wrinkled* with care]. **2.** to form wrinkles [This cloth *wrinkles* easily.] —**wrin′kled,** *p.t. & p.p.;* **wrin′kling,** *pr.p.*

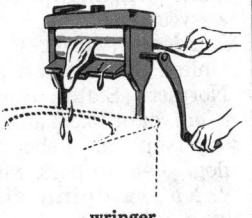

wringer

wrist (rist), *n.* the joint or part of the arm between the hand and forearm.

wrist·band (rist′band), *n.* a band around the wrist, as on the cuff of a sleeve, or a strap for a wrist watch.

writ (rit), old past tense and past participle of **write.** —*n.* **1.** a written order by a court of law [a *writ* of habeas corpus]. **2.** something written: *now seldom used except in* **Holy Writ,** meaning "the Bible."

write (rīt), *v.* **1.** to form words, letters, etc., as with a pen or pencil. **2.** to form the words, letters, etc. of [*Write* your address here.] **3.** to be the author or composer of [Dickens *wrote* novels. Mozart *wrote* symphonies.] **4.** to fill in or cover with writing [to *write* a check; to *write* ten pages]. **5.** to send a message in writing; write a letter [*Write* me every week. He *wrote* that he was ill.] **6.** to show signs of [Joy was *written* all over her face.] —**write down,** to put into writing. —**write off,** to cancel, as a debt. —**write out, 1.** to put into writing. **2.** to write in full. —**write up,** to write an account of. —**wrote,** *p.t.;* **writ′ten,** *p.p.;* **writ′ing,** *pr.p.*

writ·er (rīt′ər), *n.* a person who writes, especially one who earns his living by writing books, essays, articles, etc.; author.

write-up (rīt′up′), *n.* a written report, as in a newspaper: *used only in everyday talk.*

writhe (rīth), *v.* **1.** to twist and turn, as in pain; squirm. **2.** to suffer from shame, shyness, etc. —**writhed,** *p.t. & p.p.;* **writh′ing,** *pr.p.*

writ·ing (rīt′ing), *n.* **1.** the act of one who writes. **2.** something written, as a letter, article, poem, book, etc. [the *writings* of Thomas Jefferson]. **3.** written form [to put a request in *writing*]. **4.** handwriting [Can you read her *writing*?] **5.** the art or work of writers.

writ·ten (rit′′n), past participle of **write.**

wrong (rông), *adj.* **1.** not right, just, or good; unlawful, wicked, or bad [It is *wrong* to steal.] **2.** not the one that is true, correct, wanted, etc. [the *wrong* answer]. **3.** in error; mistaken [He's not *wrong*.] **4.** not proper or suitable [Purple is the *wrong* color for her.] **5.** not working properly; out of order [What's *wrong* with the radio?] **6.** having a rough finish and not meant to be seen [the *wrong* side of the rug]. —*n.* something wrong; especially, a wicked or unjust act [Does he know right from *wrong*? You do him a *wrong* to accuse him.] —*adv.* in a wrong way, direction, etc.; incorrectly [You did it *wrong*.] —*v.* to treat badly or unjustly [They *wronged* her by telling lies.] —**go wrong, 1.** to turn out badly. **2.** to change from being good to being bad. —**in the wrong,** at fault; wrong. —**wrong′ly,** *adv.* —**wrong′ness,** *n.*

wrong·do·ing (rông′dōō′ing), *n.* any act or behavior that is wrong, wicked, unlawful, etc. —**wrong′do′er,** *n.*

wrong·ful (rông′fəl), *adj.* wrong in a way that is unjust, unfair, unlawful, etc.

wrong·head·ed (rông′hed′id), *adj.* stubborn in sticking to wrong opinions, ideas, etc.

wrote (rōt), past tense of **write.**

wroth (rôth), *adj.* full of wrath; angry.

wrought (rôt), a past tense and past participle of **work.** —*adj.* **1.** formed or made [furniture *wrought* by craftsmen]. **2.** shaped by hammering or beating, as metals.

wrought iron, a kind of iron that contains very little carbon. It is tough and hard to break but easy to work or shape.

wrung (rung), past tense and past participle of **wring.**

wry (rī), *adj.* turned or bent to one side; twisted [a *wry* face; a *wry* smile]. —**wri′er,** *compar.;* **wri′est,** *superl.*

wt., abbreviation for **weight.**

W.Va., abbreviation for **West Virginia.**

Wy·o·ming (wī ō′ming), *n.* a State in the northwestern part of the United States: abbreviated **Wyo.**

---

fat, āpe, cär, ten, ēven, hit, bīte, gō, hôrn, tōōl, book, up, fur;
get, joy, yet, chin, she, thin, *then;* zh = s in pleasure; ′ as in able (ā′b′l)
ə = a in ago, e in agent, i in sanity, o in confess, u in focus.

X Y Z

X, x (eks), *n.* the twenty-fourth letter of the English alphabet. —**X's, x's** (eks′iz), *pl.*

X (eks), *n.* **1.** the Roman numeral for 10. **2.** something shaped like an X, as a mark used to show a place on a map, to stand for a kiss in letters, etc. **3.** a person or thing that is not known.

Xa·vi·er, Saint Francis (zā′vi·ər), 1506–1552; Spanish priest who was a missionary in Asia.

xe·bec (zē′bek), *n.* a small ship with three masts, at one time common on the Mediterranean.

Xe·rox (zir′äks), *n.* a process for copying printed material by means of a special machine, which uses light to transfer an image to paper: the image attracts dry ink particles electrically to form the copy. **Xerox** is a trademark.

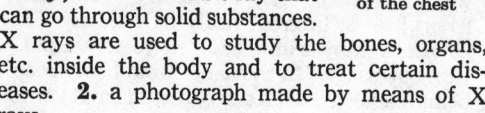
X ray *(meaning 2)* of the chest

Xer·xes I (zŭrk′sēz), 519?–465? B.C.; king of Persia from about 486 to about 465 B.C.

X·mas (kris′məs), *n.* Christmas.

X ray, 1. an invisible ray that can go through solid substances. X rays are used to study the bones, organs, etc. inside the body and to treat certain diseases. **2.** a photograph made by means of X rays.

X-ray (eks′rā′), *adj.* of, by, or having to do with X rays. —*v.* to examine, treat, or photograph with X rays.

xy·lem (zī′lem), *n.* the woody tissue of a plant.

xy·lo·phone (zī′lə fōn), *n.* a musical instrument made up of a row of wooden bars of different sizes, that are struck with wooden hammers.

xylophone

Y, y (wī), *n.* **1.** the twenty-fifth letter of the English alphabet. **2.** something shaped like a Y. —**Y's, y's** (wīz), *pl.*

-y (ē), a suffix meaning "little" or "dear" [A *dolly* is a little doll.]

-y (ē), a suffix meaning: **1.** having; full of; covered with [*Dirty* hands are covered with dirt.] **2.** somewhat; rather [A *chilly* room is somewhat chilled.] **3.** apt to [*Sticky* fingers are apt to stick to things.] **4.** somewhat like [*Wavy* hair looks somewhat like waves.]

-y (ē), a suffix meaning: **1.** the quality or condition of being [*Villainy* is the condition of being a villain.] **2.** the act or action of [An *inquiry* is the act of inquiring.]

y., abbreviation for **yard** or **year.**

yacht (yät), *n.* a boat or small ship for racing, taking pleasure cruises, etc. —*v.* to sail in a yacht. —**yacht′ing,** *n.*

yachts·man (yäts′mən), *n.* a person who owns or sails a yacht. —**yachts′men,** *pl.*

yak (yak), *n.* an ox with long hair, found wild or raised in Tibet and central Asia.

yam (yam), *n.* **1.** the starchy root of a climbing plant grown in tropical countries. It is used as food. **2.** this plant. **3.** the sweet potato: *the name used in some parts of the U.S.*

yak (5 ft. high at shoulder)

Yang·tze (yang′sē), *n.* the longest river in China, flowing from Tibet to the China Sea.

yank (yangk), *n. & v.* jerk or pull: *used only in everyday talk.*

Yan·kee (yang′kē), *n.* **1.** a citizen of the United States. **2.** a person born in one of the Northern States, especially in New England. —*adj.* of or like Yankees.

yap (yap), *n.* a short, sharp bark, as of a small dog. —*v.* to bark with yaps. —**yapped,** *p.t. & p.p.;* **yap′ping,** *pr.p.*

yard (yärd), *n.* **1.** a measure of length, equal to three feet, or 36 inches. **2.** a long pole fastened across a mast to support a sail.

yard (yärd), *n.* **1.** the ground around or next to a house or other building [a church*yard*]. **2.** a place in the open used for a special purpose, work, etc. [a lumber *yard*; a navy *yard*]. **3.** a rail center where trains are made up, switched, etc.

yard·age (yär′dij), *n.* **1.** measurement in yards. **2.** the length of something in yards.

yard·arm (yärd′ärm), *n.* either end of the yard supporting a square sail.

yard·stick (yärd′stik), *n.* **1.** a measuring stick one yard long. **2.** a standard used in judging.

yarn (yärn), *n.* **1.** fibers of wool, silk, cotton, etc. spun into strands, as for weaving or knitting. **2.** a tale or story: *used only in everyday talk.*

yar·row (yar′ō), *n.* a plant with hairy leaves, clusters of small flowers, and a strong smell.

yaw (yô), *v. & n.* turn from the course, as a boat when struck by rough waves.

yawl (yôl), *n.* **1.** a sailboat with the mainmast toward the bow and a short mast toward the stern. **2.** a ship's boat, rowed by oars.

yawn (yôn), *v.* **1.** to open the mouth wide and breathe in deeply in a way that is not controlled, as when one is sleepy or tired: *see picture on next page.* **2.** to open wide; gape [a *yawning* hole]. —*n.* the act of yawning.

yawl

yaws (yôz), *n.pl.* a serious skin disease of tropical regions, caused by a germ.

y·clept or **y·cleped** (i klept′), past participle of an old verb, no longer used, meaning "to call or name" [a knight *yclept* Sir Bors].

yd., abbreviation for **yard** or **yards.**

ye (yē), *pron.* an older form of **you,** as in the Bible.

man yawning

ye (thə), *adj.* the: *now seldom used.* *Y* was used by early printers in place of the Old English character for the sound *th*, and the word is now often incorrectly pronounced (yē).

yea (yā), *adv.* **1.** yes: *now seldom used except in poetry.* **2.** indeed; truly. —*n.* an answer or vote of "yes."

year (yir), *n.* **1.** a period of 365 days, or, in leap year, 366, divided into 12 months and beginning January 1. It is based on the time taken by the earth to go completely around the sun, about 365¼ days. **2.** any period of twelve months starting at any time [She was six *years* old in July.] **3.** a part of a year during which certain things take place [the school *year*]. **4. years,** *pl.* age [He is old for his *years*.] —**year after year,** every year.

year·book (yir′book), *n.* a book published each year, with information about the year just ended.

year·ling (yir′ling), *n.* an animal one year old or in its second year.

year·ly (yir′lē), *adj.* **1.** happening, done, etc. once a year, or every year [He sent his *yearly* greetings.] **2.** of or for a year [one's *yearly* income]. —*adv.* once a year; every year.

yearn (yûrn), *v.* **1.** to be filled with longing or desire [to *yearn* for fame]. **2.** to be filled with pity, sympathy, etc. —**yearn′ing,** *n. & adj.*

yeast (yēst), *n.* **1.** a yellow, frothy substance made up of tiny fungi, used in baking to make dough rise. **2.** yeast mixed with flour or meal, made up in small cakes: also **yeast cake.**

yell (yel), *v.* to cry out loudly; scream. —*n.* **1.** a loud shout. **2.** a cheer by a crowd, usually in rhythm, as at a football game.

yel·low (yel′ō), *adj.* **1.** having the color of ripe lemons, or of an egg yolk. **2.** having a skin that is more or less yellow. **3.** cowardly: *used only in everyday talk.* —*n.* **1.** a yellow color. **2.** a yellow paint or dye. **3.** the yolk of an egg. —*v.* to make or become yellow [linens *yellowed* with age]. —**yel′low·ish,** *adj.*

yellow fever, a tropical disease that causes fever, vomiting, and yellowing of the skin. Its virus is carried to man by certain mosquitoes.

yellow jack, 1. yellow fever. **2.** a yellow flag used as a signal of quarantine.

yellow jacket, a wasp or hornet having bright-yellow markings.

Yellow River, the Hwang Ho, a river in China.

Yellow Sea, a part of the Pacific Ocean, between China and Korea.

Yel·low·stone National Park (yel′ō stōn′), a national park mainly in northwestern Wyoming, famous for its geysers, boiling springs, petrified forests, etc.

yelp (yelp), *n.* a short, sharp cry, as of a dog in pain. —*v.* to make such a cry or cries.

Yem·en (yem′ən *or* yā′mən), *n.* a country in southwestern Arabia.

yen (yen), *n.* the basic unit of money in Japan.

yen (yen), *n.* a deep longing or desire: *used only in everyday talk.*

yeo·man (yō′mən), *n.* **1.** a petty officer in the United States Navy, who works as a clerk. **2.** a farmer who owns a small farm: *a British meaning.* —**yeo′men,** *pl.*

yes (yes), *adv.* **1.** it is so; I will, I can, I agree, I allow, etc.: opposite of **no. 2.** not only that, but more [I am ready, *yes,* eager to help you.] —*n.* **1.** the act of saying "yes"; agreement or consent. **2.** a vote for something. —**yes′es,** *pl.*

yes·ter·day (yes′tər dē *or* yes′tər dā), *adv.* on the day before today. —*n.* **1.** the day before today. **2.** some time in the past.

yes·ter·night (yes′tər nīt′), *n. & adv.* last night: *now seldom used except in poetry.*

yes·ter·year (yes′tər yir′), *n. & adv.* last year: *now seldom used except in poetry.*

yet (yet), *adv.* **1.** up to now; so far [He has not gone *yet.*] **2.** now; at the present time [We can't leave just *yet.*] **3.** still; even now [There is *yet* some hope.] **4.** at some time to come [We'll get there *yet.*] **5.** in addition; even [He was *yet* kinder.] **6.** now, after a long time [Haven't you finished *yet?*] **7.** but; nevertheless [He is comfortable, *yet* lonely.] *conj.* nevertheless; however [She seems happy, *yet* she is worried.] —**as yet,** up to now.

yew (yōo), *n.* **1.** an evergreen tree or shrub of Europe, Asia, and America. **2.** the wood of this tree, once much used in making bows for archers.

Yid·dish (yid′ish), *n.* a language spoken by many Jews in Europe and elsewhere. It developed from old German, but is written with the Hebrew alphabet.

yield (yēld), *v.* **1.** to give up; surrender [to *yield* to a demand; to *yield* a city]. **2.** to give or grant [to *yield* one's permission]. **3.** to give way [The gate would not *yield* to our pushing.] **4.** to bring forth or bring about; produce; give [The orchard *yielded* a good crop.] **5.** to give place [I *yield* to the Senator from Utah.] —*n.* the amount yielded or produced.

yield·ing (yēl′ding), *adj.* that yields or gives in easily.

Y.M.C.A., abbreviation for **Young Men's Christian Association.**

yo·del (yō′d'l), *v.* to sing with sudden changes back and forth between one's usual voice and a high, shrill voice. —*n.* the act or sound of

---

fat, āpe, cär, ten, ēven, hit, bīte, gō, hôrn, tōol, book, up, fûr; get, joy, yet, chin, she, thin, *th*en; zh = s in pleasure; ′ as in able (ā′b'l). ə = a in ago, e in agent, i in sanity, o in confess, u in focus.

yodeling. —**yo′deled** or **yo′delled,** *p.t.* & *p.p.;* **yo′del·ing** or **yo′del·ling,** *pr.p.* —**yo′del·er** or **yo′del·ler,** *n.*

yo·gurt or **yo·ghurt** (yō′goort), *n.* a thick, soft food made from fermented milk.

yoke (yōk), *n.* **1.** a wooden frame that fits around the necks of a pair of oxen, etc. to join them. **2.** a pair joined with a yoke [a *yoke* of oxen]. **3.** the condition of being under another's power or control; slavery; bondage [The peasants threw off their *yoke*.] **4.** something that binds or unites [a *yoke* of friendship]. **5.** something like a yoke, as a frame that fits over the shoulders for carrying pails. **6.** a part of a garment fitted closely around the shoulders, or sometimes the hips [the *yoke* of a shirt]. —*v.* **1.** to put a yoke on. **2.** to fasten with a yoke [to *yoke* oxen to a plow]. **3.** to join together. —**yoked,** *p.t.* & *p.p.;* **yok′ing,** *pr.p.*

yoke *(meaning 5)*

yo·kel (yō′k'l), *n.* a person who lives in the country: *used in an unfriendly way.*

Yo·ko·ha·ma (yō′kə hä′mə), *n.* a city in Japan.

yolk (yōk), *n.* the yellow part of an egg.

Yom Kip·pur (yäm′ kip′ər), a Jewish holiday and day of fasting.

yon (yän) or **yond** (yänd), *adj.* & *adv.* same as **yonder:** *now seldom used.*

yon·der (yän′dər), *adj.* at a distance, but within sight [Go to *yonder* village.] —*adv.* at or in that place; over there.

yore (yôr), *n.* time long ago: *now used only in the phrase* **of yore,** meaning "of long ago."

York·shire (yôrk′shir), *n.* the largest county of England, in the northeastern part.

Yorkshire pudding, a batter pudding served with roast beef and gravy.

York·town (yôrk′toun), *n.* a town in Virginia, where Cornwallis surrendered to Washington.

Yo·sem·i·te (yō sem′ə tē), *n.* a valley in California, part of **Yosemite National Park.**

you (yōo), *pron. sing.* & *pl.* **1.** the person or persons spoken or written to. *You* is used as the subject of a verb or as the object of a verb or preposition [*You* are right. Did I tell *you*?] **2.** a person; one [*You* seldom see a horse and buggy now.]

you'd (yōod), **1.** you had. **2.** you would.

you'll (yōol), **1.** you will. **2.** you shall.

young (yung), *adj.* **1.** being in an early part of life or growth; not old [a *young* actor; a *young* tree]. **2.** of or like a young person; youthful, fresh, vigorous, etc. [She is *young* for her age.] **3.** not so old as another of the same name or family [Do you mean *young* Bill or his father?] —*n.* young offspring [The bear defended her *young*.] —**the young,** young people. —**with young,** pregnant.

young·ster (yung′stər), *n.* a child or youth.

your (yoor), *pron.* of you or done by you: the possessive form of *you,* used before a noun and thought of as an adjective [*your* book; *your* work]. See also **yours.**

you're (yoor *or* yōōr), you are.

yours (yoorz), *pron.* the one or the ones that belong to you: the form of *your* used when it is not followed by a noun [Is this pen *yours*? *Yours* cost more than ours.] *Yours* is used as a polite closing of a letter, often with *truly, sincerely,* etc.

your·self (yoor self′), *pron.* **1.** your own self: the form of *you* that makes the subject also the object of the verb [Did you cut *yourself*?] **2.** your usual or true self [You are not *yourself* today.] *Yourself* is also used to give force to the subject [You *yourself* told me so.] —**your·selves** (yoor selvz′), *pl.*

youth (yōōth), *n.* **1.** the time when one is no longer a child but not yet an adult. **2.** an early stage of life or growth, as of a country. **3.** young people [a club for the *youth* of our town]. **4.** a young man. **5.** the quality of being young, fresh, vigorous, etc. [to recapture one's *youth*].

youth·ful (yōōth′fəl), *adj.* **1.** young. **2.** of, like, or fit for a young person [*youthful* styles; *youthful* vigor].

you've (yōov), you have.

yowl (youl), *n.* & *v.* howl.

yr., abbreviation for **year.** —**yrs.,** *pl.*

Yu·ca·tán (yōō kə tan′), *n.* a peninsula at the southeastern end of Mexico.

yuc·ca (yuk′ə), *n.* a tall plant with long, stiff, pointed leaves and large white flowers.

Yu·go·slav (yōō′gō släv′), *n.* a person born or living in Yugoslavia. —*adj.* of Yugoslavia or its people. Also **Yu′go·sla′vi·an.**

Yu·go·sla·vi·a (yōō′gō slä′vi ə), *n.* a country in southeastern Europe, on the Balkan Peninsula.

yucca

Yu·kon (yōō′kän), *n.* **1.** a territory of northwestern Canada, east of Alaska. **2.** a river flowing through this territory and Alaska into the Bering Sea.

yule (yōol), *n.* Christmas or Christmas time.

yule·tide (yōol′tīd), *n.* Christmas time.

Y.W.C.A., abbreviation for **Young Women's Christian Association.**

Z, z (zē), *n.* the twenty-sixth and last letter of the English alphabet. —**Z's, z's** (zēz), *pl.*

Zam·be·zi (zam bē′zē), *n.* a river in southern Africa, flowing into the Indian Ocean.

Zam·bi·a (zam′bi ə), *n.* a country in southern Africa.

za·ny (zā′nē), *n.* **1.** a clown, or a person who acts like a clown. **2.** a fool. —*adj.* funny, foolish, crazy, etc. [*zany* tricks]. —**za′nies,** *pl.* —**za′ni·er,** *compar.;* **za′ni·est,** *superl.*

Zan·zi·bar (zan′zə bär), *n.* an island off the eastern coast of Africa. It is part of Tanzania.

zeal (zēl), *n.* strong, eager feeling, as in working for a cause; great interest; enthusiasm.

zeal·ot (zel′ət), *n.* a person who shows zeal for something, especially too much zeal; fanatic.

zeal·ous (zel′əs), *adj.* full of zeal; very eager; enthusiastic [a *zealous* patriot]. —**zeal′ous·ly,** *adv.* —**zeal′ous·ness,** *n.*

ze·bra (zē′brə), *n.* a wild animal of Africa, related to the horse. It has dark stripes on a white or tan body.

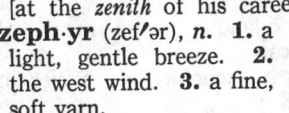
zebra (4½ ft. high at shoulder)

ze·bu (zē′byōō), *n.* a farm animal of Asia and eastern Africa, like an ox with a hump.

ze·nith (zē′nith), *n.* **1.** the point in the sky directly above one. **2.** the highest point; peak [at the *zenith* of his career]. See also **nadir.**

zeph·yr (zef′ər), *n.* **1.** a light, gentle breeze. **2.** the west wind. **3.** a fine, soft yarn.

zep·pe·lin (zep′ə lin), *n.* a former type of dirigible with a stiff framework.

zebu (4½ ft. high at shoulder)

ze·ro (zir′ō), *n.* **1.** the number or symbol 0; cipher; naught. **2.** a point marked 0, from which something is measured in degrees [It is ten below *zero* on the thermometer.] **3.** nothing [Four minus four equals *zero*.] **4.** the lowest point [His chances fell to *zero*.] —*adj.* of or at zero. —**ze′ros** or **ze′roes,** *pl.*

zero hour, the time set for beginning something, as an attack by an army.

zest (zest), *n.* **1.** exciting or interesting quality; relish [Danger adds *zest* to an acrobat's work.] **2.** keen enjoyment [to work with *zest*]. —**zest′ful,** *adj.*

Zeus (zōōs or zyōōs), *n.* the chief Greek god, ruling over all other gods. The Romans called this god *Jupiter.*

zig·zag (zig′zag), *n.* **1.** a series of short slanting lines, connected by sharp turns or angles. **2.** a design, path, etc. that looks like this [The lightning made a *zigzag* in the sky.] —*adj. & adv.* in a zigzag. —*v.* to form or move in a zigzag. —**zig′zagged,** *p.t. & p.p.*; **zig′zag·ging,** *pr.p.*

zinc (zingk), *n.* a bluish-white metal that is a chemical element. It is used to coat iron, and in making certain alloys, medicines, etc.

a zigzag trail

zing (zing), *n.* a high, whistling sound, like that made by something moving very fast: *a slang word.*

zin·ni·a (zin′i ə), *n.* a garden plant of the aster family, with brightly colored flowers having many petals.

Zi·on (zī′ən), *n.* **1.** a hill in Jerusalem where Solomon's Temple and David's palace were built. **2.** the Jewish people. **3.** heaven; the heavenly city.

Zi·on·ism (zī′ən iz'm), *n.* the movement for setting up a Jewish nation again in Palestine, that resulted in the state of Israel. —**Zi′on·ist,** *n. & adj.*

zip (zip), *v.* **1.** to make a short, sharp, hissing sound [A bullet *zipped* past.] **2.** to move fast: *used only in everyday talk* [We *zipped* through our work.] **3.** to fasten with a zipper. —*n.* **1.** a zipping sound. **2.** force or energy: *used only in everyday talk.* —**zipped,** *p.t. & p.p.*; **zip′ping,** *pr.p.*

ZIP code (zip), a system for speeding up the delivery of mail: under this system the post office has assigned a special code number to each area and place in the country.

zip·per (zip′ər), *n.* same as **slide fastener.**

zir·con (zūr′kän), *n.* a clear mineral colored yellow, brown, red, orange, etc., often used as a jewel.

zith·er (zith′ər or zith′ər), *n.* a musical instrument made up of a flat, hollow board with 30 or 40 strings stretched across it. It is played by plucking the strings.

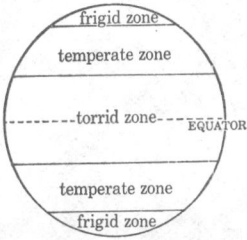
zither

Zn, the symbol for the chemical element *zinc.*

zo·di·ac (zō′di ak), *n.* an imaginary belt across the sky, along the path that the sun seems to travel. It is divided into twelve parts, each named after a different constellation. A chart showing this is used in astrology. —**zo·di·a·cal** (zō dī′ə k'l), *adj.*

zom·bi or **zom·bie** (zäm′bē), *n.* **1.** a magic power which some natives of the West Indies believe will make a dead body move and walk. **2.** a dead body with this power. —**zom′bis** or **zom′bies,** *pl.*

zone (zōn), *n.* **1.** any of the five areas into which the earth's surface is marked off by imaginary lines. They are named according to the general climate in each. *See the picture.* **2.** an area that is set apart in some special way [the Canal *Zone;* a 25 mph traffic *zone*]. **3.** a section of a city set apart by law for a particular use, as for homes or for businesses. **4.** any of the numbered sections into which a city is divided for the purpose of addressing mail; also, any of the areas marked off around a mailing point according to parcel-post rates. **5.** a belt or girdle. —*v.* to mark off into zones, as for a particular purpose [an area *zoned* for industry]. —**zoned,** *p.t. & p.p.;* **zon′ing,** *pr.p.*

zoo (zōō), *n.* a place where wild animals are kept for the public to see.

zo·o·log·i·cal (zō′ə läj′i k'l), *adj.* having to do with zoology or with animals. —**zo′o·log′i·cal·ly,** *adv.*

zoological garden, a zoo.

zo·ol·o·gy (zō äl′ə jē), *n.* the science that studies animals and animal life. —**zo·ol′o·gist,** *n.*

zoom (zōōm), *v.* **1.** to move upward at great speed with a loud, humming sound, as an airplane. **2.** to rush with this sound [cars *zooming* past]. **3.** to rise rapidly [Prices are *zooming.*] —*n.* the act or sound of zooming.

zoom lens, a system of lenses in a camera that can be adjusted very quickly so that the camera can be switched from taking a close-up picture to taking a distant picture and have the subject in focus for each picture.

Zo·ro·as·ter (zō′rō as′tər), *n.* the founder of the religion of the ancient Persians, called **Zoroastrianism.** He lived about 1000 B.C. —**Zo·ro·as·tri·an** (zō′rō as′tri ən), *adj. & n.*

zounds (zoundz), *interj.* a mild oath used in earlier times to show surprise or anger.

zuc·chi·ni (zōō kē′nē), *n.* a type of squash with a green skin, shaped like a cucumber.

zucchini

Zui·der Zee or **Zuy·der Zee** (zī′dər zē′), an arm of the North Sea that once reached into the Netherlands. It is now shut off by dikes, and much of the land that it covered has been drained.

Zu·lu (zōō′lōō), *n.* **1.** a member of a Negro people of Natal, in South Africa. **2.** their language. —*adj.* of the Zulus, their language, etc.— **Zu′lus** or **Zu′lu,** *pl.*

Zu·lu·land (zōō′lōō land′), *n.* a region of Natal in South Africa.

Zur·ich or **Zür·ich** (zoor′ik), *n.* a city in northern Switzerland.

zwie·back (tswē′bäk *or* zwē′bäk *or* swi′bak), *n.* a kind of biscuit made from a baked loaf cut into slices that are toasted brown in an oven.